TYPES of DRAMA

TYPES of DRAMA
Plays and Contexts

SEVENTH EDITION

Sylvan Barnet
Tufts University

Morton Berman
Boston University

William Burto
University of Lowell

Ren Draya
Blackburn College

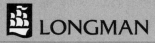
LONGMAN

An Imprint of Addison Wesley Longman, Inc.

New York•Reading, Massachusetts•Menlo Park, California•Harlow, England
Don Mills, Ontario•Sydney•Mexico City•Madrid•Amsterdam

Senior Editor: Lisa Moore

Developmental Editor: Katharine H. Glynn

Project Editor: Lois Lombardo

Design Manager: Jim Sullivan

Text Designer: Nancy Sabato

Cover Designer: Scott Russo

Cover Photo: George E. Joseph

Photo Researcher: Julie Tesser

Electronic Production Manager: Valerie Sawyer

Desktop Administrator: Jim Sullivan

Manufacturing Manager: Hilda Koparanian

Compositor: Pine Tree Composition Inc.

Printer and Binder: RR Donnelley & Sons Company

Cover Printer: The Lehigh Press, Inc.

For permission to use copyrighted material, grateful acknowledgment is made to the copyright holders on pp. 1075–1078, which are hereby made part of this copyright page.

Library of Congress Cataloging-in-Publication Data

Types of drama: plays and contexts/Sylvan Barnet . . . [et al.].—7th ed.
    p. cm.
  ISBN 0-673-52514-7
  1. Drama—Collections. 2. Drama—History and criticism.
I. Barnet, Sylvan.
PN6112.T96 1996
808.2—dc20   96-23983
                                             CIP

ISBN 0-673-52514-7
12345678910—DOW—99989796

CONTENTS

Contents

Contents

Contents

Contents

PART THREE *Writing 1037*

PREFACE

You need three things in the theater—the play, the actors, and the audience, and each must give something.

—*Kenneth Haigh (1958)*

Kenneth Haigh's statement is true. Most obviously this book gives the play—actually, 43 plays. In so far as it is possible, it also gives something of the play on the stage, since it includes 11 interviews with directors, ten reviews of productions, and numerous stage histories, all of which will give the reader a sense of the play in production. As for the third ingredient, the audience, that is where you come in. The spectator or reader, as Haigh suggests, by responding emotionally and intellectually helps to bring the play to life and indeed gives meaning to the play.

Types of Drama is divided into three parts. **Part One: Getting Started,** a quick introduction to the language of drama, moves from an examination of a play of only a few lines (the medieval *Whom Do You Seek?*) to brief discussions of basic matters such as audience awareness, plot, character, and theme. If we had to reduce all of this to a sentence, we might be tempted to quote one of Arthur Miller's remarks: "The structure of a play is always the story of how the birds come home to roost." Fortunately, however, we have space in our introductory remarks to offer a photo-essay, The Language of Drama, where we illustrate points about theaters and performance with photographs—and to invite students to test our assertions against two short plays, Susan Glaspell's *Trifles* and Lady Gregory's *Spreading the News.* Each of these plays is followed by Topics for Critical Thinking and Writing, a unit which itself is divided (like the Topics for all of the other plays in the book) into two segments, The Play on the Page and The Play on the Stage. Topics of the first sort usually concern matters of character and theme, whereas topics of the second sort usually invite students to

consider how to stage a particular scene, or ask students what gestures they might suggest actors use for particular speeches.

On the assumption that at this point most readers have read at least one short play and probably two, and have thought about specific dramatic issues and techniques, Part One next offers a review, In Brief: How to Read a Play. Then it goes on to sketch the chief traditional dramatic forms, tragedy, comedy, and tragicomedy. Because drama is not merely art but is also life—plays are supported by the public, and sometimes productions are subsidized by the government—we conclude with some questions concerning Drama and Society.

Part Two: A Collection of Plays is the heart of the book. The three short plays in Part One, with the editorial apparatus, were preliminary to the 40 plays of Part Two, ranging from plays from ancient Greece to the present. Of course (in Hamlet's words) "The play's the thing," but we also include a fair amount of pedagogical material. Of these 40 plays, 15 are pre-twentieth century (if we include Chekhov's *The Cherry Orchard,* which in fact was produced in 1903). Of the remaining 25, about a third (for instance *The Emperor Jones, The Glass Menagerie,* and *Death of a Salesman*) are classics from the middle of the twentieth century; almost all of the remaining plays are from the last three decades, with a strong representation of works by women and by minority authors (African-American, Asian-American, and Chicano).

Each play is preceded by a short biographical note and by an introductory commentary. The commentaries do not attempt to explicate the plays but they do contain, we think, useful and relevant points that will also be helpful with other plays. Thus, the introduction to *A Midsummer Night's Dream* includes a discussion of two traditions of comedy, "critical" comedy and "romantic" comedy, material that is also relevant to other plays in the book, including *The Misanthrope* and *Major Barbara*. Similarly, the commentary on *The Glass Menagerie* goes beyond the play by discussing presentational theater, a topic relevant to almost all drama before Ibsen and to a fair amount of contemporary drama. But even those commentaries that are sharply focused on a given play do not seek to utter the last word. On the contrary, they seek to provide material that will stimulate discussion in class or that may be the topic of a writing assignment. The Topics for Critical Thinking and Writing (divided, as we previously mentioned, into The Play on the Page and The Play on the Stage) are designed to assist readers to see the plays not only as literature but also as living theater—works written for the stage, or, if read, to be staged in the reader's mind.

To help readers to envision the plays on the stage, we include stage histories for most plays, ten reviews of productions, 13 discussions with directors (not only concerning productions of modern plays, such as the interviews with Jorge Huerta on Valdez's *Los Vendidos*, and with Tisa Chang and Kati Kuroda on Yamauchi's *And the Soul Shall Dance*, but also concerning productions of classical plays, such as interviews with directors who have staged Sophocles's *Oedipus* and Euripides's *Medea*). In Part Two we also include 15 discussions by playwrights, as well as four additional photoessays: Ancient Greek Drama Today, Staging Shakespeare Today, African Americans on the Stage, and Representations of Gender in the Theater. Further, Part Two includes, by way of theater history, A Note on the Greek Theater, A Note on Roman Drama, A Note on the Elizabethan Theater, A Note on the Development of the Seventeenth-Century Proscenium Theater, A Note on the Theater of the Absurd, A Note on Hispanic-American Theater, A Note on Asian-American Theater, and A Note on Women's Theater.

Part Three: Writing is devoted chiefly to writing about drama (it includes substantial advice on such matters as writing a review, finding a topic, organizing a comparison, providing documentation), but it also includes material on Writing Drama for classes in which students may be asked to write a scene or even a one-act play.

A glossary of more than two hundred dramatic terms—concludes the book. Though some of the definitions are brief, many are fairly long. Students and instructors have told us that the glossary can actually be read with interest, and that the definitions, far from perfunctory, are genuinely helpful.

New to the Seventh Edition

- **Expanded Coverage of Plays:** 43 plays are now included, 19 of which are new to this edition. The new plays are

Euripides, *Medea*; Anonymous, *Everyman*; Christopher Marlowe, *Doctor Faustus*; Aphra Behn, *The Rover*; August Strindberg, *Miss Julie*; Bernard Shaw, *Major Barbara*; Lady Gregory, *Spreading the News*; Alice Gerstenberg, *Overtones*; Eugene O'Neill, *The Emperor Jones*; Eugène Ionesco, *The Lesson*; Harold Pinter, *The Birthday Party*; Wole Soyinka, *The Strong Breed*; Adrienne Kennedy, *Funnyhouse of a Negro*; Carlos Morton, *The Many Deaths of Danny Rosales*; Wakako Yamauchi, *And the Soul Shall Dance*; Angela Jackson, *Shango Diaspora*; David Henry Hwang, *The Sound of a Voice*; David Mamet, *Oleanna*; and Timberlake Wertenbaker, *Our Country's Good*.

- **Increased coverage of Women and Contemporary Minority Authors:** The new selections increase the anthology's representation of contemporary plays, plays by women, and plays by African-American, Asian-American, and Chicano authors.

- **Perfomance Questions:** Topics for Critical Thinking and Writing include questions not only about the plays as literature (The Play on the Page) but also ask questions about the plays as they are performed (The Play on the Stage).

- **Comments by Playwrights:** In addition to remarks by Ibsen, Williams, Fugard, and Norman, there are now remarks by Harold Pinter, Eugène Ionesco, Carlos Morton, David Henry Hwang and David Mamet.

- **Discussions with Directors:** Thirteen new discussions with directors give readers first-hand views of the problems of staging not only contemporary plays but also classic plays ranging from Ancient Greece through the Middle Ages and Renaissance and on through Ibsen and Chekhov.

- **Reviews of Performance:** Eight reviews of contemporary productions of plays (from *Oedipus* and *Medea* to Adrienne Kennedy's *Funnyhouse of a Negro* and David Hwang's *The Sound of a Voice*) help students to think about the plays as works for performance.

- **Stage Histories:** Most plays are accompanied by stage histories that help students to see the plays as living theater, dynamic works that change in response to the views of each generation.

- **New Historical Notes:** Five brief essays (supplementing the essays on such topics as the origins of Greek drama and on the form of the Elizabethan playhouse) have been added—on Roman drama, the development of the proscenium stage, African-American theater, Hispanic-American theater, and women's theater.

- **Photo-Essays with Commentaries:** Five new photoessays, combining thought-provoking pictures with running commentaries, invite students to think about The Language of Drama, Ancient Greek Drama Today, Staging Shakespeare Today, African Americans on the Stage, and Representation of Gender in the Theater.

ACKNOWLEDGMENTS

We have been fortunate in getting permission to reprint important modern plays and distinguished translations of older plays; we are grateful to the authors, translators, and publishers who have cooperated. In preparing the seventh edition, we are grateful for the help we received from Charles Bachman, Buffalo State College; Leonard Berkman, Smith College; Oscar Brockett, University of Texas at Austin; Michael Cadden, Princeton University; Lou F. Caton, University of Oregon; Cynthia Clegg, Pepperdine University; Joseph J. DaCrema, Villanova University; Sherri R. Dienstfrey, Idaho State University; Anthony Graham-White, University of Illinois at Chicago; Shannon M. McGuire, Louisiana State University; Michael McVey, Miami University Middletown; Thomas J. Manning, University of Wisconsin-Oshkosh; Tim Martin, Rutgers University; Susan Vaneta Mason, California State University-Los Angeles; and Paul Wood, Villanova University.

We are also grateful to the many teachers who have given advice over the years: Jacob Adler, Purdue University; Joanne Altieri, University of Washington; David Boudreaux, Nicholls State University; Terry Browne, State University of New York, Geneseo; Leslie Phillips Butterworth, Holyoke Community College; Victor Cahn, Skidmore College; Kenneth Campbell, Virginia Commonwealth University; Douglas Cole, Northwestern University; Dorothy Crook, Central Connecticut State University; Charles L. Darn, University of Pittsburgh at Johnstown; E. T. A. Davidson, State University of New York/Oneonta; Cheryl Faraone, State University of New York, Geneseo; Jeanne Fosket, El Paso Community College; John C. Freeman, El Paso Community College; Catherine Gannon, California State University at San Bernardino; Russell Goldfarb, Western Michigan University; Charlotte Goodman, Skidmore College; John Gronbeck-Tedesco, University of Kansas; Virginia Hale, University of Hartford; Elsie Galbreath Haley, Metropolitan State College/Denver; Thomas Hatton, Southern Illinois University, Carbondale; JoAnn Holonbek, College of St. Catherine; Richard Homan, Rider College; Kathleen Klein, Southern Connecticut State University; Thomas Kranidas, State University of New York/Stony Brook; Jayne Lewis, University of California at Los Angeles; Helen Lojek, Boise State University; Mary J. McCue, College of San Mateo; Grace McLaughlin, Portland Community College; Don Moore, Louisiana State University; Lee Orchard, Northeast Missouri State University; John B. Pieters, University of Florida; Paige Price, University of Oregon; George Ray, Washington and Lee University; Bruce Robbins, Boise State University; Eric Rothstein, University of Wisconsin; Beverly Simpson, Ball State University; Gail Salo, George Mason University; David K. Sauer, Spring Hill College; Myron Simon, University of California at Irvine; Jyotsna Singh, Southern Methodist University; Keith Slocum, Montclair State College; Iris Smith, University of Kansas; Lucille Stelling, Normandale Community College; Edna M. Troiano, Charles County Community College; Robert L. Vales, Gannon University; Charles Watson, Jr., Syracuse University; and Bruce E. Woodruff, Baker University.

We also gladly acknowledge our debts to Jeanne Newlin, formerly of the Harvard Theatre Collection; Arthur Friedman, University of Lowell; Lydia Forbes, Blackburn College; Roy Graham, Blackburn College; Dan McCandless; Laurence Senelick, Tufts University; Marcia Stubbs, formerly of Wellesley College; and, at Longman, Katharine Glynn, Lynn Huddon, Lisa Moore, and Julie Tesser, all of whom made invaluable suggestions and offered support when we needed it. We wish every author such editorial assistance. Lois Lombardo effectively presided over the process of converting a manuscript into a book and Meghan Shumacher equally effectively handled the difficult job of obtaining permission for copyrighted material.

SYLVAN BARNET
MORTON BERMAN
WILLIAM BURTO
REN DRAYA

TYPES of DRAMA

PART ONE

Getting Started

WHAT IS DRAMA?

Few books on drama fail to tell the reader that *drama* comes from a Greek word meaning "a deed," and that the Greek noun itself comes from a verb, *dran,* "to do." The idea is that a drama shows something in the doing, something being done. Drama is not simply the presentation of interesting characters (Macbeth and Lady Macbeth), or a matter of preaching interesting ideas (it doesn't pay to kill a king); rather, it is the presentation of human beings engaged in action.

How is this action presented? Although a play usually tells a story, "the medium of drama," as Ezra Pound observed, "is not words, but persons moving about on a stage using words." An equally brief statement about the essence of drama is Lope de Vega's assertion (made some four hundred years ago) that the essence of drama consists of three boards, two actors, and a passion—that is, a *place* (a playing-space, three boards) where *impersonators* (two actors) engage in a *conflict* (passion). The place may be a permanent theater-building, or it may be a street corner or a flat-top truck; the impersonators may be highly paid professionals, or they may be inexperienced amateurs; the conflict may be a trivial dispute over whose dog did what, and where, or it may be a matter of life and death. When thinking about even the most sophisticated plays, it's not a bad idea to recall from time to time the statements of Pound and Lope de Vega.

A play is written to be seen and to be heard, not just to be read. We go to *see* a play in a theater (*theater* is derived from a Greek word meaning "to watch"), but in the theater we also *hear* it, thus becoming an audience (*audience* is derived from a Latin word meaning "to hear"). Hamlet was speaking the ordinary language of his day when he said, "We'll hear a play tomorrow." When we read a play rather than see and hear it in a theater, we see it in the mind's eye (Hamlet's words), and we hear it in the mind's ear.

In reading a play it's not enough mentally to hear the lines. We must try to see the characters, costumed and moving within a specified setting; costumes, sets, and gestures are parts of the language of drama. When we are in the theater, our job is much easier, of course; we have only to pay attention to the performers. But when we are readers, we must do what we can to perform the play in the theater under our hat.

A MEDIEVAL EXAMPLE OF DRAMA: "WHOM DO YOU SEEK?"

Let's look at a tiny example of early European drama—but first, a tiny bit of history. Although the ancient Greeks and Romans had developed drama to a high art, the early Christians opposed dramatic spectacles, partly because such spectacles included gladiatorial contests and naked dancing. After the Roman emperors made Christianity the official state religion, and after Rome was sacked by the Visigoths in A.D. 410, public acting was prohibited; and by the sixth century, drama had virtually disappeared from Europe, except for such rudimentary entertainments as puppet shows, minstrelsy, and acrobatics. Yet, amazingly, the drama was reborn within the church itself.

The New Testament reports that when women went to the tomb of the crucified Jesus in order to anoint the body, they found an angel, who told them that Jesus had risen from the tomb. Drawing on this narrative (chiefly Matthew 28.1–7 and Mark 16.1–8), the Church by the ninth century had developed an introductory text for the Mass on Easter Sunday morning, the anniversary of the Resurrection from the Dead of the Crucified Christ. The Latin words were chanted antiphonally, that is, with one voice or group of voices answering another. In translation the words go thus:

FIRST VOICE. Whom do you seek in the tomb?
SECOND VOICE. Jesus of Nazareth.
FIRST VOICE. He is not here; he is risen as predicted when it was prophesied that he would rise from the dead.
SECOND VOICE. Alleluia! The Lord is risen!
ALL VOICES. Come and see the place.

Now suppose we take the lines of the First Voice, and we let them be sung by a priest who represents an angel in the tomb—itself represented by the altar-table—and we take the lines of the Second Voice and we let them be sung by three priests who represent the three Marys—the three women who, according to tradition, visited the tomb in order to anoint the corpse. Exactly such a development took place in the tenth century. In a document of about 970, Ethelwold, Bishop of Winchester, England, provides dialogue and stage directions for a miniature play to be performed by priests. What follows is a translation of Ethelwold's Latin account of the work known by its first words, *Quem Quaeritis* ("Whom do you seek?").

Anonymous

WHOM DO YOU SEEK? (QUEM QUAERITIS)

While the third lesson is being chanted, let four brethren dress themselves. Let one of these, dressed in a white robe, enter as though to take part in the service, and let him go to the tomb without attracting attention and sit there quietly with a palm in his hand. While the third response is chanted, let the remaining three follow, and let them all, dressed in capes, bearing in their hand incense containers and stepping delicately as if seeking something, approach the tomb.

These things are done in imitation of the angel sitting on the tomb and the women with spices coming to anoint the body of Jesus. When, therefore, the seated one beholds the three approach him like wanderers who seek something, let him begin to sing in a sweet and moderate voice.

Whom do you seek in the tomb, O followers of Christ?

And when he has sung it to the end, let the three reply in unison:

Jesus of Nazareth who was crucified, O celestial one!

So he:

He is not here, He has risen as He foretold.
Go, announce that He is risen from the dead.

At the word of this bidding let those three turn to the choir and say:

Alleluia! The Lord is risen today,
The strong lion, Christ the Son of God! Unto God give
   thanks, eia!

This said, let the one, still sitting there and as if recalling them, say the anthem:

Come, and see the place where the Lord was laid,
Alleluia! Alleluia!

And saying this, let him rise, and lift the veil, and show them the place bare of the cross, but only the cloths laid there in which the cross was wrapped:

Go quickly, and tell the disciples that the Lord is risen.
Alleluia! Alleluia!

And when they have seen this, let them set down the incense containers which they bear in that same tomb, and take the cloth, and hold it up in the face of the clergy, and as if to demonstrate that the Lord has risen and is no longer wrapped therein, let them sing the anthem:

The Lord is risen from the tomb,
Who for us was hanged on the cross, alleluia!

and lay the cloth upon the altar. When the anthem is done, let the prior, sharing in their gladness at the triumph of Our King, in that, having vanquished death, He rose again, begin the hymn "We praise you, Lord." And this begun, all the bells chime out together.

All the elements of a play are here: an **imitation** by actors (here, priests) of an **action.** By "action" we do not mean the physical movements of the characters, but a story, a happening, in this case a story of characters moving from doubt to joyful certainty. Normally the action of a play includes a conflict; here we might say that the conflict is between the uncertainty and presumably the sorrow of the women, and the knowledge and joy of the angel. We can say, too, that the angel wins the women over to his side.

The dialogue of course is essential, but notice that the imitation is aided by scenery ("the place bare of the cross"), hand properties (incense vessels, representing the spices that the women brought to the tomb, and also the angel's palm branch), costumes (a white garment for the priest who plays the angel, and copes—capelike garments—for the priests who play the women), and gestures ("stepping delicately as if seeking something"). Even sound effects are used: "All the bells chime out together."[1]

---

[1] *Quem Quaeritis* is available on a videocassette, in *Early English Drama*, in the History of Drama series issued by Films for the Humanities and Sciences, Inc., Box 2053, Princeton, N.J. (telephone 1-800-257-5126)

MISTAKES, CONFLICTS, AND AUDIENCE-AWARENESS

MISTAKES AND CONFLICTS

If drama is the imitation of an action, an imitation of a happening, will any sort of happening do? Perhaps. Drama is so immensely varied that one is tempted to say there is no such thing as drama, only dramatists who produce dramas, plays of all sorts. Still, one notices a dominant pattern—or at least W. H. Auden, poet, librettist, and critic noticed a pattern.

> Drama is based on the Mistake. I think someone is my friend when he really is my enemy, that I am free to marry a woman when in fact she is my mother, that this person is a chambermaid when it is a young nobleman in disguise, that this well-dressed young man is rich when he is really a penniless adventurer, or that if I do this such and such a result will follow when in fact it results in something very different. All good drama has two movements, first the making of the mistake, then the discovery that it was a mistake.
>
> "NOTES ON MUSIC AND OPERA" IN *THE DYER'S HAND*
> (1962)

If we think back to "Whom Do You Seek?" we see that the three "women with spices coming to anoint the body of Jesus" are making a mistake, and as the little play progresses they discover that mistake.

The conflict is scarcely visible, but it is nevertheless present. The women have come to the tomb to anoint the body of Jesus, but instead of finding the body they find an angel. The conflict, we can say, is between the mistaken quest of the women and the knowledge of the angel.

AUDIENCE-AWARENESS

The audience of "Whom Do You Seek?" of course knows how the story will turn out. There is nothing of the suspense that we find in a mystery novel, or in a soap opera. If there is any suspense, the audience wonders not what the outcome will be, but exactly what words will be uttered—exactly what the three women will say when they are given the good news.

Obviously if you are attending a classic play, perhaps *Romeo and Juliet,* you almost surely know what mistakes are made, what conflicts are set into motion, and how it all turns out. The audience knows—but Romeo does not—that Juliet is not dead but merely asleep; the audience knows—but Macbeth does not—that by murdering King Duncan he will lose rather than gain; the audience knows—but the young lovers in *A Midsummer Night's Dream* do not—that at the end of the play, all of the competing lovers will be properly paired. Much of our pleasure, in fact, results from our superior knowledge; we see characters engaging in certain actions that we know are mistaken, and a sort of conflict is set up between us and the characters, especially between the characters with whom we most sympathize, and to whom we feel like saying, "No, no, no, don't do that; can't you see that is exactly the wrong thing to do?"

But even if you do not already know the end of the play, you may find yourself engaged in this sort of sympathetic conflict with the characters. How can this be? Easy; most dramatists—putting aside those who write plays that are essentially detective stories—usually let the audience in on facts that some of the characters do not learn until later. Later in this chapter you will read Lady Gregory's *Spreading the News* (page 25), a play based on a misunderstanding. A woman who is hard of hearing misunderstands, and innocently gives a false report, and the whole comedy depends on the audience's realization that all of the passion that the various characters express—there is shocked talk of adultery and murder—is based on a mistake. Of course Lady Gregory *could* have kept us in the dark, *could* have written a play in which we learn, at the end, that the reports of adultery and murder are unfounded, but that would be an entirely different play, and doubtless not a funny one.

PLOT, CHARACTER, THEME

Although **plot** is sometimes equated with the gist of the narrative—the story—it is sometimes reserved to denote the writer's *arrangement* of the happenings in the story. Thus, if in Lady Gregory's *Spreading the News* we learned at the end (instead of at the beginning) how the misunderstanding came about, the play would have a different plot from the play that she actually wrote, even though the basic story is the same. Similarly, all plays about the assassination of Julius Caesar have pretty much the same story, but by beginning with a scene of workmen enjoying a holiday (and thereby introducing the motif of the fickleness of the mob), Shakespeare's *Julius Caesar* has a plot different from a play that omits such a scene.

Handbooks on the drama often suggest that a plot (arrangement of happenings) should have a rising action, a climax, and a falling action. This sort of plot can be diagramed as a pyramid, the tension rising through complications, or crises, to a climax, at which point the fate of the protagonist (chief character) is firmly established; the climax is the apex, and the tension allegedly slackens as we witness the dénouement (unknotting). Shakespeare sometimes used a pyramidal structure, placing his climax neatly in the middle of what seems to us to be the third of five acts.[1] Roughly the first half of *Julius Caesar* shows Brutus rising, reaching his height in 3.1 with the death of Caesar; but later in this scene he gives Marc Antony permission to speak at Caesar's funeral and thus he sets in motion his own fall, which occupies the second half of the play. In *Macbeth*, the protagonist attains his height in 3.1 ("Thou hast it now: King"), but he soon perceives that he is going downhill:

> I am in blood
> Stepped in so far, that, should I wade no more,
> Returning were as tedious as go o'er.

Of course, no law demands such a structure, and a hunt for the pyramid usually causes the hunter to overlook all the crises but the middle one. William Butler Yeats once suggestively diagramed a good plot not as a pyramid but as a line moving diagonally upward, punctuated by several crises. Perhaps it is sufficient to say that a good plot has its moments of tension, but the location of these will vary with the play. They are the product of **conflict,** but not all conflict produces tension; there is conflict but little tension in a baseball game when the score is 10–0 in the ninth inning with two out and no one on base.

Regardless of how a plot is diagramed, the **exposition** is the part that tells the audience what it has to know about the past, the antecedent action. That is, the exposition tells the audience what the present situation is. When the three Marys say they are seeking Jesus "who was crucified," they are offering exposition, filling us in on what has already happened. In later plays, when two gossiping servants tell each other that after a year away in Paris the young master is coming home tomorrow with a new wife, they are giving the audience the exposition by introducing characters and defining relationships.

The Elizabethans and the Greeks sometimes tossed out all pretense at dialogue and began with a **prologue,** like the one spoken by the Chorus at the outset of *Romeo and Juliet*:

> Two households, both alike in dignity
>   In fair Verona, where we lay our scene.
> From ancient grudge break to new mutiny,
>   Where civil blood makes civil hands unclean.
> From forth the fatal loins of these two foes
>   A pair of star-crossed lovers take their life. . . .

And in Tennessee Williams's *The Glass Menagerie*, Tom's first speech is a sort of prologue. However, the exposition also may extend far into the play, so that the audience keeps getting bits of information that clarify the present and build suspense about the future.

Character has two meanings: someone who appears in a play (for instance, Juliet), and second, the intellectual, emotional, and moral qualities that add up to a personality (as when we say that Juliet's character is more complex than Romeo's).

When dramatic characters speak, they are doing at least two things: they are revealing themselves (if they are speaking deceitfully to their hearers, they are revealing themselves as deceivers to us), and they are also *doing things to other characters*, evoking from these characters agreement, anger, amusement, or whatever. **Dialogue,** then, is a form of action; when characters speak, they are bombarding other characters, who in turn reply and further advance the plot, perhaps by heightening the conflict.

One character may be in conflict either with another character or with a group of characters. In Susan Glaspell's *Trifles*, for instance, there is at first a subdued conflict between Mrs. Peters and Mrs. Hale (Mrs. Peters is stronger

---

[1]An **act** is a main division in a drama or opera. Act divisions probably stem from Roman theory and derive ultimately from the Greek practice of separating episodes in a play by choral interludes, but Greek (and probably Roman) plays were performed without interruption, for the choral interludes were part of the plays themselves. Elizabethan plays, too, may have been performed without breaks; the division of Elizabethan plays into five acts is usually the work of editors rather than of authors. Frequently an act division today (commonly indicated by lowering the curtain and turning up the houselights) denotes change in locale and lapse of time. A **scene** is a smaller unit, either (1) a division with no change of locale or abrupt shift of time, or (2) a division consisting of an actor or group of actors on the stage; according to the second definition, the departure or entrance of an actor changes the composition of the group and thus introduces a new scene. (In an entirely different sense, the scene is the locale where a work is set.)

on the idea of dutifully following the law than Mrs. Hale is), but later the two women join forces in a conflict with the men. Each woman is a **foil** to the other, that is, a contrasting figure, one who helps to set off or define another figure.

Finally, one may ask, What does a play add up to? What is the underlying **theme,** or meaning, of a play? Some critics, arguing that the concept of theme is meaningless, hold that any play gives us only an extremely detailed history of some imaginary people. But surely this view is desperate. Dramatists may begin by being fascinated by a particular character or by some particular happening (real or imagined), but as they work on their play they see to it that the characters and the plot add up to something. (A *plot* is what happens; a *theme* is what the happenings add up to.) *Quem Quaeritis*, for

the believer, is about the conquest of death through the sacrifice of Jesus; *Trifles* is (at least in part) about a patriarchal society that foolishly underestimates the intelligence and resourcefulness of women. To the reply that the theme, when stated, is usually banal, we can counter that the plays present these ideas in such a way that they take on life and become a part of us. And surely we are in no danger of equating the play with the theme that we sense underlies it. We never believe that our rough statement of the theme is really the equivalent of the play itself. The play, we recognize, presents the theme with such detail that our statement of the theme is only a wedge that helps us to enter the play so we may more fully (in Henry James's words) "appropriate it."

The Language of Drama

PLAYING-SPACES

Plays are meant to be seen (*theatre* is from a Greek word meaning "seeing-place") and heard (*audience* is from a Latin word connected with "to hear"). In all probability, however, if you are taking a course in drama, you will read more plays than you will see and hear. Still, when you read you will doubtless make an effort to experience the plays in the theater of your mind. This means that you will sometimes imagine the plays in the context of the distinctive theaters for which they were written. And you will (again, at least sometimes) keep in mind the dramatists' stage directions, which may describe the sets, costumes, gestures, and perhaps sound effects and lighting. Further, you will try to imagine the gestures and movements that are called for by the dialogue even if they are not specified in stage directions.

Let's look at some pictures and try to see how they clarify our experience of drama. We will begin with some playing-spaces, since the space helps to shape the kind of play performed and also the spectator's response. The audience in an ancient Greek theater (pages 12 and 46, top), sitting on a hillside and looking down on the actors, had a somewhat godlike perspective: above were the heavens; behind the actors was a facade that resembled a temple or a palace; the plot concerned the actions of legendary figures (heroes, heroines), who played their parts in a world in which the gods intervened. And since the dramas were presented at fixed times at publicly supported dramatic festivals, the experience was communal; a relatively homogeneous audience (Athenian citizens—in fact, possibly only Athenian male citizens) heard again the great stories that were part of their heritage.

The Greek theater offered three levels for performers. On the ground level was the orchestra (literally, "dance place"), where the chorus—usually representing ordinary citizens—danced. At the rear of the orchestra, on a slightly elevated stage, (there is some argument about the date when the stage was elevated above the orchestra) the actors performed with the *skene* or "scene-building" as a background. The third performing level was the roof of the *skene;* a human being might appear here, such as a watch-man, but chiefly the roof was used to represent the realm of the gods.

Elizabethan theaters (pages 12 and 186), like Greek theaters, were open to the sky. More precisely, the so-called public theaters were essentially unroofed but a canopy, called "the heaven," extended over part of the stage. (The canopy, whose underside was decorated with symbols of the zodiac, rested on two pillars that themselves rested on the stage.) Further, there were also smaller indoor theaters, customarily called "private" theaters, and plays were sometimes done at court in improvised theaters. For the most part, however, the plays of Shakespeare and his colleagues were written for theaters like the Globe—Shakespeare's theater—and the Swan, illustrated on page 12, left.

Although the Elizabethan theater, like the Greek theater, lacked a curtain at the front and therefore could not suddenly reveal elaborate settings, "discoveries" could be made by withdrawing a curtain from a doorway or perhaps from a small alcove at the back of the stage. And the architecture of the stage itself provided a degree of spectacle. Contemporary references indicate that the building itself was handsome, even splendid, and the performers thus moved against a fairly elaborate architectural background. When the Elizabethan Hamlet spoke of "this goodly frame, the earth," he moved against a sturdy and attractive background, and when (referring to the heavens) he spoke of "this majestical roof, fretted [i.e., adorned] with golden fire," he probably looked up and gestured toward the underside of the canopy. In many other scenes, spectacle was provided by colorful costumes and banners.

Further, the theater offered several levels for performers. The stage, jutting into the audience, served for most of the action, but windows above the stage could serve as Juliet's balcony in the famous scene with Romeo, or as the top of the city walls, from which residents might look down on a besieging army, or as the rigging of a ship, from which sailors would shout to those on deck below (i.e., on the main stage). In addition to the playing-spaces above the stage, there was a level below the stage called the cellarage or hell, reached by trap doors. Probably when Hamlet leaped into the grave he leapt through a trap door, and quite possibly when a ghost or devil appeared on the main stage, it entered from a trap. The illustration from Marlowe's *Doctor Faustus* (page 12, right) cannot be regarded as an accurate picture of an Elizabethan stage, but it does give a good idea of how Faustus might have been costumed, and the emerging dragon-devil may well reflect theatrical practice.

SETS

A proscenium theater (page 13, top) is a theater with a sort of picture frame separating the actors from the audience (in contrast to the theater with a thrust stage, such as the Elizabethan theater). It developed in Italy in the mid-sixteenth century and reached France and England in the next century. A proscenium stage can easily be equipped with a front curtain which can be raised to reveal actors in an elaborate setting. Further, these theaters used scenery painted on flats that ran in grooves across the breadth of the stage; the flats could be pulled off to the sides, thereby revealing another scene. Thus, the raising of the curtain revealed the performers in the first scene, who were backed by flats extending across the width of the stage; the withdrawal of the flats might reveal a second scene, and so on for a third or even a fourth scene. (For additional details, see page 322.)

The proscenium theater lends itself to the box set, which is essentially a room constructed out of flats (often equipped with working doors and sometimes windows), but with the front wall missing so the audience can see what goes on within the room. The box set, with its realistic furnishings, dominated later nineteenth-century European and American theater; it is the set in which, for instance, the plays of Ibsen and Chekhov were performed. The idea was to offer a close imitation of reality (page 13, bottom, shows a 1976 version, for Ibsen's *A Doll's House*). But the theater—any theater—is essentially a place for symbolic action, and we can now see that even a realistic set of this sort can be symbolic. For instance, it may use overstuffed furniture, heavy drapes, and moralizing paintings on the walls to symbolize the crushing bourgeois life that the characters live.

Some sets use what has been called selective realism. A famous example is Jo Mielziner's set for the original pro-duction (1947) of *Death of a Salesman* (page 14, top). The bed, the refrigerator, the chairs—all of these are just what we might find in a house of the period—but the roof of the house is indicated by a skeletallike structure. The set helps to convey both the commonplace yet oppressive world that the characters move in, and it is also suited, by its unreal aspects, to occasional scenes with flashbacks and fantasies.

The appearance of a set may have no connection, or almost no connection, with the way reality appears to our eye. Rather, it may represent a character's state of mind. For instance, Hamlet lives in a castle, but he finds not splendor but oppressiveness ("Denmark's a prison"). Hamlet's *sense of reality*, rather than optical reality, may be communicated by using a set that resembles a prison more than a palace, or for that matter by nothing much more than some clanking chains and clanging metal plates.

The director Peter Brook, wishing to convey the emptiness of the world of *King Lear*, used a set that consisted chiefly of rudimentary rather than regal furniture and large metal thunder sheets, which provided the noise of the storm but which also served to symbolize or express (rather than to imitate visually) a primitive, elemental world (see page 225). Similarly, although in Eugene O'Neill's *The Emperor Jones* the opening scene in the palace is usually represented realistically, with a throne, a red carpet, and so forth, the scenes in the jungle are represented symbolically, conveying Jones's sensations or experiences or ancient memories rather than what a dispassionate observer would actually see.

The *lighting* of course is part of the set. Here is part of the beginning stage direction in Arthur Miller's *Death of a Salesman:*

> Before us is the Salesman's house. We are aware of towering, angular shapes behind it, surrounding it on all sides. Only the blue light of the sky falls upon the house and forestage; the surrounding area shows an angry glow of orange.

Miller's lighting, especially the "angry glow of orange," is part of what we can call the language of the play. Tennessee Williams uses lighting in a similar way in *The Glass Menagerie;* while two characters quarrel, the stage "is lit with a turgid smoky red glow." These examples of symbolic lighting are obvious; less obvious are passages that at first glance seem merely naturalistic but, in fact, are also symbolic. In *A Doll's House,* as Nora's terror grows in the second act, Ibsen tells us in a brief but important stage direction, "It begins to grow dark."

Let's push the term "set" a bit far, so that we can include sound effects. After all, if a forest is part of the set, why not the sounds of the forest—whether the cheery twittering of birds or the menacing howl of the wind. In *Death of a Salesman,* before the curtain goes up, "A melody is heard, played upon a flute. It is small and fine, telling of grass and trees and the horizon." Then the curtain rises, revealing the Salesman's house, with "towering, angular shapes behind it, surrounding it on all sides." Obviously, the sound of the flute is meant to tell us about the world from which the Salesman is shut off. In *Quem Quaeritis* (page 4), the bells at the end help to communicate the joy and harmony of the action that the play sets forth.

A sound effect, however, need not be so evidently symbolic to be important. In Glaspell's *Trifles,* almost at the very end of the play we hear the "sound of a knob turning in the other room" (page 23). The sound has an electrifying effect on the audience, as it does on the two women on the stage, and it precedes a decisive action.

PERFORMERS

In the Western theater, the performers now are almost always human beings, but puppet drama has been popular in much of the world and is still esteemed in some cultures, especially in Asia. In Japan, for instance, *bunraku* uses large puppets manipulated by a principal puppeteer and two hooded assistants, who are clothed in black and regarded as invisible (page 14, middle). Outside of Asia, puppets or marionettes are rarely used today, except in entertainment for children.

But puppets and marionettes can still be used effectively, even in Western drama intended for adults. John Barton, in his 1974 production of Christopher Marlowe's *Doctor Faustus,* used two puppets—manipulated by Faustus—to represent the Good Angel and the Bad Angel (page 14, bottom). Doubtless, in Marlowe's day, two actors performed these roles, but since the characters represent (roughly speaking) Faustus's divided consciousness, it was effective to have Faustus manipulate the puppets that represented his conflicting thoughts.

Turning to human performers, we find that the use of females to play female roles is a relatively modern Western practice; in fact, it still is not the custom in Asia, where specially trained males perform the female roles in traditional drama—for instance in the Japanese No plays and Kabuki plays. Exactly *why* men have played women's roles is uncertain, but it may be related to the drama's roots in religious rituals. Although priestesses are important in many religions, some kinds of rites are off-limits to women, and it seems that males impersonated females in certain dealings with the gods. In any case, in Greece all of the performers were male, with masks making impersonation relatively easy. What is perhaps more surprising is that in medieval Christian drama—plays dramatizing biblical episodes—males took female roles, despite the injunction in the Hebrew Bible (Deuteronomy 22.5) against cross-dressing. (We have already seen, in *Quem Quaeritis* on page 4, that three priests impersonated the women who visited the tomb where they expected to find Jesus.) In the Elizabethan and Jacobean periods (the second half of the sixteenth century and the first half of the seventeenth century) highly trained boys between the ages of approximately ten and thirteen played the female roles—for instance Juliet, Lady Macbeth, and Lear's three daughters. Although the English public of the period did occasionally see actresses in visiting French companies, the English stage did not routinely use actresses until 1660, when the theaters, which had been closed for almost two decades under Puritan rule, reopened.

We have almost no evidence about how early audiences reacted to boys or men playing the parts of women. The very few extant remarks from Shakespeare's day concerning boy actors uniformly praise the boys for their skill. *Possibly* there was some sniggering, some nudging with elbows, at the sight of a hero passionately addressing a boy dressed as a girl, but if we think that this *must* have been the reaction, we may simply be imposing our ideas on earlier centuries. Probably the convention of males playing female roles was so deeply entrenched that it was not thought about—just as we do not think about the music that accompanies the action in a movie. When you think about it, music accompanying lovers walking through a field, or soldiers dying in battle, is utterly unnatural, but no one bats an eyelash. On the other hand, we know for certain that in the past when a woman played a young romantic male role—what is called a breeches part—the audience was conscious of and titillated by the cross-dressing. In ages when women wore long dresses, male attire was a way for a female performer to reveal her legs. Today the chief breeches part is Peter Pan, though occasionally women play the male roles of Ariel (in Shakespeare's *The Tempest*), Puck (in *A Midsummer Night's Dream*), and the Fool in *King Lear*.

Having so completely accepted the idea that the actor's gender determines the available roles, we read with incredulity that Sarah Bernhardt in the late nineteenth century played Hamlet. It sounds eccentric, unnatural, a bad idea. The chief exceptions have been in farce, where it is considered hilarious for a man to disguise himself as a woman and to camp it up.

Today, however, chiefly under the stimulus of the Woman's Movement and gay Liberation, gender-bending in serious drama is very much in style. A recent production of *Everyman,* for instance, cast women in the title role and in the role of Death (page 15, top left). The practice of casting against gender—having a woman play Everyman or Lear—is said to stimulate an inquiry into gender identity, making us see the plays and ourselves in a new light. (The point is briefly discussed on page 225, in connection with a production of *Lear*.)

A related issue is casting against race. How do we feel about a black actor or an Asian actor playing Lear, with three white daughters? Does it bother some or all of us? If it bothers us, *why* does it bother us? Because of the lack of verisimilitude? Or because it touches some racist notion, a notion we do not wish to acknowledge? If it does bother some of us, is this perhaps a good thing, a means of jolting us out of our accustomed ways of thinking?

COSTUMES AND GESTURES

The performers, whether puppets or human, whether male or female, are costumed, and their costumes (like our own clothes) say something. When we wear jeans, a necktie, or running shoes, we are making statements about who we are—or who we want to be. Our clothes help us to create the role of student, professor, artist, police officer, chef, or lifeguard. Hamlet's "inky cloak" tells the viewers that he is in mourning, and—by its contrast with the colorful clothes that the other courtiers are wearing—it tells us that he remembers the death of his father in a way that no one else does. A change of costume is usually highly significant. In *Everyman* (page 169), near the beginning of the play we learn that the worldly Everyman is gaily dressed, a sign of his preoccupation with material things. Later in the play, when he has seen the folly of his ways, he puts off this worldly garment and dons "a garment of sorrow," perhaps a

hair shirt. Neither garment is clearly described, but surely the change in garments symbolizes Everyman's spiritual development.

Or consider Nora Helmer's changes of costume in Ibsen's *A Doll's House.* In the first act, she wears ordinary clothing, presumably appropriate to a middle-class housewife, but in the middle of the second act, when she frantically rehearses her tarantella, a wild dance, she wears "a long, many-colored shawl." The shawl is appropriate to the Italian dance, but its multitude of colors also helps express Nora's conflicting emotions. Her extreme agitation is expressed, too, in the fact that "her hair comes loose and falls down over her shoulders," but "She doesn't notice." The shawl and her disheveled hair, then, *speak* to us as clearly as the dialogue does. In the middle of the third act, after the party and just before the showdown, Nora appears in her "Italian costume," and, her husband, Torvald, wears "evening dress" under an open black cloak. She is dressed for a masquerade (her whole life has been a masquerade, it turns out), and Torvald's formal suit and black cloak help express the stiffness and the blight that have forced her to present a false front throughout their years of marriage. (For an extremely expressive image of Torvald costumed as a Draculalike destructive being, see page 15, center.) A little later, Nora appears "in an everyday dress." The pretense is over. When she finally leaves the stage—leaves the house—she "Wraps her shawl around her." This is not the "many-colored shawl" she used in rehearsing the dance, but the "big, black shawl" she wears when she returns from the dance. The blackness of this shawl helps express the death of the old way of life.

Gestures, too, are part of the language of life, as well as of drama. Every day, in the course of countless conversations, we shrug, lean forward or draw back, thrust our hands into our pockets, cross our legs, nod or shake our heads, and engage in hundred of little actions that reveal our states of mind. And so do characters in plays. A photo on page 15 shows a young con man, in Carlos Morton's *The Many Deaths of Danny Rosales* (page 811), trying to talk his way out of trouble with the sheriff. His too eager gestures and his too engaging smile almost show that he is lying, and the sheriff's uptight posture clearly shows that he is not buying what the speaker is selling.

When we read a play can we fully envision it as though it is being performed on a stage? Of course not. But we must try, at least occasionally, to think about how we might perform a particular speech, or how we might stage a scene. In short, we must try to see and hear the play in what Shakespeare called "the mind's eye," and (to continue quoting Shakespeare) when we read what is nothing more than ink on paper, we must "give to airy nothings a local habitation."

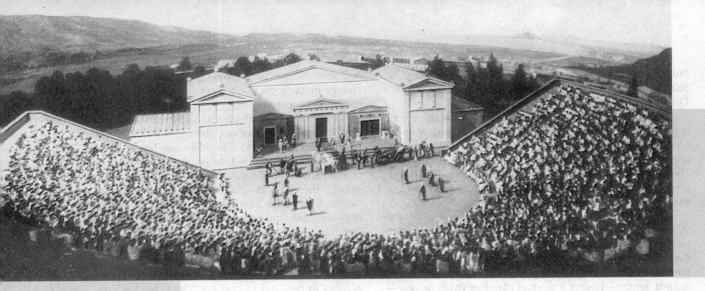

▲ This modern reconstruction of an ancient Greek theater in Athens gives a sense of the original circumstances: The audience sat on a hillside, looking down at a circular dancing place, behind which was an area where actors performed. A stone building behind the performers provided a background—its templelike or palatial facade probably implied a world governed by divine law—and it also provided a means of entering and exiting the stage. See also pages 44–46.

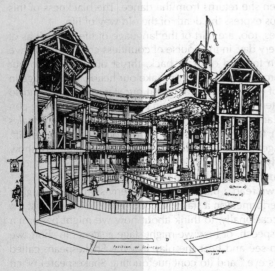

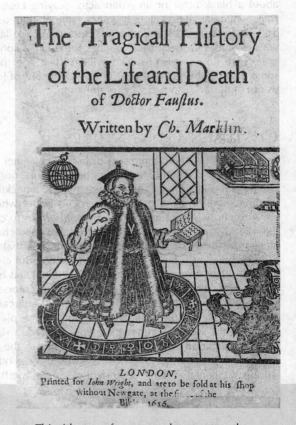

▲ This modern sketch shows what an Elizabethan theater probably looked like. The stage is a "thrust stage," jutting out into the space where the audience stands (spectators who paid an extra fee sat in the galleries). Performers chiefly used this stage, but they might also appear at higher levels, and might use a trap door for a descent to the underworld. The contract for one theater of the period specifies that the stage is to be twenty-seven and one-half feet deep and forty-three feet wide.

▲ This title page from an early seventeenth-century edition of Marlowe's play *Doctor Faustus* shows us how the title character (here conjuring up a devil) may have been costumed. In the theater, the devil probably rose through a trap door.

12

◀ The Farnese Theater, completed in 1618, uses a proscenium arch. With such a stage, elaborate sets could be revealed when a front curtain was raised, or when flats extending across the breadth of the stage were pulled to the right and left. Compared with the Elizabethan theater, which used a stage extending into the audience, this theater markedly separates the audience from the actors.

The proscenium stage is the stage that most of us are most familiar with. The theater consists of two boxes, one for the actors and one for the audience. The actors perform in their box, illuminated and separated from the audience by a frame, and the audience sits in a darkened box of its own.

A 1976 production of Ibsen's *A Doll's House* used a markedly realistic box set. But notice the doll: On a realistic level the doll is a child's toy, but in this context it is symbolic of Nora and perhaps of Torvald. ▼

Jo Mielziner's set for Arthur Miller's *Death of a Salesman* combines realism (the beds) with abstraction or highly conventional scenery (the roof). It is admirably suited to a play that is chiefly realistic but that also uses flashbacks and haunting memories. ▶

◀ The scene is from a famous *bunraku* (puppet) play, *The Double Suicide,* by Chikamatsu Monzaemon, one of Japan's greatest writers. The principal puppeteer (at the left) and his two hooded assistants are considered invisible. In Asia puppet drama is taken seriously by adults.

In John Barton's 1974 production of Marlowe's *Doctor Faustus,* the Good Angel and the Bad Angel, representing Faustus's conscience and his wicked impulses, were represented by hand puppets manipulated by Faustus. ▶

◀ In a 1996 production of *Everyman* at the Steppenwolf Theatre in Chicago, the roles of Death (left) and Everyman (center) were played by women, forcing the audience to rethink its attitudes about the issue of gender.

▲ A 1972 production of Ibsen's *A Doll's House*—a notably "realistic" play—made Torvald Helmer's formal costume into a symbol of something threatening.

◀ Body language—bodily gestures and facial expressions—is, of course, an important part of our daily behavior and also of the actor's art. In this scene from Carlos Morton's *The Many Deaths of Danny Rosales* (page 811), a young Hispanic thief (right) is trying to talk his way out of trouble with the Anglo sheriff (center). There is of course a contrast between the uptight Anglo and the expansive Hispanic, but an audience also senses that each man is putting on an act in order to impress the other.

15

IN BRIEF: HOW TO READ A PLAY

If as a reader you develop the following principles into habits, you will get far more out of a play than if you read it as though it were a novel consisting only of dialogue.

1. **Pay attention to the list of characters, and carefully read whatever descriptions the playwright has provided.** Early dramatists, such as Shakespeare, did not provide much in the way of description ("Othello, the Moor" or "Iago, a villain" is about as much as we find in Elizabethan texts), but later playwrights are often very forthcoming. Here, for instance, is Tennessee Williams introducing us to Amanda Wingfield in *The Glass Menagerie*. (We give only the beginning of his longish description.)

> *Amanda Wingfield;* the mother. A little woman of great but confused vitality clinging frantically to another time and place.

And here is Susan Glaspell introducing us to all of the characters in her one-act play, *Trifles*:

> . . . the Sheriff comes in followed by the County Attorney and Hale. The Sheriff and Hale are men in middle life, the County Attorney is a young man; all are much bundled up and go at once to the stove. They are followed by the two women—the Sheriff's wife [Mrs. Peters] first; she is a slight wiry woman, a thin nervous face. Mrs. Hale is larger and would ordinarily be called more comfortable looking, but she is disturbed now and looks fearfully about as she enters. The women have come in slowly and stand close together near the door.

Glaspell's description of her characters is not nearly so explicit as Tennessee Williams's, but Glaspell does tell a reader a good deal. What do we know about the men? They differ in age, they are bundled up, and they "go at once to the stove." What do we know about the women? Mrs. Peters is slight, and she has a "nervous face"; Mrs. Hale is "larger" but she too is "disturbed." The women enter "slowly," and they "stand close together near the door." In short, the men, who take over the warmest part of the room, are more confident than the women, who nervously huddle together near the door. It's a man's world.

2. **Pay attention to gestures and costumes that are specified in stage directions or are implied by the dialogue.** We have just seen how Glaspell distinguishes between the men and the women by what they do—the men take over the warm part of the room, the women stand insecurely near the door. Most dramatists from the late nineteenth century to the present have been fairly generous with their stage directions, but when we read the works of earlier dramatists we often have to deduce the gestures from the speeches. For instance, although Shakespeare has an occasional direction such as "She takes a sword and runs at him," for the most part he is very sparing. We must, then, infer the gestures from the dialogue. Consider this exchange between the Earl

of Gloucester and King Lear. Earlier in the play Lear has acted despotically; then he suffers so greatly that his mind becomes unhinged. Gloucester, finding the mad king, says,

> O, let me kiss that hand.

Lear replies,

> Let me wipe it first; it smells of mortality.

Surely when Gloucester speaks his line he reaches for Lear's hand (and probably he also kneels), and Lear withdraws his hand and wipes it on his tattered clothing. Exactly *how* Lear withdraws his hand—suddenly, or with some dignity—is not specified in the words. Nor is it specified whether Lear smells his hand when he says, "It smells of mortality." All readers will have to decide such matters for themselves, but we can probably agree that although the words are immensely moving, the gestures that accompany them (Gloucester's gestures of humility and Lear's unwillingness to accept those gestures) are also part of the "language" of the play.

In addition to thinking about gestures, don't forget the costumes that the characters wear. Costumes, of course, identify the characters as soldiers or farmers or whatever, and changes of costume can be especially symbolic. When we first meet King Lear, for instance, he is dressed as a king. (The text doesn't specify this, but since he is engaged in officially giving away kingdoms, he presumably wears his crown and his robe of office.) Later, driven to madness, he tears off his clothing, thus showing his realization that he is powerless; and still later, after his madness has somewhat abated, he appears dressed in fresh clothing, a sign that at least to some degree he is restored to civilization. Or consider Ibsen's *A Doll's House*. In the first act Nora wears ordinary clothing, but in the middle of the second act she puts on "a long multi-colored shawl" when she frantically rehearses her Italian dance. The shawl not only is appropriate to the tarantella dance, but also in its multitude of colors it expresses Nora's emotional turmoil. In the middle of the third act, she is wearing her Italian costume, dressed for a masquerade—her life has been a masquerade—but later she returns in her "everyday dress." The pretense is over.

3. **Keep in mind the kind of theater for which the play was written.** The plays in this book were written for various kinds of theaters. Sophocles, author of *Antigone* and *King Oedipus*, wrote for the ancient Greek theater, essentially a space where performers acted in front of an audience seated on a hillside. (See the illustration on page 12.) This theater was open to the heavens, with a structure representing a palace or temple behind the actors, in itself a kind of image of a society governed by the laws of the state and the laws of the gods. Moreover, the chorus enters the playing-space by marching down the side aisles, close to the audience, thus helping to unite the world of the audience with that of the

players. On the other hand, the audience in most modern theaters sits in a darkened area, separated by a proscenium arch from the performers, and watches them move about in a boxlike setting. The box set of Ibsen's plays or of Glaspell's *Trifles*—a room with the front wall missing—is, it often seems, an appropriate image of the confined lives of the characters of the play.

4. **If the playwright describes the locale and the furnishings, try to envision the set clearly. Pay attention also to the lighting.** Glaspell, for instance, tells us a good deal about the set. We quote only the first part.

> The kitchen in the now abandoned farmhouse of John Wright, a gloomy kitchen, and left without having been put in order. . . .

These details about a gloomy and disordered kitchen may seem to be mere realism—after all, the play has to take place somewhere—but it turns out that the disorder and, for that matter, the gloominess are extremely important. You'll have to read the play to find out why.

Another example of a setting that provides important information is Arthur Miller's, in *Death of a Salesman*. Again we quote only the beginning of the description.

> Before us is the Salesman's house. We are aware of towering, angular shapes behind it, surrounding it on all sides. Only the blue light of the sky falls upon the house and forestage; the surrounding area shows an angry glow of orange.

Here the lighting, especially the "angry glow of orange," is also a part of the language of the dramatist. Tennessee Williams uses lighting in a similar way in *The Glass Menagerie*; while two characters quarrel, the stage "is lit with a turgid smoky red glow." These examples of symbolic lighting are obvious, but what at first seems to be merely realistic lighting may also be symbolic. In *A Doll's House*, as Nora's terror grows in the second act, Ibsen tells us in a stage direction, "It begins to grow dark."

If we read older drama, we find that playwrights do not give us much help, but by paying attention to the words we can at least to some degree visualize the locale. For instance, in *King Lear* Shakespeare establishes the setting by giving Gloucester this line:

> Alack, the night comes on, and the high winds
> Do sorely ruffle. For many miles about
> There's scarce a bush.

And, again, this locale says something about the impoverished people who move in it.

5. **Pay attention to whatever sound effects are specified in the play.** As we mentioned earlier, in *Death of a Salesman*, before the curtain goes up, "A melody is heard, played upon a flute. It is small and fine, telling of grass and trees and the horizon." Then the curtain rises, revealing the Salesman's house, with "towering, angular shapes behind it, surrounding it on all sides." The sound of the flute is meant to tell us of the world from which the Salesman is shut off. In *Quem Quaeritis*, the bells at the end help to communicate the joy and harmony of the action that the play sets forth.

6. **Pay attention, at least on second reading, to silences, including pauses within speeches or between speeches.** Late in *Trifles* a stage direction tells us that "The women's eyes meet for an instant." We won't say what this exchange of looks indicates, but when you read the play you will see that the moment of silence is significant.

7. **Of course, dialogue is the most persistent sound in a play. Pay attention to what the characters say, but keep in mind that (like real people) dramatic characters are not always to be trusted.** An obvious case is Shakespeare's Edmund in *King Lear*, an utterly unscrupulous villain who knows that he is a liar, but a character may be self-deceived, or, to put it a bit differently, characters may say what they honestly think but may not know what they are talking about.

Susan Glaspell

Susan Glaspell (1882–1948) was born in Davenport, Iowa, and educated at Drake University in Des Moines. In 1903 she married George Cram Cook and, with Cook and other writers, actors, and artists, in 1915 founded the Provincetown Players, a group that remained vital until 1929. Glaspell wrote *Trifles* (1916) for the Provincetown Players, but she also wrote stories, novels, and a biography of her husband. In 1931 she won a Pulitzer Prize for *Alison's House*, a play about the family of a deceased poet who in some ways resembles Emily Dickinson.

TRIFLES

SCENE: *The kitchen in the now abandoned farmhouse of John Wright, a gloomy kitchen, and left without having been put in order—unwashed pans under the sink, a loaf of bread outside the breadbox, a dish towel on the table—other signs of incompleted work. At the rear the outer door opens, and the Sheriff comes in, followed by the County Attorney and Hale. The Sheriff and Hale are men in middle life, the County Attorney is a young man; all are much bundled up and go at once to the stove. They are followed by the two women—the Sheriff's Wife first; she is a slight wiry woman, a thin nervous face. Mrs. Hale is larger and would ordinarily be called more comfortable looking, but she is disturbed now and looks fearfully about as she enters. The women have come in slowly and stand close together near the door.*

COUNTY ATTORNEY (*rubbing his hands*). This feels good. Come up to the fire, ladies.

MRS. PETERS (*after taking a step forward*). I'm not—cold.

SHERIFF (*unbuttoning his overcoat and stepping away from the stove as if to the beginning of official business*). Now, Mr. Hale, before we move things about, you explain to Mr. Henderson just what you saw when you came here yesterday morning.

COUNTY ATTORNEY. By the way, has anything been moved? Are things just as you left them yesterday?

SHERIFF (*looking about*). It's just the same. When it dropped below zero last night, I thought I'd better send Frank out this morning to make a fire for us—no use getting pneumonia with a big case on; but I told him not to touch anything except the stove—and you know Frank.

COUNTY ATTORNEY. Somebody should have been left here yesterday.

SHERIFF. Oh—yesterday. When I had to send Frank to Morris Center for that man who went crazy—I want you to know I had my hands full yesterday. I knew you could get back from Omaha by today, and as long as I went over everything here myself—

COUNTY ATTORNEY. Well, Mr. Hale, tell just what happened when you came here yesterday morning.

HALE. Harry and I had started to town with a load of potatoes. We came along the road from my place; and as I got here, I said, "I'm going to see if I can't get John Wright to go in with me on a party telephone." I spoke to Wright about it once before, and he put me off, saying folks talked too much anyway, and all he asked was peace and quiet—I guess you know about how much he talked himself; but I thought maybe if I went to the house and talked about it before his wife, though I said to Harry that I didn't know as what his wife wanted made much difference to John—

COUNTY ATTORNEY. Let's talk about that later, Mr. Hale. I do want to talk about that, but tell now just what happened when you got to the house.

HALE. I didn't hear or see anything; I knocked at the door, and still it was all quiet inside. I knew they must be up, it was past eight o'clock. So I knocked again, and I thought I heard somebody say, "Come in." I wasn't sure, I'm not sure yet, but I opened the door—this door (*indicating the door by which the two women are still standing*), and there in that rocker—(*pointing to it*) sat Mrs. Wright. (*They all look at the rocker.*)

COUNTY ATTORNEY. What—was she doing?

HALE. She was rockin' back and forth. She had her apron in her hand and was kind of—pleating it.

COUNTY ATTORNEY. And how did she—look?

HALE. Well, she looked queer.

COUNTY ATTORNEY. How do you mean—queer?

HALE. Well, as if she didn't know what she was going to do next. And kind of done up.

COUNTY ATTORNEY. How did she seem to feel about your coming?

HALE. Why, I don't think she minded—one way or other. She didn't pay much attention. I said, "How do, Mrs. Wright, it's cold, ain't it?" And she said, "Is it?"—and went on kind of pleating at her apron. Well, I was surprised; she didn't ask me to come up to the stove, or to set down, but just sat there, not even looking at me, so I said, "I want to see John." And then she—laughed. I guess you would call it a laugh. I thought of Harry and the team outside, so I said a little sharp: "Can't I see John?" "No," she says, kind o' dull like. "Ain't he home?" says I. "Yes," says she, "he's home." "Then why can't I see him?" I asked her, out of patience. "'Cause he's dead," says she. *"Dead?"* says I. She just nodded her head, not getting a bit excited, but rockin' back and forth. "Why—where is he?" says I, not knowing what to say. She just pointed upstairs—like that (*himself pointing to the room above*). I got up, with the idea of going up there. I walked from there to here—then I says, "Why, what did he die of?" "He died of a rope around his neck," says she, and just went on pleatin' at her apron. Well, I went out and called Harry. I thought I might—need help. We went upstairs, and there he was lyin'—

COUNTY ATTORNEY. I think I'd rather have you go into that upstairs, where you can point it all out. Just go on now with the rest of the story.

HALE. Well, my first thought was to get that rope off. I looked . . . (*Stops, his face twitches.*) . . . but Harry, he went up to him, and he said, "No, he's dead all right, and we'd better not touch anything." So we went back downstairs. She was still sitting that same way. "Has anybody been notified?" I asked. "No," says she, unconcerned. "Who did this, Mrs. Wright?" said Harry. He said it businesslike—and she stopped pleatin' of her apron. "I don't know," she says. "You don't *know*?" says Harry. "No," says she, "Weren't you sleepin' in the bed with him?" says Harry. "Yes," says she, "but I was on the inside." "Somebody slipped a rope round his neck and strangled him, and you didn't wake up?" says Harry. "I didn't wake up," she said after him. We must 'a looked as if we didn't see how that could be, for after a minute she said, "I sleep sound." Harry was going to ask her more questions, but I said maybe we ought to let her tell her story first to the coroner, or the sheriff, so Harry went fast as he could to Rivers' place, where there's a telephone.

COUNTY ATTORNEY. And what did Mrs. Wright do when she knew that you had gone for the coroner?

HALE. She moved from that chair to this over here . . . (*Pointing to a small chair in the corner.*) . . . and just sat there with her hands held together and looking down. I got a feeling that I ought to make some conversation, so I said I had come in to see if John wanted to put in a telephone, and at that she started to laugh, and then she stopped and looked at me—scared. (*The County Attorney, who has had his notebook out, makes a note.*) I dunno, maybe it wasn't scared. I wouldn't like to say it was. Soon Harry got back, and then Dr. Lloyd came, and you, Mr. Peters, and so I guess that's all I know that you don't.

COUNTY ATTORNEY (*looking around*). I guess we'll go upstairs first—and then out to the barn and around there. (*To the Sheriff.*) You're convinced that there was nothing important here—nothing that would point to any motive?

SHERIFF. Nothing here but kitchen things.

(*The County Attorney, after again looking around the kitchen, opens the door of a cupboard closet. He gets up on a chair and looks on a shelf. Pulls his hand away, sticky.*)

COUNTY ATTORNEY. Here's a nice mess.

(*The women draw nearer.*)

MRS. PETERS (*to the other woman*). Oh, her fruit; it did freeze. (*To the Lawyer.*) She worried about that when it turned so cold. She said the fir'd go out and her jars would break.

SHERIFF. Well, can you beat the women! Held for murder and worryin' about her preserves.

COUNTY ATTORNEY. I guess before we're through she may have something more serious than preserves to worry about.

HALE. Well, women are used to worrying over trifles.

(*The two women move a little closer together.*)

COUNTY ATTORNEY (*with the gallantry of a young politician*). And yet, for all their worries, what would we do without the ladies? (*The women do not unbend. He goes to the sink, takes a dipperful of water from the pail and, pouring it into a basin, washes his hands. Starts to wipe them on the roller towel, turns it for a cleaner place.*) Dirty towels! (*Kicks his foot against the pans under the sink.*) Not much of a housekeeper, would you say, ladies?

MRS. HALE (*stiffly*). There's a great deal of work to be done on a farm.

COUNTY ATTORNEY. To be sure. And yet . . . (*With a little bow to her.*) . . . I know there are some Dickson county farmhouses which do not have such roller towels. (*He gives it a pull to expose its full length again.*)

MRS. HALE. Those towels get dirty awful quick. Men's hands aren't always as clean as they might be.

COUNTY ATTORNEY. Ah, loyal to your sex, I see. But you and Mrs. Wright were neighbors. I suppose you were friends, too.

MRS. HALE (*shaking her head*). I've not seen much of her of late years. I've not been in this house—it's more than a year.

COUNTY ATTORNEY. And why was that? You didn't like her?

MRS. HALE. I liked her all well enough. Farmers' wives have their hands full, Mr. Henderson. And then—

COUNTY ATTORNEY. Yes—?

MRS. HALE (*looking about*). It never seemed a very cheerful place.

COUNTY ATTORNEY. No—it's not cheerful. I shouldn't say she had the homemaking instinct.

MRS. HALE. Well, I don't know as Wright had, either.

COUNTY ATTORNEY. You mean that they didn't get on very well?

MRS. HALE. No, I don't mean anything. But I don't think a place'd be any cheerfuler for John Wright's being in it.

COUNTY ATTORNEY. I'd like to talk more of that a little later. I want to get the lay of things upstairs now. (*He goes to the left, where three steps lead to a stair door.*)

SHERIFF. I suppose anything Mrs. Peters does'll be all right. She was to take in some clothes for her, you know, and a few little things. We left in such a hurry yesterday.

COUNTY ATTORNEY. Yes, but I would like to see what you take, Mrs. Peters, and keep an eye out for anything that might be of use to us.

MRS. PETERS. Yes, Mr. Henderson.

(*The women listen to the men's steps on the stairs, then look about the kitchen.*)

MRS. HALE. I'd hate to have men coming into my kitchen, snooping around and criticizing. (*She arranges the pans under sink which the Lawyer had shoved out of place.*)

MRS. PETERS. Of course it's no more than their duty.

MRS. HALE. Duty's all right, but I guess that deputy sheriff that came out to make the fire might have got a little of this on. (*Gives the roller towel a pull.*) Wish I'd thought of that sooner. Seems mean to talk about her for not having things slicked up when she had to come away in such a hurry.

MRS. PETERS (*who has gone to a small table in the left rear corner of the room, and lifted one end of a towel that covers a pan*). She had bread set. (*Stands still.*)

MRS. HALE (*eyes fixed on a loaf of bread beside the breadbox, which is on a low shelf at the other side of the room. Moves slowly toward it*). She was going to put this in there. (*Picks up loaf, then abruptly drops it. In a manner of returning to familiar things.*) It's a shame about her fruit. I wonder if it's all gone. (*Gets up on the chair and looks.*) I think there's some here that's all right, Mrs. Peters. Yes—here; (*Holding it toward the window.*) this is cherries, too. (*Looking again.*) I declare I believe that's the only one. (*Gets down, bottle in her hand. Goes to the sink and wipes it off on the outside.*) She'll feel awful bad after all her hard work in the hot weather. I remember the afternoon I put up my cherries last summer. (*She puts the bottle on the big kitchen table, center of the room, front table. With a sigh, is about to sit down in the rocking chair. Before she is seated realizes what chair it is; with a slow look at it, steps back. The chair, which she has touched, rocks back and forth.*)

MRS. PETERS. Well, I must get those things from the front room closet. (*She goes to the door at the right, but after looking into the other room steps back.*) You coming with me, Mrs. Hale? You could help me carry them. (*They go into the other room; reappear, Mrs. Peters carrying a dress and skirt, Mrs. Hale following with a pair of shoes.*)

MRS. PETERS. My, it's cold in there. (*She puts the cloth on the big table, and hurries to the stove.*)

MRS. HALE (*examining the skirt*). Wright was close. I think maybe that's why she kept so much to herself. She didn't even belong to the Ladies' Aid. I suppose she felt she couldn't do her part, and then you don't enjoy things when you feel shabby. She used to wear pretty clothes and be lively, when she was Minnie Foster, one of the town girls singing in the choir. But that—oh, that was thirty years ago. This all you was to take in?

MRS. PETERS. She said she wanted an apron. Funny thing to want, for there isn't much to get you dirty in jail, goodness knows. But I suppose just to make her feel more natural. She said they was in the top drawer in this cupboard. Yes, here. And then her little shawl that always hung behind the door. (*Opens stair door and looks.*) Yes, here it is. (*Quickly shuts door leading upstairs.*)

MRS. HALE (*abruptly moving toward her*). Mrs. Peters?

MRS. PETERS. Yes, Mrs. Hale?

MRS. HALE. Do you think she did it?

MRS. PETERS (*in a frightened voice*). Oh, I don't know.

MRS. HALE. Well, I don't think she did. Asking for an apron and her little shawl. Worrying about her fruit.

MRS. PETERS (*starts to speak, glances up, where footsteps are heard in the room above. In a low voice*). Mr. Peters says it looks bad for her. Mr. Henderson is awful sarcastic in speech, and he'll make fun of her sayin' she didn't wake up.

MRS. HALE. Well, I guess John Wright didn't wake when they was slipping that rope under his neck.

MRS. PETERS. No, it's strange. It must have been done awful crafty and still. They say it was such a—funny way to kill a man, rigging it all up like that.

MRS. HALE. That's just what Mr. Hale said. There was a gun in the house. He says that's what he can't understand.

MRS. PETERS. Mr. Henderson said coming out that what was needed for the case was a motive; something to show anger, or—sudden feeling.

MRS. HALE (*who is standing by the table*). Well, I don't see any signs of anger around here. (*She puts her hand on the dish towel which lies on the table, stands looking down at the table, one half of which is clean, the other half messy.*) It's wiped here. (*Makes a move as if to finish work, then turns and looks at loaf of bread outside the breadbox. Drops towel. In that voice of coming back to familiar things.*) Wonder how they are finding things upstairs? I hope she had it a little more red-up there. You know, it seems kind of *sneaking*. Locking her up in town and then coming out here and trying to get her own house to turn against her!

MRS. PETERS. But, Mrs. Hale, the law is the law.

MRS. HALE. I s'pose 'tis. (*Unbuttoning her coat.*) Better loosen up your things, Mrs. Peters. You won't feel them when you go out.

(*Mrs. Peters takes off her fur tippet, goes to hang it on hook at the back of room, stands looking at the under part of the small corner table.*)

MRS. PETERS. She was piecing a quilt. (*She brings the large sewing basket, and they look at the bright pieces.*)

MRS. HALE. It's log cabin pattern. Pretty, isn't it? I wonder if she was goin' to quilt it or just knot it?

(*Footsteps have been heard coming down the stairs. The Sheriff enters, followed by Hale and the County Attorney.*)

SHERIFF. They wonder if she was going to quilt it or just knot it. (*The men laugh, the women look abashed.*)

COUNTY ATTORNEY (*rubbing his hands over the stove*). Frank's fire didn't do much up there, did it? Well, let's go out to the barn and get that cleared up.

(*The men go outside.*)

MRS. HALE (*resentfully*). I don't know as there's anything so strange, our takin' up our time with little things while we're waiting for them to get the evidence. (*She sits down at the big table, smoothing out a block with decision.*) I don't see as it's anything to laugh about.

MRS. PETERS (*apologetically*). Of course they've got awful important things on their minds. (*Pulls up a chair and joins Mrs. Hale at the table.*)

MRS. HALE (*examining another block*). Mrs. Peters, look at this one. Here, this is the one she was working on, and look at the sewing! All the rest of it has been so nice and even. And look at this! It's all over the place! Why, it looks as if she didn't know what she was about! (*After she has said this, they look at each other, then started to glance back at the door. After an instant Mrs. Hale has pulled at a knot and ripped the sewing.*)

MRS. PETERS. Oh, what are you doing, Mrs. Hale?

MRS. HALE (*mildly*). Just pulling out a stitch or two that's not sewed very good. (*Threading a needle.*) Bad sewing always made me fidgety.

MRS. PETERS (*nervously*). I don't think we ought to touch things.

MRS. HALE. I'll just finish up this end. (*Suddenly stopping and leaning forward.*) Mrs. Peters?

MRS. PETERS. Yes, Mrs. Hale?

MRS. HALE. What do you suppose she was so nervous about?

MRS. PETERS. Oh—I don't know. I don't know as she was nervous. I sometimes sew awful queer when I'm just tired. (*Mrs. Hale starts to say something, looks at Mrs. Peters, then goes on sewing.*) Well, I must get these things wrapped up. They may be through sooner than we think. (*Putting apron and other things together.*) I wonder where I can find a piece of paper, and string.

MRS. HALE. In that cupboard, maybe.

MRS. PETERS (*looking in cupboard*). Why, here's a birdcage. (*Holds it up.*) Did she have a bird, Mrs. Hale?

MRS. HALE. Why, I don't know whether she did or not—I've not been here for so long. There was a man around last year selling canaries cheap, but I don't know as she took one; maybe she did. She used to sing real pretty herself.

MRS. PETERS (*glancing around*). Seems funny to think of a bird here. But she must have had one, or why should she have a cage? I wonder what happened to it?

MRS. HALE. I s'pose maybe the cat got it.

MRS. PETERS. No, she didn't have a cat. She's got that feeling some people have about cats—being afraid of them. My cat got in her room, and she was real upset and asked me to take it out.

MRS. HALE. My sister Bessie was like that. Queer, ain't it?

MRS. PETERS (*examining the cage*). Why, look at this door. It's broke. One hinge is pulled apart.

MRS. HALE (*looking, too*). Looks as if someone must have been rough with it.

MRS. PETERS. Why, yes. (*She brings the cage forward and puts it on the table.*)

MRS. HALE. I wish if they're going to find any evidence they'd be about it. I don't like this place.

MRS. PETERS. But I'm awful glad you came with me, Mrs. Hale. It would be lonesome for me sitting here alone.

MRS. HALE. It would, wouldn't it? (*Dropping her sewing.*) But I tell you what I do wish, Mrs. Peters. I wish I had come over sometimes when *she* was here. I—(*Looking around the room.*)—wish I had.

MRS. PETERS. But of course you were awful busy, Mrs. Hale—your house and your children.

MRS. HALE. I could've come. I stayed away because it weren't cheerful—and that's why I ought to have come. I—I've never liked this place. Maybe because it's down in a hollow, and you don't see the road. I dunno what it is, but it's a lonesome place and always was. I wish I had come over to see Minnie Foster sometimes. I can see now—(*Shakes her head.*)

MRS. PETERS. Well, you mustn't reproach yourself, Mrs. Hale. Somehow we just don't see how it is with other folks until—something comes up.

MRS. HALE. Not having children makes less work—but it makes a quiet house, and Wright out to work all day, and no company when he did come in. Did you know John Wright, Mrs. Peters?

MRS. PETERS. Not to know him; I've seen him in town. They say he was a good man.

MRS. HALE. Yes—good; he didn't drink, and kept his word as well as most, I guess, and paid his debts. But he was a hard man, Mrs. Peters. Just to pass the time of day with him. (*Shivers.*) Like a raw wind that gets to the bone. (*Pauses, her eye falling on the cage.*) I should think she would 'a wanted a bird. But what do you suppose went with it?

MRS. PETERS. I don't know, unless it got sick and died. (*She reaches over and swings the broken door, swings it again; both women watch it.*)

MRS. HALE. You weren't raised round here, were you? (*Mrs. Peters shakes her head.*) You didn't know—her?

MRS. PETERS. Not till they brought her yesterday.

MRS. HALE. She—come to think of it, she was kind of like a bird herself—real sweet and pretty, but kind of timid and—fluttery. How—she—did—change. (*Silence; then as if struck by a happy thought and relieved to get back to everyday things.*) Tell you what, Mrs. Peters, why don't you take the quilt in with you? It might take up her mind.

MRS. PETERS. Why, I think that's a real nice idea, Mrs. Hale. There couldn't possibly be any objection to it, could there? Now, just what would I take? I wonder if her patches are in here—and her things. (*They look in the sewing basket.*)

MRS. HALE. Here's some red. I expect this has got sewing things in it (*Brings out a fancy box.*) What a pretty box. Looks like something somebody would give you. Maybe her scissors are in here. (*Opens box. Suddenly puts her hand to her nose.*) Why—(*Mrs. Peters bends nearer, then turns her face away.*) There's something wrapped up in this piece of silk.

MRS. PETERS. Why, this isn't her scissors.

MRS. HALE (*lifting the silk*). Oh, Mrs. Peters—it's—(*Mrs. Peters bends closer.*)

MRS. PETERS. It's the bird.

MRS. HALE (*jumping up*). But, Mrs. Peters—look at it. Its neck! Look at its neck! It's all—other side *to*.

MRS. PETERS. Somebody—wrung—its neck.

(*Their eyes meet. A look of growing comprehension of horror. Steps are heard outside. Mrs. Hale slips box under quilt pieces, and sinks into her chair. Enter Sheriff and County Attorney. Mrs. Peters rises.*)

COUNTY ATTORNEY (*as one turning from serious things to little pleasantries*). Well, ladies, have you decided whether she was going to quilt it or knot it?

MRS. PETERS. We think she was going to—knot it.

COUNTY ATTORNEY. Well, that's interesting, I'm sure. (*Seeing the birdcage.*) Has the bird flown?

MRS. HALE (*putting more quilt pieces over the box*). We think the—cat got it.

COUNTY ATTORNEY (*preoccupied*). Is there a cat?

(*Mrs. Hale glances in a quick covert way at Mrs. Peters.*)

MRS. PETERS. Well, not now. They're superstitious, you know. They leave.

COUNTY ATTORNEY (*to Sheriff Peters, continuing an interrupted conversation*). No sign at all of anyone having come from the outside. Their own rope. Now let's go up again and go over it piece by piece. (*They start upstairs.*) It would have to have been someone who knew just the—

(*Mrs. Peters sits down. The two women sit there not looking at one another, but as if peering into something and at the same time holding back. When they talk now, it is the manner of feeling their way over strange ground, as if afraid of what they are saying, but as if they cannot help saying it.*)

MRS. HALE. She liked the bird. She was going to bury it in that pretty box.

MRS. PETERS (*in a whisper*). When I was a girl—my kitten—there was a boy took a hatchet, and before my eyes—and before I could get there—(*Covers her face an instant.*) If they hadn't held me back, I would have—(*Catches herself, looks upstairs where steps are heard, falters weakly.*)—hurt him.

MRS. HALE (*with a slow look around her*). I wonder how it would seem never to have had any children around. (*Pause.*) No, Wright wouldn't like the bird—a thing that sang. She used to sing. He killed that, too.

MRS. PETERS (*moving uneasily*). We don't know who killed the bird.

MRS. HALE. I knew John Wright.

MRS. PETERS. It was an awful thing was done in this house that night, Mrs. Hale. Killing a man while he slept, slipping a rope around his neck that choked the life out of him.

MRS. HALE. His neck. Choked the life out of him.

(*Her hand goes out and rests on the birdcage.*)

MRS. PETERS (*with a rising voice*). We don't know who killed him. We don't *know*.

MRS. HALE (*her own feeling not interrupted*). If there'd been years and years of nothing, then a bird to sing to you, it would be awful—still, after the bird was still.

MRS. PETERS (*something within her speaking*). I know what stillness is. When we homesteaded in Dakota, and my first baby died—after he was two years old, and me with no other then—

MRS. HALE (*moving*). How soon do you suppose they'll be through, looking for evidence?

MRS. PETERS. I know what stillness is. (*Pulling herself back.*) The law has got to punish crime, Mrs. Hale.

MRS. HALE (*not as if answering that*). I wish you'd seen Minnie Foster when she wore a white dress with blue ribbons and stood up there in the choir and sang. (*A look around the room.*) Oh, I *wish* I'd come over here once in a while! That was a crime! That was a crime! Who's going to punish that?

MRS. PETERS (*looking upstairs*). We mustn't—take on.

MRS. HALE. I might have known she needed help! I know how things can be—for women. I tell you, it's queer, Mrs. Peters. We live close together and we live far apart. We all go through the same things—it's all just a different kind of the same thing. (*Brushes her eyes, noticing the bottle of fruit, reaches out for it.*) If I was you, I wouldn't tell her her fruit was gone. Tell her it *ain't*. Tell her it's all right. Take this in to prove it to her. She—she may never know whether it was broke or not.

MRS. PETERS (*takes the bottle, looks about for something to wrap it in; takes petticoat from the clothes brought from the other room, very nervously begins winding this around the bottle. In a false voice*). My, it's a good thing the men couldn't hear us. Wouldn't they just laugh! Getting all stirred up over a little thing like a—dead canary. As if that could have anything to do with—with—wouldn't they *laugh*!

(*The men are heard coming downstairs.*)

MRS. HALE (*under her breath*). Maybe they would—maybe they wouldn't.

COUNTY ATTORNEY. No, Peters, it's all perfectly clear except a reason for doing it. But you know juries when it comes to women. If there was some definite thing. Something to show—something to make a story about—a thing that would connect up with this strange way of doing it.

(*The women's eyes meet for an instant. Enter Hale from outer door.*)

HALE. Well, I've got the team around. Pretty cold out there.

COUNTY ATTORNEY. I'm going to stay here awhile by myself. (*To the Sheriff.*) You can send Frank out for me, can't you? I want to go over everything. I'm not satisfied that we can't do better.

SHERIFF. Do you want to see what Mrs. Peters is going to take in?

(*The Lawyer goes to the table, picks up the apron, laughs.*)

COUNTY ATTORNEY. Oh I guess they're not very dangerous things the ladies have picked up. (*Moves a few things about, disturbing the quilt pieces which cover the box. Steps back.*) No, Mrs. Peters doesn't need supervising. For that matter, a sheriff's wife is married to the law. Ever think of it that way, Mrs. Peters?

MRS. PETERS. Not—just that way.

SHERIFF (*chuckling*). Married to the law. (*Moves toward the other room.*) I just want you to come in here a minute, George. We ought to take a look at these windows.

COUNTY ATTORNEY (*scoffingly*). Oh, windows!

SHERIFF. We'll be right out, Mr. Hale.

(*Hale goes outside. The Sheriff follows the County Attorney into the other room. Then Mrs. Hale rises, hands tight together, looking intensely at Mrs. Peters, whose eyes take a slow turn, finally meeting, Mrs. Hale's. A moment Mrs. Hale holds her, then her own eyes point the way to where the box is concealed. Suddenly Mrs. Peters throws back quilt pieces and tries to put the box in the bag she is wearing. It is too big. She opens box, starts to take the bird out, cannot touch it, goes to pieces, stands there helpless. Sound of a knob turning in the other room. Mrs. Hale snatches the box and puts it in the pocket of her big coat. Enter County Attorney and Sheriff.*)

COUNTY ATTORNEY (*facetiously*). Well, Henry, at least we found out that she was not going to quilt it. She was going to—what is it you call it, ladies?

MRS. HALE (*her hand against her pocket*). We call it—knot it, Mr. Henderson.

CURTAIN

TOPICS FOR CRITICAL THINKING AND WRITING

📖 THE PLAY ON THE PAGE

1. How would you characterize Mr. Henderson, the county attorney?

2. In what way or ways are Mrs. Peters and Mrs. Hale different from each other?

3. On page 22, when Mrs. Peters tells of the boys who killed her cat, she says, "If they hadn't held me back, I would have—(*catches herself, looks upstairs where steps are heard, falters weakly.*)—hurt him." What do you think she was about to say before she faltered? Why do you suppose Glaspell included this speech about Mrs. Peters's girlhood?

4. We never see Mrs. Wright on stage. Nevertheless, by the end of *Trifles* we know a great deal about her. Explain both what we know about her—physical characteristics, habits, interests, personality, life before her marriage and after—and *how* we know these things.

5. The title of the play is ironic—the "trifles" are important. What other ironies do you find in the play. (On *irony*, see Glossary.)

6. Do you think the play is immoral? Explain.

🎭 THE PLAY ON THE STAGE

7. Briefly describe the setting, indicating what it "says" and what atmosphere it evokes.

8. Several times the men "laugh" or "chuckle." In their contexts, what do these expressions of amusement convey?

9. On page 22, "*the women's eyes meet for an instant.*" What do you think this bit of action "says"? What do you understand by the exchange of glances?

A SECOND SHORT PLAY FOR STUDY

Earlier, in a discussion of "Mistakes, Conflict, and Audience-Awareness" (page 5), we quoted W. H. Auden to the effect that mistakes are at the heart of drama. We mentioned, too, that dramatists often take the audience into their confidence, giving the audience information that the characters do not have. In *Trifles*, for instance, Susan Glaspell gives the audience information that she denies to the sheriff and the county attorney, and the audience therefore sees (and enjoys, with an ironic detachment) the mistakes made by the overly confident men. In reading or seeing *Trifles*, much of our pleasure resides in the fact that we know more than the men do.

The Greek philosopher Aristotle said that when we experience a tragedy we feel pity and terror as we watch the figures making mistakes and marching toward their destruction. Aristotle did not analyze the mistakes we see in a comedy, but surely the mistakes in comedy amuse us, partly because we know that somehow things will be cleared up and all will end happily. In comedy, the passions expressed may be just as strong as those in tragedy—jealous lovers may have murder in their eye—but we somehow know not to take the figures of comedy too seriously, and we sit back and enjoy the onstage blunders. (We will discuss the resemblances and the differences between comedy and tragedy further, on page 32.)

In the following comedy by Lady Gregory, the audience is aware of facts that the characters in the play are unaware of. That is, we hear Mrs. Tarpey—who is somewhat deaf—innocently misrepresent what she thinks she has heard. We watch the misinformation grow as each character unintentionally adds his or her own distortion, and—because the play is a comedy—we take pleasure in the mistakes of the figures on the stage, who absurdly transform an utterly innocent act into a story of adultery and murder. Perhaps, too, we see in this improbable and absurd story of misunderstandings some sort of truth, some sort of exaggerated and entertaining image of the mistakes and follies in which all of us participate.

Lady Gregory

Lady Isabella Augusta Gregory (1852–1932) was the daughter of a landowner in County Galway, Ireland. She married Sir William Gregory (who had been governor of Ceylon) in 1880, and after his death in 1892 she edited his memoirs and his grandfather's letters, but her first truly literary work was a translation of heroic Irish tales, *Cuchulain of Muirthemne* (1902), dedicated to her tenants at Kiltartan. She followed *Cuchulain* with *Gods and Fighting Men* (1904), and in the same year she turned to writing and translating plays, all the while devoting most of her energy to handling the business of the Abbey Theatre, an important force in the Irish literary renaissance of the late-nineteenth and early-twentieth century.

W. B. Yeats and John Millington Synge—and, in later days, Sean O'Casey—are usually regarded as the most important playwrights associated with the Abbey Theatre, but Lady Gregory was probably the writer whose works were most valued by the general public. She felt it was her duty to write plays that would bring audiences to the theater, while the other playwrights wrote more "literary" material.

Her modesty is evident in a note in which she explained how she came to write *Spreading the News*:

> The idea of this play first came to me as a tragedy. I kept seeing as in a picture people sitting by the roadside, and a girl passing to the market, gay and fearless. And then I saw her passing by the same place at evening, her head hanging, the heads of others turned from her, because of some sudden story that had risen out of a chance word, and had snatched away her good name.
>
> But comedy and not tragedy was wanted at our theatre to put beside the high poetic work [of Yeats]; and I let laughter have its way with the play.

SPREADING THE NEWS

Persons

BARTLEY FALLON
MRS. FALLON
JACK SMITH
SHAWN EARLY
TIM CASEY
JAMES RYAN
MRS. TARPEY
MRS. TULLY
A POLICEMAN (JO MULDOON)
A REMOVABLE MAGISTRATE[1]

SCENE: *The outskirts of a Fair. An Apple Stall. Mrs. Tarpey sitting at it. Magistrate and Policeman enter.*

MAGISTRATE. So that is the Fair Green. Cattle and sheep and mud. No system. What a repulsive sight!

POLICEMAN. That is so, indeed.

MAGISTRATE. I suppose there is a good deal of disorder in this place?

POLICEMAN. There is.

MAGISTRATE. Common assault?

POLICEMAN. It's common enough.

MAGISTRATE. Agrarian crime, no doubt?

POLICEMAN. That is so.

MAGISTRATE. Boycotting? Maiming of cattle? Firing into houses?

POLICEMAN. There was one time, and there might be again.

MAGISTRATE. That is bad. Does it go any farther than that?

POLICEMAN. Far enough, indeed.

[1]**Removable Magistrate** a magistrate who presides at various times in various places

MAGISTRATE. Homicide, then! This district has been shamefully neglected! I will change all that. When I was in the Andaman Islands, my system never failed. Yes, yes, I will change all that. What has that woman on her stall?

POLICEMAN. Apples mostly—and sweets.

MAGISTRATE. Just see if there are any unlicensed goods underneath—spirits or the like. We had evasions of the salt tax in the Andaman Islands.

POLICEMAN (*sniffing cautiously and upsetting a heap of apples*). I see no spirits here—or salt.

MAGISTRATE (*to Mrs. Tarpey*). Do you know this town well, my good woman?

MRS. TARPEY (*holding out some apples*). A penny the half-dozen, your honour.

POLICEMAN (*shouting*). The gentleman is asking do you know the town! He's the new magistrate!

MRS. TARPEY (*rising and ducking*). Do I know the town? I do, to be sure.

MAGISTRATE (*shouting*). What is its chief business?

MRS. TARPEY. Business, is it? What business would the people here have but to be minding one another's business?

MAGISTRATE. I mean what trade have they?

MRS. TARPEY. Not a trade. No trade at all but to be talking.

MAGISTRATE. I shall learn nothing here.

(*James Ryan comes in, pipe in mouth. Seeing Magistrate he retreats quickly, taking pipe from mouth.*)

MAGISTRATE. The smoke from that man's pipe had a greenish look; he may be growing unlicensed tobacco at home. I wish I had brought my telescope to this district. Come to the post-office, I will telegraph for it. I found it very useful in the Andaman Islands.

(*Magistrate and Policeman go out left.*)

MRS. TARPEY. Bad luck to Jo Muldoon, knocking my apples this way and that way. (*Begins arranging them.*) Showing off he was to the new magistrate.

(*Enter Bartley Fallon and Mrs. Fallon.*)

BARTLEY. Indeed it's a poor country and a scarce country to be living in. But I'm thinking if I went to America it's long ago the day I'd be dead!

MRS. FALLON. So you might, indeed.

(*She puts her basket on a barrel and begins putting parcels in it, taking them from under her cloak.*)

BARTLEY. And it's a great expense for a poor man to be buried in America.

MRS. FALLON. Never fear, Bartley Fallon, but I'll give you a good burying the day you'll die.

BARTLEY. Maybe it's yourself will be buried in the graveyard of Cloonmara before me, Mary Fallon, and I myself that will be dying unbeknownst some night, and no one a-near me. And the cat itself may be gone straying through the country, and the mice squealing over the quilt.

MRS. FALLON. Leave off talking of dying. It might be twenty years you'll be living yet.

BARTLEY (*with a deep sigh*). I'm thinking if I'll be living at the end of twenty years, it's a very old man I'll be then!

MRS. TARPEY (*turns and sees them*). Good morrow, Bartley Fallon; good morrow, Mrs. Fallon. Well, Bartley, you'll find no cause for complaining to-day; they are all saying it was a good fair.

BARTLEY (*raising his voice*). It was not a good fair, Mrs. Tarpey. It was a scattered sort of a fair. If we didn't expect more, we got less. That's the way with me always; whatever I have to sell goes down and whatever I have to buy goes up. If there's ever any misfortune coming to this world, it's on myself it pitches, like a flock of crows on seed potatoes.

MRS. FALLON. Leave off talking of misfortunes, and listen to Jack Smith that is coming the way, and he singing.

(*Voice of Jack Smith heard singing:*)

I thought, my first love,
  There'd be but one house between you and me,
And I thought I would find
  Yourself coaxing my child on your knee.
Over the tide
  I would leap with the leap of a swan,
Till I came to the side
  Of the wife of the Red-haired man!

(*Jack Smith comes in; he is a red-haired man, and is carrying a hayfork.*)

MRS. TARPEY. That should be a good song if I had my hearing.

MRS. FALLON (*shouting*). It's "The Red-haired Man's Wife."

MRS. TARPEY. I know it well. That's the song that has a skin on it!

(*She turns her back to them and goes on arranging her apples.*)

MRS. FALLON. Where's herself, Jack Smith?

JACK SMITH. She was delayed with her washing; bleaching the clothes on the hedge she is, and she daren't leave them, with all the tinkers that do be passing to the fair. It isn't to the fair I came myself, but up to the Five Acre Meadow I'm going, where I have a contract for the hay. We'll get a share of it into tramps to-day.

(*He lays down hayfork and lights his pipe.*)

BARTLEY. You will not get it into tramps to-day. The rain will be down on it by evening, and on myself too. It's seldom I ever started on a journey but the rain would come down on me before I'd find any place of shelter.

JACK SMITH. If it didn't itself, Bartley, it is my belief you would carry a leaky pail on your head in place of a hat, the way you'd not be without some cause of complaining.

(*A voice heard, "Go on, now, go on out o' that. Go on I say."*)

JACK SMITH. Look at that young mare of Pat Ryan's that is backing into Shaughnessy's bullocks with the dint of the crowd! Don't be daunted, Pat, I'll give you a hand with her.

(*He goes out, leaving his hayfork.*)

MRS. FALLON. It's time for ourselves to be going home. I have all I bought put in the basket. Look at there, Jack Smith's hayfork he left after him! He'll be wanting it. (*Calls.*) Jack Smith! Jack Smith!—He's gone through the crowd—hurry after him, Bartley, he'll be wanting it.

BARTLEY. I'll do that. This is no safe place to be leaving it. (*He takes up fork awkwardly and upsets the basket.*) Look at that now! If there is any basket in the fair upset, it must be our own basket!

(*He goes out to right.*)

MRS. FALLON. Get out of that! It is your own fault, it is. Talk of misfortunes and misfortunes will come. Glory be! Look at my new egg-cups rolling in every part—and my two pound of sugar with the paper broke——

MRS. TARPEY (*turning from stall*). God help us, Mrs. Fallon, what happened your basket?

MRS. FALLON. It's himself that knocked it down, bad manners to him. (*Putting things up.*) My grand sugar that's destroyed, and he'll not drink his tea without it. I had best go back to the shop for more, much good may it do him!

(*Enter Tim Casey.*)

TIM CASEY. Where is Bartley Fallon, Mrs. Fallon? I want a word with him before he'll leave the fair. I was afraid he might have gone home by this, for he's a temperate man.

MRS. FALLON. I wish he did go home! It'd be best for me if he went home straight from the fair green, or if he never came with me at all? Where is he, is it? He's gone up the road (*jerks elbow*) following Jack Smith with a hayfork.

(*She goes out to left.*)

TIM CASEY. Following Jack Smith with a hayfork! Did ever any one hear the like of that. (*Shouts.*) Did you hear that news, Mrs. Tarpey?

MRS. TARPEY. I heard no news at all.

TIM CASEY. Some dispute I suppose it was that rose between Jack Smith and Bartley Fallon, and it seems Jack made off, and Bartley is following him with a hayfork!

MRS. TARPEY. Is he now? Well, that was quick work! It's not ten minutes since the two of them were here, Bartley going home and Jack going to the Five Acre Meadow; and I had my apples to settle up, that Jo Muldoon of the police had scattered, and when I looked round again Jack Smith was gone, and Bartley Fallon was gone, and Mrs. Fallon's basket upset, and all in it strewed upon the ground—the tea here—the two pound of sugar there—the egg-cups there—Look, now, what a great hardship the deafness puts upon me, that I didn't hear the commincement of the fight! Wait till I tell James Ryan that I see below; he is a neighbour of Bartley's, it would be a pity if he wouldn't hear the news!

(*She goes out. Enter Shawn Early and Mrs. Tully.*)

TIM CASEY. Listen, Shawn Early! Listen, Mrs. Tully, to the news! Jack Smith and Bartley Fallon had a falling out, and Jack knocked Mrs. Fallon's basket into the road, and Bartley made an attack on him with a hayfork, and away with Jack, and Bartley after him. Look at the sugar here yet on the road!

SHAWN EARLY. Do you tell me so? Well, that's a queer thing, and Bartley Fallon so quiet a man!

MRS. TULLY. I wouldn't wonder at all. I would never think well of a man that would have that sort of a mouldering look. It's likely he has overtaken Jack by this.

(*Enter James Ryan and Mrs. Tarpey.*)

JAMES RYAN. That is great news Mrs. Tarpey was telling me! I suppose that's what brought the police and the magistrate up this way. I was wondering to see them in it a while ago.

SHAWN EARLY. The police after them? Bartley Fallon must have injured Jack so. They wouldn't meddle in a fight that was only for show!

MRS. TULLY. Why wouldn't he injure him? There was many a man killed with no more of a weapon than a hayfork.

JAMES RYAN. Wait till I run north as far as Kelly's bar to spread the news! (*He goes out.*)

TIM CASEY. I'll go tell Jack Smith's first cousin that is standing there south of the church after selling his lambs. (*Goes out.*)

MRS. TULLY. I'll go telling a few of the neighbours I see beyond to the west. (*Goes out.*)

SHAWN EARLY. I'll give word of it beyond at the east of the green.

(*Is going out when Mrs. Tarpey seizes hold of him.*)

MRS. TARPEY. Stop a minute, Shawn Early, and tell me did you see red Jack Smith's wife, Kitty Keary, in any place?

SHAWN EARLY. I did. At her own house she was, drying clothes on the hedge as I passed.

MRS. TARPEY. What did you say she was doing?

SHAWN EARLY (*breaking away*). Laying out a sheet on the hedge.

(*He goes.*)

MRS. TARPEY. Laying out a sheet for the dead! The Lord have mercy on us! Jack Smith dead, and his wife laying out a sheet for his burying! (*Calls out.*) Why didn't you tell me that before, Shawn Early? Isn't the deafness the great hardship? Half the world might be dead without me knowing of it or getting word of it at all! (*She sits down and rocks herself.*) O my poor Jack Smith! To be going to his work so nice and so hearty, and to be left stretched on the ground in the full light of the day!

(*Enter Tim Casey.*)

TIM CASEY. What is it, Mrs. Tarpey? What happened since?

MRS. TARPEY. O my poor Jack Smith!

TIM CASEY. Did Bartley overtake him?

MRS. TARPEY. O the poor man!

TIM CASEY. Is it killed he is?

MRS. TARPEY. Stretched in the Five Acre Meadow!

TIM CASEY. The Lord have mercy on us! Is that a fact?

MRS. TARPEY. Without the rites of the Church or a ha'porth![2]

TIM CASEY. Who was telling you?

MRS. TARPEY. And the wife laying out a sheet for his corpse. (*Sits up and wipes her eyes.*) I suppose they'll wake him the same as another?

(*Enter Mrs. Tully, Shawn Early, and James Ryan.*)

MRS. TULLY. There is great talk about this work in every quarter of the fair.

MRS. TARPEY. Ochone! cold and dead. And myself maybe the last he was speaking to!

JAMES RYAN. The Lord save us! Is it dead he is?

TIM CASEY. Dead surely, and the wife getting provision for the wake.

SHAWN EARLY. Well, now, hadn't Bartley Fallon great venom in him?

MRS. TULLY. You may be sure he had some cause. Why would he have made an end of him if he had not? (*To Mrs. Tarpey, raising her voice.*) What was it rose the dispute at all, Mrs. Tarpey?

MRS. TARPEY. Not a one of me knows. The last I saw of them, Jack Smith was standing there, and Bartley Fallon was standing there, quiet and easy, and he listening to "The Red-haired Man's Wife."

MRS. TULLY. Do you hear that, Tim Casey? Do you hear that, Shawn Early and James Ryan? Bartley Fallon was here this morning listening to red Jack Smith's wife, Kitty Keary that was! Listening to her and whispering with her! It was she started the fight so!

[2]**ha'porth** halfpennyworth

SHAWN EARLY. She must have followed him from her own house. It is likely some person roused him.

TIM CASEY. I never knew, before, Bartley Fallon was great with Jack Smith's wife.

MRS. TULLY. How would you know it? Sure it's not in the streets they would be calling it. If Mrs. Fallon didn't know of it, and if I that have the next house to them didn't know of it, and if Jack Smith himself didn't know of it, it is not likely you would know of it, Tim Casey.

SHAWN EARLY. Let Bartley Fallon take charge of her from this out so, and let him provide for her. It is little pity she will get from any person in this parish.

TIM CASEY. How can he take charge of her? Sure he has a wife of his own. Sure you don't think he'd turn souper and marry her in a Protestant church?

JAMES RYAN. It would be easy for him to marry her if he brought her to America.

SHAWN EARLY. With or without Kitty Keary, believe me it is for America he's making at this minute. I saw the new magistrate and Jo Muldoon of the police going into the post-office as I came up—there was hurry on them—you may be sure it was to telegraph they went, the way he'll be stopped in the docks at Queenstown!

MRS. TULLY. It's likely Kitty Keary is gone with him, and not minding a sheet or a wake at all. The poor man, to be deserted by his own wife, and the breath hardly gone out yet from his body that is lying bloody in the field!

(*Enter Mrs. Fallon.*)

MRS. FALLON. What is it the whole of the town is talking about? And what is it you yourselves are talking about? Is it about my man Bartley Fallon you are talking? Is it lies about him you are telling, saying that he went killing Jack Smith? My grief that ever he came into this place at all!

JAMES RYAN. Be easy now, Mrs. Fallon. Sure there is no one at all in the whole fair but is sorry for you!

MRS. FALLON. Sorry for me, is it? Why would any one be sorry for me? Let you be sorry for yourselves, and that there may be shame on you for ever and at the day of judgment, for the words you are saying and the lies you are telling to take away the character of my poor man, and to take the good name off of him, and to drive him to destruction! That is what you are doing!

SHAWN EARLY. Take comfort now, Mrs. Fallon. The police are not so smart as they think. Sure he might give them the slip yet, the same as Lynchehaun.

MRS. TULLY. If they do get him, and if they do put a rope around his neck, there is no one can say he does not deserve it!

MRS. FALLON. Is that what you are saying, Bridget Tully, and is that what you think? I tell you it's too much talk you have, making yourself out to be such a great one, and to be running down every respectable person! A rope, is it? It isn't much of a rope was needed to tie up your own fur-niture the day you came into Martin Tully's house, and you never bringing as much as a blanket, or a penny, or a suit of clothes with you and I myself bringing seventy pounds and two feather beds. And now you are stiffer than a woman would have a hundred pounds! It is too much talk the whole of you have. A rope is it? I tell you the whole of this town is full of liars and schemers that would hang you up for half a glass of whiskey. (*Turning to go.*) People they are you wouldn't believe as much as daylight from without you'd get up to have a look at it yourself. Killing Jack Smith indeed! Where are you at all, Bartley, till I bring you out of this? My nice quiet little man! My decent comrade! He that is as kind and as harmless as an innocent beast of the field! He'll be doing no harm at all if he'll shed the blood of some of you after this day's work! That much would be no harm at all. (*Calls out*) Bartley! Bartley Fallon! Where are you? (*Going out.*) Did any one see Bartley Fallon?

(*All turn to look after her.*)

JAMES RYAN. It is hard for her to believe any such a thing, God help her!

(*Enter Bartley Fallon from right, carrying hayfork.*)

BARTLEY. It is what I often said to myself, if there is ever any misfortune coming to this world it is on myself it is sure to come!

(*All turn round and face him.*)

BARTLEY. To be going about with this fork and to find no one to take it, and no place to leave it down, and I wanting to be gone out of this—Is that you, Shawn Early? (*Holds out fork.*) It's well I met you. You have no call to be leaving the fair for a while the way I have, and how can I go till I'm rid of this fork? Will you take it and keep it until such time as Jack Smith——

SHAWN EARLY (*backing*). I will not take it, Bartley Fallon, I'm very thankful to you!

BARTLEY (*turning to apple stall*). Look at it now, Mrs. Tarpey, it was here I got it; let me thrust it in under the stall. It will lie there safe enough, and no one will take notice of it until such time as Jack Smith——

MRS. TARPEY. Take your fork out of that! Is it to put trouble on me and to destroy me you want? putting it there for the police to be rooting it out maybe.

(*Thrusts him back.*)

BARTLEY. That is a very unneighbourly thing for you to do, Mrs. Tarpey. Hadn't I enough care on me with that fork before this, running up and down with it like the swinging of a clock, and afeard to lay it down in any place! I wish I never touched it or meddled with it at all!

JAMES RYAN. It is a pity, indeed, you ever did.

BARTLEY. Will you yourself take it, James Ryan? You were always a neighbourly man.

JAMES RYAN (*backing*). There is many a thing I would do for you, Bartley Fallon, but I won't do that!

SHAWN EARLY. I tell you there is no man will give you any help or any encouragement for this day's work. If it was something agrarian now——

BARTLEY. If no one at all will take it, maybe it's best to give it up to the police.

TIM CASEY. There'd be a welcome for it with them surely! (*Laughter.*)

MRS. TULLY. And it is to the police Kitty Keary herself will be brought.

MRS. TARPEY (*rocking to and fro*). I wonder now who will take the expense of the wake for poor Jack Smith?

BARTLEY. The wake for Jack Smith!

TIM CASEY. Why wouldn't he get a wake as well as another? Would you begrudge him that much?

BARTLEY. Red Jack Smith dead! Who was telling you?

SHAWN EARLY. The whole town knows of it by this.

BARTLEY. Do they say what way did he die?

JAMES RYAN. You don't know that yourself, I suppose, Bartley Fallon? You don't know he was followed and that he was laid dead with the stab of a hayfork?

BARTLEY. The stab of a hayfork!

SHAWN EARLY. You don't know, I suppose, that the body was found in the Five Acre Meadow?

BARTLEY. The Five Acre Meadow!

TIM CASEY. It is likely you don't know that the police are after the man that did it?

BARTLEY. The man that did it!

MRS. TULLY. You don't know, maybe, that he was made away with for the sake of Kitty Keary, his wife?

BARTLEY. Kitty Keary, his wife!

(*Sits down bewildered.*)

MRS. TULLY. And what have you to say now, Bartley Fallon?

BARTLEY (*crossing himself*). I to bring that fork here, and to find that news before me! It is much if I can ever stir from this place at all, or reach as far as the road!

TIM CASEY. Look, boys, at the new magistrate, and Jo Muldoon along with him! It's best for us to quit this.

SHAWN EARLY. That is so. It is best not to be mixed in this business at all.

JAMES RYAN. Bad as he is, I wouldn't like to be an informer against any man.

(*All hurry away except Mrs. Tarpey, who remains behind her stall. Enter magistrate and policeman.*)

MAGISTRATE. I knew the district was in a bad state, but I did not expect to be confronted with a murder at the first fair I came to.

POLICEMAN. I am sure you did not, indeed.

MAGISTRATE. It was well I had not gone home. I caught a few words here and there that roused my suspicions.

POLICEMAN. So they would, too.

MAGISTRATE. You heard the same story from everyone you asked?

POLICEMAN. The same story—or if it was not altogether the same, anyway it was no less than the first story.

MAGISTRATE. What is that man doing? He is sitting alone with a hayfork. He has a guilty look. The murder was done with a hayfork!

POLICEMAN (*in a whisper*). That's the very man they say did the act; Bartley Fallon himself!

MAGISTRATE. He must have found escape difficult—he is trying to brazen it out. A convict in the Andaman Islands tried the same game, but he could not escape my system! Stand aside—Don't go far—have the handcuffs ready. (*He walks up to Bartley, folds his arms, and stands before him.*) Here, my man, do you know anything of John Smith?

BARTLEY. Of John Smith! Who is he, now?

POLICEMAN. Jack Smith, sir—Red Jack Smith!

MAGISTRATE (*coming a step nearer and tapping him on the shoulder*). Where is Jack Smith?

BARTLEY (*with a deep sigh, and shaking his head slowly*). Where is he, indeed?

MAGISTRATE. What have you to tell?

BARTLEY. It is where he was this morning, standing in this spot, singing his share of songs—no, but lighting his pipe—scraping a match on the sole of his shoes——

MAGISTRATE. I ask you, for the third time, where is he?

BARTLEY. I wouldn't like to say that. It is a great mystery, and it is hard to say of any man, did he earn hatred or love.

MAGISTRATE. Tell me all you know.

BARTLEY. All that I know— Well, there are the three estates; there is Limbo, and there is Purgatory, and there is——

MAGISTRATE. Nonsense! This is trifling! Get to the point.

BARTLEY. Maybe you don't hold with the clergy so? That is the teaching of the clergy. Maybe you hold with the old people. It is what they do be saying, that the shadow goes wandering, and the soul is tired, and the body is taking a rest—The shadow! (*Starts up.*) I was nearly sure I saw Jack Smith not ten minutes ago at the corner of the forge, and I lost him again— Was it his ghost I saw, do you think?

MAGISTRATE (*to policeman*). Conscience-struck! He will confess all now!

BARTLEY. His ghost to come before me! It is likely it was on account of the fork! I to have it and he to have no way to defend himself the time he met with his death!

MAGISTRATE (*to policeman*). I must note down his words. (*Takes out notebook.*) (*To Bartley.*) I warn you that your words are being noted.

BARTLEY. If I had ha' run faster in the beginning, this terror would not be on me at the latter end! Maybe he will cast it up against me at the day of judgment— I wouldn't wonder at all at that.

MAGISTRATE (*writing*). At the day of judgment——

BARTLEY. It was soon for his ghost to appear to me—is it coming after me always by day it will be, and stripping the clothes off in the night time?— I wouldn't wonder at all at that, being as I am an unfortunate man!

MAGISTRATE (*sternly*). Tell me this truly. What was the motive of this crime?

BARTLEY. The motive, is it?

MAGISTRATE. Yes; the motive; the cause.

BARTLEY. I'd sooner not say that.

MAGISTRATE. You had better tell me truly. Was it money?

BARTLEY. Not at all! What did poor Jack Smith ever have in his pockets unless it might be his hands that would be in them?

MAGISTRATE. Any dispute about land?

BARTLEY (*indignantly*). Not at all! He never was a grabber or grabbed from any one!

MAGISTRATE. You will find it better for you if you tell me at once.

BARTLEY. I tell you I wouldn't for the whole world wish to say what it was—it is a thing I would not like to be talking about.

MAGISTRATE. There is no use in hiding it. It will be discovered in the end.

BARTLEY. Well, I suppose it will, seeing that mostly everybody knows it before. Whisper here now. I will tell no lie; where would be the use? (*Puts his hand to his mouth, and Magistrate stoops.*) Don't be putting the blame on the parish, for such a thing was never done in the parish before—it was done for the sake of Kitty Keary, Jack Smith's wife.

MAGISTRATE (*to policeman*). Put on the handcuffs. We have been saved some trouble. I knew he would confess if taken in the right way.

(*Policeman puts on handcuffs.*)

BARTLEY. Handcuffs now! Glory be! I always said, if there was ever any misfortune coming to this place it was on myself it would fall. I to be in handcuffs! There's no wonder at all in that.

(*Enter Mrs. Fallon, followed by the rest. She is looking back at them as she speaks.*)

MRS. FALLON. Telling lies the whole of the people of this town are; telling lies, telling lies as fast as a dog will trot! Speaking against my poor respectable man! Saying he made an end of Jack Smith! My decent comrade! There is no better man and no kinder man in the whole of the five parishes! It's little annoyance he ever gave to any one! (*Turns and sees him.*) What in the earthly world do I see before me? Bartley Fallon in charge of the police! Handcuffs on him! O Bartley, what did you do at all at all?

BARTLEY. O Mary, there has a great misfortune come upon me! It is what I always said, that if there is ever any misfortune——

MRS. FALLON. What did he do at all, or is it bewitched I am?

MAGISTRATE. This man has been arrested on a charge of murder.

MRS. FALLON. Whose charge is that? Don't believe them! They are all liars in this place! Give me back my man!

MAGISTRATE. It is natural you should take his part, but you have no cause of complaint against your neighbours. He has been arrested for the murder of John Smith, on his own confession.

MRS. FALLON. The saints of heaven protect us! And what did he want killing Jack Smith?

MAGISTRATE. It is best you should know all. He did it on account of a love affair with the murdered man's wife.

MRS. FALLON (*sitting down*). With Jack Smith's wife! With Kitty Keary!—Ochone, the traitor!

THE CROWD. A great shame, indeed. He is a traitor indeed.

MRS. TULLY. To America he was bringing her, Mrs. Fallon.

BARTLEY. What are you saying, Mary? I tell you——

MRS. FALLON. Don't say a word! I won't listen to any word you'll say! (*Stops her ears.*) O, isn't he the treacherous villain? Ohone go deo!

BARTLEY. Be quiet till I speak! Listen to what I say!

MRS. FALLON. Sitting beside me on the ass car coming to the town, so quiet and so respectable, and treachery like that in his heart!

BARTLEY. Is it your wits you have lost or is it I myself that have lost my wits?

MRS. FALLON. And it's hard I earned you, slaving—and you grumbling, and sighing, and coughing, and discontented, and the priest wore out anointing you, with all the times you threatened to die!

BARTLEY. Let you be quiet till I tell you!

MRS. FALLON. You to bring such a disgrace into the parish. A thing that was never heard of before!

BARTLEY. Will you shut your mouth and hear me speaking?

MRS. FALLON. And if it was for any sort of a fine handsome woman, but for a little fistful of a woman like Kitty Keary, that's not four feet high hardly, and not three teeth in her head unless she got new ones! May God reward you, Bartley Fallon, for the black treachery in your heart and the wickedness in your mind, and the red blood of poor Jack Smith that is wet upon your hand!

(*Voice of Jack Smith heard singing.*)

> The sea shall be dry,
> The earth under mourning and ban!
> Then loud shall he cry
> For the wife of the red-haired man!

BARTLEY. It's Jack Smith's voice—I never knew a ghost to sing before—. It is after myself and the fork he is coming! (*Goes back. Enter Jack Smith.*) Let one of you give him the fork and I will be clear of him now and for eternity!

MRS. TARPEY. The Lord have mercy on us! Red Jack Smith! The man that was going to be waked!

JAMES RYAN. Is it back from the grave you are come?

SHAWN EARLY. Is it alive you are, or is it dead you are?

TIM CASEY. Is it yourself at all that's in it?

MRS. TULLY. Is it letting on you were to be dead?

MRS. FALLON. Dead or alive, let you stop Kitty Keary, your wife, from bringing my man away with her to America!

JACK SMITH. It is what I think, the wits are gone astray on the whole of you. What would my wife want bringing Bartley Fallon to America?

MRS. FALLON. To leave yourself, and to get quit of you she wants, Jack Smith, and to bring him away from myself. That's what the two of them had settled together.

JACK SMITH. I'll break the head of any man that says that! Who is it says it? (*To Tim Casey.*) Was it you said it? (*To Shawn Early.*) Was it you?

ALL TOGETHER (*backing and shaking their heads*). It wasn't I said it!

JACK SMITH. Tell me the name of any man that said it!

ALL TOGETHER (*pointing to Bartley*). It was *him* that said it!

JACK SMITH. Let me at him till I break his head!

(*Bartley backs in terror. Neighbours hold Jack Smith back.*)

JACK SMITH (*trying to free himself*). Let me at him! Isn't he the pleasant sort of a scarecrow for any woman to be crossing the ocean with! It's back from the docks of New York he'd be turned (*trying to rush at him again*), with a lie in his mouth and treachery in his heart, and another man's wife by his side, and he passing her off as his own! Let me at him can't you.

(*Makes another rush, but is held back.*)

MAGISTRATE (*pointing to Jack Smith*). Policeman, put the handcuffs on this man. I see it all now. A case of false impersonation, a conspiracy to defeat the ends of justice. There was a case in the Andaman Islands, a murderer of the Mopsa tribe, a religious enthusiast——

POLICEMAN. So he might be, too.

MAGISTRATE. We must take both these men to the scene of the murder. We must confront them with the body of the real Jack Smith.

JACK SMITH. I'll break the head of any man that will find my dead body!

MAGISTRATE. I'll call more help from the barracks. (*Blows Policeman's whistle.*)

BARTLEY. It is what I am thinking, if myself and Jack Smith are put together in the one cell for the night, the handcuffs will be taken off him, and his hands will be free, and murder will be done that time surely!

MAGISTRATE. Come on! (*They turn to the right.*)

CURTAIN

TOPICS FOR CRITICAL THINKING AND WRITING

📖 THE PLAY ON THE PAGE

1. After Bartley is handcuffed he says to his wife, "O Mary, there has a great misfortune come upon me!" Consider Bartley's personality. To what extent does he exemplify the ancient Greek philosopher Heraclitus's assertion that "A man's character is his destiny"? That is, to what extent can we say that what happens *to* Bartley is largely of his own doing?

2. Very early in the play the Magistrate, exasperated with his effort to get information from Mrs. Tarpey, says, "I shall learn nothing here." How capable of learning is the Magistrate? Why?

3. Lady Gregory said of the play that at first she thought the ending—with Bartley in handcuffs—was "too harsh," but then she came to feel that she "was providing him with a happy old age in giving him the lasting glory of that great and crowning day of misfortune." Do you think the ending is too harsh? Should the play have ended with the misunderstanding cleared up, and with Bartley and Jack Smith reconciled? Or was Lady Gregory right in coming to feel that the handcuffs provide Bartley with a happy old age and a "crowning day of misfortune"?

4. William Butler Yeats, Lady Gregory's friend and collaborator at the Abbey Theatre, said of her work:

> Lady Gregory alone writes out of a spirit of pure comedy, and laughs without bitterness and with no thought but to laugh. She has a perfect sympathy with her characters, even with the worst of them, and when the curtain goes down we are so far from the mood of judgment that we do not even know that we have condoned many sins.
> (*SAMHAIN* 1905)

Evaluate Yeats's comment in the light of *Spreading the News*.

5. John Millington Synge, another of Lady Gregory's collaborators at the Abbey, in the introduction to one of his plays, *The Playboy of the Western World*, says that "In a good play every speech should be as fully flavored as a nut or apple." Take a speech or two that you like in *Spreading the News*, and call attention to qualities in the language that make the speech appealing. (One of our own favorites is the answer Mrs. Tarpey gives when the Magistrate asks her what the chief business of the town is: "Business, is it? What business would the people here have but to be minding one another's business?")

6. If you are familiar with a culture other than what can be called Irish-American or Anglo-American, rewrite a few speeches into the diction of this culture. How, for instance, might a speech sound if spoken not by Irish villagers but by Puerto Ricans in New York, or by Chicanos in California, or by Russian immigrants in Boston?

7. The journalist H. L. Mencken said, "The theater . . . is not life in miniature, but life enormously magnified, life hideously exaggerated." How well does *Spreading the News* support this view?

⚰⚱ THE PLAY ON THE STAGE

8. If you were casting the play, what sort of bodily types would you hope to find, for instance for the Magistrate, for Bartley, for Mrs. Tarpey, and for Mrs. Fallon. Do you see the Magistrate as (say) a big blustering man, or as a small, wiry, bustling fellow? Explain why you think certain types would especially fit—would be especially funny with—certain passages of dialogue.

9. Deafness is not normally today considered a fit subject for comedy. If you are not disturbed by Lady Gregory's treatment of Mrs. Tarpey, explain how Lady Gregory has made deafness an acceptable subject of comedy. You may want to begin by considering one of Mrs. Tarpey's comments: "Look, now, what a great hardship the deafness puts upon me, that I didn't hear the commencement of the fight!")

SOME KINDS OF DRAMA

TRAGEDY AND COMEDY

Whimsical assertions that all of us are Platonists or Aristotelians, or liberals or conservatives ("Nature wisely does contrive / That every boy and every gal / That's born into the world alive / Is either a little Liberal / Or else a little Conservative"), reveal a tendency to divide things into two. Two is about right: peace and war, man and woman, day and night, life and death. There may be middle cases; Edmund Burke suggested that no one can point to the precise moment that divides day from night—but Burke also suggested that everyone can make the useful distinction between day and night. The distinction between comedy and tragedy may not always be easy to make, but until the twentieth century it was usually clear enough. *Hamlet,* which in Horatio's words is concerned with "woe or wonder," is a tragedy; *A Midsummer Night's Dream,* which in Puck's words is concerned with things that pleasingly "befall preposterously," is a comedy. The best plays of our century, however, are another thing, and discussion of these plays—somewhat desperately called tragicomedy—will be postponed until later in this chapter.

What befalls—preposterous or not—is the action of the play. The gestures on the stage are, of course, "actions," but they are not the action of the play in the sense of Aristotle's use of *praxis,* or "action" in *The Poetics,* a fragmentary treatise of the fourth century B.C. that remains the starting point for most discussions of drama.

Imitation of an Action

For Aristotle, drama is the imitation (i.e., representation, re-presentation, re-creation) by impersonators, of an action. In tragedy the action is serious and important, something that matters, done by people who count (e.g., King Oedipus's discovery that he has killed his father and married his mother); in comedy (for Aristotle), the action is done by unimportant, laughable people who make mistakes that do not cause us pain. Commonly the tragic action is a man's perception of a great mistake he has made; he suffers intensely and perhaps dies, having exhausted all the possibilities of his life. (Female tragic heroes are rare.) The comic action often is

the exposure of folly and the renewal rather than the exhaustion of human nature. Crabby parents, for example, find that they cannot keep young lovers apart, and so they join in the marriage festivities. Byron jocosely put the matter thus:

> All tragedies are finished by a death,
> All comedies are ended by a marriage.

All tragedies and all comedies do not in fact end thus, but the idea is right; tragedy has the solemnity, seriousness, and finality we often associate with death,[1] and comedy has the joy and fertility and suggestion of a new life we often associate with marriage.

This concept of *an action* (i.e., an underlying motif, not merely gestures) in tragedy and in comedy makes clear that comedy is not a mere matter of jokes or funny bits of business. It also makes clear what the Greek comic playwright Menander meant when he told a friend that he had composed a play, and now had only to write the dialogue: he had worked out the happenings that would embody the action, and there remained only the slighter task of providing the spirited words. The same idea is implicit in Ibsen's comment that the drafts of his plays differed "very much from each other in characterization, not in action." The action or happening dramatized in a tragedy or a comedy may be conceived of as a single course or train of events manifested on the stage by a diversity of activities. Think of such expressions as "the closing of the frontier," or "the revival of learn-

---

[1]Shakespeare's tragedies all end with the death of the tragic hero, but a good many Greek tragedies do not. In *Oedipus the King* the hero remains alive, but he is blind and banished and seems to have exhausted the possibilities of his life. Some other Greek tragedies have what can reasonably be called a happy ending; that is, some sort of joyful reconciliation. For example, in Sophocles's *Philoctetes,* the weapon which has been taken from the sick Philoctetes is returned to him, and Heracles, a messenger from Zeus, announces that Philoctetes will be healed. But these tragedies with happy endings, like those with unhappy endings, deal with "important" people, and they are about "serious" things. If there is finally joy, it is a solemn joy.

ing"; each might be said to denote an action, though such action is seen only in its innumerable manifestations.

Happenings and Happenings

Tragic playwrights take some happening, from history (for example, the assassination of Julius Caesar) or from fiction (Shakespeare derived Othello from an Italian short story), or from their own imagination, and they make or shape or arrange episodes that clarify the action. They make (in common terminology) a *plot* that embodies the action or spiritual content. Even when playwrights draw on history, they make their own plot because they select and rearrange the available historical facts. A reenactment of everything that Julius Caesar did during his last days or hours would not be a play with an action, for drama is not so much concerned with what in fact *happened* as with some sort of typical and coherent or unified thing that *happens,* a significant action. Sometimes, of course, history provides substantial material for drama, but even Shakespeare's *Julius Caesar* takes frequent liberties with the facts as Shakespeare knew them, and Shakespeare's source, the biographer Plutarch, doubtless had already assimilated the facts to a literary form. At most we can say that history provided Shakespeare with a man whose life lent itself well to an established literary form. Not every life does lend itself thus.

Unity

We are told that Aeschylus, the earliest tragic playwright who has left us any complete plays, was killed when an eagle mistook his bald head for a rock and dropped a turtle on it to break the shell. Aeschylus's death was a great loss, but it did not have the unified significant action required of tragedy. By chance an eagle that had captured a turtle was near to Aeschylus, and Aeschylus by chance (or rather by his chemistry) was bald. There is no relation between these two circumstances; Aeschylus's death (allegedly) happened this way, and we can account for it, but the event has no intelligible unity. (A sentence from Vladimir Nabokov's *Pale Fire* comes to mind: If one is contemplating suicide, "jumping from a high bridge is not recommended even if you cannot swim, for wind and water abound in weird contingencies, and tragedy ought not to culminate in a record dive or a policeman's promotion.")

In tragedy things cohere. The hero normally does some deed and suffers as a consequence. Actions have consequences in the moral world no less than in the materialistic world of the laboratory. The tragic playwright's solemn presentation of "the remorseless working of things," Alfred North Whitehead pointed out (in his *Science and the Modern World,* 1925), is "the vision possessed by science," and it cannot be accidental that the two great periods of tragic drama, fifth-century B.C. Athens and England around 1600, were periods of scientific inquiry.

The Tragic Hero

This emphasis on causality means that the episodes are related, connected, and not merely contiguous. Generally the formula is to show the tragic hero moving toward committing some deed that will cause great unintended suffering, committing it, and then, by seeing the consequences, learning the true nature of his deed. The plot, that is, involves a credible character whose doings are related to his nature.

Hamartia

For Aristotle, in the best sort of tragedy the tragic hero is an important person, almost preeminently virtuous, who makes some sort of great mistake that entails great suffering. Calamity does not descend upon him from above, does not happen *to* him, nor does he consciously will a destructive act; he merely makes a great mistake. The mistake is Aristotle's **hamartia,** sometimes translated as "error," sometimes as "flaw." Probably Aristotle did not mean by *hamartia* a trait, such as rashness or ambition, which the translation "flaw" implies, but simply meant an action based on a mental error, a sort of false step. Oedipus, erroneously thinking that Polybus and Meropê are his parents, flees from them when he hears that he will kill his father and sleep with his mother. His action is commendable, but it happens to be a great mistake because it brings him to his real parents. Nevertheless, despite the scholarly elucidations of Aristotle, we can sometimes feel that the erring action proceeds from a particular kind of character, that a person with different traits would not have acted in the same way. The Oedipus that we see in the play, for example, is a self-assured quick-tempered man—almost a rash man, we might say—who might well have neglected to check the facts before he fled from Corinth. There are at least times, even when reading *Oedipus the King,* when one feels with George Meredith (1828–1909) that

> in tragic life, God wot,
> No villain need be! Passions spin the plot:
> We are betrayed by what is false within.

Hybris

From this it is only a short step to identifying *hamartia* with a flaw, and the flaw most often attributed to the tragic hero is **hybris,** a word that for the Greeks meant something like "bullying," "abuse of power," but in dramatic criticism usually is translated as "overweening pride." The tragic hero forgets that (in Montaigne's words) "on the loftiest throne in the world we are still sitting only on our own rear," and he believes his actions are infallible. King Lear, for example, banishes his daughter Cordelia with "Better thou / Hadst not been born than not t' have pleased me better." Macbeth, told that he will be king of Scotland, chooses to make the prophecy come true by murdering his guest, King Duncan; Brutus decides that Rome can be saved from tyranny only by killing Caesar, and he deludes himself into thinking he is not murdering Caesar but sacrificing Caesar for the welfare of Rome.

Peripeteia

We have talked of *hamartia* and *hybris* in tragedy; two more Greek words, **peripeteia** and **anagnorisis,** also common in discussions of tragedy, ought to be mentioned. A peripeteia (sometimes anglicized to *peripety* or translated as "reversal") occurs when the action takes a course not intended by the doer. Aristotle gives two examples: (1) the Messenger comes to cheer up Oedipus by freeing him from fears but the message heightens Oedipus's fears; (2) Danaus (in a lost play) prosecutes a man but is himself killed.

A few other examples may be useful: Oedipus flees from Corinth to avoid contact with his parents, but his flight brings him to them; Macbeth kills Duncan to gain the crown but his deed brings him fearful nights instead of joyful days; Lear, seeking a peaceful old age, puts himself in the hands of two daughters who maltreat him, and banishes the one daughter who later will comfort him. The Bible—especially the Hebrew Bible—is filled with such peripeties or ironic actions. For example, the Philistines brought Samson before them to entertain them, and he performed his most spectacular feat by destroying his audience. But the archetypal tragic story is that of Adam and Eve: Aiming to be like gods, they lost their immortality and the earthly paradise, and brought death to themselves.

Anagnorisis

The other Greek word, **anagnorisis,** translated as "recognition" or "discovery" or "disclosure," seems to have meant for Aristotle a clearing up of some misunderstanding, such as the proper identification of someone or the revelation of some previously unknown fact. But later critics have given it a richer meaning and used it to describe the hero's perception of his or her true nature or true plight. In the narrow sense, it is an anagnorisis or "recognition" when King Lear learns that Regan and Goneril are ungrateful and cruel. In the wider sense, the anagnorisis is in his speech in 3.4, when he confesses his former ignorance and his neglect of his realm:

> Poor naked wretches, wheresoe'er you are,
> That bide the pelting of this pitiless storm,
> How shall your houseless heads and unfed sides,
> Your looped and windowed raggedness, defend you
> From seasons such as these? O, I have ta'en
> Too little care of this! Take physic, pomp;
> Expose thyself to feel what wretches feel,
> That thou mayst shake the superflux to them,
> And show the heavens more just.

Similarly, Hamlet's "There is special providence in the fall of a sparrow," and Othello's "one that loved not wisely, but too well," may be called recognition scenes. Here is Macbeth's recognition that his purpose has been frustrated, that his deed has been ironic:

> My way of life
> Is fall'n into the sear, the yellow leaf
> And that which should accompany old age,
> As honor, love, obedience, troops of friends,
> I must not look to have.

The Social World of Comedy

"Troops of friends" abound in comedy. Where tragedy is primarily the dramatization of the single life that ripens and then can only rot, that reaches its fullest and then is destroyed, comedy is primarily the dramatization of the renewing of the self and of social relationships. Tragic heroes are isolated from society, partly by their different natures, and partly by their tragic acts; comedy suggests that selfhood is found not in assertion of individuality, but in joining in the fun, in becoming part of the flow of common humanity. Where tragedy suggests an incompatibility between the energy or surge of the individual life and the laws of life or the norms of society, comedy suggests that norms are valid and necessary.

Tragic Isolation

Tragic heroes do what they feel compelled to do; they assert themselves, and are intensely aware that they are special persons and not members of the crowd. But that their mistake always reveals that they are hybristic is not at all certain. The Greek tragic hero is commonly set against a chorus of ordinary mortals who caution him, wring their hands, and lament the hero's boldness, but these ordinary mortals are always aware that if they are law-abiding people, they are also less fully human beings than the hero. That they obey society's laws is not due to superior virtue, to the triumph of reason over will, to self-discipline; rather, their obedience is due to a lower vision, or to timidity, and indeed sometimes to a fear of what resides in their own breasts.

Tragic Virtue

Tragic heroes are, of course, in one way inferior to those about them; their actions cost them great suffering, and they are thus immobilized as the others are not. But their greatness remains indisputable; the anguish that at times paralyzes Hamlet also makes him greater than, say, Horatio and Laertes. In fact, tragic heroes are circumscribed, certainly after the deed, when they are necessarily subject to the consequences (Brutus kills Caesar and finds that he brings to Rome a turmoil that makes him flee from Rome and that ultimately makes him take his own life); even before doing the tragic deed, the heroes are circumscribed because their action proceeds from something, either from their personality or from their circumstances. Still, their action seems to them to be freely theirs, and indeed we feel that it is an action that lesser persons could not perform. This perception is almost a way of arguing that a tragic hero may err not so much from weakness as from strength. Why can Iago so easily deceive Othello? Not because Othello is an unthinking savage, or an unsophisticated foreigner, but because (as Iago admits) Othello is of a "loving noble nature," and, again,

> The Moor is of a free and open nature
> That thinks men honest that but seem to be so;
> And will as tenderly be led by th' nose
> As asses are.

Why can Claudius see to it that Laertes murders Hamlet during a fencing match? Not because Hamlet is a poor fencer, or a coward, but because Hamlet

> Most generous, and free from all contriving,
> Will not peruse the foils.

Tragic Joy

This is not to say that tragic heroes are faultless, or that they are quite happy with themselves and with their action; but they do experience a kind of exultation even in their perception that disaster is upon them. If they grieve over their deeds, we sense a glory in their grief, for they find, like Captain Ahab, that in their topmost grief lies their topmost greatness. At last they see everything and know that nothing more can be experienced. They have lived their lives to the limits. Othello put it thus:

> Here is my journey's end, here is my butt,
> And very seamark of my utmost sail.

(In a comedy Shakespeare tells us that "journeys end in lovers meeting," that is, the end is a new beginning.)

In "Under Ben Bulben" William Butler Yeats (1865–1939) suggests the sense of completeness that the tragic hero experiences when, under the influence of a great passion, he exhausts his nature and seems to be not a man among men but a partner (rather than a subject) of fate:

> Know that when all words are said
> And a man is fighting mad,
> Something drops from eyes long blind,
> He completes his partial mind,
> For an instant stands at ease,
> Laughs aloud, his heart at peace.
> Even the wisest man grows tense
> With some sort of violence
> Before he can accomplish fate,
> Know his work or choose his mate.

Elsewhere Yeats put his distinction between the tragic hero and the world the hero is up against thus: "Some French-

man[2] has said that farce is the struggle against a ridiculous object, comedy against a movable object, tragedy against an immovable; and because the will, or energy, is greatest in tragedy, tragedy is the more noble; but I add that 'will or energy is eternal delight,' and when its limit is reached it may become a pure, aimless joy, though the man, the shade, still mourns his lost object."

Comic Assertion

What of the contexts and times when we find passionate self-assertion funny? Much depends on what is being asserted, and on what or who the antagonist is. King Lear against his tigerish daughters is a tragic figure, but a pedant against a dull schoolboy may be a comic one. The lament of the tragic hero is proportionate to the event, but the effort extended by the comic figure is absurdly disproportionate. Furthermore, as Henri Bergson (1859–1941) pointed out, the comic figure usually is a sort of mechanism, repeating his actions and catch phrases with clocklike regularity in contexts where they are inappropriate. He quotes Latin on every occasion, or he never travels without his pills, or she always wants to know how much something costs, or he is forever spying on his wife. Bergson, who suggested that the comic is "the mechanical encrusted on the living," illustrated his point by telling of the customs officers who bravely rescue the crew of a sinking vessel, and then ask, the moment the shore is reached, "Have you anything to declare?" The mechanical question, inappropriate in the situation, reveals that the officers value trivial regulations as much as they do life itself. In The Circus Charlie Chaplin is dusting things off; he comes upon the magician's bowl of goldfish, takes the fish out and wipes them, and then returns them to the bowl.

Comic Joy

The comic world seems to be presided over by a genial, tolerant deity who enjoys the variety that crosses the stage. The sketchbooks of the Japanese artist Hokusai (1760–1849) wonderfully reveal this comic delight in humanity. There are pages of fat men, pages of thin men (no less engagingly drawn), pages of men making funny faces, and there is a delightful drawing of a man holding a magnifying glass in front of his face so that his nose seems enormous. Comic playwrights give us something of this range of types and grotesques, and they give us also variety in language (e.g., puns, inverted clichés, malapropisms) and variety in episodes (much hiding behind screens, dressing in disguise).

[2]Yeats is rather freely summarizing Ferdinand Brunetière's La Loi du théâtre. A translation of Brunetière's treatise is available in European Theories of the Drama, ed. Barrett H. Clark.

Comic Isolation

The characters, then, who insist on being themselves, who mechanically hold to a formula of language or of behavior, are laughably out of place in the world of varied people who live and let live. What comedy does not tolerate is intolerance; it regularly suggests that the intolerant—for example, the pedant and the ascetic—are fools and probably hypocrites. Here is the self-righteous Alceste, in Molière's *The Misanthrope:*

> Some men I hate for being rogues: the others,
> I hate because they treat the rogues like brothers,
> And, lacking a virtuous scorn for what is vile,
> Receive the villain with a complaisant smile.
> Notice how tolerant people choose to be
> Toward that bold rascal who's at law with me.

Philinte genially replies,

> Let's have an end of rantings and of railings,
> And show some leniency toward human failings.
> This world requires a pliant rectitude;
> Too stern a virtue makes one stiff and rude.

Here is the puritanical Malvolio in *Twelfth Night,* trying to quiet down some tipsy but genial revelers:

> My masters, are you mad? Or what are you? Have you no wit, manners nor honesty, but to gabble like tinkers at this time of night? Do ye make an alehouse of my lady's house? . . . Is there not respect of place, persons, nor time in you?

He is aptly answered:

> Art any more than a steward? Dost thou think, because thou art virtuous, there shall be no more cakes and ale?

This suspicion of a "virtue" that is opposed to cakes and ale runs through the history of comedy.

In Shakespeare's *Love's Labor Lost,* the young noblemen who vow to devote themselves to study, and to forgo the company of women, are laughed at until they accept their bodies and admit interest in those of the ladies. The celebration of the human body, or at least the good-natured acceptance of it which is present in comedy, is well put by the General in Anouilh's *The Waltz of the Toreadors:*

> You're in the ocean, splashing about, doing your damndest not to drown, in spite of whirlpools and cross currents. The main thing is to do the regulation breast-stroke and if you're not a clod, never to let the life-buoy ["the ideal"] out of sight. No one expects any more than that out of you. Now if you relieve yourself in the water now and then, that's your affair. The sea is big, and if the top half of your body still looks as though it's doing the breaststroke, nobody will say a word.

Detachment and Engagement

One way of distinguishing between comedy and tragedy is summarized in Horace Walpole's aphorism "This world is a comedy to those that think, a tragedy to those that feel." Life seen thoughtfully, with considerable detachment, viewed from above, as it were, is an amusing pageant, and the comic writer gives us something of this view. With Puck we look at the antics in the forest, smile tolerantly, and say with a godlike perspective, "Lord, what fools these mortals be!" But in tragedy we are to a greater degree engaged; the tragic dramatist manages to make us in large measure identify ourselves with the hero, feel his plight as if it were our own, and value his feelings as he values them.[3] Yeats noticed this when he said that "character is continuously present in comedy alone," and that "tragedy must always be a drowning and breaking of the dykes that separate man from man. . . . It is upon these dykes comedy keeps house." And Yeats again: "Nor when the tragic reverie is at its height do we say, 'How well that man is realised, I should know him were I to meet him in the street,' for it is always ourselves that we see upon the [tragic] stage."

Tragic Fate and Comic Fortune in Plots

One consequence of this distinction between tragedy and comedy, between looking-at and feeling-with, is that the comic plot is usually more intricate than the tragic plot, and less plausible. The comic plot continues to trip up its characters, bringing them into numerous situations that allow them to display their folly over and over again. The complex comic plot is often arbitrary, full of the workings of Fortune or Chance, and we delight at each new unexpected or unlikely happening. In tragedy, Fate (sometimes in the form that "character is destiny") or Necessity rules, there is the consistency and inevitability, the "remorseless working of things," that has already been mentioned. If Macbeth were struck dead by a falling roof tile while he dozed in the palace after a good meal, instead of dying on Macduff's sword, or if Brutus were to die by slipping in his bath, instead of dying on the very sword with which he killed Caesar, we would have arbitrary happenings that violate the spirit of everything that precedes. But the unexpected letters and the long-lost relatives that often turn up at the close of a comedy are thoroughly in the spirit of the comic vision, which devalues not only rigidly consistent character but rigidity of every sort, even of plot. Tragedy usually follows a straight course, comedy a delightfully twisted one.

Comic Beginnings and Endings

The rigid behavior of some of comedy's laughably serious characters (e.g., misers, jealous husbands, stern fathers) is

---

[3]Bergson's theory that a human being—an organism—is comical when it behaves mechanically requires, as Bergson said, a modification: feelings must be suppressed. A crippled man is not comic despite his mechanical limp, because we feel for him. Comedy requires, Bergson said, an "anesthesia of the heart."

paralleled in the rigid circumstances that often are sketched at the beginning of a comedy. In *A Midsummer Night's Dream* the Athenian law requires that a young woman marry the man of her father's choice, or be put to death, or live chastely in a nunnery. Gilbert and Sullivan, to draw on familiar material, afford plenty of examples of comedy's fondness for a cantankerous beginning: *The Mikado* opens with a chorus of Japanese noblemen whose code of etiquette makes them appear to be "worked by strings"; they live in a town where a law ordered that "all who flirted, leered or winked / Should forthwith be beheaded." (Comedy often begins with a society dominated by some harsh law.) Although this law has been suspended, another harsh decree is in effect: The pretty Yum-Yum is betrothed to her old guardian, Ko-Ko. We learn, too, that her appropriate wooer, Nanki-Poo, is a prince who has had to disguise himself as a humble wandering minstrel to escape his father's decree that he marry Katisha, an old and ugly lady of the court.

After various doings in a comedy, a new—presumably natural, prosperous, fertile, and free—society is formed, usually centered around young lovers who are going to be married. Yum-Yum and Nanki-Poo finally contrive to get married, evading Katisha and Ko-Ko, who make the best of things by marrying each other. The whole business is satisfactorily explained to the Mikado, who affably accepts, and ruffled tempers are soothed:

> The threatened cloud has passed away,
> And brightly shines the dawning day;
> What though the night may come too soon,
> We've years and years of afternoon!
>
> Then let the throng
> Our joy advance,
> With laughing song
> And merry dance,
> With joyous shout and ringing cheer,
> Inaugurate our new career!

The first four lines are sung by the young lovers, the remaining six are sung by "All," the new, or renewed, society, free from unnatural law. *H.M.S. Pinafore* begins with lovers who cannot marry because of disparity in rank, but ends with appropriate shifts in rank so that there can be "three loving pairs on the same day united."

Self-knowledge

In comedy there is often not only an improbable turn in events but an improbable (but agreeable) change in character—or at least in rank; troublesome persons become enlightened, find their own better nature, and join in the fun, commonly a marriage feast. Finding one's own nature is common in tragedy, too, but there self-knowledge is coterminous with death or some deathlike condition, such as blindness. *Oedipus the King* ends with a note of finality, even though Oedipus is alive at the end; the fact that twenty-five years later Sophocles decided to write a play showing Oedipus's apotheosis does not allow us to see the earlier play as less than complete. The chorus in *Oedipus the King* has the last word:

> This man was Oedipus.
> That mighty King, who knew the riddle's mystery,
> Whom all the city envied, Fortune's favorite.
> Behold, in the event, the storm of his calamities,
> And, being mortal, think on that last day of death,
> Which all must see, and speak of no man's happiness
> Till, without sorrow, he hath passed the goal of life.

Or consider the irreparable loss at the end of Shakespeare's tragedies: "This was the noblest Roman of them all"; "We that are young / Shall never see so much, nor live so long"; "The rest is silence." But comedy ends with a new beginning, a newly formed society, usually a wedding party; the tragic figure commonly awakens to the fact that he has made a big mistake and his life is over, but the comic figure commonly awakens to his better nature. He usually sheds his aberration and is restored to himself and to a renewed society. Alceste's refusal to change, at the end of *The Misanthrope*, helps to push that comedy toward the borderline between comedy and tragedy. Oedipus learns that his parents were not those whom he had supposed, and he learns that even the mighty Oedipus can be humbled. Othello comes to see himself as a man "that loved not wisely but too well," and, having reached his journey's end, he executes justice upon himself by killing himself. That is, at the end of the play he finds himself, but this finding of the self separates him forever from those around him, whereas the comic figure who finds himself usually does so by putting aside in some measure his individuality and by submitting himself to a partner or to the group.

Comedy and tragedy offer different visions and represent different psychological states. And they are equally useful. The tragic vision may have more prestige, but it is no small thing to make people laugh, to call attention amusingly to the follies and joys of life, and to help develop the sense of humor—and humility—that may be indispensable to survival in a world continually threatened by aggressive ideals that demand uncritical acceptance. Infants smile easily, and children laugh often, but growing up is often attended by a frightening seriousness. True, hostile laughter, the scarcely veiled aggressiveness that manifests itself in derision, remains an adult possession, but the laughter evoked by the best comedy is good-natured while it is critical, and it is in part directed at ourselves. We look at bumbling humanity and we recall Puck's words, "Lord, what fools these mortals be." This is not to say that the comic vision is cynical; rather, it attributes to folly what less generous visions attribute to ill will or to hopeless corruption, and when it laughs it forgives. Analyses of laughter are sometimes funny but more often they are tedious; still, they at least pay the comic spirit the compliment of recognizing it as worthy of our best efforts.

TRAGICOMEDY

Tragicomedy before 1900

The word *tragicomedy* is much newer than the words *tragedy* and *comedy*; it first appeared about 186 B.C., when Plautus spoke of *tragicocomoedia* in his *Amphitryon*, a Roman comedy in which gods assume mortal shapes in order to dupe a husband and seduce his wife. Mercury, in a joking prologue to the play, explains the author's dilemma:

> I'll make it a mixture, a tragicomedy. It wouldn't be right for me to make it all a comedy since kings and gods appear. Well, then, since there's a slave part too, I'll do as I said and make it a tragicomedy.

But the play is a traditional comedy, unalloyed with the solemnity, terror, and pity of tragedy. It shows laughable activities that finally turn out all right. It should be mentioned again, however, that although tragedy and comedy were clearly separated in the ancient world, not all ancient tragedies ended with death, or even ended unhappily. Aeschylus's trilogy, *The Oresteia*, ends with reconciliation and solemn joy (but it has been bought at the price of great suffering), and Sophocles's *Philoctetes* and Euripides's *Iphigeneia at Taurus* end with catastrophes averted. They were tragic for the Greeks because momentous issues were treated seriously, though we might say that the plots have a comic structure because they end happily.

In the Renaissance there was much fussing over the meanings of tragedy, comedy, and tragicomedy, but most theoreticians inclined to the view that tragedy dealt with noble figures engaged in serious actions, was written in a lofty style, and ended unhappily; comedy dealt with humbler figures engaged in trivial actions, was written in relatively common diction, and ended happily. Tragicomedy, whether defined as some mixture (e.g., high people in trivial actions) or as a play in which, to quote Sir Philip Sidney, the writer "thrust in the clown by head and shoulders to play a part in majestical matters," was for the most part scorned by academic critics as a mongrel. It was merely additive, bits of comedy added to a tragedy. At best the advocates for tragicomedy could argue that a play without the terror of tragedy and the absurdity of comedy can cover a good deal of life and can please a good many tastes. But this sort of play, unlike modern tragicomedy, is not so much a union of tragedy and comedy as an exclusion of both, lacking, for example, the awe we associate with tragedy and the fun we associate with comedy.

In the twentieth century the word and the form have become thoroughly respectable; indeed, it is now evident that most of the best plays of our century are best described not as tragedies or as comedies but as tragicomedies—distinctive fusions (not mere aggregations) of tragedy and comedy. For a start we can take William Hazlitt's statement that "man is the only animal that laughs and weeps; for he is the only animal that is struck with the difference between what

things are, and what they ought to be." Another way of putting it is to say that human beings have an ideal of conduct, but circumstances and human limitations prevent them from fulfilling this ideal. This pursuit of the ideal thus can seem noble, or foolish, or a mixture of the two.

Detachment and Engagement Again

Most of the best playwrights of the twentieth century have adopted the more complicated mixed view. Comedy had customarily invoked a considerable degree of detachment; in Bergson's formula (1900), already quoted, comedy requires an anesthesia of the spectators' hearts as they watch folly on the stage. Tragedy, on the other hand, has customarily invoked a considerable degree of involvement or sympathy; in Walpole's formula, also already quoted, "The world is a comedy to those that think, a tragedy to those that feel." But tragicomedy shows us comic characters for whom we feel deep sympathy. Pirandello, in his essay *Umorismo* (1908), gives an interesting example of the phenomenon. Suppose, he says, we see an elderly woman with dyed hair and much too much makeup. We find her funny; but if we realize that she is trying to hold the attention of her husband, our sympathy is aroused. Our sense of her absurdity is not totally dissipated, but we feel for her and so our laughter is combined with pity.

Theater of the Absurd

In the third quarter of the twentieth century the theater that was most vital was not the Broadway musical, the earnest problem-play, or the well-made drawing-room comedy (although these continued to be written) but a fairly unified body of drama called the absurd, whose major writers are Beckett, Genet, Ionesco, Pinter, and Albee. Their theme is human anguish, but their techniques are those of comedy: improbable situations and unheroic characters who say funny things. These writers differ, of course, and differ from play to play, but they are all preoccupied with the loneliness of people in a world without the certainties afforded by God or by optimistic rationalism. This loneliness is heightened by a sense of impotence derived partly from an awareness of our inability to communicate in a society that has made language meaningless, and partly from an awareness of the precariousness of our existence in an atomic age.

Behind this vision are some two hundred years of thinking that have conspired to make it difficult to think of any person as a hero who confronts a mysterious cosmic order. Man, Ionesco says in *Notes and Counter Notes*, is "cut off from his religious and metaphysical roots." One of the milestones in the journey toward contemporary nihilism is the bourgeois drama of the middle of the eighteenth century, which sought to show the dignity of the common people but which, negatively put, undermined the concept of a tragic hero. Instead of showing a heroic yet universal figure, it showed ordinary people in relation to their society, thus paving the way for Arthur Miller's Willy Loman, who apparently would have been okay, as we all would be, if our economic system allowed for early retirement. Miller's play makes no claim for Willy's grandeur or for the glory of life; it claims only that he is an ordinary man at the end of his rope in a deficient society and that he is entitled to a fair deal.

Diminution of Human Beings

Other landmarks on the road to our awareness of our littleness are, like bourgeois drama, developments in thinking that were believed by their builders to be landmarks on the road to our progressive conquest of fear. Among these we can name Darwin's *The Origin of Species* (1859), which, in the popular phrase, seemed to record progress "up from apes," but which, more closely read, reduced human beings to the product of "accidental variations" and left God out of the picture, substituting for a cosmic order a barbaric struggle for existence. (In the second edition, 1860, Darwin spoke of life as "breathed by the creator," but the creator was not Darwin's concern and he later abandoned all religious beliefs. Probably he retained his belief that the process of "natural selection works solely by and for the good of each being," but by 1889 his disciple T. H. Huxley saw it differently. Huxley said he knew of no study "so unutterably saddening as that of the evolution of humanity.") Karl Marx, studying the evolution of societies at about the same time, was attributing our sense of alienation to economic forces, thereby implying that we have no identity we can properly call our own. Moreover, Marxist thinking, like Darwinian thinking, suggested that human beings could not do anything of really great importance, nor could they be blamed for their misfortunes. At the end of the nineteenth century, and in the early twentieth century, Freud, also seeking to free us from tyranny, turned to the forces within our mind. Ironically, the effort to chart our unconscious drives and anarchic impulses in order to help us to know ourselves induced a profound distrust of the self: we can scarcely be confident of our behavior, for we know that apparently heroic behavior has unconscious unheroic motives rooted in the experiences of infancy. Tragic heroes are people with complexes, and religious codes are only wishful thinking.

Dissolution of Character and Plot

The result of such developments in thought seems to be that a "tragic sense" in the twentieth century commonly means a despairing or deeply uncertain view, something very different from what it meant in Greece and in Elizabethan England. This uncertainty is not merely about the cosmos but even about character or identity. In 1888, in the Preface to *Miss Julie*, August Strindberg called attention to the new sense of the instability of character:

I have made the people in my play fairly "characterless." The middle-class conception of a fixed character was transferred to the stage, where the middle class has always ruled. A character there came to mean an actor who was always one and the same, always drunk, always comic or always melancholy, and who needed to be characterized only by some physical defect such as a club foot, a wooden leg, or a red nose, or by the repetition of some such phrase such as, "That's capital," or "Barkis is willin'." . . . Since the persons in my play are modern characters, living in a transitional era more hurried and hysterical than the previous one at least, I have depicted them as more unstable, as torn and divided, a mixture of the old and the new.

In 1902, in his preface to *A Dream Play*, he is more explicit: "Anything may happen, anything seems possible and probable. . . . The characters split, double, multiply, vanish, solidify, blur, clarify." Strindberg's view of the fluidity of character—the characterlessness of character, one might say—has continued and is apparent in almost all of Pirandello's work, in the underground film, and in much of the theater of the absurd. Ionesco, in *Fragments of a Journal*, says, "I often find it quite impossible to hold an opinion about a fact, a thing or a person. Since it's all a matter of interpretation, one has to choose a particular interpretation." In *Notes and Counter Notes* Ionesco said, "chance formed us," and that we would be different if we had different experiences; characteristically, a few years later he said that he was no longer sure that he believed in chance.

Along with the sense of characterlessness, or at least of the mystery of character, there developed in the drama (and in the underground film and the novel) a sense of plotlessness, or fundamental untruthfulness of the traditional plot that moved by cause and effect. "Plots," Ionesco has said in *Conversations*, "are never interesting," and again he has said that a play should be able to stop at any point; it ends only because "the audience has to go home to bed. . . . It's true for real life. Why should it be different for art?" Ionesco has treated his own plots very casually, allowing directors to make "all the cuts needed" and suggesting that endings other than those he wrote are possibilities. After all, in a meaningless world one can hardly take a dramatic plot seriously. In Ionesco's *Victims of Duty* a character defends a new kind of irrational, anti-Aristotelian drama: "The theater of my dreams would be irrationalist. . . . The contemporary theater doesn't reflect the cultural tone of our period, it's not in harmony with the general drift of the other manifestations of the modern spirit. . . . We'll get rid of the principle of identity and unity of character. . . . Personality doesn't exist." A policeman-psychologist (a materialist who demands law and order) offers an old-fashioned view: "I don't believe in the absurd, everything hangs together, everything can be comprehended . . . thanks to the achievements of human thought and science," but he is murdered by the anti-Aristotelian.

Thus, Becket's *Waiting for Godot* ends—as the first act ended—without anything ending:

VLADIMIR. Well? Shall we go?
ESTRAGON. Yes, let's go.
They do not move.

CURTAIN

To bring an action to a completion, as drama traditionally did, is to imply an orderly world of cause and effect, of beginnings and endings, but for the dramatists of the absurd, there is no such pattern. At best it is *Hamlet* as Tom Stoppard's *Rosencrantz and Guildenstern* see it: They are supposed to do a job they don't understand, and instead of a pattern or "order" they encounter only "Incidents! Incidents! Dear God, is it too much to expect a little sustained action?" Well, yes; it is too much to expect.

The Tragedy of Comedy

There can be no tragedy, because, as Ionesco explains in *Notes,* tragedy admits the existence of fate or destiny, which is to say it admits the existence of objective (however incomprehensible) laws ruling the universe, whereas the new comic perception of incongruity is that existence itself is absurd because there is no objective law. The new comic vision is far darker than the old tragic vision; it has nothing in it of what Yeats called "tragic joy." But what is our reaction to this joyless comedy? Let Ionesco, whose plays sometimes include meaningless babble, have the last word:

> The fact of being astonishes us, in a world that now seems all illusion and pretense, in which all human behavior tells of absurdity and all history of absolute futility; all reality and all language appear to lose their articulation, to disintegrate and collapse, so what possible reaction is there left, when everything has ceased to matter, but laugh at it all.[4]

DRAMA AND SOCIETY: SIX QUESTIONS

Our government supports the arts, including the theater, by giving grants to numerous institutions. On the other hand, the amount that the government contributes (for example, through the National Endowment for the Arts and the

National Endowment for the Humanities) is extremely small when compared to the amounts given to the arts by most European governments. It is estimated that federal subsidies amount to about five percent of the funding of established arts institutions, whereas in Europe they amount to something over sixty percent. The government of Germany, for instance, gives more to its theaters than our government gives to *all* of the arts combined.

Of course one might reply that our government offers relatively little support because private philanthropies offer so much—and one can add that that is the way it ought to be. Why, after all, should the government support the arts? Why should taxpayers who have little or no interest in the arts be forced to subsidize them? Doesn't this use of tax dollars involve a sort of reverse Robin Hoodism, taking money from the poor and giving it to the rich, who go to the theaters and the museums?

Let's begin, then, by formulating a few questions:

1. Should taxpayers' dollars be used to support the arts, in particular the theater in America? Why, or why not? Is it relevant to say that even if, on principle, the arts deserve to be supported, we cannot afford to give them money when we are confronted with such problems as homelessness, AIDS, and inadequate health care?
2. What possible public benefit(s) can come from supporting the arts? Can one argue that, in effect, we should support the arts for the same reasons that we support the public schools; that is, in order to have a civilized citizenry?
3. If dollars should be given to the arts, should the political content of the works be taken into account, or only the aesthetic merit? Can we always, or sometimes, or never, separate political content from aesthetic content?
4. Is it censorship not to award public funds to artists or groups whose work is not approved of, or is it simply a matter of refusing to reward them with taxpayers' dollars?
5. Should decisions about grants be made chiefly by federal officials or chiefly by experts in the field? Why?
6. If the arts are funded, should the funds go only to bring the classics to the public—in our case, to subsidize productions of plays that have withstood the test of time, therefore becoming a part of our cultural heritage—or should funds also be used to support new playwrights?

We hope that you will occasionally think about these questions when you read the plays—and when you go to the theater.

[4]*Notes and Counter Notes: Writings on the Theatre* (New York: Grove Press, 1964), p. 163.

PART TWO

A Collection of Plays

A Note on
THE ORIGINS OF GREEK DRAMA
AND THE STRUCTURE OF GREEK TRAGEDY

THE THEORY OF AN ORIGIN IN DIONYSIAN RITUALS

Although the ancient Greeks were fairly confident that they knew the origin and history of drama, modern scholars are less certain. The Greeks—notably Aristotle (384–322 B.C.)—said that both tragedy and comedy originated in improvisations; tragedy, according to Aristotle, originated in improvisations in choral poems honoring Dionysus (the god of fertility and wine), and comedy originated in improvisations in phallic songs. Around the middle of the sixth century B.C. a man named Thespis stepped out of the chorus and, singing in a different meter, became an impersonator who sang not *about* a god but *in the role of* a god. Thespis thus was the first actor, and by taking on an identity apart from the chorus, he and his successors made possible dialogue between a character and the chorus. (The chorus numbered twelve of fifteen performers.) Later the playwright Aeschylus (525–456 B.C.) added a second actor, thus increasing the dramatic (as opposed to the lyric and narrative) element, and still later Sophocles (c. 496–406 B.C.) added the third. The number of actors became fixed at three, so in ancient Greek drama there are never more than three speaking parts onstage at one time. However, since the actors could double in roles, there may be eight or even ten speaking parts in a play.

Unfortunately, there is little evidence to support the assertion that Greek tragedy originated in festivals honoring Dionysus. The chief evidence for the theory, aside from Aristotle's assertion (made some three centuries after the supposed fact), is that tragic plays from 534 B.C. were indeed performed at a festival called the Dionysia, honoring Dionysus. But, surprisingly, Dionysus figures importantly in only one Greek tragedy, which is puzzling if Greek tragedy really did originate in songs honoring him. The old view dies hard, however, and one still usually reads that tragedy originated in choral songs sung at fertility festivals honoring Dionysus, and that at some decisive moment Thespis impersonated him or some other god, and tragic drama was born.

A sort of corollary goes thus: Since Dionysus was god of the vine, the original songs were performed during revels in honor of the rebirth of the vine, which was seen as the rebirth of the year, the renewal of life after the death of the year in winter. The celebration of the renewal of the "year spirit" involved dramatizing the death of this divine power, and that's what Greek tragedy supposedly shows, though the "divine power" or "year spirit" came to be put into the forms of Greek heroes rather than of the god Dionysus. This is all pretty imaginative; skeptics have asked not only why Dionysus virtually disappears from the plays but also why these plays, supposedly rooted in festivals honoring the renewal of the year, end with death and lamentation rather than with renewal and joy. To the second objection, the answer is sometimes made that the plays do indeed include a suggestion of renewal; the hero comes to perceive his or her fate, and in recognizing it, and in magnificently singing about it, shows a sort of spiritual rebirth. Confronted with this answer, skeptics remain (justifiably) skeptical.

THE USE OF MASKS

One other alleged connection with ritual should be mentioned. We know that Greek actors wore masks when they performed. Advocates of the ritual origin of Greek drama argue that the masks derived from masks that priests wore for two reasons: to impersonate the gods, and to disguise themselves lest the gods be displeased with them. Skeptics reply that the masks, with their bold, stylized features, were necessary in order to identify the characters to the audience in the vast theaters, since a Greek theater held some 15,000 people. That is, even a spectator at a great distance from the stage would immediately be able to know, upon seeing a character enter with a stereotyped mask, that this was a tragic king, or a young woman, or a messenger, or whatever. It is also argued that the mouths of the masks were designed to serve as megaphones, though in fact the acoustics in Greek theaters are so remarkably good that megaphones seem unnecessary.

THE STRUCTURE OF GREEK TRAGEDY

A tragedy commonly begins with a *prologue,* during which the exposition is given. Next comes the chorus's *ode* of entrance, sung while the chorus marches into the theater, through the side aisles and onto the orchestra. The ensuing *scene* is followed by a choral song or *stasimon.* Usually there are four or five scenes, alternating with odes. Each of these choral odes has a *strophe* (lines presumably sung while the chorus dances in one direction) and an *antistrophe* (lines presumably sung while the chorus retraces its steps). Sometimes a third part, an *epode,* concludes an ode. (In addition to odes that are *stasima*—the plural of stasimon—there can be odes within episodes; the fourth episode of *Antigone* contains an ode complete with *epode.*) After the last part of the last ode comes the *epilogue,* or final scene.

The actors (all male) seem to have chanted much of the play. Perhaps the total result of combining speech with music and dancing was a sort of music-drama roughly akin to opera with some spoken dialogue, such as Mozart's *Magic Flute.*

For a brief additional remark about Dionysus, see the entry on him in the Glossary.

A Note on
THE GREEK THEATER

The great age of the Greek drama was the fifth century B.C. All of the Greek plays in this book are from that period, and all were presented in the Theater of Dionysus at Athens. The audience sat on wooden benches or stone tiers of seats on a hillside (see photos, pages 12 and 46), looking down at a flat circular dancing place (the *orchestra*), about sixty-five feet in diameter, in the middle of which was an altar to Dionysus. Behind the dancing place was a stage or playing area, which logic (but almost no concrete evidence) suggests may have been slightly elevated. Visible behind the playing area was the *skene*, a wooden "scene-building" introduced about 458 B.C. that served as a background (as in our word "scenery"), as a place for actors to make entrances from and exits to (through a door or doors in the front), and as a dressing room where actors could change masks and costumes.

To speak of these elements in a little more detail: The seating area, which held some fourteen thousand people, was the *theatron* ("seeing-place"); fan-shaped or horseshoe-shaped, it swept around the orchestra in a segment greater than a semicircle. The chorus of singers and dancers, entering by an aisle (*parodos*) at each side of the *theatron*, danced in the orchestra. The *skene* or scene-building (or stage-building) was about twelve feet deep, and consisted of two stories. A god might appear on the roof, or (as in *Antigone*) even a watchman. Since most of the spectators were looking down from the hillside, a performer on the roof would be easily visible. The front (i.e., the façade) of the *skene* (or perhaps a temporary screen) and sometimes the playing area in front of it seem to have been called the *proskenion.* Though the *skene's* façade perhaps suggested the front of a temple or a palace, there were further efforts at indicating locale: Sophocles is said to have invented scene painting (a painted cloth or screen in front of the *skene?*), and there are allusions to *periaktoi,* upright prisms bearing a different decoration on each side. Apparently when a new locality in the same town was to be indicated, the *periaktos* at the right was turned; when an entirely new locality was to be indicated, both *periaktoi* were turned. Other machines were the *eccyclema,* a platform that was rolled out of the *skene* to indicate a scene indoors, and the *mechane,* a crane from which a god could descend or by means of which a character could soar through the air. (See, in the Glossary, *deus ex machina.*)

The playing area or stage in front of the *skene* was probably about twenty-five feet wide, eight or nine feet deep, and if it was elevated it was connected to the orchestra by a few steps. On the whole the actors confined themselves to the stage, backed by the *skene*, and the chorus confined itself to the *orchestra*, but there are a few instances of intermingling. For example, in *Medea*, at one point the chorus ventures onto the stage and hammers at the door of the *skene*.

STAGE SYMBOLISM

Speaking a bit broadly, we can say that the Greek theater, open to the heavens, with its orchestra representing a city square and the *skene* representing a temple or palace, is itself a symbol of the ancient Athenian worldview of a society that operates under divine and human law. Further, the diminutive size of the actors in the vast theater, and the background of trees and mountains, must also have conveyed a sense of the sublime natural world surrounding human passions.

Plays were put on chiefly during two holidays, the **Lenaea** (Feast of the Wine Press) in January, and the **Great** (or **City**) **Dionysia** in March or April. The Lenaea was chiefly associated with comedy, the Great Dionysia with tragedy. At the latter, on each of three mornings, a tragic dramatist presented three tragedies and one **satyr-play.** The expense was born by a *choregos,* a rich citizen ordered by the state to assume the financial burden. Consult Margarete Bieber, *The History of the Greek and Roman Theater;* T. B. L. Webster, *Greek Theatre Production,* 2nd ed.; Graham Ley, *A Short Introduction to the Ancient Greek Theater;* and Peter Arnott, *The Ancient Greek and Roman Theatre.*

Ancient Greek Drama Today

The ancient plays are alive and well. In Greece they are regularly performed at festivals in the surviving ancient theaters, notably at Epidaurus and Herodes. Of course, they are also performed in modern Greek theaters as well as elsewhere in Europe, and in fact throughout the world.

Speaking broadly, when the plays are staged in ancient theaters in Greece, an effort is made to produce the plays in a manner that at least somewhat resembles the manner in which they were originally done—or were thought to have been done, since we really know very little about the original productions. This means that the costuming is classical, masks may be used, the chorus is large, and there is music and dancing. But outside of Greece, where directors do not feel obligated to present the national heritage, they are less likely to aim at what has been called "museum drama."

At least five chief decisions (beyond the choice of a play and of a translation) must be made.

1. Will masks be used? If so, full masks (which most actors find very uncomfortable), or half-masks (but what is the point of a half-mask)?

2. How will the play be costumed? Here the choices usually come down to these: (a) in costumes that more or less evoke ancient Greece; (b) in contemporary dress; (c) in a period other than ancient and other than contemporary, for instance in the Victorian period; (d) in some sort of unidentifiable but perhaps evocative and seemingly archetypal dress, that is, outfits that no one ever wore, but that seem expressive of tragedy.

3. What sort of set will be used? Obviously this decision is closely connected with the decision about costuming. If one costumes the play in ancient Greek garments, probably one will want a set that evokes the ancient world, perhaps the façade of a palace or a temple. But there are other possibilities, for instance a nonrepresentational background.

4. How many people will make up the chorus? It is thought that Sophocles and Euripides used choruses of fifteen, but most modern productions reduce the chorus to a handful, often three. A large chorus makes sense in an enormous theater, but in a theater that seats only a few hundred spectators the stage is not likely to be large enough to accommodate a chorus of fifteen. On the other hand, when the number is diminished the grandeur of the play lessens. Whatever the number, should the chorus speak in unison or should the lines be distributed among the performers? In the interest of intelligibility, most modern productions distribute the lines rather than have them spoken in unison.

5. Will the chorus sing and dance, and, if so, what kinds of music and what kinds of dances will be used? Almost nothing is known about ancient music though it seems that a flute was certainly used in dramatic performances, and probably percussion instruments were also used. Even less is known for sure about ancient dance. Some modern productions use certain performers to speak the lines of the chorus, and use others—trained dancers—to dance. The dances are likely to be either something that can pass for ancient dance, or, on the other hand, they may be obviously contemporary. What is sometimes thought to be a middle position is to use Greek folk dances.

The theater at Epidaurus is the best-preserved ancient Greek theater, though the *skene* ("scene-building" or stage house) at the left is in ruins. Although the evidence is scant, it seems to indicate that the fifth-century *skene* had two stories, was about twelve feet deep, and had a double door in the center. A few comedies call for more than one point of entrance, so there probably were additional (less prominent) doors near each end of the *skene*. Whether there was an elevated stage in the fifth century has been much disputed, but the one surviving contemporary picture (about 420 B.C.) of actors and an audience shows a low stage, connected to the orchestra by four steps. The actors perform on the stage, and the chorus sings and dances in the orchestra. It is thought that during the strophe the chorus danced around the orchestra to the right, during the antistrophe it danced to the left, and during the epode it stood still. A reference to "the double dance" is taken to mean that two half-choruses faced each other. ▶

◀ Two photographs of the production of *Oedipus* directed by Tyron Guthrie at Stratford, Canada, in 1954. As Guthrie says in the essay that we reprint on page 77. Oedipus's mask was gold (the sun), Jocasta's was silver (the moon), and Creon's was bronze. The chorus wore earth-colored clothes of varying hues of grayish greens and grayish browns.▼

46

◄ Two pictures of Laurence Olivier as Oedipus, in the Old Vic production of 1945. The columns of course echo Greek architecture, and the costuming is vaguely "classical," though in its colorfulness it departs from the popular idea of classical garb. ▼

◄ A German production of *Oedipus,* directed by G. R. Sellner, in Darmstadt, 1952. Here no attempt is made to evoke the Greek world; the scenery is abstract, and although masks are used, they are clearly not used in the ancient Greek manner. Costumes and sets that more accurately represented the ancient world would (in the director's view) serve only to limit the audience's response; they might be archaeologically acceptable but they would fail to connect with some sort of universal dream-world archetype.

▲ Jane Lapotaire as Antigone, in a production directed by John Burgess and Peter Gill in London in 1984. The floor was bare, and the back wall was unadorned but vaguely suggested a stone building. Modern dress was used, but of the 1930s, thus distancing the play a bit from the contemporary world. The chorus (for the most part seated on kitchen chairs) wore gray suits and felt hats with black bands, and they held walking sticks; the guards wore berets and khaki uniforms, and Ismene and Antigone wore frocks and toques (red for Antigone, blue for Ismene). For a review of this production, see page 98.

◄ During the World War II Jean Anouilh wrote a version of *Antigone,* which was staged in Paris under the German occupation. Members of the French Resistance are said to have seen themselves as Antigone, but apparently the Germans did not mind being thought of as Creon, since Creon is presented quite sympathetically in this version. In 1946 the play was performed in New York, with Katharine Cornell in the role of Antigone. As in Paris, the actors wore contemporary formal clothing. In this photograph, the figure at the left is the Narrator, Anouilh's substitution for the Greek chorus. Antigone is seated in the center, rear; Haemon and Ismene stand in the center.

◀ Diana Rigg, in a blood-red dress, as Medea, in a production of 1992–94. The set (discussed on pages 119 and 122), consisting of massive rusting squares that clanged when struck, was abstract but nevertheless suggested a prison. In the photo on the left Medea talks with Aegeus; in the background is the chorus of three women. In the picture above Medea is about to enter the palace, shortly before the end of the play.

Judith Anderson, widely regarded as the greatest tragic actress of the American stage, played Medea in 1947. In this picture she is seated on the palace steps. The set is both realistic and abstract—it is recognizably a palace but instead of being an archaeologically accurate reproduction it seeks to evoke a world of primitive forces. ▶

49

OEDIPUS REX

Sophocles (c. 496–406 B.C.), the son of a wealthy Athenian, is one of the three Greek tragic writers whose work survives. (The other two are Aeschylus and Euripides.) Of Sophocles's more than one hundred twenty plays, we have seven. The exact dates of most of Sophocles's plays are unknown. *Antigone* probably was written about 441 B.C.; *Oedipus the King,* which deals with earlier material concerning the House of Oedipus, was written later, about 430 B.C. Some twenty-five years later, when he was almost ninety, Sophocles wrote *Oedipus at Colonus,* dramatizing Oedipus's last deeds.

COMMENTARY

Classroom discussions of *Oedipus Rex,* like discussions in books, are usually devoted to the problem of fate versus free will. Students (who ought to be filled with youthful confidence in the freedom of the will) generally argue that Oedipus is fated; instructors (who ought to be old enough to know that the inexplicable and unwilled often comes about) generally argue that Oedipus is free and of his own accord performs the actions that fulfill the prophecy. Prophecy or prediction or foreknowledge, instructors patiently explain, is not the same as foreordination. The physician who says that the newborn babe will never develop mentally beyond the age of six is predicting, not ordaining or willing. So, the argument usually runs, the oracle who predicted that Oedipus would kill his father and marry his mother was not *causing* Oedipus to do these things but was simply, in his deep knowledge, announcing what a man like Oedipus would do. But that may be too sophisticated a reading, and a reading that derives from the much later European view of human beings as creatures who can shape their destiny. It is hard for us—especially if the tragedy we know best is Shakespeare's—to recognize the possibility of another sort of tragic drama that does not relate the individual's suffering to his or her own actions but that postulates some sort of Necessity that works within an individual.

Whatever the merits of these views, the spectators or readers undeniably already know, when they set out to see or read the play, that Oedipus must end wretchedly. The story is known to all, fixed in Sophocles's text, and Oedipus cannot extricate himself from it. Something along these lines

was suggested in the middle of the fourth century B.C. when a Greek comic dramatist complained that the comic writer's task was harder than the tragic writer's: "Tragedy has the best of it since the stories are known beforehand to the spectators even before anyone speaks; so the poet only has to remind them. For if I merely say the name Oedipus, they all know the rest—his father Laius, mother Iocasta, daughters, who his sons are, what will happen to him, what he did."

Nonetheless, the tragic writer's task was not quite so easy. First of all, we have Aristotle's statement that "even the known legends are known to only a few," and, second, we have evidence that the tragic writer could vary the details. In Homer's *Iliad* we read that Oedipus continued to rule even after his dreadful history was known, but Sophocles exiles him. And a fragment of Euripides indicates that his Oedipus was blinded by Laius's followers, whereas Sophocles's Oedipus blinds himself. These are details, but they are rather important ones. Probably the ancient Greeks knew the legends in a rough sort of way, as most of us know the Bible or some nuggets of Roman history. Robert Frost and Archibald MacLeish have both drawn from the Book of Job, but their works are enormously different. Writers today who use Job can scarcely omit Job's great suffering, and they can assume that their audience will know that Job had a wife and some comforters, but they are free to go on from there.

Still, the main outline of Oedipus's life must have been fixed, and for us even the details are forever fixed in Sophocles's version. (We know that the Greeks wrote a dozen plays about Oedipus's discovery of his terrible actions, but only Sophocles's survives.) This means that as we read or watch it, each speech has for us a meaning somewhat different from the meaning it has for the speaker and the audience on the stage. Oedipus says he will hunt out the polluted man; we know, as he and the Thebans do not, that *he* is the hunted as well as the hunter. Oedipus says the killer of King Laius may well try to strike at him; we know that Oedipus will find himself out and will strike out his own eyes. A messenger from Corinth tries to allay Oedipus's fears, but instead increases them.

What we are talking about, of course, is tragic irony, or Sophoclean irony, in which words and deeds have a larger meaning for the spectator and the reader than for the dramatis personae. Because Sophocles so persistently uses this device of giving speeches a second, awesome significance, we feel the plot is a masterpiece of construction in which Oedipus is caught. If ever a man has confidence in his will, it is Oedipus, but if ever a man moves toward a predicted point, it is Oedipus. He solved the riddle of the sphinx (by himself, without the aid of birds, he somewhat hybristically boasts), but he does not yet know himself. That knowledge comes later, when he commendably pursued the quest for Laius's slayer and inevitably found himself. The thing is as inevitable as the history described in the sphinx's riddle, which in J. T. Sheppard's version goes thus:

A thing there is whose voice is one;
Whose feet are four and two and three.
So mutable a thing is none
That moves in earth or sky or sea.
When on most feet this thing doth go,
Its strength is weakest and its pace most slow.

This is the history of humanity. In Sophocles's time people grew from crawling infancy, through erect adulthood, to bent old age supported by a stick, and so they do in our time, as the child's rhyme still claims:

Walks on four feet,
On two feet, on three,
The more feet it walks on,
The weaker it be.

There was scarcely an infant weaker than the maimed Oedipus; there was scarcely a man stronger than King Oedipus at his height; and there was scarcely a man more in need of a staff than the blind exile. However free each of his actions—and we can only feel that the figure whom we see on the stage is acting freely when he abuses Teiresias and Creon—Oedipus was by fate a human being, and thus the largest pattern of his life could be predicted easily enough.

Sophocles

OEDIPUS REX

An English Version by Dudley Fitts and Robert Fitzgerald

List of Characters

OEDIPUS
A PRIEST
CREON
TEIRESIAS
IOCASTÊ
MESSENGER
SHEPHERD OF LAÏOS
SECOND MESSENGER
CHORUS OF THEBAN ELDERS

SCENE: *Before the palace of Oedipus, King of Thebes. A central door and two lateral doors open onto a platform which runs the length of the facade. On the platform, right and left, are altars; and three steps lead down into the "orchestra," or chorus-ground. At the beginning of the action these steps are crowded by Suppliants who have brought branches and chaplets of olive leaves and who lie in various attitudes of despair. Oedipus enters.*

PROLOGUE

OEDIPUS.
    My children, generations of the living
    In the line of Kadmos,° nursed at his ancient hearth;
    Why have you strewn yourselves before these altars
    In supplication, with your boughs and garlands?
5   The breath of incense rises from the city
    With a sound of prayer and lamentation.
                        Children,
    I would not have you speak through messengers,
    And therefore I have come myself to hear you—
    I, Oedipus, who bear the famous name.
10   (*To a Priest.*) You, there, since you are eldest in the company,
    Speak for them all, tell me what preys upon you,
    Whether you come in dread, or crave some blessing:
    Tell me, and never doubt that I will help you
    In every way I can; I should be heartless
15   Were I not moved to find you suppliant here.
PRIEST.
    Great Oedipus, O powerful King of Thebes!
    You see how all the ages of our people

2 **Kadmos** mythical founder of Thebes

52

    Cling to your altar steps: here are boys
    Who can barely stand alone, and here are priests
    By weight of age, as I am a priest of God,   20
    And young men chosen from those yet unmarried;
    As for the others, all that multitude,
    They wait with olive chaplets in the squares,
    At the two shrines of Pallas,° and where Apollo°
    Speaks in the glowing embers.
                     Your own eyes   25
    Must tell you: Thebes is in her extremity
    And cannot lift her head from the surge of death.
    A rust consumes the buds and fruits of the earth;
    The herds are sick; children die unborn,
    And labor is vain. The god of plague and pyre   30
    Raids like detestable lightning through the city,
    And all the house of Kadmos is laid waste,
    All emptied, and all darkened: Death alone
    Battens upon the misery of Thebes.
    You are not one of the immortal gods, we know;   35
    Yet we have come to you to make our prayer
    As to the man of all men best in adversity
    And wisest in the ways of God. You saved us
    From the Sphinx,° that flinty singer, and the tribute
    We paid to her so long; yet you were never   40
    Better informed than we, nor could we teach you:
    It was some god breathed in you to set us free.

    Therefore, O mighty King, we turn to you:
    Find us our safety, find us a remedy,
    Whether by counsel of the gods or the men.   45
    A king of wisdom tested in the past
    Can act in a time of troubles, and act well.
    Noblest of men, restore
    Life to your city! Think how all men call you
    Liberator for your triumph long ago;   50
    Ah, when your years of kingship are remembered,
    Let them not say *We rose, but later fell*—
    Keep the State from going down in the storm!

24 **Pallas** Athena, goddess of wisdom, protectress of Athens **Apollo** god of light and healing **39 Sphinx** a monster (body of a lion, wings of a bird, face of a woman) who asked the riddle, "What goes on four legs in the morning, two at noon, and three in the evening?" and who killed those who could not answer. When Oedipus responded correctly that man crawls on all fours in infancy, walks upright in maturity, and uses a staff in old age, the Sphinx destroyed herself.

55 Once, years ago, with happy augury,
You brought us fortune; be the same again!
No man questions your power to rule the land:
But rule over men, not over a dead city!
Ships are only hulls, citadels are nothing,
When no life moves in the empty passageways.

OEDIPUS.
60 Poor children! You may be sure I know
All that you longed for in your coming here.
I know that you are deathly sick; and yet,
Sick as you are, not one is as sick as I.
Each of you suffers in himself alone
65 His anguish, not another's; but my spirit
Groans for the city, for myself, for you.

I was not sleeping, you are not waking me.
No, I have been in tears for a long while
And in my restless thought walked many ways.
70 In all my search, I found one helpful course,
And that I have taken: I have sent Creon,
Son of Menoikeus, brother of the Queen,
To Delphi, Apollo's place of revelation,
To learn there, if he can,
75 What act or pledge of mine may save the city.
I have counted the days, and now, this very day,
I am troubled, for he has overstayed his time.
What is he doing? He has been gone too long.
Yet whenever he comes back, I should do ill
80 To scant whatever hint the god may give.

PRIEST.
It is a timely promise. At this instant
They tell me Creon is here.

OEDIPUS.   O Lord Apollo!
May his news be fair as his face is radiant!

PRIEST.
It could not be otherwise: he is crowned with bay,
The chaplet is thick with berries.

85 OEDIPUS.   We shall soon know;
He is near enough to hear us now.

Enter Creon.

                                    O Prince:
Brother: son of Menoikeus:
What answer do you bring us from the god?

CREON.
It is favorable. I can tell you, great afflictions
90 Will turn out well, if they are taken well.

OEDIPUS.
What was the oracle? These vague words
Leave me still hanging between hope and fear.

CREON.
Is it your pleasure to hear me with all these
Gathered around us? I am prepared to speak,
But should we not go in?

95 OEDIPUS.   Let them all hear it.
It is for them I suffer, more than myself.

CREON.
Then I will tell you what I heard at Delphi.

In plain words
The god commands us to expel from the land of Thebes
An old defilement that it seems we shelter.   100
It is a deathly thing, beyond expiation.
We must not let it feed upon us longer.

OEDIPUS.
What defilement? How shall we rid ourselves of it?

CREON.
By exile or death, blood for blood. It was
Murder that brought the plague-wind on the city.   105

OEDIPUS.
Murder of whom? Surely the god has named him?

CREON.
My lord: long ago Laïos was our king,
Before you came to govern us.

OEDIPUS.   I know;
I learned of him from others; I never saw him.

CREON.
He was murdered; and Apollo commands us now   110
To take revenge upon whoever killed him.

OEDIPUS.
Upon whom? Where are they? Where shall we find a clue
To solve that crime, after so many years?

CREON.
Here in this land, he said.

                                    If we make enquiry,
We may touch things that otherwise escape us.   115

OEDIPUS.
Tell me: Was Laïos murdered in his house,
Or in the fields, or in some foreign country?

CREON.
He said he planned to make a pilgrimage.
He did not come home again.

OEDIPUS.   And was there no one,
No witness, no companion, to tell what happened?   120

CREON.
They were all killed but one, and he got away
So frightened that he could remember one thing only.

OEDIPUS.
What was that one thing? One may be the key
To everything, if we resolve to use it.

CREON.
He said that a band of highwaymen attacked them,   125
Outnumbered them, and overwhelmed the King.

OEDIPUS.
Strange, that a highwayman should be so daring—
Unless some faction here bribed him to do it.

CREON.
We thought of that. But after Laïos' death
New troubles arose and we had no avenger.   130

OEDIPUS.
What troubles could prevent your hunting down the
      killers?

CREON.
>   The riddling Sphinx's song
>   Made us deaf to all mysteries but her own

OEDIPUS.
>   Then once more I must bring what is dark to light.
135 It is most fitting that Apollo shows,
>   As you do, this compunction for the dead.
>   You shall see how I stand by you, as I should,
>   To avenge the city and the city's god,
>   And not as though it were for some distant friend,
140 But for my own sake, to be rid of evil.
>   Whoever killed King Laïos might—who knows?—
>   Decide at any moment to kill me as well.
>   By avenging the murdered king I protect myself.
>   Come, then, my children: leave the altar steps,
>   Lift up your olive boughs!
145   One of you go
>   And summon the people of Kadmos to gather here.
>   I will do all that I can; you may tell them that.

>   (*Exit a Page.*)

>   So, with the help of God,
>   We shall be saved—or else indeed we are lost.

PRIEST.
150 Let us rise, children. It was for this we came,
>   And now the King has promised it himself.
>   Phoibos° has sent us an oracle; may he descend
>   Himself to save us and drive out the plague.

> *Exeunt Oedipus and Creon into the palace by the central
> door. The Priest and the Suppliants disperse right and left.
> After a short pause the Chorus enters the orchestra.*

PÁRODOS

CHORUS.
>   What is God singing in his profound   *Strophe 1*
>   Delphi of gold and shadow?
>   What oracle for Thebes, the sunwhipped city?
>   Fear unjoints me, the roots of my heart tremble.
5   Now I remember, O Healer, your power, and wonder;
>   Will you send doom like a sudden cloud, or weave it
>   Like nightfall of the past?
>   Speak, speak to us, issue of holy sound:
>   Dearest to our expectancy: be tender!

10   Let me pray to Athenê, the immortal   *Antistrophe 1*
>   daughter of Zeus,
>   And to Artemis her sister
>   Who keeps her famous throne in the market ring,
>   And to Apollo, bowman at the far butts of heaven—

>   O gods, descend! Like three streams leap against
15   The fires of our grief, the fires of darkness;
>   Be swift to bring us rest!

152 Phoibos Phoebus Apollo, the sun god

54

>   As in the old time from the brilliant house
>   Of air you stepped to save us, come again!

>   Now our afflictions have no end,   *Strophe 2*
>   Now all our stricken host lies down   20
>   And no man fights off death with his mind;

>   The noble plowland bears no grain,
>   And groaning mothers cannot bear—
>   See, how our lives like birds take wing,
>   Like sparks that fly when a fire soars,   25
>   To the shore of the god of evening.

>   The plague burns on, it is pitiless   *Antistrophe 2*
>   Though pallid children laden with death
>   Lie unwept in the stony ways,
>   And old gray women by every path   30
>   Flock to the strand about the altars

>   There to strike their breasts and cry
>   Worship of Phoibos in wailing prayers:
>   Be kind, God's golden child!

>   There are no swords in this attack by fire,   *Strophe 3* 35
>   No shields, but we are ringed with cries.
>   Send the besieger plunging from our homes
>   Into the vast sea-room of the Atlantic
>   Or into the waves that foam eastward of Thrace—
>   For the day ravages what the night spares—   40

>   Destroy our enemy, lord of the thunder!
>   Let him be riven by lightning from heaven!

>   Phoibos Apollo, stretch the sun's   *Antistrophe 3*
>   bowstring,
>   That golden cord, until it sing for us,
>   Flashing arrows in heaven!
>   Artemis, Huntress,   45
>   Race with flaring lights upon our mountains!
>   O scarlet god, O golden-banded brow,
>   O Theban Bacchos° in a storm of Maenads,°

> *Enter Oedipus, center.*

>   Whirl upon Death, that all the Undying hate!
>   Come with blinding cressets, come in joy!   50

SCENE I

OEDIPUS.
>   Is this your prayer? It may be answered. Come,
>   Listen to me, act as the crisis demands,
>   And you shall have relief from all these evils.

>   Until now I was a stranger to this tale,
>   As I had been a stranger to the crime.   5
>   Could I track down the murderer without a clue?
>   But now, friends,
>   As one who became a citizen after the murder,

48 Bacchos Dionysos, god of wine, thus scarlet-faced **48 Maenads** Dionysos's female attendants

I make this proclamation to all Thebans:
10 If any man knows by whose hand Laïos, son of Labdakos,
Met his death, I direct that man to tell me everything,
No matter what he fears for having so long withheld it.
Let it stand as promised that no further trouble
Will come to him, but he may leave the land in safety.

15 Moreover: If anyone knows the murderer to be foreign,
Let him not keep silent: he shall have his reward from me.
However, if he does conceal it, if any man
Fearing for his friend or for himself disobeys this edict,
Hear what I propose to do:

20 I solemnly forbid the people of this country,
Where power and throne are mine, ever to receive that
        man
Or speak to him, no matter who he is, or let him
Join in sacrifice, lustration, or in prayer.
I decree that he be driven from every house,

25 Being, as he is, corruption itself to us: the Delphic
Voice of Zeus has pronounced this revelation.
Thus I associate myself with the oracle
And take the side of the murdered king.
As for the criminal, I pray to God—

30 Whether it be a lurking thief, or one of a number—
I pray that that man's life be consumed in evil and
        wretchedness.
And as for me, this curse applies no less
If it should turn out that the culprit is my guest here,
Sharing my hearth.
                          You have heard the penalty.
35 I lay it on you now to attend to this
For my sake, for Apollo's, for the sick
Sterile city that heaven has abandoned.
Suppose the oracle had given you no command:
Should this defilement go uncleansed for ever?
40 You should have found the murderer: your king,
A noble king, had been destroyed!
                          Now I,
Having the power that he held before me,
Having his bed, begetting children there
Upon his wife, as he would have, had he lived—
45 Their son would have been my children's brother,
If Laïos had had luck in fatherhood!
(But surely ill luck rushed upon his reign)—
I say I take the son's part, just as though
I were his son, to press the fight for him
50 And see it won! I'll find the hand that brought
Death to Labdakos' and Polydoros' child,
Heir of Kadmos' and Agenor's line.
And as for those who fail me,
May the gods deny them the fruit of the earth,
55 Fruit of the womb, and may they rot utterly!
Let them be wretched as we are wretched, and worse!

For you, for loyal Thebans, and for all
Who find my actions right, I pray the favor

Of justice, and of all the immortal gods.
CHORAGOS.°
    Since I am under oath, my lord, I swear   60
    I did not do the murder, I cannot name
    The murderer. Might not the oracle
    That has ordained the search tell where to find him?
OEDIPUS.
    An honest question. But no man in the world
    Can make the gods do more than the gods will.   65
CHORAGOS.
    There is one last expedient—
OEDIPUS.   Tell me what it is.
    Though it seem slight, you must not hold it back.
CHORAGOS.
    A lord clairvoyant to the lord Apollo,
    As we all know, is the skilled Teiresias.
    One might learn much about this from him, Oedipus.   70
OEDIPUS.
    I am not wasting time:
    Creon spoke of this, and I have sent for him—
    Twice, in fact; it is strange that he is not here.
CHORAGOS.
    The other matter—that old report—seems useless.
OEDIPUS.
    Tell me. I am interested in all reports.   75
CHORAGOS.
    The King was said to have been killed by highwaymen.
OEDIPUS.
    I know. But we have no witnesses to that.
CHORAGOS.
    If the killer can feel a particle of dread,
    Your curse will bring him out of hiding!
OEDIPUS.   No.
    The man who dared that act will fear no curse.   80

Enter the blind seer Teiresias led by a Page.

CHORAGOS.
    But there is one man who may detect the criminal.
    This is Teiresias, this is the holy prophet
    In whom, alone of all men, truth was born.
OEDIPUS.
    Teiresias: seer: student of mysteries,
    Of all that's taught and all that no man tells,   85
    Secrets of Heaven and secrets of the earth:
    Blind though you are, you know the city lies
    Sick with plague; and from this plague, my lord,
    We find that you alone can guard or save us.

    Possibly you did not hear the messengers?   90
    Apollo, when we sent to him,
    Sent us back word that this great pestilence
    Would lift, but only if we established clearly
    The identity of those who murdered Laïos.
    They must be killed or exiled.

60 Choragos leader of the Chorus

95   Can you use
   Birdflight or any art of divination
   To purify yourself, and Thebes, and me
   From this contagion? We are in your hands.
   There is no fairer duty
100   Than that of helping others in distress.
   TEIRESIAS.
   How dreadful knowledge of the truth can be
   When there's no help in truth! I knew this well,
   But did not act on it: else I should not have come.
   OEDIPUS.
   What is troubling you? Why are your eyes so cold?
   TEIRESIAS.
105   Let me go home. Bear your own fate, and I'll
   Bear mine. It is better so: trust what I say.
   OEDIPUS.
   What you say is ungracious and unhelpful
   To your native country. Do not refuse to speak.
   TEIRESIAS.
   When it comes to speech, your own is neither temperate
110   Nor opportune. I wish to be more prudent.
   OEDIPUS.
   In God's name, we all beg you—
   TEIRESIAS.   You are all ignorant.
   No; I will never tell you what I know.
   Now it is my misery; then, it would be yours.
   OEDIPUS.
   What! You do know something, and will not tell us?
115   You would betray us all and wreck the State?
   TEIRESIAS.
   I do not intend to torture myself, or you.
   Why persist in asking? You will not persuade me.
   OEDIPUS.
   What a wicked man you are! You'd try a stone's
   Patience! Out with it! Have you no feeling at all?
   TEIRESIAS.
120   You call me unfeeling. If you could only see
   The nature of your feelings . . .
   OEDIPUS.   Why,
   Who would not feel as I do? Who could endure
   Your arrogance toward the city?
   TEIRESIAS.   What does it matter!
   Whether I speak or not, it is bound to come.
   OEDIPUS.
125   Then, if "it" is bound to come, you are bound to tell me.
   TEIRESIAS.
   No, I will not go on. Rage as you please
   OEDIPUS.
   Rage? Why not!
                          And I'll tell you what I think:
   You planned it, you had it done, you all but
   Killed him with your own hands: if you had eyes,
130   I'd say the crime was yours, and yours alone.
   TEIRESIAS.
   So? I charge you, then,

Abide by the proclamation you have made.
From this day forth
Never speak again to these men or to me;
You yourself are the pollution of this country.   135
OEDIPUS.
You dare say that! Can you possibly think you have
Some way of going free, after such insolence?
TEIRESIAS.
I have gone free. It is the truth sustains me.
OEDIPUS.
Who taught you shamelessness? It was not your craft.
TEIRESIAS.
You did. You made me speak. I did not want to.   140
OEDIPUS.
Speak what? Let me hear it again more clearly.
TEIRESIAS.
Was it not clear before? Are you tempting me?
OEDIPUS.
I did not understand it. Say it again.
TEIRESIAS.
I say that you are the murderer whom you seek.
OEDIPUS.
Now twice you have spat out infamy. You'll pay
   for it!   145
TEIRESIAS.
Would you care for more? Do you wish to be really
   angry?
OEDIPUS.
Say what you will. Whatever you say is worthless.
TEIRESIAS.
I say you live in hideous shame with those
Most dear to you. You cannot see the evil.
OEDIPUS.
It seems you can go on mouthing like this for ever.   150
TEIRESIAS.
I can, if there is power in truth.
OEDIPUS.   There is:
But not for you, not for you,
You sightless, witless, senseless, mad old man!
TEIRESIAS.
You are the madman. There is no one here
Who will not curse you soon, as you curse me.   155
OEDIPUS.
You child of endless night! You cannot hurt me
Or any other man who sees the sun.
TEIRESIAS.
True: it is not from me your fate will come.
That lies within Apollo's competence,
As it is his concern.
OEDIPUS.   Tell me: 160
Are you speaking for Creon, or for yourself?
TEIRESIAS.
Creon is no threat. You weave your own doom.
OEDIPUS.
Wealth, power, craft of statesmanship!

Kingly position, everywhere admired!
165   What savage envy is stored up against these,
If Creon, whom I trusted, Creon my friend,
For this great office which the city once
Put in my hands unsought—if for this power
Creon desires in secret to destroy me!

170   He has brought this decrepit fortune-teller, this
Collector of dirty pennies, this prophet fraud—
Why, he is no more clairvoyant than I am!
                                        Tell us:
Has your mystic mummery ever approached the
      truth?
When that hellcat the Sphinx was performing here,
175   What help were you to these people?
Her magic was not for the first man who came along:
It demanded a real exorcist. Your birds—
What good were they? or the gods, for the matter of that?
But I came by,
180   Oedipus, the simple man, who knows nothing—
I thought it out for myself, no birds helped me!
And this is the man you think you can destroy,
That you may be close to Creon when he's king!
Well, you and your friend Creon, it seems to me,
185   Will suffer most. If you were not an old man,
You would have paid already for your plot.

CHORAGOS.
We cannot see that his words or yours
Have spoken except in anger, Oedipus,
And of anger we have no need. How can God's will
190   Be accomplished best? That is what most concerns us.

TEIRESIAS.
You are a king. But where argument's concerned
I am your man, as much a king as you.
I am not your servant, but Apollo's.
I have no need of Creon to speak for me.

195   Listen to me. You mock my blindness, do you?
But I say that you, with both your eyes, are blind:
You cannot see the wretchedness of your life,
Not in whose house you live, no, nor with whom.
Who are your father and mother? Can you tell me?
200   You do not even know the blind wrongs
That you have done them, on earth and in the world
      below.
But the double lash of your parents' curse will whip you
Out of this land some day, with only night
Upon your precious eyes.
205   Your cries then—where will they not be heard?
What fastness of Kithairon° will not echo them?
And that bridal-descant of yours—you'll know it then,
The song they sang when you came here to Thebes
And found your misguided berthing.
210   All this, and more, that you cannot guess at now,

---

206 **fastness of Kithairon** stronghold in a mountain near Thebes

Will bring you to yourself among your children.
Be angry, then. Curse Creon. Curse my words.
I tell you, no man that walks upon the earth
Shall be rooted out more horribly than you.

OEDIPUS.
Am I to bear this from him?—Damnation   215
Take you! Out of this place! Out of my sight!

TEIRESIAS.
I would not have come at all if you had not
      asked me.

OEDIPUS.
Could I have told that you'd talk nonsense, that
You'd come here to make a fool of yourself, and
      of me?

TEIRESIAS.
A fool? Your parents thought me sane enough.   220

OEDIPUS.
My parents again!—Wait: who were my parents?

TEIRESIAS.
This day will give you a father, and break your
      heart.

OEDIPUS.
Your infantile riddles! Your damned abracadabra!

TEIRESIAS.
You were a great man once at solving riddles.

OEDIPUS.
Mock me with that if you like; you will find it true.   225

TEIRESIAS.
It was true enough. It brought about your ruin.

OEDIPUS.
But if it saved this town.

TEIRESIAS (to the Page).   Boy, give me your hand.

OEDIPUS.
Yes, boy; lead him away.
                              —While you are here
We can do nothing. Go; leave us in peace.

TEIRESIAS.
I will go when I have said what I have to say.   230
How can you hurt me? And I tell you again:
The man you have been looking for all this time,
The damned man, the murderer of Laïos,
That man is in Thebes. To your mind he is foreign-
      born,
But it will soon be shown that he is a Theban,   235
A revelation that will fail to please
                              A blind man
Who has his eyes now; a penniless man, who is
      rich now;
And he will go tapping the strange earth with his
      staff;
To the children with whom he lives now he will be
Brother and father—the very same; to her   240
Who bore him, son and husband—the very same
Who came to his father's bed, wet with his father's
      blood.

Enough. Go think that over.
If later you find error in what I have said,
245 You may say that I have no skill in prophecy.

Exit Teiresias, led by his Page. Oedipus goes into the palace.

ODE 1

CHORUS.

The Delphic stone of prophecies   *Strophe 1*
Remembers ancient regicide
And a still bloody hand.
That killer's hour of flight has come.
5   He must be stronger than riderless
Coursers of untiring wind,
For the son of Zeus° armed with his father's thunder
Leaps in lightning after him;
And the Furies° follow him, the sad Furies.

10   Holy Parnossos' peak of snow   *Antistrophe 1*
Flashes and blinds that secret man,
That all shall hunt him down:
Though he may roam the forest shade
Like a bull gone wild from pasture
15   To rage through glooms of stone.
Doom comes down on him; flight will not avail him;
For the world's heart calls him desolate,
And the immortal Furies follow, for ever follow.

But now a wilder thing is heard   *Strophe 2*
From the old man skilled at hearing Fate in
20   the wingbeat of a bird.
Bewildered as a blown bird, my soul hovers and cannot
     find
Foothold in this debate, or any reason or rest of mind.
But no man ever brought—none can bring
Proof of strife between Thebes' royal house,
25   Labdakos' line,° and the son of Polybos;°
And never until now has any man brought word
Of Laïos dark death staining Oedipus the King.

Divine Zeus and Apollo hold   *Antistrophe 2*
Perfect intelligence alone of all tales ever told;

7 **son of Zeus** Apollo 9 **Furies** avenging deities 25 **Labdakos'
line** family of Laïos **son of Polybos** Oedipus (so the Chorus
believes)

And well though this diviner works, he works in his own
     night;   30
No man can judge that rough unknown or trust in
     second sight,
For wisdom changes hands among the wise.
Shall I believe my great lord criminal.
At a raging word that a blind old man let fall?
I saw him, when the carrion woman faced him of old,   35
Prove his heroic mind! These evil words are lies.

SCENE II

CREON.

Men of Thebes:
I am told that heavy accusations
Have been brought against me by King Oedipus.
I am not the kind of man to bear this tamely.

If in these present difficulties   5
He holds me accountable for any harm to him
Through anything I have said or done—why, then,
I do not value life in this dishonor.
It is not as though this rumor touched upon
Some private indiscretion. The matter is grave.   10
The fact is that I am being called disloyal
To the State, to my fellow citizens, to my friends.
CHORAGOS.

He may have spoken in anger, not from his mind.
CREON.

But did you hear him say I was the one
Who seduced the old prophet into lying?   15
CHORAGOS.

The thing was said; I do not know how seriously.
CREON.

But you were watching him! Were his eyes steady?
Did he look like a man in his right mind?
CHORAGOS.   I do not know.
I cannot judge the behavior of great men.
But here is the King himself.

Enter Oedipus.

OEDIPUS.   So you dared come back.   20
Why? How brazen of you to come to my house,
You murderer!
               Do you think I do not know
That you plotted to kill me, plotted to steal my throne?
Tell me, in God's name: am I coward, a fool,
That you should dream you could accomplish this?   25
A fool who could not see your slippery game?
A coward, not to fight back when I saw it?
You are the fool, Creon, are you not? hoping

Without support or friends to get a throne?
30   Thrones may be won or bought: you could do neither.
CREON.
      Now listen to me. You have talked; let me talk, too.
      You cannot judge unless you know the facts.
OEDIPUS.
      You speak well: there is one fact; but I find it hard
      To learn from the deadliest enemy I have.
CREON.
35   That above all I must dispute with you.
OEDIPUS.
      That above all I will not hear you deny.
CREON.
      If you think there is anything good in being stubborn
      Against all reason, then I say you are wrong.
OEDIPUS.
      If you think a man can sin against his own kind
40   And not be punished for it, I say you are mad.
CREON.
      I agree. But tell me: what have I done to you?
OEDIPUS.
      You advised me to send for that wizard, did you not?
CREON.
      I did. I should do it again.
OEDIPUS.   Very well. Now tell me:
      How long has it been since Laïos—
CREON.   What of Laïos?
OEDIPUS.
45   Since he vanished in that onset by the road?
CREON.
      It was long ago, a long time.
OEDIPUS.   And this prophet,
      Was he practicing here then?
CREON.   He was; and with honor, as
      now.
OEDIPUS.
      Did he speak of me at that time?
CREON.   He never did;
      At least, not when I was present.
OEDIPUS.   But . . . the enquiry?
      I suppose you held one?
50   CREON.   We did, but we learned nothing.
OEDIPUS.
      Why did the prophet not speak against me then?
CREON.
      I do not know; and I am the kind of man
      Who holds his tongue when he has no facts to go on.
OEDIPUS.
      There's one fact that you know, and you could tell it.
CREON.
55   What fact is that? If I know it, you shall have it.
OEDIPUS.
      If he were not involved with you, he could not say
      That it was I who murdered Laïos.

CREON.
      If he says that, you are the one that knows it!—
      But now it is my turn to question you.
OEDIPUS.
      Put your questions. I am no murderer.   60
CREON.
      First, then: You married my sister?
OEDIPUS.   I married your sister.
CREON.
      And you rule the kingdom equally with her?
OEDIPUS.
      Everything that she wants she has from me.
CREON.
      And I am the third, equal to both of you?
OEDIPUS.
      That is why I call you a bad friend.   65
CREON.
      No. Reason it out, as I have done.
      Think of this first. Would any sane man prefer
      Power, with all a king's anxieties,
      To that same power and the grace of sleep?
      Certainly not I.   70
      I have never longed for the king's power—only his
          rights.
      Would any wise man differ from me in this?
      As matters stand, I have my way in everything
      With your consent, and no responsibilities.
      If I were king, I should be a slave to policy.   75
      How could I desire a scepter more
      Than what is now mine—untroubled influence?
      No, I have not gone mad; I need no honors,
      Except those with the perquisites I have now.
      I am welcome everywhere; every man salutes me,   80
      And those who want your favor seek my ear,
      Since I know how to manage what they ask.
      Should I exchange this ease for that anxiety?
      Besides, no sober mind is treasonable.
      I hate anarchy   85
      And never would deal with any man who likes it.

      Test what I have said. Go to the priestess
      At Delphi, ask if I quoted her correctly.
      And as for this other thing: if I am found
      Guilty of treason with Teiresias,   90
      Then sentence me to death! You have my word
      It is a sentence I should cast my vote for—
      But not without evidence!
                              You do wrong
      When you take good men for bad, bad men for good.
      A true friend thrown aside—why, life itself   95
      Is not more precious!
                              In time you will know this well:
      For time, and time alone, will show the just man,
      Though scoundrels are discovered in a day.

CHORAGOS.
   This is well said, and a prudent man would ponder it.
100   Judgments too quickly formed are dangerous.
   OEDIPUS.
   But is he not quick in his duplicity?
   And shall I not be quick to parry him?
   Would you have me stand still, hold my peace, and let
   This man win everything, through my inaction?
   CREON.
105   And you want—what is it, then? To banish me?
   OEDIPUS.
   No, not exile. It is your death I want,
   So that all the world may see what treason means.
   CREON.
   You will persist, then? You will not believe me?
   OEDIPUS.
   How can I believe you?
   CREON.   Then you are a fool.
   OEDIPUS.
   To save myself?
110   CREON.   In justice, think of me.
   OEDIPUS.
   You are evil incarnate.
   CREON.   But suppose that you are wrong?
   OEDIPUS.
   Still I must rule.
   CREON.   But not if you rule badly.
   OEDIPUS.
   O city, city!
   CREON.   It is my city, too!
   CHORAGOS.
   Now, my lords, be still. I see the Queen,
115   Iocastê, coming from her palace chambers;
   And it is time she came, for the sake of you both.
   This dreadful quarrel can be resolved through her.

   Enter Iocastê.

   IOCASTÊ.
   Poor foolish men, what wicked din is this?
   With Thebes sick to death, is it not shameful
120   That you should rake some private quarrel up?
   (*To Oedipus.*) Come into the house.
                    —And you, Creon,
      go now: Let us have no more of this tumult over
      nothing.
   CREON.
   Nothing? No, sister: what your husband plans for me
   Is one of two great evils: exile or death.
   OEDIPUS. He is right.
125   Why, woman, I have caught him squarely
   Plotting against my life.
   CREON.   No! Let me die
   Accurst if ever I have wished you harm!
   IOCASTÊ.
   Ah, believe it, Oedipus!

In the name of the gods, respect this oath of his
For my sake, for the sake of these people here!   130
CHORAGOS.
   Open your mind to her, my lord. Be ruled   *Strophe 1*
      by her, I beg you!
OEDIPUS.
   What would you have me do?
CHORAGOS.
   Respect Creon's word. He has never spoken like a fool,
   And now he has sworn an oath.
OEDIPUS.
   You know what you ask?
CHORAGOS.   I do.
OEPIDUS.   Speak on, then.   135
CHORAGOS.
   A friend so sworn should not be baited so,
   In blind malice, and without final proof.
OEDIPUS.
   You are aware, I hope, that what you say
   Means death for me, or exile at the least.
CHORAGOS.
   No, I swear by Helios,° first in Heaven!   *Strophe 2* 140
   May I die friendless and accurst,
   The worst of deaths, if ever I meant that!
      It is the withering fields
         That hurt my sick heart:
      Must we bear all these ills,   145
         And now your bad blood as well?
OEDIPUS.
   Then let him go. And let me die, if I must,
   Or be driven by him in shame from the land of Thebes.
   It is your unhappiness, and not his talk,
   That touches me.
                 As for him—   150
   Wherever he is, I will hate him as long as I live.
CREON.
   Ugly in yielding, as you were ugly in rage!
   Natures like yours chiefly torment themselves.
OEDIPUS.
   Can you not go? Can you not leave me?
CREON.   I can.
   You do not know me; but the city knows me,   155
   And in its eyes I am just, if not in yours.

                                        (*Exit Creon.*)

CHORAGOS.
   Lady Iocastê, did you not ask the King   *Antistrophe 1*
      to go to his chambers?
IOCASTÊ.
   First tell me what has happened.
CHORAGOS.
   There was suspicion without evidence; yet it rankled

140 Helios sun god

As even false charges will.
IOCASTÊ.   On both sides?
CHORAGOS.   On both.
160 IOCASTÊ.   But
what was said?
CHORAGOS.
Oh let it rest, let it be done with!
Have we not suffered enough?
OEDIPUS.
You see to what your decency has brought you:
You have made difficulties where my heart saw none.

CHORAGOS.
165 Oedipus, it is not once only I have   Antistrophe 2
        told you—
You must know I should count myself unwise
To the point of madness, should I now forsake you—
    You, under whose hand,
        In the storm of another time,
170   Our dear land sailed out free,
        But now stand fast at the helm!

IOCASTÊ.
In God's name, Oedipus, inform your wife as well:
Why are you so set in this hard anger?
OEDIPUS.
I will tell you, for none of these men deserves
175 My confidence as you do. It is Creon's work,
His treachery, his plotting against me.
IOCASTÊ.
Go on, if you can make this clear to me.
OEDIPUS.
He charges me with the murder of Laïos.
IOCASTÊ.
Has he some knowledge? Or does he speak from hearsay?
OEDIPUS.
180 He would not commit himself to such a charge,
But he has brought in that damnable soothsayer
To tell his story.
IOCASTÊ.   Set your mind at rest.
If it is a question of soothsayers, I tell you
That you will find no man whose craft gives knowledge
Of the unknowable.
185   Here is my proof.
An oracle was reported to Laïos once
(I will not say from Phoibos himself, but from
His appointed ministers, at any rate)
That his doom would be death at the hands of his own
        son—
190 His son, born of his flesh and of mine!

Now, you remember the story: Laïos was killed
By marauding strangers where three highways meet;
But his child had not been three days in this world
Before the King had pierced the baby's ankles
195 And left him to die on a lonely mountainside.

Thus, Apollo never caused that child

To kill his father, and it was not Laïos fate
To die at the hands of his son, as he had feared.
This is what prophets and prophecies are worth!
Have no dread of them.
                          It is God himself   200
Who can show us what he wills, in his own way.
OEDIPUS.
How strange a shadowy memory crossed my mind,
Just now while you were speaking; it chilled my heart.
IOCASTÊ.
What do you mean? What memory do you speak of?
OEDIPUS.
If I understand you, Laïos was killed   205
At a place where three roads meet.
IOCASTÊ.   So it was said;
We have no later story.
OEDIPUS.   Where did it happen?
IOCASTÊ.
Phokis, it is called: at a place where the Theban Way
Divides into the roads towards Delphi and Daulia.
OEDIPUS.
When?
IOCASTÊ. We had the news not long before you came   210
And proved the right to your succession here.
OEDIPUS.
Ah, what net has God been weaving for me?
IOCASTÊ.
Oedipus! Why does this trouble you?
OEDIPUS.   Do not ask me yet.
First, tell me how Laïos looked, and tell me
How old he was.
IOCASTÊ.   He was tall, his hair just touched   215
With white; his form was not unlike your own.
OEDIPUS.
I think that I myself may be accurst
By my own ignorant edict.
IOCASTÊ.   You speak strangely.
It makes me tremble to look at you, my King.
OEDIPUS.
I am not sure that the blind man cannot see.   220
But I should know better if you were to tell me—
IOCASTÊ.
Anything—though I dread to hear you ask it.
OEDIPUS.
Was the King lightly escorted, or did he ride
With a large company, as a ruler should?
IOCASTÊ.
There were five men with him in all: one was a herald;   225
And a single chariot, which he was driving.
OEDIPUS.
Alas, that makes it plain enough!
                                    But who—
Who told you how it happened?
IOCASTÊ.   A household servant,
The only one to escape.

OEDIPUS.   And is he still
　　A servant of ours?

230　IOCASTÊ.   No; for when he came back at last
　　And found you enthroned in the place of the dead king,
　　He came to me, touched my hand with his, and begged
　　That I would send him away to the frontier district
　　Where only the shepherds go—
235　As far away from the city as I could send him.
　　I granted his prayer; for although the man was a slave,
　　He had earned more than this favor at my hands.

OEDIPUS.
　　Can he be called back quickly?

IOCASTÊ.   Easily.
　　But why?

OEDIPUS.   I have taken too much upon myself
240　Without enquiry; therefore I wish to consult him.

IOCASTÊ.
　　Then he shall come.
　　　　　　　　　　But am I not one also
　　To whom you might confide these fears of yours!

OEDIPUS.
　　That is your right; it will not be denied you,
　　Now least of all; for I have reached a pitch
245　Of wild foreboding. Is there anyone
　　To whom I should sooner speak?
　　Polybos of Corinth is my father.
　　My mother is a Dorian: Meropê.
　　I grew up chief among the men of Corinth
250　Until a strange thing happened—
　　Not worth my passion, it may be, but strange.

　　At a feast, a drunken man maundering in his cups
　　Cries out that I am not my father's son!

　　I contained myself that night, though I felt anger
255　And a sinking heart. The next day I visited
　　My father and mother, and questioned them. They
　　　　stormed,
　　Calling it all the slanderous rant of a fool;
　　And this relieved me. Yet the suspicion
　　Remained always aching in my mind;
260　I knew there was talk; I could not rest;
　　And finally, saying nothing to my parents,
　　I went to the shrine at Delphi.
　　The god dismissed my question without reply;
　　He spoke of other things.
　　　　　　　　　　　Some were clear,
265　Full of wretchedness, dreadful, unbearable:
　　As, that I should lie with my own mother, breed
　　Children from whom all men would turn their eyes;
　　And that I should be my father's murderer.

　　I heard all this, and fled. And from that day
270　Corinth to me was only in the stars
　　Descending in that quarter of the sky,
　　As I wandered farther and farther on my way
　　To a land where I should never see the evil

Sung by the oracle. And I came to this country
Where, so you say, King Laïos was killed.   275
I will tell you all that happened there, my lady.

There were three highways
Coming together at a place I passed;
And there a herald came towards me, and a chariot
Drawn by horses, with a man such as you describe   280
Seated in it. The groom leading the horses
Forced me off the road at his lord's command;
But as this charioteer lurched over toward me
I struck him in my rage. The old man saw me
And brought his double goad down upon my head   285
As I came abreast.
　　　　　　　　He was paid back, and more!
Swinging my club in this right hand I knocked him
Out of his car, and he rolled on the ground.
　　　　　　　　　　　　　I killed him.
I killed them all.
Now if that stranger and Laïos were—kin,   290
Where is a man more miserable than I?
More hated by the gods? Citizen and alien alike
Must never shelter me or speak to me—
I must be shunned by all.
　　　　　　　　And I myself
Pronounced this malediction upon myself!   295

Think of it: I have touched you with these hands,
These hands that killed your husband. What defilement!

Am I all evil, then? It must be so,
Since I must flee from Thebes, yet never again
See my own countrymen, my own country,   300
For fear of joining my mother in marriage
And killing Polybos, my father.
　　　　　　　　　　Ah,
If I was created so, born to this fate,
Who could deny the savagery of God?

O holy majesty of heavenly powers!   305
May I never see that day! Never!
Rather let me vanish from the race of men
Than know the abomination destined me!

CHORAGOS.
We too, my lord, have felt dismay at this.
But there is hope: you have yet to hear the shepherd.   310

OEDIPUS.
Indeed, I fear no other hope is left me.

IOCASTÊ.
What do you hope from him when he comes?

OEDIPUS.   This much:
If his account of the murder tallies with yours,
Then I am cleared.

IOCASTÊ.   What was it that I said
Of such importance?

OEDIPUS.   Why, "marauders," you said,   315
Killed the King, according to this man's story.
If he maintains that still, if there were several,

Clearly the guilt is not mine: I was alone.
But if he says one man, singlehanded, did it,
320 Then the evidence all points to me.

IOCASTÊ.

You may be sure that he said there were several;
And can he call back that story now? He cannot.
The whole city heard it as plainly as I.
But suppose he alters some detail of it:
325 He cannot ever show that Laïos' death
Fulfilled the oracle: for Apollo said
My child was doomed to kill him; and my child—
Poor baby!—it was my child that died first.

No. From now on, where oracles are concerned,
330 I would not waste a second thought on any.

OEDIPUS.

You may be right.
                    But come: let someone go
For the shepherd at once. This matter must be settled.

IOCASTÊ.

I will send for him.
I would not wish to cross you in anything,
335 And surely not in this.—Let us go in.

(*Exeunt into the palace.*)

ODE II

CHORUS.

Let me be reverent in the ways of right,   *Strophe 1*
Lowly the paths I journey on;
Let all my words and actions keep
The laws of the pure universe
5 From highest Heaven handed down.
For Heaven is their bright nurse,
Those generations of the realms of light;
Ah, never of mortal kind were they begot,
Nor are they slaves of memory, lost in sleep:
10 Their Father is greater than Time, and ages not.

The tyrant is a child of Pride   *Antistrophe 1*
Who drinks from his great sickening cup
Recklessness and vanity,
Until from his high crest headlong
15 He plummets to the dust of hope.
That strong man is not strong.
But let no fair ambition be denied;
May God protect the wrestler for the State
In government, in comely policy,
20 Who will fear God, and on His ordinance wait.

Haughtiness and the high hand of disdain   *Strophe 2*
Tempt and outrage God's holy law;
And any mortal who dares hold
No immortal Power in awe
25 Will be caught up in a net of pain:
The price for which his levity is sold.
Let each man take due earnings, then,

And keep his hands from holy things,
And from blasphemy stand apart—
Else the crackling blast of heaven   30
Blows on his head, and on his desperate heart;
Though fools will honor impious men,
In their cities no tragic poet sings.

Shall we lose faith in Delphi's obscurities,   *Antistrophe 2*
We who have heard the world's core   35
Discredited, and the sacred wood
Of Zeus at Elis praised no more?
The deeds and the strange prophecies
Must make a pattern yet to be understood.
Zeus, if indeed you are lord of all,   40
Throned in light over night and day,
Mirror this in your endless mind:
Our masters call the oracle
Words on the wind, and the Delphic vision blind!
Their hearts no longer know Apollo,   45
And reverence for the gods has died away.

SCENE III

Enter Iocastê.

IOCASTÊ.

Princes of Thebes, it has occurred to me
To visit the altars of the gods, bearing
These branches as a suppliant, and this incense.
Our King is not himself: his noble soul
Is overwrought with fantasies of dread,   5
Else he would consider
The new prophecies in the light of the old.
He will listen to any voice that speaks disaster,
And my advice goes for nothing.

She approaches the altar, right.

                    To you, then, Apollo,
Lycean lord, since you are nearest, I turn in prayer.   10
Receive these offerings, and grant us deliverance
From defilement. Our hearts are heavy with fear
When we see our leader distracted, as helpless sailors
Are terrified by the confusion of their helmsman.

Enter messenger.

MESSENGER.

Friends, no doubt you can direct me: 15
Where shall I find the house of Oedipus,
Or, better still, where is the King himself?

CHORAGOS.

It is this very place, stranger; he is inside.
This is his wife and mother of his children.

MESSENGER.

I wish her happiness in a happy house,
Blest in all the fulfillment of her marriage.   20

IOCASTÊ.

I wish as much for you: your courtesy
Deserves a like good fortune. But now, tell me:
Why have you come? What have you to say to us?

MESSENGER.

25   Good news, my lady, for your house and your husband.

IOCASTÊ.

What news? Who sent you here?

MESSENGER.   I am from Corinth.

The news I bring ought to mean joy for you,
Though it may be you will find some grief in it.

IOCASTÊ.

What is it? How can it touch us in both ways?

MESSENGER.

30   The people of Corinth, they say,
Intend to call Oedipus to be their king.

IOCASTÊ.

But old Polybos—is he not reigning still?

MESSENGER.

No. Death holds him in his sepulchre.

IOCASTÊ.

What are you saying? Polybos is dead?

MESSENGER.

35   If I am not telling the truth, may I die myself.

IOCASTÊ (to a maidservant).

Go in, go quickly; tell this to your master.

O riddlers of God's will, where are you now!
This was the man whom Oedipus, long ago,
Feared so, fled so, in dread of destroying him—
40   But it was another fate by which he died.

Enter Oedipus, center.

OEDIPUS.

Dearest Iocastê, why have you sent for me?

IOCASTÊ.

Listen to what this man says, and then tell me
What has become of the solemn prophecies.

OEDIPUS.

Who is this man? What is his news for me?

IOCASTÊ.

He has come from Corinth to announce your father's
45   death!

OEDIPUS.

Is it true, stranger? Tell me in your own words.

MESSENGER.

I cannot say it more clearly: the King is dead.

OEDIPUS.

Was it by treason? Or by an attack of illness?

MESSENGER.

A little thing brings old men to their rest.

OEDIPUS.

It was sickness, then?

MESSENGER.   Yes, and his many years.   50

OEDIPUS.

Ah!

Why should a man respect the Pythian hearth,° or
Give heed to the birds that jangle above his head?
They prophesied that I should kill Polybos,
Kill my own father; but he is dead and buried,   55
And I am here—I never touched him, never,
Unless he died in grief for my departure,
And thus, in a sense, through me. No Polybos
Has packed the oracles off with him underground.
They are empty words.

IOCASTÊ.   Had I not told you so?   60

OEDIPUS.

You had; it was my faint heart that betrayed me.

IOCASTÊ.

From now on never think of those things again.

OEDIPUS.

And yet—must I not fear my mother's bed?

IOCASTÊ.

Why should anyone in this world be afraid,
Since Fate rules us and nothing can be foreseen?   65
A man should live only for the present day.
Have no more fear of sleeping with your mother
How many men, in dreams, have lain with their mothers!
No reasonable man is troubled by such things.

OEDIPUS.

That is true; only—   70
If only my mother were not still alive!
But she is alive. I cannot help my dread.

IOCASTÊ.

Yet this news of your father's death is wonderful.

OEDIPUS.

Wonderful. But I fear the living woman.

MESSENGER.

Tell me, who is this woman that you fear?   75

OEDIPUS.

It is Meropê, man; the wife of King Polybos.

MESSENGER.

Meropê? Why should you be afraid of her?

OEDIPUS.

An oracle of the gods, a dreadful saying.

MESSENGER.

Can you tell me about it or are you sworn to silence?

OEDIPUS.

I can tell you, and I will.   80
Apollo said through his prophet that I was the man
Who should marry his own mother, shed his father's blood
With his own hands. And so, for all these years

52 **Pythian hearth** Delphi (also called Pytho because a great snake
had lived there), where Apollo spoke through a priestess

I have kept clear of Corinth, and no harm has come—
Though it would have been sweet to see my parents
85   again.
MESSENGER.
        And is this the fear that drove you out of Corinth?
OEDIPUS.
        Would you have me kill my father?
MESSENGER.   As for that
        You must be reassured by the news I gave you.
OEDIPUS.
        If you could reassure me, I would reward you.
MESSENGER.
90   I had that in mind, I will confess: I thought
        I could count on you when you returned to Corinth.
OEDIPUS.
        No: I will never go near my parents again.
MESSENGER.
        Ah, son, you still do not know what you are doing—
OEDIPUS.
        What do you mean? In the name of God tell me!
MESSENGER.
95   —If these are your reasons for not going home—
OEDIPUS.
        I tell you, I fear the oracle may come true.
MESSENGER.
        And guilt may come upon you through your parents?
OEDIPUS.
        That is the dread that is always in my heart.
MESSENGER.
        Can you not see that all your fears are groundless?
OEDIPUS.
100   How can you say that? They are my parents, surely?
MESSENGER.
        Polybos was not your father.
OEDIPUS.   Not my father?
MESSENGER.
        No more your father than the man speaking to you.
OEDIPUS.
        But you are nothing to me!
MESSENGER.   Neither was he.
OEDIPUS.
        Then why did he call me son?
MESSENGER.   I will tell you:
105   Long ago he had you from my hands, as a gift.
OEDIPUS.
        Then how could he love me so, if I was not his?
MESSENGER.
        He had no children, and his heart turned to you.
OEDIPUS.
        What of you? Did you buy me? Did you find me by
              chance?
MESSENGER.
        I came upon you in the crooked pass of Kithairon.

OEDIPUS.
        And what were you doing there?
MESSENGER.   Tending my flocks.   110
OEDIPUS.
        A wandering shepherd?
MESSENGER.   But your savior, son, that day.
OEDIPUS.
        From what did you save me?
MESSENGER.   Your ankles should tell you
        that.
OEDIPUS.
        Ah, stranger, why do you speak of that childhood pain?
MESSENGER.
        I cut the bonds that tied your ankles together.
OEDIPUS.
        I have had the mark as long as I can remember.   115
MESSENGER.
        That was why you were given the name you bear.°
OEDIPUS.
        God! Was it my father or my mother who did it?
        Tell me!
MESSENGER.
        I do not know. The man who gave you to me
        Can tell you better than I.   120
OEDIPUS.
        It was not you that found me, but another?
MESSENGER.
        It was another shepherd gave you to me.
OEDIPUS.
        Who was he? Can you tell me who he was?
MESSENGER.
        I think he was said to be one of Laïos' people.
OEDIPUS.
        You mean the Laïos who was king here years ago?   125
MESSENGER.
        Yes; King Laïos; and the man was one of his herdsmen.
OEDIPUS.
        Is he still alive? Can I see him?
MESSENGER.   These men here
        Know best about such things.
OEDIPUS.   Does anyone here
        Know this shepherd that he is talking about?
        Have you seen him in the fields, or in the town?   130
        If you have, tell me. It is time things were made plain.
CHORAGOS.
        I think the man he means is that same shepherd
        You have already asked to see. Iocastê perhaps
        Could tell you something.
OEDIPUS.   Do you know anything
        About him, Lady? Is he the man we have summoned?   135
        Is that the man this shepherd means?

116 name you bear *Oedipus* means "swollen-foot"

IOCASTÊ.   Why think of him?
  Forget this herdsman. Forget it all.
  This talk is a waste of time.
OEDIPUS.   How can you say that,
  When the clues to my true birth are in my hands?
140 IOCASTÊ.
  For God's love, let us have no more questioning!
  Is your life nothing to you?
  My own is pain enough for me to bear.
OEDIPUS.
  You need not worry. Suppose my mother a slave,
  And born of slaves: no baseness can touch you.
145 IOCASTÊ.
  Listen to me, I beg you: do not do this thing!
OEDIPUS.
  I will not listen; the truth must be made known.
IOCASTÊ.
  Everything that I say is for your own good!
OEDIPUS.   My own good
  Snaps my patience, then: I want none of it.
IOCASTÊ.
  You are fatally wrong! May you never learn who you are!
150 OEDIPUS.
  Go, one of you, and bring the shepherd here.
  Let us leave this woman to brag of her royal name.
IOCASTÊ.
  Ah, miserable!
  That is the only word I have for you now.
  That is the only word I can ever have.
                                        (*Exit into the palace.*)
CHORAGOS.
155 Why has she left us, Oedipus? Why has she gone
  In such a passion of sorrow? I fear this silence:
  Something dreadful may come of it.
OEDIPUS.   Let it come!
  However base my birth, I must know about it.
  The Queen, like a woman, is perhaps ashamed
160 To think of my low origin. But I
  Am a child of luck; I cannot be dishonored.
  Luck is my mother; the passing months, my brothers,
  Have seen me rich and poor. If this is so,
  How could I wish that I were someone else?
165 How could I not be glad to know my birth?

ODE III

CHORUS.
  If ever the coming time were known   *Strophe*
  To my heart's pondering,
  Kithairon, now by Heaven I see the torches
  At the festival of the next full moon,
5 And see the dance, and hear the choir sing
  A grace to your gentle shade:

Mountain where Oedipus was found,
O mountain guard of a noble race!
May the god who heals us lend his aid,
And let that glory come to pass   10
For our king's cradling-ground.

Of the nymphs that flower beyond   *Antistrophe*
  the years.
Who bore you, royal child,
To Pan of the hills or the timberline Apollo,
Cold in delight where the upland clears.   15
Or Hermês for whom Kyllenê's° heights are piled?
Or flushed as evening cloud,
Great Dionysos, roamer of mountains,
He—was it he who found you there,
And caught you up in his own proud   20
Arms from the sweet god-ravisher°
Who laughed by the Muses' fountains?

SCENE IV

OEDIPUS.
  Sirs: though I do not know the man,
  I think I see him coming, this shepherd we want:
  He is old, like our friend here, and the men
  Bringing him seem to be servants of my house.
  But you can tell, if you have ever seen him.   5

  Enter shepherd escorted by servants.

CHORAGOS.
  I know him, he was Laïos' man. You can trust him.
OEDIPUS.
  Tell me first, you from Corinth: is this the shepherd
  We were discussing?
MESSENGER.   This is the very man.
OEDIPUS (*to shepherd*).
  Come here. No, look at me. You must answer
  Everything I ask.—You belonged to Laïos?   10
SHEPHERD.
  Yes: born his slave, brought up in his house.
OEDIPUS.
  Tell me: what kind of work did you do for him?
SHEPHERD.
  I was a shepherd of his, most of my life.
OEDIPUS.
  Where mainly did you go for pasturage?

16 Hermes . . . Kyllenê's Hermês, messenger of the gods, was said
to have been born on Mt. Kyllenê   **21 the sweet god-ravisher** the
presumed mother, the nymph whom the god found irresistible

SHEPHERD.

15   Sometimes Kithairon, sometimes the hills near-by.

OEDIPUS.

Do you remember ever seeing this man out there?

SHEPHERD.

What would he be doing there? This man?

OEDIPUS.

This man standing here. Have you ever seen him before?

SHEPHERD.

No. At least, not to my recollection.

MESSENGER.

20   And that is not strange, my lord. But I'll refresh
His memory: he must remember when we two
Spent three whole seasons together, March to September,
On Kithairon or thereabouts. He had two flocks;
I had one. Each autumn I'd drive mine home

25   And he would go back with his to Laïos' sheepfold.—
Is this not true, just as I have described it?

SHEPHERD.

True, yes; but it was all so long ago.

MESSENGER.

Well, then: do you remember, back in those days
That you gave me a baby boy to bring up as my own?

SHEPHERD.

30   What if I did? What are you trying to say?

MESSENGER.

King Oedipus was once that little child.

SHEPHERD.

Damn you, hold your tongue!

OEDIPUS.   No more of that!
It is your tongue needs watching, not this man's.

SHEPHERD.

My King, my Master, what is it I have done wrong?

OEDIPUS.

35   You have not answered his question about the boy.

SHEPHERD.

He does not know . . . He is only making trouble . . .

OEDIPUS.

Come, speak plainly, or it will go hard with you.

SHEPHERD.

In God's name, do not torture an old man!

OEDIPUS.

Come here, one of you; bind his arms behind him.

SHEPHERD.

40   Unhappy king! What more do you wish to learn?

OEDIPUS.

Did you give this man the child he speaks of?

SHEPHERD.   I did.
And I would to God I had died that very day.

OEDIPUS.

You will die now unless you speak the truth.

SHEPHERD.

Yet if I speak the truth, I am worse than dead.

OEDIPUS.

45   Very well; since you insist upon delaying—

SHEPHERD.

No! I have told you already that I gave him the boy.

OEDIPUS.

Where did you get him? From your house?
From somewhere else?

SHEPHERD.

Not from mine, no. A man gave him to me.

OEDIPUS.

Is that man here? Do you know whose slave he was?

SHEPHERD.

For God's love, my King, do not ask me any more!   50

OEDIPUS.

You are a dead man if I have to ask you again.

SHEPHERD.

Then . . . Then the child was from the palace of Laïos.

OEDIPUS.

A slave child? or a child of his own line?

SHEPHERD.

Ah, I am on the brink of dreadful speech!

OEDIPUS.

And I of dreadful hearing. Yet I must hear.   55

SHEPHERD.

If you must be told, then . . .
                              They said it was Laïos' child,
But it is your wife who can tell you about that.

OEDIPUS.

My wife!—Did she give it to you?

SHEPHERD.   My lord, she did.

OEDIPUS.

Do you know why?

SHEPHERD.   I was told to get rid of it.

OEDIPUS.

An unspeakable mother!

SHEPHERD.   There had been prophecies . . .   60

OEDIPUS.

Tell me.

SHEPHERD. It was said that the boy would kill his own father.

OEDIPUS.

Then why did you give him over to this old man?

SHEPHERD.

I pitied the baby, my King,
And I thought that this man would take him far away
To his own country.
                         He saved him—but for what a fate!   65
For if you are what this man says you are,
No man living is more wretched than Oedipus.

OEDIPUS.

Ah God!
         It was true!
                    All the prophecies!
                                        —Now,
O Light, may I look on you for the last time!   70
I, Oedipus,
Oedipus, damned in his birth, in his marriage damned,
Damned in the blood he shed with his own hand!

He rushes into the palace.

ODE IV

CHORUS.
> Alas for the seed of men. *Strophe 1*
>
> What measure shall I give these generations
> That breathe on the void and are void
> And exist and do not exist?
>
> 5 Who bears more weight of joy
> Than mass of sunlight shifting in images,
> Or who shall make his thought stay on
> That down time drifts away?
>
> Your splendor is all fallen.
>
> 10 O naked brow of wrath and tears,
> O change of Oedipus!
> I who saw your days call no man blest—
> Your great days like ghósts góne.
>
> That mind was a strong bow. *Antistrophe 1*
> 15 Deep, how deep you drew it then, hard archer,
> At a dim fearful range,
> And brought dear glory down!
>
> You overcame the stranger—
> The virgin with her hooking lion claws—
> 20 And though death sang, stood like a tower
> To make pale Thebes take heart.
>
> Fortress against our sorrow!
>
> Divine king, giver of laws,
> Majestic Oedipus!
> 25 No prince in Thebes had ever such renown,
> No prince won such grace of power.
>
> And now of all men ever known *Strophe 2*
> Most pitiful is this man's story:
> His fortunes are most changed, his state
> 30 Fallen to a low slave's
> Ground under bitter fate.
>
> O Oedipus, most royal one!
> The great door that expelled you to the light
> Gave it night—ah, gave night to your glory:
> 35 As to the father, to the fathering son.
>
> All understood too late.
>
> How could that queen whom Laïos won,
> The garden that he harrowed at his height,
> Be silent when that act was done?
>
> 40 But all eyes fail before time's eye, *Antistrophe 2*
> All actions come to justice there.
> Though never willed, though far down the deep past,
> Your bed, your dread sirings,
> Are brought to book at last.
> 45 Child by Laïos doomed to die,

Then doomed to lose that fortunate little death,
Would God you never took breath in this air
That with my wailing lips I take to cry:

For I weep the world's outcast.

I was blind, and now I can tell why: 50
Asleep, for you had given ease of breath
To Thebes, while the false years went by.

EXODOS

Enter, from the palace, second messenger.

SECOND MESSENGER.
> Elders of Thebes, most honored in this land,
> What horrors are yours to see and hear, what weight
> Of sorrow to be endured, if, true to your birth,
> You venerate the line of Labdakos!
> I think neither Istros nor Phasis, those great rivers, 5
> Could purify this place of the corruption
> It shelters now, or soon must bring to light—
> Evil not done unconsciously, but willed.
>
> The greatest griefs are those we cause ourselves.

CHORAGOS.
> Surely, friend, we have grief enough already; 10
> What new sorrow do you mean?

SECOND MESSENGER.   The Queen is dead.

CHORAGOS.
> Iocastê? Dead? But at whose hand?

SECOND MESSENGER.   Her own.
> The full horror of what happened you cannot know,
> For you did not see it; but I, who did, will tell you
> As clearly as I can how she met her death. 15
>
> When she had left us,
> In passionate silence, passing through the court,
> She ran to her apartment in the house,
> Her hair clutched by the fingers of both hands.
> She closed the doors behind her; then, by that bed 20
> Where long ago the fatal son was conceived—
> That son who should bring about his father's death—
> We heard her call upon Laïos, dead so many years,
> And heard her wail for the double fruit of her marriage,
> A husband by her husband, children by her child. 25
>
> Exactly how she died I do not know:
> For Oedipus burst in moaning and would not let us
> Keep vigil to the end: it was by him
> As he stormed about the room that our eyes were
>   caught.
> From one to another of us he went, begging a sword, 30
> Cursing the wife who was not his wife, the mother
> Whose womb had carried his own children and himself.
> I do not know: it was none of us aided him,
> But surely one of the gods was in control!
> For with a dreadful cry 35
> He hurled his weight, as though wrenched out of himself,

At the twin doors: the bolts gave, and he rushed in.
And there we saw her hanging, her body swaying
From the cruel cord she had noosed about her neck.
40 A great sob broke from him heartbreaking to hear,
As he loosed the rope and lowered her to the ground.

I would blot out from my mind what happened next!
For the King ripped from her gown the golden brooches
That were her ornament, and raised them, and plunged
    them down
45 Straight into his own eyeballs, crying, "No more,
No more shall you look on the misery about me,
The horrors of my own doing! Too long you have known
The faces of those whom I should never have seen,
Too long been blind to those for whom I was searching!
50 From this hour, go in darkness!" And as he spoke,
He struck at his eyes—not once, but many times;
And the blood spattered his beard,
Bursting from his ruined sockets like red hail.

So from the unhappiness of two this evil has sprung,
55 A curse on the man and woman alike. The old
Happiness of the house of Labdakos
Was happiness enough: where is it today?
It is all wailing and ruin, disgrace, death—all
The misery of mankind that has a name—
60 And it is wholly and for ever theirs.

CHORAGOS.
    Is he in agony still? Is there no rest for him?

SECOND MESSENGER.
    He is calling for someone to lead him to the gates
So that all the children of Kadmos may look upon
His father's murderer, his mother's—no,
I cannot say it!
65   And then he will leave Thebes,
Self-exiled, in order that the curse
Which he himself pronounced may depart from the
    house.
He is weak, and there is none to lead him,
So terrible is his suffering.
                But you will see:
70 Look, the doors are opening; in a moment
You will see a thing that would crush a heart of stone.

The central door is opened; Oedipus, blinded, is led in.

CHORAGOS.
    Dreadful indeed for men to see.
    Never have my own eyes
    Looked on a sight so full of fear.

75 Oedipus!
What madness came upon you, what daemon°
Leaped on your life with heavier
Punishment than a mortal man can bear?
No: I cannot even

Look at you, poor ruined one.   80
And I would speak, question, ponder,
If I were able. No.
You make me shudder.

OEDIPUS.
    God. God.
    Is there a sorrow greater?   85
    Where shall I find harbor in this world?
    My voice is hurled far on a dark wind.
    What has God done to me?

CHORAGOS.
    Too terrible to think of, or to see.

OEDIPUS.
    O cloud of night,   *Strophe 1* 90
    Never to be turned away: night coming on,
    I cannot tell how: night like a shroud!
    My fair winds brought me here.
                Oh God. Again
    The pain of the spikes where I had sight,
    The flooding pain   95
    Of memory, never to be gouged out.

CHORAGOS.
    This is not strange.
    You suffer it all twice over, remorse in pain,
    Pain in remorse.

OEDIPUS.
    Ah dear friend   *Antistrophe 1* 100
    Are you faithful even yet, you alone?
    Are you still standing near me, will you stay here,
    Patient, to care for the blind?
              The blind man!
    Yet even blind I know who it is attends me,
    By the voice's tone—   105
    Though my new darkness hide the comforter.

CHORAGOS.
    Oh fearful act!
    What god was it drove you to rake black
    Night across your eyes?

OEDIPUS.
    Apollo. Apollo. Dear   *Strophe 2* 110
    Children, the god was Apollo.
    He brought my sick, sick fate upon me.
    But the blinding hand was my own!
    How could I bear to see
    When all my sight was horror everywhere?   115

CHORAGOS.
    Everywhere; that is true.

OEDIPUS.
    And now what is left?
    Images? Love? A greeting even,
    Sweet to the senses? Is there anything?
    Ah, no, friends: lead me away.   120
    Lead me away from Thebes.
                Lead the great wreck

76 daemon a spirit, not necessarily evil

And hell of Oedipus, whom the gods hate.

CHORAGOS.
Your fate is clear, you are not blind to that.
Would God you had never found it out!

OEDIPUS.
125 Death take the man who unbound   *Antistrophe 2*
My feet on that hillside
And delivered me from death to life! What life?
If only I had died,
This weight of monstrous doom
130 Could not have dragged me and my darlings down.

CHORAGOS.
I would have wished the same.

OEDIPUS.
Oh never to have come here
With my father's blood upon me! Never
To have been the man they call his mother's husband!
135 Oh accurst! O child of evil,
To have entered that wretched bed—
                                        the selfsame one!
More primal than sin itself, this fell to me.

CHORAGOS.
I do not know how I can answer you.
You were better dead than alive and blind.

OEDIPUS.
140 Do not counsel me any more. This punishment
That I have laid upon myself is just.
If I had eyes,
I do not know how I could bear the sight
Of my father, when I came to the house of Death,
145 Or my mother: for I have sinned against them both
So vilely that I could not make my peace
By strangling my own life.
                              Or do you think my children,
Born as they were born, would be sweet to my eyes?
Ah never, never! Nor this town with its high walls,
Nor the holy images of the gods.
150   For I,
Thrice miserable—Oedipus, noblest of all the line
Of Kadmos, have condemned myself to enjoy
These things no more, by my own malediction
Expelling that man whom the gods declared
155 To be a defilement in the house of Laïos.
After exposing the rankness of my own guilt,
How could I look men frankly in the eyes?
No, I swear it,
If I could have stifled my hearing at its source,
160 I would have done it and made all this body
A tight cell of misery, blank to light and sound:
So I should have been safe in a dark agony
Beyond all recollection.
                        Ah Kithairon!
Why did you shelter me? When I was cast upon you,
165 Why did I not die? Then I should never

Have shown the world my execrable birth.

Ah Polybos! Corinth, city that I believed
The ancient seat of my ancestors: how fair
I seemed, your child! And all the while this evil
Was cancerous within me!
                        For I am sick   170
In my daily life, sick in my origin.

O three roads, dark ravine, woodland and way
Where three roads met: you, drinking my father's blood,
My own blood, spilled by my own hand: can you
     remember
The unspeakable things I did there, and the things   175
I went on from there to do?
                        O marriage, marriage!
The act that engendered me, and again the act
Performed by the son in the same bed—
                                    Ah, the net
Of incest, mingling fathers, brothers, sons,
With brides, wives, mothers: the last evil   180
That can be known by men: no tongue can say
How evil!
            No. For the love of God, conceal me
Somewhere far from Thebes; or kill me; or hurl me
Into the sea, away from men's eyes for ever.
Come, lead me. You need not fear to touch me.   185
Of all men, I alone can bear this guilt.

Enter Creon.

CHORAGOS.
We are not the ones to decide; but Creon here
May fitly judge of what you ask. He only
Is left to protect the city in your place.

OEDIPUS.
Alas, how can I speak to him? What right have I   190
To beg his courtesy whom I have deeply wronged?

CREON.
I have not come to mock you, Oedipus,
Or to reproach you, either.
(*To attendants.*)   —You, standing there:
If you have lost all respect for man's dignity,
At least respect the flame of Lord Helios: 195
Do not allow this pollution to show itself
Openly here, an affront to the earth
And Heaven's rain and the light of day. No, take him
Into the house as quickly as you can.
For it is proper   200
That only the close kindred see his grief.

OEDIPUS.
I pray you in God's name, since your courtesy
Ignores my dark expectation, visiting
With mercy this man of all men most execrable:
Give me what I ask—for your good, not for mine.   205

CREON.
And what is it that you would have me do?

OEDIPUS.
    Drive me out of this country as quickly as may be
    To a place where no human voice can ever greet me.
CREON.
    I should have done that before now—only,
210   God's will had not been wholly revealed to me.
OEDIPUS.
    But his command is plain: the parricide
    Must be destroyed. I am that evil man.
CREON.
    That is the sense of it, yes; but as things are,
    We had best discover clearly what is to be done.
OEDIPUS.
215   You would learn more about a man like me?
CREON.
    You are ready now to listen to the god.
OEDIPUS.
    I will listen. But it is to you.
    That I must turn for help. I beg you, hear me.

    The woman in there—
220   Give her whatever funeral you think proper:
    She is your sister.
             —But let me go, Creon!
    Let me purge my father's Thebes of the pollution
    Of my living here, and go out to the wild hills,
    To Kithairon, that has won such fame with me,
225   The tomb my mother and father appointed for me,
    And let me die there, as they willed I should.
    And yet I know
    Death will not ever come to me through sickness
    Or in any natural way: I have been preserved
230   For some unthinkable fate. But let that be.
    As for my sons, you need not care for them.
    They are men, they will find some way to live.
    But my poor daughters, who have shared my table,
    Who never before have been parted from their father—
235   Take care of them, Creon; do this for me.
    And will you let me touch them with my hands
    A last time, and let us weep together?
    Be kind, my lord,
    Great prince, be kind!
               Could I but touch them,
240   They would be mine again, as when I had my eyes.

Enter Antigonê and Ismenê, attended.

    Ah, God!
    Is it my dearest children I hear weeping?
    Has Creon pitied me and sent my daughters?
CREON.
    Yes, Oedipus: I knew that they were dear to you
245   In the old days, and know you must love them still.
OEDIPUS.
    May God bless you for this—and be a friendlier
    Guardian to you than he has been to me!

    Children, where are you?
    Come quickly to my hands: they are your brother's—
    Hands that have brought your father's once clear eyes   250
    To this way of seeing—
              Ah dearest ones,
    I had neither sight nor knowledge then, your father
    By the woman who was the source of his life!
    And I weep for you—having no strength to see you—,
    I weep for you when I think of the bitterness   255
    That men will visit upon you all your lives.
    What homes, what festivals can you attend
    Without being forced to depart again in tears?
    And when you come to marriageable age,
    Where is the man, my daughters, who would dare   260
    Risk the bane that lies on all my children?
    Is there any evil wanting? Your father killed
    His father; sowed the womb of her who bore him;
    Engendered you at the fount of his own existence!
    That is what they will say of you.
                 Then, whom   265
    Can you ever marry? There are no bridegrooms for you,
    And your lives must wither away in sterile dreaming.
    O Creon, son of Menoikeus!
    You are the only father my daughters have,
    Since we, their parents, are both of us gone forever.   270
    They are your own blood: you will not let them
    Fall into beggary and loneliness;
    You will keep them from the miseries that are mine!
    Take pity on them; see, they are only children,
    Friendless except for you. Promise me this,   275
    Great Prince, and give me your hand in token of it.

Creon clasps his right hand.

    Children:
    I could say much, if you could understand me,
    But as it is, I have only this prayer for you:
    Live where you can, be as happy as you can—   280
    Happier, please God, than God has made your father!
CREON.
    Enough. You have wept enough. Now go within.
OEDIPUS.
    I must; but it is hard.
CREON.
               Time eases all things.
OEDIPUS.
    But you must promise—
CREON.
               Say what you desire.
OEDIPUS.
    Send me from Thebes!
CREON.
             God grant that I may!   285
OEDIPUS.
    But since God hates me . . .
CREON.
            No, he will grant your wish.
OEDIPUS.
    You promise?

Sophocles

CREON.   I cannot speak beyond my knowledge.

OEDIPUS.
   Then lead me in.

CREON.   Come now, and leave your children.

OEDIPUS.
   No! Do not take them from me!

CREON.   Think no longer
290   That you are in command here, but rather think
   How, when you were, you served your own destruction.

(*Exeunt into the house all but the Chorus; the Choragos
chants directly to the audience.*)

CHORAGOS.
   Men of Thebes: look upon Oedipus.
   This is the king who solved the famous riddle
   And towered up, most powerful of men.
   No mortal eyes but looked on him with envy,   295

   Yet in the end ruin swept over him.
   Let every man in mankind's frailty
   Consider his last day; and let none
   Presume on his good fortune until he find
   Life, at his death, a memory without pain.   300

TOPICS FOR CRITICAL THINKING AND WRITING

 ### THE PLAY ON THE PAGE

1. On the basis on lines 1–149, characterize Oedipus. Does he seem an effective leader? What additional traits are revealed in lines 205–491?

2. In your opinion, how fair is it to say that Oedipus is morally guilty? Does he argue that he is morally innocent because he did not intend to do immoral deeds? Can it be said that he is guilty of *hybris* but that *hybris* (see page 33) has nothing to do with his fall?

3. Oedipus says that he blinds himself in order not to look upon people he should not. What further reasons can be given? Why does he not (like Iocastê) commit suicide?

4. Does the play show the futility of human efforts to act intelligently?

5. In *Oedipus* do you find the gods evil?

6. Are the choral odes lyrical interludes that serve to separate the scenes, or do they advance the dramatic action?

7. Matthew Arnold said that Sophocles saw life steadily and saw it whole. But in this play is Sophocles facing the facts of life? Or, on the contrary, is he avoiding what we think of as normal life, and presenting a series of unnatural and outrageous coincidences? In either case, do you think the play is relevant today?

8. Can you describe your emotions at the end of the play? Do they include pity for Oedipus? Pity for all human beings, including yourself? Fear that you might be punished for some unintended transgression? Awe, engendered by a perception of the interrelatedness of things? Relief that the story is only a story? Exhilaration? Explain your reaction.

9. Examine Aristotle's comments on tragedy (p. 73), and evaluate three of his points with relevance to *Oedipus*.

THE PLAY ON THE STAGE

10. During your first consideration of the play, start with a reading of lines 1–149. Choose someone from the group to stand on a chair (Oedipus), two other readers to stand nearby (the Priest and Creon) and several others to kneel or lie on the floor (Theban citizens). After this rough enactment, ask the readers how they felt about their roles. Then discuss the ways a modern staging could create a powerful opening for the play. Some questions to consider: Do the Thebans ever touch Oedipus? Should the actor playing Oedipus make eye contact with anyone on the stage?

11. Originally the Greek chorus chanted and danced. What are your recommendations for a director today? Choose a particular passage from the play to illustrate your ideas.

12. Imagine that you are directing a production of *Oedipus*. Propose a cast for the principal roles, using well-known actors or people from your own circle. Explain the reasons for your choices.

13. What might be gained or lost by performing the play in modern dress? Or is there some period other than ancient Greece—let's say the Victorian period—in which you think the play might be effectively set?

14. Alan MacVey, in his comment on a production (page 78), wishes the royalty had been clothed in "power suits." What is your response to this idea?

A CONTEXT FOR *OEDIPUS REX*

Aristotle
THE POETICS
Translated by L. J. Potts

It is no exaggeration to say that the history of tragic criticism is a series of footnotes to Aristotle. In a fragmentary treatise usually called the *Poetics*, Aristotle (384–322 B.C.) raises almost all the points that have subsequently been argued, such as the nature of the hero, the emotional effect on the spectator, the coherence of the plot. Whether or not he gave the right answers, it has seemed for more than two thousand years that he asked the right questions.

[ART IS IMITATION]

Let us talk of the art of poetry as a whole, and its different species with the particular force of each of them; how the fables must be put together if the poetry is to be well formed; also what are its elements and their different qualities; and all other matters pertaining to the subject.

To begin in the proper order, at the beginning. The making of epics and tragedies, and also comedy, and the art of the dithyramb, and most flute and lyre art, all have this in common, that they are imitations. But they differ from one another in three respects: the different kinds of medium in which they imitate, the different objects they imitate, and the different manner in which they imitate (when it does differ). . . . When the imitators imitate the doings of people, the people in the imitation must be either high or low; the characters almost always follow this line exclusively, for all men differ in character according to their degree of goodness or badness. They must therefore be either above our norm, or below it, or normal; as, in painting, Polygnōtus depicted superior, Pauson inferior, and Dionysius normal, types. It is clear that each variant of imitation that I have mentioned will have these differences, and as the object imitated varies in this way so the works will differ. Even in the ballet, and in flute and lyre music, these dissimilarities can occur; and in the art that uses prose, or verse without music. . . . This is the difference that marks tragedy out from comedy; comedy is inclined to imitate persons below the level of our world, tragedy persons above it.

[ORIGINS OF POETRY]

There seem to be two causes that gave rise to poetry in general, and they are natural. The impulse to imitate is inherent in man from his childhood; he is distinguished among the animals by being the most imitative of them, and he takes the first steps of his education by imitating. Everyone's enjoyment of imitation is also inborn. What happens with works of art demonstrates this: though a thing itself is dis-agreeable to look at, we enjoy contemplating the most accurate representations of it—for instance, figures of the most despicable animals, or of human corpses. The reason for this lies in another fact: learning is a great pleasure, not only to philosophers but likewise to everyone else, however limited his gift for it may be. He enjoys looking at these representations, because in the act of studying them he is learning—identifying the object by an inference (for instance, recognizing who is the original of a portrait); since, if he happens not to have already seen the object depicted, it will not be the imitation as such that is giving him pleasure, but the finish of the workmanship, or the colouring, or some such other cause.

And just as imitation is natural to us, so also are music and rhythm (metres, clearly, are constituent parts of rhythms). Thus, from spontaneous beginnings, mankind developed poetry by a series of mostly minute changes out of these improvisations.

[THE ELEMENTS OF TRAGEDY]

Let us now discuss tragedy, having first picked up from what has been said the definition of its essence that has so far emerged. Tragedy, then, is an imitation of an action of high importance, complete and of some amplitude; in language enhanced by distinct and varying beauties; acted not narrated; by means of pity and fear effecting its purgation of these emotions. By the beauties enhancing the language I mean rhythm and melody; by "distinct and varying" I mean that some are produced by metre alone, and others at another time by melody.

Now since the imitating is done by actors, it would follow of necessity that one element in a tragedy must be the *Mise en scène*. Others are Melody and Language, for these are the media in which the imitating is done. By Language, I mean the component parts of the verse, whereas Melody has an entirely sensuous effect. Again, since the object imitated is an action, and doings are done by persons, whose individuality will be determined by their Character and their Thought (for these are the factors we have in mind when we define the quality of their doings), it follows that there are two natural causes of these doings, Thought and Character; and these causes determine the good or ill fortune of everyone. But the Fable is the imitation of the action; and by the Fable I mean the whole structure of the incidents. By Character I mean the factor that enables us to define the particular quality of the people involved in the doings; and Thought is shown in everything they say when they are demonstrating a fact or disclosing an opinion. There are therefore necessarily six elements in every tragedy, which give it its quality; and they are the Fable, Character, Language, Thought, the *Mise en scène*, and Melody. Two of these are the media in which the imitating is done, one is the manner of imitation, and three are its objects; there is no other element besides these. Numerous poets have turned these essential components to account; all of them are always present—the *Mise en scène*, Character, the Fable, Language, Melody, and Thought.

The chief of these is the plotting of the incidents; for tragedy is an imitation not of men but of doings, life, happiness; unhappiness is located in doings, and our end is a certain kind of doing, not a personal quality; it is their characters that give men their quality, but their doings that make them happy or the opposite. So it is not the purpose of the actors to imitate character, but they include character as a factor in the doings. Thus it is the incidents (that is to say the Fable) that are the end for which tragedy exists; and the end is more important than anything else. Also, without an action there could not be a tragedy, but without Character there could. (In fact, the tragedies of most of the moderns are non-moral, and there are many non-moral poets of all periods; this also applies to the paintings of Zeuxis, if he is compared with Polygnōtus, for whereas Polygnōtus is a good portrayer of character the painting of Zeuxis leaves it out.) Again, if any one strings together moral speeches with the language and thought well worked out, he will be doing what is the business of tragedy; but it will be done much better by a tragedy that handles these elements more weakly, but has a fable with the incidents connected by a plot. Further, the chief means by which tragedy moves us, Irony of events and Disclosure, are elements in the Fable. A pointer in the same direction is that beginners in the art of poetry are able to get the language and characterization right before they can plot their incidents, and so were almost all the earliest poets.

So the source and as it were soul of tragedy is the Fable; and Character comes next. For, to instance a parallel from the art of painting, the most beautiful colours splashed on anyhow would not be as pleasing as a recognizable picture in black and white. Tragedy is an imitation of an action, and it is chiefly for this reason that it imitates the persons involved.

Third comes Thought: that is, the ability to say what circumstances allow and what is appropriate to them. It is the part played by social morality and rhetoric in making the dialogue: the old poets made their characters talk like men of the world, whereas our contemporaries make them talk like public speakers. Character is what shows a man's disposition—the kind of things he chooses or rejects when his choice is not obvious. Accordingly those speeches where the speaker shows no preferences or aversions whatever are non-moral. Thought, on the other hand, is shown in demonstrating a matter of fact or disclosing a significant opinion.

Fourth comes the Language. By Language I mean, as has already been said, words used semantically. It has the same force in verse as in prose.

Of the remaining elements, Melody is the chief of the enhancing beauties. The *Mise en scène* can excite emotion, but it is the crudest element and least akin to the art of poetry; for the force of tragedy exists even without stage and actors; besides, the fitting out of a *Mise en scène* belongs more to the wardrobe-master's art than to the poet's.

[THE TRAGIC FABLE]

So much for analysis. Now let us discuss in what sort of way the incidents should be plotted, since that is the first and chief consideration in tragedy. Our data are that tragedy is an imitation of a whole and complete action of some amplitude (a thing can be whole and yet quite lacking in amplitude). Now a whole is that which has a beginning, a middle, and an end. A beginning is that which does not itself necessarily follow anything else, but which leads naturally to another event or development; an end is the opposite, that which itself naturally (either of necessity or most commonly) follows something else, but nothing else comes after it; and a middle is that which itself follows something else and is followed by another thing. So, well-plotted fables must not begin or end casually, but must follow the pattern here described.

But, besides this, a picture, or any other composite object, if it is to be beautiful, must not only have its parts properly arranged, but be of an appropriate size; for beauty depends on size and structure. Accordingly, a minute picture cannot be beautiful (for when our vision has almost lost its sense of time it becomes confused); nor can an immense one (for we cannot take it all in together, and so our vision loses its unity and wholeness)—imagine a picture a thousand miles long! So, just as there is a proper size for bodies and pictures (a size that can be well surveyed), there is also a proper amplitude for fables (what can be kept well in one's mind). The length of the performance on the stage has nothing to do with art; if a hundred tragedies had to be produced, the length of the production would be settled by the clock, as the story goes that another kind of performance once was. But as to amplitude, the invariable rule dictated by the nature of the action is the fuller the more beautiful so long as the outline remains clear; and for a simple rule of size, the number of happenings that will make a chain of probability (or necessity) to change a given situation from misfortune to good fortune or from good fortune to misfortune is the minimum.

[UNITY]

Unity in a fable does not mean, as some think, that it has one man for its subject. To any one man many things happen—an infinite number—and some of them do not make any sort of unity; and in the same way one man has many doings which cannot be made into a unit of action. . . . Accordingly, just as in the other imitative arts the object of each imitation is a unit, so, since the fable is an imitation of an action, that action must be a complete unit, and the events of which it is made up must be so plotted that if any of these elements is moved or removed the whole is altered and upset. For when a thing can be included or not included without making any noticeable difference, that thing is no part of the whole.

[PROBABILITY]

From what has been said it is also clear that it is not the poet's business to tell what has happened, but the kind of things that would happen—what is possible according to probability or necessity. The difference between the historian and the poet is not the difference between writing in verse or prose; the work of Herodotus could be put into verse, and it would be just as much a history in verse as it is in prose. The difference is that the one tells what has happened, and the other the kind of things that would happen. It follows therefore that poetry is more philosophical and of higher value than history; for poetry unifies more, whereas history aggregates. To unify is to make a man of a certain description say or do the things that suit him, probably or necessarily, in the circumstances (this is the point of the descriptive proper names in poetry); what Alcibiades did or what happened to him is an aggregation. In comedy this has now become clear. They first plot the fable on a base of probabilities, and then find imaginary names for the people—unlike the lampooners, whose work was an aggregation of personalities. But in tragedy they keep to the names of real people. This is because possibility depends on conviction; if a thing has not happened we are not yet convinced that it is possible, but if it has happened it is clearly possible, for it would not have happened if it were impossible. Even tragedies, however, sometimes have all their persons fictitious except for one or two known names; and sometimes they have not a single known name, as in the *Anthos* of Agathon, in which both the events and the names are equally fictitious, without in the least reducing the delight it gives. It is not, therefore, requisite at all costs to keep to the traditional fables from which our tragedies draw their subject-matter. It would be absurd to insist on that, since even the known legends are known only to a few, and yet the delight is shared by everyone. . . .

[SIMPLE AND COMPLEX FABLES]

The action imitated must contain incidents that evoke fear and pity, besides being a complete action; but this effect is accentuated when these incidents occur logically as well as unexpectedly, which will be more sensational than if they happen arbitrarily, by chance. Even when events are accidental the sensation is greater if they appear to have a purpose, as when the statue of Mitys at Argos killed the man who had caused his death, by falling on him at a public entertainment. Such things appear not to have happened blindly. Inevitably, therefore, plots of this sort are finer.

Some fables are simple, others complex: for the obvious reason that the original actions imitated by the fables are the one or the other. By a simple action I mean one that leads to the catastrophe in the way we have laid down, directly and singly, without Irony of events or Disclosure.

An action is complex when the catastrophe involves Disclosure, or Irony, or both. But these complications should develop out of the very structure of the fable, so that they fit what has gone before, either necessarily or probably. To happen after something is by no means the same as to happen because of it.

[IRONY]

Irony is a reversal in the course of events, of the kind specified, and, as I say, in accordance with probability or necessity. Thus in the *Oedipus* the arrival of the messenger, which was expected to cheer Oedipus up by releasing him from his fear about his mother, did the opposite by showing him who he was; and in the *Lynceus* [Abas], who was awaiting sentence of death, was acquitted, whereas his prosecutor Dănaüs was killed, and all this arose out of what had happened previously.

A Disclosure, as the term indicates, is a change from ignorance to knowledge; if the people are marked out for good fortune it leads to affection, if for misfortune, to enmity. Disclosure produces its finest effect when it is connected with Irony, as the disclosure in the *Oedipus* is. There are indeed other sorts of Disclosure: the process I have described can even apply to inanimate objects of no significance, and mistakes about what a man has done or not done can be cleared up. But the sort I have specified is more a part of the fable and of the action than any other sort; for this coupling of Irony and Disclosure will carry with it pity or fear, which we have assumed to be the nature of the doings tragedy imitates; and further, such doings will constitute good or ill fortune. Assuming then that it is a disclosure of the identity of persons, it may be of one person only, to the other, when the former knows who the latter is; or sometimes both have to be disclosed—for instance, the sending of the letter led Orestes to the discovery of Iphigeneia, and there had to be another disclosure to make him known to her.

This then is the subject-matter of two elements in the Fable, Irony and Disclosure. A third element is the Crisis of feeling. Irony and Disclosure have been defined; the Crisis of feeling is a harmful or painful experience, such as deaths in public, violent pain, physical injuries, and everything of that sort.

[THE TRAGIC PATTERN]

Following the proper order, the next subject to discuss after this would be: What one should aim at and beware of in plotting fables; that is to say, What will produce the tragic effect. Since, then, tragedy, to be at its finest, requires a complex, not a simple, structure, and its structure should also imitate fearful and pitiful events (for that is the peculiarity of this sort of imitation), it is clear: first, that decent people must not be shown passing from good fortune to misfortune (for that is not fearful or pitiful but disgusting); again, vicious people must not be shown passing from misfortune to good fortune (for that is the most untragic situation possible—it has none of the requisites, it is neither humane, nor pitiful, nor fearful); nor again should an utterly evil man fall from good fortune into misfortune (for though a plot of that kind would be humane, it would not induce pity or fear—pity is induced by undeserved misfortune, and fear by the misfortunes of normal people, so that this situation will be neither pitiful nor fearful). So we are left with the man between these extremes: that is to say, the kind of man who neither is distinguished for excellence and virtue, nor comes to grief on account of baseness and vice, but on account of some error; a man of great reputation and prosperity, like Oedipus and Thyestes and conspicuous people of such families as theirs. So, to be well informed, a fable must be single rather than (as some say) double—there must be no change from misfortune to good fortune, but only the opposite, from good fortune to misfortune; the cause must not be vice, but a great error; and the man must be either of the type specified or better, rather than worse. This is borne out by the practice of poets; at first they picked a fable at random and made an inventory of its contents, but now the finest tragedies are plotted, and concern a few families—for example, the tragedies about Alcmeon, Oedipus, Orestes, Mĕlĕăger, Thyestes, Tēlĕphus, and any others whose lives were attended by terrible experiences or doings.

This is the plot that will produce the technically finest tragedy. Those critics are therefore wrong who censure Euripides on this very ground—because he does this in his tragedies, and many of them end in misfortune; for it is, as I have said, the right thing to do. This is clearly demonstrated on the stage in the competitions, where such plays, if they succeed, are the most tragic, and Euripides, even if he is inefficient in every other respect, still shows himself the most tragic of our poets. The next best plot, which is said by some people to be the best, is the tragedy with a double plot, like the *Odyssey*, ending in one way for the better people and in the opposite way for the worse. But it is the weakness of theatrical performances that gives priority to this kind; when poets write what the audience would like to happen, they are in leading strings. This is not the pleasure proper to tragedy, but rather to comedy, where the greatest enemies in the fable, say Orestes and Aegisthus, make friends and go off at the end, and nobody is killed by anybody.

[THE TRAGIC EMOTIONS]

The pity and fear can be brought about by the *Mise en scène*; but they can also come from the mere plotting of the incidents, which is preferable, and better poetry. For, without seeing anything, the fable ought to have been so plotted that if one heard the bare facts, the chain of circumstances would make one shudder and pity. That would happen to anyone who heard the fable of the *Oedipus*. To produce this effect by the *Mise en scène* is less artistic and puts one at the mercy of the technician; and those who use it not to frighten but merely to startle have lost touch with tragedy altogether. We should not try to get all sorts of pleasure from tragedy, but the particular tragic pleasure. And clearly, since this pleasure coming from pity and fear has to be produced by imitation, it is by his handling of the incidents that the poet must create it.

Let us, then, take next the kind of circumstances that seem terrible or lamentable. Now, doings of that kind must be between friends, or enemies, or neither. If any enemy injures an enemy, there is no pity either beforehand or at the time, except on account of the bare fact; nor is there if they are neutral; but when sufferings are engendered among the affections—for example, if murder is done or planned, or some similar outrage is committed, by brother on brother, or son on father, or mother on son, or son on mother—that is the thing to aim at.

Though it is not permissible to ruin the traditional fables—I mean, such as the killing of Clytemnestra by Orestes, or Erĭphÿle by Alcmeon—the poet should use his own invention to refine on what has been handed down to him. Let me explain more clearly what I mean by "refine." The action may take place, as the old poets used to make it, with the knowledge and understanding of the participants; this was how Euripides made Medea kill her children. Or they may do it, but in ignorance of the horror of the deed, and then afterwards discover the tie of affection, like the Oedipus of Sophocles; his act was outside the play, but there are examples where it is inside the tragedy itself—Alcmeon in the play by Astydămas, or Tēlĕgŏnus in *The Wounded Odysseus*. Besides these, there is a third possibility: when a man is about to do some fatal act in ignorance, but is enlightened before he does it. These are the only possible alternatives. One must either act or not act, and either know or not know. Of these alternatives, to know, and to be about to act, and then not to act, is thoroughly bad—it is disgusting without being tragic, for there is no emotional crisis; accordingly poets only rarely create such situations, as in the *Antigone*, when Haemon fails to kill Creon. Next in order is to act; and if the deed is done in ignorance and its nature is disclosed afterwards, so much the better—there is no bad taste in it, and the revelation is overpowering. But the last is best; I mean, like Mĕrŏpe in the *Cresphontes*, intending to kill her son, but recognizing him and not killing him; and the brother and sister in the *Iphigeneia*; and in the *Helle*, the son recognizing his mother just as he was going to betray her.—This is the reason for what was mentioned earlier: that the subject-matter of our tragedies is drawn from a few families. In their search for matter they discovered this recipe in the fables, not by cunning but by luck. So they are driven to have recourse to those families where such emotional crises have occurred. . . .

[CHARACTER]

And in the characterization, as in the plotting of the incidents, the aim should always be either necessity or probability: so that they say or do such things as it is necessary or probable that they would, being what they are; and that for this to follow that is either necessary or probable. . . . As for extravagant incidents, there should be none in the story, or if there are they should be kept outside the tragedy, as is the one in the *Oedipus* of Sophocles.

Since tragedy is an imitation of people above the normal, we must be like good portrait-painters, who follow the original model closely, but refine on it; in the same way the poet, in imitating people whose character is choleric or phlegmatic, and so forth, must keep them as they are and at the same time make them attractive. So Homer made Achilles noble, as well as a pattern of obstinacy. . . .

[CHORUS]

Treat the chorus as though it were one of the actors; it should be an organic part of the play and reinforce it, not as it is in Euripides, but as in Sophocles. In their successors the songs belong no more to the fable than to that of any other tragedy. This has led to the insertion of borrowed lyrics, an innovation for which Agathon was responsible.

THE PLAY IN PERFORMANCE

Because the story of Oedipus was ancient even in Sophocles's day, one cannot attribute all later versions of the story to the influence of Sophocles, but the version by the Roman dramatist Seneca (4 B.C.–A.D. 65) so closely resembles Sophocles's *Oedipus the King* that the influence is evident. Other famous versions of *Oedipus* are by the French writer Corneille (1659); the English writers John Dryden and Nathaniel Lee (1679; this version is noted for its combination of melodrama and low comedy); and Voltaire (1718; this version clearly puts the blame on cruel gods). In the twentieth century, Jean Cocteau's *The Infernal Machine* (1934)—the universe is conceived as a destructive and therefore infernal machine—is a four-act play about Oedipus, but only the fourth act is essentially Sophocles's play.

Sophocles's *Oedipus* has been esteemed for centuries, but Freud's comments on the Oedipus complex have given the play a special prominence in the twentieth century. *Oedipus* is often produced, not only in colleges and universities but occasionally in the professional theater. Among the most distinguished productions in the twentieth century were those by Laurence Oliver (1945) and by Tyrone Guthrie (1954). We reprint, immediately following, an essay in which Guthrie discusses some of the issues confronting a director, and an interview with Alan MacVey, who directed a more recent production.

Tyrone Guthrie
KING OEDIPUS IN CANADA

Tyrone Guthrie (1900–71), for whom the Guthrie Theatre in Minneapolis is named, achieved fame as a director in Britain, Canada, and the United States. In the following essay he discusses his 1954 production of *Oedipus the King*.

To maintain that this or that way of doing something is the Right Way is not a wise idea. Even so simple an action as hammering a nail may be done in many different ways, none of them perfectly right, but many of them defensibly reasonable, defensibly even the best possible way in given circumstances. So, in the very much more complex matter of presenting a Greek tragedy, no way can possibly be right; many ways can be reasonably defended.

Our Canadian *King Oedipus* was produced with a high degree of stylization. The great personages of the play—Oedipus, Jokasta and Creon—wore masks, one and a half times life size; and "cothurni" which made them taller than their own height by about the length of a hand. The masks designed by Tanya Moiseiwitsch, were boldly stylized and painted to represent metal—Oedipus in gold, a sun image; Jokasta, silver, like the moon; Creon, of darker baser metal than the others, in bronze. The mask of Tiresias, the Seer, resembled a great, sightless bird. The chorus masks and dresses suggested that they were very near to the earth; the head appeared to be carved out of wood, and their heavy robes were colored like lichen, brown and gray and saffron.

The verse—we used the free translation of the great Irish poet, W.B. Yeats—was declaimed in a bold, operatic fashion with few concessions to naturalism; the choruses were elaborate set-pieces of chanting and mime. Our attempt was to raise the performance to a level of religious ritual, both movement and speech being as "abstract" as we dared to make them. The reason for all this was to remove the characters and the story from the realm of the particular into something more nearly related to the universal. Oedipus, for instance, was not to be A King and A Man, but the embodiment of kingship and manhood. The great golden mask was not, of course, susceptible to fine shades of subtle expression; but it did make it possible for the actor to suggest superhuman majesty, and an extraordinarily powerful, if abstract, expression of suffering. Deliberately, we risked a production that was extreme, and might have seemed extremely pretentious. To some it may indeed have been so, but the general reaction of press and audience was markedly good.

This was four years ago. Looking back, I now wish that I had had the courage to be even more pretentious, more styl-

ized and more extreme. These dramas are, in my opinion, only reduced by concessions to the prevalent naturalistic mode in the theatre; the emotion of the audience is diminished from tragedy to pathos.

If it ever falls to my lot again to direct a Greek tragedy, I hope to be able to stage it in so bold a manner that the personages bear no more realistic resemblance to human individuals than do the people in Rouault's paintings or the sculpture of Henry Moore; and that their utterance has little in common with the bourgeois verisimilitude of the naturalistic theatre; but relates rather to the crash of waves, the sighing of the wind, or the roars of enraged or wounded beasts. The result may be absurd; but that risk must, in the theatre, always apply to any departure from current fashion.

Alan MacVey
DIRECTING OEDIPUS

Professor Alan MacVey, who teaches at the University of Iowa, in 1982 directed a production of *Oedipus* at Princeton. The play was performed by the Acting Ensemble; all principal roles were played by professional actors but the chorus consisted chiefly of students. The play was done in a small space, about sixty by forty feet, with the audience seated in two rows all around, to give the largest possible playing area. In a recent interview MacVey discussed the production.

Can you tell me something about the scenic design for your Oedipus?

I liked the scenic design of the production very much. We grappled with ways to suggest a marble landscape and the scene designer [Karen Schultz] arrived at a brilliant solution. She spread white butcher paper over the entire playing area. It was hard, cold, white, like marble, but wasn't trying to disguise itself as anything else. Each night we replaced the paper after it was scarred by blood and dirt. In the middle of the area we built an open pit out of real rocks and dirt. Above this dried, baked area hung a large bronze pan, suspended by chains from the high ceiling. It contained fire. The play began with an offering placed in it. Later Tiresius walked across the holy area, as if in defiance of its power. The remaining element of the set was composed of two white walls kitty-corner from each other. Both were as tall as we could make them in a relatively small space. They had doorways and most entrances were made from one or the other. They were functional, but weren't massive enough really to do the trick.

What about the costumes? Did you try to evoke the classical world?

After going round and round we decided to stay with a Greek design. The principal characters wore colored "togas" (for lack of a better word) that were simple and elegant and looked very beautiful. Strong, bold colors—purple, blue . . .

I can't remember what else. The chorus wore similar clothes, off-white in color, much rattier, torn with dried mud at the bottom. They wore a kind of headdress too.

At one point we debated putting the royalty in contemporary "power suits" and using a large, black round table—like a huge conference table—as the set. In hindsight I wish that we had gone this direction. Though the royal togas looked good, I wish we had been bolder. I think the suits would have looked great against the white and would have startled everyone. Given our realistic production the suits would have said power with a capital P. But we didn't do this, in part because we kept seeing togas in our minds' eyes. Since that time, in most of my Shakespeare productions, I've experimented with a kind of "modern-myth" approach to costuming that begins in the modern era and sprawls as is appropriate through other periods. I learned to do that by *not* doing it in *Oedipus*. Nonetheless, all in all the production was handsome and successful in visual terms.

Did you use masks? I suppose that everyone knows that the Greeks used masks—but modern actors aren't used to masks. What did you do?

We didn't use masks because we were exploring a more psychological approach. I think the intimate approach worked extremely well until Oedipus came out blind. Then it didn't work. Something about that scene cried out for a more distanced approach, and a mask would have been better. But we couldn't use a mask at that point in the evening. Instead we used a bloody blindfold, but it wasn't effective enough.

What about the chorus? One person or many? And did the chorus sing or speak to music?

The chorus was composed of about fifteen people, male and female, mostly students. Most of their words were sung. We hired a fine composer from Princeton to set the words to music and arrange accompaniment, et cetera. He did a fine job. The music was very powerful. It was more liturgical than I had in mind, and in some ways not as strange as it should have been. But it was complex and musically demanding, and gave a strong identity to the whole evening. Accompaniment, as I recall now, was limited. I think much of the music was sung without instrumental accompaniment—but there were surely drums on occasion.

Everyone says that Greek choruses danced, but no one knows much about ancient Greek dance. Did your chorus dance?

One of the most important things I've ever learned as a director came from dealing with the chorus and its movement. We hired a movement-choreographer to help with the chorus. She did a good job, adding movement to the singing. We tried to keep the movement fairly simple and there wasn't too much dance—mostly a kind of gesture that seemed appropriate.

Can you say a little more about the movement and its relation to the words?

At the first dress rehearsal I felt something was very wrong. It took me a while to realize what it was. It was the chorus, and specifically the movement. We were doing too much. It was a kind of meaningless layer. It made sense conceptually and looked as if it ought to be there—this was a Greek play, after all—but it was detracting from the impulse behind the words. As I thought further I realized that I hadn't really done the most important thing, which was to make sure that the chorus's words were coming from their mouths in the immediate present moment of the play for a reason that related to their experience of the events. Instead, I think we all took the chorus's words to be vaguely "choral"—that is, the words of the author, or some kind of comment on the action, or a musical interlude—something other than the direct human experience of those people in the play. After that rehearsal we simplified the movements to practically nothing. We focused the purpose of each ode directly on the immediate present, and sang directly, very intimately and personally, of fear, happiness, or whatever formed the heart of the ode. This improved the production enormously. I learned always to be sure that the words in a play come from the mouths of the characters, really from them, not from the playwright or from some "idea" of the way something was supposed to be.

It sounds as though you regard the production as quite successful.

I think the production worked very well until the closing scenes. From the blinding until the end of the play it didn't work. Perhaps the problem came from me and the actor playing Oedipus—perhaps we just weren't up to the demands of the play—but no matter what we tried, everything felt inadequate. We were stuck in a psychological approach to the material. We couldn't rise to the level of myth. The result was certainly interesting, and at times it was quite theatrical, but I felt the production failed the play at the end. Until then our approach was successful.

Did you make any cuts, or did you add anything?

We made few cuts and no additions. This was partly because we were using Bob Fagles' new translation, but also because I found the play swift and clear. The odes were not realistic, we discovered. But they too had immediacy and energy.

Did the actor playing Oedipus have to face any special difficulties?

One of the hardest things he faced was how "not to know" what the character found out until he found it out. The process of discovery is central to the play. John Doolittle (the actor) had to work hard to forget all the little details that Oedipus didn't know until he discovered them.

I imagine that the role of Tiresius is especially difficult. Did the actor seem satisfactory to you?

Yes. Paul Zimet played Tiresius brilliantly. He came up with the idea to have a woman's breasts but be dressed basically as a man. He used his amazing vocal range to move up and down the scales without ever making us feel it was technical. He barked and cried out and whispered. It was a brilliant performance because it was so bold and because it stemmed from a concept of Tiresius as man-woman.

If you were to do the play again, do you think you would pretty much repeat what you had done?

No. If I were to do the play again I'd probably try it in exactly the opposite way—nonrealistic, non-liturgical. I'm not certain any of these Greek plays can work fully for us. Who knows whether they even worked fully for the Greeks. Much of the language is mysterious for us, many of the references have little or no resonance. Even the great myths themselves, fleshed out in stories that are no longer immediate for us, are difficult to animate. The style is a mystery. Imagine doing *Oklahoma* two thousand years from now. Already that great musical is out of date, we have to find new ways to animate it. The Greeks are a giant problem. And yet I think the energy in the plays is very real and the possibility of power is there. I believe now that we need to seek the strangeness, the foreign-ness of the texts. Rather than bringing them as close to us as possible—as I tried with this production—we might look for their alien-ness. Perhaps in exploring this we'll find our way to the heart of these very strange plays.

Sophocles

ANTIGONE

Sophocles (c. 496–406 B.C.), the son of a wealthy Athenian, is one of the three Greek tragic writers whose work survives. (The other two are Aeschylus and Euripides.) Of Sophocles's more than one hundred twenty plays, we have seven. The exact dates of most of his plays are unknown. *Antigone* was written about 441 B.C.; *Oedipus the King*, which deals with earlier material concerning the house of Oedipus, was written later, probably about 430 B.C.

COMMENTARY

The German philosopher George Wilhelm Friedrich Hegel, in the early nineteenth century, offered a view that makes a good starting point for considering *Antigone*, although few have accepted it without qualification. For Hegel, the play is not a conflict of right against wrong; rather, it shows "a collision between the two highest moral powers," the rightful demands of the family versus those of the state. "The public law of the state and the instinctive family-love and duty towards a brother are here set in conflict." And elsewhere in Hegel: "Each of these two sides realizes only one of the moral powers . . . , and the meaning of eternal justice is shown in this, that both end in injustice because they are one-sided." Moreover, this conflict between ties of kinship and the claims of society reflects a conflict of divine law (the duty of the ruler to govern so as to preserve order, and of the citizen to obey). For Hegel, then, Sophocles's *Antigone* denies neither the claim of the family nor the claim of the state; what it denies is the absoluteness of either claim.

Few modern readers have agreed with Hegel that Creon and Antigone are equally right and equally wrong. Most readers find Antigone much more sympathetic than Creon. Suppose, then, we briefly make a case for Antigone. We can say, first of all, that she is right and Creon is wrong. (Even Creon's strongest defenders finally cannot say that Creon is right and Antigone is wrong.) She acts bravely, persisting in a course that she knows will bring her to suffering. And she does this not out of any hope of private gain. Moreover, she persists even though she sees that her course of action iso-

lates her from everyone else—from her sister Ismene, and from the chorus of men (Creon's counselors).

What can be said against Antigone? Some readers have found her to be a bit too eager for martyrdom, a bit too headstrong, a bit too aware of her superiority to Ismene. There is, perhaps, also some validity to Hegel's comment that "the gods she reveres are the Gods of the Underworld, the instinctive powers of feeling, love, and blood, not the daylight gods of a free, self-conscious life of nation and people."

And what of Creon? The play itself, of course, refutes his early view that he is right in denying burial to Polyneices. And he is in many ways, even from the start, unattractive. One can note, for instance, his touchy male chauvinism, in such a passage as this:

> Who is the man here,
> She or I, if this crime goes unpunished?

(page 88)

He soon comes to feel that the city is his personal property, so that his word is law—whether just or not. Can anything be said on his behalf? Perhaps at least this: First, he is new on the throne, and his inexperience apparently makes him suspicious, uneasy, and quick to act. Second, as ruler, he does indeed have the responsibility of maintaining order in a city that has recently undergone a civil war. Third, his refusal to allow Polyneices to be buried is not based on personal hatred of Polyneices; he believes (wrongly, it turns out, but perhaps understandably) that the gods cannot sympathize with a man who has come to burn their shrines. Fourth, perhaps it can be said in his behalf that the last third of the play arouses some sympathy (or at least pity) for him; although he repents, he is nevertheless terribly punished by the deaths of his son and his wife, and he must live with the knowledge that these deaths, as well as Antigone's, are his responsibility.

Much more, of course, can be said—must be said—about both Antigone and Creon; a reader of the play may well feel that not only can more be said but that less can be said, since several of the assertions just made about the two chief figures may strike some readers as scarcely relevant. For instance, one might say, "Yes, Creon is new on the throne, and, yes, he is ruling during a state of emergency, but that's of no importance since he is so clearly in the wrong." One might tentatively test this assertion by looking to see what the chorus has to say. To what degree does it support Creon, and to what degree does it support Antigone? But of course there is a problem here: the chorus is a character in the play, not simply Sophocles's spokesperson. Indeed, it is quite interesting to study this chorus of rather conventional male advisers to Creon. They give Antigone a little sympathy when she is led off to her death, but not until after they hear Teiresias (the seer) do they advise Creon to reverse his order. And, to take only one passage, we can notice that at the end of the first choral ode, celebrating civilization and the city, the chorus utters cautious words to the effect that the laws must be observed, and the "anarchic" person must be shunned. These words seem aimed at the rebel who has defied Creon, but at the end of the play the audience may well apply them not to Antigone but to Creon.

The more one reads the play and thinks about it, the more subtle it becomes. This is not to suggest that one cannot come out and say "Antigone is the tragic hero, and Creon is clearly wrong"; but it is to suggest that as soon as one has come out and said such a thing, one realizes that there is more to be said. For instance, to continue with the position just taken, one wants to see and to say exactly why and how Creon is "wrong," and even while listing his faults one finds that he holds one's attention. He acts—he believes—in the best interests of Thebes. And of course even those few who find Antigone a headstrong girl (readers familiar with *Oedipus the King* may think she has inherited her father's irritability), a bit too intent on martyrdom, must, on reading the play, admit that she compels our admiration. Scholarly books on ancient Greece rightly tell us that women played a severely limited role in Athenian society. Pericles, the Athenian statesman and general, probably summed up the average man's view when he said, "A woman's glory is not to show more weakness than is natural to her sex, and not to be talked about, for good or for evil, among men." The scholarly books on ancient Athens are probably right, in the main. Luckily, Sophocles didn't read them.

In 1849 Matthew Arnold published a splendid poem in which he said that Sophocles "saw life steadily, and saw it whole." But Arnold, no indiscriminate admirer of Sopho-

cles's work, a few years later granted that the interests of the ancient writers were sometimes so remote from ours that "we can no longer sympathize. An action like the action of the *Antigone* of Sophocles, which turns upon the conflict between the heroine's duty to her brother's corpse and that to the laws of her country, is no longer one in which it is possible that we should feel a deep interest."

One might indeed think that a play that makes a fuss about ancient Greek burial rites could be of only remote interest to later readers, and yet Sophocles's *Antigone* has seemed highly relevant to later ages. Modern writers have sometimes shown this interest by rewriting the play, finding in the old story a new meaning. For instance, during World War II, when France was occupied by the Nazis, Jean Anouilh produced his own version of *Antigone* in which it was evident that Antigone stood for the French resistance and that Creon, efficient and ruthless, stood for the Nazis. But Sophocles's play itself—not merely the gist of his plot as reinterpreted by later playwrights—continues to hold our interest, too.

Behind the story of Antigone is the story of her father, Oedipus (as told in Sophocles's *Oedipus the King;* see pp. 52–72), who unknowingly killed his own father and slept with his own mother. The curse on the house of Oedipus outlived him and descended to his children: His sons Polyneices and Eteocles quarreled and killed each other, and his daughter Antigone was put to death when she sought to confer on Polyneices the burial rites she felt were his due.

More precisely, after the fall of Oedipus his two sons inherited the rule of Thebes. They were to rule jointly, but they quarreled and Eteocles banished his brother Polyneices. Polyneices returned to Thebes, armed with allies, and in the ensuing conflict both brothers were killed. Creon, their maternal uncle (and Antigone's), thereupon set about ruling the city. One of his first acts was to order that Eteocles be given a state funeral but that Polyneices, who had come in arms against his own city and had thereby (in Creon's opinion) assaulted the gods of the city, be denied burial. For the Greeks, the denial of funeral rites—a fate reserved for the worst criminals—meant that the soul of the corpse could not enter the next world and be honored. Antigone defied her uncle's edict, gave the corpse a symbolic burial, was caught, and was sent to death. Creon ultimately relented, but his change of mind came too late: Antigone was dead, and so were Creon's wife and son.

Matthew Arnold notwithstanding, even a single reading of the play will let a reader see that it is not simply about ancient rites. Nor is it about the workings of fate, for although the household curse is several times mentioned in the play, the tragic outcome does not seem to be arbitrarily imposed on the characters. But what, then, is the play about?

Sophocles

ANTIGONE

An English Version by Dudley Fitts and Robert Fitzgerald

List of Characters

ANTIGONÊ
ISMENÊ
EURYDICÊ
CREON
HAIMON
TEIRESIAS
A SENTRY
A MESSENGER
CHORUS

SCENE: *Before the palace of Creon, King of Thebes. A central double door, and two lateral doors. A platform extends the length of the façade, and from this platform three steps lead down into the "orchestra," or chorus-ground.*

TIME: *Dawn of the day after the repulse of the Argive army from the assault on Thebes.*

PROLOGUE

Antigonê and Ismenê enter from the central door of the palace.

ANTIGONÊ.
Ismenê, dear sister,
You would think that we had already suffered enough
For the curse on Oedipus.°
I cannot imagine any grief
That you and I have not gone through. And now—   5
Have they told you of the new decree of our King
   Creon?
ISMENÊ.
I have heard nothing: I know
That two sisters lost two brothers, a double death
In a single hour; and I know that the Argive army

3 **Oedipus,** once King of Thebes, was the father of Antigonê and Ismenê, and of their brothers Polyneicês and Eteoclês. Oedipus unwittingly killed his father, Laïos, and married his own mother Iocastê. When he learned what he had done, he blinded himself and left Thebes. Eteoclês and Polyneicês quarreled; Polyneicês was driven out but returned to assault Thebes. In the battle each brother killed the other; Creon became king and ordered that Polyneicês be left to rot unburied on the battlefield as a traitor.

Fled in the night; but beyond this, nothing.   10
ANTIGONÊ.
I thought so. And this is why I wanted you
To come out here with me. There is something we must
   do.
ISMENÊ.
Why do you speak so strangely?
ANTIGONÊ.
Listen, Ismenê:
Creon buried our brother Eteoclês   15
With military honors, gave him a soldier's funeral,
And it was right that he should; but Polyneicês,
Who fought as bravely and died as miserably,—
They say that Creon has sworn
No one shall bury him, no one mourn for him,   20
But his body must lie in the fields, a sweet treasure
For carrion birds to find as they search for food.
That is what they say, and our good Creon is coming here
To announce it publicly; and the penalty—
Stoning to death in the public square!   25
                There it is,
And now you can prove what you are:
A true sister, or a traitor to your family.
ISMENÊ.
Antigonê, you are mad! What could I possibly do?
ANTIGONÊ.
You must decide whether you will help me or not.
ISMENÊ.
I do not understand you. Help you in what?   30
ANTIGONÊ.
Ismenê. I am going to bury him. Will you come?
ISMENÊ.
Bury him! You have just said the new law forbids it.
ANTIGONÊ.
He is my brother. And he is your brother, too.
ISMENÊ.
But think of the danger! Think what Creon will do!
ANTIGONÊ.
Creon is not strong enough to stand in my way.   35
ISMENÊ.
Ah sister!
Oedipus died, everyone hating him
For what his own search brought to light, his eyes
Ripped out by his own hand; and Iocastê died,
His mother and wife at once: she twisted the cords   40

That strangled her life; and our two brothers died,
Each killed by the other's sword. And we are left:
But oh, Antigonê,
Think how much more terrible than these
45 Our own death would be if we should go against Creon
And do what he has forbidden! We are only women,
We cannot fight with men, Antigonê!
The law is strong, we must give in to the law
In this thing, and in worse. I beg the Dead
50 To forgive me, but I am helpless: I must yield
To those in authority. And I think it is dangerous
        business
To be always meddling.

ANTIGONÊ.   If that is what you think,
I should not want you, even if you asked to come.
You have made your choice, you can be what you want
        to be.
55 But I will bury him; and if I must die,
I say that this crime is holy: I shall lie down
With him in death, and I shall be as dear
To him as he to me.
                    It is the dead,
Not the living, who make the longest demands:
We die for ever. . . .
60   You may do as you like.
Since apparently the laws of the gods mean nothing to
        you.

ISMENÊ.
They mean a great deal to me; but I have no strength
To break laws that were made for the public good.

ANTIGONÊ.
That must be your excuse, I suppose. But as for me,
I will bury the brother I love.

65 ISMENÊ.   Antigonê,
I am so afraid for you!

ANTIGONÊ.   You need not be:
You have yourself to consider, after all.

ISMENÊ.
But no one must hear of this, you must tell no one!
I will keep it a secret, I promise!

ANTIGONÊ.   O tell it! Tell everyone!
70 Think how they'll hate you when it all comes out
If they learn that you knew about it all the time!

ISMENÊ.
So fiery! You should be cold with fear.

ANTIGONÊ.
Perhaps. But I am doing only what I must.

ISMENÊ.
But can you do it? I say that you cannot.

ANTIGONÊ.
Very well: when my strength gives out,
75 I shall do no more.

ISMENÊ.
Impossible things should not be tried at all.

ANTIGONÊ.
Go away, Ismenê:
I shall be hating you soon, and the dead will too,
For your words are hateful. Leave me my foolish plan:
I am not afraid of the danger; if it means death,   80
It will not be the worst of deaths—death without honor.

ISMENÊ.
Go then, if you feel that you must.
You are unwise,
But a loyal friend indeed to those who love you.

*Exit into the palace. Antigonê goes off, left. Enter the
Chorus.*

PÁRODOS

CHORUS.
Now the long blade of the sun, lying   *Strophe 1*
Level east to west, touches with glory
Thebes of the Seven Gates. Open, unlidded
Eye of golden day! O marching light
Across the eddy and rush of Dircê's stream,°   5
Striking the white shields of the enemy
Thrown headlong backward from the blaze of morning!

CHORAGOS.°
Polyneicês their commander
Roused them with windy phrases,
He the wild eagle screaming   10
Insults above our land,
His wings their shields of snow,
His crest their marshalled helms.

CHORUS.
Against our seven gates in a yawning ring   *Antistrophe 1*
The famished spears came onward in the night: 15
But before his jaws were sated with our blood,
Or pinefire took the garland of our towers,
He was thrown back; and as he turned, great Thebes—
No tender victim for his noisy power—
Rose like a dragon behind him, shouting war.   20

CHORAGOS.
For God hates utterly
The bray of bragging tongues;
And when he beheld their smiling,
Their swagger of golden helms,
The frown of his thunder blasted   25
Their first man from our walls.

CHORUS.
We heard his shout of triumph high in the air   *Strophe 2*
Turn to a scream; far out in a flaming arc

5 Dircê's stream a stream west of Thebes   **8 Choragos** leader of
the Chorus

He fell with his windy torch, and the earth struck him.
30   And others storming in fury no less than his
Found shock of death in the dusty joy of battle.

CHORAGOS.
Seven captains at seven gates
Yielded their clanging arms to the god
That bends the battle-line and breaks it.
35   These two only, brothers in blood,
Face to face in matchless rage.
Mirroring each the other's death,
Clashed in long combat.

CHORUS.
But now in the beautiful morning   *Antistrophe 2*
  of victory
40   Let Thebes of the many chariots sing for joy!
With hearts for dancing we'll take leave of war:
Our temples shall be sweet with hymns of praise,
And the long nights shall echo with our chorus.

SCENE I

CHORAGOS.
But now at last our new King is coming:
Creon of Thebes, Menoikeus' son.
In this auspicious dawn of his reign
What are the new complexities
5   That shifting Fate has woven for him?
What is his counsel? Why has he summoned
The old men to hear him?

*Enter Creon from the palace, center. He addresses the
Chorus from the top step.*

CREON. Gentlemen: I have the honor to inform you that our
Ship of State, which recent storms have threatened to
10   destroy, has come safely to harbor at last, guided by the
merciful wisdom of Heaven. I have summoned you here
this morning because I know that I can depend upon you:
your devotion to King Laïos was absolute; you never hesitated in your duty to our late ruler Oedipus; and when
15   Oedipus died, your loyalty was transferred to his children.
Unfortunately, as you know, his two sons, the princes
Eteoclês and Polyneicês, have killed each other in battle;
and I, as the next in blood, have succeeded to the full
power of the throne.
20   I am aware, of course, that no Ruler can expect complete loyalty from his subjects until he has been tested in
office. Nevertheless, I say to you at the very outset that I
have nothing but contempt for the kind of Governor
who is afraid, for whatever reason, to follow the course
25   that he knows is best for the State; and as for the man
who sets private friendship above the public welfare,—I
have no use for him, either. I call God to witness that if I
saw my country headed for ruin, I should not be afraid to
speak out plainly; and I need hardly remind you that I
30   would never have any dealings with an enemy of the peo-

ple. No one values friendship more highly than I: but we
must remember that friends made at the risk of wrecking
our Ship are not real friends at all.
   These are my principles, at any rate, and that is why I
have made the following decision concerning the sons of   35
Oedipus: Eteoclês, who died as a man should die, fighting
for his country, is to be buried with full military honors,
with all the ceremony that is usual when the greatest
heroes die; but his brother Polyneicês, who broke his
exile to come back with fire and sword against his native   40
city and the shrines of his fathers' gods, whose one idea
was to spill the blood of his blood and sell his own people
into slavery—Polyneicês, I say, is to have no burial: no
man is to touch him or say the least prayer for him; he
shall lie on the plain, unburied; and the birds and the   45
scavenging dogs can do with him whatever they like.
   This is my command, and you can see the wisdom
behind it. As long as I am King, no traitor is going to be
honored with the loyal man. But whoever shows by word
and deed that he is on the side of the State—he shall   50
have my respect while he is living and my reverence
when he is dead.

CHORAGOS.
If that is your will, Creon son of Menoikeus,
You have the right to enforce it: we are yours.

CREON.
That is my will. Take care that you do your part.   55

CHORAGOS.
We are old men: let the younger ones carry it out.

CREON.
I do not mean that: the sentries have been appointed.

CHORAGOS.
Then what is it that you would have us do?

CREON.
You will give no support to whoever breaks this law.

CHORAGOS.
Only a crazy man is in love with death!   60

CREON.
And death it is; yet money talks, and the wisest
Have sometimes been known to count a few coins too
  many.

Enter Sentry from left.

SENTRY. I'll not say that I'm out of breath from running,
King, because every time I stopped to think about what I
have to tell you, I felt like going back. And all the time a   65
voice kept saying, "You fool, don't you know you're walking straight into trouble?"; and then another voice: "Yes,
but if you let somebody else get the news to Creon first, it
will be even worse than that for you!" But good sense
won out, at least I hope it was good sense, and here I am   70
with a story that makes no sense at all; but I'll tell it anyhow, because, as they say, what's going to happen's going
to happen and—

CREON. Come to the point. What have you to say?

75 SENTRY. I did not do it. I did not see who did it. You must
        not punish me for what someone else has done.
    CREON.
        A comprehensive defense! More effective, perhaps, if I
            knew its purpose. Come: what is it?
    SENTRY.
        A dreadful thing . . . I don't know how to put it—
    CREON.
        Out with it!
80 SENTRY.   Well, then;
        The dead man—
                    Polyneicês—

    *Pause. The sentry is overcome, fumbles for words. Creon
    waits impassively.*

                            out there—
                                    someone,—
        New dust on the slimy flesh!

    Pause. No sign from Creon.

        Someone has given it burial that way, and
        Gone . . . .

    Long pause. Creon finally speaks with deadly control.

    CREON.
        And the man who dared do this?
85 SENTRY.   I swear I
        Do not know! You must believe me!
                            Listen:
        The ground was dry, not a sign of digging, no,
        Not a wheeltrack in the dust, no trace of anyone.
        It was when they relieved us this morning: and one of
            them,
        The corporal, pointed to it.
90   There it was,
        The strangest—
                Look:
        The body, just mounded over with light dust: you see?
        Not buried really, but as if they'd covered it
        Just enough for the ghost's peace. And no sign
95   Of dogs or any wild animal that had been there.

        And then what a scene there was! Every man of us
        Accusing the other: we all proved the other man did it,
        We all had proof that we could not have done it.
        We were ready to take hot iron in our hands,
100   Walk through fire, swear by all the gods,
        It was not I!
        I do not know who it was, but it was not I!

    *Creon's rage has been mounting steadily, but the Sentry is
    too intent upon his story to notice it.*

        And then, when this came to nothing, someone said
        A thing that silenced us and made us stare
105   Down at the ground: you had to be told the news,
        And one of us had to do it! We threw the dice,

        And the bad luck fell to me. So here I am,
        No happier to be here than you are to have me:
        Nobody likes the man who brings bad news.
    CHORAGOS.
        I have been wondering, King: can it be that the gods   110
            have done this?
    CREON (*furiously*).
        Stop!
        Must you doddering wrecks
        Go out of your heads entirely? "The gods"!
        Intolerable!   115
        The gods favor this corpse? Why? How had he served
            them?
        Tried to loot their temples, burn their images,
        Yes, and the whole State, and its laws with it!
        Is it your senile opinion that the gods love to honor bad
            men?
        A pious thought!—
                        No, from the very beginning   120
        There have been those who have whispered together,
        Stiff-necked anarchists, putting their heads together,
        Scheming against me in alleys. These are the men,
        And they have bribed my own guard to do this thing.
        (*Sententiously.*) Money!   125
        There's nothing in the world so demoralizing as money.
        Down go your cities,
        Homes gone, men gone, honest hearts corrupted.
        Crookedness of all kinds, and all for money!
        (*To Sentry.*)   But you—!
        I swear by God and by the throne of God,   130
        The man who has done this thing shall pay for it!
        Find that man, bring him here to me, or your death
        Will be the least of your problems: I'll string you up
        Alive, and there will be certain ways to make you
        Discover your employer before you die;   135
        And the process may teach you a lesson you seem to
            have missed:
        The dearest profit is sometimes all too dear:
        That depends on the source. Do you understand me?
        A fortune won is often misfortune.
    SENTRY.
        King, may I speak?
    CREON.   Your very voice distresses me.   140
    SENTRY.
        Are you sure that it is my voice, and not your conscience?
    CREON.
        By God, he wants to analyze me now!
    SENTRY.
        It is not what I say, but what has been done, that hurts
            you.
    CREON.
        You talk too much.
    SENTRY.   Maybe; but I've done nothing.
    CREON.
        Sold your soul for some silver: that's all you've done.   145

SENTRY.

How dreadful it is when the right judge judges wrong!

CREON.

Your figures of speech
May entertain you now; but unless you bring me the man,
You will get little profit from them in the end.

Exit Creon into the palace.

SENTRY.

150 "Bring me the man"—!
I'd like nothing better than bringing him the man!
But bring him or not, you have seen the last of me here.
At any rate, I am safe!

(*Exit Sentry.*)

ODE I

CHORUS.

Numberless are the world's wonders, but not   *Strophe 1*
More wonderful than man; the stormgray sea
Yields to his prows, the huge crests bear him high;
Earth, holy and inexhaustible, is graven
5 With shining furrows where his plows have gone
Year after year, the timeless labor of stallions.

The lightboned birds and beasts that   *Antistrophe 1*
   cling to cover,
The lithe fish lighting their reaches of dim water,
All are taken, tamed in the net of his mind;
10 The lion on the hill, the wild horse windy-maned,
Resign to him; and his blunt yoke has broken
The sultry shoulders of the mountain bull.

Words also, and thought as rapid as air,   *Strophe 2*
He fashions to his good use; statecraft is his,
15 And his the skill that deflects the arrows of snow,
The spears of winter rain: from every wind
He has made himself secure—from all but one:
In the late wind of death he cannot stand.

O clear intelligence, force beyond   *Antistrophe 2*
   all measure!
20 O fate of man, working both good and evil!
When the laws are kept, how proudly his city stands!
When the laws are broken, what of his city then?
Never may the anarchic man find rest at my hearth,
Never be it said that my thoughts are his thoughts.

SCENE II

Reenter Sentry leading Antigonê.

CHORAGOS.

What does this mean? Surely this captive woman
Is the Princess, Antigonê. Why should she be taken?

SENTRY.

Here is the one who did it! We caught her
In the very act of burying him.—Where is Creon?

CHORAGOS.

Just coming from the house.

Enter Creon, center.

CREON.   What has happened?   5
Why have you come back so soon?

SENTRY (*expansively*).   O King,
A man should never be too sure of anything:
I would have sworn
That you'd not see me here again: your anger
Frightened me so, and the things you threatened me   10
   with;
But how could I tell then
That I'd be able to solve the case so soon?
No dice-throwing this time: I was only too glad to come!
Here is this woman. She is the guilty one:
We found her trying to bury him.   15
Take her, then; question her; judge her as you will.
I am through with the whole thing now, and glad of it.

CREON.

But this is Antigonê! Why have you brought her here?

SENTRY.

She was burying him, I tell you!

CREON (*severely*).   Is this the truth?

SENTRY.

I saw her with my own eyes. Can I say more?   20

CREON.

The details: come, tell me quickly!

SENTRY.   It was like this:
After those terrible threats of yours, King,
We went back and brushed the dust away from the body.
The flesh was soft by now, and stinking,
So we sat on a hill to windward and kept guard.   25
No napping this time! We kept each other awake.
But nothing happened until the white round sun
Whirled in the center of the round sky over us:
Then, suddenly,
A storm of dust roared up from the earth, and the sky   30
Went out, the plain vanished with all its trees
In the stinging dark. We closed our eyes and endured it.
The whirlwind lasted a long time, but it passed;
And then we looked, and there was Antigonê!
I have seen   35
A mother bird come back to a stripped nest, heard
Her crying bitterly a broken note or two
For the young ones stolen. Just so, when this girl
Found the bare corpse, and all her love's work wasted,
She wept, and cried on heaven to damn the hands   40
That had done this thing.
             And then she brought more dust
And sprinkled wine three times for her brother's ghost.

We ran and took her at once. She was not afraid,
Not even when we charged her with what she had done.
She denied nothing.

And this was a comfort to me,
And some uneasiness: for it is a good thing
To escape from death, but it is no great pleasure
To bring death to a friend.
                              Yet I always say
There is nothing so comfortable as your own safe skin!

CREON (*slowly, dangerously*).
And you, Antigonê,
You with your head hanging,—do you confess this thing?

ANTIGONÊ.
I do. I deny nothing.

CREON (*to Sentry*).
                      You may go.
                                            (*Exit Sentry.*)
(*To Antigonê.*) Tell me, tell me briefly:
Had you heard my proclamation touching this matter?

ANTIGONÊ.
It was public. Could I help hearing it?

CREON.
And yet you dared defy the law.

ANTIGONÊ.   I dared.
It was not God's proclamation. That final Justice
That rules the world below makes no such laws.

Your edict, King, was strong.
But all your strength is weakness itself against
The immortal unrecorded laws of God.
They are not merely now: they were, and shall be,
Operative for ever, beyond man utterly.
I knew I must die, even without your decree:
I am only mortal. And if I must die
Now, before it is my time to die,
Surely this is no hardship: can anyone
Living, as I live, with evil all about me,
Think Death less than a friend? This death of mine
Is of no importance; but if I had left my brother
Lying in death unburied, I should have suffered.
Now I do not.
              You smile at me. Ah Creon,
Think me a fool, if you like; but it may well be
That a fool convicts me of folly.

CHORAGOS.
Like father, like daughter: both headstrong, deaf to reason!
She has never learned to yield.

CREON.   She has much to learn.
The inflexible heart breaks first, the toughest iron
Cracks first, and the wildest horses bend their necks
At the pull of the smallest curb.
                                  Pride? In a slave?
This girl is guilty of a double insolence,
Breaking the given laws and boasting of it.
Who is the man here,
She or I, if this crime goes unpunished?
Sister's child, or more than sister's child,
Or closer yet in blood—she and her sister

Win bitter death for this!
(*To servants.*)   Go, some of you,
Arrest Ismenê. I accuse her equally.
Bring her: you will find her sniffling in the house there.

Her mind's a traitor: crimes kept in the dark
Cry for light, and the guardian brain shudders;
But how much worse than this
Is brazen boasting of barefaced anarchy!

ANTIGONÊ.
Creon, what more do you want than my death?

CREON.   Nothing.
That gives me everything.

ANTIGONÊ.   Then I beg you: kill me.
This talking is a great weariness: your words
Are distasteful to me, and I am sure that mine
Seem so to you. And yet they should not seem so:
I should have praise and honor for what I have done.
All these men here would praise me
Were their lips not frozen shut with fear of you.
(*Bitterly.*) Ah the good fortune of kings,
Licensed to say and do whatever they please!

CREON.
You are alone here in that opinion.

ANTIGONÊ.
No, they are with me. But they keep their tongues in
    leash.

CREON.
Maybe. But you are guilty, and they are not.

ANTIGONÊ.
There is no guilt in reverence for the dead.

CREON.
But Eteoclês—was he not your brother too?

ANTIGONÊ.
My brother too.

CREON.   And you insult his memory?

ANTIGONÊ (*softly*).
The dead man would not say that I insult it.

CREON.
He would: for you honor a traitor as much as him.

ANTIGONÊ.
His own brother, traitor or not, and equal in blood.

CREON.
He made war on his country. Eteoclês defended it.

ANTIGONÊ.
Nevertheless, there are honors due all the dead.

CREON.
But not the same for the wicked as for the just.

ANTIGONÊ.
Ah Creon, Creon,
Which of us can say what the gods hold wicked?

CREON.
An enemy is an enemy, even dead.

ANTIGONÊ.
It is my nature to join in love, not hate.

CREON (*finally losing patience*).

    Go join them then; if you must have your love,
120   Find it in hell!

CHORAGOS.

    But see, Ismenê comes:

    Enter Ismenê, guarded.

    Those tears are sisterly, the cloud
    That shadows her eyes rains down gentle sorrow.

CREON.

    You too, Ismenê,
125   Snake in my ordered house, sucking my blood
    Stealthily—and all the time I never knew
    That these two sisters were aiming at my throne!

                                 Ismenê,
    Do you confess your share in this crime, or deny it?
    Answer me.

ISMENÊ.
130   Yes, if she will let me say so. I am guilty.

ANTIGONÊ (*coldly*).

    No, Ismenê. You have no right to say so.
    You would not help me, and I will not have you help me.

ISMENÊ.

    But now I know what you meant; and I am here
    To join you, to take my share of punishment.

ANTIGONÊ.
135   The dead man and the gods who rule the dead
    Know whose act this was. Words are not friends.

ISMENÊ.

    Do you refuse me, Antigonê? I want to die with you:
    I too have a duty that I must discharge to the dead.

ANTIGONÊ.

    You shall not lessen my death by sharing it.

ISMENÊ.
140   What do I care for life when you are dead?

ANTIGONÊ.

    Ask Creon. You're always hanging on his opinions.

ISMENÊ.

    You are laughing at me. Why, Antigonê?

ANTIGONÊ.

    It's a joyless laughter, Ismenê.

ISMENÊ.   But can I do nothing?

ANTIGONÊ.

    Yes. Save yourself. I shall not envy you.
145   There are those who will praise you; I shall have honor,
        too.

ISMENÊ.

    But we are equally guilty!

ANTIGONÊ.   No more, Ismenê.
    You are alive, but I belong to Death.

CREON (*to the chorus*).

    Gentlemen, I beg you to observe these girls:
    One has just now lost her mind; the other,
150   It seems, has never had a mind at all.

ISMENÊ.

    Grief teaches the steadiest minds to waver, King.

CREON.

    Yours certainly did, when you assumed guilt with the
        guilty!

ISMENÊ.

    But how could I go on living without her?

CREON.   You are.
    She is already dead.

ISMENÊ.   But your own son's bride!

CREON.

    There are places enough for him to push his plow.   155
    I want no wicked women for my sons!

ISMENÊ.

    O dearest Haimon, how your father wrongs you!

CREON.

    I've had enough of your childish talk of marriage!

CHORAGOS.

    Do you really intend to steal this girl from your son?

CREON.

    No; Death will do that for me.

CHORAGOS.   Then she must die?   160

CREON (*ironically*).

    You dazzle me.

             —But enough of this talk!
    (*To guards.*) You, there, take them away and guard them
        well:
    For they are but women, and even brave men run
    When they see Death coming.

                (*Exeunt Ismenê, Antigonê, and guards.*)

ODE II

CHORUS.

    Fortunate is the man who has never tasted   *Strophe 1*
        God's vengeance!
    Where once the anger of heaven has struck, that house
        is shaken
    For ever: damnation rises behind each child
    Like a wave cresting out of the black northeast,
    When the long darkness under sea roars up   5
    And bursts drumming death upon the windwhipped
        sand.

    I have seen this gathering sorrow from   *Antistrophe 1*
        time long past
    Loom upon Oedipus' children: generation from generation
    Takes the compulsive rage of the enemy god.
    So lately this last flower of Oedipus' line   10
    Drank the sunlight! but now a passionate word
    And a handful of dust have closed up all its beauty.

    What mortal arrogance   *Strophe 2*
    Transcends the wrath of Zeus?
    Sleep cannot lull him nor the effortless long months   15
    Of the timeless gods: but he is young for ever,

And his house is the shining day of high Olympos.
All that is and shall be,
And all the past, is his.
20 No pride on earth is free of the curse of heaven.

The straying dreams of men   *Antistrophe 2*
May bring them ghosts of joy:
But as they drowse, the waking embers burn them;
Or they walk with fixed eyes, as blind men walk.
25 But the ancient wisdom speaks for our own time:
    Fate works most for woe
    With Folly's fairest show.
Man's little pleasure is the spring of sorrow.

SCENE III

CHORAGOS.
But here is Haimon, King, the last of all your sons.
Is it grief for Antigonê that brings him here,
And bitterness at being robbed of his bride?
    Enter Haimon.

CREON.
We shall soon see, and no need of diviners.
                                        —Son,
5   You have heard my final judgment on that girl:
Have you come here hating me, or have you come
With deference and with love, whatever I do?

HAIMON.
I am your son, father. You are my guide.
You make things clear for me, and I obey you.
No marriage means more to me than your continuing
10   wisdom.

CREON.
Good. That is the way to behave: subordinate
Everything else, my son, to your father's will.
This is what a man prays for, that he may get
Sons attentive and dutiful in his house,
15 Each one hating his father's enemies,
Honoring his father's friends. But if his sons
Fail him, if they turn out unprofitably,
What has he fathered but trouble for himself
And amusement for the malicious?
                            So you are right
20 Not to lose your head over this woman.
Your pleasure with her would soon grow cold, Haimon,
And then you'd have a hellcat in bed and elsewhere.
Let her find her husband in Hell!
Of all the people in this city, only she
25 Has had contempt for my law and broken it.

Do you want me to show myself weak before the people?
Or to break my sworn word? No, and I will not.
The woman dies.
I suppose she'll plead "family ties." Well, let her.
30 If I permit my own family to rebel,
How shall I earn the world's obedience?

Show me the man who keeps his house in hand,
He's fit for public authority.
                            I'll have no dealings
With lawbreakers, critics of the government:
Whoever is chosen to govern should be obeyed—   35
Must be obeyed, in all things, great and small,
Just and unjust! O Haimon,
The man who knows how to obey, and that man only,
Knows how to give commands when the time comes.
You can depend on him, no matter how fast   40
The spears come: he's a good soldier, he'll stick it out.

Anarchy, anarchy! Show me a greater evil!
This is why cities tumble and the great houses rain down,
This is what scatters armies!
No, no: good lives are made so by discipline.   45
We keep the laws then, and the lawmakers,
And no woman shall seduce us. If we must lose,
Let's lose to a man, at least! Is a woman stronger than we?

CHORAGOS.
Unless time has rusted my wits,
What you say, King, is said with point and dignity. 50

HAIMON (*boyishly earnest*).
Father:
Reason is God's crowning gift to man, and you are right
To warn me against losing mine. I cannot say—
I hope that I shall never want to say!—that you
Have reasoned badly. Yet there are other men   55
Who can reason, too; and their opinions might be helpful.
You are not in a position to know everything
That people say or do, or what they feel:
Your temper terrifies—everyone
Will tell you only what you like to hear.   60
But I, at any rate, can listen; and I have heard them
Muttering and whispering in the dark about this girl.
They say no woman has ever, so unreasonably,
Died so shameful a death for a generous act:
"She covered her brother's body. Is this indecent?   65
She kept him from dogs and vultures. Is this a crime?
Death?—She should have all the honor that we can give
    her!"
This is the way they talk out there in the city.

You must believe me:
Nothing is closer to me than your happiness.   70
What could be closer? Must not any son
Value his father's fortune as his father does his?
I beg you, do not be unchangeable:
Do not believe that you alone can be right.
The man who thinks that,   75
The man who maintains that only he has the power
To reason correctly, the gift to speak, the soul—
A man like that, when you know him, turns out empty.

It is not reason never to yield to reason!

In flood time you can see how some trees bend,   80
And because they bend, even their twigs are safe,

89

While stubborn trees are torn up, roots and all.
And the same thing happens in sailing:
Make your sheet fast, never slacken,—and over you go,
85 Head over heels and under: and there's your voyage.
Forget you are angry! Let yourself be moved!
I know I am young; but please let me say this:
The ideal condition
Would be, I admit, that men should be right by instinct;
90 But since we are all too likely to go astray,
The reasonable thing is to learn from those who can
teach.

CHORAGOS.
You will do well to listen to him, King,
If what he says is sensible. And you, Haimon,
Must listen to your father.—Both speak well.

CREON.
95 You consider it right for a man of my years and experience
To go to school to a boy?

HAIMON.   It is not right
If I am wrong. But if I am young, and right,
What does my age matter?

CREON.
You think it right to stand up for an anarchist?

HAIMON.
100 Not at all. I pay no respect to criminals.

CREON.
Then she is not a criminal?

HAIMON.
The City would deny it, to a man.

CREON.
And the City proposes to teach me how to rule?

HAIMON.
Ah. Who is it that's talking like a boy now?

CREON.
105 My voice is the one voice giving orders in this City!

HAIMON.
It is no City if it takes orders from one voice.

CREON.
The State is the King!

HAIMON.   Yes, if the State is a desert.
Pause.

CREON.
This boy, it seems, has sold out to a woman.

HAIMON.
If you are a woman: my concern is only for you.

CREON.
110 So? Your "concern"! In a public brawl with your father!

HAIMON.
How about you, in a public brawl with justice?

CREON.
With justice, when all that I do is within my rights?

HAIMON.
You have no right to trample on God's right.

CREON (*completely out of control*).
Fool, adolescent fool! Taken in by a woman!

HAIMON.
115 You'll never see me taken in by anything vile.

CREON.
Every word you say is for her!

HAIMON (*quietly, darkly*).   And for you.
And for me. And for the gods under the earth.

CREON.
You'll never marry her while she lives.

HAIMON.
Then she must die.—But her death will cause another.

CREON.
120 Another?
Have you lost your senses? Is this an open threat?

HAIMON.
There is no threat in speaking to emptiness.

CREON.
I swear you'll regret this superior tone of yours!
You are the empty one!

HAIMON.   If you were not my father,
125 I'd say you were perverse.

CREON.
You girlstruck fool, don't play at words with me!

HAIMON.
I am sorry. You prefer silence.

CREON.   Now, by God—
I swear, by all the gods in heaven above us,
You'll watch it, I swear you shall!
(*To the servants.*)   Bring her out!
130 Bring the woman out! Let her die before his eyes!
Here, this instant, with her bridegroom beside her!

HAIMON.
Not here, no; she will not die here, King.
And you will never see my face again.
Go on raving as long as you've a friend to endure you.

(*Exit Haimon.*)

CHORAGOS.
Gone, gone.
135 Creon, a young man in a rage is dangerous!

CREON.
Let him do, or dream to do, more than a man can.
He shall not save these girls from death.

CHORAGOS.   These girls?
You have sentenced them both?

CREON.   No, you are right.
140 I will not kill the one whose hands are clean.

CHORAGOS.
But Antigonê?

CREON (*somberly*). I will carry her far away
Out there in the wilderness, and lock her
Living in a vault of stone. She shall have food,
As the custom is, to absolve the State of her death.
145 And there let her pray to the gods of hell:
They are her only gods:
Perhaps they will show her an escape from death,
Or she may learn,

though late,
That piety shown the dead is piety in vain.

(*Exit Creon.*)

ODE III

CHORUS.

Love, unconquerable   *Strophe*
Waster of rich men, keeper
Of warm lights and all-night vigil
In the soft face of a girl:
5   Sea-wanderer, forest-visitor!
Even the pure Immortals cannot escape you,
And the mortal man, in his one day's dusk,
Trembles before your glory.

Surely you swerve upon ruin   *Antistrophe*
10   The just man's consenting heart,
As here you have made bright anger
Strike between father and son—
And none has conquered by Love!
A girl's glánce wórking the will of heaven:
15   Pleasure to her alone who mocks us,
Merciless Aphroditê.°

SCENE IV

CHORAGOS (*as Antigonê enters guarded*).
But I can no longer stand in awe of this,
Nor, seeing what I see, keep back my tears.
Here is Antigonê, passing to that chamber
Where all find sleep at last.

ANTIGONÊ.
5   Look upon me, friends, and pity me   *Strophe 1*
Turning back at the night's edge to say
Good-by to the sun that shines for me no longer;
Now sleepy Death
Summons me down to Acheron,° that cold shore:
10   There is no bridesong there, nor any music.

CHORUS.
Yet not unpraised, not without a kind of honor,
You walk at last into the underworld;
Untouched by sickness, broken by no sword.
What woman has ever found your way to death?

ANTIGONÊ.
How often I have heard the story   *Antistrophe 1*
15   of Niobê,°
Tantalos' wretched daughter, how the stone

16 Aphroditê goddess of love   **9 Acheron** a river of the underworld, which was ruled by Hades   **15 Niobê** Niobê boasted of her
numerous children, provoking Leto, the mother of Apollo, to
destroy them. Niobê wept profusely, and finally was turned to stone
on Mount Sipylus, whose streams are her tears.

Clung fast about her, ivy-close: and they say
The rain falls endlessly
And sifting soft snow; her tears are never done.
I feel the loneliness of her death in mine.   20

CHORUS.
But she was born of heaven, and you
Are woman, woman-born. If her death is yours,
A mortal woman's, is this not for you
Glory in our world and in the world beyond?

ANTIGONÊ.
You laugh at me. Ah, friends, friends   *Strophe 2*   25
Can you not wait until I am dead? O Thebes,
O men many-charioted, in love with Fortune,
Dear springs of Dircê, sacred Theban grove,
Be witnesses for me, denied all pity,
Unjustly judged! and think a word of love   30
For her whose path turns
Under dark earth, where there are no more tears.

CHORUS.
You have passed beyond human daring and come at last
Into a place of stone where Justice sits.
I cannot tell   35
What shape of your father's guilt appears in this.

ANTIGONÊ.
You have touched it at last: *Antistrophe 2*
That bridal bed
Unspeakable, horror of son and mother mingling:
Their crime, infection of all our family!   40
O Oedipus, father and brother!
Your marriage strikes from the grave to murder mine.
I have been a stranger here in my own land:
All my life
The blasphemy of my birth has followed me.   45

CHORUS.
Reverence is a virtue, but strength
Lives in established law: that must prevail.
You have made your choice,
Your death is the doing of your conscious hand.

ANTIGONÊ.
Then let me go, since all your words are bitter,   *Epode*   50
And the very light of the sun is cold to me.
Lead me to my vigil, where I must have
Neither love nor lamentation; no song, but silence.

Creon interrupts impatiently.

CREON.
If dirges and planned lamentations could put off death,
Men would be singing for ever.
(*To the servants.*)   Take her, go!   55
You know your orders: take her to the vault
And leave her alone there. And if she lives or dies,
That's her affair, not ours: our hands are clean.

ANTIGONÊ.
O tomb, vaulted bride-bed in eternal rock,
Soon I shall be with my own again   60

Where Persephonê° welcomes the thin ghosts under-
   ground:
And I shall see my father again, and you, mother,
And dearest Polyneicês—
                  dearest indeed
To me, since it was my hand
65   That washed him clean and poured the ritual wine:
And my reward is death before my time!

And yet, as men's hearts know, I have done no wrong,
I have not sinned before God. Or if I have,
I shall know the truth in death. But if the guilt
70   Lies upon Creon who judged me, then, I pray,
May his punishment equal my own.
CHORAGOS.   O passionate heart,
Unyielding, tormented still by the same winds!
CREON.
Her guards shall have good cause to regret their delaying.
ANTIGONÊ.
Ah! That voice is like the voice of death!
CREON.
75   I can give you no reason to think you are mistaken.
ANTIGONÊ.
Thebes, and you my fathers' gods,
And rulers of Thebes, you see me now, the last
Unhappy daughter of a line of kings,
Your kings, led away to death. You will remember
80   What things I suffer, and at what men's hands,
Because I would not transgress the laws of heaven.
(*To the guards, simply.*) Come: let us wait no longer.

                (*Exit Antigonê, left, guarded.*)

ODE IV

CHORUS.
All Danaê's beauty was locked away   *Strophe 1*
In a brazen cell where the sunlight could not come:
A small room still as any grave, enclosed her.
Yet she was a princess too,
5   And Zeus in a rain of gold poured love upon her.
O child, child,
No power in wealth or war
Or tough sea-blackened ships
Can prevail against untiring Destiny!

10   And Dryas' son° also, that furious king,   *Antistrophe 1*
Bore the god's prisoning anger for his pride:
Sealed up by Dionysos in deaf stone,
His madness died among echoes.
So at the last he learned what dreadful power
15   His tongue had mocked:
For he had profaned the revels,

And fired the wrath of the nine
Implacable Sisters° that love the sound of the flute.
And old men tell a half-remembered tale   *Strophe 2*
20   Of horror where a dark ledge splits the sea
And a double surf beats on the gráy shóres:
How a king's new woman,° sick
With hatred for the queen he had imprisoned,
Ripped out his two sons' eyes with her bloody hands
25   While grinning Arês° watched the shuttle plunge
Four times: four blind wounds crying for revenge,

Crying, tears and blood mingled.—   *Antistrophe 2*
    Piteously born,
Those sons whose mother was of heavenly birth!
Her father was the god of the North Wind
And she was cradled by gales,
30   She raced with young colts on the glittering hills
And walked untrammeled in the open light:
But in her marriage deathless Fate found means
To build a tomb like yours for all her joy.

SCENE V

*Enter blind Teiresias, led by a boy. The opening speeches
of Teiresias should be in singsong contrast to the realistic
lines of Creon.*

TEIRESIAS.
This is the way the blind man comes, Princes, Princes,
Lock-step, two heads lit by the eyes of one.
CREON.
What new thing have you to tell us, old Teiresias?
TEIRESIAS.
I have much to tell you: listen to the prophet, Creon.
CREON.
5   I am not aware that I have ever failed to listen.
TEIRESIAS.
Then you have done wisely, King, and ruled well.
CREON.
I admit my debt to you. But what have you to say?
TEIRESIAS.
This, Creon: you stand once more on the edge of fate.
CREON.
What do you mean? Your words are a kind of dread.
TEIRESIAS.
10   Listen, Creon:

---

61 Persephonê queen of the underworld   **10 Dryas' son** Lycurgus,
King of Thrace

18 Sisters the Muses   **22 king's new woman** Eidothea, second
wife of King Phineus, blinded her stepsons. Their mother, Cleopatra, had been imprisoned in a cave. Phineus was the son of a king,
and Cleopatra, his first wife, was the daughter of Boreas, the North
wind, but this illustrious ancestry could not protect his sons from
violence and darkness.   **25 Arês** god of war

I was sitting in my chair of augury, at the place
Where the birds gather about me. They were all a-chatter,
As is their habit, when suddenly I heard
A strange note in their jangling, a scream, a
15 Whirring fury; I knew that they were fighting,
Tearing each other, dying
In a whirlwind of wings clashing. And I was afraid.
I began the rites of burnt-offering at the altar,
But Hephaistos° failed me: instead of bright flame,
20 There was only the sputtering slime of the fat thigh-flesh
Melting: the entrails dissolved in gray smoke,
The bare bone burst from the welter. And no blaze!

This was a sign from heaven. My boy described it,
Seeing for me as I see for others.

25 I tell you, Creon, you yourself have brought
This new calamity upon us. Our hearths and altars
Are stained with the corruption of dogs and carrion birds
That glut themselves on the corpse of Oedipus' son.
The gods are deaf when we pray to them, their fire
30 Recoils from our offering, their birds of omen
Have no cry of comfort, for they are gorged
With the thick blood of the dead.
                                    O my son,
These are no trifles! Think: all men make mistakes,
But a good man yields when he knows his course is
       wrong,
35 And repairs the evil. The only crime is pride.

Give in to the dead man, then: do not fight with a
       corpse—
What glory is it to kill a man who is dead?
Think, I beg you:
It is for your own good that I speak as I do.
40 You should be able to yield for your own good.
CREON.
It seems that prophets have made me their especial
       province.
All my life long
I have been a kind of butt for the dull arrows
Of doddering fortune-tellers!
                          No, Teiresias:
45 If your birds—if the great eagles of God himself
Should carry him stinking bit by bit to heaven,
I would not yield. I am not afraid of pollution:
No man can defile the gods.
                          Do what you will,
Go into business, make money, speculate
50 In India gold or that synthetic gold from Sardis,
Get rich otherwise than by my consent to bury him.
Teiresias, it is a sorry thing when a wise man
Sells his wisdom, lets out his words for hire!
TEIRESIAS.
Ah Creon! Is there no man left in the world—

19 Hephaistos god of fire

CREON.
To do what?—Come, let's have the aphorism!   55
TEIRESIAS.
No man who knows that wisdom outweighs any wealth?
CREON.
As surely as bribes are baser than any baseness.
TEIRESIAS.
You are sick, Creon! You are deathly sick!
CREON.
As you say: it is not my place to challenge a prophet.
TEIRESIAS.
Yet you have said my prophecy is for sale.   60
CREON.
The generation of prophets has always loved gold.
TEIRESIAS.
The generation of kings has always loved brass.
CREON.
You forget yourself! You are speaking to your King.
TEIRESIAS.
I know it. You are a king because of me.
CREON.
You have a certain skill; but you have sold out.   65
TEIRESIAS.
King, you will drive me to words that—
CREON.   Say them, say them!
Only remember: I will not pay you for them.
TEIRESIAS.
No, you will find them too costly.
CREON.   No doubt. Speak:
Whatever you say, you will not change my will.
TEIRESIAS.
Then take this, and take it to heart!   70
The time is not far off when you shall pay back
Corpse for corpse, flesh of your own flesh.
You have thrust the child of this world into living night,
You have kept from the gods below the child that is
       theirs:
The one in a grave before her death, the other,   75
Dead, denied the grave. This is your crime:
And the Furies and the dark gods of Hell
Are swift with terrible punishment for you.

Do you want to buy me now, Creon?
                          Not many days,
And your house will be full of men and women weeping,   80
And curses will be hurled at you from far
Cities grieving for sons unburied, left to rot
Before the walls of Thebes.

These are my arrows, Creon: they are all for you.

(*To boy.*) But come, child: lead me home.   85
Let him waste his fine anger upon younger men.
Maybe he will learn at last
To control a wiser tongue in a better head.

(*Exit Teiresias.*)

CHORAGOS.
 The old man has gone, King, but his words
90 Remain to plague us. I am old, too,
 But I cannot remember that he was ever false.
CREON.
 That is true. . . . It troubles me.
 Oh it is hard to give in! but it is worse
 To risk everything for stubborn pride.
CHORAGOS.
 Creon: take my advice.
95 CREON.   What shall I do?
CHORAGOS.
 Go quickly: free Antigonê from her vault
 And build a tomb for the body of Polyneicês.
CREON.
 You would have me do this!
CHORAGOS.   Creon, yes!
 And it must be done at once: God moves
100 Swiftly to cancel the folly of stubborn men.
CREON.
 It is hard to deny the heart! But I
 Will do it: I will not fight with destiny.
CHORAGOS.
 You must go yourself, you cannot leave it to others.
CREON.
 I will go.
   —Bring axes, servants:
105 Come with me to the tomb. I buried her, I
 Will set her free.
     Oh quickly!
 My mind misgives—
 The laws of the gods are mighty, and a man must serve
  them
 To the last day of his life!

           (*Exit Creon.*)

PAEAN°

CHORAGOS.
 God of many names   *Strophe 1*
CHORUS.   O Iacchos
        son
 of Kadmeian Sémelê
      O born of the Thunder!
 Guardian of the West
       Regent
 of Eleusis' plain
     O Prince of maenad Thebes

Paean a hymn (here dedicated to Iacchos, also called Dionysos. His father was Zeus, his mother was Sémelê, daughter of Kadmos. Iacchos's worshipers were the Maenads, whose cry was "Evohé evohé")

and the Dragon Field by rippling Ismenós:°   5
CHORAGOS.
 God of many names   *Antistrophe 1*
CHORUS.   the flame of torches
 flares on our hills
      the nymphs of Iacchos
 dance at the spring of Castalia:°
 from the vine-close mountain
        come ah come in ivy:
 Evohé evohé! sings through the streets of Thebes 10
CHORAGOS.
 God of many names   *Strophe 2*
CHORUS.   Iacchos of Thebes
 heavenly Child
     of Sémelê bride of the Thunderer!
 The shadow of plague is upon us:
       come
 with clement feet
      oh come from Parnassos
 down the long slopes
      across the lamenting water 15
CHORAGOS.
 Iô Fire! Chorister of the throbbing stars! *Antistrophe 2*
 O purest among the voices of the night!
 Thou son of God, blaze for us!
CHORUS.
 Come with choric rapture of circling Maenads
 Who cry *Iô Iacche!*
    God of many names!   20

EXODOS

Enter Messenger from left.
MESSENGER.
 Men of the line of Kadmos,° you who live
 Near Amphion's citadel,°
      I cannot say
 Of any condition of human life "This is fixed,
 This is clearly good, or bad." Fate raises up,
 And Fate casts down the happy and unhappy alike: 5
 No man can foretell his Fate.
      Take the case of Creon:

5 Ismenós a river east of Thebes (from a dragon's teeth, sown near the river, there sprang men who became the ancestors of the Theban nobility) **8 Castalia** a spring on Mount Parnassos **1 Kadmos,** who sowed the dragon's teeth, was founder of Thebes **2 Amphion's citadel** Amphion played so sweetly on his lyre that he charmed stones to form a wall around Thebes

Creon was happy once, as I count happiness:
Victorious in battle, sole governor of the land,
Fortunate father of children nobly born.
10 And now it has all gone from him! Who can say
That a man is still alive when his life's joy fails?
He is a walking dead man. Grant him rich,
Let him live like a king in his great house:
If his pleasure is gone, I would not give
15 So much as the shadow of smoke for all he owns.
CHORAGOS.
Your words hint at sorrow: what is your news for us?
MESSENGER.
They are dead. The living are guilty of their death.
CHORAGOS.
Who is guilty? Who is dead? Speak!
MESSENGER.   Haimon.
Haimon is dead; and the hand that killed him
Is his own hand.
CHORAGOS.
20 His father's? or his own?
MESSENGER.
His own, driven mad by the murder his father had done.
CHORAGOS.
Teiresias, Teiresias, how clearly you saw it all!
MESSENGER.
This is my news: you must draw what conclusions you
can from it.
CHORAGOS.
But look: Eurydicê, our Queen:
25 Has she overheard us?

Enter Eurydicê from the palace, center.

EURYDICÊ.
I have heard something, friends:
As I was unlocking the gate of Pallas'° shrine,
For I needed her help today, I heard a voice
Telling of some new sorrow. And I fainted
30 There at the temple with all my maidens about me.
But speak again: whatever it is, I can bear it:
Grief and I are no strangers.
MESSENGER.   Dearest Lady,
I will tell you plainly all that I have seen.
I shall not try to comfort you: what is the use,
35 Since comfort could lie only in what is not true?
The truth is always best.
                 I went with Creon
To the outer plain where Polyneicês was lying,
No friend to pity him, his body shredded by dogs.
We made our prayers in the place to Hecatê

And Pluto,° that they would be merciful. And we bathed   40
The corpse with holy water, and we brought
Fresh-broken branches to burn what was left of it,
And upon the urn we heaped up a towering barrow
Of the earth of his own land.
                 When we were done, we ran
To the vault where Antigonê lay on her couch of stone.   45
One of the servants had gone ahead,
And while he was yet far off he heard a voice
Grieving within the chamber, and he came back
And told Creon. And as the King went closer,
The air was full of wailing, the words lost,   50
And he begged us to make all haste. "Am I a prophet?"
He said, weeping, "And must I walk this road,
The saddest of all that I have gone before?
My son's voice calls me on. Oh quickly, quickly!
Look through the crevice there, and tell me   55
If it is Haimon, or some deception of the gods!"

We obeyed; and in the cavern's farthest corner
We saw her lying:
She had made a noose of her fine linen veil
And hanged herself. Haimon lay beside her,   60
His arms about her waist, lamenting her,
His love lost under ground, crying out
That his father had stolen her away from him.

When Creon saw him the tears rushed to his eyes
And he called to him: "What have you done, child?
Speak to me.   65
What are you thinking that makes your eyes so strange?
O my son, my son, I come to you on my knees!"
But Haimon spat in his face. He said not a word,
Staring—
                 And suddenly drew his sword
And lunged. Creon shrank back, the blade missed; and
the boy,   70
Desperate against himself, drove it half its length
Into his own side, and fell. And as he died
He gathered Antigonê close in his arms again,
Choking, his blood bright red on her white cheek.
And now he lies dead with the dead, and she is his   75
At last, his bride in the house of the dead.
                 (*Exit Eurydicê into the palace.*)
CHORAGOS.
She has left us without a word. What can this mean?
MESSENGER.
It troubles me, too; yet she knows what is best,
Her grief is too great for public lamentation,

27 **Pallas** Pallas Athene, goddess of wisdom

40 **Hecatê / And Pluto** Hecatê and Pluto (also known as Hades) were deities of the underworld

80 And doubtless she has gone to her chamber to weep
    For her dead son, leading her maidens in his dirge.

    Pause.

    CHORAGOS.
    It may be so: but I fear this deep silence.
    MESSENGER.
    I will see what she is doing. I will go in.

    (Exit messenger into the palace.)

    Enter Creon with attendants, bearing Haimon's body.

    CHORAGOS.
    But here is the king himself: on look at him,
85 Bearing his own damnation in his arms.
    CREON.
    Nothing you say can touch me any more.
    My own blind heart has brought me
    From darkness to final darkness. Here you see
    The father murdering, the murdered son—
90 And all my civic wisdom!

    Haimon my son, so young, so young to die,
    I was the fool, not you; and you died for me.
    CHORAGOS.
    That is the truth; but you were late in learning it.
    CREON.
    This truth is hard to bear. Surely a god
95 Has crushed me beneath the hugest weight of heaven,
    And driven me headlong a barbaric way
    To trample out the thing I held most dear.

    The pains that men will take to come to pain!

    Enter Messenger from the palace.

    MESSENGER.
    The burden you carry in your hands is heavy,
100 But it is not all: you will find more in your house.
    CREON.
    What burden worse than this shall I find there?
    MESSENGER.
    The Queen is dead.
    CREON.
    O port of death, deaf world,
    Is there no pity for me? And you, Angel of evil,
105 I was dead, and your words are death again.
    Is it true, boy? Can it be true?
    Is my wife dead? Has death bred death?
    MESSENGER.
    You can see for yourself.

    The doors are opened and the body of Eurydicê is disclosed within.

    CREON.
    Oh pity!
    All true, all true, and more than I can bear!   110
    O my wife, my son!
    MESSENGER.
    She stood before the altar, and her heart
    Welcomed the knife her own hand guided,
    And a great cry burst from her lips for Megareus° dead,
    And for Haimon dead, her sons; and her last breath   115
    Was a curse for their father, the murderer of her sons.
    And she fell, and the dark flowed in through her closing
        eyes.
    CREON.
    O God, I am sick with fear.
    Are there no swords here? Has no one a blow for me?
    MESSENGER.
    Her curse is upon you for the deaths of both.   120
    CREON.
    It is right that it should be. I alone am guilty.
    I know it, and I say it. Lead me in,
    Quickly, friends.
    I have neither life nor substance. Lead me in.
    CHORAGOS.
    You are right, if there can be right in so much wrong. 125
    The briefest way is best in a world of sorrow.
    CREON.
    Let it come,
    Let death come quickly, and be kind to me.
    I would not ever see the sun again.
    CHORAGOS.
    All that will come when it will; but we, meanwhile,   130
    Have much to do. Leave the future to itself.
    CREON.
    All my heart was in that prayer!
    CHORAGOS.
    Then do not pray any more: the sky is deaf.
    CREON.
    Lead me away. I have been rash and foolish.
    I have killed my son and my wife.   135
    I look for comfort; my comfort lies here dead.
    Whatever my hands have touched has come to nothing.
    Fate has brought all my pride to a thought of dust.

    *As Creon is being led into the house, the Choragos
    advances and speaks directly to the audience.*

    CHORAGOS.
    There is no happiness where there is no wisdom;
    No wisdom but in submission to the gods.   140
    Big words are always punished,
    And proud men in old age learn to be wise.

    114 Megareus Megareus, brother of Haimon, had died in the
    assault on Thebes

TOPICS FOR CRITICAL THINKING AND WRITING

📖 THE PLAY ON THE PAGE

1. If you have read *Oedipus*, compare and contrast the Creon of *Antigone* with the Creon of *Oedipus*.

2. Although Sophocles called his play *Antigone*, many critics say that Creon is the real tragic hero, pointing out that Antigone is absent from the last third of the play. Evaluate this view.

3. In some Greek tragedies, fate plays a great role in bringing about the downfall of the tragic hero. Though there are references to the curse on the House of Oedipus in *Antigone*, do we feel that Antigone goes to her death as a result of the workings of fate? Do we feel that fate is responsible for Creon's fall? Are both Antigone and Creon the creators of their own tragedy?

4. Are the words *hamartia* and *hybris* (pages 33–34) relevant to Antigone? To Creon?

🎭 THE PLAY ON THE STAGE

8. Would you use masks for some (or all) of the characters? If so, would they be masks that fully cover the face, Greek-style, or some sort of half-masks? (A full mask enlarges the face, and conceivably the mouthpiece can amplify the voice, but only an exceptionally large theater might require such help. Perhaps half-masks are enough if the aim is chiefly to distance the actors from the audience and from daily reality, and to force the actors to develop resources other than facial gestures. One director, arguing in favor of half-masks, has said that actors who wear even a half-mask learn to act not with the eyes but with the neck.)

9. How would you costume the players? Would you dress them as the Greeks might have? Why? One argument

5. Why does Creon, contrary to the Chorus's advice (Scene 5, lines 96–97), bury the body of Polyneices before he releases Antigone? Does his action show a zeal for piety as short-sighted as his earlier zeal for law? Is his action plausible, in view of the facts that Teiresias has dwelt on the wrong done to Polyneices and that Antigone has ritual food to sustain her? Or are we not to worry about Creon's motive?

6. A *foil* is a character who, by contrast, sets off or helps define another character. To what extent is Ismene a foil to Antigone? Is she entirely without courage?

7. What function does Eurydice serve? How deeply do we feel about her fate?

sometimes used by those who hold that modern productions of Greek drama should use classical costumes is that Greek drama *ought* to be remote and ritualistic. Evaluate this view. What sort of modern dress might be effective?

10. If you were directing a college production of *Antigone*, how large a chorus would you use? (Sophocles is said to have used a chorus of fifteen.) Would you have the chorus recite (or chant) the odes in unison, or would you assign lines to single speakers? In Sophocles's day, the chorus danced. Would you use dance movements? If not, in what sorts of movements might they engage?

THE PLAY IN PERFORMANCE

Sophocles's *Antigone* has had a great influence, especially in the twentieth century, but its influence may first have manifested itself in a version of the play by his younger contemporary, Euripides. Euripides's text is known only from a few fragments, however, so a detailed comparison cannot be made. In any case, we know that Sophocles's *Antigone* was highly esteemed in the century after it was written, and that it influenced a Roman version of the play. After the collapse of the Roman Empire, however, Greek drama was absent from the public stage until the nineteenth century. When *Antigone* was produced in Greece in 1861, it had the distinction of being the first ancient Greek play to be performed for

the general public in modern times. (Earlier in the century Greek drama survived on the stage only in occasional performances by and for university students.)

In the twentieth century *Antigone* has been much in view, for instance in a pacifist version by Walter Hasenclever (1919), in a version by Jean Cocteau (1922), and especially in a version by Jean Anouilh (written in 1942 and produced in occupied France in 1944). Anouilh's version resembles Sophocles's, but it includes modern references, for instance to cigarettes, and it was done in modern dress (evening gowns and tuxedos). This version is often said to have been staged as a protest against the Nazi occupation of

Paris, and apparently those who resisted the German occupation took it that way. In fact, however, Creon is presented very sympathetically, and because the play emphasizes fulfilling the roles that fate assigns to us, it suited the Nazis quite as much as it suited the French Resistance. The version by Bertolt Brecht (1948), however, is unambiguously hostile to Creon, who is presented as a materialistic brute. Similarly, Creon is clearly presented as a villain in Athol

Michael Billington
ANTIGONE IN MODERN DRESS

The following review of a production in England by the National Theatre Company, directed by John Burgess and Peter Gill in 1984, originally appeared in *The Guardian*, May 18, 1984. For a photo, see page 48.

How does one play Greek tragedy? In ancient or modern dress? In masks or with bared faces? In dense-packed or limpid verse? Peter Hall's *Oresteia* favoured the former approach: John Burgess and Peter Gill's production of *Antigone* at the Cottesloe goes for the latter. And, while acknowledging the vast difference between the two plays and venues, I lean heavily towards the updated approach on the grounds of sheer theatrical immediacy.

What Burgess and Gill have done, with some skill, is to tread a fine line between modernity and stylisation. Taking a leaf from Peter Stein's Schaubuhne Oresteia, they turn the Chorus into old men in grey suits and felt hats (modern directors clearly like being Svengalis to their actors' trilbies). Antigone and Ismene sport red and blue Forties frocks and matching toques. The Guards wear berets and khaki uniforms. At the same time, the two sisters move with exaggeratedly long strides. The Chorus rise from their front-bench chairs to become part of the action. Staccato drumbeats punctuate the drama. The production thus manages to acquire a contemporary feel without lapsing into simple naturalism.

But the real test of any version of Sophocles's *Antigone* is whether it manages to achieve a precise balance between the two antagonists rather than becoming a crude melodrama about a brute tyrant who refuses the heroine burial rites for her brother. Maurice Bowra once suggested that the Sophoclean irony is that we start by thinking Creon must be right and then switch our sympathies to Antigone. In performance. I find the exact reverse

Fugard's *The Island* (1973), a play in which black political prisoners in a South African jail stage an abbreviated version of *Antigone*. Fugard's point obviously is that the prisoners, like Antigone, have transgressed the law of an oppressive society.

For a discussion of what *Antigone* has meant to successive generations, see George Steiner, *Antigones* (1984).

happens. Creon at first seems a narrow paternalist and Antigone the upholder of moral law. But by the end Creon seems the one who suffers more in losing both son and wife precisely because he has broken the family bonds that underpin any society.

It is a deeply complex play that asks a lot of still-pertinent questions (does one break a law if one's conscience tells one it is bad?). But Greek tragedy is also nothing without passion and this production is unafraid of gut emotion. Jane Lapotaire's Antigone is a tense, desperate woman who senses death is the penalty but who is still dragged kicking and screaming to her entombment and who instantly buckles at the knees when reminded of her father's sins: she moves one because she is specific rather than general. And Peter Sproule's bullet-headed, blue-suited Creon likewise is no vague despot but an increasingly panic-stricken figure beseechingly asking the Chorus, after prophecies of disaster, "What must I do?" Both principals, in fact, follow a basic acting-rule of playing the characters from their own point of view.

Even this production, gripping and urgent as it is, can't solve every problem. I like the way the Chorus become constantly reacting figures, emitting an audible sign at Antigone's defiance and visibly cringing at Creon's blasphemy, but their speaking of C. A. Trypanis's translation is sometimes a little furry and their canes occasionally suggest an impending soft-shoe shuffle. But it is a well-acted evening (Ron Pember and Vincenzo Nicoli as the Guards report news of fresh disasters as if they meant it), the narrative is clear and strong, and the gesture towards the present-day brings the drama home and removes the chill aura of a pious cultural event.

Euripides

MEDEA

Euripides's approximate dates (484–406 B.C.) mark him as a younger contemporary of Sophocles. Thus, while Sophocles was already old when the disastrous struggle between Greek city-states, the Peloponnesian War, began in 431 B.C., Euripides was in his maturity. In fact, 431 was the year in which he wrote *Medea*.

   More open to current intellectual trends than Sophocles, Euripides reflects a doubting, skeptical mood. Further, his extant dramas are of more varied kinds than those of Sophocles, for in addition to writing tragedies he wrote tragicomedies and melodramas. Relatively unpopular in his day (he won only five prizes, though he wrote ninety-two plays) and often maligned, he was of a retiring and bookish nature. In his last months he voluntarily left Athens and settled in Macedonia, where he may have enjoyed the excellent company of other great self-exiled Athenians, including the painter Zeuxis and the historian Thucydides.

COMMENTARY

In our introductory remarks to *Oedipus* we mention that although the Greek tragic playwrights used traditional legends, within broad limits they were free to make significant changes. In fact, the inherited legends often included contradictory details, so the dramatists had to select as well as to amplify. In the story of Medea, for instance, all of the legends indicate that her children died at Corinth, but the cause of their death was variously explained. In one version the children are killed by the Corinthians, in revenge for Medea's murder of their king and his daughter, but in Euripides's version she herself murders them. In any case, allowing for variations, we can say that the gist of the story that Euripides dramatized in *Medea* went along the following lines.

Jason was the rightful heir to the kingdom of Iolcus in western Turkey, but his uncle, Pelias, usurped the throne. When Jason tried to claim the throne, Pelias tricked him into setting out on what seemed an impossible quest—obtaining the Golden Fleece, a fleece that hung in a sacred grove at Colchis, guarded by a dragon that never slept. (Colchis was south of the Caucasus Mountains, on the Black Sea, in what is now Georgia.) Jason set out in a boat called the *Argo,* whose crew of fifty-six (the Argonauts, i.e., "those who sailed in the *Argo*") consisted of fifty-four paired heroes who served as rowers, a helmsman, and the poet Orpheus, who calmed the seas by singing to them and who called out the rhythm to the rowers. Eventually Jason reached Colchis, ruled by King Aeetes. Aeetes, who was a sorcerer and the son of Helios the sun god, sought to kill Jason by requiring him to perform impossibly dangerous tasks. For instance, he had to

harness fire-breathing bulls and plough a field with them, and he had to sow the teeth of a dragon, each of which turned into an armed soldier who strove to kill Jason.

Medea, King Aeetes's daughter and herself a sorceress, fell in love with Jason, and in exchange for his promise to marry her she enabled him to accomplish the impossible. For instance, she gave Jason a balm that made him fireproof; he anointed his body and thus was able to harness the fire-breathing bulls. But Medea did more than disobey her father in the course of helping Jason: When her father pursued her, she dismembered her brother and scattered the pieces, thereby delaying her father, who paused to gather the pieces of his murdered son.

Fleeing Colchis, Jason and Medea took refuge in Corinth, where Jason found that he could improve his lot by putting Medea aside—despite the oaths he had vowed—and by marrying the daughter of Creon, King of Corinth. Euripides's play begins at this point. Although the story of Jason and the Golden Fleece is one of the great romantic tales of the world, we will find no romance in the sequel in Corinth. True, even in Colchis the heroic Jason required Medea's aid, but the Jason we see in the play is not in any way heroic; rather, he is a petty self-server. Figures like Euripides's Jason allowed the next generation of Greeks to say that Sophocles showed men as they should be, Euripides as they are. But if the earlier legends do not prepare us for Euripides's Jason, neither do they—with their cunning sorceress—prepare us for Euripides's compelling Medea.

After the Nurse's prologue, Medea, speaking to the Chorus of Women of Corinth, utters one of the great feminist speeches (241–60) in literature. In part it runs thus:

Men say we live a lazy life at home,
while they must go to war—what fools they are!
I'd rather face the enemy three times
than undergo the pains of labor once.

(257–60)

Later, in one of the great lyrics of the play, the Chorus will celebrate women:

Let the rivers flow back to their holy sources,
Justice and all things reverse direction!
It is men whose plans are full of deceit,
and no one can trust in the gods. But now
the story is being transformed: we women
demand the respect we deserve. Our life
is just as worthy of note. We refuse
to stay imprisoned in stereotypes.

The doddering bards will stop writing their ditties
about how *mobile la donna* is.
We were not granted access to song,
were discouraged from writing what we believe.
Otherwise we would have answered back
the race of males with a tale of our own.
The past holds many things it could say
about what men *and* women have done.

(415–30)

What the Chorus is saying, in part, is of course obviously true: Men have done most of the writing, and therefore they have glorified themselves and paid little attention to the accomplishments of women. We need not say that Jason is a typical man, but if we want to know what attitudes Athenian men had toward women, probably Jason's words to Medea give us a fairly good idea. Consider, for instance, his remark that

women have gotten to such a point that you
think if your sex life's good, then everything
is perfect; but a problem in that area
makes you turn the best things people have
into a battleground.

(581–85)

We can pause here, briefly, to say a few things about the status of women in ancient Greece. According to Thucydides, Euripides's contemporary, the great statesman Pericles said that "a woman's glory is not to be mentioned, whether for good or ill." Women were married at about the age of fifteen—in arranged marriages, of course—to a man of thirty or so. Women were brought up apart from males, and, as wives, they lived in separate quarters within the household. Aristocratic women did not eat with their husbands and his male friends, and they did not go out of the house except to attend religious festivals or dramatic performances, and they were always accompanied by an attendant. Their job was to supervise the household slaves, and to produce children to inherit the land. A husband could divorce his wife merely by announcing his plan in the presence of witnesses, but a wife could divorce a husband only after a judicial proceeding and for a serious cause. Incidentally, because women rarely appeared in public, dramatists sometimes had to invent explanations to account for the presence of a woman in an outdoor scene. An example is Medea's speech in lines 226–28. Another way of surmounting the difficulty of representing an aristocratic woman was to use a go-between, such as the nurse in Medea, who would report the words and actions of her mistress.

With Euripides, we get (as we do not get from the other tragic dramatists) serious discussions of the roles of women. This is not to say, however, that the other dramatists neglected women. Quite the contrary. Although, as we have briefly seen, ancient Greece was a man's world, almost half of the extant Greek tragedies are either named for individual women (e.g., *Antigone, Medea*) or for groups of women (e.g., *The Suppliant Women, The Trojan Women*), and in most of the plays which are chiefly about women the Chorus consists of women (though not in *Antigone*, where Sophocles emphasizes Antigone's isolation by setting her against a chorus of old men). But in most of these plays by Euripides's predecessors, the women are presented—with a few notable exceptions, such as Sophocles's *Antigone*—as relatively conventional figures, and they are usually presented as pathetic creatures who undergo suffering but who scarcely initiate action.

Obviously Medea is of a different sort, strong-willed and imaginative. We can only wonder what the Greek audience—chiefly male—thought when it heard Medea denounce the traditional heroic ideas that men are important because they fight battles, and that women are unimportant because they deal with routine domestic matters. Possibly they dismissed Euripides as a gadfly, or possibly they thought that Medea's ideas were self-evidently nonsense, exactly the kind of raving that a barbarian woman was capable of—so un-Greek, so irrational. Or possibly they recognized that Euripides was a dramatist of a different sort from Sophocles, someone more like (say) Henrik Ibsen or George Bernard Shaw, dramatists who saw themselves as concerned with the problems of their day.

Certainly, if the audience was paying attention, it must have realized that although Medea is (in Greek eyes) from a primitive part of the world, Jason's arguments defending his abandonment of Medea are shallow, even despicable. He has deserted her, despite his earlier vows, in order to better his social position in Corinth. And he will learn that Medea—stimulated by his ignominious behavior—has a strength of purpose that will destroy his life, not by killing him but by killing his new wife and his children, that is, by killing everything that he wants to live for. We should remember, too, when we read or hear Medea's prediction of Jason's empty future, that in ancient Greece, where there were no pensions or insurance plans, aged people depended on their grown children for support. Notice, further, that Medea predicts an *unheroic* death for Jason. Instead of dying gloriously, he will be struck down by a timber from the rotting *Argo*, the very ship that brought him to Medea.

Euripides

MEDEA

Translated by Mary-Kay Gamel

Characters in Order of Appearance

Medea's childhood NURSE
TUTOR *of Medea's children*
CHILDREN *of Jason and Medea*
MEDEA, *formerly princess of Colchis, wife of Jason*
CREON, *King of Corinth*
JASON, *formerly prince of Iolchos, Medea's husband*
AEGEUS, *King of Athens*
MESSENGER, *slave in Creon's palace*
CHORUS *of women of Corinth*

All the action takes place in front of Medea's house in Corinth.

NURSE.
  Oh how I wish that boat the Argo had never
  flown through the dark clashing rocks to Colchis' shore!
  I wish the pine that made it had never been felled
  in the groves of Thessaly! Wish the heroes sent
5 for the Golden Fleece by Pelias never had rowed it!
  My lady Medea, battered by love for Jason,
  would never have sailed off with him to his home, Iolchos.
  She wouldn't have killed the king, by tricking his
      daughters
  to do it; she wouldn't be in exile now in this land,
10 Corinth, along with her husband and children. Here
  she's tried to please the residents of her new city,
  and gone along with Jason in everything.
  (That's stability—a wife never taking a stand
  against her husband!) That was then. But now
15 all is hatred; what's dearest to me is dying.
  Jason's betrayed his own sons, and my lady,
  by wallowing in a royal marriage bed
  with King Creon's daughter. Medea, dishonored,
  wounded, calls out "promises!" remembers how
20 he pledged his faith by clasping her hand, and asks
  the gods to see how Jason swindles her.
  She doesn't eat. Her body aches. She spends
  every moment weeping, ever since
  she found out she had been betrayed. She stares
25 at the ground, never lifts her eyes. She's like a rock,
  or the crashing surf. She can't hear the words
  of those who love her giving her advice.
  Sometimes she shakes her head, talks to herself,
  whispers her father's name, her own land,

home—all the things she gave up for Jason.   30
He gives *her* up now. In this disaster
she's found out, poor woman, what it means
to have no country. She hates her children, gets
no pleasure from seeing them. She scares me.
I'm afraid she's planning something awful,   35
awful as she can be. Someone who dares
to take her on won't leave the field alive.
But here are the children coming from their games,
completely unaware of their mother's pain.
Of course—young folks don't know what suffering is. 40

[*Enter Tutor.*]

TUTOR.
  Old fixture of my lady's household, why
  are you standing out here in front alone, fretting
  to yourself about things? How is it Medea
  is willing for you to leave her alone in the house?
NURSE.
  Old servant of Jason's children, to a good slave,   45
  troubles which fall on the master hit her too
  and bruise her heart. I'm so far gone with sadness
  I couldn't resist coming out here to tell
  all earth and heaven of my mistress' grief.
TUTOR.
  Hasn't she stopped suffering yet, poor thing?   50
NURSE.
  Far from it—the pain has only just begun.
TUTOR.
  She's a fool, then—though she is my lady.
  She doesn't know the latest awful news.
NURSE.
  What is it, old man? Don't refuse to speak!
TUTOR.
  No! Nothing! Sorry I said anything.   55
NURSE.
  I beg you, don't hold back from your fellow slave.
  I can keep my mouth shut if need be.
TUTOR.
  Down by Pirene fountain, where the old men
  play checkers in the sun, I heard someone
  (he didn't notice me) say that King Creon   60
  means to send these children out of Corinth,
  their mother too. Of course, I don't know if
  the story's true. I hope it isn't. But—

NURSE.
    Will Jason stand for this—his children exiled—
65 even if he is at odds with their mother?
TUTOR.
    Old ties give way when new ones come along.
    That man's no friend to this family any more.
NURSE.
    We're done for, then! A new disaster, before
    we've bailed out the earlier ones! We're swamped!
TUTOR.
70 Listen, you: it's no time for the mistress
    to learn this. Just keep quiet! Not a word!
NURSE.
    Children, hear what kind of father you have?
    Damn him! No—he is my master. But
    he's guilty of ignoring those he ought to love.
TUTOR.
75 So who isn't? Are you learning this just now,
    that no one loves his neighbor as himself?
    Jason's remarried. Of course he doesn't love them.
NURSE.
    Children, go inside the house, that'll be better.
    You—keep them by themselves as much as you can;
80 don't let them near their mother in her fury.
    I've already seen her staring at them like a bull,
    about to do something. She won't give up her rage,
    I know, until she rushes someone. Please,
    make it an enemy, not someone she loves.
MEDEA [within].
85   I'm so unhappy!
        I can't stand it!
        I want to die!
NURSE.
        That's it, boys!
        Mother's going
90   into a rage.
        Hurry up, get in
        the house! Keep out
        of sight, don't come
        near her! Watch out
95   for her temper—savage,
        stiff with hate.
        Go! She's a storm cloud
        gathering force,
        wounded, hurting,
100   pregnant with power,
        soon to fork lightning
        hard to put out.
        What is she going to do?
MEDEA.
        Oh God! I've suffered
105   such awful things.
        I've got a right
        to scream! Children
        of a hated mother,

        die! You're doomed!
110   Your father too!
        All of us must die!
NURSE.
        Lord, oh Lord!
        Why mix up the boys
        in their father's crime?
115   Why hate them?
        Children, I'm terrified
        you'll be destroyed.
        Powerful people
        aren't like us:
120   they get what they want,
        don't know how to give way;
        their moods are unstable.
        It's better to know
        how to live together,
125   all equal: let me
        get old in security
        rather than wealth.
        (People always
        assert that, but
130   working at it is best.)
        To try for too much
        brings no good to folks.
        When the gods get enraged
        they've got more to wreck.

[Exeunt Children and Tutor into the house.]

[Enter Chorus.]

CHORUS.
        Standing at my door   135
        I heard a voice,
        that piercing cry
        the outsider let out.
        She hasn't calmed down.
        Old lady, speak: 140
        your family troubles
        make me so sad.
        I come as a friend.
NURSE.
        Family? What family?
        That's all over with.   145
        The husband in bed
        with the princess, the wife
        in her room, weeping,
        wears herself out.
        Friendly words   150
        are not what she needs.
MEDEA [within].
        O God! Earth! Sun!
        Send a lightning flash
        through my brain! Why, why
        must I stay alive?   155
        I want to leave

this life I hate,
and find escape in death.

CHORUS.[1]

Did you hear? She called out "God! Earth! Sun!"
160 What a dreadful cry from the wretched wife!
The husband she's eager for now is Death.
But Death is already hurrying here—
don't goad him on! If your husband prefers
to sleep in a new bed, that's up to him.
165 Don't take it so hard—let God be his judge.
You're wasting away bewailing your man.

MEDEA.

O great Justice!
Mighty Artemis!
Don't you see
170 what I'm going through?
I bound my husband
with powerful oaths,
but he broke them all!
For him I abandoned
175 my father, butchered
my brother!
I want to see him,
and his bride,
and all they love,
180 lie peeled and bleeding.

NURSE.

Hear how she calls
on Justice, Zeus
who guards all contracts?
This anger will end
185 in nothing small.

CHORUS.

Then how can she see me? Hear my words?
But if she can let her anger go
and alter her mood, I'm going to be
a trustworthy friend. Won't you please go in
190 and bring her out here? You can say I've come,
and I'm anxious to help. Please hurry, before
something terrible happens inside.
Something awful is starting to stir.

NURSE.

I'll go, but I
195 don't know if she
will listen. When
someone comes near
to speak to her
she glares like a lioness
200 newly cubbed,

---

[1]At this point the chorus break into an "ode," a formal song accompanied by the flute; in the original production the chorus would have danced while singing. Medea and the Nurse continue in the movement meter, indicating that Medea is in the process of coming out. (Translator's note)

butting away
all words. Some call
those songs men sing
at banquets "life's
205 sweet sounds"—how stupid!
No one has ever
soothed away hatred
with rippling chords,
stopped death and disaster
210 with rhyme. Of course,
if poetry could
put an end to pain,
what a gift it would be.
But when there's food
215 on the table, who needs
empty words? The food
is good enough by itself.

[Exit Nurse.]

CHORUS.

Shrill with pain
she curses the liar,
220 the double-crosser.
Sailing by night
through the dangerous straits,
she made it to Greece,
and gets paid back like this.
225 God, is that justice?

[Enter Medea.]

MEDEA.

Women of Corinth, I don't want you to blame me.
So I've come out. Many people are too proud,
in public or private. Those who keep to themselves
acquire a bad reputation for being aloof.
230 It's unfair, though, when people make snap judgments,
and decide to dislike someone who's done no harm
before they even know her. A foreigner
has to work very hard not to seem odd,
but locals too become disliked if they're
stuck up and don't know how to act.

235 As for me,
this thing has fallen on me so suddenly
it's wrecked me. Giving up all joy in life,
I'm done for friends; I only want to die.
My husband, the man who could have made me know
240 a happy life, has proved the worst of men.
As women we are more abused than anything
that lives and has a mind. With a rich dowry
we first must buy a husband. Then we have
to give our bodies up to a master's control.
245 That's still more painful, but here's the worst:
he might be sweet, or abusive—we can't know.
There's no way out—we can't stay single, and
divorce makes the woman involved look bad.

250 So—you move into a stranger's house,
where things are done his way. (You can't learn that
at home—you have to read his mind.) If you
work hard, and your husband's ball and chain doesn't
      chafe,
you're lucky. But if not, you're better off dead.
255 Whenever a man gets bored with life at home,
he can go out to amuse himself with friends,
while we must set our sights on only one.
Men say we live a lazy life at home,
while they must go to war—what fools they are!
I'd rather face the enemy three times
260 than undergo the pains of labor once.

Yet your situation is very different from mine.
This is your land, your family home is here,
you get some pleasure from life, being with friends.
I am an exile, homeless, carried off
265 like a trophy from an exotic land, the victim
of my husband. Mother, brother, no one near
can harbor me in time of trouble. So
I ask you, friends, for this one favor: if
I find a way to make my husband pay
270 for what he's done, keep quiet. Other times
a woman's scared to pick up naked steel;
but when her home is threatened, then her will
grows firm and dyes itself with criminal blood.

CHORUS.
I promise to say nothing. I agree:
275 you have a right to rage, and you are right
to seek revenge. Look! I see Creon, ruler
of this land, bringing some new decision.

[Enter Creon.]

CREON.
Hey you! Yes, you, the frowning one, the one
who hates her husband, Medea: I've decreed
280 that you must leave this place, and take your children.
No delays. I came to tell you this,
and I'm not going home until I see
you've gone beyond the limit of this land.

MEDEA.
Oh, no! Please no! I'm ruined! With full sail
285 my enemies pursue me, and there's no
safe place to land. Miserable as I am,
I have to ask: why are you doing this?

CREON.
You terrify me. No need to mince my words.
You might do something awful to my daughter,
290 something I couldn't stop. I have good reason:
your nature's cunning, you have evil skills,
you're angry at being divested of your husband.
They say you threaten to harm the father-in-law
and the bridegroom and the bride herself.
295 That's what I'm taking precautions against. I'd rather

have you hate me now than soften up
and then be sorry later.

MEDEA.   Oh, my God!
This is my reputation damaging me—
not the first time it has happened. Creon,
someone who's smart should never give his children 300
too much education. First, they'll be
"overqualified" for menial jobs.
Then, your neighbors think they look down on them
and start to resent them. What a double bind:
dimwits call an unconventional thinker 305
"impractical!" "too smart for his own good!"
while those who like to think they know it all
resent someone who's smarter than they are.
This is my problem: some are jealous of me,
others find me formidable. But I 310
am not so wise. You're afraid of me?
Think I can make you suffer? I am hardly
in any position to hurt a man like you.
You needn't fear me. You've done nothing to me.
You gave your daughter to a man you liked. 315
It's my husband I hate. As for you, I think
you've acted quite correctly, and I hope
all your affairs go well. More marriages!
Many happy returns! But let me stay
here in this land. Though I'm badly treated, 320
I'll keep quiet, giving way to those in control.

CREON.
Very soft-spoken! But I shudder to think
what evil thing you're planning; your mild words
make me trust you even less than I did before.
A woman who shows her anger is easier 325
to guard against than one who holds her tongue.
No more speeches! Get out, immediately!
That's how things stand. Since you're my enemy
none of your skill can keep you here with us.

MEDEA.
No, Creon! I beg you, in your daughter's name! 330

CREON.
You're wasting your breath. You'll never change my mind.

MEDEA.
You're forcing me out? You won't hear my appeal?

CREON.
You matter less to me than my family does.

MEDEA.
The memory of my homeland comes back to me now.

CREON.
Homeland's important—but children count the most. 335

MEDEA.
Every kind of love can make you suffer.

CREON.
Of course, it all depends on the circumstances.

MEDEA.
God! Don't forget who's responsible for all this!

CREON.
    You're crazy! Get moving! Give my mind a rest!
MEDEA.
340   A rest? It's you who are arresting me!
CREON.
    Move, or my men will move you out by force.
MEDEA.
    No—not that! Creon, I beg of you—
                                            [Sinks to her knees.]
CREON.
    As usual, Medea, you're drawing a crowd.
MEDEA.
    I promise to leave. That's not what I'm asking.
CREON.
345   Why are you grovelling, then? Get up off the ground!
MEDEA.
    Just let me stay for one more day, so I
    can figure out where we can go, and get
    a new start for my children, since their father
    doesn't see the need to provide for them.
350   They're the ones who need your sympathy.
    You are a father—how can you be so hard?
    Moving on won't bother me: it's them
    I'm sorry for, involved in my bad luck.
CREON.
    My nature is hardly authoritarian. I
355   have often gotten in trouble by being too nice.
    I know I'm probably making a big mistake
    but—all right, you can stay. I warn you, though:
    you and your sons must go by dawn tomorrow.
    If you're still on my land after that,
360   you die. That's a promise. One day is all
    you get. I'm still afraid you might do something
    terrible . . . but you won't.

                                            [Exit Creon.]

CHORUS.
    Poor thing! No end
    to your problems. Where
365   will you go? Who
    will take you in?
    Where will you
    find shelter from your pain?
    In a sea of troubles
370   God has set you adrift.
MEDEA.
    Yes, all is over: who could deny it? Right?
    [Fiercely.] Don't you believe it! It's not over yet.
    The newlyweds still have some hurdles before them;
    the in-laws will have a few little problems too.
    Do you think I would ever have grovelled at that man's
375   feet
    if I didn't have something to gain, some plan in mind?
    I wouldn't have spoken one word, much less touched him.

He's such a fool! By throwing me out, he could
have blocked my entire scheme—but no, he gives me
this whole day, which is all I need. Today   380
I will make the three of them into corpses:
the father, the daughter, and the loving husband.
So many ways I can make them die! I can't
decide which one to try out first, my friends.
A little *plastique* in the bridal suite?° Or shall   385
I sneak into the house, find them in bed,
and shove a knife through both their guts? One thing
bothers me, though: if I get caught, and put
to death, that'll give them a good laugh. No—
better to use the direct method, the one   390
we women know best: poison. So—now they're dead.
Where can I go? Who will give me asylum?
Someone who doesn't know me to save my skin.
If during the short time I have left I find
someone to watch over me I'll use deceit   395
and get my revenge by secret machinations.
But if there's no way out, I'll have to run
the greater risk. Even if I must die,
I'll take up the knife and kill them with my own hands.
I swear by Hekate,° the leader whom I reverence   400
more than all others, who has been my ally,
who lives in the darkest corners of my house,
not one of them will laugh after hurting me.
I'll make this wedding taste bitter; they will weep
for making this alliance, banishing me.   405
Proceed, Medea! Leave out nothing of what
you have in mind, plotting and scheming! Go
to the awful thing! Your courage is on trial.
You know what they've done to you, and you
know how to pay them back. Will the Sisyphus family   410
laugh at Helios' grand-daughter because her man
has married their daughter? Never! Women, we
are helpless when virtue is demanded, but
incomparable architects of crime.
CHORUS.
    Let the rivers flow back to their holy sources,   415
    Justice and all things reverse direction!
    It is men whose plans are full of deceit,
    and no one can trust in the gods. But now
    the story is being transformed: we women
    demand the respect we deserve. Our life   420
    is just as worthy of note. We refuse
    to stay imprisoned in stereotypes.

    The doddering bards will stop writing their ditties
    about how *mobile la donna is.*°
    We were not granted access to song,   425

385 *plastique* bomb   400 Hekate (also Hecate) goddess of the underworld and of magic   424 how mobile la donna is how fickle a woman is

were discouraged from writing what we believe.
Otherwise we would have answered back
the race of males with a tale of our own.
The past holds many things it could say
430   about what men *and* women have done.

Medea, crazy with love, you sailed
away from your father's land, dividing
the Rocks which clash on passing ships.
Now you live in a foreign land;
435   your husband has left, your bed is abandoned,
you're driven out of your rightful place,
discarded, deprived of your legal rights.
At one time a person's word meant something;
promises were made to be kept.
440   Trustworthiness now is a thing of the past;
look for respect in this land no more.
No father's house will harbor you now
in your trouble. A woman who's stronger than you
moves into your bed and takes over your life.

[*Enter Jason.*]

JASON.
445   This isn't the first time. I have often seen
how difficult to deal with stubbornness is.
If you'd only taken it easy, you could have stayed
right here and kept the house. But no, not you—
your crazy words have gotten you thrown out.
450   And I don't give a damn: please, keep right on
calling Jason the worst man in the world.
But as for what you've said about our leaders—
be grateful all they're doing is throwing you out.
I kept trying to smoothe the royal anger,
455   kept asking them to let you stay. But you
refused to shut up, kept those stupid accusations
against them coming, and now you're exiled. Well,
I came to help you, not to write you off,
so that you and the children won't be sent off
460   without sufficient funds for your daily needs.
(I know first-hand how difficult exile is).
Even if you hate me, I'll never be
anything but quite concerned about you.

MEDEA.
Jason, I have this to say to you,
465   the worst thing one could say to a *real* man:
you have no balls! You're just a spineless coward!
You've come to see me, have you, after what you did?
To look someone in the eye who used to be dear,
someone you've hurt terribly, that isn't courage!
470   That isn't bravery! It's smug arrogance,
a cancer that poisons human relations. Still,
you did the right thing by coming. I will feel
much better after telling you how I despise you
and after hearing it you'll feel much worse.
475   I'll start from the very beginning.
As all the Greeks know, those who sailed in the ship

with you, I saved your life. Those terrible tasks
they gave you! Yoking the bulls breathing fire,
sowing the seed from which armed men sprang up,
and that great serpent coiled around the prize,   480
the Golden Fleece, never sleeping, always on guard,
was killed—by me. I delivered you from evil.
I was too eager to be prudent; I betrayed
my father, my family, and came away with you
to Iolchos. There I murdered your uncle Pelias,   485
who sent you on that trip to get you killed,
and then stole your inheritance. He died
the worst of deaths: by his own children's hands.
So I ruined the entire family. And after
I did all this for you, you bastard, you   490
betrayed me, procuring a new bride for yourself,
despite the fact that I bore you two sons.
If you were still childless, I could understand
your wanting this marriage. But as things are, where
are all those promises you proffered? Gone!   495
I can't figure it out: do you think the gods
of former times no longer rule? or that
a new code of ethics has been established?
You must, since you know you've broken your promise to
    me.
Look at my right hand—remember how often   500
you grasped it? And how you'd go right down on your
    knees?
You made me hope for things that would never happen!
Enough. I'll share with you, as if with a friend
—but why? what do I expect to gain?—
anyway, you'll look worse when I question you.   505
Where am I to turn? To my father's house,
my country, which I betrayed for you? Back
to your cousins, perhaps? No doubt they'd be delighted
to welcome their father's murderer into their home.
This is how things stand: a state of war   510
exists between the ones I loved at home,
people I never should have hurt, and me—
all because of favors I did for you.
In return, I'm blessed among Greek women:
I have you, a marvelous husband, so   515
kind and so trustworthy—the more fool I!
If we are driven out of here in exile
the children and I, completely alone, no one
whom we can turn to, what a juicy scandal—
the bridegroom's children begging on the street,   520
along with the woman who saved him. Oh, God! Why
are there simple tests that tell us whether gold
has been adulterated, yet no stamp
upon the skin to tell good men from bad?

CHORUS.
When love turns into war between two lovers,   525
that's a terrible passion which has no cure.

JASON.
I see. I have to be a rhetorician,

an expert yachtsman, furl my sails, ride out
the storm of your tongue-lashing, woman. You
530 enumerate those favors you did for me,
but I say the only one of gods and men
responsible for my salvation was—Love.°
(You do have a clever mind). It would be crude
to spell out in detail how lust took over
535 and drove you to save my body—I won't put
too fine a point on it. What service you did do
was not without its value. But you got
better than you gave from saving me.
Look at it this way. First, you now live in Greece
540 instead of that backward land. Moreover, here
you can experience justice, the rule of law
instead of brute force. Here might does not make right.
And now the Greeks all know how skilled you are.
You have a reputation! If you were still
545 out at the ends of the earth, no one would ever
have heard of you. As far as I'm concerned,
being rich, or able to strum a better tune
than Orpheus himself means less to me
than being well-known: a star, a celebrity.
550   That's what I have to say about my exploits.
(You're the one who started the debate).
As for your whining about my royal marriage,
I'll prove to you how sensible I was,
how smart . . . in fact, this marriage shows
555 how much I love you and my kids. Shut up!
When I came here from Iolchos, dragging a load
of disasters behind me, what greater streak of luck
could I have found than marrying Creon's daughter?
Me, an outcast! You think I got tired
560 of screwing you, and fell madly in love
with someone new: that's what burns you up.
But it's not true. I have no interest, either,
in seeing how many children I can father.
Ours are sufficient. I have no complaints.
565 The reason I married her was the most basic
motive anyone could have—so we
could be well off, live comfortably, and not
have any needs go unfulfilled. I know
"a friend in need is a friend indeed" but when
570 you're poor friends fade away fast. I married her
so I could raise my children in a style
appropriate to my family background, make
new brothers for them, treat them just the same
as those I have with you: and thanks to me
575 we'll be one big happy family!
Why do you need children? But I gain
if I can benefit the ones now living
by means of children who are still to come.
My plans weren't so bad, were they, wouldn't you say?

532 Love literally, "Aphrodite," the goddess who inspired sexual
desire. (Translator's note)

You would if you weren't sexually jealous. But   580
women have gotten to such a point that you
think if your sex life's good, then everything
is perfect; but a problem in that area
makes you turn the best things people have
into a battleground. There should have been   585
some other way for children to be born,
so there would be no women. In that case
men would be a carefree, happy race.

CHORUS.
Jason, your presentation was elegant.
But even though I'm contradicting you   590
I think your betrayal of your wife was wrong.

MEDEA.
I'm quite different from most people. I
think someone who does wrong, but who is slick
at speaking, gets the greatest blame. Someone
who boasts that he can always cover up   595
criminal actions with convincing words
is capable of anything. And yet
he's not so smart. Don't you come to me
with your nice getup, your deceptive speech.
A single word from me will lay you flat.   600
If you're not a coward, why marry in secret?
Why not tell the ones you love so much?

JASON.
Oh, sure! If I *had* told you of my plans,
why, you'd have jumped right on the bandwagon!
You, who can't let go of your rage even now!   605

MEDEA.
That wasn't what held you back. You're getting old.
Your unconventional marriage was starting to look
bizarre in the public eye: not good for a star.

JASON.
Just get this: it wasn't for a woman
that I made this royal marriage alliance.   610
I'm trying to help you, as I said before,
and father children, offspring to my own,
noble offspring to keep my line secure.

MEDEA.
Security like that I do not want.
That kind of money has too high a price!   615

JASON.
You know how you can change, and have more sense?
Stop looking at good luck as if it were bad;
stop agonizing when you should be glad.

MEDEA.
Go ahead, gloat: you've got your security.
I'm homeless now. I have to leave this place.   620

JASON.
The choice was yours. You can't blame anyone else.

MEDEA.
Of course! I married and abandoned *you*.

JASON.
You made terrible threats against the king.

MEDEA.
    Soon I'm going to be a threat to you.

JASON.
625   I'm not going to discuss these things any more.
    But if you want a little financial support
    for the children and yourself, just say the word.
    I'm ready to give it with an open hand.
    I have friends who can help you; I'll write them.
630   You're crazy if you don't accept. Give up
    your anger. You have everything to gain.

MEDEA.
    I'll take nothing from your friends! Nothing
    from you! Don't you offer me a cent!
    I won't let a criminal buy me off!

JASON.
635   Well, I tried to help you and the kids,
    God knows. But being nice to you's no good.
    You stubbornly push away people on your side
    and only make things worse for yourself.

                                     [Exit Jason.]

MEDEA.   Go on!
    Seized by lust, no doubt, you suddenly think
640   how long you're dawdling far from your new bride.
    Happy honeymoon! But perhaps—as God's
    my witness—you'll wish you'd never married!

CHORUS.
    When love comes on too strong, too much,
    it brings no honor, makes no one
645   look good. But nothing is so sweet
    when it goes right. Goddess of love,
    don't wound me with your golden bow
    and arrows dripping with desire.[2]

    What I want is sensible love,
650   the best the gods can give. No lust
    which drives me into a stranger's bed,
    brings arguments which never end.
    Look carefully at marriages;
    leave the peaceful ones alone.

655   My home, my country! May I never be
    a refugee, whose life drags on,
    dependent on others, miserable,

---

[2]This choral song reflects the ancient attitude towards erotic love, which was seen as a kind of frenzy sent by a god on an individual rather than as an expression of the individual self. This passion was depicted as dangerous, upsetting, undesirable rather than pleasurable and fulfilling. This song can be understood as referring both to Medea's passion for Jason and to Jason's involvement with the princess, suggesting that it was desire for her that drove him from Medea. Jason says, however (609–13) that his motive was security, not passion. (Translator's note)

pitied by all—intolerable!
I'd rather die, and end such a life!
No fate is worse than losing your home.   660
I don't say this from hearsay; I
have seen it. Medea, you've endured
the worst of trials, yet no one
consoles you. I will never respect
a man who closes his heart to a friend.   665
Let him die alone, unloved, unmourned!

    [Enter Aegeus.]

AEGEUS.
    Medea! God be with you! There is no
    more gratifying greeting between old friends.

MEDEA.
    God be with you, Aegeus, Pandion's son!
    Where do you come from, visiting this place?   670

AEGEUS.
    I come from Apollo's ancient oracle.

MEDEA.
    Why did you go to consecrated Delphi?

AEGEUS.
    To find out how I can become a father.

MEDEA.
    Good Lord! You have no children, at your age?

AEGEUS.
    No children. That's the will of God, it seems.   675

MEDEA.
    But you are married, right?

AEGEUS.   I have a wife.

MEDEA.
    What did Apollo say to you about children?

AEGEUS.
    Something too hard for a man to figure out.

MEDEA.
    Would it be all right for me to hear what it was?

AEGEUS.
    Of course—intelligence is just what's needed.   680

MEDEA.
    Well, what did he say? Tell me!

AEGEUS.   Not
    to uncork the wine in my big bottle.

MEDEA.   Till
    you did something, or reached some place?

AEGEUS.   Not till
    I came to my own home again.

MEDEA.   Then why
    are you coming this way? It's not on your route.   685

AEGEUS.
    You've heard of Pittheus, King of Troezen?

MEDEA.
    Yes—Pelops' son. They say he's very pious.

AEGEUS.
    I want to ask his advice about these words.

MEDEA.

He's a wise man, knows all about such things.

AEGEUS.

690   And he's the closest of my foreign friends.

MEDEA.

Well, good luck. I hope you get what you want.

AEGEUS.

Wait—why are you weeping? And so pale?

MEDEA.

Aegeus, my husband's the cruellest of all to me!

AEGEUS.

What's this? You're unhappy? Tell me all about it.

MEDEA.

695   I've done nothing to him, but he betrays me.

AEGEUS.

By doing what? Be more specific, please.

MEDEA.

He's made another woman mistress of his house.

AEGEUS.

Surely he didn't do such an awful thing!

MEDEA.

He did. He cares nothing for his former wife.

AEGEUS.

700   Did he fall in love, or just get tired of you?

MEDEA.

A powerful love made him turn out false to us.

AEGEUS.

Well, if he's as bad as you say, forget him.

MEDEA.

It's power he's in love with, a royal marriage.

AEGEUS.

He married a king's daughter? Tell me more.

MEDEA.

705   His father-in-law is Creon, King of Corinth.

AEGEUS.

Then I can see why you're so unhappy, Medea.

MEDEA.

I'm done for! I'm even banished from this land!

AEGEUS.

Another blow! Who's sending you away?

MEDEA.

Creon wants to drive me out of Corinth.

AEGEUS.

710   And Jason lets this happen? It's an outrage!

MEDEA.

He *says* he doesn't agree, but forces himself
to bear it like a man. At your feet
I ask, I beg you, plead with you, oh please
take pity on me in my suffering!
715   Don't let me perish as a refugee!
Take me in—to your country, to your home!
If you do this, I pray the gods may grant
your wish to father children and die happy.
You don't know what luck you've found today.

I'll make you fertile! I'm the one will end   720
your childlessness! I know certain ways . . .[3]

AEGEUS.

I have good reason to help you, Medea. First,
God blesses those who aid the needy. Next,
you bring good news about my future sons.
(Regarding that I'm utterly good for nothing.)   725
Here's what I'll do. If you come to my land
it's only right I should help you out, and I will.
But this much I must also tell you: I
will not help you get out of here. If you
come to my house, you'll stay there unmolested.   730
I won't hand you over to anyone.
Just get out of this place by yourself.
In a foreign land I don't want to offend.

MEDEA.

Fine. Now if you give me your word on this
you'll have given me everything I want.   735

AEGEUS.

What's the problem? You mean you don't trust me?

MEDEA.

I trust *you*. But Creon, and Pelias' family
are my enemies. When they come after me,
and send you threats, if you haven't sworn by the gods
you might make friends with them. But if you're held   740
by firm agreements, you won't let me go.
I'm weak, and all alone, while they control
vast wealth, and power, and a royal house.

AEGEUS.

What thorough advance planning you display!
Well, if you want me to, I won't refuse.   745
In fact, it's safer for me if I have
some kind of excuse to show your enemies,
safer for you too. By what shall I swear?

MEDEA.

Swear by Earth, and Sun my father's father;
add the whole huge race of gods as well.   750

AEGEUS.

To do or not do what? Speak.

MEDEA.   Never
cast me out yourself from your land; never,
if one of my enemies tries to drag me off,
let me go voluntarily, so long as you live.

AEGEUS.

By Earth, by Sun's holy light, by all the gods,   755
I swear I will comply with what you say.

---

[3]The obvious reference is to Medea's knowledge of magic, but she is also suggesting her own proven fertility. According to other sources Medea did marry Aegeus after arriving in Athens, but rather than help him in his quest for progeny she attempted to murder his son Theseus. (Translator's note)

MEDEA.

Good. And if you break this oath, what then?

AEGEUS.

I suffer the fate of a man who defies the gods.

MEDEA.

Be happy, proceed on your journey. All is well.
760 I'll come to you as quickly as I can,
when I've done what I intend and got what I want.

[Exit Aegeus.]

CHORUS.

May Hermes conduct
you safe to your home,
and may you achieve
765 what you're hoping for,
since to me you seem
a noble man.

MEDEA.

O God! Divine Justice! Glorious Sun!
Now I will triumph over my enemies.
770 I've taken the first step upon the road.
Now I know I'll pay my enemies back,
since this man, just when all was lost, appeared
like a safe harbor protecting all my schemes.
As soon as I get to Athens' citadel
775 I'll moor myself to him and hold him fast.
Now I can tell you everything I'll do.
Listen to me. I don't think you will laugh.
    I'll send one of my servants to Jason, ask him
nicely, please won't he come here and see me.
780 He'll come. I'll wheedle him with tender words,
agree with him completely: he was right
to make his royal marriage, abandon me.
It was a wonderful plan, so well thought out.
I'll ask that my children stay. Oh, I don't intend
785 to leave them in a hostile land, so my foes
can have their way with them. No. This
is my way to kill another child: the king's.
I'll send them holding presents in their hands,
gifts for the bride—a delicate dress, a crown
790 of finely beaten gold. If she just touches
this loveliness, lays it on her skin,
she will die the most appalling death,
and so will anyone who touches her—
so deadly the poison in which I dip my gifts.
795 Now I have to break off my strategy . . .
oh God! What a thing I have to do after this!
I'm going to kill my children! There's no one
who can take them away from me—save them from
    me.
Then, after I destroy Jason's whole world,
800 I'll leave this place, escaping from my sweetest
babies' murder—an awful, God-cursed act!
I won't stand for my enemies mocking me!
    Wait. What good is there for me in life?
I have no place to go, no family,

no refuge from my pain. When I left home,   805
that's when I made my big mistake, seduced
by a Greek man's words. But with God's help he'll pay!
He'll never see again, alive, the sons
he had with me. And he won't spawn new ones
from his new bride: she has to die, badly,   810
as she deserves, poisoned by my drugs.
No one should think I'm unimportant, weak
or lazy. Quite the opposite—kind
to my friends, implacable to my enemies.[4]
To such a character comes greatest fame.   815

CHORUS.

You have shared your thoughts with me, and I
want to help you, but still obey the law.
I'm telling you: you must not do these things!

MEDEA.

There's no other way. Of course you can't approve.
But you're not going through this pain: I am.   820

CHORUS.

Woman, will you have the heart to kill your children?

MEDEA.

To cause my husband the greatest possible pain.

CHORUS.

But *you* will be the most unhappy woman!

MEDEA.

Enough of these words! They stand between me and my
    plan.
[To the Nurse.] Go on, bring Jason here. I trust you
    completely.   825
Say nothing of what I have in mind, if you
are loyal to your mistress—and a woman.

[Exit Nurse.]

CHORUS.

Of old the Athenians prosper; the happy
descendants of blessed gods, they inhabit
a land which has never been pillaged. They feed   830
on glorious Wisdom; lightly they step
through the radiant air. It is there, people say,
the Muses conceived golden Harmony.

Beside the beautiful river of Cephisus,
Aphrodite breathes sweet gentle breezes   835
over the fertile savannahs. Wreathing
a garland of roses in fragrant hair,
she sends Love to be a companion to Wisdom;
together they give all the blessings of life.

How can a sacred city, which gives   840
sanctuary to friends, take you,
killer of children? You will infect

---

[4]This creed, quite different from the Golden Rule, was the accepted standard of Greek male behavior; Medea is here explicitly adopting a masculine code of honor. (Translator's note)

every thing that you touch. Just think
what a murder you'll carry out—
845 to gash and hack your children! No!
On my knees, I beg you, please,
somehow, anyhow, don't kill your sons!

Where will you get the courage, when
you come close to that awful deed?
850 Won't your heart and hand flinch back?
Looking them in the face, will you
carry out your role and strike,
shedding no tears? When they plead for their lives,
will you bathe your hands in innocent blood?
855 No! You won't be able to do it!

[*Enter Jason.*]

JASON.
You sent for me. I came. Though you are angry
at me, I'll always grant you this: I'll listen.
What new thing do you want from me now, woman?
MEDEA.
Jason, I beg you to forgive me for
860 the things I said. It's only right for you
to put up with my temper—I've helped you out.
Why, I've even taken myself to task
and said "You fool! Why are you crazy? Mad
at those who only wish you well! You've made
865 the ruler of this land your enemy—
your husband too, who's doing his best by us
by marrying the princess, making sons,
brothers to ours. Won't you give up your rage?
Why do you take it so hard? The gods direct
870 all well. Don't you have children? Don't you know
we're going into exile, and are short
of friends?" Thinking like this, I realized
how totally unreasonable I had been,
how useless all my furious anger was.
875 Now I agree with you. I think you're right
to make this merger for us. I was wrong
I should have shared in all your strategies,
shared in your marriage, standing by the bed,
taking pleasure in your bride with you.
880 However, we women are as we are: I
won't say we're bad. But you men should not share
our mistakes, answer our foolishness
with more stupidity. I've let that go.
I admit I was wrong before, but now
885 I've done so much more careful reasoning.[5]
    Children! Come here! Leave the house.

[*Enter Children with Tutor.*]
                            Now kiss
your father, speak to him with me. Think
of him as a friend, not an enemy,
together with your mother. We've made peace.
The anger's all gone. Take his right hand. [*Screams.*]
    Ohhh!   890
[*Recovers.*] I'm thinking awful things could always happen.
Children, all your lives long, will you stretch
your sweet hands out to me like this? Poor me—
the tears just come. I'm superstitious.
Giving up my anger towards your father   895
after such a long time makes me cry.
CHORUS.
My eyes too are filled with tears. May no
worse thing take place than what is happening now.
JASON.
Good for you, woman. I have no complaints.
It's natural for a woman to get annoyed   900
when her man smuggles in another wife.
But your heart's changed for the better—though
it did take time to see my plan was right.
Now you're acting like a sensible woman.
Children, your father has carefully provided   905
security for you—with the gods' help, of course.
I foresee in time to come you'll be
the leading men of Corinth—along with your brothers.
Just grow up. Your father will take care
of all the rest—with the gods' help, of course.   910
I want to see you coming to adolescence
strong, to triumph over my enemies.
[*To Medea.*] You there—why do you have tears in your
    eyes?
Why do you turn away your pallid face?
Aren't you pleased with what I said just now?   915
MEDEA.
It's nothing. I was just thinking about these boys.
JASON.
Oh, cheer up! I will take good care of them.
MEDEA.
I'll do that. I've no doubt of what you say.
Women are nurturers, always ready to weep.
JASON.
Why do you make such a fuss about these kids?   920
MEDEA.
I gave birth to them. When you prayed just now
that they might live, tenderness rushed on me,
uncertainty if that will ever be.
    But the reason I asked you to come,
what I wanted to say, I've covered some;   925
now I'll continue. Since the king sees fit
to send us away—I too think this is best,
I know it very clearly—not stay on,
an obstacle to you and the royal ones.
I seem to be quite dangerous to them.   930

[5]Many of Medea's comments here are not lies, but true in a different sense from the way she knows Jason will understand her. Here
her "careful reasoning" has made her realize that she was wrong to
reveal her anger previously. (Translator's note)

So I will sail off into exile, but
you should bring the children up yourself.
Ask Creon not to send them away from here.

JASON.

I don't know if I'll succeed; I'll try.

MEDEA.

935   Then order your wife to ask her father too
not to send the children away from here.

JASON.

All right—I'm pretty sure I can persuade her.

MEDEA.

You will, if she's a woman like the rest.
I'll also take a part in this attempt:
940   I'll send her gifts—the most perfect things that earth
possesses. The children will take a delicate dress,
a crown of finely beaten gold. At once!
Let one of the servants bring the treasure here.
She'll have so many reasons to rejoice—
945   you, the best of men, to sleep with her,
and now the ornaments my father's father
Helios gave to his own progeny.
Pick up these presents, children, in your hands,
and give them to the happy royal bride.
950   She won't be able to find fault with them.

JASON.

What? You're crazy to let these out of your hands!
You think the royal house is deficient in dresses?
Or golden jewelry? Keep them, don't give them away.
If my new wife thinks I'm worth anything,
955   she'll put my wishes ahead of material wealth.

MEDEA.

Don't tell me no. They say gifts can persuade
the gods themselves. To human beings they
have much more power than a thousand words.
Her star is rising, God is on her side,
960   she's young and in control. I wouldn't trade
just gold, but life, to keep my children out
of exile. Children! Carry these rich presents
to the new wife of your father—she's
my mistress too. Hurry! Ask her not
965   to send you away from here. Put the gifts
into her own hands. It's very important—
make sure she herself receives them. Go,
as fast as you can. I pray you may fare well
and come back bringing news I long to hear.

[Exeunt children, Jason, Tutor.]

CHORUS.

970   Now there is no longer hope for the children—
none! They are already walking towards death.
The new bride—unlucky!—will pick up disaster,
a curse from the golden tiara. Accepting
that loveliness, she will position Death
975   with her own hands on her shining blond hair.

That heavenly beauty, the glittering charm
of the golden dress will seduce her to try

the crown, so carefully worked, as she decks
herself as a bride—for a wedding in Hell.
What a trap she is falling into, accursed,   980
devoted to death. There is no way out.

God help you, Jason! You have made
a terrible royal marriage alliance.
You don't know it, but you've brought
an awful death on your wife and sons,   985
not even knowing what's going on!
But most of all I share your pain,
unhappy mother of the children—
the ones whom you will slaughter, since
your husband left you, wrongly. Now   990
he sleeps in another woman's bed.

[Enter Tutor and children.]

TUTOR.

Mistress! The children are set free from exile!
The princess was delighted with the gifts:
a reconciliation on their part
                     What's this?
Why are you just standing there amazed?   995

MEDEA.

Oh no!

TUTOR.

That cry is out of tune with my good news.

MEDEA.

No! No!!

TUTOR.

Maybe I don't
quite understand some part of the news? Have I   1000
made some mistake? It seemed like wonderful news.

MEDEA.

You've made your announcement. Fault's not yours.

TUTOR.

Why are you staring at the ground, in tears?

MEDEA.

Old man, I have my reasons. Gods have made
their evil machinations. So have I.   1005

TUTOR.

Cheer up! Because of your children, you'll come home.

MEDEA.

I'll send them home before me—damned as I am!

TUTOR.

You're not the only one to lose your kids.
You're human. Have to take disasters lightly.

MEDEA.

Yes. I will. Now go into the house.   1010
Get ready what they need on any day.

[Exit Tutor.]

Children, children! You have a place to go,
a house, a city. Leaving me behind,
without your mother you will live there always.

1015 I am going to another land,
exiled, before I can enjoy you, watch
you grow, adorn your brides, prepare for you
the bridal bed and lift the wedding torch . . .
it was not for this I raised you, children!
1020 not for this I struggled and took the pain,
twisting under the cruel spasms of birth.
I had such plans for you once—I thought that you
would take good care of me when I got old,
and when I died would lay me out properly—
1025 what every person hopes will happen. Now
that pleasant expectation is all gone.
Parted from you, I'll live an awful life,
filled with bitter memories. And you
won't see your mother any more; you'll go
1030 to quite another kind of life. Oh God!
Children, why are you looking at me like that?
Why are you smiling at me with your last smile?
What shall I do? My heart is giving way
as I look into my children's shining eyes.
1035 I could never do it! Goodbye, plans!
I'll take the children with me out of this land!
To make their father suffer, why should I
butcher my babies? I'll suffer twice as much!
Goodbye, my plans!
                    What's happening to me?
1040 Let my enemies get away scot-free
and earn their laughter? Is that what I want?
I have to do it. What a fool I was
putting a poultice of soft words on my heart!
Go into the house, children. If anyone here
1045 thinks it not right to attend my sacrifice,
that is your business. My hand will not fail.
        No! You cannot do this thing! You can't
Let them go, woman! Spare your children!
They can live on with you and make you happy.
1050   In the name of those punishers who dwell below
in Hell, I swear that this will never happen:
I will not deliver up my children,
victims to my enemies' abuse.
The deed is done. There's no way out.
1055 Right now the bride is putting on her crown
and melting in her dress: I see her, now.
I'm walking down the hardest road of all;
the road I send them on is harder still.
I want to speak to them. Children, give,
1060 give me your hands for Mother to hold. Oh
darling hands, and mouths I love so much,
straight bodies, and aristocratic faces!
I pray you both fare well—but not here. Here
is where your father threw it all away.
1065 How sweet you are to touch! Such tender skin,
such gentle babies' breath! Go, go away!
I can't keep looking at you any more.
The pain is stronger than I am. Now I know
what an awful thing it is I'm going to do.

But rage is stronger than this understanding— 1070
rage, the greatest cause of human pain.
CHORUS.
    I've spent time in careful thinking,
    arguments too, trying to know
    more than is right for a woman's mind.
    We too have gifts which live with us 1075
    and make us wise. Not all, perhaps
    but some of us do seek the truth.
    Women are not fools.
    And to this verdict I have come:
    those who have borne no children, who 1080
    know nothing at all of parenting
    are much better off than those who do.
    Are children a curse or a blessing?
    The childless never debate the question.
    Their lack of experience saves them pain. 1085
    But I see those with children at home,
    those sweet offshoots, worn out with care.
    They must figure out how to raise them right,
    how to get them enough to live on. Next,
    they can't know whether they're good or bad, 1090
    the ones they're spending that effort on.
    But worst of all the problems is this:
    suppose we secure a decent living,
    the children are healthy, they grow in strength,
    they turn out to have good character, too. 1095
    But if a god decides it, they're gone!
    Death carries off their bodies to Hell.
    For the gods to add this worst pain of all
    to all the others we humans have—
    what good does it do? Why bear a child? 1100
MEDEA.
    Friends, I've been standing here for a long time, waiting
    to learn how events would turn out at the palace.
    Now I see one of Jason's men coming here.
    How hard he pants! Must have some awful news.

[Enter Messenger.]

MESSENGER.
    Medea! You've done the most awful deed, illegal, 1105
    unholy! Go! Flee! You have to consider
    how to make your escape, by land or sea!
MEDEA.
    What has happened that I should take to flight?
MESSENGER.
    She's dead—the princess! Just this minute. Creon
    too, her father. Your magic poisons did it. 1110
MEDEA.
    Wonderful words! From now on I'll count you
    among my friends, who do good things for me.
MESSENGER.
    What are you saying? Are you sane, or mad?
    You've attacked the royal family,
    yet hearing this you're pleased and not afraid? 1115

MEDEA.
I have plenty to say in response to you.
But please, first tell me all, my friend. Don't hurry.
How did they die? You'll give me twice the pleasure
if their deaths were utterly horrible.

MESSENGER.

1120 When your two children arrived along with their
        father
and entered the rooms of the newly married pair,
we were all pleased, we servants who were pained
by your unhappiness. Immediately
the story went buzzing through our ears that you
1125 and Jason had settled your previous bitter feud.
Someone kissed the hand of one of the children,
another stroked a blond head. I myself
followed the children to the women's quarters,
I was so delighted. Till she saw
1130 your boys, the mistress—the one we look to now
instead of you—was casting eager eyes
on Jason. Then she went pale, and shut her eyes,
and turned her head away; she was offended,
seeing them. Your husband tried to calm
1135 her feelings, soothe the young girl's anger, saying:
"You mustn't resent the ones I care about.
Leave off this pouting. Turn your head around.
You must love the ones your husband loves.
Won't you accept these gifts, and ask your father
1140 to cancel his order banishing these boys?
You'll do it, won't you, as a favor to me?"
She said she would—as soon as she saw the gifts.
She exclaimed to him about their beauty, and
before her father and the children left
1145 the rooms, she took the delicate dress and wrapped
herself up in it. Placing the golden garland
on her curls, she arranged her hair. The mirror
showed her own dead image laughing at her.
Got up then, and walked across the room,
1150 prancing lightly on her little white feet,
so pleased with her presents, glancing back
to see just how the dress hung down behind.
But then there was a terrible sight to see.
Her color went; she staggered; body all
1155 convulsed, almost fell down, collapsed in her chair.
An old maidservant, thinking one of the gods
had sent a frenzy on her, called "God bless!"
But when she saw the white foam on her lips,
saw her eyes twisted back into her skull,
1160 saw her bloodless face, another cry
came out—a scream of terror and despair.
Off to the father's rooms ran one, another
to the new husband, telling the bride's collapse.
Whole house was thundering with running feet.
1165 It all happened fast: a runner would have turned

and been close to the finish line, when the poor girl stirred,
opening her clenchedshut eyes, and moaned.
Two kinds of pain were making war on her:
the golden crown was sending out a stream
of eerie hungry fire around her head.   1170
The delicate dress—the gift your children brought—
was lapping up her delicate flesh. She jumps
up from her chair and bursts into flame; she tries
to run away, tossing her head, her hair,
pulling, tearing the garland off—but it   1175
was a manacle of gold, it held on tight,
and when she shook her head, the fire roared up
more brightly than before. She crashes down;
the enemy wins; she's hard to recognize—
only a father would know that she was his.   1180
You couldn't see her eyes, melted into her face;
her pretty face itself was gone; her scalp
was oozing blood like lava seething flame.
The way a pine exudes its viscous tears,
the flesh was dripping off her bones: the poison   1185
had its teeth deep into her. We all
were terrified to touch the corpse: we took
a lesson from what had happened to her.
                                              And then
her father, unaware of this disaster,
comes in suddenly, sees the corpse, kneels down   1190
sobbing and gathers it into his arms, kissing,
talking to it: "My poor baby, what
demon has done this to you? Who's made me
into an orphan, an empty tomb, without you?
Oh God, I want to die with you, my child!"   1195
But then he quit his moaning and lamenting,
and tried to straighten up his body, but
the delicate dress was clutching him, like shoots
of ivy crawling over laurel. Then
there was an awful wrestling-match: he tried   1200
to rise, she grappled, pulled him down. He struggled
hard; she peeled the flesh from his old bones.
After a while, he had no more strength; he gasped
his last, extinguished by the power. Now
daughter and aged father lie together: 1205
this is an event which longs for tears.
    I'll say nothing about your situation.
You yourself will know how to find a way out.
This is not the first time I've understood
that everything people do is just a dream.   1210
I'd even say that those who seem to know
the most, who handle words so well, it's those
who get the greatest blame. Real happiness
belongs to no man. Sure, you slather on
a coating of good luck, and someone's life   1215
seems so much better than another's. But
who gets secure good fortune. No one can.

CHORUS.
 It seems a god has taken Jason's measure,
 fitting him with disaster—as he deserves.
1220 It's you we're sorry for, miserable princess,
 heading down to Hades for marrying him.
MEDEA.
 It's all decided, friends. As soon as I
 can kill my children, I will leave this land.
 I won't waste time and hand them over to
1225 some other, more sadistic murderer.
 They have to die. And since they must,
 it's I who'll kill them, I who gave them life.
 Medea, put your armor on. What
 are you waiting for? The thing that you must do
1230 is awful, but you have no choice. Come on!
 Here's your heroic, wretched hand. Pick up
 the sword. Pick it up. You're walking towards the end,
 but it's the starting-point of a painful life.
 Don't be a coward. Don't think about the children,
1235 how sweet they are, how you gave birth to them—
 Forget about them for just a few minutes now;
 later you can weep for them. Although
 you're going to kill them, they were sweet, were yours—
 I am a woman whom the gods have cursed!

           [Exit Medea.]

CHORUS.
1240 O Mother Earth! O glittering rays
 of the sun, look down and examine a woman
 who is destroyed, and destroying, before
 she can lift up her hand to slaughter her children.
 To do it is just like killing herself.
1245 They are young shoots from your own famous line;
 it is fearful for offspring of gods to be slain!
 O heavenly light, prevent her! Expel
 from the house this unhappy, murderous Fury
 whose longing for vengeance comes straight out of
  Hell!

1250 All that labor of raising the children
 all wasted, all worthless! You gave birth in vain,
 you loved them for nothing! Then was it for this
 you sailed here, defeating the sea's clashing rocks?
 Unhappy Medea, why let this resentment
1255 take over your spirit? Is murder the answer?
 To pour out the blood of your blood on the earth
 leaves a poisonous stain which can never be clean,
 and into the life of a butcher the gods
 will orchestrate an echoing pain.

 [Children scream within.]

CHORUS.
1260 A scream! Do you hear?
 The children! A scream!

CHILDREN.
 She wants to kill us![6]
 What can we do?
CHILDREN.
 I don't know, brother!
 There's no way out!   1265
CHORUS.
 Let's go in and stop
 her killing the children!
 Now! Come on![7]
CHILDREN.
 Help us, for God's sake!
CHILDREN.
 The knife's at my throat!   1270
CHORUS.
 Only one woman has done such a thing,
 killing her own dear children, and she
 was insane: when the wife of Zeus drove her out
 of her house and into the wilderness, Ino
 went raving out to the shoreline, and stepped 1275
 over a cliff to split on the rocks.
 In her arms she carried her own two babes
 She murdered them, but she died with them.
 Can something more awful than that take place?
 Marriage is so full of pain for a woman 1280
 its evils reach out to touch others too.

[Enter Jason.]

JASON.
 Women! You there, standing near the house,
 is Medea, that criminal, still inside? or has
 she already taken to flight? She'll have to hide
 beneath the earth, or lift her body on wings 1285
 and fly into the sky, to get away
 from paying the penalty to the royal house.
 Does she think she can kill the leaders of our land
 and just sail out of here, safe and secure?
 Yet it's not her I'm concerned about, but my children. 1290
 Those that she attacked will pay her back,
 but I came here to save my children's lives.
 The king's family might take out on them
 the revenge their mother's ungodly crime deserves.

[6]Children appear and even speak onstage in Euripides' plays—Alcestis' son, for example, delivers a lament over his mother's body. Given the limited number of actors used in Greek drama, most scholars assume that child actors did play the roles but did not speak, that adult actors spoke their parts. Although Medea's children are certainly old enough to speak, they have no lines until these desperate cries, which were probably spoken by an actor within the stage-building (presumably the actor playing Medea). (Translator's note)

[7]In the non-illusionistic Greek theater, the chorus almost never intervenes in the action, even at moments like this, when not to do so seems absurd. (Translator's note)

CHORUS.

1295   Jason, poor man, you don't even know how far
you've marched into misery. You wouldn't have said
      what you did.

JASON.

What's that? You mean she wants to kill me too?

CHORUS.

Your children are murdered. Their own mother did it.

JASON.

Oh, no! What are you saying? Your words destroy me.

CHORUS.

1300   You must believe it: your children are dead and gone.

JASON.

Where did she kill them? Out here, or in the house?

CHORUS.

If you open the doors, you'll see your children's bodies.

JASON.

Hurry up, slaves! Open up the locks! Shatter
the bolts! I want to see both parts of this crime:

1305   my children, dead, and her—I'll get revenge!

[*Medea appears above the palace in the Chariot of the Sun.*]

MEDEA.

Why are you rushing around and storming the doors?
Looking for your dead children and the one who killed
      them?
Give yourself a rest. If you have something
you need to say to me, just say it. But

1310   you will not lay a hand on me. The Sun,
my father's father, gave me this chariot.
It protects me from my enemies.

JASON.

You're disgusting! hated by the gods,
by me, by every human being, you

1315   dared to use a sword on your own sons.
How can you stay alive, see the sun and earth,
after you've done the most ungodly acts?
God damn you! Now I know you, but I didn't
back when I took you out of that backward land

1320   and brought you home to Greece, an evil thing,
a traitor to her father and fatherland.
The gods have set on me the punishment
which you deserved for killing your own brother
and then embarking on our beautiful ship.

1325   And that was only the beginning. Next,
after marrying me and bearing my children,
you murdered them, and why? Because of sex.
No Greek woman would dare to do such a thing,
and yet instead I chose to marry you.

1330   I made a contract with an enemy,
not a woman—a vicious lioness
more savage than the monster Scylla, who
devours ships in the Tyrrhenian Sea.
Enough! No use to gnaw at you with insults—

1335   you have no sense of shame that can be touched.

You criminal, child-killer, go to hell!
I have to weep for my own fate. I won't
ever get any profit from my bride.
I've lost my children, the ones I bore and raised.
I'll never be able to see them alive again.   134

MEDEA.

I could provide a very long rebuttal
to what you've said, but there's no reason.
God the Father knows what I have done.
He also knows what you have done. There was
no way you were going to lead a happy life   134
after disregarding our marriage and mocking me.
Not the princess either, or the father-in-law,
were about to get rid of me without paying a price.
Go right ahead and call me a lioness,
the monster Scylla in the Tyrrhenian Sea.   135
I sank my claws in your heart—as you deserved.

JASON.

You feel it too; you share the pain.

MEDEA.   You're right.
But it's worth the pain for you not to laugh at me.

JASON.

Poor children! What a bad mother you got for yourselves!

MEDEA.

Poor children! Your father infected you with death.   135

JASON.

You can't say it was my hand that killed them.

MEDEA.

No—your arrogance, and your new marriage.

JASON.

Because of my *marriage* you decided to kill them?

MEDEA.

Do you think that's such a small thing to a woman?

JASON.

To a sane one, yes. But you turn everything bad.   136

MEDEA.

This will torment you: your sons are dead and gone.

JASON.

They're not! They'll come to take revenge on you.

MEDEA.

No—the gods know who started all this pain.

JASON.

What they know is how revolting you are.

MEDEA.

Go on, hate me: I despise your pretty attacks.   136

JASON.

As I do yours. But it's easy to stop all this.

MEDEA.

Oh, really? Wonderful. What should I do?

JASON.

Give me the children's bodies to mourn and bury.

MEDEA.

Never! I'm going to bury them myself,
far off, in the shrine of Hera on the cape,   137
so that no enemy can dig up the grave

and violate their bodies. In this land
I'll establish sacred rites to last forever,
recompense for their unholy death.

1375   I myself am off to Athens; there
I'll live with Aegeus, son of Pandion.
You will die badly, just as you deserve,
hit on the head by a piece of your ship the Argo.
You've seen the bitter result of your marriage to me.

JASON.
1380   May the children's Furies
get the justice
their blood demands,
destroying you!

MEDEA.
What god listens
1385   to one who lies
and breaks his word?

JASON.
You're a disgusting
killer of children!

MEDEA.
Go to the house
1390   and bury your wife.

JASON.
I'll go, deprived
of my two sons.

MEDEA.
You don't feel it yet.
Wait till you're old.

JASON.
1395   My dearest children!

MEDEA.
Dear to their mother,
not to you.

JASON.
So why did you kill them?

MEDEA.
To make you suffer.

JASON.
I want to kiss   1400
my babies' lips.

MEDEA.
Now you talk to them.
Now you love them.
Then you ignored them.

JASON.
Please, in the gods' names,   1405
just let me touch
my children's skin.

MEDEA.
No. Your words are worthless.

                         [Exit Medea.]

JASON.
God! Do you hear
how I'm pushed aside?   1410
What this loathsome monster,
this killer of children,
is doing to me?
I'll do what I can
to mourn my children,   1415
asking the gods
to see how you killed them,
then stopped me from touching,
from burying them.
Now that I see them murdered by you,   1420
I wish they had never even been born!

CHORUS.
Zeus in Olympus
has much in store.
Gods do their work
unpredictably.   1425
What we don't expect,
the gods bring about,
and what seems sure,
doesn't happen after all.
And that is how this story turned out.   1430

TOPICS FOR CRITICAL THINKING AND WRITING

📖 THE PLAY ON THE PAGE

1. The classical scholar Gilbert Murray once summed up Medea and Jason thus: "Love to her is the whole world, to him it is a stale memory." How adequate is this summary? Explain.

2. Another classical scholar, Denys L. Page, in the preface to his edition of the Greek text of the play (1938), says:

> Here, indeed, for the first time in the Greek theatre, the power of the drama lies rather in the characters than in their actions. Medea's emotions are far more moving than her revenge; Jason's state of mind is more interest-

ing than his calamity. The murder of children, caused by jealousy and anger against their father, is mere brutality: if it moves us at all, it does so towards incredulity and horror. . . . But the emotions of the woman whose love turned to hatred, and equally those of the man who loves no longer, represent something eternal and unchangeable in human nature; here we find, what in great drama we must always seek, the universal in this particular.   (xiv–xv)

To what extent do you agree or disagree? Explain.

3. Denys L. Page, again in the preface to his edition, says (p. xiv):

> The heart of the play is the quarrel between Medea and Jason, the deserted wife and the deserting husband. It must be clearly understood that the poet does not attempt to solve the problem which they propound. The fantastic conclusion of his play—child-murder, dragon-chariot—is an end and not an answer. This is no longer a part of life, but of myth and magic; no longer about a woman, but about a barbarian sorceress.

Your view of Page's comments?

4. In popular legend and in a later play by Seneca, Medea is a cold-blooded murderer. Do you think Euripides's Medea is sufficiently human, or is she a monstrous freak? Explain. (One way to think about the issue is to ask yourself if there is any way to make sense of her murder of the children.)

5. Jason offers several arguments defending his conduct. For instance, he suggests that he has Medea's welfare in mind, in addition to his own. Do you think he is hypocritical? Or sincere but stupid? Or what? By the way, do you find any of his arguments convincing? If so, which ones?

6. Aristotle found the scene with Aegeus irrelevant. Do you agree, or do you think it serves some useful function(s)? Explain.

7. Do you think Euripides in effect is saying, "Life is sometimes like this?" or is he implying that something should be done to improve the status of women in Greek society?

❦ THE PLAY ON THE STAGE

8. Here are three translations of the opening lines of the play, spoken by the Nurse. (The first, by Mary-Kay Gamel, is the version that we print in this book.) Do the different versions require different styles of acting? If you were an actor, which version would you use? Why? (*Note:* The second and third versions, more literal than the first, mentions by name the *Symplegades* ["clashing ones"], two dark blue rocks or islands near the entrance of the Black Sea. These rocks supposedly closed and crushed ships that tried to pass between them.)

> Oh how I wish that boat the Argo had never
> flown through the dark clashing rocks to Colchis'
> shore!
> I wish the pine that made it had never been felled
> in the groves of Thessaly! Wish the heroes sent
> for the Golden Fleece by Pelias never had rowed it!
> (TRANS. MARY-KAY GAMEL)

> If only the Argo, skimming its way among
> The blue Symplegades, had never reached
> The land of Colchis, nor the ax-hewn pine
> Been felled in Pelion's glen to furnish oars
> To put into the hands of warrior princes
> Whom Pelias urged to seek the Golden Fleece!
> (TRANS. SIMON GOLDFIELD)

> How I wish the Argo never had reached the land
> Of Colchis, skimming through the blue Symplegades,
> Nor ever had fallen in the glades of Pelion
> The smitten fir-tree to furnish oars for the hands
> Of heroes who in Pelias's name attempted
> The Golden Fleece!
> (TRANS. REX WARNER)

9. Here are three versions (lines 257–60) of part of Medea's speech comparing the sufferings of women with those of men. As with the preceding question, consider whether the translations require different styles of acting, and consider, too, which translation you would prefer to speak.

> Men say we live a lazy life at home
> while they must go to war—what fools they are!
> I'd rather face the enemy three times
> than undergo the pains of labor once.
> (TRANS. MARY-KAY GAMEL)

> They say we lead a life devoid of danger
> At home while they do battle with the spear,
> But they are wrong. I'd three times rather stand
> And face a line of shields than once give birth.
> (TRANS. SIMON GOLDFIELD)

> What they say of us is that we have a peaceful time
> Living at home, while they do the fighting in war.
> How wrong they are! I would very much rather stand
> Three times in the front of battle than bear one
> child.
> (TRANS. REX WARNER)

10. Choose one key scene that includes Medea and propose two opposed ways of staging it. (Consider blocking—the director's organization of movement on the stage—lighting, gestures, and, of course, emphases.)

11. What are some difficulties (or challenges) for an actor who plays Jason? Support your answer with references to specific scenes.

12. Start by listing Medea's major one-on-one scenes (with the Nurse, with Creon, etc.). Take two of these, and indicate how the actress playing Medea should do each scene. What specific instructions would you give the actress?

13. How would you clothe, block, and choreograph the Chorus?

14. Suppose that you are the set designer for a production of *Medea*. The theater seats three hundred (not twelve

thousand), and it is not open to the heavens; the stage is a traditional proscenium arrangement, and your budget is modest. Prepare an annotated sketch of a usable one-set design. (Consider the possibility of several acting levels, and the suggestions of walls and windows, and the need for one dominant entrance.) *Or* consider an open-air site on your campus—for instance, in front of a particular building—where the play might be staged during good weather. Why did you choose this site?

THE PLAY IN PERFORMANCE

We know that when *Medea* was first performed at the festival in Athens it won third prize, but we know nothing in particular about how the play was staged. Still, we can say a few things. Almost surely Medea's costume (including the headdress on her mask) marked her as a foreigner; paintings of Medea on vases, though admittedly of a slightly later date than Euripides's play, regularly show her wearing distinctive—"foreign"—clothing.

In some Greek plays it is not always clear when a character enters or exits, but there are no such problems in *Medea*, though it is not clear at what point Medea prepares the deadly gifts. Possibly she goes inside and poisons the gifts during the choral song that begins at line 828. Or perhaps the magic poison works only on her enemies, so she and her children can handle the gifts even though they are deadly. In any case, the robe was part of the traditional story, and it therefore caused no surprise. But an audience probably was surprised to learn that Medea herself kills the children. The Chorus seems to assume that the children will be killed by the Corinthians, in retaliation for bringing destruction to the princess and to Creon. And surely there is a surprise near the end of the play, when Medea appears above the palace, in a chariot of the sun. We have heard the children scream, and we have heard the Chorus talk of murder. Jason pounds at the doors, and presumably the audience expects the doors to open and the *eccyclema* (a wheeled platform) to roll out, revealing a tableau of dead bodies, perhaps presided over by Medea. Instead, Euripides uses the Greek theater's other theatrical machine, the *mechane* or crane. Medea in the chariot, hoisted from behind the scene-building, comes into view on the roof of the scene-building, and we get, in effect, a *dea ex machina*, a "goddess out of a machine." From this elevated position Medea confronts Jason for the last time, and we see—quite literally—the great gap between the two. With her last words, presumably the crane reverses its action, lowers her out of sight, and the Chorus exits.

Medea was enormously influential on later Western literature; it was widely quoted, and several important playwrights were moved to write their own plays on the subject, notably Seneca in Rome, Corneille in France, and Grillparzer in Germany. A film (1970) by Pier Passolini, with Maria Callas as Medea, was inspired by Euripides's play, and quoted a few lines, but it cannot by any means by considered a filmed version of the play. Somewhat similarly, a New York production of *Medea* by André Serban in 1972 put so little emphasis on the words—some of it was spoken (or, rather, shouted) in Greek—and so much emphasis on physical movement that it must be regarded as a work inspired by Euripides's play rather than as a production of it.

In the United States, the poet Robinson Jeffers did a very free translation that was performed with much acclaim in 1947, with Judith Anderson—a leading classical actress—in the title role. Anderson gave a performance in a somewhat old-fashioned, highly theatrical or melodramatic style, which she managed to bring off, in part because of her reputation and in part because it seemed appropriate to an ancient Greek tragedy. John Gielgud played Jason, in a colorless manner that suited the role and allowed Anderson to dominate the play. In 1982 the role was played by Zoe Caldwell—with Judith Anderson, age eighty-four, playing the Nurse. Caldwell emphasized Medea's sexuality, with a good deal of orgiastic writhing. Reviewers who remembered Anderson in the role tended to find Caldwell lacking in power.

In 1992 a London company, with Diana Rigg as Medea, achieved acclaim and came to New York in 1994, where it received enthusiastic reviews. Rigg, her hair pulled back into a single braid, wore a blood red dress—symbolism obvious enough—but she emphasized not the sexuality of the role but the intellectuality. It was evident that Medea was the smartest person on the stage, and the ingenuity that she had used to help Jason win the Golden Fleece now was turned into an effort to destroy him, not by killing him but by killing his new wife and his children, so that he had nothing left to live for. Rigg was highly praised, but the set aroused almost as much praise. Two bronze façades, made of rusting squares, stood three stories tall, looking like the massive walls of a prison cell in a courtyard. Medea was sometimes seen in a window in a wall, a friendless foreigner, virtually in prison. And the corroded metal also suggested her tormented, burning mind. These qualities—imprisonment and mental chaos—were symbolized, too, by the clangings and groanings given out when the metal walls were struck. Two quotations from reviews may help to suggest something of the production, and something of the enthusiasm that it evoked. In the *Wall Street Journal*, April 13, 1994, Edwin Wilson commented on two aspects of staging:

> In the scene where Medea is agonizing over whether or not to carry through her infanticide, a harsh, triangular beam of light slashes across the stage, pinning her in a corner. At the

climax of the play, after Medea has murdered her sons inside her palace, three enormous metal panels break loose, falling with a clangor that lifts spectators from their seats.

William A. Henry, writing in *Time*, April 25, 1994, described the ending in more detail:

> A wall topples to reveal Diana Rigg apparently already at sea. Hunched during her period of rage and oppression, she

stands proud as a ship's figurehead, clouds streaming past, golden light burnishing her. Then she turns and looks back, toward the scene of her unrepented misdeeds and, surely, toward an audience agape at the beauty and power of this finale.

L. L. West
DIRECTING MEDEA

Director L. L. West produced *Medea* in the fall of 1994. The production was sponsored by the Utah Classical Greek Festival and toured throughout Utah, Colorado, New Mexico, and California. Venues for the production were split between indoor "traditional" proscenium stages and outdoor "classical" stages. Since the performance space changed radically with each performance, audience size varied from three hundred to fifteen hundred.

What made you decide to do a Greek play and why Medea?

Well, first off you need to know that the decision to produce a Greek play happened long before I became involved. The Utah Classical Greek Festival has produced at least one Greek play for the past twenty-four years. There is a huge classical tradition in Utah. Yes . . . Utah of all places. To my knowledge, it is the oldest festival of its kind in the country. So, as a freelance director, I was honored to be invited to direct the 1994 production. Since I had directed for the festival before—*Iphigenia at Aulis* in 1985 and *Helen* in 1988—I had some voice in the actual play selection. My first thought was to do Euripides's *Medea* . . . a brutal, raw, passionate, and loving *Medea*.

What is it about Medea?

Understand that it's more than *Medea*. It's Euripides's *Medea*. As far as Greek plays and playwrights, my taste seems to run full speed to Euripides. There is a frightening God-in-Man/Man-in-God conflict that I find very twentieth-century American. There is something brutal and passionate about Euripides's characters, especially his women. When I direct, I want to spend my time and energy with plays that touch my soul. I want to wrap myself around characters that are still a bit of an enigma. I figure if I know a character's motives and needs at the beginning of the process then what's the purpose—or the fun—of the journey? So as I looked at Euripides's *Medea*, I thought, "This play has all the stuff of a very scary ride and I'm not quite sure where it's going."

So, you decided on Euripides's Medea. *Then what?*

Finding a translation. Finding the right translation for this production.

How did you go about finding the "right" translation?

Shortly after we decided to do *Medea*, I happened to take an inhumanely long bus ride from Utah to Kansas. It was January at its bleakest. I knew the winter landscape through Wyoming and Nebraska would be flat and depressing . . . so I armed myself with at least ten translations of *Medea*. With most of the translations, I would read for a while then doze then read again. With Mary-Kay Gamel's translation, it was as if I was reading *Medea* for the first time. I started reading just outside Cheyenne and finished as we pulled into Ogalalla. Professor Gamel had managed to fill the characters—especially Medea and Jason—with a blood and a passion. There was a sense of ritual with the language that I found wonderfully dark and compelling. But the thing that impressed me most was that the story was told with painstaking clarity.

As a director, one of your biggest decisions is how to visually present the play. What did you want your audience to see?

In terms of the setting, I wanted the feel to be extremely theatrical. I felt that it was important to present an environment for the action that was unique to every theatre where we performed. We created a skeleton proscenium—very Greek-like in shape—that allowed the audience to see the surrounding space. When we performed outside, the audience saw rocks and trees; when we performed on traditional indoor stages, our audiences saw the backstage of that particular theatre.

What about costumes?

In the beginning, I knew what I didn't want. I'd seen far too many Classical white chiton productions. They all seem so pristine and bloodless. Nor did I want a twentieth-century French production with tuxedos and evening dresses . . . I wanted costumes that would capture the passion and power of the Euripides/Gamel *Medea*. Our goal with the costume design was to create an archetypal world where magic and ritual exist. It was never our desire to place our characters in a specific time frame. Consequently we borrowed from many different sources: superhero comics, ritual voodoo garb, and *Mad Max* movies.

What about masks? I imagine that everyone who goes to see a Greek play knows that originally masks were used—chiefly, it is thought, because theaters were so huge. But since the theaters where you performed were much smaller, did you feel the need to use masks?

For *Medea* I felt that some type of masking was important to set a sense of other-world-ness and ritual. Ritual played a large part in this production. We decided to avoid the traditional masks and chose instead to find other ways to hide the face. For the Chorus, each costume was designed with a cowl at the neck that could be pulled up to mask the face. In addition, each chorus member wore a headband that covered most of his or her forehead. So with the cowl up and the headband, there was a only a slit for the eyes . . . it was very much a mask. I chose not to mask the individual characters. I wanted our audiences to identify with the characters and I felt that masking would distance them.

You mentioned the Chorus. How did you use them? How many?

I used five chorus members. There was rarely a time when they were not on stage. They provided counterpoint for the action with Medea and Jason, they played music, they became Medea's friends and critics, Creon's guards, and Jason's cohorts. With the exception of Medea and Jason, all of the characters in the play—Creon, the Messenger, the Nurse, the Tutor—were pulled from the Chorus.

In all your talking about the characters, you have not mentioned the Children.

I didn't cast children. I felt that there was a more effective, more theatrical way to present the children than to have actual actors. Each time the children appeared I had the chorus leader "become" the children. She had a stylized mask on each hand that represented each boy. Her movements—again, very stylized and ritualistic—created the two children.

Of course we know virtually nothing about Greek dances and about Greek music, but it seems pretty certain that the chorus sang and—perhaps at the same time—sometimes danced. Did your chorus do any dancing? Any singing?

They probably sang more than they danced, although movement was extremely important to the overall mood and feel of the production. There was music written for all the choral odes and it was sung by the chorus. Describing the music as primitive and ritualistic is an understatement. The feel of the music was more like a voodoo incantation than a Greek ode. I would say that the music was more strident than melodic, more percussive than rhythmic. The mood that was created was dark and frightening.

The question about dance reminds me that I should have asked about musical instruments. I think scholars agree that the ancient Greeks used a flute, but there is not much more agreement than that. Sometimes in scholarly books on Greek drama one comes across statements such as "probably in addition to flute, percussion instruments were used." What musical instruments did you use?

Well, I'm sorry to disappoint the scholars . . . but we didn't use a single flute. We did, however, begin the play and end it with a saxophone solo. It had a strange and wonderful quality that we liked . . . it also kept the play in "the now." All the music within the play was vocal with a strong drum accompaniment.

One final question. At the end of the play Medea is flown away in a golden chariot. How did you accomplish that bit of Deus ex Machina—or, I guess in this case, Dea ex Machina?

Very simply and theatrically. I am a great believer in my audience's imagination. I placed Medea on one side of the stage with a chair; her focus was out and down as if she were flying. On the opposite side of the stage I grouped the Chorus and Jason; their focus was out and up as if they were looking to her rising higher and higher. The dialogue and the actors created flying chariot and the audience believed.

David Richards
MEDEA WITH DIANA RIGG

The following review of a New York production with Diana Rigg appeared in the *New York Times*, April 8, 1994. For two photographs of the production, see page 49.

Mountain climbers have Everest. Swimmers have the English Channel. Actresses have *Medea*.

The title character of Euripides' tragedy is one of the huge, ravenous roles of dramatic literature. It will take everything a performer can give, then ask for more. Sheer talent is not enough. Courage and a certain recklessness are required to conquer it. A wild and exotic creature who knows potions that cure and poisons that kill, Medea is also a forsaken wife and tortured mother. She is one of us and not like us at all.

In the London-born production that began a limited engagement last night at the Longacre Theater, Diana Rigg brings a blazing intelligence and an elegant ferocity to the part. In the course of the 90-minute production, she grovels ignominiously at the feet of men. But by the end, she stands over them like the mighty figurehead of a ship about to sail for distant lands. For the actress, who has always managed to suggest impeccable breeding even when she is behaving abominably, the evening is a triumph.

It can also be counted a considerable success for the director, Jonathan Kent, who has set the play in an abstract box that could be the courtyard of a grim prison. The three-story walls are made of rusting metal panels. Whenever someone pounds on them, they produce thunderous echoes. The doors shut with a clang. Peter J. Davison's austere design does more than convey a sense of Medea's exile in a foreign land—an incarceration, really—it is a potent image for an inhospitable universe, conceived by the gods for man's misery and pain.

Working closely, Mr. Kent and Mr. Davison have engineered a spectacular climax for a tragedy that consists primarily of a series of increasingly horrible revelations. Abandoned by Jason for a younger woman, Medea won't rest until she has poisoned her rival and her rival's father, Creon. If she spares her errant husband, it is only so she can drive him into deepest despair by slaughtering their two young sons. Atrocity follows atrocity. Then, vengeance taken, she locks herself behind the rusted walls.

The biggest jolt is still to come, however. "Unbar the doors," howls a grief-stricken Jason (Tim Oliver Woodward), desperate to see the corpses of his sons but unable to find a way in. Suddenly, as if shaken by an earthquake, the metal wall before him collapses, the panels crashing to the ground with a colossal din. There, high above, stands Medea in a blood-soaked gown: victorious, remorseless, inhuman. Jason's pleading exasperates her. The last word out of her mouth before the lights fade is "rubbish." She virtually spits it down at him.

The women of Corinth (Judith Paris, Jane Loretta Lowe, Nuala Willis), who make up the chorus, are the sorts of Greek peasants who hover like crows on the fringes of "Zorba." Their clothes are black and their faces are lined. Sometimes they sing their choral passages (Jonathan Dove has written the haunting musical line). Sometimes they speak them. But for all their grand and woeful thoughts, they mostly communicate a fearful helplessness, before taking to wooden chairs on the side lines. The play is Medea's. So is the agony.

Unlike Zoe Caldwell, who emphasized the sexuality of the character (and won a Tony Award in 1982 for her efforts), Ms.

Rigg sees Medea as a woman of restless intellect. An orgiastic fervor informed Ms. Caldwell's performance; she had a savage growl in her voice. A passionate sense of injustice propels Ms. Rigg, whose voice never entirely loses its intrinsic musicality. Her hair is swept back into a tight braid, a style that sets off her grave and handsome features. Initially, only the aggressive jut of her chin and the smolder in her eyes give her away.

While some of Paul Brown's modernistic costumes—in particular, a greatcoat for the king that seems to be growing hair—are a bit wacky, the lighting by Wayne Dowdeswell and Rui Rita is almost brutal in its directness. At one point, a merciless shaft of light actually forces Medea into a corner, even as she is wrestling with her conscience and trying to steel herself to the awful deeds ahead. In what may be the best messenger role ever written, Dan Mullane, motionless in a fierce spotlight, describes ghastly offstage events with frozen horror. He could be responding to a police grilling.

The male characters in Medea don't come off well. But then they never have, and Alistair Elliot's stripped-for-action translation of the play further emphasizes Euripides' feminist sympathies. Either the men are smug and patronizing (like John Turner's Creon) or else they're smug and self-serving (like Mr. Woodward's Jason). Although Aegeus (Donald Douglas) shows some understanding of Medea's plight and promises her asylum in Athens, he's got a prudent streak running down his back and makes it clear that she'll have to get there by herself.

None of them can hold their own against her on moral or dramatic grounds. And when Ms. Rigg allows herself to indulge in some traditional feminine wiles, their defenses prove pathetically weak. "I am clever," she admits boldly to Creon, before realizing her error and backing down. The voice softens, and she adds, "but I am not *that* clever." The qualification is shrewd, self-protective. She's not ready for the kill yet.

Let men boast that they take all of life's risks while women sit safely at home. "I'd rather stand three times in battle by my shield," she responds, "than once give birth." Ms. Rigg, who has always had a wry wit, does not forgo it here. In addition to the knife in the folds of her robe, irony is one of her weapons. Medea, a victim, is also a victimizer.

The contradictions are tantalizing.

Aristophanes

LYSISTRATA

Nothing of much interest is known about Aristophanes (c. 450–c. 385 B.C.). An Athenian, he competed for about forty years in the annual festivals of comic drama to which three playwrights each contributed one play. His first play was produced in 427 B.C., his last extant play in 388 B.C., but he is known to have written two comedies after this date. Of the forty or so plays he wrote, eleven survive. *Lysistrata* was produced in 411 B.C.

COMMENTARY

Of the hundreds of ancient Greek comedies that were written, only eleven by Aristophanes and four by Menander (c. 342–299 B.C.) are extant, and three of Menander's four survive only in long fragments. Aristophanes seems to have written about forty plays, Menander more than twice as many. Hundreds of other men wrote comedies in ancient Greece, but they are mere names, or names attached to brief fragments. This means that when we talk about Greek comedy we are really talking about a fraction of Aristophanes's work, and an even smaller fraction of Menander's.

Greek comedy is customarily divided into three kinds: Old Comedy (486 B.C., when comedy was first given official recognition at the festival called the City Dionysia, to 404 B.C., the end of the Peloponnesian War, when Athens was humbled and freedom of speech was curtailed); Middle Comedy (404 B.C.–336 B.C., the accession of Alexander, when Athens was no longer free); and New Comedy (336 B.C.–c. 250 B.C., the approximate date of the last fragments). Of Old Comedy, there are Aristophanes's plays; of Middle Comedy, there is *Plutus*, one of Aristophanes's last plays; of New Comedy, there are Menander's fragments and his recently discovered *Dyskolos* (*The Disagreeable Man*).

Old Comedy—*Lysistrata* is an example—is a curious combination of obscenity, farce, political allegory, satire, and lyricism. Puns, literary allusions, phallic jokes, and political jibes periodically give way to joyful song; Aristophanes seems to have been something of a combination of Joyce, Swift, and Shelley. Other comparisons may be helpful. Perhaps we can say that in their loosely connected episodes and

their rapid shifts from lyricism and fantasy to mockery the plays are something like a Marx Brothers movie (Harpo's musical episodes juxtaposed with Groucho's irreverent wisecracks and outrageous ogling), though the plays are more explicitly political; and they are something like the rock musical *Hair*, which combined lyricism and politics with sex. The players of male roles wore large phalluses, and all the players wore masks, usually with grotesque expressions.

Aristophanes's plays usually have the following structure:

1. *Prologos*: prologue or exposition. Someone has a bright idea and sets it forth either in monologue or dialogue. In *Lysistrata*, the prologue consists of lines 1–212, in which Lysistrata persuades the women to refrain from sex with their husbands and thus compel their husbands to give up the war.
2. *Parados*: entrance of the chorus. The twenty-four or so members of the chorus express their opinion of the idea. (The *koryphaios*, or leader of the chorus, perhaps sings some lines by himself.) *Lysistrata* is somewhat unusual in having two half-choruses (*hemichori*), one of Old Men and another of Old Women, each with its own leader. Probably each half-chorus had twelve members.
3. *Epeisodion*: episode or scene. In the first scene of *Lysistrata* the women defeat the Commissioner. (A scene in this position, that is, before the *parabasis*, is sometimes called the *agon*, or debate.)
4. *Parabasis*: usually an elaborate composition in which the leader of the chorus ordinarily sheds his dramatic character and addresses the audience on the poet's behalf, the other actors having briefly retired. The

parabasis in *Lysistrata* is unusual: it is much shorter than those in Aristophanes's earlier plays, and the chorus does not speak directly for the playwright.

5. *Epeisodia*: episodes or scenes, sometimes briefly separated by choral songs. These episodes have to do with the working out of the original bright idea. In *Lysistrata* the first scene of this group (labeled Scene II because we have already had one scene before the *parabasis*) shows the women seeking to desert the cause, the second shows Myrrhine—loyal to the idea—tormenting her husband Kinesias, the third shows the Spartan herald discomfited by an erection, and the fourth shows the Spartan ambassadors similarly discomfited.

6. *Exodos*: final scene, customarily of reconciliation and rejoicing. There is often talk of a wedding and a feast. In this play a Spartan sings in praise not only of Sparta but also of Athens, and the chorus praises the deities worshiped in both states.

Perhaps all Old Comedy was rather like this, but it should be remembered that even Aristophanes's eleven plays do not all follow the pattern exactly. *Lysistrata*, for example, is unusual in having two hemichori and in having the chorus retain its identity during the parabasis. But *Lysistrata* (the accent is on the second syllable, and the name in effect means "Disbander-of-the-Army") is typical in its political concern, in its fantasy, in its bawdiness and in its revelry. It touches on serious, destructive themes, but it is joyous and extravagant, ending with a newly unified society. These points require some explanation.

First, Aristophanes's political concern. *Lysistrata* is the last of Aristophanes's three plays opposing the Peloponnesian War (the earlier two are *Acharnians* and *Peace*). This drawn-out war (431–404 B.C.), named for a peninsula forming the southern part of Greece, was fought between Athens (with some allies) and a confederacy headed by Sparta. Though enemies when the play was performed in 411 B.C., Athens and Sparta and other communities had been allies in 478 B.C. in order to defeat a common enemy, the Persians, but once the Persian threat was destroyed, Athens deprived most of its allies of their autonomy and, in effect, Athens ruled an empire.

Moreover, Athens tried to extend its empire. The war ultimately cost Athens its overseas empire and its leadership on the mainland. In 413 B.C. Athens had suffered an especially disastrous naval defeat; it had made something of a recovery by the time of *Lysistrata*, but the cost in manpower and money was enormous. Yet Athens persisted in its dream of conquest and of colonizing.

To counter this fantastic idea Aristophanes holds up another fantastic idea: the women will end the war by a sex strike. Actually, this is not one fantastic idea but two, for the idea of a sex strike is no more fantastic (for Athenians of the fifth century B.C.) than the idea of women playing a role—not to speak of a decisive role—in national affairs. Lysis-

trata, reporting her husband's view, is reporting the view of every Athenian: "War's a man's affair." (He was quoting from Homer's *Iliad*, so the point was beyond dispute.) And so there is something wild in her suggestion that the women can save the Greek cities (her hope goes beyond Athens, to Sparta and the other combatants), and in her comparison of the state to a ball of tangled yarn:

> COMMISSIONER.
> All this is beside the point.
>   Will you be so kind
> as to tell me how you mean to save Greece?
> LYSISTRATA.   Of course.
> Nothing could be simpler.
> COMMISSIONER.   I assure you, I'm all ears.
> LYSISTRATA.
> Do you know anything about weaving?
> Say the yarn gets tangled: we thread it
> this way and that through the skein, up and down,
> until it's free. And it's like that with war.
> We'll send our envoys
> up and down, this way and that, all over Greece,
> until it's finished.
> COMMISSIONER.
> Yarn? Thread? Skein?
> Are you out of your mind? I tell you,
> war is a serious business.
> LYSISTRATA.   So serious
> that I'd like to go on talking about weaving.
> COMMISSIONER.
> All right. Go ahead.
> LYSISTRATA.   The first thing we have to do
> is to wash our yarn, get the dirt out of it.
> You see? Isn't there too much dirt here in Athens?
> You must wash those men away.
>   Then our spoiled
> wool—that's like your job-hunters, out for a life
> of no work and big pay. Back to the basket,
> citizens or not, allies or not,
> or friendly immigrants.
>   And your colonies?
> Hanks of wool lost in various places. Pull them
> together, weave them into one great whole,
> and our voters are clothed for ever.

To the Commissioner, this is utterly fantastic:

> COMMISSIONER.   It would take a
> woman to reduce state questions to a matter of
> carding and weaving.

Such is the male view, and so these fantastic women, in order to exert influence, must resort to another fantastic idea, the sex strike, and here we encounter Aristophanes's famous ribaldry. In fact the play's reputation for bawdry is grossly exaggerated. Until recently, when pornography was hard to get, *Lysistrata*—because it was literature—provided one of the few available texts that talked of erections and of female delight in sex, and Aubrey Beardsley's illustrations (1896) doubtless helped to establish the book's reputation as a sexual stimulus. But it is really pretty tame stuff compared to what is now readily available, and the play, for all its sexual jokes, is not really about sex but about peace, harmony, and union—union between husbands and wives, between all in Athens, and between Athens and the other Greek-speaking communities.

One final point: The whole play, of course, not only is utterly improbable but also is utterly impossible. The women complain that they are sex-starved because the men are away at the war, but we soon find that the women will remedy this situation by withholding sex from the men—who, we thought, were away at war. How can one withhold sex from men who are supposedly not present? But Old Comedy never worried about such consistency.

A few words should be said about Middle Comedy and New Comedy. Middle Comedy is a convenient label to apply to the lost plays that must have marked the transition from Old Comedy to New Comedy—that is, to the surviving work of Menander. In New Comedy, written when Athens's political greatness was gone, and when political invective was impossible, the chorus has dwindled to musicians and dancers who perform intermittently, characters tend to be types (the young lover, the crabby old father, etc.), and the plot is regularly a young man's wooing of a maid. Fortune seems unfair and unpredictable, but in the end the virtuous are rewarded. The personal satire and obscenity of Old Comedy are gone, and in their place is a respectably conducted tale showing how, after humorous difficulties, the young man achieves his goal. The plot steadily moves toward the happy ending, which is far more integral than the more or less elusive allegoric (or metaphoric) union at the end of Lysistrata. It was New Comedy that influenced Rome (which could scarcely have imitated the political satire of Old Comedy), and through Rome modern Europe. Shakespeare, for example, whose comedies have been described as obstacle races to the altar, was a descendant of Menander though he knew nothing of Menander's work first-hand.

Aristophanes

LYSISTRATA

English version by Dudley Fitts

List of Characters

LYSISTRATA [*pronounced* Ly SIS tra ta]
KALONIKE [*pronounced* Ka lo NI ke]
MYRRHINE [*pronounced* MYR rhi nee]
LAMPITO [*pronounced* LAM pee toe]
CHORUS
COMMISSIONER
KINESIAS [*pronounced* ki NEE see as]
SPARTAN HERALD
SPARTAN AMBASSADOR
A SENTRY

Until the exodos, *the Chorus is divided into two hemichori: the first, of Old Men; the second, of Old Women. Each of these had its Koryphaios (i.e., leader). In the* exodos, *the hemichori return as Athenians and Spartans.*

The supernumeraries include the baby son of Kinesias; Stratyllis, a member of the hemichorus of Old Women; various individual speakers, both Spartan and Athenian.

SCENE: *Athens. First, a public square; later, beneath the walls of the Akropolis; later, a courtyard within the Akropolis.*

PROLOGUE

(*Athens; a public square; early morning; Lysistrata alone.*)

LYSISTRATA.
If someone had invited them to a festival—
of Bacchos, say; or to Pan's shrine, or to Aphrodite's°
over at Kolias—, you couldn't get through the streets,
what with the drums and the dancing. But now,
not a woman in sight!
                          Except—oh, yes!   5

Enter Kalonike.

Here's one of my neighbors, at last. Good
morning, Kalonike.
KALONIKE.   Good morning, Lysistrata. Darling,
don't frown so! You'll ruin your face!

LYSISTRATA.   Never mind my face.
Kalonike,
the way we women behave! Really, I don't blame the
men
for what they say about us.   10
KALONIKE.   No; I imagine they're right.
LYSISTRATA.
For example: I call a meeting
to think out a most important matter—and what
happens?
The women all stay in bed!
KALONIKE.   Oh, they'll be along.
It's hard to get away, you know: a husband, a cook,   15
a child . . . Home life can be *so* demanding!
LYSISTRATA.
What I have in mind is even more demanding.
KALONIKE.
Tell me: what is it?
LYSISTRATA.   It's big.
KALONIKE.   Goodness! *How* big?
LYSISTRATA.
Big enough for all of us.
KALONIKE.   But we're not all here!
LYSISTRATA.
We would be, if *that's* what was up!
                            No, Kalonike,   20
this is something I've been turning over for nights,
long sleepless nights.
KALONIKE.   It must be getting worn down, then,
if you've spent so much time on it.
LYSISTRATA.   Worn down or not,
it comes to this: Only we women can save Greece!
KALONIKE.
Only we women? Poor Greece!
LYSISTRATA.   Just the same,   25
it's up to us. First, we must liquidate
the Peloponnesians—
KALONIKE.   Fun, fun!
LYSISTRATA.   —and then the Boiotians.°
KALONIKE.
Oh! But not those heavenly eels!
LYSISTRATA.   You needn't worry.
I'm not talking about eels.—But here's the point:

---

2 Bacchos, Pan, Aphrodite the first two are gods associated with wine; Aphrodite is the goddess of love

27 Boiotia a country north of Attika, noted for the crudity of its inhabitants and the excellence of its seafood

30 If we can get the women from those places—
all those Boiotians and Peloponnesians—
to join us women here, why, we can save
all Greece!
KALONIKE.   But dearest Lysistrata!
How can women do a thing so austere, so
35 political? We belong at home. Our only armor's
our perfumes, our saffron dresses and
our pretty little shoes!
LYSISTRATA.   Exactly. Those
transparent dresses, the saffron, the
perfume, those pretty shoes—
KALONIKE.   Oh?
LYSISTRATA.   Not a single man
would lift his spear—
40 KALONIKE.   I'll send my dress to the dyer's tomorrow!
LYSISTRATA.
—or grab a shield—
KALONIKE.   The sweetest little negligée—
LYSISTRATA.
—or haul out his sword.
KALONIKE.   I know where I can buy
the dreamiest sandals!
LYSISTRATA.   Well, so you see. Now shouldn't
the women have come?
KALONIKE.   Come? They should have *flown!*
LYSISTRATA.
Athenians are always late.
45   But imagine!
There's no one here from the South Shore, or from
Salamis.
KALONIKE.
Things are hard over in Salamis, I swear.
They have to get going at dawn.
LYSISTRATA.   And nobody from
Acharnai. I thought they'd be here hours ago.
KALONIKE.   Well, you'll get
50 that awful Theagenes woman: she'll be
a sheet or so in the wind.
                        But look!
Someone at last! Can you see who they are?
Enter Myrrhine and other women.
LYSISTRATA.
They're from Anagyros.
KALONIKE.   They certainly are.
You'd know them anywhere, by the scent.
MYRRHINE.
Sorry to be late, Lysistrata.
55   Oh come,
don't scowl so. Say something!
LYSISTRATA.   My dear Myrrhine,
what is there to say? After all,
you've been pretty casual about the whole thing.
MYRRHINE.   Couldn't
find my girdle in the dark, that's all.

                            But what *is*
"the whole thing"?
KALONIKE.   No, we've got to wait   60
for those Boiotians and Peloponnesians.
LYSISTRATA.
That's more like it.—But, look!
Here's Lampito!
Enter Lampito with women from Sparta.
LYSISTRATA.   Darling Lampito,
how pretty you are today! What a nice color!
Goodness, you look as though you could strangle a bull!   65
LAMPITO.
Ah think Ah could! It's the work-out
In the gym every day; and, of co'se that dance of ahs
where y' kick yo' own tail.
KALONIKE.   What an adorable figure!
LAMPITO.
Lawdy, when y' touch me lahk that,
Ah feel lahk a heifer at the altar!
LYSISTRATA.   And this young lady?   70
Where is she from?
LAMPITO.   Boiotia. Social-Register type.
LYSISTRATA.
Ah. "Boiotia of the fertile plain."
KALONIKE.   And if you look,
you'll find the fertile plain has just been mowed.
LYSISTRATA.
And this lady?
LAMPITO.   Hagh, wahd, handsome. She comes from
Korinth.
KALONIKE.
High and wide's the word for it.
LAMPITO.   Which one of you   75
called this heah meeting, and why?
LYSISTRATA.   I did.
LAMPITO.   Well, then, tell
us: What's up?
MYRRHINE.   Yes, darling, what *is* on your mind, after all?
LYSISTRATA.
I'll tell you.—But first, one little question.
MYRRHINE.   Well?
LYSISTRATA.
It's your husbands. Fathers of your children. Doesn't it
bother you
that they're always off with the Army? I'll stake my life,   80
not one of you has a man in the house this minute!
KALONIKE.
Mine's been in Thrace the last five months, keeping an
eye on that General.
MYRRHINE.   Mine's been in Pylos for seven.
LAMPITO.   And
mahn, whenever he gets a *dis*charge, he goes raht back
with that li'l ole shield of his, and enlists again!   85
LYSISTRATA.
And not the ghost of a lover to be found!

From the very day the war began—

                      those Milesians!

I could skin them alive!

                      —I've not seen so much, even,

as one of those leather consolation prizes.—

90   But there! What's important is: If I've found a way

to end the war, are you with me?

MYRRHINE.   I should *say* so!

Even if I have to pawn my best dress and

drink up the proceeds.

KALONIKE.   Me, too! Even if they split me

right up the middle, like a flounder.

LAMPITO.   Ah'm shorely with you.

95   Ah'd crawl up Taygetos° on mah knees

if that'd bring peace.

LYSISTRATA.   All right, then; here it is:

Women! Sisters!

If we really want our men to make peace,

we must be ready to give up—

MYRRHINE.   Give up what?

Quick, tell us!

LYSISTRATA.

But *will* you?

100 MYRRHINE.   We will, even if it kills us.

LYSISTRATA.

Then we must give up going to bed with our men.

(*Long silence.*)

Oh? So now you're sorry? Won't look at me?

Doubtful? Pale? All teary-eyed?

                     But come: be frank with me.

Will you do it, or not? Well? Will you do it?

MYRRHINE.   I couldn't. No.

Let the war go on.

105 KALONIKE.   Nor I. Let the war go on.

LYSISTRATA.

You, you little flounder,

ready to be split up the middle?

KALONIKE.   Lysistrata, no!

I'd walk through the fire for you—you *know* I would! but don't

ask us to give up *that*! Why, there's nothing like it!

LYSISTRATA.

And you?

110 BOIOTIAN.   No. I must say *I'd* rather walk through fire.

LYSISTRATA.

What an utterly perverted sex we women are!

No wonder poets write tragedies about us.

There's only one thing we can think of.

                     But you from Sparta:

If you stand by me, we may win yet! Will you?

It means so much!

LAMPITO.   Ah sweah, it means *too* much!   115

By the Two Goddesses, it does! Asking a girl

to sleep—Heaven knows how long!—in a great big bed

with nobody there but herself! But Ah'll stay with you!

Peace comes first!

LYSISTRATA.   Spoken like a true Spartan!

KALONIKE.

But if—

        oh dear!

                —if we give up what you tell us to,   120

will there *be* any peace?

LYSISTRATA.   Why, mercy, of course there will!

We'll just sit snug in our very thinnest gowns,

perfumed and powdered from top to bottom, and those men

simply won't stand still! And when we say No,

they'll go out of their minds! And there's your peace.   125

You can take my word for it.

LAMPITO.   Ah seem to remember

that Colonel Menelaos threw his sword away

when he saw Helen's breast all bare.

KALONIKE.   But, goodness me!

What if they just get up and leave us?

LYSISTRATA.   In that case

we'll have to fall back on ourselves, I suppose.   130

But they won't.

KALONIKE.   I must say that's not much help. But

what if they drag us into the bedroom?

LYSISTRATA.   Hang on to the door.

KALONIKE.

What if they slap us?

LYSISTRATA.   If they do, you'd better give in.

But be sulky about it. Do I have to teach you how?

You know there's no fun for men when they have to force you.   135

There are millions of ways of getting them to see reason.

Don't you worry: a man

doesn't like it unless the girl co-operates.

KALONIKE.

I suppose so. Oh, all right. We'll go along.

LAMPITO.

Ah imagine us Spahtans can arrange a peace. But you   140

Athenians! Why, you're just war-mongerers!

LYSISTRATA.   Leave that to

me. I know how to make them listen.

LAMPITO.   Ah don't see how.

After all, they've got their boats; and there's lots of money

piled up in the Akropolis.°

LYSISTRATA.   The Akropolis? Darling,

we're taking over the Akropolis today!   145

---

95 Taygetos a mountain range

144 Akropolis at the beginning of the war, Perikles stored emergency funds in the Akropolis, the citadel sacred to Athene

That's the older women's job. All the rest of us
are going to the Citadel to sacrifice—you understand
me?
And once there, we're in for good!

LAMPITO.   Whee! Up the rebels!
Ah can see you're a good strateegist.

LYSISTRATA.   Well, then, Lampito,
150   what we have to do now is take a solemn oath.

LAMPITO.
Say it. We'll sweah.

LYSISTRATA.   This is it.
—But where's our Inner Guard?
                 —Look, Guard: you see this shield?
Put it down here. Now bring me the victim's entrails.

KALONIKE.
But the oath?

LYSISTRATA.
You remember how in Aischylos' *Seven*
155   they killed a sheep and swore on a shield? Well, then?

KALONIKE.
But I don't see how you can swear for peace on a shield.

LYSISTRATA.
What else do you suggest?

KALONIKE.   Why not a white horse?
We could swear by that.

LYSISTRATA.   And where will you get a white horse?

KALONIKE.
I never thought of that. *What* can we do?

LYSISTRATA.   I have it!
160   Let's set this big black wine-bowl on the ground
and pour in a gallon or so of Thasian, and swear
not to add one drop of water.

LAMPITO.   Ah lahk *that* oath!

LYSISTRATA.
Bring the bowl and the wine-jug.

KALONIKE.   Oh, what a simply *huge* one!

LYSISTRATA.
Set it down. Girls, place your hands on the gift-offering.
165   O Goddess of Persuasion! And thou, O Loving-cup:
Look upon this our sacrifice, and
be gracious!

KALONIKE.
See the blood spill out. How red and pretty it is!

LAMPITO.
And Ah must say it smells good.

MYRRHINE.   Let me swear first!

KALONIKE.
170   No, by Aphrodite, we'll match for it!

LYSISTRATA.
Lampito: all of you women: come, touch the bowl,
and repeat after me—remember, this is an oath—:
I WILL HAVE NOTHING TO DO WITH MY
    HUSBAND OR MY LOVER

KALONIKE.
I will have nothing to do with my husband or my lover

LYSISTRATA.
THOUGH HE COME TO ME IN PITIABLE
    CONDITION   175

KALONIKE.
Though he come to me in pitiable condition
(Oh Lysistrata! This is killing me!)

LYSISTRATA.
IN MY HOUSE I WILL BE UNTOUCHABLE

KALONIKE.
In my house I will be untouchable

LYSISTRATA.
IN MY THINNEST SAFFRON SILK   180

KALONIKE.
In my thinnest saffron silk

LYSISTRATA.
AND MAKE HIM LONG FOR ME.

KALONIKE.
And make him long for me.

LYSISTRATA.
I WILL NOT GIVE MYSELF

KALONIKE.
I will not give myself   185

LYSISTRATA.
AND IF HE CONSTRAINS ME

KALONIKE.
And if he constrains me

LYSISTRATA.
I WILL BE COLD AS ICE AND NEVER MOVE

KALONIKE.
I will be cold as ice and never move

LYSISTRATA.
I WILL NOT LIFT MY SLIPPERS TOWARD THE
    CEILING   190

KALONIKE.
I will not lift my slippers toward the ceiling

LYSISTRATA.
OR CROUCH ON ALL FOURS LIKE THE LIONESS
    IN THE CARVING

KALONIKE.
Or crouch on all fours like the lioness in the carving

LYSISTRATA.
AND IF I KEEP THIS OATH LET ME DRINK FROM
    THIS BOWL

KALONIKE.
And if I keep this oath let me drink from this bowl   195

LYSISTRATA.
IF NOT, LET MY OWN BOWL BE FILLED WITH
    WATER.

KALONIKE.
If not, let my own bowl be filled with water.

LYSISTRATA.
You have all sworn?

MYRRHINE.   We have.

LYSISTRATA.   Then thus
I sacrifice the victim.

Aristophanes

(*Drinks largely.*)

KALONIKE. Save some for us!

200 Here's to you, darling, and to you, and to you!

(*Loud cries off-stage.*)

LAMPITO.
What's all *that* whoozy-goozy?

LYSISTRATA. Just what I told you.
The older women have taken the Akropolis.
Now you, Lampito,
rush back to Sparta. We'll take care of things here. Leave
these girls here for hostages.

205 The rest of you,
up to the Citadel: and mind you push in the bolts.

KALONIKE.
But the men? Won't they be after us?

LYSISTRATA. Just you leave
the men to me. There's not fire enough in the world,
or threats either, to make me open these doors
except on my own terms.

210 KALONIKE. I hope not, by Aphrodite!
After all, we've got a reputation for bitchiness to live up
to.

(*Exeunt.*)

PARADOS

CHORAL EPISODE

(*The hillside just under the Akropolis. Enter Chorus of Old Men with burning torches and braziers; much puffing and coughing.*)

KORYPHAIOS(man).
Forward march, Drakes, old friend: never mind
That damn big log banging hell down on your back.

STROPHE I

CHORUS(men).
There's this to be said for longevity:
You see things you thought that you'd never see.
    Look, Strymodoros, who would have thought it?
    We've caught it—
            the New Femininity!
The wives of our bosom, our board, our bed—
Now, by the gods, they've gone ahead
And taken the Citadel (Heaven knows why!),
Porfanéd the sacred statuar-y,
        And barred the doors,
        The subversive whores!

KORYPHAIOS(m).
Shake a leg there, Philurgos, man: the Akropolis or bust!
Put the kindling around here. We'll build one almighty
    big

130

bonfire for the whole bunch of bitches, every last one; 15
and the first we fry will be old Lykon's woman.

ANTISTROPHE I

CHORUS(m).
They're not going to give me the old horselaugh!
No, by Demeter, they won't pull this off!
    Think of Kleomenes: even he
    Didn't go free
            till he brought me his stuff. 20
A good man he was, all stinking and shaggy,
Bare as an eel except for the bag he
Covered his rear with. God, what a mess!
Never a bath in six years, I'd guess.
        Pure Sparta, man! 25
        He also ran.

KORYPHAIOS(m).
That was a siege, friends! Seventeen ranks strong
we slept at the Gate. And shall we not do as much
against these women, whom God and Euripides hate?
If we don't, I'll turn in my medals from Marathon. 30

STROPHE 2

CHORUS(m).
Onward and upward! A little push,
    And we're there.
Ouch, my shoulders! I could wish
    For a pair
Of good strong oxen. Keep your eye 35
    On the fire there, it mustn't die.
        Akh! Akh!
    The smoke would make a cadaver cough!

ANTISTROPHE 2

Holy Herakles, a hot spark
    Bit my eye! 40
Damn this hellfire, damn this work!
    So say I.
Onward and upward just the same.
(Laches, remember the Goddess: for shame!)
        Akh! Akh! 45
    The smoke would make a cadaver cough!

KORYPHAIOS(m).
At last (and let us give suitable thanks to God
for his infinite mercies) I have managed to bring
my personal flame to the common goal. It breathes, it
    lives.
Now, gentlemen, let us consider. Shall we insert 50
the torch, say, into the brazier, and thus extract
a kindling brand? And shall we then, do you think
push on to the gate like valiant sheep? On the whole,
    yes.

But I would have you consider this, too: if they—
55 I refer to the women—should refuse to open,
what then? Do we set the doors afire
and smoke them out? At ease, men. Mediate.
Akh, the smoke! Woof! What we really need
is the loan of a general or two from the Samos
        Command.
60 At least we've got this lumber off our backs.
That's something. And now let's look to our fire.
O Pot, brave Brazier, touch my torch with flame!
Victory, Goddess, I invoke thy name!
Strike down these paradigms of female pride,
65 And we shall hang our trophies up inside.

Enter Chorus of Old Women on the walls of the Akropolis,
carrying jars of water.

KORYPHAIOS(woman).
    Smoke, girls, smoke! There's smoke all over the place!
    Probably fire, too. Hurry, girls! Fire! Fire!

STROPHE I

CHORUS(women).
    Nikodike, run!
    Or Kalyke's done
70 To a turn, and poor Kritylla's
    Smoked like a ham.
            Damn
    These old men! Are we too late?
    I nearly died down at the place
    Where we fill our jars:
75   Slaves pushing and jostling—
        Such a hustling
    I never saw in all my days.

ANTISTROPHE I

    But here's water at last.
    Haste, sisters, haste!
80 Slosh it on them, slosh it down,
    The silly old wrecks!
            Sex
    Almighty! What they want's
    A hot bath? Good. Send one down.
    Athena of Athens town,
85   Trito-born!° Helm of Gold!
        Cripple the old
    Firemen! Help us help them drown!

85 **Trito-born** Athene, said to be born near Lake Tritonis, in Libya

(*The Old Men capture a woman, Stratyllis.*)

STRATYLLIS.
    Let me go! Let me go!
KORYPHAIOS(w).   You walking corpses,
    have you no shame?
KORYPHAIOS(m).   I wouldn't have believed it!
    An army of women in the Akropolis!   90
KORYPHAIOS(w).
    So we scare you, do we? Grandpa, you've seen
    only our pickets yet!
KORYPHAIOS(m).   Hey, Phaidrias!
    Help me with the necks of these jabbering hens!
KORYPHAIOS(w).
    Down with your pots, girls! We'll need both hands
    if these antiques attack us.
KORYPHAIOS(m).   Want your face kicked in?   95
KORYPHAIOS(w).
    Want your balls chewed off?
KORYPHAIOS(m).   Look out! I've got a stick!
KORYPHAIOS(w).
    You lay a half-inch of your stick on Stratyllis,
    and you'll never stick again!
KORYPHAIOS(m).
    Fall apart!
KORYPHAIOS(w). I'll spit up your guts!
KORYPHAIOS(m).   Euripedes!° Master!
    How well you knew women!
KORYPHAIOS(w).   Listen to him, Rhodippe,   100
    up with the pots!
KORYPHAIOS(m).   Demolition of God,
    what good are your pots?
KORYPHAIOS(w).   You refugee from the tomb,
    what good is your fire?
KORYPHAIOS(m).   Good enough to make a pyre
    to barbecue you!
KORYPHAIOS(w).   We'll squizzle your kindling!
KORYPHAIOS(m).
    You think so?
KORYPHAIOS(w). Yah! Just hang around a while!   105
KORYPHAIOS(m).
    Want a touch of my torch?
KORYPHAIOS(w).   It needs a good soaping.
KORYPHAIOS(m).
    How about you?
KORYPHAIOS(w).   Soap for a senile bridegroom!
KORYPHAIOS(m).
    Senile? Hold your trap!
KORYPHAIOS(w).   Just *you* try to hold it!
KORYPHAIOS(m).
    The yammer of women!
KORYPHAIOS(w).   Oh is that so?
    You're not in the jury room now, you know.   110

99 **Euripedes** a tragic dramatist

KORYPHAIOS(m).

    Gentlemen, I beg you, burn off that woman's hair!

KORYPHAIOS(w).

    Let it come down!

    (*They empty their pots on the men.*)

KORYPHAIOS(m).

    What a way to drown!

KORYPHAIOS(w).   Hot, hey?

KORYPHAIOS(m).   Say,

    enough!

KORYPHAIOS(w). Dandruff

115   needs watering. I'll make you

    nice and fresh.

KORYPHAIOS(m).   For God's sake, you,

    hold off!

SCENE I

Enter a Commissioner accompanied by four constables.

COMMISSIONER.

    These degenerate women! What a racket of little drums,

    what a yapping for Adonis on every house-top!

    It's like the time in the Assembly when I was listening

    to a speech—out of order, as usual—by that fool

5   Demostratos,° all about troops for Sicily,°

    that kind of nonsense—

                   and there was his wife

    trotting around in circles howling

    Alas for Adonis!°—

              and Demostratos insisting

    we must draft every last Zakynthian that can walk—

10   and his wife up there on the roof,

    drunk as an owl, yowling

    Oh weep for Adonis!—

             and that damned ox Demostratos

    mooing away through the rumpus. That's what we get

    for putting up with this wretched woman-business!

KORYPHAIOS(m).

15   Sir, you haven't heard the half of it. They laughed at us!

    Insulted us! They took pitchers of water

    and nearly drowned us! We're still wringing out our

        clothes,

    for all the world like unhousebroken brats.

COMMISSIONER.

    Serves you right, by Poseidon!

20   Whose fault is it if these women-folk of ours

---

5 **Demostratos** Athenian orator and jingoist politician **Sicily** a reference to the Sicilian Expedition (416 B.C.), in which Athens was decisively defeated 8 **Adonis** fertility god

get out of hand? We coddle them,

we teach them to be wasteful and loose. You'll see a

    husband

go into a jeweler's. "Look," he'll say,

"jeweler," he'll say, "you remember that gold choker

you made for my wife? Well, she went to a dance last

    night   25

and broke the clasp. Now, I've got to go to Salamis,

and can't be bothered. Run over to my house tonight,

will you, and see if you can put it together for her."

Or another one goes to a cobbler—a good strong

    workman, too,

with an awl that was never meant for child's play.

    "Here,"   30

he'll tell him, "one of my wife's shoes is pinching

her little toe. Could you come up about noon

and stretch it out for her?"

                        Well, what do you expect?

Look at me, for example, I'm a Public Officer,

and it's one of my duties to pay off the sailors.   35

And where's the money? Up there in the Akropolis!

And those blasted women slam the door in my face!

But what are we waiting for?

                   —Look here, constable,

stop sniffing around for a tavern, and get us

some crowbars. We'll force their gates! As a matter of

    fact,   40

I'll do a little forcing myself.

Enter Lysistrata, above, with Myrrhine, Kalonike, and the Boiotian.

LYSISTRATA.   No need of forcing.

Here I am, of my own accord. And all this talk

about locked doors—! We don't need locked doors,

but just the least bit of common sense.

COMMISSIONER.

Is that so, ma'am!

                —Where's my constable?

                         —Constable, 45

arrest that woman, and tie her hands behind her.

LYSISTRATA.

If he touches me, I swear by Artemis

there'll be one scamp dropped from the public payroll

    tomorrow!

COMMISSIONER.

Well constable? You're not afraid, I suppose? Grab her,

two of you, around the middle!

KALONIKE.   No, by Pandrosos! 50

Lay a hand on her, and I'll jump on you so hard

your guts will come out the back door!

COMMISSIONER.   That's what *you* think!

Where's the sergeant?—Here, you: tie up that trollop

    first,

the one with the pretty talk!

MYRRHINE.   By the Moon-Goddess,
55   just try! They'll have to scoop you up with a spoon!
COMMISSIONER.
     Another one!
                         Officer, seize that woman!
                                                  I swear
     I'll put an end to this riot!
BOIOTIAN.   By the Taurian,
     one inch closer, you'll be one screaming baldhead!
COMMISSIONER.
     Lord, what a mess! And my constables seem ineffective.
     But—women get the best of us? By God, no!
60   —Skythians!
     Close ranks and forward march!
LYSISTRATA.   "Forward," indeed!
     By the Two Goddesses, what's the sense in *that*?
     They're up against four companies of women
     armed from top to bottom.
COMMISSIONER.   Forward, my Skythians!
LYSISTRATA.
65   Forward, yourselves, dear comrades!
     You grainlettucebeanseedmarket girls!
     You garlicandonionbreadbakery girls!
     Give it to 'em! Knock 'em down! Scratch 'em!
     Tell 'em what you think of 'em!

     (*General mêlée; the Skythians yield.*)
                                    —Ah, that's enough!
70   Sound a retreat: good soldiers don't rob the dead.
COMMISSIONER.
     A nice day *this* has been for the police!
LYSISTRATA.
     Well, there you are.—Did you really think we women
     would be driven like slaves? Maybe now you'll admit
     that a woman knows something about spirit.
COMMISSIONER.   Spirit enough,
75   especially spirits in bottles! Dear Lord Apollo!
KORYPHAIOS(m).
     Your Honor, there's no use talking to them. Words
     mean nothing whatever to wild animals like these.
     Think of the sousing they gave us! and the water
     was not, I believe, of the purest.
KORYPHAIOS(w).
80   You shouldn't have come after us. And if you try it again,
     you'll be one eye short!—Although, as a matter of fact,
     what I like best is just to stay at home and read,
     like a sweet little bride: never hurting a soul, no,
     never going out. But if you *must* shake hornets' nests,
85   look out for the hornets.

STROPHE

CHORUS(m).
     Of all the beasts that God hath wrought

     What monster's worse than woman?
     Who shall encompass with his thought
          Their guile unending? No man.

     They've seized the Heights, the Rock, the Shrine—   90
          But to what end? I wot not.
     Sure there's some clue to their design!
          Have you the key? I thought not.
KORYPHAIOS(m).
     We might question them, I suppose. But I warn you sir,
     don't believe anything you hear! It would be un-   95
     Athenian
     not to get to the bottom of this plot.
COMMISSIONER.   Very well.
     My first question is this: Why, so help you God,
     did you bar the gates of the Akropolis?
LYSISTRATA.   Why?
     To keep the money, of course. No money, no war.
COMMISSIONER.
     You think that money's the cause of war?
LYSISTRATA.   I do.   100
     Money brought about that Peisandros° business
     and all the other attacks on the State. Well and good!
     They'll not get another cent here!
COMMISSIONER.   And what will you do?
LYSISTRATA.
     What a question! From now on, we intend
     to control the Treasury.
COMMISSIONER.   Control the Treasury!   105
LYSISTRATA.
     Why not? Does that seem strange? After all,
     we control our household budgets.
COMMISSIONER.   But that's different!
LYSISTRATA.
     "Different"? What do you mean?
COMMISSIONER.   I mean simply this:
     it's the Treasury that pays for National Defense.
LYSISTRATA.
     Unnecessary. We propose to abolish war.   110
COMMISSIONER.
     Good God.—And National Security?
LYSISTRATA.   Leave that to us.
COMMISSIONER.
     You?
LYSISTRATA.'
        Us.
COMMISSIONER.
              We're done for, then!
LYSISTRATA.   Never mind.
     We women will save you in spite of yourselves.

101 Peisandros a plotter against the Athenian democracy

COMMISSIONER.   What nonsense!
LYSISTRATA.
    If you like. But you must accept it, like it or not.
COMMISSIONER.
    Why, this is downright subversion!
115 LYSISTRATA.   Maybe it is.
    But we're going to save you, Judge.
COMMISSIONER.   I don't *want* to be
    saved.
LYSISTRATA.
    Tut. The death-wish. All the more reason.
COMMISSIONER.   But the idea
    of women bothering themselves about peace and war!
LYSISTRATA.
    Will you listen to me?
COMMISSIONER.   Yes. But be brief, or I'll—
LYSISTRATA.
    This is no time for stupid threats.
120 COMMISSIONER.   By the gods,
    I can't stand any more!
AN OLD WOMAN.   Can't stand? Well, well.
COMMISSIONER.
    That's enough out of you, you old buzzard!
    Now, Lysistrata: tell me what you're thinking.
LYSISTRATA.
    Glad to.
           Ever since this war began
    We women have been watching you men, agreeing with
125   you,
    keeping our thoughts to ourselves. That doesn't mean
    we were happy: we weren't, for we saw how things were
     going;
    but we'd listen to you at dinner
    arguing this way and that.
           —Oh you, and your big
    Top Secrets!—
130   And then we'd grin like little patriots
    (though goodness knows we didn't feel like grinning)
     and ask you:
    "Dear, did the Armistice come up in Assembly today?"
    And you'd say, "None of your business! Pipe down!,"
     you'd say.
    And so we would.
AN OLD WOMAN.   *I* wouldn't have, by God!
COMMISSIONER.
    You'd have taken a beating, then!
135   —Go on.
LYSISTRATA.
    Well, we'd be quiet. But then, you know, all at once
    you men would think up something worse than ever.
    Even *I* could see it was fatal. And, "Darling," I'd say,
    "have you gone completely mad?" And my husband
     would look at me
140   and say, "Wife, you've got your weaving to attend to.

Mind your tongue, if you don't want a slap. 'War's a
    man's affair!'"°
COMMISSIONER.
    Good words, and well pronounced.
LYSISTRATA.
    You're a fool if you think so.
                It was hard enough
    to put up with all this banquet-hall strategy.
    But then we'd hear you out in the public square: 145
    "Nobody left for the draft-quota here in Athens?"
    you'd say; and, "No," someone else would say, "not a
     man!"
    And so we women decided to rescue Greece.
    You might as well listen, to us now: you'll have to, later.
COMMISSIONER.
    You rescue Greece? Absurd.
LYSISTRATA.   You're the absurd one.   150
COMMISSIONER.
    You expect me to take orders from a woman?
                        I'd die first!
LYSISTRATA.
    Heavens, if that's what's bothering you, take my veil,
    here, and wrap it around your poor head.
KALONIKE.   Yes,
    and you can have my market-basket, too.
    Go home, tighten your girdle, do the washing, mind   155
    your beans! "War's
    a woman's affair!"
KORYPHAIOS[(w)].   Ground pitchers! Close ranks!

ANTISTROPHE

CHORUS[(w)].
    This is a dance that I know well,
      My knees shall never yield.
    Wobble and creak I may, but still   160
      I'll keep the well-fought field.
    Valor and grace march on before,
      Love prods us from behind.
    Our slogan is EXCELSIOR,
      Our watchword SAVE MANKIND.   165
KORYPHAIOS[(w)].
    Women, remember your grandmothers! Remember
    that little old mother of yours, what a stinger she was!
    On, on, never slacken. There's a strong wind astern!
LYSISTRATA.
    O Eros of delight! O Aphrodite! Kyprian!
    If ever desire has drenched our breasts or dreamed   170
    in our thighs, let it work so now on the men of Hellas

---

141 War's a man's affair quoted from Homer's *Iliad*, VI, 492, Hector to his wife Andromache

that they shall tail us through the land, slaves, slaves
to Woman, Breaker of Armies!
COMMISSIONER.   And if we do?
LYSISTRATA.
75   Well, for one thing, we shan't have to watch you
going to market, a spear in one hand, and heaven knows
what in the other.
KALONIKE.   Nicely said, by Aphrodite!
LYSISTRATA.
As things stand now, you're neither men nor women.
Armor clanking with kitchen pans and pots—
you sound like a pack of Korybantes!
COMMISSIONER.
A man must do what a man must do.
LYSISTRATA.
80   So I'm told.
But to see a General, complete with Gorgon-shield,
jingling along the dock to buy a couple of herrings!
KALONIKE.
I saw a Captain the other day—lovely fellow he was,
nice curly hair—sitting on his horse; and—can you
     believe it?—
85   he'd just bought some soup, and was pouring it into his
     helmet!
And there was a soldier from Thrace
swishing his lance like something out of Euripides,
and the poor fruit-store woman got so scared
that she ran away and let him have his figs free!
COMMISSIONER.
All this is beside the point
90   Will you be so kind
as to tell me how you mean to save Greece?
LYSISTRATA.   Of course.
Nothing could be simpler.
COMMISSIONER.   I assure you, I'm all ears.
LYSISTRATA.
Do you know anything about weaving?
Say the yarn gets tangled: we thread it
95   this way and that through the skein, up and down,
until it's free. And it's like that with war.
We'll send our envoys
up and down, this way and that, all over Greece,
until it's finished.
COMMISSIONER.   Yarn? Thread? Skein?
200 Are you out of your mind? I tell you,
war is a serious business.
LYSISTRATA.   So serious
that I'd like to go on talking about weaving.
COMMISSIONER.
All right. Go ahead.
LYSISTRATA.   The first thing we have to do
is to wash our yarn, get the dirt out of it.
205 You see? Isn't there too much dirt here in Athens?
You must wash those men away.
                  Then our spoiled wool—

that's like your job-hunters, out for a life
of no work and big pay. Back to the basket,
citizens or not, allies or not,
or friendly immigrants.
              And your colonies?   210
Hanks of wool lost in various places. Pull them
together, weave them into one great whole,
and our voters are clothed for ever.
COMMISSIONER.   It would take a woman
to reduce state questions to a matter of carding and
   weaving.
LYSISTRATA.
You fool! Who were the mothers whose sons sailed off   215
to fight for Athens in Sicily?
COMMISSIONER.   Enough!
I beg you, do not call back those memories.
LYSISTRATA.   And then,
instead of the love that every woman needs,
we have only our single beds, where we can dream
of our husbands off with the Army.
              Bad enough for wives! 220
But what about our girls, getting older every day,
and older, and no kisses?
COMMISSIONER.   Men get older, too.
LYSISTRATA.
Not in the same sense.
         A soldier's discharged,
and he may be bald and toothless, yet he'll find
a pretty young thing to go to bed with.
             But a woman! 225
Her beauty is gone with the first gray hair.
She can spend her time
consulting the oracles and the fortune-tellers,
but they'll never send her a husband.
COMMISSIONER.
Still, if a man can rise to the occasion— 230
LYSISTRATA.
Rise? Rise, yourself!

(*Furiously.*)

Go invest in a coffin!
           You've money enough.
                 I'll bake you
a cake for the Underworld.
            And here's your funeral
wreath!

(*She pours water upon him.*)

MYRRHINE. And here's another!

(*More water.*)

KALONIKE.   And here's
my contribution!

(*More water.*)

235 LYSISTRATA.   What are you waiting for?
All aboard Styx Ferry!
                              Charon's° calling for you!
It's sailing-time: don't disrupt the schedule!
COMMISSIONER.
The insolence of women! And to me!
No, by God, I'll go back to town and show
240 the rest of the Commission what might happen to them.
                                        (*Exit Commissioner.*)
LYSISTRATA.
Really, I suppose we should have laid out his corpse
on the doorstep, in the usual way.
                                    But never mind.
We'll give him the rites of the dead tomorrow morning.
            (*Exit Lysistrata with Myrrhine and Kalonike.*)

PARABASIS

CHORAL EPISODE

ODE I

KORYPHAIOS(m).
Sons of Liberty, awake! The day of glory is at hand.
CHORUS(m).
I smell tyranny afoot, I smell it rising from the land.
I scent a trace of Hippias,° I sniff upon the breeze
A dismal Spartan hogo that suggests King Kleisthenes.°
5   Strip, strip for action, brothers!
       Our wives, aunts, sisters, mothers
Have sold us out: the streets are full of godless female
       rages.
Shall we stand by and let our women confiscate our
       wages?

EPIRRHEMA I

KORYPHAIOS(m).
Gentlemen, it's a disgrace to Athens, a disgrace
10 to all that Athens stands for, if we allow these grandmas
to jabber about spears and shields and making friends
with the Spartans. What's a Spartan? Give me a wild
       wolf
any day. No. They want the Tyranny back, I suppose.
Are we going to take that? No. Let us look like

the innocent serpent, but be the flower under it,   15
as the poet sings. And just to begin with,
I propose to poke a number of teeth
down the gullet of that harridan over there.

ANTODE I

KORYPHAIOS(w).
Oh, is that so? When you get home, your own mammá
    won't know you!
CHORUS(w).
Who do you think we are, you senile bravos? Well, I'll
    show you.   20
I bore the sacred vessels in my eighth year, and at ten
I was pounding out the barley for Athena Goddess; then
    They made me Little Bear
    At the Braunonian Fair;
I'd held the Holy Basket by the time I was of age,   25
The Blessed Dry figs had adorned my plump décolletage.

ANTEPIRRHEMA I

KORYPHAIOS(w).
A "disgrace to Athens," am I, just at the moment
I'm giving Athens the best advice she ever had?
Don't I pay taxes to the State? Yes, I pay them
in baby boys. And what do you contribute,   30
you impotent horrors? Nothing but waste: all
our Treasury,° dating back to the Persian Wars,
gone! rifled! And not a penny out of your pockets!
Well, then? Can you cough up an answer to that?
Look out for your own gullet, or you'll get a crack   35
from this old brogan that'll make your teeth see stars!

ODE 2

CHORUS(m).
    Oh insolence!
    Am I unmanned?
    Incontinence!
    Shall my scarred hand   40
    Strike never a blow
    To curb this flow-
    ing female curse?

---

236 **Charon** god who ferried the souls of the newly dead across
the Styx to Hades   3 **Hippias** an Athenian tyrant (d. 490 B.C.)
4 **Kleisthenes** an ambisexual Athenian

32 **Treasury** money originally contributed by Athens and her
allies, intended to finance an extension of the sea-war against Persia. Since the failure of the Sicilian Expedition, the contributions
of the allies had fallen off; and the fund itself was now being raided
by Athenian politicians

Leipsydrion!°
45 Shall I betray
The laurels won
On that great day?
Come, shake a leg,
Shed old age, beg
50 The years reverse!

EPIRRHEMA 2

KORYPHAIOS⁽ᵐ⁾.

Give them an inch, and we're done for! We'll have them
launching boats next and planning naval strategy,
sailing down on us like so many Artemisias.
Or maybe they have ideas about the cavalry.
55 That's fair enough, women are certainly good
in the saddle. Just look at Mikon's paintings,
All those Amazons wrestling with all those men!
On the whole, a straitjacket's their best uniform.

ANTODE 2

CHORUS⁽ʷ⁾.

Tangle with me,
60 And you'll get cramps.
Ferocity
's no use now, Gramps!
By the Two,
I'll get through
65 To you wrecks yet!

I'll scramble your eggs,
I'll burn your beans,
With my two legs.
You'll see such scenes
70 As never yet
Your two eyes met.
A curse? You bet!

ANTEPIRRHEMA 2

KORYPHAIOS⁽ʷ⁾.

If Lampito stands by me, and that delicious Theban girl,
Ismenia—what good are *you*? You and your seven
75 Resolutions! Resolutions? Rationing Boiotian eels
and making our girls go with them at Hekate's Feast!
That was statesmanship! And we'll have to put up with it
and all the rest of your decrepit legislation
until some patriot—God give him strength!—
80 grabs you by the neck and kicks you off the Rock.

44 leipsydrion a place where patriots had gallantly fought

SCENE II

Re-enter Lysistrata and her lieutenants.

KORYPHAIOS⁽ʷ⁾ (*Tragic tone*).

Great Queen, fair Architect of our emprise,
Why lookst thou on us with foreboding eyes?

LYSISTRATA.

The behavior of these idiotic women!
There's something about the female temperament
that I can't bear!

KORYPHAIOS⁽ʷ⁾.   What in the world do you mean?   5

LYSISTRATA.

Exactly what I say.

KORYPHAIOS⁽ʷ⁾.   What dreadful thing has happened?
Come, tell us: we're all your friends.

LYSISTRATA.   It isn't easy
to say it; yet, God knows, we can't hush it up.

KORYPHAIOS⁽ʷ⁾.

Well, then? Out with it!

LYSISTRATA.   To put it bluntly,
we're dying to get laid.

KORYPHAIOS⁽ʷ⁾.   Almighty God!   10

LYSISTRATA.

Why bring God into it?—No, it's just as I say.
I can't manage them any longer: they've gone man-crazy,
they're all trying to get out.
                              Why, look:
one of them was sneaking out the back door
over there by Pan's cave; another   15
was sliding down the walls with rope and tackle;
another was climbing aboard a sparrow, ready to take off
for the nearest brothel—I dragged *her* back by the hair!
They're all finding some reason to leave.
                              Look there!
There goes another one.
                    —Just a minute, you!   20
Where are you off to so fast?

FIRST WOMAN.   I've got to get home.
I've a lot of Milesian wool, and the worms are spoiling it.

LYSISTRATA.

Oh bother you and your worms! Get back inside!

FIRST WOMAN.

I'll be back right away, I swear I will.
I just want to get it stretched out on my bed.   25

LYSISTRATA.

You'll do no such thing. You'll stay right here.

FIRST WOMAN.   And my wool?
You want it ruined?

LYSISTRATA.   Yes, for all I care.

SECOND WOMAN.

Oh dear! My lovely new flax from Amorgos—
I left it at home, all uncarded!

LYSISTRATA.   Another one!
30 And all she wants is someone to card her flax.
Get back in there!
SECOND WOMAN.   But I swear by the Moon-Goddess,
the minute I get it done, I'll be back!
LYSISTRATA.   I say No.
If you, why not all the other women as well?
THIRD WOMAN.
O Lady Eileithyia!° Radiant goddess! Thou
35 intercessor for women in childbirth! Stay, I pray thee,
oh stay this parturition. Shall I pollute
a sacred spot?
LYSISTRATA.   And what's the matter with *you*?
THIRD WOMAN.
I'm having a baby—any minute now.
LYSISTRATA.
But you weren't pregnant yesterday.
THIRD WOMAN.   Well, I am today.
40 Let me go home for a midwife, Lysistrata:
there's not much time.
LYSISTRATA.   I never heard such nonsense.
What's that bulging under your cloak?
THIRD WOMAN.   A little baby boy.
LYSISTRATA.
It certainly isn't. But it's something hollow,
like a basin or—Why, it's the helmet of Athena!
And you said you were having a baby.
45 THIRD WOMAN.   Well, I am! So there!
LYSISTRATA.
Then why the helmet?
THIRD WOMAN.   I was afraid that my pains
might begin here in the Akropolis; and I wanted
to drop my chick into it, just as the dear doves do.
LYSISTRATA.
Lies! Evasions!—But at least one thing's clear:
50 you can't leave the place before your purification.
THIRD WOMAN.
But I can't stay here in the Akropolis! Last night I
dreamed of the Snake.
FIRST WOMAN.
And those horrible owls, the noise they make!
I can't get a bit of sleep; I'm just about dead.
LYSISTRATA.
You useless girls, that's enough: Let's have no more lying.
55 Of course you want your men. But don't you imagine
that they want you just as much? I'll give you my word,
their nights must be pretty hard.
Just stick it out!
A little patience, that's all, and our battle's won.
I have heard an Oracle. Should you like to hear it?
FIRST WOMAN.
An Oracle? Yes, tell us!

34 Eileithyia goddess of childbirth

138

LYSISTRATA.   Here is what it says: 60
WHEN SWALLOWS SHALL THE HOOPOE SHUN
  AND SPURN HIS HOT DESIRE,
ZEUS WILL PERFECT WHAT THEY'VE BEGUN
  AND SET THE LOWER HIGHER.
FIRST WOMAN.
Does that mean we'll be on top?   65
LYSISTRATA.
BUT IF THE SWALLOWS SHALL FALL OUT
  AND TAKE THE HOOPOE'S BAIT,
A CURSE MUST MARK THEIR HOUR OF DOUBT,
  INFAMY SEAL THEIR FATE.
THIRD WOMAN.
I swear, *that* Oracle's all too clear.
FIRST WOMAN.   Oh the dear gods!   70
LYSISTRATA.
Let's not be downhearted, girls. Back to our places!
The god has spoken. How can we possibly fail him?

(*Exit Lysistrata with the dissident women.*)

CHORAL EPISODE

Strophe

CHORUS(m).
I know a little story that I learned way back in school.
Goes like this:
Once upon a time there was a young man—and no
  fool—   75
Named Melanion; and his
One aversion was marriage. He loathed the very
  thought.
So he ran off to the hills, and in a special grot
Raised a dog, and spent his days
Hunting rabbits. And it says   80
That he never never never did come home.
It might be called a refuge *from* the womb.
All right,
        all right,
                all right!
We're as bright as young Melanion, and we hate the very
  sight
Of you women!   85
A MAN.
How about a kiss, old lady?
A WOMAN.
Here's an onion for your eye!
A MAN.
A kick in the guts, then?
A WOMAN.
Try, old bristle-tail, just try!
A MAN.
Yet they say Myronides   90
On hands and knees
Looked just as shaggy fore and aft as I!

ANTISTROPHE

CHORUS(w).
Well, *I* know a little story, and it's just as good as yours.
Goes like this:
Once there was a man named Timon—a rough diamond, of course,
And that whiskery face of his
Looked like murder in the shrubbery. By God, he was a son
Of the Furies, let me tell you! And what did he do but run
From the world and all its ways,
Cursing mankind! And it says
That his choicest execrations as of then
Were leveled almost wholly at *old* men.
All right,
        all right,
                all right,
But there's one thing about Timon: he could always stand the sight
Of us women.
A WOMAN.
How about a crack in the jaw, Pop?
A MAN.
I can take it, Ma—no fear!
A WOMAN.
How about a kick in the face?
A MAN.
You'd reveal your old caboose?
A WOMAN.
What I'd show,
I'll have you know,
Is an instrument you're too far gone to use.

SCENE III

Re-enter Lysistrata.

LYSISTRATA.
Oh, quick, girls, quick! Come here!
A WOMAN.   What is it?
LYSISTRATA.   A man.
A man simply bulging with love.
                              O Kyprian Queen,°
O Paphian, O Kythereian! Hear us and aid us!
A WOMAN.
Where is this enemy?
LYSISTRATA.   Over there, by Demeter's shrine.

A WOMAN.
Damned if he isn't. But who *is* he?
MYRRHINE.   My husband.
Kinesias.
LYSISTRATA.
        Oh, then, get busy! Tease him! Undermine him!
Wreck him! Give him everything—kissing, tickling, nudging,
whatever you generally torture him with—: give him everything
except what we swore on the wine we would not give.
MYRRHINE.
Trust me.
LYSISTRATA. I do. But I'll help you get him started.
The rest of you women, stay back.

Enter Kinesias.

KINESIAS.   Oh God! Oh my God!
I'm stiff from lack of exercise. All I can do to stand up.
LYSISTRATA.
Halt! Who are you, approaching our lines?
KINESIAS.   Me? I.
LYSISTRATA.
A man?
KINESIAS. You have eyes, haven't you?
LYSISTRATA.   Go away.
KINESIAS.
Who says so?
LYSISTRATA.   Officer of the Day.
KINESIAS.   Officer, I beg you,
by all the gods at once, bring Myrrhine out.
LYSISTRATA.
Myrrhine? And who, my good sir, are you?
KINESIAS.
Kinesias. Last name's Pennison. Her husband.
LYSISTRATA.
Oh, of course. I beg your pardon. We're glad to see you.
We've heard so much about you. Dearest Myrrhine
is always talking about Kinesias—never nibbles an egg
or an apple without saying
"Here's to Kinesias!"
KINESIAS.   Do you really mean it?
LYSISTRATA.   I do.
When we're discussing men, she always says
"Well, after all, there's nobody like Kinesias!"
KINESIAS.
Good God.—Well, then, please send her down here.
LYSISTRATA.
And what do *I* get out of it?
KINESIAS.   A standing promise.
LYSISTRATA.
I'll take it up with her.

2 **Kyprian Queen** Aphrodite, goddess of love

(*Exit Lysistrata.*)

KINESIAS.   But be quick about it!
Lord, what's life without a wife? Can't eat. Can't sleep.
30   Every time I go home, the place is so empty, so
insufferably sad. Love's killing me, Oh,
hurry!

*Enter Manes, a slave, with Kinesias' baby; the voice of
Myrrhine is heard off-stage.*

MYRRHINE.
                    But of course I love him! Adore him—
                                                      But no,
he hates love. No. I won't go down.

Enter Myrrhine, above.

KINESIAS.   Myrrhine!
Darlingest Myrrhinette! Come down quick!
MYRRHINE.
Certainly not.
KINESIAS.
35   Not? But why, Myrrhine?
MYRRHINE.
Why? You don't need me.
KINESIAS.   Need you? My God, *look* at me!
MYRRHINE.
So long!

(Turns to go.)

KINESIAS.   Myrrhine, Myrrhine, Myrrhine!
If not for my sake, for our child!

(Pinches Baby.)

                                      —All right, you: pipe up!
BABY.
Mummie! Mummie! Mummie!
KINESIAS.   You hear that?
40   Pitiful, I call it. Six days now
with never a bath; no food; enough to break your heart!
MYRRHINE.
My darlingest child! What a father *you* acquired!
KINESIAS.
At least come down for his sake.
MYRRHINE.   I suppose I must.
Oh, this mother business!

                                                      (Exit.)

KINESIAS.   How pretty she is! And younger!
The harder she treats me, the more bothered I get.

(Myrrhine enters, below.)

45   MYRRHINE.   Dearest child,
you're as sweet as your father's horrid. Give me a kiss.
KINESIAS.
Now don't you see how wrong it was to get involved
in this scheming League of women? It's bad
for us both.
MYRRHINE.   Keep both hands to yourself!
KINESIAS.   But our house
going to rack and ruin?

MYRRHINE.   *I don't care.*
KINESIAS.   And your knitting   50
all torn to pieces by the chickens? Don't you care?
MYRRHINE.
Not at all.
KINESIAS.   And our debt to Aphrodite?
Oh, *won't* you come back?
MYRRHINE.   No.—At least, not until you men
make a treaty and stop this war.
KINESIAS.   Why, I suppose   55
that might be arranged.
MYRRHINE.   Oh? Well, I suppose
I might come down then. But meanwhile,
I've sworn not to.
KINESIAS.   Don't worry.—Now let's have fun.
MYRRHINE.
No! Stop it! I said no!
                          —Although, of course,
I *do* love you.
KINESIAS.   I know you do. Darling Myrrhine:
come, shall we?
MYRRHINE. Are you out of your mind? In front of the child?   60
KINESIAS.
Take him home, Manes.

                                      (Exit Manes with Baby.)
                          There. He's gone.
                                        Come on!
There's nothing to stop us now.
MYRRHINE.   You devil! But where?
KINESIAS.
In Pan's cave. What could be snugger than that?
MYRRHINE.
But my purification before I go back to the Citadel?
KINESIAS.
Wash in the Klepsydra.°
MYRRHINE.   And my oath?
KINESIAS.   Leave the oath to me.
After all, I'm the man.   65
MYRRHINE.   Well . . . if you say so.
                                        I'll go find a bed.
KINESIAS.
Oh, bother a bed! The ground's good enough for me.
MYRRHINE.
No. You're a bad man, but you deserve something better
    than dirt.

                                      (Exit Myrrhine.)

KINESIAS.
What a love she is! And how thoughtful!

Re-enter Myrrhine.

---

65 Klepsydra a sacred spring beneath the walls of the Akropolis.
Kinesias' suggestion has overtones of blasphemy.

MYRRHINE.   Here's your bed.
    Now let me get my clothes off.

70   But good horrors!
    We haven't a mattress.

KINESIAS.   Oh, forget the mattress!

MYRRHINE.   No.
    Just lying on blankets? Too sordid.

KINESIAS.   Give me a kiss.

MYRRHINE.
    Just a second.

                                  (*Exit Myrrhine.*)

KINESIAS.   I swear, I'll explode!

Re-enter Myrrhine.

MYRRHINE.   Here's your mattress.
    I'll just take my dress off.

                      But look—
    where's our pillow?

KINESIAS.   I don't *need* a pillow!

75 MYRRHINE.   Well, *I* do.

                                  (*Exit Myrrhine.*)

KINESIAS.
    I don't suppose even Herakles
    would stand for this!

Re-enter Myrrhine.

MYRRHINE.   There we are. Ups-a-daisy!

KINESIAS.
    So we are. Well, come to bed.

MYRRHINE.   But I wonder:
    is everything ready now?

KINESIAS.   I can swear to that. Come, darling!

MYRRHINE.
    Just getting out of my girdle.

                      But remember, now
80   what you promised about the treaty.

KINESIAS.   Yes, yes, yes!

MYRRHINE.
    But no coverlet!

KINESIAS.   Damn it, I'll be
    your coverlet!

MYRRHINE.
    Be right back.

                                (*Exit Myrrhine*)

KINESIAS.   This girl and her coverlets
    will be the death of me.

Re-enter Myrrhine.

MYRRHINE.   Here we are. Up you go!

KINESIAS.
    Up? I've been up for ages.

85 MYRRHINE.   Some perfume?

KINESIAS.
    No, by Apollo!

MYRRHINE.   Yes, by Aphrodite!
    I don't care whether you want it or not.

                             (*Exit Myrrhine.*)

KINESIAS.
    For love's sake, hurry!

Re-enter Myrrhine.

MYRRHINE.
    Here, in your hand. Rub it right in.

KINESIAS.   Never cared for perfume.
    And this is particularly strong. Still, here goes.   90

MYRRHINE.
    What a nitwit I am! I brought the Rhodian bottle.

KINESIAS.
    Forget it.

MYRRHINE.   No trouble at all. You just wait here.

                                (*Exit Myrrhine.*)

KINESIAS.
    God damn the man who invented perfume!

Re-enter Myrrhine.

MYRRHINE.
    At last! The right bottle!

KINESIAS.   I've got the rightest
    bottle of all, and it's right here waiting for you.   95
    Darling, forget everything else. Do come to bed.

MYRRHINE.
    Just let me get my shoes off.

                      —And, by the way,
    you'll vote for the treaty?

KINESIAS.   I'll think about it.

                            (*Myrrhine runs away.*)
    There! That's done it! The damned woman,
    she gets me all bothered, she half kills me,   100
    and off she runs! What'll I do? Where
    can I get laid?
                  —And you, little prodding pal,
    who's going to take care of *you*? No, you and I
    had better get down to old Foxdog's Nursing Clinic.

CHORUS[m].
    Alas for the woes of man, alas   105
      Specifically for you.
    She's brought you to a pretty pass:
      What are you going to do?
    Split, heart! Sag, flesh! Proud spirit, crack!
    Myrrhine's got you on your back.   110

KINESIAS.
    The agony, the protraction!

KORYPHAIOS[m].   Friend,
    What woman's worth a damn?
    They bitch us all, world without end.

KINESIAS.
    Yet they're so damned sweet, man!

KORYPHAIOS[m].
    Calamitous, that's what I say.   115
    You should have learned that much today.

CHORUS[m].
    O blessed Zeus, roll womankind.

Up into one great ball;
  Blast them aloft on a high wind,
120   And once there, let them fall.
  Down, down they'll come, the pretty dears,
  And split themselves on our thick spears.

(Exit Kinesias.)

SCENE IV

Enter a Spartan Herald.

HERALD.
  Gentlemen, Ah beg you will be so kind
  as to direct me to the Central Committee.
  Ah have a communication.

Re-enter Commissioner.

COMMISSIONER.   Are you a man,
  or a fertility symbol?
HERALD.   Ah refuse to answer that question!
5   Ah'm a certified herald from Spahta, and Ah've come
  to talk about an ahmistice.
COMMISSIONER.   Then why
  that spear under your cloak?
HERALD.   Ah have no speah!
COMMISSIONER.
  You don't walk naturally, with your tunic
  poked out so. You have a tumor, maybe,
  or a hernia?
HERALD.   You lost yo' mahnd, man?
10   COMMISSIONER.   Well,
  something's up, I can see that. And I don't like it.
HERALD.
  Colonel, Ah resent this.
COMMISSIONER.   So I see. But what *is* it?
HERALD.   A staff
  with a message from Spahta.
COMMISSIONER.   Oh. I know about those staffs.
  Well, then, man, speak out: How are things in Sparta?
HERALD.
15   Hahd, Colonel, hahd! We're at a standstill.
  Cain't seem to think of anything but women.
COMMISSIONER.
  How curious! Tell me, do you Spartans think
  that maybe Pan's to blame?
HERALD.
  Pan? No. Lampito and her little naked friends.
20   They won't let a man come nigh them.
COMMISSIONER.
  How are you handling it?
HERALD.   Losing our mahnds,
  if y' want to know, and walking around hunched over
  lahk men carrying candles in a gale.
  The women have swohn they'll have nothing to do with us
  until we get a treaty.

COMMISSIONER.   Yes. I know.   25
  It's a general uprising, sir, in all parts of Greece.
  But as for the answer—
                          Sir: go back to Sparta
  and have them send us your Armistice Commission.
  I'll arrange things in Athens.
                          And I may say
  that my standing is good enough to make them listen.   30
HERALD.
  A man after mah own haht! Seh, Ah thank you.

(Exit Herald.)

CHORAL EPISODE

Strophe

CHORUS[(m)].
  Oh these women! Where will you find
  A slavering beast that's more unkind? Where a hotter
      fire?
  Give me a panther, any day.
  He's not so merciless as they,   35
      And panthers don't conspire.

Antistrophe

CHORUS[(w)].
    We may be hard, you silly old ass,
        But who brought you to this stupid pass?
            You're the ones to blame.
        Fighting with us, your oldest friends,   40
        Simply to serve your selfish ends—
            Really, you have no shame!
KORYPHAIOS[(m)].
  No, I'm through with women forever.
KORYPHAIOS[(w)].   If you say so.
  Still, you might put some clothes on. You look too
      absurd
  standing around naked. Come, get into this cloak.   45
KORYPHAIOS[(m)].
  Thank you; you're right. I merely took it off
  because I was in such a temper.
KORYPHAIOS[(w)].   That's much better
  Now you resemble a man again.
                              Why have you been so horrid?
  And look: there's some sort of insect in your eye.
  Shall I take it out?
KORYPHAIOS[(m)].   An insect, is it? So that's   50
  what's been bothering me. Lord, yes: take it out!
KORYPHAIOS[(w)].
  You might be more polite.
                          —But, heavens!
  What an enormous mosquito!

KORYPHAIOS(m).   You've saved my life.
That mosquito was drilling an artesian well
in my left eye.
KORYPHAIOS (w). Let me wipe
those tears away.—And now: one little kiss?
KORYPHAIOS(m).
No, no kisses.
KORYPHAIOS(w). You're so difficult.
KORYPHAIOS(m).
You impossible women! How you do get around us!
The poet was right: Can't live with you, or without you.
But let's be friends.
And to celebrate, you might join us in an Ode.

STROPHE I

CHORUS(m and w).
          Let it never be said
          That my tongue is malicious:
          Both by word and by deed
I would set an example that's noble and gracious.
          We've had sorrow and care
          Till we're sick of the tune.
          Is there anyone here
          Who would like a small loan?
               My purse is crammed,
               As you'll soon find;
And you needn't pay me back if the Peace gets signed.

STROPHE 2

          I've invited to lunch
          Some Karystian rips—
          An esurient bunch,
But I've ordered a menu to water their lips.
          I can still make soup
          And slaughter a pig.
          You're all coming, I hope?
          But a bath first, I beg!
               Walk right up
               As though you owned the place,
And you'll get the front door slammed to in your face.

SCENE V

Enter Spartan Ambassador, with entourage.

KORYPHAIOS(m).
The Commission has arrived from Sparta.
                                        How oddly
they're walking!
                    Gentlemen, welcome to Athens!
How is life in Lakonia?
AMBASSADOR.   Need we discuss that?
Simply use your eyes.

CHORUS(m).   The poor man's right:
                        What a sight!
AMBASSADOR.   Words fail me.   5
But come, gentlemen, call in your Commissioners,
and let's get down to a Peace.
CHORAGOS(m).   The state we're in! Can't bear
a stitch below the waist. It's a kind of pelvic
paralysis.
COMMISSIONER.
          Won't somebody call Lysistrata?—Gentlemen,
we're no better off than you.
AMBASSADOR.   So I see.   10
A SPARTAN.
Seh, do y'all feel a certain strain
early in the morning?
AN ATHENIAN.   I do, sir. It's worse than a strain.
A few more days, and there's nothing for us but
          Kleisthenes,
that broken blossom.
CHORAGOS(m).   But you'd better get dressed again.
You know these people going around Athens with   15
          chisels,
looking for statues of Hermes.°
ATHENIAN.   Sir, you are right.
SPARTAN.
He certainly is! Ah'll put mah own clothes back on.
Enter Athenian Commissioners.
COMMISSIONER.
Gentlemen from Sparta, welcome. This is a sorry
          business.
SPARTAN (*To one of his own group*).
Colonel, we got dressed just in time. Ah sweah,
if they'd seen us the way we were, there'd have been a
          new wah   20
between the states.
COMMISSIONER.
Shall we call the meeting to order?
                                    Now, Lakonians,
what's your proposal?
AMBASSADOR.   We propose to consider peace.
COMMISSIONER.
Good. That's on our minds, too.
                                —Summon Lysistrata.
We'll never get anywhere without her.
AMBASSADOR.   Lysistrata?   25
Summon Lysis-*any*body! Only, summon!
KORYPHAIOS(m).   No need to summon:
here she is, herself.

---

16 statues of Hermes The statues were the Hermai, stone posts set
up in various parts of Athens. Just before the sailing of the Sicilian
Expedition, a group of anonymous vandals mutilated these statues
with chisels. This was considered an unhappy augury.

Enter Lysistrata.

COMMISSIONER.   Lysistrata! Lion of women!
This is your hour to be
hard and yielding, outspoken and shy, austere and
30 gentle. You see here
the best brains of Hellas (confused, I admit,
by your devious charming) met as one man
to turn the future over to you.

LYSISTRATA.   That's fair enough,
unless you men take it into your heads
35 to turn to each other instead of us. But I'd know
soon enough if you did.
                        —Where is Reconciliation?
Go, some of you: bring her here.

                                    (*Exeunt two women.*)

                          And now, women,
lead the Spartan delegates to me: not roughly
or insultingly, as our men handle them, but gently,
40 politely, as ladies should. Take them by the hand,
or by anything else if they won't give you their hands.

(*The Spartans are escorted over.*)

There.—The Athenians next, by any convenient
    handle.

(*The Athenians are escorted.*)

Stand there, please.—Now, all of you, listen to me.

(*During the following speech the two women reenter, carrying an enormous statue of a naked girl; this is Reconciliation.*)

I'm only a woman, I know; but I've a mind,
45 and, I think, not a bad one: I owe it to my father
and to listening to the local politicians.
So much for that.
                      Now, gentlemen,
since I have you here, I intend to give you a scolding.
We are all Greeks.
50 Must I remind you of Thermopylai,° of Olympia,
of Delphoi? names deep in all our hearts?
Are they not a common heritage?
                              Yet you men
go raiding through the country from both sides,
Greek killing Greek, storming down Greek cities—
55 and all the time the Barbarian across the sea

is waiting for his chance!
                          —That's my first point.

AN ATHENIAN.
Lord! I can hardly contain myself.

LYSISTRATA.   As for you Spartans:
Was it so long ago that Perikleides°
came here to beg our help? I can see him still,
his gray face, his sombre gown. And what did he want?   60
An army from Athens. All Messene
was hot at your heels, and the sea-god splitting your
    land.
Well, Kimon and his men,
four thousand strong, marched out and saved all Sparta.
And what thanks do we get? You come back to murder
    us.   65

AN ATHENIAN.
They're aggressors, Lysistrata!

A SPARTAN.   Ah admit it.
When Ah look at those laigs, Ah sweah Ah'll aggress
    mahself!

LYSISTRATA.
And you, Athenians: do you think you're blameless?
Remember that bad time when we were helpless,
and an army came from Sparta,   70
and that was the end of the Thessalian menace,
the end of Hippias and his allies.
                              And that was Sparta,
and only Sparta; but for Sparta, we'd be
cringing slaves today, not free Athenians.

(*From this point, the male responses are less to Lysistrata
than to the statue.*)

A SPARTAN.
A well-shaped speech.

AN ATHENIAN.   Certainly it has its points.   75

LYSISTRATA.
Why are we fighting each other? With all this history
of favors given and taken, what stands in the way
of making peace?

AMBASSADOR.   Spahta is ready, ma'am,
so long as we get that place back.

LYSISTRATA.   What place, man?

AMBASSADOR.
Ah refer to Pylos.

COMMISSIONER.   Not a chance, by God!   80

LYSISTRATA.
Give it to them, friend.

---

50 Thermopylai a narrow pass where, in 480 B.C., an army of 300
Spartans held out for three days against a vastly superior Persian
force

58 Perikleides a Spartan ambassador to Athens who successfully
urged Athenians to aid Sparta in putting down a rebellion

COMMISSIONER.   But—what shall we have to bargain with?
LYSISTRATA.
  Demand something in exchange.
COMMISSIONER.   Good idea.—Well, then:
  Cockeville first, and the Happy Hills, and the country
  between the Legs of Megara.
AMBASSADOR.   Mah government objects.
LYSISTRATA.
85 Over-ruled. Why fuss about a pair of legs?

  (*General assent. The statue is removed.*)

AN ATHENIAN.
  I want to get out of these clothes and start my plowing.
A SPARTAN.
  Ah'll fertilize mahn first, by the Heavenly Twins!
LYSISTRATA.
  And so you shall,
90 once you've made peace. If you are serious,
  go, both of you, and talk with your allies.
COMMISSIONER.
  Too much talk already. No, we'll stand together.
  We've only one end in view. All that we want
  is our women; and I speak for our allies.
AMBASSADOR.
  Mah government concurs.
AN ATHENIAN.   So does Karystos.
LYSISTRATA.
95 Good.—But before you come inside
  to join your wives at supper, you must perform
  the usual lustration. Then we'll open
  our baskets for you, and all that we have is yours.
  But you must promise upright good behavior
100 from this day on. Then each man home with his woman!
AN ATHENIAN.
  Let's get it over with.
A SPARTAN.   Lead on. Ah follow.
AN ATHENIAN.
  Quick as a cat can wink!

  (*Exeunt all but the Choruses.*)

ANTISTROPHE I

CHORUS(w).
    Embroideries and
    Twinkling ornaments and
105 Pretty dresses—I hand
  Them all over to you, and with never a qualm.
    They'll be nice for your daughters
    On festival days.
    When the girls bring the Goddess
110   The ritual prize.

  Come in, one and all:
    Take what you will.
  I've nothing here so tightly corked that you can't make
    it spill.

ANTISTROPHE 2

    You may search my house
    But you'll not find   115
    The least thing of use,
  Unless your two eyes are keener than mine.
    Your numberless brats
    Are half starved? and your slaves?
    Courage, grandpa! I've lots   120
    Of grain left, and big loaves.
      I'll fill your guts,
      I'll go the whole hog;
  But if you come too close to me, remember: 'ware the
    dog!

  (*Exeunt Choruses.*)

EXODOS

*A Drunken Citizen enters, approaches the gate, and is
halted by a sentry.*

CITIZEN.
  Open. The. Door.
SENTRY.   Now, friend, just shove along!
  —So you want to sit down. If it weren't such an old joke,
  I'd tickle your tail with this torch. Just the sort of gag
  this audience appreciates.
CITIZEN.   I. Stay. Right. Here.
SENTRY.
  Get away from there, or I'll scalp you! The gentlemen
    from Sparta   5
  are just coming back from dinner.

  (*Exit Citizen; the general company reenters; the two
    Choruses now represent Spartans and Athenians.*)

A SPARTAN.   Ah must say,
  Ah never tasted better grub.
AN ATHENIAN.   And those Lakonians!
  They're gentlemen, by the Lord! Just goes to show,
  a drink to the wise is sufficient.
COMMISSIONER.   And why not?
  A sober man's an ass.   10
  Men of Athens, mark my words: the only efficient
  Ambassador's a drunk Ambassador. Is that clear?
  Look: we go to Sparta,

and when we get there we're dead sober. The result?
15 Everyone cackling at everyone else. They make speeches;
and even if we understand, we get it all wrong
when we file our reports in Athens. But today—!
Everybody's happy. Couldn't tell the difference
between *Drink to Me Only* and
The Star-Spangled Athens.

20   What's a few lies,
washed down in good strong drink?

Re-enter the Drunken Citizen.

SENTRY.   God almighty,
he's back again!

CITIZEN.   I. Resume. My. Place.

A SPARTAN (*To an Athenian*).
Ah beg yo', seh,
take yo' instrument in yo' hand and play for us.
25 Ah'm told
yo' understand the in*tr*icacies of the floot?
Ah'd lahk to execute a song and dance
in honor of Athens,
                      and, of cohse, of Spahta.

CITIZEN.
Toot. On. Your. Flute.

(*The following song is a solo—an aria—accompanied by
the flute. The Chorus of Spartans begins a slow dance.*)

A SPARTAN.
30 O Memory,
Let the Muse speak once more
In my young voice. Sing glory.
Sing Artemision's shore,
Where Athens fluttered the Persians. *Alalai,*
35 Sing glory, that great
Victory! Sing also
Our Leonidas and his men,
Those wild boars, sweat and blood
Down in a red drench. Then, then
40 The barbarians broke, though they had stood
Numberless as the sands before!

O Artemis,°
Virgin Goddess, whose darts
Flash in our forests: approve
45 This pact of peace and join our hearts,
From this day on, in love.
Huntress, descend!

LYSISTRATA.
All that will come in time.
                      But now, Lakonians,
take home your wives. Athenians, take yours.
50 Each man be kind to his woman; and you, women,
be equally kind. Never again, pray God,

shall we lose our way in such madness.

KORYPHAIOS(Athenian).   And now
let's dance our joy.

(*From this point the dance becomes general.*)

CHORUS(Athenian).
Dance, you Graces
                      Artemis, dance
Dance, Phoibos,° Lord of dancing
                                        Dance,   55
In a scurry of Maenads, Lord Dionysos°
                      Dance, Zeus Thunderer
            Dance, Lady Hera°
Queen of the sky.
                      Dance, dance, all you gods
Dance witness everlasting of our pact
Evohí Evohé   60
Dance for the dearest
                      the Bringer of Peace
Deathless Aphrodite!

COMMISSIONER.
Now let us have another song from Sparta.

CHORUS(Spartan).
            From Taygetos, from Taygetos,
                Lakonian Muse, come down.   65
            Sing to the Lord Apollo
                Who rules Amyklai Town.

            Sing Athena of the House of Brass!°
            Sing Leda's Twins,° that chivalry
            Resplendent on the shore   70
Of our Eurotas; sing the girls
            That dance along before:
Sparkling in dust their gleaming feet,
            Their hair a Bacchant fire,
And Leda's daughter, thyrsos° raised,   75
            Leads their triumphant choir.

CHORUSES(S and A).
Evohé!
      Evohaí!
            Evohé!
                  We pass
      Dancing
            dancing
                  to greet
Athena of the House of Brass.

55 **Phoibos** god of the sun   56 **Maenads, Lord Dionysus** The
maenads were ecstatic women in the train of Dionysos, god of wine
57 **Hera** wife of Zeus   68 **Athena of the House of Brass** a temple
standing on the Akropolis of Sparta   69 **Leda's Twins** Leda, raped
by Zeus, bore quadruplets: two daughters, Helen and Klytaimnestra,
and two sons, Kastor and Polydeukes   75 **thyrsos** a staff twined
with ivy, carried by Dionysus and his followers

42 **Artemis** goddess of virginity, of the hunt, and of childbirth

TOPICS FOR CRITICAL THINKING AND WRITING

📖 THE PLAY ON THE PAGE

1. According to *Lysistrata*, what are the causes of war? What do you think are the causes of war?
2. What connection, if any, is there between the sex strike and the seizure of the Akropolis?
3. An antiwar play might be expected to call attention to cruelty, innocent suffering, and death. How much of this do you find in *Lysistrata*?

🎭 THE PLAY ON THE STAGE

4. How would you costume the play?
5. Take a passage of some fifty lines and specify the gestures and blocking that you would use if you were directing the play.
6. There is much about sex here. How much is there about love?
7. Evaluate the view that the real heroine of the play is not Lysistrata but the nude female statue, Reconciliation.

THE PLAY IN PERFORMANCE

Lysistrata requires at least four actors, in addition to the chorus and to a few mute figures.

Most ancient Greek plays require only one doorway through which actors enter and exit, but *Lysistrata* (as well as a few other comedies) seems to require two or even three doors. The *skene* or "scene-building" apparently had one permanent central entrance with double doors, but additional entrances could be created at each side. Thus, in *Lysistrata* at the end of the prologue the central door is identified as the gateway to the Acropolis. Perhaps at the start of the play Lysistrata enters from a side door, or from the *parodos*, stands in front of the central door, and then is greeted by her neighbor Kalonike, who enters from the other side door.

The play requires that actors appear not only on ground level but also at an elevation. We know that performers—usually in the role of gods—sometimes appeared on the roof of the *skene*; in *Lysistrata* the heroine appears on the roof, and so do some of the other women.

The costumes of the actors presumably resembled the costumes of the audience, that is, of contemporary society, though some of the male characters are equipped with erect phalluses. About the only other costume that requires men-

tion is that of Reconciliation, a female figure who is said to be nude. Since all of the roles were played by males, female nakedness presumably was represented by males in bodysuits adorned with female breasts and genitalia.

Probably the most important decision a director must make is whether to use actresses or (following ancient Greek practice) to use an all-male cast. It is important to realize that the parts of the women must be convincingly played; if men play the parts in drag, and camp it up, most of the joke is lost, since the male characters must be understood to be sexually aroused by the sight of the women. Or, let's say, a campy drag version becomes something very different from Aristophanes's play.

In modern times the play has occasionally been done by pacifists and also by feminists—always with women in the female roles. There are records of such productions as early as 1912. The Moscow Art Theater did a version, and brought it to the United States in 1925. In 1930 a rather free version of *Lysistrata* had a brief but successful professional run in Philadelphia and in New York, but chiefly the play is produced in college and university theaters.

A Note on
ROMAN DRAMA

The ancient Romans claimed that their drama was rooted in native material, and at least for comedy there is some evidence of skits belonging to a genre called "Atellan farce," named for the city of Attelae in southern Italy, near Naples. Atellan farce was built on stock characters (the oaf, the crabby old man, the clever slave, etc.), but it was not written down, and so we know little more than can be garnered from references to the titles of the skits. In any case, the Roman plays that exist—tragedies as well as comedies—are clearly derived from Greek plays. Greece early exerted an influence on southern Italy (the region south of Naples was called Greater Greece), and the influence spread to Rome. Around the middle of the third century B.C. Latin adaptations of Greek plays—tragedies and comedies—were performed in Rome, and these were followed by new plays, in Latin, on themes derived from ancient Greek plays.

In the first century B.C., Roman poets seem to have written tragedies not as productions for the stage but as literary exercises—works that might be read to a select group. It is customarily said that one reason serious writers now shunned the stage was that the stage was occupied by pantomime, a form in which a masked dancer (the *pantomimus*) performed all of the roles while a chorus sang the story. The dancer might use more than one mask, and on occasion two or even three dancers performed.

But Romans *did* write plays that are comedies and tragedies, and we will now glance at these. The two chief writers of comedy are Plautus (c. 254–184 B.C.) and Terence (c. 190–159 B.C.), and though their names are forever linked, they actually were very different sorts of people—like, say, Laurel and Hardy. But they did share certain qualities. They adapted their plays from Greek New Comedy, which, we have seen (page 125), is essentially a comedy of intrigue: It usually shows a young man achieving his goal—for instance outwitting an old man and getting the girl he wants. It thus combines an element of satire (ridicule for those who get in the way of the resourceful youths) and a story of intrigue (getting the girl). In Roman comedy, the names of the characters are Greek, and the settings are said to be Greek. Although the plots of Plautus and Terence resemble each other, there is a great difference in tone. A traditional comparison holds that Plautus is a blacksmith, Terence a watchmaker. That is, the twenty-one extant plays of Plautus emphasize boisterous fun, whereas the six extant plays of Terence emphasize elegant language and human tolerance.

Titus Macius Plautus ("Titus, the Flatfooted Clown") does not hesitate to allow his characters to step out of character if a laugh can be had. The plays are relatively short by today's standard—they run for about an hour—and they are built chiefly on what today is called situation comedy, with a good deal of physical humor. One situation that the Romans invented is the confusion caused by identical twins; Plautus uses this device in *Menaechmi* (*The Menaechmus Bothers*), which is the major source for Shakespeare's *The Comedy of Errors*—and also for a Rodgers and Hart musical, *The Boys from Syracuse* (1938).

Terence—more properly, Publius Terentius Afer—is said to have been a freed slave from Carthage. Six plays are attributed to him, and compared with the plays of Plautus these works are models of subtlety and restraint, with elegant language and with relatively little physical humor. Further, the follies of Terence's characters are not boisterously exposed and subjected to guffaws, but are treated genially and sympathetically. His tolerance is evident in what is his most famous line: "I am a man; nothing human is alien to me" (*Homo sum; humani nil a me alienum puto*). Consider, too, some of his other famous lines: "Moderation in all things"; "Lovers quarrels are the renewal of love"; "Time removes distress"; "Extreme law is often extreme injustice"; "Nothing is said that has not been said before." It is easy to see why school teachers have liked Terence. One unexpected product of Terence's influence is the work of Hrotsvitha of Gandersheim (c. 935–73), a German noblewoman who lived within a religious order, though she was not a nun. Hrotsvitha wrote six prose plays in Latin about martyrs and the triumph of virginity, as examples of what a Christian Terence might write. Virtually all scholars agree that she did not intend her plays for performance.

In Roman tragedy, Seneca (c. 4 B.C.– A.D. 65) is the chief name. Ten plays are ascribed to him, including a *Medea* (derived from Euripides) and an *Oedipus* (derived from Sophocles). Although the plays are derived from Greek themes, they are distinctive, partly because of a greater emphasis on the supernatural (ghosts and dreams) and especially on madness. Curiously, the mad speeches are combined with clever epigrams and with elaborate rhetorical effects. In the view of many readers—the plays are rarely staged—these tragedies dwell too lovingly on the morbid, and for all of their passionate assertion they are lacking in drama. On the other hand, Seneca has appealed to serious students who emphasize the drama's roots in ancient ritual and who believe that drama should shock an audience into primal feelings rather than merely entertain an audience. Although the issue has not been settled, it is generally believed that Seneca's plays were intended for recitation to a small private audience rather than for stage production. In any case, because in the sixteenth and seventeenth century Seneca was much read in the schools, these works had an enormous influence on the drama, evident not only in a minor work such as Shakespeare's *Titus Andronicus* but also in *Hamlet*.

A few words should be said about the Roman stage. There is evidence that in the third century B.C. the Romans sometimes erected temporary wood stages, but a permanent theater was not built until very late, 55 B.C., when Pompey the Great ordered that a stone theater be built. It no longer stands, but evidence indicates that it was semicircular, following the tradition of the Greek theater. In the next few decades several other theaters were built, including the Theater of Marcellus (13 B.C.), which seated twenty thousand spectators, and whose walls still stand in Rome. Theaters in the Roman Empire were Greek in inspiration, but instead of being built into a hillside they were built upward, on flat terrain. Thus, the *scaena* (based on the Greek *skene* or scene-building, which provided a background for the action) and the *cavea* (the auditorium) were fully surrounded. The area in front the of *scaena* was known as the *proscaena*, which gives us our word *prosecenium*. The chorus was used only rarely, and so there was no need for the *orchestra* (dancing place) of the Greek theater. Perhaps spectators in the enclosed Roman theater had a heightened feeling of being in a world apart from the real world. The opening shows at Pompey's theater consisted not of plays but of the slaughter of exotic animals. Later entertainments in Roman theaters included throwing Christian martyrs to wild beasts. Not surprisingly, when Christianity triumphed in Rome, the theater was seen as an enemy, and the theaters fell into disuse.

A Note on
THE MEDIEVAL THEATER

CHRISTIAN OPPOSITION TO DRAMA

In A.D. 410 Alaric, King of the Visigoths, crossed the Alps and sacked Rome. In the next five centuries probably no plays were written in Europe and no theaters were built there. But the drama had encountered an enemy even before Alaric entered Rome: The Christian church had long opposed theatrical entertainments, partly because they included spectacles of nudity, fights with wild beasts, and the like; partly because Christians were fed to lions or were tarred and set afire in entertainments offered to the pagan Romans; and partly because the church's hatred of "falsehood" included among the untruths—the fictions—of literature the art of acting, which involves the impersonation of one man by another, and—even worse—of a woman by a man by means of transvestism. Here is the biblical text that is usually cited: "The woman shall not wear that which pertaineth unto a man, neither shall a man put on a woman's garment; for all that do so are abomination unto the Lord God" (Deuteronomy 22.5).

THE RISE OF LITURGICAL DRAMA, AND "THE PLAY OF CORPUS CHRISTI"

In the fifth century, after a monk attempted to interfere in a gladiatorial combat and was stoned to death, the Roman emperors (who is 378 had adopted Christianity as the official state religion) prohibited public spectacles. For all practical purposes, the theater in Europe and Britain ceased to exist, except for quasi-dramatic events such as tournaments and ritual practices in pagan festivals and such meager performances as were put on by itinerant minstrels, owners of performing animals, mimes, jugglers, and puppeteers.

And yet, despite the opposition of Christianity, which held that drama is immoral because it presents false appearances, the drama was reborn within the church in what is known as liturgical drama. A liturgy is a prescribed form of worship, including the singing of the Mass, in which bread and wine are consecrated as the body and blood of Christ. Some liturgical texts were arranged in dialogue form, with choric chants divided antiphonally, that is with one voice (or set of voices) responding to another. For instance, one of the introductory antiphons for the Easter Mass consists of an exchange in song between a voice or set of voices speaking for an angel and another set of voices speaking for the women who visited Christ's tomb in order to anoint the corpse. The angel asks whom they seek, they reply that they seek Jesus, and the angel explains that Jesus has risen from the tomb. Such a service, with chanting priests and a choir—a voice or voices answering a voice or voices—resembles a dramatic exchange, but it is not quite drama since there is little or no emphasis on impersonation. Still, before the end of the tenth century it was clear that drama was reborn in the church.

Earlier in this book (pages 3–4, in our essay in which we consider the essence of drama, we discuss the liturgical drama called *Quem Quaeritis* ("Whom do you seek?"), described by Bishop Ethelwold. We need not repeat that discussion here. Suffice it to say that adaptations soon followed; for instance, similar dramatic renditions celebrated the birth of Jesus and the journey of the Magi. These compositions probably were not initially conceived of as educational, in time they must have been recognized as a means by which an illiterate congregation could better grasp the miraculous realities. In 1264, some three hundred years after Bishop Ethelwold set down his instructions, Pope Urban IV promulgated a new Feast Day, Corpus Christi (medieval

Latin, "body of Christ"), which was finally instituted by Pope Clement V in 1311. Celebrated on the Thursday following Trinity Sunday, and commemorating Christ's sacrifice of his life for the salvation of humankind, Corpus Christi Day occurred nine weeks after Easter Sunday. Although in the modern calendar it falls in late May or in June, in the Middle Ages, because the calendar was inaccurate, Corpus Christi Day fell at a time equivalent to our June or early July. It became a joyful midsummer festival, marked by a procession in which the communion chalice, escorted by local dignitaries, was carried through the streets.

Plays soon became part of the Feast of Corpus Christi, and so, for example, in Italy in the early fourteenth century Corpus Christi Day was celebrated by an almost cosmic cycle of plays on sacred history, in Latin, ranging from the Fall of Lucifer, the Crucifixion of Christ, the Harrowing of Hell, Christ's Ascension, and on up to the Day of Judgment. By the end of the fourteenth century the celebration of Corpus Christi included plays performed not in Latin but in the vernacular, on Old Testament and New Testament subjects, sponsored not only by the Church but by civic organizations. Guilds sponsored plays deemed appropriate; thus, the shipwrights were responsible for the play about Noah's Ark, the bakers for The Last Supper, and so on. The plays as a group were called "the play of Corpus Christi," and each episode was a pageant, but scholars usually call the individual episodes **miracle plays**—a term sometimes used in the Middle Ages—or **mystery plays** because they were sponsored by various trades or "mysteries," a word derived, like the French *metier,* from the Latin *minister,* "attendant," "servant."

How does one account for this widespread and vast medieval cyclical drama? Did it "develop" from *Quem Quaeritis,* or was it engendered afresh? In the late nineteenth and early twentieth centuries, scholars customarily held a sort of Darwinian view, suggesting that the late medieval cycles "evolved" out of *Quem Quaeritis.* In this view, the drama gradually but naturally grew, adding one story to another, expanding the length of the stories, inevitably shifting from Latin into the vernacular, and equally inevitably moving out of the church and into the marketplace. The current prevailing scholarly view, however, tends to deemphasize a "natural" evolution and to hold that the plays are the result of self-conscious efforts to set forth scriptural history—a history of the wonders of God—in dramatic form. That is, the plays are now seen as an effort to provide visible evidence explaining the significance of the Feast of Corpus Christi.

THE STAGING OF MIRACLE PLAYS

In England four great cycles of miracles plays are extant: forty-eight plays were done at York, thirty-two at Wakefield, twenty-four at Chester, and forty-three at an unidentified town (formerly thought to be Coventry). Moreover, this sort of medieval drama, enormously popular in the late fourteenth century and in the fifteenth, survived until well into the Renaissance, that is, for several decades after Henry VIII split with the Church of Rome and established the Church of England. The cycles were given at Chester until 1574 and at Coventry (only fourteen miles from Shakespeare's Stratford) until 1581, when Shakespeare was seventeen. They apparently were abandoned not because the people lost interest in religious drama but for two other reasons: (1) Protestantism was hostile to a drama that had developed under Roman Catholic auspices, and (2) better dramatic entertainment was becoming available. The late sixteenth century saw the rise of small companies of professional strolling players, who could put on a better show than could the local amateurs. In 1576, the last year that the plays were staged at Wakefield, James Burbage erected England's first permanent theater, in London. In York the plays were revived in 1951 to celebrate "The Festival of Britain." Much to the producers' and community's surprise, audiences found the old scripts exciting drama. Today, all around Britain the medieval plays are staged often—in medieval and in modern dress—and audiences respond to both the spiritual and theatrical elements.

Something (but not a great deal) is known about the staging of medieval plays. There is evidence of performances on temporary stages made of planks resting on trestles or barrels; there is also evidence of performances in the round (i.e., with the audience on all sides), and of performances on wagons or floats called **"pageants."** In some towns pageants were drawn to several announced localities where separate audiences waited. In this method of staging, each audience stayed in one place, seeing a succession of scenes, and the wagons traveled on to other audiences waiting at other locations. But it may also be the case, for some vast cycles, that although the wagons were first drawn through the town, they were then assembled in a circle in one place, for instance in a public square, where the plays were performed one by one with the audience in the center of the ring of wagons.

A stage, or a pageant, by the way, might simultaneously display several sets (called **sedes,** literally "seats," or **mansions**) to indicate different locales; a structure representing Hell (the head of a monster, from whose gaping mouth smoke poured forth) might be at one side, and a structure representing Heaven might be at the other. In between were structures representing various places, such as the manger where Jesus was born, the hill where he was crucified, and so forth. There is also evidence that the performers sometimes left their stages and entered the open space (the **platea**) where the audience stood. In short, the productions were closer to today's "street theater" than to what goes on in our modern playhouses.

Martial Rose, in *The Wakefield Mystery Plays* (a book with a long introduction to a modernized text of the plays), offers some conjectures about how the town of Wakefield in the mid-fifteenth century may have staged its cycle of thirty-two plays, ranging from the creation of the world through the fall of humankind, the redemption, and the judgment. (It must be remembered that the evidence is very fragmentary, and Rose's account therefore is highly conjectural, but it is as reasonable as any other that has been offered.) Perhaps, Rose says, soon after dawn on Corpus Christi Day, twenty or thirty pageants set out on the Corpus Christi procession. Sponsored by the trade guilds—each guild was associated with a particular pageant—the procession of wagons, guilds—men, minstrels, and clergy went to the parish church. Here, at the service, the Host of the Lord was raised, carried out of the church, and carried (with the procession following) to various stations in the town. At each station the pageants would produce, in pantomime, the climax of the play that they would perform in full in the following three days. During the next three days, the plays were per-formed at only one location (perhaps the market place, the common, or the land adjoining the church), where an audi-ence assembled in a circle around an open space to watch as each pageant entered through an aisle and its actors per-formed. Rose conjectures that perhaps Heaven and Hell were brought in first and remained in view throughout, while the other wagons came and went. Or possibly the audience assembled in the center, and all of the wagons were assembled around the perimeter of the circle.

The wagon for *The Second Shepherds' Play* might have used two mansions, one for Mak's house and one for Mary and Jesus. The space between and in front of the two man-sions (the *platea*) could have served for the fields, though some scholars conjecture a third mansion, a fence, to repre-sent the sheepfold.

For a further discussion of the staging of *The Second Shep-herds' Play*, see the introduction (page 152) to the play.

The Wakefield Master

THE SECOND SHEPHERDS' PLAY

The anonymous author of five plays in The Wakefield Cycle (which has a total of thirty-two plays) is called The Wakefield Master. He is thought to have been a clergyman active in the first half of the fifteenth century, but nothing is known for certain about him. (The cycle is also known as the Towneley Cycle, from the name of a family that owned the manuscript, but Wakefield is a better designation for two reasons: The manuscript specifically mentions Wakefield, a town in Yorkshire, England, and it is known that a cycle of plays was in fact performed there.)

The Wakefield Cycle probably originated in the late fourteenth century, but it was revised and amplified. The five plays attributed to the Wakefield Master are characterized by the liveliness of the roles and by a distinctive nine-line stanza. The first four lines of each stanza use identical end-rhymes and also internal rhymes. In the last five lines, lines 5 and 9 rhyme, and lines 6, 7, and 8 rhyme. The first four lines each have four stresses, line 5 has only one stress, lines 6, 7, and 8 have three stresses each, and line 9 has two stresses. This stanza is used only in the five plays attributed to the Wakefield Master and in a few passages in another play that he apparently revised.

COMMENTARY

The play that we print is called *The Second Shepherds' Play* because in the Wakefield cycle it is the second of two plays about the shepherds who received the news of the birth of Jesus, as told in the second chapter of the Gospel according to Saint Luke. Here is the biblical material, in the King James Version (1611)—a translation that appeared almost two hundred years later than the play. After reporting that Mary gave birth to Jesus in a stable, Luke says:

8 And there were in the same country shepherds abiding in the fields, keeping watch over their flock by night.

9 And, lo, the angel of the Lord came upon them, and the glory of the Lord shone round about them: and they were sore afraid.

10 And the angel said unto them, "Fear not: for behold, I bring you good tidings of great joy, which shall be to all people.

11 For unto you is born this day in the city of David a Savior, which is Christ the Lord.

12 And this shall be a sign unto you; Ye shall find the babe wrapped in swaddling clothes, lying in a manger."

13 And suddenly there was with the angel a multitude of the heavenly host praising God, and saying,

14 "Glory to God in the highest, and on earth peace, good will toward men."

15 And it came to pass, as the angels were gone away from them into heaven, the shepherds said one to another, "Let us now go even unto Bethlehem, and see this thing which is come to pass, which the Lord hath made known unto us."

16 And they came with haste, and found Mary, and Joseph, and the babe lying in a manger.

17 And when they had seen it, they made known abroad the saying which was told them concerning the child.

The life of Jesus, from his birth through his crucifixion and resurrection, underlies the numerous episodes of the cycle of plays that was known as *The Play of Corpus Christi*. The cycle begins with the Creation of the World, moves through various episodes in the Hebrew Bible, including such momentous episodes as the Fall of Adam and Eve, Abraham and Isaac, and Noah's Flood, and then gives us the turning point of history, the birth of Jesus, which, through the Crucifixion, leads to the salvation of mankind. In short, the pageants in *The Play of Corpus Christi* dramatize episodes of the Old Testament in order to show how they are fulfilled in the New Testament. But the plays often go beyond the sources, elaborating the biblical stories with invented details. Thus, Luke's ten verses concerning the shepherds are expanded in *The Second Shepherds' Play* into a drama of 794 lines—and what is more amazing, the first 637 lines of the play, concerning a stolen sheep that is disguised as an infant, are sheer invention, having nothing explicitly to do with the news of the birth of Jesus. But of course there are dramatic connections—most obviously in the contrast between the pseudo-birth scene in Mak's cottage (with the swaddled stolen sheep, horned like the devil) and the nativity of the

Christ Child, announced in the last part of the play. Similarly, the initial complaints of the laboring men in an unjust world are connected, by way of contrast, with the joy in a spiritually renewed world at the end of the play.

The Second Shepherds' Play is comic in two senses. First, it is amusing, with its grumbling figures and the sheep-stealer who adopts a dialect in order to impersonate a man of rank and who tries to pass off a stolen sheep as his newborn infant. Second, it is comic in its overall action, that is, in its movement from bad fortune to good fortune (the recovery of the stolen sheep), from sorrow to joy (the news of the birth of Jesus), from the cruelty of nature and of humankind to generosity (the giving of gifts), from winter to an anticipation of spring (in the presentation of the bunch of cherries) and renewed life.

A Note on the Translation

Something should be said about the language of the original play and about our translation. The anonymous author, writing in the middle of the fifteenth century, used an English that often is close to modern English, and often it is not. Thus, the first line of the original,

Lord, what these weders are cold! And I am ill happyd,

may be translated fairly literally as

Lord, how this weather is cold! And I am poorly clothed.

We translate it as:

Lord, but this weather is cold! And I am ill wrapped.

By substituting "wrapped" for the obscure "happyd," we can spare the reader from consulting a gloss and yet we can also preserve the rhyme of *happyd* / *nappyd* / *chappyd* of the original. Or consider the very last lines of the play:

To sing ar we bun—
Let take on loft!

Literally this means, "To sing are we bound, / Begin [the song] loudly." We render the last line as "Ring it aloft," which avoids the need to gloss "Let take" as "begin," and which yet preserves the rhyme with "Full oft," as in the original.

The Wakefield Master

THE SECOND SHEPHERDS' PLAY

Modernized version by the editors

List of Characters

FIRST SHEPHERD [*Coll*]
SECOND SHEPHERD [*Gib*]
THIRD SHEPHERD [*Daw*]
MAK [*a sheep-stealer*]
HIS WIFE [*Gill*]
ANGEL
MARY
CHRIST-CHILD

A field.

FIRST SHEPHERD.
　　Lord, but these weathers are cold! And I am ill wrapped
　　I am near-hand dold,° so long have I napped;
　　My legs they fold, my fingers are chapped.
　　It is not as I would, for I am all lapped
5　　In sorrow.
　　In storms and tempest,
　　Now in the east, now in the west,
　　Woe is him has never rest
　　Midday nor morrow!

10　　But we simple husbands° that walk on the moor,
　　In faith we are near-hands out of the door.
　　No wonder, as it stands, if we be poor,
　　For the tilth of our lands lies fallow as the floor,
　　As ye ken.°
15　　We are so lamed,
　　O'ertaxed and maimed,
　　We are made hand-tamed
　　By these gentlery men.

　　Thus they rob us our rest, our Lady them harry!
20　　These men that are lord-fast, they make the plough tarry.
　　What men say is for the best, we find it contrary.
　　Thus are husbands oppressed, about to miscarry
　　In life.
　　Thus hold they us under,
25　　Thus they bring us in blunder;
　　It were great wonder
　　If ever should we thrive.

There shall come a swain as proud as a po;°
He must borrow my wain, my plough also;
Then I am full fain° to grant ere he go.　　　　　30
Thus live we in pain, anger, and woe,
By night, and day.
He must have it for sure,
Though I remain poor;
I'll be pushed out of door　　　　　35
If I once say nay.

If he has braid on his sleeve or a badge nowadays,
Woe to him that him grieve or ever gainsays!
No complaint he'll receive, whatever his ways.
And yet may none believe one word that he says,　　　　　40
No letter.
He can make his demands
With boasts and commands,
And all because he stands
For men who are greater.　　　　　45

It does me good, as I walk thus by mine own,
Of this world for to talk in manner of moan.
To my sheep will I stalk, and hearken anon,°
And there will I halt and sit on a stone
Full soon.　　　　　50
For I trust, pardie,°
True men if there be,
We get more company
Ere it be noon.

[*Enter the Second Shepherd, who does not see the First Shepherd.*]

SECOND SHEPHERD.
　　Blessings upon us, what may this bemean?　　　　　55
　　Why fares this world thus? Such we seldom have seen.
　　Lord, these weathers are spiteous, and the winds full keen,
　　And the frosts so hideous they water mine eyne,°
　　No lie!
　　Now in dry, now in wet,　　　　　60
　　Now in snow, now in sleet,
　　When my shoes freeze to my feet

---

2 dold nearly numb　**10 husbands** husbandmen, that is, shepherds
14 ken know

28 po peacock　**30 fain** pleased　**48 anon** soon　**51 pardie** by God　**58 eyne** eyes

It is not all easy.

But as far as I've been, or yet as I know,
65 We poor wedded-men suffer great woe;
We sorrow now and again; it falls oft so.
Silly Caple, our hen, both to and fro
She cackles;
But begins she to croak,
70 To groan or to cluck,
Woe is him, our cock,
For he is in her shackles.

These men that are wed have not all their will;
When they're full hard bestead,° they sigh full still.
75 God knows they are led full hard and full ill;
In bower nor in bed they say nought theretil.°
This tide°
My part have I found,
I know my ground!
80 Woe is him that is bound,
For he must abide.

But now late in our lives—a marvel to me,
That I think my heart rives such wonders to see;
Whate'er destiny drives, it must so be—
85 Some men will have two wives, and some men three
In store;
Some are grieved that have any.
But so far ken I—
Woe is him that has many,
90 For he feels sore.

[Addresses the audience.]

But, young men, of wooing, for God who you bought,°
Be well ware of wedding, and think in your thought,
"Had I known" is a thing that serves us of nought.
Much constant mourning has wedding home brought,
95 And griefs,
With many a sharp shower;
For thou may catch in an hour
What shall savor full sour
As long as thou lives.

100 For, as e'er read I epistle, I have one for my dear
As sharp as thistle, as rough as a brier;
She is browed like a bristle, with a sour-looking cheer;°
Had she once wet her whistle, she could sing full clear
Her Paternoster.
105 She is as great as a whale,
She has a gallon of gall;
By Him that died for us all,

I would I had run till I had lost her!

[The First Shepherd interrupts him.]

FIRST SHEPHERD.
The like I never saw! Full deafly ye stand.
SECOND SHEPHERD.
Be the devil in thy maw, so tariand!°   110
Saw thou ought of Daw?
FIRST SHEPHERD.
Yea, on pasture-land
Heard I him blaw.° He comes here at hand,
Not far.
Standstill.
SECOND SHEPHERD.
Why?
FIRST SHEPHERD.
For he comes here, think I.   115
SECOND SHEPHERD.
He will tell us both a lie
Unless we beware.

[Enter the Third Shepherd, a boy, who does not see the
others.]

THIRD SHEPHERD.
Christ's cross, my creed, and Saint Nicholas!
Thereof had I need; it is worse than it was.
Whoso could take heed and let the world pass,   120
It is ever in dread and brittle as glass
And slides.
This world fared never sure,
With marvels more and more—
Now with rich, now with poor,   125
Nothing abides.

Never since Noah's flood were such floods seen,
Winds and rains so rude, and storms so keen—
Some stammered, some stood in fear, as I ween,°
Now God turn all to good! I say as I mean,   130
For, ponder:
These floods so they drown,
Both in fields and in town,
And bear all down;
And that is a wonder.   135

[He sees the others.]

We that walk in the nights, our cattle to keep,
We see sudden sights when other men sleep.
Yet methinks my heart lights; I see rogues peep.
Ye are two tall wights°—I will give my sheep
A turn.   140
But much ill have I meant;

---

74 **bestead** oppressed 76 **theretil** thereto 77 **tide** time
91 **bought** redeemed 102 **cheer** face

110 **tariand** for tarrying 112 **blaw** blow on his shepherd's pipe
129 **ween** fear 139 **wights** men

As I walk on this bent,°
I may lightly repent,
My toes if I spurn.°

[*The other two advance.*]

145 Ah, sir, God you save, and master mine!
A drink fain would I have, and somewhat to dine.

FIRST SHEPHERD.
Christ's curse, my knave, thou art lazy, I find!

SECOND SHEPHERD.
How the boy will rave!. Wait for a time;
You have fed.
150 Bad luck on your brow;
The rogue came just now,
Yet would he, I vow,
Sit down to his bread.°

THIRD SHEPHERD.
Such servants as I, that sweats and swinks,°
155 Eats our bread full dry, a sorrow methinks.
We are oft wet and weary when master-men winks;°
Yet comes full tardy both dinners and drinks.
But truly.
Both our dame and our sire,
160 When we have run in the mire,
They can nip at our hire,°
And pay us full slowly.

But hear my mind, master: for the bread that I break,
I shall toil thereafter—work as I take.
165 I shall do but little, sir, and always hold back,
For yet lay my supper never on my stomach
In fields.
Why should I complain?
With my staff I can run;
170 And men say, "A bargain
Little profit yields."

FIRST SHEPHERD.
You'd be a poor lad to go a-walking
With a man that had but little for spending.

SECOND SHEPHERD.
Peace, boy, I said. No more jangling,
175 Or I shall make thee afraid, by the heaven's king!
Thy joke—
Where are our sheep, boy?—we scorn.

THIRD SHEPHERD.
Sir, this same day at morn
I them left in the corn,°
180 When the dawn broke.

They have pasture good, they can not go wrong.

FIRST SHEPHERD.
That is right. By the rood,° these nights are long!
Ere we went, how I would, that one gave us a song.

SECOND SHEPHERD.
So I thought as I stood, to mirth us among.

THIRD SHEPHERD.
I grant.

FIRST SHEPHERD.
Let me sing the tenory.   185

SECOND SHEPHERD.
And I the treble so high.

THIRD SHEPHERD.
Then the mean falls to me.
Let see how ye chant.

[*They sing.*]

Then Mak enters with a cloak drawn over his tunic.

MAK.
Now, Lord, for Thy names seven, that made both beast
    and bird,
Well more than I can mention, Thy will leaves me
    unstirred.   190
I am all uneven; that upsets my brains.
Now would God I were in heaven, for there weep no
    bairns°
So still.°

FIRST SHEPHERD.
Who is that pipes so poor?

MAK.
Would God ye knew how I were!   195
Lo, a man that walks on the moor,
And has not all his will.

SECOND SHEPHERD.
Mak, where hast thou gone?
Tell us tiding.

THIRD SHEPHERD.
Is he come? Then each one take heed to his thing.   200

He takes the cloak from Mak.

MAK.
What! Ich° be a yeoman, I tell you, of the king,
The self and the same, agent of a lording,
And sich.
Fie on you! Go hence
Out of my presence!   205
I must have reverence.
Why, who be Ich?

FIRST SHEPHERD.
Why make ye it so quaint? Mak, ye do wrong.

---

142 **bent** heath   144 **spurn** perhaps: If I trip, I can easily expiate my
evil thoughts   154 **swinks** works   156 **winks** sleeps   161 **nip . . .
hire** reduce our wages   179 **corn** wheat

182 **rood** cross   192 **bairns** children   193 **still** continuously
201 **Ich** Mak here adopts a Southern dialect, but slips back into the
Northern dialect at times.

156

SECOND SHEPHERD.
    Mak, play ye the saint? I think not for long.
THIRD SHEPHERD.
210   I think the rogue can feign, may the devil him hang!
MAK.
    I shall make complaint, and make you all to thwang°
    At a word,
    And tell even how ye doth.
FIRST SHEPHERD.
    But, Mak, is that truth?
215   Now take out that Southern tooth,
    And put in a turd!
SECOND SHEPHERD.
    Mak, the devil in your eye! A stroke would I beat you.
THIRD SHEPHERD.
    Mak, know ye not me? By God, I could grieve you.
MAK.
    God save you all three! Me thought I had seen you.
    Ye are a fair company.
FIRST SHEPHERD.
220   What is it that mean you?
SECOND SHEPHERD.
    Shrew,° peep!
    Thus late as thou goes,
    What will men suppose?
    Thou hast a good nose
225   For stealing a sheep.
MAK.
    And I am true as steel, all men state;
    But a sickness I feel that will not abate:
    My belly fares not well; it is out of estate.
THIRD SHEPHERD.
    Seldom lies the devil dead by the gate.
MAK.
230   Therefore,
    Full sore am I and sick;
    May I stand like a stick
    If I've had a bit
    For a month and more.
FIRST SHEPHERD.
235   How fares thy wife? By the hood, what say you?
MAK.
    Lies wallowing—by the rood—by the fire, lo!
    And a house full of brood. She drinks well, too;
    There's no other good that she will do!
    But she
240   Eats as fast as may be,
    And every year that we see
    She brings forth a baby—
    And, some years, two.

    Were I even more prosperous and richer by some,
245   I were eaten out of house and even of home.

211 **thwang** be flogged   221 **shrew** rogue

Yet is she a foul souse, if ye come near;
There is none that goes or anywhere roams
Worse than she.
Now will ye see what I proffer?
To give all in my coffer,   250
Tomorrow early to offer
Her head-masspenny.°
SECOND SHEPHERD.
    I know so forwaked° is none in this shire;
    I would sleep, if I taked less for my hire.°
THIRD SHEPHERD.
    I am cold and naked, and would have a fire. 255
FIRST SHEPHERD.
    I am weary, all ached, and run in the mire—
    Watch, thou.

[*Lies down.*]

SECOND SHEPHERD.
    Nay, I will lie near by,
    For I must sleep, truly.

[*Lies down beside him.*]

THIRD SHEPHERD.
    As good a man's son was I   260
    As any of you.

[*Lies down.*]

    But, Mak, come thou here. Between us you'll stay.
MAK.
    Then could I stop you if evil you'd say,
    No dread.
    From my top to my toe,   265
    Manus tuas commendo,
    Poncio Pilato;°
    May Christ's cross me clear.

Then he gets up, the shepherds still sleeping, and says:

Now's the time for a man that lacks what he would
To stalk privily then into a fold,   270
And nimbly to work then, and be not too bold,
For he might pay for the bargain, if it were told
At the end.
Only time now will tell;
But he needs good counsel   275
Who fain would fare well,
And has little to spend.

[*Mak casts a spell over them.*]

Here about you a circle, as round as a moon,
Till I have done what I will, till that it be noon,

252 **head-masspenny** payment for funeral mass   253 **forwaked** worn out with watching   254 **taked less . . . hire** even though I accepted less wages   266–7 *Manus . . . Pilato* "Into thy hands I commend, Pontius Pilate."

280 May ye lie stone-still till that I have done;
And I shall say theretil a few good words soon:
A height,
Over your heads, my hand I lift.
Out go your eyes! Black out your sight!
285 But yet I must make better shift
If it go right.

[*The shepherds begin to snore.*]

Lord, how they sleep hard. That may ye all hear.
I was never a shepherd, but now will I lere.°
Though the flock be scared, yet shall I draw near.
290 How! Draw hitherward! Now mends our cheer
From sorrow;
A fat sheep, I dare say,
A good fleece, dare I lay.
Pay back when I may,
295 But this will I borrow.

[*He takes the sheep home.*]

How, Gill, art thou in? Get us some light.

WIFE.
Who makes such din this time of the night?
I am set for to spin; I don't think there might
Be a penny to win; I curse them, all right!
300 So fares
The housewife that has been
Called from her work by a din.
Thus I earn not a pin
For such small chores.

MAK.
305 Good wife, open the hatch! See'st thou not what I bring?

WIFE.
I will let you draw the latch. Ah, come in, my sweeting.

MAK.
Thou care not a scratch of my long standing.

WIFE.
By thy naked neck art thou like for to hang.

MAK.
Away!
310 I am worthy my meat,
For in a pinch can I get
More than they that swink and sweat
All the long day. [*Shows her the sheep.*]
Thus it fell to my lot, Gill; I had such grace.

WIFE.
315 It were a foul blot to be hanged for the case.

MAK.
I have 'scaped, Jelott, oft as hard a place.

WIFE.
"But so long goes the pot to the water," men says,
"At last
Comes it home broken."

288 **lere** learn

MAK.
Well know I the token, 320
But let it never be spoken.
But come and help fast.
I would it were slain; I would well eat.
This twelvemonth was I not so fain of one sheep-meat.

WIFE.
Come they ere it be slain, and hear the sheep bleat— 325

MAK.
Then might I be ta'en. That were a cold sweat!
Go bar
The gate-door.

WIFE.   Yes, Mak,
And if they're close at thy back—

MAK.
Then might I get, from all the pack, 330
The devil and more.

WIFE.
A good trick have I spied, since thou know none:
Here shall we him hide, till they be gone—
In my cradle abide. Let me alone,
And I shall lie beside in childbed, and groan. 335

MAK.
Good head!
And I shall say thou was light°
Of a boy-child this night.

WIFE.
For sure was the day bright
On which I was bred! 340
This is a good guise and a fair cast;
A woman's advice helps at the last.
I fear someone spies; again go thou fast.

MAK.
If I'm gone when they rise, they'll blow a cold blast.
I will go sleep. [*Returns to the shepherds.*] 345
Still they sleep, these three men,
And I shall softly creep in,
As though I had not been
He who stole their sheep.

[*He resumes his place.*]

[*The First and Second Shepherds awake.*]

FIRST SHEPHERD.
Resurrex a mortruus!° Give me a hand. 350
Judas carnas dominus!° I can not well stand;
My foot sleeps, by Jesus, and I totter on land.
I thought that we laid us full near England.

SECOND SHEPHERD.
Ah, yea?
Lord, but I have slept well! 355

337 **light** delivered   350 *Resurrex a mortruus* garbled Latin: "Resurrection from the dead"   351 *Judas carnas dominus* "Judas, lord of the flesh"

As fresh as an eel,
As light I me feel
As leaf on a tree.

[*The Third Shepherd awakes.*]

THIRD SHEPHERD.

Blessing be herein! My heart so quakes,
360 My heart is out of skin, hear how it shakes.
Who makes all this din? How my brow aches!
To the door will I spin. Hark, fellows, wake!
Four we were—
See ye ought of Mak now?

FIRST SHEPHERD.

365 We were up ere thou.

SECOND SHEPHERD.

Man, I give God a vow,
That he did not stir.

THIRD SHEPHERD.

Methought he was lapped in a wolf-skin.

FIRST SHEPHERD.

So are many wrapped now, namely within.

THIRD SHEPHERD.

370 When we had long napped, methought with a gin°
A fat sheep he trapped; but he made no din.

SECOND SHEPHERD.

Be still!
Thy dream makes thee wood;°
It is but phantom, by the rood.

FIRST SHEPHERD.

375 Now God turn all to good,
If it be his will.

[*They awaken Mak.*]

SECOND SHEPHERD.

Rise, Mak, for shame! Thou liest right long.

MAK.

Now Christ's holy name be us among.
What is this? For Saint Jame, I may not go strong.
380 I trust I be the same. Ah, my neck has lain wrong
Enough.

[*The others help him to his feet.*]

Many thanks! Since yester-even,
Now by Saint Steven,
I was scared by a dream—
385 That makes me full gruff.

I thought Gill began to croak and travail full sad,
Well-nigh at the first cock, of a young lad
To add to our flock. Then be I never glad;
I have more of my stock, more than ever I had.
390 Ah, my head!
A house full of young dolts,

The devil cut up their throats!
Woe is him has many colts,
And only little bread.

I must go home, by your leave, to Gill, as I thought.   395
I pray look up my sleeve, that I steal nought:
I am loath you to grieve, or from you take ought.

[*Leaves.*]

THIRD SHEPHERD.

Go forth, ill may'st thou 'chieve!
Now would I we sought,
This morn,
That we had all our store.   400

FIRST SHEPHERD.

But I will go before;
Let us meet.

SECOND SHEPHERD.

Where?

THIRD SHEPHERD.

At the crooked thorn. [*They go out.*]

[*Mak outside his own door.*]

MAK.

Undo this door! Who is here? How long shall I stand?

WIFE.

Who is it that's near? Go walk in the quicksand!   405

MAK.

Ah, Gill, what cheer? It is I, Mak, your husband.

WIFE.

Then may we see here the devil in a band,°
Sir Guile.
Lo, he comes with a roar,
As he were chased by a boar!   410
I may not work at my chore
A little while.

MAK.

Will ye hear what fuss she makes to get her a glose?°
And does naught but shirks, and claws her toes.

WIFE.

Why, who wanders, who wakes? Who comes, who goes?   415
Who brews, who bakes? Who makes us our hose?
And then
It is sad to behold—
Now in hot, now in cold,
Full woeful is the household   420
What lacks a woman.

What end has thou made with the shepherds, Mak?

MAK.

The last word that they said when I turned my back
They would look that they had their sheep, all the pack.
I think they will not be allayed when they their sheep
lack,   425
Pardie!

---

370 gin trap   **373 wood** crazy

407 band that is, bound up   **413 glose** explanation

But howso the ball fly,
To me they will hie,
And make a foul cry
430   And shout out upon me.
But thou must do it aright.

WIFE.   I accord me theretil;
I shall swaddle him right in my cradle.

[*Gill puts the sheep in the cradle.*]

If it were a greater sleight, yet could I help still,
I will lie down straight. Come wrap me.

MAK.   I will.

[*Covers her.*]

WIFE.
435   Behind!
Come Coll and his mate,
They will nip us full straight.

MAK.
But I may cry out, "Wait!"
The sheep if they find.

WIFE.
440   Harken well when they call; they will come anon.
Come and make ready all, and sing all alone;
Sing "Lullay" thou shall, for I must groan,
And cry out by the wall on Mary and John,
In pain
445   Sing "Lullay" so fast
When thou hearest at last;
And if I play a false cast,
Don't trust me again.

[*The shepherds meet at the thorn tree.*]

THIRD SHEPHERD.
Ah, Coll, good morn. Why sleepest thou not?

FIRST SHEPHERD.
450   Alas, that ever was I born. We have a foul blot—
Of a sheep we have been shorn.

THIRD SHEPHERD.   The devil! Say what!

SECOND SHEPHERD.
Who should do us that scorn?
That is a foul plot.

FIRST SHEPHERD.
Some shrew.
I have sought with my dogs
455   All Horbury bogs,
And of fifteen hogs°
Found all but one ewe.

THIRD SHEPHERD.
Now trust me, if ye will—by Saint Thomas of Kent,
Either Mak or Gill was at that assent.

FIRST SHEPHERD.
460   Peace, man, be still. I saw when he went.
Thou slanderest him ill; thou ought to repent

With speed.

SECOND SHEPHERD.
Now as ever might thrive I,
Though I should even here die,
It were he, I'd reply,   465
That did that same deed.

THIRD SHEPHERD.
Go we thither, let's tread, and run on our feet.
I shall never eat bread, till the truth is complete.

FIRST SHEPHERD.
No drink in my head, till him I can meet.

SECOND SHEPHERD.
I will rest in no stead till that I him greet.   470
My brother,
One pledge I will plight:
Till I see him in sight,
Shall I never sleep one night
Where I do another.   475

[*As the shepherds approach Mak's cottage, Mak's Wife
begins to groan, and Mak sings a tuneless lullaby.*]

THIRD SHEPHERD.
Will ye hear how they hack?°
Our sire can croon.

FIRST SHEPHERD.
Heard I never none crack so clear out of tune.
Call to him.

SECOND SHEPHERD.
Mak, undo your door soon!

MAK.
Who is that spake, as it were noon
Aloft?   480
Who is that, I say?

THIRD SHEPHERD.
Good fellows, were it day!

MAK.
As much as ye can, [*Opens the door.*]
Sirs, speak soft,
Over a sick woman's head that is at malaise;   485
I had rather be dead than she had any disease.

WIFE.
Go elsewhere instead. I may not well wheeze;
Each foot that ye tread makes my nose sneeze.
Ah, me!

FIRST SHEPHERD.
Tell us, Mak, if ye may,   490
How fare ye, I say?

MAK.
But are ye in this town today?
Now how fare ye?
Ye have run in the mire, and are wet yet;
I shall make you a fire, if ye will sit.   495
A nurse would I hire. Think ye on it?

456 hogs young sheep

476 hack split a note

Well paid is my hire—my dream, this is it—
In season. [*Points to the cradle.*]
I have sons, if ye knew,
500 Well more than a few;
But we must drink as we brew,
And that is but reason.

Ere ye go take some food. Me think that ye sweat.

SECOND SHEPHERD.
Nay, neither mends our mood, drink nor meat.

MAK.
505 Why, sir, is something not good?

THIRD SHEPHERD.
Yea, our sheep that we get
Were stolen as they stood. Our loss is great.

MAK.
Sirs, drink!
Had I been there,
Some should have felt it full dear.

FIRST SHEPHERD.
510 Marry, some men hold that ye were,
And that's what I think.

SECOND SHEPHERD.
Mak, some men propose that it were ye.

THIRD SHEPHERD.
Either ye or your spouse, so say
We.

MAK.
Now, if ye suppose it of Gill or of me—
515 Come and search our house, and then may ye see
Who had it.
If I any sheep got
Either cow or stot°—
And Gill, my wife, rose not
520 And here she lies yet—
As I am true in zeal, to God here I pray
That this be the first meal that I shall eat this day.

[*Points to the cradle.*]

FIRST SHEPHERD.
Mak, as have I weal, be careful, I say:
"He learned early to steal who could not say nay."

[*The shepherds begin to search.*]

WIFE.
525 I shake!
Out, thieves, from our home.
Ye come to rob us of our own.

MAK.
Hear ye not how she groans?
Your hearts should break.

[*The shepherds approach the cradle.*]

WIFE.
530 Off, thieves, from my son. Nigh him not there.

MAK.
Know ye how she had done, your hearts would have
care.
Ye do wrong, I you warn, that thus come before
To a woman that has born—but I say no more.

WIFE.
Ah, my middle!
535 I pray to God so mild,
If ever I you beguiled,
May I eat this child
That lies in this cradle.

MAK.
Peace, woman, for God's pain, and cry not so.
540 You injure your brain, and make me great woe.

SECOND SHEPHERD.
I think our sheep be slain. What find ye two?

THIRD SHEPHERD.
Our work is in vain; we may as well go.
But hatters!°
I can find no meat,
545 Salt nor sweet,
Nothing to eat—
But two bare platters.
Livestock like this, tame or wild, [*Points to cradle.*]
None, as have I bliss, has smelled so vile.

WIFE.
550 No, so God me bliss, and give me joy of my child.

FIRST SHEPHERD.
We have gone amiss; I hold us beguiled.

SECOND SHEPHERD.
We're done.
Sir—our Lady him save—
Is your child a knave?°

MAK.
555 Any lord might him have,
This child, as his son.

When he wakens he grips, such joy it's to see.

THIRD SHEPHERD.
May heirs spring from his hips, happy he be.
But who were his gossips° so soon ready?

MAK.
560 Blessings on their lips.

FIRST SHEPHERD.
[*Aside.*] Hark now, a lie!

MAK.
So God them thanks,
Parkin, and Gibbon Waller, I say,
And gentle John Horne, in good play—
He made us all gay—
565 With his great shanks.

---

518 **stot** heifer

543 **hatters** confound it 554 **knave** boy 559 **gossips** god-
parents

SECOND SHEPHERD.
    Mak, friends will we be, for we are all one.
MAK.
    We? No, I'm out for me, for help get I none.
    Farewell all three. [*Aside.*] I wish they were gone.
THIRD SHEPHERD.
    Fair words may there be, but love is there none
570 This year.

[*The shepherds leave the cottage.*]

FIRST SHEPHERD.
    Gave ye the child anything?
SECOND SHEPHERD.
    I swear not one farthing.
THIRD SHEPHERD.
    Quickly back will I fling;
    Abide ye me here. [*He runs back.*]

575 Mak, take it to no grief if I come to thy son.
MAK.
    Nay, thou dost me great mischief, and foul hast thou
        done.
THIRD SHEPHERD.
    The child will it not grieve, that daystar one?
    Mak, with your leave, let me give your son
    But sixpence.
MAK.
580 Nay, go way! He sleeps.
THIRD SHEPHERD.
    Methinks he peeps.
MAK.
    When he wakens he weeps.
    I pray you, go hence!

[*The others return.*]

THIRD SHEPHERD.
    Give me leave him to kiss, and lift up the clout.° [*He lifts
        up the cover.*]
585 What the devil is this? He has a long snout!
FIRST SHEPHERD.
    He is shapèd amiss. Let's not wait about.
SECOND SHEPHERD.
    "Ill-spun weft," iwis, "aye comes foul out."°
    A son! [*Recognizes the sheep.*]

He is like to our sheep!
THIRD SHEPHERD.
    How, Gib, may I peep?   590
FIRST SHEPHERD.
    "How nature will creep
    Where it cannot run!"
SECOND SHEPHERD.
    This was a quaint gaud and a far cast;°
    It was a high fraud.
THIRD SHEPHERD.
    Yea, sirs, was't.
    Let's burn this bawd and bind her fast.   595
    A false scold hangs at the last;
    So shalt thou.
    Will ye see how they swaddle
    His four feet in the middle?
    Saw I never in a cradle   600
    A horned lad ere now.
MAK.
    Peace, bid I. What! Leave off your care!
    I am he that begat, and yond woman him bare.
FIRST SHEPHERD.
    How named is your brat? "Mak?" Lo, God, Mak's heir.
SECOND SHEPHERD.
    Let be all that. Now God curse his fare,   605
    This boy.
WIFE.
    A pretty child is he
    As sits on a woman's knee;
    A dillydown, pardie,
    To give a man joy.   610
THIRD SHEPHERD.
    I know him by the ear-mark; that is a good token.
MAK.
    I tell you, sirs, hark!—his nose was broken.
    I was told by a clerk a spell had been spoken.
FIRST SHEPHERD.
    This is a false work; my vengeance is woken.
    Get weapon!   615
WIFE.
    He was taken by an elf,
    I saw it myself;
    When the clock struck twelve
    Was he misshapen.
SECOND SHEPHERD.
    Ye two are most deft, but we're not misled.   620
FIRST SHEPHERD.
    Since they stand by their theft, let's see them both dead.

584 **clout** cloth 587 **"Ill-spun . . . out"** "An ill-spun weft,"
indeed, "comes ever out foul," that is, the deformity of the parents
appears in the offspring.

593 **quaint . . . cast** a clever prank and a sly trick

MAK.

    If I trespass eft,° strike off my head.

    With you will I be left.

THIRD SHEPHERD.

               Sirs, let them dread:

    For this trespass

625   We will neither curse nor fight,

    Strike nor smite;

    But hold him tight,

    And cast him in canvas.

[They toss Mak in a sheet, and return to the field.]

FIRST SHEPHERD.

    Lord, how I am sore, and ready to burst.

630   Faith, I can do no more; therefore will I rest.

SECOND SHEPHERD.

    As a sheep of seven score Mak weighed in my fist.

    For to sleep anywhere me think that I must.

THIRD SHEPHERD.

    Now I pray you

    Lie on grass yonder.

FIRST SHEPHERD.

635   On these thieves I still ponder.

THIRD SHEPHERD.

    Wherefore should ye wonder?

    Do as I say.

[They lie down and fall asleep.]

An Angel sings "Gloria in excelsis," and then says:

ANGEL.

    Rise, herdsmen kind, for now is he born

    Who shall take from the fiend what from Adam was

        drawn;

640   That warlock° to rend, this night is he born.

    God is made your friend now at this morn.

    He requests

    To Bethlehem haste

    Where lies that Grace

645   In a crib low placed,

    Betwixt two beasts.

[The Angel withdraws.]

FIRST SHEPHERD.

    This was the finest voice that ever yet I heard.

    It is a marvel to rejoice, thus to be stirred.

SECOND SHEPHERD.

    Of God's son so bright he spoke the word.

622 **eft** again   640 **warlock** devil

    All the wood in a light methought that he made   650

    Appear.

THIRD SHEPHERD.

    He spoke of a bairn

    In Bethlehem born.

FIRST SHEPHERD.

    That betokens yon starn; *[Points to the star.]*

    Let us seek him there.   655

SECOND SHEPHERD.

    Say, what was his song? Heard ye not how he cracked° it,

    Three breves to a long?

THIRD SHEPHERD.

    Yea, marry, he hacked it:

    Was no crotchet wrong, nor nothing that lacked it.

FIRST SHEPHERD.

    For to sing us among, right as he knacked it,   660

    I can.

SECOND SHEPHERD.

    Let see how ye croon!

    Can ye bark at the moon?

THIRD SHEPHERD.

    Hold your tongues! Have done!

FIRST SHEPHERD.

    Hark after, then.   665

[He sings.]

SECOND SHEPHERD.

    To Bethl'em he bade that we be gone;

    I am afraid that we tarry too long.

THIRD SHEPHERD.

    Be merry and not sad—of mirth is our song.

    Now may we be glad and hasten in throng;

    Say not nay.   670

FIRST SHEPHERD.

    Go we thither quickly,

    Though we be wet and weary,

    To that child and that lady;

    We must never delay.

[He begins to sing again.]

SECOND SHEPHERD.

    The olden prophets bid—let be your din—   675

    Isaiah and David and more than I min°—

    With great learning they said that in a virgin

    Should he light and lie, to atone for our sin,

656 In the next few lines the shepherds use technical musical terms in describing the Angel's singing: **cracked,** split a note; **Three breves to a long,** three short notes to one long one; **hacked,** split a note; **crotchet,** a quarter note; **knacked,** trilled.   676 **min** remember

And slake it,
680 Our kindred, from woe;
Isaiah said so:
Ecce virgo
Concipiet° a child that is naked.

THIRD SHEPHERD.

Full glad may we be, and abide that day
685 That Glory to see, whom all things obey.
Lord, well were me, for once and for aye,
Might I kneel on my knee, some word for to say
To that child.
But the angel said
690 In a crib was he laid;
He was poorly arrayed,
So meek and so mild.

FIRST SHEPHERD.

Patriarchs that have been, and prophets beforn,
They desired to have seen this child that is born.
695 They are gone full clean—they were forlorn.
We shall see him, I ween,° ere it be morn,
As token.
When I see him and feel,
Then know I full well
700 It is true as steel
That prophets have spoken:
To so poor as we are that he would appear,
Find us, and declare by his messenger.

SECOND SHEPHERD.

Go we now, let us fare; the place is us near.

THIRD SHEPHERD.

705 I am ready, I swear; go we with cheer
To that joy.
Lord, if thy will be—
We are simple all three—
Now grant us that we
710 May comfort thy boy.

[*They enter the stable. The First Shepherd kneels.*]

FIRST SHEPHERD.

Hail, comely and clean! Hail, young child!
Hail maker, as I mean, of a maiden so mild!
Thou hast beaten, I ween, the warlock so wild:
The beguiler of men, now goes he beguiled.
715 Lo, he merries!
Lo, he laughs, my sweeting!
A welcome meeting.
I here give my greeting:
Have a bob° of cherries.

[*The Second Shepherd kneels.*]

SECOND SHEPHERD.

Hail, sovereign savior, for thou hast us sought!   720
Hail, noble child, the flower, who all thing has wrought!
Hail, full of favor, that made all of nought!
Hail! I kneel and I cower. A bird have I brought
To my bairn.
Hail, little tiny mop!°   725
Of our creed thou art crop;°
I would drink of thy cup,
Little day-starn.

[*The Third Shepherd kneels.*]

THIRD SHEPHERD.

Hail, darling dear, full of Godhead!
I pray thee be near when that I have need!   730
Hail, sweet is thy cheer! My heart would bleed
To see thee sit here in so poor weed,°
With no pennies.
Hail! Put forth thy hand small.
I bring thee but a ball: 735
Have it and play withal,
And go to the tennis.

MARY.

The father of heaven, God omnipotent,
That made all in seven, his son has he sent.
My name did he mention; I conceived ere he went.   740
I fulfilled God's intention through his might, as he
meant;
And now is he born.
He keep you from woe!
I shall pray him so.
Tell forth as ye go,   745
And mind you this morn.

FIRST SHEPHERD.

Farewell, lady, so fair to behold,
With thy child on thy knee.

SECOND SHEPHERD.

But he lies full cold.
Lord, well is me. Now we go, thou behold.   750

THIRD SHEPHERD.

Forsooth, already it seems to be told
Full oft.

FIRST SHEPHERD.

What grace we have found.

SECOND SHEPHERD.

Come forth; now are we sound.

THIRD SHEPHERD.

To sing are we bound—   755
Ring it aloft.   [*They go out singing.*]

682–3 *Ecce . . . concipiet* "Behold, a virgin shall conceive." (Isaiah 7.14)   **696 ween** know   **719 bob** bunch

725 mop moppet, babe   **726 crop** head   **732 weed** clothing

TOPICS FOR CRITICAL THINKING AND WRITING

📖 THE PLAY ON THE PAGE

1. The play presents two scenes of nativity. What details bind the two scenes together? Does the first nativity strike you as blasphemous? Does the second nativity seem to you to be tacked on? The view in the nineteenth century, and until fairly recently in the twentieth, was that in *The Second Shepherds' Play* we have an example of a virtually independent comic secular play (the business of the sheep-stealing), which is made acceptable by attaching it to a brief dramatization of Christ's nativity. The commonest scholarly view today, however, is that the comedy is subservient to the sacred theme. (For instance, some critics insist that the anachronisms—such as calling on Jesus even before the birth of Jesus has been announced—serve, during the comic

scenes, to focus the audience's attention on the profound religious meaning.) Do you find either of these views convincing? To what degree? What other view can you offer?

2. Exactly why do the shepherds return to Mak's house? Taking into account their motive for returning and the outcome of their return visit, at the risk of being a little heavy-handed, what might one say the moral is for this part of the play? How does such a moral fit with the rest of the play?

3. The medieval punishment for stealing sheep was death, but the shepherds punish Mak only by tossing him in a blanket. Why does the play depart from reality in this respect?

🎭 THE PLAY ON THE STAGE

4. Examine the references to music, chiefly song, with an eye toward seeing how music functions in the play. What sort of music would you use if you were directing the play?

5. After Mak is tossed in a blanket, we hear nothing more about him. If you were directing the play, would you have him go off to his house and watch the rest of the

play? Or might you have him sleep on the ground, as the other shepherds do, but remain sleeping, unaware of the good tidings that are granted to the other shepherds? Or should he wake with the others and join them on the journey to Bethlehem? Or can you think of some other staging? Explain your preference.

THE PLAY IN PERFORMANCE

In "A Note on the Medieval Theater" we offered a few remarks about the staging of medieval drama, but here we must add some details. First, it should be noted that although scholars have made thorough searches of medieval records and have found many documents of great interest, there is still relatively little firm information about the staging of the plays. For instance, although we know that in some locales—but probably not in all—*pageants* (wheeled playing areas, in today's terminology, *floats*) were used, because we have no contemporary picture of an English pageant, we cannot be sure of what they looked like. We do have early seventeenth-century pictures of Flemish pageants, and they deserve to be considered seriously, but we cannot be confident that the English wagons of two centuries earlier were identical to them. We do not even have any detailed contemporary verbal descriptions of the pageants. The only substantial descriptions of the English pageants are relatively late (late sixteenth century, and later), and they are not very specific. Here is one such description, from 1565: "A pageant, that is to say, a house of wainscot painted and builded on a car with four wheels. A

square top to set over the said house." Here is a second description, this one from 1609: "This pageant or carriage was a high place made like a house with two rooms, being open on the top; in the lower room they apparelled themselves, and in the higher room they played; and they stood upon six wheels." These descriptions are something—but not very much, and if (drawing on the Flemish pictures) we start to talk about the elaborate decoration of pageants, the flexibility of multiple heights for playing, and so forth, we are going beyond the hard evidence, at least so far as medieval drama goes.

Similarly, some of the English plays include very interesting stage directions, but there is much uncertainty about how typical they are. Consider, for instance, a stage direction in a medieval play on the Slaughter of the Innocents. According to the gospels of Matthew and Luke, King Herod ordered a massacre of infants in Bethlehem. The stage direction in the play says, "Here Herod rages in the pageant and in the street also." Doubtless the raging actor who played Herod leaped off the pageant, and stormed about among the spectators in the *platea* (the Latin word, translated as *place*, common in stage directions), and then climbed back onto the pageant. But we do not know how typical such an effect was. Some scholars, eager to emphasize the flexibility of the medieval stage and the intimate connection between actors and audience, assume—on very little more evidence than this stage direction—that actors often entered into the audience. So we read, in some discussions of *The Second Shepherds' Play* that when Mak steals the sheep, in order to indicate his journey from the fields to his house he climbs down from one end of the wagon, moves through the *platea,* and then climbs up the other end of the wagon, where he shows the sheep to Gill. Later we perhaps get another journey through the *platea,* when the shepherds go from Mak's house to what used to be the sheepfold but which now represents the manger where Jesus is born. Perhaps—but the text of the play does not specify even one journey through the audience.

In fact, the text does not specify that one end of the wagon represents one locale, the other end another locale. True, it is reasonable to think that the wagon is divided by two sets or *mansions,* one mansion (perhaps indicated by a fence) representing a sheepfold, the other mansion (perhaps indicated by a chair and a cradle) representing Mak's and Gill's house, but we cannot be confident about any of this.

In short, the original text of *The Second Shepherds' Play* does not include any instructions concerning properties or scenery, or any instructions concerning methods of performing. The favored view, but it is only a conjecture, is that a few props (a cradle, chair, and perhaps a table) at one end of the wagon indicated Mak's and Gill's house, and a cradle and chair at the other end indicated the manger where Jesus was born. The space between them and in front of them—the *platea*—would serve for the fields, and for the area covered by Mak's journey.

One further detail about staging should be mentioned: In today's performances, the angel who announces the birth of Jesus usually appears in an elevated place, on the assumption that in medieval times he appeared at the top of a structure on the wagon.

THE SHEPHERDS' PLAY IN SPANISH, IN THE NEW WORLD

The medieval English cycles of miracle plays were part of a European phenomenon; that is, plays on Biblical subjects were performed not only in England but in Europe. A Spanish play about the shepherds (*Los Pastores*) who were called to Bethlehem was brought by Spanish Franciscan friars to Mexico, and was performed for Spanish soldiers in what is now Mexico City at a Christmas entertainment, on January 9, 1526. Further, records indicate that in 1538 a Franciscan friar arranged for dramatic performances on the Feast of Corpus Christi, as well as on other feast days. Performed in the Nahuatl language, the plays were part of a far-reaching program to convert the native peoples to Christianity.

Although these dramatic programs were organized by churchmen, they met with opposition from other churchmen. In 1544 or 1545 a bishop denounced and banned dramatic events:

> Y cosas de gran desacato y desvergüenza parece que ante el Santisimo Sacramento vayan los hombres con máscaras y en hábitos de mujeres, danzando y saltando con meneos deshonestos y lascivos, haciendo estruendo, estorbando los cantos de Iglesia, representando profanos triunfos, como el del Dios del Amor . . . .
>
> [It is a matter of great disrespect and shame that before the Holy Sacrament men should go about with masks and in women's attire, dancing and jumping about with immodest and lascivious motions, making a racket, disrupting Church singing, performing profane celebrations, like those of the God of Love . . . .]

This translation—like all of the rest of the information contained in this note—comes from Robert Potter's fascinating article, "The Illegal Immigration of Medieval Drama to California," in *Comparative Drama* 27:1 (Spring 1993): 141–58. Potter traces the transplantation, survival (despite opposition from the bishops), and development of *Los Pastores* from Spain to Mexico and then to southern California. Thus, Potter points out that in 1585 we again encounter a prohibition against religious plays, with Nativity plays specifically mentioned—a sure sign that despite earlier bans the plays were being performed. And, as with the English *Second Shepherds' Play,* the Spanish *Los Pastores* included much humorous material that to pious eyes seemed irrelevant and even impious. In fact, the *Pastorela*—a Christmas entertainment developed around a nucleus of the story of the annunciation—spread into southern California at least as early as the late eighteenth century. One might reasonably think that this Spanish (or, better, Mexican) dramatic form would have died outside of Mexico after the Mexican-American War of 1846–48, when Mexico was forced to give up its claims to vast areas that are now part of the United States, but in fact it survived, especially in isolated villages in New Mexico and southern California. In the first half of the twentieth century anthropologists duly recorded it, with the sense that they were taking note of a dying phenomenon. In fact, however, with the recent increase of immigration from Mexico the *Pastorela* in the United States has gained new life. For instance, in 1975 it was revived by Luis Valdez and El Teatro Campesino (on Valdez, see page 799), first as a puppet show and then as an entertainment with live performers, and it has continued to thrive in California. Valdez has also made a film version. For details, see Robert Potter's article, mentioned earlier in this paragraph.

Anonymous

EVERYMAN

Everyman was published at least four times between 1508 and 1537. It closely resembles a Dutch play, *Elckerlijc* (i.e., Everyman), first printed in 1495, and although there used to be a good deal of argument as to which play was the original and which was the translation, virtually all scholars now believe that the Dutch play is the original.

COMMENTARY

The Middle Ages produced not only the numerous pageants or miracle plays such as *The Second Shepherds' Play* (page 154) that dramatized the spiritual history of the world, from the Creation to Doomsday, but also other forms of drama, notably the **morality play,** of which *Everyman* is the most impressive example in English. The morality play, a drama of ideas, uses allegorical representations—a system of equivalents—to set forth a religious or moral lesson. Thus, in a play called *The Pride of Life* (c. 1400–25), a character called the King of Life is supported by such characters as Strength, Mirth, and Health. His queen, Wisdom, warns him to live virtuously so that he can die well, that is, so that when he dies his soul will be saved. The foolish king, however, sends Mirth to proclaim that he can conquer anyone, even Death. At this point the manuscript breaks off, but we know how the play ended because a prologue tells us that Death kills the king, the king's soul is grasped by fiends, but Our Lady prays to her son for the soul's release.

Because morality plays use abstractions in order to speak about the lives of contemporary individuals, it is easy to think of them as utterly different from miracle plays, which dramatize the lives of specific biblical characters. But both forms, however different they may seem, emerge from the idea that human beings are fallen creatures who can be saved only through God's intervention in human history. Both forms—the one using specific, historical figures, the other using abstractions—seek to convey the essential truth of existence.

A morality play, through its use of abstractions such as Everyman, Goods, and Good Deeds, is about *us*; it seeks to teach us how to live. Here are the first words of the beginning of *Everyman*:

> I pray you all give your audience,
> And hear this matter with reverence,
> By figure a moral play.
> The *Summoning of Everyman* called it is,
> That of our lives and ending shows   5
> How transitory we be all day.
> This matter is wondrous precious,
> But the intent of it is more gracious,
> And sweet to bear away.

The *figure* (line 3) is the particular literary form, in this case "a moral play." The *matter* (7) is the story (Everyman's encounter with Death, and his responses) and the moral doctrine (we are saved by repentance and by God's grace); the *intent* (8) is the purport, the dramatist's hope that we will heed the lesson and live virtuously so that (like Everyman at the end of the play) we may "be crowned" (917) in heaven.

About sixty English morality plays survived, from the late fourteenth century to about 1570. They are not concerned with representing in realistic detail the complexities of human character; rather, they are concerned with representing, through allegory, what life is really about, that is, with representing the spiritual conditions of life. The largest group of moralities dramatizes the conflict between the vices and the virtues for the possession of the human soul, but some illustrate moral texts (for instance, *All for Money,* which is about avarice) or even religious or political controversy, and some, like *Everyman*, are about the coming of death.

Today we are apt to think of allegory as mechanical and lifeless—unless we remember George Orwell's *Animal Farm*, a twentieth-century classic. But to see how dramatically effective allegory can be, let's briefly look at *Everyman*'s first encounter with Death, beginning with line 87. When Death, accosting Everyman, asks if he has forgotten God, Everyman does not offer a direct answer but cagily asks, "Why askest thou?" Death says that God has sent him to Everyman, and—since few of us in the prime of life can believe that our time has come—Everyman responds incredulously, "What! Sent to me?" When Death again says that God has sent him, Everyman asks Death, "What desireth God of me?" Death explains that God wants to clear the account, now, and Everyman very humanly asks for more time: "To give a reckoning longer leisure I crave" (101). When Death presses him, Everyman blusteringly takes another tack: "I know thee not. What messenger art thou?" Death continues to press, Everyman is reduced to asking for pity, and when this fails he tries to bribe Death:

> Yet of my good will I give thee, if thou will be kind;
> Yea, a thousand pound shalt thou have. . . .
> (121–22)

We need not continue this examination; our point is the obvious but important one that the characters, though abstractions, are uncannily human. Just as Everyman's first responses to Death move through a believable sequence from denial to the plea for more time and to the attempt to bribe, similarly his spiritual progress, whereby he comes to an acceptance of death, is convincingly charted. He learns that externals (Fellowship, Kindred, Cousin, and Goods) are of no avail, and when he turns to himself, he finds that certain qualities, such as strength and Beauty, also in the end are of no avail. Even Knowledge—spiritual awareness, we might say—leaves him at the grave; only Good Deeds accompanies him on the final steps of his journey to heaven.

Morality plays exerted a profound influence on Renaissance tragic drama. This may at first sound paradoxical, since morality plays are, by virtue of their happy endings—sinners are saved—comic rather than tragic. But in their depiction of vices and virtues in conflict (let's say, material Goods versus Good Deeds) and in their dramatization of the coming of death they provided traditions that shaped Elizabethan tragedy. For instance, in Christopher Marlowe's *Doctor Faustus* (page 189) two characters called Good Angel and Bad Angel seek to guide the hero. The morality tradition is only a little less obvious in *Macbeth*, where Macbeth is flanked by a virtue and by a vice, the saintly King Duncan on one side, and the vicious Lady Macbeth and the witches on the other. Like Faustus (and unlike Everyman), Macbeth makes the wrong choice. In *Othello*, "the divine Desdemona" stands at one side of the hero, and the villainous Iago at the other. King Lear, similarly flanked, yields to his two wicked daughters and rejects the virtuous words of Kent and Cordelia.

Admittedly, the morality play puts little emphasis on the protagonist's earlier folly, but his recognition and remorse and his consequent suffering do reflect the sequence we find in tragedy. After all, the basic plot of *Everyman* concerns Everyman's recognition that he has lived the wrong sort of life. In tragedy, the hero or heroine customarily comes to a recognition of an error. (In his discussion of tragedy Aristotle uses the word *anagnorisis* for what in English is commonly called *recognition*. See page 34.) The tragic figure finds that the customary values by which he or she has lived do not suffice. The familiar world seems to drop away, the supports all collapse, and the central figure is isolated. "My dismal scene I needs must act alone," says Juliet, speaking, we might say, for Oedipus, Antigone, Hamlet, Lear, and a host of other tragic figures. In *Everyman* the sense of isolation is not given the emphasis that it is given in Greek or Elizabethan tragedies, but it is there, notably when Everyman experiences a series of desertions by aspects of the world that he had mistakenly trusted. But, again, *Everyman* has a happy ending; the desertions are subordinated to the loyalty of a few allies in a play that celebrates the salvation of the hero.

There begynneth a treatyse how þ hye fader of heuen sendeth dethe to somon euery creature to come and gyue a counte of theyr lyues in this worlde/and is in maner of a morall playe.

This woodcut of Everyman and Death is from the first printed edition (circa 1530) of the play. Although it does not illustrate an actual performance of the play—for instance, Death here holds the lid of a coffin, something not mentioned anywhere in the text—it may suggest fairly accurately the costume that Everyman wears before he changes into "a garment of sorrow." For a photograph of a recent production of Everyman, see page 15.

Anonymous

EVERYMAN

Characters

GOD
MESSENGER
DEATH
EVERYMAN
FELLOWSHIP
KINDRED
COUSIN
GOODS
GOOD DEEDS
KNOWLEDGE
CONFESSION
BEAUTY
STRENGTH

DISCRETION
FIVE WITS
ANGEL
DOCTOR

Here Beginneth a Treatise how the High Father of Heaven Sendeth Death to Summon Every Creature to Come and Give Account of their Lives in this World, and is in Manner of a Moral Play.

[Enter Messenger as a Prologue.]
MESSENGER.
    I pray you all give your audience,
    And hear this matter with reverence,

By figure° a moral play.
The *Summoning of Everyman* called it is,
5   That of our lives and ending shows
How transitory we be all day.
This matter is wondrous precious,
But the intent° of it is more gracious,
And sweet to bear away.
10   The story saith: Man, in the beginning
Look well, and take good heed to the ending,
Be you never so gay!
Ye think sin in the beginning full sweet,
Which in the end causeth the soul to weep,
15   When the body lieth in clay.
Here shall you see how Fellowship and Jollity,
Both Strength, Pleasure, and Beauty,
Will fade from thee as flower in May;
For ye shall hear how our Heaven King
20   Calleth Everyman to a general reckoning.
Give audience, and hear what he doth say.   [*Exit.*]

God speaketh.

GOD.
I perceive, here in my majesty,
How that all creatures be to me unkind,°
Living without dread in worldly prosperity.
25   Of ghostly sight° the people be so blind,
Drowned in sin, they know me not for their God.
In worldly riches is all their mind;
They fear not my rightwiseness,° the sharp rod.
My law that I showed, when I for them died,
30   They forget clean, and shedding of my blood red;
I hanged between two, it cannot be denied;
To get them life I suffered° to be dead;
I healed their feet, with thorns hurt was my head.
I could do no more than I did, truly;
35   And now I see the people do clean forsake me.
They use the seven deadly sins° damnable,
As pride, covetise, wrath, and lechery
Now in the world be made commendable;
And thus they leave of angels, the heavenly company.
40   Every man liveth so after his own pleasure,
And yet of their life they be nothing sure.
I see the more that I them forbear
The worse they be from year to year.
All that liveth appaireth° fast;
45   Therefore I will, in all the haste,
Have a reckoning of every man's person;

For, and° I leave the people thus alone
In their life and wicked tempests,
Verily they will become much worse than beasts;
50   For now one would by envy another up eat;
Charity° they do all clean forget.
I hoped well that every man
In my glory should make his mansion,
And thereto I had them all elect.
55   But now I see, like traitors deject,
They thank me not for the pleasure that I to them
        meant,
Nor yet for their being that I them have lent.
I proffered the people great multitude of mercy,
And few there be that asketh it heartily.
60   They be so cumbered with worldly riches
That needs on them I must do justice,
On every man living, without fear.
Where art thou, Death, thou mighty messenger?

[*Enter Death.*]

DEATH.
Almighty God, I am here at your will,
65   Your commandment to fulfill.
GOD.
Go thou to Everyman,
And show him, in my name,
A pilgrimage he must on him take,
Which he in no wise may escape;
70   And that he bring with him a sure reckoning
Without delay or any tarrying.   [*Exit God*]
DEATH.
Lord, I will in the world go run overall,°
And cruelly outsearch both great and small.
Every man will I beset that liveth beastly
75   Out of God's laws, and dreadeth not folly.
He that loveth riches I will strike with my dart,
His sight to blind, and from heaven to depart°—
Except that alms be his good friend—
In hell for to dwell, world without end.
80   Lo, yonder I see Everyman walking.
Full little he thinketh on my coming;
His mind is on fleshly lusts and his treasure,
And great pain it shall cause him to endure
Before the Lord, Heaven King.

[*Enter Everyman.*]

85   Everyman, stand still! Whither art thou going
Thus gaily? Hast thou thy Maker forget?
EVERYMAN.
Why askest thou?
Wouldest thou wit?°

2–3 matter . . . figure the *matter* is the story and the moral doctrine;
the *figure* is the literary form, in this case a play   **8 intent** meaning
22 unkind (1) unnatural (2) ungrateful   **25 ghostly sight** spiritual
insight   **28 rightwiseness** righteousness   **32 suffered** allowed
36 seven deadly sins four are named in the next line; the other
three are envy, gluttony, and sloth   **44 appaireth** becomes worse

47 and if   **51 Charity** love (of God and of one's fellows)
72 overall everywhere   **77 depart** sunder   **88 wit** know

DEATH.

Yea, sir; I will show you:

90 In great haste I am sent to thee

From God out of his majesty.

EVERYMAN.

What, sent to me?

DEATH.

Yea, certainly.

Though thou have forget him here,

95 He thinketh on thee in the heavenly sphere,

As, ere we depart, thou shalt know.

EVERYMAN.

What desireth God of me?

DEATH.

That shall I show thee:

A reckoning he will needs have

100 Without any longer respite.

EVERYMAN.

To give a reckoning longer leisure I crave;

This blind° matter troubleth my wit.

DEATH.

On thee thou must take a long journey;

Therefore thy book of count° with thee thou bring,

105 For turn again° thou cannot by no way.

And look thou be sure of thy reckoning,

For before God thou shalt answer, and show

Thy many bad deeds, and good but a few;

How thou hast spent thy life, and in what wise,

110 Before the chief Lord of paradise.

Have ado that we were in that way,°

For, wit thou well, thou shalt make none attorney.°

EVERYMAN.

Full unready I am such reckoning to give.

I know thee not. What messenger art thou?

DEATH.

115 I am Death, that no man dreadeth,°

For every man I rest,° and no man spareth;

For it is God's commandment

That all to me shall be obedient.

EVERYMAN.

O Death, thou comest when I had thee least in mind!

120 In thy power it lieth me to save;

Yet of my good° will I give thee, if thou will be kind;

Yea, a thousand pound shalt thou have,

And defer this matter till another day.

DEATH.

Everyman, it may not be, by no way.

125 I set not by gold, silver, nor riches,

Ne° by pope, emperor, king, duke, ne princes;

For, and I would receive gifts great,

All the world I might get;

But my custom is clean contrary.

I give thee no respite. Come hence, and not tarry. 130

EVERYMAN.

Alas, shall I have no longer respite?

I may say Death giveth no warning!

To think on thee, it maketh my heart sick,

For all unready is my book of reckoning.

But twelve year and I might have abiding, 135

My counting-book I would make so clear

That my reckoning I should not need to fear.

Wherefore, Death, I pray thee, for God's mercy,

Spare me till I be provided of remedy.

DEATH.

Thee availeth not to cry, weep, and pray; 140

But haste thee lightly° that thou were gone that journey,

And prove thy friends, if thou can;

For, wit thou well, the tide° abideth no man,

And in the world each living creature

For Adam's sin must die of nature.° 145

EVERYMAN.

Death, if I should this pilgrimage take,

And my reckoning surely make,

Show me, for° Saint Charity,

Should I not come again shortly?

DEATH.

No, Everyman; and thou be once there, 150

Thou mayst never more come here,

Trust me verily.

EVERYMAN.

O gracious God in the high seat celestial,

Have mercy on me in this most need!

Shall I have no company from this vale terrestrial 155

Of mine acquaintance, that way me to lead?

DEATH.

Yea, if any be so hardy

That would go with thee and bear thee company.

Hie° thee that thou were gone to God's magnificence,

Thy reckoning to give before his presence. 160

What, weenest° thou thy life is given thee,

And thy worldly goods also?

EVERYMAN.

I had wend° so, verily.

DEATH.

Nay, nay; it was but lent thee;

For as soon as thou art go, 165

Another a while shall have it, and then go therefro,°

Even as thou hast done.

Everyman, thou art mad! Thou hast thy wits five,

---

102 **blind** obscure   104 **book of count** account book   105 **turn again** return   111 **Have . . . way** Get ready that we may be on that road   112 **make none attorney** have no attorney   115 **no man dreadeth** dreads no man   116 **rest** arrest   121 **good** wealth   126 **Ne** Nor

141 **lightly** quickly   143 **tide** time   145 **of nature** as a natural thing   148 **for** in the name of   159 **Hie** Hurry   161 **weenest** think   163 **wend** thought   166 **therefro** from it

And here on earth will not amend thy life;
170   For suddenly I do come.

EVERYMAN.

    O wretched caitiff,° whither shall I flee,
    That I might scape this endless sorrow?
    Now, gentle Death, spare me till tomorrow,
    That I may amend me
175   With good advisement.°

DEATH.

    Nay, thereto I will not consent,
    Nor no man will I respite;
    But to the heart suddenly I shall smite
    Without any advisement.
180   And now out of thy sight I will me hie.
    See thou make thee ready shortly,
    For thou mayst say this is the day
    That no man living may scape away.   [Exit Death.]

EVERYMAN.

    Alas, I may well weep with sighs deep!
185   Now have I no manner of company
    To help me in my journey, and me to keep;
    And also my writing is full unready.
    How shall I do now for to excuse me?
    I would to God I had never be get!°
190   To my soul a full great profit it had be;
    For now I fear pains huge and great.
    The time passeth. Lord, help, that all wrought!
    For though I mourn it availeth nought.
    The day passeth, and is almost ago.°
195   I wot° not well what for to do.
    To whom were I best my complaint to make?
    What and I to Fellowship thereof spake,
    And showed him of this sudden chance?
    For in him is all mine affiance;°
200   We have in the world so many a day
    Be good friends in sport and play.
    I see him yonder certainly.
    I trust that he will bear me company;
    Therefore to him will I speak to ease my sorrow.
205   Well met, good Fellowship, and good morrow!

    Fellowship speaketh.

FELLOWSHIP.

    Everyman, good morrow, by this day!
    Sir, why lookest thou so piteously?
    If any thing be amiss, I pray thee me say,
    That I may help to remedy.

EVERYMAN.

210   Yea, good Fellowship, yea;
    I am in great jeopardy.

FELLOWSHIP.

    My true friend, show to me your mind;
    I will not forsake thee to my life's end
    In the way of good company.

EVERYMAN.

215   That was well spoken, and lovingly.

FELLOWSHIP.

    Sir, I must needs know your heaviness;°
    I have pity to see you in any distress.
    If any have you wronged, ye shall revenged be,
    Though I on the ground be slain for thee,
220   Though that I know before that I should die.

EVERYMAN.

    Verily, Fellowship, gramercy.°

FELLOWSHIP.

    Tush! by thy thanks I set not a straw.
    Show me your grief, and say no more.

EVERYMAN.

    If I my heart should to you break,°
225   And then you to turn your mind from me,
    And would not me comfort when ye hear me speak,
    Then should I ten times sorrier be.

FELLOWSHIP.

    Sir, I say as I will do, indeed.

EVERYMAN.

    Then be you a good friend at need!
230   I have found you true here before.

FELLOWSHIP.

    And so ye shall evermore;
    For, in faith, and thou go to hell,
    I will not forsake thee by the way.

EVERYMAN.

    Ye speak like a good friend; I believe you well.
235   I shall deserve it, and I may.

FELLOWSHIP.

    I speak of no deserving, by this day!
    For he that will say, and nothing do,
    Is not worthy with good company to go;
    Therefore show me the grief of your mind,
240   As to your friend most loving and kind.

EVERYMAN.

    I shall show you how it is:
    Commanded I am to go a journey—
    A long way, hard and dangerous—
    And give a strait count, without delay,
245   Before the high Judge, Adonai.°
    Wherefore, I pray you, bear me company,
    As ye have promised, in this journey.

FELLOWSHIP.

    That is matter indeed. Promise is duty;
    But, and I should take such a voyage on me,

---

171 wretched caitiff captive wretch   **175 good advisement** proper reflection   **189 be get** been born   **194 ago** gone by   **195 wot** know   **199 affiance** trust

216 heaviness sorrow   **221 gramercy** thanks   **224 break** open   **245 Adonai** a Hebrew name for God; in Christian liturgy, Christ

250 I know it well, it should be to my pain.
Also it maketh me afeard, certain.
But let us take counsel here as well as we can,
For your words would fear° a strong man.

EVERYMAN.
Why, ye said if I had need
255 Ye would me never forsake, quick° ne dead,
Though it were to hell, truly.

FELLOWSHIP.
So I said, certainly,
But such pleasures be set aside, the sooth° to say.
And also, if we took such a journey,
260 When should we come again?

EVERYMAN.
Nay, never again, till the day of doom.

FELLOWSHIP.
In faith, then will not I come there!
Who hath you these tidings brought?

EVERYMAN.
Indeed, Death was with me here.

FELLOWSHIP.
265 Now, by God that all hath bought,°
If Death were the messenger,
For no man that is living today
I will not go that loath journey—
Not for the father that begat me!

EVERYMAN.
270 Ye promised otherwise, pardie.°

FELLOWSHIP.
I wot well I said so, truly.
And yet if thou wilt eat, and drink, and make good cheer,
Or haunt to women the lusty company,°
I would not forsake you while the day is clear,
275 Trust me verily.

EVERYMAN.
Yea, thereto ye would be ready!
To go to mirth, solace, and play,
Your mind will sooner apply,
Than to bear me company in my long journey.

FELLOWSHIP.
280 Now, in good faith, I will not that way.
But and thou will murder, or any man kill,
In that I will help thee with a good will.

EVERYMAN.
O, that is a simple advice, indeed.
Gentle fellow, help me in my necessity!
285 We have loved long, and now I need;
And now, gentle Fellowship, remember me.

FELLOWSHIP.
Whether ye have loved me or no,
By Saint John, I will not with thee go.

EVERYMAN.
Yet, I pray thee, take the labor, and do so much for me
290 To bring me forward,° for Saint Charity,
And comfort me till I come without the town.

FELLOWSHIP.
Nay, and thou would give me a new gown,
I will not a foot with thee go;
But, and thou had tarried, I would not have left thee so.
295 And as now God speed thee in thy journey,
For from thee I will depart as fast as I may.

EVERYMAN.
Whither away, Fellowship? Will you forsake me?

FELLOWSHIP.
Yea, by my fay!° To God I betake° thee.

EVERYMAN.
Farewell, good Fellowship; for thee my heart is sore.
300 Adieu for ever! I shall see thee no more.

FELLOWSHIP.
In faith, Everyman, farewell now at the end,
For you I will remember that parting is mourning.

[Exit Fellowship.]

EVERYMAN.
Alack! shall we thus depart° indeed—
Ah, Lady, help!—without any more comfort?
305 Lo, Fellowship forsaketh me in my most need.
For help in this world whither shall I resort?
Fellowship here before with me would merry make,
And now little sorrow for me doth he take.
It is said, "In prosperity men friends may find,
310 Which in adversity be full unkind."
Now whither for succor shall I flee,
Sith that° Fellowship hath forsaken me?
To my kinsmen I will, truly,
Praying them to help me in my necessity.
315 I believe that they will do so,
For "kind° will creep where it may not go."
I will go say,° for yonder I see them go.
Where be ye now, my friends and kinsmen?

[Enter Kindred and Cousin.]

KINDRED.
Here be we now at your commandment.
320 Cousin, I pray you show us your intent
In any wise, and do not spare.°

COUSIN.
Yea, Everyman, and to us declare
If ye be disposed to go any whither;
For, wit you well, we will live and die together.

---

253 **fear** frighten   255 **quick** alive   258 **sooth** truth   265 **bought** redeemed   270 **pardie** by God   273 **haunt . . . company** frequent the delightful company of women

290 **bring me forward** accompany me   298 **fay** faith   **betake** commend   303 **depart** separate   312 **Sith that** Since   316 **kind** kinship, family (the idea is that blood ties will find a way) 317 **say** try, essay   321 **spare** hold back

KINDRED.

325   In wealth and woe we will with you hold,
     For over his kin a man may be bold.°

EVERYMAN.

     Gramercy, my friends and kinsmen kind.
     Now shall I show you the grief of my mind:
     I was commanded by a messenger,
330   That is a high king's chief officer;
     He bade me go a pilgrimage, to my pain,
     And I know well I shall never come again;
     Also I must give a reckoning strait,
     For I have a great enemy° that hath me in wait,
335   Which intendeth me for to hinder.

KINDRED.

     What account is that which ye must render?
     That would I know.

EVERYMAN.

     Of all my works I must show
     How I have lived and my days spent;
340   Also of ill deeds that I have used°
     In my time sith life was me lent;
     And of all virtues that I have refused.
     Therefore, I pray you, go thither with me
     To help to make mine account, for Saint Charity.

COUSIN.

345   What, to go thither? Is that the matter?
     Nay, Everyman, I had leifer fast° bread and water
     All this five year and more.

EVERYMAN.

     Alas, that ever I was bore!°
     For now shall I never be merry,
350   If that you forsake me.

KINDRED.

     Ah, sir, what, ye be a merry man!
     Take good heart to you, and make no moan.
     But one thing I warn you, by Saint Anne—
     As for me, ye shall go alone.

EVERYMAN.

355   My Cousin, will you not with me go?

COUSIN.

     No, by Our Lady! I have the cramp in my toe.
     Trust not to me, for, so God me speed,°
     I will deceive you in your most need.

KINDRED.

     It availeth not us to tice.°
360   Ye shall have my maid with all my heart;
     She loveth to go to feasts, there to be nice,°
     And to dance, and abroad to start.°

I will give her leave to help you in that journey,
If that you and she may agree.

EVERYMAN.

     Now show me the very effect of your mind: 365
     Will you go with me, or abide behind?

KINDRED.

     Abide behind? Yea, that will I, and I may!
     Therefore farewell till another day.   [Exit Kindred.]

EVERYMAN.

     How should I be merry or glad?
     For fair promises men to me make,   370
     But when I have most need they me forsake.
     I am deceived; that maketh me sad.

COUSIN.

     Cousin Everyman, farewell now,
     For verily I will not go with you.
     Also of mine own an unready reckoning   375
     I have to account; therefore I make tarrying.
     Now God keep thee, for now I go.   [Exit Cousin.]

EVERYMAN.

     Ah, Jesus, is all come hereto?°
     Lo, fair words maketh fools fain;°
     They promise, and nothing will do certain.   380
     My kinsmen promised me faithfully
     For to abide with me steadfastly;
     And now fast away do they flee.
     Even so Fellowship promised me.
     What friend were best me of to provide?°   385
     I lose my time here longer to abide.
     Yet in my mind a thing there is;
     All my life I have loved riches;
     If that my Good° now help me might,
     He would make my heart full light.   390
     I will speak to him in this distress.
     Where art thou, my Goods and riches?

GOODS.

     [Within.] Who calleth me? Everyman? What! hast thou
        haste?
     I lie here in corners, trussed and piled so high,
     And in chests I am locked so fast,   395
     Also sacked in bags. Thou mayst see with thine eye
     I cannot stir; in packs low I lie.
     What would ye have? Lightly me say.

EVERYMAN.

     Come hither, Good, in all the haste thou may,
     For of counsel I must desire thee.   400

     [Enter Goods.]

GOODS.

     Sir, and ye in the world have sorrow or adversity,
     That can I help you to remedy shortly.

---

326 **over his kin . . . hold** a man may command his kinsmen
334 **enemy** that is, the Devil   340 **used** practiced   344 **leifer fast**
would rather have nothing but   348 **bore** born   357 **so God me
speed** so may God cause me to prosper   359 **tice** entice   361 **nice**
wanton   362 **abroad to start** go gadding about

378 **hereto** to this   379 **fain** glad   385 **of me to provide** to provide me with   389 **Good** wealth

EVERYMAN.
　　It is another disease that grieveth me;
　　In this world it is not, I tell thee so.
405　I am sent for another way to go,
　　To give a strait count general
　　Before the highest Jupiter of all;
　　And all my life I have had joy and pleasure in thee,
　　Therefore, I pray thee, go with me;
410　For, peradventure, thou mayst before God Almighty
　　My reckoning help to clean and purify;
　　For it is said ever among°
　　That "money maketh all right that is wrong."
GOODS.
　　Nay, Everyman, I sing another song.
415　I follow no man in such voyages;
　　For, and I went with thee,
　　Thou shouldst fare much the worse for me;
　　For because on me thou did set thy mind,
　　Thy reckoning I have made blotted and blind,
420　That thine account thou cannot make truly—
　　And that hast thou for the love of me.
EVERYMAN.
　　That would grieve me full sore,
　　When I should come to that fearful answer.
　　Up, let us go thither together.
GOODS.
425　Nay, not so! I am too brittle, I may not endure.
　　I will follow no man one foot, be ye sure.
EVERYMAN.
　　Alas, I have thee loved, and had great pleasure
　　All my life-days on good and treasure.
GOODS.
　　That is to thy damnation, without lesing,°
430　For my love is contrary to the love everlasting.
　　But if thou had me loved moderately during,
　　As to the poor to give part of me,
　　Then shouldst thou not in this dolor be,
　　Nor in this great sorrow and care.
EVERYMAN.
435　Lo, now was I deceived ere I was ware,
　　And all I may wite° misspending of time.
GOODS.
　　What, weenest thou that I am thine?
EVERYMAN.
　　I had wend so.
GOODS.
　　Nay, Everyman, I say no.
440　As for a while I was lent thee;
　　A season thou hast had me in prosperity.
　　My condition is man's soul to kill;
　　If I save one, a thousand I do spill.°

　　Weenest thou that I will follow thee?
　　Nay, not from this world, verily.　　　　　　445
EVERYMAN.
　　I had wend otherwise.
GOODS.
　　Therefore to thy soul Good is a thief;
　　For when thou art dead, this is my guise°—
　　Another to deceive in this same wise
　　As I have done thee, and all to his soul's reprief.°　450
EVERYMAN.
　　O false Good, cursed may thou be,
　　Thou traitor to God, that hast deceived me
　　And caught me in thy snare!
GOODS.
　　Mary!° thou brought thyself in care,
　　Whereof I am right glad;　　　　　　　　　455
　　I must needs laugh, I cannot be sad.
EVERYMAN.
　　Ah, Good, thou hast had long my heartly° love;
　　I gave thee that which should be the Lord's above.
　　But wilt thou not go with me indeed?
　　I pray thee truth to say.　　　　　　　　460
GOODS.
　　No, so God me speed!
　　Therefore farewell, and have good day.　[Exit Goods.]
EVERYMAN.
　　O, to whom shall I make my moan
　　For to go with me in that heavy journey?
　　First Fellowship said he would with me gone—　465
　　His words were very pleasant and gay,
　　But afterward he left me alone.
　　Then spake I to my kinsmen, all in despair,
　　And also they gave me words fair—
　　They lacked no fair speaking,　　　　　　470
　　But all forsook me in the ending.
　　Then went I to my Goods, that I loved best,
　　In hope to have comfort, but there had I least;
　　For my Goods sharply did me tell
　　That he bringeth many into hell.　　　　　475
　　Then of myself I was ashamed,
　　And so I am worthy to be blamed.
　　Thus may I well myself hate.
　　Of whom shall I now counsel take?
　　I think that I shall never speed　　　　　480
　　Till that I go to my Good Deed.
　　But, alas, she is so weak
　　That she can neither go° nor speak.
　　Yet will I venture on her now.
　　My Good Deeds, where be you?　　　　　485

[Good Deeds speaks from the ground.]

---

412 **ever among** every now and then　429 **lesing** lying　436 **wite**
blame on　443 **spill** destroy

448 **guise** custom, practice　450 **reprief** reproof　454 **Mary** By
Mary (an expletive)　456 **heartly** hearty　483 **go** walk

GOOD DEEDS.
Here I lie, cold in the ground.
Thy sins hath me sore bound,
That I cannot stir.
EVERYMAN.
O Good Deeds, I stand in fear!
490　I must you pray of counsel,
For help now should come right well.
GOOD DEEDS.
Everyman, I have understanding
That ye be summoned account to make
Before Messias, of Jerusalem King;
495　And you do by me,° that journey with you will I take.
VERYMAN.
Therefore I come to you, my moan to make.
I pray you that ye will go with me.
GOOD DEEDS.
I would full fain, but I cannot stand, verily.
EVERYMAN.
Why, is there anything on you fall?
GOOD DEEDS.
500　Yea, sir, I may thank you of° all;
If ye had perfectly cheered me,
Your book of count full ready had be.
Look, the books of your works and deeds eke!°
Behold how they lie under the feet
505　To your soul's heaviness.
EVERYMAN.
Our Lord Jesus help me!
For one letter here I cannot see.
GOOD DEEDS.
There is a blind reckoning in time of distress.
EVERYMAN.
Good Deeds, I pray you help me in this need,
510　Or else I am for ever damned indeed;
Therefore help me to make reckoning
Before the Redeemer of all thing,
That King is, and was, and ever shall.
GOOD DEEDS.
Everyman, I am sorry of your fall,
515　And fain would I help you, and I were able.
EVERYMAN.
Good Deeds, your counsel I pray you give me
GOOD DEEDS.
That shall I do verily;
Though that on my feet I may not go,
I have a sister that shall with you also,
520　Called Knowledge,° which shall with you abide,
To help you to make that dreadful reckoning.

[Enter Knowledge.]

KNOWLEDGE.
Everyman, I will go with thee, and be thy guide,
In thy most need to go by thy side.
EVERYMAN.
In good condition I am now in every thing,
And am wholly content with this good thing,　525
Thanked be God my creator.
GOOD DEEDS.
And when she hath brought you there
Where thou shalt heal thee of thy smart,°
Then go you with your reckoning and your Good Deeds
　　together,
For to make you joyful at heart　530
Before the Blessed Trinity.
EVERYMAN.
My Good Deeds, gramercy!
I am well content, certainly,
With your words sweet.
KNOWLEDGE.
Now go we together lovingly　535
To Confession, that cleansing river.
EVERYMAN.
For joy I weep; I would we were there!
But, I pray you give me cognition
Where dwelleth that holy man, Confession?
KNOWLEDGE.
In the House of Salvation:　540
We shall find him in that place,
That shall us comfort, by God's grace.

[Knowledge leads Everyman to Confession.]

Lo, this is Confession. Kneel down and ask mercy,
For he is in good conceit° with God Almighty.
EVERYMAN.
O glorious fountain, that all uncleanness doth clarify,　545
Wash from me the spots of vice unclean,
That on me no sin may be seen.
I come with Knowledge for my redemption,
Redempt with heart and full contrition;
For I am commanded a pilgrimage to take,　550
And great accounts before God to make.
Now I pray you, Shrift,° mother of Salvation,
Help my Good Deeds for my piteous exclamation.
CONFESSION.
I know your sorrow well, Everyman.
Because with Knowledge ye come to me,　555
I will you comfort as well as I can,
And a precious jewel I will give thee,
Called penance, voider of adversity;
Therewith shall your body chastised be,

---

495 **And you do by me** If you do as I advise　500 **of** for　503 **eke** also　520 **Knowledge** acknowledgement of sin, the first step to contrition (*Knowledge* is not scientific knowledge, but is knowledge of Christianity—the knowledge that tells us we are dependent on God's grace)

528 **smart** pain　544 **good conceit** high esteem　552 **Shrift** Confession

560　With abstinence and perseverance in God's service.
　　Here shall you receive that scourge of me,
　　Which is penance strong that ye must endure,
　　To remember thy Savior was scourged for thee
　　With sharp scourges, and suffered it patiently;
565　So must thou, ere thou scape that painful pilgrimage.
　　Knowledge, keep him in this voyage,
　　And by that time Good Deeds will be with thee.
　　But in any wise be siker° of mercy,
　　For your time draweth fast; and° ye will saved be,
570　Ask God mercy, and he will grant truly.
　　When with the scourge of penance man doth him° bind,
　　The oil of forgiveness then shall he find.

EVERYMAN.
　　Thanked be God for his gracious work!
　　For now I will my penance begin;
575　This hath rejoiced and lighted my heart,
　　Though the knots be painful and hard within.

KNOWLEDGE.
　　Everyman, look your penance that ye fulfill,
　　What pain that ever it to you be;
　　And Knowledge shall give you counsel at will
580　How your account ye shall make clearly.

EVERYMAN.
　　O eternal God, O heavenly figure,
　　O way of rightwiseness, O goodly vision,
　　Which descended down in a virgin pure
　　Because he would every man redeem,
585　Which Adam forfeited by his disobedience,
　　O blessed Godhead, elect and high divine,
　　Forgive my grievous offense;
　　Here I cry thee mercy in this presence.
　　O ghostly treasure, O ransomer and redeemer,
590　Of all the world hope and conductor,°
　　Mirror of joy, and founder of mercy,
　　Which enlumineth heaven and earth thereby,
　　Hear my clamorous complaint, though it late be;
　　Receive my prayers, unworthy of thy benignity.
595　Though I be a sinner most abominable,
　　Yet let my name be written in Moses' table.
　　O Mary, pray to the Maker of all thing,
　　Me for to help at my ending,
　　And save me from the power of my enemy,
600　For Death assaileth me strongly.
　　And, Lady, that I may by mean of thy prayer
　　Of your Son's glory to be partner,
　　By the means of his passion, I it crave.
　　I beseech you help my soul to save.
605　Knowledge, give me the scourge of penance;
　　My flesh therewith shall give acquittance.°
　　I will now begin, if God give me grace.

KNOWLEDGE.
　　Everyman, God give you time and space!
　　Thus I bequeath you in the hands of our Savior.
　　Now may you make your reckoning sure.　610

EVERYMAN.
　　In the name of the Holy Trinity,
　　My body sore punished shall be.
　　Take this, body, for the sin of the flesh! [Scourges himself.]
　　Also thou delightest to go gay and fresh,
　　And in the way of damnation thou did me bring;　615
　　Therefore suffer now strokes of punishing.
　　Now of penance I will wade the water clear,
　　To save me from purgatory, that sharp fire.

[Good Deeds rises from the floor.]

GOOD DEEDS.
　　I thank God, now I can walk and go,
　　And am delivered of my sickness and woe.　620
　　Therefore with Everyman I will go, and not spare;
　　His good works I will help him to declare.

KNOWLEDGE.
　　Now, Everyman, be merry and glad!
　　Your Good Deeds cometh now; ye may not be sad.
　　Now is your Good Deeds whole and sound,　625
　　Going upright upon the ground.

EVERYMAN.
　　My heart is light, and shall be evermore;
　　Now will I smite faster than I did before.

GOOD DEEDS.
　　Everyman, pilgrim, my special friend,
　　Blessed be thou without end;　630
　　For thee is preparate° the eternal glory.
　　Ye have me made whole and sound,
　　Therefore I will bide by thee in every stound.°

EVERYMAN.
　　Welcome, my Good Deeds! Now I hear thy voice,
　　I weep for very sweetness of love.　635

KNOWLEDGE.
　　Be no more sad, but ever rejoice;
　　God seeth thy living in his throne above.
　　Put on this garment to thy behove,°
　　Which is wet with your tears,
　　Or else before God you may it miss,　640
　　When ye to your journey's end come shall.

EVERYMAN.
　　Gentle Knowledge, what do ye it call?

KNOWLEDGE.
　　It is a garment of sorrow;
　　From pain it will you borrow;°
　　Contrition it is,　645
　　That getteth forgiveness;
　　It pleaseth God passing well.

---

568 siker certain　**569 and** if　**571 him** himself　**590 conductor** guide　**606 acquittance** atonement

631 preparate prepared　**633 stound** moment (i.e., in every fierce attack)　**638 behove** benefit　**644 borrow** redeem

GOOD DEEDS.
Everyman, will you wear it for your heal?
EVERYMAN.
Now blessed be Jesu, Mary's Son,
650   For now have I on true contrition.
And let us go now without tarrying.
Good Deeds, have we clear our reckoning?
GOOD DEEDS.
Yea, indeed, I have here.
EVERYMAN.
Then I trust we need not fear.
655   Now, friends, let us not part in twain.
KNOWLEDGE.
Nay, Everyman, that will we not, certain.
GOOD DEEDS.
Yet must thou lead with thee
Three persons of great might.
EVERYMAN.
Who should they be?
GOOD DEEDS.
660   Discretion and Strength they hight,°
And thy Beauty may not abide behind.
KNOWLEDGE.
Also ye must call to mind
Your Five Wits° as for your counselors.
GOOD DEEDS.
You must have them ready at all hours.
EVERYMAN.
665   How shall I get them hither?
KNOWLEDGE.
You must call them all together,
And they will hear you incontinent.°
EVERYMAN.
My friends, come hither and be present,
Discretion, Strength, my Five Wits, and Beauty.

[*Enter Beauty, Strength, Discretion, and Five Wits.*]

BEAUTY.
670   Here at your will we be all ready.
What will ye that we should do?
GOOD DEEDS.
That ye would with Everyman go,
And help him in his pilgrimage.
Advise you, will ye with him or not in that voyage?
STRENGTH.
675   We will bring him all thither,
To his help and comfort, ye may believe me.
DISCRETION.
So will we go with him all together.

EVERYMAN.
Almighty God, loved may thou be!
I give thee laud that I have hither brought
Strength, Discretion, Beauty, and Five Wits. Lack I
    nought.   680
And my Good Deeds, with Knowledge clear,
All be in my company at my will here.
I desire no more to° my business.
STRENGTH.
And I, Strength, will by you stand in distress,
Though thou would in battle fight on the ground.   685
FIVE WITS.
And though it were through the world round,
We will not depart for sweet ne sour.
BEAUTY.
No more will I unto death's hour,
Whatsoever thereof befall.
DISCRETION.
Everyman, advise you° first of all;   690
Go with a good advisement and deliberation.
We all give you virtuous monition°
That all shall be well.
EVERYMAN.
My friends, harken what I will tell:
I pray God reward you in his heavenly sphere.   695
Now harken, all that be here,
For I will make my testament
Here before you all present:
In alms half my good I will give with my hands twain
In the way of charity with good intent,   700
And the other half still shall remain
In queth,° to be returned there° it ought to be.
This I do in despite of the fiend of hell,
To go quite out of his peril
Ever after and this day.   705
KNOWLEDGE.
Everyman, harken what I say:
Go to Priesthood, I you advise,
And receive of him in any wise
The holy sacrament and ointment together.
Then shortly see ye turn again hither;   710
We will all abide you here.
FIVE WITS.
Yea, Everyman, hie you that ye ready were.
There is no emperor, king, duke, ne baron,
That of God hath commission
As hath the least priest in the world being;°   715
For of the blessed sacraments pure and benign
He bareth the keys, and thereof hath the cure°
For man's redemption—it is ever sure—

---

660 hight are called   **663 Five Wits** five physical senses (they are Everyman's "counselors" because they provide him with sensory data on which Discretion, that is, reason, operates) **667 incontinent** immediately

683 to for   **690 advise you** consider the matter   **692 monition** admonition   **702 queth** bequest   **there** where   **715 being** living **717 cure** charge, spiritual responsibility (with a pun on medical healing, indicated in 719)

Which God for our soul's medicine
720 Gave us out of his heart with great pain
Here in this transitory life, for thee and me.
The blessed sacraments seven there be:
Baptism, confirmation, with priesthood good,
And the sacrament of God's precious flesh and blood,
725 Marriage, the holy extreme unction, and penance.
These seven be good to have in remembrance,
Gracious sacraments of high divinity.

EVERYMAN.
Fain would I receive that holy body,
And meekly to my ghostly° father I will go.

FIVE WITS.
730 Everyman, that is the best that ye can do.
God will you to salvation bring,
For priesthood exceedeth all other thing:
To us Holy Scripture they do teach,
And converteth man from sin heaven to reach;
735 God hath to them more power given
Than to any angel that is in heaven.
With five words° he may consecrate,
God's body in flesh and blood to make,
And handleth his Maker between his hands.
740 The priest bindeth and unbindeth all bands,
Both in earth and in heaven.
Thou ministers° all the sacraments seven;
Though we kissed thy feet, thou were worthy;
Thou art surgeon that cureth sin deadly;
745 No remedy we find under God
But all only° priesthood.
Everyman, God gave priests that dignity,
And setteth them in his stead among us to be.
Thus be they above angels in degree.

[Exit Everyman to receive the last sacraments
from the priest.]

KNOWLEDGE.
750 If priests be good, it is so,° surely.
But when Jesus hanged on the cross with great smart,
There he gave out of his blessed heart
The same sacrament in great torment.
He sold them not to us, that Lord omnipotent.
755 Therefore Saint Peter the apostle doth say
That Jesu's curse hath all they
Which God their Savior do buy or sell,
Or they for any money do take or tell.°
Sinful priests giveth the sinners example bad;
760 Their children sitteth by other men's fires, I have heard;
And some haunteth women's company

With unclean life, as lusts of lechery:
These be with sin made blind.

FIVE WITS.
I trust to God no such may we find.
Therefore let us priesthood honor, 765
And follow their doctrine for our souls' succor.
We be their sheep, and they shepherds be,
By whom we all be kept in surety.
Peace, for yonder I see Everyman come,
Which hath made true satisfaction. 770

GOOD DEEDS.
Methink it is he indeed.

[Re-enter Everyman.]

EVERYMAN.
Now Jesu be your alder speed!°
I have received the sacrament for my redemption,
And then mine extreme unction.
Blessed be all they that counseled me to take it! 775
And now, friends, let us go without longer respite;
I thank God that ye have tarried so long.
Now set each of you on this rod° your hand,
And shortly follow me.
I go before there° I would be; God be our guide! 780

STRENGTH.
Everyman, we will not from you go
Till ye have done this voyage long.

DISCRETION.
I, Discretion, will bide by you also.

KNOWLEDGE.
And though this pilgrimage be never so strong,°
I will never part you fro. 785

STRENGTH.
Everyman, I will be as sure by thee
As ever I did by Judas Maccabee.°

[They go together to the grave.]

EVERYMAN.
Alas, I am so faint I may not stand;
My limbs under me doth fold.
Friends, let us not turn again to this land, 790
Not for all the world's gold;
For into this cave must I creep
And turn to earth, and there to sleep.

BEAUTY.
What, into this grave? Alas!

EVERYMAN.
Yea, there shall ye consume, more and less.° 795

BEAUTY.
And what, should I smother here?

---

729 **ghostly** spiritual   737 **five words** *Hoc est enim corpus meum* (For this is my body), from the sacrament of the Eucharist   742 **ministers** administers   746 **only** except   750 **it is so** that is, "above angels in degree"   758 **tell** count

772 **Now Jesu . . . speed** Now may Jesus let you all prosper 778 **rod** cross   780 **there** where   784 **strong** hard   787 **Judas Maccabee** Judas Maccabeus, ancient Jewish leader noted for his military exploits   795 **more and less** high and low, that is, people of all ranks

EVERYMAN.
    Yea, by my faith, and never more appear.
    In this world live no more we shall,
    But in heaven before the highest Lord of all.
BEAUTY.
800   I cross out all this! Adieu, by Saint John!
    I take my cap in my lap, and am gone.
EVERYMAN.
    What, Beauty, whither will ye?
BEAUTY.
    Peace, I am deaf; I look not behind me,
    Not and thou wouldest give me all the gold in thy chest.

                                    [Exit Beauty.]

EVERYMAN.
805   Alas, whereto may I trust?
    Beauty goeth fast away from me;
    She promised with me to live and die.
STRENGTH.
    Everyman, I will thee also forsake and deny;
    Thy game liketh° me not at all.
EVERYMAN.
810   Why, then, ye will forsake me all?
    Sweet Strength, tarry a little space.
STRENGTH.
    Nay, sir, by the rood of grace!
    I will hie me from thee fast,
    Though thou weep till they heart to-brast.°
EVERYMAN.
815   Ye would ever bide by me, ye said.
STRENGTH.
    Yea, I have you far enough conveyed.
    Ye be old enough, I understand,
    Your pilgrimage to take on hand;
    I repent me that I hither came.
EVERYMAN.
820   Strength, you to displease I am to blame;
    Yet promise is debt, this ye well wot.
STRENGTH.
    In faith, I care not.
    Thou are but a fool to complain;
    You spend your speech and waste your brain.
825   Go, thrust thee into the ground!   [Exit Strength.]
EVERYMAN.
    I had wend surer I should you have found.
    He that trusteth in his Strength
    She him deceiveth at the length.
    Both Strength and Beauty forsaketh me;
830   Yet they promised me fair and lovingly.
DISCRETION.
    Everyman, I will after Strength be gone;
    As for me, I will leave you alone.

809 liketh pleases   **814 to-brast** burst to pieces

180

EVERYMAN.
    Why, Discretion, will ye forsake me?
DISCRETION.
    Yea, in faith, I will go from thee,
    For when Strength goeth before   835
    I follow after evermore.
EVERYMAN.
    Yet, I pray thee, for the love of the Trinity,
    Look in my grave once piteously.
DISCRETION.
    Nay, so nigh will I not come;
    Farewell, everyone!   [Exit Discretion.]   840
EVERYMAN.
    O, all thing faileth, save God alone—
    Beauty, Strength, and Discretion;
    For when Death bloweth his blast,
    They all run from me full fast.
FIVE WITS.
    Everyman, my leave now of thee I take;   845
    I will follow the other, for here I thee forsake.
EVERYMAN.
    Alas, then may I wail and weep,
    For I took you for my best friend.
FIVE WITS.
    I will no longer thee keep;
    Now farewell, and there an end.   [Exit Five Wits.] 850
EVERYMAN.
    O Jesu, help! All hath forsaken me.
GOOD DEEDS.
    Nay, Everyman; I will bide with thee.
    I will not forsake thee indeed;
    Thou shalt find me a good friend at need.
EVERYMAN.
    Gramercy, Good Deeds! Now may I true friends see. 855
    They have forsaken me, every one;
    I loved them better than my Good Deeds alone.
    Knowledge, will ye forsake me also?
KNOWLEDGE.
    Yea, Everyman, when ye to Death shall go;
    But not yet, for no manner of danger.   860
EVERYMAN.
    Gramercy, Knowledge, with all my heart.
KNOWLEDGE.
    Nay, yet I will not from hence depart
    Till I see where ye shall be come.
EVERYMAN.
    Methink, alas, that I must be gone
    To make my reckoning and my debts pay,   865
    For I see my time is nigh spent away.
    Take example, all ye that this do hear or see,
    How they that I loved best do forsake me,
    Except my Good Deeds that bideth truly.
GOOD DEEDS.
    All earthly things is but vanity: 870
    Beauty, Strength, and Discretion do man forsake,

Foolish friends, and kinsmen, that fair spake—
All fleeth save Good Deeds, and that am I.

EVERYMAN.
Have mercy on me, God most mighty;
875 And stand by me, thou mother and maid, Holy Mary.

GOOD DEEDS.
Fear not; I will speak for thee.

EVERYMAN.
Here I cry God mercy.

GOOD DEEDS.
Short° our end, and minish° our pain;
Let us go and never come again.

EVERYMAN.
880 Into thy hands, Lord, my soul I commend;
Receive it, Lord, that it be not lost.
As thou me boughtest, so me defend,
And save me from the fiend's boast,
That I may appear with that blessed host
885 That shall be saved at the day of doom.
In manus tuas, of might's most
For ever, *commendo spiritum meum*.°

[*Everyman and Good Deeds descend into the grave.*]

KNOWLEDGE.
Now hath he suffered that we all shall endure;
The Good Deeds shall make all sure.
890 Now hath he made ending.
Methinketh that I hear angels sing,
And make great joy and melody
Where Everyman's soul received shall be.

[*Enter Angel.*]

ANGEL.
Come, excellent elect spouse, to Jesu!
895 Here above thou shalt go

Because of thy singular virtue.
Now the soul is taken the body fro,
Thy reckoning is crystal clear.
Now shalt thou in to the heavenly sphere,
Unto the which all ye shall come   900
That liveth well before the day of doom.

[*Exit Knowledge.*]

Enter Doctor [*of Theology*]

DOCTOR.
This moral men may have in mind.
Ye hearers, take it of worth,° old and young,
And forsake Pride, for he deceiveth you in the end;
And remember Beauty, Five Wits, Strength, and Discre-
    tion,   905
They all at the last do every man forsake,
Save° his Good Deeds there doth he take.
But beware, and they be small
Before God, he hath no help at all;
None excuse may be there for every man.   910
Alas, how shall he do then?
For after death amends may no man make,
For then mercy and pity doth him forsake.
If his reckoning be not clear when he doth come,
God will say: "*Ite, maledicti, in ignem eternum.*"°   915
And he that hath his account whole and sound,
High in heaven he shall be crowned;
Unto which place God bring us all thither,
That we may live body and soul together.
Thereto help the Trinity!   920
Amen, say ye, for Saint Charity.   [*Exit Doctor.*]

THUS ENDETH THIS MORAL PLAY OF *Everyman*.

TOPICS FOR CRITICAL THINKING AND WRITING

 THE PLAY ON THE PAGE

1. The Messenger's speech at the beginning of *Everyman* announces the theme and suggests the gist of the plot. Do you think that by giving this information the speech diminishes the possibility of suspense, and thereby weakens the play? Explain.

2. In the play, Death is an abstraction, of course, but what characteristics does the author give him?

---

878 **Short** Shorten **minish** diminish **886–87 In manus . . . meum** "Into thy hands I commit my spirit"; Christ's last words, according to Luke 23.46

903 **take it of worth** value it   907 **Save** Only   915 **Ite . . . eternum** "Depart from me, ye cursed, into everlasting fire" (Christ's words in Matthew 25.41)

🎭 THE PLAY ON THE STAGE

3. If you were producing *Everyman*, how would you costume Death? As a skeleton, wearing a cloak? As a businessman in a three-piece suit? Or what? Do you think a woman can perform the role effectively? Explain.

4. Take one of the abstractions other than Death and Everyman and examine the degree to which it is made concrete and interesting. Suggest appropriate stage business for several speeches of this character. And how would you costume him or her? By the way, do you assume that certain roles should necessarily be played by a male (e.g., Strength) and certain roles by a woman (e.g., Beauty)? (Note that in line 828 strength is spoken of as "she.") Or can we disregard the sex of the actor? Explain.

5. If you were staging the play would you use the same actor for the Messenger (who opens the play) and the Doctor (who closes it), in the same costume? Why, or why not?

6. Lines 707–49, on the powers of the priesthood, are sometimes deleted from modern productions. What arguments can you offer, pro or con?

THE PLAY IN PERFORMANCE

Because *Everyman* was printed four times early in the sixteenth century, we can infer that it probably was performed as well as read, but we do not have a single reference to a performance before William Poel's revival in 1901, which we will discuss later. We do not know, therefore, if it was performed outdoors, perhaps on some sort of booth-and-trestle stage, or indoors, in a castle, court, or school. Probably it was performed under a variety of circumstances, sometimes perhaps by students, sometimes by amateurs or semiprofessional actors—let's say a group of talented part-time actors who took their local productions to neighboring towns—but all of this is only conjecture. What we do know is that the required stage properties are few (perhaps a cross, and a chair or two), that with some doubling of roles it can be done by a cast of seven, and that from about 1400 there were indeed small touring companies of actors. The trouble is, we do not know which plays these companies performed; the records that prove their existence are for the most part records of payments for "a play" or payments to "players of interludes."

In *Everyman*, we have no hard evidence concerning the methods of production; in fact, we have only four stage directions in the entire play: "God speketh," after line 21; "Dethe" (i.e., "enter Death"), after line 63; "Euery Man" (i.e., "enter Everyman"), after 86 (but we place it a bit earlier), and "Felawshyp speketh," after 205. We must examine the text, then, with an eye toward what *might* have been done, but with the understanding that we cannot speak with certainty.

COSTUMES

The first character to speak is a Messenger. Perhaps he wore some sort of garb that identified him as such, but nothing is specified. The next character to speak is God. We know, from a few medieval records of performances, that in miracle plays God was distinctively costumed. One document speaks of "five sheep-skins for God's coat," and another, concerning a late (1565) production of *Creation of Eve and Expulsion from Eden,* calls for "A face [i.e., a mask] and hair [a wig] for the Father." Perhaps, then, in *Everyman* God wore a mask and a wig. In any case, because in his very first line God refers to his "majesty," probably he is dressed as a king or emperor. If today we wish to stage *Everyman* in a way that might resemble its original staging, we can easily find pictures of monarchs. On the other hand, although in the Middle Ages troupes did not hesitate to use actors to impersonate God, some modern directors prefer to keep God offstage, and to represent him only by his voice. Similarly, although we are told nothing about the appearance of the angel who speaks in line 894, he probably was represented much as angels appear in medieval paintings—winged, white-robed, with gold hair. And, again, some modern directors prefer to have the angel heard but not seen.

God calls on Death. What does Death look like? In the Middle Ages Death was often depicted as a skeleton, sometimes holding a scythe (the Grim Reaper), or holding an hourglass (to symbolize the passage of time), or holding a dart (to strike down his prey), or holding a coffin-lid. It happens that in his first speech in *Everyman*, Death actually mentions his dart (line 76), and in line 178 he says he will "smite" Everyman to the heart, but the dart is never again mentioned, so Death probably did not carry a dart in sixteenth-century productions. The illustration in one of the earliest editions of the play shows Death carrying a board for a coffin (see page 169), but the play makes no reference to such a prop, so again we can assume it probably was not used. In fact, since Everyman does not at first recognize Death, perhaps Death is *not* immediately identifiable by his costume or by a hand prop; perhaps he is identifiable only when, saying "I am Death that no man dredeth" (i.e., "I am Death, who dreads no man"), he removes a hood or cloak and reveals a skull or skeleton. In short, we can offer ideas, but we cannot say with any certainty what Death looked like in *Everyman*.

Similarly, we cannot say for sure what the various personified abstractions, such as Kindred and Good Deeds looked like, though we can guess that Goods held a money bag or a money box, and Beauty doubtless was beautiful. Finally, the Doctor at the end of the play presumably wore an academic robe, indicating that he was a learned man.

Looking further at the text, still with an eye toward the costumes, we find that Death ask Everyman, "Whither are thou going / Thus gaily?" (85–86). From this line we may infer that Everyman is dressed in some sort of colorful, fashionably tailored apparel. In line 638, when Everyman is in "the House of Salvation," Knowledge says to him, "Put on this garment," and a few lines later Knowledge explains that it is "a garment of sorrow." Here, most likely, Everyman changes from his worldly garments to some sort of austere garment, thus *visibly* communicating the change in his spiritual condition.

SCENERY AND LOCALES

But what is this "House of Salvation" (540) where Confession dwells? It stands for the Church, but how was it represented on the stage? We do not know. Possibly a cross, or a cross and a chair would be enough, but possibly there was some further indication of a house, for instance a framework covered with canvas. We know that in other plays painted or constructed scenery was used to represent such things as "the city of Jerusalem, with towers and pinnacles," "a prison," and "a fiery cloud." Perhaps to help represent the House of Salvation, God stood there, or even sat atop it.

If the staging of the House of Salvation is uncertain, so too is the staging of other locales. It seems reasonable to assume that, at the beginning of the play, God appears on some sort of elevated structure, indicating heaven, and that most of the action takes place beneath him. God's "I perceive" and his repeated "I see" add to the likelihood that he is aloft, looking down on his creation. Possibly from a lofty position he watches the entire action; possibly, however, he joins Everyman in the House of Salvation; or possibly we see God only at the start of the play. It is even possible, as we have already said, that we do not see him but only hear his voice. Let's assume, however, that at least at the start God stands or sits above the other players: The audience sees two realms, the spiritual and the earthly. When Everyman dies, does he descend into a lower realm? Consider these lines:

For into this cave must I creep / And turn to earth (792–93)

What, into this grave? (794)

Look in my grave once piteously (838)

Good Deeds says he will go with Everyman, and the editors of this text have added a stage direction, "Everyman and Good Deeds descend into the grave." We have added this direction (887) because the text strongly suggests that they descend through a trap door, but possibly they simply walk offstage, that is, disappear behind a curtain or screen.

Before looking briefly at the play's stage history, we want to mention one other conjectural bit of staging, and our comments may strike readers as extremely eccentric. Many medieval illustrations show, just above a dying man's head, Mary holding—receiving—a small, naked figure. This figure represents the soul of the dying man, which has escaped from the gesticulating devils at the bottom of the illustration. Now, such pictures illustrate what all morality plays are essentially about, the salvation of the repentant soul. And the happy ending, in art, is almost always shown by a depiction of the soul, symbolized by an infant, in the arms of Mary, or in heaven. And so, when at the end of the play Knowledge says that he hears angels sing (891), and the angel says, "Come, excellent spouse, to Jesu" (894), it is possible or (we think) even probable that the audience heard music and actually saw a representation of Everyman's soul rise out of the grave and go to the angel, presumably in an elevated place.

STAGE HISTORY

Solid information about *Everyman* on the stage begins in 1901, with a production by William Poel, an Englishman who founded the Elizabethan Stage Society. Poel tried to stage early plays in the way that (he thought) they were originally staged. He therefore rejected the elaborate sets, with realistic scenery, common in the Victorian period. The late nineteenth-century use of illusionistic sets—trees that looked like trees, rooms with substantial walls, and so forth—had two consequences: (1) Intermissions were introduced, so that the sets could be changed, and (2) the original sequence of scenes was altered, in an effort to reduce the number of changes. For instance, two forest scenes that had been separated by, say, a scene in court were run together. Poel assumed that early plays should be performed without cuts, without transpositions of scenes, and without interruptions. The stage thus was kept relatively bare, with a few props brought on as needed.

On July 13, 1901, Poel produced *Everyman*. He wanted to stage it in the cloisters of Westminster Abbey, but he had been turned down, and turned down again when he had asked for permission to use Canterbury Cathedral. He then settled for the Master's Court (an old gray quadrangle) of the Charterhouse, a former monastery but in Poel's day a home for the aged. Poel played God (Adonai), and a famous actress, Edith Wynne Mathison, played Everyman, the idea being that a woman's voice would make an effective contrast against the male voices of God and Death. Death, a skeleton, carried a drum. Otherwise the costumes were derived chiefly from Flemish tapestries of the fifteenth century, and from the two woodcuts that appear in some copies of the earliest editions of *Everyman* (see illustration 169).

Poel's staging involved two levels, an upper level (a battlement) for God, and a main level, for the rest of the action. His production was very popular, and Poel staged it elsewhere in England and also in Scotland and Ireland. His company also played in America, where it opened in New York on October 13, 1902. It toured the United States, and

Anonymous

in fact the British company returned again and again, with changes in the cast, of course, until the 1930s.

Poel's *Everyman* engendered a more famous version, *Jedermann* (Everyman), a German version produced by Max Reinhardt. Reinhardt saw Poel's production, and commissioned the German writer Hugo von Hofmannsthal to write a version of the play. Hofmannsthal complied, and his *Jedermann* achieved fame, especially in its annual productions at the Salzburg Festival (1920 to the present, except for 1937–45), where it was staged in front of the cathedral.

Everyman is occasionally performed by students and by religious groups. It requires only a fairly small company (the actors who play Fellowship, Kindred, Cousin, and Goods usually double as Discretion, Strength, Five Wits, and Beauty),

and only a few props, for instance a scourge, and perhaps some money bags or a money box for Goods. Most productions today are performed either within a church or against the façade of a church, thereby borrowing a religious background, though for outdoor staging almost any stone building seems to provide an adequate background. When the play is staged, directors often use artificial light to reveal the characters to whom Everyman appeals for help, and then cause them to disappear with a blackout. Costumes tend to be either medieval or contemporary. Sometimes masks are used for the various abstractions (e.g., Goods, Beauty, Strength) to whom Everyman turns for help, but the mouth-openings have to be almost grotesquely large to make sure that the speeches can be heard, and, in any case, amateurs usually find masks uncomfortable.

John Astington
EVERYMAN IN TORONTO

In 1979 John Astington staged *Everyman* in Toronto. Music was incorporated at two points in the play—at Everyman's entrance (treated as a kind of dance, accompanied by a dance-song played on a recorder by a seated actor) and, second, during Knowledge's final speech (the Antiphon from the Office of the Dead, sung by the Angel).

A plain modern style was chosen for this production. The play was acted in three-quarter round, on and around a simple wooden platform ten feet square and eighteen inches high. The stage had a central hinged trap, with crawl spaces to gain access to it from below. A small square platform three feet in height, with steps down to floor level, represented both heaven and the house of salvation. General area lighting illuminated the audience and acting area, with the stage slightly brighter, lit by spotlights.

The generally austere, spare style of the production was intended to place stress on the action and words of the play. The doubling of parts, and the presence of the actors before and after they appeared on the stage as specific characters were intended to stimulate the imaginative involvement of the audience with the play, by limiting the fiction that the actors "were" the characters they played.

The actors were dressed alike in plain modern clothes in dark colours, predominantly black: cloth shoes, trousers, and leotard tops or T-shirts. The actresses playing Good Deeds and Knowledge wore long skirts. The only other items of costume were the robe of contrition, a simple, full-length, sleeveless gown, and two long, coloured sashes, one red and one gold, which were used at Everyman's entrance to symbolise his rich clothing. Death carried a staff, one end of which was sharpened and the other surmounted by a hooded skull.

The actors entered together before the start of the play and sat in a ring on the floor, facing inward towards the stage, where they remained throughout the play when they were not

on stage. Entrances were made from these positions, and exits simply required the actor to move to his or her place and sit.

Staging of particular passages conformed to the general style dictated by this approach. God was not revealed, but the actor simply rose and took a standing position on the platform as the Messenger ended his speech, extending his arms as he began to speak. After the command to Death, the actor unobtrusively dropped his pose and returned to his place. The entry of Everyman was made into a tableau: to a dance tune Everyman was teasingly pulled around the edge of the stage by two companions, who wrapped and entangled him in long, coloured sashes. At Death's summons this dance abruptly stopped, the companions fled, and the cloth sashes dropped to the ground around Everyman's feet. The trap was not used for the entry of Death, but was opened by Everyman himself as he searched for Goods, and thereafter remained open. Goods was played primarily by one actress, who crawled into the trap from below, but the opening lines were split up among four other actors, who crept and rolled into positions roughly at the four corners of the stage. Goods thus became multiple, as his name suggests: he spoke from many places and with different voices, and the laughter at the end of the scene could build and echo as the actors rolled and staggered back to their positions. During the activity of the opening of this scene the actress playing Good Deeds could slip under the edge of the stage unnoticed, to be ready for her entrance. There was a deliberate visual contrast between the two entrances from the trap.

The play was managed with seven actors rather than eight by having the actor playing Discretion, who had already played Confession, simply leave the group around Everyman after l. 705 and mount the higher platform to become Priesthood. The extreme unction was played with Everyman kneeling on the steps; once Everyman returned to

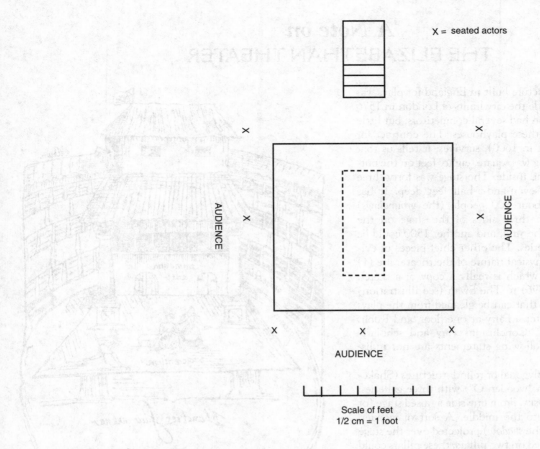

X = seated actors

AUDIENCE

AUDIENCE

AUDIENCE

Scale of feet
1/2 cm = 1 foot

the central platform, about l. 775, Priesthood moved down to resume his role as Discretion. Beauty was played by a man; it is Everyman's beauty, after all, and though the character is referred to as 'she,' so is Strength (l. 828). The line that does indicate a female dress and occupation, 'I take my cap in my lap and am gone,' is fairly obscure to a modern audience.

The journey of the soul to heaven (l. 894 ff) was not staged; the Angel spoke towards the grave into which Everyman had sunk. The Angel remained in position, and Knowledge remained kneeling at the head of the grave as the Doctor delivered the final speech.

A deliberate effect of the visual austerity of the production was that properties had a strong visual emphasis. The

book particularly was made into a central property. The Messenger carried it as he came on to the stage, and left it lying there, whence it was picked up by Death, and subsequently delivered to Everyman. Everyman tried to rid himself of it by throwing it at Death's feet on l. 113; it was roughly thrust back at him on l. 130. Thereafter it always lay in view on the stage, liable to catch Everyman's eye as he looked about him, and was picked up to be shown to Kindred, and then to Good Deeds, who took it from him and carried it until he required it to recite his testament. He then laid it at the foot of the grave, where it remained until the entrance of the Doctor, who picked it up and carried it during his final speech.

A Note on
THE ELIZABETHAN THEATER

The first permanent structure built in England for plays was The Theatre, built outside the city limits of London in 1576 by James Burbage. It soon had several competitors, but little is known about any of these playhouses. The contract for one, The Fortune (built in 1600), survives; it tells us that the three-storied building was square, eighty feet on the outside, fifty-five feet on the inside. The stage was forty-three feet broad and twenty-seven-and-a-half feet deep. It has been calculated that about 800 people (the *groundlings*) could stand around the three sides of the stage on the ground that was called the *yard,* and another 1500 could be seated in the three galleries. The other chief pieces of evidence concerning the physical nature of the theater are (1) the "de Witt drawing," which is really a copy of a sketch made by a visitor (c. 1596) to The Swan (see illustration) and (2) bits of evidence that can be gleaned from the plays themselves, such as "Enter a Fairy at one door, and Robin Goodfellow at another." Conclusions vary and scholarly tempers run high; the following statements are not indisputable.

Most theaters were polygonal or round structures (Shakespeare calls the theater a "wooden O") with three galleries; the yard was open to the sky. From one side a raised stage (or open *platform*) jutted into the middle. A sort of wooden canopy (the *heavens,* or the *shadow*) projected over the stage and in some theaters rested on two pillars; these pillars could conveniently serve as a hiding place for an actor supposed to be unseen by the other characters. At the rear of the stage there sometimes was a curtained alcove or booth, which when uncurtained might represent a room or a cave. The curtain is often called an *arras,* and it was probably behind this curtain that Polonius hid, only to be stabbed. At the rear of the stage (flanking the curtained space?) there were perhaps also two or three doors, through which entrances and exits were made. Probably the *tiring house* ("attiring house," i.e., dressing room) was behind the stage. Above the alcove or booth was an area that could be used for an *upper stage* (for example, in scenes of people standing on a city's walls); flanking the upper stage were windows, one of which may have served Juliet for her misnamed balcony scene. Some scholars argue that in a yet higher place were musicians, and at the very top—called the *top*—was an opening from which an actor could look; in *Henry VI, Part I,* Joan of Arc appears "on the top, thrusting out a torch burning."

Most of the acting was done on the main stage (the platform), but the "inner stage," "upper stage," "windows," and "top" must have been useful occasionally (if they existed). The *cellar* (beneath the stage) was used, for example, for the voice of the ghost in *Hamlet* and for Ophelia's grave. Though some scenery was used, the absence of a front cur-

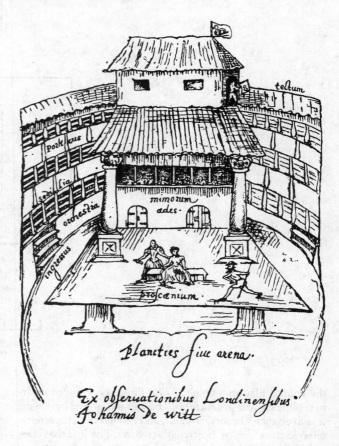

Arend Van Buchel's copy of a drawing of the Swan Theater, made by Johannes de Witt about 1596. The absence of spectators is puzzling; perhaps Van Buchel attended a rehearsal, or perhaps he didn't bother to attempt to draw a crowd. For a modern drawing based chiefly on de Witt's drawing, see page 12.

tain precluded many elaborate scenic effects (much, however, could be done by carrying banners) and encouraged continuous action. The stage that was a battlefield could in an instant, by the introduction of a throne, become a room in a palace. Two readable books are A. M. Nagler, *Shakespeare's Stage,* and C. Walter Hodges, *The Globe Restored.* Nagler (Ch. 12) also gives information about a second kind of Elizabethan theater—basically a platform at one end of a hall—that catered to a courtly group. For a more detailed study, see Andrew Gurr, *The Shakespearean Stage, 1542–1642,* third edition.

Christopher Marlowe

DOCTOR FAUSTUS

Christopher Marlowe (1564–1593) was born in Canterbury, England, in the year of Shakespeare's birth. Like Shakespeare, he was of a prosperous middle-class family (his father was a shoemaker), but unlike Shakespeare he went to a university, Corpus Christi College, Cambridge, where he received his B.A. degree in 1584 and his M.A. in 1587. The terms of his scholarship implied that he was preparing for the clergy, but he did not become a clergyman. Shortly before he received his M.A., the university seems to have wished to withhold it, apparently suspecting him of conversion to Roman Catholicism, but the queen's Privy Council intervened on his behalf, stating that he "had done her majesty good service" and had been employed "in matters touching the benefit of his country." His precise service is unknown. Marlowe's first play, *Tamburlaine the Great* (c. 1587), in blank verse (unrhymed iambic pentameter) inaugurated the great age of Elizabethan drama with its "mighty" line. While continuing his career as dramatist, he apparently lived a turbulent life in London: In 1589, involved in a brawl in which a man was killed, Marlowe was jailed (though later released); in 1593 he was again arrested, this time accused of atheism. He was not imprisoned, but before his case could be decided, he was dead, only six years after having left Cambridge, stabbed in a tavern fight. Marlowe wrote seven plays—the dates are uncertain—the most important of which, besides *Doctor Faustus* (c. 1593), were *The Jew of Malta* (c. 1588) and *Edward II* (c. 1591). He did a verse translation of Ovid's *Amores* and left unfinished at the time of his death the long poem *Hero and Leander*.

COMMENTARY

The exact date of *Doctor Faustus* is unknown, but the play was probably written not long before Marlowe was stabbed to death in 1593. It is universally acknowledged as the first great English tragedy (Shakespeare was barely starting at the time), but behind *Doctor Faustus* stands the tradition of the morality play, a form that had originated in the late fourteenth century and survived until the latter part of the sixteenth. As readers of *Everyman* (page 169) know, the morality play uses allegorical figures to dramatize a representative person's struggle in a world of deceitful appearances. Thus, *Everyman* (late fifteenth century) shows a figure called Everyman who has put his trust in Goods, Kindred, Fellowship, and so forth, but who learns—when faced with Death—that these are false friends who will abandon him; he rightly turns to Good Deeds, who assists him to achieve eternal felicity after death. Despite its happy ending, then, the morality play dramatizes guilt, suffering, and sometimes even death, and thus it approaches tragedy.

In a morality play, good and evil are sharply delineated and the spectator never doubts which is which. Wicked deeds are repaid with suffering, virtuous deeds with eternal happiness. Performers portraying good and bad angels sometimes engage in lively struggles—visible demonstrations of the conscience being tempted by the agents of Satan. In tragedy, however, the issues may be more complicated; the suffering hero may say, with King Lear, "I am a man more sinned against than sinning," and the audience may feel the truth of his assertion. Or the tragic hero may act in defiance of the conventional good, and the audience may not find it in their hearts to condemn the action, partly because the conventional good may seem severely limited, and the defiant act may seem, at least in some degree, noble. We leave it to you to think about whether Faustus's acts are noble, ignoble, or a mixture.

Textual Note

The earliest edition of *Doctor Faustus* was published in 1604, eleven years after Marlowe's death. Scholars call it the A-text, or A1. The text was reprinted in 1609 (A2) and again in 1611 (A3); A2 and A3 differ from A only by virtue of small errors that they introduce. In 1616, however, a very different version of *Doctor Faustus* was published, conventionally called the B-text. Whereas the A-text contains 1,517 lines, the B-text contains 2,121 lines. The B-text has:

some passages that are very close to A;
some episodes that are broadly parallel to A, but with little verbal similarity;
some deletions of material found in A, especially material that might be thought blasphemous;
approximately 600 more lines than A, chiefly devoted to comic scenes; the last act is notably fuller in B, which has a final visit of the angels, and the discovery of Faustus's mangled body. But although longer than A, B lacks some material found in A.

Because it is known that in 1602 a theatrical entrepreneur named Philip Henslowe paid William Bird and Samuel Rowley "for their adicyones in doctor fostes," it was believed until fairly recently that all or nearly all of the new material in B consisted of un-Marlovian additions, and that A, the shorter text, therefore was closer to Marlowe's own play. But today most scholars believe that B is closer to Marlowe's play. Instead of seeing B as containing un-Marlovian additions to an authentic text represented by A, scholars now see A as being an abridged version of Marlowe's play. That is, some or much of the material found only in B is now thought to be Marlowe's.

But even if it is agreed that A is abridged, and that B is closer to Marlowe's final manuscript, it is evident that some passages in B are not by Marlowe. For example, B prints "O mercy heauen," which almost surely is a censored version of A's "My God, my God." The text that follows is essentially the B text, but the "blasphemy" of A has been restored, and in a few other places, where A makes better sense than B, we print the A version.

For convenience in reference, we add act and scene divisions in square brackets [ ], though no edition of the play was so divided until relatively recent times.

The photograph illustrates Clifford Williams's Royal Shakespeare Company production (1968–1969) of Doctor Faustus, with Eric Porter (extreme right) in the title role. Faustus is watching the antics of the Seven Deadly Sins (2.2). This production did not seek to recreate an Elizabethan performance, but purists who object to introducing highly spectacular elements in modern production of Elizabethan plays should remember that the Elizabethan theater did as much as possible to introduce striking visual effects. Marlowe's text, for instance, calls for splendidly costumed figures (e.g., the pope), and it includes scenes with fireworks. For pictures of other productions of Doctor Faustus, see pages 14 and 902.

Christopher Marlowe

DOCTOR FAUSTUS

Edited by Sylvan Barnet

Speaking Characters

CHORUS
DOCTOR FAUSTUS
WAGNER, *his student and servant*
GOOD ANGEL
BAD ANGEL
VALDES ⎫
CORNELIUS ⎭ *magicians*
Three SCHOLARS
LUCIFER, *prince of devils*
MEPHOSTOPHILIS, *a devil*

ROBIN, *a clown*
BELZEBUB, *a devil*
DICK, *a clown*
POPE ADRIAN
PRIDE ⎫
COVETOUSNESS ⎪
ENVY ⎪
WRATH ⎬ *the Seven Deadly Sins*
GLUTTONY ⎪
SLOTH ⎪
LECHERY ⎭

RAYMOND, *King of Hungary*
BRUNO, *rival Pope appointed by the Emperor*
Two CARDINALS
ARCHBISHOP OF RHEIMS
FRIARS
VINTNER
The German Emperor, CHARLES THE FIFTH
MARTINO
FREDERICK } *gentlemen at the Emperor's court*
BENVOLIO
DUKE OF SAXONY
Two SOLDIERS
HORSE-COURSER, *a clown*

Mute Characters

DARIUS OF PERSIA
ALEXANDER THE GREAT
ALEXANDER'S PARAMOUR
HELEN OF TROY
DEVILS
PIPER
CARDINALS
CARTER, *a clown*
HOSTESS *of a Tavern*
DUKE OF VANHOLT
DUCHESS OF VANHOLT
SERVANT
OLD MAN

MONKS
FRIARS
ATTENDANTS
SOLDIERS
SERVANTS
Two CUPIDS

[PROLOGUE]

(*Enter Chorus.*°)

Not marching in the fields of Trasimene°
Where Mars did mate° the warlike Carthagens,
Nor sporting in the dalliance of love
In courts of kings where state° is overturned,
Nor in the pomp of proud audacious deeds   5
Intends our muse° to vaunt° his heavenly verse.
Only this, gentles—We must now perform

The form of Faustus' fortunes, good or bad:
And now to patient judgments we appeal
And speak for Faustus in his infancy.   10
Now is he born of parents base of stock
In Germany within a town called Rhode;°
At riper years to Wittenberg he went
Whereas° his kinsmen chiefly brought him up.
So much he profits in divinity   15
That shortly he was graced° with doctor's name,
Excelling all, and sweetly can dispute
In th' heavenly matters of theology;
Till swoll'n with cunning, of a self-conceit,°
His waxen wings° did mount above his reach   20
And melting, heavens conspired his overthrow!
For falling to a devilish exercise
And glutted now with learning's golden gifts
He surfeits upon cursèd necromancy:°
Nothing so sweet as magic is to him   25
Which he prefers before his chiefest bliss°—
And this the man that in his study sits.

                                          (*Exit.*)

[1.1] (*Faustus in his study.*°)

FAUSTUS.
Settle thy studies Faustus, and begin
To sound the depth of that thou wilt profess.°
Having commenced,° be a divine in show—
Yet level° at the end of every art
And live and die in Aristotle's works.   5
Sweet *Analytics,*° 'tis thou hast ravished me.
Bene disserere est finis logices.°
Is to dispute well logic's chiefest end?
Affords this art no greater miracle?
Then read no more, thou hast attained that end.   10
A greater subject fitteth Faustus' wit:°
Bid *on kai me on*° farewell, and Galen° come:
Be a physician Faustus, heap up gold,
And be eternized for some wondrous cure.

15 *Summum bonum medicinae sanitas,*°
   The end of physic° is our body's health.
   Why Faustus hast thou not attained that end?
   Are not thy bills° hung up as monuments
   Whereby whole cities have escaped the plague
20 And thousand desperate maladies been cured?
   Yet art thou still but Faustus and a man.
   Could'st thou make men to live eternally
   Or being dead raise them to life again,
   Then this profession were to be esteemed.
25 Physic farewell! Where is Justinian?°
   Si una eademque res legatur duobus, alter rem, alter valorem
        rei, et cetera.°
   A petty case of paltry legacies.
   Exhereditare filium non potest pater, nisi°—
30 Such is the subject of the *Institute*
   And universal body of the law!
   This study fits a mercenary drudge
   Who aims at nothing but external trash,
   Too servile and illiberal for me.
35 When all is done, divinity is best.
   Jerome's Bible,° Faustus, view it well.
   Stipendium peccati mors est.° Ha! *Stipendium et cetera.* The
        reward of sin is death? That's hard: *Si peccasse nega-*
        mus, fallimur, et nulla est in nobis veritas.° If we say
40   that we have no sin, we deceive ourselves, and there
        is no truth in us. Why, then belike, we must sin, and
        so consequently die.
   Ay, we must die an everlasting death.
   What doctrine call you this? *Che serà, serà:*°
45 What will be, shall be! Divinity, adieu!
   These metaphysics° of magicians
   And negromantic° books are heavenly;
   Lines, circles, letters, characters—

Ay, these are those that Faustus most desires.
O, what a world of profit and delight,   50
Of power, of honor, and omnipotence
Is promised to the studious artisan!°
All things that move between the quiet° poles
Shall be at my command: emperors and kings
Are but obeyed in their several provinces   55
But his dominion that exceeds in this°
Stretcheth as far as doth the mind of man:
A sound magician is a demi-god!
Here tire my brains to get° a deity!

(*Enter Wagner.*)

Wagner, commend me to my dearest friends,   60
The German Valdes and Cornelius.
Request them earnestly to visit me.
WAGNER. I will, sir. (*Exit.*)
FAUSTUS.
  Their conference° will be a greater help to me
  Than all my labors, plod I ne'er so fast.   65

(*Enter the [Good] Angel and the [Evil] Spirit.*°)

GOOD ANGEL.
  O Faustus, lay that damnèd book aside
  And gaze not on it lest it tempt thy soul
  And heap God's heavy wrath upon thy head!
  Read, read the Scriptures—that° is blasphemy!
BAD ANGEL.
  Go forward Faustus, in that famous art   70
  Wherein all nature's treasure is contained.
  Be thou on earth as Jove is in the sky,
  Lord and commander of these elements!

(*Exeunt Angels.*)

FAUSTUS.
  How am I glutted with conceit of this!°
  Shall I make spirits fetch me what I please?   75
  Resolve me of° all ambiguities?
  Perform what desperate enterprise I will?
  I'll have them fly to India° for gold,
  Ransack the ocean for orient° pearl,
  And search all corners of the new-found world   80
  For pleasant fruits and princely delicates;
  I'll have them read me strange philosophy
  And tell the secrets of all foreign kings;
  I'll have them wall all Germany with brass

---

15 *Summum . . . sanitas* health is the greatest good of medicine
(Latin, translated from Aristotle's *Nichomachean Ethics*)
16 physic medicine 18 bills prescriptions 25 Justinian Roman
emperor and authority on law (483–565) who ordered the compila-
tion of the *Institutes* (see line 30) 26–27 *Si . . . et cetera* if one
thing is willed to two persons, one of them shall have the thing
itself, the other the value of the thing, and so forth (Latin)
29 *Exhereditare . . . nisi* a father cannot disinherit his son unless
(Latin) 36 Jerome's Bible the Latin translation made by St.
Jerome (c. 340–420) 37 *Stipendium . . . est* the wages of sin is
death (Romans 6.23; if Faustus had gone on to read the rest of the
verse, he would have found that "the gift of God is eternal life
through Jesus Christ our Lord") 38–39 *Si . . . veritas* from I John
1.8, translated in the next two lines; Faustus neglects the following
verse: "If we confess our sins, He is faithful and just to forgive us our
sins, and to cleanse us from all unrighteousness" 44 *Che serà,*
serà (Italian, translated in the first half of the next line)
46 metaphysics subjects lying beyond (or studied after) physics
47 negromantic black magical (though probably here also associated with "necromantic," that is, concerned with raising the spirits
of the dead)

52 artisan that is, expert 53 quiet motionless 56 this that is,
magic 59 get beget 64 conference conversation 65 s.d. Spirit
Bad Angel, devil (the two angels probably enter the stage from separate doors) 69 that that is, the book of magic 74 conceit of
this that is, the conception of being a magician 76 Resolve me of
explain to me 78 India either the West Indies (America) or the
East Indies 79 orient lustrous and precious

85 And make swift Rhine circle fair Wittenberg;
I'll have them fill the public schools° with silk
Wherewith the students shall be bravely° clad.
I'll levy soldiers with the coin they bring
And chase the Prince of Parma° from our land
90 And reign sole king of all the provinces!
Yea, stranger engines for the brunt° of war
Than was the fiery keel° at Antwerp bridge
I'll make my servile spirits to invent.

(Enter Valdes and Cornelius.)

Come German Valdes and Cornelius
95 And make me blest with your sage conference.
Valdes, sweet Valdes, and Cornelius,
Know that your words have won me at the last
To practice magic and concealèd arts.
Philosophy is odious and obscure,
100 Both law and physic are for petty wits,
Divinity is basest of the three—
Unpleasant, harsh, contemptible, and vile.
'Tis magic, magic, that hath ravished me!
Then, gentle friends, aid me in this attempt
105 And I, that have with subtle syllogisms
Graveled° the pastors of the German church
And made the flow'ring pride of Wittenberg
Swarm to my problems° as th' infernal spirits
On sweet Musaeus° when he came to hell,
110 Will be as cunning as Agrippa° was,
Whose shadows made all Europe honor him.

VALDES.

Faustus, these books, thy wit, and our experience
Shall make all nations to canonize us.
As Indian Moors° obey their Spanish lords,
115 So shall the spirits of every element
Be always serviceable to us three:
Like lions shall they guard us when we please,
Like Almain rutters° with their horsemen's staves
Or Lapland giants trotting by our sides;
120 Sometimes like women or unwedded maids
Shadowing° more beauty in their airy brows
Than has the white breasts of the queen of love;
From Venice shall they drag huge argosies

And from America the golden fleece
That yearly stuffs old Philip's° treasury,   125
If learnèd Faustus will be resolute.

FAUSTUS.

Valdes, as resolute am I in this
As thou to live; therefore object it not.

CORNELIUS.

The miracles that magic will perform
Will make thee vow to study nothing else.   130
He that is grounded in astrology,
Enriched with tongues, well seen° in minerals,
Hath all the principles magic doth require.
Then doubt not Faustus but to be renowned
And more frequented for this mystery°   135
Than heretofore the Delphian oracle.°
The spirits tell me they can dry the sea
And fetch the treasure of all foreign wracks,
Yea, all the wealth that our forefathers hid
Within the massy° entrails of the earth.   140
Then tell me Faustus, what shall we three want?°

FAUSTUS.

Nothing, Cornelius. O, this cheers my soul!
Come, show me some demonstrations magical
That I may conjure° in some bushy grove
And have these joys in full possession.   145

VALDES.

Then haste thee to some solitary grove,
And bear wise Bacon's° and Albanus'° works,
The Hebrew Psalter, and New Testament;
And whatsoever else is requisite
We will inform thee ere our conference cease.   150

CORNELIUS.

Valdes, first let him know the words of art,
And then, all other ceremonies learned,
Faustus may try his cunning by himself.

VALDES.

First I'll instruct thee in the rudiments,
And then wilt thou be perfecter than I.   155

FAUSTUS.

Then come and dine with me, and after meat
We'll canvass every quiddity° thereof,
For ere I sleep I'll try what I can do:
This night I'll conjure though I die therefor!

(Exeunt omnes.°)

86 **public schools** universities   87 **bravely** splendidly   89 **Prince of Parma** Spanish governor-general of the Low Countries during 1579–92   91 **brunt** assault   92 **fiery keel** burning ship sent by the Netherlanders in 1585 against a bridge erected by Parma to blockade Antwerp (Antwerp here is an adjective, not genitive)   106 **Graveled** confounded   108 **problems** questions proposed for disputation   109 **Musaeus** legendary Greek poet   110 **Agrippa** Cornelius Agrippa of Nettesheim (1486–1535), German author of *De occulta philosophia*, a survey of Renaissance magic; Agrippa was believed to have raised spirits ("shadows") from the dead   114 **Indian Moors** American Indians   118 **Almain rutters** German cavalrymen   121 **Shadowing** sheltering

125 **Philip** King Philip II of Spain (1527–98)   132 **well seen** skilled   135 **frequented for this mystery** resorted to for this art   136 **Delphian oracle** oracle of Apollo at Delphi   140 **massy** massive   141 **want** lack   144 **conjure** raise spirits   147 **Bacon** Roger Bacon, medieval friar and scientist   **Albanus** perhaps Pietro d'Abano, medieval writer on medicine and philosophy   157 **canvass every quiddity** discuss every essential detail   159 **s.d. omnes** all (Latin)

[1.2] (*Enter two Scholars.*)

I SCHOLAR. I wonder what's become of Faustus that was
wont to make our schools ring with *sic probo*.°

(*Enter Wagner.*)

II SCHOLAR. That shall we presently° know. Here comes his
boy.°

I SCHOLAR. How now sirrah,° where's thy master?

WAGNER. God in heaven knows.

I SCHOLAR. Why, dost not thou know then?

WAGNER. Yes, I know, but that follows not.

I SCHOLAR. Go to° sirrah, leave your jesting and tell us
where he is.

WAGNER. That follows not by force of argument, which you,
being licentiates,° should stand upon;° therefore
acknowledge your error and be attentive.

II SCHOLAR. Then you will not tell us?

WAGNER. You are deceived, for I will tell you. Yet if you were
not dunces,° you would never ask me such a question. For
is he not *corpus naturale*? And is not that *mobile*?° Then
wherefore should you ask me such a question? But that I
am by nature phlegmatic,° slow to wrath, and prone to
lechery—to love, I would say—it were not for you to
come within forty foot of the place of execution°—
although I do not doubt but to see you both hanged the
next sessions.° Thus, having triumphed over you, I will set
my countenance like a precisian° and begin to speak thus:
Truly, my dear brethren, my master is within at dinner,
with Valdes and Cornelius, as this wine, if it could speak,
would inform your worships; and so, the Lord bless you,
preserve you, and keep you, my dear brethren.   (*Exit.*)

I SCHOLAR.
O Faustus, then I fear that which I have long suspected,
That thou art fall'n into that damnèd art
For which they two are infamous through the world.

II SCHOLAR.
Were he a stranger, not allied to me,
The danger of his soul would make me mourn.
But come, let us go and inform the rector.°
It may be his grave counsel may reclaim him.

I SCHOLAR.
I fear me nothing will reclaim him now.

II SCHOLAR.
Yet let us see what we can do.   (*Exeunt.*)

[1.3] (*Thunder. Enter Lucifer and four Devils.° Faustus to them with this speech.*)

FAUSTUS.
Now that the gloomy shadow of the night,
Longing to view Orion's° drizzling look,
Leaps from th' antarctic world unto the sky
And dims the welkin° with her pitchy breath,
Faustus, begin thine incantations   5
And try if devils will obey thy hest,
Seeing thou hast prayed and sacrificed to them.
Within this circle° is Jehovah's name
Forward and backward anagrammatized,
Th' abbreviated names of holy saints,   10
Figures of every adjunct to° the heavens,
And characters of signs and erring stars,°
By which the spirits are enforced to rise:
Then fear not, Faustus, to be resolute
And try the utmost magic can perform.   15

(*Thunder.*)

*Sint mihi dei Acherontis propitii! Valeat numen triplex Ieho-
vae! Ignei, aerii, aquatici, spiritus, salvete! Orientis princeps,
Belzebub inferni ardentis monarcha, et Demogorgon, propiti-
amus vos ut appareat et surgat Mephostophilis! Quid tu
moraris? Per Iehovam, Gehennam, et consecratam aquam*   20
*quam nunc spargo, signumque crucis quod nunc facio, et per
vota nostra, ipse nunc surgat nobis dicatus Mephostophilis!*°

(*Enter a Devil.°*)

1.3.s.d. Enter . . . Devils (they are invisible to Faustus; perhaps they
enter through a trapdoor and climb to the upper playing area, as
implied in V.ii.s.d.)   **2 Orion** constellation appearing at the beginning of winter, associated with rain   **4 welkin** sky   **8 circle** circle
the conjuror draws around him on the ground, to call the spirits and
to protect himself from them   **11 adjunct to** heavenly body fixed to
12 signs and erring stars signs of the Zodiac and planets
16–22 Sint . . . Mephostophilis may the gods of the lower region be
favorable to me. Away with the trinity of Jehovah. Hail, spirits of
fire, air, water. Prince of the east, Belzebub monarch of burning hell,
and Demogorgon, we pray to you that Mephostophilis may appear
and rise. Why do you delay? By Jehovah, Gehenna, and the holy
water which now I sprinkle, and the sign of the cross which now I
make, and by our vows, may Mephostophilis himself now rise to
serve us (Latin)   **22 s.d. Devil** (the word "dragon" oddly appears,
after "surgat Mephostophilis," in the preceding conjuration. It
makes no sense in the sentence, and it has therefore been omitted
from the present text, but perhaps it indicates that a dragon briefly
appears at that point, or perhaps the devil referred to in the present
stage direction is disguised as a dragon)

1.2.2 sic probo thus I prove it (Latin)   **3 presently** at once
4 boy servant (an impoverished student)   **5 sirrah** (term of
address used to an inferior)   **9 Go to** (exclamation of impatience)
12 licentiates possessors of a degree preceding the master's degree
stand upon make much of   **16 dunces** (1) fools (2) hairsplitters
17 corpus naturale . . . mobile natural matter . . . movable (Latin,
scholastic definition of the subject-matter of physics)
19 phlegmatic sluggish   **21 the place of execution** the place of
action, that is, the dining room (with quibble on gallows)
23 sessions sittings of a court   **24 precisian** Puritan (Wagner goes
on to parody the style of the Puritans)   **34 rector** head of the university

I charge thee to return and change thy shape,
Thou art too ugly to attend on me.
25 Go, and return an old Franciscan friar:
That holy shape becomes a devil best.

(*Exit Devil.*)

I see there's virtue in my heavenly words.
Who would not be proficient in this art?
How pliant is this Mephostophilis,
30 Full of obedience and humility,
Such is the force of magic and my spells.

(*Enter Mephostophilis.*)

MEPHOSTOPHILIS.
Now Faustus, what wouldst thou have me do?
FAUSTUS.
I charge thee wait upon me whilst I live
To do whatever Faustus shall command,
35 Be it to make the moon drop from her sphere
Or the ocean to overwhelm the world.
MEPHOSTOPHILIS.
I am a servant to great Lucifer
And may not follow thee without his leave.
No more than he commands must we perform.
FAUSTUS.
40 Did not he charge thee to appear to me?
MEPHOSTOPHILIS.
No, I came now hither of mine own accord.
FAUSTUS.
Did not my conjuring raise thee? Speak.
MEPHOSTOPHILIS.
That was the cause, but yet *per accidens:*°
For when we hear one rack° the name of God,
45 Abjure the Scriptures and his savior Christ,
We fly in hope to get his glorious° soul.
Nor will we come unless he use such means
Whereby he is in danger to be damned.
Therefore the shortest cut for conjuring
50 Is stoutly to abjure the Trinity
And pray devoutly to the prince of hell.
FAUSTUS.
So Faustus hath already done, and holds this principle,
There is no chief but only Belzebub:
To whom Faustus doth dedicate himself.
55 This word "damnation" terrifies not me
For I confound hell in Elysium:°
My ghost° be with the old° philosophers!
But leaving these vain trifles of men's souls,
Tell me, what is that Lucifer thy lord?
MEPHOSTOPHILIS.
60 Arch-regent and commander of all spirits.°

FAUSTUS.
Was not that Lucifer an angel once?
MEPHOSTOPHILIS.
Yes Faustus, and most dearly loved of God.
FAUSTUS.
How comes it then that he is prince of devils?
MEPHOSTOPHILIS.
O, by aspiring pride and insolence,
For which God threw him from the face of heaven.   65
FAUSTUS.
And what are you that live with Lucifer?
MEPHOSTOPHILIS.
Unhappy spirits that fell with Lucifer,
Conspired against our God with Lucifer,
And are forever damned with Lucifer.
FAUSTUS.
Where are you damned?   70
MEPHOSTOPHILIS.
In hell.
FAUSTUS.
How comes it then that thou art out of hell?
MEPHOSTOPHILIS.
Why this is hell, nor am I out of it.
Think'st thou that I who saw the face of God
And tasted the eternal joys of heaven   75
Am not tormented with ten thousand hells
In being deprived of everlasting bliss?
O Faustus, leave these frivolous demands
Which strikes° a terror to my fainting soul!
FAUSTUS.
What, is great Mephostophilis so passionate°   80
For being deprivèd of the joys of heaven?
Learn thou of Faustus manly fortitude
And scorn those joys thou never shalt possess.
Go bear these tidings to great Lucifer:
Seeing Faustus hath incurred eternal death   85
By desperate thoughts against Jove's deity,
Say he surrenders up to him his soul
So he will spare him four and twenty years,
Letting him live in all voluptuousness,
Having thee ever to attend on me,   90
To give me whatsoever I shall ask,
To tell me whatsoever I demand,
To slay mine enemies and to aid my friends
And always be obedient to my will.
Go and return to mighty Lucifer   95
And meet me in my study at midnight,
And then resolve° me of thy master's mind.
MEPHOSTOPHILIS.
I will, Faustus.

---

43 *per accidens* the immediate (but not ultimate) cause (Latin)
44 rack torture **46 glorious** (1) splendid (2) presumptuous
56 confound hell in Elysium do not distinguish between hell and
Elysium **57 ghost** spirit **old** pre-Christian **60 spirits** devils

79 strikes (it is not unusual to have a plural subject—especially when
it has a collective force—take a verb ending in -s) **80 passionate**
emotional **97 resolve** inform

FAUSTUS.

Had I as many souls as there be stars
100 I'd give them all for Mephostophilis.
By him I'll be great emperor of the world,
And make a bridge through° the moving air
To pass the ocean with a band of men;
I'll join the hills that bind the Afric shore
105 And make that country continent to° Spain,
And both contributary to my crown;
The Emperor shall not live but by my leave,
Nor any potentate of Germany.
Now that I have obtained what I desired
110 I'll live in speculation° of this art
Till Mephostophilis return again.   (Exit.)

[Exeunt Lucifer and Devils.]

[1.4] (Enter Wagner and [Robin] the Clown.°)

WAGNER. Come hither, sirrah boy.
ROBIN. Boy! O, disgrace to my person! Zounds,° boy in your
face! You have seen many boys with such pickadevants,°
I am sure.
5 WAGNER. Sirrah, hast thou no comings in?°
ROBIN. Yes, and goings out too, you may see sir.
WAGNER. Alas, poor slave! See how poverty jests in his
nakedness. I know the villain's out of service, and so hun-
gry that I know he would give his soul to the devil for a
10 shoulder of mutton, though it were blood-raw.
ROBIN. Not so, neither! I had need to have it well roasted,
and good sauce to it, if I pay so dear, I can tell you.
WAGNER. Sirrah, wilt thou be my man and wait on me? And
I will make thee go like Qui mihi discipulus.°
15 ROBIN. What, in verse?
WAGNER. No, slave, in beaten° silk and stavesacre.°
ROBIN. Stavesacre? That's good to kill vermin! Then, belike,
if I serve you I shall be lousy.
WAGNER. Why, so thou shalt be, whether thou dost it or no;
20 for sirrah, if thou dost not presently bind thyself to me for
seven years, I'll turn all the lice about thee into familiars°
and make them tear thee in pieces.
ROBIN. Nay sir, you may save yourself a labor, for they are as
familiar with me as if they paid for their meat and drink, I
25 can tell you.

WAGNER. Well sirrah, leave your jesting and take these
guilders.°
ROBIN. Yes marry° sir, and I thank you too.
WAGNER. So, now thou art to be at an hour's warning when-
soever and wheresoever the devil shall fetch thee.   30
ROBIN. Here, take your guilders, I'll none of 'em!
WAGNER. Not I, thou art pressed.° Prepare thyself, for I will
presently raise up two devils to carry thee away. Banio!
Belcher!
ROBIN. Belcher! And° Belcher come here I'll belch him. I   35
am not afraid of a devil!

(Enter two Devils.)

WAGNER. How now sir, will you serve me now?
ROBIN. Ay, good Wagner, take away the devil then.
WAGNER. Spirits, away! [Exeunt Devils.] Now sirrah, follow
me.   40
ROBIN. I will sir! But hark you master, will you teach me this
conjuring occupation?
WAGNER. Ay sirrah, I'll teach thee to turn thyself to a dog or
a cat or a mouse or a rat or anything.
ROBIN. A dog or a cat or a mouse or a rat? O brave° Wagner!   45
WAGNER. Villain, call me Master Wagner. And see that you
walk attentively, and let your right eye be always diame-
trally° fixed upon my left heel, that thou mayst quasi vestigiis nostris insistere.°
ROBIN. Well sir, I warrant you.   (Exeunt.)   50

[2.1] (Enter Faustus in his study.)

FAUSTUS.

Now, Faustus, must thou needs be damned;
Canst thou not be saved!
What boots° it then to think on God or heaven?
Away with such vain fancies, and despair—
Despair in God and trust in Belzebub!   5
Now go not backward. Faustus, be resolute!
Why waver'st thou? O something soundeth in mine ear,
"Abjure this magic, turn to God again."
Ay, and Faustus will turn to God again.
To God? He loves thee not;   10
The god thou serv'st is thine own appetite
Wherein is fixed the love of Belzebub!
To him I'll build an altar and a church
And offer lukewarm blood of newborn babes!

(Enter the two Angels.)

BAD ANGEL.

Go forward, Faustus, in that famous art.   15

GOOD ANGEL.

Sweet Faustus, leave that execrable art.

---

102 **through** (pronounced "thorough")   105 **continent to** continuous with   110 **speculation** contemplation
1.4.s.d. Clown buffoon **2 Zounds** by God's wounds
3 pickadevants pointed beards **5 comings in** income (the Clown
then quibbles on "goings out," i.e., expenses and also holes in his
clothes through which his body pokes) **14 Qui mihi discipulus**
one who is my disciple, that is, like the servant of a learned man (the
Latin is the beginning of a poem, familiar to Renaissance schoolboys,
on proper behavior) **16 beaten** embroidered (leading to the quibble on the sense "hit") **stavesacre** preparation from seeds of del-
phinium, used to kill vermin **21 familiars** attendant demons

27 **guilders** Dutch coins **28 marry** indeed (a mild oath, from "by
the Virgin Mary") **32 pressed** enlisted into service **35 And** if
45 brave splendid **47–48 diametrally** directly **48–49 quasi
vestigiis nostris insistere** as if to step in our footsteps
2.1.3 boots avails

FAUSTUS.
    Contrition, prayer, repentance, what of these?
GOOD ANGEL.
    O, they are means to bring thee unto heaven.
BAD ANGEL.
    Rather illusions, fruits of lunacy,
20   That make men foolish that do use them most.
GOOD ANGEL.
    Sweet Faustus, think of heaven and heavenly things.
BAD ANGEL.
    No Faustus, think of honor and of wealth.

                              (Exeunt Angels.)
FAUSTUS.
    Wealth!
    Why, the signory of Emden° shall be mine!
25   When Mephostophilis shall stand by me
    What power can hurt me? Faustus, thou art safe.
    Cast no more doubts! Mephostophilis, come,
    And bring glad tidings from great Lucifer.
    Is't not midnight? Come Mephostophilis,
30   *Veni, veni, Mephostophile!*°

    (Enter Mephostophilis.)
    Now tell me, what saith Lucifer thy lord?
MEPHOSTOPHILIS.
    That I shall wait on Faustus whilst he lives,
    So he will buy my service with his soul.
FAUSTUS.
    Already Faustus hath hazarded that for thee.
MEPHOSTOPHILIS.
35   But now thou must bequeath it solemnly
    And write a deed of gift with thine own blood,
    For that security craves Lucifer.
    If thou deny it I must back to hell.
FAUSTUS.
    Stay Mephostophilis and tell me
40   What good will my soul do thy lord?
MEPHOSTOPHILIS.
    Enlarge his kingdom.
FAUSTUS.
    Is that the reason why he tempts us thus?
MEPHOSTOPHILIS.
    Solamen miseris socios habuisse doloris.°
FAUSTUS.
    Why, have you any pain that torture other?°
MEPHOSTOPHILIS.
45   As great as have the human souls of men.
    But tell me, Faustus, shall I have thy soul—
    And I will be thy slave and wait on thee
    And give thee more than thou hast wit to ask?

FAUSTUS.
    Ay Mephostophilis, I'll give it him.°
MEPHOSTOPHILIS.
    Then, Faustus, stab thy arm courageously   50
    And bind thy soul that at some certain day
    Great Lucifer may claim it as his own.
    And then be thou as great as Lucifer!
FAUSTUS.
    Lo, Mephostophilis, for love of thee
    Faustus hath cut his arm and with his proper° blood   55
    Assures° his soul to be great Lucifer's,
    Chief lord and regent of perpetual night.
    View here this blood that trickles from mine arm
    And let it be propitious for my wish.
MEPHOSTOPHILIS.
    But Faustus,   60
    Write it in manner of a deed of gift.
FAUSTUS.
    Ay so I do—But Mephostophilis,
    My blood congeals and I can write no more.
MEPHOSTOPHILIS.
    I'll fetch thee fire to dissolve it straight.

                                (Exit.)
FAUSTUS.
    What might the staying of my blood portend?   65
    Is it unwilling I should write this bill?°
    Why streams it not that I may write afresh:
    "Faustus gives to thee his soul"? O there it stayed.
    Why shouldst thou not? Is not thy soul thine own?
    Then write again: "Faustus gives to thee his soul."   70

    (Enter Mephostophilis with the chafer° of fire.)

MEPHOSTOPHILIS.
    See Faustus, here is fire. Set it° on.
FAUSTUS.
    So, now the blood begins to clear again.
    Now will I make an end immediately.
MEPHOSTOPHILIS [*aside*].
    What will not I do to obtain his soul!
FAUSTUS.
    Consummatum est!° This bill is ended: 75
    And Faustus hath bequeathed his soul to Lucifer.
    —But what is this inscription on mine arm?
    Homo fuge!° Whither should I fly?
    If unto God, He'll throw me down to hell.
    My senses are deceived, here's nothing writ.   80
    O yes, I see it plain! Even here is writ
    Homo fuge! Yet shall not Faustus fly!

---

24 **signory of Emden** lordship of the rich German port at the mouth of the Ems 30 *Veni, veni, Mephostophile* come, come, Mephostophilis (Latin) 43 *Solamen . . . doloris* misery loves company (Latin) 44 **other** others

49 **him** that is, to Lucifer 55 **proper** own 56 **Assures** conveys by contract 66 **bill** contract 70 **s.d. chafer** portable grate 71 **it** that is, the receptacle containing the congealed blood 75 *Consummatum est* it is finished (Latin; a blasphemous repetition of Christ's words on the Cross; see John 19.30) 78 *Homo fuge* fly, man (Latin)

MEPHOSTOPHILIS [*aside*].
  I'll fetch him somewhat to delight his mind.

                                                          (*Exit.*)

(*Enter Devils giving crowns and rich apparel to Faustus.
They dance and then depart.*)

(*Enter Mephostophilis.*)

FAUSTUS.
  What means this show? Speak, Mephostophilis.
MEPHOSTOPHILIS.
85 Nothing Faustus, but to delight thy mind
  And let thee see what magic can perform.
FAUSTUS.
  But may I raise such spirits when I please?
MEPHOSTOPHILIS.
  Ay Faustus, and do greater things than these.
FAUSTUS.
  Then, Mephostophilis, receive this scroll,
90 A deed of gift of body and of soul:
  But yet conditionally that thou perform
  All covenants and articles between us both.
MEPHOSTOPHILIS.
  Faustus, I swear by hell and Lucifer
  To effect all promises between us both.
FAUSTUS.
95 Then hear me read it, Mephostophilis:
  "On these conditions following:
  First, that Faustus may be a spirit° in form and substance.
  Secondly, that Mephostophilis shall be his servant and
    be by him commanded.
100 Thirdly, that Mephostophilis shall do for him and bring
    him whatsoever.
  Fourthly, that he shall be in his chamber or house
    invisible.
  Lastly, that he shall appear to the said John Faustus at all
105   times in what form or shape soever he please:
  I, John Faustus of Wittenberg, Doctor, by these presents,
    do give both body and soul to Lucifer, prince of the
    east, and his minister Mephostophilis, and further-
    more grant unto them that, four and twenty years
110   being expired, and these articles above written being
    inviolate,° full power to fetch or carry the said John
    Faustus, body and soul, flesh, blood, or goods, into
    their habitation wheresoever.
                                    By me John Faustus.
MEPHOSTOPHILIS. Speak Faustus, do you deliver this as your
115 deed?
FAUSTUS. Ay, take it, and the devil give thee good of it!

MEPHOSTOPHILIS. So now Faustus, ask me what thou wilt.
FAUSTUS. First will I question with thee about hell. Tell me,
  where is the place that men call hell?   120
MEPHOSTOPHILIS. Under the heavens.
FAUSTUS.
  Ay, so are all things else, but whereabouts?
MEPHOSTOPHILIS.
  Within the bowels of these elements
  Where we are tortured and remain forever.
  Hell hath no limits nor is circumscribed   125
  In one self place, but where we are is hell,
  And where hell is there must we ever be.
  And to be short, when all the world dissolves
  And every creature shall be purified
  All places shall be hell that is not heaven!   130
FAUSTUS.
  I think hell's a fable.
MEPHOSTOPHILIS.
  Ay, think so still—till experience change thy mind!
FAUSTUS.
  Why, dost thou think that Faustus shall be damned?
MEPHOSTOPHILIS.
  Ay, of necessity, for here's the scroll
  In which thou hast given thy soul to Lucifer.   135
FAUSTUS.
  Ay, and body too; but what of that?
  Think'st thou that Faustus is so fond° to imagine
  That after this life there is any pain?
  No, these are trifles and mere old wives' tales.
MEPHOSTOPHILIS.
  But I am an instance to prove the contrary,   140
  For I tell thee I am damned and now in hell!
FAUSTUS.
  Nay, and this be hell, I'll willingly be damned—
  What, sleeping, eating, walking, and disputing?
  But leaving this, let me have a wife, the fairest maid in
    Germany, for I am wanton and lascivious and cannot   145
    live without a wife.
MEPHOSTOPHILIS.
  Well Faustus, thou shalt have a wife.

(*He fetches in a woman Devil* [*with fireworks*].)

FAUSTUS.
  What sight is this?
MEPHOSTOPHILIS.
  Now Faustus, wilt thou have a wife?
FAUSTUS.
  Here's a hot whore indeed! No, I'll no wife.   150
MEPHOSTOPHILIS.
  Marriage is but a ceremonial toy,°

                                          [*Exit She-Devil.*]
  And if thou lovest me, think no more of it.

---

97 spirit evil spirit, devil (but to see Faustus as transformed now
into a devil deprived of freedom to repent is to deprive the remainder of the play of much of its meaning)   **111 inviolate** unviolated

137 fond foolish   **151 toy** trifle

I'll cull thee out° the fairest courtesans
And bring them every morning to thy bed.
155 She whom thine eye shall like thy heart shall have,
Were she as chaste as was Penelope,°
As wise as Saba,° or as beautiful
As was bright Lucifer before his fall.
Here, take this book and peruse it well.
160 The iterating° of these lines brings gold;
The framing° of this circle on the ground
Brings thunder, whirlwinds, storm, and lightning;
Pronounce this thrice devoutly to thyself,
And men in harness° shall appear to thee,
165 Ready to execute what thou command'st.

FAUSTUS.
Thanks Mephostophilis for this sweet book.
This will I keep as chary as my life.

(*Exeunt.°*)

[2.2] (*Enter Faustus in his study and Mephostophilis.*)

FAUSTUS.
When I behold the heavens, then I repent
And curse thee, wicked Mephostophilis,
Because thou has deprived me of those joys.

MEPHOSTOPHILIS.
'Twas thine own seeking Faustus, thank thyself.
5 But think'st thou heaven is such a glorious thing?
I tell thee, Faustus, it is not half so fair
As thou or any man that breathe on earth.

FAUSTUS.
How prov'st thou that?

MEPHOSTOPHILIS.
'Twas made for man; then he's more excellent.

FAUSTUS.
10 If heaven was made for man, 'twas made for me!
I will renounce this magic and repent.

(*Enter the two Angels.*)

GOOD ANGEL.
Faustus, repent: yet° God will pity thee!

BAD ANGEL.
Thou art a spirit: God cannot pity thee!

FAUSTUS.
Who buzzeth in mine ears I am a spirit?
15 Be I a devil, yet God may pity me—
Yea, God will pity me if I repent.

BAD ANGEL.
Ay, but Faustus never shall repent.

(*Exit Angels.*)

FAUSTUS.
My heart is hardened, I cannot repent.
Scarce can I name salvation, faith, or heaven,
Swords, poison, halters, and envenomed steel 20
Are laid before me to dispatch myself.
And long ere this I should have done the deed
Had not sweet pleasure conquered deep despair.
Have not I made blind Homer sing to me
Of Alexander's love and Oenon's° death? 25
And hath not he° that built the walls of Thebes
With ravishing sound of his melodious harp
Made music with my Mephostophilis?
Why should I die then or basely despair?
I am resolved, Faustus shall not repent! 30
Come Mephostophilis, let us dispute again
And reason of divine astrology.
Speak, are there many spheres above the moon?
Are all celestial bodies but one globe
As is the substance of this centric° earth? 35

MEPHOSTOPHILIS.
As are the elements, such° are the heavens,
Even from the moon unto the empyreal orb
Mutually folded in each others' spheres,
And jointly move upon one axle-tree,
Whose terminè° is termed the world's wide pole. 40
Nor are the names of Saturn, Mars, or Jupiter
Feigned but are erring stars.°

FAUSTUS.
But have they all one motion,
Both *situ et tempore?*°

MEPHOSTOPHILIS. All move from east to west in four and 45
twenty hours upon the poles of the world but differ in
their motions upon the poles of the zodiac.

FAUSTUS.
These slender questions Wagner can decide.
Hath Mephostophilis no greater skill?
Who knows not the double motion of the planets? 50
That the first is finished in a natural day.°
The second thus: Saturn in thirty years;
Jupiter in twelve; Mars in four; the sun, Venus, and Mer-
cury in a year; the moon in twenty-eight days. These

---

153 **cull thee out** select for you   156 **Penelope** wife of Ulysses, famed for her fidelity   157 **Saba** the Queen of Sheba   160 **iterating** repetition   161 **framing** drawing   164 **harness** armor   167 **s.d. Exeunt** (a scene following this stage direction has probably been lost. Earlier Wagner hired the Clown; later the Clown is an ostler possessed of one of Faustus' conjuring books. Possibly, then, the lost scene was a comic one, showing the Clown stealing a book and departing)
II.ii.12 yet still, even now

25 **Alexander . . . Oenone** Paris, also called Alexander, was Oenone's lover, but he later deserted her for Helen of Troy, causing the Trojan War, the subject of Homer's *Iliad*   26 **he** Amphion, whose music charmed stones to form the walls of Thebes   35 **centric** central   36 **such** that is, separate but combined; the idea is that the heavenly bodies are separate but their spheres are concentric ("folded"), and all—from the nearest (the moon) to the farthest ("the empyreal orb" or empyrean)—move on one axletree   40 **terminè** end, extremity   42 **erring stars** planets   44 *situ et tempore* in place and in time   51 **natural day** twenty-four hours

are freshmen's suppositions.° But tell me, hath every
sphere a dominion or *intelligentia?*°

MEPHOSTOPHILIS. Ay.

FAUSTUS. How many heavens or spheres are there?

MEPHOSTOPHILIS. Nine: the seven planets, the firmament,
and the empyreal heaven.

FAUSTUS. But is there not *coelum igneum et crystallinum?*°

MEPHOSTOPHILIS. No Faustus, they be but fables.

FAUSTUS. Resolve me then in this one question. Why are
not conjunctions, oppositions, aspects, eclipses all at one
time,° but in some years we have more, in some less?

MEPHOSTOPHILIS. *Per inaqualem motum respectu totius.*°

FAUSTUS. Well, I am answered. Now tell me, who made the
world?

MEPHOSTOPHILIS. I will not.

FAUSTUS. Sweet Mephostophilis, tell me.

MEPHOSTOPHILIS. Move° me not, Faustus!

FAUSTUS. Villain, have not I bound thee to tell me anything?

MEPHOSTOPHILIS. Ay, that is not against our kingdom.
This is. Thou are damned. Think thou of hell!

FAUSTUS.
Think, Faustus, upon God, that made the world.

MEPHOSTOPHILIS.
Remember this!   (*Exit.*)

FAUSTUS.
Ay, go accursèd spirit to ugly hell!
'Tis thou hast damned distressèd Faustus' soul.—
Is't not too late?

(*Enter the two Angels.*)

BAD ANGEL.
Too late.

GOOD ANGEL.
Never too late, if Faustus will repent.

BAD ANGEL.
If thou repent, devils will tear thee in pieces.

GOOD ANGEL.
Repent, and they shall never raze° thy skin.

(*Exeunt Angels.*)

FAUSTUS.
O Christ, my savior, my savior!
Help to save distressèd Faustus' soul.

(*Enter Lucifer, Belzebub, and Mephostophilis.*)

LUCIFER.
Christ cannot save thy soul, for He is just.
There's none but I have interest in° the same.

FAUSTUS.
O, what art thou that look'st so terribly?

LUCIFER.
I am Lucifer   90
And this is my companion prince in hell.

FAUSTUS.
O Faustus, they are come to fetch thy soul!

BELZEBUB.
We are come to tell thee thou dost injure us.

LUCIFER.
Thou call'st on Christ contrary to thy promise.

BELZEBUB.
Thou should'st not think on God.   95

LUCIFER.   Think on the Devil.

BELZEBUB.
And his dam° too.

FAUSTUS.
Nor will Faustus henceforth. Pardon him for this,
And Faustus vows never to look to heaven!
Never to name God or to pray to Him,   100
To burn His Scriptures, slay His ministers,
And make my spirits pull His churches down.

LUCIFER.
So shalt thou show thyself an obedient servant,
And we will highly gratify thee for it.

BELZEBUB. Faustus, we are come from hell in person to show   105
thee some pastime. Sit down and thou shalt behold the
Seven Deadly Sins° appear to thee in their own proper
shapes and likeness.

FAUSTUS. That sight will be as pleasant to me as Paradise
was to Adam the first day of his creation.   110

LUCIFER. Talk not of Paradise or creation but mark the show.
Go Mephostophilis, fetch them in.

(*Enter the Seven Deadly Sins [led by a Piper].*)

BELZEBUB. Now Faustus, question them of their names and
dispositions.

FAUSTUS. That shall I soon. What art thou, the first?   115

PRIDE. I am Pride. I disdain to have any parents. I am like to
Ovid's flea,° I can creep into every corner of a wench:
sometimes, like a periwig I sit upon her brow; next, like a
necklace I hang about her neck; then, like a fan of feathers I kiss her; and then, turning myself to a wrought   120
smock,° do what I list—But fie, what a smell is here! I'll
not speak a word more for a king's ransom unless the
ground be perfumed and covered with cloth of arras.°

FAUSTUS. Thou art a proud knave indeed.
What art thou, the second?   125

---

55 suppositions premises   **56 dominion or intelligentia** governing
angel or intelligence (believed to impart motion to the sphere)
61 *coelum igneum et crystallinum* a heaven of fire and a crystalline sphere (Latin)   **64–65 at one time** that is, at regular intervals   **66 *Per . . . totius*** because of unequal speed within the system (Latin)   **71 Move** anger   **84 raze** scratch   **88 interest in**
legal claim on

97 dam mother   **107 Seven Deadly Sins** (so called because they
cause spiritual death; they are Pride, Covetousness, Envy, Wrath,
Gluttony, Sloth, Lechery)   **117 Ovid's flea** flea in *Carmen de pulce*,
a lewd poem mistakenly attributed to Ovid   **120–121 wrought
smock** decorated petticoat   **123 cloth of arras** Flemish cloth used
for tapestries

COVETOUSNESS. I am Covetousness, begotten of an old churl in a leather bag;° and might I now obtain my wish, this house, you and all, should turn to gold that I might lock you safe into my chest. O my sweet gold!

130 FAUSTUS. And what art thou, the third?

ENVY. I am Envy, begotten of a chimney-sweeper and an oyster-wife.° I cannot read and therefore wish all books burned. I am lean with seeing others eat. O, that there would come a famine over all the world that all might die

135 and I live alone! Then thou shouldst see how fat I'd be. But must thou sit and I stand? Come down, with a vengeance!

FAUSTUS. Out, envious wretch! But what art thou, the fourth?

140 WRATH. I am Wrath. I had neither father nor mother. I leapt out of a lion's mouth when I was scarce an hour old and ever since have run up and down the world with these case° of rapiers, wounding myself when I could get none to fight withal. I was born in hell! And look to it, for

145 some of you shall be my father.

FAUSTUS. And what art thou, the fifth?

GLUTTONY. I am Gluttony. My parents are all dead, and the devil a penny they have left me, but a small pension: and that buys me thirty meals a day and ten bevers,° a small

150 trifle to suffice nature. I come of a royal pedigree. My father was a gammon° of bacon, and my mother was a hogshead of claret wine. My godfathers were these: Peter Pickled-herring and Martin Martlemas-beef.° But my godmother, O, she was an ancient gentlewoman: her

155 name was Margery March-beer.° Now Faustus, thou hast heard all my progeny,° wilt thou bid me to supper?

FAUSTUS. Not I.

GLUTTONY. Then the devil choke thee!

FAUSTUS. Choke thyself, glutton! What art thou, the sixth?

160 SLOTH. Heigh-ho!° I am Sloth. I was begotten on a sunny bank. Heigh-ho, I'll not speak a word more for a king's ransom.

FAUSTUS. And what are you, Mistress Minx, the seventh and last?

165 LECHERY. Who, I, I sir? I am one that loves an inch of raw mutton° better than an ell of fried stockfish,° and the first letter of my name begins with Lechery.

LUCIFER. Away to hell, away! On, piper!

(Exeunt the Seven Sins.)

---

127 **leather bag** moneybag (?)   131–132 **chimney-sweeper . . . oyster-wife** that is, dirty and smelly   142–143 **these case** this pair   149 **bevers** snacks (literally drinks)   151 **gammon** haunch   153 **Martlemas-beef** cattle slaughtered at Martinmas (11 November) and salted for winter consumption   155 **March-beer** strong beer brewed in March   156 **progeny** ancestry   160 **Heigh-ho** (a yawn or tired greeting)   165–166 **inch of raw mutton** that is, penis ("mutton" in a bawdy sense commonly alludes to a prostitute, but since here the speaker is a woman, the allusion must be to a male)   166 **an ell of . . . stockfish** forty-five inches of dried cod

FAUSTUS.
O, how this sight doth delight my soul!

LUCIFER.
But Faustus, in hell is all manner of delight.   170

FAUSTUS.
O, might I see hell and return again safe, how happy were I then!

LUCIFER.
Faustus, thou shalt. At midnight I will send for thee. Meanwhile peruse this book and view it thoroughly, And thou shalt turn thyself into what shape thou wilt.   175

FAUSTUS.
Thanks mighty Lucifer.
This will I keep as chary° as my life.

LUCIFER.
Now Faustus, farewell.

FAUSTUS.
Farewell great Lucifer. Come Mephostophilis.

(Exeunt omnes several° ways.)

[2.3] (Enter [Robin] the Clown.)

ROBIN. What, Dick, look to the horses there till I come again! I have gotten one of Doctor Faustus' conjuring books, and now we'll have such knavery as't passes.

(Enter Dick.)

DICK. What, Robin, you must come away and walk the horses.   5

ROBIN. I walk the horses? I scorn't, 'faith. I have other matters in hand. Let the horses walk themselves an° they will. [Reading] A per se°—a; t, h, e—the; o per se—o; deny orgon—gorgon.° Keep further from me, O thou illiterate and unlearned hostler!   10

DICK. 'Snails,° what hast thou got there, a book? Why, thou canst not tell ne'er a word on't.

ROBIN. That thou shalt see presently. Keep out of the circle, I say, lest I send you into the hostry° with a vengeance.

DICK. That's like, 'faith! You had best leave your foolery, for   15 an my master come, he'll conjure you, 'faith.

ROBIN. My master conjure me? I'll tell thee what. An my master come here, I'll clap as fair a pair of horns° on's head as e'er thou sawest in thy life.

DICK. Thou need'st not do that, for my mistress hath   20 done it.

ROBIN. Ay, there be of us here that have waded as deep into matters as other men—if they were disposed to talk.

---

177 **chary** carefully   179 **s.d. several** various
2.3.7 **an** if   8 **per se** by itself (Latin; the idea is, "A by itself spells A")   8–9 **deny orgon—gorgon** (Robin is trying to read the name "Demogorgon")   11 **'Snails** by God's nails   14 **hostry** hostelry, inn   18 **horns** (as the next speech indicates, horns were said to adorn the head of a man whose wife was unfaithful)

DICK. A plague take you! I thought you did not sneak up
    and down after her for nothing. But I prithee tell me in
    good sadness° Robin, is that a conjuring book?

ROBIN. Do but speak what thou't have me to do, and I'll
    do't. If thou't dance naked, put off thy clothes, and I'll
    conjure thee about presently. Or if thou't go but to the
    tavern with me, I'll give thee white wine, red wine, claret
    wine, sack,° muscadine, malmsey, and whippincrust°—
    hold-belly-hold. And we'll not pay one penny for it.

DICK. O brave! Prithee let's to it presently, for I am as dry as
    a dog.

ROBIN. Come then, let's away.   (*Exeunt.*)

[3] (*Enter the Chorus.*)

Learnèd Faustus,
To find the secrets of astronomy
Graven in the book of Jove's high firmament,
Did mount him up to scale Olympus' top:
Where, sitting in a chariot burning bright
Drawn by the strength of yokèd dragons' necks,
He views the clouds, the planets, and the stars,
The tropics, zones,° and quarters of the sky,
From the bright circle° of the hornèd moon
Even to the height of *primum mobile:*°
And whirling round with this circumference
Within the concave compass of the pole,
From east to west his dragons swiftly glide
And in eight days did bring him home again.
Not long he stayed within his quiet house
To rest his bones after his weary toil
But new exploits do hale him out again.
And mounted then upon a dragon's back,
That with his wings did part the subtle air,
He now is gone to prove cosmography,°
That measures coasts and kingdoms of the earth,
And as I guess will first arrive at Rome
To see the Pope and manner of his court
And take some part of holy Peter's feast,
The which this day is highly solemnized.

                       (*Exit.*)

[3.1] (*Enter Faustus and Mephostophilis.*)

FAUSTUS.
Having now, my good Mephostophilis,
Passed with delight the stately town of Trier,°
Environed round with airy mountain tops,

With walls of flint, and deep-entrenchèd lakes,°
Not to be won by any conquering prince:
From Paris next, coasting the realm of France,
We saw the river Main fall into Rhine,
Whose banks are set with groves of fruitful vines:
Then up to Naples, rich Campania,
Whose buildings fair and gorgeous to the eye,
The streets straight forth and paved with finest brick,
Quarters the town in four equivalents.
There saw we learnèd Maro's° golden tomb,
The way he cut an English mile in length
Through° a rock of stone in one night's space.
From thence to Venice, Padua, and the rest,
In one of which a sumptuous temple stands
That threats the stars with her aspiring top,
Whose frame is paved with sundry colored stones
And roofed aloft with curious work in gold.
Thus hitherto hath Faustus spent his time.
But tell me now, what resting-place is this?
Hast thou, as erst I did command,
Conducted me within the walls of Rome?

MEPHOSTOPHILIS.
I have, my Faustus, and for proof thereof
This is the goodly palace of the Pope,
And 'cause we are no common guests
I choose his privy chamber for our use.

FAUSTUS.
I hope his Holiness will bid us welcome.

MEPHOSTOPHILIS.
All's one, for we'll be bold with his venison.
But now my Faustus, that thou may'st perceive
What Rome contains for to delight thine eyes,
Know that this city stands upon seven hills
That underprop the groundwork of the same:
Just through the midst runs flowing Tiber's stream
With winding banks that cut it in two parts,
Over the which four stately bridges lean°
That make safe passage to each part of Rome.
Upon the bridge called Ponte Angelo
Erected is a castle passing strong
Where thou shalt see such store of ordinance
As that the double cannons forged of brass
Do match the number of the days contained
Within the compass of one complete year,
Beside the gates and high pyramides°
That Julius Caesar brought from Africa.

FAUSTUS.
Now, by the kingdoms of infernal rule,
Of Styx, of Acheron, and the fiery lake
Of ever-burning Phlegethon,° I swear
That I do long to see the monuments

25
30
35

5
10
15
20
25
30
35
40
45
50

25–26 **in good sadness** seriously   31 **sack** sherry   **whippincrust**
illiterate pronunciation of "hippocras," a spiced wine   3 **Chorus**
8 **zones** segments of the sky   9 **circle** orbit   10 **primum mobile** the
outermost sphere, the empyrean   20 **prove cosmography** test maps,
that is, explore the universe
3.1.2 **Trier** German city on the Moselle, also known as Trèves

4 **deep-entrenchèd lakes** moats   13 **Maro** Vergil (Publius Vergilius
Maro, 70–19 B.C.)   15 **Through** (pronounced "thorough")
37 **lean** bend   45 **pyramides** obelisk (pronounced py-ràm-i-des)
48–49 **Styx, Acheron, Phlegethon** rivers of the underworld

And situation of bright-splendent Rome.
Come therefore, let's away.

MEPHOSTOPHILIS.
Nay stay my Faustus. I know you'd see the Pope
And take some part of holy Peter's feast,
55 The which this day with high solemnity,
This day, is held through Rome and Italy
In honor of the Pope's triumphant victory.

FAUSTUS.
Sweet Mephostophilis, thou pleasest me.
Whilst I am here on earth let me be cloyed
60 With all things that delight the heart of man.
My four and twenty years of liberty
I'll spend in pleasure and in dalliance,
That Faustus' name, whilst this bright frame doth stand,
May be admirèd through the furthest land.

MEPHOSTOPHILIS.
65 'Tis well said, Faustus, come then, stand by me
And thou shalt see them come immediately.

FAUSTUS.
Nay stay my Faustus. I know you'd see the Pope
And grant me my request, and then I go.
Thou know'st, within the compass of eight days
70 We viewed the face of heaven, of earth, and hell.
So high our dragons soared into the air
That looking down the earth appeared to me
No bigger than my hand in quantity—
There did we view the kingdoms of the world,
75 And what might please mine eye I there beheld.
Then in this show let me an actor be
That this proud Pope may Faustus' cunning see!

MEPHOSTOPHILIS.
Let it be so, my Faustus, but first stay
And view their triumphs° as they pass this way.
80 And then devise what best contents thy mind
By cunning in thine art to cross the Pope
Or dash the pride of this solemnity—
To make his monks and abbots stand like apes
And point like antics° at his triple crown,
85 To beat the beads about the friars' pates,
Or clap huge horns upon the cardinals' heads,
Or any villainy thou canst devise—
And I'll perform it, Faustus. Hark, they come!
This day shall make thee be admired° in Rome!

(*Enter the Cardinals and Bishops, some bearing crosiers,
some the pillars; Monks and Friars singing their procession; then the Pope and Raymond King of Hungary, with
Bruno° led in chains.*)

POPE.
Cast down our footstool.   90

RAYMOND.   Saxon Bruno, stoop,
Whilst on thy back his Holiness ascends
Saint Peter's chair and state° pontifical.

BRUNO.
Proud Lucifer, that state belongs to me—
But thus I fall to Peter, not to thee.   95

POPE.
To me and Peter shalt thou grov'lling lie
And crouch before the papal dignity!
Sound trumpets then, for thus Saint Peter's heir
From Bruno's back ascends Saint Peter's chair!

(*A flourish° while he ascends.*)

Thus as the gods creep on with feet of wool   100
Long ere with iron hands they punish men,
So shall our sleeping vengeance now arise
And smite with death thy hated enterprise.
Lord Cardinals of France and Padua,
Go forthwith to our holy consistory°   105
And read amongst the statutes decretal°
What by the holy council held at Trent°
The sacred synod° hath decreed for him
That doth assume the papal government
Without election and a true consent.   110
Away, and bring us word with speed!

I CARDINAL.
We go my lord.   (*Exeunt [two] Cardinals.*)

POPE.
Lord Raymond—   [*Talks to him apart.*]

FAUSTUS.
Go haste thee, gentle Mephostophilis,
Follow the cardinals to the consistory   115
And as they turn their superstitious books
Strike them with sloth and drowsy idleness
And make them sleep so sound that in their shapes
Thyself and I may parley with this Pope,
This proud confronter of the Emperor!   120
—And in despite of all his holiness
Restore this Bruno to his liberty
And bear him to the states of Germany!

MEPHOSTOPHILIS.
Faustus, I go.

FAUSTUS.
Dispatch it soon.   125
The Pope shall curse that Faustus came to Rome.

(*Exit Faustus and Mephostophilis.*)

---

79 triumphs spectacular displays **84 antics** grotesque figures, buffoons **89 admired** wondered at **s.d. Raymond King of Hungary . . . Bruno** (unhistorical figures; Bruno is the emperor's nominee for the papal throne)

93 state throne **99 s.d. flourish** trumpet fanfare **105 consistory** that is, meeting-place of the papal consistory or senate **106 statutes decretal** that is, ecclesiastical laws **107 council held at Trent** (intermittently from 1545 to 1563) **108 synod** council

BRUNO.

    Pope Adrian, let me have some right of law:
    I was elected by the Emperor.

POPE.

    We will depose the Emperor for that deed
130   And curse the people that submit to him.
    Both he and thou shalt stand excommunicate
    And interdict from church's privilege
    And all society of holy men.
    He grows too proud in his authority,
135   Lifting his lofty head above the clouds,
    And like a steeple overpeers the church.
    But we'll pull down his haughty insolence.
    And as Pope Alexander,° our progenitor,°
    Trod on the neck of German Frederick,
140   Adding this golden sentence to our praise:
    "That Peter's heirs should tread on emperors
    And walk upon the dreadful adder's back,
    Treading the lion and the dragon down,
    And fearless spurn the killing basilisk"°—
145   So will we quell that haughty schismatic
    And by authority apostolical
    Depose him from his regal government.

BRUNO.

    Pope Julius swore to princely Sigismond,
    For him and the succeeding Popes of Rome,
150   To hold the emperors their lawful lords.

POPE.

    Pope Julius did abuse the church's rites
    And therefore none of his decrees can stand.
    Is not all power on earth bestowed on us?
    And therefore though we would, we cannot err.
155   Behold this silver belt whereto is fixed
    Seven golden keys fast sealed with seven seals
    In token of our sevenfold power from heaven
    To bind or loose, lock fast, condemn, or judge,
    Resign° or seal, or whatso pleaseth us.
160   Then he and thou and all the world shall stoop—
    Or be assured of our dreadful curse
    To light as heavy as the pains of hell.

(Enter Faustus and Mephostophilis like the cardinals.)

MEPHOSTOPHILIS [*aside*].

    Now tell me Faustus, are we not fitted well?

FAUSTUS [*aside*].

    Yes Mephostophilis, and two such cardinals
165   Ne'er served a holy Pope as we shall do.
    But whilst they sleep within the consistory
    Let us salute his reverend Fatherhood.

RAYMOND.

    Behold my lord, the cardinals are returned.

POPE.

    Welcome grave fathers, answer presently,°
    What have our holy council there decreed   170
    Concerning Bruno and the Emperor
    In quittance of° their late conspiracy
    Against our state and papal dignity?

FAUSTUS.

    Most sacred patron of the church of Rome,
    By full consent of all the synod   175
    Of priests and prelates it is thus decreed:
    That Bruno and the German Emperor
    Be held as lollards° and bold schismatics
    And proud disturbers of the church's peace.
    And if that Bruno by his own assent,   180
    Without enforcement of the German peers,
    Did seek to wear the triple diadem
    And by your death to climb Saint Peter's chair,
    The statutes decretal have thus decreed:
    He shall be straight condemned of heresy   185
    And on a pile of fagots burnt to death.

POPE.

    It is enough. Here, take him to your charge
    And bear him straight to Ponte Angelo
    And in the strongest tower enclose him fast.
    Tomorrow, sitting in our consistory   190
    With all our college of grave cardinals
    We will determine of his life or death.
    Here, take his triple crown along with you
    And leave it in the church's treasury.
    Make haste again,° my good lord cardinals,   195
    And take our blessing apostolical.

MEPHOSTOPHILIS [*aside*].

    So, so! Was never devil thus blessed before.

FAUSTUS [*aside*].

    Away sweet Mephostophilis, be gone!
    The cardinals will be plagued for this anon.

(Exeunt Faustus and Mephostophilis [with Bruno].)

POPE.

    Go presently and bring a banquet forth,   200
    That we may solemnize Saint Peter's feast
    And with Lord Raymond, King of Hungary,
    Drink to our late and happy victory.

(Exeunt.)

[3.2] (*A sennet° while the banquet is brought in, and
then enter Faustus and Mephostophilis in their own shapes.*)

MEPHOSTOPHILIS.

    Now Faustus, come prepare thyself for mirth.
    The sleepy cardinals are hard at hand

---

138 Pope Alexander Pope Alexander III (d. 1181) compelled the
emperor Frederick Barbarossa to kneel before him **progenitor** predecessor **144 basilisk** fabulous monster said to kill with a glance
159 Resign unseal

169 presently immediately **172 quittance of** requital for
178 lollards heretics **195 again** that is, to return
3.2.s.d. sennet set of notes played on a trumpet signaling an
approach or a departure

To censure Bruno, that is posted hence,
And on a proud-paced steed as swift as thought
5 Flies o'er the Alps to fruitful Germany,
There to salute the woeful Emperor.

FAUSTUS.
The Pope will curse them for their sloth today
That slept both Bruno and his crown away.
But now, that Faustus may delight his mind
10 And by their folly make some merriment,
Sweet Mephostophilis, so charm me here
That I may walk invisible to all
And do whate'er I please unseen of any.

MEPHOSTOPHILIS.
Faustus, thou shalt. Then kneel down presently,
15   Whilst on thy head I lay my hand
And charm thee with this magic wand.
First wear this girdle, then appear
Invisible to all are here:
The planets seven, the gloomy air,
20   Hell, and the Furies' forkèd hair,°
Pluto's blue fire, and Hecat's° tree
With magic spells so compass thee
That no eye may thy body see.

So Faustus, now for all their holiness,
25   Do what thou wilt, thou shalt not be discerned.

FAUSTUS.
Thanks Mephostophilis. Now friars, take heed
Lest Faustus make your shaven crowns to bleed.

MEPHOSTOPHILIS.
Faustus, no more. See where the cardinals come.

(Enter Pope [and Friars] and all the Lords [with King
Raymond and the Archbishop of Rheims]. Enter the [two]
Cardinals with a book.)

POPE.
Welcome lord cardinals. Come, sit down.
30 Lord Raymond, take your seat. Friars, attend,
And see that all things be in readiness
As best beseems this solemn festival.

I CARDINAL.
First may it please your sacred Holiness
To view the sentence of the reverend synod
35 Concerning Bruno and the Emperor.

POPE.
What needs this question? Did I not tell you
Tomorrow we would sit i' th' consistory
And there determine of his punishment?
You brought us word, even now, it was decreed
40 That Bruno and the cursèd Emperor

Were by the holy council both condemned
For loathèd lollards and base schismatics.
Then wherefore would you have me view that book?

I CARDINAL.
Your Grace mistakes. You gave us no such charge.

RAYMOND.
Deny it not; we all are witnesses   45
That Bruno here was late delivered you
With his rich triple crown to be reserved
And put into the church's treasury.

BOTH CARDINALS.
By holy Paul we saw them not.

POPE.
By Peter you shall die   50
Unless you bring them forth immediately.
Hale them to prison, lade their limbs with gyves.°
False prelates, for this hateful treachery
Cursed be your souls to hellish misery.

[Exeunt Attendants with two Cardinals.]

FAUSTUS.
So, they are safe. Now Faustus, to the feast.   55
The Pope had never such a frolic guest.

POPE.
Lord Archbishop of Rheims, sit down with us.

ARCHBISHOP.
I thank your Holiness.

FAUSTUS.
Fall to,° the devil choke you an you spare!

POPE.
Who's that spoke? Friars, look about.
Lord Raymond, pray fall to. I am beholding   60
To the Bishop of Milan for this so rare a present.

FAUSTUS [aside].
I thank you, sir!   [Snatches the dish.]

POPE.
How now! Who snatched the meat from me?
Villains, why speak you not?   65
My good Lord Archbishop, here's a most dainty dish
Was sent me from a cardinal in France.

FAUSTUS [aside].
I'll have that too!   [Snatches the dish.]

POPE.
What lollards do attend our Holiness
That we receive such great indignity!   70
Fetch me some wine.

FAUSTUS [aside].
Ay, pray do, for Faustus is adry.

POPE.
Lord Raymond, I drink unto your Grace.

FAUSTUS [aside].
I pledge your Grace.   [Snatches the goblet.]

---

20 **Furies' forkèd hair** (the hair of the Furies consisted of snakes, whose forked tongues may be implied here) 21 **Hecat** Hecate, goddess of magic (possibly her "tree" is the gallows-tree, but possibly "tree" is a slip for "three," Hecate being the triple goddess of heaven, earth, and hell)

52 **gyves** fetters 59 **Fall to** set to work (here, as commonly, "start eating")

POPE.
  My wine gone too? Ye lubbers, look about
  And find the man that doth this villainy,
  Or by our sanctitude you all shall die.
  I pray, my lords, have patience at this troublesome ban-
    quet.

ARCHBISHOP.
  Please it your Holiness, I think it be some ghost crept
    out of purgatory, and now is come unto your Holiness
    for his pardon.

POPE.
  It may be so:
  Go then, command our priests to sing a dirge
  To lay the fury of this same troublesome ghost.
                            [*Exit Attendant.*]

[*The Pope crosses himself before eating.*]

FAUSTUS.
  How now! Must every bit be spiced with a cross?
  Nay then, take that! [*Strikes the Pope.*]

POPE.
  O, I am slain! Help me my lords!
  O come and help to bear my body hence.
  Damned be this soul forever for this deed.
                (*Exeunt the Pope and his train.*)

MEPHOSTOPHILIS.
  Now Faustus, what will you do now?
  For I can tell you, you'll be cursed with bell, book, and
    candle.°

FAUSTUS.
  Bell, book, and candle. Candle, book, and bell.
  Forward and backward, to curse Faustus to hell!

(*Enter the Friars, with bell, book, and candle for the dirge.*)

1 FRIAR.
  Come brethren, let's about our business with good devo-
    tion.
  Cursèd be he that stole his Holiness' meat from the
    table.
      Maledicat Dominus!°
  Cursèd be he that struck his Holiness a blow on the face.
      Maledicat Dominus!

                     [*Faustus strikes a Friar.*]
  Cursèd be he that took Friar Sandelo a blow on the pate.
      Maledicat Dominus!
  Cursèd be he that disturbeth our holy dirge.
      Maledicat Dominus!
  Cursèd be he that took away his Holiness' wine.
      Maledicat Dominus!

([*Faustus and Mephostophilis*] *beat the Friars, fling fireworks among them and exeunt.*)

[3.3] (*Enter* [*Robin the*] *Clown and Dick with a cup.*)

DICK. Sirrah Robin, we were best look that your devil can
answer the stealing of this same cup, for the vintner's boy
follows us at the hard heels.°

ROBIN. 'Tis no matter, let him come! An he follow us I'll so
conjure him as he was never conjured in his life, I warrant him. Let me see the cup.

(*Enter Vintner.*)

DICK. Here 'tis. Yonder he comes. Now Robin, now or never
show thy cunning.

VINTNER. O, are you here? I am glad I have found you. You
are a couple of fine companions!° Pray, where's the cup
you stole from the tavern?

ROBIN. How, how! We steal a cup? Take heed what you say.
We look not like cup-stealers, I can tell you.

VINTNER. Never deny't, for I know you have it, and I'll
search you.

ROBIN. Search me? Ay, and spare not! [*Aside.*] Hold the cup,
Dick.—Come, come. Search me, search me.

                      [*Vintner searches him.*]
VINTNER. Come on sirrah, let me search you now.

DICK. Ay ay, do do. [*Aside.*] Hold the cup, Robin.—I fear
not your searching. We scorn to steal your cups, I can tell
you.

                      [*Vintner searches him.*]
VINTNER. Never outface me for the matter, for sure the cup
is between you two.

ROBIN. Nay, there you lie! 'Tis beyond us both.°

VINTNER. A plague take you. I thought 'twas your knavery to
take it away. Come, give it me again.

ROBIN. Ay, much! When, can you tell?° [*Aside.*] Dick, make
me a circle and stand close at my back and stir not for thy
life. Vintner, you shall have your cup anon. [*Aside.*] Say
nothing, Dick! O *per se,* o; Demogorgon, Belcher, and
Mephostophilis!

(*Enter Mephostophilis.* [*Exit Vintner.*])

MEPHOSTOPHILIS.
  You princely legions of infernal rule,
  How am I vexèd by these villains' charms!
  From Constantinople have they brought me now
  Only for pleasure of these damnèd slaves.

---

91 bell, book, and candle implements used in excommunicating (the bell was tolled, the book closed, the candle extinguished) **96 Maledicat Dominus** may the Lord curse him (Latin)

3.3.3 at the hard heels hard at heel, closely **10 companions** fellows (contemptuous) **24 beyond us both** (apparently Robin has managed to place the cup at some distance from where he now stands) **27 When, can you tell** (a scornful reply)

ROBIN. By lady sir, you have had a shrewd° journey of it.
  Will it please you to take a shoulder of mutton to supper
  and a tester° in your purse and go back again?

DICK. Ay, I pray you heartily, sir. For we called you but in
40   jest, I promise you.

MEPHOSTOPHILIS.
  To purge the rashness of this cursèd deed,
  First be thou turnèd to this ugly shape,
  For apish° deeds transformèd to an ape.

ROBIN. O brave! An ape! I pray sir, let me have the carrying
45   of him about to show some tricks.

MEPHOSTOPHILIS. And so thou shalt. Be thou transformed to
  a dog and carry him upon thy back. Away, be gone!

ROBIN. A dog! That's excellent. Let the maids look well to
  their porridge-pots, for I'll into the kitchen presently.
50   Come Dick, come.

(Exeunt the two Clowns.)

MEPHOSTOPHILIS.
  Now with the flames of ever-burning fire
  I'll wing myself and forthwith fly amain
  Unto my Faustus, to the Great Turk's court.

(Exit.)

[4] *(Enter Chorus.)*

  When Faustus had with pleasure ta'en the view
  Of rarest things and royal courts of kings,
  He stayed his course and so returnèd home,
  Where such as bare his absence but with grief,
5   I mean his friends and nearest companions,
  Did gratulate° his safety with kind words.
  And in their conference° of what befell
  Touching his journey through the world and air
  They put forth questions of astrology
10   Which Faustus answered with such learnèd skill
  As they admired and wondered at his wit.
  Now is his fame spread forth in every land.
  Amongst the rest the Emperor is one,
  Carolus the Fifth,° at whose palace now
15   Faustus is feasted 'mongst his noblemen.
  What there he did in trial of his art
  I leave untold, your eyes shall see performed.

(Exit.)

[4.1] *(Enter Martino and Frederick at several° doors.)*

MARTINO.
  What ho, officers, gentlemen!
  Hie to the presence° to attend the Emperor.

Good Frederick, see the rooms be voided straight,°
  His Majesty is coming to the hall.
  Go back and see the state° in readiness.

FREDERICK.   5
  But where is Bruno, our elected Pope,
  That on a fury's back came post from Rome?
  Will not his Grace consort° the Emperor?

MARTINO.
  O yes, and with him comes the German conjurer,
  The learnèd Faustus, fame of Wittenberg,
  The wonder of the world for magic art: 10
  And he intends to show great Carolus
  The race of all his stout progenitors
  And bring in presence of his Majesty
  The royal shapes and warlike semblances
  Of Alexander and his beauteous paramour.°   15

FREDERICK.
  Where is Benvolio?

MARTINO.   Fast asleep, I warrant you.
  He took his rouse with stoups° of Rhenish wine
  So kindly yesternight to Bruno's health
  That all this day the sluggard keeps his bed.

FREDERICK.   20
  See, see, his window's ope. We'll call to him.

MARTINO.
  What ho, Benvolio!

*(Enter Benvolio above at a window, in his nightcap,
buttoning.)*

BENVOLIO.
  What a devil ail you two?

MARTINO.
  Speak softly sir, lest the devil hear you,
  For Faustus at the court is late arrived
  And at his heels a thousand furies wait   25
  To accomplish whatsoever the doctor please.

BENVOLIO.
  What of this?

MARTINO.
  Come, leave thy chamber first, and thou shalt see
  This conjurer perform such rare exploits
  Before the Pope° and royal Emperor   30
  As never yet was seen in Germany.

BENVOLIO.
  Has not the Pope enough of conjuring yet?
  He was upon the devil's back late enough!
  And if he be so far in love with him
  I would he would post with him to Rome again.   35

---

36 shrewd bad   **38 tester** sixpence   **43 apish** (1) foolish (2) imitative
4 Chorus 6 gratulate express joy in   **7 conference** discussion
14 Carolus the Fifth Charles V (1500–58), Holy Roman Emperor
4.1.s.d. several separate   **2 presence** presence-chamber

3 voided straight emptied immediately   **5 state** chair of state, throne   **8 consort** attend   **16 Alexander and his beauteous paramour** Alexander the Great and his mistress Thaïs   **18 took his rouse with stoups** had drinking bouts with full goblets   **31 the Pope** that is, Bruno

206

FREDERICK.
   Speak, wilt thou come and see this sport?
BENVOLIO.   Not I.
MARTINO.
   Wilt thou stand in thy window and see it then?
BENVOLIO.
   Ay, and I fall not asleep i' th' meantime.
MARTINO.
   The Emperor is at hand, who comes to see
   What wonders by black spells may compassed be.
BENVOLIO. Well, go you attend the Emperor. I am content
   for this once to thrust my head out at a window, for they
   say if a man be drunk overnight the devil cannot hurt
   him in the morning. If that be true, I have a charm in my
   head shall control him as well as the conjurer, I warrant
   you.

                      (*Exit [Martino with Frederick. Benvolio remains at*
                                                          window].°)

   [4.2] (*A sennet.° Charles the German Emperor,*
   Bruno, [Duke of] Saxony, Faustus, Mephostophilis,
   Frederick, Martino, and Attendants.)

EMPEROR.
   Wonder of men, renownèd magician,
   Thrice-learnèd Faustus, welcome to our court.
   This deed of thine in setting Bruno free
   From his and our professèd enemy,
   Shall add more excellence unto thine art
   Than if by powerful necromantic spells
   Thou could'st command the world's obedience.
   For ever be beloved of Carolus!
   And if this Bruno thou hast late redeemed°
   In peace possess the triple diadem
   And sit in Peter's chair despite of chance,
   Thou shalt be famous through all Italy
   And honored of the German Emperor.
FAUSTUS.
   These gracious words, most royal Carolus,
   Shall make poor Faustus to his utmost power
   Both love and serve the German Emperor
   And lay his life at holy Bruno's feet.
   For proof whereof, if so your Grace be pleased,
   The doctor stands prepared by power of art
   To cast his magic charms that shall pierce through

   The ebon gates of ever-burning hell,
   And hale the stubborn furies from their caves
   To compass whatsoe'er your Grace commands.
BENVOLIO. Blood! He speaks terribly. But for all that I do
   not greatly believe him. He looks as like a conjurer as the   25
   Pope to a costermonger.°
EMPEROR.
   Then Faustus, as thou late didst promise us,
   We would behold that famous conqueror
   Great Alexander and his paramour
   In their true shapes and state majestical,   30
   That we may wonder at their excellence.
FAUSTUS.
   Your Majesty shall see them presently.—
   Mephostophilis away,
   And with a solemn noise of trumpets' sound
   Present before this royal Emperor   35
   Great Alexander and his beauteous paramour.
MEPHOSTOPHILIS.
   Faustus, I will.   [*Exit.*]
BENVOLIO. Well master doctor, an your devils come not
   away quickly, you shall have me asleep presently.
   Zounds,° I could eat myself for anger to think I have been   40
   such an ass all this while to stand gaping after the devils'
   governor and can see nothing.
FAUSTUS.
   I'll make you feel something anon if my art fail me not!
   My lord, I must forewarn your Majesty
   That when my spirits present the royal shapes   45
   Of Alexander and his paramour,
   Your Grace demand no questions of the King
   But in dumb silence let them come and go.
EMPEROR.
   Be it as Faustus please; we are content.
BENVOLIO. Ay, ay, and I am content too. And thou bring   50
   Alexander and his paramour before the Emperor, I'll be
   Actaeon° and turn myself to a stag.
FAUSTUS [*aside*]. And I'll play Diana and send you the horns
   presently.

   (*Sennet. Enter at one [door] the Emperor Alexander, at*
   the other Darius.° They meet. Darius is thrown down.
   Alexander kills him, takes off his crown, and offering to
   go out, his Paramour meets him. He embraceth her and
   sets Darius' crown upon her head, and coming back both
   salute the Emperor; who leaving his state offers to
   embrace them, which Faustus seeing suddenly stays him.
   Then trumpets cease and music sounds.)

   My gracious lord, you do forget yourself.   55
   These are but shadows, not substantial.

48 s.d. Benvolio remains at window (because Benvolio does not
leave the stage, this scene cannot properly be said to be ended. But
the present edition, following its predecessors for convenience of
reference, begins a new scene)
4.2.s.d. sennet trumpet fanfare (the absence of a verb in the rest of
the stage direction perhaps indicates that the Emperor and his party
do not enter but rather are "discovered," as Faustus may have been
discovered at the beginning of I.i, if the Chorus drew back a curtain) **9 redeemed** freed

26 costermonger fruit-seller **40 Zounds** by God's wounds
52 Actaeon legendary hunter who saw the naked goddess Diana
bathing. She transformed him into a stag, and he was torn to pieces
by his own hounds **54 s.d. Darius** King of Persia, defeated by
Alexander in 334 B.C.

EMPEROR.

    O pardon me, my thoughts are so ravished

    With sight of this renownèd Emperor,

    That in mine arms I would have compassed° him.

60   But Faustus, since I may not speak to them,

    To satisfy my longing thoughts at full,

    Let me this tell thee: I have heard it said

    That this fair lady whilst she lived on earth,

    Had on her neck a little wart or mole.

65   How may I prove that saying to be true?

FAUSTUS.

    Your Majesty may boldly go and see.

EMPEROR.

    Faustus, I see it plain!

    And in this sight thou better pleasest me

    Than if I gained another monarchy.

FAUSTUS.

70   Away, be gone!   (Exit show.)

    See, see, my gracious lord, what strange beast is yon that

        thrusts his head out at the window!

EMPEROR.

    O wondrous sight! See, Duke of Saxony,

    Two spreading horns most strangely fastened

75   Upon the head of young Benvolio.

SAXONY.

    What, is he asleep or dead?

FAUSTUS.

    He sleeps my lord, but dreams not of his horns.

EMPEROR.

    This sport is excellent. We'll call and wake him.

    What ho, Benvolio!

80 BENVOLIO. A plague upon you! Let me sleep awhile.

EMPEROR. I blame thee not to sleep much, having such a

    head of thine own.

SAXONY. Look up Benvolio! 'Tis the Emperor calls.

BENVOLIO. The Emperor! Where? O zounds, my head!

85 EMPEROR. Nay, and thy horns hold, 'tis no matter for thy

    head, for that's armed sufficiently.

FAUSTUS. Why, how now Sir Knight? What, hanged by the

    horns?° This is most horrible! Fie fie, pull in your head

    for shame! Let not all the world wonder at you.

90 BENVOLIO. Zounds doctor, is this your villainy?

FAUSTUS.

    Oh, say not so sir: The doctor has no skill,

    No art, no cunning to present these lords

    Or bring before this royal Emperor

    The mighty monarch, warlike Alexander.

95   If Faustus do it, you are straight resolved

    In bold Actaeon's shape to turn a stag.

    And therefore my lord, so please your Majesty,

    I'll raise a kennel of hounds shall hunt him so

    As all his footmanship shall scarce prevail

    To keep his carcass from their bloody fangs.   100

    Ho, Belimote, Argiron, Asterote!

BENVOLIO. Hold, hold! Zounds, he'll raise up a kennel of

    devils I think, anon. Good my lord, entreat for me.

    'Sblood,° I am never able to endure these torments.

EMPEROR.

    Then good master doctor,   105

    Let me entreat you to remove his horns.

    He has done penance now sufficiently.

FAUSTUS. My gracious lord, not so much for injury done to

    me, as to delight your Majesty with some mirth, hath

    Faustus justly requited this injurious° knight; which   110

    being all I desire, I am content to remove his horns.

    Mephostophilis, transform him. And hereafter sir, look

    you speak well of scholars.

BENVOLIO [aside]. Speak well of ye! 'Sblood, and scholars be

    such cuckold-makers to clap horns of honest men's heads   115

    o' this order, I'll ne'er trust smooth faces and small ruffs°

    more. But an I be not revenged for this, would I might be

    turned to a gaping oyster and drink nothing but salt

    water.   [Exit.]

EMPEROR.

    Come Faustus, while the Emperor lives,   120

    In recompense of this thy high desert,

    Thou shalt command the state of Germany

    And live beloved of mighty Carolus.

                                   (Exeunt omnes.)

[4.3] (Enter Benvolio, Martino, Frederick, and Soldiers.)

MARTINO.

    Nay, sweet Benvolio, let us sway thy thoughts

    From this attempt against the conjurer.

BENVOLIO.

    Away! You love me not to urge me thus.

    Shall I let slip° so great an injury

    When every servile groom jests at my wrongs   5

    And in their rustic gambols proudly say,

    "Benvolio's head was graced with horns today"?

    O, may these eyelids never close again

    Till with my sword I have that conjurer slain!

    If you will aid me in this enterprise,   10

    Then draw your weapons and be resolute;

    If not, depart. Here will Benvolio die

    But° Faustus' death shall quit° my infamy.

FREDERICK.

    Nay, we will stay with thee, betide what may,

    And kill that doctor if he come this way.   15

---

59 compassed encompassed, embraced   **87–88 hanged by the
horns** (the spreading horns prevent Benvolio from pulling his head
inside the window)

104 'Sblood by God's blood   **110 injurious** insulting   **116 small
ruffs** (worn by scholars, in contrast to the large ruffs worn by
courtiers)

4.3.4 let slip ignore   **13 But** unless   **quit** avenge

BENVOLIO.
    Then, gentle Frederick, hie thee to the grove
    And place our servants and our followers
    Close in an ambush there behind the trees.
    By this, I know, the conjurer is near.
    I saw him kneel and kiss the Emperor's hand
    And take his leave laden with rich rewards.
    Then soldiers, boldly fight. If Faustus die,
    Take you the wealth, leave us the victory.
FREDERICK.
    Come soldiers, follow me unto the grove.
    Who kills him shall have gold and endless love.

                            (*Exit Frederick with the Soldiers.*)

BENVOLIO.
    My head is lighter than it was by th' horns—
    But yet my heart more ponderous than my head,
    And pants until I see that conjurer dead.
MARTINO.
    Where shall we place ourselves, Benvolio?
BENVOLIO.
    Here will we stay to bide the first assault.
    O, were that damnèd hell-hound but in place
    Thou soon should'st see me quit my foul disgrace.

(*Enter Frederick.*)

FREDERICK.
    Close, close! The conjurer is at hand
    And all alone comes walking in his gown.
    Be ready then and strike the peasant° down!
BENVOLIO.
    Mine be that honor then! Now sword, strike home!
    For horns he gave I'll have his head anon.

(*Enter Faustus with the false head.*)

MARTINO.
    See see, he comes.
BENVOLIO.   No words. This blow ends all!

                            [*Strikes Faustus.*]
    Hell take his soul, his body thus must fall.
FAUSTUS.
    O!
FREDERICK.
    Groan you, master doctor?
BENVOLIO.
    Break may his heart with groans! Dear Frederick, see,
    Thus will I end his griefs immediately.

[*Cuts off Faustus's false head.*]

MARTINO.
    Strike with a willing hand! His head is off.
BENVOLIO.
    The devil's dead, the furies now may laugh.

FREDERICK.
    Was this that stern aspect, that awful frown,
    Made the grim monarch of infernal spirits
    Tremble and quake at his commanding charms?
MARTINO.
    Was this that damnèd head whose heart conspired
    Benvolio's shame before the Emperor?   50
BENVOLIO.
    Ay, that's the head, and here the body lies
    Justly rewarded for his villainies.
FREDERICK.
    Come let's devise how we may add more shame
    To the black scandal of his hated name.
BENVOLIO.
    First, on his head in quittance of my wrongs   55
    I'll nail huge forkèd horns and let them hang
    Within the window where he yoked me first
    That all the world may see my just revenge.
MARTINO.
    What use shall we put his beard to?
BENVOLIO. We'll sell it to a chimney-sweeper. It will wear 60
    out ten birchen brooms, I warrant you.
FREDERICK. What shall eyes do?
BENVOLIO. We'll put out his eyes, and they shall serve for
    buttons to his lips to keep his tongue from catching cold.
MARTINO. An excellent policy! And now sirs, having di- 65
    vided him, what shall the body do?

                            [*Faustus rises.*]

BENVOLIO. Zounds, the devil's alive again!
FREDERICK. Give him his head for God's sake!
FAUSTUS.
    Nay keep it. Faustus will have heads and hands,
    Ay, all your hearts, to recompense this deed.   70
    Knew you not, traitors, I was limited
    For four and twenty years to breathe on earth?
    And had you cut my body with your swords
    Or hewed this flesh and bones as small as sand,
    Yet in a minute had my spirit returned   75
    And I had breathed a man made free from harm.
    But wherefore do I dally my revenge?
    Asteroth, Belimoth, Mephostophilis!

(*Enter Mephostophilis and other Devils.*)

    Go horse these traitors on your fiery backs
    And mount aloft with them as high as heaven,   80
    Thence pitch them headlong to the lowest hell.
    Yet stay, the world shall see their misery,
    And hell shall after plague their treachery.
    Go Belimoth, and take this caitiff° hence
    And hurl him in some lake of mud and dirt: 85
    Take thou this other, drag him through the woods
    Amongst the pricking thorns and sharpest briars:

---

35 peasant low fellow   **84 caitiff** wretch

Whilst with my gentle Mephostophilis
This traitor flies unto some steepy rock
90 That rolling down may break the villain's bones
As he intended to dismember me.
Fly hence, dispatch my charge immediately!

FREDERICK.
Pity us, gentle Faustus, save our lives!

FAUSTUS.
Away!

FREDERICK.
95 He must needs go that the devil drives.

                                    (*Exeunt Spirits with the Knights.*)

(*Enter the ambushed Soldiers.*)

I SOLDIER.
Come sirs, prepare yourselves in readiness.
Make haste to help these noble gentlemen.
I heard them parley with the conjurer.

II SOLDIER.
See where he comes, dispatch, and kill the slave!

FAUSTUS.
100 What's here, an ambush to betray my life?
Then Faustus, try thy skill. Base peasants, stand!
For lo, these trees remove° at my command
And stand as bulwarks 'twixt yourselves and me
To shield me from your hated treachery!
105 Yet to encounter this your weak attempt
Behold an army comes incontinent.°

(*Faustus strikes the door, and enter a Devil playing on a drum, after him another bearing an ensign, and divers with weapons: Mephostophilis with fireworks: they set upon the Soldiers and drive them out.*)

                                                    [*Exeunt all.*]

[4.4] (*Enter at several doors Benvolio, Frederick, and Martino, their heads and faces bloody and besmeared with mud and dirt, all having horns on their heads.*)

MARTINO.
What ho, Benvolio!

BENVOLIO.   Here! What, Frederick, ho!

FREDERICK.
O, help me gentle friend. Where is Martino?

MARTINO.
Dear Frederick, here,
Half smothered in a lake of mud and dirt,
5 Through which the furies dragged me by the heels.

FREDERICK.
Martino, see, Benvolio's horns again.

MARTINO.
O misery! How now Benvolio?

BENVOLIO.
Defend me, heaven! Small I be haunted° still?

MARTINO.
Nay fear not man, we have no power to kill.

BENVOLIO.
My friends transformèd thus! O hellish spite,   10
Your heads are all set with horns.

FREDERICK.   You hit it right:
It is your own you mean. Feel on your head.

BENVOLIO.
Zounds, horns again!

MARTINO.   Nay chafe° not man, we all are sped.°

BENVOLIO.
What devil attends this damned magician,
That spite of spite our wrongs are doubled?   15

FREDERICK.
What may we do that we may hide our shames?

BENVOLIO.
If we should follow him to work revenge
He'd join long asses' ears to these huge horns
And make us laughing-stocks to all the world.

MARTINO.
What shall we then do, dear Benvolio?   20

BENVOLIO.
I have a castle joining near these woods,
And thither we'll repair and live obscure
Till time shall alter this our brutish shapes.
Sith° black disgrace hath thus eclipsed our fame,
We'll rather die with grief than live with shame.   25

                                        (*Exeunt omnes.*)

[4.5] (*Enter Faustus and the Horse-Courser.°*)

HORSE-COURSER. I beseech your worship, accept of these forty dollars.°

FAUSTUS. Friend, thou canst not buy so good a horse for so small a price. I have no great need to sell him, but if thou likest him for ten dollars more, take him, because I see   5
thou hast a good mind to him.

HORSE-COURSER. I beseech you sir, accept of this. I am a very poor man and have lost very much of late by horse-flesh,° and this bargain will set me up again.

FAUSTUS. Well, I will not stand° with thee. Give me the   10
money. Now sirrah, I must tell you that you may ride him o'er hedge and ditch and spare him not. But, do you hear, in any case ride him not into the water.

HORSE-COURSER. How sir, not into the water! Why, will he not drink of all waters?°   15

4.4.8 **haunted** (the following line suggests that there is a quibble on "hunted," Benvolio now resembling a stag)   **13 chafe** fret   **sped** done for, ruined (because of the horns)   **24 Sith** since
4.5.s.d. Horse-Courser horse trader   **2 dollars** German coins
9 horse-flesh (the possibility of a quibble on "whores' flesh" is increased by "set me up" and "stand" in the ensuing dialogue)
10 stand haggle   **15 drink of all waters** that is, go anywhere

102 remove move   **106 incontinent** immediately

FAUSTUS. Yes, he will drink of all waters, but ride him not into the water: o'er hedge and ditch or where thou wilt, but not into the water. Go bid the hostler deliver him unto you, and remember what I say.

HORSE-COURSER. I warrant you sir. O joyful day! Now am I a made man forever.   (*Exit.*)

FAUSTUS.
What art thou, Faustus, but a man condemned to die?
Thy fatal time° draws to a final end;
Despair doth drive distrust into my thoughts.
Confound these passions with a quiet sleep.
Tush, Christ did call the thief upon the cross!°
Then rest thee Faustus, quiet in conceit.°

(*He sits to sleep.*)

(*Enter the Horse-Courser wet.*)

HORSE-COURSER. O what a cozening° doctor was this! I riding my horse into the water, thinking some hidden mystery had been in the horse, I had nothing under me but a little straw and had much ado to escape drowning. Well, I'll go rouse him and make him give me my forty dollars again. Ho, sirrah doctor, you cozening scab! Master doctor, awake and rise, and give me my money again, for your horse is turned to a bottle° of hay. Master doctor!

(*He pulls off his leg.*)
Alas, I am undone! What shall I do? I have pulled off his leg.

FAUSTUS. O help, help! The villain hath murdered me!

HORSE-COURSER. Murder or not murder, now he has but one leg I'll outrun him, and cast this leg into some ditch or other.   [*Exit.*]

FAUSTUS. Stop him, stop him, stop him!—Ha, ha, ha! Faustus hath his leg again, and the horse-courser a bundle of hay for his forty dollars.

(*Enter Wagner.*)

How now, Wagner? What news with thee?

WAGNER. If it please you, the Duke of Vanholt doth earnestly entreat your company, and hath sent some of his men to attend you with provision fit for your journey.

FAUSTUS. The Duke of Vanholt's an honorable gentleman, and one to whom I must be no niggard of my cunning. Come, away!

(*Exeunt.*)

[4.6] (*Enter [Robin the] Clown, Dick, Horse-courser, and a Carter.*)

CARTER. Come my masters, I'll bring you to the best beer in Europe. What ho, hostess! Where be these whores?

(*Enter Hostess.*)

HOSTESS. How now? What lack you? What, my old guests, welcome.

ROBIN [*aside*]. Sirrah Dick, dost thou know why I stand so mute?

DICK [*aside*]. No Robin, why is't?

ROBIN [*aside*]. I am eighteen pence on the score.° But say nothing. See if she have forgotten me.

HOSTESS. Who's this that stands so solemnly by himself? What, my old guest!

ROBIN. O, hostess, how do you? I hope my score stands still.

HOSTESS. Ay, there's no doubt of that, for methinks you make no haste to wipe it out.

DICK. Why hostess, I say, fetch us some beer!

HOSTESS. You shall, presently.—Look up into th' hall there, ho!   (*Exit.*)

DICK. Come sirs, what shall we do now till mine hostess comes?

CARTER. Marry sir, I'll tell you the bravest tale how a conjurer served me. You know Doctor Fauster?

HORSE-COURSER. Ay, a plague take him! Here's some on's have cause to know him. Did he conjure thee too?

CARTER. I'll tell you how he served me. As I was going to Wittenberg t'other day with a load of hay, he met me and asked me what he should give me for as much hay as he could eat. Now sir, I thinking that a little would serve his turn, bad him take as much as he would for three farthings. So he presently gave me my money and fell to eating; and as I am a cursen° man, he never left eating till he had eat up all my load of hay.

ALL. O monstrous, eat a whole load of hay!

ROBIN. Yes yes, that may be, for I have heard of one that has eat a load of logs.°

HORSE-COURSER. Now sirs, you shall hear how villainously he served me. I went to him yesterday to buy a horse of him, and he would by no means sell him under forty dollars. So sir, because I knew him to be such a horse as would run over hedge and ditch and never tire, I gave him his money. So, when I had my horse, Doctor Fauster bade me ride him night and day and spare him no time. "But," quoth he, "in any case ride him not into the water." Now sir, I thinking the horse had had some quality that he would not have me know of, what did I but rid him into a great river—and when I came just in the midst, my horse vanished away and I sate straddling upon a bottle of hay.

ALL. O brave doctor!

HORSE-COURSER. But you shall hear how bravely I served him for it. I went me home to his house, and there I found him asleep. I kept ahallowing and whooping in his ears, but all could not wake him. I seeing that, took him

---

23 **fatal time** life span   26 **Christ . . . cross** (in Luke 23.39–43 Christ promised one of the thieves that he would be with Christ in paradise)   27 **quiet in conceit** with a quiet mind   28 **cozening** deceiving   35 **bottle** bundle

4.6.8 **on the score** in debt   30 **cursen** that is, Christian (dialect form)   34 **eat a load of logs** been drunk

by the leg and never rested pulling till I had pulled me his
leg quite off, and now 'tis at home in mine hostry.°

55   DICK. And has the doctor but one leg then? That's excellent, for one of his devils turned me into the likeness of
an ape's face.

CARTER. Some more drink, hostess!

ROBIN. Hark you, we'll into another room and drink awhile,
60   and then we'll go seek out the doctor.   (*Exeunt omnes*.)

[4.7] (*Enter the Duke of Vanholt, his [Servants,]*
Duchess, Faustus, and Mephostophilis.)

DUKE. Thanks master doctor, for these pleasant sights. Nor
know I how sufficiently to recompense your great deserts
in erecting that enchanted castle in the air, the sight
whereof so delighted me,
5   As nothing in the world could please me more.

FAUSTUS. I do think myself, my good lord, highly recom-
pensed in that it pleaseth your Grace to think but well of
that which Faustus hath performed.—But gracious lady,
it may be that you have taken no pleasure in those sights.
10   Therefore I pray you tell me what is the thing you most
desire to have: be it in the world it shall be yours. I have
heard that great-bellied° women do long for things are
rare and dainty.

DUCHESS. True master doctor, and since I find you so kind, I
15   will make known unto you what my heart desires to have:
and were it now summer, as it is January, a dead time of
the winter, I would request no better meat° than a dish of
ripe grapes.

FAUSTUS.
This is but a small matter. Go Mephostophilis, away!
(*Exit Mephostophilis*.)
20   Madam, I will do more than this for your content.

(*Enter Mephostophilis again with the grapes*.)

Here, now taste ye these. They should be good,
For they come from a far country, I can tell you.

DUKE. This makes me wonder more than all the rest, that at
this time of the year when every tree is barren of his fruit,
25   from whence you had these ripe grapes.

FAUSTUS. Please it your Grace, the year is divided into two
circles° over the whole world, so that when it is winter
with us, in the contrary circle it is likewise summer with
them, as in India, Saba,° and such countries that lie far
30   east, where they have fruit twice a year. From whence, by
means of a swift spirit that I have, I had these grapes
brought as you see.

DUCHESS. And trust me, they are the sweetest grapes that
e'er I tasted.

(*The Clowns [Robin, Dick, Carter, and Horse-Courser]*
bounce° at the gate within.)

DUKE.
What rude disturbers have we at the gate?   35
Go pacify their fury, set it ope,
And then demand of them what they would have.

(*They knock again and call out to talk with Faustus*.)

SERVANT.
Why, how now masters, what a coil° is there!
What is the reason° you disturb the Duke?

DICK. We have no reason for it, therefore a fig for him!   40

SERVANT.
Why saucy varlets, dare you be so bold!

HORSE-COURSER. I hope sir, we have wit enough to be more
bold than welcome.

SERVANT.
It appears so. Pray be bold elsewhere   45
And trouble not the Duke.

DUKE. What would they have?

SERVANT.
They all cry out to speak with Doctor Faustus.

CARTER. Ay, and we will speak with him.

DUKE. Will you sir? Commit° the rascals.   50

DICK. Commit with us! He were as good commit with his
father as commit with us!

FAUSTUS.
I do beseech your Grace, let them come in.
They are good subject for a merriment.

DUKE.
Do as thou wilt, Faustus, I give thee leave.

FAUSTUS.   55
I thank your Grace.

(*Enter [Robin] the Clown, Dick, Carter, and Horse-*
courser.)

Why, how now my good friends?
'Faith, you are too outrageous; but come near,
I have procured your pardons. Welcome all.

ROBIN. Nay sir, we will be welcome for our money, and we
will pay for what we take. What ho, give's half a dozen of   60
beer here, and be hanged!

FAUSTUS.
Nay, hark you, can you tell me where you are?

CARTER. Ay, marry can I, we are under heaven.

SERVANT.
Ay, but Sir Sauce-box, know you in what place?

---

54 **hostry** inn
4.7.12 **great-bellied** that is, pregnant   17 **meat** food   27 **two cir-**
cles that is, the northern and the southern hemispheres (though
later in the speech he talks of east and west rather than of north
and south)   29 **Saba** Sheba

34 s.d. **bounce** knock   38 **coil** turmoil   39 **reason** (pronounced
like "raisin," leading to the quibble on "fig"; a "fig" here is an
obscene contemptuous gesture in which the hand is clenched and
the thumb is thrust between the first and second fingers, making
the thumb resemble the stem of a fig, or a penis)   49 **Commit**
imprison (Dick proceeds to quibble on the idea of committing adultery)

HORSE-COURSER. Ay ay, the house is good enough to drink
in. Zounds, fill us some beer, or we'll break all the barrels
in the house and dash out all your brains with your bottles.

FAUSTUS.
Be not so furious. Come, you shall have beer.
My lord, beseech you give me leave awhile;
I'll gage° my credit 'twill content your Grace.

DUKE.
With all my heart, kind doctor, please thyself.
Our servants and our court's at thy command.

FAUSTUS.
I humbly thank your Grace.—Then fetch some beer.

HORSE-COURSER. Ay marry, there spake a doctor indeed!
And 'faith, I'll drink a health to thy wooden leg for that
word.

FAUSTUS.
My wooden leg? What dost thou mean by that?

CARTER. Ha, ha, ha, dost hear him Dick? He has forgot his
leg.

HORSE-COURSER. Ay ay, he does not stand much upon° that.

FAUSTUS.
No, 'faith, not much upon a wooden leg.

CARTER. Good lord, that flesh and blood should be so frail
with your worship! Do not you remember a horse-courser
you sold a horse to?

FAUSTUS. Yes, I remember I sold one a horse.

CARTER. And do you remember you bid he should not ride
into the water?

FAUSTUS. Yes, I do very well remember that.

CARTER. And do you remember nothing of your leg?

FAUSTUS. No, in good sooth.

CARTER. Then I pray remember your curtsy.°

FAUSTUS. I thank you sir.

CARTER. 'Tis not so much worth. I pray you tell me one
thing.

FAUSTUS. What's that?

CARTER. Be both your legs bedfellows every night together?

FAUSTUS. Would'st thou make a colossus° of me that thou
askest me such questions?

CARTER. No, truly sir, I would make nothing of you, but I
would fain know that.

(*Enter Hostess with drink.*)

FAUSTUS. Then I assure thee certainly they are.

CARTER. I thank you, I am fully satisfied.

FAUSTUS. But wherefore dost thou ask?

CARTER. For nothing, sir, but methinks you should have a
wooden bedfellow of one of 'em.

HORSE-COURSER. Why, do you hear sir, did not I pull off one
of your legs when you were asleep?

FAUSTUS. But I have it again now I am awake. Look you
here sir.

ALL. O horrible! Had the doctor three legs?

CARTER. Do you remember sir, how you cozened me and eat
up my load of—

(*Faustus charms him dumb.*)

DICK. Do you remember how you made me wear an ape's—
[*Faustus charms him.*]

HORSE-COURSER. You whoreson conjuring scab! Do you
remember how you cozened me with a ho—

[*Faustus charms him.*]

ROBIN. Ha' you forgotten me? You think to carry it away
with your "hey-pass" and "re-pass"?° Do you remember
the dog's fa—

([*Faustus charms him.*] *Exeunt Clowns.*)

HOSTESS. Who pays for the ale? Hear you master doctor,
now you have sent away my guests, I pray who shall pay
me for my a—

([*Faustus charms her.*] *Exit Hostess.*)

DUCHESS.
My lord,
We are much beholding to this learnèd man.

DUKE.
So are we madam, which we will recompense
With all the love and kindness that we may:
His artful sport drives all sad thoughts away.

(*Exeunt.*)

[5.1] (*Thunder and lightning. Enter Devils with covered dishes: Mephostophilis leads them into Faustus's
study. Then enter Wagner.*)

WAGNER. I think my master means to die shortly. He has
made his will and given me his wealth: his house, his
goods, and store of golden plate—besides two thousand
ducats ready coined. I wonder what he means. If death
were nigh, he would not frolic thus. He's now at supper
with the scholars, where there's such belly-cheer as Wagner in his life ne'er saw the like! And see where they
come. Belike° the feast is done.°   (*Exit.*)

(*Enter Faustus, Mephostophilis, and two or three Scholars.*)

1 SCHOLAR. Master Doctor Faustus, since our conference
about fair ladies, which was the beautifulest in all the
world, we have determined with ourselves that Helen of
Greece was the admirablest lady that ever lived. Therefore master doctor, if you will do us so much favor as to

---

70 gage pledge   **80 stand much upon** (quibble on "attach much
importance to")   **91 curtsy** (also called "a leg," hence there is a quibble on the Carter's previous speech)   **97 colossus** huge statue in the
harbor at Rhodes, between whose legs ships were said to have sailed

117 hey-pass, re-pass conjuring expressions
5.1.8 Belike most likely   **1–8 I think . . . done** (though printed as
prose in the quarto, as here, perhaps this speech should be verse,
the lines ending *shortly, wealth, plate, coined, nigh, supper, belly-
cheer, like, done*)

15 let us see that peerless dame of Greece, whom all the
world admires for majesty, we should think ourselves
much beholding unto you.

FAUSTUS.
Gentlemen,
For that I know your friendship is unfeigned,
It is not Faustus' custom to deny
20 The just request of those that wish him well:
You shall behold that peerless dame of Greece
No otherwise for pomp or majesty
Than when Sir Paris crossed the seas with her
And brought the spoils° to rich Dardania.°
25 Be silent then, for danger is in words.

(*Music sounds. Mephostophilis brings in Helen: she passeth over the stage.*)

II SCHOLAR.
Was this fair Helen, whose admired worth
Made Greece with ten years' wars afflict poor Troy?

III SCHOLAR.
Too simple is my wit to tell her worth,
Whom all the world admires for majesty.

SCHOLAR.
30 Now we have seen the pride of nature's work,
We'll take our leaves, and for this blessèd sight
Happy and blest be Faustus evermore.

FAUSTUS.
Gentlemen, farewell, the same wish I to you.

(*Exeunt Scholars.*)

(*Enter an Old Man.*)

OLD MAN.
O gentle Faustus, leave this damnèd art,
35 This magic that will charm thy soul to hell
And quite bereave° thee of salvation.
Though thou hast now offended like a man,
Do not persever° in it like a devil.
Yet, yet, thou hast an amiable soul°
40 If sin by custom grow not into nature.
Then, Faustus, will repentance come too late!
Then, thou art banished from the sight of heaven!
No mortal can express the pains of hell!
It may be this my exhortation
45 Seems harsh and all unpleasant. Let it not.
For gentle son, I speak it not in wrath
Or envy of thee but in tender love
And pity of thy future misery:
And so have hope that this my kind rebuke,
50 Checking° thy body, may amend thy soul.

FAUSTUS.
Where art thou, Faustus? Wretch, what hast thou done!

(*Mephostophilis gives him a dagger.*)

Hell claims his right and with a roaring voice
Says "Faustus, come, thine hour is almost come!"
And Faustus now will come to do thee right!

OLD MAN.
O stay, good Faustus, stay thy desperate steps!   55
I see an angel hover o'er thy head,
And with a vial full of precious grace
Offers to pour the same into thy soul:
Then call for mercy and avoid despair.

FAUSTUS.
O friend,   60
I feel thy words to comfort my distressèd soul:
Leave me awhile to ponder on my sins.

OLD MAN.
Faustus, I leave thee, but with grief of heart,
Fearing the enemy of thy hapless soul.

(*Exit.*)

FAUSTUS.
Accursèd Faustus! Wretch, what hast thou done!   65
I do repent, and yet I do despair:
Hell strives with grace for conquest in my breast!
What shall I do to shun the snares of death?

MEPHOSTOPHILIS.
Thou traitor Faustus, I arrest thy soul
For disobedience to my sovereign lord.   70
Revolt,° or I'll in piecemeal tear thy flesh.

FAUSTUS.
I do repent I e'er offended him.
Sweet Mephostophilis, entreat thy lord
To pardon my unjust presumption,
And with my blood again I will confirm   75
The former vow I made to Lucifer.

MEPHOSTOPHILIS.
Do it then, Faustus, with unfeignèd heart
Lest greater dangers do attend thy drift.

FAUSTUS.
Torment, sweet friend, that base and agèd man
That durst dissuade me from thy Lucifer,   80
With greatest torment that our hell affords.

MEPHOSTOPHILIS.
His faith is great. I cannot touch his soul.
But what I may afflict his body with
I will attempt, which is but little worth.

FAUSTUS.
One thing, good servant, let me crave of thee   85
To glut the longing of my heart's desire:
That I may have unto my paramour
That heavenly Helen which I saw of late,
Whose sweet embraces may extinguish clear
Those thoughts that do dissuade me from my vow,   90
And keep mine oath I made to Lucifer.

---

24 spoils booty (including Helen) **Dardania** Troy **36 bereave**
deprive **38 persever** (accent on second syllable) **39 an amiable
soul** a soul worthy of love **50 Checking** rebuking

71 Revolt return (to your allegiance)

MEPHOSTOPHILIS.
      This or what else my Faustus shall desire
      Shall be performed in twinkling of an eye.

      (*Enter Helen again, passing over between two Cupids.*)

FAUSTUS.
      Was this the face that launched a thousand ships
95   And burnt the topless° towers of Ilium?°
      Sweet Helen, make me immortal with a kiss.
      Her lips suck forth my soul. See where it flies!
      Come Helen, come, give me my soul again.
      Here will I dwell, for heaven is in these lips
100   And all is dross that is not Helena.
      I will be Paris, and for love of thee
      Instead of Troy shall Wittenberg be sacked;
      And I will combat with weak Menelaus°
      And wear thy colors on my plumèd crest.
105   Yea, I will wound Achilles° in the heel
      And then return to Helen for a kiss.
      O, thou art fairer than the evening's air
      Clad in the beauty of a thousand stars,
      Brighter art thou than flaming Jupiter
110   When he appeared to hapless Semele,°
      More lovely than the monarch of the sky
      In wanton Arethusa's° azure arms,
      And none but thou shalt be my paramour.

                                                        (*Exeunt.*)

[5.2] (*Thunder, Enter Lucifer, Belzebub, and
Mephostophilis.*°)

LUCIFER.
      Thus from infernal Dis° do we ascend
      To view the subjects of our monarchy,
      Those souls which sin seals the black sons of hell.
      'Mong which as chief, Faustus, we come to thee,
5   Bringing with us lasting damnation
      To wait upon thy soul. The time is come
      Which makes it forfeit.
MEPHOSTOPHILIS.   And this gloomy night
      Here in this room will wretched Faustus be.
BELZEBUB.
      And here we'll stay
10   To mark him how he doth demean himself.

---

95 **topless** that is, so tall their tops are beyond sight   **Ilium** Troy
103 **Menelaus** Greek king, deserted by Helen for Paris
105 **Achilles** greatest of the Greek warriors   110 **Semele** beloved
by Jupiter, who promised to do whatever she wished; she asked to
see him in his full splendor, and the sight incinerated her
112 **Arethusa** a nymph, here apparently loved by Jupiter, "the
monarch of the sky"
5.2.s.d. Enter Lucifer, Belzebub, and Mephostophilis (probably
they rise out of a trapdoor and ascend to the upper stage,
Mephostophilis descending to the main stage at line 108)
1 infernal Dis the underworld (named for its ruler)

MEPHOSTOPHILIS.
      How should he but in desperate lunacy?
      Fond° worldling, now his heart blood dries with grief,
      His conscience kills it, and his laboring brain
      Begets a world of idle fantasies
15   To overreach the devil; but all in vain:
      His store of pleasures must be sauced with pain!
      He and his servant Wagner are at hand.
      Both come from drawing Faustus' latest will.
      See where they come.

      (*Enter Faustus and Wagner.*)

FAUSTUS.
      Say Wagner, thou hast perused my will;   20
      How dost thou like it?
WAGNER.   Sir, so wondrous well
      As in all humble duty I do yield
      My life and lasting service for your love.

      (*Enter the Scholars.*)

FAUSTUS.
      Gramercies,° Wagner.—Welcome gentlemen.

                                          [*Exit Wagner.*]
I SCHOLAR. Now worthy Faustus, methinks your looks are   25
   changed.
FAUSTUS.
      O gentlemen!
II SCHOLAR.
      What ails Faustus?
FAUSTUS. Ah my sweet chamber-fellow, had I lived with
   thee, then had I lived still!—But now must die eternally.   30
   Look sirs, comes he not, comes he not?
I SCHOLAR. O my dear Faustus, what imports this fear?
II SCHOLAR. Is all our pleasure turned to melancholy?
III SCHOLAR. He is not well with being oversolitary.
II SCHOLAR. If it be so, we'll have physicians and Faustus   35
   shall be cured.
III SCHOLAR. 'Tis but a surfeit° sir, fear nothing.
FAUSTUS. A surfeit of deadly sin that hath damned both
   body and soul!
II SCHOLAR. Yet Faustus, look up to heaven and remember   40
   mercy is infinite.
FAUSTUS. But Faustus' offense can ne'er be pardoned. The
   serpent that tempted Eve may be saved, but not Faustus!
   O gentlemen, hear with patience and tremble not at my
   speeches. Though my heart pant and quiver to remember   45
   that I have been a student here these thirty years, O,
   would I had never seen Wittenberg, never read book.—
   And what wonders I have done all Germany can witness,
   yea all the world, for which Faustus hath lost both Ger-

---

12 **Fond** foolish   24 **Gramercies** thank you   37 **a surfeit** indigestion

50 many and the world, yea heaven itself—heaven, the seat
of God, the throne of the blessèd, the kingdom of joy—
and must remain in hell forever! hell, O hell forever!
Sweet friends, what shall become of Faustus being in hell
forever?

55 II SCHOLAR. Yet Faustus, call on God.

FAUSTUS. On God, whom Faustus hath abjured? On God,
whom Faustus hath blasphemed? O my God, I would
weep, but the devil draws in my tears! Gush forth blood
instead of tears, yea life and soul! O, he stays my tongue!
60 I would lift up my hands, but see, they hold 'em, they
hold 'em!

ALL. Who, Faustus?

FAUSTUS. Why, Lucifer and Mephostophilis. O gentlemen, I
gave them my soul for my cunning.

65 ALL. O, God forbid!

FAUSTUS. God forbade it indeed, but Faustus hath done it.
For the vain pleasure of four and twenty years hath Faustus lost eternal joy and felicity. I writ them a bill with
mine own blood. The date is expired. This is the time.
70 And he will fetch me.

I SCHOLAR. Why did not Faustus tell us of this before, that
divines might have prayed for thee?

FAUSTUS. Oft have I thought to have done so, but the devil
threatened to tear me in pieces if I named God—to fetch
75 me body and soul if I once gave ear to divinity; and now
'tis too late! Gentlemen, away, lest you perish with me.

II SCHOLAR. O, what may we do to save Faustus?

FAUSTUS. Talk not of me but save yourselves and depart.

III SCHOLAR. God will strengthen me. I will stay with Faus-
80 tus.

I SCHOLAR. Tempt not God, sweet friend, but let us into the
next room and pray for him.

FAUSTUS. Ay, pray for me, pray for me. And what noise
soever you hear, come not unto me, for nothing can res-
85 cue me.

II SCHOLAR. Pray thou, and we will pray that God may have
mercy upon thee.

FAUSTUS. Gentlemen, farewell! If I live till morning, I'll
visit you. If not, Faustus is gone to hell.

90 ALL. Faustus, farewell.   (*Exeunt Scholars.*)

MEPHOSTOPHILIS.
Ay, Faustus, now thou hast no hope of heaven.
Therefore, despair! Think only upon hell,
For that must be thy mansion, there to dwell.

FAUSTUS.
O thou bewitching fiend, 'twas thy temptation
95 Hath robbed me of eternal happiness.

MEPHOSTOPHILIS.
I do confess it Faustus, and rejoice.
'Twas I, that when thou wert i' the way to heaven
Dammed up thy passage. When thou took'st the book
To view the Scriptures, then I turned the leaves
100 And led thine eye.
What, weep'st thou! 'Tis too late, despair, farewell!

Fools that will laugh on earth, most weep in hell.

                                                   (*Exit.*)

(*Enter the Good Angel and the Bad Angel at several
doors.*)

GOOD ANGEL.
O Faustus, if thou hadst given ear to me
Innumerable joys had followèd thee.
But thou did'st love the world.   105

BAD ANGEL.   Gave ear to me,
And now must taste hell's pains perpetually.

GOOD ANGEL.
O, what will all thy riches, pleasures, pomps
Avail thee now?

BAD ANGEL.   Nothing but vex thee more,
To want in hell, that had on earth such store.

(*Music while the throne° descends.*)

GOOD ANGEL.
O, thou hast lost celestial happiness,   110
Pleasures unspeakable, bliss without end.
Had'st thou affected° sweet divinity,
Hell or the devil had had no power on thee.
Had'st thou kept on that way, Faustus behold
In what resplendent glory thou had'st sat   115
In yonder throne, like those bright shining saints,
And triumphed over hell! That hast thou lost.

                                        [*Throne ascends.*]
And now, poor soul, must thy good angel leave thee,
The jaws of hell are open to receive thee.

                                                   (*Exit.*)

(*Hell is discovered.*)

BAD ANGEL.
Now Faustus, let thine eyes with horror stare   120
Into that vast perpetual torture-house.
There are the furies, tossing damnèd souls
On burning forks. Their bodies boil in lead.
There are live quarters° broiling on the coals,
That ne'er can die: this ever-burning chair   125
Is for o'er-tortured souls to rest them in.
These that are fed with sops of flaming fire
Were gluttons and loved only delicates
And laughed to see the poor starve at their gates.
But yet all these are nothing. Thou shalt see   130
Ten thousand tortures that more horrid be.

FAUSTUS.
O, I have seen enough to torture me.

BAD ANGEL.
Nay, thou must feel them, taste the smart of all:
He that loves pleasure must for pleasure fall.
And so I leave thee Faustus, till anon: 135

109 s.d. **throne** (symbolic of heaven) 112 **affected** preferred
124 **quarters** bodies

Then wilt thou tumble in confusion.°   (*Exit.*)

(*The clock strikes eleven.*)

FAUSTUS.
    O Faustus!
    Now hast thou but one bare hour to live
    And then thou must be damned perpetually.
140 Stand still, you ever-moving spheres of Heaven
    That time may cease and midnight never come:
    Fair nature's eye, rise, rise again and make
    Perpetual day, or let this hour be but a year,
    A month, a week, a natural day—
145 That Faustus may repent and save his soul.
    O lente lente currite noctis equi!°
    The stars move still, time runs, the clock will strike:
    The devil will come, and Faustus must be damned!
    O, I'll leap up to my God! Who pulls me down?
150 See, see where Christ's blood streams in the firmament!
    One drop of blood will save me. O my Christ!—
    Rend not my heart for naming of my Christ!
    Yet will I call on Him! O spare me, Lucifer!—
    Where is it now? 'Tis gone: and see where God
155 Stretcheth out His arm and bends His ireful brows!
    Mountains and hills, come, come and fall on me
    And hide me from the heavy wrath of God!
    No?
    Then will I headlong run into the earth.
160 Gape earth! O no, it will not harbor me.
    You stars that reigned at my nativity,
    Whose influence hath allotted death and hell,
    Now draw up Faustus like a foggy mist
    Into the entrails of yon laboring cloud
165 That when you vomit forth into the air,
    My limbs may issue from your smoky mouths—
    But let my soul mount and ascend to heaven!

(*The watch strikes.*)

    O half the hour is passed! 'Twill all be passed anon!
    O God,
170 If thou wilt not have mercy on my soul,
    Yet for Christ's sake, whose blood hath ransomed me,
    Impose some end to my incessant pain!
    Let Faustus live in hell a thousand years,
    A hundred thousand, and at last be saved!
175 No end is limited to° damnèd souls!
    Why wert thou not a creature wanting soul?
    Or why is this immortal that thou hast?
    O, Pythagoras' metempsychosis,° were that true

This soul should fly from me and I be changed
Into some brutish beast.   180
All beasts are happy, for when they die
Their souls are soon dissolved in elements.
But mine must live still° to be plagued in hell!
Cursed be the parents that engendered me!
No Faustus, curse thyself, curse Lucifer   185
That hath deprived thee of the joys of heaven.

(*The clock strikes twelve.*)

It strikes, it strikes! Now body, turn to air,
Or Lucifer will bear thee quick° to hell!
O soul, be changed into small water-drops
And fall into the ocean, ne'er be found.   190

(*Thunder, and enter the Devils.*)

My God, my God! Look not so fierce on me!
Adders and serpents, let me breathe awhile!
Ugly Hell, gape not! Come not Lucifer!
I'll burn my books!—O Mephostophilis!

(*Exeunt [Devils with Faustus.]°*)

[5.3] (*Enter the Scholars.*)

I SCHOLAR.
    Come gentlemen, let us go visit Faustus,
    For such a dreadful night was never seen
    Since first the world's creation did begin!
    Such fearful shrieks and cries were never heard!
    Pray heaven, the doctor have escaped the danger.   5
II SCHOLAR.
    O, help us heaven, see, here are Faustus' limbs
    All torn asunder by the hand of death!
III SCHOLAR.
    The devils whom Faustus served have torn him thus:
    For 'twixt the hours of twelve and one, methought
    I heard him shriek and call aloud for help,   10
    At which self° time the house seemed all on fire
    With dreadful horror of these damnèd fiends.
II SCHOLAR.
    Well gentlemen, though Faustus' end be such
    As every Christian heart laments to think on,
    Yet for he was a scholar once admired   15
    For wondrous knowledge in our German schools,
    We'll give his mangled limbs due burial;
    And all the students, clothed in mourning black,
    Shall wait upon° his heavy° funeral.

(*Exeunt.*)

---

136 **confusion** destruction   146 **O . . . *equi*** slowly, slowly run, O
horses of the night (Latin, adapted from Ovid's *Amores*, I.xiii.40,
where a lover regretfully thinks of the coming of the dawn)
175 **limited to** set for   178 **metempsychosis** transmigration of
souls (a doctrine held by Pythagoras, philosopher of the sixth century B.C.)

183 **still** always   188 **quick** alive   194 **s.d. Exeunt [Devils with
Faustus]** (possibly the devils drag Faustus into the "hell" that was
"discovered" at 5.2.119, and then toss his limbs onto the stage, or
possibly the limbs are revealed in V.iii.6 by withdrawing a curtain at
the rear of the stage)
5.3.11 **self** same   19 **wait upon** attend   **heavy** sad

(*Enter Chorus.*)

20 Cut is the branch that might have grown full straight
And burnèd is Apollo's laurel bough°
That sometime grew within this learnèd man.
Faustus is gone: regard his hellish fall,
Whose fiendful fortune may exhort the wise
25 Only to wonder at° unlawful things,
Whose deepness doth entice such forward wits

To practice more than heavenly power permits.

[*Exit.*]

Terminat hora diem; terminat Author opus.°

FINIS

TOPICS FOR CRITICAL THINKING AND WRITING

 ### THE PLAY ON THE PAGE

1. Characterize Faustus, calling attention to his virtues (if any) and to his weaknesses. In 1.1.74–93, for instance, how mixed are his motives? Elsewhere in the play do you find evidence of *hybris* (see Glossary)? In Faustus's last scene (5.2) do you find indications that he has grown morally? Explain.

2. What evidence can you offer to support the idea that Faustus is a victim, trapped by diabolic forces?

3. What evidence can you offer to support the idea that Faustus freely chooses damnation?

4. In 1.3.23–24 Faustus says to a devil, "I charge thee to return and change thy shape, / Thou art too ugly to attend on me." What does this statement tell us about Faustus?

5. Take at least two comic scenes and examine them with the idea that perhaps these scenes can be justified in one way or another as related to the story of Faustus. Or are the scenes irrelevant material added to fill out the play?

6. Faustus often engages in low fooling, rather than in heroic errors. Can we satisfactorily explain this comic stuff? How?

7. Do you find the final scene integral to the dramatic wholeness of the play? Provide specific arguments.

THE PLAY ON THE STAGE

8. If you were directing the play, exactly what blocking and what gestures would you prescribe for the Chorus at the beginning of the play and for Faustus in his first speech?

9. Do you think the devils can be played in such a way that at least in some scenes they are genuinely terrifying, or do you think that a modern audience can see them only as absurd? Explain.

10. Much of the fooling, especially with the Horse-courser and with the Pope, is deleted in most modern productions, on the grounds that it is unfunny and that it trivializes the tragic hero. Are there certain comic scenes that you would cut, and others that you would retain? Why?

11. If you were staging the play would you try to suggest that Faustus is basically a heroic figure who finds himself in conflict with an oppressive morality, or would you try to suggest that Faustus is essentially a talented but shallow person, overly fond of coarse fun? Or a neurotic? Or would you try to develop some other view? (One way to think about the problem is this: Does Faustus *enjoy* the jokes—in which case he is shallow and vulgar—or does Marlowe somehow distance Faustus from the comedy, perhaps even suggesting that Faustus's clowning represents his unsatisfactory attempt to alleviate his painful awareness of the limitations imposed upon humanity.)

12. Clifford Williams, in his 1968 production (discussed in Gareth Lloyd Evans's essay, which follows), used a nude Helen. If you were directing the play, and if you thought that the law would allow you to present Helen nude, would you do so? Why, or why not?

13. In some modern productions, the role of Helen has been played by a man, thus making clear that the devils have duped Faustus. What do you think of this idea?

14. In John Barton's 1974 production, a devil—rather than the Chorus—spoke the final lines of the play. How do you feel about this?

---

21 **laurel bough** symbol of wisdom, here associated with Apollo, god of divination   25 **Only to wonder at** that is, merely to observe at a distance, with awe

28 **Terminat . . . opus** the hour ends the day; the author ends his work (this Latin tag probably is not Marlowe's but the printer's, though it is engaging to believe Marlowe wrote it, ending his play at midnight, the hour of Faustus' death)

THE PLAY IN PERFORMANCE

The date of the composition of *Doctor Faustus* is uncertain, but it probably was first performed during the winter of 1592–93, and it was certainly performed in September 1594, with Edward Alleyn—the leading tragic actor of the period—in the title role. We know that it was popular for the next few years, and we know that in 1602 Philip Henslowe, a theater owner and manager, paid William Bird and William Rowley for "additions" to the play. Subsequent performances, therefore—including those of today—surely include some material that Marlowe did not write. Unfortunately, it is not certain which scenes or lines are the "additions."

The play was popular until the theaters were closed in 1642, at the outbreak of the English Civil War. We can get some idea of what these early performances were like from Sir John Melton, who in a work published in 1620 says that at a production of *Doctor Faustus*

> a man may behold shagge-hayr'd Deuills runne roaring ouer the Stage with Squibs [i.e., firecrackers] in their mouthes, while Drummers make thunder in the Tyring-house [i.e., the area at the back of the projecting stage], and the twelue-penny Hirelings [i.e., stagehands] make artificiall Lightning in their heauens.

The text of the play supports Melton's comment. For instance, 1.3 begins with "thunder"; in 2.1 when Faustus calls for a wife, Mephostophilis provides a female devil with fireworks; 3.2 tells us that Faustus and Mephostophilis "fling fireworks" at the friars. We know for certain that the stage effects were not only frightening but also were comic, since (for instance) when Faustus gives up his desire for a wife, he jokes that the fireworks-throwing female devil is "a hot whore indeed." (With the word "hot," he is punning on her lasciviousness and also suggesting that she is burning with venereal disease.) It may be hard for some of us to take seriously the spectacular events and the talk of the supernatural, but apparently the Elizabethans were impressed. For instance, stories circulated that during a performance the actors suddenly found one devil more on the stage than there should have been. According to one report, when the actors perceived that the devil himself was among them, they were so unnerved that they terminated the performance. Edward Alleyn's retirement was traditionally attributed to the appearance of a devil during the play.

Beyond the fact that drums provided the thunder, and firecrackers and lightning were used, what do we know about the earliest productions of the play? Not a great deal for sure, but we probably can make some safe guesses. The Chorus, who opens the play, probably wore a black cloak—traditional for such a role—and possibly he wore a crown of bays, emblematic of the poet. When he ends his first speech with "And this the man that in his study sits," he probably pulls back a curtain at the rear of the stage, revealing Faustus in his study.

From here, however, we enter upon less firm ground. Probably the study was equipped with some books and with some magic symbols, for instance a magic circle on the floor, as is seen on the title page of an edition of the play. (This picture shows a dragon emerging from the floor; possibly in the play a devil appeared in the form of a dragon.) Faustus probably wore a scholar's robe—maybe the fur-trimmed gown of a Doctor of Divinity—and he may have held a magician's wand, again as in the woodcut on the title page. Probably when Faustus dismissed each field of learning in his first speech (philosophy, medicine, law, theology) he read from a different book, and then cast it aside. With the entrance of Wagner in the first scene, Faustus probably came forth from the alcove at the rear and moved forward, onto the platform stage, in a sense bringing his locale with him. The audience would then understand that (so long as Faustus was on the stage) the scene was still within his study, even though whatever scenery there was—for instance an astrological chart—probably was confined to the alcove at the rear of the platform.

The Good Angel and the Bad Angel entered and exited through different doors (the text says they enter "at several doors"); possibly some or all devils showed their underworld nature by entering onto the stage through a trapdoor. Perhaps during his last speech, when he says he will burn his books, Faustus rushed into his study, an alcove at the rear of the stage, and perhaps devils then pulled him down into an opened trap. In keeping with the other medieval aspects of the play, this trap may have been covered by a conventional medieval hellmouth, a gaping mouth of a monster or a devil, from which infernal smoke issued. The curtain could then have been pulled closed, the hellmouth removed, and when the curtain was drawn back the limbs of Faustus would be discovered.

We know, of course, that the Elizabethan stage not only made use of traps, but it also made use of playing spaces *above* the stage. When Lucifer begins 5.2 by saying, "Thus from infernal Dis [the underworld] do we ascend," he and his cohorts may have climbed out of a trapdoor and then continued climbing onto an elevated position above the stage, where for a while they looked down on their victim. An area above the platform stage is also indicated by a stage direction in 5.2, which tells us that "the throne descends," that is, a symbol from heaven manifests itself on the stage.

From 1642 to 1660, during the Civil War between the Parliamentarians and the Royalists (1642–52) and during the Commonwealth Period (1649–60) when Oliver Cromwell and his son were dictators, the theaters were closed, but in 1662, during the Restoration, *Doctor Faustus* was revived. The play was performed again in 1675, and then it disappeared from the stage for more than two hundred years, until July 1896, when William Poel, founder of the Elizabethan Stage Society, revived it on a stage that approximated an Elizabethan stage. (Poel's revival of *Everyman* in 1901 is discussed on page 183.)

Perhaps a director's first act of interpretation is the decision about which text to use—the 1604 text, or the longer (chiefly because of comic scenes) 1616 text. The choice makes a big difference not only in the playing time but also in the interpretation of the central figure, because the abundant comic scenes of 1616 tend to trivialize Faustus. Directors who wish to suggest that Faustus is a grand Renaissance hero whose fault—let's say an overly aspiring mind—is tragic, usually choose the shorter text.

For the 1896 production (and again for a revival in 1906), William Poel relied chiefly on the shorter text, partly because he believed that the longer text included additions not by Marlowe, and partly because he saw Faustus as a heroic figure, driven by a quest for knowledge. In keeping with the ideals of the Elizabethan Stage Society—the idea was to produce the plays as they might have been done in the sixteenth century, with relatively little scenery and therefore with no intervals between changes of scene—Poel dispensed with the usual Victorian scenery that clearly established the particular setting as a room or a forest or whatever. The players merely entered the stage through curtains, in effect establishing the particular locale by their dialogue and their costumes (for instance, the costumes of cardinals or of a pope indicated that the scene was Rome). A reviewer of Poel's production tells us that for some scenes, however, a curtain at the rear was drawn back to reveal "a great dragon's mouth wide open, representing the mouth of hell. Out of this mouth came Mephostophilis, and under his escort the Seven Deadly Sins, Alexander and his paramour, and Helen."

Three other points about Poel's production should be mentioned. (1) The Chorus was a woman (odd, since the Elizabethan Stage Society sought to imitate Elizabethan practice, and the Elizabethan stage did not use actresses). (2) Faustus's encounter with Helen was very chaste (Helen kissed his forehead, and he kissed her hand), though in the 1906 revival, Poel—or Faustus—was a little bolder, since Faustus brushed Helen's cheek with his lips. (3) The devilwife of 2.1, seen from the front, seemed a beautiful woman, but when she turned around the audience perceived a skeleton—an interesting idea that to the best of our knowledge has not been used in later productions.

We cannot discuss all of the subsequent productions, but a few deserve special mention. In 1937 Orson Welles—not yet twenty-two and therefore still regarded as a boy genius—produced the play under the auspices of the Federal Theatre Project (part of Franklin Delano Roosevelt's Works Project Administration, a plan to find work for the unemployed during the Depression). John Houseman (later known to a vast public as the law professor in the television series, *Paper Chase*) was the director of the unit in which Welles worked, and the two staged an impressive version. In fact, Welles was a devoted amateur magician, and—given his high estimate of himself and his fondness for breaking rules—he must have identified strongly with the role of Faustus. He cut much of the comedy and stressed the heroic aspects of Faustus, but he did retain some of the comedy where he could indulge in conjuring. Thus, the cardinals' hats flew through the air, the pope's miter arose, splendidly dressed papal servants carrying dishes of food were astonished to find the food—a side of beef, a pudding, roasted chickens—fly through the air and disappear. Welles's set appeared to be not much more than a background of black velvet, but this set was the key to the magic. Houseman, in *Run-Through*, an autobiography, explains a system that professional magicians call "black magic."

> Used for vanishing acts and miraculous appearances, it exploits the absorbent properties of black velvet so that, under certain lighting conditions, not only do black surfaces become totally invisible against each other, but all normal sense of space, depth and perspective becomes lost and confused in the eye of the spectator.... By using almost no front light and crisscrossing the stage with parallel light curtains and clusters of units carefully focused from the sides and overhead, [Welles] was able to achieve mystifications that would have impressed the great Thurston....
>
> This mystification was accomplished with the aid of eight dancers, dressed from head to foot in black velvet, moving alongside the procession [of servants carrying food], just far enough upstage to be out of the blaze of the light curtain and thus completely invisible to the audience against the darkness of black velvet. In their black-gloved hands, they held . . . thin, black, flexible steel rods whose ends were affixed to the meats, the pudding and the episcopal headgear that were marked for flight. On cue the boys in black swung those loaded rods up over their heads and brought them down behind them where their own black costumes formed a screen for them till they were able to leave the stage unobserved in the confusion of the dissolving parade.
>
> (233–34)

Although most of the comedy was cut, those clown scenes that were staged were played strictly for comedy—Faustus was just fooling around—and they did not seem to interfere with Welles's heroic interpretation of the role. The Seven Deadly Sins were puppets that appeared onstage by wriggling up through openings in the floor; as we will see in a moment, later productions follow Welles in tending to use puppets rather than human actors for the Seven Deadly Sins.

One other point should be made about this production. Welles used an African-American actor, Jack Carter, in the role of Mephostophilis. The employment of a single black actor in the role of a devil today scarcely seems to be daring, but it was an innovation in the 1930s, when casts were almost never integrated.

In 1968 Clifford Williams directed the Royal Shakespeare Company's production of *Doctor Faustus*, with Eric Porter in the title role. Because this production is discussed in Gareth Lloyd Evans's essay, which follows, we need not comment at length here, but we do want briefly to describe the staging of Faustus's last exit. Faustus grovelled in terror as he made his final speech, but when the clock finished striking twelve and nothing happened, he raised his head, looked at the emptiness around, and then laughed. At this point, sections of the back wall fell away, revealing a red glow, through which were seen steel spikes, the teeth of a hellmouth. Devils slowly came forward, surrounded Faustus, and then carried him screaming back into the hellmouth, which then closed.

The 1974 production by John Barton, first in Edinburgh and then in London, starred Ian McKellen as Faustus. Barton cut almost all of the comedy, replacing some of it with passages from the source of the play, a prose account of Faus-

tus. All of the action took place within Faustus's study, and Barton gave the final lines of the play, in the original spoken by the Chorus, to a devil. Despite the deletion of the comic material, which might indicate that the director was aiming at an heroic Faustus, Barton's Faustus was not a grand figure but rather struck most viewers as a neurotic pedant. He peered through spectacles, twitched, grimaced, and hugged himself with glee. All of the magical figures—the Seven Deadly Sins, Helen, and so forth—were puppets or dummies of one sort or another. The Good Angel and Bad Angel, for instance, were hand puppets manipulated by Faustus, who spoke their lines. Helen of Troy was merely a blonde wig, a mask, and a bit of cloth, which Faustus caressed and took to bed. The effect was to diminish Faustus. After all, what sort of a man would be delighted with these toys? Reviews tended to be unfavorable, with much severe talk about the director who dared to cut the text and to impose his views on what was left of it, but, as we have seen, no one really knows what Marlowe's original text was like.

For further discussion of these and of other productions, see Michael Hattaway, *Elizabethan Popular Theatre* (1982, chiefly on the earliest productions), and William Tydeman, *Doctor Faustus: Text and Performance* (1984, on productions in the later twentieth century).

Gareth Lloyd Evans
THE ROYAL SHAKESPEARE COMPANY PRODUCTION OF *DOCTOR FAUSTUS*

Gareth Lloyd Evans, a distinguished specialist in Eliza-bethan drama, here reviews a 1968 production at Stratford-upon-Avon.

Stratford made its most explicit committal to the era of per-missiveness when it announced that Helen in *Doctor Faustus* was to appear naked. The result of this decision and of the attention it incited was a mere confirmation that she did, in fact, appear naked—and that is all. It is a respectable and traditional view that a sweet disorder in dress kindles wantonness, and that total exposure has an anesthetic effect. Helen's appearance proved this. At one stroke the expectations of the lascivious were dampened and the wan-ton and desperate passion of Faustus's speech to Helen reduced to superfluous triviality. The best answer to any theory the director may have had that a naked Helen was essential to his interpretation is the fact that the understudy appeared fully clothed and Eric Porter's speech gained immensely in evocative power.

This production is, indeed, noteworthy for other quali-ties. Visually it was the most inventive of the whole season, and often successfully. The claustrophobic and dark recesses of Faustus's study were exactly and economically achieved—the designer had resisted the usual temptation of depicting

'Elizabethanism' by a vast clutter of dusty books, skulls, astrolabes and olde mappes. Hell enclosed about Faustus in a sensational explosion of colour, noise and shape—a medieval conception boosted by twentieth-century techni-cal aids. The Seven Deadly Sins, out of Bosch by Gerald Scarfe, cavorted and shrieked. They were startlingly ugly and malformed and had a great theatrical impact. At the same time they raised the question, 'Would Faustus or any-one be tempted by such grotesque ugliness?' In a way Faustus is a demonstration of Wilde's dictum that the only way to resist temptation is to yield to it. These Sins made a mock-ery of any urge to yield. Perhaps the director had concluded that their appearance is calculated less to allure Faustus than to convince him of Lucifer's theatrical inventiveness; if this is so, it begs many questions about the relationship of Faus-tus to the Devil and, more pertinently, of the meaning of the bond.

Eric Porter, in the name part, created, with thoughtful precision, the various stages of Faustus's spiritual and physi-cal journey—the curiosity, the doubt, the urge for more and yet more sensation, the regret, the terror. Technically and intellectually, his reading of the text was excellent. What was lacking (and this where it was most needed—in the final monologue) was passion. At any point in this performance one could sense a strong intellectual engagement with the character, but missed the sense of a heart and soul moving in parallel with the mind's experience. The pathos of this play comes from our observation of a man wasting great gifts and entering into a trap. It was Terrence Hardiman's Mephistopheles, rather than Faustus, who induced the pity of it in a performance characterized by quiet grief, mor-

dant humour, and resigned dignity. His performance was the more touching since the overall interpretation stressed wryness and grim humour—this was increased by the brilliantly controlled and realized comic scenes. These did not attempt comic relief (for which Marlowe's text is not conspicuously well equipped) but underlined the dangerous absurdity of playing with the devil's fire.

Staging Shakespeare Today

Although many details remain unclear, we have a pretty good idea of how Shakespeare's plays were originally staged. We know that although there were properties (chairs, tables, torches, and so on) there was no bulky scenery. This is not to say, however, that the stage seemed barren. The architecture of the playing area itself was attractive, and costumes and banners would add color. We know, too, that the action could take place on several levels, and we know that the actors—all were male, boys taking the female parts—for the most part wore Elizabethan clothing. If they were performing a play set in ancient times, the chief actors wore something that passed for a toga, but much of the clothing nevertheless was Elizabethan.

Contemporary clothing continued to be used in the seventeenth century and well into the eighteenth: In the late eighteenth century David Garrick played King Lear in black satin knee-breeches and a velvet coat—this in a play set in pre-Christian Britain. At the very end of the eighteenth century however, and through much of the nineteenth, the emphasis shifted to historical accuracy, both in costumes and in stage sets. (A problem, of course, is this: What *is* the dress and architecture of the period of *King Lear?* Or, for that matter, what is the architecture in the Athens of *A Midsummer Night's Dream,* and what is the bower of a fairy queen?)

The early twentieth century saw a reaction to realism and efforts at historical accuracy. One form of the reaction was to stage the plays in what was thought to be the Elizabethan manner, on a relatively bare stage, and in Elizabethan costume. (We have already briefly discussed Elizabethan revivalism in our comments on William Poel's productions of *Everyman* [page 183] and *Doctor Faustus* [page 220].) But soon this antiquarianism seemed inadequate, and directors turned toward more imaginative kinds of staging—sometimes using symbolic decor, and sometimes using modern dress. But these solutions introduce problems of their own, as we shall see in a moment.

◀ Henry Irving's London production (1892) of *King Lear,* showing Lear's explosion in the first scene of the play. The costumes and the elaborate set were thought to present accurate representations of life in ancient Britain. The use of such sets, which of course could not quickly be dismantled and then set up again for a later scene, meant that some scenes were deleted, and that the surviving scenes might be rearranged; scenes with the same set, though separated in the original play, were run together in order to avoid time-consuming shifts of scenery. A further disadvantage of a highly realistic (i.e., illusionistic) set, offered in the name of historical accuracy, is that its very detail may obscure what we may call the universal qualities of the play.

The Oregon Shakespeare Festival Theater, in Ashland, Oregon, opened in 1935. Scholarly efforts to stage plays in the Elizabethan manner inevitably produced some new theaters that were based at least in part on Elizabethan theaters. The Oregon theater more or less imitates the façade and the thrust stage of what we think an Elizabethan theater was like. Doors right and left, pillars, windows, and a musicians' gallery on the third level all can be justified on the basis of Elizabethan evidence, but the "inner stage" and the "upper stage" are less certain. The building itself is the chief element in the set of any play staged here; obviously one would not use the sort of set that Henry Irving used (see above). Equally obviously, this stage is better suited to performances in which the performers wear Elizabethan costume than to performances in modern dress. ▶

◀ Whereas some directors such as Henry Irving (top of page) aimed at evoking a specific historical period, others have sought to avoid the particular, arguing that the plays finally are not about specific periods but are about archetypal issues. In 1955 George Devine directed John Gielgud in *King Lear,* with sets and costumes by the Japanese-American artist, Isamu Noguchi. Devine and Noguchi said that their aim was "to find a setting and costumes which would be free of historical or decorative associations, so that the timeless, universal and mythical quality of the story may be clear." The set consisted of blocks of contrasting colors and shapes, which on occasion seemed to move under their own power. There were also symbolic forms: Thus, an arch represented Lear's world, and a black shape stood for doom. Many viewers found that the sets and costumes evoked the world of science fiction, not the world of tragedy.

Antiquarian productions—whether the antiquarianism took the form of accuracy in representing the costumes and architecture of the period of the play or, on the other hand, accuracy in capturing Elizabethan methods of staging—did not long survive in the twentieth century. Inevitably some directors wished to use new kinds of symbolism, and wished to respond to new conceptions of drama. In 1962 Peter Brook staged *King Lear* at Stratford-upon-Avon, in a production much influenced by the plays of Samuel Beckett. "*Lear* for me," Brook said, "is the prime example of the Theatre of the Absurd, from which everything in good modern drama has been drawn." Brook's set was relatively bare—not in an attempt to imitate Elizabethan staging but rather as a metaphor for the emptiness of life. For the storm scenes Brook lowered from the flies three rusty thunder sheets. He explained why he chose to make the thunder visible as well as audible: "The vibrations of a large sheet of rusty metal have, as anybody knows who has watched a stage manager shaking a thunder sheet, a curiously disturbing quality. The noise is, of course, disturbing but so also is the fact that you see it vibrating. The thunder sheets on view in this production of *Lear,* then, give the King a firm source of conflict without at the same time attempting to stage the storm realistically, which never really works" (*The Shifting Point* [1987], pp. 90–91). And of course the rusty sheets are also a visible sign of a decaying world. In Brook's film version (1969) he retained his overall interpretation—he used a film stock that was grainy and that sometimes showed washed-out images—but the film nevertheless has a more sensuous appeal than the stage production had.

◄ Modern productions often use modern dress, or something approaching modern dress. In this 1990 production by the American Repertory Theater, directed by Adrian Hall, the dress seems to be something like that of Russia, about 1900. Perhaps the idea behind using modern but not contemporary dress is that such costumes help to prevent the play from being a museum piece and they also provide some element of the strange. Thus, the play is supposed to become more real to the audience (presumably this means that the audience can more fully experience the play, can get more out of it) if the action is set in a real (easily identifiable) period. In practice, however, spectators often are distracted by the novelty of the costumes and occasionally by the incongruity between the action (say, a duel) and the later setting (say, the 1920s).

◄ In 1990 Mabou Mines staged a play called *Lear* (not *King Lear*), in which the sex of most of the roles was switched, and the scene and time were shifted to Georgia in the 1950s. Lear was a queen, not a king, and she had three sons, not daughters. Here we see (from left to right) Edna (equivalent to Shakespeare's Edgar in the role of Mad Tom), Lear, and the Fool (the Fool was played by a man in drag). For some additional details about this production, see page 319. Persons who commented favorably on the Mabou Mines version talked about the ways in which it forced them to see the play afresh, and forced them to think about the role of gender in society.

Sir Herbert Beerbohm Tree's production (1900) of *A Midsummer Night's Dream* is close in time to Henry Irving's production of *King Lear* (page 224), and like Irving's production it used elaborate sets, seeking to evoke a forest that looked as real as possible. Such sets could be impressive in themselves, but in order to eliminate intervals during which sets were erected, taken down, and again erected, directors rearranged the sequence of scenes, or simply deleted some scenes. ▶

◀ Harley Granville Barker's production (1914) of *A Midsummer Night's Dream* marked a striking departure from the traditional staging. For the palace of Theseus, in Athens, Granville Barker used a relatively realistic, solidly built structure in black and silver, but for the forest he used stylized scenery. In the center of the stage was a green velvet mound—clearly artificial and therefore quite different from the grasslike textures and real plants commonly used in Victorian productions (e.g.,Beerbohm Tree's)—and at the rear was a spangled backcloth, green at the bottom and bluish-purple toward the top. Trees were suggested by bands of green, blue, and violet hanging cloth. Suspended above the green velvet mound was a wreath of flowers, ten feet in diameter, from which hung a gauze curtain that constituted Titania's bower. In order to further emphasize the contrast between the two worlds—the world of the mortals (represented by Theseus's palace) and the world of the fairies (represented by Titania's bower)—Granville Barker dressed the fairies in bronze-colored tights and he gilded their faces and hands. Further, instead of moving with the childlike skipping steps of the cute fairies of Victorian productions, his fairies moved in a jerky fashion—causing some uneasiness even among his admirers. On the whole, Granville Barker was the chief force in moving early twentieth-century Shakespearean production away from realism and toward stylization.

Peter Brook's production (1970) at Stratford-upon-Avon was for the second half of the twentieth century what Granville Barker's production (page 226) was for the first half. Brook has said that after failing to find a symbol for the fairy world, he "turned to the arts of the circus, the tumblers, the acrobats, the jugglers and the slapstick comedy of the clowns. I wanted to make it a joyful production and I felt a display of sheer physical virtuosity would achieve this." The setting consisted of simple white flats surrounded by a catwalk, with trapezes. In one scene Oberon and Puck were on trapezes, and the magic flower that Oberon gave to Puck was a disk spinning on a wand, passed from Oberon's wand to Puck's. The fairies—chiefly males wearing pajamalike garb or track suits—sometimes seemed to be doing gymnastics, and at other times acted as stagehands or circus roustabouts, for instance sweeping up confetti. (For additional comments about this production, see page 262.) ▶

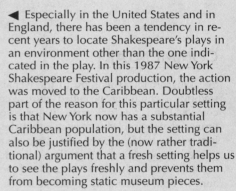

◀ Especially in the United States and in England, there has been a tendency in recent years to locate Shakespeare's plays in an environment other than the one indicated in the play. In this 1987 New York Shakespeare Festival production, the action was moved to the Caribbean. Doubtless part of the reason for this particular setting is that New York now has a substantial Caribbean population, but the setting can also be justified by the (now rather traditional) argument that a fresh setting helps us to see the plays freshly and prevents them from becoming static museum pieces.

◀ In 1991 the Asian/Experimental Theater Program—a group that uses Asian methods of physical training—produced *A Midsummer Night's Dream* in Madison, Wisconsin. The theater was renovated to resemble a bar; spectators entered through the lighted proscenium and then sat at café tables around a raised dance floor. The performers wore modern clothing (an Armani suit for Theseus, a purple lycra mini-dress for Hippolyta), and there was much interaction with the audience, especially by Puck, a black male who often moved from the stage to the tables. There were also implications of homoeroticism: Egeus had a special fondness for Demetrius, and Helena and Hermia seemed more than good friends. In further connecting the play with today's chief concerns, a touch of racism was introduced; Lysander was played by a Nigerian actor, and it seemed that Egeus's dislike for him was at least partly attributable to Lysander's color. The wood was a gay disco, and the fairies were two visions of homosexuals—"radical fairies" (drag queens) aligned with Oberon (played by a mustached woman in a suit), and ACT-UP activists (in jeans and T-shirts), aligned with Titania (a man in high-heeled shoes and a leather mini-skirt). In the scene in which Helena invites Demetrius to beat her, the fairies took over her role and Demetrius's, wearing masks to indicate the switch. The overall implication was that the play revealed not only the irrational love found in the real world but also other irrationalities, such as the construction of gender and the oppression of women.

227

William Shakespeare

A Midsummer Night's Dream

William Shakespeare (1564–1616) was born in Stratford, England, of middle-class parents. Nothing of interest is known about his early years, but by 1590 he was acting and writing plays in London. He worked early in all three Elizabethan dramatic genres—tragedy, comedy, and history. *Romeo and Juliet,* for example, was written about 1595, the year of *Richard II,* and in the following year he wrote *A Midsummer Night's Dream*. Other major comedies are *The Merchant of Venice* (1596–97), *As You Like It* (1599–1600), and *Twelfth Night* (1599–1600). His last major works, *The Winter's Tale* (1610–11) and *The Tempest* (1611), are usually called "romances"; these plays have happy endings but they seem more meditative and less joyful than the earlier comedies.

COMMENTARY

Speaking broadly, there are in the Renaissance two comic traditions, which may be called "critical comedy" (or "bitter comedy") and "romantic comedy" (or "sweet comedy"). The former claims, in Hamlet's words, that the "purpose of playing . . . is to hold, as 'twere, the mirror up to nature; to show virtue her own feature, scorn her own image, and the very age and body of the time his form and pressure." Because it aims to hold a mirror up to the audience, its dramatis personae are usually urban citizens—jealous husbands, foolish merchants, and the like. These are ultimately punished, at times merely by exposure, at times by imprisonment or fines or some such thing. The second kind of comedy, romantic comedy, seeks less to correct than to delight with scenes of pleasant behavior. It does not hold a mirror to the audience: Rather, it leads the audience into an elegant dream world where charming gentlefolk live in a timeless world. Thomas Heywood, a playwright contemporary with Shakespeare, briefly set forth the characteristics of both traditions in *An Apology for Actors* (1612). A comedy, he said,

is pleasantly contrived with merry accidents, and intermixed with apt and witty jests. . . . and what then is the subject of this harmless mirth? Either in the shape of a clown to show others their slovenly behavior, that they may reform that simplicity in themselves, which others make their sport, . . . or to refresh such weary spirits as are tired with labors or study, to moderate the cares and heaviness of the mind, that they may return to their trades and faculties with more zeal and earnestness, after some small soft and pleasant retirement.

When we think of *A Midsummer Night's Dream*, we think not of critical comedy that seeks to reform "slovenly behavior" but of romantic comedy that offers "harmless mirth," "sport," and the refreshing of "such weary spirits as are tired with labors or study." Yet even *A Midsummer Night's Dream* has its touches of critical comedy, its elements that, in Heywood's words, "may reform" by holding up a mirror to unsocial behavior. There is some satire—a little satire of the crabby father, Egeus, and rather more of the young lovers and of the well-meaning rustics who bumblingly stage a play in an effort to please their duke (and to win pensions), but mostly the play is pervaded by genial spirits and a humane vision that make it moral without moralizing. The first book on Shakespeare's morality, Elizabeth Griffith's *The Morality of Shakespeare's Dramas* (1775), rather impatiently dismissed *A Midsummer Night's Dream*: "I shall not trouble my readers with the Fable of this piece, as I can see no general moral that can be deducted from the Argument."

For one thing, all of the people—including the fairies—in *A Midsummer Night's Dream* are basically decent creatures. Egeus is at first irascible, but at the end of the play we hear no more of his insistence that his daughter marry the young man of his choice; Theseus had engaged in youthful indiscretions, but that was long ago and in another country, and now he is the very model of a benevolent ruler; the fairy king and queen bicker, but at the end they are reconciled and they bless the bridal beds of the newlyweds. The rustics, though inept actors and sometimes too impressed by their own theatrical abilities, are men of good intentions. And if in the last act the young aristocratic lovers are a little too confident of their superiority to the rustic actors, we nevertheless feel that they are fundamentally decent; after all, their comments on the performance are more or less in tune with our own.

If *A Midsummer Night's Dream*, then, employs satire only sparingly, what does it do, and what is it about? Perhaps we can get somewhere near to an answer by briefly looking at some of the interrelationships of the stories that make up the intricate plot. There is the story of Theseus and Hippolyta, who will be married in four days; the story of the four young lovers; the story of Bottom and his fellow craftsmen, who are rehearsing a play; and the story of the quarreling fairies. All these stories are related, and eventually come together: the lovers marry on the same day as Theseus and Hippolyta; the craftsmen perform their play at the wedding; the fairies come to witness the wedding and bless it.

One of the play's themes, of course, is love, as shown in the contrasts between the stately love of Theseus and Hippolyta, the changeable romantic love of the four young Athenians, the love of Pyramus and Thisby in the play that the craftsmen are rehearsing, the quarrel between the fairy king and queen, and even Titania's infatuation with Bottom. All these stories play against one another, sometimes very subtly, and sometimes explicitly, as when Lysander, having shifted his affection from Hermia to Helena, says, "Reason says you are the worthier maid" (2.2.122), and Bottom in the next scene accepts Titania's love, saying, "Reason and love keep little company together nowadays" (3.1.143–44). The nature of reason is also implicitly discussed in the play, in the numerous references to "fantasy" and "fancy," or imagination. There is scarcely a scene that does not touch on the matter of the power of the imagination. In the opening scene, for example, Egeus says that Lysander has corrupted Hermia's fantasy (1.1.32), and Duke Theseus tells Hermia that she must perceive her suitors as her father perceives them. The most famous of these references is Theseus's speech on "the lunatic, the lover, and the poet" (5.1.7). In addition to setting the time and place, the images help to define the nature of fantasy: There is an emphasis on night and moonlight during the period of confusion, and then references to the "morning lark," "day," and so on, when Theseus (the spokesman for reason) enters the woods and the lovers are properly paired (4.1.102 ff.). The last scene reintroduces night, and the lovers have moved from the dark wood back to the civilized world of Athens, and the night will bring them to bed. The plot of *A Midsummer Night's Dream*, then, juxtaposes speech against speech, image against image, and scene against scene, telling not simply a story but a story that "grows to something of great constancy, . . . strange and admirable."[1]

---

[1]The last two paragraphs of commentary are from *The Complete Signet Classic Shakespeare*, edited by Sylvan Barnet. Copyright © 1972 by Harcourt Brace Jovanovich. Reprinted by permission.

Shakespeare's A Midsummer Night's Dream *is a common offering in outdoor summer dramatic festivals. Among the most successful versions was this elegant modern-dress production at the Colorado Shakespeare Festival in 1988, directed by Robert Cohen, with scenery by Douglas-Scott Goheen. The circular stage and a large white marble disk (with a door in it) kept the moon themes in view. For the forest, the disk slid to stage right, revealing an opening in which hung ropes suggestive of vines and foliage.*

William Shakespeare

A MIDSUMMER NIGHT'S DREAM*

Edited by David Bevington

[Dramatis Personae

THESEUS, *Duke of Athens*
HIPPOLYTA, *Queen of the Amazons, betrothed to Theseus*
PHILOSTRATE, *Master of the Revelsy*
EGEUS, *father of Hermia*

HERMIA, *daughter of Egeus, in love with Lysander*
LYSANDER, *in love with Hermia*
DEMETRIUS, *in love with Hermia and favored by Egeus*
HELENA, *in love with Demetrius*

OBERON, *King of the Fairies*
TITANIA, *Queen of the Fairies*
PUCK, *or* ROBIN GOODFELLOW
PEASEBLOSSOM,
COBWEB,
MOTE, } *fairies attending Titania*
MUSTARDSEED,
Other FAIRIES *attending*

PETER QUINCE, *a carpenter,*   PROLOGUE
NICK BOTTOM, *a weaver,*   PYRAMUS
FRANCIS FLUTE, *a bellows mender,*   THISBE
TOM SNOUT, *a tinker,* } *representing*   WALL
SNUG, *a joiner,*   LION
ROBIN STARVELING, *a tailor,*   MOONSHINE
Lords and Attendants on Theseus and Hippolyta

SCENE: *Athens, and a wood near it*]

[1.1] *Enter Theseus, Hippolyta, [and Philostrate,] with others.*

THESEUS.
Now, fair Hippolyta, our nuptial hour
Draws on apace. Four happy days bring in
Another moon; but, O, methinks, how slow
This old moon wanes! She lingers° my desires,
Like to a stepdame° or a dowager°   5
Long withering out° a young man's revenue.
HIPPOLYTA.
Four days will quickly steep themselves in night,
Four nights will quickly dream away the time;
And then the moon, like to a silver bow
New bent in heaven, shall behold the night   10
Of our solemnities.
THESEUS.   Go, Philostrate,
Stir up the Athenian youth to merriments,
Awake the pert and nimble spirit of mirth,
Turn melancholy forth to funerals;
The pale companion° is not for our pomp.°   15
                              [Exit Philostrate.]
Hippolyta, I wooed thee with my sword°
And won thy love doing thee injuries;
But I will wed thee in another key,
With pomp, with triumph,° and with reveling.

Enter Egeus and his daughter Hermia, and Lysander, and Demetrius.

EGEUS.
Happy be Theseus, our renowned duke!   20
THESEUS.
Thanks, good Egeus. What's the news with thee?
EGEUS.
Full of vexation come I, with complaint
Against my child, my daughter Hermia.
Stand forth, Demetrius. My noble lord,
This man hath my consent to marry her.   25
Stand forth, Lysander. And, my gracious Duke,

A Midsummer Night's Dream was first published in 1600 in a small book of a type called a quarto. A second quarto edition, printed in 1616 but based on the 1600 text, introduces a few corrections, but it also introduces many errors. The 1619 text in turn was the basis for the text in the first collected edition of Shakespeare's plays, the First Folio (1623). Bevington's edition is of course based on the text of 1600, but it includes a few corrections, and it modifies the punctuation in accordance with modern usage. Material added by the editor, such as amplifications in the *dramatis personae*, is enclosed within square brackets [ ].

1.1 Location: Athens, Theseus' court **4 lingers** postpones, delays the fulfillment of **5 stepdame** stepmother. **dowager** i.e., a widow (whose right of inheritance from her dead husband is eating into her son's estate) **6 withering out** causing to dwindle **15 companion** fellow. **pomp** ceremonial magnificence **16 with my sword** i.e., in a military engagement against the Amazons, when Hippolyta was taken captive **19 triumph** public festivity

This man hath bewitched the bosom of my child.
Thou, thou, Lysander, thou hast given her rhymes
And interchanged love tokens with my child.
30　Thou hast by moonlight at her window sung
With feigning voice verses of feigning° love,
And stol'n the impression of her fantasy°
With bracelets of thy hair, rings, gauds,° conceits,°
Knacks,° trifles, nosegays, sweetmeats—messengers
35　Of strong prevailment in° unhardened youth.
With cunning hast thou filched my daughter's heart,
Turned her obedience, which is due to me,
To stubborn harshness. And, my gracious Duke,
Be it so° she will not here before Your Grace
40　Consent to marry with Demetrius,
I beg the ancient privilege of Athens:
As she is mine, I may dispose of her,
Which shall be either to this gentleman
Or to her death, according to our law
45　Immediately° provided in that case.
THESEUS.
What say you, Hermia? Be advised, fair maid.
To you your father should be as a god—
One that composed your beauties, yea, and one
To whom you are but as a form in wax
50　By him imprinted, and within his power
To leave° the figure or disfigure° it.
Demetrius is a worthy gentleman.
HERMIA.
So is Lysander.
THESEUS.　　　　In himself he is;
But in this kind,° wanting° your father's voice,°
55　The other must be held the worthier.
HERMIA.
I would my father looked but with my eyes.
THESEUS.
Rather your eyes must with his judgment look.
HERMIA.
I do entreat Your Grace to pardon me.
I know not by what power I am made bold,
60　Nor how it may concern° my modesty
In such a presence here to plead my thoughts;
But I beseech Your Grace that I may know
The worst that may befall me in this case
If I refuse to wed Demetrius.
THESEUS.
65　Either to die the death or to abjure

Forever the society of men.
Therefore, fair Hermia, question your desires,
Know of your youth, examine well your blood,°
Whether, if you yield not to your father's choice,
You can endure the livery° of a nun,　　　　　70
For aye° to be in shady cloister mewed,°
To live a barren sister all your life,
Chanting faint hymns to the cold fruitless moon.
Thrice blessèd they that master so their blood
To undergo such maiden pilgrimage;　　　　　75
But earthlier happy° is the rose distilled
Than that which, withering on the virgin thorn,
Grows, lives, and dies in single blessedness.
HERMIA.
So will I grow, so live, so die, my lord,
Ere I will yield my virgin patent° up　　　　　80
Unto his lordship, whose unwishèd yoke
My soul consents not to give sovereignty.
THESEUS.
Take time to pause, and by the next new moon—
The sealing day betwixt my love and me
For everlasting bond of fellowship—　　　　　85
Upon that day either prepare to die
For disobedience to your father's will,
Or° else to wed Demetrius, as he would,
Or on Diana's altar to protest°
For aye austerity and single life.　　　　　90
DEMETRIUS.
Relent, sweet Hermia, and, Lysander, yield
Thy crazèd° title to my certain right.
LYSANDER.
You have her father's love, Demetrius;
Let me have Hermia's. Do you marry him.
EGEUS.
Scornful Lysander! True, he hath my love,　　　95
And what is mine my love shall render him.
And she is mine, and all my right of her
I do estate unto° Demetrius.
LYSANDER.
I am, my lord, as well derived° as he,
As well possessed;° my love is more than his;　　100
My fortunes every way as fairly° ranked,
If not with vantage,° as Demetrius';
And, which is more than all these boasts can be,
I am beloved of beauteous Hermia.
Why should not I then prosecute my right?　　105
Demetrius, I'll avouch it to his head,°

---

31 **feigning** (1) counterfeiting (2) faining, desirous　**32 And . . .
fantasy** and made her fall in love with you (imprinting your image
on her imagination) by stealthy and dishonest means　**33 gauds**
playthings. **conceits** fanciful trifles　**34 Knacks** knickknacks
35 prevailment in influence on　**39 Be it so** if　**45 Immediately**
directly, with nothing intervening　**51 leave** i.e., leave unaltered.
disfigure obliterate　**54 kind** respect. **wanting** lacking. **voice**
approval　**60 concern** befit

68 blood passions　**70 livery** habit　**71 aye** ever. **mewed** shut
in. (Said of a hawk, poultry, etc.)　**76 earthlier happy** happier as
respects this world　**80 patent** privilege　**88 Or** either
89 protest vow　**92 crazèd** cracked, unsound　**98 estate unto** settle or bestow upon　**99 derived** descended, i.e., as well born
100 possessed endowed with wealth　**101 fairly** handsomely
102 vantage superiority　**106 head** i.e., face

Made love to Nedar's daughter, Helena
And won her soul; and she, sweet lady, dotes,
Devoutly dotes, dotes in idolatry,
110   Upon this spotted° and inconstant man.
THESEUS.
I must confess that I have heard so much,
And with Demetrius thought to have spoke thereof;
But, being overfull of self-affairs,°
My mind did lose it. But, Demetrius, come,
115   And come, Egeus, you shall go with me;
I have some private schooling° for you both.
For you, fair Hermia, look you arm° yourself
To fit your fancies° to your father's will;
Or else the law of Athens yields you up—
120   Which by no means we may extenuate°—
To death or to a vow of single life.
Come, my Hippolyta. What cheer, my love?
Demetrius and Egeus, go° along.
I must employ you in some business
125   Against° our nuptial and confer with you
Of something nearly that° concerns yourselves.
EGEUS.
With duty and desire we follow you.

       Exeunt [all but Lysander and Hermia].
LYSANDER.
How now, my love, why is your cheek so pale?
How chance the roses there do fade so fast?
HERMIA.
130   Belike° for want of rain, which I could well
Beteem° them from the tempest of my eyes.
LYSANDER.
Ay me! For aught that I could ever read,
Could ever hear by tale or history,
The course of true love never did run smooth
135   But either it was different in blood°—
HERMIA.
O cross!° Too high to be enthralled to low.
LYSANDER.
Or else misgrafted° in respect of years—
HERMIA.
O spite! Too old to be engaged to young.
LYSANDER.
Or else it stood upon the choice of friends°—
HERMIA.
140   O hell, to choose love by another's eyes!

LYSANDER.
Or if there were a sympathy° in choice,
War, death, or sickness did lay siege to it,
Making it momentany° as a sound,
Swift as a shadow, short as any dream,
Brief as the lightning in the collied° night,   145
That in a spleen° unfolds° both heaven and earth,
And ere a man hath power to say "Behold!"
The jaws of darkness do devour it up.
So quick° bright things come to confusion.°
HERMIA.
If then true lovers have been ever crossed,°   150
It stands as an edict in destiny.
Then let us teach our trial patience,°
Because it is a customary cross,
As due to love as thoughts and dreams and sighs,
Wishes and tears, poor fancy's° followers.   155
LYSANDER.
A good persuasion.° Therefore, hear me, Hermia:
I have a widow aunt, a dowager
Of great revenue, and she hath no child.
From Athens is her house remote seven leagues;
And she respects° me as her only son.   160
There, gentle Hermia, may I marry thee,
And to that place the sharp Athenian law
Cannot pursue us. If thou lovest me, then,
Steal forth thy father's house tomorrow night;
And in the wood, a league without the town,   165
Where I did meet thee once with Helena
To do observance to a morn of May,°
There will I stay for thee.
HERMIA.   My good Lysander!
I swear to thee by Cupid's strongest bow,
By his best arrow° with the golden head,   170
By the simplicity° of Venus' doves,°
By that which knitteth souls and prospers loves,
And by that fire which burned the Carthage queen°
When the false Trojan° under sail was seen,
By all the vows that ever men have broke,   175
In number more than ever women spoke,

---

110 **spotted** i.e., morally stained   113 **self-affairs** my own concerns   116 **schooling** admonition   117 **look you arm** take care you prepare   118 **fancies** likings, thoughts of love   120 **extenuate** mitigate   123 **go** i.e., come   125 **Against** in preparation for   126 **nearly that** that closely   130 **Belike** very likely   131 **Beteem** grant, afford   135 **blood** hereditary station   136 **cross** vexation   137 **misgrafted** ill grafted, badly matched   139 **friends** relatives

141 **sympathy** agreement   143 **momentany** lasting but a moment   145 **collied** blackened (as with coal dust), darkened   146 **in a spleen** in a swift impulse, in a violent flash. **unfolds** discloses   149 **quick** quickly; or, perhaps, living, alive. **confusion** ruin   150 **ever crossed** always thwarted   152 **teach . . . patience** i.e., teach ourselves patience in this trial   155 **fancy's** amorous passion's   156 **persuasion** conviction   160 **respects** regards   167 **do . . . May** perform the ceremonies of May Day   170 **best arrow** (Cupid's best gold-pointed arrows were supposed to induce love; his blunt leaden arrows, aversion.)   171 **simplicity** innocence. **doves** i.e., those that drew Venus' chariot   173, 174 **Carthage queen, false Trojan** (Dido, Queen of Carthage, immolated herself on a funeral pyre after having been deserted by the Trojan hero Aeneas.)

In that same place thou hast appointed me
Tomorrow truly will I meet with thee.

LYSANDER.
Keep promise, love. Look, here comes Helena.

Enter Helena.

HERMIA.
180   God speed, fair° Helena! Whither away?

HELENA.
Call you me fair? That "fair" again unsay.
Demetrius loves your fair.° O happy fair!°
Your eyes are lodestars,° and your tongue's sweet air°
More tunable° than lark to shepherd's ear
185   When wheat is green, when hawthorn buds appear.
Sickness is catching. O, were favor° so!
Yours would I catch, fair Hermia, ere I go;
My ear should catch your voice, my eye your eye,
My tongue should catch your tongue's sweet melody.
190   Were the world mine, Demetrius being bated,°
The rest I'd give to be to you translated.°
O, teach me how you look and with what art
You sway the motion° of Demetrius' heart.

HERMIA.
I frown upon him, yet he loves me still.

HELENA.
195   O, that your frowns would teach my smiles such skill!

HERMIA.
I give him curses, yet he gives me love.

HELENA.
O, that my prayers could such affection° move!°

HERMIA.
The more I hate, the more he follows me.

HELENA.
The more I love, the more he hateth me.

HERMIA.
200   His folly, Helena, is no fault of mine.

HELENA.
None but your beauty. Would that fault were mine!

HERMIA.
Take comfort. He no more shall see my face.
Lysander and myself will fly this place.
Before the time I did Lysander see
205   Seemed Athens as a paradise to me.
O, then, what graces in my love do dwell
That he hath turned a heaven unto a hell!

LYSANDER.
Helen, to you our minds we will unfold.

Tomorrow night, when Phoebe° doth behold
Her silver visage in the watery glass,°   210
Decking with liquid pearl the bladed grass,
A time that lovers' flights doth still° conceal,
Through Athens' gates have we devised to steal.

HERMIA.
And in the wood, where often you and I
Upon faint° primrose beds were wont to lie,   215
Emptying our bosoms of their counsel° sweet,
There my Lysander and myself shall meet;
And thence from Athens turn away our eyes,
To seek new friends and stranger companies.
Farewell, sweet playfellow. Pray thou for us,   220
And good luck grant thee thy Demetrius!
Keep word, Lysander. We must starve our sight
From lovers' food till morrow deep midnight.

LYSANDER.
I will, my Hermia. *Exit Hermia.*
                    Helena, adieu.
As you on him, Demetrius dote on you!   *Exit Lysander.*   225

HELENA.
How happy some o'er other some can be!°
Through Athens I am thought as fair as she.
But what of that? Demetrius thinks not so;
He will not know what all but he do know.
And as he errs, doting on Hermia's eyes,   230
So I, admiring of° his qualities.
Things base and vile, holding no quantity,°
Love can transpose to form and dignity.
Love looks not with the eyes, but with the mind,
And therefore is winged Cupid painted blind.   235
Nor hath Love's mind of any judgment taste;°
Wings, and no eyes, figure° unheedy haste.
And therefore is Love said to be a child,
Because in choice he is so oft beguiled.
As waggish° boys in game° themselves forswear,   240
So the boy Love is perjured everywhere.
For ere Demetrius looked on Hermia's eyne,°
He hailed down oaths that he was only mine;
And when this hail some heat from Hermia felt,
So he dissolved, and showers of oaths did melt.   245
I will go tell him of fair Hermia's flight.
Then to the wood will he tomorrow night
Pursue her; and for this intelligence°
If I have thanks, it is a dear expense.°

---

180 **fair** fair-complexioned (generally regarded by the Elizabethans as more beautiful than dark complexioned) 182 **your fair** your beauty (even though Hermia is dark-complexioned). **happy fair** lucky fair one 183 **lodestars** guiding stars. **air** music 184 **tunable** tuneful, melodious 186 **favor** appearance, looks 190 **bated** excepted 191 **translated** transformed 193 **motion** impulse 197 **affection** passion. **move** arouse

209 **Phoebe** Diana, the moon 210 **glass** mirror 212 **still** always 215 **faint** pale 216 **counsel** secret thought 226 **o'er . . . can be** can be in comparison to some others 231 **admiring of** wondering at 232 **holding no quantity** i.e., unsubstantial, unshapely 236 **Nor . . . taste** i.e., nor has Love, which dwells in the fancy or imagination, any *taste* or least bit of judgment or reason 237 **figure** are a symbol of 240 **waggish** playful, mischievous. **game** sport, jest 242 **eyne** eyes. (Old form of plural.) 248 **intelligence** information 249 **a dear expense** i.e., a trouble worth taking (**dear** costly)

250   But herein mean I to enrich my pain,
       To have his sight thither and back again.

                                                        Exit.

       [1.2] *Enter Quince the carpenter, and Snug the joiner,*
       and Bottom the weaver, and Flute the bellows mender,
       and Snout the tinker, and Starveling the tailor.

       QUINCE. Is all our company here?
       BOTTOM. You were best to call them generally,° man by
          man, according to the scrip.°
5   QUINCE. Here is the scroll of every man's name which is
          thought fit, through all Athens, to play in our interlude
          before the Duke and the Duchess on his wedding day at
          night.
       BOTTOM. First, good Peter Quince, say what the play treats
10   on, then read the names of the actors, and so grow to° a
          point.
       QUINCE. Marry,° our play is "The most lamentable comedy
          and most cruel death of Pyramus and Thisbe."
       BOTTOM. A very good piece of work, I assure you, and a
15   merry. Now, good Peter Quince, call forth your actors by
          the scroll. Masters, spread yourselves.
       QUINCE. Answer as I call you. Nick Bottom,° the weaver.
       BOTTOM. Ready. Name what part I am for, and proceed.
       QUINCE. You, Nick Bottom, are set down for Pyramus.
       BOTTOM. What is Pyramus? A lover or a tyrant?
20   QUINCE. A lover, that kills himself most gallant for love.
       BOTTOM. That will ask some tears in the true performing of
          it. If I do it, let the audience look to their eyes. I will
          move storms; I will condole° in some measure. To the
          rest—yet my chief humor° is for a tyrant. I could play
25   Ercles° rarely, or a part to tear a cat° in, to make all split.°

              "The raging rocks
              And shivering shocks
              Shall break the locks
                 Of prison gates:
              And Phibbus' car°
30   Shall shine from far
              And make and mar
                 The foolish Fates."

       This was lofty! Now name the rest of the players. This is
       Ercles' vein, a tyrant's vein. A lover is more condoling.

       QUINCE. Francis Flute, the bellows mender.
       FLUTE. Here, Peter Quince.   35
       QUINCE. Flute, you must take Thisbe on you.
       FLUTE. What is Thisbe? A wandering knight?
       QUINCE. It is the lady that Pyramus must love.
       FLUTE. Nay, faith, let not me play a woman. I have a beard
          coming.   40
       QUINCE. That's all one.° You shall play it in a mask, and you
          may speak as small° as you will.
       BOTTOM. An° I may hide my face, let me play Thisbe too.
          I'll speak in a monstrous little voice, "Thisne, Thisne!"
          "Ah Pyramus, my lover dear! Thy Thisbe dear, and lady   45
          dear!"
       QUINCE. No, no, you must play Pyramus, and, Flute, you
          Thisbe.
       BOTTOM. Well, proceed.
       QUINCE. Robin Starveling, the tailor.   50
       STARVELING. Here, Peter Quince.
       QUINCE. Robin Starveling, you must play Thisbe's mother.
          Tom Snout, the tinker.
       SNOUT. Here, Peter Quince.
       QUINCE. You, Pyramus' father; myself, Thisbe's father; Snug, 55
          the joiner, you, the lion's part, and I hope here is a play
          fitted.
       SNUG. Have you the lion's part written? Pray you, if it be,
          give it me, for I am slow of study.
       QUINCE. You may do it extempore, for it is nothing but roar- 60
          ing.
       BOTTOM. Let me play the lion too. I will roar that I will do
          any man's heart good to hear me. I will roar that I will
          make the Duke say, "Let him roar again, let him roar
          again."   65
       QUINCE. An you should do it too terribly, you would fright
          the Duchess and the ladies, that they would shriek; and
          that were enough to hang us all.
       ALL. That would hang us, every mother's son.
       BOTTOM. I grant you, friends, if you should fright the ladies 70
          out of their wits, they would have no more discretion but
          to hang us; but I will aggravate° my voice so that I will
          roar you° as gently as any sucking dove;° I will roar you
          an 'twere any nightingale.
       QUINCE. You can play no part but Pyramus; for Pyramus is a 75
          sweet-faced man, a proper° man as one shall see in a sum-
          mer's day, a most lovely gentlemanlike man. Therefore
          you must needs play Pyramus.
       BOTTOM. Well, I will undertake it. What beard were I best
          to play it in?   80
       QUINCE. Why, what you will.

1.2 Location: Athens   2 generally (Bottom's blunder for *individu-*
ally.)   **3 scrip** scrap. (Bottom's error for *script*.)   **9 grow to** come
to   **11 Marry** (A mild oath; originally the name of the Virgin
Mary.)   **16 Bottom** (As a weaver's term, a *bottom* was an object
around which thread was wound.)   **23 condole** lament, arouse pity
24 humor inclination, whim   **25 Ercles** Hercules. (The tradition
of ranting came from Seneca's *Hercules Furens*.)   **tear a cat** i.e.,
rant   **make all split** i.e., cause a stir, bring the house down   **29
Phibbus' car** Phoebus', the sun-god's, chariot

41 That's all one it makes no difference   **42 small** high-pitched
43 An if (also at l. 66)   **72 aggravate** (Bottom's blunder for *moder-*
ate.)   **73 roar you** i.e., roar for you.   **sucking dove** (Bottom con-
flates *sitting dove* and *sucking lamb*, two proverbial images of innocence.)   **76 proper** handsome

BOTTOM. I will discharge° it in either your° straw-color
beard, your orange-tawny beard, your purple-in-grain°
beard, or your French-crown-color° beard, your perfect
85 yellow.

QUINCE. Some of your French crowns° have no hair at all,
and then you will play barefaced. But, masters, here are
your parts. [*He distributes parts.*] And I am to entreat you,
request you, and desire you to con° them by tomorrow
90 night; and meet me in the palace wood, a mile without
the town, by moonlight. There will we rehearse; for if we
meet in the city, we shall be dogged with company, and
our devices° known. In the meantime I will draw a bill°
of properties, such as our play wants. I pray you, fail me
95 not.

BOTTOM. We will meet, and there we may rehearse most
obscenely° and courageously. Take pains, be perfect;°
adieu.

QUINCE. At the Duke's oak we meet.

100 BOTTOM. Enough. Hold, or cut bowstrings.°   *Exeunt.*

[2.1] *Enter a Fairy at one door, and Robin Goodfellow
[Puck] at another.*

PUCK.
  How now, spirit, whither wander you?

FAIRY.
        Over hill, over dale,
          Thorough° bush, thorough brier,
        Over park, over pale,°
5   Thorough flood, thorough fire,
        I do wander everywhere,
        Swifter than the moon's sphere;°
        And I serve the Fairy Queen,
        To dew her orbs° upon the green.
10   The cowslips tall her pensioners° be.
        In their gold coats spots you see:
        Those be rubies, fairy favors;°
        In those freckles live their savors.°

I must go seek some dewdrops here
And hang a pearl in every cowslip's ear.   15
Farewell, thou lob° of spirits: I'll be gone.
Our Queen and all her elves come here anon.°

PUCK.
The King doth keep his revels here tonight.
Take heed the Queen come not within his sight.
For Oberon is passing fell° and wrath,°   20
Because that she as her attendant hath
A lovely boy, stolen from an Indian king;
She never had so sweet a changeling.°
And jealous Oberon would have the child
Knight of his train, to trace° the forests wild.   25
But she perforce° withholds the lovèd boy,
Crowns him with flowers, and makes him all her joy.
And now they never meet in grove or green,
By fountain° clear, or spangled starlight sheen,°
But they do square,° that all their elves for fear   30
Creep into acorn cups and hide them there.

FAIRY.
Either I mistake your shape and making quite,
Or else you are that shrewd° and knavish sprite°
Called Robin Goodfellow. Are not you he
That frights the maidens of the villagery,°   35
Skim milk, and sometimes labor in the quern,°
And bootless° make the breathless huswife° churn,
And sometimes make the drink to bear no barm,°
Mislead night wanderers, laughing at their harm?
Those that "Hobgoblin" call you, and "Sweet Puck,"   40
You do their work, and they shall have good luck.
Are you not he?

PUCK.   Thou speakest aright;
I am that merry wanderer of the night.
I jest to Oberon and make him smile
When I a fat and bean-fed horse beguile,   45
Neighing in likeness of a filly foal;
And sometimes lurk I in a gossip's° bowl,
In very likeness of a roasted crab,°
And when she drinks, against her lips I bob
And on her withered dewlap° pour the ale.   50
The wisest aunt,° telling the saddest° tale,
Sometimes for three-foot stool mistaketh me;
Then slip I from her bum, down topples she,
And "Tailor"° cries, and falls into a cough;

82 discharge perform. **your** i.e., you know the kind I mean
83 purple-in-grain dyed a very deep red. (From *grain*, the name
applied to the dried insect used to make the dye.) **84 French-
crown-color** i.e., color of a French crown, a gold coin **86 crowns**
heads bald from syphilis, the "French disease" **89 con** learn by
heart **93 devices** plans **bill** list **97 obscenely** (An unintentionally funny blunder, whatever Bottom meant to say.) **perfect**
i.e., letter-perfect in memorizing your parts **100 Hold . . . bowstrings** (An archers' expression not definitely explained, but probably meaning here "keep your promises, or give up the play.")
2.1 Location: A wood near Athens 3 Thorough through
4 pale enclosure **7 sphere** orbit **9 orbs** circles, i.e., fairy rings
(circular bands of grass, darker than the surrounding area, caused by
fungi enriching the soil) **10 pensioners** retainers, members of the
royal bodyguard **12 favors** love tokens **13 savors** sweet smells

16 lob country bumpkin **17 anon** at once **20 passing fell**
exceedingly angry. **wrath** wrathful **23 changeling** child
exchanged for another by the fairies **25 trace** range through
26 perforce forcibly **29 fountain** spring. **starlight sheen** shining starlight **30 square** quarrel **33 shrewd** mischievous. **sprite**
spirit **35 villagery** village population **36 quern** handmill
37 bootless in vain. **huswife** housewife **38 barm** yeast, head on
the ale **47 gossip's** old woman's **48 crab** crab apple **50 dewlap**
loose skin on neck **51 aunt** old woman. **saddest** most serious
54 Tailor (possibly because she ends up sitting cross-legged on the
floor, looking like a tailor.)

And then the whole choir° hold their hips and laugh,
And waxen° in their mirth, and neeze,° and swear
A merrier hour was never wasted there.
But, room,° fairy! Here comes Oberon.

FAIRY.
And here my mistress. Would that he were gone!

Enter [Oberon] the King of Fairies at one door, with his
train; and [Titania] the Queen at another, with hers.

OBERON.
Ill met by moonlight, proud Titania.

TITANIA.
What, jealous Oberon? Fairies, skip hence.
I have forsworn his bed and company.

OBERON.
Tarry, rash wanton.° Am not I thy lord?

TITANIA.
Then I must be thy lady; but I know
When thou hast stolen away from Fairyland
And in the shape of Corin° sat all day,
Playing on pipes of corn° and versing love
To amorous Phillida.° Why art thou here
Come from the farthest step° of India
But that, forsooth, the bouncing Amazon,
Your buskined° mistress and your warrior love,
To Theseus must be wedded, and you come
To give their bed joy and prosperity.

OBERON.
How canst thou thus for shame, Titania,
Glance at my credit with Hippolyta,°
Knowing I know thy love to Theseus?
Didst not thou lead him through the glimmering night
From Perigenia,°whom he ravishèd?
And make him with fair Aegles° break his faith,
With Ariadne° and Antiopa?°

TITANIA.
These are the forgeries of jealousy;
And never, since the middle summer's spring,°

Met we on hill, in dale, forest, or mead,
By pavèd° fountain or by rushy° brook,
Or in° the beachèd margent° of the sea,   85
To dance our ringlets° to the whistling wind,
But with thy brawls thou hast disturbed our sport.
Therefore the winds, piping to us in vain,
As in revenge, have sucked up from the sea
Contagious° fogs; which, falling in the land,   90
Hath every pelting° river made so proud
That they have overborne their continents.°
The ox hath therefore stretched his yoke in vain,
The plowman lost his sweat, and the green corn°
Hath rotted ere his youth attained a beard;   95
The fold° stands empty in the drownèd field,
And crows are fatted with the murrain° flock;
The nine-men's-morris° is filled up with mud,
And the quaint mazes° in the wanton° green
For lack of tread are undistinguishable.   100
The human mortals want° their winter° here;
No night is now with hymn or carol blessed.
Therefore° the moon, the governess of floods,
Pale in her anger, washes all the air,
That rheumatic diseases° do abound.   105
And thorough this distemperature° we see
The seasons alter: hoary-headed frosts
Fall in the fresh lap of the crimson rose,
And on old Hiems'° thin and icy crown
An odorous chaplet of sweet summer buds   110
Is, as in mockery, set. The spring, the summer,
The childing° autumn, angry winter, change
Their wonted liveries,° and the mazèd° world
By their increase° now knows not which is which.
And this same progeny of evils comes   115
From our debate,° from our dissension;
We are their parents and original.°

OBERON.
Do you amend it, then; it lies in you.
Why should Titania cross her Oberon?

---

55 choir company **56 waxen** increase. **neeze** sneeze **58 room** stand aside, make room **63 wanton** headstrong creature **66, 68 Corin, Phillida** (Conventional names of pastoral lovers.) **67 corn** (Here, oat stalks.) **69 step** farthest limit of travel, or, perhaps, *steep*, mountain range **71 buskined** wearing half-boots called buskins **75 Glance . . . Hippolyta** make insinuations about my favored relationship with Hippolyta **78 Perigenia** i.e., Perigouna, one of Theseus' conquests. (This and the following women are named in Thomas North's translation of Plutarch's "Life of Theseus.") **79 Aegles** i.e., Aegle, for whom Theseus deserted Ariadne according to some accounts **80 Ariadne** the daughter of Minos, King of Crete, who helped Theseus to escape the labyrinth after killing the Minotaur; later she was abandoned by Theseus. **Antiopa** Queen of the Amazons and wife of Theseus; elsewhere identified with Hippolyta, but here thought of as a separate woman **82 middle summer's spring** beginning of midsummer

84 pavèd with pebbled bottom. **rushy** bordered with rushes **85 in** on. **margent** edge, border **86 ringlets** dances in a ring. (See *orbs* in line 9.) **90 Contagious** noxious **91 pelting** paltry **92 continents** banks that contain them **94 corn** grain of any kind **96 fold** pen for sheep or cattle **97 murrain** having died of the plague **98 nine-men's-morris** i.e., portion of the village green marked out in a square for a game played with nine pebbles or pegs **99 quaint mazes** i.e., intricate paths marked out on the village green to be followed rapidly on foot as a kind of contest. **wanton** luxuriant **101 want** lack. **winter** i.e., regular winter season; or, proper observances of winter, such as the *hymn or carol* in the next line (?) **103 Therefore** i.e., as a result of our quarrel **105 rheumatic diseases** colds, flu, and other respiratory infections **106 distemperature** disturbance in nature **109 Hiems'** the winter god's **112 childing** fruitful, pregnant **113 wonted liveries** usual apparel. **mazèd** bewildered **114 their increase** their yield, what they produce **116 debate** quarrel **117 original** origin

120   I do but beg a little changeling boy
      To be my henchman.°
TITANIA.   Set your heart at rest.
      The fairy land buys not the child of me.
      His mother was a vot'ress of my order,
      And in the spicèd Indian air by night
125   Full often hath she gossiped by my side
      And sat with me on Neptune's yellow sands,
      Marking th' embarkèd traders° on the flood,°
      When we have laughed to see the sails conceive
      And grow big-bellied with the wanton° wind;
130   Which she, with pretty and with swimming° gait,
      Following—her womb then rich with my young squire—
      Would imitate, and sail upon the land
      To fetch me trifles, and return again
      As from a voyage, rich with merchandise.
135   But she, being mortal, of that boy did die;
      And for her sake do I rear up her boy,
      And for her sake I will not part with him.
OBERON.
      How long within this wood intend you stay?
TITANIA.
      Perchance till after Theseus' wedding day.
140   If you will patiently dance in our round°
      And see our moonlight revels, go with us;
      If not, shun me, and I will spare° your haunts.
OBERON.
      Give me that boy and I will go with thee.
TITANIA.
      Not for thy fairy kingdom. Fairies, away!
145   We shall chide downright if I longer stay.

                Exeunt [Titania with her train].
OBERON.
      Well, go thy way. Thou shalt not from° this grove
      Till I torment thee for this injury.
      My gentle Puck, come hither. Thou rememb'rest
      Since° once I sat upon a promontory,
150   And heard a mermaid on a dolphin's back
      Uttering such dulcet and harmonious breath°
      That the rude° sea grew civil at her song,
      And certain stars shot madly from their spheres
      To hear the sea-maid's music?
PUCK.   I remember.
OBERON.
155   That very time I saw, but thou couldst not,
      Flying between the cold moon and the earth,
      Cupid all° armed. A certain aim he took

      At a fair vestal° thronèd by the west,
      And loosed° his love shaft smartly from his bow
      As° it should pierce a hundred thousand hearts;   160
      But I might° see young Cupid's fiery shaft
      Quenched in the chaste beams of the watery moon,
      And the imperial vot'ress passèd on
      In maiden meditation, fancy-free.°
      Yet marked I where the bolt° of Cupid fell: 165
      It fell upon a little western flower,
      Before milk-white, now purple with love's wound,
      And maidens call it "love-in-idleness."°
      Fetch me that flower; the herb I showed thee once.
      The juice of it on sleeping eyelids laid   170
      Will make or man or° woman madly dote
      Upon the next live creature that it sees.
      Fetch me this herb, and be thou here again
      Ere the leviathan° can swim a league.
PUCK.
      I'll put a girdle round about the earth   175
      In forty° minutes.   *[Exit.]*
OBERON.   Having once this juice,
      I'll watch Titania when she is asleep
      And drop the liquor of it in her eyes.
      The next thing then she waking looks upon,
      Be it on lion, bear, or wolf, or bull,   180
      On meddling monkey, or on busy ape,
      She shall pursue it with the soul of love.
      And ere I take this charm from off her sight,
      As I can take it with another herb,
      I'll make her render up her page to me.   185
      But who comes here? I am invisible,
      And I will overhear their conference.

Enter Demetrius, Helena following him.

DEMETRIUS.
      I love thee not; therefore pursue me not.
      Where is Lysander and fair Hermia?
      The one I'll slay; the other slayeth me.   190
      Thou toldst me they were stol'n unto this wood;
      And here am I, and wode° within this wood,
      Because I cannot meet my Hermia.
      Hence, get thee gone, and follow me no more.
HELENA.
      You draw me, you hardhearted adamant!°   195

158 vestal vestal virgin. (Contains a complimentary allusion to Queen Elizabeth as a votaress of Diana and probably refers to an actual entertainment in her honor at Elvetham in 1591.) **159 loosed** released   **160 As** as if   **161 might** could   **164 fancy-free** free of love's spell   **165 bolt** arrow   **168 love-in-idleness** pansy, heartsease   **171 or . . . or** either . . . or   **174 leviathan** sea monster, whale   **176 forty** (Used indefinitely.)   **192 wode** mad. (Pronounced "wood" and often spelled so.)   **195 adamant** lodestone, magnet (with pun on *hardhearted*, since adamant was also thought to be the hardest of all stones and was confused with the diamond)

121 henchman attendant, page   **127 traders** trading vessels. **flood** flood tide   **129 wanton** sportive   **130 swimming** smooth, gliding   **140 round** circular dance   **142 spare** shun   **146 from** go from   **149 Since** when   **151 breath** voice, song   **152 rude** rough   **157 all** fully

But yet you draw not iron, for my heart
Is true as steel. Leave° you your power to draw,
And I shall have no power to follow you.
DEMETRIUS.
   Do I entice you? Do I speak you fair?°
200   Or rather do I not in plainest truth
   Tell you I do not nor I cannot love you?
HELENA.
   And even for that do I love you the more.
   I am your spaniel; and, Demetrius,
   The more you beat me, I will fawn on you.
205   Use me but as your spaniel, spurn me, strike me,
   Neglect me, lose me; only give me leave,
   Unworthy as I am, to follow you.
   What worser place can I beg in your love—
   And yet a place of high respect with me—
210   Than to be usèd as you use your dog?
DEMETRIUS.
   Tempt not too much the hatred of my spirit,
   For I am sick when I do look on thee.
HELENA.
   And I am sick when I look not on you.
DEMETRIUS.
   You do impeach° your modesty too much
215   To leave the city and commit yourself
   Into the hands of one that loves you not,
   To trust the opportunity of night
   And the ill counsel of a desert° place
   With the rich worth of your virginity.
HELENA.
220   Your virtue° is my privilege°. For that°
   It is not night when I do see your face,
   Therefore I think I am not in the night;
   Nor doth this wood lack worlds of company,
   For you, in my respect,° are all the world.
225   Then how can it be said I am alone
   When all the world is here to look on me?
DEMETRIUS.
   I'll run from thee and hide me in the brakes,°
   And leave thee to the mercy of wild beasts.
HELENA.
   The wildest hath not such a heart as you.
230   Run when you will, the story shall be changed:
   Apollo flies and Daphne holds the chase,°
   The dove pursues the griffin,° the mild hind°

Makes speed to catch the tiger—bootless° speed,
When cowardice pursues and valor flies!
DEMETRIUS.
   I will not stay° thy questions.° Let me go!   235
   Or if thou follow me, do not believe
   But I shall do thee mischief in the wood.
HELENA.
   Ay, in the temple, in the town, the field,
   You do me mischief. Fie, Demetrius!
   Your wrongs do set a scandal on my sex.°   240
   We cannot fight for love, as men may do;
   We should be wooed and were not made to woo.
                          [Exit Demetrius.]
   I'll follow thee and make a heaven of hell,
   To die upon° the hand I love so well.   *[Exit.]*
OBERON.
   Fare thee well, nymph. Ere he do leave this grove,   245
   Thou shalt fly him and he shall seek thy love.
   Enter Puck.
   Hast thou the flower there? Welcome, wanderer.
PUCK.
   Ay, there it is.   *[He offers the flower.]*
OBERON.   I pray thee, give it me.
   I know a bank where the wild thyme blows,°
   Where oxlips° and the nodding violet grows,   250
   Quite overcanopied with luscious woodbine,°
   With sweet muskroses° and with eglantine.°
   There sleeps Titania sometimes of the night,
   Lulled in these flowers with dances and delight;
   And there the snake throws° her enameled skin,   255
   Weed° wide enough to wrap a fairy in.
   And with the juice of this I'll streak° her eyes
   And make her full of hateful fantasies.
   Take thou some of it, and seek through this grove.
                      [He gives some love juice.]
   A sweet Athenian lady is in love   260
   With a disdainful youth. Anoint his eyes,
   But do it when the next thing he espies
   May be the lady. Thou shalt know the man
   By the Athenian garments he hath on.
   Effect it with some care, that he may prove   265
   More fond on° her than she upon her love;
   And look thou meet me ere the first cock crow.
PUCK.
   Fear not, my lord, your servant shall do so.
                               Exeunt.

---

197 Leave give up   **199 fair** courteously   **214 impeach** call into question   **218 desert** deserted   **220 virtue** goodness or power to attract. **privilege** safeguard; warrant. **For that** because **224 in my respect** as far as I am concerned **227 brakes** thickets **231 Apollo . . . chase** (In the ancient myth, Daphne fled from Apollo and was saved from rape by being transformed into a laurel tree; here it is the female *who holds the chase*, or pursues, instead of the male.) **232 griffin** a fabulous monster with the head of an eagle and the body of a lion. **hind** female deer

---

233 bootless fruitless **235 stay** wait for. **questions** talk or argument **240 Your . . . sex** i.e., the wrongs that you do me cause me to act in a manner that disgraces my sex **244 upon** by **249 blows** blooms **250 oxlips** flowers resembling cowslip and primrose **251 woodbine** honeysuckle **252 muskroses** a kind of large, sweet-scented rose. **eglantine** sweetbrier, another kind of rose **255 throws** sloughs off, sheds **256 Weed** garment **257 streak** anoint, touch gently **266 fond on** doting on

[2.2] *Enter Titania, Queen of Fairies, with her train.*

TITANIA.
Come, now a roundel° and a fairy song;
Then, for the third part of a minute, hence—
Some to kill cankers° in the muskrose buds,
Some war with reremice° for their leathern wings
5 To make my small elves coats, and some keep back
The clamorous owl, that nightly hoots and wonders
At our quaint° spirits. Sing me now asleep.
Then to your offices, and let me rest.
Fairies sing.

FIRST FAIRY.
You spotted snakes with double° tongue,
10 Thorny hedgehogs, be not seen;
Newts° and blindworms, do no wrong,
Come not near our Fairy Queen.

CHORUS.
Philomel,° with melody
Sing in our sweet lullaby;
15 Lulla, lulla, lullaby, lulla, lulla, lullaby.
Never harm
Nor spell nor charm
Come our lovely lady nigh.
So good night, with lullaby.

FIRST FAIRY.
20 Weaving spiders, come not here;
Hence, you long-legged spinners, hence!
Beetles black, approach not near;
Worm nor snail, do no offense.

CHORUS.
Philomel, with melody
25 Sing in our sweet lullaby;
Lulla, lulla, lullaby, lulla, lulla, lullaby.
Never harm
Nor spell nor charm
Come our lovely lady nigh.
30 So good night, with lullaby.
[Titania sleeps.]

SECOND FAIRY.
Hence, away! Now all is well.
One aloof stand sentinel. *[Exeunt Fairies.]*

Enter Oberon [and squeezes the flower on Titania's eyelids].

OBERON.
What thou seest when thou dost wake,
Do it for thy true love take;
Love and languish for his sake. 35
Be it ounce,° or cat, or bear,
Pard,° or boar with bristled hair,
In thy eye that shall appear
When thou wak'st, it is thy dear.
Wake when some vile thing is near. *[Exit.]* 40

Enter Lysander and Hermia.

LYSANDER.
Fair love, you faint with wandering in the wood;
And to speak truth, I have forgot our way.
We'll rest us, Hermia, if you think it good,
And tarry for the comfort of the day.

HERMIA.
Be it so, Lysander. Find you out a bed, 45
For I upon this bank will rest my head.

LYSANDER.
One turf shall serve as pillow for us both;
One heart, one bed, two bosoms, and one troth.°

HERMIA.
Nay, good Lysander, for my sake, my dear,
Lie further off yet; do not lie so near. 50

LYSANDER.
O, take the sense, sweet, of my innocence!°
Love takes the meaning in love's conference.°
I mean that my heart unto yours is knit
So that but one heart we can make of it;
Two bosoms interchainéd with an oath— 55
So then two bosoms and a single troth.
Then by your side no bed-room me deny,
For lying so, Hermia, I do not lie.°

HERMIA.
Lysander riddles very prettily.
Now much beshrew° my manners and my pride 60
If Hermia meant to say Lysander lied.
But, gentle friend, for love and courtesy
Lie further off, in human° modesty;
Such separation as may well be said
Becomes a virtuous bachelor and a maid, 65
So far be distant; and good night, sweet friend.
Thy love ne'er alter till thy sweet life end!

2.2 Location: The wood   1 roundel dance in a ring   **3 cankers** cankerworms (i.e., caterpillars or grubs)   **4 reremice** bats   **7 quaint** dainty   **9 double** forked   **11 Newts** water lizards (considered poisonous, as were *blindworms*—small snakes with tiny eyes—and spiders)   **13 Philomel** the nightingale. (Philomela, daughter of King Pandion, was transformed into a nightingale, according to Ovid's *Metamorphoses* 6, after she had been raped by her sister Procne's husband, Tereus.)

36 ounce lynx   **37 Pard** leopard   **48 troth** faith, trothplight   **51 take . . . innocence** i.e., interpret my intention as innocent   **52 Love . . . conference** i.e., when lovers confer, love teaches each lover to interpret the other's meaning lovingly   **58 lie** tell a falsehood (with a riddling pun on *lie*, recline)   **60 beshrew** curse. (But mildly meant.)   **63 human** courteous

LYSANDER.

Amen, amen, to that fair prayer, say I,
And then end life when I end loyalty!
Here is my bed. Sleep give thee all his rest!

HERMIA.

With half that wish the wisher's eyes be pressed!°

[*They sleep, separated by a short distance.*]

Enter Puck.

PUCK.

Through the forest have I gone,
But Athenian found I none
On whose eyes I might approve°
This flower's force in stirring love.
Night and silence.—Who is here?
Weeds of Athens he doth wear.
This is he, my master said,
Despisèd the Athenian maid;
And here the maiden, sleeping sound,
On the dank and dirty ground.
Pretty soul, she durst not lie
Near this lack-love, this kill-courtesy.
Churl, upon thy eyes I throw
All the power this charm doth owe.°

[*He applies the love juice.*]

When thou wak'st, let love forbid
Sleep his seat on thy eyelid.
So awake when I am gone,
For I must now to Oberon.   *Exit.*

Enter Demetrius and Helena, running.

HELENA.

Stay, though thou kill me, sweet Demetrius!

DEMETRIUS.

I charge thee, hence, and do not haunt me thus.

HELENA.

O, wilt thou darkling° leave me? Do not so.

DEMETRIUS.

Stay, on thy peril!° I alone will go.   [*Exit.*]

HELENA.

O, I am out of breath in this fond° chase!
The more my prayer, the lesser is my grace.°
Happy is Hermia, wheresoe'er she lies,
For she hath blessèd and attractive eyes.
How came her eyes so bright? Not with salt tears;
If so, my eyes are oftener washed than hers.
No, no, I am as ugly as a bear;
For beasts that meet me run away for fear.
Therefore no marvel though Demetrius

Do, as a monster, fly my presence thus.°
What wicked and dissembling glass of mine
Made me compare° with Hermia's sphery eyne?°   105
But who is here? Lysander, on the ground?
Dead, or asleep? I see no blood, no wound.
Lysander, if you live, good sir, awake.

LYSANDER [*Awaking*].

And run through fire I will for thy sweet sake.
Transparent° Helena! Nature shows art,   110
That through thy bosom makes me see thy heart.
Where is Demetrius? O, how fit a word
Is that vile name to perish on my sword!

HELENA.

Do not say so, Lysander, say not so.
What though he love your Hermia? Lord, what though? 115
Yet Hermia still loves you. Then be content.

LYSANDER.

Content with Hermia? No! I do repent
The tedious minutes I with her have spent.
Not Hermia but Helena I love.
Who will not change a raven for a dove?   120
The will of man is by his reason swayed,
And reason says you are the worthier maid.
Things growing are not ripe until their season;
So I, being young, till now ripe not° to reason.
And touching° now the point° of human skill,°   125
Reason becomes the marshal to my will
And leads me to your eyes, where I o'erlook°
Love's stories written in love's richest book.

HELENA.

Wherefore° was I to this keen mockery born?
When at your hands did I deserve this scorn?   130
Is 't not enough, is 't not enough, young man,
That I did never, no, nor never can,
Deserve a sweet look from Demetrius' eye,
But you must flout my insufficiency?
Good troth,° you do me wrong, good sooth,° you do, 135
In such disdainful manner me to woo.
But fare you well. Perforce I must confess
I thought you lord of° more true gentleness.°
O, that a lady, of° one man refused,
Should of another therefore be abused!°   *Exit.* 140

LYSANDER.

She sees not Hermia. Hermia, sleep thou there,
And never mayst thou come Lysander near!
For as a surfeit of the sweetest things

102–103 **no marvel . . . thus** i.e., no wonder that Demetrius flies from me as from a monster   105 **compare** vie.   **sphery eyne** eyes as bright as stars in their spheres   110 **Transparent** (1) radiant (2) able to be seen through   124 **ripe not** (am) not ripened   125 **touching** reaching.   **point** summit.   **skill** judgment   127 **o'erlook** read   129 **Wherefore** why   135 **Good troth, good sooth** i.e., indeed, truly   138 **lord of** i.e., possessor of. **gentleness** courtesy   139 **of** by   140 **abused** ill treated

The deepest loathing to the stomach brings,
145   Or as the heresies that men do leave
      Are hated most of those they did deceive,°
      So thou, my surfeit and my heresy,
      Of all be hated, but the most of me!
      And, all my powers, address° your love and might
150   To honor Helen and to be her knight!   *Exit.*
      HERMIA [*Awaking*].
      Help me, Lysander, help me! Do thy best
      To pluck this crawling serpent from my breast!
      Ay me, for pity! What a dream was here!
      Lysander, look how I do quake with fear.
155   Methought a serpent ate my heart away,
      And you sat smiling at his cruel prey.°
      Lysander! What, removed? Lysander! Lord!
      What, out of hearing? Gone? No sound, no word?
      Alack, where are you? Speak, an if° you hear;
160   Speak, of all loves!° I swoon almost with fear.
      No? Then I well perceive you are not nigh.
      Either death, or you, I'll find immediately.

                      Exit. [*The sleeping Titania remains.*]

[3.1] *Enter the clowns* [*Quince, Snug, Bottom, Flute,*
Snout, and Starveling].

BOTTOM. Are we all met?
QUINCE. Pat, pat;° and here's a marvelous convenient place
      for our rehearsal. This green plot shall be our stage, this
      hawthorn brake° our tiring-house,° and we will do it in
5   action as we will do it before the Duke.
BOTTOM. Peter Quince?
QUINCE. What sayest thou, bully° Bottom?
BOTTOM. There are things in this comedy of Pyramus and
      This be that will never please. First, Pyramus must draw a
10   sword to kill himself, which the ladies cannot abide. How
      answer you that?
SNOUT. By 'r lakin,° a parlous° fear.
STARVELING. I believe we must leave the killing out, when
      all is done.°
15   BOTTOM. Not a whit. I have a device to make all well. Write
      me° a prologue, and let the prologue seem to say we will
      do no harm with our swords, and that Pyramus is not
      killed indeed; and for the more better assurance, tell

them that I, Pyramus, am not Pyramus but Bottom the
weaver. This will put them out of fear.   20
QUINCE. Well, we will have such a prologue, and it shall be
      written in eight and six.°
BOTTOM. No, make it two more; let it be written in eight
      and eight.
SNOUT. Will not the ladies be afeard of the lion?   25
STARVELING. I fear it, I promise you.
BOTTOM. Masters, you ought to consider with yourselves, to
      bring in—God shield us!—a lion among ladies° is a most
      dreadful thing. For there is not a more fearful° wildfowl
      than your lion living; and we ought to look to 't.   30
SNOUT. Therefore another prologue must tell he is not a
      lion.
BOTTOM. Nay, you must name his name, and half his face
      must be seen through the lion's neck, and he himself
      must speak through, saying thus, or to the same defect:° 35
      "Ladies"—or "Fair ladies—I would wish you"—or "I
      would request you"—or "I would entreat you—not to
      fear, not to tremble; my life for yours.° If you think I
      come hither as a lion, it were pity of my life.° No, I am no
      such thing: I am a man as other men are." And there   40
      indeed let him name his name and tell them plainly he is
      Snug the joiner.
QUINCE. Well, it shall be so. But there is two hard things:
      that is, to bring the moonlight into a chamber; for, you
      know, Pyramus and Thisbe meet by moonlight.   45
SNOUT. Doth the moon shine that night we play our play?
BOTTOM. A calendar, a calendar! Look in the almanac. Find
      out moonshine, find out moonshine.
                              [*They consult an almanac.*]
QUINCE. Yes, it doth shine that night.
BOTTOM. Why, then, may you leave a casement of the great   50
      chamber window, where we play, open, and the moon
      may shine in at the casement.
QUINCE. Ay; or else one must come in with a bush of thorns°
      and a lantern and say he comes to disfigure,° or to pre-
      sent,° the person of Moonshine. Then there is another   55
      thing: we must have a wall in the great chamber; for
      Pyramus and Thisbe, says the story, did talk through the
      chink of a wall.

145–146 as . . . deceive as renounced heresies are hated most by
those persons who formerly were deceived by them   **149 address**
direct, apply   **156 prey** act of preying   **159 an if** if   **160 of all
loves** for all love's sake
3.1. Location: The action is continuous.   **2 Pat** on the dot, punctually   **4 brake** thicket   **tiring-house** attiring area, hence backstage   **7 bully** i.e., worthy, jolly, fine fellow   **12 By 'r lakin** by our
ladykin, i.e., the Virgin Mary.   **parlous** alarming   **13–14 when
all is done** i.e., when all is said and done   **15–16 Write me** i.e.,
write at my suggestion. (*Me* is used colloquially.)

22 eight and six alternate lines of eight and six syllables, a common
ballad measure   **28 lion among ladies** (A contemporary pamphlet
tells how at the christening in 1594 of Prince Henry, eldest son of
King James VI of Scotland, later James I of England, a "black-
amoor" instead of a lion drew the triumphal chariot, since the lion's
presence might have "brought some fear to the nearest.")
29 fearful fear inspiring   **35 defect** (Bottom's blunder for *effect*.)
38 my life for yours i.e., I pledge my life to make your lives safe
39 it were . . . life my life would be endangered   **53 bush of
thorns** bundle of thornbush faggots (part of the accoutrements of
the man in the moon, according to the popular notions of the time,
along with his lantern and his dog)   **54 disfigure** (Quince's blunder for *figure.*)   **54–55 present** represent

SNOUT. You can never bring in a wall. What say you, Bottom?

BOTTOM. Some man or other must present Wall. And let him have some plaster, or some loam, or some roughcast° about him, to signify wall; or let him hold his fingers thus, and through that cranny shall Pyramus and Thisbe whisper.

QUINCE. If that may be, then all is well. Come, sit down, every mother's son, and rehearse your parts. Pyramus, you begin. When you have spoken your speech, enter into that brake, and so everyone according to his cue.

Enter Robin [Puck].

PUCK.
What hempen homespuns° have we swaggering here
    So near the cradle° of the Fairy Queen?
What, a play toward?° I'll be an auditor;
    An actor too perhaps, if I see cause.

QUINCE. Speak, Pyramus. Thisbe, stand forth.

BOTTOM [*As Pyramus*]. "Thisbe, the flowers of odious savors sweet—"

QUINCE. Odors, odors.

BOTTOM. "—Odors savors sweet;
    So hath thy breath, my dearest Thisbe dear.
    But hark, a voice! Stay thou but here awhile,
    And by and by I will to thee appear."   *Exit.*

PUCK. A stranger Pyramus than e'er played here.°   [*Exit.*]

FLUTE. Must I speak now?

QUINCE. Ay, marry, must you; for you must understand he goes but to see a noise that he heard, and is to come again.

FLUTE [*As Thisbe*].
"Most radiant Pyramus, most lily-white of hue,
    Of color like the red rose on triumphant° brier,
Most brisky juvenal° and eke° most lovely Jew,°
    As true as truest horse, that yet would never tire.
I'll meet thee, Pyramus, at Ninny's tomb."

QUINCE. "Ninus'° tomb," man. Why, you must not speak that yet. That you answer to Pyramus. You speak all your part° at once, cues and all. Pyramus, enter. Your cue is past; it is "never tire."

FLUTE. O—"As true as truest horse, that yet would never tire."

[*Enter Puck, and Bottom as Pyramus with the ass head.°*]

BOTTOM. "If I were fair,° Thisbe, I were° only thine."

QUINCE. O, monstrous! O, strange! We are haunted. Pray, masters! Fly, masters! Help!

[*Exeunt Quince, Snug, Flute, Snout, and Starveling.*]

PUCK.
I'll follow you, I'll lead you about a round,°
    Through bog, through bush, through brake, through brier.
Sometimes a horse I'll be, sometimes a hound,
    A hog, a headless bear, sometimes a fire;°
And neigh, and bark, and grunt, and roar, and burn,
Like horse, hound, hog, bear, fire, at every turn.   *Exit.*

BOTTOM. Why do they run away? This is a knavery of them to make me afeard.

Enter Snout.

SNOUT. O Bottom, thou art changed! What do I see on thee?

BOTTOM. What do you see? You see an ass head of your own, do you?

[*Exit Snout.*]

Enter Quince.

QUINCE. Bless thee, Bottom, bless thee! Thou art translated.°   *Exit.*

BOTTOM. I see their knavery. This is to make an ass of me, to fright me, if they could. But I will not stir from this place, do what they can. I will walk up and down here, and will sing, that they shall hear I am not afraid.   [*Sings.*]

The ouzel cock° so black of hue,
    With orange-tawny bill,
The throstle° with his note so true,
    The wren with little quill°—

TITANIA [*Awaking*].
What angel wakes me from my flowery bed?

BOTTOM [*Sings*].
The finch, the sparrow, and the lark,
    The plainsong° cuckoo gray,
Whose note full many a man doth mark,
    And dares not answer nay°—

---

62 **roughcast** a mixture of lime and gravel used to plaster the outside of buildings   70 **hempen homespuns** i.e., rustics dressed in clothes woven of coarse, homespun fabric made from hemp   71 **cradle** i.e., Titania's bower   72 **toward** about to take place   82 **A stranger . . . here** (Puck indicates that he has conceived of his plan to present a "stranger" Pyramus than ever seen before, and so Puck exits to put his plan into effect.)   88 **triumphant** magnificent   89 **brisky juvenal** lively youth. **eke** also. **Jew** (Probably an absurd repetition of the first syllable of *juvenal*, or Flute's error for *jewel*.)   92 **Ninus** mythical founder of Nineveh (whose wife, Semiramis, was supposed to have built the walls of Babylon where the story of Pyramus and Thisbe takes place)   94 **part** (An actor's *part* was a script consisting only of his speeches and their cues.)

97 **s.d. with the ass head** (This stage direction, taken from the Folio, presumably refers to a standard stage property.)   98 **fair** handsome. **were** would be   101 **about a round** roundabout   105 **fire** will-o'-the-wisp   119–120 **translated** transformed   125 **ouzel cock** male blackbird   127 **throstle** song thrush   128 **quill** (Literally, a reed pipe; hence, the bird's piping song.)   131 **plainsong** singing a melody without variations   133 **dares . . . nay** i.e., cannot deny that he is a cuckold

For, indeed, who would set his wit to so foolish a bird?
135 Who would give a bird the lie,° though he cry "cuckoo"
     never so?°
TITANIA.
     I pray thee, gentle mortal, sing again.
     Mine ear is much enamored of thy note;
     So is mine eye enthrallèd to thy shape;
140 And thy fair virtue's force° perforce doth move me
     On the first view to say, to swear, I love thee.
BOTTOM. Methinks, mistress, you should have little reason
     for that. And yet, to say the truth, reason and love keep
     little company together nowadays. The more the pity
145 that some honest neighbors will not make them friends.
     Nay, I can gleek° upon occasion.
TITANIA.
     Thou art as wise as thou art beautiful.
BOTTOM. Not so, neither. But if I had wit enough to get out
     of this wood, I have enough to serve mine own turn.°
TITANIA.
150 Out of this wood do not desire to go.
     Thou shalt remain here, whether thou wilt or no.
     I am a spirit of no common rate.°
     The summer still° doth tend upon my state,°
     And I do love thee. Therefore go with me.
155 I'll give thee fairies to attend on thee
     And they shall fetch thee jewels from the deep,
     And sing while thou on pressèd flowers dost sleep.
     And I will purge thy mortal grossness° so
     That thou shalt like an airy spirit go.
160 Peaseblossom, Cobweb, Mote,° and Mustardseed!

     Enter four Fairies [Peaseblossom, Cobweb, Mote, and
     Mustardseed].

PEASEBLOSSOM.
     Ready.
COBWEB.
     And I.
MOTE.   And I.
MUSTARDSEED. And I.
ALL.   Where shall we go?
TITANIA.
     Be kind and courteous to this gentleman.
165 Hop in his walks and gambol in his eyes;°
     Feed him with apricots and dewberries,°
     With purple grapes, green figs, and mulberries;
     The honey bags steal from the humble-bees,

     And for night tapers crop their waxen thighs
     And light them at the fiery glowworms' eyes,   170
     To have my love to bed and to arise;
     And pluck the wings from painted butterflies
     To fan the moonbeams from his sleeping eyes.
     Nod to him, elves, and do him courtesies.
PEASEBLOSSOM.
     Hail, mortal!   175
COBWEB.
     Hail!
MOTE.
     Hail!
MUSTARDSEED.
     Hail!
BOTTOM. I cry your worships mercy, heartily. I beseech your
     worship's name.   180
COBWEB.
     Cobweb.
BOTTOM. I shall desire you of more acquaintance, good Mas-
     ter Cobweb. If I cut my finger, I shall make bold with
     you.°—Your name, honest gentleman?
PEASEBLOSSOM.
     Peaseblossom.   185
BOTTOM. I pray you, commend me to Mistress Squash,° your
     mother, and to Master Peascod,° your father. Good Mas-
     ter Peaseblossom, I shall desire you of more acquaintance
     too.—Your name, I beseech you, sir?
MUSTARDSEED.
     Mustardseed.   190
BOTTOM. Good Master Mustardseed I know your patience°
     well. That same cowardly giantlike ox-beef hath
     devoured many a gentleman of your house. I promise you,
     your kindred hath made my eyes water° ere now. I desire
     you of more acquaintance, good Master Mustardseed.   195
TITANIA.
     Come, wait upon him; lead him to my bower.
        The moon methinks looks with a watery eye;
     And when she weeps,° weeps every little flower,
        Lamenting some enforcèd° chastity.
     Tie up my lover's tongue,° bring him silently.   200

                                              [Exeunt.]

[3.2] *Enter [Oberon,] King of Fairies.*

OBERON.
     I wonder if Titania be awaked;

---

135 **give . . . lie** call the bird a liar.   136 **never so** ever so much
140 **thy . . . force** the power of your beauty   146 **gleek** scoff, jest
149 **serve . . . turn** answer my purpose   152 **rate** rank, value
153 **still** ever, always.   **doth . . . state** waits upon me as a part of
my royal retinue   158 **mortal grossness** materiality (i.e., the corporal nature of a mortal being)   160 **Mote** i.e., speck. (The two
words *moth* and *mote* were pronounced alike, and both meanings
may be present.)   165 **in his eyes** in his sight (i.e., before him)
166 **dewberries** blackberries

183–184 **If . . . you** (Cobwebs were used to stanch bleeding.)
186 **Squash** unripe pea pod   187 **Peascod** ripe pea pod
191 **your patience** what you have endured   194 **water** (1) weep
for sympathy (2) smart, sting   198 **she weeps** i.e., she causes dew
199 **enforcèd** forced, violated; or, possibly, constrained (since Titania at this moment is hardly concerned about chastity)   200 **Tie
. . . tongue** (Presumably Bottom is braying like an ass.)
3.2. Location: The wood

Then what it was that next came in her eye,
Which she must dote on in extremity.

[*Enter*] *Robin Goodfellow* [*Puck*].

Here comes my messenger. How now, mad spirit?
What night-rule° now about this haunted° grove?

PUCK.
My mistress with a monster is in love.
Near to her close° and consecrated bower,
While she was in her dull° and sleeping hour,
A crew of patches,° rude mechanicals,°
That work for bread upon Athenian stalls,°
Were met together to rehearse a play
Intended for great Theseus' nuptial day.
The shallowest thick-skin of that barren sort,°
Who Pyramus presented° in their sport,
Forsook his scene° and entered in a brake.
When I did him at this advantage take,
An ass's noll° I fixèd on his head.
Anon his Thisbe must be answered,
And forth my mimic° comes. When they him spy,
As wild geese that the creeping fowler° eye,
Or russet-pated choughs,° many in sort,°
Rising and cawing at the gun's report,
Sever° themselves and madly sweep the sky,
So, at his sight, away his fellows fly;
And, at our stamp, here o'er and o'er one falls;
He "Murder!" cries and help from Athens calls.
Their sense thus weak, lost with their fears thus strong,
Made senseless things begin to do them wrong,
For briers and thorns at their apparel snatch;
Some, sleeves—some, hats; from yielders all things
    catch.°
I led them on in this distracted fear
And left sweet Pyramus translated there,
When in that moment, so it came to pass,
Titania waked and straightway loved an ass.

OBERON.
This falls out better than I could devise.
But hast thou yet latched° the Athenian's eyes
With the love juice, as I did bid thee do?

PUCK.
I took him sleeping—that is finished too—
And the Athenian woman by his side,
That, when he waked, of force° she must be eyed.

Enter Demetrius and Hermia.

OBERON.
Stand close. This is the same Athenian.

PUCK.
This is the woman, but not this the man.

[*They stand aside.*]

DEMETRIUS.
O, why rebuke you him that loves you so?
Lay breath so bitter on your bitter foe.   45

HERMIA.
Now I but chide; but I should use thee worse,
For thou, I fear, hast given me cause to curse.
If thou hast slain Lysander in his sleep,
Being o'er shoes° in blood, plunge in the deep,
And kill me too.   50
The sun was not so true unto the day
As he to me. Would he have stolen away
From sleeping Hermia? I'll believe as soon
This whole° earth may be bored, and that the moon
May through the center creep, and so displease   55
Her brother's° noontide with th' Antipodes.°
It cannot be but thou hast murdered him;
So should a murderer look, so dead,° so grim.

DEMETRIUS.
So should the murdered look, and so should I
Pierced through the heart with your stern cruelty.   60
Yet you, the murderer, look as bright, as clear,
As yonder Venus in her glimmering sphere.

HERMIA.
What's this to° my Lysander? Where is he?
Ah, good Demetrius, wilt thou give him me?

DEMETRIUS.
I had rather give his carcass to my hounds.   65

HERMIA.
Out, dog! Out, cur! Thou driv'st me past the bounds
Of maiden's patience. Hast thou slain him, then?
Henceforth be never numbered among men.
O, once tell true, tell true, even for my sake:
Durst thou have looked upon him being awake?   70
And hast thou killed him sleeping? O brave touch!°
Could not a worm,° an adder, do so much?
An adder did it; for with doubler tongue
Than thine, thou serpent, never adder stung.

DEMETRIUS.
You spend your passion° on a misprised mood.°   75
I am not guilty of Lysander's blood,
Nor is he dead, for aught that I can tell.

---

5 **night-rule** diversion for the night. **haunted** much frequented
7 **close** secret, private 8 **dull** drowsy 9 **patches** clowns, fools.
rude mechanicals ignorant artisans 10 **stalls** market booths
13 **barren sort** stupid company or crew 14 **presented** acted
15 **scene** playing area 17 **noll** noddle, head 19 **mimic** burlesque
actor 20 **fowler** hunter of game birds 21 **russet-pated choughs**
reddish brown or gray-headed jackdaws. **in sort** in a flock
23 **Sever** i.e., scatter 30–31 **from . . . catch** i.e., everything preys
on those who yield to fear 37 **latched** fastened, snared 41 **of
force** perforce

49 **o'er shoes** i.e., so far gone 54 **whole** solid 56 **Her brother's**
i.e., the sun's. **th' Antipodes** the people on the opposite side of
the earth (where the moon is imagined bringing night to noon-
time) 58 **dead** deadly, or deathly pale 63 **to** to do with
71 **brave touch** noble exploit. (Said ironically.) 72 **worm** serpent
75 **passion** violent feelings. **misprised mood** anger based on misconception

HERMIA.
 I pray thee, tell me then that he is well.
DEMETRIUS.
 An if I could, what should I get therefor?
HERMIA.
80 A privilege never to see me more.
 And from thy hated presence part I so.
 See me no more, whether he be dead or no.   *Exit.*
DEMETRIUS.
 There is no following her in this fierce vein.
 Here therefore for a while I will remain.
85 So sorrow's heaviness doth heavier° grow
 For debt that bankrupt° sleep doth sorrow owe;
 Which now in some slight measure it will pay,
 If for his tender here I make some stay.°
        Lie[s] down [and sleeps].
OBERON.
 What hast thou done? Thou hast mistaken quite
90 And laid the love juice on some true love's sight.
 Of thy misprision° must perforce ensue
 Some true love turned, and not a false turned true.
PUCK.
 Then fate o'errules, that, one man holding troth,°
 A million fail, confounding oath on oath.°
OBERON.
95 About the wood go swifter than the wind,
 And Helena of Athens look° thou find.
 All fancy-sick° she is and pale of cheer°
 With sighs of love, that cost the fresh blood° dear.
 By some illusion see thou bring her here.
100 I'll charm his eyes against she do appear.°
PUCK.
 I go. I go, look how I go,
 Swifter than arrow from the Tartar's bow.° *[Exit].*
OBERON *[Applying love juice to Demetrius' eyes].*
 Flower of this purple dye,
 Hit with Cupid's archery,
105 Sink in apple of his eye.
 When his love he doth espy,
 Let her shine as gloriously
 As the Venus of the sky.
 When thou wak'st, if she be by,
110 Beg of her for remedy.

Enter Puck.

PUCK.
 Captain of our fairy band,
 Helena is here at hand,
 And the youth, mistook by me,
 Pleading for a lover's fee.°
 Shall we their fond pageant° see?   115
 Lord, what fools these mortals be!
OBERON.
 Stand aside. The noise they make
 Will cause Demetrius to awake.
PUCK.
 Then will two at once woo one;
 That must needs be sport alone.°   120
 And those things do best please me
 That befall preposterously.°

         [They stand aside.]

Enter Lysander and Helena.

LYSANDER.
 Why should you think that I should woo in scorn?
  Scorn and derision never come in tears.
 Look when° I vow, I weep; and vows so born, 125
  In their nativity all truth appears.°
 How can these things in me seem scorn to you,
 Bearing the badge° of faith to prove them true?
HELENA.
 You do advance° your cunning more and more.
  When truth kills truth,° O, devilish-holy fray! 130
 These vows are Hermia's. Will you give her o'er?
  Weigh oath with oath, and you will nothing weigh.
 Your vows to her and me, put in two scales,
 Will even weigh, and both as light as tales.°
LYSANDER.
 I had no judgment when to her I swore.   135
HELENA.
 Nor none, in my mind, now you give her o'er.
LYSANDER.
 Demetrius loves her, and he loves not you.
DEMETRIUS *[Awaking].*
 O Helen, goddess, nymph, perfect, divine!
 To what, my love, shall I compare thine eyne?
 Crystal is muddy. O, how ripe in show°   140
 Thy lips, those kissing cherries, tempting grow!
 That pure congealèd white, high Taurus'° snow,

---

85 heavier (1) harder to bear (2) more drowsy **86 bankrupt**
(Demetrius is saying that his sleepiness adds to the weariness caused
by sorrow.) **87–88 Which . . . stay** i.e., to a small extent I will be
able to "pay back" and hence find some relief from sorrow, if I pause
here awhile (*make some stay*) while sleep "tenders" or offers itself by
way of paying the debt owed to sorrow **91 misprision** mistake
93 troth faith **94 confounding . . . oath** i.e., invalidating one
oath with another **96 look** i.e., be sure **97 fancy-sick** lovesick.
cheer face **98 sighs . . . blood** (An allusion to the physiological
theory that each sigh costs the heart a drop of blood.)
100 against . . . appear in anticipation of her coming
102 Tartar's bow (Tartars were famed for their skill with the bow.)

114 fee privilege, reward **115 fond pageant** foolish exhibition
120 alone unequaled **122 preposterously** out of the natural order
125 Look when whenever **125–126 vows . . . appears** i.e., vows
made by one who is weeping give evidence thereby of their sincerity **128 badge** identifying device such as that worn on servants'
livery (here, his tears) **129 advance** carry forward, display
130 truth kills truth i.e., one of Lysander's vows must invalidate
the other **134 tales** lies **140 show** appearance **142 Taurus** a
lofty mountain range in Asia Minor

Fanned with the eastern wind, turns to a crow°
When thou hold'st up thy hand. O, let me kiss
45 This princess of pure white, this seal° of bliss!

HELENA.
O spite! O hell! I see you all are bent
To set against° me for your merriment.
If you were civil and knew courtesy,
You would not do me thus much injury.
50 Can you not hate me, as I know you do,
But you must join in souls to mock me too?
If you were men, as men you are in show,
You would not use a gentle lady so—
To vow, and swear, and superpraise° my parts,°
55 When I am sure you hate me with your hearts.
You both are rivals, and love Hermia;
And now both rivals, to mock Helena.
A trim° exploit, a manly enterprise,
To conjure tears up in a poor maid's eyes
60 With your derision! None of noble sort°
Would so offend a virgin and extort°
A poor soul's patience, all to make you sport.

LYSANDER.
You are unkind, Demetrius. Be not so;
For you love Hermia; this you know I know.
65 And here, with all good will, with all my heart,
In Hermia's love I yield you up my part;
And yours of Helena to me bequeath,
Whom I do love and will do till my death.

HELENA.
Never did mockers waste more idle breath.

DEMETRIUS.
170 Lysander, keep thy Hermia; I will none.°
If e'er I loved her, all that love is gone.
My heart to her but as guest-wise sojourned,°
And now to Helen is it home returned,
There to remain.

LYSANDER.   Helen, it is not so.

DEMETRIUS.
175 Disparage not the faith thou dost not know,
Lest, to thy peril, thou aby° it dear.
Look where thy love comes; yonder is thy dear.

Enter Hermia.

HERMIA.
Dark night, that from the eye his° function takes,
The ear more quick of apprehension makes;
180 Wherein it doth impair the seeing sense
It pays the hearing double recompense.

Thou art not by mine eye, Lysander, found;
Mine ear, I thank it, brought me to thy sound.
But why unkindly didst thou leave me so?

LYSANDER.
Why should he stay whom love doth press to go?   185

HERMIA.
What love could press Lysander from my side?

LYSANDER.
Lysander's love, that would not let him bide—
Fair Helena, who more engilds° the night
Than all yon fiery oes° and eyes of light.
Why seek'st thou me? Could not this make thee know,   190
The hate I bear thee made me leave thee so?

HERMIA.
You speak not as you think. It cannot be.

HELENA.
Lo, she is one of this confederacy!
Now I perceive they have conjoined all three
To fashion this false sport in spite of me.°   195
Injurious Hermia, most ungrateful maid!
Have you conspired, have you with these contrived°
To bait° me with this foul derision?
Is all the counsel° that we two have shared,
The sisters' vows, the hours that we have spent,   200
When we have chid the hasty-footed time
For parting us—O, is all forgot?
All schooldays' friendship, childhood innocence?
We, Hermia, like two artificial° gods,
Have with our needles created both one flower,   205
Both on one sampler, sitting on one cushion,
Both warbling of one song, both in one key,
As if our hands, our sides, voices, and minds
Had been incorporate.° So we grew together
Like to a double cherry, seeming parted   210
But yet an union in partition,
Two lovely° berries molded on one stem;
So with two seeming bodies but one heart,
Two of the first, like coats in heraldry,
Due but to one and crownèd with one crest.°   215
And will you rend our ancient love asunder
To join with men in scorning your poor friend?
It is not friendly, 'tis not maidenly.
Our sex, as well as I, may chide you for it,
Though I alone do feel the injury.   220

---

188 **engilds** brightens with a golden light   189 **oes** spangles (here, stars)   195 **in spite of me** to vex me   197 **contrived** plotted   198 **bait** torment, as one sets on dogs to bait a bear   199 **counsel** confidential talk   204 **artificial** skilled in art or creation   209 **incorporate** of one body   212 **lovely** loving   214–215 **Two . . . crest** i.e., we have two separate bodies, just as a coat of arms in heraldry can be represented twice on a shield but surmounted by a single crest

---

143 **turns to a crow** i.e., seems black by contrast   145 **seal** pledge   147 **set against** attack   154 **superpraise** overpraise. **parts** qualities   158 **trim** pretty, fine. (Said ironically.)   160 **sort** character, quality   161 **extort** twist, torture   170 **will none** i.e., want no part of her   172 **to . . . sojourned** only visited with her   176 **aby** pay for   178 **his** its

HERMIA.
    I am amazèd at your passionate words.
    I scorn you not. It seems that you scorn me.
HELENA.
    Have you not set Lysander, as in scorn,
    To follow me and praise my eyes and face?
225   And made your other love, Demetrius,
    Who even but now did spurn me with his foot,
    To call me goddess, nymph, divine and rare,
    Precious, celestial? Wherefore speaks he this
    To her he hates? And wherefore doth Lysander
230   Deny your love, so rich within his soul,
    And tender° me, forsooth, affection,
    But by your setting on, by your consent?
    What though I be not so in grace° as you,
    So hung upon with love, so fortunate,
235   But miserable most, to love unloved?
    This you should pity rather than despise.
HERMIA.
    I understand not what you mean by this.
HELENA.
    Ay, do! Persever, counterfeit sad° looks,
    Make mouths° upon° me when I turn my back.
240   Wink each at other, hold the sweet jest up.°
    This sport, well carried,° shall be chronicled.
    If you have any pity, grace, or manners,
    You would not make me such an argument.°
    But fare ye well. 'Tis partly my own fault,
245   Which death, or absence, soon shall remedy.
LYSANDER.
    Stay, gentle Helena; hear my excuse,
    My love, my life, my soul, fair Helena!
HELENA.
    O excellent!
HERMIA [To Lysander].
    Sweet, do not scorn her so.
DEMETRIUS.
250   If she cannot entreat,° I can compel.
LYSANDER.
    Thou canst compel no more than she entreat.
    Thy threats have no more strength than her weak
        prayers.
    Helen, I love thee, by my life I do!
255   I swear by that which I will lose for thee,
    To prove him false that says I love thee not.
DEMETRIUS.
    I say I love thee more than he can do.
LYSANDER.
    If thou say so, withdraw, and prove it too.

DEMETRIUS.
    Quick, come!
HERMIA.   Lysander, whereto tends all this?
LYSANDER.
    Away, you Ethiop!°   260
                [He tries to break away from Hermia.]
DEMETRIUS. No, no; he'll
    Seem to break loose; take on as° you would follow,
    But yet come not. You are a tame man, go!
LYSANDER.
    Hang off,° thou cat, thou burr! Vile thing, let loose,
    Or I will shake thee from me like a serpent!   265
HERMIA.
    Why are you grown so rude? What change is this,
    Sweet love?
LYSANDER.   Thy love? Out, tawny Tartar, out!
    Out, loathèd med'cine!° O hated potion, hence!
HERMIA.
    Do you not jest?
HELENA.   Yes, sooth,° and so do you.
LYSANDER.
    Demetrius, I will keep my word with thee.   270
DEMETRIUS.
    I would I had your bond, for I perceive
    A weak bond° holds you. I'll not trust your word.
LYSANDER.
    What, should I hurt her, strike her, kill her dead?
    Although I hate her, I'll not harm her so.
HERMIA.
    What, can you do me greater harm than hate?   275
    Hate me? Wherefore? O me, what news,° my love?
    Am not I Hermia? Are not you Lysander?
    I am as fair now as I was erewhile.°
    Since night you loved me; yet since night you left me.
    Why, then you left me—O, the gods forbid!—   280
    In earnest, shall I say?
LYSANDER.   Ay, by my life!
    And never did desire to see thee more.
    Therefore be out of hope, of question, of doubt;
    Be certain, nothing truer. 'Tis no jest
    That I do hate thee and love Helena.   285
HERMIA [to Helena].
    O me! You juggler! You cankerblossom!°
    You thief of love! What, have you come by night
    And stol'n my love's heart from him?
HELENA.   Fine, i' faith!
    Have you no modesty, no maiden shame,

---

231 **tender** offer 233 **grace** favor 238 **sad** grave, serious 239 **mouths** i.e., mows, faces, grimaces. **upon** at 240 **hold . . . up** keep up the joke 241 **carried** managed 243 **argument** subject for a jest 250 **entreat** i.e., succeed by entreaty

260 **Ethiop** (Referring to Hermia's relatively dark hair and complexion; see also *tawny Tartar* six lines later.) 262 **take on as** act as if 264 **Hang off** let go 268 **med'cine** i.e., poison 269 **sooth** truly 272 **weak bond** i.e., Hermia's arm (with a pun on *bond*, oath, in the previous line) 276 **what news** what is the matter 278 **erewhile** just now 286 **cankerblossom** worm that destroys the flower bud (?)

290   No touch of bashfulness? What, will you tear
    Impatient answers from my gentle tongue?
    Fie, fie! You counterfeit, you puppet,° you!
    HERMIA.
    "Puppet"? Why, so!° Ay, that way goes the game.
    Now I perceive that she hath made compare
295   Between our statures: she hath urged her height,
    And with her personage, her tall personage,
    Her height, forsooth, she hath prevailed with him.
    And are you grown so high in his esteem
    Because I am so dwarfish and so low?
300   How low am I, thou painted maypole? Speak!
    How low am I? I am not yet so low
    But that my nails can reach unto thine eyes.

                  [*She flails at Helena but is restrained.*]

    HELENA.
    I pray you, though you mock me, gentlemen,
    Let her not hurt me. I was never curst;°
305   I have no gift at all in shrewishness;
    I am a right° maid for my cowardice.
    Let her not strike me. You perhaps may think,
    Because she is something° lower than myself,
    That I can match her.
    HERMIA.   Lower? Hark, again!
    HELENA.
310   Good Hermia, do not be so bitter with me.
    I evermore did love you, Hermia,
    Did ever keep your counsels, never wronged you;
    Save that, in love unto Demetrius,
    I told him of your stealth° unto this wood.
315   He followed you; for love I followed him.
    But he hath chid me hence° and threatened me
    To strike me, spurn me, nay, to kill me too.
    And now, so° you will let me quiet go,
    To Athens will I bear my folly back
320   And follow you no further. Let me go.
    You see how simple and how fond° I am.
    HERMIA.
    Why, get you gone. Who is 't that hinders you?
    HELENA.
    A foolish heart, that I leave here behind.
    HERMIA.
    What, with Lysander?
    HELENA.   With Demetrius.
    LYSANDER.
325   Be not afraid; she shall not harm thee, Helena.
    DEMETRIUS.
    No, sir, she shall not, though you take her part.

    HELENA.
    O, when she is angry, she is keen° and shrewd.°
    She was a vixen when she went to school,
    And though she be but little, she is fierce.
    HERMIA.
    "Little" again? Nothing but "low" and "little"?   330
    Why will you suffer her to flout me thus?
    Let me come to her.
    LYSANDER.   Get you gone, you dwarf!
    You minimus,° of hindering knotgrass° made!
    You bead, you acorn!
    DEMETRIUS.   You are too officious   335
    In her behalf that scorns your services.
    Let her alone. Speak not of Helena;
    Take not her part. For, if thou dost intend°
    Never so little show of love to her,
    Thou shalt aby° it.
    LYSANDER.   Now she holds me not;   340
    Now follow, if thou dar'st, to try whose right,
    Of thine or mine, is most in Helena.   [*Exit.*]
    DEMETRIUS.
    Follow? Nay, I'll go with thee, cheek by jowl.°

                  [*Exit, following Lysander.*]

    HERMIA.
    You, mistress, all this coil° is 'long of° you.
    Nay, go not back.°
    HELENA.   I will not trust you, I,   345
    Nor longer stay in your curst company.
    Your hands than mine are quicker for a fray;
    My legs are longer, though, to run away.   [*Exit.*]
    HERMIA.
    I am amazed and know not what to say.   *Exit.*

    [*Oberon and Puck come forward.*]

    OBERON.
    This is thy negligence. Still thou mistak'st,   350
    Or else committ'st thy knaveries willfully.
    PUCK.
    Believe me, king of shadows, I mistook.
    Did not you tell me I should know the man
    By the Athenian garments he had on?
    And so far blameless proves my enterprise   355
    That I have 'nointed an Athenian's eyes;
    And so far am I glad it so did sort,°
    As° this their jangling I esteem a sport.
    OBERON.
    Thou seest these lovers seek a place to fight.

---

292 puppet (1) counterfeit (2) dwarfish woman (in reference to
Hermia's smaller stature)   **293 Why, so** i.e., Oh, so that's how it is
304 curst shrewish   **306 right** true   **308 something** somewhat
314 stealth stealing away   **316 chid me hence** driven me away
with his scolding   **318 so** if only   **321 fond** foolish

327 keen fierce, cruel.   **shrewd** shrewish   **333 minimus** diminutive creature.   **knotgrass** a weed, an infusion of which was thought
to stunt the growth   **338 intend** give sign of   **340 aby** pay for
343 cheek by jowl i.e., side by side   **344 coil** turmoil, dissension.
'long of on account of   **345 go not back** i.e., don't retreat. (Hermia is again proposing a fight.)   **357 sort** turn out   **358 As** that
(also at l. 359)

360   Hie° therefore, Robin, overcast the night;
        The starry welkin° cover thou anon
        With drooping fog as black as Acheron,°
        And lead these testy rivals so astray
        As one come not within another's way.
365   Like to Lysander sometimes frame thy tongue,
        Then stir Demetrius up with bitter wrong;°
        And sometimes rail thou like Demetrius.
        And from each other look thou lead them thus,
        Till o'er their brows death-counterfeiting sleep
370   With leaden legs and batty° wings doth creep.
        Then crush this herb° into Lysander's eye,   [*Giving herb*]
        Whose liquor hath this virtuous° property,
        To take from thence all error with his° might
        And make his eyeballs roll with wonted° sight.
375   When they next wake, all this derision°
        Shall seem a dream and fruitless vision,
        And back to Athens shall the lovers wend
        With league whose date° till death shall never end.
        Whiles I in this affair do thee employ,
380   I'll to my queen and beg her Indian boy;
        And then I will her charmèd eye release
        From monster's view, and all things shall be peace.
     PUCK.
        My fairy lord, this must be done with haste,
        For night's swift dragons° cut the clouds full fast,
385   And yonder shines Aurora's harbinger,°
        At whose approach, ghosts, wand'ring here and there,
        Troop home to churchyards. Damnèd spirits all,
        That in crossways and floods have burial,°
        Already to their wormy beds are gone.
390   For fear lest day should look their shames upon,
        They willfully themselves exile from light
        And must for aye° consort with black-browed night.
     OBERON.
        But we are spirits of another sort.
        I with the Morning's love° have oft made sport,
395   And, like a forester,° the groves may tread
        Even till the eastern gate, all fiery red,

        Opening on Neptune with fair blessèd beams,
        Turns into yellow gold his salt green streams.
        But notwithstanding, haste, make no delay.
        We may effect this business yet ere day.   [*Exit.*]   400
     PUCK.
        Up and down, up and down,
        I will lead them up and down.
        I am feared in field and town.
        Goblin, lead them up and down.
        Here comes one.   405
     Enter Lysander.
     LYSANDER.
        Where art thou, proud Demetrius? Speak thou now.
     PUCK [*Mimicking Demetrius*].
        Here, villain, drawn° and ready. Where art thou?
     LYSANDER.
        I will be with thee straight.°
     PUCK.   Follow me, then,
        To plainer° ground.
             [*Lysander wanders about,° following the voice.*]
     Enter Demetrius.
     DEMETRIUS.   Lysander! Speak again!   410
        Thou runaway, thou coward, art thou fled?
        Speak! In some bush? Where dost thou hide thy head?
     PUCK [*Mimicking Lysander*].
        Thou coward, art thou bragging to the stars,
        Telling the bushes that thou look'st for wars,
        And wilt not come? Come, recreant;° come, thou child,   415
        I'll whip thee with a rod. He is defiled
        That draws a sword on thee.
     DEMETRIUS.   Yea, art thou there?
     PUCK.
        Follow my voice. We'll try° no manhood here.
                                Exeunt.
     [*Lysander returns.*]
     LYSANDER.
        He goes before me and still dares me on.   420
        When I come where he calls, then he is gone.
        The villain is much lighter-heeled than I.
        I followed fast, but faster he did fly,
        That fallen am I in dark uneven way,
        And here will rest me. [*He lies down.*] Come, thou gentle   425
          day!
        For if but once thou show me thy gray light,
        I'll find Demetrius and revenge this spite. [*He sleeps.*]

---

360 Hie hasten   **361 welkin** sky   **362 Acheron** river of Hades (here representing Hades itself)   **366 wrong** insults   **370 batty** batlike   **371 this herb** i.e., the antidote (mentioned in 2.1.184) to love-in-idleness   **372 virtuous** efficacious   **373 his** its   **374 wonted** accustomed   **375 derision** laughable business   **378 date** term of existence   **384 dragons** (Supposed by Shakespeare to be yoked to the car of the goddess of night.)   **385 Aurora's harbinger** the morning star, precursor of dawn   **388 crossways . . . burial** (Those who had committed suicide were buried at crossways, with a stake driven through them; those drowned, i.e., buried in floods or great waters, would be condemned to wander disconsolate for want of burial rites.)   **392 for aye** forever   **394 Morning's love** Cephalus, a beautiful youth beloved by Aurora; or perhaps the goddess of the dawn herself   **395 forester** keeper of a royal forest

407 drawn with drawn sword   **408 straight** immediately   **409 plainer** more open   **s.d. Lysander wanders about** (It is not clearly necessary that Lysander exit at this point; neither exit nor reentrance is indicated in the early texts.)   **415 recreant** cowardly wretch   **419 try** test

[Enter] Robin [Puck] and Demetrius.

PUCK.
  Ho, ho, ho! Coward, why com'st thou not?

DEMETRIUS.
430 Abide° me, if thou dar'st; for well I wot°
  Thou runn'st before me, shifting every place,
  And dar'st not stand nor look me in the face.
  Where art thou now?

PUCK.
              Come hither. I am here.

DEMETRIUS.
  Nay, then, thou mock'st me. Thou shalt buy° this dear,°
435 If ever I thy face by daylight see.
  Now, go thy way. Faintness constraineth me
  To measure out my length on this cold bed.
  By day's approach look to be visited.

          [He lies down and sleeps.]

Enter Helena.

HELENA.
  O weary night, O long and tedious night,
440   Abate° thy hours! Shine comforts from the east,
  That I may back to Athens by daylight,
    From these that my poor company detest;
  And sleep, that sometimes shuts up sorrow's eye,
  Steal me awhile from mine own company.

        [She lies down and] sleep[s].

PUCK.
445 Yet but three? Come one more;
  Two of both kinds makes up four.
  Here she comes, curst° and sad.
  Cupid is a knavish lad,
  Thus to make poor females mad.

[Enter Hermia.]

HERMIA.
450 Never so weary, never so in woe,
    Bedabbled with the dew and torn with briers
  I can no further crawl, no further go;
    My legs can keep no pace with my desires.
  Here will I rest me till the break of day.
455 Heavens shield Lysander, if they mean a fray!

        [She lies down and sleeps.]

PUCK.
    On the ground
    Sleep sound.
    I'll apply
    To your eye,
  Gentle lover, remedy.

460   *[Squeezing the juice on Lysander's eyes.]*

  When thou wak'st,
  Thou tak'st
  True delight
  In the sight
  Of thy former lady's eye;   465
  And the country proverb known,
  That every man should take his own,
  In your waking shall be shown:
    Jack shall have Jill;°
    Naught shall go ill;   470

The man shall have his mare again, and all shall be well.

    [Exit. The four sleeping lovers remain.]

[4.1] *Enter [Titania] Queen of Fairies, and [Bottom the] clown, and Fairies; and [Oberon,] the King, behind them.*

TITANIA.
  Come, sit thee down upon this flowery bed,
    While I thy amiable° cheeks do coy,°
  And stick muskroses in thy sleek smooth head,
    And kiss thy fair large ears, my gentle joy.

        [They recline.]

BOTTOM. Where's Peaseblossom?   5
PEASEBLOSSOM.
  Ready.
BOTTOM. Scratch my head, Peaseblossom. Where's Monsieur Cobweb?
COBWEB.
  Ready.
BOTTOM. Monsieur Cobweb, good monsieur, get you your   10
weapons in your hand, and kill me a red-hipped humble-
bee on the top of a thistle; and, good monsieur, bring me
the honey bag. Do not fret yourself too much in the
action, monsieur, and, good monsieur, have a care the
honey bag break not; I would be loath to have you over-   15
flown with a honey bag, signor. *[Exit Cobweb.]* Where's
Monsieur Mustardseed?
MUSTARDSEED.
  Ready.
BOTTOM. Give me your neaf,° Monsieur Mustardseed. Pray
you, leave your courtesy,° good monsieur.   20
MUSTARDSEED.
  What's your will?

---

469 **Jack shall have Jill** (Proverbial for "boy gets girl.")
4.1 Location: The action is continuous. The four lovers are still asleep onstage. **2 amiable** lovely. **coy** caress **19 neaf** fist **20 leave your courtesy** i.e., stop bowing, or put on your hat

---

430 **Abide** confront, face. **wot** know **434 buy** aby, pay for.
dear dearly **440 Abate** lessen, shorten **447 curst** ill-tempered

BOTTOM. Nothing, good monsieur, but to help Cavalery°
Cobweb° to scratch. I must to the barber's, monsieur, for
methinks I am marvelous hairy about the face; and I am
25   such a tender ass, if my hair do but tickle me, I must
scratch.

TITANIA.
What, wilt thou hear some music, my sweet love?

BOTTOM. I have a reasonable good ear in music. Let's have
the tongs and the bones.°

[*Music: tongs, rural music.°*]

TITANIA.
30   Or say, sweet love, what thou desirest to eat.

BOTTOM. Truly, a peck of provender.° I could munch your
good dry oats. Methinks I have a great desire to a bottle°
of hay. Good hay, sweet hay, hath no fellow.°

TITANIA.
I have a venturous fairy that shall seek
35   The squirrel's hoard, and fetch thee new nuts.

BOTTOM. I had rather have a handful or two of dried peas.
But, I pray you, let none of your people stir° me. I have
an exposition° of sleep come upon me.

TITANIA.
Sleep thou, and I will wind thee in my arms.
40   Fairies, begone, and be all ways° away.

[*Exeunt Fairies.*]

So doth the woodbine the sweet honeysuckle
Gently entwist; the female ivy so
Enrings the barky fingers of the elm.
O, how I love thee! How I dote on thee!

[*They sleep.*]

Enter Robin Goodfellow [Puck].

OBERON [*Coming forward*].
45   Welcome, good Robin. Seest thou this sweet sight?
Her dotage now I do begin to pity.
For, meeting her of late behind the wood,
Seeking sweet favors° for this hateful fool,
I did upbraid her and fall out with her.
50   For she his hairy temples then had rounded
With coronet of fresh and fragrant flowers;
And that same dew, which sometime° on the buds
Was wont to swell like round and orient pearls,°

Stood now within the pretty flowerets' eyes
Like tears that did their own disgrace bewail.   55
When I had at my pleasure taunted her,
And she in mild terms begged my patience,
I then did ask of her her changeling child,
Which straight she gave me, and her fairy sent
To bear him to my bower in Fairyland.   60
And, now I have the boy, I will undo
This hateful imperfection of her eyes.
And, gentle Puck, take this transformèd scalp
From off the head of this Athenian swain,
That he, awaking when the other° do,   65
May all to Athens back again repair,°
And think no more of this night's accidents
But as the fierce vexation of a dream.
But first I will release the Fairy Queen.

[*He squeezes a herb on her eyes.*]

Be as thou wast wont to be;   70
See as thou wast wont to see.
Dian's bud° o'er Cupid's flower
Hath such force and blessèd power.

Now, my Titania, wake you, my sweet queen.

TITANIA [*Waking*].
My Oberon! What visions have I seen!   75
Methought I was enamored of an ass.

OBERON.
There lies your love.

TITANIA.   How came these things to pass?
O, how mine eyes do loathe his visage now!

OBERON.
Silence awhile. Robin, take off this head.
Titania, music call, and strike more dead   80
Than common sleep of all these five° the sense.

TITANIA.
Music, ho! Music, such as charmeth° sleep!

[*Music.*]

PUCK [*Removing the ass head*].
Now, when thou wak'st, with thine own fool's eyes peep.

OBERON.
Sound, music! Come, my queen, take hands with me,
And rock the ground whereon these sleepers be.   85

[*They dance.*]

Now thou and I are new in amity,
And will tomorrow midnight solemnly°
Dance in Duke Theseus' house triumphantly,

---

22 **Cavalery** cavalier. (Form of address for a gentleman.)
23 **Cobweb** (Seemingly an error, since Cobweb has been sent to
bring honey while Peaseblossom has been asked to scratch.)
29 **tongs . . . bones** instruments for rustic music. (The tongs were
played like a triangle, whereas the bones were held between the fingers and used as clappers.) **s.d. Music . . . music** (This stage direction is added from the Folio.) 31 **peck of provender** one-quarter
bushel of grain 32 **bottle** bundle 33 **fellow** equal 37 **stir** disturb 38 **exposition** (Bottom's word for *disposition*.) 40 **all ways**
in all directions 48 **favors** i.e., gifts of flowers 52 **sometime** formerly 53 **orient pearls** i.e., the most beautiful of all pearls, those
coming from the Orient

65 **other** others 66 **repair** return 72 **Dian's bud** (Perhaps the
flower the flower of the *agnus castus* or chaste-tree, supposed to preserve chastity; or perhaps referring simply to Oberon's herb by
which he can undo the effects of "Cupid's flower," the love-in-idleness of 2.1.166–168.) 81 **these five** i.e., the four lovers and Bottom 82 **charmeth** brings about, as though by a charm
87 **solemnly** ceremoniously

     And bless it to all fair prosperity.
90   There shall the pairs of faithful lovers be
     Wedded, with Theseus, all in jollity.

PUCK.
     Fairy King, attend, and mark:
     I do hear the morning lark.

OBERON.
     Then, my queen, in silence sad,°
95   Trip we after night's shade.
     We the globe can compass soon,
     Swifter than the wandering moon.

TITANIA.
     Come, my lord, and in our flight
     Tell me how it came this night
100 That I sleeping here was found
     With these mortals on the ground.   *Exeunt.*

                     Wind horn [within].

Enter Theseus and all his train; [Hippolyta, Egeus].

THESEUS.
     Go, one of you, find out the forester,
     For now our observation° is performed;
     And since we have the vaward° of the day,
105 My love shall hear the music of my hounds.
     Uncouple° in the western valley, let them go.
     Dispatch, I say, and find the forester.   *[Exit an Attendant.]*
     We will, fair queen, up to the mountain's top
     And mark the musical confusion
110 Of hounds and echo in conjunction.

HIPPOLYTA.
     I was with Hercules and Cadmus° once,
     When in a wood of Crete they bayed° the bear
     With hounds of Sparta.° Never did I hear
     Such gallant chiding;° for, besides the groves,
115 The skies, the fountains, every region near
     Seemed all one mutual cry. I never heard
     So musical a discord, such sweet thunder.

THESEUS.
     My hounds are bred out of the Spartan kind,°
     So flewed,° so sanded;° and their heads are hung
120 With ears that sweep away the morning dew;
     Crook-kneed, and dewlapped° like Thessalian bulls;

Slow in pursuit, but matched in mouth like bells,
Each under each.° A cry° more tunable°
Was never holloed to, nor cheered° with horn,
In Crete, in Sparta, nor in Thessaly.   125
Judge when you hear. [*He sees the sleepers.*] But, soft!
     What nymphs are these?

EGEUS.
     My lord, this is my daughter here asleep,
     And this Lysander; this Demetrius is,
     This Helena, old Nedar's Helena.   130
     I wonder of° their being here together.

THESEUS.
     No doubt they rose up early to observe
     The rite of May, and hearing our intent,
     Came here in grace of our solemnity.°
     But speak, Egeus. Is not this the day   135
     That Hermia should give answer of her choice?

EGEUS.
     It is, my lord.

THESEUS.
     Go, bid the huntsmen wake them with their horns.

                     [Exit an Attendant.]

Shout within. Wind horns. They all start up.

     Good morrow, friends. Saint Valentine°is past.
     Begin these woodbirds but to couple now?   140

LYSANDER.
     Pardon, my lord.   *[They kneel.]*

THESEUS.   I pray you all, stand up.
     I know you two are rival enemies;
     How comes this gentle concord in the world,
     That hatred is so far from jealousy°
     To sleep by hate and fear no enmity?   145

LYSANDER.
     My lord, I shall reply amazedly,
     Half sleep, half waking; but as yet, I swear,
     I cannot truly say how I came here.
     But, as I think—for truly would I speak,
     And now I do bethink me, so it is—   150
     I came with Hermia hither. Our intent
     Was to be gone from Athens, where° we might,
     Without° the peril of the Athenian law—

EGEUS.
     Enough, enough, my lord; you have enough.
     I beg the law, the law, upon his head.   155
     They would have stol'n away; they would, Demetrius,

---

94 **sad** sober   103 **observation** i.e., observance to a morn of May (1.1.167)   104 **vaward** vanguard, i.e., earliest part   106 **Uncouple** set free for the hunt   111 **Cadmus** mythical founder of Thebes. (This story about him is unknown.)   112 **bayed** brought to bay   113 **hounds of Sparta** (A breed famous in antiquity for their hunting skill.)   114 **chiding** i.e., yelping   118 **kind** strain, breed   119 **So flewed** similarly having large hanging chaps or fleshly covering of the jaw. **sanded** of sandy color   121 **dewlapped** having pendulous folds of skin under the neck

122–123 **matched . . . each** i.e., harmoniously matched in their various cries like a set of bells, from treble down to bass   123 **cry** pack of hounds. **tunable** well tuned, melodious   124 **cheered** encouraged   131 **wonder of** wonder at   134 **in . . . solemnity** in honor of our wedding   139 **Saint Valentine** (Birds were supposed to choose their mates on Saint Valentine's Day.)   144 **jealousy** suspicion   152 **where** wherever; or, to where   153 **Without** outside of, beyond

Thereby to have defeated° you and me,
You of your wife and me of my consent,
Of my consent that she should be your wife.

DEMETRIUS.
160   My lord, fair Helen told me of their stealth,
Of this their purpose hither° to this wood,
And I in fury hither followed them,
Fair Helena in fancy following me.
But, my good lord, I wot not by what power—
165   But by some power it is—my love to Hermia,
Melted as the snow, seems to me now
As the remembrance of an idle gaud°
Which in my childhood I did dote upon;
And all the faith, the virtue of my heart,
170   The object and the pleasure of mine eye,
Is only Helena. To her, my lord,
Was I betrothed ere I saw Hermia,
But like a sickness did I loathe this food;
But, as in health, come to my natural taste,
175   Now I do wish it, love it, long for it,
And will for evermore be true to it.

THESEUS.
Fair lovers, you are fortunately met.
Of this discourse we more will hear anon.
Egeus, I will overbear your will;
180   For in the temple, by and by, with us
These couples shall eternally be knit.
And, for° the morning now is something° worn,
Our purposed hunting shall be set aside.
Away with us to Athens. Three and three,
185   We'll hold a feast in great solemnity.
Come, Hippolyta.

     [Exeunt Theseus, Hippolyta, Egeus, and train.]

DEMETRIUS.
These things seem small and undistinguishable,
Like far-off mountains turnèd into clouds.

HERMIA.
Methinks I see these things with parted° eye,
When everything seems double.

190 HELENA.   So methinks;
And I have found Demetrius like a jewel,
Mine own, and not mine own.°

DEMETRIUS.   Are you sure
That we are awake? It seems to me
195   That yet we sleep, we dream. Do not you think
The Duke was here, and bid us follow him?

HERMIA.
Yea, and my father.

HELENA.   And Hippolyta.

LYSANDER.
And he did bid us follow to the temple.

DEMETRIUS.
Why, then, we are awake. Let's follow him,
And by the way let us recount our dreams.   *[Exeunt.]* 200

BOTTOM *[Awaking].* When my cue comes, call me, and I will
answer. My next is, "Most fair Pyramus." Heigh—ho!
Peter Quince! Flute, the bellows mender! Snout, the tinker! Starveling! God's° my life, stolen hence and left me
asleep! I have had a most rare vision. I have had a dream, 205
past the wit of man to say what dream it was. Man is but
an ass if he go about° to expound this dream. Methought
I was—there is no man can tell what. Methought I was—
and methought I had—but man is but a patched° fool if
he will offer° to say what methought I had. The eye of 210
man hath not heard, the ear of man hath not seen, man's
hand is not able to taste, his tongue to conceive, nor his
heart to report,° what my dream was. I will get Peter
Quince to write a ballad of this dream. It shall be called
"Bottom's Dream," because it hath no bottom; and I will 215
sing it in the latter end of a play, before the Duke. Peradventure, to make it the more gracious, I shall sing it at
her° death.   *[Exit.]*

[4.2] *Enter Quince, Flute, [Snout, and Starveling].*

QUINCE. Have you sent to Bottom's house? Is he come home
yet?

STARVELING. He cannot be heard of. Out of doubt he is
transported.°

FLUTE. If he come not, then the play is marred. It goes not 5
forward, doth it?

QUINCE. It is not possible. You have not a man in all Athens
able to discharge° Pyramus but he.

FLUTE. No, he hath simply the best wit° of any handicraft
man in Athens. 10

QUINCE. Yea, and the best person° too, and he is a very paramour for a sweet voice.

FLUTE. You must say "paragon." A paramour is, God bless us,
a thing of naught.°

---

157 **defeated** defrauded   161 **hither** in coming hither   167 **idle
gaud** worthless trinket   182 **for** since. **something** somewhat
189 **parted** improperly focused   191–192 **like . . . mine own** i.e.,
like a jewel that one finds by chance and therefore possesses but
cannot certainly consider one's own property

204 **God's** may God save   207 **go about** attempt   209 **patched**
wearing motley, i.e., a dress of various colors.   210 **offer** venture
210–213 **The eye . . . report** (Bottom garbles the terms of 1
Corinthians 2:9)   218 **her** Thisbe's (?)
4.2 **Location:** Athens   4 **transported** carried off by fairies; or, possibly, transformed   8 **discharge** perform   9 **wit** intellect
11 **person** appearance   14 **a . . . naught** a shameful thing

Enter Snug the joiner.

15 SNUG. Masters, the Duke is coming from the temple and there is two or three lords and ladies more married. If our sport had gone forward, we had all been made men.°

FLUTE. O sweet bully Bottom! Thus hath he lost sixpence a
20 day during his life; he could not have scaped sixpence a day. An the Duke had not given him sixpence a day° for playing Pyramus, I'll be hanged. He would have deserved it. Sixpence a day in Pyramus, or nothing.

Enter Bottom.

BOTTOM. Where are these lads? Where are these hearts?°

QUINCE. Bottom! O most courageous day! O most happy
25 hour!

BOTTOM. Masters, I am to discourse wonders.° But ask me not what; for if I tell you, I am no true Athenian. I will tell you everything, right as it fell out.

QUINCE. Let us hear, sweet Bottom.

30 BOTTOM. Not a word of° me. All that I will tell you is—that the Duke hath dined. Get your apparel together, good strings° to your beards, new ribbons to your pumps;° meet presently° at the palace; every man look o'er his part; for the short and the long is, our play is preferred.° In any
35 case, let Thisbe have clean linen; and let not him that plays the lion pare his nails, for they shall hang out for the lion's claws. And, most dear actors, eat no onions nor garlic, for we are to utter sweet breath; and I do not doubt but to hear them say it is a sweet comedy. No more
40 words. Away! Go, away!

                                         [Exeunt.]

[5.1] *Enter Theseus, Hippolyta, and Philostrate,
[lords, and attendants].*

HIPPOLYTA.
  'Tis strange, my Theseus, that° these lovers speak of.

THESEUS.
  More strange than true. I never may° believe
  These antique° fables nor these fairy toys.°
  Lovers and madmen have such seething brains,
  Such shaping fantasies,° that apprehend°
5 More than cool reason ever comprehends.°

The lunatic, the lover, and the poet
Are of imagination all compact.°
One sees more devils than vast hell can hold;
That is the madman. The lover, all as frantic,   10
Sees Helen's° beauty in a brow of Egypt.°
The poet's eye, in a fine frenzy rolling,
Doth glance from heaven to earth, from earth to heaven;
And as imagination bodies forth
The forms of things unknown, the poet's pen   15
Turns them to shapes and gives to airy nothing
A local habitation and a name.
Such tricks hath strong imagination
That, if it would but apprehend some joy,
It comprehends some bringer° of that joy;   20
Or in the night, imagining some fear,°
How easy is a bush supposed a bear!

HIPPOLYTA.
  But all the story of the night told over,
  And all their minds transfigured so together,
  More witnesseth than fancy's images°   25
  And grows to something of great constancy;°
  But, howsoever,° strange and admirable.°

Enter lovers: Lysander, Demetrius, Hermia, and Helena.

THESEUS.
  Here come the lovers, full of joy and mirth.
  Joy, gentle friends! Joy and fresh days of love
  Accompany your hearts!

LYSANDER.   More than to us   30
  Wait in your royal walks, your board, your bed!

THESEUS.
  Come now, what masques,° what dances shall we have
  To wear away this long age of three hours
  Between our after-supper and bedtime?
  Where is our usual manager of mirth?   35
  What revels are in hand? Is there no play
  To ease the anguish of a torturing hour?
  Call Philostrate.

PHILOSTRATE.   Here, mighty Theseus.

THESEUS.
  Say what abridgment° have you for this evening?
  What masque? What music? How shall we beguile   40
  The lazy time, if not with some delight?

PHILOSTRATE [*Giving him a paper*].
  There is a brief° how many sports are ripe.
  Make choice of which Your Highness will see first.

---

17 we . . . men i.e., we would have had our fortunes made
20 sixpence a day i.e., as a royal pension   **23 hearts** good fellows
26 am . . . wonders have wonders to relate   **30 of** out of
32 strings (to attach the beards)   **pumps** light shoes or slippers.
33 presently immediately   **34 preferred** selected for consideration
5.1 Location: Athens. The palace of Theseus. 1 that that which   **2 may** can   **3 antique** old-fashioned (punning too on *antic*, strange, grotesque).   **fairy toys** trifling stories about fairies
5 fantasies imaginations. **apprehend** conceive, imagine
6 comprehends understands

8 compact formed, composed   **11 Helen's** i.e., of Helen of Troy, pattern of beauty.   **brow of Egypt** i.e., face of a gypsy   **20 bringer** i.e., source   **21 fear** object of fear   **25 More . . . images** testifies to something more substantial than mere imaginings
26 constancy certainty   **27 howsoever** in any case   **admirable** a source of wonder   **32 masques** courtly entertainments
39 abridgment pastime (to abridge or shorten the evening)
42 brief short written statement, summary

THESEUS [*Reads*].
　　"The battle with the Centaurs,° to be sung
45　　By an Athenian eunuch to the harp"?
　　We'll none of that. That have I told my love,
　　In glory of my kinsman° Hercules.
　　[*Reads*.] "The riot of the tipsy Bacchanals,
　　Tearing the Thracian singer in their rage"?°
50　　That is an old device;° and it was played
　　When I from Thebes came last a conqueror.
　　[*Reads*.] "The thrice three Muses mourning for the death
　　Of Learning, late deceased in beggary"?°
　　That is some satire, keen and critical,
55　　Not sorting with° a nuptial ceremony.
　　[*Reads*.] "A tedious brief scene of young Pyramus
　　And his love Thisbe; very tragical mirth"?
　　Merry and tragical? Tedious and brief?
　　That is hot ice and wondrous strange° snow.
60　　How shall we find the concord of this discord?
PHILOSTRATE.
　　A play there is, my lord, some ten words long,
　　Which is as brief as I have known a play;
　　But by ten words, my lord, it is too long,
　　Which makes it tedious. For in all the play
65　　There is not one word apt, one player fitted.
　　And tragical, my noble lord, it is,
　　For Pyramus therein doth kill himself.
　　Which, when I saw rehearsed, I must confess,
　　Made mine eyes water; but more merry tears
70　　The passion of loud laughter never shed.
THESEUS.
　　What are they that do play it?
PHILOSTRATE.
　　Hard-handed men that work in Athens here,
　　Which never labored in their minds till now,
　　And now have toiled° their unbreathed° memories
75　　With this same play, against° your nuptial.
THESEUS.
　　And we will hear it.
PHILOSTRATE.　　　　　No, my noble lord,
　　It is not for you. I have heard it over,

And it is nothing, nothing in the world;
Unless you can find sport in their intents,
Extremely stretched° and conned° with cruel pain　　80
To do you service.
THESEUS.　　　　　　I will hear that play;
For never anything can be amiss
When simpleness° and duty tender it.
Go bring them in; and take your places, ladies.

　　　　　　　　[*Philostrate goes to summon the players*.]
HIPPOLYTA.
　　I love not to see wretchedness o'ercharged,°　　85
　　And duty in his service° perishing.
THESEUS.
　　Why, gentle sweet, you shall see no such thing.
HIPPOLYTA.
　　He says they can do nothing in this kind.°
THESEUS.
　　The kinder we, to give them thanks for nothing.
　　Our sport shall be to take what they mistake;　　90
　　And what poor duty cannot do, noble respect°
　　Takes it in might, not merit.°
　　Where I have come, great clerks° have purposèd
　　To greet me with premeditated welcomes;
　　Where I have seen them shiver and look pale,　　95
　　Make periods in the midst of sentences,
　　Throttle their practiced accent° in their fears,
　　And in conclusion dumbly have broke off,
　　Not paying me a welcome. Trust me, sweet,
　　Out of this silence yet I picked a welcome;　　100
　　And in the modesty of fearful duty
　　I read as much as from the rattling tongue
　　Of saucy and audacious eloquence.
　　Love, therefore, and tongue-tied simplicity
　　In least° speak most, to my capacity.°　　105
[*Philostrate returns*.]

PHILOSTRATE. So please Your Grace, the Prologue° is
　　addressed.°
THESEUS. Let him approach.　　　[*A flourish of trumpets*.]
　　Enter the Prologue [*Quince*].
PROLOGUE.
　　If we offend, it is with our good will.
　　That you should think, we come not to offend,　　110

44 battle . . . Centaurs (Probably refers to the battle of the Centaurs and the Lapithae, when the Centaurs attempted to carry off Hippodamia, bride of Theseus' friend Pirothous.) 47 kinsman (Plutarch's "Life of Theseus" states that Hercules and Theseus were near kinsmen. Theseus is referring to a version of the battle of the Centaurs in which Hercules was said to be present.) 48–49 The riot . . . rage (This was the story of the death of Orpheus, as told in *Metamorphoses* 9.) 50 device show, performance 52–53 The thrice . . . beggary (Possibly an allusion to Spenser's *Tears of the Muses*, 1591, though "satires" deploring the neglect of learning and the creative arts were commonplace.) 55 sorting with befitting 59 strange (Sometimes emended to an adjective that would contrast with *snow*, just as *hot* contrasts with *ice*.) 74 toiled taxed. unbreathed unexercised 75 against in preparation for

80 stretched strained. conned memorized 83 simpleness simplicity 85 wretchedness o'ercharged incompetence overburdened 86 his service its attempt to serve 88 kind kind of thing 91 respect evaluation, consideration 92 Takes . . . merit values it for the effort made rather than for the excellence achieved 93 clerks learned men 97 practiced accent i.e., rehearsed speech; or, usual way of speaking 105 least i.e., saying least. to my capacity in my judgment and understanding 106 Prologue speaker of the prologue. 107 addressed ready

But with good will. To show our simple skill,
    That is the true beginning of our end.
Consider then, we come but in despite.
    We do not come, as minding° to content you,
115 Our true intent is. All for your delight.
    We are not here. That you should here repent you,
The actors are at hand, and, by their show,
You shall know all that you are like to know.
THESEUS. This fellow doth not stand upon points.°
120 LYSANDER. He hath rid° his prologue like a rough° colt; he
    knows not the stop.° A good moral, my lord: it is not
    enough to speak, but to speak true.
HIPPOLYTA. Indeed he hath played on his prologue like a
    child on a recorder°; a sound, but not in government.°
125 THESEUS. His speech was like a tangled chain: nothing°
    impaired, but all disordered. Who is next?

    *Enter Pyramus [Bottom] and Thisbe [Flute], and Wall
    [Snout], and Moonshine [Starveling], and Lion [Snug].*

PROLOGUE.
    Gentles, perchance you wonder at this show,
        But wonder on, till truth makes all things plain.
    This man is Pyramus, if you would know;
130   This beauteous lady Thisbe is certain.
    This man with lime and roughcast doth present
        Wall, that vile Wall which did these lovers sunder;
    And through Wall's chink, poor souls, they are content
        To whisper. At the which let no man wonder.
135 This man, with lantern, dog, and bush of thorn,
        Presenteth Moonshine; for, if you will know,
    By moonshine did these lovers think no scorn°
        To meet at Ninus' tomb, there, there to woo.
    This grisly beast, which Lion hight° by name,
140   The trusty Thisbe coming first by night
    Did scare away, or rather did affright;
    And as she fled, her mantle she did fall,°
        Which Lion vile with bloody mouth did stain.
    Anon comes Pyramus, sweet youth and tall,°
145   And finds his trusty Thisbe's mantle slain;
    Whereat, with blade, with bloody blameful blade,
        He bravely broached° his boiling bloody breast.
    And Thisbe, tarrying in mulberry shade,
        His dagger drew, and died. For all the rest,
150 Let Lion, Moonshine, Wall, and lovers twain
    At large° discourse while here they do remain.

    Exeunt Lion, Thisbe, and Moonshine.
THESEUS. I wonder if the lion be to speak.
DEMETRIUS. No wonder, my lord. One lion may, when many
    asses do.
WALL.
    In this same interlude° it doth befall   155
    That I, one Snout by name, present a wall;
    And such a wall as I would have you think
    That had in it a crannied hole or chink,
    Through which the lovers, Pyramus and Thisbe,
    Did whisper often, very secretly.   160
    This loam, this roughcast, and this stone doth show
    That I am that same wall; the truth is so.
    And this the cranny is, right and sinister,°
    Through which the fearful lovers are to whisper.
THESEUS. Would you desire lime and hair to speak better?   165
DEMETRIUS. It is the wittiest partition° that ever I heard dis-
    course, my lord.

    [Pyramus comes forward.]
THESEUS. Pyramus draws near the wall. Silence!
PYRAMUS.
    O grim-looked° night! O night with hue so black!
        O night, which ever art when day is not!   170
    O night, O night! Alack, alack, alack,
        I fear my Thisbe's promise is forgot.
    And thou, O wall, O sweet, O lovely wall,
        That stand'st between her father's ground and mine,
    Thou wall, O wall, O sweet and lovely wall,   175
        Show me thy chink to blink through with mine eyne!

        [Wall makes a chink with his fingers.]
    Thanks, courteous wall. Jove shield thee well for this.
        But what see I? No Thisbe do I see.
    O wicked wall, through whom I see no bliss!
        Cursed by they stones for thus deceiving me!   180
THESEUS. The wall, methinks, being sensible,° should curse
    again.
PYRAMUS. No, in truth, sir, he should not. "Deceiving me" is
    Thisbe's cue: she is to enter now, and I am to spy her
    through the wall. You shall see, it will fall pat° as I told   185
    you. Yonder she comes.

    Enter Thisbe.
THISBE.
    O wall, full often hast thou heard my moans,
        For parting my fair Pyramus and me.
    My cherry lips have often kissed thy stones,
        Thy stones with lime and hair knit up in thee.   190

---

114 minding intending   **119 stand upon points** (1) heed niceties
or small points (2) pay attention to punctuation in his reading.
(The humor of Quince's speech is in the blunders of its punctuation.)   **120 rid** ridden.   **rough** unbroken   **121 stop** (1) the stopping of a colt by reining it in (2) punctuation mark   **124 recorder**
a wind instrument like a flute or flageolet   **government** control
125 nothing not at all   **137 think no scorn** think it no disgraceful
matter   **139 hight** is called   **142 fall** let fall   **144 tall** courageous
147 broached stabbed   **151 At large** in full, at length

155 interlude play   **163 right and sinister** i.e., the right side of it
and the left; or, running from right to left, horizontally
166 partition (1) wall (2) section of a learned treatise or oration
169 grim-looked grim-looking   **181 sensible** capable of feeling
185 pat exactly

PYRAMUS.
    I see a voice. Now will I to the chink,
        To spy an° I can hear my Thisbe's face.
    Thisbe!

THISBE.
    My love! Thou art my love, I think.

PYRAMUS.
195   Think what thou wilt, I am thy lover's grace,°
    And like Limander° am I trusty still.

THISBE.
    And I like Helen,° till the Fates me kill.

PYRAMUS.
    Not Shafalus to Procrus° was so true.

THISBE.
    As Shafalus to Procrus, I to you.

PYRAMUS.
200   O, kiss me through the hole of this vile wall!

THISBE.
    I kiss the wall's hole, not your lips at all.

PYRAMUS.
    Wilt thou at Ninny's tomb meet me straightway?

THISBE.
    'Tide° life, 'tide death, I come without delay.

                        [*Exeunt Pyramus and Thisbe.*]

WALL.
    Thus have I, Wall, my part dischargèd so;
205   And, being done, thus Wall away doth go.   [*Exit.*]

THESEUS. Now is the mural down between the two neighbors.

DEMETRIUS. No remedy, my lord, when walls are so willful°
    to hear without warning.°

210 HIPPOLYTA. This is the silliest stuff that ever I heard.

THESEUS. The best in this kind° are but shadows;° and the
    worst are no worse, if imagination amend them.

HIPPOLYTA. It must be your imagination then, and not
    theirs.

215 THESEUS. If we imagine no worse of them than they of
    themselves, they may pass for excellent men. Here come
    two noble beasts in, a man and a lion.

    Enter Lion and Moonshine.

LION.
    You, ladies, you whose gentle hearts do fear
        The smallest monstrous mouse that creeps on floor,
220   May now perchance both quake and tremble here,
        When lion rough in wildest rage doth roar.

    Then know that I, as Snug the joiner, am
    A lion fell,° nor else no lion's dam;
    For, if I should as lion come in strife
    Into this place, 'twere pity on my life.   225

THESEUS. A very gentle beast, and of a good conscience.

DEMETRIUS. The very best at a beast, my lord, that e'er I saw.

LYSANDER. This lion is a very fox for his valor.°

THESEUS. True; and a goose for his discretion.°

DEMETRIUS. Not so, my lord; for his valor cannot carry his 230
    discretion; and the fox carries the goose.

THESEUS. His discretion, I am sure, cannot carry his valor;
    for the goose carries not the fox. It is well. Leave it to his
    discretion, and let us listen to the moon.

MOON.
    This lanthorn° doth the hornèd moon present—   235

DEMETRIUS. He should have worn the horns on his head.°

THESEUS. He is no crescent, and his horns are invisible
    within the circumference.

MOON.
    This lanthorn doth the hornèd moon present;
    Myself the man i' the moon do seem to be.   240

THESEUS. This is the greatest error of all the rest. The man
    should be put into the lanthorn. How is it else the man i'
    the moon?

DEMETRIUS. He dares not come there for the° candle, for
    you see, it is already in snuff.°   245

HIPPOLYTA. I am aweary of this moon. Would he would
    change!

THESEUS. It appears, by his small light of discretion, that he
    is in the wane; but yet, in courtesy, in all reason, we must
    stay the time.   250

LYSANDER. Proceed, Moon.

MOON. All that I have to say is to tell you that the lanthorn
    is the moon, the man i' the moon, this thornbush my
    thornbush, and this dog my dog.

DEMETRIUS. Why, all these should be in the lanthorn, for all 255
    these are in the moon. But silence! Here comes Thisbe.

    Enter Thisbe.

THISBE.
    This is old Ninny's tomb. Where is my love?

LION [*Roaring*].
    O!

DEMETRIUS. Well roared, Lion.

               [*Thisbe runs off, dropping her mantle.*]

---

223 **lion fell** fierce lion (with a play on the idea of "lion skin")
228 **is . . . valor** i.e., his valor consists of craftiness and discretion
229 **goose . . . discretion** i.e., as discreet as a goose, that is, more
foolish than discreet 235 **lanthorn** (This original spelling, *lanthorn*, may suggest a play on the *horn* of which lanterns were made,
and also on a cuckold's horns; but the spelling *lanthorn* is not used
consistently for comic effect in this play or elsewhere. At 5.1.135,
for example, the word is *lantern* in the original.) 236 **on his head**
(as a sign of cuckoldry) 244 **for the** because of the 245 **in snuff**
(1) offended (2) in need of snuffing or trimming

---

192 **an** if 195 **lover's grace** i.e., gracious lover 196,
197 **Limander, Helen** (Blunders for *Leander* and *Hero.*)
198 **Shafalus, Procrus** (Blunders for *Cephalus* and *Procris*, also
famous lovers.) 203 **'Tide** betide, come 208 **willful** willing
209 **without warning** i.e., without warning the parents. (Demetrius
makes a joke on the proverb "Walls have ears.") 211 **in this kind**
of this sort. **shadows** likenesses, representations

260 THESEUS. Well run, Thisbe.

HIPPOLYTA. Well shone, Moon. Truly, the moon shines with
    a good grace.

                                      [The Lion worries Thisbe's mantle.]

THESEUS. Well moused,° Lion.

    Enter Pyramus.   *[Exit Lion.]*

DEMETRIUS. And then came Pyramus.

265 LYSANDER. And so the lion vanished.

PYRAMUS.

    Sweet Moon, I thank thee for thy sunny beams;
      I thank thee, Moon, for shining now so bright;
    For, by thy gracious, golden, glittering gleams,
    I trust to take of truest Thisbe sight.

270   But stay, O spite!
      But mark, poor knight,
    What dreadful dole° is here?
      Eyes, do you see?
      How can it be?
275   O dainty duck! O dear!
      Thy mantle good,
      What, stained with blood!
    Approach, ye Furies° fell!°
      O Fates,° come, come,
280   Cut thread and thrum;°
    Quail,° crush, conclude, and quell!°

THESEUS. This passion, and the death of a dear friend, would
    go near to make a man look sad.°

HIPPOLYTA. Beshrew my heart, but I pity the man.

PYRAMUS.

285   O, wherefore, Nature, didst thou lions frame?
    Since lion vile hath here deflowered my dear,
    Which is—no, no, which was—the fairest dame
    That lived, that loved, that liked, that looked with
      cheer.°

290   Come, tears, confound,
      Out, sword, and wound
    The pap° of Pyramus;
      Ay, that left pap,
      Where heart doth hop.   *[He stabs himself.]*
295   Thus die I, thus, thus, thus.
      Now am I dead,
      Now am I fled;

    My soul is in the sky.
      Tongue, lose thy light;
      Moon, take thy flight.   *[Exit Moonshine.]* 300
    Now die, die, die, die, die.   *[Pyramus dies.]*

DEMETRIUS. No die, but an ace,° for him; for he is but one.°

LYSANDER. Less than an ace, man; for he is dead, he is noth-
    ing.

THESEUS. With the help of a surgeon he might yet recover, 305
    and yet prove an ass.°

HIPPOLYTA. How chance Moonshine is gone before Thisbe
    comes back and finds her lover?

THESEUS. She will find him by starlight.

    [Enter Thisbe.]

    Here she comes, and her passion ends the play. 310

HIPPOLYTA. Methinks she should not use a long one for such
    a Pyramus. I hope she will be brief.

DEMETRIUS. A mote° will turn the balance, which Pyramus,
    which° Thisbe, is the better: he for a man, God warrant
    us; she for a woman, God bless us. 315

LYSANDER. She hath spied him already with those sweet
    eyes.

DEMETRIUS. And thus she means,° videlicet:°

THISBE.

      Asleep, my love?
      What, dead, my dove? 320
    O Pyramus, arise!
      Speak, speak. Quite dumb?
      Dead, dead? A tomb
    Must cover thy sweet eyes.
      These lily lips, 325
      This cherry nose,
    These yellow cowslip cheeks,
      Are gone, are gone!
      Lovers, make moan.
    His eyes were green as leeks. 330
      O Sisters Three,°
      Come, come to me,
    With hands as pale as milk;
      Lay them in gore,
      Since you have shore° 335
    With shears his thread of silk.
      Tongue, not a word.
      Come, trusty sword,
    Come, blade, my breast imbrue!°   *[Stabs herself.]*
      And farewell, friends. 340
      Thus Thisbe ends.
    Adieu, adieu, adieu.   *[She dies.]*

263 **moused** shaken, torn, bitten 272 **dole** grievous event
278 **Furies** avenging goddesses of Greek myth. **fell** fierce
279 **Fates** the three goddesses (Clotho, Lachesis, Atropos) of
Greek myth who drew and cut the thread of human life
280 **thread and thrum** the warp in weaving and the loose end of
the warp 281 **Quail** overpower. **quell** kill, destroy
282–283 **This . . . sad** i.e., if one had other reason to grieve, one
might be sad, but not from this absurd portrayal of passion
289 **cheer** countenance 292 **pap** breast

302 **ace** the side of the die featuring the single pip, or spot. (The
pun is on *die* as a singular of *dice*; Bottom's performance is not worth
a whole *die* but rather one single face of it, one small portion.)
one (1) an individual person (2) unique 306 **ass** (with a pun on
ace) 313 **mote** small particle. **which . . . which** whether . . . or
318 **means** moans, laments. **videlicet** to wit 331 **Sisters Three**
the Fates 335 **shore** shorn 339 **imbrue** stain with blood

THESEUS. Moonshine and Lion are left to bury the dead.

DEMETRIUS. Ay, and Wall too.

345 BOTTOM [*Starting up, as Flute does also*]. No, I assure you, the wall is down that parted their fathers. Will it please you to see the epilogue, or to hear a Bergomask dance° between two of our company?

[*The other players enter.*]

THESEUS. No epilogue, I pray you; for your play needs no
350 excuse. Never excuse; for when the players are all dead, there need none to be blamed. Marry, if he that writ it had played Pyramus and hanged himself in Thisbe's garter, it would have been a fine tragedy; and so it is, truly, and very notably discharged. But, come, your
355 Bergomask. Let your epilogue alone.   [*A dance.*]

The iron tongue° of midnight hath told° twelve.
Lovers, to bed, 'tis almost fairy time.
I fear we shall outsleep the coming morn
As much as we this night have overwatched.°
360 This palpable-gross° play hath well beguiled
The heavy° gait of night. Sweet friends, to bed.
A fortnight hold we this solemnity,
In nightly revels and new jollity.   *Exeunt.*

Enter Puck [*carrying a broom*].

PUCK.
Now the hungry lion roars,
365   And the wolf behowls the moon;
Whilst the heavy° plowman snores,
    All with weary task fordone.°
Now the wasted brands° do glow,
    Whilst the screech owl, screeching loud
370 Puts the wretch that lies in woe
    In remembrance of a shroud.
Now it is the time of night
    That the graves, all gaping wide,
Every one lets forth his sprite,°
375   In the church-way paths to glide.
And we fairies, that do run
    By the triple Hecate's° team
From the presence of the sun,
    Following darkness like a dream,
380 Now are frolic.° Not a mouse
    Shall disturb this hallowed house.

I am sent with broom before,
To sweep the dust behind° the door.

Enter [*Oberon and Titania,*] *King and Queen of Fairies,
with all their train.*

OBERON.
Through the house give glimmering light,
    By the dead and drowsy fire;   385
Every elf and fairy sprite
    Hop as light as bird from brier;
And this ditty, after me,
Sing, and dance it trippingly.

TITANIA.
First, rehearse your song by rote,   390
To each word a warbling note.
Hand in hand, with fairy grace,
Will we sing, and bless this place.

[*Song and dance.*]

OBERON.
Now, until the break of day,
Through this house each fairy stray.   395
To the best bride-bed will we,
Which by us shall blessèd be;
And the issue there create°
Ever shall be fortunate.
So shall all the couples three   400
Ever true in loving be;
And the blots of Nature's hand
Shall not in their issue stand;
Never mole, harelip, nor scar,
Nor mark prodigious,° such as are   405
Despisèd in nativity,
Shall upon their children be.
With this field dew consecrate°
Every fairy take his gait,°
And each several° chamber bless,   410
Through this palace, with sweet peace;
And the owner of it blest
Ever shall in safety rest.
Trip away; make no stay;
Meet me all by break of day.   415

Exeunt [*Oberon, Titania, and train*].

PUCK [*To the audience*].
If we shadows have offended,
Think but this, and all is mended,
That you have but slumbered here°
While these visions did appear.
And this weak and idle theme,   420

347 **Bergomask dance** a rustic dance named from Bergamo, a province in the state of Venice   355 **iron tongue** i.e., of a bell. **told** counted, struck ("tolled")   359 **overwatched** stayed up too late 360 **palpable-gross** gross, obviously crude   361 **heavy** drowsy, dull 366 **heavy** tired   367 **fordone** exhausted   368 **wasted brands** burned-out logs   374 **Every . . . sprite** every grave lets forth its ghost   377 **triple Hecate's** (Hecate ruled in three capacities: as Luna or Cynthia in heaven, as Diana on earth, and as Proserpina in hell.)   380 **frolic** merry

383 **behind** from behind. (Robin Goodfellow was a household spirit who helped good housemaids and punished lazy ones.)   398 **create** created   405 **prodigious** monstrous, unnatural   408 **consecrate** consecrated   409 **take his gait** go his way   410 **several** separate 418 **That . . . here** i.e., that it is a "midsummer night's dream"

No more yielding but° a dream,
Gentles, do not reprehend.
If you pardon, we will mend.°
And, as I am an honest Puck,
425   If we have unearnèd luck
Now to scape the serpent's tongue,°

We will make amends ere long;
Else the Puck a liar call.
So, good night unto you all.
Give me your hands,° if we be friends,   430
And Robin shall restore amends.°   [*Exit.*]

TOPICS FOR CRITICAL THINKING AND WRITING

📖 THE PLAY ON THE PAGE

1. What impression do you get of Theseus in the first scene?
2. Characterize Bottom in the second scene.
3. The love story is really complete by the end of the fourth act. What does the fifth act contribute to the play?

4. What ironies (see the Glossary) do you find in the play?
5. What do you find funny about *A Midsummer Night's Dream?*

🎭 THE PLAY ON THE STAGE

6. Take one scene and compose detailed stage directions for it, indicating exactly how you would stage the scene.
7. What challenges do the roles of Lysander, Demetrius, Hermia, and Helena offer the actors? Take either the pair of men or the pair of women and set forth the suggestions you would give to the performers if you were directing a production.
8. If a small company were producing the play, which roles might be double- (or triple-) cast?
9. If you were directing and had decided on modern dress, what costumes and stage actions might be suitable for

Theseus and Hippolyta in the first scene? For the Rude Mechanicals when they stage *Pyramus and Thisby?*
10. Propose three very different stage or film actors or actresses who might play Puck, and explain the strengths each would bring to the role.
11. When the St. Louis Shakespeare Company staged the play recently, they cast a young child to play the changeling over whom Oberon and Titania quarrel. He appeared on stage in all the relevant scenes. What do you think of this decision? Why?

THE PLAY IN PERFORMANCE

In the last few decades, the productions of *A Midsummer Night's Dream* that have aroused the most interest are the ones that have emphasized the dark aspects of the comedy. This concern with "the fierce vexation of a dream" (Oberon's words, in 4.1.68) makes a marked contrast with the sweet, opulent productions that from the middle of the nineteenth century until the second decade of the twentieth century prettified the play with butterfly-winged child fairies, gauzy sets, and Mendelssohn's music. When Theseus smoothly says to Hippolyta, "I wooed thee with my sword," directors and spectators—heirs to Brecht, and to Artaud's Theater of Cruelty—can easily perceive the violence of rape. And so a play that a century ago was thought to be an airy trifle, full of high jinks and lovely sentiments about love, is now seen largely as an image of brutality. Thus, in

John Hancock's production (San Francisco, 1965, New York, 1967), Hippolyta in leopard skins was brought onstage as a captive, Hermia was a transvestite, Demetrius wore an electrified codpiece; the emphasis was on the malevolence of the fairies, and the cruelty and lust of the humans. Mendelssohn's music was used—but ironically, since it blared from a jukebox.

It is not puzzling that our time should emphasize the eroticism and the violence of the play, just as it is not puzzling that the second half of the nineteenth century emphasized the lyricism; what is puzzling is that *A Midsummer Night's Dream*—Shakespeare's play as opposed to operatic versions of it—was in effect banished from the theater from the second half of the seventeenth century until 1840, when Madame Vestris staged a fairly full text at Covent Garden in

---

421 No...but yielding no more than   **423 mend** improve
426 serpent's tongue i.e., hissing

430 Give...hands applaud   **431 restore amends** give satisfaction in return

London. Her version served as the basis for all productions of the play until Harley Granville Barker staged an uncut version in 1914. Rejecting the realistic scenery that had characterized productions of the late nineteenth and early twentieth centuries, Barker used what he called "decorative" settings. (See page 226 for an illustration, and for a brief additional account of his production.)

For the next fifty years most productions seemed either to echo Granville Barker or to react against him. One production, however, neither echoed nor answered him: this was Louis Armstrong's and Benny Goodman's *Swingin' the Dream*, done in 1939 with a predominantly black cast that included Armstrong as Bottom, Butterfly McQueen as Puck, Maxine Sullivan as Titania, and the Dandridge Sisters as three fairies. The book was by Gilbert Seldes and Erik Charell, the locale was New Orleans in the late nineteenth century, and the scenery was indebted to Walt Disney. Despite all of this talent, it was unsuccessful, running for only thirteen performances.

Of all the productions of Shakespeare's play since Barker's the most widely discussed was Peter Brook's Stratford version, given in 1970. Brook has said that he was influenced by Jan Kott's *Shakespeare Our Contemporary*, which emphasizes the night world of sex and violence. In the spirit of Kott, Brook said that Oberon furnishes Titania with "the crudest sex machine he can find"—though one might pedantically point out that Oberon doesn't choose Bottom, or anyone, for it is only by chance that Bottom enters Titania's line of sight.

Curiously, given the stimulus of Kott, the production was in many ways attractive and elegant, with a brightly lit box set consisting of three white walls surrounded by a catwalk. Brook has said that he was influenced by the circus, and the circus element was evident from the start, when the entire company entered to a roll of drums, removed their white capes and revealed their costumes. (For an illustration and a further comment on this production, see page 227.)

Most productions of A *Midsummer Night's Dream* are somewhat more traditional than Brook's, but the emphasis on anti-illusionism and on aggressive sexuality continue, and since 1964, when Kott's book was published in English, most productions have been influenced by Kott's vision of the play as a work concerned with violence and power. For instance, Liviu Ciulei at the Guthrie Theater in Minneapolis in 1985, and in Purchase, New York, in 1986, used a blood-red vinyl set in order, he said, to represent passion in a play about a society in which males dominate. His Hippolyta, a black woman, in an opening dumb show at first appeared in dark battle fatigues. Female attendants removed her clothes, tossed them onto a glowing brazier, and then wrapped her in white clothes taken from mannequins. (Thus Ciulei gave the play racial overtones too.) Theseus then entered and offered casual approval of the transformation of a passionate black into a tamed pseudo-white. Violence of a less subtle sort was provided by the switchblades of the lovers, which are more threatening to a twentieth-century audience than swords would have been.

Alan MacVey
DIRECTING A MIDSUMMER NIGHT'S DREAM

Alan MacVey teaches at the University of Iowa. In the following interview he discusses a production he directed in 1980 at the Bread Loaf School of English. The cast included Equity actors, faculty, and students from the school.

It's my impression that A Midsummer Night's Dream *is a special favorite in our time. Do you agree?*

Yes. One of the reasons this play has been so popular on the contemporary stage is that it gives directors great opportunities to play. It can work as a romantic comedy, as an investigation of unconscious desires, as an explosion of sexual energy (violent or not), as an exploration of gender roles, or as a dark rumination on power. I've done the play three times in three different ways. In each case the production was very much about the power of sex to change individuals and determine relationships, but the style and feel of each production was quite different.

What was the conception behind the productions?

In each of the productions I began with the same image: a rock in the forest. The top of the rock is rubbed clean. It's

nearly white. Lift the rock up, however, and you find insects, mold, and all kinds of things you wouldn't have imagined.

Which of the three productions pleased you most?

I was happy with all three productions, but I'll discuss the middle one, done at Bread Loaf in 1980. I set the play in the modern world. Costumes were white with bits of color here and there; they included a few Elizabethan touches (in design) and a hint of Greek (in color), but were basically modern. Much of the first part of the play was done in front of a white wall. Later, when the characters entered the forest, the wall spun away and revealed a deep, dark setting inhabited by strange beings. Arriving back in the palace at the end of the play we repeated the wall, now divided into smaller sections that gave both space and organization.

In addition to visual effects, you must have been concerned with aural effects, for instance with music.

Yes. Music is important in *Midsummer*. It can arise from almost any period and can be romantic, mysterious, strange, even violent. Perhaps it's best if it touches all these bases. Our production used a mixture of classical music (for the court scenes) and electronic/computer music for the forest scenes. The forest music was based on recordings of spoken poetry. It was extraordinarily beautiful but also very strange, and drew us into a subconscious world where words and the meaning of words were turned into pure sound—yet where something remained of the words themselves. The fairies added to the strangeness with their own "natural sounds," twisted and turned by the human voice. The final scene of the play, in which Oberon and Titania blessed the house, was graced by simple, beautiful music whose rhythm matched that of the verse.

Did some central idea dominate your presentation?

The central conflict in the play—between Titania and Oberon—requires the director to decide what's really going on here. Does Oberon have any right to the changeling child, or is he just muscling in on Titania? If we say that he has no right to the child except that he's king and he wants it, then the play spins out as the victory of male over female, king over queen, sexual dominance over another kind of love. This journey will strongly influence all the other scenes in the forest and the end of the play; in our day, it can't help but have dark overtones. On the other hand, if Oberon has some right to the child—if, for example, he's the father—then the play can become a journey in which the male feels what it's like to be abandoned (Oberon can feel jealousy, envy, even sorrow as he watches Titania with Bottom), and the female can feel what it's like to be irrationally and powerfully attracted to someone she shouldn't like. In this reading, each learns something about the other's experience of life.

Did you use a particular kind of acting style?

We played most of the lovers' exchanges (as well as those of Titania and Oberon) very physically. We kept the comedy, permitted violent colors to arise as they do in the text, and allowed the play to move very quickly from physical comedy to threatening situation. We didn't cross the boundary to violence, though we suggested it was possible at any moment.

In almost every production I've seen the mechanicals are very funny. Audiences don't have to pretend to find them funny. Did your mechanicals succeed in this way?

They did, and they did so by playing their parts very straight. They never "hammed it up." The characters weren't very bright and were very inexperienced on the stage, but the

actors never pushed for laughs. They were very real and while we laughed at them we didn't make fun of them because they, too, changed over the course of the evening. They arrived in the first act on a truck with a keg of beer; five acts later, transformed into a little troupe of fledgling artists, they left the stage proud of their work and aware, for the first time, of how little they knew. Their artistry, in the end, came from their simplicity. Though Thisby's death is funny, for example, we found it also to be very moving. Here was a person—Thisby—ready to die for love. And when she died she did it simply, gently, next to Bottom. The stage-audience was touched, though they didn't know what to do with those feelings.

But earlier, during the play-within-a-play, what did you do with the stage audience?

That's a very good question. It opens up a series of complex possibilities. Neither Hermia nor Helena says a word, and that's a clue. The men work very hard to be clever. Their jokes aren't too successful and I believe that's what Shakespeare intended. Hippolyta seems to make a transition from sarcasm to appreciation, and I believe she leads the others to experience the play in a surprising way. The "audience" should not be central to our experience of the scene—the mechanicals are the most important element—but their interruptions should not be cut because they suggest how difficult it is for art (yes, even Pyramus and Thisby is art) to get through to people. In our production the "art" did finally have its effect and the "audience" was moved by the simple presentation of a love story not very different from their own.

How did you play the final scene?

We did the final scene—as many productions do—as a blessing. A senior colleague at Bread Loaf had drowned that summer and the community was very shaken. So in the last scene Oberon and Titania blessed the audience and the community. They did it with great simplicity. Reeds were dipped into a bowl of field dew and waved gently above the audience, with beautiful music beneath. I believe Shakespeare intended us to travel a great distance in this play and experience all the anticipation, fear, excitement, and danger of a first sexual encounter (perhaps on a wedding night). At the end of the journey we bless the moment, in hope, simplicity, and love. We acknowledge all the dark places of the spirit, and, in the finest moment of any comedy ever written, unite with the generative forces of the universe in an act that is both physical and spiritual.

William Shakespeare

THE TRAGEDY OF KING LEAR

William Shakespeare (1564–1616) was born in Stratford, England, of middle-class parents. Nothing of interest is known about his early years, but by 1590 he was acting and writing plays in London. He early worked in all three Elizabethan dramatic genres—tragedy, comedy, and history. *Romeo and Juliet,* for example, was written about 1595, the year of *Richard II*, and in the following year he wrote *A Midsummer Night's Dream. Julius Caesar* (1599) probably preceded *As You Like It* by one year, and *Hamlet* probably followed *As You Like It* by less than a year. Among the plays that followed *King Lear* (1605–06) were *Macbeth* (1605–06) and several "romances"—plays that have happy endings but that seem more meditative and closer to tragedy than such comedies as *A Midsummer Night's Dream, As You Like It,* and *Twelfth Night.*

COMMENTARY

The best way to understand Shakespeare's tragic vision is, of course, to see and read the tragedies receptively, but some help may be gained from a brief consideration of two speeches in *Hamlet*. In the final scene, when Fortinbras and others enter the stage looking for Claudius, they find to their amazement the corpses of Claudius, Gertrude, Laertes, and Hamlet. Horatio, Hamlet's friend, endeavors to bring the visitors up to date:

> What is it you would see?
> If aught of woe or wonder, cease your search.

Fortinbras and his associates are indeed struck with woe and wonder:

> FORTINBRAS.   O proud Death,
>   What feast is toward in thine eternal cell
>   That thou so many princes at a shot
>   So bloodily hast struck?
> AMBASSADOR.   The sight is dismal.

Horatio seeks to explain: the visitors will hear

> Of carnal, bloody, and unnatural acts,
> Of accidental judgments, casual slaughters,
> Of deaths put on by cunning and forced cause,
> And, in this upshot, purposes mistook
> Fall'n on th'inventors' heads.

The spectators of the play itself have indeed seen "unnatural acts," "deaths put on by cunning," and so on, and presumably these spectators have experienced the "woe" and "wonder" that the new arrivals will experience as Horatio sets forth the details.

Let us now look at a second passage from *Hamlet*. The speaker is the despicable Rosencrantz, and there is some flattery of King Claudius in his speech, but the gist of his argument about the death of a king rings true, makes sense:

>   The cess of majesty
> Dies not alone, but like a gulf doth draw
> What's near it with it; or it is a massy wheel
> Fixed on the summit of the highest mount.
> To whose huge spokes ten thousand lesser things
> Are mortised and adjoined, which when it falls,
> Each small annexment, petty consequence,
> Attends the boist'rous ruin. Never alone
> Did the King sigh, but with a general groan.

Surely it is understandable that the deaths of, say, Lincoln and Kennedy had a vastly greater effect upon America than the deaths of any number of private citizens. Put crudely, they mattered more—hence the "general groan."

Together, the speeches afford some justification of the Elizabethan view that tragedy is concerned with violence done to and by people of high rank. The fall of a person in high position evokes deeper woe and wonder than the snuffing out of a nonentity. The latter may evoke pity, but scarcely awe at the terrifying power of destructiveness or at the weakness that is at the heart of power.

Shakespeare does not merely slap the label of king or prince or general on a character and then assume that greatness has been established. His characters speak great language and perform great deeds. (And, no less important, they have the capacity to suffer greatly.) Lear, in the first scene, gives away—almost seems to create—fertile kingdoms:

Of all these bounds, even from this line to this.
With shadowy forests, and with champains riched,
With plenteous rivers, and wide-skirted meads,
We make thee lady.

Even in injustice, when he banishes his daughter, Cordelia, for speaking the truth as she sees it, he has a kind of terrible grandeur:

Let it be so, thy truth then be thy dower!
For, by the sacred radiance of the sun,
The mysteries of Hecate and the night,
By all the operation of the orbs
From whom we do exist and cease to be,
Here I disclaim all my paternal care,
Propinquity and property of blood,
And as a stranger to my heart and me
Hold thee from this for ever.

Finally, even in his madness—"a sight most pitiful in the meanest wretch, / Past speaking of in a king"—he has grandeur. To Gloucester's "Is't not the king?" he replies:

Ay, every inch a king.
When I do stare, see how the subject quakes.
I pardon that man's life. What was thy cause?
Adultery?
Thou shalt not die: die for adultery! No:
The wren goes to 't, and the small gilded fly
Does lecher in my sight.
Let copulation thrive . . . .

We might contrast Lear's noble voice with Edmund's materialistic comment on the way of the world:

This is the excellent foppery of the world, that when we are sick in fortune, often the surfeits of our own behavior, we make guilty of our disasters the sun, the moon, and stars; as if we were villains on necessity; fools by heavenly compulsion; knaves, thieves, and treachers by spherical predominance; drunkards, liars, and adulterers by an enforced obedience of planetary influence; and all that we are evil in, by a divine thrusting on. An admirable evasion of whoremaster man, to

lay his goatish disposition on the charge of a star. . . . Fut! I should have been that I am, had the maidenliest star in the firmament twinkled on my bastardizing.

Lear seems to be displacing *Hamlet* as the play that speaks to our time. *Hamlet* was especially popular with nineteenth-century audiences, who often found in the uncertain prince an image of their own doubts in a world in which belief in a benevolent divine order was collapsing under the influence of scientific materialism and bourgeois aggressiveness. Many audiences in our age find in *Lear*—where "for many miles about / There's scarce a bush"—a play thoroughly in the spirit of Beckett's *Waiting for Godot*, where the scenery consists of a single tree. Moreover, Lear denounces the hypocrisy of the power structure and exposes the powerlessness of the disenfranchised: "Robes and furred gowns hide all. Plate sin with gold, / And the strong lance of justice hurtless breaks; / Arm it in rags, a pygmy's straw does pierce it." And what of the gods? There are several comments about their nature, but perhaps the most memorable reference to the gods is not a mere comment but one followed by an action: Learning that Cordelia is in danger, Albany cries out, "The gods defend her!" and immediately his words are mocked by Lear's entrance on the stage, with the dead Cordelia in his arms.

But the interpretation of *King Lear* as a revelation of the emptiness of life fails to consider at least two things. First, there is an affirmation in those passages in which Lear comes, through heart-rending anguish, to see that he was not what he thought he was. Second, this anagnorisis or recognition is several times associated with love or charity, as when (3.4) Lear invites the Fool to enter the hovel first and then confesses his guilt in having cared too little for humanity. And this care for humanity is seen in Cordelia, who comes—though ineffectually in the long run—to the aid of her father. It is seen, too, in the nameless servant who at the end of 3.7 promises to apply medicine to Gloucester's eyeless sockets; it is seen even in the villainous Edmund, who in dying repents and says, "Some good I mean to do, / Despite mine own nature" (5.3), and who thereupon tries, unsuccessfully, to save Cordelia. No one would say that these actions turn *King Lear* into a happy vision, but it is perverse to ignore them and to refuse to see that in this play love humanizes as surely as egoism dehumanizes. If the play dramatizes human desolation, it also dramatizes the love that, while providing no protection against pain or death, makes a human being's life different from the life of "a dog, a horse, a rat."

William Shakespeare

KING LEAR

Edited by David Bevington

[*Dramatis Personae*

KING LEAR
GONERIL,
REGAN,⎫ *Lear's daughters*
CORDELIA,⎭
DUKE OF ALBANY, *Goneril's husband*
DUKE OF CORNWALL, *Regan's husband*
KING OF FRANCE, *Cordelia's suitor and husband*
DUKE OF BURGUNDY, *suitor to Cordelia*

EARL OF KENT, *later disguised as Caius*
EARL OF GLOUCESTER (*pronounced "Gloster"*)
EDGAR, *Gloucester's son and heir, later disguised as poor Tom*
EDMUND, *Gloucester's bastard son*

OSWALD, *Goneril's steward*
A KNIGHT *serving King Lear*
Lear's FOOL
CURAN, *in Gloucester's household*
GENTLEMEN
Three SERVANTS
OLD MAN, *a tenant of Gloucester*
Three MESSENGERS
DOCTOR *attending Cordelia*
Two CAPTAINS
HERALD

Knights, Gentlemen, Attendants, Servants, Officers, Soldiers, Trumpeters

SCENE: *Britain*]

1.1 *Enter Kent, Gloucester, and Edmund.*

KENT. I thought the King had more affected° the Duke of Albany° than Cornwall.
GLOUCESTER. It did always seem so to us; but now in the division of the kingdom it appears not which of the dukes he values most, for equalities are so weighed that curiosity in neither can make choice of either's moiety.° 5
KENT. Is not this your son, my lord?

1.1. Location: King Lear's palace. 1 more affected better liked **2 Albany** that is, Scotland **5–6 equalities . . . moiety** the shares balance so equally that close scrutiny cannot find advantage in either's portion

---

GLOUCESTER. His breeding,° sir, hath been at my charge.° I have so often blushed to acknowledge him that now I am brazed° to 't. 10
KENT. I cannot conceive° you.
GLOUCESTER. Sir, this young fellow's mother could; whereupon she grew round-wombed and had indeed, sir, a son for her cradle ere she had a husband for her bed. Do you smell a fault?° 15
KENT. I cannot wish the fault undone, the issue° of it being so proper.°
GLOUCESTER. But I have a son, sir, by order of law,° some year° elder than this, who yet is no dearer in my account.° Though this knave° came something° saucily 20 to the world before he was sent for, yet was his mother fair, there was good sport at his making, and the whoreson° must be acknowledged.—Do you know this noble gentleman, Edmund?
EDMUND. No, my lord. 25
GLOUCESTER. My lord of Kent. Remember him hereafter as my honorable friend.
EDMUND. My services° to your lordship.
KENT. I must love you, and sue° to know you better.
EDMUND. Sir, I shall study deserving.° 30
GLOUCESTER. He hath been out° nine years, and away he shall again. The King is coming.

Sennet.° Enter [one bearing a coronet, then°] King Lear, Cornwall, Albany, Goneril, Regan, Cordelia, and attendants.

LEAR.
Attend° the lords of France and Burgundy, Gloucester.

---

8 breeding raising, care. **charge** expense **10 brazed** hardened **11 conceive** understand. (But Gloucester puns in the sense of "become pregnant.") **15 fault** (1) sin (2) loss of scent by the hounds **16 issue** (1) result (2) offspring **17 proper** (1) excellent (2) handsome **18 by order of law** legitimate **18–19 some year** about a year **20 account** estimation **knave** young fellow (not said disapprovingly, though the word is ironic). **something** somewhat **23 whoreson** low fellow; suggesting bastardy, but (like *knave* earlier) used with affectionate condescension **28 services** duty **29 sue** petition, beg **30 study deserving** strive to be worthy (of your esteem) **31 out** that is, abroad, absent **32 s.d. Sennet** trumpet signal heralding a procession. **one . . . then** (This direction is from the Quarto. The *coronet* is perhaps intended for Cordelia or her betrothed. A coronet signifies nobility below the rank of king.) **33 Attend** that is wait on them ceremonially, usher them into our presence

---

GLOUCESTER.
    I shall, my liege.   *Exit.*
LEAR.
35   Meantime we° shall express our° darker purpose.°
    Give me the map there. [*He takes a map.*] Know that we
        have divided
    In three our kingdom; and 'tis our fast° intent
40   To shake all cares and business from our age,
    Conferring them on younger strengths while we
    Unburdened crawl toward death. Our son of Cornwall,
    And you, our no less loving son of Albany,
    We have this hour a constant will to publish°
    Our daughters' several° dowers, that future strife
    May be prevented now. The princes, France and Bur-
        gundy,
45   Great rivals in our youngest daughter's love,
    Long in our court have made their amorous sojourn
    And here are to be answered. Tell me, my daughters—
    Since now we will divest us both of rule,
    Interest° of territory, cares of state—
50   Which of you shall we say doth love us most,
    That we our largest bounty may extend
    Where nature doth with merit challenge?° Goneril,
    Our eldest born, speak first.
GONERIL.
    Sir, I love you more than words can wield the matter,
55   Dearer than eyesight, space,° and liberty,
    Beyond what can be valued, rich or rare,
    No less than life, with grace, health, beauty, honor;
    As much as child e'er loved, or father found;°
    A love that makes breath° poor and speech unable.°
60   Beyond all manner of so much I love you.
CORDELIA [*aside*].
    What shall Cordelia speak? Love and be silent.
LEAR [*indicating on map*].
    Of all these bounds, even from this line to this,
    With shadowy° forests and with champains riched,°
    With plenteous rivers and wide-skirted meads,°
65   We make thee lady. To thine and Albany's issue
    Be this perpetual.—What says our second daughter,
    Our dearest Regan, wife of Cornwall? Speak.
REGAN.
    I am made of that self° mettle° as my sister,

And prize me at her worth.° In my true heart
I find she names my very deed of love;°   70
Only she comes too short, that° I profess
Myself an enemy to all other joys
Which the most precious square of sense possesses,°
And find I am alone felicitate°
In your dear Highness' love.
CORDELIA [*aside*].   Then poor Cordelia!   75
And yet not so, since I am sure my love's
More ponderous° than my tongue.
LEAR.
To thee and thine hereditary ever
Remain this ample third of our fair kingdom,
No less in space, validity,° and pleasure°   80
Than that conferred on Goneril.—Now, our joy,
Although our last and least,° to whose young love
The vines° of France and milk° of Burgundy
Strive to be interessed,° what can you say to draw°
A third more opulent than your sisters'? Speak.   85
CORDELIA. Nothing, my lord.
LEAR. Nothing?
CORDELIA. Nothing.
LEAR.
Nothing will come of nothing. Speak again.
CORDELIA.
Unhappy that I am, I cannot heave   90
My heart into my mouth. I love Your Majesty
According to my bond,° no more nor less.
LEAR.
How, how, Cordelia? Mend your speech a little,
Lest you may mar your fortunes.
CORDELIA.   Good my lord,
You have begot me, bred me, loved me. I   95
Return those duties back as are right fit,°
Obey you, love you, and most honor you.
Why have my sisters husbands if they say
They love you all?° Haply,° when I shall wed,
That lord whose hand must take my plight° shall carry   100
Half my love with him, half my care and duty.
Sure I shall never marry like my sisters,
To love my father all.
LEAR.
But goes thy heart with this?
CORDELIA.   Ay, my good lord.

---

35 **we, our** (The royal plural; also in lines, etc.) **darker purpose** undeclared intention 37 **fast** firm 42 **constant . . . publish** firm resolve to proclaim 43 **several** individual 49 **Interest of** right or title to, possession of 52 **Where . . . challenge** where both natural affection and merit claim it as due 55 **space** freedom from confinement 58 **found** that is, found himself to be loved 59 **breath** voice, speech. **unable** incompetent, inadequate 63 **shadowy** shady **champains riched** fertile plains 64 **wide-skirted meads** extensive, spread out meadows 68 **self** same **mettle** spirit, temperament. (But with the meaning also of *metal,* "substance," continued in the metaphor of *prize* and *worth,* line 69.)

69 **prize . . . worth** value myself as her equal (in love for you). (*Prize* suggests "price.") 70 **names . . . love** describes my love in action 71 **that** in that 73 **most . . . possesses** most delicate test of my sensibility, most delicately sensitive part of my nature, can enjoy 74 **felicitate** made happy 77 **ponderous** weighty 80 **validity** value. **pleasure** pleasing features 82 **least** youngest 83 **vines** vineyards. **milk** pastures (?) 84 **be interessed** be affiliated, establish a claim, be admitted as to a privilege **draw** win 92 **bond** filial obligation 96 **right fit** proper and fitting 99 **all** exclusively, and with all of themselves. **Haply** perhaps, with luck 100 **plight** pledge in marriage

105 LEAR. So young, and so untender?
      CORDELIA. So young, my lord, and true.
      LEAR.
        Let it be so! Thy truth then be thy dower!
        For, by the sacred radiance of the sun,
        The mysteries° of Hecate° and the night,
110   By all the operation° of the orbs°
        From whom° we do exist and cease to be,
        Here I disclaim all my paternal care,
        Propinquity, and property of blood,°
        And as a stranger to my heart and me
115   Hold thee from this° forever. The barbarous Scythian,°
        Or he that makes his generation messes°
        To gorge his appetite, shall to my bosom
        Be as well neighbored, pitied, and relieved
        As thou my sometime° daughter.
      KENT.   Good my liege—
120 LEAR. Peace, Kent!
        Come not between the dragon and his wrath.
        I loved her most, and thought to set my rest°
        On her kind nursery.° [*To Cordelia.*] Hence, and avoid
          my sight!—
        So be my grave my peace,° as here I give
125   Her father's heart from her. Call France. Who stirs?°
        Call Burgundy. [*Exit one.*] Cornwall and Albany,
        With my two daughters' dowers digest° the third.
        Let pride, which she calls plainness, marry her.°
        I do invest you jointly with my power,
130   Preeminence, and all the large effects°
        That troop° with majesty. Ourself° by monthly course,
        With reservation of° an hundred knights
        By you to be sustained, shall our abode
        Make with you by due turns. Only we shall retain
135   The name and all th' addition° to a king.
        The sway,° revenue, execution of the rest,
        Belovèd sons, be yours, which to confirm,
        This coronet° part between you.

      KENT.   Royal Lear,
        Whom I have ever honored as my king,
        Loved as my father, as my master followed,   140
        As my great patron thought on in my prayers—
      LEAR.
        The bow is bent and drawn. Make from° the shaft.
      KENT.
        Let it fall° rather, though the fork° invade
        The region of my heart. Be Kent unmannerly
        When Lear is mad. What wouldst thou do, old man?   145
        Think'st thou that duty shall have dread to speak
        When power to flattery bows?
        To plainness honor's bound°
        When majesty falls to folly. Reserve thy state,°
        And in thy best consideration° check°   150
        This hideous rashness. Answer my life my judgment,°
        Thy youngest daughter does not love thee least,
        Nor are those emptyhearted whose low sounds
        Reverb no hollowness.°
      LEAR.   Kent, on thy life, no more.
      KENT.
        My life I never held° but as a pawn°   155
        To wage° against thine enemies, nor fear to lose it,
        Thy safety being motive.°
      LEAR.   Out of my sight!
      KENT.
        See better, Lear, and let me still° remain
        The true blank of thine eye.°
      LEAR. Now, by Apollo—
      KENT. Now, by Apollo, King,   160
        Thou swear'st thy gods in vain.
      LEAR. O, vassal!° Miscreant!°

                   [*Laying his hand on his sword.*]
      ALBANY, CORNWALL. Dear sir, forbear.
      KENT.
        Kill thy physician, and the fee bestow   165
        Upon the foul disease. Revoke thy gift,
        Or whilst I can vent clamor from my throat
        I'll tell thee thou dost evil.
      LEAR.
        Hear me, recreant,° on thine allegiance hear me!

---

109 mysteries secret rites. **Hecate** goddess of witchcraft and the moon **110 operation** influence. **orbs** planets and stars **111 From whom** under whose influence **113 Propinquity... blood** close kinship **115 this** this time forth. **Scythian** (Scythians were famous in antiquity for savagery.) **116 makes... messes** makes meals of his children or parents **119 sometime** former **122 set my rest** rely wholly. (A phrase from a game of cards, meaning "to stake all.") **123 nursery** nursing, care. **avoid** leave **124 So... peace, as** as I hope to rest peacefully in my grave **125 Who stirs?** that is, somebody do something; don't just stand there **127 digest** assimilate, incorporate **128 Let... her** let her pride be her dowry and get her a husband **130 effects** outward shows **131 troop with** accompany, serve. **Ourself** (The royal "we.") **132 With reservation of** reserving to myself the right to be attended by **135 addition** honors and prerogatives **136 sway** sovereign authority **138 coronet** (Perhaps Lear gestures toward this coronet that was to have symbolized Cordelia's dowry and marriage, hands it to his sons-in-law, or actually attempts to divide it.)

142 Make from get out of the way of **143 fall** strike. **fork** barbed head of an arrow **148 To... bound** loyalty demands frankness **149 Reserve thy state** retain your royal authority **150 in... consideration** with wise deliberation **check** restrain, withhold **151 Answer... judgment** I wager my life on my judgment that **154 Reverb no hollowness** do not reverberate like a hollow drum, insincerely **155 held** regarded. **pawn** weakest chess piece **156 wage** wager, hazard in warfare **157 motive** that which prompts me to act **158 still** always **159 The true... eye** that is, the means to enable you to see better. (*Blank* means "the white center of the target," or, more probably, "the true direct aim," as in "point-blank," traveling in a straight line.) **163 vassal** that is, wretch. **Miscreant** (Literally, infidel; hence, villain, rascal.) **169 recreant** traitor

70 That° thou hast sought to make us break our vows,
    Which we durst never yet, and with strained° pride
    To come betwixt our sentence and our power,°
    Which nor our nature nor our place° can bear,
    Our potency made good,° take thy reward.
75 Five days we do allot thee for provision
    To shield thee from disasters of the world,
    And on the sixth to turn thy hated back
    Upon our kingdom. If on the tenth day following
    Thy banished trunk° be found in our dominions,
80 The moment is thy death. Away! By Jupiter,
    This shall not be revoked.

KENT.
    Fare thee well, King. Sith° thus thou wilt appear,
    Freedom lives hence and banishment is here.
    [To Cordelia.] The gods to their dear shelter take thee,
        maid,
85 That justly think'st and hast most rightly said!
    [To Regan and Goneril.] And your large speeches may
        your deeds approve,°
    That good effects may spring from words of love.
    Thus Kent, O princes, bids you all adieu.
    He'll shape his old course° in a country new.   Exit.

    Flourish.° Enter Gloucester, with France and Burgundy;
    attendants.

GLOUCESTER.
90 Here's France and Burgundy, my noble lord.

LEAR. My lord of Burgundy,
    We first address° toward you, who with this king
    Hath rivaled° for our daughter. What in the least°
    Will you require in present dower with her
    Or cease your quest of love?

95 BURGUNDY.   Most royal Majesty,
    I crave no more than hath Your Highness offered,
    Nor will you tender° less.

LEAR.   Right noble Burgundy,
    When she was dear to us we did hold her so,°
    But now her price is fallen. Sir, there she stands.
00 If aught within that little-seeming substance,°
    Or all of it, with our displeasure pieced,°
    And nothing more, may fitly like° Your Grace,
    She's there, and she is yours.

BURGUNDY.   I know no answer.

LEAR.
    Will you, with those infirmities she owes,°
    Unfriended, new-adopted to our hate,   205
    Dowered with our curse and strangered with° our oath,
    Take her, or leave her?

BURGUNDY.   Pardon me, royal sir.
    Election makes not up in such conditions.°

LEAR.
    Then leave her, sir, for by the power that made me,
    I tell you° all her wealth. [To France.] For° you, great
        King,   210
    I would not from your love make such a stray°
    To° match you where I hate; therefore beseech° you
    T' avert your liking° a more worthier way
    Than on a wretch whom Nature is ashamed
    Almost t' acknowledge hers.

FRANCE.   This is most strange,   215
    That she whom even but now was your best object,
    The argument° of your praise, balm of your age,
    The best, the dearest, should in this trice° of time
    Commit a thing so monstrous to° dismantle
    So many folds of favor. Sure her offense   220
    Must be of such unnatural degree
    That monsters° it, or your forevouched affection
    Fall into taint,° which° to believe of her
    Must be a faith that reason without miracle
    Should° never plant in me.   225

CORDELIA. I yet beseech Your Majesty—
    If for I want° that glib and oily art
    To speak and purpose not,° since what I well intend
    I'll do 't before I speak—that you make known
    It is no vicious blot, murder, or foulness,   230
    No unchaste action or dishonored step
    That hath deprived me of your grace, and favor,
    But even for want of that for which° I am richer:
    A still-soliciting° eye and such a tongue
    That I am glad I have not, though not to have it   235
    Hath lost me in your liking.

LEAR.   Better thou
    Hadst not been born than not t' have pleased me better.

---

170 **That** in that, since 171 **strained** excessive 172 **To . . .
power** that is, to block my power to command and judge
173 **Which . . . place** which neither my temperament nor my office
as king 174 **Our . . . good** my power enacted, demonstrated
179 **trunk** body 182 **Sith** since 186 **your . . . approve** may your
deeds confirm your speeches with their vast claims 189 **shape . . .
course** follow his traditional plainspoken ways **s.d. Flourish** trumpet fanfare used for the entrance or exit of important persons
192 **address** address myself 193 **rivaled** competed. **in the least**
at the lowest 197 **tender** offer 198 **so** that is, *dear*, beloved and
valued at a high price. 200 **little-seeming substance** one who
seems substantial but whose substance is, in fact, little, or, one who
refuses to flatter 201 **pieced** added, joined 202 **like** please

204 **owes** owns 206 **strangered with** made a stranger by
208 **Election . . . conditions** no choice is possible under such conditions 210 **tell you** (1) inform you of (2) enumerate for you.
For as for 211 **make such a stray** stray so far 212 **To** as to.
beseech I beseech 213 **avert your liking** turn your affections
217 **argument** theme 218 **trice** moment 219 **to** as to
222 **monsters it** makes it monstrous 222–223 **or . . . taint** or else
the affection for her you have hitherto affirmed (*forevouched*) must
fall into suspicion (*taint*), or, before (ere, *or*) your hitherto-pro-
claimed affection could have fallen into decay 223 **which** that is,
that her offense is monstrous 225 **Should** could 227 **for I want**
because I lack 228 **purpose not** not intend to do what I say
233 **for which** for want of which 234 **still-soliciting** ever begging

FRANCE.
        Is it but this? A tardiness in nature
        Which often leaves the history unspoke°
240   That it intends to do? My lord of Burgundy,
        What say you to the lady? Love's not love
        When it is mingled with regards that stands
        Aloof from th' entire point.° Will you have her?
        She is herself a dowry.
BURGUNDY.   Royal King,
245   Give but that portion which yourself proposed,
        And here I take Cordelia by the hand,
        Duchess of Burgundy.
LEAR.
        Nothing. I have sworn. I am firm.
BURGUNDY [to Cordelia].
        I am sorry, then, you have so lost a father
        That you must lose a husband.
250   CORDELIA.   Peace be with Burgundy!
        Since that° respects of fortune° are his love,
        I shall not be his wife.
FRANCE.
        Fairest Cordelia, that art most rich being poor,
        Most choice, forsaken, and most loved, despised,
255   Thee and thy virtues here I seize upon,
        Be it lawful° I take up what's cast away.
        [He takes her hand.]
        Gods, gods! 'Tis strange that from their cold'st neglect°
        My love should kindle to inflamed respect.°—
        Thy dowerless daughter, King, thrown to my chance,°
260   Is queen of us, of ours, and our fair France.
        Not all the dukes of waterish° Burgundy
        Can buy this unprized° precious maid of me.—
        Bid them farewell, Cordelia, though unkind.°
        Thou losest here,° a better where° to find.
LEAR.
265   Thou hast her, France. Let her be thine, for we
        Have no such daughter, nor shall ever see
        That face of hers again. Therefore begone
        Without our grace, our love, our benison.°
        Come, noble Burgundy.
            Flourish. Exeunt [all but France, Goneril, Regan, and
                                                        Cordelia].

FRANCE. Bid farewell to your sisters.   270
CORDELIA.
        Ye jewels of our father, with washed° eyes
        Cordelia leaves you. I know you what you are,
        And like a sister° am most loath to call
        Your faults as they are named.° Love well our father.
        To your professèd bosoms° I commit him.   275
        But yet, alas, stood I within his grace,
        I would prefer° him to a better place.
        So, farewell to you both.
REGAN.
        Prescribe not us our duty.
GONERIL.   Let your study
        Be to content your lord, who hath received you   280
        At Fortune's alms.° You have obedience scanted,
        And well are worth the want that you have wanted.°
CORDELIA.
        Time shall unfold what plighted° cunning hides;
        Who covers faults, at last shame them derides.°
        Well may you prosper!
FRANCE.   Come, my fair Cordelia.   285
                        Exeunt France and Cordelia.
GONERIL. Sister, it is not little I have to say of what most
    nearly appertains to us both. I think our father will hence
    tonight.
REGAN. That's most certain, and with you; next month with
    us.   290
GONERIL. You see how full of changes his age is; the observa-
    tion we have made of it hath not been little. He always
    loved our sister most, and with what poor judgment he
    hath now cast her off appears too grossly.°
REGAN. 'Tis the infirmity of his age. Yet he hath ever but 295
    slenderly known himself.
GONERIL. The best and soundest of his time hath been but
    rash.° Then must we look from his age to receive not
    alone the imperfections of long-ingraffed condition,° but
    therewithal° the unruly waywardness that infirm and   300
    choleric years bring with them.
REGAN. Such unconstant starts° are we like° to have from
    him as this of Kent's banishment.

239 leaves . . . unspoke does not speak aloud the action
242–243 regards . . . point irrelevant considerations 251 Since
that since. respects of fortune concern for wealth and position
256 Be it lawful if it be lawful that 257 from . . . neglect that is,
because the gods seem to have deserted Cordelia 258 inflamed
respect ardent affection 259 chance lot 261 waterish (1) well-
watered with rivers (2) feeble, watery 262 unprized not appreciated (with perhaps a sense also of "priceless") 263 though
unkind though they have behaved unnaturally 264 here this
place. where place elsewhere 267–268 Therefore . . . benison
(Said perhaps to Cordelia and to the King of France.) benison
blessing

271 washed tear-washed 273 like a sister that is, because I am
your sister 274 as . . . named by their true names 275 professèd
bosoms publicly avowed love 277 prefer advance, recommend
281 At . . . alms as a pittance or dole from Fortune 282 well . . .
wanted well deserve the lack of affection which you yourself have
shown. (Want may also refer to her dowry.) 283 plighted pleated,
enfolded 284 Who . . . derides those who hide their faults may
do so for a while, but in time they will be exposed and derided
294 grossly obviously 297–298 The best . . . rash even in the
prime of his life, he was stormy and unpredictable 299–300 long-
ingraffed condition long-implanted habit 300 therewithal added
thereto 302 unconstant starts impulsive outbursts. (A term from
horsemanship.) like likely

GONERIL. There is further compliment° of leave-taking
　　between France and him. Pray you, let us hit° together. If
　　our father carry authority with such disposition as he
　　bears,° this last surrender° of his will but offend° us.
REGAN.　We shall further think of it.
GONERIL.　We must do something, and i' the heat.°

Exeunt.

1.2　*Enter Bastard [Edmund, with a letter].*

EDMUND.
　　Thou, Nature,° art my goddess; to thy law
　　My services are bound. Wherefore should I
　　Stand in the plague of custom° and permit
　　The curiosity° of nations° to deprive me,
　　For that° I am some twelve or fourteen moonshines°
　　Lag of° a brother? Why bastard? Wherefore base?
　　When my dimensions° are as well compact,°
　　My mind as generous,° and my shape as true,
　　As honest° madam's issue? Why brand they us
　　With base? With baseness? Bastardy? Base, base?
　　Who in the lusty stealth of nature take
　　More composition and fierce quality°
　　Than doth within a dull, stale, tirèd bed
　　Go to th' creating a whole tribe of fops°
　　Got° 'tween asleep and wake? Well, then,
　　Legitimate Edgar, I must have your land.
　　Our father's love is to the bastard Edmund
　　As to th' legitimate. Fine word, "legitimate"!
　　Well, my legitimate, if this letter speed°
　　And my invention thrive,° Edmund the base
　　Shall top th' legitimate. I grow, I prosper.
　　Now, gods, stand up for bastards!

Enter Gloucester.

GLOUCESTER.
　　Kent banished thus? And France in choler parted?
　　And the King gone tonight?° Prescribed° his power,

Confined to exhibition?° All this done
Upon the gad?° Edmund, how now? What news?
EDMUND.　So please your lordship, none.

[Putting up the letter.]

GLOUCESTER.　Why so earnestly seek you to put up that let-
　　ter?
EDMUND.　I know no news, my lord.
GLOUCESTER.　What paper were you reading?
EDMUND.　Nothing, my lord.
GLOUCESTER.　No? What needed then that terrible dispatch°
　　of it into your pocket? The quality of nothing hath not
　　such need to hide itself. Let's see. Come, if it be nothing I
　　shall not need spectacles.
EDMUND.　I beseech you, sir, pardon me. It is a letter from my
　　brother, that I have not all o'erread; and for° so much as I
　　have perused, I find it not fit for your o'erlooking.°
GLOUCESTER.　Give me the letter, sir.
EDMUND.　I shall offend either to detain or give it. The con-
　　tents, as in part I understand them, are to blame.°
GLOUCESTER.　Let's see, let's see.

[Edmund gives the letter.]

EDMUND.　I hope for my brother's justification he wrote this
　　but as an essay or taste° of my virtue.
GLOUCESTER (*reads*).　"This policy and reverence° of age
　　makes the world bitter to the best of our times,° keeps
　　our fortunes from us till our oldness cannot relish them. I
　　begin to find an idle° and fond° bondage in the oppres-
　　sion of aged tyranny, who sways° not as it hath power but
　　as it is suffered.° Come to me, that of this I may speak
　　more. If our father would sleep till I waked him, you
　　should enjoy half his revenue forever and live the
　　beloved of your brother,　　　　　　　　　　Edgar."
Hum! Conspiracy! "Sleep till I waked him, you should
　　enjoy half his revenue." My son Edgar! Had he a hand to
　　write this? A heart and brain to breed it in? When came
　　you to this?° Who brought it?
EDMUND.　It was not brought me, my lord; there's the cun-
　　ning of it. I found it thrown in at the casement° of my
　　closet.°
GLOUCESTER.　You know the character° to be your brother's?

---

304 compliment ceremony　**305 hit** agree　**306–307 with . . .
bears** that is, with the arrogance he has just shown　**307 last surrender** just-completed abdication.　**offend** harm, injure　**309 i'
the heat** that is, while the iron is hot
1.2. The Earl of Gloucester's house.　**1 Nature** that is, the sanction that governs the material world through mechanistic amoral
forces　**3 Stand . . . custom** submit to the vexatious injustice of
convention　**4 curiosity** fastidious distinctions.　**nations** societies
5 For that because.　**moonshines** months　**6 Lag of** lagging
behind　**7 dimensions** proportions.　**compact** knit together, fitted
8 generous noble, refined　**9 honest** chaste　**11–12 Who . . .
quality** whose begetting in the sexual act both requires and engen-
ders a fuller mixture and more energetic force　**14 fops** fools
15 Got begotten　**19 speed** succeed, prosper　**20 invention
thrive** scheme prosper　**24 tonight** last night.　**Prescribed** limited

25 exhibition an allowance, pension　**26 Upon the gad** suddenly,
as if pricked by a gad or spur　**33 terrible dispatch** fearful haste
38 for as for　**39 o'erlooking** perusal　**42 to blame** (The Folio
reading, *too blame*, "too blameworthy to be shown," may be correct.)　**45 essay or taste** assay, test　**46 policy and reverence of**
policy of reverencing　**47 the best . . . times** the best years of our
lives, that is, our youth　**49 idle** useless　**fond** foolish　**50 who
sways** which rules　**51 suffered** permitted (by the young, who
could seize power if they wished)　**58 to this** upon this (letter)
60 casement window　**61 closet** private room　**62 character**
handwriting

EDMUND. If the matter° were good, my lord, I durst swear it were his; but in respect of that° I would fain° think it were not.

GLOUCESTER. It is his.

EDMUND. It is his hand, my lord, but I hope his heart is not in the contents.

GLOUCESTER. Has he never before sounded you in this business?

EDMUND. Never, my lord. But I have heard him oft maintain it to be fit° that, sons at perfect age° and fathers declined,° the father should be as ward to the son, and the son manage his revenue.

GLOUCESTER. O villain,° villain! His very opinion in the letter! Abhorred° villain! Unnatural, detested,° brutish villain! Worse than brutish! Go, sirrah,° seek him. I'll apprehend him. Abominable villain! Where is he?

EDMUND. I do not well know, my lord. If it shall please you to suspend your indignation against my brother till you can derive from him better testimony of his intent, you should run a certain course;° where,° if you violently proceed against him, mistaking his purpose, it would make a great gap in your own honor and shake in pieces the heart of his obedience. I dare pawn down° my life for him that he hath writ this to feel° my affection to your honor, and to no other pretense of danger.°

GLOUCESTER. Think you so?

EDMUND. If your honor judge it meet,° I will place you where you shall hear us confer of this, and by an auricular assurance have your satisfaction,° and that without any further delay than this very evening.

GLOUCESTER. He cannot be such a monster—

EDMUND. Nor is not, sure.

GLOUCESTER. To his father, that so tenderly and entirely loves him. Heaven and earth! Edmund, seek him out; wind me into him,° I pray you. Frame° the business after your own wisdom.° I would unstate myself to be in a due resolution.°

EDMUND. I will seek him, sir, presently;° convey° the business as I shall find means, and acquaint you withal.°

GLOUCESTER. These late° eclipses in the sun and moon portend no good to us. Though the wisdom of nature° can reason it thus and thus, yet nature finds itself scourged by the sequent effects.° Love cools, friendship falls off, brothers divide; in cities, mutinies; in countries, discord; in palaces, treason; and the bond cracked twixt son and father. This villain of mine comes under the prediction; there's son against father. The King falls from bias of nature;° there's father against child. We have seen the best of our time. Machinations, hollowness, treachery, and all ruinous disorders follow us disquietly to our graves. Find out this villain, Edmund; it shall lose thee nothing.° Do it carefully. And the noble and truehearted Kent banished! His offense, honesty! 'Tis strange. *Exit.*

EDMUND. This is the excellent foppery° of the world, that when we are sick in fortune—often the surfeits of our own behavior°—we make guilty of our disasters the sun, the moon, and stars, as if we were villains on° necessity, fools by heavenly compulsion, knaves, thieves, and treachers° by spherical predominance,° drunkards, liars, and adulterers by an enforced obedience of planetary influence, and all that we are evil in, by a divine° thrusting on. An admirable evasion of whoremaster man, to lay his goatish disposition° on the charge° of a star! My father compounded with my mother under the Dragon's tail° and my nativity was under Ursa Major,° so that it follows I am rough and lecherous. Fut,° I should have been that° I am, had the maidenliest star in the firmament twinkled on my bastardizing. Edgar—

Enter Edgar.

and pat° he comes like the catastrophe° of the old comedy. My cue is villainous melancholy, with a sigh like Tom o' Bedlam.°—O, these eclipses do portend these divisions!° Fa, sol, la, mi.

EDGAR. How now, brother Edmund, what serious contemplation are you in?

---

63 **matter** contents   64 **in . . . that** considering what the contents are **fain** gladly   72 **fit** fitting, appropriate   **perfect age** full maturity   73 **declined** having become feeble   75 **villain** vile wretch, diabolical schemer   76 **Abhorred** abhorrent   **detested** hated and hateful   77 **sirrah** (Form of address used to inferiors or children.)   82 **run a certain course** proceed with safety and certainty.   **where** whereas   85 **pawn down** stake   86 **feel** feel out   87 **pretense of danger** dangerous purpose   89 **meet** fitting, proper   90–91 **by an . . . satisfaction** satisfy yourself as to the truth by what you hear   97 **wind me into him** insinuate yourself into his confidence. (*Me* is used colloquially.)   **Frame** arrange   98 **after your own wisdom** as you think best   98–99 **unstate . . . resolution** give up anything and everything to know the truth, have my doubts resolved   100 **presently** immediately.   **convey** manage   101 **withal** therewith

102 **late** recent   103 **the wisdom of nature** natural science   105 **sequent effects** that is, devastating consequences   109–110 **bias of nature** natural inclination   113–114 **lose thee nothing** that is, earn you a reward   116 **foppery** foolishness   117–118 **surfeits . . . behavior** consequences of our own overindulgence   119 **on** by   121 **treachers** traitors.   **spherical predominance** astrological determinism, because a certain planet was ascendant at the hour of our birth   123 **divine** supernatural   125 **goatish disposition** lecherous   **on the charge** to the responsibility   126–127 **compounded . . . Dragon's tail** had sex with my mother under the constellation Draco   127 **Ursa Major** the big bear   128 **Fut** that is, 'sfoot, by Christ's foot.   129 **that** what   131 **pat** on cue.   **catastrophe** conclusion, resolution (of a play)   132–133 **Tom o' Bedlam** a lunatic patient of Bethlehem Hospital in London turned out to beg for his bread   133–134 **divisions** social and family conflicts (but with a musical sense also of florid variations on a theme, thus prompting Edmund's singing)

EDMUND. I am thinking, brother, of a prediction I read this other day,° what should follow these eclipses.

EDGAR. Do you busy yourself with that?

40 EDMUND. I promise° you, the effects he writes of succeed unhappily,° as of unnaturalness between the child and the parent, death, dearth, dissolutions of ancient amities, divisions in state, menaces and maledictions against king and nobles, needless diffidences° banishment of friends,
45 dissipation of cohorts,° nuptial breaches, and I know not what.

EDGAR. How long have you been a sectary astronomical?°

EDMUND. Come, come, when saw you my father last?

EDGAR. The night gone by.

50 EDMUND. Spake you with him?

EDGAR. Ay, two hours together.

EDMUND. Parted you in good terms? Found you no displeasure in him by word nor countenance?°

EDGAR. None at all.

55 EDMUND. Bethink yourself wherein you may have offended him, and at my entreaty forbear his presence° until some little time hath qualified° the heat of his displeasure, which at this instant so rageth in him that with the mischief of your person° it would scarcely allay.°

60 EDGAR. Some villain hath done me wrong.

EDMUND. That's my fear. I pray you, have a continent forbearance° till the speed of his rage goes slower; and, as I say, retire with me to my lodging, from whence I will fitly° bring you to hear my lord speak. Pray ye, go! There's
65 my key. [He gives a key.] If you do stir abroad, go armed.

EDGAR. Armed, brother?

EDMUND. Brother, I advise you to the best. I am no honest man if there be any good meaning° toward you. I have told you what I have seen and heard, but faintly,° noth-
70 ing like the image and horror° of it. Pray you, away.

EDGAR. Shall I hear from you anon?

EDMUND.
I do serve you in this business.

                                        Exit [Edgar].

A credulous father and a brother noble,
Whose nature is so far from doing harms
75 That he suspects none; on whose foolish honesty

My practices° ride easy. I see the business.°
Let me, if not by birth, have lands by wit.°
All with me's meet° that I can fashion fit.°   *Exit.*

1.3 *Enter Goneril, and [Oswald, her] steward.*

GONERIL. Did my father strike my gentleman for chiding of his fool?

OSWALD. Ay, madam.

GONERIL.
By day and night he wrongs me! Every hour
He flashes into one gross crime° or other   5
That sets us all at odds. I'll not endure it.
His knights grow riotous, and himself upbraids us
On every trifle. When he returns from hunting
I will not speak with him. Say I am sick.
If you come slack° of former services   10
You shall do well; the fault of it I'll answer.°

[*Horns within.*]

OSWALD. He's coming, madam. I hear him.

GONERIL.
Put on what weary negligence you please,
You and your fellows. I'd have it come to question.°
If he distaste° it, let him to my sister,   15
Whose mind and mine, I know, in that are one,
Not to be overruled. Idle° old man,
That still would manage those authorities°
That he hath given away! Now, by my life,
Old fools are babes again, and must be used   20
With checks as flatteries, when they are seen abused.°
Remember what I have said.

OSWALD. Well, madam.

GONERIL.
And let his knights have colder looks among you.
What grows of it, no matter. Advise your fellows so.   25
I would breed from hence occasions, and I shall,
That I may speak.° I'll write straight° to my sister
To hold my very course. Prepare for dinner.   *Exeunt.*

137–138 **this other day** the other day 140 **promise** assure 140–141 **succeed unhappily** follow unluckily 144 **needless diffidences** groundless distrust of others 145 **dissipation of cohorts** breaking up of military companies, large-scale desertions 147 **sectary astronomical** believer in astrology 153 **countenance** demeanor 156 **forbear his presence** avoid meeting him 157 **qualified** moderated 158–159 **with . . . person** with the harmful effect of your presence; or, even if there were injury done to you **allay** be allayed 161–162 **have . . . forbearance** keep a wary distance 164 **fitly** at a fit time 168 **meaning** intention 169 **but faintly** only with a faint impression 170 **image and horror** horrid reality

176 **practices** plots. **the business** that is, how my plots should proceed 177 **wit** intelligence 178 **meet** justifiable. **fit** to my purpose **1.3. Location:** The Duke of Albany's palace. 5 **crime** offense 10 **come slack** fall short 11 **answer** be answerable for 14 **come to question** be made an issue 15 **distaste** dislike 17 **Idle** foolish 18 **manage those authorities** exercise those prerogatives 21 **With . . . abused** with rebukes instead of flattery, when they (old men) are seen to be deceived by, or too apt to take advantage of, flatteries 26–27 **I would . . . speak** I wish to create from these incidents the opportunity to speak out 27 **straight** immediately

1.4 *Enter Kent [disguised].*

KENT.
      If but as well° I other accents borrow
      That can my speech diffuse,° my good intent
      May carry through itself to that full issue°
      For which I razed my likeness.° Now, banished Kent,
5   If thou canst serve where thou dost stand condemned,
      So may it come° thy master, whom thou lov'st,
      Shall find thee full of labors.

      Horns within. Enter Lear, [Knights,] and attendants.

LEAR. Let me not stay° a jot for dinner. Go get it ready. *[Exit
      an Attendant.°]* How now, what art thou?
10   KENT. A man, sir.
LEAR. What dost thou profess?° What wouldst thou with us?
KENT. I do profess to be no less than I seem: to serve him
      truly that will put me in trust, to love him that is honest,°
      to converse° with him that is wise and says little, to fear
15   judgment,° to fight when I cannot choose,° and to eat no
      fish.°
LEAR. What art thou?
KENT. A very honest-hearted fellow, and as poor as the
      King.
20   LEAR. If thou be'st as poor for a subject as he's for a king,
      thou'rt poor enough. What wouldst thou?
KENT. Service.
LEAR. Who wouldst thou serve?
KENT. You.
25   LEAR. Dost thou know me, fellow?
KENT. No, sir, but you have that in your countenance°
      which I would fain call master.
LEAR. What's that?
KENT. Authority.
30   LEAR. What services canst do?
KENT. I can keep honest counsel,° ride, run, mar a curious°
      tale in telling it, and deliver a plain message bluntly.
      That which ordinary men are fit for I am qualified in, and
      the best of me is diligence.
35   LEAR. How old art thou?

KENT. Not so young, sir, to love° a woman for singing, nor so
      old to dote on her for anything. I have years on my back
      forty-eight.
LEAR. Follow me; thou shalt serve me. If I like thee no worse
      after dinner, I will not part from thee yet. Dinner, ho,   40
      dinner! Where's my knave, my fool? Go you and call my
      fool hither.   *[Exit one.]*

Enter steward [Oswald].

      You! You, sirrah, where's my daughter?
OSWALD. So please you—   *Exit.*
LEAR. What says the fellow there? Call the clodpoll° back.   45
      [Exit a Knight.] Where's my fool, ho? I think the world's
      asleep.

[Enter Knight.]

      How now? Where's that mongrel?
KNIGHT. He says, my lord, your daughter is not well.
LEAR. Why came not the slave back to me when I called   50
      him?
KNIGHT. Sir, he answered me in the roundest° manner, he
      would not.
LEAR. He would not?
KNIGHT. My lord, I know not what the matter is, but to my   55
      judgment Your Highness is not entertained with that
      ceremonious affection as you were wont. There's a great
      abatement of kindness appears as well in the general
      dependents° as in the Duke himself also and your
      daughter.   60
LEAR. Ha? Sayst thou so?
KNIGHT. I beseech you, pardon me, my lord, if I be mistaken,
      for my duty cannot be silent when I think Your Highness
      wronged.
LEAR. Thou but rememberest° me of mine own   65
      conception.° I have perceived a most faint° neglect of
      late, which I have rather blamed as mine own jealous
      curiosity° than as a very pretense° and purpose of
      unkindness. I will look further into 't. But where's my
      fool? I have not seen him this° two days.   70
KNIGHT. Since my young lady's going into France, sir, the
      Fool hath much pined away.
LEAR. No more of that. I have noted it well. Go you and tell
      my daughter I would speak with her.   *[Exit one.]*
      Go you call hither my fool.   *[Exit one.]*   75

Enter steward [Oswald].

      O, you, sir, you, come you hither, sir. Who am I, sir?
OSWALD. My lady's father.

**1.4. Location: The Duke of Albany's palace still. The sense of
time is virtually continuous.**   **1 as well** that is, as well as I have
disguised myself by means of costume   **2 diffuse** render confused
or indistinct   **3 carry...issue** succeed to that perfect result
4 razed my likeness scraped off my beard, erased my outward
appearance   **6 come** come to pass that   **8 stay** wait   **9 s.d.
Attendant** (This attendant may be a knight; certainly the one who
speaks at line 49 is a knight.)   **11 What...profess** what is your
special calling? (But Kent puns in his answer on *profess* meaning to
"claim.")   **13 honest** honorable.   **14 converse** associate
15 judgment that is, God's judgment.   **choose** that is, choose but
to fight   **15–16 eat no fish** that is, eat a manly diet (?), be a good
Protestant (?)   **26 countenance** face and bearing   **31 keep honest counsel** respect confidences   **curious** ornate, elaborate

36 to love as to love   **45 clodpoll** blockhead   **52 roundest** bluntest
58–59 general dependents servants generally   **65 rememberest**
remind   **66 conception** idea, thought   **67 faint** halfhearted
67–68 jealous curiosity overscrupulous regard for matters of etiquette   **68 very pretense** true intention   **70 this** these

LEAR. "My lady's father"? My lord's knave! You whoreson dog, you slave, you cur!

OSWALD. I am none of these, my lord, I beseech your pardon.

LEAR. Do you bandy° looks with me, you rascal?

[*He strikes Oswald.*]

OSWALD. I'll not be strucken,° my lord.

KENT. Nor tripped neither, you base football° player.

[*He trips up Oswald's heels.*]

LEAR. I thank thee, fellow. Thou serv'st me, and I'll love thee.

KENT. Come, sir, arise, away! I'll teach you differences.° Away, away! If you will measure your lubber's length again,° tarry; but away! Go to. Have you wisdom?° So.

[*He pushes Oswald out.*]

LEAR. Now, my friendly knave, I thank thee. There's earnest° of thy service.   [*He gives Kent money.*]

Enter Fool.

FOOL. Let me hire him too. Here's my coxcomb.°

[*Offering Kent his cap.*]

LEAR. How now, my pretty knave, how dost thou?

FOOL [*to Kent*]. Sirrah, you were best° take my coxcomb.

KENT. Why, Fool?

FOOL. Why? For taking one's part that's out of favor. Nay, an thou canst not smile as the wind sits,° thou'lt catch cold° shortly. There, take my coxcomb. Why, this fellow has banished° two on 's° daughters and did the third a blessing° against his will. If thou follow him, thou must needs wear my coxcomb.—How now, nuncle?° Would I had two coxcombs and two daughters.

LEAR. Why, my boy?

FOOL. If I gave them all my living,° I'd keep my coxcombs° myself. There's mine; beg another° of thy daughters.

LEAR. Take heed, sirrah—the whip.

FOOL. Truth's a dog must to kennel. He must be whipped out, when the Lady Brach° may stand by the fire and stink.

LEAR. A pestilent gall° to me!   110

FOOL. Sirrah, I'll teach thee a speech.

LEAR. Do.

FOOL. Mark it, nuncle:

Have more than thou showest,°
Speak less than thou knowest,   115
Lend less than thou owest,°
Ride more than thou goest,°
Learn° more than thou trowest,°
Set less than thou throwest;°
Leave thy drink and thy whore,   120
And keep in-a-door,°
And thou shalt have more
Than two tens to a score.°

KENT. This is nothing, Fool.

FOOL. Then 'tis like the breath° of an unfee'd lawyer; you   125
gave me nothing for 't. Can you make no use of nothing, nuncle?

LEAR. Why, no, boy. Nothing can be made out of nothing.

FOOL [*to Kent*]. Prithee, tell him; so much the rent° of his land comes to. He will not believe a fool.   130

LEAR. A bitter° fool!

FOOL. Dost know the difference, my boy, between a bitter fool and a sweet one?

LEAR. No, lad. Teach me.

FOOL.

That lord that counseled thee   135
   To give away thy land,
Come place him here by me;
   Do thou for him stand.°
The sweet and bitter fool
   Will presently° appear: 140
The one in motley° here,
   The other found out there.°

LEAR. Dost thou call me fool, boy?

FOOL. All thy other titles thou hast given away; that thou wast born with.   145

KENT. This is not altogether fool, my lord.

---

82 bandy volley, exchange (as in tennis)   **83 strucken** struck
84 football (A raucous street game played by the lower classes.)
87 differences distinctions in rank   **88–89 If . . . again** that is, if you want to be laid out flat again, you clumsy ox   **89 Have you wisdom** that is, are you smart enough to make a quick retreat?
91 earnest partial advance payment   **92 coxcomb** fool's cap, crested with a red comb   **94 you were best** you had better   **96–97 an . . . sits** that is, if you can't play along with those in power   **98 catch cold** that is, find yourself out in the cold   **99 banished** (i.e., paradoxically, by giving Goneril and Regan his kingdom, Lear has lost them, given them power over him.)   **on 's** of his   **99–100 blessing** that is, bestowing Cordelia on France and saving her from the curse of insolent prosperity   **101 nuncle** (Contraction of "mine uncle," the Fool's way of addressing Lear.)   **104 living** property   **keep my coxcombs** (as proof of my folly)   **105 another** (Lear's folly deserves two coxcombs.)   **108 Brach** hound bitch (here suggesting flattery)

110 gall irritation, bitterness—literally, a painful swelling, or bile. (Lear is stung by the Fool's gibe because it is so true.)   **114 Have . . . showest** don't display your wealth ostentatiously   **116 owest** own   **117 goest** that is, on foot. (Travel prudently on horseback, not afoot.)   **118 Learn** that is, listen to.   **trowest** believe   **119 Set . . . throwest** don't stake everything on a single throw   **121 in-a-door** indoors, at home   **122–123 shalt . . . score** that is, will do better than break even (since a *score* equals two tens, or twenty)   **125 breath** speech, counsel   **129 rent** (Lear has no land, hence no rent.)   **131 bitter** satirical   **138 for him stand** impersonate him   **140 presently** immediately   **141 motley** the parti-colored dress of the professional fool. (The Fool identifies himself as the sweet fool, Lear as the bitter fool who counseled himself to give away his kingdom.)   **142 found out there** discovered there. (The Fool points at Lear.)

FOOL. No, faith, lords and great men will not let me;° if I
had a monopoly out,° they would have part on 't.° And
ladies too, they will not let me have all the fool to myself;
150   they'll be snatching.° Nuncle, give me an egg and I'll
give thee two crowns.

LEAR. What two crowns shall they be?

FOOL. Why, after I have cut the egg i' the middle and eat°
up the meat,° the two crowns of the egg. When thou
155   clovest thy crown i' the middle and gav'st away both
parts, thou bor'st thine ass on thy back o'er the dirt.°
Thou hadst little wit in thy bald crown when thou gav'st
thy golden one away. If I speak like myself° in this, let
him be whipped° that first finds it so.°

160   [Sings.] "Fools had ne'er less grace in a year,°
           For wise men are grown foppish°
        And know not how their wits to wear,°
           Their manners are so apish."

LEAR. When were you wont to be so full of songs, sirrah?

165 FOOL. I have used° it, nuncle, e'er since thou mad'st thy
daughters thy mothers; for when thou gav'st them the rod
and putt'st down thine own breeches,

        [Sings] "Then they for sudden joy did weep,
           And I for sorrow sung,
170   That such a king should play bo-peep°
           And go the fools among."

Prithee, nuncle, keep a schoolmaster that can teach thy
fool to lie. I would fain learn to lie.

LEAR. An° you lie, sirrah, we'll have you whipped.

175 FOOL. I marvel what kin thou and thy daughters are. They'll
have me whipped for speaking true, thou'lt have me
whipped for lying, and sometimes I am whipped for holding my peace. I had rather be any kind o' thing than a
fool. And yet I would not be thee, nuncle. Thou hast
180   pared thy wit o' both sides and left nothing i' the middle.
Here comes one o' the parings.

Enter Goneril.

LEAR.
How now, daughter? What makes° that frontlet° on?
You are too much of late i' the frown.

FOOL. Thou wast a pretty fellow when thou hadst no need
to care for her frowning; now thou art an O without a fig- 185
ure.° I am better than thou art now; I am a fool, thou art
nothing. [*To Goneril.*] Yes, forsooth, I will hold my
tongue; so your face bids me, though you say nothing.

    Mum, mum,
    He that keeps nor crust nor° crumb,   190
    Weary of all, shall want° some.°

[*Pointing to Lear.*] That's a shelled peascod.°

GONERIL.
Not only, sir, this your all-licensed° fool,
But other of your insolent retinue
Do hourly carp° and quarrel, breaking forth   195
In rank° and not-to-be-endurèd riots. Sir,
I had thought by making this well known unto you
To have found a safe° redress, but now grow fearful,
By what yourself too late° have spoke and done,
That you protect this course and put it on°   200
By your allowance;° which if you should, the fault
Would not scape censure, nor the redresses sleep°
Which in the tender of a wholesome weal°
Might in their working do you that offense,
Which else were° shame, that then necessity°   205
Will call discreet° proceeding.

FOOL. For you know, nuncle,

    "The hedge sparrow fed the cuckoo° so long
    That it had its head bit off by its young."°

So, out went the candle, and we were left darkling.° 210

LEAR. Are you our daughter?

GONERIL.
I would you would make use of your good wisdom,
Whereof I know you are fraught,° and put away

---

147 No . . . let me that is, great persons at court will not let me
monopolize folly; I am not *altogether fool* in the sense of being "all
the fool there is" **148 a monopoly out** a corner on the market
(The granting of monopolies was a common abuse under King
James and Queen Elizabeth.) **on 't** of it **150 snatching** seizing
their share; perhaps snatching at the Fool's phallic bauble or crotch
153 eat eaten, et **154 the meat** the edible part **156 bor'st . . .
dirt** that is, bore the ass instead of letting the ass bear you
158 like myself that is, like a fool **159 whipped** that is, as a fool
finds it so discovers from his experience that it is true (as Lear is
now discovering) **160 Fools . . . year** fools have never enjoyed
less favor; that is, they are made obsolete by the folly of supposed
wise men **161 foppish** foolish, vain **162 wear** use **165 used**
practiced **170 bo-peep** (a child's game) **174 An** if

182 makes is doing.   **frontlet** a band worn on the forehead; here,
frown **185–186 O without a figure** zero, cipher of no value
unless preceded by a digit **190–191 He . . . some** that is, that
person who, having grown weary of his possessions, gives all away,
will find himself in need of part of what is gone **190 nor . . . nor**
neither . . . nor **191 want** lack **192 shelled peascod** shelled pea
pod, empty of its contents **193 all-licensed** allowed to speak or
act as he pleases **195 carp** find fault **196 rank** gross, excessive
198 safe certain **199 too late** all too recently **200 put it on**
encourage it **201 allowance** approval **202 redresses sleep** pun-
ishments (for the riotous conduct of Lear's attendants) lie dormant
203 tender . . . weal care for preservation of the peace of the state
205 else were in other circumstances would be regarded as.   **then
necessity** the necessity of the times **206 discreet** prudent
208 cuckoo a bird that lays its eggs in other birds' nests **209 its
young** that is, the young cuckoo **210 darkling** in the dark
213 fraught freighted, laden

These dispositions° which of late transport you
15   From what you rightly are.
FOOL. May not an ass know when the cart draws the horse?°
Whoop, Jug!° I love thee.
LEAR.
Does any here know me? This is not Lear.
Does Lear walk thus, speak thus? Where are his eyes?
20   Either his notion° weakens, his discernings
Are lethargied°—Ha! Waking?° 'Tis not so.
Who is it that can tell me who I am?
FOOL. Lear's shadow.
LEAR.
I would learn that;° for, by the marks of sovereignty,°
25   Knowledge, and reason, I should be false persuaded
I had daughters.°
FOOL. Which° they will make an obedient father.
LEAR. Your name, fair gentlewoman?
GONERIL.
This admiration,° sir, is much o' the savor
30   Of other° your new pranks. I do beseech you
To understand my purposes aright.
As you are old and reverend, should° be wise.
Here do you keep a hundred knights and squires,
Men so disordered,° so debauched° and bold°
35   That this our court, infected with their manners,
Shows° like a riotous inn. Epicurism° and lust
Makes it more like a tavern or a brothel
Than a graced° palace. The shame itself doth speak
For instant remedy. Be then desired,°
40   By her that else will take the thing she begs,
A little to disquantity your train,°
And the remainders that shall still depend°
To be such men as may besort° your age,
Which know themselves and you.
LEAR.   Darkness and devils!
45   Saddle my horses! Call my train together!   [Exit one.]

214 dispositions states of mind, moods   216 May . . . horse that
is, may not even a fool see that matters are backwards when a
daughter lectures her father?   217 Jug that is, Joan. (The origin of
this phrase is uncertain.)   220 notion intellectual power
220–221 discernings Are lethargied faculties are asleep
221 Waking that is, am I really awake?   224 that that is, who I
am. marks of sovereignty outward and visible evidence of being
king   225–226 I should . . . daughters that is, all these outward
signs of sanity and status would seem to suggest (falsely) that I am
the king who had obedient daughters   227 Which whom
229 admiration (guise of) wonderment   230 other other of
232 should that is, you should   233 disordered disorderly.
debauched (1) led away from proper service and allegiance (2)
depraved. bold impudent   236 Shows appears. Epicurism
excess, hedonism   238 graced honorable, graced by a royal presence   239 desired requested   241 disquantity your train diminish the number of your attendants   242 the remainders . . .
depend those who remain to attend you   243 besort befit

Degenerate bastard, I'll not trouble thee.
Yet have I left a daughter.
GONERIL.
You strike my people, and your disordered rabble
Make servants of their betters.

Enter Albany.

LEAR.
Woe, that° too late repents!—O, sir, are you come?   250
Is it your will? Speak, sir.—Prepare my horses.

[*Exit one.*]

Ingratitude, thou marble-hearted fiend,
More hideous when thou show'st thee in a child
Than the sea monster!
ALBANY. Pray, sir, be patient.   255
LEAR [*to Goneril*]. Detested kite,° thou liest!
My train are men of choice and rarest parts,°
That all particulars of duty know
And in the most exact regard° support
The worships° of their name. O most small fault,   260
How ugly didst thou in Cordelia show!
Which, like an engine,° wrenched my frame of nature
From the fixed place, drew from my heart all love,
And added to the gall. O Lear, Lear, Lear!
Beat at this gate [*striking his head*] that let thy folly in   265
And thy dear° judgment out! Go, go, my people.

[*Exeunt some.*]

ALBANY.
My lord, I am guiltless as I am ignorant
Of what hath moved you.
LEAR.   It may be so, my lord.
Hear, Nature, hear! Dear goddess, hear!
Suspend thy purpose if thou didst intend   270
To make this creature fruitful!
Into her womb convey sterility;
Dry up in her the organs of increase,
And from her derogate° body never spring
A babe to honor her! If she must teem,°   275
Create her child of spleen,° that it may live
And be a thwart disnatured° torment to her!
Let it stamp wrinkles in her brow of youth,
With cadent° tears fret° channels in her cheeks,
Turn all her mother's pains and benefits°   280

250 Woe, that woe to the person who   256 kite bird of prey
257 parts qualities   259 in . . . regard with close attention to
detail   260 worships honors, reputations   262 engine powerful
mechanical contrivance, able to wrench Lear's *frame of nature* or
natural self from his *fixed place* or foundation, like a building being
torn from its foundation   266 dear precious   274 derogate
debased   275 teem increase the species   276 of spleen consisting
only of malice   277 thwart disnatured obstinate, perverse, and
unnatural, unfilial   279 cadent falling. fret wear   280 benefits
kind offerings

To laughter and contempt, that she may feel
How sharper than a serpent's tooth it is
To have a thankless child! Away, away!

          Exit [with Kent and the rest of Lear's followers].

ALBANY.
  Now, gods that we adore, whereof comes this?

GONERIL.
285 Never afflict yourself to know more of it,
But let his disposition° have that scope
As° dotage gives it.

    Enter Lear.

LEAR.
  What, fifty of my followers at a clap?
Within a fortnight?

ALBANY.   What's the matter, sir?

LEAR.
290 I'll tell thee. [*To Goneril.*] Life and death! I am ashamed
That thou hast power to shake my manhood thus,
That these hot tears, which break from me perforce,
Should make thee worth them.° Blasts and fogs° upon
    thee!
Th' untented° woundings of a father's curse
295 Pierce every sense about thee! Old fond° eyes,
Beweep° this cause again, I'll pluck ye out
And cast you, with the waters that you loose,°
To temper° clay. Yea, is 't come to this?
Ha! Let it be so. I have another daughter,
300 Who, I am sure, is kind and comfortable.°
When she shall hear this of thee, with her nails
She'll flay thy wolvish visage. Thou shalt find
That I'll resume the shape which thou dost think
I have cast off forever.   *Exit.*

GONERIL.   Do you mark that?°

ALBANY.
305 I cannot be so partial, Goneril,
To° the great love I bear you—

GONERIL.
  Pray you, content.—What, Oswald, ho!
[*To the Fool.*] You, sir, more knave than fool, after your
    master.

FOOL. Nuncle Lear, nuncle Lear! Tarry, take the Fool with
310 thee.°

A fox, when one has caught her,
And such a daughter
Should sure° to the slaughter,
If my cap would buy a halter.
So the Fool follows after.   *Exit.* 31

GONERIL.
This man hath had good counsel. A hundred knights?
'Tis politic° and safe to let him keep
At point° a hundred knights—yes, that on every dream,°
Each buzz,° each fancy, each complaint, dislike,
He may enguard his dotage with their powers 32●
And hold our lives in mercy.°—Oswald, I say!

ALBANY. Well, you may fear too far.°

GONERIL. Safer than trust too far.
Let me still take away° the harms I fear,
Not fear still to be taken.° I know his heart. 32
What he hath uttered I have writ my sister.
If she sustain him and his hundred knights
When I have showed th' unfitness—

    Enter steward [Oswald].

                    How now, Oswald?
What, have you writ that letter to my sister?

OSWALD. Ay, madam.   330

GONERIL.
Take you some company and away to horse.
Inform her full of my particular fear,
And thereto add such reasons of your own
As may compact° it more. Get you gone,
And hasten your return. [*Exit Oswald.*] No, no, my lord, 33●
This milky gentleness and course° of yours
Though I condemn not, yet, under pardon,°
You're much more attasked° for want of wisdom
Than praised for harmful mildness.°

ALBANY.
How far your eyes may pierce° I cannot tell. 340
Striving to better, oft we mar what's well.

GONERIL. Nay, then—

ALBANY. Well, well, th' event.°   *Exeunt.*

---

286 disposition humor, mood **287 As** which **293 Should . . .
them** should seem to suggest that you are worth a king's tears.
Blasts and fogs infectious blights and disease-bearing fogs
294 untented too deep to be probed and cleansed **295 fond** foolish **296 Beweep** if you weep for **297 loose** let loose
298 temper soften, bring to a proper consistency for use. (Lear will
throw away his tears on a lowly object.) **300 comfortable** willing
to comfort **304 Do . . . that** that is, did you hear his threat to
resume royal power? **306 To** because of **309–310 take . . . thee**
(1) take me with you (2) take the name "fool" with you. (A stock
phrase of taunting farewell.)

313 Should sure should certainly be sent **317 politic** prudent.
(Said ironically.) **318 At point** under arms. **dream** that is,
imagined wrong **319 buzz** idle rumor **321 in mercy** at his
mercy **322 fear too far** overestimate the danger **324 still take
away** always remove **325 Not . . . taken** rather than dwell continually in the fear of being overtaken (by the *harms*)
334 compact confirm **336 milky . . . course** effeminate and gentle way **337 under pardon** if you'll excuse my saying so
338 attasked taken to task for, blamed **339 harmful mildness**
mildness that causes harm **340 pierce** that is, see into matters
343 th' event that is, time will show

1.5 *Enter Lear, Kent [disguised as Caius], and Fool.*

LEAR *[giving a letter to Kent]*. Go you before to Gloucester°
with these letters.° Acquaint my daughter no further
with anything you know than comes from her demand°
out of° the letter. If your diligence be not speedy, I shall
be there afore you.

KENT. I will not sleep, my lord, till I have delivered your let-
ter.   *Exit.*

FOOL. If a man's brains were in 's heels, were 't not in danger
of kibes?°

LEAR. Ay, boy.

FOOL. Then, I prithee, be merry. Thy wit shall not go slipshod.°

LEAR. Ha, ha, ha!

FOOL. Shalt° see thy other daughter will use thee kindly,°
for though she's as like this as a crab's° like an apple, yet
I can tell what I can tell.

LEAR. What canst tell, boy?

FOOL. She will taste as like this as a crab does to a crab.
Thou canst tell why one's nose stands i' the middle on 's°
face?

LEAR. No.

FOOL. Why, to keep one's eyes of either side 's° nose, that
what a man cannot smell out he may spy into.

LEAR. I did her° wrong.

FOOL. Canst tell how an oyster makes his shell?

LEAR. No.

FOOL. Nor I neither. But I can tell why a snail has a house.

LEAR. Why?

FOOL. Why, to put's head in, not to give it away to his
daughters and leave his horns° without a case.

LEAR. I will forget my nature.° So kind a father!—Be my
horses ready?

FOOL. Thy asses are gone about 'em.° The reason why the
seven stars° are no more than seven is a pretty reason.

LEAR. Because they are not eight.

FOOL. Yes, indeed. Thou wouldst make a good fool.

LEAR. To take 't again perforce!° Monster ingratitude!

FOOL. If thou wert my fool, nuncle, I'd have thee beaten for
being old before thy time.

LEAR. How's that?   40

FOOL. Thou shouldst not have been old till thou hadst been
wise.

LEAR.
O, let me not be mad, not mad, sweet heaven!
Keep me in temper; I would not be mad!

[Enter Gentleman.]

How now, are the horses ready?   45

GENTLEMAN. Ready, my lord.

LEAR. Come, boy.   *[Exeunt Lear and Gentleman.]*

FOOL.
She that's a maid now, and laughs at my departure,
Shall not be a maid long, unless things° be cut shorter.°
                                                                           Exit.

2.1 *Enter Bastard [Edmund] and Curan, severally.°*

EDMUND. Save° thee, Curan.

CURAN. And you, sir. I have been with your father and
given him notice that the Duke of Cornwall and Regan
his duchess will be here with him this night.

EDMUND. How comes that?   5

CURAN. Nay, I know not. You have heard of the news
abroad—I mean the whispered ones,° for they are yet but
ear-kissing arguments?°

EDMUND. Not I. Pray you, what are they?

CURAN. Have you heard of no likely wars toward° twixt the   10
Dukes of Cornwall and Albany?

EDMUND. Not a word.

CURAN. You may do, then, in time. Fare you well, sir.
                                                                           Exit.

EDMUND.
The Duke be here tonight? The better! Best!°
This weaves itself perforce into my business.   15
My father hath set guard to take my brother,
And I have one thing, of a queasy question,°
Which I must act. Briefness and fortune,° work!—
Brother, a word. Descend. Brother, I say!

1.5. Location: Before Albany's palace. 1 Gloucester that is, the
place in Gloucestershire **2 these letters** this letter **3 demand**
inquiry **4 out of** prompted by **9 kibes** chilblains
11–12 slipshod in slippers, worn because of chilblains. (There are
no brains, says the Fool, in the heels of one who is on his way to visit
Regan.) **14 Shalt** thou shalt. **kindly** (1) according to filial
nature. (Said ironically.) (2) according to her own nature **15 crab**
crab apple **19 on 's** of his **22 of either side 's** on either side of his
24 her that is, Cordelia **30 horns** (Suggests cuckold's horns, as
though Lear were figuratively not the father of Goneril and Regan.)
31 forget my nature (Compare this with 1.4.222: "Who is it that
can tell me who I am?" Lear can no longer recognize the kind,
beloved father he thought himself to be.) **33 Thy . . . 'em** that is,
your servants (who labor like asses) have gone about 'readying the
horses **34 seven stars** Pleiades

37 To take . . . perforce that is, to think that Goneril would
forcibly take back again the privileges guaranteed to me. (Some
editors suggest, less persuasively, that Lear is meditating an armed
restoration of his monarchy.) **49 things** that is, penises. **cut
shorter** (A bawdy joke addressed to the audience.)
2.1. Location: The Earl of Gloucester's house. s.d. severally
separately **1 Save** God save **7 ones** that is, the news, regarded as
plural **8 ear-kissing arguments** lightly whispered topics
10 toward impending **14 The better! Best** so much the better; in
fact, the best that could happen **17 queasy question** matter not
for queasy stomachs **18 Briefness and fortune** expeditious dispatch and good luck

Enter Edgar.

20 My father watches. O sir, fly this place!
Intelligence is given where you are hid.
You have now the good advantage of the night.
Have you not spoken 'gainst the Duke of Cornwall?
He's coming hither, now, i' the night, i' the haste,°
25 And Regan with him. Have you nothing said
Upon his party 'gainst° the Duke of Albany?
Advise yourself.°

EDGAR.   I am sure on 't,° not a word.

EDMUND.
I hear my father coming. Pardon me;
In cunning I must draw my sword upon you.
30 Draw. Seem to defend yourself. Now, quit you° well.—
                              [*They draw.*]
Yield! Come before my father!—Light, ho, here!—
Fly, brother.—Torches, torches!—So, farewell.°

                              Exit Edgar.

Some blood drawn on me would beget opinion
Of my more fierce endeavor.° I have seen drunkards
Do more than this in sport. [*He wounds himself in the*
35   *arm.*] Father, Father!
Stop, stop! No help?

Enter Gloucester, and servants with torches.

GLOUCESTER.   Now, Edmund, where's the villain?

EDMUND.
Here stood he in the dark, his sharp sword out,
Mumbling of wicked charms, conjuring the moon
To stand 's° auspicious mistress.

GLOUCESTER.   But where is he?

EDMUND.
Look, sir, I bleed.

40 GLOUCESTER.   Where is the villain, Edmund?

EDMUND.
Fled this way, sir. When by no means he could—

GLOUCESTER.
Pursue him, ho! Go after. [*Exeunt some servants.*] By no
   means what?

EDMUND.
Persuade me to the murder of your lordship,
But that° I told him the revenging gods
45 'Gainst parricides did all the thunder bend,°
Spoke with how manifold and strong a bond

The child was bound to th' father; sir, in fine,°
Seeing how loathly opposite° I stood
To his unnatural purpose, in fell motion°
With his preparèd° sword he charges home°   50
My unprovided° body, latched° ine arm;
And when he saw my best alarumed° spirits,
Bold in the quarrel's right,° roused to th' encounter,
Or whether gasted° by the noise I made,
Full suddenly he fled.

GLOUCESTER.   Let him fly far.°   55
Not in this land shall he remain uncaught;
And found—dispatch.° The noble Duke my master,
My worthy arch and patron,° comes tonight.
By his authority I will proclaim it
That he which finds him shall deserve our thanks,   60
Bringing the murderous coward to the stake;°
He that conceals him, death.

EDMUND.
When I dissuaded him from his intent
And found him pight° to do it, with curst° speech
I threatened to discover° him. He replied,   65
"Thou unpossessing° bastard, dost thou think,
If I would stand against thee, would the reposal°
Of any trust, virtue, or worth in thee
Make thy words faithed?° No. What° I should deny—
As this I would, ay, though thou didst produce   70
My very character°—I'd turn° it all
To thy suggestion,° plot, and damnèd practice;°
And thou must make a dullard of the world°
If they not thought° the profits of my death°
Were very pregnant and potential spirits°   75
To make thee seek it."

GLOUCESTER.   O strange° and fastened° villain!
Would he deny his letter, said he? I never got° him.

Tucket° within.

47 **in fine** in conclusion   48 **loathly opposite** loathingly opposed
49 **fell motion** deadly thrust   50 **preparèd** unsheathed and ready.
home to the very heart   51 **unprovided** unprotected.   **latched**
nicked, lanced   52 **best alarumed** thoroughly aroused to action, as
by a trumpet   53 **quarrel's right** justice of the cause   54 **gasted**
frightened   55 **Let him fly far** that is, any fleeing, no matter how
far, will be in vain   57 **dispatch** that is, that will be the end for
him   58 **arch and patron** chief patron   61 **to the stake** that is, to
reckoning   64 **pight** determined.   **curst** angry   65 **discover**
expose   66 **unpossessing** unable to inherit, beggarly   67 **reposal**
placing   69 **faithed** believed.   **What** that which, whatever
71 **character** written testimony, handwriting.   **turn** attribute
72 **suggestion** instigation.   **practice** plot   73 **make . . . world**
think everyone idiotic   74 **not thought** did not think.   **of my**
death that you would gain through my death   75 **pregnant . . .**
spirits fertile and potent tempters   76 **strange** unnatural.
fastened hardened   77 **got** begot.   **s.d. Tucket** series of notes on
the trumpet, here indicating Cornwall's arrival

24 **i' the haste** in great haste   26 **Upon his party 'gainst** that is,
(too zealously) on Cornwall's behalf, or, (too critically) on the subject of his antagonism toward. (It would be dangerous to speak on
either side.)   27 **Advise yourself** think it over carefully.   **on 't** of
it   30 **quit you** defend, acquit yourself   31–32 **Yield . . . farewell**
(Edmund speaks loudly as though trying to arrest Edgar, calls for
others to help, and privately bids Edgar to flee.)   33–34 **beget . . .**
endeavor create an impression of my having fought fiercely
39 **stand 's** stand his, act as his   44 **that** when   45 **bend** aim

Hark, the Duke's trumpets! I know not why he comes.
All ports° I'll bar; the villain shall not scape.
80   The Duke must grant me that. Besides, his picture
I will send far and near, that all the kingdom
May have due note of him; and of my land,
Loyal and natural° boy, I'll work the means
To make thee capable.°

Enter Cornwall, Regan, and attendants.

CORNWALL.
85   How now, my noble friend? Since I came hither,
Which I can call but now, I have heard strange news.
REGAN.
If it be true, all vengeance comes too short
Which can pursue th' offender. How dost, my lord?
GLOUCESTER.
O madam, my old heart is cracked, it's cracked!
REGAN.
90   What, did my father's godson seek your life?
He whom my father named? Your Edgar?
GLOUCESTER.
O, lady, lady, shame would have it hid!
REGAN.
Was he not companion with the riotous knights
That tended upon my father?
GLOUCESTER.
95   I know not, madam. 'Tis too bad, too bad.
EDMUND.
Yes, madam, he was of that consort.°
REGAN.
No marvel, then, though° he were ill affected.°
'Tis they have put him on° the old man's death,
To have th' expense and spoil° of his revenues.
100   I have this present evening from my sister
Been well informed of them, and with such cautions
That if they come to sojourn at my house
I'll not be there.
CORNWALL.   Nor I, assure thee, Regan.
Edmund, I hear that you have shown your father
A childlike° office.
105   EDMUND.   It was my duty, sir.
GLOUCESTER [*to Cornwall*].
He did bewray his practice,° and received
This hurt you see striving to apprehend° him.
CORNWALL. Is he pursued?
GLOUCESTER. Ay, my good lord.

CORNWALL.
If he be taken, he shall never more   110
Be feared of doing harm. Make your own purpose,
How in my strength you please.° For° you, Edmund,
Whose virtue and obedience doth this instant
So much commend itself, you shall be ours.
Natures of such deep trust we shall much need;   115
You we first seize on.
EDMUND.   I shall serve you, sir,
Truly, however else.°
GLOUCESTER. For him I thank Your Grace.
CORNWALL.
You know not why we came to visit you—
REGAN.
—Thus out of season, threading dark-eyed night: 120
Occasions, noble Gloucester, of some poise,°
Wherein we must have use of your advice.
Our father he hath writ, so hath our sister,
Of differences,° which° I least thought it fit
To answer from our home.° The several messengers   125
From hence attend dispatch.° Our good old friend,
Lay comforts to your bosom, and bestow
Your needful° counsel to our businesses,
Which craves the instant use.°
GLOUCESTER. I serve you, madam.   130
Your Graces are right welcome.   *Flourish. Exeunt.*

2.2 *Enter Kent [disguised as Caius] and steward
[Oswald], severally.°*

OSWALD. Good dawning° to thee, friend. Art of this house?
KENT. Ay.
OSWALD. Where may we set our horses?
KENT. I' the mire.
OSWALD. Prithee, if thou lov'st me,° tell me.   5
KENT. I love thee not.
OSWALD. Why then, I care not for thee.
KENT. If I had thee in Lipsbury pinfold,° I would make thee
care for° me.

111–112 **Make . . . please** form your plans, making free use of my
authority and resources 112 **For** as for 117 **however else** that
is, whether capably or not 121 **poise** weight 124 **differences**
quarrels. **which** that is, which letters 125 **from our home** while
still at our palace in Cornwall 126 **attend dispatch** wait to be dispatched 127 **needful** necessary 128 **the instant use** immediate
attention
2.2 Location: Before Gloucester's house. **s.d. severally** at separate doors 1 **dawning** (It is not yet day.) 5 **if thou lov'st me** that
is, if you bear good will toward me. (But Kent deliberately takes the
phrase in its literal, not courtly, sense.) 8 **in Lipsbury pinfold**
that is, within the pinfold of the lips, between my teeth. (A *pinfold*
is a pound for stray animals.) 7–9 **care not for . . . care for** do not
like . . . have an anxious regard for

79 **ports** seaports, or gateways 83 **natural** (1) prompted by natural feelings of loyalty and affection (2) bastard 84 **capable** legally able to become the inheritor 96 **consort** crew 97 **though** if.
ill affected ill-disposed, disloyal 98 **put him on** incited him to
99 **expense and spoil** squandering 105 **childlike** filial
106 **bewray his practice** expose his (Edgar's) plot 107 **apprehend**
arrest

10 OSWALD. Why dost thou use me thus? I know thee not.
    KENT. Fellow, I know thee.°
    OSWALD. What dost thou know me for?
    KENT. A knave, a rascal, an eater of broken meats;° a base,
    proud, shallow, beggarly, three-suited,° hundred-pound,°
15 filthy worsted-stocking° knave; a lily-livered,° action-
    taking,° whoreson, glass-gazing,° superserviceable,° fini-
    cal° rogue; one-trunk-inheriting° slave; one that wouldst
    be a bawd in way of good service,° and art nothing but
    the composition° of a knave, beggar, coward, pander, and
20 the son and heir of a mongrel bitch; one whom I will beat
    into clamorous whining if thou deny'st the least syllable
    of thy addition.°
    OSWALD. Why, what a monstrous fellow art thou thus to rail
    on one that is neither known of thee nor knows thee!
25 KENT. What a brazen-faced varlet art thou to deny thou
    knowest me! Is it two days since I tripped up thy heels
    and beat thee before the King? Draw, you rogue, for
    though it be night, yet the moon shines. I'll make a sop o'
    the moonshine° of you, you whoreson, cullionly barber-
30 monger.° Draw!   [He brandishes his sword.]
    OSWALD. Away! I have nothing to do with thee.
    KENT. Draw, you rascal! You come with letters against the
    King, and take Vanity the puppet's part° against the roy-
    alty of her father. Draw, you rogue, or I'll so carbonado°
35 your shanks—draw, you rascal! Come your ways.°
    OSWALD. Help, ho! Murder! Help!
    KENT. Strike, you slave! Stand, rogue, stand, you neat°
    slave, strike!   [He beats him.]
    OSWALD. Help, ho! Murder! Murder!

    Enter Bastard [Edmund, with his rapier drawn], Corn-
    wall, Regan, Gloucester, servants.

EDMUND. How now, what's the matter?° Part!   40
KENT. With you,° goodman boy, an° you please! Come, I'll
    flesh° ye. Come on, young master.
GLOUCESTER. Weapons? Arms? What's the matter here?
CORNWALL. Keep peace, upon your lives! [Kent and Oswald
    are parted.] He dies that strikes again. What is the matter? 45
REGAN. The messengers from our sister and the King.
CORNWALL. What's your difference?° Speak.
OSWALD. I am scarce in breath, my lord.
KENT. No marvel, you have so bestirred your valor. You cow-
    ardly rascal, nature disclaims° in thee. A tailor made   50
    thee.
CORNWALL. Thou art a strange fellow. A tailor make a man?
KENT. A tailor, sir. A stonecutter or a painter could not have
    made him so ill, though they had been but two years o'
    the trade.   55
CORNWALL. Speak yet, how grew your quarrel?
OSWALD. This ancient ruffian, sir, whose life I have spared at
    suit of his gray beard—
KENT. Thou whoreson zed!° Thou unnecessary letter!—My
    lord, if you'll give me leave, I will tread this unbolted°   60
    villain into mortar and daub° the wall of a jakes° with
    him.—Spare my gray beard, you wagtail?°
CORNWALL. Peace, sirrah!
    You beastly knave, know you no reverence?
KENT.
    Yes, sir, but anger hath a privilege.   65
CORNWALL. Why art thou angry?
KENT.
    That such a slave as this should wear a sword,
    Who wears no honesty. Such smiling rogues as these,
    Like rats, oft bite the holy cords° atwain
    Which are too intrinse° t' unloose; smooth° every pas-   70
        sion
    That in the natures of their lords rebel,
    Bring oil to fire,° snow to their colder moods,
    Renege,° affirm, and turn their halcyon beaks°
    With every gale and vary° of their masters,   75

10–11 know thee not . . . know thee am unacquainted with you
. . . can see through you   13 broken meats scraps of food (such as
were passed out to the most lowly)   14 three-suited (Three suits a
year were allowed to servants.)   hundred-pound (Possible allusion
to the fee paid by some parvenus to be knighted by James I.)
15 worsted-stocking that is, too poor and menial to wear silk
stockings   lily-livered cowardly (the liver being pale through lack
of blood)   15–16 action-taking settling quarrels by resort to law
instead of arms, cowardly.   16 glass-gazing fond of looking in the
mirror   superserviceable officious.   16–17 finical foppish, fastidious   17 one-trunk-inheriting possessing effects sufficient for one
trunk only   18 bawd . . . service that is, pimp or pander as a way
of providing whatever is wanted   19 composition compound
22 thy addition the titles I've given you   28–29 sop o' the moonshine something so perforated that it will soak up moonshine as a
sop (floating piece of toast) soaks up liquor   29–30 cullionly bar-
bermonger base frequenter of barber shops, fop. (Cullion originally
meant "testicle.")   33 Vanity . . . part that is, the part of Goneril
(here personified as a character in a morality play)   34 carbonado
cut crosswise, like meat for broiling   35 Come your ways come on
37 neat (1) foppish (2) calflike. (Neat means "horned cattle.")

40 matter that is, trouble. (But Kent takes the meaning "cause for
quarrel.")   41 With you I'll fight with you; my quarrel is with you.
goodman boy (A contemptuous epithet, a title of mock respect,
addressed seemingly to Edmund.)   an if   42 flesh initiate into combat   47 difference quarrel   50 disclaims in disowns   59 zed the
letter z, regarded as unnecessary and often not included in dictio-
naries of the time   60 unbolted unsifted; hence, coarse   61 daub
plaster.   jakes privy   62 wagtail that is, bird wagging its tail
feathers in pert obsequiousness   69 holy cords sacred bonds of
affection and order   70 intrinse intrinsicate, tightly knotted.
smooth flatter, humor   73 Bring oil to fire that is, flattering servants fuel the flame of their masters' angry passions   74 Renege
deny   halcyon beaks (The halcyon or kingfisher, if hung up,
would supposedly turn its beak into the wind.)   75 gale and vary
variation in the wind

Knowing naught, like dogs, but following.—
A plague upon your epileptic° visage!
Smile you° my speeches, as° I were a fool?
Goose, an° I had you upon Sarum° plain,
30   I'd drive ye cackling home to Camelot.°
CORNWALL. What, art thou mad, old fellow?
GLOUCESTER. How fell you out? Say that.
KENT.
    No contraries hold more antipathy
    Than I and such a knave.
CORNWALL.
35   Why dost thou call him knave? What is his fault?
KENT. His countenance likes° me not.
CORNWALL.
    No more, perchance, does mine, nor his, nor hers.
KENT.
    Sir, 'tis my occupation to be plain:
    I have seen better faces in my time
90   Than stands on any shoulder that I see
    Before me at this instant.
CORNWALL.   This is some fellow
    Who, having been praised for bluntness, doth affect°
    A saucy roughness, and constrains the garb
    Quite from his nature.° He cannot flatter, he;
95   An honest mind and plain, he must speak truth!
    An they will take 't, so; if not, he's plain.°
    These kind of knaves I know, which in this plainness
    Harbor more craft and more corrupter ends
    Than twenty silly-ducking observants°
100   That stretch their duties nicely.°
    KENT.
        Sir, in good faith,° in sincere verity,
        Under th' allowance° of your great aspect,°
        Whose influence,° like the wreath of radiant fire
        On flickering Phoebus' front°—

CORNWALL.   What mean'st by this?
KENT. To go out of my dialect, which you discommend so   105
    much. I know, sir, I am no flatterer. He that beguiled you
    in a plain accent° was a plain knave, which for my part I
    will not be, though I should win your displeasure to
    entreat me to 't.°
CORNWALL. What was th' offense you gave him?   110
OSWALD. I never gave him any.
    It pleased the King his master very late°
    To strike at me, upon his misconstruction;°
    When he,° compact,° and flattering his displeasure,°
    Tripped me behind; being down, insulted,° railed,   115
    And put upon him such a deal of man°
    That worthied° him, got praises of the King
    For him attempting who was self-subdued;°
    And, in the fleshment° of this dread exploit,°
    Drew on me here again.   120
KENT. None of these rogues and cowards
    But Ajax is their fool.°
CORNWALL.   Fetch forth the stocks!
    You stubborn, ancient knave, you reverend° braggart,
    We'll teach you.
KENT.   Sir, I am too old to learn.
    Call not your stocks for me. I serve the King,   125
    On whose employment I was sent to you.
    You shall do small respect, show too bold malice
    Against the grace° and person of my master,
    Stocking his messenger.
CORNWALL.
    Fetch forth the stocks! As I have life and honor,   130
    There shall he sit till noon.
REGAN.
    Till noon? Till night, my lord, and all night too.

77 **epileptic** that is, trembling and pale with fright and distorted with a grin 78 **Smile you** do you smile at **as** as if 79 **an** if. **Sarum** Salisbury. 79–80 **Goose . . . Camelot** (The reference is obscure, but the general sense is that Kent scorns Oswald as a cackling goose.) **Camelot** legendary seat of King Arthur and his Round Table, said to have been at Cadbury and at Winchester, and hence in the general vicinity of Salisbury and Gloucester 86 **likes** pleases 92 **affect** adopt the style of 93–94 **constrains . . . nature** that is, distorts plainness to the point of caricature, away from its true purpose 96 **An . . . plain** if people will take his rudeness, fine; if not, his excuse is that he speaks plain truth 99 **silly-ducking observants** foolishly bowing, obsequious attendants 100 **stretch . . . nicely** exert themselves in their courtly duties punctiliously 101 **Sir, in good faith,** and so on (Kent assumes the wordy mannerisms of courtly flattery.) 102 **allowance** approval. **aspect** (1) countenance (2) astrological positions 103 **influence** astrological power 104 **Phoebus' front** that is, the sun's forehead

106–107 **He . . . accent** that is, the man who used plain speech to you craftily (see lines 97–100 and thereby taught you to suspect plain speakers of being deceitful 107–109 **which . . . me to 't** that is, I will no longer use plain speech, despite the incentive of incurring your displeasure by doing so. (Kent prefers to displease Cornwall, since Cornwall is pleased only by flatterers, and Kent has assumed until now that plain speech was the best way to offend, but he now argues mockingly that he can no longer speak plainly, since his honest utterance will be interpreted as duplicity.) 112 **late** recently 113 **upon his misconstruction** as a result of the King's misunderstanding (me) 114 **he** that is, Kent. **compact** joined, united with the King. **flattering his displeasure** gratifying the King's anger (at me) 115 **being down, insulted** that is, when I was down, he exulted over me 116 **put . . . man** acted like such a hero 117 **worthied** won a reputation for 118 **For . . . self-subdued** for assailing one (i.e., myself) who chose not to resist 119 **fleshment** excitement resulting from a first success. **dread exploit** (Said ironically.) 121–122 **None . . . fool** that is, you never find any rogues and cowards of this sort who do not outdo the blustering Ajax in their boasting 123 **reverend** (because old) 128 **grace** sovereignty, royal grace

KENT.
    Why, madam, if I were your father's dog
    You should° not use me so.
135 REGAN. Sir, being° his knave, I will.
CORNWALL.
    This is a fellow of the selfsame color°
    Our sister speaks of.—Come, bring away° the stocks!
    Stocks brought out.
GLOUCESTER.
    Let me beseech Your Grace not to do so.
    His fault is much, and the good King his master
140   Will check° him for 't. Your purposed low correction
    Is such as basest and contemned'st° wretches
    For pilferings and most common trespasses
    Are punished with. The King must take it ill
    That he, so slightly valued in his messenger,
    Should have him thus restrained.
145 CORNWALL.   I'll answer° that.
REGAN.
    My sister may receive it much more worse
    To have her gentleman abused, assaulted,
    For following her affairs. Put in his legs.
    [Kent is put in the stocks.]
    Come, my good lord, away.
              Exeunt [all but Gloucester and Kent].
GLOUCESTER.
150   I am sorry for thee, friend. 'Tis the Duke's pleasure,
    Whose disposition, all the world well knows,
    Will not be rubbed° nor stopped. I'll entreat for thee.
KENT.
    Pray, do not, sir. I have watched° and traveled hard.
    Some time I shall sleep out; the rest I'll whistle.
155   A good man's fortune may grow out at heels.°
    Give you° good morrow!
GLOUCESTER.
    The Duke's to blame in this. 'Twill be ill taken.   *Exit.*
KENT.
    Good King, that must approve° the common saw,°
    Thou out of heaven's benediction com'st
160   To the warm sun! *[He takes out a letter.]*

Approach, thou beacon to this under globe,°
That by thy comfortable° beams I may
Peruse this letter. Nothing almost sees miracles
But misery.° I know 'tis from Cordelia,
Who hath most fortunately been informed   165
Of my obscurèd° course, and shall find time
From this enormous state,° seeking to give
Losses° their remedies.° All weary and o'erwatched,°
Take vantage,° heavy eyes, not to behold
This shameful lodging.°   170
Fortune, good night. Smile once more; turn thy wheel!°
                     [He sleeps.]

2.3 *Enter Edgar.*

EDGAR. I heard myself proclaimed,
And by the happy° hollow of a tree
Escaped the hunt. No port° is free, no place
That° guard and most unusual vigilance
Does not attend my taking.° Whiles I may scape   5
I will preserve myself, and am bethought°
To take the basest and most poorest shape
That ever penury, in contempt of man,°
Brought near to beast. My face I'll grime with filth,
Blanket my loins, elf° all my hairs in knots,   10
And with presented° nakedness outface
The winds and persecutions of the sky.
The country gives me proof° and precedent
Of Bedlam° beggars who with roaring voices
Strike° in their numbed and mortifièd° arms   15
Pins, wooden pricks,° nails, sprigs of rosemary;

161 **beacon . . . globe** that is, the sun (?). (Some editors believe that Kent means the moon, since it is night at lines 28 and 171, but he probably is saying that he hopes for daylight soon in order that he can read the letter from Cordelia.) 162 **comfortable** useful, aiding 163–164 **Nothing . . . misery** scarcely anything can make one appreciate miracles like being in a state of misery; to the miserable, any relief seems miraculous 166 **obscurèd** disguised 167 **From . . . state** that is, to provide relief from this monstrous state of affairs, this enormity (?) 168 **Losses** reversals of fortune. 166–168 **and . . . remedies** (This seemingly incoherent passage may be textually corrupt or may be meant to represent fragments from the letter Kent is reading.) 168 **o'erwatched** exhausted with staying awake 169 **vantage** advantage (of sleep) 170 **lodging** that is, the stocks 171 **wheel** (Since Kent is at the bottom of Fortune's wheel, any turning will improve his situation.)
2.3. Location: Scene continues. Kent is dozing in the stocks.
2 **happy** luckily found 3 **port** (See 2.1.79 and note.) 4 **That** which 5 **attend my taking** lie in wait to capture me 6 **bethought** resolved 8 **in . . . man** in order to show how contemptible humankind is 10 **elf** tangle into elflocks 11 **presented** exposed to view, displayed 13 **proof** example 14 **Bedlam** (See the note to 1.2.133.) 15 **Strike** stick. **mortifièd** deadened 16 **wooden pricks** skewers

134 **should** would 135 **being** since you are 136 **color** complexion, character 137 **away** along 140 **check** rebuke, correct 141 **contemned'st** most despised 145 **answer** be answerable for 152 **rubbed** hindered, obstructed. (A term from bowls.) 153 **watched** gone sleepless 155 **A . . . heels** that is, even good men suffer decline in fortune at times. (To be out at heels is literally to be threadbare, coming through one's stockings.) 156 **Give you** that is, God give you 158 **approve** prove true. **saw** proverb (that is, "To run out of God's blessing into the warm sun," meaning "to go from better to worse," from a state of bliss into the pitiless world. Kent sees Lear as heading for trouble.)

And with this horrible object,° from low° farms,
Poor pelting° villages, sheepcotes, and mills,
Sometimes with lunatic bans,° sometimes with prayers,
20 Enforce their charity.° Poor Turlygod!° Poor Tom!°
That's something yet.° Edgar I nothing am.°   *Exit.*

2.4 *Enter Lear, Fool, and Gentleman.*

LEAR.
'Tis strange that they should so depart from home
And not send back my messenger.
GENTLEMAN.   As I learned,
The night before there was no purpose in them
Of this remove.°
KENT.   Hail to thee, noble master!
5 LEAR. Ha?
Mak'st thou this shame thy pastime?
KENT.   No, my lord.
FOOL. Ha, ha, he wears cruel° garters. Horses are tied by the
heads, dogs and bears by the neck, monkeys by the loins,
and men by the legs. When a man's overlusty at legs,°
10   then he wears wooden netherstocks.°
LEAR.
What's he that hath so much thy place mistook
To° set thee here?
KENT.   It is both he and she:
Your son and daughter.
LEAR. No.
15 KENT. Yes.
LEAR. No, I say.
KENT. I say yea.
LEAR. No, no, they would not.
KENT. Yes, they have.
20 LEAR. By Jupiter, I swear no.
KENT.
By Juno, I swear ay.
LEAR.   They durst not do 't!
They could not, would not do 't. 'Tis worse than murder
To do upon respect° such violent outrage.

Resolve° me with all modest° haste which way
Thou mightst deserve, or they impose, this usage,   25
Coming from us.
KENT.   My lord, when at their home°
I did commend° Your Highness' letters to them,
Ere I was risen from the place that showed
My duty kneeling,° came there a reeking° post,
Stewed° in his haste, half breathless, panting forth   30
From Goneril his mistress salutations;
Delivered letters, spite of intermission,°
Which presently° they read; on° whose contents
They summoned up their meiny,° straight took horse,
Commanded me to follow and attend   35
The leisure of their answer, gave me cold looks;
And meeting here the other messenger,
Whose welcome, I perceived, had poisoned mine—
Being the very fellow which of late
Displayed so saucily° against Your Highness—   40
Having more man° than wit about me, drew.
He raised the house with loud and coward cries.
Your son and daughter found this trespass worth
The shame which here it suffers.
FOOL. Winter's not gone yet if the wild geese fly that way.° 45

Fathers that wear rags
    Do make their children blind,°
But fathers that bear bags°
    Shall see their children kind.
Fortune, that arrant whore,   50
Ne'er turns the key° to the poor.

But, for all this, thou shalt have as many dolors° for° thy
daughters as thou canst tell° in a year.
LEAR.
O, how this mother° swells up toward my heart!
Hysterica passio,° down, thou climbing sorrow!   55
Thy element's° below.—Where is this daughter?

17 **object** spectacle. **low** lowly   18 **pelting** paltry   19 **bans** curses
20 **Enforce their charity** manage to beg something.   **Turlygod**
(Meaning unknown.)   **Poor . . . Tom** (Edgar practices the begging
role he is about to adopt. Beggars were known as "poor Toms.")
21 **That's something yet** there's some kind of existence still for me
as poor Tom.   **Edgar . . . am** as Edgar, I'm done for. (Suggesting
also, "I am Edgar no longer.")
2.4. Location: Scene continues before Gloucester's house. Kent
still dozing in the stocks.   4 **remove** change of residence   7 **cruel**
(1) unkind (2) crewel (compare the Quarto spelling, *crewell*), a thin
yarn of which garters were made   9 **overlusty at legs** given to running away   10 **netherstocks** stockings   12 **To** as to   23 **upon
respect** that is, against my officers (who deserve respect)

24 **Resolve** enlighten.   **modest** moderate   26 **their home** (Kent
and Oswald went first to Cornwall's palace after leaving Albany's
palace.)   27 **commend** deliver   28–29 **from . . . kneeling** from
the kneeling posture that showed my duty   29 **reeking** steaming
(with heat of travel)   30 **Stewed** that is, thoroughly heated,
soaked   32 **spite of intermission** in disregard of interrupting me,
or, in spite of the interruptions caused by his being out of breath
33 **presently** instantly.   **on** on the basis of   34 **meiny** retinue of
servants, household   40 **Displayed so saucily** behaved so insolently   41 **man** manhood, courage. **wit** discretion, sense
45 **Winter's . . . way** that is, the signs still point to continued and
worsening fortune; the wild geese are still flying south   47 **blind**
that is, indifferent to their father's needs   48 **bags** that is, of gold
51 **turns the key** opens the door   52 **dolors** griefs (with pun on
"dollars," English word for an Austrian or Spanish coin).   **for** (1)
on account of (2) in exchange for   53 **tell** (1) relate (2) count
54, 55 **mother, Hysterica passio** that is, hysteria, giving the sensation of choking or suffocating   56 **element's** proper place is.
(Hysteria, from the Greek *hystera,* womb, was thought to be produced by vapors ascending from the uterus or abdomen.)

KENT. With the Earl, sir, here within.

LEAR. Follow me not. Stay here. *Exit.*

GENTLEMAN.
Made you no more offense but what you speak of?

60 KENT. None.

How chance° the King comes with so small a number?

FOOL. An° thou hadst been set i' the stocks for that question, thou'dst well deserved it.

KENT. Why, Fool?

65 FOOL. We'll set thee to school to an ant to teach thee there's
no laboring i' the winter.° All that follow their noses are
led by their eyes but blind men, and there's not a nose
among twenty but can smell him that's stinking.° Let go
thy hold when a great wheel runs down a hill lest it break
70 thy neck with following; but the great one that goes
upward, let him draw thee after. When a wise man gives
thee better counsel, give me mine again. I would have
none but knaves follow it, since a fool gives it.

That sir which serves and seeks for gain,
75   And follows but for form,
Will pack° when it begins to rain
    And leave thee in the storm.
But I will tarry; the fool will stay,
    And let the wise man fly.
80 The knave turns fool that runs away;°
    The fool no knave, pardie.°

Enter Lear and Gloucester.

KENT. Where learned you this, Fool?

FOOL. Not i' the stocks, fool.

LEAR.
Deny to speak with me? They are sick? They are weary?
85 They have traveled all the night? Mere fetches,°
The images° of revolt and flying off.°
Fetch me a better answer.

GLOUCESTER.   My dear lord,
You know the fiery quality of the Duke,
How unremovable and fixed he is
90 In his own course.

LEAR.
Vengeance! Plague! Death! Confusion!°
Fiery? What quality? Why, Gloucester, Gloucester,
I'd speak with the Duke of Cornwall and his wife.

GLOUCESTER.
Well, my good lord, I have informed them so.

LEAR.
Informed them? Dost thou understand me, man?   95

GLOUCESTER. Ay, my good lord.

LEAR.
The King would speak with Cornwall. The dear father
Would with his daughter speak, commands, tends° ser-
vice.
Are they informed of this? My breath and blood!°   100
Fiery? The fiery Duke? Tell the hot Duke that—
No, but not yet. Maybe he is not well.
Infirmity doth still° neglect all office
Whereto our health is bound;° we are not ourselves
When nature, being oppressed, commands the mind   105
To suffer with the body. I'll forbear,
And am fallen out with my more headier will,
To take° the indisposed and sickly fit
For the sound man. [*Looking at Kent.*] Death on my
    state!° Wherefore   110
Should he sit here? This act persuades me
That this remotion° of the Duke and her
Is practice° only. Give me my servant forth.°
Go tell the Duke and 's wife I'd speak with them,
Now, presently.° Bid them come forth and hear me,   115
Or at their chamber door I'll beat the drum
Till it cry sleep to death.°

GLOUCESTER. I would have all well betwixt you.   *Exit.*

LEAR.
O me, my heart, my rising heart! But down!

FOOL. Cry to it, nuncle, as the cockney° did to the eels   120
when she put 'em i' the paste° alive. She knapped° 'em o'
the coxcombs° with a stick and cried, "Down, wantons,°
down!" 'Twas her brother° that, in pure kindness to his
horse, buttered his hay.°

Enter Cornwall, Regan, Gloucester, [and] servants.

---

61 **chance** chances it   62 **An** if   65–66 **We'll . . . winter** that is,
just as the ant knows not to labor in the winter, the wise man
knows not to labor for one whose fortunes are fallen   66–68 **All
. . . stinking** that is, one who is out of favor can be easily detected
(he smells of misfortune) and so is easily avoided by timeservers
76 **pack** be off   80 **The knave . . . away** that is, deserting one's
master is the greatest folly   81 **pardie** *par Dieu* (French), "by God"
85 **fetches** pretexts, dodges   86 **images** signs. **flying off** deser-
tion   91 **Confusion** destruction

98 **tends** attends, waits for   100 **My . . . blood** that is, by my very
life. (An oath.)   103 **still** always   103–104 **all . . . bound** all
duties which in good health we are bound to perform
107–108 **am . . . take** now disapprove of my more impetuous will
in having rashly taken   119–110 **Death on my state** may death
come to my royal authority. (An oath with ironic appropriateness.)
112 **remotion** removal, inaccessibility   113 **practice** deception.
forth out of the stocks   115 **presently** at once   117 **cry sleep to
death** that is, put an end to sleep by the noise   120 **cockney** that
is, a Londoner, ignorant of ways of cooking eels   121 **paste** pastry
pie. **knapped** rapped   122 **coxcombs** heads   122 **wantons** playful creatures, sexy rogues. (A term of affectionate abuse.) **brother**
that is, fellow creature, foolishly tenderhearted in the same way
123–124 **'Twas . . . hay** (Another city ignorance; the act is well
intended, but horses do not like greasy hay. As with Lear, good
intentions are not enough.)

125 LEAR. Good morrow to you both.
CORNWALL. Hail to Your Grace!

Kent here set at liberty.

REGAN. I am glad to see Your Highness.
LEAR.
Regan, I think you are. I know what reason
I have to think so. If thou shouldst not be glad,
130 I would divorce me from° thy mother's tomb,
Sepulch'ring° an adultress. [*To Kent.*] O, are you free?
Some other time for that.—Belovèd Regan,
Thy sister's naught.° O Regan, she hath tied
Sharp-toothed unkindness, like a vulture, here.

[*He lays his hand on his heart.*]

135 I can scarce speak to thee. Thou'lt not believe
With how depraved a quality°—O Regan!
REGAN.
I pray you, sir, take patience. I have hope
You less know how to value her desert
Than she to scant her duty.°
LEAR.   Say?° How is that?
REGAN.
140 I cannot think my sister in the least
Would fail her obligation. If, sir, perchance
She have restrained the riots of your followers,
'Tis on such ground and to such wholesome end
As clears her from all blame.
145 LEAR. My curses on her!
REGAN. O, sir, you are old;
Nature in you stands on the very verge
Of his confine.° You should be ruled and led
By some discretion° that discerns your state°
150 Better than you yourself. Therefore, I pray you,
That to our sister you do make return.
Say you have wronged her.
LEAR.   Ask her forgiveness?
Do you but mark how this becomes the house:°
[*Kneeling*] "Dear daughter, I confess that I am old;
155 Age is unnecessary.° On my knees I beg
That you'll vouchsafe me raiment, bed, and food."

REGAN.
Good sir, no more. These are unsightly tricks.
Return you to my sister.
LEAR [*rising*].   Never, Regan.
She hath abated° me of half my train,
Looked black upon me, struck me with her tongue   160
Most serpentlike upon the very heart.
All the stored vengeances of heaven fall
On her ingrateful top!° Strike her young bones,
You taking° airs, with lameness!
CORNWALL.   Fie, sir, fie!
LEAR.
You nimble lightnings, dart your blinding flames   165
Into her scornful eyes! Infect her beauty,
You fen-sucked° fogs drawn by the powerful sun
To fall and blister!°
REGAN.
O the blest gods! So will you wish on me
When the rash mood is on.   170
LEAR.
No, Regan, thou shalt never have my curse.
Thy tender-hafted° nature shall not give
Thee o'er to harshness. Her eyes are fierce, but thine
Do comfort and not burn. 'Tis not in thee
To grudge my pleasures, to cut off my train,   175
To bandy° hasty words, to scant my sizes,°
And, in conclusion, to oppose the bolt°
Against my coming in. Thou better know'st
The offices of nature,° bond of childhood,°
Effects° of courtesy, dues of gratitude.   180
Thy half o' the kingdom hast thou not forgot,
Wherein I thee endowed.
REGAN.   Good sir, to the purpose.°
LEAR.
Who put my man i' the stocks?

Tucket within.

CORNWALL.   What trumpet's that?
REGAN.
I know 't—my sister's. This approves° her letter,
That she would soon be here.

Enter steward [Oswald].

                    Is your lady come?   185

130 **divorce me from** that is, refuse to be buried beside
131 **Sepulch'ring** that is, since it would surely contain the dead
body of 133 **naught** wicked 136 **quality** disposition
137–139 **I have . . . duty** I trust this is more a matter of your
undervaluing her merit than of her falling slack in her duty to you
139 **Say?** come again? 147–148 **Nature . . . confine** that is, your
life has almost completed its allotted scope 149 **discretion** discreet person. **discerns your state** understands your dependent situation and aged condition (with an ironic reminder that *state* also
means "royal power") 153 **becomes the house** suits domestic
decorum, is suited to the family or household and its dutiful relationships. (Said with bitter irony.) 155 **Age is unnecessary** old
people are useless

159 **abated** deprived 163 **ingrateful top** ungrateful head
164 **taking** infectious 167 **fen-sucked** (It was supposed that the
sun sucked up poisons from fens or marshes.) 168 **To fall and
blister** to fall upon her and blister her beauty 172 **tender-hafted**
set in a tender *haft*, that is, "handle" or "frame"; moved by a tender
feeling, gently disposed 176 **bandy** volley, exchange. **scant my
sizes** diminish my allowances 177 **oppose the bolt** lock the door
179 **offices of nature** natural duties. **bond of childhood** filial
obligations due to parents 180 **Effects** actions, manifestations
182 **purpose** point 184 **approves** confirms

LEAR.
　　This is a slave, whose easy-borrowed° pride
　　Dwells in the fickle grace° of her he follows.
　　Out, varlet,° from my sight!
CORNWALL.　　　　　　　　　What means Your Grace?
LEAR.
　　Who stocked my servant? Regan, I have good hope
190　　Thou didst not know on 't.

　　　　Enter Goneril.

　　Who comes here? O heavens,
　　If you do love old men, if your sweet sway
　　Allow° obedience, if you yourselves are old,
　　Make it your cause; send down, and take my part!
195　　[_To Goneril._] Art not ashamed to look upon this beard?°
　　　　[_Goneril and Regan join hands._]
　　O Regan, will you take her by the hand?
GONERIL.
　　Why not by th' hand, sir? How have I offended?
　　All's not offense that indiscretion finds°
　　And dotage terms so.
LEAR.　　　　　　　　　O sides,° you are too tough!
200　　Will you yet hold?—How came my man i' the stocks?
CORNWALL.
　　I set him there, sir; but his own disorders
　　Deserved much less advancement.°
LEAR.　　　　　　　　　　You? Did you?
REGAN.
　　I pray you, Father, being weak, seem so.°
　　If till the expiration of your month
205　　You will return and sojourn with my sister,
　　Dismissing half your train, come then to me.
　　I am now from home, and out of that provision
　　Which shall be needful for your entertainment.°
LEAR.
　　Return to her? And fifty men dismissed?
210　　No! Rather I abjure all roofs, and choose
　　To wage° against the enmity o' th' air,
　　To be a comrade with the wolf and owl—
　　Necessity's sharp pinch. Return with her?
　　Why, the hot-blooded° France, that dowerless took
215　　Our youngest born—I could as well be brought
　　To knee° his throne and, squirelike, pension beg

To keep base life afoot. Return with her?
Persuade me rather to be slave and sumpter°
To this detested groom.　　　　[_He points to Oswald._]
GONERIL.　　　　　　　　At your choice, sir.
LEAR.
　　I prithee, daughter, do not make me mad.　　　　220
　　I will not trouble thee, my child. Farewell.
　　We'll no more meet, no more see one another.
　　But yet thou art my flesh, my blood, my daughter—
　　Or rather a disease that's in my flesh,
　　Which I must needs call mine. Thou art a boil,　　225
　　A plague-sore, or embossèd° carbuncle
　　In my corrupted blood. But I'll not chide thee;
　　Let shame come when it will, I do not call° it.
　　I do not bid the thunder-bearer° shoot,
　　Nor tell tales of thee to high-judging° Jove.　　230
　　Mend when thou canst; be better at thy leisure.
　　I can be patient. I can stay with Regan,
　　I and my hundred knights.
REGAN.　　Not altogether so.
　　I looked not for° you yet, nor am provided　　235
　　For your fit welcome. Give ear, sir, to my sister;
　　For those that mingle reason with your passion°
　　Must be content to° think you old, and so—
　　But she knows what she does.
LEAR.　　　　　　　　　Is this well spoken?
REGAN.
　　I dare avouch° it, sir. What, fifty followers?　　240
　　Is it not well? What should you need of more?
　　Yea, or so many, sith that° both charge° and danger
　　Speak 'gainst so great a number? How in one house
　　Should many people under two commands
　　Hold amity? 'Tis hard, almost impossible.　　245
GONERIL.
　　Why might not you, my lord, receive attendance
　　From those that she calls servants, or from mine?
REGAN.
　　Why not, my lord? If then they chanced to slack° ye,
　　We could control° them. If you will come to me—
　　For now I spy a danger—I entreat you　　250
　　To bring but five-and-twenty. To no more
　　Will I give place or notice.°

---

186 easy-borrowed that is, acquired with little effort at deserving and with weak commitment　**187 grace** favor　**188 varlet** worthless fellow　**193 Allow** approve, sanction　**195 beard** (A sign of age and presumed entitlement to respect.)　**196 indiscretion finds** poor judgment deems to be so　**197 sides** that is, sides of the chest (stretched by the swelling heart)　**202 much less advancement** far less honor, that is, far worse treatment　**203 seem so** that is, don't act as if you were strong　**208 entertainment** proper reception　**211 wage** wage war　**214 hot-blooded** choleric. (Compare this with 1.2.23.)　**216 knee** fall on my knees before

218 sumpter packhorse; hence, drudge　**226 embossèd** swollen, tumid　**228 call** summon　**229 the thunder-bearer** that is, Jove　**230 high-judging** judging from on high　**235 looked not for** did not expect　**237 mingle . . . passion** consider your passionate behavior with the cold eye of reason　**238 Must . . . to** must inevitably　**240 avouch** vouch for　**242 sith that** since.　**charge** expense　**248 slack** neglect　**249 control** correct　**252 notice** recognition, acknowledgment

LEAR.
　　I gave you all—
REGAN. 　　　　　　　And in good time you gave it.
LEAR.
　　Made you my guardians, my depositaries,°
255　But kept a reservation° to be followed
　　With such a number. What, must I come to you
　　With five-and-twenty? Regan, said you so?
REGAN.
　　And speak 't again, my lord. No more with me.
LEAR.
　　Those wicked creatures yet do look well-favored°
260　When others are more wicked; not being the worst
　　Stands in some rank of praise.° [To Goneril.] I'll go with
　　　　thee.
　　Thy fifty yet doth double five-and-twenty,
　　And thou art twice her love.
GONERIL. 　　　　　　　　Hear me, my lord:
　　What need you five-and-twenty, ten, or five,
265　To follow° in a house where twice so many
　　Have a command to tend you?
REGAN. 　　　　　　　　What need one?
LEAR.
　　O, reason not° the need! Our basest° beggars
　　Are in the poorest thing superfluous.°
　　Allow not° nature more than nature needs,°
270　Man's life is cheap as beast's. Thou art a lady;
　　If only to go warm were gorgeous,
　　Why, nature needs not what thou gorgeous wear'st,
　　Which scarcely keeps thee warm.° But, for° true need—
　　You heavens, give me that patience, patience I need!
275　You see me here, you gods, a poor old man,
　　As full of grief as age, wretched in both.
　　If it be you that stirs these daughters' hearts
　　Against their father, fool me not so much
　　To° bear it tamely; touch me with noble anger,
280　And let not women's weapons, water drops,
　　Stain my man's cheeks. No, you unnatural hags,
　　I will have such revenges on you both
　　That all the world shall—I will do such things—
　　What they are yet I know not, but they shall be

The terrors of the earth. You think I'll weep;　285
No, I'll not weep.
Storm and tempest.
　　I have full cause of weeping; but this heart
　　Shall break into a hundred thousand flaws°
　　Or ere° I'll weep. O Fool, I shall go mad!
　　　　Exeunt [Lear, Gloucester, Kent, Gentleman, and Fool].
CORNWALL.
　　Let us withdraw. 'Twill be a storm.　290
REGAN.
　　This house is little. The old man and 's people
　　Cannot be well bestowed.°
GONERIL.
　　'Tis his own blame° hath° put himself from rest,°
　　And must needs taste° his folly.
REGAN.
　　For his particular,° I'll receive him gladly,　295
　　But not one follower.
GONERIL.
　　So am I purposed. Where is my Lord of Gloucester?
CORNWALL.
　　Followed the old man forth.
　　Enter Gloucester.
　　　　　　　　　　He is returned.
GLOUCESTER.
　　The King is in high rage.
CORNWALL. 　　　　　Whither is he going?　300
GLOUCESTER.
　　He calls to horse, but will I know not whither.
CORNWALL.
　　'Tis best to give him way. He leads himself.°
GONERIL [to Gloucester].
　　My lord, entreat him by no means to stay.
GLOUCESTER.
　　Alack, the night comes on, and the bleak winds
　　Do sorely ruffle.° For many miles about　305
　　There's scarce a bush.
REGAN. 　　　　　　O, sir, to willful men
　　The injuries that they themselves procure
　　Must be their schoolmasters. Shut up your doors.
　　He is attended with a desperate train,
　　And what they may incense him to, being apt　310
　　To have his ear abused,° wisdom bids fear.

---

254 **depositaries** trustees　255 **kept a reservation** reserved a right
259 **well-favored** attractive, fair of feature　261 **Stands . . . praise**
achieves, by necessity, some relative deserving of praise
265 **follow** be your attendants　267 **reason not** do not dispassionately analyze.　**Our basest** even our most wretched　268 **Are . . .**
superfluous have some wretched possessions beyond what they
absolutely need　269 **Allow not** if you do not allow.　**needs** that
is, to survive　271–273 **If . . . warm** if fashions in clothes were
determined only by the need for warmth, this natural standard
wouldn't justify the rich robes you wear to be gorgeous—which
don't serve well for warmth in any case　273 **for** as for
278–279 **fool . . . To** do not make me so foolish as to

288 **flaws** fragments　289 **Or ere** before　292 **bestowed** lodged
293 **blame** fault.　**hath** that he has, or, that has.　**from rest** that
is, out of the house; also, lacking peace of mind　294 **taste** experience　295 **For his particular** as for him individually　301 **give**
. . . himself give him his own way. He is guided only by his own
willfulness.　305 **ruffle** bluster　310–311 **being . . . abused** (he)
being inclined to hearken to wild counsel

CORNWALL.
　　Shut up your doors, my lord; 'tis a wild night.
　　My Regan counsels well. Come out o' the storm.

　　　　　　　　　　　　　　　　　　　　Exeunt.

3.1 *Storm still. Enter Kent [disguised as Caius] and a Gentleman, severally.*°

KENT.　Who's there, besides foul weather?
GENTLEMAN.
　　One minded like the weather, most unquietly.
KENT.　I know you. Where's the King?
GENTLEMAN.
　　Contending with the fretful elements;
5　　Bids the wind blow the earth into the sea
　　Or swell the curlèd waters 'bove the main,°
　　That things° might change or cease; tears his white hair,
　　Which the impetuous blasts with eyeless rage
　　Catch in their fury and make nothing° of;
10　　Strives in his little world of man° to outstorm
　　The to-and-fro-conflicting wind and rain.
　　This night, wherein the cub-drawn° bear would couch,°
　　The lion and the belly-pinchèd wolf
　　Keep their fur dry, unbonneted he runs
　　And bids what will take all.°
15　KENT.　　　　　　　　　　　　But who is with him?
GENTLEMAN.
　　None but the Fool, who labors to outjest°
　　His heart-struck injuries.°
KENT.　　　　　　　　　　　　Sir, I do know you,
　　And dare upon the warrant of my note°
　　Commend a dear thing° to you. There is division,
20　　Although as yet the face of it is covered
　　With mutual cunning, twixt Albany and Cornwall;
　　Who have—as who have not, that° their great stars°
　　Throned and set high?—servants, who seem no less,°
　　Which are to France the spies and speculations°
25　　Intelligent of° our state. What hath been seen,
　　Either in snuffs° and packings° of the Dukes,

Or the hard rein which both of them hath borne
Against the old kind King, or something deeper,
Whereof perchance these are but furnishings°—
But true it is, from France there comes a power°　　30
Into this scattered° kingdom, who already,
Wise in° our negligence, have secret feet°
In some of our best ports and are at point°
To show their open banner. Now to you:
If on my credit° you dare build so far°　　35
To make your speed to Dover, you shall find
Some that will thank you, making just report°
Of how unnatural and bemadding sorrow
The King hath cause to plain.°
I am a gentleman of blood and breeding,　　40
And from some knowledge and assurance offer
This office° to you.
GENTLEMAN.
　　I will talk further with you.
KENT.　　　　　　　　　　　　No, do not.
　　For confirmation that I am much more
　　Than my outwall,° open this purse and take　　45
　　What it contains. [*He gives a purse and a ring.*] If you
　　　　shall see Cordelia—
　　As fear not but you shall—show her this ring,
　　And she will tell you who that fellow° is
　　That yet you do not know. Fie on this storm!
　　I will go seek the King.　　　　　　　　　　50
GENTLEMAN.
　　Give me your hand. Have you no more to say?
KENT.
　　Few words, but, to effect,° more than all yet:
　　That when we have found the King—in which your pain
　　That way, I'll this°—he that first lights on him
　　Holla the other　　　　　　　　　*Exeunt [separately].*

3.2 *Storm still. Enter Lear and Fool.*

LEAR.
　　Blow, winds, and crack your cheeks! Rage, blow!
　　You cataracts and hurricanoes,° spout
　　Till you have drenched° our steeples, drowned the
　　　　cocks!°

3.1. Location: An open place in Gloucestershire.　s.d. severally
at separate doors　**6 main** mainland　**7 things** all things　**9 make nothing of** treat disrespectfully　**10 little world of man** that is, microcosm, which is an epitome of the macrocosm or universe **12 cub-drawn** famished, with udders sucked dry (and hence ravenous).　**couch** lie close in its den　**15 bids . . . all** (A cry of desperate defiance; "take all" is the cry of a gambler in staking his last.) **16 outjest** exorcise or relieve by jesting　**17 heart-struck injuries** injuries that strike to the very heart　**18 upon . . . note** on the strength of what I know (about you)　**19 Commend . . . thing** entrust a precious undertaking　**22 that** whom.　**stars** destinies **23 no less** that is, no other than servants　**24 speculations** scouts, spies　**25 Intelligent of** supplying intelligence pertinent to **26 snuffs** quarrels.　**packings** intrigues

29 furnishings outward shows　**30 power** army　**31 scattered** divided　**32 Wise in** taking advantage of.　**feet** footholds　**33 at point** ready　**35 credit** trustworthiness.　**so far** so far as **37 making just report** for making an accurate report　**39 plain** complain　**42 office** assignment　**45 outwall** exterior appearance **48 fellow** that is, Kent　**52 to effect** in their consequences **53–54 in which . . . this** in which task, you search in that direction while I go this way
3.2. Location: An open place, as before.　2 hurricanoes waterspouts　**3 drenched** drowned.　**cocks** weathercocks

You sulfurous and thought-executing° fires,°
5 Vaunt-couriers° of oak-cleaving thunderbolts,
Singe my white head! And thou, all-shaking thunder,
Strike flat the thick rotundity o' the world!
Crack nature's molds,° all germens° spill° at once
That makes ingrateful man!

10 FOOL. O nuncle, court holy water° in a dry house is better
than this rainwater out o' door. Good nuncle, in, ask thy
daughters blessing.° Here's a night pities neither wise
men nor fools.

LEAR.
Rumble thy bellyful! Spit, fire! Spout, rain!
15 Nor rain, wind, thunder, fire are my daughters.
I tax° not you, you elements, with° unkindness;
I never gave you kingdom, called you children.
You owe me no subscription.° Then let fall
Your horrible pleasure. Here I stand your slave,
20 A poor, infirm, weak, and despised old man.
But yet I call you servile ministers,°
That will with two pernicious daughters join
Your high-engendered battles° 'gainst a head
So old and white as this. O, ho! 'Tis foul!

25 FOOL. He that has a house to put 's head in has a good headpiece.°

       The codpiece° that will house
         Before the head has any,
       The head and he shall louse;
30   So beggars marry many.
       The man that makes his toe
         What he his heart should make
       Shall of a corn cry woe,
         And turn his sleep to wake.°

35 For there was never yet fair woman but she made mouths
in a glass.°

LEAR.
No, I will be the pattern of all patience;
I will say nothing.

Enter Kent, [disguised as Caius].

KENT. Who's there?

FOOL. Marry,° here's grace° and a codpiece;° that's a wise 40
man and a fool.

KENT.
Alas, sir, are you here? Things that love night
Love not such nights as these. The wrathful skies
Gallow° the very wanderers of the dark°
And make them keep° their caves. Since I was man, 45
Such sheets of fire, such bursts of horrid thunder,
Such groans of roaring wind and rain I never
Remember to have heard. Man's nature cannot carry°
Th' affliction° nor the fear.

LEAR.   Let the great gods,
That keep this dreadful pother° o'er our heads, 50
Find out their enemies now.° Tremble, thou wretch,
That hast within thee undivulgèd crimes
Unwhipped of° justice! Hide thee, thou bloody hand,
Thou perjured,° and thou simular° of virtue
That art incestuous! Caitiff,° to pieces shake, 55
That under covert and convenient seeming°
Has practiced on° man's life! Close° pent-up guilts,
Rive your concealing continents° and cry
These dreadful summoners grace!° I am a man
More sinned against than sinning.

KENT.   Alack, bareheaded? 60
Gracious my lord, hard by here is a hovel;
Some friendship will it lend you 'gainst the tempest.
Repose you there while I to this hard house—
More harder than the stones whereof 'tis raised,
Which° even but now, demanding° after you, 65
Denied me to come in—return and force
Their scanted° courtesy.

LEAR.   My wits begin to turn.
Come on, my boy. How dost, my boy? Art cold?
I am cold myself.—Where is this straw, my fellow?

---

4 thought-executing acting with the quickness of thought. **fires**
that is, lightning **5 Vaunt-couriers** forerunners **8 nature's
molds** the molds in which nature makes all life. **germens** germs,
seeds. **spill** destroy **10 court holy water** flattery **12 ask . . .
blessing** (For Lear to do so would be to acknowledge their authority.) **16 tax** accuse. **with** of **18 subscription** allegiance
21 ministers agents **23 high-engendered battles** battalions
engendered in the heavens **25–26 headpiece** (1) helmetlike covering for the head (2) head for common sense **27–34 The codpiece . . . wake** that is, a man who houses his genitals in a sexual
embrace before he provides a roof for his head can expect the lice-
infested penury of a penniless marriage; and one who cherishes an
ignoble part of his body above what is noble (as Lear has done with
his daughters) can expect misery and wakeful tossing from that very
part he has so foolishly favored. **codpiece** covering for the genitals
worn by men with their close-fitting hose; here, representing the
genitals themselves **35–36 made . . . glass** practiced making
attractive faces in a mirror

40 Marry (An oath, originally "by the Virgin Mary.") **grace** royal
grace. **codpiece** (Often prominent in the Fool's costume.)
44 Gallow that is, gally, frighten. **wanderers of the dark** noctur-
nal wild beasts **45 keep** occupy, remain inside **48 carry** endure
49 affliction physical affliction **50 pother** hubbub, turmoil
51 Find . . . now that is, expose criminals (by the criminals' terrified response to this storm) **53 of** by **54 perjured** perjurer.
simular pretender **55 Caitiff** wretch **56 seeming** hypocrisy
57 practiced on plotted against. **58 Rive . . . continents** split open the covering that contains you **58–59 cry . . .
grace** pray for mercy at the hands of these officers of divine justice.
(*Summoners* are the police officers of an ecclesiastical court.)
65 Which that is, the occupants of which. **demanding** I inquiring
67 scanted stinted

70   The art of our necessities is strange,
      And can make vile things precious. Come, your hovel.—
      Poor fool and knave, I have one part in my heart
      That's sorry yet for thee.
      FOOL [*sings*].
         "He that has and a little tiny wit,
75   With heigh-ho, the wind and the rain,
         Must make content with his fortunes fit,
            Though the rain it raineth every day."°
      LEAR.
         True, boy.—Come, bring us to this hovel.

                                    Exit [with Kent].

      FOOL. This is a brave° night to cool a courtesan.° I'll speak a
80   prophecy ere I go:

         When priests are more in word than matter;°
         When brewers mar° their malt with water;
         When nobles are their tailors' tutors,°
         No heretics burned but wenches' suitors,°
85   Then shall the realm of Albion°
         Come to great confusion.

         When every case in law is right,°
         No squire in debt, nor no poor knight;
         When slanders do not live in tongues,
90   Nor cutpurses come not to throngs;
         When usurers tell° their gold i' the field,°
         And bawds and whores do churches build,
         Then comes the time, who lives to see 't,
         That going shall be used with feet.°

95   This prophecy Merlin° shall make, for I live before his
      time.   *Exit.*

3.3 *Enter Gloucester and Edmund [with lights].*

      GLOUCESTER. Alack, alack, Edmund, I like not this unnatur-
      al dealing. When I desired their leave that I might pity°

him, they took from me the use of mine own house,
charged me on pain of perpetual displeasure neither to
speak of him, entreat for him, or any way sustain him.   5
      EDMUND.
         Most savage and unnatural!
      GLOUCESTER. Go to;° say you nothing. There is division
between the Dukes, and a worse matter than that. I have
received a letter this night; 'tis dangerous to be spoken; I
have locked the letter in my closet.° These injuries the   10
King now bears will be revenged home;° there is part of a
power° already footed.° We must incline to° the King. I
will look° him and privily relieve him. Go you and maintain talk with the Duke, that my charity be not of° him
perceived. If he ask for me, I am ill and gone to bed. If I   15
die for 't, as no less is threatened me, the King my old
master must be relieved. There is strange things toward,°
Edmund. Pray you, be careful.   *Exit.*
      EDMUND.
         This courtesy forbid thee° shall the Duke
         Instantly know, and of that letter too.   20
         This seems a fair deserving,° and must draw me
         That which my father loses—no less than all.
         The younger rises when the old doth fall.   *Exit.*

3.4 *Enter Lear, Kent [disguised as Caius], and Fool.*

      KENT.
         Here is the place, my lord. Good my lord, enter.
         The tyranny of the open night's too rough
         For nature° to endure.
         Storm still.
      LEAR.   Let me alone.
      KENT.
         Good my lord, enter here.
      LEAR.   Wilt break my heart?°
      KENT.
         I had rather break mine own. Good my lord, enter.   5
      LEAR.
         Thou think'st 'tis much that this contentious storm
         Invades us to the skin. So 'tis to thee,
         But where the greater malady is fixed°

74–77 He . . . day (Derived from the popular song that Feste sings in *Twelfth Night*, 5.1.389 ff.)   **79 This . . . courtesan** that is, this wretched night might put courtesans off from streetwalking (?) **brave** fine   **81 more . . . matter** better as talkers about virtue than as practitioners of it. (This and the next three lines satirize the present state of affairs.)   **82 mar** adulterate   **83 are . . . tutors** can instruct their own tailors about fashion   **84 No . . . suitors** when heresy is a matter, not of religious faith, but of perjured lovers (whose burning is not at the stake but in catching venereal disease) **85 realm of Albion** kingdom of England. (The Fool is parodying a pseudo-Chaucerian prophetic verse.)   **87 right** just. (This and the next five lines offer a utopian vision of justice and charity that will never be realized in this corrupted world.)   **91 tell** count. **i' the field** that is, openly, without fear   **94 going . . . feet** walking will be done on foot   **95 Merlin** (A great wizard of the court of King Arthur, who came after Lear.)
3.3. Location: Gloucester's house.   **2 pity** be merciful to, relieve

7 Go to that is, no more of that   **10 closet** private chamber **11 home** thoroughly   **12 power** armed force. **footed** landed **incline to** side with   **13 look** look for   **14 of** by   **17 toward** impending   **19 courtesy forbid thee** kindness (to Lear) which you were forbidden to show   **21 fair deserving** meritorious action
3.4. Location: An open place. Before a hovel.   **3 nature** human nature   **4 break my heart** that is, cause me anguish by relieving my physical wants and thus forcing me to confront again my *greater malady* (line 8)   **8 fixed** lodged, implanted

The lesser is scarce felt. Thou'dst shun a bear,
10 But if thy flight lay toward the roaring sea
Thou'dst meet the bear i' the mouth.° When the mind's
   free,°
The body's delicate.° This tempest in my mind
Doth from my senses take all feeling else
Save what beats there. Filial ingratitude!
15 Is it not as° this mouth should tear this hand
For lifting food to 't? But I will punish home.°
No, I will weep no more. In such a night
To shut me out? Pour on; I will endure.
In such a night as this? O Regan, Goneril,
20 Your old kind father, whose frank° heart gave all—
O, that way madness lies; let me shun that!
No more of that.
KENT.   Good my lord, enter here.
LEAR.
Prithee, go in thyself; seek thine own ease.
This tempest will not give me leave° to ponder
25 On things would° hurt me more. But I'll go in.
[To the Fool.] In, boy; go first. You houseless poverty—
Nay, get thee in. I'll pray, and then I'll sleep.

                      Exit [Fool into the hovel].

Poor naked wretches, wheresoe'er you are,
That bide° the pelting of this pitiless storm,
30 How shall your houseless heads and unfed sides,°
Your looped and windowed° raggedness, defend you
From seasons such as these? O, I have ta'en
Too little care of this! Take physic, pomp;°
Expose thyself to feel what wretches feel,
35 That thou mayst shake the superflux° to them
And show the heavens more just.
EDGAR [within] Fathom and half,° fathom and half!
Poor Tom!

              Enter Fool [from the hovel].

FOOL. Come not in here, nuncle; here's a spirit. Help me,
40   help me!
KENT. Give me thy hand. Who's there?
FOOL. A spirit, a spirit! He says his name's poor Tom.
KENT.
What art thou that dost grumble° there i' the straw?
Come forth.

          Enter Edgar [disguised as a madman].

EDGAR. Away!° The foul fiend follows me! Through the   45
sharp hawthorn blows the cold wind.° Hum! Go to thy
bed and warm thee.
LEAR. Didst thou give all to thy daughters? And art thou
come to this?
EDGAR. Who gives anything to poor Tom? Whom the foul   50
fiend hath led through fire and through flame, through
ford and whirlpool, o'er bog and quagmire; that hath laid
knives° under his pillow and halters° in his pew,° set rats-
bane° by his porridge,° made him proud of heart to ride
on a bay trotting horse over four-inched bridges° to   55
course° his own shadow for° a traitor. Bless thy five wits!°
Tom's a-cold. O, do de, do de, do de. Bless thee from
whirlwinds, star-blasting,° and taking!° Do poor Tom
some charity, whom the foul fiend vexes. There° could I
have him now—and there—and there again—and there.   60

        Storm still.

LEAR.
Has his daughters brought him to this pass?°—
Couldst thou save nothing? Wouldst thou give 'em all?
FOOL. Nay, he reserved a blanket,° else we had been all
shamed.
LEAR.
Now, all the plagues that in the pendulous° air   65
Hang fated° o'er men's faults light on thy daughters!
KENT. He hath no daughters, sir.
LEAR.
Death, traitor! Nothing could have subdued nature
To such a lowness but his unkind daughters.
Is it the fashion that discarded fathers   70
Should have thus little mercy on their flesh?°
Judicious° punishment! 'Twas this flesh begot
Those pelican° daughters.
EDGAR. Pillicock sat on Pillicock° Hill. Alow, alow, loo, loo!

---

45 Away keep away **45–46 Through . . . wind** (Possibly a line
from a ballad.) **53–54 knives, halters, ratsbane** (Like knives,
nooses, and rat poison are means to commit suicide and hence are
damned.) **53 pew** gallery, place (?) **54 porridge** soup **55 over
four-inched bridges** that is, taking mad risks on narrow bridges with
the devil's assistance **56 course** chase. **for** as **57 five wits** either
the five senses, or common wit, imagination, fantasy, estimation, and
memory **58 star-blasting** being blighted by influence of the stars
taking infection, evil influence, enchantment **59 There** (Perhaps
he slaps at lice and other vermin as if they were devils.) **61 pass**
miserable plight **63 reserved a blanket** kept a wrap (for his nakedness) **65 pendulous** suspended, overhanging **66 fated** having the
power of fate **71 have . . . flesh** that is, punish themselves, as Edgar
has done (probably with pins and thorns stuck in his flesh)
72 Judicious appropriate to the crime **73 pelican** greedy. (Young
pelicans supposedly smote their parents and fed on the blood of their
mothers' breasts.) **74 Pillicock** (From an old rhyme, suggested by
the sound of *pelican. Pillicock* in nursery rhyme seems to have been a
euphemism for penis; *Pillicock Hill*, for the Mount of Venus.)

---

11 i' the mouth that is, head-on. **free** free of anxiety **12 The
body's delicate** that is, the body's importunate needs can assert
themselves **15 as** as if **16 home** fully **20 frank** liberal
24 will . . . leave that is, keeps me too preoccupied **25 things
would** things (such as filial ingratitude) that would **29 bide**
endure **30 unfed sides** that is, lean ribs **31 looped and win-
dowed** full of openings like windows and loopholes **33 Take
physic, pomp** cure yourself, O distempered great ones
35 superflux superfluity (with suggestion of *flux*, "bodily discharge," introduced by *physic*, "purgative," in line 33) **37 Fathom
and half** (A sailor's cry while taking soundings, hence appropriate
to a deluge.) **43 grumble** utter inarticulate sounds

75 FOOL. This cold night will turn us all to fools and madmen.

EDGAR. Take heed o' the foul fiend. Obey thy parents; keep thy word's justice;° swear not; commit not° with man's sworn spouse; set not thy sweet heart on proud array. Tom's a-cold.

80 LEAR. What hast thou been?

EDGAR. A servingman,° proud in heart and mind, that curled my hair, wore gloves° in my cap, served the lust of my mistress' heart, and did the act of darkness with her; swore as many oaths as I spake words, and broke them in 85 the sweet face of heaven. One that slept in the contriving of lust and waked to do it. Wine loved I deeply, dice dearly, and in woman out-paramoured the Turk.° False of heart, light of ear,° bloody of hand; hog in sloth, fox in stealth, wolf in greediness, dog in madness, lion in prey.° 90 Let not the creaking of shoes nor the rustling of silks betray thy poor heart to woman. Keep thy foot out of brothels, thy hand out of plackets,° thy pen from lenders' books,° and defy the foul fiend. Still through the hawthorn blows the cold wind; says suum, mun, nonny.° 95 Dolphin my boy,° boy, sessa!° Let him trot by.

Storm still.

LEAR. Thou wert better in a grave than to answer with thy uncovered body this extremity of the skies. Is man no more than this? Consider him well. Thou ow'st° the worm no silk, the beast no hide, the sheep no wool, the 100 cat° no perfume. Ha! Here's three on's are sophisticated.° Thou art the thing itself; unaccommodated° man is no more but such a poor, bare, forked animal as thou art. Off, off, you lendings! Come, unbutton here.

[Tearing off his clothes.]

FOOL. Prithee, nuncle, be contented; 'tis a naughty° night to 105 swim in. Now a little fire in a wild° field were like an old lecher's heart—a small spark, all the rest on 's° body cold.

Enter Gloucester, with a torch.

Look, here comes a walking fire.

EDGAR. This is the foul fiend Flibbertigibbet!° He begins at curfew and walks till the first cock;° he gives the web and the pin,° squinnies° the eye and makes the harelip, 110 mildews the white° wheat, and hurts the poor creature of earth.

Swithold° footed thrice the 'old;°
He met the nightmare and her ninefold;°
    Bid her alight,   115
    And her troth plight,
And aroint thee,° witch, aroint thee!

KENT. How fares Your Grace?

LEAR. What's he?

KENT. Who's there? What is 't you seek?   120

GLOUCESTER. What are you there? Your names?

EDGAR. Poor Tom, that eats the swimming frog, the toad, the tadpole, the wall newt and the water;° that in the fury of his heart, when the foul fiend rages, eats cow dung for salads, swallows the old rat and the ditch-dog,° drinks 125 the green mantle° of the standing° pool; who is whipped from tithing to tithing° and stock-punished° and imprisoned; who hath had three suits° to his back, six shirts to his body,

Horse to ride, and weapon to wear;   130
But mice and rats and such small deer°
Have been Tom's food for seven long year.

Beware my follower.° Peace, Smulkin!° Peace, thou fiend!

GLOUCESTER.
What, hath Your Grace no better company?   135

EDGAR. The Prince of Darkness is a gentleman. Modo° he's called, and Mahu.°

---

77 **justice** integrity.   **commit not** that is, do not commit adultery. (Edgar's mad catechism contains fragments of the Ten Commandments.)   81 **servingman** either a "servant" in the language of courtly love or an ambitious servant in a household   82 **gloves** that is, my mistress's favors   87 **out-paramoured the Turk** outdid the Sultan in keeping mistresses   88 **light of ear** credulous in believing malicious talk   89 **prey** preying   92 **plackets** slits in skirts or petticoats   92–93 **thy pen . . . books** that is, do not sign a contract for a loan   94 **suum . . . nonny** (Imitative of the wind?)   95 **Dolphin my boy** (A slang phrase or bit of song?)   **sessa** that is, away, cease (?)   98 **ow'st** have borrowed from   100 **cat** civet cat   **sophisticated** clad in the trappings of civilized life; adulterated   101 **unaccommodated** unfurnished with the trappings of civilization   104 **naughty** bad   105 **wild** barren, uncultivated   106 **on 's** of his

108 **Flibbertigibbet** (A devil from Elizabethan folklore whose name appears in Samuel Harsnett's *Declaration of Egregious Popish Impostures,* 1603, and elsewhere.)   109 **first cock** midnight   109–110 **web and the pin** cataract of the eye   110 **squinnies** causes to squint   111 **white** ripening   113 **Swithold** Saint Withold, an Anglo-Saxon exorcist, who here provides defense against the *nightmare,* or demon thought to afflict sleepers, by commanding the nightmare to *alight,* that is, stop riding over the sleeper, and *plight* her *troth,* that is, vow true faith, promise to do no harm. (Or, an error for *Swithin.*)   **footed . . . 'old** thrice traversed the wold (tract of hilly upland)   114 **ninefold** nine offspring (with possible pun on *fold, foal*)   117 **aroint thee** begone   123 **water** that is, water newt   125 **ditch-dog** that is, dead dog in a ditch.   126 **mantle** scum.   **standing** stagnant   127 **tithing to tithing** that is, one ward or parish to another   **stock-punished** placed in the stocks   128 **three suits** (Like the menial servant at 2.2.14.)   131 **deer** animals   133 **follower** familiar, attendant devil   133, 136, 137 **Smulkin, Modo, Mahu** (Shakespeare found these Elizabethan devils in Samuel Harsnett's *Declaration.*)

GLOUCESTER.
    Our flesh and blood, my lord, is grown so vile
    That it doth hate what gets it.°
140 EDGAR. Poor Tom's a-cold.
GLOUCESTER.
    Go in with me. My duty cannot suffer°
    T' obey in all your daughters' hard commands.
    Though their injunction be to bar my doors
    And let this tyrannous night take hold upon you,
145   Yet have I ventured to come seek you out
    And bring you where both fire and food is ready.
LEAR.
    First let me talk with this philosopher.
    [*To Edgar.*] What is the cause of thunder?
KENT.   Good my lord,
    Take his offer. Go into the house.
LEAR.
150   I'll talk a word with this same learnèd Theban.°
    [*To Edgar.*] What is your study?°
EDGAR. How to prevent° the fiend, and to kill vermin.
LEAR Let me ask you one word in private.

                             [*Lear and Edgar talk apart.*]

KENT [*to Gloucester*].
    Importune him once more to go, my lord.
    His wits begin t' unsettle.
155 GLOUCESTER.   Canst thou blame him?

                                 Storm still.

    His daughters seek his death. Ah, that good Kent!
    He said it would be thus, poor banished man.
    Thou sayest the King grows mad; I'll tell thee, friend,
    I am almost mad myself. I had a son,
160   Now outlawed from my blood;° he sought my life
    But lately, very late. I loved him, friend,
    No father his son dearer. True to tell thee,
    The grief hath crazed my wits. What a night's this!—
    I do beseech Your Grace—
165 LEAR. O, cry you mercy,° sir.
    [*To Edgar.*] Noble philosopher, your company.
EDGAR. Tom's a-cold.
GLOUCESTER [*to Edgar*].
    In, fellow, there, in th' hovel. Keep thee warm.
LEAR [*starting toward the hovel*].
    Come, let's in all.
KENT.   This way, my lord.
LEAR.   With him!
170   I will keep still with my philosopher.

KENT [*to Gloucester*].
    Good my lord, soothe° him. Let him take the fellow.
GLOUCESTER [*to Kent*]. Take him you on.°
KENT [*to Edgar*].
    Sirrah, come on. Go along with us.
LEAR. Come, good Athenian.°
GLOUCESTER. No words, no words! Hush.   175
EDGAR.
    Child Rowland° to the dark tower came;
    His word° was still,° "Fie, foh, and fum,
      I smell the blood of a British man."°   *Exeunt.*

3.5 *Enter Cornwall and Edmund [with a letter].*

CORNWALL. I will have my revenge ere I depart his house.
EDMUND. How, my lord, I may be censured,° that nature°
    thus gives way to loyalty, something fears° me to think of.
CORNWALL. I now perceive it was not altogether your broth-
    er's evil disposition made him seek his° death, but a pro- 5
    voking merit set awork by a reprovable badness in himself.°
EDMUND. How malicious is my fortune, that I must repent to
    be just!° This is the letter he spoke of, which approves°
    him an intelligent party to the advantages° of France. O
    heavens! That this treason were not, or not I the detector! 10
CORNWALL. Go with me to the Duchess.
EDMUND. If the matter of this paper be certain, you have
    mighty business in hand.
CORNWALL. True or false, it hath made thee Earl of Glouces-
    ter. Seek out where thy father is, that he may be ready for 15
    our apprehension.°
EDMUND [*aside*]. If I find him° comforting° the King, it will
    stuff his suspicion° more fully.—I will persevere in my
    course of loyalty, though the conflict be sore between
    that and my blood.°   20
CORNWALL. I will lay trust upon thee, and thou shalt find a
    dearer father in my love.   *Exeunt.*

---

171 soothe humor **172 Take . . . on** that is, go on ahead with
Edgar **174 Athenian** that is, philosopher **176 Child Rowland,**
and so on (Probably a fragment of a ballad about the hero of the
Charlemagne legends. A *child* is a candidate for knighthood.)
177 word watchword. **still** always **177–178 Fie . . . man** (This
is essentially what the Giant says in "Jack, the Giant Killer.")
3.5 Location: Gloucester's house. **2 censured** judged. **nature**
attachment to family **3 something fears** somewhat frightens
5 his that is, his father's **6 provoking . . . himself** that is, the badness of Gloucester which deserved punishment, set awork by an evil
propensity in Edgar himself **7–8 How . . . just** that is, how cruel
of fate to oblige me to be upright and loyal by betraying my own
father, which breaks my heart **8 approves** proves. **9 an intelligent . . . advantages** a spy in the service **16 apprehension** arrest
17 him that is, Gloucester. **comforting** offering aid and comfort
to, helping **18 his suspicion** the suspicion of Gloucester
20 blood family loyalty, filial instincts

138–139 Our . . . gets it (1) life is so wretched that it cries out
against having been born (2) our children hate their parents. **gets**
begets **141 suffer** permit me **150 Theban** that is, one deeply
versed in "philosophy" or natural science **151 study** special competence **152 prevent** thwart **160 outlawed . . . blood** dis-
owned, disinherited, and legally outlawed **165 cry you mercy** I
beg your pardon

3.6 *Enter Kent [disguised as Caius] and Gloucester.*

GLOUCESTER. Here is better than the open air; take it thankfully. I will piece° out the comfort with what addition I
can. I will not be long from you.
KENT. All the power of his wits have given way to his impa-
5 tience.° The gods reward your kindness!

Exit [Gloucester].

Enter Lear, Edgar [as poor Tom], and Fool.

EDGAR. Fraretto° calls me, and tells me Nero is an angler°
in the lake of darkness. Pray, innocent,° and beware the
foul fiend.
FOOL. Prithee, nuncle, tell me whether a madman be a gen-
10 tleman or a yeoman?°
LEAR. A king, a king!
FOOL. No, he's a yeoman that has a gentleman to his son; for
he's a mad yeoman that sees his son a gentleman before
him.
LEAR.
15 To have a thousand with red burning spits
Come hizzing° in upon 'em—
EDGAR. The foul fiend bites° my back.
FOOL. He's mad that trusts in the tameness of a wolf, a
horse's health,° a boy's love, or a whore's oath.
LEAR.
20 It shall be done; I will arraign them° straight.
[*To Edgar.*] Come, sit thou here, most learnèd justicer.°
[*To the Fool.*] Thou, sapient sir, sit here. Now, you she-
foxes!
EDGAR. Look where he° stands and glares! Want'st thou
25 eyes at trial,° madam?
[*Sings.*] "Come o'er the burn, Bessy, to me—"°

**3.6. Location: Within a building on Gloucester's estate, near or
adjoining his house, or part of the house itself. See 3.4.150–69.
Cushions are provided, and stools. 2 piece eke 4–5 impatience**
rage, inability to endure more **6 Fraretto** (Another of the fiends
from Harsnett.) **Nero is an angler** (Chaucer's "Monk's Tale,"
lines 2474–2475, tells how Nero fished in the Tiber with nets of
gold thread; in Rabelais, 2.30, Nero is described as a hurdy-gurdy
player and Trajan an angler for frogs in the underworld.)
7 innocent simpleton, fool (i.e., the Fool) **10 yeoman** property
owner below the rank of gentleman. (The Fool's bitter jest in lines
12–14 is that such a man might go mad to see his son advanced
over him.) **16 hizzing** hissing. (Lear imagines his wicked daughters suffering torments in hell or being attacked by enemies.)
17 bites (i.e., in the shape of a louse) **18–19 tameness . . . health**
(Wolves are untamable, and horses are prone to disease.)
20 arraign them (Lear now imagines the trial of his cruel daughters.) **21 justicer** judge, justice **24 he** (Probably one of Edgar's
devils, or, Lear.) **24–25 Want'st . . . trial** do you lack spectators at
your trial? or, can't you see who's looking at you? **26 Come . . . me**
(First line of a ballad by William Birche, 1558. A *burn* is a brook.
The Fool makes a ribald reply, in which the *leaky boat* suggests her
easy virtue or perhaps her menstrual period.)

FOOL [*sings*].
Her boat hath a leak,
And she must not speak
Why she dares not come over to thee.
EDGAR. The foul fiend haunts poor Tom in the voice of a   30
nightingale.° Hoppedance° cries in Tom's belly for two
white° herring. Croak° not, black angel; I have no food
for thee.
KENT.
How do you, sir? Stand you not so amazed.°
Will you lie down and rest upon the cushions?   35
LEAR.
I'll see their trial first. Bring in their evidence.°
[*To Edgar.*] Thou robèd man° of justice, take thy place;
[*To the Fool.*] And thou, his yokefellow of equity,°
Bench° by his side. [*To Kent.*] You are o' the
commission;°
Sit you, too.   [*They sit.*] 40
EDGAR. Let us deal justly.   [*He sings.*]

Sleepest or wakest thou, jolly shepherd?
Thy sheep be in the corn;°
And for one blast of thy minikin° mouth,
Thy sheep shall take no harm.°   45

Purr the cat° is gray.
LEAR. Arraign her first; 'tis Goneril, I here take my oath
before this honorable assembly, kicked° the poor King
her father.
FOOL. Come hither, mistress. Is your name Goneril?   50
LEAR. She cannot deny it.
FOOL. Cry you mercy, I took you for a joint stool.°
LEAR.
And here's another, whose warped looks proclaim
What store° her heart is made on.° Stop her there!
Arms, arms, sword, fire! Corruption in the place!°   55
False justicer, why hast thou let her scape?

---

31 nightingale (Edgar pretends to take the Fool's singing for that of a
fiend disguised as a nightingale.) **Hoppedance** (Harsnett mentions
"Hoberdidance.") **32 white** unsmoked (contrasted with *black
angel*, a demon.) **Croak** (Refers to the rumbling in Edgar's stomach, denoting hunger.) **34 amazed** bewildered **36 their evidence**
the witnesses against them **37 robèd man** that is, Edgar, with his
blanket **38 yokefellow of equity** partner in the law **39 Bench**
take your place on the bench. **39–40 o' the commission** one commissioned to be a justice **43 corn** grainfield **44–45 And . . .
harm** (This may mean that, if the shepherd recalls his sheep by piping to them before they consume the grainfield, they will not be put
in the pound.) **44 minikin** dainty, pretty **46 Purr the cat** (A
devil or familiar from Harsnett; see the note for 3.4.108. *Purr* may be
the sound the familiar makes.) **48 kicked** who kicked **52 joint
stool** low stool made by a joiner, or maker of furniture with joined
parts. (Proverbially, the phrase "I took . . . stool" meant "I beg your
pardon for failing to notice you." The reference is also presumably to
a real stool onstage.) **54 store** material. **on** of **55 Corruption
in the place** that is, there is iniquity or bribery in this court

EDGAR. Bless thy five wits!

KENT.
O, pity! Sir, where is the patience now
That you so oft have boasted to retain?

EDGAR [aside].
My tears begin to take his part so much
They mar my counterfeiting.

LEAR. The little dogs and all,
Tray, Blanch, and Sweetheart, see, they bark at me.

EDGAR. Tom will throw his head° at them. Avaunt, you
curs!

Be thy mouth or black° or white,
Tooth that poisons if it bite,
Mastiff, greyhound, mongrel grim,
Hound or spaniel, brach° or lym,°
Bobtail tike° or trundle-tail,°
Tom will make him weep and wail;
For, with throwing thus my head,
Dogs leapt the hatch,° and all are fled.

Do de, de, de. Sessa!° Come, march to wakes° and fairs
and market towns. Poor Tom, thy horn° is dry.

LEAR. Then let them anatomize° Regan; see what breeds
about her heart. Is there any cause in nature that makes
these hard hearts? [To Edgar.] You, sir, I entertain° for one
of my hundred; only I do not like the fashion of your garments. You will say they are Persian;° but let them be
changed.

KENT.
Now, good my lord, lie here and rest awhile.

LEAR [lying on cushions°]. Make no noise, make no noise.
Draw the curtains. So, so. We'll go to supper i' the morning.   [He sleeps.]

FOOL. And I'll go to bed at noon.

Enter Gloucester.

GLOUCESTER.
Come hither, friend. Where is the King my master?

KENT.
Here, sir, but trouble him not; his wits are gone.

GLOUCESTER.
Good friend, I prithee, take him in thy arms.
I have o'erheard a plot of death upon° him.
There is a litter ready; lay him in 't

And drive toward Dover, friend, where thou shalt meet
Both welcome and protection. Take up thy master.
If thou shouldst dally half an hour, his life,
With thine and all that offer to defend him,   95
Stand in assurèd loss.° Take up, take up,
And follow me, that will to some provision°
Give thee quick conduct.°

KENT.   Oppressèd nature sleeps.
This rest might yet have balmed° thy broken sinews,°
Which, if convenience° will not allow,   100
Stand in hard cure.° [To the Fool.] Come, help to bear
thy master.
Thou must not stay behind.   [They pick up Lear.]

GLOUCESTER.   Come, come, away!

Exeunt [all but Edgar].

EDGAR.
When we our betters see bearing our woes,°
We scarcely think our miseries our foes.°
Who alone suffers suffers most i' the mind,   105
Leaving free things and happy shows behind;°
But then the mind much sufferance° doth o'erskip
When grief hath mates, and bearing fellowship.°
How light and portable° my pain seems now,
When that which makes me bend makes the King bow—
He childed as I fathered.° Tom, away!   110
Mark the high noises,° and thyself bewray°
When false opinion, whose wrong thoughts defile thee,
In thy just proof repeals and reconciles thee.°
What will hap more tonight, safe scape the King!°
Lurk, lurk.   [Exit.]   115

3.7 Enter Cornwall, Regan, Goneril, Bastard
[Edmund], and Servants.

CORNWALL [to Goneril]. Post speedily° to my lord your husband; show him this letter. [He gives a letter.] The army of
France is landed.—Seek out the traitor Gloucester.

---

64 **throw his head at** that is, threaten   66 **or black** either black
69 **brach** hound bitch.   **lym** bloodhound   70 **Bobtail tike** short-
tailed, small cur.   **trundle-tail** long-tailed dog   73 **hatch** lower
half of a divided door   74 **Sessa** that is, away, cease (?)   **wakes**
(Here, parish festivals.)   75 **horn** that is, horn bottle, used by beggars to beg for drinks   76 **anatomize** dissect   78 **entertain** take
into my service   80 **Persian** (Lear madly asks if Edgar's wretched
blanket is a rich Persian fabric.)   83 **curtains** bed curtains. (They
presumably exist only in Lear's mad imagination.)   90 **upon**
against

96 **Stand . . . loss** will assuredly be lost   97 **provision** supplies, or,
means of providing for safety   98 **conduct** guidance   99 **balmed**
cured, healed.   **sinews** nerves   100 **convenience** circumstances
101 **Stand . . . cure** will be hard to cure   103 **our woes** woes like
ours   104 **We . . . foes** we almost forget our own miseries (since we
see how human suffering afflicts even the great)   105–106 **Who
. . . behind** when we think of our own misfortunes as unique, we suffer the mental anguish of reflecting on all the carefree joys and happy
scenes that were once ours   107 **sufferance** suffering   108 **bearing
fellowship** tribulation (has) company   **portable** bearable, endurable
110 **He . . . fathered** that is, he suffering cruelty from his children as
I from my father   111 **Mark . . . noises** that is, observe what is
being said about those in high places or about great events.   **bewray**
reveal   113 **In . . . thee** upon your being proved innocent recalls
you and restores you to favor   114 **What . . . King** whatever else
happens tonight, may the King escape safely
3.7. Location: Gloucester's house.   1 **Post speedily** hurry

[Exeunt some Servants.]

REGAN. Hang him instantly.

5 GONERIL. Pluck out his eyes.

CORNWALL. Leave him to my displeasure. Edmund, keep you
our sister° company. The revenges we are bound° to take
upon your traitorous father are not fit for your beholding.
Advise the Duke,° where you are going, to a most festi-
10 nate° preparation; we are bound° to the like. Our posts°
shall be swift and intelligent° betwixt us. Farewell, dear
sister; farewell, my lord of Gloucester.°

Enter steward [Oswald].

How now? Where's the King?

OSWALD.

My lord of Gloucester hath conveyed him hence.
15 Some five- or six-and-thirty of his° knights,
Hot questrists after him,° met him at gate,
Who, with some other of the lord's° dependents,
Are gone with him toward Dover, where they boast
To have well-armèd friends.

20 CORNWALL. Get horses for your mistress.   *[Exit Oswald.]*

GONERIL. Farewell, sweet lord, and sister.

CORNWALL.

Edmund, farewell.   *Exeunt [Goneril and Edmund].*
Go seek the traitor Gloucester.
Pinion him like a thief; bring him before us.

[Exeunt Servants.]

Though well we may not pass upon his life°
25 Without the form of justice, yet our power
Shall do a court'sy° to our wrath, which men
May blame but not control.

Enter Gloucester, and Servants [leading him].

Who's there? The traitor?

REGAN. Ingrateful fox! 'Tis he.

CORNWALL. Bind fast his corky° arms.

GLOUCESTER.

30 What means Your Graces? Good my friends, consider
You are my guests. Do me no foul play, friends.

CORNWALL.

Bind him, I say.   *[Servants bind him.]*

REGAN.   Hard, hard. O filthy traitor!

GLOUCESTER.

Unmerciful lady as you are, I'm none.

CORNWALL.

To this chair bind him.—Villain, thou shalt find—

[Regan plucks Gloucester's beard.]

GLOUCESTER.

By the kind gods, 'tis most ignobly done   35
To pluck me by the beard.

REGAN.

So white,° and such a traitor?

GLOUCESTER.   Naughty° lady,
These hairs which thou dost ravish from my chin
Will quicken° and accuse thee. I am your host.
With robbers' hands my hospitable favors°   40
You should not ruffle° thus. What will you do?

CORNWALL.

Come, sir, what letters had you late° from France?

REGAN.

Be simple-answered,° for we know the truth.

CORNWALL.

And what confederacy have you with the traitors
Late footed° in the kingdom?

REGAN.   To whose hands   45
You have sent the lunatic King. Speak.

GLOUCESTER.

I have a letter guessingly set down,°
Which came from one that's of a neutral heart,
And not from one opposed.

CORNWALL. Cunning.   50

REGAN. And false.

CORNWALL. Where hast thou sent the King?

GLOUCESTER. To Dover.

REGAN.

Wherefore to Dover? Wast thou not charged at peril°—

CORNWALL.

Wherefore to Dover? Let him answer that.   55

GLOUCESTER.

I am tied to th' stake,° and I must stand the course.°

REGAN. Wherefore to Dover?

GLOUCESTER.

Because I would not see thy cruel nails
Pluck out his poor old eyes, nor thy fierce sister
In his anointed° flesh rash° boarish fangs.   60
The sea, with such a storm as his bare head
In hell-black night endured, would have buoyed up

---

7 **sister** that is, sister-in-law, Goneril **bound** intending; obliged
9 **the Duke** that is, Albany **9–10 festinate** hasty. **10 are bound**
intend, are committed **posts** messengers. **11 intelligent** serviceable in bearing information, knowledgeable **12 my . . . Gloucester** that is, Edmund, the recipient now of his father's forfeited estate
and title. (Two lines later, Oswald uses the same title to refer to
Edmund's father.) **15 his** Lear's **16 questrists after him**
searchers for Lear **17 the lord's** that is, Gloucester's **24 pass
upon his life** pass the death sentence upon him **26 do a court'sy**
that is, bow before, yield precedence **29 corky** withered with age

37 **white** that is, white-haired, venerable. **Naughty** wicked
39 **quicken** come to life **40 my hospitable favors** the features of
me, your host **41 ruffle** tear or snatch at, treat with such violence
42 **late** lately **43 simple-answered** straightforward in your
answers **45 footed** landed **47 guessingly set down** which was
tentatively stated **54 charged at peril** commanded on peril of
your life **56 tied to th' stake** that is, like a bear to be baited with
dogs. **the course** the dogs' attack **60 anointed** consecrated with
holy oil. **rash** slash sideways with

And quenched the stellèd° fires;°
Yet, poor old heart, he holp° the heavens to rain.
55 If wolves had at thy gate howled that dern° time,
Thou shouldst have said, "Good porter, turn the key."°
All cruels else subscribe.° But I shall see
The wingèd Vengeance° overtake such children.
CORNWALL.
See 't shalt thou never. Fellows, hold the chair.
70 Upon these eyes of thine I'll set my foot.
GLOUCESTER.
He that will think° to live till he be old,
Give me some help!

[*Servants hold the chair as Cornwall grinds out one of Gloucester's eyes with his boot.*]

O cruel! O you gods!
REGAN.
One side will mock another. Th' other too.
CORNWALL.
If you see Vengeance—
FIRST SERVANT.   Hold your hand, my lord!
75 I have served you ever since I was a child;
But better service have I never done you
Than now to bid you hold.
REGAN.   How now, you dog?
FIRST SERVANT [*to Regan*].
If you did wear a beard upon your chin,
I'd shake it on this quarrel.°—What do you mean?°
80 CORNWALL. My villain?°   [*He draws his sword.*]
FIRST SERVANT [*drawing*].
Nay, then, come on, and take the chance of anger.°

[*They fight. Cornwall is wounded.*]

REGAN [*to another Servant*].
Give me thy sword. A peasant stand up thus?

[*She takes a sword and runs at him behind.*°]

FIRST SERVANT.
O, I am slain! My lord, you have one eye left
To see some mischief° on him. O!   [*He dies.*]
CORNWALL.
85 Lest it see more, prevent it. Out, vile jelly!

[*He puts out Gloucester's other eye.*]
Where is thy luster now?
GLOUCESTER.
All dark and comfortless. Where's my son Edmund?
Edmund, enkindle all the sparks of nature°
To quit° this horrid act.
REGAN.   Out,° treacherous villain!
90 Thou call'st on him that hates thee. It was he
That made the overture° of thy treasons to us,
Who is too good to pity thee.
GLOUCESTER.
O my follies! Then Edgar was abused.°
Kind gods, forgive me that, and prosper him!
REGAN.
95 Go thrust him out at gates and let him smell
His way to Dover.

Exit [*a Servant*] *with Gloucester.*
How is 't, my lord? How look you?°
CORNWALL.
I have received a hurt. Follow me, lady.—
Turn out that eyeless villain. Throw this slave
Upon the dunghill.—Regan, I bleed apace.
100 Untimely comes this hurt. Give me your arm.

Exeunt [*Cornwall, supported by Regan*].
SECOND SERVANT.
I'll never care what wickedness I do,
If this man come to good.
THIRD SERVANT.   If she live long,
And in the end meet the old° course of death,
Women will all turn monsters.
SECOND SERVANT.
105 Let's follow the old Earl, and get the Bedlam
To lead him where he would. His roguish madness
Allows itself to anything.°
THIRD SERVANT.
Go thou. I'll fetch some flax and whites of eggs
To apply to his bleeding face. Now, heaven help him!

Exeunt° [*with the body*].

4.1 *Enter Edgar* [*as poor Tom*].

EDGAR.
Yet better thus,° and known° to be contemned,°

62–63 **would . . . fires** would have swelled high enough, like a wave-lifted buoy, to quench the stars. (The storm was monstrous in its scope and in its assault on order.) **stellèd** starry, or fixed **64 holp** helped **65 dern** dire, dread **66 turn the key** that is, let them in **67 All . . . subscribe** all other cruel creatures would show forgiveness except you; this cruelty is unparalleled **68 The wingèd Vengeance** the swift vengeance of the avenging angel of divine wrath **71 will think** hopes **79 I'd . . . quarrel** that is, I'd pull your beard in vehement defiance in this cause. **What do you mean** that is, what are you thinking of, what do you think you're doing? (Said perhaps to Cornwall.) **80 villain** servant, bondman. (Cornwall's question implies, "How dare you do such a thing?") **81 the chance of anger** the risks of an angry encounter **82 s.d. She . . . behind** (This stage direction appears in the Quarto.) **84 mischief** injury

88 **nature** that is, filial love **89 quit** requite. **Out** (An exclamation of anger or impatience.) **91 overture** disclosure **93 abused** wronged **96 How look you** how is it with you? **103 old** customary, natural **106–107 His . . . anything** that is, his being a madman and derelict allows him to do anything **109 s.d. Exeunt** (At some point after lines 98–99, the body of the slain First Servant must be removed.)
4.1. Location: An open place. **1 Yet better thus** that is, it is better to be a beggar. **known** know what it is. **contemned** despised

Than still contemned and flattered.° To be worst,
The lowest and most dejected thing of° fortune,
Stands still in esperance,° lives not in fear.°

5 The lamentable change is from the best;
The worst returns to laughter.° Welcome, then,
Thou unsubstantial air that I embrace!
The wretch that thou hast blown unto the worst
Owes nothing° to thy blasts.

Enter Gloucester, and an Old Man [leading him].

                But who comes here?

10 My father, poorly led? World, world, O world!
But that thy strange mutations make us hate thee,
Life would not yield to age.°

OLD MAN.
    O, my good lord, I have been your tenant
And your father's tenant these fourscore years.

GLOUCESTER.

15 Away, get thee away! Good friend, begone.
Thy comforts° can do me no good at all;
Thee they may hurt.

OLD MAN.   You cannot see your way.

GLOUCESTER.
I have no way and therefore want no eyes;
I stumbled when I saw. Full oft 'tis seen

20 Our means secure us,° and our mere defects°
Prove our commodities.° O dear son Edgar,
The food of thy abusèd father's wrath!°
Might I but live to see thee in° my touch,
I'd say I had eyes again!

OLD MAN.   How now? Who's there?

EDGAR [*aside*].

25 O gods! Who is 't can say, "I am at the worst"?
I am worse than e'er I was.

OLD MAN.   'Tis poor mad Tom.

EDGAR [*aside*].
And worse I may be yet. The worst is not
So long as we can say, "This is the worst."°

OLD MAN.
Fellow, where goest?

---

2 contemned and flattered despised behind your back and flattered
to your face **3 dejected . . . of** debased or humbled by
4 esperance hope. **fear** that is, of something worse happening
5–6 The lamentable . . . laughter any change from the best is
grievous, just as any change from the worst is bound to be for the
better **9 Owes nothing** can pay no more, is free of obligation
11–12 But . . . age if it were not for your hateful inconstancy, we
would never be reconciled to old age and death **16 comforts**
kindnesses **20 Our means secure us** our prosperity makes us
overconfident **mere defects** sheer afflictions **21 commodities**
benefits **22 The . . . wrath** on whom thy deceived father's wrath
fed, the object of his anger **23 in** that is, by means of
27–28 The worst . . . worst so long as we can speak and act and
delude ourselves with false hopes, our fortunes can, in fact, grow
worse

GLOUCESTER.   Is it a beggar-man?

OLD MAN. Madman and beggar too.   30

GLOUCESTER.
He has some reason,° else he could not beg.
I' the last night's storm I such a fellow saw,
Which made me think a man a worm. My son
Came then into my mind, and yet my mind
Was then scarce friends with him. I have heard more
    since.   35
As flies to wanton° boys are we to th' gods;
They kill us for their sport.

EDGAR [*aside*].   How should this be?°
Bad is the trade that must play fool to sorrow,°
Ang'ring° itself and others.—Bless thee, master!

GLOUCESTER.
Is that the naked fellow?

OLD MAN.   Ay, my lord.   40

GLOUCESTER.
Then, prithee, get thee gone. If for my sake
Thou wilt o'ertake us° hence a mile or twain
I' the way toward Dover, do it for ancient love,°
And bring some covering for this naked soul,
Which I'll entreat to lead me.

OLD MAN.   Alack, sir, he is mad.   45

GLOUCESTER
'Tis the time's plague,° when madmen lead the blind.
Do as I bid thee, or rather do thy pleasure;
Above the rest,° begone.

OLD MAN.
I'll bring him the best 'parel that I have,
Come on 't° what will.   *Exit.*

GLOUCESTER.   Sirrah, naked fellow—   50

EDGAR. Poor Tom's a-cold. [*Aside*]. I cannot daub it further.°

GLOUCESTER. Come hither, fellow.

EDGAR [*aside*].
And yet I must.—Bless thy sweet eyes, they bleed.

GLOUCESTER. Know'st thou the way to Dover?

EDGAR. Both stile and gate, horseway and footpath. Poor 55
Tom hath been scared out of his good wits. Bless thee,
good man's son, from the foul fiend! Five fiends have
been in poor Tom at once: of lust, as Obidicut;° Hobbidi-
dance, prince of dumbness; Mahu, of stealing; Modo, of

---

31 reason power of reason **36 wanton** playful **37 How . . . be**
that is, how can he have suffered so much, changed so much?
38 Bad . . . sorrow that is, it's a bad business to have to play the
fool to my sorrowing father **39 Ang'ring** offending, distressing
42 o'ertake us catch up to us (after you have found clothing for
Tom o' Bedlam) **43 ancient love** that is, the mutually trusting
relationship of master and tenant that Gloucester and the Old Man
have long enjoyed **46 'Tis the time's plague** that is, it well
expresses the spreading sickness of our present state **48 the rest**
all **50 on 't** of it **51 daub it further** that is, keep up this pretense

murder; Flibbertigibbet,° of mopping and mowing,° who
since° possesses chambermaids and waiting women. So,
bless thee, master!

GLOUCESTER [*giving a purse*].
Here, take this purse, thou whom the heavens' plagues
Have humbled to all strokes.° That I am wretched
Makes thee the happier. Heavens, deal so still!
Let the superfluous° and lust-dieted° man,
That slaves your ordinance,° that will not see
Because he does not feel,° feel your pow'r quickly!
So distribution should undo excess
And each man have enough. Dost thou know Dover?

EDGAR. Ay, master.

GLOUCESTER.
There is a cliff, whose high and bending° head
Looks fearfully in the confinèd deep.°
Bring me but to the very brim of it
And I'll repair the misery thou dost bear
With something rich about me. From that place
I shall no leading need.

EDGAR.   Give me thy arm.
Poor Tom shall lead thee.   *Exeunt.*

4.2 *Enter Goneril [and] Bastard [Edmund].*

GONERIL.
Welcome,° my lord. I marvel our mild husband
Not met° us on the way.
[*Enter*] *steward [Oswald].*
                         Now, where's your master?

OSWALD.
Madam, within, but never man so changed.
I told him of the army that was landed;
He smiled at it. I told him you were coming;
His answer was "The worse." Of Gloucester's treachery
And of the loyal service of his son
When I informed him, then he called me sot°
And told me I had turned the wrong side out.
What most he should dislike seems pleasant to him;
What like, offensive.

GONERIL [*to Edmund*].
Then shall you go no further.
It is the cowish° terror of his spirit,
That dares not undertake.° He'll not feel wrongs
Which tie him to an answer.° Our wishes on the way   15
May prove effects.° Back, Edmund, to my brother;°
Hasten his musters° and conduct his powers.°
I must change names° at home and give the distaff°
Into my husband's hands. This trusty servant
Shall pass between us. Ere long you are like° to hear,   20
If you dare venture in your own behalf,
A mistress's° command. Wear this; spare speech.

[*She gives him a favor.*]

Decline your head. [*She kisses him.*] This kiss, if it durst
    speak,
Would stretch thy spirits up into the air.
Conceive,° and fare thee well.   25

EDMUND.
Yours in the ranks of death.   *Exit.*

GONERIL.   My most dear Gloucester!
O, the difference of man and man!
To thee a woman's services are due;
My fool usurps my body.°

OSWALD.
Madam, here comes my lord.   [*Exit.*°]   30
Enter Albany.

GONERIL.
I have been worth the whistling.°

ALBANY.   O Goneril,
You are not worth the dust which the rude wind
Blows in your face. I fear your disposition;°
That nature which contemns° its origin

58–60 **Obidicut . . . Flibbertigibbet** (Fiends borrowed, as before in
3.4.108 and 133–37, from Harsnett.) 60 **mopping and mowing**
making grimaces and mouths 61 **since** since that time 64 **Have
. . . strokes** have brought so low as to be prepared to accept every
blow of Fortune 66 **superfluous** immoderate, gluttonous. **lust-
dieted** feeding luxuriously 67 **slaves your ordinance** makes the
laws of heaven his slaves 68 **feel** feel sympathy or fellow feeling;
suffer 72 **bending** overhanging 73 **in . . . deep** that is, into the
sea below, which is confined by its shores
4.2. Location: Before the Duke of Albany's palace. 1 **Welcome**
(Goneril, who has just arrived home from Gloucestershire escorted
by Edmund, bids him brief welcome before he must return.)
2 **Not met** has not met 8 **sot** fool

13 **cowish** cowardly 14 **undertake** venture 14–15 **He'll . . .
answer** he will ignore insults that, if he took notice, would oblige
him to respond, to fight 15–16 **Our . . . effects** the hopes we discussed on our journey here (presumably concerning the supplanting
of Albany by Edmund) may come to pass 16 **brother** that is,
brother-in-law, Cornwall 17 **musters** assembling of troops.
powers armed forces 18 **change names** that is, exchange the roles
of master and mistress of the household, and exchange the insignia
of man and woman: the sword and the *distaff*. **distaff** spinning
staff, symbolizing the wife's role 20 **like** likely 22 **mistress's**
(With sexual double meaning.) 25 **Conceive** understand, take my
meaning (with sexual double entendre, continuing from *stretch thy
spirits* in the previous line and continued in *death*, line 26, and a
woman's services, line 28) 29 **My fool . . . body** that is, my husband claims possession of me but is unfitted to do so 30 **s.d. Exit**
(Oswald could exit later with Goneril, at line 89.) 31 **worth the
whistling** that is, worth the attentions of men. (Alludes to the
proverb, "it is a poor dog that is not worth the whistling.")
33 **fear your disposition** mistrust your nature 34 **contemns**
despises

35 Cannot be bordered certain° in itself.
She that herself will sliver° and disbranch
From her material sap° perforce must wither
And come to deadly use.°
GONERIL. No more. The text° is foolish.
ALBANY.
40 Wisdom and goodness to the vile seem vile;
Filths savor but themselves.° What have you done?
Tigers, not daughters, what have you performed?
A father, and a gracious agèd man,
Whose reverence even the head-lugged° bear would lick,
45 Most barbarous, most degenerate, have you madded.°
Could my good brother° suffer you to do it?
A man, a prince, by him so benefited?
If that the heavens do not their visible° spirits
Send quickly down to tame these vile offenses,
50 It will come,
Humanity must perforce prey on itself,
Like monsters of the deep.
GONERIL.   Milk-livered° man,
That bear'st a cheek for blows, a head for wrongs,
Who hast not in thy brows an eye discerning
55 Thine honor from thy suffering,° that not know'st
Fools° do those villains pity who are punished
Ere they have done their mischief. Where's thy drum?°
France spreads his banners in our noiseless° land,
With plumèd helm thy state begins to threat,°
60 Whilst thou, a moral° fool, sits still and cries,
"Alack, why does he so?"°
ALBANY.   See thyself, devil!
Proper deformity° shows not in the fiend
So horrid as in woman.

GONERIL.   O vain fool!
ALBANY.
Thou changèd° and self-covered° thing, for shame,
Bemonster not thy feature.° Were 't my fitness°   65
To let these hands obey my blood,°
They are apt° enough to dislocate and tear
Thy flesh and bones. Howe'er thou art a fiend,°
A woman's shape doth shield° thee.
GONERIL. Marry, your manhood! Mew!°   70

Enter a Messenger.

ALBANY. What news?
MESSENGER.
O, my good lord, the Duke of Cornwall's dead,
Slain by his servant, going to put out
The other eye of Gloucester.
ALBANY.   Gloucester's eyes!
MESSENGER.
A servant that he bred,° thrilled with remorse,°   75
Opposed° against the act, bending his sword
To° his great master, who, thereat enraged,
Flew on him and amongst them° felled him dead,
But not without that harmful stroke which since
Hath plucked him after.°
ALBANY.   This shows you are above,   80
You justicers,° that these our nether° crimes
So speedily can venge! But, O poor Gloucester!
Lost he his other eye?
MESSENGER.   Both, both, my lord.—
This letter, madam, craves a speedy answer;
'Tis from your sister.   [*He gives her a letter.*]
GONERIL. [*aside*].   One way° I like this well;   85
But being widow, and my Gloucester with her,
May all the building in my fancy pluck
Upon my hateful life.° Another way
The news is not so tart.°—I'll read, and answer.

[*Exit.*]

---

35 bordered certain safely restrained, kept within bounds
36 sliver tear off   **37 material sap** nourishing substance, the stock
from which she grew   **38 to deadly use** to destruction, like firewood   **39 The text** that is, on which you have been preaching
41 savor but themselves hunger only for that which is filthy
44 head-lugged dragged by the head (or by the ring in its nose) and
infuriated   **45 madded** driven mad   **46 brother** brother-in-law
(Cornwall)   **48 visible** made visible   **52 Milk-livered** white-liv-
ered, cowardly   **54–55 discerning . . . suffering** able to tell the
difference between an insult to your honor and something you
should tolerate   **56 Fools** that is, only fools. (Goneril goes on to
say that only fools are so tenderhearted as to worry about injustices
to potential troublemakers, like Lear and Gloucester, instead of
applauding measures taken to insure order.)   **57 thy drum** that is,
your military preparations   **58 noiseless** peaceful, having none of
the bustle of war   **59 thy state . . . threat** (France) begins to
threaten your kingdom   **60 moral** moralizing   **61 why does he so**
that is, why does the King of France invade England?   **62 Proper
deformity** that is, the deformity appropriate to the fiend. (Such
deformity seems even uglier in a woman's features than in a fiend's,
since it is appropriate in a fiend's.)

64 changèd transformed.   **self-covered** having the true nature
concealed   **65 Bemonster . . . feature** do not, however evil you
are, take on the outward form of a monster or a fiend.   **my fitness**
suitable for me   **66 blood** passion   **67 apt** ready   **68 Howe'er
. . . fiend** however much you may be a fiend in reality   **69 shield**
(Since I, as a gentleman, cannot lay violent hands on a lady.)
70 Mew (An exclamation of disgust, a derisive catcall: You speak of
manhood in shielding me as a woman. Some manhood!)   **75 bred**
kept in his household.   **thrilled with remorse** deeply moved with
pity   **76 Opposed** opposed himself   **76–77 bending . . . To**
directing his sword against   **78 amongst them** together with the
others (?) in their midst (?) out of their number (?)   **80 after** along
(to death)   **81 justicers** (heavenly judges).   **nether** that is, committed here below, on earth   **85 One way** that is, because Edmund
is now Duke of Gloucester, and Cornwall, a dangerous rival for the
throne, is dead   **87–88 May . . . life** that is, may pull down my
imagined happiness (of possessing the entire kingdom with
Edmund) and make hateful my life   **89 tart** bitter, sour

ALBANY.
Where was his son when they did take his eyes?
MESSENGER.
Come with my lady hither.
ALBANY.   He is not here.
MESSENGER.
No, my good lord. I met him back° again.
ALBANY. Knows he the wickedness?
MESSENGER.
Ay, my good lord. 'Twas he informed against him,
And quit the house on purpose that their punishment
Might have the freer course.
ALBANY.   Gloucester, I live
To thank thee for the love thou show'dst the King
And to revenge thine eyes.—Come hither, friend.
Tell me what more thou know'st.   *Exeunt.*

4.3 *Enter Kent [disguised] and a Gentleman.*

KENT. Why the King of France is so suddenly gone back
    know you no reason?
GENTLEMAN. Something he left imperfect in the state,°
    which since his coming forth is thought of, which
    imports° to the kingdom so much fear and danger that
    his personal return was most required and necessary.
KENT.
Who hath he left behind him general?
GENTLEMAN.
The Marshal of France, Monsieur la Far.
KENT. Did your letters pierce the Queen to any demonstra-
    tion of grief?
GENTLEMAN.
Ay, sir. She took them, read them in my presence,
And now and then an ample tear trilled° down
Her delicate cheek. It seemed she was a queen
Over her passion,° who, most rebel-like,
Sought to be king o'er her.
KENT.   O, then it moved her?
GENTLEMAN.
Not to a rage. Patience and sorrow strove
Who should express her goodliest.° You have seen
Sunshine and rain at once. Her smiles and tears
Were like a better way;° those happy smilets
That played on her ripe lip seemed not to know
What guests were in her eyes, which° parted thence
As pearls from diamonds dropped. In brief,

Sorrow would be a rarity° most beloved
If all could so become it.°
KENT. Made she no verbal° question?   25
GENTLEMAN.
Faith, once or twice she heaved° the name of "father"
Pantingly forth, as if it pressed her heart;
Cried, "Sisters, sisters! Shame of ladies, sisters!
Kent! Father! Sisters! What, i' the storm, i' the night?
Let pity not be believed!"° There she shook   30
The holy water from her heavenly eyes,
And, clamor-moistened,° then away she started°
To deal with grief alone.
KENT.   It is the stars,
The stars above us, govern our conditions,°
Else one self mate and make° could not beget   35
Such different issues.° You spoke not with her since?
GENTLEMAN. No.
KENT.
Was this before the King° returned?
GENTLEMAN.   No, since.
KENT.
Well, sir, the poor distressèd Lear's i' the town,
Who sometimes in his better tune° remembers   40
What we are come about, and by no means
Will yield to see his daughter.
GENTLEMAN.   Why, good sir?
KENT.
A sovereign° shame so elbows him°—his own unkind-
    ness
That stripped her from his benediction, turned her°
To foreign casualties,° gave her dear rights   45
To his dog-hearted daughters—these things sting
His mind so venomously that burning shame
Detains him from Cordelia.
GENTLEMAN. Alack, poor gentleman!
KENT.
Of Albany's and Cornwall's powers° you heard not?   50
GENTLEMAN. 'Tis so. They are afoot.°
KENT.
Well, sir, I'll bring you to our master Lear
And leave you to attend him. Some dear cause°
Will in concealment wrap me up awhile.

---

92 back going back
4.3. Location: The French camp near Dover.   3 imperfect in the state unsettled in state affairs **5 imports** portends **12 trilled** trickled **14 passion, who** emotion, which **17 Who . . . goodliest** which of the two could make her appear more lovely **19 like a better way** better than that, though similar **21 which** that is, which *guests* or tears

23 a rarity that is, a precious thing, like a jewel **24 If . . . it** that is, if all persons were as attractive in sorrow as she **25 verbal** that is, as distinguished from her tears and looks **26 heaved** breathed out with difficulty **30 believed** that is, believed to be extant **32 clamor-moistened** that is, her outcry of grief assuaged by tears. **started** that is, went **34 conditions** characters **35 Else . . . make** otherwise, one couple (husband and wife) **36 issues** offspring **38 the King** the King of France **40 better tune** more composed state **43 sovereign** overruling. **elbows him** that is, prods his memory, jostles him, thrusts him back **44 turned her** turned her out **45 foreign casualties** chances of fortune abroad **50 powers** troops, armies **51 afoot** on the march **53 dear cause** important purpose

55 When I am known aright, you shall not grieve
Lending me this acquaintance.° I pray you, go
Along with me.   *Exeunt.*

4.4 *Enter, with drum and colors, Cordelia, Doctor, and soldiers.*

CORDELIA.
Alack, 'tis he! Why, he was met even now
As mad as the vexed sea, singing aloud,
Crowned with rank fumiter° and furrow weeds,
With hardocks,° hemlock, nettles, cuckooflowers,
5 Darnel,° and all the idle° weeds that grow
In our sustaining° corn. A century° send forth!
Search every acre in the high-grown field
And bring him to our eye. [*Exit a soldier or soldier.*]
     What can man's wisdom°
10 In the restoring his bereavèd sense?
He that helps him take all my outward° worth.
DOCTOR.
There is means, madam.
Our foster nurse of nature is repose,
The which he lacks. That to provoke° in him
15 Are many simples° operative,° whose power
Will close the eye of anguish.
CORDELIA.   All blest secrets,
All you unpublished virtues° of the earth,
Spring° with my tears! Be aidant and remediate°
In the good man's distress! Seek, seek for him,
20 Lest his ungoverned rage° dissolve the life
That wants° the means° to lead it.
     Enter Messenger.
MESSENGER.   News, madam.
The British powers° are marching hitherward.
CORDELIA.
'Tis known before. Our preparation stands
In expectation of them. O dear Father,
25 It is thy business that I go about;
Therefore great France
My mourning and importuned° tears hath pitied.

No blown° ambition doth our arms incite,
But love, dear love, and our aged father's right.
Soon may I hear and see him!   *Exeunt.* 30

4.5 *Enter Regan and steward [Oswald].*

REGAN. But are my brother's powers° set forth?
OSWALD. Ay, madam.
REGAN. Himself in person there?
OSWALD. Madam, with much ado.°
     Your sister is the better soldier.   5
REGAN.
Lord Edmund spake not with your lord at home?
OSWALD. No, madam.
REGAN.
What might import° my sister's letters to him?
OSWALD. I know not, lady.
REGAN.
Faith, he is posted° hence on serious matter.   10
It was great ignorance,° Gloucester's eyes being out,
To let him live. Where he arrives he moves
All hearts against us. Edmund, I think, is gone,
In pity of his misery, to dispatch
His nighted° life; moreover to descry   15
The strength o' th' enemy.
OSWALD.
I must needs after him, madam, with my letter.
REGAN.
Our troops set forth tomorrow. Stay with us;
The ways are dangerous.
OSWALD.   I may not, madam.
My lady charged my duty° in this business.   20
REGAN.
Why should she write to Edmund? Might not you
Transport her purposes by word? Belike°
Something—I know not what. I'll love thee much;
Let me unseal the letter.
OSWALD.   Madam, I had rather—
REGAN.
I know your lady does not love her husband,   25
I am sure of that; and at her late° being here
She gave strange oeillades° and most speaking looks
To noble Edmund. I know you are of her bosom.°
OSWALD. I, madam?

55–56 grieve . . . acquaintance regret having made my acquaintance **4.4. Location: The French camp.** **3 fumiter** that is, fumitory, a weed or herb **4 hardocks** that is, burdocks or hoardocks, white-leaved (?) (Identity uncertain.) **5 Darnel** (A weed of the grass kind.) **idle** worthless **6 sustaining** giving sustenance. **corn** grain. **century** troop of one hundred men **9 What . . . wisdom** that is, what can medical knowledge accomplish **11 outward** material **14 That to provoke** to induce that **15 simples** medicinal plants. **operative** effective **17 unpublished virtues** little-known benign herbs **18 Spring** grow. **aidant and remediate** helpful and remedial **20 rage** frenzy **21 wants** lacks. **means** that is, his reason **22 powers** armies **27 importuned** importunate

28 blown puffed up with pride
4.5. Location: Gloucester's house. **1 my brother's powers** that is, Albany's forces **4 with much ado** after much fuss and persuasion **8 import** bear as its purport, express **10 is posted** has hurried **11 ignorance** error, folly **15 nighted** benighted, blinded **20 charged my duty** laid great stress on my obedience **22 Belike** it may be **26 late** recently **27 oeillades** amorous glances **28 of her bosom** in her confidence

REGAN.

30   I speak in understanding; y' are,° I know 't.
   Therefore I do advise you, take this note:°
   My lord is dead; Edmund and I have talked,° and more
     convenient° is he for my hand
   Than for your lady's. You may gather more.°
35   If you do find him, pray you, give him this;°
   And when your mistress hears thus much° from you,
   I pray, desire her call her wisdom to her.°
   So, fare you well.
   If you do chance to hear of that blind traitor,
40   Preferment° falls on him that cuts him off.

OSWALD.
   Would I could meet him, madam! I should show
   What party I do follow.

REGAN.   Fare thee well.

                                Exeunt [separately].

4.6 *Enter Gloucester, and Edgar [in peasant's clothes, leading his father].*

GLOUCESTER.
   When shall I come to th' top of that same hill?°

EDGAR.
   You do climb up it now. Look how we labor.

GLOUCESTER.
   Methinks the ground is even.

EDGAR.   Horrible steep.
   Hark, do you hear the sea?

GLOUCESTER.   No, truly.

EDGAR.
5   Why, then, your other senses grow imperfect
   By your eyes' anguish.

GLOUCESTER.   So may it be, indeed.
   Methinks thy voice is altered, and thou speak'st
   In better phrase and matter than thou didst.

EDGAR.
   You're much deceived. In nothing am I changed
   But in my garments.

10 GLOUCESTER.   Methinks you're better spoken.

EDGAR.
   Come on, sir, here's the place. Stand still. How fearful
   And dizzy 'tis to cast one's eyes so low!
   The crows and choughs° that wing the midway° air

   Show scarce so gross° as beetles. Halfway down
   Hangs one that gathers samphire°—dreadful trade!   15
   Methinks he seems no bigger than his head.
   The fishermen that walk upon the beach
   Appear like mice, and yond tall anchoring bark
   Diminished to her cock;° her cock, a buoy
   Almost too small for sight. The murmuring surge,   20
   That on th' unnumbered idle pebble° chafes,
   Cannot be heard so high. I'll look no more,
   Lest my brain turn, and the deficient sight
   Topple° down headlong.

GLOUCESTER.   Set me where you stand.

EDGAR.
   Give me your hand. You are now within a foot   25
   Of th' extreme verge. For all beneath the moon
   Would I not leap upright.°

GLOUCESTER.   Let go my hand.
   Here, friend, 's another purse; in it a jewel
   Well worth a poor man's taking. [*He gives a purse*]. Fairies
     and gods
   Prosper it with thee!° Go thou further off.   30
   Bid me farewell, and let me hear thee going.

EDGAR [*moving away*].
   Now fare ye well, good sir.

GLOUCESTER.   With all my heart.

EDGAR [*aside*].
   Why I do trifle thus with his despair
   Is done to cure it.

GLOUCESTER [*kneeling*].   O you mighty gods!   35
   This world I do renounce, and in your sights
   Shake patiently my great affliction off.
   If I could bear it longer, and not fall
   To quarrel with° your great opposeless° wills,
   My snuff° and loathèd part of nature° should   40
   Burn itself out. If Edgar live, O, bless him!
   Now, fellow, fare thee well.   [*He falls forward.*]

EDGAR.   Gone, sir. Farewell.—
   And yet I know not how conceit° may rob
   The treasury of life, when life itself
   Yields° to the theft. Had he been where he thought,   45
   By this had thought been past. Alive or dead?—
   Ho, you, sir! Friend! Hear you, sir! Speak!—

---

30 y' are you are   **31 take this note** take note of this   **32 have talked** have come to an understanding   **33 convenient** fitting   **34 gather more** infer what I am trying to suggest   **35 this** that is, this information, or a love token, or possibly a letter (though only one letter, Goneril's, is found on his dead body at 4.6.261)   **36 thus much** what I have told you   **37 call . . . to her** recall her to her senses   **40 Preferment** advancement   **4.6. Location:** Open place near Dover.   **1 that same hill** that is, the cliff we talked about (4.1.72–77)   **13 choughs** jackdaws. **midway** halfway down

14 gross large   **15 samphire** (A herb used in pickling.) **19 Diminished . . . cock** reduced to the size of her cockboat, small ship's boat   **21 unnumbered idle pebble** innumerable, randomly shifting, pebbles   **23–24 the deficient sight Topple** my failing sight topple me   **27 upright** that is, up and down, much less forward   **29–30 Fairies . . . thee** may the fairies and gods cause this to multiply in your possession   **39 To quarrel with** into rebellion against. **opposeless** irresistible   **40 snuff** that is, useless residue. (Literally, the smoking wick of a candle.)   **of nature** that is, of my life   **43 conceit** imagination   **45 Yields** consents

Thus might he pass° indeed; yet he revives.—
What° are you, sir?
GLOUCESTER.   Away, and let me die.
EDGAR.
50 Hadst thou been aught but gossamer, feathers, air,
So many fathom down precipitating,
Thou'dst shivered like an egg; but thou dost breathe,
Hast heavy substance,° bleed'st not, speak'st, art sound.
Ten masts at each° make not the altitude
55 Which thou hast perpendicularly fell.
Thy life's a miracle. Speak yet again.
GLOUCESTER. But have I fallen or no?
EDGAR.
From the dread summit of this chalky bourn.°
Look up aheight;° the shrill-gorged° lark so far
60 Cannot be seen or heard. Do but look up.
GLOUCESTER. Alack, I have no eyes.
Is wretchedness deprived that benefit
To end itself by death? 'Twas yet some comfort
When misery could beguile° the tyrant's rage
And frustrate his proud will.
65 EDGAR.   Give me your arm.
[He lifts him up.]
Up—so. How is 't? Feel you your legs? You stand.
GLOUCESTER.
Too well, too well.
EDGAR.   This is above all strangeness.
Upon the crown o' the cliff what thing was that
Which parted from you?
GLOUCESTER.   A poor unfortunate beggar.
EDGAR.
70 As I stood here below, methought his eyes
Were two full moons; he had a thousand noses,
Horns whelked° and waved like the enridgèd° sea.
It was some fiend. Therefore, thou happy father,°
Think that the clearest° gods, who make them honors
75 Of men's impossibilities,° have preserved thee.
GLOUCESTER.
I do remember now. Henceforth I'll bear
Affliction till it do cry out itself
"Enough, enough," and die.° That thing you speak of,
I took it for a man; often 'twould say
80 "The fiend, the fiend." He led me to that place.

EDGAR.
Bear free° and patient thoughts.
Enter Lear [mad, fantastically dressed with wild flowers].
But who comes here?
The safer sense will ne'er accommodate
His master° thus.°
LEAR. No, they cannot touch° me for coining.° I am the   85
King himself.
EDGAR. O thou side-piercing° sight!
LEAR. Nature's above art in that respect.° There's your press
money.° That fellow handles his bow like a crow-keeper.°
Draw me° a clothier's yard. Look, look, a mouse! Peace,   90
peace; this piece of toasted cheese will do't.° There's my
gauntlet;° I'll prove it on° a giant. Bring up the brown
bills.° O, well flown, bird!° I' the clout,° i' the clout—
hewgh!° Give the word.°
EDGAR. Sweet marjoram.°   95
LEAR. Pass.
GLOUCESTER. I know that voice.
LEAR. Ha! Goneril with a white beard? They flattered me
like a dog° and told me I had white hairs in my beard° ere
the black ones were there. To say ay and no to everything   100
that I said ay and no to was no good divinity.° When the
rain came to wet me once and the wind to make me chatter, when the thunder would not peace at my bidding,
there I found 'em,° there I smelt 'em out. Go to,° they are
not men o' their words. They told me I was everything.   105
'Tis a lie; I am not ague-proof.°
GLOUCESTER.
The trick° of that voice I do well remember.
Is 't not the King?

81 **free** that is, free from despair   84 **His master** the owner of the
safer sense or sane mind. (*His* means "its.")   83–84 **The safer …
thus** that is, a person in his right senses would never dress himself in
such a fashion.   85 **touch** arrest, prosecute. **coining** minting
coins. (A royal prerogative; the King wants money for his imaginary
soldiers, lines 89–93.)   87 **side-piercing** heartrending (with a suggestion also of Christ's suffering on the cross)   88 **Nature's …
respect** that is, a born king is superior to anything art (or counterfeiting) can produce (?)   88–89 **press money** enlistment bonus
89 **crowkeeper** laborer hired to scare away the crows   90 **me** for me
Draw … yard that is, draw your bow to the full length of the arrow,
a cloth-yard long.   91 **do 't** that is, capture the mouse, an imagined
enemy.   92 **gauntlet** armored glove thrown down as a challenge.
prove it on maintain it against   92–93 **brown bills** soldiers carrying
pikes (painted brown), or the pikes themselves.   93 **well flown,
bird** (Lear uses the language of hawking to describe the flight of an
arrow.) **clout** target, bull's-eye   94 **hewgh** (The arrow's noise.)
word password   95 **Sweet marjoram** (A herb used to cure madness.)
99 **like a dog** as a dog fawns **had … beard** that is, had wisdom
101 **To … divinity** that is, to agree flatteringly with everything I
said was not good theology, since the Bible teaches us to "let your yea
be yea and your nay, nay" (James 5:12; see also Matthew 5:37 and 2
Cor. 1:18)   104 **found 'em** found them out **Go to** (An expression
of impatience.)   106 **ague-proof** immune against illness (literally,
fever)   107 **trick** peculiar characteristic

48 **pass** die   49 **What** who. (Edgar now speaks in a new voice, differing from that of "poor Tom" and also from the "altered" voice he
used at the start of this scene; see lines 7–10.)   53 **heavy substance** the substance of the flesh   54 **at each** end to end
58 **bourn** limit, boundary (that is, the edge of the sea)   59 **aheight**
on high **shrill-gorged** shrill-throated   64 **beguile** outwit
72 **whelked** twisted, convoluted. **enridgèd** furrowed (by the
wind)   73 **happy father** lucky old man   74 **clearest** purest, most
righteous   74–75 **who … impossibilities** who win our awe and
reverence by doing things impossible to men   77–78 **till … die**
that is, until affliction itself has had enough, or until I die

LEAR.   Ay, every inch a king.
When I do stare, see how the subject quakes.
110 I pardon that man's life. What was thy cause?°
Adultery?
Thou shalt not die. Die for adultery? No.
The wren goes to 't, and the small gilded fly
Does lecher in my sight.
115 Let copulation thrive; for Gloucester's bastard son
Was kinder to his father than my daughters
Got 'tween the lawful sheets.
To 't, luxury,° pell-mell, for I lack soldiers.
Behold yond simpering dame,
120 Whose face between her forks presages snow,°
That minces° virtue and does shake the head
To hear of pleasure's name;°
The fitchew° nor the soilèd horse° goes to 't
With a more riotous appetite.
125 Down from the waist they're centaurs,°
Though women all above.
But° to the girdle° do the gods inherit;°
Beneath is all the fiends'.
There's hell, there's darkness, there is the sulfurous pit,
130 burning, scalding, stench, consumption. Fie, fie, fie! Pah,
pah! Give me an ounce of civet,° good apothecary,
sweeten my imagination. There's money for thee.
GLOUCESTER. O, let me kiss that hand!
LEAR. Let me wipe it first; it smells of mortality.
GLOUCESTER.
135 O ruined piece° of nature! This great world°
Shall so° wear out to naught. Dost thou know me?
LEAR. I remember thine eyes well enough. Dost thou
squinny° at me? No, do thy worst, blind Cupid; I'll not
love. Read thou this challenge. Mark but the penning of it.
GLOUCESTER.
140 Were all thy letters suns, I could not see.
EDGAR [aside].
I would not take° this from report. It is,°
And my heart breaks at it.
LEAR. Read.
GLOUCESTER. What, with the case° of eyes?
145 LEAR Oho, are you there with me?° No eyes in your head,
nor no money in your purse? Your eyes are in a heavy

case,° your purse in a light, yet you see how this world
goes.
GLOUCESTER. I see it feelingly.°
LEAR. What, art mad? A man may see how this world goes 150
with no eyes. Look with thine ears. See how yond justice
rails upon yond simple° thief. Hark in thine ear: change
places and, handy-dandy,° which is the justice, which is
the thief? Thou hast seen a farmer's dog bark at a beggar?
GLOUCESTER. Ay, sir. 155
LEAR. And the creature° run from the cur? There thou
mightst behold the great image of authority: a dog's
obeyed in office.°
Thou rascal beadle,° hold thy bloody hand!
Why dost thou lash that whore? Strip thine own back; 160
Thou hotly lusts to use her in that kind°
For which thou whipp'st her. The usurer° hangs the coz-
ener.°
Through tattered clothes small vices do appear;
Robes and furred gowns hide all. Plate° sin with gold,
And the strong lance of justice hurtless breaks;° 165
Arm it in rags, a pygmy's straw does pierce it.
None does offend, none, I say, none. I'll able° 'em.
Take that° of me, my friend, who have the power
To seal th' accuser's lips. Get thee glass eyes,°
And like a scurvy politician seem 170
To see the things thou dost not. Now, now, now, now!
Pull off my boots. Harder, harder! So.
EDGAR [aside].
O, matter and impertinency° mixed,
Reason in madness!
LEAR.
If thou wilt weep my fortunes, take my eyes. 175
I know thee well enough; thy name is Gloucester.
Thou must be patient. We came crying hither.
Thou know'st the first time that we smell the air
We wawl and cry. I will preach to thee. Mark.
GLOUCESTER. Alack, alack the day! 180

110 **cause** offense   118 **luxury** lechery   120 **Whose . . . snow**
whose frosty countenance seems to suggest frigidity between her
legs   121 **minces** affects, mimics   122 **of pleasure's name** the
very name of pleasure   123 **The fitchew** neither the polecat.
soilèd horse horse turned out to grass, well-fed and hence wanton
125 **centaurs** fabulous creatures with the head, trunk, and arms of a
man joined to the body and legs of a horse   127 **But** only.   **girdle**
waist.   **inherit** possess   131 **civet** musk perfume   135 **piece** masterpiece.   **This great world** that is, the macrocosm, of which
humanity, the masterpiece of nature, is the microcosm   136 **so**
similarly   138 **squinny** squint   141 **take** believe, credit.   **It is** it
is taking place, incredibly enough   144 **case** mere sockets
145 **are . . . me** is that your meaning, the point you are making?

146–147 **heavy case** sad plight (with pun on *case* in line 144)
149 **feelingly** (1) by touch (2) keenly, painfully   152 **simple** of
humble station   153 **handy-dandy** take your choice of hands (as
in a well-known child's game)   156 **creature** poor fellow
157–158 **a dog's . . . office** that is, even currish power commands
submission   159 **beadle** parish officer, responsible for giving whippings   161 **kind** way   162 **The usurer** that is, a judge guilty of
lending money at usurious rates.   **cozener** petty cheater
164 **Plate** arm in plate armor   165 **hurtless breaks** splinters
harmlessly   167 **able** give warrant to   168 **that** that is, a guarantee of immunity   169 **glass eyes** (With glass eyes, possibly spectacles, Gloucester could pretend to see or understand what he does
not comprehend, like a vile *politician* governing through oppor-
tunism and trickery, hiding his blindness behind his glass eyes.)
173 **matter and impertinency** sense and nonsense

LEAR.
When we are born, we cry that we are come
To this great stage of fools.—This'° a good block.°
It were a delicate° stratagem to shoe
A troop of horse with felt.° I'll put 't in proof,°
185   And when I have stol'n upon these son-in-laws,
Then, kill, kill, kill, kill, kill, kill!

Enter a Gentleman [with attendants].

GENTLEMAN.
O, here he is. Lay hand upon him.—Sir,
Your most dear daughter—
LEAR.
No rescue? What, a prisoner? I am even
190   The natural fool° of fortune. Use me well;
You shall have ransom. Let me have surgeons;
I am cut° to th' brains.
GENTLEMAN.   You shall have anything.
LEAR.   No seconds?° All myself?
Why, this would make a man a man of salt°
195   To use his eyes for garden waterpots,
Ay, and laying autumn's dust.
I will die bravely,° like a smug° bridegroom. What?
I will be jovial. Come, come, I am a king,
Masters, know you that?
GENTLEMAN.
200   You are a royal one, and we obey you.
LEAR.   Then there's life° in 't. Come, an° you get it, you shall
get it by running. Sa, sa, sa, sa.°

Exit [running, followed by attendants].

GENTLEMAN.
A sight most pitiful in the meanest wretch,
Past speaking of in a king! Thou hast one daughter
205   Who redeems nature from the general curse°
Which twain have brought her to.
EDGAR.   Hail, gentle° sir.
GENTLEMAN.   Sir, speed° you. What's your will?
EDGAR.
Do you hear aught, sir, of a battle toward?°
GENTLEMAN.
210   Most sure and vulgar.° Everyone hears that
Which° can distinguish sound.

EDGAR.   But, by your favor,
How near's the other army?
GENTLEMAN.
Near and on speedy foot. The main descry
Stands on the hourly thought.°
EDGAR.   I thank you, sir; that's all.   215
GENTLEMAN.
Though that the Queen on special cause° is here,
Her army is moved on.
EDGAR.   I thank you, sir.

Exit [Gentleman].

GLOUCESTER.
You ever-gentle gods, take my breath from me;
Let not my worser spirit° tempt me again
To die before you please!   220
EDGAR.   Well pray you, father.°
GLOUCESTER.   Now, good sir, what° are you?
EDGAR.
A most poor man, made tame° to fortune's blows,
Who, by the art of known° and feeling° sorrows,
Am pregnant° to good pity. Give me your hand.   225
I'll lead you to some biding.°   [He offers his arm.]
GLOUCESTER.   Hearty thanks.
The bounty and the benison of heaven
To boot, and boot!°

Enter steward [Oswald].

OSWALD.   A proclaimed prize!° Most happy!°
[He draws his sword.]
That eyeless head of thine was first framed flesh°
To raise my fortunes. Thou old unhappy traitor,   230
Briefly thyself remember.° The sword is out
That must destroy thee.
GLOUCESTER.   Now let thy friendly° hand
Put strength enough to 't.   [Edgar intervenes.]
OSWALD.   Wherefore, bold peasant,
Durst thou support a published° traitor? Hence,
Lest that° th' infection of his fortune take   235
Like° hold on thee. Let go his arm.

213–214 **The main . . . thought** the full view of the main body is
expected any hour now   216 **on special cause** for a special reason,
that is, to minister to Lear   219 **worser spirit** bad angel, or ill
thoughts   221 **father** (A term of respect to older men, as also in
lines 73, 258, and 288, though with ironic double meaning
throughout the scene.)   222 **what** who. (Again, Edgar alters his
voice to personate a new stranger assisting Gloucester. See line 49
above, and note.)   223 **tame** submissive   224 **known** personally
experienced. **feeling** heartfelt, deep   225 **pregnant** prone
226 **biding** abode   227–228 **The bounty . . . and boot** in addition to my thanks, I wish you the bounty and blessings of heaven
228 **proclaimed prize** one with a price on his head.   **happy** fortunate   229 **framed flesh** born   231 **thyself remember** that is, confess your sins   232 **friendly** that is, welcome, since I desire death
234 **published** proclaimed   235 **Lest that** lest   236 **Like** similar

182 **This'** this is.   **block** felt hat (?) (Lear may refer to the weeds
strewn in his hair, which he removes as though doffing a hat before
preaching a sermon.)   183 **delicate** subtle   184 **felt** that is,
padding to deaden the sound of the footfall.   **in proof** to the test
190 **natural fool** born plaything   192 **cut** wounded
193 **seconds** supporters   194 **of salt** of salt tears   197 **bravely** (1)
courageously (2) splendidly attired.   **smug** trimly dressed. (*Bridegroom* continues the punning sexual suggestion of *die bravely*, "have
sex successfully.")   201 **life** that is, hope still.   **an if**   202 **Sa . . .
sa** (A hunting cry.)   205 **general curse** fallen condition of the
human race   207 **gentle** noble   208 **speed** Godspeed
209 **toward** imminent   210 **vulgar** in everyone's mouth, generally
known   211 **Which** who

EDGAR. 'Chill° not let go, zir, without vurther 'cagion.°

OSWALD. Let go, slave, or thou diest!

EDGAR. Good gentleman, go your gait,° and let poor volk
240   pass. An 'chud° ha' bin zwaggered° out of my life, 'twould
       not ha' bin zo long as 'tis by a vortnight.° Nay, come not
       near the old man; keep out, 'che vor ye,° or Ise° try
       whether your costard° or my ballow° be the harder. 'Chill
       be plain with you.

245 OSWALD. Out, dunghill!

EDGAR. 'Chill, pick your teeth, zir. Come, no matter vor
       your foins.°

       [*They fight. Edgar fells him with his cudgel.*]

OSWALD.
       Slave, thou hast slain me. Villain,° take my purse.
       If ever thou wilt thrive, bury my body
250   And give the letters° which thou find'st about me°
       To Edmund, Earl of Gloucester. Seek him out
       Upon° the English party.° O, untimely death!
       Death!   [*He dies.*]

EDGAR.
       I know thee well: a serviceable° villain,
255   As duteous to the vices of thy mistress
       As badness would desire.

GLOUCESTER. What, is he dead?

EDGAR. Sit you down, father. Rest you. [*Gloucester sits.*]
       Let's see these pockets; the letters that he speaks of
260   May be my friends. He's dead; I am only sorry
       He had no other deathsman.° Let us see.

       [*He finds a letter and opens it.*]

       Leave,° gentle wax,° and, manners, blame us not.
       To know our enemies' minds we rip their hearts;
       Their papers is more lawful. (*Reads the letter.*)

265   "Let our reciprocal vows be remembered. You have
       many opportunities to cut him off; if your will want not,°
       time and place will be fruitfully° offered. There is noth-
       ing done° if he return the conqueror. Then am I the pris-
       oner, and his bed my jail, from the loathed warmth
270   whereof deliver me and supply the place for your labor.°

       Your—wife, so I would say—affectionate servant, and
       for you her own for venture,°   Goneril."
       O indistinguished space of woman's will!°
       A plot upon her virtuous husband's life,
       And the exchange my brother! Here in the sands   275
       Thee I'll rake up,° the post unsanctified°
       Of murderous lechers; and in the mature time°
       With this ungracious° paper strike° the sight
       Of the death-practiced° Duke. For him 'tis well
       That of thy death and business I can tell.   280

                                    [*Exit with the body.*]

GLOUCESTER.
       The King is mad. How stiff° is my vile sense,°
       That I stand up and have ingenious° feeling
       Of my huge sorrows! Better I were distract;°
       So should my thoughts be severed from my griefs,
       And woes by wrong imaginations° lose   285
       The knowledge of themselves.   *Drum afar off.*

[*Enter Edgar.*]

EDGAR.   Give me your hand.
       Far off, methinks, I hear the beaten drum.
       Come, father, I'll bestow° you with a friend.

                          Exeunt, [Edgar leading his father].

4.7 *Enter Cordelia, Kent [dressed still in his disguise
costume, and Doctor].*

CORDELIA.
       O thou good Kent, how shall I live and work
       To match thy goodness? My life will be too short,
       And every measure fail me.°

KENT.
       To be acknowledged, madam, is o'erpaid.
       All my reports° go with the modest truth,   5
       Nor more nor clipped,° but so.

---

237 **'Chill** I will. (Literally, a contraction of *Ich will*. Edgar adopts Somerset dialect, a stage convention regularly used for peasants.) **vurther 'cagion** further occasion   239 **go your gait** go your own way   240 **An 'chud** if I could.   **zwaggered** swaggered, bluffed 240–241 **'twould ... vortnight** it (my life) wouldn't have lasted as long as it has   242 **'che vor ye** I warrant you   **Ise** I shall 243 **costard** head. (Literally, an apple.)   **ballow** cudgel 247 **foins** thrusts   248 **Villain** serf   250 **letters** letter. **about me** upon my person   252 **Upon** on.   **party** side   254 **serviceable** officious   261 **deathsman** executioner   262 **Leave** by your leave. **wax** wax seal on the letter   266 **want not** is not lacking 267 **fruitfully** plentifully and with results   267–268 **There is nothing done** that is, we will have accomplished nothing   270 **for your labor** (1) as recompense for your efforts (2) as a place for your amorous labors

271–272 **and for ... venture** and one ready to venture her own fortunes for your sake   273 **indistinguished ... will** limitless and incalculable range of woman's appetite   276 **rake up** cover up. **post unsanctified** unholy messenger   277 **in ... time** when the time is ripe   278 **ungracious** wicked.   **strike** blast   279 **death-practiced** whose death is plotted   281 **stiff** obstinate   **sense** consciousness, sane mental powers   282 **ingenious** conscious. (Gloucester laments that he remains sane and hence fully conscious of his troubles, unlike Lear.)   283 **distract** distracted, crazy 285 **wrong imaginations** delusions   288 **bestow** lodge. (At the scene's end, Edgar leads off Gloucester; presumably, here or at line 280, he must also dispose of Oswald's body in the trapdoor or by lugging it offstage.)
4.7. Location: The French camp   3 **every ... me** every attempt (to match your goodness) will fall short   5 **All my reports** go let all reports (of my service as Caius to Lear) conform   6 **Nor ... clipped** that is, neither more nor less.

CORDELIA.   Be better suited.°
    These weeds° are memories° of those worser hours;
    I prithee, put them off.
KENT.   Pardon, dear madam;
    Yet to be known shortens my made intent.°
10 My boon I make it° that you know° me not
    Till time and I think meet.°
CORDELIA.
    Then be 't so, my good lord. [To the Doctor.] How does
        the King?
DOCTOR. Madam, sleeps still.
CORDELIA. O you kind gods,
15   Cure this great breach in his abusèd nature!
    Th' untuned and jarring senses, O, wind up°
    Of this child-changèd° father!
DOCTOR. So please Your Majesty
    That we may wake the King? He hath slept long.
CORDELIA.
20   Be governed by your knowledge, and proceed
    I' the sway° of your own will.—Is he arrayed?

    *Enter Lear in a chair carried by servants, [attended by a
    Gentleman].*

GENTLEMAN.
    Ay, madam. In the heaviness of sleep
    We put fresh garments on him.
DOCTOR.
    Be by, good madam, when we do awake him.
    I doubt not of his temperance.°
25 CORDELIA.   Very well.   [Music.]
DOCTOR.
    Please you, draw near.—Louder the music there!
CORDELIA [kissing him].
    O my dear Father! Restoration hang
    Thy medicine on my lips, and let this kiss
    Repair those violent harms that my two sisters
    Have in thy reverence made!
30 KENT.   Kind and dear princess!
CORDELIA.
    Had you° not been their father, these white flakes°
    Did challenge° pity of them. Was this a face
    To be opposed against the warring winds?
    To stand against the deep° dread-bolted° thunder
35   In the most terrible and nimble stroke

    Of quick cross° lightning? To watch°—poor perdu!°—
    With this thin helm?° Mine enemy's dog,
    Though he had bit me, should have stood that night
    Against° my fire; and wast thou fain,° poor Father,
    To hovel thee with swine and rogues forlorn°   40
    In short° and musty straw? Alack, alack!
    'Tis wonder that thy life and wits at once
    Had not concluded all.°—He wakes! Speak to him.
DOCTOR. Madam, do you; 'tis fittest.
CORDELIA.
    How does my royal lord? How fares Your Majesty?   45
LEAR.
    You do me wrong to take me out o' the grave.
    Thou art a soul in bliss; but I am bound
    Upon a wheel of fire,° that° mine own tears
    Do scald like molten lead.
CORDELIA.   Sir, do you know me?
LEAR.
    You are a spirit, I know. Where did you die?   50
CORDELIA. Still, still, far wide!°
DOCTOR.
    He's scarce awake. Let him alone awhile.
LEAR.
    Where have I been? Where am I? Fair daylight?
    I am mightily abused.° I should ev'n die with pity
    To see another thus.° I know not what to say.   55
    I will not swear these are my hands. Let's see;
    I feel this pinprick. Would I were assured
    Of my condition!
CORDELIA [kneeling]. O, look upon me, sir,
    And hold your hands in benediction o'er me. [He   60
        attempts to kneel.]
    No, sir, you must not kneel.
LEAR.   Pray, do not mock me.
    I am a very foolish fond° old man,
    Fourscore and upward, not an hour more nor less;
    And, to deal plainly,
    I fear I am not in my perfect mind.   65
    Methinks I should know you, and know this man,
    Yet I am doubtful; for I am mainly° ignorant
    What place this is, and all the skill I have

---

suited dressed **7 weeds** garments. **memories** remembrances
9 Yet . . . intent to reveal my true identity now would alter my
carefully made plan **10 My . . . it** the favor I seek is. **know**
acknowledge **11 meet** appropriate **16 wind up** tune (as by
winding the slackened string of an instrument) **17 child-changèd**
changed (in mind) by children's cruelty **21 I' the sway** under the
direction **25 temperance** self-control, calm behavior **31 Had
you** even if you had. **flakes** locks of hair **32 Did challenge**
would have demanded **34 deep** bass-voiced. **dread-bolted** furnished with the dreadful thunderbolt

36 cross zigzag. **watch** stay awake (like a sentry on duty). **perdu**
lost one; a sentinel placed in a position of peculiar danger
37 helm helmet, that is, his scanty hair **39 Against** before, in
front of. **fain** glad, constrained **40 rogues forlorn** abandoned
vagabonds **41 short** broken up and hence uncomfortable
43 concluded all come to an end altogether **48 wheel of fire** (A
hellish torment for the eternally damned.) **that** so that **51 wide**
wide of the mark, wandering **54 abused** confused, deluded
55 thus that is, thus confused, bewildered **62 fond** foolish
67 mainly perfectly

Remembers not these garments, nor I know not
70   Where I did lodge last night. Do not laugh at me,
      For, as I am a man, I think this lady
      To be my child Cordelia.
CORDELIA [*weeping*].   And so I am, I am.
LEAR.
      Be your tears wet? Yes, faith. I pray, weep not.
75   If you have poison for me I will drink it.
      I know you do not love me, for your sisters
      Have, as I do remember, done me wrong.
      You have some cause, they have not.
CORDELIA.   No cause, no cause.
80   LEAR.   Am I in France?
KENT.   In your own kingdom, sir.
LEAR.   Do not abuse° me.
DOCTOR.
      Be comforted, good madam. The great rage,°
      You see, is killed in him, and yet it is danger
85   To make him even o'er° the time he has lost.
      Desire him to go in. Trouble him no more
      Till further settling.°
CORDELIA.   Will 't please Your Highness walk?°
LEAR.   You must bear with me.
90   Pray you now, forget and forgive.
      I am old and foolish.

                    Exeunt [*all but Kent and Gentleman*].
GENTLEMAN.   Holds it true,° sir, that the Duke of Cornwall
      was so slain?
KENT.   Most certain, sir.
95   GENTLEMAN.   Who is conductor° of his people?
KENT.   As 'tis said, the bastard son of Gloucester.
GENTLEMAN.   They say Edgar, his banished son, is with the
      Earl of Kent in Germany.
KENT.   Report is changeable. 'Tis time to look about;° the
100   powers of the kingdom° approach apace.
GENTLEMAN.   The arbitrament° is like to be bloody. Fare you
      well, sir.   [*Exit.*]
KENT.
      My point and period will be throughly wrought,°
      Or° well or ill, as° this day's battle's fought.   *Exit.*

5.1   *Enter, with drum and colors, Edmund, Regan,*
Gentlemen, and soldiers.

EDMUND [*to a Gentleman*].
      Know° of the Duke if his last purpose hold,°
      Or whether since° he is advised by aught°
      To change the course. He's full of alteration°
      And self-reproving. Bring his constant pleasure.°

                                        [*Exit Gentleman.*]
REGAN.
      Our sister's man° is certainly miscarried.°   5
EDMUND.
      'Tis to be doubted,° madam.
REGAN.   Now, sweet lord,
      You know the goodness I intend° upon you.
      Tell me, but truly—but then speak the truth—
      Do you not love my sister?
EDMUND.   In honored° love.
REGAN.
      But have you never found my brother's way   10
      To the forfended° place?
EDMUND.
      That thought abuses° you.
REGAN.
      I am doubtful that you have been conjunct
      And bosomed with her, as far as we call hers.°
EDMUND.   No, by mine honor, madam.   15
REGAN.
      I never shall endure her. Dear my lord,
      Be not familiar° with her.
EDMUND.
      Fear me not.°—She and the Duke her husband!
      Enter, with drum and colors, Albany, Goneril, [*and*] *sol-*
      diers.
GONERIL [*aside*].
      I had rather lose the battle than that sister
      Should loosen him and me.   20
ALBANY.
      Our very loving sister, well bemet.°
      Sir, this I heard: the King is come to his daughter,
      With others whom the rigor of our state°

---

82 **abuse** deceive. (Or perhaps Lear feels hurt by the reminder of
his having divided the kingdom.)   83 **rage** frenzy   85 **even o'er**
fill in, go over in his mind   87 **settling** composing of his mind
88 **walk** withdraw   92 **Holds it true** is it still held to be true
95 **conductor** leader, general   99 **look about** be wary
100 **powers of the kingdom** British armies (marching against the
French invaders)   101 **arbitrament** decision by arms, decisive
encounter   103 **My . . . wrought** that is, the conclusion of my
destiny (literally, the full stop at the end of my life's sentence) will
be thoroughly brought about   104 **Or** either   **as** according as

5.1. Location: The British camp near Dover.   **1 Know** inquire.
last purpose hold most recent intention (to fight) remains firm
2 since since then   **advised by aught** persuaded by any consideration   **3 alteration** vacillation   **4 constant pleasure** settled decision   **5 man** that is, Oswald. **miscarried** lost, perished
6 doubted feared   **7 intend** intend to confer   **9 honored** honorable   **11 forfended** forbidden (by the commandment against adultery)   **12 abuses** degrades, wrongs   **13–14 I am . . . hers** I fear
that you have been sexually intimate with her   **17 familiar** intimate   **18 Fear me not** don't worry about me on that score
21 bemet met   **23 rigor of our state** harshness of our rule

Forced to cry out. Where° I could not be honest,°
25 I never yet was valiant. For° this business,
It touches us as° France invades our land,
Not bolds° the King, with others whom, I fear,
Most just and heavy causes make oppose.°
EDMUND. Sir, you speak nobly.
30 REGAN. Why is this reasoned?°
GONERIL.
Combine together 'gainst the enemy;
For these domestic and particular broils°
Are not the question here.
ALBANY.   Let's then determine
With th' ancient of war° on our proceeding.
EDMUND.
35 I shall attend you presently° at your tent.
REGAN. Sister, you'll go with us?
GONERIL. No.
REGAN.
'Tis most convenient.° Pray, go with us.
GONERIL [aside].
Oho, I know the riddle.°—I will go.

[As they are going out,] enter Edgar [disguised].

EDGAR [to Albany].
40 If e'er Your Grace had speech with man so poor,
Hear me one word.
ALBANY [to the others].
                              I'll overtake you.

                              Exeunt both the armies.
                              Speak.

EDGAR [giving a letter].
Before you fight the battle, ope this letter.°
If you have victory, let the trumpet sound°
For him that brought it. Wretched though I seem,
45 I can produce a champion that will prove°
What is avouchèd° there. If you miscarry,°
Your business of the world hath so an end,
And machination° ceases. Fortune love you!
ALBANY. Stay till I have read the letter.

EDGAR. I was forbid it.   50
When time shall serve, let but the herald cry
And I'll appear again.   Exit [Edgar].
ALBANY.
Why, fare thee well. I will o'erlook° thy paper.

Enter Edmund.

EDMUND.
The enemy's in view. Draw up your powers.

[He offers Albany a paper.]

Here is the guess° of their true strength and forces   55
By diligent discovery,° but your haste
Is now urged on you
ALBANY.   We will greet the time.°   Exit.
EDMUND.
To both these sisters have I sworn my love,
Each jealous° of the other as the stung
Are of the adder. Which of them shall I take?   60
Both? One? Or neither? Neither can be enjoyed
If both remain alive. To take the widow
Exasperates, makes mad her sister Goneril,
And hardly shall I carry out my side,°
Her husband being alive. Now then, we'll use   65
His countenance° for the battle, which being done,
Let her who would be rid of him devise
His speedy taking off.° As for the mercy
Which he intends to Lear and to Cordelia,
The battle done and they within our power,   70
Shall° never see his pardon, for my state
Stands on me to defend, not to debate.°

                                                        Exit.

5.2 Alarum° within. Enter, with drum and colors,
Lear, Cordelia, and soldiers, over the stage; and exeunt.
Enter Edgar and Gloucester.
EDGAR.
Here, father,° take the shadow of this tree
For your good host.° Pray that the right may thrive.
If ever I return to you again,
I'll bring you comfort.
GLOUCESTER.   Grace go with you, sir!

                                        Exit [Edgar].

Alarum and retreat° within. Enter Edgar.

---

24 **Where** in a case where **honest** honorable 25 **For** as for
26 **touches us as** concerns us insofar as 27–28 **Not . . . oppose**
not because France encourages the King and others who, I fear, are
driven into opposition by just and weighty grievances. **bolds**
emboldens by offering encouragement and support 30 **Why . . .
reasoned** that is, why are we arguing about reasons for fighting,
instead of fighting? 32 **particular broils** private quarrels
34 **ancient of war** veteran officers 35 **presently** at once
38 **convenient** proper, befitting 39 **know the riddle** that is,
understand the reason for Regan's enigmatic demand that Goneril
accompany her, which is that Regan wants to keep Goneril from
Edmund 42 **this letter** that is, Goneril's letter to Edmund found
on Oswald's body 43 **sound** sound a summons 45 **prove** that is,
in trial by combat 46 **avouchèd** maintained. **miscarry** perish,
come to destruction 48 **machination** plotting (against your life)

53 **o'erlook** peruse 55 **guess** estimate 56 **discovery** reconnoi-
tering 57 **greet the time** meet the occasion 59 **jealous** suspicious 64 **carry out my side** fulfill my ambition and satisfy her
(Goneril) 66 **countenance** backing, authority of his name
68 **taking off** killing 71 **Shall** they shall 71–72 **my state . . .
debate** my position depends upon maintenance by forceful action,
not by talk
5.2. Location: The battlefield. s.d. Alarum trumpet call to arms
1 **father** that is, reverend old man 2 **host** shelterer 4 **s.d. retreat**
trumpet signal for withdrawal

EDGAR.
Away, old man! Give me thy hand. Away!
King Lear hath lost, he and his daughter ta'en.
Give me thy hand. Come on.

GLOUCESTER.
No further, sir. A man may rot even here.

EDGAR.
What, in ill thoughts again? Men must endure
Their going hence, even as their coming hither;
Ripeness° is all. Come on.

GLOUCESTER.　　　　　　　　　　And that's true too.

Exeunt.

5.3 *Enter, in conquest, with drum and colors, Edmund;*
Lear and Cordelia, as prisoners; soldiers, Captain.

EDMUND.
Some officers take them away. Good guard,°
Until their greater pleasures° first be known
That are to censure° them.

CORDELIA [*to Lear*].　　　　　　We are not the first
Who with best meaning° have incurred the worst.
For thee, oppressèd King, I am cast down;
Myself could else outfrown false Fortune's frown.
Shall we not see these daughters and these sisters?°

LEAR.
No, no, no, no! Come, let's away to prison.
We two alone will sing like birds i' the cage.
When thou dost ask me blessing, I'll kneel down
And ask of thee forgiveness. So we'll live,
And pray, and sing, and tell old tales, and laugh
At gilded butterflies,° and hear poor rogues
Talk of court news; and we'll talk with them too—
Who loses and who wins; who's in, who's out—
And take upon 's° the mystery of things,
As if we were God's spies;° and we'll wear out,°
In a walled prison, packs and sects of great ones,
That ebb and flow by th' moon.°

EDMUND.　　　　　　　　　　　　Take them away.

LEAR.
Upon such sacrifices, my Cordelia,　　　　　　　20
The gods themselves throw incense.° Have I caught
　　thee?
He that parts us shall bring a brand from heaven
And fire us hence like foxes.° Wipe thine eyes;
The goodyears° shall devour them, flesh and fell,°
Ere they shall make us weep. We'll see 'em starved first.　25
Come.　　　　　　　　*Exit [with Cordelia, guarded].*

EDMUND.　Come hither, Captain. Hark.
Take thou this note. [*He gives a paper.*] Go follow them
　　to prison.
One step I have advanced thee; if thou dost
As this instructs thee, thou dost make thy way　　　30
To noble fortunes. Know thou this: that men
Are as the time is. To be tender-minded
Does not become a sword.° Thy great employment
Will not bear question;° either say thou'lt do 't
Or thrive by other means.

CAPTAIN.　　　　　　　　I'll do 't, my lord.　　　35

EDMUND.
About it, and write "happy"° when th'° hast done.
Mark, I say, instantly, and carry it° so
As I have set it down.

CAPTAIN.
I cannot draw a cart, nor eat dried oats;
If it be man's work, I'll do 't.　　　*Exit Captain.*　　40

Flourish. Enter Albany, Goneril, Regan, [another Cap-
tain, and] soldiers.

ALBANY.
Sir, you have showed today your valiant strain,
And fortune led you well. You have the captives
Who were the opposites° of this day's strife;
I do require them of you, so to use them
As we shall find their merits and our safety　　　45
May equally determine.

EDMUND.
Sir, I thought it fit
To send the old and miserable King
To some retention° and appointed guard,
Whose° age had charms in it, whose title more,°　　50

---

11 Ripeness (Humans shouldn't die before their time, just as fruit
doesn't fall until it's ripe.)
5.3. Location: The British camp. **1 Good guard** guard them well
2 their greater pleasures the wishes of those in command
3 censure judge **4 meaning** intentions **7 Shall . . . sisters** that
is, aren't we even allowed to speak to Goneril and Regan before
they order to prison their own father and sister? **13 gilded butter-**
flies that is, gaily dressed courtiers and other ephemeral types, or
perhaps actual butterflies **16 take upon 's** assume the burden of,
or profess to understand **17 God's spies** that is, detached
observers surveying the deeds of humanity from an eternal vantage
point. **wear out** outlast **18–19 packs . . . moon** that is, followers and cliques attached to persons of high station, whose fortunes
change erratically and constantly

21 throw incense participate as celebrants **22–23 He . . . foxes**
that is, anyone seeking to part us will have to employ a heavenly
firebrand to drive us out of our prison refuge, as foxes are driven out
of their holes by fire and smoke. (Suggests that only death will part
them.) **24 goodyears** (Apparently a word connoting evil or conceivably the passage of time.) **flesh and fell** flesh and skin, completely **33 become a sword** that is, suit a warrior **34 bear ques-**
tion admit of discussion **36 write "happy"** call yourself fortunate.
th' thou **37 carry it** carry it out **43 opposites** enemies
49 retention confinement **50 Whose** that is, the King's. **whose**
title more and whose title as king is even more of a magic spell

To pluck the common bosom° on his side
And turn our impressed lances in our eyes
Which° do command them.° With him I sent the
    Queen,
My reason all the same; and they are ready
55 Tomorrow, or at further space,° t' appear
Where you shall hold your session. At this time
We sweat and bleed; the friend hath lost his friend,
And the best quarrels in the heat are cursed
By those that feel their sharpness.°
60 The question of Cordelia and her father
Requires a fitter place.
    ALBANY.   Sir, by your patience,
I hold you but a subject of° this war,
Not as a brother.
    REGAN.   That's as we list° to grace him.
65 Methinks our pleasure° might have been demanded°
Ere you had spoke so far. He led our powers,
Bore the commission of my place and person,
The which immediacy° may well stand up
And call itself your brother.
    GONERIL.   Not so hot!
In his own grace he doth exalt himself
More than in your addition.°
70 REGAN.   In my rights,
By me invested, he compeers° the best.
    GONERIL.
That were the most° if he should husband you.
    REGAN.
Jesters do oft prove° prophets.
    GONERIL.   Holla, holla!
That eye that told you so looked but asquint.°
75 REGAN.
Lady, I am not well, else I should answer
From a full-flowing stomach.° [*To Edmund.*] General,
Take thou my soldiers, prisoners, patrimony;°
Dispose of them, of me; the walls is thine.°
Witness the world that I create thee here
My lord and master.

    GONERIL.   Mean you to enjoy him?   80
    ALBANY.
The let-alone° lies not in your good will.
    EDMUND.
Nor in thine, lord.
    ALBANY.   Half-blooded° fellow, yes.
    REGAN [*to Edmund*].
Let the drum strike° and prove my title thine.
    albany.
Stay yet; hear reason. Edmund, I arrest thee
On capital treason; and, in thy attaint°   85
This gilded serpent. [*Pointing to Goneril.*] For your claim,
    fair sister,
I bar it in the interest of my wife;
'Tis she is subcontracted to this lord,
And I, her husband, contradict your banns.°
If you will marry, make your loves to me;   90
My lady is bespoke.
    GONERIL.   An interlude!°
    ALBANY.
Thou art armed, Gloucester. Let the trumpet sound.
If none appear to prove upon thy person
Thy heinous, manifest, and many treasons,
There is my pledge. [*He throws down a glove.*] I'll make°
    it on thy heart,   95
Ere I taste bread, thou art in nothing less°
Than I have here proclaimed thee.
    REGAN. Sick, O, sick!
    GONERIL [*aside*]. If not, I'll ne'er trust medicine.°
    EDMUND [*throwing down a glove*].
There's my exchange. What° in the world he is   100
That names me traitor, villain-like he lies.
Call by the trumpet. He that dares approach,
On him, on you—who not?—I will maintain
My truth and honor firmly.
    ALBANY.
A herald, ho!
    EDMUND.   A herald, ho, a herald!   105
Enter a Herald.
    ALBANY.
Trust to thy single virtue;° for thy soldiers,
All levied in my name, have in my name
Took their discharge.

---

51 common bosom affection of the multitude **53 Which** of us who **52–53 turn . . . them** that is, turn against us the weapons of those very troops whom we impressed into service **55 space** interval of time **58–59 And . . . sharpness** and even the best of causes, at this moment when the passions of battle have not cooled, are viewed with hatred by those who have suffered the painful consequences. (Edmund pretends to worry that Lear and Cordelia would not receive a fair trial.) **62 subject of** subordinate in **63 list** please **64 pleasure** wish. **demanded** asked about **67 immediacy** nearness of connection **70 your addition** the titles you confer **71 compeers** is equal with **72 That . . . most** that investiture would be most complete **73 prove** turn out to be **74 asquint** (Jealousy proverbially makes the eye look *asquint*, "furtively, suspiciously.") **76 full-flowing stomach** full tide of angry rejoinder **77 patrimony** inheritance **78 the walls is thine** that is, the citadel of my heart and body surrenders completely to you

81 let-alone preventing, denying **82 Half-blooded** only partly of noble blood, bastard **83 Let . . . strike** that is, to announce our banns (?) **85 in thy attaint** that is, as partner in your corruption and as one who has (unwittingly) provided the *attaint* or impeachment against you **89 banns** public announcement of a proposed marriage **91 An interlude** a play; that is, you are being melodramatic, or, what a farce this is **95 make** prove **96 in nothing less** in no respect less guilty **99 medicine** that is, poison **100 What** whoever **106 single virtue** unaided prowess

REGAN.   My sickness grows upon me.
ALBANY.
   She is not well. Convey her to my tent.

                                   [*Exit Regan, supported.*]

110   Come hither, herald. Let the trumpet sound,
   And read out this.   [*He gives a paper.*]
CAPTAIN.   Sound, trumpet!   *A trumpet sounds.*
HERALD (*reads*). "If any man of quality or degree° within the
   lists of the army will maintain upon Edmund, supposed
115   Earl of Gloucester, that he is a manifold traitor, let him
   appear by the third sound of the trumpet. He is bold in
   his defense."
EDMUND.   Sound!   *First trumpet.*
HERALD.   Again!   *Second trumpet.*
120 HERALD.   Again!   *Third trumpet.*

                                Trumpet answers within.

   Enter Edgar, armed, [*with a trumpeter before him*].

ALBANY.
   Ask him his purposes, why he appears
   Upon this call o' the trumpet.
HERALD.   What° are you?
   Your name, your quality, and why you answer
   This present summons?
EDGAR.   Know my name is lost,
125   By treason's tooth bare-gnawn and canker-bit.°
   Yet am I noble as the adversary
   I come to cope.°
ALBANY.   Which is that adversary?
EDGAR.
   What's he that speaks for Edmund, Earl of Gloucester?
EDMUND.
   Himself. What sayst thou to him?
EDGAR.   Draw thy sword,
130   That, if my speech offend a noble heart,
   Thy arm may do thee justice. Here is mine.

   [*He draws his sword.*]

   Behold, it is the privilege of mine honors,°
   My oath, and my profession.° I protest,
   Maugre° thy strength, place, youth, and eminence,
135   Despite thy victor° sword and fire-new° fortune,
   Thy valor, and thy heart,° thou art a traitor—
   False to thy gods, thy brother, and thy father,
   Conspirant 'gainst this high-illustrious prince,
   And from th' extremest upward° of thy head
140   To the descent° and dust below thy foot

A most toad-spotted° traitor. Say thou° no,
This sword, this arm, and my best spirits are bent°
To prove upon thy heart, whereto I speak,
Thou liest.
EDMUND.   In wisdom° I should ask thy name.
But since thy outside looks so fair and warlike,   145
And that thy tongue some say° of breeding breathes,
What safe and nicely° I might well delay
By rule of knighthood, I disdain and spurn.°
Back do I toss those treasons to thy head,°
With the hell-hated° lie o'erwhelm thy heart,   150
Which—for they yet glance by and scarcely bruise°—
This sword of mine shall give them instant way,°
Where they shall rest forever.° Trumpets, speak!

[*He draws.*] *Alarums. Fight.* [*Edmund falls.*]

ALBANY [*to Edgar*].
   Save° him, save him!
GONERIL.   This is practice,° Gloucester.
By th' law of arms thou wast not bound to answer   155
An unknown opposite. Thou art not vanquished,
But cozened° and beguiled.
ALBANY.   Shut your mouth, dame,
Or with this paper shall I stopple° it.—Hold, sir.°—
[*To Goneril.*] Thou worse than any name, read thine own
   evil.

[*He shows her the letter.*]

No tearing, lady; I perceive you know it.   160
GONERIL.
Say if I do, the laws are mine, not thine.
Who can arraign me for 't?
ALBANY.   Most monstrous! O!
Know'st thou this paper?
GONERIL.   Ask me not what I know.

                                        Exit.

ALBANY.
Go after her. She's desperate; govern° her.

                                   [*Exit a soldier.*]

141 toad-spotted venomous, or having spots of infamy. **Say thou**
if you say   **142 bent** prepared   **144 wisdom** prudence   **146 say**
smack, taste, indication   **147 safe and nicely** prudently and punctiliously   **148 I . . . spurn** that is, I disdain to insist on my right to
refuse combat with one of lower rank   **149 treasons . . . head** that
is, accusations of treason in your teeth   **150 hell-hated** hated as
hell is hated   **151 Which . . . bruise** that is, which charges of treason—since as yet they merely glance off your armor and do no harm
152 give . . . way provide them an immediate pathway (to your
heart)   **153 Where . . . forever** that is, my victory in trial by combat will prove forever that the charges of treason apply to you
154 Save spare. (Albany wishes to spare Edmund's life so that he
may confess and be found guilty.)   **practice** trickery, or (said sardonically),   astute   management   **157   cozened**   tricked
158 stopple stop up.   **Hold, sir** (Perhaps addressed to Edgar; see
line 154 and note.)   **164 govern** restrain

113 degree rank   **122 What** who   **125 canker-bit** eaten as by the
caterpillar   **127 cope** encounter   **132 of mine honors** that is, of
my   knighthood   **133   profession**   that   is,   knighthood
134 Maugre in spite of   **135 victor** victorious.   **fire-new** newly
minted   **136 heart** courage   **139 upward** top   **140 descent** lowest extreme

EDMUND.
165 What you have charged me with, that have I done,
And more, much more. The time will bring it out.
'Tis past, and so am I. But what art thou
That hast this fortune on° me? If thou'rt noble,
I do forgive thee.

EDGAR.   Let's exchange charity.°
170 I am no less in blood than thou art, Edmund;
If more, the more th'° hast wronged me.
My name is Edgar, and thy father's son.
The gods are just, and of our pleasant° vices
Make instruments to plague us.
175 The dark and vicious place where thee he got°
Cost him his eyes.

EDMUND.   Th' hast spoken right. 'Tis true.
The wheel° is come full circle; I am here.°

ALBANY [to Edgar].
Methought thy very gait did prophesy
A royal nobleness. I must embrace thee.

[They embrace.]

180 Let sorrow split my heart if ever I
Did hate thee or thy father!

EDGAR. Worthy prince, I know 't.

ALBANY. Where have you hid yourself?
How have you known the miseries of your father?

EDGAR.
185 By nursing them, my lord. List° a brief tale,
And when 'tis told, O, that my heart would burst!
The bloody proclamation to escape°
That followed me so near—O, our lives' sweetness,
That we the pain of death would hourly die
190 Rather than die at once!—taught me to shift
Into a madman's rags, t' assume a semblance
That very dogs disdained; and in this habit
Met I my father with his bleeding rings,°
Their precious stones new lost; became his guide,
195 Led him, begged for him, saved him from despair;
Never—O fault!°—revealed myself unto him
Until some half hour past, when I was armed.
Not sure, though hoping, of this good success,°
I asked his blessing, and from first to last
200 Told him our pilgrimage. But his flawed° heart—
Alack, too weak the conflict to support—
Twixt two extremes of passion, joy and grief,
Burst smilingly.

EDMUND.   This speech of yours hath moved me,
And shall perchance do good. But speak you on;
You look as you had something more to say.   205

ALBANY.
If there be more, more woeful, hold it in,
For I am almost ready to dissolve,°
Hearing of this.

EDGAR.   This would have seemed a period°
To such as love not° sorrow; but another,
To amplify too much, would make much more   210
And top extremity.° Whilst I
Was big in clamor,° came there in a man
Who, having seen me in my worst estate,
Shunned my abhorred society; but then, finding
Who 'twas that so endured, with his strong arms   215
He fastened on my neck and bellowed out
As° he'd burst heaven, threw him on my father,°
Told the most piteous tale of Lear and him
That ever ear received, which in recounting
His° grief grew puissant,° and the strings of life°   220
Began to crack. Twice then the trumpets sounded,
And there I left him tranced.°

ALBANY.   But who was this?

EDGAR.
Kent, sir, the banished Kent, who in disguise
Followed his enemy king° and did him service
Improper for a slave.   225

Enter a Gentleman [with a bloody knife].

GENTLEMAN.
Help, help, O, help!

EDGAR.   What kind of help?

ALBANY.   Speak, man.

EDGAR.
What means this bloody knife?

GENTLEMAN.   'Tis hot, it smokes.°
It came even from the heart of—O, she's dead!

ALBANY. Who dead? Speak, man.

GENTLEMAN.
Your lady, sir, your lady! And her sister   230
By her is poisoned; she confesses it.

EDMUND.
I was contracted to them both. All three
Now marry in an instant.

---

168 **fortune on** victory over 169 **charity** forgiveness (for Edmund's wickedness toward Edgar and Edgar's having slain Edmund) 171 **th'** thou 173 **pleasant** pleasurable 175 **got** begot 177 **wheel** that is, wheel of fortune. **here** that is, at its bottom 185 **List** listen to 187 **The...escape** in order to escape the death-threatening proclamation 193 **rings** sockets 196 **fault** mistake 198 **success** outcome 200 **flawed** cracked

207 **dissolve** that is, in tears 208 **a period** the limit 209 **love not** are not in love with 209–211 **but...extremity** that is, but another sorrowful circumstance, adding to what is already too much, would increase it and exceed the limit 212 **big in clamor** loud in my lamenting 217 **As** as if. **threw...father** threw himself on my father's body 220 **His** that is, Kent's. **puissant** powerful. **strings of life** heartstrings 222 **tranced** entranced, senseless 224 **his enemy king** that is, the king who had rejected and banished him 227 **smokes** steams

EDGAR.   Here comes Kent.

Enter Kent.

ALBANY.
Produce the bodies, be they alive or dead.

[*Exit Gentleman.*]

235 This judgment of the heavens, that makes us tremble,
Touches us not with pity.—O, is this he?
[*To Kent.*] The time will not allow the compliment°
Which very manners urges.°

KENT.   I am come
To bid my king and master aye good night.°
Is he not here?

240 ALBANY.   Great thing of us forgot!
Speak, Edmund, where's the King? And where's
    Cordelia?

Goneril's and Regan's bodies [are] brought out.

Seest thou this object,° Kent?

KENT. Alack, why thus?

EDMUND. Yet° Edmund was beloved.
245 The one the other poisoned for my sake
And after slew herself.

ALBANY. Even so. Cover their faces.

EDMUND.
I pant for life. Some good I mean to do,
Despite of mine own nature. Quickly send—
250 Be brief in it—to th' castle, for my writ
Is on the life of Lear and on Cordelia.
Nay, send in time.

ALBANY.   Run, run, O, run!

EDGAR.
To who, my lord? Who has the office?° Send
Thy token of reprieve.

EDMUND. Well thought on. Take my sword. The captain!
Give it the Captain.

EDGAR.   Haste thee, for thy life.

255
[*Exit one with Edmund's sword.*]

EDMUND.
He hath commission from thy wife and me
To hang Cordelia in the prison and
To lay the blame upon her own despair,
That she fordid° herself.

ALBANY.
260 The gods defend her! Bear him hence awhile.

[*Edmund is borne off.*]

Enter Lear, with Cordelia in his arms; [Captain].

LEAR.
Howl, howl, howl! O, you are men of stones!

Had I your tongues and eyes, I'd use them so
That heaven's vault should crack. She's gone forever.
I know when one is dead and when one lives;
She's dead as earth. Lend me a looking glass;   265
If that her breath will mist or stain the stone,°
Why, then she lives.

KENT.   Is this the promised end?°

EDGAR.
Or image of that horror?

ALBANY.   Fall and cease!°

LEAR.
This feather stirs; she lives! If it be so,
It is a chance which does redeem all sorrows   270
That ever I have felt.

KENT [*kneeling*].   O my good master!

LEAR.
Prithee, away.

EDGAR.   'Tis noble Kent, your friend.

LEAR.
A plague upon you, murderers, traitors all!
I might have saved her; now she's gone forever!
Cordelia, Cordelia! Stay a little. Ha?   275
What is 't thou sayst? Her voice was ever soft,
Gentle, and low, an excellent thing in woman.
I killed the slave that was a-hanging thee.

CAPTAIN.
'Tis true, my lords, he did.

LEAR.   Did I not, fellow?
I have seen the day, with my good biting falchion°   280
I would have made them skip. I am old now,
And these same crosses spoil me.°—Who are you?
Mine eyes are not o' the best; I'll tell you straight.°

KENT.
If Fortune brag of two° she loved and hated,°
One of them we behold.   285

LEAR.
This is a dull sight.° Are you not Kent?

KENT.   The same,
Your servant Kent. Where is your servant Caius?°

LEAR.
He's a good fellow, I can tell you that;
He'll strike, and quickly too. He's dead and rotten.

KENT.
No, my good lord, I am the very man—   290

---

237 **compliment** ceremony   238 **very manners urges** mere decency requires   239 **aye good night** farewell forever. (Kent believes he himself is near death, his heartstrings having begun to crack.)   242 **object** sight   244 **Yet** despite everything   253 **office** commission   259 **fordid** destroyed

266 **stone** crystal or polished stone of which the mirror is made   267 **promised end** that is, Last Judgment   268 **image** representation. **Fall and cease** that is, let heavens fall and all things cease   280 **falchion** light sword   282 **crosses spoil me** adversities take away my strength   283 **I'll . . . straight** I'll recognize you in a moment   284 **two** that is, Lear and a hypothetical individual whose misfortunes are without parallel. **loved and hated** that is, first raised and then lowered   286 **This . . . sight** that is, my vision is clouding, or, this is a dismal spectacle   287 **Caius** (Kent's disguise name)

LEAR. I'll see that straight.°

KENT.
That from your first of difference° and decay°
Have followed your sad steps—

LEAR.   You are welcome hither.

KENT.
Nor no man else.° All's cheerless, dark, and deadly.
295 Your eldest daughters have fordone° themselves,
And desperately° are dead.

LEAR.   Ay, so I think.

ALBANY.
He knows not what he says, and vain is it
That we present us to him.

EDGAR.   Very bootless.°

Enter a Messenger.

MESSENGER. Edmund is dead, my lord.

300 ALBANY. That's but a trifle here.
You lords and noble friends, know our intent:
What comfort to this great decay may come°
Shall be applied. For° us, we will resign,
During the life of this old majesty,
To him our absolute power; [*to Edgar and Kent*] you, to
305   your rights,
With boot° and such addition° as your honors
Have more than merited. All friends shall taste
The wages of their virtue, and all foes
The cup of their deservings.–O, see, see!

LEAR.
310 And my poor fool° is hanged! No, no, no life?
Why should a dog, a horse, a rat have life,
And thou no breath at all? Thou'lt come no more,
Never, never, never, never, never!

Pray you, undo this button. Thank you, sir.
Do you see this? Look on her, look, her lips,   315
Look there, look there!

He dies.

EDGAR.   He faints. My lord, my lord!

KENT.
Break, heart, I prithee, break!

EDGAR.   Look up, my lord.

KENT.
Vex not his ghost.° O, let him pass! He hates him
That would upon the rack° of this tough world
Stretch him out longer.

EDGAR.   He is gone indeed.   320

KENT.
The wonder is he hath endured so long.
He but usurped his life.

ALBANY.
Bear them from hence. Our present business
Is general woe. [*To Kent and Edgar.*] Friends of my soul,
      you twain
Rule in this realm, and the gored state sustain.   325

KENT.
I have a journey,° sir, shortly to go.
My master calls me; I must not say no.

EDGAR.
The weight of this sad time we must obey;
Speak what we feel, not what we ought to say.
The oldest hath borne most; we that are young
Shall never see so much nor live so long.   330

Exeunt,° with a dead march.

TOPICS FOR CRITICAL THINKING AND WRITING

 ### THE PLAY ON THE PAGE

1. On the basis of his remarks in the first thirty-six lines of
the play, how would you characterize Gloucester?

2. Coleridge found in Cordelia's "Nothing" (1.1.86) "some
little, faulty admixture of pride or sullenness." Do you
think that Cordelia is blameworthy here, or can she be
exonerated?

3. Characterize the Lear of the first act. Regan and Goneril offer a characterization in 1.1.291–301. Do you find
their description acceptable?

4. Explain in a sentence or two what Edmund means by
"Nature" in 1.2.1–22. On the basis of 1.2, characterize
Edmund.

---

291 see that straight attend to that in a moment, or, comprehend
that soon   **292 first of difference** beginning of your quarrel (with
Cordelia).   **decay** decline of fortune   **294 Nor . . . else** no, not I
nor anyone else, or, I am *the very man* (line 290), him and no one
else   **295 fordone** destroyed   **296 desperately** in despair
298 bootless in vain   **302 What . . . come** that is, whatever
means of comforting this ruined king may present themselves
303 For as for   **306 boot** advantage, good measure.   **addition**
titles, further distinctions   **310 poor fool** that is, Cordelia. (*Fool* is
here a term of endearment.)

318 ghost departing spirit   **319 rack** torture rack (with suggestion, in the Folio and Quarto spelling *wracke*, of shipwreck, disaster)   **326 journey** that is, to another world   **331 s.d. Exeunt**
(Presumably the dead bodies are borne out in procession.)

5. In 1.4, what evidence is there that Lear is perceiving a "recognition" or *anagnorisis* (see Glossary)? On the other hand, which of his speeches in this scene especially indicate that he still has much to learn?

6. At the end of 2.2, Kent is put in the stocks. In a sentence, characterize him on the basis of the last speech in the scene.

7. Characterize Lear in 3.2 and 3.4.

8. In 4.1.19, what does Gloucester mean when he says, "I stumbled when I saw"?

9. In 5.3 why does Edmund confess and tell of the plan to murder Lear and Cordelia?

10. What motives do Goneril and Regan have for their behavior? What motive does Edmund have for his?

11. How much self-knowledge do you think Lear achieves?

12. What function does the Fool perform?

13. Some critics insist that Lear dies joyfully, but others insist that he dies angrily and blindly. What can be said on behalf of each of these views? Which view strikes you as truer?

14. In what ways is the subplot (Gloucester and his sons) related to the main plot of Lear and his daughters?

15. Gloucester says: "As flies to wanton boys, are we to th' gods; / They kill us for their sport" (4.1.36–37). Do you think that this is an adequate summary of the theme of *King Lear*?

🎭 THE PLAY ON THE STAGE

16. In 1990, Mabou Mines, an experimental theater troupe in New York, staged *King Lear* with a woman in the title role (and simply called the play *Lear*). What do you think of this casting? Could—or should—a woman play Lear? (A reviewer in *Theatre Journal,* December 1990, wrote of the production, "Mabou Mines has made maternal vanity, rage, and pain the stuff of high tragedy and that alone merits interest.")

17. Among other changes that Mabou Mines made were these: Lear's three daughters became sons, Cornwall and Albany became daughters-in-law, and Kent became the Queen's loyal woman. Gloucester, Edgar, and Edmund were all turned into female roles, and a racial element was added: Gloucester and the legitimate daughter were played by African Americans, the illegitimate daughter by a white. The fool was played by a man in drag. (For a photo of the production, see page 225.)

18. In 4.1.36–37 Gloucester says, "As flies to wanton boys are we to the gods; / They kill us for their sport." How would you want this line spoken? (Obviously your response will depend on your conception of Gloucester.)

19. If you were directing a production, how would you suggest Kent perform 2.4.1–21? Exactly what tone(s) would you like him to use?

20. The last two lines of 2.4 (Cornwall's speech) are often deleted in performances. Why? What do you think is gained or lost?

21. Have a group of readers try 4.7. Discuss the shifts of emotion throughout the scene.

THE PLAY IN PERFORMANCE

In 1808 Charles Lamb wrote an essay that has become infamous, "On the Tragedies of Shakespeare, Considered with Reference to Their Fitness for Stage Representation." The most controversial portion runs as follows:

> To see Lear acted—to see an old man tottering about the stage with a walking-stick, turned out of doors by his daughters in a rainy night, has nothing in it but what is painful and disgusting. We want to take him into shelter and relieve him. That is all the feeling which the acting of Lear ever produced in me. But the Lear of Shakespeare cannot be acted. The contemptible machinery by which they mimic the storm which he goes out in, is not more inadequate to represent the horrors of the real elements, than any actor can be to represent Lear. . . . The greatness of Lear is not in corporal dimension, but in intellectual: the explosions of his passion are terrible as a volcano; they are storms turning up and disclosing to the bottom that sea, his mind, with all its vast riches. It is his mind which is laid bare. . . . On the stage we see nothing but corporal infirmities and weakness, the impotence of rage.

Many play readers and theatergoers have tested Lamb's response against their own; those who believe that even the best production of a play (if the play is great literature) is reductive have sided with Lamb; others, who believe that a play—even the greatest play—is essentially a script that achieves its fullest life only in performance, have dismissed him.

The earliest recorded performance is at the court of King James I in Whitehall Palace, London, on December 26, 1606. A few references to the play during the first seventy-five years of its existence assure us that it was occasionally acted, but tell us nothing about how it was performed or how it was received. Performances of *Lear* ceased when civil war broke out in England in 1642 (the theaters were soon closed by Act of Parliament), but after Charles II was restored to the throne in 1660 the theaters were reopened, and we know that *Lear* was among the plays acted in the 1660s. In 1681 Nahum Tate presented his adaptation of the play in London, an adaptation that was to hold the stage for more than a century and a half.

In his dedication, Tate says that he found in Shakespeare's *Lear*

> a heap of jewels unstrung and unpolished, yet so dazzling in their disorder that I soon perceived I had seized a treasure. 'Twas my good fortune to light on one expedient to rectify what was wanting in the regularity and probability of the tale, which was to run through the whole a love betwixt Edgar and Cordelia . . . .

And so, as Shakespeare had freely rewritten the old anonymous play of *King Leir*, Tate now rewrote Shakespeare's play. He made changes throughout, for example modifications in Lear's curses, but the verbal changes seem small when compared with structural changes:

1. Tate manufactured a love interest for Edgar and Cordelia (Edgar, by the way, in this version saves Cordelia from an attempted rape by Edmund) and therefore eliminated the King of France;
2. he deleted the Fool;
3. he added a happy ending, keeping Lear, Cordelia, and Gloucester alive, and marrying Cordelia and Edgar.

This version persisted on the stage throughout the eighteenth century and well into the nineteenth. Thus, even when David Garrick played *Lear* in 1756 with "restorations from Shakespeare," that is, with the restoration of some of Shakespeare's lines, he nevertheless followed Tate in dropping the Fool, and in retaining not only Tate's love affair between Cordelia and Edgar but also Tate's happy ending. Not until 1838, in William Macready's production, were all three of Tate's basic changes eliminated. That is, Macready eliminated the love story, restored the Fool (though he assigned the role to a woman) and restored the tragic ending.

Productions of *Lear* in the middle and later nineteenth century were given to emphasizing lavish spectacle that was said to be historically accurate. The aim (again, speaking roughly) was theatrical illusionism: The viewer looked, through the proscenium, at a highly detailed scene that was alleged to be an authentic reproduction of the past. Thus, Charles Kean's production in 1858 was said to be set in eighth-century Anglo-Saxon England. Architecture (a great raftered hall for the palace), decor (skins and heads of animals on the walls, gigantic crimson banners with pictures of animals on them), and costumes (for instance, Lear in a floor-length robe of gold, blue and purple, and France in a blue and red robe decorated with gold fleur-de-lys) were based on historical research—though today it is recognized that the sources Kean drew on range from the sixth through the eleventh centuries. Because it could take ten or fifteen minutes to erect on the stage a highly illusionistic set, scenes employing the same set were grouped together; intervening scenes with a different locale were either transposed or completely omitted, thus seriously distorting the rhythm of the play. Henry Irving's production of 1892 (see the illustration on page 224) was in this tradition.

Most productions of *King Lear* evoke some vaguely medieval setting, usually by means of furs and leather, but one difficulty with this approach is that Lear's society may seem so primitive to begin with that as the play progresses there is little sense of a stripping away of conventional codes of behavior, with a descent into the depths. Partly to avoid a sense of primitiveness or remoteness that a medieval setting may be thought to convey, an occasional production uses modern dress or something close to it. For instance, Trevor Nunn's production for the Royal Shakespeare Company, in 1976, with Donald Sinden as Lear, was set in Victorian or Edwardian times: The King (smoking a cigar, to indicate that the division of the kingdom was a rather informal, private affair) wore a military uniform, with medals; Kent wore a frock coat; and others wore tweeds and riding boots. Modern dress is of course supposed to make the plays relevant to the audience, but it is not unusual for spectators to be distracted by the modern costumes and setting.

An alternative approach, also seeking to dislocate the plays from the Elizabethan period and also from the period in which they are supposed to be set, is to use costumes and sets that do not suggest any particular period. For an example, see page 224.

Among the most important productions of the twentieth century is the version performed in 1962 at Stratford-upon-Avon, starring Paul Scofield and directed by Peter Brook. (The production became the basis for a film, but the film was not identical to the stage performance.) Brook saw *Lear* as an anticipation of the work of Beckett and other dramatists of the Theater of the Absurd. (For further information, see page 225.)

Alan MacVey
DIRECTING KING LEAR

Alan MacVey teaches drama at the University of Iowa. In this interview he discusses a production presented by the Acting Ensemble at the Bread Loaf School of English in 1991.

One sometimes hears it said that Hamlet *was the play for the nineteenth century and that* Lear *is the play for the twentieth century. Do you agree—at least about* Lear?

Is *Lear* a play for this century? I believe so. Our century has seen the release of horribly chaotic forces. Human beings have struggled to learn from these forces and justify the terrible experience of them. At the heart of *King Lear* are these same forces of chaos, the same violence and destruction, the same urgency to find meaning. At the end of the play, as at the end of our century, we discover that the questions we've asked and the meaning we've tried to ascribe to these experiences are met with silence. Neither Shakespeare nor our contemporary world gives any indication that pain is justified.

How did you costume the play? Did you think of modern dress?

I believe modern dress is often a viable option for Shakespeare's works. Our production of *King Lear* was anchored deep in the past. Clothing was made of leather, fur, and rich but heavy materials. Yet these clothes were often constructed from modern garments. The robe Lear wore out onto the heath, for example, was adapted from a heavy overcoat. Beneath it was another, lighter coat, and beneath that a shirt which could have been worn a thousand years ago, in the Renaissance, or today. The set, a great round slab with high walls, transformed to the heath as the walls disappeared and left nothing but blackness all around.

But wouldn't you agree that Lear *also has some very intimate scenes? I've heard you say you think Olivier's TV version was strong here.*

I believe the finest moment in Olivier's television version is the scene in which Lear awakens from his madness to find Cordelia. On stage, this scene can be difficult because Lear must either be carried into view or be revealed behind a curtain or wall—often upstage and far from the audience. The intimacy between Cordelia and Lear is difficult to achieve on a large stage, especially as Cordelia bends close to her father to comfort him. Our production brought Lear onto the stage in a primitive chair—not very comfortable but interesting-looking. The scene possessed a strange quality because of it, but even in a small theater we couldn't achieve the delicacy that is called for. Olivier plays the scene in bed. His slow recognition of Cordelia is played very intimately. Whispering to his daughter (as I recall—I haven't seen the film in a while) he and Cordelia gently embrace as the camera draws in close to them. Such quiet scenes may play best on screen.

I know a director in a university theater who says he will never do Lear *because undergraduates are not up to the play.*

It may be true that the play is difficult to teach and even to see, but not because students are too young to understand it. I've rarely encountered a work of art about which there is so much to say and about which all words seem insufficient. What is there to say about Mt. Everest? A great deal, of course—the location of paths to the top, descriptions of rock faces, warnings of danger. But the experience of the mountain has little to do with such descriptions. The mountain doesn't *mean* anything, nor does the experience of climbing it. As with *Lear*, one encounters the mountain and comes away sobered, humbled. As a director I began rehearsal aided by hundreds of pages of notes I'd written over several months. By our final performance these words seemed like an old map, which bore no relation to the journey. The play, like a mountain, dictated the territory; words could not describe it.

A Note on
THE DEVELOPMENT OF THE
SEVENTEENTH-CENTURY PROSCENIUM THEATER

In our discussion of the Greek theater (page 44) we mentioned that the actors performed in front of the *skene*, literally a hut or tent, but in this case a "scene-building," a structure that served two purposes: It served as a place from which the actors entered onto the performing areas and into which they exited, and it also served as a background for the actors (*skene* gives us our word *scene*).

The word *proscenium*, a Latinized form of a Greek word, is made up of *pro* = in front of, *skene* = hut, and *-ion*, a diminutive suffix, rather like the *-ette* in *kitchenette*. The *proscenium*, then, is a little something in front of the *skene*. In the Hellenistic world (Greece after the death of Alexander, in 323 B.C.), the word could refer to decorated panels set against the *skene*, or it could refer to the raised stage in front of the *skene*. For the ancient Romans, it almost always meant the raised stage, but in Italy in the sixteenth century it began to take on another meaning, *something in front of the scenery*—in particular, an arch that acted somewhat like a frame around a picture, in this case the picture being the set on the stage.

Such an arch has come to separate the actors from the audience, but in the early proscenium theaters the division was not sharp. True, the stage was no longer the *thrust stage* (or *platform stage*) of the Elizabethan theater (see page 186), but it did extend beyond the proscenium, allowing actors to perform in what can be thought of as the audience's space. (This protruding segment of the stage is called the *apron*, and today's proscenium theaters retain a trace of the apron, though it is scarcely deep enough to allow for much action. It is now chiefly used when actors take curtain calls at the end of a performance.

Theaters of course varied from decade to decade, and from country to country—an Italian theater of 1550 can scarcely be expected to be identical with a French theater of 1600 or with an English theater of 1670—but we can say that the development of the proscenium theater allowed for increasingly pictorial effects, and it also reduced the intimacy between performers and audience. In the English theaters of the late seventeenth century—the theaters of Aphra Behn, one of whose plays we include in this book—two doors were built into each side of the proscenium, and above the doors were windows or balconies. Because actors entered and exited through the doors, they were indeed in front of the proscenium, but much of the action nevertheless took place behind the proscenium. These theaters were equipped with **wings** and with **shutter settings.** Wings—rectangular painted canvases in wooden frames, often set into grooves—were used at the sides to help decorate the stage setting. Shutters were similar contrivances, usually in pairs, extending from one side of the stage to the other. Thus, when a pair

of shutters was pulled back, another scene could be revealed. The depth of the space between one pair of shutters and the pair behind it varied, but the space could be considerable. The withdrawing of the front pair could reveal, for instance, a fairly large group of actors, thus changing the scene from, say, a street in front of a house to a banquet hall within the house. The use of fairly elaborate painted scenery means that actors did not have to announce—as they did in the Elizabethan theater—what the scene was. You will recall that in *King Lear*, for instance, we get such helpful dialogue as this (2.4.304–06), and we know what time of day it is and what the setting is:

> Alack, the night comes on, and the high winds
> Do sorely ruffle. For many miles about
> There's scarce a bush.

With painted scenery—although the characters will still have to tell us what time of day it is—we know where we are, without dialogue. Further, a theater that uses painted scenery is likely to use it a good deal. The stage directions in Behn's *The Rover* indicate that the scene often changes. For instance, 3.2 is set in "Lucetta's house," but Lucetta soon exits, and after a few lines spoken by two other characters we are told that the scene changes. That is, 3.3 begins thus:

> The scene changes to a chamber with an alcove bed in it, a table, etc. Lucetta in bed. Enter Sancho and Blunt, who takes the candle of Sancho at the door.

The change was accomplished by drawing back the shutters, thereby revealing Lucetta's bedchamber. Perhaps the alcove specified in the stage direction was simply painted on a shutter at the rear. The bedroom scene then yields to a scene (3.4) that begins with Blunt pulling himself up out a sewer (a "common-shore"):

> The scene changes, and discovers Blunt, creeping out of a common-shore, his face, etc. all dirty.

The sharp changes of locale are immediately evident, even without dialogue. Sometimes even the change from one street to another is marked by a change of scenery, whereas in the Elizabethan theater the audience would have been given nothing more than the entrance of new characters, and perhaps a few words indicating where they are. In *The Rover*, however, 4.3, which is set in "A street," is followed by a scene which is set in "Another street." Presumably at the end of 4.3 shutters were withdrawn to mark the change.

For additional details about the English theater in the late seventeenth century, see Jocelyn Powell, *Restoration Theater Production* (1984); John Loftis et al., *The Revels History of Drama in English*, vol. 5 (1976); J. L. Styan, *Restoration Comedy in Performance* (1986).

Molière

THE MISANTHROPE

Jean Baptiste Poquelin (1622–73), who took the name Molière, was born into a prosperous middle-class family. For a while he studied law and philosophy, but by 1643 he was acting. He became the head of a theatrical company that had initial difficulties but later, thanks largely to Molière's comedies, had great successes. In 1662 he married Armande Béjart. The marriage apparently was unhappy, but the capricious and flirtatious Armande proved to be an accomplished actress. Molière continued to act, with great success in comedy, until his death. In one of those improbable things that happen in real life but that are too strange for art, Molière died of a hemorrhage that he suffered while playing the title role in his comedy *The Hypochondriac*. The early plays are highly farcical; among the later and greater plays are *The Highbrow Ladies* (1659), *Tartuffe* (1664), *Don Juan* (1665), *The Misanthrope* (1666), and *The Miser* (1668).

COMMENTARY

The introduction to this book makes the rather obvious point that in both tragedy and comedy we have characters who are motivated by some ideal and that (for example) the tragic hero who hunts out the polluted man in Thebes or who kills his wife because he thinks she is unfaithful is neither more nor less impassioned than the comic lover who writes sonnets to his mistress's eyebrow. Whether the passion is noble or comic depends not on its depth, or its persistence, but on its context, and especially on its object.

The passion for honesty that drives Molière's misanthrope, Alceste, is said by the equable Éliante to have "its noble, heroic side," and her view has found wide acceptance among audiences and readers. Alceste is sometimes seen as a tragic figure caught in a comic world, and the play is sometimes said to be a sort of tragic comedy. Alceste demands honesty, and he fulminates against flattery and other forms of insincerity that apparently compose the entire life of the other figures. Surrounded by trimmers and gossips and worse, he alone (if we except the gentle Éliante) seems to hold to a noble ideal. The only other ideal given much prominence is Philinte's, a code of such easy tolerance that it is at times almost indistinguishable from mere passive acceptance of everything.

What case can be made that Alceste is comic, not tragic? A few points suggest themselves. First, this champion of honesty is in love (or thinks he is) with a coquette. What can be more comic than the apostle of plain-dealing being himself in the power of the irrational, especially when this power deposits him at the feet of Célimène, a woman who employs all the devices that in others infuriate him? Second, his demand for honesty is indiscriminate; he is as offended at trivial courtesies as at the law's injustice. Philinte "ought to die of self-disgust" for his "crime" of effusively greeting a casual acquaintance whose name he cannot even recall. So disproportionate is Alceste's passion that when he pops onstage in 4.2, saying to Éliante, "Avenge me, Madam," he is funny, though the words in themselves are scarcely amusing.

Alceste's remark about joking provides a thread that may be followed usefully. He cannot take a joke. Whenever he is laughed at, he becomes indignant, but indignation (when motivated by a desire to protect the self from criticism) itself evokes further laughter because of the gap between the indignant man's presentation of himself and his real worth. Comedy does not allow people to strike attitudes. The man who protests that his argument *is* valid, dammit, or that he has a sense of humor, or that his opponent is a fool, is likely to evoke laughter by his monolithic insistence on his merit. When Philinte laughs at the old poem Alceste quotes, Alceste resorts to bitter irony, and when told that his frankness has made him ridiculous, he irritably replies:

> So much the better; just what I wish to hear.
> No news could be more grateful to my ear.
> All men are so detestable in my eyes.
> I should be sorry if they thought me otherwise.

When his persistent refusal to praise a trivial poem moves two auditors to laughter, he again employs frigid irony, and concludes the scene ominously:

> By heavens, Sir, I really didn't know
> That I was being humorous
> CÉLIMÈNE.   Go, Sir; go;
> Settle your business.
> ALCESTE.   I shall, and when I'm through,
> I shall return to settle things with you.

Alceste, unable to laugh at the folly of others, cannot, of course, tolerate laughter at himself. When Philinte puts into practice the frankness Alceste stormily advocates, Alceste's response is the indignation we have been commenting on. A sense of humor (as distinct from derisive laughter) involves the ability to laugh at what one values, and among the things one values is the self. Children can laugh at surprises and at the distress of other children, but they cannot laugh at themselves because they cannot see themselves in perspective, at a distance, as it were. Mature people can laugh at (for example) mimicry of themselves, but the child or the immature adult will, like Alceste, sulk or fly into a rage.

In *The Misanthrope* Molière may in some degree be mimicking himself. In 1662 Molière at forty married Armande Béjart, a woman less than half his age. The marriage seems to have been unhappy, apparently because his wife enjoyed attracting the attentions of other men. Some critics, pressing this point, assume that if the play is autobiographical, Alceste must be expressing Molière's point of view, and therefore he cannot be a comic figure. If anything, the autobiographic origin shows only that Molière had (which no one has doubted) a sense of humor. He could laugh at himself. Alceste's courtship of Célimène may in some degree represent Molière's unhappy marriage to a flirtatious and unappreciative woman, but the point is that Molière apparently could stand back and laugh at his own exasperation, which Alceste cannot do. (Molière subtitled the play "The Atrabilious Man in Love"; one cannot hear Alceste speaking thus of himself.) Alceste can only, rather childishly, try

to maintain his way, and demand that his special merit be noted and rewarded:

> However high the praise, there's nothing worse
> Than sharing honors with the universe.
> Esteem is founded on comparison:
> To honor all men is to honor none.
> Since you embrace this indiscriminate vice,
> Your friendship comes at far too cheap a price;
> I spurn the easy tribute of a heart
> Which will not set the worthy man apart:
> I choose, Sir, to be chosen; and in fine,
> The friend of mankind is no friend of mine.

Once or twice, when he confesses that his love for Célimène is irrational, he seems to have some perspective, but mostly the scenes of Alceste as lover serve to reveal again and again his consuming egotism. His love is so great, he tells Célimène, that he wishes she were in some peril so that he could prove his love by saving her. Célimène aptly replies that Alceste's is "a strange benevolence indeed."

The argument thus far has tried to make the point that Alceste is funny—funny because (among other things) his anger is indiscriminate and disproportionate, because he is a sort of philosopher and yet is in love, and because his *idée fixe*, frankness, when turned against him, exasperates him. But when we return to Éliante's reference to his "noble, heroic side," and we recall his passion for honesty and his passionate desire to be himself, and when we see the hollowness all about him, the comic figure begins to take on a tragic aspect; and when at the end he departs from the stage unrepentant and bitter, banishing himself from society, we feel that the usual comic plot too has taken on a tragic aspect. But this is hardly to say that Alceste is tragic and *The Misanthrope* a tragedy. One cannot, for example, imagine Alceste committing suicide. He is not a Romeo or an Othello.

Molière

THE MISANTHROPE

English Version by Richard Wilbur

List of Characters

ALCESTE, *in love with Célimène*
PHILINTE, *Alceste's friend*
ORONTE, *in love with Célimène*
CÉLIMÈNE, *Alceste's beloved*
ÉLIANTE, *Célimène's cousin*
ARSINOÉ, *a friend of Célimène's*
ACASTE }
CLITANDRE } *Marquesses*
BASQUE, *Célimène's servant*
A GUARD *of the Marshalsea*
DUBOIS, *Alceste's valet*

The scene throughout is in Célimène's house at Paris.

ACT 1

SCENE 1

[*Philinte, Alceste*]

PHILINTE.
    Now, what's got into you?

ALCESTE (*seated*).   Kindly leave me alone.

PHILINTE.
    Come, come, what is it? This lugubrious tone . . .

ALCESTE.
    Leave me, I said; you spoil my solitude.

PHILINTE.
    Oh, listen to me, now, and don't be rude.

ALCESTE.
    I choose to be rude, Sir, and to be hard of hearing.

PHILINTE.
    These ugly moods of yours are not endearing;
    Friends though we are, I really must insist . . .

ALCESTE (*abruptly rising*).
    Friends? Friends, you say? Well, cross me off your list.
    I've been your friend till now, as you well know;
    But after what I saw a moment ago
    I tell you flatly that our ways must part.
    I wish no place in a dishonest heart.

PHILINTE.
    Why, what have I done, Alceste? Is this quite just?

ALCESTE.
    My God, you ought to die of self-disgust.
    I call your conduct inexcusable, Sir,
    And every man of honor will concur.

    I see you almost hug a man to death,
    Exclaim for joy until you're out of breath,
    And supplement these loving demonstrations
    With endless offers, vows, and protestations;   20
    Then when I ask you "Who was that?" I find
    That you can barely bring his name to mind!
    Once the man's back is turned, you cease to love him,
    And speak with absolute indifference of him!
    By God, I say it's base and scandalous   25
    To falsify the heart's affections thus;
    If I caught myself behaving in such a way,
    I'd hang myself for shame, without delay.

PHILINTE.
    It hardly seems a hanging matter to me;
    I hope that you will take it graciously   30
    If I extend myself a slight reprieve,
    And live a little longer, by your leave.

ALCESTE.
    How dare you joke about a crime so grave?

PHILINTE.
    What crime? How else are people to behave?

ALCESTE.
    I'd have them be sincere, and never part   35
    With any word that isn't from the heart.

PHILINTE.
    When someone greets us with a show of pleasure,
    It's but polite to give him equal measure,
    Return his love the best that we know how,
    And trade him offer for offer, vow for vow.   40

ALCESTE.
    No, no, this formula you'd have me follow,
    However fashionable, is false and hollow,
    And I despise the frenzied operations
    Of all these barterers of protestations,
    These lavishers of meaningless embraces,   45
    These utterers of obliging commonplaces,
    Who court and flatter everyone on earth
    And praise the fool no less than the man of worth.
    Should you rejoice that someone fondles you,
    Offers his love and service, swears to be true,   50
    And fills your ears with praises of your name,
    When to the first damned fop he'll say the same?
    No, no: no self-respecting heart would dream
    Of prizing so promiscuous an esteem;
    However high the praise, there's nothing worse   55
    Than sharing honors with the universe.

Esteem is founded on comparison:
To honor all men is to honor none.
Since you embrace this indiscriminate vice,
60   Your friendship comes at far too cheap a price;
I spurn the easy tribute of a heart
Which will not set the worthy man apart:
I choose, Sir, to be chosen; and in fine,
The friend of mankind is no friend of mine.

PHILINTE.
65   But in polite society, custom decrees
That we show certain outward courtesies . . .

ALCESTE.
Ah, no! we should condemn with all our force
Such false and artificial intercourse.
Let men behave like men; let them display
70   Their inmost hearts in everything they say;
Let the heart speak, and let our sentiments
Not mask themselves in silly compliments.

PHILINTE.
In certain cases it would be uncouth
And most absurd to speak the naked truth;
75   With all respect for your exalted notions,
It's often best to veil one's true emotions.
Wouldn't the social fabric come undone
If we were wholly frank with everyone?
Suppose you met with someone you couldn't bear;
80   Would you inform him of it then and there?

ALCESTE.
Yes.

PHILINTE.   Then you'd tell old Emilie it's pathetic
The way she daubs her features with cosmetic
And plays the gay coquette at sixty-four?

ALCESTE.
I would.

PHILINTE.   And you'd call Dorilas a bore,
85   And tell him every ear at court is lame
From hearing him brag about his noble name?

ALCESTE.
Precisely.

PHILINTE.   Ah, you're joking.

ALCESTE.   Au contraire:
In this regard there's none I'd choose to spare.
All are corrupt; there's nothing to be seen
90   In court or town but aggravates my spleen.
I fall into deep gloom and melancholy
When I survey the scene of human folly,
Finding on every hand base flattery,
Injustice, fraud, self-interest, treachery. . . .
95   Ah, it's too much; mankind has grown so base,
I mean to break with the whole human race.

PHILINTE.
This philosophic rage is a bit extreme;
You've no idea how comical you seem;
Indeed, we're like those brothers in the play
100   Called *School for Husbands*, one of whom was prey . . .

ALCESTE.
Enough, now! None of your stupid similes.

PHILINTE.
Then let's have no more tirades, if you please.
The world won't change, whatever you say or do;
And since plain speaking means so much to you,
I'll tell you plainly that by being frank   10
You've earned the reputation of a crank,
And that you're thought ridiculous when you rage
And rant against the manners of the age.

ALCESTE.
So much the better; just what I wish to hear.
No news could be more grateful to my ear.   11
All men are so detestable in my eyes,
I should be sorry if they thought me wise.

PHILINTE.
Your hatred's very sweeping, is it not?

ALCESTE.
Quite right: I hate the whole degraded lot.

PHILINTE.
Must all poor human creatures be embraced,   11
Without distinction, by your vast distaste?
Even in these bad times, there are surely a few . . .

ALCESTE.
No, I include all men in one dim view:
Some men I hate for being rogues: the others
I hate because they treat the rogues like brothers,   120
And, lacking a virtuous scorn for what is vile,
Receive the villain with a complaisant smile.
Notice how tolerant people choose to be
Toward that bold rascal who's at law with me.
His social polish can't conceal his nature;   12
One sees at once that he's a treacherous creature;
No one could possibly be taken in
By those soft speeches and that sugary grin.
The whole world knows the shady means by which
The low-brow's grown so powerful and rich,   130
And risen to a rank so bright and high
That virtue can but blush, and merit sigh.
Whenever his name comes up in conversation,
None will defend his wretched reputation;
Call him knave, liar, scoundrel, and all the rest,   135
Each head will nod, and no one will protest.
And yet his smirk is seen in every house,
He's greeted everywhere with smiles and bows,
And when there's any honor that can be got
By pulling strings, he'll get it, like as not.   140
My God! It chills my heart to see the ways
Men come to terms with evil nowadays;
Sometimes, I swear, I'm moved to flee and find
Some desert land unfouled by humankind.

PHILINTE.
Come, let's forget the follies of the times   145
And pardon mankind for its petty crimes;
Let's have an end of rantings and of railings,

And show some leniency toward human failings.
This world requires a pliant rectitude;
50 Too stern a virtue makes one stiff and rude;
Good sense views all extremes with detestation,
And bids us to be noble in moderation.
The rigid virtues of the ancient days
Are not for us; they jar with all our ways
55 And ask of us too lofty a perfection.
Wise men accept their times without objection,
And there's no greater folly, if you ask me,
Than trying to reform society.
Like you, I see each day a hundred and one
60 Unhandsome deeds that might be better done,
But still, for all the faults that meet my view,
I'm never known to storm and rave like you.
I take men as they are, or let them be,
And teach my soul to bear their frailty;
65 And whether in court or town, whatever the scene,
My phlegm's as philosophic as your spleen.

ALCESTE.
This phlegm which you so eloquently commend,
Does nothing ever rile it up, my friend?
Suppose some man you trust should treacherously
70 Conspire to rob you of your property,
And do his best to wreck your reputation?
Wouldn't you feel a certain indignation?

PHILINTE.
Why, no. These faults of which you so complain
Are part of human nature, I maintain,
75 And it's no more a matter for disgust
That men are knavish, selfish and unjust,
Than that the vulture dines upon the dead,
And wolves are furious, and apes ill-bred.

ALCESTE.
Shall I see myself betrayed, robbed, torn to bits,
80 And not. . . . Oh, let's be still and rest our wits.
Enough of reasoning, now. I've had my fill.

PHILINTE.
Indeed, you would do well, Sir, to be still.
Rage less at your opponent, and give some thought
To how you'll win this lawsuit that he's brought.

ALCESTE.
85 I assure you I'll do nothing of the sort.

PHILINTE.
Then who will plead your case before the court?

ALCESTE.
Reason and right and justice will plead for me.

PHILINTE.
Oh, Lord. What judges do you plan to see?

ALCESTE.
Why, none. The justice of my cause is clear.

PHILINTE.
190 Of course, man; but there's politics to fear . . .

ALCESTE.
No, I refuse to lift a hand. That's flat.

I'm either right, or wrong.

PHILINTE.   Don't count on that.

ALCESTE.
No, I'll do nothing.

PHILINTE.   Your enemy's influence
Is great, you know . . .

ALCESTE.   That makes no difference.

PHILINTE.
It will; you'll see.

ALCESTE.   Must honor bow to guile?   195
If so, I shall be proud to lose the trial.

PHILINTE.
O, really . . .

ALCESTE.   I'll discover by this case
Whether or not men are sufficiently base
And impudent and villainous and perverse
To do me wrong before the universe.   200

PHILINTE.
What a man!

ALCESTE.   Oh, I could wish, whatever the cost,
Just for the beauty of it, that my trial were lost.

PHILINTE.
If people heard you talking so, Alceste,
They'd split their sides. Your name would be a jest.

ALCESTE.
So much the worse for jesters.

PHILINTE.   May I enquire   205
Whether this rectitude you so admire,
And these hard virtues you're enamored of
Are qualities of the lady whom you love?
It much surprises me that you, who seem
To view mankind with furious disesteem,   210
Have yet found something to enchant your eyes
Amidst a species which you so despise.
And what is more amazing, I'm afraid,
Is the most curious choice your heart has made.
The honest Éliante is fond of you,   215
Arsinoé, the prude, admires you too;
And yet your spirit's been perversely led
To choose the flighty Célimène instead,
Whose brittle malice and coquettish ways
So typify the manners of our days.   220
How is it that the traits you most abhor
Are bearable in this lady you adore?
Are you so blind with love that you can't find them?
Or do you contrive, in her case, not to mind them?

ALCESTE.
My love for that young widow's not the kind   225
That can't perceive defects; no, I'm not blind.
I see her faults, despite my ardent love,
And all I see I fervently reprove.
And yet I'm weak; for all her falsity,
That woman knows the art of pleasing me,   230
And though I never cease complaining of her,
I swear I cannot manage not to love her.

Her charm outweighs her faults; I can but aim
To cleanse her spirit in my love's pure flame.

PHILINTE.
235   That's no small task; I wish you all success.
You think then that she loves you?

ALCESTE.   Heavens, yes!
I wouldn't love her did she not love me.

PHILINTE.
Well, if her taste for you is plain to see,
Why do these rivals cause you such despair?

ALCESTE.
240   True love, Sir, is possessive, and cannot bear
To share with all the world. I'm here today
To tell her she must send that mob away.

PHILINTE.
If I were you, and had your choice to make,
Éliante, her cousin, would be the one I'd take;
245   That honest heart, which cares for you alone,
Would harmonize far better with your own.

ALCESTE.
True, true: each day my reason tells me so;
But reason doesn't rule in love, you know.

PHILINTE.
I fear some bitter sorrow is in store;
250   This love . . .

SCENE 2

[Oronte, Alceste, Philinte]

ORONTE (*to Alceste*). The servants told me at the door
That Éliante and Célimène were out,
But when I heard, dear Sir, that you were about,
I came to say, without exaggeration,
5   That I hold you in the vastest admiration,
And that it's always been my dearest desire
To be the friend of one I so admire.
I hope to see my love of merit requited,
And you and I in friendship's bond united.
10   I'm sure you won't refuse—if I may be frank—
A friend of my devotedness—and rank.

*During this speech of Oronte's, Alceste is abstracted, and
seems unaware that he is being spoken to. He only breaks
off his reverie when Oronte says:*

It was for you, if you please, that my words were
    intended.

ALCESTE.
For me, Sir?

ORONTE.   Yes, for you. You're not offended?

ALCESTE.
By no means. But this much surprises me . . .
15   The honor comes most unexpectedly . . .

ORONTE.
My high regard should not astonish you;
The whole world feels the same. It is your due.

ALCESTE.
Sir . . .

ORONTE. Why, in all the State there isn't one
Can match your merits; they shine, Sir, like the sun.

ALCESTE.
Sir . . .

ORONTE. You are higher in my estimation   20
Than all that's most illustrious in the nation.

ALCESTE.
Sir . . .

ORONTE. If I lie, may heaven strike me dead!
To show you that I mean what I have said,
Permit me, Sir, to embrace you most sincerely,
And swear that I will prize our friendship dearly.   25
Give me your hand. And now, Sir, if you choose,
We'll make our vows.

ALCESTE.   Sir . . .

ORONTE.   What! You refuse?

ALCESTE.
Sir, it's a very great honor you extend:
But friendship is a sacred thing, my friend;
It would be profanation to bestow   30
The name of friend on one you hardly know.
All parts are better played when well-rehearsed;
Let's put off friendship, and get acquainted first.
We may discover it would be unwise
To try to make our natures harmonize.   35

ORONTE.
By heaven! You're sagacious to the core;
This speech has made me admire you even more.
Let time, then, bring us closer day by day;
Meanwhile, I shall be yours in every way.
If, for example, there should be anything   40
You wish at court, I'll mention it to the King.
I have his ear, of course; it's quite well known
That I am much in favor with the throne.
In short, I am your servant. And now, dear friend,
Since you have such fine judgment, I intend   45
To please you, if I can, with a small sonnet
I wrote not long ago. Please comment on it,
And tell me whether I ought to publish it.

ALCESTE.
You must excuse me, Sir; I'm hardly fit
To judge such matters.

ORONTE.   Why not?

ALCESTE.   I am, I fear,   50
Inclined to be unfashionably sincere.

ORONTE.
Just what I ask; I'd take no satisfaction
In anything but your sincere reaction.
I beg you not to dream of being kind.

ALCESTE.
Since you desire it, Sir, I'll speak my mind.   55

ORONTE.
Sonnet. It's a sonnet. . . . *Hope.* . . . The poem's addressed

To a lady who wakened hopes within my breast.
Hope . . . this is not the pompous sort of thing,
Just modest little verses, with a tender ring.

ALCESTE.
    Well, we shall see.

ORONTE.   *Hope . . .* I'm anxious to hear
    Whether the style seems properly smooth and clear,
    And whether the choice of words is good or bad.

ALCESTE.
    We'll see, we'll see.

ORONTE.   Perhaps I ought to add
    That it took me only a quarter-hour to write it.

ALCESTE.
    The time's irrelevant, Sir: kindly recite it.

ORONTE (*reading*).

> *Hope comforts us awhile, 'tis true,*
> *Lulling our cares with careless laughter,*
> *And yet such joy is full of rue,*
> *My Phyllis, if nothing follows after.*

PHILINTE.
    I'm charmed by this already; the style's delightful.

ALCESTE (*sotto voce, to Philinte*).
    How can you say that? Why, the thing is frightful.

ORONTE.

> *Your fair face smiled on me awhile,*
> *But was it kindness so to enchant me?*
> *'Twould have been fairer not to smile,*
> *If hope was all you meant to grant me.*

PHILINTE.
    What a clever thought! How handsomely you phrase it!

ALCESTE (*sotto voce, to Philinte*).
    You know the thing is trash. How dare you praise it?

ORONTE.

> *If it's to be my passion's fate.*
> *Thus everlastingly to wait,*
> *Then death will come to set me free:*
> *For death is fairer than the fair;*
> *Phyllis, to hope is to despair*
> *When one must hope eternally.*

PHILINTE.
    The close is exquisite—full of feeling and grace.

ALCESTE (*sotto voce, aside*).
    Oh, blast the close; you'd better close your face
    Before you send your lying soul to hell.

PHILINTE.
    I can't remember a poem I've liked so well.

ALCESTE (*sotto voce, aside*).
    Good Lord!

ORONTE (*to Philinte*).   I fear you're flattering me a bit.

PHILINTE.
    Oh, no!

ALCESTE (*sotto voce, aside*). What else d'you call it, you
    hypocrite?

ORONTE (*to Alceste*).
    But you, Sir, keep your promise now: don't shrink   90
    From telling me sincerely what you think.

ALCESTE.
    Sir, these are delicate matters; we all desire
    To be told that we've the true poetic fire.
    But once, to one whose name I shall not mention,
    I said, regarding some verse of his invention,   95
    That gentlemen should rigorously control
    That itch to write which often afflicts the soul;
    That one should curb the heady inclination
    To publicize one's little avocation;
    And that in showing off one's works of art   100
    One often plays a very clownish part.

ORONTE.
    Are you suggesting in a devious way
    That I ought not . . .

ALCESTE.   Oh, that I do not say.
    Further, I told him that no fault is worse
    Than that of writing frigid, lifeless verse,   105
    And that the merest whisper of such a shame
    Suffices to destroy a man's good name.

ORONTE.
    D'you mean to say my sonnet's dull and trite?

ALCESTE.
    I don't say that. But I went on to cite
    Numerous cases of once-respected men   110
    Who came to grief by taking up the pen.

ORONTE.
    And am I like them? Do I write so poorly?

ALCESTE.
    I don't say that. But I told this person, "Surely
    You're under no necessity to compose;
    Why you should wish to publish, heaven knows.   115
    There's no excuse for printing tedious rot
    Unless one writes for bread, as you do not.
    Resist temptation, then, I beg of you;
    Conceal your pastimes from the public view;
    And don't give up, on any provocation,   120
    Your present high and courtly reputation,
    To purchase at a greedy printer's shop
    The name of silly author and scribbling fop."
    These were the points I tried to make him see.

ORONTE.
    I sense that they are also aimed at me;   125
    But now—about my sonnet—I'd like to be told . . .

ALCESTE.
    Frankly, that sonnet should be pigeonholed.
    You've chosen the worst models to imitate.
    The style's unnatural. Let me illustrate:
    For example, *Your fair face smiled on me awhile,*   130
    Followed by, *'Twould have been fairer not to smile!*
    Or this: *such joy is full of rue;*

Or this: *For death is fairer than the fair;*
Or, *Phyllis, to hope is to despair*
135 *When one must hope eternally!*
This artificial style, that's all the fashion,
Has neither taste, nor honesty, nor passion;
It's nothing but a sort of wordy play,
And nature never spoke in such a way.
140 What, in this shallow age, is not debased?
Our fathers, though less refined, had better taste;
I'd barter all that men admire today
For one old love song I shall try to say:

If the King had given me for my own
145 *Paris, his citadel,*
And I for that must leave alone
Her whom I love so well,
I'd say then to the Crown,
Take back your glittering town;
150 *My darling is more fair, I swear,*
My darling is more fair.

The rhyme's not rich, the style is rough and old,
But don't you see that it's the purest gold
Beside the tinsel nonsense now preferred,
155 And that there's passion in its every word?

If the King had given me for my own
Paris, his citadel,
And I for that must leave alone
Her whom I love so well,
160 *I'd say then to the Crown,*
Take back your glittering town;
My darling is more fair, I swear,
My darling is more fair.

There speaks a loving heart. (*To Philinte.*) You're laugh-
ing, eh?
165 Laugh on, my precious wit. Whatever you say,
I hold that song's worth all the bibelots
That people hail today with ah's and oh's.
ORONTE.
And I maintain my sonnet's very good.
ALCESTE.
It's not at all surprising that you should.
170 You have your reasons; permit me to have mine
For thinking that you cannot write a line.
ORONTE.
Others have praised my sonnet to the skies.
ALCESTE.
I lack their art of telling pleasant lies.
ORONTE.
You seem to think you've got no end of wit.
ALCESTE.
175 To praise your verse, I'd need still more of it.

ORONTE.
I'm not in need of your approval, Sir.
ALCESTE.
That's good; you couldn't have it if you were.
ORONTE.
Come now, I'll lend you the subject of my sonnet;
I'd like to see you try to improve upon it.
ALCESTE.
I might, by chance, write something just as shoddy;   180
But then I wouldn't show it to everybody.
ORONTE.
You're most opinionated and conceited.
ALCESTE.
Go find your flatterers, and be better treated.
ORONTE.
Look here, my little fellow, pray watch your tone.
ALCESTE.
My great big fellow, you'd better watch your own.   185
PHILINTE (*stepping between them*).
Oh, please, please, gentlemen! This will never do.
ORONTE.
The fault is mine, and I leave the field to you.
I am your servant, Sir, in every way.
ALCESTE.
And I, Sir, am your most abject valet.

SCENE 3

[*Philinte, Alceste*]

PHILINTE.
Well, as you see, sincerity in excess
Can get you into a very pretty mess;
Oronte was hungry for appreciation. . . .
ALCESTE.
Don't speak to me.
PHILINTE.   What?
ALCESTE.   No more conversation.
PHILINTE.
Really, now . . .
ALCESTE.   Leave me alone.
PHILINTE.   If I . . .
ALCESTE.   Out of my sight!   5
PHILINTE.
But what . . .
ALCESTE.   I won't listen.
PHILINTE.   But . . .
ALCESTE.   Silence!
PHILINTE.
Now, is it polite . . .
ALCESTE.
By heaven, I've had enough. Don't follow me.

PHILINTE.
Ah, you're just joking. I'll keep you company.

ACT 2

SCENE 1

[*Alceste, Célimène*]

ALCESTE.
Shall I speak plainly, Madam? I confess
Your conduct gives me infinite distress,
And my resentment's grown too hot to smother.
Soon, I foresee, we'll break with one another.
If I said otherwise, I should deceive you;
Sooner or later, I shall be forced to leave you,
And if I swore that we shall never part,
I should misread the omens of my heart.

CÉLIMÈNE.
You kindly saw me home, it would appear,
So as to pour invectives in my ear.

ALCESTE.
I've no desire to quarrel. But I deplore
Your inability to shut the door
On all these suitors who beset you so.
There's what annoys me, if you care to know.

CÉLIMÈNE.
Is it my fault that all these men pursue me?
Am I to blame if they're attracted to me?
And when they gently beg an audience,
Ought I to take a stick and drive them hence?

ALCESTE.
Madam, there's no necessity for a stick;
A less responsive heart would do the trick.
Of your attractiveness I don't complain;
But those your charms attract, you then detain
By a most melting and receptive manner,
And so enlist their hearts beneath your banner.
It's the agreeable hopes which you excite
That keep these lovers round you day and night;
Were they less liberally smiled upon,
That sighing troop would very soon be gone.
But tell me, Madam, why is it that lately
This man Clitandre interests you so greatly?
Because of what high merits do you deem
Him worthy of the honor of your esteem?
Is it that your admiring glances linger
On the splendidly long nail of his little finger?
Or do you share the general deep respect
For the blond wig he chooses to affect?
Are you in love with his embroidered hose?
Do you adore his ribbons and his bows?

Or is it that this paragon bewitches
Your tasteful eye with his vast German breeches? 40
Perhaps his giggle, or his falsetto voice,
Makes him the latest gallant of your choice?

CÉLIMÈNE.
You're much mistaken to resent him so.
Why I put up with him you surely know:
My lawsuit's very shortly to be tried, 45
And I must have his influence on my side.

ALCESTE.
Then lose your lawsuit, Madam, or let it drop;
Don't torture me by humoring such a fop.

CÉLIMÈNE.
You're jealous of the whole world, Sir.

ALCESTE.   That's true,
Since the whole world is well-received by you. 50

CÉLIMÈNE.
That my good nature is so unconfined
Should serve to pacify your jealous mind;
Were I to smile on one, and scorn the rest,
Then you might have some cause to be distressed.

ALCESTE.
Well, if I mustn't be jealous, tell me, then, 55
Just how I'm better treated than other men.

CÉLIMÈNE.
You know you have my love. Will that not do?

ALCESTE.
What proof have I that what you say is true?

CÉLIMÈNE.
I would expect, Sir, that my having said it
Might give the statement a sufficient credit. 60

ALCESTE.
But how can I be sure that you don't tell
The selfsame thing to other men as well?

CÉLIMÈNE.
What a gallant speech! How flattering to me!
What a sweet creature you make me out to be!
Well then, to save you from the pangs of doubt, 65
All that I've said I hereby cancel out;
Now, none but yourself shall make a monkey of you:
Are you content?

ALCESTE.   Why, why am I doomed to love you?
I swear that I shall bless the blissful hour
When this poor heart's no longer in your power! 70
I make no secret of it: I've done my best
To exorcise this passion from my breast;
But thus far all in vain; it will not go;
It's for my sins that I must love you so.

CÉLIMÈNE.
Your love for me is matchless, Sir; that's clear. 75

ALCESTE.
Indeed, in all the world it has no peer;
Words can't describe the nature of my passion,

And no man ever loved in such a fashion.

CÉLIMÈNE.

Yes, it's a brand-new fashion, I agree:
80   You show your love by castigating me,
And all your speeches are enraged and rude.
I've never been so furiously wooed.

ALCESTE.

Yet you could calm that fury, if you chose.
Come, shall we bring our quarrels to a close?
85   Let's speak with open hearts, then, and begin . . .

SCENE 2

[*Célimène, Alceste, Basque*]

CÉLIMÈNE.

What is it?

BASQUE.   Acaste is here.

CÉLIMÈNE.   Well, send him in.

SCENE 3

[*Célimène, Alceste*]

ALCESTE.

What! Shall we never be alone at all?
You're always ready to receive a call,
And you can't bear, for ten ticks of the clock,
Not to keep open house for all who knock.

CÉLIMÈNE.

5   I couldn't refuse him: he'd be most put out.

ALCESTE.

Surely that's not worth worrying about.

CÉLIMÈNE.

Acaste would never forgive me if he guessed.
That I consider him a dreadful pest.

ALCESTE.

If he's a pest, why bother with him then?

CÉLIMÈNE.

10   Heavens! One can't antagonize such men;
Why, they're the chartered gossips of the court,
And have a say in things of every sort.
One must receive them, and be full of charm;
They're no great help, but they can do you harm,
15   And though your influence be ever so great,
They're hardly the best people to alienate.

ALCESTE.

I see, dear lady, that you could make a case
For putting up with the whole human race;
These friendships that you calculate so nicely . . .

SCENE 4

[*Alceste, Célimène, Basque*]

BASQUE.

Madam, Clitandre is here as well.

ALCESTE.   Precisely.

CÉLIMÈNE.

Where are you going?

ALCESTE.   Elsewhere.

ÉLIMÈNE.   Stay.

ALCESTE.   No, no.

CÉLIMÈNE.

Stay, Sir.

ALCESTE.   I can't.

CÉLIMÈNE.   I wish it.

ALCESTE.   No, I must go.

I beg you, Madam, not to press the matter;
You know I have no taste for idle chatter.   5

CÉLIMÈNE.

Stay. I command you.

ALCESTE.   No, I cannot stay.

CÉLIMÈNE.

Very well; you have my leave to go away.

SCENE 5

[*Éliante, Philinte, Acaste, Clitandre, Alceste, Célimène, Basque*]

ÉLIANTE (*to Célimène*).

The Marquesses have kindly come to call.
Were they announced?

CÉLIMÈNE.   Yes. Basque, bring chairs for all.

Basque provides the chairs, and exits.

(*To Alceste.*) You haven't gone?

ALCESTE.   No; and I shan't depart
Till you decide who's foremost in your heart.

CÉLIMÈNE.

Oh, hush.

ALCESTE.   It's time to choose; take them, or me.   5

CÉLIMÈNE.

You're mad.

ALCESTE.   I'm not, as you shall shortly see.

CÉLIMÈNE.

Oh?

ALCESTE.   You'll decide.

CÉLIMÈNE.   You're joking now, dear friend.

ALCESTE.

No, no; you'll choose; my patience is at an end.

CLITANDRE.

Madam, I come from court, where poor Cléonte
Behaved like a perfect fool, as is his wont.   10
Has he no friend to counsel him, I wonder,
And teach him less unerringly to blunder?

CÉLIMÈNE.

It's true, the man's a most accomplished dunce;
His gauche behavior charms the eye at once;
And every time one sees him, on my word,
His manner's grown a trifle more absurd.   15

ACASTE.

    Speaking of dunces, I've just now conversed
    With old Damon, who's one of the very worst;
    I stood a lifetime in the broiling sun
    Before his dreary monologue was done.

CÉLIMÈNE.

    Oh, he's a wondrous talker, and has the power
    To tell you nothing hour after hour:
    If, by mistake, he ever came to the point,
    The shock would put his jawbone out of joint.

ÉLIANTE (*to Philinte*).

    The conversation takes its usual turn,
    And all our dear friends' ears will shortly burn.

CLITANDRE.

    Timante's a character, Madam.

CÉLIMÈNE.   Isn't he, though?

    A man of mystery from top to toe,
    Who moves about in a romantic mist
    On secret missions which do not exist.
    His talk is full of eyebrows and grimaces;
    How tired one gets of his momentous faces;
    He's always whispering something confidential
    Which turns out to be quite inconsequential;
    Nothing's too slight for him to mystify;
    He even whispers when he says "good-bye."

ACASTE.

    Tell us about Géralde.

CÉLIMÈNE.   That tiresome ass.

    He mixes only with the titled class,
    And fawns on dukes and princes, and is bored
    With anyone who's not as least a lord.
    The man's obsessed with rank, and his discourses
    Are all of hounds and carriages and horses;
    He uses Christian names with all the great,
    And the word Milord, with him, is out of date.

CLITANDRE.

    He's very taken with Bélise, I hear.

CÉLIMÈNE.

    She is the dreariest company, poor dear.
    Whenever she comes to call, I grope about
    To find some topic which will draw her out,
    But, owing to her dry and faint replies,
    The conversation wilts, and droops, and dies.
    In vain one hopes to animate her face
    By mentioning the ultimate commonplace;
    But sun or shower, even hail or frost
    Are matters she can instantly exhaust.
    Meanwhile her visit, painful though it is,
    Drags on and on through mute eternities,
    And though you ask the time, and yawn, and yawn,
    She sits there like a stone and won't be gone.

ACASTE.

    Now for Adraste.

CÉLIMÈNE.   Oh, that conceited elf
    Has a gigantic passion for himself;

He rails against the court, and cannot bear it
That none will recognize his hidden merit;
All honors given to others give offense
To his imaginary excellence.

CLITANDRE.

    What about young Cléon? His house, they say,   65
    Is full of the best society, night and day.

CÉLIMÈNE.

    His cook has made him popular, not he:
    It's Cléon's table that people come to see.

ÉLIANTE.

    He gives a splendid dinner, you must admit.

CÉLIMÈNE.

    But must he serve himself along with it?   70
    For my taste, he's a most insipid dish
    Whose presence sours the wine and spoils the fish.

PHILINTE.

    Damis, his uncle, is admired no end.
    What's your opinion, Madam?

CÉLIMÈNE.   Why, he's my friend.

PHILINTE.

    He seems a decent fellow, and rather clever.   75

CÉLIMÈNE.

    He works too hard at cleverness, however.
    I hate to see him sweat and struggle so
    To fill his conversation with bons mots.
    Since he's decided to become a wit
    His taste's so pure that nothing pleases it;   80
    He scolds at all the latest books and plays,
    Thinking that wit must never stoop to praise,
    That finding fault's a sign of intellect,
    That all appreciation is abject,
    And that by damning everything in sight   85
    One shows oneself in a distinguished light.
    He's scornful even of our conversations:
    Their trivial nature sorely tries his patience;
    He folds his arms, and stands above the battle,
    And listens sadly to our childish prattle.   90

ACASTE.

    Wonderful, Madam! You've hit him off precisely.

CLITANDRE.

    No one can sketch a character so nicely.

ALCESTE.

    How bravely, Sirs, you cut and thrust at all
    These absent fools, till one by one they fall:
    But let one come in sight, and you'll at once   95
    Embrace the man you lately called a dunce,
    Telling him in a tone sincere and fervent
    How proud you are to be his humble servant.

CLITANDRE.

    Why pick on us? *Madame's* been speaking, Sir.
    And you should quarrel, if you must, with her.   100

ALCESTE.

    No, no, by God, the fault is yours, because
    You lead her on with laughter and applause,

And make her think that she's the more delightful
The more her talk is scandalous and spiteful.
105   Oh, she would stoop to malice far, far less
If no such claque approved her cleverness.
It's flatterers like you whose foolish praise
Nourishes all the vices of these days.

PHILINTE.
But why protest when someone ridicules
110   Those you'd condemn, yourself, as knaves or fools?

CÉLIMÈNE.
Why, Sir? Because he loves to make a fuss.
You don't expect him to agree with us,
When there's an opportunity to express
His heaven-sent spirit of contrariness?
115   What other people think, he can't abide;
Whatever they say, he's on the other side;
He lives in deadly terror of agreeing;
'Twould make him seem an ordinary being.
Indeed, he's so in love with contradiction,
120   He'll turn against his most profound conviction
And with a furious eloquence deplore it,
If only someone else is speaking for it.

ALCESTE.
Go on, dear lady, mock me as you please;
You have your audience in ecstasies.

PHILINTE.
125   But what she says is true: you have a way
Of bridling at whatever people say;
Whether they praise or blame, your angry spirit
Is equally unsatisfied to hear it.

ALCESTE.
Men, Sir, are always wrong, and that's the reason
130   That righteous anger's never out of season;
All that I hear in all their conversation
Is flattering praise or reckless condemnation.

CÉLIMÈNE.
But . . .

ALCESTE. No, no, Madam, I am forced to state
That you have pleasures which I deprecate,
135   And that these others, here, are much to blame
For nourishing the faults which are your shame.

CLITANDRE.
I shan't defend myself, Sir; but I vow
I'd thought this lady faultless until now.

ACASTE.
I see her charms and graces, which are many;
140   But as for faults, I've never noticed any.

ALCESTE.
I see them, Sir; and rather than ignore them,
I strenuously criticize her for them.
The more one loves, the more one should object
To every blemish, every least defect.
145   Were I this lady, I would soon get rid
Of lovers who approved of all I did,
And by their slack indulgence and applause

Endorsed my follies and excused my flaws.

CÉLIMÈNE.
If all hearts beat according to your measure,
150   The dawn of love would be the end of pleasure;
And love would find its perfect consummation
In ecstasies of rage and reprobation.

ÉLIANTE.
Love, as a rule, affects men otherwise,
And lovers rarely love to criticize.
155   They see their lady as a charming blur,
And find all things commendable in her.
If she has any blemish, fault, or shame,
They will redeem it by a pleasing name.
The pale-faced lady's lily-white, perforce;
160   The swarthy one's a sweet brunette, of course;
The spindly lady has a slender grace;
The fat one has a most majestic pace;
The plain one, with her dress in disarray,
They classify as *beauté negligée*;
165   The hulking one's a goddess in their eyes,
The dwarf, a concentrate of Paradise;
The haughty lady has a noble mind;
The mean one's witty, and the dull one's kind;
The chatterbox has liveliness and verve,
170   The mute one has a virtuous reserve.
So lovers manage, in their passion's cause,
To love their ladies even for their flaws.

ALCESTE.
But I still say . . .

CÉLIMÈNE.   I think it would be nice
To stroll around the gallery once or twice.
What! You're not going, Sirs?

CLITANDRE AND ACASTE.   No, Madam, no. 175

ALCESTE.
You seem to be in terror lest they go.
Do what you will, Sirs; leave, or linger on,
But I shan't go till after you are gone.

ACASTE.
I'm free to linger, unless I should perceive
Madame is tired, and wishes me to leave. 180

CLITANDRE.
And as for me, I needn't go today
Until the hour of the King's *coucher*.

CÉLIMÈNE (*to Alceste*).
You're joking, surely?

ALCESTE.   Not in the least; we'll see
Whether you'd rather part with them, or me.

SCENE 6

[*Alceste, Célimène, Éliante, Acaste, Philinte, Clitandre,
Basque*]

BASQUE (*to Alceste*).
Sir, there's a fellow here who bids me state

That he must see you, and that it can't wait.
ALCESTE.
    Tell him that I have no such pressing affairs.
BASQUE.
    It's a long tailcoat that this fellow wears,
    With gold all over.
CÉLIMÈNE (to Alceste). You'd best go down and see.
    Or—have him enter.

SCENE 7

[Alceste, Célimène, Éliante, Acaste, Philinte, Clitandre, Guard]

ALCESTE (confronting the Guard). Well, what do you want
        with me?
    Come in, Sir.
GUARD.   I've a word, Sir, for your ear.
ALCESTE.
    Speak it aloud, Sir; I shall strive to hear.
GUARD.
    The Marshals have instructed me to say
    You must report to them without delay.
ALCESTE.
    Who? Me, Sir?
GUARD.   Yes, Sir; you.
ALCESTE.   But what do they want?
PHILINTE (to Alceste).
    To scotch your silly quarrel with Oronte.
CÉLIMÈNE (to Philinte).
    What quarrel?
PHILINTE.   Oronte and he have fallen out
    Over some verse he spoke his mind about;
    The Marshals wish to arbitrate the matter.
ALCESTE.
    Never shall I equivocate or flatter!
PHILINTE.
    You'd best obey their summons; come, let's go.
ALCESTE.
    How can they mend our quarrel, I'd like to know?
    Am I to make a cowardly retraction,
    And praise those jingles to his satisfaction?
    I'll not recant; I've judged that sonnet rightly.
    It's bad.
PHILINTE. But you might say so more politely . . .
ALCESTE.
    I'll not back down; his verses make me sick.
PHILINTE.
    If only you could be more politic!
    But come, let's go.
ALCESTE.   I'll go, but I won't unsay
    A single word.
PHILINTE.   Well, let's be on our way.
ALCESTE.
    Till I am ordered by my lord the King

To praise that poem, I shall say the thing
Is scandalous, by God, and that the poet
Ought to be hanged for having the nerve to show it.   25
(To Clitandre and Acaste, who are laughing.) By heaven,
    Sirs, I really didn't know
That I was being humorous.
CÉLIMÈNE.   Go, Sir, go;
    Settle your business.
ALCESTE.   I shall, and when I'm through,
    I shall return to settle things with you.

ACT 3

SCENE 1

[Clitandre, Acaste]

CLITANDRE.
    Dear Marquess, how contented you appear;
    All things delight you, nothing mars your cheer.
    Can you, in perfect honesty, declare
    That you've a right to be so debonair?
ACASTE.
    By Jove, when I survey myself, I find   5
    No cause whatever for distress of mind.
    I'm young and rich; I can in modesty
    Lay claim to an exalted pedigree;
    And owing to my name and my condition
    I shall not want for honors and position.   10
    Then as to courage, that most precious trait,
    I seem to have it, as was proved of late
    Upon the field of honor, where my bearing,
    They say, was very cool and rather daring.
    I've wit, of course; and taste in such perfection   15
    That I can judge without the least reflection,
    And at the theater, which is my delight,
    Can make or break a play on opening night,
    And lead the crowd in hisses or bravos,
    And generally be known as one who knows.   20
    I'm clever, handsome, gracefully polite;
    My waist is small, my teeth are strong and white.
    As for my dress, the world's astonished eyes
    Assure me that I bear away the prize.
    I find myself in favor everywhere,   25
    Honored by men, and worshiped by the fair;
    And since these things are so, it seems to me
    I'm justified in my complacency.
CLITANDRE.
    Well, if so many ladies hold you dear,
    Why do you press a hopeless courtship here?   30
ACASTE.
    Hopeless, you say? I'm not the sort of fool
    That likes his ladies difficult and cool.
    Men who are awkward, shy, and peasantish
    May pine for heartless beauties, if they wish,

35   Grovel before them, bear their cruelties,
       Woo them with tears and sighs and bended knees,
       And hope by dogged faithfulness to gain
       What their poor merits never could obtain.
       For men like me, however, it makes no sense
40   To love on trust, and foot the whole expense.
       Whatever any lady's merits be,
       I think, thank God, that I'm as choice as she;
       That if my heart is kind enough to burn
       For her, she owes me something in return;
45   And that in any proper love affair
       The partners must invest an equal share.
  CLITANDRE.
       You think, then, that our hostess favors you?
  ACASTE.
       I've reason to believe that that is true.
  CLITANDRE.
       How did you come to such a mad conclusion?
50   You're blind, dear fellow. This is sheer delusion.
  ACASTE.
       All right, then: I'm deluded and I'm blind.
  CLITANDRE.
       Whatever put the notion in your mind?
  ACASTE.
       Delusion.
  CLITANDRE. What persuades you that you're right?
  ACASTE.
       I'm blind.
  CLITANDRE. But have you any proofs to cite?
  ACASTE.
       I tell you I'm deluded.
55 CLITANDRE.   Have you, then,
       Received some secret pledge from Célimène?
  ACASTE.
       Oh, no: she scorns me.
  CLITANDRE.   Tell me the truth, I beg.
  ACASTE.
       She just can't bear me.
  CLITANDRE.   Ah, don't pull my leg.
       Tell me what hope she's given you, I pray.
  ACASTE.
60   I'm hopeless, and it's you who win the day.
       She hates me thoroughly, and I'm so vexed
       I mean to hang myself on Tuesday next.
  CLITANDRE.
       Dear Marquess, let us have an armistice
       And make a treaty. What do you say to this?
65   If ever one of us can plainly prove
       That Célimène encourages his love,
       The other must abandon hope, and yield,
       And leave him in possession of the field.
  ACASTE.
       Now there's a bargain that appeals to me;
70   With all my heart, dear Marquess, I agree.
       But hush.

SCENE 2

[Célimène, Acaste, Clitandre]

CÉLIMÈNE.   Still here?
CLITANDRE.   'Twas love that stayed our feet.
CÉLIMÈNE.
    I think I heard a carriage in the street.
    Whose is it? D'you know?

SCENE 3

[Célimène, Acaste, Clitandre, Basque]

BASQUE.   Arsinoé is here,
    Madame.
CÉLIMÈNE.   Arsinoé, you say? Oh, dear.
BASQUE.
    Éliante is entertaining her below.
CÉLIMÈNE.
    What brings the creature here, I'd like to know?
ACASTE.
    They say she's dreadfully prudish, but in fact   5
    I think her piety . . .
CÉLIMÈNE.   It's all an act.
    At heart she's worldly, and her poor success
    In snaring men explains her prudishness.
    It breaks her heart to see the beaux and gallants
    Engrossed by other women's charms and talents,   10
    And so she's always in a jealous rage
    Against the faulty standards of the age.
    She lets the world believe that she's a prude
    To justify her loveless solitude,
    And strives to put a brand of moral shame   15
    On all the graces that she cannot claim.
    But still she'd love a lover; and Alceste
    Appears to be the one she'd love the best.
    His visits here are poison to her pride;
    She seems to think I've lured him from her side;   20
    And everywhere, at court or in the town,
    The spiteful, envious woman runs me down.
    In short, she's just as stupid as can be,
    Vicious and arrogant in the last degree,
    And . . .   25

SCENE 4

[Arsinoé, Célimène, Clitandre, Acaste]

CÉLIMÈNE. Ah! What happy chance has brought you here?
    I've thought about you ever so much, my dear.
ARSINOÉ.
    I've come to tell you something you should know.
CÉLIMÈNE.
    How good of you to think of doing so!

Clitandre and Acaste go out, laughing.

SCENE 5

[*Arsinoé, Célimène*]

ARSINOÉ.
   It's just as well those gentlemen didn't tarry.
CÉLIMÈNE.
   Shall we sit down?
ARSINOÉ.   That won't be necessary.
   Madam, the flame of friendship ought to burn
   Brightest in matters of the most concern,
   And as there's nothing which concerns us more
   Than honor, I have hastened to your door
   To bring you, as your friend, some information
   About the status of your reputation.
   I visited, last night, some virtuous folk,
   And, quite by chance, it was of you they spoke;
   There was, I fear, no tendency to praise
   Your light behavior and your dashing ways.
   The quantity of gentlemen you see
   And your by now notorious coquetry
   Were both so vehemently criticized
   By everyone, that I was much surprised.
   Of course, I needn't tell you where I stood;
   I came to your defense as best I could,
   Assured them you were harmless, and declared
   Your soul was absolutely unimpaired.
   But there are some things, you must realize,
   One can't excuse, however hard one tries,
   And I was forced at last into conceding
   That your behavior, Madam, is misleading,
   That it makes a bad impression, giving rise
   To ugly gossip and obscene surmise,
   And that if you were more *overtly* good,
   You wouldn't be so much misunderstood.
   Not that I think you've been unchaste—no! no!
   The saints preserve me from a thought so low!
   But mere good conscience never did suffice:
   One must avoid the outward show of vice.
   Madam, you're too intelligent, I'm sure,
   To think my motives anything but pure
   In offering you this counsel—which I do
   Out of a zealous interest in you.
CÉLIMÈNE.
   Madam, I haven't taken you amiss;
   I'm very much obliged to you for this;
   And I'll at once discharge the obligation
   By telling you about *your* reputation.
   You've been so friendly as to let me know
   What certain people say of me, and so
   I mean to follow your benign example
   By offering you a somewhat similar sample.
   The other day, I went to an affair

And found some most distinguished people there
Discussing piety, both false and true.
The conversation soon came round to you.
Alas! Your prudery and bustling zeal
Appeared to have a very slight appeal.
Your affectation of a grave demeanor,
Your endless talk of virtue and of honor,
The aptitude of your suspicious mind
For finding sin where there is none to find,
Your towering self-esteem, that pitying face
With which you contemplate the human race,
Your sermonizings and your sharp aspersions
On people's pure and innocent diversions—
All these were mentioned, Madam, and, in fact,
Were roundly and concertedly attacked.
"What good," they said, "are all these outward shows,
When everything belies her pious pose?
She prays incessantly; but then, they say,
She beats her maids and cheats them of their pay;
She shows her zeal in every holy place,
But still she's vain enough to paint her face;
She holds that naked statues are immoral,
But with a naked *man* she'd have no quarrel."
Of course, I said to everybody there
That they were being viciously unfair;
But still they were disposed to criticize you,
And all agreed that someone should advise you
To leave the morals of the world alone,
And worry rather more about your own.
They felt that one's self-knowledge should be great
Before one thinks of setting others straight;
That one should learn the art of living well
Before one threatens other men with hell,
And that the Church is best equipped, no doubt,
To guide our souls and root our vices out.
Madam, you're too intelligent, I'm sure,
To think my motives anything but pure
In offering you this counsel—which I do
Out of a zealous interest in you.
ARSINOÉ.
   I dared not hope for gratitude, but I
   Did not expect so acid a reply;
   I judge, since you've been so extremely tart,
   That my good counsel pierced you to the heart.
CÉLIMÈNE.
   Far from it, Madam. Indeed, it seems to me
   We ought to trade advice more frequently.
   One's vision of oneself is so defective
   That it would be an excellent corrective.
   If you are willing, Madam, let's arrange
   Shortly to have another frank exchange
   In which we'll tell each other, *entre nous*,
   What you've heard tell of me, and I of you.
ARSINOÉ.
   Oh, people never censure you, my dear;

It's me they criticize. Or so I hear.

CÉLIMÈNE.
Madam, I think we either blame or praise
100   According to our taste and length of days.
There is a time of life for coquetry,
And there's a season, too, for prudery.
When all one's charms are gone, it is, I'm sure,
Good strategy to be devout and pure:
105   It makes one seem a little less forsaken.
Some day, perhaps, I'll take the road you've taken:
Time brings all things. But I have time aplenty,
And see no cause to be a prude at twenty.

ARSINOÉ.
You give your age in such a gloating tune
110   That one would think I was an ancient crone;
We're not so far apart, in sober truth,
That you can mock me with a boast of youth!
Madam, you baffle me. I wish I knew
What moves you to provoke me as you do.

CÉLIMÈNE.
115   For my part, Madam, I should like to know
Why you abuse me everywhere you go.
Is it my fault, dear lady, that your hand
Is not, alas, in very great demand?
If men admire me, if they pay me court
120   And daily make me offers of the sort
You'd dearly love to have them make to you,
How can I help it? What would you have me do?
If what you want is lovers, please feel free
To take as many as you can from me.

ARSINOÉ.
125   Oh, come. D'you think the world is losing sleep
Over the flock of lovers which you keep,
Or that we find it difficult to guess
What price you pay for their devotedness?
Surely you don't expect us to suppose
130   Mere merit could attract so many beaux?
It's not your virtue that they're dazzled by;
Nor is it virtuous love for which they sigh.
You're fooling no one, Madam; the world's not blind;
There's many a lady heaven has designed
135   To call men's noblest, tenderest feelings out,
Who has no lovers dogging her about;
From which it's plain that lovers nowadays
Must be acquired in bold and shameless ways,
And only pay one court for such reward
140   As modesty and virtue can't afford.
Then don't be quite so puffed up, if you please,
About your tawdry little victories;
Try, if you can, to be a shade less vain,
And treat the world with somewhat less disdain.
145   If one were envious of your amours,
One soon could have a following like yours;
Lovers are no great trouble to collect
If one prefers them to one's self-respect.

CÉLIMÈNE.
Collect them then, my dear; I'd love to see
You demonstrate that charming theory;   150
Who knows, you might . . .

ARSINOÉ.   Now, Madam, that will do;
It's time to end this trying interview.
My coach is late in coming to your door,
Or I'd have taken leave of you before.

CÉLIMÈNE.
Oh, please don't feel that you must rush away;   155
I'd be delighted, Madam, if you'd stay.
However, lest my conversation bore you,
Let me provide some better company for you;
This gentleman, who comes most apropos,
Will please you more than I could do, I know.   160

SCENE 6

[Alceste, Célimène, Arsinoé]

CÉLIMÈNE.
Alceste, I have a little note to write
Which simply must go out before tonight;
Please entertain Madame; I'm sure that she
Will overlook my incivility.

SCENE 7

[Alceste, Arsinoé]

ARSINOÉ.
Well, Sir, our hostess graciously contrives
For us to chat until my coach arrives;
And I shall be forever in her debt
For granting me this little tête-à-tête.
We women very rightly give our hearts   5
To men of noble character and parts,
And your especial merits, dear Alceste,
Have roused the deepest sympathy in my breast.
Oh, how I wish they had sufficient sense
At court, to recognize your excellence!   10
They wrong you greatly, Sir. How it must hurt you
Never to be rewarded for your virtue!

ALCESTE.
Why, Madam, what cause have I to feel aggrieved?
What great and brilliant thing have I achieved?
What service have I rendered to the King   15
That I should look to him for anything?

ARSINOÉ.
Not everyone who's honored by the State
Has done great services. A man must wait
Till time and fortune offer him the chance.
Your merit, Sir, is obvious at a glance,   20
And . . .

ALCESTE.   Ah, forget my merit; I am not neglected.
The court, I think, can hardly be expected

To mine men's souls for merit, and unearth
Our hidden virtues and our secret worth.

ARSINOÉ.

Some virtues, though are far too bright to hide;
Yours are acknowledged, Sir, on every side.
Indeed, I've heard you warmly praised of late
By persons of considerable weight.

ALCESTE.

This fawning age has praise for everyone,
And all distinctions, Madam, are undone.
All things have equal honor nowadays,
And no one should be gratified by praise.
To be admired, one only need exist,
And every lackey's on the honors list.

ARSINOÉ.

I only wish, Sir, that you had your eye
On some position at court, however high;
You'd only have to hint at such a notion
For me to set the proper wheels in motion;
I've certain friendships I'd be glad to use
To get you any office you might choose.

ALCESTE.

Madam, I fear that any such ambition
Is wholly foreign to my disposition.
The soul God gave me isn't of the sort
That prospers in the weather of a court.
It's all too obvious that I don't possess
The virtues necessary for success.
My one great talent is for speaking plain;
I've never learned to flatter or to feign;
And anyone so stupidly sincere
Had best not seek a courtier's career.
Outside the court, I know, one must dispense
With honors, privilege, and influence;
But still one gains the right, forgoing these,
Not to be tortured by the wish to please.
One needn't live in dread of snubs and slights,
Nor praise the verse that every idiot writes,
Nor humor silly Marquesses, nor bestow
Politic sighs on Madam So-and-So.

ARSINOÉ.

Forget the court, then; let the matter rest.
But I've another cause to be distressed
About your present situation, Sir.
It's to your love affair that I refer.
She whom you love, and who pretends to love you,
Is, I regret to say, unworthy of you.

ALCESTE.

Why, Madam? Can you seriously intend
To make so grave a charge against your friend?

ARSINOÉ.

Alas, I must. I've stood aside too long
And let that lady do you grievous wrong;
But now my debt to conscience shall be paid:
I tell you that your love has been betrayed.

ALCESTE.

I thank you, Madam; you're extremely kind.
Such words are soothing to a lover's mind.

ARSINOÉ.

Yes, though she *is* my friend, I say again
You're very much too good for Célimène.
She's wantonly misled you from the start.

ALCESTE.

You may be right; who knows another's heart?
But ask yourself if it's the part of charity
To shake my soul with doubts of her sincerity.

ARSINOÉ.

Well, if you'd rather be a dupe than doubt her,
That's your affair. I'll say no more about her.

ALCESTE.

Madam, you know that doubt and vague suspicion
Are painful to a man in my position;
It's most unkind to worry me this way
Unless you've some real proof of what you say.

ARSINOÉ.

Sir, say no more: all doubts shall be removed,
And all that I've been saying shall be proved.
You've only to escort me home, and there
We'll look into the heart of this affair.
I've ocular evidence which will persuade you
Beyond a doubt, that Célimène's betrayed you.
Then, if you're saddened by that revelation,
Perhaps I can provide some consolation.

ACT 4

SCENE 1

[Éliante, Philinte]

PHILINTE.

Madam, he acted like a stubborn child;
I thought they never would be reconciled;
In vain we reasoned, threatened, and appealed;
He stood his ground and simply would not yield.
The Marshals, I feel sure, have never heard
An argument so splendidly absurd.
"No, gentlemen," said he, "I'll not retract.
His verse is bad: extremely bad, in fact.
Surely it does the man no harm to know it.
Does it disgrace him, not to be a poet?
A gentleman may be respected still,
Whether he writes a sonnet well or ill.
That I dislike his verse should not offend him;
In all that touches honor, I commend him;
He's noble, brave, and virtuous—but I fear
He can't in truth be called a sonneteer.
I'll gladly praise his wardrobe; I'll endorse
His dancing, or the way he sits a horse;
But, gentlemen, I cannot praise his rhyme.

20 In fact, it ought to be a capital crime
    For anyone so sadly unendowed
    To write a sonnet, and read the thing aloud."
    At length he fell into a gentler mood
    And, striking a concessive attitude,
25 He paid Oronte the following courtesies.
    "Sir, I regret that I'm so hard to please,
    And I'm profoundly sorry that your lyric
    Failed to provoke me to a panegyric."
    After these curious words, the two embraced,
30 And then the hearing was adjourned—in haste.

ÉLIANTE.
    His conduct has been very singular lately;
    Still, I confess that I respect him greatly.
    The honesty in which he takes such pride
    Has—to my mind—its noble, heroic side.
35 In this false age, such candor seems outrageous;
    But I could wish that it were more contagious.

PHILINTE.
    What most intrigues me in our friend Alceste
    Is the grand passion that rages in his breast.
    The sullen humors he's compounded of
40 Should not, I think, dispose his heart to love;
    But since they do, it puzzles me still more
    That he should choose your cousin to adore.

ÉLIANTE.
    It does, indeed, belie the theory
    That love is born of gentle sympathy,
45 And that the tender passion must be based
    On sweet accords of temper and of taste.

PHILINTE.
    Does she return his love, do you suppose?

ÉLIANTE.
    Ah, that's a difficult question, Sir. Who knows?
    How can we judge the truth of her devotion?
50 Her heart's a stranger to its own emotion.
    Sometimes it thinks it loves, when no love's there;
    At other times it loves quite unaware.

PHILINTE.
    I rather think Alceste is in for more
    Distress and sorrow than he's bargained for;
55 Were he of my mind, Madam, his affection
    Would turn in quite a different direction,
    And we would see him more responsive to
    The kind regard which he receives from you.

ÉLIANTE.
    Sir, I believe in frankness, and I'm inclined,
60 In matters of the heart, to speak my mind.
    I don't oppose his love for her; indeed,
    I hope with all my heart that he'll succeed,
    And were it in my power, I'd rejoice
    In giving him the lady of his choice.
65 But if, as happens frequently enough
    In love affairs, he meets with a rebuff—
    If Célimène should grant some rival's suit—

    I'd gladly play the role of substitute;
    Nor would his tender speeches please me less
    Because they'd once been made without success.   70

PHILINTE.
    Well, Madam, as for me, I don't oppose
    Your hopes in this affair; and heaven knows
    That in my conversations with the man
    I plead your cause as often as I can.
    But if those two should marry, and so remove   75
    All chance that he will offer you his love,
    Then I'll declare my own, and hope to see
    Your gracious favor pass from him to me.
    In short, should you be cheated of Alceste,
    I'd be most happy to be second best.   80

ÉLIANTE.
    Philinte, you're teasing.

PHILINTE.   Ah, Madam, never fear;
    No words of mine were ever so sincere,
    And I shall live in fretful expectation
    Till I can make a fuller declaration.

SCENE 2

[Alceste, Éliante, Philinte]

ALCESTE.
    Avenge me, Madam! I must have satisfaction,
    Or this great wrong will drive me to distraction!

ÉLIANTE.
    Why, what's the matter? What's upset you so?

ALCESTE.
    Madam, I've had a mortal, mortal blow.
    If Chaos repossessed the universe,   5
    I swear I'd not be shaken any worse.
    I'm ruined. . . . I can say no more. . . . My soul . . .

ÉLIANTE.
    Do try, Sir, to regain your self-control.

ALCESTE.
    Just heaven! Why were so much beauty and grace
    Bestowed on one so vicious and so base?   10

ÉLIANTE.
    Once more, Sir, tell us . . .

ALCESTE.   My world has gone to wrack;
    I'm—I'm betrayed; she's stabbed me in the back.
    Yes, Célimène (who would have thought it of her?)
    Is false to me, and has another lover.

ÉLIANTE.
    Are you quite certain? Can you prove these things?   15

PHILINTE.
    Lovers are prey to wild imaginings
    And jealous fancies. No doubt there's some mistake. . . .

ALCESTE.
    Mind your own business, Sir, for heaven's sake.
    (To Éliante.) Madam, I have the proof that you demand
    Here in my pocket, penned by her own hand.   20

Yes, all the shameful evidence one could want
Lies in this letter written to Oronte—
Oronte! whom I felt sure she couldn't love,
And hardly bothered to be jealous of.

PHILINTE.
Still, in a letter, appearances may deceive;   5
This may not be so bad as you believe.

ALCESTE.
Once more I beg you, Sir, to let me be;
Tend to your own affairs; leave mine to me.

ÉLIANTE.
Compose yourself, this anguish that you feel . . .

ALCESTE.
Is something, Madam, you alone can heal.   10
My outraged heart, beside itself with grief,
Appeals to you for comfort and relief.
Avenge me on your cousin, whose unjust
And faithless nature has deceived my trust;
Avenge a crime your pure soul must detest.   15

ÉLIANTE.
But how, Sir?

ALCESTE.   Madam, this heart within my breast
Is yours; pray take it; redeem my heart from her,
And so avenge me on my torturer.
Let her be punished by the fond emotion,
The ardent love, the bottomless devotion,   20
The faithful worship which this heart of mine
Will offer up to yours as to a shrine.

ÉLIANTE.
You have my sympathy, Sir, in all you suffer;
Nor do I scorn the noble heart you offer;
But I suspect you'll soon be mollified,   25
And this desire for vengeance will subside.
When some beloved hand has done us wrong
We thirst for retribution—but not for long;
However dark the deed that she's committed,
A lovely culprit's very soon acquitted.   30
Nothing's so stormy as an injured lover,
And yet no storm so quickly passes over.

ALCESTE.
No, Madam, no—this is no lovers' spat;
I'll not forgive her; it's gone too far for that;
My mind's made up; I'll kill myself before   35
I waste my hopes upon her any more.
Ah, here she is. My wrath intensifies.
I shall confront her with her tricks and lies,
And crush her utterly, and bring you then
A heart no longer slave to Célimène.   40

SCENE 3

[Célimène, Alceste]

ALCESTE (aside).
Sweet heaven, help me to control my passion.

CÉLIMÈNE (aside).
Oh, Lord.
(To Alceste.) Why stand there staring in that fashion?
And what d'you mean by those dramatic sighs,
And that malignant glitter in your eyes?

ALCESTE.
I mean that sins which cause the blood to freeze   5
Look innocent beside your treacheries;
That nothing Hell's or Heaven's wrath could do
Ever produced so bad a thing as you.

CÉLIMÈNE.
Your compliments were always sweet and pretty.

ALCESTE.
Madam, it's not the moment to be witty.   10
No, blush and hang your head; you've ample reason,
Since I've the fullest evidence of your treason.
Ah, this is what my sad heart prophesied;
Now all my anxious fears are verified;
My dark suspicion and my gloomy doubt   15
Divined the truth, and now the truth is out.
For all your trickery, I was not deceived;
It was my bitter stars that I believed.
But don't imagine that you'll go scot-free;
You shan't misuse me with impunity.   20
I know that love's irrational and blind;
I know the heart's not subject to the mind,
And can't be reasoned into beating faster;
I know each soul is free to choose its master;
Therefore had you but spoken from the heart,   25
Rejecting my attention from the start,
I'd have no grievance, or at any rate
I could complain of nothing but my fate.
Ah, but so falsely to encourage me—
That was a treason and a treachery   30
For which you cannot suffer too severely,
And you shall pay for that behavior dearly.
Yes, now I have no pity, not a shred;
My temper's out of hand; I've lost my head.
Shocked by the knowledge of your double-dealings,   35
My reason can't restrain my savage feelings;
A righteous wrath deprives me of my senses,
And I won't answer for the consequences.

CÉLIMÈNE.
What does this outburst mean? Will you please explain?
Have you, by any chance, gone quite insane?   40

ALCESTE.
Yes, yes, I went insane the day I fell
A victim to your black and fatal spell,
Thinking to meet with some sincerity
Among the treacherous charms that beckoned me.

CÉLIMÈNE.
Pooh. Of what treachery can you complain?   45

ALCESTE.
How sly you are, how cleverly you feign!
But you'll not victimize me any more.

Look: here's a document you've seen before.
This evidence, which I acquired today,
50 Leaves you, I think, without a thing to say.

CÉLIMÈNE.
Is this what sent you into such a fit?

ALCESTE.
You should be blushing at the sight of it.

CÉLIMÈNE.
Ought I to blush? I truly don't see why.

ALCESTE.
Ah, now you're being bold as well as sly;
55 Since there's no signature, perhaps you'll claim . . .

CÉLIMÈNE.
I wrote it, whether or not it bears my name.

ALCESTE.
And you can view with equanimity
This proof of your disloyalty to me!

CÉLIMÈNE.
Oh, don't be so outrageous and extreme.

ALCESTE.
60 You take this matter lightly, it would seem.
Was it no wrong to me, no shame to you,
That you should send Oronte this billet-doux?

CÉLIMÈNE.
Oronte! Who said it was for him?

ALCESTE.   Why, those
Who brought me this example of your prose.
65 But what's the difference? If you wrote the letter
To someone else, it pleases me no better.
My grievance and your guilt remain the same.

CÉLIMÈNE.
But need you rage, and need I blush for shame,
If this was written to a *woman* friend?

ALCESTE.
70 Ah! Most ingenious. I'm impressed no end;
And after that incredible evasion
Your guilt is clear. I need no more persuasion.
How dare you try so clumsy a deception?
D'you think I'm wholly wanting in perception?
75 Come, come, let's see how brazenly you'll try
To bolster up so palpable a lie:
Kindly construe this ardent closing section
As nothing more than sisterly affection!
Here, let me read it. Tell me, if you dare to,
That this is for a woman . . .

CÉLIMÈNE.   I don't care to.
80 What right have you to badger and berate me,
And so highhandedly interrogate me?

ALCESTE.
Now, don't be angry; all I ask of you
Is that you justify a phrase or two . . .

CÉLIMÈNE.
85 No, I shall not. I utterly refuse,
And you may take those phrases as you choose.

ALCESTE.
Just show me how this letter could be meant
For a woman's eyes, and I shall be content.

CÉLIMÈNE.
No, no, it's for Oronte; you're perfectly right.
90 I welcome his attentions with delight,
I prize his character and his intellect,
And everything is just as you suspect.
Come, do your worst now; give your rage free rein;
But kindly cease to bicker and complain.

ALCESTE (aside).
95 Good God! Could anything be more inhuman?
Was ever a heart so mangled by a woman?
When I complain of how she has betrayed me,
She bridles, and commences to upbraid me!
She tries my tortured patience to the limit;
100 She won't deny her guilt; she glories in it!
And yet my heart's too faint and cowardly
To break these chains of passion, and be free,
To scorn her as it should, and rise above
This unrewarded, mad, and bitter love.
105 (To Célimène.) Ah, traitress, in how confident a fashion
You take advantage of my helpless passion,
And use my weakness for your faithless charms
To make me once again throw down my arms!
But do at least deny this black transgression;
110 Take back that mocking and perverse confession;
Defend this letter and your innocence,
And I, poor fool, will aid in your defense.
Pretend, pretend, that you are just and true,
And I shall make myself believe in you.

CÉLIMÈNE.
115 Oh, stop it. Don't be such a jealous dunce,
Or I shall leave off loving you at once.
Just why should I *pretend?* What could impel me
To stoop so low as that? And kindly tell me
Why, if I loved another, I shouldn't merely
120 Inform you of it, simply and sincerely!
I've told you where you stand, and that admission
Should altogether clear me of suspicion;
After so generous a guarantee,
What right have you to harbor doubts of me?
125 Since women are (from natural reticence)
Reluctant to declare their sentiments,
And since the honor of our sex requires
That we conceal our amorous desires,
Ought any man for whom such laws are broken
130 To question what the oracle has spoken?
Should he not rather feel an obligation
To trust that most obliging declaration?
Enough, now. Your suspicions quite disgust me;
Why should I love a man who doesn't trust me?
135 I cannot understand why I continue,
Fool that I am, to take an interest in you.

I ought to choose a man less prone to doubt,
And give you something to be vexed about.

ALCESTE.
40   Ah, what a poor enchanted fool I am;
       These gentle words, no doubt, were all a sham,
       But destiny requires me to entrust
       My happiness to you, and so I must.
       I'll love you to the bitter end, and see
       How false and treacherous you dare to be.

CÉLIMÈNE.
45   No, you don't really love me as you ought.

ALCESTE.
       I love you more than can be said or thought;
       Indeed, I wish you were in such distress
       That I might show my deep devotedness.
       Yes, I could wish that you were wretchedly poor,
150   Unloved, uncherished, utterly obscure;
       That fate had set you down upon the earth
       Without possessions, rank, or gentle birth;
       Then, by the offer of my heart, I might
       Repair the great injustice of your plight;
155   I'd raise you from the dust, and proudly prove
       The purity and vastness of my love.

CÉLIMÈNE.
       This is a strange benevolence indeed!
       God grant that I may never be in need. . . .
       Ah, here's Monsier Dubois, in quaint disguise.

SCENE 4

[Célimène, Alceste, Dubois]

ALCESTE.
       Well, why this costume? Why those frightened eyes?
       What ails you?

DUBOIS.   Well, Sir, things are most mysterious.

ALCESTE.
       What do you mean?

DUBOIS.   I fear they're very serious.

ALCESTE.
       What?

DUBOIS. Shall I speak more loudly?

ALCESTE.   Yes; speak out.

DUBOIS.
       Isn't there someone here, Sir?

5   ALCESTE.   Speak, you lout!
       Stop wasting time.

DUBOIS.   Sir, we must slip away.

ALCESTE.
       How's that?

DUBOIS.   We must decamp without delay.

ALCESTE.
       Explain yourself.

DUBOIS.   I tell you we must fly.

ALCESTE.
       What for?

DUBOIS.   We mustn't pause to say good-by.

ALCESTE.
       Now what d'you mean by all of this, you clown?   10

DUBOIS.
       I mean, Sir, that we've got to leave this town.

ALCESTE.
       I'll tear you limb from limb and joint from joint
       If you don't come more quickly to the point.

DUBOIS.
       Well, Sir, today a man in a black suit,
       Who wore a black and ugly scowl to boot,   15
       Left us a document scrawled in such a hand
       As even Satan couldn't understand.
       It bears upon your lawsuit, I don't doubt;
       But all hell's devils couldn't make it out.

ALCESTE.
       Well, well, go on. What then? I fail to see   20
       How this event obliges us to flee.

DUBOIS.
       Well, Sir, an hour later, hardly more,
       A gentleman who's often called before
       Came looking for you in an anxious way.
       Not finding you, he asked me to convey   25
       (Knowing I could be trusted with the same)
       The following message. . . . Now, what *was* his name?

ALCESTE.
       Forget his name, you idiot. What did he say?

DUBOIS.
       Well, it was one of your friends, Sir, anyway.
       He warned you to begone, and he suggested   30
       That if you stay, you may well he arrested.

ALCESTE.
       What? Nothing more specific? Think, man, think!

DUBOIS.
       No, Sir. He had me bring him pen and ink,
       And dashed you off a letter which, I'm sure,
       Will render things distinctly less obscure.   35

ALCESTE.
       Well—let me have it!

CÉLIMÈNE.   What *is* this all about?

ALCESTE.
       God knows; but I have hopes of finding out.
       How long am I to wait, you blitherer?

DUBOIS (*after a protracted search for the letter*).
       I must have left it on your table, Sir.

ALCESTE.
       I ought to . . .

CÉLIMÈNE.   No, no, keep your self-control;   40
       Go find out what's behind this rigmarole.

ALCESTE.
       It seems that fate, no matter what I do,

Has sworn that I may not converse with you;
But, Madam, pray permit your faithful lover
45 To try once more before the day is over.

ACT 5

SCENE 1

[Alceste, Philinte]

ALCESTE.
    No, it's too much. My mind's made up, I tell you.
PHILINTE.
    Why should this blow, however hard, compel you . . .
ALCESTE.
    No, no, don't waste your breath in argument;
    Nothing you say will alter my intent;
5   This age is vile, and I've made up my mind
    To have no further commerce with mankind.
    Did not truth, honor, decency, and the laws
    Oppose my enemy and approve my cause?
    My claims were justified in all men's sight;
10 I put my trust in equity and right;
    Yet, to my horror and the world's disgrace,
    Justice is mocked, and I have lost my case!
    A scoundrel whose dishonesty is notorious
    Emerges from another lie victorious!
15 Honor and right condone his brazen fraud,
    While rectitude and decency applaud!
    Before his smirking face, the truth stands charmed,
    And virtue conquered, and the law disarmed!
    His crime is sanctioned by a court decree!
20 And not content with what he's done to me,
    The dog now seeks to ruin me by stating
    That I composed a book now circulating,
    A book so wholly criminal and vicious
    That even to speak its title is seditious!
25 Meanwhile Oronte, my rival, lends his credit
    To the same libelous tale, and helps to spread it!
    Oronte! a man of honor and of rank,
    With whom I've been entirely fair and frank;
    Who sought me out and forced me, willy-nilly,
30 To judge some verse I found extremely silly;
    And who, because I properly refused
    To flatter him, or see the truth abused,
    Abets my enemy in a rotten slander!
    There's the reward of honesty and candor!
35 The man will hate me to the end of time
    For failing to commend his wretched rhyme!
    And not this man alone, but all humanity
    Do what they do from interest and vanity;
    They prate of honor, truth, and righteousness,
40 But lie, betray, and swindle nonetheless.
    Come then: man's villainy is too much to bear;

Let's leave this jungle and this jackal's lair.
Yes! treacherous and savage race of men,
You shall not look upon my face again.
PHILINTE.
    Oh, don't rush into exile prematurely;   45
    Things aren't as dreadful as you make them, surely.
    It's rather obvious, since you're still at large,
    That people don't believe your enemy's charge.
    Indeed, his tale's so patently untrue
    That it may do more harm to him than you.   50
ALCESTE.
    Nothing could do that scoundrel any harm:
    His frank corruption is his greatest charm,
    And, far from hurting him, a further shame
    Would only serve to magnify his name.
PHILINTE.
    In any case, his bald prevarication   55
    Has done no injury to your reputation,
    And you may feel secure in that regard.
    As for your lawsuit, it should not be hard
    To have the case reopened, and contest
    This judgment . . .
ALCESTE.   No, no, let the verdict rest.   60
    Whatever cruel penalty it may bring,
    I wouldn't have it changed for anything.
    It shows the times' injustice with such clarity
    That I shall pass it down to our posterity
    As a great proof and signal demonstration   65
    Of the black wickedness of this generation.
    It may cost twenty thousand francs; but I
    Shall pay their twenty thousand, and gain thereby
    The right to storm and rage at human evil,
    And send the race of mankind to the devil.   70
PHILINTE.
    Listen to me . . .
ALCESTE.   Why? What can you possibly say?
    Don't argue, Sir; your labor's thrown away.
    Do you propose to offer lame excuses
    For men's behavior and the times' abuses?
PHILINTE.
    No, all you say I'll readily concede.   75
    This is a low, conniving age indeed;
    Nothing but trickery prospers nowadays,
    And people ought to mend their shabby ways.
    Yes, man's a beastly creature; but must we then
    Abandon the society of men?   80
    Here in the world, each human frailty
    Provides occasion for philosophy,
    And that is virtue's noblest exercise;
    If honesty shone forth from all men's eyes,
    If every heart were frank and kind and just,   85
    What could our virtues do but gather dust
    (Since their employment is to help us bear
    The villainies of men without despair)?
    A heart well-armed with virtue can endure . . .

ALCESTE.

Sir, you're a matchless reasoner, to be sure;
Your words are fine and full of cogency;
But don't waste time and eloquence on me.
My reason bids me go, for my own good.
My tongue won't lie and flatter as it should;
God knows what frankness it might next commit,
And what I'd suffer on account of it.
Pray let me wait for Célimène's return
In peace and quiet. I shall shortly learn,
By her response to what I have in view,
Whether her love for me is feigned or true.

PHILINTE.

Till then, let's visit Éliante upstairs.

ALCESTE.

No, I am too weighed down with somber cares.
Go to her, do; and leave me with my gloom
Here in the darkened corner of this room.

PHILINTE.

Why, that's no sort of company, my friend;
I'll see if Éliante will not descend.

SCENE 2

[Célimène, Oronte, Alceste]

ORONTE.

Yes, Madam, if you wish me to remain
Your true and ardent lover, you must deign
To give me some more positive assurance.
All this suspense is quite beyond endurance.
If your heart shares the sweet desires of mine,
Show me as much by some convincing sign;
And here's the sign I urgently suggest:
That you no longer tolerate Alceste,
But sacrifice him to my love, and sever
All your relations with the man forever.

CÉLIMÈNE.

Why do you suddenly dislike him so?
You praised him to the skies not long ago.

ORONTE.

Madam, that's not the point. I'm here to find
Which way your tender feelings are inclined.
Choose, if you please, between Alceste and me,
And I shall stay or go accordingly.

ALCESTE (emerging from the corner).

Yes, Madam, choose; this gentleman's demand
Is wholly just, and I support his stand.
I too am true and ardent; I too am here
To ask you that you make your feelings clear.
No more delays, now; no equivocation;
The time has come to make your declaration.

ORONTE.

Sir, I've no wish in any way to be
An obstacle to your felicity.

ALCESTE.

Sir, I've no wish to share her heart with you;
That may sound jealous, but at least it's true.

ORONTE.

If, weighing us, she leans in your direction . . .

ALCESTE.

If she regards you with the least affection . . .

ORONTE.

I swear I'll yield her to you there and then.

ALCESTE.

I swear I'll never see her face again.

ORONTE.

Now, Madam, tell us what we've come to hear.

ALCESTE.

Madam, speak openly and have no fear.

ORONTE.

Just say which one is to remain your lover.

ALCESTE.

Just name one name, and it will all be over.

ORONTE.

What! Is it possible that you're undecided?

ALCESTE.

What! Can your feelings possibly be divided?

CÉLIMÈNE.

Enough: this inquisition's gone too far:
How utterly unreasonable you are!
Not that I couldn't make the choice with ease;
My heart has no conflicting sympathies;
I know full well which one of you I favor,
And you'd not see me hesitate or waver.
But how can you expect me to reveal
So cruelly and bluntly what I feel?
I think it altogether too unpleasant
To choose between two men when both are present;
One's heart has means more subtle and more kind
Of letting its affections be divined,
Nor need one be uncharitably plain
To let a lover know he loves in vain.

ORONTE.

No, no, speak plainly; I for one can stand it.
I beg you to be frank.

ALCESTE.   And I demand it.
The simple truth is what I wish to know,
And there's no need for softening the blow.
You've made an art of pleasing everyone,
But now your days of coquetry are done.
You have no choice now, Madam, but to choose,
For I'll know what to think if you refuse;
I'll take your silence for a clear admission
That I'm entitled to my worst suspicion.

ORONTE.

I thank you for this ultimatum, Sir,
And I may say I heartily concur.

CÉLIMÈNE.

Really, this foolishness is very wearing.

Must you be so unjust and overbearing?
65 Haven't I told you why I must demur?
Ah, here's Éliante; I'll put the case to her.

SCENE 3

[*Éliante, Philinte, Célimène, Oronte, Alceste*]

CÉLIMÈNE.
Cousin, I'm being persecuted here
By these two persons, who, it would appear,
Will not be satisfied till I confess
Which one I love the more, and which the less,
5 And tell the latter to his face that he
Is henceforth banished from my company.
Tell me, has ever such a thing been done?
ÉLIANTE.
You'd best not turn to me; I'm not the one
To back you in a matter of this kind.
10 I'm all for those who frankly speak their mind.
ORONTE.
Madam, you'll search in vain for a defender.
ALCESTE.
You're beaten, Madam, and may as well surrender.
ORONTE.
Speak, speak, you must; and end this awful strain.
ALCESTE.
Or don't, and your position will be plain.
ORONTE.
15 A single word will close this painful scene.
ALCESTE.
But if you're silent, I'll know what you mean.

SCENE 4

[*Arsinoé, Célimène, Éliante, Alceste, Philinte, Acaste,
Clitandre, Oronte*]

ACASTE (*to Célimène*).
Madam, with all due deference, we two
Have come to pick a little bone with you.
CLITANDRE (*to Oronte and Alceste*).
I'm glad you're present, Sirs, as you'll soon learn,
Our business here is also your concern.
ARSINOÉ (*to Célimène*).
5 Madam, I visit you so soon again
Only because of these two gentlemen,
Who came to me indignant and aggrieved
About a crime too base to be believed.
Knowing your virtue, having such confidence in it,
10 I couldn't think you guilty for a minute,
In spite of all their telling evidence;
And, rising above our little difference,
I've hastened here in friendship's name to see
You clear yourself of this great calumny.

ACASTE.
Yes, Madam, let us see with what composure   15
You'll manage to respond to this disclosure.
You lately sent Clitandre this tender note.
CLITANDRE.
And this one, for Acaste, you also wrote.
ACASTE (*to Oronte and Alceste*).
You'll recognize this writing, Sirs, I think;
The lady is so free with pen and ink   20
That you must know it all too well, I fear.
But listen: this is something you should hear.

"How absurd you are to condemn my light-heart-
edness in society, and to accuse me of being happiest in the company of others. Nothing could be   25
more unjust; and if you do not come to me instantly
and beg pardon for saying such a thing, I shall
never forgive you as long as I live. Our big bumbling friend the Viscount . . ."

What a shame that he's not here.   30

"Our big bumbling friend the Viscount, whose name
stands first in your complaint, is hardly a man to my
taste; and ever since the day I watched him spend
three-quarters of an hour spitting into a well, so as
to make circles in the water, I have been unable to   35
think highly of him. As for the little Marquess . . ."

In all modesty, gentlemen, that is I.

"As for the little Marquess, who sat squeezing my
hand for such a long while yesterday, I find him in
all respects the most trifling creature alive; and the   40
only things of value about him are his cape and his
sword. As for the man with the green ribbons . . ."

(*To Alceste.*) It's your turn now, Sir.

"As for the man with the green ribbons, he amuses
me now and then with his bluntness and his bear-   45
ish ill-humor; but there are many times indeed
when I think him the greatest bore in the world.
And as for the sonneteer . . ."

(*To Oronte.*) Here's your helping.

"And as for the sonneteer, who has taken it into   50
his head to be witty, and insists on being an author
in the teeth of opinion, I simply cannot be bothered to listen to him, and his prose wearies me
quite as much as his poetry. Be assured that I am
not always so well-entertained as you suppose; that   55
I long for your company more than I dare to say, at
all these entertainments to which people drag me;
and that the presence of those one loves is the true
and perfect seasoning to all one's pleasures."

CLITANDRE.
And now for me.   60

"Clitandre, whom you mention, and who so pesters
me with his saccharine speeches, is the last man on

earth for whom I could feel any affection. He is
quite mad to suppose that I love him, and so are
you, to doubt that you are loved. Do come to your
senses; exchange your suppositions for his; and
visit me as often as possible, to help me bear the
annoyance of his unwelcome attentions."

It's sweet character that these letters show,
And what to call it, Madam, you well know.
Enough. We're off to make the world acquainted
With this sublime self-portrait that you've painted.

ACASTE.
Madam I'll make no farewell oration;
No, you're not worthy of my indignation.
Far choicer hearts than yours, as you'll discover,
Would like this little Marquess for a lover.

SCENE 5

[*Célimène, Éliante, Arsinoé, Alceste, Oronte, Philinte*]

ORONTE.
So! After all those loving letters you wrote,
You turn on me like this and cut my throat!
And your dissembling faithless heart, I find,
Has pledged itself by turns to all mankind!
How blind I've been! But now I clearly see;
I thank you, Madam, for enlightening me.
My heart is mine once more, and I'm content;
The loss of it shall be your punishment.
(*To Alceste.*) Sir, she is yours; I'll seek no more to stand
Between your wishes and this lady's hand.

SCENE 6

[*Célimène, Éliante, Arsinoé, Alceste, Philinte*]

ARSINOÉ (*to Célimène*).
Madam I'm forced to speak. I'm far too stirred
To keep my counsel after what I've heard.
I'm shocked and staggered by your want of morals.
It's not my way to mix in others' quarrels;
But really, when this fine and noble spirit,
This man of honor and surpassing merit,
Laid down the offering of his heart before you,
How *could* you . . .

ALCESTE.   Madam, permit me, I implore you,
To represent myself in this debate.
Don't bother, please, to be my advocate.
My heart, in any case, could not afford
To give your services their due reward;
And if I chose, for consolation's sake,
Some other lady, 'twould not be you I'd take.

ARSINOÉ.
What makes you think you could, Sir? And how dare you
Imply that I've been trying to ensnare you?

If you can for a moment entertain
Such flattering fancies, you're extremely vain.
I'm not so interested as you suppose
In Célimène's discarded gigolos.
Get rid of that absurd illusion, do.
Women like me are not for such as you.
Stay with this creature, to whom you're so attached;
I've never seen two people better matched.

SCENE 7

[*Célimène, Éliante, Alceste, Philinte*]

ALCESTE (*to Célimène*).
Well, I've been still throughout this exposé,
Till everyone but me has said his say.
Come, have I shown sufficient self-restraint?
And may I now . . .

CÉLIMÈNE.   Yes, make your just complaint.
Reproach me freely, call me what you will;
You've every right to say I've used you ill.
I've wronged you, I confess it; and in my shame
I'll make no effort to escape the blame.
The anger of those others I could despise;
My guilt toward you I sadly recognize.
Your wrath is wholly justified, I fear;
I know how culpable I must appear,
I know all things bespeak my treachery,
And that, in short, you've grounds for hating me.
Do so; I give you leave.

ALCESTE.   Ah, traitress—how,
How should I cease to love you, even now?
Though mind and will were passionately bent
On hating you, my heart would not consent.
(*To Éliante and Philinte.*) Be witness to my madness, both
    of you;
See what infatuation drives one to;
But wait; my folly's only just begun,
And I shall prove to you before I'm done
How strange the human heart is, and how far
From rational we sorry creatures are.
(*To Célimène.*) Woman, I'm willing to forget your shame,
And clothe your treacheries in a sweeter name;
I'll call them youthful errors, instead of crimes,
And lay the blame on these corrupting times.
My one condition is that you agree
To share my chosen fate, and fly with me
To that wild, trackless, solitary place
In which I shall forget the human race.
Only by such a course can you atone
For those atrocious letters; by that alone
Can you remove my present horror of you,
And make it possible for me to love you.

CÉLIMÈNE.
What! *I* renounce the world at my young age,

And die of boredom in some hermitage?

ALCESTE.

    Ah, if you really loved me as you ought,
40   You wouldn't give the world a moment's thought;
    Must you have me, and all the world beside?

CÉLIMÈNE.

    Alas, at twenty one is terrified
    Of solitude. I fear I lack the force
    And depth of soul to take so stern a course.
45   But if my hand in marriage will content you,
    Why, there's a plan which I might well consent to,
    And . . .

ALCESTE.   No, I detest you now. I could excuse
    Everything else, but since you thus refuse
    To love me wholly as a wife should do,
50   And see the world in me, as I in you,
    Go! I reject your hand and disenthrall
    My heart from your enchantments, once for all.

SCENE 8

[*Éliante, Alceste, Philinte*]

ALCESTE (*to Éliante*).

    Madam, your virtuous beauty has no peer;
    Of all this world you only are sincere;

    I've long esteemed you highly, as you know;
    Permit me ever to esteem you so,
    And if I do not now request your hand,   5
    Forgive me, Madam, and try to understand.
    I feel unworthy of it; I sense that fate
    Does not intend me for the married state,
    That I should do you wrong by offering you
    My shattered heart's unhappy residue,   10
    And that in short . . .

ÉLIANTE.   Your argument's well taken:
    Nor need you fear that I shall feel forsaken.
    Were I to offer him this hand of mine,
    Your friend Philinte, I think, would not decline.

PHILINTE.

    Ah, Madam, that's my heart's most cherished goal,   15
    For which I'd gladly give my life and soul.

ALCESTE (*to Éliante and Philinte*).

    May you be true to all you now profess,
    And so deserve unending happiness.
    Meanwhile betrayed and wronged in everything,
    I'll flee this bitter world where vice is king,   20
    And seek some spot unpeopled and apart
    Where I'll be free to have an honest heart.

PHILINTE.

    Come, Madam, let's do everything we can
    To change the mind of this unhappy man.

TOPICS FOR CRITICAL THINKING AND WRITING

📖 THE PLAY ON THE PAGE

1. Does Alceste want to win or lose his lawsuit? Why?
2. Alceste bases his claims on reason. Do you think his own tone is always reasonable? Is his love of Célimène reasonable?
3. Jean-Jacques Rousseau said (in 1758) that Alceste is a man "who detests the morals of his age . . . who precisely because he loves mankind, despises in them the wrong they inflict upon one another." In somewhat the same vein, Jean-Louis Barrault, who often performed the role of Alceste, said that Alceste "loved people too well. That was why he couldn't stand them as they were." How much evidence do you find of this love?
4. Evaluate François Mauriac's comment:
   > In a world where a decent man . . . has so many reasons if not for protest, at least for examining his own conscience, Alceste only attacks the most harmless practices, those "lies" which do not take anyone in but which are necessary if social life is to go on at all. . . . In a world where injustice is rife, where crime is everywhere, he is up in arms against trivialities. He feels no horror for what is really horrible—beginning with himself. All his attacks are directed to things outside himself; he only compares himself with other people in order to demonstrate his own superiority.

5. Like King Lear, Alceste is greatly distressed at the discrepancy between reality and appearance, between what is said and what is believed or felt. But why—at least to some degree—does Alceste's distress strike you as funny?
6. Alceste scarcely appears in the third act. Is there any decline of interest? If not, why not? Is it reasonable to argue that Molière has not lost sight of the issues, that (for example) Acaste in 3.1 gives us something of Alceste and that Arsinoé in 3.5 gives us a sample of the outspokenness Alceste desires? Do you find Arsinoé's sincerity engaging?
7. What is the difference between Éliante's view of Alceste and Philinte's view? What do you think are the strengths and weaknesses of Philinte's speech on "philosophy" and "virtue" in 5.1.81–89?
8. Philinte's marriage to Éliante is in accord with the usual ending of comedy, but what is the dramatic relevance of Molière's emphasis on the unromantic aspects of the marriage?
9. If we grant that Alceste's sincerity is at least in part rooted in self-love, does it follow that an audience sees no validity in his indictment of society?

🎭 THE PLAY ON THE STAGE

10. Molière's play is set in Paris, in the time of its first audience. Clearly it is concerned with the values of the people who are at the social and political center. Should (or can) we update it to our day and to some other place, for instance to Washington, D.C., or perhaps to New York or Dallas or Los Angeles? Explain.

11. In our comment that follows on the Play in Performance we mention that a contemporary engraving shows little difference in the costumes of Alceste and Philinte. In today's productions, however, Alceste is almost always costumed austerely, in contrast to the other characters, who are costumed elaborately. How would you costume the play? Why?

12. Arsinoe is usually cast as an older woman, perhaps because of Célimène's comment about her grotesque make-up (3.5.66). But she has also been played as young. Your choice? Why?

13. Choosing from among well-known actors, or perhaps college actors who are known on the campus for their performances, whom might you cast as Oronte? Why?

14. Assume that you are the set designer for a theater-in-the-round production of *The Misanthrope*. Provide a sketch of your design, with explanations for its various features.

15. Would you suggest a staging with one or two intermissions? Why? At which point(s) in the script? Why?

16. If you were directing a production, what gestures and movements would you prescribe for the first hundred and one lines of the play?

17. In the first thirty-four lines of 1.2, what gestures and movements would you use for Oronte and Alceste?

18. As a director, provide full blocking for 2.5.

19. In 3.4 Célimène and Arsiné duel verbally. Is the scene offensive—a male author winking at his audience, assuring them that women engage in cutthroat competition—or is the scene amusing? If you think it is amusing, what gestures would you use in a production?

20. Offer a reading or memorization of 5.8, using three actors. Would there be any physical contact? Why, or why not?

21. The final couplet, spoken by Philinte, is sometimes omitted in performances. Why might a director omit it? Why might a director retain it?

THE PLAY IN PERFORMANCE

The Misanthrope had its premiére in 1666 in front of an aristocratic audience in a theater with a proscenium arch and a drop curtain. A tradition, first reported some forty years later, says that the play was not successful, but theatrical records of the time indicate that it had a respectable (though not an outstanding) run. In the succeeding decades it has gained in popularity, and for at least a century *The Misanthrope* has been among the most widely produced premodern plays in the world.

In the year that *The Misanthrope* was first performed, Molière published another of his plays, *L'Amour medecin* (Love's the Best Doctor), with a preface in which he wrote,

> It is not necessary to caution you that much depends on the acting: Everybody knows that plays are made only to be performed, and I do not advise anyone to read this one unless he has the eyes to discover in the printed word all the business of the stage.

Obviously readers who had seen the play on the stage could have the pleasure of recalling the stage business as they read and reread the play. Even if they had not already seen this play but had seen other plays, they would have been able to imagine some of the business because certain kinds of things are repeated from play to play. Molière had learned much from a troupe of *commedia dell'arte* players, an Italian company that shared the theater where his company regularly performed. The *commedia dell'arte* ("comedy of the profession") specialized in improvising on plot outlines that used stock characters, so there would be fairly standard bits of business called *lazi* (perhaps from *l'azione* = action; singular: *lazzo*). Take, as an obvious example of a *lazzo* in *The Misanthrope*, the business in 4.4, when Dubois frantically searches his pockets for a letter that, it turns out, he has forgotten to bring. One can imagine the search from pocket to pocket, and then perhaps a search of more improbable parts of his clothing. Molière did not provide stage directions, but a reader could deduce the comic search from a few lines of dialogue. Alceste says to Dubois, "Well—let me have it!"—and presumably Dubois begins the comic search—and a few seconds later says, "How long am I to wait, you blitherer?" Ultimately Dubois confesses, "I must have left it on your table, Sir," at which point Alceste presumably engages in some stage business of his own, perhaps what comedians call a slow burn.

The evidence indicates that in its own day—the late seventeenth century—*The Misanthrope* was regarded as a comedy, which is to say that Alceste was played as a laughable figure, a grouch whose crazy idealism has led him to scorn not simply most members of his society, but much of the pleasure and business of living; and at the same time this eccentric is ridiculously in love with a flirt. In such an interpretation, Philinte is the voice of reason. But in the late eighteenth century critical attention shifted from a satirical presentation of Alceste—a warped idealist in love—to a sympathetic presentation of the suffering man. Yes (the argument went), he is too easily angered, yes, he is extreme in his demands, yes, his love for Célimène is odd, but see how much he suffers. The nineteenth century continued the late eighteenth-century view, and pushed it further: Alceste is not a comic eccentric but a man who, seeing the sinfulness of the world, is (quite naturally) driven into a rage. Philinte, on the other hand, far from being a voice of reason, is a shallow, self-satisfied egoist.

One of the most important productions of the second half of the twentieth century, Pierre Dux's 1977 production at the Comédie-Française, took the tragic or semitragic line. The costumes alone set the tone, indicating Alceste's isolation from his society. In an age of highly beribboned garments and of elaborate wigs, Alceste wore a gray costume with only a few ribbons, and he wore his own hair, iron-gray, pulled back at the forehead. He was thus contrasted with the three fools in the play, Oronte, Acaste, and Clitandre, who were bewigged and tricked out in colorful costumes (blue, yellow, pink). Philinte was somewhere in between; his hair was his own, but it was curled (i.e., it was both natural and artificial), and he wore a brown garment (i.e., something less austere that Alceste's gray, but more austere than the costumes of the other men). Interestingly, an engraving of 1666—the year of the first performance—shows Alceste and Philinte in costumes that are barely distinguishable. Obviously, directors who want to present Alceste as comic, may choose to follow the engraving, showing that this man who rails against society is himself—though (comically) he doesn't seem to realize it—very much a part of the society.

It is of course impossible to discuss all of the major recent productions of the play, but two other productions require mention. In 1975 Britain's National Theatre staged *The Misanthrope* in London (and the next year in New York and in Washington, D.C., at the Kennedy Center), setting it in 1966, in De Gaulle's France. Alec McCowen was Alceste, and Diana Rigg was Célimène. At the end of the play Célimène—despite a stage direction in Molière's text indicating that she exits—remained onstage after Alceste left her. She watched all of her friends leave—the party was moving elsewhere—and thus she remained alone, an abandoned figure in her luxurious apartment.

The other production that requires at least mention is Ingmar Bergman's production in 1995—Bergman's third version of the play (he had done it in 1955 and 1973). The costumes were very elaborate, preventing the wearers from sitting, standing, or even breathing naturally, but the stage was almost bare. The idea was that these people, moving within a barren world, have encased themselves within conventions that almost overwhelm them and that make natural behavior virtually impossible. Alceste, though costumed austerely, is as artificial as the figures whom he condemns; his denunciations of society are a mask to cover his absurd sexual jealousy. He castigates the world because he can't have what he wants. At the end, when Célimène starts to offer a counterproposal to Alceste's proposal that they marry and leave society, Alceste rejects her violently. A moment later he talks of proposing marriage to Éliante. Rejected by Éliante, he announces that he will go to "some spot unpeopled and apart, / Where I'll be free to have an honest heart," but the audience knows that he will be plagued by his own egotism. (For a fuller discussion of Bergman's production, see the *New Yorker* magazine, May 8, 1995.)

Aphra Behn

THE ROVER

Very little is known for certain about Aphra Behn. We are not sure of the year or the place of her birth in England, her maiden name, the date of her marriage or the nationality and the profession of her husband, or even of the exact number of plays that she wrote. Some biographers, however, have been quick to report as fact what is really conjecture. She is usually said to have been born about 1640, probably into a family named Johnson. It is commonly asserted that her father was appointed Lieutenant General of Surinam, then a British colony and now Dutch Guiana, but that he died on the voyage to Surinam, and that Aphra lived only briefly there and then returned to England. In fact, the chief authority for her visit to Surinam is a passage in her novel, *Oroonoko* (1688), which was then reported as a biographical fact in the first (anonymous) biography of Behn issued after her death. There is no compelling reason, however, to assume that *Oroonoko* is in any way autobiographical—such details as it does include about Surinam could well have been derived from other books—and there is no compelling reason to believe that the anonymous biography is authoritative, though some scholars believe it is by Behn herself. The biography may or my not be by Behn, and if it is by Behn it may or may not be truthful.

Still, there are some facts. In 1666 Aphra Behn served in Antwerp as a spy for England, but her services were deemed of no value and she was not paid. In 1667 she returned to England, impoverished, and in 1668 she was imprisoned for debt. She began her career as a playwright in 1670, with a tragicomedy called *The Forced Marriage*. It ran for six performances, which means that it was a success, although today a play must run far longer if it is to earn any money for the author. At least fifteen more of her plays were produced during her lifetime, including *The Rover* (1677), *The Second Part of the Rover* (1681), and *The Emperor of the Moon* (1687). It is not known how she became associated with the theater, but perhaps it was through Thomas Killigrew, a playwright and later a theatrical entrepreneur, with whom Behn had corresponded when she was in Antwerp. (*The Rover* is partly based on a play by Killigrew, *Thomaso*.) Behn also wrote an important antislavery novel, *Oronooko* (1688), which was dramatized by Thomas Southerne in 1695 and was popular throughout the eighteenth century.

Behn was not the first woman in England to write plays, but she was the first to make a living as a playwright. (Two women who were her contemporaries must be mentioned: The Marchioness of Newcastle published two collections of plays, in 1662 and 1668, but they were never performed; Catherine Phillips [or Katherine Philips] did have a play performed, *Pompey*, but she was not a professional playwright.) Behn died in 1689, and is buried in Westminster Abbey.

COMMENTARY

Let's begin with words by Aphra Behn herself, though not words from *The Rover*. In the preface to another of her plays, *The Lucky Chance* (1686), she complained that her plays were given low marks simply because it was known that they were by a woman, and the age believed that it took a man to write a good play:

> Had the Plays I have writ come forth under any Mans Name, and never known to have been mine, I appeal to all unbyast Judges of Sense, if they had not said that Person had made as many good Comedies, as any one Man that has writ in our Age; but a Devil on't the Woman damns the Poet. . . . All I ask, is the Priviledge for my Masculine Part the Poet in me.

Behn is asking that she be judged on her work, not on her gender. When she writes, she is (she says) doing what is usually done only by men. She is using what the age would think of as her "Masculine Part"—for instance the power to

imagine characters, or the power to organize episodes into a coherent plot. But if some readers of Behn's day were skeptical that a woman could write a play, some readers of our day are skeptical that a woman can write the same sort of play that a man can write. The idea is this: Given the fact that the experience of being a woman is different from the experience of being a man, men and women must in some degree see things differently.

Take, for instance, the common use of women as commodities in marriage. An impoverished male aristocrat might marry a rich middle-class woman in order to improve his finances, and a shopkeeper might marry in order to have a cheap housekeeper. A woman usually married in order to have economic security. All of this may have seemed perfectly natural to the men and the women involved, but clearly marriage had one meaning for men and another for women. A related point: Prostitution is accepted by many men because it is an institution that affords them pleasure, but for women prostitution is a means of livelihood. In

Behn's day, women had few choices: marriage (arranged by men, for business reasons), the cloister (again arranged by men), domestic service, and prostitution.

Speaking of prostitution, we should mention that when the theaters in England reopened in 1660, after the period of Puritan rule, actresses appeared on the English stage in place of young boys who had taken the female roles in earlier years. These actresses were widely regarded—with some justification—as prostitutes; some of them were the mistresses of courtiers, and Nell Gwynne, perhaps the most famous actress of her day, for a while was the mistress of King Charles II. It is not entirely surprising, then, that prostitution becomes a topic for discussion in the plays, as we will see in a moment.

Although some men have profited financially from prostitution, it is largely a woman's business. Partly for this reason, as well as for moral reasons, prostitution has been scorned by men and has been regarded as the antithesis of marriage, which was regarded as an institution that offered a respectable career for women. But some women have been quick to point out a connection between the business of marriage and the business of prostitution. For instance, Polly Adler, a brothel-keeper, in a book called *A House Is Not a Home* (1953), wrote:

> The women who take husbands not out of love but out of greed, to get their bills paid, to get a fine house and clothes and jewels; the women who marry to get out of a tiresome job, or to get away from disagreeable relatives, or to avoid being called an old maid—these are whores in everything but in name.

In several passages in *The Rover* Aphra Behn raises a similar point. For instance, when Willmore, in 2.2, rebukes Angellica for demanding money for her services, Angellica replies by commenting on the financial aspects of respectable marriage:

> Pray tell me, sir, are not you guilty of the same mercenary crime? When a lady is proposed to you for a wife, you never ask how fair, discreet, or virtuous she is, but what's her fortune—which if but small, you cry, "She will not do my business" and basely leave her, though she languish for you. . . .

Because we know that *The Rover* was written by a woman, it is hard not to hear a distinctive female sensibility in such a passage, and indeed it would be hard to find comparable lines in the work of a male dramatist of the period. On the other hand, we should make two points about dramatic traditions that Behn is working in. First, there is the tradition of "the love-game comedy," in which a witty young man and a witty young woman engage in verbal combat. A famous example is Shakespeare's *Much Ado about Nothing*, in which Beatrice and Benedict enjoy themselves and give enjoyment to audiences by putting each other down, and then, at last find what everyone has long known—that they love each other and will make an excellent couple. In Behn's play, Willmore and Angellica do *not* marry, and the business

aspect of what passes as respectable marriage is subjected to an irony not found in Shakespeare's comedies, but Behn was by no means the first dramatist to present a clever woman who speaks hard truths.

Second, the skeptical view of marriage that Behn offers is found in many other comic writers of the time. Consider, for instance, this song from a comedy by John Dryden, *Marriage a-la-Mode*, written in 1671:

> Why should a foolish marriage vow,
>   Which long ago was made,
> Oblige us to each other now
>   When passion is decayed?
> We loved, and we loved, as long as we could,
>   Till our love was loved out in us both:
> But our marriage is dead, when the pleasure is fled:
>   'Twas pleasure first made it an oath.

If we go back a century from Dryden and Behn to Shakespeare's songs about marriage—delightful lyrics about true love and undying passion—in the last decade of the sixteenth century and the first decade or so of the seventeenth, we realize how greatly the English theater had changed.

Even in Shakespeare's day, the English theater can be said to have been divided between two theatrical publics. There was the broad, general public that paid a penny to enter a large theater which was open to the elements, and there was a smaller, richer public that paid sixpence to enter an indoor theater, a so-called private theater. The difference can be exaggerated—certain authors wrote for both theaters, and the richer members of the theater-going public could go to both theaters—but, still, the price of admission meant that there was a difference. For one thing, English history plays were more popular with the general Elizabethan public than with the smaller, richer public.

What we are saying about the effect of an audience's taste on those who make a living by satisfying that taste is nothing new. Dr. Samuel Johnson in 1747 made the point memorably, in a verse prologue he wrote in honor of his former pupil David Garrick—the greatest actor of the day—who had just became joint owner of a theater. After sketching the history of English drama, Johnson says that the playwrights and actors respond to the public—"The stage but echoes back the public voice." Then he goes on to offer this memorable formula:

> The drama's laws the drama's patrons give,
> For we that live to please, must please to live.

But who were "the drama's patrons" when Aphra Behn was writing, in the 1670s and 1680s? A bit of historical background must be offered. King Charles I (reigned 1625–49) sought to limit the powers of Parliament and in particular to suppress the Puritans, but in 1642 Parliament passed legislation limiting the power of the throne. One of Parliament's actions was to close the London theaters, and though there were some surreptitious performances, for all practical purposes theatrical activity ceased in England. The civil war which in 1642 broke out between the Parliamentary and the Royalist forces more or less ended with the capture of Charles in 1646, and it decisively ended in 1649, when Charles was executed. His wife and children (including the future Charles II) escaped to France, where they were joined by some loyal followers, called the cavaliers. (*The Rover* is about such followers, though it is set in Naples rather than in France.) The management of what had been the kingdom but now was called the Commonwealth fell chiefly into the hands of Oliver Cromwell, a Puritan who held the title of Lord Protector of the Realm.

Cromwell died in 1658, and in 1660, when the monarchy was restored, Charles II returned from the Continent. Even in exile he had lived a life of ease and pleasure, and when he was restored to the throne one of the first actions of "The Merry Monarch" was to give patents or licenses to William Davenant and Thomas Killigrew, each of whom was permitted to operate a theater—the so-called theaters-royal. Each of the two theater buildings held fewer spectators than an Elizabethan theater had held, but even so, the new theaters did not prosper, and from 1682 until 1695 the two companies survived only by uniting into a single company. This means that a relatively small group of performers did all of the acting, and a relatively small audience witnessed the plays. The composition of the audience cannot be determined exactly, but we know that the king himself attended the first recorded performance of *The Rover*, and where the king is, courtiers are not far behind. And we can notice in the plays a mild contempt for bourgeois values—for the values of "the cits," as they are called. We are told that Angellica Bianca, a courtesan, is "the only adored beauty of all the youth in Naples," something that perhaps gives us pause if we think of the beautiful, chaste women in Shakespeare's comedies. In *The Rover*, all of the men except Belvile attempt to rape women, but no one seems to think this activity is especially reprehensible; alcohol and youth are considered sufficient excuses for such assaults. Willmore, the hero, is lust incarnate, and he therefore finds it difficult to believe that any woman can be virtuous:

> A virtuous mistress? Death, what a thing thou has found out for me! Why, what the devil should I do with a virtuous woman, a sort of ill-natured creature that take a pride to torment a lover. Virtue is but an infirmity in woman, a disease that renders even the handsome ungrateful; whilst the ill-favored, for want of solicitations and address, only fancy themselves so. I have lain with a woman of quality who has all the while been railing at whores. (4.2)

Presumably the audience that enjoyed this speech regarded itself as highly sophisticated—witty, skeptical, enlightened, adventurous—especially sexually adventurous, which gets us back to the passage by Dryden, asking why "a foolish marriage vow" should oblige a couple to stay together, and the passage by Behn, asking if prostitution is much different from marriage.

What are we to make of this world of rovers, of men and women who condone adultery, and who, speaking broadly, live in a world in which the values seem utterly remote from traditional values—or at least from the values expressed earlier on the English stage, say in *A Midsummer Night's Dream*? (*A Midsummer Night's Dream* ends with fairies blessing the marriage bed; *The Rover* ends with Willmore talking of "the storms o' th' marriage bed.") In 1822, in a famous essay called "On the Artificial Comedy of the Last Century," Charles Lamb offered one way of thinking about this. Lamb's word "artificial" is the key. According to Lamb, the comic world that we see on the Restoration stage has no connection with our world, the real world. Rather, the characters belong to a fairy-tale world of utterly unreal—but thoroughly entertaining—people. These characters do not offend our moral sense because they are not moving in a moral world:

> They seem engaged in their proper element. They break through no laws or conscientious restraints. They know of none. They have got out of Christendom into the land—what shall I call it?—of cuckoldry—the Utopia of gallantry, where pleasure is duty, and the manners perfect freedom. It is altogether a speculative scene of things, which has no reference whatever to the world that is. No good person can be justly offended as a spectator, because no good person suffers on the stage. Judged morally, every character in these plays—the few exceptions only are *mistakes*—is alike essentially vain and worthless. . . . The whole is a passing pageant, where we should sit as unconcerned at the issues, for life or death, as at the battle of the frogs and mice.

Whereas the moralist might say that plays are morally damaging to spectators if (as in *The Rover*) characters who think that rape is fun go unpunished, Lamb says that these plays—far from damaging us—have a beneficial effect, at least on him, since they entertain him and therefore allow him to return to his job refreshed. "I come back to my cage and my restraint the fresher and more healthy for it. I wear my shackles more contentedly for having respired the breath of an imaginary freedom."

Today, most scholars of Restoration drama believe that Lamb was mistaken when he said that the plays had no connection with real life. On the other hand, even if he was mistaken on this point, we probably cannot simply dismiss his view that a certain amount of imaginative liberty—let's say fantasizing—is actually healthful. Lamb's assertion that after witnessing a Restoration comedy we return, refreshed, to the "cage" of the real world, can be tested against your own response to, say, a Marx Brothers movie, where mayhem rules, or even your response to a Chaplin movie, since in the films Chaplin engages in all sorts of deceits that in the real world would be reprehensible. Lamb's theory can also be related to Aristotle's theory of catharsis, which holds that we somehow are made better by seeing on the stage actions—let's say an action such as the suffering of Oedipus—that in real life would pain us.

If we accept Lamb's view that the world in a Restoration comedy is unrelated to our world, we undermine the view that the comedy probes our social institutions and sets out to make us think. In particular, Lamb's view would diminish the idea that because Behn was a woman—an outsider, so to speak, in the man's world of playwrighting—she was in a particularly good position to examine male values, and to stimulate skeptical thought in her audience. Perhaps the twentieth century offers a synthesis: We can hold both views, sometimes with Lamb seeing *The Rover* as a play that offers a never-never land in which fantasy reigns, and sometimes with today's critics seeing *The Rover* as a searching criticism of patriarchy.

Aphra Behn

THE ROVER; OR, THE BANISHED CAVALIERS*

PROLOGUE

Wits, like physicians, never can agree,
When of a different society.
And Rabel's drops[1] were never more cried down
By all the learned doctors of the town,
Than a new play whose author is unknown.
Nor can those doctors with more malice sue
(And powerful purses) the dissenting few,
Than those, with an insulting pride, do rail
At all who are not of their own cabal.[2]
    If a young poet hit your humor[3] right,
You judge him then out of revenge and spite.
So amongst men there are ridiculous elves,
Who monkeys hate for being too like themselves.
So that the reason of the grand debate
Why wit so oft is damned when good plays take,
Is that you censure as you love, or hate.
    Thus like a learned conclave poets sit,
Catholic judges[4] both of sense and wit,
And damn or save as they themselves think fit.
Yet those who to others' faults are so severe,
Are not so perfect but themselves may err.
Some write correct, indeed, but then the whole
(Bating[5] their own dull stuff i'th' play) is stole:
As bees do suck from flowers their honeydew,
So they rob others striving to please you.
    Some write their characters genteel and fine,
But then they do so toil for every line,
That what to you does easy seem, and plain,
Is the hard issue of their laboring brain.
And some th' effects of all their pains, we see,
Is but to mimic good extempore.[6]
Others, by long converse about the town,
Have wit enough to write a lewd lampoon,
But their chief skill lies in a bawdy song.
In short, the only wit that's now in fashion,
Is but the gleanings of good conversation.
As for the author of this coming play,
I asked him[7] what he thought fit I should say
In thanks for your good company today:
He called me fool, and said it was well known
You came not here for our sakes, but your own.
New plays are stuffed with wits, and with deboches,[8]
That crowd and sweat like cits[9] in May-Day coaches.[10]

WRITTEN BY A PERSON OF QUALITY

The Actors' Names

[Men]

DON ANTONIO, *the Viceroy's son*
DON PEDRO, *a noble Spaniard, his friend*
BELVILE, *an English colonel in love with Florinda*
WILLMORE, *the Rover*[11]
FREDERICK, *an English gentleman, and friend to Belvile and Blunt*
BLUNT, *an English country gentleman*
STEPHANO, *servant to Don Pedro*
PHILIPPO, *Lucetta's gallant*
SANCHO, *pimp to Lucetta*
BISKEY *and* SEBASTIAN, *two Bravos*[12] *to Angellica*
OFFICER *and* SOLDIERS
[DIEGO,] *Page to Don Antonio*

[Women]

FLORINDA, *sister to Don Pedro*
HELLENA, *a gay young woman designed for a nun, and sister to Florinda*
VALERIA, *a kinswoman to Florinda*
ANGELLICA BIANCA, *a famous courtesan*
MORETTA, *her woman*
CALLIS, *governess to Florinda and Hellena*
LUCETTA, *a jilting wench*
SERVANTS, *other* MASQUERADERS, MEN *and* WOMEN

THE SCENE: *Naples, in Carnival time.*

---

*Cavaliers supporters of the English monarchy during the English civil war. After the execution of Charles I in 1649, many cavaliers left England. [1]**Rabel's drops** a patent medicine [2]**cabal** secret group [3]**hit your humor** accurately portray your characteristics [4]**Catholic judges** broadminded judges [5]**Bating** excepting [6]**extempore** that is, a performance given without adequate preparation

[7]**him** the play was published anonymously, and the writer of the prologue speaks of the author as a male [8]**deboches** dissipations [9]**Cits** tradesman and their families (a mildly contemptuous term) [10]**May-Day coaches** on May 1, pretentious "cits" customarily took a carriage ride through Hyde Park [11]**Rover** wanderer (also *pirate*) [12]**Bravos** hired ruffians

ACT 1

SCENE 1

(*A Chamber. Enter Florinda and Hellena.*)

FLORINDA. What an impertinent thing is a young girl bred in a nunnery! How full of questions! Prithee no more, Hellena; I have told thee more than thou understand'st already.

HELLENA. The more's my grief. I would fain[13] know as much as you, which makes me so inquisitive; nor is't enough I know you're a lover, unless you tell me too who 'tis you sigh for.

FLORINDA. When you're a lover I'll think you fit for a secret of that nature.

HELLENA. 'Tis true, I never was a lover yet, but I begin to have a shrewd guess what 'tis to be so, and fancy it very pretty to sigh, and sing, and blush, and wish, and dream and wish, and long and wish to see the man, and when I do, look pale and tremble, just as you did when my brother brought home the fine English colonel to see you. What do you call him? Don Belvile?

FLORINDA. Fie, Hellena.

HELLENA. That blush betrays you. I am sure 'tis so. Or is it Don Antonio the Viceroy's son? Or perhaps the rich old Don Vincentio, whom my father designs you for a husband? Why do you blush again?

FLORINDA. With indignation; and how near soever my father thinks I am to marrying that hated object, I shall let him see I understand better what's due to my beauty, birth, and fortune, and more to my soul, than to obey those unjust commands.

HELLENA. Now hang me, if I don't love thee for that dear disobedience. I love mischief strangely, as most of our sex do who are come to love nothing else. But tell me, dear Florinda, don't you love that fine *Anglese?*[14] For I vow, next to loving him myself, 'twill please me most that you do so, for he is so gay and so handsome.

FLORINDA. Hellena, a maid designed for a nun ought not to be so curious in a discourse of love.

HELLENA. And dost thou think that ever I'll be a nun? Or at least till I'm so old I'm fit for nothing else? Faith no, sister; and that which makes me long to know whether you love Belvile, is because I hope he has some mad companion or other that will spoil my devotion. Nay, I'm resolved to provide myself this Carnival, if there be e'er a handsome proper fellow of my humor[15] above ground, though I ask first.

FLORINDA. Prithee be not so wild.

HELLENA. Now you have provided yourself of a man you take no care of poor me. Prithee tell me, what dost thou

see about me that is unfit for love? Have I not a world of youth? A humor gay? A beauty passable? A vigor desirable? Well shaped? Clean limbed? Sweet breathed? And sense enough to know how all these ought to be employed to the best advantage? Yes, I do and will; therefore lay aside your hopes of my fortune by my being a devote,[16] and tell me how you came acquainted with this Belvile. For I perceive you knew him before he came to Naples.

FLORINDA. Yes, I knew him at the siege of Pamplona;[17] he was then a colonel of French horse,[18] who when the town was ransacked, nobly treated my brother and myself, preserving us from all insolences. And I must own, besides great obligations, I have I know not what that pleads kindly for him about my heart, and will suffer no other to enter. But see, my brother.

(*Enter Don Pedro, Stephano with a masking habit,[19] and Callis.*)

PEDRO. Good morrow, sister. Pray when saw you your lover Don Vincentio?

FLORINDA. I know not, sir. Callis, when was he here? For I consider it so little I know not when it was.

PEDRO. I have a command from my father here to tell you you ought not to despise him, a man of so vast a fortune, and such a passion for you.—Stephano, my things.

(*Puts on his masking habit.*)

FLORINDA. A passion for me? 'Tis more than e'er I saw, or he had a desire should be known. I hate Vincentio, sir, and I would not have a man so dear to me as my brother follow the ill customs of our country and make a slave of his sister. And, sir, my father's will I'm sure you may divert.

PEDRO. I know not how dear I am to you, but I wish only to be ranked in your esteem equal with the English colonel Belvile. Why do you frown and blush? Is there any guilt belongs to the name of that cavalier?

FLORINDA. I'll not deny I value Belvile. When I was exposed to such dangers as the licensed lust of common soldiers threatened when rage and conquest flew through the city, then Belvile, this criminal for my sake, threw himself into all dangers to save my honor. And will you not allow him my esteem?

PEDRO. Yes, pay him what you will in honor, but you must consider Don Vincentio's fortune, and the jointure[20] he'll make you.

FLORINDA. Let him consider my youth, beauty, and fortune, which ought not to be thrown away on his age and jointure.

---

[13]**fain** gladly [14]***Anglese*** Englishman, that is, Belvile [15]**Humor** mood

[16]**devote** nun [17]**Pamplona** town in northern Spain [18]**of French horse** in the French cavalry [19]**masking habit** masquerade costume for the Carnival [20]**jointure** a marriage settlement providing for the wife's support after her husband's death

PEDRO. 'Tis true, he's not so young and fine a gentleman as that Belvile. But what jewels will that cavalier present you with? Those of his eyes and heart?

HELLENA. And are not those better than any Don Vincentio has brought from the Indies?

PEDRO. Why, how now! Has your nunnery breeding taught you to understand the value of hearts and eyes?

HELLENA. Better than to believe Vincentio's deserve value from any woman. He may perhaps increase her bags, but not her family.[21]

PEDRO. This is fine! Go! Up to your devotion! You are not designed for the conversation of lovers.

HELLENA (aside). Nor saints yet a while, I hope.—Is't not enough you make a nun of me, but you must cast my sister away too, exposing her to a worse confinement than a religious life?

PEDRO. The girl's mad! It is a confinement to be carried into the country to an ancient villa belonging to the family of the Vincentios these five hundred years, and have no other prospect than that pleasing one of seeing all her own that meets her eyes: a fine air, large fields, and gardens where she may walk and gather flowers?

HELLENA. When, by moonlight? For I am sure she dares not encounter with the heat of the sun; that were a task only for Don Vincentio and his Indian breeding, who loves it in the dog days.[22] And if these be her daily divertissements,[23] what are those of the night? To lie in a wide moth-eaten bedchamber with furniture in fashion in the reign of King Sancho the First; the bed, that which his forefathers lived and died in.

PEDRO. Very well.

HELLENA. This apartment, new furbrushed[24] and fitted out for the young wife, he out of freedom makes his dressing room; and being a frugal and a jealous coxcomb,[25] instead of a valet to uncase[26] his feeble carcass, he desires you to do that office. Signs of favor, I'll assure you, and such as you must not hope for unless your woman be out of the way.

PEDRO. Have you done yet?

HELLENA. That honor being past, the giant stretches itself, yawns and sighs a belch or two loud as a musket, throws himself into bed, and expects you in his foul sheets; and ere you can get yourself undressed, calls you with a snore or two. And are not these fine blessings to a young lady?

PEDRO. Have you done yet?

HELLENA. And this man you must kiss, nay you must kiss none but him too, and nuzzle through his beard to find his lips. And this you must submit to for threescore years, and all for a jointure.

PEDRO. For all your character of Don Vincentio, she is as like to marry him as she was before.

HELLENA. Marry Don Vincentio! Hang me, such a wedlock would be worse than adultery with another man. I had rather see her in the *Hostel de Dieu*,[27] to waste her youth there in vows, and be a handmaid to lazars[28] and cripples, than to lose it in such a marriage.

PEDRO. You have considered, sister, that Belvile has no fortune to bring you to; banished his country, despised at home, and pitied abroad.

HELLENA. What then? The Viceroy's son is better than that old Sir Fifty. Don Vincentio! Don Indian! He thinks he's trading to Gambo[29] still, and would barter himself—that bell and bauble—for your youth and fortune.

PEDRO. Callis, take her hence and lock her up all this Carnival, and at Lent she shall begin her everlasting penance in a monastery.

HELLENA. I care not; I had rather be a nun than be obliged to marry as you would have me if I were designed for't.

PEDRO. Do not fear the blessing of that choice. You shall be a nun.

HELLENA (aside). Shall I so? You may chance to be mistaken in my way of devotion. A nun! Yes, I am like to make a fine nun! I have an excellent humor for a grate![30] No, I'll have a saint of my own to pray to shortly, if I like any that dares venture on me.

PEDRO. Callis, make it your business to watch this wildcat.—As for you, Florinda, I've only tried you all this while and urged my father's will; but mine is that you would love Antonio: He is brave and young, and all that can complete the happiness of a gallant maid. This absence of my father will give us opportunity to free you from Vincentio by marrying here, which you must do tomorrow.

FLORINDA. Tomorrow!

PEDRO. Tomorrow, or 'twill be too late. 'Tis not my friendship to Antonio which makes me urge this, but love to thee and hatred to Vincentio; therefore resolve upon tomorrow.

FLORINDA. Sir, I shall strive to do as shall become your sister.

PEDRO. I'll both believe and trust you. Adieu.

(*Exeunt*[31] *Pedro and Stephano.*)

HELLENA. As becomes his sister! That is to be as resolved your way as he is his.

(*Hellena goes to Callis.*)

FLORINDA.
I ne'er till now perceived my ruin near.
I've no defense against Antonio's love,
For he has all the advantages of nature,
The moving arguments of youth and fortune.

---

[21]**increase . . . family** that is he may make her rich but he is too old to make her pregnant   [22]**dog days** hot summer days   [23]**divertissements** diversions   [24]**new furbrushed** refurbished   [25]**coxcomb** conceited fop   [26]**uncase** undress

[27]**Hostel de Dieu** hospital run by nuns   [28]**lazars** lepers   [29]**Gambo** Gambia, in West Africa   [30]**grate** a grille covering a convent window (i.e., the convent)   [31]**Exeunt** they go out (Latin)

HELLENA. But hark you, Callis, you will not be so cruel to lock me up indeed, will you?

CALLIS. I must obey the commands I have. Besides, do you consider what a life you are going to lead?

HELLENA. Yes, Callis, that of a nun; and till then I'll be indebted a world of prayers to you if you'll let me now see what I never did, the divertissements of a Carnival.

CALLIS. What, go in masquerade? 'Twill be a fine farewell to the world, I take it. Pray what would you do there?

HELLENA. That which all the world does, as I am told: Be as mad as the rest and take all innocent freedoms. Sister, you'll go too, will you not? Come, prithee be not sad. We'll outwit twenty brothers if you'll be ruled by me. Come, put off this dull humor with your clothes, and assume one as gay and as fantastic as the dress my cousin Valeria and I have provided, and let's ramble.

FLORINDA. Callis, will you give us leave to go?

CALLIS (aside). I have a youthful itch of going myself.— Madam, if I thought your brother might not know it, and I might wait on you; for by my troth I'll not trust young girls alone.

FLORINDA. Thou seest my brother's gone already, and thou shalt attend and watch us.

(Enter Stephano.)

STEPHANO. Madam, the habits[32] are come, and your cousin Valeria is dressed and stays for you.

FLORINDA (aside). 'Tis well. I'll write a note, and if I chance to see Belvile and want an opportunity to speak to him, that shall let him know what I've resolved in favor of him.

HELLENA. Come, let's in and dress us.

(Exeunt.)

SCENE 2

(A long street. Enter Belvile, melancholy; Blunt and Frederick.)

FREDERICK. Why, what the devil ails the colonel, in a time when all the world is gay to look like mere Lent thus? Hadst thou been long enough in Naples to have been in love, I should have sworn some such judgment had befallen thee.

BELVILE. No, I have made no new amours since I came to Naples.

FREDERICK. You have left none behind you in Paris?

BELVILE. Neither.

FREDERICK. I cannot divine the cause then, unless the old cause, the want of money.

BLUNT. And another old cause, the want of a wench. Would not that revive you?

BELVILE. You are mistaken, Ned.

BLUNT. Nay, 'adsheartlikins,[33] then thou'rt past cure.

FREDERICK. I have found it out: Thou hast renewed thy acquaintance with the lady that cost thee so many sighs at the siege of Pamplona—pox on't, what d'ye call her— her brother's a noble Spaniard, nephew to the dead general. Florinda. Ay, Florinda. And will nothing serve thy turn but that damned virtuous woman, whom on my conscience thou lov'st in spite too, because thou seest little or no possibility of gaining her.

BELVILE. Thou art mistaken; I have int'rest enough in that lovely virgin's heart to make me proud and vain, were it not abated by the severity of a brother, who, perceiving my happiness—

FREDERICK. Has civilly forbid thee the house?

BELVILE. 'Tis so, to make way for a powerful rival, the Viceroy's son, who has the advantage of me in being a man of fortune, a Spaniard, and her brother's friend; which gives him liberty to make his court, whilst I have recourse only to letters and distant looks from her window, which are as soft and kind as those which heaven sends down on penitents.

BLUNT. Heyday! 'Adsheartlikins, simile! By this light the man is quite spoiled. Fred, what the devil are we made of that we cannot be thus concerned for a wench? 'Adsheartlikins, our Cupids are like the cooks of the camp: They can roast or boil a woman, but they have none of the fine tricks to set 'em off; no hogoes[34] to make the sauce pleasant and the stomach sharp.

FREDERICK. I dare swear I have had a hundred as young, kind, and handsome as this Florinda; and dogs eat me if they were not as troublesome to me i'th' morning as they were welcome o'er night.

BLUNT. And yet I warrant he would not touch another woman if he might have her for nothing.

BELVILE. That's thy joy, a cheap whore.

BLUNT. Why, 'adsheartlikins, I love a frank soul. When did you ever hear of an honest woman that took a man's money? I warrant 'em good ones. But gentlemen, you may be free; you have been kept so poor with parliaments and protectors[35] that the little stock you have is not worth preserving. But I thank my stars I had more grace than to forfeit my estate by cavaliering.

BELVILE. Me thinks only following the court should be sufficient to entitle 'em to that.

BLUNT. 'Adsheartlikins, they know I follow it to do it no good, unless they pick a hole in my coat for lending you money now and then, which is a greater crime to my conscience, gentlemen, than to the Commonwealth.[36]

---

[32]**habits** costumes (of a religious order)

[33]**'adsheartlikins** God's little heart (a mild oath)   [34]**hogoes** relishes   [35]**protectors** Oliver Cromwell used this title   [36]**Commonwealth** the republican government of England, 1649–53, replaced by the Proctorate

(*Enter Willmore.*)

WILLMORE. Ha! Dear Belvile! Noble colonel!

BELVILE. Willmore! Welcome ashore, my dear rover! What happy wind blew us this good fortune?

WILLMORE. Let me salute my dear Fred, and then command me.—How is't, honest lad?

FREDERICK. Fair, sir, the old compliment, infinitely the better to see my dear mad Willmore again. Prithee, why camest thou ashore? And where's the Prince?[37]

WILLMORE. He's well, and reigns still lord of the wat'ry element. I must aboard again within a day or two, and my business ashore was only to enjoy myself a little this Carnival.

BELVILE. Pray know our new friend, sir; he's but bashful, a raw traveler, but honest, stout, and one of us. (*Embraces Blunt.*)

WILLMORE. That you esteem him gives him an int'rest[38] here.

BLUNT. Your servant, sir.

WILLMORE. But well, faith, I'm glad to meet you again in a warm climate, where the kind sun has its godlike power still over the wine and women. Love and mirth are my business in Naples, and if I mistake not the place, here's an excellent market for chapmen[39] of my humor.

BELVILE. See, here be those kind merchants of love you look for.

(*Enter several men in masking habits, some playing on music, others dancing after; women dressed like courtesans, with papers pinned on their breasts, and baskets of flowers in their hands.*)

BLUNT. 'Adsheartlikins, what have we here?

FREDERICK. Now the game begins.

WILLMORE. Fine pretty creatures! May a stranger have leave to look and love? What's here? "Roses for every month"? (*Reads the papers.*)

BLUNT. Roses for every month? What means that?

BELVILE. They are, or would have you think they're courtesans, who here in Naples are to be hired by the month.

WILLMORE. Kind and obliging to inform us, pray where do these roses grow? I would fain plant some of 'em in a bed of mine.

WOMAN. Beware such roses, sir.

WILLMORE. A pox of fear:[40] I'll be baked with thee between a pair of sheets, and that's thy proper still;[41] so I might but strew such roses over me and under me. Fair one, would you would give me leave to gather at your bush

this idle month; I would go near to make somebody smell of it all the year after.

BELVILE. And thou hast need of such a remedy, for thou stink'st of tar and ropes' ends like a dock or pesthouse.

(*The Woman puts herself into the hands of a man and exeunt.*)

WILLMORE. Nay, nay, you shall not leave me so.

BELVILE. By all means use no violence here.

WILLMORE. Death! Just as I was going to be damnably in love, to have her led off! I could pluck that rose out of his hand, and even kiss the bed the bush grew in.

FREDERICK. No friend to love like a long voyage at sea.

BLUNT. Except a nunnery, Fred.

WILLMORE. Death! But will they not be kind? Quickly be kind? Thou know'st I'm no tame sigher, but a rampant lion of the forest.

(*Advances from the farther end of the scenes two men dressed all over with horns[42] of several sorts, making grimaces at one another, with papers pinned on their backs.*)

BELVILE. Oh the fantastical rogues, how they're dressed! 'Tis a satire against the whole sex.

WILLMORE. Is this a fruit that grows in this warm country?

BELVILE. Yes, 'tis pretty to see these Italians start, swell, and stab at the word cuckold, and yet stumble at horns on every threshold.

WILLMORE. See what's on their back. (*Reads.*) "Flowers of every night." Ah, rogue! And more sweet than roses of every month! This is a gardener of Adam's own breeding.

(*They dance.*)

BELVILE. What think you of these grave people? Is a wake[43] in Essex half so mad or extravagant?

WILLMORE. I like their sober grave way; 'tis a kind of legal authorized fornication, where the men are not chid[44] for't, nor the women despised, as amongst our dull English. Even the monsieurs[45] want[46] that part of good manners.

BELVILE. But here in Italy, a monsieur is the humblest best-bred gentleman: Duels are so baffled by bravos that an age shows not one but between a French man and a hangman, who is as much too hard for him on the Piazza as they are for a Dutchman on the New Bridge.[47] But see, another crew.

(*Enter Florinda, Hellena, and Valeria, dressed like gypsies; Callis and Stephano, Lucetta, Philippo, and Sancho in masquerade.*)

---

[37]**Prince** Charles II, who was in exile on the Continent during Cromwell's reign in England [38]**int'rest** recommendation [39]**chapmen** merchants (of love) [40]**pox of fear** a curse on fear [41]**baked . . . still** a bawdy joke comparing women to roses, which are distilled to make rose water; the bawdiness continues in *bush*, that is, pubic hair

[42]**horns** allusion to the old belief that a cuckolded husband sprouted horns on his forehead that could be seen by everyone but himself [43]**wake** vigil over a corpse [44]**chid** chided [45]**monsieurs** Frenchmen [46]**want** lack [47]**Dutchman . . . Bridge** a reference to recent French military successes in Flanders

HELLENA. Sister, there's your Englishman, and with him a handsome proper fellow. I'll to him, and instead of telling him his fortune, try my own.

WILLMORE. Gypsies, on my life. Sure these will prattle if a man cross their hands.[48] (*Goes to Hellena.*)—Dear, pretty, and, I hope, young devil, will you tell an amorous stranger what luck he's like to have?

HELLENA. Have a care how you venture with me, sir, lest I pick your pocket, which will more vex your English humor than an Italian fortune will please you.

WILLMORE. How the devil cam'st thou to know my country and humor?

HELLENA. The first I guess by a certain forward impudence, which does not displease me at this time; and the loss of your money will vex you because I hope you have but very little to lose.

WILLMORE. Egad, child, thou'rt i'th' right; it is so little I dare not offer it thee for a kindness. But cannot you divine what other things of more value I have about me that I would more willingly part with?

HELLENA. Indeed no, that's the business of a witch, and I am but a gypsy yet. Yet without looking in your hand, I have a parlous guess[49] 'tis some foolish heart you mean, an inconstant English heart, as little worth stealing as your purse.

WILLMORE. Nay, then thou dost deal with the devil, that's certain. Thou hast guessed as right as if thou hadst been one of that number it has languished for. I find you'll be better acquainted with it, nor can you take it in a better time; for I am come from sea, child, and Venus not being propitious to me in her own element,[50] I have a world of love in store. Would you would be good-natured and take some on't[51] off my hands.

HELLENA. Why, I could be inclined that way, but for a foolish vow I am going to make to die a maid.

WILLMORE. Then thou art damned without redemption, and as I am a good Christian, I ought in charity to divert so wicked a design. Therefore prithee, dear creature, let me know quickly when and where I shall begin to set a helping hand to so good a work.

HELLENA. If you should prevail with my tender heart, as I begin to fear you will, for you have horrible loving eyes, there will be difficulty in't that you'll hardly undergo for my sake.

WILLMORE. Faith, child, I have been bred in dangers, and wear a sword that has been employed in a worse cause than for a handsome kind woman. Name the danger; let it be anything but a long siege, and I'll undertake it.

HELLENA. Can you storm?[52]

WILLMORE. Oh, most furiously.

HELLENA. What think you of a nunnery wall? For he that wins me must gain that first.

WILLMORE. A nun! Oh, now I love thee for't! There's no sinner like a young saint. Nay, now there's no denying me; the old law had no curse to a woman like dying a maid: Witness Jeptha's daughter.[53]

HELLENA. A very good text this, if well handled; and I perceive, Father Captain, you would impose no severe penance on her who were inclined to console herself before she took orders.[54]

WILLMORE. If she be young and handsome.

HELLENA. Ay, there's it. But if she be not—

WILLMORE. By this hand, child, I have an implicit faith, and dare venture on thee with all faults. Besides, 'tis more meritorious to leave the world when thou hast tasted and proved the pleasure on't. Then 'twill be a virtue in thee, which now will be pure ignorance.

HELLENA. I perceive, good Father Captain, you design only to make me fit for heaven. But if, on the contrary, you should quite divert me from it, and bring me back to the world again, I should have a new man to seek, I find. And what a grief that will be; for when I begin, I fancy I shall love like anything; I never tried yet.

WILLMORE. Egad, and that's kind! Prithee, dear creature, give me credit for a heart, for faith, I'm a very honest fellow. Oh, I long to come first to the banquet of love! And such a swinging appetite I bring. Oh, I'm impatient. Thy lodging, sweetheart, thy lodging, or I'm a dead man!

HELLENA. Why must we be either guilty of fornication or murder if we converse with you men? And is there no difference between leave to love me, and leave to lie with me?

WILLMORE. Faith, child, they were made to go together.

LUCETTA (*pointing to Blunt*). Are you sure this is the man?

SANCHO. When did I mistake your game?

LUCETTA. This is a stranger, I know by his gazing; if he be brisk he'll venture to follow me, and then, if I understand my trade, he's mine. He's English, too, and they say that's a sort of good-natured loving people, and have generally so kind an opinion of themselves that a woman with any wit may flatter 'em into any sort of fool she pleases.

(*She often passes by Blunt and gazes on him; he struts and cocks, and walks and gazes on her.*)

BLUNT. 'Tis so, she is taken; I have beauties which my false glass[55] at home did not discover.[56]

FLORINDA (*aside*). This woman watches me so, I shall get no opportunity to discover myself to him, and so miss the intent of my coming.—[*To Belvile.*] But as I was saying, sir, by this line you should be a lover.

---

[48]**prattle . . . hands** tell his fortune if he gives them silver   [49]**a parlous guess** a hunch   [50]**Venus . . . element** Venus, the goddess of love, was born from sea foam   [51]**on't** of it   [52]**storm** attack

[53]**Jeptha's daughter** the virgin daughter of a Hebrew judge who rashly sacrificed her. See Judges 11:39–40.   [54]**took orders** entered a convent   [55]**false glass** lying mirror   [56]**discover** reveal

(Looking in his hand.)

BELVILE. I thought how right you guessed: All men are in love, or pretend to be so. Come, let me go; I'm weary of this fooling.   *(Walks away.)*

FLORINDA. I will not, sir, till you have confessed whether the passion that you have vowed Florinda be true or false.

(She holds him; he strives to get from her.)

BELVILE. Florinda!   *(Turns quick toward her.)*

FLORINDA. Softly.

BELVILE. Thou hast nam'd one will fix me here forever.

FLORINDA. She'll be disappointed then, who expects you this night at the garden gate. And if you fail not, as— *(Looks on Callis, who observes 'em.)* Let me see the other hand—you will go near to do, she vows to die or make you happy.

BELVILE. What canst thou mean?

FLORINDA. That which I say. Farewell.

(Offers to go.)

BELVILE. O charming sibyl,[57] stay; complete that joy which as it is will turn into distraction! Where must I be? At the garden gate? I know it. At night, you say? I'll sooner forfeit heaven than disobey.

(Enter Don Pedro and other maskers, and pass over the stage.)

CALLIS. Madam, your brother's here.

FLORINDA. Take this to instruct you farther.

(Gives him a letter, and goes off.)

FREDERICK. Have a care, sir, what you promise; this may be a trap laid by her brother to ruin you.

BELVILE. Do not disturb my happiness with doubts.

(Opens the letter.)

WILLMORE. My dear pretty creature, a thousand blessings on thee! Still in this habit, you say? And after dinner at this place?

HELLENA. Yes, if you will swear to keep your heart and not bestow it between this and that.

WILLMORE. By all the little gods of love, I swear; I'll leave it with you, and if you run away with it, those deities of justice[58] will revenge me.

(Exeunt all the women [except Lucetta].)

FREDERICK. Do you know the hand?

BELVILE. 'Tis Florinda's.

All blessings fall upon the virtuous maid.

FREDERICK. Nay, no idolatry; a sober sacrifice I'll allow you.

BELVILE. Oh friends, the welcom'st news! The softest letter! Nay, you shall all see it. And could you now be serious, I might be made the happiest man the sun shines on!

WILLMORE. The reason of this mighty joy?

BELVILE. See how kindly she invites me to deliver her from the threatened violence of her brother. Will you not assist me?

WILLMORE. I know not what thou mean'st, but I'll make one at any mischief where a woman's concerned. But she'll be grateful to us for the favor, will she not?

BELVILE. How mean you?

WILLMORE. How should I mean? Thou know'st there's but one way for a woman to oblige me.

BELVILE. Do not profane; the maid is nicely virtuous.

WILLMORE. Who, pox,[59] then she's fit for nothing but a husband. Let her e'en go, colonel.

FREDERICK. Peace, she's the colonel's mistress, sir.

WILLMORE. Let her be the devil; if she be thy mistress, I'll serve her. Name the way.

BELVILE. Read here this postscript.

(Gives him a letter.)

WILLMORE *(reads).* "At ten at night, at the garden gate, of which, if I cannot get the key, I will contrive a way over the wall. Come attended with a friend or two."—Kind heart, if we three cannot weave a string to let her down a garden wall, 'twere pity but the hangman wove one for us all.

FREDERICK. Let her alone for that; your woman's wit, your fair kind woman, will outtrick a broker or a Jew, and contrive like a Jesuit[60] in chains. But see, Ned Blunt is stolen out after the lure of a damsel.

(Exeunt Blunt and Lucetta.)

BELVILE. So, he'll scarce find his way home again unless we get him cried by the bellman[61] in the market place. And 'twould sound prettily: "A lost English boy of thirty."

FREDERICK. I hope 'tis some common crafty sinner, one that will fit him. It may be she'll sell him for Peru:[62] The rogue's sturdy, and would work well in a mine. At least I hope she'll dress him for our mirth, cheat him of all, then have him well-favoredly banged, and turned out at midnight.

WILLMORE. Prithee what humor is he of, that you wish him so well?

BELVILE. Why, of an English elder brother's humor: educated in a nursery, with a maid to tend him till fifteen, and lies with his grandmother till he's of age; one that knows no pleasure beyond riding to the next fair, or going up to London with his right worshipful father in parliament time, wearing gay clothes, or making honorable love to his lady mother's laundry maid; gets drunk at a hunting match, and ten to one then gives some proofs of his prowess. A pox upon him, he's our banker, and has all our cash about him; and if he fail, we are all broke.

FREDERICK. Oh, let him alone for that matter; he's of a damned stingy quality that will secure our stock. I know

---

[57]**sybil** prophetess, here a fortuneteller   [58]**deities of justice** in Greek mythology, the Erynys, avenging spirits

[59]**pox** damn   [60]**Jew . . . Jesuit** Jews and Jesuits were widely distrusted and feared in this period   [61]**the bellman** town crier   [62]**sell . . . Peru** sell him as a slave to Peru

not in what danger it were indeed if the jilt[63] should pretend she's in love with him, for 'tis a kind believing coxcomb; otherwise, if he part with more than a piece of eight,[64] geld him—for which offer he may chance to be beaten if she be a whore of the first rank.

BELVILE. Nay, the rogue will not be easily beaten; he's stout enough. Perhaps if they talk beyond his capacity he may chance to exercise his courage upon some of them, else I'm sure they'll find it as difficult to beat as to please him.

WILLMORE. 'Tis a lucky devil to light upon so kind a wench!

FREDERICK. Thou hadst a great deal of talk with thy little gypsy; couldst thou do no good upon her? For mine was hardhearted.

WILLMORE. Hang her, she was some damned honest person of quality, I'm sure, she was so very free and witty. If her face be but answerable to her wit and humor, I would be bound to constancy this month to gain her. In the meantime, have you made no kind acquaintance since you came to town? You do not use to be honest[65] so long, gentlemen.

FREDERICK. Faith, love has kept us honest: We have been all fir'd with a beauty newly come to town, the famous Paduana[66] Angellica Bianca.

WILLMORE. What, the mistress of the dead Spanish general?

BELVILE. Yes, she's now the only ador'd beauty of all the youth in Naples, who put on all their charms to appear lovely in her sight: Their coaches, liveries, and themselves all gay as on a monarch's birthday to attract the eyes of this fair charmer, while she has the pleasure to behold all languish for her that see her.

FREDERICK. 'Tis pretty to see with how much love the men regard her, and how much envy the women.

WILLMORE. What gallant has she?

BELVILE. None; she's exposed to sale, and four days in the week she's yours, for so much a month.

WILLMORE. The very thought of it quenches all manner of fire in me. Yet prithee, let's see her.

BELVILE. Let's first to dinner, and after that we'll pass the day as you please. But at night ye must all be at my devotion.

WILLMORE. I will not fail you.

[Exeunt.]

ACT 2

SCENE 1

(*The long street. Enter Belvile and Frederick in masking habits, and Willmore in his own clothes, with a vizard[67] in his hand.*)

WILLMORE. But why thus disguised and muzzled?

BELVILE. Because whatever extravagances we commit in these faces, our own may not be obliged to answer 'em.

WILLMORE. I should have changed my eternal buff,[68] too; but no matter, my little gypsy would not have found me out then. For if she should change hers, it is impossible I should know her unless I should hear her prattle. A pox on't, I cannot get her out of my head. Pray heaven, if ever I do see her again, she prove damnably ugly, that I may fortify myself against her tongue.

BELVILE. Have a care of love, for o' my conscience she was not of a quality to give thee any hopes.

WILLMORE. Pox on 'em, why do they draw a man in then? She has played with my heart so, that 'twill never lie still till I have met with some kind wench that will play the game out with me. Oh, for my arms full of soft, white, kind woman—such as I fancy Angellica.

BELVILE. This is her house, if you were but in stock to get admittance. They have not dined yet; I perceive the picture is not out.[69]

(*Enter Blunt.*)

WILLMORE. I long to see the shadow of the fair substance; a man may gaze on that for nothing.

BLUNT. Colonel, thy hand. And thine, Fred. I have been an ass, a deluded fool, a very coxcomb from my birth till this hour, and heartily repent my little faith.

BELVILE. What the devil's the matter with thee, Ned?

BLUNT. Oh, such a mistress, Fred! Such a girl!

WILLMORE. Ha! Where?

FREDERICK. Ay, where?

BLUNT. So fond, so amorous, so toying, and so fine! And all for sheer love, ye rogue! Oh, how she looked and kissed! And soothed my heart from my bosom! I cannot think I was awake, and yet methinks I see and feel her charms still. Fred, try if she have not left the taste of her balmy kisses upon my lips.   (*Kisses him.*)

BELVILE. Ha! Ha! Ha!

WILLMORE. Death, man, where is she?

BLUNT. What a dog was I to stay in dull England so long! How have I laughed at the colonel when he sighed for love! But now the little archer[70] has revenged him! And by this one dart I can guess at all his joys, which then I took for fancies, mere dreams and fables. Well, I'm resolved to sell all in Essex and plant here forever.

BELVILE. What a blessing 'tis, thou hast a mistress thou dar'st boast of; for I know thy humor is rather to have a proclaimed clap[71] than a secret amour.

WILLMORE. Dost know her name?

BLUNT. Her name? No, 'adsheartlikins. What care I for names? She's fair, young, brisk and kind, even to ravishment! And what a pox care I for knowing her by any other title?

---

[63]**jilt** whore   [64]**piece of eight** obsolete Spanish coin   [65]**honest** chaste   [66]**Paduana** Angellica comes from Padua   [67]**vizard** mask

[68]**buff** leather military coat   [69]**the picture . . . out** when Angellica's picture is hung, she is open for business; see stage direction line later in the scene, referring to a great picture of Angellica   [70]**the little archer** Cupid   [71]**proclaimed clap** sexual disease that everyone knows of

WILLMORE. Didst give her anything?

BLUNT. Give her? Ha! Ha! Ha! Why, she's a person of quality. That's a good one! Give her? 'Adsheartlikins, dost think such creatures are to be bought? Or are we provided for such a purchase? Give her, quoth ye? Why, she presented me with this bracelet for the toy of a diamond I used to wear. No, gentlemen, Ned Blunt is not everybody. She expects me again tonight.

WILLMORE. Egad, that's well; we'll all go.

BLUNT. Not a soul! No, gentlemen, you are wits; I am a dull country rogue, I.

FREDERICK. Well, sir, for all your person of quality, I shall be very glad to understand your purse be secure; 'tis our whole estate at present, which we are loath to hazard in one bottom.[72] Come sir, unlade.

BLUNT. Take the necessary trifle useless now to me, that am beloved by such a gentlewoman. 'Adsheartlikins, money! Here, take mine too.

FREDERICK. No, keep that to be cozened,[73] that we may laugh.

WILLMORE. Cozened? Death! Would I could meet with one that would cozen me of all the love I could spare tonight.

FREDERICK. Pox, 'tis some common whore, upon my life.

BLUNT. A whore? Yes, with such clothes, such jewels, such a house, such furniture, and so attended! A whore!

BELVILE. Why yes, sir, they are whores, though they'll neither entertain you with drinking, swearing, or bawdry; are whores in all those gay clothes and right[74] jewels; are whores with those great houses richly furnished with velvet beds, store of plate,[75] handsome attendance, and fine coaches; are whores, and errant[76] ones.

WILLMORE. Pox on't, where do these fine whores live?

BELVILE. Where no rogues in office, ycleped[77] constables, dare give 'em laws, nor the wine-inspired bullies of the town break their windows; yet they are whores though this Essex calf[78] believe 'em persons of quality.

BLUNT. 'Adsheartlikins, y'are all fools. There are things about this Essex calf that shall take with the ladies, beyond all your wit and parts. This shape and size, gentlemen, are not to be despised; my waist, too, tolerably long, with other inviting signs that shall be nameless.

WILLMORE. Egad, I believe he may have met with some person of quality that may be kind to him.

BELVILE. Dost thou perceive any such tempting things about him that should make a fine woman, and of quality, pick him out from all mankind to throw away her youth and beauty upon; nay, and her dear heart, too? No, no, Angellica has raised the price too high.

WILLMORE. May she languish for mankind till she die, and be damned for that one sin alone.

(*Enter two Bravos and hang up a great picture of Angellica's against the balcony, and two little ones at each side of the door.*)

BELVILE. See there the fair sign to the inn where a man may lodge that's fool enough to give her price.

(*Willmore gazes on the picture.*)

BLUNT. 'Adsheartlikins, gentlemen, what's this?

BELVILE. A famous courtesan, that's to be sold.

BLUNT. How? To be sold? Nay, then I have nothing to say to her. Sold? What impudence is practiced in this country; with what order and decency whoring's established here by virtue of the Inquisition![79] Come, let's be gone; I'm sure we're no chapmen[80] for this commodity.

FREDERICK. Thou art none, I'm sure, unless thou couldst have her in thy bed at a price of a coach in the street.

WILLMORE. How wondrous fair she is! A thousand crowns a month? By heaven, as many kingdoms were too little! A plague of this poverty, of which I ne'er complain but when it hinders my approach to beauty which virtue ne'er could purchase.

(*Turns from the picture.*)

BLUNT. What's this? (*Reads.*) "A thousand crowns a month"! 'Adsheartlikins, here's a sum! Sure 'tis a mistake.—[To one of the Bravos.] Hark you, friend, does she take or give so much by the month?

FREDERICK. A thousand crowns! Why, 'tis a portion for the Infanta![81]

BLUNT. Hark ye, friends, won't she trust?[82]

BRAVO. This is a trade, sir, that cannot live by credit.

(*Enter Don Pedro in masquerade, followed by Stephano.*)

BELVILE. See, here's more company; let's walk off a while.

(*Exeunt English;[83] Pedro reads.*)

PEDRO. Fetch me a thousand crowns; I never wished to buy this beauty at an easier rate. (*Passes off.*)

(*Enter Angellica and Moretta in the balcony, and draw a silk curtain.*)

ANGELLICA. Prithee, what said those fellows to thee?

BRAVO. Madam, the first were admirers of beauty only, but no purchasers; they were merry with your price and picture, laughed at the sum, and so passed off.

ANGELLICA. No matter, I'm not displeased with their rallying; their wonder feeds my vanity, and he that wishes but to buy gives me more pride than he that gives my price can make my pleasure.

---

[72]**loath . . . bottom** reluctant to risk cargo in one ship [73]**cozened** cheated [74]**right** real [75]**plate** silverware [76]**errant** arrant, unmitigated [77]**ycleped** called [78]**Essex calf** fool from Essex (Blunt's county in England)

[79]**Inquisition** prostitutes forced out of Spain by the Spanish Inquisition came to Italy [80]**chapmen** merchants [81]**portion . . . Infanta** dowry for the Spanish princess [82]**trust** extend credit [83]**English** all the Englishmen

BRAVO. Madam, the last I knew through all his disguises to be Don Pedro, nephew to the general, and who was with him in Pamplona.

ANGELLICA. Don Pedro? My old gallant's nephew? When his uncle died he left him a vast sum of money; it is he who was so in love with me at Padua, and who used to make the general so jealous.

MORETTA. Is this he that used to prance before our window, and take such care to show himself an amorous ass? If I am not mistaken, he is the likeliest man to give your price.

ANGELLICA. The man is brave and generous, but of a humor so uneasy and inconstant that the victory over his heart is as soon lost as won; a slave that can add little to the triumph of the conqueror. But inconstancy's the sin of all mankind, therefore I'm resolved that nothing but gold shall charm my heart.

MORETTA. I'm glad on't; 'tis only interest that women of our profession ought to consider, though I wonder what has kept you from that general disease of our sex so long; I mean, that of being in love.

ANGELLICA. A kind but sullen star under which I had the happiness to be born. Yet I have had no time for love; the bravest and noblest of mankind have purchased my favors at so dear a rate, as if no coin but gold were current with our trade. But here's Don Pedro again; fetch me my lute, for 'tis for him or Don Antonio the Viceroy's son that I have spread my nets.

(*Enter at one door Don Pedro, Stephano; Don Antonio and Diego [his page] at the other door, with people following him in masquerade, antically attired, some with music. They both go up to the picture.*)

ANTONIO. A thousand crowns! Had not the painter flattered her, I should not think it dear.[84]

PEDRO. Flattered her? By heaven, he cannot. I have seen the original, nor is there one charm here more than adorns her face and eyes; all this soft and sweet, with a certain languishing air that no artist can represent.

ANTONIO. What I heard of her beauty before had fired my soul, but this confirmation of it has blown it to a flame.

PEDRO. Ha!

PAGE. Sir, I have known you throw away a thousand crowns on a worse face, and though y'are near your marriage, you may venture a little love here; Florinda will not miss it.

PEDRO (*aside*). Ha! Florinda! Sure 'tis Antonio.

ANTONIO. Florinda! Name not those distant joys; there's not one thought of her will check my passion here.

PEDRO [*aside*]. Florinda scorned! (*A noise of a lute above.*) And all my hopes defeated of the possession of Angellica! (*Antonio gazes up.*) Her injuries, by heaven, he shall not boast of!

(*Song to a lute above.*)

SONG
[I]
When Damon first began to love
He languished in a soft desire,
And knew not how the gods to move,
To lessen or increase his fire.
For Caelia in her charming eyes
Wore all love's sweets, and all his cruelties.

II
But as beneath a shade he lay,
Weaving of flowers for Caelia's hair,
She chanced to lead her flock that way,
And saw the am'rous shepherd there.
She gazed around upon the place,
And saw the grove, resembling night,
To all the joys of love invite,
Whilst guilty smiles and blushes dressed her face.
At this the bashful youth all transport grew,
And with kind force he taught the virgin how
To yield what all his sighs could never do.

(*Angellica throws open the curtains and bows to Antonio, who pulls off his vizard and bows and blows up kisses. Pedro, unseen, looks in's face. [The curtains close.]*)

ANTONIO. By heaven, she's charming fair!

PEDRO (*aside*). 'Tis he, the false Antonio!

ANTONIO (*to the Bravo*[85]).
Friend, where must I pay my off'ring of love?
My thousand crowns I mean.

PEDRO.
That off'ring I have designed to make,
And yours will come too late.

ANTONIO.
Prithee begone; I shall grow angry else,
And then thou art not safe.

PEDRO.
My anger may be fatal, sir, as yours,
And he that enters here may prove this truth.

ANTONIO. I know not who thou art, but I am sure thou'rt worth my killing, for aiming at Angellica.

(*They draw and fight.*)
(*Enter Willmore and Blunt, who draw and part 'em.*)

BLUNT. 'Adsheartlikins, here's fine doings.

WILLMORE. Tilting[86] for the wench, I'm sure. Nay, gad, if that would win her I have as good a sword as the best of ye. Put up, put up, and take another time and place, for this is designed for lovers only.   (*They all put up.*)

---

[84]**dear** expensive

[85]**Bravo** ruffian   [86]**Tilting** fighting (normally charging on horseback, with a lance)

PEDRO.
    We are prevented; dare you meet me tomorrow on the
        Molo?[87]
    For I've a title to a better quarrel,
    That of Florinda, in whose credulous heart
    Thou'st made an int'rest, and destroyed my hopes.
ANTONIO. Dare!
    I'll meet thee there as early as the day.
PEDRO. We will come thus disguised, that whosoever chance
    to get the better, he may escape unknown.
ANTONIO. It shall be so.

                    (*Exeunt Pedro and Stephano.*)

    —Who should this rival be? Unless the English colonel,
    of whom I've often heard Don Pedro speak. It must be he,
    and time he were removed who lays a claim to all my
    happiness.
(*Willmore, having gazed all this while on the picture*[s],
pulls down a little one.)

WILLMORE.
    This posture's loose and negligent;
    The sight on't would beget a warm desire
    In souls whom impotence and age had chilled.
    This must along with me.
BRAVO. What means this rudeness, sir? Restore the picture.
ANTONIO. Ha! Rudeness committed to the fair Angellica!—
    Restore the picture, sir.
WILLMORE. Indeed I will not, sir.
ANTONIO. By heaven, but you shall.
WILLMORE. Nay, do not show your sword; if you do, by this
    dear beauty, I will show mine too.
ANTONIO. What right can you pretend to't?
WILLMORE. That of possession, which I will maintain. You,
    perhaps, have a thousand crowns to give for the original.
ANTONIO. No matter, sir, you shall restore the picture.

    ([*The curtains open.*] *Angellica and Moretta above.*)

ANGELLICA. Oh, Moretta, what's the matter?
ANTONIO. Or leave your life behind.
WILLMORE. Death! You lie; I will do neither.

    ([*Willmore and Antonio*] *fight. The Spaniards join with
    Antonio, Blunt* [*joins with Willmore,*] *laying on like
    mad.*)

ANGELLICA. Hold, I command you, if for me you fight.

    (*They leave off and bow.*)

WILLMORE [*aside*]. How heavenly fair she is! Ah, plague of
    her price!
ANGELLICA. You sir, in buff, you that appear a soldier, that
    first began this insolence—
WILLMORE. 'Tis true, I did so, if you call it insolence for a
    man to preserve himself. I saw your charming picture and
    was wounded; quite through my soul each pointed beauty

ran; and wanting a thousand crowns to procure my remedy, I laid this little picture to my bosom, which, if you
cannot allow me, I'll resign.
ANGELLICA. No, you may keep the trifle.
ANTONIO. You shall first ask me leave, and this.

                    (*Fight again as before.*)

(*Enter Belvile and Frederick, who join with the English.*)

ANGELLICA. Hold! Will you ruin me?—Biskey! Sebastian!
    Part 'em!

                    (*The Spaniards are beaten off.*)

MORETTA. Oh, madam, we're undone. A pox upon that rude
    fellow; he's set on to ruin us. We shall never see good
    days again till all these fighting poor rogues are sent to
    the galleys.

(*Enter Belvile, Blunt, Frederick, and Willmore with's shirt
bloody.*)

BLUNT. 'Adsheartlikins, beat me at this sport and I'll ne'er
    wear sword more.
BELVILE (*to Willmore*). The devil's in thee for a mad fellow;
    thou art always one at an unlucky adventure. Come, let's
    be gone whilst we're safe, and remember these are
    Spaniards, a sort of people that know how to revenge an
    affront.
FREDERICK. You bleed! I hope you are not wounded.
WILLMORE. Not much. A plague on your dons; if they fight
    no better they'll ne'er recover Flanders.[88] What the devil
    was't to them that I took down the picture?
BLUNT. Took it! 'Adsheartlikins, we'll have the great one
    too; 'tis ours by conquest. Prithee help me up and I'll pull
    it down.
ANGELLICA [*to Willmore*]. Stay, sir, and ere you affront me
    farther let me know how you durst commit this outrage.
    To you I speak, sir, for you appear a gentleman.
WILLMORE. To me, madam?—Gentlemen, your servant.

    (*Belvile stays him.*)

BELVILE. Is the devil in thee? Dost know the danger of
    ent'ring the house of an incensed courtesan?
WILLMORE. I thank you for your care, but there are other
    matters in hand, there are, though we have no great
    temptation. Death! Let me go!
FREDERICK. Yes, to your lodging if you will, but not in here.
    Damn these gay harlots; by this hand I'll have as sound
    and handsome a whore for a patacoon.[89] Death, man,
    she'll murder thee!
WILLMORE. Oh, fear me not. Shall I not venture where a
    beauty calls? A lovely charming beauty! For fear of dan-
    ger? When, by heaven, there's none so great as to long for
    her whilst I want money to purchase her.

---

[87]**Molo** stone pier

[88]**Flanders** in 1659 Spain ceded the Netherlands to France
[89]**patacoon** Spanish coin

FREDERICK. Therefore 'tis loss of time unless you had the thousand crowns to pay.

WILLMORE. It may be she may give a favor; at least I shall have the pleasure of saluting her when I enter and when I depart.

BELVILE. Pox, she'll as soon lie with thee as kiss thee, and sooner stab than do either. You shall not go.

ANGELLICA. Fear not, sir, all I have to wound with is my eyes.

BLUNT. Let him go. 'Adsheartlikins, I believe the gentlewoman means well.

BELVILE. Well, take thy fortune; we'll expect you in the next street. Farewell, fool, farewell.

WILLMORE. 'Bye, colonel.   (*Goes in.*)

FREDERICK. The rogue's stark mad for a wench.

(*Exeunt.*)

SCENE 2

(*A fine chamber. Enter Willmore, Angellica, and Moretta.*)

ANGELLICA. Insolent sir, how durst you pull down my picture?

WILLMORE. Rather, how durst you set it up to tempt poor am'rous mortals with so much excellence, which I find you have but too well consulted by the unmerciful price you set upon't. Is all this heaven of beauty shown to move despair in those that cannot buy? And can you think th'effects of that despair should be less extravagant than I have shown?

ANGELLICA. I sent for you to ask my pardon, sir, not to aggravate your crime. I thought I should have seen you at my feet imploring it.

WILLMORE. You are deceived. I came to rail at you, and rail such truths too, as shall let you see the vanity of that pride which taught you how to set such price on sin.
For such it is whilst that which is love's due
Is meanly bartered for.

ANGELLICA. Ha! Ha! Ha! Alas, good captain, what pity 'tis your edifying doctrine will do no good upon me. Moretta, fetch the gentleman a glass,[90] and let him survey himself to see what charms he has.—(*Aside, in a soft tone.*) And guess my business.

MORETTA. He knows himself of old: I believe those breeches and he have been acquainted ever since he was beaten at Worcester.[91]

ANGELLICA. Nay, do not abuse the poor creature.

MORETTA. Good weather-beaten corporal, will you march off? We have no need of your doctrine, though you have of our charity. But at present we have no scraps; we can afford no kindness for God's sake. In fine, sirrah, the price is too high i'th' mouth[92] for you, therefore troop, I say.

WILLMORE. Here, good forewoman of the shop, serve me and I'll be gone.

MORETTA. Keep it to pay your laundress; your linen stinks of the gun room. For here's no selling by retail.

WILLMORE. Thou hast sold plenty of thy stale ware at a cheap rate.

MORETTA. Ay, the more silly kind heart I, but this is an age wherein beauty is at higher rates. In fine, you know the price of this.

WILLMORE. I grant you 'tis here set down, a thousand crowns a month. Pray, how much may come to my share for a pistole? Bawd, take your black lead[93] and sum it up, that I may have a pistole's worth[94] of this vain gay thing, and I'll trouble you no more.

MORETTA. Pox on him, he'll fret me to death! Abominable fellow, I tell thee we only sell by the whole piece.

WILLMORE. 'Tis very hard, the whole cargo or nothing. Faith, madam, my stock will not reach it; I cannot be your chapman. Yet I have countrymen in town, merchants of love like me; I'll see if they'll put in for a share. We cannot lose much by it, and what we have no use for, we'll sell upon the Friday's mart at "Who gives more?"—I am studying, madam, how to purchase you, though at present I am unprovided of money.

ANGELLICA (*aside*). Sure this from any other man would anger me; nor shall he know the conquest he has made.—Poor angry man, how I despise this railing.

WILLMORE.
Yes, I am poor. But I'm a gentleman,
And one that scorns this baseness which you practice.
Poor as I am I would not sell myself,
No, not to gain your charming high-prized person.
Though I admire you strangely for your beauty,
Yet I contemn your mind.
And yet I would at any rate enjoy you;
At your own rate; but cannot. See here
The only sum I can command on earth:
I know not where to eat when this is gone.
Yet such a slave I am to love and beauty
This last reserve I'll sacrifice to enjoy you.
Nay, do not frown, I know you're to be bought,
And would be bought by me. By me,
For a meaning trifling sum, if I could pay it down.
Which happy knowledge I will still repeat,
And lay it to my heart: It has a virtue in't,
And soon will cure those wounds your eyes have made.
And yet, there's something so divinely powerful there—
Nay, I will gaze, to let you see my strength.

(*Holds her, looks on her, and pauses and sighs.*)

---

[90]**glass** mirror [91]**Worcester** Cromwell defeated Charles II at Worcester and forced him into exile

[92]**high i'th' mouth** expensive [93]**black lead** pencil [94]**a pistole's worth** as much as a Spanish gold coin will buy

By heav'n, bright creature, I would not for the world
Thy fame were half so fair as is thy face.

(Turns her away from him.)

ANGELLICA *(aside).*
His words go through me to the very soul.—
If you have nothing else to say to me—

WILLMORE.
Yes, you shall hear how infamous you are—
For which I do not hate thee—
But that secures my heart, and all the flames it feels
Are but so many lusts:
I know it by their sudden bold intrusion.
The fire's impatient and betrays; 'tis false.
For had it been the purer flame of love,
I should have pined and languished at your feet,
Ere found the impudence to have discovered it.
I now dare stand your scorn and your denial.

MORETTA. Sure she's bewitched, that she can stand thus tamely and hear his saucy railing.—Sirrah, will you be gone?

ANGELLICA *(to Moretta).* How dare you take this liberty! Withdraw!—Pray tell me, sir, are not you guilty of the same mercenary crime? When a lady is proposed to you for a wife, you never ask how fair, discreet, or virtuous she is, but what's her fortune; which, if but small, you cry "She will not do my business," and basely leave her, though she languish for you. Say, is not this as poor?

WILLMORE. It is a barbarous custom, which I will scorn to defend in our sex, and do despise in yours.

ANGELLICA.
Thou'rt a brave fellow! Put up thy gold, and know,
That were thy fortune as large as is thy soul,
Thou shouldst not buy my love
Couldst thou forget those mean effects of vanity
Which set me out to sale,
And as a lover prize my yielding joys.
Canst thou believe they'll be entirely thine,
Without considering they were mercenary?

WILLMORE.
I cannot tell, I must bethink me first.
(Aside.) Ha! Death, I'm going to believe her.

ANGELLICA.
Prithee confirm that faith, or if thou canst not,
Flatter me a little: 'Twill please me from thy mouth.

WILLMORE *(aside).*
Curse on thy charming tongue! Dost thou return
My feigned contempt with so much subtlety?—
Thou'st found the easiest way into my heart,
Though I yet know that all thou say'st is false.

(Turning from her in rage.)

ANGELLICA.
By all that's good, 'tis real;
I never loved before, though oft a mistress.
Shall my first vows be slighted?

WILLMORE *(aside).*
What can she mean?

ANGELLICA *(in an angry tone).*
I find you cannot credit me.

WILLMORE.
I know you take me for an errant ass,
An ass that may be soothed into belief,
And then be used at pleasure;
But, madam, I have been so often cheated
By perjured, soft, deluding hypocrites,
That I've no faith left for the cozening sex,
Especially for women of your trade.

ANGELLICA.
The low esteem you have of me perhaps
May bring my heart again:
For I have pride that yet surmounts my love.

(She turns with pride; he holds her.)

WILLMORE.
Throw off this pride, this enemy to bliss,
And show the power of love: 'Tis with those arms
I can be only vanquished, made a slave.

ANGELLICA.
Is all my mighty expectation vanished?
No, I will not hear thee talk; thou hast a charm
In every word that draws my heart away,
And all the thousand trophies I designed
Thou hast undone. Why art thou soft?
Thy looks are bravely rough, and meant for war.
Couldst thou not storm on still?
I then perhaps had been as free as thou.

WILLMORE *(aside).*
Death, how she throws her fire about my soul!—
Take heed, fair creature, how you raise my hopes,
Which once assumed pretends to all dominion:
There's not a joy thou hast in store
I shall not then command.
For which I'll pay you back my soul, my life!
Come, let's begin th'account this happy minute!

ANGELLICA.
And will you pay me then the price I ask?

WILLMORE.
Oh, why dost thou draw me from an awful worship,
By showing thou art no divinity.
Conceal the fiend, and show me all the angel!
Keep me but ignorant, and I'll be devout
And pay my vows forever at this shrine.

(Kneels and kisses her hand.)

ANGELLICA.
The pay I mean is but thy love for mine.
Can you give that?

WILLMORE. Entirely. Come, let's withdraw where I'll renew my vows, and breathe 'em with such ardor thou shalt not doubt my zeal.

ANGELLICA. Thou hast a power too strong to be resisted.

(Exeunt Willmore and Angellica.)

MORETTA. Now my curse go with you! Is all our project fallen to this? To love the only enemy to our trade? Nay, to love such a shameroon;[95] a very beggar; nay, a pirate beggar, whose business is to rifle and be gone; a no-purchase, no-pay tatterdemalion, and English picaroon;[96] a rogue that fights for daily drink, and takes a pride in being loyally lousy? Oh, I could curse now, if I durst. This is the fate of most whores.

> *Trophies, which from believing fops we win,*
> *Are spoils to those who cozen us again.*

[*Exit.*]

ACT 3

SCENE 1

(A street. Enter Florinda, Valeria, Hellena, in antic[97] different dresses from what they were in before; Callis attending.)

FLORINDA. I wonder what should make my brother in so ill a humor? I hope he has not found out our ramble this morning.

HELLENA. No, if he had, we should have heard on't at both ears, and have been mew'd up[98] this afternoon, which I would not for the world should have happened. Hey ho, I'm as sad as a lover's lute.

VALERIA. Well, methinks we have learnt this trade of gypsies as readily as if we had been bred upon the road to Loretto, and yet I did so fumble when I told the stranger his fortune that I was afraid I should have told my own and yours by mistake. But methinks Hellena has been very serious ever since.

FLORINDA. I would give my garters she were in love, to be revenged upon her for abusing me. How is't, Hellena?

HELLENA. Ah, would I had never seen my mad monsieur. And yet, for all your laughing, I am not in love. And yet this small acquaintance, o' my conscience, will never out of my head.

VALERIA. Ha! Ha! Ha! I laugh to think how thou art fitted with a lover, a fellow that I warrant loves every new face he sees.

HELLENA. Hum, he has not kept his word with me here, and may be taken up. That thought is not very pleasant to me. What the deuce should this be now that I feel?

VALERIA. What is't like?

HELLENA. Nay, the Lord knows, but if I should be hanged I cannot choose but be angry and afraid when I think that mad fellow should be in love with anybody but me. What

to think of myself I know not: Would I could meet with some true damned gypsy, that I might know my fortune.

VALERIA. Know it! Why there's nothing so easy: Thou wilt love this wand'ring inconstant till thou find'st thyself hanged about his neck, and then be as mad to get free again.

FLORINDA. Yes, Valeria, we shall see her bestride his baggage horse and follow him to the campaign.

HELLENA. So, so, now you are provided for there's no care taken of poor me. But since you have set my heart a-wishing, I am resolved to know for what; I will not die of the pip,[99] so I will not.

FLORINDA. Art thou mad to talk so? Who will like thee well enough to have thee, that hears what a mad wench thou art?

HELLENA. Like me? I don't intend every he that likes me shall have me, but he that I like. I should have stayed in the nunnery still if I had liked my lady abbess as well as she liked me. No, I came thence not, as my wise brother imagines, to take an eternal farewell of the world, but to love and to be beloved; and I will be beloved, or I'll get one of your men, so I will.

VALERIA. Am I put into[100] the number of lovers?

HELLENA. You? Why, coz, I know thou'rt too good-natured to leave us in any design; thou wouldst venture a cast[101] though thou comest off a loser, especially with such a gamester. I observed your man, and your willing ear incline that way; and if you are not a lover, 'tis an art soon learnt—that I find.   (*Sighs.*)

FLORINDA. I wonder how you learnt to love so easily. I had a thousand charms to meet my eyes and ears ere I could yield, and 'twas the knowledge of Belvile's merit, not the surprising person, took my soul. Thou art too rash, to give a heart at first sight.

HELLENA. Hang your considering lover! I never thought beyond the fancy that 'twas a very pretty, idle, silly kind of pleasure to pass one's time with: to write little soft nonsensical billets,[102] and with great difficulty and danger receive answers in which I shall have my beauty praised, my wit admired, though little or none, and have the vanity and power to know I am desirable. Then I have the more inclination that way because I am to be a nun, and so shall not be suspected to have any such earthly thoughts about me; but when I walk thus—and sigh thus—they'll think my mind's upon my monastery, and cry, "How happy 'tis she's so resolved." But not a word of man.

FLORINDA. What a mad creature's this!

HELLENA. I'll warrant, if my brother hears either of you sigh, he cries gravely, "I fear you have the indiscretion to be in love, but take heed of the honor of our house, and your

---

[95]**shameroon** deceiver   [96]**picaroon** rogue   [97]**antic** grotesque   [98]**mew'd up** confined

[99]**die of the pip** die of some minor ailment   [100]**into** among   [101]**venture a cast** throw dice   [102]**billets** love notes

own unspotted fame"; and so he conjures on till he has laid the soft winged god in your hearts, or broke the bird's nest.[103] But see, here comes your lover, but where's my inconstant? Let's step aside, and we may learn something.

(Go aside.)

(Enter Belvile, Frederick, and Blunt.)

BELVILE. What means this! The picture's taken in.

BLUNT. It may be the wench is good-natured, and will be kind gratis.[104] Your friend's a proper handsome fellow.

BELVILE. I rather think she has cut his throat and is fled; I am mad he should throw himself into dangers. Pox on't, I shall want him, too, at night. Let's knock and ask for him.

HELLENA. My heart goes a-pit, a-pat, for fear 'tis my man they talk of.

(Knock; Moretta above.)

MORETTA. What would you have?

BELVILE. Tell the stranger that entered here about two hours ago that his friends stay here for him.

MORETTA. A curse upon him for Moretta: Would he were at the devil! But he's coming to you.

(Enter Willmore.)

HELLENA. Ay, ay 'tis he. Oh, how this vexes me!

BELVILE. And how and how, dear lad, has fortune smiled? Are we to break her windows, or raise up altars to her, hah?

WILLMORE. Does not my fortune sit triumphant on my brow? Dost not see the little wanton god there all gay and smiling? Have I not an air about my face and eyes that distinguish me from the crowd of common lovers? By heaven, Cupid's quiver has not half so many darts as her eyes! Oh, such a *bona roba*![105] To sleep in her arms is lying *in fresco*,[106] all perfumed air about me.

HELLENA *(aside)*. Here's fine encouragement for me to fool on!

WILLMORE. Hark'ee, where didst thou purchase that rich Canary[107] we drank today? Tell me, that I may adore the spigot and sacrifice to the butt.[108] The juice was divine; into which I must dip my rosary, and then bless all things that I would have bold or fortunate.

BELVILE. Well, sir, let's go take a bottle and hear the story of your success.

FREDERICK. Would not French wine do better?

WILLMORE. Damn the hungry balderdash![109] Cheerful sack[110] has a generous virtue in't inspiring a successful

confidence, gives eloquence to the tongue and vigor to the soul, and has in a few hours completed all my hopes and wishes! There's nothing left to raise a new desire in me. Come, let's be gay and wanton. And, gentlemen, study; study what you want, for here are friends that will supply gentlemen. *[Jingles gold coins.]* Hark what a charming sound they make! 'Tis he and she gold whilst here, and shall beget new pleasures every moment.

BLUNT. But hark'ee, sir, you are not married, are you?

WILLMORE. All the honey of matrimony but none of the sting, friend.

BLUNT. 'Adsheartlikins, thou'rt a fortunate rogue!

WILLMORE. I am so, sir: let these inform you! Ha, how sweetly they chime! Pox of poverty: It makes a man a slave, makes wit and honor sneak. My soul grew lean and rusty for want of credit.

BLUNT. 'Adsheartlikins, this I like well; it looks like my lucky bargain! Oh, how I long for the approach of my squire, that is to conduct me to her house again. Why, here's two provided for!

FREDERICK. By this light, y'are happy men.

BLUNT. Fortune is pleased to smile on us, gentlemen, to smile on us.

(Enter Sancho and pulls down Blunt by the sleeve; they go aside.)

SANCHO. Sir, my lady expects you. She has removed all that might oppose your will and pleasure, and is impatient till you come.

BLUNT. Sir, I'll attend you.—Oh the happiest rogue! I'll take no leave, lest they either dog me or stay me.

(Exit with Sancho.)

BELVILE. But then the little gypsy is forgot?

WILLMORE. A mischief on thee for putting her into my thoughts! I had quite forgot her else, and this night's debauch had drunk her quite down.

HELLENA. Had it so, good captain!

(Claps him on the back.)

WILLMORE *(aside)*. Ha! I hope she did not hear me!

HELLENA. What, afraid of such a champion?

WILLMORE. Oh, you're a fine lady of your word, are you not? To make a man languish a whole day—

HELLENA. In tedious search of me.

WILLMORE. Egad, child, thou'rt in the right. Hadst thou seen what a melancholy dog I have been ever since I was a lover, how I have walked the streets like a Capuchin,[111] with my hands in my sleeves—faith, sweetheart, thou wouldst pity me.

HELLENA *[aside]*. Now if I should be hanged I can't be angry with him, he dissembles so heartily.—Alas, good captain, what pains you have taken; now were I ungrateful not to reward so true a servant.

---

[103]**laid . . . bird's nest** stimulated your love, or destroyed the place where love dwells (*bird* = Cupid)   [104]**gratis** freely   [105]***bona roba*** courtesan   [106]***in fresco*** outdoors   [107]**Canary** sweet wine, from the Canary Islands   [108]**butt** large cask   [109]**hungry balderdash** cheap mixture of liquor   [110]**sack** dry wine from Spain

[111]**Capuchin** monk

WILLMORE. Poor soul, that's kindly said; I see thou barest a conscience. Come then, for a beginning show my thy dear face.

HELLENA. I'm afraid, my small acquaintance, you have been staying that swinging stomach you boasted of this morning. I then remember my little collation[112] would have gone down with you without the sauce of a handsome face. Is your stomach so queasy now?

WILLMORE. Faith, long fasting, child, spoils a man's appetite. Yet if you durst treat, I could so lay about me still—

HELLENA. And would you fall to before a priest says grace?

WILLMORE. O fie, fie, what an old out-of-fashioned thing hast thou named? Thou couldst not dash me more out of countenance shouldst thou show me an ugly face.

(*Whilst he is seemingly courting Hellena, enter Angellica, Moretta, Biskey, and Sebastian, all in masquerade. Angellica sees Willmore and stares.*)

ANGELLICA. Heavens, 'tis he! And passionately fond to see another woman!

MORETTA. What could you less expect from such a swaggerer?

ANGELLICA.
Expect? As much as I paid him: a heart entire,
Which I had pride enough to think when'er I gave,
It would have raised the man above the vulgar,
Made him all soul, and that all soft and constant.

HELLENA. You see, captain, how willing I am to be friends with you, till time and ill luck make us lovers; and ask you the question first rather than put your modesty to the blush by asking me. For alas, I know you captains are such strict men, and such severe observers of your vows to chastity, that 'twill be hard to prevail with your tender conscience to marry a young willing maid.

WILLMORE. Do not abuse me, for fear I should take thee at thy word and marry thee indeed, which I'm sure will be revenge sufficient.

HELLENA. O' my conscience, that will be our destiny, because we are both of one humor: I am as inconstant as you, for I have considered, captain, that a handsome woman has a great deal to do whilst her face is good. For then is our harvest-time to gather friends, and should I in these days of my youth catch a fit of foolish constancy, I were undone: 'tis loitering by daylight in our great journey. Therefore, I declare I'll allow but one year for love, one year for indifference, and one year for hate; and then go hang yourself, for I profess myself the gay, the kind, and the inconstant. The devil's in't if this won't please you!

WILLMORE. Oh, most damnably. I have a heart with a hole quite through it too; no prison mine, to keep a mistress in.

ANGELLICA (*aside*). Perjured man! How I believe thee now!

HELLENA. Well, I see our business as well as humors are alike: yours to cozen as many maids as will trust you, and I as many men as have faith. See if I have not as desperate a lying look as you can have for the heart of you. (*Pulls off her vizard; he starts.*) How do you like it, captain?

WILLMORE. Like it! By heaven, I never saw so much beauty! Oh, the charms of those sprightly black eyes! That strangely fair face, full of smiles and dimples! Those soft round melting cherry lips and small even white teeth! Not to be expressed, but silently adored! [*She replaces her mask.*] Oh, one look more, and strike me dumb, or I shall repeat nothing else till I'm mad.

(*He seems to court her to pull off her vizard; she refuses.*)

ANGELLICA. I can endure no more. Nor is it fit to interrupt him, for if I do, my jealousy has so destroyed my reason I shall undo him. Therefore I'll retire, and you, Sebastian (*to one of her Bravos*), follow that woman and learn who 'tis; while you (*to the other Bravo*) tell the fugitive I would speak to him instantly.   (*Exit.*)

(*This while Florinda is talking to Belvile, who stands sullenly; Frederick courting Valeria.*)

VALERIA [*to Belvile*]. Prithee, dear stranger, be not so sullen, for though you have lost your love you see my friend frankly offers you hers to play with in the meantime.

BELVILE. Faith, madam, I am sorry I can't play at her game.

FREDERICK [*to Valeria*]. Pray leave your intercession and mind your own affair. They'll better agree apart: He's a modest sigher in company, but alone no woman 'scapes him.

FLORINDA [*aside*]. Sure he does but rally. Yet, if it should be true? I'll tempt him farther.—Believe me, noble stranger, I'm no common mistress. And for a little proof on't, wear this jewel. Nay, take it, sir, 'tis right, and bills of exchange may sometimes miscarry.

BELVILE. Madam, why am I chose out of all mankind to be the object of your bounty?

VALERIA. There's another civil question asked.

FREDERICK [*aside*]. Pox of's modesty; it spoils his own markets and hinders mine.

FLORINDA. Sir, from my window I have often seen you, and women of my quality have so few opportunities for love that we ought to lose none.

FREDERICK [*to Valeria*]. Ay, this is something! Here's a woman! When shall I be blest with so much kindness from your fair mouth?—(*Aside to Belvile.*) Take the jewel, fool!

BELVILE. You tempt me strangely, madam, every way—

FLORINDA (*aside*). So, if I find him false, my whole repose is gone.

BELVILE. And but for a vow I've made to a very fair lady, this goodness had subdued me.

[112]**collation** light meal

FREDERICK [*aside to Belvile*]. Pox on't, be kind, in pity to me be kind. For I am to thrive here but as you treat her friend.

HELLENA. Tell me what you did in yonder house, and I'll unmask.

WILLMORE. Yonder house? Oh, I went to a—to—why, there's a friend of mine lives there.

HELLENA. What, a she or a he friend?

WILLMORE. A man, upon honor, a man. A she friend? No, no, madam, you have done my business, I thank you.

HELLENA. And was't your man friend that had more darts in's eyes than Cupid carries in's whole budget[113] of arrows?

WILLMORE. So—

HELLENA. "Ah, such a *bona roba!* To be in her arms is lying *in fresco,* all perfumed air about me." Was this your man friend too?

WILLMORE. So—

HELLENA. That gave you the he and the she gold, that begets young pleasures?

WILLMORE. Well, well, madam, then you can see there are ladies in the world that will not be cruel. There are, madam, there are.

HELLENA. And there be men, too, as fine, wild, inconstant fellows as yourself. There be, captain, there be, if you go to that now. Therefore, I'm resolved—

WILLMORE. Oh!

HELLENA. To see your face no more—

WILLMORE. Oh!

HELLENA. Till tomorrow.

WILLMORE. Egad, you frighted me.

HELLENA. Nor then neither, unless you'll swear never to see that lady more.

WILLMORE. See her! Why, never to think of womankind again.

HELLENA. Kneel and swear.

(*Kneels; she gives him her hand.*)

WILLMORE. I do, never to think, to see, to love, nor lie, with any but thyself.

HELLENA. Kiss the book.

WILLMORE. Oh, most religiously.   (*Kisses her hand.*)

HELLENA. Now what a wicked creature am I, to damn a proper fellow.

CALLIS (*to Florinda*). Madam, I'll stay no longer: 'tis e'en dark.

FLORINDA [*to Belvile*]. However, sir, I'll leave this with you, that when I'm gone you may repent the opportunity you have lost by your modesty.

(*Gives him the jewel, which is her picture, and exits. He gazes after her.*)

WILLMORE [*to Hellena*]. 'Twill be an age till tomorrow, and till then I will most impatiently expect you. Adieu, my dear pretty angel.

(*Exeunt all the women.*)

BELVILE. Ha! Florinda's picture! 'Twas she herself. What a dull dog was I! I would have given the world for one minute's discourse with her.

FREDERICK. This comes of your modesty. Ah, pox o' your vow; 'twas ten to one but we had lost the jewel by't.

BELVILE. Willmore, the blessed'st opportunity lost! Florinda, friends, Florinda!

WILLMORE. Ah, rogue! Such black eyes! Such a face! Such a mouth! Such teeth! And so much wit!

BELVILE. All, all, and a thousand charms besides.

WILLMORE. Why, dost thou know her?

BELVILE. Know her! Ay, ay, and a pox take me with all my heart for being so modest.

WILLMORE. But hark'ee, friend of mine, are you my rival? And have I been only beating the bush all this while?

BELVILE. I understand thee not. I'm mad! See here—
(*Shows the picture.*)

WILLMORE. Ha! Whose picture's this? 'Tis a fine wench!

FREDERICK. The colonel's mistress, sir.

WILLMORE. Oh, oh, here. (*Gives the picture back.*) I thought't had been another prize. Come, come, a bottle will set thee right again.

BELVILE. I am content to try, and by that time 'twill be late enough for our design.

WILLMORE. Agreed.

Love does all day the soul's great empire keep,
But wine at night lulls the soft god asleep.

(*Exeunt.*)

SCENE 2

(*Lucetta's house. Enter Blunt and Lucetta with a light.*)

LUCETTA. Now we are safe and free: no fears of the coming home of my old jealous husband, which made me a little thoughtful when you came in first. But now love is all the business of my soul.

BLUNT. I am transported!—(*Aside.*) Pox on't, that I had but some fine things to say to her, such as lovers use. I was a fool not to learn of Fred a little by heart before I came. Something I must say.—'Adsheartlikins, sweet soul, I am not used to compliment, but I'm an honest gentleman, and thy humble servant.

LUCETTA. I have nothing to pay for so great a favor, but such a love as cannot but be great, since at first sight of that sweet face and shape it made me your absolute captive.

BLUNT (*aside*). Kind heart, how prettily she talks! Egad, I'll show her husband a Spanish trick: Send him out of the world and marry her; she's damnably in love with me,

---

[113]**budget** bag, quiver

and will ne'er mind settlements,[114] and so there's that saved.

LUCETTA. Well, sir, I'll go and undress me, and be with you instantly.

BLUNT. Make haste then, for 'adsheartlikins, dear soul, thou canst not guess at the pain of a longing lover when his joys are drawn within the compass of a few minutes.

LUCETTA. You speak my sense, and I'll make haste to prove it.   (*Exit*.)

BLUNT. 'Tis a rare girl, and this one night's enjoyment with her will be worth all the days I ever passed in Essex. Would she would go with me into England, though to say truth, there's plenty of whores already. Put a pox on 'em, they are such mercenary prodigal whores that they want such a one as this, that's free and generous, to give 'em good examples. Why, what a house she has, how rich and fine!

(*Enter Sancho.*)

SANCHO. Sir, my lady has sent me to conduct you to her chamber.

BLUNT. Sir, I shall be proud to follow.—(*Aside*.) Here's one of her servants too; 'adsheartlikins, by this garb and gravity he might be a justice of peace in Essex, and is but a pimp here.

                                                        (*Exeunt*.)

SCENE 3

(*The scene changes to a chamber with an alcove bed in't, a table, etc.; Lucetta in bed. Enter Sancho and Blunt, who takes the candle of Sancho at the door.*)

SANCHO. Sir, my commission reaches no farther.

BLUNT. Sir, I'll excuse your compliment.

                                                [*Exit Sancho.*]

—What, in bed, my sweet mistress?

LUCETTA. You see, I still outdo you in kindness.

BLUNT. And thou shalt see what haste I'll make to quit scores. Oh, the luckiest rogue!

(*He undresses himself.*)

LUCETTA. Should you be false or cruel now—

BLUNT. False! 'Adsheartlikins, what dost thou take me for, a Jew? An insensible heathen? A pox of thy old jealous husband: An[115] he were dead, egad,[116] sweet soul, it should be none of my fault if I did not marry thee.

LUCETTA. It never should be mine.

BLUNT. Good soul! I'm the fortunatest dog!

LUCETTA. Are you not undressed yet?

BLUNT. As much as my impatience will permit.

(*Goes toward the bed in his shirt, drawers, etc.*)

LUCETTA. Hold, sir, put out the light; it may betray us else.

BLUNT. Anything; I need no other light but that of thine eyes.—(*Aside*.) 'Adsheartlikins, there I think I had it.

(*Puts out the candle; the bed descends; he gropes about to find it.*)

Why, why, where am I got? What, not yet? Where are you, sweetest?—Ah, the rogue's silent now. A pretty love-trick this; how she'll laugh at me anon!—You need not, my dear rogue, you need not! I'm all on fire already; come, come, now call me, in pity.—Sure I'm enchanted! I have been round the chamber, and can find neither woman nor bed. I locked the door; I'm sure she cannot go that way, or if she could, the bed could not.—Enough, enough, my pretty wanton; do not carry the jest too far! (*Lights on a trap, and is let down.*)—Ha! Betrayed! Dogs! Rogues! Pimps! Help! Help!

(*Enter Lucetta, Philippo, and Sancho with a light.*)

PHILIPPO. Ha! Ha! Ha! He's dispatched finely.

LUCETTA. Now, sir, had I been coy, we had missed of this booty.

PHILIPPO. Nay, when I saw 'twas a substantial fool, I was mollified. But when you dote upon a serenading coxcomb, upon a face, fine clothes, and a lute, it makes me rage.

LUCETTA. You know I was never guilty of that folly, my dear Philippo, but with yourself. But come, let's see what we have got by this.

PHILIPPO. A rich coat; sword and hat; these breeches, too, are well lined! See here, a gold watch! A purse—Ha! Gold! At least two hundred pistoles! A bunch of diamond rings, and one with the family arms! A gold box, with a medal of his king, and his lady mother's picture! These were sacred relics, believe me. See, the waistband of his breeches have a mine of gold—old queen Bess's![117] We have a quarrel to her ever since eighty-eight,[118] and may therefore justify the theft: The Inquisition might have committed it.

LUCETTA. See, a bracelet of bowed[119] gold! These his sisters tied about his arm at parting. But well, for all this, I fear his being a stranger may make a noise and hinder our trade with them hereafter.

PHILIPPO. That's our security: He is not only a stranger to us, but to the country too. The common shore[120] into which he is descended, thou know'st, conducts him into another street, which this light will hinder him from ever finding again. He knows neither your name, nor that of the street where your house is; nay, nor the way to his own lodgings.

---

[114]**settlements** prenuptial agreement settling property on a wife
[115]**An if**   [116]**egad** a mild oath

[117]**old queen Bess** Queen Elizabeth I (reigned 1558–1603)   [118]**eighty-eight** 1588, the year the English defeated the Spanish Armada
[119]**bowed** curved(?) braided(?)   [120]**common shore** sewer

LUCETTA. And art thou not an unmerciful rogue, not to afford him one night for all this? I should not have been such a Jew.

PHILIPPO. Blame me not, Lucetta, to keep as much of thee as I can to myself. Come, that thought makes me wanton; let's to bed.—Sancho, lock up these.

> This is the fleece which fools do bear,
> Designed for witty men to shear.

(Exeunt.)

SCENE 4

(The scene changes, and discovers Blunt creeping out of a common shore; his face, etc., all dirty.)

BLUNT (climbing up). Oh, Lord, I am got out at last, and, which is a miracle, without a clue. And now to damning and cursing! But if that would ease me, where shall I begin? With my fortune, myself, or the quean[121] that cozened me? What a dog was I to believe in woman! Oh, coxcomb! Ignorant conceited coxcomb! To fancy she could be enamored with my person! At first sight enamored! Oh, I'm a cursed puppy! 'Tis plain, fool was writ upon my forehead! She perceived it; saw the Essex calf there. For what allurements could there be in this countenance, which I can endure because I'm acquainted with it. Oh dull, silly dog, to be thus soothed into a cozening! Had I been drunk, I might fondly have credited the young quean; but as I was in my right wits to be thus cheated, confirms it: I am a dull believing English country fop. But my comrades! Death and the devil, there's the worst of all! Then a ballad will be sung tomorrow on the Prado,[122] to a lousy tune of the enchanted squire and the annihilated damsel. But Fred—that rogue—and the colonel will abuse me beyond all Christian patience. Had she left me my clothes, I have a bill of exchange at home would have saved my credit. But now all hope is taken from me. Well, I'll home, if I can find the way, with this consolation: that I am not the first kind believing coxcomb; but there are, gallants, many such good natures amongst ye.

> And though you've better arts to hide your follies,
> 'Adsheartlikins, y'are all as errant cullies.[123]

(Exit.)

SCENE 5

(Scene: the garden in the night. Enter Florinda in an undress,[124] with a key and a little box.)

FLORINDA. Well, thus far I'm in my way to happiness. I have got myself free from Callis; my brother too, I find by yonder light, is got into his cabinet,[125] and thinks not of me; I have by good fortune got the key of the garden back door. I'll open it to prevent Belvile's knocking: A little noise will now alarm my brother. Now am I as fearful as a young thief. (Unlocks the door.) Hark! What noise is that? Oh, 'twas the wind that played amongst the boughs. Belvile stays long, methinks; it's time. Stay, for fear of a surprise, I'll hide these jewels in yonder jasmine.

(She goes to lay down the box.)

(Enter Willmore, drunk.)

WILLMORE. What the devil is become of these fellows Belvile and Frederick? They promised to stay at the next corner for me, but who the devil knows the corner of a full moon? Now, whereabouts am I? Ha, what have we here? A garden! A very convenient place to sleep in. Ha! What has God sent us here? A female! By this light, a woman! I'm a dog if it be not a very wench!

FLORINDA. He's come! Ha! Who's there?

WILLMORE. Sweet soul, let me salute thy shoestring.

FLORINDA [aside]. 'Tis not my Belvile. Good heavens, I know him not!—Who are you, and from whence come you?

WILLMORE. Prithee, prithee, child, not so many hard questions! Let is suffice I am here, child. Come, come kiss me.

FLORINDA. Good gods! What luck is mine?

WILLMORE. Only good luck, child, parlous[126] good luck. Come hither.—'Tis a delicate shining wench. By this hand, she's perfumed, and smells like any nosegay.— Prithee, dear soul, let's not play the fool and lose time— precious time. For as Gad shall save me, I'm as honest a fellow as breathes, though I'm a little disguised[127] at present. Come, I say. Why, thou mayst be free with me: I'll be very secret. I'll not boast who 'twas obliged me, not I; for hang me if I know thy name.

FLORINDA. Heavens! What a filthy beast is this!

WILLMORE. I am so, and thou ought'st the sooner to lie with me for that reason. For look you, child, there will be no sin in't, because 'twas neither designed nor premeditated: 'Tis pure accident on both sides. That's a certain thing now. Indeed, should I make love to you, and you vow fidelity, and swear and lie till you believed and yielded— that were to make it willful fornication, the crying sin of the nation. Thou art, therefore, as thou art a good Christian, obliged in conscience to deny me nothing. Now, come be kind without any more idle prating.

FLORINDA. Oh, I am ruined! Wicked man, unhand me!

WILLMORE. Wicked? Egad, child, a judge, were he young and vigorous, and saw those eyes of thine, would know 'twas they gave the first blow, the first provocation. Come, prithee let's lose no time, I say. This is a fine convenient place.

---

[121]**quean** harlot   [122]**Prado** promenade   [123]**errant cullies** arrant fools   [124]**undress** informal clothing

[125]**cabinet** private room   [126]**parlous** excessively, with pun on perilous   [127]**disguised** drunk

FLORINDA. Sir, let me go, I conjure[128] you, or I'll call out.

WILLMORE. Ay, ay, you were best to call witness to see how finely you treat me. Do!

FLORINDA. I'll cry murder, rape, or anything, if you do not instantly let me go!

WILLMORE. A rape? Come, come, you lie, you baggage, you lie. What! I'll warrant you would fain have the world believe now that you are not so forward as I. No, not you. Why at this time of night was your cobweb door set open, dear spider, but to catch flies? Ha! Come, or I shall be damnably angry. Why, what a coil[129] is here!

FLORINDA. Sir, can you think—

WILLMORE. That you would do't for nothing? Oh, oh, I find what you would be at. Look here, here's a pistole[130] for you. Here's a work indeed! Here, take it, I say!

FLORINDA. For heaven's sake, sir, as you're a gentleman—

WILLMORE. So now, now, she would be wheedling me for more! What, you will not take it then? You are resolved you will not? Come, come, take it or I'll put it up again, for look ye, I never give more. Why, how now, mistress, are you so high i'th' mouth[131] a pistole won't down with you? Ha! Why, what a work's here! In good time! Come, no struggling to be gone. But an y'are good at a dumb wrestle, I'm for ye. Look ye, I'm for ye.

(*She struggles with him.*)

(*Enter Belvile and Frederick.*)

BELVILE. The door is open. A pox of this mad fellow! I'm angry that we've lost him; I durst have sworn he had followed us.

FREDERICK. But you were so hasty, colonel, to be gone.

FLORINDA. Help! Help! Murder! Help! Oh, I am ruined!

BELVILE. Ha! Sure that's Florinda's voice (*Comes up to them.*) A man!—Villain, let go that lady!

(*A noise; Willmore turns and draws; Frederick interposes.*)

FLORINDA. Belvile! Heavens! My brother too is coming, and 'twill be impossible to escape. Belvile, I conjure you to walk under my chamber window, from whence I'll give you some instructions what to do. This rude man has undone us.   (*Exit.*)

WILLMORE. Belvile!

(*Enter Pedro, Stephano, and other servants, with lights.*)

PEDRO. I'm betrayed! Run, Stephano, and see if Florinda be safe.

(*Exit Stephano.*)

(*They fight, and Pedro's party beats 'em out.*)

—So, whoe'er they be, all is not well. I'll to Florinda's chamber.   (*Going out, meets Stephano.*)

STEPHANO. You need not, sir: The poor lady's fast asleep, and thinks no harm. I would not awake her, sir, for fear of frighting her with your danger.

PEDRO. I'm glad she's there.—Rascals, how came the garden door open?

STEPHANO. That question comes too late, sir. Some of my fellow servants masquerading, I'll warrant.

PEDRO. Masquerading! A lewd custom to debauch our youth! There's something more in this than I imagine.

(*Exeunt.*)

SCENE 6

(*Scene changes to the street. Enter Belvile in rage, Frederick holding him, Willmore melancholy.*)

WILLMORE. Why, how the devil should I know Florinda?

BELVILE. Ah, plague of your ignorance! If it had not been Florinda, must you be a beast? A brute? A senseless swine?

WILLMORE. Well, sir, you see I am endued[132] with patience: I can bear. Though egad, y'are very free with me, methinks. I was in good hopes the quarrel would have been on my side, for so uncivilly interrupting me.

BELVILE. Peace, brute, whilst thou'rt safe. Oh, I'm distracted!

WILLMORE. Nay, nay, I'm an unlucky dog, that's certain.

BELVILE. Ah, curse upon the star that ruled my birth, or whatsoever other influence that makes me still so wretched.

WILLMORE. Thou break'st my heart with these complaints. There is no star in fault, no influence but sack, the cursed sack I drunk.

FREDERICK. Why, how the devil came you so drunk?

WILLMORE. Why, how the devil came you so sober?

BELVILE. A curse upon his thin skull, he was always beforehand that way.

FREDERICK. Prithee, dear colonel, forgive him; he's sorry for his fault.

BELVILE. He's always so after he has done a mischief. A plague on all such brutes!

WILLMORE. By this light, I took her for an errant harlot.

BELVILE. Damn your debauched opinion! Tell me, sot, hadst thou so much sense and light about thee to distinguish her woman, and couldst not see something about her face and person to strike an awful reverence into thy soul?

WILLMORE. Faith no, I considered her as mere a woman as I could wish.

BELVILE. 'Sdeath, I have no patience. Draw, or I'll kill you!

WILLMORE. Let that alone till tomorrow, and if I set not all right again, use your pleasure.

---

[128]**conjure** implore [129]**coil** disturbance [130]**pistole** gold coin
[131]**high i'th' mouth** stuck up

[132]**endued** endowed

BELVILE. Tomorrow! Damn it,
  The spiteful light will lead me to no happiness.
  Tomorrow is Antonio's, and perhaps
  Guides him to my undoing. Oh, that I could meet
  This rival, this powerful fortunate!

WILLMORE. What then?

BELVILE. Let thy own reason, or my rage, instruct thee.

WILLMORE. I shall be finely informed then, no doubt. Hear me, colonel, hear me; show me the man and I'll do his business.

BELVILE. I know him no more than thou, or if I did I should not need thy aid.

WILLMORE. This you say is Angellica's house; I promised the kind baggage to lie with her tonight.

(Offers to go in.)

(Enter Antonio and his Page. Antonio knocks on the hilt of's sword.)

ANTONIO. You paid the thousand crowns I directed?

PAGE. To the lady's old woman, sir, I did.

WILLMORE. Who the devil have we here?

BELVILE. I'll now plant myself under Florinda's window, and if I find no comfort there, I'll die.

(Exeunt Belvile and Frederick.)

(Enter Moretta.)

MORETTA. Page?

PAGE. Here's my lord.

WILLMORE. How is this? A picaroon[133] going to board my frigate?—Here's one chase gun for you!

(Drawing his sword, justles Antonio, who turns and draws. They fight; Antonio falls.)

MORETTA. Oh, bless us! We're all undone!

(Runs in and shuts the door.)

PAGE. Help! Murder!

(Belvile returns at the noise of fighting.)

BELVILE. Ha! The mad rogue's engaged in some unlucky adventure again.

(Enter two or three Masqueraders.)

MASQUERADER. Ha! A man killed!

WILLMORE. How, a man killed? Then I'll go home to sleep.

(Puts up and reels out. Exeunt Masqueraders another way.)

BELVILE. Who should it be? Pray heaven the rogue is safe, for all my quarrel to him.

(As Belvile is groping about, enter an Officer and six Soldiers.)

SOLDIER. Who's there?

OFFICER. So, here's one dispatched. Secure the murderer.

BELVILE. Do not mistake my charity for murder! I came to his assistance!

(Soldiers seize on Belvile.)

OFFICER. That shall be tried, sir. St. Jago! Swords drawn in the Carnival time!   (Goes to Antonio.)

ANTONIO. Thy hand, prithee.

OFFICER. Ha! Don Antonio! Look well to the villain there.—How is it, sir?

ANTONIO. I'm hurt.

BELVILE. Has my humanity made me a criminal?

OFFICER. Away with him!

BELVILE. What a curst chance is this!

(Exeunt soldiers with Belvile.)

ANTONIO [aside]. This is the man that has set upon me twice.—(To the officer.) Carry him to my apartment till you have further orders from me.

(Exit Antonio, led.)

ACT 4

SCENE 1

(A fine room. Discovers Belvile as by dark alone.)

BELVILE. When shall I be weary of railing on fortune, who is resolved never to turn with smiles upon me? Two such defeats in one night none but the devil and that mad rogue could have contrived to have plagued me with. I am here a prisoner. But where, heaven knows. And if there be murder done, I can soon decide the fate of a stranger in a nation without mercy. Yet this is nothing to the torture my soul bows with when I think of losing my fair, my dear Florinda. Hark, my door opens. A light! A man, and seems of quality. Armed, too! Now shall I die like a dog, without defense.

(Enter Antonio in a nightgown, with a light; his arm in a scarf, and a sword under his arm. He sets the candle on the table.)

ANTONIO. Sir, I come to know what injuries I have done you, that could provoke you to so mean an action as to attack me basely without allowing time for my defense?

BELVILE. Sir, for a man in my circumstances to plead innocence would look like fear. But view me well, and you will find no marks of coward on me, nor anything that betrays that brutality you accuse me with.

ANTONIO. In vain, sir, you impose upon my sense. You are not only he who drew on me last night, but yesterday before the same house, that of Angellica. Yet there is something in your face and mien[134] that makes me wish I were mistaken.

BELVILE. I own I fought today in the defense of a friend of mine with whom you, if you're the same, and your party were first engaged. Perhaps you think this crime enough to kill me; but if you do, I cannot fear you'll do it basely.

---

[133]**picaroon** pirate

[134]**mien** manner

ANTONIO. No sir, I'll make you fit for a defense with this. (*Gives him the sword.*)

BELVILE. This gallantry surprises me, nor know I how to use this present, sir, against a man so brave.

ANTONIO. You shall not need. For know, I come to snatch you from a danger that is decreed against you: perhaps your life, or long imprisonment. And 'twas with so much courage you offended, I cannot see you punished.

BELVILE. How shall I pay this generosity?

ANTONIO. It had been safer to have killed another than have attempted me. To show your danger, sir, I'll let you know my quality:[135] And 'tis the Viceroy's son whom you have wounded.

BELVILE. The Viceroy's son!—(*Aside.*) Death and confusion! Was this plague reserved to complete all the rest? Obliged by[136] him, the man of all the world I would destroy!

ANTONIO. You seem disordered, sir.

BELVILE. Yes, trust me, I am, and 'tis with pain that man receives such bounties who wants the power to pay 'em back again.

ANTONIO. To gallant spirits 'tis indeed uneasy, but you may quickly overpay me, sir.

BELVILE (*aside*). Then I am well. Kind heaven, but set us even, that I may fight with him and keep my honor safe.—Oh, I'm impatient, sir, to be discounting the mighty debt I owe you. Command me quickly.

ANTONIO. I have a quarrel with a rival, sir, about the maid we love.

BELVILE (*aside*). Death, 'tis Florinda he means! That thought destroys my reason, and I shall kill him.

ANTONIO. My rival, sir, is one has all the virtues man can boast of—

BELVILE (*aside*). Death, who should this be?

ANTONIO. He challenged me to meet him on the Molo[137] as soon as day appeared, but last night's quarrel has made my arm unfit to guide a sword.

BELVILE. I apprehend you, sir. You'd have me kill the man that lays a claim to the maid you speak of. I'll do't. I'll fly to do't!

ANTONIO. Sir, do you know her?

BELVILE. No, sir, but 'tis enough she is admired by you.

ANTONIO. Sir, I shall rob you of the glory on't, for you must fight under my name and dress.

BELVILE. That opinion must be strangely obliging that makes you think I can personate the brave Antonio, whom I can but strive to imitate.

ANTONIO. You say too much to my advantage. Come, sir, the day appears that calls you forth. Within, sir, is the habit.[138] (*Exit Antonio.*)

BELVILE.
Fantastic fortune, thou deceitful light,

That cheats the wearied traveler by night,
Though on a precipice each step you tread,
I am resolved to follow where you lead.

(*Exit.*)

SCENE 2

(*The Molo. Enter Florinda and Callis in masks, with Stephano.*)

FLORINDA (*aside*). I'm dying with my fears: Belvile's not coming as I expected under my window makes me believe that all those fears are true.—Canst thou not tell with whom my brother fights?

STEPHANO. No, madam, they were both in masquerade. I was by when they challenged one another, and they had decided the quarrel then, but were prevented by some cavaliers; which made 'em put it off till now. But I am sure 'tis about you they fight.

FLORINDA (*aside*). Nay, then, 'tis with Belvile, for what other lover have I that dares fight for me except Antonio, and he is too much in favor with my brother. If it be he, for whom shall I direct my prayers to heaven?

STEPHANO. Madam, I must leave you, for if my master see me, I shall be hanged for being your conductor. I escaped narrowly for the excuse I made for you last night i'th' garden.

FLORINDA. I'll reward thee for't. Prithee, no more.

(*Exit Stephano.*)

(*Enter Don Pedro in his masking habit.*)

PEDRO. Antonio's late today; the place will fill, and we may be prevented.[139]

(*Walks about.*)

FLORINDA (*aside*). Antonio? Sure I heard amiss.

PEDRO.
But who will not excuse a happy lover
When soft fair arms confine the yielding neck,
And the kind whisper languishingly breathes
"Must you be gone so soon?"
Sure I had dwelt forever on her bosom—
But stay, he's here.

(*Enter Belvile dressed in Antonio's clothes.*)

FLORINDA [*aside*]. 'Tis not Belvile; half my fears are vanished.

PEDRO. Antonio!

BELVILE (*aside*). This must be he.—You're early, sir; I do not use to be outdone this way.

PEDRO.
The wretched, sir, are watchful, and 'tis enough
You've the advantage of me in Angellica.

BELVILE (*aside*).
Angellica! Or[140] I've mistook my man, or else Antonio!
Can he forget his interest in Florinda

And fight for common prize?

PEDRO.

Come, sir, you know our terms.

BELVILE (*aside*).

By heaven, not I.
No talking; I am ready, sir.

(*Offers to fight; Florinda runs in.*)

FLORINDA (*to Belvile*).

Oh, hold! Whoe'er you be, I do conjure you hold!
If you strike here, I die!

PEDRO. Florinda!

BELVILE. Florinda imploring for my rival!

PEDRO.

Away; this kindness is unseasonable.

(*Puts her by; they fight; she runs in just as Belvile disarms Pedro.*)

FLORINDA.

Who are you, sir, that dares deny my prayers?

BELVILE.

Thy prayers destroy him; if thou wouldst preserve him,
Do that thou'rt unacquainted with, and curse him.

(*She holds him.*)

FLORINDA.

By all you hold most dear, by her you love,
I do conjure you, touch him not.

BELVILE.

By her I love?
See, I obey, and at your feet resign
The useless trophy of my victory.

(*Lays his sword at her feet.*)

PEDRO. Antonio, you've done enough to prove you love
Florinda.

BELVILE. Love Florinda! Does heaven love adoration, prayer,
or penitence? Love her? Here, sir, your sword again.

(*Snatches up the sword and gives it to him.*)

Upon this truth I'll fight my life away.

PEDRO. No, you've redeemed my sister, and my friendship.

(*He gives him Florinda, and pulls off his vizard to show his
face, and puts it on again.*)

BELVILE. Don Pedro!

PEDRO.

Can you resign your claims to other women,
And give your heart entirely to Florinda?

BELVILE.

Entire, as dying saints' confessions are!
I can delay my happiness no longer:
This minute let me make Florinda mine.

PEDRO.

This minute let it be. No time so proper:
This night my father will arrive from Rome,
And possibly may hinder what we purpose.

FLORINDA. O, heavens! This minute?

(*Enter Masqueraders and pass over.*)

BELVILE. Oh, do not ruin me!

PEDRO. The place begins to fill, and that we may not be
observed, do you walk off to St. Peter's church, where I
will meet you and conclude your happiness.

BELVILE. I'll meet you there.—(*Aside.*) If there be no more
saints' churches in Naples.

FLORINDA.

Oh, stay, sir, and recall your hasty doom!
Alas, I have not yet prepared my heart
To entertain so strange a guest.

PEDRO.

Away; this silly modesty is assumed too late.

BELVILE.

Heaven, madam, what do you do?

FLORINDA.

Do? Despise the man that lays a tyrant's claim
To what he ought to conquer by submission.

BELVILE.

You do not know me. Move a little this way.

(*Draws her aside.*)

FLORINDA.

Yes, you may force me even to the altar,
But not the holy man that offers there
Shall force me to be thine.

(*Pedro talks to Callis this while.*)

BELVILE.

Oh, do not lose so blest an opportunity!

(*Pulls off his vizard.*)

See, 'tis your Belvile, not Antonio,
Whom your mistaken scorn and anger ruins.

FLORINDA. Belvile!

Where was my soul it could not meet thy voice,
And take this knowledge in.

(*As they are talking, enter Willmore, finely dressed, and
Frederick.*)

WILLMORE. No intelligence? No news of Belvile yet? Well, I
am the most unlucky rascal in nature. Ha! Am I
deceived, or is it he? Look, Fred! 'Tis he, my dear Belvile!

(*Runs and embraces him; Belvile's vizard falls out on's
hand.*)

BELVILE. Hell and confusion seize thee!

PEDRO. Ha! Belvile! I beg your pardon, sir.

(*Takes Florinda from him.*)

BELVILE.

Nay, touch her not. She's mine by conquest, sir;
I won her by my sword.

WILLMORE.

Didst thou so? And egad, child, we'll keep her by the
sword.

(*Draws on Pedro; Belvile goes between.*)

BELVILE. Stand off!

Thou'rt so profanely lewd, so curst by heaven,
All quarrels thou espousest must be fatal.

WILLMORE.

Nay, an you be so hot, my valor's coy,
And shall be courted when you want it next.

(*Puts up his sword.*)

BELVILE (*to Pedro*).

You know I ought to claim a victor's right,
But you're the brother to divine Florinda,
To whom I'm such a slave. To purchase her
I durst not hurt the man she holds so dear.

PEDRO.

Twas by Antonio's, not by Belvile's sword
This question should have been decided, sir.
I must confess much to your bravery's due,
Both now and when I met you last in arms;
But I am nicely punctual in my word,
As men of honor ought, and beg your pardon:
For this mistake another time shall clear.

(*Aside to Florinda as they are going out.*)

—This was some plot between you and Belvile,
But I'll prevent you.

[*Exeunt Pedro and Florinda.*]

(*Belvile looks after her and begins to walk up and down in rage.*)

WILLMORE. Do not be modest now and lose the woman. But if we shall fetch her back so—

BELVILE. Do not speak to me!

WILLMORE. Not speak to you? Egad, I'll speak to you, and will be answered, too.

BELVILE. Will you, sir?

WILLMORE. I know I've done some mischief, but I'm so dull a puppy that I'm the son of a whore if I know how or where. Prithee inform my understanding.

BELVILE. Leave me, I say, and leave me instantly!

WILLMORE. I will not leave you in this humor, nor till I know my crime.

BELVILE. Death, I'll tell you, sir—

(*Draws and runs at Willmore; he runs out, Belvile after him; Frederick interposes.*)

(*Enter Angellica, Moretta, and Sebastian.*)

ANGELLICA. Ha! Sebastian, is that not Willmore? Haste! haste and bring him back.

[*Exit Sebastian.*]

FREDERICK [*aside*]. The colonel's mad: I never saw him thus before. I'll after 'em lest he do some mischief, for I am sure Willmore will not draw on him.   (*Exit.*)

ANGELLICA.

I am all rage! My first desires defeated!
For one for aught he knows that has no
Other merit than her quality,
Her being Don Pedro's sister. He loves her!
I know 'tis so. Dull, dull, insensible,

He will not see me now, though oft invited,
And broke his word last night. False perjured man!
He that but yesterday fought for my favors,
And would have made his life a sacrifice
To've gained one night with me,
Must now be hired and courted to my arms.

MORETTA. I told you what would come on't, but Moretta's an old doting fool. Why did you give him five hundred crowns, but to set himself out for other lovers? You should have kept him poor if you had meant to have had any good from him.

ANGELLICA.

Oh, name not such mean trifles! Had I given
Him all my youth has earned from sin,
I had not lost a thought nor sigh upon't.
But I have given him my eternal rest,
My whole repose, my future joys, my heart!
My virgin heart, Moretta! Oh, 'tis gone!

MORETTA. Curse on him, here he comes. How fine she has made him, too.

(*Enter Willmore and Sebastian; Angellica turns and walks away.*)

WILLMORE.

How now, turned shadow?
Fly when I pursue, and follow when I fly?   (*Sings.*)

Stay, gentle shadow of my dove,
    And tell me ere I go,
Whether the substance may not prove
    A fleeting thing like you.

(*As she turns she looks on him.*)

There's a soft kind look remaining yet.

ANGELLICA. Well, sir, you may be gay: All happiness, all joys pursue you still. Fortune's your slave, and gives you every hour choice of new hearts and beauties, till you are cloyed[141] with the repeated bliss which others vainly languish for. But know, false man, that I shall be revenged.

(*Turns away in rage.*)

WILLMORE. So, gad, there are of those faint-hearted lovers, whom such a sharp lesson next their hearts would make as impotent as fourscore.[142] Pox o' this whining; my business is to laugh and love. A pox on't, I hate your sullen lover: A man shall lose as much time to put you in humor now as would serve to gain a new woman.

ANGELLICA.

I scorn to cool that fire I cannot raise,
Or do the drudgery of your virtuous mistress.

WILLMORE. A virtuous mistress? Death, what a thing thou hast found out for me! Why, what the devil should I do with a virtuous woman, a sort of ill-natured creatures that

---

[141]**cloyed** sickened   [142]**as fourscore** as an eighty-year old

take a pride to torment a lover. Virtue is but an infirmity in woman, a disease that renders even the handsome ungrateful; whilst the ill-favored, for want of solicitations and address, only fancy themselves so. I have lain with a woman of quality who has all the while been railing at whores.

ANGELLICA.
  I will not answer for your mistress's virtue,
  Though she be young enough to know no guilt;
  And I could wish you would persuade my heart
  'Twas the two hundred thousand crowns you courted.

WILLMORE. Two hundred thousand crowns! What story's this? What trick? What woman, ha?

ANGELLICA. How strange you make it. Have you forgot the creature you entertained on the Piazzo last night?

WILLMORE (aside). Ha! My gypsy worth two hundred thousand crowns! Oh, how I long to be with her! Pox, I knew she was of quality.

ANGELLICA.
  False man! I see my ruin in thy face.
  How many vows you breathed upon my bosom
  Never to be unjust. Have you forgot so soon?

WILLMORE. Faith, no; I was just coming to repeat 'em. But here's a humor indeed would make a man a saint.—(Aside.) Would she would be angry enough to leave me, and command me not to wait on her.

(Enter Hellena dressed in man's clothes.)

HELLENA. This must be Angellica: I know it by her mumping[143] matron here. Ay, ay, 'tis she. My mad captain's with her, too, for all his swearing. How this unconstant humor makes me love him!—Pray, good grave gentlewoman, is not this Angellica?

MORETTA. My too young sir, it is.—[Aside.] I hope 'tis one from Don Antonio.   (Goes to Angellica.)

HELLENA (aside). Well, something I'll do to vex him for this.

ANGELLICA. I will not speak with him. Am I in humor to receive a lover?

WILLMORE. Not speak with him? Why, I'll be gone, and wait your idler minutes. Can I show less obedience to the thing I love so fondly?

                                                   (Offers to go.)

ANGELLICA. A fine excuse this! Stay—

WILLMORE. And hinder your advantage? Should I repay your bounties so ungratefully?

ANGELLICA [to Hellena].
  Come hither, boy.—[To Willmore.] That I may let you see
  How much above the advantages you name
  I prize one minute's joy with you.

WILLMORE (impatient to be gone). Oh, you destroy me with this endearment.—[Aside.] Death, how shall I get away?—Madam, 'twill not be fit I should be seen with you. Besides, it will not be convenient. And I've a friend—that's dangerously sick.

ANGELLICA. I see you're impatient. Yet you shall stay.

WILLMORE (aside). And miss my assignation with my gypsy.

(Walks about impatiently; Moretta brings Hellena, who addresses herself to Angellica.)

HELLENA. Madam,
  You'll hardly pardon my instrusion
  When you shall know my business,
  And I'm too young to tell my tale with art;
  But there must be a wondrous store of goodness
  Where so much beauty dwells.

ANGELLICA.
  A pretty advocate, whoever sent thee.
  Prithee proceed. (To Willmore, who is stealing off.)—Nay,
    sir, you shall not go.

WILLMORE (aside). Then I shall lose my dear gypsy forever.
  Pox on't, she stays me out of spite.

HELLENA.
  I am related to a lady, madam,
  Young, rich, and nobly born, but has the fate
  To be in love with a young English gentleman.
  Strangely she loves him, at first sight she loved him,
  But did adore him when she heard him speak;
  For he, she said, had charms in every word
  That failed not to surprise, to wound and conquer.

WILLMORE (aside). Ha! Egad, I hope this concerns me.

ANGELLICA (aside).
  'Tis my false man he means. Would he were gone:
  This praise will raise his pride, and ruin me. (To
    Willmore.)—Well,
  Since you are so impatient to be gone,
  I will release you, sir.

WILLMORE (aside). Nay, then I'm sure 'twas me he spoke of:
  This cannot be the effects of kindness in her.—No,
  Madam, I've considered better on't, and will not give you
  cause of jealousy.

ANGELLICA. But sir, I've business that—

WILLMORE. This shall not do; I know 'tis but to try me.

ANGELLICA. Well, to your story, boy.—(Aside). Though
  'twill undo me.

HELLENA.
  With this addition to his other beauties,
  He won her unresisting tender heart.
  He vowed, and sighed, and swore he loved her dearly;
  And she believed the cunning flatterer,
  And thought herself the happiest maid alive.
  Today was the appointed time by both
  To consummate their bliss:
  The virgin, altar, and the priest were dressed;
  And whilst she languished for th'expected bridegroom,
  She heard he paid his broken vows to you.

WILLMORE (*aside*). So, this is some dear rogue that's in love
   with me, and this way lets me know it. Or, if it be not me,
   he means someone whose place I may supply.
ANGELLICA. Now I perceive
   The cause of thy impatience to be gone,
   And all the business of this glorious dress.
WILLMORE. Damn the young prater; I know not what he
   means.
HELLENA. Madam,
   In your fair eyes I read too much concern
   To tell my further business.
ANGELLICA.
   Prithee, sweet youth, talk on: Thou mayst perhaps
   Raise here a storm that may undo my passion,
   And then I'll grant thee anything.
HELLENA.
   Madam, 'tis to entreat you (oh unreasonable)
   You would not see this stranger.
   For if you do, she vows you are undone;
   Though nature never made a man so excellent,
   And sure he 'ad been a god, but for inconstancy.
WILLMORE (*aside*). Ah, rogue, how finely he's instructed! 'Tis
   plain, some woman that has seen me *en passant*.[144]
ANGELLICA. Oh, I shall burst with jealousy! Do you know
   the man you speak of?
HELLENA. Yes, madam, he used to be in buff and scarlet.
ANGELLICA (*to Willmore*). Thou false as hell, what canst
   thou say to this?
WILLMORE. By heaven—
ANGELLICA. Hold, do not damn thyself—
HELLENA. Nor hope to be believed.

   (*He walks about; they follow.*)

ANGELLICA. Oh perjured man!
   Is't thus you pay my generous passion back?
HELLENA. Why would you, sir, abuse my lady's faith?
ANGELLICA. And use me so unhumanely.
HELLENA. A maid so young, so innocent—
WILLMORE. Ah, young devil!
ANGELLICA. Dost thou not know thy life is in my power?
HELLENA. Or think my lady cannot be revenged?
WILLMORE (*aside*). So, so, the storm comes finely on.
ANGELLICA.
   Now thou art silent: Guilt has struck thee dumb.
   Oh, hadst thou still been so, I'd lived in safety.

                              (*She turns away and weeps.*)

WILLMORE (*aside to Hellena*). Sweetheart, the lady's name
   and house—quickly! I'm impatient to be with her.

   (*Looks toward Angellica to watch her turning, and as she
   comes towards them he meets her.*)

HELLENA (*aside*). So, now is he for another woman.
WILLMORE.
   The impudent'st young thing in nature:
   I cannot persuade him out of his error, madam.
ANGELLICA.
   I know he's in the right; yet thou'st a tongue
   That would persuade him to deny his faith.

                              (*In rage walks away.*)

WILLMORE (*said softly to Hellena*). Her name, her name, dear
   boy!
HELLENA. Have you forgot it, sir?
WILLMORE (*aside*). Oh, I perceive he's not to know I am a
   stranger to his lady.—Yes, yes, I do know, but I have forgot the—
   (*Angellica turns.*)

   By heaven, such early confidence I never saw.
ANGELLICA.
   Did I not charge you with this mistress, sir?
   Which you denied, though I beheld your perjury.
   This little generosity of thine has rendered back my
      heart.   (*Walks away.*)
WILLMORE (*to Hellena*). So, you have made sweet work here,
   my little mischief. Look your lady be kind and good-
   natured now, or I shall have but a cursed bargain on't.

   (*Angellica turns toward them.*)

   —The rogue's bred up to mischief;
   Art thou so great a fool to credit him?
ANGELLICA.
   Yes, I do, and you in vain impose upon me.
   Come hither, boy. Is not this he you spake of?
HELLENA. I think it is. I cannot swear, but I vow he has just
   such another lying lover's look.

   (*Hellena looks in his face; he gazes on her.*)

WILLMORE (*aside*).
   Ha! Do I not know that face?
   By heaven, my little gypsy! What a dull dog was I:
   Had I but looked that way I'd known her.
   Are all my hopes of a new woman banished?—
   Egad, if I do not fit thee for this, hang me.—
   [*To Angellica.*] Madam, I have found out the plot.
HELLENA [*aside*]. Oh lord, what does he say? Am I discovered
   now?
WILLMORE. Do you see this young spark here?
HELLENA [*aside*]. He'll tell her who I am.
WILLMORE. Who do you think this is?
HELLENA [*aside*]. Ay, ay, he does know me.—
   Nay, dear captain, I am undone if you discover me.
WILLMORE. Nay, nay, no cogging;[145] she shall know what a
   precious mistress I have.

HELLENA. Will you be such a devil?

WILLMORE. Nay, nay, I'll teach you to spoil sport you will not make.—This small ambassador comes not from a person of quality, as you imagine and he says, but from a very errant gypsy: the talking'st, prating'st, canting'st little animal thou ever saw'st.

ANGELLICA. What news you tell me, that's the thing I mean.

HELLENA (*aside*). Would I were well off the place! If ever I go a-captain-hunting again—

WILLMORE. Mean that thing? That gypsy thing? Thou mayst as well be jealous of thy monkey or parrot as of her. A German motion[146] were worth a dozen of her, and a dream were a better enjoyment—a creature of a constitution fitter for heaven than man.

HELLENA (*aside*). Though I'm sure he lies, yet this vexes me.

ANGELLICA. You are mistaken: she's a Spanish woman made up of no such dull materials.

WILLMORE. Materials? Egad, and she be made of any that will either dispense or admit of love, I'll be bound to continence.

HELLENA (*aside to him*). Unreasonable man, do you think so?

WILLMORE. You may return, my little brazen head, and tell your lady, that till she be handsome enough to be beloved, or I dull enough to be religious, there will be small hopes of me.

ANGELLICA. Did you not promise, then, to marry her?

WILLMORE. Not I, by heaven.

ANGELLICA. You cannot undeceive my fears and torments, till you have vowed you will not marry her.

HELLENA (*aside*). If he swears that, he'll be revenged on me indeed for all my rogueries.

ANGELLICA. I know what arguments you'll bring against me: fortune and honor.

WILLMORE. Honor! I tell you, I hate it in your sex; and those that fancy themselves possessed of that foppery are the most impertinently troublesome of all womankind, and will transgress nine commandments to keep one. And to satisfy your jealousy, I swear—

HELLENA (*aside to him*). Oh, no swearing, dear captain.

WILLMORE. If it were possible I should ever be inclined to marry, it should be some kind young sinner: one that has generosity enough to give a favor handsomely to one that can ask it discreetly, one that has wit enough to manage an intrigue of love. Oh, how civil such a wench is to a man that does her the honor to marry her.

ANGELLICA. By heaven, there's no faith in anything he says.

(*Enter Sebastian.*)

SEBASTIAN. Madam, Don Antonio—

ANGELLICA. Come hither.

HELLENA [*aside*]. Ha! Antonio! He may be coming hither, and he'll certainly discover me. I'll therefore retire without a ceremony.   (*Exit Hellena.*)

ANGELLICA. I'll see him. Get my coach ready.

SEBASTIAN. It waits you, madam.

WILLMORE [*aside*]. This is lucky.—What, madam, now I may be gone and leave you to the enjoyment of my rival?

ANGELLICA.
Dull man, that canst not see how ill, how poor,
That false dissimulation looks. Be gone,
And never let me see thy cozening face again,
Lest I relapse and kill thee.

WILLMORE. Yes, you can spare me now. Farewell, till you're in better humor.—[*Aside.*] I'm glad of this release.
Now for my gypsy:
For though to worse we change, yet still we find
New joys, new charms, in a new miss that's kind.
                                            (*Exit Willmore.*)

ANGELLICA.
He's gone, and in this ague[147] of my soul
The shivering fit returns.
Oh, with what willing haste he took his leave,
As if the longed-for minute were arrived
Of some blest assignation.
In vain I have consulted all my charms,
In vain this beauty prized, in vain believed
My eyes could kindle any lasting fires;
I had forgot my name, my infamy,
And the reproach that honor lays on those
That dare pretend a sober passion here.
Nice[148] reputation, though it leave behind
More virtues than inhabit where that dwells,
Yet that once gone, those virtues shine no more.
Then since I am not fit to be beloved,
I am resolved to think on a revenge
On him that soothed[149] me thus to my undoing.

                                            (*Exeunt.*)

SCENE 3

(*A street. Enter Florinda and Valeria in habits different from what they have been seen in.*)

FLORINDA. We're happily escaped, and yet I tremble still.

VALERIA. A lover, and fear? Why, I am but half an one, and yet I have courage for any attempt. Would Hellena were here: I would fain have had her as deep in this mischief as we; she'll fare but ill else, I doubt.

FLORINDA. She pretended a visit to the Augustine nuns; but I believe some other design carried her out; pray heaven we light on her. Prithee, what didst do with Callis?

VALERIA. When I saw no reason would do good on her, I followed her into the wardrobe, and as she was looking for something in a great chest, I toppled her in by the heels,

---

[146]**motion** puppet show

[147]**ague** fever   [148]**nice** scrupulous   [149]**soothed** flattered

snatched the key of the apartment where you were confined, locked her in, and left her bawling for help.

FLORINDA. 'Tis well you resolve to follow my fortunes, for
thou darest never appear at home again after such an
action.

VALERIA. That's according as the young stranger and I shall
agree. But to our business. I delivered your note to
Belvile when I got out under pretense of going to mass. I
found him at his lodging, and believe me it came season-
ably, for never was man in so desperate a condition. I told
him of your resolution of making your escape today if
your brother would be absent long enough to permit you;
if not, to die rather than be Antonio's.

FLORINDA. Thou should'st have told him I was confined to
my chamber upon my brother's suspicion that the business on the Molo was a plot laid between him and I.

VALERIA. I said all this, and told him your brother was now
gone to his devotion; and he resolves to visit every
church till he find him, and not only undeceive him in
that, but caress him so as shall delay his return home.

FLORINDA. Oh heavens! He's here, and Belvile with him,
too.

(They put on their vizards.)

(Enter Don Pedro, Belvile, Willmore; Belvile and Don
Pedro seeming in serious discourse.)

VALERIA. Walk boldly by them, and I'll come at a distance,
lest he suspect us.

(She walks by them and looks back on them.)

WILLMORE. Ha! A woman, and of excellent mien!

PEDRO. She throws a kind look back on you.

WILLMORE. Death, 'tis a likely wench, and that kind look
shall not be cast away. I'll follow her.

BELVILE. Prithee do not.

WILLMORE. Do not? By heavens, to the antipodies,[150] with
such an invitation.

(She goes out, and Willmore follows her.)

BELVILE. 'Tis a mad fellow for a wench.

(Enter Frederick.)

FREDERICK. Oh, colonel, such news!

BELVILE. Prithee what?

FREDERICK. News that will make you laugh in spite of fortune.

BELVILE. What, Blunt has had some damned trick put upon
him? Cheated, banged, or clapped?[151]

FREDERICK. Cheated, sir, rarely cheated of all but his shirt
and drawers; the unconscionable whore too turned him
out before consummation, so that, traversing the streets
at midnight, the watch found him in this *fresco* and conducted him home. By heaven, 'tis such a sight, and yet I

durst as well been hanged as laughed at him or pity him:
He beats all that do but ask him a question, and is in such
an humor.

PEDRO. Who is't has met with this ill usage, sir?

BELVILE. A friend of ours whom you must see for mirth's
sake.—(Aside.) I'll employ him to give Florinda time for
an escape.

PEDRO. What is he?

BELVILE. A young countryman of ours, one that has been
educated at so plentiful a rate he yet ne'er knew the want
of money; and 'twill be a great jest to see how simply he'll
look without it. For my part, I'll lend him none: And the
rogue know not how to put on a borrowing face and ask
first, I'll let him see how good 'tis to play our parts whilst
I play his. Prithee, Fred, do you go home and keep him in
that posture till we come.   (Exeunt.)

(Enter Florinda from the farther end of the scene, looking
behind her.)

FLORINDA. I am followed still. Ha! My brother too advancing this way! Good heavens defend me from being seen
by him! (She goes off.)

(Enter Willmore, and after him Valeria, at a little distance.)

WILLMORE. Ah, there she sails! She looks back as she were
willing to be boarded; I'll warrant her prize.[152]

(He goes out, Valeria following.)

(Enter Hellena, just as he goes out, with a page.)

HELLENA. Ha, is not that my captain that has a woman in
chase? 'Tis not Angellica.—Boy, follow those people at a
distance, and bring me an account where they go in.
(Exit Page.)—I'll find his haunts, and plague him everywhere. Ha! My brother!

(Belvile, Willmore, Pedro cross the stage; Hellena runs off.)

SCENE 4

(Scene changes to another street. Enter Florinda.)

FLORINDA.
What shall I do? My brother now pursues me.
Will no kind power protect me from his tyranny?
Ha! Here's a door open; I'll venture in, since nothing can
be worse than to fall into his hands. My life and honor
are at stake, and my necessity has no choice.

(She goes in.)

(Enter Valeria, Hellena's Page peeping after Florinda.)

PAGE. Here she went in; I shall remember this house.

(Exit Boy.)

---

[150]**antipodies** Antipodes, on the opposite side of the earth   [151]**clapped**
(1) beaten; or (2) infected with a venereal disease

[152]**warrant her prize** consider her worthy of pursuing

VALERIA. This is Belvile's lodging; she's gone in as readily as if she knew it. Ha! Here's that mad fellow again; I dare not venture in. I'll watch my opportunity.   (*Goes aside.*)

(*Enter Willmore, gazing about him.*)

WILLMORE. I have lost her hereabouts. Pox on't, she must not 'scape me so.   (*Goes out.*)

SCENE 5

(*Scene changes to Blunt's chamber, discovers him sitting on a couch in his shirt and drawers, reading.*)

BLUNT. So, now my mind's a little at peace, since I have resolved revenge. A pox on this tailor, though, for not bringing home the clothes I bespoke. And a pox of all poor cavaliers: A man can never keep a spare suit for 'em, and I shall have these rogues come in and find me naked, and then I'm undone. But I'm resolved to arm myself: The rascals shall not insult over me too much. (*Puts on an old rusty sword and buff belt.*) Now, how like a morris dancer[153] I am equipped! A fine ladylike whore to cheat me thus without affording me a kindness for my money! A pox light on her, I shall never be reconciled to the sex more; she has made me as faithless as a physician, as uncharitable as a churchman, and as ill-natured as a poet. Oh, how I'll use all womankind hereafter! What would I give to have one of 'em within my reach now! Any mortal thing in petticoats, kind fortune, send me, and I'll forgive thy last night's malice.—Here's a cursed book, too— a warning to all young travelers—that can instruct me how to prevent such mischiefs now 'tis too late. Well, 'tis a rare convenient thing to read a little now and then, as well as hawk and hunt.

(*Sits down again and reads.*)

(*Enter to him Florinda.*)

FLORINDA. This house is haunted, sure: 'Tis well furnished, and no living thing inhabits it. Ha! A man! Heavens, how he's attired! Sure 'tis some rope dancer, or fencing master. I tremble now for fear, and yet I must venture now to speak to him.—Sir, if I may not interrupt your meditations—

(*He starts up and gazes.*)

BLUNT. Ha, what's here? Are my wishes granted? And is not that a she creature? 'Adsheartlikins, 'tis.—What wretched thing art thou, ha?

FLORINDA. Charitable sir, you've told yourself already what I am: a very wretched maid, forced by a strange unlucky accident to seek a safety here, and must be ruined if you do not grant it.

BLUNT. Ruined! Is there any ruin so inevitable as that which now threatens thee? Dost thou know, miserable woman, into what den of mischiefs thou art fallen; what abyss of confusion, ha? Dost not see something in my looks that frights thy guilty soul, and makes thee wish to change that shape of woman for any humble animal, or devil? For those were safer for thee, and less mischievous.

FLORINDA. Alas, what mean you, sir? I must confess, your looks have something in 'em makes me fear, but I beseech you, as you seem a gentleman, pity a harmless virgin that takes your house for sanctuary.

BLUNT. Talk on, talk on; and weep, too, till my faith return. Do, flatter me out of my senses again. A harmless virgin with a pox; as much one as t'other, 'adsheartlikins. Why, what the devil, can I not be safe in my house for you, not in my chamber? Nay, not even being naked too cannot secure me? This is an impudence greater than has invaded me yet. Come, no resistance.   (*Pulls her rudely.*)

FLORINDA. Dare you be so cruel?

BLUNT. Cruel? 'Adsheartlikins, as a galley slave, or a Spanish whore. Cruel? Yes, I will kiss and beat thee all over, kiss and see thee all over; thou shalt lie with me too, not that I care for the enjoyment, but to let thee see I have ta'en deliberated malice to thee, and will be revenged on one whore for the sins of another. I will smile and deceive thee; flatter thee, and beat thee; embrace thee and rob thee, as she did me; fawn on thee, and strip thee stark naked; then hang thee out at my window by the heels, with a paper of scurvy verses fastened to thy breast in praise of damnable women. Come, come, along.

FLORINDA. Alas, sir, must I be sacrificed for the crimes of the most infamous of my sex? I never understood the sins you name.

BLUNT. Do, persuade the fool you love him, or that one of you can be just or honest; tell me I was not an easy coxcomb, or any strange impossible tale: It will be believed sooner than thy false showers or protestations. A generation of damned hypocrites! To flatter my very clothes from my back! Dissembling witches! Are these the returns you make an honest gentleman that trusts, believes, and loves you? But if I be not even with you— Come along, or I shall—   (*Pulls her again.*)

(*Enter Frederick.*)

FREDERICK. Ha, what's here to do?

BLUNT. 'Adsheartlikins, Fred, I am glad thou art come, to be a witness of my dire revenge.

FREDERICK. What's this, a person of quality too, who is upon the ramble[154] to supply the defects of some grave impotent husband?

BLUNT. No, this has another pretense: Some very unfortunate accident brought her hither, to save a life pursued by

---

[153]**morris dancer** fantastically attired dancer

[154]**upon the ramble** wandering

I know not who or why, and forced to take sanctuary here at fool's haven. 'Adsheartlikins, to me of all mankind for protection? Is the ass to be cajoled again, think ye? No, young one, no prayers or tears shall mitigate my rage; therefore prepare for both my pleasures of enjoyment and revenge. For I am resolved to make up my loss here on thy body: I'll take it out in kindness and in beating.

FREDERICK. Now, mistress of mine, what do you think of this?

FLORINDA. I think he will not, dares not be so barbarous.

FREDERICK. Have a care, Blunt, she fetched a deep sigh; she is enamored with thy shirt and drawers. She'll strip thee even of that; there are of her calling such unconscionable baggages and such dexterous thieves, they'll flea[155] a man and he shall ne'er miss his skin till he feels the cold. There was a countryman of ours robbed of a row of teeth whilst he was a-sleeping, which the jilt made him buy again when he waked. You see, lady, how little reason we have to trust you.

BLUNT. 'Adsheartlikins, why this is most abominable!

FLORINDA. Some such devils there may be, but by all that's holy, I am none such. I entered here to save a life in danger.

BLUNT. For no goodness, I'll warrant her.

FREDERICK. Faith, damsel, you had e'en confessed the plain truth, for we are fellows not to be caught twice in the same trap. Look on that wreck: a tight vessel when he set out of haven, well trimmed and laden. And see how a female picaroon of this island of rogues has shattered him, and canst thou hope for any mercy?

BLUNT. No, no, gentlewoman, come along; 'adsheartlikins, we must be better acquainted.—We'll both lie with her, and then let me along to bang her.

FREDERICK. I'm ready to serve you in matters of revenge that has a double pleasure in't.

BLUNT. Well said.—You hear, little one, how you are condemned by public vote to the bed within; there's no resisting your destiny, sweetheart.

(Pulls her.)

FLORINDA. Stay, sir. I have seen you with Belvile, an English cavalier. For his sake, use me kindly. You know him, sir.

BLUNT. Belvile? Why yes, sweeting, we do know Belvile, and wish he were with us now. He's a cormorant at whore and bacon:[156] He'd have a limb or two of thee, my virgin pullet. But 'tis no matter; we'll leave him the bones to pick.

FLORINDA. Sir, if you have any esteem for that Belvile, I conjure you to treat me with more gentleness; he'll thank you for the justice.

FREDERICK. Hark'ee, Blunt, I doubt we are mistaken in this matter.

FLORINDA. Sir, if you find me not worth Belvile's care, use me as you please. And that you may think I merit better treatment than you threaten, pray take this present.

(Gives him a ring; he looks on it.)

BLUNT. Hum, a diamond! Why, 'tis a wonderful virtue now that lies in this ring, a mollifying virtue. 'Adsheartlikins, there's more persuasive rhetoric in't than all her sex can utter.

FREDERICK. I begin to suspect something, and 'twould anger us vilely to be trussed up for a rape upon a maid of quality, when we only believe we ruffle a harlot.

BLUNT. Thou art a credulous fellow, but 'adsheartlikins, I have no faith yet. Why, my saint prattled as parlously as this does; she gave me a bracelet, too, a devil on her! But I sent my man to sell it today for necessaries, and it proved as counterfeit as her vows of love.

FREDERICK. However, let it reprieve her till we see Belvile.

BLUNT. That's hard, yet I will grant it.

(Enter a Servant.)

SERVANT. Oh, sir, the colonel is just come in with his new friend and a Spaniard of quality, and talks of having you to dinner with 'em.

BLUNT. 'Adsheartlikins, I'm undone! I would not see 'em for the world. Hark'ee, Fred, lock up the wench in your chamber.

FREDERICK. Fear nothing, madam: Whate'er he threatens, you are safe whilst in my hands.

(Exeunt Frederick and Florinda.)

BLUNT. And sirrah, upon your life, say I am not at home, or that I'm asleep, or—or—anything. Away; I'll prevent their coming this way.

(Locks the door, and exeunt.)

ACT 5

(Blunt's chamber. After a great knocking as at his chamber door, enter Blunt softly crossing the stage, in his shirt and drawers as before.)

[voices] (CALL WITHIN). NED! NED BLUNT! NED BLUNT!

BLUNT. The rogues are up in arms. 'Adsheartlikins, this villainous Frederick has betrayed me: They have heard of my blessed fortune.

[voices] (AND KNOCKING WITHIN). NED BLUNT! NED! NED!

BELVILE [within]. Why, he's dead, sir, without dispute dead; he has not been seen today. Let's break open the door. Here, boy—

BLUNT. Ha, break open the door? 'Adsheartlikins, that mad fellow will be as good as his word.

BELVILE [within]. Boy, bring something to force the door.

(A great noise within, at the door again.)

---

[155]**flea** flay   [156]**cormorant . . . bacon** glutton for sex

BLUNT. So, now must I speak in my own defense; I'll try what rhetoric will do.—Hold, hold! What do you mean, gentlemen, what do you mean?

BELVILE (*within*). Oh, rogue, art alive? Prithee open the door and convince us.

BLUNT. Yes, I am alive, gentlemen, but at present a little busy.

BELVILE (*within*). How, Blunt grown a man of business? Come, come, open and let's see this miracle.

BLUNT. No, no, no, no, gentlemen, 'tis no great business. But—I am—at—my devotion. 'Adsheartlikins, will you not allow a man time to pray?

BELVILE (*within*). Turned religious? A greater wonder than the first! Therefore open quickly, or we shall unhinge, we shall.

BLUNT [*aside*]. This won't do.—Why hark'ee, colonel, to tell you the truth, I am about a necessary affair of life: I have a wench with me. You apprehend me?—The devil's in't if they be so uncivil as to disturb me now.

WILLMORE [*within*]. How, a wench? Nay then, we must enter and partake. No resistance. Unless it be your lady of quality, and then we'll keep our distance.

BLUNT. So, the business is out.

WILLMORE [*within*]. Come, come, lend's more hands to the door. Now heave, all together. (*Breaks open the door.*) So, well done, my boys.

(*Enter Belvile [and his Page], Willmore, Frederick, and Pedro. Blunt looks simply,[157] they all laugh at him; he lays his hand on his sword, and comes up to Willmore.*)

BLUNT. Hark'ee, sir, laugh out your laugh quickly, d'ye hear, and be gone. I shall spoil your sport else, 'adsheartlikins, sir. I shall. The jest has been carried on too long.— (*Aside.*) A plague upon my tailor!

WILLMORE. 'Sdeath, how the whore has dressed him! Faith, sir, I'm sorry.

BLUNT. Are you so, sir? Keep't to yourself then, sir, I advise you, d'ye hear, for I can as little endure your pity as his mirth.

(*Lays his hand on's sword.*)

BELVILE. Indeed, Willmore, thou wert a little too rough with Ned Blunt's mistress. Call a person of quality whore, and one so young, so handsome, and so eloquent? Ha, ha, he.

BLUNT. Hark'ee, sir, you know me, and know I can be angry. Have a care, for 'adsheartlikins, I can fight, too, I can, sir. Do you mark me? No more.

BELVILE. Why so peevish, good Ned? Some disappointments, I'll warrant. What, did the jealous count, her husband, return just in the nick?

BLUNT. Or the devil, sir. (*They laugh.*) D'ye laugh? Look ye settle me a good sober countenance, and that quickly, too, or you shall know Ned Blunt is not—

BELVILE. Not everybody, we know that.

BLUNT. Not an ass to be laughed at, sir.

WILLMORE. Unconscionable sinner! To bring a lover so near his happiness—a vigorous passionate lover—and then not only cheat him of his movables, but his very desires, too.

BELVILE. Ah, sir, a mistress is a trifle with Blunt; he'll have a dozen the next time he looks abroad. His eyes have charms not to be resisted; there needs no more than to expose that taking person to the view of the fair, and he leads 'em all in triumph.

PEDRO. Sir, though I'm a stranger to you, I am ashamed at the rudeness of my nation; and could you learn who did it, would assist you to make an example of 'em.

BLUNT. Why ay, there's one speaks sense now, and handsomely. And let me tell you, gentlemen, I should not have showed myself like a jack pudding[158] thus to have made you mirth, but that I have revenge within my power. For know, I have got into my possession a female, who had better have fallen under any curse than the ruin I design her. 'Adsheartlikins, she assaulted me here in my own lodgings, and had doubtless committed a rape upon me, had not this sword defended me.

FREDERICK. I know not that, but o' my conscience thou had ravished her, had she not redeemed herself with a ring. Let's see't, Blunt.

(*Blunt shows the ring.*)

BELVILE [*aside*]. Ha! The ring I gave Florinda when we exchanged our vows!—Hark'ee, Blunt—

(*Goes to whisper to him.*)

WILLMORE. No whispering, good colonel, there's a woman in the case. No whispering.

BELVILE [*aside to Blunt*]. Hark'ee, fool, be advised, and conceal both the ring and the story for your reputation's sake. Do not let people know what despised cullies[159] we English are; to be cheated and abused by one whore, and another rather bribe thee than be kind to thee, is an infamy to our nation.

WILLMORE. Come, come, where's the wench? We'll see her; let her be what she will, we'll see her.

PEDRO. Ay, ay, let us see her. I can soon discover whether she be of quality, or for your diversion.

BLUNT. She's in Fred's custody.

WILLMORE. Come, come, the key—

(*To Frederick, who gives him the key; they are going.*)

BELVILE [*aside*]. Death, what shall I do?—Stay, gentlemen.— [*Aside.*] Yet if I hinder 'em, I shall discover all.—Hold, let's go one at once.[160] Give me the key.

---

[157]**simply** foolishly

[158]**jack pudding** clown   [159]**cullies** dupes   [160]**one at once** one after the other

WILLMORE. Nay, hold there, colonel, I'll go first.

FREDERICK. Nay, no dispute, Ned and I have the propriety of her.

WILLMORE. Damn propriety! Then we'll draw cuts. (*Belvile goes to whisper [to] Willmore.*) Nay, no corruption, good colonel. Come, the longest sword carries her.

(*They all draw, forgetting Don Pedro, being a Spaniard, had the longest.*)

BLUNT. I yield up my interest to you, gentlemen, and that will be revenge sufficient.

WILLMORE (*to Pedro*). The wench is yours.—[*Aside.*] Pox of his Toledo,[161] I had forgot that.

FREDERICK. Come, sir, I'll conduct you to the lady.

(*Exeunt Frederick and Pedro.*)

BELVILE (*aside*). To hinder him will certainly discover her.— Dost know, dull beast, what mischief thou hast done?

(*Willmore walking up and down, out of humor.*)

WILLMORE. Ay, ay, to trust our fortune to lots! A devil on't, 'twas madness, that's the truth on't.

BELVILE. Oh, intolerable sot—

(*Enter Florinda running, masked, Pedro after her; Willmore gazing round her.*)

FLORINDA (*aside*). Good heaven defend me from discovery!

PEDRO. 'Tis but in vain to fly me; you're fallen to my lot.

BELVILE [*aside*]. Sure she's undiscovered yet, but now I fear there is no way to bring her off.

WILLMORE [*aside*]. Why, what a pox, is not this my woman, the same I followed but now?

(*Pedro talking to Florinda, who walks up and down.*)

PEDRO. As if I did not know ye, and your business here.

FLORINDA (*aside*). Good heaven, I fear he does indeed!

PEDRO. Come, pray be kind; I know you meant to be so when you entered here, for these are proper gentlemen.

WILLMORE. But sir, perhaps the lady will not be imposed upon: She'll choose her man.

PEDRO. I am better bred than not to leave her choice free.

(*Enter Valeria, and is surprised at sight of Don Pedro.*)

VALERIA (*aside*). Don Pedro here! There's no avoiding him.

FLORINDA (*aside*). Valeria! Then I'm undone.

VALERIA (*to Pedro, running to him*). Oh, I have found you, sir! The strangest accident—if I had breath—to tell it.

PEDRO. Speak! Is Florinda safe? Hellena well?

VALERIA. Ay, ay, sir. Florinda is safe.—[*Aside.*] From any fears of you.

PEDRO. Why, where's Florinda? Speak!

VALERIA. Ay, where indeed, sir; I wish I could inform you. But to hold you no longer in doubt—

FLORINDA (*aside*). Oh, what will she say?

VALERIA. She's fled away in the habit—of one of her pages, sir. But Callis thinks you may retrieve her yet, if you make haste away. She'll tell you, sir, the rest.—(*Aside.*) If you can find her out.

PEDRO. Dishonorable girl, she has undone my aim.—[*To Belvile.*] Sir, you see my necessity of leaving you, and I hope you'll pardon it. My sister, I know, will make her flight to you; and if she do, I shall expect she should be rendered back.

BELVILE. I shall consult my love and honor, sir.

(*Exit Pedro.*)

FLORINDA (*to Valeria*). My dear preserver, let me embrace thee.

WILLMORE. What the devil's all this?

BLUNT. Mystery, by this light.

VALERIA. Come, come, make haste and get yourselves married quickly, for your brother will return again.

BELVILE. I'm so surprised with fears and joys, so amazed to find you here in safety, I can scarce persuade my heart into a faith of what I see.

WILLMORE. Hark'ee, colonel, is this that mistress who has cost you so many sighs, and me so many quarrels with you?

BELVILE. It is.—[*To Florinda.*] Pray give him the honor of your hand.

WILLMORE. Thus it must be received, then. (*Kneels and kisses her hand.*) And with it give your pardon, too.

FLORINDA. The friend to Belvile may command me anything.

WILLMORE (*aside*). Death, would I might; 'tis a surprising beauty.

BELVILE. Boy, run and fetch a father[162] instantly.

(*Exit Boy.*)

FREDERICK. So, now do I stand like a dog, and have not a syllable to plead my own cause with. By this hand, madam, I was never thoroughly confounded before, nor shall I ever more dare look up with confidence, till you are pleased to pardon me.

FLORINDA. Sir, I'll be reconciled to you on one condition: that you'll follow the example of your friend in marrying a maid that does not hate you, and whose fortune, I believe, will not be unwelcome to you.

FREDERICK. Madam, had I no inclinations that way, I should obey your kind commands.

BELVILE. Who, Fred marry? He has so few inclinations for womankind that had he been possessed of paradise he might have continued there to this day, if no crime but love could have disinherited him.

FREDERICK. Oh, I do not use to boast of my intrigues.

BELVILE. Boast! Why, thou dost nothing but boast. And I dare swear, wert thou as innocent from the sin of the grape as thou art from the apple, thou might'st yet claim

---

[161]**Toledo** sword made in Toledo

[162]**father** priest

that right in Eden which our first parents lost by too much loving.

FREDERICK. I wish this lady would think me so modest a man.

VALERIA. She would be sorry then, and not like you half so well. And I should be loath to break my word with you, which was, that if your friend and mine agreed, it should be a match between you and I.   (*She gives him her hand.*)

FREDERICK. Bear witness, colonel, 'tis a bargain.

(*Kisses her hand.*)

BLUNT (*to Florinda*). I have a pardon to beg, too; but 'adsheartlikins, I am so out of countenance that I'm a dog if I can say anything to purpose.

FLORINDA. Sir, I heartily forgive you all.

BLUNT. That's nobly said, sweet lady.—Belvile, prithee present her her ring again, for I find I have not courage to approach her myself.

(*Gives him the ring; he gives it to Florinda.*)

(*Enter Boy.*)

BOY. Sir, I have brought the father that you sent for.

[*Exit Boy.*]

BELVILE. 'Tis well. And now, my dear Florinda, let's fly to complete that mighty joy we have so long wished and signed for.—Come, Fred, you'll follow?

FREDERICK. Your example, sir, 'twas ever my ambition in war, and must be so in love.

WILLMORE. And must not I see this juggling[163] knot tied?

BELVILE. No, thou shalt do us better service and be our guard, lest Don Pedro's sudden return interrupt the ceremony.

WILLMORE. Content; I'll secure this pass.

(*Exeunt Belvile, Florinda, Frederick, and Valeria.*)

(*Enter Boy.*)

BOY (*to Willmore*). Sir, there's a lady without would speak to you.

WILLMORE. Conduct her in; I dare not quit my post.

BOY [*to Blunt*]. And sir, your tailor waits you in your chamber.

BLUNT. Some comfort yet: I shall not dance naked at the wedding.

(*Exeunt Blunt and Boy.*)

(*Enter again the Boy, conducting in Angellica in a masking habit and a vizard. Willmore runs to her.*)

WILLMORE [*aside*]. This can be none but my pretty gypsy.—Oh, I see you can follow as well as fly. Come, confess thyself the most malicious devil in nature; you think you have done my business with Angellica—

ANGELLICA. Stand off, base villain!

(*She draws a pistol and holds it to his breast.*)

WILLMORE. Ha, 'tis not she! Who art thou, and what's thy business?

ANGELLICA. One thou hast injured, and who comes to kill thee for't.

WILLMORE. What the devil canst thou mean?

ANGELLICA. By all my hopes to kill thee—

(*Holds still the pistol to his breast; he going back, she following still.*)

WILLMORE. Prithee, on what acquaintance? For I know thee not.

ANGELLICA.
Behold this face so lost to thy remembrance,

(*Pulls off her vizard.*)

And then call all thy sins about thy soul,
And let 'em die with thee.

WILLMORE. Angellica!

ANGELLICA. Yes, traitor!
Does not thy guilty blood run shivering through thy veins?
Hast thou no horror at this sight, that tells thee
Thou hast not long to boast thy shameful conquest?

WILLMORE. Faith, no, child. My blood keeps its old ebbs and flows still, and that usual heat too, that could oblige thee with a kindness, had I but opportunity.

ANGELLICA. Devil! Dost wanton with my pain? Have at thy heart!

WILLMORE. Hold, dear virago![164] Hold thy hand a little; I am not now at leisure to be killed. Hold and hear me.—(*Aside.*) Death, I think she's in earnest.

ANGELLICA (*aside, turning from him*).
Oh, if I take not heed,
My coward heart will leave me to his mercy.—
What have you, sir, to say?—But should I hear thee,
Thoud'st talk away all that is brave about me,
And I have vowed thy death by all that's sacred.

(*Follows him with the pistol to his breast.*)

WILLMORE.
Why then, there's an end of a proper handsome fellow,
That might 'a lived to have done good service yet.
That's all I can say to't.

ANGELLICA (*pausingly*).
Yet—I would give thee time for—penitence.

WILLMORE.
Faith, child, I thank God I have ever took
Care to lead a good, sober, hopeful life, and am of a religion
That teaches me to believe I shall depart in peace.

ANGELLICA.
So will the devil! Tell me,
How many poor believing fools thou hast undone?
How many hearts thou hast betrayed to ruin?

[163]**juggling** deceptive

[164]**virago** dominating woman

Yet these are little mischiefs to the ills
Thou'st taught mine to commit: Thou'st taught it love.

WILLMORE.

Egad, 'twas shrewdly hurt the while.

ANGELLICA.

Love, that has robbed it of its unconcern,
Of all that pride that taught me how to value it.
And in its room
A mean submissive passion was conveyed,
That made me humbly bow, which I ne'er did
To anything but heaven.
Thou, perjured man, didst this; and with thy oaths,
Which on thy knees thou didst devoutly make,
Softened my yielding heart, and then I was a slave.
Yet still had been content to've worn my chains,
Worn 'em with vanity and joy forever,
Hadst thou not broke those vows that put them on.
'Twas then I was undone.

(All this while follows him with the pistol to his breast.)

WILLMORE. Broke my vows? Why, where hast thou lived?
Amongst the gods? For I never heard of mortal man that
has not broke a thousand vows.

ANGELLICA. Oh, impudence!

WILLMORE. Angellica, that beauty has been too long tempting, not to have made a thousand lovers languish; who,
in the amorous fever, no doubt have sworn like me. Did
they all die in that faith, still adoring? I do not think they
did.

ANGELLICA. No, faithless man; had I repaid their vows, as I
did thine, I would have killed the ingrateful that had
abandoned me.

WILLMORE. This old general has quite spoiled thee: Nothing
makes a woman so vain as being flattered. Your old lover
ever supplies the defects of age with intolerable dotage,
vast charge, and that which you call constancy; and
attributing all this to your own merits, you domineer, and
throw your favors in's teeth, upbraiding him still with the
defects of age, and cuckold him as often as he deceives
your expectations. But the gay, young, brisk lover, that
brings his equal fires, and can give you dart for dart, you'll
find will be as nice as you sometimes.

ANGELLICA.

All this thou'st made me know, for which I hate thee.
Had I remained in innocent security,
I should have thought all men were born my slaves,
And worn my power like lightning in my eyes,
To have destroyed at pleasure when offended.
But when love held the mirror, the undeceiving glass
Reflected all the weakness of my soul, and made me know
My richest treasure being lost, my honor,
All the remaining spoil could not be worth
The conqueror's care or value.
Oh, how I feel, like a long-worshiped idol,
Discovering all the cheat.
Would not the incense and rich sacrifice

Which blind devotion offered at my altars
Have fallen to thee?
Why wouldst thou then destroy my fancied power?

WILLMORE.

By heaven, thou'rt brave, and I admire thee strangely.
I wish I were that dull, that constant thing
Which thou wouldst have, and nature never meant me.
I must, like cheerful birds, sing in all groves,
And perch on every bough,
Billing the next kind she that flies to meet me;
Yet, after all, could build my nest with thee,
Thither repairing when I'd loved my round,
And still reserve a tributary flame.
To gain your credit, I'll pay you back your charity,
And be obliged for nothing but for love.

(Offers her a purse of gold.)

ANGELLICA.

Oh, that thou wert in earnest!
So mean a thought of me
Would turn my rage to scorn, and I should pity thee,
And give thee leave to live;
Which for the public safety of our sex,
And my own private injuries, I dare not do.
Prepare—*(Follows still, as before.)*
I will no more be tempted with replies.

WILLMORE. Sure—

ANGELLICA. Another word will damn thee! I've heard thee
talk too long.

*(She follows him with the pistol ready to shoot; he retires,
still amazed. Enter Don Antonio, his arm in a scarf, and
lays hold on the pistol.)*

ANTONIO. Ha! Angellica!

ANGELLICA. Antonio! What devil brought thee hither?

ANTONIO.

Love and curiosity, seeing your coach at door.
Let me disarm you of this unbecoming instrument of
death.

(Takes away the pistol.)

Amongst the number of your slaves was there not one
worthy the honor to have fought your quarrel?—
[*To Willmore.*] Who are you, sir, that are so very
wretched
To merit death from her?

WILLMORE. One, sir, that could have made a better end of an
amorous quarrel without you, than with you.

ANTONIO. Sure 'tis some rival. Ha! The very man took
down her picture yesterday; the very same that set on me
last night! Blessed opportunity—

(Offers to shoot him.)

ANGELLICA. Hold, you're mistaken, sir.

ANTONIO. By heaven, the very same!—Sir, what preten-
sions have you to this lady?

WILLMORE. Sir, I do not use to be examined, and am ill at all
disputes but this—

(Draws; Antonio offers to shoot.)

ANGELLICA *(to Willmore)*.

Oh, hold! You see he's armed with certain death.

—And you, Antonio, I command you hold,

By all the passion you've so lately vowed me.

(Enter Don Pedro, sees Antonio, and stays.)

PEDRO *(aside)*. Ha! Antonio! And Angellica!

ANTONIO.

When I refuse obedience to your will,

May you destroy me with your mortal hate.

By all that's holy, I adore you so,

That even my rival, who has charms enough

To make him fall a victim to my jealousy,

Shall live; nay, and have leave to love on still.

PEDRO *(aside)*. What's this I hear?

ANGELLICA *(pointing to Willmore)*.

Ah thus, 'twas thus he talked, and I believed.

Antonio, yesterday

I'd not have sold my interest in his heart

For all the sword has won and lost in battle.

—But now, to show my utmost of contempt,

I give thee life; which, if thou wouldst preserve,

Live where my eyes may never see thee more.

Live to undo someone whose soul may prove

So bravely constant to revenge my love.

(Goes out. Antonio follows, but Pedro pulls him back.)

PEDRO. Antonio, stay.

ANTONIO. Don Pedro!

PEDRO.

What coward fear was that prevented thee

From meeting me this morning on the Molo?

ANTONIO. Meet thee?

PEDRO. Yes, me; I was the man that dared thee to't.

ANTONIO.

Hast thou so often seen me fight in war,

To find no better cause to excuse my absence?

I sent my sword and one to do thee right,

Finding myself uncapable to use a sword.

PEDRO.

But 'twas Florinda's quarrel that we fought,

And you, to show how little you esteemed her,

Sent me your rival, giving him your interest.

But I have found the cause of this affront,

And when I meet you fit for the dispute,

I'll tell you my resentment.

ANTONIO.

I shall be ready, sir, ere long, to do you reason.

(Exit Antonio.)

PEDRO. If I could find Florinda, now whilst my anger's high, I think I should be kind, and give her to Belvile in revenge.

WILLMORE. Faith, sir, I know not what you would do, but I believe the priest within has been so kind.

PEDRO. How? My sister married?

WILLMORE. I hope by this time he is, and bedded too, or he has not my longings about him.

PEDRO. Dares he do this? Does he not fear my power?

WILLMORE. Faith, not at all; if you will go in and thank him for the favor he has done your sister, so; if not, sir, my power's greater in this house than yours: I have a damned surly crew here that will keep you till the next tide, and then clap you on board for prize. My ship lies but a league off the Molo, and we shall show your donship a damned Tramontana[165] rover's trick.

(Enter Belvile.)

BELVILE. This rogue's in some new mischief. Ha! Pedro returned!

PEDRO. Colonel Belvile, I hear you have married my sister.

BELVILE. You have heard truth then, sir.

PEDRO. Have I so? Then, sir, I wish you joy.

BELVILE. How?

PEDRO. By this embrace I do, and I am glad on't.

BELVILE. Are you in earnest?

PEDRO.

By our long friendship and my obligations to thee, I am;

The sudden change I'll give you reasons for anon.

Come, lead me to my sister,

That she may know I now approve her choice.

(Exit Belvile with Pedro.)

(Willmore goes to follow them. Enter Hellena, as before in boy's clothes, and pulls him back.)

WILLMORE. Ha! My gypsy! Now a thousand blessings on thee for this kindness. Egad, child, I was e'en in despair of ever seeing thee again; my friends are all provided for within, each man his kind woman.

HELLENA. Ha! I thought they had served me some such trick!

WILLMORE. And I was e'en resolved to go aboard, and condemn myself to my lone cabin, and the thoughts of thee.

HELLENA. And could you have left me behind? Would you have been so ill natured?

WILLMORE. Why, 'twould have broke my heart, child. But since we are met again, I defy foul weather to part us.

HELLENA. And would you be a faithful friend now, if a maid should trust you?

WILLMORE. For a friend I cannot promise: Thou art of a form so excellent, a face and humor too good for cold dull friendship. I am parlously afraid of being in love, child; and you have not forgotten how severely you have used me?

HELLENA. That's all one; such usage you must still look for: to find out all your haunts, to rail at you to all that love

---

[165]**Tramontana** in Northern Italy (literally: beyond the mountains)

you, till I have made you love only me in your own defense, because nobody else will love you.

WILLMORE. But hast thou no better quality to recommend thyself by?

HELLENA. Faith, none, captain. Why, 'twill be the greater charity to take me for thy mistress. I am a lone child, a kind of orphan lover; and why I should die a maid, and in a captain's hands too, I do not understand.

WILLMORE. Egad, I was never clawed away with broadsides from any female before. Thou hast one virtue I adore— good nature. I hate a coy demure mistress, she's as troublesome as a colt; I'll break none. No, give me a mad mistress when mewed, and in flying, one I dare trust upon the wing, that whilst she's kind will come to the lure.[166]

HELLENA. Nay, as kind as you will, good captain, whilst it lasts. But let's lose no time.

WILLMORE. My time's as precious to me as thine can be. Therefore, dear creature, since we are so well agreed, let's retire to my chamber; and if ever thou wert treated with such savory love! Come, my bed's prepared for such a guest all clean and sweet as thy fair self. I love to steal a dish and a bottle with a friend, and hate long graces. Come, let's retire and fall to.

HELLENA. 'Tis but getting my consent, and the business is soon done. Let but old gaffer Hymen[167] and his priest say amen to't, and I dare lay my mother's daughter by as proper a fellow as your father's son, without fear or blushing.

WILLMORE. Hold, hold, no bug words,[168] child. Priest and Hymen? Prithee add a hangman to 'em to make up the consort. No, no, we'll have no vows but love, child, nor witness but the lover: The kind deity enjoins naught but love and enjoy. Hymen and priest wait still upon portion and jointure; love and beauty have their own ceremonies. Marriage is as certain a bane to love as lending money is to friendship. I'll neither ask nor give a vow, though I could be content to turn gypsy and become a left-handed bridegroom to have the pleasure of working that great miracle of making a maid a mother, if you durst venture. 'Tis upse gypsy[169] that, and if I miss I'll lose my labor.

HELLENA. And if you do not lose, what shall I get? A cradle full of noise and mischief, with a pack of repentance at my back? Can you teach me to weave incle[170] to pass my time with? 'Tis upse gypsy that, too.

WILLMORE. I can teach thee to weave a true love's knot better.

HELLENA. So can my dog.

WILLMORE. Well, I see we are both upon our guards, and I see there's no way to conquer good nature but by yielding. Here, give me thy hand: One kiss, and I am thine.

HELLENA. One kiss! How like my page he speaks! I am resolved you shall have none, for asking such a sneaking sum. He that will be satisfied with one kiss will never die of that longing. Good friend single-kiss, is all your talking come to this? A kiss, a caudle![171] Farewell, captain single-kiss.

(Going out; he stays her.)

WILLMORE. Nay, if we part so, let me die like a bird upon a bough, at the sheriff's charge. By heaven, both the Indies shall not buy thee from me. I adore thy humor and will marry thee, and we are so of one humor it must be a bargain. Give me thy hand. (Kisses her hand.) And now let the blind ones, love and fortune, do their worst.

HELLENA. Why, god-a-mercy, captain!

WILLMORE. But hark'ee: the bargain is now made, but is it not fit we should know each other's names, that when we have reason to curse one another hereafter, and people ask me who 'tis I give to the devil, I may at least be able to tell what family you came of?

HELLENA. Good reason, captain; and where I have cause, as I doubt not but I shall have plentiful, that I may know at whom to throw my—blessings, I beseech ye your name.

WILLMORE. I am called Robert the Constant.

HELLENA. A very fine name! Pray was it your faulkner[172] or butler that christened you? Do they not use to whistle when they call you?

WILLMORE. I hope you have a better, that a man may name without crossing himself—you are so merry with mine.

HELLENA. I am called Hellena the Inconstant.

(Enter Pedro, Belvile, Florinda, Frederick, Valeria.)

PEDRO. Ha! Hellena!

FLORINDA. Hellena!

HELLENA. The very same. Ha! My brother! Now, captain, show your love and courage; stand to your arms and defend me bravely, or I am lost forever.

PEDRO. What's this I hear? False girl, how came you hither, and what's your business? Speak!

(Goes roughly to her.)

WILLMORE. Hold off, sir; you have leave to parley[173] only.

(Puts himself between.)

HELLENA. I had e'en as good tell it, as you guess it. Faith, brother, my business is the same with all living creatures of my age: to love and be beloved—and here's the man.

PEDRO. Perfidious maid, hast thou deceived me too; deceived thyself and heaven?

HELLENA.
'Tis time enough to make my peace with that;
Be you but kind, let me alone with heaven.

PEDRO. Belvile, I did not expect this false play from you. Was't not enough you'd gain Florinda, which I pardoned,

---

[166]**whilst . . . lure** will follow her nature and will do what she should(?); while she is happy with him she will be faithful(?)
[167]**gaffer Hymen** old Hymen, God of Marriage [168]**bug words** frightening words, threats [169]**upse gypsy** like a gypsy [170]**incle** linen tape

[171]**caudle** warm drink given to the sick [172]**faulkner** falconer, a trainer of falcons [173]**parley** speak

but your lewd friends too must be enriched with the spoils of a noble family?

BELVILE. Faith, sir, I am as much surprised at this as you can be. Yet, sir, my friends are gentlemen, and ought to be esteemed for their misfortunes, since they have the glory to suffer with the best of men and kings. 'Tis true, he's a rover of fortune, yet a prince aboard his little wooden world.

PEDRO. What's this to the maintenance of a woman of her birth and quality?

WILLMORE. Faith, sir, I can boast of nothing but a sword which does me right where'er I come, and has defended a worse cause than a woman's; and since I loved her before I either knew her birth or name, I must pursue my resolution and marry her.

PEDRO. And is all your holy intent of becoming a nun debauched into a desire of man?

HELLENA. Why, I have considered the matter, brother, and find the three hundred thousand crowns my uncle left me, and you cannot keep from me, will be better laid out in love than in religion, and turn to as good an account. Let most voices carry it: for heaven or the captain?

ALL CRY. A captain! A captain!

HELLENA. Look ye, sir, 'tis a clear case.

PEDRO. Oh, I am mad!—(*Aside.*) If I refuse, my life's in danger.—Come, there's one motive induces me. Take her; I shall now be free from fears of her honor. Guard it you now, if you can; I have been a slave to't long enough.

(*Gives her to him.*)

WILLMORE. Faith, sir, I am of a nation that are of opinion a woman's honor is not worth guarding when she has a mind to part with it.

HELLENA. Well said, captain.

PEDRO (*to Valeria*). This was your plot, mistress, but I hope you have married one that will revenge my quarrel to you.

VALERIA. There's no altering destiny, sir.

PEDRO. Sooner than a woman's will; therefore I forgive you all, and wish you may get my father's pardon as easily, which I fear.

(*Enter Blunt dressed in a Spanish habit, looking very ridiculous; his Man adjusting his band.*[174])

MAN. 'Tis very well, sir.

BLUNT. Well, sir! 'Adsheartlikins, I tell you 'tis damnable ill, sir. A Spanish habit! Good Lord! Could the devil and my tailor devise no other punishment for me but the mode of a nation I abominate?

BELVILE. What's the matter, Ned?

BLUNT. Pray view me round, and judge.

(*Turns round.*)

BELVILE. I must confess thou art a kind of an odd figure.

BLUNT. In a Spanish habit with a vengeance! I had rather be in the Inquisition for Judaism[175] than in this doublet and breeches; a pillory were an easy collar to this, three handfuls high; and these shoes, too, are worse than the stocks, with the sole an inch shorter than my foot. In fine, gentlemen, methinks I look like a bag of bays[176] stuffed full of fool's flesh.

BELVILE. Methinks 'tis well, and makes thee look e'en cavalier. Come, sir, settle your face and salute our friends. Lady—

BLUNT (*to Hellena*). Ha! Sayst thou so, my little rover? Lady, if you be one, give me leave to kiss your hand, and tell you, 'adsheartlikins, for all I look so, I am your humble servant. A pox of my Spanish habit!

(*Music is heard to play.*)

WILLMORE. Hark! What's this?

(*Enter Boy.*)

BOY. Sir, as the custom is, the gay people in masquerade, who make every man's house their own, are coming up.

(*Enter several men and women in masking habits, with music; they put themselves in order and dance.*)

BLUNT. 'Adsheartlikins, would 'twere lawful to pull off their false faces, that I might see if my doxy[177] were not amongst 'em.

BELVILE (*to the maskers*). Ladies and gentlemen, since you are come so *a propos*,[178] you must take a small collation with us.

WILLMORE (*to Hellena*). Whilst we'll to the good man within, who stays to give us a cast of his office.[179] Have you no trembling at the near approach?

HELLENA. No more than you have in an engagement or a tempest.

WILLMORE. Egad, thou'rt a brave girl, and I admire thy love and courage.

Lead on; no other dangers they can dread,
Who venture in the storms o'th' marriage bed.

(*Exeunt.*)

EPILOGUE

The banished cavaliers! A roving blade!
A popish carnival! A masquerade!
The devil's in't if this will please the nation
In these our blessed times of reformation,
When conventickling[180] is so much in fashion.

---

[175]**Inquisition for Judaism** the Spanish Inquisition persecuted Jews as well as heretics   [176]**bag of bays** bag of spices used in cooking   [177]**doxy** prostitute   [178]*a propos* opportunely   [179]**cast of office** sample of his work (in marrying people)   [180]**conventickling** attending conventicles, that is, participating in secret meetings of religious dissenters (with a pun on *tickling*)

[174]**band** neckband

And yet—
That mutinous tribe[181] less factions do beget,
Than your continual differing in wit.
Your judgment's, as your passion's, a disease:
Nor muse nor miss your appetite can please;
You're grown as nice as queasy consciences,
Whose each convulsion, when the spirit moves,
Damns everything that maggot[182] disapproves.

With canting[183] rule you would the stage refine,
And to dull method all our sense confine.
With th'insolence of commonwealths you rule,
Where each gay fop and politic grave fool
On monarch wit impose, without control.
As for the last, who seldom sees a play,
Unless it be the old Blackfriars[184] way;
Shaking his empty noddle[185] o'er bamboo,[186]
He cries, "Good faith, these plays will never do!
Ah, sir, in my young days, what lofty wit,
What high-strained scenes of fighting there were writ.
These are slight airy toys. But tell me, pray,
What has the House of Commons done today?"
Then shows his politics, to let you see
Of state affairs he'll judge as notably
As he can do of wit and poetry.
The younger sparks, who hither do resort,
Cry,
"Pox o' your genteel things! Give us more sport!
Damn me, I'm sure 'twill never please the court."

Such fops are never pleased, unless the play
Be stuffed with fools as brisk and dull as they.
Such might the half-crown[187] spare, and in a glass
At home behold a more accomplished ass.
Where they may set their cravats, wigs, and faces,
And practice all their buffoonry grimaces:
See how this huff becomes, this damny,[188] stare,
Which they at home may act because they dare,

But must with prudent caution do elsewhere.
Oh that our Nokes, or Tony Lee,[189] could show
A fop but half so much to th' life as you.

POSTSCRIPT

This play had been sooner in print, but for a report about the town (made by some either very malicious or very ignorant) that 'twas *Thomaso*[190] altered; which made the booksellers fear some trouble from the proprietor of that admirable play, which indeed has wit enough to stock a poet, and is not to be pieced or mended by any but the excellent author himself. That I have stolen some hints from it, may be a proof that I valued it more than to pretend to alter it, had I the dexterity of some poets, who are not more expert in stealing than in the art of concealing, and who even that way outdo the Spartan boys.[191] I might have appropriated all to myself; but I, vainly proud of my judgment, hang out the sign of Angellica (the only stolen object) to give notice where a great part of the wit dwelt; though if the *Play of the Novella*[192] were as well worth remembering as *Thomaso*, they might (bating[193] the name) have as well said I took it from thence. I will only say the plot and business (not to boast on't) is my own; as for the words and characters, I leave the reader to judge and compare 'em with *Thomaso*, to whom I recommend the great entertainment of reading it. Though had this succeeded ill, I should have had no need of imploring that justice from the critics, who are naturally so kind to any that pretend to usurp their dominion, especially of our sex: They would doubtless have given me the whole honor on't. Therefore I will only say in English what the famous Vergil does in Latin: I make verses, and others have the fame.

TOPICS FOR CRITICAL THINKING AND WRITING

 ### THE PLAY ON THE PAGE

1. What (if anything) makes Blunt's pursuit of Lucetta different from Willmore's pursuit of Angellica?
2. Angellica falls in love with Willmore. Do you think he is convincing enough for her to love him as the play indicates?

3. How disturbed are we by Willmore's rejection of Angellica's love? Is his rejection of Angellica so disturbing that the play *as a comedy* suffers? Explain.
4. Angellica and Hellena both comment on Willmore's eloquence. How eloquent do you find him? Is it impor-

---

[181]**mutinous tribe** dissenters   [182]**maggot** the inner light (the *spirit* of the preceding line) that guides dissenters   [183]**canting** hypocritical   [184]**Blackfriars** a London theater, closed in 1642   [185]**noddle** head   [186]**bamboo** a cane, that is, an infirm man is shaking his head   [187]**half-crown** coin   [188]**damny** damn me

[189]**Nokes . . . Lee** James Nokes and Anthony Leigh, two comedians of the period   [190]**Thomaso** play by Thomas Killigrew, *Thomaso; or, The Wanderer* (1654)   [191]**Spartan boys** soldiers who hid in the Trojan horse   [192]**Play of the Novella** Richard Brome's *The Novella* (1632)   [193]**bating** excepting

tant that we find him eloquent, or is it enough for the characters to say that *they* find him eloquent? (Cite several speeches to support your point.)

5. Angellica's future is left unresolved at the end of the play. Some critics take this to mean that Aphra Behn is suggesting that in the real world there is no place for

women like Angellica. Do you agree with this interpretation? Explain. Two related questions: (a) Is Angellica too rounded a figure—too convincing a figure—for a comedy? (b) Do you think Behn is signalling readers that Angellica Bianca is her spokesperson by using a character whose initials—A. B.—correspond with her own?

🎭 THE PLAY ON THE STAGE

6. Two questions about Blunt: (a) We laugh at him, but do we also sometimes feel that he is badly treated? Support your answer by pointing to specific episodes; (b) since Blunt is companion of Belvile and Willmore, does the role need to portray him as something more than a buffoon?

7. It is customary to stage Restoration comedies (English comedies of the late seventeenth century) in the costume of the period—women draped under yards of

heavy material, men in clothing adorned with gold braid and lace, and men and women with towering wigs. In short, the usual costuming emphasizes the artifice of the behavior. What might be gained or lost by staging the play in another period, for instance in the 1920s?

8. Suggest a casting for *The Rover*, choosing from today's film or stage performers, or from your own circle of friends. Explain your reasons.

THE PLAY IN PERFORMANCE

The Rover was first performed at the Dorset Garden Theatre in 1677, with King Charles II present. We cannot be certain of every performance, but we know that it was revived in 1680, 1685, and in 1696, and throughout the first half of the eighteenth century it was a regular part of the repertory, with several performances in almost every year. After 1761, however, it disappeared, until it was brought back in 1790 in a shortened and somewhat moralized form (*Love in Many Masks*) by John Philip Kemble. In Kemble's version, Willmore is less often in pursuit of women, and the final lines of the play suggest that the marriage may turn out well. *Love in Many Masks*, however, did not see many productions, and the original went unproduced for well over a century. A new interest in Behn, begun by feminist literary historians in the 1970s, brought *The Rover* (with some cuts) back to the stage. It is now again fairly popular, especially on college campuses but also occasionally in the professional theater. In 1986 John Barton, directing the Royal Shakespeare Company, with Jeremy Irons as Willmore, did a heavily revised version at Stratford-upon-Avon. Barton cut about five hundred fifty lines and added about three hundred fifty lines, some of them from Behn's chief source, Thomas Killigrew's *Thomaso*.

In Barton's version, Belvile is a black soldier of fortune, and the setting is an unspecified Spanish colony in the Caribbean, rather than Naples. Because the production met with considerable popular success at Stratford-upon-Avon, it was produced in London in the following year, but on a different kind of stage. In the Stratford production Barton used a bare thrust—such a stage would have seemed terribly old-fashioned to Behn and her audience, who valued the relatively new invention of painted scenery—thereby bringing the actors into close contact with the audience. In fact, the actors sometimes addressed the audience, as when Florinda appealed to the audience to stop the fight between Pedro and Belvile.

In 1987 the Williamstown Theater in Massachusetts staged a more conventional production, with Christopher Reeve as Willmore and Kate Burton (Richard Burton's daughter) as Florinda. Finally, it should be mentioned that although most productions emphasize the high spirits and energy of the play, in 1991 the New Cross Theatre in London emphasized the darker aspects of the play; the desperation of the characters seemed not so much funny as disturbing.

Carol Elliott MacVey
DIRECTING *THE ROVER*

Carol Elliott MacVey, a member of the Department of Theatre at the University of Iowa, directed *The Rover* at Princeton University in 1985. In this interview, she discusses the production.

Why did you choose to stage The Rover?

I found it satisfied my needs for an undergraduate production—many young roles for college-aged actors, lots of comic shenanigans, sword fights, and women who prevailed. I recognized an innate sense of theatricality in Behn's script and prayed I could find enough actors who loved long sentences and had breath enough to speak them.

What did you cut, and what did you add?

I did a lot of cutting—of speeches, of scenes, whole pages. I also interpolated events in the carnival scenes. As it turned out, the carnival scenes played a major role in my production, providing a mother lode of theatrical energy which both dazzled and entertained. Every time the setting shifted to the carnival, two events happened. First, there was a explosion of Dionysian activity with carnival acts being performed everywhere: dancing, juggling, fire-swallowing, singing, acrobatics, whatever. This was followed, center stage, by an episode of an ongoing commedia dumbshow entitled *Marriage a-la-Mode* (or as one of the actors renamed it, *Marriage with Ice Cream*). These episodes depicted a series of arranged marriages in one woman's lifetime.

Episode 1: youth—she is physically dragged by her father to the altar to marry a very senile, very old man.
Episode 2: woman—she is carrying ten bambinos and is forced to marry a very ugly old man with ten bambinos of his own. He has two bags of gold.
Episode 3: midlife—she is carrying thirty bambinos and is forced to marry a very old, very mean man with multo bambinos of his own. He has many bags of gold.
Episode 4: old age—she is carrying several bags of gold, has no bambinos, no teeth, no hair, sans everything, and a very handsome young man is being physically dragged to the altar to marry her.

Willmore's initial entrance into the carnival conveyed much about what one might expect from his character. One of the many carnival figures was a giantess, a hoop-skirted woman on stilts. She was huge and grotesque. Suddenly she screamed, no one knowing if the scream was a result of surprise or of pleasure. All activity stopped and everyone focused on her. Then, out from under her skirts, smug and satisfied, strutted Willmore. She picked him up, smothered him in her oversized balloon breasts and hurled him to the ground, much to everyone's delight. Let's ramble!

Are you familiar with Peter Hall's adaptation of The Rover?

Yes. I regret to say that it is the version that is popularly done. Behn's original script opens with two sisters discussing how to solve their respective problems. Florinda is in love but is being forced to marry a septuagenarian while Hellena

is being forced to go to a convent. Hall's script, on the other hand, opens with a band of Cavaliers entering Naples trying to figure out how, while they are ashore, they will woo and win women in order to satisfy their long-delayed sexual yearnings. What Behn gives us in the original version is unusual and ought to be fiercely protected—a play that opens with women's energies generating the machinations of the plot and creating a landscape into which the men will enter. What Hall gives us is the usual "good ole boy" formula: Let the men create and organize the world and then let women enter into it as devices for their pleasure. Even though much of the rest of Hall's script reflects Behn's original version, the damage has been done: He has sabotaged and violated and subverted all the primal female energy with which Behn obviously intended the play to begin.

Do you think the original version ends satisfactorily?

I'm interested in the unresolved tensions at the end of a play. I find Angellica's problem to be a curious one. The courtesan, for the first time, falls in love. She loves Willmore with a passion she has never experienced with any other man and yet she, unlike the other lovers in the play, ends up rejected, alone. The final image in my production was of Angellica on a balcony, alone, watching the paired lovers exit as the festive carnival music brought the play to an end.

What design decisions did you make about The Rover?

The action took place on a three-quarter-round stage, with the audience quite close to the actors; there was a balcony upstage. The only set pieces were huge pillows which were used in various ways throughout, allowing the playing to be extremely physical, even for the women. At the opening of the first scene, the pillows were piled center stage and we heard raucous screaming offstage. Then, Florinda ran in, wildly pursued by Hellena, who eventually tackled her sister, threw her onto the piles of pillows, straddled her, and pinned her down. Florinda, struggling to be free, exclaims, "What an impertinent thing is a young girl bred in a nunnery! Prithee, no more Hellena! I have told you more than thou understand'st already." From the outset, Hellena is someone to reckon with, not only verbally, but physically.

The costume design was modified Restoration, which meant that one could easily identify the period but there was enough flexibility and physical freedom for the women to cavort when needed. Although the women do prevail primarily by their wits I also wanted to provide them with other options.

Henrik Ibsen

A DOLL'S HOUSE

Henrik Ibsen (1828–1906) was born in Skien, Norway, of wealthy parents who soon after his birth lost their money. Ibsen worked as a pharmacist's apprentice, but at the age of twenty-two he had written his first play, a promising melodrama entitled *Cataline*. He engaged in theater work first in Norway and then in Denmark and Germany. By 1865 his plays had won him a state pension that enabled him to settle in Rome. After writing romantic, historic, and poetic plays, he turned to realistic drama with *The League of Youth* (1869). Among the major realistic "problem plays" are *A Doll's House* (1879), *Ghosts* (1881), and *An Enemy of the People* (1882). In *The Wild Duck* (1884) he moved toward a more symbolic tragic comedy, and his last plays, written in the nineties, are highly symbolic.

COMMENTARY

Before he was forty Ibsen had written two masterpieces of poetic drama, *Brand* (1866) and *Peer Gynt* (1867). But a few years later he came to feel, along with many others, that the future of dramatic literature was not in poetic language, but in language that closely resembled ordinary speech. He devoted his subsequent efforts to prose drama, and we find him, in his letters, occasionally prophesying that poetic drama has no future and warning his translators to avoid all expressions that depart from "everyday speech." In the 1870s and 1880s he wrote the so-called problem plays (including *A Doll's House*, *Ghosts*, and *An Enemy of the People*) that for the next seventy-five years made his name familiar to the English-speaking world. A problem play, or "play of ideas," or *pièce à thèse*, is concerned with a serious political or social issue, its author hoping to arouse the audience to do something about the problem (for example, to modify the divorce laws, to extend the ballot, to alter the tax structure). The more successful the play, the more it ensures its own demise, for when the social institutions have been altered and the problem has been solved, the play has no relevance to experience; it is merely a thing of historical importance, a museum curio. The violent reviews that *A Doll's House*, *Ghosts*, and some of Ibsen's other plays engendered are evidence that more was at stake than aesthetic matters; discussions of the plays inevitably became discussions of divorce, venereal disease, incest, and so forth. A century later, we see readers have found that Ibsen has something more to offer than thoughts on how to improve society.

First of all, we have come to see that Ibsen's prose dramas, which he said were written in "the straightforward plain language spoken in daily life," are more than realistic copies of aspects of behavior. With Ibsen, realism often becomes a form of symbolism. Let's begin with the stage and its setting. When the curtain goes up on a performance of *A Doll's House*, the audience sees "a comfortably and tastefully but not expensively furnished room." Additional details, such as "engravings on the walls," and "a small bookcase with leather-bound books," tell us much about the kind of people who live here. We shall learn more about these people when we see the clothes that they wear and hear the words that they speak, but even now—from seeing their living room— we know that they are people who hold the conventional middle-class values. The leather-bound books in the bookcase, for example, are more for show than for reading.

In some plays there are several sets—sometimes in sharp contrast—but in *A Doll's House* there is only one set, and perhaps we come to feel that this omnipresent room is a sort of prison that stifles its inhabitants or, as the title of the play implies, that this room keeps its inhabitants at a distance from the realities of life. At the end of the play, Nora escapes from this box and enters the real world. We might look, too, at the ways in which some of the furniture and the properties work in the play. Very early, when Torvald begins to lecture Nora about incurring debts, she "goes over towards the stove." It is scarcely too subtle to conclude that she is seeking a place of warmth or security when confronted by Torvald's chilling words. We may not *consciously* come to this conclusion, but that doesn't matter. Indeed, later in this act,

Torvald, sitting near the stove, says quite naturally, "Ah, how cozy and peaceful it is here."

Or consider the use Ibsen makes of the Christmas tree. In the first act, when Nora's world is still relatively undisturbed, the tree, adorned with candles and flowers, is in the center of the stage. By the end of this act Nora is terrified, and when the curtain goes up for the second act, we see the tree thrust into a corner, "stripped and disheveled," with burnt-down candles. Again, we may not consciously concede that Ibsen, through the tree, is telling us something about Nora, but surely the tree—at first gay, then forlorn—somehow has an impact on us.

It would be easy to go on at length, discussing the ways in which Ibsen as a dramatist produces meanings, but we now should step back and ask a large question: What does the play add up to? Before we try to answer such a question, it may be useful to mention that Ibsen actually knew a woman who had forged a check to pay for a trip that her husband's health required. When the husband learned the truth, he turned on her and had her committed to an asylum, though later, for the sake of their children, he allowed her to return to their home. This episode apparently set Ibsen thinking, and when he set to work on A Doll's House he jotted down some "Notes for a Modern Tragedy":

> There are two kinds of moral law, two kinds of conscience, one in man and a completely different one in woman. They do not understand each other; but in matters of practical living the woman is judged by man's law, as if she were not a woman but a man.
>
> The wife in the play ends up quite bewildered and not knowing right from wrong; her natural instincts on the one side and her faith in authority on the other leave her completely confused.

Of course, Ibsen probably began by thinking about the real woman who forged a check to pay for the trip to save her sick husband, but the passage just quoted is the earliest writing relevant to the play. As Ibsen worked on the play, he (not surprisingly) produced characters and a plot that have a life of their own; but even if they depart from his preliminary note, these characters and this plot add up to something. (A *plot* is what happens; a *theme* is what the happenings add up to.) Some readers see in A Doll's House a play about a woman's place in a man's world, or a play about women's rights, but Ibsen himself (years after writing the play) said he had a larger theme: "I am not even sure what women's rights really are. To me it has been a question of human rights." Certainly the play deals, as Ibsen implies, with the enslavement of one person by another. At last Torvald dimly seems to recognize that Nora is a human being, not a doll; and Nora perceives that such a recognition could lead to "a true marriage."

Ingmar Bergman's 1989 production of A Doll's House *at the Royal Dramatic Theatre in Stockholm kept all of the characters on stage throughout the play, or, more precisely, those characters who were not speaking were seated, in view of the audience, at the side of the stage. In the illustrated scene we see Nora taking leave of her husband, Torvald. Bergman emphasized Torvald's vulnerability by having him in bed, nude. For additional photographs of productions of* A Doll's House, *see pages 13 and 15.*

Henrik Ibsen

A DOLL'S HOUSE

Translated by Michael Meyer

List of Characters

TORVALD HELMER, *a lawyer*
NORA, *his wife*
DR. RANK
MRS. LINDE
NILS KROGSTAD, *also a lawyer*
The Helmers' three small children
ANNE-MARIE, *their nurse*
HELEN, *the maid*
A Porter

SCENE: *The action takes place in the Helmers' apartment.*

ACT 1

A comfortably and tastefully, but not expensively furnished room. Backstage right a door leads out to the hall; backstage left, another door to Helmer's study. Between these two doors stands a piano. In the middle of the left-hand wall is a door, with a window downstage of it. Near the window, a round table with armchairs and a small sofa. In the right-hand wall, slightly upstage, is a door, downstage of this, against the same wall, a stove lined with porcelain tiles, with a couple of armchairs and a rocking-chair in front of it. Between the stove and the side door is a small table. Engravings on the wall. A what-not with china and other bric-a-brac; a small bookcase with leather-bound books. A carpet on the floor; a fire in the stove. A winter day.

A bell rings in the hall outside. After a moment, we hear the front door being opened. Nora enters the room, humming contentedly to herself. She is wearing outdoor clothes and carrying a lot of parcels, which she puts down on the table right. She leaves the door to the hall open; through it, we can see a Porter carrying a Christmas tree and a basket. He gives these to the Maid, who has opened the door for them.

NORA. Hide that Christmas tree away, Helen. The children mustn't see it before I've decorated it this evening. (*To the porter, taking out her purse.*) How much—?

PORTER. A shilling.

NORA. Here's half a crown. No, keep it.

The Porter touches his cap and goes. Nora closes the door. She continues to laugh happily to herself as she removes her coat, etc. She takes from her pocket a bag containing macaroons and eats a couple. Then, she tiptoes across and listens at her husband's door.

NORA. Yes, he's here. (*Starts humming again as she goes over to the table, right.*)

HELMER (*from his room*). Is that my skylark twittering out there?

NORA (*opening some of the parcels*). It is!

HELMER. Is that my squirrel rustling?

NORA. Yes!

HELMER. When did my squirrel come home?

NORA. Just now. (*Pops the bag of macaroons in her pocket and wipes her mouth.*) Come out here, Torvald, and see what I've bought.

HELMER. You mustn't disturb me! (*Short pause; then he opens the door and looks in, his pen in his hand.*) Bought, did you say? All that? Has my little squanderbird been overspending again?

NORA. Oh, Torvald, surely we can let ourselves go a little this year! It's the first Christmas we don't have to scrape.

HELMER. Well, you know, we can't afford to be extravagant.

NORA. Oh yes, Torvald, we can be a little extravagant now. Can't we? Just a tiny bit? You've got a big salary now, and you're going to make lots and lots of money.

HELMER. Next year, yes. But my new salary doesn't start till April.

NORA. Pooh; we can borrow till then.

HELMER. Nora! (*Goes over to her and takes her playfully by the ear.*) What a little spendthrift you are! Suppose I were to borrow fifty pounds today, and you spent it all over Christmas, and then on New Year's Eve a tile fell off a roof onto my head—

NORA (*puts her hand over his mouth*). Oh, Torvald! Don't say such dreadful things!

HELMER. Yes, but suppose something like that did happen? What then?

NORA. If any thing as frightful as that happened, it wouldn't make much difference whether I was in debt or not.

HELMER. But what about the people I'd borrowed from?

NORA. Them? Who cares about them? They're strangers.

HELMER. Oh, Nora, Nora, how like a woman! No, but seriously, Nora, you know how I feel about this. No debts! Never borrow! A home that is founded on debts can never be a place of freedom and beauty. We two have stuck it out bravely up to now; and we shall continue to do so for the short time we still have to.

NORA (*goes over towards the stove*). Very well, Torvald. As you say.

HELMER (*follows her*). Now, now! My little songbird mustn't droop her wings. What's this? Is little squirrel sulking? (*Takes out his purse.*) Nora; guess what I've got here!

NORA (*turns quickly*). Money!

HELMER. Look. (*Hands her some banknotes.*) I know how these small expenses crop up at Christmas.

NORA (*counts them*). One—two—three—four. Oh, thank you, Torvald, thank you! I should be able to manage with this.

HELMER. You'll have to.

NORA. Yes, yes, of course I will. But come over here, I want to show you everything I've bought. And so cheaply! Look, here are new clothes for Ivar—and a sword. And a horse and a trumpet for Bob. And a doll and a cradle for Emmy—they're nothing much, but she'll pull them apart in a few days. And some bits of material and handkerchiefs for the maids. Old Anne-Marie ought to have had something better, really.

HELMER. And what's in that parcel?

NORA (*cries*). No, Torvald, you mustn't see that before this evening!

HELMER. Very well. But now, tell me, you little spendthrift, what do you want for Christmas?

NORA. Me? Oh, pooh, I don't want anything.

HELMER. Oh, yes, you do. Now tell me, what, within reason, would you most like?

NORA. No, I really don't know. Oh, yes—Torvald—!

HELMER. Well?

NORA (*plays with his coat-buttons; not looking at him*). If you really want to give me something, you could—you could—

HELMER. Come on, out with it.

NORA (*quickly*). You could give me money, Torvald. Only as much as you feel you can afford; then later I'll buy something with it.

HELMER. But, Nora—

NORA. Oh yes, Torvald dear, please! Please! Then I'll wrap up the notes in pretty gold paper and hang them on the Christmas tree. Wouldn't that be fun?

HELMER. What's the name of that little bird that can never keep any money?

NORA. Yes, yes, squanderbird; I know. But let's do as I say, Torvald; then I'll have time to think about what I need most. Isn't that the best way? Mm?

HELMER (*smiles*). To be sure it would be, if you could keep what I give you and really buy yourself something with it. But you'll spend it on all sorts of useless things for the house, and then I'll have to put my hand in my pocket again.

NORA. Oh, but Torvald—

HELMER. You can't deny it, Nora dear. (*Puts his arm round her waist.*) The squanderbird's a pretty little creature, but she gets through an awful lot of money. It's incredible what an expensive pet she is for a man to keep.

NORA. For shame! How can you say such a thing? I save every penny I can.

HELMER (*laughs*). That's quite true. Every penny you can. But you can't.

NORA (*hums and smiles, quietly gleeful*). Hm. If you only knew how many expenses we larks and squirrels have, Torvald.

HELMER. You're a funny little creature. Just like your father used to be. Always on the look-out for some way to get money, but as soon as you have any it just runs through your fingers, and you never know where it's gone. Well, I suppose I must take you as you are. It's in your blood. Yes, yes, yes, these things are hereditary, Nora.

NORA. Oh, I wish I'd inherited more of Papa's qualities.

HELMER. And I wouldn't wish my darling little songbird to be any different from what she is. By the way, that reminds me. You look awfully—how shall I put it?— awfully guilty today.

NORA. Do I?

HELMER. Yes, you do. Look me in the eyes.

NORA (*looks at him*). Well?

HELMER (*wags his finger*). Has my little sweet-tooth been indulging herself in town today, by any chance?

NORA. No, how can you think such a thing?

HELMER. Not a tiny little digression into a pastry shop?

NORA. No, Torvald, I promise—

HELMER. Not just a wee jam tart?

NORA. Certainly not.

HELMER. Not a little nibble at a macaroon?

NORA. No, Torvald—I promise you, honestly—

HELMER. There, there. I was only joking.

NORA (*goes over to the table, right*). You know I could never act against your wishes.

HELMER. Of course not. And you've given me your word— (*Goes over to her.*) Well, my beloved Nora, you keep your little Christmas secrets to yourself. They'll be revealed this evening, I've no doubt, once the Christmas tree has been lit.

NORA. Have you remembered to invite Dr. Rank?

HELMER. No. But there's no need; he knows he'll be dining with us. Anyway, I'll ask him when he comes this morn-ing. I've ordered some good wine. Oh Nora, you can't imagine how I'm looking forward to this evening.

NORA. So am I. And, Torvald, how the children will love it!

HELMER. Yes, it's a wonderful thing to know that one's position is assured and that one has an ample income. Don't you agree? It's good to know that, isn't it?

NORA. Yes, it's almost like a miracle.

HELMER. Do you remember last Christmas? For three whole weeks you shut yourself away every evening to make flowers for the Christmas tree, and all those other things you were going to surprise us with. Ugh, it was the most boring time I've ever had in my life.

NORA. I didn't find it boring.

HELMER (*smiles*). But it all came to nothing in the end, didn't it?

NORA. Oh, are you going to bring that up again? How could I help the cat getting in and tearing everything to bits?

HELMER. No, my poor little Nora, of course you couldn't. You simply wanted to make us happy, and that's all that matters. But it's good that those hard times are past.

NORA. Yes, it's wonderful.

HELMER. I don't have to sit by myself and be bored. And you don't have to tire your pretty eyes and your delicate little hands—

NORA (*claps her hands*). No, Torvald, that's true, isn't it—I don't have to any longer? Oh, it's really all just like a mir-acle. (*Takes his arm.*) Now, I'm going to tell you what I thought we might do, Torvald. As soon as Christmas is over—(*A bell rings in the hall.*) Oh, there's the doorbell. (*Tidies up one or two things in the room.*) Someone's com-ing. What a bore.

HELMER. I'm not at home to any visitors. Remember!

MAID (*in the doorway*). A lady's called, madam. A stranger.

NORA. Well, ask her to come in.

MAID. And the doctor's here too, sir.

HELMER. Has he gone to my room?

MAID. Yes, sir.

Helmer goes into his room. The Maid shows in Mrs. Linde, who is dressed in traveling clothes, and closes the door.

MRS. LINDE (*shyly and a little hesitantly*). Good evening, Nora.

NORA (*uncertainly*). Good evening—

MRS. LINDE. I don't suppose you recognize me.

NORA. No, I'm afraid I—Yes, wait a minute—surely— (*Exclaims.*) Why, Christine! Is it really you?

MRS. LINDE. Yes, it's me.

NORA. Christine! And I didn't recognize you! But how could I—? (*More quietly.*) How you've changed, Chris-tine!

MRS. LINDE. Yes, I know. It's been nine years—nearly ten—

NORA. Is it so long? Yes, it must be. Oh, these last eight years have been such a happy time for me! So you've come to town? All that way in winter! How brave of you!

MRS. LINDE. I arrived by the steamer this morning.

NORA. Yes, of course—to enjoy yourself over Christmas. Oh, how splendid! We'll have to celebrate! But take off your coat. You're not cold, are you? (*Helps her off with it.*) There! Now let's sit down here by the stove and be comfortable. No, you take the armchair. I'll sit here in the rocking-chair. (*Clasps Mrs. Linde's hands.*) Yes, now you look like your old self. It was just at first that—you've got a little paler, though, Christine. And perhaps a bit thinner.

MRS. LINDE. And older, Nora. Much, much older.

NORA. Yes, perhaps a little older. Just a tiny bit. Not much. (*Checks herself suddenly and says earnestly.*) Oh, but how thoughtless of me to sit here and chatter away like this! Dear, sweet Christine, can you forgive me?

MRS. LINDE. What do you mean, Nora?

NORA (*quietly*). Poor Christine, you've become a widow.

MRS. LINDE. Yes. Three years ago.

NORA. I know, I know—I read it in the papers. Oh, Christine, I meant to write to you so often, honestly. But I always put it off, and something else always cropped up.

MRS. LINDE. I understand, Nora dear.

NORA. No, Christine, it was beastly of me. Oh, my poor darling, what you've gone through! And he didn't leave you anything?

MRS. LINDE. No.

NORA. No children, either?

MRS. LINDE. No.

NORA. Nothing at all, then?

MRS. LINDE. Not even a feeling of loss or sorrow.

NORA (*looks incredulously at her*). But, Christine, how is that possible?

MRS. LINDE (*smiles sadly and strokes Nora's hair*). Oh, these things happen, Nora.

NORA. All alone. How dreadful that must be for you. I've three lovely children. I'm afraid you can't see them now, because they're out with nanny. But you must tell me everything—

MRS. LINDE. No, no, no. I want to hear about you.

NORA. No, you start. I'm not going to be selfish today, I'm just going to think about you. Oh, but there's one thing I *must* tell you. Have you heard of the wonderful luck we've just had?

MRS. LINDE. No. What?

NORA. Would you believe it—my husband's just been made manager of the bank!

MRS. LINDE. Your husband? Oh, how lucky—!

NORA. Yes, isn't it? Being a lawyer is so uncertain, you know, especially if one isn't prepared to touch any case that isn't—well—quite nice. And of course Torvald's been very firm about that—and I'm absolutely with him. Oh, you can imagine how happy we are! He's joining the bank in the New Year, and he'll be getting a big salary, and lots of percentages too. From now on we'll be able to live quite differently—we'll be able to do whatever we want. Oh, Christine, it's such a relief! I feel so happy!

Well, I mean, it's lovely to have heaps of money and not to have to worry about anything. Don't you think?

MRS. LINDE. It must be lovely to have enough to cover one's needs, anyway.

NORA. Not just our needs! We're going to have heaps and heaps of money!

MRS. LINDE (*smiles*). Nora, Nora, haven't you grown up yet? When we were at school you were a terrible little spendthrift.

NORA (*laughs quietly*). Yes, Torvald still says that. (*Wags her finger.*) But "Nora, Nora" isn't as silly as you think. Oh, we've been in no position for me to waste money. We've both had to work.

MRS. LINDE. You too?

NORA. Yes, little things—fancy work, crocheting, embroidery and so forth. (*Casually.*) And other things too. I suppose you know Torvald left the Ministry when we got married? There were no prospects of promotion in his department, and of course he needed more money. But the first year he overworked himself quite dreadfully. He had to take on all sorts of extra jobs, and worked day and night. But it was too much for him, and he became frightfully ill. The doctors said he'd have to go to a warmer climate.

MRS. LINDE. Yes, you spent a whole year in Italy, didn't you?

NORA. Yes. It wasn't easy for me to get away, you know. I'd just had Ivar. But of course we had to do it. Oh, it was a marvelous trip! And it saved Torvald's life. But it cost an awful lot of money, Christine.

MRS. LINDE. I can imagine.

NORA. Two hundred and fifty pounds. That's a lot of money, you know.

MRS. LINDE. How lucky you had it.

NORA. Well, actually, we got it from my father.

MRS. LINDE. Oh, I see. Didn't he die just about that time?

NORA. Yes, Christine, just about then. Wasn't it dreadful, I couldn't go and look after him. I was expecting little Ivar any day. And then I had my poor Torvald to care for—we really didn't think he'd live. Dear, kind Papa! I never saw him again, Christine. Oh, it's the saddest thing that's happened to me since I got married.

MRS. LINDE. I know you were very fond of him. But you went to Italy—?

NORA. Yes. Well, we had the money, you see, and the doctors said we mustn't delay. So we went the month after Papa died.

MRS. LINDE. And your husband came back completely cured?

NORA. Fit as a fiddle!

MRS. LINDE. But—the doctor?

NORA. How do you mean?

MRS. LINDE. I thought the maid said that the gentleman who arrived with me was the doctor.

NORA. Oh yes, that's Doctor Rank, but he doesn't come because anyone's ill. He's our best friend, and he looks us up at least once every day. No, Torvald hasn't had a moment's illness since we went away. And the children are fit and healthy and so am I. (*Jumps up and claps her hands.*) Oh God, oh God, Christine, isn't it a wonderful thing to be alive and happy! Oh, but how beastly of me! I'm only talking about myself. (*Sits on a footstool and rests her arms on Mrs. Linde's knee.*) Oh, please don't be angry with me! Tell me, is it really true you didn't love your husband? Why did you marry him, then?

MRS. LINDE. Well, my mother was still alive; and she was helpless and bedridden. And I had my two little brothers to take care of. I didn't feel I could say no.

NORA. Yes, well, perhaps you're right. He was rich then, was he?

MRS. LINDE. Quite comfortably off, I believe. But his business was unsound, you see, Nora. When he died it went bankrupt, and there was nothing left.

NORA. What did you do?

MRS. LINDE. Well, I had to try to make ends meet somehow, so I started a little shop, and a little school, and anything else I could turn my hand to. These last three years have been just one endless slog for me, without a moment's rest. But now it's over, Nora. My poor dear mother doesn't need me any more; she's passed away. And the boys don't need me either; they've got jobs now and can look after themselves.

NORA. How relieved you must feel—

MRS. LINDE. No, Nora. Just unspeakably empty. No one to live for any more. (*Gets up restlessly.*) That's why I couldn't bear to stay out there any longer, cut off from the world. I thought it'd be easier to find some work here that will exercise and occupy my mind. If only I could get a regular job—office work of some kind—

NORA. Oh, but Christine, that's dreadfully exhausting; and you look practically finished already. It'd be much better for you if you could go away somewhere.

MRS. LINDE (*goes over to the window*). I have no Papa to pay for my holidays, Nora.

NORA (*gets up*). Oh, please don't be angry with me.

MRS. LINDE. My dear Nora, it's I who should ask you not to be angry. That's the worst thing about this kind of situation—it makes one so bitter. One has no one to work for; and yet one has to be continually sponging for jobs. One has to live; and so one becomes completely egocentric. When you told me about this luck you've just had with Torvald's new job—can you imagine?—I was happy not so much on your account, as on my own.

NORA. How do you mean? Oh, I understand. You mean Torvald might be able to do something for you?

MRS. LINDE. Yes, I was thinking that.

NORA. He will too, Christine. Just you leave it to me. I'll lead up to it so delicately, so delicately; I'll get him in the right mood. Oh, Christine, I do so want to help you.

MRS. LINDE. It's sweet of you to bother so much about me, Nora. Especially since you know so little of the worries and hardships of life.

NORA. I? You say *I* know little of—?

MRS. LINDE (*smiles*). Well, good heavens—those bits of fancy work of yours—well, really—! You're a child, Nora.

NORA (*tosses her head and walks across the room*). You shouldn't say that so patronizingly.

MRS. LINDE. Oh?

NORA. You're like the rest. You all think I'm incapable of getting down to anything serious—

MRS. LINDE. My dear—

NORA. You think I've never had any worries like the rest of you.

MRS. LINDE. Nora dear, you've just told me about all your difficulties—

NORA. Pooh—that! (*Quietly.*) I haven't told you about the big thing.

MRS. LINDE. What big thing? What do you mean?

NORA. You patronize me, Christine; but you shouldn't. You're proud that you've worked so long and so hard for your mother.

MRS. LINDE. I don't patronize anyone, Nora. But you're right—I am both proud and happy that I was able to make my mother's last months on earth comparatively easy.

NORA. And you're also proud of what you've done for your brothers.

MRS. LINDE. I think I have a right to be.

NORA. I think so too. But let me tell you something, Christine. I too have done something to be proud and happy about.

MRS. LINDE. I don't doubt it. But—how do you mean?

NORA. Speak quietly! Suppose Torvald should hear! He mustn't, at any price—no one must know, Christine—no one but you.

MRS. LINDE. But what is this?

NORA. Come over here. (*Pulls her down on to the sofa beside her.*) Yes, Christine—I too have done something to be happy and proud about. It was I who saved Torvald's life.

MRS. LINDE. Saved his—? How did you save it?

NORA. I told you about our trip to Italy. Torvald couldn't have lived if he hadn't managed to get down there—

MRS. LINDE. Yes, well—your father provided the money—

NORA (*smiles*). So Torvald and everyone else thinks. But—

MRS. LINDE. Yes?

NORA. Papa didn't give us a penny. It was I who found the money.

MRS. LINDE. You? All of it?

NORA. Two hundred and fifty pounds. What do you say to that?

MRS. LINDE. But Nora, how could you? Did you win a lottery or something?

NORA (*scornfully*). Lottery? (*Sniffs.*) What would there be to be proud of in that?

MRS. LINDE. But where did you get it from, then?

NORA (*hums and smiles secretively*). Hm; tra-la-la-la.

MRS. LINDE. You couldn't have borrowed it.

NORA. Oh? Why not?

MRS. LINDE. Well, a wife can't borrow money without her husband's consent.

NORA (*tosses her head*). Ah, but when a wife has a little business sense, and knows how to be clever—

MRS. LINDE. But Nora, I simply don't understand—

NORA. You don't have to. No one has said I borrowed the money. I could have got it in some other way. (*Throws herself back on the sofa.*) I could have got it from an admirer. When a girl's as pretty as I am—

MRS. LINDE. Nora, you're crazy!

NORA. You're dying of curiosity now, aren't you, Christine?

MRS. LINDE. Nora dear, you haven't done anything foolish?

NORA (*sits up again*). Is it foolish to save one's husband's life?

MRS. LINDE. I think it's foolish if without his knowledge, you—

NORA. But the whole point was that he mustn't know! Great heavens, don't you see? He hadn't to know how dangerously ill he was. I was the one they told that his life was in danger and that only going to a warm climate could save him. Do you suppose I didn't try to think of other ways of getting him down there? I told him how wonderful it would be for me to go abroad like other young wives; I cried and prayed; I asked him to remember my condition, and said he ought to be nice and tender to me; and then I suggested he might quite easily borrow the money. But then he got almost angry with me, Christine. He said I was frivolous, and that it was his duty as a husband not to pander to my moods and caprices—I think that's what he called them. Well, well, I thought, you've got to be saved somehow. And then I thought of a way—

MRS. LINDE. But didn't your husband find out from your father that the money hadn't come from him?

NORA. No, never. Papa died just then. I'd thought of letting him into the plot and asking him not to tell. But since he was so ill—! And as things turned out, it didn't become necessary.

MRS. LINDE. And you've never told your husband about this?

NORA. For heaven's sake, no! What an idea! He's frightfully strict about such matters. And besides—he's so proud of being a *man*—it'd be so painful and humiliating for him to know that he owed anything to me. It'd completely wreck our relationship. This life we have built together would no longer exist.

MRS. LINDE. Will you never tell him?

NORA (*thoughtfully, half-smiling*). Yes—some time, perhaps. Years from now, when I'm no longer pretty. You mustn't laugh! I mean of course, when Torvald no longer loves me as he does now; when it no longer amuses him to see me dance and dress up and play the fool for him. Then it might be useful to have something up my sleeve. (*Breaks off.*) Stupid, stupid, stupid! That time will never come. Well, what do you think of my big secret, Christine? I'm not completely useless, am I? Mind you, all this has caused me a frightful lot of worry. It hasn't been easy for

me to meet my obligations punctually. In case you don't know, in the world of business there are things called quarterly installments and interest, and they're a terrible problem to cope with. So I've had to scrape a little here and save a little there as best I can. I haven't been able to save much on the housekeeping money, because Torvald likes to live well; and I couldn't let the children go short of clothes—I couldn't take anything out of what he gives me for them. The poor little angels!

MRS. LINDE. So you've had to stint yourself, my poor Nora?

NORA. Of course. Well, after all, it was my problem. Whenever Torvald gave me money to buy myself new clothes, I never used more than half of it; and I always bought what was cheapest and plainest. Thank heaven anything suits me, so that Torvald's never noticed. But it made me a bit sad sometimes, because it's lovely to wear pretty clothes. Don't you think?

MRS. LINDE. Indeed it is.

NORA. And then I've found one or two other sources of income. Last winter I managed to get a lot of copying to do. So I shut myself away and wrote every evening, late into the night. Oh, I often got so tired, so tired. But it was great fun, though, sitting there working and earning money. It was almost like being a man.

MRS. LINDE. But how much have you managed to pay off like this?

NORA. Well, I can't say exactly. It's awfully difficult to keep an exact check on these kind of transactions. I only know I've paid everything I've managed to scrape together. Sometimes I really didn't know where to turn. (*Smiles.*) Then I'd sit here and imagine some rich old gentleman had fallen in love with me—

MRS. LINDE. What! What gentleman?

NORA. Silly! And that now he'd died and when they opened his will it said in big letters: "Everything I possess is to be paid forthwith to my beloved Mrs. Nora Helmer in cash."

MRS. LINDE. But, Nora dear, who was this gentleman?

NORA. Great heavens, don't you understand? There wasn't any old gentleman, he was just something I used to dream up as I sat here evening after evening wondering how on earth I could raise some money. But what does it matter? The old bore can stay imaginary as far as I'm concerned, because now I don't have to worry any longer! (*Jumps up.*) Oh, Christine, isn't it wonderful? I don't have to worry any more! No more troubles! I can play all day with the children, I can fill the house with pretty things, just the way Torvald likes. And, Christine, it will soon be spring, and the air will be fresh and the skies blue—and then perhaps we'll be able to take a little trip somewhere. I shall be able to see the sea again. Oh, yes, yes, it's a wonderful thing to be alive and happy!

The bell rings in the hall.

MRS. LINDE (*gets up*). You've a visitor. Perhaps I'd better go.

NORA. No stay. It won't be for me. It's someone for Torvald—

MAID (*in the doorway*). Excuse me, madam, a gentleman's called who says he wants to speak to the master. But I didn't know—seeing as the doctor's with him—

NORA. Who is this gentleman?

KROGSTAD (*in the doorway*). It's me, Mrs. Helmer.

Mrs. Linde starts, composes herself; and turns away to the window.

NORA (*takes a step toward him and whispers tensely*). You? What is it? What do you want to talk to my husband about?

KROGSTAD. Business—you might call it. I hold a minor post in the bank, and I hear your husband is to become our new chief—

NORA. Oh—then it isn't—?

KROGSTAD. Pure business, Mrs. Helmer. Nothing more.

NORA. Well, you'll find him in his study.

Nods indifferently as she closes the hall door behind him. Then she walks across the room and sees to the stove.

MRS. LINDE. Nora, who was that man?

NORA. A lawyer called Krogstad.

MRS. LINDE. It was him, then.

NORA. Do you know that man?

MRS. LINDE. I used to know him—some years ago. He was a solicitor's clerk in our town, for a while.

NORA. Yes, of course, so he was.

MRS. LINDE. How he's changed!

NORA. He was very unhappily married, I believe.

MRS. LINDE. Is he a widower now?

NORA. Yes, with a lot of children. Ah, now it's alight.

She closes the door of the stove and moves the rocking-chair a little to one side.

MRS. LINDE. He does—various things now, I hear?

NORA. Does he? It's quite possible—I really don't know. But don't let's talk about business. It's so boring.

Dr. Rank enters from Helmer's study.

RANK (*still in the doorway*). No, no, my dear chap, don't see me out. I'll go and have a word with your wife. (*Closes the door and notices Mrs. Linde.*) Oh, I beg your pardon. I seem to be *de trop* here too.

NORA. Not in the least. (*Introduces them.*) Dr. Rank. Mrs. Linde.

RANK. Ah! A name I have often heard in this house. I believe I passed you on the stairs as I came up.

MRS. LINDE. Yes. Stairs tire me; I have to take them slowly.

RANK. Oh, have you hurt yourself?

MRS. LINDE. No, I'm just a little run down.

RANK. Ah, is that all? Then I take it you've come to town to cure yourself by a round of parties?

MRS. LINDE. I have come here to find work.

RANK. Is that an approved remedy for being run down?

MRS. LINDE. One has to live, Doctor.

RANK. Yes, people do seem to regard it as a necessity.

NORA. Oh, really, Dr. Rank. I bet you want to stay alive.

RANK. You bet I do. However miserable I sometimes feel, I still want to go on being tortured for as long as possible. It's the same with all my patients; and with people who are morally sick, too. There's a moral cripple in with Helmer at this very moment—

MRS. LINDE (*softly*). Oh!

NORA. Whom do you mean?

RANK. Oh, a lawyer fellow called Krogstad—you wouldn't know him. He's crippled all right; morally twisted. But even he started off by announcing, as though it were a matter of enormous importance, that he had to live.

NORA. Oh? What did he want to talk to Torvald about?

RANK. I haven't the faintest idea. All I heard was something about the bank.

NORA. I didn't know that Krog—that this man Krogstad had any connection with the bank.

RANK. Yes, he's got some kind of job down there. (*To Mrs. Linde.*) I wonder if in your part of the world you too have a species of human being that spends its time fussing around trying to smell out moral corruption? And when they find a case they give him some nice, comfortable position so that they can keep a good watch on him. The healthy ones just have to lump it.

MRS. LINDE. But surely it's the sick who need care most?

RANK (*shrugs his shoulders*). Well, there we have it. It's that attitude that's turning human society into a hospital.

Nora, lost in her own thoughts, laughs half to herself and claps her hands.

RANK. Why are you laughing? Do you really know what society is?

NORA. What do I care about society? I think it's a bore. I was laughing at something else—something frightfully funny. Tell me, Dr. Rank—will everyone who works at the bank come under Torvald now?

RANK. Do you find that particularly funny?

NORA (*smiles and hums*). Never you mind! Never you mind! (*Walks around the room.*) Yes, I find it very amusing to think that we—I mean, Torvald—has obtained so much influence over so many people. (*Takes the paper bag from her pocket.*) Dr. Rank, would you like a small macaroon?

RANK. Macaroons! I say! I thought they were forbidden here.

NORA. Yes, well, these are some Christine gave me.

MRS. LINDE. What? I—?

NORA. All right, all right, don't get frightened. You weren't to know Torvald had forbidden them. He's afraid they'll ruin my teeth. But, dash it—for once—! Don't you agree, Dr. Rank? Here! (*Pops a macaroon into his mouth.*) You too, Christine. And I'll have one too. Just a little one. Two at the most. (*Begins to walk round again.*) Yes, now I feel really, really happy. Now there's just one thing in the world I'd really love to do.

RANK. Oh? And what is that?

NORA. Just something I'd love to say to Torvald.

RANK. Well, why don't you say it?

NORA. No, I daren't. It's too dreadful.

MRS. LINDE. Dreadful?

RANK. Well, then, you'd better not. But you can say it to us. What is it you'd so love to say to Torvald?

NORA. I've the most extraordinary longing to say: "Bloody hell!"

RANK. Are you mad?

MRS. LINDE. My dear Nora—!

RANK. Say it. Here he is.

NORA (*hiding the bag of macaroons*). Ssh! Ssh!

Helmer, with his overcoat on his arm and his hat in his hand, enters from his study.

NORA (*goes to meet him*). Well, Torvald dear, did you get rid of him?

HELMER. Yes, he's just gone.

NORA. May I introduce you—? This is Christine. She's just arrived in town.

HELMER. Christine—? Forgive me, but I don't think—

NORA. Mrs. Linde, Torvald dear. Christine Linde.

HELMER. Ah. A childhood friend of my wife's, I presume?

MRS. LINDE. Yes, we knew each other in earlier days.

NORA. And imagine, now she's traveled all this way to talk to you.

HELMER. Oh?

MRS. LINDE. Well, I didn't really—

NORA. You see, Christine's frightfully good at office work, and she's mad to come under some really clever man who can teach her even more than she knows already—

HELMER. Very sensible, madam.

NORA. So when she heard you'd become head of the bank—it was in her local paper—she came here as quickly as she could and—Torvald, you will, won't you? Do a little something to help Christine? For my sake?

HELMER. Well, that shouldn't be impossible. You are a widow, I take it, Mrs. Linde?

MRS. LINDE. Yes.

HELMER. And you have experience of office work?

MRS. LINDE. Yes, quite a bit.

HELMER. Well then, it's quite likely I may be able to find some job for you—

NORA (*claps her hands*). You see, you see!

HELMER. You've come at a lucky moment, Mrs. Linde.

MRS. LINDE. Oh, how can I ever thank you—?

HELMER. There's absolutely no need. (*Puts on his overcoat.*) But now I'm afraid I must ask you to excuse me—

RANK. Wait. I'll come with you.

He gets his fur coat from the hall and warms it at the stove.

NORA. Don't be long, Torvald dear.

HELMER. I'll only be an hour.

NORA. Are you going too, Christine?

MRS. LINDE (*puts on her outdoor clothes*). Yes, I must start to look round for a room.

HELMER. Then perhaps we can walk part of the way together.

NORA (*helps her*). It's such a nuisance we're so cramped here—I'm afraid we can't offer to—

MRS. LINDE. Oh, I wouldn't dream of it. Goodbye, Nora dear, and thanks for everything.

NORA. *Au revoir.* You'll be coming back this evening, of course. And, you too, Dr. Rank. What? If you're well enough? Of course you'll be well enough. Wrap up warmly, though.

They go out, talking, into the hall. Children's voices are heard from the stairs.

NORA. Here they are! Here they are!

She runs out and opens the door. Anne-Marie, the nurse, enters with the children.

NORA. Come in, come in! (*Stoops down and kisses them.*) Oh, my sweet darlings—! Look at them, Christine! Aren't they beautiful?

RANK. Don't stand here chattering in this draught!

HELMER. Come, Mrs. Linde. This is for mothers only.

Dr. Rank, Helmer, and Mrs. Linde go down the stairs. The Nurse brings the children into the room. Nora follows, and closes the door to the hall.

NORA. How well you look! What red cheeks you've got! Like apples and roses! (*The children answer her inaudibly as she talks to them.*) Have you had fun? That's splendid. You gave Emmy and Bob a ride on the sledge? What, both together? I say! What a clever boy you are, Ivar! Oh, let me hold her for a moment, Anne-Marie! My sweet little baby doll! (*Takes the smallest child from the nurse and dances with her.*) Yes, yes, Mummy will dance with Bob too. What? Have you been throwing snowballs? Oh, I wish I'd been there! No, don't—I'll undress them myself, Anne-Marie. No, please let me; it's such fun. Go inside and warm yourself; you look frozen. There's some hot coffee on the stove. (*The nurse goes into the room on the left. Nora takes off the children's outdoor clothes and throws them anywhere while they all chatter simultaneously.*) What? A big dog ran after you? But he didn't bite you? No, dogs don't bite lovely little baby dolls. Leave those parcels alone, Ivar. What's in them? Ah, wouldn't you like to know! No, no; it's nothing nice. Come on, let's play a game. What shall we play? Hide and seek. Yes, let's play hide and seek. Bob shall hide first. You want me to? All right, let me hide first.

Nora and the children play around the room, and in the adjacent room to the left, laughing and shouting. At length Nora hides under the table. The children rush in, look, but cannot find her. Then they hear her half-stifled laughter, run to the table, lift up the cloth, and see her. Great excitement. She crawls out as though to frighten them. Further excitement. Meanwhile, there has been a knock on the door leading from the hall, but no one has noticed it. Now the door is half-opened and Krogstad enters. He waits for a moment; the game continues.

KROGSTAD. Excuse me, Mrs. Helmer—

NORA (*turns with a stifled cry and half jumps up*). Oh! What do you want?

KROGSTAD. I beg your pardon; the front door was ajar. Someone must have forgotten to close it.

NORA (*gets up*). My husband is not at home, Mr. Krogstad.

KROGSTAD. I know.

NORA. Well, what do want here, then?

KROGSTAD. A word with you.

NORA. With—? (*To the children, quietly.*) Go inside to Anne-Marie. What? No, the strange gentleman won't do anything to hurt Mummy. When he's gone we'll start playing again.

She takes the children into the room on the left and closes the door behind them.

NORA (*uneasy, tense*). You want to speak to me?

KROGSTAD. Yes.

NORA. Today? But it's not the first of the month yet.

KROGSTAD. No, it is Christmas Eve. Whether or not you have a merry Christmas depends on you.

NORA. What do you want? I can't give you anything today—

KROGSTAD. We won't talk about that for the present. There's something else. You have a moment to spare?

NORA. Oh, yes. Yes, I suppose so; though—

KROGSTAD. Good. I was sitting in the café down below and I saw your husband cross the street—

NORA. Yes.

KROGSTAD. With a lady.

NORA. Well?

KROGSTAD. Might I be so bold as to ask: was not that lady a Mrs. Linde?

NORA. Yes.

KROGSTAD. Recently arrived in town?

NORA. Yes, today.

KROGSTAD. She is a good friend of yours, is she not?

NORA. Yes, she is. But I don't see—

KROGSTAD. I used to know her too once.

NORA. I know.

KROGSTAD. Oh? You've discovered that. Yes, I thought you would. Well then, may I ask you a straight question: is Mrs. Linde to be employed at the bank?

NORA. How dare you presume to cross-examine me, Mr. Krogstad? You, one of my husband's employees? But since you ask, you shall have an answer. Yes, Mrs. Linde is to be employed by the bank. And I arranged it, Mr. Krogstad. Now you know.

KROGSTAD. I guessed right, then.

NORA (*walks up and down the room*). Oh, one has a little influence, you know. Just because one's a woman it doesn't necessarily mean that—When one is in a humble position, Mr. Krogstad, one should think twice before offending someone who—hm—

KROGSTAD. —who has influence?

NORA. Precisely.

KROGSTAD (*changes his tone*). Mrs. Helmer, will you have the kindness to use your influence on my behalf?

NORA. What? What do you mean?

KROGSTAD. Will you be so good as to see that I keep my humble position at the bank?

NORA. What do you mean? Who is thinking of removing you from your position?

KROGSTAD. Oh, you don't need to play innocent with me. I realize it can't be very pleasant for your friend to risk bumping into me; and now I also realize whom I have to thank for being hounded out like this.

NORA. But I assure you—

KROGSTAD. Look, let's not beat about the bush. There's still time, and I'd advise you to use your influence to stop it.

NORA. But, Mr. Krogstad, I have no influence—

KROGSTAD. Oh? I thought you just said—

NORA. But I didn't mean it like that! I? How on earth could you imagine that I would have any influence over my husband?

KROGSTAD. Oh, I've known your husband since we were students together. I imagine he has his weaknesses like other married men.

NORA. If you speak impertinently of my husband, I shall show you the door.

KROGSTAD. You're a bold woman, Mrs. Helmer.

NORA. I'm not afraid of you any longer. Once the New Year is in, I'll soon be rid of you.

KROGSTAD (*more controlled*). Now listen to me, Mrs. Helmer. If I'm forced to, I shall fight for my little job at the bank as I would fight for my life.

NORA. So it sounds.

KROGSTAD. It isn't just the money; that's the last thing I care about. There's something else—well, you might as well know. It's like this, you see. You know of course, as every one else does, that some years ago I committed an indiscretion.

NORA. I think I did hear something—

KROGSTAD. It never came into court; but from that day, every opening was barred to me. So I turned my hand to the kind of business you know about. I had to do something; and I don't think I was one of the worst. But now I want to give up all that. My sons are growing up; for their sake, I must try to regain what respectability I can. This job in the bank was the first step on the ladder. And now your husband wants to kick me off that ladder back into the dirt.

NORA. But my dear Mr. Krogstad, it simply isn't in my power to help you.

KROGSTAD. You say that because you don't want to help me. But I have the means to make you.

NORA. You don't mean you'd tell my husband that I owe you money?

KROGSTAD. And if I did?

NORA. That'd be a filthy trick! (*Almost in tears.*) This secret that is my pride and my joy—that he should hear about it in such a filthy, beastly way—hear about it from you! It'd involve me in the most dreadful unpleasantness—

KROGSTAD. Only—unpleasantness?

NORA (*vehemently*). All right, do it! You'll be the one who'll suffer. It'll show my husband the kind of man you are, and then you'll never keep your job.

KROGSTAD. I asked you whether it was merely domestic unpleasantness you were afraid of.

NORA. If my husband hears about it, he will of course immediately pay you whatever is owing. And then we shall have nothing more to do with you.

KROGSTAD (*takes a step closer*). Listen, Mrs. Helmer. Either you've a bad memory or else you know very little about financial transactions. I had better enlighten you.

NORA. What do you mean?

KROGSTAD. When your husband was ill, you came to me to borrow two hundred and fifty pounds.

NORA. I didn't know anyone else.

KROGSTAD. I promised to find that sum for you—

NORA. And you did find it.

KROGSTAD. I promised to find that sum for you on certain conditions. You were so worried about your husband's illness and so keen to get the money to take him abroad that I don't think you bothered much about the details. So it won't be out of place if I refresh your memory. Well—I promised to get you the money in exchange for an I.O.U., which I drew up.

NORA. Yes, and which I signed.

KROGSTAD. Exactly. But then I added a few lines naming your father as security for the debt. This paragraph was to be signed by your father.

NORA. Was to be? He did sign it.

KROGSTAD. I left the date blank for your father to fill in when he signed this paper. You remember, Mrs. Helmer?

NORA. Yes, I think so—

KROGSTAD. Then I gave you back this I.O.U. for you to post to your father. Is that not correct?

NORA. Yes.

KROGSTAD. And of course you posted it at once; for within five or six days you brought it along to me with your father's signature on it. Whereupon I handed you the money.

NORA. Yes, well. Haven't I repaid the installments as agreed?

KROGSTAD. Mm—yes, more or less. But to return to what we were speaking about—that was a difficult time for you just then, wasn't it, Mrs. Helmer?

NORA. Yes, it was.

KROGSTAD. And your father was very ill, if I am not mistaken.

NORA. He was dying.

KROGSTAD. He did in fact die shortly afterwards?

NORA. Yes.

KROGSTAD. Tell me, Mrs. Helmer, do you by any chance remember the date of your father's death? The day of the month, I mean.

NORA. Papa died on the twenty-ninth of September.

KROGSTAD. Quite correct; I took the trouble to confirm it. And that leaves me with a curious little problem—(*Takes out a paper.*)—which I simply cannot solve.

NORA. Problem? I don't see—

KROGSTAD. The problem, Mrs. Helmer, is that your father signed this paper three days after his death.

NORA. What? I don't understand—

KROGSTAD. Your father died on the twenty-ninth of September. But look at this. Here your father has dated his signature the second of October. Isn't that a curious little problem, Mrs. Helmer? (*Nora is silent.*) Can you suggest any explanation? (*She remains silent.*) And there's another curious thing. The words "second of October" and the year are written in a hand which is not your father's, but which I seem to know. Well, there's a simple explanation to that. Your father could have forgotten to write in the date when he signed, and someone else could have added it before the news came of his death. There's nothing criminal about that. It's the signature itself I'm wondering about. It is genuine, I suppose, Mrs. Helmer? It was your father who wrote his name here?

NORA (*after a short silence, throws back her head and looks defiantly at him*). No, it was not. It was I who wrote Papa's name there.

KROGSTAD. Look, Mrs. Helmer, do you realize this is a dangerous admission?

NORA. Why? You'll get your money.

KROGSTAD. May I ask you a question? Why didn't you send this paper to your father?

NORA. I couldn't. Papa was very ill. If I'd asked him to sign this, I'd have had to tell him what the money was for. But I couldn't have told him in his condition that my husband's life was in danger. I couldn't have done that!

KROGSTAD. Then you would have been wiser to have given up your idea of a holiday.

NORA. But I couldn't! It was to save my husband's life. I couldn't put it off.

KROGSTAD. But didn't it occur to you that you were being dishonest towards me?

NORA. I couldn't bother about that. I didn't care about you. I hated you because of all the beastly difficulties you'd put in my way when you knew how dangerously ill my husband was.

KROGSTAD. Mrs. Helmer, you evidently don't appreciate exactly what you have done. But I can assure you that it is no bigger nor worse a crime than the one I once committed, and thereby ruined my whole social position.

NORA. You? Do you expect me to believe that you would have taken a risk like that to save your wife's life?

KROGSTAD. The law does not concern itself with motives.

NORA. Then the law must be very stupid.

KROGSTAD. Stupid or not, if I show this paper to the police, you will be judged according to it.

NORA. I don't believe that. Hasn't a daughter the right to shield her father from worry and anxiety when he's old and dying? Hasn't a wife the right to save her husband's life? I don't know much about the law but there must be something somewhere that says that such things are allowed. You ought to know about that, you're meant to be a lawyer, aren't you? You can't be a very good lawyer, Mr. Krogstad.

KROGSTAD. Possibly not. But business, the kind of business we two have been transacting—I think you'll admit I understand something about that? Good. Do as you please. But I tell you this. If I get thrown into the gutter for a second time, I shall take you with me.

He bows and goes out through the hall.

NORA (*stands for a moment in thought, then tosses her head*). What nonsense! He's trying to frighten me! I'm not that stupid. (*Busies herself gathering together the children's clothes; then she suddenly stops.*) But—? No, it's impossible. I did it for love, didn't I?

CHILDREN (*in the doorway, left*). Mummy, the strange gentleman's gone out into the street.

NORA. Yes, yes, I know. But don't talk to anyone about the strange gentleman. You hear? Not even to Daddy.

CHILDREN. No, Mummy. Will you play with us again now?

NORA. No, no. Not now.

CHILDREN. Oh but, Mummy, you promised!

NORA. I know, but I can't just now. Go back to the nursery. I've a lot to do. Go away, my darlings, go away. (*She pushes them gently into the other room and closes the door behind them. She sits on the sofa, takes up her embroidery, stitches for a few moments, but soon stops.*) No! (*Throws the embroidery aside, gets up, goes to the door leading to the hall, and calls.*) Helen! Bring in the Christmas tree! (*She goes to the table on the left and opens the drawer in it; then pauses again.*) No, but it's utterly impossible!

MAID (*enters with the tree*). Where shall I put it, madam?

NORA. There, in the middle of the room.

MAID. Will you be wanting anything else?

NORA. No, thank you, I have everything I need.

The Maid puts down the tree and goes out.

NORA (*busy decorating the tree*). Now—candles here—and flowers here. That loathsome man! Nonsense, nonsense, there's nothing to be frightened about. The Christmas tree must be beautiful. I'll do everything that you like. Torvald. I'll sing for you, dance for you—

Helmer, with a bundle of papers under his arm, enters.

NORA. Oh—are you back already?

HELMER. Yes. Has anyone been here?

NORA. Here? No.

HELMER. That's strange. I saw Krogstad come out of the front door.

NORA. Did you? Oh yes, that's quite right—Krogstad was here for a few minutes.

HELMER. Nora, I can tell from your face, he's been here and asked you to put in a good word for him.

NORA. Yes.

HELMER. And you were to pretend you were doing it of your own accord? You weren't going to tell me he'd been here? He asked you to do that too, didn't he?

NORA. Yes, Torvald. But—

HELMER. Nora, Nora! And you were ready to enter into such a conspiracy? Talking to a man like that, and making him promises—and then, on top of it all, to tell me an untruth!

NORA. An untruth?

HELMER. Didn't you say no one had been here? (*Wags his finger.*) My little songbird must never do that again. A songbird must have a clean beak to sing with; otherwise she'll start twittering out of tune. (*Puts his arm round her waist.*) Isn't that the way we want things? Yes, of course it is. (*Lets go of her.*) So let's hear no more about that. (*Sits down in front of the stove.*) Ah, how cozy and peaceful it is here. (*Glances for a few moments at his papers.*)

NORA (*busy with the tree; after a short silence*). Torvald.

HELMER. Yes.

NORA. I'm terribly looking forward to that fancy dress ball at the Stenborgs on Boxing Day.

HELMER. And I'm terribly curious to see what you're going to surprise me with.

NORA. Oh, it's so maddening.

HELMER. What is?

NORA. I can't think of anything to wear. It all seems so stupid and meaningless.

HELMER. So my little Nora's come to that conclusion, has she?

NORA (*behind his chair, resting her arms on its back*). Are you very busy, Torvald?

HELMER. Oh—

NORA. What are those papers?

HELMER. Just something to do with the bank.

NORA. Already?

HELMER. I persuaded the trustees to give me authority to make certain immediate changes in the staff and organization. I want to have everything straight by the New Year.

NORA. Then that's why this poor man Krogstad—

HELMER. Hm.

NORA (*still leaning over his chair, slowly strokes the back of his head*). If you hadn't been so busy, I was going to ask you an enormous favor, Torvald.

HELMER. Well, tell me. What was it to be?

NORA. You know I trust your taste more than anyone's. I'm so anxious to look really beautiful at the fancy dress ball. Torvald, couldn't you help me to decide what I shall go as, and what kind of costume I ought to wear?

HELMER. Aha! So little Miss Independent's in trouble and needs a man to rescue her, does she?

NORA. Yes, Torvald. I can't get anywhere without your help.

HELMER. Well, well, I'll give the matter thought. We'll find something.

NORA. Oh, how kind of you! (*Goes back to the tree. Pause.*) How pretty these red flowers look! But, tell me, is it so dreadful, this thing that Krogstad's done?

HELMER. He forged someone else's name. Have you any idea what that means?

NORA. Mightn't he have been forced to do it by some emergency?

HELMER. He probably just didn't think—that's what usually happens. I'm not so heartless as to condemn a man for an isolated action.

NORA. No, Torvald, of course not!

HELMER. Men often succeed in re-establishing themselves if they admit their crime and take their punishment.

NORA. Punishment?

HELMER. But Krogstad didn't do that. He chose to try and trick his way out of it; and that's what has morally destroyed him.

NORA. You think that would—?

HELMER. Just think how a man with that load on his conscience must always be lying and cheating and dissembling; how he must wear a mask even in the presence of those who are dearest to him, even his own wife and children! Yes, the children. That's the worst danger, Nora.

NORA. Why?

HELMER. Because an atmosphere of lies contaminates and poisons every corner of the home. Every breath that the children draw in such a house contains the germs of evil.

NORA (*comes closer behind him*). Do you really believe that?

HELMER. Oh, my dear, I've come across it so often in my work at the bar. Nearly all young criminals are the children of mothers who are constitutional liars.

NORA. Why do you say mothers?

HELMER. It's usually the mother; though of course the father can have the same influence. Every lawyer knows that only too well. And yet this fellow Krogstad has been sitting at home all these years poisoning his children with

his lies and pretenses. That's why I say that, morally speaking, he is dead. (*Stretches out his hands towards her.*) So my pretty little Nora must promise me not to plead his case. Your hand on it. Come, come, what's this? Give me your hand. There. That's settled, now. I assure you it'd be quite impossible for me to work in the same building as him. I literally feel physically ill in the presence of a man like that.

NORA (*draws her hand from his and goes over to the other side of the Christmas tree*). How hot it is in here! And I've so much to do.

HELMER (*gets up and gathers his papers*). Yes, and I must try to get some of this read before dinner. I'll think about your costume too. And I may even have something up my sleeve to hang in gold paper on the Christmas tree. (*Lays his hand on her head.*) My precious little songbird!

He goes into his study and closes the door.

NORA (*softly, after a pause*). It's nonsense. It must be. It's impossible. It *must* be impossible!

NURSE (*in the doorway, left*). The children are asking if they can come in to Mummy.

NORA. No, no, no; don't let them in! You stay with them, Anne-Marie.

NURSE. Very good, madam. (*Closes the door.*)

NORA (*pale with fear*). Corrupt my little children—! Poison my home! (*Short pause. She throws back her head.*) It isn't true! It *couldn't* be true!

ACT 2

The same room. In the corner by the piano the Christmas tree stands, stripped and disheveled, its candles burned to their sockets. Nora's outdoor clothes lie on the sofa. She is alone in the room, walking restlessly to and fro. At length she stops by the sofa and picks up her coat.

NORA (*drops the coat again*). There's someone coming! (*Goes to the door and listens.*) No, it's no one. Of course—no one'll come today, it's Christmas Day. Nor tomorrow. But perhaps—! (*Opens the door and looks out.*) No. Nothing in the letter-box. Quite empty. (*Walks across the room.*) Silly, silly. Of course he won't do anything. It couldn't happen. It isn't possible. Why, I've three small children.

The Nurse, carrying a large cardboard box, enters from the room on the left.

NURSE. I found those fancy dress clothes at last, madam.

NORA. Thank you. Put them on the table.

NURSE (*does so*). They're all rumpled up.

NORA. Oh, I wish I could tear them into a million pieces!

NURSE. Why, madam! They'll be all right. Just a little patience.

NORA. Yes, of course. I'll go and get Mrs. Linde to help me.

NURSE. What, out again? In this dreadful weather? You'll catch a chill, madam.

NORA. Well, that wouldn't be the worst. How are the children?

NURSE. Playing with their Christmas presents, poor little dears. But—

NORA. Are they still asking to see me?

NURSE. They're so used to having their Mummy with them.

NORA. Yes, but, Anne-Marie, from now on I shan't be able to spend so much time with them.

NURSE. Well, children get used to anything in time.

NORA. Do you think so? Do you think they'd forget their mother if she went away from them—for ever?

NURSE. Mercy's sake, madam! For ever!

NORA. Tell me, Anne-Marie—I've so often wondered. How could you bear to give your child away—to strangers?

NURSE. But I had to when I came to nurse my little Miss Nora.

NORA. Do you mean you wanted to?

NURSE. When I had the chance of such a good job? A poor girl what's got into trouble can't afford to pick and choose. That good-for-nothing didn't lift a finger.

NORA. But your daughter must have completely forgotten you.

NURSE. Oh no, indeed she hasn't. She's written to me twice, once when she got confirmed and then again when she got married.

NORA (hugs her). Dear old Anne-Marie, you were a good mother to me.

NURSE. Poor little Miss Nora, you never had any mother but me.

NORA. And if my little ones had no one else, I know you would—no, silly, silly, silly! (Opens the cardboard box.) Go back to them, Anne-Marie. Now I must—Tomorrow you'll see how pretty I shall look.

NURSE. Why, there'll be no one at the ball as beautiful as my Miss Nora.

She goes into the room, left.

NORA (begins to unpack the clothes from the box, but soon throws them down again). Oh, if only I dared to go out! If I could be sure no one would come, and nothing would happen while I was away! Stupid, stupid! No one will come. I just mustn't think about it. Brush this muff. Pretty gloves, pretty gloves! Don't think about it, don't think about it! One, two, three, four, five, six—(Cries.) Ah—they're coming—!

She begins to run toward the door, but stops uncertainly. Mrs. Linde enters from the hall, where she has been taking off her outdoor clothes.

NORA. Oh, it's you, Christine. There's no one else out there, is there? Oh, I'm so glad you've come.

MRS. LINDE. I hear you were at my room asking for me.

NORA. Yes, I just happened to be passing. I want to ask you to help me with something. Let's sit down here on the sofa. Look at this. There's going to be a fancy dress ball tomorrow night upstairs at Consul Stenborg's, and Tor-vald wants me to go as a Neapolitan fisher-girl and dance the tarantella. I learned it on Capri.

MRS. LINDE. I say, are you going to give a performance?

NORA. Yes, Torvald says I should. Look, here's the dress. Torvald had it made for me in Italy; but now it's all so torn, I don't know—

MRS. LINDE. Oh, we'll soon put that right; the stitching's just come away. Needle and thread? Ah, here we are.

NORA. You're being awfully sweet.

MRS. LINDE (sews). So you're going to dress up tomorrow, Nora? I must pop over for a moment to see how you look. Oh, but I've completely forgotten to thank you for that nice evening yesterday.

NORA (gets up and walks across the room). Oh, I didn't think it was as nice as usual. You ought to have come to town a little earlier, Christine. . . . Yes, Torvald understands how to make a home look attractive.

MRS. LINDE. I'm sure you do, too. You're not your father's daughter for nothing. But, tell me. Is Dr. Rank always in such low spirits as he was yesterday?

NORA. No, last night it was very noticeable. But he's got a terrible disease; he's got spinal tuberculosis, poor man. His father was a frightful creature who kept mistresses and so on. As a result Dr. Rank has been sickly ever since he was a child—you understand—

MRS. LINDE (puts down her sewing). But, my dear Nora, how on earth did you get to know about such things?

NORA (walks about the room). Oh, don't be silly, Christine—when one has three children, one comes into contact with women who—well, who know about medical matters, and they tell one a thing or two.

MRS. LINDE (sews again; a short silence). Does Dr. Rank visit you every day?

NORA. Yes, every day. He's Torvald's oldest friend, and a good friend to me too. Dr. Rank's almost one of the family.

MRS. LINDE. But, tell me—is he quite sincere? I mean, doesn't he rather say the sort of thing he thinks people want to hear?

NORA. No, quite the contrary. What gave you that idea?

MRS. LINDE. When you introduced me to him yesterday, he said he'd often heard my name mentioned here. But later I noticed your husband had no idea who I was. So how could Dr. Rank—?

NORA. Yes, that's quite right, Christine. You see, Torvald's so hopelessly in love with me that he wants to have me all to himself—those were his very words. When we were first married, he got quite jealous if I as much as mentioned any of my old friends back home. So naturally I stopped talking about them. But I often chat with Dr. Rank about that kind of thing. He enjoys it, you see.

MRS. LINDE. Now listen, Nora. In many ways you're still a child; I'm a bit older than you and have a little more experience of the world. There's something I want to say to you. You ought to give up this business with Dr. Rank.

NORA. What business?

MRS. LINDE. Well, everything. Last night you were speaking about this rich admirer of yours who was going to give you money—

NORA. Yes, and who doesn't exist—unfortunately. But what's that got to do with—?

MRS. LINDE. Is Dr. Rank rich?

NORA. Yes.

MRS. LINDE. And he has no dependents?

NORA. No, no one. But—

MRS. LINDE. And he comes here to see you every day?

NORA. Yes, I've told you.

MRS. LINDE. But how dare a man of his education be so forward?

NORA. What on earth are you talking about?

MRS. LINDE. Oh, stop pretending, Nora. Do you think I haven't guessed who it was who lent you that two hundred pounds?

NORA. Are you out of your mind? How could you imagine such a thing? A friend, someone who comes here every day! Why, that'd be an impossible situation!

MRS. LINDE. Then it really wasn't him?

NORA. No, of course not. I've never for a moment dreamed of—anyway, he hadn't any money to lend then. He didn't come into that till later.

MRS. LINDE. Well, I think that was a lucky thing for you, Nora dear.

NORA. No, I could never have dreamed of asking Dr. Rank—Though I'm sure that if I ever did ask him—

MRS. LINDE. But of course you won't.

NORA. Of course not. I can't imagine that it should ever become necessary. But I'm perfectly sure that if I did speak to Dr. Rank—

MRS. LINDE. Behind your husband's back?

NORA. I've got to get out of this other business; and *that's* been going on behind his back. I've *got* to get out of it.

MRS. LINDE. Yes, well, that's what I told you yesterday. But—

NORA (*walking up and down*). It's much easier for a man to arrange these things than a woman—

MRS. LINDE. One's own husband, yes.

NORA. Oh, bosh. (*Stops walking.*) When you've completely repaid a debt, you get your I.O.U. back, don't you?

MRS. LINDE. Yes, of course.

NORA. And you can tear it into a thousand pieces and burn the filthy, beastly thing!

MRS. LINDE (*looks hard at her, puts down her sewing, and gets up slowly*). Nora, you're hiding something from me.

NORA. Can you see that?

MRS. LINDE. Something has happened since yesterday morning. Nora, what is it?

NORA (*goes toward her*). Christine! (*Listens.*) Ssh! There's Torvald. Would you mind going into the nursery for a few minutes? Torvald can't bear to see sewing around. Anne-Marie'll help you.

MRS. LINDE (*gathers some of her things together*). Very well. But I shan't leave this house until we've talked this matter out.

She goes into the nursery, left. As she does so, Helmer enters from the hall.

NORA (*runs to meet him*). Oh, Torvald dear, I've been so longing for you to come back!

HELMER. Was that the dressmaker?

NORA. No, it was Christine. She's helping me mend my costume. I'm going to look rather splendid in that.

HELMER. Yes, that was quite a bright idea of mine, wasn't it?

NORA. Wonderful! But wasn't it nice of me to give in to you?

HELMER (*takes her chin in his hand*). Nice—to give in to your husband? All right, little silly, I know you didn't mean it like that. But I won't disturb you. I expect you'll be wanting to try it on.

NORA. Are you going to work now?

HELMER. Yes. (*Shows her a bundle of papers.*) Look at these. I've been down to the bank—(*Turns to go into his study.*)

NORA. Torvald.

HELMER (*stops*). Yes.

NORA. If little squirrel asked you really prettily to grant her a wish—

HELMER. Well?

NORA. Would you grant it to her?

HELMER. First I should naturally have to know what it was.

NORA. Squirrel would do lots of pretty tricks for you if you granted her wish.

HELMER. Out with it, then.

NORA. Your little skylark would sing in every room—

HELMER. My little skylark does that already.

NORA. I'd turn myself into a little fairy and dance for you in the moonlight, Torvald.

HELMER. Nora, it isn't that business you were talking about this morning?

NORA (*comes closer*). Yes, Torvald—oh, please! I beg of you!

HELMER. Have you really the nerve to bring that up again?

NORA. Yes, Torvald, yes, you must do as I ask! You must let Krogstad keep his place at the bank!

HELMER. My dear Nora, his is the job I'm giving to Mrs. Linde.

NORA. Yes, that's terribly sweet of you. But you can get rid of one of the other clerks instead of Krogstad.

HELMER. Really, you're being incredibly obstinate. Just because you thoughtlessly promised to put in a word for him, you expect me to—

NORA. No, it isn't that, Helmer. It's for your own sake. That man writes for the most beastly newspapers—you said so yourself. He could do you tremendous harm. I'm so dreadfully frightened of him—

HELMER. Oh, I understand. Memories of the past. That's what's frightening you.

NORA. What do you mean?

HELMER. You're thinking of your father, aren't you?

NORA. Yes, yes. Of course. Just think what those dreadful men wrote in the papers about Papa! The most frightful slanders. I really believe it would have lost him his job if the Ministry hadn't sent you down to investigate, and you hadn't been so kind and helpful to him.

HELMER. But my dear little Nora, there's a considerable difference between your father and me. Your father was not a man of unassailable reputation. But I am; and I hope to remain so all my life.

NORA. But no one knows what spiteful people may not dig up. We could be so peaceful and happy now, Torvald—we could be free from every worry—you and I and the children. Oh, please, Torvald, please—!

HELMER. The very fact of your pleading his cause makes it impossible for me to keep him. Everyone at the bank already knows that I intend to dismiss Krogstad. If the rumor got about that the new manager had allowed his wife to persuade him to change his mind—

NORA. Well, what then?

HELMER. Oh, nothing, nothing. As long as my little Miss Obstinate gets her way—Do you expect me to make a laughing-stock of myself before my entire staff—give people the idea that I am open to outside influence? Believe me, I'd soon feel the consequences! Besides—there's something else that makes it impossible for Krogstad to remain in the bank while I am its manager.

NORA. What is that?

HELMER. I might conceivably have allowed myself to ignore his moral obloquies—

NORA. Yes, Torvald, surely?

HELMER. And I hear he's quite efficient at his job. But we—well, we were school friends. It was one of those friendships that one enters into over hastily and so often comes to regret later in life. I might as well confess the truth. We—well, we're on Christian name terms. And the tactless idiot makes no attempt to conceal it when other people are present. On the contrary, he thinks it gives him the right to be familiar with me. He shows off the whole time, with "Torvald this," and "Torvald that." I can tell you, I find it damned annoying. If he stayed, he'd make my position intolerable.

NORA. Torvald, you can't mean this seriously.

HELMER. Oh? And why not?

NORA. But it's so petty.

HELMER. What did you say? Petty? You think I am petty?

NORA. No, Torvald dear, of course you're not. That's just why—

HELMER. Don't quibble! You call my motives petty. Then I must be petty too. Petty! I see. Well, I've had enough of this. (Goes to the door and calls into the hall.) Helen!

NORA. What are you going to do?

HELMER (searching among his papers). I'm going to settle this matter once and for all. (The Maid enters.) Take this letter downstairs at once. Find a messenger and see that he delivers it. Immediately! The address is on the envelope. Here's the money.

MAID. Very good, sir. (Goes out with the letter.)

HELMER (putting his papers in order). There now, little Miss Obstinate.

NORA (tensely). Torvald—what was in that letter?

HELMER. Krogstad's dismissal.

NORA. Call her back, Torvald! There's still time. Oh, Torvald, call her back! Do it for my sake—for your own sake—for the children! Do you hear me, Torvald? Please do it! You don't realize what this may do to us all!

HELMER. Too late.

NORA. Yes. Too late.

HELMER. My dear Nora, I forgive you this anxiety. Though it is a bit of an insult to me. Oh, but it is! Isn't it an insult to imply that I should be frightened by the vindictiveness of a depraved hack journalist? But I forgive you, because it so charmingly testifies to the love you bear me. (Takes her in his arms.) Which is as it should be, my own dearest Nora. Let what will happen, happen. When the real crisis comes, you will not find me lacking in strength or courage. I am man enough to bear the burden for us both.

NORA (fearfully). What do you mean?

HELMER. The whole burden, I say—

NORA (calmly). I shall never let you do that.

HELMER. Very well. We shall share it, Nora—as man and wife. And that is as it should be. (Caresses her.) Are you happy now? There, there, there; don't look at me with those frightened little eyes. You're simply imagining things. You go ahead now and do your tarantella, and get some practice on that tambourine. I'll sit in my study and close the door. Then I won't hear anything, and you can make all the noise you want. (Turns in the doorway.) When Dr. Rank comes, tell him where to find me. (He nods to her, goes into his room with his papers, and closes the door.)

NORA (desperate with anxiety, stands as though transfixed, and whispers). He said he'd do it. He will do it. He will do it, and nothing'll stop him. No, never that. I'd rather anything. There must be some escape—Some way out—! (The bell rings in the hall.) Dr. Rank—! Anything but that! Anything, I don't care—!

She passes her hand across her face, composes herself, walks across, and opens the door to the hall. Dr. Rank is standing there, hanging up his fur coat. During the following scene, it begins to grow dark.

NORA. Good evening, Dr. Rank. I recognized your ring. But you mustn't go to Torvald yet. I think he's busy.

RANK. And—you?

NORA (as he enters the room and she closes the door behind him). Oh, you know very well I've always time to talk to you.

RANK. Thank you. I shall avail myself of that privilege as long as I can.

NORA. What do you mean by that? As long as you *can*?

RANK. Yes. Does that frighten you?

NORA. Well, it's rather a curious expression. Is something going to happen?

RANK. Something I've been expecting to happen for a long time. But I didn't think it would happen quite so soon.

NORA (*seizes his arm*). What is it? Dr. Rank, you must tell me!

RANK (*sits down by the stove*). I'm on the way out. And there's nothing to be done about it.

NORA (*sighs with relief*). Oh, it's you—?

RANK. Who else? No, it's no good lying to oneself. I am the most wretched of all my patients, Mrs. Helmer. These last few days I've been going through the books of this poor body of mine, and I find I am bankrupt. Within a month I may be rotting up there in the churchyard.

NORA. Ugh, what a nasty way to talk!

RANK. The facts aren't exactly nice. But the worst is that there's so much else that's nasty to come first. I've only one more test to make. When that's done I'll have a pretty accurate idea of when the final disintegration is likely to begin. I want to ask you a favour. Helmer's a sensitive chap, and I know how he hates anything ugly. I don't want him to visit me when I'm in hospital—

NORA. Oh but, Dr. Rank—

RANK. I don't want him there. On any pretext. I shan't have him allowed in. As soon as I know the worst, I'll send you my visiting card with a black cross on it, and then you'll know that the final filthy process has begun.

NORA. Really, you're being quite impossible this evening. And I did hope you'd be in a good mood.

RANK. With death on my hands? And all this to atone for someone else's sin? Is there justice in that? And in every single family, in one way or another, the same merciless law of retribution is at work—

NORA (*holds her hands to her ears*). Nonsense! Cheer up! Laugh!

RANK. Yes, you're right. Laughter's all the damned thing's fit for. My poor innocent spine must pay for the fun my father had as a gay young lieutenant.

NORA (*at the table, left*). You mean he was too fond of asparagus and *foie gras*?

RANK. Yes, and truffles too.

NORA. Yes, of course, truffles, yes. And oysters too, I suppose?

RANK. Yes, oysters, oysters. Of course.

NORA. And all that port and champagne to wash them down. It's too sad that all those lovely things should affect one's spine.

RANK. Especially a poor spine that never got any pleasure out of them.

NORA. Oh yes, that's the saddest thing of all.

RANK (*looks searchingly at her*). Hm—

NORA (*after a moment*). Why did you smile?

RANK. No, it was you who laughed.

NORA. No, it was you who smiled, Dr. Rank!

RANK (*gets up*). You're a worse little rogue than I thought.

NORA. Oh, I'm full of stupid tricks today.

RANK. So it seems.

NORA (*puts both her hands on his shoulders*). Dear, dear Dr. Rank, you mustn't die and leave Torvald and me.

RANK. Oh, you'll soon get over it. Once one is gone, one is soon forgotten.

NORA (*looks at him anxiously*). Do you believe that?

RANK. One finds replacements, and then—

NORA. Who will find a replacement?

RANK. You and Helmer both will, when I am gone. You seem to have made a start already, haven't you? What was this Mrs. Linde doing here yesterday evening?

NORA. Aha! But surely you can't be jealous of poor Christine?

RANK. Indeed I am. She will be my successor in this house. When I have moved on, this lady will—

NORA. Ssh—don't speak so loud! She's in there!

RANK. Today again? You see!

NORA. She's only come to mend my dress. Good heavens, how unreasonable you are! (*Sits on the sofa.*) Be nice now, Dr. Rank. Tomorrow you'll see how beautifully I shall dance; and you must imagine that I'm doing it just for you. And for Torvald of course; obviously. (*Takes some things out of the box.*) Dr. Rank, sit down here and I'll show you something.

RANK (*sits*). What's this?

NORA. Look here! Look!

RANK. Silk stockings!

NORA. Flesh-colored. Aren't they beautiful? It's very dark in here now, of course, but tomorrow—No, no, no; only the soles. Oh well, I suppose you can look a bit higher if you want to.

RANK. Hm—

NORA. Why are you looking so critical? Don't you think they'll fit me?

RANK. I can't really give you a qualified opinion on that.

NORA (*looks at him for a moment*). Shame on you! (*Flicks him on the ear with the stockings.*) Take that. (*Puts them back in the box.*)

RANK. What other wonders are to be revealed to me?

NORA. I shan't show you anything else. You're being naughty.

She hums a little and looks among the things in the box.

RANK (*after a short silence*). When I sit here like this being so intimate with you, I can't think—I cannot imagine what would have become of me if I had never entered this house.

NORA (*smiles*). Yes, I think you enjoy being with us, don't you?

RANK (*more quietly, looking into the middle distance*). And now to have to leave it all—

NORA. Nonsense. You're not leaving us.

RANK (*as before*). And not to be able to leave even the most wretched token of gratitude behind; hardly even a passing sense of loss; only an empty place, to be filled by the next comer.

NORA. Suppose I were to ask you to—? No—

RANK. To do what?

NORA. To give me proof of your friendship—

RANK. Yes, yes?

NORA. No, I mean—to do me a very great service—

RANK. Would you really for once grant me that happiness?

NORA. But you've no idea what it is.

RANK. Very well, tell me, then.

NORA. No, but, Dr. Rank, I can't. It's far too much—I want your help and advice, and I want you to do something for me.

RANK. The more the better. I've no idea what it can be. But tell me. You do trust me, don't you?

NORA. Oh, yes, more than anyone. You're my best and truest friend. Otherwise I couldn't tell you. Well then, Dr. Rank—there's something you must help me to prevent. You know how much Torvald loves me—he'd never hesitate for an instant to lay down his life for me—

RANK (*leans over towards her*). Nora—do you think he is the only one—?

NORA (*with a slight start*). What do you mean?

RANK. Who would gladly lay down his life for you?

NORA (*sadly*). Oh, I see.

RANK. I swore to myself I would let you know that before I go. I shall never have a better opportunity. . . . Well, Nora, now you know that. And now you also know that you can trust me as you can trust nobody else.

NORA (*rises; calmly and quietly*). Let me pass, please.

RANK (*makes room for her but remains seated*). Nora—

NORA (*in the doorway to the hall*). Helen, bring the lamp. (*Goes over to the stove.*) Oh, dear Dr. Rank, this was really horrid of you.

RANK (*gets up*). That I have loved you as deeply as anyone else has? Was that horrid of me?

NORA. No—but that you should go and tell me. That was quite unnecessary—

RANK. What do you mean? Did you know, then—?

The Maid enters with the lamp, puts it on the table, and goes out.

RANK. Nora—Mrs. Helmer—I am asking you, did you know this?

NORA. Oh, what do I know, what did I know, what didn't I know—I really can't say. How could you be so stupid, Dr. Rank? Everything was so nice.

RANK. Well, at any rate now you know that I am ready to serve you, body and soul. So—please continue.

NORA (*looks at him*). After this?

RANK. Please tell me what it is.

NORA. I can't possibly tell you now.

RANK. Yes, yes! You mustn't punish me like this. Let me be allowed to do what I can for you.

NORA. You can't do anything for me now. Anyway; I don't need any help. It was only my imagination—you'll see. Yes, really. Honestly. (*Sits in the rocking-chair, looks at him, and smiles.*) Well, upon my word you *are* a fine gentleman, Dr. Rank. Aren't you ashamed of yourself, now that the lamp's been lit?

RANK. Frankly, no. But perhaps I ought to say—*adieu?*

NORA. Of course not. You will naturally continue to visit us as before. You know quite well how Torvald depends on your company.

RANK. Yes, but you?

NORA. Oh, I always think it's enormous fun having you here.

RANK. That was what misled me. You're a riddle to me, you know. I'd often felt you'd just as soon be with me as with Helmer.

NORA. Well, you see, there are some people whom one loves, and others whom it's almost more fun to be with.

RANK. Oh yes, there's some truth in that.

NORA. When I was at home, of course I loved Papa best. But I always used to think it was terribly amusing to go down and talk to the servants; because they never told me what I ought to do; and they were such fun to listen to.

RANK. I see. So I've taken their place?

NORA (*jumps up and runs over to him*). Oh, dear, sweet Dr. Rank, I didn't mean that at all. But I'm sure you understand—I feel the same about Torvald as I did about Papa.

MAID (*enters from the hall*). Excuse me, madam. (*Whispers to her and hands her a visiting card.*)

NORA (*glances at the card*). Oh! (*Puts it quickly in her pocket.*)

RANK. Anything wrong?

NORA. No, no, nothing at all. It's just something that—it's my new dress.

RANK. What? But your costume is lying over there.

NORA. Oh—that, yes—but there's another—I ordered it specially—Torvald mustn't know—

RANK. Ah, so that's your big secret?

NORA. Yes, yes. Go in and talk to him—he's in his study—keep him talking for a bit—

RANK. Don't worry. He won't get away from me. (*Goes into Helmer's study.*)

NORA (*to the Maid*). Is he waiting in the kitchen?

MAID. Yes, madam, he came up the back way—

NORA. But didn't you tell him I had a visitor?

MAID. Yes, but he wouldn't go.

NORA. Wouldn't go?

MAID. No, madam, not until he'd spoken with you.

NORA. Very well, show him in; but quietly. Helen, you mustn't tell anyone about this. It's a surprise for my husband.

MAID. Very good, madam. I understand. (*Goes.*)

NORA. It's happening. It's happening after all. No, no, no, it can't happen, it mustn't happen.

She walks across and bolts the door of Helmer's study. The Maid opens the door from the hall to admit Krogstad, and closes it behind him. He is wearing an overcoat, heavy boots, and a fur cap.

NORA (*goes towards him*). Speak quietly. My husband's at home.

KROGSTAD. Let him hear.

NORA. What do you want from me?

KROGSTAD. Information.

NORA. Hurry up, then. What is it?

KROGSTAD. I suppose you know I've been given the sack.

NORA. I couldn't stop it, Mr. Krogstad. I did my best for you, but it didn't help.

KROGSTAD. Does your husband love you so little? He knows what I can do to you, and yet he dares to—

NORA. Surely you don't imagine I told him?

KROGSTAD. No. I didn't really think you had. It wouldn't have been like my old friend Torvald Helmer to show that much courage—

NORA. Mr. Krogstad, I'll trouble you to speak respectfully of my husband.

KROGSTAD. Don't worry, I'll show him all the respect he deserves. But since you're so anxious to keep this matter hushed up, I presume you're better informed than you were yesterday of the gravity of what you've done?

NORA. I've learned more than you could ever teach me.

KROGSTAD. Yes, a bad lawyer like me—

NORA. What do you want from me?

KROGSTAD. I just wanted to see how things were with you, Mrs. Helmer. I've been thinking about you all day. Even duns and hack journalists have hearts, you know.

NORA. Show some heart, then. Think of my little children.

KROGSTAD. Have you and your husband thought of mine? Well, let's forget that. I just wanted to tell you, you don't need to take this business too seriously. I'm not going to take any action, for the present.

NORA. Oh, no—you won't, will you? I knew it.

KROGSTAD. It can all be settled quite amicably. There's no need for it to become public. We'll keep it among the three of us.

NORA. My husband must never know about this.

KROGSTAD. How can you stop him? Can you pay the balance of what you owe me?

NORA. Not immediately.

KROGSTAD. Have you any means of raising the money during the next few days?

NORA. None that I would care to use.

KROGSTAD. Well, it wouldn't have helped anyway. However much money you offered me now I wouldn't give you back that paper.

NORA. What are you going to do with it?

KROGSTAD. Just keep it. No one else need ever hear about it. So in case you were thinking of doing anything desperate—

NORA. I am.

KROGSTAD. Such as running away—

NORA. I am.

KROGSTAD. Or anything more desperate—

NORA. How did you know?

KROGSTAD. —just give up the idea.

NORA. How did you know?

KROGSTAD. Most of us think of that at first. I did. But I hadn't the courage—

NORA (*dully*). Neither have I.

KROGSTAD (*relieved*). It's true, isn't it? You haven't the courage either?

NORA. No. I haven't. I haven't.

KROGSTAD. It'd be a stupid thing to do anyway. Once the first little domestic explosion is over. . . . I've got a letter in my pocket here addressed to your husband—

NORA. Telling him everything?

KROGSTAD. As delicately as possible.

NORA (*quickly*). He must never see that letter. Tear it up. I'll find the money somehow—

KROGSTAD. I'm sorry, Mrs. Helmer, I thought I'd explained—

NORA. Oh, I don't mean the money I owe you. Let me know how much you want from my husband, and I'll find it for you.

KROGSTAD. I'm not asking your husband for money.

NORA. What do you want, then?

KROGSTAD. I'll tell you. I want to get on my feet again, Mrs. Helmer. I want to get to the top. And your husband's going to help me. For eighteen months now my record's been clean. I've been in hard straits all that time; I was content to fight my way back inch by inch. Now I've been chucked back into the mud, and I'm not going to be satisfied with just getting back my job. I'm going to get to the top, I tell you. I'm going to get back into the bank, and it's going to be higher up. Your husband's going to create a new job for me—

NORA. He'll never do that!

KROGSTAD. Oh, yes he will. I know him. He won't dare to risk a scandal. And once I'm in there with him, you'll see! Within a year I'll be his right-hand man. It'll be Nils Krogstad who'll be running that bank, not Torvald Helmer!

NORA. That will never happen.

KROGSTAD. Are you thinking of—?

NORA. Now I *have* the courage.

KROGSTAD. Oh, you can't frighten me. A pampered little pretty like you—

NORA. You'll see! You'll see!

KROGSTAD. Under the ice? Down in the cold, black water? And then, in the spring, to float up again, ugly, unrecognizable, hairless—?

NORA. You can't frighten me.

KROGSTAD. And you can't frighten me. People don't do such things, Mrs. Helmer. And anyway, what'd be the use? I've got him in my pocket.

NORA. But afterwards? When I'm no longer—?

KROGSTAD. Have you forgotten that then your reputation will be in my hands? (*She looks at him speechlessly.*) Well, I've warned you. Don't do anything silly. When Helmer's read my letter, he'll get in touch with me. And remember, it's your husband who's forced me to act like this. And for that I'll never forgive him. Goodbye, Mrs. Helmer. (*He goes out through the hall.*)

NORA (*runs to the hall door, opens it a few inches, and listens*). He's going. He's not going to give him the letter. Oh, no, no, it couldn't possibly happen. (*Opens the door a little wider.*) What's he doing? Standing outside the front door. He's not going downstairs. Is he changing his mind? Yes, he—!

A letter falls into the letter-box. Krogstad's footsteps die away down the stairs.

NORA (*with a stifled cry runs across the room towards the table by the sofa. A pause*). In the letter-box. (*Steals timidly over towards the hall door.*) There it is! Oh, Torvald, Torvald! Now we're lost!

MRS. LINDE (*enters from the nursery with Nora's costume*). Well, I've done the best I can. Shall we see how it looks—?

NORA (*whispers hoarsely*). Christine, come here.

MRS. LINDE (*throws the dress on the sofa*). What's wrong with you? You look as though you'd seen a ghost!

NORA. Come here. Do you see that letter? There—look—through the glass of the letter-box.

MRS. LINDE. Yes, yes, I see it.

NORA. That letter's from Krogstad—

MRS. LINDE. Nora! It was Krogstad who lent you the money!

NORA. Yes. And now Torvald's going to discover everything.

MRS. LINDE. Oh, believe me, Nora, it'll be best for you both.

NORA. You don't know what's happened. I've committed a forgery—

MRS. LINDE. But, for heaven's sake—!

NORA. Christine, all I want is for you to be my witness.

MRS. LINDE. What do you mean? Witness what?

NORA. If I should go out of my mind—and it might easily happen—

MRS. LINDE. Nora!

NORA. Or if anything else should happen to me—so that I wasn't here any longer—

MRS. LINDE. Nora, Nora, you don't know what you're saying!

NORA. If anyone should try to take the blame, and say it was all his fault—you understand—?

MRS. LINDE. Yes, yes—but how can you think?

NORA. Then you must testify that it isn't true, Christine. I'm not mad—I know exactly what I'm saying—and I'm telling you, no one else knows anything about this. I did it entirely on my own. Remember that.

MRS. LINDE. All right. But I simply don't understand—

NORA. Oh, how could you understand? A—miracle—is about to happen.

MRS. LINDE. Miracle?

NORA. Yes. A miracle. But it's so frightening. Christine. It *mustn't* happen, not for anything in the world.

MRS. LINDE. I'll go over and talk to Krogstad.

NORA. Don't go near him. He'll only do something to hurt you.

MRS. LINDE. Once upon a time he'd have done anything for my sake.

NORA. He?

MRS. LINDE. Where does he live?

NORA. Oh, how should I know—? Oh, yes, wait a moment—! (*Feels in her pocket.*) Here's his card. But the letter, the letter—!

HELMER (*from his study, knocks on the door*). Nora!

NORA (*cries in alarm*). What is it?

HELMER. Now, now, don't get alarmed. We're not coming in; you've closed the door. Are you trying on your costume?

NORA. Yes, yes—I'm trying on my costume. I'm going to look so pretty for you, Torvald.

MRS. LINDE (*who has been reading the card*). Why, he lives just around the corner.

NORA. Yes; but it's no use. There's nothing to be done now. The letter's lying there in the box.

MRS. LINDE. And your husband has the key?

NORA. Yes, he always keeps it.

MRS. LINDE. Krogstad must ask him to send the letter back unread. He must find some excuse—

NORA. But Torvald always opens the box at just about this time—

MRS. LINDE. You must stop him. Go in and keep him talking. I'll be back as quickly as I can.

She hurries out through the hall.

NORA (*goes over to Helmer's door, opens it and peeps in*). Torvald!

HELMER (*offstage*). Well, may a man enter his own drawing-room again? Come on, Rank, now we'll see what—(*In the doorway.*) But what's this?

NORA. What, Torvald dear?

HELMER. Rank's been preparing me for some great transformation scene.

RANK (*in the doorway*). So I understood. But I seem to have been mistaken.

NORA. Yes, no one's to be allowed to see me before tomorrow night.

HELMER. But, my dear Nora, you look quite worn out. Have you been practicing too hard?

NORA. No, I haven't practiced at all yet.

HELMER. Well, you must.

NORA. Yes, Torvald, I must, I know. But I can't get anywhere without your help. I've completely forgotten everything.

HELMER. Oh, we'll soon put that to rights.

NORA. Yes, help me, Torvald. Promise me you will? Oh, I'm so nervous. All those people—! You must forget everything except me this evening. You mustn't think of business—I won't even let you touch a pen. Promise me, Torvald?

HELMER. I promise. This evening I shall think of nothing but you—my poor, helpless little darling. Oh, there's just one thing I must see to—(*Goes towards the hall door.*)

NORA. What do you want out there?

HELMER. I'm only going to see if any letters have come.

NORA. No, Torvald, no!

HELMER. Why, what's the matter?

NORA. Torvald, I beg you. There's nothing there.

HELMER. Well, I'll just make sure.

He moves towards the door. Nora runs to the piano and plays the first bars of the tarantella.

HELMER (*at the door, turns*). Aha!

NORA. I can't dance tomorrow if I don't practice with you now.

HELMER (*goes over to her*). Are you really so frightened, Nora dear?

NORA. Yes, terribly frightened. Let me start practicing now, at once—we've still time before dinner. Oh, do sit down and play for me, Torvald dear. Correct me, lead me, the way you always do.

HELMER. Very well, my dear, if you wish it.

He sits down at the piano. Nora seizes the tambourine and a long multi-colored shawl from the cardboard box, wraps the latter hastily around her, then takes a quick leap into the center of the room.

NORA. Play for me! I want to dance!

Helmer plays and Nora dances. Dr. Rank stands behind Helmer at the piano and watches her.

HELMER (*as he plays*). Slower, slower!

NORA. I can't!

HELMER. Not so violently, Nora.

NORA. I must!

HELMER (*stops playing*). No, no, this won't do at all.

NORA (*laughs and swings her tambourine*). Isn't that what I told you?

RANK. Let me play for her.

HELMER (*gets up*). Yes, would you? Then it'll be easier for me to show her.

Rank sits down at the piano and plays. Nora dances more and more wildly. Helmer has stationed himself by the stove and tries repeatedly to correct her, but she seems not to hear him. Her hair works loose and falls over her shoulders; she ignores it and continues to dance. Mrs. Linde enters.

MRS. LINDE (*stands in the doorway as though tongue-tied*). Ah—!

NORA (*as she dances*). Oh, Christine, we're having such fun!

HELMER. But, Nora darling, you're dancing as if your life depended on it.

NORA. It does.

HELMER. Rank, stop it! This is sheer lunacy. Stop it, I say!

Rank ceases playing. Nora suddenly stops dancing.

HELMER (*goes over to her*). I'd never have believed it. You've forgotten everything I taught you.

NORA (*throws away the tambourine*). You see!

HELMER. I'll have to show you every step.

NORA. You see how much I need you! You must show me every step of the way. Right to the end of the dance. Promise me you will, Torvald?

HELMER. Never fear. I will.

NORA. You mustn't think about anything but me—today or tomorrow. Don't open any letters—don't even open the letter-box—

HELMER. Aha, you're still worried about that fellow—

NORA. Oh, yes, yes, him too.

HELMER. Nora, I can tell from the way you're behaving, there's a letter from him already lying there.

NORA. I don't know. I think so. But you mustn't read it now. I don't want anything ugly to come between us till it's all over.

RANK (*quietly, to Helmer*). Better give her her way.

HELMER (*puts his arm round her*). My child shall have her way. But tomorrow night, when your dance is over—

NORA. Then you will be free.

MAID (*appears in the doorway, right*). Dinner is served, madam.

NORA. Put out some champagne, Helen.

MAID. Very good, madam. (*Goes.*)

HELMER. I say! What's this, a banquet?

NORA. We'll drink champagne until dawn! (*Calls.*) And, Helen! Put out some macaroons! Lots of macaroons—for once!

HELMER (*takes her hands in his*). Now, now, now. Don't get so excited. Where's my little songbird, the one I know?

NORA. All right. Go and sit down—and you too, Dr. Rank. I'll be with you in a minute. Christine, you must help me put my hair up.

RANK (*quietly, as they go*). There's nothing wrong, is there? I mean, she isn't—er—expecting—?

HELMER Good heavens no, my dear chap. She just gets scared like a child sometimes—I told you before—

They go out right.

NORA. Well?

MRS. LINDE. He's left town.

NORA. I saw it from your face.

MRS. LINDE. He'll be back tomorrow evening. I left a note for him.

NORA. You needn't have bothered. You can't stop anything now. Anyway, it's wonderful really, in a way—sitting here and waiting for the miracle to happen.

MRS. LINDE. Waiting for what?

NORA. Oh, you wouldn't understand. Go in and join them. I'll be with you in a moment.

Mrs. Linde goes into the dining-room.

NORA (*stands for a moment as though collecting herself. Then she looks at her watch*). Five o'clock. Seven hours till midnight. Then another twenty-four hours till midnight tomorrow. And then the tarantella will be finished. Twenty-four and seven? Thirty-one hours to live.

HELMER (*appears in the doorway, right*). What's happened to my little songbird?

NORA (*runs to him with her arms wide*). Your songbird is here!

ACT 3

The same room. The table which was formerly by the sofa has been moved into the center of the room; the chairs surround it as before. The door to the hall stands open. Dance music can be heard from the floor above. Mrs. Linde is seated at the table, absent-mindedly glancing through a book. She is trying to read, but seems unable to keep her mind on it. More than once she turns and listens anxiously towards the front door.

MRS. LINDE (*looks at her watch*). Not here yet. There's not much time left. Please God he hasn't—! (*Listens again.*) Ah, here he is. (*Goes out into the hall and cautiously opens the front door. Footsteps can be heard softly ascending the stairs. She whispers.*) Come in. There's no one here.

KROGSTAD (*in the doorway*). I found a note from you at my lodgings. What does this mean?

MRS. LINDE. I must speak with you.

KROGSTAD. Oh? And must our conversation take place in this house?

MRS. LINDE. We couldn't meet at my place; my room has no separate entrance. Come in. We're quite alone. The maid's asleep, and the Helmers are at the dance upstairs.

KROGSTAD (*comes into the room*). Well, well! So the Helmers are dancing this evening? Are they indeed?

MRS. LINDE. Yes, why not?

KROGSTAD. True enough. Why not?

MRS. LINDE. Well, Krogstad. You and I must have a talk together.

KROGSTAD. Have we two anything further to discuss?

MRS. LINDE. We have a great deal to discuss.

KROGSTAD. I wasn't aware of it.

MRS. LINDE. That's because you've never really understood me.

KROGSTAD. Was there anything to understand? It's the old story, isn't it—a woman chucking a man because something better turns up?

MRS. LINDE. Do you really think I'm so utterly heartless? You think it was easy for me to give you up?

KROGSTAD. Wasn't it?

MRS. LINDE. Oh, Nils, did you really believe that?

KROGSTAD. Then why did you write to me the way you did?

MRS. LINDE. I had to. Since I had to break with you, I thought it my duty to destroy all the feelings you had for me.

KROGSTAD (*clenches his fists*). So that was it. And you did this for money!

MRS. LINDE. You mustn't forget I had a helpless mother to take care of, and two little brothers. We couldn't wait for you, Nils. It would have been so long before you'd had enough to support us.

KROGSTAD. Maybe. But you had no right to cast me off for someone else.

MRS. LINDE. Perhaps not. I've often asked myself that.

KROGSTAD (*more quietly*). When I lost you, it was just as though all solid ground had been swept from under my feet. Look at me. Now I am a shipwrecked man, clinging to a spar.

MRS. LINDE. Help may be near at hand.

KROGSTAD. It was near. But then you came, and stood between it and me.

MRS. LINDE. I didn't know, Nils. No one told me till today that this job I'd found was yours.

KROGSTAD. I believe you, since you say so. But now you know, won't you give it up?

MRS. LINDE. No—because it wouldn't help you even if I did.

KROGSTAD. Wouldn't it? I'd do it all the same.

MRS. LINDE. I've learned to look at things practically. Life and poverty have taught me that.

KROGSTAD. And life has taught me to distrust fine words.

MRS. LINDE. Then it's taught you a useful lesson. But surely you still believe in actions?

KROGSTAD. What do you mean?

MRS. LINDE. You said you were like a shipwrecked man clinging to a spar.

KROGSTAD. I have good reason to say it.

MRS. LINDE. I'm in the same position as you. No one to care about, no one to care for.

KROGSTAD. You made your own choice.

MRS. LINDE. I had no choice—then.

KROGSTAD. Well?

MRS. LINDE. Nils, suppose we two shipwrecked souls could join hands?

KROGSTAD. What are you saying?

MRS. LINDE. Castaways have a better chance of survival together than on their own.

KROGSTAD. Christine!

MRS. LINDE. Why do you suppose I came to this town?

KROGSTAD. You mean—you came because of me?

MRS. LINDE. I must work if I'm to find life worth living. I've always worked, for as long as I can remember; it's been the greatest joy of my life—my only joy. But now I'm alone in the world, and I feel so dreadfully lost and empty. There's no joy in working just for oneself. Oh, Nils, give me something—someone—to work for.

KROGSTAD. I don't believe all that. You're just being hysterical and romantic. You want to find an excuse for self-sacrifice.

MRS. LINDE. Have you ever known me to be hysterical?

KROGSTAD. You mean you really—? Is it possible? Tell me—you know all about my past?

MRS. LINDE. Yes.

KROGSTAD. And you know what people think of me here?

MRS. LINDE. You said just now that with me you might have become a different person.

KROGSTAD. I know I could have.

MRS. LINDE. Couldn't it still happen?

KROGSTAD. Christine—do you really mean this? Yes—you do—I see it in your face. Have you really the courage—?

MRS. LINDE. I need someone to be a mother to; and your children need a mother. And you and I need each other. I believe in you, Nils. I am afraid of nothing—with you.

KROGSTAD (clasps her hands). Thank you, Christine—thank you! Now I shall make the world believe in me as you do! Oh—but I'd forgotten—

MRS. LINDE (listens). Ssh! The tarantella! Go quickly, go!

KROGSTAD. Why? What is it?

MRS. LINDE. You hear that dance? As soon as it's finished, they'll be coming down.

KROGSTAD. All right, I'll go. It's no good, Christine. I'd forgotten—you don't know what I've just done to the Helmers.

MRS. LINDE. Yes, Nils. I know.

KROGSTAD. And yet you'd still have the courage to—?

MRS. LINDE. I know what despair can drive a man like you to.

KROGSTAD. Oh, if only I could undo this!

MRS. LINDE. You can. Your letter is still lying in the box.

KROGSTAD. Are you sure?

MRS. LINDE. Quite sure. But—

KROGSTAD (looks searchingly at her). Is that why you're doing this? You want to save your friend at any price? Tell me the truth. Is that the reason?

MRS. LINDE. Nils, a woman who has sold herself once for the sake of others doesn't make the same mistake again.

KROGSTAD. I shall demand my letter back.

MRS. LINDE. No, no.

KROGSTAD. Of course I shall. I shall stay here till Helmer comes down. I'll tell him he must give me back my letter—I'll say it was only to do with my dismissal, and that I don't want him to read it—

MRS. LINDE. No, Nils, you mustn't ask for that letter back.

KROGSTAD. But—tell me—wasn't that the real reason you asked me to come here?

MRS. LINDE. Yes—at first, when I was frightened. But a day has passed since then, and in that time I've seen incredi-

ble things happen in this house. Helmer must know the truth. This unhappy secret of Nora's must be revealed. They must come to a full understanding; there must be an end of all these shiftings and evasions.

KROGSTAD. Very well. If you're prepared to risk it. But one thing I can do—and at once—

MRS. LINDE (listens). Hurry! Go, go! The dance is over. We aren't safe here another moment.

KROGSTAD. I'll wait for you downstairs.

MRS. LINDE. Yes, do. You can see me home.

KROGSTAD. I've never been so happy in my life before!

He goes out through the front door. The door leading from the room into the hall remains open.

MRS. LINDE (tidies the room a little and gets her hat and coat). What a change! Oh, what a change! Someone to work for—to live for! A home to bring joy into! I won't let this chance of happiness slip through my fingers. Oh, why don't they come? (Listens.) Ah, here they are. I must get my coat on.

She takes her hat and coat. Helmer's and Nora's voices become audible outside. A key is turned in the lock and Helmer leads Nora almost forcibly into the hall. She is dressed in an Italian costume with a large black shawl. He is in evening dress, with a black cloak.

NORA (still in the doorway, resisting him). No, no, no—not in here! I want to go back upstairs. I don't want to leave so early.

HELMER. But my dearest Nora—

NORA. Oh, please, Torvald, please! Just another hour!

HELMER. Not another minute, Nora, my sweet. You know what we agreed. Come along, now. Into the drawing-room. You'll catch cold if you stay out here.

He leads her, despite her efforts to resist him, gently into the room.

MRS. LINDE. Good evening.

NORA. Christine!

HELMER. Oh, hullo, Mrs. Linde. You still here?

MRS. LINDE. Please forgive me. I did so want to see Nora in her costume.

NORA. Have you been sitting here waiting for me?

MRS. LINDE. Yes. I got here too late, I'm afraid. You'd already gone up. And I felt I really couldn't go back home without seeing you.

HELMER (takes off Nora's shawl). Well, take a good look at her. She's worth looking at, don't you think? Isn't she beautiful, Mrs. Linde?

MRS. LINDE. Oh, yes, indeed—

HELMER. Isn't she unbelievably beautiful? Everyone at the party said so. But dreadfully stubborn she is, bless her pretty little heart. What's to be done about that? Would you believe it, I practically had to use force to get her away!

NORA. Oh, Torvald, you're going to regret not letting me stay—just half an hour longer.

HELMER. Hear that, Mrs. Linde? She dances her tarantella—makes a roaring success—and very well deserved—though possibly a trifle too realistic—more so than was aesthetically necessary, strictly speaking. But never mind that. Main thing is—she had a success—roaring success. Was I going to let her stay on after that and spoil the impression? No, thank you. I took my beautiful little Capri signorina—my capricious little Capricienne, what?—under my arm—a swift round of the ballroom, a curtsey to the company, and, as they say in novels, the beautiful apparition disappeared! An exit should always be dramatic, Mrs. Linde. But unfortunately that's just what I can't get Nora to realize. I say, it's hot in here. (*Throws his cloak on a chair and opens the door to his study.*) What's this? It's dark in here. Ah, yes, of course—excuse me. (*Goes in and lights a couple of candles.*)

NORA (*whispers swiftly, breathlessly*). Well?

MRS. LINDE (*quietly*). I've spoken to him.

NORA. Yes?

MRS. LINDE. Nora—you must tell your husband everything.

NORA (*dully*). I knew it.

MRS. LINDE. You've nothing to fear from Krogstad. But you must tell him.

NORA. I shan't tell him anything.

MRS. LINDE. Then the letter will.

NORA. Thank you, Christine. Now I know what I must do. Ssh!

HELMER (*returns*). Well, Mrs. Linde, finished admiring her?

MRS. LINDE. Yes. Now I must say good night.

HELMER. Oh, already? Does this knitting belong to you?

MRS. LINDE (*takes it*). Thank you, yes. I nearly forgot it.

HELMER. You knit, then?

MRS. LINDE. Why, yes.

HELMER. Know what? You ought to take up embroidery.

MRS. LINDE. Oh? Why?

HELMER. It's much prettier. Watch me, now. You hold the embroidery in your left hand, like this, and then you take the needle in your right hand and go in and out in a slow, easy movement—like this. I am right, aren't I?

MRS. LINDE. Yes, I'm sure—

HELMER. But knitting, now—that's an ugly business—can't help it. Look—arms all huddled up—great clumsy needles going up and down—makes you look like a damned Chinaman. I say, that really was a magnificent champagne they served us.

MRS. LINDE. Well, good night, Nora. And stop being stubborn. Remember!

HELMER. Quite right, Mrs. Linde!

MRS. LINDE. Good night, Mr. Helmer.

HELMER (*accompanies her to the door*). Good night, good night! I hope you'll manage to get home all right? I'd gladly—but you haven't far to go, have you? Good night, good night. (*She goes. He closes the door behind her and returns.*) Well, we've got rid of her at last. Dreadful bore that woman is!

NORA. Aren't you very tired, Torvald?

HELMER. No, not in the least.

NORA. Aren't you sleepy?

HELMER. Not a bit. On the contrary, I feel extraordinarily exhilarated. But what about you? Yes, you look very sleepy and tired.

NORA. Yes, I am very tired. Soon I shall sleep.

HELMER. You see, you see! How right I was not to let you stay longer!

NORA. Oh, you're always right, whatever you do.

HELMER (*kisses her on the forehead*). Now my little songbird's talking just like a real big human being. I say, did you notice how cheerful Rank was this evening?

NORA. Oh? Was he? I didn't have a chance to speak with him.

HELMER. I hardly did. But I haven't seen him in such a jolly mood for ages. (*Looks at her for a moment, then comes closer.*) I say, it's nice to get back to one's home again, and be all alone with you. Upon my word, you're a distractingly beautiful young woman.

NORA. Don't look at me like that, Torvald!

HELMER. What, not look at my most treasured possession? At all this wonderful beauty that's mine, mine alone, all mine.

NORA (*goes round to the other side of the table*). You mustn't talk to me like that tonight.

HELMER (*follows her*). You've still the tarantella in your blood, I see. And that makes you even more desirable. Listen! Now the other guests are beginning to go. (*More quietly.*) Nora—soon the whole house will be absolutely quiet.

NORA. Yes, I hope so.

HELMER. Yes, my beloved Nora, of course you do! Do you know—when I'm out with you among other people like we were tonight, do you know why I say so little to you, why I keep so aloof from you, and just throw you an occasional glance? Do you know why I do that? It's because I pretend to myself that you're my secret mistress, my clandestine little sweetheart, and that nobody knows there's anything at all between us.

NORA. Oh, yes, yes, yes—I know you never think of anything but me.

HELMER. And then when we're about to go, and I wrap the shawl round your lovely young shoulders, over this wonderful curve of your neck—then I pretend to myself that you are my young bride, that we've just come from the wedding, that I'm taking you to my house for the first time—that, for the first time, I am alone with you—quite alone with you, as you stand there young and trembling and beautiful. All evening I've had no eyes for anyone but you. When I saw you dance the tarantella, like a huntress, a temptress, my blood grew hot, I couldn't stand it any longer! That was why I seized you and dragged you down here with me—

NORA. Leave me, Torvald! Get away from me! I don't want all this.

HELMER. What? Now, Nora, you're joking with me. Don't want, don't want—? Aren't I your husband—?

There is a knock on the front door.

NORA (*starts*). What was that?

HELMER (*goes towards the hall*). Who is it?

RANK (*outside*). It's me. May I come in for a moment?

HELMER (*quietly, annoyed*). Oh, what does he want now? (*Calls.*) Wait a moment. (*Walks over and opens the door.*) Well! Nice of you not to go by without looking in.

RANK. I thought I heard your voice, so I felt I had to say goodbye. (*His eyes travel swiftly around the room.*) Ah, yes—these dear rooms, how well I know them. What a happy, peaceful home you two have.

HELMER. You seemed to be having a pretty happy time yourself upstairs.

RANK. Indeed I did. Why not? Why shouldn't one make the most of this world? As much as one can, and for as long as one can. The wine was excellent—

HELMER. Especially the champagne.

RANK. You noticed that too? It's almost incredible how much I managed to get down.

NORA. Torvald drank a lot of champagne too, this evening.

RANK. Oh?

NORA. Yes. It always makes him merry afterwards.

RANK. Well, why shouldn't a man have a merry evening after a well-spent day?

HELMER. Well-spent? Oh, I don't know that I can claim that.

RANK (*slaps him across the back*). I can though, my dear fellow!

NORA. Yes, of course, Dr. Rank—you've been carrying out a scientific experiment today, haven't you?

RANK. Exactly.

HELMER. Scientific experiment! Those are big words for my little Nora to use!

NORA. And may I congratulate you on the finding?

RANK. You may indeed.

NORA. It was good, then?

RANK. The best possible finding—both for the doctor and the patient. Certainty.

NORA (*quickly*). Certainty?

RANK. Absolute certainty. So aren't I entitled to have a merry evening after that?

NORA. Yes, Dr. Rank. You were quite right to.

HELMER. I agree. Provided you don't have to regret it tomorrow.

RANK. Well, you never get anything in this life without paying for it.

NORA. Dr. Rank—you like masquerades, don't you?

RANK. Yes, if the disguises are sufficiently amusing.

NORA. Tell me. What shall we two wear at the next masquerade?

HELMER. You little gadabout! Are you thinking about the next one already?

RANK. We two? Yes, I'll tell you. You must go as the Spirit of Happiness—

HELMER. You try to think of a costume that'll convey that.

RANK. Your wife need only appear as her normal, everyday self—

HELMER. Quite right! Well said! But what are you going to be? Have you decided that?

RANK. Yes, my dear friend. I have decided that.

HELMER. Well?

RANK. At the next masquerade, I shall be invisible.

HELMER. Well, that's a funny idea.

RANK. There's a big, black hat—haven't you heard of the invisible hat? Once it's over your head, no one can see you any more.

HELMER (*represses a smile*). Ah yes, of course.

RANK. But I'm forgetting what I came for. Helmer, give me a cigar. One of your black Havanas.

HELMER. With the greatest pleasure. (*Offers him the box.*)

RANK (*takes one and cuts off the tip*). Thank you.

NORA (*strikes a match*). Let me give you a light.

RANK. Thank you. (*She holds out the match for him. He lights his cigar.*) And now—goodbye.

HELMER. Goodbye, my dear chap, goodbye.

NORA. Sleep well, Dr. Rank.

RANK. Thank you for that kind wish.

NORA. Wish me the same.

RANK. You? Very well—since you ask. Sleep well. And thank you for the light. (*He nods to them both and goes.*)

HELMER (*quietly*). He's been drinking too much.

NORA (*abstractedly*). Perhaps.

Helmer takes his bunch of keys from his pocket and goes out into the hall.

NORA. Torvald, what do you want out there?

HELMER. I must empty the letter-box. It's absolutely full. There'll be no room for the newspapers in the morning.

NORA. Are you going to work tonight?

HELMER. You know very well I'm not. Hullo, what's this? Someone's been at the lock.

NORA. At the lock—?

HELMER. Yes, I'm sure of it. Who on earth—? Surely not one of the maids? Here's a broken hairpin. Nora, it's yours—

NORA (*quickly*). Then it must have been the children.

HELMER. Well, you'll have to break them of that habit. Hm, hm. Ah, that's done it. (*Takes out the contents of the box and calls into the kitchen.*) Helen! Put out the light on the staircase. (*Comes back into the drawing-room with the letters in his hand and closes the door to the hall.*) Look at this! You see how they've piled up? (*Glances through them.*) What on earth's this?

NORA (*at the window*). The letter! Oh, no, Torvald, no!

HELMER. Two visiting cards—from Rank.

NORA. From Dr. Rank?

HELMER (*looks at them*). Peter Rank, M.D. They were on top. He must have dropped them in as he left.

NORA. Has he written anything on them?

HELMER. There's a black cross above his name. Look. Rather gruesome, isn't it? It looks just as though he was announcing his death.

NORA. He is.

HELMER. What? Do you know something? Has he told you anything?

NORA. Yes. When these cards come, it means he's said goodbye to us. He wants to shut himself up in his house and die.

HELMER. Ah, poor fellow. I knew I wouldn't be seeing him for much longer. But so soon—! And now he's going to slink away and hide like a wounded beast.

NORA. When the time comes, it's best to go silently. Don't you think so, Torvald?

HELMER (*walks up and down*). He was so much a part of our life. I can't realize that he's gone. His suffering and loneliness seemed to provide a kind of dark background to the happy sunlight of our marriage. Well, perhaps it's best this way. For him, anyway. (*Stops walking.*) And perhaps for us too, Nora. Now we have only each other. (*Embraces her.*) Oh, my beloved wife—I feel as though I could never hold you close enough. Do you know, Nora, often I wish some terrible danger might threaten you, so that I could offer my life and my blood, everything, for your sake.

NORA (*tears herself loose and says in a clear, firm voice*). Read your letters now, Torvald.

HELMER. No, no. Not tonight. Tonight I want to be with you, my darling wife—

NORA. When your friend is about to die—?

HELMER. You're right. This news has upset us both. An ugliness has come between us; thoughts of death and dissolution. We must try to forget them. Until then—you go to your room; I shall go to mine.

NORA (*throws her arms around his neck*). Good night, Torvald! Good night!

HELMER (*kisses her on the forehead*). Good night, my darling little songbird. Sleep well, Nora. I'll go and read my letters.

He goes into the study with the letters in his hand, and closes the door.

NORA (*wild-eyed, fumbles around, seizes Helmer's cloak, throws it round herself and whispers quickly, hoarsely*). Never see him again. Never. Never. Never. (*Throws the shawl over her head.*) Never see the children again. Them too. Never. Never. Oh—the icy black water! Oh—that bottomless—that—! Oh, if only it were all over! Now he's got it—he's reading it. Oh, no, no! Not yet! Goodbye, Torvald! Goodbye, my darlings!

She turns to run into the hall. As she does so, Helmer throws open his door and stands there with an open letter in his hand.

HELMER. Nora!

NORA (*shrieks*). Ah—!

HELMER. What is this? Do you know what is in this letter?

NORA. Yes, I know. Let me go! Let me go!

HELMER (*holds her back*). Go? Where?

NORA (*tries to tear herself loose*). You mustn't try to save me, Torvald!

HELMER (*staggers back*). Is it true? Is it true, what he writes? Oh, my God! No, no—it's impossible, it can't be true!

NORA. It *is* true. I've loved you more than anything else in the world.

HELMER. Oh, don't try to make silly excuses.

NORA (*takes a step towards him*). Torvald—

HELMER. Wretched woman! What have you done?

NORA. Let me go! You're not going to suffer for my sake. I won't let you!

HELMER. Stop being theatrical. (*Locks the front door.*) You're going to stay here and explain yourself. Do you understand what you've done? Answer me! Do you understand?

NORA (*looks unflinchingly at him and, her expression growing colder, says*). Yes. Now I am beginning to understand.

HELMER (*walking around the room*). Oh, what a dreadful awakening! For eight whole years—she who was my joy and my pride—a hypocrite, a liar—worse, worse—a criminal! Oh, the hideousness of it! Shame on you, shame!

Nora is silent and stares unblinkingly at him.

HELMER (*stops in front of her*). I ought to have guessed that something of this sort would happen. I should have foreseen it. All your father's recklessness and instability—be quiet!—I repeat, all your father's recklessness and instability he has handed on to you. No religion, no morals, no sense of duty! Oh, how I have been punished for closing my eyes to his faults! I did it for your sake. And now you reward me like this.

NORA. Yes. Like this.

HELMER. Now you have destroyed all my happiness. You have ruined my whole future. Oh, it's too dreadful to contemplate! I am in the power of a man who is completely without scruples. He can do what he likes with me, demand what he pleases, order me to do anything—I dare not disobey him. I am condemned to humiliation and ruin simply for the weakness of a woman.

NORA. When I am gone from this world, you will be free.

HELMER. Oh, don't be melodramatic. Your father was always ready with that kind of remark. How would it help me if you were "gone from this world," as you put it? It wouldn't assist me in the slightest. He can still make all the facts public; and if he does, I may quite easily be suspected of having been an accomplice in your crime. People may think that I was behind it—that it was I who encouraged you! And for all this I have to thank you, you whom I have carried on my hands through all the years of our marriage! Now do you realize what you've done to me?

NORA (*coldly calm*). Yes.

HELMER. It's so unbelievable I can hardly credit it. But we must try to find some way out. Take off that shawl. Take it off, I say! I must try to buy him off somehow. This thing must be hushed up at any price. As regards our relationship—we must appear to be living together just as before. Only *appear,* of course. You will therefore continue to reside here. That is understood. But the children shall be taken out of your hands. I dare no longer entrust them to you. Oh, to have to say this to the woman I once loved so dearly—and whom I still—! Well, all that must be finished. Henceforth there can be no question of happiness; we must merely strive to save what shreds and tatters— (*The front door bell rings. Helmer starts.*) What can that be? At this hour? Surely not—? He wouldn't—? Hide yourself, Nora. Say you're ill.

Nora does not move. Helmer goes to the door of the room and opens it. The Maid is standing half-dressed in the hall.

MAID. A letter for madam.

HELMER. Give it to me. (*Seizes the letter and shuts the door.*) Yes, it's from him. You're not having it. I'll read this myself.

NORA. Read it.

HELMER (*by the lamp*). I hardly dare to. This may mean the end for us both. No, I must know. (*Tears open the letter hastily; reads a few lines; looks at a piece of paper which is enclosed with it; utters a cry of joy.*) Nora! (*She looks at him questioningly.*) Nora! No—I must read it once more. Yes, yes, it's true! I am saved! Nora, I am saved!

NORA. What about me?

HELMER. You too, of course. We're both saved, you and I. Look! He's returning your I.O.U. He writes that he is sorry for what has happened—a happy accident has changed his life—oh, what does it matter what he writes? We are saved, Nora! No one can harm you now. Oh, Nora, Nora—no, first let me destroy this filthy thing. Let me see—! (*Glances at the I.O.U.*) No, I don't want to look at it. I shall merely regard the whole business as a dream. (*He tears the I.O.U. and both letters into pieces, throws them into the stove, and watches them burn.*) There. Now they're destroyed. He wrote that ever since Christmas Eve you've been—oh, these must have been three dreadful days for you, Nora.

NORA. Yes. It's been a hard fight.

HELMER. It must have been terrible—seeing no way out except—no, we'll forget the whole sordid business. We'll just be happy and go on telling ourselves over and over again: "It's over! It's over!" Listen to me. Nora. You don't seem to realize. It's over! Why are you looking so pale? Ah, my poor little Nora, I understand. You can't believe

that I have forgiven you. But I have, Nora. I swear it to you. I have forgiven you everything. I know that what you did you did for your love of me.

NORA. That is true.

HELMER. You have loved me as a wife should love her husband. It was simply that in your inexperience you chose the wrong means. But do you think I love you any the less because you don't know how to act on your own initiative? No, no. Just lean on me. I shall counsel you. I shall guide you. I would not be a true man if your feminine helplessness did not make you doubly attractive in my eyes. You mustn't mind the hard words I said to you in those first dreadful moments when my whole world seemed to be tumbling about my ears. I have forgiven you, Nora. I swear it to you; I have forgiven you.

NORA. Thank you for your forgiveness.

She goes out through the door, right.

HELMER. No, don't go—(*Looks in.*) What are you doing there?

NORA (*offstage*). Taking off my fancy dress.

HELMER (*by the open door*). Yes, do that. Try to calm yourself and get your balance again, my frightened little songbird. Don't be afraid. I have broad wings to shield you. (*Begins to walk around near the door.*) How lovely and peaceful this little home of ours is, Nora. You are safe here; I shall watch over you like a hunted dove which I have snatched unharmed from the claws of the falcon. Your wildly beating little heart shall find peace with me. It will happen, Nora; it will take time, but it will happen, believe me. Tomorrow all this will seem quite different. Soon everything will be as it was before. I shall no longer need to remind you that I have forgiven you; your own heart will tell you that it is true. Do you really think I could ever bring myself to disown you, or even to reproach you? Ah, Nora, you don't understand what goes on in a husband's heart. There is something indescribably wonderful and satisfying for a husband in knowing that he has forgiven his wife—forgiven her unreservedly, from the bottom of his heart. It means that she has become his property in a double sense; he has, as it were, brought her into the world anew; she is now not only his wife but also his child. From now on that is what you shall be to me, my poor, helpless, bewildered little creature. Never be frightened of anything again, Nora. Just open your heart to me. I shall be both your will and your conscience. What's this? Not in bed? Have you changed?

NORA (*in her everyday dress*). Yes, Torvald. I've changed.

HELMER. But why now—so late—?

NORA. I shall not sleep tonight.

HELMER. But, my dear Nora—

NORA (*looks at her watch*). It isn't that late. Sit down here, Torvald. You and I have a lot to talk about.

She sits down on one side of the table.

HELMER. Nora, what does this mean? You look quite drawn—

NORA. Sit down. It's going to take a long time. I've a lot to say to you.

HELMER (*sits down on the other side of the table*). You alarm me, Nora. I don't understand you.

NORA. No, that's just it. You don't understand me. And I've never understood you—until this evening. No, don't interrupt me. Just listen to what I have to say. You and I have got to face facts, Torvald.

HELMER. What do you mean by that?

NORA (*after a short silence*). Doesn't anything strike you about the way we're sitting here?

HELMER. What?

NORA. We've been married for eight years. Does it occur to you that this is the first time that we two, you and I, man and wife, have ever had a serious talk together?

HELMER. Serious? What do you mean, serious?

NORA. In eight whole years—no, longer—ever since we first met—we have never exchanged a serious word on a serious subject.

HELMER. Did you expect me to drag you into all my worries—worries you couldn't possibly have helped me with?

NORA. I'm not talking about worries. I'm simply saying that we have never sat down seriously to try to get to the bottom of anything.

HELMER. But, my dear Nora, what on earth has that got to do with you?

NORA. That's just the point. You have never understood me. A great wrong has been done to me, Torvald. First by Papa, and then by you.

HELMER. What? But we two have loved you more than anyone in the world!

NORA (*shakes her head*). You have never loved me. You just thought it was fun to be in love with me.

HELMER. Nora, what kind of a way is this to talk?

NORA. It's the truth, Torvald. When I lived with Papa, he used to tell me what he thought about everything, so that I never had any opinions but his. And if I did have any of my own, I kept them quiet, because he wouldn't have liked them. He called me his little doll, and he played with me just the way I played with my dolls. Then I came here to live in your house—

HELMER. What kind of a way is that to describe our marriage?

NORA (*undisturbed*). I mean, then I passed from Papa's hands into yours. You arranged everything the way you wanted it, so that I simply took over your taste in everything—or pretended I did—I don't really know—I think it was a little of both—first one and then the other. Now I look back on it, it's as if I've been living here like a pauper, from hand to mouth. I performed tricks for you, and you

gave me food and drink. But that was how you wanted it. You and Papa have done me a great wrong. It's your fault that I have done nothing with my life.

HELMER. Nora, how can you be so unreasonable and ungrateful? Haven't you been happy here?

NORA. No; never. I used to think I was; but I haven't ever been happy.

HELMER. Not—not happy?

NORA. No. I've just had fun. You've always been very kind to me. But our home has never been anything but a playroom. I've been your doll-wife, just as I used to be Papa's doll-child. And the children have been my dolls. I used to think it was fun when you came in and played with me, just as they think it's fun when I go in and play games with them. That's all our marriage has been, Torvald.

HELMER. There may be a little truth in what you say, though you exaggerate and romanticize. But from now on it'll be different. Playtime is over. Now the time has come for education.

NORA. Whose education? Mine or the children's?

HELMER. Both yours and the children's, my dearest Nora.

NORA. Oh, Torvald, you're not the man to educate me into being the right wife for you.

HELMER. How can you say that?

NORA. And what about me? Am I fit to educate the children?

HELMER. Nora!

NORA. Didn't you say yourself a few minutes ago that you dare not leave them in my charge?

HELMER. In a moment of excitement. Surely you don't think I meant it seriously?

NORA. Yes. You were perfectly right. I'm not fitted to educate them. There's something else I must do first. I must educate myself. And you can't help me with that. It's something I must do by myself. That's why I'm leaving you.

HELMER (*jumps up*). What did you say?

NORA. I must stand on my own feet if I am to find out the truth about myself and about life. So I can't go on living here with you any longer.

HELMER. Nora, Nora!

NORA. I'm leaving you now, at once. Christine will put me up for tonight—

HELMER. You're out of your mind! You can't do this! I forbid you!

NORA. It's no use your trying to forbid me any more. I shall take with me nothing but what is mine. I don't want anything from you, now or ever.

HELMER. What kind of madness is this?

NORA. Tomorrow I shall go home—I mean, to where I was born. It'll be easiest for me to find some kind of a job there.

HELMER. But you're blind! You've no experience of the world—

NORA. I must try to get some, Torvald.

HELMER. But to leave your home, your husband, your children! Have you thought what people will say?

NORA. I can't help that. I only know that I must do this.

HELMER. But this is monstrous! Can you neglect your most sacred duties?

NORA. What do you call my most sacred duties?

HELMER. Do I have to tell you? Your duties towards your husband, and your children.

NORA. I have another duty which is equally sacred.

HELMER. You have not. What on earth could that be?

NORA. My duty towards myself.

HELMER. First and foremost you are a wife and a mother.

NORA. I don't believe that any longer. I believe that I am first and foremost a human being, like you—or anyway, that I must try to become one. I know most people think as you do, Torvald, and I know there's something of the sort to be found in books. But I'm no longer prepared to accept what people say and what's written in books. I must think things out for myself, and try to find my own answer.

HELMER. Do you need to ask where your duty lies in your own home? Haven't you an infallible guide in such matters—your religion?

NORA. Oh, Torvald, I don't really know what religion means.

HELMER. What are you saying?

NORA. I only know what Pastor Hansen told me when I went to confirmation. He explained that religion meant this and that. When I get away from all this and can think things out on my own, that's one of the questions I want to look into. I want to find out whether what Pastor Hansen said was right—or anyway, whether it is right for me.

HELMER. But it's unheard of for so young a woman to behave like this! If religion cannot guide you, let me at least appeal to your conscience. I presume you have some moral feelings left? Or—perhaps you haven't? Well, answer me.

NORA. Oh, Torvald, that isn't an easy question to answer. I simply don't know. I don't know where I am in these matters. I only know that these things mean something quite different to me from what they do to you. I've learned now that certain laws are different from what I'd imagined them to be; but I can't accept that such laws can be right. Has a woman really not the right to spare her dying father pain, or save her husband's life? I can't believe that.

HELMER. You're talking like a child. You don't understand how society works.

NORA. No, I don't. But now I intend to learn. I must try to satisfy myself which is right, society or I.

HELMER. Nora, you're ill; you're feverish. I almost believe you're out of your mind.

NORA. I've never felt so sane and sure in my life.

HELMER. You feel sure that it is right to leave your husband and your children?

NORA. Yes. I do.

HELMER. Then there is only one possible explanation.

NORA. What?

HELMER. That you don't love me any longer.

NORA. No, that's exactly it.

HELMER. Nora! How can you say this to me?

NORA. Oh, Torvald, it hurts me terribly to have to say it, because you've always been so kind to me. But I can't help it. I don't love you any longer.

HELMER (controlling his emotions with difficulty). And you feel quite sure about this too?

NORA. Yes, absolutely sure. That's why I can't go on living here any longer.

HELMER. Can you also explain why I have lost your love?

NORA. Yes, I can. It happened this evening, when the miracle failed to happen. It was then that I realized you weren't the man I'd thought you to be.

HELMER. Explain more clearly. I don't understand you.

NORA. I've waited so patiently, for eight whole years—well, good heavens, I'm not such a fool as to suppose that miracles occur every day. Then this dreadful thing happened to me, and then I knew: "Now the miracle will take place!" When Krogstad's letter was lying out there, it never occurred to me for a moment that you would let that man trample over you. I knew that you would say to him: "Publish the facts to the world." And when he had done this—

HELMER. Yes, what then? When I'd exposed my wife's name to shame and scandal—

NORA. Then I was certain that you would step forward and take all the blame on yourself, and say: "I am the one who is guilty!"

HELMER. Nora!

NORA. You're thinking I wouldn't have accepted such a sacrifice from you? No, of course I wouldn't! But what would my word have counted for against yours? That was the miracle I was hoping for, and dreading. And it was to prevent it happening that I wanted to end my life.

HELMER. Nora, I would gladly work for you night and day, and endure sorrow and hardship for your sake. But no man can be expected to sacrifice his honor, even for the person he loves.

NORA. Millions of women have done it.

HELMER. Oh, you think and talk like a stupid child.

NORA. That may be. But you neither think nor talk like the man I could share my life with. Once you'd got over your fright—and you weren't frightened of what might threaten me, but only of what threatened you—once the danger was past, then as far as you were concerned it was exactly as though nothing had happened. I was your little songbird just as before—your doll whom henceforth you would take particular care to protect from the world because she was so weak and fragile. (*Gets up.*) Torvald, in that moment I realized that for eight years I had been living here with a complete stranger, and had borne him three children—! Oh, I can't bear to think of it! I could tear myself to pieces!

HELMER (*sadly*). I see it, I see it. A gulf has indeed opened between us. Oh, but Nora—couldn't it be bridged?

NORA. As I am now, I am no wife for you.

HELMER. I have the strength to change.

NORA. Perhaps—if your doll is taken from you.

HELMER. But to be parted—to be parted from you! No, no, Nora, I can't conceive of it happening!

NORA (*goes into the room, right*). All the more necessary that it should happen.

She comes back with her outdoor things and a small traveling-bag, which she puts down on a chair by the table.

HELMER. Nora, Nora, not now! Wait till tomorrow!

NORA (*puts on her coat*). I can't spend the night in a strange man's house.

HELMER. But can't we live here as brother and sister, then—?

NORA (*fastens her hat*). You know quite well it wouldn't last. (*Puts on her shawl.*) Goodbye, Torvald. I don't want to see the children. I know they're in better hands than mine. As I am now, I can be nothing to them.

HELMER. But some time, Nora—some time—?

NORA. How can I tell? I've no idea what will happen to me.

HELMER. But you are my wife, both as you are and as you will be.

NORA. Listen, Torvald. When a wife leaves her husband's house, as I'm doing now, I'm told that according to the law he is freed of any obligations towards her. In any case, I release you from any such obligations. You mustn't feel bound to me in any way, however small, just as I shall not feel bound to you. We must both be quite free. Here is your ring back. Give me mine.

HELMER. That too?

NORA. That too.

HELMER. Here it is.

NORA. Good. Well, now it's over. I'll leave the keys here. The servants know about everything to do with the house—much better than I do. Tomorrow, when I have left town, Christine will come to pack the things I brought here from home. I'll have them sent on after me.

HELMER. This is the end then! Nora, will you never think of me any more?

NORA. Yes, of course. I shall often think of you and the children and this house.

HELMER. May I write to you, Nora?

NORA. No, never. You mustn't do that.

HELMER. But at least you must let me send you—

NORA. Nothing. Nothing.

HELMER. But if you should need help?—

NORA. I tell you, no. I don't accept things from strangers.

HELMER. Nora—can I never be anything but a stranger to you?

NORA (*picks up her bag*). Oh, Torvald! Then the miracle of miracles would have to happen.

HELMER. The miracle of miracles?

NORA. You and I would both have to change so much that—oh, Torvald, I don't believe in miracles any longer.

HELMER. But I want to believe in them. Tell me. We should have to change so much that—?

NORA. That life together between us two could become a marriage. Goodbye.

She goes out through the hall.

HELMER (*sinks down on a chair by the door and buries his face in his hands*). Nora! Nora! (*Looks round and gets up.*) Empty! She's gone! (*A hope strikes him.*) The miracle of miracles—?

The street door is slammed shut downstairs.

TOPICS FOR CRITICAL THINKING AND WRITING

 ### THE PLAY ON THE PAGE

1. Near the beginning of the play, how does Mrs. Linde's presence help to define Nora's character? How does Nora's response to Krogstad's entrance tell us something about Nora?

2. What does Dr. Rank contribute to the play? If he were eliminated, what would be lost?

3. In view of the fact that the last act several times seems to be moving toward a "happy ending" (e.g., Krogstad promises to recall his letter), what is wrong with the alternate ending (see page 427) that Ibsen reluctantly provided for a German production?

4. Can it be argued that although at the end Nora goes out to achieve self-realization, her abandonment of her children—especially to Torvald's loathsome conventional morality—is a crime? (By the way, exactly why does Nora leave the children? She seems to imply, in some passages, that because she forged a signature she is unfit to bring them up. But do you agree with her?)

Henrik Ibsen

5. Michael Meyer, in his splendid biography *Henrik Ibsen*, says that the play is not so much about women's rights as about "the need of every individual to find out the kind of person he or she really is, and to strive to become that person." What evidence can you offer to support or refute this interpretation?

6. In *The Quintessence of Ibsenism* Bernard Shaw says that Ibsen, reacting against a common theatrical preference for strange situations, "saw that . . . the more familiar the situation, the more interesting the play. Shakespear had put ourselves on the stage but not our situations.

Our uncles seldom murder our fathers and . . . marry our mothers. . . . Ibsen . . . gives us not only ourselves, but ourselves in our own situations. The things that happen to his stage figures are things that happen to us. One consequence is that his plays are much more important to us than Shakespear's. Another is that they are capable both of hurting us cruelly and of filling us with excited hopes of escape from idealistic tyrannies, and with visions of intenser life in the future." How much of this do you believe?

🎭 THE PLAY ON THE STAGE

7. In some interpretations, Nora is at the start a ninny, who matures during the play. In other interpretations, she is cunning at the start. If you were directing the play, would you lean toward one or the other of these interpretations, and if so, how would you direct the actress playing Nora? What specific bits of business might you give her?

8. Does it matter if Helmer is especially handsome or not? And whatever his physical appearance, should he display any signs of weakness? Actors often emphasize one trait, for instance his silliness, or his brutality, or his affection. Do you think one trait is dominant, and should be evident to the audience?

9. As costume designer for a staging of *A Doll's House*, what colors and fabrics would you use for Torvald, Nora, Mrs. Linde, Krogstad, and Dr. Rank?

10. If you were directing a production, what gestures and movements would you give to Nora and Krogstad when they first meet in the play?

11. Nora's tarantella is usually performed as an attempt to distract Helmer from the letterbox. In Bergman's production (see page 428), the dance—performed on top of the dining room table—expressed Nora's anger, and it ended with Nora dropping her tambourine, indicating that the masquerade was over. How would you stage the dance?

12. Working from the last three pages of the script, do you suggest any physical contact between Nora and her husband? If so, point to the specific passages and describe the contact. If you think there should be no physical contact, explain why.

13. Keeping in mind Ibsen's wintry setting—specifically, Christmastime—what kinds of sound effects might be effective in a production?

14. The play is occasionally updated, for instance to an Indiana farm in the 1950s, or to suburban San Diego in the 1990s. What might be gained by some such updating? Do you think that more would be lost than gained? Explain.

CONTEXTS FOR *A DOLL'S HOUSE*

Henrik Ibsen
NOTES FOR THE TRAGEDY OF MODERN TIMES

[The University Library, Oslo, has the following preliminary notes for *A Doll's House*:]

Rome 19.10.78

There are two kinds of moral law, two kinds of conscience, one in man and a completely different one in woman. They do not understand each other; but in matters of practical living the woman is judged by man's law, as if she were not a woman but a man.

The wife in the play ends up quite bewildered and not knowing right from wrong; her natural instincts on the one

side and her faith in authority on the other leave her completely confused.

A woman cannot be herself in contemporary society, it is an exclusively male society with laws drafted by men, and with counsel and judges who judge feminine conduct from the male point of view.

She has committed a crime, and she is proud of it; because she did it for love of her husband and to save his life. But the husband, with his conventional views of honor, stands on the side of the law and looks at the affair with male eyes.

Mental conflict. Depressed and confused by her faith in authority, she loses faith in her moral right and ability to bring up her children. Bitterness. A mother in contemporary society, just as certain insects go away and die when she has done her duty in the propagation of the race [*sic*]. Love of life, of home and husband and children and family. Now and then, woman-like, she shrugs off her thoughts. Sudden return of dread and terror. Everything must be borne alone. The catastrophe approaches, ineluctably, inevitably. Despair, resistance, defeat.

[The following note was later added in the margin:]

Krogstad has done some dishonest business, and thus made a bit of money; but his prosperity does not help him, he cannot recover his honour.

Henrik Ibsen
ADAPTATION OF *A DOLL'S HOUSE* FOR A GERMAN PRODUCTION

[Because Norwegian works were not copyrighted in Germany, German theaters could stage and freely adapt Ibsen's works without his consent. When he heard that a German director was going to change the ending to a happy one, Ibsen decided that he had better do the adaptation himself, though he characterized it as "a barbaric outrage" against the play.]

NORA. . . . Where we could make a real marriage out of our lives together. Goodbye. (*Begins to go.*)
HELMER. Go then! (*Seizes her arm.*) But first you shall see your children for the last time!
NORA. Let me go! I will not see them! I cannot!
HELMER (*draws her over to the door, left*). You shall see them. (*Opens the door and says softly.*) Look, there

they are asleep, peaceful and carefree. Tomorrow, when they wake up and call for their mother, they will be—motherless.
NORA (*trembling*). Motherless . . . !
HELMER. As you once were.
NORA. Motherless! (*Struggles with herself, lets her travelling bag fall, and says.*) Oh, this is a sin against myself, but I cannot leave them. (*Half sinks down by the door.*)
HELMER (*joyfully, but softly*). Nora!

(THE CURTAIN FALLS.)

Henrik Ibsen
SPEECH AT THE BANQUET OF THE NORWEGIAN LEAGUE FOR WOMEN'S RIGHTS

[A month after the official birthday celebrations were over, Ibsen and his wife were invited to a banquet in his honor given by the leading Norwegian feminist society.]

Christiania, May 26, 1898

I am not a member of the Women's Rights League. Whatever I have written has been without any conscious thought of making propaganda. I have been more the poet and less the social philosopher than people generally seem inclined to believe. I thank you for the toast, but must disclaim the honor of having consciously worked for the women's rights movement. I am not even quite clear as to just what this

women's rights movement really is. To me it has seemed a problem of mankind in general. And if you read my books carefully you will understand this. True enough, it is desirable to solve the woman problem, along with all the others; but that has not been the whole purpose. My task has been the *description of humanity*. To be sure, whenever such a description is felt to be reasonably true, the reader will read his own feelings and sentiments into the work of the poet. These are then attributed to the poet; but incorrectly so. Every reader remolds the work beautifully and neatly, each according to his own personality. Not only those who write but also those who read are poets. They are collaborators. They are often more poetical than the poet himself.

THE PLAY IN PERFORMANCE

A Doll's House is probably Ibsen's most frequently staged play, which means that it is probably the most frequently staged modern drama, and probably only the major plays of Shakespeare are more frequently performed.

A Doll's House had its premiére in Copenhagen, in 1879; as early as 1882 it was produced in English (under the title of *The Child Wife*) in Milwaukee, but with a revised ending in which Nora remained with her family. In the first London production (an amateur production, in 1884), too, Nora did not leave home, and for a German production of 1880 Ibsen himself reluctantly wrote a happy ending, rather than allow someone else to write it (see page 427).

It is inconceivable today that the ending would be revised thus, and indeed most productions probably can be characterized as traditional. That is to say, the play is regarded as a classic of realistic drama, and it is staged appropriately, with characters in the dress of the period, and with the appropriate setting. But there have been some notable departures. In Stockholm in 1967 Peter Zadek used a bare room (in contrast to the usual room full of overstuffed furniture), and he rearranged the text into a series of scenes each of which ended with a blackout. In a 1972 production in Stockholm, transferred to Frankfurt in 1973, Hans Neunfels directed a production with surrealistic qualities. The set was an immense room, which of course diminished the characters. At the rear were tall glass doors topped by a kitten (at the left) and a lioness (at the right), symbolizing Nora's dual nature. (For a photograph from this production, see page 15.)

In 1981 the Swedish director Ingmar Bergman offered a severely cut version in Munich, entitled *Nora,* which with some changes was repeated (again called *Nora*) in 1989 in Stockholm. In his first version Bergman omitted the children in order to concentrate on the adult couple, but he later regretted this decision and in the Stockholm version he used one child. Bergman's Helmer was the traditional stuffy figure, but his Nora was from the start an angry woman, and his Dr. Rank was a warmer man than the usual rank. In the stocking scene, each of these characters brought to the other a warmth that was nowhere else to be found in the play.

Bergman's staging was highly unusual. He used three sets: a living room, with a massive dark sofa, a chair, and in the background a Christmas tree with two dolls, a doll's bed, and other presents; a dining room, with a large round table and four chairs; and a bedroom, with a brass bed that resembled a miniature doll's bed that was among the toys in the first scene. But the use of several rooms instead of only one, far from making the Helmer household seem relatively open, made it more oppressive than the usual living room set does,

since none of the rooms had windows or door, except in the final scene when a door appeared in the background. Each set appeared on a platform, and the platform itself was surrounded by high walls with small barred windows at the top. The platform thus was a sort of inner stage, and each room was itself imprisoned within the tall outer walls. The actors were always in view of the audience; in the first (Munich) version, when called upon to perform, they stepped onto the platform from the background (in effect, they entered the inner stage), performed their parts, and then returned to the background. In the Stockholm version, they sat in simple chairs at the sides, and, when called upon to perform in the action, they stepped up onto the platform, played their parts, and then returned to their chairs, where they watched the others perform. Thus the actors were spectators as well as actors, with the implication that life is a matter of role-playing.

Most astounding was Bergman's ending. He did not, of course, use the happy ending that in earlier days some directors had foisted on the play, but he did something almost as daring—he staged the scene in the Helmer bedroom. Helmer was asleep (presumably he had gone to bed thinking that he and Nora were reconciled), when Nora entered, carrying a small suitcase. Helmer awakened, flooded with light (Nora was in the dark), sat up, and the audience realized that he was naked. (See the photo on page 397.) Moving in and out of the light Nora spoke to Helmer, who—for reasons of modesty dared not get out of bed, despite years of marriage. Nora exited and was replaced by her daughter, who carried the doll—a Christmas present—that the audience had seen at the start. Nora reentered, and then made a final exit from the platform, walking past Mrs. Linde and Krogstad, who were sitting offstage, and she then walked through the auditorium.

For an extended discussion of productions of the play, see Egil Tornqvist, *Ibsen: A Doll's House* (1995). For a briefer discussion, see Frederick J. Marker and Lise-Lone Marker, *Ibsen's Lively Art* (1989). On Bergman's *Nora,* see Ingmar Bergman, *A Project for the Theatre,* ed. Frederick J. Marker and Lise-Lone Marker (1983).

Carol Elliot MacVey
DIRECTING A DOLL'S HOUSE

Carol Elliot MacVey, a member of the theater department at the University of Iowa, directed *A Doll's House* at Princeton in 1991.

Did you make any cuts? If so, why?

When asked about cutting an Ibsen text the question ought to be, almost *has* to be, "If you made any cuts, *how* did you manage to do so?" My own rule: if you're going to cut, *cut big.* Ibsen's dialogue is so finely crafted that it is often virtually

impossible to excise a sentence without confusing what directly follows. There is a verbal dependency between speaker's sentences. Many responses repeat a word mentioned in the previous sentence, frustrating the possibility of doing much interdialogue cutting. This pattern is consistent throughout the text. This careful forging of each link to form a whole is quintessentially Ibsen, his characteristic rhythm. It isn't surprising to read that once on meeting an architect Ibsen commented, "Yes; it is, as you know, my own trade."

And wouldn't you agree that some very brief passages of dialogue are highly important to the plot and to connections between characters?

There is a weighty history to the personal and relational events of the play. Ibsen might well have entitled this play *Ghosts* too, since each of the characters in this play is haunted by sins of the past. The actors, directors, and designers must be vigilant in detecting clues to what these sins of the past might be and how they relate to the other characters. What appears to be a casual or cryptic comment by one character can actually turn out to be significant in decoding that character's past.

What might be an example?

When Krogstad confronts Nora with having forged her father's signature, Krogstad says,

> "But business, the kind of business we two have been transacting—I think you'll admit I understand something about that?"

Precisely what does he mean by "the kind of business"? With some research and poetic license I deduced from that comment something along these lines: When, years earlier, Torvald and Krogstad, both government legal inspectors, investigated Nora's father's firm, they found the old gentleman guilty of improprieties. But because Torvald was then engaged to Nora he didn't want to bring charges against her father so he "turned a blind eye"; Krogstad, out of friendship to Torvald, submitted a false report and altered one or more bank documents that might have incriminated Nora's father. I assume that Krogstad falsified these documents by forging the old man's signature. Meanwhile, Torvald resigned his government job, married Nora, and within months Nora's father died. Later there was some questioning about one of the aforementioned bank documents and Krogstad was accused of forgery and subsequently fired. Therefore, when Krogstad says to Nora that he knows about "the kind of business," he is alluding to his own experience with forgery, ironically linking him and Nora in a similar crime motivated by the same reason: Torvald's salvation. So aside from violating the exact verbal architecture of the play, it is also difficult to cut text without excising some of the irony, morality, history, and complexity of the characters.

What are some other ways in which you see connections between characters?

There is a kind of incestuousness with these characters' lives, each one having been connected with another at some time in his or her past. With Ibsen's own words those relationships may also be projected into the future as well. Consider the relationship between Nora and Mrs. Linde. As a character construct, Christine is somewhat of a doppelganger for Nora: When they first meet in Act I, Christine is needy, Nora has everything; at the end Christine is poised for security, Nora is practically destitute. Imagine that some time has passed since Nora's departure at the end of the play and the two friends meet. The exchange from their first meeting in Act I, as scripted by Ibsen, could be recycled almost word for word except that the speakers would be switched and the resonances of their pasts altered. It would read as follows:

NORA (*shyly and a little hesitantly*). Good evening, Christine.
MRS. LINDE (*uncertainly*). Good evening—
NORA. I don't suppose you recognize me.
MRS. LINDE. No, I'm afraid I—Yes, wait a minute— surely—(*Exclaims.*) Why, Nora! Is it really you?
NORA. Yes, it's me.
MRS. LINDE. And I didn't recognize you! But how could I—? (*More quietly.*) How you've changed, Nora!
NORA. Yes, I know. It's been nine years—nearly ten—
MRS. LINDE. Is it so long? Yes, it must be. Oh, these last eight years have been such a happy time for me! So you've come to town? All that way in winter! How brave of you!
NORA. I arrived by the steamer this morning.
MRS. LINDE. Yes, of course—to enjoy yourself over Christmas. Oh, how splendid! We'll have to celebrate! But take off your coat. You're not cold, are you? (*Helps her off with it.*) There! Now let's sit down here by the stove and be comfortable. No, you take the armchair. I'll sit here in the rocking-chair. (*Clasps Nora's hands.*) Yes, now you look like your old self. It was just at first that—you've got a little paler, though, Nora. And perhaps a bit thinner.
NORA. And older, Christine. Much, much older.

This is one of several examples I could point out. We actually used these character/line reversals in rehearsal as improvisations to discover character relationships. I contend that the incestuousness of the characters' past lives also extends to their very words. Again, any cutting would have to be judicious.

But you did make a big cut late in the play, didn't you?

Yes. Once Nora stood up and said, "Torvald, in that moment I realized that for eight years I had been living here with a complete stranger and had borne him three children! Oh, I can't bear to think of it. I could tear myself to pieces!" the actors spoke no more lines from the text. Originally the actors had memorized and spoken all of the text and we had rehearsed it intact. But one day, as a rehearsal technique—a favorite of mine—we played the scene (from the time Nora stands to the end of play) as a silent movie, without any words. It turned out that everything essential was conveyed in movement and sound and that in the process we had gained tremendous emotional resonances. As a result of bypassing the literal word, we discovered firsthand what Peter Brook says about a word being "a small visible portion of a gigantic unseen formation." We drew from a primordial stratum of human sounds that we associate with a life and death situation, which is what the ending is for Nora and Torvald, and it yielded a powerful spectacle.

Did you do anything special with Nora's departure at the end? Everyone expects the door to slam.

Oh yes, the door did slam in our production, the climax of a litany of orchestrated sounds—not arbitrary sounds but ones suggested by the text. One such sequence played especially well. At the very end of the play when Nora walked to the door to exit she found that the door was locked. Torvald had locked it earlier (via Ibsen's stage directions), but he had not yet unlocked it (Ibsen never indicated that he should have) and he still had the key. Nora desperately tried to pull and kick the door open. That didn't work. Torvald refused to give her the key. And in one of the more powerful images of the production she tried climbing out up over the walls of the room but was not successful. Finally, in desperation, she had to assault Torvald physically in order to extricate the key from him. Throughout all of this, there were no words, but there was language and sound: Nora's footsteps, the grappling with the doorknob, her kicking the door, her heaving and panting, her fingernails and feet scratching the walls, her pummelling Torvald, their cries as they struggled. It was a brutal fight, but she prevailed and got the key. Some evenings the audience actually applauded and cheered at this point. When, at last, we finally heard the sound of the key in the door and saw the door open wide and heard her hard footsteps go into the hall and heard the final slam of the outside door we knew it was not only an act of will but also a result of great courage and we felt that she could and would survive. I hoped as much.

Purists are shocked that I cut those final last exchanges about "the miracle of miracles" but I felt we lost nothing essential and gained a visual and visceral power that the words never unpacked. To this day, when asked what I feel most successful about as a director I always reply, "The last act of *A Doll's House*."

What design decisions did you make about A Doll's House? *How did you costume it?*

One particular costume was the lynchpin for our thinking about the rest of the costume design: Nora's Neapolitan dress. What a theatrical genius Ibsen is! He built into this play a truly stunning stage image executed by a costume; unfortunately, it's easy to miss since it's buried in a stage direction: *Nora removes the dress from a box.* We wanted to underscore the drama and import of that event so we consciously chose to color-starve our audience up until that moment of unpacking the dress. Our palette for the set and costumes was combinations of mauves, tans, and endless shades of off-white. When Nora took her tarantella dress out of its box and all that brilliant redness ignited the stage, it was a thrilling event. Each night, when that dress appeared, there were audible gasps from the audience. I wish I could take sole credit for the idea, but I can't; it's right there in Ibsen's text.

What was the set like?

We started our set design discussions with a principle, a fact, and a question—principle: Space is destiny; fact: The only object Ibsen insisted be present on the set of *A Doll's House* was a painting of the Madonna and Child; question: What, if anything, should be visible outside the room's windows? We ended up fusing those three elements. The walls of the room, which were papered in a delicate Victorian design, were rounded and very, very high. There were three doors, which were also wallpapered like the walls, an idea inspired by Strindberg's design for *The Father*. When these doors were closed they created one continuous seamless wall and the sense of confinement was total: Nora's space was the physical correlative of Nora's character. The only other objects in the room were three chairs, a small table, and a stove. But the most visually exciting and dominating aspect of the design was Ibsen's called-for portrait of the Virgin and Infant. In the center of the room was a very large window— maybe eight feet high—outside of which was hung a bigger than life-size painting of the Madonna and Child. We believed that if there was a single image of what that society held up as the model for motherhood, femininity, and womanhood it was the image of the Madonna. We intended that the image be pervasive. It was. For the last act the painting of the Madonna was covered in black velvet, giving the effect of an ominous bleakness and void "out there" to which Nora would exit. There were no models of womanhood or femininity or motherhood for Nora at the end of the play.

Do you think that the play may come across as a melodrama?

In the reading of it, yes. I had always been daunted by Ibsen. In part I feared the inherent melodrama—you know, those coincidences that make one want to snicker aloud and roll one's eyes in disbelief as one reads the stage directions announcing a knock at the door and—gasp!—the entrance of the very person just whispered about and least expected. But much to my surprise, what was melodramatic on the page most often became simply dramatic on the stage. And the truth is that each of our lives, when reduced to a plot summary, sounds very melodramatic, doesn't it? Often in recounting important moments in our lives, don't we tell about unbelievable coincidences? So I embraced the artifice of those selected coincidences and constructed events and constricted time and concentrated on making the characters real people, which is where the actual power of the performance lies. Plays are artifices; people aren't.

Two questions: Is this a feminist piece? And, is it dated?

As a director, I have always been interested in the unresolved tensions at the end of a play: What remains in that final moment? Of equal theatrical importance are the two final events of the play: Nora's leaving and Torvald's remaining. Consider the final image in our production: Nora has exited and the door has slammed. But that's not the end of the play, not in my imagination, not in Ibsen's text. The final image belongs to Torvald. He is alone on stage as the sound of Nora's door slamming reverberates (and in our production he was on the floor in a totally empty room, weeping, distraught, bewildered, rocking himself in a prenatal position). It is the single most powerful image I know of in dramatic literature which suggests both the 1880's as well as the 1990's response of the majority of men vis-à-vis the feminist movement: silence and perhaps an unspoken "How could this have happened?" What was and remains both feminist and timely then is Nora's struggle to achieve the miracle of miracles, which has yet to be achieved in any culture, and Torvald's reaction to his wife's departure which has yet, sad to say, been fully processed and understood by many men and even by many women.

August Strindberg

MISS JULIE

August Strindberg (1849–1912) was born in Sweden two months after the marriage of his parents (who already had three children). After a desperately unhappy childhood and youth, he turned to playwrighting; King Charles XV of Sweden was impressed by one drama and granted Strindberg a small scholarship to the university. The king, however, soon died, and Strindberg found employment in the Royal Library, where he studied Chinese. In 1877, he married a divorced baroness, but the marriage was extremely stormy and they separated in 1891. During the period when he was married, however, he wrote his great naturalistic plays, all of which deal with sexual conflict: *The Father* (1887), *Miss Julie* (1888), and *The Creditors* (1889). (*Miss Julie* includes autobiographical elements—Strindberg's mother was a servant, yet he married a baroness.) In 1893 he married an Austrian woman and again separated, and lastly, after a period in a sanatorium, he married and separated for a third time. During and between marriages he worked fiercely at Chinese, dramaturgy, and, for a while, chemistry.

His early plays are mostly either historical (on Swedish history from the thirteenth to the eighteenth century) or realistic; his later ones, notably *The Dance of Death* (1901), wherein he tries to dramatize the conflict of the soul, are symbolic and expressionistic; that is, they present not life as we all see it but life as the artist passionately feels it to be. In all, he wrote some seventy plays, as well as several autobiographical novels.

COMMENTARY

Realism, as practiced by Ibsen, insists that the drama ought to be a close copy of life. People on the stage should sound pretty much like people off the stage, the scenery and the properties should look like the real thing—if the set is a kitchen, the pots and pans should not be obviously painted on the wall but should be real pots and pans—and the story dramatized should be one in which we ourselves might participate. But realism is not allied to any particular philosophy, and in this it is unlike naturalism.

Naturalism is an artistic movement characterized not merely by an attempt to imitate life and life's dialogue, but also by a basic assumption about the nature of existence. Heavily influenced by scientific—especially biological—research, the naturalists believed that human actions are less free than had generally been supposed, and are in fact the results of influences exerted by heredity and environment. In this view, genetics (our biological inheritance) and history (the shape of our society, and our assigned role in it) largely determine what we are and what we do. As early as the second quarter of the nineteenth century, for example, Balzac in his novels had examined human beings partly by examining their environment, working on the biological assumption that the creature's nature is partly determined by its surroundings. But, as Strindberg points out in his preface to *Miss Julie*, though naturalism has, by appealing to factors outside of man's control, abolished guilt, the consequences of man's actions nevertheless remain.

Naturalism, then, aims not merely at presenting a "slice of life," but, assuming that we are motivated by our biological inheritance and our milieu, it has a definite attitude as to what life is like. It thus dethrones reason, and for free will it substitutes biological drives (notably hunger and sex) and sometimes economic pressures. In 1881 Zola published a collection of essays, *Naturalism in the Theater,* demanding that the drama not only set aside old theatrical conventions such as unconvincing scenery but that it also take account of scientific research—meaning the influence of heredity and environment—and in 1887 Andre Antoine, founder of the Theatre Libre, a dramatic group dedicated to realism—illusionism in costume and setting—and to serious drama rather than to farce and melodrama, staged a dramatization of one of Zola's naturalistic stories. Because it emphasizes environment, naturalism tends to concentrate on what used to be called the lower classes, whose basic drives and economic pressures are most obviously manifested in actions. (Strindberg closely followed newspapers reports of Antoine's activities.) Zola, in his novel, *L'Assommoir* (The Tavern), for example, using the appropriate slang, describes the influence of a lazy drunkard (who ultimately dies in an asylum) on his mistress (who ultimately dies of starvation). But Zola, despite the protests he evoked, was basically moral; although he depicted the influence of environment, he nevertheless held his characters morally responsible for their actions. In early twentieth-century America, Theodore Dreiser's characters range, in a series of novels, from frightened young men to ruthless financiers, but Dreiser excuses their crimes and lies by assuming that, given their "chemistry" and their situation, they could do nothing else.

Because naturalism generally explores an environment, and in addition often traces actions back to one's ancestors, the novel, by virtue of its breadth, is more suited to its needs than is the drama. Strindberg, however, found its philosophy congenial to his own obviously irrational nature and sought to write plays for the naturalistic theater. He succeeded admirably, and Eugene O'Neill called him "the greatest interpreter in the theater of the characteristic spiritual conflicts which constitute the drama—the blood—of our lives today." *Miss Julie* (1888), written as Strindberg's contribution to the new drama promoted by Antoine, characterized by Strindberg in a letter to his publisher as "the Swedish drama's first naturalistic tragedy," is among the most important products of naturalism. It has had much success on the stage, and a Swedish motion picture version has recently brought *Miss Julie* to an even wider public than before. The germ of the play, Strindberg claimed, was a real story of which he had heard, though he admitted altering the ending. (Incidentally, if his account is accurate, by reworking the facts he violated one of the tenets of naturalism.)

Technically, the play (which lasts about an hour-and-a-half) has no intermission; Strindberg, in his concern with realism, did not want to destroy the dramatic illusion by a break, which would allow the spectators to be reminded that they are watching a play, not life itself. But we move from realism to naturalism in the tragic outcome of the conflict of wills, where Strindberg gives us a conflict equivalent to the Darwinian struggle for existence. The actions, Strindberg insists in his preface (see page 449), are not the outcome of this or that obvious motive but are the products of a number of forces, some almost invisible, uniting with a particular circumstance to produce deeds not rationally willed. Julie's motives, he says, are deliberately complex, for whereas (he claims) older drama falsely suggests that a character is motivated by one trait, such as pride, or love, or hate, Strindberg's figures have all the complexity of life itself. Jean, the count's valet, on Midsummer Eve (a night, when the sun does not set, devoted to festive dancing and celebration) seduces Julie, his master's daughter, and then drives her to suicide. Why does Julie yield? As a matter of fact, a reading of the play will show that this summary is misleading, for Jean is seduced by Julie as much as she is by him. Strindberg states that she is undone by many causes: her father's faulty care of her; his absence; the aphrodisiacal influence of flowers; the excitement of the dance; and chance, which happens to bring her into proximity with an excited, aggressive man.

Coupled with this picture of human beings as victims of heredity, environment, and chance is Strindberg's assumption that, in addition to the conflict between individuals and more especially between the male and the female, there is a larger battle, the class struggle. Thus, Julie and Jean represent not only the struggle between the sexes but also the clash between a decaying aristocracy and a rising working class. Strindberg himself reports in one of his autobiographies how delighted he was by the thought that he, the son of poor parents, had married—conquered—a daughter of the aristocracy, Baron Wrangel's wife. But whether the conflict is sexual or economic, behind the struggle of the individual looms Fate, now composed of heredity and environment, absolving human beings from moral responsibility. Furthermore, Strindberg assumes that the conflicts are irreconcilable; no compromise can be worked out in these struggles, which must be to the death. Drawing on his own unhappy marital experiences, he assumed that each individual is propelled by a desire to dominate, and though life is ghastly, we irrationally desire to prolong it. Why, then, does Julie commit suicide? Because, Strindberg explained in a letter to a friend, she is ashamed, depressed, under the influence of a will stronger than her own, and near a razor. Her tragedy, Strindberg implies, is pathetic as she struggles against a destiny that cannot be averted, and at last yields, semivoluntarily.

Jean (played by Peter Francis James) seduces—or is seduced by—Miss Julie (Kim Catrall), in a production at the McCarter Theatre, in Princeton, New Jersey. Like most productions of Miss Julie, this one used sets and costumes that evoked the period in which the play was written and set.

August Strindberg

MISS JULIE

Translated by Harry G. Carlson

Characters

MISS JULIE, 25 years old
JEAN, her father's valet, 30 years old
KRISTINE, her father's cook, 35 years old

(The action takes place in the Count's kitchen on midsummer eve.)

SETTING: (A large kitchen, the ceiling and side walls of which are hidden by draperies. The rear wall runs diagonally from down left to up right. On the wall down left are two shelves with copper, iron, and pewter utensils; the shelves are lined with scalloped paper. Visible to the right is most of a set of large, arched glass doors, through which can be seen a fountain with a statue of Cupid, lilac bushes in bloom, and the tops of some Lombardy poplars. At down left is the corner of a large tiled stove; a portion of its hood is showing. At right, one end of the servants' white pine dining table juts out; several chairs stand around it. The stove is decorated with birch branches; juniper twigs are strewn on the floor. On the end of the table stands a large Japanese spice jar, filled with lilac blossoms. An ice box, a sink, and a wash-stand. Above the door is an old-fashioned bell on a spring; to the left of the door, the mouthpiece of a speaking tube is visible.)

(Kristine is frying something on the stove. She is wearing a light-colored cotton dress and an apron. Jean enters. He is wearing livery and carries a pair of high riding boots with spurs, which he puts down on the floor where they can be seen by the audience.)

JEAN. Miss Julie's crazy again tonight; absolutely crazy!

KRISTINE. So you finally came back?

JEAN. I took the Count to the station and when I returned past the barn I stopped in for a dance. Who do I see but Miss Julie leading off the dance with the gamekeeper! But as soon as she saw me she rushed over to ask me for the next waltz. And she's been waltzing ever since—I've never seen anything like it. She's crazy!

KRISTINE. She always has been, but never as bad as the last two weeks since her engagement was broken off.

JEAN. Yes, I wonder what the real story was there. He was a gentleman, even if he wasn't rich. Ah! These people have such romantic ideas. (Sits at the end of the table.) Still, it's strange, isn't it? I mean that she'd rather stay home with the servants on midsummer eve instead of going with her father to visit relatives?

KRISTINE. She's probably embarrassed after that row with her fiancé.

JEAN. Probably! He gave a good account of himself, though. Do you know how it happened, Kristine? I saw it, you know, though I didn't let on I had.

KRISTINE. No! You saw it?

JEAN. Yes, I did.——That evening they were out near the stable, and she was "training" him—as she called it. Do you know what she did? She made him jump over her riding crop, the way you'd teach a dog to jump. He jumped twice and she hit him each time. But the third time he grabbed the crop out of her hand, hit her with it across the cheek, and broke it in pieces. Then he left.

KRISTINE. So, that's what happened! I can't believe it!

JEAN. Yes, that's the way it went!——What have you got for me that's tasty, Kristine?

KRISTINE (serving him from the pan). Oh, it's only a piece of kidney I cut from the veal roast.

JEAN (smelling the food). Beautiful! That's my favorite délice.[1] (Feeling the plate.) But you could have warmed the plate!

KRISTINE. You're fussier than the Count himself, once you start! (She pulls his hair affectionately.)

JEAN (angry). Stop it, leave my hair alone! You know I'm touchy about that.

KRISTINE. Now, now, it's only love, you know that. (Jean eats. Kristine opens a bottle of beer.)

JEAN. Beer? On midsummer eve? No thank you! I can do better than that. (Opens a drawer in the table and takes out a bottle of red wine with yellow sealing wax.) See that? Yellow seal! Give me a glass! A wine glass! I'm drinking this pur.[2]

KRISTINE (returns to the stove and puts on a small saucepan). God help the woman who gets you for a husband! What a fussbudget.

JEAN. Nonsense! You'd be damned lucky to get a man like me. It certainly hasn't done you any harm to have people call me your sweetheart. (Tastes the wine.) Good! Very good! Just needs a little warming. (Warms the glass between his hands.) We bought this in Dijon. Four francs a liter, not counting the cost of the bottle, or the customs duty.——What are you cooking now? It stinks like hell!

KRISTINE. Oh, some slop Miss Julie wants to give Diana.

JEAN. Watch your language, Kristine. But why should you have to cook for that damn mutt on midsummer eve? Is she sick?

KRISTINE. Yes, she's sick! She sneaked out with the gatekeeper's dog—and now there's hell to pay. Miss Julie won't have it!

JEAN. Miss Julie has too much pride about some things and not enough about others, just like her mother was. The Countess was most at home in the kitchen and the cowsheds, but a one-horse carriage wasn't elegant enough for her. The cuffs of her blouse were dirty, but she had to have her coat of arms on her cufflinks.——And Miss Julie won't take proper care of herself either. If you ask me, she just isn't refined. Just now, when she was dancing in the barn, she pulled the gamekeeper away from Anna and made him dance with her. We wouldn't behave like that, but that's what happens when aristocrats pretend they're common people—they get common!——But she is quite a woman! Magnificent! What shoulders, and what—et cetera!

KRISTINE. Oh, don't overdo it! I've heard what Clara says, and she dresses her.

JEAN. Ha, Clara! You're all jealous of each other! I've been out riding with her. . . . And the way she dances!

KRISTINE. Listen, Jean! You're going to dance with me, when I'm finished here, aren't you?

JEAN. Of course I will.

KRISTINE. Promise?

JEAN. Promise? When I say I'll do something, I do it! By the way, the kidney was very good. (Corks the bottle.)

JULIE (in the doorway to someone outside). I'll be right back! You go ahead for now! (Jean sneaks the bottle back into the table drawer and gets up respectfully. Miss Julie enters and crosses to Kristine by the stove.) Well? Is it ready? (Kristine indicates that Jean is present.)

JEAN (gallantly). Are you ladies up to something secret?

JULIE (flicking her handkerchief in his face). None of your business!

JEAN. Hmm! I like the smell of violets!

JULIE (coquettishly). Shame on you! So you know about perfumes, too? You certainly know how to dance. Ah, ah! No peeking! Go away.

JEAN (boldly but respectfully). Are you brewing up a magic potion for midsummer eve? Something to prophesy by

---

[1]délice delight [2]pur pure; without water

under a lucky star, so you'll catch a glimpse of your future husband!

JULIE (*caustically*). You'd need sharp eyes to see him! (*To Kristine.*) Pour out half a bottle and cork it well.——Come and dance a schottische[3] with me, Jean . . .

JEAN (*hesitating*). I don't want to be impolite to anyone, and I've already promised this dance to Kristine . . .

JULIE. Oh, she can have another one—can't you, Kristine? Won't you lend me Jean?

KRISTINE. It's not up to me, ma'am. (*To Jean.*) If the mistress is so generous, it wouldn't do for you to say no. Go on, Jean, and thank her for the honor.

JEAN. To be honest, and no offense intended, I wonder whether it's wise for you to dance twice running with the same partner, especially since these people are quick to jump to conclusions . . .

JULIE (*flaring up*). What's that? What sort of conclusions? What do you mean?

JEAN (*submissively*). If you don't understand, ma'am, I must speak more plainly. It doesn't look good to play favorites with your servants. . . .

JULIE. Play favorites! What an idea! I'm astonished! As mistress of the house, I honor your dance with my presence. And when I dance, I want to dance with someone who can lead, so I won't look ridiculous.

JEAN. As you order, ma'am! I'm at your service!

JULIE (*gently*). Don't take it as an order! On a night like this we're all just ordinary people having fun, so we'll forget about rank. Now, take my arm!——Don't worry, Kristine! I won't steal your sweetheart! (*Jean offers his arm and leads Miss Julie out.*)

MIME

(*The following should be played as if the actress playing Kristine were really alone. When she has to, she turns her back to the audience. She does not look toward them, nor does she hurry as if she were afraid they would grow impatient. Schottische music played on a fiddle sounds in the distance. Kristine hums along with the music. She clears the table, washes the dishes, dries them, and puts them away. She takes off her apron. From a table drawer she removes a small mirror and leans it against the bowl of lilacs on the table. She lights a candle, heats a hairpin over the flame, and uses it to set a curl on her forehead. She crosses to the door and listens, then returns to the table. She finds the handkerchief Miss Julie left behind, picks it up, and smells it. Then, preoccupied, she spreads it out, stretches it, smoothes out the wrinkles, and folds it into quarters, and so forth.*)

JEAN (*enters alone*). God, she really *is* crazy! What a way to dance! Everybody's laughing at her behind her back. What do you make of it, Kristine?

KRISTINE. Ah! It's that time of the month for her, and she always gets peculiar like that. Are you going to dance with me now?

JEAN. You're not mad at me, are you, for leaving . . . ?

KRISTINE. Of course not!——Why should I be, for a little thing like that? Besides, I know my place . . .

JEAN (*puts his arm around her waist*). You're a sensible girl, Kristine, and you'd make a good wife . . .

JULIE (*entering; uncomfortably surprised; with forced good humor*). What a charming escort—running away from his partner.

JEAN. On the contrary, Miss Julie. Don't you see how I rushed back to the partner I abandoned!

JULIE (*changing her tone*). You know, you're a superb dancer!——But why are you wearing livery on a holiday? Take it off at once!

JEAN. Then I must ask you to go outside for a moment. You see, my black coat is hanging over here . . . (*Gestures and crosses right.*)

JULIE. Are you embarrassed about changing your coat in front of me? Well, go in your room then. Either that or stay and I'll turn my back.

JEAN. With your permission, ma'am! (*He crosses right. His arm is visible as he changes his jacket.*)

JULIE (*to Kristine*). Tell me, Kristine—you two are so close—. Is Jean your fiancé?

KRISTINE. Fiancé? Yes, if you wish. We can call him that.

JULIE. What do you mean?

KRISTINE. You had a fiancé yourself, didn't you? So . . .

JULIE. Well, we were properly engaged . . .

KRISTINE. But nothing came of it, did it? (*Jean returns dressed in a frock coat and bowler hat.*)

JULIE. *Très gentil, monsieur Jean! Très gentil!*

JEAN. *Vous voulez plaisanter, madame!*

JULIE. *Et vous voulez parler français!*[4] Where did you learn that?

JEAN. In Switzerland, when I was wine steward in one of the biggest hotels in Lucerne!

JULIE. You look like a real gentleman in that coat! *Charmant!*[5] (*Sits at the table.*)

JEAN. Oh, you're flattering me!

JULIE (*offended*). Flattering you?

JEAN. My natural modesty forbids me to believe that you would really compliment someone like me, and so I took the liberty of assuming that you were exaggerating, which polite people call flattering.

---

[3]**schottische** a Scottish round dance

[4]**Très gentil . . . français!** Very nice, Mr. Jean. You are joking, madam! And you want to speak French!   [5]**Charmant** charming

JULIE. Where did you learn to talk like that? You must have been to the theater often.

JEAN. Of course. And I've done a lot of traveling.

JULIE. But you come from here, don't you?

JEAN. My father was a farmhand on the district attorney's estate nearby. I used to see you when you were little, but you never noticed me.

JULIE. No! Really?

JEAN. Sure. I remember one time especially . . . but I can't talk about that.

JULIE. Oh, come now! Why not? Just this once!

JEAN. No, I really couldn't, not now. Some other time, perhaps.

JULIE. Why some other time? What's so dangerous about now?

JEAN. It's not dangerous, but there are obstacles.——Her, for example. (*Indicating Kristine, who has fallen asleep in a chair by the stove.*)

JULIE. What a pleasant wife she'll make! She probably snores, too.

JEAN. No, she doesn't, but she talks in her sleep.

JULIE (*cynically*). How do *you* know?

JEAN (*audaciously*). I've heard her! (*Pause, during which they stare at each other.*)

JULIE. Why don't you sit down?

JEAN. I couldn't do that in your presence.

JULIE. But if I order you to?

JEAN. Then I'd obey.

JULIE. Sit down, then.——No, wait. Can you get me something to drink first?

JEAN. I don't know what we have in the ice box. I think there's only beer.

JULIE. Why do you say "only"? My tastes are so simple I prefer beer to wine. (*Jean takes a bottle of beer from the ice box and opens it. He looks for a glass and a plate in the cupboard and serves her.*)

JEAN. Here you are, ma'am.

JULIE. Thank you. Won't you have something yourself?

JEAN. I'm not partial to beer, but if it's an order . . .

JULIE. An order?——Surely a gentleman can keep his lady company.

JEAN. You're right, of course. (*Opens a bottle and gets a glass.*)

JULIE. Now, drink to my health! (*He hesitates.*) What? A man of the world—and shy?

JEAN (*in mock romantic fashion, he kneels and raises his glass*). Skål to my mistress!

JULIE. Bravo!——Now kiss my shoe, to finish it properly. (*Jean hesitates, then boldly seizes her foot and kisses it lightly.*) Perfect! You should have been an actor.

JEAN (*rising*). That's enough now, Miss Julie! Someone might come in and see us.

JULIE. What of it?

JEAN. People talk, that's what! If you knew how their tongues were wagging just now at the dance, you'd . . .

JULIE. What were they saying? Tell me!——Sit down!

JEAN (*sits*). I don't want to hurt you, but they were saying things——suggestive things, that, that . . . well, you can figure it out for yourself! You're not a child. If a woman is seen drinking alone with a man—let alone a servant—at night—then . . .

JULIE. Then what? Besides, we're not alone. Kristine is here.

JEAN. Asleep!

JULIE. Then I'll wake her up. (*Rising.*) Kristine! Are you asleep? (*Kristine mumbles in her sleep.*)

JULIE. Kristine!——She certainly can sleep!

KRISTINE (*in her sleep*). The Count's boots are brushed—put the coffee on—right away, right away—uh, huh—oh!

JULIE (*grabbing Kristine's nose*). Will you wake up!

JEAN (*severely*). Leave her alone—let her sleep!

JULIE (*sharply*). What?

JEAN. Someone who's been standing over a stove all day has a right to be tired by now. Sleep should be respected . . .

JULIE (*changing her tone*). What a considerate thought—it does you credit—thank you! (*Offering her hand.*) Come outside and pick some lilacs for me! (*During the following, Kristine awakens and shambles sleepily off right to bed.*)

JEAN. Go with you?

JULIE. With me!

JEAN. We couldn't do that! Absolutely not!

JULIE. I don't understand. Surely you don't imagine . . .

JEAN. No, I don't, but the others might.

JULIE. What? That I've fallen in love with a servant?

JEAN. I'm not a conceited man, but such things happen— and for these people, nothing is sacred.

JULIE. I do believe you're an aristocrat!

JEAN. Yes, I am.

JULIE. And I'm stepping down . . .

JEAN. Don't step down, Miss Julie, take my advice. No one'll believe you stepped down voluntarily. People will always say you fell.

JULIE. I have a higher opinion of people than you. Come and see!——Come! (*She stares at him broodingly.*)

JEAN. You're very strange, do you know that?

JULIE. Perhaps! But so are you!——For that matter, everything is strange. Life, people, everything. Like floating scum, drifting on and on across the water, until it sinks down and down! That reminds me of a dream I have now and then. I've climbed up on top of a pillar. I sit there and see no way of getting down. I get dizzy when I look down, and I must get down, but I don't have the courage to jump. I can't hold on firmly, and I long to be able to fall, but I don't fall. And yet I'll have no peace until I get down, no rest unless I get down, down on the ground! And if I did get down to the ground, I'd want to be under the earth . . . Have you ever felt anything like that?

JEAN. No. I dream that I'm lying under a high tree in a dark forest. I want to get up, up on top, and look out over the bright landscape, where the sun is shining, and plunder the bird's nest up there, where the golden eggs lie. And I climb and climb, but the trunk's so thick and smooth, and it's so far to the first branch. But I know if I just reached that first branch, I'd go right to the top, like up a ladder. I haven't reached it yet, but I will, even if it's only in a dream!

JULIE. Here I am chattering with you about dreams. Come, let's go out! Just into the park! (*She offers him her arm, and they start to leave.*)

JEAN. We'll have to sleep on nine midsummer flowers, Miss Julie, to make our dreams come true! (*They turn at the door. Jean puts his hand to his eye.*)

JULIE. Did you get something in your eye?

JEAN. It's nothing—just a speck—it'll be gone in a minute.

JULIE. My sleeve must have brushed against you. Sit down and let me help you. (*She takes him by the arm and seats him. She tilts his head back and with the tip of a handkerchief tries to remove the speck.*) Sit still, absolutely still! (*She slaps his hand.*) Didn't you hear me?——Why, you're trembling; the big, strong man is trembling! (*Feels his biceps.*) What muscles you have!

JEAN (*warning*). Miss Julie!

JULIE. Yes, *monsieur* Jean.

JEAN. *Attention! Je ne suis qu'un homme!*[6]

JULIE. Will you sit still!——There! Now it's gone! Kiss my hand and thank me.

JEAN (*rising*). Miss Julie, listen to me!——Kristine has gone to bed!——Will you listen to me!

JULIE. Kiss my hand first!

JEAN. Listen to me!

JULIE. Kiss my hand first!

JEAN. All right, but you've only yourself to blame!

JULIE. For what?

JEAN. For what? Are you still a child at twenty-five? Don't you know that it's dangerous to play with fire?

JULIE. Not for me. I'm insured.

JEAN (*boldly*). No, you're not! But even if you were, there's combustible material close by.

JULIE. Meaning you?

JEAN. Yes! Not because it's me, but because I'm young——

JULIE. And handsome—what incredible conceit! A Don Juan perhaps! Or a Joseph![7] Yes, that's it, I do believe you're a Joseph!

JEAN. Do you?

JULIE. I'm almost afraid so. (*Jean boldly tries to put his arm around her waist and kiss her. She slaps his face.*) How dare you?

JEAN. Are you serious or joking?

JULIE. Serious.

JEAN. Then so was what just happened. You play games too seriously, and that's dangerous. Well, I'm tired of games.

You'll excuse me if I get back to work. I haven't done the Count's boots yet and it's long past midnight.

JULIE. Put the boots down!

JEAN. No! It's the work I have to do. I never agreed to be your playmate, and never will. It's beneath me.

JULIE. You're proud.

JEAN. In certain ways, but not in others.

JULIE. Have you ever been in love?

JEAN. We don't use that word, but I've been fond of many girls, and once I was sick because I couldn't have the one I wanted. That's right, sick, like those princes in the Arabian Nights—who couldn't eat or drink because of love.

JULIE. Who was she? (*Jean is silent.*) Who was she?

JEAN. You can't force me to tell you that.

JULIE. But if I ask you as an equal, as a—friend! Who was she?

JEAN. You!

JULIE (*sits*). How amusing . . .

JEAN. Yes, if you like! It was ridiculous!——You see, that was the story I didn't want to tell you earlier. Maybe I will now. Do you know how the world looks from down below?——Of course you don't. Neither do hawks and falcons, whose backs we can't see because they're usually soaring up there above us. I grew up in a shack with seven brothers and sisters and a pig, in the middle of a wasteland, where there wasn't a single tree. But from our window I could see the tops of apple trees above the wall of your father's garden. That was the Garden of Eden, guarded by angry angels with flaming swords. All the same, the other boys and I managed to find our way to the Tree of Life.——Now you think I'm contemptible, I suppose.

JULIE. Oh, all boys steal apples.

JEAN. You say that, but you think I'm contemptible anyway. Oh well! One day I went into the Garden of Eden with my mother, to weed the onion beds. Near the vegetable garden was a small Turkish pavilion in the shadow of jasmine bushes and overgrown with honeysuckle. I had no idea what it was used for, but I'd never seen such a beautiful building. People went in and came out again, and one day the door was left open. I sneaked close and saw walls covered with pictures of kings and emperors, and red curtains with fringes at the windows—now you know the place I mean. I——(*Breaks off a sprig of lilac and holds it in front of Miss Julie's nose.*)——I'd never been inside the manor house, never seen anything except the church—but this was more beautiful. From then on, no matter where my thoughts wandered, they returned—there. And gradually I got a longing to experience, just once, the full pleasure of—*enfin*,[8] I sneaked in, saw, and marveled! But then I heard someone coming! There was only one exit for ladies and gentlemen, but for me there was

[6]**Attention!...homme!** Watch out! I am only a man! [7]**Don Juan...Joseph:** Don Juan is a seducer of women; in the Hebrew Bible (Genesis 39.6–20) Joseph resists the advances of Potiphar's wife

[8]**enfin** finally

another, and I had no choice but to take it! (*Miss Julie, who has taken the lilac sprig, lets it fall on the table.*) Afterwards, I started running. I crashed through a raspberry bush, flew over a strawberry patch, and came up onto the rose terrace. There I caught sight of a pink dress and a pair of white stockings—it was you. I crawled under a pile of weeds, and I mean under—under thistles that pricked me and wet dirt that stank. And I looked at you as you walked among the roses, and I thought: If it's true that a thief can enter heaven and be with the angels, then why can't a farmhand's son here on God's earth enter the manor house garden and play with the Count's daughter?

JULIE (*romantically*). Do you think all poor children would have thought the way you did?

JEAN (*at first hesitant, then with conviction*). If *all* poor—yes—of course. Of course!

JULIE. It must be terrible to be poor!

JEAN (*with exaggerated suffering*). Oh, Miss Julie! Oh!——A dog can lie on the Countess's sofa, a horse can have his nose patted by a young lady's hand, but a servant—— (*Changing his tone.*)——oh, I know—now and then you find one with enough stuff in him to get ahead in the world, but how often?—Anyhow, do you know what I did then?—I jumped in the millstream with my clothes on, was pulled out, and got a beating. But the following Sunday, when my father and all the others went to my grandmother's, I arranged to stay home. I scrubbed myself with soap and water, put on my best clothes, and went to church so that I could see you! I saw you and returned home, determined to die. But I wanted to die beautifully and pleasantly, without pain. And then I remembered that it was dangerous to sleep under an elder bush. We had a big one, and it was in full flower. I plundered its treasures and bedded down under them in the oat bin. Have you ever noticed how smooth oats are?—and soft to the touch, like human skin . . . ! Well, I shut the lid and closed my eyes. I fell asleep and woke up feeling very sick. But I didn't die, as you can see. What was I after?——I don't know. There was no hope of winning you, of course.——You were a symbol of the hopelessness of ever rising out of the class in which I was born.

JULIE. You're a charming storyteller. Did you ever go to school?

JEAN. A bit, but I've read lots of novels and been to the theater often. And then I've listened to people like you talk—that's where I learned most.

JULIE. Do you listen to what we say?

JEAN. Naturally! And I've heard plenty, too, driving the carriage or rowing the boat. Once I heard you and a friend . . .

JULIE. Oh?——What did you hear?

JEAN. I'd better not say. But I was surprised a little. I couldn't imagine where you learned such words. Maybe at bottom there isn't such a great difference between people as we think.

JULIE. Shame on you! We don't act like you when we're engaged.

JEAN (*staring at her*). Is that true?——You don't have to play innocent with me, Miss . . .

JULIE. The man I gave my love to was a swine.

JEAN. That's what you all say—afterwards.

JULIE. All?

JEAN. I think so. I know I've heard that phrase before, on similar occasions.

JULIE. What occasions?

JEAN. Like the one I'm talking about. The last time . . .

JULIE (*rising*). Quiet! I don't want to hear any more!

JEAN. That's interesting—that's what *she* said, too. Well, if you'll excuse me, I'm going to bed.

JULIE (*gently*). To bed? On midsummer eve?

JEAN. Yes! Dancing with the rabble out there doesn't amuse me much.

JULIE. Get the key to the boat and row me out on the lake. I want to see the sun come up.

JEAN. Is that wise?

JULIE. Are you worried about your reputation?

JEAN. Why not? Why should I risk looking ridiculous and getting fired without a reference, just when I'm trying to establish myself. Besides, I think I owe something to Kristine.

JULIE. So, now it's Kristine . . .

JEAN. Yes, but you, too.——Take my advice, go up and go to bed!

JULIE. Am I to obey you?

JEAN. Just this once—for your own good! Please! It's very late. Drowsiness makes people giddy and liable to lose their heads! Go to bed! Besides—unless I'm mistaken—I hear the others coming to look for me. And if they find us together, you'll be lost!

(*The Chorus approaches, singing.*)

The swineherd found his true love
a pretty girl so fair,
The swineherd found his true love
but let the girl beware.

For then he saw the princess
the princess on the golden hill,
but then saw the princess,
so much fairer still.

So the swineherd and the princess
they danced the whole night through,
and he forgot his first love,
to her he was untrue.

And when the long night ended,
and in the light of day, of day,
the dancing too was ended,
and the princess could not stay.

Then the swineherd lost his true love,
and the princess grieves him still,
and never more she'll wander
from atop the golden hill.

JULIE. I know all these people and I love them, just as they love me. Let them come in and you'll see.

JULIE (listening). What are they singing?

JEAN. It's a dirty song! About you and me!

JULIE. Disgusting! Oh! How deceitful!——

JEAN. The rabble is always cowardly! And in a battle like this, you don't fight; you can only run away!

JULIE. Run away? But where? We can't go out—or into Kristine's room.

JEAN. True. But there's my room. Necessity knows no rules. Besides, you can trust me. I'm your friend and I respect you.

JULIE. But suppose—suppose they look for you in there?

JEAN. I'll bolt the door, and if anyone tries to break in, I'll shoot!——Come! (On his knees.) Come!

JULIE (urgently). Promise me . . . ?

JEAN. I swear! (Miss Julie runs off right. Jean hastens after her.)

BALLET

(Led by a fiddler, the servants and farm people enter, dressed festively, with flowers in their hats. On the table they place a small barrel of beer and a keg of schnapps, both garlanded. Glasses are brought out, and the drinking starts. A dance circle is formed and "The Swineherd and the Princess" is sung. When the dance is finished, everyone leaves, singing.)

(Miss Julie enters alone. She notices the mess in the kitchen, wrings her hands, then takes out her powder puff and powders her nose.)

JEAN (enters, agitated). There, you see? And you heard them. We can't possibly stay here now, you know that.

JULIE. Yes, I know. But what can we do?

JEAN. Leave, travel, far away from here.

JULIE. Travel? Yes, but where?

JEAN. To Switzerland, to the Italian lakes. Have you ever been there?

JULIE. No. Is it beautiful?

JEAN. Oh, an eternal summer—oranges growing everywhere, laurel trees, always green . . .

JULIE. But what'll we do there?

JEAN. I'll open a hotel—with first-class service for first-class people.

JULIE. Hotel?

JEAN. That's the life, you know. Always new faces, new languages. No time to worry or be nervous. No hunting for something to do—there's always work to be done: bells ringing night and day, train whistles blowing, carriages coming and going, and all the while gold rolling into the till! That's the life!

JULIE. Yes, it sounds wonderful. But what'll I do?

JEAN. You'll be mistress of the house: the jewel in our crown! With your looks . . . and your manner—oh—success is guaranteed! It'll be wonderful! You'll sit in your office like a queen and push an electric button to set your slaves in motion. The guests will file past your throne and timidly lay their treasures before you.——You have no idea how people tremble when they get their bill.——I'll salt the bills and you'll sweeten them with your prettiest smile.——Let's get away from here——(Takes a timetable out of his pocket.)——Right away, on the next train!—— We'll be in Malmö six-thirty tomorrow morning, Hamburg at eight-forty; from Frankfort to Basel will take a day, then on to Como by way of the St. Gotthard Tunnel, in, let's see, three days. Three days!

JULIE. That's all very well! But Jean—you must give me courage!——Tell me you love me! Put your arms around me!

JEAN (hesitating). I want to—but I don't dare. Not in this house, not again. I love you—never doubt that—you don't doubt it, do you, Miss Julie?

JULIE (shy; very feminine). "Miss!"——Call me Julie! There are no barriers between us anymore. Call me Julie!

JEAN (tormented). I can't! There'll always be barriers between us as long as we stay in this house.——There's the past and there's the Count. I've never met anyone I had such respect for.——When I see his gloves lying on a chair, I feel small.——When I hear that bell up there ring, I jump like a skittish horse.——And when I look at his boots standing there so stiff and proud, I feel like bowing! (Kicking the boots.) Superstitions and prejudices we learned as children—but they can easily be forgotten. If I can just get to another country, a republic, people will bow and scrape when they see my livery—they'll bow and scrape, you hear, not me! I wasn't born to cringe. I've got stuff in me, I've got character, and if I can only grab onto that first branch, you watch me climb! I'm a servant today, but next year I'll own my own hotel. In ten years I'll have enough to retire. Then I'll go to Rumania and be decorated. I could—mind you I said could—end up a count!

JULIE. Wonderful, wonderful!

JEAN. Ah, in Rumania you just buy your title, and so you'll be a countess after all. My countess!

JULIE. But I don't care about that—that's what I'm putting behind me! Show me you love me, otherwise—otherwise, what am I?

JEAN. I'll show you a thousand times—afterwards! Not here! And whatever you do, no emotional outbursts, or we'll both be lost! We must think this through coolly, like sensible people. (He takes out a cigar, snips the end, and lights *it.*) You sit there, and I'll sit here. We'll talk as if nothing happened.

JULIE (*desperately*). Oh, my God! Have you no feelings?

JEAN. Me? No one has more feelings than I do, but I know how to control them.

JULIE. A little while ago you could kiss my shoe—and now!

JEAN (*harshly*). Yes, but that was before. Now we have other things to think about.

JULIE. Don't speak harshly to me!

JEAN. I'm not—just sensibly! We've already done one foolish thing, let's not have any more. The Count could return any minute, and by then we've got to decide what to do with our lives. What do you think of my plans for the future? Do you approve?

JULIE. They sound reasonable enough. I have only one question: For such a big undertaking you need capital—do you have it?

JEAN (*chewing on the cigar*). Me? Certainly! I have my professional expertise, my wide experience, and my knowledge of languages. That's capital enough, I should think!

JULIE. But all that won't even buy a train ticket.

JEAN. That's true. That's why I'm looking for a partner to advance me the money.

JULIE. Where will you find one quickly enough?

JEAN. That's up to you, if you want to come with me.

JULIE. But I can't; I have no money of my own. (*Pause.*)

JEAN. Then it's all off . . .

JULIE. And . . .

JEAN. Things stay as they are.

JULIE. Do you think I'm going to stay in this house as your lover? With all the servants pointing their fingers at me? Do you imagine I can face my father after this? No! Take me away from here, away from shame and dishonor——Oh, what have I done! My God, my God! (*She cries.*)

JEAN. Now, don't start that old song!——What have you done? The same as many others before you.

JULIE (*screaming convulsively*). And now you think I'm contemptible!——I'm falling, I'm falling!

JEAN. Fall down to my level and I'll lift you up again.

JULIE. What terrible power drew me to you? The attraction of the weak to the strong? The falling to the rising? Or was it love? Was this love? Do you know what love is?

JEAN. Me? What do you take me for? You don't think this was my first time, do you?

JULIE. The things you say, the thoughts you think!

JEAN. That's the way I was taught, and that's the way I am! Now don't get excited and don't play the grand lady, because we're in the same boat now!——Come on, Julie, I'll pour you a glass of something special! (*He opens a drawer in the table, takes out a wine bottle, and fills two glasses already used.*)

JULIE. Where did you get that wine?

JEAN. From the cellar.

JULIE. My father's burgundy!

JEAN. That'll do for his son-in-law, won't it?

JULIE. And I drink beer! Beer!

JEAN. That only shows I have better taste.

JULIE. Thief!

JEAN. Planning to tell?

JULIE. Oh, oh! Accomplice of a common thief! Was I drunk? Have I been walking in a dream the whole evening? Midsummer eve! A time of innocent fun!

JEAN. Innocent, eh?

JULIE (*pacing back and forth*). Is there anyone on earth more miserable than I am at this moment?

JEAN. Why should you be? After such a conquest? Think of Kristine in there. Don't you think she has feelings, too?

JULIE. I thought so awhile ago, but not any more. No, a servant is a servant . . .

JEAN. And a whore is a whore!

JULIE (*on her knees, her hands clasped*). Oh, God in heaven, end my wretched life! Take me away from the filth I'm sinking into! Save me! Save me!

JEAN. I can't deny I feel sorry for you. When I lay in that onion bed and saw you in the rose garden, well . . . I'll be frank . . . I had the same dirty thoughts all boys have.

JULIE. And you wanted to die for me!

JEAN. In the oat bin? That was just talk.

JULIE. A lie, in other words!

JEAN (*beginning to feel sleepy*). More or less! I got the idea from a newspaper story about a chimney sweep who curled up in a firewood bin full of lilacs because he got a summons for not supporting his illegitimate child . . .

JULIE. So, that's what you're like . . .

JEAN. I had to think of something. And that's the kind of story women always go for.

JULIE. Swine!

JEAN. *Merde!*

JULIE. And now you've seen the hawk's back . . .

JEAN. Not exactly its *back* . . .

JULIE. And I was to be the first branch . . .

JEAN. But the branch was rotten . . .

JULIE. I was to be the sign on the hotel . . .

JEAN. And I the hotel . . .

JULIE. Sit at your desk, entice your customers, pad their bills . . .

JEAN. That I'd do myself . . .

JULIE. How can anyone be so thoroughly filthy?

JEAN. Better clean up then!

JULIE. You lackey, you menial, stand up, when I speak to you!

JEAN. Menial's strumpet, lackey's whore, shut up and get out of here! Who are you to lecture me on coarseness? None of my kind is ever as coarse as you were tonight. Do you think one of your maids would throw herself at a man the way you did? Have you ever seen any girl of my class offer herself like that? I've only seen it among animals and streetwalkers.

JULIE (*crushed*). You're right. Hit me, trample on me. I don't deserve any better. I'm worthless. But help me! If you see any way out of this, help me, Jean, please!

JEAN (*more gently*). I'd be lying if I didn't admit to a sense of triumph in all this, but do you think that a person like me would have dared even to look at someone like you if you hadn't invited it? I'm still amazed . . .

JULIE. And proud . . .

JEAN. Why not? Though I must say it was too easy to be really exciting.

JULIE. Go on, hit me, hit me harder!

JEAN (*rising*). No! Forgive me for what I've said! I don't hit a man when he's down, let alone a woman. I can't deny though, that I'm pleased to find out that what looked so dazzling to us from below was only tinsel, that the hawk's back was only gray, after all, that the lovely complexion was only powder, that those polished fingernails had black edges, and that a dirty handkerchief is still dirty, even if it smells of perfume . . . ! On the other hand, it hurts me to find out that what I was striving for wasn't finer, more substantial. It hurts me to see you sunk so low that you're inferior to your own cook. It hurts like watching flowers beaten down by autumn rains and turned into mud.

JULIE. You talk as if you were already above me.

JEAN. I am. You see, I could make you a countess, but you could never make me a count.

JULIE. But I'm the child of a count—something you could never be!

JEAN. That's true. But I could be the father of counts—if . . .

JULIE. But you're a thief. I'm not.

JEAN. There are worse things than being a thief! Besides, when I'm working in a house, I consider myself sort of a member of the family, like one of the children. And you don't call it stealing when a child snatches a berry off a full bush. (*His passion is aroused again.*) Miss Julie, you're a glorious woman, much too good for someone like me! You were drinking and you lost your head. Now you want to cover up your mistake by telling yourself that you love me! You don't. Maybe there was a physical attraction—but then your love is no better than mine.——I could never be satisfied to be no more than an animal to you, and I could never arouse real love in you.

JULIE. Are you sure of that?

JEAN. You're suggesting it's possible——Oh, I could fall in love with you, no doubt about it. You're beautiful, you're refined——(*approaching and taking her hand*)——cultured, lovable when you want to be, and once you start a fire in a man, it never goes out. (*Putting his arm around her waist.*) You're like hot, spicy wine, and one kiss from you . . . (*He tries to lead her out, but she slowly frees herself.*)

JULIE. Let me go!?——You'll never win me like that.

JEAN. *How* then?——Not like that? Not with caresses and pretty speeches. Not with plans about the future or rescue from disgrace! *How* then?

JULIE. How? How? I don't know!——I have no idea!——I detest you as I detest rats, but I can't escape from you.

JEAN. Escape with me!

JULIE (*pulling herself together*). Escape? Yes, we must escape!——But I'm so tired. Give me a glass of wine? (*Jean pours the wine. She looks at her watch.*) But we must talk first. We still have a little time. (*She drains the glass, then holds it out for more.*)

JEAN. Don't drink so fast. It'll go to your head.

JULIE. What does it matter?

JEAN. What does it matter? It's vulgar to get drunk! What did you want to tell me?

JULIE. We must escape! But first we must talk, I mean I must talk. You've done all the talking up to now. You told about your life, now I want to tell about mine, so we'll know all about each other before we go off together.

JEAN. Just a minute! Forgive me! If you don't want to regret it afterwards, you'd better think twice before revealing any secrets about yourself.

JULIE. Aren't you my friend?

JEAN. Yes, sometimes! But don't rely on me.

JULIE. You're only saying that.——Besides, everyone already knows my secrets.——You see, my mother was a commoner—very humble background. She was brought up believing in social equality, women's rights, and all that. The idea of marriage repelled her. So, when my father proposed, she replied that she would never become his wife, but he could be her lover. He insisted that he didn't want the woman he loved to be less respected than he. But his passion ruled him, and when she explained that the world's respect meant nothing to her, he accepted her conditions. But now his friends avoided him and his life was restricted to taking care of the estate, which couldn't satisfy him. I came into the world—against my mother's wishes, as far as I can understand. She wanted to bring me up as a child of nature, and, what's more, to learn everything a boy had to learn, so that I might be an example of how a woman can be as good as a man. I had to wear boy's clothes and learn to take care of horses, but I was never allowed in the cowshed. I had to groom and harness the horses and go hunting—and even had to watch them slaughter animals—that was disgusting! On the estate men were put on women's jobs and women on men's jobs—with the result that the property became run down and we became the laughingstock of the district. Finally, my father must have awakened from his trance because he rebelled and changed everything his way. My parents were then married quietly. Mother became ill—I don't know what illness it was—but she often had convulsions, hid in the attic and in the garden, and sometimes stayed out all night. Then came the great fire, which you've heard about. The house, the stables, and the cowshed all burned down, under very curious circumstances, suggesting arson, because the accident happened the day after the insurance had expired. The quarterly premium my father sent in was delayed because of a messenger's carelessness and didn't arrive in time. (*She fills her glass and drinks.*)

JEAN. Don't drink any more!

JULIE. Oh, what does it matter.——We were left penniless and had to sleep in the carriages. My father had no idea where to find money to rebuild the house because he had so slighted his old friends that they had forgotten him. Then my mother suggested that he borrow from a childhood friend of hers, a brick manufacturer who lived nearby. Father got the loan without having to pay interest, which surprised him. And that's how the estate was rebuilt.—— (*Drinks again.*) Do you know who started the fire?

JEAN. The Countess, your mother.

JULIE. Do you know who the brick manufacturer was?

JEAN. Your mother's lover?

JULIE. Do you know whose money it was?

JEAN. Wait a moment—no, I don't.

JULIE. It was my mother's.

JEAN. You mean the Count's, unless they didn't sign an agreement when they were married.

JULIE. They didn't.——My mother had a small inheritance which she didn't want under my father's control, so she entrusted it to her—friend.

JEAN. Who stole it!

JULIE. Exactly! He kept it.——All this my father found out, but he couldn't bring it to court, couldn't repay his wife's lover, couldn't prove it was his wife's money! It was my mother's revenge for being forced into marriage against her will. It nearly drove him to suicide—there was a rumor that he tried with a pistol, but failed. So, he managed to live through it and my mother had to suffer for what she'd done. You can imagine that those were a terrible five years for me. I loved my father, but I sided with my mother because I didn't know the circumstances. I learned from her to hate men—you've heard how she hated the whole male sex—and I swore to her I'd never be a slave to any man.

JEAN. But you got engaged to that lawyer.

JULIE. In order to make him my slave.

JEAN. And he wasn't willing?

JULIE. He was willing, all right, but I wouldn't let him. I got tired of him.

JEAN. I saw it—out near the stable.

JULIE. What did you see?

JEAN. I saw—how he broke off the engagement.

JULIE. That's a lie! I was the one who broke it off. Has he said that he did? That swine . . .

JEAN. He was no swine, I'm sure. So, you hate men, Miss Julie?

JULIE. Yes!——Most of the time! But sometimes—when the weakness comes, when passion burns! Oh, God, will the fire never die out?

JEAN. Do you hate me, too?

JULIE. Immeasurably! I'd like to have you put to death, like an animal . . .

JEAN. I see—the penalty for bestiality—the woman gets two years at hard labor and the animal is put to death. Right?

JULIE. Exactly!

JEAN. But there's no prosecutor here—and no animal. So, what'll we do?

JULIE. Go away!

JEAN. To torment each other to death?

JULIE. No! To be happy for—two days, a week, as long as we can be happy, and then—die . . .

JEAN. Die? That's stupid! It's better to open a hotel!

JULIE (*without listening*). ——on the shore of Lake Como, where the sun always shines, where the laurels are green at Christmas and the oranges glow.

JEAN. Lake Como is a rainy hole, and I never saw any oranges outside the stores. But tourists are attracted there because there are plenty of villas to be rented out to lovers, and that's a profitable business.——Do you know why? Because they sign a lease for six months—and then leave after three weeks!

JULIE (*naively*). Why after three weeks?

JEAN. They quarrel, of course! But they still have to pay the rent in full! And so you rent the villas out again. And that's the way it goes, time after time. There's never a shortage of love—even if it doesn't last long!

JULIE. You don't want to die with me?

JEAN. I don't want to die at all! For one thing, I like living, and for another, I think suicide is a crime against the Providence which gave us life.

JULIE. You believe in God? *You?*

JEAN. Of course I do. And I go to church every other Sunday.——To be honest, I'm tired of all this, and I'm going to bed.

JULIE. Are you? And do you think I can let it go at that? A man owes something to the woman he's shamed.

JEAN (*taking out his purse and throwing a silver coin on the table*). Here! I don't like owing anything to anybody.

JULIE (*pretending not to notice the insult*). Do you know what the law states . . .

JEAN. Unfortunately the law doesn't state any punishment for the woman who seduces a man!

JULIE (*as before*). Do you see any way out but to leave, get married, and then separate?

JEAN. Suppose I refuse such a *mésalliance?*[9]

---

[9]**mésalliance** mismatch

JULIE. *Mésalliance . . .*

JEAN. Yes, for me! You see, I come from better stock than you. There's no arsonist in my family.

JULIE. How do you know?

JEAN. You can't prove otherwise. We don't keep charts on our ancestors—there's just the police records! But I've read about your family. Do you know who the founder was? He was a miller who let the king sleep with his wife one night during the Danish War. I don't have any noble ancestors like that. I don't have any noble ancestors at all, but I could become one myself.

JULIE. This is what I get for opening my heart to someone unworthy, for giving my family's honor . . .

JEAN. Dishonor!——Well, I told you so: When people drink, they talk, and talk is dangerous!

JULIE. Oh, how I regret it!——How I regret it!——If you at least loved me.

JEAN. For the last time—what do you want? Shall I cry; shall I jump over your riding crop? Shall I kiss you and lure you off to Lake Como for three weeks, and then God knows what . . . ? What shall I do? What do you want? This is getting painfully embarrassing! But that's what happens when you stick your nose in women's business. Miss Julie! I see that you're unhappy. I know you're suffering, but I can't understand you. We don't have such romantic ideas; there's not this kind of hate between us. Love is a game we play when we get time off from work, but we don't have all day and night, like you. I think you're sick, really sick. Your mother was crazy, and her ideas have poisoned your life.

JULIE. Be kind to me. At least now you're talking like a human being.

JEAN. Be human yourself, then. You spit on me, and you won't let me wipe myself off——

JULIE. Help me! Help me! Just tell me what to do, where to go!

JEAN. In God's name, if I only knew myself!

JULIE. I've been crazy, out of my mind, but isn't there any way out?

JEAN. Stay here and keep calm! No one knows anything!

JULIE. Impossible! The others know and Kristine knows.

JEAN. No they don't, and they'd never believe a thing like that!

JULIE (*hesitantly*). But—it could happen again!

JEAN. That's true!

JULIE. And then?

JEAN (*frightened*). Then?——Why didn't I think about that? Yes, there is only one thing to do—get away from here! Right away! I can't come with you, then we'd be finished, so you'll have to go alone—away—anywhere!

JULIE. Alone?——Where?——I can't do that!

JEAN. You must! And before the Count gets back! If you stay, you know what'll happen. Once you make a mistake like this, you want to continue because the damage has already been done. . . . Then you get bolder and bolder—

until finally you're caught! So leave! Later you can write to the Count and confess everything—except that it was me! He'll never guess who it was, and he's not going to be eager to find out, anyway.

JULIE. I'll go if you come with me.

JEAN. Are you out of your head? Miss Julie runs away with her servant! In two days it would be in the newspapers, and that's something your father would never live through.

JULIE. I can't go and I can't stay! Help me! I'm so tired, so terribly tired.——Order me! Set me in motion—I can't think or act on my own . . .

JEAN. What miserable creatures you people are! You strut around with your noses in the air as if you were the lords of creation! All right, I'll order you. Go upstairs and get dressed! Get some money for the trip, and then come back down!

JULIE (*in a half-whisper*). Come up with me!

JEAN. To your room?——Now you're crazy again! (*Hesitates for a moment.*) No! Go, at once! (*Takes her hand to lead her out.*)

JULIE (*as she leaves*). Speak kindly to me, Jean!

JEAN. An order always sounds unkind—now you know how it feels. (*Jean, alone, sighs with relief. He sits at the table, takes out a notebook and pencil, and begins adding up figures, counting aloud as he works. He continues in dumb show until Kristine enters, dressed for church. She is carrying a white tie and shirt front.*)

KRISTINE. Lord Jesus, what a mess! What have you been up to?

JEAN. Oh, Miss Julie dragged everybody in here. You mean you didn't hear anything? You must have been sleeping soundly.

KRISTINE. Like a log.

JEAN. And dressed for church already?

KRISTINE. Of course! You remember you promised to come with me to communion today!

JEAN. Oh, yes, that's right.——And you brought my things. Come on, then! (*He sits down. Kristine starts to put on his shirt front and tie. Pause. Jean begins sleepily.*) What's the gospel text for today?

KRISTINE. On St. John's Day?—the beheading of John the Baptist, I should think!

JEAN. Ah, that'll be a long one, for sure.——Hey, you're choking me!——Oh, I'm sleepy, so sleepy!

KRISTINE. Yes, what have you been doing, up all night? Your face is absolutely green.

JEAN. I've been sitting here gabbing with Miss Julie.

KRISTINE. She has no idea what's proper, that one! (*Pause.*)

JEAN. You know, Kristine . . .

KRISTINE. What?

JEAN. It's really strange when you think about it.——Her!

KRISTINE. What's so strange?

JEAN. Everything! (*Pause.*)

KRISTINE (*looking at the half-empty glasses standing on the table*). Have you been drinking together, too?

JEAN. Yes.

KRISTINE. Shame on you!——Look me in the eye!

JEAN. Well?

KRISTINE. Is it possible? Is it possible?

JEAN (*thinking it over for a moment*). Yes, it is.

KRISTINE. Ugh! I never would have believed it! No, shame on you, shame!

JEAN. You're not jealous of her, are you?

KRISTINE. No, not of her! If it had been Clara or Sofie I'd have scratched your eyes out!——I don't know why, but that's the way I feel.——Oh, it's disgusting!

JEAN. Are you angry at her, then?

KRISTINE. No, at you! That was an awful thing to do, awful! Poor girl!——No, I don't care who knows it—I won't stay in a house where we can't respect the people we work for.

JEAN. Why should we respect them?

KRISTINE. You're so clever, you tell me! Do you want to wait on people who can't behave decently? Do you? You disgrace yourself that way, if you ask me.

JEAN. But it's a comfort to know they aren't any better than us.

KRISTINE. Not for me. If they're no better, what do we have to strive for to better ourselves.——And think of the Count! Think of him! As if he hasn't had enough misery in his life! Lord Jesus! No, I won't stay in this house any longer!——And it had to be with someone like you! If it had been that lawyer, if it had been a real gentleman . . .

JEAN. What do you mean?

KRISTINE. Oh, you're all right for what you are, but there are men and gentlemen, after all!——No, this business with Miss Julie I can never forget. She was so proud, so arrogant with men, you wouldn't have believed she could just go and give herself—and to someone like you! And she was going to have poor Diana shot for running after the gatekeepers' mutt!——Yes, I'm giving my notice, I mean it—I won't stay here any longer. On the twenty-fourth of October, I leave!

JEAN. And then?

KRISTINE. Well, since the subject has come up, it's about time you looked around for something since we're going to get married, in any case.

JEAN. Where am I going to look? I couldn't find a job like this if I was married.

KRISTINE. No, that's true. But you can find work as a porter or as a caretaker in some government office. The state doesn't pay much, I know, but it's secure, and there's a pension for the wife and children . . .

JEAN (*grimacing*). That's all very well, but it's a bit early for me to think about dying for a wife and children. My ambitions are a little higher than that.

KRISTINE. Your ambitions, yes! Well, you have obligations, too! Think about them!

JEAN. Don't start nagging me about obligations. I know what I have to do! (*Listening for something outside.*)

Besides, this is something we have plenty of time to think over. Go and get ready for church.

KRISTINE. Who's that walking around up there?

JEAN. I don't know, unless it's Clara.

KRISTINE (*going*). You don't suppose it's the Count, who came home without us hearing him?

JEAN (*frightened*). The Count? No, I don't think so. He'd have rung.

KRISTINE (*going*). Well, God help us! I've never seen anything like this before. (*The sun has risen and shines through the treetops in the park. The light shifts gradually until it slants in through the windows. Jean goes to the door and signals. Miss Julie enters, dressed in travel clothes and carrying a small bird cage, covered with a cloth, which she places on a chair.*)

JULIE. I'm ready now.

JEAN. Shh! Kristine is awake.

JULIE (*very nervous during the following*). Does she suspect something?

JEAN. She doesn't know anything. But my God, you look awful!

JULIE. Why? How do I look?

JEAN. You're pale as a ghost and—excuse me, but your face is dirty.

JULIE. Let me wash up then.——(*She goes to the basin and washes her hands and face.*) Give me a towel!——Oh—the sun's coming up.

JEAN. Then the goblins will disappear.

JULIE. Yes, there must have been goblins out last night!——Jean, listen, come with me! I have some money now.

JEAN (*hesitantly*). Enough?

JULIE. Enough to start with. Come with me! I just can't travel alone on a day like this—midsummer day on a stuffy train—jammed in among crowds of people staring at me. Eternal delays at every station, while I'd wish I had wings. No, I can't, I can't! And then there'll be memories, memories of midsummer days when I was little. The church—decorated with birch leaves and lilacs; dinner at the big table with relatives and friends; the afternoons in the park, dancing, music, flowers, and games. Oh, no matter how far we travel, the memories will follow in the baggage car, with remorse and guilt!

JEAN. I'll go with you—but right away, before it's too late. Right this minute!

JULIE. Get dressed, then! (*Picking up the bird cage.*)

JEAN. But no baggage! It would give us away!

JULIE. No, nothing! Only what we can have in the compartment with us.

JEAN (*has taken his hat*). What've you got there? What is it?

JULIE. It's only my greenfinch. I couldn't leave her behind.

JEAN. What? Bring a bird cage with us? You're out of your head! Put it down!

JULIE. It's the only thing I'm taking from my home—the only living being that loves me, since Diana was unfaithful. Don't be cruel! Let me take her!

JEAN. Put the cage down, I said!——And don't talk so loudly—Kristine will hear us!

JULIE. No, I won't leave her in the hands of strangers! I'd rather you killed her.

JEAN. Bring the thing here, then, I'll cut its head off!

JULIE. Oh! But don't hurt her! Don't . . . no, I can't.

JEAN. Bring it here! I can!

JULIE (*taking the bird out of the cage and kissing it*). Oh, my little Serena, must you die and leave your mistress?

JEAN. Please don't make a scene! Your whole future is at stake! Hurry up! (*He snatches the bird from her, carries it over to the chopping block, and picks up a meat cleaver. Miss Julie turns away.*) You should have learned how to slaughter chickens instead of how to fire pistols. (*He chops off the bird's head.*) Then you wouldn't feel faint at the sight of blood.

JULIE (*screaming*). Kill me, too! Kill me! You, who can slaughter an innocent animal without blinking an eye! Oh, how I hate, how I detest you! There's blood between us now! I curse the moment I set eyes on you! I curse the moment I was conceived in my mother's womb!

JEAN. What good does cursing do? Let's go!

JULIE (*approaching the chopping block, as if drawn against her will*). No, I don't want to go yet. I can't . . . until I see . . . Shh! I hear a carriage——(*She listens, but her eyes never leave the cleaver and the chopping block.*) Do you think I can't stand the sight of blood? You think I'm so weak . . . Oh—I'd like to see your blood and your brains on a chopping block!——I'd like to see your whole sex swimming in a sea of blood, like my little bird . . . I think I could drink from your skull! I'd like to bathe my feet in your open chest and eat your heart roasted whole!——You think I'm weak. You think I love you because my womb craved your seed. You think I want to carry your spawn under my heart and nourish it with my blood—bear your child and take your name! By the way, what is your family name? I've never heard it.——Do you have one? I was to be Mrs. Bootblack—or Madame Pigsty.——You dog, who wears my collar, you lackey, who bears my coat of arms on your buttons—do I have to share you with my cook, compete with my own servant? Oh! Oh! Oh!—— You think I'm a coward who wants to run away! No, now I'm staying—and let the storm break! My father will come home . . . to find his desk broken open . . . and his money gone! Then he'll ring—that bell . . . twice for his valet—and then he'll send for the police . . . and then I'll tell everything! Everything! Oh, what a relief it'll be to have it all end—if only it will end!——And then he'll have a stroke and die . . . That'll be the end of all of us— and there'll be peace . . . quiet . . . eternal rest!—And then our coat of arms will be broken against his coffin— the family title extinct—but the valet's line will go on in an orphanage . . . win laurels in the gutter, and end in jail!

JEAN. There's the blue blood talking! Very good, Miss Julie! Just don't let that miller out of the closet! (*Kristine enters, dressed for church, with a psalmbook in her hand.*)

JULIE (*rushing to Kristine and falling into her arms, as if seeking protection*). Help me, Kristine! Help me against this man!

KRISTINE (*unmoved and cold*). What a fine way to behave on a Sunday morning! (*Sees the chopping block.*) And look at this mess!——What does all this mean? Why all this screaming and carrying on?

JULIE. Kristine! You're a woman and my friend! Beware of this swine!

JEAN (*uncomfortable*). While you ladies discuss this, I'll go in and shave. (*Slips off right.*)

JULIE. You must listen to me so you'll understand!

KRISTINE. No, I could never understand such disgusting behavior! Where are you off to in your traveling clothes?—— And he had his hat on.——Well?——Well?——

JULIE. Listen to me, Kristine! Listen, and I'll tell you everything——

KRISTINE. I don't want to hear it . . .

JULIE. But you must listen to me . . .

KRISTINE. What about? If it's about this silliness with Jean, I'm not interested, because it's none of my business. But if you're thinking of tricking him into running out, we'll soon put a stop to that!

JULIE (*extremely nervous*). Try to be calm now, Kristine, and listen to me! I can't stay here, and neither can Jean—so we must go away . . .

KRISTINE. Hm, hm!

JULIE (*brightening*). You see, I just had an idea——What if all three of us go—abroad—to Switzerland and start a hotel together?——I have money, you see—and Jean and I could run it—and I thought you, you could take care of the kitchen . . . Wouldn't that be wonderful?——Say yes! And come with us, and then everything will be settled!——Oh, do say yes! (*Embracing Kristine and patting her warmly.*)

KRISTINE (*coolly, thoughtfully*). Hm, hm!

JULIE (*presto tempo*)[10]. You've never traveled, Kristine.—— You must get out and see the world. You can't imagine how much fun it is to travel by train—always new faces—new countries.——And when we get to Hamburg, we'll stop off at the zoo—you'll like that.——and then we'll go to the theater and the opera—and when we get to Munich, dear, there we have museums, with Rubens and Raphael, the great painters, as you know.—— You've heard of Munich, where King Ludwig lived—the king who went mad.——And then we'll see his castles— they're still there and they're like castles in fairy tales.—— And from there it isn't far to Switzerland—and the Alps.——Imagine—the Alps have snow on them even in the middle of summer!——And oranges grow there and laurel trees that are green all year round——(*Jean*

[10]**presto tempo** quickly

can be seen in the wings right, sharpening his razor on a strop which he holds with his teeth and his left hand. He listens to the conversation with satisfaction, nodding now and then in approval. Miss Julie continues tempo prestissimo.)[11] And then we'll start a hotel—and I'll be at the desk, while Jean greets the guests . . . does the shopping . . . writes letters.——You have no idea what a life it'll be—the train whistles blowing and the carriages arriving and the bells ringing in the rooms and down in the restaurant.—— And I'll make out the bills—and I know how to salt them! . . . You'll never believe how timid travelers are when they have to pay their bills!——And you—you'll be in charge of the kitchen.——Naturally, you won't have to stand over the stove yourself.——And since you're going to be seen by people, you'll have to wear beautiful clothes.——And you, with your looks—no, I'm not flattering you—one fine day you'll grab yourself a husband!——You'll see!——A rich Englishman— they're so easy to——(*Slowing down.*)——catch—and then we'll get rich—and build ourselves a villa on Lake Como.——It's true it rains there a little now and then, but——(*Dully.*)——the sun has to shine sometimes— although it looks dark—and then . . . of course we could always come back home again——(*Pause.*)——here—or somewhere else——

KRISTINE. Listen, Miss Julie, do you believe all this?

JULIE (*crushed*). Do I believe it?

KRISTINE. Yes!

JULIE (*wearily*). I don't know. I don't believe in anything anymore. (*She sinks down on the bench and cradles her head in her arms on the table.*) Nothing! Nothing at all!

KRISTINE (*turning right to where Jean is standing*). So, you thought you'd run out!

JEAN (*embarrassed; puts the razor on the table*). Run out? That's no way to put it. You hear Miss Julie's plan, and even if she is tired after being up all night, it's still a practical plan.

KRISTINE. Now you listen to me! Did you think I'd work as a cook for that . . .

JEAN (*sharply*). You watch what you say in front of your mistress! Do you understand?

KRISTINE. Mistress!

JEAN. Yes!

KRISTINE. Listen to him! Listen to him!

JEAN. Yes, you listen! It'd do you good to listen more and talk less! Miss Julie is your mistress. If you despise her, you have to despise yourself for the same reason!

KRISTINE. I've always had enough self-respect——

JEAN. ——to be able to despise other people!

KRISTINE. ——to stop me from doing anything that's beneath me. You can't say that the Count's cook has been up to something with the groom or the swineherd! Can you?

JEAN. No, you were lucky enough to get hold of a gentleman!

[11]**tempo prestissimo** very quickly

KRISTINE. Yes, a gentleman who sells the Count's oats from the stable.

JEAN. You should talk—taking a commission from the grocer and bribes from the butcher.

KRISTINE. What?

JEAN. And you say you can't respect your employers any longer. You, you, you!

KRISTINE. Are you coming to church with me, now? You could use a good sermon after your fine deed!

JEAN. No, I'm not going to church today. You'll have to go alone and confess what you've been up to.

KRISTINE. Yes, I'll do that, and I'll bring back enough forgiveness for you, too. The Savior suffered and died on the Cross for all our sins, and if we go to Him with faith and a penitent heart, He takes all our sins on Himself.

JEAN. Even grocery sins?

JULIE. And do you believe that, Kristine?

KRISTINE. It's my living faith, as sure as I stand here. It's the faith I learned as a child, Miss Julie, and kept ever since. "Where sin abounded, grace did much more abound!"

JULIE. Oh, if I only had your faith. If only . . .

KRISTINE. Well, you see, we can't have it without God's special grace, and that isn't given to everyone——

JULIE. Who is it given to then?

KRISTINE. That's the great secret of the workings of grace, Miss Julie, and God is no respecter of persons, for the last shall be the first . . .

JULIE. Then He does respect the last.

KRISTINE (*continuing*). . . . and it is easier for a camel to go through the eye of a needle, than for a rich man to enter the Kingdom of God. That's how it is, Miss Julie! Anyhow, I'm going now—alone, and on the way I'm going to tell the groom not to let any horses out, in case anyone wants to leave before the Count gets back!——Goodbye! (*Leaves.*)

JEAN. What a witch!——And all this because of a greenfinch!——

JULIE (*dully*). Never mind the greenfinch!——Can you see any way out of this? Any end to it?

JEAN (*thinking*). No!

JULIE. What would you do in my place?

JEAN. In your place? Let's see—as a person of position, as a woman who had—fallen. I don't know—wait, now I know.

JULIE (*taking the razor and making a gesture*). You mean like this?

JEAN. Yes! But—understand—*I* wouldn't do it! That's the difference between us!

JULIE. Because you're a man and I'm a woman? What sort of difference is that?

JEAN. The usual difference—between a man and a woman.

JULIE (*with the razor in her hand*). I want to, but I can't!—— My father couldn't either, the time he should have done it.

JEAN. No, he shouldn't have! He had to revenge himself first.

JULIE. And now my mother is revenged again, through me.

JEAN. Didn't you ever love your father, Miss Julie?

JULIE. Oh yes, deeply, but I've hated him, too. I must have done so without realizing it! It was he who brought me up to despise my own sex, making me half woman, half man. Whose fault is what's happened? My father's, my mother's, my own? My own? I don't have anything that's my own. I don't have a single thought that I didn't get from my father, not an emotion that I didn't get from my mother, and this last idea—that all people are equal—I got that from my fiancé.——That's why I called him a swine! How can it be my fault? Shall I let Jesus take on the blame, the way Kristine does?——No, I'm too proud to do that and too sensible—thanks to my father's teachings.——And as for someone rich not going to heaven, that's a lie. But Kristine won't get in—how will she explain the money she has in the savings bank? Whose fault is it?——What does it matter whose fault it is? I'm still the one who has to bear the blame, face the consequences . . .

JEAN. Yes, but . . . (*The bell rings sharply twice. Miss Julie jumps up. Jean changes his coat.*) The Count is back! Do you suppose Kristine— (*He goes to the speaking tube, taps the lid, and listens.*)

JULIE. He's been to his desk!

JEAN. It's Jean, sir! (*Listening, the audience cannot hear the Count's voice.*) Yes, sir! (*Listening.*) Yes, sir! Right away! (*Listening.*) At once, sir! (*Listening.*) I see, in half an hour!

JULIE (*desperately frightened*). What did he say? Dear Lord, what did he say?

JEAN. He wants his boots and his coffee in half an hour.

JULIE. So, in half an hour! Oh, I'm so tired. I'm not able to do anything. I can't repent, can't run away, can't stay, can't live—can't die! Help me now! Order me, and I'll obey like a dog! Do me this last service, save my honor, save his name! You know what I *should* do, but don't have the will to . . . You will it, you order me to do it!

JEAN. I don't know why——but now I can't either——I don't understand.——It's as if this coat made it impossible for me to order you to do anything.——And now, since the Count spoke to me—I—I can't really explain it—but—ah, it's the damn lackey in me!——I think if the Count came down here now—and ordered me to cut my throat, I'd do it on the spot.

JULIE. Then pretend you're he, and I'm you!——You gave such a good performance before when you knelt at my feet.——You were a real nobleman.——Or—have you ever seen a hypnotist in the theater? (*Jean nods.*) He says to his subject: "Take the broom," and he takes it. He says: "Sweep," and he sweeps——

JEAN. But the subject has to be asleep.

JULIE (*ecstatically*). I'm already asleep.——The whole room is like smoke around me . . . and you look like an iron stove . . . shaped like a man in black, with a tall hat— and your eyes glow like coals when the fire is dying— and your face is a white patch, like ashes——(*The sunlight has reached the floor and now shines on Jean.*)——it's so warm and good——(*She rubs her hands as if warming them before a fire.*)——and bright—and so peaceful!

JEAN (*taking the razor and putting it in her hand*). Here's the broom! Go now while it's bright—out to the barn— and . . . (*Whispers in her ear.*)

JULIE (*awake*). Thank you. I'm going now to rest! But just tell me—that those who are first can also receive the gift of grace. Say it, even if you don't believe it.

JEAN. The first? No, I can't——But wait—Miss Julie—now I know! You're no longer among the first—you're now among—the last!

JULIE. That's true.——I'm among the last. I'm the last one of all! Oh!——But now I can't go!——Tell me once more to go!

JEAN. No, now I can't either! I can't!

JULIE. And the first shall be the last!

JEAN. Don't think, don't think! You're taking all my strength from me, making me a coward.——What was that? I thought the bell moved!——No! Shall we stuff paper in it?—To be so afraid of a bell!——But it isn't just a bell.——There's someone behind it—a hand sets it in motion—and something else sets the hand in motion.——Maybe if you cover your ears—cover your ears! But then it rings even louder! rings until someone answers.——And then it's too late! And then the police come—and—then——(*The bell rings twice loudly. Jean flinches, then straightens up.*) It's horrible! But there's no other way!——Go! (*Miss Julie walks firmly out through the door.*)

TOPICS FOR CRITICAL THINKING AND WRITING

 THE PLAY ON THE PAGE

1. In his preface, Strindberg emphasizes that the play is realistic, but many readers and viewers have found it highly symbolic. What symbolic elements, if any, do you find? Do you consider, for instance, the "statue of Cupid" (specified in the opening stage direction) to be symbolic?

2. Do you think the ending of *Miss Julie* is plausible? (Some contemporary critics found Julie's suicide improbable because she cannot know if she is pregnant. Strindberg argued that she would have killed herself because of her sense of honor.) Support your response with reasons.

3. Do you think the play is a tragedy? Explain?

🎭 THE PLAY ON THE STAGE

4. Reread Strindberg's opening stage direction, and make a rough sketch of the set. Notice that "the rear wall runs diagonally from down left to up right." Usually the rear wall of a box set runs parallel to the rear wall of the theater. What effect do you think this diagonal has on the spectators?

5. Usually directors ignore Strindberg's wishes and place an intermission after the interlude of the dancing peas-

ants. If you were staging the play would you include an intermission? Explain.

6. In a 1985 production in South Africa, Jean was played by a black, Julie by a white. What is your response to this decision? Explain.

A CONTEXT FOR MISS JULIE

SELECTIONS FROM STRINDBERG'S PREFACE

In the following play, instead of trying to do anything new—which is impossible—I have simply modernized the form in accordance with demands I think contemporary audiences make upon this art. Toward this end, I have chosen, or let myself be moved by, a theme that can be said to lie outside partisan politics since the problem of social climbing or falling, of higher or lower, better or worse, man or woman, are, have been, and will be of lasting interest. When I took this theme from a true story I heard told some years ago, which made a strong impression on me, I found it appropriate for tragedy, for it still seems tragic to see someone favored by fortune go under, much more to see a family die out. Perhaps the time will come when we will be so advanced, so enlightened, that we can witness with indifference what now seem the coarse, cynical, heartless dramas life has to offer, when we have closed down those lower, unreliable mechanisms of thought called feelings, because better developed organs of judgment will have found them superfluous and harmful. The fact that the heroine arouses compassion is because we are too weak to resist the fear that the same fate could overtake us. A hypersensitive spectator may not be satisfied with compassion alone, while a man with faith in the future may demand some positive proposals to remedy the evil, in other words, a program of some kind. But for one thing there is no absolute evil. The fall of one family can mean a chance for another family to rise, and the alternation of rising and falling fortunes is one of life's greatest delights since happiness lies only in comparison. And to the man who wants a program to remedy the unpleasant fact that the bird of prey eats the dove and the louse eats the bird of prey I ask: why should it be remedied? Life is not so idiotically mathematical that only the great eat the small; it is just as common for a bee to kill a lion or at least drive it mad.

If my tragedy depresses many people, it is their own fault. When we become as strong as the first French revolutionaries, it will afford nothing but pleasure and relief to witness the thinning out in royal parks of overage, decaying trees that have long stood in the way of others equally entitled to

their time in the sun, the kind of relief we feel when we see someone incurably ill die!

. . .

I have motivated Miss Julie's tragic fate by a great number of circumstances: her mother's primary instincts, her father raising her incorrectly, her own nature, and the influence of her fiancé on her weak and degenerate brain. Also, more particularly: the festive atmosphere of midsummer night, her father's absence, her monthly indisposition, her preoccupation with animals, the provocative effect of the dancing, the magical midsummer twilight, the powerfully aphrodisiac influence of flowers, and, finally, the chance that drives the couple together into a room alone—plus the boldness of the aroused man.

My treatment of the subject has thus been neither one-sidedly physiological nor exclusively psychological. I have not put the entire blame on what she inherited from her mother, nor on her monthly indisposition, nor on immorality. I have not even preached morality—this I left to the cook in the absence of a minister.

. . .

Miss Julie is a modern character. Not that the man-hating half-woman has not existed in all ages but because now that she has been discovered, she has come out in the open to make herself heard. The half-woman is a type who pushes her way ahead, selling herself nowadays for power, decorations, honors, and diplomas, as formerly she used to do for money. The type implies a retrogressive step in evolution, an inferior species who cannot endure. Unfortunately, they are able to pass on their wretchedness; degenerate men seem unconsciously to choose their mates from among them. And so they breed, producing an indeterminate sex for whom life is a torture. Fortunately, the offspring go under either because they are out of harmony with reality or because their repressed instincts break out uncontrollably or because their hopes of achieving equality with men are crushed. The type is tragic, revealing the drama of a desperate struggle against

Nature, tragic as the romantic heritage now being dissipated by naturalism, which has a contrary aim: happiness, and happiness belongs only to the strong and skillful species.

But Miss Julie is also: a relic of the old warrior nobility now giving way to a new nobility of nerve and intellect, a victim of her own flawed constitution, a victim of the discord caused in a family by a mother's "crime," a victim of the delusions and conditions of her age—and together these are the equivalent of the concept of Destiny, or Universal Law, of antiquity. Guilt has been abolished by the naturalist, along with God, but the consequences of an action—punishment, imprisonment or the fear of it—that he cannot erase, for the simple reason that they remain, whether he pronounces acquittal or not. Those who have been injured are not as kind and understanding as an unscathed outsider can afford to be. Even if her father felt constrained not to seek revenge, his daughter would wreak vengeance upon herself, as she does here, out of an innate or acquired sense of honor, which the upper classes inherit—from where? From barbarism, from the ancient Aryan home of the race, from medieval chivalry. It is a beautiful thing, but nowadays a hindrance to the survival of the race. It is the nobleman's harikari, which compels him to slit open his own stomach when someone insults him and which survives in a modified form in the duel, that privilege of the nobility. That is why Jean, the servant, lives, while Miss Julie cannot live without honor. The slave's advantage over the nobleman is that he lacks this fatal preoccupation with honor. But in all of us Aryans there is something of the nobleman, or a Don Quixote. And so we sympathize with the suicide, whose act means a loss of honor. We are noblemen enough to be pained when we see the mighty fallen and as superfluous as a corpse, yes, even if the fallen should rise again and make amends through an honorable act. The servant Jean is a race-founder, someone in whom the process of differentiation can be detected. Born the son of a tenant farmer, he has educated himself in the things a gentleman should know. He has been quick to learn, has finely developed senses (smell, taste, sight) and a feeling for what is beautiful. He is already moving up in the world and is not embarrassed about using other people's help. He is alienated from his fellow servants, despising them as parts of a past he has already put behind him. He fears and flees them because they know his secrets, pry into his intentions, envy his rise, and look forward eagerly to his fall. Hence his dual, indecisive nature, vacillating between sympathy for people in high social positions and hatred for those who currently occupy those positions. He is an aristocrat, as he himself says, has learned the secrets of good society, is polished on the surface but coarse beneath, wears a frock coat tastefully but without any guarantee that his body is clean.

He has respect for Miss Julie, but is afraid of Kristine because she knows his dangerous secrets. He is sufficiently callous not to let the night's events disturb his plans for the future. With both a slave's brutality and a master's lack of squeamishness, he can see blood without fainting and shake off misfortune easily. Consequently, he comes through the struggle unscathed and will probably end up an innkeeper. And even if *he* does not become a Rumanian count, his son will become a university student and possibly a county police commissioner.

. . .

Apart from the fact that Jean is rising in the world, he is superior to Miss Julie because he is a man. Sexually, he is an aristocrat because of his masculine strength, his more keenly developed senses, and his capacity for taking the initiative. His sense of inferiority is mostly due to the social circumstances in which he happens to be living, and he can probably shed it along with his valet's jacket.

His slave mentality expresses itself in the fearful respect he has for the Count (the boots) and his religious superstition; but he respects the Count mainly as the occupant of the kind of high position to which he himself aspires; and the respect remains even after he has conquered the daughter of the house and seen how empty the lovely shell was. I do not believe that love in any "higher" sense can exist between two people of such different natures, and so I have Miss Julie's love as something she fabricates in order to protect and excuse herself; and I have Jean suppose himself capable of loving her under other social circumstances. I think it is the same with love as with the hyacinth, which must take root in darkness *before* it can produce a sturdy flower. Here a flower shoots up, blooms, and goes to seed all at once, and that is why it dies so quickly.

Kristine, finally, is a female slave. Years standing over the stove have made her conventional and lethargic; instinctively hypocritical, she uses morality and religion as cloaks and scapegoats. A strong person would not need these because he can either bear his guilt or reason it away. Kristine goes to church as a quick and easy way to unload her household thefts on Jesus and to take on a new charge of innocence.

THE PLAY IN PERFORMANCE

Miss Julie—Strindberg's most popular play—exists in at least twenty English translations, and it has been made into a film, an opera, and a ballet. It has been staged countless times throughout the world—chiefly in Europe and the United States, of course, but also in Latin America, Asia, and Africa.

Miss Julie had its world premiere Copenhagen in 1889, performed by the Scandinavian Experimental Theater, a small group that Strindberg had organized under the influence of Andre Antoine's Theatre Libre. Because the Danish censor had banned the play, it was performed privately for an invited audience rather than publicly staged. Four years later, in 1893, Antoine staged *Miss Julie* in his theater in Paris, where it received mixed reviews, because some critics considered that naturalistic drama was already old-fashioned. The early productions of course used realistic settings and a style of acting that was thought to be realistic, in accordance with Strindberg's wishes, and indeed most productions continue to be realistic, but in recent decades productions have departed very far from Strindberg's vision. For instance, in a German production of 1974 five old women in black moved about on the stage, a sort of silent chorus. Further, all three of Strindberg's characters were visible throughout the play; when a character was not onstage, he or she sat on a chair at the side and watched the performance. In the following year, another German production offered a different variant: The scene in which Julie says she would like to see Jean's blood and his brains on the chopping block was played as an affectionate love scene between bantering lovers. In 1979 a production in London set the play in South Africa, using a black Jean and a white Julie—an idea repeated by a company in South Africa, where for the first time in South African history a black man was seen to kiss a white woman on the stage. In this production, it was clear that all talk about class was really talk about race. A 1982 production in Gothenburg (Sweden) took a strong feminist line: Jean was made up to look like Strindberg, Julie was quite pleasant, and in the final scene a woman came onstage and silently watched the ending, implicitly condemning the misogynistic author.

A highly praised English production in 1983 was much more traditional. It opened in the tiny (one hundred and twenty seats) Lyric Theatre, Hammersmith, but after a few weeks it was transferred to a theater whose capacity was five times greater. Strindberg would have been delighted with the highly realistic set, which included a dripping faucet that unnerved the spectators. The director had wanted to set the play in nineteenth-century Ireland—the servants were to have Irish accents, Julie an English accent—but the actress playing Kristine could not produce an acceptable accent, and so this interpretation was not put onto the stage until that play had changed theaters and the actress in question had been replaced.

The next major production was in Tokyo in 1984, where Strindberg's demand that the set be naturalistic was ignored. The set was not the usual room without a fourth wall but was a birdcage without a fourth wall, and the characters perched on pedestals. The play began with a flirtation between Jean and Kristine, with Jean holding a boot between his legs as a phallus. A 1986 Swedish production was even less faithful to the letter of the play, which was updated to the 1920s and presented with a highly symbolic set—a glowing stove, a table that was a block for slaughtering an animal, and huge meat hooks. Even more obvious was the symbolism used when Julie and Jean left the stage for Jean's room—a peasant came by and placed a midsummer wreath over the tip of a maypole.

The Swedish director Ingmar Bergman staged the play, under the title *Julie*, in Stockholm in 1981, as part of a program that included *Nora*—Bergman's version of Ibsen's *A Doll's House*. Bergman's interpretation of the play was heavily based on a detail that Strindberg deleted from his manuscript. In the manuscript version of the speech in which Kristine tells Jean that Julie made her lover jump over her whip, there is a sentence—never published—to the effect that the lover jumped twice, but on the third command he "grabbed the whip from her and slashed her face with it, leaving a long scratch on her left cheek." In Bergman's production, it was evident that Julie was heavily made up, but after the sexual encounter with Jean the make-up has come off, and a bleeding scar was evident on her cheek. As Bergman explains in his account of the production, *A Project for the Theatre*, he wanted to show that Julie had already been wounded. "Then, you see, when Jean gives her this second 'wound'—her second physical humiliation at the hands of a man—it destroys her" (15).

For brief discussions of numerous productions, see Egil Tornqvist and Barry Jacobs, *Strindberg's "Miss Julie": A Play and Its Transpositions* (1988). For an interview with Ingmar Bergman concerning his production, as well as a discussion of his *Julie*, see Bergman's *A Project for the Theatre*, ed. Frederick J. Marker and Lise-Lone Marker (1993).

Oscar Wilde

THE IMPORTANCE OF BEING EARNEST

A Trivial Comedy for Serious People

Oscar Wilde (1854–1900) was born in Dublin. He distinguished himself as a student at Trinity College, Dublin, and at Oxford and then turned to a career of writing, lecturing, and in other ways making himself a public figure in England: His posture as an aesthete (he was alleged to have walked down Piccadilly with a flower in his hand) was caricatured by Gilbert and Sullivan in *Patience*. But it became no laughing matter when in 1895 he was arrested and convicted of homosexuality. After serving two years at hard labor, he was released from jail. He then went to France, where he lived under an assumed name until he died. His Irish birth did not ally him to the Irish Renaissance at the end of the nineteenth century; when W. B. Yeats was writing plays on Irish legends, Wilde was writing drawing-room comedies.

COMMENTARY

The gist of the plot of *The Importance of Being Earnest* is the gist of the plot of many comedies: A young man and a young woman wish to marry, but an apparently insurmountable obstacle interposes. The obstacle, however, is surmounted, and so at the end we get a happy, united society. Wilde doubles the lovers, giving us two young men and two young women, but this is scarcely an innovation, for we get two pairs of lovers in several of Shakespeare's comedies, including *A Midsummer Night's Dream*, which, after what has been called an obstacle race to the altar, similarly concludes with all of the lovers happily paired.

Our entry on *farce* in the Glossary suggests that farce is "a sort of comedy based not on clever language or subtleties of character, but on broadly humorous situations," such as a man mistakenly entering the ladies' locker room. Generally the emphasis in farce is on surprise and on swift physical action, with much frantic hiding under beds, desperate putting on of absurd disguises, and so forth. But it is widely (though not universally) agreed that *The Importance of Being Earnest* is a farce, an utterly improbable play with virtually no connection with life as we know or feel it. Those who hold this view, however, see this play as unique, the one farce that depends on language rather than physical action. Writing in 1902, of a revival staged seven years after the original production of *The Importance of Being Earnest*, Max Beerbohm said:

> In scheme, of course, it is a hackneyed farce—the story of a young man coming up to London "on the spree," and of another young man going down conversely to the country, and of the complications that ensue. . . . [But] the fun depends mainly on what the characters say, rather than on what they do. They speak a kind of beautiful nonsense—the language of high comedy, twisted into fantasy. Throughout the dialogue is the horseplay of a distinguished intellect and a distinguished imagination—a horse-play among words and ideas, conducted with poetic dignity.

A few critics, however, have insisted that under the glittering but apparently trivial surface (Wilde said this play was "written by a butterfly for butterflies") there are serious topics, and that Wilde is indeed saying serious things—disguised as nonsense—about society. He is, in this view, joking in earnest; that is, he is writing satirically and only pretending to be playful. (On *satire*, see the Glossary entry.) Among the topics that critics have singled out are marriage, money, education, sincerity (the importance—or unimportance—of being earnest), class relationships, and death. In effect, the question comes down to this: When we hear, for instance, Lady Bracknell commenting on the absurd circumstances of Jack's infancy, do our minds turn to a criticism of the snobbish speaker, or do they (delighting in the absurd speech) relish the lines themselves and take pleasure in the speaker? Here is the passage in question:

> To be born, or at any rate, bred in a handbag, whether it had handles or not, seems to me to display a contempt for the ordinary decencies of family life that reminds one of the worst excesses of the French Revolution. And I presume you know what that unfortunate movement led to?

Readers are invited to try thinking about the play both ways—as a work of art divorced from reality, and as a work of art that repeatedly if indirectly comments on life—and to come to their own conclusions about the truth of the two views we have set forth. Possibly they will conclude, with Algernon, that "The truth is rarely pure, and never simple."

Oscar Wilde

THE IMPORTANCE OF BEING EARNEST

Characters

JOHN WORTHING, J.P.
ALGERNON MONCRIEFF
REV. CANON CHASUBLE, D.D.
MERRIMAN (*butler*)
LANE (*manservant*)
LADY BRACKNELL
HON. GWENDOLEN FAIRFAX
CECILY CARDEW
MISS PRISM (*governess*)

THE SCENES OF THE PLAY

ACT I: *Algernon Moncrieff's flat in Half-Moon Street, W.*
ACT II: *The garden at the Manor House, Woolton*
ACT III: *Drawing-room of the Manor House, Woolton*

TIME: *The present*   PLACE: *London*

ACT 1

SCENE: *Morning-room in Algernon's flat in Half-Moon Street. The room is luxuriously and artistically furnished. The sound of a piano is heard in the adjoining room. (Lane is arranging afternoon tea on the table, and after the music has ceased, Algernon enters.)*

ALGERNON. Did you hear what I was playing, Lane?

LANE. I didn't think it polite to listen, sir.

ALGERNON. I'm sorry for that, for your sake. I don't play accurately—anyone can play accurately—but I play with wonderful expression. As far as the piano is concerned, sentiment is my forte. I keep science for Life.

LANE. Yes, sir.

ALGERNON. And, speaking of the science of Life, have you got the cucumber sandwiches cut for Lady Bracknell?

LANE. Yes, sir. (*Hands them on a salver.*)

ALGERNON (*inspects them, takes two, and sits down on the sofa*). Oh!... by the way, Lane, I see from your book that on Thursday night, when Lord Shoreman and Mr. Worthing were dining with me, eight bottles of champagne are entered as having been consumed.

LANE. Yes, sir; eight bottles and a pint.

ALGERNON. Why is it that at a bachelor's establishment the servants invariably drink the champagne? I ask merely for information.

LANE. I attribute it to the superior quality of the wine, sir. I have often observed that in married households the champagne is rarely of a first-rate brand.

ALGERNON. Good Heavens! Is marriage so demoralizing as that?

LANE. I believe it *is* a very pleasant state, sir. I have had very little experience of it myself up to the present. I have only been married once. That was in consequence of a misunderstanding between myself and a young woman.

ALGERNON (*languidly*). I don't know that I am much interested in your family life, Lane.

LANE. No, sir; it is not a very interesting subject. I never think of it myself.

ALGERNON. Very natural, I am sure. That will do, Lane, thank you.

LANE. Thank you, sir. (*Lane goes out.*)

ALGERNON. Lane's views on marriage seem somewhat lax. Really, if the lower orders don't set us a good example, what on earth is the use of them? They seem, as a class, to have absolutely no sense of moral responsibility.

(*Enter Lane.*)

LANE. Mr. Ernest Worthing.

(*Enter Jack. Lane goes out.*)

ALGERNON. How are you, my dear Ernest? What brings you up to town?

JACK. Oh, pleasure, pleasure! What else should bring one anywhere? Eating as usual, I see, Algy!

ALGERNON (*stiffly*). I believe it is customary in good society to take some slight refreshment at five o'clock. Where have you been since last Thursday?

JACK (*sitting down on the sofa*). In the country.

ALGERNON. What on earth do you do there?

JACK (*pulling off his gloves*). When one is in town one amuses oneself. When one is in the country one amuses other people. It is excessively boring.

ALGERNON. And who are the people you amuse?

JACK (*airily*). Oh, neighbours, neighbours.

ALGERNON. Got nice neighbours in your part of Shropshire?

JACK. Perfectly horrid! Never speak to one of them.

ALGERNON. How immensely you must amuse them! (*Goes over and takes sandwich.*) By the way, Shropshire is your county, is it not?

JACK. Eh? Shropshire? Yes, of course. Hallo! Why all these cups? Why cucumber sandwiches? Why such reckless extravagance in one so young? Who is coming to tea?

ALGERNON. Oh! merely Aunt Augusta and Gwendolen.

JACK. How perfectly delightful!

ALGERNON. Yes, that is all very well; but I am afraid Aunt Augusta won't quite approve of your being here.

JACK. May I ask why?

ALGERNON. My dear fellow, the way you flirt with Gwendolen is perfectly disgraceful. It is almost as bad as the way Gwendolen flirts with you.

JACK. I am in love with Gwendolen. I have come up to town expressly to propose to her.

ALGERNON. I thought you had come up for pleasure? . . . I call that business.

JACK. How utterly unromantic you are!

ALGERNON. I really don't see anything romantic in proposing. It is very romantic to be in love. But there is nothing romantic about a definite proposal. Why, one may be accepted. One usually is, I believe. Then the excitement is all over. The very essence of romance is uncertainty. If ever I get married, I'll certainly try to forget the fact.

JACK. I have no doubt about that, dear Algy. The Divorce Court was specially invented for people whose memories are so curiously constituted.

ALGERNON. Oh! there is no use speculating on that subject. Divorces are made in Heaven--(*Jack puts out his hand to take a sandwich. Algernon at once interferes.*) Please don't touch the cucumber sandwiches. They are ordered specially for Aunt Augusta. (*Takes one and eats it.*)

JACK. Well, you have been eating them all the time.

ALGERNON. That is quite a different matter. She is my aunt. (*Takes plate from below.*) Have some bread and butter. The bread and butter is for Gwendolen. Gwendolen is devoted to bread and butter.

JACK (*advancing to table and helping himself*). And very good bread and butter it is, too.

ALGERNON. Well, my dear fellow, you need not eat as if you were going to eat it all. You behave as if you were married to her already. You are not married to her already, and I don't think you ever will be.

JACK. Why on earth do you say that?

ALGERNON. Well, in the first place girls never marry the men they flirt with. Girls don't think it right.

JACK. Oh, that is nonsense!

ALGERNON. It isn't. It is a great truth. It accounts for the extraordinary number of bachelors that one sees all over the place. In the second place, I don't give my consent.

JACK. Your consent!

ALGERNON. My dear fellow, Gwendolen is my first cousin. And before I allow you to marry her, you will have to clear up the whole question of Cecily. (*Rings bell.*)

JACK. Cecily! What on earth do you mean? What do you mean, Algy, by Cecily? I don't know anyone of the name of Cecily.

(*Enter Lane.*)

ALGERNON. Bring me that cigarette case Mr. Worthing left in the smoking-room the last time he dined here.

LANE. Yes, sir. (*Lane goes out.*)

JACK. Do you mean to say you have had my cigarette case all this time? I wish to goodness you had let me know. I have been writing frantic letters to Scotland Yard about it. I was very nearly offering a large reward.

ALGERNON. Well, I wish you would offer one. I happen to be more than usually hard up.

JACK. There is no good offering a large reward now that the thing is found.

(*Enter Lane with the cigarette case on a salver. Algernon takes it at once. Lane goes out.*)

ALGERNON. I think that is rather mean of you, Ernest, I must say. (*Opens case and examines it.*) However, it makes no matter, for, now that I look at the inscription, I find that the thing isn't yours after all.

JACK. Of course it's mine. (*Moving to him.*) You have seen me with it a hundred times, and you have no right whatsoever to read what is written inside. It is a very ungentlemanly thing to read a private cigarette case.

ALGERNON. Oh! it is absurd to have a hard-and-fast rule about what one should read and what one shouldn't. More than half of modern culture depends on what one shouldn't read.

JACK. I am quite aware of the fact, and I don't propose to discuss modern culture. It isn't the sort of thing one should talk of in private. I simply want my cigarette case back.

ALGERNON. Yes; but this isn't your cigarette case. This cigarette case is a present from someone of the name of Cecily, and you said you didn't know anyone of that name.

JACK. Well, if you want to know, Cecily happens to be my aunt.

ALGERNON. Your aunt!

JACK. Yes. Charming old lady she is, too. Lives at Tunbridge Wells. Just give it back to me, Algy.

ALGERNON (*retreating to back of sofa*). But why does she call herself little Cecily if she is your aunt and lives at Tunbridge Wells? (*Reading.*) "From little Cecily with her fondest love."

JACK (*moving to sofa and kneeling upon it*). My dear fellow, what on earth is there in that? Some aunts are tall, some aunts are not tall. That is a matter that surely an aunt may be allowed to decide for herself. You seem to think that every aunt should be exactly like your aunt! That is absurd! For Heaven's sake give me back my cigarette case. (*Follows Algernon round the room.*)

ALGERNON. Yes. But why does your aunt call you her uncle? "From little Cecily, with her fondest love to her dear Uncle Jack." There is no objection, I admit, to an aunt being a small aunt, but why an aunt, no matter what her size may be, should call her own nephew her uncle, I can't quite make out. Besides, your name isn't Jack at all; it is Ernest.

JACK. It isn't Ernest; it's Jack.

ALGERNON. You have always told me it was Ernest. I have introduced you to everyone as Ernest. You answer to the name of Ernest. You look as if your name was Ernest. You are the most ernest looking person I ever saw in my life. It is perfectly absurd your saying that your name isn't Ernest. It's on your cards. Here is one of them. (*Taking it from case.*) "Mr. Ernest Worthing, B 4, The Albany." I'll keep this as a proof your name is Ernest if ever you attempt to deny it to me, or to Gwendolen, or to anyone else. (*Puts the card in his pocket.*)

JACK. Well, my name is Ernest in town and Jack in the country, and the cigarette case was given to me in the country.

ALGERNON. Yes, but that does not account for the fact that your small Aunt Cecily, who lives at Tunbridge Wells, calls you her dear uncle. Come, old boy, you had much better have the thing out at once.

JACK. My dear Algy, you talk exactly as if you were a dentist. It is very vulgar to talk like a dentist when one isn't a dentist. It produces a false impression.

ALGERNON. Well, that is exactly what dentists always do. Now, go on! Tell me the whole thing. I may mention that I have always suspected you of being a confirmed and secret Bunburyist; and I am quite sure of it now.

JACK. Bunburyist? What on earth do you mean by a Bunburyist?

ALGERNON. I'll reveal to you the meaning of that incomparable expression as soon as you are kind enough to inform me why you are Ernest in town and Jack in the country.

JACK. Well, produce my cigarette case first.

ALGERNON. Here it is. (*Hands cigarette case.*) Now produce your explanation, and pray make it improbable. (*Sits on sofa.*)

JACK. My dear fellow, there is nothing improbable about my explanation at all. In fact it's perfectly ordinary. Old Mr. Thomas Cardew, who adopted me when I was a little boy, made me in his will guardian to his granddaughter, Miss Cecily Cardew. Cecily, who addresses me as her uncle from motives of respect that you could not possibly appreciate, lives at my place in the country under the charge of her admirable governess, Miss Prism.

ALGERNON. Where is that place in the country, by the way?

JACK. That is nothing to you, dear boy. You are not going to be invited. . . . I may tell you candidly that the place is not in Shropshire.

ALGERNON. I suspected that, my dear fellow! I have Bunburyed all over Shropshire on two separate occasions. Now, go on. Why are you Ernest in town and Jack in the country?

JACK. My dear Algy, I don't know whether you will be able to understand my real motives. You are hardly serious enough. When one is placed in the position of guardian,

one has to adopt a very high moral tone on all subjects. It's one's duty to do so. And as a high moral tone can hardly be said to conduce very much to either one's health or one's happiness, in order to get up to town I have always pretended to have a younger brother of the name of Ernest, who lives in the Albany, and gets into the most dreadful scrapes. That, my dear Algy, is the whole truth pure and simple.

ALGERNON. The truth is rarely pure and never simple. Modern life would be very tedious if it were either, and modern literature a complete impossibility!

JACK. That wouldn't be at all a bad thing.

ALGERNON. Literary criticism is not your forte, my dear fellow. Don't try it. You should leave that to people who haven't been at a University. They do it so well in the daily papers. What you really are is a Bunburyist. I was quite right in saying you were a Bunburyist. You are one of the most advanced Bunburyists I know.

JACK. What on earth do you mean?

ALGERNON. You have invented a very useful younger brother called Ernest, in order that you may be able to come up to town as often as you like. I have invented an invaluable permanent invalid called Bunbury, in order that I may be able to go down into the country whenever I choose. Bunbury is perfectly invaluable. If it wasn't for Bunbury's extraordinary bad health, for instance, I wouldn't be able to dine with you at Willis's to-night, for I have been really engaged to Aunt Augusta for more than a week.

JACK. I haven't asked you to dine with me anywhere tonight.

ALGERNON. I know. You are absolutely careless about sending out invitations. It is very foolish of you. Nothing annoys people so much as not receiving invitations.

JACK. You had much better dine with your Aunt Augusta.

ALGERNON. I haven't the smallest intention of doing anything of the kind. To begin with, I dined there on Monday, and once a week is quite enough to dine with one's own relatives. In the second place, whenever I do dine there I am always treated as a member of the family, and sent down with either no woman at all, or two. In the third place, I know perfectly well whom she will place me next to, tonight. She will place me next Mary Farquhar, who always flirts with her own husband across the dinner-table. That is not very pleasant. Indeed, it is not even decent . . . and that sort of thing is enormously on the increase. The amount of women in London who flirt with their own husbands is perfectly scandalous. It looks so bad. It is simply washing one's clean linen in public. Besides, now that I know you to be a confirmed Bunburyist I naturally want to talk to you about Bunburying. I want to tell you the rules.

JACK. I'm not a Bunburyist at all. If Gwendolen accepts me, I am going to kill my brother, indeed I think I'll kill him in any case. Cecily is a little too much interested in him.

It is rather a bore. So I am going to get rid of Ernest. And I strongly advise you to do the same with Mr. . . . with your invalid friend who has the absurd name.

ALGERNON. Nothing will induce me to part with Bunbury, and if you ever get married, which seems to me extremely problematic, you will be very glad to know Bunbury. A man who marries without knowing Bunbury has a very tedious time of it.

JACK. That is nonsense. If I marry a charming girl like Gwendolen, and she is the only girl I ever saw in my life that I would marry, I certainly won't want to know Bunbury.

ALGERNON. Then your wife will. You don't seem to realize, that in married life three is company and two is none.

JACK (*sententiously*). That, my dear young friend, is the theory that the corrupt French Drama has been propounding for the last fifty years.

ALGERNON. Yes; and that the happy English home has proved in half the time.

JACK. For heaven's sake, don't try to be cynical. It's perfectly easy to be cynical.

ALGERNON. My dear fellow, it isn't easy to be anything now-a-days. There's such a lot of beastly competition about. (*The sound of an electric bell is heard.*) Ah! that must be Aunt Augusta. Only relatives, or creditors, ever ring in that Wagnerian manner. Now, if I get her out of the way for ten minutes, so that you can have an opportunity for proposing to Gwendolen, may I dine with you to-night at Willis's?"

JACK. I suppose so if you want to.

ALGERNON. Yes, but you must be serious about it. I hate people who are not serious about meals. It is so shallow of them.

(*Enter Lane.*)

LANE. Lady Bracknell and Miss Fairfax. (*Algernon goes forward to meet them. Enter Lady Bracknell and Gwendolen.*)

LADY BRACKNELL. Good afternoon, dear Algernon, I hope you are behaving very well.

ALGERNON. I'm feeling very well, Aunt Augusta.

LADY BRACKNELL. That's not quite the same thing. In fact the two things rarely go together. (*Sees Jack and bows to him with icy coldness.*)

ALGERNON (*to Gwendolen*). Dear me, you are smart!

GWENDOLEN. I am always smart! Aren't I, Mr. Worthing?

JACK. You're quite perfect, Miss Fairfax.

GWENDOLEN. Oh! I hope I am not that. It would leave no room for developments, and I intend to develop in *many directions*. (*Gwendolen and Jack sit down together in the corner.*)

LADY BRACKNELL. I'm sorry if we are a little late, Algernon, but I was obliged to call on dear Lady Harbury. I hadn't been there since her poor husband's death. I never saw a woman so altered; she looks quite twenty years younger.

And now I'll have a cup of tea, and one of those nice cucumber sandwiches you promised me.

ALGERNON. Certainly, Aunt Augusta. (*Goes over to tea-table.*)

LADY BRACKNELL. Won't you come and sit here, Gwendolen?

GWENDOLEN. Thanks, mamma, I'm quite comfortable where I am.

ALGERNON (*picking up empty plate in horror*). Good heavens! Lane! Why are there no cucumber sandwiches? I ordered them specially.

LANE (*gravely*). There were no cucumbers in the market this morning, sir. I went down twice.

ALGERNON. No cucumbers!

LANE. No, sir. Not even for ready money.

ALGERNON. That will do, Lane, thank you.

LANE. Thank you sir. (*Goes out.*)

ALGERNON. I am greatly distressed, Aunt Augusta, about there being no cucumbers, not even for ready money.

LADY BRACKNELL. It really makes no matter, Algernon. I had some crumpets with Lady Harbury, who seems to me to be living entirely for pleasure now.

ALGERNON. I hear her hair has turned quite gold from grief.

LADY BRACKNELL. It certainly has changed its colour. From what cause I, of course, cannot say. (*Algernon crosses and hands tea.*) Thank you. I've quite a treat for you to-night, Algernon. I am going to send you down with Mary Farquhar. She is such a nice woman, and so attentive to her husband. It's delightful to watch them.

ALGERNON. I am afraid, Aunt Augusta, I shall have to give up the pleasure of dining with you to-night after all.

LADY BRACKNELL (*frowning*). I hope not, Algernon. It would put my table completely out. Your uncle would have to dine upstairs. Fortunately he is accustomed to that.

ALGERNON. It is a great bore, and, I need hardly say, a terrible disappointment to me, but the fact is I have just had a telegram to say that my poor friend Bunbury is very ill again. (*Exchanges glances with Jack.*) They seem to think I should be with him.

LADY BRACKNELL. It is very strange. This Mr. Bunbury seems to suffer from curiously bad health.

ALGERNON. Yes; poor Bunbury is a dreadful invalid.

LADY BRACKNELL. Well, I must say, Algernon, that I think it is high time that Mr. Bunbury made up his mind whether he was going to live or to die. This shilly-shallying with the question is absurd. Nor do I in any way approve of the modern sympathy with invalids. I consider it morbid. Illness of any kind is hardly a thing to be encouraged in others. Health is the primary duty of life. I am always telling that to your poor uncle, but he never seems to take much notice . . . as far as any improvement in his ailments goes. I should be much obliged if you would ask Mr. Bunbury, from me, to be kind enough not to have a relapse on Saturday, for I rely on you to arrange my music for me. It is my last reception and one wants something that will encouraged conversation, particularly at the end of the season when everyone has practically said whatever they had to say, which, in most cases, was probably not much.

ALGERNON. I'll speak to Bunbury, Aunt Augusta, if he is still conscious, and I think I can promise you he'll be all right by Saturday. You see, if one plays good music, people don't listen, and if one plays bad music people don't talk. But I'll run over the programme I've drawn out, if you will kindly come into the next room for a moment.

LADY BRACKNELL. Thank you, Algernon. It is very thoughtful of you. (*Rising, and following Algernon.*) I'm sure the programme will be delightful, after a few expurgations. French songs I cannot possibly allow. People always seem to think that they are improper, and either look shocked, which is vulgar, or laugh, which is worse. But German sounds a thoroughly respectable language, and indeed, I believe is so. Gwendolen, you will accompany me.

GWENDOLEN. Certainly, mamma. (*Lady Bracknell and Algernon go into the music-room, Gwendolen remains behind.*)

JACK. Charming day it has been, Miss Fairfax.

GWENDOLEN. Pray don't talk to me about the weather, Mr. Worthing. Whenever people talk to me about the weather, I always feel quite certain that they mean something else. And that makes me so nervous.

JACK. I do mean something else.

GWENDOLEN. I thought so. In fact, I am never wrong.

JACK. And I would like to be allowed to take advantage of Lady Bracknell's temporary absence . . .

GWENDOLEN. I would certainly advise you to do so. Mamma has a way of coming back suddenly into a room that I have often had to speak to her about.

JACK (*nervously*). Miss Fairfax, ever since I met you I have admired you more than any girl . . . I have ever met since . . . I met you.

GWENDOLEN. Yes, I am quite aware of the fact. And I often wish that in public, at any rate, you had been more demonstrative. For me you have always had an irresistible fascination. Even before I met you I was far from indifferent to you. (*Jack looks at her in amazement.*) We live, as I hope you know, Mr. Worthing, in an age of ideals. The fact is constantly mentioned in the more expensive monthly magazines, and has reached the provincial pulpits I am told: and my ideal has always been to love some one of the name of Ernest. There is something in that name that inspires absolute confidence. The moment Algernon first mentioned to me that he had a friend called Ernest, I knew I was destined to love you.

JACK. You really love me, Gwendolen?

GWENDOLEN. Passionately!

JACK. Darling! You don't know how happy you've made me.

GWENDOLEN. My own Ernest!

JACK. But you don't really mean to say that you couldn't love me if my name wasn't Ernest?

GWENDOLEN. But your name is Ernest.

JACK. Yes, I know it is. But supposing it was something else? Do you mean to say you couldn't love me then?

GWENDOLEN (*glibly*). Ah! that is clearly a metaphysical speculation, and like most metaphysical speculations has very little reference at all to the actual facts of real life, as we know them.

JACK. Personally, darling, to speak quite candidly, I don't much care about the name of Ernest . . . I don't think that name suits me at all.

GWENDOLEN. It suits you perfectly. It is a divine name. It has a music of its own. It produces vibrations.

JACK. Well, really, Gwendolen, I must say that I think there are lots of other much nicer names. I think, Jack, for instance, a charming name.

GWENDOLEN. Jack? . . . No, there is very little music in the name Jack, if any at all, indeed. It does not thrill. It produces absolutely no vibration. . . . I have known several Jacks, and they all, without exception, were more than usually plain. Besides, Jack is a notorious domesticity for John! And I pity any woman who is married to a man called John. She would probably never be allowed to know the entrancing pleasure of a single moment's solitude. The only really safe name is Ernest.

JACK. Gwendolen, I must get christened at once—I mean we must get married at once. There is no time to be lost.

GWENDOLEN. Married, Mr. Worthing?

JACK (*astounded*). Well . . . surely. You know that I love you, and you led me to believe, Miss Fairfax, that you were not absolutely indifferent to me.

GWENDOLEN. I adore you. But you haven't proposed to me yet. Nothing has been said at all about marriage. The subject has not even been touched on.

JACK. Well . . . may I propose to you now?

GWENDOLEN. I think it would be an admirable opportunity. And to spare you any possible disappointment, Mr. Worthing, I think it only fair to tell you quite frankly beforehand that I am fully determined to accept you.

JACK. Gwendolen!

GWENDOLEN. Yes, Mr. Worthing, what have you got to say to me?

JACK. You know what I have got to say to you.

GWENDOLEN. Yes, but you don't say it.

JACK. Gwendolen, will you marry me? (*Goes on his knees.*)

GWENDOLEN. Of course I will, darling. How long you have been about it! I am afraid you have had very little experience in how to propose.

JACK. My own one, I have never loved anyone in the world but you.

GWENDOLEN. Yes, but men often propose for practice. I know my brother Gerald does. All my girl-friends tell me so. What wonderfully blue eyes you have, Ernest! They are quite, quite blue. I hope you will always look at me just like that, especially when there are other people present.

(*Enter Lady Bracknell.*)

LADY BRACKNELL. Mr. Worthing! Rise, sir, from this semi-recumbent posture. It is most indecorous.

GWENDOLEN. Mamma! (*He tried to rise; she restrains him.*) I must beg you to retire. This is no place for you. Besides, Mr. Worthing has not quite finished yet.

LADY BRACKNELL. Finished what, may I ask?

GWENDOLEN. I am engaged to Mr. Worthing, mamma. (*They rise together.*)

LADY BRACKNELL. Pardon me, you are not engaged to anyone. When you do become engaged to some one, I, or your father, should his health permit him, will inform you of the fact. An engagement should come on a young girl as a surprise, pleasant or unpleasant, as the case may be. It is hardly a matter that she could be allowed to arrange for herself. . . . And now I have a few questions to put to you, Mr. Worthing. While I am making these inquiries, you, Gwendolen, will wait for me below in the carriage.

GWENDOLEN (*reproachfully*). Mamma!

LADY BRACKNELL. In the carriage, Gwendolen! (*Gwendolen goes to the door. She and Jack blow kisses to each other behind Lady Bracknell's back. Lady Bracknell looks vaguely about as if she could not understand what the noise was. Finally turns round.*) Gwendolen, the carriage!

GWENDOLEN. Yes, mamma. (*Goes out, looking back at Jack.*)

LADY BRACKNELL (*sitting down*). You can take a seat, Mr. Worthing. (*Looks in her pocket for note-book and pencil.*)

JACK. Thank you, Lady Bracknell, I prefer standing.

LADY BRACKNELL (*pencil and notebook in hand*). I feel bound to tell you that you are not down on my list of eligible young men, although I have the same list as the dear Duchess of Bolton has. We work together, in fact. However, I am quite ready to enter your name, should your answers be what a really affectionate mother requires. Do you smoke?

JACK. Well, yes, I must admit I smoke.

LADY BRACKNELL. I am glad to hear it. A man should always have an occupation of some kind. There are far too many idle men in London as it is. How old are you?

JACK. Twenty-nine.

LADY BRACKNELL. A very good age to be married at. I have always been of opinion that a man who desires to get married should know either everything or nothing. Which do you know?

JACK (*after some hesitation*). I know nothing, Lady Bracknell.

LADY BRACKNELL. I am pleased to hear it. I do not approve of anything that tampers with natural ignorance. Ignorance is like a delicate exotic fruit; touch it and the bloom is gone. The whole theory of modern education is radically unsound. Fortunately in England, at any rate, education produces no effect whatsoever. If it did, it would prove a serious danger to the upper classes, and probably lead to acts of violence in Grosvenor Square. What is your income?

JACK. Between seven and eight thousand a year.

LADY BRACKNELL (*makes a note in her book*). In land, or in investments?

JACK. In investments, chiefly.

LADY BRACKNELL. That is satisfactory. What between the duties expected of one during one's life-time, and the duties exacted from one after one's death, land has ceased to be either a profit or a pleasure. It gives one position, and prevents one from keeping it up. That's all that can be said about land.

JACK. I have a country house with some land, of course, attached to it, about fifteen hundred acres, I believe; but I don't depend on that for my real income. In fact, as far as I can make out, the poachers are the only people who make anything out of it.

LADY BRACKNELL. A country house! How many bedrooms? Well, that point can be cleared up afterwards. You have a town house, I hope? A girl with a simple, unspoiled nature, like Gwendolen, could hardly be expected to reside in the country.

JACK. Well, I own a house in Belgrave Square, but it is let by the year to Lady Bloxham. Of course, I can get it back whenever I like, at six months' notice.

LACY BRACKNELL. Lady Bloxham? I don't know her.

JACK. Oh, she goes about very little. She is a lady considerably advanced in years.

LADY BRACKNELL. Ah, now-a-days that is no guarantee of respectability of character. What number in Belgrave Square?

JACK. 149.

LADY BRACKNELL (*shaking her head*). The unfashionable side. I thought there was something. However, that could easily be altered.

JACK. Do you mean the fashion, or the side?

LADY BRACKNELL (*sternly*). Both, if necessary, I presume. What are your politics?

JACK. Well, I am afraid I really have none. I am a Liberal Unionist.

LADY BRACKNELL. Oh, they count as Tories. They dine with us. Or come in the evening, at any rate. Now to minor matters. Are your parents living?

JACK. I have lost both my parents.

LADY BRACKNELL. Both? . . . That seems like carelessness. Who was your father? He was evidently a man of some wealth. Was he born in what the Radical papers call the purple of commerce, or did he rise from the ranks of the aristocracy?

JACK. I am afraid I really don't know. The fact is, Lady Bracknell, I said I had lost my parents. It would be nearer the truth to say that my parents seem to have lost me . . . I don't actually know who I am by birth. I was . . . well, I was found.

LADY BRACKNELL. Found!

JACK. The late Mr. Thomas Cardew, an old gentleman of a very charitable and kindly disposition, found me, and gave me the name of Worthing, because he happened to have a first-class ticket for Worthing in his pocket at the time. Worthing is a place in Sussex. It is a seaside resort.

LADY BRACKNELL. Where did the charitable gentleman who had a first-class ticket for this seaside resort find you?

JACK (*gravely*). In a hand-bag.

LADY BRACKNELL. A hand-bag?

JACK (*very seriously*). Yes, Lady Bracknell. I was in a hand-bag—a somewhat large, black leather hand-bag, with handles to it—an ordinary hand-bag in fact.

LADY BRACKNELL. In what locality did Mr. James, or Thomas, Cardew come across this ordinary hand-bag?

JACK. In the cloak-room at Victoria Station. It was given to him in mistake for his own.

LADY BRACKNELL. The cloak-room at Victoria Station?

JACK. Yes. The Brighton line.

LADY BRACKNELL. The line is immaterial. Mr. Worthing, I confess I feel somewhat bewildered by what you have just told me. To be born, or at any rate bred, in a hand-bag, whether it had handles or not, seems to me to display a contempt for the ordinary decencies of family life that remind one of the worst excesses of the French Revolution. And I presume you know what that unfortunate movement led to? As for the particular locality in which the hand-bag was found, a cloak-room at a railway station might serve to conceal a social indiscretion—has probably, indeed, been used for the purpose before now—but it could hardly be regarded as an assured basis for a recognized position in good society.

JACK. May I ask you then what you would advise me to do? I need hardly say I would do anything in the world to ensure Gwendolen's happiness.

LADY BRACKNELL. I would strongly advise you, Mr. Worthing, to try and acquire some relations as soon as possible, and to make a definite effort to produce at any rate one parent, of either sex, before the season is quite over.

JACK. Well, I don't see how I could possibly manage to do that. I can produce the hand-bag at any moment. It is in my dressing-room at home. I really think that should satisfy you, Lady Bracknell.

LADY BRACKNELL. Me, sir! What has it to do with me? You can hardly imagine that I and Lord Bracknell would dream of allowing our only daughter—a girl brought up with the utmost care—to marry into a cloak-room, and form an alliance with a parcel? Good morning, Mr. Worthing! (*Lady Bracknell sweeps out in majestic indignation.*)

JACK. Good morning! (*Algernon, from the other room, strikes up the Wedding March. Jack looks perfectly furious, and goes to the door.*) For goodness' sake don't play that ghastly tune, Algy! How idiotic you are! (*The music stops, and Algernon enters cheerily.*)

ALGERNON. Didn't it go off all right, old boy? You don't mean to say Gwendolen refused you? I know it is a way she has. She is always refusing people. I think it is most ill-natured of her.

JACK. Oh, Gwendolen is as right as a trivet. As far as she is concerned, we are engaged. Her mother is perfectly unbearable. Never met such a Gorgon . . . I don't really know what a Gorgon is like, but I am quite sure that Lady Bracknell is one. In any case, she is a monster, without being a myth, which is rather unfair. . . . I beg your pardon, Algy, I suppose I shouldn't talk about your own aunt in that way before you.

ALGERNON. My dear boy, I love hearing my relations abused. It is the only thing that makes me put up with them at all. Relations are simply a tedious pack of people, who haven't got the remotest knowledge of how to live, nor the smallest instinct about when to die.

JACK. Oh, that is nonsense!

ALGERNON. It isn't!

JACK. Well, I won't argue about the matter. You always want to argue about things.

ALGERNON. That is exactly what things were originally made for.

JACK. Upon my word, if I thought that, I'd shoot myself . . . (*A pause.*) You don't think there is any chance of Gwendolen becoming like her mother in about a hundred and fifty years, do you, Algy?

ALGERNON. All women become like their mothers. That is their tragedy. No man does. That's his.

JACK. Is that clever?

ALGERNON. It is perfectly phrased! and quite as true as any observation in civilized life should be.

JACK. I am sick to death of cleverness. Everybody is clever now-a-days. You can't go anywhere without meeting clever people. The thing has become an absolute public nuisance. I wish to goodness we had a few fools left.

ALGERNON. We have.

JACK. I should extremely like to meet them. What do they talk about?

ALGERNON. The fools? Oh! about the clever people, of course.

JACK. What fools!

ALGERNON. By the way, did you tell Gwendolen the truth about your being Ernest in town, and Jack in the country?

JACK (*in a very patronising manner*). My dear fellow, the truth isn't quite the sort of thing one tells to a nice, sweet, refined girl. What extraordinary ideas you have about the way to behave to a woman!

ALGERNON. The only way to behave to a woman is to make love to her, if she is pretty, and to someone else if she is plain.

JACK. Oh, that is nonsense.

ALGERNON. What about your brother? What about the profligate Ernest?

JACK. Oh, before the end of the week I shall have got rid of him. I'll say he died in Paris of apoplexy. Lots of people die of apoplexy, quite suddenly, don't they?

ALGERNON. Yes, but it's hereditary, my dear fellow. It's a sort of thing that runs in families. You had much better say a severe chill.

JACK. You are sure a severe chill isn't hereditary, or anything of that kind?

ALGERNON. Of course it isn't!

JACK. Very well, then. My poor brother Ernest is carried off suddenly in Paris, by a severe chill. That gets rid of him.

ALGERNON. But I thought you said that . . . Miss Cardew was a little too much interested in your poor brother Ernest? Won't she feel his loss a good deal?

JACK. Oh, that is all right. Cecily is not a silly, romantic girl, I am glad to say. She has got a capital appetite, goes for long walks, and pays no attention at all to her lessons.

ALGERNON. I would rather like to see Cecily.

JACK. I will take very good care you never do. She is excessively pretty, and she is only just eighteen.

ALGERNON. Have you told Gwendolen yet that you have an excessively pretty ward who is only just eighteen?

JACK. Oh! one doesn't blurt these things out to people. Cecily and Gwendolen are perfectly certain to be extremely great friends. I'll bet you anything you like that half an hour after they have met, they will be calling each other sister.

ALGERNON. Women only do that when they have called each other a lot of other things first. Now, my dear boy, if we want to get a good table at Willis's, we really must go and dress. Do you know it is nearly seven?

JACK (*irritably*). Oh! it always is nearly seven.

ALGERNON. Well, I'm hungry.

JACK. I never knew you when you weren't . . . .

ALGERNON. What shall we do after dinner? Go to a theatre?

JACK. Oh, no! I loathe listening.

ALGERNON. Well, let us go to the Club?

JACK. Oh, no! I hate talking.

ALGERNON. Well, we might trot round to the Empire at ten?

JACK. Oh, no! can't bear looking at things. It is so silly.

ALGERNON. Well, what shall we do?

JACK. Nothing!

ALGERNON. It is awfully hard work doing nothing. However, I don't mind hard work where there is no definite object of any kind.

(*Enter Lane.*)

LANE. Miss Fairfax.

(*Enter Gwendolen. Lane goes out.*)

ALGERNON. Gwendolen, upon my word!

GWENDOLEN. Algy, kindly turn your back. I have something very particular to say to Mr. Worthing.

ALGERNON. Really, Gwendolen, I don't think I can allow this at all.

GWENDOLEN. Algy, you always adopt a strictly immoral attitude towards life. You are not quite old enough to do that. (*Algernon retires to the fireplace.*)

JACK. My own darling!

GWENDOLEN. Ernest, we may never be married. From the expression on mamma's face I fear we never shall. Few parents now-a-days pay any regard to what their children say to them. The old-fashioned respect for the young is fast dying out. Whatever influence I ever had over

mamma, I lost at the age of three. But although she may prevent us from becoming man and wife, and I may marry someone else, and marry often, nothing that she can possibly do can alter my eternal devotion to you.

JACK. Dear Gwendolen.

GWENDOLEN. The story of your romantic origin, as related to me by mamma, with unpleasing comments, has naturally stirred the deeper fibers of my nature. Your Christian name has an irresistible fascination. The simplicity of your character makes you exquisitely incomprehensible to me. Your town address at the Albany I have. What is your address in the country?

JACK. The Manor House, Woolton, Hertfordshire. (*Algernon, who has been carefully listening, smiles to himself, and writes the address on his shirt-cuff. Then picks up the Railway Guide.*)

GWENDOLEN. There is a good postal service, I suppose? It may be necessary to do something desperate. That, of course, will require serious consideration. I will communicate with you daily.

JACK. My own one!

GWENDOLEN. How long do you remain in town?

JACK. Till Monday.

GWENDOLEN. Good! Algy, you may turn round now.

ALGERNON. Thanks, I've turned round already.

GWENDOLEN. You may also ring the bell.

JACK. You will let me see you to your carriage, my own darling?

GWENDOLEN. Certainly.

JACK (*to Lane, who now enters*). I will see Miss Fairfax out.

LANE. Yes, sir. (*Jack and Gwendolen go off. Lane presents several letters on a salver to Algernon. It is to be surmised that they are bills, as Algernon, after looking at the envelopes, tears them up.*)

ALGERNON. A glass of sherry, Lane.

LANE. Yes, sir.

ALGERNON. To-morrow, Lane, I'm going Bunburying.

LANE. Yes, sir.

ALGERNON. I shall probably not be back till Monday. You can put up my dress clothes, my smoking jacket, and all the Bunbury suits . . .

LANE. Yes, sir. (*Handing sherry.*)

ALGERNON. I hope to-morrow will be a fine day, Lane.

LANE. It never is, sir.

ALGERNON. Lane, you're a perfect pessimist.

LANE. I do my best to give satisfaction, sir.

(*Enter Jack. Lane goes off.*)

JACK. There's a sensible, intellectual girl! the only girl I ever cared for in my life. (*Algernon is laughing immoderately.*) What on earth are you so amused at?

ALGERNON. Oh, I'm a little anxious about poor Bunbury, that's all.

JACK. If you don't take care, your friend Bunbury will get you into a serious scrape some day.

ALGERNON. I love scrapes. They are the only things that are never serious.

JACK. Oh, that's nonsense, Algy. You never talk anything but nonsense.

ALGERNON. Nobody ever does. (*Jack looks indignantly at him, and leaves the room. Algernon lights a cigarette, reads his shirt-cuff and smiles.*)

ACT 2

SCENE: *Garden at the Manor House. A flight of gray stone steps leads up to the house. The garden, an old-fashioned one, full of roses. Time of year, July. Basket chairs, and a table covered with books, are set under a large yew tree.*

(*Miss Prism discovered seated at the table. Cecily is at the back watering flowers.*)

MISS PRISM (*calling*). Cecily, Cecily! Surely such a utilitarian occupation as the watering of flowers is rather Moulton's duty than yours? Especially at a moment when intellectual pleasures await you. Your German grammar is on the table. Pray open it at page fifteen. We will repeat yesterday's lesson.

CECILY (*coming over very slowly*). But I don't like German. It isn't at all a becoming language. I know perfectly well that I look quite plain after my German lesson.

MISS PRISM. Child, you know how anxious your guardian is that you should improve yourself in every way. He laid particular stress on your German, as he was leaving for town yesterday. Indeed, he always lays stress on your German when he is leaving for town.

CECILY. Dear Uncle Jack is so very serious! Sometimes he is so serious that I think he cannot be quite well.

MISS PRISM (*drawing herself up*). Your guardian enjoys the best of health, and his gravity of demeanour is especially to be commended in one so comparatively young as he is. I know no one who has a higher sense of duty and responsibility.

CECILY. I suppose that is why he often looks a little bored when we three are together.

MISS PRISM. Cecily! I am surprised at you. Mr. Worthing has many troubles in his life. Idle merriment and triviality would be out of place in his conversation. You must remember his constant anxiety about that unfortunate young man, his brother.

CECILY. I wish Uncle Jack would allow the unfortunate young man, his brother, to come down here sometimes. We might have a good influence over him, Miss Prism. I am sure you certainly would. You know German, and geology, and things of that kind influence a man very much. (*Cecily begins to write in her diary.*)

MISS PRISM (*shaking her head*). I do not think that even I could produce any effect on a character that, according to his own brother's admission, is irretrievably weak and

vacillating. Indeed, I am not sure that I would desire to reclaim him. I am not in favour of this modern mania for turning bad people into good people at a moment's notice. As a man sows so let him reap. You must put away your diary, Cecily. I really don't see why you should keep a diary at all.

CECILY. I keep a diary in order to enter the wonderful secrets of my life. If I didn't write them down I should probably forget all about them.

MISS PRISM. Memory, my dear Cecily, is the diary that we all carry about with us.

CECILY. Yes, but it usually chronicles the things that have never happened, and couldn't possibly have happened. I believe that Memory is responsible for nearly all the three-volume novels that Mudie sends us.

MISS PRISM. Do not speak slightingly of the three-volume novel, Cecily. I wrote one myself in earlier days.

CECILY. Did you really, Miss Prism? How wonderfully clever you are! I hope it did not end happily? I don't like novels that end happily. They depress me so much.

MISS PRISM. The good ended happily, and the bad unhappily. That is what Fiction means.

CECILY. I suppose so. But it seems very unfair. And was your novel ever published?

MISS PRISM. Alas! no. The manuscript unfortunately was abandoned. I use the word in the sense of lost or mislaid. To your work, child, these speculations are profitless.

CECILY (*smiling*). But I see dear Dr. Chasuble coming up through the garden.

MISS PRISM (*rising and advancing*). Dr. Chasuble! This is indeed a pleasure.

(*Enter Canon Chasuble.*)

CHASUBLE. And how are we this morning? Miss Prism, you are, I trust, well?

CECILY. Miss Prism has just been complaining of a slight headache. I think it would do her so much good to have a short stroll with you in the park, Dr. Chasuble.

MISS PRISM. Cecily, I have not mentioned anything about a headache.

CECILY. No, dear Miss Prism, I know that, but I felt instinctively that you had a headache. Indeed I was thinking about that, and not about my German lesson, when the Rector came in.

CHASUBLE. I hope, Cecily, you are not inattentive.

CECILY. Oh, I am afraid I am.

CHASUBLE. That is strange. Were I fortunate enough to be Miss Prism's pupil, I would hang upon her lips. (*Miss Prism glares.*) I spoke metaphorically.—My metaphor was drawn from bees. Ahem! Mr. Worthing, I suppose, has not returned from town yet?

MISS PRISM. We do not expect him till Monday afternoon.

CHASUBLE. Ah, yes, he usually likes to spend his Sunday in London. He is not one of those whose sole aim is enjoyment, as by all accounts, that unfortunate young man, his brother, seems to be. But I must not disturb Egeria and her pupil any longer.

MISS PRISM. Egeria? My name is Lætitia, Doctor.

CHASUBLE (*bowing*). A classical allusion merely, drawn from the Pagan authors. I shall see you both no doubt at Evensong.

MISS PRISM. I think, dear Doctor, I will have a stroll with you. I find I have a headache after all, and a walk might do it good.

CHASUBLE. With pleasure, Miss Prism, with pleasure. We might go as far as the schools and back.

MISS PRISM. That would be delightful. Cecily, you will read your Political Economy in my absence. The chapter on the Fall of the Rupee you may omit. It is somewhat too sensational. Even these metallic problems have their melodramatic side.

(*Goes down the garden with Dr. Chasuble.*)

CECILY (*picks up books and throws them back on table*). Horrid Political Economy! Horrid Geography! Horrid, horrid German!

(*Enter Merriman with a card on a salver.*)

MERRIMAN. Mr. Ernest Worthing has just driven over from the station. He has brought his luggage with him.

CECILY (*takes the card and reads it*). "Mr. Ernest Worthing, B 4 The Albany, W." Uncle Jack's brother! Did you tell him Mr. Worthing was in town?

MERRIMAN. Yes, Miss. He seemed very much disappointed. I mentioned that you and Miss Prism were in the garden. He said he was anxious to speak to you privately for a moment.

CECILY. Ask Mr. Ernest Worthing to come here. I suppose you had better talk to the housekeeper about a room for him.

MERRIMAN. Yes, Miss.   (*Merriman goes off.*)

CECILY. I have never met any really wicked person before. I feel rather frightened. I am so afraid he will look just like everyone else.

(*Enter Algernon, very gay and debonair.*)

He does!

ALGERNON (*raising his hat*). You are my little cousin Cecily, I'm sure.

CECILY. You are under some strange mistake. I am not little. In fact, I am more than usually tall for my age. (*Algernon is rather taken aback.*) But I am your cousin Cecily. You, I see from your card, are Uncle Jack's brother, my cousin Ernest, my wicked cousin Ernest.

ALGERNON. Oh! I am not really wicked at all, cousin Cecily. You mustn't think that I am wicked.

CECILY. If you are not, then you have certainly been deceiving us all in a very inexcusable manner. I hope you have not been leading a double life, pretending to be wicked and being really good all the time. That would be hypocrisy.

ALGERNON (*looks at her in amazement*). Oh! of course I have been rather reckless.

CECILY. I am glad to hear it.

ALGERNON. In fact, now you mention the subject, I have been very bad in my own small way.

CECILY. I don't think you should be so proud of that, though I am sure it must have been very pleasant.

ALGERNON. It is much pleasanter being here with you.

CECILY. I can't understand how you are here at all. Uncle Jack won't be back till Monday afternoon.

ALGERNON. That is a great disappointment. I am obliged to go up by the first train on Monday morning. I have a business appointment that I am anxious . . . to miss.

CECILY. Couldn't you miss it anywhere but in London?

ALGERNON. No; the appointment is in London.

CECILY. Well, I know, of course, how important it is not to keep a business engagement, if one wants to retain any sense of the beauty of life, but still I think you had better wait till Uncle Jack arrives. I know he wants to speak to you about your emigrating.

ALGERNON. About my what?

CECILY. Your emigrating. He has gone up to buy your outfit.

ALGERNON. I certainly wouldn't let Jack buy my outfit. He has no taste in neckties at all.

CECILY. I don't think you will require neckties. Uncle Jack is sending you to Australia.

ALGERNON. Australia! I'd sooner die.

CECILY. Well, he said at dinner on Wednesday night, that you would have to choose between this world, the next world, and Australia.

ALGERNON. Oh, well! The accounts I have received of Australia and the next world, are not particularly encouraging. This world is good enough for me, cousin Cecily.

CECILY. Yes, but are you good enough for it?

ALGERNON. I'm afraid I'm not that. That is why I want you to reform me. You might make that your mission, if you don't mind, cousin Cecily.

CECILY. I'm afraid I've not time, this afternoon.

ALGERNON. Well, would you mind my reforming myself this afternoon?

CECILY. That is rather Quixotic of you. But I think you should try.

ALGERNON. I will. I feel better already.

CECILY. You are looking a little worse.

ALGERNON. That is because I am hungry.

CECILY. How thoughtless of me. I should have remembered that when one is going to lead an entirely new life, one requires regular and wholesome meals. Won't you come in?

ALGERNON. Thank you. Might I have a button-hole first? I never have any appetite unless I have a button-hole first.

CECILY. A Maréchal Niel? (*Picks up scissors.*)

ALGERNON. No, I'd sooner have a pink rose.

CECILY. Why? (*Cuts a flower.*)

ALGERNON. Because you are like a pink rose, cousin Cecily.

CECILY. I don't think it can be right for you to talk to me like that. Miss Prism never says such things to me.

ALGERNON. Then Miss Prism is a short-sighted old lady. (*Cecily puts the rose in his button-hole*.) You are the prettiest girl I ever saw.

CECILY. Miss Prism says that all good looks are a snare.

ALGERNON. They are a snare that every sensible man would like to be caught in.

CECILY. Oh! I don't think I would care to catch a sensible man. I shouldn't know what to talk to him about. (*They pass into the house. Miss Prism and Dr. Chasuble return.*)

MISS PRISM. You are too much alone, dear Dr. Chasuble. You should get married. A misanthrope I can understand—a womanthrope, never!

CHASUBLE (*with a scholar's shudder*). Believe me, I do not deserve so neologistic a phrase. The precept as well as the practice of the Primitive Church was distinctly against matrimony.

MISS PRISM (*sententiously*). That is obviously the reason why the Primitive Church has not lasted up to the present day. And you do not seem to realize, dear Doctor, that by persistently remaining single, a man converts himself into a permanent public temptation. Men should be careful; this very celibacy leads weaker vessels astray.

CHASUBLE. But is a man not equally attractive when married?

MISS PRISM. No married man is ever attractive except to his wife.

CHASUBLE. And often, I've been told, not even to her.

MISS PRISM. That depends on the intellectual sympathies of the woman. Maturity can always be depended on. Ripeness can be trusted. Young women are green. (*Dr. Chasuble starts*.) I spoke horticulturally. My metaphor was drawn from fruits. But where is Cecily?

CHASUBLE. Perhaps she followed us to the schools.

(*Enter Jack slowly from the back of the garden. He is dressed in the deepest mourning, with crepe hatband and black gloves.*)

MISS PRISM. Mr. Worthing!

CHASUBLE. Mr. Worthing?

MISS PRISM. This is indeed a surprise. We did not look for you till Monday afternoon.

JACK (*shakes Miss Prism's hand in a tragic manner*). I have returned sooner than I expected. Dr. Chasuble, I hope you are well?

CHASUBLE. Dear Mr. Worthing, I trust this garb of woe does not betoken some terrible calamity?

JACK. My brother.

MISS PRISM. More shameful debts and extravagance?

CHASUBLE. Still leading his life of pleasure?

JACK (*shaking his head*). Dead!

CHASUBLE. Your brother Ernest dead?

JACK. Quite dead.

MISS PRISM. What a lesson for him! I trust he will profit by it.

CHAUSBLE. Mr. Worthing, I offer you my sincere condolence. You have at least the consolation of knowing that you were always the most generous and forgiving of brothers.

JACK. Poor Ernest! He had many faults, but it is a sad, sad blow.

CHASUBLE. Very sad indeed. Were you with him at the end?

JACK. No. He died abroad; in Paris, in fact. I had a telegram last night from the manager of the Grand Hotel.

CHAUSBLE. Was the cause of death mentioned?

JACK. A severe chill, it seems.

MISS PRISM. As a man sows, so shall he reap.

CHASUBLE (*raising his hand*). Charity, dear Miss Prism, charity! None of us are perfect. I myself am peculiarly susceptible to draughts. Will the interment take place here?

JACK. No. He seems to have expressed a desire to be buried in Paris.

CHASUBLE. In Paris! (*Shakes his head.*) I fear that hardly points to any very serious state of mind at the last. You would no doubt wish me to make some slight allusion to this tragic domestic affliction next Sunday. (*Jack presses his hand convulsively.*) My sermon on the meaning of the manna in the wilderness can be adapted to almost any occasion, joyful, or, as in the present case, distressing. (*All sigh.*) I have preached it at harvest celebrations, christenings, confirmations, on days of humiliation and festal days. The last time I delivered it was in the Cathedral, as a charity sermon on behalf of the Society for the Prevention of Discontentment among the Upper Orders. The Bishop, who was present, was much struck by some of the analogies I drew.

JACK. Ah, that reminds me, you mentioned christenings I think, Dr. Chasuble? I suppose you know how to christen all right? (*Dr. Chasuble looks astounded.*) I mean, of course, you are continually christening, aren't you?

MISS PRISM. It is, I regret to say, one of the Rector's most constant duties in this parish. I have often spoken to the poorer classes on the subject. But they don't seem to know what thrift is.

CHASUBLE. But is there any particular infant in whom you are interested, Mr. Worthing? Your brother was, I believe, unmarried, was he not?

JACK. Oh, yes.

MISS PRISM (*bitterly*). People who live entirely for pleasure usually are.

JACK. But it is not for any child, dear Doctor. I am very fond of children. No! the fact is, I would like to be christened myself, this afternoon, if you have nothing better to do.

CHASUBLE. But surely, Mr. Worthing, you have been christened already?

JACK. I don't remember anything about it.

CHASUBLE. But have you any grave doubts on the subject?

JACK. I certainly intend to have. Of course, I don't know if the thing would bother you in any way, or if you think I am a little too old now.

CHASUBLE. Not at all. The sprinkling, and, indeed, the immersion of adults is a perfectly canonical practice.

JACK. Immersion!

CHASUBLE. You need have no apprehensions. Sprinkling is all that is necessary, or indeed I think advisable. Our weather is so changeable. At what hour would you wish the ceremony performed?

JACK. Oh, I might trot around about five if that would suit you.

CHASUBLE. Perfectly, perfectly! In fact I have two similar ceremonies to perform at that time. A case of twins that occurred recently in one of the outlying cottages on your own estate. Poor Jenkins the carter, a most hard-working man.

JACK. Oh! I don't see much fun in being christened along with other babies. It would be childish. Would half-past five do?

CHASUBLE. Admirably! Admirably! (*Takes out watch.*) And now, dear Mr. Worthing, I will not intrude any longer into a house of sorrow. I would merely beg you not to be too much bowed down by grief. What seem to us bitter trials at the moment are often blessings in disguise.

MISS PRISM. This seems to me a blessing of an extremely obvious kind.

(*Enter Cecily from the house.*)

CECILY. Uncle Jack! Oh, I am pleased to see you back. But what horrid clothes you have on! Do go and change them.

MISS PRISM. Cecily!

CHASUBLE. My child! my child! (*Cecily goes towards Jack; he kisses her brow in a melancholy manner.*)

CECILY. What is the matter, Uncle Jack? Do look happy! You look as if you had a toothache and I have such a surprise for you. Who do you think is in the dining-room? Your brother!

JACK. Who?

CECILY. Your brother Ernest. He arrived about half an hour ago.

JACK. What nonsense! I haven't got a brother.

CECILY. Oh, don't say that. However badly he may have behaved to you in the past he is still your brother. You couldn't be so heartless as to disown him. I'll tell him to come out. And you will shake hands with him, won't you, Uncle Jack? (*Runs back into the house.*)

CHASUBLE. There are very joyful tidings.

MISS PRISM. After we had all been resigned to his loss, his sudden return seems to me peculiarly distressing.

JACK. My brother is in the dining-room? I don't know what it all means. I think it is perfectly absurd.

(*Enter Algernon and Cecily hand in hand. They come slowly up to Jack.*)

JACK. Good heavens! (*Motions Algernon away.*)

ALGERNON. Brother John, I have come down from town to tell you that I am very sorry for all the trouble I have given you, and that I intend to lead a better life in the future. (*Jack glares at him and does not take his hand.*)

CECILY. Uncle Jack, you are not going to refuse your own brother's hand.

JACK. Nothing will induce me to take his hand. I think his coming down here disgraceful. He knows perfectly well why.

CECILY. Uncle Jack, do be nice. There is good in everyone. Ernest has just been telling me about his poor invalid friend, Mr. Bunbury, whom he goes to visit so often. And surely there must be much good in one who is kind to an invalid, and leaves the pleasures of London to sit by a bed of pain.

JACK. Oh, he has been talking about Bunbury, has he?

CECILY. Yes, he has told me all about poor Mr. Bunbury, and his terrible state of health.

JACK. Bunbury! Well, I won't have him talk to you about Bunbury or about anything else. It is enough to drive one perfectly frantic.

ALGERNON. Of course I admit that the faults were all on my side. But I must say that I think that Brother John's coldness to me is peculiarly painful. I expected a more enthusiastic welcome, especially considering it is the first time I have come here.

CECILY. Uncle Jack, if you don't shake hands with Ernest I will never forgive you.

JACK. Never forgive me?

CECILY. Never, never, never!

JACK. Well, this is the last time I shall ever do it. (*Shakes hands with Algernon and glares.*)

CHASUBLE. It's pleasant, is it not, to see so perfect a reconciliation? I think we might leave the two brothers together.

MISS PRISM. Cecily, you will come with us.

CECILY. Certainly, Miss Prism. My little task of reconciliation is over.

CHASUBLE. You have done a beautiful action to-day, dear child.

MISS PRISM. We must not be premature in our judgments.

CECILY. I feel very happy. (*They all go off.*)

JACK. You young scoundrel, Algy, you must get out of this place as soon as possible. I don't allow any Bunburying here.

(*Enter Merriman.*)

MERRIMAN. I have put Mr. Ernest's things in the room next to yours, sir. I suppose that is all right?

JACK. What?

MERRIMAN. Mr. Ernest's luggage, sir. I have unpacked it and put it in the room next to your own.

JACK. His luggage?

MERRIMAN. Yes, sir. Three portmanteaus, a dressing-case, two hat-boxes, and a large luncheon-basket.

ALGERNON. I am afraid I can't stay more than a week this time.

JACK. Merriman, order the dog-cart at once. Mr. Ernest has been suddenly called back to town.

MERRIMAN. Yes, sir. (*Goes back into the house.*)

ALGERNON. What a fearful liar you are, Jack. I have not been called back to town at all.

JACK. Yes, you have.

ALGERNON. I haven't heard anyone call me.

JACK. Your duty as a gentleman calls you back.

ALGERNON. My duty as a gentleman has never interfered with my pleasures in the smallest degree.

JACK. I can quite understand that.

ALGERNON. Well, Cecily is a darling.

JACK. You are not to talk of Miss Cardew like that. I don't like it.

ALGERNON. Well, I don't like your clothes. You look perfectly ridiculous in them. Why on earth don't you go up and change? It is perfectly childish to be in deep mourning for a man who is actually staying for a whole week with you in your house as a guest. I call it grotesque.

JACK. You are certainly not staying with me for a whole week as a guest or anything else. You have got to leave . . . by the four-five train.

ALGERNON. I certainly won't leave you so long as you are in mourning. It would be most unfriendly. If I were in mourning you would stay with me, I suppose. I should think it very unkind if you didn't.

JACK. Well, will you go if I change my clothes?

ALGERNON. Yes, if you are not too long. I never saw anybody take so long to dress, and with such little result.

JACK. Well, at any rate, that is better than being always over-dressed as you are.

ALGERNON. If I am occasionally a little over-dressed, I make up for it by being always immensely over-educated.

JACK. Your vanity is ridiculous, your conduct an outrage, and your presence in my garden utterly absurd. However, you have got to catch the four-five, and I hope you will have a pleasant journey back to town. This Bunburying, as you call it, has not been a great success for you. (*Goes into the house.*)

ALGERNON. I think it has been a great success. I'm in love with Cecily, and that is everything. (*Enter Cecily at the back of the garden. She picks up the can and begins to water the flowers.*) But I must see her before I go, and make arrangements for another Bunbury. Ah, there she is.

CECILY. Oh, I merely came back to water the roses. I thought you were with Uncle Jack.

ALGERNON. He's gone to order the dog-cart for me.

CECILY. Oh, is he going to take you for a nice drive?

ALGERNON. He's going to send me away.

CECILY. Then have we got to part?

ALGERNON. I am afraid so. It's a very painful parting.

CECILY. It is always painful to part from people whom one has known for a very brief space of time. The absence of old friends one can endure with equanimity. But even a momentary separation from anyone to whom one has just been introduced is almost unbearable.

ALGERNON. Thank you.

(*Enter Merriman.*)

MERRIMAN. The dog-cart is at the door, sir. (*Algernon looking appealingly at Cecily.*)

CECILY. It can wait, Merriman . . . for . . . five minutes.

MERRIMAN. Yes, miss.   (*Exit Merriman.*)

ALGERNON. I hope, Cecily, I shall not offend you if I state quite frankly and openly that you seem to me to be in every way the visible personification of absolute perfection.

CECILY. I think your frankness does you great credit, Ernest. If you will allow me I will copy your remarks into my diary. (*Goes over to table and begins writing in diary.*)

ALGERNON. Do you really keep a diary? I'd give any thing to look at it. May I?

CECILY. Oh, no. (*Puts her hand over it.*) You see, it is simply a very young girl's record of her own thoughts and impressions, and consequently meant for publication. When it appears in volume form I hope you will order a copy. But pray, Ernest, don't stop. I delight in taking down from dictation. I have reached "absolute perfection." You can go on. I am quite ready for more.

ALGERNON (*somewhat taken aback*). Ahem! Ahem!

CECILY. Oh, don't cough, Ernest. When one is dictating one should speak fluently and not cough. Besides I don't know how to spell a cough. (*Writes as Algernon speaks.*)

ALGERNON (*speaking very rapidly*). Cecily, ever since I first looked upon your wonderful and incomparable beauty, I have dared to love you wildly, passionately, devotedly, hopelessly.

CECILY. I don't think that you should tell me that you love me wildly, passionately, devotedly, hopelessly. Hopelessly doesn't seem to make much sense, does it?

ALGERNON. Cecily!

(*Enter Merriman.*)

MERRIMAN. The dog-cart is waiting, sir.

ALGERNON. Tell it to come round next week, at the same hour.

MERRIMAN (*looks at Cecily, who makes no sign*). Yes, sir.

(*Merriman retires.*)

CECILY. Uncle Jack would be very much annoyed if he knew you were staying on till next week, at the same hour.

ALGERNON. Oh, I don't care about Jack. I don't care for anybody in the whole world but you. I love you, Cecily. You will marry me, won't you?

CECILY. You silly you! Of course. Why, we have been engaged for the last three months.

ALGERNON. For the last three months?

CECILY. Yes, it will be exactly three months on Thursday.

ALGERNON. But how did we become engaged?

CECILY. Well, ever since dear Uncle Jack first confessed to us that he had a younger brother who was very wicked and bad, you of course have formed the chief topic of conversation between myself and Miss Prism. And of course a man who is much talked about is always very attractive. One feels there must be something in him after all. I daresay it was foolish of me, but I fell in love with you, Ernest.

ALGERNON. Darling! And when was the engagement actually settled?

CECILY. On the 14th of February last. Worn out by your entire ignorance of my existence, I determined to end the matter one way or the other, and after a long struggle with myself I accepted you under this dear old tree here. The next day I bought this little ring in your name, and this is the little bangle with the true lovers' knot I promised you always to wear.

ALGERNON. Did I give you this? It's very pretty, isn't it?

CECILY. Yes, you've wonderfully good taste, Ernest. It's the excuse I've always given for your leading such a bad life. And this is the box in which I keep all your dear letters. (*Kneels at table, opens box, and produces letters tied up with blue ribbon.*)

ALGERNON. My letters! But my own sweet Cecily, I have never written you any letters.

CECILY. You need hardly remind me of that, Ernest. I remember only too well that I was forced to write your letters for you. I wrote always three times a week, and sometimes oftener.

ALGERNON. Oh, do let me read them, Cecily?

CECILY. Oh, I couldn't possibly. They would make you far too conceited. (*Replaces box.*) The three you wrote me after I had broken off the engagement are so beautiful, and so badly spelled, that even now I can hardly read them without crying a little.

ALGERNON. But was our engagement ever broken off?

CECILY. Of course it was. On the 22nd of last March. You can see the entry if you like. (*Shows diary.*) "Today I broke off my engagement with Ernest. I feel it is better to do so. The weather still continues charming."

ALGERNON. But why on earth did you break it off? What had I done? I had done nothing at all, Cecily. I am very much hurt indeed to hear you broke it off. Particularly when the weather was so charming.

CECILY. It would hardly have been a really serious engagement if it hadn't been broken off at least once. But I forgave you before the week was out.

ALGERNON (*crossing to her, and kneeling*). What a perfect angel you are, Cecily.

CECILY. You dear romantic boy. (*He kisses her, she puts her fingers through his hair.*) I hope your hair curls naturally, does it?

ALGERNON. Yes, darling, with a little help from others.

CECILY. I am so glad.

ALGERNON. You'll never break off our engagement again, Cecily?

CECILY. I don't think I could break it off now that I have actually met you. Besides, of course, that is the question of your name.

ALGERNON. Yes, of course. (*Nervously.*)

CECILY. You must not laugh at me, darling, but it had always been a girlish dream of mine to love some one whose name was Ernest. (*Algernon rises, Cecily also.*) There is something in that name that seems to inspire absolute confidence. I pity any poor married woman whose husband is not called Ernest.

ALGERNON. But, my dear child, do you mean to say you could not love me if I had some other name?

CECILY. But what name?

ALGERNON. Oh, any name you like—Algernon, for instance. . . .

CECILY. But I don't like the name of Algernon.

ALGERNON. Well, my own dear, sweet, loving little darling, I really can't see why you should object to the name of Algernon. It is not at all a bad name. In fact, it is rather an aristocratic name. Half of the chaps who get into the Bankruptcy Court are called Algernon. But seriously, Cecily . . . (*Moving to her*) . . . if my name was Algy, couldn't you love me?

CECILY (*rising*). I might respect you, Ernest, I might admire your character, but I fear that I should not be able to give you my undivided attention.

ALGERNON. Ahem! Cecily! (*Picking up hat.*) Your Rector here is, I suppose, thoroughly experienced in the practice of all the rites and ceremonials of the church?

CECILY. Oh, yes. Dr. Chasuble is a most learned man. He has never written a single book, so you can imagine how much he knows.

ALGERNON. I must see him at once on a most important christening—I mean on most important business.

CECILY. Oh!

ALGERNON. I sha'n't be away more than half an hour.

CECILY. Considering that we have been engaged since February the 14th, and that I only met you to-day for the first time, I think it is rather hard that you should leave me for so long a period as half an hour. Couldn't you make it twenty minutes?

ALGERNON. I'll be back in no time. (*Kisses her and rushes down the garden.*)

CECILY. What an impetuous boy he is. I like his hair so much. I must enter his proposal in my diary.

(*Enter Merriman.*)

MERRIMAN. A Miss Fairfax has just called to see Mr. Worthing. On very important business, Miss Fairfax states.

CECILY. Isn't Mr. Worthing in his library?

MERRIMAN. Mr. Worthing went over in the direction of the Rectory some time ago.

CECILY. Pray ask the lady to come out here; Mr. Worthing is sure to be back soon. And you can bring tea.

MERRIMAN. Yes, miss.   (*Goes out.*)

CECILY. Miss Fairfax! I suppose one of the many good elderly women who are associated with Uncle Jack in some of his philanthropic work in London. I don't quite like women who are interested in philanthropic work. I think it is so forward of them.

(*Enter Merriman.*)

MERRIMAN. Miss Fairfax.

(*Enter Gwendolen. Exit Merriman.*)

CECILY (*advancing to meet her*). Pray let me introduce myself to you. My name is Cecily Cardew.

GWENDOLEN. Cecily Cardew? (*Moving to her and shaking hands.*) What a very sweet name! Something tells me that we are going to be great friends. I like you already more than I can say. My first impressions of people are never wrong.

CECILY. How nice of you to like me so much after we have known each other such a comparatively short time. Pray sit down.

GWENDOLEN (*still standing up*). I may call you Cecily, may I not?

CECILY. With pleasure!

GWENDOLEN. And you will always call me Gwendolen, won't you?

CECILY. If you wish.

GWENDOLEN. Then that is all quite settled, is it not?

CECILY. I hope so. (*A pause. They both sit down together.*)

GWENDOLEN. Perhaps this might be a favourable opportunity for my mentioning who I am. My father is Lord Bracknell. You have never heard of papa, I suppose?

CECILY. I don't think so.

GWENDOLEN. Outside the family circle, papa, I am glad to say, is entirely unknown. I think that is quite as it should be. The home seems to me to be the proper sphere for the man. And certainly once a man begins to neglect his domestic duties he becomes painfully effeminate, does he not? And I don't like that. It makes men so very attractive. Cecily, mamma, whose views on education are remarkably strict, has brought me up to be extremely short-sighted; it is part of her system; so do you mind my looking at you through my glasses?

CECILY. Oh, not at all, Gwendolen. I am very fond of being looked at.

GWENDOLEN (*after examining Cecily carefully through a lorgnette*). You are here on a short visit, I suppose.

CECILY. Oh, no, I live here.

GWENDOLEN (*severely*). Really? Your mother, no doubt, or some female relative of advanced years, resides here also?

CECILY. Oh, no. I have no mother, nor, in fact, any relations.

GWENDOLEN. Indeed?

CECILY. My dear guardian, with the assistance of Miss Prism, has the arduous task of looking after me.

GWENDOLEN. Your guardian?

CECILY. Yes, I am Mr. Worthing's ward.

GWENDOLEN. Oh! It is strange he never mentioned to me that he had a ward. How secretive of him! He grows more interesting hourly. I am not sure, however, that the news inspires me with feelings of unmixed delight. (*Rising and going to her.*) I am very fond of you, Cecily; I have liked you ever since I met you. But I am bound to state that now that I know that you are Mr. Worthing's ward, I cannot help expressing a wish you were—well, just a little older than you seem to be—and not quite so very alluring in appearance. In fact, if I may speak candidly—

CECILY. Pray do! I think that whenever one has anything unpleasant to say, one should always be quite candid.

GWENDOLEN. Well, to speak with perfect candour, Cecily, I wish that you were fully forty-two, and more than usually plain for your age. Ernest has a strong upright nature. He is the very soul of truth and honour. Disloyalty would be as impossible to him as deception. But even men of the noblest possible moral character are extremely susceptible to the influence of the physical charms of others. Modern, no less than Ancient History, supplies us with many most painful examples of what I refer to. If it were not so, indeed, History would be quite unreadable.

CECILY. I beg your pardon, Gwendolen, did you say Ernest?

GWENDOLEN. Yes.

CECILY. Oh, but it is not Mr. Ernest Worthing who is my guardian. It is his brother—his elder brother.

GWENDOLEN (*sitting down again*). Ernest never mentioned to me that he had a brother.

CECILY. I am sorry to say they have not been on good terms for a long time.

GWENDOLEN. Ah! that accounts for it. And now that I think of it I have never heard any man mention his brother. The subject seems distasteful to most men. Cecily, you have lifted a load from my mind. I was growing almost anxious. It would have been terrible if any cloud had come across a friendship like ours, would it not? Of course you are quite, quite sure that it is not Mr. Ernest Worthing who is your guardian?

CECILY. Quite sure. (*A pause.*) In fact, I am going to be his.

GWENDOLEN (*enquiringly*). I beg your pardon?

CECILY (*rather shy and confidingly*). Dearest Gwendolen, there is no reason why I should make a secret of it to you. Our little county newspaper is sure to chronicle the fact next week. Mr. Ernest Worthing and I are engaged to be married.

GWENDOLEN (*quite politely, rising*). My darling Cecily, I think there must be some slight error. Mr. Ernest Worthing is engaged to me. The announcement will appear in the *Morning Post* on Saturday at the latest.

CECILY (*very politely, rising*). I am afraid you must be under some misconception. Ernest proposed to me exactly ten minutes ago. (*Shows diary.*)

GWENDOLEN (*examines diary through her lorgnette carefully*). It is certainly very curious, for he asked me to be his wife yesterday afternoon at 5.30. If you would care to verify the incident, pray do so. (*Produces diary of her own.*) I never travel without my diary. One should always have something sensational to read in the train. I am so sorry, dear Cecily, if it is any disappointment to you, but I am afraid *I* have the prior claim.

CECILY. It would distress me more than I can tell you, dear Gwendolen, if it caused you any mental or physical anguish, but I feel bound to point out that since Ernest proposed to you he clearly has changed his mind.

GWENDOLEN (*meditatively*). If the poor fellow has been entrapped into any foolish promise I shall consider it my duty to rescue him at once, and with a firm hand.

CECILY (*thoughtfully and sadly*). Whatever unfortunate entanglement my dear boy may have got into, I will never reproach him with it after we are married.

GWENDOLEN. Do you allude to me, Miss Cardew, as an entanglement? You are presumptuous. On an occasion of this kind it becomes more than a moral duty to speak one's mind. It becomes a pleasure.

CECILY. Do you suggest, Miss Fairfax, that I entrapped Ernest into an engagement? How dare you? This is no time for wearing the shallow mask of manners. When I see a spade I call it a spade.

GWENDOLEN (*satirically*). I am glad to say that I have never seen a spade. It is obvious that our social spheres have been widely different.

(*Enter Merriman, followed by the footman. He carries a salver, tablecloth, and plate-stand. Cecily is about to retort. The presence of the servants exercises a restraining influence, under which both girls chafe.*)

MERRIMAN. Shall I lay tea here as usual, miss?

CECILY (*sternly, in a calm voice*). Yes, as usual. (*Merriman begins to clear and lay cloth. A long pause. Cecily and Gwendolen glare at each other.*)

GWENDOLEN. Are there many interesting walks in the vicinity, Miss Cardew?

CECILY. Oh, yes, a great many. From the top of one of the hills quite close one can see five counties.

GWENDOLEN. Five counties! I don't think I should like that. I hate crowds.

CECILY (*sweetly*). I suppose that is why you live in town? (*Gwendolen bites her lip, and beats her foot nervously with her parasol.*)

GWENDOLEN (*looking round*). Quite a well-kept garden this is, Miss Cardew.

CECILY. So glad you like it, Miss Fairfax.

GWENDOLEN. I had no idea there were any flowers in the country.

CECILY. Oh, flowers are as common here, Miss Fairfax, as people are in London.

GWENDOLEN. Personally I cannot understand how anybody manages to exist in the country, if anybody who is anybody does. The country always bores me to death.

CECILY. Ah! This is what the newspapers call agricultural depression, is it not? I believe the aristocracy are suffering very much from it just at present. It is almost an epidemic amongst them, I have been told. May I offer you some tea, Miss Fairfax?

GWENDOLEN (*with elaborate politeness*). Thank you. (*Aside.*) Detestable girl! But I require tea!

CECILY (*sweetly*). Sugar?

GWENDOLEN (*superciliously*). No, thank you. Sugar is not fashionable any more. (*Cecily looks angrily at her, takes up the tongs and puts four lumps of sugar into the cup.*)

CECILY (*severely*). Cake or bread and butter?

GWENDOLEN (*in a bored manner*). Bread and butter, please. Cake is rarely seen at the best houses nowadays.

CECILY (*cuts a very large slice of cake, and puts it on the tray*). Hand that to Miss Fairfax. (*Merriman does so, and goes out with footman. Gwendolen drinks the tea and makes a grimace. Puts down cup at once, reaches out her hand to the bread and butter, looks at it, and finds it is cake. Rises in indignation.*)

GWENDOLEN. You have filled my tea with lumps of sugar, and though I asked most distinctly for bread and butter, you have given me cake. I am known for the gentleness of my disposition, and the extraordinary sweetness of my nature, but I warn you, Miss Cardew, you may go too far.

CECILY (*rising*). To save my poor, innocent, trusting boy from the machinations of any other girl there are no lengths to which I would not go.

GWENDOLEN. From the moment I saw you I distrusted you. I felt that you were false and deceitful. I am never deceived in such matters. My first impressions of people are invariably right.

CECILY. It seems to me, Miss Fairfax, that I am trespassing on your valuable time. No doubt you have many other calls of a similar character to make in the neighbourhood.

(*Enter Jack.*)

GWENDOLEN (*catching sight of him*). Ernest! My own Ernest!

JACK. Gwendolen! Darling! (*Offers to kiss her.*)

GWENDOLEN (*drawing back*). A moment! May I ask if you are engaged to be married to this young lady? (*Points to Cecily.*)

JACK (*laughing*). To dear little Cecily! Of course not! What could have put such an idea into your pretty little head?

GWENDOLEN. Thank you. You may. (*Offers her cheek.*)

CECILY (*very sweetly*). I knew there must be some misunderstanding, Miss Fairfax. The gentleman whose arm is at present around your waist is my dear guardian, Mr. John Worthing.

GWENDOLEN. I beg your pardon?

CECILY. This is Uncle Jack.

GWENDOLEN (*receding*). Jack! Oh!

(*Enter Algernon.*)

CECILY. Here is Ernest.

ALGERNON (*goes straight over to Cecily without noticing anyone else*). My own love! (*Offers to kiss her.*)

CECILY (*drawing back*). A moment, Ernest! May I ask you— are you engaged to be married to this young lady?

ALGERNON (*looking round*). To what young lady? Good heavens! Gwendolen!

CECILY. Yes, to good heavens, Gwendolen, I mean to Gwendolen.

ALGERNON (*laughing*). Of course not! What could have put such an idea into your pretty little head?

CECILY. Thank you. (*Presenting her cheek to be kissed.*) You may. (*Algernon kisses her.*)

GWENDOLEN. I felt there was some slight error, Miss Cardew. The gentleman who is now embracing you is my cousin, Mr. Algernon Moncrieff.

CECILY (*breaking away from Algernon*). Algernon Moncrieff! Oh! (*The two girls move towards each other and put their arms round each other's waists as if for protection.*)

CECILY. Are you called Algernon?

ALGERNON. I cannot deny it.

CECILY. Oh!

GWENDOLEN. Is your name really John?

JACK (*standing rather proudly*). I could deny it if I liked. I could deny anything if I liked. But my name certainly is John. It has been John for years.

CECILY (*to Gwendolen*). A gross deception has been practised on both of us.

GWENDOLEN. My poor wounded Cecily!

CECILY. My sweet, wronged Gwendolen!

GWENDOLEN (*slowly and seriously*). You will call me sister, will you not? (*They embrace. Jack and Algernon groan and walk up and down.*)

CECILY (*rather brightly*). There is just one question I would like to be allowed to ask my guardian.

GWENDOLEN. An admirable idea! Mr. Worthing, there is just one question I would like to be permitted to put to you. Where is your brother Ernest? We are both engaged to be married to your brother Ernest, so it is a matter of some importance to us to know where your brother Ernest is at present.

JACK (*slowly and hesitatingly*). Gwendolen—Cecily—it is very painful for me to be forced to speak the truth. It is the first time in my life that I have ever been reduced to such a painful position, and I am really quite inexperienced in doing anything of the kind. However I will tell you quite frankly that I have no brother Ernest. I have no brother at all. I never had a brother in my life, and I certainly have not the smallest intention of ever having one in the future.

CECILY (*surprised*). No brother at all?

JACK (*cheerily*). None!

GWENDOLEN (*severely*). Had you never a brother of any kind?

JACK (*pleasantly*). Never. Not even of any kind.

GWENDOLEN. I am afraid it is quite clear, Cecily, that neither of us is engaged to be married to anyone.

CECILY. It is not a very pleasant position for a young girl suddenly to find herself in. Is it?

GWENDOLEN. Let us go into the house. They will hardly venture to come after us there.

CECILY. No, men are so cowardly, aren't they? (*They retire into the house with scornful looks.*)

JACK. This ghastly state of things is what you call Bunburying, I suppose?

ALGERNON. Yes, and a perfectly wonderful Bunbury it is. The most wonderful Bunbury I have ever had in my life.

JACK. Well, you've no right whatsoever to Bunbury here.

ALGERNON. That is absurd. One has a right to Bunbury anywhere one chooses. Every serious Bunburyist knows that.

JACK. Serious Bunburyist! Good heavens!

ALGERNON. Well, one must be serious about something, if one wants to have any amusement in life. I happen to be serious about Bunburying. What on earth you are serious about I haven't got the remotest idea. About everything, I should fancy. You have such an absolutely trivial nature.

JACK. Well, the only small satisfaction I have in the whole of this wretched business is that your friend Bunbury is quite exploded. You won't be able to run down to the country quite so often as you used to do, dear Algy. And a very good thing, too.

ALGERNON. Your brother is a little off colour, isn't he, dear Jack? You won't be able to disappear to London quite so frequently as your wicked custom was. And not a bad thing, either.

JACK. As for your conduct towards Miss Cardew, I must say that your taking in a sweet, simple, innocent girl like that is quite inexcusable. To say nothing of the fact that she is my ward.

ALGERNON. I can see no possible defence at all for your deceiving a brilliant, clever, thoroughly experienced young lady like Miss Fairfax. To say nothing of the fact that she is my cousin.

JACK. I wanted to be engaged to Gwendolen, that is all. I love her.

ALGERNON. Well, I simply wanted to be engaged to Cecily. I adore her.

JACK. There is certainly no chance of your marrying Miss Cardew.

ALGERNON. I don't think there is much likelihood, Jack, of you and Miss Fairfax being united.

JACK. Well, that is no business of yours.

ALGERNON. If it was my business, I wouldn't talk about it. (*Begins to eat muffins.*) It is very vulgar to talk about one's business. Only people like stock-brokers do that, and then merely at dinner parties.

JACK. How you can sit there, calmly eating muffins, when we are in this horrible trouble, I can't make out. You seem to me to be perfectly heartless.

ALGERNON. Well, I can't eat muffins in an agitated manner. The butter would probably get on my cuffs. One should always eat muffins quite calmly. It is the only way to eat them.

JACK. I say it's perfectly heartless your eating muffins at all, under the circumstances.

ALGERNON. When I am in trouble, eating is the only thing that consoles me. Indeed, when I am in really great trouble, as anyone who knows me intimately will tell you, I refuse everything except food and drink. At the present moment I am eating muffins because I am unhappy. Besides, I am particularly fond of muffins. (*Rising.*)

JACK (*rising*). Well, that is no reason why you should eat them all in that greedy way. (*Takes muffin from Algernon.*)

ALGERNON (*offering tea-cake*). I wish you would have tea-cake instead. I don't like tea-cake.

JACK. Good heavens! I suppose a man may eat his own muffins in his own garden.

ALGERNON. But you have just said it was perfectly heartless to eat muffins.

JACK. I said it was perfectly heartless of you, under the circumstances. That is a very different thing.

ALGERNON. That may be. But the muffins are the same. (*He seizes the muffin dish from Jack.*)

JACK. Algy, I wish to goodness you would go.

ALGERNON. You can't possibly ask me to go without having some dinner. It's absurd. I never go without my dinner. No one ever does, except vegetarians and people like that. Besides I have just made arrangements with Dr. Chasuble to be christened at a quarter to six under the name of Ernest.

JACK. My dear fellow, the sooner you give up that nonsense the better. I made arrangements this morning with Chasuble to be christened myself at 5:30, and I naturally will take the name of Ernest. Gwendolen would wish it. We can't both be christened Ernest. It's absurd. Besides, I have a perfect right to be christened if I like. There is no evidence at all that I ever have been christened by anybody. I should think it extremely probable I never was, and so does Dr. Chasuble. It is entirely different in your case. You have been christened already.

ALGERNON. Yes, but I have not been christened for years.

JACK. Yes, but you have been christened. That is the important thing.

ALGERNON. Quite so. So I know my constitution can stand it. If you are not quite sure about your ever having been christened, I must say I think it rather dangerous your venturing on it now. It might make you very unwell. You can hardly have forgotten that someone very closely connected with you was very nearly carried off this week in Paris by a severe chill.

JACK. Yes, but you said yourself that a severe chill was not hereditary.

ALGERNON. It usedn't to be, I know—but I daresay it is now. Science is always making wonderful improvements in things.

JACK (*picking up the muffin-dish*). Oh, that is nonsense; you are always talking nonsense.

ALGERNON. Jack, you are at the muffins again! I wish you wouldn't. There are only two left. (*Takes them.*) I told you I was particularly fond of muffins.

JACK. But I hate tea-cake.

ALGERNON. Why on earth then do you allow tea-cake to be served up for your guests? What ideas you have of hospitality!

JACK. Algernon! I have already told you to go. I don't want you here. Why don't you go?

ALGERNON. I haven't quite finished my tea yet, and there is still one muffin left. (*Jack groans, and sinks into a chair. Algernon still continues eating.*)

CURTAIN

ACT 3

SCENE: *Morning-room at the Manor House. Gwendolen and Cecily are at the window, looking out into the garden.*

GWENDOLEN. The fact that they did not follow us at once into the house, as anyone else would have done, seems to me to show that they have some sense of shame left.

CECILY. They have been eating muffins. That looks like repentance.

GWENDOLEN (*after a pause*). They don't seem to notice us at all. Couldn't you cough?

GWENDOLEN. They're looking at us. What effrontery!

CECILY. They're approaching. That's very forward of them.

GWENDOLEN. Let us preserve a dignified silence.

CECILY. Certainly, it's the only thing to do now.

(*Enter Jack, followed by Algernon. They whistle some dreadful popular air from a British opera.*)

GWENDOLEN. This dignified silence seems to produce an unpleasant effect.

CECILY. A most distasteful one.

GWENDOLEN. But we will not be the first to speak.

CECILY. Certainly not.

GWENDOLEN. Mr. Worthing, I have something very particular to ask you. Much depends on your reply.

CECILY. Gwendolen, your common sense is invaluable. Mr. Moncrieff, kindly answer me the following question. Why did you pretend to be my guardian's brother?

ALGERNON. In order that I might have an opportunity of meeting you.

CECILY (*to Gwendolen*). That certainly seems a satisfactory explanation, does it not?

GWENDOLEN. Yes, dear, if you can believe him.

CECILY. I don't. But that does not affect the wonderful beauty of his answer.

GWENDOLEN. True. In matters of grave importance, style, not sincerity, is the vital thing. Mr. Worthing, what explanation can you offer to me for pretending to have a brother? Was it in order that you might have an opportunity of coming up to town to see me as often as possible?

JACK. Can you doubt it, Miss Fairfax?

GWENDOLEN. I have the gravest doubts upon the subject. But I intend to crush them. This is not the moment for German scepticism. (*Moving to Cecily.*) Their explanations appear to be quite satisfactory, especially Mr. Worthing's. That seems to me to have the stamp of truth upon it.

CECILY. I am more than content with what Mr. Moncrieff said. His voice alone inspires one with absolute credulity.

GWENDOLEN. Then you think we should forgive them?

CECILY. Yes. I mean no.

GWENDOLEN. True! I had forgotten. There are principles at stake that one cannot surrender. Which of us should tell them? The task is not a pleasant one.

CECILY. Could we not both speak at the same time?

GWENDOLEN. An excellent idea! I nearly always speak at the same time as other people. Will you take the time from me?

CECILY. Certainly. (*Gwendolen beats time with uplifted finger.*)

GWENDOLEN and CECILY (*speaking together*). Your Christian names are still an insuperable barrier. That is all!

JACK and ALGERNON (*speaking together*). Our Christian names! Is that all? But we are going to be christened this afternoon.

GWENDOLEN (*to Jack*). For my sake you are prepared to do this terrible thing?

JACK. I am.

CECILY (*to Algernon*). To please me you are ready to face this fearful ordeal?

ALGERNON. I am!

GWENDOLEN. How absurd to talk of the equality of the sexes! Where questions of self-sacrifice are concerned, men are infinitely beyond us.

JACK. We are. (*Clasps hands with Algernon.*)

CECILY. They have moments of physical courage of which we women know absolutely nothing.

GWENDOLEN (*to Jack*). Darling!

ALGERNON (*to Cecily*). Darling! (*They fall into each other's arms.*)

(*Enter Merriman. When he enters he coughs loudly, seeing the situation.*)

MERRIMAN. Ahem! Ahem! Lady Bracknell!

JACK. Good heavens!

(*Enter Lady Bracknell. The couples separate in alarm. Exit Merriman.*)

LADY BRACKNELL. Gwendolen! What does this mean?

GWENDOLEN. Merely that I am engaged to be married to Mr. Worthing, Mamma.

LADY BRACKNELL. Come here. Sit down. Sit down immediately. Hesitation of any kind is a sign of mental decay in the young, of physical weakness in the old. (*Turns to Jack.*) Apprised, sir, of my daughter's sudden flight by her trusty maid, whose confidence I purchased by means of a small coin, I followed her at once by a luggage train. Her unhappy father is, I am glad to say, under the impression that she is attending a more than usually lengthy lecture by the University Extension Scheme on the Influence of a Permanent Income on Thought. I do not propose to undeceive him. Indeed I have never undeceived him on any question. I would consider it wrong. But of course, you will clearly understand that all communication between yourself and my daughter must cease immediately from this moment. On this point, as indeed on all points, I am firm.

JACK. I am engaged to be married to Gwendolen, Lady Bracknell!

LADY BRACKNELL. You are nothing of the kind, sir. And now, as regards Algernon! . . . Algernon!

ALGERNON. Yes, Aunt Augusta.

LADY BRACKNELL. May I ask if it is in this house that your invalid friend Mr. Bunbury resides?

ALGERNON (*stammering*). Oh no! Bunbury doesn't live here. Bunbury is somewhere else at present. In fact, Bunbury is dead.

LADY BRACKNELL. Dead! When did Mr. Bunbury die? His death must have been extremely sudden.

ALGERNON (*airily*). Oh, I killed Bunbury this afternoon. I mean poor Bunbury died this afternoon.

LADY BRACKNELL. What did he die of?

ALGERNON. Bunbury? Oh, he was quite exploded.

LADY BRACKNELL. Exploded! Was he the victim of a revolutionary outrage? I was not aware that Mr. Bunbury was interested in social legislation. If so, he is well punished for his morbidity.

ALGERNON. My dear Aunt Augusta, I mean he was found out! The doctors found out that Bunbury could not live, that is what I mean—so Bunbury died.

LADY BRACKNELL. He seems to have had great confidence in the opinion of his physicians. I am glad, however, that he made up his mind at the last to some definite course of action, and acted under proper medical advice. And now that we have finally got rid of this Mr. Bunbury, may I ask, Mr. Worthing, who is that young person whose hand my nephew Algernon is now holding in what seems to me a peculiarly unnecessary manner?

JACK. That lady is Miss Cecily Cardew, my ward. (*Lady Bracknell bows coldly to Cecily.*)

ALGERNON. I am engaged to be married to Cecily, Aunt Augusta.

LADY BRACKNELL. I beg your pardon?

CECILY. Mr. Moncrieff and I are engaged to be married, Lady Bracknell.

LADY BRACKNELL (*with a shiver, crossing to the sofa and sitting down*). I do not know whether there is anything peculiarly exciting in the air of this particular part of Hertfordshire, but the number of engagements that go on seems to me considerably above the proper average that statistics have laid down for our guidance. I think some preliminary enquiry on my part would not be out of place. Mr. Worthing, is Miss Cardew at all connected with any of the larger railway stations in London? I merely desire information. Until yesterday I had no idea that there were any families or persons whose origin was a Terminus. (*Jack looks perfectly furious, but restrains himself.*)

JACK (*in a clear, cold voice*). Miss Cardew is the granddaughter of the late Mr. Thomas Cardew of 149, Belgrave Square, S.W.; Gervase Park, Dorking, Surrey; and the Sporran, Fifeshire, N.B.

LADY BRACKNELL. That sounds not unsatisfactory. Three addresses always inspire confidence, even in tradesmen. But what proof have I of their authenticity?

JACK. I have carefully preserved the Court Guide of the period. They are open to your inspection, Lady Bracknell.

LADY BRACKNELL (*grimly*). I have known strange errors in that publication.

JACK. Miss Cardew's family solicitors are Messrs. Markby, Markby, and Markby.

LADY BRACKNELL. Markby, Markby, and Markby? A firm of the very highest position in their profession. Indeed I am told that one of the Mr. Markbys is occasionally to be seen at dinner parties. So far I am satisfied.

JACK (*very irritably*). How extremely kind of you, Lady Bracknell! I have also in my possession, you will be pleased to hear, certificates of Miss Cardew's birth, baptism, whooping cough, registration, vaccination, confirmation, and the measles; both the German and the English variety.

LADY BRACKNELL. Ah! A life crowded with incident, I see; though perhaps somewhat too exciting for a young girl. I am not myself in favor of premature experiences. (*Rises, looks at her watch.*) Gwendolen! the time approaches for our departure. We have not a moment to lose. As a matter of form, Mr. Worthing, I had better ask you if Miss Cardew has any little fortune?

JACK. Oh, about a hundred and thirty thousand pounds in the Funds. That is all. Good-bye, Lady Bracknell. So pleased to have seen you.

LADY BRACKNELL (*sitting down again*). A moment, Mr. Worthing. A hundred and thirty thousand pounds! And in the Funds! Miss Cardew seems to me a most attractive young lady, now that I look at her. Few girls of the present day have any really solid qualities, any of the qualities that last, and improve with time. We live, I regret to say, in an age of surfaces. (*To Cecily.*) Come over here, dear. (*Cecily goes across.*) Pretty child! your dress is sadly simple, and your hair seems almost as Nature might have left it. But we can soon alter all that. A thoroughly experienced French maid produces a really marvellous result in a very brief space of time. I remember recommending one to young Lady Lancing, and after three months her own husband did not know her.

JACK (*aside*). And after six months nobody knew her.

LADY BRACKNELL (*glares at Jack for a few moments. Then bends, with a practised smile, to Cecily*). Kindly turn round, sweet child. (*Cecily turns completely round.*) No, the side view is what I want. (*Cecily presents her profile.*) Yes, quite as I expected. There are distinct social possibilities in your profile. The two weak points in our age are its want of principle and its want of profile. The chin a little higher, dear. Style largely depends on the way the chin is worn. They are worn very high, just at present. Algernon!

ALGERNON. Yes, Aunt Augusta!

LADY BRACKNELL. There are distinct social possibilities in Miss Cardew's profile.

ALGERNON. Cecily is the sweetest, dearest, prettiest girl in the whole world. And I don't care twopence about social possibilities.

LADY BRACKNELL. Never speak disrespectfully of society, Algernon. Only people who can't get into it do that. (*To Cecily.*) Dear child, of course you know that Algernon has nothing but his debts to depend upon. But I do not approve of mercenary marriages. When I married Lord Bracknell I had no fortune of any kind. But I never dreamed for a moment of allowing that to stand in my way. Well, I suppose I must give my consent.

ALGERNON. Thank you, Aunt Augusta.

LADY BRACKNELL. Cecily, you may kiss me!

CECILY (*kisses her*). Thank you, Lady Bracknell.

LADY BRACKNELL. You may also address me as Aunt Augusta for the future.

CECILY. Thank you, Aunt Augusta.

LADY BRACKNELL. The marriage, I think, had better take place quite soon.

ALGERNON. Thank you, Aunt Augusta.

CECILY. Thank you, Aunt Augusta.

LADY BRACKNELL. To speak frankly, I am not in favour of long engagements. They give people the opportunity of finding out each other's character before marriage, which I think is never advisable.

JACK. I beg your pardon for interrupting you, Lady Bracknell, but this engagement is quite out of the question. I am Miss Cardew's guardian, and she cannot marry without my consent until she comes of age. That consent I absolutely decline to give.

LADY BRACKNELL. Upon what grounds, may I ask? Algernon is an extremely, I may almost say an ostentatiously, eligible young man. He has nothing, but he looks everything. What more can one desire?

JACK. It pains me very much to have to speak frankly to you, Lady Bracknell, about your nephew, but the fact is that I do not approve at all of his moral character. I suspect him of being untruthful. (*Algernon and Cecily look at him in indignant amazement.*)

LADY BRACKNELL. Untruthful! My nephew Algernon? Impossible! He is an Oxonian.

JACK. I fear there can be no possible doubt about the matter. This afternoon, during my temporary absence in London on an important question of romance, he obtained admission to my house by means of the false pretence of being my brother. Under an assumed name he drank, I've just been informed by my butler, an entire pint bottle of my Perrier-Jouet, Brut, '89; a wine I was specially reserving for myself. Continuing his disgraceful deception, he succeeded in the course of the afternoon in alienating the affections of my only ward. He subsequently stayed to tea, and devoured every single muffin. And what makes his conduct all the more heartless is, that he was perfectly well aware from the first that I have no brother, that I never had a brother, and that I don't intend to have a brother, not even of any kind. I distinctly told him so myself yesterday afternoon.

LADY BRACKNELL. Ahem! Mr. Worthing, after careful consideration I have decided entirely to overlook my nephew's conduct to you.

JACK. That is very generous of you, Lady Bracknell. My own decision, however, is unalterable. I decline to give my consent.

LADY BRACKNELL (*to Cecily*). Come here, sweet child. (*Cecily goes over.*) How old are you, dear?

CECILY. Well, I am really only eighteen, but I always admit to twenty when I go to evening parties.

LADY BRACKNELL. You are perfectly right in making some slight alteration. Indeed, no woman should ever be quite accurate about her age. It looks so calculating. . . . (*In meditative manner.*) Eighteen, but admitting to twenty at evening parties. Well, it will not be very long before you are of age and free from the restraints of tutelage. So I don't think your guardian's consent is, after all, a matter of any importance.

JACK. Pray excuse me, Lady Bracknell, for interrupting you again, but it is only fair to tell you that according to the terms of her grandfather's will Miss Cardew does not come legally of age till she is thirty-five.

LADY BRACKNELL. That does not seem to me to be a grave objection. Thirty-five is a very attractive age. London society is full of women of the very highest birth who have, of their own free choice, remained thirty-five for years. Lady Dumbleton is an instance in point. To my own knowledge she had been thirty-five ever since she arrived at the age of forty, which was many years ago now. I see no reason why our dear Cecily should not be even still more attractive at the age you mention than she is at present. There will be a large accumulation of property.

CECILY. Algy, could you wait for me till I was thirty-five?

ALGERNON. Of course I could, Cecily. You know I could.

CECILY. Yes, I felt it instinctively, but I couldn't wait all that time. I hate waiting even five minutes for anybody. It always makes me rather cross. I am not punctual myself, I know, but I do like punctuality in others, and waiting, even to be married, is quite out of the question.

ALGERNON. Then what is to be done, Cecily?

CECILY. I don't know, Mr. Moncrieff.

LADY BRACKNELL. My dear Mr. Worthing, as Miss Cardew states positively that she cannot wait till she is thirty-five—a remark which I am bound to say seems to me to show a somewhat impatient nature—I would beg of you to reconsider your decision.

JACK. But my dear Lady Bracknell, the matter is entirely in your own hands. The moment you consent to my marriage with Gwendolen, I will most gladly allow your nephew to form an alliance with my ward.

LADY BRACKNELL (*rising and drawing herself up*). You must be quite aware that what you propose is out of the question.

JACK. Then a passionate celibacy is all that any of us can look forward to.

LADY BRACKNELL. That is not the destiny I propose for Gwendolen. Algernon, of course, can choose for himself. (*Pulls out her watch.*) Come, dear, (*Gwendolen rises*) we have already missed five, if not six, trains. To miss any more might expose us to comment on the platform.

(*Enter Dr. Chasuble.*)

CHASUBLE. Everything is quite ready for the christenings.

LADY BRACKNELL. The christenings, sir! Is not that somewhat premature?

CHASUBLE (*looking rather puzzled, and pointing to Jack and Algernon*). Both these gentlemen have expressed a desire for immediate baptism.

LADY BRACKNELL. At their age? The idea is grotesque and irreligious! Algernon, I forbid you to be baptised. I will not hear of such excesses. Lord Bracknell would be highly displeased if he learned that that was the way in which you wasted your time and money.

CHASUBLE. Am I to understand then that there are to be no christenings at all this afternoon?

JACK. I don't think that, as things are now, it would be of much practical value to either of us, Dr. Chasuble.

CHASUBLE. I am grieved to hear such sentiments from you, Mr. Worthing. They savour of the heretical views of the Anabaptists, views that I have completely refuted in four of my unpublished sermons. However, as your present mood seems to be one peculiarly secular, I will return to the church at once. Indeed, I have just been informed by the pew-opener that for the last hour and a half Miss Prism has been waiting for me in the vestry.

LADY BRACKNELL (*starting*). Miss Prism! Did I hear you mention a Miss Prism?

CHASUBLE. Yes, Lady Bracknell. I am on my way to join her.

LADY BRACKNELL. Pray allow me to detain you for a moment. This matter may prove to be one of vital importance to Lord Bracknell and myself. Is this Miss Prism a female of repellent aspect, remotely connected with education?

CHASUBLE (*somewhat indignantly*). She is the most cultivated of ladies, and the very picture of respectability.

LADY BRACKNELL. It is obviously the same person. May I ask what position she holds in your household?

CHASUBLE (*severely*). I am a celibate, madam.

JACK (*interposing*). Miss Prism, Lady Bracknell, has been for the last three years Miss Cardew's esteemed governess and valued companion.

LADY BRACKNELL. In spite of what I hear of her, I must see her at once. Let her be sent for.

CHASUBLE (*looking off*). She approaches; she is nigh.

(*Enter Miss Prism hurriedly.*)

MISS PRISM. I was told you expected me in the vestry, dear Canon. I have been waiting for you there for an hour and three-quarters. (*Catches sight of Lady Bracknell, who has fixed her with a stony glare. Miss Prism grows pale and quails. She looks anxiously round as if desirous to escape.*)

LADY BRACKNELL (*in a severe, judicial voice*). Prism! (*Miss Prism bows her head in shame.*) Come here, Prism! (*Miss Prism approaches in a humble manner.*) Where is that baby? (*General consternation. The Canon starts back in horror. Algernon and Jack pretend to be anxious to shield Cecily and Gwendolen from hearing the details of a terrible public scandal.*) Twenty-eight years ago, Prism, you left Lord Bracknell's house, Number 104, Upper Grosvenor Street, in charge of a perambulator that contained a baby, of the male sex. You never returned. A few weeks later, through the elaborate investigations of the Metropolitan police, the perambulator was discovered at midnight, standing by itself in a remote corner of Bayswater. It contained the manuscript of a three-volume novel of more than usually revolting sentimentality. (*Miss Prism starts in involuntary indignation.*) But the baby was not there! (*Everyone looks at Miss Prism.*) Prism, where is that baby? (*A pause.*)

MISS PRISM. Lady Bracknell, I admit with shame that I do not know. I only wish I did. The plain facts of the case are these. On the morning of the day you mention, a day that is forever branded on my memory, I prepared as usual to take the baby out in its perambulator. I had also with me a somewhat old but capacious hand-bag in which I had intended to place the manuscript of a work of fiction that I had written during my few unoccupied hours. In a moment of mental abstraction, for which I never can forgive myself, I deposited the manuscript in the bassinette, and placed the baby in the hand-bag.

JACK (*who had been listening attentively*). But where did you deposit the hand-bag?

MISS PRISM. Do not ask me, Mr. Worthing.

JACK. Miss Prism, this is a matter of no small importance to me. I insist on knowing where you deposited the handbag that contained that infant.

MISS PRISM. I left it in the cloak-room of one of the larger railway stations in London.

JACK. What railway station?

MISS PRISM (*quite crushed*). Victoria. The Brighton line. (*Sinks into a chair.*)

JACK. I must retire to my room for a moment. Gwendolen, wait here for me.

GWENDOLEN. If you are not too long, I will wait here for you all my life.

(*Exit Jack in great excitement.*)

CHASUBLE. What do you think this means, Lady Bracknell?

LADY BRACKNELL. I dare not even suspect, Dr. Chasuble. I need hardly tell you that in families of high position strange coincidences are not supposed to occur. They are hardly considered the thing. (*Noises heard overhead as if someone was throwing trunks about. Everybody looks up.*)

CECILY. Uncle Jack seems strangely agitated.

CHASUBLE. Your guardian has a very emotional nature.

LADY BRACKNELL. This noise is extremely unpleasant. It sounds as if he was having an argument. I dislike arguments of any kind. They are always vulgar, and often convincing.

CHASUBLE (*looking up*). It has stopped now. (*The noise is redoubled.*)

LADY BRACKNELL. I wish he would arrive at some conclusion.

GWENDOLEN. The suspense is terrible. I hope it will last.

(*Enter Jack with a hand-bag of black leather in his hand.*)

JACK (*rushing over to Miss Prism*). Is this the hand-bag, Miss Prism? Examine it carefully before you speak. The happiness of more than one life depends on your answers.

MISS PRISM (*calmly*). It seems to be mine. Yes, here is the injury it received through the upsetting of a Gower Street omnibus in younger and happier days. Here is the stain on the lining caused by the explosion of a temperance beverage, an incident that occurred at Leamington.

And here, on the lock, are my initials. I had forgotten that in an extravagant mood I had had them placed there. The bag is undoubtedly mine. I am delighted to have it so unexpectedly restored to me. It has been a great inconvenience being without it all these years.

JACK (*in a pathetic voice*). Miss Prism, more is restored to you than this hand-bag. I was the baby you placed in it.

MISS PRISM (*amazed*). You?

JACK (*embracing her*). Yes . . . mother!

MISS PRISM (*recoiling in indignant astonishment*). Mr. Worthing! I am unmarried!

JACK. Unmarried! I do not deny that is a serious blow. But after all, who has the right to cast a stone against one who has suffered? Cannot repentance wipe out an act of folly? Why should there be one law for men and another for women? Mother, I forgive you. (*Tries to embrace her again.*)

MISS PRISM (*still more indignant*). Mr. Worthing, there is some error. (*Pointing to Lady Bracknell.*) There is the lady who can tell you who you really are.

JACK (*after a pause*). Lady Bracknell, I hate to seem inquisitive, but would you kindly inform me who I am?

LADY BRACKNELL. I am afraid that the news I have to give you will not altogether please you. You are the son of my poor sister, Mrs. Moncrieff, and consequently Algernon's elder brother.

JACK. Algy's elder brother! Then I have a brother after all. I knew I had a brother! I always said I had a brother! Cecily,—how could you have ever doubted that I had a brother? (*Seizes hold of Algernon.*) Dr. Chasuble, my unfortunate brother. Miss Prism, my unfortunate brother. Gwendolen, my unfortunate brother. Algy, you young scoundrel, you will have to treat me with more respect in the future. You have never behaved to me like a brother in all your life.

ALGERNON. Well, not till to-day, old boy, I admit. I did my best, however, though I was out of practice. (*Shakes hands.*)

GWENDOLEN (*to Jack*). My own! But what own are you? What is your Christian name, now that you have become someone else?

JACK. Good heavens! . . . I had quite forgotten that point. Your decision on the subject of my name is irrevocable, I suppose?

GWENDOLEN. I never change, except in my affections.

CECILY. What a noble nature you have, Gwendolen!

JACK. Then the question had better be cleared up at once. Aunt Augusta, a moment. At the time when Miss Prism left me in the hand-bag, had I been christened already?

LADY BRACKNELL. Every luxury that money could buy, including christening, had been lavished on you by your fond and doting parents.

JACK. Then I was christened! That is settled. Now, what name was I given? Let me know the worst.

LADY BRACKNELL. Being the eldest son you were naturally christened after your father.

JACK (*irritably*). Yes, but what was my father's Christian name?

LADY BRACKNELL (*meditatively*). I cannot at the present moment recall what the General's Christian name was. But I have no doubt he had one. He was eccentric, I admit. But only in later years. And that was the result of the Indian climate, and marriage, and indigestion, and other things of that kind.

JACK. Algy! Can't you recollect what our father's Christian name was?

ALGERNON. My dear boy, we were never even on speaking terms. He died before I was a year old.

JACK. His name would appear in the Army Lists of the period, I suppose, Aunt Augusta?

LADY BRACKNELL. The general was essentially a man of peace, except in his domestic life. But I have no doubt his name would appear in any military directory.

JACK. The Army Lists of the last forty years are here. These delightful records should have been my constant study. (*Rushes to bookcase and tears the books out.*) M. Generals . . . Mallham, Maxbohm, Magley, what ghastly names they have—Markby, Migsby, Mobbs, Moncrieff! Lieutenant 1840, Captain, Lieutenant-Colonel, Colonel, General 1869, Christian names, Ernest John. (*Puts book very quietly down and speaks quite calmly.*) I always told you, Gwendolen, my name was Ernest, didn't I? Well, it is Ernest after all, I mean it naturally is Ernest.

LADY BRACKNELL. Yes, I remember the General was called Ernest. I knew I had some particular reason for disliking the name.

GWENDOLEN. Ernest! My own Ernest! I felt from the first that you could have no other name!

JACK. Gwendolen, it is a terrible thing for a man to find out suddenly that all his life he has been speaking nothing but the truth. Can you forgive me?

GWENDOLEN. I can. For I feel sure that you are sure to change.

JACK. My own one!

CHASUBLE (*to Miss Prism*). Lætitia! (*Embraces her.*)

MISS PRISM (*enthusiastically*). Frederick! At last!

ALGERNON. Cecily! (*Embraces her.*) At last!

JACK. Gwendolen! (*Embraces her.*) At last!

LADY BRACKNELL. My nephew, you seem to be displaying signs of triviality.

JACK. On the contrary, Aunt Augusta, I've now realized for the first time in my life the vital Importance of Being Earnest.

TABLEAU

CURTAIN

TOPICS FOR CRITICAL THINKING AND WRITING

📖 THE PLAY ON THE PAGE

1. Speaking of this play, Wilde said in an interview: "It has as its philosophy . . . that we should treat all the trivial things of life seriously, and all the serious things of life with sincere and studied triviality." Was he kidding? To what extent does the play dramatize such a view?

2. Can it be argued that the play presents a fanciful world utterly remote from the real world, and that attempts to see it as in any way related to our world do it an injustice? If this is the case, what value does the play have?

🎭 THE PLAY ON THE STAGE

5. Take one part of one act—Lady Bracknell's examination of Jack in Act I would be a good choice—and indicate what stage business you would use if you were directing the play. A simple example: When Lady Bracknell finishes questioning Jack about his finances and his social standing, she might close her notebook and invitingly pat the seat beside her as she says, "Now to minor matters. Are your parents living?" A little later, when Jack confesses that he cannot identify his parents, she might tear the page out of her notebook.

6. If you were directing a production, what suggestions would you offer the actors for the first fifteen lines of the play? Consider, for instance, "Did you hear what I was playing, Lane?" Which word(s) should be stressed? What facial movements are appropriate, what gestures, what voice qualities? What sort of eye contact? Would you aim for the maximum humorous effect? For delineation of social class? Or what?

7. List all of Miss Prism's appearances, and then put into writing the advice you would give to an actress playing the role. For each appearance indicate how she might stand, how her face should be set, at whom she should

3. Describe some of Wilde's chief devices of verbal humor. One such device, for instance, is to turn a proverb inside out, as with the proverbial "Marriages are made in heaven." What other examples of this device do you find? And what other kinds of humor?

4. What are Lady Bracknell's values? What is your response to her—not to her values, but to her? Why?

look, when she should show emotion, and so forth. Suggest an actress—either well-known or known within the class or college—whom you would nominate for the role, and give your reasons.

8. Should Cecily and Gwendolen seem interchangeable—that is, are they both sweet, young, vain, spoiled? If so, point to evidence supporting your view. If not, indicate the ways in which they differ, and point to the supporting evidence.

9. As costume designer, what colors would you choose for each of the young women? What accessories?

10. Wilde's opening instructions merely call for the sound of a piano. If you were the sound designer for *The Importance of Being Earnest*, what musical piece (specific title and composer) would you propose for a production set in the 1890s? For a production set in the 1990s? Explain your choices.

11. The original production (1895) used a contemporary setting. What arguments might you advance for and against the idea of setting the play in a period other than the original, for instance in the 1920s, or the 1990s?

THE PLAY IN PERFORMANCE

When *The Importance of Being Earnest* had its premiere performance in London in 1895 it was an immediate hit with audiences and with critics. Three months later, when the author was convicted of indecency and was sentenced to two years of hard labor, the play was withdrawn from the stage. In 1899 Wilde arranged for the publication of the play, but, such was his disgrace, reviewers ignored the book.

There were revivals in London in 1898 and 1902, but not until the revival of 1909 did the play have a long run. By the

1920s it was a staple of the theater, and probably not a week now goes by that it is not produced somewhere. Between the 1920s and the 1970s most productions probably were set in the 1890s, and they were more or less in the tradition of museum theater, that is, they sought to perform the play in the way that (in the director's view) it was originally performed. The set, for instance, re-created an elegant Victorian bachelor's apartment. Such productions are often still seen today, though there are variations. In 1982 Sir Peter

Hall staged *Earnest* with minimal sets—two white cane chairs and a few pots of roses for the garden in Act II, for instance—and the production was well received.

But the difference between *Earnest* in 1895 and *Earnest* today is something larger than the set. The original audience knew that Wilde was a dandy—a man who pays too much attention to his clothes and too little attention to bourgeois morality—but until the trial they did not know that he was a homosexual. Dandyism, it should be mentioned, was by no means associated with homosexuality. It was associated with the idle rich, or the would-be idle rich, and the hard-working middle-class male regarded it with disapproval because Victorian men were supposed to work hard and leave such things as attention to clothing to women, who (in the common view) were not suited for serious work. When Wilde's homosexuality became public knowledge, for a while his name could scarcely be mentioned in decent society, and the play could not be staged. With the passage of a few years, however, the play could be staged so long as one did not mention homosexuality. And this was not hard to do, because in fact the two young men in the play are in love with women.

But since homosexuality has come out of the closet (around the 1970s), today it is common to read discussions of the play as a gay play (which we can define as a play about gay life), a sort of closet revelation of homosexuality. One reads, for example, that *bunburying* is a thinly veiled pun on *burying in the buns*, that is, on penetrating the buttocks. At the risk of being spoilsports, we must mention that no one has bothered to offer evidence that in Wilde's day the word *buns* was used in England to refer to buttocks. (In fact, the earliest recorded use of *buns* in this sense is in mid-twentieth-century American English.) The published critical interpre-

tations of course are paralleled by an occasional gay production, and so we have been given versions in which Algy and Jack are presented as lovers (they kiss) who only pretend to be interested in women. There has also been at least one all-male production of the play (the Berlin Actors, in New York in 1987), and many productions in which Lady Bracknell is played by a man in drag.

Was Wilde in fact setting forth his secret life in a code that the initiate could read? Was he saying that *The Importance of Being Earnest* is autobiographical when, writing from prison to his former lover, he said, "I took the drama, the most objective form known to art, and made it as personal a mode of expression as the lyric or the sonnet?" In the play was he talking in code about his secret double life when he had Cecily say, "I hope you have not been leading a double life, pretending to be wicked and being really good all the time. That would be hypocrisy"? Conceivably. Even so, one can ask if a "gay" production makes sense. And one can ask if it does not lose more than it gains. Gay productions usually strike audiences as unfunny, or at least as far less funny than versions that are done straight.

One last point about the play in production: Wilde wrote a four-act version, but his director insisted that it be cut to three acts. Wilde protested, but the director prevailed. One might ask, then, if Wilde's "real" play is the four-act version rather than the three-act version. The answer probably is no. When Wilde published the play, he published the three-act version, and so we can assume that he ultimately decided that the revised version was indeed preferable. The four-act version is occasionally produced out of academic piety, but audiences familiar with the three-act version regard the longer version as less successful.

Anton Chekhov

THE CHERRY ORCHARD

Anton Chekhov (1860–1904) received his medical degree from the University of Moscow in 1884, but he had already published some stories. His belief that his medical training assisted him in writing about people caused some people to find him cold, but on the whole the evidence suggests that he was a genial, energetic young man with considerable faith in reason and (as befitted a doctor) in science, and with very little faith in religion and in heroics. His major plays are *The Seagull* (1896), *Uncle Vanya* (1899), *Three Sisters* (1901), and, finally, *The Cherry Orchard* (1903), written during his last illness.

COMMENTARY

At the end of *The Cherry Orchard*, the old servant Firs, forgotten by the family he has long served, wanders onto the stage, locked within the house that is no longer theirs. Is he comic, in his mutterings, in his old-maidish frettings about Leonid Andreevich's inadequate coat, and in his implicit realization that although he is concerned about the aristocrats the aristocrats are unconcerned about him? Or is he tragic, dying in isolation? Or neither? The comedy is scarcely uproarious; if there is humor in his realization that his life has been trivial, this humor is surely tinged with melancholy. And the "tragic" reading is also ambiguous: First, the text does not say that he dies; second, if it can be assumed that he dies, the death of an ill eighty-seven-year-old man can scarcely seem untimely; and third, Firs does not seem particularly concerned about dying.

If this play ends with a death, then, it is not the sort of death that Byron had in mind when he said, "All tragedies are finished by a death, / All comedies are ended by a marriage." We are in the dramatic world that Shaw spoke of when he said that "the curtain no longer comes down on a hero slain or married: it comes down when the audience has seen enough of the life presented to it, . . . and must either leave the theatre or miss its last train."

Chekhov insisted that *The Cherry Orchard* was a comedy, but what sort of comedy? In the latter part of the last act there is almost a proposal of marriage, but, typically, it never gets made. For two years everyone has joked about the anticipated marriage between Lopakhin and Varya, but when these two are thrust together they are overcome by embarrassment, and the interview is dissipated in small talk. Not that (of course) a comedy must end with a marriage; marriage is only the conventional way of indicating a happy union, or reunion, that symbolizes the triumph of life. But in this play we *begin* with a reunion—the family is reunited in the ancestral home—and we end with a separation, the inhabitants scattering when the home is sold.

Another way of getting at *The Cherry Orchard* is to notice that in this play, although there are innumerable references to Time between the first speech, when Lopakhin says "Train's in, thank God! What's the time?" and the last act, where there is much talk about catching the outbound train, Time does not function as it usually functions either in tragedy or in comedy. In tragedy we usually feel: if there had only been more time. . . . For example, in *Romeo and Juliet* Friar Laurence writes a letter to Romeo, explaining that Juliet will take a potion that will put her in a temporary, deathlike trance, but the letter is delayed, Romeo mistakenly hears that Juliet is dead, and he kills himself. A few moments after his suicide Juliet revives. Had Friar Laurence's message arrived on schedule, or had Romeo not been so quick to commit suicide, no great harm would have been done. In *King Lear*, Edmund repents that he has ordered a soldier to kill Cordelia, and a messenger hurries out to change the order, but he is too late.

If in tragedy we usually feel the pressure of time, in comedy there is usually a sense of leisure. Things are difficult now, but in the course of time they will work themselves out. Sooner or later people will realize that the strange goings-on are due to the existence of identical twins; sooner or later the stubborn parents will realize that they cannot forever stand in the way of young lovers; sooner or later the money will turn up and all will be well. In the world of comedy, one is always safe in relying on time. In *The Cherry Orchard*, Lopakhin insists, correctly enough, that the family must act *now* if it is to save the orchard: "You've got to decide once and for all—time won't stand still." There is ample time to act on Lopakhin's suggestion that the orchard be leased for summer houses, and the play covers a period from May to October; but the plan is not acted on because to the aristocrats any sort of selling is unthinkable, and although one Pishchik is in the course of time miraculously redeemed from financial ruin by some Englishmen who discover and buy "some kind of white clay" on *his* land, time brings Mme. Ranevskaya and her brother Gaev no such good fortune. So far as the main happenings in the play are concerned, time neither presses nor preserves; it only passes.

During the passage of time in this play, the orchard is lost (tragic?) and the characters reveal themselves to be funny (comic?). The loss of the orchard is itself a happening of an uncertain kind. It stands, partly, for the end of an old way of life. But if that way once included intelligent and gracious aristocrats, it also included slavery, and in any case it now is embodied in the irresponsible heirs we see on the stage—Mme. Ranevskaya and her brother Gaev, along with their deaf and near-senile servant Firs. For Gaev the orchard is important chiefly because it lends prestige, since it is mentioned in the encyclopedia. Mme. Ranevskaya sees more to it. For her it is "all white" and it is "young again, full of happiness"; we are momentarily touched by her vision, but there is yet another way of seeing the orchard: For Trofimov, a student who envisions a new society as an orchard for all people, the ancestral cherry orchard is haunted by the serfs of the bad old days. Moreover, although the orchard is much talked about, it seems to have decayed to a trivial ornament. Long ago its crop was regularly harvested, pickled, and sold, thus providing food and income, but now "nobody remembers" the pickling formula and nobody buys the crop. There seems to be some truth to Lopakhin's assertion that "the only remarkable thing about this cherry orchard is that it's very big," and although one must point out that this remark is made by a despised merchant, Lopakhin is neither a fool nor the "money grubber" that Gaev thinks he is. Lopakhin delights in nature put to use. He "cleared forty thousand net" from poppies, "And when my poppies bloomed, it was like a picture!" His enthusiasm for the flowers is undercut for us only a little, if at all, by the fact that they were of use to him and to others.

Lopakhin's serious concern, whether for his poppies or for the future of the cherry orchard, contrasts interestingly with Mme. Ranevskaya's and with Gaev's sporadic passion for the orchard. Mme. Ranevskaya says, "Without the cherry orchard, I couldn't make sense of my life," and she doubtless means what she says; but that her words have not much relation to reality is indicated by her meaningless addition, "If it really has to be sold, then sell me along with the orchard."

After the orchard has been sold, Gaev confesses, "everything's fine now. Until the sale of the cherry orchard, we were all upset, distressed, but then, when the dilemma was settled, finally, irrevocably, everyone calmed down, even became cheerful . . . I'm a bank employee. . . . Lyuba, anyway, you're looking better, that's for sure." His sister agrees: "Yes. My nerves are better, that's true. . . . I'm sleeping well. Carry my things out, Yasha. It's time." She returns to her lover in Paris, Gaev goes off to a job in the bank, and though we can imagine that the orchard will continue to be an occasional topic of conversation, we cannot imagine that the loss has in any way changed them. The play ends, but things will go on in the same way; neither a tragic nor a comic action has been completed.

The characters no less than the action are tragicomic. Their longings would touch the heart if only these people did not so quickly digress or engage in little actions that call their depth into doubt. Charlotta laments that she had no proper passport and that her deceased parents may not have been married: "Where I came from and who I am I don't know." And then, having touched on the mighty subject of one's identity, the subject that is the stuff of tragedy in which heroes endure the worst in order to know who they are, she begins to eat a cucumber, and somehow that simple and entirely necessary act diminishes her dignity—though it does not totally dissipate our glimpse of her alienation. In the same scene, when Yepikhodov confesses that although he reads "all kinds of remarkable books" he "cannot discover [his] own inclinations," we hear another echo of the tragic hero's quest for self-knowledge, but we also hear an echo from the world of comedy, say of the pedant who guides his life by a textbook. Yepikhodov, perhaps like a tragic hero, is particularly concerned with whether to live or to shoot himself; but this racking doubt is diminished by his prompt explanation that since he may someday decide on suicide, he always carries a revolver, which he proceeds to show to his listeners. Almost all of the characters bare their souls, but their slightly addled minds and their hungry bodies expose them to a gentle satirical treatment so that they evoke a curious amused pathos. One can, for example, sympathize with Mme. Ranevskaya's despair—but one cannot forget that she is scatterbrained and that domestic duties and local pieties occupy her mind only occasionally and that her disreputable lover in Paris means as much as the orchard she thinks she cannot live without. And when Gaev says, "Word of honor I'll swear, by whatever you like, that the estate won't be sold," we know that he has very little honor and even less ability to focus on the problem (mostly he takes refuge in thoughts about billiards, and somehow his habit of eating candy does not enhance his status in our eyes) and that the estate will be sold.

Finally, something must be said about the ambiguous treatment of the future. We know, from his correspondence, that Chekhov looked forward to a new and happier society. Russia, like much of the rest of Europe, was ceasing to be an agrarian society, but if the death throes were evident, one could not be so confident about the birth pangs. Something of the presence of two worlds is hinted at in the stage direction at the beginning of the second act, where we see the estate with its orchard, and also "Further off are telegraph poles, and way in the distance, dimly sketched on the horizon, is a large town." The telegraph poles and the town silently represent the new industrial society, but Trofimov the student speaks at length of the glorious possibilities of the future, and his speeches were sufficiently close to the bone for the censor to delete two passages sharply critical of the present. But we cannot take Trofimov's speeches quite at face value. He is a student, but he is almost thirty and still has not received his degree. His speeches in Act 2 are moving, especially those on the need to work rather than to talk if the future is to be better than the past, but we cannot quite rid ourselves of the suspicion that Trofimov talks rather than works. Certainly he is contemptuous of the merchant Lopakhin, who delights in work. And, worse, Trofimov frets too much about his overshoes, thinks he is "above love," and is so confounded by Mme. Ranevskaya's remark, "At your age, not to have a mistress!" that he falls down a flight of stairs. None of these personal failings invalidates his noble view of the future; certainly none of them turns this view into a comic pipedream, and yet all of these things, along with a certain nostalgia that we feel for the past, do suffuse even his noblest statements about the future with a delicate irony that puts them, along with the much praised but totally neglected cherry orchard, firmly in the tragicomic world. One understands why Chekhov called the play a comedy, and one understands why Stanislavsky (who directed the first production and played the part of Gaev) told Chekhov, "It is definitely not a comedy . . . but a tragedy." Perhaps neither of the men fully wanted to see the resonant ambiguities in the play.

The premiere production of The Cherry Orchard *in 1904 was highly realistic, but recent productions usually mix realistic costumes—to evoke the period—with stylized or symbolic elements, as in this photograph of a 1990 production by the Seattle Repertory company, where, behind and above the characters, a miniature of the house stands for the world that is being lost.*

Anton Chekhov

THE CHERRY ORCHARD

Translated by Laurence Senelick

List of Characters[1]

RANEVSKAYA, LYUBOV ANDREEVNA, *a landowner* (Lyoo-BAWFF Ahn-DRAY-eff-nah Rahn-YEHFF-skei-ah)

ANYA, *her daughter, age 17* (AHN-yah)

VARYA, *her adopted daughter, age 24* (VAHR-yah)

GAEV, LEONID ANDREEVICH, *Ranevskaya's brother* (Lyaw-NEED Ahn-DRAY-eech GEI-ehff)

LOPAKHIN, YERMOLAI ALEKSEICH, *a businessman* (Yehr-mah-LEI Ah-lihk-SAY-eech Lah-PAH-kheen)

TROFIMOV, PYOTR SERGEEVICH, *a student* (PYAW-tr Ser-GAY-veech Trah-FEE-mawff)

SIMEONOV-PISHCHIK, BORIS BORISOVICH, *a landowner* (Seem-YAWN-awff PEESH-cheek)

CHARLOTTA IVANOVNA, *a governess* (Sharh-LAW-tah Ee-VAHN-awff-nah)

YEPIKHODOV, SEMYON PANTELEEVICH, *a bookkeeper* (Sim-YAHN Pahn-til-YAY-eech Ippy-KHAW-dawff)

DUNYASHA, *a parlor-maid* (Doon-YAH-shah)

[1]Unlike earlier dramatists like Gogol or Ostrovsky, Chekhov seldom resorts to word play in naming the characters in his full-length pieces, but to a Russian ear, certain associations can be made. *Lyubov* means "love" (perhaps Amy is the English equivalent), and a kind of indiscriminate love is indeed the soul of Ranevskaya's character. *Gaev* suggests *gaer,* buffoon, while *Lopakhin* may be derived from either *lopata,* a shovel, or *lopat',* to shovel food down one's gullet—both words of the earth, earthy. *Simeonov-Pishchik* is a Dickensian combination of a noble boyar name and a silly one reminiscent of *pishchat',* to chirp. A similar English appellation might be Montmorency-Tweet. [All notes are by the translator.]

482

FIRS NIKOLAEVICH, *a footman, an old fellow of 87* (FEERRSS *Nee-kaw-LEI-yeh-veech*)

YASHA, *a young manservant* (YAH-*shah*)
A TRAMP
THE STATIONMASTER
A POSTAL CLERK
GUESTS, SERVANTS

The action takes place on Madam Ranevskaya's estate.

ACT 1

A room, which is still known as the Nursery. One of the doors opens into Anya's bedroom. Dawn, soon the sun will be up. It is already May, the cherry trees are in blossom, but it is chilly in the orchard, there is a frost. The windows in the room are shut.

(*Enter Dunyasha carrying a candle, and Lopakhin holding a book.*)

LOPAKHIN. Train's in, thank God. What's the time?

DUNYASHA. Almost two. (*Blows out the candle.*) Daylight already.

LOPAKHIN. But just how late was the train? Must have been two hours at least. (*Yawns and stretches.*) I'm a fine one, made quite a fool of myself! Drove over here on purpose, so as to meet them at the station, and fell asleep just like that . . . dozed off in a chair. Annoying . . . but you should have woken me up.

DUNYASHA. I thought you'd gone. (*Listening.*) Listen, it sounds like they're coming.

LOPAKHIN (*listening*). No . . . the luggage has to be brought in, and what-have-you. . . . (*Pause.*) Lyubov Andreevna's been living abroad five years now. I wonder what she's like these days. . . . She's a good sort of person. An easy-going, unpretentious person. I remember, when I was a lad of about fifteen, my late father—at that time he kept a shop here in the village—punched me in the face with his fist, blood was pouring from my nose. . . . We'd come into the yard for some reason or other, and he was tipsy. Lyubov Andreevna, I remember as if it were yesterday, she was still a young lady, so slender, led me to the wash-basin, right here in this very room, the nursery. "Don't cry," says she "peasant boy, it'll heal in time for your wedding . . ." (*Pause.*) Peasant boy. . . . My father, it's true, was a peasant, and here am I in a white waistcoat and tan shoes. Like a pig rooting in a pastry shop. . . . Now here am I, rich, plenty of money, but if you think it over and consider, once a peasant, always a peasant. . . . (*Leafs through the book.*) I was reading this book and couldn't make head or tail of it. Reading and dozed off.

(*Pause.*)

DUNYASHA. The dogs didn't sleep all night, they sense the mistress coming home.

LOPAKHIN. What's got into you, Dunyasha, you're such a . . .

DUNYASHA. My hands are trembling. I'm going to swoon.

LOPAKHIN. You're much too delicate, Dunyasha. Dressing up like a lady, fixing your hair like one too. Mustn't do that. Mustn't forget who you are.

(*Yepikhodov enters with a bouquet; he is wearing a jacket and brightly polished boots, which squeak noisily. On entering, he drops the bouquet.*)

YEPIKHODOV (*picks up the bouquet*). Here, the gardener sent them, he says to stick 'em in the dining room. (*He hands Dunyasha the bouquet.*)

LOPAKHIN. And bring me some beer.

DUNYASHA. Very good. (*She exits.*)

YEPIKHODOV. Three degrees of frost this morning, but the cherries are all in bloom. I can't condone our climate. (*He sighs.*) I can't. I mean, it doesn't seem to make an effort. Look, Yermolai Alekseich, allow me to append, I bought myself some boots the day before yesterday, and they, I make bold to assert, squeak so much, it's quite out of the question. What should I grease them with?

LOPAKHIN. Leave me alone. You're a pest.

YEPIKHODOV. Every day something unlucky happens to me. But I don't complain, I'm used to it. I even smile.

(*Dunyasha enters and gives Lopakhin some beer.*)

YEPIKHODOV. I'm on my way. (*Bumps into a chair which falls over.*) There. . . . (*As if triumphant*) You see, pardon the expression, what a circumstance, incidentally. . . . It's simply, you might say conspicuous! (*He exits.*)

DUNYASHA. Just let me tell you, Yermolai Alekseich, Yepikhodov proposed to me.

LOPAKHIN. Ah!

DUNYASHA. I don't know what to do. . . . He's a quiet sort, but sometimes he starts talking away, and you can't understand a thing. It's nice and it's sensitive, only you can't understand it. I kind of like him. He's madly in love with me. He's an unlucky sort of fellow, something happens every day. So we've nicknamed him: twenty-two troubles. . . .

LOPAKHIN (*hearkening*). Listen, I think they're coming. . . .

DUNYASHA. Coming! What's the matter with me . . . I'm all over chills.

LOPAKHIN. They are coming. Let's go meet them. Will she recognize me? We haven't set eyes on one another for five years.

DUNYASHA (*in a flurry*). I'll faint this minute. . . . Ach, I'll faint!

(*We hear the sounds of two carriages drawing up to the house. Lopakhin and Dunyasha exeunt quickly. The stage is empty. Noises begin in the adjoining rooms. Firs, leaning on a stick, hurries across the stage; he has just been to meet Lyubov Andreevna: he is wearing an old suit of livery and a top hat; he mutters something to himself but no words can be made out. The offstage noises keep growing louder. A voice: "Let's go through here." Lyubov*)

Andreevna, Anya, and Charlotta Ivanovna with a lapdog on a leash, the three dressed in travelling clothes, Varya in an overcoat and kerchief, Gaev, Simeonov-Pishchik, Lopakhin, Dunyasha with a bundle and a parasol, servants carrying suitcases—all pass through the room.)

ANYA. Let's go through here. Mama, do you remember what room this was?

LYUBOV ANDREEVNA (*joyously, through tears*). The nursery!

VARYA. It's cold, my hands are numb. (*To Lyubov Andreevna*) Your rooms, the white and the violet, are still the same as ever, Mama dear.

LYUBOV ANDREEVNA. The nursery, my darling, beautiful room. . . . I slept here when I was a little girl. . . . (*She weeps.*) And now I'm like a little girl. . . . (*She kisses her brother and Varya and then her brother again.*) And Varya is just the same as before, looks like a nun. And I recognized Dunyasha. . . . (*Kisses Dunyasha.*)

GAEV. The train was two hours late. What's going on? What kind of organization is that?

CHARLOTTA (*to Pishchik*). My dog, he even eats nuts.

PISHCHIK (*astounded*). Can you imagine!

(*They all go out, except for Anya and Dunyasha.*)

DUNYASHA. We've been waiting and waiting. (*Helps to remove Anya's overcoat and hat.*)

ANYA. I couldn't sleep the four nights on the train . . . now I'm so frozen.

DUNYASHA. You left during Lent, then there was snow, frost, and now? My darling! (*She laughs and kisses her.*) We kept waiting for you, my sweet, my precious . . . I'll tell you now, I can't keep it back another minute. . . .

ANYA (*weary*). Now what . . .

DUNYASHA. Yepikhodov the bookkeeper proposed to me right after Easter.

ANYA. You've got a one-track mind. . . . (*Setting her hair to rights.*) I've lost all my hair-pins. . . . (*She is very tired, practically staggering.*)

DUNYASHA. I just don't know what to think. He loves me, loves me so much!

ANYA (*peering through the door to her room, tenderly*). My room, my windows, as if I'd never gone away. I'm home! Tomorrow morning I'll get up, I'll run through the orchard. . . . Oh, if only I could get some sleep! I couldn't sleep the whole way. I was worried to death.

DUNYASHA. Day before yesterday, Pyotr Sergeich arrived.

ANYA (*joyfully*). Petya!

DUNYASHA. Sleeping in the bathhouse, practically lives there. "I'm afraid," says he, "of being a bother." (*Looking at her pocket watch*) Somebody ought to wake him up, but Varvara Mikhailovna gave the order not to. "You mustn't wake him up," she says.

(*Enter Varya, with a key-ring on her belt.*)

VARYA. Dunyasha, coffee immediately. . . . Mama dear is asking for coffee.

DUNYASHA. Right this minute. (*She exits.*)

VARYA. Well, thank God, you've come back. You're home again. (*Caressing her.*) My darling's come back! My beauty's come back!

ANYA. I've had so much to put up with.

VARYA. I can imagine!

ANYA. I left during Holy Week, it was so cold then. Charlotta kept on talking the whole way, performing card tricks. Why you stuck me with Charlotta. . . .

VARYA. You couldn't have travelled by yourself, precious. Seventeen years old!

ANYA. We got to Paris, it was cold there too, snowing. I speak awful French. Mama was living on a fifth floor walkup, she had all sorts of French visitors, ladies, some old Catholic priest with a little book, so smoky and tawdry. And all of a sudden I started pitying Mama, pitying her so, I took her head between my hands and couldn't let go. Then Mama kept hugging me, crying. . . .

VARYA (*through tears*). Don't talk about it, don't talk about it . . .

ANYA. The villa near Menton she'd already sold, she had nothing left, nothing. And I hadn't a kopek left either, we barely got this far. And Mama doesn't understand! We sit down to dine at a station, and she orders the most expensive meal and gives each waiter a ruble tip. Charlotta's the same way. And Yasha insists on his share too, it's simply horrible. Of course Mama has her own valet Yasha, we brought him back. . . .

VARYA. I saw the loafer. . . .

ANYA. Well, how is everything? Have we paid off the interest?

VARYA. What with?

ANYA. Oh dear, oh dear. . . .

VARYA. In August the estate's to be auctioned off. . . .

ANYA. Oh dear. . . .

LOPAKHIN (*sticking his head in the door and bleating*). Me-e-eh. . . . (*Exits.*)

VARYA (*through tears*). I'd like to smack him one. . . . (*Shakes her fist.*)

ANYA (*embraces Varya, quietly*). Varya, has he proposed? (*Varya shakes her head.*) He *does* love you. . . . Why don't you talk it over, what are you waiting for?

VARYA. I don't think anything will come of it for us. He's got so much work, no time for me . . . and pays me no attention. May he go with God, it's hard for me even to get to see him . . . Everybody talks about our wedding, everybody's congratulating us, but as a matter of fact, there's nothing to it, it's all like a dream. . . . (*In a different tone*) You've got a new brooch like a bumble-bee.

ANYA (*sadly*). Mama bought it. (*Goes to her room, speaks merrily, like a child.*) And in Paris I went up in a balloon!

VARYA. My darling's come back! My beauty's come back!

(*Dunyasha has returned with a coffee-pot and is making coffee.*)

VARYA (*stands near the door*). I go about the whole day, darling, with my household chores and dream and dream. If only there were a rich man for you to marry, I'd be at peace too, I'd go to a hermitage, then to Kiev . . . to Moscow, and so I'd keep on going to holy places . . . I'd go on and on. Glorious! . . .

ANYA. Birds are singing in the orchard. What's the time now?

VARYA. Must be three. Time for you to be asleep, dearest. (*Going into Anya's room*.) Glorious!

(*Yasha enters with a lap rug, and a travelling bag*.)

YASHA (*crosses the stage; affectedly*). May I pass through here?

DUNYASHA. A body'd hardly recognize you, Yasha. How you've changed abroad.

YASHA. Mm. . . . Who are you?

DUNYASHA. When you left here, I was so high. . . . (*Measures from the floor*.) Dunyasha, Fyodor Kozoedov's daughter. You don't remember!

YASHA. Mm . . . some tomato! (*Glances around, embraces her; she shrieks and drops a saucer. Yasha hurriedly exits*.)

VARYA (*in the doorway, crossly*). Now what was that?

DUNYASHA (*through tears*). I broke a saucer. . . .

VARYA. That's good luck.

ANYA (*entering from her room*). We ought to warn Mama that Petya's here. . . .

VARYA. I gave orders not to wake him.

ANYA (*pensively*). Six years ago, a month after father died, brother Grisha drowned in the river, a sweet little boy, seven years old. Mama couldn't stand it, she went away, went away without looking back. . . . (*Shivers*.) How I understand her, if she only knew! (*Pause*.) And Petya Trofimov was Grisha's tutor, he might remind . . .

(*Enter Firs in a jacket and white vest*.)

FIRS (*goes to the coffee pot; preoccupied*). The mistress will take her coffee in here. . . . (*Putting on white gloves*) Coffee ready? (*Sternly to Dunyasha*) You! where's the cream?

DUNYASHA. Ach, my God. . . . (*Exits hurriedly*.)

FIRS (*fussing with the coffee-pot*). Ech, you're half-baked. . . . (*Mumbles to himself*) Come home from Paris. . . . And the master went to Paris once upon a time . . . by coach. . . . (*Laughs*.)

VARYA. Firs, what are you on about?

FIRS. What's wanted? (*Joyfully*) My mistress has come home! I've been waiting! Now I can die. . . . (*Weeps with joy*.)

(*Enter Lyubov Andreevna, Gaev, and Simeonov-Pishchik, the last in a peasant coat of excellent cloth and wide trousers. Gaev, on entering, moves his arms and torso as if he were playing billiards*.)

LYUBOV ANDREEVNA. How does it go? Let me remember. . . . Yellow to the corner! Doublet to the center!

GAEV. Red to the corner! Once upon a time, sister we used to sleep together in this very room, and now I'm already fifty-one years old, strange as it seems. . . .

LOPAKHIN. Yes, time flies.

GAEV. How's that?

LOPAKHIN. Time, I say, flies.

GAEV. It smells of cheap perfume in here.

ANYA. I'm going to bed. Good night, Mama. (*Kisses her mother*.)

LYUBOV ANDREEVNA. My precious little princess. (*Kisses her hands*.) Are you glad you're home? I can't pull myself together.

ANYA. Good night, Uncle.

GAEV (*kisses her face, hands*). God bless you. How like your mother you are! (*To his sister*) Lyuba, you were just the same at her age.

(*Anya gives her hand to Lopakhin and Pishchik, exits, and shuts the door behind her*.)

LYUBOV ANDREEVNA. She's very tired.

PISHCHIK. Must be a long trip.

VARYA (*to Lopakhin and Pishchik*). Well, gentlemen? Three o'clock, by this time you've worn out your welcome.

LYUBOV ANDREEVNA (*laughing*). You never change, Varya. (*Draws Varya to her and kisses her*.) First I'll have some coffee, then everybody will go. (*Firs puts a cushion under her feet*.) Thank you, dear. I've grown accustomed to coffee. I drink it night and day. Thank you, old dear. (*Kisses Firs*.)

VARYA. I'll see if all the luggage was brought in. . . . (*Exits*.)

LYUBOV ANDREEVNA. Can I really be sitting here? (*Laughs*.) I feel like jumping up and down and swinging my arms. (*Hides her face in her hands*.) But suppose I'm dreaming! God knows, I love my country, love it tenderly. I couldn't look at it from the carriage, couldn't stop crying. (*Through tears*) However, must drink some coffee. Thank you, Firs, thank you, my old dear. I'm so glad you're still alive.

FIRS. Day before yesterday.

GAEV. He doesn't hear well.

LOPAKHIN. I've got to leave for Kharkov around five. What a nuisance! I wanted to have a look at you, to talk. . . . You're still as lovely as ever.

PISHCHIK (*breathing hard*). Even gotten prettier. . . . Dressed in Parisian fashions. . . . "Lost my cart with all four wheels. Lost my heart head over heels."

LOPAKHIN. Your brother, Leonid Andreich here, says that I'm a boor, a money-grubbing peasant, but it doesn't make the least bit of difference to me. Let him talk. The only thing I want is for you to believe in me as you once did, for your wonderful, heart-breaking eyes to look at me as they once did. Merciful God! My father was your grandfather's serf and your father's, but you, you personally, did so much for me once that I forgot it all and love you like my own kin—more than my own kin.

LYUBOV ANDREEVNA. I can't sit still. I just can't. . . . (*Leaps up and walks about in great excitement*.) I won't survive the joy. . . . Laugh at me, I'm silly. . . . My dear bookcase! (*Kisses the bookcase*.) My little table.

GAEV. While you were away, Nanny died.

LYUBOV ANDREEVNA (*sits and drinks coffee*). Yes, may she rest in peace. They wrote me.

GAEV. And Anastasy died. Cross-eyed Petrusha left me and now he's working in town for the police. (*Takes a box from his pocket and eats caramels out of it.*)

PISHCHIK. My dear daughter Dashenka . . . says to say hello. . . .

LOPAKHIN. I'd like to tell you something very enjoyable, cheery. (*Looking at his watch.*) I have to go now, never time for a chat . . . well, here it is in two or three words. As you already know, the cherry orchard will be sold to pay your debts, the auction is set for August 22nd but don't you fret, dear lady, don't lose any sleep, there's a way out. . . . Here's my plan. Please pay attention! Your estate lies only thirteen miles from town, the railroad runs alongside it, and if the cherry orchard were divided into building lots and then leased out for summer cottages, you'd be making at the very least twenty-five thousand a year.

GAEV. Excuse me, what poppycock!

LYUBOV ANDREEVNA. I don't quite understand you, Yermolai Alekseich.

LOPAKHIN. You'll get out of the tenants about twenty-five rubles a year per two-and-a-half acres at the very least, and if you advertise now, I'll willingly bet anything that by fall there won't be a single unoccupied plot, it'll all be grabbed up. In a word, congratulations, you're saved. Wonderful location, deep river. Only, of course, we'll have to put it to rights, fix it up . . . for example, say, pull down all the old sheds, and this house, which is absolutely worthless, chop down the old cherry orchard.

LYUBOV ANDREEVNA. Chop it down? My dear, forgive me, but you don't understand anything. If there's one thing of interest in the entire district, even outstanding, it's none other than our cherry orchard.

LOPAKHIN. The only outstanding thing about this orchard is that it's enormous. The cherries grow once in two years, and there's no way of getting rid of them, nobody buys them.

GAEV. This orchard is cited in the Encyclopedia.

LOPAKHIN (*glancing at his watch*). If we don't think up something and come to some decision, then on the twenty-second of August the cherry orchard and the whole estate will be sold at auction. Make up your mind! There's no other way out, I promise you. Absolutely none!

FIRS. In the old days, some forty–fifty years back—cherries were dried, preserved, pickled, made into jam, and sometimes . . .

GAEV. Be quiet, Firs.

FIRS. And sometimes whole cartloads of dried cherries were sent to Moscow and Kharkov. Then there was money! And in those days the dried cherries were soft, juicy, sweet, tasty. . . . They knew a recipe then. . . .

LYUBOV ANDREEVNA. And where's that recipe today?

FIRS. Forgotten. Nobody remembers.

PISHCHIK (*to Lyubov*). What's going on in Paris? How was it? You ate frogs?

LYUBOV ANDREEVNA. I ate crocodiles.

PISHCHIK. Can you imagine . . .

LOPAKHIN. Up till now there were only gentry and peasants in the country, but now the summer tourists have sprung up. Every town, even the smallest, is surrounded these days by summer cottages. And I'll bet that during the next twenty-odd years the summer tourist will multiply fantastically. Now he only drinks tea on his veranda, but it might just happen that on his puny two-and-a-half acres, he goes in for farming and then your cherry orchard will become happy, rich, lush. . . .

GAEV (*getting indignant*). What poppycock!

(*Enter Varya and Yasha.*)

VARYA. Mama dear, here are two telegrams for you. (*Selects a key; with a jangle opens the old bookcase.*) Here they are.

LYUBOV ANDREEVNA. This is from Paris. (*Tears up the telegrams, without reading them.*) I'm through with Paris.

GAEV. Lyuba, do you know how old that bookcase is? A week ago I pulled out the bottom drawer, and I looked, and there were numbers burnt into it. This bookcase was built exactly one hundred years ago. How do you like that? Maybe we ought to celebrate its anniversary. An inanimate object, but all the same, any way you look at it, a case to hold books.

PISHCHIK (*astounded*). A hundred years. . . . Can you imagine! . . .

GAEV. Yes. . . . This thing. . . . (*Clasping the bookcase*) Dear, venerable bookcase! I salute your existence, which for over a century has been dedicated to the enlightened idealism of virtue and justice. Your mute appeal to constructive endeavor has not faltered in the course of a century, upholding (*through tears*) in generations of our line, courage, faith in a better future and nurturing within us ideals of decency and social consciousness.

(*Pause.*)

LOPAKHIN. Yes. . . .

LYUBOV ANDREEVNA. You're still the same, Lyonya.

GAEV (*somewhat embarrassed*). Carom to the right corner! Red to the center!

LOPAKHIN (*glancing at his watch*). Well, my time's up.

YASHA (*handing medicine to Lyubov*). Maybe you'll take your pills now. . . .

PISHCHIK. Shouldn't take medicine, dearest lady. . . . It does no good, or harm. . . . Give that here . . . most respected lady. (*He takes the pills, shakes them into his palm, blows on them, pops them into his mouth and drinks some beer.*) There!

LYUBOV ANDREEVNA (*alarmed*). You've gone crazy!

PISHCHIK. I took all the pills.

LOPAKHIN. What a glutton!

(*They all laugh.*)

FIRS. The gentleman stayed with us during Holy Week, ate half-a-bucket of cucumbers. . . . (*Mumbles.*)

LYUBOV ANDREEVNA. What is he on about?

VARYA. For three years now he's been mumbling like that. We're used to it.

YASHA. Senility.

(*Charlotta Ivanovna crosses the stage in a white dress. She is very slender, tightly laced, with a pair of pincenez on a cord at her belt.*)

LOPAKHIN. Excuse me, Charlotta Ivanovna, I haven't yet had time to say hello to you. (*Tries to kiss her hand.*)

CHARLOTTA (*pulling her hand away*). If I let you kiss a hand, then next you'd be after a elbow, then a shoulder. . . .

LOPAKHIN. My unlucky day. (*Everybody laughs.*) Charlotta Ivanovna, show us a trick!

LYUBOV ANDREEVNA. Charlotta, show us a trick!

CHARLOTTA. No reason. I want to go to bed. (*Exits.*)

LOPAKHIN. We'll see each other again in three weeks. (*Kisses Lyubov Andreevna's hand.*) Meanwhile good-bye. It's time. (*To Gaev*) Be seeing you. (*Exchanges kisses with Pishchik*) Be seeing you. (*Gives his hand to Varya, then to Firs and Yasha*) I don't want to go. (*To Lyubov Andreevna*) If you think over this business of the cottages and decide, then let me know, I'll arrange a loan of fifty thousand or so. Give it some serious thought.

VARYA (*angrily*). Well, go once and for all!

LOPAKHIN. I'm going, I'm going. . . . (*He leaves.*)

GAEV. Boor. However, I apologize. . . . Varya's going to marry him, that's Varya's little fiancé!

VARYA. Don't say anything uncalled for, Uncle dear.

LYUBOV ANDREEVNA. Anyway, Varya, I shall be delighted. He's a good man.

PISHCHIK. A man, you've got to tell the truth . . . most worthy. . . . And my Dashenka . . . also says that . . . says all sorts of things. (*Snores but immediately wakes up.*) But by the way, most respected lady, will you lend me . . . two hundred forty rubles . . . tomorrow I've got to pay the interest on the mortgage.

VARYA (*alarmed*). We haven't got any, we haven't got any!

LYUBOV ANDREEVNA. As a matter of fact, I haven't a thing.

PISHCHIK. It'll turn up. (*Laughs.*) I never lose hope. There, I think, all is lost, I'm ruined, lo and behold!—the railroad runs across my land and . . . pays me for it. And then, watch, something else will happen, if not today, tomorrow . . . Dashenka will win two hundred thousand . . . she's got a lottery ticket.

LYUBOV ANDREEVNA. The coffee's finished, now we can go to bed.

FIRS (*brushes Gaev's clothes, scolding*). You didn't put on them trousers again. What am I going to do with you!

VARYA (*quietly*). Anya's asleep. (*Quietly opens a window.*) The sun's up already, it's not so cold. Look, Mama dear:

what wonderful trees! My God, the air! The starlings are singing.

GAEV (*opens another window*). The orchard's all white. You haven't forgotten, Lyuba? There's that long pathway leading straight on, straight on, like a stretched ribbon, it glistens on moonlit nights. You remember? You haven't forgotten?

LYUBOV ANDREEVNA (*looks through the window at the orchard*). O my childhood, my innocence! I slept in this nursery, gazed out at the orchard, happiness awoke with me every morning, and it was just the same then, nothing has changed. (*Laughs with joy.*) All, all white! O my orchard! After the dark, drizzly autumn and the cold winter, you're young again, full of happiness, the heavenly angels haven't forsaken you. . . . If only I could lift this heavy stone from off my chest and shoulders, if only I could forget my past!

GAEV. Yes, and the orchard will be sold for debts, strange as it seems.

LYUBOV ANDREEVNA. Look, our poor Mama is walking through the orchard . . . in a white dress! (*Laughs with joy.*) There she is.

GAEV. Where?

VARYA. God be with you, Mama dear.

LYUBOV ANDREEVNA. There's nobody there, it just seemed so to me. At the right, by the turning to the summerhouse, a white sapling is bent over, looking like a woman. . . . (*Enter Trofimov in a shabby student's uniform and eyeglasses.*) What a marvelous orchard! White bunches of blossoms, blue sky . . .

TROFIMOV. Lyubov Andreevna! (*She stares round at him.*) I'll only pay my respects and then leave at once. (*Kisses her hand fervently.*) They told me to wait till morning, but I didn't have the patience. . . .

(*Lyubov Andreevna stares in bewilderment.*)

VARYA (*through tears*). This is Petya Trofimov.

TROFIMOV. Petya Trofimov, one-time tutor to your Grisha. . . . Can I have changed so much?

(*Lyubov Andreevna embraces him and weeps quietly.*)

GAEV (*embarrassed*). Come, come, Lyuba.

VARYA (*weeps*). Didn't I tell you, Petya, to wait till tomorrow.

LYUBOV ANDREEVNA. My Grisha . . . my little boy . . . Grisha . . . son. . . .

VARYA. There's no help for it, Mama dear. God's will be done.

TROFIMOV (*gently, through tears*). All right, all right. . . .

LYUBOV ANDREEVNA (*quietly weeping*). A little boy lost, drowned. . . . What for? What for, my friend? (*More quietly*) Anya's asleep in there, and I'm shouting . . . making noise. . . . Well now, Petya? Why have you become so homely? Why have you aged so?

TROFIMOV. On the train an old peasant woman called me "the mangy gent."

LYUBOV ANDREEVNA. You were just a boy in those days, a dear little student, but now your hair is thinning, eyeglasses. Are you really still a student? (*Goes to the door.*)

TROFIMOV. I suppose I'll be a perpetual student.

LYUBOV ANDREEVNA (*kisses her brother, then Varya*). Well, let's go to bed. . . . You've aged too, Leonid.

PISHCHIK (*follows her*). That means it's time for bed. . . . Och, my gout. I'll stay over with you. . . . And if you would, Lyubov Andreevna, my soul, tomorrow morning early . . . two hundred forty rubles. . . .

GAEV. He never gives up.

PISHCHIK. Two hundred forty rubles . . . to pay the interest on the mortgage.

LYUBOV ANDREEVNA. I haven't any money, dovie.

PISHCHIK. We'll pay it back, dear lady. . . . A trifling sum. . . .

LYUBOV ANDREEVNA. Well, all right, Leonid will let you have it. . . . You give it to him, Leonid.

GAEV. I'll give it to him all right, hold out your pockets.

LYUBOV ANDREEVNA. What can we do, give it to him. . . . He needs it. . . . He'll pay it back.

(*Lyubov Andreevna, Trofimov, Pishchik, and Firs exeunt. Gaev, Varya and Yasha remain.*)

GAEV. My sister still hasn't outgrown the habit of squandering money. (*To Yasha.*) Out of the way, my good man, you smell like a chicken-coop.

YASHA (*with a sneer*). But you're just the same as you always were, Leonid Andreich.

GAEV. How's that? (*To Varya*) What did he say?

VARYA (*to Yasha*). Your mother's come from the village, ever since yesterday she's been sitting in the servant's hall, wanting to see you. . . .

YASHA. To hell with her!

VARYA. Ach, disgraceful!

YASHA. That's all I need. She might have come tomorrow. (*Exits.*)

VARYA. Mama dear is just as she was before, she hasn't changed a bit. If it were in her power, she'd give away everything.

GAEV. Yes. . . . (*Pause.*) If a large number of cures is suggested for a particular disease, that means the disease is incurable. I think, wrack my brains, I've come up with all sorts of solutions, all sorts, and that means, actually, none. It would be nice to inherit a fortune from somebody, nice if we married off our Anya to a very rich man, nice to go off to Yaroslavl and try our luck with our auntie the Countess. Auntie's really very, very wealthy.

VARYA (*weeps*). If only God would help us.

GAEV. Stop snivelling. Auntie's very wealthy, but she isn't fond of us. In the first place, Sister married a courtroom lawyer, not a nobleman. . . . (*Anya appears in the doorway.*) Married a commoner and behaved herself, well, you can't say very virtuously. She's a good, kind, splendid person, I love her very much, but, no matter how much you consider the extenuating circumstances, even so, it must be admitted she's depraved. You can feel it in her slightest movement.

VARYA (*whispering*). Anya's standing in the doorway.

GAEV. How's that? (*Pause.*) Extraordinary, something's got in my right eye. . . . My sight's beginning to fail. And Thursday, when I was at the County Court . . .

(*Anya enters.*)

VARYA. Why aren't you asleep, Anya?

ANYA. I can't fall asleep. I can't.

GAEV. My little tadpole. (*Kisses Anya's face, hands.*) My little girl. . . . (*Through tears*) You're not my niece, you're my angel, you're everything to me. Believe me, believe . . .

ANYA. I believe you, Uncle. Everybody loves you, respects you . . . but, dear Uncle, you must keep still, simply keep still. What were you saying just now about my Mama, your own sister? Why did you say that?

GAEV. Yes, yes. . . . (*Hides his face in his hands.*) In fact, it was terrible! My God! God, save me! And today I made a speech to the bookcase . . . like a fool! And as soon as I'd finished, I realized what a fool I'd been.

VARYA. True, Uncle dear, you ought to keep still. Just keep still. That's all.

ANYA. If you keep still, you'll be more at peace with yourself.

GAEV. I'll keep still. (*Kisses Anya's and Varya's hands.*) I'll keep still. Only this is business. Thursday I was at the County Court, well, some friends gathered around, started a conversation about this and that, six of one, half a dozen of the other, and it turns out it's possible to borrow money on an I.O.U. to pay the interest to the bank.

VARYA. If only God would help us!

GAEV. I'll go there on Tuesday and have another talk. (*To Varya*) Stop snivelling. (*To Anya*) Your Mama will talk to Lopakhin, he won't refuse her, of course. . . . And you, when you're rested up, will go to Yaroslavl to your grandmother the Countess. That way we'll have action in three directions—and our business is in the bag! We'll pay off the interest. I'm positive. . . . (*Pops a caramel into his mouth.*) Word of honor. I'll swear by whatever you like, the estate won't be sold! (*Excited*) I swear by my happiness! Here's my hand on it, call me a trashy, dishonorable man if I permit that auction! I swear with all my heart!

ANYA (*a more peaceful mood comes over her, she is happy*). You're so good, Uncle, so clever! (*Embraces her uncle.*) Now I feel calm! I'm calm! I'm happy!

(*Enter Firs.*)

FIRS (*scolding*). Leonid Andreich, have you no fear of God? When are you going to bed?

GAEV. Right now, right now. Go along, Firs. I'll even undress myself, how about that. Well, children, beddy-bye. . . . Details tomorrow, but for now go to bed. (*Kisses*

Anya and Varya.) I'm a man of the 'eighties.[2] . . . People don't put much stock in that period, but all the same I can say I've suffered considerably for my convictions in my time. It's not for nothing I'm loved by the peasant. You've got to know the peasant! You've got to know with what . . .

ANYA. You're at it again, Uncle!

VARYA. You must keep still, Uncle dear.

FIRS (*angrily*). Leonid Andreich!

GAEV. Coming, coming. . . . Go to bed. Two cushion carom to the center! I pocket the white . . . (*Exits followed by Firs, hobbling.*)

ANYA. Now I'm calm. I don't want to go to Yaroslavl. I don't like Grandmama, but just the same, I'm calm. Thanks to Uncle. (*Sits down.*)

VARYA. I must get some sleep. I'm off. Oh, there was some unpleasantness while you were away. As you probably know, only the old servants live in the old quarters; Yefimushka, Polya, Yevstignei, oh, and Karp. They started letting certain tramps spend the night with them—I held my peace. Only then, I hear they're spreading the rumor that I gave orders to feed them nothing but peas. Out of stinginess, you see. . . . And this was all Yevstignei's doing. . . . Fine, thinks I. If that's how things are, thinks I, then just you wait. I send for Yevstignei. . . . (*Yawns.*) Up he trots. . . . What's wrong with you, I say, Yevstignei . . . you're such a nincompoop. . . . (*Glancing at Anya.*) Anechka! (*Pause.*) Fallen asleep! . . . (*Takes Anya by the arm.*) Let's go to bed. . . . Let's go! . . . (*Leads her.*) My darling has fallen asleep! Let's go. . . .

(*They exeunt. Far beyond the orchard a shepherd is playing his pipes. Trofimov crosses the stage and, seeing Anya and Varya, stops short.*)

VARYA. Ssh. . . . She's asleep . . . asleep. . . . Let's go, dearest.

ANYA (*softly, half-asleep*). I'm so tired. . . . all the bells. . . . Uncle . . . dear . . . and mama and uncle . . .

VARYA. Let's go, dearest, let's go. . . . (*Exits into Anya's room.*)

TROFIMOV (*moved*). My sunshine! My springtime!

ACT 2

A field. An old, long-abandoned shrine leaning to one side. Beside it a well, large stones which were once, obvi-

ously, tombstones, and an old bench. At one side, towering poplars cast their shadows; here the cherry orchard begins. Further off are telegraph poles, and way in the distance, dimly sketched on the horizon, is a large town, which can be seen only in the best and clearest weather. A road to Gaev's estate can be seen. Soon the sun will set. Charlotta, Yasha, and Dunyasha are sitting on the bench. Yepikhodov stands nearby and strums a guitar; everyone sits rapt in thought. Charlotta is wearing an old peaked cap; she has taken a rifle off her shoulder and is adjusting a buckle on the strap.

CHARLOTTA (*pensively*). I haven't got a proper passport. I don't know how old I am, and I always have the impression I'm still a young thing. When I was a little girl, my father and Mama used to go from fairground to fairground, giving performances, rather good ones. And I would jump the *salto mortale*[3] and do all sorts of different stunts. And when Papa and Mama died, a German lady took me to her house and started teaching me. Fine. I grew up, then turned into a governess. But where I'm from and who I am—I don't know. . . . Who my parents were, maybe they weren't married. . . . I don't know. (*Pulls a cucumber from her pocket and eats it.*) I don't know anything. (*Pause.*) I would so like to talk, but there's no one to talk with. . . . No one.

YEPIKHODOV (*strums his guitar and sings*). "What care I for the noisy world, what are friends and foes to me. . . ." How pleasant to play the mandolin!

DUNYASHA. That's a guitar, not a mandolin. (*Looks in a hand-mirror and powders her nose.*)

YEPIKHODOV. To a lovesick lunatic, this is a mandolin. . . . (*Sings quietly*) "Were but my heart aflame with the spark of requited love. . . ."

(*Yasha joins in.*)

CHARLOTTA. These people are rotten singers. . . . Fooey! A pack of hyenas.

DUNYASHA (*to Yasha*). Anyway, how lucky you were to live abroad.

YASHA. Yes, of course. I can't disagree with you there. (*Yawns, then lights a cigar.*)

YEPIKHODOV. Stands to reason. Abroad everything has long since attained its complete maturation point.

YASHA. Goes without saying.

YEPIKHODOV. I'm a cultured fellow, I read all kinds of remarkable books, but somehow I can't figure out my own inclinations, what I personally want, to live or to shoot myself, strictly speaking, but nevertheless I always carry a revolver on my person. Here it is. . . . (*Displays a revolver.*)

CHARLOTTA. I'm done. Now I'll go. (*Slips the gun over her shoulder.*) Yepikhodov, you're a very clever fellow and a very frightening one; the women ought to love you

---

[2]**A man of the 'eighties** The 1880s, when Russia was ruled by the reactionary Alexander III, was a period of intensive political repression. Revolutionary movements were forcibly suppressed, as were the more liberal journals, and social activism virtually ceased. The intelligentsia took refuge in the passive resistance of Tolstoyanism and a tame dabbling in "art for art's sake" (which explains Gaev's chatter about the decadents, mentioned in Act 2). The feeling of social and political impotence led to the torpid aimlessness that is a common theme in Chekhov's works.

[3]***salto mortale*** death-defying leap

madly. Brr! (*Exiting*) These clever people are all so stupid there's no one for me to talk to.... No one.... All alone, alone, I've got no one and ... who I am, why I am, I don't know. (*Exits.*)

YEPIKHODOV. Strictly speaking, not flying off on tangents, I must declare concerning myself, by the way, that Fate treats me ruthlessly, as a storm does a rowboat. If, suppose, I'm wrong about this, then why when I woke up this morning, to give but a single example, I look and there on my chest is a terrifically huge spider.... This big. (*Uses both hands to show.*) Or then again, I'll take some beer, so as to drink it, and there, lo and behold, is something in the highest degree improper, such as a cockroach.... (*Pause.*) Have you read Buckle?[4] (*Pause.*) I should like to trouble you with a couple of words, Avdotya Fyodorovna.

DUNYASHA. Go ahead.

YEPIKHODOV. I'm desirous of seeing you in private.... (*Sighs.*)

DUNYASHA (*embarrassed*). All right ... only first bring me my shawl ... It's next to the cupboard ... it's getting damp.

YEPIKHODOV. All right, ma'am ... I'll fetch it, ma'am.... Now I know what I must do with my revolver.... (*Takes the guitar and exits playing it.*)

YASHA. Twenty-two troubles! Pretty stupid, take it from me. (*Yawns.*)

DUNYASHA. God forbid he should shoot himself. (*Pause.*) I've gotten jittery, always worrying. When I was still a little girl, they took me to the master's house, now I'm out of touch with the simple life, and my hands are white, as white as can be, like a young lady's. I've gotten sensitive, so delicate, ladylike, afraid of everything.... Awfully so. And, Yasha, if you deceive me, then I don't know what'll happen to my nerves.

YASHA (*kisses her*). Some tomato! Of course, every girl ought to know just how far to go, and if there's one thing I hate, it's a girl who misbehaves herself.

DUNYASHA. I love you ever so much, you're educated, you can discuss anything.

(*Pause.*)

YASHA (*yawns*). Yes'm.... The way I look at it, it's like this: if a girl loves somebody, that means she's immoral.

[4] **Buckle** Henry Thomas Buckle—pronounced Bucklee—(1821–62), whose *History of Civilization in England* (1857, 1861) posited that skepticism was the handmaiden of progress and that credulity (for which, read religion) retarded civilization's advance. He enjoyed immense popularity among progressive Russians in the 1860s, but by the end of the century seemed outmoded. Chekhov himself had read Buckle when a youth and quoted him approvingly in his early correspondence; as the years wore on, however, he began to take issue with many of Buckle's contentions. In *The Cherry Orchard,* he uses the reference to indicate that Yepikhodov's attempts at self-education are jejune and far behind the times.

(*Pause.*) Nice smoking a cigar in the fresh air.... (*Listening*) Someone's coming this way.... The gentry.... (*Dunyasha impulsively embraces him.*) Go home, as if you'd been to the river for a swim, take this road or you'll run into them and they'll think I've been going out with you. I couldn't stand that.

DUNYASHA (*coughs quietly*). I've got a headache from your cigar.... (*Exits.*)

(*Yasha remains sitting beside the shrine. Enter Lyubov Andreevna, Gaev, and Lopakhin.*)

LOPAKHIN. You've got to decide once and for all—time won't stand still. It's really quite a dead issue. Do you agree to rent land for cottages or not? Answer in one word: yes or no? Just one word!

LYUBOV ANDREEVNA. Who's been smoking those revolting cigars here? ... (*Sits.*)

GAEV. Now that the railroad's in operation it's become convenient. (*Sits.*) You ride to town and have lunch ... yellow to the center! I ought to stop off at home, play one game....

LYUBOV ANDREEVNA. You'll have time.

LOPAKHIN. Just one word! (*Pleading.*) Give me an answer!

GAEV (*yawning*). Hows that?

LYUBOV ANDREEVNA (*looking into her purse*). Yesterday I had lots of money, but today there's very little. My poor Varya for economy's sake feeds everybody milk soup, in the kitchen the old people get nothing but peas, and somehow I'm spending recklessly.... (*Drops the purse, scattering gold coins.*) Oh dear, spilled all over the place.... (*Annoyed.*)

YASHA. Allow me, I'll pick them up at once. (*Gathers the money.*)

LYUBOV ANDREEVNA. That's sweet of you, Yasha. And why did I go into town for lunch.... That shabby restaurant of yours with its music, the tablecloths smelt of soap.... Why drink so much, Lyonya? Why eat so much? Why talk so much? Today in the restaurant you started in talking a lot again and all off the subject. About the 'seventies, about the decadents. And who to? Talking to waiters about the decadents!

LOPAKHIN. Yes.

GAEV (*waves his hands*). I'm incorrigible, it's obvious.... (*Irritably, to Yasha*) What's the matter, forever whirling around in front of us....

YASHA (*laughing*). I can't hear your voice without laughing.

GAEV (*to his sister*). Either he goes, or I do....

LYUBOV ANDREEVNA. Go away, Yasha, run along.

YASHA (*handing the purse to Lyubov Andreevna*). I'll go right now. (*Barely restraining his laughter.*) This very minute.... (*Exits.*)

LOPAKHIN. Rich old Deriganov intends to purchase your estate. They say he's coming to the auction.

LYUBOV ANDREEVNA. Where did you hear that?

LOPAKHIN. They were discussing it in town.

GAEV. Our aunt in Yaroslavl promised to send something, but when and how much she'll send I don't know.

LOPAKHIN. How much is she sending? A hundred thousand? Two hundred?

LYUBOV ANDREEVNA. Well . . . ten or fifteen thousand—and we're grateful for that much.

LOPAKHIN. Excuse me, but such frivolous people as you, my friends, such unbusinesslike, peculiar people I never encountered before. Somebody tells you in plain Russian your estate is going to be sold, but you simply refuse to understand.

LYUBOV ANDREEVNA. But what are we going to do? Inform us, what?

LOPAKHIN. I inform you every day. Every day I tell you one and the same thing. Both the cherry orchard and the land have got to be leased as lots for cottages, do it right now, immediately—the auction is staring you in the face! Will you understand! Decide once and for all that there'll be cottages, they'll lend you as much money as you want, and then you'll be saved.

LYUBOV ANDREEVNA. Summer cottages and summer tourists—it's so vulgar, excuse me.

GAEV. I agree with you wholeheartedly.

LOPAKHIN. I'll either burst into tears or scream or fall down in a faint. It's too much for me! You're wearing me out! (*To Gaev*) You old woman!

GAEV. How's that?

LOPAKHIN. Old woman! (*Starts to exit.*)

LYUBOV ANDREEVNA (*frightened*). No, don't go, stay, dovie. Please! Maybe we'll think of something.

LOPAKHIN. What's there to think about?

LYUBOV ANDREEVNA. Don't go, please. With you here somehow it's jollier. . . . (*Pause.*) I keep anticipating something, as if the house were about to collapse on top of us.

GAEV (*in deep meditation*). Off the cushion to the corner . . . double to the center. . . .

LYUBOV ANDREEVNA. We've sinned so very much. . . .

LOPAKHIN. What kind of sins have you got. . . .

GAEV (*pops a caramel into his mouth*). They say I've eaten up my whole estate in caramels. . . . (*Laughs*)

LYUBOV ANDREEVNA. Oh, my sins. . . . I've always thrown money around recklessly, like a maniac, and married a man who produced nothing but debts. My husband died of champagne—he drank frightfully—and then, to my misfortune, I fell in love with another man, had an affair, and just at that time—this was my first punishment, dropped right on my head—the river over there . . . my little boy drowned, and I went abroad, went for good, so as never to return, never see that river again . . . I shut my eyes, ran away, beside myself, and *he* came after me . . . cruelly, brutally. I bought a villa near Menton, because *he* fell ill there, and for three years I didn't know what it was to rest day or night: the invalid exhausted me, my heart shrivelled up. But the next year, when the villa was sold for debts, I went to Paris, and there he robbed me, ran off

and had an affair with another woman, I tried to poison myself . . . so silly, so shameful . . . and suddenly I had a longing for Russia, for my country, my little girl. . . . (*Wipes away her tears.*) Lord, Lord, be merciful, forgive me my sins! Don't punish me anymore! (*Takes a telegram out of her pocket.*) I received this today from Paris. . . . He begs my forgiveness, implores me to come back. . . . (*Tears up telegram.*) Sounds like music somewhere. (*Listens.*)

GAEV. That's our famous Jewish orchestra. You remember, four fiddles, a flute and a double bass.

LYUBOV ANDREEVNA. Does it still exist? We ought to hire them sometime and throw a party.

LOPAKHIN (*listening*). I don't hear it. . . . (*Sings softly*) "And for cash the Prussians will Frenchify the Russians." (*Laughs.*) What a play I saw at the theatre yesterday, very funny.

LYUBOV ANDREEVNA. And most likely there was nothing funny about it. It's not for you to look at plays, you should look at yourselves more. You all lead such gray lives, you talk such utter nonsense.

LOPAKHIN. That's true. I've got to admit, our life is idiotic. . . . (*Pause.*) My daddy was a peasant, an ignoramus, he didn't understand anything, didn't teach me but kept getting drunk and beating me with a stick. When you come down to it, I'm the same kind of idiot and ignoramus. I never studied anything, my handwriting is terrible, I write, I'm ashamed to show it to people, like a pig.

LYUBOV ANDREEVNA. You ought to get married, my friend.

LOPAKHIN. Yes . . . that's true.

LYUBOV ANDREEVNA. You should marry our Varya; she's a good girl.

LOPAKHIN. Yes.

LYUBOV ANDREEVNA. I adopted her from the common folk, she works the livelong day, but the main thing is she loves you. Yes and you've cared for her for a long time.

LOPAKHIN. Why not? I'm not against it. . . . She's a good girl.

(*Pause.*)

GAEV. They've offered me a position at the bank. Six thousand a year. . . . Did you hear?

LYUBOV ANDREEVNA. You indeed! Stay where you are. . . .

(*Firs enters; he is carrying an overcoat.*)

FIRS (*to Gaev*). Please, sir, put it on, it's damp here.

GAEV (*putting on the overcoat*). You're a pest, my man.

FIRS. Never you mind. . . . You went out this morning, didn't tell me. (*Inspects him.*)

LYUBOV ANDREEVNA. How old you're getting, Firs!

FIRS. What's wanted?

LOPAKHIN. The mistress says, you're getting very old!

FIRS. I've lived a long time. They were planning my wedding, long before your daddy was even born. . . .

(*Laughs.*) And when the serfs was freed,[5] I was already head valet. Those days I didn't hanker to be freed, I stayed by the masters. . . . (*Pause.*) And I remember, everybody was glad, but what they was glad about, they didn't know themselves.

LOPAKHIN. It used to be nice all right. For instance, you got flogged.

FIRS (*not having heard*). I'll say. The peasants stood by the masters, the masters stood by the peasants, but now everything is topsy-turvy, can't figure out nothing.

GAEV. Keep quiet, Firs. Tomorrow I have to go to town. They promised to introduce me to some general, who might make us a loan on an I.O.U.

LOPAKHIN. Nothing'll come of it. And you won't pay the interest, you can be sure.

LYUBOV ANDREEVNA. He's raving. There are no such generals.

(*Enter Trofimov, Anya, and Varya.*)

GAEV. And here comes our crowd.

ANYA. Mama's sitting down.

LYUBOV ANDREEVNA (*tenderly*). Come, come. . . . My darlings. . . . (*kissing Anya and Varya.*) If only you both knew how much I love you. Sit beside me, that's right.

(*Everyone sits down.*)

LOPAKHIN. Our perpetual student is always stepping out with the ladies.

TROFIMOV. None of your business.

LOPAKHIN. Soon he'll be fifty and he'll still be a student.

TROFIMOV. Stop your idiotic jokes.

LOPAKHIN. What are you getting angry about, you crank?

TROFIMOV. Stop pestering me.

LOPAKHIN (*laughs*). May I ask, what's your opinion of me?

TROFIMOV. Here's my opinion, Yermolai Alekseich. You're a rich man, soon you'll be a millionaire. And in the same way a wild beast that devours everything that crosses its path is necessary to the conversion of matter, *you're* necessary.

(*Everyone laughs.*)

VARYA. Petya, tell us about the planets instead.

LYUBOV ANDREEVNA. No, let's go with yesterday's conversation.

TROFIMOV. What was that about?

GAEV. About human pride.

TROFIMOV. Yesterday we talked for quite a while, but we didn't get anywhere. In a proud man, according to you,

there's something mystical. It may be your viewpoint's the right one, but if we reason it out simply, without frills, what pride can there be, is there any sense to it, if Man is poorly constructed physiologically, if the vast majority is crude, unthinking, profoundly wretched? We ought to stop admiring ourselves. We should just work.

GAEV. You'll die nonetheless.

TROFIMOV. Who knows? What does that mean—you'll die? Maybe Man has a hundred senses and with death only five, the ones known to us, perish, but the remaining ninety-five live on.

LYUBOV ANDREEVNA. Aren't you clever, Petya. . . .

LOPAKHIN (*ironically*). Awfully!

TROFIMOV. Mankind moves forward, perfecting its powers. Everything that's unattainable for us now will some day come within our grasp and our understanding, only we've got to work to help the Truth seekers with all our might. Here in Russia very few people do any work at the moment. The vast majority of educated people, as I know them, are searching for nothing, do nothing, and so far aren't capable of work. They call themselves intellectuals, but they refer to their servants by pet names, treat the peasants like animals, are poorly informed, read nothing serious, do absolutely nothing, just talk about science, barely understand art. They're all intense, they all have glum faces, and all they talk about is major concerns, they philosophize, but meanwhile anybody can see that the working class is abominably fed, sleeps without pillows, thirty or forty to a single room, everywhere bedbugs, foul odors, dampness, moral filth. . . . And obviously all our nice chitchat serves only to shut our own eyes and other people's. Show me, where are the day-care centers we do so much talking about so often, where are the reading rooms? People only write about them in novels, in fact there aren't any. There's only dirt, vulgarity, Asiatic bestiality. . . . I distrust and don't care for very intense faces, I distrust intense conversations. It's better to keep still!

LOPAKHIN. Take me, I get up before five every morning, I work from dawn to dusk, well, I always have money on hand, my own and other people's, and I notice what the people around me are like. You only have to start in business to find out how few honest, decent people there are. Sometimes, when I can't sleep, I think: "Lord, you gave us vast forests, boundless fields, the widest horizons, and living here, we ourselves ought to be regular giants."

LYUBOV ANDREEVNA. What do you need giants for? . . . They're only useful in fairy tales, anywhere else they're scary.

(*Far upstage Yepikhodov crosses and plays his guitar.*)

LYUBOV ANDREEVNA (*dreamily*). There goes Yepikhodov. . . .

ANYA (*dreamily*). There goes Yepikhodov. . . .

GAEV. The sun is setting ladies and gentlemen.

TROFIMOV. Yes.

---

[5]**When the serfs was freed** The serfs were emancipated by Alexander II in 1861, two years before Lincoln followed suit. Under the terms of the Emancipation Act, peasants were allotted land but had to pay back the government in annual installments, the sum used to indemnify former landowners. House serfs, on the other hand, were allotted no land. Both these conditions caused tremendous hardship and were responsible for great unrest among the newly manumitted. So there is more than a grain of truth in Firs's jeremiad.

GAEV (*quietly, as if declaiming*). Oh, Nature, wondrous creature, aglow with eternal radiance, beautiful yet impassive, you, whom we call Mother, merging within yourself Life and Death, you vitalize and you destroy. . . .

VARYA (*pleading*). Uncle dear!

ANYA. Uncle, you're at it again!

TROFIMOV. You'd better bank the yellow to the center doublet.

GAEV. I'll keep still, keep still.

(*Everyone sits down, absorbed in thought. The only sound is Firs softly muttering. Suddenly a distant sound is heard, as if from the sky, the sound of a snapped string, dying away, mournfully.*)

LYUBOV ANDREEVNA. What's that?

LOPAKHIN. I don't know. Somewhere far off in a mineshaft a bucket dropped. But somewhere very far off.

GAEV. Or perhaps it was some kind of bird . . . such as a heron.

TROFIMOV. Or an owl . . .

LYUBOV ANDREEVNA (*shivers*). Unpleasant anyway.

(*Pause.*)

FIRS. Before the disaster it was the same: the screech-owl hooted and the samovar hummed non-stop.

GAEV. Before what disaster?

FIRS. Before the serfs were freed.

(*Pause.*)

LYUBOV ANDREEVNA. Come everyone, let's go home. Evening's coming on. (*To Anya*) You've got tears in your eyes. . . . What is it, my little girl? (*Kisses her.*)

ANYA. Nothing special, Mama. Never mind.

TROFIMOV. Someone's coming.

(*A Tramp appears, in a shabby white peaked cap, and an overcoat; he's tipsy.*)

TRAMP. Allow me to inquire, can I reach the station straight on from here?

GAEV. You can. Follow that road.

TRAMP. I'm extremely obliged to you. (*Coughs.*) Splendid weather. . . . (*Declaiming*) "Brother mine, suffering brother. . . . come to Volga, whose laments . . ." (*To Varya*) Mademoiselle, bestow some thirty kopeks on a famished fellow Russian. . . .

(*Varya is alarmed, screams.*)

LOPAKHIN (*angrily*). That'll be enough of that!

LYUBOV ANDREEVNA (*flustered*). Take this . . . here you are. . . . (*Looks in her purse.*) No silver. . . . Never mind, here's a gold-piece for you. . . .

TRAMP. Extremely obliged to you! (*Exits.*)

(*Laughter.*)

VARYA (*frightened*). I'm going. . . . I'm going. . . . Ach, Mama dear, there's nothing in the house for people to eat, and you gave him a gold-piece.

LYUBOV ANDREEVNA. What can you do with a silly like me! I'll let you have everything I've got when we get home. Yermolai Alekseich, lend me some more!

LOPAKHIN. Gladly.

LYUBOV ANDREEVNA. Come along, ladies and gentlemen, it's time. And look, Varya, we've made quite a match for you, congratulations.

VARYA (*through tears*). You mustn't joke about this, Mama.

LOPAKHIN. Oldphelia, get thee to a nunnery.[6] . . .

GAEV. My hands are trembling: it's been a long time since I played billiards.

LOPAKHIN. Oldphelia, oh nymph, in thy horizons be all my sins remembered!

LYUBOV ANDREEVNA. Come along, ladies and gentlemen. Almost time for supper.

VARYA. He scared me. My heart's pounding so.

LOPAKHIN. I remind you, ladies and gentlemen, on the twenty-second of August the estate will be auctioned off. Think about that! . . . Think! . . .

(*Exeunt everyone except Trofimov and Anya.*)

ANYA (*laughing*). Thank the tramp, he scared off Varya, now we're alone.

TROFIMOV. Varya's afraid we'll suddenly fall in love with one another, so she hangs around us all day long. Her narrow mind can't comprehend that we're above love. Avoiding the petty and specious that keeps us from being free and happy, that's the goal and meaning of our life. Forward! We march irresistibly toward the shining star, glowing there in the distance! Forward! No dropping behind, friends!

ANYA (*stretching up her arms*). You speak so well! (*Pause.*) It's wonderful here today.

TROFIMOV. Yes, superb weather.

ANYA. What you have done to me, Petya, why have I stopped loving the cherry orchard as I did? I loved it so tenderly, there seemed to me no finer place on earth than our orchard.

TROFIMOV. All Russia is our orchard. The world is wide and beautiful and there are many wonderful places in it. (*Pause.*) Just think, Anya: your grandfather, great-grandfather and all your ancestors were slave-owners, owners of living souls, and from every cherry in the orchard, every leaf, every tree trunk there must be human beings watching you, you must hear voices. . . . To own living souls—it's really corrupted all of you, those who lived before and those living now, so that your mother, you, your uncle, no longer notice that you're living in debt, at other peoples' expense, at the expense of those people whom you wouldn't even let beyond your front hall. . . . We're at least two hundred years behind the times, we've still got absolutely nothing, no definite attitude to the

---

[6]**Oldphelia** Lopakhin is apparently an avid theatre-goer and misquotes from one of the many bad Russian translations of Shakespeare. The reference is to Hamlet's admonition to Ophelia.

past, we just philosophize, complain we're depressed or drink vodka. Yet it's so clear that before we start living in the present, we must first atone for our past, finish with it, and we can atone for it only through suffering, only through extraordinary, incessant labor. Understand that, Anya.

ANYA. The house we live in hasn't been our house for a long time, and I'll go away, I give you my word.

TROFIMOV. If you have the housekeeper's keys, throw them down the well and go away. Be free as the wind.

ANYA (*enraptured*). You speak so well!

TROFIMOV. Believe me, Anya, believe! I'm not yet thirty, I'm young. I'm still a student, but I've already undergone so much! When winter comes, I'm starved, sick, worried, poor as a beggar, and—where haven't I been chased by Fate, where haven't I been! And yet, always, every moment of the day and night, my soul has been full of inexplicable presentiments. I foresee happiness, Anya, I can see it already. . . .

ANYA (*dreamily*). The moon's on the rise.

(*We can hear Yepikhodov playing the same gloomy tune as before on his guitar. The moon comes up. Somewhere near the poplars Varya is looking for Anya and calling: "Anya! Where are you?"*)

TROFIMOV. Yes, the moon's on the rise. (*Pause.*) Here's happiness, here it comes, drawing closer and closer, I can already hear its footsteps. And if we don't see it, can't recognize it, what's wrong with that? Others will see it!

VARYA'S VOICE. Anya! Where are you?

TROFIMOV. That Varya again! (*Angrily*) Appalling!

ANYA. So what? Let's go down to the river. It's nice there.

TROFIMOV. Let's go. (*They exit.*)

VARYA'S VOICE. Anya! Anya!

ACT 3

The drawing room, separated from the ballroom by an arch. A chandelier is alight. We can hear, as if in the hallway, a Jewish orchestra, the same mentioned in Act 2. Evening. Grand-rond is being played in the ballroom. Simeonov-Pishchik's voice: "Promenade à une paire!" Enter the drawing room: in the first couple Pishchik and Charlotta Ivanovna, in the second Trofimov and Lyubov Andreevna, in the third Anya and the Postal Clerk, in the fourth Varya and the Stationmaster, etc. Varya is weeping quietly and while dancing, wipes away the tears. In the last couple Dunyasha. They go through the drawing-room. Pishchik calls out: "Grand-rond balancez!" and "Les cavaliers à genoux et remerciez vos dames!" Firs in a tail-coat crosses the room with seltzer bottle on a tray. Pishchik and Trofimov enter the room.

PISHCHIK. I've got high blood pressure, I've already had two strokes, it's tough dancing, but as the saying goes, when you run with the pack, bark or don't bark, but keep on wagging your tail. Actually I've got the constitution of a horse. My late father, what a cut-up, rest in peace, used to talk of our ancestry as if our venerable line, the Simeonov-Pishchiks, were descended from the very horse Caligula made a Senator. . . . (*Sits down.*) But here's my problem: no money! A hungry dog believes only in meat. . . . (*Snores and immediately wakes up.*) Just like me. . . . I can't think of anything but money. . . .

TROFIMOV. As a matter of fact, there is something horsey about your build.

PISHCHIK. So what . . . a horse is a fine beast . . . you could sell a horse. . . .

(*We hear billiards played in the next room. Varya appears under the arch in the ballroom.*)

TROFIMOV (*teasing*). Madam Lopakhin! Madam Lopakhin!

VARYA (*angrily*). Mangy gent!

TROFIMOV. Yes, I'm a mangy gent and proud of it!

VARYA (*brooding bitterly*). Here we've hired musicians and what are we going to pay them with? (*Exits.*)

TROFIMOV (*to Pishchik*). If the energy you've wasted in the course of a lifetime tracking down money to pay off interest had gone into something else, then you probably could have turned the world upside-down.

PISHCHIK. Nietzsche[7] . . . a philosopher . . . the greatest, most famous . . . a man of immense intellect, says in his works it's justifiable to counterfeit money.

TROFIMOV. So you've read Nietzsche?

PISHCHIK. Well . . . Dashenka told me. But now I'm in such straits that if it came to counterfeiting money . . . Day after tomorrow three hundred rubles to pay . . . I've already borrowed a hundred and thirty. . . . (*Feeling his pockets, alarmed.*) The money's gone! I've lost the money! (*Through tears*) Where's the money? (*Gleefully*) Here it is, in the lining. . . . I was really sweating for a minute.

(*Enter Lyubov Andreevna and Charlotta Ivanovna.*)

LYUBOV ANDREEVNA (*humming a lively dance*). Why is Lyonya taking so long? What's he doing in town? (*To Dunyasha*) Dunyasha, offer the musicians some tea. . . .

TROFIMOV. The auction didn't come off, in all likelihood.

LYUBOV ANDREEVNA. And the musicians arrived at the wrong time and we started the ball at the wrong time. . . . Well, never mind. . . . (*Sits down and hums softly.*)

CHARLOTTA (*hands Pishchik a deck of cards*). Here's a deck of cards for you, think of one particular card.

PISHCHIK. I've got one.

CHARLOTTA. Now shuffle the deck. Very good. Hand it over. O my dear Mister Pishchik. Ein, zwei, drei! Now look at it, it's in your breast pocket. . . .

---

[7]**Nietzsche** Friedrich Wilhelm Nietzsche (1844–1900), whose philosophy encourages a new "master" morality for Supermen and instigates revolt against the conventional constraints of Western civilization

PISHCHIK (*pulling a card from his breast pocket*). Eight of spades, absolutely right! (*Astounded*) Can you imagine!

CHARLOTTA (*holds deck of cards on her palm, to Trofimov*). Tell me quick, which card's on top.

TROFIMOV. What? Well, the queen of spades.

CHARLOTTA. Right! (*To Pishchik*) Well? Which card's on top?

PISHCHIK. The ace of hearts.

CHARLOTTA. Right! (*Claps her hand over her palm, the deck of cards disappears.*) Isn't it lovely weather today! (*She is answered by a mysterious feminine voice, as if from beneath the floor: "Oh yes, marvellous weather, Madam."*) You're so nice, my ideal. . . .

VOICE. Madam, I been liking you ferry much.

STATIONMASTER (*applauding*). Lady ventriloquist, bravo!

PISHCHIK (*astounded*). Can you imagine! Bewitching Charlotta Ivanovna. . . . I'm simply in love with you. . . .

CHARLOTTA. In love? (*Shrugging*) What do you know about love? *Guter Mensch, aber schlechter Musikant.*[8]

TROFIMOV (*claps Pishchik on the shoulder*). Good old horse. . . .

CHARLOTTA. Please pay attention, one more trick. (*Takes a rug from a chair.*) Here is a very nice rug. I'd like to sell it . . . (*Shakes it out.*) What am I offered?

PISHCHIK (*astounded*). Can you imagine!

CHARLOTTA. Ein, zwei, drei! (*Quickly lifts the lowered rug.*)

(*Behind the rug stands Anya, who curtsies, runs to her mother, embraces her, and runs back to the ballroom amid the general delight.*)

LYUBOV ANDREEVNA (*applauding*). Bravo, bravo!

CHARLOTTA. One more! Ein, zwei, drei! (*Raises the rug.*)

(*Behind the rug stands Varya, who bows.*)

PISHCHIK (*astounded*). Can you imagine!

CHARLOTTA. The end! (*Throws the rug at Pishchik, curtsies, and runs into the ballroom.*)

PISHCHIK (*scurrying after her*). You little rascal! . . . How do you like that! How do you like that! (*Exits.*)

LYUBOV ANDREEVNA. And Leonid still isn't back. I don't understand what he can be doing in town all this time! Everything must be over there, either the estate is sold or the auction didn't take place, but why keep us in suspense so long?

VARYA (*trying to solace her*). Uncle dear bought it, I'm sure of it.

TROFIMOV (*sarcastically*). Sure.

VARYA. Granny sent him power of attorney, so he could buy it in her name and transfer the debt. She did it for Anya. And I'm sure, God willing, that Uncle dear bought it.

LYUBOV ANDREEVNA. Granny in Yaroslavl sent fifty thousand to buy the estate in her name—she doesn't trust

us—but that money won't even manage to pay off the interest. (*Hides her face in her hands.*) Today my fate will be decided, my fate. . . .

TROFIMOV (*teases Varya*). Madam Lopakhin!

VARYA (*angrily*). Perpetual student! Twice already you've been expelled from the university.

LYUBOV ANDREEVNA. Why are you getting angry, Varya? He teases you about Lopakhin, what of it? You want to— then marry Lopakhin, he's a good man, an interesting person. You don't want to—don't get married; nobody's forcing you, sweetheart. . . .

VARYA. I regard this as a serious matter, Mama dear, I've got to speak frankly. He's a good man, I like him.

LYUBOV ANDREEVNA. Then marry him. I don't understand what you're waiting for!

VARYA. Mama dear, I can't propose to him myself. It's been two years now they've talked about him, everyone's talking, but he either keeps still or makes jokes. I understand. He's getting rich, involved in business, no time for me. If only I'd had some money, even a little, just a hundred rubles, I'd have dropped everything and gone far away. I'd have gone to a convent.

TROFIMOV. Glorious!

VARYA (*to Trofimov*). A student ought to act intelligent! (*In a soft voice, tearfully*) How homely you've become, Petya. How old you've grown! (*To Lyubov Andreevna, no longer weeping*) Only I can't do without work, Mama dear. I have to do something every minute.

(*Enter Yasha.*)

YASHA (*barely restraining his laughter*). Yepikhodov broke a billiard cue!

(*He exits.*)

VARYA. What's Yepikhodov doing here? Who allowed him to play billiards? I don't understand these people. (*She exits.*)

LYUBOV ANDREEVNA. Don't tease her, Petya, can't you see she's sad enough without that?

TROFIMOV. She's just too officious, poking her nose in other people's business. All summer long she couldn't leave us alone, me or Anya. She was afraid a romance might spring up between us. What concern is it of hers? And anyway, I didn't show any signs of it, I'm so removed from banality. We're above love!

LYUBOV ANDREEVNA. Well then, I must be beneath love. (*Extremely upset*) Why isn't Leonid back? If only I knew whether the estate were sold or not. Calamity seems so incredible to me that I don't even know what to think, I'm at a loss. . . . I could scream right this minute. . . . I could do something absurd. Save me, Petya. Say something, tell me. . . .

TROFIMOV. Whether the estate's sold today or not—what's the difference? It's been over and done with for a long time now, no turning back, the bridges are burnt. Calm

---

[8]*Guter Mensch, aber schlechter Musikant* a good man, but a poor musician

down, dear lady. You mustn't deceive yourself, for once in your life you've got to look the truth straight in the eye.

LYUBOV ANDREEVNA. What truth? You can see where truth is and where falsehood is, but I seem to have lost my sight. I can't see anything. You boldly settle all the important questions, but tell me, dovie, isn't that because you're young, because you haven't had time to suffer through any of your problems? You boldly look forward, but isn't that because you don't see and don't expect anything awful, because life is still concealed from your young eyes? You're more courageous and more sincere and more profound than we are, but stop and think, be indulgent if only in your fingertips, spare me. Why, I was born here, here lived my father and my mother, my grandfather, I love this house, without the cherry orchard, I couldn't make sense of my life, and if it really has to be sold, then sell me along with the orchard. . . . (*Embraces Trofimov, kisses him on the forehead.*) Why, my son was drowned here. . . . (*Weeps.*) Show me some pity, dear, kind man.

TROFIMOV. You know I sympathize wholeheartedly.

LYUBOV ANDREEVNA. But you should say so differently, differently. . . . (*Takes out a handkerchief, a telegram falls to the floor.*) My heart is so heavy today, you can't imagine. Here it's too noisy for me, my soul shudders at every sound, I shudder all over, but I can't go off by myself, it would terrify me to be alone in silence. Don't blame me, Petya . . . I love you like my own flesh-and-blood. I'd gladly have given you Anya's hand, believe me, only, dovie, you've got to study, got to finish your course. You don't do anything, Fate simply hustles you from place to place, it's so odd. . . . Isn't that right? Isn't it? And something's got to be done about your beard, to make it grow somehow. . . . (*Laughs.*) You look funny!

TROFIMOV (*picks up telegram*). I've no desire to be a fashionplate.

LYUBOV ANDREEVNA. This telegram's from Paris. Every day I get one. Yesterday too and today. That wild man has fallen ill again, something's wrong with him again. . . . He begs my forgiveness, implores me to come back, and actually I feel I ought to go to Paris, stay with him for a while. You look so stern, Petya, but what's to be done, dove, what am I to do, he's ill, he's lonely, unhappy, and who's there to look after him, who'll keep him out of mischief, who'll give him his medicine at the right time? And what's there to hide or keep mum about, I love him, it's obvious. I love him, I love him. . . . It's a millstone around my neck, it's dragging me to the depths, but I love that stone and I can't live without it. (*Presses Trofimov's hand.*) Don't think harshly of me, Petya, don't say anything, don't talk. . . .

TROFIMOV (*through tears*). Forgive my frankness, for God's sake: but he robbed you blind!

LYUBOV ANDREEVNA. No, no, no, don't talk that way. . . . (*Puts her hands over her ears.*)

TROFIMOV. Why, he's a scoundrel, you're the only one who doesn't realize it! He's an insignificant scoundrel, a nonentity. . . .

LYUBOV ANDREEVNA (*getting angry, but restraining herself*). You're twenty-six or twenty-seven, but you're still a sophomoric schoolboy!

TROFIMOV. So what!

LYUBOV ANDREEVNA. You should act like a man, at your age you should understand people in love. And you should be in love yourself . . . you should fall in love! (*Angrily*) Yes, yes! And there's no purity in you, you're simply "puritanical," a ridiculous crank, a freak. . . .

TROFIMOV (*horrified*). What is she saying!

LYUBOV ANDREEVNA. "I am above love!" You're not above love, but simply, as our Firs here says, you're half-baked. At your age not to have a mistress! . . .

TROFIMOV (*horrified*). This is horrible! What is she saying! (*Rushes to the ballroom clutching his head.*) This is horrible . . . I can't stand it, I'm going. . . . (*Exits, but immediately returns.*) All is over between us! (*Exits into the hall.*)

LYUBOV ANDREEVNA (*shouting after him*). Petya, wait! You funny man, I was joking! Petya!

(*We hear in the hallway, someone running up the stairs and suddenly falling back down with a crash. Anya and Varya shriek, but immediately laughter is heard.*)

LYUBOV ANDREEVNA. What's going on in there?

(*Anya runs in.*)

ANYA (*laughing*). Petya fell down the stairs! (*Runs out.*)

LYUBOV ANDREEVNA. What a character that Petya is! . . .

(*The Stationmaster stops in the center of the ballroom and recites Aleksei Tolstoi's "The Fallen Woman." The guests listen, but barely has he recited a few lines, when the strains of a waltz reach them from the hallway, and the recitation breaks off. Everyone dances. Enter from the hall, Trofimov, Anya, Varya, and Lyubov Andreevna.*)

LYUBOV ANDREEVNA. Well, Petya. . . . well, my pure-in-heart. I apologize . . . let's go dance. . . . (*Dances with Trofimov.*)

(*Anya and Varya dance.*)

(*Firs enters, leaves his stick by the side-door. Yasha also enters the drawing room, watching the dancers.*)

YASHA. How're you doing, Gramps?

FIRS. I'm none too well. In the old days we had generals, barons, admirals dancing at our parties, but now we send for the postal clerk and the stationmaster, yes and they don't come a-running. Somehow I've gotten weak. The late master, the grandfather, doctored everybody with sealing wax for every ailment. I've took sealing wax every day now for twenty-odd years, and maybe more; maybe that's why I'm still alive.

YASHA. You bore me stiff, Gramps. (*Yawns.*) How about dropping dead.

FIRS. Ech, you're . . . half-baked! (*Mutters.*)

(*Trofimov and Lyubov Andreevna dance in the ballroom, then in the drawing-room.*)

LYUBOV ANDREEVNA. Merci, I'm going to sit down a bit. . . . (*Sits down.*) I'm tired.

(*Enter Anya.*)

ANYA (*agitated*). Just now in the kitchen some man was saying that the cherry orchard has already been sold.

LYUBOV ANDREEVNA. Sold to whom?

ANYA. He didn't say. He left. (*Dances with Trofimov.*)

(*They both exeunt into the ballroom.*)

YASHA. It was some old coot babbling away there. A stranger.

FIRS. And Leonid Andreich still isn't back, still not returned. He's got on a light topcoat, for between seasons, see if he don't catch cold. Ech, these striplings!

LYUBOV ANDREEVNA. I'll die this instant. Yasha, go and find out whom it's been sold to.

YASHA. He went away a long time ago, that old man. (*Laughs.*)

LYUBOV ANDREEVNA (*somewhat annoyed*). Well, what are you laughing about? What's made you so happy?

YASHA. Yepikhodov's awfully funny. Empty-headed fellow. Twenty-two troubles.

LYUBOV ANDREEVNA. Firs, if the estate is sold, then where will you go?

FIRS. Wherever you order, there I'll go.

LYUBOV ANDREEVNA. Why do you look like that? Aren't you well? You know you ought to go to bed. . . .

FIRS. Yes—(*With a grin*) I go to bed, and with me gone, who'll serve, who'll take care of things? I'm the only one in the whole house.

YASHA (*to Lyubov Andreevna*). Lyubov Andreevna! Let me ask you a favor, be so kind! If you go off to Paris again, take me with you, please. For me to stay around here is absolutely out of the question. (*Glances around, lowers his voice*) Why bring it up, you see for yourself, an uncivilized country, immoral people, besides it's boring, in the kitchen they feed us disgusting stuff and there's that Firs going around, muttering all sorts of uncalled-for remarks. Take me with you, be so kind!

(*Enter Pishchik.*)

PISHCHIK. Allow me to request . . . a little waltz, loveliest of ladies. . . . (*Lyubov Andreevna goes with him.*) Enchanting lady, I'll borrow that hundred and eighty rubles off you just the same . . . I'll borrow . . . (*Dances*) a hundred and eighty rubles. . . .

(*They pass into the ballroom.*)

YASHA (*singing softly*). "Wilt thou learn my soul's unrest . . ."

(*In the ballroom a figure in a gray top-hat and checked trousers waves its arms and jumps up and down; shouts of "Bravo, Charlotta Ivanovna!"*)

DUNYASHA (*stops to powder her nose*). The young mistress orders me to dance—lots of gentlemen and few ladies—but dancing makes my head swim, my heart pound. Firs Nikolaevich, just now the clerk from the post-office told me something that took my breath away.

(*The music subsides.*)

FIRS. Well, what did he tell you?

DUNYASHA. You, he says, are like a flower.

YASHA (*yawns*). Ignorance. . . . (*Exits.*)

DUNYASHA. Like a flower. . . . I'm such a sensitive girl, I'm frightfully fond of compliments.

FIRS. You'll get your head turned.

(*Enter Yepikhodov.*)

YEPIKHODOV. Avdotya Fyodorovna, you refuse to see me . . . as if I were some sort of bug. (*Sighs.*) Ech, life!

DUNYASHA. What can I do for you?

YEPIKHODOV. No doubt you may be right. (*Sighs.*) But, of course, if it's considered from a standpoint, then you, I venture to express myself thus, pardon my outspokenness, positively drove me into a state of mind. I know my fate, every day something unlucky happens to me, and I've grown accustomed to that long ago, so that I look upon my destiny with a smile. You gave me your word, and although I . . .

DUNYASHA. Please, we'll talk later on, but now leave me alone. I'm dreaming now. (*Plays with her fan.*)

YEPIKHODOV. I suffer misfortune every day, and I, I venture to express myself thus, merely smile, even laugh.

(*Enter Varya from the ballroom.*)

VARYA. Haven't you gone yet, Semyon? What a really disrespectful person you are. (*To Dunyasha.*) Clear out of here, Dunyasha. (*To Yepikhodov.*) First you play billiards and break the cue, and now you're strolling around the drawing room like a guest.

YEPIKHODOV. To make demands on me, allow me to inform you, you can't.

VARYA. I'm not making demands on you, I'm just telling you. The only thing you know is walking from place to place, instead of attending to business. We keep a bookkeeper but nobody knows what for.

YEPIKHODOV (*offended*). Whether I work or whether I walk or whether I eat or whether I play billiards may only be discussed by people of understanding, my elders.

VARYA. You dare to talk to me that way? (*Flying into a rage*) You dare? You mean I don't understand anything? Get out of here! This minute!

YEPIKHODOV (*alarmed*). I request you to express yourself in a tactful fashion.

VARYA (*beside herself*). This very minute, out of here! Out! (*He goes to the door, she follows him.*) Twenty-two troubles! Don't draw another breath here! Don't let me set eyes on you! (*Yepikhodov exits, behind the door his voice:*)

YEPIKHODOV'S VOICE. I'm going to complain about you.

VARYA. So, you're coming back? (*Seizes the stick, left near the door by Firs.*) Come on . . . come on . . . come on, I'll show you. . . . Well, are you coming? Are you coming? So take this. . . . (*Swings the stick.*)

(*At the same moment, Lopakhin enters.*)

LOPAKHIN. My humble thanks.

VARYA (*angrily and sarcastically*). My fault!

LOPAKHIN. Don't mention it. Thank you kindly for the pleasant surprise.

VARYA. It's not worth thanks. (*Starts out, then looks back and asks gently.*) I didn't hurt you?

LOPAKHIN. No, it's nothing. Raised an enormous bump though.

(*Voices in the ballroom: "Lopakhin's arrived! Yermolai Alekseich!"*)

PISHCHIK. Sights to be seen, sounds to be heard. . . . (*He and Lopakhin kiss.*) You smell a little of cognac, my dear boy, my bucko. But we were making merry here too.

(*Enter Lyubov Andreevna.*)

LYUBOV ANDREEVNA. Is that you, Yermolai Alekseich? Why so long? Where's Leonid?

LOPAKHIN. Leonid Andreich returned with me, he's on his way. . . .

LYUBOV ANDREEVNA (*agitated*). Well, what? Was there an auction? Tell me!

LOPAKHIN (*embarrassed, afraid to display his joy*). The auction was over by four o'clock. . . . We missed the train, had to wait till half-past nine. (*Sighs heavily.*) Oof! My head's in a bit of a whirl. . . .

(*Enter Gaev; his right hand is holding packages, his left is wiping away tears.*)

LYUBOV ANDREEVNA. Lyonya, what? Well, Lyonya? (*Impatiently, tearfully*) Hurry up, for God's sake. . . .

GAEV (*not answering her, only waves his hand, to Firs, weeping*). Here, take this. . . . There's anchovies, Kerch herring. . . . I didn't eat a thing all day. . . . What I've been through!

(*The door to the billiard room opens. We hear the sounds of the balls and Yasha's voice: "Seven and Eighteen!" Gaev's expression shifts, he stops crying.*)

GAEV. I'm awfully tired. Firs, help me change. (*Exits through the ballroom, followed by Firs.*)

PISHCHIK. What happened at the auction? Tell us!

LYUBOV ANDREEVNA. Is the cherry orchard sold?

LOPAKHIN. Sold.

LYUBOV ANDREEVNA. Who bought it?

LOPAKHIN. I bought it.

(*Pause. Lyubov Andreevna is overcome; she would fall, were she not standing beside an armchair and a table. Varya takes the keys from her belt, throws them on the floor in the middle of the drawing room and exits.*)

LOPAKHIN. I bought it! Wait, ladies and gentlemen, please for a minute, my head's in a muddle, I can't talk. . . . (*Laughs.*) We showed up at the auction, Deriganov was there already. Leonid Andreich only had fifty thousand, and Deriganov right off bid thirty over and above the mortgage. I get the picture, I pitched into him, bid forty. He forty-five. I fifty-five. I mean, he kept adding by fives, I by tens. . . . Well, it ended. Over and above the mortgage I bid ninety thousand, it was knocked down to me. Now the cherry orchard's mine. Mine! (*Chuckling.*) My God, Lord, the cherry orchard's mine! Tell me I'm drunk, out of my mind, that I'm imagining it all. . . . (*Stamps his feet.*) Don't laugh at me! If only my father and grandfather could rise up from their graves and see all that's happened, how their Yermolai, beaten, half-literate Yermolai, who used to run around barefoot in the wintertime; how this same Yermolai bought the estate, the most beautiful thing in the world. I bought the estate where grandfather and father were slaves, where they weren't even allowed in the kitchen. I'm asleep, this is only one of my dreams, it only looks this way. . . . This is a figment of your imagination, hidden by the shadows of ignorance. . . . (*Picks up the keys, smiles gently.*) She threw down the keys, she wants to show that she's no longer mistress here. . . . (*Jingles the keys.*) Well, it's all the same. (*We hear the orchestra tuning up.*) Hey, musicians, play, I want to hear you! Come on, everybody, see how Yermolai Lopakhin will swing an axe in the cherry orchard, how the trees'll come tumbling to the ground!! We'll build cottages, and our grandchildren and great-grandchildren will see a new life here. . . . Music, play! (*The music plays, Lyubov Andreevna has sunk into a chair, crying bitterly.*) (*Reproachfully*) Why, oh, why didn't you listen to me? My poor, dear lady, you can't undo it now. (*Tearfully*) Oh, if only this were all over quickly, if somehow our clumsy, unhappy life could be changed quickly.

PISHCHIK (*takes him by the arm; in an undertone*). She's crying. Let's go into the ballroom, leave her alone. . . . Let's go. . . . (*Drags him by the arm and leads him into the ballroom.*)

LOPAKHIN. So what? Music, play louder! Let everything be the way I want it! (*Ironically*) Here comes the new landlord, the owner of the cherry orchard! (*He accidentally bumps into a small table and almost knocks over the candelabrum.*) I can pay for everything! (*Exits with Pishchik.*)

(*No one is left in the ballroom or drawing room except Lyubov Andreevna, who is sitting, all bunched up, weeping bitterly. The music is playing, softly. Anya and Trofimov hurry in. Anya goes up to her mother and kneels before her. Trofimov remains at the entrance to the ballroom.*)

ANYA. Mama! . . . Mama, you're crying? Dear, kind, good Mama, my own, my beautiful, I love you . . . I bless you. The cherry orchard's sold, there isn't any more, that's true, true, true, but don't cry, Mama, you've got your life ahead of you, you've got your good, pure heart . . . Come with me, come, dearest, away from here, come! . . . We'll plant a new orchard, more splendid than this one, you'll see it, you'll understand, and joy, peaceful, profound joy will sink into your heart, like the sun at nightfall, and you'll smile, Mama! Come, dearest! Come! . . .

ACT 4

First act set. Neither curtains on the windows, nor pictures on the walls, a few sticks of furniture remain, piled up in a corner, as if for sale. A feeling of emptiness. Near the door to the outside and at the back of the stage are piled suitcases, travelling bags, etc. At the left the door is open, and through it we can hear the voices of Varya and Anya. Lopakhin stands waiting. Yasha is holding a tray of champagne glasses. In the hallway, Yepikhodov is tying up a carton. Offstage, at the back, a hum. It's the peasants come to say good-bye. Gaev's voice: "Thank you, friends, thank you."

YASHA. The common folk have come to say good-bye. I'm of the opinion, Yermolai Alekseich, they're decent enough people, but they aren't too bright.

(*The hum subsides. Enter through the hall Lyubov Andreevna and Gaev. She isn't crying, but is pale, her face twitches, she can't talk.*)

GAEV. You gave them your purse, Lyuba. You mustn't! You mustn't!

LYUBOV ANDREEVNA. I couldn't help it! I couldn't help it!

(*Both exit.*)

LOPAKHIN (*through the door, after them*). Please, I humbly beseech you! A little drink at parting. It didn't occur to me to bring any from town, and at the station I only found one bottle. Please! (*Pause.*) How about it, ladies and gentlemen? Don't you want any? (*Walks away from the door.*) Had I known, I wouldn't have bought it. Well, I won't drink any either. (*Yasha carefully sets the tray on a chair.*) You drink up, Yasha, anyway.

YASHA. To those departing! And happy days to the stay-at-homes! (*Drinks.*) This champagne isn't the genuine article, you can take it from me.

LOPAKHIN. Eight rubles a bottle. (*Pause.*) It's cold as hell in here.

YASHA. They didn't stoke up today, it doesn't matter, we're leaving. (*Laughs.*)

LOPAKHIN. What's that for?

YASHA. Sheer satisfaction.

LOPAKHIN. Outside it's October, but sunny and mild, like summer. Good building weather. (*Glances at his watch, at the door.*) Ladies and gentlemen, remember, until the train leaves, there's forty-seven minutes in all! Which means, in twenty minutes we start for the station. Get a move on.

(*Enter from outdoors Trofimov in an overcoat.*)

TROFIMOV. Seems to me it's time to go now. The horses are at the door. Where the hell are my galoshes? Disappeared. (*Through the door*) Anya, my galoshes aren't here! I can't find them!

LOPAKHIN. And I have to be in Kharkov. I'll accompany you on the same train. I'm staying all winter in Kharkov. I've been hanging around here with you, I'm worn out doing nothing. I can't be without work, I don't even know what to do with my hands. They dangle something strange, like somebody else's.

TROFIMOV. We'll be going soon, and you can return to your productive labor.

LOPAKHIN. Do have a little drink.

TROFIMOV. None for me.

LOPAKHIN. Looks like off to Moscow now?

TROFIMOV. Yes, I'll see them as far as town, but tomorrow off to Moscow.

LOPAKHIN. Yes. . . . Hey, the professors are holding off on lectures, I'll bet they're waiting for your arrival!

TROFIMOV. None of your business.

LOPAKHIN. How many years have you been studying at the University?

TROFIMOV. Think up something fresher. That's old and stale. (*Looks for his galoshes.*) By the way, we probably won't see each other again, so let me give you a piece of advice as a farewell: don't wave your arms! Break yourself of that habit—arm-waving. And also cottage-building, figuring that eventually tourists will turn into private householders, figuring in that way is just the same as arm-waving. . . . When you come down to it, I'm fond of you anyhow. You've got delicate, gentle fingers, like an artist, you've got a delicate, gentle soul. . . .

LOPAKHIN (*embraces him*). Good-bye, dear boy. Thanks for everything. If you need it, borrow some money from me for the road.

TROFIMOV. What for? No need.

LOPAKHIN. But you've got none!

TROFIMOV. I do. Thank you. I received some for a translation. Here it is, in my pocket. (*Anxiously*) But my galoshes are gone!

VARYA (*from the next room*). Take your nasty things! (*She flings a pair of rubber galoshes on stage.*)

TROFIMOV. What are you upset about, Varya? Hm. . . . But these aren't *my* galoshes!

LOPAKHIN. Last spring I planted twenty-seven hundred acres of poppies, and now I've cleared forty thousand net. And when my poppies bloomed, it was like a picture! Here's what I'm driving at, I cleared forty thousand, which means I offer you a loan because I'm able to. Why turn up your nose? I'm a peasant . . . plain and simple.

TROFIMOV. Your father was a peasant, mine, a druggist, but from that absolutely nothing follows. (*Lopakhin pulls out his wallet.*) Don't bother, don't bother. . . . Even if you gave me two hundred thousand, I wouldn't take it. I'm a free man. And everything that's valued so highly and fondly by all of you, rich men and beggars, hasn't the slightest sway over me, it's like fluff floating in the air. I can manage without you, I can pass you by. I'm strong and proud. Humanity is moving toward the most exalted truth, the most exalted happiness possible on earth, and I'm in the front ranks!

LOPAKHIN. Will you get there?

TROFIMOV. I'll get there. (*Pause.*) I'll get there, or I'll show others the way to get there.

(*We hear in the distance an axe striking a tree.*)

LOPAKHIN. Well, good-bye, my boy. Time to go. We turn up our noses at each other, but life keeps slipping by. When I work a long time nonstop, then my thoughts are sharper, and even I seem to know why I exist. But, brother, how many people there are in Russia who have no reason to exist. Well, what's the difference, that's not what makes the world go round. Leonid Andreich, they say, took a position, he'll be in the bank, six thousand a year. . . . Only he won't keep at it, too lazy. . . .

ANYA (*in the doorway*). Mama begs you: until she's gone, not to chop down the orchard.

TROFIMOV. I mean really, haven't you got any tact. . . . (*Exits through the hall.*)

LOPAKHIN. Right away, right away. . . . These people, honestly! (*Exits after him.*)

ANYA. Did they take Firs to the hospital?

YASHA. I told them to this morning. They took him, I should think.

ANYA (*to Yepikhodov, who is crossing through the ballroom*). Semyon Panteleich, please find out whether Firs was taken to the hospital.

YASHA (*offended*). I told Yegor this morning. Why ask ten times?

YEPIKHODOV. Superannuated Firs, in my conclusive opinion, is past all repairing, he should be gathered to his fathers. And I can only envy him. (*Sets a suitcase on top of a cardboard hatbox and crushes it.*) Well, look at that, naturally. I should have known. (*Exits.*)

YASHA (*mocking*). Twenty-two troubles. . . .

YEPIKHODOV. Well, it could have happened to anybody.

VARYA (*from behind door*). Have they sent Firs to the hospital?

ANYA. They have.

VARYA. Then why didn't they take the letter to the doctor?

ANYA. We'll have to send someone after them. . . . (*Exits.*)

VARYA (*from the adjoining room*). Where's Yasha? Tell him his mother's arrived, wants to say good-bye to him.

YASHA (*waves his hand*). They simply try my patience.

(*Dunyasha in the meantime has been fussing with the luggage; now that Yasha is alone, she comes up to him.*)

DUNYASHA. If only you'd take one little look at me, Yasha. You're going away . . . you're leaving me behind. . . . (*Weeps and throws herself around his neck.*)

YASHA. What's to cry about? (*Drinks champagne.*) In six days I'll be in Paris again. Tomorrow we'll board an express train and dash away, just try and spot us. Somehow I can't believe it. Vive la France! . . . It doesn't suit me, here, I can't live . . . nothing going on. I've seen enough ignorance—fed up. (*Drinks champagne.*) What's there to cry about? Behave respectably, then you won't have to cry.

DUNYASHA (*powdering her nose, looks in a hand-mirror*). Drop me a line from Paris. I really loved you, Yasha, loved you so! I'm a soft-hearted creature, Yasha!

YASHA. Someone's coming in here. (*Fusses around with the luggage, humming softly.*)

(*Enter Lyubov Andreevna, Gaev, Anya, and Charlotta Ivanovna.*)

GAEV. We should be off. Not much time left. (*Looking at Yasha*) Who's that smelling of herring?

LYUBOV ANDREEVNA. In about ten minutes we ought to be getting into the carriages . . . (*Casting a glance around the room.*) Good-bye, dear old house, old grandfather. Winter will pass, spring will come again, but you won't be here anymore, they'll tear you down. How much these walls have seen! (*Kissing her daughter ardently.*) My precious, you're radiant, your eyes are sparkling like two diamonds. Are you glad? Very?

ANYA. Very! A new life is beginning, Mama!

GAEV. As a matter of fact, everything's fine now. Until the sale of the cherry orchard, we were all upset, distressed, but then, when the dilemma was settled, finally, irrevocably, everyone calmed down, even became cheerful. . . . I'm a bank employee, now; I'm a financier . . . yellow to the center, and you, Lyuba, anyway, you're looking better, that's for sure.

LYUBOV ANDREEVNA. Yes. My nerves are better, that's true. (*They help her on with her hat and coat.*) I'm sleeping well. Carry my things out, Yasha. It's time. (*To Anya*) My little girl, we'll see each other soon. . . . I'm off to Paris, I'll live there on that money your granny in Yaroslavl sent us to buy the estate—hurray for Granny!—but that money won't last long.

ANYA. Mama, you'll come back soon . . . won't you? I'll study, pass the examination at the high school, and then I'll work to help you. Mama, we'll be together and read all sorts of books . . . won't we? (*Kisses her mother's hand.*) We'll read in the autumn evenings, we'll read lots of books, and before us a new, wonderful world will open up. . . . (*Dreaming*) Mama, come back. . . .

LYUBOV ANDREEVNA. I'll come back, my treasure. (*Embraces her daughter.*)

(Enter Lopakhin. Charlotta is quietly singing a song.)

GAEV. Charlotta's happy! She's singing.

CHARLOTTA *(picks up a bundle that looks like a swaddled baby)*. Rock-a-bye, baby, on-the-tree-top. *(We hear a baby crying: "Waa! Waa!")* Hush, my sweet, my dear little boy. *("Waa! Waa!")* I'm so sorry for you! *(Tossing back the bundle.)* Will you please find me a position! I can't keep on this way.

LOPAKHIN. We'll find one, Charlotta Ivanovna, don't worry.

GAEV. Everyone's dropping us, Varya's leaving . . . we've suddenly become superfluous.

CHARLOTTA. There's no place to live in town. Have to go away. . . . *(Hums.)* It doesn't matter.

(Enter Pishchik.)

LOPAKHIN. The freak of nature! . . .

PISHCHIK *(out of breath)*. Oy, let me catch my breath. . . . I'm winded . . . my most honored. . . . Give me some water. . . .

GAEV. After money, I suppose? Your humble servant, I'll keep out of temptation's way. . . . *(Exits.)*

PISHCHIK *(out of breath)*. I haven't been to see you for a long time . . . loveliest of ladies. . . . *(To Lopakhin)* You here . . . glad to see you . . . a man of the widest intellect . . . take . . . go on. . . . *(Hands money to Lopakhin.)* Four hundred rubles. . . . I still owe you eight hundred and forty. . . .

LOPAKHIN *(bewildered, shrugs)*. It's like a dream. . . . Where did you get this?

PISHCHIK. Wait. . . . Hot. . . . Most amazing thing happened. Some Englishmen stopped by my place and found some kind of white clay on the land. . . . *(To Lyubov Andreevna)* And four hundred for you . . . beautiful lady, divine. . . . *(Hands her money.)* The rest later. *(Drinks water.)* Just now some young man on the train was relating that a certain . . . great philosopher recommends jumping off roofs . . . "Jump!"—he says, and in that lies the whole problem. *(Astounded.)* Can you imagine! Water! . . .

LOPAKHIN. Who were these Englishmen?

PISHCHIK. I leased them the lot with the clay for twenty-four years. . . . But now, excuse me, no time. . . . Have to run along . . . I'm going to Znoikov's . . . Kardamonov's . . . I owe everybody. . . . *(Drinks.)* I wish you health. . . . On Thursday I'll drop by. . . .

LYUBOV ANDREEVNA. We're just about to move to town, and tomorrow I'll be abroad.

PISHCHIK. What? *(Agitated)* Why to town? Goodness, look at the furniture . . . the suitcases . . . well, never mind. . . . *(Through tears)* Never mind. Persons of the highest intelligence . . . those Englishmen. . . . Never mind. . . . Be happy. . . . God will aid you. . . . Never mind. . . . Everything in this world comes to an end. . . . *(Kisses Lyubov Andreevna's hand.)* And should rumor reach you that my end has come, just remember this very thing—a horse, and say: "There was on earth thus-and-such . . . Simeonov-Pishchik . . . rest in peace." . . . Incredible weather . . . yes. . . . *(Exits, overcome with emotion, but immediately reappears in the doorway and says)* Dashenka says to say hello! *(Exits.)*

LYUBOV ANDREEVNA. Now we can go. I'm leaving with two things on my mind. First—that Firs is ill. *(Glancing at her watch.)* There's still five minutes. . . .

ANYA. Mama, they've already sent Firs to the hospital. Yasha sent him this morning.

LYUBOV ANDREEVNA. My second anxiety is Varya. She's used to early rising and working, and now without work, she's like a fish out of water. She's got thin, she's got pale, she cries, poor thing. . . . *(Pause.)* You know this perfectly well, Yermolai Alekseich: I had dreamt . . . of marrying her to you, yes and it certainly looked as if you were ready to get married. *(Whispers to Anya, who nods to Charlotta, and both leave.)* She loves you, you're fond of her, I don't know, I just don't know why you seem to avoid each other. I don't understand.

LOPAKHIN. Personally I don't understand either, I admit. It's all sort of strange. . . . If there's still time, then I'm ready right now. . . . Let's settle it right away—and there's an end to it, but if it weren't for you I feel I wouldn't propose.

LYUBOV ANDREEVNA. That's excellent. All it takes is one little minute. I'll call her right now. . . .

LOPAKHIN. And there's champagne for the occasion. *(Looks in the glasses.)* Empty, somebody drank it already. *(Yasha coughs.)* I should say, lapped it up. . . .

LYUBOV ANDREEVNA *(lively)*. Fine! We'll leave . . . Yasha, allez! I'll call her. . . . *(In the doorway)* Varya, drop everything, come here. Come on! *(Exits with Yasha.)*

LOPAKHIN *(glancing at his watch)*. Yes. . . . *(Pause. Behind the door a stifled laugh, whispering, finally Varya enters.)*

VARYA *(scrutinizes the luggage for a long time)*. That's odd, I just can't find it. . . .

LOPAKHIN. What are you looking for?

VARYA. I packed it myself and can't remember. *(Pause.)*

LOPAKHIN. Where are you off to now, Varvara Mikhailovna?

VARYA. Me? To the Ragulins'. . . . I've agreed to take charge of their household . . . as a housekeeper, or something.

LOPAKHIN. That's in Yashnevo? On to seventy miles from here. *(Pause.)* So ends life in this house. . . .

VARYA *(examining the luggage)*. Where in the world is it. . . . Or maybe I packed it in the trunk. . . . Yes, life in this house is ended . . . there won't be any more.

LOPAKHIN. And I'll be riding to Kharkov soon . . . by the same train. Lots of business. But I'm leaving Yepikhodov on the grounds . . . I hired him.

VARYA. That so!

LOPAKHIN. Last year by this time it was snowing already, if you remember, but now it's mild, sunny. Except that it's cold. . . . About three degrees of frost.

VARYA. I haven't noticed. (*Pause.*) And besides our thermometer is broken. . . .

(*Pause. Voice from the yard through the door: "Yermolai Alekseich!"*)

LOPAKHIN (*as if expecting this call for a long time*). Right away! (*Rushes out.*)

(*Varya, sitting on the floor, laying her head on a pile of dresses, quietly sobs. The door opens, Lyubov Andreevna enters cautiously.*)

LYUBOV ANDREEVNA. Well? (*Pause.*) We've got to go.

VARYA (*has stopped crying, wipes her eyes*). Yes, it's time, Mama dear. I'll get to the Ragulins today, if only I don't miss the train. . . .

LYUBOV ANDREEVNA (*in the doorway*). Anya, put your things on!

(*Enter Anya, then Gaev, Charlotta Ivanovna. Gaev has on a heavy overcoat with a hood. The servants and coachman foregather. Yepikhodov fusses around with the luggage.*)

LYUBOV ANDREEVNA. Now we can be on our way.

ANYA (*joyously*). On our way!

GAEV. My friends, beloved friends! Leaving this house forever, can I be silent, can I restrain myself from expressing at parting those feelings which now fill my whole being . . .

ANYA (*entreating*). Uncle!

VARYA. Uncle dear, you mustn't!

GAEV (*depressed*). Bank the yellow to the center . . . I'll keep still. . . .

(*Enter Trofimov, then Lopakhin.*)

TROFIMOV. Well, ladies and gentlemen, time to go!

LOPAKHIN. Yepikhodov, my overcoat!

LYUBOV ANDREEVNA. I'll sit just one more minute. It's as if I'd never before seen what the walls are like in this house, what the ceilings are like, and now I gaze at them greedily, with such tender love. . . .

GAEV. I remember when I was six, on Trinity Sunday I sat in this window and watched my father driving to church. . . .

LYUBOV ANDREEVNA. Is all the luggage loaded?

LOPAKHIN. Everything, I think. (*Putting on his overcoat, to Yepikhodov*) You there, Yepikhodov, see that everything's in order.

YEPIKHODOV (*talks in a hoarse voice*). Don't worry, Yermolai Alekseich!

LOPAKHIN. What's the matter with your voice?

YEPIKHODOV. I just drank some water, swallowed something.

YASHA (*contemptuously*). Ignorance. . . .

LYUBOV ANDREEVNA. We're leaving—and not a soul will be left here. . . .

LOPAKHIN. Until next spring.

VARYA (*pulls a parasol out of a bundle, looking as if she were about to hit somebody. Lopakhin pretends to be scared*). What are you . . . what are you doing . . . it never crossed my mind. . . .

TROFIMOV. Ladies and gentlemen, let's get into the carriages. . . . It's high time! The train'll be here any minute!

VARYA. Petya, here they are, your galoshes, next to the suitcase. (*Tearfully*) And yours are so muddy, so old. . . .

TROFIMOV (*putting on his galoshes*). Let's go, ladies and gentlemen! . . .

GAEV (*overcome with emotion, afraid he'll cry*). The train . . . the station. . . . Followshot to the center, white doublet to the corner. . . .

LYUBOV ANDREEVNA. Let's go!

LOPAKHIN. Everybody here? Nobody there? (*Locking the side door on the left.*) Things stored here, have to lock up. Let's go! . . .

ANYA. Good-bye, house! Good-bye, old life!

TROFIMOV. Hello, new life! (*Exits with Anya.*)

(*Varya casts a glance around the room and exits unhurriedly. Exeunt Yasha and Charlotta with a lapdog.*)

LOPAKHIN. Which means, till spring. Come along, ladies and gentlemen. . . . Till we meet again! . . . (*Exits.*)

(*Lyubov Andreevna and Gaev are left alone. As if they had been waiting for this, they throw themselves around one another's neck and sob with restraint, quietly, afraid of someone hearing them.*)

GAEV (*in despair*). Sister dear, sister dear. . . .

LYUBOV ANDREEVNA. Oh, my darling, my sweet, beautiful orchard! . . . My life, my youth, my happiness, good-bye! . . . Good-bye! . . .

(*Anya's voice, gaily, appealing: "Mama!" Trofimov's voice, gaily, excited: "Yoo-hoo!"*)

LYUBOV ANDREEVNA. One last look at the walls, the windows. . . . Our poor mother loved to walk about in this room. . . .

GAEV. Sister dear, sister dear! . . .

ANYA'S VOICE. Mama! . . .

TROFIMOV'S VOICE. Yoo-hoo! . . .

LYUBOV ANDREEVNA. We're coming!

(*They exeunt. The stage is empty. We hear the doors being locked with a key, then the carriages driving off. It grows quiet. In the silence there is the dull thud of the axe against a tree, sounding forlorn and doleful. We hear footsteps. From the door at right Firs appears. He's dressed as always, in a jacket and white vest, slippers on his feet. He is ill.*)

FIRS (*crosses to the door, tries the knob*). Locked. They've gone. . . . (*Sits on the sofa.*) Forgot about me. . . . Never mind. . . . I'll sit here a bit. . . . And I guess Leonid Andreich didn't put on his fur-coat, went out in his top-coat. . . . (*Sighs, anxiously.*) I didn't see to it. . . . Young striplings! (*Mutters something that cannot be understood.*) This life's gone by like I hadn't lived. (*Lies down.*) I'll lie down a bit. . . . Ain't no strength in you, nothing left, nothing. . . . Ech, you're . . . half-baked! . . . (*Lies immobile.*)

(*We hear the distant sound, as if from the sky, the sound of a snapped string, dying away mournfully. Silence ensues, and all we hear far away in the orchard is the thud of an axe on a tree.*)

TOPICS FOR CRITICAL THINKING AND WRITING

📖 THE PLAY ON THE PAGE

1. What do you make of the fact that the opening stage directions specify that the setting for the first act is a room that "is still known as the Nursery"?
2. Characterize Lyubov Andreevna.
3. Can some of the characters clearly be called comic? Do some of these characters help to make Lyubov Andreevna less comic?

4. How might the theme of the play be stated?
5. Chekhov said that he wrote "a comedy, in places even a farce." But the director, Stansilavsky, replied, "This is not a comedy or a farce. . . . It is a tragedy." What can be said for each of these views? Try to specify speeches or scenes that can be used to support these judgments. For instance, when Trofimov falls downstairs, is the episode farcical?

🎭 THE PLAY ON THE STAGE

6. What do the costumes, as specified by Chekhov, communicate? (Consider, for example, the brief description of Lopakhin's costume, p. 483.)
7. In a letter to his wife, Olga Knipper, who was preparing to play the role of Mme. Ranevskaya, Chekhov wrote, "It's not hard to play Ranevskaya. It's only necessary to strike the right note from the very beginning. It's necessary to invent a smile and a way of smiling, and it's necessary to know how to dress." How would you dress her?
8. In at least one production, Firs was played with great dignity, providing a contrast to the frantic and absurd behavior of the others. What do you think of this interpretation of the character?

9. What do you make of the sound of the broken string at the end of the play?
10. Do you think the setting of the play might effectively be transferred to the United States? One production, for instance, set it in the South in the late nineteenth century. What might be gained or lost by such a transfer?
11. Imagine that you are casting *The Cherry Orchard*. For three or four roles, choose several well-known actors, and explain why you are choosing them. (Incidentally, directors often succeed with surprising choices. For the role of Lopakhin, Peter Brook chose Brian Dennehy, a bearish man known for his work in cop dramas on television.)

THE PLAY IN PERFORMANCE

Our introduction mentions that although Chekhov said *The Cherry Orchard* was a comedy, Constantin Stanislavsky (cofounder of the Moscow Art Theatre in 1898, the first director of Chekhov's plays, and the performer of the role of Gaev) insisted it was a tragedy. With the productions of Stanislavsky, we are in the world of "director's theater"—theater in which the director rather than the author is the dominant voice.

The director, it should be mentioned, is a relatively recent invention. There is no sign of the director in Shake-

speare's day, for instance; presumably the company of actors—Shakespeare of course was himself an actor—put on the play in accordance with what the author told them. But of course in a theater such as today's, which offers modern productions of classic plays, it is impossible to consult the author, and we are rarely certain about the author's intentions. Chekhov, however, though dying, *was* available for consultation. Still, one can argue that even if the author is alive, the author's views are by no means definitive. The creator of a play may not be consciously aware of what he or she is including in it, and artists—however independent they may think they are—to some degree unconsciously participate in the ideological conflicts of their age. (In the terminology of modern critical theory, to accept the artist's statements about his or her intentions in the work is "to privilege intentionalism.") The idea that the seeming creator of the work cannot comment definitively on it is especially associated with Roland Barthes (1915–80), author of "The Death of the Author," in *Image-Music-Text* (1977), and with Michel Foucault (1926–84), author of "What Is an Author?," in *The Foucault Reader* (1984). For example, Foucault assumes that the concept of the author (we can say the playwright) is a repressive invention designed to impede the free circulation of ideas. In Foucault's view, the work does not belong to the alleged maker; rather, it belongs—or ought to belong—to the *perceivers*, who of course interpret it variously, according to their historical, social, and psychological circumstances. These ideas are especially relevant to drama, particularly for a live performance.

How has *The Cherry Orchard* been perceived? If one reads the several dozen reviews of early productions (from 1911 to 1944) reprinted in *Chekhov: The Critical Heritage*, ed. Victor Emeljanow (1981), one notices that most of the productions have leaned toward tragedy, or toward an emphasis on a tragic mood. This is true not only of the Moscow Art Theatre productions at home and abroad (the company made several visits to London and New York, performing in Russian) but it is true also of most later productions. Inevitably the Russian Revolution—the overthrow of the czarist government and the old aristocracy in 1917—gave the play a meaning it had not had in Chekhov's day; after the revolution the play had to be seen in the light of history. Most productions emphasized the melancholy implicit in the fate that the unwitting characters were about to undergo. But even putting aside the historical developments, the characters' present situation was seen as melancholy. Here is Edmund Wilson commenting on the Moscow Art Theatre's production in New York in 1923:

> In *The Cherry Orchard*, for example, not only is a whole complex of social relations presented with the most con-

vincing exactitude, but *The Cherry Orchard* itself, the sort of beauty which Mme Ranevskaya represents, the charm which hangs about the Russian gentry even in decay is somehow put upon the stage in a way that their futility is never dreary, but moving, their ineptitude touched with the tragedy of all human failure.

> (CHEKHOV: THE CRITICAL HERITAGE, 236)

Or consider a statement made by a reviewer of a 1925 London production: "A sense of beauty now and again steals through the miasma of misery." Remember, these remarks are made about a play that Chekhov insisted was a comedy.

True, occasional productions—notably those of Tyrone Guthrie in 1933 and again in 1941—labored hard to emphasize the comic aspects of the play, but, judging from the reviews, most audiences were not much entertained, partly because the productions were not what audiences expected of Chekhov. A 1977 production in New York, directed by Andrei Serban, however, did emphasize the comedy, and did play to enthusiastic audiences. This production was very much an example of "director's theater"; for instance, in the third act Chekhov tells us that a dance is going on, and we hear the offstage music, but in Serban's version the dance was elaborately staged, eclipsing the actors.

The most recent professional production to achieve national attention was by Peter Brook, a director known for his unconventional presentations. Thus, Brook's *King Lear* was in large measure *Lear* as Samuel Beckett might have conceived it, a Lear of the Absurd. And Brook's *Midsummer Night's Dream* was not the usual amiable play about the delightful tribulations of engaging lovers, but was a disturbing play about deep sexual and class conflicts. To take a single example: In *A Midsummer Night's Dream* the set is usually a pretty thing showing realistic or pleasantly stylized greenery, but in Brook's production it consisted of jangling coils. Not surprisingly, then, Brook's production of *The Cherry Orchard* dispensed with the usual realistic box set filled with furniture. The rear wall was not the wall of a room, with pictures, windows, draperies, and so forth, but was the dilapidated real wall of the theater, and the characters sat not on chairs but on a rug on the floor. (We reprint, in the following, a review of Brook's production.)

Alan MacVey
DIRECTING *THE CHERRY ORCHARD*

Alan MacVey is a member of the theater department at the University of Iowa. In 1991 he directed a production of *The Cherry Orchard* at the Bread Loaf School of English. The cast included Equity actors, staff, and students from the school.

In the course of directing the play, did your conception change?

It deepened. Going into rehearsal I considered the play to be about change. As the social and political world alters around them, the characters face changes in their relationships and

in themselves. A director may decide that the lives of the characters are quite different at the end than they were at the beginning, or that their lives are really much the same; either way, however, the characters are dealing with change all around them. This is where I began.

Well, you said "going into rehearsal." So your ideas did change?

I'm getting there. The first act takes place in a nursery, so our set contained a large toy box. When the lid was opened a tune played as if from a music box; when the lid closed the tune stopped. Planning the production, I thought it would be good to open the box at one point and have music play beneath the action for perhaps five minutes. In the course of rehearsal, though, I found myself closing the box earlier and earlier because the music provided too coherent a mood; though it was quite soft, the music subtly forced all the action and dialogue to fit into a certain tone. This didn't work because we were discovering that things did not fit together—characters were in very different psychological states, much of the time they hardly heard each other, and they changed their actions and moods very quickly. We discovered that the play was indeed about change, but at a microscopic level: Nothing lasts longer than a few seconds. Internal stimulation (from thoughts, memories, etc.) combined with external stimulation (the other characters, the set, the music, etc.) so that each character's internal landscape changed very quickly. Thus "mood music" was an imposition on the scene. By the first performance we simply opened the toy box, listened to its music for five seconds and closed it again. Nothing lasts long in the world of this play.

I heard your staging of the end of the play was especially effective. What did you do?

You'll recall that at the end of Act 4 Firs is left alone on stage. Chekhov has beautifully created the sounds of the scene, which include the cutting of cherry trees and the famous breaking string. We took a hint from Chekhov and added something of our own. The set made use of real French doors that opened west, out to the Vermont mountains. As Firs was left alone on stage, a workman passed by the doors outside and locked them all, just as Chekhov suggests. But our theater also had doors behind the audience, opening to the east. As the last stage door to the west was locked and Firs sat alone, forgotten, a second workman slowly locked the remaining doors behind the audience. We were all locked in the abandoned old house with Firs. The string broke for us as it did for him. Something had happened—but like Firs we could hardly say when or how.

Frank Rich
REVIEW OF PETER BROOK'S *THE CHERRY ORCHARD*

It is not until the final act of *The Cherry Orchard* that the malevolent thud of an ax signals the destruction of a family's ancestral estate and, with it, the traumatic uprooting of a dozen late-nineteenth-century Russian lives. But in Peter Brook's production of Chekhov's play, the landscape seems to have been cleared before Act I begins. Mr. Brook has stripped *The Cherry Orchard* of its scenery, its front curtain, its intermissions. Even the house in which the play unfolds—the Brooklyn Academy of Music's semirestored Majestic Theater—looks half-demolished, a once-genteel palace of gilt and plush now a naked, faded shell of crumbling brick, chipped paint and forgotten hopes.

What little decorative elegance remains can be found on the vast stage floor, which Mr. Brook has covered, as is his wont, with dark Oriental rugs. And that—plus an extraordinary international cast, using a crystalline new translation by Elisaveta Lavrova—proves to be all that's needed. On this director's magic carpets, *The Cherry Orchard* flies. By banishing all forms of theatrical realism except the only one that really matters—emotional truth—Mr. Brook has found the pulse of a play that its author called "not a drama but a comedy, in places almost a farce." That pulse isn't to be confused with the somber metronomic beat of the Act IV ax—the Stanislavskian gloom that Chekhov so despised—and it isn't the kinetic, too frequently farcical gait of Andrei Serban's fascinating 1977 production at Lincoln Center. The real tone of *The Cherry Orchard* is that of a breaking string—that mysterious unidentifiable offstage sound that twice interrupts the action, unnerving the characters and audience alike with the sensation that unfathomable life is inexorably rushing by.

We feel that strange tingle, an exquisite pang of joy and suffering, again and again. When the beautiful Natasha Parry, as the bankrupt landowner Lyubov, returns to her estate from Paris, her brimming eyes take in the vast reaches of the auditorium in a single sweeping glance of nostalgic longing. But when she says, "I feel like a little girl again," the husky darkness of her voice fills in the scarred decades since childhood, relinquishing the girlishness even as it is reclaimed. Later, Miss Parry will simply sit in a chair, quietly crying, as Brian Dennehy, in the role of the merchant Lopakhin, announces that he has purchased her estate at auction. Lopakhin, whose ancestors were serfs on the land he now owns, can't help celebrating his purchase, but his half-jig of victory is slowly tempered by the realization that he has forfeited any chance of affection from the aristocratic woman he has just bought out. A bear of a man, Mr. Dennehy ends up prostrate on the floor behind Miss Parry's chair, tugging ineffectually at her hem. We're left with an indelible portrait of not one but two well-meaning souls who have lost what they most loved by recognizing their own desires too late.

That Lopakhin is as sympathetic and complex a figure as Lyubov, rather than a malicious arriviste, is a tribute not just to Mr. Dennehy's performance but also to Mr. Brook's entire approach to the play. When Trofimov (Zeljko Ivanek), the eternal student, angrily tells Miss Parry to "face the truth" for once in her life, she responds rhetorically, "What truth?"

The director, like Chekhov, recognizes that there is no one truth. Each character must be allowed his own truth—a mixture of attributes and convictions that can't easily be typed or judged. Mr. Dennehy gives us both sides (and more) of the man whom Trofimov variously calls a "beast of prey" and "a fine, sensitive soul." Mr. Ivanek does the same with Trofimov, providing a rounded view of the sometimes foolish but fundamentally idealistic young man whose opinions swing so wildly. Though the student may look immature telling off Lyubov or Lopakhin, his vision of a happier future is so stirring that Mr. Ivanek quite rightly prompts the moon to rise while proclaiming it ("I can feel my happiness coming—I can see it!") at the end of Act II.

Miss Parry, Mr. Dennehy and Mr. Ivanek are all brilliant under Mr. Brook's guidance, and they're not alone. As Lyubov's brother, Gaev—a forlorn representative of Czarist Russia's obsolete, decaying nobility—the Swedish actor Erland Josephson embodies the fossilized remains of a civilization. Elegant of bearing yet fuzzy of expression, his voice mellifluous yet childlike, he snaps into focus only when drifting into imaginary billiard games. One of the evening's comic high points is his absurdly gratuitous tribute to a century-old family bookcase, but the hilarity of his futility is matched by the poignance of his Act III entrance, in which his exhausted posture and sad, dangling bundle of anchovy and herring tins announce the estate's sale to his sister well before Lopakhin does.

As Firs, the octogenarian family retainer, Roberts Blossom is a tall, impish, bearded figure in formal black, stooping over his cane—a spindly, timeless ghost from the past, as rooted to the soil as the trees we never see. Stephanie Roth is a revelation as Varya, whose fruitless religious piety is balanced by a bravery that saves her from despair when her last prayer for happiness, a marriage proposal from Lopakhin, flickers and then dies in Mr. Dennehy's eyes. Linda Hunt (Charlotta), Jan Triska (Yepikhodov) and Mike Nussbaum (Pishchik) find the melancholy humor of true Old World clowns in their subsidiary, more broadly conceived roles. If the play's younger generation—Rebecca Miller (Anya), Kate Mailer (Dunyasha) and David Pierce (Yasha)—is not of the same class, holding one's own with a company of this stature is no small achievement in itself.

In keeping with his work with the actors, Mr. Brook's staging has a supple, airy flow that avoids cheap laughs or sentimentality yet is always strikingly theatrical. In Act III,

the reveling dancers twirl around velvet screens in choreographic emulation of the ricocheting rumors of the estate's sale. Throughout the evening, the transitions of mood are lightning fast. In an instant, Miss Parry's reminiscence of her son's drowning can be dispelled by the jaunty strains of a nearby band. Neither Lyubov nor anyone else is allowed the self-pity that would plunge *The Cherry Orchard* from the flickering tearfulness of regret into the maudlin sobs of phony high drama.

The mood that is achieved instead, though not tragic, recalls Mr. Brook's *Endgame*-inspired *King Lear* of the 1960s. Beckett is definitely on the director's mind, as is evident not just from the void in which he sets the play but also by his explicit evocation of the Beckett humor in several scenes. When Miss Hunt's governess gives her monologue describing her utter lack of identity—she doesn't know who she is or where she came from—it's a cheeky, center-stage effusion of existential verbal slapstick, with a vegetable for a prop, right out of *Waiting for Godot* or *Happy Days*. When, at evening's end, old Firs is locked by accident in the mansion, we're keenly aware of the repetition of the word "nothing" in his final speech. As Mr. Blossom falls asleep in his easy chair, illuminated by a bare shaft of light and accompanied by the far-off sound of the ax, one can't be blamed for thinking of Krapp reviewing his last tape.

But the delicate connections Mr. Brook draws between Beckett and Chekhov are inevitable and to the point, not arch and pretentious, and they help explain why this *Cherry Orchard* is so right. Though Chekhov was dying when he wrote this play, he didn't lose his perspective on existence and the people who endure it. Horrible, inexplicable things happen to the characters in *The Cherry Orchard*—the shadow of death is always cloaking their shoulders, as it does Beckett's lost souls—but, as Mr. Brook writes in the program, "they have not given up." They simply trudge on, sometimes with their senses of humor intact, sometimes with a dogged faith in the prospects for happiness.

That's the human comedy, and, if it isn't riotously funny, one feels less alone in the solitary plight, indeed exhilarated, watching it unfold on stage as honestly and buoyantly and poetically as a dream. This is a *Cherry Orchard* that pauses for breath only when life does, for people to recoup after dying a little. I think Mr. Brook has given us the Chekhov production that every theatergoer fantasizes about but, in my experience, almost never finds.

John Millington Synge

RIDERS TO THE SEA

John Millington Synge (1871–1909) was born in Dublin of Protestant English stock. After his graduation from Trinity College, Dublin, where he specialized in languages—Gaelic, Latin, Greek, Hebrew—he went to Paris and tried to eke out a living by writing criticism of French literature. William Butler Yeats, in Paris in 1896, urged him to return to Ireland so that he might steep himself in the speech of the common people and record a life never described in literature. Synge took the advice and then in his few remaining years wrote six plays, three of which are masterpieces: *Riders to the Sea* (1904), *The Playboy of the Western World* (1907), and *Deidre of the Sorrows* (1909). He died of cancer in his thirty-eighth year.

COMMENTARY

Synge first visited the Aran Islands (three rocky places off the west coast of Ireland, inhabited by Gaelic-speaking fishermen) in the summer of 1898. From this visit and subsequent ones he derived the material for *The Aran Islands*, an account of life there, full of observations and bits of folklore he had picked up. In it one can find something of the origins of *Riders to the Sea*: descriptions of bringing horses across the sound, including an account of an old woman who had a vision of her drowned son riding on a horse; a reference to a coffin untimely made out of boards prepared for another person; and a reference to a body that floated ashore some weeks after the man drowned.

In writing the play Synge chose among the innumerable things he saw and heard, selecting (as any artist does) from the welter or chaos of experience to put together a unified story. One need not compare *Riders to the Sea* (in which everything is related to everything else) with *The Aran Islands* (in which we have a wonderful grab bag of scarcely related details) to see that the careful arrangement of physical happenings and dialogue gives us more than a slice of life, more than a picture of a certain kind of Irish life. Synge's art extends beyond his plot to his language. The islanders spoke Gaelic, and Synge claimed that his English was close to a translation of their language; but the speeches—as distinct from the words—are Synge's, just as Macbeth's "I am in blood / Stepped in so far, that, should I wade no more, / Returning were as tedious as go o'er" is Shakespeare's creation although the individual words are pretty much the property of any literate American or Eng-

lishman. The speeches Synge creates, no less than his plot, belong to the world of art, though the speeches and the events are made up of the materials of Aran life.

Synge chose the peasant idiom because it seemed to him to have beauty and even grandeur, while at the same time it was rooted in people who lived an elemental existence. He saw no need to choose between beauty and truth: Beauty without truth led writers of the late nineteenth century (he believed) to highly wrought yet trivial or even meaningless verse, and truth without beauty to dull pictures of humankind's insignificance. It is partly by making "every speech . . . as fully flavored as a nut or apple" that Synge produced a work that (although it deals with multiple deaths) is not depressing but is, like every work of art, stimulating: "Let you go down each day, and see the sheep aren't jumping in on the rye, and if the jobber comes you can sell the pig with the black feet if there is a good price going." Even the speeches on the inevitable end of humankind have, while they call attention to a person's ignominious remains, richness and dignity: "And isn't it a pitiful thing when there is nothing left of a man who was a great rower and fisher, but a bit of an old shirt and a plain stocking?" Throughout the play this artful use of language communicates a picture of heroism and humbleness that is reassuring as well as grievous, nowhere more so than in Maurya's final speech, which calls attention to the hardness of life and the inevitability of death in such a way as almost to offer a kind of reassurance.

Early in the play Maurya speaks "querulously" and rakes the fire "aimlessly." Finally, after the death of Bartley, Maurya derives some comfort from the thought that "Bartley will have a fine coffin out of the white boards," and Michael "a clean burial in the far north." She has been "hard set," known despair, seen the worst that can happen ("They're all gone now, and there isn't anything more the sea can do to me"), and now from the vantage point of one stripped of all that one has cherished, she can utter with dignity the most terrible facts of life. This is the heart of Synge's drama. The word *drama* is from the Greek verb *dran*, "to do," "to accomplish"; in *Riders to the Sea* the thing accomplished is not only the identification of Michael's clothing and the death of Bartley, but the shift in Maurya's mind.

We have been talking at some length about *Riders to the Sea* as a drama, but we have said nothing about it as a tragedy. Two of Synge's fellow Irishmen have left brief interesting comments on the play, especially on the play's relation to classical tragedy. William Butler Yeats, Synge's older contemporary, called it "quite Greek"; but James Joyce, Synge's younger contemporary, who regarded himself as one who adhered to Aristotle's *Poetics*, after reading *Riders to the Sea* sniffily remarked that "Synge isn't an Aristotelian." Joyce was especially bothered by the brevity of the play; in a program note to a production of the play, he wondered "whether a brief tragedy be possible or not (a point on which Aristotle had some doubts)," though he did go on to say that *Riders to the Sea* is "the work of a tragic poet." One might learn something by considering the play in the light of some of Aristotle's remarks. This is not to say that if the play doesn't hew to Aristotle's prescriptions it is defective—and indeed Aristotle is sometimes confusing and sometimes contradictory. Still, here are a few of his comments, extracted from the fuller text of *The Poetics* that we print on pages 73–77. You may want to evaluate their relevance to *Riders to the Sea*, partly in an effort to see the strengths or weaknesses of the play, partly in an effort to see the strengths or weaknesses of *The Poetics*.

1. "Tragedy is an imitation of people above the normal" (page 77).
2. "Tragedy . . . is an imitation of an action of high importance, complete and of some amplitude; in language enhanced by . . . beauties. . . . By the beauties enhancing the language I mean rhythm and melody" (page 73).
3. "[One of] the chief means by which tragedy moves us [is] Irony of events. . . . Irony is a reversal in the course of events, . . . and, as I say, in accordance with probability or necessity" (page 75).
4. ". . . tragedy is an imitation of a whole and complete action of some amplitude. . . . as to amplitude, the invariable rule dictated by the nature of the action is the fuller the more beautiful so long as the outline remains clear" (pages 73–74).
5. ". . . it is not the poet's business to tell what has happened, but the kind of things that would happen— what is possible according to probability or necessity" (page 75).
6. "The action imitated must contain incidents that evoke fear and pity, besides being a complete action; but this effect is accentuated when these incidents occur logically as well as unexpectedly, which will be more sensational if they happen arbitrarily, by chance" (page 75).
7. ". . . tragedy, to be at its finest, . . . should . . . imitate fearful and pitiful events. . . . pity is induced by undeserved misfortune, and fear by the misfortunes of normal people" (page 76).
8. "[Tragedy shows] the kind of man who neither is distinguished for excellence and virtue, nor comes to grief on account of baseness and vice, but on account of some error" (page 76).

John Millington Synge

RIDERS TO THE SEA

List of Characters

MAURYA, *an old woman*
BARTLEY, *her son*
CATHLEEN, *her daughter*
NORA, *a younger daughter*
MEN *and* WOMEN

SCENE: *An island off the West of Ireland.*

Cottage kitchen, with nets, oil-skins, spinning-wheel, some new boards standing by the wall, etc. Cathleen, a girl of about twenty, finishes kneading cake, and puts it down in the pot-oven by the fire; then wipes her hands, and begins to spin at the wheel. Nora, a young girl, puts her head in at the door.

NORA (*in a low voice*). Where is she?

CATHLEEN. She's lying down, God help her, and may be sleeping, if she's able.

Nora comes in softly, and takes a bundle from under her shawl.

CATHLEEN (*spinning the wheel rapidly*). What is it you have?

NORA. The young priest is after bringing them. It's a shirt and a plain stocking were got off a drowned man in Donegal.

Cathleen stops her wheel with a sudden movement, and leans out to listen.

NORA. We're to find out if it's Michael's they are, some time herself will be down looking by the sea.

CATHLEEN. How would they be Michael's, Nora? How would he go the length of that way to the far north?

NORA. The young priest says he's known the like of it. "If it's Michael's they are," says he, "you can tell herself he's got a clean burial by the grace of God, and if they're not his, let no one say a word about them, for she'll be getting her death," says he, "with crying and lamenting."

The door which Nora half-closed is blown open by a gust of wind.

CATHLEEN (*looking out anxiously*). Did you ask him would he stop Bartley going this day with the horses to the Galway fair?

NORA. "I won't stop him," says he, "but let you not be afraid. Herself does be saying prayers half through the night, and the Almighty God won't leave her destitute," says he, "with no son living."

CATHLEEN. Is the sea bad by the white rocks, Nora?

NORA. Middling bad, God help us. There's a great roaring in the west, and it's worse it'll be getting when the tide's turned to the wind. (*She goes over to the table with the bundle.*) Shall I open it now?

CATHLEEN. Maybe she'd wake up on us, and come in before we'd done. (*Coming to the table.*) It's a long time we'll be, and the two of us crying.

NORA (*goes to the inner door and listens*). She's moving about on the bed. She'll be coming in a minute.

CATHLEEN. Give me the ladder, and I'll put them up in the turf-loft, the way she won't know of them at all, and maybe when the tide turns she'll be going down to see would he be floating from the east.

They put the ladder against the gable of the chimney; Cathleen goes up a few steps and hides the bundle in the turf-loft. Maurya comes from the inner room.

MAURYA (*looking up at Cathleen and speaking querulously*). Isn't it turf enough you have for this day and evening?

CATHLEEN. There's a cake baking at the fire for a short space (*throwing down the turf*) and Bartley will want it when the tide turns if he goes to Connemara.

Nora picks up the turf and puts it round the pot-oven.

MAURYA (*sitting down on a stool at the fire*). He won't go this day with the wind rising from the south and west. He won't go this day, for the young priest will stop him surely.

NORA. He'll not stop him, mother, and I heard Eamon Simon and Stephen Pheety and Colum Shawn saying he would go.

MAURYA. Where is he itself?

NORA. He went down to see would there be another boat sailing in the week, and I'm thinking it won't be long till he's here now, for the tide's turning at the green head, and the hooker's[1] tacking from the east.

CATHLEEN. I hear some one passing the big stones.

NORA (*looking out*). He's coming now, and he in a hurry.

BARTLEY (*comes in and looks round the room. Speaking sadly and quietly*). Where is the bit of new rope, Cathleen, was bought in Connemara?

CATHLEEN (*coming down*). Give it to him, Nora; it's on a nail by the white boards. I hung it up this morning, for the pig with the black feet was eating it.

NORA (*giving him a rope*). Is that it, Bartley?

MAURYA. You'd do right to leave that rope, Bartley, hanging by the boards. (*Bartley takes the rope.*) It will be wanting in this place, I'm telling you, if Michael is washed up to-morrow morning, or the next morning, or any morning

[1]**hooker** sailing boat

in the week, for it's a deep grave we'll make him by the grace of God.

BARTLEY (*beginning to work with the rope*). I've no halter the way I can ride down on the mare, and I must go now quickly. This is the one boat going for two weeks or beyond it, and the fair will be a good fair for horses I heard them saying below.

MAURYA. It's a hard thing they'll be saying below if the body is washed up and there's no man in it to make the coffin, and I after giving a big price for the finest white boards you'd find in Connemara.

She looks round at the boards.

BARTLEY. How would it be washed up, and we after looking each day for nine days, and a strong wind blowing a while back from the west and south?

MAURYA. If it wasn't found itself, that wind is raising the sea, and there was a star up against the moon, and it rising in the night. If it was a hundred horses, or a thousand horses you had itself, what is the price of a thousand horses against a son where there is one son only?

BARTLEY (*working at the halter, to Cathleen*). Let you go down each day, and see the sheep aren't jumping in on the rye, and if the jobber comes you can sell the pig with the black feet if there is a good price going.

MAURYA. How would the like of her get a good price for a pig?

BARTLEY (*to Cathleen*). If the west wind holds with the last bit of the moon let you and Nora get up weed enough for another cock for the kelp.[2] It's hard set we'll be from this day with no one in it but one man to work.

MAURYA. It's hard set we'll be surely the day you're drownd'd with the rest. What way will I live and the girls with me, and I an old woman looking for the grave?

Bartley lays down the halter, takes off his old coat, and puts on a newer one of the same flannel.

BARTLEY (*to Nora*). Is she coming to the pier?

NORA (*looking out*). She's passing the green head and letting fall her sails.

BARTLEY (*getting his purse and tobacco*). I'll have half an hour to go down, and you'll see me coming again in two days, or in three days, or maybe in four days if the wind is bad.

MAURYA (*turning round to the fire, and putting her shawl over her head*). Isn't it a hard and cruel man won't hear a word from an old woman, and she holding him from the sea?

CATHLEEN. It's the life of a young man to be going on the sea, and who would listen to an old woman with one thing and she saying it over?

BARTLEY (*taking the halter*). I must go now quickly. I'll ride down on the red mare, and the gray pony'll run behind me. . . . The blessing of God on you.

He goes out.

[2]**kelp** seaweed (used for fertilizer)

MAURYA (*crying out as he is in the door*). He's gone now, God spare us, and we'll not see him again. He's gone now, and when the black night is falling I'll have no son left me in the world.

CATHLEEN. Why wouldn't you give him your blessing and he looking round in the door? Isn't it sorrow enough is on every one in this house without your sending him out with an unlucky word behind him, and a hard word in his ear?

Maurya takes up the tongs and begins raking the fire aimlessly without looking round.

NORA (*turning towards her*). You're taking away the turf from the cake.

CATHLEEN (*crying out*). The Son of God forgive us, Nora, we're after forgetting his bit of bread.

She comes over to the fire.

NORA. And it's destroyed he'll be going till dark night, and he after eating nothing since the sun went up.

CATHLEEN (*turning the cake out of the oven*). It's destroyed he'll be, surely. There's no sense left on any person in a house where an old woman will be talking for ever.

Maurya sways herself on her stool.

CATHLEEN (*cutting off some of the bread and rolling it in a cloth; to Maurya*). Let you go down now to the spring well and give him this and he passing. You'll see him then and the dark word will be broken, and you can say "God speed you," the way he'll be easy in his mind.

MAURYA (*taking the bread*). Will I be in it as soon as himself?

CATHLEEN. If you go now quickly.

MAURYA (*standing up unsteadily*). It's hard set I am to walk.

CATHLEEN (*looking at her anxiously*). Give her the stick, Nora, or maybe she'll slip on the big stones.

NORA. What stick?

CATHLEEN. The stick Michael brought from Connemara.

MAURYA (*taking a stick Nora gives her*). In the big world the old people do be leaving things after them for their sons and children, but in this place it is the young men do be leaving things behind for them that do be old.

She goes out slowly. Nora goes over to the ladder.

CATHLEEN. Wait, Nora, maybe she'd turn back quickly. She's that sorry, God help her, you wouldn't know the thing she'd do.

NORA. Is she gone around by the bush?

CATHLEEN (*looking out*). She's gone now. Throw it down quickly, for the Lord knows when she'll be out of it again.

NORA (*getting the bundle from the loft*). The young priest said he'd be passing to-morrow, and we might go down and speak to him below if it's Michael's they are surely.

CATHLEEN (*taking the bundle*). Did he say what way they were found?

NORA (*coming down*). "There were two men," says he, "and they rowing round with poteen[3] before the cocks crowed, and the oar of one of them caught the body, and they passing the black cliffs of the north."

CATHLEEN (*trying to open the bundle*). Give me a knife, Nora, the strings perished with the salt water, and there's a black knot on it you wouldn't loosen in a week.

NORA (*giving her a knife*). I've heard tell it was a long way to Donegal.

CATHLEEN (*cutting the string*). It is surely. There was a man in here a while ago—the man sold us that knife—and he said if you set off walking from the rock beyond, it would be seven days you'd be in Donegal.

NORA. And what time would a man take, and he floating?

Cathleen opens the bundle and takes out a bit of a stocking. They look at them eagerly.

CATHLEEN (*in a low voice*). The Lord spare us, Nora! isn't it a queer hard thing to say if it's his they are surely?

NORA. I'll get his shirt off the hook the way we can put the one flannel on the other. (*She looks through some clothes hanging in the corner.*) It's not with them, Cathleen, and where will it be?

CATHLEEN. I'm thinking Bartley put it on him in the morning, for his own shirt was heavy with the salt in it. (*Pointing to the corner.*) There's a bit of a sleeve was of the same stuff. Give me that and it will do.

Nora brings it to her and they compare the flannel.

CATHLEEN. It's the same stuff, Nora; but if it is itself aren't there great rolls of it in the shops of Galway, and isn't it many another man may have a shirt of it as well as Michael himself?

NORA (*who has taken up the stocking and counted the stitches, crying out*). It's Michael, Cathleen, it's Michael; God spare his soul, and what will herself say when she hears this story, and Bartley on the sea?

CATHLEEN (*taking the stocking*). It's a plain stocking.

NORA. It's the second one of the third pair I knitted, and I put up three score stitches, and I dropped four of them.

CATHLEEN (*counts the stitches*). It's that number is in it. (*Crying out.*) Ah, Nora, isn't it a bitter thing to think of him floating that way to the far north, and no one to keen[4] him but the black hags that do be flying on the sea?

NORA (*swinging herself round, and throwing out her arms on the clothes*). And isn't it a pitiful thing when there is nothing left of a man who was a great rower and fisher, but a bit of an old shirt and a plain stocking?

CATHLEEN (*after an instant*). Tell me is herself coming, Nora? I hear a little sound on the path.

NORA (*looking out*). She is, Cathleen. She's coming up to the door.

---

³**poteen** illegal whiskey ⁴**keen** lament

CATHLEEN. Put these things away before she'll come in. Maybe it's easier she'll be after giving her blessing to Bartley, and we won't let on we've heard anything the time he's on the sea.

NORA (*helping Cathleen to close the bundle*). We'll put them here in the corner.

They put them into a hole in the chimney corner. Cathleen goes back to the spinning-wheel.

NORA. Will she see it was crying I was?

CATHLEEN. Keep your back to the door the way the light'll not be on you.

Nora sits down at the chimney corner, with her back to the door. Maurya comes in very slowly, without looking at the girls, and goes over to her stool at the other side of the fire. The cloth with the bread is still in her hand. The girls look at each other, and Nora points to the bundle of bread.

CATHLEEN (*after spinning for a moment*). You didn't give him his bit of bread?

Maurya begins to keen softly, without turning round.

CATHLEEN. Did you see him riding down?

Maurya goes on keening.

CATHLEEN (*a little impatiently*). God forgive you; isn't it a better thing to raise your voice and tell what you seen, than to be making lamentation for a thing that's done? Did you see Bartley, I'm saying to you.

MAURYA (*with a weak voice*). My heart's broken from this day.

CATHLEEN (*as before*). Did you see Bartley?

MAURYA. I seen the fearfulest thing.

CATHLEEN (*leaves her wheel and looks out*). God forgive you; he's riding the mare now over the green head, and the gray pony behind him.

MAURYA (*starts, so that her shawl falls back from her head and shows her white tossed hair. With a frightened voice*). The gray pony behind him.

CATHLEEN (*coming to the fire*). What is it ails you, at all?

MAURYA (*speaking very slowly*). I've seen the fearfulest thing any person has seen, since the day Bride Dara seen the dead man with the child in his arms.

CATHLEEN AND NORA. Uah.

They crouch down in front of the old woman at the fire.

NORA. Tell us what it is you seen.

MAURYA. I went down to the spring well, and I stood there saying a prayer to myself. Then Bartley came along, and he riding on the red mare with the gray pony behind him. (*She puts up her hands, as if to hide something from her eyes.*) The Son of God spare us, Nora!

CATHLEEN. What is it you seen?

MAURYA. I seen Michael himself.

CATHLEEN (*speaking softly*). You did not, mother; it wasn't Michael you seen, for his body is after being found in the far north, and he's got a clean burial by the grace of God.

MAURYA (*a little defiantly*). I'm after seeing him this day, and he riding and galloping. Bartley came first on the red mare; and I tried to say "God speed you," but something choked the words in my throat. He went by quickly; and "the blessing of God on you," says he, and I could say nothing. I looked up then, and I crying, at the gray pony, and there was Michael upon it—with fine clothes on him, and new shoes on his feet.

CATHLEEN (*begins to keen*). It's destroyed we are from this day. It's destroyed, surely.

NORA. Didn't the young priest say the Almighty God wouldn't leave her destitute with no son living?

MAURYA (*in a low voice, but clearly*). It's little the like of him knows of the sea. . . . Bartley will be lost now, and let you call in Eamon and make me a good coffin out of the white boards, for I won't live after them. I've had a husband, and a husband's father, and six sons in this house—six fine men, though it was a hard birth I had with every one of them and they coming to the world—and some of them were found and some of them were not found, but they're gone now the lot of them. . . . There were Stephen, and Shawn, were lost in the great wind, and found after in the Bay of Gregory of the Golden Mouth, and carried up the two of them on the one plank, and in by that door.

She pauses for a moment, the girls start as if they heard something through the door that is half open behind them.

NORA (*in a whisper*). Did you hear that, Cathleen? Did you hear a noise in the north-east?

CATHLEEN (*in a whisper*). There's some one after crying out by the seashore.

MAURYA (*continues without hearing anything*). There was Sheamus and his father, and his own father again, were lost in a dark night, and not a stick or sign was seen of them when the sun went up. There was Patch after was drowned out of a curagh[5] that turned over. I was sitting here with Bartley, and he a baby, lying on my two knees, and I seen two women, and three women, and four women coming in, and they crossing themselves, and not saying a word. I looked out then, and there were men coming after them, and they holding a thing in the half of a red sail, and water dripping out of it—it was a dry day, Nora—and leaving a track to the door.

She pauses again with her hand stretched out towards the door. It opens softly and old women begin to come in, crossing themselves on the threshold, and kneeling down in front of the stage with red petticoats over their heads.

MAURYA (*half in a dream, to Cathleen*). Is it Patch, or Michael, or what is it at all?

CATHLEEN. Michael is after being found in the far north, and when he is found there how could he be here in this place?

MAURYA. There does be a power of young men floating round in the sea, and what way would they know if it was Michael they had, or another man like him, for when a man is nine days in the sea, and the wind blowing, it's hard set his own mother would be to say what man was it.

CATHLEEN. It's Michael, God spare him, for they're after sending us a bit of his clothes from the far north.

She reaches out and hands Maurya the clothes that belonged to Michael. Maurya stands up slowly and takes them in her hand. Nora looks out.

NORA. They're carrying a thing among them and there's water dripping out of it and leaving a track by the big stones.

CATHLEEN (*in a whisper to the women who have come in*). Is it Bartley it is?

ONE OF THE WOMEN. It is surely, God rest his soul.

Two younger women come in and pull out the table. Then men carry in the body of Bartley, laid on a plank, with a bit of sail over it, and lay it on the table.

CATHLEEN (*to the women, as they are doing so*). What way was he drowned?

ONE OF THE WOMEN. The gray pony knocked him into the sea, and he was washed out where there is a great surf on the white rocks.

Maurya has gone over and knelt down at the head of the table. The women are keening softly and swaying themselves with a slow movement. Cathleen and Nora kneel at the other end of the table. The men kneel near the door.

MAURYA (*raising her head and speaking as if she did not see the people around her*). They're all gone now, and there isn't anything more the sea can do to me. . . . I'll have no call now to be up crying and praying when the wind breaks from the south, and you can hear the surf is in the east, and the surf is in the west, making a great stir with the two noises, and they hitting one on the other. I'll have no call now to be going down and getting Holy Water in the dark nights after Samhain,[6] and I won't care what way the sea is when the other women will be keening. (*To Nora.*) Give me the Holy Water, Nora, there's a small sup still on the dresser.

Nora gives it to her.

MAURYA (*drops Michael's clothes across Bartley's feet, and sprinkles the Holy Water over him*). It isn't that I haven't prayed for you, Bartley, to the Almighty God. It isn't that I haven't said prayers in the dark night till you wouldn't know what I'd be saying; but it's a great rest I'll have now, and it's time surely. It's a great rest I'll have now, and great sleeping in the long nights after Samhain, if it's only a bit of wet flour we do have to eat, and maybe a fish that would be stinking.

---

[5]**curagh** unstable vessel of tarred canvas on a wood frame; canoe

[6]**Samhain** November 1, All Saints' Day

She kneels down again, crossing herself, and saying prayers under her breath.

CATHLEEN (*to an old man*). Maybe yourself and Eamon would make a coffin when the sun rises. We have fine white boards herself bought, God help her, thinking Michael would be found, and I have a new cake you can eat while you'll be working.

THE OLD MAN (*looking at the boards*). Are there nails with them?

CATHLEEN. There are not, Colum; we didn't think of the nails.

ANOTHER MAN. It's a great wonder she wouldn't think of the nails, and all the coffins she's seen made already.

CATHLEEN. It's getting old she is, and broken.

Maurya stands up again very slowly and spreads out the pieces of Michael's clothes beside the body, sprinkling them with the last of the Holy Water.

NORA (*in a whisper to Cathleen*). She's quiet now and easy; but the day Michael was drowned you could hear her crying out from this to the spring well. It's fonder she was of Michael, and would any one have thought that?

CATHLEEN (*slowly and clearly*). An old woman will be soon tired with anything she will do, and isn't it nine days herself is after crying and keening, and making great sorrow in the house?

MAURYA (*puts the empty cup mouth downwards on the table, and lays her hands together on Bartley's feet*). They're all together this time, and the end is come. May the Almighty God have mercy on Bartley's soul, and on Michael's soul, and on the souls of Sheamus and Patch, and Stephen and Shawn (*bending her head*); and may He have mercy on my soul, Nora, and on the soul of every one is left living in the world.

She pauses, and the keen rises a little more loudly from the women, then sinks away.

MAURYA (*continuing*). Michael has a clean burial in the far north, by the grace of the Almighty God. Bartley will have a fine coffin out of the white boards, and a deep grave surely. What more can we want than that? No man at all can be living for ever, and we must be satisfied.

She kneels down again and the curtain falls slowly.

TOPICS FOR CRITICAL THINKING AND WRITING

THE PLAY ON THE PAGE

1. What is revealed about Maurya's state of mind by her speech (page 509): "He won't go this day with the wind rising from the south and west. He won't go this day, for the young priest will stop him surely." Why is her reference to the need for the rope (page 509) one of the strongest arguments she can propose for Bartley's staying?
2. Characterize the priest. What is his function in the play?
3. What is implied by Maurya's vision of Michael "with fine clothes on him, and new shoes on his feet" (page 512)?
4. Trace the foreshadowing of Bartley's death.
5. Nora and Cathleen hear someone calling out by the seashore (page 512). Why doesn't Maurya hear the noise? Why does Synge not have a stage direction calling for a cry?
6. Does the fact that Maurya has forgotten the coffin-nails indicate (as Cathleen says, page 513) that she is "broken"?
7. Evaluate James Joyce's complaint that the catastrophe is brought about by a pony rather than by the sea. It has been suggested that a reply can be made to Joyce: Bartley is knocked into the sea by the gray pony, but this is not an accident, for the ghost of his brother Michael is riding the pony, and Irish ghosts commonly seek to bring the living into the realm of the dead. Do you think this reply is satisfactory, or does it introduce a red herring?
8. In addition to the conflict between human beings and nature, what conflicts do you find in the play?

THE PLAY ON THE STAGE

9. Synge insisted on authentic stage properties—for instance the distinctive leather footwear worn by the Aran Islanders, and an old spinning wheel. Do you think that the play requires realistic detail? Explain.
10. If you were casting the play, what well-known actors might you use for two or three of the parts? Why?

THE PLAY IN PERFORMANCE

Synge drafted the play in the summer of 1902, and in the fall he read it to Lady Gregory and W. B. Yeats, two important figures in the Irish dramatic movement. They were enthusiastic and recommended it to their associates in the Irish National Theatre Society, which produced the play in 1904. Joseph Holloway, an avid theatergoer, was present on the opening night, and the next day he reported his response in his diary:

> *Friday, February 26.* I have come to the conclusion that a more gruesome and harrowing play than *Riders to the Sea* has seldom if ever, been staged before. The thoroughly in-earnest playing of the company made the terribly depressing wake episode so realistic and weirdly doleful that some of the audience could not stand the painful horror of the scene, and had to leave the hall during its progress. . . . The audience was so deeply moved by the tragic gloom of the terrible scene on which the curtains close in, that it could not applaud.
>
> JOSEPH HOLLOWAY'S *ABBEY THEATRE* (1965), ED. ROBERT HOGAN AND MICHAEL J. O'NEILL, PAGE 35

The professional reviewers, however, were less moved. The *Irish Times* complained that "the long exposure of the dead body before an audience may be realistic, but it certainly is not artistic. There are some things which are lifelike, and yet are quite unfit for presentation on the stage . . . ." The *New Leader* called the play "hideous in its realism," and the *Freeman's Journal* objected to Maurya's sense of relief at the end. On the other hand, when the Irish company brought the play to London, Max Beerbohm, a far more distinguished literary critic than the reviewers whom we have just quoted, praised *Riders to the Sea* as a masterpiece. The play has been widely performed, and it is probably the best-known Irish play, or, if not, it is second in reputation only to another play by Synge, *The Playboy of the Western World*.

A NOTE ON THE ABBEY THEATRE

It should be mentioned that Irish drama and the Abbey Theatre in Dublin are almost synonymous—almost but not quite, since the earliest plays of Lady Gregory (see page 25), Synge, W. B. Yeats, and others were produced before the group acquired the Abbey. The Irish National Theatre Society, founded by Lady Gregory and Yeats, staged its earliest works in a variety of rooms and halls, and acquired the Abbey Theatre a few months after the premiere of Synge's *Riders to the Sea*. The theater, purchased by Annie Horniman and put at the disposal of Yeats and Lady Gregory, is named after the street it is on. In 1910 a public subscription enabled the Irish National Theatre Society to buy the theater, but in 1951 a fire destroyed the building, forcing the company to play elsewhere for fifteen years. It now plays in a new building on the original site.

Bernard Shaw

MAJOR BARBARA

Bernard Shaw (1856–1950) was born in Dublin of Anglo-Irish stock. His father drank too much, his mother—something of an Ibsenite "new woman"—went to London to make her way as singer and voice teacher. Shaw worked in a Dublin real estate office for a while (he did not attend a college or university), and then followed his mother to London, where he wrote critical reviews, and five novels (1879–1883) before turning playwright. His first play, begun with William Archer (playwright and translator of Ibsen), was abandoned in 1885, and then entirely revised by Shaw into *Widowers' Houses* (1892). He had already shown, in a critical study entitled *The Quintessence of Ibsenism* (1891), that he regarded the stage as a pulpit and soapbox; before the nineteenth century was over, he wrote nine more plays, in order (he said) to espouse socialism effectively. *Major Barbara* (1905) is his comic masterpiece, but at least a dozen of his plays have established themselves in the repertoire, including one tragedy, *Saint Joan* (1924).

COMMENTARY

One of the earliest English remarks about comedy, Sir Philip Sidney's written about 1580, runs thus:

> Comedy is an imitation of the common errors of our life, which he representeth in the most ridiculous and scornful sort that may be; so that it is impossible that any beholder can be content to be such a one.

Sidney is indebted to Italian commentators, who in turn are indebted to Roman commentators, and behind them are the Greeks, notably Aristotle. Along the way there are lots of variations, but the basic ideas may fairly be said to constitute the "classical" theory of comedy:

1. The characters are ignoble
2. Their actions arouse derision (rather than, say, terror or pity)
3. The spectators, if they have resembled the dramatis personae, leave the theater morally improved after seeing the absurdity of such behavior.

The "classical" theory, often stated before Sidney, has since been restated at least as often. Almost every comic dramatist who has commented on his work has offered it as his justification. Shaw, in a preface to his *Complete Plays*, put it thus:

> If I make you laugh at yourself, remember that my business as a classic writer of comedies is "to chasten morals with ridicule"; and if I sometimes make you feel like a fool, remember that I have by the same action cured your folly, just as the dentist cures your toothache by pulling out your

tooth. And I never do it without giving you plenty of laughing gas.

To begin with the laughing gas in *Major Barbara:* The first act suggests that the play is a drawing-room comedy, full of aristocratic people bouncing elegant lines off each other. (Lady Brit, of course, affects innocence, but she is accomplished at getting what she wants.) Sample:

> I am not a Pharisee, I hope; and I should not have minded his merely doing wrong things: we are none of us perfect. But your father didnt exactly do wrong things: he said them and thought them: that was what was so dreadful. He really had a sort of religion of wrongness. Just as one doesnt mind men practising immorality so long as they own that they are in the wrong by preaching morality; so I couldnt forgive Andrew for preaching immorality while he practised morality.

Another sample:

> CUSINS. Let me advise you to study Greek, Mr. Undershaft. Greek scholars are privileged men. Few of them know Greek; and none of them know anything else; but their position is unchallengeable. Other languages are the qualifications of waiters and commercial travellers: Greek is to a man of position what the hallmark is to silver.

If Shaw had been content to write a comedy in the classical tradition, he would have contrived a plot that would probably have involved an unsuitable wooer of Barbara, maybe a rich old aristocrat, maybe a parvenu, maybe a fortune hunter, who would finally be unmasked and then displaced by an appropriately young and charming and socially acceptable bridegroom. But Shaw turned to comedy as a propagandist. He had been deeply impressed by Ibsen's plays, and he saw in the drama an opportunity to preach his economic ideas to a wider audience than is normally reached by the pamphleteer. For Shaw, the heart of Ibsen's plays lies in such a "discussion" as the one in *A Doll's House*, in which Nora explains to her husband that things are all wrong in their apparently happy marriage. (The interested reader is advised to look at Shaw's *The Quintessence of Ibsenism*, especially the next to the last chapter, "The Technical Novelty," which insists that post-Ibsen plays must replace the old formula of exposition-situation-unraveling with "exposition, situation, and discussion; and the discussion is the test of the playwright. . . . The serious playwright recognizes not only the main test of his highest powers, but also the real center of his play's interest.")

What Shaw does, then, is introduce massive discussions into a comedy that at first seems to be doing little more than spoofing Lady Brit and holding her son Stephen up to rather obvious ridicule. Stephen is not merely an ass; he is made to serve as a sort of straightman for Undershaft, who expounds at length unconventional ideas about munitions, sin, power, and poverty. These ideas require discussion because Shaw, unlike most comic writers, is not content with the traditional views. Comic playwrights usually criticize eccentric behavior, and at least implicitly suggest that there is a reasonable norm, known to all men of sense, from which fools depart. But because Shaw believed that society's norm is itself foolish, he devotes much of his play to expounding a new creed. Shaw reverses the old joke about the entire platoon being out of step except Johnny; for Shaw, the deviant, Johnny, *is* in step, and the rest of the platoon is laughably out of step. During the central part of *Major Barbara*, then, Undershaft, the eccentric, is for Shaw the least laughable

character. Even Barbara, the heroine, is exposed as a fool, though with great tenderness, and is forced to shed her conventional illusions. So great is the tenderness that as we see her world collapse, she seems almost a tragic figure:

> I stood on the rock I thought eternal; and without a word of warning it reeled and crumbled under me.

But Undershaft dispels the tragedy, harshly but necessarily, with, "Come, come, my daughter! dont make too much of your little tinpot tragedy. . . . Dont persist in that folly. If your old religion broke down yesterday, get a newer and a better one for tomorrow."

Enough has been said to give some idea of the novelty of Shaw's comic practice, however conventional his theory. But one should note, too, that in one important way his practice is conventional: his plays have the stock quack doctors, pompous statesmen, dragonlike matrons, and young lovers of traditional comedy. And in *Major Barbara* he even uses the ancient motif of the foundling who proves to be a suitable husband for the heroine.

Something more, however, must be said of Undershaft. Having allowed Undershaft to triumph over Barbara, Shaw does not stop; very late in the play Undershaft himself is threatened with the loss of *his* illusions when Barbara and Adolphus Cusins will make their presence felt in the munitions factory. The play ends with the usual marriage, joy, and promise of a newly organized society; in its suggestion, however, that this new society is not a return to a sensible world that was lost before the play began (think, for example, of the end of *As You Like It*, where the duke is restored to his realm), but rather is the beginning of a totally new sort of world, it marks a departure from comic practice. Maybe that is why the end of the play has seemed to most audiences the least amusing part.

Bernard Shaw

MAJOR BARBARA*

ACT 1

It is after dinner in January 1906, in the library in Lady Britomart Undershaft's house in Wilton Crescent. A large and comfortable settee is in the middle of the room, upholstered in dark leather. A person sitting on it (it is vacant at present) would have, on his right, Lady Britomart's writing table, with the lady herself busy at it; a smaller writing table behind him on his left; the door behind him on Lady Britomart's side; and a window with a window seat directly on his left. Near the window is an armchair.

Lady Britomart is a woman of fifty or thereabouts, well dressed and yet careless of her dress, well bred and quite reckless of her breeding, well mannered and yet appallingly outspoken and indifferent to the opinion of her interlocutors, amiable and yet peremptory, arbitrary, and high-tempered to the last bearable degree, and withal a very typical managing matron of the upper class, treated as a naughty child until she grew into a scolding mother, and finally settling down with plenty of practical ability and worldly experience, limited in the oddest way with domestic and class limitations, conceiving the universe exactly as if it were a large house in Wilton Crescent, though handling her corner of it very effectively on that assumption, and being quite enlightened and liberal as to the books in the library, the pictures on the walls, the music in the portfolios, and the articles in the papers.

Her son, Stephen, comes in. He is a gravely correct young man under 25, taking himself very seriously, but still in some awe of his mother, from childish habit and bachelor shyness rather than from any weakness of character.

STEPHEN. Whats the matter?

LADY BRITOMART. Presently, Stephen.

Stephen submissively walks to the settee and sits down. He takes up a Liberal weekly called The Speaker.

LADY BRITOMART. Dont begin to read, Stephen. I shall require all your attention.

STEPHEN. It was only while I was waiting—

*N.B. The Euripidean verses in the second act of *Major Barbara* are not by me, nor even directly by Euripides. They are by Professor Gilbert Murray, whose English version of *The Bacchae* came into our dramatic literature with all the impulsive power of an original work shortly before *Major Barbara* was begun. The play, indeed, stands indebted to him in more ways than one.—G.B.S.

LADY BRITOMART. Dont make excuses, Stephen. (*He puts down The Speaker.*) Now! (*She finishes her writing; rises; and comes to the settee.*) I have not kept you waiting very long, I think.

STEPHEN. Not at all, mother.

LADY BRITOMART. Bring me my cushion. (*He takes the cushion from the chair at the desk and arranges it for her as she sits down on the settee.*) Sit down. (*He sits down and fingers his tie nervously.*) Dont fiddle with your tie, Stephen: there is nothing the matter with it.

STEPHEN. I beg your pardon. (*He fiddles with his watch chain instead.*)

LADY BRITOMART. Now are you attending to me, Stephen?

STEPHEN. Of course, mother.

LADY BRITOMART. No: it's not of course. I want something much more than your everyday matter-of-course attention. I am going to speak to you very seriously, Stephen. I wish you would let that chain alone.

STEPHEN (*hastily relinquishing the chain*). Have I done anything to annoy you, mother? If so, it was quite unintentional.

LADY BRITOMART (*astonished*). Nonsense! (*With some remorse.*) My poor boy, did you think I was angry with you?

STEPHEN. What is it, then, mother? You are making me very uneasy.

LADY BRITOMART (*squaring herself at him rather aggressively*). Stephen: may I ask how soon you intend to realize that you are a grown-up man, and that I am only a woman?

STEPHEN (*amazed*). Only a—

LADY BRITOMART. Dont repeat my words, please: it is a most aggravating habit. You must learn to face life seriously, Stephen. I really cannot bear the whole burden of our family affairs any longer. You must advise me; you must assume the responsibility.

STEPHEN. I!

LADY BRITOMART. Yes, you, of course. You were 24 last June. Youve been at Harrow and Cambridge. Youve been to India and Japan. You must know a lot of things, now; unless you have wasted your time most scandalously. Well, advise me.

STEPHEN (*much perplexed*). You know I have never interfered in the household—

LADY BRITOMART. No: I should think not. I dont want you to order the dinner.

STEPHEN. I mean in our family affairs.

LADY BRITOMART. Well, you must interfere now; for they are getting quite beyond me.

STEPHEN (*troubled*). I have thought sometimes that perhaps I ought; but really, mother, I know so little about them; and what I do know is so painful! it is so impossible to mention some things to you—(*He stops, ashamed.*)

LADY BRITOMART. I suppose you mean your father.

STEPHEN (*almost inaudibly*). Yes.

LADY BRITOMART. My dear: we cant go on all our lives not mentioning him. Of course you were quite right not to open the subject until I asked you to; but you are old enough now to be taken into my confidence, and to help me to deal with him about the girls.

STEPHEN. But the girls are all right. They are engaged.

LADY BRITOMART (*complacently*). Yes: I have made a very good match for Sarah. Charles Lomax will be a millionaire at 35. But that is ten years ahead; and in the meantime his trustees cannot under the terms of his father's will allow him more than £800 a year.

STEPHEN. But the will says also that if he increases his income by his own exertions, they may double the increase.

LADY BRITOMART. Charles Lomax's exertions are much more likely to decrease his income than to increase it. Sarah will have to find at least another £800 a year for the next ten years; and even then they will be as poor as church mice. And what about Barbara? I thought Barbara was going to make the most brilliant career of all of you. And what does she do? Joins the Salvation Army; discharges her maid; lives on a pound a week; and walks in one evening with a professor of Greek whom she has picked up in the street, and who pretends to be a Salvationist, and actually plays the big drum for her in public because he has fallen head over ears in love with her.

STEPHEN. I was certainly rather taken aback when I heard they were engaged. Cusins is a very nice fellow, certainly: nobody would ever guess that he was born in Australia; but—

LADY BRITOMART. Oh, Adolphus Cusins will make a very good husband. After all, nobody can say a word against Greek: it stamps a man at once as an educated gentleman. And my family, thank Heaven, is not a pig-headed Tory one. We are Whigs, and believe in liberty. Let snobbish people say what they please: Barbara shall marry, not the man they like, but the man *I* like.

STEPHEN. Of course I was thinking only of his income. However, he is not likely to be extravagant.

LADY BRITOMART. Dont be too sure of that, Stephen. I know your quiet, simple, refined, poetic people like Adolphus: quite content with the best of everything! They cost more than your extravagant people, who are always as mean as they are second rate. No: Barbara will need at least £2000 a year. You see it means two additional households. Besides, my dear, you must marry soon. I dont approve of the present fashion of philandering bachelors and late marriages; and I am trying to arrange something for you.

STEPHEN. It's very good of you, mother; but perhaps I had better arrange that for myself.

LADY BRITOMART. Nonsense! you are much too young to begin matchmaking: you would be taken in by some pretty little nobody. Of course I dont mean that you are not to be consulted: you know that as well as I do. (*Stephen closes his lips and is silent.*) Now dont sulk, Stephen.

STEPHEN. I am not sulking, mother. What has all this got to do with—with—with my father?

LADY BRITOMART. My dear Stephen: where is the money to come from? It is easy enough for you and the other children to live on my income as long as we are in the same house; but I cant keep four families in four separate houses. You know how poor my father is: he has barely seven thousand a year now; and really, if he were not the Earl of Stevenage, he would have to give up society. He can do nothing for us. He says, naturally enough, that it is absurd that he should be asked to provide for the children of a man who is rolling in money. You see, Stephen, your father must be fabulously wealthy, because there is always a war going on somewhere.

STEPHEN. You need not remind me of that, mother. I have hardly ever opened a newspaper in my life without seeing our name in it. The Undershaft torpedo! The Undershaft quick firers! The Undershaft ten inch! the Undershaft disappearing rampart gun! the Undershaft submarine! and now the Undershaft aerial battleship! At Harrow they called me the Woolwich Infant. At Cambridge it was the same. A little brute at King's who was always trying to get up revivals, spoilt my Bible—your first birthday present to me—by writing under my name, "Son and heir to Undershaft and Lazarus, Death and Destruction Dealers: address, Christendom and Judea." But that was not so bad as the way I was kowtowed to everywhere because my father was making millions by selling cannons.

LADY BRITOMART. It is not only the cannons, but the war loans that Lazarus arranges under cover of giving credit for the cannons. You know, Stephen, it's perfectly scandalous. Those two men, Andrew Undershaft and Lazarus, positively have Europe under their thumbs. That is why your father is able to behave as he does. He is above the law. Do you think Bismarck or Gladstone or Disraeli could have openly defied every social and moral obligation all their lives as your father has? They simply wouldnt have dared. I asked Gladstone to take it up. I asked The Times to take it up. I asked the Lord Chamberlain to take it up. But it was just like asking them to declare war on the Sultan. They wouldnt. They said they couldnt touch him. I believe they were afraid.

STEPHEN. What could they do? He does not actually break the law.

LADY BRITOMART. Not break the law! He is always breaking the law. He broke the law when he was born: his parents were not married.

STEPHEN. Mother! Is that true?

LADY BRITOMART. Of course it's true: that was why we separated.

STEPHEN. He married without letting you know this!

LADY BRITOMART (*rather taken aback by this inference*). Oh no. To do Andrew justice, that was not the sort of thing he did. Besides, you know the Undershaft motto: Unashamed. Everybody knew.

STEPHEN. But you said that was why you separated.

LADY BRITOMART. Yes, because he was not content with being a foundling himself: he wanted to disinherit you for another foundling. That was what I couldnt stand.

STEPHEN (*ashamed*). Do you mean for—for—for—

LADY BRITOMART. Dont stammer, Stephen. Speak distinctly.

STEPHEN. But this is so frightful to me, mother. To have to speak to you about such things!

LADY BRITOMART. It's not pleasant for me, either, especially if you are still so childish that you must make it worse by a display of embarrassment. It is only in the middle classes, Stephen, that people get into a state of dumb helpless horror when they find that there are wicked people in the world. In our class, we have to decide what is to be done with wicked people; and nothing should disturb our self-possession. Now ask your question properly.

STEPHEN. Mother: have you no consideration for me? For Heaven's sake either treat me as a child, as you always do, and tell me nothing at all; or tell me everything and let me take it as best I can.

LADY BRITOMART. Treat you as a child! What do you mean? It is most unkind and ungrateful of you to say such a thing. You know I have never treated any of you as children. I have always made you my companions and friends, and allowed you perfect freedom to do and say whatever you liked, so long as you liked what I could approve of.

STEPHEN (*desperately*). I daresay we have been the very imperfect children of a very perfect mother; but I do beg you to let me alone for once, and tell me about this horrible business of my father wanting to set me aside for another son.

LADY BRITOMART (*amazed*). Another son! I never said anything of the kind. I never dreamt of such a thing. This is what comes of interrupting me.

STEPHEN. But you said—

LADY BRITOMART (*cutting him short*). Now be a good boy, Stephen, and listen to me patiently. The Undershafts are descended from a foundling in the parish of St Andrew Undershaft in the city. That was long ago, in the reign of James the First. Well, this foundling was adopted by an armorer and gun-maker. In the course of time the foundling succeeded to the business; and from some notion of gratitude, or some vow or something, he adopted another foundling, and left the business to him. And that foundling did the same. Ever since that, the cannon business has always been left to an adopted foundling named Andrew Undershaft.

STEPHEN. But did they never marry? Were there no legitimate sons?

LADY BRITOMART. Oh yes: they married just as your father did; and they were rich enough to buy land for their own children and leave them well provided for. But they always adopted and trained some foundling to succeed them in the business; and of course they always quarrelled with their wives furiously over it. Your father was adopted in that way; and he pretends to consider himself bound to keep up the tradition and adopt somebody to leave the business to. Of course I was not going to stand that. There may have been some reason for it when the Undershafts could only marry women in their own class, whose sons were not fit to govern great estates. But there could be no excuse for passing over my son.

STEPHEN (*dubiously*). I am afraid I should make a poor hand of managing a cannon foundry.

LADY BRITOMART. Nonsense! you could easily get a manager and pay him a salary.

STEPHEN. My father evidently had no great opinion of my capacity.

LADY BRITOMART. Stuff, child! you were only a baby: it had nothing to do with your capacity. Andrew did it on principle, just as he did every perverse and wicked thing on principle. When my father remonstrated, Andrew actually told him to his face that history tells us of only two successful institutions: one the Undershaft firm, and the other the Roman Empire under the Antonines. That was because the Antonine emperors all adopted their successors. Such rubbish! The Stevenages are as good as the Antonines, I hope; and you are a Stevenage. But that was Andrew all over. There you have the man! Always clever and unanswerable when he was defending nonsense and wickedness: always awkward and sullen when he had to behave sensibly and decently!

STEPHEN. Then it was on my account that your home life was broken up, mother. I am sorry.

LADY BRITOMART. Well, dear, there were other differences. I really cannot bear an immoral man. I am not a Pharisee, I hope; and I should not have minded his merely doing wrong things: we are none of us perfect. But your father didnt exactly do wrong things: he said them and thought them: that was what was so dreadful. He really had a sort of religion of wrongness. Just as one doesnt mind men practising immorality so long as they own that they are in the wrong by preaching morality; so I couldnt forgive Andrew for preaching immorality while he practised morality. You would all have grown up without principles, without any knowledge of right and wrong, if he had been in the house. You know, my dear, your father was a very attractive man in some ways. Children did not dislike him; and he took advantage of it to put the wickedest ideas into their heads, and make them quite unmanageable. I did not dislike him myself: very far from it; but nothing can bridge over moral disagreement.

STEPHEN. All this simply bewilders me, mother. People may differ about matters of opinion, or even about religion; but how can they differ about right and wrong? Right is right; and wrong is wrong; and if a man cannot distinguish them properly, he is either a fool or a rascal: thats all.

LADY BRITOMART (*touched*). Thats my own boy! (*She pats his cheek.*) Your father never could answer that: he used to laugh and get out of it under cover of some affectionate nonsense. And now that you understand the situation, what do you advise me to do?

STEPHEN. Well, what can you do?

LADY BRITOMART. I must get the money somehow.

STEPHEN. We cannot take money from him. I had rather go and live in some cheap place like Bedford Square or even Hampstead[1] than take a farthing of his money.

LADY BRITOMART. But after all, Stephen, our present income comes from Andrew.

STEPHEN (*shocked*). I never knew that.

LADY BRITOMART. Well, you surely didnt suppose your grandfather had anything to give me. The Stevenages could not do everything for you. We gave you social position. Andrew had to contribute something. He had a very good bargain, I think.

STEPHEN (*bitterly*). We are utterly dependent on him and his cannons, then?

LADY BRITOMART. Certainly not: the money is settled. But he provided it. So you see it is not a question of taking money from him or not: it is simply a question of how much. I dont want any more for myself.

STEPHEN. Nor do I.

LADY BRITOMART. But Sarah does; and Barbara does. That is, Charles Lomax and Adolphus Cusins will cost them more. So I must put my pride in my pocket and ask for it, I suppose. That is your advice, Stephen, is it not?

STEPHEN. No.

LADY BRITOMART (*sharply*). Stephen!

STEPHEN. Of course if you are determined—

LADY BRITOMART. I am not determined: I ask your advice; and I am waiting for it. I will not have all the responsibility thrown on my shoulders.

STEPHEN (*obstinately*). I would die sooner than ask him for another penny.

LADY BRITOMART (*resignedly*). You mean that *I* must ask him. Very well, Stephen: it shall be as you wish. You will be glad to know that your grandfather concurs. But he thinks I ought to ask Andrew to come here and see the girls. After all, he must have some natural affection for them.

STEPHEN. Ask him here!!!

LADY BRITOMART. Do not repeat my words, Stephen. Where else can I ask him?

---

[1] **Bedford Square . . . Hampstead** Good neighborhoods but not at the very top.

STEPHEN. I never expected you to ask him at all.

LADY BRITOMART. Now dont tease, Stephen. Come! you see that it is necessary that he should pay us a visit, dont you?

STEPHEN (*reluctantly*). I suppose so, if the girls cannot do without his money.

LADY BRITOMART. Thank you, Stephen: I knew you would give me the right advice when it was properly explained to you. I have asked your father to come this evening. (*Stephen bounds from his seat.*) Dont jump, Stephen: it fidgets me.

STEPHEN (*in utter consternation*). Do you mean to say that my father is coming here tonight—that he may be here at any moment?

LADY BRITOMART (*looking at her watch*). I said nine. (*He gasps. She rises.*) Ring the bell, please. (*Stephen goes to the smaller writing table; presses a button on it; and sits at it with his elbows on the table and his head in his hands, outwitted and overwhelmed.*) It is ten minutes to nine yet; and I have to prepare the girls. I asked Charles Lomax and Adolphus to dinner on purpose that they might be here. Andrew had better see them in case he should cherish any delusions as to their being capable of supporting their wives. (*The butler enters: Lady Britomart goes behind the settee to speak to him.*) Morrison: go up to the drawing room and tell everybody to come down here at once. (*Morrison withdraws. Lady Britomart turns to Stephen.*) Now remember, Stephen: I shall need all your countenance and authority. (*He rises and tries to recover some vestige of these attributes.*) Give me a chair, dear. (*He pushes a chair forward from the wall to where she stands, near the smaller writing table. She sits down; and he goes to the armchair, into which he throws himself.*) I dont know how Barbara will take it. Ever since they made her a major in the Salvation Army she has developed a propensity to have her own way and order people about which quite cows me sometimes. It's not ladylike: I'm sure I dont know where she picked it up. Anyhow, Barbara shant bully me; but still it's just as well that your father should be here before she has time to refuse to meet him or make a fuss. Dont look nervous, Stephen: it will only encourage Barbara to make difficulties. *I* am nervous enough, goodness knows; but I dont shew it.

Sarah and Barbara come in with their respective young men, Charles Lomax and Adolphus Cusins. Sarah is slender, bored, and mundane. Barbara is robuster, jollier, much more energetic. Sarah is fashionably dressed: Barbara is in Salvation Army uniform. Lomax, a young man about town, is like many other young men about town. He is afflicted with a frivolous sense of humor which plunges him at the most inopportune moments into paroxysms of imperfectly suppressed laughter. Cusins is a spectacled student, slight, thin haired, and sweet voiced, with a more complex form of Lomax's complaint. His sense of humor is intellectual and subtle, and is complicated by an appalling temper. The lifelong struggle of a benevolent temperament and a high conscience against impulses of inhuman ridicule and fierce impatience has set up a chronic strain which has visibly wrecked his constitution. He is a most implacable, determined, tenacious, intolerant person who by mere force of character presents himself as—and indeed actually is—considerate, gentle, explanatory, even mild and apologetic, capable possibly of murder, but not of cruelty or coarseness. By the operation of some instinct which is not merciful enough to blind him with the illusions of love, he is obstinately bent on marrying Barbara. Lomax likes Sarah and thinks it will be rather a lark to marry her. Consequently he has not attempted to resist Lady Britomart's arrangements to that end.

All four look as if they had been having a good deal of fun in the drawing room. The girls enter first, leaving the swains outside. Sarah comes to the settee. Barbara comes in after her and stops at the door.

BARBARA. Are Cholly and Dolly to come in?

LADY BRITOMART (*forcibly*). Barbara: I will not have Charles called Cholly: the vulgarity of it positively makes me ill.

BARBARA. It's all right, mother: Cholly is quite correct nowadays. Are they to come in?

LADY BRITOMART. Yes, if they will behave themselves.

BARBARA (*through the door*). Come in, Dolly; and behave yourself.

Barbara comes to her mother's writing table. Cusins enters smiling, and wanders towards Lady Britomart.

SARAH (*calling*). Come in, Cholly. (*Lomax enters, controlling his features very imperfectly, and places himself vaguely between Sarah and Barbara.*)

LADY BRITOMART (*peremptorily*). Sit down, all of you. (*They sit. Cusins crosses to the window and seats himself there. Lomax takes a chair. Barbara sits at the writing table and Sarah on the settee.*) I dont in the least know what you are laughing at, Adolphus. I am surprised at you, though I expected nothing better from Charles Lomax.

CUSINS (*in a remarkably gentle voice*). Barbara has been trying to teach me the West Ham Salvation March.

LADY BRITOMART. I see nothing to laugh at in that; nor should you if you are really converted.

CUSINS (*sweetly*). You were not present. It was really funny, I believe.

LOMAX. Ripping.

LADY BRITOMART. Be quiet, Charles. Now listen to me, children. Your father is coming here this evening.

General stupefaction. Lomax, Sarah, and Barbara rise: Sarah scared, and Barbara amused and expectant.

LOMAX (*remonstrating*). Oh I say!

LADY BRITOMART. You are not called on to say anything, Charles.

SARAH. Are you serious, mother?

LADY BRITOMART. Of course I am serious. It is on your account, Sarah, and also on Charles's. (*Silence. Sarah sits,*

with a shrug. Charles looks painfully unworthy.) I hope you are not going to object, Barbara.

BARBARA. I! why should I? My father has a soul to be saved like anybody else. He's quite welcome as far as I am concerned. (*She sits on the table, and softly whistles 'Onward, Christian Soldiers.'*)

LOMAX (*still remonstrant*). But really, dont you know! Oh I say!

LADY BRITOMART (*frigidly*). What do you wish to convey, Charles?

LOMAX. Well, you must admit that this is a bit thick.

LADY BRITOMART (*turning with ominous suavity to Cusins*). Adolphus: you are a professor of Greek. Can you translate Charles Lomax's remarks into reputable English for us?

CUSINS (*cautiously*). If I may say so, Lady Brit, I think Charles has rather happily expressed what we all feel. Homer, speaking of Autolycus, uses the same phrase. πυκινὸν δόμον ἐλθεῖν[2] means a bit thick.

LOMAX (*handsomely*). Not that I mind, you know, if Sarah dont. (*He sits.*)

LADY BRITOMART (*crushingly*). Thank you. Have I your permission, Adolphus, to invite my own husband to my own house?

CUSINS (*gallantly*). You have my unhesitating support in everything you do.

LADY BRITOMART. Tush! Sarah: have you nothing to say?

SARAH. Do you mean that he is coming regularly to live here?

LADY BRITOMART. Certainly not. The spare room is ready for him if he likes to stay for a day or two and see a little more of you; but there are limits.

SARAH. Well, he cant eat us, I suppose. I dont mind.

LOMAX (*chuckling*). I wonder how the old man will take it.

LADY BRITOMART. Much as the old woman will, no doubt, Charles.

LOMAX (*abashed*). I didn't mean—at least—

LADY BRITOMART. You didnt think, Charles. You never do; and the result is, you never mean anything. And now please attend to me, children. Your father will be quite a stranger to us.

LOMAX. I suppose he hasnt seen Sarah since she was a little kid.

LADY BRITOMART. Not since she was a little kid, Charles, as you express it with that elegance of diction and refinement of thought that seem never to desert you. Accordingly—er—(*impatiently*). Now I have forgotten what I was going to say. That comes of your provoking me to be sarcastic, Charles. Adolphus: will you kindly tell me where I was.

CUSINS (*sweetly*). You were saying that as Mr Undershaft has not seen his children since they were babies, he will form

---

[2]πυκινὸν δόμον ἐλθεῖν "Pukinon domon elthein." In Homer, the phrase refers to a fortified house.

his opinion of the way you have brought them up from their behavior tonight, and that therefore you wish us all to be particularly careful to conduct ourselves well, especially Charles.

LADY BRITOMART (*with emphatic approval*). Precisely.

LOMAX. Look here, Dolly: Lady Brit didnt say that.

LADY BRITOMART (*vehemently*). I did, Charles. Adolphus's recollection is perfectly correct. It is most important that you should be good; and I do beg you for once not to pair off into opposite corners and giggle and whisper while I am speaking to your father.

BARBARA. All right, mother. We'll do you credit. (*She comes off the table, and sits in her chair with ladylike elegance.*)

LADY BRITOMART. Remember, Charles, that Sarah will want to feel proud of you instead of ashamed of you.

LOMAX. Oh I say! theres nothing to be exactly proud of, dont you know.

LADY BRITOMART. Well, try and look as if there was.

Morrison, pale and dismayed, breaks into the room in unconcealed disorder.

MORRISON. Might I speak a word to you, my lady?

LADY BRITOMART. Nonsense! Shew him up.

MORRISON. Yes, my lady. (*He goes.*)

LOMAX. Does Morrison know who it is?

LADY BRITOMART. Of course. Morrison has always been with us.

LOMAX. It must be a regular corker for him, dont you know.

LADY BRITOMART. Is this a moment to get on my nerves, Charles, with your outrageous expressions?

LOMAX. But this is something out of the ordinary, really—

MORRISON (*at the door*). The—er—Mr Undershaft. (*He retreats in confusion.*)

Andrew Undershaft comes in. All rise. Lady Britomart meets him in the middle of the room behind the settee.

    Andrew is, on the surface, a stoutish, easygoing elderly man, with kindly patient manners, and an engaging simplicity of character. But he has a watchful, deliberate, waiting, listening face, and formidable reserves of power, both bodily and mental, in his capacious chest and long head. His gentleness is partly that of a strong man who has learnt by experience that his natural grip hurts ordinary people unless he handles them very carefully, and partly the mellowness of age and success. He is also a little shy in his present very delicate situation.

LADY BRITOMART. Good evening, Andrew.

UNDERSHAFT. How d'ye do, my dear.

LADY BRITOMART. You look a good deal older.

UNDERSHAFT (*apologetically*). I am somewhat older. (*Taking her hand with a touch of courtship.*) Time has stood still with you.

LADY BRITOMART (*throwing away his hand*). Rubbish! This is your family.

UNDERSHAFT (*surprised*). Is it so large? I am sorry to say my memory is failing very badly in some things. (*He offers his hand with paternal kindness to Lomax.*)

LOMAX (*jerkily shaking his hand*). Ahdedoo.

UNDERSHAFT. I can see you are my eldest. I am very glad to meet you again, my boy.

LOMAX (*remonstrating*). No, but look here dont you know—(*Overcome.*) Oh I say!

LADY BRITOMART (*recovering from momentary speechlessness*). Andrew: do you mean to say that you dont remember how many children you have?

UNDERSHAFT. Well, I am afraid I—. They have grown so much—er. Am I making any ridiculous mistake? I may as well confess: I recollect only one son. But so many things have happened since, of course—er—

LADY BRITOMART (*decisively*). Andrew: you are talking nonsense. Of course you have only one son.

UNDERSHAFT. Perhaps you will be good enough to introduce me, my dear.

LADY BRITOMART. That is Charles Lomax, who is engaged to Sarah.

UNDERSHAFT. My dear sir, I beg your pardon.

LOMAX. Notatall. Delighted, I assure you.

LADY BRITOMART. This is Stephen.

UNDERSHAFT (*bowing*). Happy to make your acquaintance, Mr Stephen. Then (*going to Cusins*) you must be my son. (*Taking Cusins' hands in his.*) How are you, my young friend? (*To Lady Britomart.*) He is very like you, my love.

CUSINS. You flatter me, Mr Undershaft. My name is Cusins: engaged to Barbara. (*Very explicitly.*) That is Major Barbara Undershaft, of the Salvation Army. That is Sarah, your second daughter. This is Stephen Undershaft, your son.

UNDERSHAFT. My dear Stephen, I beg your pardon.

STEPHEN. Not at all.

UNDERSHAFT. Mr Cusins: I am much indebted to you for explaining so precisely. (*Turning to Sarah.*) Barbara, my dear—

SARAH (*prompting him*). Sarah.

UNDERSHAFT. Sarah, of course. (*They shake hands. He goes over to Barbara.*) Barbara—I am right this time, I hope?

BARBARA. Quite right. (*They shake hands.*)

LADY BRITOMART (*resumimg command*). Sit down, all of you. Sit down, Andrew. (*She comes forward and sits on the settee. Cusins also brings his chair forward on her left. Barbara and Stephen resume their seats. Lomax gives his chair to Sarah and goes for another.*)

UNDERSHAFT. Thank you, my love.

LOMAX (*conversationally, as he brings a chair forward between the writing table and the settee, and offers it to Undershaft*). Takes you some time to find out exactly where you are, dont it?

UNDERSHAFT (*accepting the chair, but remaining standing*). That is not what embarrasses me, Mr Lomax. My difficulty is that if I play the part of a father, I shall produce the effect of an intrusive stranger; and if I play the part of a discreet stranger, I may appear a callous father.

LADY BRITOMART. There is no need for you to play any part at all, Andrew. You had much better be sincere and natural.

UNDERSHAFT (*submissively*). Yes, my dear: I daresay that will be best. (*He sits down comfortably.*) Well, here I am. Now what can I do for you all?

LADY BRITOMART. You need not do anything, Andrew. You are one of the family. You can sit with us and enjoy yourself.

A painfully conscious pause. Barbara makes a face at Lomax, whose too long suppressed mirth immediately explodes in agonized neighings.

LADY BRITOMART (*outraged*). Charles Lomax: if you can behave yourself, behave yourself. If not, leave the room.

LOMAX. I'm awfully sorry, Lady Brit; but really you know, upon my soul! (*He sits on the settee between Lady Britomart and Undershaft, quite overcome.*)

BARBARA. Why dont you laugh if you want to, Cholly? It's good for your inside.

LADY BRITOMART. Barbara: you have had the education of a lady. Please let your father see that; and dont talk like a street girl.

UNDERSHAFT. Never mind me, my dear. As you know, I am not a gentleman; and I was never educated.

LOMAX (*encouragingly*). Nobody'd know it, I assure you. You look all right, you know.

CUSINS. Let me advise you to study Greek, Mr Undershaft. Greek scholars are privileged men. Few of them know Greek; and none of them know anything else; but their position is unchallengeable. Other languages are the qualifications of waiters and commercial travellers: Greek is to a man of position what the hallmark is to silver.

BARBARA. Dolly: dont be insincere. Cholly: fetch your concertina and play something for us.

LOMAX (*jumps up eagerly, but checks himself to remark doubtfully to Undershaft*). Perhaps that sort of thing isnt in your line, eh?

UNDERSHAFT. I am particularly fond of music.

LOMAX (*delighted*). Are you? Then I'll get it. (*He goes upstairs for the instrument.*)

UNDERSHAFT. Do you play, Barbara?

BARBARA. Only the tambourine. But Cholly's teaching me the concertina.

UNDERSHAFT. Is Cholly also a member of the Salvation Army?

BARBARA. No: he says it's bad form to be a dissenter. But I dont despair of Cholly. I made him come yesterday to a meeting at the dock gates, and take the collection in his hat.

UNDERSHAFT (*looks whimsically at his wife*)!!

LADY BRITOMART. It is not my doing, Andrew. Barbara is old enough to take her own way. She has no father to advise her.

BARBARA. Oh yes she has. There are no orphans in the Salvation Army.

UNDERSHAFT. Your father there has a great many children and plenty of experience, eh?

BARBARA (*looking at him with quick interest and nodding*). Just so. How did you come to understand that? (*Lomax is heard at the door trying the concertina.*)

LADY BRITOMART. Come in, Charles. Play us something at once.

LOMAX. Righto! (*He sits down in his former place, and preludes.*)

UNDERSHAFT. One moment, Mr Lomax. I am rather interested in the Salvation Army. Its motto might be my own: Blood and Fire.

LOMAX (*shocked*). But not your sort of blood and fire, you know.

UNDERSHAFT. My sort of blood cleanses: my sort of fire purifies.

BARBARA. So do ours. Come down tomorrow to my shelter—the West Ham shelter—and see what we're doing. We're going to march to a great meeting in the Assembly Hall at Mile End. Come and see the shelter and then march with us: it will do you a lot of good. Can you play anything?

UNDERSHAFT. In my youth I earned pennies, and even shillings occasionally, in the streets and in public house parlors by my natural talent for stepdancing. Later on, I became a member of the Undershaft orchestral society, and performed passably on the tenor trombone.

LOMAX (*scandalized—putting down the concertina*). Oh I say!

BARBARA. Many a sinner has played himself into heaven on the trombone, thanks to the Army.

LOMAX (*to Barbara, still rather shocked*). Yes; but what about the cannon business, dont you know? (*To Undershaft.*) Getting into heaven is not exactly in your line, is it?

LADY BRITOMART. Charles!!!

LOMAX. Well; but it stands to reason, dont it? The cannon business may be necessary and all that: we cant get on without cannons; but it isnt right, you know. On the other hand, there may be a certain amount of tosh about the Salvation Army—I belong to the Established Church myself—but still you cant deny that it's religion; and you cant go against religion, can you? At least unless youre downright immoral, dont you know.

UNDERSHAFT. You hardly appreciate my position, Mr Lomax—

LOMAX (*hastily*). I'm not saying anything against you personally—

UNDERSHAFT. Quite so, quite so. But consider for a moment. Here I am, a profiteer in mutilation and murder. I find myself in a specially amiable humor just now because, this morning, down at the foundry, we blew twenty-seven dummy soldiers into fragments with a gun which formerly destroyed only thirteen.

LOMAX (*leniently*). Well, the more destructive war becomes, the sooner it will be abolished, eh?

UNDERSHAFT. Not at all. The more destructive war becomes the more fascinating we find it. No, Mr Lomax: I am obliged to you for making the usual excuse for my trade; but I am not ashamed of it. I am not one of those men who keep their morals and their business in water-tight compartments. All the spare money my trade rivals spend on hospitals, cathedrals, and other receptacles for conscience money, I devote to experiments and researches in improved methods of destroying life and property. I have always done so; and I always shall. Therefore your Christmas card moralities of peace on earth and goodwill among men are of no use to me. Your Christianity, which enjoins you to resist not evil, and to turn the other cheek, would make me a bankrupt. My morality—my religion—must have a place for cannons and torpedoes in it.

STEPHEN (*coldly—almost sullenly*). You speak as if there were half a dozen moralities and religions to choose from, instead of one true morality and one true religion.

UNDERSHAFT. For me there is only one true morality; but it might not fit you, as you do not manufacture aerial battleships. There is only one true morality for every man; but every man has not the same true morality.

LOMAX (*overtaxed*). Would you mind saying that again? I didnt quite follow it.

CUSINS. It's quite simple. As Euripides says, one man's meat is another man's poison morally as well as physically.

UNDERSHAFT. Precisely.

LOMAX. Oh, that! Yes, yes, yes. True. True.

STEPHEN. In other words, some men are honest and some are scoundrels.

BARBARA. Bosh! There are no scoundrels.

UNDERSHAFT. Indeed? Are there any good men?

BARBARA. No. Not one. There are neither good men nor scoundrels: there are just children of one Father; and the sooner they stop calling one another names the better. You neednt talk to me: I know them. Ive had scores of them through my hands: scoundrels, criminals, infidels, philanthropists, missionaries, county councillors, all sorts. Theyre all just the same sort of sinner; and theres the same salvation ready for them all.

UNDERSHAFT. May I ask have you ever saved a maker of cannons?

BARBARA. No. Will you let me try?

UNDERSHAFT. Well, I will make a bargain with you. If I go to see you tomorrow in your Salvation Shelter, will you come the day after to see me in my cannon works?

BARBARA. Take care. It may end in your giving up the cannons for the sake of the Salvation Army.

UNDERSHAFT. Are you sure it will not end in your giving up the Salvation Army for the sake of the cannons?

BARBARA. I will take my chance of that.

UNDERSHAFT. And I will take my chance of the other. (*They shake hands on it.*) Where is your shelter?

BARBARA. In West Ham. At the sign of the cross. Ask anybody in Canning Town. Where are your works?

UNDERSHAFT. In Perivale St Andrews. At the sign of the sword. Ask anybody in Europe.

LOMAX. Hadnt I better play something?

BARBARA. Yes. Give us Onward, Christian Soldiers.

LOMAX. Well, thats rather a strong order to begin with, dont you know. Suppose I sing Thourt passing hence, my brother. It's much the same tune.

BARBARA. It's too melancholy. You get saved, Cholly; and youll pass hence, my brother, without making such a fuss about it.

LADY BRITOMART. Really, Barbara, you go on as if religion were a pleasant subject. Do have some sense of propriety.

UNDERSHAFT. I do not find it an unpleasant subject, my dear. It is the only one that capable people really care for.

LADY BRITOMART (*looking at her watch*). Well, if you are determined to have it, I insist on having it in a proper and respectable way. Charles: ring for prayers.

General amazement. Stephen rises in dismay.

LOMAX (*rising*). Oh I say!

UNDERSHAFT (*rising*). I am afraid I must be going.

LADY BRITOMART. You cannot go now, Andrew: it would be most improper. Sit down. What will the servants think?

UNDERSHAFT. My dear: I have conscientious scruples. May I suggest a compromise? If Barbara will conduct a little service in the drawing room, with Mr Lomax as organist, I will attend it willingly. I will even take part, if a trombone can be procured.

LADY BRITOMART. Dont mock, Andrew.

UNDERSHAFT (*shocked—to Barbara*). You dont think I am mocking, my love, I hope.

BARBARA. No, of course not; and it wouldnt matter if you were: half the Army came to their first meeting for a lark. (*Rising.*) Come along. (*She throws her arm round her father and sweeps him out, calling to the others from the threshold.*) Come, Dolly. Come, Cholly.

Cusins rises.

LADY BRITOMART. I will not be disobeyed by everybody. Adolphus: sit down. (*He does not.*) Charles: you may go. You are not fit for prayers: you cannot keep your countenance.

LOMAX. Oh I say! (*He goes out.*)

LADY BRITOMART (*continuing*). But you, Adolphus, can behave yourself if you choose to. I insist on your staying.

CUSINS. My dear Lady Brit: there are things in the family prayer book that I couldnt bear to hear you say.

LADY BRITOMART. What things, pray?

CUSINS. Well, you would have to say before all the servants that we have done things we ought not to have done, and left undone things we ought to have done, and that there is no health in us. I cannot bear to hear you doing yourself such an injustice, and Barbara such an injustice. As for myself, I flatly deny it: I have done my best. I shouldnt dare to marry Barbara—I couldnt look you in the face—if it were true. So I must go to the drawing room.

LADY BRITOMART (*offended*). Well, go. (*He starts for the door.*) And remember this, Adolphus: (*He turns to listen.*) I have a very strong suspicion that you went to the Salvation Army to worship Barbara and nothing else. And I quite appreciate the very clever way in which you systematically humbug me. I have found you out. Take care Barbara doesnt. Thats all.

CUSINS (*with unruffled sweetness*). Dont tell on me. (*He steals out.*)

LADY BRITOMART. Sarah: if you want to go, go. Anything's better than to sit there as if you wished you were a thousand miles away.

SARAH (*languidly*). Very well, mamma. (*She goes.*)

Lady Britomart, with a sudden flounce, gives way to a little gust of tears.

STEPHEN (*going to her*). Mother: whats the matter?

LADY BRITOMART (*swishing away her tears with her handkerchief*). Nothing. Foolishness. You can go with him, too, if you like, and leave me with the servants.

STEPHEN. Oh, you mustnt think that, mother. I—I dont like him.

LADY BRITOMART. The others do. That is the injustice of a woman's lot. A woman has to bring up her children; and that means to restrain them, to deny them things they want, to set them tasks, to punish them when they do wrong, to do all the unpleasant things. And then the father, who has nothing to do but pet them and spoil them, comes in when all her work is done and steals their affection from her.

STEPHEN. He has not stolen our affection from you. It is only curiosity.

LADY BRITOMART (*violently*). I wont be consoled, Stephen. There is nothing the matter with me. (*She rises and goes towards the door.*)

STEPHEN. Where are you going, mother?

LADY BRITOMART. To the drawing room, of course. (*She goes out. Onward, Christian Soldiers, on the concertina, with tambourine accompaniment, is heard when the door opens.*) Are you coming, Stephen?

STEPHEN. No. Certainly not. (*She goes. He sits down on the settee, with compressed lips and an expression of strong dislike.*)

ACT 2

The yard of the West Ham shelter of the Salvation Army is a cold place on a January morning. The building itself, an old warehouse, is newly whitewashed. Its gabled end projects into the yard in the middle, with a door on the ground floor, and another in the loft above it without any balcony or ladder, but with a pulley rigged over it for hoisting sacks. Those who come from this central gable end into the yard have the gateway leading to the street on their left, with a stone horse-trough just beyond it, and, on the right, a penthouse shielding a table from the weather. There are forms at the table; and on them are seated a man and a woman, both much down on their luck, finishing a meal of bread (one thick slice each, with margarine and golden syrup) and diluted milk.

The man, a workman out of employment, is young, agile, a talker, a poser, sharp enough to be capable of anything in reason except honesty or altruistic considerations of any kind. The woman is a commonplace old bundle of poverty and hard-worn humanity. She looks sixty and probably is forty-five. If they were rich people, gloved and muffed and well wrapped up in furs and overcoats, they would be numbed and miserable; for it is a grindingly cold raw January day; and a glance at the background of grimy warehouses and leaden sky visible over the whitewashed walls of the yard would drive any idle rich person straight to the Mediterranean. But these two, being no more troubled with visions of the Mediterranean than of the moon, and being compelled to keep more of their clothes in the pawnshop, and less on their persons, in winter than in summer, are not depressed by the cold: rather are they stung into vivacity, to which their meal has just now given an almost jolly turn. The man takes a pull at his mug, and then gets up and moves about the yard with his hands deep in his pockets, occasionally breaking into a stepdance.

THE WOMAN. Feel better arter your meal, sir?

THE MAN. No. Call that a meal! Good enough for you, praps; but wot is it to me, an intelligent workin man.

THE WOMAN. Workin man! Wot are you?

THE MAN. Painter.

THE WOMAN (*sceptically*). Yus, I dessay.

THE MAN. Yus, you dessay! I know. Every loafer that cant do nothink calls isself a painter. Well, I'm a real painter: grainer, finisher, thirty-eight bob a week when I can get it.

THE WOMAN. Then why dont you go and get it?

THE MAN. I'll tell you why. Fust: I'm intelligent—fffff! it's rotten cold here—(*He dances a step or two.*) yes: intelligent beyond the station o life into which it has pleased the capitalists to call me; and they dont like a man that sees through em. Second, an intelligent bein needs a doo share of appiness; so I drink somethink cruel when I get the chawnce. Third, I stand by my class and do as little as I can so's to leave arf the job for me fellow workers. Fourth, I'm fly enough to know wots inside the law and wots outside it; and inside it I do as the capitalists do: pinch wot I can lay me ands on. In a proper state of society I am sober, industrious and honest: in Rome, so to speak, I do as the Romans do. Wots the consequence? When trade is bad—and it's rotten bad just now—and the employers az to sack arf their men, they generally start on me.

THE WOMAN. Whats your name?

THE MAN. Price. Bronterre O'Brien Price. Usually called Snobby Price, for short.

THE WOMAN. Snobby's a carpenter, aint it? You said you was a painter.

PRICE. Not that kind of snob, but the genteel sort. I'm too uppish, owing to my intelligence, and my father being a Chartist[3] and a reading, thinking man: a stationer, too. I'm none of your common hewers of wood and drawers of water; and dont you forget it. (*He returns to his seat at the table, and takes up his mug.*) Wots your name?

THE WOMAN. Rummy Mitchens, sir.

PRICE (*quaffing the remains of his milk to her*). Your elth, Miss Mitchens.

RUMMY (*correcting him*). Missis Mitchens.

PRICE. Wot! Oh Rummy, Rummy! Respectable married woman, Rummy, gittin rescued by the Salvation Army by pretendin to be a bad un. Same old game!

RUMMY. What am I to do? I cant starve. Them Salvation lasses is dear good girls; but the better you are, the worse they likes to think you were before they rescued you. Why shouldnt they av a bit o credit, poor loves? theyre worn to rags by their work. And where would they get the money to rescue us if we was to let on we're no worse than other people? You know what ladies and gentlemen are.

PRICE. Thievin swine! Wish I ad their job, Rummy, all the same. Wot does Rummy stand for? Pet name praps?

RUMMY. Short for Romola.[4]

PRICE. For wot!?

RUMMY. Romola. It was out of a new book. Somebody me mother wanted me to grow up like.

PRICE. We're companions in misfortune, Rummy. Both on us got names that nobody cawnt pronounce. Conse-quently I'm Snobby and youre Rummy because Bill and Sally wasnt good enough for our parents. Such is life!

RUMMY. Who saved you, Mr Price? Was it Major Barbara?

PRICE. No: I come here on my own. I'm going to be Bronterre O'Brien Price, the converted painter. I know wot they like. I'll tell em how I blasphemed and gambled and wopped my poor old mother—

RUMMY (*shocked*). Used you to beat your mother?

PRICE. Not likely. She used to beat me. No matter: you come and listen to the converted painter, and youll hear how she was a pious woman that taught me me prayers at er knee, an how I used to come home drunk and drag her out o bed be er snow white airs, an lam into er with the poker.

RUMMY. That whats so unfair to us women. Your confessions is just as big lies as ours: you dont tell what you really done no more than us; but you men can tell your lies right out at the meetins and be made much of for it; while the sort o confessions we az to make az to be wispered to one lady at a time. It aint right, spite of all their piety.

PRICE. Right! Do you spose the Army'd be allowed if it went and did right? Not much. It combs out air and makes us good little blokes to be robbed and put upon. But I'll play the game as good as any of em. I'll see somebody struck by lightnin, or hear a voice sayin "Snobby Price: where will you spend eternity?" I'll av a time of it, I tell you.

RUMMY. You wont be let drink, though.

PRICE. I'll take it out in gorspellin, then. I dont want to drink if I can get fun enough any other way.

Jenny Hill, a pale, overwrought, pretty Salvation lass of 18, comes in through the yard gate, leading Peter Shirley, a half hardened, half worn-out elderly man, weak with hunger.

JENNY (*supporting him*). Come! pluck up. I'll get you something to eat. Youll be all right then.

PRICE (*rising and hurrying officiously to take the old man off Jenny's hands*). Poor old man! Cheer up, brother: youll find rest and peace and appiness ere. Hurry up with the food, miss: e's fair done (*Jenny hurries into the shelter.*) Ere, buck up, daddy! she's fetchin y'a thick slice o breadn trea-cle,[5] an a mug o skyblue. (*He seats him at the corner of the table.*)

RUMMY (*gaily*). Keep up your old art! Never say die!

SHIRLEY. I'm not an old man. I'm only 46. I'm as good as ever I was. The grey patch come in my hair before I was thirty. All it wants is three pennorth o hair dye: am I to be turned on the streets to starve for it? Holy God! Ive worked ten to twelve hours a day since I was thirteen, and paid my way all through; and now am I to be thrown into the gutter and my job given to a young man that can

---

[3]**Chartist** a member of an English workers' reform movement of the 1840's. [4]**Romola** the idealistic heroine of George Eliot's novel, 1863.

[5]**treacle** molasses.

do it better than me because Ive black hair that goes white at the first change?

PRICE (*cheerfully*). No good jawrin about it. Youre ony a jumped-up, jerked-off, orspittle-turned-out incurable of an ole workin man: who cares about you? Eh? Make the thievin swine give you a meal: theyve stole many a one from you. Get a bit o your own back (*Jenny returns with the usual meal.*) There you are, brother. Awsk a blessin an tuck that into you.

SHIRLEY (*looking at it ravenously but not touching it, and crying like a child*). I never took anything before.

JENNY (*petting him*). Come, come! the Lord sends it to you: he wasnt above taking bread from his friends; and why should you be? Besides, when we find you a job you can pay us for it if you like.

SHIRLEY (*eagerly*). Yes, yes: thats true. I can pay you back: it's only a loan. (*Shivering.*) Oh Lord! oh Lord! (*He turns to the table and attacks the meal ravenously.*)

JENNY. Well, Rummy, are you more comfortable now?

RUMMY. God bless you, lovey! youve fed my body and saved my soul, havnt you? (*Jenny, touched, kisses her.*) Sit down and rest a bit: you must be ready to drop.

JENNY. Ive been going hard since morning. But theres more work than we can do. I mustnt stop.

RUMMY. Try a prayer for just two minutes. Youll work all the better after.

JENNY (*her eyes lighting up*). Oh isnt it wonderful how a few minutes prayer revives you! I was quite lightheaded at twelve o'clock, I was so tired; but Major Barbara just sent me to pray for five minutes; and I was able to go on as if I had only just begun. (*To Price.*) Did you have a piece of bread?

PRICE (*with unction*). Yes, miss; but Ive got the piece that I value more; and thats the peace that passeth hall hannerstennin.

RUMMY (*fervently*). Glory Hallelujah!

Bill Walker, a rough customer of about 25, appears at the yard gate and looks malevolently at Jenny.

JENNY. That makes me so happy. When you say that, I feel wicked for loitering here. I must get to work again.

She is hurrying to the shelter, when the new-comer moves quickly up to the door and intercepts her. His manner is so threatening that she retreats as he comes at her truculently, driving her down the yard.

BILL. Aw knaow you. Youre the one that took away maw girl. Youre the one that set er agen me. Well, I'm gowin to ev er aht. Not that Aw care a carse for er or you: see? Bat Aw'll let er knaow; and Aw'll let you knaow. Aw'm gowing to give her a doin thatll teach er to cat away from me. Nah in wiv you and tell er to cam aht afore Aw cam in and kick er aht. Tell er Bill Walker wants er. She'll knaow wot thet means; and if she keeps me witin itll be worse. You stop to jawr beck at me; and Aw'll stawt on you: d'ye eah? Theres your wy. In you gow. (*He takes her*

by the arm and slings her towards the door of the shelter. She falls on her hand and knee. Rummy helps her up again.*)

PRICE (*rising, and venturing irresolutely towards Bill*). Easy there, mate. She aint doin you no arm.

BILL. Oo are you callin mite? (*Standing over him threateningly.*) Youre gowin to stend ap for er, aw yer? Put ap your ends.

RUMMY (*running indignantly to him to scold him*). Oh, you great brute—(*He instantly swings his left hand back against her face. She screams and reels back to the trough, where she sits down, covering her bruised face with her hands and rocking herself and moaning with pain.*)

JENNY (*going to her*). Oh, God forgive you! How could you strike an old woman like that?

BILL (*seizing her by the hair so violently that she also screams, and tearing her away from the old woman*). You Gawd forgimme again an Aw'll Gawd forgive you one on the jawr thetll stop you pryin for a week. (*Holding her and turning fiercely on Price.*) Ev you ennything to sy agen it?

PRICE (*intimidated*). No, matey: she aint anything to do with me.

BILL. Good job for you! Aw'd pat two meals into you and fawt you with one finger arter, you stawved cur. (*To Jenny.*) Nah are you gowin to fetch aht Mog Ebbijem; or em Aw to knock your fice off you and fetch her meself?

JENNY (*writhing in his grasp*). Oh please someone go in and tell Major Barbara—(*She screams again as he wrenches her head down; and Price and Rummy flee into the shelter.*)

BILL. You want to gow in and tell your Mijor of me, do you?

JENNY. Oh please dont drag my hair. Let me go.

BILL. Do you or downt you? (*She stifles a scream.*) Yus or nao?

JENNY. God give me strength—

BILL (*striking her with his fist in the face*). Gow an shaow her thet, and tell her if she wants one lawk it to cam and interfere with me. (*Jenny, crying with pain, goes into the shed. He goes to the form and addresses the old man.*) Eah: finish your mess; an git aht o maw wy.

SHIRLEY (*springing up and facing him fiercely, with the mug in his hand*). You take a liberty with me, and I'll smash you over the face with the mug and cut your eye out. Aint you satisfied—young whelps like you—with takin the bread out o the mouths of your elders that have brought you up and slaved for you, but you must come shovin and cheekin and bullyin in here, where the bread o charity is sickenin in our stummicks?

BILL (*contemptuously, but backing a little*). Wot good are you, you aold palsy mag?[6] Wot good are you?

SHIRLEY. As good as you and better. I'll do a day's work agen you or any fat young soaker of your age. Go and take my job at Horrockses, where I worked for ten year. They want young men there: they cant afford to keep men over forty-five. Theyre very sorry—give you a character and

6**palsy mag** drunkard.

happy to help you to get anything suited to your years—
sure a steady man wont be long out of a job. Well, let em
try you. Theyll find the differ. What do you know? Not as
much as how to beeyave yourself—layin your dirty fist
across the mouth of a respectable woman!

BILL. Downt provowk me to ly it acrost yours: d'ye eah?

SHIRLEY (*with blighting contempt*). Yes: you like an old man to
hit, dont you, when youve finished with the women. I
aint seen you hit a young one yet.

BILL (*stung*). You loy, you aold soupkitchener, you. There was
a yang menn eah. Did Aw offer to itt him or did Aw not?

SHIRLEY. Was he starvin or was he not? Was he a man or
only a crosseyed thief an a loafer? Would you hit my son-
in-law's brother?

BILL. Oo's ee?

SHIRLEY. Todger Fairmile o Balls Pond. Him that won £20
off the Japanese wrastler at the music hall by standin out
17 minutes 4 seconds agen him.

BILL (*sullenly*). Aw'm nao music awl wrastler. Ken he box?

SHIRLEY. Yes: an you cant.

BILL. Wot! Aw cawnt, cawnt Aw? Wots thet you sy? (*Threatening him.*)

SHIRLEY (*not budging an inch*). Will you box Todger Fairmile
if I put him on to you? Say the word.

BILL (*subsiding with a slouch*). Aw'll stend ap to enny menn
alawv, if he was ten Todger Fairmawls. But Aw dont set
ap to be a perfeshnal.

SHIRLEY (*looking down on him with unfathomable disdain*). You
box! Slap an old woman with the back o your hand! You
hadnt even the sense to hit her where a magistrate couldnt
see the mark of it, you silly young lump of conceit and
ignorance. Hit a girl in the jaw and ony make her cry! If
Todger Fairmile'd done it, she wouldnt a got up inside o
ten minutes, no more than you would if he got on to you.
Yah! I'd set about you myself if I had a week's feedin in
me instead o two months' starvation. (*He turns his back
on him and sits down moodily at the table.*)

BILL (*following him and stooping over him to drive the taunt in*).
You loy! youve the bread and treacle in you that you cam
eah to beg.

SHIRLEY (*bursting into tears*). Oh God! it's true: I'm only an
old pauper on the scrap heap. (*Furiously.*) But youll come
to it yourself; and then youll know. Youll come to it sooner
than a teetotaller like me, fillin yourself with gin at this
hour o the mornin!

BILL. Aw'm nao gin drinker, you oald lawr; bat wen Aw want
to give my girl a bloomin good awdin Aw lawk to ev a bit
o devil in me: see? An eah Aw emm, talkin to a rotten
aold blawter like you sted o givin her wot for. (*Working
himself into a rage.*) Aw'm gowin in there to fetch her aht.
(*He makes vengefully for the shelter door.*)

SHIRLEY. Youre goin to the station on a stretcher, more likely;
and theyll take the gin and the devil out of you there
when they get you inside. You mind what youre about:
the major here is the Earl o Stevenage's granddaughter.

BILL (*checked*). Garn!

SHIRLEY. Youll see.

BILL (*his resolution oozing*). Well, Aw aint dan nathin to er.

SHIRLEY. Spose she said you did! who'd believe you?

BILL (*very uneasy, skulking back to the corner of the penthouse*).
Gawd! theres no jastice in this cantry. To think wot them
people can do! Aw'm as good as er.

SHIRLEY. Tell her so. It's just what a fool like you would do.

*Barbara, brisk and businesslike, comes from the shelter
with a note book, and addresses herself to Shirley. Bill,
cowed, sits down in the corner on a form, and turns his
back on them.*

BARBARA. Good morning.

SHIRLEY (*standing up and taking off his hat*). Good morning,
miss.

BARBARA. Sit down: make yourself at home. (*He hesitates;
but she puts a friendly hand on his shoulder and makes him
obey.*) Now then! since youve made friends with us, we
want to know all about you. Names and addresses and
trades.

SHIRLEY. Peter Shirley. Fitter. Chucked out two months
ago because I was too old.

BARBARA (*not at all surprised*). Youd pass still. Why didnt
you dye your hair?

SHIRLEY. I did. Me age come out at a coroner's inquest on me
daughter.

BARBARA. Steady?

SHIRLEY. Teetotaller. Never out of a job before. Good worker.
And sent to the knackers[7] like an old horse!

BARBARA. No matter: if you did your part God will do his.

SHIRLEY (*suddenly stubborn*). My religion's no concern of
anybody but myself.

BARBARA (*guessing*). I know. Secularist?[8]

SHIRLEY (*hotly*). Did I offer to deny it?

BARBARA. Why should you? My own father's a Secularist, I
think. Our Father—yours and mine—fulfils himself in
many ways; and I daresay he knew what he was about
when he made a Secularist of you. So buck up, Peter! we
can always find a job for a steady man like you. (*Shirley,
disarmed and a little bewildered, touches his hat. She turns
from him to Bill.*) Whats your name?

BILL (*insolently*). Wots thet to you?

BARBARA (*calmly making a note*). Afraid to give his name.
Any trade?

BILL. Oo's afride to give is nime? (*Doggedly, with a sense of
heroically defying the House of Lords in the person of Lord
Stevenage.*) If you want to bring a chawge agen me, bring
it. (*She waits, unruffled.*) Moy nime's Bill Walker.

BARBARA (*as if the name were familiar: trying to remember
how*). Bill Walker? (*Recollecting.*) Oh, I know: youre the

---

[7]**Knackers** buyers and slaughterers of old animals.   [8]**Secularist** an
atheist.

man that Jenny Hill was praying for inside just now. (*She enters his name in her note book.*)

BILL. Oo's Jenny Ill? And wot call as she to pry for me?

BARBARA. I dont know. Perhaps it was you that cut her lip.

BILL (*defiantly*). Yus, it was me that cat her lip. Aw aint afride o you.

BARBARA. How could you be, since youre not afraid of God? Youre a brave man, Mr Walker. It takes some pluck to do our work here; but none of us dare lift our hand against a girl like that, for fear of her father in heaven.

BILL (*sullenly*). I want nan o your kentin jawr. I spowse you think Aw cam eah to beg from you, like this demmiged lot eah. Not me. Aw downt want your bread and scripe and ketlep.[9] Aw dont blieve in your Gawd, no more than you do yourself.

BARBARA (*sunnily apologetic and ladylike, as on a new footing with him*). Oh, I beg your pardon for putting your name down, Mr Walker. I didnt understand. I'll strike it out.

BILL (*taking this as a slight, and deeply wounded by it*). Eah! you let maw nime alown. Aint it good enaff to be in your book?

BARBARA (*considering*). Well, you see, theres no use putting down your name unless I can do something for you, is there? Whats your trade?

BILL (*still smarting*). Thets nao concern o yours.

BARBARA. Just so. (*Very businesslike.*) I'll put you down as (*writing*) the man who—struck—poor little Jenny Hill—in the mouth.

BILL (*rising threateningly*). See eah. Awve ed enaff o this.

BARBARA (*quite sunny and fearless*). What did you come to us for?

BILL. Aw cam for maw gel, see? Aw cam to tike her aht o this and to brike er jawr for er.

BARBARA (*complacently*). You see I was right about your trade. (*Bill, on the point of retorting furiously, finds himself, to his great shame and terror, in danger of crying instead. He sits down again suddenly.*) Whats her name?

BILL (*dogged*). Er nime's Mog Ebbijem: thets wot her nime is.

BARBARA. Mog Habbijam! Oh, she's gone to Canning Town, to our barracks there.

BILL (*fortified by his resentment of Mog's perfidy*). Is she? (*Vindictively.*) Then Aw'm gowin to Kennintahn arter her. (*He crosses to the gate; hesitates; finally comes back at Barbara.*) Are you loyin to me to git shat o me?

BARBARA. I dont want to get shut of you. I want to keep you here and save your soul. Youd better stay: youre going to have a bad time today, Bill.

BILL. Oo's gowin to give it to me? You, preps?

BARBARA. Someone you dont believe in. But youll be glad afterwards.

BILL (*slinking off*). Aw'll gow to Kennintahn to be aht o reach o your tangue. (*Suddenly turning on her with intense

malice.*) And if Aw downt fawnd Mog there, Aw'll cam beck and do two years for you, selp me Gawd if Aw downt!

BARBARA (*a shade kindlier, if possible*). It's no use, Bill. She's got another bloke.

BILL. Wot!

BARBARA. One of her own converts. He fell in love with her when he saw her with her soul saved, and her face clean, and her hair washed.

BILL (*surprised*). Wottud she wash it for, the carroty slat? It's red.

BARBARA. It's quite lovely now, because she wears a new look in her eyes with it. It's a pity youre too late. The new bloke has put your nose out of joint, Bill.

BILL. Aw'll put his nowse aht o joint for him. Not that Aw care a carse for er, mawnd thet. But Aw'll teach her to drop me as if Aw was dirt. And Aw'll teach him to meddle with maw judy. Wots iz bleedin nime?

BARBARA. Sergeant Todger Fairmile.

SHIRLEY (*rising with grim joy*). I'll go with him, miss. I want to see them two meet. I'll take him to the infirmary when it's over.

BILL (*to Shirley, with undissembled misgiving*). Is thet im you was speakin on?

SHIRLEY. Thats him.

BILL. Im that wrastled in the music awl?

SHIRLEY. The competitions at the National Sportin Club was worth nigh a hundred a year to him. He's gev em up now for religion; so he's a bit fresh for want of the exercise he was accustomed to. He'll be glad to see you. Come along.

BILL. Wots is wight?

SHIRLEY. Thirteen four.[10] (*Bill's last hope expires.*)

BARBARA. Go and talk to him, Bill. He'll convert you.

SHIRLEY. He'll convert your head into a mashed potato.

BILL (*sullenly*). Aw aint afride of im. Aw aint afride of ennybody. Bat e can lick me. She's dan me. (*He sits down moodily on the edge of the horse trough.*)

SHIRLEY. You aint goin. I thought not. (*He resumes his seat.*)

BARBARA (*calling*). Jenny!

JENNY (*appearing at the shelter door with a plaster on the corner of her mouth*). Yes, Major.

BARBARA. Send Rummy Mitchens out to clear away here.

JENNY. I think she's afraid.

BARBARA (*her resemblance to her mother flashing out for a moment*). Nonsense! she must do as she's told.

JENNY (*calling into the shelter*). Rummy: the Major says you must come.

Jenny comes to Barbara, purposely keeping on the side next Bill, lest he should suppose that she shrank from him or bore malice.

---

[9]**Scripe and ketlep** "scrape," that is, thinly spread butter, and "catlap," a diluted drink.

[10]**Thirteen four** Thirteen stone, four pounds, i.e. 186 pounds.

BARBARA. Poor little Jenny! Are you tired? (*Looking at the wounded cheek.*) Does it hurt?

JENNY. No: it's all right now. It was nothing.

BARBARA (*critically*). It was as hard as he could hit, I expect. Poor Bill! You dont feel angry with him, do you?

JENNY. Oh no, no, no: indeed I dont, Major, bless his poor heart! (*Barbara kisses her; and she runs away merrily into the shelter. Bill writhes with an agonizing return of his new and alarming symptoms, but says nothing. Rummy Mitchens comes from the shelter.*)

BARBARA (*going to meet Rummy*). Now Rummy, bustle. Take in those mugs and plates to be washed; and throw the crumbs about for the birds.

Rummy takes the three plates and mugs; but Shirley takes back his mug from her, as there is still some milk left in it.

RUMMY. There aint any crumbs. This aint a time to waste good bread on birds.

PRICE (*appearing at the shelter door*). Gentleman come to see the shelter, Major. Says he's your father.

BARBARA. All right. Coming. (*Snobby goes back into the shelter, followed by Barbara.*)

RUMMY (*stealing across to Bill and addressing him in a subdued voice, but with intense conviction*). I'd av the lor of you, you flat eared pignosed potwalloper,[11] if she'd let me. Youre no gentleman, to hit a lady in the face. (*Bill, with greater things moving in him, takes no notice.*)

SHIRLEY (*following her*). Here! in with you and dont get yourself into more trouble by talking.

RUMMY (*with hauteur*). I aint ad the pleasure o being hintroduced to you, as I can remember. (*She goes into the shelter with the plates.*)

SHIRLEY. Thats the—

BILL (*savagely*). Downt you talk to me, d'ye eah? You lea me alown, or Aw'll do you a mischief. Aw'm not dirt under your feet, ennyway.

SHIRLEY (*calmly*). Dont you be afeerd. You aint such prime company that you need expect to be sought after. (*He is about to go into the shelter when Barbara comes out, with Undershaft on her right.*)

BARBARA. Oh, there you are, Mr Shirley! (*Between them.*) This is my father: I told you he was a Secularist, didnt I? Perhaps youll be able to comfort one another.

UNDERSHAFT (*startled*). A Secularist! Not the least in the world: on the contrary, a confirmed mystic.

BARBARA. Sorry, I'm sure. By the way, papa, what is your religion? in case I have to introduce you again.

UNDERSHAFT. My religion? Well, my dear, I am a Millionaire. That is my religion.

BARBARA. Then I'm afraid you and Mr Shirley wont be able to comfort one another after all. Youre not a Millionaire, are you, Peter?

SHIRLEY. No; and proud of it.

[11]**potwalloper** a pot-washer, a menial servant.

UNDERSHAFT (*gravely*). Poverty, my friend, is not a thing to be proud of.

SHIRLEY (*angrily*). Who made your millions for you? Me and my like. Whats kep us poor? Keepin you rich. I wouldnt have your conscience, not for all your income.

UNDERSHAFT. I wouldnt have your income, not for all your conscience, Mr Shirley. (*He goes to the penthouse and sits down on a form.*)

BARBARA (*stopping Shirley adroitly as he is about to retort*). You wouldnt think he was my father, would you, Peter? Will you go into the shelter and lend the lasses a hand for a while: we're worked off our feet.

SHIRLEY (*bitterly*). Yes: I'm in their debt for a meal, aint I?

BARBARA. Oh, not because youre in their debt, but for love of them, Peter, for love of them. (*He cannot understand, and is rather scandalized.*) There! dont stare at me. In with you; and give that conscience of yours a holiday (*bustling him into the shelter*).

SHIRLEY (*as he goes in*). Ah! it's a pity you never was trained to use your reason, miss. Youd have been a very taking lecturer on Secularism.

Barbara turns to her father.

UNDERSHAFT. Never mind me, my dear. Go about your work; and let me watch it for a while.

BARBARA. All right.

UNDERSHAFT. For instance, whats the matter with that outpatient over there?

BARBARA (*looking at Bill, whose attitude has never changed, and whose expression of brooding wrath has deepened*). Oh, we shall cure him in no time. Just watch. (*She goes over to Bill and waits. He glances up at her and casts his eyes down again, uneasy, but grimmer than ever.*) It would be nice to just stamp on Mog Habbijam's face, wouldnt it, Bill?

BILL (*starting up from the trough in consternation*). It's a loy: Aw never said so. (*She shakes her head.*) Oo taold you wot was in moy mawnd?

BARBARA. Only your new friend.

BILL. Wot new friend?

BARBARA. The devil, Bill. When he gets round people they get miserable, just like you.

BILL (*with a heartbreaking attempt at devil-may-care cheerfulness*). Aw aint miserable. (*He sits down again, and stretches his legs in an attempt to seem indifferent.*)

BARBARA. Well, if youre happy, why dont you look happy, as we do?

BILL (*his legs curling back in spite of him*). Aw'm eppy enaff, Aw tell you. Woy cawnt you lea me alown? Wot ev I dan to you? Aw aint smashed y o u r fice, ev Aw?

BARBARA (*softly: wooing his soul*). It's not me thats getting at you, Bill.

BILL. Oo else is it?

BARBARA. Somebody that doesn't intend you to smash women's faces, I suppose. Somebody or something that wants to make a man of you.

BILL (*blustering*). Mike a menn o m e! Aint Aw a menn? eh? Oo sez Aw'm not a menn?

BARBARA. Theres a man in you somewhere, I suppose. But why did he let you hit poor little Jenny Hill? That wasnt very manly of him, was it?

BILL (*tormented*). Ev dan wiv it, Aw tell you. Chack it. Aw'm sick o your Jenny Ill and er silly little fice.

BARBARA. Then why do you keep thinking about it? Why does it keep coming up against you in your mind? Youre not getting converted, are you?

BILL (*with conviction*). Not ME. Not lawkly.

BARBARA. Thats right, Bill. Hold out against it. Put out your strength. Dont lets get you cheap. Todger Fairmile said he wrestled for three nights against his salvation harder than he ever wrestled with the Jap at the music hall. He gave in to the Jap when his arm was going to break. But he didnt give in to his salvation until his heart was going to break. Perhaps youll escape that. You havnt any heart, have you?

BILL. Wot d'ye mean? Woy aint Aw got a awt the sime as ennybody else?

BARBARA. A man with a heart wouldnt have bashed poor little Jenny's face, would he?

BILL (*almost crying*). Ow, will you lea me alown? Ev Aw ever offered to meddle with you, that you cam neggin and provowkin me lawk this? (*He writhes convulsively from his eyes to his toes.*)

BARBARA (*with a steady soothing hand on his arm and a gentle voice that never lets him go*). It's your soul thats hurting you, Bill, and not me. Weve been through it all ourselves. Come with us, Bill. (*He looks wildly round.*) To brave manhood on earth and eternal glory in heaven. (*He is on the point of breaking down.*) Come. (*A drum is heard in the shelter; and Bill, with a gasp, escapes from the spell as Barbara turns quickly. Adolphus enters from the shelter with a big drum.*) Oh! there you are, Dolly. Let me introduce a new friend of mine, Mr Bill Walker. This is my bloke, Bill: Mr Cusins. (*Cusins salutes with his drumstick.*)

BILL. Gowin to merry im?

BARBARA. Yes.

BILL (*fervently*). Gawd elp im! Gaw-aw-aw-awd elp im!

BARBARA. Why? Do you think he wont be happy with me?

BILL. Awve aony ed to stend it for a mawnin: e'll ev to stend it for a lawftawm.

CUSINS. That is a frightful reflection, Mr Walker. But I cant tear myself away from her.

BILL. Well, Aw ken. (*To Barbara.*) Eah! do you knaow where Aw'm gowin to, and wot Aw'm gowin to do?

BARBARA. Yes: youre going to heaven; and youre coming back here before the week's out to tell me so.

BILL. You loy. Aw'm gowin to Kennintahn, to spit in Todger Fairmawl's eye. Aw beshed Jenny Ill's fice; an nar Aw'll git me aown fice beshed and cam beck and shaow it to er. Ee'll itt me ardern Aw itt er. Thatll mike us square. (*To Adolphus.*) Is thet fair or is it not? Youre a genlmn: you oughter knaow.

BARBARA. Two black eyes wont make one white one, Bill.

BILL. Aw didnt awst you. Cawnt you never keep your mahth shat? Oy awst the genlmn.

CUSINS (*reflectively*). Yes: I think youre right, Mr Walker. Yes: I should do it. It's curious: it's exactly what an ancient Greek would have done.

BARBARA. But what good will it do?

CUSINS. Well, it will give Mr Fairmile some exercise; and it will satisfy Mr Walker's soul.

BILL. Rot! there aint nao sach a thing as a saoul. Ah kin you tell wevver Awve a saoul or not? You never seen it.

BARBARA. Ive seen it hurting you when you went against it.

BILL (*with compressed aggravation*). If you was maw gel and took the word aht o me mahth lawk thet, Aw'd give you sathink youd feel urtin, Aw would. (*To Adolphus.*) You tike maw tip, mite. Stop er jawr; or youll doy afoah your tawm (*With intense expression.*) Wore aht: thets wot youll be: wore aht. (*He goes away through the gate.*)

CUSINS (*looking after him*). I wonder!

BARBARA. Dolly! (*Indignant, in her mother's manner.*)

CUSINS. Yes, my dear, it's very wearing to be in love with you. If it lasts, I quite think I shall die young.

BARBARA. Should you mind?

CUSINS. Not at all. (*He is suddenly softened, and kisses her over the drum, evidently not for the first time, as people cannot kiss over a big drum without practice. Undershaft coughs.*)

BARBARA. It's all right, papa, weve not forgotten you. Dolly: explain the place to papa: I havnt time. (*She goes busily into the shelter.*)

Undershaft and Adolphus now have the yard to themselves. Undershaft, seated on a form, and still keenly attentive, looks hard at Adolphus. Adolphus looks hard at him.

UNDERSHAFT. I fancy you guess something of what is in my mind, Mr Cusins. (*Cusins flourishes his drumsticks as if in the act of beating a lively rataplan, but makes no sound.*) Exactly so. But suppose Barbara finds you out!

CUSINS. You know, I do not admit that I am imposing on Barbara. I am quite genuinely interested in the views of the Salvation Army. The fact is, I am a sort of collector of religions; and the curious thing is that I find I can believe them all. By the way, have you any religion?

UNDERSHAFT. Yes.

CUSINS. Anything out of the common?

UNDERSHAFT. Only that there are two things necessary to Salvation.

CUSINS (*disappointed, but polite*). Ah, the Church Catechism. Charles Lomax also belongs to the Established Church.

UNDERSHAFT. The two things are—

CUSINS. Baptism and—

UNDERSHAFT. No. Money and gunpowder.

CUSINS (*surprised, but interested*). That is the general opinion of our governing classes. The novelty is in hearing any man confess it.

UNDERSHAFT. Just so.

CUSINS. Excuse me: is there any place in your religion for honor, justice, truth, love, mercy and so forth?

UNDERSHAFT. Yes: they are the graces and luxuries of a rich, strong, and safe life.

CUSINS. Suppose one is forced to choose between them and money or gunpowder?

UNDERSHAFT. Choose money and gunpowder; for without enough of both you cannot afford the others.

CUSINS. That is your religion?

UNDERSHAFT. Yes.

The cadence of this reply makes a full close in the conversation. Cusins twists his face dubiously and contemplates Undershaft. Undershaft contemplates him.

CUSINS. Barbara wont stand that. You will have to choose between your religion and Barbara.

UNDERSHAFT. So will you, my friend. She will find out that that drum of yours is hollow.

CUSINS. Father Undershaft: you are mistaken: I am a sincere Salvationist. You do not understand the Salvation Army. It is the army of joy, of love, of courage: it has banished the fear and remorse and despair of the old hell-ridden evangelical sects: it marches to fight the devil with trumpet and drum, with music and dancing, with banner and palm, as becomes a sally from heaven by its happy garrison. It picks the waster out of the public house and makes a man of him: it finds a worm wriggling in a back kitchen, and lo! a woman! Men and women of rank too, sons and daughters of the Highest. It takes the poor professor of Greek, the most artificial and self-suppressed of human creatures, from his meal of roots, and lets loose the rhapsodist in him; reveals the true worship of Dionysos to him; sends him down the public street drumming dithyrambs. (*He plays a thundering flourish on the drum.*)

UNDERSHAFT. You will alarm the shelter.

CUSINS. Oh, they are accustomed to these sudden ecstasies. However, if the drum worries you— (*He pockets the drumsticks; unhooks the drum; and stands it on the ground opposite the gateway.*)

UNDERSHAFT. Thank you.

CUSINS. You remember what Euripides says about your money and gunpowder?

UNDERSHAFT. No.

CUSINS (*declaiming*).

> One and another
> In money and guns may outpass his brother;
> And men in their millions float and flow
> And seethe with a million hopes as leaven;
> And they win their will; or they miss their will;
> And their hopes are dead or are pined for still;
>   But who'er can know
>   As the long days go
> That to live is happy, has found his heaven.

My translation: what do you think of it?

UNDERSHAFT. I think, my friend, that if you wish to know, as the long days go, that to live is happy, you must first acquire money enough for a decent life, and power enough to be your own master.

CUSINS. You are damnably discouraging. (*He resumes his declamation.*)

>   Is it so hard a thing to see
>   That the spirit of God—whate'er it be—
> The law that abides and changes not, ages long,
> The Eternal and Nature-born: these things be strong?
> What else is Wisdom? What of Man's endeavor,
> Or God's high grace so lovely and so great?
> To stand from fear set free? to breathe and wait?
> To hold a hand uplifted over Fate?
> And shall not Barbara be loved for ever?

UNDERSHAFT. Euripides mentions Barbara, does he?

CUSINS. It is a fair translation. The word means Loveliness.

UNDERSHAFT. May I ask—as Barbara's father—how much a year she is to be loved for ever on?

CUSINS. As Barbara's father, that is more your affair than mine. I can feed her by teaching Greek: that is about all.

UNDERSHAFT. Do you consider it a good match for her?

CUSINS (*with polite obstinacy*). Mr Undershaft: I am in many ways a weak, timid, ineffectual person; and my health is far from satisfactory. But whenever I feel that I must have anything, I get it, sooner or later. I feel that way about Barbara. I dont like marriage: I feel intensely afraid of it; and I dont know what I shall do with Barbara or what she will do with me. But I feel that I and nobody else must marry her. Please regard that as settled.—Not that I wish to be arbitrary; but why should I waste your time in discussing what is inevitable?

UNDERSHAFT. You mean that you will stick at nothing: not even the conversion of the Salvation Army to the worship of Dionysos.

CUSINS. The business of the Salvation Army is to save, not to wrangle about the name of the pathfinder. Dionysos or another: what does it matter?

UNDERSHAFT (*rising and approaching him*). Professor Cusins: you are a young man after my own heart.

CUSINS. Mr Undershaft: you are, as far as I am able to gather, a most infernal old rascal; but you appeal very strongly to my sense of ironic humor.

Undershaft mutely offers his hand. They shake.

UNDERSHAFT (*suddenly concentrating himself*). And now to business.

CUSINS. Pardon me. We are discussing religion. Why go back to such an uninteresting and unimportant subject as business?

UNDERSHAFT. Religion is our business at present, because it is through religion alone that we can win Barbara.

CUSINS. Have you, too, fallen in love with Barbara?

UNDERSHAFT. Yes, with a father's love.

CUSINS. A father's love for a grown-up daughter is the most dangerous of all infatuations. I apologize for mentioning my own pale, coy, mistrustful fancy in the same breath with it.

UNDERSHAFT. Keep to the point. We have to win her; and we are neither of us Methodists.

CUSINS. That doesnt matter. The power Barbara wields here—the power that wields Barbara herself—is not Calvinism, not Presbyterianism, not Methodism—

UNDERSHAFT. Not Greek Paganism either, eh?

CUSINS. I admit that. Barbara is quite original in her religion.

UNDERSHAFT (*triumphantly*). Aha! Barbara Undershaft would be. Her inspiration comes from within herself.

CUSINS. How do you suppose it got there?

UNDERSHAFT (*in towering excitement*). It is the Undershaft inheritance. I shall hand on my torch to my daughter. She shall make my converts and preach my gospel—

CUSINS. What! Money and gunpowder!

UNDERSHAFT. Yes, money and gunpowder. Freedom and power. Command of life and command of death.

CUSINS (*urbanely: trying to bring him down to earth*). This is extremely interesting, Mr Undershaft. Of course you know that you are mad.

UNDERSHAFT (*with redoubled force*). And you?

CUSINS. Oh, mad as a hatter. You are welcome to my secret since I have discovered yours. But I am astonished. Can a madman make cannons?

UNDERSHAFT. Would anyone else than a madman make them? And now (*with surging energy*) question for question. Can a sane man translate Euripides?

CUSINS. No.

UNDERSHAFT (*seizing him by the shoulder*). Can a sane woman make a man of a waster or a woman of a worm?

CUSINS (*reeling before the storm*). Father Colossus—Mammoth Millionaire—

UNDERSHAFT (*pressing him*). Are there two mad people or three in this Salvation shelter today?

CUSINS. You mean Barbara is as mad as we are?

UNDERSHAFT (*pushing him lightly off and resuming his equanimity suddenly and completely*). Pooh, Professor! let us call things by their proper names. I am a millionaire; you are a poet; Barbara is a savior of souls. What have we three to do with the common mob of slaves and idolaters? (*He sits down again with a shrug of contempt for the mob.*)

CUSINS. Take care! Barbara is in love with the common people. So am I. Have you never felt the romance of that love?

UNDERSHAFT (*cold and sardonic*). Have you ever been in love with Poverty, like St Francis? Have you ever been in love with Dirt, like St Simeon? Have you ever been in love with disease and suffering, like our nurses and philanthropists? Such passions are not virtues, but the most unnatural of all the vices. This love of the common people may please an earl's granddaughter and a university professor; but I have been a common man and a poor man; and it has no romance for me. Leave it to the poor to pretend that poverty is a blessing: leave it to the coward to make a religion of his cowardice by preaching humility: we know better than that. We three must stand together above the common people: how else can we help their children to climb up beside us? Barbara must belong to us, not to the Salvation Army.

CUSINS. Well, I can only say that if you think you will get her away from the Salvation Army by talking to her as you have been talking to me, you dont know Barbara.

UNDERSHAFT. My friend: I never ask for what I can buy.

CUSINS (*in a white fury*). Do I understand you to imply that you can buy Barbara?

UNDERSHAFT. No; but I can buy the Salvation Army.

CUSINS. Quite impossible.

UNDERSHAFT. You shall see. All religious organizations exist by selling themselves to the rich.

CUSINS. Not the Army. That is the Church of the poor.

UNDERSHAFT. All the more reason for buying it.

CUSINS. I dont think you quite know what the Army does for the poor.

UNDERSHAFT. Oh yes I do. It draws their teeth: that is enough for me as a man of business.

CUSINS. Nonsense! It makes them sober—

UNDERSHAFT. I prefer sober workmen. The profits are larger.

CUSINS. —honest—

UNDERSHAFT. Honest workmen are the most economical.

CUSINS. —attached to their homes—

UNDERSHAFT. So much the better: they will put up with anything sooner than change their shop.

CUSINS. —happy—

UNDERSHAFT. An invaluable safeguard against revolution.

CUSINS. —unselfish—

UNDERSHAFT. Indifferent to their own interests, which suits me exactly.

CUSINS. —with their thoughts on heavenly things—

UNDERSHAFT (*rising*). And not on Trade Unionism nor Socialism. Excellent.

CUSINS (*revolted*). You really are an infernal old rascal.

UNDERSHAFT (*indicating Peter Shirley, who has just come from the shelter and strolled dejectedly down the yard between them*). And this is an honest man!

SHIRLEY. Yes; and what av I got by it? (*He passes on bitterly and sits on the form, in the corner of the penthouse.*)

Snobby Price, beaming sanctimoniously, and Jenny Hill, with a tambourine full of coppers, come from the shelter and go to the drum, on which Jenny begins to count the money.

UNDERSHAFT (*replying to Shirley*). Oh, your employers must have got a good deal by it from first to last. (*He sits on the table, with one foot on the side form. Cusins, overwhelmed, sits down on the same form nearer the shelter. Barbara comes from the shelter to the middle of the yard. She is excited and a little overwrought.*)

BARBARA. Weve just had a splendid experience meeting at the other gate in Cripps's lane. Ive hardly ever seen them so much moved as they were by your confession, Mr Price.

PRICE. I could almost be glad of my past wickedness if I could believe that it would elp to keep hathers stright.

BARBARA. So it will, Snobby. How much, Jenny?

JENNY. Four and tenpence, Major.

BARBARA. Oh Snobby, if you had given your poor mother just one more kick, we should have got the whole five shillings!

PRICE. If she heard you say that, miss, she'd be sorry I didnt. But I'm glad. Oh what a joy it will be to her when she hears I'm saved!

UNDERSHAFT. Shall I contribute the odd twopence, Barbara? The millionaire's mite, eh? (*He takes a couple of pennies from his pocket.*)

BARBARA. How did you make that twopence?

UNDERSHAFT. As usual. By selling cannons, torpedoes, submarines, and my new patent Grand Duke hand grenade.

BARBARA. Put it back in your pocket. You cant buy your salvation here for twopence: you must work it out.

UNDERSHAFT. Is twopence not enough? I can afford a little more, if you press me.

BARBARA. Two million millions would not be enough. There is bad blood on your hands; and nothing but good blood can cleanse them. Money is no use. Take it away. (*She turns to Cusins.*) Dolly: you must write another letter for me to the papers. (*He makes a wry face.*) Yes: I know you dont like it; but it must be done. The starvation this winter is beating us: everybody is unemployed. The General says we must close this shelter if we cant get more money. I force the collections at the meetings until I am ashamed: dont I, Snobby?

PRICE. It's a fair treat to see you work it, miss. The way you got them up from three-and-six to four-and-ten with that hymn, penny by penny and verse by verse, was a caution. Not a Cheap Jack on Mile End Waste[12] could touch you at it.

BARBARA. Yes; but I wish we could do without it. I am getting at last to think more of the collection than of the people's souls. And what are those hatfuls of pence and halfpence? We want thousands! tens of thousands! hundreds of thousands! I want to convert people, not to be always begging for the Army in a way I'd die sooner than beg for myself.

UNDERSHAFT (*in profound irony*). Genuine unselfishness is capable of anything, my dear.

BARBARA (*unsuspectingly, as she turns away to take the money from the drum and put it in a bag she carries*). Yes, isnt it? (*Undershaft looks sardonically at Cusins.*)

CUSINS (*aside to Undershaft*). Mephistopheles! Machiavelli!

[12]**Cheap Jack . . . Waste** a peddler at fairs.

BARBARA (*tears coming into her eyes as she ties the bag and pockets it*). How are we to feed them? I cant talk religion to a man with bodily hunger in his eyes. (*Almost breaking down.*) It's frightful.

JENNY (*running to her*). Major, dear—

BARBARA (*rebounding*). No: dont comfort me. It will be all right. We shall get the money.

UNDERSHAFT. How?

JENNY. By praying for it, of course. Mrs Baines says she prayed for it last night; and she has never prayed for it in vain: never once. (*She goes to the gate and looks out into the street.*)

BARBARA (*who has dried her eyes and regained her composure*). By the way, dad, Mrs Baines has come to march with us to our big meeting this afternoon; and she is very anxious to meet you, for some reason or other. Perhaps she'll convert you.

UNDERSHAFT. I shall be delighted, my dear.

JENNY (*at the gate: excitedly*). Major! Major! heres that man back again.

BARBARA. What man?

JENNY. The man that hit me. Oh, I hope he's coming back to join us.

Bill Walker, with frost on his jacket, comes through the gate, his hands deep in his pockets and his chin sunk between his shoulders, like a cleaned-out gambler. He halts between Barbara and the drum.

BARBARA. Hullo, Bill! Back already!

BILL (*nagging at her*). Bin talkin ever sence, ev you?

BARBARA. Pretty nearly. Well, has Todger paid you out for poor Jenny's jaw?

BILL. Nao e aint.

BARBARA. I thought your jacket looked a bit snowy.

BILL. Sao it is snaowy. You want to knaow where the snaow cam from, downt you?

BARBARA. Yes.

BILL. Well, it cam from orf the grahnd in Pawkinses Corner in Kennintahn. It got rabbed orf be maw shaoulders: see?

BARBARA. Pity you didnt rub some off with your knees, Bill! That would have done you a lot of good.

BILL (*with sour mirthless humor*). Aw was sivin anather menn's knees at the tawm. E was kneelin on moy ed, e was.

JENNY. Who was kneeling on your head?

BILL. Todger was. E was pryin for me: pryin camfortable wiv me as a cawpet. Sow was Mog. Sao was the aol bloomin meetin. Mog she sez "Ow Lawd brike is stabborn sperrit; bat downt urt is dear art." Thet was wot she said. "Downt urt is dear art"! An er blowk—thirteen stun four!—kneelin wiv all is wight on me. Fanny, aint it?

JENNY. Oh no. We're sorry, Mr Walker.

BARBARA (*enjoying it frankly*). Nonsense! of course it's funny. Served you right, Bill! You must have done something to him first.

BILL (*doggedly*). Aw did wot Aw said Aw'd do. Aw spit in is eye. E looks ap at the skoy and sez, "Ow that Aw should be fahnd worthy to be spit upon for the gospel's sike!" e sez; an Mog sez "Glaory Allelloolier!"; an then e called me Braddher, an dahned me as if Aw was a kid and e was me mather worshin me a Setterda nawt. Aw ednt jast nao shaow wiv im at all. Arf the street pryed; an the tather arf larfed fit to split theirselves. (*To Barbara.*) There! are you settisfawd nah?

BARBARA (*her eyes dancing*). Wish I'd been there, Bill.

BILL. Yus: youd a got in a hextra bit o talk on me, wouldnt you?

JENNY. I'm so sorry, Mr Walker.

BILL (*fiercely*). Downt you gow bein sorry for me: youve no call. Listen eah. Aw browk your jawr.

JENNY. No, it didn't hurt me: indeed it didnt, except for a moment. It was only that I was frightened.

BILL. Aw downt want to be forgive be you, or be ennybody. Wot Aw did Aw'll py for. Aw trawd to gat me aown jawr browk to settisfaw you—

JENNY (*distressed*). Oh no—

BILL (*impatiently*). Tell y Aw did: cawnt you listen to wots bein taold you? All Aw got be it was being mide a sawt of in the pablic street for me pines. Well, if Aw cawnt settisfaw you one wy, Aw ken anather. Listen eah! Aw ed two quid[13] sived agen the frost; an Awve a pahnd of it left. A mite o mawn last week ed words with the judy e's gowin to merry. E give er wot-for; an e's bin fawnd fifteen bob.[14] E ed a rawt to itt er cause they was gowin to be merrid; but Aw ednt nao rawt to itt you; sao put anather fawv bob on an call it a pahnd's worth. (*He produces a sovereign.*)[15] Eahs the manney. Tike it; and lets ev no more o your forgivin an pryin and your Mijor jawrin me. Let wot Aw dan be dan an pide for; and let there be a end of it.

JENNY. Oh, I couldnt take it, Mr Walker. But if you would give a shilling or two to poor Rummy Mitchens! you really did hurt her; and she's old.

BILL (*contemptuously*). Not lawkly. Aw'd give her anather as soon as look at er. Let her ev the lawr o me as she threatened! She aint forgiven me: not mach. Wot Aw dan to er is not on me mawnd—wot she (*indicating Barbara*) mawt call on me conscience—no more than stickin a pig. It's this Christian gime o yours that Aw wownt ev plyed agen me: this bloomin forgivin an neggin an jawrin that mikes a menn thet sore that iz lawf's a burdn to im. Aw wownt ev it, Aw tell you; sao tike your manney and stop thraowin your silly beshed fice hap agen me.

JENNY. Major: may I take a little of it for the Army?

BARBARA. No: the Army is not to be bought. We want your soul, Bill; and we'll take nothing less.

BILL (*bitterly*). Aw knaow. Me an maw few shillins is not good enaff for you. Youre a earl's grendorter, you are. Nathink less than a andered pahnd for you.

UNDERSHAFT. Come, Barbara! you could do a great deal of good with a hundred pounds. If you will set this gentleman's mind at ease by taking his pound, I will give the other ninety-nine.

Bill, dazed by such opulence, instinctively touches his cap.

BARBARA. Oh, youre too extravagant, papa. Bill offers twenty pieces of silver. All you need offer is the other ten.[16] That will make the standard price to buy anybody who's for sale. I'm not; and the Army's not. (*To Bill.*) Youll never have another quiet moment, Bill, until you come round to us. You cant stand out against your salvation.

BILL (*sullenly*). Aw cawnt stand aht agen music awl wrastlers and awtful tangued women. Awve offered to py. Aw can do no more. Tike it or leave it. There it is. (*He throws the sovereign on the drum, and sits down on the horse-trough. The coin fascinates Snobby Price, who takes an early opportunity of dropping his cap on it.*)

Mrs Baines comes from the shelter. She is dressed as a Salvation Army Commissioner. She is an earnest looking woman of about 40, with a caressing, urgent voice, and an appealing manner.

BARBARA. This is my father, Mrs Baines (*Undershaft comes from the table, taking his hat off with marked civility.*) Try what you can do with him. He wont listen to me, because he remembers what a fool I was when I was a baby. (*She leaves them together and chats with Jenny.*)

MRS BAINES. Have you been shewn over the shelter Mr Undershaft? You know the work we're doing, of course.

UNDERSHAFT (*very civilly*). The whole nation knows it, Mrs Baines.

MRS BAINES. No, sir: the whole nation does not know it, or we should not be crippled as we are for want of money to carry our work through the length and breadth of the land. Let me tell you that there would have been rioting this winter in London but for us.

UNDERSHAFT. You really think so?

MRS BAINES. I know it. I remember 1886, when you rich gentlemen hardened your hearts against the cry of the poor. They broke the windows of your clubs in Pall Mall.

UNDERSHAFT (*gleaming with approval of their method*). And the Mansion House Fund went up next day from thirty thousand pounds to seventy-nine thousand! I remember quite well.

MRS BAINES. Well, wont you help me to get at the people? They wont break windows then. Come here, Price. Let me shew you to this gentleman. (*Price comes to be inspected.*) Do you remember the window breaking?

---

[13]**quid** slang for a pound note.   [14]**bob** a shilling, or one-twentieth of a pound.   [15]**sovereign** a gold coin worth a pound.

[16]Bill's sovereign is twenty silver shillings; the thirty "pieces of silver" was Judas' reward for betraying Jesus.

PRICE. My ole father thought it was the revolution, maam.

MRS BAINES. Would you break windows now?

PRICE. Oh no, maam. The windows of eaven av bin opened to me. I know now that the rich man is a sinner like myself.

RUMMY (*appearing above at the loft door*). Snobby Price!

SNOBBY. Wot is it?

RUMMY. Your mother's askin for you at the other gate in Cripps's Lane. She's heard about your confession. (*Price turns pale.*)

MRS BAINES. Go, Mr Price; and pray with her.

JENNY. You can go through the shelter, Snobby.

PRICE (*to Mrs. Baines*). I couldnt face her now, maam, with all the weight of my sins fresh on me. Tell her she'll find her son at ome, waitin for her in prayer. (*He skulks off through the gate, incidentally stealing the sovereign on his way out by picking up his cap from the drum.*)

MRS BAINES (*with swimming eyes*). You see how we take the anger and the bitterness against you out of their hearts, Mr Undershaft.

UNDERSHAFT. It is certainly most convenient and gratifying to all large employers of labor, Mrs Baines.

MRS BAINES. Barbara: Jenny: I have good news: most wonderful news. (*Jenny runs to her.*) My prayers have been answered. I told you they would, Jenny, didnt I?

JENNY. Yes, yes.

BARBARA (*moving nearer to the drum*). Have we got money enough to keep the shelter open?

MRS BAINES. I hope we shall have enough to keep all the shelters open. Lord Saxmundham has promised us five thousand pounds—

BARBARA. Hooray!

JENNY. Glory!

MRS BAINES. —if—

BARBARA. "If!" If what?

MRS BAINES. —if five other gentlemen will give a thousand each to make it up to ten thousand.

BARBARA. Who is Lord Saxmundham? I never heard of him.

UNDERSHAFT (*who has pricked up his ears at the peer's name, and is now watching Barbara curiously*). A new creation, my dear. You have heard of Sir Horace Bodger?

BARBARA. Bodger! Do you mean the distiller? Bodger's whisky!

UNDERSHAFT. That is the man. He is one of the greatest of our public benefactors. He restored the cathedral at Hakington. They made him a baronet for that. He gave half a million to the funds of his party: they made him a baron for that.

SHIRLEY. What will they give him for the five thousand?

UNDERSHAFT. There is nothing left to give him. So the five thousand, I should think, is to save his soul.

MRS BAINES. Heaven grant it may! Oh Mr Undershaft, you have some very rich friends. Cant you help us towards the other five thousand? We are going to hold a great meeting this afternoon at the Assembly Hall in the Mile End Road. If I could only announce that one gentleman had come forward to support Lord Saxmundham, others would follow. Dont you know somebody? couldnt you? wouldnt you? (*Her eyes fill with tears.*) oh, think of those poor people, Mr Undershaft: think of how much it means to them, and how little to a great man like you.

UNDERSHAFT (*sardonically gallant*). Mrs Baines: you are irresistible. I cant disappoint you; and I cant deny myself the satisfaction of making Bodger pay up. You shall have your five thousand pounds.

MRS BAINES. Thank God!

UNDERSHAFT. You dont thank me?

MRS BAINES. Oh sir, dont try to be cynical: dont be ashamed of being a good man. The Lord will bless you abundantly; and our prayers will be like a strong fortification round you all the days of your life. (*With a touch of caution.*) You will let me have the cheque to shew at the meeting, wont you? Jenny: go in and fetch a pen and ink. (*Jenny runs to the shelter door.*)

UNDERSHAFT. Do not disturb Miss Hill: I have a fountain pen. (*Jenny halts. He sits at the table and writes the cheque. Cusins rises to make room for him. They all watch him silently.*)

BILL (*cynically, aside to Barbara, his voice and accent horribly debased*). Wot prawce selvytion nah?

BARBARA. Stop. (*Undershaft stops writing: they all turn to her in surprise.*) Mrs Baines: are you really going to take this money?

MRS BAINES (*astonished*). Why not, dear?

BARBARA. Why not! Do you know what my father is? Have you forgotten that Lord Saxmundham is Bodger the whisky man? Do you remember how we implored the County Council to stop him from writing Bodger's Whisky in letters of fire against the sky; so that the poor drink-ruined creatures on the Embankment could not wake up from their snatches of sleep without being reminded of their deadly thirst by that wicked sky sign? Do you know that the worst thing I have had to fight here is not the devil, but Bodger, Bodger, Bodger, with his whisky, his distilleries, and his tied houses?[17] Are you going to make our shelter another tied house for him, and ask me to keep it?

BILL. Rotten dranken whisky it is too.

MRS BAINES. Dear Barbara: Lord Saxmundham has a soul to be saved like any of us. If heaven has found the way to make a good use of his money, are we to set ourselves up against the answer to our prayers?

BARBARA. I know he has a soul to be saved. Let him come down here; and I'll do my best to help him to his salva-

[17]**tied houses** taverns owned by brewing firms.

tion. But he wants to send his cheque down to buy us, and go on being as wicked as ever.

UNDERSHAFT (*with a reasonableness which Cusins alone perceives to be ironical*). My dear Barbara: alcohol is a very necessary article. It heals the sick—

BARBARA. It does nothing of the sort.

UNDERSHAFT. Well, it assists the doctor: that is perhaps a less questionable way of putting it. It makes life bearable to millions of people who could not endure their existence if they were quite sober. It enables Parliament to do things at eleven at night that no sane person would do at eleven in the morning. Is it Bodger's fault that this inestimable gift is deplorably abused by less than one per cent of the poor? (*He turns again to the table; signs the cheque; and crosses it.*)

MRS BAINES. Barbara: will there be less drinking or more if all those poor souls we are saving come tomorrow and find the doors of our shelters shut in their faces? Lord Saxmundham gives us the money to stop drinking—to take his own business from him.

CUSINS (*impishly*). Pure self-sacrifice on Bodger's part, clearly! Bless dear Bodger! (*Barbara almost breaks down as Adolphus, too, fails her.*)

UNDERSHAFT (*tearing out the cheque and pocketing the book as he rises and goes past Cusins to Mrs Baines*). I also, Mrs Baines, may claim a little disinterestedness. Think of my business! think of the widows and orphans! the men and lads torn to pieces with shrapnel and poisoned with lyddite![18] (*Mrs Baines shrinks; but he goes on remorselessly*) the oceans of blood, not one drop of which is shed in a really just cause! the ravaged crops! the peaceful peasant forced, women and men, to till their fields, under the fire of opposing armies on pain of starvation! the bad blood of the fierce little cowards at home who egg on others to fight for the gratification of their national vanity! All this makes money for me: I am never richer, never busier than when the papers are full of it. Well, it is your work to preach peace on earth and goodwill to men. (*Mrs Baines's face lights up again.*) Every convert you make is a vote against war. (*Her lips move in prayer.*) Yet I give you this money to help you to hasten my own commercial ruin. (*He gives her the cheque.*)

CUSINS (*mounting the form in an ecstasy of mischief*). The millennium will be inaugurated by the unselfishness of Undershaft and Bodger. Oh be joyful! (*He takes the drumsticks from his pocket and flourishes them.*)

MRS BAINES (*taking the cheque*). The longer I live the more proof I see that there is an Infinite Goodness that turns everything to the work of salvation sooner or later. Who would have thought that any good could have come out

of war and drink? And yet their profits are brought today to the feet of salvation to do its blessed work. (*She is affected to tears.*)

JENNY (*running to Mrs Baines and throwing her arms around her*). Oh dear! how blessed, how glorious it all is!

CUSINS (*in a convulsion of irony*). Let us seize this unspeakable moment. Let us march to the great meeting at once. Excuse me just an instant. (*He rushes into the shelter. Jenny takes her tambourine from the drum head.*)

MRS BAINES. Mr Undershaft: have you ever seen a thousand people fall on their knees with one impulse and pray? Come with us to the meeting. Barbara shall tell them that the Army is saved, and saved through you.

CUSINS (*returning impetuously from the shelter with a flag and a trombone, and coming between Mrs Baines and Undershaft*). You shall carry the flag down the first street, Mrs Baines. (*He gives her the flag.*) Mr Undershaft is a gifted trombonist: he shall intone an Olympian diapason to the West Ham Salvation March. (*Aside to Undershaft, as he forces the trombone on him.*) Blow, Machiavelli, blow.

UNDERSHAFT (*aside to him, as he takes the trombone*). The trumpet in Zion! (*Cusins rushes to the drum, which he takes up and puts on. Undershaft continues, aloud.*) I will do my best. I could vamp a bass if I knew the tune.

CUSINS. It is a wedding chorus from one of Donizetti's operas; but we have converted it. We convert everything to good here, including Bodger. You remember the chorus. "For thee immense rejoicing—immenso giubilo— immenso giubilo." (*With drum obbligato.*) Rum tum ti tum, tum tum ti ta—

BARBARA. Dolly: you are breaking my heart.

CUSINS. What is a broken heart more or less here? Dionysos Undershaft has descended. I am possessed.

MRS BAINES. Come, Barbara: I must have my dear Major to carry the flag with me.

JENNY. Yes, yes, Major darling.

CUSINS (*snatches the tambourine out of Jenny's hand and mutely offers it to Barbara*).

BARBARA (*coming forward a little as she puts the offer behind her with a shudder, whilst Cusins recklessly tosses the tambourine back to Jenny and goes to the gate*). I cant come.

JENNY. Not come!

MRS BAINES (*with tears in her eyes*). Barbara: do you think I am wrong to take the money?

BARBARA (*impulsively going to her and kissing her*). No, no: God help you, dear, you must: you are saving the Army. Go; and may you have a great meeting!

JENNY. But arnt you coming?

BARBARA. No. (*She begins taking off the silver S brooch from her collar.*)

MRS BAINES. Barbara: what are you doing?

JENNY. Why are you taking your badge off? You cant be going to leave us, Major.

BARBARA (*quietly*). Father: come here.

---

[18]**lyddite** an explosive.

UNDERSHAFT (*coming to her*). My dear! (*Seeing that she is going to pin the badge on his collar, he retreats to the penthouse in some alarm.*)

BARBARA (*following him*). Dont be frightened. (*She pins the badge on and steps back towards the table, shewing him to the others.*) There! It's not much for £5000, is it?

MRS BAINES. Barbara: if you wont come and pray with us, promise me you will pray for us.

BARBARA. I cant pray now. Perhaps I shall never pray again.

MRS BAINES. Barbara!

JENNY. Major!

BARBARA (*almost delirious*). I cant bear any more. Quick march!

CUSINS (*calling to the procession in the street outside*). Off we go. Play up, there! I m m e n s o g i u b i l o. (*He gives the time with his drum; and the band strikes up the march, which rapidly becomes more distant as the procession moves briskly away.*)

MRS BAINES. I must go, dear. Youre overworked: you will be all right tomorrow. We'll never lose you. Now Jenny: step out with the old flag. Blood and Fire! (*She marches out through the gate with her flag.*)

JENNY. Glory Hallelujah! (*Flourishing her tambourine and marching.*)

UNDERSHAFT (*to Cusins, as he marches out past him easing the slide of his trombone*). "My ducats and my daughter"!

CUSINS (*following him out*). Money and gunpowder!

BARBARA. Drunkenness and Murder! My God: why hast thou forsaken me?

She sinks on the form with her face buried in her hands. The march passes away into silence. Bill Walker steals across to her.

BILL (*taunting*). Wot prawce selvytion nah?

SHIRLEY. Dont you hit her when she's down.

BILL. She itt me wen aw wiz dahn. Waw shouldnt Aw git a bit o me aown beck?

BARBARA (*raising her head*). I didnt take your money, Bill. (*She crosses the yard to the gate and turns her back on the two men to hide her face from them.*)

BILL (*sneering after her*). Naow, it warnt enaff for you. (*Turning to the drum, he misses the money.*) Ellow! If you aint took it sammun else ez. Weres it gorn? Bly me if Jenny Ill didnt tike it arter all!

RUMMY (*screaming at him from the loft*). You lie, you dirty blackguard! Snobby Price pinched it off the drum when he took up his cap. I was up here all the time an see im do it.

BILL. Wot! Stowl maw manney! Waw didnt you call thief on him, you silly aold macker you?

RUMMY. To serve you aht for ittin me across the fice. It's cost y'pahnd, that az. (*Raising a paean of squalid triumph.*) I done you. I'm even with you. Ive ad it aht o y——(*Bill snatches up Shirley's mug and hurls it at her. She slams the loft

door and vanishes. The mug smashes against the door and falls in fragments.*)

BILL (*beginning to chuckle*). Tell us, aol menn, wot o'clock this mawnin was it wen im as they call Snobby Prawce was sived?

BARBARA (*turning to him more composedly, and with unspoiled sweetness*). About half past twelve, Bill. And he pinched your pound at a quarter to two. I know. Well, you cant afford to lose it. I'll send it to you.

BILL (*his voice and accent suddenly improving*). Not if Aw wiz to stawve for it. Aw aint to be bought.

SHIRLEY. Aint you? Youd sell yourself to the devil for a pint o beer; only there aint no devil to make the offer.

BILL (*unshamed*). Sao Aw would, mite, and often ev, cheerful. But she cawnt baw me. (*Approaching Barbara.*) You wanted maw saoul, did you? Well, you aint got it.

BARBARA. I nearly got it, Bill. But weve sold it back to you for ten thousand pounds.

SHIRLEY. And dear at the money!

BARBARA. No, Peter: it was worth more than money.

BILL (*salvationproof*). It's nao good: you cawnt get rahnd me nah. Aw downt blieve in it; and Awve seen tody that Aw was rawt. (*Going.*) Sao long, aol soupkitchener! Ta, ta, Mijor Earl's Grendorter! (*Turning at the gate.*) Wot prawce selvytion nah? Snobby Prawce! Ha! ha!

BARBARA (*offering her hand*). Goodbye, Bill.

BILL (*taken aback, half plucks his cap off; then shoves it on again defiantly*). Git aht. (*Barbara drops her hand, discouraged. He has a twinge of remorse.*) But thets aw rawt, you knaow. Nathink pasnl. Naow mellice. Sao long, Judy. (*He goes.*)

BARBARA. No malice. So long, Bill.

SHIRLEY (*shaking his head*). You make too much of him, miss, in your innocence.

BARBARA (*going to him*). Peter: I'm like you now. Cleaned out, and lost my job.

SHIRLEY. Youve youth an hope. Thats two better than me.

BARBARA. I'll get you a job, Peter. Thats hope for you: the youth will have to be enough for me. (*She counts her money.*) I have just enough left for two teas at Lockharts, a Rowton doss[19] for you, and my tram and bus home. (*He frowns and rises with offended pride. She takes his arm.*) Dont be proud, Peter: it's sharing between friends. And promise me youll talk to me and not let me cry. (*She draws him towards the gate.*)

SHIRLEY. Well, I'm not accustomed to talk to the like of you——

BARBARA (*urgently*). Yes, yes: you must talk to me. Tell me about Tom Paine's books and Bradlaugh's lectures.[20] Come along.

SHIRLEY. Ah, if you would only read Tom Paine in the proper spirit, miss! (*They go out through the gate together.*)

[19] **a Rowton doss** a bed in one of Rowton's cheap rooming houses.
[20] **Charles Bradlaugh,** a secularist, died in 1891.

ACT 3

Next day after lunch Lady Britomart is writing in the library in Wilton Crescent. Sarah is reading in the armchair near the window. Barbara, in ordinary fashionable dress, pale and brooding, is on the settee. Charles Lomax enters. He starts on seeing Barbara fashionably attired and in low spirits.

LOMAX. Youve left off your uniform!

Barbara says nothing; but an expression of pain passes over her face.

LADY BRITOMART (*warning him in low tones to be careful*). Charles!

LOMAX (*much concerned, coming behind the settee and bending sympathetically over Barbara*). I'm awfully sorry, Barbara. You know I helped you all I could with the concertina and so forth. (*Momentously.*) Still, I have never shut my eyes to the fact that there is a certain amount of tosh about the Salvation Army. Now the claims of the Church of England—

LADY BRITOMART. Thats enough, Charles. Speak of something suited to your mental capacity.

LOMAX. But surely the Church of England is suited to all our capacities.

BARBARA (*pressing his hand*). Thank you for your sympathy, Cholly. Now go and spoon with Sarah.

LOMAX (*dragging a chair from the writing table and seating himself affectionately by Sarah's side*). How is my ownest today?

SARAH. I wish you wouldnt tell Cholly to do things, Barbara. He always comes straight and does them. Cholly: we're going to the works this afternoon.

LOMAX. What works?

SARAH. The cannon works.

LOMAX. What? your governor's shop!

SARAH. Yes.

LOMAX. Oh I say!

Cusins enters in poor condition. He also starts visibly when he sees Barbara without her uniform.

BARBARA. I expected you this morning, Dolly. Didn't you guess that?

CUSINS (*sitting down beside her*). I'm sorry. I have only just breakfasted.

SARAH. But weve just finished lunch.

BARBARA. Have you had one of your bad nights?

CUSINS. No: I had rather a good night: in fact, one of the most remarkable nights I have ever passed.

BARBARA. The meeting?

CUSINS. No: after the meeting.

LADY BRITOMART. You should have gone to bed after the meeting. What were you doing?

CUSINS. Drinking.

LADY BRITOMART. ⎱ ⎰Adolphus!
SARAH.   ⎱ ⎰Dolly!
BARBARA.   ⎱ ⎰Dolly!
LOMAX.   ⎰ ⎱Oh I say!

LADY BRITOMART. What were you drinking, may I ask?

CUSINS. A most devilish kind of Spanish burgundy, warranted free from added alcohol: a Temperance burgundy in fact. Its richness in natural alcohol made any addition superfluous.

BARBARA. Are you joking, Dolly?

CUSINS (*patiently*). No. I have been making a night of it with the nominal head of this household: that is all.

LADY BRITOMART. Andrew made you drunk!

CUSINS. No: he only provided the wine. I think it was Dionysos who made me drunk. (*To Barbara.*) I told you I was possessed.

LADY BRITOMART. Youre not sober yet. Go home to bed at once.

CUSINS. I have never before ventured to reproach you, Lady Brit; but how could you marry the Prince of Darkness?

LADY BRITOMART. It was much more excusable to marry him than to get drunk with him. That is a new accomplishment of Andrew's, by the way. He usent to drink.

CUSINS. He doesnt now. He only sat there and completed the wreck of my moral basis, the rout of my convictions, the purchase of my soul. He cares for you, Barbara. That is what makes him so dangerous to me.

BARBARA. That has nothing to do with it, Dolly. There are larger loves and diviner dreams than the fireside ones. You know that, dont you?

CUSINS. Yes: that is our understanding. I know it. I hold to it. Unless he can win me on that holier ground he may amuse me for a while; but he can get no deeper hold, strong as he is.

BARBARA. Keep to that; and the end will be right. Now tell me what happened at the meeting?

CUSINS. It was an amazing meeting. Mrs Baines almost died of emotion. Jenny Hill simply gibbered with hysteria. The Prince of Darkness played his trombone like a madman: its brazen roarings were like the laughter of the damned. 117 conversions took place then and there. They prayed with the most touching sincerity and gratitude for Bodger, and for the anonymous donor of the £5000. Your father would not let his name be given.

LOMAX. That was rather fine of the old man, you know. Most chaps would have wanted the advertisement.

CUSINS. He said all the charitable institutions would be down on him like kites on a battle-field if he gave his name.

LADY BRITOMART. Thats Andrew all over. He never does a proper thing without giving an improper reason for it.

CUSINS. He convinced me that I have all my life been doing improper things for proper reasons.

LADY BRITOMART. Adolphus: now that Barbara has left the Salvation Army, you had better leave it too. I will not have you playing that drum in the streets.

CUSINS. Your orders are already obeyed, Lady Brit.

BARBARA. Dolly: were you ever really in earnest about it? Would you have joined if you had never seen me?

CUSINS (*disingenuously*). Well—er—well, possibly, as a collector of religions—

LOMAX (*cunningly*). Not as a drummer, though, you know. You are a very clearheaded brainy chap, Dolly; and it must have been apparent to you that there is a certain amount of tosh about—

LADY BRITOMART. Charles: if you must drivel, drivel like a grown-up man and not like a schoolboy.

LOMAX (*out of countenance*). Well, drivel is drivel, dont you know, whatever a man's age.

LADY BRITOMART. In good society in England, Charles, men drivel at all ages by repeating silly formulas with an air of wisdom. Schoolboys make their own formulas out of slang, like you. When they reach your age, and get political private secretaryships and things of that sort, they drop slang and get their formulas out of The Spectator or The Times. You had better confine yourself to The Times. You will find that there is a certain amount of tosh about The Times; but at least its language is reputable.

LOMAX (*overwhelmed*). You are so awfully strong-minded, Lady Brit—

LADY BRITOMART. Rubbish! (*Morrison comes in.*) What is it?

MORRISON. If you please, my lady, Mr Undershaft has just drove up to the door.

LADY BRITOMART. Well, let him in. (*Morrison hesitates.*) Whats the matter with you?

MORRISON. Shall I announce him, my lady; or is he at home here, so to speak, my lady?

LADY BRITOMART. Announce him.

MORRISON. Thank you, my lady. You wont mind my asking, I hope. The occasion is in a manner of speaking new to me.

LADY BRITOMART. Quite right. Go and let him in.

MORRISON. Thank you, my lady. (*He withdraws.*)

LADY BRITOMART. Children: go and get ready. (*Sarah and Barbara go upstairs for their out-of-door wraps.*) Charles: go and tell Stephen to come down here in five minutes: you will find him in the drawing room. (*Charles goes.*) Adolphus: tell them to send round the carriage in about fifteen minutes. (*Adolphus goes.*)

MORRISON (*at the door*). Mr Undershaft.

Undershaft comes in. Morrison goes out.

UNDERSHAFT. Alone! How fortunate!

LADY BRITOMART (*rising*). Dont be sentimental, Andrew. Sit down. (*She sits on the settee: he sits beside her, on her left. She comes to the point before he has time to breathe.*) Sarah must have £800 a year until Charles Lomax comes into

his property. Barbara will need more, and need it permanently, because Adolphus hasnt any property.

UNDERSHAFT (*resignedly*). Yes, my dear: I will see to it. Anything else? for yourself, for instance?

LADY BRITOMART. I want to talk to you about Stephen.

UNDERSHAFT (*rather wearily*). Dont, my dear. Stephen doesnt interest me.

LADY BRITOMART. He does interest me. He is our son.

UNDERSHAFT. Do you really think so? He has induced us to bring him into the world; but he chose his parents very incongruously, I think. I see nothing of myself in him, and less of you.

LADY BRITOMART. Andrew: Stephen is an excellent son, and a most steady, capable, highminded young man. You are simply trying to find an excuse for disinheriting him.

UNDERSHAFT. My dear Biddy: the Undershaft tradition disinherits him. It would be dishonest of me to leave the cannon foundry to my son.

LADY BRITOMART. It would be most unnatural and improper of you to leave it to anyone else, Andrew. Do you suppose this wicked and immoral tradition can be kept up for ever? Do you pretend that Stephen could not carry on the foundry just as well as all the other sons of the big business houses?

UNDERSHAFT. Yes: he could learn the office routine without understanding the business, like all the other sons; and the firm would go on by its own momentum until the real Undershaft—probably an Italian or a German—would invent a new method and cut him out.

LADY BRITOMART. There is nothing that any Italian or German could do that Stephen could not do. And Stephen at least has breeding.

UNDERSHAFT. The son of a foundling! Nonsense!

LADY BRITOMART. My son, Andrew! And even you may have good blood in your veins for all you know.

UNDERSHAFT. True. Probably I have. That is another argument in favor of a foundling.

LADY BRITOMART. Andrew: dont be aggravating. And dont be wicked. At present you are both.

UNDERSHAFT. This conversation is part of the Undershaft tradition, Biddy. Every Undershaft's wife has treated him to it ever since the house was founded. It is a mere waste of breath. If the tradition be ever broken it will be for an abler man than Stephen.

LADY BRITOMART (*pouting*). Then go away.

UNDERSHAFT (*deprecatory*). Go away!

LADY BRITOMART. Yes: go away. If you will do nothing for Stephen, you are not wanted here. Go to your foundling, whoever he is; and look after him.

UNDERSHAFT. The fact is, Biddy—

LADY BRITOMART. Dont call me Biddy. I dont call you Andy.

UNDERSHAFT. I will not call my wife Britomart: it is not good sense. Seriously, my love, the Undershaft tradition has landed me in a difficulty. I am getting on in years; and my partner Lazarus has at last made a stand and insisted that the succession must be settled one way or the other; and of course he is quite right. You see, I havnt found a fit successor yet.

LADY BRITOMART (*obstinately*). There is Stephen.

UNDERSHAFT. Thats just it: all the foundlings I can find are exactly like Stephen.

LADY BRITOMART. Andrew!!

UNDERSHAFT. I want a man with no relations and no schooling: that is, a man who would be out of the running altogether if he were not a strong man. And I cant find him. Every blessed foundling nowadays is snapped up in his infancy by Barnardo homes, or School Board officers, or Boards of Guardians; and if he shews the least ability he is fastened on by schoolmasters; trained to win scholarships like a racehorse; crammed with secondhand ideas; drilled and disciplined in docility and what they call good taste; and lamed for life so that he is fit for nothing but teaching. If you want to keep the foundry in the family, you had better find an eligible foundling and marry him to Barbara.

LADY BRITOMART. Ah! Barbara! Your pet! You would sacrifice Stephen to Barbara.

UNDERSHAFT. Cheerfully. And you, my dear, would boil Barbara to make soup for Stephen.

LADY BRITOMART. Andrew: this is not a question of our likings and dislikings: it is a question of duty. It is your duty to make Stephen your successor.

UNDERSHAFT. Just as much as it is your duty to submit to your husband. Come, Biddy! these tricks of the governing class are of no use with me. I am one of the governing class myself; and it is a waste of time giving tracts to a missionary. I have the power in this matter; and I am not to be humbugged into using it for your purposes.

LADY BRITOMART. Andrew: you can talk my head off; but you cant change wrong into right. And your tie is all on one side. Put it straight.

UNDERSHAFT (*disconcerted*). It wont stay unless it's pinned— (*He fumbles at it with childish grimaces.*)

Stephen comes in.

STEPHEN (*at the door*). I beg your pardon. (*About to retire.*)

LADY BRITOMART. No: come in, Stephen. (*Stephen comes forward to his mother's writing table.*)

UNDERSHAFT (*not very cordially*). Good afternoon.

STEPHEN (*coldly*). Good afternoon.

UNDERSHAFT (*to Lady Britomart*). He knows all about the tradition, I suppose?

LADY BRITOMART. Yes. (*To Stephen.*) It is what I told you last night, Stephen.

UNDERSHAFT (*sulkily*). I understand you want to come into the cannon business.

STEPHEN. *I* go into trade! Certainly not.

UNDERSHAFT (*opening his eyes, greatly eased in mind and manner*). Oh! in that case—

LADY BRITOMART. Cannons are not trade, Stephen. They are enterprise.

STEPHEN. I have no intention of becoming a man of business in any sense. I have no capacity for business and no taste for it. I intend to devote myself to politics.

UNDERSHAFT (*rising*). My dear boy: this is an immense relief to me. And I trust it may prove an equally good thing for the country. I was afraid you would consider yourself disparaged and slighted. (*He moves towards Stephen as if to shake hands with him.*)

LADY BRITOMART (*rising and interposing*). Stephen: I cannot allow you to throw away an enormous property like this.

STEPHEN (*stiffly*). Mother: there must be an end of treating me as a child, if you please. (*Lady Britomart recoils, deeply wounded by his tone.*) Until last night I did not take your attitude seriously, because I did not think you meant it seriously. But I find now that you left me in the dark as to matters which you should have explained to me years ago. I am extremely hurt and offended. Any further discussion of my intentions had better take place with my father, as between one man and another.

LADY BRITOMART. Stephen! (*She sits down again, her eyes filling with tears.*)

UNDERSHAFT (*with grave compassion*). You see, my dear, it is only the big men who can be treated as children.

STEPHEN. I am sorry, mother, that you have forced me—

UNDERSHAFT (*stopping him*). Yes, yes, yes, yes: thats all right, Stephen. She wont interfere with you any more: your independence is achieved: you have won your latchkey. Dont rub it in; and above all, dont apologize. (*He resumes his seat.*) Now what about your future, as between one man and another—I beg your pardon, Biddy: as between two men and a woman.

LADY BRITOMART (*who has pulled herself together strongly*). I quite understand, Stephen. By all means go your own way if you feel strong enough. (*Stephen sits down magisterially in the chair at the writing table with an air of affirming his majority.*)

UNDERSHAFT. It is settled that you do not ask for the succession to the cannon business.

STEPHEN. I hope it is settled that I repudiate the cannon business.

UNDERSHAFT. Come, come! dont be so devilishly sulky: it's boyish. Freedom should be generous. Besides, I owe you a fair start in life in exchange for disinheriting you. You cant become prime minister all at once. Havnt you a turn for something? What about literature, art, and so forth?

STEPHEN. I have nothing of the artist about me, either in faculty or character, thank Heaven!

UNDERSHAFT. A philosopher, perhaps? Eh?

STEPHEN. I make no such ridiculous pretension.

UNDERSHAFT. Just so. Well, there is the army, the navy, the Church, the Bar. The Bar requires some ability. What about the Bar?

STEPHEN. I have not studied law. And I am afraid I have not the necessary push—I believe that is the name barristers give to their vulgarity—for success in pleading.

UNDERSHAFT. Rather a difficult case, Stephen. Hardly anything left but the stage, is there? (*Stephen makes an impatient movement.*) Well, come! is there anything you know or care for?

STEPHEN (*rising and looking at him steadily*). I know the difference between right and wrong.

UNDERSHAFT (*hugely tickled*). You dont say so! What! no capacity for business, no knowledge of law, no sympathy with art, no pretension to philosophy; only a simple knowledge of the secret that has puzzled all the philosophers, baffled all the lawyers, muddled all the men of business, and ruined most of the artists: the secret of right and wrong. Why, man, youre a genius, a master of masters, a god! At twentyfour, too!

STEPHEN (*keeping his temper with difficulty*). You are pleased to be facetious. I pretend to nothing more than any honorable English gentleman claims as his birthright (*He sits down angrily.*)

UNDERSHAFT. Oh, thats everybody's birthright. Look at poor little Jenny Hill, the Salvation lassie! she would think you were laughing at her if you asked her to stand up in the street and teach grammar or geography or mathematics or even drawing room dancing; but it never occurs to her to doubt that she can teach morals and religion. You are all alike, you respectable people. You cant tell me the bursting strain of a ten-inch gun, which is a very simple matter; but you all think you can tell me the bursting strain of a man under temptation. You darent handle high explosives; but youre all ready to handle honesty and truth and justice and the whole duty of man, and kill one another at that game. What a country! What a world!

LADY BRITOMART (*uneasily*). What do you think he had better do, Andrew?

UNDERSHAFT. Oh, just what he wants to do. He knows nothing and he thinks he knows everything. That points clearly to a political career. Get him a private secretaryship to someone who can get him an Under Secretaryship; and then leave him alone. He will find his natural and proper place in the end on the Treasury Bench.

STEPHEN (*springing up again*). I am sorry, sir, that you force me to forget the respect due to you as my father. I am an Englishman and I will not hear the Government of my country insulted. (*He thrusts his hands in his pockets, and walks angrily across to the window.*)

UNDERSHAFT (*with a touch of brutality*). The government of your country! *I* am the government of your country: I, and Lazarus. Do you suppose that you and half a dozen amateurs like you, sitting in a row in that foolish gabble shop, can govern Undershaft and Lazarus? No, my friend: you will do what pays us. You will make war when it suits us, and keep peace when it doesnt. You will find out that

trade requires certain measures when we have decided on those measures. When I want anything to keep my dividends up, you will discover that my want is a national need. When other people want something to keep my dividends down, you will call out the police and military. And in return you shall have the support and applause of my newspapers, and the delight of imagining that you are a great statesman. Government of your country! Be off with you, my boy, and play with your caucuses and leading articles and historic parties and great leaders and burning questions and the rest of your toys. *I* am going back to my counting-house to pay the piper and call the tune.

STEPHEN (*actually smiling, and putting his hand on his father's shoulder with indulgent patronage*). Really, my dear father, it is impossible to be angry with you. You dont know how absurd all this sounds to me. You are very properly proud of having been industrious enough to make money; and it is greatly to your credit that you have made so much of it. But it has kept you in circles where you are valued for your money and deferred to for it, instead of in the doubtless very old-fashioned and behind-the-times public school and university where I formed my habits of mind. It is natural for you to think that money governs England; but you must allow me to think I know better.

UNDERSHAFT. And what does govern England, pray?

STEPHEN. Character, father, character.

UNDERSHAFT. Whose character? Yours or mine?

STEPHEN. Neither yours nor mine, father, but the best elements in the English national character.

UNDERSHAFT. Stephen: Ive found your profession for you. Youre a born journalist. I'll start you with a high-toned weekly review. There!

Before Stephen can reply Sarah, Barbara, Lomax, and Cusins come in ready for walking. Barbara crosses the room to the window and looks out. Cusins drifts amiably to the armchair. Lomax remains near the door, whilst Sarah comes to her mother.

Stephen goes to the smaller writing table and busies himself with his letters.

SARAH. Go and get ready, mama: the carriage is waiting. (*Lady Britomart leaves the room.*)

UNDERSHAFT (*to Sarah*). Good day, my dear. Good afternoon, Mr Lomax.

LOMAX (*vaguely*). Ahdedoo.

UNDERSHAFT (*to Cusins*). Quite well after last night, Euripides, eh?

CUSINS. As well as can be expected.

UNDERSHAFT. Thats right. (*To Barbara.*) So you are coming to see my death and devastation factory, Barbara?

BARBARA (*at the window*). You came yesterday to see my salvation factory. I promised you a return visit.

LOMAX (*coming forward between Sarah and Undershaft*). Youll find it awfully interesting. Ive been through the Woolwich Arsenal; and it gives you a ripping feeling of security, you know, to think of the lot of beggars we could kill if it came to fighting. (*To Undershaft, with sudden solemnity.*) Still, it must be rather an awful reflection for you, from the religious point of view as it were. Youre getting on, you know, and all that.

SARAH. You dont mind Cholly's imbecility, papa, do you?

LOMAX (*much taken aback*). Oh I say!

UNDERSHAFT. Mr Lomax looks at the matter in a very proper spirit, my dear.

LOMAX. Just so. Thats all I meant, I assure you.

SARAH. Are you coming, Stephen?

STEPHEN. Well, I am rather busy—er—(*Magnanimously.*) Oh well, yes: I'll come. That is, if there is room for me.

UNDERSHAFT. I can take two with me in a little motor I am experimenting with for field use. You wont mind its being rather unfashionable. It's not painted yet; but it's bullet proof.

LOMAX (*appalled at the prospect of confronting Wilton Crescent in an unpainted motor*). Oh I say!

SARAH. The carriage for me, thank you. Barbara doesnt mind what she's seen in.

LOMAX. I say, Dolly, old chap: do you really mind the car being a guy? Because of course if you do I'll go in it. Still—

CUSINS. I prefer it.

LOMAX. Thanks awfully, old man. Come, my ownest. (*He hurries to secure his seat in the carriage. Sarah follows him.*)

CUSINS (*moodily walking across to Lady Britomart's writing table*). Why are we two coming to this Works Department of Hell? that is what I ask myself.

BARBARA. I have always thought of it as a sort of pit where lost creatures with blackened faces stirred up smoky fires and were driven and tormented by my father? Is it like that, dad?

UNDERSHAFT (*scandalized*). My dear! It is a spotlessly clean and beautiful hillside town.

CUSINS. With a Methodist chapel? Oh do say theres a Methodist chapel.

UNDERSHAFT. There are two: a Primitive one and a sophisticated one. There is even an Ethical Society; but it is not much patronized, as my men are all strongly religious. In the High Explosives Sheds they object to the presence of Agnostics as unsafe.

CUSINS. And yet they dont object to you!

BARBARA. Do they obey all your orders?

UNDERSHAFT. I never give them any orders. When I speak to one of them it is "Well, Jones, is the baby doing well? and has Mrs Jones made a good recovery?" "Nicely, thank you, sir." And thats all.

CUSINS. But Jones has to be kept in order. How do you maintain discipline among your men?

UNDERSHAFT. I dont. They do. You see, the one thing Jones wont stand is any rebellion from the man under him, or any assertion of social equality between the wife of the man with 4 shillings a week less than himself, and Mrs Jones! Of course they all rebel against me, theoretically. Practically, every man of them keeps the man just below him in his place. I never meddle with them. I never bully them. I dont even bully Lazarus. I say that certain things are to be done; but I dont order anybody to do them. I dont say, mind you, that there is no ordering about and snubbing and even bullying. The men snub the boys and order them about; the carmen snub the sweepers; the artisans snub the unskilled laborers; the foremen drive and bully both the laborers and artisans; the assistant engineers find fault with the foremen; the chief engineers drop on the assistants; the departmental managers worry the chiefs; and the clerks have tall hats and hymnbooks and keep up the social tone by refusing to associate on equal terms with anybody. The result is a colossal profit, which comes to me.

CUSINS (*revolted*). You really are a—well, what I was saying yesterday.

BARBARA. What was he saying yesterday?

UNDERSHAFT. Never mind, my dear. He thinks I have made you unhappy. Have I?

BARBARA. Do you think I can be happy in this vulgar silly dress? I! who have worn the uniform. Do you understand what you have done to me? Yesterday I had a man's soul in my hand. I set him in the way of life with his face to salvation. But when we took your money he turned back to drunkenness and derision. (*With intense conviction.*) I will never forgive you that. If I had a child, and you destroyed its body with your explosives—if you murdered Dolly with your horrible guns—I could forgive you if my forgiveness would open the gates of heaven to you. But to take a human soul from me, and turn it into the soul of a wolf! that is worse than any murder.

UNDERSHAFT. Does my daughter despair so easily? Can you strike a man to the heart and leave no mark on him?

BARBARA (*her face lighting up*). Oh, you are right: he can never be lost now: where was my faith?

CUSINS. Oh, clever clever devil!

BARBARA. You may be a devil; but God speaks through you sometimes (*She takes her father's hands and kisses them.*) You have given me back my happiness: I feel it deep down now, though my spirit is troubled.

UNDERSHAFT. You have learnt something. That always feels at first as if you had lost something.

BARBARA. Well, take me to the factory of death; and let me learn something more. There must be some truth or other behind all this frightful irony. Come, Dolly. (*She goes out.*)

CUSINS. My guardian angel! (*To Undershaft.*) Avaunt! (*He follows Barbara.*)

STEPHEN (*quietly, at the writing table*). You must not mind Cusins, father. He is a very amiable good fellow; but he is a Greek scholar and naturally a little eccentric.

UNDERSHAFT. Ah, quite so. Thank you, Stephen. Thank you. (*He goes out.*)

Stephen smiles patronizingly; buttons his coat responsibly; and crosses the room to the door. Lady Britomart, dressed for out-of-doors, opens it before he reaches it. She looks round for the others; looks at Stephen; and turns to go without a word.

STEPHEN (*embarrassed*). Mother—

LADY BRITOMART. Dont be apologetic, Stephen. And dont forget that you have outgrown your mother. (*She goes out.*)

Perivale St Andrews lies between two Middlesex hills, half climbing the northern one. It is an almost smokeless town of white walls, roofs of narrow green slates or red tiles, tall trees, domes, campaniles, and slender chimney shafts, beautifully situated and beautiful in itself. The best view of it is obtained from the crest of a slope about half a mile to the east, where the high explosives are dealt with. The foundry lies hidden in the depths between, the tops of its chimneys sprouting like huge skittles into the middle distance. Across the crest runs an emplacement of concrete, with a firestep, and a parapet which suggests a fortification, because there is a huge cannon of the obsolete Woolwich Infant pattern peering across it at the town. The cannon is mounted on an experimental gun carriage: possibly the original model of the Undershaft disappearing rampart gun alluded to by Stephen. The firestep, being a convenient place to sit, is furnished here and there with straw disc cushions; and at one place there is the additional luxury of a fur rug.

Barbara is standing on the firestep, looking over the parapet towards the town. On her right is the cannon; on her left the end of a shed raised on piles, with a ladder of three or four steps up to the door, which opens outwards and has a little wooden landing at the threshold, with a fire bucket in the corner of the landing. Several dummy soldiers more or less mutilated, with straw protruding from their gashes, have been shoved out of the way under the landing. A few others are nearly upright against the shed; and one has fallen forward and lies, like a grotsque corpse, on the emplacement. The parapet stops short of the shed, leaving a gap which is the beginning of the path down the hill through the foundry to the town. The rug is on the firestep near this gap. Down on the emplacement behind the cannon is a trolley carrying a huge conical bombshell with a red band painted on it. Further to the right is the door of an office, which, like the sheds, is of the lightest possible construction.

Cusins arrives by the path from the town.

BARBARA. Well?

CUSINS. Not a ray of hope. Everything perfect! wonderful! real! It only needs a cathedral to be a heavenly city instead of a hellish one.

BARBARA. Have you found out whether they have done anything for old Peter Shirley?

CUSINS. They have found him a job as gatekeeper and timekeeper. He's frightfully miserable. He calls the time-keeping brainwork, and says he isnt used to it; and his gate lodge is so splendid that he's ashamed to use the rooms, and skulks in the scullery.

BARBARA. Poor Peter!

Stephen arrives from the town. He carries a fieldglass.

STEPHEN (*enthusiastically*). Have you two seen the place? Why did you leave us?

CUSINS. I wanted to see everything I was not intended to see; and Barbara wanted to make the men talk.

STEPHEN. Have you found anything discreditable?

CUSINS. No. They call him Dandy Andy and are proud of his being a cunning old rascal; but it's all horribly, frightfully, immorally, unanswerably perfect.

Sarah arrives.

SARAH. Heavens! what a place! (*She crosses to the trolley.*) Did you see the nursing home!? (*She sits down on the shell.*)

STEPHEN. Did you see the libraries and schools!?

SARAH. Did you see the ball room and the banqueting chamber in the Town Hall!?

STEPHEN. Have you gone into the insurance fund, the pension fund, the building society, the various applications of cooperation!?

Undershaft comes from the office, with a sheaf of telegrams in his hand.

UNDERSHAFT. Well, have you seen everything? I'm sorry I was called away. (*Indicating the telegrams.*) Good news from Manchuria.

STEPHEN. Another Japanese victory?

UNDERSHAFT. Oh, I dont know. Which side wins does not concern us here. No: the good news is that the aerial battleship is a tremendous success. At the first trial it has wiped out a fort with three hundred soldiers in it.

CUSINS (*from the platform*). Dummy soldiers?

UNDERSHAFT (*striding across to Stephen and kicking the prostrate dummy brutally out of his way*). No: the real thing.

Cusins and Barbara exchange glances. Then Cusins sits on the step and buries his face in his hands. Barbara gravely lays her hand on his shoulder. He looks up at her in whimsical desperation.

UNDERSHAFT. Well, Stephen, what do you think of the place?

STEPHEN. Oh, magnificent. A perfect triumph of modern industry. Frankly, my dear father, I have been a fool: I had no idea of what it all meant: of the wonderful forethought, the power of organization, the administrative capacity, the financial genius, the colossal capital it represents. I have been repeating to myself as I came through your streets "Peace hath her victories no less renowned than War." I have only one misgiving about it all.

UNDERSHAFT. Out with it.

STEPHEN. Well, I cannot help thinking that all this provision for every want of your workmen may sap their independence and weaken their sense of responsibility. And greatly as we enjoyed our tea at that splendid restaurant—how they gave us all that luxury and cake and jam and cream for threepence I really cannot imagine!—still you must remember that restaurants break up home life. Look at the continent, for instance! Are you sure so much pampering is really good for the men's characters?

UNDERSHAFT. Well you see, my dear boy, when you are organizing civilization you have to make up your mind whether trouble and anxiety are good things or not. If you decide that they are, then, I take it, you simply dont organize civilization; and there you are, with trouble and anxiety enough to make us all angels! But if you decide the other way, you may as well go through with it. However, Stephen, our characters are safe here. A sufficient dose of anxiety is always provided by the fact that we may be blown to smithereens at any moment.

SARAH. By the way, papa, where do you make the explosives?

UNDERSHAFT. In separate little sheds, like that one. When one of them blows up, it costs very little; and only the people quite close to it are killed.

Stephen, who is quite close to it, looks at it rather scaredly, and moves away quickly to the cannon. At the same moment the door of the shed is thrown abruptly open; and a foreman in overalls and list slippers[21] comes out on the little landing and holds the door for Lomax, who appears in the doorway.

LOMAX (*with studied coolness*). My good fellow: you neednt get into a state of nerves. Nothing's going to happen to you; and I suppose it wouldnt be the end of the world if anything did. A little bit of British pluck is what you want, old chap. (*He descends and strolls across to Sarah.*)

UNDERSHAFT (*to the foreman*). Anything wrong, Bilton?

BILTON (*with ironic calm*). Gentleman walked into the high explosives shed and lit a cigaret, sir: thats all.

UNDERSHAFT. Ah, quite so. (*Going over to Lomax.*) Do you happen to remember what you did with the match?

LOMAX. Oh come! I'm not a fool. I took jolly good care to blow it out before I chucked it away.

BILTON. The top of it was red hot inside, sir.

LOMAX. Well, suppose it was! I didn't chuck it into any of your messes.

UNDERSHAFT. Think no more of it, Mr Lomax. By the way, would you mind lending me your matches.

LOMAX (*offering his box*). Certainly.

UNDERSHAFT. Thanks. (*He pockets the matches.*)

LOMAX (*lecturing to the company generally*). You know, these high explosives dont go off like gunpowder, except when theyre in a gun. When theyre spread loose, you can put a match to them without the least risk: they just burn quietly like a bit of paper. (*Warming to the scientific interest of the subject.*) Did you know that, Undershaft? Have you ever tried?

UNDERSHAFT. Not on a large scale, Mr Lomax. Bilton will give you a sample of gun cotton when you are leaving if you ask him. You can experiment with it at home. (*Bilton looks puzzled.*)

SARAH. Bilton will do nothing of the sort, papa. I suppose it's your business to blow up the Russians and Japs; but you might really stop short of blowing up poor Cholly. (*Bilton gives it up and retires into the shed.*)

LOMAX. My ownest, there is no danger. (*He sits beside her on the shell.*)

Lady Britomart arrives from the town with a bouquet.

LADY BRITOMART (*impetuously*). Andrew: you shouldnt have let me see this place.

UNDERSHAFT. Why, my dear?

LADY BRITOMART. Never mind why: you shouldnt have: thats all. To think of all that (*indicating the town*) being yours! and that you have kept it to yourself all these years!

UNDERSHAFT. It does not belong to me. I belong to it. It is the Undershaft inheritance.

LADY BRITOMART. It is not. Your ridiculous cannons and that noisy banging foundry may be the Undershaft inheritance; but all that plate and linen, all that furniture and those houses and orchards and gardens belong to us. They belong to me: they are not a man's business. I wont give them up. You must be out of your senses to throw them all away; and if you persist in such folly, I will call in a doctor.

UNDERSHAFT (*stooping to smell the bouquet*). Where did you get the flowers, my dear?

LADY BRITOMART. Your men presented them to me in your William Morris Labor Church.[22]

CUSINS. Oh! It needed only that. A Labor Church! (*He mounts the firestep distractedly, and leans with his elbows on the parapet, turning his back to them.*)

LADY BRITOMART. Yes, with Morris's words in mosaic letters ten feet high round the dome. NO MAN IS GOOD ENOUGH TO BE ANOTHER MAN'S MASTER. The cynicism of it!

UNDERSHAFT. It shocked the men at first, I am afraid. But now they take no more notice of it than of the ten commandments in church.

LADY BRITOMART. Andrew: you are trying to put me off the subject of the inheritance by profane jokes. Well, you shant. I dont ask it any longer for Stephen: he has inherited far too much of your perversity to be fit for it. But

---

[21]**list slippers** cloth overshoes.

[22]**Labor church** the Labor church, founded in 1891, was part of an attempt to transform the Labor movement into a kind of religious organization.

Barbara has rights as well as Stephen. Why should not Adolphus succeed to the inheritance? I could manage the town for him; and he can look after the cannons, if they are really necessary.

UNDERSHAFT. I should ask nothing better if Adolphus were a foundling. He is exactly the sort of new blood that is wanted in English business. But he's not a foundling; and theres an end of it. (*He makes for the office door.*)

CUSINS (*turning to them*). Not quite. (*They all turn and stare at him.*) I think—Mind! I am not committing myself in any way as to my future course—but I think the foundling difficulty can be got over. (*He jumps down to the emplacement.*)

UNDERSHAFT (*coming back to him*). What do you mean?

CUSINS. Well, I have something to say which is in the nature of a confession.

SARAH.
LADY BRITOMART.   } Confession!
BARBARA.
STEPHEN.

LOMAX. Oh I say!

CUSINS. Yes, a confession. Listen, all. Until I met Barbara I thought myself in the main an honorable, truthful man, because I wanted the approval of my conscience more than I wanted anything else. But the moment I saw Barbara, I wanted her far more than the approval of my conscience.

LADY BRITOMART. Adolphus!

CUSINS. It is true. You accused me yourself, Lady Brit, of joining the Army to worship Barbara; and so I did. She bought my soul like a flower at a street corner; but she bought it for herself.

UNDERSHAFT. What! Not for Dionysos or another?

CUSINS. Dionysos and all the others are in herself. I adored what was divine in her, and was therefore a true worshipper. But I was romantic about her too. I thought she was a woman of the people, and that a marriage with a professor of Greek would be far beyond the wildest social ambitions of her rank.

LADY BRITOMART. Adolphus!!

LOMAX. Oh I say!!!

CUSINS. When I learnt the horrible truth—

LADY BRITOMART. What do you mean by the horrible truth, pray?

CUSINS. That she was enormously rich; that her grandfather was an earl; that her father was the Prince of Darkness—

UNDERSHAFT. Chut!

CUSINS. —and that I was only an adventurer trying to catch a rich wife, then I stooped to deceive her about my birth.

BARBARA (*rising*). Dolly!

LADY BRITOMART. Your birth! Now Adolphus, dont dare to make up a wicked story for the sake of these wretched cannons. Remember: I have seen photographs of your parents; and the Agent General for South Western Aus-

tralia knows them personally and has assured me that they are most respectable married people.

CUSINS. So they are in Australia; but here they are outcasts. Their marriage is legal in Australia, but not in England. My mother is my father's deceased wife's sister; and in this island I am consequently a foundling.[23] (*Sensation.*)

BARBARA. Silly! (*She climbs to the cannon, and leans, listening, in the angle it makes with the parapet.*)

CUSINS. Is the subterfuge good enough, Machiavelli?

UNDERSHAFT (*thoughtfully*). Biddy: this may be a way out of the difficulty.

LADY BRITOMART. Stuff! A man cant make cannons any the better for being his own cousin instead of his proper self. (*She sits down on the rug with a bounce that expresses her downright contempt for their casuistry.*)

UNDERSHAFT (*to Cusins*). You are an educated man. That is against the tradition.

CUSINS. Once in ten thousand times it happens that the schoolboy is a born master of what they try to teach him. Greek has not destroyed my mind: it has nourished it. Besides, I did not learn it at an English public school.

UNDERSHAFT. Hm! Well, I cannot afford to be too particular: you have cornered the foundling market. Let it pass. You are eligible, Euripides: you are eligible.

BARBARA. Dolly: yesterday morning, when Stephen told us all about the tradition, you became very silent; and you have been strange and excited ever since. Were you thinking of your birth then?

CUSINS. When the finger of Destiny suddenly points at a man in the middle of his breakfast, it makes him thoughtful.

UNDERSHAFT. Aha! You have had your eye on the business, my young friend, have you?

CUSINS. Take care! There is an abyss of moral horror between me and your accursed aerial battleships.

UNDERSHAFT. Never mind the abyss for the present. Let us settle the practical details and leave your final decision open. You know that you will have to change your name. Do you object to that?

CUSINS. Would any man named Adolphus—any man called Dolly!—object to be called something else?

UNDERSHAFT. Good. Now, as to money! I propose to treat you handsomely from the beginning. You shall start at a thousand a year.

CUSINS (*with sudden heat, his spectacles twinkling with mischief*). A thousand! You dare offer a miserable thousand to the son-in-law of a millionaire! No, by Heavens, Machiavelli! you shall not cheat me. You cannot do without me; and I can do without you. I must have two thousand five hundred a year for two years. At the end of

---

[23]**The Deceased Wife's Sister Act,** later repealed, forbade marriage of a widower with his late wife's sister.

that time, if I am a failure, I go. But if I am a success, and stay on, you must give me the other five thousand.

UNDERSHAFT. What other five thousand?

CUSINS. To make the two years up to five thousand a year. The two thousand five hundred is only half pay in case I should turn out a failure. The third year I must have ten per cent on the profits.

UNDERSHAFT (taken aback). Ten per cent! Why, man, do you know what my profits are?

CUSINS. Enormous, I hope: otherwise I shall require twenty-five per cent.

UNDERSHAFT. But, Mr Cusins, this is a serious matter of business. You are not bringing any capital into the concern.

CUSINS. What! no capital! Is my mastery of Greek no capital? Is my access to the subtlest thought, the loftiest poetry yet attained by humanity, no capital? My character! my intellect! my life! my career! what Barbara calls my soul! are these no capital? Say another word; and I double my salary.

UNDERSHAFT. Be reasonable—

CUSINS (permptorily). Mr Undershaft: you have my terms. Take them or leave them.

UNDERSHAFT (recovering himself). Very well. I note your terms; and I offer you half.

CUSINS (disgusted). Half!

UNDERSHAFT (firmly). Half.

CUSINS. You call yourself a gentleman; and you offer me half!!

UNDERSHAFT. I do not call myself a gentleman; but I offer you half.

CUSINS. This to your future partner! your successor! your son-in-law!

BARBARA. You are selling your own soul, Dolly, not mine. Leave me out of the bargain, please.

UNDERSHAFT. Come! I will go a step further for Barbara's sake. I will give you three fifths; but that is my last word.

CUSINS. Done!

LOMAX. Done in the eye! Why, I get only eight hundred, you know.

CUSINS. By the way, Mac, I am a classical scholar, not an arithmetical one. Is three fifths more than half or less?

UNDERSHAFT. More, of course.

CUSINS. I would have taken two hundred and fifty. How you can succeed in business when you are willing to pay all that money to a University don who is obviously not worth a junior clerk's wages!—well! What will Lazarus say?

UNDERSHAFT. Lazarus is a gentle romantic Jew who cares for nothing but string quartets and stalls at fashionable theatres. He will be blamed for your rapacity in money matters, poor fellow! as he has hitherto been blamed for mine. You are a shark of the first order, Euripides. So much the better for the firm!

BARBARA. Is the bargain closed, Dolly? Does your soul belong to him now?

CUSINS. No: the price is settled: that is all. The real tug of war is still to come. What about the moral question?

LADY BRITOMART. There is no moral question in the matter at all, Adolphus. You must simply sell cannons and weapons to people whose cause is right and just, and refuse them to foreigners and criminals.

UNDERSHAFT (determinedly). No: none of that. You must keep the true faith of an Armorer, or you dont come in here.

CUSINS. What on earth is the true faith of an Armorer?

UNDERSHAFT. To give arms to all men who offer an honest price for them, without respect of persons or principles: to aristocrat and republican, to Nihilist and Tsar, to Capitalist and Socialist, to Protestant and Catholic, to burglar and policeman, to black man, white man and yellow man, to all sorts and conditions, all nationalities, all faiths, all follies, all causes and all crimes. The first Undershaft wrote up in his shop IF GOD GAVE THE HAND, LET NOT MAN WITHHOLD THE SWORD. The second wrote up ALL HAVE THE RIGHT TO FIGHT: NONE HAVE THE RIGHT TO JUDGE. The third wrote up TO MAN THE WEAPON: TO HEAVEN THE VICTORY. The fourth had no literary turn; so he did not write up anything; but he sold cannons to Napoleon under the nose of George the Third. The fifth wrote up PEACE SHALL NOT PREVAIL SAVE WITH A SWORD IN HER HAND. The sixth, my master, was the best of all. He wrote up NOTHING IS EVER DONE IN THIS WORLD UNTIL MEN ARE PREPARED TO KILL ONE ANOTHER IF IT IS NOT DONE. After that, there was nothing left for the seventh to say. So he wrote up, simply, UNASHAMED.

CUSINS. My good Machiavelli, I shall certainly write something up on the wall; only, as I shall write it in Greek, you wont be able to read it. But as to your Armorer's faith, if I take my neck out of the noose of my own morality I am not going to put it into the noose of yours. I shall sell cannons to whom I please and refuse them to whom I please. So there!

UNDERSHAFT. From the moment when you become Andrew Undershaft, you will never do as you please again. Dont come here lusting for power, young man.

CUSINS. If power were my aim I should not come here for it. You have no power.

UNDERSHAFT. None of my own, certainly.

CUSINS. I have more power than you, more will. You do not drive this place: it drives you. And what drives the place?

UNDERSHAFT (enigmatically). A will of which I am a part.

BARBARA (startled). Father! Do you know what you are saying; or are you laying a snare for my soul?

CUSINS. Dont listen to his metaphysics, Barbara. The place is driven by the most rascally part of society, the money hunters, the pleasure hunters, the military promotion hunters; and he is their slave.

UNDERSHAFT. Not necessarily. Remember the Armorer's Faith. I will take an order from a good man as cheerfully as from a bad one. If you good people prefer preaching and shirking to buying my weapons and fighting the rascals, dont blame me. I can make cannons: I cannot make courage and conviction. Bah! you tire me, Euripides, with your morality mongering. Ask Barbara: she understands. (*He suddenly reaches up and takes Barbara's hands, looking powerfully into her eyes.*) Tell him, my love, what power really means.

BARBARA (*hypnotized*). Before I joined the Salvation Army, I was in my own power; and the consequence was that I never knew what to do with myself. When I joined it, I had not time enough for all the things I had to do.

UNDERSHAFT (*approvingly*). Just so. And why was that, do you suppose?

BARBARA. Yesterday I should have said, because I was in the power of God. (*She resumes her self-possession, withdrawing her hands from his with a power equal to his own.*) But you came and shewed me that I was in the power of Bodger and Undershaft. Today I feel—oh! how can I put it into words? Sarah: do you remember the earthquake at Cannes, when we were little children?—how little the surprise of the first shock mattered compared to the dread and horror of waiting for the second? That is how I feel in this place today. I stood on the rock I thought eternal; and without a word of warning it reeled and crumbled under me. I was safe with an infinite wisdom watching me, an army marching to Salvation with me; and in a moment, at a stroke of your pen in a cheque book, I stood alone; and the heavens were empty. That was the first shock of the earthquake: I am waiting for the second.

UNDERSHAFT. Come, come, my daughter! dont make too much of your little tinpot tragedy. What do we do here when we spend years of work and thought and thousands of pounds of solid cash on a new gun or an aerial battleship that turns out just a hairsbreadth wrong after all? Scrap it. Scrap it without wasting another hour or another pound on it. Well, you have made for yourself something that you call a morality or a religion or what not. It doesnt fit the facts. Well, scrap it. Scrap it and get one that does fit. That is what is wrong with the world at present. It scraps its obsolete steam engines and dynamos; but it wont scrap its old prejudices and its old moralities and its old religions and its old political constitutions. Whats the result? In machinery it does very well; but in morals and religion and politics it is working at a loss that brings it nearer bankruptcy every year. Dont persist in that folly. If your old religion broke down yesterday, get a newer and a better one for tomorrow.

BARBARA. Oh how gladly I would take a better one to my soul! But you offer me a worse one. (*Turning on him with sudden vehemence.*) Justify yourself: shew me some light through the darkness of this dreadful place, with its beautifully clean workshops, and respectable workmen, and model homes.

UNDERSHAFT. Cleanliness and respectability do not need justification, Barbara: they justify themselves. I see no darkness here, no dreadfulness. In your Salvation shelter I saw poverty, misery, cold and hunger. You gave them bread and treacle and dreams of heaven. I give them thirty shillings a week to twelve thousand a year. They find their own dreams; but I look after the drainage.

BARBARA. And their souls?

UNDERSHAFT. I save their souls just as I saved yours.

BARBARA (*revolted*). You saved my soul! What do you mean?

UNDERSHAFT. I fed you and clothed you and housed you. I took care that you should have money enough to live handsomely—more than enough; so that you could be wasteful, careless, generous. That saved your soul from the seven deadly sins.

BARBARA (*bewildered*). The seven deadly sins!

UNDERSHAFT. Yes, the deadly seven. (*Counting on his fingers.*) Food, clothing, firing, rent, taxes, respectability and children. Nothing can lift those seven millstones from Man's neck but money; and the spirit cannot soar until the millstones are lifted. I lifted them from your spirit. I enabled Barbara to become Major Barbara; and I saved her from the crime of poverty.

CUSINS. Do you call poverty a crime?

UNDERSHAFT. The worst of crimes. All the other crimes are virtues beside it: all the other dishonors are chivalry itself by comparison. Poverty blights whole cities; spreads horrible pestilences; strikes dead the very souls of all who come within sight, sound, or smell of it. What you call crime is nothing: a murder here and a theft there, a blow now and a curse then: what do they matter? they are only the accidents and illnesses of life: there are not fifty genuine professional criminals in London. But there are millions of poor people, abject people, dirty people, ill fed, ill clothed people. They poison us morally and physically: they kill the happiness of society: they force us to do away with our own liberties and to organize unnatural cruelties for fear they should rise against us and drag us down into their abyss. Only fools fear crime: we all fear poverty. Pah! (*Turning on Barbara.*) you talk of your half-saved ruffian in West Ham: you accuse me of dragging his soul back to perdition. Well, bring him to me here; and I will drag his soul back again to salvation for you. Not by words and dreams; but by thirtyeight shillings a week, a sound house in a handsome street, and a permanent job. In three weeks he will have a fancy waistcoat; in three months a tall hat and a chapel sitting; before the end of the year he will shake hands with a duchess at a Primrose League meeting, and join the Conservative Party.

BARBARA. And will he be the better for that?

UNDERSHAFT. You know he will. Dont be a hypocrite, Barbara. He will be better fed, better housed, better clothed, better behaved; and his children will be pounds heavier and bigger. That will be better than an American cloth mattress in a shelter, chopping firewood, eating bread and treacle, and being forced to kneel down from time to time to thank heaven for it: knee drill, I think you call it. It is cheap work converting starving men with a Bible in one hand and a slice of bread in the other. I will undertake to convert West Ham to Mahometanism on the same terms. Try your hand on my men: their souls are hungry because their bodies are full.

BARBARA. And leave the east end to starve?

UNDERSHAFT (*his energetic tone dropping into one of bitter and brooding remembrance*). I was an east ender. I moralized and starved until one day I swore that I would be a full-fed free man at all costs; that nothing should stop me except a bullet, neither reason nor morals nor the lives of other men. I said "Thou shalt starve ere I starve"; and with that word I became free and great. I was a dangerous man until I had my will: now I am a useful, beneficent, kindly person. That is the history of most self-made millionaires, I fancy. When it is the history of every Englishman we shall have an England worth living in.

LADY BRITOMART. Stop making speeches, Andrew. This is not the place for them.

UNDERSHAFT (*punctured*). My dear: I have no other means of conveying my ideas.

LADY BRITOMART. Your ideas are nonsense. You got on because you were selfish and unscrupulous.

UNDERSHAFT. Not at all. I had the strongest scruples about poverty and starvation. Your moralists are quite unscrupulous about both: they make virtues of them. I had rather be a thief than a pauper. I had rather be a murderer than a slave. I dont want to be either; but if you force the alternative on me, then, by Heaven, I'll choose the braver and more moral one. I hate poverty and slavery worse than any other crimes whatsoever. And let me tell you this. Poverty and slavery have stood up for centuries to your sermons and leading articles: they will not stand up to my machine guns. Dont preach at them: dont reason with them. Kill them.

BARBARA. Killing. Is that your remedy for everything?

UNDERSHAFT. It is the final test of conviction, the only lever strong enough to overturn a social system, the only way of saying Must. Let six hundred and seventy fools loose in the streets; and three policemen can scatter them. But huddle them together in a certain house in Westminster; and let them go through certain ceremonies and call themselves certain names until at last they get the courage to kill; and your six hundred and seventy fools become a government. Your pious mob fills up ballot papers and imagines it is governing its masters; but the ballot paper that really governs is the paper that has a bullet wrapped up in it.

CUSINS. That is perhaps why, like most intelligent people, I never vote.

UNDERSHAFT. Vote! Bah! When you vote, you only change the names of the cabinet. When you shoot, you pull down governments, inaugurate new epochs, abolish old orders and set up new. Is that historically true, Mr Learned Man, or is it not?

CUSINS. It is historically true. I loathe having to admit it. I repudiate your sentiments. I abhor your nature. I defy you in every possible way. Still, it is true. But it ought not to be true.

UNDERSHAFT. Ought! ought! ought! ought! ought! Are you going to spend your life saying ought, like the rest of our moralists? Turn your oughts into shalls, man. Come and make explosives with me. Whatever can blow men up can blow society up. The history of the world is the history of those who had courage enough to embrace this truth. Have you the courage to embrace it, Barbara?

LADY BRITOMART. Barbara: I positively forbid you to listen to your father's abominable wickedness. And you, Adolphus, ought to know better than to go about saying that wrong things are true. What does it matter whether they are true if they are wrong?

UNDERSHAFT. What does it matter whether they are wrong if they are true?

LADY BRITOMART (*rising*). Children: come home instantly. Andrew: I am exceedingly sorry I allowed you to call on us. You are wickeder than ever. Come at once.

BARBARA (*shaking her head*). It's no use running away from wicked people, mamma.

LADY BRITOMART. It is every use. It shews your disapprobation of them.

BARBARA. It does not save them.

LADY BRITOMART. I can see that you are going to disobey me. Sarah: are you coming home or are you not?

SARAH. I daresay it's very wicked of papa to make cannons; but I dont think I shall cut him on that account.

LOMAX (*pouring oil on the troubled waters*). The fact is, you know, there is a certain amount of tosh about this notion of wickedness. It doesnt work. You must look at facts. Not that I would say a word in favor of anything wrong; but then, you see, all sorts of chaps are always doing all sorts of things; and we have to fit them in somehow, dont you know. What I mean is that you cant go cutting everybody; and thats about what it comes to. (*Their rapt attention to his eloquence makes him nervous.*) Perhaps I dont make myself clear.

LADY BRITOMART. You are lucidity itself, Charles. Because Andrew is successful and has plenty of money to give to Sarah, you will flatter him and encourage him in his wickedness.

LOMAX (*unruffled*). Well, where the carcase is, there will the eagles be gathered, dont you know. (*To Undershaft.*) Eh? What?

UNDERSHAFT. Precisely. By the way, may I call you Charles?

LOMAX. Delighted. Cholly is the usual ticket.

UNDERSHAFT (*to Lady Britomart*). Biddy—

LADY BRITOMART (*violently*). Dont dare call me Biddy. Charles Lomax: you are a fool. Adolphus Cusins: you are a Jesuit. Stephen: you are a prig. Barbara: you are a lunatic. Andrew: you are a vulgar tradesman. Now you all know my opinion; and my conscience is clear, at all events. (*She sits down with a vehemence that the rug fortunately softens.*)

UNDERSHAFT. My dear: you are the incarnation of morality. (*She snorts.*) Your conscience is clear and your duty done when you have called everybody names. Come, Euripides! it is getting late; and we all want to go home. Make up your mind.

CUSINS. Understand this, you old demon—

LADY BRITOMART. Adolphus!

UNDERSHAFT. Let him alone, Biddy. Proceed, Euripides.

CUSINS. You have me in a horrible dilemma. I want Barbara.

UNDERSHAFT. Like all young men, you greatly exaggerate the difference between one young woman and another.

BARBARA. Quite true, Dolly.

CUSINS. I also want to avoid being a rascal.

UNDERSHAFT (*with biting contempt*). You lust for personal righteousness, for self-approval, for what you call a good conscience, for what Barbara calls salvation, for what I call patronizing people who are not so lucky as yourself.

CUSINS. I do not: all the poet in me recoils from being a good man. But there are things in me that I must reckon with. Pity—

UNDERSHAFT. Pity! The scavenger of misery.

CUSINS. Well, love.

UNDERSHAFT. I know. You love the needy and the outcast: you love the oppressed races, the negro, the Indian ryot,[24] the underdog everywhere. Do you love the Japanese? Do you love the French? Do you love the English?

CUSINS. No. Every true Englishman detests the English. We are the wickedest nation on earth; and our success is a moral horror.

UNDERSHAFT. That is what comes of your gospel of love, is it?

CUSINS. May I not love even my father-in-law?

UNDERSHAFT. Who wants your love, man? By what right do you take the liberty of offering it to me? I will have your due heed and respect, or I will kill you. But your love! Damn your impertinence!

CUSINS (*grinning*). I may not be able to control my affections, Mac.

UNDERSHAFT. You are fencing, Euripides. You are weakening: your grip is slipping. Come! try your last weapon. Pity and love have broken in your hand: forgiveness is still left.

CUSINS. No: forgiveness is a beggar's refuge. I am with you there: we must pay our debts.

UNDERSHAFT. Well said. Come! you will suit me. Remember the words of Plato.

CUSINS (*starting*). Plato! You dare quote Plato to me!

UNDERSHAFT. Plato says, my friend, that society cannot be saved until either the Professors of Greek take to making gunpowder, or else the makers of gunpowder become Professors of Greek.

CUSINS. Oh, tempter, cunning tempter!

UNDERSHAFT. Come! choose, man, choose.

CUSINS. But perhaps Barbara will not marry me if I make the wrong choice.

BARBARA. Perhaps not.

CUSINS (*desperately perplexed*). You hear!

BARBARA. Father: do you love nobody?

UNDERSHAFT. I love my best friend.

LADY BRITOMART. And who is that, pray?

UNDERSHAFT. My bravest enemy. That is the man who keeps me up to the mark.

CUSINS. You know, the creature is really a sort of poet in his way. Suppose he is a great man, after all!

UNDERSHAFT. Suppose you stop talking and make up your mind, my young friend.

CUSINS. But you are driving me against my nature. I hate war.

UNDERSHAFT. Hatred is the coward's revenge for being intimidated. Dare you make war on war? Here are the means: my friend Mr. Lomax is sitting on them.

LOMAX (*springing up*). Oh I say! You dont mean that this thing is loaded, do you? My ownest: come off it.

SARAH (*sitting placidly on the shell*). If I am to be blown up, the more thoroughly it is done the better. Dont fuss, Cholly.

LOMAX (*to Undershaft, strongly remonstrant*). Your own daughter, you know!

UNDERSHAFT. So I see. (*To Cusins.*) Well, my friend, may we expect you here at six tomorrow morning?

CUSINS (*firmly*). Not on any account. I will see the whole establishment blown up with its own dynamite before I will get up at five. My hours are healthy, rational hours: eleven to five.

UNDERSHAFT. Come when you please: before a week you will come at six and stay until I turn you out for the sake of your health. (*Calling.*) Bilton! (*He turns to Lady Britomart, who rises.*) My dear: let us leave these two young people to themselves for a moment. (*Bilton comes from the shed.*) I am going to take you through the gun cotton shed.

BILTON (*barring the way*). You cant take anything explosive in here, sir.

LADY BRITOMART. What do you mean? Are you alluding to me?

BILTON (*unmoved*). No, maam. Mr Undershaft has the other gentleman's matches in his pocket.

LADY BRITOMART (*abruptly*). Oh! I beg your pardon. (*She goes into the shed.*)

---

[24]**ryot** tenant farmer.

UNDERSHAFT. Quite right, Bilton, quite right: here you are. (*He gives Bilton the box of matches.*) Come, Stephen. Come, Charles. Bring Sarah. (*He passes into the shed.*)

Bilton opens the box and deliberately drops the matches into the fire-bucket.

LOMAX. Oh! I say. (*Bilton stolidly hands him the empty box.*) Infernal nonsense! Pure scientific ignorance! (*He goes in.*)

SARAH. Am I all right, Bilton?

BILTON. Youll have to put on list slippers, miss: thats all. Weve got em inside. (*She goes in.*)

STEPHEN (*very seriously to Cusins*). Dolly, old fellow, think. Think before you decide. Do you feel that you are a sufficiently practical man? It is a huge undertaking, an enormous responsibility. All this mass of business will be Greek to you.

CUSINS. Oh, I think it will be much less difficult than Greek.

STEPHEN. Well, I just want to say this before I leave you to yourselves. Dont let anything I have said about right and wrong prejudice you against this great chance in life. I have satisfied myself that the business is one of the highest character and a credit to our country. (*Emotionally.*) I am very proud of my father. I—(*Unable to proceed, he presses Cusins' hand and goes hastily into the shed, followed by Bilton.*)

Barbara and Cusins, left alone together, look at one another silently.

CUSINS. Barbara: I am going to accept this offer.

BARBARA. I thought you would.

CUSINS. You understand, dont you, that I had to decide without consulting you. If I had thrown the burden of the choice on you, you would sooner or later have despised me for it.

BARBARA. Yes; I did not want you to sell your soul for me any more than for this inheritance.

CUSINS. It is not the sale of my soul that troubles me: I have sold it too often to care about that. I have sold it for a professorship. I have sold it for an income. I have sold it to escape being imprisoned for refusing to pay taxes for hangmen's ropes and unjust wars and things that I abhor. What is all human conduct but the daily and hourly sale of our souls for trifles? What I am now selling it for is neither money nor position nor comfort, but for reality and for power.

BARBARA. You know that you will have no power, and that he has none.

CUSINS. I know. It is not for myself alone. I want to make power for the world.

BARBARA. I want to make power for the world too; but it must be spiritual power.

CUSINS. I think all power is spiritual: these cannons will not go off by themselves. I have tried to make spiritual power by teaching Greek. But the world can never be really touched by a dead language and a dead civilization. The people must have power; and the people cannot have Greek. Now the power that is made here can be wielded by all men.

BARBARA. Power to burn women's houses down and kill their sons and tear their husbands to pieces.

CUSINS. You cannot have power for good without having power for evil too. Even mother's milk nourishes murderers as well as heroes. This power which only tears men's bodies to pieces has never been so horribly abused as the intellectual power, the imaginative power, the poetic, religious power that can enslave men's souls. As a teacher of Greek I gave the intellectual man weapons against the common man. I now want to give the common man weapons against the inellectual man. I love the common people. I want to arm them against the lawyers, the doctors, the priests, the literary men, the professors, the artists, and the politicians, who, once in authority, are more disastrous and tyrannical than all the fools, rascals, and impostors. I want a power simple enough for common men to use, yet strong enough to force the intellectual oligarchy to use its genius for the general good.

BARBARA. Is there no higher power than that? (*Pointing to the shell.*)

CUSINS. Yes; but that power can destroy the higher powers just as a tiger can destroy a man: therefore Man must master that power first. I admitted this when the Turks and Greeks were last at war. My best pupil went out to fight for Hellas. My parting gift to him was not a copy of Plato's Republic, but a revolver and a hundred Undershaft cartridges. The blood of every Turk he shot—if he shot any—is on my head as well as on Undershaft's. That act committed me to this place for ever. Your father's challenge has beaten me. Dare I make war on war? I dare. I must. I will. And now, is it all over between us?

BARBARA (*touched by his evident dread of her answer*). Silly baby Dolly! How could it be!

CUSINS (*overjoyed*). Then you—you—you—Oh for my drum! (*He flourishes imaginary drumsticks.*)

BARBARA (*angered by his levity*). Take care, Dolly, take care. Oh, if only I could get away from you and from father and from it all! if I could have the wings of a dove and fly away to heaven!

CUSINS. And leave me!

BARBARA. Yes, you, and all the other naughty mischievous children of men. But I cant. I was happy in the Salvation Army for a moment. I escaped from the world into a paradise of enthusiasm and prayer and soul saving; but the moment our money ran short, it all came back to Bodger: it was he who saved our people: he, and the Prince of Darkness, my papa. Undershaft and Bodger: their hands stretch everywhere: when we feed a starving fellow creature, it is with their bread, because there is no other bread; when we tend the sick, it is in the hospitals they endow; if we turn from the churches they build, we must kneel on the stones of the streets they pave. As long as that lasts, there is no getting away from them. Turning our backs on Bodger and Undershaft is turning our backs on life.

CUSINS. I thought you were determined to turn your back on the wicked side of life.

BARBARA. There is no wicked side: life is all one. And I never wanted to shirk my share in whatever evil must be endured, whether it be sin or suffering. I wish I could cure you of middle-class ideas, Dolly.

CUSINS (*gasping*). Middle cl—! A snub! A social snub to me! from the daughter of a foundling!

BARBARA. That is why I have no class, Dolly: I come straight out of the heart of the whole people. If I were middle-class I should turn my back on my father's business; and we should both live in an artistic drawing room, with you reading the reviews in one corner, and I in the other at the piano, playing Schumann: both very superior persons, and neither of us a bit of use. Sooner than that, I would sweep out the guncotton shed, or be one of Bodger's barmaids. Do you know what would have happened if you had refused papa's offer?

CUSINS. I wonder!

BARBARA. I should have given you up and married the man who accepted it. After all, my dear old mother has more sense than any of you. I felt like her when I saw this place—felt that I must have it—that never, never, never could I let it go; only she thought it was the houses and the kitchen ranges and the linen and china, when it was really all the human souls to be saved: not weak souls in starved bodies, sobbing with gratitude for a scrap of bread and treacle, but fullfed, quarrelsome, snobbish, uppish creatures, all standing on their little rights and dignities, and thinking that my father ought to be greatly obliged to them for making so much money for him—and so he ought. That is where salvation is really wanted. My father shall never throw it in my teeth again that my converts were bribed with bread. (*She is transfigured.*) I have got rid of the bribe of bread. I have got rid of the bribe of heaven. Let God's work be done for its own sake: the work he had to create us to do because it cannot be done except by living men and women. When I die, let

him be in my debt, not I in his; and let me forgive him as becomes a woman of my rank.

CUSINS. Then the way of life lies through the factory of death?

BARBARA. Yes, through the raising of hell to heaven and of man to God, through the unveiling of an eternal light in the Valley of The Shadow. (*Seizing him with both hands.*) Oh, did you think my courage would never come back? did you believe that I was a deserter? that I, who have stood in the streets, and taken my people to my heart, and talked of the holiest and greatest things with them, could ever turn back and chatter foolishly to fashionable people about nothing in a drawing room? Never, never, never, never: Major Barbara will die with the colors. Oh! and I have my dear little Dolly boy still; and he has found me my place and my work. Glory Hallelujah! (*She kisses him.*)

CUSINS. My dearest: consider my delicate health. I cannot stand as much happiness as you can.

BARBARA. Yes: it is not easy work being in love with me, is it? But it's good for you. (*She runs to the shed, and calls, childlike.*) Mamma! Mamma! (*Bilton comes out of the shed, followed by Undershaft.*) I want Mamma.

UNDERSHAFT. She is taking off her list slippers, dear. (*He passes on to Cusins.*) Well? What does she say?

CUSINS. She has gone right up into the skies.

LADY BRITOMART (*coming from the shed and stopping on the steps, obstructing Sarah, who follows with Lomax. Barbara clutches like a baby at her mother's skirt*). Barbara: when will you learn to be independent and to act and think for yourself? I know as well as possible what that cry of "Mamma, Mamma," means. Always running to me!

SARAH (*touching Lady Britomart's ribs with her finger tips and imitating a bicycle horn*). Pip! pip!

LADY BRITOMART (*highly indignant*). How dare you say Pip! pip! to me, Sarah? You are both very naughty children. What do you want, Barbara?

BARBARA. I want a house in the village to live in with Dolly. (*Dragging at the skirt.*) Come and tell me which one to take.

UNDERSHAFT (*to Cusins*). Six o'clock tomorrow morning, Euripides.

THE END

TOPICS FOR CRITICAL THINKING AND WRITING

 ### THE PLAY ON THE PAGE

1. What is the basic comic situation in Lady Britomart's dialogue with Stephen at the beginning of the play? Do we laugh with her or at her, or both? Explain.

2. When Undershaft is confused about which persons are his children, do we laugh with him or at him, or both? Explain. What sort of man had we expected? What sort of man does he seem to be in this scene?

3. In a paragraph characterize Barbara on the basis of her lines in Act 1.

4. The opening dialogue in Act 2, between Snobby Price and Rummy Mitchens, suggests that those who seek help from the Salvation Army are hypocrites. How does Shaw make Rummy likeable, and how does he prevent us from seeing Jenny and Barbara as mere dupes?

5. Is it a defect that Stephen, who was prominent in Act 1, plays only a small part in Act 3? Should his rebellion against his mother, in a way foreshadowed in the first act, have been made more of? Or did Shaw rightly move to bigger game? Explain.

6. What arguments can be offered to support the view that Cusins, and not Barbara or Undershaft, is the central figure in the play? Do these arguments convince us that Cusins is as successfully created as Barbara and Undershaft, or do we find him less memorable?

7. Aristotle's terms *peripeteia* (reversal) and *anagnorisis* (recognition), are commonly used in discussions of tragedy (see p. 34), but they can also be useful in discussions of comedy. What reversals and recognitions occur in *Major Barbara?* When Bill Walker says, "Wot prawce selvytion nah?" is this recognition the point toward which the play has been moving? Has he a point? The whole point?

8. Shaw once said, "It is the business of a writer of comedy to wound the susceptibilities of his audience. The classic definition of his function is 'the chastening of morals by ridicule.'" Does *Major Barbara* wound susceptibilities? If so, to any purpose? Is the play a serious examination of capitalism, charity, and religion, or does the clowning (e.g., Lady Britomart's "I know your quiet, simple, refined, poetic people like Adolphus: quite content with the best of everything," obliterate the ideological content? Explain. Consider Undershaft's speeches on power on pages 542 and 547. Are they contradictory? If so, do they indicate that Shaw is writing amusing speeches but is not seriously concerned with the development of an idea? Consider, too, Cusins' assertion (p. 551) that he wishes to help the common man by arming him against the lawyer, the doctor, the priest, the literary man, the professor, and so on. How will the manufacture of weapons help the common man?

9. One of the chief theories of laughter is neatly stated in Thomas Hobbes's *Leviathan* (1651):

> *Sudden Glory,* is the passion which maketh those *Grimaces* called Laughter; and is caused either by some sudden act of their own, that pleaseth them; or by the apprehension of some deformed thing in another, in comparison whereof they suddenly applaud themselves.

If *Major Barbara* evokes laughter, is the laughter of Hobbes's sort? Does Hobbes's theory cover any or all laughable occurrences?

☻☻ THE PLAY ON THE STAGE

10. Shaw is known for his detailed stage directions, but of course he can specify only a relatively few of a performer's actions. Take the first fifteen or so speeches, and prepare a detailed commentary on how you would hope the actors would deliver them.

11. On one occasion Shaw said that the scene in which Barbara pits herself against Bill is a love scene. Reread the scene and think about staging it in a way that would bring out Shaw's view.

12. At the beginning of the final act, attention is drawn to the fact that Barbara is not wearing the Salvation Army uniform. Nothing is said of Cusins's garment. If you were directing the play, would you have him wear the uniform? Explain.

13. What actors—or persons known to your classmates—would you cast in the chief roles in the play?

A CONTEXT FOR *MAJOR BARBARA*

SELECTIONS FROM SHAW'S PREFACE

[Shaw usually equipped the published versions of his plays with lengthy prefaces, not so much discussing the plays themselves as discussing issues associated with the plays. His preface to *Major Barbara* was no exception. We reprint here some of the most relevant comments.]

THE GOSPEL OF ST. ANDREW UNDERSHAFT

In the millionaire Undershaft I have represented a man who has become intellectually and spiritually as well as practically conscious of the irresistible natural truth which we all abhor and repudiate; to wit, that the greatest of our evils, and the worst of our crimes is poverty, and that our first duty, to which every other consideration should be sacrificed, is not to be poor. "Poor but honest," "the respectable poor," and such phrases are as intolerable and as immoral as "drunken but amiable," "fraudulent but a good after-dinner speaker," "splendidly criminal," or the like. Security, the chief pretense of civilization, cannot exist where the worst of dangers, the danger of poverty, hangs over everyone's head, and where the alleged protection of our persons from violence is only an accidental result of the existence of a police force whose real business is to force the poor man to see his children starve whilst idle people overfeed pet dogs with the money that might feed and clothe them.

. . .

Now what does this Let Him Be Poor mean? It means let him be weak. Let him be ignorant. Let him become a nucleus of disease. Let him be a standing exhibition and example of ugliness and dirt. Let him have rickety children. Let him be cheap, and drag his fellows down to his own price by selling himself to do their work. Let his habitations turn our cities into poisonous congeries of slums. Let his daughters infect our young men with the diseases of the streets, and his sons revenge him by turning the nation's manhood into scrofula, cowardice, cruelty, hypocrisy, political imbecility, and all the other fruits of oppression and malnutrition. Let the undeserving become still less deserving; and let the deserving lay up for himself, not treasures in heaven, but horrors in hell upon earth. This being so, is it really wise to let him be poor? Would he not do ten times less harm as a prosperous burglar, incendiary, ravisher or murderer, to the utmost limits of humanity's comparatively negligible impulses in these directions? Suppose we were to abolish all penalties for such activities, and decide that poverty is the one thing we will not tolerate—that every adult with less than, say, £365 a year, shall be painlessly but inexorably killed, and every hungry half naked child forcibly fattened and clothed, would not that be an enormous improvement on our existing system, which has already destroyed so many civilizations, and is visibly destroying ours in the same way?

Is there any radicle of such legislation in our parliamentary system? Well, there are two measures just sprouting in the political soil, which may conceivably grow to something valuable. One is the institution of a Legal Minimum Wage. The other, Old Age Pensions. But there is a better plan than either of these. Some time ago I mentioned the subject of Universal Old Age Pensions to my fellow Socialist Cobden-Sanderson, famous as an artist-craftsman in bookbinding and printing. "Why not Universal Pensions for Life?" said Cobden-Sanderson. In saying this, he solved the industrial problem at a stroke. At present we say callously to each citizen "If you want money, earn it" as if his having or not having it were a matter that concerned himself alone. We do not even secure for him the opportunity of earning it: on the contrary, we allow our industry to be organized in open dependence on the maintenance of "a reserve army of unemployed" for the sake of "elasticity." The sensible course would be Cobden-Sanderson's: that is, to give every man enough to live well on, so as to guarantee the community against the possibility of a case of the malignant disease of poverty, and then (necessarily) to see that he earned it.

Undershaft, the hero of Major Barbara, is simply a man who, having grasped the fact that poverty is a crime, knows that when society offered him the alternative of poverty or a lucrative trade in death and destruction, it offered him, not a choice between opulent villainy and humble virtue, but

between energetic enterprise and cowardly infamy. His conduct stands the Kantian test, which Peter Shirley's does not. Peter Shirley is what we call the honest poor man. Undershaft is what we call the wicked rich one: Shirley is Lazarus, Undershaft Dives. Well, the misery of the world is due to the fact that the great mass of men act and believe as Peter Shirley acts and believes. If they acted and believed as Undershaft acts and believes, the immediate result would be a revolution of incalculable beneficence. To be wealthy, says Undershaft, is with me a point of honor for which I am prepared to kill at the risk of my own life. This preparedness is, as he says, the final test of sincerity. Like Froissart's medieval hero, who saw that "to rob and pill was a good life," he is not the dupe of that public sentiment against killing which is propagated and endowed by people who would otherwise be killed themselves, or of the mouth-honor paid to poverty and obedience by rich and insubordinate do-nothings who want to rob the poor without courage and command them without superiority. Froissart's knight, in placing the achievement of a good life before all the other duties—which indeed are not duties at all when they conflict with it, but plain wickedness—behaved bravely, admirably, and, in the final analysis, public-spiritedly. Medieval society, on the other hand, behaved very badly indeed in organizing itself so stupidly that a good life could be achieved by robbing and pilling. If the knight's contemporaries had been all as resolute as he, robbing and pilling would have been the shortest way to the gallows, just as, if we were all as resolute and clearsighted as Undershaft, an attempt to live by means of what is called "an independent income" would be the shortest way to the lethal chamber. But as, thanks to our political imbecility and personal cowardice (fruits of poverty, both), the best imitation of a good life now procurable is life on an independent income, all sensible people aim at securing such an income, and are, of course, careful to legalize and moralize both it and all the actions and sentiments which lead to it and support it as an institution. What else can they do? They know, of course, that they are rich because others are poor. But they cannot help that: it is for the poor to repudiate poverty when they have had enough of it. The thing can be done easily enough: the demonstrations to the contrary made by the economists, jurists, moralists and sentimentalists hired by the rich to defend them, or even doing the work gratuitously out of sheer folly and abjectness, impose only on those who want to be imposed on.

. . .

THE SALVATION ARMY

When *Major Barbara* was produced in London, the second act was reported in an important northern newspaper as a withering attack on the Salvation Army, and the despairing ejaculation of Barbara deplored by a London daily as a tasteless blasphemy. And they were set right, not by the professed critics of the theater, but by religious and philosophical publicists like Sir Oliver Lodge and Dr. Stanton Coit, and strenuous Nonconformist journalists like William Stead, who not only understood the act as well as the Salvationists themselves, but also saw it in its relation to the religious life of the nation, a life which seems to lie not only outside the sympathy of many of our theater critics, but actually outside their knowledge of society. Indeed nothing could be more ironically curious than the confrontation Major Barbara effected of the theater enthusiasts with the religious enthusiasts. On the one hand was the playgoer, always seeking pleasure, paying exorbitantly for it, suffering unbearable discomforts for it, and hardly ever getting it. On the other hand was the Salvationist, repudiating gaiety and courting effort and sacrifice, yet always in the wildest spirits, laughing, joking, singing, rejoicing, drumming, and tambourining: his life flying by in a flash of excitement, and his death arriving as a climax of triumph. And, if you please, the playgoer despising the Salvationist as a joyless person, shut out from the heaven of the theater, self-condemned to a life of hideous gloom; and the Salvationist mourning over the playgoer as over a prodigal with vine leaves in his hair, careering outrageously to hell amid the popping of champagne corks and the ribald laughter of sirens! Could misunderstanding be more complete, or sympathy worse misplaced?

Fortunately, the Salvationists are more accessible to the religious character of the drama than the playgoers to the gay energy and artistic fertility of religion. They can see, when it is pointed out to them, that a theater, as a place where two or three are gathered together, takes from that divine presence an inalienable sanctity of which the grossest and profanest farce can no more deprive it than a hypocritical sermon by a snobbish bishop can desecrate Westminster Abbey. But in our professional playgoers this indispensable preliminary conception of sanctity seems wanting. They talk of actors as mimes and mummers, and I fear, think of dramatic authors as liars and pandars, whose main business is the voluptuous soothing of the tired city speculator when what he calls the serious business of the day is over. Passion, the life of drama, means nothing to them but primitive sexual excitement: such phrases as "impassioned poetry" or "passionate love of truth" have fallen quite out of their vocabulary and been replaced by "passional crime" and the like. They assume, as far as I can gather, that people in whom passion has a larger scope are passionless and therefore uninteresting. Consequently they come to think of religious people as people who are not interesting and not amusing. And so, when Barbara cuts the regular Salvation Army jokes, and snatches a kiss from her lover across his drum, the devotees of the theater think they ought to appear shocked, and conclude that the whole play is an elaborate mockery of the Army. And then

either hypocritically rebuke me for mocking, or foolishly take part in the supposed mockery!

Even the handful of mentally competent critics got into difficulties over my demonstration of the economic deadlock in which the Salvation Army finds itself. Some of them thought that the Army would not have taken money from a distiller and a cannon founder: others thought it should not have taken it: all assumed more or less definitely that it reduced itself to absurdity or hypocrisy by taking it. On the first point the reply of the Army itself was prompt and conclusive. As one of its officers said, they would take money from the devil himself and be only too glad to get it out of his hands and into God's. They gratefully acknowledged that publicans not only give them money but allow them to collect it in the bar—sometimes even when there is a Salvation meeting outside preaching teetotalism. In fact, they questioned the verisimilitude of the play, not because Mrs Baines took the money, but because Barbara refused it.

On the point that the Army ought not to take such money, its justification is obvious. It must take the money because it cannot exist without money, and there is no other money to be had. Practically all the spare money in the country consists of a mass of rent, interest, and profit, every penny of which is bound up with crime, drink, prostitution, disease, and all the evil fruits of poverty, as inextricably as with enterprise, wealth, commercial probity, and national prosperity. The notion that you can earmark certain coins as tainted is an unpractical individualist superstition. Nonetheless the fact that all our money is tainted gives a very severe shock to earnest young souls when some dramatic instance of the taint first makes them conscious of it.

...

WEAKNESSES OF THE SALVATION ARMY

For the present, however, it is not my business to flatter the Salvation Army. Rather must I point out to it that it has almost as many weaknesses as the Church of England itself. It is building up a business organization which will compel it eventually to see that its present staff of enthusiast-commanders shall be succeeded by a bureaucracy of men of business who will be no better than bishops, and perhaps a good deal more unscrupulous. That has always happened sooner or later to great orders founded by saints; and the order founded by St William Booth is not exempt from the same danger. It is even more dependent than the Church on rich people who would cut off supplies at once if it began to preach that indispensable revolt against poverty which must also be a revolt against riches. It is hampered by a heavy contingent of pious elders who are not really Salvationists at all, but Evangelicals of the old school. It still, as Commissioner Howard affirms, "sticks to Moses," which is flat nonsense at this time of day if the Commissioner means, as I am afraid he does, that the

Book of Genesis contains a trustworthy scientific account of the origin of species, and that the god to whom Jephthah sacrificed his daughter is any less obviously a tribal idol than Dagon or Chemosh.

Further, there is still too much other-worldliness about the Army. Like Frederick's grenadier, the Salvationist wants to live forever (the most monstrous way of crying for the moon); and though it is evident to anyone who has ever heard General Booth and his best officers that they would work as hard for human salvation as they do at present if they believed that death would be the end of them individually, they and their followers have a bad habit of talking as if the Salvationists were heroically enduring a very bad time on earth as an investment which will bring them in dividends later on in the form, not of a better life to come for the whole world, but of an eternity spent by themselves personally in a sort of bliss which would bore any active person to a second death. Surely the truth is that the Salvationists are unusually happy people. And is it not the very diagnostic of true salvation that it shall overcome the fear of death? Now the man who has come to believe that there is no such thing as death, the change so called being merely the transition to an exquisitely happy and utterly careless life, has not overcome the fear of death at all: on the contrary, it has overcome him so completely that he refuses to die on any terms whatever. I do not call a Salvationist really saved until he is ready to lie down cheerfully on the scrap heap, having paid scot and lot and something over, and let his eternal life pass on to renew its youth in the battalions of the future.

Then there is the nasty lying habit called confession, which the Army encourages because it lends itself to dramatic oratory, with plenty of thrilling incident. For my part, when I hear a convert relating the violences and oaths and blasphemies he was guilty of before he was saved, making out that he was a very terrible fellow then and is the most contrite and chastened of Christians now, I believe him no more than I believe the millionaire who says he came up to London or Chicago as a boy with only three halfpence in his pocket.

. . .

And here my disagreement with the Salvation Army, and with all propagandists of the Cross (which I loathe as I loathe all gibbets) becomes deep indeed. Forgiveness, absolution, atonement, are figments: punishment is only a pretense of canceling one crime by another; and you can no more have forgiveness without vindictiveness than you can have a cure without a disease. You will never get a high morality from people who conceive that their misdeeds are revocable and pardonable, or in a society where absolution and expiation are officially provided for us all. The demand may be very real; but the supply is spurious. Thus Bill Walker, in my play, having assaulted the Salvation Lass, presently finds himself overwhelmed with an intolerable conviction of sin under the skilled treatment of Barbara. Straightway he begins to try to

unassault the lass and deruffianize his deed, first by getting punished for it in kind, and, when that relief is denied him, by fining himself a pound to compensate the girl. He is foiled both ways. He finds the Salvation Army is inexorable as fact itself. It will not punish him: it will not take his money. It will not tolerate a redeemed ruffian: it leaves him no means of salvation except ceasing to be a ruffian. In doing this, the Salvation Army instinctively grasps the central truth of Christianity, and discards its central superstition: that central truth being the vanity of revenge and punishment, and that central superstition the salvation of the world by the gibbet.

For, be it noted, Bill has assaulted an old and starving woman also; and for this worse offense he feels no remorse whatever, because she makes it clear that her malice is as great as his own. "Let her have the law of me, as she said she would," says Bill: "what I done to her is no more on what you might call my conscience than sticking a pig." This shows a perfectly natural and wholesome state of mind on his part. The old woman, like the law she threatens him with, is perfectly ready to play the game of retaliation with him: to rob him if he steals, to flog him if he strikes, to murder him if he kills. By example and precept the law and public opinion teach him to impose his will on others by anger, violence, and cruelty, and to wipe off the moral score by punishment. That is sound Crosstianity. But his Crosstianity has got entangled with something which Barbara calls Christianity, and which unexpectedly causes her to refuse to play the hangman's game of Satan casting out Satan. She refuses to prosecute a drunken ruffian; she converses on equal terms with a blackguard to whom no lady should be seen speaking in the public street: in short, she imitates Christ. Bill's conscience reacts to this just as naturally as it does to the old woman's threats. He is placed in a position of unbearable moral inferiority, and strives by every means in his power to escape from it, whilst he is still quite ready to meet the abuse of the old woman by attempting to smash a mug on her face. And that is the triumphant justification of Barbara's Christianity as against our system of judicial punishment and the vindictive villain-thrashings and "poetic justice" of the romantic stage.

. . .

In short, when Major Barbara says that there are no scoundrels, she is right: there are no absolute scoundrels, though there are impracticable people of whom I shall treat presently. Every reasonable man (and woman) is a potential scoundrel and a potential good citizen. What a man is depends on his character; but what he does, and what we think of what he does, depends on his circumstances. The characteristics that ruin a man in one class make him eminent in another. The characters that behave differently in different circumstances behave alike in similar circumstances. Take a common English character like that of Bill Walker. We meet Bill everywhere: on the judicial bench, on the episcopal bench, in the Privy Council, at the War Office and Admiralty, as well as in the Old Bailey dock or in the ranks of casual unskilled labor. And the morality of Bill's characteristics varies with these various circumstances. The faults of the burglar are the qualities of the financier: the manners and habits of a duke would cost a city clerk his situation. In short, though character is independent of circumstances, conduct is not; and our moral judgments of character are not: both are circumstantial. Take any condition of life in which the circumstances are for a mass of men practically alike: felony, the House of Lords, the factory, the stables, the gipsy encampment or where you please! In spite of diversity of character and temperament, the conduct and morals of the individuals in each group are as predicable and as alike in the main as if they were a flock of sheep, morals being mostly only social habits and circumstantial necessities.

THE PLAY IN PERFORMANCE

When *Major Barbara* opened in London in 1905, Shaw was a well-known dramatist and the play inevitably attracted much comment. The reviews were mixed—a good deal of praise for its brilliance, a good deal of regret for its talkiness, and a good deal of anger at its message, sometimes all in a single review. The reviewer in the *Daily Telegraph*, for instance, spoke of the play's "desolating cleverness . . . that is purely destructive and never constructive."

Throughout his life Shaw heard pretty much the same kinds of judgements. He was willing to accept the praise for his "cleverness," but he customarily replied to charges that he was destructive by arguing that his critics were stuck in some sort of old-fashioned thinking and simply could not bring themselves to see that the destructiveness was a prelude to a new way of thinking and of living. As for the common complaint that his plays were all talk, he replied that of course his plays were full of talk, "just as Raphael's pictures are all paint, Michael Angelo's statues all marble, Beethoven's symphonies all noise." (This particular witty response, much later than *Major Barbara,* comes from "The Play of Ideas," an essay of 1950.) But the talk, Shaw insisted, has ideas behind it. Further, the talk *is* highly dramatic he argued, but in a special way. Here we quote again from the essay of 1950:

> Opera taught me to shape my plays into recitatives, arias, duets, trios, ensemble finales, and bravura pieces to display the technical accomplishments of the executants . . . .

Consider, as an example, this duet from *Major Barbara.* Undershaft has offered to take into his business Cusins, and in the course of bargaining Cusins demands ten percent of the profit:

> UNDERSHAFT (*taken aback*). Ten per cent! Why, man, do you know what my profits are?

CUSINS. Enormous, I hope: otherwise I shall require twenty-five per cent.
UNDERSHAFT. But, Mr. Cusins, this is a serious matter of business. You are not bringing any capital into the concern.
CUSINS. What! No capital! Is my mastery of Greek no capital? Is my access to the subtlest thought, the loftiest poetry yet attained by humanity, no capital? My character! my intellect! my life! my career! what Barbara calls my soul! are these no capital? say another word, and I double my salary.
UNDERSHAFT. Be reasonable—
CUSINS. Mr. Undershaft: you have my terms. Take them or leave them.
UNDERSHAFT (*recovering himself*). Very well. I note your terms; and I offer you half.
CUSINS (*disgusted*). Half!
UNDERSHAFT (*firmly*). Half.
CUSINS. You call yourself a gentleman; and you offer me half!!
UNDERSHAFT. I do not call myself a gentleman; but I offer you half.

Given dialogue like this, it is easy to see the truth of Shaw's statement that he learned from opera, and hard to see how anyone can regard the play as undramatic or talky.

The fact, however, is (as we have said) that the play received mixed reviews. But even the most negative critics and spectators—chiefly those who were deeply offended by the shocking ideas—recognized its brilliance, and the play has had a very strong stage history. It is of course often staged in colleges and universities, and perhaps every eight or ten years it receives a major professional production. A film version in 1941 starred Wendy Hiller and Rex Harrison.

Alice Gerstenberg

OVERTONES

Playwright, novelist, and director Alice Gerstenberg (1885–1972) was born in Chicago. With a group of actors and writers, she organized the Experimental Theatre Workshop in Chicago and developed many scripts for this group. Later, Gerstenberg founded the Playwrights Theatre in Chicago. *Overtones* (1913), first performed by New York City's Washington Square Players in 1915, is one of a number of one-act plays that she wrote. Gerstenberg's adaptation of *Alice in Wonderland*, one of several scripts for children, proved particularly popular.

COMMENTARY

Traditionally, European and American drama sought to imitate human behavior. The speakers might speak in blank verse, as many of Shakespeare's characters do, but the dramatist still aimed at giving us the illusion of life. In the words of Hamlet (advising an actor, but probably voicing Shakespeare's own opinion), the aim of drama was "to hold the mirror up to nature"—nature meaning, of course, human nature. Although Hamlet is many things we are not (he is a prince, he lives in medieval Denmark, he broods about his mother's hasty remarriage to his uncle), we think of this fictional character as real. His personality seems utterly believable; and his struggles, confusions, worries, and mistakes mirror many of our own. We come to an understanding of Hamlet—or of any dramatic character—by assessing his actions and his relationships with other characters, but primarily by considering what he says, that is, his speeches (including soliloquies and asides).

In a staging of *Hamlet*, a director might decide to emphasize Hamlet's contemplation of suicide ("To be or not to be . . .") by having the actor pace back and forth, use certain gestures, or change the pitch of his voice. Perhaps the actor dresses entirely in black; perhaps the lighting dims, and we see Hamlet as a stark, solitary figure caught in a single spotlight; perhaps a drumroll or eerie flute melody accentuates each movement. In such a situation, through the use of music and lighting, theater departs from an exact depiction of reality. In the real world—that is, one's day-to-day existence—our speeches and actions are seldom accompanied by special lighting effects and carefully selected music or sound effects. Suppose the director and technical crew go even further: The

stage abruptly tilts or a recorded voice echoes or horrible sirens scream. Devices such as these do more than "hold the mirror up to nature," for they deliberately exaggerate what happens—or what could happen—in life. An unhappy person might *feel* as if the very foundations of his or her life are unstable (and an audience would see this awful moment represented by the tilting floor), but in actual life floors don't tilt. These devices are called **expressionistic;** that is, they are ways to express (or reveal) a character's inner feelings.

Expressionistic devices are not, of course, limited to drama. For example, on a television situation comedy, a character might speak sweetly to his date, but in a split-screen image he might snarl, and viewers will realize that he actually hates this woman. Alternatively, in an advertisement, a toddler races through a house, little feet whirling in a blur, and jumps huge distances. Even though viewers know that a child this age cannot possess superhuman capabilities, the idea of liveliness and good health has been communicated, and we just might buy the brand of cereal being touted.

In drama, **expressionism** refers to a movement that emerged from playwrights in Germany and Austria around the time of World War I. It attempted to reveal to an audience the inner feelings of the characters rather than simply portray outer events. To a certain extent, we can say that expressionism is the antithesis of realism or naturalism. Plot details merely skate the surface of "what is really going on" inside these characters' minds. For example, in *Overtones*, one woman politely offers another woman a piece of cake, and the second accepts. Externally, it would seem that the two women are cordial and calm. If we relied only on the polite lines of these "cultured" women, we wouldn't know that, in fact, their relationship is one of jealousy and mistrust.

In an expressionistic play, subjective truths (for example, characters' true emotions, conflicts, and judgments) are revealed through such devices as the speeches of an alter ego, stylized movements, visual projections, musical representations, distortions in lighting or set, and piercing or unusual sounds. George Kaiser (in Germany), August Strindberg (in Sweden), and Eugene O'Neill are among the best-known playwrights who experimented with expressionism or incorporated expressionistic techniques. In O'Neill's 1920 play, *The Emperor Jones* (see p. 569), scenes shift rapidly, as if in dream sequences, and seem to have a pulsating rhythm that is almost dancelike in intensity. Colors for the set are used symbolically, dazzling reds and yellows suggesting heat and fiery passions. For further comment on expressionism, see page 1065 in the Glossary.

It is no accident that expressionism and Freudian psychology are by-products of the same era. Sigmund Freud (1856–1939) is considered the father of psychoanalysis, which is the method of investigating mental processes Freud developed in the final decade of the nineteenth century and the first decade of the twentieth century. Freud introduced the idea that the human personality can be divided into three functional parts. Put briefly, we can summarize his terms as follows:

The *id* is the reservoir of instinctual drives; dominated by the pleasure principle and irrational desires, the id seeks immediate gratification.

The *ego* experiences the external world through the senses and organizes thought processes rationally; the ego makes up most of what we think of as consciousness.

The *superego* originates in the child through identification with parents and other older persons; the superego is critical of the ego, enforces moral standards, and (on an unconscious level) blocks the unacceptable impulses of the id.

Freud's theories—and the controversies surrounding them—provide an interesting perspective for thinking about the power of expressionism in the creative arts.

Alice Gerstenberg is one of the first American expressionists. In *Overtones* she seems to be using some of Freud's ideas as a springboard for characterization. She gives each of the two main characters an outer and an inner persona so that four actresses are needed. Harriet and Margaret, each described as "a cultured woman," maintain the social properties: They do and say "the right thing" at all times. If we read only their lines—or, if an audience were to hear and see only their "proper" responses of cordial social chitchat—we would have no access to their true, seething, passionate feelings. However, each character has "a primitive self." Even the informal nicknames (Hetty for Harriet and Maggie for Margaret) match the primitives' lack of social restraint. Gerstenberg's technique is different from what is known as an *aside*. On Shakespeare's stage, for example, a character can utter a brief speech revealing inner feelings, but, by convention, the audience understands that the other characters on stage do not hear this speech. For example, in *King Lear* Edgar assures us (4.6.33–44) that although he deceives his father, it is for a good purpose. The actor playing Edgar might tilt his head in a conspiratorial way toward the audience and change his tone slightly for this aside. In *Overtones*, however, the primitive selves are separate beings. Within the first few moments, we realize the tacit rules Gerstenberg establishes: Harriet and Margaret (the two cultured selves) can speak to each other, each cultured self can speak to her primitive self (Harriet to Hetty, Margaret to Maggie), the primitive selves can speak to each other (Hetty to Maggie, Maggie to Hetty), but Harriet cannot hear Maggie nor can Margaret hear Hetty.

Staging the play requires ensemble work, that is, four actresses attuned to each other (and to the script) who are capable of split-second timing, careful modulations of expression, and (for the actresses playing the cultured selves) the ability to feign unawareness during a raging quarrel.

Two features of *Overtones* mark it as expressionistic: costuming and characterization. Gerstenberg indicates that Harriet's and Margaret's dresses are of the same design, suggesting that they share a love for the same man. Harriet's dress is green to symbolize jealousy. Each primitive self also wears a dress of this design, but the colors are deeper, suggesting the deeper, more genuine passions of Hetty and Maggie. As for characterization, Gerstenberg's invention of the cultured and primitive selves (we might substitute Freud's terms *ego* and *id*) makes this a chilling play on stage. The psychological intensity in *Overtones* is a product of the tension between repressed feelings (Harriet's and Margaret's social charade) and the subjective truth (Hetty's and Maggie's "down and dirty" bluntness).

Overtones is significant not only because it is an early expressionistic play by an American but also because it is written by a woman. True, there are other and earlier female playwrights. A very brief list would include the British dramatists Aphra Behn and Susanna Centlivre (seventeenth century); Sarah Gardner, Elizabeth Griffith, Eliza Haywood, Elizabeth Inchbald, Dorothy Jordon, and Mary O'Brien (eighteenth century); and the American dramatists Margaretta Faugeres, Charlotte Lennox, and Judith Murray (eighteenth century). Nevertheless, the roll call of well-known playwrights over the centuries is certainly not equally represented by male and female authors. Although many female playwrights are now being staged—and garnering awards—the theater world is still dominated by men. Students interested in the social and political reasons behind this inequity may wish to start by reading some of the following:

Heilbrun, Carolyn. *Writing a Woman's Life* (1988).

Millett, Kate. *Sexual Politics* (1990).

Weldon, Fay. *Letters to Alice* (1984).

Woolf, Virginia. "Professions for Women," in *Women and Writing* (1979); *Three Guineas* (1938); and *A Room of One's Own* (1929).

Alice Gerstenberg

OVERTONES

TIME: *The present.*

SCENE: *Harriet's fashionable living room. The door at the back leads to the hall.*

In the center a tea table with a high-backed chair at each side. Harriet's gown is a light, "jealous" green. Her counterpart, Hetty, wears a gown of the same design but in a darker shade. Margaret wears a gown of lavender chiffon while her counterpart, Maggie, wears a gown of the same design in purple, a purple scarf veiling her face. Chiffon is used to give a sheer effect, suggesting a possibility of primitive and cultured selves merging into one woman. The primitive and cultured selves never come into actual physical contact but try to sustain the impression of mental conflict. Harriet never sees Hetty, never talks to her but rather thinks aloud looking into space. Hetty, however, looks at Harriet, talks intently and shadows her continually. The same is true of Margaret and Maggie. The voices of the cultured women are affected and lingering, the voices of the primitive impulsive and more or less staccato. When the curtain rises Harriet is seated right of tea table, busying herself with the tea things.

HETTY. Harriet. (*There is no answer.*) Harriet, my other self. (*There is no answer.*) My trained self.

HARRIET (*listens intently*). Yes?

(*From behind Harriet's chair Hetty rises slowly.*)

HETTY. I want to talk to you.

HARRIET. Well?

HETTY (*looking at Harriet admiringly*). Oh, Harriet, you are beautiful today.

HARRIET. Am I presentable, Hetty?

HETTY. Suits me.

HARRIET. I've tried to make the best of the good points.

HETTY. My passions are deeper than yours. I can't keep on the mask as you do. I'm crude and real, you are my appearance in the world.

HARRIET. I am what you wish the world to believe you are.

HETTY. You are the part of me that has been trained.

HARRIET. I am your educated self.

HETTY. I am the rushing river; you are the ice over the current.

HARRIET. I am your subtle overtones.

HETTY. But together we are one woman, the wife of Charles Goodrich.

HARRIET. There I disagree with you, Hetty, I alone am his wife.

HETTY (*indignantly*). Harriet, how can you say such a thing!

HARRIET. Certainly. I am the one who flatters him. I have to be the one who talks to him. If I gave you a chance you would tell him at once that you dislike him.

HETTY (*moving away*). I don't love him, that's certain.

HARRIET. You leave all the fibbing to me. He doesn't suspect that my calm, suave manner hides your hatred. Considering the amount of scheming it causes me it can safely be said that he is my husband.

HETTY. Oh, if you love him—

HARRIET. I? I haven't any feelings. It isn't my business to love anybody.

HETTY. Then why need you object to calling him my husband?

HARRIET. I resent your appropriation of a man who is managed only through the cleverness of my artifice.

HETTY. You may be clever enough to deceive him, Harriet, but I am still the one who suffers. I can't forget he is my husband. I can't forget that I might have married John Caldwell.

HARRIET. How foolish of you to remember John, just because we met his wife by chance.

HETTY. That's what I want to talk to you about. She may be here at any moment. I want to advise you about what to say to her this afternoon.

HARRIET. By all means tell me now and don't interrupt while she is here. You have a most annoying habit of talking to me when people are present. Sometimes it is all I can do to keep my poise and appear *not* to be listening to you.

HETTY. Impress her.

HARRIET. Hetty, dear, is it not my custom to impress people?

HETTY. I hate her.

HARRIET. I can't let her see that.

HETTY. I hate her because she married John.

HARRIET. Only after you had refused him.

HETTY (*turning to Harriet*). Was it my fault that I refused him?

HARRIET. That's right, blame me.

HETTY. It was your fault. You told me he was too poor and never would be able to do anything in painting. Look at him now, known in Europe, just returned from eight years in Paris, famous.

HARRIET. It was too poor a gamble at the time. It was much safer to accept Charles's money and position.

HETTY. And then John married Margaret within the year.

HARRIET. Out of spite.

HETTY. Freckled, gauky-looking thing she was, too.

HARRIET (*a little sadly*). Europe improved her. She was stunning the other morning.

HETTY. Make her jealous today.

HARRIET. Shall I be haughty or cordial or caustic or—

HETTY. Above all else you must let her know that we are rich.

HARRIET. Oh, yes, I do that quite easily now.

HETTY. You must put it on a bit.

HARRIET. Never fear.

HETTY. Tell her I love my husband.

HARRIET. My husband—

HETTY. Are you going to quarrel with me?

HARRIET (*moves away*). No, I have no desire to quarrel with you. It is quite too uncomfortable. I couldn't get away from you if I tried.

HETTY (*stamping her foot and following Harriet*). You were a stupid fool to make me refuse John, I'll never forgive you—never—

HARRIET (*stopping and holding up her hand*). Don't get me all excited. I'll be in no condition to meet her properly this afternoon.

HETTY (*passionately*). I could choke you for robbing me of John.

HARRIET (*retreating*). Don't muss me!

HETTY. You don't know how you have made me suffer.

HARRIET (*beginning to feel the strength of Hetty's emotion surge through her and trying to conquer it*). It is not my business to have heartaches.

HETTY. You're bloodless. Nothing but sham—sham—while I—

HARRIET (*emotionally*). Be quiet! I can't let her see that I have been fighting with my inner self.

HETTY. And now after all my suffering you say it has cost you more than it has cost me to be married to Charles. But it's the pain here in my heart—I've paid the price— I've paid—Charles is not your husband!

HARRIET (*trying to conquer emotion*). He is.

HETTY (*follows Harriet*). He isn't.

HARRIET (*weakly*). He is.

HETTY (*towering over Harriet*). He isn't! I'll kill you!

HARRIET (*overpowered, sinks into a chair*). Don't—don't you're stronger than I—you're—

HETTY. Say he's mine.

HARRIET. He's ours.

HETTY. (*The telephone rings.*) There she is now.

(*Hetty hurries to 'phone but Harriet regains her supremacy.*)

HARRIET (*authoritatively*). Wait! I can't let the telephone girl down there hear my real self. It isn't proper. (*At phone.*) Show Mrs. Caldwell up.

HETTY. I'm so excited, my heart's in my mouth.

HARRIET (*at the mirror*). A nice state you've put my nerves into.

HETTY. Don't let her see you're nervous.

HARRIET. Quick, put the veil on, or she'll see you shining through me.

(*Harriet takes a scarf of chiffon that has been lying over the back of a chair and drapes it on Hetty, covering her face. The chiffon is the same color of their gowns but paler in shade so that it pales Hetty's darker gown to match Harriet's lighter one. As Hetty moves in the following scene the chiffon falls away revealing now and then the gown of deeper dye underneath.*)

HETTY. Tell her Charles is rich and fascinating—boast of our friends, make her feel she needs us.

HARRIET. I'll make her ask John to paint us.

HETTY. That's just my thought—if John paints our portrait—

HARRIET. We can wear an exquisite gown—

HETTY. And make him fall in love again and—

HARRIET (*schemingly*). Yes. (*Margaret parts the portières back center and extends her hand. Margaret is followed by her counterpart Maggie.*) Oh, Margaret, I'm so glad to see you!

HETTY (*to Maggie*). That's a lie.

MARGARET (*in superficial voice throughout*). It's enchanting to see you, Harriet.

MAGGIE (*in emotional voice throughout*). I'd bite you, if I dared.

HARRIET (*to Margaret*). Wasn't our meeting a stroke of luck?

MARGARET (*coming down left of table*). I've thought of you so often, Harriet; and to come back and find you living in New York.

HARRIET (*coming down right of table*). Mr. Goodrich has many interests here.

MAGGIE (*to Margaret*). Flatter her.

MARGARET. I know, Mr. Goodrich is so successful.

HETTY (*to Harriet*). Tell her we're rich.

HARRIET (*to Margaret*). Won't you sit down?

MARGARET (*takes a chair*). What a beautiful cabinet!

HARRIET. Do you like it? I'm afraid Charles paid an extravagant price.

MAGGIE (*to Hetty*). I don't believe it.

MARGARET (*sitting down; to Harriet*). I am sure he must have.

HARRIET (*sitting down*). How well you are looking, Margaret.

HETTY. Yes, you are not. There are circles under your eyes.

MAGGIE (*to Hetty*). I haven't eaten since breakfast and I'm hungry.

MARGARET (*to Harriet*). How well you are looking, too.

MAGGIE (*to Hetty*). You have hard lines about your lips, are you happy?

HETTY (*to Harriet*). Don't let her know that I'm unhappy.

HARRIET (*to Margaret*). Why shouldn't I look well? My life is full, happy, complete—

561

MAGGIE. I wonder.

HETTY (*in Harriet's ear*). Tell her we have an automobile.

MARGARET (*to Harriet*). My life is complete, too.

MAGGIE. My heart is torn with sorrow; my husband cannot make a living. He will kill himself if he does not get an order for a painting.

MARGARET (*laughs*). You must come and see us in our studio. John has been doing some excellent portraits. He cannot begin to fill his orders.

HETTY (*to Harriet*). Tell her we have an automobile.

HARRIET (*to Margaret*). Do you take lemon in your tea?

MAGGIE. Take cream. It's more filling.

MARGARET (*looking nonchalantly at tea things*). No, cream, if you please. How cozy!

MAGGIE (*glaring at tea things*). Only cakes! I could eat them all!

HARRIET (*to Margaret*). How many lumps?

MAGGIE (*to Margaret*). Sugar is nourishing.

MARGARET (*to Harriet*). Three, please. I used to drink very sweet coffee in Turkey and ever since I've—

HETTY. I don't believe you were ever in Turkey.

MAGGIE. I wasn't, but it is none of your business.

HARRIET (*pouring tea*). Have you been in Turkey? Do tell me about it.

MAGGIE (*to Margaret*). Change the subject.

MARGARET (*to Harriet*). You must go there. You have so much taste in dress you would enjoy seeing their costumes.

MAGGIE. Isn't she going to pass the cake?

MARGARET (*to Harriet*). John painted several portraits there.

HETTY (*to Harriet*). Why don't you stop her bragging and tell her we have an automobile?

HARRIET (*offers cake across the table to Margaret*). Cake?

MAGGIE (*stands back of Margaret, shadowing her as Hetty shadows Harriet; Maggie reaches claws out for the cake and groans with joy*). At last!

(*But her claws do not touch the cake.*)

MARGARET (*with a graceful, nonchalant hand places cake upon her plate and bites at it slowly and delicately*). Thank you.

HETTY (*to Harriet*). Automobile!

MAGGIE (*to Margaret*). Follow up the costumes with the suggestion that she would make a good model for John. It isn't too early to begin getting what you came for.

MARGARET (*ignoring Maggie*). What delicious cake.

HETTY (*excitedly to Harriet*). There's your chance for the auto.

HARRIET (*nonchalantly to Margaret*). Yes, it is good cake, isn't it? There are always a great many people buying it at Harper's. I sat in my automobile fifteen minutes this morning waiting for my chauffeur to get it.

MAGGIE (*to Margaret*). Make her order a portrait.

MARGARET (*to Harriet*). If you stopped at Harper's you must have noticed the new gowns at Henderson's. Aren't the shop windows alluring these days?

HARRIET. Even my chauffeur notices them.

MAGGIE. I know you have an automobile, I heard you the first time.

MARGARET. I notice gowns now with an artist's eye as John does. The one you have on, my dear, is very paintable.

HETTY. Don't let her see you're anxious to be painted.

HARRIET (*nonchalantly*). Oh, it's just a little model.

MAGGIE (*to Margaret*). Don't seem anxious to get the order.

MARGARET (*nonchalantly*). Perhaps it isn't the gown itself but the way you wear it that pleases the eye. Some people can wear anything with grace.

HETTY. Yes, I'm very graceful.

HARRIET (*to Margaret*). You flatter me, my dear.

MARGARET. On the contrary, Harriet, I have an intense admiration for you. I remember how beautiful you were— as a girl. In fact, I was quite jealous when John was paying you so much attention.

HETTY. She is gloating because I lost him.

HARRIET. Those were childhood days in a country town.

MAGGIE (*to Margaret*). She's trying to make you feel that John was only a country boy.

MARGARET. Most great men have come from the country. There is a fair chance that John will be added to the list.

HETTY. I know it and I am bitterly jealous of you.

HARRIET. Undoubtedly he owes much of his success to you. Margaret, your experience in economy and your ability to endure hardship. Those first few years in Paris must have been a struggle.

MAGGIE. She is sneering at your poverty.

MARGARET. Yes, we did find life difficult at first, not the luxurious start a girl has who marries wealth.

HETTY (*to Harriet*). Deny that you married Charles for his money.

(*Harriet deems it wise to ignore Hetty's advice.*)

MARGARET. But John and I are so congenial in our tastes, that we were impervious to hardship or unhappiness.

HETTY (*in anguish*). Do you love each other? Is it really true?

HARRIET (*sweetly*). Did you have all the romance of starving for his art?

MAGGIE (*to Margaret*). She's taunting you. Get even with her.

MARGARET. Not for long. Prince Rier soon discovered John's genius, and introduced him royally to wealthy Parisians who gave him many orders.

HETTY (*to Maggie*). Are you telling the truth or are you lying?

HARRIET. If he had so many opportunities there, you must have had great inducements to come back to the States.

MAGGIE (*to Hetty*). We did, but not the kind you think.

MARGARET. John became the rage among Americans traveling in France, too, and they simply insisted upon his coming here.

HARRIET. Whom is he going to paint here?

MAGGIE (*frightened*). What names dare I make up?

MARGARET (*calmly*). Just at present Miss Dorothy Ainsworth of Oregon is posing. You may not know the name, but she is the daughter of a wealthy miner who found gold in Alaska.

HARRIET. I dare say there are many Western people we have never heard of.

MARGARET. You must have found social life in New York very interesting, Harriet, after the simplicity of our home town.

HETTY (*to Maggie*). There's no need to remind us that our beginnings were the same.

HARRIET. Of course Charles's family made everything delightful for me. They are so well connected.

MAGGIE (*to Margaret*). Flatter her.

MARGARET. I heard it mentioned yesterday that you had made yourself very popular. Some one said you were very clever!

HARRIET (*pleased*). Who told you that?

MAGGIE. Nobody!

MARGARET (*pleasantly*). Oh, confidences should be suspected—respected, I mean. They said, too, that you are gaining some reputation as a critic of art.

HARRIET. I make no pretences.

MARGARET. Are you and Mr. Goodrich interested in the same things, too?

HETTY. No!

HARRIET. Yes, indeed, Charles and I are inseparable.

MAGGIE. I wonder.

HARRIET. Do have another cake.

MAGGIE (*in relief*). Oh, yes.

(*Again her claws extend but do not touch the cake.*)

MARGARET (*takes cake delicately*). I really shouldn't—after my big luncheon. John took me to the Ritz and we are invited to the Bedfords' for dinner—they have such a magnificent house near the drive—I really shouldn't, but the cakes are so good.

MAGGIE. Starving!

HARRIET (*to Margaret*). More tea?

MAGGIE. Yes!

MARGARET. No, thank you. How wonderfully life has arranged itself for you. Wealth, position, a happy marriage, every opportunity to enjoy all pleasures; beauty, art—how happy you must be.

HETTY (*in anguish*). Don't call me happy. I've never been happy since I gave up John. All these years without him—a future without him—no—no—I shall win him back—away from you—away from you—

HARRIET (*does not see Maggie pointing to cream and Margaret stealing some*). I sometimes think it is unfair for anyone to be as happy as I am. Charles and I are just as much in love now as when we married. To me he is just the dearest man in the world.

MAGGIE (*passionately*). My John is. I love him so much I could die for him. I'm going through hunger and want to make him great and he loves me. He worships me!

MARGARET (*leisurely to Harriet*). I should like to meet Mr. Goodrich. Bring him to our studio. John has some sketches to show. Not many, because all the portraits have been purchased by the subjects. He gets as much as four thousand dollars now.

HETTY (*to Harriet*). Don't pay that much.

HARRIET (*to Margaret*). As much as that?

MARGARET. It is not really too much when one considers that John is in the foremost ranks of artists today. A picture painted by him now will double and treble in value.

MAGGIE. It's a lie. He is growing weak with despair.

HARRIET. Does he paint all day long?

MAGGIE. No, he draws advertisements for our bread.

MARGARET (*to Harriet*). When you and your husband come to see us, telephone first—

MAGGIE. Yes, so he can get the advertisements out of the way.

MARGARET. Otherwise you might arrive while he has a sitter, and John refuses to let me disturb him then.

HETTY. Make her ask for an order.

HARRIET (*to Margaret*). Le Grange offered to paint me for a thousand.

MARGARET. Louis Le Grange's reputation isn't worth more than that.

HARRIET. Well, I've heard his work well mentioned.

MAGGIE. Yes, he is doing splendid work.

MARGARET. Oh, dear me, no. He is only praised by the masses. He is accepted not at all by artists themselves.

HETTY (*anxiously*). Must I really pay the full price?

HARRIET. Le Grange thought I would make a good subject.

MAGGIE (*to Margaret*). Let her fish for it.

MARGARET. Of course you would. Why don't you let Le Grange paint you, if you *trust* him?

HETTY. She doesn't seem anxious to have John do it.

HARRIET. But if Le Grange isn't accepted by artists, it would be a waste of time to pose for him, wouldn't it?

MARGARET. Yes, I think it would.

MAGGIE (*passionately to Hetty across back of table*). Give us the order. John is so despondent he can't endure much longer. Help us! Help me! Save us!

HETTY (*to Harriet*). Don't seem too eager.

HARRIET. And yet if he charges only a thousand one might consider it.

MARGARET. If you really wish to be painted, why don't you give a little more and have a portrait really worth while? John might be induced to do you for a little below his usual price considering that you used to be such good friends.

HETTY (*in glee*). Hurrah!

HARRIET (*quietly to Margaret*). That's very nice of you to suggest—of course I don't know—

MAGGIE (*in fear*). For God's sake, say yes.

MARGARET (*quietly to Harriet*). Of course, I don't know whether John would. He is very peculiar in these matters. He sets his value on his work and thinks it beneath him to discuss price.

HETTY (*to Maggie*). You needn't try to make us feel small.

MARGARET. Still, I might quite delicately mention to him that inasmuch as you have many influential friends you would be very glad to—to—

MAGGIE (*to Hetty*). Finish what I don't want to say.

HETTY (*to Harriet*). Help her out.

HARRIET. Oh, yes, introductions will follow the exhibition of my portrait. No doubt I—

HETTY (*to Harriet*). Be patronizing.

HARRIET. No doubt I shall be able to introduce your husband to his advantage.

MAGGIE (*relieved*). Saved.

MARGARET. If I find John in a propitious mood I shall take pleasure, for your sake, in telling him about your beauty. Just as you are sitting now would be a lovely pose.

MAGGIE (*to Margaret*). We can go now.

HETTY (*to Harriet*). Don't let her think she is doing us a favor.

HARRIET. It will give me pleasure to add my name to your husband's list of patronesses.

MAGGIE (*excitedly to Margaret*). Run home and tell John the good news.

MARGARET (*leisurely to Harriet*). I little guessed when I came for a pleasant chat about old times that it would develop into business arrangements. I had no idea, Harriet, that you had any intention of being painted. By Le Grange, too. Well, I came just in time to rescue you.

MAGGIE (*to Margaret*). Run home and tell John. Hurry, hurry!

HETTY (*to Harriet*). You managed the order very neatly. She doesn't suspect that you wanted it.

HARRIET. Now if I am not satisfied with my portrait I shall blame you. Margaret, dear. I am relying upon your opinion of John's talent.

MAGGIE (*to Margaret*). She doesn't suspect what you came for. Run home and tell John!

HARRIET. You always had a brilliant mind, Margaret.

MARGARET. Ah, it is you who flatter, now.

MAGGIE (*to Margaret*). You don't have to stay so long. Hurry home!

HARRIET. Ah, one does not flatter when one tells the truth.

MARGARET (*smiles*). I must be going or you will have me completely under your spell.

HETTY (*looks at clock*). Yes, do go. I have to dress for dinner.

HARRIET (*to Margaret*). Oh, don't hurry.

MAGGIE (*to Hetty*). I hate you!

MARGARET (*to Harriet*). No, really I must, but I hope we shall see each other often at the studio. I find you so stimulating.

HETTY (*to Maggie*). I hate you!

HARRIET (*to Margaret*). It is indeed gratifying to find a kindred spirit.

MAGGIE (*to Hetty*). I came for your gold.

MARGARET (*to Harriet*). How delightful it is to know you again.

HETTY (*to Maggie*). I am going to make you and your husband suffer.

HARRIET. My kind regards to John.

MAGGIE (*to Hetty*). He has forgotten all about you.

MARGARET (*rises*). He will be so happy to receive them.

HETTY (*to Maggie*). I can hardly wait to talk to him again.

HARRIET. I shall wait, then, until you send me word?

MARGARET (*offering her hand*). I'll speak to John about it as soon as I can and tell you when to come.

(*Harriet takes Margaret's hand affectionately. Hetty and Maggie rush at each other, throw back their veils, and fling their speeches fiercely at each other.*)

HETTY. I love him—I love him—

MAGGIE. He's starving—I'm starving—

HETTY. I'm going to take him away from you—

MAGGIE. I want your money—and your influence.

HETTY and MAGGIE. I'm going to rob you—rob you.

(*There is a cymbal crash, the lights go out and come up again slowly, leaving only Margaret and Harriet visible.*)

MARGARET (*quietly to Harriet*). I've had such a delightful afternoon.

HARRIET (*offering her hand*). It has been a joy to see you.

MARGARET (*sweetly to Harriet*). Good-bye.

HARRIET (*sweetly to Margaret as she kisses her*). Good-bye, my dear.

CURTAIN

TOPICS FOR CRITICAL THINKING AND WRITING

📖 THE PLAY ON THE PAGE

1. Provide a definition of *feminism*, either using your own words or the terms from a standard source. (If you use a source, be sure to provide documentation, preferably in the MLA style.) Then analyze characterization and plot to assess whether or not we can dub *Overtones* a feminist play.

2. John is talked about but never makes an appearance. Do you find the play weakened or strengthened by John's absence?

3. Because Gerstenberg has set the play in Harriet's house and opens with Hetty, do you think Harriet should be considered the most important character? Why or why not?

4. Gerstenberg describes Harriet and Margaret as "cultured." What do you think she means by this word? Has Gerstenberg offered any social criticism through these so-called society ladies?

5. Would *Undertones* have been a more appropriate title?

🎭 THE PLAY ON THE STAGE

6. Medieval morality plays sometimes included the device of a good angel and a bad angel, each vying for a character's attention. Christopher Marlowe's sixteenth-century play, *Doctor Faustus* (p. 189) includes this device, too. Compare Marlowe's method of staging an internal conflict with Gerstenberg's.

7. For a modern staging, what changes in costuming, lighting, and sound would you suggest?

8. Do you think today's audiences would find *Overtones* a dated play? Are its issues still relevant? Provide specific reasons for your answer.

9. List the various adjectives you would apply to Harriet and to Margaret. Cite speeches that make you aware of specific differences between the two women, and suggest ways (for instance, characteristic gestures) in which the actresses on stage could relay the distinctions between the two characters.

THE PLAY IN PERFORMANCE

Overtones was given its first production by the Washington Square Players in 1915. The "cultured" women were impeccably attired, with Margaret (the caller) wearing a hat and an afternoon dress, and Harriet in a looser style befitting the woman at home. Although Gerstenberg in her first stage direction specifies that Harriet and Hetty are costumed fairly similarly, as are Margaret and Maggie (though Maggie was to wear a veil), the New York production chose a different method of representing the "inner" or "primitive" selves: Hetty and Maggie wore voluminous, hooded costumes that concealed them, thus visually symbolizing their mysterious and invisible natures. In addition to these two methods of staging the play, at least one other method can be used, the one Eugene O'Neill later used in *The Great God Brown* (1926): Each woman can hold a mask before her face when she speaks in her public role (Harriet and Margaret) and can remove it when speaking private thoughts, representing her inner self (Hetty and Maggie).

Overtones has been a popular one-act play for university and community theaters. Recent productions include performances at Butler University in Indianapolis in 1987 and at the Boston Conservatory in 1993.

Eugene O'Neill

THE EMPEROR JONES

Eugene O'Neill (1888–1953), the son of an actor, was born in a hotel room near New York City's Broadway and spent his early years traveling with his parents throughout the United States. He entered Princeton University in 1906 but left before the end of the first year. In 1909 he traveled to Honduras looking for gold, contracted malaria, and returned to the United States in 1910. After touring briefly with his father's company, he shipped to Buenos Aires, jumped ship there, did odd jobs, shipped to South Africa, and returned to the United States in 1911. The following year he learned that he had tuberculosis. In a sanatorium he began seriously reading plays, and in 1916 he joined the Provincetown Players, who put on some of his one-act plays. *The Emperor Jones* (1920), produced by the Provincetown Players in New York City, was his first major play. In time he was awarded four Pulitzer Prizes (one, given posthumously was for *A Long Day's Journey into Night*, written in 1940 but not produced until 1955), and a Nobel Prize.

COMMENTARY

The gist of the story of *The Emperor Jones* is simply this: Jones, a black fugitive from a chain gang, has turned up on an island in the West Indies and established himself as emperor. By his own admission he has tyrannized his subjects, and he was able to get away with it because they believed that he could be killed only by a silver bullet. (This is the *antecedent action*; we learn it during the play, but it reports what happened before the play begins.) At the beginning of the play, hearing that a rebellion is in progress, Jones confidently sets out to leave the island; he becomes increasingly terrified, and at the end of the play he is shot with a silver bullet.

This is moderately interesting and not totally different from some historical episodes. For example, President Guillaume Sam of Haiti boasted he would kill himself with a silver bullet, but he was hacked to pieces by his oppressed subjects in 1915, only five years before O'Neill wrote *The Emperor Jones*. A century earlier, Henri Christophe, a slave who had become the merciless ruler of part of Haiti, shot himself when confronted with an insurrection. O'Neill knew these bits of history and used them to shape *The Emperor Jones*. However, even if he had not changed some facts, a play about Sam or Christophe inevitably would—if it were any good—be very different from an encyclopedia entry on them because, in Ezra Pound's words, a play is made not out of words but out of "persons moving about on a stage using words."

Let's begin with the stage and its setting. When the curtain goes up on a performance of *The Emperor Jones*, the audience sees "the audience chamber in the palace of the Emperor." It is furnished solely with "one huge chair . . . painted a dazzling, eye-smiting scarlet," a cushion that serves as a footstool, and two scarlet mats that go "from the foot of the throne to the two entrances." This stage, at least in the context of what follows, "says" a lot. It conveys Jones's dominance, for he alone can sit in the room, and it conveys something of his bloody career, for if the scarlet throne on which Jones sits at first suggests royalty, it also (in retrospect) suggests the blood that surrounds his career. Whether or not O'Neill was conscious of the fact when he was writing the play, the huge scarlet chair, which at the start is boldly emblematic of Jones both as Emperor and as murderer, makes a notable contrast to the "little reddish-purple hole under his left breast" when his corpse is brought onstage at the end of the play. The imperial murderer has diminished to this.

The play uses only two other sets, and these are almost one: the edge of the Great Forest and within the Great Forest. The Forest, in the context of the action, says something. O'Neill tells us, in his first description of it, that it gives an impression of "relentless immobility" and of "brooding, implacable silence." Fleeing through the forest Jones becomes terrified, and we see that the dark forest is, in part at least, the jungle of the human mind, the world of inarticulate, elemental passions that seethe beneath the fragile surface of reason. (*The Emperor Jones* belongs, at least roughly,

566

to the movement called **expressionism,** in which scenery is commonly used not to give a character's state of mind but rather to present an image of the external world—see the Glossary.) The darkness of the jungle, a strong contrast to the brightly illuminated throne room where Jones was the confident master, provides us with an example of the way in which a dramatist uses lighting—or, rather, darkness—symbolically.

Among the stock dramatic types of the black man available to O'Neill in 1920, the chief were the Tom (faithful black retainer), the Buffoon (clownish lazy servant), the Bull (villain who wants to rape white women), and the Tragic Mulatto (hovering between two races.) Almost all depictions of blacks on the American stage of the time fell into these classifications. O'Neill, in a remarkable step forward in the history of American drama and, therefore, in the history of American thought, used none of these stereotypes. (In *The Emperor Jones* the lazy man is not the black, who has diligently learned the language of the islanders and who for two years worked hard and efficiently at his job of robbing his subjects; the lazy man is the white man, Smithers, who in ten years has not bothered to learn the language.)

Today, some seventy years after O'Neill wrote the play, inevitably we are disturbed by some of its racist implications, especially by what seems to be the implication that a black more quickly than a white reverts to the condition of the "primitive" human being. Indeed, we can find traces of racism in the play. For instance, O'Neill's first description of Jones says that "his features are typically negroid, yet there is something decidedly distinctive about his face—an underlying strength of will, a hardy, self-reliant confidence in himself that inspires respect." The "yet" is very troublesome, and we can all wish that O'Neill had written "and" instead of "yet." Nevertheless, the actor Paul Robeson, the African American who knew O'Neill best, never suggested that O'Neill was a racist. On the contrary, Robeson had nothing but praise for O'Neill, whom he called his "dear friend," and who, in *Paul Robeson Speaks,* says that O'Neill "has had many Negro friends and appreciated them for their true worth" (p. 71). Langston Hughes and W. E. B. Du Bois were among the other African Americans who praised O'Neill.

In fact, O'Neill was far ahead of most whites of his time in presenting a black whose face showed "an underlying strength of will, a hardy, self-reliant confidence," and whose eyes showed "a keen, cunning intelligence." If these words put us in mind of any type, it is, paradoxically, the rugged white individualist who was so worshiped in the nineteenth and early twentieth centuries. O'Neill gives us not a stereotypical black man (and none of the stereotypes was flattering) but a fresh conception, a black who has the virtues and faults of white society, of America as it was and is, and perhaps of mankind. (The very name *Jones* suggests Every-

man—though *Brutus* adds to it a sense of high Roman dignity, a sense of grotesque incongruity, as well as a hint of the "brute" that is beneath the clothes of every person, white or black.) Jones is quite explicit about his code: His aim is to get rich in the great white man's way by hard work and by cunning immorality on a grand scale.

> JONES. . . . You heah what I tells you, Smithers. Dere's little stealin' like you does, and dere's big stealin' like I does. For de little stealin' dey gits you in jail soon or late. For de big stealin' dey makes you Emperor and puts you in de Hall o' Fame when you croaks. (*Reminiscently.*) If dey's one thing I learns in ten years on de Pullman ca's listenin' to de white quality talk, it's dat same fact. And when I gits a chance to use it I winds up Emperor in two years.

Smithers is no less unscrupulous or cruel than Jones is, but he simply does not have Jones's courage, perseverance, intelligence, and vision. In short, O'Neill gives us a fresh, fully realized picture of believable human beings, and we should not be deceived by the funny spelling into thinking that Jones is the conventional black man that existed on the stage up to O'Neill's time.

It should be mentioned, too, that O'Neill strongly and successfully urged that the role be played by Charles Gilpin, a black actor who had played only minor parts in essentially white plays. For instance, he had played the small role of a slave in John Drinkwater's *Abraham Lincoln.* O'Neill somehow became acquainted with him, and Gilpin became the first Emperor Jones—and the first black man to play a major role in an integrated cast. Today, when all casts are integrated, we can hardly imagine how astounding it was not to use a white actor in blackface, but even as late as 1943, when Paul Robeson was playing Othello, there were surprised murmurs about a black man doing the role.

In any case—and this is perhaps the central point— although it sounds astounding to say so, O'Neill did not see the play as essentially about a black man. He was deeply influenced by the psychology of C. G. Jung, who in *Psychology of the Unconscious* (1912, translated 1917) argued that "each individual inherits a residue from the significant memories of the human race." The operative words are "the human race." Of course, Jung granted that the individual is also influenced by his or her particular culture, but essentially, he said, we all share an instinctual life. We draw, he claimed, on some sort of human collective memory, hence, the communal fear of night and the need for a god. In Jones's case the memory of a god takes the form of a crocodile god (not surprising for someone of African origin), but in someone else it would take a different form, such as a storm god for an Icelander. In short, O'Neill was writing about what he considered to be a universal condition, though of course to set forth this condition he had to use individuals. It should be mentioned that the idea that *all* of us, under certain kinds of conditions, will revert to our "primitive" origins was fairly widespread from the late nineteenth century and can be seen in the white man Kurtz's degeneration in Joseph Conrad's *Heart of Darkness* and in many works by Jack London, most notably in *Call of the Wild*.

Finally, something should be said about O'Neill's use of Black English Vernacular, or, rather, about his use of spelling

to indicate Jones's pronunciation, for instance "dat" for "that" and "dis" for "this." Today such spelling offends many readers, but in O'Neill's day it was regularly used by African-American writers as well as by white writers. One has only to look at the works of Charles Waddell Chestnutt, Paul Laurence Dunbar, Zora Neale Hurston, and Langston Hughes to verify this assertion. O'Neill's spelling, like the spelling of these black authors, was an effort at realism—an effort to catch distinctive speech.

Paul Robeson was not the first actor to play Brutus Jones in O'Neill's The Emperor Jones—that honor goes to another African-American actor, Charles Gilpin—but Robeson was the first to play it on Broadway. For a picture of Robeson as Othello, see page 784.

Eugene O'Neill

THE EMPEROR JONES

Characters

BRUTUS JONES, *emperor*
HENRY SMITHERS, *a Cockney trader*
AN OLD NATIVE WOMAN
LEM, *a native chief*
SOLDIERS, *adherents of Lem*
THE LITTLE FORMLESS FEARS
JEFF
THE NEGRO CONVICTS

THE PRISON GUARD
THE PLANTERS
THE AUCTIONEER
THE SLAVES
THE CONGO WITCH-DOCTOR
THE CROCODILE GOD

The action of the play takes place on an island in the West Indies as yet not self-determined by white Marines. The form of native government is, for the time being, an empire.

SCENE 1

SCENE: *The audience chamber in the palace of the Emperor—a spacious, high-ceilinged room with bare, white-washed walls. The floor is of white tiles. In the rear, to the left of center, a wide archway giving out on a portico with white pillars. The palace is evidently situated on high ground for beyond the portico nothing can be seen but a vista of distant hills, their summits crowned with thick groves of palm trees. In the right wall, center, a smaller arched doorway leading to the living quarters of the palace. The room is bare of furniture with the exception of one huge chair made of uncut wood which stands at center, its back to rear. This is very apparently the Emperor's throne. It is painted a dazzling, eye-smiting scarlet. There is a brilliant orange cushion on the seat and another smaller one is placed on the floor to serve as a footstool. Strips of matting, dyed scarlet, lead from the foot of the throne to the two entrances.*

It is late afternoon but the sunlight still blazes yellowly beyond the portico and there is an oppressive burden of exhausting heat in the air.

As the curtain rises, a native Negro woman sneaks in cautiously from the entrance on the right. She is very old, dressed in cheap calico, bare-footed, a red bandana handkerchief covering all but a few stray wisps of white hair. A bundle bound in colored cloth is carried over her shoulder on the end of a stick. She hesitates beside the doorway, peering back as if in extreme dread of being discovered. Then she begins to glide noiselessly, a step at a time, toward the doorway in the rear. At this moment, Smithers appears beneath the portico.

Smithers is a tall, stoop-shouldered man about forty. His bald head, perched on a long neck with an enormous Adam's apple, looks like an egg. The tropics have tanned his naturally pasty face with its small, sharp features to a sickly yellow, and native rum has painted his pointed nose to a startling red. His little, washy-blue eyes are red-rimmed and dart about him like a ferret's. His expression is one of unscrupulous meanness, cowardly and dangerous. He is dressed in a worn riding suit of dirty white drill, puttees, spurs, and wears a white cork helmet. A cartridge belt with an automatic revolver is around his waist. He carries a riding whip in his hand. He sees the woman and stops to watch her suspiciously. Then, making up his mind, he steps quickly on tiptoe into the room. The woman, looking back over her shoulder continually, does not see him until it is too late. When she does Smithers springs forward and grabs her firmly by the shoulder. She struggles to get away, fiercely but silently.

SMITHERS (*tightening his grasp—roughly*). Easy! None o' that, me birdie. You can't wriggle out now. I got me 'ooks on yer.

WOMAN (*seeing the uselessness of struggling, gives way to frantic terror, and sinks to the ground, embracing his knees supplicatingly*). No tell him! No tell him, Mister!

SMITHERS (*with great curiosity*). Tell 'im? (*Then scornfully.*) Oh, you mean 'is bloomin' Majesty. What's the gaime, any 'ow? What are you sneakin' away for? Been stealin' a bit, I s'pose. (*He taps her bundle with his riding whip significantly.*)

WOMAN (*shaking her head vehemently*). No, me no steal.

SMITHERS. Bloody liar! But tell me what's up. There's somethin' funny goin' on. I smelled it in the air first thing I got up this mornin'. You blacks are up to some devilment. This palace of 'is is like a bleedin' tomb. Where's all the 'ands?

(*The woman keeps sullenly silent. Smithers raises his whip threateningly.*)

Ow, yer won't, won't yer? I'll show yer what's what.

WOMAN (*coweringly*). I tell, Mister. You no hit. They go—all go. (*She makes a sweeping gesture toward the hills in the distance.*)

SMITHERS. Run away—to the 'ills?

WOMAN. Yes, Mister. Him Emperor—Great Father. (*She touches her forehead to the floor with a quick mechanical jerk.*) Him sleep after eat. Then they go—all go. Me old woman. Me left only. Now me go too.

SMITHERS (*his astonishment giving way to an immense, mean satisfaction*). Ow! So that's the ticket! Well, I know bloody well wot's in the air—when they runs orf to the 'ills. The tom-tom 'll be thumping out there bloomin' soon. (*With extreme vindictiveness.*) And I'm bloody glad of it, for one! Serve 'im right! Puttin' on airs, the stinkin' nigger! 'Is Majesty! Gawd blimey! I only 'opes I'm there when they takes 'im out to shoot 'im. (*Suddenly.*) 'E's still 'ere all right, ain't 'e?

WOMAN. Yes. Him sleep.

SMITHERS. 'E's bound to find out soon as 'e wakes up. 'E's cunnin' enough to know when 'is time's come.

(*He goes to the doorway on right and whistles shrilly with his fingers in his mouth. The old woman springs to her feet and runs out of the doorway, rear. Smithers goes after her, reaching for his revolver.*)

Stop or I'll shoot! (*Then stopping—indifferently.*) Pop orf then, if yer like, yer black cow. (*He stands in the doorway, looking after her.*)

(*Jones enters from the right. He is a tall, powerfully-built, full-blooded Negro of middle age. His features are typically negroid, yet there is something decidedly distinctive about his face—an underlying strength of will, a hardy, self-reliant confidence in himself that inspires respect. His eyes are alive with a keen, cunning intelligence. In manner he is shrewd, suspicious, evasive. He wears a light blue uniform coat, sprayed with brass buttons, heavy gold* chevrons on his shoulders, gold braid on the collar, cuffs, etc. His pants are bright red with a light blue stripe down the side. Patent-leather laced boots with brass spurs, and a belt with a long-barreled, pearl-handled revolver in a holster complete his make up. Yet there is something not altogether ridiculous about his grandeur. He has a way of carrying it off.)

JONES (*not seeing anyone—greatly irritated and blinking sleepily—shouts*). Who dare whistle dat way in my palace? Who dare wake up de Emperor? I'll git de hide fravled off some o' you niggers sho'!

SMITHERS (*showing himself—in a manner half-afraid and half-defiant*). It was me whistled to yer. (*As Jones frowns angrily.*) I got news for yer.

JONES (*putting on his suavest manner, which fails to cover up his contempt for the white man*). Oh, it's you, Mister Smithers. (*He sits down on his throne with easy dignity.*) What news you got to tell me?

SMITHERS (*coming close to enjoy his discomfiture*). Don't yer notice nothin' funny today?

JONES (*coldly*). Funny? No. I ain't perceived nothin' of de kind!

SMITHERS. Then yer ain't so foxy as I thought yer was. Where's all your court? (*Sarcastically.*) The Generals and the Cabinet Ministers and all?

JONES (*imperturbably*). Where dey mostly runs de minute I closes my eyes—drinkin' rum and talkin' big down in de town. (*Sarcastically.*) How come you don't know dat? Ain't you sousin' with 'em most every day?

SMITHERS (*stung but pretending indifference—with a wink*). That's part of the day's work. I got ter—ain't I—in my business?

JONES (*contemptuously*). Yo' business!

SMITHERS (*imprudently enraged*). Gawd blimey, you was glad enough for me ter take yer in on it when you landed here first. You didn' 'ave no 'igh and mighty airs in them days!

JONES (*his hand going to his revolver like a flash—menacingly*). Talk polite, white man! Talk polite, you heah me! I'm boss heah now, is you fergettin'? (*The Cockney seems about to challenge this last statement with the facts but something in the other's eyes holds and cows him.*)

SMITHERS (*in a cowardly whine*). No 'arm meant, old top.

JONES (*condescendingly*). I accepts yo' apology. (*Lets his hand fall from his revolver.*) No use'n you rakin' up ole times. What I was den is one thing. What I is now 's another. You didn't let me in on yo' crooked work out o' no kind feelin's dat time. I done de dirty work fo' you—and most o' de brain work, too, fo' dat matter—and I was wu'th money to you, dat's de reason.

SMITHERS. Well, blimey, I give yer a start, didn't I—when no one else would. I wasn't afraid to 'ire yer like the rest was—'count of the story about your breakin' jail back in the States.

JONES. No, you didn't have no s'cuse to look down on me fo' dat. You been in jail you'self more'n once.

SMITHERS (*furiously*). It's a lie! (*Then trying to pass it off by an attempt at scorn.*) Garn! Who told yer that fairy tale?

JONES. Dey's some tings I ain't got to be tole. I kin see 'em in folk's eyes. (*Then after a pause—meditatively.*) Yes, you sho' give me a start. And it didn't take long from dat time to git dese fool, woods' niggers right where I wanted dem. (*With pride.*) From stowaway to Emperor in two years! Dat's goin' some!

SMITHERS (*with curiosity*). And I bet you got yer pile o' money 'id safe some place.

JONES (*with satisfaction*). I sho' has! And it's in a foreign bank where no pusson don't ever git it out but me no matter what come. You didn't s'pose I was holdin' down dis Emperor job for de glory in it, did you? Sho'! De fuss and glory part of it, dat's only to turn de heads o' de low-flung, bush niggers dat's here. Dey wants de big circus show for deir money. I gives it to 'em an' I gits de money. (*With a grin.*) De long green, dat's me every time! (*Then rebukingly.*) But you ain't got no kick agin me, Smithers. I'se paid you back all you done for me many times. Ain't I pertected you and winked at all de crooked tradin' you been doin' right out in de broad day? Sho' I has—and me makin' laws to stop it at de same time! (*He chuckles.*)

SMITHERS (*grinning*). But, meanin' no 'arm, you been grabbin' right and left yourself, ain't yer? Look at the taxes you've put on 'em! Blimey! You've squeezed 'em dry!

JONES (*chuckling*). No, dey ain't *all* dry yet. I'se still heah, ain't I?

SMITHERS (*smiling at his secret thought*). They're dry right now, you'll find out. (*Changing the subject abruptly.*) And as for me breakin' laws, you've broke 'em all yerself just as fast as yer made 'em.

JONES. Ain't I de Emperor? De laws don't go for him. (*Judicially.*) You heah what I tells you, Smithers. Dere's little stealin' like you does, and dere's big stealin' like I does. For de little stealin' dey gits you in jail soon or late. For de big stealin' dey makes you Emperor and puts you in de Hall o' Fame when you croaks. (*Reminiscently.*) If dey's one thing I learns in ten years on de Pullman ca's listenin' to de white quality talk, it's dat same fact. And when I gits a chance to use it I winds up Emperor in two years.

SMITHERS (*unable to repress the genuine admiration of the small fry for the large*). Yes, yer turned the bleedin' trick, all right. Blimey, I never seen a bloke 'as 'ad the bloomin' luck you 'as.

JONES (*severely*). Luck? What you mean—luck?

SMITHERS. I suppose you'll say as that swank about the silver bullet ain't luck—and that was what first got the fool blacks on yer side the time of the revolution, wasn't it?

JONES (*with a laugh*). Oh, dat silver bullet! Sho' was luck! But I makes dat luck, you heah? I loads de dice! Yessuh! When dat murderin' nigger ole Lem hired to kill me takes aim ten feet away and his gun misses fire and I shoots him dead, what you heah me say?

SMITHERS. You said yer'd got a charm so's no lead bullet'd kill yer. You was so strong only a silver bullet could kill yer, you told 'em. Blimey, wasn't that swank for yer—and plain, fat-'eaded luck?

JONES (*proudly*). I got brains and I uses 'em quick. Dat ain't luck.

SMITHERS. Yer know they wasn't 'ardly liable to get no silver bullets. And it was luck 'e didn't 'it you that time.

JONES (*laughing*). And dere all dem fool, bush niggers was kneelin' down and bumpin' deir heads on de ground like I was a miracle out o' de Bible. Oh Lawd, from dat time on I has dem all eatin' out of my hand. I cracks de whip and dey jumps through.

SMITHERS (*with a sniff*). Yankee bluff done it.

JONES. Ain't a man's talkin' big what makes him big—long as he makes folks believe it? Sho', I talks large when I ain't got nothin' to back it up, but I ain't talkin' wild just de same. I knows I kin fool 'em—I *knows* it—and dat's backin' enough fo' my game. And ain't I got to learn deir lingo and teach some of dem English befo' I kin talk to 'em? Ain't dat wuk? You ain't never learned ary word er it, Smithers, in de ten years you been heah, dough yo' knows it's money in yo' pocket tradin' wid 'em if you does. But you'se too shiftless to take de trouble.

SMITHERS (*flushing*). Never mind about me. What's this I've 'eard about yer really 'avin' a silver bullet moulded for yourself?

JONES. It's playin' out my bluff. I has de silver bullet moulded and I tells 'em when de time comes I kills myself wid it. I tells 'em dat's 'cause I'm de on'y man in de world big enuff to git me. No use'n deir tryin'. And dey falls down and bumps deir heads. (*He laughs.*) I does dat so's I kin take a walk in peace widout no jealous nigger gunnin' at me from behind de trees.

SMITHERS (*astonished*). Then you 'ad it made—'onest?

JONES. Sho' did. Heah she be. (*He takes out his revolver, breaks it, and takes the silver bullet out of one chamber.*) Five lead an' dis silver baby at de last. Don't she shine pretty? (*He holds it in his hand, looking at it admiringly, as if strangely fascinated.*)

SMITHERS. Let me see. (*Reaches out his hand for it.*)

JONES (*harshly*). Keep yo' hands whar dey b'long, white man. (*He replaces it in the chamber and puts the revolver back on his hip.*)

SMITHERS (*snarling*). Gawd blimey! Think I'm a bleedin' thief, you would.

JONES. No, 'tain't dat. I knows you'se scared to steal from me. On'y I ain't 'lowin' nary body to touch dis baby. She's my rabbit's foot.

SMITHERS (*sneering*). A bloomin' charm, wot? (*Venomously.*) Well, you'll need all the bloody charms you 'as before long, s' 'elp me!

JONES (*judicially*). Oh, I'se good for six months yit 'fore dey gits sick o' my game. Den, when I sees trouble comin', I makes my getaway.

SMITHERS. Ho! You got it all planned, ain't yer?

JONES. I ain't no fool. I knows dis Emperor's time is sho't. Dat why I make hay when de sun shine. Was you thinkin' I'se aimin' to hold down dis job for life? No, suh! What good is gittin' money if you stays back in dis raggedy country? I wants action when I spends. And when I sees dese niggers gittin' up deir nerve to tu'n me out, and I'se got all de money in sight, I resigns on de spot and beats it quick.

SMITHERS. Where to?

JONES. None o' yo' business.

SMITHERS. Not back to the bloody States, I'll lay my oath.

JONES (*suspiciously*). Why don't I? (*Then with an easy laugh.*) You mean 'count of dat story 'bout me breakin' from jail back dere? Dat's all talk.

SMITHERS (*skeptically*). Ho, yes!

JONES (*sharply*). You ain't 'sinuatin' I'se a liar, is you?

SMITHERS (*hastily*). No, Gawd strike me! I was only thinkin' o' the bloody lies you told the blacks 'ere about killin' white men in the States.

JONES (*angered*). How come dey're lies?

SMITHERS. You'd 'ave been in jail if you 'ad, wouldn't yer then? (*With venom.*) And from what I've 'eard, it ain't 'ealthy for a black to kill a white man in the States. They burns 'em in oil, don't they?

JONES (*with cool deadliness*). You mean lynchin' 'd scare me? Well, I tells you, Smithers, maybe I does kill one white man back dere. Maybe I does. And maybe I kills another right heah 'fore long if he don't look out.

SMITHERS (*trying to force a laugh*). I was on'y spoofin' yer. Can't yer take a joke? And you was just sayin' you'd never been in jail.

JONES (*in the same tone—slightly boastful*). Maybe I goes to jail dere for gettin' in an argument wid razors ovah a crap game. Maybe I gits twenty years when dat colored man die. Maybe I gits in 'nother argument wid de prison guard was overseer ovah us when we're wukin' de roads. Maybe he hits me wid a whip and I splits his head wid a shovel and runs away and files de chain off my leg and gits away safe. Maybe I does all dat an' maybe I don't. It's a story I tells you so's you knows I'se de kind of man dat if you evah repeats one word of it, I ends yo' stealin' on dis yearth mighty damn quick!

SMITHERS (*terrified*). Think I'd peach on yer? Not me! Ain't I always been yer friend?

JONES (*suddenly relaxing*). Sho' you has—and you better be.

SMITHERS (*recovering his composure—and with it his malice*). And just to show yer I'm yer friend, I'll tell yer that bit o' news I was goin' to.

JONES. Go ahead! Shoot de piece. Must be bad news from de happy way you look.

SMITHERS (*warningly*). Maybe it's gettin' time for you to resign—with that bloomin' silver bullet, wot? (*He finishes with a mocking grin.*)

JONES (*puzzled*). What's dat you say? Talk plain.

SMITHERS. Ain't noticed any of the guards or servants about the place today, I 'aven't.

JONES (*carelessly*). Dey're all out in de garden sleepin' under de trees. When I sleeps, dey sneaks a sleep, too, and I pretends I never suspicions it. All I got to do is to ring de bell and dey come flyin', makin' a bluff dey was wukin' all de time.

SMITHERS (*in the same mocking tone*). Ring the bell now an' you'll bloody well see what I means.

JONES (*startled to alertness, but preserving the same careless tone*). Sho' I rings. (*He reaches below the throne and pulls out a big, common dinner bell which is painted the same vivid scarlet as the throne. He rings this vigorously—then stops to listen. Then he goes to both doors, rings again, and looks out.*)

SMITHERS (*watching him with malicious satisfaction, after a pause—mockingly*). The bloody ship is sinkin' an' the bleedin' rats 'as slung their 'ooks.

JONES (*in a sudden fit of anger flings the bell clattering into a corner*). Low-flung, woods' niggers! (*Then catching Smithers' eye on him, he controls himself and suddenly bursts into a low chuckling laugh.*) Reckon I overplays my hand dis once! A man can't take de pot on a bob-tailed flush all de time. Was I sayin' I'd sit in six months mo'? Well, I'se changed my mind den. I cashes in and resigns de job of Emperor right dis minute.

SMITHERS (*with real admiration*). Blimey, but you're a cool bird, and no mistake.

JONES. No use'n fussin'. When I knows de game's up I kisses it good-bye widout no long waits. Dey've all run off to de hills, ain't dey?

SMITHERS. Yes—every bleedin' man jack of 'em.

JONES. Den de revolution is at de post. And de Emperor better git his feet smokin' up de trail. (*He starts for the door in rear.*)

SMITHERS. Goin' out to look for your 'orse? Yer won't find any. They steals the 'orses first thing. Mine was gone when I went for 'im this mornin'. That's wot first give me a suspicion of wot was up.

JONES (*alarmed for a second, scratches his head, then philosophically*). Well, den I hoofs it. Feet, do yo' duty! (*He pulls out a gold watch and looks at it.*) Three-thuty. Sundown's at six-thuty or dereabouts. (*Puts his watch back—with cool confidence.*) I got plenty o' time to make it easy.

SMITHERS. Don't be so bloomin' sure of it. They'll be after you 'ot and 'eavy. Ole Lem is at the bottom o' this business an' 'e 'ates you like 'ell. 'E'd rather do for you than eat 'is dinner, 'e would!

JONES (*scornfully*). Dat fool no-count nigger! Does you think I'se scared o' him? I stands him on his thick head more'n once befo' dis, and I does it again if he come in my way . . . (*Fiercely.*) And dis time I leave him a dead nigger fo' sho'!

SMITHERS. You'll 'ave to cut through the big forest—an' these blacks 'ere can sniff and follow a trail in the dark like 'ounds. You'd 'ave to 'ustle to get through that forest in twelve hours even if you knew all the bloomin' trails like a native.

JONES (*with indignant scorn*). Look-a-heah, white man! Does you think I'se a natural bo'n fool? Give me credit fo' havin' some sense, fo' Lawd's sake! Don't you s'pose I'se looked ahead and made sho' of all de chances? I'se gone out in dat big forest, pretendin' to hunt, so many times dat I knows it high an' low like a book. I could go through on dem trails wid my eyes shut. (*With great contempt.*) Think dese ign'rent bush niggers dat ain't got brains enuff to know deir own names even can catch Brutus Jones? Huh, I s'pects not! Not on yo' life! Why, man, de white men went after me wid bloodhounds where I come from an' I jes' laughs at 'em. It's a shame to fool dese black trash around heah, dey're so easy. You watch me, man! I'll make dem look sick, I will. I'll be 'cross de plain to de edge of de forest by time dark comes. Once in de woods in de night, dey got a swell chance o' findin' dis baby! Dawn tomorrow I'll be out at de oder side and on de coast whar dat French gunboat is stayin'. She picks me up, take me to Martinique when she go dar, and dere I is safe wid a mighty big bankroll in my jeans. It's easy as rollin' off a log.

SMITHERS (*maliciously*). But s'posin' somethin' 'appens wrong an' they do nab yer?

JONES (*decisively*). Dey don't—dat's de answer.

SMITHERS. But, just for argyment's sake—what'd you do?

JONES (*frowning*). I'se got five lead bullets in dis gun good enuff fo' common bush niggers—and after dat I got de silver bullet left to cheat 'em out o' gittin' me.

SMITHERS (*jeeringly*). Ho, I was fergettin' that silver bullet. You'll bump yourself orf in style, won't yer? Blimey!

JONES (*gloomily*). You kin bet yo' whole roll on one thing, white man. Dis baby plays out his string to de end and when he quits, he quits wid a bang de way he ought. Silver bullet ain't none too good for him when he go, dat's a fac'! (*Then shaking off his nervousness—with a confident laugh.*) Sho'! What is I talkin' about? Ain't come to dat yit and I never will—not wid trash niggers like dese yere. (*Boastfully.*) Silver bullet bring me luck anyway. I kin outguess, outrun, outfight, an' outplay de whole lot o' dem all ovah de board any time o' de day er night! You watch me!

(*From the distant hills comes the faint, steady thump of a tom-tom, low and vibrating. It starts at a rate exactly corresponding to normal pulse beat—72 to the minute—and continues at a gradually accelerating rate from this point uninterruptedly to the very end of the play.*

Jones starts at the sound. A strange look of apprehension creeps into his face for a moment as he listens. Then he asks, with an attempt to regain his most casual manner.)

What's dat drum beatin' fo'?

SMITHERS (*with a mean grin*). For you. That means the bleedin' ceremony 'as started. I've 'eard it before and I knows.

JONES. Cer'mony? What cer'mony?

SMITHERS. The blacks is 'oldin' a bloody meetin', 'avin' a war dance, gettin' their courage worked up b'fore they starts after you.

JONES. Let dem! Dey'll sho' need it!

SMITHERS. And they're there 'oldin' their 'eathen religious service—makin' no end of devil spells and charms to 'elp 'em against your silver bullet. (*He guffaws loudly.*) Blimey, but they're balmy as 'ell!

JONES (*a tiny bit awed and shaken in spite of himself*). Huh! Takes more'n dat to scare dis chicken!

SMITHERS (*scenting the other's feeling—maliciously*). Ternight when it's pitch black in the forest, they'll 'ave their pet devils and ghosts 'oundin' after you. You'll find yer bloody 'air 'll be standin' on end before termorrow mornin'. (*Seriously.*) It's a bleedin' queer place, that stinkin' forest, even in daylight. Yer don't know what might 'appen in there, it's that rotten still. Always sends the cold shivers down my back minute I gets in it.

JONES (*with a contemptuous sniff*). I ain't no chicken-liver like you is. Trees an' me, we'se friends, and dar's a full moon comin' bring me light. And let dem po' niggers make all de fool spells dey'se a min' to. Does yo' s'pect I'se silly enuff to b'lieve in ghosts an' ha'nts an' all dat ole woman's talk? G'long, white man! You ain't talkin' to me. (*With a chuckle.*) Doesn't you know dey's got to do wid a man was member in good standin' o' de Baptist Church? Sho' I was dat when I was porter on de Pullmans, befo' I gits into my little trouble. Let dem try deir heathen tricks. De Baptist Church done pertect me and land dem all in hell. (*Then with more confident satisfaction.*) And I'se got little silver bullet o' my own, don't forgit.

SMITHERS. Ho! You 'aven't give much 'eed to your Baptist Church since you been down 'ere. I've 'eard myself you 'ad turned yer coat an' was takin' up with their blarsted witch-doctors, or whatever the 'ell yer calls the swine.

JONES (*vehemently*). I pretends to! Sho' I pretends! Dat's part o' my game from de fust. If I finds out dem niggers believes dat black is white, den I yells it out louder 'n deir loudest. It don't git me nothin' to do missionary work for de Baptist Church. I'se after de coin, an' I lays my Jesus on de shelf for de time bein'. (*Stops abruptly to look at his watch—alertly.*) But I ain't got de time to waste no more fool talk wid you. I'se gwine away from heah dis secon'. (*He reaches in under the throne and pulls out an expensive Panama hat with a bright multi-colored band and sets it jaun-*

tily on his head.) So long, white man! (*With a grin.*) See you in jail sometime, maybe!

SMITHERS. Not me, you won't. Well, I wouldn't be in yer bloody boots for no bloomin' money, but 'ere's wishin' yer luck just the same.

JONES (*contemptuously*). Yo're de frightenedest man evah I see! I tells you I'se safe's 'f I was in New York City. It takes dem niggers from now to dark to git up de nerve to start somethin'. By dat time, I'se got a head start dey never kotch up wid.

SMITHERS (*maliciously*). Give my regards to any ghosts yer meets up with.

JONES (*grinning*). If dat ghost got money, I'll tell him never ha'nt you less'n he wants to lose it.

SMITHERS (*flattered*). Garn! (*Then curiously.*) Ain't yer takin' no luggage with yer?

JONES. I travels light when I wants to move fast. And I got tinned grub buried on de edge o' de forest. (*Boastfully.*) Now say dat I don't look ahead an' use my brains! (*With a wide, liberal gesture.*) I will all dat's left in de palace to you—and you better grab all you kin sneak away wid befo' dey gits here.

SMITHERS (*gratefully*). Righto—and thanks ter yer. (*As Jones walks toward the door in rear—cautioningly.*) Say! Look 'ere, you ain't goin' out that way, are yer?

JONES. Does you think I'd slink out de back door like a common nigger? I'se Emperor yit, ain't I? And de Emperor Jones leaves de way he comes, and dat black trash don't dare stop him—not yit, leastways. (*He stops for a moment in the doorway, listening to the far-off but insistent beat of the tom-tom.*) Listen to dat roll-call, will you? Must be mighty big drum carry dat far. (*Then with a laugh.*) Well, if dey ain't no whole brass band to see me off, I sho' got de drum part of it. So long, white man. (*He puts his hands in his pockets and with studied carelessness, whistling a tune, he saunters out of the doorway and off to the left.*)

SMITHERS (*looks after him with a puzzled admiration*). 'E's got 'is bloomin' nerve with 'im, s'elp me! (*Then angrily.*) Ho—the bleedin' nigger—puttin' on 'is bloody airs! I 'opes they nabs 'im an' gives 'im what's what! (*Then putting business before the pleasure of this thought, looking around him with cupidity.*) A bloke ought to find a 'ole lot in this palace that'd go for a bit of cash. Let's take a look, 'Arry, me lad. (*He starts for the doorway on right as*

THE CURTAIN FALLS

SCENE 2

SCENE: *Nightfall. The end of the plain where the Great Forest begins. The foreground is sandy, level ground dotted by a few stones and clumps of stunted bushes covering close against the earth to escape the buffeting of the trade wind. In the rear the forest is a wall of darkness dividing the world. Only when the eye becomes accustomed to the gloom can the outlines of separate trunks of the nearest trees be made out, enormous pillars of deeper blackness. A somber monotone of wind lost in the leaves moans in the air. Yet this sound serves but to intensify the impression of the forest's relentless immobility, to form a background throwing into relief its brooding, implacable silence.*

Jones enters from the left, walking rapidly. He stops as he nears the edge of the forest, looks around him quickly, peering into the dark as if searching for some familiar landmark. Then, apparently, satisfied that he is where he ought to be, he throws himself on the ground, dog-tired.

Well, heah I is. In de nick o' time, too! Little mo' an' it'd be blacker'n de ace of spades heahabouts. (*He pulls a bandana handkerchief from his hip pocket and mops off his perspiring face.*) Sho'! Gimme air! I'se tuckered out sho' nuff. Dat soft Emperor job ain't no trainin' fo' a long hike ovah dat plain in de brilin' sun. (*Then with a chuckle.*) Cheah up, nigger, de worst is yet to come. (*He lifts his head and stares at the forest. His chuckle peters out abruptly. In a tone of awe.*) My goodness, look at dem woods, will you? Dat no-count Smithers said dey'd be black an' he sho' called de turn. (*Turning away from them quickly and looking down at his feet, he snatches at a chance to change the subject— solicitously.*) Feet, you is holdin' up yo' end fine an' I sutinly hopes you ain't blisterin' none. It's time you git a rest. (*He takes off his shoes, his eyes studiously avoiding the forest. He feels of the soles of his feet gingerly.*) You is still in de pink—on'y a little mite feverish. Cool yo'selfs. Remember you done got a long journey yit befo' you. (*He sits in a weary attitude, listening to the rhythmic beating of the tom-tom. He grumbles in a loud tone to cover up a growing uneasiness.*) Bush niggers! Wonder dey wouldn' get sick o' beatin' dat drum. Sound louder, seem like. I wonder if dey's startin' after me? (*He scrambles to his feet, looking back across the plain.*) Couldn't see dem now, nohow, if dey was hundred feet away. (*Then shaking himself like a wet dog to get rid of these depressing thoughts.*) Sho', dey's miles an' miles behind. What you gittin' fidgety about? (*But he sits down and begins to lace up his shoes in great haste, all the time muttering reassuringly.*) You know what? Yo' belly is empty, dat's what's de matter wid you. Come time to eat! Wid nothin' but wind on yo' stumach, o' course you feels jiggedy. Well, we eats right heah an' now soon's I gits dese pesky shoes laced up! (*He finishes lacing up his shoes.*) Dere! Now le's see. (*Gets on his hands and knees and searches the ground around him with his eyes.*) White stone, white stone, where is you? (*He sees the first white stone and crawls to it—with satisfaction.*) Heah you is! I knowed dis was de right place. Box of grub, come to me. (*He turns over the stone and feels in under it—in a tone of dismay.*) Ain't heah! Gorry, is I in de right place or isn't I? Dere's 'nother stone. Guess dat's it. (*He scrambles to the next stone and turns it over.*) Ain't heah, neither! Grub, whar is you? Ain't heah. Gorry, has I got to go hungry into dem woods—all de night? (*While he is talking he scrambles from*

one stone to another, turning them over in frantic haste. Finally, he jumps to his feet excitedly.*) Is I lost de place? Must have! But how dat happen when I was followin' de trail across de plain in broad daylight? (*Almost plaintively.*) I'se hungry, I is! I gotta git my feed. Whar's my strength gonna come from if I doesn't? Gorry, I gotta find dat grub high an' low somehow! Why it come dark so quick like dat? Can't see nothin'. (*He scratches a match on his trousers and peers about him. The rate of the beat of the far-off tom-tom increases perceptibly as he does so. He mutters in a bewildered voice.*) How come all dese white stones come heah when I only remembers one? (*Suddenly, with a frightened gasp, he flings the match on the ground and stamps on it.*) Nigger, is you gone crazy mad? Is you lightin' matches to show dem whar you is? Fo' Lawd's sake, use yo' haid. Gorry, I'se got to be careful! (*He stares at the plain behind him apprehensively, his hand on his revolver.*) But how come all dese white stones? And whar's dat tin box o' grub I had all wrapped up in oil cloth?

(*While his back is turned, the Little Formless Fears creep out from the deeper blackness of the forest. They are black, shapeless, only their glittering little eyes can be seen. If they have any describable form at all it is that of a grubworm about the size of a creeping child. They move noiselessly, but with deliberate, painful effort, striving to raise themselves on end, failing and sinking prone again. Jones turns about to face the forest. He stares up at the tops of the trees, seeking vainly to discover his whereabouts by their conformation.*)

Can't tell nothin' from dem trees! Gorry, nothin' 'round heah look like I evah seed befo'. I'se done lost de place sho' 'nuff! (*With mournful foreboding.*) It's mighty queer! It's mighty queer! (*With sudden forced defiance—in an angry tone.*) Woods, is you tryin' to put somethin' ovah on me?

(*From the formless creatures on the ground in front of him comes a tiny gale of low mocking laughter like a rustling of leaves. They squirm upward toward him in twisted attitudes. Jones looks down, leaps backward with a yell of terror, yanking out his revolver as he does so—in a quavering voice.*)

What's dat? Who's dar? What is you? Git away from me befo' I shoots you up! You don't? . . .

(*He fires. There is a flash, a loud report, then silence broken only by the far-off, quickened throb of the tom-tom. The formless creatures have scurried back into the forest. Jones remains fixed in his position, listening intently. The sound of the shot, the reassuring feel of the revolver in his hand, have somewhat restored his shaken nerve. He addresses himself with renewed confidence.*)

Dey're gone. Dat shot fix 'em. Dey was only little animals—little wild pigs, I reckon. Dey've maybe rooted out yo' grub an' eat it. Sho', you fool nigger, what you think dey is—ha'nts? (*Excitedly.*) Gorry, you give de game away when you fire dat shot. Dem niggers heah dat fo' su'tin! Time you beat it in de woods widout no long waits. (*He starts for the forest—hesitates before the plunge—then urging himself in with manful resolution.*) Git in, nigger! What you skeered at? Ain't nothin' dere but de trees! Git in! (*He plunges boldly into the forest.*)

SCENE 3

SCENE: *Nine o'clock. In the forest. The moon has just risen. Its beams, drifting through the canopy of leaves, make a barely perceptible, suffused, eerie glow. A dense low wall of underbrush and creepers is in the nearer foreground, fencing in a small triangular clearing. Beyond this is the massed blackness of the forest like an encompassing barrier. A path is dimly discerned leading down to the clearing from left, rear, and winding away from it again toward the right. As the scene opens nothing can be distinctly made out. Except for the beating of the tom-tom, which is a trifle louder and quicker than in the previous scene, there is silence, broken every few seconds by a queer, clicking sound. Then gradually the figure of the Negro, Jeff, can be discerned crouching on his haunches at the rear of the triangle. He is middle-aged, thin, brown in color, is dressed in a Pullman porter's uniform, cap, etc. He is throwing a pair of dice on the ground before him, picking them up, shaking them, casting them out with the regular, rigid, mechanical movements of an automaton. The heavy, plodding footsteps of someone approaching along the trail from the left are heard and Jones' voice, pitched in a slightly higher key and strained in a cheering effort to overcome its own tremors.*

De moon's rizen. Does you heah dat, nigger? You gits more light from dis out. No mo' buttin' yo' fool head agin' de trunks an' scratchin' de hide off yo' legs in de bushes. Now you sees whar yo'se gwine. So cheer up! From now on you has a snap. (*He steps just to the rear of the triangular clearing and mops off his face on his sleeve. He has lost his Panama hat. His face is scratched, his brilliant uniform shows several large rents.*) What time's it gittin' to be, I wonder? I dassent light no match to find out. Phoo'. It's wa'm an' dat's a fac'! (*Wearily.*) How long I been makin' tracks in dese woods? Must be hours an' hours. Seems like fo'evah! Yit can't be, when de moon's jes' riz. Dis am a long night fo' yo', yo' Majesty! (*With a mournful chuckle.*) Majesty! Der ain't much majesty 'bout dis baby now. (*With attempted cheerfulness.*) Never min'. It's all part o' de game. Dis night come to an end like everything else. And when you gits dar safe and has dat bankroll in yo' hands you laughs at all dis. (*He starts to whistle but checks himself abruptly.*) What yo' whistlin' for, you po' dope! Want all de worl' to heah you? (*He stops talking to listen.*) Heah dat ole drum! Sho' gits nearer from de

sound. Dey're packin' it along wid 'em. Time fo' me to move. (*He takes a step forward, then stops—worriedly.*) What's dat odder queer clickety sound I heah? Dere it is! Sound close! Sound like—sound like—Fo' God sake, sound like some nigger was shootin' crap! (*Frightenedly.*) I better beat it quick when I gits dem notions. (*He walks quickly into the clear space—then stands transfixed as he sees Jeff—in a terrified gasp.*) Who dar? Who dat? Is dat you, Jeff? (*Starting toward the other, forgetful for a moment of his surroundings and really believing it is a living man that he sees—in a tone of happy relief.*) Jeff! I'se sho' mighty glad to see you! Dey tol' me you done died from dat razor cut I gives you. (*Stopping suddenly, bewilderedly.*) But how you come to be heah, nigger? (*He stares fascinatedly at the other who continues his mechanical play with the dice. Jones' eyes begin to roll wildly. He stutters.*) Ain't you gwine—look up—can't you speak to me? Is you—is you—a ha'nt? (*He jerks out his revolver in a frenzy of terrified rage.*) Nigger, I kills you dead once. Has I got to kill you again? You take it den. (*He fires. When the smoke clears away Jeff has disappeared. Jones stands trembling—then with a certain reassurance.*) He's gone, anyway. Ha'nt or no ha'nt, dat shot fix him. (*The beat of the far-off tom-tom is perceptibly louder and more rapid. Jones becomes conscious of it—with a start, looking back over his shoulder.*) Dey's gittin' near! Dey's comin' fast! And heah I is shootin' shots to let 'em know jes' whar I is. Oh, Gorry, I'se got to run. (*Forgetting the path he plunges wildly into the underbrush in the rear and disappears in the shadow.*)

SCENE 4

SCENE: *Eleven o'clock. In the forest. A wide dirt road runs diagonally from right, front, to left, rear. Rising sheer on both sides the forest walls it in. The moon is now up. Under its light the road glimmers ghastly and unreal. It is as if the forest had stood aside momentarily to let the road pass through and accomplish its veiled purpose. This done, the forest will fold in upon itself again and the road will be no more. Jones stumbles in from the forest on the right. His uniform is ragged and torn. He looks about him with numbed surprise when he sees the road, his eyes blinking in the bright moonlight. He flops down exhaustedly and pants heavily for a while. Then with sudden anger.*

I'm meltin' wid heat! Runnin' an' runnin' an' runnin'! Damn dis heah coat! Like a strait-jacket! (*He tears off his coat and flings it away from him, revealing himself stripped to the waist.*) Dere! Dat's better! Now I kin breathe! (*Looking down at his feet, the spurs catch his eye.*) And to hell wid dese high-fangled spurs. Dey're what's been a-trippin' me up an' breakin' my neck. (*He unstraps them and flings them away disgustedly.*) Dere! I gits rid o' dem frippety Emperor trappin's an' I travels lighter. Lawd! I'se tired! (*After a pause, listening to the insistent beat of the tom-tom in* the distance.) I must 'a put some distance between myself an' dem—runnin' like dat—and yit—dat damn drum sound jes' de same—nearer, even. Well, I guess I a'most holds my lead anyhow. Dey won't never catch up. (*With a sigh.*) If on'y my fool legs stands up. Oh, I'se sorry I evah went in for dis. Dat Emperor job is sho' hard to shake. (*He looks around him suspiciously.*) How'd dis road evah git heah? Good level road, too. I never remembers seein' it befo'. (*Shaking his head apprehensively.*) Dese woods is sho' full o' de queerest things at night. (*With a sudden terror.*) Lawd God, don't let me see no more o' dem ha'nts! Dey gits my goat! (*Then trying to talk himself into confidence.*) Ha'nts! You fool nigger, dey ain't no such things! Don't de Baptist parson tell you dat many time? Is you civilized, or is you like dese ign'rent black niggers heah? Sho'! Dat was all in yo' own head. Wasn't nothin' dere. Wasn't no Jeff! Know what? You jus' get seein' dem things 'cause yo' belly's empty and you's sick wid hunger inside. Hunger 'fects yo' head and yo' eyes. Any fool know dat. (*Then pleading fervently.*) But bless God, I don't come across no more o' dem, whatever dey is! (*Then cautiously.*) Rest! Don't talk! Rest! You needs it. Den you gits on yo' way again. (*Looking at the moon.*) Night's half gone a'most. You hits de coast in de mawning! Den you'se all safe.

(*From the right forward a small gang of Negroes enter. They are dressed in striped convict suits, their heads are shaven, one leg drags limpingly, shackled to a heavy ball and chain. Some carry picks, the others shovels. They are followed by a white man dressed in the uniform of a prison guard. A Winchester rifle is slung across his shoulders and he carries a heavy whip. At a signal from the Guard they stop on the road opposite where Jones is sitting. Jones, who has been staring up at the sky, unmindful of their noiseless approach, suddenly looks down and sees them. His eyes pop out, he tries to get to his feet and fly, but sinks back, too numbed by fright to move. His voice catches in a choking prayer.*)

Lawd Jesus!

(*The Prison Guard cracks his whip—noiselessly—and at that signal all the convicts start to work on the road. They swing their picks, they shovel, but not a sound comes from their labor. Their movements, like those of Jeff in the preceding scene, are those of automatons,—rigid, slow, and mechanical. The Prison Guard points sternly at Jones with his whip, motions him to take his place among the other shovelers. Jones gets to his feet in a hypnotized stupor. He mumbles subserviently.*)

Yes, suh! Yes, suh! I'se comin'.

(*As he shuffles, dragging one foot, over to his place, he curses under his breath with rage and hatred.*)

God damn yo' soul, I gits even wid you yit, sometime.

(*As if there were a shovel in his hands he goes through weary, mechanical gestures of digging up dirt, and throwing it to the roadside. Suddenly the Guard approaches him angrily, threateningly. He raises his whip and lashes Jones viciously across the shoulders with it. Jones winces with pain and cowers abjectly. The Guard turns his back on him and walks away contemptuously. Instantly Jones straightens up. With arms upraised as if his shovel were a club in his hands he springs murderously at the unsuspecting Guard. In the act of crashing down his shovel on the white man's skull, Jones suddenly becomes aware that his hands are empty. He cries despairingly.*)

Whar's my shovel? Gimme my shovel till I splits his damn head! (*Appealing to his fellow convicts.*) Gimme a shovel, one o' you, fo' God's sake!

(*They stand fixed in motionless attitudes, their eyes on the ground. The Guard seems to wait expectantly, his back turned to the attacker. Jones bellows with baffled, terrified rage, tugging frantically at his revolver.*)

I kills you, you white debil, if it's de last thing I evah does! Ghost or debil, I kill you again!

(*He frees the revolver and fires point blank at the Guard's back. Instantly the walls of the forest close in from both sides, the road and the figures of the convict gang are blotted out in an enshrouding darkness. The only sounds are a crashing in the underbrush as Jones leaps away in mad flight and the throbbing of the tom-tom, still far distant, but increased in volume of sound and rapidity of beat.*)

SCENE 5

SCENE: *One o'clock. A large circular clearing, enclosed by the serried ranks of gigantic trunks of tall trees whose tops are lost to view. In the center is a big dead stump worn by time into a curious resemblance to an auction block. The moon floods the clearing with a clear light. Jones forces his way in through the forest on the left. He looks wildly about the clearing with hunted, fearful glances. His pants are in tatters, his shoes cut and misshapen, flapping about his feet. He slinks cautiously to the stump in the center and sits down in a tense position, ready for instant flight. Then he holds his head in his hands and rocks back and forth, moaning to himself miserably.*

Oh Lawd, Lawd! Oh Lawd, Lawd! (*Suddenly he throws himself on his knees and raises his clasped hands to the sky—in a voice of agonized pleading.*) Lawd Jesus, heah my prayer! I'se a po' sinner, a po' sinner! I knows I done wrong, I knows it! When I cotches Jeff cheatin' wid loaded dice my anger overcomes me and I kills him dead! Lawd, I done wrong! When dat guard hits me wid de whip, my anger overcomes me, and I kills him dead. Lawd, I done wrong! And down heah whar dese fool bush niggers raises me up to the seat o' de mighty, I steals all I could grab. Lawd, I done wrong! I knows it! I'se sorry! Forgive me, Lawd! Forgive dis po' sinner! (*Then beseeching terrifiedly.*) And keep dem away, Lawd! Keep dem away from me! And stop dat drum soundin' in my ears! Dat begin to sound ha'nted, too. (*He gets to his feet, evidently slightly reassured by his prayer—with attempted confidence.*) De Lawd'll preserve me from dem ha'nts after dis. (*Sits down on the stump again.*) I ain't skeered o' real men. Let dem come. But dem odders . . . (*He shudders—then looks down at his feet, working his toes inside the shoes—with a groan.*) Oh, my po' feet! Dem shoes ain't no use no more 'ceptin' to hurt. I'se better off widout dem. (*He unlaces them and pulls them off—holds the wrecks of the shoes in his hands and regards them mournfully.*) You was real, A-one patin' leather, too. Look at you now. Emperor, you'se gittin' mighty low!

(*He sits dejectedly and remains with bowed shoulders, staring down at the shoes in his hands as if reluctant to throw them away. While his attention is thus occupied, a crowd of figures silently enter the clearing from all sides. All are dressed in Southern costumes of the period of the fifties of the last century. There are middle-aged men who are evidently well-to-do planters. There is one spruce, authoritative individual—the Auctioneer. There is a crowd of curious spectators, chiefly young belles and dandies who have come to the slave-market for diversion. All exchange courtly greetings in dumb show and chat silently together. There is something stiff, rigid, unreal, marionettish about their movements. They group themselves about the stump. Finally a batch of slaves are led in from the left by an attendant—three men of different ages, two women, one with a baby in her arms, nursing. They are placed to the left of the stump, beside Jones.*)

The white planters look them over appraisingly as if they were cattle, and exchange judgments on each. The dandies point with their fingers and make witty remarks. The belles titter bewitchingly. All this in silence save for the ominous throb of the tom-tom. The Auctioneer holds up his hand, taking his place at the stump. The group strain forward attentively. He touches Jones on the shoulder peremptorily, motioning for him to stand on the stump—the auction block.

Jones looks up, sees the figures on all sides, looks wildly for some opening to escape, sees none, screams and leaps madly to the top of the stump to get as far away from them as possible. He stands there, cowering, paralyzed with horror. The Auctioneer begins his silent spiel. He points to Jones appeals to the planters to see for themselves. Here is a good field hand, sound in wind and limb as they can see. Very strong still in spite of his being middle-aged. Look at that back. Look at those shoulders. Look at the muscles in his arms and his sturdy legs. Capable of any amount of hard labor. Moreover, of a good disposition, intelligent and tractable. Will any gentleman start the bidding? The Planters raise their fingers, make their bids. They are ap-

parently all eager to posses Jones. The bidding is lively, the crowd interested. While this has been going on, Jones has been seized by the courage of desperation. He dares to look down and around him. Over his face abject terror gives way to mystification, to gradual realization—stutteringly.)

What you all doin', white folks? What's all dis? What you all lookin' at me fo'? What you doin' wid me, anyhow? (*Suddenly convulsed with raging hatred and fear.*) Is dis a auction? Is you sellin' me like dey uster befo' de war? (*Jerking out his revolver just as the Auctioneer knocks him down to one of the planters—glaring from him to the purchaser.*) And you sells me? And you buys me? I shows you I'se a free nigger, damn yo' souls!

(*He fires at the Auctioneer and at the Planter with such rapidity that the two shots are almost simultaneous. As if this were a signal the walls of the forest fold in. Only blackness remains and silence broken by Jones as he rushes off, crying with fear—and by the quickened, ever louder beat of the tom-tom.*)

SCENE 6

SCENE: *Three o'clock. A cleared space in the forest. The limbs of the trees meet over it forming a low ceiling about five feet from the ground. The interlocked ropes of creepers reaching upward to entwine the tree trunks give an arched appearance to the sides. The space thus enclosed is like the dark, noisome hold of some ancient vessel. The moonlight is almost completely shut out and only a vague, wan light filters through. There is the noise of someone approaching from the left, stumbling and crawling through the undergrowth. Jones' voice is heard between chattering moans.*

Oh, Lawd, what I gwine do now? Ain't got no bullet left on'y de silver one. If mo' o' dem ha'nts come after me, how I gwine skeer dem away? Oh, Lawd, on'y de silver one left—an' I gotta save dat fo' luck. If I shoots dat one I'm a goner sho'! Lawd, it's black heah! Whar's de moon? Oh, Lawd, don't dis night evah come to an end? (*By the sounds, he is feeling his way cautiously forward.*) Dere! Dis feels like a clear space. I gotta lie down an' rest. I don't care if dem niggers does cotch me. I gotta rest.

(*He is well forward now where his figure can be dimly made out. His pants have been so torn away that what is left of them is no better than a breech cloth. He flings himself full length, face downward on the ground, panting with exhaustion. Gradually it seems to grow lighter in the enclosed space and two rows of seated figures can be seen behind Jones. They are sitting in crumpled, despairing attitudes, hunched, facing one another with their backs touching the forest walls as if they were shackled to them. All are Negroes, naked save for loin cloths. At first they are silent and motionless. Then they begin to sway slowly for-*)

ward toward each other and back again in unison, as if they were laxly letting themselves follow the long roll of a ship at sea. At the same time, a low, melancholy murmur rises among them, increasing gradually by rhythmic degrees which seem to be directed and controlled by the throb of the tom-tom in the distance, to a long, tremulous wail of despair that reaches a certain pitch, unbearably acute, then falls by slow gradations of tone into silence and is taken up again. Jones starts, looks up, sees the figures, and throws himself down again to shut out the sight. A shudder of terror shakes his whole body as the wail rises up about him again. But the next time, his voice, as if under some uncanny compulsion, starts with the others. As their chorus lifts he rises to a sitting posture similar to the others, swaying back and forth. His voice reaches the highest pitch of sorrow, of desolation. The light fades out, the other voices cease, and only darkness is left. Jones can be heard scrambling to his feet and running off, his voice sinking down the scale and receding as he moves farther and farther away in the forest. The tom-tom beats louder, quicker, with a more insistent, triumphant pulsation.)

SCENE 7

SCENE: *Five o'clock. The foot of a gigantic tree by the edge of a great river. A rough structure of boulders, like an altar, is by the tree. The raised river bank is in the nearer background. Beyond this the surface of the river spreads out, brilliant and unruffled in the moonlight, blotted out and merged into a veil of bluish mist in the distance. Jones' voice is heard from the left rising and falling in the long, despairing wail of the chained slaves, to the rhythmic beat of the tom-tom. As his voice sinks into silence, he enters the open space. The expression of his face is fixed and stony, his eyes have an obsessed glare, he moves with a strange deliberation like a sleepwalker or one in a trance. He looks around at the tree, the rough stone altar, the moonlit surface of the river beyond, and passes his hand over his head with a vague gesture of puzzled bewilderment. Then, as if in obedience to some obscure impulse, he sinks into a kneeling, devotional posture before the altar. Then he seems to come to himself partly, to have an uncertain realization of what he is doing, for he straightens up and stares about him horrifiedly—in an incoherent mumble.*

What—what is I doin'? What is—dis place? Seems like—seems like I know dat tree—an' dem stones—an' de river. I remember—seems like I been heah befo'. *(Tremblingly.)* Oh, Gorry, I'se skeered in dis place! I'se skeered! Oh, Lawd, pertect dis sinner!

(Crawling away from the altar, he cowers close to the ground, his face hidden, his shoulders heaving with sobs of hysterical fright. From behind the trunk of the tree, as if he

had sprung out of it, the figure of the Congo Witch-doctor appears. He is wizened and old, naked except for the fur of some small animal tied about his waist, its bushy tail hanging down in front. His body is stained all over a bright red. Antelope horns are on each side of his head, branching upward. In one hand he carries a bone rattle, in the other a charm stick with a bunch of white cockatoo feathers tied to the end. A great number of glass beads and bone ornaments are about his neck, ears, wrists, and ankles. He struts noiselessly with a queer prancing step to a position in the clear ground between Jones and the altar. Then with a preliminary, summoning stamp of his foot on the earth, he begins to dance and to chant. As if in response to his summons the beating of the tom-tom grows to a fierce, exultant boom whose throbs seem to fill the air with vibrating rhythm. Jones looks up, starts to spring to his feet, reaches a half-kneeling, half-squatting position and remains rigidly fixed there, paralyzed with awed fascination by this new apparition. The Witch-doctor sways, stamping with his foot, his bone rattle clicking the time. His voice rises and falls in a weird, monotonous croon, without articulate word divisions. Gradually his dance becomes clearly one of a narrative in pantomime, his croon is an incantation, a charm to allay the fierceness of some implacable deity demanding sacrifice. He flees, he is pursued by devils, he hides, he flees again. Ever wilder and wilder becomes his flight, nearer and nearer draws the pursuing evil, more and more the spirit of terror gains possession of him. His croon, rising to intensity, is punctuated by shrill cries. Jones has become completely hypnotized. His voice joins in the incantation, in the cries, he beats time with his hands and sways his body to and fro from the waist. The whole spirit and meaning of the dance has entered into him, has become his spirit. Finally the theme of the pantomime halts on a howl of despair, and is taken up again in a note of savage hope. There is a salvation. The forces of evil demand sacrifice. They must be appeased. The Witch-doctor points with his wand to the sacred tree, to the river beyond, to the altar, and finally to Jones with a ferocious command. Jones seems to sense the meaning of this. It is he who must offer himself for sacrifice. He beats his forehead abjectly to the ground, moaning hysterically.)

Mercy, Oh Lawd! Mercy! Mercy on dis po' sinner.

(The Witch-doctor springs to the river bank. He stretches out his arms and calls to some god within its depths. Then he starts backward slowly, his arms remaining out. A huge head of a crocodile appears over the bank and its eyes, glittering greenly, fasten upon Jones. He stares into them fascinatedly. The Witch-doctor prances up to him, touches him with his wand, motions with hideous command toward the waiting monster. Jones squirms on his belly nearer and nearer, moaning continually.)

Mercy, Lawd! Mercy!

(The crocodile heaves more of his enormous bulk onto the land. Jones squirms toward him. The Witch-doctor voice shrills out in furious exultation, the tom-tom beats madly. Jones cries out in a fierce, exhausted spasm of anguished pleading.)

Lawd, save me! Lawd Jesus, heah my prayer!

(Immediately, in answer to his prayer, comes the thought of the one bullet left him. He snatches at his hip, shouting defiantly.)

De silver bullet! You don't git me yit!

(He fires at the green eyes in front of him. The head of the crocodile sinks back behind the river bank, the Witch-doctor springs behind the sacred tree and disappears. Jones lies with his face to the ground, his arms outstretched, whimpering with fear as the throb of the tom-tom fills the silence about him with a somber pulsation, a baffled but revengeful power.)

SCENE 8

SCENE: *Dawn. Same as Scene II, the dividing line of forest and plain. The nearest tree trunks are dimly revealed but the forest behind them is still a mass of glooming shadows. The tom-tom seems on the very spot, so loud and continuously vibrating are its beats. Lem enters from the left, followed by a small squad of his soldiers, and by the Cockney trader, Smithers. Lem is a heavy-set, ape-faced old savage of the extreme African type, dressed only in a loin cloth. A revolver and cartridge belt are about his waist. His soldiers are in different degrees of rag-concealed nakedness. All wear broad palm-leaf hats. Each one carries a rifle. Smithers is the same as in Scene I. One of the soldiers, evidently a tracker, is peering about keenly on the ground. He grunts and points to the spot where Jones entered the forest. Lem and Smithers come to look.*

SMITHERS *(after a glance, turns away in disgust)*. That's where 'e went in right enough. Much good it'll do yer. 'E's miles orf by this an' safe to the Coast, damn 'is 'ide! I tole yer yer'd lose 'im, didn't I?—wastin' the 'ole bloomin' night beatin' yer bloody drum and castin' yer silly spells! Gawd blimey, wot a pack!

LEM *(gutturally)*. We cotch him. You see. *(He makes a motion to his soldiers who squat down on their haunches in a semi-circle.)*

SMITHERS *(exasperatedly)*. Well, ain't yer goin' in an' 'unt 'im in the woods? What the 'ell's the good of waitin'?

LEM *(imperturbably—squatting down himself)*. We cotch him.

SMITHERS *(turning away from him contemptuously)*. Aw! Garn! 'E's a better man than the lot o' you put together. I 'ates the sight o' 'im but I'll say that for 'im.

(A sound of snapping twigs comes from the forest. The soldiers jump to their feet, cocking their rifles alertly. Lem remains sitting with an imperturbable expression, but listening intently. The sound from the woods is repeated. Lem makes a quick signal with his hand. His followers creep quickly but noiselessly into the forest, scattering so that each enters at a different spot.)

SMITHERS *(in the silence that follows—in a contemptuous whisper)*. You ain't thinkin' that would be 'im, I 'ope?

LEM *(calmly)*. We cotch him.

SMITHERS. Blarsted fat 'eads! *(Then after a second's thought—wonderingly.)* Still an' all, it might 'appen. If 'e lost 'is bloody way in these stinkin' woods 'e'd likely turn in a circle without 'is knowin' it. They all does.

LEM *(peremptorily)*. Sssh!

(The reports of several rifles sound from the forest, followed a second later by savage, exultant yells. The beating of the tom-tom abruptly ceases. Lem looks up at the white man with a grin of satisfaction.)

We cotch him. Him dead.

SMITHERS *(with a snarl)*. 'Ow d'yer know it's 'im an' 'ow d'yer know 'e's dead?

LEM. My mens dey got 'um silver bullets. Dey kill him shore.

SMITHERS *(astonished)*. They got silver bullets?

LEM. Lead bullet no kill him. He got um strong charm. I cook um money, make um silver bullet, make um strong charm, too.

SMITHERS *(light breaking upon him)*. So that's wot you was up to all night, wot? You was scared to put after 'im till you'd moulded silver bullets, eh?

LEM *(simply stating a fact)*. Yes. Him got strong charm. Lead no good.

SMITHERS *(slapping his thigh and guffawing)*. Haw-haw! If yer don't beat all 'ell! *(Then recovering himself—scornfully.)* I'll bet yer it ain't 'im they shot at all, yer bleedin' looney!

LEM *(calmly)*. Dey come bring him now.

(The soldiers come out of the forest, carrying Jones' limp body. There is a little reddish-purple hole under his left breast. He is dead. They carry him to Lem, who examines his body with great satisfaction. Smithers over his shoulder—in a tone of frightened awe.)

Well, they did for yer right enough, Jonsey, me lad! Dead as a 'erring! *(Mockingly.)* Where's yer 'igh an' mighty airs now, yer bloomin' Majesty? *(Then with a grin.)* Silver bullets! Gawd blimey, but yer died in the 'eighth o' style, any'ow!

(*Lem makes a motion to the soldiers to carry the body out left. Smithers speaks to him sneeringly.*)

SMITHERS. And I s'pose you think it's yer bleedin' charms and yer silly beatin' the drum that made 'im run in a circle when 'e'd lost 'imself, don't yer?

(*But Lem makes no reply, does not seem to hear the question, walks out left after his men. Smithers looks after him with contemptuous scorn.*)

Stupid as 'ogs, the lot of 'em! Blarsted niggers!

CURTAIN FALLS

TOPICS FOR CRITICAL THINKING AND WRITING

📖 THE PLAY ON THE PAGE

1. Smithers is essentially a coward. Why, then, does he talk impudently and even angrily to Jones at the start of the play?

2. Discuss the organization of the six scenes in the jungle. (O'Neill gives us, first, the "little formless fears," then the memory of the murder of Jeff, the memory of the murder of the prison guard, the slave auction, the slave ship, and the African ceremony.) How are the last three of these fundamentally different from the first three? Dramatically speaking, could the last three be given before the first three? Explain.

3. Jones runs in a circle. Smithers sees in this only a simple fact, but can one say that the symmetry is meaningful? Do you think it is appropriate, for instance, to see in it a return to our inarticulate and mysterious origin? Explain.

4. If you don't recall the time scheme of the play, look again to see at what time of day the play begins and at what time it ends. What do you make out of this structure?

5. How relevant to the play do you find the concepts of *hybris* and *hamartia* (see p. 33 and Glossary)? Explain.

6. The play was enthusiastically received in 1920. Heywood Broun, however, writing in the *New York Tribune* (see p. 582), offered one objection in an otherwise ecstatic review: "We cannot understand just why he [O'Neill] has allowed the Emperor to die to the sound of off-stage shots. It is our idea that he should come crawling to the very spot where he meets his death and that the natives should be molding silver bullets there and waiting without so much as stretching out a finger for him." What do you think of Broun's suggestion?

🎭 THE PLAY ON THE STAGE

7. O'Neill's stage direction concerning the tom-tom is inaccurate. He says that it "continues . . . uninterruptedly to the very end of the play," but in the middle of Scene 8 O'Neill writes, "The beating of the tom-tom abruptly ceases." Why does O'Neill stop the tom-tom here? Would it be more effective if it continued until the end of the play? Explain.

8. In addition to the tom-tom, other sound effects are used. What are they, and how effective do you think they are?

9. *The Emperor Jones* has eight scenes, a large number for a short play. What is the effect of so large a number? After all, the six central, expressionistic scenes between the realistic opening and closing scenes could, with a little rewriting, have been one long scene, but O'Neill chose to put the material into six scenes. Why? Hint: Expressionistic drama (see Glossary) often uses a lot of scenes—but why?

10. Some years after the original production, O'Neill said, "All the figures in Jones's flight through the forest should be masked. Masks would dramatically stress their phantasmal quality, as contrasted with the unmasked Jones, intensify the supernatural menace of the tomtom, give the play a more complete and vivid expression." If you were staging the play, would you use masks, as O'Neill suggests? Why?

THE PLAY IN PERFORMANCE

The Emperor Jones opened on November 4, 1920, at the Provincetown Playhouse, in Greenwich Village, New York. (The theater derived its name from a town on Cape Cod, Massachusetts, where in the summer of 1915 a group of amateurs staged some of their own plays. In the following year—the year that O'Neill joined them—they moved to Greenwich Village, in New York City, but they kept their original name.) Although not every review was highly favorable, several reviewers were extremely enthusiastic, and on the whole the reviews were good. Early in the run the play moved to a larger theater, and what was scheduled for a run of two weeks turned into a run of two hundred four performances.

For the first run, O'Neill and the other members of the company selected an African-American actor, Charles Gilpin (1878–1930). The choice of a black seems unexceptional now (indeed, any other choice is almost unthinkable), but in 1920, when blacks played only minor roles in plays with white companies, the choice was highly daring. Ordinarily, the role would have gone to a white actor who would play it in blackface. O'Neill himself had acted in blackface in an earlier play. Gilpin was immensely successful, and many years later O'Neill said that Gilpin was the only actor who ever performed an O'Neill role to O'Neill's fullest satisfaction. However, a strain developed during the course of the run. Gilpin felt uneasy speaking the word *nigger*, and so he began to substitute words such as *colored man* and *Negro* for *nigger*. O'Neill was furious and insisted that Gilpin follow the text.

When the play was revived in 1924, O'Neill turned with some relief to Paul Robeson (1898–1976), who also played in the London production of 1925. In later years Robeson performed in revivals in Europe and the United States until 1940. Robeson also played Jones in a film version of 1933 and in a concert version of an opera (1933), though in the full production of the opera the baritone Lawrence Tibbett sang Jones in blackface.

In 1964 *The Emperor Jones* was performed at the Boston Arts Festival, starring James Earl Jones, in a production that used no scenery other than a few platforms and some backing flats. A dozen dancers were used for the phantoms. On the whole, the play was rarely seen in the 1960s and 1970s, doubtless because the advanced thinking of 1920 seemed to be racist thinking forty or fifty years later, but an off-Broadway revival in 1977 was greeted favorably. A current (spring 1996) revival has been going on, with many changes during the process, in New York, offered by the Wooster Group, which is known for its utterly untraditional methods. Any description of one of its productions (especially a brief description) is bound to sound puzzling and more than a little eccentric, but audiences who experience the plays find the productions exciting. Kate Valk, a white woman, played Jones in blackface. More precisely, in the opening sequence her head appears on a large television screen, in blackface, but because a negative is projected, her face is white and her lips are dark. In the dialogue with Smithers, she addressed the audience, not Smithers; Smithers, offstage, spoke to a video camera, and his image was reproduced on an up-center stage screen. Again, we can say only that the production caught the *excitement* that (judging from the original reviews) animated the Provincetown Players when they produced the play in 1920. Something of the Wooster production can be ascertained from a discussion in *The Eugene O'Neill Review* 16.2 (1992): 114–22.

We have already mentioned that Robeson starred in a film version of 1933. The film is a very free adaptation, apparently constructed chiefly to allow Robeson to show his talents as a singer. Louis Gruenberg's opera (1933) had a very limited success in New York, Los Angeles, and San Francisco when it was first done and probably has not been heard since. José Limon, the Mexican-born dancer and choreographer who grew up in the United States, choreographed the play in 1956 and often performed it in later years. The play also exists as a recording. In 1971 Caedmon issued an album of two long-playing records starring James Earl Jones. The records include comments by Jones, who expresses the suspicion that O'Neill was a racist and that he used "Niggerisms" in order to make the play acceptable to a white audience of the 1920s. Jones does grant that younger blacks, seeing the play as a "study of power," may find it acceptable. We should add that Jones's performance on the recording is extremely effective.

Heywood Broun
A REVIEW OF *THE EMPEROR JONES*

Heywood Broun (1888–1939), a newspaper columnist and critic, wrote a syndicated column, "It Seems to Me." We reprint his influential review of the first production of *The Emperor Jones*.

Subject to later reservations and revisions, when all the missing districts are in, Eugene O'Neill's *The Emperor Jones* seems to us just about the most interesting play which has yet come from the most promising playwright in America.

Perhaps we ought to be a little more courageous and say right out the best of American playwrights, but somehow or other a superlative carries the implication of a certain static quality. We never see a play by O'Neill without feeling that something of the sort will be done better within a season or so, and that O'Neill will do it.

As gorgeous a piece as *The Emperor Jones* has loose ends fluttering here and there as they trail along with the clouds of glory. This is a play of high trajectory and up above the country stores and the lobby of the Palace Hotel, Wuppinger Falls, ten months later and Yvette's boudoir there is a rarer atmosphere which makes it difficult to avoid an occasional slip this way and that.

The Emperor Jones tells of an American negro, a Pullman porter, who, by some chance or other, comes to an island in the West Indies, "not yet self-determined by white marines." In two years Jones has made himself emperor. Luck has played a part, but he has been quick to take advantage of it. Once a native tried to shoot him at point-blank range, but the gun missed fire, whereupon Jones announced that he was protected by a charm and that only silver bullets could harm him. When the play begins he has been emperor long enough to amass a fortune by imposing heavy taxes on the islanders and carrying on all sorts of large-scale graft. Rebellion is brewing. When Emperor Jones rings the bell which should summon his servants no one appears. The palace is deserted, but from deep in the jungle there comes the sound of the steady beat of a big drum. The islanders are whipping up their courage to the fighting point by calling on the local gods and demons of the forest.

Jones, realizing that his reign is over, starts to make his escape to the coast where a French gunboat is anchored. First it is necessary for him to travel through the jungle and as time presses he must go through at night. Back in the States he was a good Baptist and he begins the journey through the dark places unafraid. But under the dim moonlight he cannot recognize any familiar landmarks and, hard as he runs, the continuous drumbeat never grows any less in his ears. Then demons and apparitions begin to torment him. First it is the figure of a negro he killed back in the States. He fires and the dim thing vanishes, but immediately he reproaches himself, for in his revolver now he has only five shots left. Four are lead bullets and the fifth is a silver one which he has reserved for himself, if by any chance capture seems imminent.

Other little "formless fears" creep in upon him. As his panic increases the fears become not things in his own life, but old race fears. He sees himself being sold in a slave market and then, most horrible of all, a Congo witch doctor tries to lure him to death in a river where a crocodile god is waiting. It is at this point that he fires his last bullet, the silver one.

During the night he has discarded his big patent leather boots and most of his clothes in order to run faster from the drumbeat. But it is louder now than ever and in the last scene we find the natives sitting about in a circle weaving spells and molding bullets. And it is to this spot that the defenseless and exhausted emperor crawls, having made a complete circle in the jungle as his panic whipped him on.

The play is of eight scenes and it is largely a monologue by one character, the Emperor Jones. Unfortunately, production in the tiny Provincetown Theatre is difficult and the waits between these scenes are often several minutes in length. Each wait is a vulture which preys upon the attention. With the beginning of each new scene, contact must again be established and all this unquestionably hurts. Still we have no disposition to say, "If only the play had been done in 'the commercial theatre'!" This is a not infrequent comment whenever a little theatre does a fine piece of work and it seems to us to have in it something of the spirit of a man standing on the deck of a great liner who should remark, "Wasn't Columbus a bally ass to come over in such a little tub!"

The Emperor Jones is so unusual in its technique that it might wait in vain for a production anywhere except in so adventurous a playhouse as the Provincetown Theatre. As a matter of fact, the setting of the play on the little stage is fine and imaginative and the lighting effects uncommonly beautiful. There is nothing for complaint but the delays. Also, if *The Emperor Jones* were taken elsewhere we have little doubt that the manager would engage a white man with a piece of burnt cork to play Brutus Jones. They have done better in Macdougal Street. The Emperor is played by a negro actor named Charles S. Gilpin, who gives the most thrilling performance we have seen any place this season. He sustains the succession of scenes in monologue not only because his voice is one of gorgeous natural quality, but because he knows just what to do with it. All the notes are there and he has also the extraordinary facility for being in the right place at the right time. Generally he seems fairly painted into the scenic design. One performance is not enough to entitle a player to the word great even from a not too careful critic, but there can be no question whatever that in *The Emperor Jones* Gilpin is great. It is a performance of heroic stature. It is so good that the fact that it is enormously skillful seems only incidental.

Aside from difficulties of production there are some faults in O'Neill's play. He has almost completely missed the opportunities of his last scene, which should blaze with a vast tinder spark of irony. Instead, he rounds it off with a snap of the fingers, a little O. Henry dido. We cannot understand just why he has allowed the Emperor to die to the sound of off-stage shots. It is our idea that he should come crawling to the very spot where he meets his death and that the natives should be molding silver bullets there and waiting without so much as stretching out a finger for him. Of course all this goes to show that *The Emperor Jones* is truly a fine play. It is only such which tempt the spectator to leap in himself as a collaborator.

Bertolt Brecht

THE GOOD WOMAN
OF SETZUAN

Bertolt Brecht (1898–1956) was born in Germany of middle-class parents, attended public schools, and then entered the University of Munich to study medicine. However, after one year he was drafted for military service in World War I and served as a medical orderly for about a year. At the end of the war, he returned to a shattered Germany, and during most of the twenties he seems to have been more or less an anarchist. His earliest poems and plays (e.g., *The Threepenny Opera*, 1928) cannot be called communist, although around 1928 he seems to have become a believer in communism. With the rise of Hitler, Brecht left Germany (1933), spending most of the years 1933 to 1939 in Denmark, 1940 in Finland, and 1941 to 1948 in the United States. Most of his best-known plays (including *The Good Woman of Setzuan*, 1938–1941) were written during these fifteen years of exile. His return in 1948 to Germany—to East Berlin—was somewhat equivocal, for he obtained Austrian citizenship (1950) and arranged for the copyright to his work to be held by a publisher in West Berlin. He died suddenly, of a thrombosis, in 1956.

COMMENTARY

Earlier drama interested Brecht enormously. However, he believed it was obsolete and devoted a fair amount of his time to trying to adapt it to the twentieth century. (His most popular play, *The Threepenny Opera*, is an adaptation of John Gay's *The Beggar's Opera*, and at the time of his death Brecht was working on an adaptation of Shakespeare's *Coriolanus*. Accused of plagiarism, he replied that in literature as in life he did not recognize the idea of private property.)

Roughly speaking, Brecht saw early forms of tragedy as depicting a hero who, inevitably driven to the wall, performs some terrible deed and then becomes aware of all of its implications, thus achieving full understanding of himself and his fate. Interpreting Aristotle's comments on tragedy, Brecht went on to say that early tragedy customarily seeks to cause the audience to identify itself with the tragic hero, thereby undergoing an emotional cleansing, or catharsis. Here is one of Brecht's characteristically earthy and acerbic comments:

> The drama of our time still follows Aristotle's recipe for achieving what he calls catharsis (the spiritual cleansing of the spectator). In Aristotelian drama the plot leads the hero into situations where he reveals his innermost being. All the incidents shown have the object of driving the hero into spiritual conflicts. It is a possibly blasphemous but quite useful comparison if one turns one's mind to the burlesque shows on Broadway, where the public, with yells of "Take it off!" forces the girls to expose their bodies more and more.

The individual whose innermost being is thus driven into the open then of course comes to stand for Man with a capital M. Everyone (including every spectator) is then carried away by the momentum of the events portrayed, so that in a performance of *Oedipus* one has for all practical purposes an auditorium full of little Oedipuses, an auditorium full of Emperor Joneses for a performance of *The Emperor Jones*.[1]

Now, in opposition to what he called "Aristotelian drama," Brecht, drawing partly on German critical theories about the difference between drama and epic, developed the idea of "non-Aristotelian drama," or "epic drama." Whereas the usual play is set in the present and implies that what is happening on the stage happens *now*, to all of us, the epic drama traditionally is set in the past and is quite frankly about how things *used to be*. The readers of an epic, the argument goes, are detached individuals capable of using their minds critically, but the spectators at a performance of an Aristotelian drama are part of a mob, their reason having been subordinated to a communal emotion. Epic drama, then, in opposition to traditional Aristotelian drama, seeks to create a detachment comparable to that which the epic creates.

Brecht's word for this quality is *Verfremdung*, that is, detachment, estrangement, alienation. The reason for estranging the dramatic action from the audience is to make the audience regard it critically and thus see it more clearly,

[1]*Brecht on Theatre*, translated by John Willett (New York: Hill and Wang; London: Methuen & Co., 1964), p. 87.

unobscured by emotional prejudices. To induce this estrangement, to shatter a sense of community between actors and audience, Brecht interrupted the action of his plays with such devices as songs, addresses to the audience, and slogans projected onto the stage, and he insisted on highly stylized acting (Chaplin was one of his heroes) and unrealistic scenery. Brecht's ideal audience at an epic drama is critically aware of—not emotionally overcome by—what it sees on the stage. Brecht thus rejected tragedy of the sort that Yeats characterized as "a drowning and breaking of the dykes that separate man from man," and he insisted, in contrast to Yeats, that detachment is not limited to the spectator at a comedy.

Every play gives some image of the world. According to Brecht, the Aristotelian play shows a static world, for in the hero's agony it claims to reveal with increasing clarity how things inevitably are. The epic play, however, shows a dynamic, or changing, world—a world that can be, must be, changed. (The direction in which Brecht wanted the change to go is clear enough; he was a communist.)

> The dramatic [i.e., Aristotelian] theatre's spectator says: Yes, I have felt like that too—Just like me—It's only natural—It'll never change—The sufferings of this man appall me, because they are inescapable—That's great art; it all seems the most obvious thing in the world—I weep when they weep, I laugh when they laugh.
>
> The epic theatre's spectator says: I'd never have thought it—That's not the way—That's extraordinary, hardly believable—It's got to stop—The sufferings of this man appall me, because they are unnecessary—That's great art: nothing obvious in it—I laugh when they weep, I weep when they laugh.[2]

Brecht put the distinctions between the two kinds of drama into the following tabular form, but one should keep in mind that he was talking about emphases, not utter opposites:[3]

DRAMATIC THEATRE	EPIC THEATRE
plot	narrative
implicates the spectator in a stage situation	turns the spectator into an observer, but
wears down his capacity for action	arouses his capacity for action
provides him with sensations	forces him to take decisions
experience	picture of the world
the spectator is involved in something	he is made to face something

[2]*Brecht on Theatre*, p. 71.

[3]The list is reprinted from *Brecht on Theatre*, translated by John Willett, p. 37. Copyright © 1957, 1963 and 1964 by Suhrkamp Verlag, Frankfurt am Main.

This translation and notes © 1964 by John Willett. Reprinted by permission of Hill and Wang, Inc., and Methuen & Co. Ltd.

DRAMATIC THEATRE	EPIC THEATRE
suggestion	argument
instinctive feelings are preserved	brought to the point of recognition
the spectator is in the thick of it, shares the experience	the spectator stands outside, studies
the human being is taken for granted	the human being is the object of the inquiry
he is unalterable	he is alterable and able to alter
eyes on the finish	eyes on the course
one scene makes another	each scene for itself
growth	montage
linear development	in curves
evolutionary determinism	jumps
man as a fixed point	man as a process
thought determines being	social being determines thought
feeling	reason

It was with this scaffolding that Brecht built his plays. His interest was not in passionate tragic heroes who reveal their greatness when they assert themselves and do a deed of horror that affronts a mysterious metaphysical order that demands their life in expiation. Nevertheless, Brecht dealt with no less momentous issues than these: How do we survive? Must little people be imposed on? Above all, What is to be done?

Such plays do not seek to evoke the woe or wonder that Shakespeare spoke of in connection with tragedy, for these emotions induce a sense of the inevitability of guilt and suffering and send us out of the theater reconciled to the naturalness of our present condition. For Brecht, what is "natural" is not guilty actions but generous actions. (Brecht would argue that the following speech is counterbalanced by many other speeches, because epic drama shows several sides, but it seems evident that the speech represents Brecht's own thinking.) Shen Te, the charitable prostitute, says in another version of *The Good Woman of Setzuan*:

> Why are you so bad?
> You tread on your fellow man.
> Isn't it a strain?
> Your veins swell with your efforts to be greedy.
> Extended naturally, a hand gives and receives with equal ease.

Somehow, according to Brecht, in our present (i.e., capitalistic) society, we find that we are forced into unnatural postures. For example, Shen Te finds that she cannot continue to be charitable without the aid of a cruel "cousin" (she is so torn by the problem that she invents this person in order to protect herself from her own generous impulses). Moreover, in our society love itself must become savage. For instance, Shen Te so loves her child and so fears that he may encounter a life of poverty that she determines for his sake to be ruthless in her business dealings, and she determines also (further irony) to shield the child from knowledge of her activities so that he will grow up to be good—in a world in which goodness cannot survive.

These life-and-death issues are treated tragicomically. First, and least importantly, the play mingles gods and mortals, as does Plautus' *Amphitryon,* a mixture which caused Plautus to introduce the word *tragicomedy.* And what gods they are, mouthing amiable pieties; getting a black eye when they intervene in a mortal quarrel; and, finally, in a concluding scene that is funny and terrible, ascending to heaven on a cloud, singing, smiling, and waving to Shen Te, who is crying for help. More importantly, in this immensely earnest play that seeks to face some of the darkest facts of our life as it is, there are a good many comic figures and there is a good deal of wry wit. One example will have to suffice. Yang Sun wants to be sure that his wife will be frugal.

YANG SUN. Can you sleep on a straw mattress the size of that book?
SHEN TE. The two of us?
YANG SUN. The one of you.
SHEN TE. In that case, no.

More broadly, *The Good Woman of Setzuan,* like all comedies, calls attention to incongruity, but here the incongruity is not from some sort of unlovely behavior needlessly adopted in a smiling world where things will work out all right; rather, the incongruity is generosity in a corrupt world. Shen Te is funny in her persistent innocence and goodness—but she is not only funny, she is also compelling (despite Brecht's theories?) and deeply sympathetic, as when she persists in loving the deceitful Yang Sun:

SHEN TE.
When I heard his cunning laugh, I was afraid
But when I saw the holes in his shoes, I loved him dearly.

At the end, the play does not let us rest content, as tragedy and comedy in their different ways traditionally do. An epilogue invites us to work out a sequel:

We feel deflated too. We too are nettled
To see the curtain down and nothing settled.
How could a better ending be arranged?
Could one change people? Can the world be changed?
Would new gods do the trick? Will atheism?
Moral rearmament? Materialism?
It is for you to find a way, my friends,
To help good men arrive at happy ends.
You write the happy ending to the play!
There must, there must, there's got to be a way!

Probably Brecht assumed that Marx had shown us the way out: Change the economic basis of society, and you will find a new human nature. Still, at rehearsals of his plays Brecht sometimes quoted his own Galileo: "I'm not trying to show that I'm in the right, but to find out whether."

Bertolt Brecht

THE GOOD WOMAN OF SETZUAN

Translated by Eric Bentley

List of Characters

WONG, *a water seller*
THREE GODS
SHEN TE, *a prostitute, later a shopkeeper*
MRS. SHIN, *former owner of Shen Te's shop*
A FAMILY OF EIGHT (*husband, wife, brother, sister-in-law, grandfather, nephew, niece, boy*)
AN UNEMPLOYED MAN
A CARPENTER
MRS. MI TZU, *Shen Te's landlady*
YANG SUN, *an unemployed pilot, later a factory manager*
AN OLD WHORE
A POLICEMAN
AN OLD MAN
AN OLD WOMAN, *his wife*
MR. SHU FU, *a barber*
MRS. YANG, *mother of Yang Sun*
GENTLEMEN, VOICES, CHILDREN (*three*), *etc.*

PROLOGUE

(*At the gates of the half-westernized city of Setzuan.* Evening. Wong the Water Seller introduces himself to the audience.*)

WONG. I sell water here in the city of Setzuan. It isn't easy. When water is scarce, I have long distances to go in search of it, and when it is plentiful, I have no income. But in our part of the world there is nothing unusual about poverty. Many people think only the gods can save the situation. And I hear from a cattle merchant—who travels a lot—that some of the highest gods are on their way here at this very moment. Informed sources have it that heaven is quite disturbed at all the complaining. I've been coming out here to the city gates for three days now to bid these gods welcome. I want to be the first to greet them. What about those fellows over there? No, no, they *work.* And that one there has ink on his fingers, he's no god, he must be a clerk from the cement factory. *Those* two are another story. They look as though they'd like to beat you. But gods don't need to beat you, do they? (*Enter*

---

*"So Brecht's first manuscript. Brecht must later have learned that Setzuan (usually spelled Szechwan) is not a city but a province, and he adjusted the printed German text. I have kept the earlier reading since such mythology seems to me more Brechtian than Brecht's own second thoughts."—E.B.

Three Gods.) What about those three? Old-fashioned clothes—dust on their feet—they *must* be gods! (*He throws himself at their feet.*) Do with me what you will, illustrious ones!

FIRST GOD (*with an ear trumpet*). Ah! (*He is pleased.*) So we were expected?

WONG (*giving them water*). Oh, yes. And I *knew* you'd come.

FIRST GOD. We need somewhere to stay the night. You know of a place?

WONG. The whole town is at your service, illustrious ones! What sort of a place would you like?

(*The Gods eye each other.*)

FIRST GOD. Just try the first house you come to, my son.

WONG. That would be Mr. Fo's place.

FIRST GOD. Mr. Fo.

WONG. One moment! (*He knocks at the first house.*)

VOICE FROM MR. FO'S. No!

(*Wong returns a little nervously.*)

WONG. It's too bad. Mr. Fo isn't in. And his servants don't dare do a thing without his consent. He'll have a fit when he finds out who they turned away, won't he?

FIRST GOD (*smiling*). He will, won't he?

WONG. One moment! The next house is Mr. Cheng's. Won't he be thrilled?

FIRST GOD. Mr. Cheng.

(*Wong knocks.*)

VOICE FROM MR. CHENG'S. Keep your gods. We have our own troubles!

WONG (*back with the Gods*). Mr. Cheng is very sorry, but he has a houseful of relations. I think some of them are a bad lot, and naturally, he wouldn't like you to see them.

THIRD GOD. Are we so terrible?

WONG. Well, only with bad people, of course. Everyone knows the province of Kwan is always having floods.

SECOND GOD. Really? How's *that?*

WONG. Why, because they're so irreligious.

SECOND GOD. Rubbish. It's because they neglected the dam.

FIRST GOD (*to Second*). Sh! (*To Wong.*) You're still in hopes, aren't you, my son?

WONG. Certainly. All Setzuan is competing for the honor! What happened up to now is pure coincidence. I'll be back. (*He walks away, but then stands undecided.*)

SECOND GOD. What did I tell you?

THIRD GOD. It *could* be pure coincidence.

SECOND GOD. The same coincidence in Shun, Kwan, and Setzuan? People just aren't religious any more, let's face the fact. Our mission has failed!

FIRST GOD. Oh come, we might run into a good person any minute.

THIRD GOD. How did the resolution read? (*Unrolling a scroll and reading from it.*) "The world can stay as it is if enough people are found living lives worthy of human beings." Good people, that is. Well, what about this Water Seller himself? *He's* good, or I'm very much mistaken.

SECOND GOD. You're very much mistaken. When he gave us a drink, I had the impression there was something odd about the cup. Well, look! (*He shows the cup to the First God.*)

FIRST GOD. A false bottom!

SECOND GOD. The man is a swindler.

FIRST GOD. Very well, count *him* out. That's one man among millions. And as a matter of fact, we only need one on *our* side. These atheists are saying, "The world must be changed because no one can *be* good and *stay* good." No one, eh? I say: let us find one—just one—and we have those fellows where we want them!

THIRD GOD (*to Wong*). Water Seller, is it so hard to find a place to stay?

WONG. Nothing could be easier. It's just me. I don't go about it right.

THIRD GOD. Really? (*He returns to the others. A Gentleman passes by.*)

WONG. Oh dear, they're catching on. (*He accosts the Gentleman.*) Excuse the intrusion, dear sir, but three Gods have just turned up. Three of the very highest. They need a place for the night. Seize this rare opportunity—to have real gods as your guests!

GENTLEMAN (*laughing*). A new way of finding free rooms for a gang of crooks.

(*Exit Gentleman.*)

WONG (*shouting at him*). Godless rascal! Have you no religion, gentlemen of Setzuan? (*Pause.*) Patience, illustrious ones! (*Pause.*) There's only one person left. Shen Te, the prostitute. She *can't* say no. (*Calls up to a window.*) Shen Te!

(*Shen Te opens the shutters and looks out.*)

WONG. *They're* here, and nobody wants them. Will you take them?

SHEN TE. Oh, no, Wong, I'm expecting a gentleman.

WONG. Can't you forget about him for tonight?

SHEN TE. The rent has to be paid by tomorrow or I'll be out on the street.

WONG. This is no time for calculation, Shen Te.

SHEN TE. Stomachs rumble even on the Emperor's birthday, Wong.

WONG. Setzuan is one big dung hill!

SHEN TE. Oh, very well! I'll hide till my gentleman has come and gone. Then I'll take them. (*She disappears.*)

WONG. They mustn't see her gentleman or they'll know what she is.

FIRST GOD (*who hasn't heard any of this*). I think it's hopeless.

(*They approach Wong.*)

WONG (*jumping, as he finds them behind him*). A room has been found, illustrious ones! (*He wipes sweat off his brow.*)

SECOND GOD. Oh, good.

THIRD GOD. Let's see it.

WONG (*nervously*). Just a minute. It has to be tidied up a bit.

THIRD GOD. Then we'll sit down here and wait.

WONG (*still more nervous*). No, no! (*Holding himself back.*) Too much traffic, you know.

THIRD GOD (*with a smile*). Of course, if you *want* us to move.

(*They retire a little. They sit on a doorstep. Wong sits on the ground.*)

WONG (*after a deep breath*). You'll be staying with a single girl—the finest human being in Setzuan!

THIRD GOD. That's nice.

WONG (*to the audience*). They gave me such a look when I picked up my cup just now.

THIRD GOD. You're worn out, Wong.

WONG. A little, maybe.

FIRST GOD. Do people here have a hard time of it?

WONG. The good ones do.

FIRST GOD. What about yourself?

WONG. You mean I'm not good. That's true. And I don't have an easy time either!

(*During this dialogue, a Gentleman has turned up in front of Shen Te's house, and has whistled several times. Each time Wong has given a start.*)

THIRD GOD (*to Wong, softly*). Psst! I think he's gone now.

WONG (*confused and surprised*). Ye-e-es.

(*The Gentleman has left now, and Shen Te has come down to the street.*)

SHEN TE (*softly*). Wong!

(*Getting no answer, she goes off down the street. Wong arrives just too late, forgetting his carrying pole.*)

WONG (*softly*). Shen Te! Shen Te! (*To himself.*) So she's gone off to earn the rent. Oh dear, I can't go to the gods *again* with no room to offer them. Having failed in the service of the gods, I shall run to my den in the sewer pipe down by the river and hide from their sight!

(*He rushes off. Shen Te returns, looking for him, but finding the gods. She stops in confusion.*)

SHEN TE. You are the illustrious ones? My name is Shen Te. It would please me very much if my simple room could be of use to you.

THIRD GOD. Where is the Water Seller, Miss . . . Shen Te?

SHEN TE. I missed him, somehow.

FIRST GOD. Oh, he probably thought you weren't coming, and was afraid of telling us.

THIRD GOD (*picking up the carrying pole*). We'll leave this with you. He'll be needing it.

(*Led by Shen Te, they go into the house. It grows dark, then light. Dawn. Again escorted by Shen Te, who leads them through the half-light with a little lamp, the Gods take their leave.*)

FIRST GOD. Thank you, thank you, dear Shen Te, for your elegant hospitality! We shall not forget! And give our thanks to the Water Seller—he showed us a good human being.

SHEN TE. Oh, *I'm* not good. Let me tell you something: when Wong asked me to put you up, I hesitated.

FIRST GOD. It's all right to hesitate if you then go ahead! And in giving us that room you did much more than you knew. You proved that good people still exist, a point that has been disputed of late—even in heaven. Farewell!

SECOND GOD. Farewell!

THIRD GOD. Farewell!

SHEN TE. Stop, illustrious ones! I'm not sure you're right. I'd like to be good, it's true, but there's the rent to pay. And that's not all: I sell myself for a living. Even so I can't make ends meet, there's too much competition. I'd like to honor my father and mother and speak nothing but the truth and not covet my neighbor's house. I should love to stay with one man. But how? How is it done? Even breaking only a *few* of your commandments, I can hardly manage.

FIRST GOD (*clearing his throat*). These thoughts are but, um, the misgivings of an unusually good woman!

THIRD GOD. Goodbye, Shen Te! Give our regards to the Water Seller!

SECOND GOD. And above all: be good! Farewell!

FIRST GOD. Farewell!

THIRD GOD. Farewell!

(*They start to wave good-bye.*)

SHEN TE. But everything is so expensive, I don't feel sure I can do it!

SECOND GOD. That's not in our sphere. We never meddle with economics.

THIRD GOD. One moment.

(*They stop.*)

Isn't it true she might do better if she had more money?

SECOND GOD. Come, come! How could we ever account for it Up Above?

FIRST GOD. Oh, there are ways.

(*They put their heads together and confer in dumb show.*)

(*To Shen Te, with embarrassment.*) As you say you can't pay your rent, well, um, we're not paupers, so of course we *insist* on paying for our room. (*Awkwardly thrusting money into her hands.*) There! (*Quickly.*) But don't tell anyone! The incident is open to misinterpretation.

SECOND GOD. It certainly is!

FIRST GOD (*defensively*). But there's no law against it! It was never decreed that a god mustn't pay hotel bills!

(*The Gods leave.*)

SCENE 1

(*A small tobacco shop. The shop is not as yet completely furnished and hasn't started doing business.*)

SHEN TE (*to the audience*). It's three days now since the gods left. When they said they wanted to pay for the room, I looked down at my hand, and there was more than a thousand silver dollars! I bought a tobacco shop with the money, and moved in yesterday. I don't own the building, of course, but I can pay the rent, and I hope to do a lot of good here. Beginning with Mrs. Shin, who's just coming across the square with her pot. She had the shop before me, and yesterday she dropped in to ask for rice for her children.

(*Enter Mrs. Shin. Both women bow.*)

How do you do, Mrs. Shin.

MRS. SHIN. How do you do, Miss Shen Te. You like your new home?

SHEN TE. Indeed, yes. Did your children have a good night?

MRS. SHIN. In that hovel? The youngest is coughing already.

SHEN TE. Oh, dear!

MRS. SHIN. You're going to learn a thing or two in these slums.

SHEN TE. Slums? That's not what you said when you sold me the shop!

MRS. SHIN. Now don't start nagging! Robbing me and my innocent children of their home and then calling it a slum! That's the limit! (*She weeps.*)

SHEN TE (*tactfully*). I'll get your rice.

MRS. SHIN. And a little cash while you're at it.

SHEN TE. I'm afraid I haven't sold anything yet.

MRS. SHIN (*screeching*). I've got to have it. Strip the clothes from my back and then cut my throat, will you? I know what I'll do: I'll leave my children on your doorstep! (*She snatches the pot out of Shen Te's hands.*)

SHEN TE. Please don't be angry. You'll spill the rice.

(*Enter an elderly Husband and Wife with their shabbily-dressed Nephew.*)

WIFE. Shen Te, dear! You've come into money, they tell me. And we haven't a roof over our heads! A tobacco shop. We had one too. But it's gone. Could we spend the night here, do you think?

NEPHEW (*appraising the shop*). Not bad!

WIFE. He's our nephew. We're inseparable!

MRS. SHIN. And who are these . . . ladies and gentlemen?

SHEN TE. They put me up when I first came in from the country. (*To the audience.*) Of course, when my small purse was empty, they put me out on the street, and they may be afraid I'll do the same to them. (*To the newcomers,*

kindly.) Come in, and welcome, though I've only one little room for you—it's behind the shop.

HUSBAND. That'll do. Don't worry.

WIFE (*bringing Shen Te some tea*). We'll stay over here, so we
won't be in your way. Did you make it a tobacco shop in
memory of your first real home? We can certainly give
you a hint or two! That's one reason we came.

MRS. SHIN (*to Shen Te*). Very nice! As long as you have a few
customers too!

HUSBAND. Sh! A customer!

(*Enter an Unemployed Man, in rags.*)

UNEMPLOYED MAN. Excuse me. I'm unemployed.

(*Mrs. Shin laughs.*)

SHEN TE. Can I help you?

UNEMPLOYED MAN. Have you any damaged cigarettes? I
thought there might be some damage when you're
unpacking.

WIFE. What nerve, begging for tobacco! (*Rhetorically.*) Why
don't they ask for bread?

UNEMPLOYED MAN. Bread is expensive. One cigarette butt
and I'll be a new man.

SHEN TE (*giving him cigarettes*). That's very important—to be
a new man. You'll be my first customer and bring me
luck.

(*The Unemployed Man quickly lights a cigarette, inhales,
and goes off, coughing.*)

WIFE. Was that right, Shen Te, dear?

MRS. SHIN. If this is the opening of a shop, you can hold the
closing at the end of the week.

HUSBAND. I bet he had money on him.

SHEN TE. Oh, no, he said he hadn't!

NEPHEW. How d'you know he wasn't lying?

SHEN TE (*angrily*). How do you know he was?

WIFE (*wagging her head*). You're too good, Shen Te, dear. If
you're going to keep this shop, you'll have to learn to say
No.

HUSBAND. Tell them the place isn't yours to dispose of.
Belongs to . . . some relative who insists on all accounts
being strictly in order . . .

MRS. SHIN. That's right! What do you think you are—a phil-
anthropist?

SHEN TE (*laughing*). Very well, suppose I ask you for my rice
back, Mrs. Shin?

WIFE (*combatively, at Mrs. Shin*). So that's *her* rice?

(*Enter the Carpenter, a small man.*)

MRS. SHIN (*who, at the sight of him, starts to hurry away*). See
you tomorrow, Miss Shen Te! (*Exit Mrs. Shin.*)

CARPENTER. Mrs. Shin, it's you I want!

WIFE (*to Shen Te*). Has she some claim on you?

SHEN TE. She's hungry. That's a claim.

CARPENTER. Are you the new tenant? And filling up the
shelves already? Well, they're not yours, till they're paid
for, ma'am. I'm the carpenter, so I should know.

SHEN TE. I took the shop "furnishings included."

CARPENTER. You're in league with that Mrs. Shin, of course.
All right: I demand my hundred silver dollars.

SHEN TE. I'm afraid I haven't got a hundred silver dollars.

CARPENTER. Then you'll find it. Or I'll have you arrested.

WIFE (*whispering to Shen Te*). That relative: make it a cousin.

SHEN TE. Can't it wait till next month?

CARPENTER. No!

SHEN TE. Be a little patient, Mr. Carpenter, I can't settle all
claims at once.

CARPENTER. Who's patient with me? (*He grabs a shelf from
the wall.*) Pay up—or I take the shelves back!

WIFE. Shen Te! Dear! Why don't you let your . . . cousin settle this affair? (*To Carpenter.*) Put your claim in writing.
Shen Te's cousin will see you get paid.

CARPENTER (*derisively*). Cousin, eh?

HUSBAND. Cousin, yes.

CARPENTER. I know these cousins!

NEPHEW. Don't be silly. He's a personal friend of mine.

HUSBAND. What a man! Sharp as a razor!

CARPENTER. All right. I'll put my claim in writing. (*Puts
shelf on floor, sits on it, writes out bill.*)

WIFE (*to Shen Te*). He'd tear the dress off your back to get his
shelves. Never recognize a claim! That's my motto.

SHEN TE. He's done a job, and wants something in return.
It's shameful that I can't give it to him. What will the
gods say?

HUSBAND. You did your bit when you took *us* in.

(*Enter the Brother, limping, and the Sister-in-Law, pregnant.*)

BROTHER (*to Husband and Wife*). So this is where you're hiding out! There's family feeling for you! Leaving us on the
corner!

WIFE (*embarrassed, to Shen Te*). It's my brother and his wife.
(*To them.*) Now stop grumbling, and sit quietly in that
corner. (*To Shen Te.*) It can't be helped. She's in her fifth
month.

SHEN TE. Oh, yes. Welcome!

WIFE (*to the couple*). Say thank you.

(*They mutter something.*)

The cups are there. (*To Shen Te.*) Lucky you bought this
shop when you did!

SHEN TE (*laughing and bringing tea*). Lucky indeed!

(*Enter Mrs. Mi Tzu, the landlady.*)

MRS. MI TZU. Miss Shen Te? I am Mrs. Mi Tzu, your landlady. I hope our relationship will be a happy one? I like to
think I give my tenants modern, personalized service.
Here is your lease. (*To the others, as Shen Te reads the
lease.*) There's nothing like the opening of a little shop, is
there? A moment of true beauty! (*She is looking around.*)
Not very much on the shelves, of course. But everything
in the gods' good time! Where are your references, Miss
Shen Te?

SHEN TE. Do I *have* to have references?

MRS. MI TZU. After all, I haven't a notion who you are!

HUSBAND. Oh, *we'd* be glad to vouch for Miss Shen Te! We'd go through fire for her!

MRS. MI TZU. And who may *you* be?

HUSBAND (*stammering*). Ma Fu, tobacco dealer.

MRS. MI TZU. Where is your shop, Mr. . . . Ma Fu?

HUSBAND. Well, um, I haven't a shop—I've just sold it.

MRS. MI TZU. I see. (*To Shen Te.*) Is there no one else that knows you?

WIFE (*whispering to Shen Te*). Your cousin! Your cousin!

MRS. MI TZU. This is a respectable house, Miss Shen Te. I never sign a lease without certain assurances.

SHEN TE (*slowly, her eyes downcast*). I have . . . a cousin.

MRS. MI TZU. On the square? Let's go over and see him. What does he do?

SHEN TE (*as before*). He lives . . . in another city.

WIFE (*prompting*). Didn't you say he was in Shung?

SHEN TE. That's right. Shung.

HUSBAND (*prompting*). I had his name on the tip of my tongue. Mr. . . .

SHEN TE (*with an effort*). Mr. . . . Shui . . . Ta.

HUSBAND. That's it! Tall, skinny fellow!

SHEN TE. Shui Ta!

NEPHEW (*to Carpenter*). You were in touch with him, weren't you? About the shelves?

CARPENTER (*surlily*). Give him this bill. (*He hands it over.*) I'll be back in the morning. (*Exit Carpenter.*)

NEPHEW (*calling after him, but with his eyes on Mrs. Mi Tzu*). Don't worry! Mr. Shui Ta pays on the nail!

MRS. MI TZU (*looking closely at Shen Te*). I'll be happy to make his acquaintance, Miss Shen Te. (*Exit Mrs. Mi Tzu.*)

(*Pause.*)

WIFE. By tomorrow morning she'll know more about you than you do yourself.

SISTER-IN-LAW (*to Nephew*). This thing isn't built to last.

(*Enter Grandfather.*)

WIFE. It's Grandfather! (*To Shen Te.*) Such a good old soul!

(*The Boy enters.*)

BOY (*over his shoulder*). Here they are!

WIFE. And the boy, how he's grown! But he always could eat enough for ten.

(*Enter the Niece.*)

WIFE (*to Shen Te*). Our little niece from the country. There are more of us now than in your time. The less we had, the more there were of us; the more there were of us, the less we had. Give me the key. We must protect ourselves from unwanted guests. (*She takes the key and locks the door.*) Just make yourself at home. I'll light the little lamp.

NEPHEW (*a big joke*). I hope her cousin doesn't drop in tonight! The strict Mr. Shui Ta!

(*Sister-in-Law laughs.*)

BROTHER (*reaching for a cigarette*). One cigarette more or less . . .

HUSBAND. One cigarette more or less.

(*They pile into the cigarettes. The Brother hands a jug of wine round.*)

NEPHEW. Mr. Shui Ta'll pay for it!

GRANDFATHER (*gravely, to Shen Te*). How do you do?

(*Shen Te, a little taken aback by the belatedness of the greeting, bows. She has the Carpenter's bill in one hand, the landlady's lease in the other.*)

WIFE. How about a bit of a song? To keep Shen Te's spirits up?

NEPHEW. Good idea. Grandfather: you start!

Song of the Smoke

GRANDFATHER.

> I used to think (before old age beset me)
>> That brains could fill the pantry of the poor.
> But where did all my cerebration get me?
>> I'm just as hungry as I was before.
>>> So what's the use?
>>>> See the smoke float free
>>>> Into ever colder coldness!
>>>> It's the same with me.

HUSBAND.

> The straight and narrow path leads to disaster
>> And so the crooked path I tried to tread.
> That got me to disaster even faster.
>> (They say we shall be happy when we're dead.)
>>> So what's the use, etc.

NIECE.

> You older people, full of expectation,
>> At any moment now you'll walk the plank!
> The future's for the younger generation!
>> Yes, even if that future is a blank.
>>> So what's the use, etc.

NEPHEW (*to the Brother*). Where'd you get that wine?

SISTER-IN-LAW (*answering for the Brother*). He pawned the sack of tobacco.

HUSBAND (*stepping in*). What? That tobacco was all we had to fall back on! You pig!

BROTHER. *You'd* call a man a pig because your wife was frigid! Did you refuse to drink it?

(*They fight. The shelves fall over.*)

SHEN TE (*imploringly*). Oh, don't! Don't break everything! Take it, take it all, but don't destroy a gift from the gods!

WIFE (*disparagingly*). This shop isn't big enough. I should never have mentioned it to Uncle and the others. When *they* arrive, it's going to be disgustingly overcrowded.

SISTER-IN-LAW. And did you hear our gracious hostess? She cools off quick!

(*Voices outside. Knocking at the door.*)

UNCLE'S VOICE. Open the door!

WIFE. Uncle? Is that you, Uncle?

UNCLE'S VOICE. Certainly, it's me. Auntie says to tell you she'll have the children here in ten minutes.

WIFE (*to Shen Te*). I'll have to let him in.

SHEN TE (*who scarcely hears her*).

> The little lifeboat is swiftly sent down
> Too many men too greedily
> Hold on to it as they drown.

SCENE 1A

(*Wong's den in a sewer pipe.*)

WONG (*crouching there*). All quiet! It's four days now since I left the city. The gods passed this way on the second day. I heard their steps on the bridge over there. They must be a long way off by this time, so I'm safe.

(*Breathing a sigh of relief, he curls up and goes to sleep. In his dream the pipe becomes transparent, and the Gods appear.*)

(*Raising an arm, as if in self-defense.*) I know, I know, illustrious ones! I found no one to give you a room—not in all Setzuan! There, it's out. Please continue on your way!

FIRST GOD (*mildly*). But you did find someone. Someone who took us in for the night, watched over us in our sleep, and in the early morning lighted us down to the street with a lamp.

WONG. It was . . . Shen Te, that took you in?

THIRD GOD. Who else?

WONG. And I ran away! "She isn't coming," I thought, "she just can't afford it."

GODS (*singing*).

> O you feeble, well-intentioned, and yet feeble chap!
> Where there's need the fellow thinks there is no
> goodness!
> When there's danger he thinks courage starts to ebb
> away!
> Some people only see the seamy side!
> What hasty judgment! What premature desperation!

WONG. I'm *very* ashamed, illustrious ones.

FIRST GOD. Do us a favor, Water Seller. Go back to Setzuan. Find Shen Te, and give us a report on her. We hear that she's come into a little money. Show interest in her goodness—for no one can be good for long if goodness is not in demand. Meanwhile we shall continue the search, and find other good people. After which, the idle chatter about the impossibility of goodness will stop!

(*The Gods vanish.*)

SCENE 2

(*A knocking.*)

WIFE. Shen Te! Someone at the door. Where is she anyway?

NEPHEW. She must be getting the breakfast. Mr. Shui Ta will pay for it.

(*The Wife laughs and shuffles to the door. Enter Mr. Shui Ta and the Carpenter.*)

WIFE. Who is it?

SHUI TA. I am Miss Shen Te's cousin.

WIFE. What?

SHUI TA. My name is Shui Ta.

WIFE. Her cousin?

NEPHEW. Her cousin?

NIECE. But that was a joke. She hasn't got a cousin.

HUSBAND. So early in the morning?

BROTHER. What's all the noise?

SISTER-IN-LAW. This fellow says he's her cousin.

BROTHER. Tell him to prove it.

NEPHEW. Right. If you're Shen Te's cousin, prove it by getting the breakfast.

SHUI TA (*whose regime begins as he puts out the lamp to save oil. Loudly, to all present, asleep or awake*). Would you all please get dressed! Customers will be coming! I wish to open my shop!

HUSBAND. *Your* shop? Doesn't it belong to our good friend Shen Te?

(*Shui Ta shakes his head.*)

SISTER-IN-LAW. So we've been cheated. Where *is* the little liar?

SHUI TA. Miss Shen Te has been delayed. She wishes me to tell you there will be nothing she can do—now I am here.

WIFE (*bowled over*). I thought she was *good!*

NEPHEW. Do you have to believe *him?*

HUSBAND. *I* don't.

NEPHEW. Then do something.

HUSBAND. Certainly! I'll send out a search party at once. You, you, you, and you, go out and look for Shen Te.

(*As the Grandfather rises and makes for the door.*)

Not you, Grandfather, you and I will hold the fort.

SHUI TA. You won't find Miss Shen Te. She has suspended her hospitable activity for an unlimited period. There are too many of you. She asked me to say: this is a tobacco shop, not a gold mine.

HUSBAND. Shen Te never said a thing like that. Boy, food! There's a bakery on the corner. Stuff your shirt full when they're not looking!

SISTER-IN-LAW. Don't overlook the raspberry tarts.

HUSBAND. And don't let the policeman see you.

(*The Boy leaves.*)

SHUI TA. Don't you depend on this shop now? Then why give it a bad name, by stealing from the bakery?

NEPHEW. Don't listen to him. Let's find Shen Te. She'll give him a piece of her mind.

SISTER-IN-LAW. Don't forget to leave us some breakfast.

(*Brother, Sister-in-Law, and Nephew leave.*)

SHUI TA (*to the Carpenter*). You see, Mr. Carpenter, nothing has changed since the poet, eleven hundred years ago, penned these lines:

> A governor was asked what was needed
> To save the freezing people in the city.
> He replied:
> "A blanket ten thousand feet long
> To cover the city and all its suburbs."

(*He starts to tidy up the shop.*)

CARPENTER. Your cousin owes me money. I've got witnesses. For the shelves.

SHUI TA. Yes, I have your bill. (*He takes it out of his pocket.*) Isn't a hundred silver dollars rather a lot?

CARPENTER. No deductions! I have a wife and children.

SHUI TA. How many children?

CARPENTER. Three.

SHUI TA. I'll make you an offer. Twenty silver dollars.

(*The Husband laughs.*)

CARPENTER. You're crazy. Those shelves are real walnut.

SHUI TA. Very well. Take them away.

CARPENTER. What?

SHUI TA. They cost too much. Please take them away.

WIFE. Not bad! (*And she, too, is laughing.*)

CARPENTER (*a little bewildered*). Call Shen Te, someone! (*To Shui Ta.*) She's good!

SHUI TA. Certainly. She's ruined.

CARPENTER (*provoked into taking some of the shelves*). All right, you can keep your tobacco on the floor.

SHUI TA (*to the Husband*). Help him with the shelves.

HUSBAND (*grins and carries one shelf over to the door where the Carpenter now is*). Goodbye, shelves!

CARPENTER (*to the Husband*). You dog! You want my family to starve?

SHUI TA. I repeat my offer. I have no desire to keep my tobacco on the floor. Twenty silver dollars.

CARPENTER (*with desperate aggressiveness*). One hundred!

(*Shui Ta shows indifference, looks through the window. The Husband picks up several shelves.*)

(*To Husband.*) You needn't smash them against the door-post, you idiot! (*To Shui Ta.*) These shelves were made to measure. They're no use anywhere else!

SHUI TA. Precisely.

(*The Wife squeals with pleasure.*)

CARPENTER (*giving up, sullenly*). Take the shelves. Pay what you want to pay.

SHUI TA (*smoothly*). Twenty silver dollars.

(*He places two large coins on the table. The Carpenter picks them up.*)

HUSBAND (*brings the shelves back in*). And quite enough too!

CARPENTER (*slinking off*). Quite enough to get drunk on.

HUSBAND (*happily*). Well, we got rid of *him*!

WIFE (*weeping with fun, gives a rendition of the dialogue just spoken*). "Real walnut," says he. "Very well, take them away," says his lordship. "I have children," says he. "Twenty silver dollars," says his lordship. "They're no use anywhere else," says he. "Precisely," said his lordship! (*She dissolves into shrieks of merriment.*)

SHUI TA. And now: go!

HUSBAND. What's that?

SHUI TA. You're thieves, parasites. I'm giving you this chance. Go!

HUSBAND (*summoning all his ancestral dignity*). That sort deserves no answer. Besides, one should never shout on an empty stomach.

WIFE. Where's that boy?

SHUI TA. Exactly. The boy. I want no stolen goods in this shop. (*Very loudly.*) I strongly advise you to leave! (*But they remain seated, noses in the air. Quietly.*) As you wish.

(*Shui Ta goes to the door. A Policeman appears. Shui Ta bows.*)

I am addressing the officer in charge of this precinct?

POLICEMAN. That's right, Mr., um . . . what was the name, sir?

SHUI TA. Mr. Shui Ta.

POLICEMAN. Yes, of course, sir.

(*They exchange a smile.*)

SHUI TA. Nice weather we're having.

POLICEMAN. A little on the warm side, sir.

SHUI TA. Oh, a little on the warm side.

HUSBAND (*whispering to the Wife*). If he keeps it up till the boy's back, we're done for. (*Tries to signal Shui Ta.*)

SHUI TA (*ignoring the signal*). Weather, of course, is one thing indoors, another out on the dusty street!

POLICEMAN. Oh, quite another, sir!

WIFE (*to the Husband*). It's all right as long as he's standing in the doorway—the boy will see him.

SHUI TA. Step inside for a moment! It's quite cool indoors. My cousin and I have just opened the place. And we attach the greatest importance to being on good terms with the, um, authorities.

POLICEMAN (*entering*). Thank you, Mr. Shui Ta. It *is* cool!

HUSBAND (*whispering to the Wife*). And now the boy *won't* see him.

SHUI TA (*showing Husband and Wife to the Policeman*). Visitors, I think my cousin knows them. They were just leaving.

HUSBAND (*defeated*). Ye-e-es, we were . . . just leaving.

SHUI TA. I'll tell my cousin you couldn't wait.

(*Noise from the street. Shouts of "Stop, thief!"*)

POLICEMAN. What's that?

(*The Boy is in the doorway with cakes and buns and rolls spilling out of his shirt. The Wife signals desperately to him to leave. He gets the idea.*)

No, you don't! (*He grabs the Boy by the collar.*) Where's all this from?

BOY (*vaguely pointing*). Down the street.

POLICEMAN (*grimly*). So that's it. (*Prepares to arrest the Boy.*)

WIFE (*stepping in*). And *we* knew nothing about it. (*To the Boy.*) Nasty little thief!

POLICEMAN (*dryly*). Can you clarify the situation, Mr. Shui Ta?

(*Shui Ta is silent.*)

POLICEMAN (*who understands silence*). Aha. You're all coming with me—to the station.

SHUI TA. I can hardly say how sorry I am that *my* establishment . . .

WIFE. Oh, he saw the boy leave not ten minutes ago!

SHUI TA. And to conceal the theft asked a policeman in?

POLICEMAN. Don't listen to her, Mr. Shui Ta, I'll be happy to relieve you of their presence one and all! (*To all three.*) Out! (*He drives them before him.*)

GRANDFATHER (*leaving last. Gravely*). Good morning!

POLICEMAN. Good morning!

(*Shui Ta, left alone, continues to tidy up. Mrs. Mi Tzu breezes in.*)

MRS. MI TZU. *You're* her cousin, are you? Then have the goodness to explain what all this means—police dragging people from a respectable house! By what right does your Miss Shen Te turn my property into a house of assignation?—Well, as you see, I know all!

SHUI TA. Yes. My cousin has the worst possible reputation: that of being poor.

MRS. MI TZU. No sentimental rubbish, Mr. Shui Ta. Your cousin was a common . . .

SHUI TA. Pauper. Let's use the uglier word.

MRS. MI TZU. I'm speaking of her conduct, not her earnings. But there must have *been* earnings, or how did she buy all this? Several elderly gentlemen took care of it, I suppose. I repeat: this is a respectable house! I have tenants who prefer not to live under the same roof with such a person.

SHUI TA (*quietly*). How much do you want?

MRS. MI TZU (*he is ahead of her now*). I beg your pardon.

SHUI TA. To reassure yourself. To reassure your tenants. How much will it cost?

MRS. MI TZU. You're a cool customer.

SHUI TA (*picking up the lease*). The rent is high. (*He reads on.*) I assume it's payable by the month?

MRS. MI TZU. Not in her case.

SHUI TA (*looking up*). What?

MRS. MI TZU. Six months rent payable in advance. Two hundred silver dollars.

SHUI TA. Six . . . ! Sheer usury! And where am I to find it?

MRS. MI TZU. You should have thought of that before.

SHUI TA. Have you no heart, Mrs. Mi Tzu? It's true Shen Te acted foolishly, being kind to all those people, but she'll improve with time. I'll see to it she does. She'll work her fingers to the bone to pay her rent, and all the time be as quiet as a mouse, as humble as a fly.

MRS. MI TZU. Her social background . . .

SHUI TA. Out of the depths! She came out of the depths! And before she'll go back there, she'll work, sacrifice, shrink from nothing. . . . Such a tenant is worth her weight in gold, Mrs. Mi Tzu.

MRS. MI TZU. It's silver we were talking about, Mr. Shui Ta. Two hundred silver dollars or . . .

(*Enter the Policeman.*)

POLICEMAN. Am I intruding, Mr. Shui Ta?

MRS. MI TZU. This tobacco shop is well-known to the police, I see.

POLICEMAN. Mr. Shui Ta has done us a service, Mrs. Mi Tzu. I am here to present our official felicitations!

MRS. MI TZU. That means less than nothing to me, sir. Mr. Shui Ta, all I can say is: I hope your cousin will find my terms acceptable. Good day, gentlemen. (*Exit.*)

SHUI TA. Good day, ma'am.

(*Pause.*)

POLICEMAN. Mrs. Mi Tzu a bit of a stumbling block, sir?

SHUI TA. She wants six months' rent in advance.

POLICEMAN. And you haven't got it, eh?

(*Shui Ta is silent.*)

But surely you can get it, sir? A man like you?

SHUI TA. What about a woman like Shen Te?

POLICEMAN. You're not staying, sir?

SHUI TA. No, and I won't be back. Do you smoke?

POLICEMAN (*taking two cigars, and placing them both in his pocket*). Thank you, sir—I see your point. Miss Shen Te—let's mince no words—Miss Shen Te lived by selling herself. "What else could she have done?" you ask. "How else was she to pay the rent?" True. But the fact remains, Mr. Shui Ta, it is not respectable. Why not? A very deep question. But, in the first place, love—love isn't bought and sold like cigars, Mr. Shui Ta. In the second place, it isn't respectable to go waltzing off with someone that's paying his way, so to speak—it must be for love! Thirdly and lastly, as the proverb has it: not for a handful of rice but for love! (*Pause. He is thinking hard.*) "Well," you may say, "and what good is all this wisdom if the milk's already spilt?" Miss Shen Te is what she is. Is *where* she is. We have to face the fact that if she doesn't get hold of six months' rent pronto, she'll be back on the streets. The question then as I see it—everything in this world is a matter of opinion—the question as I see it is: *how* is she to get hold of this rent? How? Mr. Shui Ta: I don't know. (*Pause.*) I take that back, sir. It's just come to me. A husband. We must find her a husband!

(*Enter a little Old Woman.*)

OLD WOMAN. A good cheap cigar for my husband, we'll have been married forty years tomorrow and we're having a little celebration.

SHUI TA. Forty years? And you still want to celebrate?

OLD WOMAN. As much as we can afford to. We have the carpet shop across the square. We'll be good neighbors, I hope?

SHUI TA. I hope so too.

POLICEMAN (*who keeps making discoveries*). Mr. Shui Ta, you know what we need? We need capital. And how do we acquire capital? We get married.

SHUI TA (*to Old Woman*). I'm afraid I've been pestering this gentleman with my personal worries.

POLICEMAN (*lyrically*). We can't pay six months' rent, so what do we do? We marry money.

SHUI TA. That might not be easy.

POLICEMAN. Oh, I don't know. She's a good match. Has a nice, growing business. (*To the Old Woman.*) What do you think?

OLD WOMAN (*undecided*). Well—

POLICEMAN. Should she put an ad in the paper?

OLD WOMAN (*not eager to commit herself*). Well, if *she* agrees—

POLICEMAN. I'll write it for her. *You* lend us a hand, and *we* write an ad for you! (*He chuckles away to himself, takes out his notebook, wets the stump of a pencil between his lips, and writes away.*)

SHUI TA (*slowly*). Not a bad idea.

POLICEMAN. "What . . . *respectable* . . . man . . . with small capital . . . widower . . . not excluded . . . desires . . . marriage . . . into flourishing . . . tobacco shop?" And now let's add: "am . . . pretty . . ." No! . . . "Prepossessing appearance."

SHUI TA. If you don't think that's an exaggeration?

OLD WOMAN. Oh, not a bit. I've seen her.

(*The Policeman tears the page out of his notebook, and hands it over to Shui Ta.*)

SHUI TA (*with horror in his voice*). How much luck we need to keep our heads above water! How many ideas! How many friends! (*To the Policeman.*) Thank you, sir. I think I see my way clear.

SCENE 3

(*Evening in the municipal park. Noise of a plane overhead. Yang Sun, a young man in rags, is following the plane with his eyes: one can tell that the machine is describing a curve above the park. Yang Sun then takes a rope out of his pocket, looking anxiously about him as he does so. He moves toward a large willow. Enter Two Prostitutes, one old, the other the Niece whom we have already met.*)

NIECE. Hello. Coming with me?

YANG SUN (*taken aback*). If you'd like to buy me a dinner.

OLD WHORE. Buy you a dinner! (*To the Niece.*) Oh, we know him—it's the unemployed pilot. Waste no time on him!

NIECE. But he's the only man left in the park. And it's going to rain.

OLD WHORE. Oh, how do you know?

(*And they pass by. Yang Sun again looks about him, again takes his rope, and this time throws it round a branch of the willow tree. Again he is interrupted. It is the Two Prostitutes returning—and in such a hurry they don't notice him.*)

NIECE. It's going to pour!

(*Enter Shen Te.*)

OLD WHORE. There's that *gorgon* Shen Te! That *drove* your family out into the cold!

NIECE. It wasn't her. It was that cousin of hers. She offered to *pay* for the cakes. I've nothing against her.

OLD WHORE. I have, though. (*So that Shen Te can hear.*) Now where could the little lady be off to? She may be rich now but that won't stop her snatching our young men, will it?

SHEN TE. I'm going to the tearoom by the pond.

NIECE. Is it true what they say? You're marrying a widower—with three children?

SHEN TE. Yes, I'm just going to see him.

YANG SUN (*his patience at breaking point*). Move on there! This is a park, not a whorehouse!

OLD WHORE. Shut your mouth!

(*But the Two Prostitutes leave.*)

YANG SUN. Even in the farthest corner of the park, even when it's raining, you can't get rid of them! (*He spits.*)

SHEN TE (*overhearing this*). And what right have you to scold them? (*But at this point she sees the rope.*) Oh!

YANG SUN. Well, what are you staring at?

SHEN TE. That rope. What is it for?

YANG SUN. Think! Think! I haven't a penny. Even if I had, I wouldn't spend it on you. I'd buy a drink of water.

(*The rain starts.*)

SHEN TE (*still looking at the rope*). What is the rope for? You mustn't!

YANG SUN. What's it to you? Clear out!

SHEN TE (*irrelevantly*). It's raining.

YANG SUN. Well, don't try to come under this tree.

SHEN TE. Oh, no. (*She stays in the rain.*)

YANG SUN. Now go away. (*Pause.*) For one thing, I don't like your looks, you're bow-legged.

SHEN TE (*indignantly*). That's not true!

YANG SUN. Well, don't show 'em to me. Look, it's raining. You better come under this tree.

(*Slowly, she takes shelter under the tree.*)

SHEN TE. Why did you want to do it?

YANG SUN. You really want to know? (*Pause.*) To get rid of you! (*Pause.*) You know what a flyer is?

SHEN TE. Oh yes, I've met a lot of pilots. At the tearoom.

YANG SUN. You call *them* flyers? Think they know what a machine *is*? Just 'cause they have leather helmets? They gave the airfield director a bribe, that's the way *those* fellows got up in the air! Try one of them out sometime. "Go up to two thousand feet," tell him, "then let it fall, then pick it up again with a flick of the wrist at the last moment." Know what he'll say to that? "It's not in my contract." Then again, there's the landing problem. It's like landing on your own backside. It's no different, planes are human. Those fools don't understand. (*Pause.*) And I'm the biggest fool for reading the book on flying in the Peking school and skipping the page where it says: "we've got enough flyers and we don't need you." I'm a mail pilot and no mail. You understand that?

SHEN TE (*shyly*). Yes. I do.

YANG SUN. No, you don't. You'd never understand that.

SHEN TE. When we were little we had a crane with a broken wing. He made friends with us and was very good-natured about our jokes. He would strut along behind us and call out to stop us going too fast for him. But every spring and autumn when the cranes flew over the villages in great swarms, he got quite restless. (*Pause.*) I understood that. (*She bursts out crying.*)

YANG SUN. Don't!

SHEN TE (*quieting down*). No.

YANG SUN. It's bad for the complexion.

SHEN TE (*sniffing*). I've stopped.

(*She dries her tears on her big sleeve. Leaning against the tree, but not looking at her, he reaches for her face.*)

YANG SUN. You can't even wipe your own face. (*He is wiping it for her with his handkerchief. Pause.*)

SHEN TE (*still sobbing*). I don't know *anything!*

YANG SUN. You interrupted me! What for?

SHEN TE. It's such a rainy day. You only wanted to do . . . *that* because it's such a rainy day.

(*To the audience.*)

In our country
The evenings should never be somber
High bridges over rivers
The grey hour between night and morning
And the long, long winter:
Such things are dangerous
For, with all the misery,
A very little is enough
And men throw away an unbearable life.

(*Pause.*)

YANG SUN. Talk about yourself for a change.

SHEN TE. What about me? I have a shop.

YANG SUN (*incredulous*). You have a shop, do you? Never thought of walking the streets?

SHEN TE. I *did* walk the streets. Now I have a shop.

YANG SUN (*ironically*). A gift of the gods, I suppose!

SHEN TE. How did you know?

YANG SUN (*even more ironical*). One fine evening the gods turned up saying: here's some money!

SHEN TE (*quickly*). One fine morning.

YANG SUN (*fed up*). This isn't much of an entertainment.

(*Pause.*)

SHEN TE. I can play the zither a little. (*Pause.*) And I can mimic men. (*Pause.*) I got the shop, so the first thing I did was to give my zither away. I can be as stupid as a fish now, I said to myself, and it won't matter.

I'm rich now, I said
I walk alone, I sleep alone
For a whole year, I said
I'll have nothing to do with a man.

YANG SUN. And now you're marrying one! The one at the tearoom by the pond?

(*Shen Te is silent.*)

YANG SUN. What do you know about love?

SHEN TE. Everything.

YANG SUN. Nothing. (*Pause.*) Or d'you just mean you enjoyed it?

SHEN TE. No.

YANG SUN (*again without turning to look at her, he strokes her cheek with his hand*). You like that?

SHEN TE. Yes.

YANG SUN (*breaking off*). You're easily satisfied, I must say. (*Pause.*) What a town!

SHEN TE. You have no friends?

YANG SUN (*defensively*). Yes, I have! (*Change of tone.*) But they don't want to hear I'm still unemployed. "What?" they ask. "Is there still water in the sea?" You have friends?

SHEN TE (*hesitating*). Just a . . . cousin.

YANG SUN. Watch him carefully.

SHEN TE. He only came once. Then he went away. He won't be back.

(*Yang Sun is looking away.*)

But to be without hope, they say, is to be without goodness!

(*Pause.*)

YANG SUN. Go on talking. A voice is a voice.

SHEN TE. Once, when I was a little girl, I fell, with a load of brushwood. An old man picked me up. He gave me a penny too. Isn't it funny how people who don't have very much like to give some of it away? They must like to show what they can do, and how could they show it better than by being kind? Being wicked is just like being clumsy. When we sing a song, or build a machine, or plant some rice, we're being kind. You're kind.

YANG SUN. You make it sound easy.

SHEN TE. Oh, no. (*Little pause.*) Oh! A drop of rain!

YANG SUN. Where'd you feel it?

SHEN TE. Between the eyes.

YANG SUN. Near the right eye? Or the left?

SHEN TE. Near the left eye.

YANG SUN. Oh, good. (*He is getting sleepy.*) So you're through with men, eh?

SHEN TE (*with a smile*). But I'm not bow-legged.

YANG SUN. Perhaps not.

SHEN TE. Definitely not.

(*Pause.*)

YANG SUN (*leaning wearily against the willow*). I haven't had a drop to drink all day, I haven't eaten anything for *two* days. I couldn't love you if I tried.

(*Pause.*)

SHEN TE. I like it in the rain.

(*Enter Wong the Water Seller, singing.*

The Song of the Water Seller in the Rain

"Buy my water," I am yelling
And my fury restraining
For no water I'm selling
'Cause it's raining, 'cause it's raining!
    I keep yelling: "Buy my water!"
    But no one's buying
    Athirst and dying
    And drinking and paying!
    Buy water!
    Buy water, you dogs!

Nice to dream of lovely weather!
Think of all the consternation
Were there no precipitation
Half a dozen years together!
Can't you hear them shrieking: "Water!"
Pretending they adore me!
They all would go down on their knees before me!
Down on your knees!
Go down on your knees, you dogs!

What are lawns and hedges thinking?
What are fields and forests saying?
"At the cloud's breast we are drinking!
And we've no idea who's paying!"
    I keep yelling: "Buy my water!"
    But no one's buying
    Athirst and dying
    And drinking and paying!
    Buy water!
    Buy water, you dogs!

(*The rain has stopped now. Shen Te sees Wong and runs toward him.*)

SHEN TE. Wong! You're back! Your carrying pole's at the shop.

WONG. Oh, thank you, Shen Te. And how is life treating *you*?

SHEN TE. I've just met a brave and clever man. And I want to buy him a cup of your water.

WONG (*bitterly*). Throw back your head and open your mouth and you'll have all the water you need—

SHEN TE (*tenderly*).

I want *your* water, Wong
The water that has tired you so
The water that you carried all this way
The water that is hard to sell because it's been raining
I need it for the young man over there—he's a flyer!
    A flyer is a bold man:
    Braving the storms
    In company with the clouds
    He crosses the heavens
    And brings to friends in far-away lands
    The friendly mail!

(*She pays Wong, and runs over to Yang Sun with the cup. But Yang Sun is fast asleep.*)

(*Calling to Wong, with a laugh.*) He's fallen asleep! Despair and rain and I have worn him out!

SCENE 3A

(*Wong's den. The sewer pipe is transparent, and the Gods again appear to Wong in a dream.*)

WONG (*radiant*). I've seen her, illustrious ones! And she hasn't changed!

FIRST GOD. That's good to hear.

WONG. She loves someone.

FIRST GOD. Let's hope the experience gives her the strength to stay good!

WONG. It does. She's doing good deeds all the time.

FIRST GOD. Ah? What sort? What sort of good deeds, Wong?

WONG. Well, she has a kind word for everybody.

FIRST GOD (*eagerly*). And then?

WONG. Hardly anyone leaves her shop without tobacco in his pocket—even if he can't pay for it.

FIRST GOD. Not bad at all. Next?

WONG. She's putting up a family of eight.

FIRST GOD (*gleefully, to the Second God*). Eight! (*To Wong.*) And that's not all, of course!

WONG. She bought a cup of water from me even though it was raining.

FIRST GOD. Yes, yes, yes, all these smaller good deeds!

WONG. Even they run into money. A little tobacco shop doesn't make so much.

FIRST GOD (*sententiously*). A prudent gardener works miracles on the smallest plot.

WONG. She hands out rice every morning. That eats up half her earnings.

FIRST GOD (*a little disappointed*). Well, as a beginning . . .

WONG. They call her the Angel of the Slums—whatever the Carpenter may say!

FIRST GOD. What's this? A carpenter speaks ill of her?

WONG. Oh, he only says her shelves weren't paid for in full.

SECOND GOD (*who has a bad cold and can't pronounce his n's and m's*). What's this? Not paying a carpenter? Why was that?

WONG. I suppose she didn't have the money.

SECOND GOD (*severely*). One pays what one owes, that's in our book of rules! First the letter of the law, then the spirit!

WONG. But it wasn't Shen Te, illustrious ones, it was her cousin. She called *him* in to help.

SECOND GOD. Then her cousin must never darken her threshold again!

WONG. Very well, illustrious ones! But in fairness to Shen Te, let me say that her cousin is a businessman.

FIRST GOD. Perhaps we should inquire what is customary? I find business quite unintelligible. But everybody's doing it. Business! Did the Seven Good Kings do business? Did Kung the Just sell fish?

SECOND GOD. In any case, such a thing must not occur again!

(*The Gods start to leave.*)

THIRD GOD. Forgive us for taking this tone with you, Wong, we haven't been getting enough sleep. The rich recommend us to the poor, and the poor tell us they haven't enough room.

SECOND GOD. Feeble, feeble, the best of them!

FIRST GOD. No great deeds! No heroic daring!

THIRD GOD. On such a *small* scale!

SECOND GOD. Sincere, yes, but what is actually *achieved*?

(*One can no longer hear them.*)

WONG (*calling after them*). I've thought of something, illustrious ones: Perhaps you shouldn't ask—too—much—all—at—once!

SCENE 4

(*The square in front of Shen Te's tobacco shop. Beside Shen Te's place, two other shops are seen: the carpet shop and a barber's. Morning. Outside Shen Te's the Grandfather, the Sister-in-Law, the Unemployed Man, and Mrs. Shin stand waiting.*)

SISTER-IN-LAW. She's been out all night again.

MRS. SHIN. No sooner did we get rid of that crazy cousin of hers than Shen Te herself starts carrying on! Maybe she does give us an ounce of rice now and then, but can you depend on her? Can you depend on her?

(*Loud voices from the Barber's.*)

VOICE OF SHU FU. What are you doing in my shop? Get out—at once!

VOICE OF WONG. But sir. They all let me sell . . .

(*Wong comes staggering out of the barber's shop pursued by Mr. Shu Fu, the barber, a fat man carrying a heavy curling iron.*)

SHU FU. Get out, I said! Pestering my customers with your slimy old water! Get out! Take your cup!

(*He holds out the cup. Wong reaches out for it. Mr. Shu Fu strikes his hand with the curling iron, which is hot. Wong howls.*)

You had it coming, my man!

(*Puffing, he returns to his shop. The Unemployed Man picks up the cup and gives it to Wong.*)

UNEMPLOYED MAN. You can report that to the police.

WONG. My hand! It's smashed up!

UNEMPLOYED MAN. Any bones broken?

WONG. I can't move my fingers.

UNEMPLOYED MAN. Sit down. I'll put some water on it.

(*Wong sits.*)

MRS. SHIN. The water won't cost you anything.

SISTER-IN-LAW. You might have got a bandage from Miss Shen Te till she took to staying out all night. It's a scandal.

MRS. SHIN (*despondently*). If you ask me, she's forgotten we ever existed!

(*Enter Shen Te down the street, with a dish of rice.*)

SHEN TE (*to the audience*). How wonderful to see Setzuan in the early morning! I always used to stay in bed with my dirty blanket over my head afraid to wake up. This morning I saw the newspapers being delivered by little boys, the streets being washed by strong men, and fresh vegetables coming in from the country on ox carts. It's a long walk from where Yang Sun lives, but I feel lighter at every step. They say you walk on air when you're in love, but it's even better walking on the rough earth, on the hard cement. In the early morning, the old city looks like a great rubbish heap. Nice, though—with all its little lights. And the sky, so pink, so transparent, before the dust comes and muddies it! What a lot you miss if you never see your city rising from its slumbers like an honest old craftsman pumping his lungs full of air and reaching for his tools, as the poet says! (*Cheerfully, to her waiting guests.*) Good morning, everyone, here's your rice! (*Distributing the rice, she comes upon Wong.*) Good morning, Wong, I'm quite lightheaded today. On my way over, I looked at myself in all the shop windows. I'd love to be beautiful.

(*She slips into the carpet shop. Mr. Shu Fu has just emerged from his shop.*)

SHU FU (*to the audience*). It surprises me how beautiful Miss Shen Te is looking today! I never gave her a passing thought before. But now I've been gazing upon her comely form for exactly three minutes! I begin to suspect I am in love with her. She is overpoweringly attractive! (*Crossly, to Wong.*) Be off with you, rascal!

(*He returns to his shop. Shen Te comes back out of the carpet shop with the Old Man, its proprietor, and his*) *wife—whom we have already met—the Old Woman. Shen Te is wearing a shawl. The Old Man is holding up a looking glass for her.*)

OLD WOMAN. Isn't it lovely? We'll give you a reduction because there's a little hole in it.

SHEN TE (*looking at another shawl on the Old Woman's arm*). The other one's nice too.

OLD WOMAN (*smiling*). Too bad there's no hole in that!

SHEN TE. That's right. My shop doesn't make very much.

OLD WOMAN. And your good deeds eat it all up! Be more careful, my dear . . .

SHEN TE (*trying on the shawl with the hole*). Just now, I'm lightheaded! Does the color suit me?

OLD WOMAN. You'd better ask a man.

SHEN TE (*to the Old Man*). Does the color suit me?

OLD MAN. You'd better ask your young friend.

SHEN TE. I'd like to have your opinion.

OLD MAN. It suits you, very well. But wear it this way: the dull side out.

(*Shen Te pays up.*)

OLD WOMAN. If you decide you don't like it, you can exchange it. (*She pulls Shen Te to one side.*) Has he got money?

SHEN TE (*with a laugh*). Yang Sun? Oh, no.

OLD WOMAN. Then how're you going to pay your rent?

SHEN TE. I'd forgotten about that.

OLD WOMAN. And next Monday is the first of the month! Miss Shen Te, I've got something to say to you. After we (*indicating her husband*) got to know you, we had our doubts about that marriage ad. We thought it would be better if you'd let *us* help you. Out of our savings. We reckon we could lend you two hundred silver dollars. We don't need anything in writing—you could pledge us your tobacco stock.

SHEN TE. You're prepared to lend money to a person like me?

OLD WOMAN. It's folks like you that need it. We'd think twice about lending anything to your cousin.

OLD MAN (*coming up*). All settled, my dear?

SHEN TE. I wish the gods could have heard what your wife was just saying, Mr. Ma. They're looking for good people who're happy—and helping me makes you happy because you know it was love that got me into difficulties!

(*The old couple smile knowingly at each other.*)

OLD MAN. And here's the money, Miss Shen Te.

(*He hands her an envelope. Shen Te takes it. She bows. They bow back. They return to their shop.*)

SHEN TE (*holding up her envelope*). Look, Wong, here's six months' rent! Don't you believe in miracles now? And how do you like my new shawl?

WONG. For the young fellow I saw you with in the park?

(*Shen Te nods.*)

MRS. SHIN. Never mind all that. It's time you took a look at his hand!

SHEN TE. Have you hurt your hand?

MRS. SHIN. That barber smashed it with his hot curling iron. Right in front of our eyes.

SHEN TE (*shocked at herself*). And I never noticed! We must get you to a doctor this minute or who knows what will happen?

UNEMPLOYED MAN. It's not a doctor he should see, it's a judge. He can ask for compensation. The barber's filthy rich.

WONG. You think I have a chance?

MRS. SHIN (*with relish*). If it's really good and smashed. But is it?

WONG. I think so. It's very swollen. Could I get a pension?

MRS. SHIN. You'd need a witness.

WONG. Well, you all saw it. You could all testify.

(*He looks round. The Unemployed Man, the Grandfather, and the Sister-in-Law are all sitting against the wall of the shop eating rice. Their concentration on eating is complete.*)

SHEN TE (*to Mrs. Shin*). You saw it yourself.

MRS. SHIN. I want nothin' to do with the police. It's against my principles.

SHEN TE (*to Sister-in-Law*). What about you?

SISTER-IN-LAW. Me? I wasn't looking.

SHEN TE (*to the Grandfather, coaxingly*). Grandfather, *you'll* testify, won't you?

SISTER-IN-LAW. And a lot of good that will do. He's simpleminded.

SHEN TE (*to the Unemployed Man*). You seem to be the only witness left.

UNEMPLOYED MAN. My testimony would only hurt him. I've been picked up twice for begging.

SHEN TE. Your brother is assaulted, and you shut your eyes?

He is hit, cries out in pain, and you are silent?
The beast prowls, chooses and seizes his victim, and
    you say:
"Because we showed no displeasure, he has spared us."

If no one present will be a witness, I will. I'll say *I* saw it.

MRS. SHIN (*solemnly*). The name for that is perjury.

WONG. I don't know if I can accept that. Though maybe I'll have to. (*Looking at his hand.*) Is it swollen enough, do you think? The swelling's not going down?

UNEMPLOYED MAN. No, no, the swelling's holding up well.

WONG. Yes. It's *more* swollen if anything. Maybe my wrist is broken after all. I'd better see a judge at once.

(*Holding his hand very carefully, and fixing his eyes on it, he runs off. Mrs. Shin goes quickly into the barber's shop.*)

UNEMPLOYED MAN (*seeing her*). She is getting on the right side of Mr. Shu Fu.

SISTER-IN-LAW. You and I can't change the world, Shen Te.

SHEN TE. Go away! Go away all of you!

(*The Unemployed Man, the Sister-in-Law, and the Grandfather stalk off, eating and sulking.*)

(To the audience.)

> They've stopped answering
> They stay put
> They do as they're told
> They don't care
> Nothing can make them look up
> But the smell of food.

(Enter Mrs. Yang, Yang Sun's mother, out of breath.)

MRS. YANG. Miss. Shen Te. My son has told me everything. I am Mrs. Yang, Sun's mother. Just think. He's got an offer. Of a job as a pilot. A letter has just come. From the director of the airfield in Peking!

SHEN TE. So he can fly again? Isn't that wonderful!

MRS. YANG *(less breathlessly all the time)*. They won't give him the job for nothing. They want five hundred silver dollars.

SHEN TE. We can't let money stand in his way, Mrs. Yang!

MRS. YANG. If only you could help him out!

SHEN TE. I have the shop. I can try! *(She embraces Mrs. Yang.)* I happen to have two hundred with me now. Take it. *(She gives her the old couple's money.)* It was a loan but they said I could repay it with my tobacco stock.

MRS. YANG. And they were calling Sun the Dead Pilot of Setzuan! A friend in need!

SHEN TE. We must find another three hundred.

MRS. YANG. How?

SHEN TE. Let me think. *(Slowly.)* I know someone who can help. I didn't want to call on his services again, he's hard and cunning. But a flyer must fly. And I'll make this the last time.

(Distant sound of a plane.)

MRS. YANG. If the man you mentioned can do it. . . . Oh, look, there's the morning mail plane, heading for Peking!

SHEN TE. The pilot can see us, let's wave!

(They wave. The noise of the engine is louder.)

MRS. YANG. You know that pilot up there?

SHEN TE. Wave, Mrs. Yang! I know the pilot who *will* be up there. He gave up hope. But he'll do it now. One man to raise himself above the misery, above us all.

(To the audience.)

> Yang Sun, my lover:
> Braving the storms
> In company with the clouds
> Crossing the heavens
> And bringing to friends in far-away lands
> The friendly mail!

SCENE 4A

(In front of the inner curtain. Enter Shen Te, carrying Shui Ta's mask. She sings.)

The Song of Defenselessness

> In our country
> A useful man needs luck
> Only if he finds strong backers can he prove himself
>   useful
> The good can't defend themselves and
> Even the gods are defenseless.

> Oh, why don't the gods have their own ammunition
> And launch against badness their own expedition
> Enthroning the good and preventing sedition
> And bringing the world to a peaceful condition?

> Oh, why don't the gods do the buying and selling
> Injustice forbidding, starvation dispelling
> Give bread to each city and joy to each dwelling?
> Oh, why don't the gods do the buying and selling?

(She puts on Shui Ta's mask and sings in his voice.)

> You can only help one of your luckless brothers
> By trampling down a dozen others

> Why is it the gods do not feel indignation
> And come down in fury to end exploitation
> Defeat all defeat and forbid desperation
> Refusing to tolerate such toleration?

> Why is it?

SCENE 5

(Shen Te's tobacco shop. Behind the counter, Mr. Shui Ta, reading the paper. Mrs. Shin is cleaning up. She talks and he takes no notice.)

MRS. SHIN. And when certain' rumors get about, what *happens* to a little place like this? It goes to pot. *I* know. So, if you want my advice, Mr. Shui Ta, find out just what exactly has been going on between Miss Shen Te and that Yang Sun from Yellow Street. And remember: a certain interest in Miss Shen Te has been expressed by the barber next door, a man with twelve houses and only one wife, who, for that matter, is likely to drop off at any time. A certain interest has been expressed. *(She relishes the phrase.)* He was even inquiring about her means and, if *that* doesn't prove a man is getting serious, what would? *(Still getting no response, she leaves with her bucket.)*

YANG SUN'S VOICE. Is that Miss Shen Te's tobacco shop?

MRS. SHIN'S VOICE. Yes, it is, but it's Mr. Shui Ta who's here today.

(Shui Ta runs to the looking glass with the short, light steps of Shen Te, and is just about to start primping, when he realizes his mistake, and turns away, with a short laugh. Enter Yang Sun. Mrs. Shin enters behind him and slips into the back room to eavesdrop.)

YANG SUN. I am Yang Sun.

(*Shui Ta bows.*)

Is Miss Shen Te in?

SHUI TA. No.

YANG SUN. I guess you know our relationship? (*He is inspecting the stock.*) Quite a place! And I thought she was just talking big. I'll be flying again, all right. (*He takes a cigar, solicits and receives a light from Shui Ta.*) You think we can squeeze the other three hundred out of the tobacco stock?

SHUI TA. May I ask if it is your intention to sell at once?

YANG SUN. It was decent of her to come out with the two hundred but they aren't much use with the other three hundred still missing.

SHUI TA. Shen Te was overhasty promising so much. She might have to sell the shop itself to raise it. Haste, they say, is the wind that blows the house down.

YANG SUN. Oh, she isn't a girl to keep a man waiting. For one thing or the other, if you take my meaning.

SHUI TA. I take your meaning.

YANG SUN (*leering*). Uh, huh.

SHUI TA. Would you explain what the five hundred silver dollars are for?

YANG SUN. Trying to sound me out? Very well. The director of the Peking airfield is a friend of mine from flying school. I give him five hundred: he gets me the job.

SHUI TA. The price is high.

YANG SUN. Not as these things go. He'll have to fire one of the present pilots—for negligence. Only the man he has in mind isn't negligent. Not easy, you understand. You needn't mention that part of it to Shen Te.

SHUI TA (*looking intently at Yang Sun*). Mr. Yang Sun, you are asking my cousin to give up her possessions, leave her friends, and place her entire fate in your hands. I presume you intend to marry her?

YANG SUN. I'd be prepared to.

(*Slight pause.*)

SHUI TA. Those two hundred silver dollars would pay the rent here for six months. If you were Shen Te wouldn't you be tempted to continue in business?

YANG SUN. What? Can you imagine Yang Sun the Flyer behind a counter? (*In an oily voice.*) "A strong cigar or a mild one, worthy sir?" Not in this century!

SHUI TA. My cousin wishes to follow the promptings of her heart, and, from her own point of view, she may even have what is called the right to love. Accordingly, she has commissioned me to help you to this post. There is nothing here that I am not empowered to turn immediately into cash. Mrs. Mi Tzu, the landlady, will advise me about the sale.

(*Enter Mrs. Mi Tzu.*)

MRS. MI TZU. Good morning, Mr. Shui Ta, you wish to see me about the rent? As you know it falls due the day after tomorrow.

SHUI TA. Circumstances have changed, Mrs. Mi Tzu: my cousin is getting married. Her future husband here, Mr. Yang Sun, will be taking her to Peking. I am interested in selling the tobacco stock.

MRS. MI TZU. How much are you asking, Mr. Shui Ta?

YANG SUN. Three hundred sil—

SHUI TA. Five hundred silver dollars.

MRS. MI TZU. How much did she pay for it, Mr. Shui Ta?

SHUI TA. A thousand. And very little has been sold.

MRS. MI TZU. She was robbed. But I'll make you a special offer if you'll promise to be out by the day after tomorrow. Three hundred silver dollars.

YANG SUN (*shrugging*). Take it, man, take it.

SHUI TA. It is not enough.

YANG SUN. Why not? Why not? Certainly, it's enough.

SHUI TA. Five hundred silver dollars.

YANG SUN. But why? We only need three!

SHUI TA (*to Mrs. Mi Tzu*). Excuse me. (*Takes Yang Sun on one side.*) The tobacco stock is pledged to the old couple who gave my cousin the two hundred.

YANG SUN. Is it in writing?

SHUI TA. No.

YANG SUN (*to Mrs. Mi Tzu*). Three hundred will do.

MRS. MI TZU. Of course, I need an assurance that Miss Shen Te is not in debt.

YANG SUN. Mr. Shui Ta?

SHUI TA. She is not in debt.

YANG SUN. When can you let us have the money?

MRS. MI TZU. The day after tomorrow. And remember: I'm doing this because I have a soft spot in my heart for young lovers! (*Exit.*)

YANG SUN (*calling after her*). Boxes, jars and sacks—three hundred for the lot and the pain's over! (*To Shui Ta.*) Where else can we raise money by the day after tomorrow?

SHUI TA. Nowhere. Haven't you enough for the trip and the first few weeks?

YANG SUN. Oh, certainly.

SHUI TA. How much, exactly?

YANG SUN. Oh, I'll dig it up, if I have to steal it.

SHUI TA. I see.

YANG SUN. Well, don't fall off the roof. I'll get to Peking somehow.

SHUI TA. Two people can't travel for nothing.

YANG SUN (*not giving Shui Ta a chance to answer*). I'm leaving *her* behind. No millstones round *my* neck!

SHUI TA. Oh.

YANG SUN. Don't look at me like that!

SHUI TA. How precisely is my cousin to live?

YANG SUN. Oh, you'll think of something.

SHUI TA. A small request, Mr. Yang Sun. Leave the two hundred silver dollars here until you can show me two tickets for Peking.

YANG SUN. You learn to mind your own business, Mr. Shui Ta.

SHUI TA. I'm afraid Miss Shen Te may not wish to sell the shop when she discovers that . . .

YANG SUN. You don't know women. She'll want to. Even then.

SHUI TA (*a slight outburst*). She is a human being, sir! And not devoid of common sense!

YANG SUN. Shen Te is a woman: she *is* devoid of common sense. I only have to lay my hand on her shoulder, and church bells ring.

SHUI TA (*with difficulty*). Mr. Yang Sun!

YANG SUN. Mr. Shui Whatever-it-is!

SHUI TA. My cousin is devoted to you . . . because . . .

YANG SUN. Because I have my hands on her breasts. Give me a cigar. (*He takes one for himself, stuffs a few more in his pocket, then changes his mind and takes the whole box.*) Tell her I'll marry her, then bring me the three hundred. Or let her bring it. One or the other. (*Exit.*)

MRS. SHIN (*sticking her head out of the back room*). Well, he has your cousin under his thumb, and doesn't care if all Yellow Street knows it!

SHUI TA (*crying out*). I've lost my shop! And he doesn't love me! (*He runs berserk through the room, repeating these lines incoherently. Then stops suddenly, and addresses Mrs. Shin.*) Mrs. Shin, you grew up in the gutter, like me. Are we lacking in hardness? I doubt it. If you steal a penny from me, I'll take you by the throat till you spit it out! You'd do the same to me. The times are bad, this city is hell, but we're like ants, we keep coming, up and up the walls, however smooth! Till bad luck comes. Being in love, for instance. *One* weakness is enough, and love is the deadliest.

MRS. SHIN (*emerging from the back room*). You should have a little talk with Mr. Shu Fu the Barber. He's a real gentleman and just the thing for your cousin. (*She runs off.*)

SHUI TA.

A caress becomes a stranglehold
A sigh of love turns to a cry of fear
Why are there vultures circling in the air?
A girl is going to meet her lover.

(*Shui Ta sits down and Mr. Shu Fu enters with Mrs. Shin.*)

Mr. Shu Fu?

SHU FU. Mr. Shui Ta.

(*They both bow.*)

SHUI TA. I am told that you have expressed a certain interest in my cousin Shen Te. Let me set aside all propriety and confess: she is at this moment in grave danger.

SHU FU. Oh, dear!

SHUI TA. She has lost her shop, Mr. Shu Fu.

SHU FU. The charm of Miss Shen Te, Mr. Shui Ta, derives from the goodness, not of her shop, but of her heart. Men call her the Angel of the Slums.

SHUI TA. Yet her goodness has cost her two hundred silver dollars in a single day: we must put a stop to it.

SHU FU. Permit me to differ, Mr. Shui Ta. Let us rather, open wide the gates to such goodness! Every morning, with pleasure tinged by affection, I watch her charitable ministrations. For they are hungry, and she giveth them to eat! Four of them, to be precise. Why only four? I ask. Why not four hundred? I hear she has been seeking shelter for the homeless. What about my humble cabins behind the cattle run? They are at her disposal. And so forth. And so on. Mr. Shui Ta, do you think Miss Shen Te could be persuaded to listen to certain ideas of mine? Ideas like these?

SHUI TA. Mr. Shu Fu, she would be honored.

(*Enter Wong and the Policeman. Mr. Shu Fu turns abruptly away and studies the shelves.*)

WONG. Is Miss Shen Te here?

SHUI TA. No.

WONG. I am Wong the Water Seller. You are Mr. Shui Ta?

SHUI TA. I am.

WONG. I am a friend of Shen Te's.

SHUI TA. An intimate friend, I hear.

WONG (*to the Policeman*). You see? (*To Shui Ta.*) It's because of my hand.

POLICEMAN. He hurt his hand, sir, that's a fact.

SHUI TA (*quickly*). You need a sling, I see. (*He takes a shawl from the back room, and throws it to Wong.*)

WONG. But that's her new shawl!

SHUI TA. She has no more use for it.

WONG. But she bought it to please someone!

SHUI TA. It happens to be no longer necessary.

WONG (*making the sling*). She is my only witness.

POLICEMAN. Mr. Shui Ta, your cousin is supposed to have seen the Barber hit the Water Seller with a curling iron.

SHUI TA. I'm afraid my cousin was not present at the time.

WONG. But she was, sir! Just ask her! Isn't she in?

SHUI TA (*gravely*). Mr. Wong, my cousin has her own troubles. You wouldn't wish her to add to them by committing perjury?

WONG. But it was she that told me to go to the judge!

SHUI TA. Was the judge supposed to heal your hand?

(*Mr. Shu Fu turns quickly around. Shui Ta bows to Shu Fu, and vice versa.*)

WONG (*taking the sling off, and putting it back*). I see how it is.

POLICEMAN. Well, I'll be on my way. (*To Wong.*) And you be careful. If Mr. Shu Fu wasn't a man who tempers justice with mercy, as the saying is, you'd be in jail for libel. Be off with you!

(*Exit Wong, followed by Policeman.*)

SHUI TA. Profound apologies, Mr. Shu Fu.

SHU FU. Not at all, Mr. Shui Ta. (*Pointing to the shawl.*) The episode is over?

SHUI TA. It may take her time to recover. There are some fresh wounds.

SHU FU. We shall be discreet. Delicate. A short vacation could be arranged . . .

SHUI TA. First, of course, you and she would have to talk things over.

SHU FU. At a small supper in a small, but high-class, restaurant.

SHUI TA. I'll go and find her. (*Exit into back room.*)

MRS. SHIN (*sticking her head in again*). Time for congratulations, Mr. Shu Fu?

SHU FU. Ah, Mrs. Shin! Please inform Miss Shen Te's guests they may take shelter in the cabins behind the cattle run!

(*Mrs. Shin nods, grinning.*)

(*To the audience.*) Well? What do you think of me, ladies and gentlemen? What could a man do more? Could he be less selfish? More farsighted? A small supper in a small but . . . Does that bring rather vulgar and clumsy thoughts into your mind? Ts, ts, ts. Nothing of the sort will occur. She won't even be touched. Not even accidentally while passing the salt. An exchange of ideas only. Over the flowers on the table—white chrysanthemums, by the way (*He writes down a note of this.*)—yes, over the white chrysanthemums, two young souls will . . . shall I say "find each other"? We shall NOT exploit the misfortune of others. Understanding? Yes. An offer of assistance? Certainly. But quietly. Almost inaudibly. Perhaps with a single glance. A glance that could also—mean more.

MRS. SHIN (*coming forward*). Everything under control, Mr. Shu Fu?

SHU FU. Oh, Mrs. Shin, what do you know about this worthless rascal Yang Sun?

MRS. SHIN. Why, he's the most worthless rascal . . .

SHU FU. Is he really? You're sure? (*As she opens her mouth.*) From now on, he doesn't exist! Can't be found anywhere!

(*Enter Yang Sun.*)

YANG SUN. What's been going on here?

MRS. SHIN. Shall I call Mr. Shui Ta, Mr. Shu Fu? He wouldn't want strangers in here!

SHU FU. Mr. Shui Ta is in conference with Miss Shen Te. Not to be disturbed!

YANG SUN. Shen Te here? I didn't see her come in. What kind of conference?

SHU FU (*not letting him enter the back room*). Patience, dear sir! And if by chance I have an inkling who you are, pray take note that Miss Shen Te and I are about to announce our engagement.

YANG SUN. What?

MRS. SHIN. You didn't expect that, did you?

(*Yang Sun is trying to push past the barber into the back room when Shen Te comes out.*)

SHU FU. My dear Shen Te, ten thousand apologies! Perhaps you . . .

YANG SUN. What is it, Shen Te? Have you gone crazy?

SHEN TE (*breathless*). My cousin and Mr. Shu Fu have come to an understanding. They wish me to hear Mr. Shu Fu's plans for helping the poor.

YANG SUN. Your cousin wants to part us.

SHEN TE. Yes.

YANG SUN. And you've agreed to it?

SHEN TE. Yes.

YANG SUN. They told you I was bad.

(*Shen Te is silent.*)

And suppose I am. Does that make me need you less? I'm low, Shen Te, I have no money, I don't do the right thing but at least I put up a fight! (*He is near her now, and speaks in an undertone.*) Have you no eyes? Look at him. Have you forgotten already?

SHEN TE. No.

YANG SUN. How it was raining?

SHEN TE. No.

YANG SUN. How you cut me down from the willow tree? Bought me water? Promised me money to fly with?

SHEN TE (*shakily*). Yang Sun, what do you want?

YANG SUN. I want you to come with me.

SHEN TE (*in a small voice*). Forgive me, Mr. Shu Fu, I want to go with Mr. Yang Sun.

YANG SUN. We're lovers you know. Give me the key to the shop.

(*Shen Te takes the key from around her neck. Yang Sun puts it on the counter. To Mrs. Shin.*)

Leave it under the mat when you're through. Let's go, Shen Te.

SHU FU. But this is rape! Mr. Shui Ta!!

YANG SUN (*to Shen Te*). Tell him not to shout.

SHEN TE. Please don't shout for my cousin, Mr. Shu Fu. He doesn't agree with me, I know, but he's wrong. (*To the audience.*)

I want to go with the man I love
I don't want to count the cost
I don't want to consider if it's wise
I don't want to know if he loves me
I want to go with the man I love

YANG SUN. That's the spirit.

(*And the couple leave.*)

SCENE 5A

(*In front of the inner curtain. Shen Te in her wedding clothes, on the way to her wedding.*)

SHEN TE. Something terrible has happened. As I left the shop with Yang Sun, I found the old carpet dealer's wife waiting in the street, trembling all over. She told me her husband had taken to his bed—sick with all the worry and excitement over the two hundred silver dollars they lent me. She said it would be best if I gave it back now. Of course, I had to say I would. She said she couldn't quite trust my cousin Shui Ta or even my fiancé Yang Sun. There were tears in her eyes. With my emotions in an uproar, I threw myself into Yang Sun's arms, I couldn't resist him. The things he'd said to Shui Ta had taught Shen Te nothing. Sinking into his arms, I said to myself:

> To let no one perish, not even oneself
> To fill everyone with happiness, even oneself
> Is so good

How could I have forgotten those two old people? Yang Sun swept me away like a small hurricane. But he's not a bad man, and he loves me. He'd rather work in the cement factory than owe his flying to a crime. Though, of course, flying *is* a great passion with Sun. Now, on the way to my wedding, I waver between fear and joy.

SCENE 6

(*The "private dining room" on the upper floor of a cheap restaurant in a poor section of town. With Shen Te: the Grandfather, the Sister-in-Law, the Niece, Mrs. Shin, the Unemployed Man. In a corner, alone, a Priest. A Waiter pouring wine. Downstage, Yang Sun talking to his mother. He wears a dinner jacket.*)

YANG SUN. Bad news, Mamma. She came right out and told me she can't sell the shop for me. Some idiot is bringing a claim because he lent her the two hundred she gave you.

MRS. YANG. What did *you* say? Of course, you can't marry her now.

YANG SUN. It's no use saying anything to *her*. I've sent for her cousin, Mr. Shui Ta. He said there was nothing in writing.

MRS. YANG. Good idea. I'll go out and look for him. Keep an eye on things.

(*Exit Mrs. Yang. Shen Te has been pouring wine.*)

SHEN TE (*to the audience, pitcher in hand*). I wasn't mistaken in him. He's bearing up well. Though it must have been an awful blow—giving up flying. I do love him so. (*Calling across the room to him.*) Sun, you haven't drunk a toast with the bride!

YANG SUN. What do we drink to?

SHEN TE. Why, to the future!

YANG SUN. When the bridegroom's dinner jacket won't be a hired one!

SHEN TE. But when the bride's dress will still get rained on sometimes!

YANG SUN. To everything we ever wished for!

SHEN TE. May all our dreams come true!

(*They drink.*)

YANG SUN (*with loud conviviality*). And now, friends, before the wedding gets under way, I have to ask the bride a few questions. I've no idea what kind of a wife she'll make, and it worries me. (*Wheeling on Shen Te.*) For example. Can you make five cups of tea with three tea leaves?

SHEN TE. No.

YANG SUN. So I won't be getting very much tea. Can you sleep on a straw mattress the size of that book? (*He points to the large volume the Priest is reading.*)

SHEN TE. The two of us?

YANG SUN. The one of you.

SHEN TE. In that case, no.

YANG SUN. What a wife! I'm shocked!

(*While the audience is laughing, his mother returns. With a shrug of her shoulders, she tells Yang Sun the expected guest hasn't arrived. The Priest shuts the book with a bang, and makes for the door.*)

MRS. YANG. Where are *you* off to? It's only a matter of minutes.

PRIEST (*watch in hand*). Time goes on, Mrs. Yang, and I've another wedding to attend to. Also a funeral.

MRS. YANG (*irately*). D'you think we planned it this way? I was hoping to manage with one pitcher of wine, and we've run through two already. (*Points to empty pitcher. Loudly.*) My dear Shen Te, I don't know where your cousin can be keeping himself!

SHEN TE. My cousin?

MRS. YANG. Certainly. I'm old fashioned enough to think such a close relative should attend the wedding.

SHEN TE. Oh, Sun, is it the three hundred silver dollars?

YANG SUN (*not looking her in the eye*). Are you deaf? Mother says she's old fashioned. And I say I'm considerate. We'll wait another fifteen minutes.

HUSBAND. Another fifteen minutes.

MRS. YANG (*addressing the company*). Now you all know, don't you, that my son is getting a job as a mail pilot?

SISTER-IN-LAW. In Peking, too, isn't it?

MRS. YANG. In Peking, too! The two of us are moving to Peking!

SHEN TE. Sun, tell your mother Peking is out of the question now.

YANG SUN. Your cousin'll tell her. If he agrees. I don't agree.

SHEN TE (*amazed, and dismayed*). Sun!

YANG SUN. I hate this godforsaken Setzuan. What people! Know what they look like when I half close my eyes? Horses! Whinnying, fretting, stamping, screwing their necks up! (*Loudly.*) And what is it the thunder says? They are su-per-flu-ous! (*He hammers out the syllables.*) They've run their last race! They can go trample themselves to death! (*Pause.*) I've got to get out of here.

SHEN TE. But I've promised the money to the old couple.

YANG SUN. And since you always do the wrong thing, it's lucky your cousin's coming. Have another drink.

SHEN TE (*quietly*). My cousin can't be coming.

YANG SUN. How d'you mean?

SHEN TE. My cousin can't be where I am.

YANG SUN. Quite a conundrum!

SHEN TE (*desperately*). Sun, I'm the one that loves you. Not my cousin. He was thinking of the job in Peking when he promised you the old couple's money—

YANG SUN. Right. And that's why he's bringing the three hundred silver dollars. Here—to my wedding.

SHEN TE. He is not bringing the three hundred silver dollars.

YANG SUN. Huh? What makes you think that?

SHEN TE (*looking into his eyes*). He says you only bought one ticket to Peking.

(*Short pause.*)

YANG SUN. That was yesterday. (*He pulls two tickets part way out of his inside pocket, making her look under his coat.*) Two tickets. I don't want Mother to know. She'll get left behind. I sold her furniture to buy these tickets, so you see . . .

SHEN TE. But what's to become of the old couple?

YANG SUN. What's to become of me? Have another drink. Or do you believe in moderation? If I drink, I fly again. And if you drink, you may learn to understand me.

SHEN TE. You want to fly. But I can't help you.

YANG SUN. "Here's a plane, my darling—but it's only got one wing!"

(*The Waiter enters.*)

WAITER. Mrs. Yang! Mrs. Yang!

MRS. YANG. Yes?

WAITER. Another pitcher of wine, ma'am?

MRS. YANG. We have enough, thanks. Drinking makes me sweat.

WAITER. Would you mind paying, ma'am?

MRS. YANG (*to everyone*). Just be patient a few moments longer, everyone, Mr. Shui Ta is on his way over! (*To the Waiter.*) Don't be a spoilsport.

WAITER. I can't let you leave till you've paid your bill, ma'am.

MRS. YANG. But they know me here!

WAITER. That's just it.

PRIEST (*ponderously getting up*). I humbly take my leave. (*And he does.*)

MRS. YANG (*to the others, desperately*). Stay where you are, everybody! The priest says he'll be back in two minutes!

YANG SUN. It's no good, Mamma. Ladies and gentlemen, Mr. Shui Ta still hasn't arrived and the priest has gone home. We won't detain you any longer.

(*They are leaving now.*)

GRANDFATHER (*in the doorway, having forgotten to put his glass down*). To the bride! (*He drinks, puts down the glass, and follows the others.*)

(*Pause.*)

SHEN TE. Shall I go too?

YANG SUN. You? Aren't you the bride? Isn't this your wedding? (*He drags her across the room, tearing her wedding dress.*) If we can wait, you can wait. Mother calls me her falcon. She wants to see me in the clouds. But I think it may be St. Nevercome's Day before she'll go to the door and see my plane thunder by. (*Pause. He pretends the guests are still present.*) Why such a lull in the conversa-

tion, ladies and gentlemen? Don't you like it here? The ceremony is only slightly postponed—because an important guest is expected at any moment. Also because the bride doesn't know what love is. While we're waiting, the bridegroom will sing a little song. (*He does so.*)

The Song of St. Nevercome's Day

On a certain day, as is generally known,
    One and all will be shouting: Hooray, hooray!
For the beggar maid's son has a solid-gold throne
    And the day is St. Nevercome's Day
On St. Nevercome's, Nevercome's, Nevercome's Day
    He'll sit on his solid-gold throne

Oh, hooray, hooray! That day goodness will pay!
    That day badness will cost you your head!
And merit and money will smile and be funny
    While exchanging salt and bread
On St. Nevercome's, Nevercome's, Nevercome's Day
    While exchanging salt and bread

And the grass, oh, the grass will look down at the sky
    And the pebbles will roll up the stream
And all men will be good without batting an eye
    They will make of our earth a dream
On St. Nevercome's, Nevercome's, Nevercome's Day
    They will make of our earth a dream

And as for me, that's the day I shall be
    A flyer and one of the best
Unemployed man, you will have work to do
    Washerwoman, you'll get your rest
On St. Nevercome's, Nevercome's, Nevercome's Day
    Washerwoman, you'll get your rest

MRS. YANG. It looks like he's not coming.

(*The three of them sit looking at the door.*)

SCENE 6A

(*Wong's den. The sewer pipe is again transparent and again the Gods appear to Wong in a dream.*)

WONG. I'm so glad you've come, illustrious ones. It's Shen Te. She's in great trouble from following the rule about loving thy neighbor. Perhaps she's *too* good for this world!

FIRST GOD. Nonsense! You are eaten up by lice and doubts!

WONG. Forgive me, illustrious one, I only meant you might deign to intervene.

FIRST GOD. Out of the question! My colleague here intervened in some squabble or other only yesterday. (*He points to the Third God who has a black eye.*) The results are before us!

WONG. She had to call on her cousin again. But not even he could help. I'm afraid the shop is done for.

THIRD GOD (*a little concerned*). Perhaps we should help after all?

FIRST GOD. The gods help those that help themselves.

WONG. What if we *can't* help ourselves, illustrious ones?

(*Slight pause.*)

SECOND GOD. Try, anyway! Suffering ennobles!

FIRST GOD. Our faith in Shen Te is unshaken!

THIRD GOD. We certainly haven't found any *other* good people. You can see where we spend our nights from the straw on our clothes.

WONG. You might help her find her way by—

FIRST GOD. The good man finds his own way here below!

SECOND GOD. The good woman too.

FIRST GOD. The heavier the burden, the greater her strength!

THIRD GOD. We're only onlookers, you know.

FIRST GOD. And everything will be all right in the end, O ye of little faith!

(*They are gradually disappearing through these last lines.*)

SCENE 7

(*The yard behind Shen Te's shop. A few articles of furniture on a cart. Shen Te and Mrs. Shin are taking the washing off the line.*)

MRS. SHIN. If you ask me, you should fight tooth and nail to keep the shop.

SHEN TE. How can I? I have to sell the tobacco to pay back the two hundred silver dollars today.

MRS. SHIN. No husband, no tobacco, no house and home! What are you going to live on?

SHEN TE. I can work. I can sort tobacco.

MRS. SHIN. Hey, look, Mr. Shui Ta's trousers! He must have left here stark naked!

SHEN TE. Oh, he may have another pair, Mrs. Shin.

MRS. SHIN. But if he's gone for good as you say, why has he left his pants behind?

SHEN TE. Maybe he's thrown them away.

MRS. SHIN. Can I take them?

SHEN TE. Oh, no.

(*Enter Mr. Shu Fu, running.*)

SHU FU. Not a word! Total silence! I know all. You have sacrificed your own love and happiness so as not to hurt a dear old couple who had put their trust in you! Not in vain does this district—for all its malevolent tongues!—call you the Angel of the Slums! That young man couldn't rise to your level, so you left him. And now, when I see you closing up the little shop, that veritable haven of rest for the multitude, well, I cannot, I cannot let it pass. Morning after morning I have stood watching in the doorway not unmoved—while you graciously handed out rice to the wretched. Is that never to happen again? Is the good woman of Setzuan to disappear? If only you would

allow *me* to assist you! Now don't say anything! No assurances, no exclamations of gratitude! (*He has taken out his check book.*) Here! A blank check. (*He places it on the cart.*) Just my signature. Fill it out as you wish. Any sum in the world. I herewith retire from the scene, quietly, unobtrusively, making no claims, on tiptoe, full of veneration, absolutely selflessly . . . (*He has gone.*)

MRS. SHIN. Well! You're saved. There's always some idiot of a man . . . Now hurry! Put down a thousand silver dollars and let me fly to the bank before he comes to his senses.

SHEN TE. I can pay you for the washing without any check.

MRS. SHIN. What? You're not going to cash it just because you might have to marry him? Are you crazy? Men like him *want* to be led by the nose! Are you still thinking of that flyer? All Yellow Street knows how he treated you!

SHEN TE.

When I heard his cunning laugh, I was afraid

But when I saw the holes in his shoes, I loved him dearly.

MRS. SHIN. Defending that good for nothing after all that's happened!

SHEN TE (*staggering as she holds some of the washing*). Oh!

MRS. SHIN (*taking the washing from her, dryly*). So you feel dizzy when you stretch and bend? There couldn't be a little visitor on the way? If that's it, you can forget Mr. Shu Fu's blank check: it wasn't meant for a christening present!

(*She goes to the back with a basket. Shen Te's eyes follow Mrs. Shin for a moment. Then she looks down at her own body, feels her stomach, and a great joy comes into her eyes.*)

SHEN TE. O joy! A new human being is on the way. The world awaits him. In the cities the people say: he's got to be reckoned with, this new human being! (*She imagines a little boy to be present, and introduces him to the audience.*)

This is my son, the well-known flyer!

Say: Welcome

To the conqueror of unknown mountains and unreachable regions

Who brings us our mail across the impassable deserts!

(*She leads him up and down by the hand.*) Take a look at the world, my son. That's a tree. Tree, yes. Say: "Hello, tree!" And bow. Like this. (*She bows.*) Now you know each other. And, look, here comes the Water Seller. He's a friend, give him your hand. A cup of fresh water for my little son, please. Yes, it *is* a warm day. (*Handing the cup.*) Oh dear, a policeman, we'll have to make a circle round *him*. Perhaps we can pick a few cherries over there in the rich Mr. Pung's garden. But we mustn't be seen. You want cherries? Just like children with fathers. No, no, you can't go straight at them like that. Don't pull. We must learn to be reasonable. Well, have it your own way. (*She has let him make for the cherries.*) Can you reach? Where to put them? Your mouth is the best place. (*She tries one herself.*)

Mmm, they're good. But the policeman, we must run! (*They run.*) Yes, back to the street. Calm now, so no one will notice us. (*Walking the street with her child, she sings.*)

Once a plum—'twas in Japan—
Made a conquest of a man
But the man's turn soon did come
For he gobbled up the plum

(*Enter Wong, with a Child by the hand. He coughs.*)

SHEN TE. Wong!

WONG. It's about the Carpenter, Shen Te. He's lost his shop, and he's been drinking. His children are on the streets. This is one. Can you help?

SHEN TE (*to the child*). Come here, little man. (*Takes him down to the footlights. To the audience.*)

You there! A man is asking you for shelter!
A man of tomorrow says: what about today?
His friend the conqueror, whom you know,
Is his advocate!

(*To Wong.*) He can live in Mr. Shu Fu's cabins. I may have to go there myself. I'm going to have a baby. That's a secret—don't tell Yang Sun—we'd only be in his way. Can you find the Carpenter for me?

WONG. I knew you'd think of something. (*To the Child.*) Goodbye, son, I'm going for your father.

SHEN TE. What about your hand, Wong? I wanted to help, but my cousin . . .

WONG. Oh, I can get along with one hand, don't worry. (*He shows how he can handle his pole with his left hand alone.*)

SHEN TE. But your right hand! Look, take this cart, sell everything that's on it, and go to the doctor with the money . . .

WONG. She's still good. But first I'll bring the Carpenter. I'll pick up the cart when I get back. (*Exit Wong.*)

SHEN TE (*to the Child*). Sit down over here, son, till your father comes.

(*The Child sits crosslegged on the ground. Enter the Husband and Wife, each dragging a large, full sack.*)

WIFE (*furtively*). You're alone, Shen Te, dear?

(*Shen Te nods. The Wife beckons to the Nephew offstage. He comes on with another sack.*)

Your cousin's away?

(*Shen Te nods.*)

He's not coming back?

SHEN TE. No. I'm giving up the shop.

WIFE. That's why we're here. We want to know if we can leave these things in your new home. Will you do us this favor?

SHEN TE. Why, yes, I'd be glad to.

HUSBAND (*cryptically*). And if anyone asks about them, say they're yours.

SHEN TE. Would anyone ask?

WIFE (*with a glance back at her Husband*). Oh, someone might. The police, for instance. They don't seem to like us. Where can we put it?

SHEN TE. Well, I'd rather not get in any more trouble . . .

WIFE. Listen to her! The good woman of Setzuan!

(*Shen Te is silent.*)

HUSBAND. There's enough tobacco in those sacks to give us a new start in life. We could have our own tobacco factory!

SHEN TE (*slowly*). You'll have to put them in the back room.

(*The sacks are taken offstage, where the Child is left alone. Shyly glancing about him, he goes to the garbage can, starts playing with the contents, and eating some of the scraps. The others return.*)

WIFE. We're counting on you, Shen Te!

SHEN TE. Yes. (*She sees the Child and is shocked.*)

HUSBAND. We'll see you in Mr. Shu Fu's cabins.

NEPHEW. The day after tomorrow.

SHEN TE. Yes. Now, go. Go! I'm not feeling well.

(*Exeunt all three, virtually pushed off.*)

He is eating the refuse in the garbage can!
Only look at his little grey mouth!

(*Pause. Music.*)

As this is the world my son will enter
I will study to defend him.
To be good to you, my son,
I shall be a tigress to all others
If I have to.
And I shall have to.

(*She starts to go.*) One more time, then. I hope really the last.

(*Exit Shen Te, taking Shui Ta's trousers. Mrs. Shin enters and watches her with marked interest. Enter the Sister-in-Law and the Grandfather.*)

SISTER-IN-LAW. So it's true, the shop has closed down. And the furniture's in the back yard. It's the end of the road!

MRS. SHIN (*pompously*). The fruit of high living, selfishness, and sensuality! Down the primrose path to Mr. Shu Fu's cabins—with you!

SISTER-IN-LAW. Cabins? Rat holes! He gave them to us because his soap supplies only went mouldy there!

(*Enter the Unemployed Man.*)

UNEMPLOYED MAN. Shen Te is moving?

SISTER-IN-LAW. Yes. She was sneaking away.

MRS. SHIN. She's ashamed of herself, and no wonder!

UNEMPLOYED MAN. Tell her to call Mr. Shui Ta or she's done for this time!

SISTER-IN-LAW. Tell her to call Mr. Shui Ta or *we're* done for this time!

(*Enter Wong and Carpenter, the latter with a Child on each hand.*)

CARPENTER. So we'll have a roof over our heads for a change!

MRS. SHIN. Roof? Whose roof?

CARPENTER. Mr. Shu Fu's cabins. And we have little Feng to thank for it. (*Feng, we find, is the name of the child already there; his Father now takes him. To the other two.*) Bow to your little brother, you two! (*The Carpenter and the two new arrivals bow to Feng.*)

(*Enter Shui Ta.*)

UNEMPLOYED MAN. Sst! Mr. Shui Ta!

(*Pause.*)

SHUI TA. And what is this crowd here for, may I ask?

WONG. How do you do, Mr. Shui Ta? This is the Carpenter. Miss Shen Te promised him space in Mr. Shu Fu's cabins.

SHUI TA. That will not be possible.

CARPENTER. We can't go there after all?

SHUI TA. All the space is needed for other purposes.

SISTER-IN-LAW. You mean we have to get out? But we've got nowhere to go.

SHUI TA. Miss Shen Te finds it possible to provide employment. If the proposition interests you, you may stay in the cabins.

SISTER-IN-LAW (*with distaste*). You mean *work?* Work for Miss Shen Te?

SHUI TA. Making tobacco, yes. There are three bales here already. Would you like to get them?

SISTER-IN-LAW (*trying to bluster*). We have our own tobacco! We were in the tobacco business before you were born!

SHUI TA (*to the Carpenter and the Unemployed Man*). You don't have your own tobacco. What about you?

(*The Carpenter and the Unemployed Man get the point, and go for the sacks. Enter Mrs. Mi Tzu.*)

MRS. MI TZU. Mr. Shui Ta? I've brought you your three hundred silver dollars.

SHUI TA. I'll Sign your lease instead. I've decided not to sell.

MRS. MI TZU. What? You don't need the money for that flyer?

SHUI TA. No.

MRS. MI TZU. And you can pay six months' rent?

SHUI TA (*takes the barber's blank check from the cart and fills it out*). Here is a check for ten thousand silver dollars. On Mr. Shu Fu's account. Look! (*He shows her the signature on the check.*) Your six months' rent will be in your hands by seven this evening. And now, if you'll excuse me.

MRS. MI TZU. So it's Mr. Shu Fu now. The flyer has been given his walking papers. These modern girls! In my day they'd have said she was flighty. That poor, deserted Mr. Yang Sun!

(*Exit Mrs. Mi Tzu. The Carpenter and the Unemployed Man drag the three sacks back on the stage.*)

CARPENTER (*to Shui Ta*). I don't know why I'm doing this for you.

SHUI TA. Perhaps your children want to eat, Mr. Carpenter.

SISTER-IN-LAW (*catching sight of the sacks*). Was my brother-in-law here?

MRS. SHIN. Yes, he was.

SISTER-IN-LAW. I thought as much. I know those sacks! That's our tobacco!

SHUI TA. Really? I thought it came from my back room? Shall we consult the police on the point?

SISTER-IN-LAW (*defeated*). No.

SHUI TA. Perhaps you will show me the way to Mr. Shu Fu's cabins?

(*Shui Ta goes off, followed by the Carpenter and his two older children, the Sister-in-Law, the Grandfather, and the Unemployed Man. Each of the last three drags a sack. Enter Old Man and Old Woman.*)

MRS. SHIN. A pair of pants—missing from the clothes line one minute—and next minute on the honorable backside of Mr. Shu Ta!

OLD WOMAN. We thought Miss Shen Te was here.

MRS. SHIN (*preoccupied*). Well, she's not.

OLD MAN. There was something she was going to give us.

WONG. She was going to help me too. (*Looking at his hand.*) It'll be too late soon. But she'll be back. This cousin has never stayed long.

MRS. SHIN (*approaching a conclusion*). No, he hasn't, has he?

SCENE 7A

(*The sewer pipe: Wong asleep. In his dream, he tells the Gods his fears. The Gods seem tired from all their travels. They stop for a moment and look over their shoulders at the Water Seller.*)

WONG. Illustrious ones, I've been having a bad dream. Our beloved Shen Te was in great distress in the rushes down by the rivers—the spot where the bodies of suicides are washed up. She kept staggering and holding her head down as if she was carrying something and it was dragging her down into the mud. When I called out to her, she said she had to take your Book of Rules to the other side, and not get it wet, or the ink would all come off. You had talked to her about the virtues, you know, the time she gave you shelter in Setzuan.

THIRD GOD. Well, but what do you suggest, my dear Wong?

WONG. Maybe a little relaxation of the rules, Benevolent One, in view of the bad times.

THIRD GOD. As for instance?

WONG. Well, um, good-will, for instance, might do instead of love?

THIRD GOD. I'm afraid that would create new problems.

WONG. Or, instead of justice, good sportsmanship?

THIRD GOD. That would only mean more work.

WONG. Instead of honor, outward propriety?

THIRD GOD. Still more work! No, no! The rules will have to stand, my dear Wong!

(*Wearily shaking their heads, all three journey on.*)

SCENE 8

(*Shui Ta's tobacco factory in Shu Fu's cabins. Huddled together behind bars, several families, mostly women and children. Among these people the Sister-in-Law, the Grandfather, the Carpenter, and his three children. Enter Mrs. Yang followed by Yang Sun.*)

MRS. YANG (*to the audience*). There's something I just *have* to tell you: strength and wisdom are wonderful things. The strong and wise Mr. Shui Ta has transformed my son from a dissipated good-for-nothing into a model citizen. As you may have heard, Mr. Shui Ta opened a small tobacco factory near the cattle runs. It flourished. Three months ago—I shall never forget it—I asked for an appointment, and Mr. Shui Ta agreed to see us—me and my son. I can see him now as he came through the door to meet us . . .

(*Enter Shui Ta, from a door.*)

SHUI TA. What can I do for you, Mrs. Yang?

MRS. YANG. This morning the police came to the house. We find you've brought an action for breach of promise of marriage. In the name of Shen Te. You also claim that Sun came by two hundred silver dollars by improper means.

SHUI TA. That is correct.

MRS. YANG. Mr. Shui Ta, the money's all gone. When the Peking job didn't materialize, he ran through it all in three days. I know he's a good-for-nothing. He sold my furniture. He was moving to Peking without me. Miss Shen Te thought highly of him at one time.

SHUI TA. What do *you* say, Mr. Yang Sun?

YANG SUN. The money's gone.

SHUI TA (*to Mrs. Yang*). Mrs. Yang, in consideration of my cousin's incomprehensible weakness for your son, I am prepared to give him another chance. He can have a job—here. The two hundred silver dollars will be taken out of his wages.

YANG SUN. So it's the factory or jail?

SHUI TA. Take your choice.

YANG SUN. May I speak with Shen Te?

SHUI TA. You may not.

(*Pause.*)

YANG SUN (*sullenly*). Show me where to go.

MRS. YANG. Mr. Shui Ta, you are kindness itself: the gods will reward you! (*To Yang Sun.*) And honest work will make a man of you, my boy.

(*Yang Sun follows Shui Ta into the factory. Mrs. Yang comes down again to the footlights.*)

Actually, honest work didn't agree with him—at first. And he got no opportunity to distinguish himself till—in the third week—when the wages were being paid. . . .

(*Shui Ta has a bag of money. Standing next to his foreman—the former Unemployed Man—he counts out the wages. It is Yang Sun's turn.*)

UNEMPLOYED MAN (*reading*). Carpenter, six silver dollars. Yang Sun, six silver dollars.

YANG SUN (*quietly*). Excuse me, sir. I don't think it can be more than five. May I see? (*He takes the foreman's list.*) It says six working days. But that's a mistake, sir. I took a day off for court business. And I won't take what I haven't earned, however miserable the pay is!

UNEMPLOYED MAN. Yang Sun. Five silver dollars. (*To Shui Ta.*) A rare case, Mr. Shui Ta!

SHUI TA. How is it the book says six when it should say five?

UNEMPLOYED MAN. I must've made a mistake, Mr. Shui Ta. (*With a look at Yang Sun.*) It won't happen again.

SHUI TA (*taking Yang Sun aside*). You don't hold back, do you? You give your all to the firm. You're even honest. Do the foreman's mistakes always favor the workers?

YANG SUN. He does have . . . friends.

SHUI TA. Thank you. May I offer you any little recompense?

YANG SUN. Give me a trial period of one week, and I'll prove my intelligence is worth more to you than my strength.

MRS. YANG (*still down at the footlight*). Fighting words, fighting words! That evening, I said to Sun: "If you're a flyer, then fly, my falcon! Rise in the world!" And he got to be foreman. Yes, in Mr. Shui Ta's tobacco factory, he worked real miracles.

(*We see Yang Sun with his legs apart standing behind the workers who are handing along a basket of raw tobacco above their heads.*)

YANG SUN. Faster! Faster! You there, d'you think you can just stand around now you're not foreman any more? It'll be your job to lead us in song. Sing!

(*Unemployed Man starts singing. The others join in the refrain.*)

Song of the Eighth Elephant

Chang had seven elephants—all much the same—
But then there was Little Brother
The seven, they were wild, Little Brother, he was tame
And to guard them Chang chose Little Brother
Run faster!
Mr. Chang has a forest park
Which must be cleared before tonight
And already it's growing dark!

When the seven elephants cleared that forest park
Mr. Chang rode high on Little Brother
While the seven toiled and moiled till dark
On his big behind sat Little Brother
Dig faster!
Mr. Chang has a forest park
Which must be cleared before tonight
And already it's growing dark!

And the seven elephants worked many an hour

Till none of them could work another
Old Chang, he looked sour, on the seven, he did
    glower
    But gave a pound of rice to Little Brother
        What was that?
        Mr. Chang has a forest park
        Which must be cleared before tonight
        And already it's growing dark!

And the seven elephants hadn't any tusks
    The one that had the tusks was Little Brother!
Seven are no match for one, if the one has a gun!
    How old Chang did laugh at Little Brother!
        Keep on digging!
        Mr. Chang has a forest park
        Which must be cleared before tonight
        And already it's growing dark!

(*Smoking a cigar, Shui Ta strolls by. Yang Sun, laughing, has joined in the refrain of the third stanza and speeded up the tempo of the last stanza by clapping his hands.*)

MRS. YANG. And that's why I say: strength and wisdom are wonderful things. It took the strong and wise Mr. Shui Ta to bring out the best in Yang Sun. A real superior man is like a bell. If you ring it, it rings, and if you don't, it don't, as the saying is.

SCENE 9

(*Shen Te's shop, now an office with club chairs and fine carpets. It is raining. Shui Ta, now fat, is just dismissing the Old Man and Old Woman. Mrs. Shin, in obviously new clothes, looks on, smirking.*)

SHUI TA. No! I can NOT tell you when we expect her back.

OLD WOMAN. The two hundred silver dollars came today. In an envelope. There was no letter, but it must be from Shen Te. We want to write and thank her. May we have her address?

SHUI TA. I'm afraid I haven't got it.

OLD MAN (*pulling Old Woman's sleeve*). Let's be going.

OLD WOMAN. She's got to come back some time! (*They move off, uncertainly, worried. Shui Ta bows.*)

MRS. SHIN. They lost the carpet shop because they couldn't pay their taxes. The money arrived too late.

SHUI TA. They could have come to me.

MRS. SHIN. People don't like coming to you.

SHUI TA (*sits suddenly, one hand to his head*). I'm dizzy.

MRS. SHIN. After all, you *are* in your seventh month. But old Mrs. Shin will be there in your hour of trial! (*She cackles feebly.*)

SHUI TA (*in a stifled voice*). Can I count on that?

MRS. SHIN. We all have our price, and mine won't be too high for the great Mr. Shui Ta! (*She opens Shui Ta's collar.*)

SHUI TA. It's for the child's sake. All of this.

MRS. SHIN. "All for the child," of course.

SHUI TA. I'm so fat. People must notice.

MRS. SHIN. Oh no, they think it's 'cause you're rich.

SHUI TA (*more feelingly*). What will happen to the child?

MRS. SHIN. You ask that nine times a day. Why, it'll have the best that money can buy!

SHUI TA. He must never see Shui Ta.

MRS. SHIN. Oh, no. Always Shen Te.

SHUI TA. What about the neighbors? There are rumors, aren't there?

MRS. SHIN. As long as Mr. Shu Fu doesn't find out, there's nothing to worry about. Drink this.

(*Enter Yang Sun in a smart business suit, and carrying a businessman's brief case. Shui Ta is more or less in Mrs. Shin's arms.*)

YANG SUN (*surprised*). I seem to be in the way.

SHUI TA (*ignoring this, rises with an effort*). Till tomorrow, Mrs. Shin.

(*Mrs. Shin leaves with a smile, putting her new gloves on.*)

YANG SUN. Gloves now! She couldn't be fleecing you? And since when did *you* have a private life? (*Taking a paper from the brief case.*) You haven't been at your best lately, and things are getting out of hand. The police want to close us down. They say that at the most they can only permit twice the lawful number of workers.

SHUI TA (*evasively*). The cabins are quite good enough.

YANG SUN. For the workers maybe, not for the tobacco. They're too damp. We must take over some of Mrs. Mi Tzu's buildings.

SHUI TA. Her price is double what I can pay.

YANG SUN. Not unconditionally. If she has me to stroke her knees she'll come down.

SHUI TA. I'll never agree to that.

YANG SUN. What's wrong? Is it the rain? You get so irritable whenever it rains.

SHUI TA. Never! I will never . . .

YANG SUN. Mrs. Mi Tzu'll be here in five minutes. *You* fix it. And Shu Fu will be with her. . . . What's all that noise?

(*During the above dialogue, Wong is heard off stage calling: "The good Shen Te, where is she? Which of you has seen Shen Te, good people? Where is Shen Te?" A knock. Enter Wong.*)

WONG. Mr. Shui Ta, I've come to ask when Miss Shen Te will be back, it's six months now . . . There are rumors. People say something's happened to her.

SHUI TA. I'm busy. Come back next week.

WONG (*excited*). In the morning there was always rice on her doorstep—for the needy. It's been there again lately!

SHUI TA. And what do people conclude from this?

WONG. That Shen Te is still in Setzuan! She's been . . . (*He breaks off.*)

SHUI TA. She's been what? Mr. Wong, if you're Shen Te's friend, talk a little less about her, that's my advice to you.

WONG. I don't want your advice! Before she disappeared, Miss Shen Te told me something very important—she's pregnant!

YANG SUN. What? What was that?

SHUI TA (*quickly*). The man is lying.

WONG. A good woman isn't so easily forgotten. Mr. Shui Ta.

(*He leaves. Shui Ta goes quickly into the back room.*)

YANG SUN (*to the audience*). Shen Te pregnant? So that's why. Her cousin sent her away, so I wouldn't get wind of it. I have a son, a Yang appears on the scene, and what happens? Mother and child vanish into thin air! That scoundrel, that unspeakable . . . (*The sound of sobbing is heard from the back room.*) What was that? Someone sobbing? Who was it? Mr. Shui Ta the Tobacco King doesn't weep his heart out. And where does the rice come from that's on the doorstep in the morning?

(*Shui Ta returns. He goes to the door and looks out into the rain.*)

Where is she?

SHUI TA. Sh! It's nine o'clock. But the rain's so heavy, you can't hear a thing.

YANG SUN. What do you want to hear?

SHUI TA. The mail plane.

YANG SUN. What?

SHUI TA. I've been told *you* wanted to fly at one time. Is that all forgotten?

YANG SUN. Flying mail is night work. I prefer the daytime. And the firm is very dear to me—after all it belongs to my ex-fiancée, even if she's not around. And she's not, is she?

SHUI TA. What do you mean by that?

YANG SUN. Oh, well, let's say I haven't altogether—lost interest.

SHUI TA. My cousin might like to know that.

YANG SUN. I might not be indifferent—if I found she was being kept under lock and key.

SHUI TA. By whom?

YANG SUN. By you.

SHUI TA. What could you do about it?

YANG SUN. I could submit for discussion—my position in the firm.

SHUI TA. You are now my Manager. In return for a more appropriate position, you might agree to drop the enquiry into your ex-fiancée's whereabouts?

YANG SUN. I might.

SHUI TA. What position *would* be more appropriate?

YANG SUN. The one at the top.

SHUI TA. My own? (*Silence.*) And if I preferred to throw you out on your neck?

YANG SUN. I'd come back on my feet. With suitable escort.

SHUI TA. The police?

YANG SUN. The police.

SHUI TA. And when the police found no one?

YANG SUN. I might ask them not to overlook the back room. (*Ending the pretense.*) In short, Mr. Shui Ta, my interest in this young woman has not been officially terminated. I should like to see more of her. (*Into Shui Ta's face.*) Besides, she's pregnant and needs a friend. (*He moves to the door.*) I shall talk about it with the Water Seller. (*Exit.*)

(*Shui Ta is rigid for a moment, then he quickly goes into the back room. He returns with Shen Te's belongings: underwear, etc. He takes a long look at the shawl of the previous scene. He then wraps the things in a bundle which, upon hearing a noise, he hides under the table. Enter Mrs. Mi Tzu and Mr. Shu Fu. They put away their umbrellas and galoshes.*)

MRS. MI TZU. I thought your manager was here, Mr. Shui Ta. He combines charm with business in a way that can only be to the advantage of all of us.

SHU FU. You sent for us, Mr. Shui Ta?

SHUI TA. The factory is in trouble.

SHU FU. It always is.

SHUI TA. The police are threatening to close us down unless I can show that the extension of our facilities is imminent.

SHU FU. Mr. Shui Ta, I'm sick and tired of your constantly expanding projects. I place cabins at your cousin's disposal; you make a factory of them. I hand your cousin a check; you present it. Your cousin disappears and you find the cabins too small and talk of yet more . . .

SHUI TA. Mr. Shu Fu, I'm authorized to inform you that Miss Shen Te's return is now imminent.

SHU FU. Imminent? It's becoming his favorite word.

MRS. MI TZU. Yes, what does it mean?

SHUI TA. Mrs. Mi Tzu, I can pay you exactly half what you asked for your buildings. Are you ready to inform the police that I am taking them over?

MRS. MI TZU. Certainly, if I can take over your manager.

SHU FU. What?

MRS. MI TZU. He's so efficient.

SHUI TA. I'm afraid I need Mr. Yang Sun.

MRS. MI TZU. So do I.

SHUI TA. He will call on you tomorrow

SHU FU. So much the better. With Shen Te likely to turn up at any moment, the presence of that young man is hardly in good taste.

SHUI TA. So we have reached a settlement. In what was once the good Shen Te's little shop we are laying the foundations for the great Mr. Shui Ta's twelve magnificent super tobacco markets. You will bear in mind that though they call me the Tobacco King of Setzuan, it is my cousin's interests that have been served . . .

VOICES (*off*). The police, the police! Going to the tobacco shop! Something must have happened! (*et cetera.*)

(*Enter Yang Sun, Wong, and the Policeman.*)

POLICEMAN. Quiet there, quiet, quiet! (*They quiet down.*) I'm sorry, Mr. Shui Ta, but there's a report that you've been depriving Miss Shen Te of her freedom. Not that I believe all I hear, but the whole city's in an uproar.

SHUI TA. That's a lie.

POLICEMAN. Mr. Yang Sun has testified that he heard someone sobbing in the back room.

SHU FU. Mrs. Mi Tzu and myself will testify that no one here has been sobbing.

MRS. MI TZU. We have been quietly smoking our cigars.

POLICEMAN. Mr. Shui Ta, I'm afraid I shall have to take a look at that room. (*He does so. The room is empty.*) No one there, of course, sir.

YANG SUN. But I hear sobbing. What's that? (*He finds the clothes.*)

WONG. Those are Shen Te's things. (*To crowd.*) Shen Te's clothes are here!

VOICES (*Off. In sequence*). Shen Te's clothes! They've been found under the table! Body of murdered girl still missing! Tobacco King suspected!

POLICEMAN. Mr. Shui Ta, unless you can tell us where the girl is, I'll have to ask you to come along.

SHUI TA. I do not know.

POLICEMAN. I can't say how sorry I am, Mr. Shui Ta. (*He shows him the door.*)

SHUI TA. Everything will be cleared up in no time. There are still judges in Setzuan.

YANG SUN. I heard sobbing!

SCENE 9A

(*Wong's den. For the last time, the Gods appear to the Water Seller in his dream. They have changed and show signs of a long journey, extreme fatigue, and plenty of mishaps. The First no longer has a hat; the Third has lost a leg; all Three are barefoot.*)

WONG. Illustrious ones, at last you're here. Shen Te's been gone for months and today her cousin's been arrested. They think he murdered her to get the shop. But I had a dream and in this dream Shen Te said her cousin was keeping her prisoner. You must find her for us, illustrious ones!

FIRST GOD. We've found very few good people anywhere, and even they didn't keep it up. Shen Te is still the only one that stayed good.

SECOND GOD. If she *has* stayed good.

WONG. Certainly she has. But she's vanished.

FIRST GOD. That's the last straw. All is lost!

SECOND GOD. A little moderation, dear colleague!

FIRST GOD (*plaintively*). What's the good of moderation now? If she can't be found, we'll have to resign! The world is a terrible place! Nothing but misery, vulgarity, and waste! Even the countryside isn't what it used to be. The trees are getting their heads chopped off by telephone wires, and there's such a noise from all the gunfire, and I can't stand those heavy clouds of smoke, and—

THIRD GOD. The place is absolutely unlivable! Good intentions bring people to the brink of the abyss, and good deeds push them over the edge. I'm afraid our book of rules is destined for the scrap heap—

SECOND GOD. It's people! They're a worthless lot!

THIRD GOD. The world is too cold!

SECOND GOD. It's people! They are too weak!

FIRST GOD. Dignity, dear colleagues, dignity! Never despair! As for this world, didn't we agree that we only have to find one human being who can stand the place? Well, we found her. True, we lost her again. We must find her again, that's all! And at once!

(*They disappear.*)

SCENE 10

(*Courtroom. Groups: Shu Fu and Mrs. Mi Tzu; Yang Sun and Mrs. Yang; Wong, the Carpenter, the Grandfather, the Niece, the Old Man, the Old Woman; Mrs. Shin, the Policeman; the Unemployed Man, the Sister-in-Law.*)

OLD MAN. So much power isn't good for one man.

UNEMPLOYED MAN. And he's going to open twelve super tobacco markets!

WIFE. One of the judges is a friend of Mr. Shu Fu's.

SISTER-IN-LAW. Another one accepted a present from Mr. Shui Ta only last night. A great fat goose.

OLD WOMAN (*to Wong*). And Shen Te is nowhere to be found.

WONG. Only the gods will ever know the truth.

POLICEMAN. Order in the court! My lords the judges!

(*Enter the Three Gods in judges' robes. We overhear their conversation as they pass along the footlights to their bench.*)

THIRD GOD. We'll never get away with it, our certificates were so badly forged.

SECOND GOD. My predecessor's "sudden indigestion" will certainly cause comment.

FIRST GOD. But he *had* just eaten a whole goose.

UNEMPLOYED MAN. Look at that! *New* judges!

WONG. New judges. And what good ones!

(*The Third God hears this, and turns to smile at Wong. The Gods sit. The First God beats on the bench with his gavel. The Policeman brings in Shui Ta who walks with lordly steps. He is whistled at.*)

POLICEMAN (*to Shui Ta*). Be prepared for a surprise. The judges have been changed.

(*Shui Ta turns quickly round, looks at them, and staggers.*)

NIECE. What's the matter now?

WIFE. The great Tobacco King nearly fainted.

HUSBAND. Yes, as soon as he saw the new judges.

WONG. Does *he* know who they are?

(*Shui Ta picks himself up, and the proceedings open.*)

FIRST GOD. Defendant Shui Ta, you are accused of doing away with your cousin Shen Te in order to take possession of her business. Do you plead guilty or not guilty?

SHUI TA. Not guilty, my lord.

FIRST GOD (*thumbing through the documents of the case*). The first witness is the Policeman. I shall ask him to tell us something of the respective reputations of Miss Shen Te and Mr. Shui Ta.

POLICEMAN. Miss Shen Te was a young lady who aimed to please, my lord. She liked to live and let live, as the saying goes. Mr. Shui Ta, on the other hand, is a man of principle. Though the generosity of Miss Shen Te forced him at times to abandon half measures, unlike the girl, he was always on the side of the law, my lord. One time, he even unmasked a gang of thieves to whom his too trustful cousin had given shelter. The evidence, in short, my lord, proves that Mr. Shui Ta was *incapable* of the crime of which he stands accused!

FIRST GOD. I see. And are there others who could testify along, shall we say, the same lines?

(*Shu Fu rises.*)

POLICEMAN (*whispering to Gods*). Mr. Shu Fu—a very important person.

FIRST GOD (*inviting him to speak*). Mr. Shu Fu!

SHU FU. Mr. Shui Ta is a businessman, my lord. Need I say more?

FIRST GOD. Yes.

SHU FU. Very well, I will. He is Vice President of the Council of Commerce and is about to be elected a Justice of the Peace. (*He returns to his seat.*)

WONG. Elected! *He* gave him the job!

(*With a gesture the First God asks who Mrs. Mi Tzu is.*)

POLICEMAN. Another very important person. Mrs. Mi Tzu.

FIRST GOD (*inviting her to speak*). Mrs. Mi Tzu!

MRS. MI TZU. My lord, as Chairman of the Committee on Social Work, I wish to call attention to just a couple of eloquent facts: Mr. Shui Ta not only has erected a model factory with model housing in our city, he is a regular contributor to our home for the disabled. (*She returns to her seat.*)

POLICEMAN (*whispering*). And she's a great friend of the judge that ate the goose!

FIRST GOD (*to the* Policeman). Oh, thank you. What next? (*To the Court, genially.*) Oh, yes. We should find out if any of the evidence is less favorable to the Defendant.

(*Wong, the Carpenter, the Old Man, the Old Woman, the Unemployed Man, the Sister-in-Law, and the Niece come forward.*)

POLICEMAN (*whispering*). Just the riff raff, my lord.

FIRST GOD (*addressing the "riff raff"*). Well, um, riff raff—do you know anything of the Defendant, Mr. Shui Ta?

WONG. Too much, my lord.

UNEMPLOYED MAN. What don't we know, my lord?

CARPENTER. He ruined us.

SISTER-IN-LAW. He's a cheat.

NIECE. Liar.

WIFE. Thief.

BOY. Blackmailer.

BROTHER. Murderer.

FIRST GOD. Thank you. We should now let the Defendant state his point of view.

SHUI TA. I only came on the scene when Shen Te was in danger of losing what I had understood was a gift from the gods. Because I did the filthy jobs which someone had to do, they hate me. My activities were held down to the minimum, my lord.

SISTER-IN-LAW. He had us arrested!

SHUI TA. Certainly. You stole from the bakery!

SISTER-IN-LAW. Such concern for the bakery! You didn't want the shop for yourself, I suppose!

SHUI TA. I didn't want the shop overrun with parasites.

SISTER-IN-LAW. We had nowhere else to go.

SHUI TA. There were too many of you.

WONG. What about this old couple: Were *they* parasites?

OLD MAN. We lost our shop because of you!

SISTER-IN-LAW. And we gave your cousin money!

SHUI TA. My cousin's fiancé was a flyer. The money had to go to *him*.

WONG. Did you care whether he flew or not? Did you care whether she married him or not? You wanted her to marry someone else! (*He points at Shu Fu.*)

SHUI TA. The flyer unexpectedly turned out to be a scoundrel.

YANG SUN (*jumping up*). Which was the reason you made him your Manager?

SHUI TA. Late on he improved.

WONG. And when he improved, you sold him to her? (*He points out Mrs. Mi Tzu.*)

SHUI TA. She wouldn't let me have her premises unless she had him to stroke her knees!

MRS. MI TZU. What? The man's a pathological liar. (*To him.*) Don't mention my property to me as long as you live! Murderer! (*She rustles off, in high dudgeon.*)

YANG SUN (*pushing in*). My lord, I wish to speak for the Defendant.

SISTER-IN-LAW. Naturally. He's your employer.

UNEMPLOYED MAN. And the worst slave driver in the country.

MRS. YANG. That's a lie! My lord, Mr. Shui Ta is a great man. He . . .

YANG SUN. He's this and he's that, but he is not a murderer, my lord. Just fifteen minutes before his arrest I heard Shen Te's voice in his own back room.

FIRST GOD. Oh? Tell us more!

YANG SUN. I heard sobbing, my lord!

FIRST GOD. But lots of women sob, we've been finding.

YANG SUN. Could I fail to recognize her voice?

SHU FU. No, you made her sob so often yourself, young man!

YANG SUN. Yes. But I also made her happy. Till he (*pointing at Shui Ta*) decided to sell her to you!

SHUI TA. Because you didn't love her.

WONG. Oh, no: it was for the money, my lord!

SHUI TA. And what was the money for, my lord? For the poor! And for Shen Te so she could go on being good!

WONG. For the poor? That he sent to his sweatshops? And why didn't you let Shen Te be good when you signed the big check?

SHUI TA. For the child's sake, my lord.

CARPENTER. What about *my* children? What did he do about them?

(*Shui Ta is silent.*)

WONG. The shop was to be a fountain of goodness. That was the gods' idea. You came and spoiled it!

SHUI TA. If I hadn't, it would have run dry!

MRS. SHIN. There's a lot in that, my lord.

WONG. What have you done with the good Shen Te, bad man? She *was* good, my lords, she was, I swear it! (*He raises his hand in an oath.*)

THIRD GOD. What's happened to your hand, Water Seller?

WONG (*pointing to Shui Ta*). It's all his fault, my lord, *she* was going to send me to a doctor—(*To Shui Ta.*) You were her worst enemy!

SHUI TA. I was her only friend!

WONG. Where is she then? Tell us where your good friend is!

(*The excitement of this exchange has run through the whole crowd.*)

ALL. Yes, where is she? Where is Shen Te? (*et cetera.*)

SHUI TA. Shen Te had to go.

WONG. Where? Where to?

SHUI TA. I cannot tell you! I cannot tell you!

ALL. Why? Why did she have to go away? (*et cetera.*)

WONG (*into the din with the first words, but talking on beyond the others*). Why not, why not? Why did she have to go away?

SHUI TA (*shouting*). Because you'd all have torn her to shreds, that's why! My lords, I have a request. Clear the court! When only the judges remain, I will make a confession.

ALL (*except Wong, who is silent, struck by the new turn of events*). So he's guilty? He's confessing! (*et cetera.*)

FIRST GOD (*using the gavel*). Clear the court!

POLICEMAN. Clear the court!

WONG. Mr. Shui Ta has met his match this time.

MRS. SHIN (*with a gesture toward the judges*). You're in for a little surprise.

(*The court is cleared. Silence.*)

SHUI TA. Illustrious ones!

(*The Gods look at each other, not quite believing their ears.*)

SHUI TA. Yes, I recognize you!

SECOND GOD (*taking matters in hand, sternly*). What have you done with our good woman of Setzuan?

SHUI TA. I have a terrible confession to make: I am she! (*He takes off his mask, and tears away his clothes. Shen Te stands there.*)

SECOND GOD. Shen Te!

SHEN TE. Shen Te, yes. Shui Ta *and* Shen Te. Both.

Your injunction
To be good and yet to live
Was a thunderbolt:
It has torn me in two
I can't tell how it was
But to be good to others
And myself at the same time
I could not do it
Your world is not an easy one, illustrious ones!
When we extend our hand to a beggar, he tears it off
    for us
When we help the lost, we are lost ourselves.
And so
Since not to eat is to die
Who can long refuse to be bad?
As I lay prostrate beneath the weight of good
    intentions
Ruin stared me in the face
It was when I was unjust that I ate good meat
And hobnobbed with the mighty
Why?
Why are bad deeds rewarded?
Good ones punished?
I enjoyed giving
I truly wished to be the Angel of the Slums
But washed by a foster-mother in the water of the
    gutter
I developed a sharp eye
The time came when pity was a thorn in my side
And, later, when kind words turned to ashes in my
    mouth
And anger took over
I became a wolf
Find me guilty, then, illustrious ones,
But know:
All that I have done I did
To help my neighbor
To love my lover
And to keep my little one from want
For your great, godly deeds, I was too poor, too small.

(*Pause.*)

FIRST GOD (*shocked*). Don't go on making yourself miserable, Shen Te! We're overjoyed to have found you!

SHEN TE. I'm telling you I'm the bad man who committed all those crimes!

FIRST GOD (*using—or failing to use—his ear trumpet*). The good woman who did all those good deeds?

SHEN TE. Yes, but the bad man too!

FIRST GOD (*as if something had dawned*). Unfortunate coincidences! Heartless neighbors!

THIRD GOD (*shouting in his ear*). But how is she to continue?

FIRST GOD. Continue? Well, she's a strong, healthy girl . . .

SECOND GOD. You didn't hear what she said!

FIRST GOD. I heard every word! She is confused, that's all! (*He begins to bluster.*) And what about this book of rules—we can't renounce our rules, can we? (*More quietly.*) Should the world be changed? How? By whom? The world should *not* be changed! (*At a sign from him, the lights turn pink, and music plays.*)

> And now the hour of parting is at hand.
> Dost thou behold, Shen Te, yon fleecy cloud?
> It is our chariot. At a sign from me
> 'Twill come and take us back from whence we came
> Above the azure vault and silver stars . . .

SHEN TE. No! Don't go, illustrious ones!

FIRST GOD.

> Our cloud has landed now in yonder field
> From whence it will transport us back to heaven.
> Farewell, Shen Te, let not thy courage fail thee . . .

(*Exeunt Gods.*)

SHEN TE. What about the old couple? They've lost their shop! What about the Water Seller and his hand? And I've got to defend myself against the barber, because I don't love him! And against Sun, because I do love him! How? How?

(*Shen Te's eyes follow the Gods as they are imagined to step into a cloud which rises and moves forward over the orchestra and up beyond the balcony*)

FIRST GOD (*from on high*). We have faith in you, Shen Te!

SHEN TE. There'll be a child. And he'll have to be fed. I can't stay here. Where shall I go?

FIRST GOD. Continue to be good, good woman of Setzuan!

SHEN TE. I need my bad cousin!

FIRST GOD. But not very often!

SHEN TE. Once a week at least!

FIRST GOD. Once a month will be quite enough!

SHEN TE (*shrieking*). No, no! Help!

(*But the cloud continues to recede as the Gods sing.*)

Valedictory Hymn

> What rapture, oh, it is to know
>   A good thing when you see it
> And having seen a good thing, oh,
>   What rapture 'tis to flee it
>
> Be good, sweet maid of Setzuan
>   Let Shui Ta be clever
> Departing, we forget the man
>   Remember your endeavor
>
> Ò Because through all the length of days
>   Her goodness faileth never
> Sing hallelujah! May Shen Te's
>   Good name live on forever!

SHEN TE. Help!

EPILOGUE

> You're thinking, aren't you, that this is no right
> Conclusion to the play you've seen tonight?
> After a tale, exotic, fabulous,
> A nasty ending was slipped up on us.
> We feel deflated too. We too are nettled
> To see the curtain down and nothing settled.
> How could a better ending be arranged?
> Could one change people? Can the world be
>   changed?
> Would new gods do the trick? Will atheism?
> Moral rearmament? Materialism?
> It is for you to find a way, my friends,
> To help good men arrive at happy ends.
> *You* write the happy ending to the play!
> There must, there must, there's got to be a way!

TOPICS FOR CRITICAL THINKING AND WRITING

📖 THE PLAY ON THE PAGE

1. It has been said that Brecht's "characters are social types without a private psychological side." Do you agree? If so, do you think this is a shortcoming in his work? Explain.

2. In your opinion, why does Shen Te assume the mask of Shui Ta?

3. It has been said that drama is the art of preparation—meaning that speeches and scenes generate suspense that is interestingly fulfilled. How important would you say suspense is in *The Good Woman*?

4. Brecht was a didactic writer, unashamed of preaching. What would you say is his message in this play? How acceptable to you is the message? Why? Would you say that Brecht presents the message interestingly? Explain.

5. Originally Brecht set the play in the Berlin of the 1920s. What do you think is gained or lost by setting it in a rather mythical China?

6. What do the gods stand for? What do you think Brecht's attitude is toward them?

7. Is Shui Ta bad or merely realistic? Explain.

8. What, if anything, is Brecht saying about the causes of evil?

THE PLAY ON THE STAGE

9. Imagine that you are directing a production of the play. Select a passage of some fifty to one hundred lines, such as the interlude that follows Scene 6, and indicate what instructions you would give about how to deliver the lines.

10. Select one of the songs, for instance "The Song of St. Nevercome's Day" in Scene 6, and explain what sort of music you would want it set to. Jazz? Rock? Country? What?

11. How would you costume the gods? Would they wear the same costumes throughout, or might they change costumes?

12. In some productions almost all of the lines are delivered in a sort of a chant. What do you think of this idea? Why?

THE PLAY IN PERFORMANCE

First, it must be mentioned that because Brecht kept tinkering with the play, it exists in several versions. The translations, too, differ not only because different translators inevitably translated speeches somewhat differently (for example, titles include *The Good Woman of Setzuan*, *The Good Person of Setzuan*, and *The Good Soul of Setzuan*) but also because they may draw on different manuscripts. Furthermore, Brecht sometimes told a translator to omit this speech or that for political reasons.

The play had its world premiere in Zurich in 1943; the American premiere was at Carleton College in Northfield, Minnesota, in the spring of 1948; and the first professional American production was at the Hedgerow Theatre, near Philadelphia, in the summer of 1948. It was not performed by the Berliner Ensemble (a company established in the Soviet section of Berlin to promote Brecht's works) until 1957, a year after Brecht's death.

Because of his leftist politics, the commercial theater has been leery of producing Brecht, but he has been popular on campuses, and *The Good Woman* is probably the Brecht play most often staged. Perhaps because Brecht himself did not hesitate to adapt plays freely, modern productions of Brecht often are very free. A 1984 production at Indiana University Theatre, for instance, dared to turn the gods into Jesus Christ look-alikes. A production in Santa Monica had the gods enter on roller skates. And Brecht left it up to the director to decide who should speak the Epilogue. It is usually spoken by the actress who plays Shen Te, or by the actor who plays Wong. In any case, in most productions whichever actor speaks it usually drops the role and appears as an actor rather than as a character in the play.

Tennessee Williams

THE GLASS MENAGERIE

Tennessee Williams (1914–1983) was born Thomas Lanier Williams in Columbus, Mississippi. During his childhood his family moved to St. Louis, where his father had accepted a job as manager of a shoe company. Williams has written that neither he nor his sister, Rose, could adjust to the change from the South to the Midwest, but the children had already been deeply troubled. Nevertheless, at the age of sixteen he achieved some distinction as a writer when his prize-winning essay in a nationwide contest was published. After high school he attended the University of Missouri but flunked ROTC and was, therefore, withdrawn from school by his father. He worked in a shoe factory for a while, and then attended Washington University, where he wrote several plays. He finally graduated from the University of Iowa with a major in playwrighting. After graduation he continued to write, supporting himself with odd jobs such as waiting on tables and running elevators. His first commercial success was *The Glass Menagerie* (produced in Chicago in 1944 and in New York in 1945). Among his other plays are *A Streetcar Named Desire* (1947), *Cat on a Hot Tin Roof* (1955), and *Suddenly Last Summer* (1958).

COMMENTARY

Broadly speaking, drama has been divided into two sorts, *conventional* (also called presentational, stylized, or symbolic) and *realistic* (or naturalistic). Conventional drama, such as the ancient Greek plays of Sophocles or the Elizabethan plays of Shakespeare, makes little pretense of offering an accurate transcription of the surface reality. For instance, in real life we all speak prose, but in Sophocles' *Oedipus the King* it is conventional for the characters to speak verse. The play's lack of realism can be further seen in the way in which the action takes place. A man living in a remote region is summoned and appears on stage a few minutes later; moments after blinding himself, Oedipus enters, not writhing in pain but speaking eloquently. Similarly, in Shakespeare's plays, which were staged during the daytime in an unroofed theater, if a character enters carrying a torch, the audience understands, by means of this convention, that the scene—even though acted in full light—is taking place at night. (A *convention* is literally a "coming together"; the audience and the theatrical personnel come together—that is, reach an understanding—and pretend that what is shown onstage is real.)

Most drama before the middle of the nineteenth century was highly conventional, partly because it had to be. The vast size of a Greek theater required the actors to gesticulate broadly and to speak loudly, even if they were supposed to be whispering inconspicuously. Similarly, before the development of advanced techniques of lighting, night scenes necessarily were played in the daylight, or if played in roofed theaters that used artificial illumination, they were played with only a suggestion of darkness. If a character looked upward and spoke of the moon, the audience agreed to pretend that the moon was visible. Then around the middle of the nineteenth century, new techniques of lighting allowed for relatively realistic effects, such as, the breaking of dawn or the gradual coming of night. Moreover, the temper of the times (largely dominated by a scientific spirit—which, for instance, invented the art of photography) favored an art that seemed close to the surface of life. The announced aim of art, at least for some artists, was to give "a slice of life."

Of course, even the most realistic play is in some ways conventional. For two and a half hours the characters do not digress, and they never seem to have to go to the bathroom. The audience looks at "real" furniture displayed in what seems to be a "real" room, but in fact most of the furniture faces the footlights, and the room is missing a wall (see, for instance, the illustration of the set for *A Doll's House* on p. 13) so that the audience may see what goes on in it. At the end of the act, the curtain drops, and the audience, knowing that there will be an intermission of fifteen minutes, troops out into the lobby. When the audience returns, it understands from the dialogue (and maybe from the program notes) that the time is now the next day or the next week. We are scarcely aware of these conventions because, having grown up with them, we have assimilated them, just as we hardly think it is odd that a photograph in a newspaper is black and white, when in real life the images are colored.

Similarly, in film and on television—media that are largely realistic—we are not surprised when we get a close-up of a head, even though such a shot is a convention, since in real life we don't suddenly see heads without bodies.

Although the conventions of realism dominated the serious theater in the later nineteenth century, the very end of the century and the first third of the twentieth century saw a vigorous rebellion against them. Just as the realism of the nineteenth century owed much to a new spirit of scientific thinking (especially to studies of the influence of the environment on the individual), so this new movement owed much to a new science, psychology. Some plays now sought to give not the external reality or surface appearance of life but the inner reality, that is, life as *felt* rather than as seen. Thus, instead of the setting closely imitating a room as the scientific eye sees it, the walls might veer crazily to represent (or symbolize) the way the main character perceives his or her irrational or oppressive world. (For a bit more on this, see the entry on *expressionism* in the Glossary.)

Tennessee Williams's *The Glass Menagerie* is largely in this expressionistic tradition. Its link to psychology—to feeling rather than seeing—is suggested in the first sentence of the Production Notes, where Williams calls it a "memory play." Notice, too, that in the Production Notes he says that the play "can be presented with unusual freedom of convention." He does not mean that the play is free from conventions; rather, he means that the conventions are not the old established ones but are relatively fresh ones, invented for the moment. Similarly, when he speaks of expressionist plays as being "unconventional," he does not mean that they do not employ conventions. Rather, he means that the ones used are untraditional and relatively novel. "Expressionism," he says,

> and all other unconventional techniques in drama have only one valid aim, and that is a closer approach to truth. When a play employs unconventional techniques, it is not, or certainly shouldn't be, trying to escape its responsibility of dealing with reality, or interpreting experience, but is actually or should be attempting to find a closer approach, a more penetrating and vivid expression of things as they are.

In fact, when *The Glass Menagerie* was staged in New York, the conspicuously unrealistic convention of projecting words on a screen was not used, but the New York production, nevertheless, was essentially unrealistic, following, for instance, Williams's comment that "[t]he lighting in the play is not realistic. . . . Shafts of light are focused on selected areas or actors . . . The light upon Laura should be distinct from the others, having a peculiar pristine clarity such as light used in early religious portraits of female saints or madonnas." Jo Mielziner, who did the sets for this play and for many of Williams's other plays, makes a helpful comment in *Designing for the Theatre*:

> If he had written plays in the days before the technical development of translucent and transparent scenery, I believe he would have invented it. . . . My use of translucent and transparent scenic interior walls was not just another trick. It was a true reflection of the contemporary playwright's interest in—and at times obsession with—the exploration of the inner man. Williams was writing not only a memory play but a play of influences that were not confined within the walls of a room.

Tennessee Williams

THE GLASS MENAGERIE

nobody, not even the rain, has such small hands.
        —e. e. cummings

List of Characters

AMANDA WINGFIELD, *the mother. A little woman of great but confused vitality clinging frantically to another time and place. Her characterization must be carefully created, not copied from type. She is not paranoiac, but her life is paranoia. There is much to admire in Amanda, and as much to love and pity as there is to laugh at. Certainly she has endurance and a kind of heroism, and though her foolishness makes her unwittingly cruel at times, there is tenderness in her slight person.*

LAURA WINGFIELD, *her daughter. Amanda, having failed to establish contact with reality, continues to live vitally in her illusions, but Laura's situation is even graver. A childhood illness has left her crippled, one leg slightly shorter than the other, and held in a brace. This defect need not be more than suggested on the stage. Stemming from this, Laura's separation increases till she is like a piece of her own glass collection, too exquisitely fragile to move from the shelf.*

TOM WINGFIELD, *her son. And the narrator of the play. A poet with a job in a warehouse. His nature is not remorseless, but to escape from a trap he has to act without pity.*

JIM O'CONNOR, *the gentleman caller. A nice, ordinary, young man.*

SCENE. *An alley in St. Louis.*

PART I. *Preparation for a Gentleman Caller.*
PART II. *The Gentleman Calls.*

TIME. *Now and the Past.*

SCENE 1

The Wingfield apartment is in the rear of the building, one of those vast hive-like conglomerations of cellular living-units that flower as warty growths in overcrowded urban centers of lower middle-class population and are symptomatic of the impulse of this largest and fundamentally enslaved section of American society to avoid fluidity and differentiation and to exist and function as one interfused mass of automatism.

The apartment faces an alley and is entered by a fire-escape, a structure whose name is a touch of accidental poetic truth, for all of these huge buildings are always burning with the slow and implacable fires of human desperation. The fire-escape is included in the set—that is, the landing of it and steps descending from it.

The scene is memory and is therefore nonrealistic. Memory takes a lot of poetic license. It omits some details; others are exaggerated, according to the emotional value of the articles it touches, for memory is seated predominantly in the heart. The interior is therefore rather dim and poetic.

At the rise of the curtain, the audience is faced with the dark, grim rear wall of the Wingfield tenement. This building, which runs parallel to the footlights, is flanked on both sides by dark, narrow alleys which run into murky canyons of tangled clotheslines, garbage cans and the sinister latticework of neighboring fire-escapes. It is up and down these side alleys that exterior entrances and exits are made, during the play. At the end of Tom's opening commentary, the dark tenement wall slowly reveals (by means of a transparency) the interior of the ground floor Wingfield apartment.

Downstage is the living room, which also serves as a sleeping room for Laura, the sofa unfolding to make her bed. Upstage, center, and divided by a wide arch or second proscenium with transparent faded portieres (or second curtain), is the dining room. In an old-fashioned what-not in the living room are seen scores of transparent glass animals. A blown-up photograph of the father hangs on the wall of the living room, facing the audience, to the left of the archway. It is the face of a very handsome young man in a doughboy's First World War cap. He is gallantly smiling, ineluctably smiling, as if to say, "I will be smiling forever."

The audience hears and sees the opening scene in the dining room through both the transparent fourth wall of the building and the transparent gauze portieres of the dining-room arch. It is during this revealing scene that the fourth wall slowly ascends, out of sight.

This transparent exterior wall is not brought down again until the very end of the play, during Tom's final speech.

The narrator is an undisguised convention of the play. He takes whatever license with dramatic convention as is convenient to his purposes.

Tom enters dressed as a merchant sailor from alley, stage left, and strolls across the front of the stage to the fire-escape. There he stops and lights a cigarette. He addresses the audience.

TOM. Yes, I have tricks in my pocket, I have things up my sleeve. But I am the opposite of a stage magician. He gives you illusion that has the appearance of truth. I give you truth in the pleasant disguise of illusion. To begin with, I turn back time. I reverse it to that quaint period, the thirties, when the huge middle class of America was matriculating in a school for the blind. Their eyes had failed them, or they had failed their eyes, and so they were having their fingers pressed forcibly down on the fiery Braille alphabet of a dissolving economy. In Spain there was revolution. Here there was only shouting and confusion. In Spain there was Guernica. Here there were disturbances of labor, sometimes pretty violent, in otherwise peaceful cities such as Chicago, Cleveland, Saint Louis. . . . This is the social background of the play.

(*Music.*)

The play is memory. Being a memory play, it is dimly lighted, it is sentimental, it is not realistic. In memory everything seems to happen to music. That explains the fiddle in the wings. I am the narrator of the play, and also a character in it. The other characters are my mother, Amanda, my sister, Laura, and a gentleman caller who appears in the final scenes. He is the most realistic character in the play, being an emissary from a world of reality that we were somehow set apart from. But since I have a poet's weakness for symbols, I am using this character also as a symbol; he is the long delayed but always expected something that we live for. There is a fifth character in the play who doesn't appear except in this larger-than-life photograph over the mantel. This is our father who left us a long time ago. He was a telephone man who fell in love with long distances; he gave up his job with the telephone company and skipped the light fantastic out of town. . . . The last we heard of him was a picture post-card from Mazatlan, on the Pacific coast of Mexico, containing a message of two words—"Hello—Goodbye!" and no address. I think the rest of the play will explain itself. . . .

Amanda's voice becomes audible through the portieres.

(*Legend on Screen: "Où Sont les Neiges?"*)

He divides the portieres and enters the upstage area.
    Amanda and Laura are seated at a drop-leaf table. Eating is indicated by gestures without food or utensils. Amanda faces the audience. Tom and Laura are seated in profile.
    The interior has lit up softly and through the scrim we see Amanda and Laura seated at the table in the upstage area.

AMANDA (*calling*). Tom?

TOM. Yes, Mother.

AMANDA. We can't say grace until you come to the table!

TOM. Coming, Mother. (*He bows slightly and withdraws, reappearing a few moments later in his place at the table.*)

AMANDA (*to her son*). Honey, don't *push* with your *fingers*. If you have to push with something, the thing to push with is a crust of bread. And chew—chew! Animals have sections in their stomachs which enable them to digest food without mastication, but human beings are supposed to chew their food before they swallow it down. Eat food leisurely, son, and really enjoy it. A well-cooked meal has lots of delicate flavors that have to be held in the mouth for appreciation. So chew your food and give your salivary glands a chance to function!

Tom deliberately lays his imaginary fork down and pushes his chair back from the table.

TOM. I haven't enjoyed one bite of this dinner because of your constant directions on how to eat it. It's you that makes me rush through meals with your hawk-like attention to every bite I take. Sickening—spoils my appetite—all this discussion of animals' secretion—salivary glands—mastication!

AMANDA (*lightly*). Temperament like a Metropolitan star! (*He rises and crosses downstage.*) You're not excused from the table.

TOM. I am getting a cigarette.

AMANDA. You smoke too much.

Laura rises.

LAURA. I'll bring in the blanc mange.

He remains standing with his cigarette by the portieres during the following.

AMANDA (*rising*). No, sister, no, sister—you be the lady this time and I'll be the darky.

LAURA. I'm already up.

AMANDA. Resume your seat, little sister—I want you to stay fresh and pretty—for gentlemen callers!

LAURA. I'm not expecting any gentlemen callers.

AMANDA (*crossing out to kitchenette. Airily*). Sometimes they come when they are least expected! Why, I remember one Sunday afternoon in Blue Mountain—(*Enters kitchenette.*)

TOM. I know what's coming!

LAURA. Yes. But let her tell it.

TOM. Again?

LAURA. She loves to tell it.

Amanda returns with bowl of dessert.

AMANDA. One Sunday afternoon in Blue Mountain—your mother received—*seventeen!*—gentlemen callers! Why, sometimes there weren't chairs enough to accommodate them all. We had to send the nigger over to bring in folding chairs from the parish house.

TOM (*remaining at portieres*). How did you entertain those gentlemen callers?

AMANDA. I understood the art of conversation!

TOM. I bet you could talk.

AMANDA. Girls in those days *knew* how to talk, I can tell you.

TOM. Yes?

(*Image: Amanda as a Girl on a Porch Greeting Callers.*)

AMANDA. They knew how to entertain their gentlemen callers. It wasn't enough for a girl to be possessed of a pretty face and a graceful figure—although I wasn't slighted in either respect. She also needed to have a nimble wit and a tongue to meet all occasions.

TOM. What did you talk about?

AMANDA. Things of importance going on in the world! Never anything coarse or common or vulgar. (*She addresses Tom as though he were seated in the vacant chair at the table though he remains by portieres. He plays this scene as though he held the book.*) My callers were gentlemen—all! Among my callers were some of the most prominent young planters of the Mississippi Delta—planters and sons of planters!

Tom motions for music and a spot of light on Amanda.

Her eyes lift, her face glows, her voice becomes rich and elegiac.

(*Screen Legend: "Où Sont les Neiges?"*)

There was young Champ Laughlin who later became vice-president of the Delta Planters Bank. Hadley Stevenson who was drowned in Moon Lake and left his widow one hundred and fifty thousand in Government bonds. There were the Cutrere brothers, Wesley and Bates. Bates was one of my bright particular beaux! He got in a quarrel with that wild Wainright boy. They shot it out on the floor of Moon Lake Casino. Bates was shot through the stomach. Died in the ambulance on his way to Memphis. His widow was also well-provided for, came into eight or ten thousand acres, that's all. She married him on the rebound—never loved her—carried my picture on him the night he died! And there was that boy that every girl in Delta had set her cap for! That beautiful, brilliant young Fitzhugh boy from Green County!

TOM. What did he leave his widow?

AMANDA. He never married! Gracious, you talk as though all of my old admirers had turned up their toes to the daisies!

TOM. Isn't this the first you mentioned that still survives?

AMANDA. That Fitzhugh boy went North and made a fortune—came to be known as the Wolf of Wall Street! He had the Midas touch, whatever he touched turned to gold! And I could have been Mrs. Duncan J. Fitzhugh, mind you! But—I picked your *father*!

LAURA (*rising*). Mother, let me clear the table.

AMANDA. No dear, you go in front and study your typewriter chart. Or practice your shorthand a little. Stay fresh and pretty!—It's almost time for our gentlemen callers to start arriving. (*She flounces girlishly toward the kitchenette.*) How many do you suppose we're going to entertain this afternoon?

Tom throws down the paper and jumps up with a groan.

LAURA (*alone in the dining room*). I don't believe we're going to receive any, Mother.

AMANDA (*reappearing, airily*). What? No one—not one? You must be joking! (*Laura nervously echoes her laugh. She slips in a fugitive manner through the half-open portieres and draws them gently behind her. A shaft of very clear light is thrown on her face against the faded tapestry of the curtains.*) (*Music: "The Glass Menagerie" Under Faintly.*) (*Lightly.*) Not one gentleman caller? It can't be true! There must be a flood, there must have been a tornado!

LAURA. It isn't a flood, it's not a tornado, Mother. I'm just not popular like you were in Blue Mountain. . . . (*Tom utters another groan. Laura glances at him with a faint, apologetic smile. Her voice catching a little.*) Mother's afraid I'm going to be an old maid.

(*The Scene Dims Out with "Glass Menagerie" Music.*)

SCENE 2

"Laura, Haven't You Ever Liked Some Boy?"

On the dark stage the screen is lighted with the image of blue roses. Gradually Laura's figure becomes apparent and the screen goes out. The music subsides.

Laura is seated in the delicate ivory chair at the small clawfoot table.

She wears a dress of soft violet material for a kimono—her hair tied back from her forehead with a ribbon.

She is washing and polishing her collection of glass.

Amanda appears on the fire-escape steps. At the sound of her ascent, Laura catches her breath, thrusts the bowl of ornaments away and seats herself stiffly before the diagram of the typewriter keyboard as though it held her spellbound. Something has happened to Amanda. It is written in her face as she climbs to the landing: a look that is grim and hopeless and a little absurd.

She has on one of those cheap or imitation velvety-looking cloth coats with imitation fur collar. Her hat is five or six years old, one of those dreadful cloche hats that were worn in the late twenties, and she is clasping an enormous black patent-leather pocketbook with nickel clasp and initials. This is her full-dress outfit, the one she usually wears to the D.A.R.

Before entering she looks through the door.

She purses her lips, opens her eyes wide, rolls them upward and shakes her head.

Then she slowly lets herself in the door. Seeing her mother's expression Laura touches her lips with a nervous gesture.

LAURA. Hello, Mother, I was—(*She makes a nervous gesture toward the chart on the wall. Amanda leans against the shut door and stares at Laura with a martyred look.*)

AMANDA. Deception? Deception? (*She slowly removes her hat and gloves, continuing the swift suffering stare. She lets the hat and gloves fall on the floor—a bit of acting.*)

LAURA (*shakily*). How was the D.A.R. meeting? (*Amanda slowly opens her purse and removes a dainty white handkerchief which she shakes out delicately and delicately touches to her lips and nostrils.*) Didn't you go to the D.A.R. meeting, Mother?

AMANDA (*faintly, almost inaudibly*). —No.—No. (*Then more forcibly.*) I did not have the strength—to go to the D.A.R. In fact, I did not have the courage! I wanted to find a hole in the ground and hide myself in it forever! (*She crosses slowly to the wall and removes the diagram of the typewriter keyboard. She holds it in front of her for a second, staring at it sweetly and sorrowfully—then bites her lips and tears it in two pieces.*)

LAURA (*faintly*). Why did you do that, Mother? (*Amanda repeats the same procedure with the chart of the Gregg Alphabet.*) Why are you—

AMANDA. Why? Why? How old are you, Laura?

LAURA. Mother, you know my age.

AMANDA. I thought that you were an adult; it seems that I was mistaken. (*She crosses slowly to the sofa and sinks down and stares at Laura.*)

LAURA. Please don't stare at me, Mother.

Amanda closes her eyes and lowers her head. Count ten.

AMANDA. What are we going to do, what is going to become of us, what is the future?

Count ten.

LAURA. Has something happened, Mother? (*Amanda draws a long breath and takes out the handkerchief again. Dabbing process.*) Mother, has—something happened?

AMANDA. I'll be all right in a minute. I'm just bewildered— (*count five*)—by life. . . .

LAURA. Mother, I wish that you would tell me what's happened.

AMANDA. As you know, I was supposed to be inducted into my office at the D.A.R. this afternoon. (*Image: A Swarm of Typewriters.*) But I stopped off at Rubicam's Business College to speak to your teachers about your having a cold and ask them what progress they thought you were making down there.

LAURA. Oh. . . .

AMANDA. I went to the typing instructor and introduced myself as your mother. She didn't know who you were. Wingfield, she said. We don't have any such student enrolled at the school! I assured her she did, that you had been going to classes since early in January. "I wonder," she said, "if you could be talking about that terribly shy little girl who dropped out of school after only a few days' attendance?" "No," I said, "Laura, my daughter, has been going to school every day for the past six weeks!" "Excuse me," she said. She took the attendance book out and there was your name, unmistakably printed, and all the dates you were absent until they decided that you had dropped out of school. I still said, "No, there must have been some mistake! There must have been some mix-up

in the records!" And she said, "No—I remember her perfectly now. Her hand shook so that she couldn't hit the right keys! The first time we gave a speed-test, she broke down completely—was sick at the stomach and almost had to be carried into the wash-room! After that morning she never showed up any more. We phoned the house but never got any answer"—while I was working at Famous and Barr, I suppose, demonstrating those—Oh! I felt so weak I could barely keep on my feet. I had to sit down while they got me a glass of water! Fifty dollars' tuition, all of our plans—my hopes and ambitions for you—just gone up the spout, just gone up the spout like that. (*Laura draws a long breath and gets awkwardly to her feet. She crosses to the victrola and winds it up.*) What are you doing?

LAURA. Oh! (*She releases the handle and returns to her seat.*)

AMANDA. Laura, where have you been going when you've gone out pretending that you were going to business college?

LAURA. I've just been going out walking.

AMANDA. That's not true.

LAURA. It is. I just went walking.

AMANDA. Walking? Walking? In winter? Deliberately courting pneumonia in that light coat? Where did you walk to, Laura?

LAURA. It was the lesser of two evils, Mother. (*Image: Winter Scene in Park.*) I couldn't go back up. I—threw up—on the floor!

AMANDA. From half past seven till after five every day you mean to tell me you walked around in the park, because you wanted to make me think that you were still going to Rubicam's Business College?

LAURA. It wasn't as bad as it sounds. I went inside places to get warmed up.

AMANDA. Inside where?

LAURA. I went in the art museum and the bird-houses at the Zoo. I visited the penguins every day! Sometimes I did without lunch and went to the movies. Lately I've been spending most of my afternoons in the Jewel-box, that big glass house where they raise the tropical flowers.

AMANDA. You did all this to deceive me, just for the deception? (*Laura looks down.*) Why?

LAURA. Mother, when you're disappointed, you get that awful suffering look on your face, like the picture of Jesus' mother in the museum!

AMANDA. Hush!

LAURA. I couldn't face it.

Pause. A whisper of strings.

(*Legend: "The Crust of Humility."*)

AMANDA (*hopelessly fingering the huge pocketbook*). So what are we going to do the rest of our lives? Stay home and watch the parades go by? Amuse ourselves with the glass menagerie, darling? Eternally play those worn-out phonograph records your father left as a painful reminder of him? We won't have a business career—we've given that up because it gave us nervous indigestion! (*Laughs wearily.*) What is there left but dependency all our lives? I know so well what becomes of unmarried women who aren't prepared to occupy a position. I've seen such pitiful cases in the South—barely tolerated spinsters living upon the grudging patronage of sister's husband or brother's wife!—stuck away in some little mousetrap of a room— encouraged by one in-law to visit another—little birdlike women without any nest—eating the crust of humility all their life! Is that the future that we've mapped out for ourselves? I swear it's the only alternative I can think of! It isn't a very pleasant alternative, is it? Of course—some girls *do* marry. (*Laura twists her hands nervously.*) Haven't you ever liked some boy?

LAURA. Yes. I liked one once. (*Rises.*) I came across his picture a while ago.

AMANDA (*with some interest*). He gave you his picture?

LAURA. No, it's in the year-book.

AMANDA (*disappointed*). Oh—a high-school boy.

(*Screen Image: Jim as a High-School Hero Bearing a Silver Cup.*)

LAURA. Yes. His name was Jim. (*Laura lifts the heavy annual from the clawfoot table.*) Here he is in *The Pirates of Penzance*.

AMANDA (*absently*). The what?

LAURA. The operetta the senior class put on. He had a wonderful voice and we sat across the aisle from each other Mondays, Wednesdays and Fridays in the Aud. Here he is with the silver cup for debating! See his grin?

AMANDA (*absently*). He must have had a jolly disposition.

LAURA. He used to call me—Blue Roses.

(*Image: Blue Roses.*)

AMANDA. Why did he call you such a name as that?

LAURA. When I had that attack of pleurosis—he asked me what was the matter when I came back. I said pleurosis— he thought that I said Blue Roses! So that's what he always called me after that. Whenever he saw me, he'd holler, "Hello, Blue Roses!" I didn't care for the girl that he went out with. Emily Meisenbach. Emily was the best-dressed girl at Soldan. She never struck me, though, as being sincere. . . . It says in the Personal Section— they're engaged. That's—six years ago! They must be married by now.

AMANDA. Girls that aren't cut out for business careers usually wind up married to some nice man. (*Gets up with a spark of revival.*) Sister, that's what you'll do!

Laura utters a startled, doubtful laugh. She reaches quickly for a piece of glass.

LAURA. But, Mother—

AMANDA. Yes? (*Crossing to photograph.*)

LAURA (*in a tone of frightened apology*). I'm—crippled!

(*Image: Screen.*)

AMANDA. Nonsense! Laura, I've told you never, never to use that word. Why, you're not crippled, you just have a little defect—hardly noticeable, even! When people have some slight disadvantage like that, they cultivate other things to make up for it—develop charm—and viva-city—and—*charm!* That's all you have to do! (*She turns again to the photograph.*) One thing your father had *plenty of*—was *charm!*

Tom motions to the fiddle in the wings.

(*The Scene Fades out with Music.*)

SCENE 3

(*Legend on the Screen: "After the Fiasco—"*)

Tom speaks from the fire-escape landing.

TOM. After the fiasco at Rubicam's Business College, the idea of getting a gentleman caller for Laura began to play a more important part in Mother's calculations. It became an obsession. Like some archetype of the universal unconscious, the image of the gentleman caller haunted our small apartment. . . . (*Image: Young Man at Door with Flowers.*) An evening at home rarely passed without some allusion to this image, this specter, this hope. . . . Even when he wasn't mentioned, his presence hung in Mother's preoccupied look and in my sister's frightened, apologetic manner—hung like a sentence passed upon the Wingfields! Mother was a woman of action as well as words. She began to take logical steps in the planned direction. Late that winter and in the early spring—realizing that extra money would be needed to properly feather the nest and plume the bird—she conducted a vigorous campaign on the telephone, roping in subscribers to one of those magazines for matrons called *The Home-maker's Companion*, the type of journal that features the serialized sublimations of ladies of letters who think in terms of delicate cuplike breasts, slim, tapering waists, rich, creamy thighs, eyes like wood-smoke in autumn, fingers that soothe and caress like strains of music, bodies as powerful as Etruscan sculpture.

(*Screen Image: Glamor Magazine Cover.*)

Amanda enters with phone on long extension cord. She is spotted in the dim stage.

AMANDA. Ida Scott? This is Amanda Wingfield! We *missed* you at the D.A.R. last Monday! I said to myself: She's probably suffering with that sinus condition! How is that sinus condition? Horrors! Heaven have mercy!—You're a Christian martyr, yes, that's what you are, a Christian martyr! Well, I just now happened to notice that your subscription to the *Companion's* about to expire! Yes, it expires with the next issue, honey!—just when that wonderful new serial by Bessie Mae Hopper is getting off to such an exciting start. Oh, honey, it's something that you can't miss! You remember how *Gone With the Wind* took everybody by storm? You simply couldn't go out if you hadn't read it. All everybody *talked* was Scarlett O'Hara. Well, this is a book that critics already compare to *Gone With the Wind*. It's the *Gone With the Wind* of the post–World War generation!—What?—Burning?—Oh, honey, don't let them burn, go take a look in the oven and I'll hold the wire! Heavens—I think she's hung up!

(*Dim Out.*)

(*Legend on Screen: "You Think I'm in Love with Continental Shoemakers?"*)

Before the stage is lighted, the violent voices of Tom and Amanda are heard. They are quarreling behind the portieres. In front of them stands Laura with clenched hands and panicky expression.

A clear pool of light on her figure throughout this scene.

TOM. What in Christ's name am I—

AMANDA (*shrilly*). Don't you use that—

TOM. Supposed to do!

AMANDA. Expression! Not in my—

TOM. Ohhh!

AMANDA. Presence! Have you gone out of your senses?

TOM. I have, that's true, *driven* out!

AMANDA. What is the matter with you, you—big—big— IDIOT!

TOM. Look—I've got *no thing,* no single thing—

AMANDA. Lower your voice!

TOM. In my life here that I can call my OWN! Everything is—

AMANDA. Stop that shouting!

TOM. Yesterday you confiscated my books! You had the nerve to—

AMANDA. I took that horrible novel back to the library— yes! That hideous book by that insane Mr. Lawrence. (*Tom laughs wildly.*) I cannot control the output of diseased minds or people who cater to them—(*Tom laughs still more wildly.*) BUT I WON'T ALLOW SUCH FILTH BROUGHT INTO MY HOUSE! No, no, no, no, no!

TOM. House, house! Who pays rent on it, who makes a slave of himself to—

AMANDA (*fairly screeching*). Don't you DARE to—

TOM. No, no, *I* mustn't say things! *I've* got to just—

AMANDA. Let me tell you—

TOM. I don't want to hear any more! (*He tears the portieres open. The upstage area is lit with a turgid smoky red glow.*)

Amanda's hair is in metal curlers and she wears a very old bathrobe, much too large for her slight figure, a relic of the faithless Mr. Wingfield.

An upright typewriter and a wild disarray of manuscripts are on the dropleaf table. The quarrel was probably precipitated by Amanda's interruption of his creative labor. A chair lying overthrown on the floor.

Their gesticulating shadows are cast on the ceiling by the fiery glow.

AMANDA. You *will* hear more, you—

TOM. No, I won't hear more, I'm going out!

AMANDA. You come right back in—

TOM. Out, out, out! Because I'm—

AMANDA. Come back here, Tom Wingfield! I'm not through talking to you!

TOM. Oh, go—

LAURA (*desperately*). Tom!

AMANDA. You're going to listen, and no more insolence from you! I'm at the end of my patience! (*He comes back toward her.*)

TOM. What do you think I'm at? Aren't I supposed to have any patience to reach the end of, Mother? I know, I know. It seems unimportant to you, what I'm *doing*— what I *want* to do—having a little *difference* between them! You don't think that—

AMANDA. I think you've been doing things that you're ashamed of. That's why you act like this. I don't believe that you go every night to the movies. Nobody goes to the movies night after night. Nobody in their right minds goes to the movies as often as you pretend to. People don't go to the movies at nearly midnight, and movies don't let out at two A.M. Come in stumbling. Muttering to yourself like a maniac! You get three hours' sleep and then go to work. Oh, I can picture the way you're doing down there. Moping, doping, because you're in no condition.

TOM (*wildly*). No, I'm in no condition!

AMANDA. What right have you got to jeopardize your job? Jeopardize the security of us all? How do you think we'd manage if you were—

TOM. Listen! You think I'm crazy *about* the *warehouse?* (*He bends fiercely toward her slight figure.*) You think I'm in love with the Continental Shoemakers? You think I want to spend fifty-five years down there in that—celotex interior! with—fluorescent—tubes! Look! I'd rather somebody picked up a crowbar and battered out my brains—than go back mornings! *I go!* Every time you come in yelling that God damn *"Rise and Shine!" "Rise and Shine!"* I say to myself *"How lucky dead people are!"* But I get up. I *go!* For sixty-five dollars a month I give up all that I dream of doing and being *ever!* And you say self—*self's* all I ever think of. Why, listen, if self is what I thought of, Mother, I'd be where he is—GONE! (*Pointing to father's picture.*) As far as the system of transportation reaches! (*He starts past her. She grabs his arm.*) Don't grab at me, Mother!

AMANDA. Where are you going?

TOM. I'm going to the *movies!*

AMANDA. I don't believe that lie!

TOM (*crouching toward her, overtowering her tiny figure. She backs away, gasping*). I'm going to opium dens! Yes, opium dens, dens of vice and criminals' hang-outs, Mother. I've joined the Hogan gang, I'm a hired assassin, I carry a Tommy-gun in a violin case! I run a string of cat-houses in the Valley! They call me Killer, Killer Wingfield, I'm leading a double-life, a simple, honest warehouse worker by day, by night a dynamic *czar* of the *underworld*, Mother. I go to gambling casinos, I spin away fortunes on the roulette table! I wear a patch over one eye and a false mustache, sometimes I put on green whiskers. On those occasions they call me—*El Diablo!* Oh, I could tell you things to make you sleepless! My enemies plan to dynamite this place. They're going to blow us all sky-high some night! I'll be glad, very happy, and so will you! You'll go up, up on a broomstick, over Blue Mountain with seventeen gentlemen callers! You ugly—babbling old—*witch.* . . . (*He goes through a series of violent, clumsy movements, seizing his overcoat, lunging to the door, pulling it fiercely open. The women watch him, aghast. His arm catches in the sleeve of the coat as he struggles to pull it on. For a moment he is pinioned by the bulky garment. With an outraged groan he tears the coat off again, splitting the shoulders of it, and hurls it across the room. It strikes against the shelf of Laura's glass collection, there is a tinkle of shattering glass. Laura cries out as if wounded.*)

(*Music Legend: "The Glass Menagerie."*)

LAURA (*shrilly*). My glass!—menagerie. . . . (*She covers her face and turns away.*)

But Amanda is still stunned and stupefied by the "ugly witch" so that she barely notices this occurrence. Now she recovers her speech.

AMANDA (*in an awful voice*). I won't speak to you—until you apologize! (*She crosses through portieres and draws them together behind her. Tom is left with Laura. Laura clings weakly to the mantel with her face averted. Tom stares at her stupidly for a moment. Then he crosses to shelf. Drops awkwardly to his knees to collect the fallen glass, glancing at Laura as if he would speak but couldn't.*)

"The Glass Menagerie" steals in as

(*The Scene Dims Out.*)

SCENE 4

The interior is dark. Faint light in the alley.

A deep-voiced bell in a church is tolling the hour of five as the scene commences.

Tom appears at the top of the alley. After each solemn boom of the bell in the tower, he shakes a little noise-maker or rattle as if to express the tiny spasm of man in contrast to the sustained power and dignity of the Almighty. This and the unsteadiness of his advance make it evident that he has been drinking.

As he climbs the few steps to the fire-escape landing light steals up inside. Laura appears in night-dress, observing Tom's empty bed in the front room.

Tom fishes in his pockets for the door-key, removing a motley assortment of articles in the search, including a perfect shower of movie-ticket stubs and an empty bottle. At last he finds the key, but just as he is about to insert it, it slips from his fingers. He strikes a match and crouches below the door.

TOM (*bitterly*). One crack—and it falls through!

Laura opens the door.

LAURA. Tom! Tom, what are you doing?

TOM. Looking for a door-key.

LAURA. Where have you been all this time?

TOM. I have been to the movies.

LAURA. All this time at the movies?

TOM. There was a very long program. There was a Garbo picture and a Mickey Mouse and a travelogue and a newsreel and a preview of coming attractions. And there was an organ solo and a collection for the milk-fund—simultaneously—which ended up in a terrible fight between a fat lady and an usher!

LAURA (*innocently*). Did you have to stay through everything?

TOM. Of course! And, oh, I forgot! There was a big stage show! The headliner on this stage show was Malvolio the Magician. He performed wonderful tricks, many of them, such as pouring water back and forth between pitchers. First it turned to wine and then it turned to beer and then it turned to whiskey. I know it was whiskey it finally turned into because he needed somebody to come up out of the audience to help him, and I came up—both shows! It was Kentucky Straight Bourbon. A very generous fellow, he gave souvenirs. (*He pulls from his back pocket a shimmering rainbow-colored scarf.*) He gave me this. This is his magic scarf. You can have it, Laura. You wave it over a canary cage and you get a bowl of gold-fish. You wave it over the gold-fish bowl and they fly away canaries. . . . But the wonderfullest trick of all was the coffin trick. We nailed him into a coffin and he got out of the coffin without removing one nail. (*He has come inside.*) There is a trick that would come in handy for me—get me out of this 2 by 4 situation! (*Flops onto bed and starts removing shoes.*)

LAURA. Tom—Shhh!

TOM. What you shushing me for?

LAURA. You'll wake up Mother.

TOM. Goody, goody! Pay 'er back for all those "Rise an' Shines." (*Lies down, groaning.*) You know it don't take much intelligence to get yourself into a nailed-up coffin, Laura. But who in hell ever got himself out of one without removing one nail?

As if in answer, the father's grinning photograph lights up.

(*Scene Dims Out.*)

Immediately following: The church bell is heard striking six. At the sixth stroke the alarm clock goes off in Amanda's room, and after a few moments we hear her calling: "Rise and Shine! Rise and Shine! Laura, go tell your brother to rise and shine!"

TOM (*sitting up slowly*). I'll rise—but I won't shine.

The light increases.

AMANDA. Laura, tell your brother his coffee is ready.

Laura slips into front room.

LAURA. Tom! it's nearly seven. Don't make Mother nervous. (*He stares at her stupidly. Beseechingly.*) Tom, speak to Mother this morning. Make up with her, apologize, speak to her!

TOM. She won't to me. It's her that started not speaking.

LAURA. If you just say you're sorry she'll start speaking.

TOM. Her not speaking—is that such a tragedy?

LAURA. Please—please!

AMANDA (*calling from kitchenette*). Laura, are you going to do what I asked you to do, or do I have to get dressed and go out myself?

LAURA. Going, going—soon as I get on my coat! (*She pulls on a shapeless felt hat with nervous, jerky movement, pleadingly glancing at Tom. Rushes awkwardly for coat. The coat is one of Amanda's, inaccurately made-over, the sleeves too short for Laura.*) Butter and what else?

AMANDA (*entering upstage*). Just butter. Tell them to charge it.

LAURA. Mother, they make such faces when I do that.

AMANDA. Sticks and stones may break my bones, but the expression on Mr. Garfinkel's face won't harm us! Tell your brother his coffee is getting cold.

LAURA (*at door*). Do what I asked you, will you, will you, Tom?

He looks sullenly away.

AMANDA. Laura, go now or just don't go at all!

LAURA (*rushing out*). Going—going! (*A second later she cries out. Tom springs up and crosses to the door. Amanda rushes anxiously in. Tom opens the door.*)

TOM. Laura?

LAURA. I'm all right. I slipped, but I'm all right.

AMANDA (*peering anxiously after her*). If anyone breaks a leg on those fire-escape steps, the landlord ought to be sued for every cent he possesses! (*She shuts door. Remembers she isn't speaking and returns to other room.*)

As Tom enters listlessly for his coffee, she turns her back to him and stands rigidly facing the window on the gloomy gray vault of the areaway. Its light on her face with its aged but childish features is cruelly sharp, satirical as a Daumier print.

(*Music Under: "Ave Maria."*)

Tom glances sheepishly but sullenly at her averted figure and slumps at the table. The coffee is scalding hot; he sips it and gasps and spits it back in the cup. At his gasp, Amanda catches her breath and half turns. Then catches herself and turns back to window.

Tom blows on his coffee, glancing sidewise at his mother. She clears her throat. Tom clears his. He starts to rise. Sinks back down again, scratches his head, clears his

throat again. Amanda coughs. Tom raises his cup in both hands to blow on it, his eyes staring over the rim of it at his mother for several moments. Then he slowly sets the cup down and awkwardly and hesitantly rises from the chair.

TOM (*hoarsely*). Mother. I—I apologize. Mother. (*Amanda draws a quick, shuddering breath. Her face works grotesquely. She breaks into childlike tears.*) I'm sorry for what I said, for everything that I said, I didn't mean it.

AMANDA (*sobbingly*). My devotion has made me a witch and so I make myself hateful to my children!

TOM. No, you *don't*.

AMANDA. I worry so much, don't sleep, it makes me nervous!

TOM (*gently*). I understand that.

AMANDA. I've had to put up a solitary battle all these years. But you're my right-hand bower! Don't fall down, don't fail!

TOM (*gently*). I try, Mother.

AMANDA (*with great enthusiasm*). Try and you will SUCCEED! (*The notion makes her breathless.*) Why, you—you're just *full* of natural endowments! Both of my children— they're *unusual* children! Don't you think I know it? I'm so—*proud*! Happy and—feel I've—so much to be thankful for but—Promise me one thing, son!

TOM. What, Mother?

AMANDA. Promise, son, you'll—never be a drunkard!

TOM (*turns to her grinning*). I will never be a drunkard, Mother.

AMANDA. That's what frightened me so, that you'd be drinking! Eat a bowl of Purina!

TOM. Just coffee, Mother.

AMANDA. Shredded wheat biscuit?

TOM. No. No, Mother, just coffee.

AMANDA. You can't put in a day's work on an empty stomach. You've got ten minutes—don't gulp! Drinking too-hot liquids makes cancer of the stomach.... Put cream in.

TOM. No, thank you.

AMANDA. To cool it.

TOM. No! No, thank you, I want it black.

AMANDA. I know, but it's not good for you. We have to do all that we can to build ourselves up. In these trying times we live in, all that we have to cling to is—each other.... That's why it's so important to—Tom, I—I sent out your sister so I could discuss something with you. If you hadn't spoken I would have spoken to you. (*Sits down.*)

TOM (*gently*). What is it, Mother, that you want to discuss?

AMANDA. Laura!

Tom puts his cup down slowly.

(*Legend on Screen: "Laura."*)

(*Music: "The Glass Menagerie."*)

TOM. —Oh.—Laura ...

AMANDA (*touching his sleeve*). You know how Laura is. So quiet but—still water runs deep! She notices things and I think she—broods about them. (*Tom looks up.*) A few days ago I came in and she was crying.

TOM. What about?

AMANDA. You.

TOM. Me?

AMANDA. She has an idea that you're not happy here.

TOM. What gave her that idea?

AMANDA. What gives her any idea? However, you do act strangely. I—I'm not criticizing, understand *that!* I know your ambitions do not lie in the warehouse, that like everybody in the whole wide world—you've had to—make sacrifices, but—Tom—Tom—life's not easy, it calls for—Spartan endurance! There's so many things in my heart that I cannot describe to you! I've never told you but I—*loved* your father. . . .

TOM (*gently*). I know that, Mother.

AMANDA. And you—when I see you taking after his ways! Staying out late—and—well, you *had* been drinking the night you were in that—terrifying condition! Laura says that you hate the apartment and that you go out nights to get away from it! Is that true, Tom?

TOM. No. You say there's so much in your heart that you can't describe to me. That's true of me, too. There's so much in my heart that I can't describe to *you!* So let's respect each other's—

AMANDA. But, why—*why*, Tom—are you always so *restless?* Where do you go to, nights?

TOM. I—go to the movies.

AMANDA. Why do you go to the movies so much, Tom?

TOM. I go to the movies because—I like adventure. Adventure is something I don't have much of at work, so I go to the movies.

AMANDA. But, Tom, you go to the movies *entirely too much!*

TOM. I like a lot of adventure.

Amanda looks baffled, then hurt. As the familiar inquisition resumes he becomes hard and impatient again. Amanda slips back into her querulous attitude toward him.

(*Image on Screen: Sailing Vessel with Jolly Roger.*)

AMANDA. Most young men find adventure in their careers.

TOM. Then most young men are not employed in a warehouse.

AMANDA. The world is full of young men employed in warehouses and offices and factories.

TOM. Do all of them find adventure in their careers?

AMANDA. They do or they do without it! Not everybody has a craze for adventure.

TOM. Man is by instinct a lover, a hunter, a fighter, and none of those instincts are given much play at the warehouse!

AMANDA. Man is by instinct! Don't quote instinct to me! Instinct is something that people have got away from! It belongs to animals! Christian adults don't want it!

TOM. What do Christian adults want, then, Mother?

AMANDA. Superior things! Things of the mind and the spirit! Only animals have to satisfy instincts! Surely your aims are somewhat higher than theirs! Than monkeys—pigs—

TOM. I reckon they're not.

AMANDA. You're joking. However, that isn't what I wanted to discuss.

TOM (*rising*). I haven't much time.

AMANDA (*pushing his shoulders*). Sit down.

TOM. You want me to punch in red at the warehouse, Mother?

AMANDA. You have five minutes. I want to talk about Laura.

(*Legend: "Plans and Provisions."*)

TOM. All right! What about Laura?

AMANDA. We have to be making plans and provisions for her. She's older than you, two years, and nothing has happened. She just drifts along doing nothing. It frightens me terribly how she just drifts along.

TOM. I guess she's the type that people call home girls.

AMANDA. There's no such type, and if there is, it's a pity! That is unless the home is hers, with a husband!

TOM. What?

AMANDA. Oh, I can see the handwriting on the wall as plain as I see the nose in the front of my face! It's terrifying! More and more you remind me of your father! He was out all hours without explanation—Then *left!* Goodbye! And me with the bag to hold. I saw that letter you got from the Merchant Marine. I know what you're dreaming of. I'm not standing here blindfolded. Very well, then. Then *do* it! But not till there's somebody to take your place.

TOM. What do you mean?

AMANDA. I mean that as soon as Laura has got somebody to take care of her, married, a home of her own, independent—why, then you'll be free to go wherever you please, on land, on sea, whichever way the wind blows! But until that time you've got to look out for your sister. I don't say me because I'm old and don't matter! I say for your sister because she's young and dependent. I put her in business college—a dismal failure! Frightened her so it made her sick to her stomach. I took her over to the Young People's League at the church. Another fiasco. She spoke to nobody, nobody spoke to her. Now all she does is fool with those pieces of glass and play those worn-out records. What kind of a life is that for a girl to lead!

TOM. What can I do about it?

AMANDA. Overcome selfishness! Self, self, self is all that you ever think of! (*Tom springs up and crosses to get his coat. It is ugly and bulky. He pulls on a cap with earmuffs.*) Where is your muffler? Put your wool muffler on! (*He snatches it angrily from the closet and tosses it around his neck and pulls both ends tight.*) Tom! I haven't said what I had in mind to ask you.

TOM. I'm too late to—

AMANDA (*catching his arms—very importunately. Then shyly*). Down at the warehouse, aren't there some—nice young men?

TOM. No!

AMANDA. There *must* be—some.

TOM. Mother—

Gesture.

AMANDA. Find out one that's clean-living—doesn't drink and—ask him out for sister!

TOM. What?

AMANDA. For *sister!* To meet! Get *acquainted!*

TOM (*stamping to door*). Oh, my go-osh!

AMANDA. Will you? (*He opens door. Imploringly.*) Will you? (*He starts down.*) Will you? *Will* you dear?

TOM (*calling back*). YES!

Amanda closes the door hesitantly and with a troubled but faintly hopeful expression.

(*Screen Image: Glamor Magazine Cover.*)

Spot Amanda at phone.

AMANDA. Ella Cartwright? This is Amanda Wingfield! How are you honey? How is that kidney condition? (*Count five.*) Horrors! (*Count five.*) You're a Christian martyr, yes, honey, that's what you are, a Christian martyr! Well, I just happened to notice in my little red book that your subscription to the *Companion* has just run out! I knew that you wouldn't want to miss out on the wonderful serial starting in this new issue. It's by Bessie Mae Hopper, the first thing she's written since *Honeymoon for Three*. Wasn't that a strange and interesting story? Well, this one is even lovelier, I believe. It has a sophisticated society background. It's all about the horsey set on Long Island!

(*Fade Out.*)

SCENE 5

(*Legend on Screen: "Annunciation."*) *Fade with music.*

It is early dusk of a spring evening. Supper has just been finished at the Wingfield apartment. Amanda and Laura in light colored dresses are removing dishes from the table, in the upstage area, which is shadowy, their movements formalized almost as a dance or ritual, their moving forms as pale and silent as moths.

Tom, in white shirt and trousers, rises from the table and crosses toward the fire-escape.

AMANDA (*as he passes her*). Son, will you do me a favor?

TOM. What?

AMANDA. Comb your hair! You look so pretty when your hair is combed! (*Tom slouches on sofa with evening paper. Enormous caption "Franco Triumphs."*) There is only one respect in which I would like you to emulate your father.

TOM. What respect is that?

AMANDA. The care he always took of his appearance. He never allowed himself to look untidy. (*He throws down the paper and crosses to fire-escape.*) Where are you going?

TOM. I'm going out to smoke.

AMANDA. You smoke too much. A pack a day at fifteen cents a pack. How much would that amount to in a month? Thirty times fifteen is how much, Tom? Figure it out and you will be astounded at what you could save. Enough to give you a night-school course in accounting at Washington U! Just think what a wonderful thing that would be for you, son!

Tom is unmoved by the thought.

TOM. I'd rather smoke. (*He steps out on landing, letting the screen door slam.*)

AMANDA (*sharply*). I know! That's the tragedy of it.... (*Alone, she turns to look at her husband's picture.*)

(*Dance Music: "All the World Is Waiting for the Sunrise!"*)

TOM (*to the audience*). Across the alley from us was the Paradise Dance Hall. On evenings in spring the windows and doors were open and the music came outdoors. Sometimes the lights were turned out except for a large glass sphere that hung from the ceiling. It would turn slowly about and filter the dusk with delicate rainbow colors. Then the orchestra played a waltz or a tango, something that had a slow and sensuous rhythm. Couples would come outside, to the relative privacy of the alley. You could see them kissing behind ashpits and telephone poles. This was the compensation for lives that passed like mine, without any change or adventure. Adventure and change were imminent in this year. They were waiting around the corner for all these kids. Suspended in the mist over Berchtesgaden, caught in the folds of Chamberlain's umbrella—In Spain there was Guernica! But here there was only hot swing music and liquor, dance halls, bars, and movies, and sex that hung in the gloom like a chandelier and flooded the world with brief, deceptive rainbows.... All the world was waiting for bombardments!

Amanda turns from the picture and comes outside.

AMANDA (*sighing*). A fire-escape landing's a poor excuse for a porch. (*She spreads a newspaper on a step and sits down, gracefully and demurely as if she were settling into a swing on a Mississippi veranda.*) What are you looking at?

TOM. The moon.

AMANDA. Is there a moon this evening?

TOM. It's rising over Garfinkel's Delicatessen.

AMANDA. So it is! A little silver slipper of a moon. Have you made a wish on it yet?

TOM. Um-hum.

AMANDA. What did you wish for?

TOM. That's a secret.

AMANDA. A secret, huh? Well, I won't tell mine either. I will be just as mysterious as you.

TOM. I bet I can guess what yours is.

AMANDA. Is my head so transparent?

TOM. You're not a sphinx.

AMANDA. No, I don't have secrets. I'll tell you what I wished for on the moon. Success and happiness for my precious children! I wish for that whenever there's a moon, and when there isn't a moon, I wish for it, too.

TOM. I thought perhaps you wished for a gentleman caller.

AMANDA. Why do you say that?

TOM. Don't you remember asking me to fetch one?

AMANDA. I remember suggesting that it would be nice for your sister if you brought some nice young man from the warehouse. I think I've made that suggestion more than once.

TOM. Yes, you have made it repeatedly.

AMANDA. Well?

TOM. We are going to have one.

AMANDA. *What?*

TOM. A gentleman caller!

(*The Annunciation Is Celebrated with Music.*)

Amanda rises.

(*Image on Screen: Caller with Bouquet.*)

AMANDA. You mean you have asked some nice young man to come over?

TOM. Yep. I've asked him to dinner.

AMANDA. You really did?

TOM. I did!

AMANDA. You did, and did he—*accept?*

TOM. He did!

AMANDA. Well, well—well, well! That's—lovely!

TOM. I thought that you would be pleased.

AMANDA. It's definite, then?

TOM. Very definite.

AMANDA. Soon?

TOM. Very soon.

AMANDA. For heaven's sake, stop putting on and tell me some things, will you?

TOM. What things do you want me to tell you?

AMANDA. Naturally I would like to know when he's *coming!*

TOM. He's coming tomorrow.

AMANDA. *Tomorrow?*

TOM. Yep. Tomorrow.

AMANDA. But, Tom!

TOM. Yes, Mother?

AMANDA. Tomorrow gives me no time!

TOM. Time for what?

AMANDA. Preparations! Why didn't you phone me at once, as soon as you asked him, the minute that he accepted? Then, don't you see, I could have been getting ready!

TOM. You don't have to make any fuss.

AMANDA. Oh, Tom, Tom, Tom, of course I have to make a fuss! I want things nice, not sloppy! Not thrown together. I'll certainly have to do some fast thinking, won't I?

TOM. I don't see why you have to think at all.

AMANDA. You just don't know. We can't have a gentleman caller in a pigsty! All my wedding silver has to be polished, the monogrammed table linen ought to be laundered! The windows have to be washed and fresh curtains put up. And how about clothes? We have to *wear* something, don't we?

TOM. Mother, this boy is no one to make a fuss over!

AMANDA. Do you realize he's the first young man we've introduced to your sister? It's terrible, dreadful, disgraceful that poor little sister has never received a single gentleman caller! Tom, come inside! (*She opens the screen door.*)

TOM. What for?

AMANDA. I want to ask you some things.

TOM. If you're going to make such a fuss, I'll call it off, I'll tell him not to come.

AMANDA. You certainly won't do anything of the kind. Nothing offends people worse than broken engagements. It simply means I'll have to work like a Turk! We won't be brilliant, but we'll pass inspection. Come on inside. (*Tom follows, groaning.*) Sit down.

TOM. Any particular place you would like me to sit?

AMANDA. Thank heavens I've got that new sofa! I'm also making payments on a floor lamp I'll have sent out! And put the chintz covers on, they'll brighten things up! Of course I'd hoped to have these walls repapered. . . . What is the young man's name?

TOM. His name is O'Connor.

AMANDA. That, of course, means fish—tomorrow is Friday! I'll have that salmon loaf—with Durkee's dressing! What does he do? He works at the warehouse?

TOM. Of course! How else would I—

AMANDA. Tom, he—doesn't drink?

TOM. Why do you ask me that?

AMANDA. Your father *did!*

TOM. Don't get started on that!

AMANDA. He *does* drink, then?

TOM. Not that I know of!

AMANDA. Make sure, be certain! The last thing I want for my daughter's a boy who drinks!

TOM. Aren't you being a little premature? Mr. O'Connor has not yet appeared on the scene!

AMANDA. But will tomorrow. To meet your sister, and what do I know about his character? Nothing! Old maids are better off than wives of drunkards!

TOM. Oh, my God!

AMANDA. Be still!

TOM (*leaning forward to whisper*). Lots of fellows meet girls whom they don't marry!

AMANDA. Oh, talk sensibly, Tom—and don't be sarcastic! (*She has gotten a hairbrush.*)

TOM. What are you doing?

AMANDA. I'm brushing that cow-lick down! What is this young man's position at the warehouse?

TOM (*submitting grimly to the brush and the interrogation*). This young man's position is that of a shipping clerk, Mother.

AMANDA. Sounds to me like a fairly responsible job, the sort of a job *you* would be in if you just had more *get-up.* What is his salary? Have you got any idea?

TOM. I would judge it to be approximately eighty-five dollars a month.

AMANDA. Well—not princely, but—

TOM. Twenty more than I make.

AMANDA. Yes, how well I know! But for a family man, eighty-five dollars a month is not much more than you can just get by on. . . .

TOM. Yes, but Mr. O'Connor is not a family man.

AMANDA. He might be, mightn't he? Some time in the future?

TOM. I see. Plans and provisions.

AMANDA. You are the only man that I know of who ignores the fact that the future becomes the present, the present the past, and the past turns into everlasting regret if you don't plan for it!

TOM. I will think that over and see what I can make of it.

AMANDA. Don't be supercilious with your mother! Tell me some more about this—what do you call him?

TOM. James D. O'Connor. The D. is for Delaney.

AMANDA. Irish on *both* sides! *Gracious!* And doesn't drink?

TOM. Shall I call him up and ask him right this minute?

AMANDA. The only way to find out about those things is to make discreet inquiries at the proper moment. When I was a girl in Blue Mountain and it was suspected that a young man drank, the girl whose attentions he had been receiving, if any girl *was*, would sometimes speak to the minister of his church, or rather her father would if her father was living, and sort of feel him out on the young man's character. That is the way such things are discreetly handled to keep a young woman from making a tragic mistake!

TOM. Then how did you happen to make a tragic mistake?

AMANDA. That innocent look of your father's had everyone fooled! He *smiled*—the world was *enchanted!* No girl can do worse than put herself at the mercy of a handsome appearance! I hope that Mr. O'Connor is not too good-looking.

TOM. No, he's not too good-looking. He's covered with freckles and hasn't too much of a nose.

AMANDA. He's not right-down homely, though?

TOM. Not right-down homely. Just medium homely, I'd say.

AMANDA. Character's what to look for in a man.

TOM. That's what I've always said, Mother.

AMANDA. You've never said anything of the kind and I suspect you would never give it a thought.

TOM. Don't be suspicious of me.

AMANDA. At least I hope he's the type that's up and coming.

TOM. I think he really goes in for self-improvement.

AMANDA. What reason have you to think so?

TOM. He goes to night school.

AMANDA (*beaming*). Splendid! What does he do, I mean study?

TOM. Radio engineering and public speaking!

AMANDA. Then he has visions of being advanced in the world! Any young man who studies public speaking is aiming to have an executive job some day! And radio engineering? A thing for the future! Both of these facts are very illuminating. Those are the sort of things that a mother should know concerning any young man who comes to call on her daughter. Seriously or—not.

TOM. One little warning. He doesn't know about Laura. I didn't let on that we had dark ulterior motives. I just said, why don't you come have dinner with us? He said okay and that was the whole conversation.

AMANDA. I bet it was! You're eloquent as an oyster. However, he'll know about Laura when he gets here. When he sees how lovely and sweet and pretty she is, he'll thank his lucky stars he was asked to dinner.

TOM. Mother, you mustn't expect too much of Laura.

AMANDA. What do you mean?

TOM. Laura seems all those things to you and me because she's ours and we love her. We don't even notice she's crippled any more.

AMANDA. Don't say crippled! You know that I never allow that word to be used!

TOM. But face facts, Mother. She is and—that's not all—

AMANDA. What do you mean "not all"?

TOM. Laura is very different from other girls.

AMANDA. I think the difference is all to her advantage.

TOM. Not quite all—in the eyes of others—strangers—she's terribly shy and lives in a world of her own and those things make her seem a little peculiar to people outside the house.

AMANDA. Don't say peculiar.

TOM. Face the facts. She is.

(*The Dance-Hall Music Changes to a Tango that Has a Minor and Somewhat Ominous Tone.*)

AMANDA. In what way is she peculiar—may I ask?

TOM (*gently*). She lives in a world of her own—a world of—little glass ornaments, Mother. . . . (*Gets up. Amanda remains holding brush, looking at him, troubled.*) She plays old phonograph records and—that's about all—(*He glances at himself in the mirror and crosses to door.*)

AMANDA (*sharply*). Where are you going?

TOM. I'm going to the movies. (*Out screen door.*)

AMANDA. Not to the movies, every night to the movies! (*Follows quickly to screen door.*) I don't believe you always go to the movies! (*He is gone. Amanda looks worriedly after him for a moment. Then vitality and optimism return and she turns from the door. Crossing to portieres.*) Laura! Laura! (*Laura answers from kitchenette.*)

LAURA. Yes, Mother.

AMANDA. Let those dishes go and come in front! (*Laura appears with dish towel. Gaily.*) Laura, come here and make a wish on the moon!

LAURA (*entering*). Moon—moon?

AMANDA. A little silver slipper of a moon. Look over your left shoulder, Laura, and make a wish! (*Laura looks faintly puzzled as if called out of sleep. Amanda seizes her shoulders and turns her at angle by the door.*) Now! Now, darling, wish!

LAURA. What shall I wish for, Mother?

AMANDA (*her voice trembling and her eyes suddenly filling with tears*). Happiness! Good Fortune!

The violin rises and the stage dims out.

SCENE 6

(*Image: High School Hero.*)

TOM. And so the following evening I brought Jim home to dinner. I had known Jim slightly in high school. In high school Jim was a hero. He had tremendous Irish good nature and vitality with the scrubbed and polished look of white chinaware. He seemed to move in a continual spotlight. He was a star in basketball, captain of the debating club, president of the senior class and the glee club and he sang the male lead in the annual light operas. He was always running or bounding, never just walking. He seemed always at the point of defeating the law of gravity. He was shooting with such velocity through his adolescence that you would logically expect him to arrive at nothing short of the White House by the time he was thirty. But Jim apparently ran into more interference after his graduation from Soldan. His speed had definitely slowed. Six years after he left high school he was holding a job that wasn't much better than mine.

(*Image: Clerk.*)

He was the only one at the warehouse with whom I was on friendly terms. I was valuable to him as someone who could remember his former glory, who had seen him win basketball games and the silver cup in debating. He knew of my secret practice of retiring to a cabinet of the washroom to work on poems when business was slack in the warehouse. He called me Shakespeare. And while the other boys in the warehouse regarded me with suspicious hostility, Jim took a humorous attitude toward me. Gradually his attitude affected the others, their hostility wore off and they also began to smile at me as people smile at an oddly fashioned dog who trots across their path at some distance.

I knew that Jim and Laura had known each other at Soldan, and I had heard Laura speak admiringly of his voice. I didn't know if Jim remembered her or not. In high school Laura had been as unobtrusive as Jim had been astonishing. If he did remember Laura, it was not as my sister, for when I asked him to dinner, he grinned and said, "You know, Shakespeare, I never thought of you as having folks!"

He was about to discover that I did. . . .

(*Light up Stage.*)

(*Legend on Screen: "The Accent of a Coming Foot."*)

Friday evening. It is about five o'clock of a late spring evening which comes "scattering poems in the sky."

A delicate lemony light is in the Wingfield apartment.

Amanda has worked like a Turk in preparation for the gentleman caller. The results are astonishing. The new floor lamp with its rose-silk shade is in place, a colored paper lantern conceals the broken light fixture in the ceiling, new billowing white curtains are at the windows, chintz covers are on chairs and sofa, a pair of new sofa pillows make their initial appearance.

Open boxes and tissue paper are scattered on the floor.

Laura stands in the middle with lifted arms while Amanda crouches before her, adjusting the hem of the new dress, devout and ritualistic. The dress is colored and designed by memory. The arrangement of Laura's hair is changed; it is softer and more becoming. A fragile, unearthly prettiness has come out in Laura: she is like a piece of translucent glass touched by light, given a momentary radiance, not actual, not lasting.

AMANDA (*impatiently*). Why are you trembling?

LAURA. Mother, you've made me so nervous!

AMANDA. How have I made you nervous?

LAURA. By all this fuss! You make it seem so important!

AMANDA. I don't understand you, Laura. You couldn't be satisfied with just sitting home, and yet whenever I try to arrange something for you, you seem to resist it. (*She gets up.*) Now take a look at yourself. No, wait! Wait just a moment—I have an idea!

LAURA. What is it now?

Amanda produces two powder puffs which she wraps in handkerchiefs and stuffs in Laura's bosom.

LAURA. Mother, what are you doing?

AMANDA. They call them "Gay Deceivers"!

LAURA. I won't wear them!

AMANDA. You will!

LAURA. Why should I?

AMANDA. Because, to be painfully honest, your chest is flat.

LAURA. You make it seem like we were setting a trap.

AMANDA. All pretty girls are a trap, a pretty trap, and men expect them to be. (*Legend: "A Pretty Trap."*) Now look at yourself, young lady. This is the prettiest you will ever be! I've got to fix myself now! You're going to be surprised by your mother's appearance! (*She crosses through portieres, humming gaily.*)

Laura moves slowly to the long mirror and stares solemnly at herself. A wind blows the white curtains inward in a slow, graceful motion and with a faint, sorrowful sighing.

AMANDA (*off stage*). It isn't dark enough yet. (*She turns slowly before the mirror with a troubled look.*)

(*Legend on Screen: "This Is My Sister: Celebrate Her with Strings!" Music.*)

AMANDA (*laughing, off*). I'm going to show you something. I'm going to make a spectacular appearance!

LAURA. What is it, Mother?

AMANDA. Possess your soul in patience—you will see! Something I've resurrected from that old trunk! Styles haven't changed so terribly much after all. . . . (*She parts the portieres.*) Now just look at your mother! (*She wears a girlish frock of yellowed voile with a blue silk sash. She carries a bunch of jonquils—the legend of her youth is nearly revived. Feverishly.*) This is the dress in which I led the cotillion. Won the cakewalk twice at Sunset Hill, wore one spring to the Governor's ball in Jackson! See how I sashayed around the ballroom, Laura? (*She raises her skirt and does a mincing step around the room.*) I wore it on Sundays for my gentlemen callers! I had it on the day I met your father— I had malaria fever all that spring. The change of climate from East Tennessee to the Delta—weakened resistance—I had a little temperature all the time—not enough to be serious—just enough to make me restless and giddy! Invitations poured in—parties all over the Delta!—"Stay in bed," said Mother, "you have fever!"— but I just wouldn't.—I took quinine but kept on going, going!—Evenings, dances!—Afternoons, long, long rides! Picnics—lovely!—So lovely, that country in May.—All lacy with dogwood, literally flooded with jonquils!—That was the spring I had the craze for jonquils. Jonquils became an absolute obsession. Mother said, "Honey, there's no more room for jonquils." And still I kept bringing in more jonquils. Whenever, wherever I saw them, I'd say, "Stop! Stop! I see jonquils!" I made the young men help me gather the jonquils! It was a joke, Amanda and her jonquils! Finally there were no more vases to hold them, every available space was filled with jonquils. No vases to hold them? All right, I'll hold them myself! And then I—(*She stops in front of the picture.*) (*Music.*) met your father! Malaria fever and jonquils and then—this—boy. . . . (*She switches on the rose-colored lamp.*) I hope they get here before it starts to rain. (*She crosses upstage and places the jonquils in bowl on table.*) I gave your brother a little extra change so he and Mr. O'Connor could take the service car home.

LAURA (*with altered look*). What did you say his name was?

AMANDA. O'Connor.

LAURA. What is his first name?

AMANDA. I don't remember. Oh, yes, I do. It was—Jim!

Laura sways slightly and catches hold of a chair.

(*Legend on Screen: "Not Jim!"*)

LAURA (*faintly*). Not—Jim!

AMANDA. Yes, that was it, it was Jim! I've never known a Jim that wasn't nice!

(*Music: Ominous.*)

LAURA. Are you sure his name is Jim O'Connor?

AMANDA. Yes. Why?

LAURA. Is he the one that Tom used to know in high school?

AMANDA. He didn't say so. I think he just got to know him at the warehouse.

LAURA. There was a Jim O'Connor we both knew in high school—(*Then, with effort.*) If that is the one that Tom is bringing to dinner—you'll have to excuse me, I won't come to the table.

AMANDA. What sort of nonsense is this?

LAURA. You asked me once if I'd ever liked a boy. Don't you remember I showed you this boy's picture?

AMANDA. You mean the boy you showed me in the year book?

LAURA. Yes, that boy.

AMANDA. Laura, Laura, were you in love with that boy?

LAURA. I don't know, Mother. All I know is I couldn't sit at the table if it was him!

AMANDA. It won't be him! It isn't the least bit likely. But whether it is or not, you will come to the table. You will not be excused.

LAURA. I'll have to be, Mother.

AMANDA. I don't intend to humor your silliness, Laura. I've had too much from you and your brother, both! So just sit down and compose yourself till they come. Tom has forgotten his key so you'll have to let them in, when they arrive.

LAURA (*panicky*). Oh, Mother—*you* answer the door!

AMANDA (*lightly*). I'll be in the kitchen—busy!

LAURA. Oh, Mother, please answer the door, don't make me do it!

AMANDA (*crossing into kitchenette*). I've got to fix the dressing for the salmon. Fuss, fuss—silliness!—over a gentleman caller!

Door swings shut. Laura is left alone.

(*Legend: "Terror!"*)

She utters a low moan and turns off the lamp—sits stiffly on the edge of the sofa, knotting her fingers together.

(*Legend on Screen: "The Opening of a Door!"*)

Tom and Jim appear on the fire-escape steps and climb to landing. Hearing their approach, Laura rises with a panicky gesture. She retreats to the portieres.

The doorbell. Laura catches her breath and touches her throat. Low drums.

AMANDA (*calling*). Laura, sweetheart! The door!

Laura stares at it without moving.

JIM. I think we just beat the rain.

TOM. Uh-huh. (*He rings again, nervously. Jim whistles and fishes for a cigarette.*)

AMANDA (*very, very gaily*). Laura, that is your brother and Mr. O'Connor! Will you let them in, darling?

Laura crosses toward kitchenette door.

LAURA (*breathlessly*). Mother—you go to the door!

Amanda steps out of kitchenette and stares furiously at Laura. She points imperiously at the door.

LAURA. Please, please!

AMANDA (*in a fierce whisper*). What is the matter with you, you silly thing?

LAURA (*desperately*). Please, you answer it, *please*!

AMANDA. I told you I wasn't going to humor you, Laura. Why have you chosen this moment to lose your mind?

LAURA. Please, please, please, you go!

AMANDA. You'll have to go to the door because I can't!

LAURA (*despairingly*). I can't either!

AMANDA. Why?

LAURA. I'm *sick*!

AMANDA. I'm sick, too—of your nonsense! Why can't you and your brother be normal people? Fantastic whims and behavior! (*Tom gives a long ring.*) Preposterous goings on! Can you give me one reason—(*Calls out lyrically.*) COMING! JUST ONE SECOND!—why should you be afraid to open a door? Now you answer it, Laura!

LAURA. Oh, oh, oh . . . (*She returns through the portieres. Darts to the victrola and winds it frantically and turns it on.*)

AMANDA. Laura Wingfield, you march right to that door!

LAURA. Yes—yes, Mother!

A faraway, scratchy rendition of "Dardanella" softens the air and gives her strength to move through it. She slips to the door and draws it cautiously open.

Tom enters with caller, Jim O'Connor.

TOM. Laura, this is Jim. Jim, this is my sister, Laura.

JIM (*stepping inside*). I didn't know that Shakespeare had a sister!

LAURA (*retreating stiff and trembling from the door*). How—how do you do?

JIM (*heartily extending his hand*). Okay!

Laura touches it hesitantly with hers.

JIM. Your hand's cold, Laura!

LAURA. Yes, well—I've been playing the victrola. . . .

JIM. Must have been playing classical music on it! You ought to play a little hot swing music to warm you up!

LAURA. Excuse me—I haven't finished playing the victrola. . . .

She turns awkwardly and hurries into the front room. She pauses a second by the victrola. Then catches her breath and darts through the portieres like a frightened deer.

JIM (*grinning*). What was the matter?

TOM. Oh—with Laura? Laura is—terribly shy.

JIM. Shy, huh? It's unusual to meet a shy girl nowadays. I don't believe you ever mentioned you had a sister.

TOM. Well, now you know. I have one. Here is the *Post Dispatch*. You want a piece of it?

JIM. Uh-huh.

TOM. What piece? The comics?

JIM. Sports! (*Glances at it.*) Ole Dizzy Dean is on his bad behavior.

TOM (*disinterest*). Yeah? (*Lights cigarette and crosses back to fire-escape door.*)

JIM. Where are *you* going?

TOM. I'm going out on the terrace.

JIM (*goes after him*). You know, Shakespeare—I'm going to sell you a bill of goods!

TOM. What goods?

JIM. A course I'm taking.

TOM. Huh?

JIM. In public speaking! You and me, we're not the warehouse type.

TOM. Thanks—that's good news. But what has public speaking got to do with it?

JIM. It fits you for—executive positions!

TOM. Awww.

JIM. I tell you it's done a helluva lot for me.

(*Image: Executive at Desk.*)

TOM. In what respect?

JIM. In every! Ask yourself what is the difference between you an' me and men in the office down front? Brains?—No!—Ability?—No! Then what? Just one little thing—

TOM. What is that one little thing?

JIM. Primarily it amounts to—social poise! Being able to square up to people and hold your own on any social level!

AMANDA (*off stage*). Tom?

TOM. Yes, Mother?

AMANDA. Is that you and Mr. O'Connor?

TOM. Yes, Mother.

AMANDA. Well, you just make yourselves comfortable in there.

TOM. Yes, Mother.

AMANDA. Ask Mr. O'Connor if he would like to wash his hands.

JIM. Aw—no—no—thank you—I took care of that at the warehouse. Tom—

TOM. Yes?

JIM. Mr. Mendoza was speaking to me about you.

TOM. Favorably?

JIM. What do you think?

TOM. Well—

JIM. You're going to be out of a job if you don't wake up.

TOM. I am waking up—

JIM. You show no signs.

TOM. The signs are interior.

(*Image on Screen: The Sailing Vessel with Jolly Roger Again.*)

TOM. I'm planning to change. (*He leans over the rail speaking with quiet exhilaration. The incandescent marquees and signs of the first-run movie houses light his face from across the alley. He looks like a voyager.*) I'm right at the point of committing myself to a future that doesn't include the warehouse and Mr. Mendoza or even a night-school course in public speaking.

JIM. What are you gassing about?

TOM. I'm tired of the movies.

JIM. Movies!

TOM. Yes, movies! Look at them—(*A wave toward the marvels of Grand Avenue.*) All of those glamorous people—having adventures—hogging it all, gobbling the whole thing up! You know what happens? People go to the *movies* instead of *moving*! Hollywood characters are supposed to have all the adventures for everybody in America, while everybody in America sits in a dark room and watches them have them! Yes, until there's a war. That's when adventure becomes available to the masses! *Everyone's* dish, not only Gable's! Then the people in the dark room come out of the dark room to have some adventures themselves—Goody, goody—It's our turn now, to go to the South Sea Island—to make a safari—to be exotic, far-off—But I'm not patient. I don't want to wait till then. I'm tired of the *movies* and I am *about to move*!

JIM (*incredulously*). Move?

TOM. Yes.

JIM. When?

TOM. Soon!

JIM. Where? Where?

(*Theme Three: Music Seems to Answer the Question, while Tom Thinks it Over. He Searches among his Pockets.*)

TOM. I'm starting to boil inside. I know I seem dreamy, but inside—well, I'm boiling! Whenever I pick up a shoe, I shudder a little thinking how short life is and what I am doing!—Whatever that means. I know it doesn't mean shoes—except as something to wear on a traveler's feet (*Finds paper.*) Look—

JIM. What?

TOM. I'm a member.

JIM (*reading*). The Union of Merchant Seamen.

TOM. I paid my dues this month, instead of the light bill.

JIM. You will regret it when they turn the lights off.

TOM. I won't be here.

JIM. How about your mother?

TOM. I'm like my father. The bastard son of a bastard! See how he grins? And he's been absent going on sixteen years!

JIM. You're just talking, you drip. How does your mother feel about it?

TOM. Shhh—Here comes Mother! Mother is not acquainted with my plans!

AMANDA (*enters portieres*). Where are you all?

TOM. On the terrace, Mother.

They start inside. She advances to them. Tom is distinctly shocked at her appearance. Even Jim blinks a little. He is making his first contact with girlish Southern vivacity and in spite of the night-school course in public speaking is somewhat thrown off the beam by the unexpected outlay of social charm.

Certain responses are attempted by Jim but are swept aside by Amanda's gay laughter and chatter. Tom is em-

barrassed but after the first shock Jim reacts very warmly. Grins and chuckles, is altogether won over.

(*Image: Amanda as a Girl.*)

AMANDA (*coyly smiling, shaking her girlish ringlets*). Well, well, well, so this is Mr. O'Connor. Introductions entirely unnecessary. I've heard so much about you from my boy. I finally said to him, Tom—good gracious!—why don't you bring this paragon to supper? I'd like to meet this nice young man at the warehouse!—Instead of just hearing him sing your praises so much! I don't know why my son is so standoffish—that's not Southern behavior! Let's sit down and—I think we could stand a little more air in here! Tom, leave the door open. I felt a nice fresh breeze a moment ago. Where has it gone? Mmm, so warm already! And not quite summer, even. We're going to burn up when summer really gets started. However, we're having—we're having a very light supper. I think light things are better fo' this time of year. The same as light clothes are. Light clothes an' light food are what warm weather calls fo'. You know our blood gets so thick during th' winter—it takes a while fo' us to *adjust* ou'selves!—when the season changes. . . . It's come so quick this year. I wasn't prepared. All of a sudden—heavens! Already summer!—I ran to the trunk an' pulled out this light dress—Terribly old! Historical almost! But feels so good—so good an' co-ol, y'know. . . .

TOM. Mother—

AMANDA. Yes, honey?

TOM. How about—supper?

AMANDA. Honey, you go ask Sister if supper is ready! You know that Sister is in full charge of supper! Tell her you hungry boys are waiting for it. (*To Jim.*) Have you met Laura?

JIM. She—

AMANDA. Let you in? Oh, good, you've met already! It's rare for a girl as sweet an' pretty as Laura to be domestic! But Laura is, thank heavens, not only pretty but also very domestic. I'm not at all. I never was a bit. I never could make a thing but angel-food cake. Well, in the South we had so many servants. Gone, gone, gone. All vestiges of gracious living! Gone completely! I wasn't prepared for what the future brought me. All of my gentlemen callers were sons of planters and so of course I assumed that I would be married to one and raise my family on a large piece of land with plenty of servants. But man proposes—and woman accepts the proposal!—To vary that old, old saying a little bit—I married no planter! I married a man who worked for the telephone company!—that gallantly smiling gentleman over there! (*Points to the picture.*) A telephone man who—fell in love with long distance!—Now he travels and I don't even know where!—But what am I going on for about my—tribulations! Tell me yours—I hope you don't have any! Tom?

TOM (*returning*). Yes, Mother?

AMANDA. Is supper nearly ready?

TOM. It looks to me like supper is on the table.

AMANDA. Let me look—(*She rises prettily and looks through portieres.*) Oh, lovely—But where is Sister?

TOM. Laura is not feeling well and she says that she thinks she'd better not come to the table.

AMANDA. What?—Nonsense!—Laura? Oh, Laura!

LAURA (*off stage, faintly*). Yes, Mother.

AMANDA. You really must come to the table. We won't be seated until you come to the table! Come in, Mr. O'Connor. You sit over there and I'll—Laura? Laura Wingfield! You're keeping us waiting, honey! We can't say grace until you come to the table!

The back door is pushed weakly open and Laura comes in. She is obviously quite faint, her lips trembling, her eyes wide and staring. She moves unsteadily toward the table.

(*Legend: "Terror!"*)

Outside a summer storm is coming abruptly. The white curtains billow inward at the windows and there is a sorrowful murmur and deep blue dusk.

Laura suddenly stumbles—She catches a chair with a faint moan.

TOM. Laura!

AMANDA. Laura! (*There is a clap of thunder.*) (*Legend: "Ah!"*) (*Despairingly.*) Why, Laura, you *are* sick, darling! Tom, help your sister into the living room, dear! Sit in the living room, Laura—rest on the sofa. Well! (*To the gentleman caller.*) Standing over the hot stove made her ill!—I told her that it was just too warm this evening, but—(*Tom comes back in. Laura is on the sofa.*) Is Laura all right now?

TOM. Yes.

AMANDA. What is that? Rain? A nice cool rain has come up! (*She gives the gentleman caller a frightened look.*) I think we may—have grace—now . . . (*Tom looks at her stupidly.*) Tom, honey—you say grace!

TOM. Oh . . . "For these and all thy mercies—" (*They bow their heads, Amanda stealing a nervous glance at Jim. In the living room Laura, stretched on the sofa, clenches her hand to her lips, to hold back a shuddering sob.*) God's Holy Name be praised—

(*The Scene Dims Out.*)

SCENE 7

A Souvenir

Half an hour later. Dinner is just being finished in the upstage area which is concealed by the drawn portieres.

As the curtain rises Laura is still huddled upon the sofa, her feet drawn under her, her head resting on a pale blue pillow, her eyes wide and mysteriously watchful. The new floor lamp with its shade of rose-colored silk gives a soft,

becoming light to her face, bringing out the fragile, unearthly prettiness which usually escapes attention. There is a steady murmur of rain, but it is slackening and stops soon after the scene begins; the air outside becomes pale and luminous as the moon breaks out.

A moment after the curtain rises, the lights in both rooms flicker and go out.

JIM. Hey, there, Mr. Light Bulb!

Amanda laughs nervously.

(*Legend: "Suspension of a Public Service."*)

AMANDA. Where was Moses when the lights went out? Haha. Do you know the answer to that one, Mr. O'Connor?

JIM. No, Ma'am, what's the answer?

AMANDA. In the dark! (*Jim laughs appreciatively.*) Everybody sit still. I'll light the candles. Isn't it lucky we have them on the table? Where's a match? Which of you gentlemen can provide a match?

JIM. Here.

AMANDA. Thank you, sir.

JIM. Not at all, Ma'am!

AMANDA. I guess the fuse has burnt out. Mr. O'Connor, can you tell a burnt-out fuse? I know I can't and Tom is a total loss when it comes to mechanics. (*Sound: Getting Up: Voices Recede a Little to Kitchenette.*) Oh, be careful you don't bump into something. We don't want our gentleman caller to break his neck. Now wouldn't that be a fine howdy-do?

JIM. Ha-ha! Where is the fuse-box?

AMANDA. Right here next to the stove. Can you see anything?

JIM. Just a minute.

AMANDA. Isn't electricity a mysterious thing? Wasn't it Benjamin Franklin who tied a key to a kite? We live in such a mysterious universe, don't we? Some people say that science clears up all the mysteries for us. In my opinion it only creates more! Have you found it yet?

JIM. No, Ma'am. All these fuses look okay to me.

AMANDA. Tom!

TOM. Yes, Mother?

AMANDA. That light bill I gave you several days ago. The one I told you we got the notices about?

TOM. Oh.—Yeah.

(*Legend: "Ha!"*)

AMANDA. You didn't neglect to pay it by any chance?

TOM. Why, I—

AMANDA. Didn't! I might have known it!

JIM. Shakespeare probably wrote a poem on that light bill, Mrs. Wingfield.

AMANDA. I might have known better than to trust him with it! There's such a high price for negligence in this world!

JIM. Maybe the poem will win a ten-dollar prize.

AMANDA. We'll just have to spend the remainder of the evening in the nineteenth century, before Mr. Edison made the Mazda lamp!

JIM. Candlelight is my favorite kind of light.

AMANDA. That shows you're romantic! But that's no excuse for Tom. Well, we got through dinner. Very considerate of them to let us get through dinner before they plunged us into everlasting darkness, wasn't it, Mr. O'Connor?

JIM. Ha-ha!

AMANDA. Tom, as a penalty for your carelessness you can help me with the dishes.

JIM. Let me give you a hand.

AMANDA. Indeed you will not!

JIM. I ought to be good for something.

AMANDA. Good for something? (*Her tone is rhapsodic.*) You? Why, Mr. O'Connor, nobody, *nobody's* given me this much entertainment in years—as you have!

JIM. Aw, now, Mrs. Wingfield!

AMANDA. I'm not exaggerating, not one bit! But Sister is all by her lonesome. You go keep her company in the parlor! I'll give you this lovely old candelabrum that used to be on the altar at the church of the Heavenly Rest. It was melted a little out of shape when the church burnt down. Lightning struck it one spring. Gypsy Jones was holding a revival at the time and he intimated that the church was destroyed because the Episcopalians gave card parties.

JIM. Ha-ha.

AMANDA. And how about coaxing Sister to drink a little wine? I think it would be good for her! Can you carry both at once?

JIM. Sure. I'm Superman!

AMANDA. Now, Thomas, get into this apron!

The door of kitchenette swings closed on Amanda's gay laughter; the flickering light approaches the portieres.

Laura sits up nervously as he enters. Her speech at first is low and breathless from the almost intolerable strain of being alone with a stranger.

(*Legend: "I Don't Suppose You Remember Me at All!"*)

In her first speeches in this scene, before Jim's warmth overcomes her paralyzing shyness, Laura's voice is thin and breathless as though she has run up a steep flight of stairs.

Jim's attitude is gently humorous. In playing this scene it should be stressed that while the incident is apparently unimportant, it is to Laura the climax of her secret life.

JIM. Hello, there, Laura.

LAURA (*faintly*). Hello. (*She clears her throat.*)

JIM. How are you feeling now? Better?

LAURA. Yes. Yes, thank you.

JIM. This is for you. A little dandelion wine. (*He extends it toward her with extravagant gallantry.*)

LAURA. Thank you.

JIM. Drink it—but don't get drunk! (*He laughs heartily. Laura takes the glass uncertainly; laughs shyly.*) Where shall I set the candles?

LAURA. Oh—oh, anywhere . . .

JIM. How about here on the floor? Any objections?

LAURA. No.

JIM. I'll spread a newspaper under to catch the drippings. I like to sit on the floor. Mind if I do?

LAURA. Oh, no.

JIM. Give me a pillow?

LAURA. What?

JIM. A pillow!

LAURA. Oh . . . (*Hands him one quickly.*)

JIM. How about you? Don't you like to sit on the floor?

LAURA. Oh—yes.

JIM. Why don't you, then?

LAURA. I—will.

JIM. Take a pillow! (*Laura does. Sits on the other side of the candelabrum. Jim crosses his legs and smiles engagingly at her.*) I can't hardly see you sitting way over there.

LAURA. I can—see you.

JIM. I know, but that's not fair, I'm in the limelight. (*Laura moves her pillow closer.*) Good! Now I can see you! Comfortable?

LAURA. Yes.

JIM. So am I. Comfortable as a cow. Will you have some gum?

LAURA. No, thank you.

JIM. I think that I will indulge, with your permission. (*Musingly unwraps it and holds it up.*) Think of the fortune made by the guy that invented the first piece of chewing gum. Amazing, huh? The Wrigley Building is one of the sights of Chicago.—I saw it summer before last when I went up to the Century of Progress. Did you take in the Century of Progress?

LAURA. No, I didn't.

JIM. Well, it was quite a wonderful exposition. What impressed me most was the Hall of Science. Gives you an idea of what the future will be in America, even more wonderful than the present time is! (*Pause. Smiling at her.*) Your brother tells me you're shy. Is that right, Laura?

LAURA. I—don't know.

JIM. I judge you to be an old-fashioned type of girl. Well, I think that's a pretty good type to be. Hope you don't think I'm being too personal—do you?

LAURA (*hastily, out of embarrassment*). I believe I *will* take a piece of gum, if you—don't mind. (*Clearing her throat.*) Mr. O'Connor, have you—kept up with your singing?

JIM. Singing? Me?

LAURA. Yes. I remember what a beautiful voice you had.

JIM. When did you hear me sing?

(*Voice Offstage in the Pause*)

VOICE (*offstage*).
O blow, ye winds, heigh-ho.
A-roving I will go!
I'm off to my love
With a boxing glove—
Ten thousand miles away!

JIM. You say you've heard me sing?

LAURA. Oh, yes! Yes, very often . . . I—don't suppose you remember me—at all?

JIM (*smiling doubtfully*). You know I have an idea I've seen you before. I had that idea soon as you opened the door. It seemed almost like I was about to remember your name. But the name that I started to call you—wasn't a name! And so I stopped myself before I said it.

LAURA. Wasn't it—Blue Roses?

JIM (*springs up, grinning*). Blue Roses! My gosh, yes—Blue Roses! That's what I had on my tongue when you opened the door! Isn't it funny what tricks your memory plays? I didn't connect you with the high school some-how or other. But that's where it was; it was high school. I didn't even know you were Shakespeare's sister! Gosh, I'm sorry.

LAURA. I didn't expect you to. You—barely knew me!

JIM. But we did have a speaking acquaintance, huh?

LAURA. Yes, we—spoke to each other.

JIM. When did you recognize me?

LAURA. Oh, right away!

JIM. Soon as I came in the door?

LAURA. When I heard your name I thought it was probably you. I knew that Tom used to know you a little in high school. So when you came in the door—Well, then I was—sure.

JIM. Why didn't you *say* something, then?

LAURA (*breathlessly*). I didn't know what to say, I was—too surprised!

JIM. For goodness' sakes! You know, this sure is funny!

LAURA. Yes! Yes, isn't it, though. . . .

JIM. Didn't we have a class in something together?

LAURA. Yes, we did.

JIM. What class was that?

LAURA. It was—singing—Chorus!

JIM. Aw!

LAURA. I sat across the aisle from you in the Aud.

JIM. Aw.

LAURA. Mondays, Wednesdays and Fridays.

JIM. Now I remember—you always came in late.

LAURA. Yes, it was so hard for me, getting upstairs. I had a brace on my leg—it clumped so loud!

JIM. I never heard any clumping.

LAURA (*wincing at the recollection*). To me it sounded like—thunder!

JIM. Well, well, well. I never even noticed.

LAURA. And everybody was seated before I came in. I had to walk in front of all those people. My seat was in the back row. I had to go clumping all the way up the aisle with everyone watching!

JIM. You shouldn't have been self-conscious.

LAURA. I know, but I was. It was always such a relief when the singing started.

JIM. Aw, yes, I've placed you now! I used to call you Blue Roses. How was it that I got started calling you that?

LAURA. I was out of school a little while with pleurosis. When I came back you asked me what was the matter. I said I had pleurosis—you thought I said Blue Roses. That's what you always called me after that!

JIM. I hope you didn't mind.

LAURA. Oh, no—I liked it. You see, I wasn't acquainted with many—people. . . .

JIM. As I remember you sort of stuck by yourself.

LAURA. I—I—never had much luck at—making friends.

JIM. I don't see why you wouldn't.

LAURA. Well, I—started out badly.

JIM. You mean being—

LAURA. Yes, it sort of—stood between me—

JIM. You shouldn't have let it!

LAURA. I know, but it did, and—

JIM. You were shy with people!

LAURA. I tried not to be but never could—

JIM. Overcome it?

LAURA. No, I—I never could!

JIM. I guess being shy is something you have to work out of kind of gradually.

LAURA (*sorrowfully*). Yes—I guess it—

JIM. Takes time!

LAURA. Yes—

JIM. People are not so dreadful when you know them. That's what you have to remember! And everybody has prob-lems, not just you, but practically everybody has got some problems. You think of yourself as having the only prob-lems, as being the only one who is disappointed. But just look around you and you will see lots of people as disap-pointed as you are. For instance, I hoped when I was going to high school that I would be further along at this time, six years after, than I am now—You remember that wonderful write-up I had in *The Torch*?

LAURA. Yes! (*She rises and crosses to table.*)

JIM. It said I was bound to succeed in anything I went into! (*Laura returns with the annual.*) Holy Jeez! *The Torch!* (*He accepts it reverently. They smile across it with mutual won-der. Laura crouches beside him and they begin to turn through it. Laura's shyness is dissolving in his warmth.*)

LAURA. Here you are in *Pirates of Penzance!*

JIM (*wistfully*). I sang the baritone lead in that operetta.

LAURA (*rapidly*). So—*beautifully!*

JIM (*protesting*). Aw—

LAURA. Yes, yes—beautifully—beautifully!

JIM. You heard me?

LAURA. All three times!

JIM. No!

LAURA. Yes!

JIM. All three performances?

LAURA (*looking down*). Yes.

JIM. Why?

LAURA. I—wanted to ask you to—autograph my program.

JIM. Why didn't you ask me to?

LAURA. You were always surrounded by your own friends so much that I never had a chance to.

JIM. You should have just—

LAURA. Well, I—thought you might think I was—

JIM. Thought I might think you was—what?

LAURA. Oh—

JIM (*with reflective relish*). I was beleaguered by females in those days.

LAURA. You were terribly popular!

JIM. Yeah—

LAURA. You had such a—friendly way—

JIM. I was spoiled in high school.

LAURA. Everybody—liked you!

JIM. Including you?

LAURA. I—yes, I—I did, too—(*She gently closes the book in her lap.*)

JIM. Well, well, well!—Give me that program, Laura. (*She hands it to him. He signs it with a flourish.*) There you are—better late than never!

LAURA. Oh, I—what a—surprise!

JIM. My signature isn't worth very much right now. But some day—maybe—it will increase in value! Being disappointed is one thing and being discouraged is something else. I am disappointed but I'm not discouraged. I'm twenty-three years old. How old are you?

LAURA. I'll be twenty-four in June.

JIM. That's not old age!

LAURA. No, but—

JIM. You finished high school?

LAURA (*with difficulty*). I didn't go back.

JIM. You mean you dropped out?

LAURA. I made bad grades in my final examinations. (*She rises and replaces the book and the program. Her voice strained.*) How is—Emily Meisenbach getting along?

JIM. Oh, that kraut-head!

LAURA. Why do you call her that?

JIM. That's what she was.

LAURA. You're not still—going with her?

JIM. I never see her.

LAURA. It said in the Personal Section that you were—engaged!

JIM. I know, but I wasn't impressed by that—propaganda!

LAURA. It wasn't—the truth?

JIM. Only in Emily's optimistic opinion!

LAURA. Oh—

(*Legend: "What Have You Done since High School?"*)

Jim lights a cigarette and leans indolently back on his elbows smiling at Laura with a warmth and charm which light her inwardly with altar candles. She remains by the table and turns in her hands a piece of glass to cover her tumult.

JIM (*after several reflective puffs on a cigarette*). What have you done since high school? (*She seems not to hear him.*) Huh? (*Laura looks up.*) I said what have you done since high school, Laura?

LAURA. Nothing much.

JIM. You must have been doing something these six long years.

LAURA. Yes.

JIM. Well, then, such as what?

LAURA. I took a business course at business college—

JIM. How did that work out?

LAURA. Well, not very—well—I had to drop out, it gave me—indigestion—

Jim laughs gently.

JIM. What are you doing now?

LAURA. I don't do anything—much. Oh, please don't think I sit around doing nothing! My glass collection takes up a good deal of my time. Glass is something you have to take good care of.

JIM. What did you say—about glass?

LAURA. Collection I said—I have one—(*She clears her throat and turns away again, acutely shy.*)

JIM (*abruptly*). You know what I judge to be the trouble with you? Inferiority complex! Know what that is? That's what they call it when someone low-rates himself! I understand it because I had it, too. Although my case was not so aggravated as yours seems to be. I had it until I took up public speaking, developed my voice, and learned that I had an aptitude for science. Before that time I never thought of myself as being outstanding in any way whatsoever! Now I've never made a regular study of it, but I have a friend who says I can analyze people better than doctors that make a profession of it. I don't claim that to be necessarily true, but I can sure guess a person's psychology, Laura! (*Takes out his gum.*) Excuse me, Laura. I always take it out when the flavor is gone. I'll use this scrap of paper to wrap it in. I know how it is to get it stuck on a shoe. Yep—that's what I judge to be your principal trouble. A lack of confidence in yourself as a person. You don't have the proper amount of faith in yourself. I'm basing that fact on a number of your remarks and also on certain observations I've made. For instance that clumping you thought was so awful in high school. You say that you even dreaded to walk into class. You see what you did? You dropped out of school, you gave up an education because of a clump, which as far as I know was practically nonexistent! A little physical defect is what you have. Hardly noticeable even! Magnified thousands of times by imagination! You know what my strong advice to you is? Think of yourself as *superior* in some way!

LAURA. In what way would I think?

JIM. Why, man alive, Laura! Just look about you a little. What do you see? A world full of common people! All of 'em born and all of 'em going to die! Which of them has one-tenth of your good points! Or mine! Or anyone else's, as far as that goes—Gosh! Everybody excels in some one thing. Some in many! (*Unconsciously glances at himself in the mirror.*) All you've got to do is discover in *what!* Take me, for instance. (*He adjusts his tie at the mirror.*) My interest happens to lie in electrodynamics. I'm taking a course in radio engineering at night school, Laura, on top of a fairly responsible job at the warehouse. I'm taking that course and studying public speaking.

LAURA. Ohhhh.

JIM. Because I believe in the future of television! (*Turning back to her.*) I wish to be ready to go up right along with it. Therefore I'm planning to get in on the ground floor. In fact, I've already made the right connections and all that remains is for the industry itself to get under way! Full steam—(*His eyes are starry.*) Knowledge—Zzzzzp! Money—Zzzzzzp!—Power! That's the cycle democracy is built on! (*His attitude is convincingly dynamic. Laura stares at him, even her shyness eclipsed in her absolute wonder. He suddenly grins.*) I guess you think I think a lot of myself!

LAURA. No—o-o-o, I—

JIM. Now how about you? Isn't there something you take more interest in than anything else?

LAURA. Well, I do—as I said—have my—glass collection—

A peal of girlish laughter from the kitchen.

JIM. I'm not right sure I know what you're talking about. What kind of glass is it?

LAURA. Little articles of it, they're ornaments mostly! Most of them are little animals made out of glass, the tiniest little animals in the world. Mother calls them a glass menagerie! Here's an example of one, if you'd like to see it! This one is one of the oldest. It's nearly thirteen. (*He stretches out his hand.*) (*Music: "The Glass Menagerie."*) Oh, be careful—if you breathe, it breaks!

JIM. I'd better not take it. I'm pretty clumsy with things.

LAURA. Go on, I trust you with him! (*Places it in his palm.*) There now—you're holding him gently! Hold him over the light, he loves the light! You see how the light shines through him?

JIM. It sure does shine!

LAURA. I shouldn't be partial, but he is my favorite one.

JIM. What kind of a thing is this one supposed to be?

LAURA. Haven't you noticed the single horn on his forehead?

JIM. A unicorn, huh?

LAURA. Mmm-hmmm!

JIM. Unicorns, aren't they extinct in the modern world?

LAURA. I know!

JIM. Poor little fellow, he must feel sort of lonesome.

LAURA (*smiling*). Well, if he does he doesn't complain about it. He stays on a shelf with some horses that don't have horns and all of them seem to get along nicely together.

JIM. How do you know?

LAURA (*lightly*). I haven't heard any arguments among them!

JIM (*grinning*). No arguments, huh? Well, that's a pretty good sign! Where shall I set him?

LAURA. Put him on the table. They all like a change of scenery once in a while!

JIM (*stretching*). Well, well, well, well—Look how big my shadow is when I stretch!

LAURA. Oh, oh, yes—it stretches across the ceiling!

JIM (*crossing to door*). I think it's stopped raining. (*Opens fire-escape door.*) Where does the music come from?

LAURA. From the Paradise Dance Hall across the alley.

JIM. How about cutting the rug a little, Miss Wingfield?

LAURA. Oh, I—

JIM. Or is your program filled up? Let me have a look at it. (*Grasps imaginary card.*) Why, every dance is taken! I'll just have to scratch some out. (*Waltz Music: "La Golondrina."*) Ahhh, a waltz! (*He executes some sweeping turns by himself then holds his arms toward Laura.*)

LAURA (*breathlessly*). I—can't dance!

JIM. There you go, that inferiority stuff!

LAURA. I've never danced in my life!

JIM. Come on, try!

LAURA. Oh, but I'd step on you!

JIM. I'm not made out of glass.

LAURA. How—how—how do we start?

JIM. Just leave it to me. You hold your arms out a little.

LAURA. Like this?

JIM. A little bit higher. Right. Now don't tighten up, that's the main thing about it—relax.

LAURA (*laughing breathlessly*). It's hard not to.

JIM. Okay.

LAURA. I'm afraid you can't budge me.

JIM. What do you bet I can't? (*He swings her into motion.*)

LAURA. Goodness, yes, you can!

LAURA. Let yourself go, now, Laura, just let yourself go.

LAURA. I'm—

JIM. Come on!

LAURA. Trying!

JIM. Not so stiff—Easy does it!

LAURA. I know but I'm—

JIM. Loosen th' backbone! There now, that's a lot better.

LAURA. Am I?

JIM. Lots, lots better! (*He moves her about the room in a clumsy waltz.*)

LAURA. Oh, my!

JIM. Ha-ha!

LAURA. Goodness, yes you can!

JIM. Ha-ha-ha! (*They suddenly bump into the table. Jim stops.*) What did we hit on?

LAURA. Table.

JIM. Did something fall off it? I think—

LAURA. Yes.

JIM. I hope that it wasn't the little glass horse with the horn!

LAURA. Yes.

JIM. Aw, aw, aw. Is it broken?

LAURA. Now it is just like all the other horses.

JIM. It's lost its—

LAURA. Horn! It doesn't matter. Maybe it's a blessing in disguise.

JIM. You'll never forgive me. I bet that that was your favorite piece of glass.

LAURA. I don't have favorites much. It's no tragedy, Freckles. Glass breaks so easily. No matter how careful you are. The traffic jars the shelves and things fall off them.

JIM. Still I'm awfully sorry that I was the cause.

LAURA (*smiling*). I'll just imagine he had an operation. The horn was removed to make him feel less—freakish! (*They both laugh.*) Now he will feel more at home with the other horses, the ones that don't have horns . . .

JIM. Ha-ha, that's very funny! (*Suddenly serious.*) I'm glad to see that you have a sense of humor. You know—you're—well—very different! Surprisingly different from anyone else I know! (*His voice becomes soft and hesitant with a genuine feeling.*) Do you mind me telling you that? (*Laura is abashed beyond speech.*) You make me feel sort of—I don't know how to put it! I'm usually pretty good at expressing things, but—This is something that I don't know how to say! (*Laura touches her throat and clears it—turns the broken unicorn in her hands.*) (*Even softer.*) Has anyone ever told you that you were pretty? (*Pause: Music.*) (*Laura looks up slowly, with wonder, and shakes her head.*) Well, you are! In a very different way from anyone else. And all the nicer because of the difference, too. (*His voice becomes low and husky. Laura turns away, nearly faint with the novelty of her emotions.*) I wish that you were my sister. I'd teach you to have some confidence in yourself. The different people are not like other people, but being different is nothing to be ashamed of. Because other people are not such wonderful people. They're one hundred times one thousand. You're one times one! They walk all over the earth. You just stay here. They're common as—weeds, but—you—well, you're *Blue Roses*!

(*Image on Screen: Blue Roses.*)

(*Music Changes.*)

LAURA. But blue is wrong for—roses . . .

JIM. It's right for you—You're—pretty!

LAURA. In what respect am I pretty?

JIM. In all respects—believe me! Your eyes—your hair—are pretty! Your hands are pretty! (*He catches hold of her hand.*) You think I'm making this up because I'm invited to dinner and have to be nice. Oh, I could do that! I could put on an act for you, Laura, and say lots of things without being very sincere. But this time I am. I'm talking to you sincerely. I happened to notice you had this inferiority complex that keeps you from feeling comfortable with people. Somebody needs to build your confidence up and make you proud instead of shy and turning away and—blushing—Somebody ought to—ought to—kiss you. Laura! (*His hand slips slowly up her arm to her shoulder.*) (*Music Swells Tumultuously.*) (*He suddenly turns her about and kisses her on the lips. When he releases her Laura sinks on the sofa with a bright, dazed look. Jim backs away and fishes in his pocket for a cigarette.*) (*Legend on Screen: "Souvenir."*) Stumble-john! (*He lights the cigarette, avoiding her look. There is a peal of girlish laughter from Amanda in the kitchen. Laura slowly raises and opens her hand. It still contains the little broken glass animal. She looks at it with a tender, bewildered expression.*) Stumble-john! I shouldn't have done that—That was way off the beam. You don't smoke, do you? (*She looks up, smiling, not hearing the question. He sits beside her a little gingerly. She looks at him speechlessly—waiting. He coughs decorously and moves a little farther aside as he considers the situation and senses her feelings, dimly, with perturbation. Gently.*) Would you—care for a—mint? (*She doesn't seem to hear him but her look grows brighter even.*) Peppermint—Life Saver? My pocket's a regular drug store—wherever I go . . . (*He pops a mint in his mouth. Then gulps and decides to make a clean breast of it. He speaks slowly and gingerly.*) Laura, you know, if I had a sister like you, I'd do the same thing as Tom. I'd bring out fellows—introduce her to them. The right type of boys of a type to—appreciate her. Only—well—he made a mistake about me. Maybe I've got no call to be saying this. That may not have been the idea in having me over. But what if it was? There's nothing wrong about that. The only trouble is that in my case—I'm not in a situation to—do the right thing. I can't take down your number and say I'll phone. I can't call up next week and—ask for a date. I thought I had better explain the situation in case you misunderstood it and—hurt your feelings. . . . (*Pause. Slowly, very slowly, Laura's look changes, her eyes returning slowly from his to the ornament in her palm.*)

Amanda utters another gay laugh in the kitchen.

LAURA (*faintly*). You—won't—call again?

JIM. No, Laura, I can't. (*He rises from the sofa.*) As I was just explaining, I've—got strings on me, Laura, I've—been going steady! I go out all the time with a girl named Betty. She's a home-girl like you, and Catholic, and Irish, and in a great many ways we—get along fine. I met her last summer on a moonlight boat trip up the river to Alton, on the *Majestic*. Well—right away from the start it was—love! (*Legend: Love!*) (*Laura sways slightly forward and grips the arm of the sofa. He fails to notice, now enrapt in his own comfortable being.*) Being in love has made a new man of me! (*Leaning stiffly forward, clutching the arm of the sofa, Laura struggles visibly with her storm. But Jim is oblivious, she is a long way off.*) The power of love is really pretty tremendous! Love is something that—changes the whole world, Laura! (*The storm abates a little and Laura leans back. He notices her again.*) It happened that Betty's aunt took sick, she got a wire and had to go to Centralia. So Tom—when he asked me to dinner—I naturally just accepted the invitation, not knowing that you—that he—that I—(*He stops awkwardly.*) Huh—I'm a stumble-john! (*He flops back on the sofa. The holy candles in the altar of Laura's face have been snuffed out! There is a look of almost infinite desolation. Jim glances at her uneasily.*) I wish that you would—say something. (*She bites her lip which was trembling and then bravely smiles. She opens her hand again on the broken glass ornament. Then she gently takes his hand and raises it level with her own. She carefully places the unicorn in the palm of his hand, then pushes his fingers closed upon it.*) What are you—doing that for? You want me to have him?—Laura? (*She nods.*) What for?

LAURA. A—souvenir . . .

She rises unsteadily and crouches beside the victrola to wind it up.

(*Legend on Screen: "Things Have a Way of Turning Out So Badly."*)

(*Or Image: "Gentleman Caller Waving Good-Bye!—Gaily."*)

At this moment Amanda rushes brightly back in the front room. She bears a pitcher of fruit punch in an old-fashioned cut-glass pitcher and a plate of macaroons. The plate has a gold border and poppies painted on it.

AMANDA. Well, well, well! Isn't the air delightful after the shower? I've made you children a little liquid refreshment. (*Turns gaily to the gentleman caller.*) Jim, do you know that song about lemonade?

"Lemonade, lemonade
Made in the shade and stirred with a spade—
Good enough for any old maid!"

JIM (*uneasily*). Ha-ha! No—I never heard it.
AMANDA. Why, Laura! You look so serious!
JIM. We were having a serious conversation.
AMANDA. Good! Now you're better acquainted!
JIM (*uncertainly*). Ha-ha! Yes.
AMANDA. You modern young people are much more serious-minded than my generation. I was so gay as a girl!

JIM. You haven't changed, Mrs. Wingfield.
AMANDA. Tonight I'm rejuvenated! The gaiety of the occasion, Mr. O'Connor! (*She tosses her head with a peal of laughter. Spills lemonade.*) Oooo! I'm baptizing myself!
JIM. Here—let me—
AMANDA (*setting the pitcher down*). There now. I discovered we had some maraschino cherries. I dumped them in, juice and all!
JIM. You shouldn't have gone to that trouble, Mrs. Wingfield.
AMANDA. Trouble, trouble? Why it was loads of fun! Didn't you hear me cutting up in the kitchen? I bet your ears were burning! I told Tom how outdone with him I was for keeping you to himself so long a time! He should have brought you over much, much sooner! Well, now that you've found your way, I want you to be a very frequent caller! Not just occasional but all the time. Oh, we're going to have a lot of gay times together! I see them coming! Mmm, just breathe that air! So fresh, and the moon's so pretty! I'll skip back out—I know where my place is when young folks are having a—serious conversation!
JIM. Oh, don't go out, Mrs. Wingfield. The fact of the matter is I've got to be going.
AMANDA. Going, now? You're joking! Why, it's only the shank of the evening, Mr. O'Connor!
JIM. Well, you know how it is.
AMANDA. You mean you're a young workingman and have to keep workingmen's hours. We'll let you off early tonight. But only on the condition that next time you stay later. What's the best night for you? Isn't Saturday night the best night for you workingmen?
JIM. I have a couple of time-clocks to punch, Mrs. Wingfield. One at morning, another one at night!
AMANDA. My, but you *are* ambitious! You work at night, too?
JIM. No, Ma'am, not work but—Betty! (*He crosses deliberately to pick up his hat. The band at the Paradise Dance Hall goes into a tender waltz.*)
AMANDA. Betty? Betty? Who's—Betty! (*There is an ominous cracking sound in the sky.*)
JIM. Oh, just a girl. The girl I go steady with! (*He smiles charmingly. The sky falls.*)

(*Legend: "The Sky Falls."*)

AMANDA (*a long-drawn exhalation*). Ohhh . . . Is it a serious romance, Mr. O'Connor?
JIM. We're going to be married the second Sunday in June.
AMANDA. Ohhhh—how nice! Tom didn't mention that you were engaged to be married.
JIM. The cat's not out of the bag at the warehouse yet. You know how they are. They call you Romeo and stuff like that. (*He stops at the oval mirror to put on his hat. He carefully shapes the brim and the crown to give a discreetly dashing effect.*) It's been a wonderful evening, Mrs. Wingfield. I guess this is what they mean by Southern hospitality.

AMANDA. It really wasn't anything at all.

JIM. I hope it don't seem like I'm rushing off. But I promised Betty I'd pick her up at the Wabash depot, an' by the time I get my jalopy down there her train'll be in. Some women are pretty upset if you keep 'em waiting.

AMANDA. Yes, I know—The tyranny of women! (*Extends her hand.*) Good-bye, Mr. O'Connor. I wish you luck—and happiness—and success! All three of them, and so does Laura!—Don't you, Laura?

LAURA. Yes!

JIM (*taking her hand*). Good-bye, Laura. I'm certainly going to treasure that souvenir. And don't you forget the good advice I gave you. (*Raises his voice to a cheery shout.*) So long, Shakespeare! Thanks again, ladies—good night!

He grins and ducks jauntily out.
    Still bravely grimacing, Amanda closes the door on the gentleman caller. Then she turns back to the room with a puzzled expression. She and Laura don't dare to face each other. Laura crouches beside the victrola to wind it.

AMANDA (*faintly*). Things have a way of turning out so badly. I don't believe that I would play the victrola. Well, well—well—Our gentleman caller was engaged to be married! Tom!

TOM (*from back*). Yes, Mother?

AMANDA. Come in here a minute. I want to tell you something awfully funny.

TOM (*enters with macaroon and a glass of the lemonade*). Has the gentleman caller gotten away already?

AMANDA. The gentleman caller has made an early departure. What a wonderful joke you played on us!

TOM. How do you mean?

AMANDA. You didn't mention that he was engaged to be married.

TOM. Jim? Engaged?

AMANDA. That's what he just informed us.

TOM. I'll be jiggered! I didn't know about that.

AMANDA. That seems very peculiar.

TOM. What's peculiar about it?

AMANDA. Didn't you call him your best friend down at the warehouse?

TOM. He is, but how did I know?

AMANDA. It seems extremely peculiar that you wouldn't know your best friend was going to be married!

TOM. The warehouse is where I work, not where I know things about people!

AMANDA. You don't know things anywhere! You live in a dream; you manufacture illusions! (*He crosses to door.*) Where are you going?

TOM. I'm going to the movies.

AMANDA. That's right, now that you've had us make such fools of ourselves. The effort, the preparations, all the expense! The new floor lamp, the rug, the clothes for

Laura! All for what? To entertain some other girl's fiancé! Go to the movies, go! Don't think about us, a mother deserted, an unmarried sister who's crippled and has no job! Don't let anything interfere with your selfish pleasure! Just go, go, go—to the movies!

TOM. All right, I will! The more you shout about my selfishness to me the quicker I'll go, and I won't go to the movies!

AMANDA. Go, then! Then go to the moon—you selfish dreamer!

Tom smashes his glass on the floor. He plunges out on the fire-escape, slamming the door. Laura screams—cut by door.
    Dance-hall music up. Tom goes to the rail and grips it desperately, lifting his face in the chill white moonlight penetrating the narrow abyss of the alley.

(*Legend on Screen: "And So Good-Bye . . ."*)

Tom's closing speech is timed with the interior pantomime. The interior scene is played as though viewed through sound-proof glass. Amanda appears to be making a comforting speech to Laura who is huddled upon the sofa. Now that we cannot hear the mother's speech, her silliness is gone and she has dignity and tragic beauty. Laura's dark hair hides her face until at the end of the speech she lifts it to smile at her mother. Amanda's gestures are slow and graceful, almost dancelike, as she comforts the daughter. At the end of her speech she glances a moment at the father's picture—then withdraws through the portieres. At close of Tom's speech, Laura blows out the candles, ending the play.

TOM. I didn't go to the moon, I went much further—for time is the longest distance between two places—Not long after that I was fired for writing a poem on the lid of a shoe-box. I left Saint Louis. I descended the steps of this fire-escape for a last time and followed, from then on, in my father's footsteps, attempting to find in motion what was lost in space—I traveled around a great deal. The cities swept about me like dead leaves, leaves that were brightly colored but torn away from the branches. I would have stopped, but I was pursued by something. It always came upon me unawares, taking me altogether by surprise. Perhaps it was a familiar bit of music. Perhaps it was only a piece of transparent glass—Perhaps I am walking along a street at night, in some strange city, before I have found companions. I pass the lighted window of a shop where perfume is sold. The window is filled with pieces of colored glass, tiny transparent bottles in delicate colors, like bits of a shattered rainbow. Then all at once my sister touches my shoulder. I turn around and look into her eyes . . . Oh, Laura, Laura, I tried to leave you behind me, but I am more faithful than I intended to be! I reach for a cigarette, I cross the street, I run into the movies or a bar, I buy a drink, I speak to the nearest stranger—anything that can blow your candles out! (*Laura bends over the candles.*)—for nowadays the world is lit by lightning! Blow out your candles, Laura—and so good-bye . . .

She blows the candles out.

(*The Scene Dissolves.*)

Topics for Critical Thinking and Writing

📖 The Play on the Page

1. What does the victrola offer to Laura? Why is the typewriter a better symbol (for the purposes of the play) than, for example, a piano? After all, Laura could have been taking piano lessons.

2. What do you understand of Laura's glass menagerie? Why is it especially significant that the unicorn is Laura's favorite? How do you interpret the loss of the unicorn's horn? What is Laura saying to Jim in the gesture of giving him the unicorn?

3. Laura escapes to her glass menagerie. To what do Tom and Amanda escape? How complete do you think Tom's escape is at the end of the play?

4. Jim is described as "a nice, ordinary young man." To what extent can it be said that he, like the Wingfields, lives in a dream world? Tom says (speaking of the time of the play, 1939) that "The huge middle class was matriculating in a school for the blind." Does the play suggest that Jim, apparently a spokesperson for the American dream, is one of the pupils in this school?

5. There is an implication that had Jim not been going steady he might have rescued Laura, but Jim also seems to represent (for example, in his lines about money and power) the corrupt outside world that no longer values humanity. Is this a slip on Williams's part, or is it an interesting complexity?

6. How do you interpret the episode at the end when Laura blows out the candles? Is she blowing out illusions? her own life? both? Explain.

7. Some readers have seen great importance in the religious references in the play. To cite only a few examples: Scene 5 is called (on the screen) "Annunciation"; Amanda is associated with the music "Ave Maria"; Laura's candelabrum, from the altar of the Church of Heavenly Rest, was melted out of shape when the church burned down. Do you think these references add up to anything? If so, to what?

8. On page 642 Williams says, in a stage direction, "Now that we cannot hear the mother's speech, her silliness is gone and she has dignity and tragic beauty." Is Williams simply dragging in the word "tragic" because of its prestige, or is it legitimate? *Tragedy* is often distinguished from *pathos:* in tragedy, suffering is experienced by persons who act and are in some measure responsible for their suffering; in pathos, suffering is experienced by the passive and the innocent. For example, in discussing *The Suppliants,* a play by the ancient Greek dramatist Aeschylus, H. D. F. Kitto (in *Greek Tragedy*) says, "The Suppliants are not only pathetic, as the victims of outrage, but also tragic, as the victims of their own misconceptions." Given this distinction, to what extent are Amanda and Laura tragic? pathetic? You might take into account the following quote from an interview with Williams, reprinted in *Conversations with Tennessee Williams* (ed. Albert J. Devlin): "The mother's valor is the *core* of *The Glass Menagerie.* . . . She's confused, pathetic, even stupid, but everything has *got* to be all right. She fights to make it that way in the only way she knows how."

9. Before writing *The Glass Menagerie,* Williams wrote a short story with the same plot, "Portrait of a Girl in Glass" (later published in his *Collected Stories*). You may want to compare the two works, noticing especially the ways in which Williams has turned a story into a play.

🎭 The Play on the Stage

10. In what ways is the setting relevant to the issues raised in the play?

11. In his Production Notes (p. 644) Williams called for the use of a "screen device." Over the years, some productions have incorporated it and some have not. If you were involved in producing *The Glass Menagerie,* would you use this device? Explain your reasons.

12. As director, would you want the actress playing Laura to limp? Give reasons for your decision, and provide additional comments on the ways in which you would ask an actress to portray the role.

13. List the various emotions that you find for Amanda in Scenes 2 and 3. If you were advising an actress playing this role, how would you suggest she convey these different feelings? Following are some questions to consider: In what ways does she reveal her own sadnesses? Should her speeches to Tom be delivered differently from her speeches to Laura? When she looks at Laura's yearbook,

should there be any physical contact between the two women? What effect would you wish to achieve at the close of Scene 3?

14. At the end of Scene 5, after an exasperated exchange between Tom and Amanda, Laura and her mother make a wish on the new moon. Three students can memorize this brief section and present it to the group. Then examine each speech, and discuss its emotion. Offer suggestions to the three actors—for instance, changes in emphasis, a slight difference in tone, a certain stance for the mother and daughter—and repeat the scene.

A CONTEXT FOR *THE GLASS MENAGERIE*

Tennessee Williams
PRODUCTION NOTES

Being a "memory play," *The Glass Menagerie* can be presented with unusual freedom of convention. Because of its considerably delicate or tenuous material, atmospheric touches and subtleties of direction play a particularly important part. Expressionism and all other unconventional techniques in drama have only one valid aim, and that is a closer approach to truth. When a play employs unconventional techniques, it is not, or certainly shouldn't be, trying to escape its responsibility of dealing with reality, or interpreting experience, but is actually or should be attempting to find a closer approach, a more penetrating and vivid expression of things as they are. The straight realistic play with its genuine frigidaire and authentic ice cubes, its characters that speak exactly as its audience speaks, corresponds to the academic landscape and has the same virtue of a photographic likeness. Everyone should know nowadays the unimportance of the photographic in art: that truth, life, or reality is an organic thing which the poetic imagination can represent or suggest, in essence, only through transformation, through changing into other forms than those which were merely present in appearance.

These remarks are not meant as comments only on this particular play. They have to do with a conception of a new, plastic theater which must take the place of the exhausted theater of realistic conventions if the theater is to resume vitality as a part of our culture.

THE SCREEN DEVICE

There is *only one important difference between the original and acting version of the play* and that is the *omission* in the latter of the device which I tentatively included in my *original* script. This device was the use of a screen on which were projected magic-lantern slides bearing images or titles. I do not regret the omission of this device from the . . . Broadway production. The extraordinary power of Miss Taylor's performance made it suitable to have the utmost simplicity in the physical production. But I think it may be interesting to some readers to see how this device was conceived. So I am putting it into the published manuscript. These images and legends, projected from behind, were cast on a section of wall between the front-room and dining-room areas, which should be indistinguishable from the rest when not in use.

The purpose of this will probably be apparent. It is to give accent to certain values in each scene. Each scene contains a particular point (or several) which is structurally the most important. In an episodic play, such as this, the basic structure or narrative line may be obscured from the audience; the effect may seem fragmentary rather than architectural. This may not be the fault of the play so much as a lack of attention in the audience. The legend or image upon the screen will strengthen the effect of what is merely allusion in the writing and allow the primary point to be made more simply and lightly than if the entire responsibility were on the spoken lines. Aside from this structural value, I think the screen will have a definite emotional appeal, less definable but just as important. An imaginative producer or director may invent many other uses for this device than those indicated in the present script. In fact the possibilities of the device seem much larger to me than the instance of this play can possibly utilize.

THE MUSIC

Another extra-literary accent in this play is provided by the use of music. A single recurring tune, "The Glass Menagerie," is used to give emotional emphasis to suitable passages. This tune is like circus music, not when you are on the grounds or in the immediate vicinity of the parade, but when you are at some distance and very likely thinking of something else. It seems under those circumstances to continue almost interminably and it weaves in and out of your preoccupied consciousness; then it is the lightest, most delicate music in the world and perhaps the saddest. It expresses the surface vivacity of life with the underlying strain of immutable and inexpressible sorrow. When you look at a piece of delicately spun glass you think of two things: how beautiful it is and how easily it can be broken. Both of those ideas should be woven into the recurring tune, which dips in and out of the play as if it were carried on a wind that changes. It serves as a thread of connection and allusion between the narrator with his separate point in time and space and the subject of his story. Between each episode it returns as reference to the emotion, nostalgia, which is the first condition of the play. It is primarily Laura's music and therefore comes out most clearly when the play focuses upon her and the lovely fragility of glass which is her image.

THE LIGHTING

The lighting in the play is not realistic. In keeping with the atmosphere of memory, the stage is dim. Shafts of light are focused on selected areas or actors, sometimes in contradistinction to what is the apparent center. For instance, in the quarrel scene between Tom and Amanda, in which Laura has no active part, the clearest pool of light is on her figure. This is also true of the supper scene. The light upon Laura should be distinct from the others, having a peculiar pristine clarity such as light used in early religious portraits of female saints or madonnas. A certain correspondence to light in religious paintings, such as El Greco's, where the figures are radiant in atmosphere that is relatively dusky, could be effectively used throughout the play. (It will also permit a more effective use of the screen.) A free, imaginative use of light can be of enormous value in giving a mobile, plastic quality to plays of a more or less static nature.

THE PLAY IN PERFORMANCE

Because *The Glass Menagerie* reads so well and plays so well, it is hard to believe that Williams had a great deal of trouble getting it into its final form. It began as a short story, "Portrait of a Girl in Glass," which was reworked into a one-act play, "If You Breathe, It Breaks! or Portrait of a Girl in Glass." Subsequently, it was modified into a screenplay called *The Gentleman Caller* and then (when the screenplay was rejected) into another version of a stage play. Williams extensively revised this stage play (a manuscript now in the C. Waller Barrett Library at the University of Virginia shows that he used at least six typewriters and added at least four layers of handwritten alterations), but he finally sent it to his agent. It reached the desk of Margo Jones, a director who knew there was (or ought to be) life in the theater outside of New York. Jones liked the script and checked with Eddie Dowling, an actor-director-producer. Dowling liked what he read and agreed to codirect the play with Jones. Dowling played Tom, Julie Haydon played Laura, and Laurette Taylor played Amanda. The choice of Laurette Taylor was bold. She had once been a well-regarded actress, but her career seemed to end when she became an alcoholic, and now she was trying to make a comeback. Jo Mielziner was hired as the designer. A producer was found who put up the money—Louis J. Singer, a man who had never before backed a play—and *The Glass Menagerie* was booked to open in Chicago on December 26, 1944.

Rehearsals did not go well; Taylor had trouble with her lines and with her Southern accent, and as late as Christmas Eve Williams was busy rewriting. At the opening, the theater was only half filled, and applause was polite rather than enthusiastic. The reviews were highly favorable, but for about two weeks the audiences were thin, even though two of the drama critics returned to see the play and again wrote about it enthusiastically. There was talk of closing the play, but eventually the campaign of the critics was successful, and attendance picked up for the remaining performances in Chicago. When *The Glass Menagerie* opened in New York on March 31, 1945, its reputation had preceded it. Tickets were hard to get, and the New York reviews—and audiences—were so favorable that the play ran for 563 performances on Broadway. No one was surprised that *The Glass Menagerie* won the New York Drama Critics' Circle Award as the best American play of the 1944–1945 season, though some people believed that the success was largely due to Laurette Taylor, who won universal applause.

It was soon produced abroad—in 1948 Helen Hayes played the role of Amanda in London, directed by John Gielgud—and in 1950 a film version was made. Among notable New York revivals were those of 1956 with Helen Hayes and 1965 with Maureen Stapleton (both as Amanda), and that of 1980 with Julie Haydon (the original Laura) as Amanda. A New York production in 1983 was rare in the sense that it flashed some lines on a scrim, in accordance with the author's own recommendation in his Production Notes (see p. 644). *The Glass Menagerie* has been made into a film (1950) and into two television versions (CBS in 1966, with Shirley Booth as Amanda, and ABC in 1973, with Katharine Hepburn as Amanda).

The play remains a favorite; quite possibly in the last forty years it has been produced more times in college and university theaters than any other play.

L. L. West
DIRECTING *THE GLASS MENAGERIE*

In April 1982 Larry L. West directed the production of *The Glass Menagerie* at the opening of the Margo Jones Theater on the campus of Texas Woman's University in Denton, Texas. Jones, a graduate of the school and a major figure in the regional theater movement, was a codirector of the first production of *The Glass Menagerie*. In West's production, Maureen Stapleton, who had played Amanda on Broadway, again played the role.

Interviewer: Mr. West, I saw your production of The Glass Menagerie *and I admit that I'm somewhat concerned and confused. Having read the play previously, I fully expected to see the play as it was envisioned by the playwright. What happened?*

West: I think we stayed extremely close to Tennessee Williams' vision.

But he talks about screens and projections. Why did you ignore his stage directions?

We didn't ignore Williams' stage directions, but we were much more interested in his intent—his vision. The original Chicago production was staged in 1944 with the screens; the New York production was reworked in 1945 and again in 1948. Although the screens were removed, the Broadway production held to the playwright's earlier statement that "[t]he play is memory. Being a memory play, it is dimly lighted, it is sentimental, it is not realistic." With great respect for the Broadway production—Margo Jones's production—I felt strongly that our *Glass Menagerie* should be memory-like, even dream-like. At the same time, I felt no obligation or need to incorporate the screens.

Although I was confused about the screens, my concern with your production was what seemed to be a disregard for the play itself.

What do you mean? Can you give me an example?

Sure. When Tom promises to look for a gentleman caller for Laura, Amanda sits down at the telephone with renewed vigor to sell magazine subscriptions. In her speech to Ella Cartwright she is supposed to describe the new serial by Bessie Mae Harper, as the lights fade. Instead, with your production, the scene ends with Amanda apologizing for the hour of the day (7:00 in the morning) and then saying, "You'll take the subscription anyway? Bless you! Bless you!"

But that's the scene . . .

Not the scene I know . . . not the scene I read and re-read after seeing your production. There were lines that I didn't recognize. I can only conclude that something went wrong, that your Amanda (Maureen Stapleton) forgot her lines and was ad-libbing.

Nothing went wrong . . .

The point of the scene is that Amanda, like Laura, is a failure, too, and can't make a living. If she is as aggressive as you interpret her—and Miss Stapleton played her—there is no need for her dependence on Tom.

Again, I need to remind you that the script you "re-read" was the 1944 version of the play. In that edition, Amanda doesn't quite finish her conversation with Ella Cartwright. In 1948 Tennessee Williams expanded the script to include an apology to Ella for the hour of the call and the sale of a magazine subscription. The line reads, "You're going to take that subscription from me anyhow? Well, bless you, Ella, bless you, bless you, bless you." In my opinion, the playwright's choice to expand the scene shows that Amanda's dependence on Tom is more emotional than financial. I believe that makes for better theater.

So, you're telling me that there are two versions of The Glass Menagerie?

At least.

Are they both published?

Although the 1944 edition is the version most commonly published, it doesn't mean that it is the version most frequently performed. In 1948, Tennessee Williams published an "acting edition" of the play that was designed for performance. And just to set the record straight, Maureen Stapleton's memorization was near word-perfect to the 1948 edition.

Be that as it may, I'm not sure that I completely agreed with the casting of Miss Stapleton in the role of Amanda. It is difficult to see her as aggressive. I have always seen her as a vestige of the Old South, unable to cope with the present world and still living in the past. In my mind she has always been frail rather than robust.

Great plays allow actors and directors the wonderful freedom to see characters and plays from a variety of vantage points. Is Hamlet truly mad or merely feigning madness? Is Antigone a spoiled brat or a noble heroine? There is enough "stuff" in *Hamlet* and *Antigone* to warrant hundreds of interpretations. Do you agree?

Of course.

Well, I believe *The Glass Menagerie* is a great play; I might even go so far as to call it a "classic." I think there's abundant "stuff" in the script to buttress myriad interpretations of Amanda. For the 1945 Broadway production, Tennessee Williams selected the wispy and frail Laurette Taylor to play

Amanda. Thirty years later, Tennessee Williams singled out the robust and aggressive Maureen Stapleton to star in the Circle in the Square's revival of his classic play. From all accounts, both productions were equally successful—vastly different, but equally successful. The mark of a superior work of art is in its ability to endure the test of time . . . that, and its capacity to sustain criticism and interpretation. In the years—decades—even centuries to come—I hope that the character of Amanda is a topic of interpretation and debate . . . And I further hope that *The Glass Menagerie* is subject to criticism and illumination.

Arthur Miller

DEATH OF A SALESMAN

Arthur Miller (1915–   ) was born in New York. In 1938 he graduated from the University of Michigan, where he won several prizes for drama. Six years later he had his first Broadway production, *The Man Who Had All the Luck,* but the play was unlucky and closed after four days. By the time of his first commercial success, *All My Sons* (1947), he had already written eight or nine plays. In 1949 he won a Pulitzer Prize with *Death of a Salesman* and achieved an international reputation. Among his other works are an adaptation (1950) of Ibsen's *Enemy of the People* and a play about the Salem witch trials, *The Crucible* (1953), both containing political implications, and *The Misfits* (1961, a screenplay), *After the Fall* (1964), and *Incident at Vichy* (1965).

COMMENTARY

For the ancient Greeks, at least for Aristotle, *pathos* was the destructive or painful act common in tragedy. In English, however, *pathos* refers to an element in art or life that evokes tenderness or sympathetic pity. Modern English critical usage distinguishes between tragic figures and pathetic figures by recognizing some element either of strength or of regeneration in the former that is not in the latter. The tragic protagonists perhaps act so that they bring their destruction upon themselves, or if their destruction comes from outside, they resist it. In either case, they come to at least a partial understanding of the causes of their suffering. Pathetic figures, however, are largely passive, unknowing, and unresisting innocents. In such a view, Macbeth is tragic, but Duncan pathetic. Lear is tragic; Cordelia pathetic. Othello is tragic; Desdemona pathetic. Hamlet is tragic (the situation is not of his making, but he does what he can to alter it); Ophelia pathetic. (Note, by the way, that of the four pathetic figures named, the first is old and the remaining three are women. Pathos is more likely to be evoked by persons assumed to be relatively defenseless than by those who are able-bodied.)

That the spectators were not themselves heroic figures seems to have been assumed by the Greeks and by the Elizabethans; the lesser choral figures or nameless citizens interpret the action and call attention to the fact that even highly placed great heroes are not exempt from pain. Indeed, high place and strenuous activity invite pain: the lofty pine tree or the mariner who ventures far from the coast is more likely to meet destruction than the lowly shrub or the fair-weather sailor. For Greeks of the fifth century B.C. and for Elizabethans, high place was not a mere matter of rank, but of worth. In both ages, it was of course known that a king may be unkingly, but it was assumed that kingship required a special nature—though that nature was not always forthcoming. In other words, tragedy deals with kings, not because they are men with a certain title (though of course the title does give them special power), but because they are men with a certain nature. This nature is an extraordinary capacity for action and for feeling; when they make an error, its consequences are enormous, and they themselves feel it as lesser people would not. When Oedipus is polluted, all of Thebes feels it. Arthur Miller is somewhat misleading when he argues (p. 686) that because Oedipus has given his name to a complex that the common man may have, the common man is therefore "as apt a subject for tragedy." It is not Oedipus's "complex" but his unique importance that is the issue in the play. Moreover, even if one argues that a person of no public importance may suffer as much as one of public importance (and surely nobody doubts this), one may be faced with the fact that unimportant people by their ordinariness are not particularly good material for drama, and we are here concerned with drama rather than with life. In *Death of a Salesman* Willy Loman's wife says, rightly, "A small man can be just as exhausted as a great man." Yes, but is his exhaustion itself interesting, and do his activities (and this includes the words he utters) before his exhaustion have interesting dramatic possibilities? Isn't there a colorlessness that may weaken the play, an impoverishment of what John Milton called "gorgeous tragedy"?

Inevitably, the rise of the bourgeoisie brought about the rise of bourgeois drama, and in the eighteenth century we get a fair number of tragedies with prologues that insist that characters like ourselves deserve our *pity:*

No fustian hero rages here tonight,
No armies fall, to fix a tyrant's right.
From lower life we draw our scene's distress:
—Let not your equals move your pity less.
GEORGE LILLO, *FATAL CURIOSITY* (1733)

Note the deflation of older tragedy, the implication that its heroes were "fustian" (bombastic, pretentious) rather than genuinely heroic persons of deep feelings and high aspirations. Put differently, in the bourgeois view older tragedy dealt with persons of high rank, but rank (in this view) is not significant; therefore one may as well show persons of middle rank with whom the middle-class audience may readily identify. At the same time, the dismissal of heroic activities ("no fustian hero *rages*," "no armies *fall*") and the substitution of "distress" indicates that we are well on the road to the hero as victim.

And we have kept on that road. As early as the sixteenth century Copernicus had shown that humanity and its planet were not the center of the universe, but the thought did not distress most people until much later. In 1859 Darwin published *The Origin of Species,* arguing that human beings are not a special creation but creatures that have evolved because "accidental variations" have aided them in the struggle for survival. At about the same time, Marx (who wished to dedicate *Capital* to Darwin) argued that economic forces guide our lives. Early in the twentieth century Freud seemed to argue that we are conditioned by infantile experiences and are enslaved by the dark forces of the id. All in all, by the time of the depression of the 1930s, it was difficult to have much confidence in our ability to shape our destiny. The human condition was a sorry one; we were insignificant, lust-ridden, soulless creatures in a terrifying materialistic universe. A human being was no Oedipus whose moral pollution infected a great city, no Brutus whose deed might bring civil war to Rome. A human being was really not much of anything, except perhaps to a few immediate dependents.

Arthur Miller accurately noted (*Theatre Arts,* October 1953) that American drama "has been a steady year by year documentation of the frustration of man," and it is evident that Miller has set out to restore a sense of importance if not greatness to the individual. In "Tragedy and the Common Man" (see p. 686), published in the same year that *Death of a Salesman* was produced and evidently a defense of the play, he argues on behalf of the common man as a tragic figure and he insists that tragedy and pathos are very different: "Pathos truly is the mode of the pessimist. . . . [T]he plays we revere, century after century, are the tragedies. In them, and in them alone, lies the belief—optimistic, if you will—in the perfectibility of man."

Curiously, however, many spectators and readers find that by Miller's own terms Willy Loman fails to be a tragic figure; he seems to them pathetic rather than tragic, a victim rather than a man who acts and who wins our esteem. True, he is partly the victim of his own actions (although he could have chosen to be a carpenter, he chose to live by the bourgeois code that values a white collar), but he seems in larger part to be a victim of the system itself, a system of ruthless competition that has no place for the man who can no longer produce. (Here is an echo of the social-realist drama of the thirties.) Willy had believed in this system. Although his son Biff comes to the realization that Willy "had the wrong dreams," Willy himself seems not to achieve this insight. Of course he knows that he is out of a job, that the system does not value him any longer, but he still seems not to question the values he had subscribed to. Even in the last minutes of the play, when he is planning his suicide in order to provide money for his family—really for Biff—he says such things as, "Can you imagine his magnificence with twenty thousand dollars in his pocket?" and "When the mail comes he'll be ahead of Bernard again." In the preface to his *Collected Plays,* Miller comments on the "exultation" with which Willy faces the end, but it is questionable whether an audience shares it. Many people find that despite the gulf in rank, they can share King Lear's feelings more easily than Willy's.

Perhaps, however, tradition has been too arbitrary in its use of the word *tragedy.* Perhaps we should be as liberal as the ancient Greeks who did not withhold it from any play that was serious and dignified.

Arthur Miller

DEATH OF A SALESMAN

Certain Private Conversations in Two Acts and a Requiem

List of Characters

WILLY LOMAN
LINDA
BIFF
HAPPY
BERNARD
THE WOMAN
CHARLEY
UNCLE BEN
HOWARD WAGNER
JENNY
STANLEY
MISS FORSYTHE
LETTA

SCENE: *The action takes place in Willy Loman's house and yard and in various places he visits in the New York and Boston of today.*

ACT 1

SCENE: *A melody is heard, played upon a flute. It is small and fine, telling of grass and trees and the horizon. The curtain rises.*

Before us is the Salesman's house. We are aware of towering, angular shapes behind it, surrounding it on all sides. Only the blue light of the sky falls upon the house and forestage; the surrounding area shows an angry glow of orange. As more light appears, we see a solid vault of apartment houses around the small, fragile-seeming home. An air of the dream clings to the place, a dream rising out of reality. The kitchen at center seems actual enough, for there is a kitchen table with three chairs, and a refrigerator. But no other fixtures are seen. At the back of the kitchen there is a draped entrance, which leads to the living room. To the right of the kitchen, on a level raised two feet, is a bedroom furnished only with a brass bedstead and a straight chair. On a shelf over the bed a silver athletic trophy stands. A window opens onto the apartment house at the side.

Behind the kitchen, on a level raised six and a half feet, is the boys' bedroom, at present barely visible. Two beds are dimly seen, and at the back of the room a dormer window. (This bedroom is above the unseen living room.) At the left a stairway curves up to it from the kitchen.

The entire setting is wholly or, in some places, partially transparent. The roof-line of the house is one-dimensional; under and over it we see the apartment buildings. Before the house lies an apron, curving beyond the forestage into the orchestra. This forward area serves as the back yard as well as the locale of all Willy's imaginings and of his city scenes. Whenever the action is in the present the actors observe the imaginary wall-lines, entering the house only through its door at the left. But in the scenes of the past these boundaries are broken, and characters enter or leave a room by stepping "through" a wall onto the forestage.

From the right, Willy Loman, the Salesman, enters, carrying two large sample cases. The flute plays on. He hears but is not aware of it. He is past sixty years of age, dressed quietly. Even as he crosses the stage to the doorway of the house, his exhaustion is apparent. He unlocks the door, comes into the kitchen, and thankfully lets his burden down, feeling the soreness of his palms. A word-sigh escapes his lips—it might be "Oh, boy, oh, boy." He closes the door, then carries his cases out into the living room, through the draped kitchen doorway.

Linda, his wife, has stirred in her bed at the right. She gets out and puts on a robe, listening. Most often jovial, she has developed an iron repression of her exceptions to Willy's behavior—she more than loves him, she admires him, as though his mercurial nature, his temper, his massive dreams and little cruelties, served her only as sharp reminders of the turbulent longings within him, longings which she shares but lacks the temperament to utter and follow to their end.

LINDA [*hearing Willy outside the bedroom, calls with some trepidation*]. Willy!
WILLY. It's all right. I came back.
LINDA. Why? What happened? (*Slight pause.*) Did something happen, Willy?
WILLY. No, nothing happened.
LINDA. You didn't smash the car, did you?
WILLY (*with casual irritation*). I said nothing happened. Didn't you hear me?
LINDA. Don't you feel well?

WILLY. I'm tired to the death. (*The flute has faded away. He sits on the bed beside her, a little numb.*) I couldn't make it. I just couldn't make it, Linda.

LINDA (*very carefully, delicately*). Where were you all day? You look terrible.

WILLY. I got as far as a little above Yonkers. I stopped for a cup of coffee. Maybe it was the coffee.

LINDA. What?

WILLY (*after a pause*). I suddenly couldn't drive any more. The car kept going off onto the shoulder, y'know?

LINDA (*helpfully*). Oh. Maybe it was the steering again. I don't think Angelo knows the Studebaker.

WILLY. No, it's me, it's me. Suddenly I realize I'm goin' sixty miles an hour and I don't remember the last five minutes. I'm—I can't seem to—keep my mind to it.

LINDA. Maybe it's your glasses. You never went for your new glasses.

WILLY. No, I see everything. I came back ten miles an hour. It took me nearly four hours from Yonkers.

LINDA (*resigned*). Well, you'll just have to take a rest, Willy, you can't continue this way.

WILLY. I just got back from Florida.

LINDA. But you didn't rest your mind. Your mind is overactive, and the mind is what counts, dear.

WILLY. I'll start out in the morning. Maybe I'll feel better in the morning. (*She is taking off his shoes.*) These goddam arch supports are killing me.

LINDA. Take an aspirin. Should I get you an aspirin? It'll soothe you.

WILLY (*with wonder*). I was driving along, you understand? And I was fine. I was even observing the scenery. You can imagine, me looking at scenery, on the road every week of my life. But it's so beautiful up there, Linda, the trees are so thick, and the sun is warm. I opened the windshield and just let the warm air bathe over me. And then all of a sudden I'm goin' off the road! I'm tellin' ya, I absolutely forgot I was driving. If I'd've gone the other way over the white line I might've killed somebody. So I went on again—and five minutes later I'm dreamin' again, and I nearly . . . (*He presses two fingers against his eyes.*) I have such thoughts, I have such strange thoughts.

LINDA. Willy, dear. Talk to them again. There's no reason why you can't work in New York.

WILLY. They don't need me in New York. I'm the New England man. I'm vital in New England.

LINDA. But you're sixty years old. They can't expect you to keep traveling every week.

WILLY. I'll have to send a wire to Portland. I'm supposed to see Brown and Morrison tomorrow morning at ten o'clock to show the line. Goddammit, I could sell them! (*He starts putting on his jacket.*)

LINDA (*taking the jacket from him*). Why don't you go down to the place tomorrow and tell Howard you've simply got to work in New York? You're too accommodating, dear.

WILLY. If old man Wagner was alive I'd a been in charge of New York now! That man was a prince, he was a masterful man. But that boy of his, that Howard, he don't appreciate. When I went north the first time, the Wagner Company didn't know where New England was!

LINDA. Why don't you tell those things to Howard, dear?

WILLY (*encouraged*). I will, I definitely will. Is there any cheese?

LINDA. I'll make you a sandwich.

WILLY. No, go to sleep. I'll take some milk. I'll be up right away. The boys in?

LINDA. They're sleeping. Happy took Biff on a date tonight.

WILLY (*interested*). That so?

LINDA. It was so nice to see them shaving together, one behind the other, in the bathroom. And going out together. You notice? The whole house smells of shaving lotion.

WILLY. Figure it out. Work a lifetime to pay off a house. You finally own it, and there's nobody to live in it.

LINDA. Well, dear, life is a casting off. It's always that way.

WILLY. No, no, some people—some people accomplish something. Did Biff say anything after I went this morning?

LINDA. You shouldn't have criticized him, Willy, especially after he just got off the train. You mustn't lose your temper with him.

WILLY. When the hell did I lose my temper? I simply asked him if he was making any money. Is that a criticism?

LINDA. But, dear, how could he make any money?

WILLY (*worried and angered*). There's such an undercurrent in him. He became a moody man. Did he apologize when I left this morning?

LINDA. He was crestfallen, Willy. You know how he admires you. I think if he finds himself, then you'll both be happier and not fight any more.

WILLY. How can he find himself on a farm? Is that a life? A farm hand? In the beginning, when he was young, I thought, well, a young man, it's good for him to tramp around, take a lot of different jobs. But it's more than ten years now and he has yet to make thirty-five dollars a week!

LINDA. He's finding himself, Willy.

WILLY. Not finding yourself at the age of thirty-four is a disgrace!

LINDA. Shh!

WILLY. The trouble is he's lazy, goddammit!

LINDA. Willy, please!

WILLY. Biff is a lazy bum!

LINDA. They're sleeping. Get something to eat. Go on down.

WILLY. Why did he come home? I would like to know what brought him home.

LINDA. I don't know. I think he's still lost, Willy. I think he's very lost.

WILLY. Biff Loman is lost. In the greatest country in the world a young man with such—personal attractiveness, gets lost. And such a hard worker. There's one thing about Biff—he's not lazy.

LINDA. Never.

WILLY (*with pity and resolve*). I'll see him in the morning; I'll have a nice talk with him. I'll get him a job selling. He could be big in no time. My God! Remember how they used to follow him around in high school? When he smiled at one of them their faces lit up. When he walked down the street . . . (*He loses himself in reminiscences.*)

LINDA (*trying to bring him out of it*). Willy, dear, I got a new kind of American-type cheese today. It's whipped.

WILLY. Why do you get American when I like Swiss?

LINDA. I just thought you'd like a change . . .

WILLY. I don't want a change! I want Swiss cheese. Why am I always being contradicted?

LINDA (*with a covering laugh*). I thought it would be a surprise.

WILLY. Why don't you open a window in here, for God's sake?

LINDA (*with infinite patience*). They're all open, dear.

WILLY. The way they boxed us in here. Bricks and windows, windows and bricks.

LINDA. We should've bought the land next door.

WILLY. The street is lined with cars. There's not a breath of fresh air in the neighborhood. The grass don't grow any more, you can't raise a carrot in the back yard. They should've had a law against apartment houses. Remember those two beautiful elm trees out there? When I and Biff hung the swing between them?

LINDA. Yeah, like being a million miles from the city.

WILLY. They should've arrested the builder for cutting those down. They massacred the neighborhood. (*Lost.*) More and more I think of those days, Linda. This time of year it was lilac and wisteria. And then the peonies would come out, and the daffodils. What fragrance in this room!

LINDA. Well, after all, people had to move somewhere.

WILLY. No, there's more people now.

LINDA. I don't think there's more people. I think . . .

WILLY. There's more people! That's what's ruining this country! Population is getting out of control. The competition is maddening! Smell the stink from that apartment house! And another one on the other side . . . How can they whip cheese?

On Willy's last line, Biff and Happy raise themselves up in their beds, listening.

LINDA. Go down, try it. And be quiet.

WILLY (*turning to Linda, guiltily*). You're not worried about me, are you, sweetheart?

BIFF. What's the matter?

HAPPY. Listen!

LINDA. You've got too much on the ball to worry about.

WILLY. You're my foundation and my support, Linda.

LINDA. Just try to relax, dear. You make mountains out of molehills.

WILLY. I won't fight with him any more. If he wants to go back to Texas, let him go.

LINDA. He'll find his way.

WILLY. Sure. Certain men just don't get started till later in life. Like Thomas Edison, I think. Or B. F. Goodrich. One of them was deaf. (*He starts for the bedroom doorway.*) I'll put my money on Biff.

LINDA. And Willy—if it's warm Sunday we'll drive in the country. And we'll open the windshield, and take lunch.

WILLY. No, the windshields don't open on the new cars.

LINDA. But you opened it today.

WILLY. Me? I didn't. (*He stops.*) Now isn't that peculiar! Isn't that a remarkable . . . (*He breaks off in amazement and fright as the flute is heard distantly.*)

LINDA. What, darling?

WILLY. That is the most remarkable thing.

LINDA. What, dear?

WILLY. I was thinking of the Chevvy. (*Slight pause.*) Nineteen twenty-eight . . . when I had that red Chevvy . . . (*Breaks off:*) That funny? I coulda sworn I was driving that Chevvy today.

LINDA. Well, that's nothing. Something must've reminded you.

WILLY. Remarkable. Ts. Remember those days? The way Biff used to simonize that car? The dealer refused to believe there was eighty thousand miles on it. (*He shakes his head.*) Heh! (*To Linda.*) Close your eyes, I'll be right up. (*He walks out of the bedroom.*)

HAPPY (*to Biff*). Jesus, maybe he smashed up the car again!

LINDA (*calling after Willy*). Be careful on the stairs, dear! The cheese is on the middle shelf. (*She turns, goes over to the bed, takes his jacket, and goes out of the bedroom.*)

Light has risen on the boys' room. Unseen, Willy is heard talking to himself; "Eighty thousand miles," and a little laugh. Biff gets out of bed, comes downstage a bit, and stands attentively. Biff is two years older than his brother Happy, well built, but in these days bears a worn air and seems less self-assured. He has succeeded less, and his dreams are stronger and less acceptable than Happy's. Happy is tall, powerfully made. Sexuality is like a visible color on him, or a scent that many women have discovered. He, like his brother, is lost, but in a different way, for he has never allowed himself to turn his face toward defeat and is thus more confused and hard-skinned, although seemingly more content.

HAPPY (*getting out of bed*). He's going to get his license taken away if he keeps that up. I'm getting nervous about him, y'know, Biff?

BIFF. His eyes are going.

HAPPY. No, I've driven with him. He sees all right. He just doesn't keep his mind on it. I drove into the city with

him last week. He stops at a green light and then it turns
red and he goes. (*He laughs.*)

BIFF. Maybe he's color-blind.

HAPPY. Pop? Why he's got the finest eye for color in the
business. You know that.

BIFF (*sitting down on his bed*). I'm going to sleep.

HAPPY. You're not still sour on Dad, are you, Biff?

BIFF. He's all right, I guess.

WILLY (*underneath them, in the living room*). Yes, sir, eighty
thousand miles—eighty-two thousand!

BIFF. You smoking?

HAPPY (*holding out a pack of cigarettes*). Want one?

BIFF (*taking a cigarette*). I can never sleep when I smell it.

WILLY. What a simonizing job, heh!

HAPPY (*with deep sentiment*). Funny, Biff, y'know? Us sleeping in here again? The old beds. (*He pats his bed affectionately.*) All the talk that went across those beds, huh? Our
whole lives.

BIFF. Yeah. Lotta dreams and plans.

HAPPY (*with a deep and masculine laugh*). About five hundred
women would like to know what was said in this room.
(*They share a soft laugh.*)

BIFF. Remember that big Betsy something—what the hell
was her name—over on Bushwick Avenue?

HAPPY (*combing his hair*). With the collie dog!

BIFF. That's the one. I got you in there, remember?

HAPPY. Yeah, that was my first time—I think. Boy, there was
a pig. (*They laugh, almost crudely.*) You taught me everything I know about women. Don't forget that.

BIFF. I bet you forgot how bashful you used to be. Especially
with girls.

HAPPY. Oh, I still am, Biff.

BIFF. Oh, go on.

HAPPY. I just control it, that's all. I think I got less bashful
and you got more so. What happened, Biff? Where's the
old humor, the old confidence? (*He shakes Biff's knee. Biff
gets up and moves restlessly about the room.*) What's the
matter?

BIFF. Why does Dad mock me all the time?

HAPPY. He's not mocking you, he . . .

BIFF. Everything I say there's a twist of mockery on his face. I
can't get near him.

HAPPY. He just wants you to make good, that's all. I wanted
to talk to you about Dad for a long time, Biff. Something's—happening to him. He—talks to himself.

BIFF. I noticed that this morning. But he always mumbled.

HAPPY. But not so noticeable. It got so embarrassing I sent
him to Florida. And you know something? Most of the
time he's talking to you.

BIFF. What's he say about me?

HAPPY. I can't make it out.

BIFF. What's he say about me?

HAPPY. I think the fact that you're not settled, that you're
still kind of up in the air . . .

BIFF. There's one or two other things depressing him, Happy.

HAPPY. What do you mean?

BIFF. Never mind. Just don't lay it all to me.

HAPPY. But I think if you just got started—I mean—is there
any future for you out there?

BIFF. I tell ya, Hap, I don't know what the future is. I don't
know—what I'm supposed to want.

HAPPY. What do you mean?

BIFF. Well, I spent six or seven years after high school trying
to work myself up. Shipping clerk, salesman, business of
one kind or another. And it's a measly manner of existence. To get on that subway on the hot mornings in
summer. To devote your whole life to keeping stock, or
making phone calls, or selling or buying. To suffer fifty
weeks of the year for the sake of a two-week vacation,
when all you really desire is to be outdoors, with your
shirt off. And always to have to get ahead of the next
fella. And still—that's how you build a future.

HAPPY. Well, you really enjoy it on a farm? Are you content
out there?

BIFF (*with rising agitation*). Hap, I've had twenty or thirty different kinds of jobs since I left home before the war, and
it always turns out the same. I just realized it lately. In
Nebraska when I herded cattle, and the Dakotas, and
Arizona, and now in Texas. It's why I came home now, I
guess, because I realized it. This farm I work on, it's spring
there now, see? And they've got about fifteen new colts.
There's nothing more inspiring or—beautiful than the
sight of a mare and a new colt. And it's cool there now,
see? Texas is cool now, and it's spring. And whenever
spring comes to where I am, I suddenly get the feeling,
my God, I'm not gettin' anywhere! What the hell am I
doing, playing around with horses, twenty-eight dollars a
week! I'm thirty-four years old, I oughta be makin' my
future. That's when I come running home. And now, I
get here, and I don't know what to do with myself. (*After
a pause.*) I've always made a point of not wasting my life,
and everytime I come back here I know that all I've done
is to waste my life.

HAPPY. You're a poet, you know that, Biff? You're a—you're
an idealist!

BIFF. No, I'm mixed up very bad. Maybe I oughta get married. Maybe I oughta get stuck into something. Maybe
that's my trouble. I'm like a boy. I'm not married, I'm not
in business, I just—I'm like a boy. Are you content, Hap?
You're a success, aren't you? Are you content?

HAPPY. Hell, no!

BIFF. Why? You're making money, aren't you?

HAPPY (*moving about with energy, expressiveness*). All I can
do now is wait for the merchandise manager to die. And
suppose I get to be merchandise manager? He's a good
friend of mine, and he just built a terrific estate on Long
Island. And he lived there about two months and sold it,
and now he's building another one. He can't enjoy it
once it's finished. And I know that's just what I would do.
I don't know what the hell I'm workin' for. Sometimes I

sit in my apartment—all alone. And I think of the rent I'm paying. And it's crazy. But then, it's what I always wanted. My own apartment, a car, and plenty of women. And still, goddammit, I'm lonely.

BIFF (*with enthusiasm*). Listen, why don't you come out West with me?

HAPPY. You and I, heh?

BIFF. Sure, maybe we could buy a ranch. Raise cattle, use our muscles. Men built like we are should be working out in the open.

HAPPY (*avidly*). The Loman Brothers, heh?

BIFF (*with vast affection*). Sure, we'd be known all over the counties!

HAPPY (*enthralled*). That's what I dream about, Biff. Sometimes I want to just rip my clothes off in the middle of the store and outbox that goddam merchandise manager. I mean I can outbox, outrun, and outlift anybody in that store, and I have to take orders from those common, petty sons-of-bitches till I can't stand it any more.

BIFF. I'm tellin' you, kid, if you were with me I'd be happy out there.

HAPPY (*enthused*). See, Biff, everybody around me is so false that I'm constantly lowering my ideals . . .

BIFF. Baby, together we'd stand up for one another, we'd have someone to trust.

HAPPY. If I were around you . . .

BIFF. Hap, the trouble is we weren't brought up to grub for money. I don't know how to do it.

HAPPY. Neither can I!

BIFF. Then let's go!

HAPPY. The only thing is—what can you make out there?

BIFF. But look at your friend. Builds an estate and then hasn't the peace of mind to live in it.

HAPPY. Yeah, but when he walks into the store the waves part in front of him. That's fifty-two thousand dollars a year coming through the revolving door, and I got more in my pinky finger than he's got in his head.

BIFF. Yeah, but you just said . . .

HAPPY. I gotta show some of those pompous, self-important executives over there that Hap Loman can make the grade. I want to walk into the store the way he walks in. Then I'll go with you, Biff. We'll be together yet, I swear. But take those two we had tonight. Now weren't they gorgeous creatures?

BIFF. Yeah, yeah, most gorgeous I've had in years.

HAPPY. I get that any time I want, Biff. Whenever I feel disgusted. The only trouble is, it gets like bowling or something. I just keep knockin' them over and it doesn't mean anything. You still run around a lot?

BIFF. Naa. I'd like to find a girl—steady, somebody with substance.

HAPPY. That's what I long for.

BIFF. Go on! You'd never come home.

HAPPY. I would! Somebody with character, with resistance! Like Mom, y'know? You're gonna call me a bastard when

I tell you this. That girl Charlotte I was with tonight is engaged to be married in five weeks. (*He tries on his new hat.*)

BIFF. No kiddin'!

HAPPY. Sure, the guy's in line for the vice-presidency of the store. I don't know what gets into me, maybe I just have an over-developed sense of competition or something, but I went and ruined her, and furthermore I can't get rid of her. And he's the third executive I've done that to. Isn't that a crummy characteristic? And to top it all, I go to their weddings! (*Indignantly, but laughing.*) Like I'm not supposed to take bribes. Manufacturers offer me a hundred-dollar bill now and then to throw an order their way. You know how honest I am, but it's like this girl, see. I hate myself for it. Because I don't want the girl, and, still, I take it and—I love it!

BIFF. Let's go to sleep.

HAPPY. I guess we didn't settle anything, heh?

BIFF. I just got one idea that I think I'm going to try.

HAPPY. What's that?

BIFF. Remember Bill Oliver?

HAPPY. Sure, Oliver is very big now. You want to work for him again?

BIFF. No, but when I quit he said something to me. He put his arm on my shoulder, and he said, "Biff, if you ever need anything, come to me."

HAPPY. I remember that. That sounds good.

BIFF. I think I'll go to see him. If I could get ten thousand or even seven or eight thousand dollars I could buy a beautiful ranch.

HAPPY. I bet he'd back you. 'Cause he thought highly of you, Biff. I mean, they all do. You're well liked, Biff. That's why I say to come back here, and we both have the apartment. And I'm tellin' you, Biff, any babe you want . . .

BIFF. No, with a ranch I could do the work I like and still be something. I just wonder though. I wonder if Oliver still thinks I stole that carton of basketballs.

HAPPY. Oh, he probably forgot that long ago. It's almost ten years. You're too sensitive. Anyway, he didn't really fire you.

BIFF. Well, I think he was going to. I think that's why I quit. I was never sure whether he knew or not. I know he thought the world of me, though. I was the only one he'd let lock up the place.

WILLY (*below*). You gonna wash the engine, Biff?

HAPPY. Shh!

Biff looks at Happy, who is gazing down, listening. Willy is mumbling in the parlor.

HAPPY. You hear that?

They listen. Willy laughs warmly.

BIFF (*growing angry*). Doesn't he know Mom can hear that?

WILLY. Don't get your sweater dirty, Biff!

A look of pain crosses Biff's face.

HAPPY. Isn't that terrible? Don't leave again, will you? You'll find a job here. You gotta stick around. I don't know what to do about him, it's getting embarrassing.

WILLY. What a simonizing job!

BIFF. Mom's hearing that!

WILLY. No kiddin', Biff, you got a date? Wonderful!

HAPPY. Go on to sleep. But talk to him in the morning, will you?

BIFF (*reluctantly getting into bed*). With her in the house. Brother!

HAPPY (*getting into bed*). I wish you'd have a good talk with him.

The light on their room begins to fade.

BIFF (*to himself in bed*). That selfish, stupid . . .

HAPPY. Sh . . . Sleep, Biff.

Their light is out. Well before they have finished speaking, Willy's form is dimly seen below in the darkened kitchen. He opens the refrigerator, searches in there, and takes out a bottle of milk. The apartment houses are fading out, and the entire house and surroundings become covered with leaves. Music insinuates itself as the leaves appear.

WILLY. Just wanna be careful with those girls, Biff, that's all. Don't make any promises. No promises of any kind. Because a girl, y'know, they always believe what you tell 'em, and you're very young, Biff, you're too young to be talking seriously to girls.

Light rises on the kitchen. Willy, talking, shuts the refrigerator door and comes downstage to the kitchen table. He pours milk into a glass. He is totally immersed in himself, smiling faintly.

WILLY. Too young entirely, Biff. You want to watch your schooling first. Then when you're all set, there'll be plenty of girls for a boy like you. (*He smiles broadly at a kitchen chair.*) That so? The girls pay for you? (*He laughs.*) Boy, you must really be makin' a hit.

Willy is gradually addressing—physically—a point offstage, speaking through the wall of the kitchen, and his voice has been rising in volume to that of a normal conversation.

WILLY. I been wondering why you polish the car so careful. Ha! Don't leave the hubcaps, boys. Get the chamois to the hubcaps. Happy, use newspaper on the windows, it's the easiest thing. Show him how to do it, Biff! You see, Happy? Pad it up, use it like a pad. That's it, that's it, good work. You're doin' all right, Hap. (*He pauses, then nods in approbation for a few seconds, then looks upward.*) Biff, first thing we gotta do when we get time is clip that big branch over the house. Afraid it's gonna fall in a storm and hit the roof. Tell you what. We get a rope and sling her around, and then we climb up there with a couple of saws and take her down. Soon as you finish the car, boys, I wanna see ya. I got a surprise for you, boys.

BIFF (*offstage*). Whatta ya got, Dad?

WILLY. No, you finish first. Never leave a job till you're finished—remember that. (*Looking toward the "big trees."*) Biff, up in Albany I saw a beautiful hammock. I think I'll buy it next trip, and we'll hang it right between those two elms. Wouldn't that be something? Just swingin' there under those branches. Boy, that would be . . .

Young Biff and Young Happy appear from the direction Willy was addressing. Happy carries rags and a pail of water. Biff, wearing a sweater with a block "S," carries a football.

BIFF (*pointing in the direction of the car offstage*). How's that, Pop, professional?

WILLY. Terrific. Terrific job, boys. Good work, Biff.

HAPPY. Where's the surprise, Pop?

WILLY. In the back seat of the car.

HAPPY. Boy! (*He runs off.*)

BIFF. What is it, Dad? Tell me, what'd you buy?

WILLY (*laughing, cuffs him*). Never mind, something I want you to have.

BIFF (*turns and starts off*). What is it, Hap?

HAPPY (*offstage*). It's a punching bag!

BIFF. Oh, Pop!

WILLY. It's got Gene Tunney's signature on it!

Happy runs onstage with a punching bag.

BIFF. Gee, how'd you know we wanted a punching bag?

WILLY. Well, it's the finest thing for the timing.

HAPPY (*lies down on his back and pedals with his feet*). I'm losing weight, you notice, Pop?

WILLY (*to Happy*). Jumping rope is good too.

BIFF. Did you see the new football I got?

WILLY (*examining the ball*). Where'd you get a new ball?

BIFF. The coach told me to practice my passing.

WILLY. That so? And he gave you the ball, heh?

BIFF. Well, I borrowed it from the locker room. (*He laughs confidentially.*)

WILLY (*laughing with him at the theft*). I want you to return that.

HAPPY. I told you he wouldn't like it!

BIFF (*angrily*). Well, I'm bringing it back!

WILLY (*stopping the incipient argument, to Happy*). Sure, he's gotta practice with a regulation ball, doesn't he? (*To Biff.*) Coach'll probably congratulate you on your initiative!

BIFF. Oh, he keeps congratulating my initiative all the time, Pop.

WILLY. That's because he likes you. If somebody else took that ball there'd be an uproar. So what's the report, boys, what's the report?

BIFF. Where'd you go this time, Dad? Gee we were lonesome for you.

WILLY (*pleased, puts an arm around each boy and they come down to the apron*). Lonesome, heh?

BIFF. Missed you every minute.

WILLY. Don't say? Tell you a secret, boys. Don't breathe it to a soul. Someday I'll have my own business, and I'll never have to leave home any more.

HAPPY. Like Uncle Charley, heh?

WILLY. Bigger than Uncle Charley! Because Charley is not—liked. He's liked, but he's not—well liked.

BIFF. Where'd you go this time, Dad?

WILLY. Well, I got on the road, and I went north to Providence. Met the Mayor.

BIFF. The Mayor of Providence!

WILLY. He was sitting in the hotel lobby.

BIFF. What'd he say?

WILLY. He said, "Morning!" And I said, "Morning!" And I said, "You got a fine city here, Mayor." And then he had coffee with me. And then I went to Waterbury. Waterbury is a fine city. Big clock city, the famous Waterbury clock. Sold a nice bill there. And then Boston—Boston is the cradle of the Revolution. A fine city. And a couple of other towns in Mass., and on to Portland and Bangor and straight home!

BIFF. Gee, I'd love to go with you sometime, Dad.

WILLY. Soon as summer comes.

HAPPY. Promise?

WILLY. You and Hap and I, and I'll show you all the towns. America is full of beautiful towns and fine, upstanding people. And they know me, boys, they know me up and down New England. The finest people. And when I bring you fellas up, there'll be open sesame for all of us, 'cause one thing, boys: I have friends. I can park my car in any street in New England, and the cops protect it like their own. This summer, heh?

BIFF AND HAPPY (together). Yeah! You bet!

WILLY. We'll take our bathing suits.

HAPPY. We'll carry your bags, Pop!

WILLY. Oh, won't that be something! Me comin' into the Boston stores with you boys carryin' my bags. What a sensation!

Biff is prancing around, practicing passing the ball.

WILLY. You nervous, Biff, about the game?

BIFF. Not if you're gonna be there.

WILLY. What do they say about you in school, now that they made you captain?

HAPPY. There's a crowd of girls behind him everytime the classes change.

BIFF (taking Willy's hand). This Saturday, Pop, this Saturday—just for you, I'm going to break through for a touchdown.

HAPPY. You're supposed to pass.

BIFF. I'm takin' one play for Pop. You watch me, Pop, and when I take off my helmet, that means I'm breakin' out. Then you watch me crash through that line!

WILLY (kisses Biff). Oh, wait'll I tell this in Boston!

Bernard enters in knickers. He is younger than Biff, earnest and loyal, a worried boy.

BERNARD. Biff, where are you? You're supposed to study with me today.

WILLY. Hey, looka Bernard. What're you lookin' so anemic about, Bernard?

BERNARD. He's gotta study, Uncle Willy. He's got Regents next week.

HAPPY (tauntingly, spinning Bernard around). Let's box, Bernard!

BERNARD. Biff! (He gets away from Happy.) Listen, Biff, I heard Mr. Birnbaum say that if you don't start studyin' math he's gonna flunk you, and you won't graduate. I heard him!

WILLY. You better study with him, Biff. Go ahead now.

BERNARD. I heard him!

BIFF. Oh, Pop, you didn't see my sneakers! (He holds up a foot for Willy to look at.)

WILLY. Hey, that's a beautiful job of printing!

BERNARD (wiping his glasses). Just because he printed University of Virginia on his sneakers doesn't mean they've got to graduate him, Uncle Willy!

WILLY (angrily). What're you talking about? With scholarships to three universities they're gonna flunk him?

BERNARD. But I heard Mr. Birnbaum say . . .

WILLY. Don't be a pest, Bernard! (To his boys.) What an anemic!

BERNARD. Okay, I'm waiting for you in my house, Biff.

Bernard goes off. The Lomans laugh.

WILLY. Bernard is not well liked, is he?

BIFF. He's liked, but he's not well liked.

HAPPY. That's right, Pop.

WILLY. That's just what I mean. Bernard can get the best marks in school, y'understand, but when he gets out in the business world, y'understand, you are going to be five times ahead of him. That's why I thank Almighty God you're both built like Adonises. Because the man who makes an appearance in the business world, the man who creates personal interest, is the man who gets ahead. Be liked and you will never want. You take me, for instance. I never have to wait in line to see a buyer. "Willy Loman is here!" That's all they have to know, and I go right through.

BIFF. Did you knock them dead, Pop?

WILLY. Knocked 'em cold in Providence, slaughtered 'em in Boston.

HAPPY (on his back, pedaling again). I'm losing weight, you notice, Pop?

Linda enters as of old, a ribbon in her hair, carrying a basket of washing.

LINDA (with youthful energy). Hello, dear!

WILLY. Sweetheart!

LINDA. How'd the Chevvy run?

WILLY. Chevrolet, Linda, is the greatest car ever built. (To the boys.) Since when do you let your mother carry wash up the stairs?

BIFF. Grab hold there, boy!

HAPPY. Where to, Mom?

LINDA. Hang them up on the line. And you better go down to your friends, Biff. The cellar is full of boys. They don't know what to do with themselves.

BIFF. Ah, when Pop comes home they can wait!

WILLY (*laughs appreciatively*). You better go down and tell them what to do. Biff.

BIFF. I think I'll have them sweep out the furnace room.

WILLY. Good work, Biff.

BIFF (*goes through wall-line of kitchen to doorway at back and calls down*). Fellas! Everybody sweep out the furnace room! I'll be right down!

VOICES. All right! Okay, Biff.

BIFF. George and Sam and Frank, come out back! We're hangin' up the wash! Come on, Hap, on the double! (*He and Happy carry out the basket.*)

LINDA. The way they obey him!

WILLY. Well, that's training, the training. I'm tellin' you, I was sellin' thousands and thousands, but I had to come home.

LINDA. Oh, the whole block'll be at that game. Did you sell anything?

WILLY. I did five hundred gross in Providence and seven hundred gross in Boston.

LINDA. No! Wait a minute. I've got a pencil. (*She pulls pencil and paper out of her apron pocket.*) That makes your commission . . . Two hundred—my God! Two hundred and twelve dollars!

WILLY. Well, I didn't figure it yet, but . . .

LINDA. How much did you do?

WILLY. Well, I—I did—about a hundred and eighty gross in Providence. Well, no—it came to—roughly two hundred gross on the whole trip.

LINDA (*without hesitation*). Two hundred gross. That's . . . (*She figures.*)

WILLY. The trouble was that three of the stores were half-closed for inventory in Boston. Otherwise I woulda broke records.

LINDA. Well, it makes seventy dollars and some pennies. That's very good.

WILLY. What do we owe?

LINDA. Well, on the first there's sixteen dollars on the refrigerator . . .

WILLY. Why sixteen?

LINDA. Well, the fan belt broke, so it was a dollar eighty.

WILLY. But it's brand new.

LINDA. Well, the man said that's the way it is. Till they work themselves in, y'know.

They move through the wall-line into the kitchen.

WILLY. I hope we didn't get stuck on that machine.

LINDA. They got the biggest ads of any of them!

WILLY. I know, it's a fine machine. What else?

LINDA. Well, there's nine-sixty for the washing machine. And for the vacuum cleaner there's three and a half due on the fifteenth. Then the roof, you got twenty-one dollars remaining.

WILLY. It don't leak, does it?

LINDA. No, they did a wonderful job. Then you owe Frank for the carburetor.

WILLY. I'm not going to pay that man! That goddam Chevrolet, they ought to prohibit the manufacture of that car!

LINDA. Well, you owe him three and a half. And odds and ends, comes to around a hundred and twenty dollars by the fifteenth.

WILLY. A hundred and twenty dollars! My God, if business don't pick up I don't know what I'm gonna do!

LINDA. Well, next week you'll do better.

WILLY. Oh, I'll knock 'em dead next week. I'll go to Hartford. I'm very well liked in Hartford. You know, the trouble is, Linda, people don't seem to take to me.

They move onto the forestage.

LINDA. Oh, don't be foolish.

WILLY. I know it when I walk in. They seem to laugh at me.

LINDA. Why? Why would they laugh at you? Don't talk that way, Willy.

Willy moves to the edge of the stage. Linda goes into the kitchen and starts to darn stockings.

WILLY. I don't know the reason for it, but they just pass me by. I'm not noticed.

LINDA. But you're doing wonderful, dear. You're making seventy to a hundred dollars a week.

WILLY. But I gotta be at it ten, twelve hours a day. Other men—I don't know—they do it easier. I don't know why—I can't stop myself—I talk too much. A man oughta come in with a few words. One thing about Charley. He's a man of few words, and they respect him.

LINDA. You don't talk too much, you're just lively.

WILLY (*smiling*). Well, I figure, what the hell, life is short, a couple of jokes. (*To himself:*) I joke too much! (*The smile goes.*)

LINDA. Why? You're . . .

WILLY. I'm fat. I'm very—foolish to look at, Linda. I didn't tell you, but Christmas time I happened to be calling on F. H. Stewarts, and a salesman I know, as I was going in to see the buyer I heard him say something about—walrus. And I—I cracked him right across the face. I won't take that. I simply will not take that. But they do laugh at me. I know that.

LINDA. Darling . . .

WILLY. I gotta overcome it. I know I gotta overcome it. I'm not dressing to advantage, maybe.

LINDA. Willy, darling, you're the handsomest man in the world . . .

WILLY. Oh, no, Linda.

LINDA. To me you are. (*Slight pause.*) The handsomest.

From the darkness is heard the laughter of a woman. Willy doesn't turn to it, but it continues through Linda's lines.

LINDA. And the boys, Willy. Few men are idolized by their children the way you are.

Music is heard as behind a scrim, to the left of the house; The Woman, dimly seen, is dressing.

WILLY (*with great feeling*). You're the best there is. Linda, you're a pal, you know that? On the road—on the road I want to grab you sometimes and just kiss the life outa you.

The laughter is loud now, and he moves into a brightening area at the left, where The Woman has come from behind the scrim and is standing, putting on her hat, looking into a "mirror" and laughing.

WILLY. 'Cause I get so lonely—especially when business is bad and there's nobody to talk to. I get the feeling that I'll never sell anything again, that I won't make a living for you, or a business, a business for the boys. (*He talks through The Woman's subsiding laughter; The Woman primps at the "mirror."*) There's so much I want to make for . . .

THE WOMAN. Me? You didn't make me, Willy. I picked you.

WILLY (*pleased*). You picked me?

THE WOMAN (*who is quite proper-looking, Willy's age*). I did. I've been sitting at that desk watching all the salesmen go by, day in, day out. But you've got such a sense of humor, and we do have such a good time together, don't we?

WILLY. Sure, sure. (*He takes her in his arms.*) Why do you have to go now?

THE WOMAN. It's two o'clock . . .

WILLY. No, come on in! (*He pulls her.*)

THE WOMAN. . . . my sisters'll be scandalized. When'll you be back?

WILLY. Oh, two weeks about. Will you come up again?

THE WOMAN. Sure thing. You do make me laugh. It's good for me. (*She squeezes his arm, kisses him.*) And I think you're a wonderful man.

WILLY. You picked me, heh?

THE WOMAN. Sure. Because you're so sweet. And such a kidder.

WILLY. Well, I'll see you next time I'm in Boston.

THE WOMAN. I'll put you right through to the buyers.

WILLY (*slapping her bottom*). Right. Well, bottoms up!

THE WOMAN (*slaps him gently and laughs*). You just kill me, Willy. (*He suddenly grabs her and kisses her roughly.*) You kill me. And thanks for the stockings. I love a lot of stockings. Well, good night.

WILLY. Good night. And keep your pores open!

THE WOMAN. Oh, Willy!

The Woman bursts out laughing, and Linda's laughter blends in. The Woman disappears into the dark. Now the area at the kitchen table brightens. Linda is sitting where she was at the kitchen table, but now is mending a pair of her silk stockings.

LINDA. You are, Willy. The handsomest man. You've got no reason to feel that . . .

WILLY (*coming out of The Woman's dimming area and going over to Linda*). I'll make it all up to you, Linda, I'll . . .

LINDA. There's nothing to make up, dear. You're doing fine, better than . . .

WILLY (*noticing her mending*). What's that?

LINDA. Just mending my stockings. They're so expensive . . .

WILLY (*angrily, taking them from her*). I won't have you mending stockings in this house! Now throw them out!

Linda puts the stockings in her pocket.

BERNARD (*entering on the run*). Where is he? If he doesn't study!

WILLY (*moving to the forestage, with great agitation*). You'll give him the answers!

BERNARD. I do, but I can't on a Regents! That's a state exam! They're liable to arrest me!

WILLY. Where is he? I'll whip him, I'll whip him!

LINDA. And he'd better give back that football, Willy, it's not nice.

WILLY. Biff! Where is he? Why is he taking everything?

LINDA. He's too rough with the girls, Willy. All the mothers are afraid of him!

WILLY. I'll whip him!

BERNARD. He's driving the car without a license!

The Woman's laugh is heard.

WILLY. Shut up!

LINDA. All the mothers . . .

WILLY. Shut up!

BERNARD (*backing quietly away and out*). Mr. Birnbaum says he's stuck up.

WILLY. Get outa here!

BERNARD. If he doesn't buckle down he'll flunk math! (*He goes off.*)

LINDA. He's right, Willy, you've gotta . . .

WILLY (*exploding at her*). There's nothing the matter with him! You want him to be a worm like Bernard? He's got spirit, personality . . .

As he speaks, Linda, almost in tears, exits into the living room. Willy is alone in the kitchen, wilting and staring. The leaves are gone. It is night again, and the apartment houses look down from behind.

WILLY. Loaded with it. Loaded! What is he stealing? He's giving it back, isn't he? Why is he stealing? What did I tell him? I never in my life told him anything but decent things.

Happy in pajamas has come down the stairs; Willy suddenly becomes aware of Happy's presence.

HAPPY. Let's go now, come on.

WILLY (*sitting down at the kitchen table*). Huh! Why did she have to wax the floors herself? Everytime she waxes the floors she keels over. She knows that!

HAPPY. Shh! Take it easy. What brought you back tonight?

WILLY. I got an awful scare. Nearly hit a kid in Yonkers. God! Why didn't I go to Alaska with my brother Ben that time! Ben! That man was a genius, that man was success incarnate! What a mistake! He begged me to go.

HAPPY. Well, there's no use in . . .

WILLY. You guys! There was a man started with the clothes on his back and ended up with diamond mines!

HAPPY. Boy, someday I'd like to know how he did it.

WILLY. What's the mystery? The man knew what he wanted and went out and got it! Walked into a jungle, and comes out, the age of twenty-one, and he's rich! The world is an oyster, but you don't crack it open on a mattress!

HAPPY. Pop, I told you I'm gonna retire you for life.

WILLY. You'll retire me for life on seventy goddam dollars a week? And your women and your car and your apartment, and you'll retire me for life! Christ's sake, I couldn't get past Yonkers today! Where are you guys, where are you? The woods are burning! I can't drive a car!

Charley has appeared in the doorway. He is a large man, slow of speech, laconic, immovable. In all he says, despite what he says, there is pity, and, now, trepidation. He has a robe over pajamas, slippers on his feet. He enters the kitchen.

CHARLEY. Everything all right?

HAPPY. Yeah, Charley, everything's . . .

WILLY. What's the matter?

CHARLEY. I heard some noise. I thought something happened. Can't we do something about the walls? You sneeze in here, and in my house hats blow off.

HAPPY. Let's go to bed, Dad. Come on.

Charley signals to Happy to go.

WILLY. You go ahead, I'm not tired at the moment.

HAPPY (*to Willy*). Take it easy, huh? (*He exits.*)

WILLY. What're you doin' up?

CHARLEY (*sitting down at the kitchen table opposite Willy*). Couldn't sleep good. I had a heartburn.

WILLY. Well, you don't know how to eat.

CHARLEY. I eat with my mouth.

WILLY. No, you're ignorant. You gotta know about vitamins and things like that.

CHARLEY. Come on, let's shoot. Tire you out a little.

WILLY (*hesitantly*). All right. You got cards?

CHARLEY (*taking a deck from his pocket*). Yeah, I got them. Someplace. What is it with those vitamins?

WILLY (*dealing*). They build up your bones. Chemistry.

CHARLEY. Yeah, but there's no bones in a heartburn.

WILLY. What are you talkin' about? Do you know the first thing about it?

CHARLEY. Don't get insulted.

WILLY. Don't talk about something you don't know anything about.

They are playing. Pause.

CHARLEY. What're you doin' home?

WILLY. A little trouble with the car.

CHARLEY. Oh. (*Pause.*) I'd like to take a trip to California.

WILLY. Don't say.

CHARLEY. You want a job?

WILLY. I got a job, I told you that. (*After a slight pause.*) What the hell are you offering me a job for?

CHARLEY. Don't get insulted.

WILLY. Don't insult me.

CHARLEY. I don't see no sense in it. You don't have to go on this way.

WILLY. I got a good job. (*Slight pause.*) What do you keep comin' in here for?

CHARLEY. You want me to go?

WILLY (*after a pause, withering*). I can't understand it. He's going back to Texas again. What the hell is that?

CHARLEY. Let him go.

WILLY. I got nothin' to give him, Charley, I'm clean, I'm clean.

CHARLEY. He won't starve. None a them starve. Forget about him.

WILLY. Then what have I got to remember?

CHARLEY. You take it too hard. To hell with it. When a deposit bottle is broken you don't get your nickel back.

WILLY. That's easy enough for you to say.

CHARLEY. That ain't easy for me to say.

WILLY. Did you see the ceiling I put up in the living room?

CHARLEY. Yeah, that's a piece of work. To put up a ceiling is a mystery to me. How do you do it?

WILLY. What's the difference?

CHARLEY. Well, talk about it.

WILLY. You gonna put up a ceiling?

CHARLEY. How could I put up a ceiling?

WILLY. Then what the hell are you bothering me for?

CHARLEY. You're insulted again.

WILLY. A man who can't handle tools is not a man. You're disgusting.

CHARLEY. Don't call me disgusting, Willy.

Uncle Ben, carrying a valise and an umbrella, enters the forestage from around the right corner of the house. He is a stolid man, in his sixties, with a mustache and an authoritative air. He is utterly certain of his destiny, and there is an aura of far places about him. He enters exactly as Willy speaks.

WILLY. I'm getting awfully tired, Ben.

Ben's music is heard. Ben looks around at everything.

CHARLEY. Good, keep playing; you'll sleep better. Did you call me Ben?

Ben looks at his watch.

WILLY. That's funny. For a second there you reminded me of my brother Ben.

BEN. I only have a few minutes. (*He strolls, inspecting the place. Willy and Charley continue playing.*)

CHARLEY. You never heard from him again, heh? Since that time?

WILLY. Didn't Linda tell you? Couple of weeks ago we got a letter from his wife in Africa. He died.

CHARLEY. That so.

BEN (*chuckling*). So this is Brooklyn, eh?

CHARLEY. Maybe you're in for some of his money.

WILLY. Naa, he had seven sons. There's just one opportunity I had with that man . . .

BEN. I must make a train, William. There are several properties I'm looking at in Alaska.

WILLY. Sure, sure! If I'd gone with him to Alaska that time, everything would've been totally different.

CHARLEY. Go on, you'd froze to death up there.

WILLY. What're you talking about?

BEN. Opportunity is tremendous in Alaska, William. Surprised you're not up there.

WILLY. Sure, tremendous.

CHARLEY. Heh?

WILLY. There was the only man I ever met who knew the answers.

CHARLEY. Who?

BEN. How are you all?

WILLY (*taking a pot, smiling*). Fine, fine.

CHARLEY. Pretty sharp tonight.

BEN. Is Mother living with you?

WILLY. No, she died a long time ago.

CHARLEY. Who?

BEN. That's too bad. Fine specimen of a lady, Mother.

WILLY (*to Charley*). Heh?

BEN. I'd hoped to see the old girl.

CHARLEY. Who died?

BEN. Heard anything from Father, have you?

WILLY (*unnerved*). What do you mean, who died?

CHARLEY (*taking a pot*). What're you talkin' about?

BEN (*looking at his watch*). William, it's half-past eight!

WILLY (*as though to dispel his confusion he angrily stops Charley's hand*). That's my build!

CHARLEY. I put the ace . . .

WILLY. If you don't know how to play the game I'm not gonna throw my money away on you!

CHARLEY (*rising*). It was my ace, for God's sake!

WILLY. I'm through, I'm through!

BEN. When did Mother die?

WILLY. Long ago. Since the beginning you never knew how to play cards.

CHARLEY (*picks up the cards and goes to the door*). All right! Next time I'll bring a deck with five aces.

WILLY. I don't play that kind of game!

CHARLEY (*turning to him*). You ought to be ashamed of yourself!

WILLY. Yeah?

CHARLEY. Yeah! (*He goes out.*)

WILLY (*slamming the door after him*). Ignoramus!

BEN (*as Willy comes toward him through the wall-line of the kitchen*). So you're William.

WILLY (*shaking Ben's hand*). Ben! I've been waiting for you so long! What's the answer? How did you do it?

BEN. Oh, there's a story in that.

Linda enters the forestage, as of old, carrying the wash basket.

LINDA. Is this Ben?

BEN (*gallantly*). How do you do, my dear.

LINDA. Where've you been all these years? Willy's always wondered why you . . .

WILLY (*pulling Ben away from her impatiently*). Where is Dad? Didn't you follow him? How did you get started?

BEN. Well, I don't know how much you remember.

WILLY. Well, I was just a baby, of course, only three or four years old . . .

BEN. Three years and eleven months.

WILLY. What a memory, Ben!

BEN. I have many enterprises, William, and I have never kept books.

WILLY. I remember I was sitting under the wagon in—was it Nebraska?

BEN. It was South Dakota, and I gave you a bunch of wild flowers.

WILLY. I remember you walking away down some open road.

BEN (*laughing*). I was going to find Father in Alaska.

WILLY. Where is he?

BEN. At that age I had a very faulty view of geography, William. I discovered after a few days that I was heading due south, so instead of Alaska, I ended up in Africa.

LINDA. Africa!

WILLY. The Gold Coast!

BEN. Principally diamond mines.

LINDA. Diamond mines!

BEN. Yes, my dear. But I've only a few minutes . . .

WILLY. No! Boys! Boys! (*Young Biff and Happy appear.*) Listen to this. This is your Uncle Ben, a great man! Tell my boys, Ben!

BEN. Why, boys, when I was seventeen I walked into the jungle, and when I was twenty-one I walked out. (*He laughs.*) And by God I was rich.

WILLY (*to the boys*). You see what I been talking about? The greatest things can happen!

BEN (*glancing at his watch*). I have an appointment in Ketchikan Tuesday week.

WILLY. No, Ben! Please tell about Dad. I want my boys to hear. I want them to know the kind of stock they spring from. All I remember is a man with a big beard, and I was in Mamma's lap, sitting around a fire, and some kind of high music.

BEN. His flute. He played the flute.

WILLY. Sure, the flute, that's right!

New music is heard, a high, rollicking tune.

BEN. Father was a very great and a very wild-hearted man. We would start in Boston, and he'd toss the whole family into the wagon, and then he'd drive the team right across the country; through Ohio, and Indiana, Michigan, Illinois, and all the Western states. And we'd stop in the towns and sell the flutes that he'd made on the way. Great inventor, Father. With one gadget he made more in a week than a man like you could make in a lifetime.

WILLY. That's just the way I'm bringing them up, Ben—rugged, well liked, all-around.

BEN. Yeah? (*To Biff.*) Hit that, boy—hard as you can. (*He pounds his stomach.*)

BIFF. Oh, no, sir!

BEN (*taking boxing stance*). Come on, get to me! (*He laughs.*)

WILLY. Go to it. Biff! Go ahead, show him!

BIFF. Okay! (*He cocks his fists and starts in.*)

LINDA (*to Willy*). Why must he fight, dear?

BEN (*sparring with Biff*). Good boy! Good boy!

WILLY. How's that, Ben, heh?

HAPPY. Give him the left, Biff!

LINDA. Why are you fighting?

BEN. Good boy! (*Suddenly comes in, trips Biff, and stands over him, the point of his umbrella poised over Biff's eye.*)

LINDA. Look out, Biff!

BIFF. Gee!

BEN (*patting Biff's knee*). Never fight fair with a stranger, boy. You'll never get out of the jungle that way. (*Taking Linda's hand and bowing.*) It was an honor and a pleasure to meet you, Linda.

LINDA (*withdrawing her hand coldly, frightened*). Have a nice—trip.

BEN (*to Willy*). And good luck with your—what do you do?

WILLY. Selling.

BEN. Yes. Well . . . (*He raises his hand in farewell to all.*)

WILLY. No, Ben, I don't want you to think . . . (*He takes Ben's arm to show him.*) It's Brooklyn, I know, but we hunt too.

BEN. Really, now.

WILLY. Oh, sure, there's snakes and rabbits and—that's why I moved out here. Why, Biff can fell any one of these trees in no time! Boys! Go right over to where they're building the apartment house and get some sand. We're gonna rebuild the entire front stoop right now! Watch this, Ben!

BIFF. Yes, sir! On the double, Hap!

HAPPY (*as he and Biff run off*). I lost weight, Pop, you notice?

Charley enters in knickers, even before the boys are gone.

CHARLEY. Listen, if they steal any more from that building the watchman'll put the cops on them!

LINDA (*to Willy*). Don't let Biff . . .

Ben laughs lustily.

WILLY. You shoulda seen the lumber they brought home last week. At least a dozen six-by-tens worth all kinds a money.

CHARLEY. Listen, if that watchman . . .

WILLY. I gave them hell, understand. But I got a couple of fearless characters there.

CHARLEY. Willy, the jails are full of fearless characters.

BEN (*clapping Willy on the back, with a laugh at Charley*). And the stock exchange, friend!

WILLY (*joining in Ben's laughter*). Where are the rest of your pants?

CHARLEY. My wife bought them.

WILLY. Now all you need is a golf club and you can go upstairs and go to sleep. (*To Ben.*) Great athlete! Between him and his son Bernard they can't hammer a nail!

BERNARD (*rushing in*). The watchman's chasing Biff!

WILLY (*angrily*). Shut up! He's not stealing anything!

LINDA (*alarmed, hurrying off left*). Where is he? Biff, dear! (*She exits.*)

WILLY (*moving toward the left, away from Ben*). There's nothing wrong. What's the matter with you?

BEN. Nervy boy. Good!

WILLY (*laughing*). Oh, nerves of iron, that Biff!

CHARLEY. Don't know what it is. My New England man comes back and he's bleedin', they murdered him up there.

WILLY. It's contacts, Charley, I got important contacts!

CHARLEY (*sarcastically*). Glad to hear it, Willy. Come in later, we'll shoot a little casino. I'll take some of your Portland money. (*He laughs at Willy and exits.*)

WILLY (*turning to Ben*). Business is bad, it's murderous. But not for me, of course.

BEN. I'll stop by on my way back to Africa.

WILLY (*longingly*). Can't you stay a few days? You're just what I need, Ben, because I—I have a fine position here, but I—well, Dad left when I was such a baby and I never had a chance to talk to him and I still feel—kind of temporary about myself.

BEN. I'll be late for my train.

They are at opposite ends of the stage.

WILLY. Ben, my boys—can't we talk? They'd go into the jaws of hell for me, see, but I . . .

BEN. William, you're being first-rate with your boys. Outstanding, manly chaps!

WILLY (*hanging on to his words*). Oh, Ben, that's good to hear! Because sometimes I'm afraid that I'm not teaching them the right kind of—Ben, how should I teach them?

BEN (*giving great weight to each word, and with a certain vicious audacity*). William, when I walked into the jungle, I was seventeen. When I walked out I was twenty-one. And, by God, I was rich! (*He goes off into darkness around the right corner of the house.*)

WILLY. . . . was rich! That's just the spirit I want to imbue them with! To walk into a jungle! I was right! I was right! I was right!

Ben is gone, but Willy is still speaking to him as Linda, in nightgown and robe, enters the kitchen, glances around for

Willy, then goes to the door of the house, looks out and sees him. Comes down to his left. He looks at her.

LINDA. Willy, dear? Willy?

WILLY. I was right!

LINDA. Did you have some cheese? (*He can't answer.*) It's very late, darling. Come to bed, heh?

WILLY (*looking straight up*). Gotta break your neck to see a star in this yard.

LINDA. You coming in?

WILLY. Whatever happened to that diamond watch fob? Remember? When Ben came from Africa that time? Didn't he give me a watch fob with a diamond in it?

LINDA. You pawned it, dear. Twelve, thirteen years ago. For Biff's radio correspondence course.

WILLY. Gee, that was a beautiful thing. I'll take a walk.

LINDA. But you're in your slippers.

WILLY (*starting to go around the house at the left*). I was right! I was! (*Half to Linda, as he goes, shaking his head.*) What a man! There was a man worth talking to. I was right!

LINDA (*calling after Willy*). But in your slippers, Willy!

Willy is almost gone when Biff, in his pajamas, comes down the stairs and enters the kitchen.

BIFF. What is he doing out there?

LINDA. Sh!

BIFF. God Almighty, Mom, how long has he been doing this?

LINDA. Don't, he'll hear you.

BIFF. What the hell is the matter with him?

LINDA. It'll pass by morning.

BIFF. Shouldn't we do anything?

LINDA. Oh, my dear, you should do a lot of things, but there's nothing to do, so go to sleep.

Happy comes down the stair and sits on the steps.

HAPPY. I never heard him so loud, Mom.

LINDA. Well, come around more often; you'll hear him. (*She sits down at the table and mends the lining of Willy's jacket.*)

BIFF. Why didn't you ever write me about this, Mom?

LINDA. How would I write to you? For over three months you had no address.

BIFF. I was on the move. But you know I thought of you all the time. You know that, don't you, pal?

LINDA. I know, dear, I know. But he likes to have a letter. Just to know that there's still a possibility for better things.

BIFF. He's not like this all the time, is he?

LINDA. It's when you come home he's always the worst.

BIFF. When I come home?

LINDA. When you write you're coming, he's all smiles, and talks about the future, and—he's just wonderful. And then the closer you seem to come, the more shaky he gets, and then, by the time you get here, he's arguing, and he seems angry at you. I think it's just that maybe he can't bring himself to—to open up to you. Why are you so hateful to each other? Why is that?

BIFF (*evasively*). I'm not hateful, Mom.

LINDA. But you no sooner come in the door than you're fighting!

BIFF. I don't know why. I mean to change. I'm tryin', Mom, you understand?

LINDA. Are you home to stay now?

BIFF. I don't know. I want to look around, see what's doin'.

LINDA. Biff, you can't look around all your life, can you?

BIFF. I just can't take hold, Mom. I can't take hold of some kind of a life.

LINDA. Biff, a man is not a bird, to come and go with the spring time.

BIFF. Your hair . . . (*He touches her hair.*) Your hair got so gray.

LINDA. Oh, it's been gray since you were in high school. I just stopped dyeing it, that's all.

BIFF. Dye it again, will ya? I don't want my pal looking old. (*He smiles.*)

LINDA. You're such a boy! You think you can go away for a year and . . . You've got to get it into your head now that one day you'll knock on this door and there'll be strange people here . . .

BIFF. What are you talking about? You're not even sixty, Mom.

LINDA. But what about your father?

BIFF (*lamely*). Well, I meant him too.

HAPPY. He admires Pop.

LINDA. Biff, dear, if you don't have any feeling for him, then you can't have any feeling for me.

BIFF. Sure I can, Mom.

LINDA. No. You can't just come to see me, because I love him. (*With a threat, but only a threat, of tears.*) He's the dearest man in the world to me, and I won't have anyone making him feel unwanted and low and blue. You've got to make up your mind now, darling, there's no leeway any more. Either he's your father and you pay him that respect, or else you're not to come here. I know he's not easy to get along with—nobody knows that better than me—but . . .

WILLY (*from the left, with a laugh*). Hey, hey, Biffo!

BIFF (*starting to go out after Willy*). What the hell is the matter with him? (*Happy stops him.*)

LINDA. Don't—don't go near him!

BIFF. Stop making excuses for him! He always, always wiped the floor with you. Never had an ounce of respect for you.

HAPPY. He's always had respect for . . .

BIFF. What the hell do you know about it?

HAPPY (*surlily*). Just don't call him crazy!

BIFF. He's got no character—Charley wouldn't do this. Not in his own house—spewing out that vomit from his mind.

HAPPY. Charley never had to cope with what he's got to.

BIFF. People are worse off than Willy Loman. Believe me, I've seen them!

LINDA. Then make Charley your father, Biff. You can't do that, can you? I don't say he's a great man. Willy Loman never made a lot of money. His name was never in the paper. He's not the finest character that ever lived. But he's a human being, and a terrible thing is happening to him. So attention must be paid. He's not to be allowed to fall into his grave like an old dog. Attention, attention must be finally paid to such a person. You called him crazy . . .

BIFF. I didn't mean . . .

LINDA. No, a lot of people think he's lost his—balance. But you don't have to be very smart to know what his trouble is. The man is exhausted.

HAPPY. Sure!

LINDA. A small man can be just as exhausted as a great man. He works for a company thirty-six years this March, opens up unheard-of territories to their trademark, and now in his old age they take his salary away.

HAPPY (*indignantly*). I didn't know that, Mom.

LINDA. You never asked, my dear! Now that you get your spending money someplace else you don't trouble your mind with him.

HAPPY. But I gave him money last . . .

LINDA. Christmas time, fifty dollars! To fix the hot water it cost ninety-seven fifty! For five weeks he's been on straight commission, like a beginner, an unknown!

BIFF. Those ungrateful bastards!

LINDA. Are they any worse than his sons? When he brought them business, when he was young, they were glad to see him. But now his old friends, the old buyers that loved him so and always found some order to hand him in a pinch—they're all dead, retired. He used to be able to make six, seven calls a day in Boston. Now he takes his valises out of the car and puts them back and takes them out again and he's exhausted. Instead of walking he talks now. He drives seven hundred miles, and when he gets there no one knows him any more, no one welcomes him. And what goes through a man's mind, driving seven hundred miles home without having earned a cent? Why shouldn't he talk to himself? Why? When he has to go to Charley and borrow fifty dollars a week and pretend to me that it's his pay? How long can that go on? How long? You see what I'm sitting here and waiting for? And you tell me he has no character? The man who never worked a day but for your benefit? When does he get the medal for that? Is this his reward—to turn around at the age of sixty-three and find his sons, who he loved better than his life, one a philandering bum . . .

HAPPY. Mom!

LINDA. That's all you are, my baby! (*To Biff.*) And you! What happened to the love you had for him? You were such pals! How you used to talk to him on the phone every night! How lonely he was till he could come home to you!

BIFF. All right, Mom. I'll live here in my room, and I'll get a job. I'll keep away from him, that's all.

LINDA. No, Biff. You can't stay here and fight all the time.

BIFF. He threw me out of this house, remember that.

LINDA. Why did he do that? I never knew why.

BIFF. Because I know he's a fake and he doesn't like anybody around who knows!

LINDA. Why a fake? In what way? What do you mean?

BIFF. Just don't lay it all at my feet. It's between me and him—that's all I have to say. I'll chip in from now on. He'll settle for half my paycheck. He'll be all right. I'm going to bed. (*He starts for the stairs.*)

LINDA. He won't be all right.

BIFF (*turning on the stairs, furiously*). I hate this city and I'll stay here. Now what do you want?

LINDA. He's dying, Biff.

Happy turns quickly to her, shocked.

BIFF (*after a pause*). Why is he dying?

LINDA. He's been trying to kill himself.

BIFF (*with great horror*). How?

LINDA. I live from day to day.

BIFF. What're you talking about?

LINDA. Remember I wrote you that he smashed up the car again? In February?

BIFF. Well?

LINDA. The insurance inspector came. He said that they have evidence. That all these accidents in the last year—weren't—weren't—accidents.

HAPPY. How can they tell that? That's a lie.

LINDA. It seems there's a woman . . . (*She takes a breath as:*)

BIFF (*sharply but contained*). What woman?

LINDA (*simultaneously*). . . . and this woman . . .

LINDA. What?

BIFF. Nothing. Go ahead.

LINDA. What did you say?

BIFF. Nothing. I just said what woman?

HAPPY. What about her?

LINDA. Well, it seems she was walking down the road and saw his car. She says that he wasn't driving fast at all, and that he didn't skid. She says he came to that little bridge, and then deliberately smashed into the railing, and it was only the shallowness of the water that saved him.

BIFF. Oh, no, he probably just fell asleep again.

LINDA. I don't think he fell asleep.

BIFF. Why not?

LINDA. Last month . . . (*With great difficulty.*) Oh, boys, it's so hard to say a thing like this! He's just a big stupid man to you, but I tell you there's more good in him than in many other people. (*She chokes, wipes her eyes.*) I was looking for a fuse. The lights blew out, and I went down the cellar. And behind the fuse box—it happened to fall out—was a length of rubber pipe—just short.

HAPPY. No kidding!

LINDA. There's a little attachment on the end of it. I knew right away. And sure enough, on the bottom of the water heater there's a new little nipple on the gas pipe.

HAPPY (*angrily*). That—jerk.

BIFF. Did you have it taken off?

LINDA. I'm—I'm ashamed to. How can I mention it to him? Every day I go down and take away that little rubber pipe. But, when he comes home, I put it back where it was. How can I insult him that way? I don't know what to do. I live from day to day, boys. I tell you, I know every thought in his mind. It sounds so old-fashioned and silly, but I tell you he put his whole life into you and you've turned your backs on him. (*She is bent over in the chair, weeping, her face in her hands.*) Biff, I swear to God! Biff, his life is in your hands!

HAPPY (*to Biff*). How do you like that damned fool!

BIFF (*kissing her*). All right, pal, all right. It's all settled now. I've been remiss. I know that, Mom. But now I'll stay, and I swear to you, I'll apply myself. (*Kneeling in front of her, in a fever of self-reproach.*) It's just—you see, Mom, I don't fit in business. Not that I won't try. I'll try, and I'll make good.

HAPPY. Sure you will. The trouble with you in business was you never tried to please people.

BIFF. I know, I . . .

HAPPY. Like when you worked for Harrison's. Bob Harrison said you were tops, and then you go and do some damn fool thing like whistling whole songs in the elevator like a comedian.

BIFF (*against Happy*). So what? I like to whistle sometimes.

HAPPY. You don't raise a guy to a responsible job who whistles in the elevator!

LINDA. Well, don't argue about it now.

HAPPY. Like when you'd go off and swim in the middle of the day instead of taking the line around.

BIFF (*his resentment rising*). Well, don't you run off? You take off sometimes, don't you? On a nice summer day?

HAPPY. Yeah, but I cover myself!

LINDA. Boys!

HAPPY. If I'm going to take a fade the boss can call any number where I'm supposed to be and they'll swear to him that I just left. I'll tell you something that I hate to say, Biff, but in the business world some of them think you're crazy.

BIFF (*angered*). Screw the business world!

HAPPY. All right, screw it! Great, but cover yourself!

LINDA. Hap, Hap!

BIFF. I don't care what they think! They've laughed at Dad for years, and you know why? Because we don't belong in this nuthouse of a city! We should be mixing cement on some open plain or—or carpenters. A carpenter is allowed to whistle!

Willy walks in from the entrance of the house, at left.

WILLY. Even your grandfather was better than a carpenter. (*Pause. They watch him.*) You never grew up. Bernard does not whistle in the elevator, I assure you.

BIFF (*as though to laugh Willy out of it*). Yeah, but you do, Pop.

WILLY. I never in my life whistled in an elevator! And who in the business world thinks I'm crazy?

BIFF. I didn't mean it like that, Pop. Now don't make a whole thing out of it, will ya?

WILLY. Go back to the West! Be a carpenter, a cowboy, enjoy yourself!

LINDA. Willy, he was just saying . . .

WILLY. I heard what he said!

HAPPY (*trying to quiet Willy*). Hey, Pop, come on now . . .

WILLY (*continuing over Happy's line*). They laugh at me, heh? Go to Filene's, go to the Hub, go to Slattery's, Boston. Call out the name Willy Loman and see what happens! Big shot!

BIFF. All right, Pop.

WILLY. Big!

BIFF. All right!

WILLY. Why do you always insult me?

BIFF. I didn't say a word. (*To Linda.*) Did I say a word?

LINDA. He didn't say anything, Willy.

WILLY (*going to the doorway of the living room*). All right, good night, good night.

LINDA. Willy, dear, he just decided . . .

WILLY (*to Biff*). If you get tired hanging around tomorrow, paint the ceiling I put up in the living room.

BIFF. I'm leaving early tomorrow.

HAPPY. He's going to see Bill Oliver, Pop.

WILLY (*interestedly*). Oliver? For what?

BIFF (*with reserve, but trying; trying*). He always said he'd stake me. I'd like to go into business, so maybe I can take him up on it.

LINDA. Isn't that wonderful?

WILLY. Don't interrupt. What's wonderful about it? There's fifty men in the City of New York who'd stake him. (*To Biff.*) Sporting goods?

BIFF. I guess so. I know something about it and . . .

WILLY. He knows something about it! You know sporting goods better than Spalding, for God's sake! How much is he giving you?

BIFF. I don't know, I didn't even see him yet, but . . .

WILLY. Then what're you talkin' about?

BIFF (*getting angry*). Well, all I said was I'm gonna see him, that's all!

WILLY (*turning away*). Ah, you're counting your chickens again.

BIFF (*starting left for the stairs*). Oh, Jesus, I'm going to sleep!

WILLY (*calling after him*). Don't curse in this house!

BIFF (*turning*). Since when did you get so clean?

HAPPY (*trying to stop them*). Wait a . . .

WILLY. Don't use that language to me! I won't have it!

HAPPY (*grabbing Biff, shouts*). Wait a minute! I got an idea. I got a feasible idea. Come here, Biff, let's talk this over now, let's talk some sense here. When I was down in Florida last time, I thought of a great idea to sell sporting goods. It just came back to me. You and I, Biff—we have a line, the Loman Line. We train a couple of weeks, and put on a couple of exhibitions, see?

WILLY. That's an idea!

HAPPY. Wait! We form two basketball teams, see? Two water-polo teams. We play each other. It's a million dollars' worth of publicity. Two brothers, see? The Loman Brothers. Displays in the Royal Palms—all the hotels. And banners over the ring and the basketball court: "Loman Brothers." Baby, we could sell sporting goods!

WILLY. That is a one-million-dollar idea!

LINDA. Marvelous!

BIFF. I'm in great shape as far as that's concerned.

HAPPY. And the beauty of it is, Biff, it wouldn't be like a business. We'd be out playin' ball again.

BIFF (*enthused*). Yeah, that's . . .

WILLY. Million-dollar . . .

HAPPY. And you wouldn't get fed up with it, Biff. It'd be the family again. There'd be the old honor, and comradeship, and if you wanted to go off for a swim or somethin'—well, you'd do it! Without some smart cooky gettin' up ahead of you!

WILLY. Lick the world! You guys together could absolutely lick the civilized world.

BIFF. I'll see Oliver tomorrow. Hap, if we could work that out . . .

LINDA. Maybe things are beginning to . . .

WILLY (*widely enthused, to Linda*). Stop interrupting! (*To Biff.*) But don't wear sport jacket and slacks when you see Oliver.

BIFF. No, I'll . . .

WILLY. A business suit, and talk as little as possible, and don't crack any jokes.

BIFF. He did like me. Always liked me.

LINDA. He loved you!

WILLY (*to Linda*). Will you stop! (*To Biff.*) Walk in very serious. You are not applying for a boy's job. Money is to pass. Be quiet, fine, and serious. Everybody likes a kidder, but nobody lends him money.

HAPPY. I'll try to get some myself, Biff. I'm sure I can.

WILLY. I see great things for you kids, I think your troubles are over. But remember, start big and you'll end big. Ask for fifteen. How much you gonna ask for?

BIFF. Gee, I don't know . . .

WILLY. And don't say "Gee." "Gee" is a boy's word. A man walking in for fifteen thousand dollars does not say "Gee!"

BIFF. Ten, I think, would be top though.

WILLY. Don't be so modest. You always started too low. Walk in with a big laugh. Don't look worried. Start off with a couple of your good stories to lighten things up. It's not what you say, it's how you say it—because personality always wins the day.

LINDA. Oliver always thought the highest of him . . .

WILLY. Will you let me talk?

BIFF. Don't yell at her, Pop, will ya?

WILLY (*angrily*). I was talking, wasn't I?

BIFF. I don't like you yelling at her all the time, and I'm tellin' you, that's all.

WILLY. What're you, takin' over this house?

LINDA. Willy . . .

WILLY (*turning to her*). Don't take his side all the time, goddammit!

BIFF (*furiously*). Stop yelling at her!

WILLY (*suddenly pulling on his cheek, beaten down, guilt ridden*). Give my best to Bill Oliver—he may remember me. (*He exits through the living room doorway.*)

LINDA (*her voice subdued*). What'd you have to start that for? (*Biff turns away.*) You see how sweet he was as soon as you talked hopefully? (*She goes over to Biff.*) Come up and say good night to him. Don't let him go to bed that way.

HAPPY. Come on, Biff, let's buck him up.

LINDA. Please, dear. Just say good night. It takes so little to make him happy. Come. (*She goes through the living room doorway, calling upstairs from within the living room.*) Your pajamas are hanging in the bathroom, Willy!

HAPPY (*looking toward where Linda went out*). What a woman! They broke the mold when they made her. You know that, Biff?

BIFF. He's off salary. My God, working on commission!

HAPPY. Well, let's face it: he's no hot-shot selling man. Except that sometimes, you have to admit, he's a sweet personality.

BIFF (*deciding*). Lend me ten bucks, will ya? I want to buy some new ties.

HAPPY. I'll take you to a place I know. Beautiful stuff. Wear one of my striped shirts tomorrow.

BIFF. She got gray. Mom got awful old. Gee, I'm gonna go in to Oliver tomorrow and knock him for a . . .

HAPPY. Come on up. Tell that to Dad. Let's give him a whirl. Come on.

BIFF (*steamed up*). You know, with ten thousand bucks, boy!

HAPPY (*as they go into the living room*). That's the talk, Biff, that's the first time I've heard the old confidence out of you! (*From within the living room, fading off*) You're gonna live with me, kid, and any babe you want just say the word . . . (*The last lines are hardly heard. They are mounting the stairs to their parents' bedroom.*)

LINDA (*entering her bedroom and addressing Willy, who is in the bathroom. She is straightening the bed for him*). Can you do anything about the shower? It drips.

WILLY (*from the bathroom*). All of a sudden everything falls to pieces. Goddam plumbing, oughta be sued, those people. I hardly finished putting it in and the thing . . . (*His words rumble off.*)

LINDA. I'm just wondering if Oliver will remember him. You think he might?

WILLY (*coming out of the bathroom in his pajamas*). Remember him? What's the matter with you, you crazy? If he'd've stayed with Oliver he'd be on top by now! Wait'll Oliver gets a look at him. You don't know the average caliber any more. The average young man today—(*he is getting into bed*)—is got a caliber of zero. Greatest thing in the world for him was to bum around.

Biff and Happy enter the bedroom. Slight pause.

WILLY (*stops short, looking at Biff*). Glad to hear it, boy.

HAPPY. He wanted to say good night to you, sport.

WILLY (*to Biff*). Yeah. Knock him dead, boy. What'd you want to tell me?

BIFF. Just take it easy, Pop. Good night. (*He turns to go.*)

WILLY (*unable to resist*). And if anything falls off the desk while you're talking to him—like a package or something—don't you pick it up. They have office boys for that.

LINDA. I'll make a big breakfast . . .

WILLY. Will you let me finish? (*To Biff.*) Tell him you were in the business in the West. Not farm work.

BIFF. All right, Dad.

LINDA. I think everything . . .

WILLY (*going right through her speech*). And don't undersell yourself. No less than fifteen thousand dollars.

BIFF (*unable to bear him*). Okay. Good night, Mom. (*He starts moving.*)

WILLY. Because you got a greatness in you, Biff, remember that. You got all kinds of greatness . . . (*He lies back, exhausted. Biff walks out.*)

LINDA (*calling after Biff*). Sleep well, darling!

HAPPY. I'm gonna get married, Mom. I wanted to tell you.

LINDA. Go to sleep, dear.

HAPPY (*going*). I just wanted to tell you.

WILLY. Keep up the good work. (*Happy exits.*) God . . . remember that Ebbets Field game? The championship of the city?

LINDA. Just rest. Should I sing to you?

WILLY. Yeah. Sing to me. (*Linda hums a soft lullaby.*) When that team came out—he was the tallest, remember?

LINDA. Oh, yes. And in gold.

Biff enters the darkened kitchen, takes a cigarette, and leaves the house. He comes downstage into a golden pool of light. He smokes, staring at the night.

WILLY. Like a young god. Hercules—something like that. And the sun, the sun all around him. Remember how he waved to me? Right up from the field, with the representatives of three colleges standing by? And the buyers I brought, and the cheers when he came out—Loman, Loman, Loman! God Almighty, he'll be great yet. A star like that, magnificent, can never really fade away!

The light on Willy is fading. The gas heater begins to glow through the kitchen wall, near the stairs, a blue flame beneath red coils.

LINDA (*timidly*). Willy dear, what has he got against you?

WILLY. I'm so tired. Don't talk any more.

Biff slowly returns to the kitchen. He stops, stares toward the heater.

LINDA. Will you ask Howard to let you work in New York?

WILLY. First thing in the morning. Everything'll be all right.

Biff reaches behind the heater and draws out a length of rubber tubing. He is horrified and turns his head toward Willy's room, still dimly lit, from which the strains of Linda's desperate but monotonous humming rise.

WILLY (*staring through the window into the moonlight*). Gee, look at the moon moving between the buildings!

Biff wraps the tubing around his hand and quickly goes up the stairs.

ACT 2

SCENE: *Music is heard, gay and bright. The curtain rises as the music fades away. Willy, in shirt sleeves, is sitting at the kitchen table, sipping coffee, his hat in his lap. Linda is filling his cup when she can.*

WILLY. Wonderful coffee. Meal in itself.

LINDA. Can I make you some eggs?

WILLY. No. Take a breath.

LINDA. You look so rested, dear.

WILLY. I slept like a dead one. First time in months. Imagine, sleeping till ten on a Tuesday morning. Boys left nice and early, heh?

LINDA. They were out of here by eight o'clock.

WILLY. Good work!

LINDA. It was so thrilling to see them leaving together. I can't get over the shaving lotion in this house!

WILLY (*smiling*). Mmm . . .

LINDA. Biff was very changed this morning. His whole attitude seemed to be hopeful. He couldn't wait to get downtown to see Oliver.

WILLY. He's heading for a change. There's no question, there simply are certain men that take longer to get—solidified. How did he dress?

LINDA. His blue suit. He's so handsome in that suit. He could be a—anything in that suit!

Willy gets up from the table. Linda holds his jacket for him.

WILLY. There's no question, no question at all. Gee, on the way home tonight I'd like to buy some seeds.

LINDA (*laughing*). That'd be wonderful. But not enough sun gets back there. Nothing'll grow any more.

WILLY. You wait, kid, before it's all over we're gonna get a little place out in the country, and I'll raise some vegetables, a couple of chickens . . .

LINDA. You'll do it yet, dear.

Willy walks out of his jacket. Linda follows him.

WILLY. And they'll get married, and come for a weekend. I'd build a little guest house. 'Cause I got so many fine tools, all I'd need would be a little lumber and some peace of mind.

LINDA (*joyfully*). I sewed the lining . . .

WILLY. I could build two guest houses, so they'd both come. Did he decide how much he's going to ask Oliver for?

LINDA (*getting him into the jacket*). He didn't mention it, but I imagine ten or fifteen thousand. You going to talk to Howard today?

WILLY. Yeah. I'll put it to him straight and simple. He'll just have to take me off the road.

LINDA. And Willy, don't forget to ask for a little advance, because we've got the insurance premium. It's the grace period now.

WILLY. That's a hundred . . . ?

LINDA. A hundred and eight, sixty-eight. Because we're a little short again.

WILLY. Why are we short?

LINDA. Well, you had the motor job on the car . . .

WILLY. That goddam Studebaker!

LINDA. And you got one more payment on the refrigerator . . .

WILLY. But it just broke again!

LINDA. Well, it's old, dear.

WILLY. I told you we should've bought a well-advertised machine. Charley bought a General Electric and it's twenty years old and it's still good, that son-of-a-bitch.

LINDA. But, Willy . . .

WILLY. Whoever heard of a Hastings refrigerator? Once in my life I would like to own something outright before it's broken! I'm always in a race with the junkyard! I just finished paying for the car and it's on its last legs. The refrigerator consumes belts like a goddam maniac. They time those things. They time them so when you finally paid for them, they're used up.

LINDA (*buttoning up his jacket as he unbuttons it*). All told, about two hundred dollars would carry us, dear. But that includes the last payment on the mortgage. After this payment, Willy, the house belongs to us.

WILLY. It's twenty-five years!

LINDA. Biff was nine years old when we bought it.

WILLY. Well, that's a great thing. To weather a twenty-five year mortgage is . . .

LINDA. It's an accomplishment.

WILLY. All the cement, the lumber, the reconstruction I put in this house! There ain't a crack to be found in it any more.

LINDA. Well, it served its purpose.

WILLY. What purpose? Some stranger'll come along, move in, and that's that. If only Biff would take this house, and raise a family . . . (*He starts to go.*) Good-by, I'm late.

LINDA (*suddenly remembering*). Oh, I forgot! You're supposed to meet them for dinner.

WILLY. Me?

LINDA. At Frank's Chop House on Forty-eighth near Sixth Avenue.

WILLY. Is that so! How about you?

LINDA. No, just the three of you. They're gonna blow you to a big meal!

WILLY. Don't say! Who thought of that?

LINDA. Biff came to me this morning, Willy, and he said, "Tell Dad, we want to blow him to a big meal." Be there six o'clock. You and your two boys are going to have dinner.

WILLY. Gee whiz! That's really somethin'. I'm gonna knock Howard for a loop, kid. I'll get an advance, and I'll come home with a New York job. Goddammit, now I'm gonna do it!

LINDA. Oh, that's the spirit, Willy!

WILLY. I will never get behind a wheel the rest of my life!

LINDA. It's changing, Willy, I can feel it changing!

WILLY. Beyond a question. G'by, I'm late. (*He starts to go again.*)

LINDA (*calling after him as she runs to the kitchen table for a handkerchief*). You got your glasses?

WILLY (*feels for them, then comes back in*). Yeah, yeah, got my glasses.

LINDA (*giving him the handkerchief*). And a handkerchief.

WILLY. Yeah, handkerchief.

LINDA. And your saccharine?

WILLY. Yeah, my saccharine.

LINDA. Be careful on the subway stairs.

She kisses him, and a silk stocking is seen hanging from her hand. Willy notices it.

WILLY. Will you stop mending stockings? At least while I'm in the house. It gets me nervous. I can't tell you. Please.

Linda hides the stocking in her hand as she follows Willy across the forestage in front of the house.

LINDA. Remember, Frank's Chop House.

WILLY (*passing the apron*). Maybe beets would grow out there.

LINDA (*laughing*). But you tried so many times.

WILLY. Yeah. Well, don't work hard today. (*He disappears around the right corner of the house.*)

LINDA. Be careful!

As Willy vanishes, Linda waves to him. Suddenly the phone rings. She runs across the stage and into the kitchen and lifts it.

LINDA. Hello? Oh, Biff! I'm so glad you called, I just . . . Yes, sure, I just told him. Yes, he'll be there for dinner at six o'clock, I didn't forget. Listen, I was just dying to tell you. You know that little rubber pipe I told you about? That he connected to the gas heater? I finally decided to go down the cellar this morning and take it away and destroy it. But it's gone! Imagine? He took it away himself, it isn't there! (*She listens.*) When? Oh, then you took it. Oh—nothing, it's just that I'd hoped he'd taken it away himself. Oh, I'm not worried, darling, because this morning he left in such high spirits, it was like the old

days! I'm not afraid any more. Did Mr. Oliver see you?
. . . Well, you wait there then. And make a nice impression on him, darling. Just don't perspire too much before
you see him. And have a nice time with Dad. He may
have big news too! . . . That's right, a New York job. And
be sweet to him tonight, dear. Be loving to him. Because
he's only a little boat looking for a harbor. (*She is trembling with sorrow and joy.*) Oh, that's wonderful, Biff,
you'll save his life. Thanks, darling. Just put your arm
around him when he comes into the restaurant. Give
him a smile. That's the boy . . . Good-by, dear. . . . You
got your comb? . . . That's fine. Good-by, Biff dear.

*In the middle of her speech, Howard Wagner, thirty-six,
wheels in a small typewriter table on which is a wire-
recording machine and proceeds to plug it in. This is on the
left forestage. Light slowly fades on Linda as it rises on
Howard. Howard is intent on threading the machine and
only glances over his shoulder as Willy appears.*

WILLY. Pst! Pst!

HOWARD. Hello, Willy, come in.

WILLY. Like to have a little talk with you, Howard.

HOWARD. Sorry to keep you waiting. I'll be with you in a
minute.

WILLY. What's that, Howard?

HOWARD. Didn't you ever see one of these? Wire recorder.

WILLY. Oh. Can we talk a minute?

HOWARD. Records things. Just got delivery yesterday. Been
driving me crazy, the most terrific machine I ever saw in
my life. I was up all night with it.

WILLY. What do you do with it?

HOWARD. I bought it for dictation, but you can do anything
with it. Listen to this. I had it home last night. Listen to
what I picked up. The first one is my daughter. Get this.
(*He flicks the switch and "Roll Out the Barrel" is heard being
whistled.*) Listen to that kid whistle.

WILLY. That is lifelike, isn't it?

HOWARD. Seven years old. Get that tone.

WILLY. Ts, ts. Like to ask a little favor if you . . .

*The whistling breaks off, and the voice of Howard's
daughter is heard.*

HIS DAUGHTER. "Now you, Daddy."

HOWARD. She's crazy for me! (*Again the same song is whistled.*) That's me! Ha! (*He winks.*)

WILLY. You're very good!

*The whistling breaks off again. The machine runs silent
for a moment.*

HOWARD. Sh! Get this now, this is my son.

HIS SON. "The capital of Alabama is Montgomery; the capital of Arizona is Phoenix; the capital of Arkansas is Little
Rock; the capital of California is Sacramento . . ." (*and
on, and on.*)

HOWARD (*holding up five fingers*). Five years old, Willy!

WILLY. He'll make an announcer some day!

HIS SON (*continuing*). "The capital . . ."

HOWARD. Get that—alphabetical order! (*The machine breaks
off suddenly.*) Wait a minute. The maid kicked the plug
out.

WILLY. It certainly is a . . .

HOWARD. Sh, for God's sake!

HIS SON. "It's nine o'clock, Bulova watch time. So I have to
go to sleep."

WILLY. That really is . . .

HOWARD. Wait a minute! The next is my wife.

They wait.

HOWARD'S VOICE. "Go on, say something." (*Pause.*) "Well,
you gonna talk?"

HIS WIFE. "I can't think of anything."

HOWARD'S VOICE. "Well, talk—it's turning."

HIS WIFE (*shyly, beaten*). "Hello." (*Silence.*) "Oh, Howard, I
can't talk into this . . ."

HOWARD (*snapping the machine off*). That was my wife.

WILLY. That is a wonderful machine. Can we . . .

HOWARD. I tell you, Willy, I'm gonna take my camera, and
my bandsaw, and all my hobbies, and out they go. This is
the most fascinating relaxation I ever found.

WILLY. I think I'll get one myself.

HOWARD. Sure, they're only a hundred and a half. You can't
do without it. Supposing you wanna hear Jack Benny,
see? But you can't be at home at that hour. So you tell the
maid to turn the radio on when Jack Benny comes on,
and this automatically goes on with the radio . . .

WILLY. And when you come home you . . .

HOWARD. You can come home twelve o'clock, one o'clock,
any time you like, and you get yourself a Coke and sit
yourself down, throw the switch, and there's Jack Benny's
program in the middle of the night!

WILLY. I'm definitely going to get one. Because lots of times
I'm on the road, and I think to myself, what I must be
missing on the radio!

HOWARD. Don't you have a radio in the car?

WILLY. Well, yeah, but who ever thinks of turning it on?

HOWARD. Say, aren't you supposed to be in Boston?

WILLY. That's what I want to talk to you about, Howard. You
got a minute? (*He draws a chair in from the wing.*)

HOWARD. What happened? What're you doing here?

WILLY. Well . . .

HOWARD. You didn't crack up again, did you?

WILLY. Oh, no. No . . .

HOWARD. Geez, you had me worried there for a minute.
What's the trouble?

WILLY. Well, tell you the truth, Howard. I've come to the
decision that I'd rather not travel any more.

HOWARD. Not travel! Well, what'll you do?

WILLY. Remember, Christmas time, when you had the party
here? You said you'd try to think of some spot for me here
in town.

HOWARD. With us?

WILLY. Well, sure.

HOWARD. Oh, yeah, yeah. I remember. Well, I couldn't think of anything for you, Willy.

WILLY. I tell ya, Howard. The kids are all grown up, y'know. I don't need much any more. If I could take home—well, sixty-five dollars a week, I could swing it.

HOWARD. Yeah, but Willy, see I . . .

WILLY. I tell ya why, Howard. Speaking frankly and between the two of us, y'know—I'm just a little tired.

HOWARD. Oh, I could understand that, Willy. But you're a road man, Willy, and we do a road business. We've only got a half-dozen salesmen on the floor here.

WILLY. God knows, Howard. I never asked a favor of any man. But I was with the firm when your father used to carry you in here in his arms.

HOWARD. I know that, Willy, but . . .

WILLY. Your father came to me the day you were born and asked me what I thought of the name Howard, may he rest in peace.

HOWARD. I appreciate that, Willy, but there just is no spot here for you. If I had a spot I'd slam you right in, but I just don't have a single solitary spot.

He looks for his lighter. Willy has picked it up and gives it to him. Pause.

WILLY (*with increasing anger*). Howard, all I need to set my table is fifty dollars a week.

HOWARD. But where am I going to put you, kid?

WILLY. Look, it isn't a question of whether I can sell merchandise, is it?

HOWARD. No, but it's business, kid, and everybody's gotta pull his own weight.

WILLY (*desperately*). Just let me tell you a story, Howard . . .

HOWARD. 'Cause you gotta admit, business is business.

WILLY (*angrily*). Business is definitely business, but just listen for a minute. You don't understand this. When I was a boy—eighteen, nineteen—I was already on the road. And there was a question in my mind as to whether selling had a future for me. Because in those days I had a yearning to go to Alaska. See, there were three gold strikes in one month in Alaska, and I felt like going out. Just for the ride, you might say.

HOWARD (*barely interested*). Don't say.

WILLY. Oh, yeah, my father lived many years in Alaska. He was an adventurous man. We've got quite a little streak of self-reliance in our family. I thought I'd go out with my older brother and try to locate him, and maybe settle in the North with the old man. And I was almost decided to go, when I met a salesman in the Parker House. His name was Dave Singleman. And he was eighty-four years old, and he'd drummed merchandise in thirty-one states. And old Dave, he'd go up to his room, y'understand, put on his green velvet slippers—I'll never forget—and pick up his phone and call the buyers, and without ever leaving his room, at the age of eighty-four, he made his living.

And when I saw that, I realized that selling was the greatest career a man could want. 'Cause what could be more satisfying than to be able to go, at the age of eight-four, into twenty or thirty different cities, and pick up a phone, and be remembered and loved and helped by so many different people? Do you know? when he died—and by the way he died the death of a salesman, in his green velvet slippers in the smoker of the New York, New Haven and Hartford, going into Boston—when he died, hundreds of salesmen and buyers were at his funeral. Things were sad on a lotta trains for months after that. (*He stands up, Howard has not looked at him.*) In those days there was personality in it, Howard. There was respect, and comradeship, and gratitude in it. Today, it's all cut and dried, and there's no chance for bringing friendship to bear—or personality. You see what I mean? They don't know me any more.

HOWARD (*moving away, to the right*). That's just the thing, Willy.

WILLY. If I had forty dollars a week—that's all I'd need. Forty dollars, Howard.

HOWARD. Kid, I can't take blood from a stone, I . . .

WILLY (*desperation is on him now*). Howard, the year Al Smith was nominated, your father came to me and . . .

HOWARD (*starting to go off*). I've got to see some people, kid.

WILLY (*stopping him*). I'm talking about your father! There were promises made across this desk! You mustn't tell me you've got people to see—I put thirty-four years into this firm, Howard, and now I can't pay my insurance! You can't eat the orange and throw the peel away—a man is not a piece of fruit! (*After a pause.*) Now pay attention. Your father—in 1928 I had a big year. I averaged a hundred and seventy dollars a week in commissions.

HOWARD (*impatiently*). Now, Willy, you never averaged . . .

WILLY (*banging his hand on the desk*). I averaged a hundred and seventy dollars a week in the year of 1928! And your father came to me—or rather, I was in the office here—it was right over this desk—and he put his hand on my shoulder . . .

HOWARD (*getting up*). You'll have to excuse me, Willy, I gotta see some people. Pull yourself together. (*Going out.*) I'll be back in a little while.

On Howard's exit, the light on his chair grows very bright and strange.

WILLY. Pull myself together! What the hell did I say to him? My God, I was yelling at him! How could I? (*Willy breaks off, staring at the light, which occupies the chair, animating it. He approaches this chair, standing across the desk from it.*) Frank, Frank, don't you remember what you told me that time? How you put your hand on my shoulder, and Frank . . . (*He leans on the desk and as he speaks the dead man's name he accidentally switches on the recorder, and instantly*)

HOWARD'S SON. ". . . of New York is Albany. The capital of Ohio is Cincinnati, the capital of Rhode Island is . . ." (*The recitation continues.*)

WILLY (*leaping away with fright, shouting*). Ha! Howard! Howard! Howard!

HOWARD (*rushing in*). What happened?

WILLY (*pointing at the machine, which continues nasally, childishly, with the capital cities*). Shut it off! Shut it off!

HOWARD (*pulling the plug out*). Look, Willy . . .

WILLY (*pressing his hands to his eyes.*) I gotta get myself some coffee. I'll get some coffee . . .

Willy starts to walk out. Howard stops him.

HOWARD (*rolling up the cord*). Willy, look . . .

WILLY. I'll go to Boston.

HOWARD. Willy, you can't go to Boston for us.

WILLY Why can't I go?

HOWARD. I don't want you to represent us. I've been meaning to tell you for a long time now.

WILLY. Howard, are you firing me?

HOWARD. I think you need a good long rest, Willy.

WILLY. Howard . . .

HOWARD. And when you feel better, come back, and we'll see if we can work something out.

WILLY. But I gotta earn money, Howard. I'm in no position to . . .

HOWARD. Where are your sons? Why don't your sons give you a hand?

WILLY. They're working on a very big deal.

HOWARD. This is no time for false pride, Willy. You go to your sons and you tell them that you're tired. You've got two great boys, haven't you?

WILLY. Oh, no question, no question, but in the meantime . . .

HOWARD. Then that's that, heh?

WILLY. All right, I'll go to Boston tomorrow.

HOWARD. No, no.

WILLY. I can't throw myself on my sons. I'm not a cripple!

HOWARD. Look, kid, I'm busy this morning.

WILLY (*grasping Howard's arm*). Howard, you've got to let me go to Boston!

HOWARD (*hard, keeping himself under control*). I've got a line of people to see this morning. Sit down, take five minutes, and pull yourself together, and then go home, will ya? I need the office, Willy. (*He starts to go, turns, remembering the recorder, starts to push off the table holding the recorder.*) Oh, yeah. Whenever you can this week, stop by and drop off the samples. You'll feel better, Willy, and then come back and we'll talk. Pull yourself together, kid, there's people outside.

Howard exits, pushing the table off left. Willy stares into space, exhausted. Now the music is heard—Ben's music—first distantly, then closer, closer. As Willy speaks, Ben enters from the right. He carries valise and umbrella.

WILLY. Oh, Ben, how did you do it? What is the answer? Did you wind up the Alaska deal already?

BEN. Doesn't take much time if you know what you're doing. Just a short business trip. Boarding ship in an hour. Wanted to say good-by.

WILLY. Ben, I've got to talk to you.

BEN (*glancing at his watch*). Haven't the time, William.

WILLY (*crossing the apron to Ben*). Ben, nothing's working out. I don't know what to do.

BEN. Now, look here, William. I've bought timberland in Alaska and I need a man to look after things for me.

WILLY. God, timberland! Me and my boys in those grand outdoors!

BEN. You've a new continent at your doorstep, William. Get out of these cities, they're full of talk and time payments and courts of law. Screw on your fists and you can fight for a fortune up there.

WILLY. Yes, yes! Linda, Linda!

Linda enters as of old, with the wash.

LINDA. Oh, you're back?

BEN. I haven't much time.

WILLY. No, wait! Linda, he's got a proposition for me in Alaska.

LINDA. But you've got . . . (*To Ben.*) He's got a beautiful job here.

WILLY. But in Alaska, kid, I could . . .

LINDA. You're doing well enough, Willy!

BEN (*to Linda*). Enough for what, my dear?

LINDA (*frightened of Ben and angry at him*). Don't say those things to him! Enough to be happy right here, right now. (*To Willy, while Ben laughs.*) Why must everybody conquer the world? You're well liked, and the boys love you, and someday—(*To Ben*)—why, old man Wagner told him just the other day that if he keeps it up he'll be a member of the firm, didn't he, Willy?

WILLY. Sure, sure. I am building something with this firm, Ben, and if a man is building something he must be on the right track, mustn't he?

BEN. What are you building? Lay your hand on it. Where is it?

WILLY (*hesitantly*). That's true, Linda, there's nothing.

LINDA. Why? (*To Ben.*) There's a man eighty-four years old . . .

WILLY. That's right, Ben, that's right. When I look at that man I say, what is there to worry about?

BEN. Bah!

WILLY. It's true, Ben. All he has to do is go into any city, pick up the phone, and he's making his living and you know why?

BEN (*picking up his valise*). I've got to go.

WILLY (*holding Ben back*). Look at this boy!

Biff, in his high school sweater, enters carrying suitcase. Happy carries Biff's shoulder guards, gold helmet, and football pants.

WILLY. Without a penny to his name, three great universities are begging for him, and from there the sky's the limit, because it's not what you do, Ben. It's who you know and the smile on your face! It's contacts, Ben, contacts! The whole wealth of Alaska passes over the lunch table at the Commodore Hotel, and that's the wonder, the wonder of this country, that a man can end with diamonds here on the basis of being liked! (*He turns to Biff.*) And that's why when you get out on that field today it's important. Because thousands of people will be rooting for you and loving you. (*To Ben, who has again begun to leave.*) And Ben! when he walks into a business office his name will sound out like a bell and all the doors will open to him! I've seen it, Ben, I've seen it a thousand times! You can't feel it with your hand like timber, but it's there!

BEN. Good-by, William.

WILLY. Ben, am I right? Don't you think I'm right? I value your advice.

BEN. There's a new continent at your doorstep, William. You could walk out rich. Rich! (*He is gone.*)

WILLY. We'll do it here, Ben! You hear me? We're gonna do it here!

Young Bernard rushes in. The gay music of the Boys is heard.

BERNARD. Oh, gee, I was afraid you left already!

WILLY. Why? What time is it?

BERNARD. It's half-past one!

WILLY. Well, come on, everybody! Ebbets Field next stop! Where's the pennants? (*He rushes through the wall-line of the kitchen and out into the living room.*)

LINDA (*to Biff*). Did you pack fresh underwear?

BIFF (*who has been limbering up*). I want to go!

BERNARD. Biff, I'm carrying your helmet, ain't I?

HAPPY. No, I'm carrying the helmet.

BERNARD. Oh, Biff, you promised me.

HAPPY. I'm carrying the helmet.

BERNARD. How am I going to get in the locker room?

LINDA. Let him carry the shoulder guards. (*She puts her coat and hat on in the kitchen.*)

BERNARD. Can I, Biff? 'Cause I told everybody I'm going to be in the locker room.

HAPPY. In Ebbets Field it's the clubhouse.

BERNARD. I meant the clubhouse. Biff!

HAPPY. Biff!

BIFF (*grandly, after a slight pause*). Let him carry the shoulder guards.

HAPPY (*as he gives Bernard the shoulder guards*). Stay close to us now.

Willy rushes in with the pennants.

WILLY (*handing them out*). Everybody wave when Biff comes out on the field. (*Happy and Bernard run off.*) You set now, boy?

The music has died away.

BIFF. Ready to go, Pop. Every muscle is ready.

WILLY (*at the edge of the apron*). You realize what this means?

BIFF. That's right, Pop.

WILLY (*feeling Biff's muscles*). You're comin' home this afternoon captain of the All-Scholastic Championship Team of the City of New York.

BIFF. I got it, Pop. And remember, pal, when I take off my helmet, that touchdown is for you.

WILLY. Let's go! (*He is starting out, with his arm around Biff, when Charley enters, as of old, in knickers.*) I got no room for you, Charley.

CHARLEY. Room? For what?

WILLY. In the car.

CHARLEY. You goin' for a ride? I wanted to shoot some casino.

WILLY (*furiously*). Casino! (*Incredulously.*) Don't you realize what today is?

LINDA. Oh, he knows, Willy. He's just kidding you.

WILLY. That's nothing to kid about!

CHARLEY. No, Linda, what's goin' on?

LINDA. He's playing in Ebbets Field.

CHARLEY. Baseball in this weather?

WILLY. Don't talk to him. Come on, come on! (*He is pushing them out.*)

CHARLEY. Wait a minute, didn't you hear the news?

WILLY. What?

CHARLEY. Don't you listen to the radio? Ebbets Field just blew up.

WILLY. You go to hell! (*Charley laughs. Pushing them out.*) Come on, come on! We're late.

CHARLEY (*as they go*). Knock a homer, Biff, knock a homer!

WILLY (*the last to leave, turning to Charley*). I don't think that was funny, Charley. This is the greatest day of his life.

CHARLEY. Willy, when are you going to grow up?

WILLY. Yeah, heh? When this game is over, Charley, you'll be laughing out of the other side of your face. They'll be calling him another Red Grange. Twenty-five thousand a year.

CHARLEY (*kidding*). Is that so?

WILLY. Yeah, that's so.

CHARLEY. Well, then, I'm sorry, Willy. But tell me something.

WILLY. What?

CHARLEY. Who is Red Grange?

WILLY. Put up your hands. Goddam you, put up your hands!

Charley, chuckling, shakes his head and walks away, around the left corner of the stage. Willy follows him. The music rises to a mocking frenzy.

WILLY. Who the hell do you think you are, better than everybody else? You don't know everything, you big, ignorant, stupid . . . Put up your hands!

Light rises, on the right side of the forestage, on a small table in the reception room of Charley's office. Traffic sounds are heard. Bernard, now mature, sits whistling to himself. A pair of tennis rackets and an old overnight bag are on the door beside him.

WILLY (*offstage*). What are you walking away for? Don't walk away! If you're going to say something say it to my face! I

know you laugh at me behind my back. You'll laugh out
of the other side of your goddam face after this game.
Touchdown! Touchdown! Eighty thousand people!
Touchdown! Right between the goal posts.

*Bernard is a quiet, earnest, but self-assured young man.
Willy's voice is coming from right upstage now. Bernard
lowers his feet off the table and listens. Jenny, his father's
secretary, enters.*

JENNY (*distressed*). Say, Bernard, will you go out in the hall?

BERNARD. What is that noise? Who is it?

JENNY. Mr. Loman. He just got off the elevator.

BERNARD (*getting up*). Who's he arguing with?

JENNY. Nobody. There's nobody with him. I can't deal with
him any more, and your father gets all upset every time
he comes. I've got a lot of typing to do, and your father's
waiting to sign it. Will you see him?

WILLY (*entering*). Touchdown! Touch—(*He sees Jenny.*)
Jenny, Jenny, good to see you. How're ya? Workin'? Or
still honest?

JENNY. Fine. How've you been feeling?

WILLY. Not much any more, Jenny. Ha, ha! (*He is surprised to
see the rackets.*)

BERNARD. Hello, Uncle Willy.

WILLY (*almost shocked*). Bernard! Well, look who's here! (*He
comes quickly, guiltily, to Bernard and warmly shakes his
hand.*)

BERNARD. How are you? Good to see you.

WILLY. What are you doing here?

BERNARD. Oh, just stopped by to see Pop. Get off my feet till
my train leaves. I'm going to Washington in a few minutes.

WILLY. Is he in?

BERNARD. Yes, he's in his office with the accountant. Sit
down.

WILLY (*sitting down*). What're you going to do in Washington?

BERNARD. Oh, just a case I've got there, Willy.

WILLY. That so? (*Indicating the rackets.*) You going to play
tennis there?

BERNARD. I'm staying with a friend who's got a court.

WILLY. Don't say. His own tennis court. Must be fine people,
I bet.

BERNARD. They are, very nice. Dad tells me Biff's in town.

WILLY (*with a big smile*). Yeah, Biff's in. Working on a very
big deal, Bernard.

BERNARD. What's Biff doing?

WILLY. Well, he's been doing very big things in the West.
But he decided to establish himself here. Very big. We're
having dinner. Did I hear your wife had a boy?

BERNARD. That's right. Our second.

WILLY. Two boys! What do you know!

BERNARD. What kind of a deal has Biff got?

WILLY. Well, Bill Oliver—very big sporting-goods man—he
wants Biff very badly. Called him in from the West. Long

distance, carte blanche, special deliveries. Your friends
have their own private tennis court?

BERNARD. You still with the old firm, Willy?

WILLY (*after a pause*). I'm—I'm overjoyed to see how you
made the grade, Bernard, overjoyed. It's an encouraging
thing to see a young man really—really . . . Looks very
good for Biff—very . . . (*He breaks off, then.*) Bernard . . .
(*He is so full of emotion, he breaks off again.*)

BERNARD. What is it, Willy?

WILLY (*small and alone*). What—what's the secret?

BERNARD. What secret?

WILLY. How—how did you? Why didn't he ever catch on?

BERNARD. I wouldn't know that, Willy.

WILLY (*confidentially, desperately*). You were his friend, his
boyhood friend. There's something I don't understand
about it. His life ended after that Ebbets Field game.
From the age of seventeen nothing good ever happened
to him.

BERNARD. He never trained himself for anything.

WILLY. But he did, he did. After high school he took so
many correspondence courses. Radio mechanics; television; God knows what, and never made the slightest
mark.

BERNARD (*taking off his glasses*). Willy, do you want to talk
candidly?

WILLY (*rising, faces Bernard*). I regard you as a very brilliant
man, Bernard. I value your advice.

BERNARD. Oh, the hell with the advice, Willy. I couldn't
advise you. There's just one thing I've always wanted to
ask you. When he was supposed to graduate, and the
math teacher flunked him . . .

WILLY. Oh, that son-of-a-bitch ruined his life.

BERNARD. Yeah, but, Willy, all he had to do was go to summer school and make up that subject.

WILLY. That's right, that's right.

BERNARD. Did you tell him not to go to summer school?

WILLY. Me? I begged him to go. I ordered him to go!

BERNARD. Then why wouldn't he go?

WILLY. Why? Why! Bernard, that question has been trailing
me like a ghost for the last fifteen years. He flunked the
subject, and laid down and died like a hammer hit him!

BERNARD. Take it easy, kid.

WILLY. Let me talk to you—I got nobody to talk to. Bernard,
Bernard, was it my fault? Y'see? It keeps going around in
my mind, maybe I did something to him. I got nothing to
give him.

BERNARD. Don't take it so hard.

WILLY. Why did he lay down? What is the story there? You
were his friend!

BERNARD. Willy, I remember, it was June, and our grades
came out. And he'd flunked math.

WILLY. That son-of-a-bitch!

BERNARD. No, it wasn't right then. Biff just got very angry, I
remember, and he was ready to enroll in summer school.

WILLY (*surprised*). He was?

BERNARD. He wasn't beaten by it at all. But then, Willy, he disappeared from the block for almost a month. And I got the idea that he'd gone up to New England to see you. Did he have a talk with you then?

Willy stares in silence.

BERNARD. Willy?

WILLY (*with a strong edge of resentment in his voice*). Yeah, he came to Boston. What about it?

BERNARD. Well, just that when he came back—I'll never forget this, it always mystifies me. Because I'd thought so well of Biff, even though he'd always taken advantage of me. I loved him, Willy, y'know? And he came back after that month and took his sneakers—remember those sneakers with "University of Virginia" printed on them? He was so proud of those, wore them every day. And he took them down in the cellar, and burned them up in the furnace. We had a fist fight. It lasted at least half an hour. Just the two of us, punching each other down the cellar, and crying right through it. I've often thought of how strange it was that I knew he'd given up his life. What happened in Boston, Willy?

Willy looks at him as at an intruder.

BERNARD. I just bring it up because you asked me.

WILLY (*angrily*). Nothing. What do you mean, "What happened?" What's that got to do with anything?

BERNARD. Well, don't get sore.

WILLY. What are you trying to do, blame it on me? If a boy lays down is that my fault?

BERNARD. Now, Willy, don't get . . .

WILLY. Well, don't—don't talk to me that way! What does that mean, "What happened?"

Charley enters. He is in his vest, and he carries a bottle of bourbon.

CHARLEY. Hey, you're going to miss that train. (*He waves the bottle.*)

BERNARD. Yeah, I'm going. (*He takes the bottle.*) Thanks, Pop. (*He picks up his rackets and bag.*) Good-by, Willy, and don't worry about it. You know, "If at first you don't succeed . . ."

WILLY. Yes, I believe in that.

BERNARD. But sometimes, Willy, it's better for a man just to walk away.

WILLY. Walk away?

BERNARD. That's right.

WILLY. But if you can't walk away?

BERNARD (*after a slight pause*). I guess that's when it's tough. (*Extending his hand.*) Good-by, Willy.

WILLY (*shaking Bernard's hand*). Good-by, boy.

CHARLEY (*an arm on Bernard's shoulder*). How do you like this kid? Gonna argue a case in front of the Supreme Court.

BERNARD (*protesting*). Pop!

WILLY (*genuinely shocked, pained, and happy*). No! The Supreme Court!

BERNARD. I gotta run. 'By, Dad!

CHARLEY. Knock 'em dead, Bernard!

Bernard goes off.

WILLY (*as Charley takes out his wallet*). The Supreme Court! And he didn't even mention it!

CHARLEY (*counting out money on the desk*). He don't have to—he's gonna do it.

WILLY. And you never told him what to do, did you? You never took any interest in him.

CHARLEY. My salvation is that I never took any interest in anything. There's some money—fifty dollars. I got an accountant inside.

WILLY. Charley, look . . . (*with difficulty.*) I got my insurance to pay. If you can manage it—I need a hundred and ten dollars.

Charley doesn't reply for a moment; merely stops moving.

WILLY. I'd draw it from my bank but Linda would know, and I . . .

CHARLEY. Sit down, Willy.

WILLY (*moving toward the chair*). I'm keeping an account of everything, remember. I'll pay every penny back. (*He sits.*)

CHARLEY. Now listen to me, Willy.

WILLY. I want you to know I appreciate . . .

CHARLEY (*sitting down on the table*). Willy, what're you doin'? What the hell is going on in your head?

WILLY. Why? I'm simply . . .

CHARLEY. I offered you a job. You make fifty dollars a week. And I won't send you on the road.

WILLY. I've got a job.

CHARLEY. Without pay? What kind of a job is a job without pay? (*He rises.*) Now, look, kid, enough is enough. I'm no genius but I know when I'm being insulted.

WILLY. Insulted!

CHARLEY. Why don't you want to work for me?

WILLY. What's the matter with you? I've got a job.

CHARLEY. Then what're you walkin' in here every week for?

WILLY (*getting up*). Well, if you don't want me to walk in here . . .

CHARLEY. I'm offering you a job.

WILLY. I don't want your goddam job!

CHARLEY. When the hell are you going to grow up?

WILLY (*furiously*). You big ignoramus, if you say that to me again I'll rap you one! I don't care how big you are! (*He's ready to fight.*)

Pause.

CHARLEY (*kindly, going to him*). How much do you need, Willy?

WILLY. Charley, I'm strapped. I'm strapped. I don't know what to do. I was just fired.

CHARLEY. Howard fired you?

WILLY. That snotnose. Imagine that? I named him. I named him Howard.

CHARLEY. Willy, when're you gonna realize that them things don't mean anything? You named him Howard, but you can't sell that. The only thing you got in this world is what you can sell. And the funny thing is that you're a salesman, and you don't know that.

WILLY. I've always tried to think otherwise, I guess. I always felt that if a man was impressive, and well liked, that nothing . . .

CHARLEY. Why must everybody like you? Who liked J. P. Morgan? Was he impressive? In a Turkish bath he'd look like a butcher. But with his pockets on he was very well liked. Now listen, Willy, I know you don't like me, and nobody can say I'm in love with you, but I'll give you a job because—just for the hell of it, put it that way. Now what do you say?

WILLY. I—I just can't work for you, Charley.

CHARLEY. What're you, jealous of me?

WILLY. I can't work for you, that's all, don't ask me why.

CHARLEY (angered, takes out more bills). You been jealous of me all your life, you damned fool! Here, pay your insurance. (He puts the money in Willy's hand.)

WILLY. I'm keeping strict accounts.

CHARLEY. I've got some work to do. Take care of yourself. And pay your insurance.

WILLY (moving to the right). Funny, y'know? After all the highways, and the trains, and the appointments, and the years, you end up worth more dead than alive.

CHARLEY. Willy, nobody's worth nothin' dead. (After a slight pause.) Did you hear what I said?

Willy stands still, dreaming.

CHARLEY. Willy!

WILLY. Apologize to Bernard for me when you see him. I didn't mean to argue with him. He's a fine boy. They're all fine boys, and they'll end up big—all of them. Someday they'll all play tennis together. Wish me luck, Charley. He saw Bill Oliver today.

CHARLEY. Good luck.

WILLY (on the verge of tears). Charley, you're the only friend I got. Isn't that a remarkable thing? (He goes out.)

CHARLEY. Jesus!

Charley stares after him a moment and follows. All light blacks out. Suddenly raucous music is heard, and a red glow rises behind the screen at right. Stanley, a young waiter, appears, carrying a table, followed by Happy, who is carrying two chairs.

STANLEY (putting the table down). That's all right, Mr. Loman, I can handle it myself. (He turns and takes the chairs from Happy and places them at the table.)

HAPPY (glancing around). Oh, this is better.

STANLEY. Sure, in the front there you're in the middle of all kinds of noise. Whenever you got a party, Mr. Loman, you just tell me and I'll put you back here. Y'know, there's a lotta people they don't like it private, because when they go out they like to see a lotta action around them because they're sick and tired to stay in the house by theirself. But I know you, you ain't from Hackensack. You know what I mean?

HAPPY (sitting down). So how's it coming, Stanley?

STANLEY. Ah, it's a dog life. I only wish during the war they'd a took me in the Army. I coulda been dead by now.

HAPPY. My brother's back, Stanley.

STANLEY. Oh, he come back, heh? From the Far West.

HAPPY. Yeah, big cattle man, my brother, so treat him right. And my father's coming too.

STANLEY. Oh, your father too!

HAPPY. You got a couple of nice lobsters?

STANLEY. Hundred per cent, big.

HAPPY. I want them with the claws.

STANLEY. Don't worry, I don't give you no mice. (Happy laughs.) How about some wine? It'll put a head on the meal.

HAPPY. No. You remember, Stanley, that recipe I brought you from overseas? With the champagne in it?

STANLEY. Oh, yeah, sure. I still got it tacked up yet in the kitchen. But that'll have to cost a buck apiece anyways.

HAPPY. That's all right.

STANLEY. What'd you, hit a number or somethin'?

HAPPY. No, it's a little celebration. My brother is—I think he pulled off a big deal today. I think we're going into business together.

STANLEY. Great! That's the best for you. Because a family business, you know what I mean?—that's the best.

HAPPY. That's what I think.

STANLEY. 'Cause what's the difference? Somebody steals? It's in the family. Know what I mean? (Sotto voce.) Like this bartender here. The boss is goin' crazy what kinda leak he's got in the cash register. You put it in but it don't come out.

HAPPY (raising his head). Sh!

STANLEY. What?

HAPPY. You notice I wasn't lookin' right or left, was I?

STANLEY. No.

HAPPY. And my eyes are closed.

STANLEY. So what's the . . . ?

HAPPY. Strudel's comin'.

STANLEY (catching on, looks around). Ah, no, there's no . . .

He breaks off as a furred, lavishly dressed Girl enters and sits at the next table. Both follow her with their eyes.

STANLEY. Geez, how'd ya know?

HAPPY. I got radar or something. (Staring directly at her profile.) Oooooooo . . . Stanley.

STANLEY. I think that's for you, Mr. Loman.

HAPPY. Look at that mouth. Oh, God. And the binoculars.

STANLEY. Geez, you got a life, Mr. Loman.

HAPPY. Wait on her.

STANLEY (going to the Girl's table). Would you like a menu, ma'am?

GIRL. I'm expecting someone, but I'd like a . . .

HAPPY. Why don't you bring her—excuse me, miss, do you mind? I sell champagne, and I'd like you to try my brand. Bring her a champagne, Stanley.

GIRL. That's awfully nice of you.

HAPPY. Don't mention it. It's all company money. (*He laughs.*)

GIRL. That's a charming product to be selling, isn't it?

HAPPY. Oh, gets to be like everything else. Selling is selling, y'know.

GIRL. I suppose.

HAPPY. You don't happen to sell, do you?

GIRL. No, I don't sell.

HAPPY. Would you object to a compliment from a stranger? You ought to be on a magazine cover.

GIRL (*looking at him a little archly*). I have been.

Stanley comes in with a glass of champagne.

HAPPY. What'd I say before, Stanley? You see? She's a cover girl.

STANLEY. Oh, I could see, I could see.

HAPPY (*to the Girl*). What magazine?

GIRL. Oh, a lot of them. (*She takes the drink.*) Thank you.

HAPPY. You know what they say in France, don't you? "Champagne is the drink of the complexion"—Hya, Biff!

Biff has entered and sits with Happy.

BIFF. Hello, kid. Sorry I'm late.

HAPPY. I just got here. Uh, Miss . . . ?

GIRL. Forsythe.

HAPPY. Miss Forsythe, this is my brother.

BIFF. Is Dad here?

HAPPY. His name is Biff. You might've heard of him. Great football player.

GIRL. Really? What team?

HAPPY. Are you familiar with football?

GIRL. No, I'm afraid I'm not.

HAPPY. Biff is quarterback with the New York Giants.

GIRL. Well, that is nice, isn't it? (*She drinks.*)

HAPPY. Good health.

GIRL. I'm happy to meet you.

HAPPY. That's my name. Hap. It's really Harold, but at West Point they called me Happy.

GIRL (*now really impressed*). Oh, I see. How do you do? (*She turns her profile.*)

BIFF. Isn't Dad coming?

HAPPY. You want her?

BIFF. Oh, I could never make that.

HAPPY. I remember the time that idea would never come into your head. Where's the old confidence, Biff?

BIFF. I just saw Oliver . . .

HAPPY. Wait a minute. I've got to see that old confidence again. Do you want her? She's on call.

BIFF. Oh, no. (*He turns to look at the Girl.*)

HAPPY. I'm telling you. Watch this. (*Turning to the Girl.*) Honey? (*She turns to him.*) Are you busy?

GIRL. Well, I am . . . but I could make a phone call.

HAPPY. Do that, will you, honey? And see if you can get a friend. We'll be here for a while. Biff is one of the greatest football players in the country.

GIRL (*standing up*). Well, I'm certainly happy to meet you.

HAPPY. Come back soon.

GIRL. I'll try.

HAPPY. Don't try, honey, try hard.

The Girl exits. Stanley follows, shaking his head in bewildered admiration.

HAPPY. Isn't that a shame now? A beautiful girl like that? That's why I can't get married. There's not a good woman in a thousand. New York is loaded with them, kid!

BIFF. Hap, look . . .

HAPPY. I told you she was on call!

BIFF (*strangely unnerved*). Cut it out, will ya? I want to say something to you.

HAPPY. Did you see Oliver?

BIFF. I saw him all right. Now look, I want to tell Dad a couple of things and I want you to help me.

HAPPY. What? Is he going to back you?

BIFF. Are you crazy? You're out of your goddam head, you know that?

HAPPY. Why? What happened?

BIFF (*breathlessly*). I did a terrible thing today, Hap. It's been the strangest day I ever went through. I'm all numb, I swear.

HAPPY. You mean he wouldn't see you?

BIFF. Well, I waited six hours for him, see? All day. Kept sending my name in. Even tried to date his secretary so she'd get me to him, but no soap.

HAPPY. Because you're not showin' the old confidence, Biff. He remembered you, didn't he?

BIFF (*stopping Happy with a gesture*). Finally, about five o'clock, he comes out. Didn't remember who I was or anything. I felt like such an idiot, Hap.

HAPPY. Did you tell him my Florida idea?

BIFF. He walked away. I saw him for one minute. I got so mad I could've torn the walls down! How the hell did I ever get the idea I was a salesman there? I even believed myself that I'd been a salesman for him! And then he gave me one look and—I realized what a ridiculous lie my whole life has been! We've been talking in a dream for fifteen years. I was a shipping clerk.

HAPPY. What'd you do?

BIFF (*with great tension and wonder*). Well, he left, see. And the secretary went out. I was all alone in the waiting room. I don't know what came over me, Hap. The next thing I know I'm in his office—paneled walls, everything. I can't explain it. I—Hap. I took his fountain pen.

HAPPY. Geez, did he catch you?

BIFF. I ran out. I ran down all eleven flights. I ran and ran and ran.

HAPPY. That was an awful dumb—what'd you do that for?

BIFF (*agonized*). I don't know, I just—wanted to take something, I don't know. You gotta help me, Hap. I'm gonna tell Pop.

HAPPY. You crazy? What for?

BIFF. Hap, he's got to understand that I'm not the man somebody lends that kind of money to. He thinks I've been spiting him all these years and it's eating him up.

HAPPY. That's just it. You tell him something nice.

BIFF. I can't.

HAPPY. Say you got a lunch date with Oliver tomorrow.

BIFF. So what do I do tomorrow?

HAPPY. You leave the house tomorrow and come back at night and say Oliver is thinking it over. And he thinks it over for a couple of weeks, and gradually it fades away and nobody's the worse.

BIFF. But it'll go on forever!

HAPPY. Dad is never so happy as when he's looking forward to something!

Willy enters.

HAPPY. Hello, scout!

WILLY. Gee, I haven't been here in years!

Stanley has followed Willy in and sets a chair for him. Stanley starts off but Happy stops him.

HAPPY. Stanley!

Stanley stands by, waiting for an order.

BIFF (*going to Willy with guilt, as to an invalid*). Sit down, Pop. You want a drink?

WILLY. Sure, I don't mind.

BIFF. Let's get a load on.

WILLY. You look worried.

BIFF. N-no. (*To Stanley.*) Scotch all around. Make it doubles.

STANLEY. Doubles, right. (*He goes.*)

WILLY. You had a couple already, didn't you?

BIFF. Just a couple, yeah.

WILLY. Well, what happened, boy? (*Nodding affirmatively, with a smile.*) Everything go all right?

BIFF (*takes a breath, then reaches out and grasps Willy's hand*). Pal . . . (*He is smiling bravely, and Willy is smiling too.*) I had an experience today.

HAPPY. Terrific, Pop.

WILLY. That so? What happened?

BIFF (*high, slightly alcoholic, above the earth*). I'm going to tell you everything from first to last. It's been a strange day. (*Silence. He looks around, composes himself as best he can, but his breath keeps breaking the rhythm of his voice.*) I had to wait quite a while for him, and . . .

WILLY. Oliver?

BIFF. Yeah, Oliver. All day, as a matter of cold fact. And a lot of—instances—facts, Pop, facts about my life came back to me. Who was it, Pop? Who ever said I was a salesman with Oliver?

WILLY. Well, you were.

BIFF. No, Dad, I was a shipping clerk.

WILLY. But you were practically . . .

BIFF (*with determination*). Dad, I don't know who said it first, but I was never a salesman for Bill Oliver.

WILLY. What're you talking about?

BIFF. Let's hold on to the facts tonight, Pop. We're not going to get anywhere bullin' around. I was a shipping clerk.

WILLY (*angrily*). All right, now listen to me . . .

BIFF. Why don't you let me finish?

WILLY. I'm not interested in stories about the past or any crap of that kind because the woods are burning, boys, you understand? There's a big blaze going on all around. I was fired today.

BIFF (*shocked*). How could you be?

WILLY. I was fired, and I'm looking for a little good news to tell your mother, because the woman has waited and the woman has suffered. The gist of it is that I haven't got a story left in my head, Biff. So don't give me a lecture about facts and aspects. I am not interested. Now what've you got to say to me?

Stanley enters with three drinks. They wait until he leaves.

WILLY. Did you see Oliver?

BIFF. Jesus, Dad!

WILLY. You mean you didn't go up there?

HAPPY. Sure he went up there.

BIFF. I did. I—saw him. How could they fire you?

WILLY (*on the edge of his chair*). What kind of a welcome did he give you?

BIFF. He won't even let you work on commission?

WILLY. I'm out! (*Driving.*) So tell me, he gave you a warm welcome?

HAPPY. Sure, Pop, sure!

BIFF (*driven*). Well, it was kind of . . .

WILLY. I was wondering if he'd remember you. (*To Happy.*) Imagine, man doesn't see him for ten, twelve years and gives him that kind of a welcome!

HAPPY. Damn right!

BIFF (*trying to return to the offensive*). Pop, look . . .

WILLY. You know why he remembered you, don't you? Because you impressed him in those days.

BIFF. Let's talk quietly and get this down to the facts, huh?

WILLY (*as though Biff had been interrupting*). Well, what happened? It's great news, Biff. Did he take you into his office or'd you talk in the waiting room?

BIFF. Well, he came in, see, and . . .

WILLY (*with a big smile*). What'd he say? Betcha he threw his arm around you.

BIFF. Well, he kinda . . .

WILLY. He's a fine man. (*To Happy.*) Very hard man to see, y'know.

HAPPY (*agreeing*). Oh, I know.

WILLY (*to Biff*). Is that where you had the drinks?

BIFF. Yeah, he gave me a couple of—no, no!

HAPPY (*cutting in*). He told him my Florida idea.

WILLY. Don't interrupt. (*To Biff.*) How'd he react to the Florida idea?

BIFF. Dad, will you give me a minute to explain?

WILLY. I've been waiting for you to explain since I sat down here! What happened? He took you into his office and what?

BIFF. Well—I talked. And—and he listened, see.

WILLY. Famous for the way he listens, y'know. What was his answer?

BIFF. His answer was—(*He breaks off, suddenly angry.*) Dad, you're not letting me tell you what I want to tell you!

WILLY (*accusing, angered*). You didn't see him, did you?

BIFF. I did see him!

WILLY. What'd you insult him or something? You insulted him, didn't you?

BIFF. Listen, will you let me out of it, will you just let me out of it!

HAPPY. What the hell!

WILLY. Tell me what happened!

BIFF (*to Happy*). I can't talk to him!

A single trumpet note jars the ear. The light of green leaves stains the house, which holds the air of night and a dream. Young Bernard enters and knocks on the door of the house.

YOUNG BERNARD (*frantically*). Mrs. Loman, Mrs. Loman!

HAPPY. Tell him what happened!

BIFF (*to Happy*). Shut up and leave me alone!

WILLY. No, no! You had to go and flunk math!

BIFF. What math? What're you talking about?

YOUNG BERNARD. Mrs. Loman, Mrs. Loman!

Linda appears in the house, as of old.

WILLY (*wildly*). Math, math, math!

BIFF. Take it easy, Pop!

YOUNG BERNARD. Mrs. Loman!

WILLY (*furiously*). If you hadn't flunked you'd've been set by now!

BIFF. Now, look, I'm gonna tell you what happened, and you're going to listen to me.

YOUNG BERNARD. Mrs. Loman!

BIFF. I waited six hours . . .

HAPPY. What the hell are you saying?

BIFF. I kept sending in my name but he wouldn't see me. So finally he . . . (*He continues unheard as light fades low on the restaurant.*)

YOUNG BERNARD. Biff flunked math!

LINDA. No!

YOUNG BERNARD. Birnbaum flunked him! They won't graduate him!

LINDA. But they have to. He's gotta go to the university. Where is he? Biff! Biff!

YOUNG BERNARD. No, he left. He went to Grand Central.

LINDA. Grand—You mean he went to Boston!

YOUNG BERNARD. Is Uncle Willy in Boston?

LINDA. Oh, maybe Willy can talk to the teacher. Oh, the poor, poor boy!

Light on house area snaps out.

BIFF (*at the table, now audible, holding up a gold fountain pen*). . . . so I'm washed up with Oliver, you understand? Are you listening to me?

WILLY (*at a loss*). Yeah, sure. If you hadn't flunked . . .

BIFF. Flunked what? What're you talking about?

WILLY. Don't blame everything on me! I didn't flunk math— you did! What pen?

HAPPY. That was awful dumb, Biff, a pen like that is worth—

WILLY (*seeing the pen for the first time*). You took Oliver's pen?

BIFF (*weakening*). Dad, I just explained it to you.

WILLY. You stole Bill Oliver's fountain pen!

BIFF. I didn't exactly steal it! That's just what I've been explaining to you!

HAPPY. He had it in his hand and just then Oliver walked in, so he got nervous and stuck it in his pocket!

WILLY. My God, Biff!

BIFF. I never intended to do it, Dad!

OPERATOR'S VOICE. Standish Arms, good evening!

WILLY (*shouting*). I'm not in my room!

BIFF (*frightened*). Dad, what's the matter? (*He and Happy stand up.*)

OPERATOR. Ringing Mr. Loman for you!

WILLY. I'm not there, stop it!

BIFF (*horrified, gets down on one knee before Willy*). Dad, I'll make good, I'll make good. (*Willy tries to get to his feet. Biff holds him down.*) Sit down now.

WILLY. No, you're no good, you're no good for anything.

BIFF. I am, Dad, I'll find something else, you understand? Now don't worry about anything. (*He holds up Willy's face.*) Talk to me, Dad.

OPERATOR. Mr. Loman does not answer. Shall I page him?

WILLY (*attempting to stand, as though to rush and silence the Operator*). No, no, no!

HAPPY. He'll strike something, Pop.

WILLY. No, no . . .

BIFF (*desperately, standing over Willy*). Pop, listen! Listen to me! I'm telling you something good. Oliver talked to his partner about the Florida idea. You listening? He—he talked to his partner, and he came to me . . . I'm going to be all right, you hear? Dad, listen to me, he said it was just a question of the amount!

WILLY. Then you . . . got it?

HAPPY. He's gonna be terrific, Pop!

WILLY (*trying to stand*). Then you got it, haven't you? You got it! You got it!

BIFF (*agonized, holds Willy down*). No, no. Look, Pop. I'm supposed to have lunch with them tomorrow. I'm just telling you this so you'll know that I can still make an impression, Pop. And I'll make good somewhere, but I can't go tomorrow, see.

WILLY. Why not? You simply . . .

BIFF. But the pen, Pop!

WILLY. You give it to him and tell him it was an oversight!

HAPPY. Sure, have lunch tomorrow!

BIFF. I can't say that . . .

WILLY. You were doing a crossword puzzle and accidentally used his pen!

BIFF. Listen, kid, I took those balls years ago, now I walk in with his fountain pen? That clinches it, don't you see? I can't face him like that! I'll try elsewhere.

PAGE'S VOICE. Paging Mr. Loman!

WILLY. Don't you want to be anything?

BIFF. Pop, how can I go back?

WILLY. You don't want to be anything, is that what's behind it?

BIFF (*now angry at Willy for not crediting his sympathy*). Don't take it that way! You think it was easy walking into that office after what I'd done to him? A team of horses couldn't have dragged me back to Bill Oliver!

WILLY. Then why'd you go?

BIFF. Why did I go? Why did I go! Look at you! Look at what's become of you!

Off left, The Woman laughs.

WILLY. Biff, you're going to go to that lunch tomorrow, or . . .

BIFF. I can't go. I've got no appointment!

HAPPY. Biff, for . . . !

WILLY. Are you spiting me?

BIFF. Don't take it that way! Goddammit!

WILLY (*strikes Biff and falters away from the table*). You rotten little louse! Are you spiting me?

THE WOMAN. Someone's at the door, Willy!

BIFF. I'm no good, can't you see what I am?

HAPPY (*separating them*). Hey, you're in a restaurant! Now cut it out, both of you! (*The girls enter.*) Hello, girls, sit down.

The Woman laughs, off left.

MISS FORSYTHE. I guess we might as well. This is Letta.

THE WOMAN. Willy, are you going to wake up?

BIFF (*ignoring Willy*). How're ya, miss, sit down. What do you drink?

MISS FORSYTHE. Letta might not be able to stay long.

LETTA. I gotta get up very early tomorrow. I got jury duty. I'm so excited! Were you fellows ever on a jury?

BIFF. No, but I been in front of them! (*The girls laugh.*) This is my father.

LETTA. Isn't he cute? Sit down with us, Pop.

HAPPY. Sit him down, Biff!

BIFF (*going to him*). Come on, slugger, drink us under the table. To hell with it! Come on, sit down, pal.

On Biff's last insistence, Willy is about to sit.

THE WOMAN (*now urgently*). Willy, are you going to answer the door!

The Woman's call pulls Willy back. He starts right, befuddled.

BIFF. Hey, where are you going?

WILLY. Open the door.

BIFF. The door?

WILLY. The washroom . . . the door . . . where's the door?

BIFF (*leading Willy to the left*). Just go straight down.

Willy moves left.

THE WOMAN. Willy, Willy, are you going to get up, get up, get up, get up?

Willy exits left.

LETTA. I think it's sweet you bring your daddy along.

MISS FORSYTHE. Oh, he isn't really your father!

BIFF (*at left, turning to her resentfully*). Miss Forsythe, you've just seen a prince walk by. A fine, troubled prince. A hardworking, unappreciated prince. A pal, you understand? A good companion. Always for his boys.

LETTA. That's so sweet.

HAPPY. Well, girls, what's the program? We're wasting time. Come on, Biff. Gather round. Where would you like to go?

BIFF. Why don't you do something for him?

HAPPY. Me!

BIFF. Don't you give a damn for him, Hap?

HAPPY. What're you talking about? I'm the one who . . .

BIFF. I sense it, you don't give a good goddam about him. (*He takes the rolled-up hose from his pocket and puts it on the table in front of Happy.*) Look what I found in the cellar, for Christ's sake. How can you bear to let it go on?

HAPPY. Me? Who goes away? Who runs off and . . .

BIFF. Yeah, but he doesn't mean anything to you. You could help him—I can't! Don't you understand what I'm talking about? He's going to kill himself, don't you know that?

HAPPY. Don't know it! Me!

BIFF. Hap, help him! Jesus . . . help him . . . Help me, help me, I can't bear to look at his face! (*Ready to weep, he hurries out, up right.*)

HAPPY (*starting after him*). Where are you going?

MISS FORSYTHE. What's he so mad about?

HAPPY. Come on, girls, we'll catch up with him.

MISS FORSYTHE (*as Happy pushes her out*). Say, I don't like that temper of his!

HAPPY. He's just a little overstrung, he'll be all right!

WILLY (*off left, as The Woman laughs*). Don't answer! Don't answer!

LETTA. Don't you want to tell your father . . .

HAPPY. No, that's not my father. He's just a guy. Come on, we'll catch Biff, and, honey, we're going to paint this town! Stanley, where's the check! Hey, Stanley!

They exit. Stanley looks toward left.

STANLEY (*calling to Happy indignantly*). Mr. Loman! Mr. Loman!

Stanley picks up a chair and follows them off. Knocking is heard off left. The Woman enters, laughing. Willy follows her. She is in a black slip; he is buttoning his shirt. Raw, sensuous music accompanies their speech:

WILLY. Will you stop laughing? Will you stop?

THE WOMAN. Aren't you going to answer the door? He'll wake the whole hotel.

WILLY. I'm not expecting anybody.

THE WOMAN. Whyn't you have another drink, honey, and stop being so damn self-centered?

WILLY. I'm so lonely.

THE WOMAN. You know you ruined me, Willy? From now on, whenever you come to the office, I'll see that you go right through to the buyers. No waiting at my desk anymore, Willy. You ruined me.

WILLY. That's nice of you to say that.

THE WOMAN. Gee, you are self-centered! Why so sad? You are the saddest, self-centeredest soul I ever did see-saw. (*She laughs. He kisses her.*) Come on inside, drummer boy. It's silly to be dressing in the middle of the night. (*As knocking is heard.*) Aren't you going to answer the door?

WILLY. They're knocking on the wrong door.

THE WOMAN. But I felt the knocking. And he heard us talking in here. Maybe the hotel's on fire!

WILLY (*his terror rising*). It's a mistake.

THE WOMAN. Then tell him to go away!

WILLY. There's nobody there.

THE WOMAN. It's getting on my nerves, Willy. There's somebody standing out there and it's getting on my nerves!

WILLY (*pushing her away from him*). All right, stay in the bathroom here, and don't come out. I think there's a law in Massachusetts about it, so don't come out. It may be that new room clerk. He looked very mean. So don't come out. It's a mistake, there's no fire.

The knocking is heard again. He takes a few steps away from her, and she vanishes into the wing. The light follows him, and now he is facing Young Biff, who carries a suitcase. Biff steps toward him. The music is gone.

BIFF. Why didn't you answer?

WILLY. Biff! What are you doing in Boston?

BIFF. Why didn't you answer? I've been knocking for five minutes, I called you on the phone . . .

WILLY. I just heard you. I was in the bathroom and had the door shut. Did anything happen home?

BIFF. Dad—I let you down.

WILLY. What do you mean?

BIFF. Dad . . .

WILLY. Biffo, what's this about? (*Putting his arm around Biff.*) Come on, let's go downstairs and get you a malted.

BIFF. Dad, I flunked math.

WILLY. Not for the term?

BIFF. The term. I haven't got enough credits to graduate.

WILLY. You mean to say Bernard wouldn't give you the answers?

BIFF. He did, he tried, but I only got a sixty-one.

WILLY. And they wouldn't give you four points?

BIFF. Birnbaum refused absolutely. I begged him, Pop, but he won't give me those points. You gotta talk to him before they close the school. Because if he saw the kind of man you are, and you just talked to him in your way, I'm sure he'd come through for me. The class came right before practice, see, and I didn't go enough. Would you talk to him? He'd like you, Pop. You know the way you could talk.

WILLY. You're on. We'll drive right back.

BIFF. Oh, Dad, good work! I'm sure he'll change it for you!

WILLY. Go downstairs and tell the clerk I'm checkin' out. Go right down.

BIFF. Yes, sir! See, the reason he hates me, Pop—one day he was late for class so I got up at the blackboard and imitated him. I crossed my eyes and talked with a lithp.

WILLY (*laughing*). You did? The kids like it?

BIFF. They nearly died laughing!

WILLY. Yeah? What'd you do?

BIFF. The thquare root of thixthy twee is . . . (*Willy bursts out laughing; Biff joins.*) And in the middle of it he walked in!

Willy laughs and The Woman joins in offstage.

WILLY (*without hesitation*). Hurry downstairs and . . .

BIFF. Somebody in there?

WILLY. No, that was next door.

The Woman laughs offstage.

BIFF. Somebody got in your bathroom!

WILLY. No, it's the next room, there's a party . . .

THE WOMAN (*enters, laughing; she lisps this*). Can I come in? There's something in the bathtub, Willy, and it's moving!

Willy looks at Biff; who is staring open-mouthed and horrified at The Woman.

WILLY. Ah—you better go back to your room. They must be finished painting by now. They're painting her room so I let her take a shower here. Go back, go back . . . (*He pushes her.*)

THE WOMAN (*resisting*). But I've got to get dressed, Willy, I can't . . .

WILLY. Get out of here! Go back, go back . . . (*Suddenly striving for the ordinary.*) This is Miss Francis, Biff, she's a buyer. They're painting her room. Go back, Miss Francis, go back . . .

THE WOMAN. But my clothes, I can't go out naked in the hall!

WILLY (*pushing her offstage*). Get outa here! Go back, go back!

Biff slowly sits down on his suitcase as the argument continues offstage.

THE WOMAN. Where's my stockings? You promised me stockings, Willy!

WILLY. I have no stockings here!

THE WOMAN. You had two boxes of size nine sheers for me, and I want them!

WILLY. Here, for God's sake, will you get outa here!

THE WOMAN (*enters holding a box of stockings*). I just hope there's nobody in the hall. That's all I hope. (*To Biff.*) Are you football or baseball?

BIFF. Football.

THE WOMAN (*angry, humiliated*). That's me too. G'night. (*She snatches her clothes from Willy, and walks out.*)

WILLY (*after a pause*). Well, better get going. I want to get to the school first thing in the morning. Get my suits out of the closet. I'll get my valise. (*Biff doesn't move.*) What's the matter! (*Biff remains motionless, tears falling.*) She's a buyer. Buys for J. H. Simmons. She lives down the hall—they're painting. You don't imagine—(*He breaks off. After a pause.*) Now listen, pal, she's just a buyer. She sees merchandise in her room and they have to keep it looking just so . . . (*Pause. Assuming command.*) All right, get my suits. (*Biff doesn't move.*) Now stop crying and do as I say. I gave you an order. Biff, I gave you an order! Is that what you do when I give you an order? How dare you cry! (*Putting his arm around Biff.*) Now look, Biff, when you grow up you'll understand about these things. You mustn't—you mustn't overemphasize a thing like this. I'll see Birnbaum first thing in the morning.

BIFF. Never mind.

WILLY (*getting down beside Biff*). Never mind! He's going to give you those points. I'll see to it.

BIFF. He wouldn't listen to you.

WILLY. He certainly will listen to me. You need those points for the U. of Virginia.

BIFF. I'm not going there.

WILLY. Heh? If I can't get him to change that mark you'll make it up in summer school. You've got all summer to . . .

BIFF (*his weeping breaking from him*). Dad . . .

WILLY (*infected by it*). Oh, my boy . . .

BIFF. Dad . . .

WILLY. She's nothing to me, Biff. I was lonely, I was terribly lonely.

BIFF. You—you gave her Mama's stockings! (*His tears break through and he rises to go.*)

WILLY (*grabbing for Biff*). I gave you an order!

BIFF. Don't touch me, you—liar!

WILLY. Apologize for that!

BIFF. You fake! You phony little fake! You fake! (*Overcome, he turns quickly and weeping fully goes out with his suitcase. Willy is left on the floor on his knees.*)

WILLY. I gave you an order! Biff, come back here or I'll beat you! Come back here! I'll whip you!

Stanley comes quickly in from the right and stands in front of Willy.

WILLY (*shouts at Stanley*). I gave you an order . . .

STANLEY. Hey, let's pick it up, pick it up, Mr. Loman. (*He helps Willy to his feet.*) Your boys left with the chippies. They said they'll see you home.

A second waiter watches some distance away.

WILLY. But we were supposed to have dinner together.

Music is heard, Willy's theme.

STANLEY. Can you make it?

WILLY. I'll—sure, I can make it. (*Suddenly concerned about his clothes.*) Do I—I look all right?

STANLEY. Sure, you look all right. (*He flicks a speck off Willy's lapel.*)

WILLY. Here—here's a dollar.

STANLEY. Oh, your son paid me. It's all right.

WILLY (*putting it in Stanley's hand*). No, take it. You're a good boy.

STANLEY. Oh, no, you don't have to . . .

WILLY. Here—here's some more, I don't need it any more. (*After a slight pause.*) Tell me—is there a seed store in the neighborhood?

STANLEY. Seeds? You mean like to plant?

As Willy turns, Stanley slips the money back into his jacket pocket.

WILLY. Yes. Carrots, peas . . .

STANLEY. Well, there's hardware stores on Sixth Avenue, but it may be too late now.

WILLY (*anxiously*). Oh, I'd better hurry. I've got to get some seeds. (*He starts off to the right.*) I've got to get some seeds, right away. Nothing's planted. I don't have a thing in the ground.

Willy hurries out as the light goes down. Stanley moves over to the right after him, watches him off. The other waiter has been staring at Willy.

STANLEY (*to the waiter*). Well, whatta you looking at?

The waiter picks up the chairs and moves off right. Stanley takes the table and follows him. The light fades on this area. There is a long pause, the sound of the flute coming over. The light gradually rises on the kitchen, which is empty. Happy appears at the door of the house, followed by Biff. Happy is carrying a large bunch of long-stemmed roses. He enters the kitchen, looks around for Linda. Not seeing her, he turns to Biff, who is just outside the house door, and makes a gesture with his hands, indicating "Not here, I guess." He looks into the living room and freezes. Inside, Linda, unseen, is seated, Willy's coat on her lap. She rises ominously and quietly and moves toward Happy, who backs up into the kitchen, afraid.

HAPPY. Hey, what're you doing up? (*Linda says nothing but moves toward him implacably.*) Where's Pop? (*He keeps backing to the right, and now Linda is in full view in the doorway to the living room.*) Is he sleeping?

LINDA. Where were you?

HAPPY (*trying to laugh it off*). We met two girls, Mom, very fine types. Here, we brought you some flowers. (*Offering them to her.*) Put them in your room, Ma.

She knocks them to the floor at Biff's feet. He has now come inside and closed the door behind him. She stares at Biff, silent.

HAPPY. Now what'd you do that for? Mom, I want you to have some flowers . . .

LINDA (*cutting Happy off, violently to Biff*). Don't you care whether he lives or dies?

HAPPY (*going to the stairs*). Come upstairs, Biff.

BIFF (*with a flare of disgust, to Happy*). Go away from me! (*To Linda.*) What do you mean, lives or dies? Nobody's dying around here, pal.

LINDA. Get out of my sight! Get out of here!

BIFF. I wanna see the boss.

LINDA. You're not going near him!

BIFF. Where is he? (*He moves into the living room and Linda follows.*)

LINDA (*shouting after Biff.*) You invite him for dinner. He looks forward to it all day—(*Biff appears in his parents' bedroom, looks around, and exits*)—and then you desert him there. There's no stranger you'd do that to!

HAPPY. Why? He had a swell time with us. Listen, when I—(*Linda comes back into the kitchen*)—desert him I hope I don't outlive the day!

LINDA. Get out of here!

HAPPY. Now look, Mom . . .

LINDA. Did you have to go to women tonight? You and your lousy rotten whores!

Biff re-enters the kitchen.

HAPPY. Mom, all we did was follow Biff around trying to cheer him up! (*To Biff.*) Boy, what a night you gave me!

LINDA. Get out of here, both of you, and don't come back! I don't want you tormenting him any more. Go on now, get your things together! (*To Biff.*) You can sleep in his apartment. (*She starts to pick up the flowers and stops herself.*) Pick up this stuff, I'm not your maid any more. Pick it up, you bum, you!

Happy turns his back to her in refusal. Biff slowly moves over and gets down on his knees, picking up the flowers.

LINDA. You're a pair of animals! Not one, not another living soul would have had the cruelty to walk out on that man in a restaurant!

BIFF (*not looking at her*). Is that what he said?

LINDA. He didn't have to say anything. He was so humiliated he nearly limped when he came in.

HAPPY. But, Mom, he had a great time with us . . .

BIFF (*cutting him off violently*). Shut up!

Without another word, Happy goes upstairs.

LINDA. You! You didn't even go in to see if he was all right!

BIFF (*still on the floor in front of Linda, the flowers in his hand; with self-loathing*). No. Didn't. Didn't do a damned thing. How do you like that, heh? Left him babbling in a toilet.

LINDA. You louse. You . . .

BIFF. Now you hit it on the nose! (*He gets up, throws the flowers in the wastebasket.*) The scum of the earth, and you're looking at him!

LINDA. Get out of here!

BIFF. I gotta talk to the boss, Mom. Where is he?

LINDA. You're not going near him. Get out of this house!

BIFF (*with absolute assurance, determination*). No. We're gonna have an abrupt conversation, him and me.

LINDA. You're not talking to him.

Hammering is heard from outside the house, off right. Biff turns toward the noise.

LINDA (*suddenly pleading*). Will you please leave him alone?

BIFF. What's he doing out there?

LINDA. He's planting the garden!

BIFF (*quietly*). Now? Oh, my God!

Biff moves outside, Linda following. The light dies down on them and comes up on the center of the apron as Willy walks into it. He is carrying a flashlight, a hoe, and a handful of seed packets. He raps the top of the hoe sharply to fix it firmly, and then moves to the left, measuring off the distance with his foot. He holds the flashlight to look at the seed packets, reading off the instructions. He is in the blue of night.

WILLY. Carrots . . . quarter-inch apart. Rows . . . one-foot rows. (*He measures it off.*) One foot. (*He puts down a package and measures off.*) Beets. (*He puts down another package and measures again.*) Lettuce. (*He reads the package, puts it down.*) One foot—(*He breaks off as Ben appears at the right and moves slowly down to him.*) What a proposition, ts, ts. Terrific, terrific. 'Cause she's suffered, Ben, the woman has suffered. You understand me? A man can't go out the way he came in, Ben, a man has got to add up to something. You can't, you can't—(*Ben moves toward him as though to interrupt.*) You gotta consider now. Don't answer so quick. Remember, it's a guaranteed twenty-thousand-dollar proposition. Now look, Ben, I want you to go through the ins and outs of this thing with me. I've got nobody to talk to, Ben, and the woman has suffered, you hear me?

BEN (*standing still, considering*). What's the proposition?

WILLY. It's twenty thousand dollars on the barrelhead. Guaranteed, gilt-edged, you understand?

BEN. You don't want to make a fool of yourself. They might not honor the policy.

WILLY. How can they dare refuse? Didn't I work like a coolie to meet every premium on the nose? And now they don't pay off? Impossible!

BEN. It's called a cowardly thing, William.

WILLY. Why? Does it take more guts to stand here the rest of my life ringing up a zero?

BEN (*yielding*). That's a point, William. (*He moves, thinking, turns.*) And twenty thousand—that is something one can feel with the hand, it is there.

WILLY (*now assured, with rising power*). Oh, Ben, that's the whole beauty of it! I see it like a diamond, shining in the dark, hard and rough, that I can pick up and touch in my hand. Not like—like an appointment! This would not be another damned-fool appointment, Ben, and it changes all the aspects. Because he thinks I'm nothing, see, and so he spites me. But the funeral . . . (*Straightening up.*) Ben, that funeral will be massive! They'll come from Maine, Massachusetts, Vermont, New Hampshire! All the old-timers with the strange license plates—that boy will be thunderstruck, Ben, because he never realized—I am known! Rhode Island, New York, New Jersey—I am known, Ben, and he'll see it with his eyes once and for all. He'll see what I am, Ben! He's in for a shock, that boy!

BEN (*coming down to the edge of the garden*). He'll call you a coward.

WILLY (*suddenly fearful*). No, that would be terrible.

BEN. Yes. And a damned fool.

WILLY. No, no, he mustn't, I won't have that! (*He is broken and desperate.*)

BEN. He'll hate you, William.

The gay music of the Boys is heard.

WILLY. Oh, Ben, how do we get back to all the great times? Used to be so full of light, and comradeship, the sleigh-riding in winter, and the ruddiness on his cheeks. And always some kind of good news coming up, always something nice coming up ahead. And never even let me carry the valises in the house, and simonizing, simonizing that little red car! Why, why can't I give him something and not have him hate me?

BEN. Let me think about it. (*He glances at his watch.*) I still have a little time. Remarkable proposition, but you've got to be sure you're not making a fool of yourself.

Ben drifts off upstage and goes out of sight. Biff comes down from the left.

WILLY (*suddenly conscious of Biff, turns and looks up at him, then begins picking up the packages of seeds in confusion*). Where the hell is that seed? (*Indignantly.*) You can't see nothing out here! They boxed in the whole goddam neighborhood!

BIFF. There are people all around here. Don't you realize that?

WILLY. I'm busy. Don't bother me.

BIFF (*taking the hoe from Willy*). I'm saying good-by to you, Pop. (*Willy looks at him, silent, unable to move.*) I'm not coming back any more.

WILLY. You're not going to see Oliver tomorrow?

BIFF. I've got no appointment, Dad.

WILLY. He put his arm around you, and you've got no appointment?

BIFF. Pop, get this now, will you? Everytime I've left it's been a—fight that sent me out of here. Today I realized something about myself and I tried to explain it to you and I—I think I'm just not smart enough to make any sense out of it for you. To hell with whose fault it is or anything like that. (*He takes Willy's arm.*) Let's just wrap it up, heh? Come on in, we'll tell Mom. (*He gently tries to pull Willy to left.*)

WILLY (*frozen, immobile, with guilt in his voice*). No, I don't want to see her.

BIFF. Come on! (*He pulls again, and Willy tries to pull away.*)

WILLY (*highly nervous*). No, no, I don't want to see her.

BIFF (*tries to look into Willy's face, as if to find the answer there*). Why don't you want to see her?

WILLY (*more harshly now*). Don't bother me, will you?

BIFF. What do you mean, you don't want to see her? You don't want them calling you yellow, do you? This isn't your fault; it's me, I'm a bum. Now come inside! (*Willy strains to get away.*) Did you hear what I said to you?

Willy pulls away and quickly goes by himself into the house. Biff follows.

LINDA (*to Willy*). Did you plant, dear?

BIFF (*at the door, to Linda*). All right, we had it out. I'm going and I'm not writing any more.

LINDA (*going to Willy in the kitchen*). I think that's the best way, dear. 'Cause there's no use drawing it out, you'll just never get along.

Willy doesn't respond.

BIFF. People ask where I am and what I'm doing, you don't know, and you don't care. That way it'll be off your mind and you can start brightening up again. All right? That clears it, doesn't it? (*Willy is silent, and Biff goes to him.*) You gonna wish me luck, scout? (*He extends his hand.*) What do you say?

LINDA. Shake his hand, Willy.

WILLY (*turning to her, seething with hurt*). There's no necessity—to mention the pen at all, y'know.

BIFF (*gently*). I've got no appointment, Dad.

WILLY (*erupting fiercely*). He put his arm around . . . ?

BIFF. Dad, you're never going to see what I am, so what's the use of arguing? If I strike oil I'll send you a check. Meantime forget I'm alive.

WILLY (*to Linda*). Spite, see?

BIFF. Shake hands, Dad.

WILLY. Not my hand.

BIFF. I was hoping not to go this way.

WILLY. Well, this is the way you're going. Good-by.

Biff looks at him a moment, then turns sharply and goes to the stairs.

WILLY (*stops him with*). May you rot in hell if you leave this house!

BIFF (*turning*). Exactly what is it that you want from me?

WILLY. I want you to know, on the train, in the mountains, in the valleys, wherever you go, that you cut down your life for spite!

BIFF. No, no.

WILLY. Spite, spite, is the word of your undoing! And when you're down and out, remember what did it. When you're rotting somewhere beside the railroad tracks, remember, and don't you dare blame it on me!

BIFF. I'm not blaming it on you!

WILLY. I won't take the rap for this, you hear?

Happy comes down the stairs and stands on the bottom step, watching.

BIFF. That's just what I'm telling you!

WILLY (*sinking into a chair at a table, with full accusation*). You're trying to put a knife in me—don't think I don't know what you're doing!

BIFF. All right, phony! Then let's lay it on the line. (*He whips the rubber tube out of his pocket and puts it on the table.*)

HAPPY. You crazy . . .

LINDA. Biff! (*She moves to grab the hose, but Biff holds it down with his hand.*)

BIFF. Leave it there! Don't move it!

WILLY (*not looking at it*). What is that?

BIFF. You know goddam well what that is.

WILLY (*caged, wanting to escape*). I never saw that.

BIFF. You saw it. The mice didn't bring it into the cellar! What is this supposed to do, make a hero out of you? This supposed to make me sorry for you?

WILLY. Never heard of it.

BIFF. There'll be no pity for you, you hear it? No pity!

WILLY (*to Linda*). You hear the spite!

BIFF. No, you're going to hear the truth—what you are and what I am!

LINDA. Stop it!

WILLY. Spite!

HAPPY (*coming down toward Biff*). You cut it now!

BIFF (*to Happy*). The man don't know who we are! The man is gonna know! (*To Willy.*) We never told the truth for ten minutes in this house!

HAPPY. We always told the truth!

BIFF (*turning on him*). You big blow, are you the assistant buyer? You're one of the two assistants to the assistant, aren't you?

HAPPY. Well, I'm practically . . .

BIFF. You're practically full of it! We all are! and I'm through with it. (*To Willy.*) Now hear this, Willy, this is me.

WILLY. I know you!

BIFF. You know why I had no address for three months? I stole a suit in Kansas City and I was in jail. (*To Linda, who is sobbing.*) Stop crying. I'm through with it.

Linda turns away from them, her hands covering her face.

WILLY. I suppose that's my fault!

BIFF. I stole myself out of every good job since high school!

WILLY. And whose fault is that?

BIFF. And I never got anywhere because you blew me so full of hot air I could never stand taking orders from any-body! That's whose fault it is!

WILLY. I hear that!

LINDA. Don't, Biff!

BIFF. It's goddam time you heard that! I had to be boss big shot in two weeks, and I'm through with it!

WILLY. Then hang yourself! For spite, hang yourself!

BIFF. No! Nobody's hanging himself, Willy! I ran down eleven flights with a pen in my hand today. And sud-denly I stopped, you hear me? And in the middle of that office building, do you hear this? I stopped in the middle of that building and I saw—the sky. I saw the things that I love in this world. The work and the food and time to sit and smoke. And I looked at the pen and said to myself, what the hell am I grabbing this for? Why am I trying to become what I don't want to be? What am I doing in an office, making a contemptuous, begging fool of myself, when all I want is out there, waiting for me the minute I say I know who I am! Why can't I say that, Willy? (*He tries to make Willy face him, but Willy pulls away and moves to the left.*)

WILLY (*with hatred, threateningly*). The door of your life is wide open!

BIFF. Pop! I'm a dime a dozen, and so are you!

WILLY (*turning on him now in an uncontrolled outburst*). I am not a dime a dozen! I am Willy Loman, and you are Biff Loman!

Biff starts for Willy, but is blocked by Happy. In his fury, Biff seems on the verge of attacking his father.

BIFF. I am not a leader of men, Willy, and neither are you. You were never anything but a hard-working drummer who landed in the ash can like all the rest of them! I'm one dollar an hour, Willy! I tried seven states and couldn't raise it. A buck an hour! Do you gather my meaning? I'm not bringing home any prizes any more, and you're going to stop waiting for me to bring them home!

WILLY (*directly to Biff*). You vengeful, spiteful mutt!

Biff breaks from Happy. Willy, in fright, starts up the stairs. Biff grabs him.

BIFF (*at the peak of his fury*). Pop! I'm nothing! I'm nothing, Pop. Can't you understand that? There's no spite in it any more. I'm just what I am, that's all.

Biff's fury has spent itself and he breaks down, sobbing, holding on to Willy, who dumbly fumbles for Biff's face.

WILLY (*astonished*). What're you doing? What're you doing? (*To Linda.*) Why is he crying?

BIFF (*crying, broken*). Will you let me go, for Christ's sake? Will you take that phony dream and burn it before some-thing happens? (*Struggling to contain himself, he pulls away and moves to the stairs.*) I'll go in the morning. Put him—put him to bed. (*Exhausted, Biff moves up the stairs to his room.*)

WILLY (*after a long pause, astonished, elevated*). Isn't that—isn't that remarkable? Biff—he likes me!

LINDA. He loves you, Willy!

HAPPY (*deeply moved*). Always did, Pop.

WILLY. Oh, Biff! (*Staring wildly.*) He cried! Cried to me. (*He is choking with his love, and now cries out his promise.*) That boy—that boy is going to be magnificent!

Ben appears in the light just outside the kitchen.

BEN. Yes, outstanding, with twenty thousand behind him.

LINDA (*sensing the racing of his mind, fearfully, carefully*). Now come to bed, Willy. It's all settled now.

WILLY (*finding it difficult not to rush out of the house*). Yes, we'll sleep. Come on. Go to sleep, Hap.

BEN. And it does take a great kind of a man to crack the jungle.

In accents of dread, Ben's idyllic music starts up.

HAPPY (*his arm around Linda*). I'm getting married, Pop, don't forget it. I'm changing everything. I'm gonna run that department before the year is up. You'll see, Mom. (*He kisses her.*)

BEN. The jungle is dark but full of diamonds, Willy.

Willy turns, moves, listening to Ben.

LINDA. Be good. You're both good boys, just act that way, that's all.

HAPPY. 'Night, Pop. (*He goes upstairs.*)

LINDA (*to Willy*). Come, dear.

BEN (*with greater force*). One must go in to fetch a diamond out.

WILLY (*to Linda, as he moves slowly along the edge of the kitchen, toward the door*). I just want to get settled down, Linda. Let me sit alone for a little.

LINDA (*almost uttering her fear*). I want you upstairs.

WILLY (*taking her in his arms*). In a few minutes, Linda. I couldn't sleep right now. Go on, you look awful tired. (*He kisses her.*)

BEN. Not like an appointment at all. A diamond is rough and hard to the touch.

WILLY. Go on now. I'll be right up.

LINDA. I think this is the only way, Willy.

WILLY. Sure, it's the best thing.

BEN. Best thing!

WILLY. The only way. Everything is gonna be—go on, kid, get to bed. You look so tired.

LINDA. Come right up.

WILLY. Two minutes.

Linda goes into the living room, then reappears in her bedroom. Willy moves just outside the kitchen door.

WILLY. Loves me. (*Wonderingly.*) Always loved me. Isn't that a remarkable thing? Ben, he'll worship me for it!

BEN (*with promise*). It's dark there, but full of diamonds.

WILLY. Can you imagine that magnificence with twenty thousand dollars in his pocket?

LINDA (*calling from her room*). Willy! Come up!

WILLY (*calling into the kitchen*). Yes! Yes. Coming! It's very smart, you realize that, don't you, sweetheart? Even Ben sees it. I gotta go, baby. 'By! 'By! (*Going over to Ben, almost dancing.*) Imagine? When the mail comes he'll be ahead of Bernard again!

BEN. A perfect proposition all around.

WILLY. Did you see how he cried to me? Oh, if I could kiss him, Ben!

BEN. Time, William, time!

WILLY. Oh, Ben, I always knew one way or another we were gonna make it, Biff and I.

BEN (*looking at his watch*). The boat. We'll be late. (*He moves slowly off into the darkness.*)

WILLY (*elegiacally, turning to the house*). Now when you kick off, boy, I want a seventy-yard boot, and get right down the field under the ball, and when you hit, hit low and hit hard, because it's important, boy. (*He swings around and faces the audience.*) There's all kinds of important people in the stands, and the first thing you know . . . (*Suddenly realizing he is alone.*) Ben! Ben, where do I . . . ? (*He makes a sudden movement of search.*) Ben, how do I . . . ?

LINDA (*calling*). Willy, you coming up?

WILLY (*uttering a gasp of fear, whirling about as if to quiet her*). Sh! (*He turns around as if to find his way; sounds, faces, voices, seem to be swarming in upon him and he flicks at them, crying.*) Sh! Sh! (*Suddenly music, faint and high, stops him. It rises in intensity, almost to an unbearable scream. He goes up and down on his toes, and rushes off around the house.*) Shhh!

LINDA. Willy?

There is no answer. Linda waits. Biff gets up off his bed. He is still in his clothes. Happy sits up. Biff stands listening.

LINDA (*with real fear*). Willy, answer me! Willy!

There is the sound of a car starting and moving away at full speed.

LINDA. No!

BIFF (*rushing down the stairs*). Pop!

As the car speeds off the music crashes down in a frenzy of sound, which becomes the soft pulsation of a single cello string. Biff slowly returns to his bedroom. He and Happy gravely don their jackets. Linda slowly walks out of her room. The music has developed into a dead march. The leaves of day are appearing over everything. Charley and Bernard, somberly dressed, appear and knock on the kitchen door. Biff and Happy slowly descend the stairs to the kitchen as Charley and Bernard enter. All stop a moment when Linda, in clothes of mourning, bearing a little bunch of roses, comes through the draped doorway into the kitchen. She goes to Charley and takes his arm. Now all move toward the audience, through the wall-line of the kitchen. At the limit of the apron, Linda lays down the flowers, kneels, and sits back on her heels. All stare down at the grave.

REQUIEM

CHARLEY. It's getting dark, Linda.

Linda doesn't react. She stares at the grave.

BIFF. How about it, Mom? Better get some rest, heh? They'll be closing the gate soon.

Linda makes no move. Pause.

HAPPY (*deeply angered*). He had no right to do that. There was no necessity for it. We would've helped him.

CHARLEY (*grunting*). Hmmm.

BIFF. Come along, Mom.

LINDA. Why didn't anybody come?

CHARLEY. It was a very nice funeral.

LINDA. But where are all the people he knew? Maybe they blame him.

CHARLEY. Naa. It's a rough world, Linda. They wouldn't blame him.

LINDA. I can't understand it. At this time especially. First time in thirty-five years we were just about free and clear. He only needed a little salary. He was even finished with the dentist.

CHARLEY. No man only needs a little salary.

LINDA. I can't understand it.

BIFF. There were a lot of nice days. When he'd come home from a trip; or on Sundays, making the stoop; finishing the cellar; putting on the new porch; when he built the extra bathroom; and put up the garage. You know something, Charley, there's more of him in that front stoop than in all the sales he ever made.

CHARLEY. Yeah. He was a happy man with a batch of cement.

LINDA. He was so wonderful with his hands.

BIFF. He had the wrong dreams. All, all, wrong.

HAPPY (*almost ready to fight Biff*). Don't say that!

BIFF. He never knew who he was.

CHARLEY (*stopping Happy's movement and reply; to Biff*). Nobody dast blame this man. You don't understand: Willy was a salesman. And for a salesman, there is no rock bottom to the life. He don't put a bolt to a nut, he don't tell you the law or give you medicine. He's a man way out there in the blue, riding on a smile and a shoeshine. And when they start not smiling back—that's an earthquake. And then you get yourself a couple of spots on your hat, and you're finished. Nobody dast blame this man. A salesman is got to dream, boy. It comes with the territory.

BIFF. Charley, the man didn't know who he was.

HAPPY (*infuriated*). Don't say that!

BIFF. Why don't you come with me, Happy?

HAPPY. I'm not licked that easily. I'm staying right in this city, and I'm gonna beat this racket! (*He looks at Biff, his chin set.*) The Loman Brothers!

BIFF. I know who I am, kid.

HAPPY. All right, boy. I'm gonna show you and everybody else that Willy Loman did not die in vain. He had a good dream. It's the only dream you can have—to come out number-one man. He fought it out here, and this is where I'm gonna win it for him.

BIFF (*with a hopeless glance at Happy, bends toward his mother*). Let's go, Mom.

LINDA. I'll be with you in a minute. Go on, Charley. (*He hesitates.*) I want to, just for a minute. I never had a chance to say good-by.

Charley moves away, followed by Happy. Biff remains a slight distance up and left of Linda. She sits there, summoning herself. The flute begins, not far away, playing behind her speech.

LINDA. Forgive me, dear. I can't cry. I don't know what it is, but I can't cry. I don't understand it. Why did you ever do that? Help me, Willy, I can't cry. It seems to me that you're just on another trip. I keep expecting you. Willy, dear, I can't cry. Why did you do it? I search and search and I search, and I can't understand it, Willy. I made the last payment on the house today. Today, dear. And there'll be nobody home. (*A sob rises in her throat.*) We're free and clear. (*Sobbing mournfully, released.*) We're free. (*Biff comes slowly toward her.*) We're free . . . We're free . . .

Biff lifts her to her feet and moves out up right with her in his arms. Linda sobs quietly. Bernard and Charley come together and follow them, followed by Happy. Only the music of the flute is left on the darkening stage as over the house the hard towers of the apartment buildings rise into sharp focus and the curtain falls.

TOPICS FOR CRITICAL THINKING AND WRITING

📖 THE PLAY ON THE PAGE

1. Miller said in the *New York Times* (February 27, 1949, Sec. II, p. 1) that tragedy shows man's struggle to secure "his sense of personal dignity" and that "his destruction in the attempt posits a wrong or an evil in his environment." Does this make sense when applied to some earlier tragedy (for example, *Oedipus Rex* or *Hamlet*), and does it apply convincingly to *Death of a Salesman*? Is this the tragedy of an individual's own making? Or is society at fault for corrupting and exploiting Willy? Or both?

2. Is Willy pathetic rather than tragic? If pathetic, does this imply that the play is less worthy than if he is tragic?

3. Do you feel that Miller is straining too hard to turn a play about a little man into a big, impressive play? For example, do the musical themes, the unrealistic setting, the appearances of Ben, and the speech at the grave seem out of keeping in a play about the death of a salesman?

4. We don't know what Willy sells, and we don't know whether or not the insurance will be paid after his death. Do you consider these uncertainties to be faults in the play?

5. Is Howard a villain?

6. Characterize Linda.

🎭 THE PLAY ON THE STAGE

7. It is sometimes said that in this realistic play that includes symbolic and expressionistic elements (on expressionism, see p. 558 and the Glossary), Biff and Happy can be seen as two aspects of Willy. In this view, Biff more or less represents Willy's spiritual needs, and Happy represents his materialism and his sexuality. If you were directing the play, would you adopt this point of view? Whatever your interpretation, how would you costume the brothers?

8. As we indicate on page 689, although Miller envisioned Willy as a small man (literally small), the role was first performed by Lee J. Cobb, a large man. If you were casting the play, what actor would you select? Why? Whom would you choose for Linda, Biff, Happy, Bernard, and Charley?

9. Select roughly thirty lines of dialogue, and discuss the movements (gestures and blocking) that as a director you would suggest to the performers.

CONTEXTS FOR *DEATH OF A SALESMAN*

Arthur Miller
TRAGEDY AND THE COMMON MAN

In this age few tragedies are written. It has often been held that the lack is due to a paucity of heroes among us, or else that modern man has had the blood drawn out of his organs of belief by the skepticism of science, and the heroic attack on life cannot feed on an attitude of reserve and circumspection. For one reason or another, we are often held to be below tragedy—or tragedy above us. The inevitable conclusion is, of course, that the tragic mode is archaic, fit only for the very highly placed, the kings or the kingly, and where this admission is not made in so many words it is most often implied.

I believe that the common man is as apt a subject for tragedy in its highest sense as kings were. On the face of it this ought to be obvious in the light of modern psychiatry, which bases its analysis upon classic formulations, such as the Oedipus and Orestes complexes, for instances, which were enacted by royal beings, but which apply to everyone in similar emotional situations.

More simply, when the question of tragedy in art is not at issue, we never hesitate to attribute to the well-placed and the exalted the very same mental processes as the lowly. And finally, if the exaltation of tragic action were truly a property of the high-bred character alone, it is inconceivable that the mass of mankind should cherish tragedy above all other forms, let alone be capable of understanding it.

As a general rule, to which there may be exceptions unknown to me, I think the tragic feeling is evoked in us when we are in the presence of a character who is ready to lay down his life, if need be, to secure one thing—his sense of personal dignity. From Orestes to Hamlet, Medea to Macbeth, the underlying struggle is that of the individual attempting to gain his "rightful" position in his society.

Sometimes he is one who has been displaced from it, sometimes one who seeks to attain it for the first time, but the fateful wound from which the inevitable events spiral is the wound of indignity, and its dominant force is indignation. Tragedy, then, is the consequence of a man's total compulsion to evaluate himself justly.

In the sense of having been initiated by the hero himself, the tale always reveals what has been called his "tragic flaw," a failing that is not peculiar to grand or elevated characters. Nor is it necessarily a weakness. The flaw, or crack in the character, is really nothing—and need be nothing, but his inherent unwillingness to remain passive in the face of what he conceives to be a challenge to his dignity, his image of his rightful status. Only the passive, only those who accept their lot without active retaliation, are "flawless." Most of us are in that category.

But there are among us today, as there always have been, those who act against the scheme of things that degrades them, and in the process of action everything we have accepted out of fear or insensitivity or ignorance is shaken before us and examined, and from this total onslaught by an individual against the seemingly stable cosmos surrounding us—from this total examination of the "unchangeable" environment—comes the terror and the fear that is classically associated with tragedy.

More important, from this total questioning of what has previously been unquestioned, we learn. And such a process is not beyond the common man. In revolutions around the world, these past thirty years, he has demonstrated again and again this inner dynamic of all tragedy.

Insistence upon the rank of the tragic hero, or the so-called nobility of his character, is really but a clinging to the outward forms of tragedy. If rank or nobility of character was indispensable, then it would follow that the problems of those with rank were the particular problems of tragedy. But surely the right of one monarch to capture the domain from another no longer raises our passions, nor are our concepts of justice what they were to the mind of an Elizabethan king.

The quality in such plays that does shake us, however, derives from the underlying fear of being displaced, the disaster inherent in being torn away from our chosen image of what and who we are in this world. Among us today this fear is as strong, and perhaps stronger, than it ever was. In fact, it is the common man who knows this fear best.

Now, if it is true that tragedy is the consequence of a man's total compulsion to evaluate himself justly, his destruction in the attempt posits a wrong or an evil in his environment. And this is precisely the morality of tragedy and its lesson. The discovery of the moral law, which is what the enlightenment of tragedy consists of, is not the discovery of some abstract or metaphysical quantity.

The tragic right is a condition of life, a condition in which the human personality is able to flower and realize itself. The wrong is the condition which suppresses man, perverts the flowing out of his love and creative instinct. Tragedy enlightens—and it must, in that it points the heroic finger at the enemy of man's freedom. The thrust for freedom is the quality in tragedy which exalts. The revolutionary questioning of the stable environment is what terrifies.

In no way is the common man debarred from such thoughts or such actions.

Seen in this light, our lack of tragedy may be partially accounted for by the turn which modern literature has taken toward the purely psychiatric view of life, or the purely sociological. If all our miseries, our indignities, are born and bred within our minds, then all action, let alone the heroic action, is obviously impossible.

And if society alone is responsible for the cramping of our lives, then the protagonist must needs be so pure and faultless as to force us to deny his validity as a character. From neither of these views can tragedy derive, simply because neither represents a balanced concept of life. Above all else, tragedy requires the finest appreciation by the writer of cause and effect.

No tragedy can therefore come about when its author fears to question absolutely everything, when he regards any institution, habit or custom as being either everlasting, immutable or inevitable. In the tragic view the need of man to wholly realize himself is the only fixed star, and whatever it is that hedges his nature and lowers it is ripe for attack and examination. Which is not to say that tragedy must preach revolution.

The Greeks could probe the very heavenly origin of their ways and return to confirm the rightness of laws. And Job could face God in anger, demanding his right, and end in submission. But for a moment everything is in suspension, nothing is accepted, and in this stretching and tearing apart of the cosmos, in the very action of so doing, the character gains "size," the tragic stature which is spuriously attached to the royal or the high-born in our minds. The commonest of men may take on that stature to the extent of his willingness to throw all he has into the contest, the battle to secure his rightful place in his world.

There is a misconception of tragedy with which I have been struck in review after review, and in many conversations with writers and readers alike. It is the idea that tragedy is of necessity allied to pessimism. Even the dictionary says nothing more about the word than that it means a story with a sad or unhappy ending. This impression is so firmly fixed that I almost hesitate to claim that in truth tragedy implies more optimism in its author than does comedy, and that its final result ought to be the reinforcement of the onlooker's brightest opinions of the human animal.

For, if it is true to say that in essence the tragic hero is intent upon claiming his whole due as a personality, and if this struggle must be total and without reservation, then it automatically demonstrates the indestructible will of man to achieve his humanity.

The possibility of victory must be there in tragedy. Where pathos rules, where pathos is finally derived, a character has fought a battle he could not possibly have won. The pathetic is achieved when the protagonist is, by virtue of his witlessness, his insensitivity or the very air he gives off, incapable of grappling with a much superior force.

Arthur Miller

Pathos truly is the mode for the pessimist. But tragedy requires a nicer balance between what is possible and what is impossible. And it is curious, although edifying, that the plays we revere, century after century, are the tragedies. In them, and in them alone, lies the belief—optimistic, if you will—in the perfectibility of man.

Arthur Miller
WILLY LOMAN'S IDEALS

[In 1958 Arthur Miller made these comments during the course of a symposium on *Death of a Salesman*. The title is the editors'.]

Miller. The trouble with Willy Loman is that he has tremendously powerful ideals. We're not accustomed to speaking of ideals in his terms; but, if Willy Loman, for instance, had not had a very profound sense that his life as lived had left him hollow, he would have died contentedly polishing his car on some Sunday afternoon at a ripe old age. The fact is he has values. The fact that they cannot be realized is what is driving him mad—just as, unfortunately, it's driving a lot of other people mad. The truly valueless man, a man without ideals, is always perfectly at home anywhere . . . because there cannot be a conflict between nothing and something. Whatever negative qualities there are in the society or in

It is time, I think, that we who are without kings, took up this bright thread of our history and followed it to the only place it can possibly lead in our time—the heart and spirit of the average man.

the environment don't bother him, because they are not in conflict with what positive sense one may have. I think Willy Loman, on the other hand, is seeking for a kind of ecstasy in life, which the machine-civilization deprives people of. He's looking for his selfhood, for his immortal soul, so to speak. People who don't know the intensity of that quest, possibly, think he's odd. Now an extraordinarily large number of salesmen particularly, who are in a line of work where a large measure of ingenuity and individualism are required, have a very intimate understanding of this problem. More so, I think, than literary critics who probably need strive less after a certain point. A salesman is a kind of creative person (it's possibly idiotic to say so on a literary program, but they are), they have to get up in the morning and conceive a plan of attack and use all kinds of ingenuity all day long, just the way a writer does.

THE PLAY IN PERFORMANCE

When Miller began working on the play that became *Death of a Salesman,* he tells us in his introduction to *Collected Plays* (1957) that he tentatively thought of calling it *The Inside of His Head.* The audience would see "an enormous face the height of the proscenium arch which would appear and then open up, and we would see the inside of a man's head . . . It was conceived half in laughter, for the inside of his head was a mass of contradictions." However, as he worked on the play, he reports in his autobiography *Timebends* (1987), he toyed with using only "three bare platforms and only the minimum necessary furniture for a kitchen and two bedrooms, with the Boston hotel room as well as Howard's office to be played in open space" (188).

Miller found a producer relatively quickly. Elia Kazan directed the play, Joel Mielziner designed the set, and the rest is history. (The set, depicted on p. 14, combined realism—for instance the period-piece refrigerator—along with expressionistic elements, such as the skeletal roof that suggests vulnerability. The opening stage direction clearly indicates some expressionistic elements, that is, elements that express the states of mind of the characters. The house, we are told, is surrounded by an "angry glow of orange," and as the light increases "we see a solid vault of apartment houses around the small, fragile-seeming house." In the second act,

in the restaurant scene, "a red glow rises behind the screen at right," and still later in the act "[a] single trumpet note jars the ear. The light of green leaves stains the house, which holds the air of night and a dream.") In January 1949 *Death of a Salesman* was enthusiastically received by reviewers and by the general public in its pre-Broadway run in Philadelphia, and it was received with at least equal enthusiasm when it opened in New York City in February. In the autumn a touring company visited cities throughout the United States, and by 1950 it had played in a dozen countries in Europe, the Middle East, and South America. It has been said that since its first performance in Philadelphia in 1949, there probably has not been a single day when *Death of a Salesman* has not been produced somewhere in the world. As early as 1959 it was produced in the Soviet Union, where it was taken as a condemnation of American capitalism, and in 1983 it was produced in Beijing under Miller's own direction, where, of course, the play was seen through Marxist eyes. The Chinese audiences (and the actors, too) expected to find a hero and a villain—not a man of mingled qualities. In his account of the production, in *Salesman in Beijing* (1983), Miller says that he had considerable difficulty getting the actor who played Willy to think of Willy sympathetically, since Willy is not a symbol of the virtuous man.

Furthermore, Miller had trouble getting the actors who, of course were trained in a Chinese style of operatic acting, to act realistically. For instance, in the Chinese theater, characters may address the audience rather than each other. Similarly, the Chinese actors wanted to wear the light-colored wigs and white makeup that they customarily used when playing Caucasians. Miller felt, however, that these devices made the play seem *unreal*, and he persuaded them to perform the play in a more Western manner. The result, he reports, was that the spectators, seeing Asian faces instead of Asians made up to look like whites, were able to identify with the actors and thus with the Westerners for whom the actors stood.

In the early days most productions of *Death of a Salesman* used the highly praised set (or an adaptation of it) that Jo Mielziner had designed for the original production. However, at least as early as 1963 grumblings were heard. Mielziner's set

was now said (by some) to be too elaborate, too attention getting, and it was argued that the play would benefit from a stripped-down set, perhaps just some multilevel platforms and a few pieces of furniture. Most sets continue, however, to be realistic and, at the same time, at least mildly expressionistic.

The first Willy Loman was Lee J. Cobb, a large man (he is usually described as "bearish"). Miller was at first uncertain about this choice, because he had envisioned the role as being played by a small man, but Cobb was enormously successful. Over the years, there have been two kinds of Willy Lomans—big men such as Cobb and George C. Scott, and small men (almost always described as "feisty bantams") such as Dustin Hoffman and Hume Cronyn. Actors of both sorts have received favorable reviews, and, in fact, it is a rare production that does stir an audience.

For a readable history of the play on the stage and screen, see Brenda Murphy, *Miller: Death of a Salesman* (1995).

A Note on the
THEATER OF THE ABSURD

What does it mean if a writer is called an "absurdist" or if certain works of literature are labeled "absurdist"? The term is derived from "theater of the absurd," a phrase first used by Martin Esslin in 1961 to describe works by such playwrights as Eugène Ionesco (Romanian), Samuel Beckett (Irish), Jean Genet (French), Edward Albee (American), and Harold Pinter (British). These writers did not run a theater together, nor did they meet regularly or decide to call themselves absurdists. Like many other people in the years following the devastation of World War II, they felt a deep sense of loss, despair, and hopelessness—a feeling that our world is an absurd, meaningless one. Writing in his journal in 1967, Ionesco described the effect of World War II on people's beliefs:

> There was a time, long, long ago, when the world seemed to man to be so charged with meanings that he didn't have *time* to ask himself questions, the manifestation was so spectacular. The whole world was like a theater in which the elements, the forest, the oceans and the rivers, the mountains and the plains, the bushes and each plant played a role that man tried to explain to himself, and gave an explanation of. But the explanations were less important: what was essential, what was satisfying, was the evidence of the presence of the gods, it was plenitude, everything was a series of glorious epiphanies. The world was full of meaning. . . . Now we are abandoned to ourselves, to our solitude, to our fear, and the problem was born. What is this world? Who are we?[1]

Although absurdist plays reflect different responses to this stripped-down world and this feeling of abandonment, they share a number of traits:

- The plays are "theatrical" rather than realistic, often setting forth obviously impossible situations with obviously unreal characters.
- The plays are serious but often (or at least intermittently) comic, especially satiric.
- The basic themes are (a) human loneliness in a world without God, (b) the inability to communicate, (c) the dehumanization and impotence of individuals in a bourgeois society, and (d) the meaninglessness of life.

The French writer/philosopher Albert Camus often referred to the feeling of absurdity, not as a conclusion to be drawn about the human condition but as a premise for contemplating human existence. In one of his essays, "The Myth of Sisyphus" (1940), Camus says:

This world in itself is not reasonable, that is all that can be said. But what is absurd is the confrontation of this irrational and the wild longing for clarity whose call echoes in the human heart. The absurd depends as much on man as on the world. For the moment it is all that links them together.[2]

It is in this sense that a discussion of the absurd helps us in our reading of Pinter, Beckett, Albee, and the others. We are going beyond the dictionary definition of absurd (ridiculously senseless, illogical, or untrue; contrary to all reason or common sense) to a meaning suggested by Ionesco: "that which is devoid of purpose. . . . Cut off from his religious, metaphysical, and transcendental roots, man is lost; all his actions become senseless, absurd, useless." In the late 1960s the American social-protest singer Bob Dylan captured this feeling of absurdity and alientation, for instance, in "Ballad of a Thin Man":

> You raise up your head
> and you ask 'Is this where it is?'
> and somebody points to you and says 'It's his,'
> and you say 'What's mine?'

The confusion expressed in Dylan's song is similar to the confusion and uncertainty felt by characters such as Stanley Webber, in Pinter's chilling *The Birthday Party* (p. 712). Something is very definitely happening to Stanley—he is the passive "victim" of two thugs come to do a job—yet he is a grown man incapable of taking care of himself and uncertain as to his fate. In *The Lesson* (p. 694), Ionesco shows us how even a confident individual can be destroyed because of the confusion and uncertainty caused by an unyielding tyrannical force. The 1990s catchword *clueless* expresses a similar lack of certainty and direction.

Of course, the "newness" of absurdist drama, even for the post–World War II era, is debatable. Absurdist elements are apparent in some early Greek drama (think of the nonsensical word play and farcical slapstick in *Lysistrata*) and in Shakespeare (think of Poor Tom in *King Lear* and Lear's own ravings during the storm scene). Throughout the ages people may have assumed the structure and existence of a force greater than humankind—God, fate, some divine and larger purpose. Nonetheless, there has always been much in human experience for which reason and logic, sometimes even faith, seem inadequate. Terrible accidents, the bombing in Oklahoma City, a severely disabled child, the deaths of millions of people during the Holocaust—how does one explain or rationalize these events?

---

[1] *Present Past, Past Present: A Personal Memoir* (New York: Grove, 1971), p. 116.

[2] *The Myth of Sisyphus and Other Essays,* translated by Justin O'Brien (New York: Knopf, 1967), p. 21.

Absurdity does not necessarily divorce itself from the world of reason; it can parody the forms and appearances of logic, norms, or accepted morality. Examine Meg and Petey's opening conversation in *The Birthday Party* as an example of this kind of parody, and think about their relationship as a representation of the complacency and banality possible in a marriage. The dialogue of an absurdist play often includes puns, nonsequiturs, nonsense patter, jokes, or babble that seem unrelated to the stage action. The characters may be tramps or misfits—almost subhuman types who seem to live outside law and society. Theatrical effects may be achieved through the use of comic gestures, exaggeration, repetitive actions, and grotesque or incongruous props. For example, imagine the effect for an audience watching the opening moments of Adrienne Kennedy's *Funnyhouse of a Negro* (p. 788)

Before the closed curtain a woman dressed in a white nightgown walks across the stage carrying before her a bald head. She moves as one in a trance and is mumbling something inaudible to herself. She appears faceless, wearing a yellow whitish maskover over her face, with no apparent eyes.

Finally, we need to mention that bawdy elements, such as obscenities interwoven in "normal" speech or vulgar sexual acts portrayed (consider the tableau of Lulu spread on the table at the close of Act Two in *The Birthday Party* or the professor at the conclusion of *The Lesson*—p. 706), may be part of an absurdist play. The absurdists deliberately create a mood of menace and threat; they produce a body of work that makes us uncomfortable, uneasy, unsure of whether there is any order, sense, or meaning in existence.

Eugène Ionesco

THE LESSON

Eugène Ionesco (1912–1994) was born in Romania of a Romanian father and a French mother. He spent his childhood in France and did not return to Romania, or learn Romanian, until he was thirteen. (He has said that his view of the world as a place where almost nothing can be known is partly due to the fact that until he was thirteen he heard that the French were the bravest in the world, and after thirteen he heard that Romanians were the bravest.) After university training in Romania, he taught French there, but in 1939 he returned to France and worked for a publisher. He did not write his first play, *The Bald Soprano*, until about 1948, and he did not become well known as a dramatist until 1956, when a revival of *The Chairs* (1951) attracted critical attention. Other major plays are *The Lesson* (1950), *Amédée* (1953), *The Killer* (1957), *Rhinoceros* (1959), and *The King Dies* (1962).

COMMENTARY

The remarks on theater of the absurd (pp. 690–91) will help provide a perspective for understanding Eugène Ionesco's unusual, disturbing play, *The Lesson*. Originally written in French, Ionesco's first four plays (all short scripts) baffled and outraged their initial audiences in Paris. The plays' titles and subtitles may give you an indication of Ionesco's vision: *The Bald Soprano, Anti-play* (1948); *The Lesson, a Comic Drama* (1950); *The Chairs, a Tragic Farce* (1951); *Jack, or the Submission, a Naturalistic Comedy* (1955). Critics attacked—but eventually praised—Ionesco's plays with labels such as "surreal fantasies," "grotesque practical jokes," "anti-realistic parodies," "bourgeois satires," "maniacal parodies," and "comic revelations."

How do we approach these perplexing descriptions? Perhaps some comments by Ionesco himself, written in 1957 about *The Bald Soprano* but equally applicable to *The Lesson*, provide insight into his serious concerns:

> We can no longer avoid asking ourselves what we are doing here on earth, and how, having no deep sense of our destiny, we can endure the crushing weight of the material world. This is the *eternal problem* if ever there was one; for living means alienation. . . . [I]f man is not tragic, he is ridiculous and painful, "comic" in fact, and by revealing his absurdity one can achieve a sort of tragedy.

In *The Lesson*, Ionesco demonstrates this ridiculous and painful condition through means that may seem very cruel: a pupil who is at first enthusiastic and confident degenerates into dullness, while her professor changes from timidity to aggression and sadism. Clearly, we must not take the portrait of the professor as Ionesco's indictment against all educators. Rather it is Ionesco's reaction against all brutal figures of authority. In a 1960 memoir, Ionesco recalled an event from the 1920s when his family had returned to Romania:

> I saw a man, still young, big and strong, attack an old man with his fists and kick him with his boots . . . I have no other images of the world except those of evanscence and brutality, vanity and rage, nothingness or hideous, useless hatred.

In common with so many people who witnessed the catastrophic events of the 1940s in Europe, Ionesco was deeply affected by the destruction wrought by the Nazis and Facists.

Despite his habit of journal writing and his rage against totalitarianism, Ionesco's first play, *The Bald Soprano*, came about almost by accident. As he memorized and wrote out sentences in an effort to teach himself English, he noted that the dialogues in his English primer seemed like a play—characters asked questions of each other, answers were given, and perfectly obvious facts stated. His script parodied those simple, inane dialogues. *The Bald Soprano* ran for six weeks, often with only a handful of people in attendance. However, for Ionesco—who had not intended to be a writer, much less a playwright—the experience of live theater was a turning point. He was deeply moved by seeing his own creations on stage. Writing in 1958 he explained, "One cannot resist the desire of making appear, on a stage, characters that are at the same time real and invented." Perhaps recalling his fascination with the Punch-and-Judy puppet shows when he was a child in Paris, Ionesco decided that characters needed to be exaggerated in order for playwrights to make the points they intended:

[I]f the essence of the theatre lay in the enlargement of effects, it was necessary to enlarge them even more, to underline them, to emphasize them as much as possible. To push the theatre beyond that intermediary zone that is neither theatre nor literature was to put it back into its proper framework . . . What was needed was not to disguise the strings that moved the puppets but to make them even more visible, deliberately apparent, to go right down to the very basis of the grotesque, the realms of caricature. . . . To create a theatre of violence—violently comic, violently dramatic.

This quotation should help you assess the professor's violence and the overall effect of *The Lesson*. As we think about the various types of drama, it is clear that Ionesco's contribution—call it outrageous, inventive, avant-garde, absurdist—is an innovative one.

Max Adrian, a distinguished comic actor, here plays the professor, lecturing his student, Joan Plowright, while the maid (Paula Bauersmith) looks on, in a 1958 Phoenix Theatre (London) production, directed by Tony Richardson.

Eugène Ionesco

THE LESSON

Translated by Donald M. Allen

The Characters

THE PROFESSOR, *aged 50 to 60*
THE YOUNG PUPIL, *aged 18*
THE MAID, *aged 45 to 50*

SCENE: *The office of the old professor, which also serves as a dining room. To the left, a door opens onto the apartment stairs; upstage, to the right, another door opens onto a corridor of the* apartment. *Upstage, a little left of center, a window, not very large, with plain curtains; on the outside sill of the window are ordinary potted plants. The low buildings with red roofs of a small town can be seen in the distance. The sky is grayish-blue. On the right stands a provincial buffet. The table doubles as a desk; it stands at stage center. There are three chairs around the table, and two more stand on each side of the window. Light-colored wallpaper, some shelves with books.*

(*When the curtain rises the stage is empty, and it remains so for a few moments. Then we hear the doorbell ring.*)

VOICE OF THE MAID (*from the corridor*). Yes. I'm coming.

(*The Maid comes in, after having run down the stairs. She is stout, aged 45 to 50, red-faced, and wears a peasant woman's cap. She rushes in, slamming the door to the right behind her, and dries her hands on her apron as she runs towards the door on the left. Meanwhile we hear the doorbell ring again.*)

MAID. Just a moment, I'm coming.

(*She opens the door. A young Pupil, aged 18, enters. She is wearing a gray student's smock, a small white collar, and carries a student's satchel under her arm.*)

MAID. Good morning, miss.

PUPIL. Good morning, madam. Is the Professor at home?

MAID. Have you come for the lesson?

PUPIL. Yes, I have.

MAID. He's expecting you. Sit down for a moment. I'll tell him you're here.

PUPIL. Thank you.

(*She seats herself near the table, facing the audience; the hall door is to her left; her back is to the other door, through which the Maid hurriedly exists, calling.*)

MAID. Professor, come down please, your pupil is here.

VOICE OF THE PROFESSOR (*rather reedy*). Thank you. I'm coming . . . in just a moment . . .

(*The Maid exits; the Pupil draws in her legs, holds her satchel on her lap, and waits demurely. She casts a glance or two around the room, at the furniture, at the ceiling too. Then she takes a notebook out of her satchel, leafs through it, and stops to look at a page for a moment as though reviewing a lesson, as though taking a last look at her homework. She seems to be a well-brought-up girl, polite, but lively, gay, dynamic; a fresh smile is on her lips. During the course of the play she progressively loses the lively rhythm of her movement and her carriage, she becomes withdrawn. From gay and smiling she becomes progressively sad and morose; from very lively at the beginning, she becomes more and more fatigued and somnolent. Towards the end of the play her face must clearly express a nervous depression; her way of speaking shows the effects of this, her tongue becomes thick, words come to her memory with difficulty and emerge from her mouth with as much difficulty; she comes to have a manner vaguely paralyzed, the beginning of aphasia. Firm and determined at the beginning, so much so as to appear to be almost aggressive, she becomes more and more passive, until she is almost a mute and inert object, seemingly inanimate in the Professor's hands, to such an extent that when he makes his final gesture, she no longer reacts. Insensible, her reflexes deadened, only her eyes in an expressionless face will show inexpressible astonishment and fear. The transi-*tion from one manner to the other must of course be made imperceptibly.*

The Professor enters. He is a little old man with a little white beard. He wears pince-nez, a black skull cap, a long black school-master's coat, trousers and shoes of black, detachable white collar, a black tie. Excessively polite, very timid, his voice deadened by his timidity, very proper, very much the teacher. He rubs his hands together constantly; occasionally a lewd gleam comes into his eyes and is quickly repressed.

During the course of the play his timidity will disappear progressively, imperceptibly; and the lewd gleams in his eyes will become a steady devouring flame in the end. From a manner that is inoffensive at the start, the Professor becomes more and more sure of himself, more and more nervous, aggressive, dominating, until he is able to do as he pleases with the Pupil, who has become, in his hands, a pitiful creature. Of course, the voice of the Professor must change too, from thin and reedy, to stronger and stronger, until at the end it is extremely powerful, ringing, sonorous, while the Pupil's voice changes from the very clear and ringing tones that she has at the beginning of the play until it is almost inaudible. In these first scenes the Professor might stammer very slightly.)

PROFESSOR. Good morning, young lady. You . . . I expect that you . . . that you are the new pupil?

PUPIL (*turns quickly with a lively and self-assured manner; she gets up, goes towards the Professor, and gives him her hand*). Yes, Professor. Good morning, Professor. As you see, I'm on time. I didn't want to be late.

PROFESSOR. That's fine, miss. Thank you, you didn't really need to hurry. I am very sorry to have kept you waiting . . . I was just finishing up . . . well . . . I'm sorry . . . You will excuse me, won't you? . . .

PUPIL. Oh, certainly, Professor. It doesn't matter at all, Professor.

PROFESSOR. Please excuse me . . . Did you have any trouble finding the house?

PUPIL. No . . . Not at all. I just asked the way. Everybody knows you around here.

PROFESSOR. For thirty years I've lived in this town. You've not been here for long? How do you find it?

PUPIL. It's all right. The town is attractive and even agreeable, there's a nice park, a boarding school, a bishop, nice shops and streets . . .

PROFESSOR. That's very true, young lady. And yet, I'd just as soon live somewhere else. In Paris, or at least Bordeaux.

PUPIL. Do you like Bordeaux?

PROFESSOR. I don't know. I've never seen it.

PUPIL. But you know Paris?

PROFESSOR. No, I don't know it either, young lady, but if you'll permit me, can you tell me, Paris is the capital city of . . . miss?

PUPIL (*searching her memory for a moment, then, happily guessing*). Paris is the capital city of . . . France?

PROFESSOR. Yes, young lady, bravo, that's very good, that's perfect. My congratulations. You have your French geography at your finger tips. You know your chief cities.

PUPIL. Oh! I don't know them all yet, Professor, it's not quite that easy, I have trouble learning them.

PROFESSOR. Oh! it will come . . . you mustn't give up . . . young lady . . . I beg your pardon . . . have patience . . . little by little . . . You will see, it will come in time . . . What a nice day it is today . . . or rather, not so nice . . . Oh! but then yes it is nice. In short it's not too bad a day, that's the main thing . . . ahem . . . ahem . . . it's not raining and it's not snowing either.

PUPIL. That would be most unusual, for it's summer now.

PROFESSOR. Excuse me, miss, I was just going to say so . . . but as you will learn, one must be ready for anything.

PUPIL. I guess so, Professor.

PROFESSOR. We can't be sure of anything, young lady, in this world.

PUPIL. The snow falls in the winter. Winter is one of the four seasons. The other three are . . . uh . . . spr . . .

PROFESSOR. Yes?

PUPIL. . . . ing, and then summer . . . and . . . uh . . .

PROFESSOR. It begins like "automobile," miss.

PUPIL. Ah, yes, autumn . . .

PROFESSOR. That's right, miss. That's a good answer, that's perfect. I am convinced that you will be a good pupil. You will make real progress. You are intelligent, you seem to me to be well informed, and you've a good memory.

PUPIL. I know my seasons, don't I, Professor?

PROFESSOR. Yes, indeed, miss . . . or almost. But it will come in time. In any case, you're coming along. Soon you'll know all the seasons, with your eyes closed. Just as I do.

PUPIL. It's hard.

PROFESSOR. Oh, no. All it takes is a little effort, a little good will, miss. You will see. It will come, you may be sure of that.

PUPIL. Oh, I do hope so, Professor. I have a great thirst for knowledge. My parents also want me to get an education. They want me to specialize. They consider a little general culture, even if it is solid, is no longer enough, in these times.

PROFESSOR. Your parents, miss, are perfectly right. You must go on with your studies. Forgive me for saying so, but it is very necessary. Our contemporary life has become most complex.

PUPIL. And so very complicated too . . . My parents are fairly rich, I'm lucky. They can help me in my work, help me in my very advanced studies.

PROFESSOR. And you wish to qualify for . . . ?

PUPIL. Just as soon as possible, for the first doctor's orals. They're in three weeks' time.

PROFESSOR. You already have your high school diploma, if you'll pardon the question?

PUPIL. Yes, Professor, I have my science diploma and my arts diploma, too.

PROFESSOR. Ah, you're very far advanced, even perhaps too advanced for your age. And which doctorate do you wish to qualify for? In the physical sciences or in moral philosophy?

PUPIL. My parents are very much hoping—if you think it will be possible in such a short time—they very much hope that I can qualify for the total doctorate.

PROFESSOR. The total doctorate? . . . You have great courage, young lady, I congratulate you sincerely. We will try, miss, to do our best. In any case, you already know quite a bit, and at so young an age too.

PUPIL. Oh, Professor.

PROFESSOR. Then, if you'll permit me, pardon me, please, I do think that we ought to get to work. We have scarcely any time to lose.

PUPIL. Oh, but certainly, Professor, I want to. I beg you to.

PROFESSOR. Then, may I ask you to sit down . . . there . . . Will you permit me, miss, that is if you have no objections, to sit down opposite you?

PUPIL. Oh, of course, Professor, please do.

PROFESSOR. Thank you very much, miss. (*They sit down facing each other at the table, their profiles to the audience.*) There we are. Now have you brought your books and notebooks?

PUPIL (*taking notebooks and books out of her satchel*). Yes, Professor. Certainly, I have brought all that we'll need.

PROFESSOR. Perfect, miss. This is perfect. Now, if this doesn't bore you . . . shall we begin?

PUPIL. Yes, indeed, Professor, I am at your disposal.

PROFESSOR. At my disposal? (*A gleam comes into his eyes and is quickly extinguished; he begins to make a gesture that he suppresses at once.*) Oh, miss, it is I who am at *your* disposal. I am only your humble servant.

PUPIL. Oh, Professor . . .

PROFESSOR. If you will . . . now . . . we . . . we . . . I . . . I will begin by making a brief examination of your knowledge, past and present, so that we may chart our future course . . . Good. How is your perception of plurality?

PUPIL. It's rather vague . . . confused.

PROFESSOR. Good. We shall see.

(*He rubs his hands together. The Maid enters, and this appears to irritate the Professor. She goes to the buffet and looks for something, lingering.*)

PROFESSOR. Now, miss, would you like to do a little arithmetic, that is if you want to . . .

PUPIL. Oh, yes, Professor. Certainly, I ask nothing better.

PROFESSOR. It is rather a new science, a modern science, properly speaking, it is more a method than a science . . . And it is also a therapy. (*To the Maid:*) Have you finished, Marie?

MAID. Yes, Professor, I've found the plate. I'm just going . . .

PROFESSOR. Hurry up then. Please go along to the kitchen, if you will.

MAID. Yes, Professor, I'm going. (*She starts to go out.*) Excuse me. Professor, but take care, I urge you to remain calm.

PROFESSOR. You're being ridiculous, Marie. Now, don't worry.

MAID. That's what you always say.

PROFESSOR. I will not stand for your insinuations. I know perfectly well how to comport myself. I am old enough for that.

MAID. Precisely, Professor. You will do better not to start the young lady on arithmetic. Arithmetic is tiring, exhausting.

PROFESSOR. Not at my age. And anyhow, what business is it of yours? This is my concern. And I know what I'm doing. This is not your department.

MAID. Very well, Professor. But you can't say that I didn't warn you.

PROFESSOR. Marie, I can get along without your advice.

MAID. As you wish, Professor. (*She exits.*)

PROFESSOR. Miss, I hope you'll pardon this absurd interruption . . . Excuse this woman . . . She is always afraid that I'll tire myself. She fusses over my health.

PUPIL. Oh, that's quite all right, Professor. It shows that she's very devoted. She loves you very much. Good servants are rare.

PROFESSOR. She exaggerates. Her fears are stupid. But let's return to our arithmetical knitting.

PUPIL. I'm following you, Professor.

PROFESSOR (*wittily*). Without leaving your seat!

PUPIL (*appreciating his joke*). Like you, Professor.

PROFESSOR. Good. Let us arithmetize a little now.

PUPIL. Yes, gladly, Professor.

PROFESSOR. It wouldn't be too tiresome for you to tell me . . .

PUPIL. Not at all, Professor, go on.

PROFESSOR. How much are one and one?

PUPIL. One and one make two.

PROFESSOR (*marveling at the Pupil's knowledge*). Oh, but that's very good. You appear to me to be well along in your studies. You should easily achieve the total doctorate, miss.

PUPIL. I'm so glad. Especially to have someone like you tell me this.

PROFESSOR. Let's push on: how much are two and one?

PUPIL. Three.

PROFESSOR. Three and one?

PUPIL. Four.

PROFESSOR. Four and one?

PUPIL. Five.

PROFESSOR. Five and one?

PUPIL. Six.

PROFESSOR. Six and one?

PUPIL. Seven.

PROFESSOR. Seven and one?

PUPIL. Eight.

PROFESSOR. Seven and one?

PUPIL. Eight again.

PROFESSOR. Very well answered. Seven and one?

PUPIL. Eight once more.

PROFESSOR. Perfect. Excellent. Seven and one?

PUPIL. Eight again. And sometimes nine.

PROFESSOR. Magnificent. You are magnificent. You are exquisite. I congratulate you warmly, miss. There's scarcely any point in going on. At addition you are a past master. Now, let's look at subtraction. Tell me, if you are not exhausted, how many are four minus three?

PUPIL. Four minus three? . . . Four minus three?

PROFESSOR. Yes. I mean to say: subtract three from four.

PUPIL. That makes . . . seven?

PROFESSOR. I am sorry but I'm obliged to contradict you. Four minus three does not make seven. You are confused: four plus three makes seven, four minus three does not make seven . . . This is not addition anymore, we must subtract now.

PUPIL (*trying to understand*). Yes . . . yes . . .

PROFESSOR. Four minus three makes . . . How many? . . . How many?

PUPIL. Four?

PROFESSOR. No, miss, that's not it.

PUPIL. Three, then.

PROFESSOR. Not that either, miss . . . Pardon, I'm sorry . . . I ought to say, that's not it . . . excuse me.

PUPIL. Four minus three . . . Four minus three . . . Four minus three? . . . But now doesn't that make ten?

PROFESSOR. Oh, certainly not, miss. It's not a matter of guessing, you've got to think it out. Let's try to deduce it together. Would you like to count?

PUPIL. Yes, Professor. One . . . two . . . uh . . .

PROFESSOR. You know how to count? How far can you count up to?

PUPIL. I can count to . . . to infinity.

PROFESSOR. That's not possible, miss.

PUPIL. Well then, let's say to sixteen.

PROFESSOR. That is enough. One must know one's limits. Count then, if you will, please.

PUPIL. One . . . two . . . and after two, comes three . . . then four . . .

PROFESSOR. Stop there, miss. Which number is larger? Three or four?

PUPIL. Uh . . . three or four? Which is the larger? The larger of three or four? In what sense larger?

PROFESSOR. Some numbers are smaller and others are larger. In the larger numbers there are more units than in the smaller . . .

PUPIL. Than in the small numbers?

PROFESSOR. Unless the small ones have smaller units. If they are very small, then there might be more units in the small numbers than in the large . . . if it is a question of other units . . .

PUPIL. In that case, the small numbers can be larger than the large numbers?

PROFESSOR. Let's not go into that. That would take us much too far. You must realize simply that more than numbers are involved here . . . there are also magnitudes, totals, there are groups, there are heaps, heaps of such things as plums, trucks, geese, prune pits, etc. To facilitate our work, let's merely suppose that we have only equal numbers, then the bigger numbers will be those that have the most units.

PUPIL. The one that has the most is the biggest? Ah, I understand. Professor, you are identifying quality with quantity.

PROFESSOR. That is too theoretical, miss, too theoretical. You needn't concern yourself with that. Let us take an example and reason from a definite case. Let's leave the general conclusions for later. We have the number four and the number three, and each has always the same number of units. Which number will be larger, the smaller or the larger?

PUPIL. Excuse me, Professor . . . What do you mean by the larger number? Is it the one that is not so small as the other?

PROFESSOR. That's it, miss, perfect. You have understood me very well.

PUPIL. Then, it is four.

PROFESSOR. What is four—larger or smaller than three?

PUPIL. Smaller . . . no, larger.

PROFESSOR. Excellent answer. How many units are there between three and four? . . . Or between four and three, if you prefer?

PUPIL. There aren't any units, Professor, between three and four. Four comes immediately after three; there is nothing at all between three and four!

PROFESSOR. I haven't made myself very well understood. No doubt, it is my fault. I've not been sufficiently clear.

PUPIL. No, Professor, it's my fault.

PROFESSOR. Look here. Here are three matches. And here is another one, that makes four. Now watch carefully—we have four matches. I take one away, now how many are left?

(*We don't see the matches, nor any of the objects that are mentioned. The Professor gets up from the table, writes on the imaginary blackboard with an imaginary piece of chalk, etc.*)

PUPIL. Five. If three and one make four, four and one make five.

PROFESSOR. That's not it. That's not it at all. You always have a tendency to add. But one must be able to subtract too. It's not enough to integrate, you must also disintegrate. That's the way life is. That's philosophy. That's science. That's progress, civilization.

PUPIL. Yes, Professor.

PROFESSOR. Let's return to our matches. I have four of them. You see, there are really four. I take one away, and there remain only . . .

PUPIL. I don't know, Professor.

PROFESSOR. Come now, think. It's not easy, I admit. Nevertheless, you've had enough training to make the intellectual effort required to arrive at an understanding. So?

PUPIL. I can't get it, Professor. I don't know, Professor.

PROFESSOR. Let us take a simpler example. If you had two noses, and I pulled one of them off . . . how many would you have left?

PUPIL. None.

PROFESSOR. What do you mean, none?

PUPIL. Yes, it's because you haven't pulled off any, that's why I have one now. If you had pulled it off, I wouldn't have it anymore.

PROFESSOR. You've not understood my example. Suppose that you have only one ear.

PUPIL. Yes, and then?

PROFESSOR. If I gave you another one, how many would you have then?

PUPIL. Two.

PROFESSOR. Good. And if I gave you still another ear. How many would you have then?

PUPIL. Three ears.

PROFESSOR. Now, I take one away . . . and there remain . . . how many ears?

PUPIL. Two.

PROFESSOR. Good. I take away still another one, how many do you have left?

PUPIL. Two.

PROFESSOR. No. You have two, I take one away, I eat one up, then how many do you have left?

PUPIL. Two.

PROFESSOR. I eat one of them . . . one.

PUPIL. Two.

PROFESSOR. One.

PUPIL. Two.

PROFESSOR. One!

PUPIL. Two!

PROFESSOR. One!!!

PUPIL. Two!!!

PROFESSOR. One!!!

PUPIL. Two!!!

PROFESSOR. One!!!

PUPIL. Two!!!

PROFESSOR. No. No. That's not right. The example is not . . . it's not convincing. Listen to me.

PUPIL. Yes, Professor.

PROFESSOR. You've got . . . you've got . . . you've got . . .

PUPIL. Ten fingers!

PROFESSOR. If you wish. Perfect. Good. You have then ten fingers.

PUPIL. Yes, Professor.

PROFESSOR. How many would you have if you had only five of them?

PUPIL. Ten, Professor.

PROFESSOR. That's not right!

PUPIL. But it is, Professor.

PROFESSOR. I tell you it's not!

PUPIL. You just told me that I had ten . . .

PROFESSOR. I also said, immediately afterwards, that you had five!

PUPIL. I don't have five, I've got ten!

PROFESSOR. Let's try another approach . . . for purposes of subtraction let's limit ourselves to the numbers from one to five . . . Wait now, miss, you'll soon see. I'm going to make you understand.

(*The Professor begins to write on the imaginary blackboard. He moves it closer to the Pupil, who turns around in order to see it.*)

PROFESSOR. Look here, miss . . . (*He pretends to draw a stick on the blackboard and the number 1 below the stick; then two sticks and the number 2 below, then three sticks and the number 3 below, then four sticks with the number 4 below.*) You see . . .

PUPIL. Yes, Professor.

PROFESSOR. These are sticks, miss, sticks. This is one stick, these are two sticks, and three sticks, then four sticks, then five sticks. One stick, two sticks, three sticks, four and five sticks, these are numbers. When we count the sticks, each stick is a unit, miss . . . What have I just said?

PUPIL. "A unit, miss! What have I just said?"

PROFESSOR. Or a figure! Or a number! One, two, three, four, five, these are the elements of numeration, miss.

PUPIL (*hesitant*). Yes, Professor. The elements, figures, which are sticks, units and numbers . . .

PROFESSOR. At the same time . . . that's to say, in short—the whole of arithmetic is there.

PUPIL. Yes, Professor. Good, Professor. Thanks, Professor.

PROFESSOR. Now, count, if you will please, using these elements . . . add and subtract . . .

PUPIL (*as though trying to impress them on her memory*). Sticks are really figures and numbers are units?

PROFESSOR. Hmm . . . so to speak. And then?

PUPIL. One could subtract two units from three units, but can one subtract two twos from three threes? And two figures from four numbers? And three numbers from one unit?

PROFESSOR. No, miss.

PUPIL. Why, Professor?

PROFESSOR. Because, miss.

PUPIL. Because why, Professor? Since one is the same as the other?

PROFESSOR. That's the way it is, miss. It can't be explained. This is only comprehensible through internal mathematical reasoning. Either you have it or you don't.

PUPIL. So much the worse for me.

PROFESSOR. Listen to me, miss, if you don't achieve a profound understanding of these principles, these arithmetical archetypes, you will never be able to perform correctly the functions of a polytechnician. Still less will you be able to teach a course in a polytechnical school . . . or the primary grades. I realize that this is not easy, it is very, very abstract . . . obviously . . . but unless you can comprehend the primary elements, how do you expect to be able to calculate mentally—and this is the least of the things that even an ordinary engineer must be able to do—how much, for example, are three billion seven hundred fifty-five million nine hundred ninety-eight thousand two hundred fifty-one, multiplied by five billion one hundred sixty-two million three hundred and three thousand five hundred and eight?

PUPIL (*very quickly*). That makes nineteen quintillion three hundred ninety quadrillion two trillion eight hundred forty-four billion two hundred nineteen million one hundred sixty-four thousand five hundred and eight . . .

PROFESSOR (*astonished*). No. I don't think so. That must make nineteen quintillion three hundred ninety quadrillion two trillion eight hundred forty-four billion two hundred nineteen million one hundred sixty-four thousand five hundred and nine . . .

PUPIL. . . . No . . . five hundred and eight . . .

PROFESSOR (*more and more astonished, calculating mentally*). Yes . . . you are right . . . the result is indeed . . . (*He mumbles unintelligibly:*) . . . quintillion, quadrillion, trillion, billion, million . . . (*Clearly:*) one hundred sixty-four thousand five hundred and eight . . . (*Stupefied:*) But how did you know that, if you don't know the principles of arithmetical reasoning?

PUPIL. It's easy. Not being able to rely on my reasoning, I've memorized all the products of all possible multiplications.

PROFESSOR. That's pretty good . . . However, permit me to confess to you that that doesn't satisfy me, miss, and I do not congratulate you: in mathematics and in arithmetic especially, the thing that counts—for in arithmetic it is always necessary to count—the thing that counts is, above all, understanding . . . It is by mathematical reasoning, simultaneously inductive and deductive, that you ought to arrive at this result—as well as at any other result. Mathematics is the sworn enemy of memory, which is excellent otherwise, but disastrous, arithmetically speaking! . . . That's why I'm not happy with this . . . this won't do, not at all . . .

PUPIL (*desolated*). No, Professor.

PROFESSOR. Let's leave it for the moment. Let's go on to another exercise . . .

PUPIL. Yes, Professor.

MAID (*entering*). Hmm, hmm, Professor . . .

PROFESSOR (*who doesn't hear her*). It is unfortunate, miss, that you aren't further along in specialized mathematics . . .

MAID (*taking him by the sleeve*). Professor! Professor!

PROFESSOR. I fear that you will not be able to qualify for the total doctor's orals . . .

PUPIL. Yes, Professor, it's too bad!

PROFESSOR. Unless you . . . (*To the Maid:*) Let me be, Marie . . . Look here, why are you bothering me? Go back to the kitchen! To your pots and pans! Go away! Go away! (*To the Pupil:*) We will try to prepare you at least for the partial doctorate . . .

MAID. Professor! . . . Professor! . . . (*She pulls his sleeve.*)

PROFESSOR (*to the Maid*). Now leave me alone! Let me be! What's the meaning of this . . . (*To the Pupil:*) I must therefore teach you, if you really do insist on attempting the partial doctorate . . .

PUPIL. Yes, Professor.

PROFESSOR. . . . The elements of linguistics and of comparative philology . . .

MAID. No, Professor, no! . . . You mustn't do that! . . .

PROFESSOR. Marie, you're going too far!

MAID. Professor, especially not philology, philology leads to calamity . . .

PUPIL (*astonished*). To calamity? (*Smiling a little stupidly.*) That's hard to believe.

PROFESSOR (*to the Maid*). That's enough now! Get out of here!

MAID. All right, Professor, all right. But you can't say that I didn't warn you! Philology leads to calamity!

PROFESSOR. I'm an adult, Marie!

PUPIL. Yes, Professor.

MAID. As you wish. (*She exits.*)

PROFESSOR. Let's continue, miss.

PUPIL. Yes, Professor.

PROFESSOR. I want you to listen now with the greatest possible attention to a lecture I have prepared . . .

PUPIL. Yes, Professor!

PROFESSOR. . . . Thanks to which, in fifteen minutes' time, you will be able to acquire the fundamental principles of the linguistic and comparative philology of the neo-Spanish languages.

PUPIL. Yes, Professor, oh good! (*She claps her hands.*)

PROFESSOR (*with authority*). Quiet! What do you mean by that?

PUPIL. I'm sorry, Professor. (*Slowly, she replaces her hands on the table.*)

PROFESSOR. Quiet! (*He gets up, walks up and down the room, his hands behind his back; from time to time he stops at stage center or near the Pupil, and underlines his words with a gesture of his hand; he orates, but without being too emotional. The Pupil follows him with her eyes, occasionally with some difficulty, for she has to turn her head far around; once or twice, not more, she turns around completely.*) And now, miss, Spanish is truly the mother tongue which gave birth to all the neo-Spanish languages, of which Spanish, Latin, Italian, our own French, Portuguese, Romanian, Sardinian or Sardanapalian, Spanish and neo-Spanish—and also, in certain of its aspects, Turkish which is otherwise very close to Greek, which is only logical, since it is a fact that Turkey is a neighbor of Greece and Greece is even closer to Turkey than you are to me—this is only one more illustration of the very important linguistic law

which states that geography and philology are twin sisters . . . You may take notes, miss.

PUPIL (*in a dull voice*). Yes, Professor!

PROFESSOR. That which distinguishes the neo-Spanish languages from each other and their idioms from the other linguistic groups, such as the group of languages called Austrian and neo-Austrian or Hapsburgian, as well as the Esperanto, Helvetian, Monacan, Swiss, Andorran, Basque, and jai alai groups, and also the groups of diplomatic and technical languages—that which distinguishes them, I repeat, is their striking resemblance which makes it so hard to distinguish them from each other—I'm speaking of the neo-Spanish languages which one is able to distinguish from each other, however, only thanks to their distinctive characteristics, absolutely indisputable proofs of their extraordinary resemblance, which renders indisputable their common origin, and which, at the same time, differentiates them profoundly—through the continuation of the distinctive traits which I've just cited.

PUPIL. Oooh! Ye-e-e-s-s, Professor!

PROFESSOR. But let's not linger over generalities . . .

PUPIL (*regretfully, but won over*). Oh, Professor . . .

PROFESSOR. This appears to interest you. All the better, all the better.

PUPIL. Oh, yes, Professor . . .

PROFESSOR. Don't worry, miss. We will come back to it later . . . That is if we come back to it at all. Who can say?

PUPIL (*enchanted in spite of everything*). Oh, yes, Professor.

PROFESSOR. Every tongue—you must know this, miss, and remember it *until the hour of your death* . . .

PUPIL. Oh! yes, Professor, until the hour of my death . . . Yes, Professor . . .

PROFESSOR. . . . And this, too, is a fundamental principle, every tongue is at bottom nothing but language, which necessarily implies that it is composed of sounds, or . . .

PUPIL. Phonemes . . .

PROFESSOR. Just what I was going to say. Don't parade your knowledge. You'd do better to listen.

PUPIL. All right, Professor. Yes, Professor.

PROFESSOR. The sounds, miss, must be seized on the wing as they fly so that they'll not fall on deaf ears. As a result, when you set out to articulate, it is recommended, insofar as possible, that you lift up your neck and chin very high, and rise up on the tips of your toes, you see, this way . . .

PUPIL. Yes, Professor.

PROFESSOR. Keep quiet. Remain seated, don't interrupt me . . . And project the sounds very loudly with all the force of your lungs in conjunction with that of your vocal cords. Like this, look: "Butterfly," "Eureka," "Trafalgar," "Papaya." This way, the sounds become filled with a warm air that is lighter than the surrounding air so that they can fly without danger of falling on deaf ears, which are veritable voids, tombs of sonorities. If you utter several sounds at an accelerated speed, they will automatically cling to each other, constituting thus syllables, words, even sentences, that is to say groupings of various importance, purely irrational assemblages of sounds, denuded of all sense, but for that very reason the more capable of maintaining themselves without danger at a high altitude in the air. By themselves, words charged with significance will fall, weighted down by their meaning, and in the end they always collapse, fall . . .

PUPIL. . . . On deaf ears.

PROFESSOR. That's it, but don't interrupt . . . and into the worst confusion . . . Or else burst like balloons. Therefore, miss . . . (*The Pupil suddenly appears to be unwell.*) What's the matter?

PUPIL. I've got a toothache, Professor.

PROFESSOR. That's not important. We're not going to stop for anything so trivial. Let us go on . . .

PUPIL (*appearing to be in more and more pain*). Yes, Professor.

PROFESSOR. I draw your attention in passing to the consonants that change their nature in combinations. In this case *f* becomes *v*, *d* becomes *t*, *g* becomes *k*, and vice versa, as in these examples that I will cite for you: "That's all right," "hens and chickens," "Welsh rabbit," "lots of nothing," "not at all."[1]

PUPIL. I've got a toothache.

PROFESSOR. Let's continue.

PUPIL. Yes.

PROFESSOR. To resume: it takes years and years to learn to pronounce. Thanks to science, we can achieve this in a few minutes. In order to project words, sounds and all the rest, you must realize that it is necessary to pitilessly expel air from the lungs, and make it pass delicately, caressingly, over the vocal cords, which, like harps or leaves in the wind, will suddenly shake, agitate, vibrate, vibrate, vibrate or uvulate, or fricate or jostle against each other, or sibilate, sibilate, placing everything in movement, the uvula, the tongue, the palate, the teeth . . .

PUPIL. I have a toothache.

PROFESSOR. . . . And the lips . . . Finally the words come out through the nose, the mouth, the ears, the pores, drawing along with them all the organs that we have named, torn up by the roots, in a powerful, majestic flight, which is none other than what is called, improperly, the voice, whether modulated in singing or transformed into a terrible symphonic storm with a whole procession . . . of garlands of all kinds of flowers, of sonorous artifices: labials, dentals, occlusives, palatals, and others, some caressing, some bitter or violent.

PUPIL. Yes, Professor, I've got a toothache.

PROFESSOR. Let's go on, go on. As for the neo-Spanish languages, they are closely related, so closely to each other,

that they can be considered as true second cousins. Moreover, they have the same mother: Spanishe, with a mute *e*. That is why it is so difficult to distinguish them from one another. That is why it is so useful to pronounce carefully, and to avoid errors in pronunciation. Pronunciation itself is worth a whole language. A bad pronunciation can get you into trouble. In this connection, permit me, parenthetically, to share a personal experience with you. (*Slight pause. The Professor goes over his memories for a moment; his features mellow, but he recovers at once.*) I was very young, little more than a child. It was during my military service. I had a friend in the regiment, a vicomte, who suffered from a rather serious defect in his pronunciation: he could not pronounce the letter *f*. Instead of *f*, he said *f*. Thus, instead of "Birds of a feather flock together," he said: "Birds of a feather flock together." He pronounced filly instead of filly, Firmin instead of Firmin, French bean instead of French bean, go frig yourself instead of go frig yourself, farrago instead of farrago, fee fi fo fum instead of fee fi fo fum, Philip instead of Philip, fictory instead of fictory, February instead of February, March-April instead of March-April, Gérard de Nerval and not as is correct—Gérard de Nerval, Mirabeau instead of Mirabeau, etc., instead of etc., and thus instead of etc., instead of etc., and thus and so forth. However, he managed to conceal his fault so effectively that, thanks to the hats he wore, no one ever noticed it.

PUPIL. Yes, I've got a toothache.

PROFESSOR (*abruptly changing his tone, his voice hardening*). Let's go on. We'll first consider the points of similarity in order the better to apprehend, later on, that which distinguishes all these languages from each other. The differences can scarcely be recognized by people who are not aware of them. Thus, all the words of all the languages . . .

PUPIL. Uh, yes? . . . I've got a toothache.

PROFESSOR. Let's continue . . . are always the same, just as all the suffixes, all the prefixes, all the terminations, all the roots . . .

PUPIL. Are the roots of words square?

PROFESSOR. Square or cube. That depends.

PUPIL. I've got a toothache.

PROFESSOR. Let's go on. Thus, to give you an example which is little more than an illustration, take the word "front" . . .

PUPIL. How do you want me to take it?

PROFESSOR. However you wish, so long as you take it, but above all do not interrupt.

PUPIL. I've got a toothache.

PROFESSOR. Let's continue . . . I said: Let's continue. Take now the word "front." Have you taken it?

PUPIL. Yes, yes, I've got it. My teeth, my teeth . . .

PROFESSOR. The word "front" is the root of "frontispiece." It is also to be found in "affronted." "Ispiece" is the suffix,

---

[1] All to be heavily elided. [Translator's note.]

and "af" the prefix. They are so called because they do not change. They don't want to.

PUPIL. I've got a toothache.

PROFESSOR. Let's go on. (*Rapidly:*) These prefixes are of Spanish origin. I hope you noticed that, did you?

PUPIL. Oh, how my tooth aches.

PROFESSOR. Let's continue. You've surely also noticed that they've not changed in French. And now, young lady, nothing has succeeded in changing them in Latin either, nor in Italian, nor in Portuguese, nor in Sardanapalian, nor in Sardanapali, nor in Romanian, nor in neo-Spanish, nor in Spanish, nor even in the Oriental: front, frontispiece, affronted, always the same word, invariably with the same root, the same suffix, the same prefix, in all the languages I have named. And it is always the same for all words.

PUPIL. In all languages, these words mean the same thing? I've got a toothache.

PROFESSOR. Absolutely. Moreover, it's more a notion than a word. In any case, you have always the same signification, the same composition, the same sound structure, not only for this word, but for all conceivable words, in all languages. For one single notion is expressed by one and the same word, and its synonyms, in all countries. Forget about your teeth.

PUPIL. I've got a toothache. Yes, yes, yes.

PROFESSOR. Good, let's go on. I tell you, let's go on . . . How would you say, for example, in French: the roses of my grandmother are as yellow as my grandfather who was Asiatic?

PUPIL. My teeth ache, ache, ache.

PROFESSOR. Let's go on, let's go on, go ahead and answer, anyway.

PUPIL. In French?

PROFESSOR. In French.

PUPIL. Uhh . . . I should say in French: the roses of my grandmother are . . . ?

PROFESSOR. As yellow as my grandfather who was Asiatic . . .

PUPIL. Oh well, one would say, in French, I believe, the roses . . . of my . . . how do you say "grandmother" in French?

PROFESSOR. In French? Grandmother.

PUPIL. The roses of my grandmother are as yellow—in French, is it "yellow"?

PROFESSOR. Yes, of course!

PUPIL. Are as yellow as my grandfather when he got angry.

PROFESSOR. No . . . who was A . . .

PUPIL. . . . siatic . . . I've got a toothache.

PROFESSOR. That's it.

PUPIL. I've got a tooth . . .

PROFESSOR. Ache . . . so what . . . let's continue! And now translate the same sentence into Spanish, then into neo-Spanish . . .

PUPIL. In Spanish . . . this would be: the roses of my grandmother are as yellow as my grandfather who was Asiatic.

PROFESSOR. No. That's wrong.

PUPIL. And in neo-Spanish: the roses of my grandmother are as yellow as my grandfather who was Asiatic.

PROFESSOR. That's wrong. That's wrong. That's wrong. You have inverted it, you've confused Spanish with neo-Spanish, and neo-Spanish with Spanish . . . Oh . . . no . . . it's the other way around . . .

PUPIL. I've got a toothache. You're getting mixed up.

PROFESSOR. You're the one who is mixing me up. Pay attention and take notes. I will say the sentence to you in Spanish, then in neo-Spanish, and finally, in Latin. You will repeat after me. Pay attention, for the resemblances are great. In fact, they are identical resemblances. Listen, follow carefully . . .

PUPIL. I've got a tooth . . .

PROFESSOR. . . . Ache.

PUPIL. Let us go on . . . Ah! . . .

PROFESSOR. . . . In Spanish: the roses of my grandmother are as yellow as my grandfather who was Asiatic; in Latin: the roses of my grandmother are as yellow as my grandfather who was Asiatic. Do you detect the differences? Translate this into . . . Romanian.

PUPIL. The . . . how do you say "roses" in Romanian?

PROFESSOR. But "roses," what else?

PUPIL. It's not "roses"? Oh, how my tooth aches!

PROFESSOR. Certainly not, certainly not, since "roses" is a translation in Oriental of the French word "roses," in Spanish "roses," do you get it? In Sardanapali, "roses" . . .

PUPIL. Excuse me, Professor, but . . . Oh, my toothache! . . . I don't get the difference.

PROFESSOR. But it's so simple! So simple! It's a matter of having a certain experience, a technical experience and practice in these diverse languages, which are so diverse in spite of the fact that they present wholly identical characteristics. I'm going to try to give you a key . . .

PUPIL. Toothache . . .

PROFESSOR. That which differentiates these languages, is neither the words, which are absolutely the same, nor the structure of the sentence which is everywhere the same, nor the intonation, which does not offer any differences, nor the rhythm of the language . . . that which differentiates them . . . are you listening?

PUPIL. I've got a toothache.

PROFESSOR. Are you listening to me, young lady? Aah! We're going to lose our temper.

PUPIL. You're bothering me, Professor. I've got a toothache.

PROFESSOR. Son of a cocker spaniel! Listen to me!

PUPIL. Oh well . . . yes . . . yes . . . go on . . .

PROFESSOR. That which distinguishes them from each other, on the one hand, and from their mother, Spanishe with its mute *e*, on the other hand . . . is . . .

PUPIL (*grimacing*). Is what?

PROFESSOR. Is an intangible thing. Something intangible that one is able to perceive only after very long study, with a great deal of trouble and after the broadest experience . . .

PUPIL. Ah?

PROFESSOR. Yes, young lady. I cannot give you any rule. One must have a feeling for it, and well, that's it. But in order to have it, one must study, study, and then study some more.

PUPIL. Toothache.

PROFESSOR. All the same, there are some specific cases where words differ from one language to another . . . but we cannot base our knowledge on these cases, which are, so to speak, exceptional.

PUPIL. Oh, yes? . . . Oh, Professor, I've got a toothache.

PROFESSOR. Don't interrupt! Don't make me lose my temper! I can't answer for what I'll do. I was saying, then . . . Ah, yes, the exceptional cases, the so-called easily distinguished . . . or facilely distinguished . . . or conveniently . . . if you prefer . . . I repeat, if you prefer, for I see that you're not listening to me . . .

PUPIL. I've got a toothache.

PROFESSOR. I say then: in certain expressions in current usage, certain words differ totally from one language to another, so much so that the language employed is, in this case, considerably easier to identify. I'll give you an example: the neo-Spanish expression, famous in Madrid: "My country is the new Spain," becomes in Italian: "My country is . . ."

PUPIL. The new Spain.

PROFESSOR. No! "My country is Italy." Tell me now, by simple deduction, how do you say "Italy" in French?

PUPIL. I've got a toothache.

PROFESSOR. But it's so easy: for the word "Italy," in French we have the word "France," which is an exact translation of it. My country is France. And "France" in Oriental: "Orient!" My country is the Orient. And "Orient" in Portuguese: "Portugal!" The Oriental expression: My country is the Orient is translated then in the same fashion into Portuguese: My country is Portugal! And so on . . .

PUPIL. Oh, no more, no more. My teeth . . .

PROFESSOR. Ache! ache! ache! . . . I'm going to pull them out, I will! One more example. The word "capital"—it takes on, according to the language one speaks, a different meaning. That is to say that when a Spaniard says: "I reside in the capital," the word "capital" does not mean at all the same thing that a Portuguese means when he says: "I reside in the capital." All the more so in the case of a Frenchman, a neo-Spaniard, a Romanian, a Latin, a Sardanapali . . . Whenever you hear it, young lady—young lady, I'm saying this for you! Pooh! Whenever you hear the expression: "I reside in the capital," you will immediately and easily know whether this is Spanish or Spanish, neo-Spanish, French, Oriental, Romanian, or Latin, for it is enough to know which metropolis is referred to by the person who pronounces the sentence . . . at the very moment he pronounces it . . . But these are almost the only precise examples that I can give you . . .

PUPIL. Oh dear! My teeth . . .

PROFESSOR. Silence! Or I'll bash in your skull!

PUPIL. Just try to! Skulldugger!

(*The Professor seizes her wrist and twists it.*)

PUPIL. Oww!

PROFESSOR. Keep quiet now! Not a word!

PUPIL (*whimpering*). Toothache . . .

PROFESSOR. One thing that is the most . . . how shall I say it? . . . the most paradoxical . . . yes . . . that's the word . . . the most paradoxical thing, is that a lot of people who are completely illiterate speak these different languages . . . do you understand? What did I just say?

PUPIL. . . . "Speak these different languages! What did I just say?"

PROFESSOR. You were lucky that time! . . . The common people speak a Spanish full of neo-Spanish words that they are entirely unaware of, all the while believing that they are speaking Latin . . . or they speak Latin, full of Oriental words, all the while believing that they're speaking Romanian . . . or Spanish, full of neo-Spanish, all the while believing that they're speaking Sardanapali, or Spanish . . . Do you understand?

PUPIL. Yes! yes! yes! yes! What more do you want . . . ?

PROFESSOR. No insolence, my pet, or you'll be sorry . . . (*In a rage:*) But the worst of all, young lady, is that certain people, for example, in a Latin that they suppose is Spanish, say: "Both my kidneys are of the same kidney," in addressing themselves to a Frenchman who does not know a word of Spanish, but the latter understands it as if it were his own language. For that matter he thinks it is his own language. And the Frenchman will reply, in French: "Me too, sir, mine are too," and this will be perfectly comprehensible to a Spaniard, who will feel certain that the reply is in pure Spanish and that Spanish is being spoken . . . when, in reality, it was neither Spanish nor French, but Latin in the neo-Spanish dialect . . . Sit still, young lady, don't fidget, stop tapping your feet . . .

PUPIL. I've got a toothache.

PROFESSOR. How do you account for the fact that, in speaking without knowing which language they speak, or even while each of them believes that he is speaking another, the common people understand each other at all?

PUPIL. I wonder.

PROFESSOR. It is simply one of the inexplicable curiosities of the vulgar empiricism of the common people—not to be confused with experience!—a paradox, a non-sense, one of the aberrations of human nature, it is purely and simply instinct—to put it in a nutshell . . . That's what is involved here.

PUPIL. Hah! hah!

PROFESSOR. Instead of staring at the flies while I'm going to all this trouble . . . you would do much better to try to be more attentive . . . it is not I who is going to qualify for the partial doctor's orals . . . I passed mine a long time ago . . . and I've won my total doctorate, too . . . and my supertotal diploma . . . Don't you realize that what I'm saying is for your own good?

PUPIL. Toothache!

PROFESSOR. Ill-mannered . . . It can't go on like this, it won't do, it won't do, it won't do . . .

PUPIL. I'm . . . listening . . . to you . . .

PROFESSOR. Ahah! In order to learn to distinguish all the different languages, as I've told you, there is nothing better than practice . . . Let's take them up in order. I am going to try to teach you all the translations of the word "knife."

PUPIL. Well, all right . . . if you want . . .

PROFESSOR (calling the Maid). Marie! Marie! She's not there . . . Marie! Marie! . . . Marie, where are you? (He opens the door on the right.) Marie! . . . (He exits.)

(The Pupil remains alone several minutes, staring into space, wearing a stupefied expression.)

PROFESSOR (offstage, in a shrill voice). Marie! What are you up to? Why don't you come! When I call you, you must come! (He reenters, followed by the Maid.) It is I who gives the orders, do you hear? (He points at the Pupil:) She doesn't understand anything, that girl. She doesn't understand!

MAID. Don't get into such a state, sir, you know where it'll end! You're going to go too far, you're going to go too far.

PROFESSOR. I'll be able to stop in time.

MAID. That's what you always say. I only wish I could see it.

PUPIL. I've got a toothache.

MAID. You see, it's starting, that's the symptom!

PROFESSOR. What symptom? Explain yourself! What do you mean?

PUPIL (in a spiritless voice). Yes, what do you mean? I've got a toothache.

MAID. The final symptom! The chief symptom!

PROFESSOR. Stupid! stupid! stupid! (The Maid starts to exit.) Don't go away like that! I called you to help me find the Spanish, neo-Spanish, Portuguese, French, Oriental, Romanian, Sardanapali, Latin and Spanish knives.

MAID (severely). Don't ask me. (She exits.)

PROFESSOR (makes a gesture as though to protest, then refrains, a little helpless. Suddenly, he remembers). Ah! (He goes quickly to the drawer where he finds a big knife, invisible or real according to the preference of the director. He seizes it and brandishes it happily.) Here is one, young lady, here is a knife. It's too bad that we only have this one, but we're going to try to make it serve for all the languages, anyway! It will be enough if you will pronounce the word "knife" in all the languages, while looking at the object, very closely, fixedly, and imagining that it is in the language that you are speaking.

PUPIL. I've got a toothache.

PROFESSOR (almost singing, chanting). Now, say "kni," like "kni," "fe," like "fe" . . . And look, look, look at it, watch it . . .

PUPIL. What is this one in? French, Italian or Spanish?

PROFESSOR. That doesn't matter now . . . That's not your concern. Say: "kni."

PUPIL. "Kni."

PROFESSOR. . . . "fe" . . . Look. (He brandishes the knife under the Pupil's eyes.)

PUPIL. "fe" . . .

PROFESSOR. Again . . . Look at it.

PUPIL. Oh, no! My God! I've had enough. And besides, I've got a toothache, my feet hurt me, I've got a headache.

PROFESSOR (abruptly). Knife . . . look . . . knife . . . look . . . knife . . . look . . .

PUPIL. You're giving me an earache, too. Oh, your voice! It's so piercing!

PROFESSOR. Say: knife . . . kni . . . fe . . .

PUPIL. No! My ears hurt, I hurt all over . . .

PROFESSOR. I'm going to tear them off, your ears, that's what I'm going to do to you, and then they won't hurt you anymore, my pet.

PUPIL. Oh . . . you're hurting me, oh, you're hurting me . . .

PROFESSOR. Look, come on, quickly, repeat after me: "kni" . . .

PUPIL. Oh, since you insist . . . knife . . . knife . . . (In a lucid moment, ironically:) Is that neo-Spanish . . . ?

PROFESSOR. If you like, yes, it's neo-Spanish, but hurry up . . . we haven't got time . . . And then, what do you mean by that insidious question? What are you up to?

PUPIL (becoming more and more exhausted, weeping, desperate, at the same time both exasperated and in a trance). Ah!

PROFESSOR. Repeat, watch. (He imitates a cuckoo:) Knife, knife . . . knife, knife . . . knife, knife . . . knife, knife . . .

PUPIL. Oh, my head . . . aches . . . (With her hand she caressingly touches the parts of her body as she names them:) . . . My eyes . . .

PROFESSOR (like a cuckoo). Knife, knife . . . knife, knife . . .

(They are both standing. The Professor still brandishes his invisible knife, nearly beside himself, as he circles around her in a sort of scalp dance, but it is important that this not be exaggerated and that his dance steps be only suggested. The Pupil stands facing the audience, then recoils in the direction of the window, sickly, languid, victimized.)

PROFESSOR. Repeat, repeat: knife . . . knife . . . knife . . .

PUPIL. I've got a pain . . . my throat, neck . . . oh, my shoulders . . . my breast . . . knife . . .

PROFESSOR. Knife . . . knife . . . knife . . .

PUPIL. My hips . . . knife . . . my thighs . . . kni . . .

PROFESSOR. Pronounce it carefully . . . knife . . . knife . . .

PUPIL. Knife . . . my throat . . .

PROFESSOR. Knife . . . knife . . .

PUPIL. Knife . . . my shoulders . . . my arms, my breast, my hips . . . knife . . . knife . . .

PROFESSOR. That's right . . . Now, you're pronouncing it well . . .

PUPIL. Knife . . . my breast . . . my stomach . . .

PROFESSOR (*changing his voice*). Pay attention . . . don't break my window . . . the knife kills . . .

PUPIL (*in a weak voice*). Yes, yes . . . the knife kills?

PROFESSOR (*striking the Pupil with a very spectacular blow of the knife*). Aaah! That'll teach you!

(*The Pupil also cries "Aaah!" then falls, flopping in an immodest position onto a chair which, as though by chance, is near the window. The murderer and his victim shout "Aaah!" at the same moment. After the first blow of the knife, The Pupil flops onto the chair, her legs spread wide and hanging over both sides of the chair. The Professor remains standing in front of her, his back to the audience. After the first blow, he strikes her dead with a second slash of the knife, from bottom to top. After that blow a noticeable convulsion shakes his whole body.*)

PROFESSOR (*winded, mumbling*). Bitch . . . Oh, that's good, that does me good . . . Ah! Ah! I'm exhausted . . . I can scarcely breathe . . . Aah! (*He breathes with difficulty; he falls—fortunately a chair is there; he mops his brow, mumbles some incomprehensible words; his breathing becomes normal. He gets up, looks at the knife in his hand, looks at the young girl, then as though he were waking up, in a panic:*) What have I done! What's going to happen to me now! What's going to happen! Oh! dear! Oh dear, I'm in trouble! Young lady, young lady, get up! (*He is agitated, still holding onto the invisible knife, which he doesn't know what to do with.*) Come now, young lady, the lesson is over . . . you may go . . . you can pay another time . . . Oh! she is dead . . . dea-ead . . . And by my knife . . . She is dea-ead . . . It's terrible. (*He calls the Maid:*) Marie! Marie! My good Marie, come here! Ah! ah! (*The door on the right opens a little and the Maid appears.*) No . . . don't come in . . . I made a mistake . . . I don't need you, Marie . . . I don't need you anymore . . . do you understand? . . .

(*The Maid enters wearing a stern expression, without saying a word. She sees the corpse.*)

PROFESSOR (*in a voice less and less assured*). I don't need you, Marie . . .

MAID (*sarcastic*). Then, you're satisfied with your pupil, she's profited by your lesson?

PROFESSOR (*holding the knife behind his back*). Yes, the lesson is finished . . . but . . . she . . . she's still there . . . she doesn't want to leave . . .

MAID (*very harshly*). Is that a fact? . . .

PROFESSOR (*trembling*). It wasn't I . . . it wasn't I . . . Marie . . . No . . . I assure you . . . it wasn't I, my little Marie . . .

MAID. And who was it? Who was it then? Me?

PROFESSOR. I don't know . . . maybe . . .

MAID. Or the cat?

PROFESSOR. That's possible . . . I don't know . . .

MAID. And today makes it the fortieth time! . . . And every day it's the same thing! Every day! You should be ashamed, at your age . . . and you're going to make yourself sick! You won't have any pupils left. That will serve you right.

PROFESSOR (*irritated*). It wasn't my fault! She didn't want to learn! She was disobedient! She was a bad pupil! She didn't want to learn!

MAID. Liar! . . .

PROFESSOR (*craftily approaching the Maid, holding the knife behind his back*). It's none of your business! (*He tries to strike her with a blow of the knife; the Maid seizes his wrist in mid-gesture and twists it; the Professor lets the knife fall to the floor:*) . . . I'm sorry!

MAID (*gives him two loud, strong slaps; the Professor falls onto the floor, on his prat; he sobs*). Little murderer! bastard! You're disgusting! You wanted to do that to me? I'm not one of your pupils, not me! (*She pulls him up by the collar, picks up his skullcap and puts it on his head; he's afraid she'll slap him again and holds his arm up to protect his face, like a child.*) Put the knife back where it belongs, go on! (*The Professor goes and puts it back in the drawer of the buffet, then comes back to her.*) Now didn't I warn you, just a little while ago: arithmetic leads to philology, and philology leads to crime . . .

PROFESSOR. You said "to calamity"!

MAID. It's the same thing.

PROFESSOR. I didn't understand you. I thought that "calamity" was a city and that you meant that philology leads to the city of Calamity . . .

MAID. Liar! Old fox! An intellectual like you is not going to make a mistake in the meanings of words. Don't try to pull the wool over my eyes.

PROFESSOR (*sobbing*). I didn't kill her on purpose!

MAID. Are you sorry at least?

PROFESSOR. Oh, yes, Marie, I swear it to you!

MAID. I can't help feeling sorry for you! Ah! you're a good boy in spite of everything! I'll try to fix this. But don't start it again . . . It could give you a heart attack . . .

PROFESSOR. Yes, Marie! What are we going to do, now?

MAID. We're going to bury her . . . along with the thirty-nine others . . . that will make forty coffins . . . I'll call the undertakers and my lover, Father Auguste . . . I'll order the wreaths . . .

PROFESSOR. Yes, Marie, thank you very much.

MAID. Well, that's that. And perhaps it won't be necessary to call Auguste, since you yourself are something of a priest at times, if one can believe the gossip.

PROFESSOR. In any case, don't spend too much on the wreaths. She didn't pay for her lesson.

MAID. Don't worry . . . The least you can do is cover her up with her smock, she's not decent that way. And then we'll carry her out . . .

PROFESSOR. Yes, Marie, yes. (*He covers up the body.*) There's a chance that we'll get pinched . . . with forty coffins . . . Don't you think . . . people will be surprised . . . Suppose they ask us what's inside them?

MAID. Don't worry so much. We'll say that they're empty. And besides people won't ask questions, they're used to it.

PROFESSOR. Even so . . .

MAID (*she takes out an armband with an insignia, perhaps the Nazi swastika*). Wait, if you're afraid, wear this, then you won't have anything more to be afraid of. (*She puts the armband around his arm.*) . . . That's good politics.

PROFESSOR. Thanks, my little Marie. With this, I won't need to worry . . . You're a good girl, Marie . . . very loyal . . .

MAID. That's enough. Come on, sir. Are you all right?

PROFESSOR. Yes, my little Marie. (*The Maid and the Professor take the body of the young girl, one by the shoulders, the other by the legs, and move towards the door on the right.*) Be careful. We don't want to hurt her. (*They exit.*)

(*The stage remains empty for several moments. We hear the doorbell ring at the left.*)

VOICE OF THE MAID. Just a moment, I'm coming!

(*She appears as she was at the beginning of the play, and goes towards the door. The doorbell rings again.*)

MAID (*aside*). She's certainly in a hurry, this one! (*Aloud:*) Just a moment! (*She goes to the door on the left, and opens it.*) Good morning, miss! You are the new pupil? You have come for the lesson? The Professor is expecting you. I'll go tell him that you've come. He'll be right down. Come in, miss, come in!

TOPICS FOR CRITICAL THINKING AND WRITING

📖 THE PLAY ON THE PAGE

1. Why do you suppose Ionesco included the role of the maid in this play? Why a maid instead of, for example, the professor's daughter?

2. Propose three alternative endings for *The Lesson*, and then, in this context, evaluate Ionesco's ending. (You will need to supply a set of criteria so that your reader will know why you regard one ending as better than the others.)

3. Read Kenneth Tynan and Ionesco's "debate" (pp. 707–09), and analyze their key points. What artistic points does each make? What large issue is at stake? Would most critics in the late 1990s echo Tynan's points?

4. What application to *The Lesson* can you make of the following lines, written by Ionesco in a 1967 journal entry?

Language is thought. It is also the manifestation of thought. It is at the same time thought and its manifestation. Language is one thing, ways of speaking are another. A way of speaking may be mere trickery; it should not be confused with language, which is certain.

You might also apply the quotation to one or all of the following plays: *The Birthday Party* (p. 712), *Funnyhouse of a Negro* (p. 788), *Happy Days* (p. 749), and *The Sandbox* (p. 743).

5. At one point the pupil demonstrates that she has memorized all possible multiplications, but she cannot subtract three from four. Is Ionesco making a point about education? If so, what is the point?

6. For you, what is the lesson in *The Lesson*?

🎭 THE PLAY ON THE STAGE

7. If the plot of *The Lesson* were graphed as the intersection of two lines—the pupil's descending line intersecting with the professor's ascending line—decide on the exact point in the play at which this intersection occurs. Then describe the minute changes (for example, stance, gestures, pitch of voice, hesitations, and emphases) you would recommend for the actors over the next few speeches.

8. A critic remarked of Ionesco, "Contradiction and antagonism are at the foundation of his vision." As costumer, how would you express contradiction and antagonism? Provide details (for instance, color, fabric, styling, accessories) for costuming *The Lesson*.

9. Would you recommend that an actor tackle both the role of the professor in *The Lesson* and the professor in David Mamet's *Oleanna* (see p. 987). Why or why not?

10. Discuss the ways the dynamics of *The Lesson* change if the roles are cast as follows: the professor as a woman and the pupil as a girl, the professor as a woman and the pupil as a boy, the professor as a man and the pupil as a boy. In each case, what if the maid were a manservant?

THE PLAY IN PERFORMANCE

A DEBATE: KENNETH TYNAN VERSUS EUGÈNE IONESCO

The Lesson (in French, *Le Leçon*) was written in June 1950 and first produced in February 1951 at a tiny theater in Paris called Théâtre de Poche. As did his earlier play, *The Bald Soprano* (in French, *La Cantatrice Chauve*), *The Lesson* proved baffling to its first audiences. Because no bald person (much less, a soprano) had appeared in *The Bald Soprano*, theatergoers didn't know what to expect in the second play and were surprised to find that *The Lesson* is, in fact, about a lesson. (A few years later, in a 1954 preface to the first collection of Ionesco's plays, Jacques Lemarchand deemed the play "almost a faithful reproduction of a lesson" actually given at the *École de Guerre*.) Faced with the play's final tableau, the first audiences tended to boo, shake their heads in bewilderment, or be uncertain that the play had actually ended. If they did not leave the theater, the cast began the play again, with a different actress playing the student. Usually, upon realizing that they were hearing the same speeches, audiences would finally catch on and would leave. If not, the cast would start up a third time.

Ionesco struggled, financially and artistically, for several years as the public slowly came to understand—or, at least, to begin to accept—absurdist drama. Martin Esslin, in *The Theatre of the Absurd*, remarked:

> Not only in France but in other countries as well, performances of Ionesco's plays became more frequent. There were still scandals like the one in Brussels where the audience at a performance of *The Lesson* demanded their money back, and the leading actor had to escape through a back door. . . .

Kenneth Tynan
IONESCO: MAN OF DESTINY

Ever since the fry-eliot "poetic revival" caved in on them, the ostriches of our theatrical intelligentsia have been seeking another faith. Anything would do as long as it shook off what are known as "the fetters of realism." Now the broad definition of a realistic play is that its characters and events have traceable roots in life. Gorki and Chekhov, Arthur Miller and Tennessee Williams, Brecht and O'Casey, Osborne and Sartre have all written such plays. They express one man's view of the world in terms of people we can all recognize. Like all hard disciplines, realism can easily be corrupted. It can sink into sentimentality . . . , half truth . . . , or mere photographic reproduction of the trivia of human behavior. Even so, those who have mastered it have created the lasting body of twentieth century drama; and I have been careful not to except Brecht, who employed stylized production techniques to set off eventually realistic characters.

In 1957 *The Lesson* and *The Bald Soprano* were produced at Théâtre de la Huchette (it seats seventy-eight people), in the Left Bank area of Paris, and ran for more than ten years. During the 1950s *The Lesson* was often produced in the United States, including a 1957 staging at Tempo Playhouse and a 1958 staging at the Phoenix Theater (both in New York City). At the Phoenix, the play was paired with another one-act play by Ionesco, *The Chairs*, and directed by Tony Richardson. Brooks Atkinson, drama critic for the *New York Times*, praised the production and spoke of Ionesco's plays as "odd, elliptical fantastifications . . . amusing and provocative." He also remarked that a play such as *The Lesson* required "audiences that are willing to collaborate with the author." Given the rather conventional nature of much drama produced in the 1950s, Atkinson seemed to be warning audiences that they couldn't sit back and expect, merely, to be entertained.

To give you a sense of the artistic and dramatic controversies Ionesco provoked in his first decade as a playwright, we reprint two statements from 1958: the first one by the London-based critic, Kenneth Tynan, who rails against what he terms the "anti-theatre" of Ionesco; the second one by Ionesco, who defends both himself and all playwrights who venture beyond the "main road of the theatre."

Since the early 1960s the play, generally paired with one or two other absurdist pieces, is often performed by college, community, and professional groups. Because of its brevity, small cast, and simple set, *The Lesson* is a favorite in acting classes.

That, for the ostriches, was what ruled him out of court. He was too real. Similarly, they preferred Beckett's "Endgame," in which the human element was minimal, to "Waiting for Godot," which not only contained two tramps of mephitic reality but even seemed to regard them, as human beings, with love. Veiling their disapproval, the ostriches seized on Beckett's more blatant verbal caprices and called them "authentic images of a disintegrated society." But it was only when M. Ionesco arrived that they hailed a messiah. Here at last was a self-proclaimed advocate of *anti-theatre*: explicitly anti-realist, and by implication anti-reality as well. Here was a writer ready to declare that words were meaningless and that all communication between human beings was impossible. The aged (as in "The Chairs") are wrapped in an impenetrable cocoon of hallucinatory memories; they can speak intelligibly neither to each other nor to the world. The teacher in "The Lesson" can

Eugène Ionesco

"get through" to his pupil only by means of sexual assault, followed by murder. Words, the magic innovation of our species, are dismissed as useless and fraudulent.

Ionesco's is a world of isolated robots, conversing in cartoon-strip balloons of dialogue that are sometimes hilarious, sometimes evocative, and quite often neither, on which occasions they become profoundly tiresome. . . . This world is not mine, but I recognize it to be a valid personal vision, presented with great imaginative aplomb and verbal audacity. The peril arises when it is held up for general emulation as the gateway to the theatre of the future, that bleak new world from which the humanist heresies of faith in logic and belief in man will forever be banished.

M. Ionesco certainly offers an "escape from realism"; but an escape into what? A blind alley, perhaps, adorned with *tachiste* murals. Or a self-imposed vacuum, wherein the author ominously bids us observe the absence of air. Or, best of all, a funfair ride on a ghost train, all skulls and hooting waxworks, from which we emerge into the far more intimidating clamor of diurnal reality. M. Ionesco's theatre is pungent and exciting, but it remains a diversion. It is not on the main road; and we do him no good, nor the drama at large, to pretend that it is. . . .

Eugène Ionesco
A REPLY TO KENNETH TYNAN: THE PLAYWRIGHT'S ROLE

I was of course honored by the article Mr. Tynan devoted to my two plays, "The Chairs" and "The Lesson," in spite of the strictures it contained, which a critic has a perfect right to make. However, since some of his objections seem to me to be based on premises that are not only false but, strictly speaking, outside the domain of the theatre, I think I have the right to make certain comments.

In effect, Mr. Tynan says that it has been claimed, and that I myself have approved or supported this claim, that I was a sort of "messiah" of the theatre. This is doubly untrue because I do not like messiahs and I certainly do not consider the vocation of the artist or the playwright to lie in that direction. I have a distinct impression that it is Mr. Tynan who is in search of messiahs. But to deliver a message to the world, to wish to direct its course, to save it, is the business of the founders of religions, of the moralists or the politicians who, incidentally, as we know only too well, make a pretty poor job of it. A playwright simply writes plays, in which he can offer only a testimony, not a didactic message, a personal, affective testimony of his anguish and the anguish of others or, which is rare, of his happiness—or he can express his feelings, comic or tragic, about life.

A work of art has nothing to do with doctrine. I have already written elsewhere that any work of art which was ideological and nothing else would be pointless, tautological, inferior to the doctrine it claimed to illustrate, which would already have been expressed in its proper language, that of discursive demonstration. An ideological play can be no more than the vulgarization of an ideology. In my view, a work of art has its own unique system of expression, its own means of directly apprehending the real.

Mr. Tynan seems to accuse me of being deliberately, explicitly, anti-realist; of having declared that words have no meaning and that all language is incommunicable. That is only partly true, for the very fact of writing and presenting plays is surely incompatible with such a view. I simply hold that it is difficult to make oneself understood, not absolutely

impossible, and my play "The Chairs" is a plea, pathetic perhaps, for mutual understanding. As for the idea of reality, Mr. Tynan seems . . . to acknowledge only one plane of reality: what is called the "social" plane, which seems to me to be the most external, in other words, the most superficial. That is why I think that writers like Sartre. . . , Osborne, Miller, Brecht, etc., are simply the new *auteurs du boulevard*, representatives of a left-wing conformism which is just as lamentable as the right-wing sort. These writers offer nothing that one does not know already, through books and political speeches.

But that is not all; it is not enough to be a social realist writer, one must also, apparently, be a militant believer in what is known as progress. The only worthwhile authors, those who are on the "main road" of the theatre, would be those who thought in a certain clearly defined way, obeying certain pre-established principles or directives. This would be to make the "main road" a very narrow one; it would considerably restrict the planes of reality (which are innumerable) and limit the field open to the investigation of artistic research and creation.

I believe that what separates us all from one another is simply society itself, or, if you like, politics. This is what raises barriers between men, this is what creates misunderstanding.

If I may be allowed to express myself paradoxically, I should say that the true society, the authentic human community, is extra-social—a wider, deeper society, that which is revealed by our common anxieties, our desires, our secret nostalgias. The whole history of the world has been governed by these nostalgias and anxieties, which political action does no more than reflect and interpret, very imperfectly. No society has been able to abolish human sadness, no political system can deliver us from the pain of living, from our fear of death, our thirst for the absolute; it is the human condition that directs the social condition, not vice versa.

This "reality" seems to me much vaster and more complex than the one to which Mr. Tynan and many others want to limit themselves. The problem is to get to the source of our malady, to find the non-conventional language of this anguish, perhaps by breaking down this "social" language which is nothing but clichés, empty formulas, and slogans. The "robot" characters Mr. Tynan disapproves of seem to me to be precisely those who belong *solely* to this or that *milieu* or social "reality," who are prisoners of it, and who—being no more than social, seeking a solution to their problems only by so-called social means—have become impoverished, alienated, empty. It is precisely the conformist, the *petit-bourgeois,* the ideologist of *every* society who is lost and dehumanized. If anything needs demystifying it is our ideologies, which offer ready-made solutions . . . in a language that congeals *as soon as it is formulated.* It is these ideologies which must be continually re-examined in the light of our anxieties and dreams, and their congealed language must be relentlessly split apart in order to find the living sap beneath.

To discover the fundamental problem common to all mankind, I must ask myself what *my* fundamental problem is, what *my* most ineradicable fear is. I am certain, then, to find the problems and fears of literally everyone. That is the true road, into my own darkness, our darkness, which I try to bring to the light of day.

It would be amusing to try an experiment, which I have no room for here but which I hope to carry out some day. I could take almost any work of art, any play, and guarantee to give it in turn a Marxist, a Buddhist, a Christian, an Existen-

tialist, psycho-analytical interpretation and "prove" that the work subjected to each interpretation is a perfect and exclusive illustration of each creed, that it confirms this or that ideology beyond all doubt. For me this proves another thing: that every work of art (unless it is a pseudo-intellectualist work, a work already comprised in some ideology that it merely illustrates, as with Brecht) is outside ideology, is not reducible to ideology. Ideology circumscribes without penetrating it. The absence of ideology in a work does not mean an absence of ideas; on the contrary it fertilizes them. In other words, it was not Sophocles who was inspired by Freud but, obviously, the other way round. Ideology is not the source of art. A work of art is the source and the raw material of ideologies to come.

What, then, should the critic do? Where should he look for his criteria? Inside the work itself, its universe and its mythology. He must look at it, listen to it, and simply say whether it is true to its own nature. The best judgment is a careful exposition of the work itself. For that, the work must be allowed to speak, uncolored by preconceptions or prejudices.

Whether or not it is on the "main road"; whether or not it is what you would like it to be—to consider this is already to pass judgment, a judgment that is external, pointless and false. A work of art is the expression of an incommunicable reality that one tries to communicate—and which sometimes can be communicated. That is its paradox, and its truth.

Harold Pinter

THE BIRTHDAY PARTY

Harold Pinter, born in London in 1930 to a working-class family, left school at sixteen and drifted into a career as an actor. In 1957 a friend suggested that he write a play, which he completed in four days. This play, *The Room*, was immediately produced, and it was followed by *The Dumb Waiter, The Birthday Party* (1958), and *The Caretaker* (1960). Since then, he has written a steady stream of one-act plays, full-length plays, short stories, a novel, and a number of screenplays, including *The French Lieutenant's Woman* (from John Fowles's novel) and *The Trial* (from Franz Kafka's novel). His most recent play is *Moonlight* (1995). With some twelve years' of experience as a radio and stage actor before he became a playwright, Pinter is especially attuned to gestures, stances, pauses, silences.

COMMENTARY

The Birthday Party, Harold Pinter's first full-length play, was originally performed in 1958. In the introduction to his *Complete Works*, Pinter gives us an idea of how he writes a play. He says that he generally begins a play by imagining a room with two people: "The context has always been concrete and particular, and the characters concrete also. I've never started a play from any kind of abstract idea or theory and never envisaged my own characters as messengers of death, doom, heaven or the milky way or, in other words, as allegorical representations. . . ." Thus, *The Birthday Party* is set in the living room of a seaside boarding house. Petey and Meg are the simple, middle-aged couple who run this rather off-the-beaten-track place. Their sole boarder, Stanley Webber, seems a fearful, nervous man—a former pianist who suffered some kind of breakdown and who is now recuperating (or hiding). Other characters include a sexy neighbor, Lulu, and two hired thugs (Goldberg and McCann), who look and sound a lot like the stereotypical Jew and Irishman, respectively, from comedy acts.

The play follows a conventional three-act pattern, and each act ends with a particularly terrifying or chilling moment. As for plot, it seems to be a standard, almost gangster-type melodrama: a man is hiding out, and two thugs have come to get him. However, as Act One unfolds, we sense that some very odd things are happening—or are about to happen. A mood of menace prevails; characters' speeches and motivations are ambiguous. Could Meg really be as childish as she sounds? Is the inane conversation about cornflakes masking something sinister? Is Meg's affection for

Stanley warmhearted and maternal? Alternatively, is there something sexual about her words and actions? By Act Two, we also feel uneasy about Goldberg and McCann; their interrogation of Stanley is harsh and brutal:

> GOLDBERG. Where was your wife?
> STANLEY. In—
> GOLDBERG. Answer.
> STANLEY (*turning, crouched*). What wife?
> GOLDBERG. What have you done with your wife?
> MCCANN. He's killed his wife!
> GOLDBERG. Why did you kill your wife?
> STANLEY (*sitting, his back to the audience*). What wife?

The stage directions help us imagine the frightening effect on stage. Act Two includes Stanley's birthday party—a horrible parody of celebration and fun (and a brilliantly effective scene on stage). By Act Three, the "job" the thugs have come to do is accomplished, and Stanley leaves with them.

Summarized in this way, the play hints of politics and treason, but Pinter does not provide clear or definite answers. Instead, we sense intimations of guilt, fear, and ambiguity. Pinter is, of course, an absurdist (you may find it helpful to review the remarks on the theater of the absurd, pp. 690–91). Although the action of *The Birthday Party* seems quite straightforward, a reader or audience member perceives the action as complicated and unsettling. Part of the unsettling effect is a product of the variety and the swift changes of language in *The Birthday Party*. For example, much of the dialogue requires a rapid-fire delivery by the actors, such as in the interrogation scene, and this staccato hammering usually prompts nervous giggles for audiences and readers. Pinter also makes use of a kind of rhythmic pattern—filled with clichés and twists—that reminds us of vaudeville (in Britain, the music hall). For example, the following sample could be from a Laurel and Hardy routine:

GOLDBERG. From now on, we'll be the hub of your wheel.
MCCANN. We'll renew your season ticket.
GOLDBERG. We'll take tuppence off your morning tea.
MCCANN. We'll give you a discount on all inflammable goods.
GOLDBERG. We'll watch over you.
MCCANN. Advise you.
GOLDBERG. Give you proper care and treatment.
MCCANN. Let you use the club bar.
GOLDBERG. Keep a table reserved.

Pinter is known, also, for the silences and pauses that punctuate his characters' speeches:

STANLEY. I feel like something cooked.

MEG. Well, I'm not going to give it to you.
PETEY. Give it to him.
MEG (*sitting at the table, right*). I'm not going to.
(*Pause*).
STANLEY. No breakfast.
(*Pause*).
   All night long I've been dreaming about this breakfast.
MEG. I thought you said you didn't sleep.

Although some reviewers have said that Pinter writes about the "failure of communication," he has rejected this comment and its implication about human relationships: "I think that we communicate only too well, in our silence, in what is unsaid, and that what takes place is a continual evasion, desperate rearguard attempts to keep ourselves to ourselves. Communication is too alarming" (*Complete Works*, I. 15).

Harold Pinter

THE BIRTHDAY PARTY

Characters

PETEY, *a man in his sixties*
MEG, *a woman in her sixties*
STANLEY, *a man in his late thirties*
LULU, *a girl in her twenties*
GOLDBERG, *a man in his fifties*
MCCANN, *a man of thirty*

ACT I: *A morning in summer*
ACT II: *Evening of the same day*
ACT III: *The next morning*

The living-room of a house in a seaside town. Door leading to hall D.L. Back door and small window U.L. Kitchen hatch centre back. Kitchen door U.R. Table and chairs centre. Two ordinary chairs above and left table, one armchair right table. Sideboard above small fireplace on Right wall. Stool and wooden box for shoe-brushes in fireplace.

ACT 1

Petey enters from door left with paper and sits at table. He begins to read. Meg's voice comes through the kitchen hatch.

MEG. Is that you, Petey?

(*Pause.*)

Petey, is that you?

(*Pause.*)

Petey?

PETEY. What?

MEG. Is that you?

PETEY. Yes, it's me.

MEG. What? (*Her face appears at hatch.*) Are you back?

PETEY. Yes.

MEG. I've got your cornflakes ready. (*She disappears and reappears.*) Here's your cornflakes.

(*He rises and takes the plate from her, sits at table, props paper and begins to eat. Meg enters by the kitchen door*).

Are they nice?

PETEY. Very nice.

MEG. I thought they'd be nice. (*She sits at table.*) You got your paper?

PETEY. Yes.

MEG. Is it good?

PETEY. Not bad.

MEG. What does it say?

PETEY. Nothing much.

MEG. You read me out some nice bits yesterday.

PETEY. Yes, well, I haven't finished this one yet.

MEG. Will you tell me when you come to something good?

PETEY. Yes.

(*Pause.*)

MEG. Have you been working hard this morning?

PETEY. No. Just stacked a few of the old chairs. Cleaned up a bit.

MEG. Is it nice out?

PETEY. Very nice.

(*Pause.*)

MEG. Is Stanley up yet?

PETEY. I don't know. Is he?

MEG. I don't know. I haven't seen him down yet.

PETEY. Well then, he can't be up.

MEG. Haven't you seen him down?

PETEY. I've only just come in.

MEG. He must be still asleep.

(*She looks round the room, stands, goes to sideboard and takes pair of socks from drawer, collects wool and needle and goes back to table.*)

What time did you go out this morning, Petey?

PETEY. Same time as usual.

MEG. Was it dark?

PETEY. No, it was light.

MEG (*beginning to darn*). But sometimes you go out in the morning and it's dark.

PETEY. That's in the winter.

MEG. Oh, in winter.

PETEY. Yes, it gets light later in winter.

MEG. Oh.

(*Pause.*)

What are you reading?

PETEY. Someone's just had a baby.

MEG. Oh, they haven't! Who?

PETEY. Some girl.

MEG. Who, Petey, who?

PETEY. I don't think you'd know her.

MEG. What's her name?

PETEY. Lady Mary Platt.

MEG. I don't know her.

PETEY. No.

MEG. What is it?

PETEY (*studying paper*). Er—a girl.

MEG. Not a boy?

PETEY. No.

MEG. Oh, what a shame. I'd be sorry. I'd much rather have a little boy.

PETEY. A little girl's all right.

MEG. I'd much rather have a little boy.

(*Pause.*)

(*Vaguely.*) Is it nice out?

PETEY. Yes, it's a nice day.

MEG. Is the sun shining?

PETEY. Yes.

MEG. I wish Stanley would take me for a walk along the front one day. When was I last along the front? Why don't you ask him to take me for a walk one day, Petey?

PETEY. Why don't you ask him yourself?

MEG. No. You ask him.

(*Pause.*)

He goes through his socks terrible.

PETEY. Why? He's in bed half the week.

MEG. That boy should be up. Why isn't he up? What's the time?

PETEY. About half past ten.

MEG. He should be down. He's late for his breakfast.

PETEY. I've finished my cornflakes.

MEG. Were they nice?

PETEY. Very nice.

MEG. I've got something else for you.

PETEY. Good.

(*She rises, takes his plate and exits into kitchen. Appears at hatch with two pieces of fried bread on a plate.*)

MEG. Here you are, Petey.

(*He rises, collects plate, looks at it, sits at table. Meg re-enters.*)

Is it nice?

PETEY. I haven't tasted it yet.

MEG. I bet you don't know what it is.

PETEY. Yes, I do.

MEG. What is it, then?

PETEY. Fried bread.

MEG. That's right.

(*He begins to eat.*)

PETEY. No bacon?

MEG. I've run out.

PETEY. Ah.

MEG. I'm going out soon, to do some shopping.

(*She watches him eat.*)

PETEY. Very nice.

MEG. I knew it was.

PETEY (*turning to her*). Oh, Meg, two men came up to me on the beach last night.

MEG. Two men?

PETEY. Yes. They wanted to know if we could put them up for a couple of nights.

MEG. Put them up? Here?

PETEY. Yes.

MEG. How many men?

PETEY. Two.

MEG. What did you say?

PETEY. Well, I said I didn't know. So they said they'd come round to find out.

MEG. Are they coming?

PETEY. Well, they said they would.

MEG. Had they heard about us, Petey?

PETEY. They must have done.

MEG. Yes, they must have done. They must have heard this was a very good boarding house. It is. This house is on the list.

PETEY. It is.

MEG. I know it is.

PETEY. They might turn up today. Can you do it?

MEG. Oh, I've got that lovely room they can have.

PETEY. You've got a room ready?

MEG. I've got the room with the armchair all ready for visitors.

PETEY. You're sure?

MEG. Yes, that'll be all right then, if they come today.

PETEY. Good.

(*She takes socks, etc. back to sideboard drawer.*)

MEG. I'm going to wake that boy.

PETEY. There's a new show coming to the Palace.

MEG. On the pier?

PETEY. No. The Palace, in the town.

MEG. Stanley could have been in it, if it was on the pier.

PETEY. This is a straight show.

MEG. What do you mean?

PETEY. No dancing or singing.

MEG. What do they do then?

PETEY. They just talk.

(*Pause.*)

MEG. Oh.

PETEY. You like a song, eh, Meg?

MEG. I like listening to the piano. I used to like watching Stanley play the piano. Of course, he didn't sing. (*Looking at right door.*) I'm going to call that boy.

PETEY. Didn't you take him up his cup of tea?

MEG. I always take him up his cup of tea. But that was a long time ago.

PETEY. Did he drink it?

MEG. I made him. I stood there till he did. I tried to get him up then. But he wouldn't, the little monkey. I'm going to call him. (*She goes to door right.*) Stan! Stanny! (*She listens.*) Stan! I'm coming up to fetch you if you don't come down! I'm coming up! I'm going to count three! One! Two! Three! I'm coming to get you! (*She exits and goes upstairs. In a moment, shouts from Stanley, wild laughter from Meg. Petey takes his plate to the hatch. Shouts. Laughter. Petey sits at table. Silence. She returns.)*

He's coming down. (*She is panting and arranges her hair.*) I told him if he didn't hurry up he'd get no breakfast.

PETEY. That did it, eh?

MEG. I'll get his cornflakes.

(*Meg exits to kitchen. Petey reads paper. Stanley enters right. He is unshaven, in his pyjama jacket and wears glasses. He sits at table.*)

PETEY. Morning, Stanley.

STAN. Morning.

(*Silence. Meg enters with bowl of cornflakes, which she sets on table.*)

MEG. So he's come down at last, has he? He's come down at last for his breakfast. But he doesn't deserve any, does he, Petey?

(*Stanley stares at the cornflakes.*)

Did you sleep well?

STAN. I didn't sleep at all.

MEG. You didn't sleep at all? Did you hear that, Petey? Too tired to eat your breakfast, I suppose? Now you eat up those cornflakes like a good boy. Go on.

(*He begins to eat.*)

STAN. What's it like out today?

PETEY. Very nice.

STAN. Warm?

PETEY. Well, there's a good breeze blowing.

STAN. Cold?

PETEY. No, no, I wouldn't say it was cold.

MEG. What are the cornflakes like, Stan?

STAN. Horrible.

MEG. Those flakes? Those lovely flakes? You're a liar, a little liar. They're refreshing. It says so. For people when they get up late.

STAN. The milk's off.

MEG. It's not. Petey ate his, didn't you, Petey?

PETEY. That's right.

MEG. There you are then.

STAN. All right, I'll go on to the second course.

MEG. He hasn't finished the first course and he wants to go on to the second course!

STAN. I feel like something cooked.

MEG. Well, I'm not going to give it to you.

PETEY. Give it to him.

MEG (*sitting right table*). I'm not going to.

(*Pause.*)

STAN. No breakfast.

(*Pause.*)

All night long I've been dreaming about this breakfast.

MEG. I thought you said you didn't sleep.

STAN. Day dreaming. All night long. And now she won't give me any. Not even a crust of bread on the table.

(*Pause.*)

Well, I can see I'll have to go down to one of those smart hotels on the front.

MEG (*rising quickly*). You won't get a better breakfast there than here.

(*She exits kitchen. Stanley yawns broadly. Meg appears at hatch with plate.*)

Here you are. You'll like this.

(*Petey rises, collects plate, brings it to table and puts it in front of Stanley, sits.*)

STAN. What's this?

PETEY. Fried bread.

MEG (*entering*). Well, I bet you don't know what it is.

STAN. Oh yes I do.

MEG. What?

STAN. Fried bread.

MEG. He knew.

STAN. What a wonderful surprise.

MEG. You didn't expect that, did you?

STAN. I bloody-well didn't.

PETEY (*rising*). Well, I'm off.

MEG. You going back to work?

PETEY. Yes.

MEG. Your tea! You haven't had your tea!

PETEY. That's all right. No time now.

MEG. I've got it made inside.

PETEY. No, never mind. See you later. Ta-ta, Stan.

STAN. Ta-ta.

(*Petey exits left.*)

Tch, tch, tch, tch.

MEG (*defensively*). What do you mean?

STAN. You're a bad wife.

MEG. I'm not. Who said I am?

STAN. Not to make your husband a cup of tea. Terrible.

MEG. He knows I'm not a bad wife.

STAN. Giving him sour milk instead.

MEG. It wasn't sour.

STAN. Disgraceful.

MEG. You mind your own business, anyway. (*Stanley eats.*) You won't find many better wives than me, I can tell you. I keep a very nice house and I keep it clean.

STAN. Whoo!

MEG. Yes! And this house is very well known, for a very good boarding house for visitors.

STAN. Visitors? Do you know how many visitors you've had since I've been here?

MEG. How many?

STAN. One.

MEG. Who?

STAN. Me! I'm your visitor.

MEG. You're a liar. This house is on the list.

STAN. I bet it is.

MEG. I know it is.

(*He pushes his plate away and picks up the paper.*)

Was it nice?

STAN. What?

MEG. The fried bread.

STAN. Succulent.

MEG. You shouldn't say that word.

STAN. What word?

MEG. That word you said.

STAN. What, succulent—?

MEG. Don't say it!

STAN. What's the matter with it?

MEG. You shouldn't say that word to a married woman.

STAN. Is that a fact?

MEG. Yes.

STAN. Well, I never knew that.

MEG. Well, it's true.

STAN. Who told you that?

MEG. Never you mind.

STAN. Well, if I can't say it to a married woman who can I say it to?

MEG. You're bad.

STAN. What about some tea?

MEG. Do you want some tea? (*Stanley reads the paper.*) Say please.

STAN. Please.

MEG. Say sorry first.

STAN. Sorry first.

MEG. No. Just sorry.

STAN. Just sorry!

MEG. You deserve the strap.

(*She takes his plate, ruffles his hair as she passes. Stanley exclaims and throws her arm away. She goes into the kitchen. He rubs his eyes under his glasses, picks up paper. She enters.*)

I brought the pot in.

STAN (*absently*). I don't know what I'd do without you.

MEG. You don't deserve it though.

STAN. Why not?

MEG (*pouring tea, coyly*). Go on. Calling me that.

STAN. How long has that tea been in the pot?

MEG. It's good tea. Good strong tea.

STAN. This isn't tea. It's gravy!

MEG. It's not.

STAN. Get out of it. You succulent old washing bag.

MEG. I am not! And it isn't your place to tell me if I am!

STAN. And it isn't your place to come into a man's bedroom and—wake him up.

MEG. Stanny! Don't you like your cup of tea of a morning—the one I bring you?

STAN. I can't drink this muck. Didn't anyone ever tell you to warm the pot, at least?

MEG. My father wouldn't let you insult me the way you do.

STAN. Your father? Who was he when he was at home?

MEG. He would report you.

STAN (*sleepily*). Now would I insult you, Meg? Would I do a terrible thing like that?

MEG. You did.

STAN (*putting his head in his hands*). Oh God, I'm tired.

(*Silence. Meg goes to sideboard, collects duster, vaguely dusts room, watching him. She comes to table and dusts it.*)

Not the bloody table!

(*Pause.*)

MEG. Stan?

STAN. What?

MEG (*shyly*). Am I really succulent?

STAN. Oh, you are. I'd rather have you than a cold in the nose any day.

MEG. You're just saying that.

STAN (*violently*). Look, why don't you get this place cleared up! It's a pig-sty. And another thing, what about my room? It needs sweeping. It needs papering. I need a new room!

MEG (*sensual, stroking his arm*). Oh, Stan, that's a lovely room. I've had some lovely afternoons in that room.

(*He recoils from her hand in disgust, stands and exits quickly by door left. She collects his cup and the teapot and takes them to hatch shelf. The street door slams. Stanley returns.*)

MEG. Is the sun shining?

(*He crosses up to the window, takes cigarette and matches from his pyjama jacket, lights cigarette.*)

What are you smoking, Stan?

STAN. A cigarette.

MEG. Are you going to give me one?

STAN. No.

MEG. I like cigarettes. (*He stands at the window, smoking. She crosses behind him and tickles the back of his neck.*) Tickle, tickle.

STAN (*pushing her*). Get away from me.

MEG. Are you going out?

STAN. Not with you.

MEG. But I'm going shopping in a minute.

STAN. Go.

MEG. You'll be lonely, all by yourself.

STAN. Will I?

MEG. Without your old Meg. I've got to get things in for the two gentlemen.

(*A pause. Stanley slowly raises his head. He speaks without turning.*)

STAN. What two gentlemen?

MEG. I'm expecting visitors.

(*He turns.*)

STAN. What?

MEG. You didn't know that, did you?

STAN. What are you talking about?

MEG. Two gentlemen asked Petey if they could come and stay for a couple of nights. I'm expecting them. (*She picks up the duster and begins to wipe the cloth on the table.*)

STAN. I don't believe it.

MEG. It's true.

STAN (*moving to her*). You're saying it on purpose.

MEG. Petey told me this morning.

STAN (*grinding his cigarette*). When was this? When did he see them?

MEG. Last night.

STAN. Who are they?

MEG. I don't know.

STAN. Didn't he tell you their names?

MEG. No.

STAN (*pacing the room*). Here? They wanted to come here?

MEG. Yes, they did. (*She takes the curlers out of her hair.*)

STAN. Why?

MEG. This house is on the list.

STAN. But who are they? I mean, why . . . ?

MEG. You'll see when they come.

STAN (*decisively*). They won't come.

MEG. Why not?

STAN (*quickly*). I tell you they won't come. Why didn't they come last night, if they were coming?

MEG. Perhaps they couldn't find the place in the dark. It's not easy to find in the dark.

STAN. They won't come. Someone's taking the Michael. Forget all about it. It's a false alarm. A false alarm. (*He sits at table.*) Where's my tea?

MEG. I took it away. You didn't want it.

STAN. What do you mean, you took it away?

MEG. I took it away.

STAN. What did you take it away for?

MEG. You didn't want it!

STAN. Who said I didn't want it?

MEG. You did!

STAN. Who gave you the right to take away my tea?

MEG. You wouldn't drink it.

(*Stanley stares at her.*)

STAN (*quietly*). Who do you think you're talking to?

MEG (*uncertainly*). What?

STAN. Come here.

MEG. What do you mean?

STAN. Come over here.

MEG. No.

STAN. I want to ask you something. (*Meg fidgets nervously. She does not go to him.*) Come on. (*Pause.*) All right. I can ask it from here just as well. (*Deliberately.*) Tell me, Mrs. Boles, when you address yourself to me, do you ever ask yourself who exactly you are talking to? Eh?

(*Silence. He groans, his trunk falls forward, his head falls into his hands.*)

MEG (*in a small voice*). Didn't you enjoy your breakfast, Stan? (*She approaches the table.*) Stan? When are you going to play the piano again? (*Stanley grunts.*) Like you used to? (*Stanley grunts.*) I used to like watching you play the piano. When are you going to play it again?

STAN. I can't, can I?

MEG. Why not?

STAN. I haven't got a piano, have I?

MEG. No, I meant like when you were working. That piano.

STAN. Go and do your shopping.

MEG. But you wouldn't have to go away if you got a job, would you? You could play the piano on the pier.

(*He looks at her, then speaks airily.*)

STAN. I've . . . er . . . I've been offered a job, as a matter of fact.

MEG. What?

STAN. Yes. I'm considering a job at the moment.

MEG. You're not.

STAN. A good one, too. A night club. In Berlin.

MEG. Berlin?

STAN. Berlin. A night club. Playing the piano. A fabulous salary. And all found.

MEG. How long for?

STAN. We don't stay in Berlin. Then we go to Athens.

MEG. How long for?

STAN. Yes. Then we pay a flying visit to . . . er . . . whatsisname . . .

MEG. Where?

STAN. Constantinople. Zagreb. Vladivostock. It's a round the world tour.

MEG (*sitting table*). Have you played the piano in those places before?

STAN. Played the piano? I've played the piano all over the world. All over the country. (*Pause.*) I once gave a concert.

MEG. A concert?

STAN (*reflectively*). Yes. It was a good one, too. They were all there that night. Every single one of them. It was a great success. Yes. A concert. At Lower Edmonton.

MEG. What did you wear?

STAN (*to himself*). I had a unique touch. Absolutely unique. They came up to me. They came up to me and said they were grateful. Champagne we had that night, the lot. (*Pause.*) My father nearly came down to hear me. Well, I dropped him a card anyway. But I don't think he could make it. No, I—I lost the address, that was it. (*Pause.*) Yes. Lower Edmonton. Then after that, you know what they did? They carved me up. Carved me up. It was all arranged, it was all worked out. My next concert. Somewhere else it was. In winter. I went down there to play. Then, when I got there, the hall was closed, the place was shuttered up, not even a caretaker. They'd locked it up. (*Takes off glasses and wipes them on his pyjama jacket.*) A fast one. They pulled a fast one. I'd like to know who was responsible for that. (*Bitterly.*) All right, Jack, I can take a tip. They want me to crawl down on my bended knees. Well, I can take a tip . . . any day of the week. (*He replaces his glasses, then looks at Meg.*) Look at her. You're just an old piece of rock cake, aren't you? (*He rises and leans across the table to her.*) That's what you are, aren't you?

MEG. Don't you go away again, Stan. You stay here. You'll be better off. You stay with your old Meg.

(*He groans and lies across the table.*)

Aren't you feeling well this morning, Stan? Did you pay a visit this morning?

(*He stiffens, then lifts himself slowly, turns to face her and speaks low and meaningfully.*)

STAN. Meg. Do you know what?

MEG. What?

STAN. Have you heard the latest?

MEG. No.

STAN. I'll bet you have.

MEG. I haven't.

STAN. Shall I tell you?

MEG. What latest?

STAN. You haven't heard it?

MEG. No.

STAN (*advancing*). They're coming today.

MEG. Who?

STAN. They're coming in a van.

MEG. Who?

STAN. And do you know what they've got in that van?

MEG. What?

STAN. They've got a wheelbarrow in that van.

MEG (*breathlessly*). They haven't.

STAN. Oh yes they have.

MEG. You're a liar.

STAN (*advancing upon her*). A big wheelbarrow. And when the van stops they wheel it out, and they wheel it up the garden path, and then they knock at the front door.

MEG. They don't.

STAN. They're looking for someone.

MEG. They're not.

STAN. They're looking for someone. A certain person.

MEG (*hoarsely*). No, they're not!

STAN. Shall I tell you who they're looking for?

MEG. No!

STAN. You don't want me to tell you?

MEG. You're a liar!

(*A sudden knock on the front door. Meg edges past Stanley and collects her shopping bag. Another knock on the door. Meg goes out left. Stanley sidles to the door and listens.*)

VOICE. Hullo Mrs. Boles. It's come.

MEG. Oh, has it come?

VOICE. Yes, it's just come.

MEG. What, is that it?

VOICE. Yes. I thought I'd bring it round.

MEG. Is it nice?

VOICE. Very nice. What shall I do with it?

MEG. Well, I don't . . . (*whispers*).

VOICE. No, of course not . . . (*whispers*).

MEG. All right, but . . . (*whispers*).

VOICE. I won't . . . (*whispers*). Ta-ta, Mrs. Boles.

(*Stanley quickly sits at table. Enter Lulu.*)

LULU. Oh, hullo.

STAN. Ay-ay.

LULU. I just want to leave this in here.

STAN. Do.

(*Lulu crosses to sideboard and puts a solid, round parcel upon it.*)

That's a bulky object.

LULU. You're not to touch it.

STAN. Why would I want to touch it?

LULU. Well, you're not to, anyway.

STAN. Sit down a minute.

(*Lulu walks upstage.*)

LULU. Why don't you open the door? It's all stuffy in here.

(*She opens the back door.*)

STAN (*rising*). Stuffy? What are you talking about? I disinfected the place this morning.

LULU (*at the door*). Oh, that's better.

STAN. Don't you believe me, then?

LULU. What?

STAN. Don't you believe I scrubbed the place out with Dettol this morning?

LULU. You didn't scrub yourself, I suppose?

STAN. I was in the sea at half past six.

LULU. Were you?

STAN. Sit down.

LULU. A minute.

(*She sits, takes out compact, powders her nose.*)

STAN. So you're not going to tell me what's in that parcel?

LULU. Who said I knew?

STAN. Don't you?

LULU. I never said so.

STAN (*triumphantly*). Well, how can you tell me what's in it if you don't know what's in it?

LULU. I'm not going to tell you.

STAN. I think it's going to rain today, what do you think?

LULU. Why don't you have a shave?

STAN. Don't you believe me then, when I tell you I was in the sea at half past six this morning?

LULU. I'd rather not discuss it.

STAN. You think I'm a liar then?

LULU (*offering him compact*). Do you want to have a look at your face? (*Stanley withdraws from the table.*) You could do with a shave, do you know that? Stanley sits right table.) Don't you ever go out? (*He does not answer.*) I mean, what do you do, just sit around the house like this all day long? (*Pause.*) Hasn't Mrs. Boles got enough to do without having you under her feet all day long?

STAN. I always stand on the table when she sweeps the floor.

LULU. Why don't you ever go out?

STAN. I was out—this morning—before breakfast—

LULU. I've never seen you out, not once.

STAN. Well, perhaps you're never out when I'm out.

LULU. I'm always out.

STAN. We've just never met, that's all.

LULU. Why don't you have a wash? You look terrible.

STAN. A wash wouldn't make any difference.

LULU (*rising*). Come out and get a bit of air. You depress me, looking like that.

STAN. Air? Oh, I don't know about that.

LULU. It's lovely out. And I've got a few sandwiches.

STAN. What sort of sandwiches?

LULU. Cheese.

STAN. I'm a big eater, you know.

LULU. That's all right. I'm not hungry.

STAN (*abruptly*). How would you like to go away with me?

LULU. Where?

STAN. Nowhere. Still, we could go.

LULU. But where could we go?

STAN. Nowhere. There's nowhere to go. So we could just go. It wouldn't matter.

LULU. We might as well stay here.

STAN. No. It's no good here.

LULU. Well, where else is there?

STAN. Nowhere.

LULU. Well, that's a charming proposal. (*He gets up.*) Are you going to wash?

STAN (*round to her*). Listen. I want to ask you something.

LULU. You've just asked me.

STAN. No. Listen. (*Urgently.*) Has Meg had many guests staying in this house, besides me, I mean, before me?

LULU. Besides you?

STAN (*impatiently*). Was she very busy, in the old days?

LULU. Why should she be?

STAN. What do you mean? This used to be a boarding house, didn't it?

LULU. Did it?

STAN. Didn't it?

LULU. Did it?

STAN. Didn't . . . oh, skip it.

LULU. Why do you want to know?

STAN. She's expecting two guests, for the first time since I've been here.

LULU. Oh. Do you have to wear those glasses?

STAN. Yes.

LULU. So you're not coming out for a walk?

STAN. I can't at the moment.

LULU. You're a bit of a washout, aren't you?

(*She exits left. Stanley stands. He then goes to mirror and looks in it. He goes into kitchen, takes off his glasses and begins to wash his face. A pause. Enter, by the back door, Goldberg and McCann. McCann carries two suitcases, Goldberg a briefcase. They halt inside the door, then walk downstage. Stanley, wiping his face, glimpses their backs through the hatch. Goldberg and McCann look round the room. Stanley slips on his glasses, sidles through the kitchen door and out the back door.*)

MCCANN. Is this it?

GOLDBERG. This is it.

MCCANN. Are you sure?

GOLDBERG. Sure I'm sure.

(*Pause.*)

MCCANN. What now?

GOLDBERG. Don't worry yourself, McCann. Take a seat.

MCCANN. What about you?

GOLDBERG. What about me?

MCCANN. Are you going to take a seat?

GOLDBERG. We'll both take a seat.

(*McCann puts down suitcases and sits left of table.*)

Sit back, McCann. Relax. What's the matter with you? I bring you down for a few days to the seaside. Take a holiday. Do yourself a favour. Learn to relax, McCann, or you'll never get anywhere.

MCCANN. Ah sure, I do try, Nat.

GOLDBERG (*sitting right table*). The secret is breathing. Take my tip. It's a well-known fact. Breathe in, breathe out, take a chance, let yourself go, what can you lose? Look at me. When I was an apprentice yet, McCann, every second Friday of the month my Uncle Barney used to take me to the seaside, regular as clockwork. Brighton, Canvey Island, Rottingdean—Uncle Barney wasn't particular. After lunch on Shabbuss we'd go and sit in a couple of deck-chairs—you know, the ones with canopies—we'd have a little paddle, we'd watch the tide coming in, going out, the sun coming down—golden days, believe me, McCann. (*Reminiscent.*) Uncle Barney. Of course, he was an impeccable dresser. One of the old school. He had a house just outside Basingstoke at the time. Respected by the whole community. Culture? Don't talk to me about culture. He was an all-round man, what do you mean? He was a cosmopolitan.

MCCANN. Hey, Nat . . .

GOLDBERG (*reflectively*). Yes. One of the old school.

MCCANN. Nat. How do we know this is the right house?

GOLDBERG. What?

MCCANN. How do we know this is the right house?

GOLDBERG. What makes you think it's the wrong house?

MCCANN. I didn't see a number on the gate.

GOLDBERG. I wasn't looking for a number.

MCCANN. No?

GOLDBERG (*settling in the armchair*). You know one thing Uncle Barney taught me? Uncle Barney taught me that the word of a gentleman is enough. That's why, when I had to go away on business I never carried any money. One of my sons used to come with me. He used to carry a few coppers. For a paper, perhaps, to see how the M.C.C. was getting on overseas. Otherwise my name was good. Besides, I was a very busy man.

MCCANN. I didn't know you had any sons.

GOLDBERG. But of course. I've been a family man.

MCCANN. How many did you have?

GOLDBERG. I lost my last two—in an accident. But the first, the first grew up to be a fine boy.

MCCANN. What's he doing now?

GOLDBERG. I often wonder that myself. Yes. Emanuel. A quiet fellow. He never said much. Timmy I used to call him.

MCCANN. Emanuel?

GOLDBERG. That's right. Manny.

MCCANN. Manny?

GOLDBERG. Sure. It's short for Emanuel.

MCCANN. I thought you called him Timmy.

GOLDBERG. I did.

MCCANN. What about this, Nat? Isn't it about time someone came in?

GOLDBERG. McCann, what are you so nervous about? Pull yourself together. Everywhere you go these days it's like a funeral.

MCCANN. That's true.

GOLDBERG. True? Of course it's true. It's more than true. It's a fact.

MCCANN. You may be right.

GOLDBERG. What is it, McCann? You don't trust me like you did in the old days?

MCCANN. Sure I trust you, Nat.

GOLDBERG. I'm glad. But why is it that before you do a job you're all over the place, and when you're doing the job you're as cool as a whistle?

MCCANN. I don't know, Nat. I'm just all right once I know what I'm doing. When I know what I'm doing I'm all right.

GOLDBERG. Well, you do it very well.

MCCANN. Thank you, Nat.

GOLDBERG. As a matter of fact I was talking about you only the other day. I gave you a very good name.

MCCANN. That was kind of you, Nat.

GOLDBERG. And then this job came up out of the blue. Naturally they approached me to take care of it. And you know who I asked for?

MCCANN. Who?

GOLDBERG. You.

MCCANN. That was very good of you, Nat.

GOLDBERG. No, it was nothing. You're a capable man, McCann.

MCCANN. That's a great compliment, Nat, coming from a man in your position.

GOLDBERG. Well, I've got a position, I won't deny it.

MCCANN. You certainly have.

GOLDBERG. I would never deny that I had a position.

MCCANN. And what a position!

GOLDBERG. It's not a thing I would deny.

MCCANN. Yes, it's true, you've done a lot for me. I appreciate it.

GOLDBERG. Say no more.

MCCANN. You've always been a true Christian.

GOLDBERG. In a way.

MCCANN. No, I just thought I'd tell you that I appreciate it.

GOLDBERG. It's unnecessary to recapitulate.

MCCANN. You're right there.

GOLDBERG. Quite unnecessary.

(*Pause. McCann leans forward.*)

MCCANN. Hey Nat, just one thing . . .

GOLDBERG. What now?

MCCANN. This job—no, listen—this job, is it going to be like anything we've ever done before?

GOLDBERG. Tch, tch, tch.

MCCANN. No, just tell me that. Just that, and I won't ask any more.

(*Goldberg sighs, stands, goes behind the table, ponders, looks at McCann, and then speaks in a quiet, fluent, official tone.*)

GOLDBERG. The main issue is a singular issue and quite distinct from your previous work. Certain elements, however, might well approximate in points of procedure to some of your other activities. All is dependent on the attitude of our subject. At all events, McCann, I can assure you that the assignment will be carried out and the mission accomplished with no excessive aggravation to you or myself. Satisfied?

MCCANN. Sure. Thank you, Nat.

(*Meg enters left.*)

GOLDBERG. Ah, Mrs. Boles?

MEG. Yes?

GOLDBERG. We spoke to your husband last night. Perhaps he mentioned us? We heard that you kindly let rooms for gentlemen. So I brought my friend along with me. We were after a nice place, you understand. So we came to you. I'm Mr. Goldberg and this is Mr. McCann.

MEG. Very pleased to meet you.

(*They shake hands.*)

GOLDBERG. We're pleased to meet you, too.

MEG. That's very nice.

GOLDBERG. You're right. How often do you meet someone it's a pleasure to meet?

MCCANN. Never.

GOLDBERG. But today it's different. How are you keeping, Mrs. Boles?

MEG. Oh very well, thank you.

GOLDBERG. Yes? Really?

MEG. Oh yes, really.

GOLDBERG. I'm glad. What do you say, McCann? Oh, Mrs. Boles, would you mind if my friend went into your kitchen and had a little gargle?

MEG. (*To McCann.*) Why, have you got a sore throat?

MCCANN. Er—yes.

MEG. Do you want some salt?

MCCANN. Salt?

MEG. Salt's good.

GOLDBERG. Good? It's wonderful. Go on, off you go, McCann.

MCCANN. Where is the kitchen?

MEG. Over there. (*McCann goes to the kitchen.*) There's some salt on the shelf.

(*McCann exits. Goldberg sits right table.*)

GOLDBERG. So you can manage to put us up, eh, Mrs. Boles?

MEG. Well, it would have been easier last week.

GOLDBERG. Last week.

MEG. Or next week.

GOLDBERG. Next week.

MEG. Yes.

GOLDBERG. How many have you got here at the moment?

MEG. Just one at the moment.

GOLDBERG. Just one?

MEG. Yes. Just one. Until you came.

GOLDBERG. And your husband, of course?

MEG. Yes, but he sleeps with me.

GOLDBERG. What does he do, your husband?

MEG. He's a deck-chair attendant.

GOLDBERG. Oh, very nice.

MEG. Yes, he's out in all weathers.

(*She begins to take her purchases from her bag.*)

GOLDBERG. Of course. And your guest? Is he a man?

MEG. A man?

GOLDBERG. Or a woman?

MEG. No. A man.

GOLDBERG. Been here long?

MEG. He's been here about a year now.

GOLDBERG. Oh yes. A resident. What's his name?

MEG. Stanley Webber.

GOLDBERG. Oh yes? Does he work here?

MEG. He used to work. He used to be a pianist. In a concert party on the pier.

GOLDBERG. Oh yes? On the pier, eh? Does he play a nice piano?

MEG. Oh, lovely. (*She sits at table.*) He once gave a concert.

GOLDBERG. Oh? Where?

MEG (*falteringly*). In . . . a big hall. His father gave him champagne. But then they locked the place up and he couldn't get out. The caretaker had gone home. So he had to wait until the morning before he could get out. (*With confidence.*) They were very grateful. (*Pause.*) And then they all wanted to give him a tip. And so he took the tip. And then he got a fast train and he came down here.

GOLDBERG. Really?

MEG. Oh yes. Straight down.

(*Pause.*)

MEG. I wish he could have played tonight.

GOLDBERG. Why tonight?

MEG. It's his birthday today.

GOLDBERG. His birthday?

MEG. Yes. Today. But I'm not going to tell him until tonight.

GOLDBERG. Doesn't he know it's his birthday?

MEG. He hasn't mentioned it.

GOLDBERG (*thoughtfully*). Well, well, well. Tell me. Are you going to have a party?

MEG. A party?

GOLDBERG. Weren't you going to have one?

MEG (*her eyes wide*). No.

GOLDBERG. Well, of course, you must have one. (*He stands.*) We'll have a party, eh? What do you say?

MEG. Oh yes!

GOLDBERG. Sure. We'll give him a party. Leave it to me.

MEG. Oh, that's wonderful, Mr. Gold—

GOLDBERG. Berg.

MEG. Berg.

GOLDBERG. You like the idea?

MEG. Oh, I'm so glad you came today.

GOLDBERG. If we hadn't come today we'd have come tomorrow. Still, I'm glad we came today. Just in time for his birthday.

MEG. I wanted to have a party. But you must have people for a party.

GOLDBERG. And now you've got McCann and me. McCann's the life and soul of any party.

(*McCann enters from the kitchen.*)

MEG. I'll invite Lulu this afternoon. (*To McCann.*) We're going to have a party tonight.

MCCANN. What?

GOLDBERG. There's a gentleman living here, McCann, who's got a birthday today, and he's forgotten all about it. So we're going to remind him. We're going to give him a party.

MCCANN. Oh, is that a fact?

MEG. Tonight.

GOLDBERG. Tonight. Did you have a good gargle?

MCCANN. Yes, thanks.

MEG. I'll put on my party dress.

GOLDBERG. And I'll get some bottles.

MEG. Oh, this is going to cheer Stanley up. It will. He's been down in the dumps lately.

GOLDBERG. We'll bring him out of himself.

MEG. I hope I look nice in my dress.

GOLDBERG. Madam, you'll look like a tulip.

MEG. What colour?

GOLDBERG. Er—well, I'll have to see the dress first.

MCCANN. Could I go up to my room?

MEG. Oh, I've put you both together. Do you mind being both together?

GOLDBERG. I don't mind. Do you mind, McCann?

MCCANN. No.

MEG. What time shall we have the party?

GOLDBERG. Nine o'clock.

MCCANN (*at door*). Is this the way?

MEG (*rising*). I'll show you. If you don't mind coming upstairs.

GOLDBERG. With a tulip? It's a pleasure.

(*Meg and Goldberg exit laughing, followed by McCann. Stanley appears at window. He enters by the back door. He goes to door left, opens it, listens. Silence. He walks to table. He stands. He sits, as Meg enters. She crosses and hangs her shopping bag on a hook. He lights a match and watches it burn.*)

STAN. Who is it?

MEG. The two gentlemen.

STAN. Who two gentlemen?

MEG. The ones that were coming. I just took them to their room. They were thrilled with their room.

STAN. They've come?

MEG. They're very nice, Stan.

STAN. Why didn't they come last night?

MEG. They said the beds were wonderful.

STAN. Who are they?

MEG (*sitting*). They're very nice, Stanley.

STAN. I said, who are they?

MEG. I've told you, the two gentlemen.

STAN. I didn't think they'd come.

(*He rises, walks to window.*)

MEG. They have. They were here when I came in.

STAN. What do they want here?

MEG. They want to stay.

STAN. How long for?

MEG. They didn't say.

STAN (*turning*). But why here? Why not somewhere else?

MEG. This house is on the list.

STAN (*coming down*). What are they called? What are their names?

MEG. Oh, Stanley, I can't remember.

STAN. They told you, didn't they? Or didn't they tell you?

MEG. Yes, they . . .

STAN. Then what are they? Come on. Try to remember.

MEG. Why, Stan? Do you know them?

STAN. How do I know if I know them until I know their names?

MEG. Well . . . he told me, I remember.

STAN. Well?

(*She thinks.*)

MEG. Gold—something.

STAN. Goldsomething?

MEG. Yes. Gold . . .

STAN. Yes?

MEG. Goldberg.

STAN. Goldberg?

MEG. That's right. That was one of them.

(*Stanley slowly sits at table, left.*)

Do you know them?

(*Stanley does not answer.*)

Stan, they won't wake you up, I promise. I'll tell them they must be quiet.

(*Stanley sits still.*)

They won't be here long, Stan. I'll still bring you up your early morning tea.

(*Stanley sits still.*)

You mustn't be sad today. It's your birthday.

(*A pause.*)

STAN (*dumbly*). Uh?

MEG. It's your birthday, Stan. I was going to keep it a secret until tonight.

STAN. No.

MEG. It is. I've brought you a present.

(*She goes to sideboard, picks up parcel, places it on the table in front of him.*)

Here. Go on. Open it.

STAN. What's this?

MEG. It's your present.

STAN. This isn't my birthday, Meg.

MEG. Of course it is. Open your present.

(*He stares at the parcel, slowly stands, and opens it. He takes out a boy's drum.*)

STAN (*flatly*). It's a drum. A boy's drum.

MEG (*tenderly*). It's because you haven't got a piano.

(*He stares at her, then turns and walks towards door left.*)

Aren't you going to give me a kiss?

(*He turns sharply, stops. He walks back towards her slowly. He stops at her chair, looking down upon her. Pause. His shoulders sag, he bends and kisses her on the cheek.*)

There are some sticks in there.

(*Stanley looks into the parcel. He takes out two drumsticks. He taps them together. He looks at her.*)

STAN. Shall I put it round my neck?

(*She watches him, uncertainly. He hangs the drum around his neck, taps it gently with the sticks, then marches round the table, beating it regularly. Meg, pleased, watches him. Still beating it regularly, he begins to go round the table a second time. Halfway round the beat becomes erratic, uncontrolled. Meg expresses dismay. He arrives at her chair, banging the drum, his face and the drumbeat now savage and possessed.*)

CURTAIN

ACT 2

(*McCann is sitting at the table tearing a sheet of newspaper into five equal strips. It is evening. After a few*

moments Stanley enters from the left. He stops upon see-
ing McCann, and watches him. He then walks towards
the kitchen, stops, speaks.)

STAN. Evening.

MCCANN. Evening.

(*Chuckles are heard from outside the back door, which is*
open.)

STAN. Very warm tonight. (*He turns towards back door, and*
back.) Someone out there?

(*McCann tears another length of paper. Stanley goes into*
the kitchen and pours a glass of water. He drinks it looking
through the hatch. He puts the glass down, comes out of
kitchen and walks quickly towards door left. McCann rises
and intercepts him.)

MCCANN. I don't think we've met.

STAN. No we haven't.

MCCANN. My name's McCann.

STAN. Staying here long?

MCCANN. Not long. What's your name?

STAN. Webber.

MCCANN. I'm glad to meet you, sir.

(*He offers his hand. Stanley takes it, and McCann holds*
the grip.)

Many happy returns of the day.

(*Stanley withdraws his hand. They face each other.*)

Were you going out?

STAN. Yes.

MCCANN. On your birthday?

STAN. Yes. Why not?

MCCANN. But they're holding a party here for you tonight.

STAN. Oh really? That's unfortunate.

MCCANN. Ah no. It's very nice.

(*Voices from outside the back door.*)

STAN. I'm sorry. I'm not in the mood for a party tonight.

MCCANN. Oh, is that so? I'm sorry.

STAN. Yes, I'm going out to celebrate quietly, on my own.

MCCANN. That's a shame.

(*They stand.*)

STAN. Well, if you'd move out of my way—

MCCANN. But everything's laid on. The guests are expected.

STAN. Guests? What guests?

MCCANN. Myself for one. I had the honour of an invitation.

(*McCann begins to whistle 'The Mountains of Morne.'*)

STAN (*moving away*). I wouldn't call it an honour, would
you? It'll just be another booze-up.

(*Stanley joins McCann in whistling 'The Mountains of*
Morne.' During the next five lines the whistling is continu-
ous, one whistling while the other speaks, both whistling
together.)

MCCANN. But it is an honour.

STAN. I'd say you were exaggerating.

MCCANN. Oh no. I'd say it was an honour.

STAN. I'd say that was plain stupid.

MCCANN. Oh no.

(*They stare at each other.*)

STAN. Who are the other guests?

MCCANN. A young lady.

STAN. Oh yes? And . . . ?

MCCANN. My friend.

STAN. Your friend?

MCCANN. That's right. It's all laid on.

(*Stanley walks below the table towards the door. McCann*
meets him.)

STAN. Excuse me.

MCCANN. Where are you going?

STAN. I want to go out.

MCCANN. Why don't you stay here?

(*Stanley moves away, to right of table.*)

STAN. So you're down here on holiday?

MCCANN. A short one.

(*Stanley picks up a strip of paper.*)

(*Moving in.*) Mind that.

STAN. What is it?

MCCANN. Mind it. Leave it.

STAN. I've got a feeling we've met before.

MCCANN. No we haven't.

STAN. Ever been anywhere near Maidenhead?

MCCANN. No.

STAN. There's a Fuller's teashop. I used to have my tea there.

MCCANN. I don't know it.

STAN. And a Boots Library. I seem to connect you with the
High Street.

MCCANN. Yes?

STAN. A charming town, don't you think?

MCCANN. I don't know it.

STAN. Oh no. A quiet, thriving community. I was born and
brought up there. I lived well away from the main road.

MCCANN. Yes?

(*Pause.*)

STAN. You're here on a short stay?

MCCANN. That's right.

STAN. You'll find it very bracing.

MCCANN. Do you find it bracing?

STAN. Me? No. But you will. (*He sits at table.*) I like it here,
but I'll be moving soon. Back home. I'll stay there too,
this time. No place like home. (*He laughs.*) I wouldn't
have left, but business calls. Business called, and I had to
leave for a bit. You know how it is.

MCCANN (*sitting left table*). You in business?

STAN. No. I think I'll give it up. I've got a small private
income, you see. I think I'll give it up. Don't like being
away from home. I used to live very quietly—played
records, that's about all. Everything delivered to the door.
Then I started a little private business, in a small way,

and it compelled me to come down here—kept me longer than I expected. You never get used to living in someone else's house. Don't you agree? I lived so quietly. You can only appreciate what you've had when things change. That's what they say, isn't it? Cigarette?

MCCANN. I don't smoke.

(*Stanley lights a cigarette. Voices from the back.*)

STAN. Who's out there?

MCCANN. My friend and the man of the house.

STAN. You know what? To look at me, I bet you wouldn't think I'd led such a quiet life. The lines on my face, eh? It's the drink. Been drinking a bit down here. But what I mean is . . . you know how it is . . . away from your own . . . all wrong, of course . . . I'll be all right when I get back . . . but what I mean is, the way some people look at me you'd think I was a different person. I suppose I have changed, but I'm still the same man that I always was. I mean, you wouldn't think, to look at me, really . . . I mean, not really, that I was the sort of bloke to—to cause any trouble, would you?

(*McCann looks at him.*)

Do you know what I mean?

MCCANN. No. (*As Stanley picks up a strip of paper.*) Mind that.

STAN (*quickly*). Why are you down here?

MCCANN. A short holiday.

STAN. This is a ridiculous house to pick on. (*He rises.*)

MCCANN. Why?

STAN. Because it's not a boarding house. It never was.

MCCANN. Sure it is.

STAN. Why did you choose this house?

MCCANN. You know, sir, you're a bit depressed for a man on his birthday.

STAN (*sharply*). Why do you call me sir?

MCCANN. You don't like it?

STAN (*to table*). Listen. Don't call me sir.

MCCANN. I won't, if you don't like it.

STAN (*moving away*). No. Anyway, this isn't my birthday.

MCCANN. No?

STAN. No. It's not till next month.

MCCANN. Not according to the lady.

STAN. Her? She's crazy. Round the bend.

MCCANN. That's a terrible thing to say.

STAN (*to table*). Haven't you found that out yet? There's a lot you don't know. I think someone's leading you up the garden path.

MCCANN. Who would do that?

STAN (*leaning across table*). That woman is mad!

MCCANN. That's slander.

STAN. And you don't know what you're doing.

MCCANN. Your cigarette is near that paper.

(*Voices from the back.*)

STAN. Where the hell are they? (*Stubbing his cigarette.*) Why don't they come in? What are they doing out there?

MCCANN. You want to steady yourself.

(*Stanley crosses to him and grips his arm.*)

STAN (*urgently*). Look—

MCCANN. Don't touch me.

STAN. Look. Listen a minute.

MCCANN. Let go my arm.

STAN. Look. Sit down a minute.

MCCANN (*savagely, hitting his arm*). Don't do that!

(*Stanley backs across the stage, holding his arm.*)

STAN. Listen. You knew what I was talking about before, didn't you?

MCCANN. I don't know what you're at at all.

STAN. It's a mistake! Do you understand?

MCCANN. You're in a bad state, man.

STAN (*whispering, advancing*). Has he told you anything? Do you know what you're here for? Tell me. You needn't be frightened of me. Or hasn't he told you?

MCCANN. Told me what?

STAN (*hissing*). I've explained to you, damn you, that all those years I lived in Basingstoke I never stepped outside the door.

MCCANN. You know, I'm flabbergasted with you.

STAN (*reasonably*). Look. You look an honest man. You're being made a fool of, that's all. You understand? Where do you come from?

MCCANN. Where do you think?

STAN. I know Ireland very well. I've many friends there. I love that country and I admire and trust its people. I trust them. They respect the truth and they have a sense of humour. I think their policemen are wonderful. I've been there. I've never seen such sunsets. What about coming out to have a drink with me? There's a pub down the road serves Draught Guinness. Very difficult to get in these parts—

(*He breaks off. The voices draw nearer. Goldberg and Petey enter from U.L.*)

GOLDBERG (*as he enters*). A mother in a million. (*Sees Stanley.*) Ah.

PETEY. Oh hullo, Stan. You haven't met Stanley, have you, Mr. Goldberg?

GOLDBERG. I haven't had the pleasure.

PETEY. Oh well, this is Mr. Goldberg, this is Mr. Webber.

GOLDBERG. Pleased to meet you.

PETEY. We were just getting a bit of air in the garden.

GOLDBERG. I was telling Mr. Boles about my old mum. What days. (*He sits right table.*) Yes. When I was a youngster, of a Friday, I used to go for a walk down the canal with a girl who lived down my road. A beautiful girl. What a voice that bird had! A nightingale, my word of honour. Good? Pure? She wasn't a Sunday school teacher for nothing. Anyway, I'd leave her with a little kiss on the cheek—I never took liberties—we weren't like the young men these days in those days. We knew the meaning of respect. So I'd give her a peck and I'd bowl back home.

Humming away I'd be, past the children's playground. I'd tip my hat to the toddlers, I'd give a helping hand to a couple of stray dogs, everything came natural. I can see it like yesterday. The sun falling behind the dog stadium. Ah! (*He leans back contentedly.*)

MCCANN. Like behind the town hall.

GOLDBERG. What town hall?

MCCANN. In Carrikmacross.

GOLDBERG. There's no comparison. Up the street, into my gate, inside the door, home. 'Simey!' my old mum used to shout, 'quick before it gets cold.' And there on the table what would I see? The nicest piece of gefilte fish you could wish to find on a plate.

MCCANN. I thought your name was Nat.

GOLDBERG. She called me Simey.

PETEY. Yes, we all remember our childhood.

GOLDBERG. Too true. Eh, Mr. Webber, what do you say? Childhood. Hot water bottles. Hot milk. Pancakes. Soap suds. What a life.

(*Pause.*)

PETEY (*rising from above table*). Well, I'll have to be off.

GOLDBERG. Off?

PETEY. It's my chess night.

GOLDBERG. You're not staying for the party?

PETEY. No, I'm sorry, Stan. I didn't know about it till just now. And we've got a game on. I'll try and get back early.

GOLDBERG. We'll save some drink for you, all right? Oh, that reminds me. You'd better go and collect the bottles.

MCCANN. Now?

GOLDBERG. Of course, now. Time's getting on. Round the corner, remember? Mention my name.

PETEY. I'm coming your way.

GOLDBERG. Beat him quick and come back, Mr. Boles.

PETEY. Do my best. See you later, Stan.

(*Petey and McCann go out left. Stanley moves U.C.*)

GOLDBERG. A warm night.

STAN (*turning*). Don't mess me about!

GOLDBERG. I beg your pardon?

STAN (*moving down*). I'm afraid there's been a mistake. We're booked out. Your room is taken. Mrs. Boles forgot to tell you. You'll have to find somewhere else.

GOLDBERG. Are you the manager here?

STAN. That's right.

GOLDBERG. Is is a good game?

STAN. I run the house. I'm afraid you and your friend will have to find other accommodation.

GOLDBERG (*rising*). Oh, I forgot, I must congratulate you on your birthday. (*Offering his hand.*) Congratulations.

STAN (*ignoring hand.*) Perhaps you're deaf.

GOLDBERG. No, what makes you think that? As a matter of fact, every single one of my senses is at its peak. Not bad going, eh? For a man past fifty. But a birthday, I always feel, is a great occasion, taken too much for granted these days. What a thing to celebrate—birth! Like getting up in the morning. Marvellous! Some people don't like the idea of getting up in the morning. I've heard them. Getting up in the morning, they say, what is it? Your skin's crabby, you need a shave, your eyes are full of muck, your mouth is like a boghouse, the palms of your hands are full of sweat, your nose is clogged up, your feet stink, what are you but a corpse waiting to be washed? Whenever I hear that point of view I feel cheerful. Because I know what it is to wake up with the sun shining, to the sound of the lawnmower, all the little birds, the smell of the grass, church bells, tomato juice—

STAN. Get out.

(*Enter McCann, with bottles.*)

Get that drink out. These are unlicensed premises.

GOLDBERG. You're in a terrible humor today, Mr. Webber. And on your birthday too, with the good lady getting her strength up to give you a party.

(*McCann puts the bottles on the sideboard.*)

STAN. I told you to get those bottles out.

GOLDBERG. Mr. Webber, sit down a minute.

STAN. Let me—just make this clear. You don't bother me. To me, you're nothing but a dirty joke. But I have a responsibility towards the people in this house. They've been down here too long. They've lost their sense of smell. I haven't. And nobody's going to take advantage of them while I'm here. (*A little less forceful.*) Anyway, this house isn't your cup of tea. There's nothing here for you, from any angle. Any angle. So why don't you just go, without any more fuss?

GOLDBERG. Mr. Webber, sit down.

STAN. It's no good starting any kind of trouble.

GOLDBERG. Sit down.

STAN. Why should I?

GOLDBERG. If you want to know the truth, Webber, you're beginning to get on my breasts.

STAN. Really? Well, that's—

GOLDBERG. Sit down.

STAN. No.

(*Goldberg sighs, sits right table.*)

GOLDBERG. McCann.

MCCANN. Nat?

GOLDBERG. Ask him to sit down.

MCCANN. Yes, Nat. (*McCann moves to Stanley.*) Do you mind sitting down?

STAN. Yes, I do mind.

MCCANN. Yes now, but—it'd be better if you did.

STAN. Why don't you sit down?

MCCANN. No, not me—you.

STAN. No thanks.

(*Pause.*)

MCCANN. Nat.

GOLDBERG. What?

MCCANN. He won't sit down.

GOLDBERG. Well, ask him.

MCCANN. I've asked him.

GOLDBERG. Ask him again.

MCCANN (*to Stanley*). Sit down.

STAN. Why?

MCCANN. You'd be more comfortable.

STAN. So would you.

(*Pause.*)

MCCANN. All right. If you will I will.

STAN. You first.

(*McCann slowly sits left table.*)

MCCANN. Well?

STAN. Right. Now you've both had a rest you can get out!

MCCANN (*rising*). That's a dirty trick! I'll kick the shite out of him!

GOLDBERG (*rising*). No! I have stood up.

MCCANN. Sit down again!

GOLDBERG. Once I'm up I'm up.

STAN. Same here.

MCCANN (*moving to Stanley*). You've made Mr. Goldberg stand up.

STAN (*his voice still rising*). It'll do him good!

MCCANN. Get in that seat.

GOLDBERG. McCann.

MCCANN. Get down in that seat!

GOLDBERG (*crossing to him*). Webber. (*Quietly*). SIT DOWN.

(*Silence. Stanley begins to whistle 'The Mountains of Morne.' He strolls casually to chair above the table. They watch him. He stops whistling. Silence. He sits.*)

STAN. You'd better be careful.

GOLDBERG. Webber, what were you doing yesterday?

STAN. Yesterday?

GOLDBERG. And the day before. What did you do the day before that?

STAN. What do you mean?

GOLDBERG. Why are you wasting everybody's time Webber? Why are you getting in everybody's way?

STAN. Me? What are you—

GOLDBERG. I'm telling you, Webber. You're a washout. Why are you getting on everybody's wick? Why are you driving that old lady off her conk?

MCCANN. He likes to do it!

GOLDBERG. Why do you behave so badly, Webber? Why do you force that old man out to play chess?

STAN. Me?

GOLDBERG. Why do you treat that young lady like a leper? She's not the leper, Webber!

STAN. What the—

GOLDBERG. What did you wear last week, Webber? Where do you keep your suits?

MCCANN. Why did you leave the organisation?

GOLDBERG. What would your old mum say, Webber?

MCCANN. Why did you betray us?

GOLDBERG. You hurt me, Webber. You're playing a dirty game.

MCCANN. That's a Black and Tan fact.

GOLDBERG. Who does he think he is?

MCCANN. Who do you think you are?

STAN. You're on the wrong horse.

GOLDBERG. When did you come to this place?

STAN. Last year.

GOLDBERG. Where did you come from?

STAN. Somewhere else.

GOLDBERG. Why did you come here?

STAN. My feet hurt!

GOLDBERG. Why did you stay?

STAN. I had a headache!

GOLDBERG. Did you take anything for it?

STAN. Yes.

GOLDBERG. What?

STAN. Fruit salts!

GOLDBERG. Enos or Andrews?

STAN. En—An—

GOLDBERG. Did you stir properly? Did they fizz?

STAN. Now, now, wait, you—

GOLDBERG. Did they fizz? Did they fizz or didn't they fizz?

MCCANN. He doesn't know!

GOLDBERG. You don't know. What's happened to your memory, Webber? When did you last have a bath?

STAN. I have one every—

GOLDBERG. Don't lie.

MCCANN. You betrayed the organisation. I know him!

STAN. You don't!

GOLDBERG. What can you see without your glasses?

STAN. Anything.

GOLDBERG. Take off his glasses.

(*McCann snatches his glasses and as Stanley rises, reaching for them, takes his chair downstage centre, below the table, Stanley stumbling following. Stanley clutches the chair and stays bent over it.*)

Webber, you're a fake.

(*They stand each side of the chair.*)

When did you last wash up a cup?

STAN. The Christmas before last.

GOLDBERG. Where?

STAN. Lyons Corner House.

GOLDBERG. Which one?

STAN. Marble Arch.

GOLDBERG. Where was your wife?

STAN. In—

GOLDBERG. Answer.

STAN (*turning, crouched*). What wife?

GOLDBERG. What have you done with your wife?

MCCANN. He's killed his wife!

GOLDBERG. Why did you kill your wife?

STAN (*sitting, his back to the audience*). What wife?

MCCANN. How did he kill her?

GOLDBERG. How did you kill her?

MCCANN. You throttled her.

GOLDBERG. With arsenic.

MCCANN. There's your man!

GOLDBERG. Where's your old mum?

STAN. In the sanatorium.

MCCANN. Yes!

GOLDBERG. Why did you never get married?

MCCANN. She was waiting at the porch.

GOLDBERG. You skedaddled from the wedding.

MCCANN. He left her in the lurch.

GOLDBERG. You left her in the pudding club.

MCCANN. She was waiting at the church.

GOLDBERG. Webber! Why did you change your name?

STAN. I forgot the other one.

GOLDBERG. What's your name now?

STAN. Joe Soap.

GOLDBERG. You stink of sin.

MCCANN. I can smell it.

GOLDBERG. Do you recognise an external force?

STAN. What?

GOLDBERG. Do you recognise an external force?

MCCANN. That's the question!

GOLDBERG. Do you recognise an external force, responsible for you, suffering for you?

STAN. It's late.

GOLDBERG. Late! Late enough! When did you last pray?

MCCANN. He's sweating!

GOLDBERG. When did you last pray?

MCCANN. He's sweating!

GOLDBERG. Is the number 846 possible or necessary?

STAN. Neither.

GOLDBERG. Wrong! Is the number 846 possible or necessary?

STAN. Both.

GOLDBERG. Wrong! It's necessary but not possible.

STAN. Both.

GOLDBERG. Wrong! Why do you think the number 846 is necessarily possible?

STAN. Must be.

GOLDBERG. Wrong! It's only necessarily necessary! We admit possibility only after we grant necessity. It is possible because necessary but by no means necessary through possibility. The possibility can only be assumed after the proof of necessity.

MCCANN. Right!

GOLDBERG. Right? Of course right! We're right and you're wrong, Webber, all along the line.

MCCANN. All along the line!

GOLDBERG. Where is your lechery leading you?

MCCANN. You'll pay for this.

GOLDBERG. You stuff yourself with dry toast.

MCCANN. You contaminate womankind.

GOLDBERG. Why don't you pay the rent?

MCCANN. Mother defiler!

GOLDBERG. Why do you pick your nose?

MCCANN. I demand justice!

GOLDBERG. What's your trade?

MCCANN. What about Ireland?

GOLDBERG. What's your trade?

STAN. I play the piano.

GOLDBERG. How many fingers do you use?

STAN. No hands!

GOLDBERG. No society would touch you. Not even a building society.

MCCANN. You're a traitor to the cloth.

GOLDBERG. What do you use for pyjamas?

STAN. Nothing.

GOLDBERG. You verminate the sheet of your birth.

MCCANN. What about the Albigensenist heresy?

GOLDBERG. Who watered the wicket in Melbourne?

MCCANN. What about the blessed Oliver Plunkett?

GOLDBERG. Speak up Webber. Why did the chicken cross the road?

STAN. He wanted to—he wanted to—he wanted to . . .

MCCANN. He doesn't know!

GOLDBERG. Why did the chicken cross the road?

STAN. He wanted to—he wanted to . . .

GOLDBERG. Why did the chicken cross the road?

STAN. He wanted . . .

MCCANN. He doesn't know. He doesn't know which came first!

GOLDBERG. Which came first?

MCCANN. Chicken? Egg? Which came first?

GOLDBERG and MCCANN. Which came first? Which came first? Which came first?

(*Stanley screams.*)

GOLDBERG. He doesn't know. Do you know your own face?

MCCANN. Wake him up. Stick a needle in his eye.

GOLDBERG. You're a plague, Webber. You're an overthrow.

MCCANN. You're what's left!

GOLDBERG. But we've got the answer to you. We can sterilize you.

MCCANN. What about Drogheda?

GOLDBERG. Your bite is dead. Only your pong is left.

MCCANN. You betrayed our land.

GOLDBERG. You betray our breed.

MCCANN. Who are you, Webber?

GOLDBERG. What makes you think you exist?

MCCANN. You're dead.

GOLDBERG. You're dead. You can't live, you can't think, you can't love. You're dead. You're a plague gone bad. There's no juice in you. You're nothing but an odour!

(*Silence. They stand over him. He is crouched in the chair. He looks up slowly and kicks Goldberg in the stomach. Goldberg falls. Stanley stands. McCann seizes a chair and lifts it above his head. Stanley seizes a chair and covers his head with it. McCann and Stanley circle.*)

GOLDBERG. Steady, McCann.

STAN (*circling*). Uuuuuhhhhh!

MCCANN. Right, Judas.

GOLDBERG (*rising*). Steady, McCann.

MCCANN. Come on!

STAN. Uuuuuuuhhhhh!

MCCANN. He's sweating.

GOLDBERG. Easy, McCann.

MCCANN. The bastard sweatpig is sweating.

(*A loud drumbeat off right, descending the stairs. Goldberg takes chair from Stanley. They put chairs down. They stop still. Enter Meg, in evening dress, holding sticks and drum.*)

MEG. I brought the drum down. I'm dressed for the party.

GOLDBERG. Wonderful.

MEG. You like my dress?

GOLDBERG. Wonderful. Out of this world.

MEG. I know. My father gave it to me. (*Placing drum on table.*) Doesn't it make a beautiful noise?

GOLDBERG. It's a fine piece of work. Maybe Stan'll play us a little tune afterwards.

MEG. Oh yes. Will you, Stan?

STAN. Could I have my glasses?

GOLDBERG. Ah yes. (*He holds his hand out to McCann. McCann passes him glasses.*) Here they are. (*He holds them out for Stanley, who reaches for them.*) Here they are. (*Stanley takes them.*) Now. What have we got here? Enough to scuttle a liner. We've got four bottles of Scotch and one bottle of Irish.

MEG. Oh, Mr. Goldberg, what should I drink?

GOLDBERG. Glasses, glasses first. Open the Scotch, McCann.

MEG (*at sideboard*). Here's my very best glasses in here.

MCCANN. I don't drink Scotch.

GOLDBERG. You drink that one.

MEG (*bringing glasses*). Here they are.

GOLDBERG. Good. Mrs. Boles, I think Stanley should pour the toast, don't you?

MEG. Oh yes. Come on, Stanley. (*Stanley walks slowly to the table.*) Do you like my dress, Mr. Goldberg?

GOLDBERG. It's out on its own. Turn yourself round a minute. I used to be in the business. Go on, walk up there.

MEG. Oh no.

GOLDBERG. Don't be shy. (*He slaps her bottom.*)

MEG. Oooh!

GOLDBERG. Walk up the boulevard. Let's have a look at you. What a carriage. What's your opinion, McCann? Like a Countess, nothing less. Madam, now turn about and promenade to the kitchen. What a deportment!

MCCANN (*to Stanley*). You can pour my Irish too.

GOLDBERG. You look like a Gladiola.

MEG. Stan, what about my dress?

GOLDBERG. One for the lady, one for the lady. Now madam—your glass.

MEG. Thank you.

GOLDBERG. Lift your glasses, ladies and gentlemen. We'll drink a toast.

MEG. Lulu isn't here.

GOLDBERG. It's past the hour. Now—who's going to propose the toast? Mrs. Boles, it can only be you.

MEG. Me?

GOLDBERG. Who else?

MEG. But what do I say?

GOLDBERG. Say what you feel. What you honestly feel. (*Meg looks uncertain.*) It's Stanley's birthday. Your Stanley. Look at him. Look at him and it'll come. Wait a minute, the light's too strong. Let's have proper lighting. McCann, have you got your torch?

MCCANN (*bringing small torch from his pocket*). Here.

GOLDBERG. Switch out the light and put on your torch.

(*McCann goes to door, switches off light, comes back, shines torch on Meg. Outside the window there is still a faint light.*)

Not on the lady, on the gentleman! You must shine it on the birthday boy.

(*McCann shines torch in Stanley's face.*)

Now, Mrs. Boles, it's all yours.

(*Pause.*)

MEG. I don't know what to say.

GOLDBERG. Look at him. Just look at him.

MEG. Isn't the light in his eyes?

GOLDBERG. No, no. Go on.

MEG. Well—it's very, very nice to be here tonight, in my house, and I want to propose a toast to Stanley, because it's his birthday, and he's lived here for a long while now, and he's my Stanley now. And I think he's a good boy, although sometimes he's bad. (*Appreciative laugh from Goldberg.*) And he's the only Stanley I know, and I know him better than all the world, although he doesn't think so. (*"Hear—hear" from Goldberg.*) Well, I could cry because I'm so happy, having him here and not gone away, on his birthday, and there isn't anything I wouldn't do for him, and all you good people here tonight. . . . (*She sobs.*)

GOLDBERG. Beautiful! A beautiful speech. Put the light on, McCann. (*McCann goes to door. Stanley remains still.*) That was a lovely toast. (*The light goes on. Lulu enters door left.*) (*Comforting Meg.*) Buck up now. Come on, smile at the birdy. That's better. We've got to drink yet. Ah, look who's here.

MEG. Lulu.

GOLDBERG. How do you do, Lulu? I'm Nat Goldberg. Stanley, a drink for your guest. You just missed the toast, my dear, and what a toast.

LULU. Did I?

GOLDBERG. Stanley, a drink for your guest. Stanley. (*Stanley hands a glass to Lulu.*) Right. Now raise your glasses.

Everyone standing up? No, not you, Stanley. You must sit down.

MCCANN. Yes, that's right. He must sit down.

GOLDBERG. You don't mind sitting down a minute? We're going to drink to you.

MEG. Come on!

(*Stanley sits in chair above table.*)

GOLDBERG. Right. Now Stanley's sat down. (*Taking the stage.*) Well, I want to say first that I've never been so touched to the heart as by the toast we've just heard. How often, in this day and age, do you come across real, true warmth? Once in a lifetime. Until a few minutes ago, ladies and gentlemen, I, like all of you, was asking the same question. What's happened to the love, the bonhomie, the unashamed expression of affection of the day before yesterday, that our mums taught us in the nursery?

MCCANN. Gone with the wind.

GOLDBERG. That's what I thought, until today. I believe in a good laugh, a day's fishing, a bit of gardening. I was very proud of my old greenhouse, made out of my own spit and faith. That's the sort of man I am. Not size but quality. A little Austin, tea in Fullers, a library book from Boots, and I'm satisfied. But just now, I say just now, the lady of the house said her piece and I for one am knocked over by the sentiments she expressed. Lucky is the man who's at the receiving end, that's what I say. (*Pause.*) How can I put it to you? We all wander on our tod through this world. It's a lonely pillow to kip on. Right!

LULU (*admiringly*). Right!

GOLDBERG. Agreed. But tonight, Lulu, McCann, we've known a great fortune. We've heard a lady extend the sum total of her devotion, in all its pride, plume and peacock, to a member of her own living race. Stanley, my heartfelt congratulations. I wish you, on behalf of us all a happy birthday. I'm sure you've never been a prouder man than you are today. Mazoltov! And may we only meet at Simchahs!

(*Lulu and Meg applaud.*)

Turn out the light, McCann, while we drink the toast.

LULU. That was a wonderful speech.

(*McCann switches out the light, comes back, shines torch in Stanley's face. The light outside the window is fainter.*)

GOLDBERG. Lift your glasses. Stanley—happy birthday.

MCCANN. Happy birthday.

LULU. Happy birthday.

MEG. Many happy returns of the day, Stan.

GOLDBERG. And well over the fast.

(*They all drink.*)

MEG (*kissing him*). Oh, Stanny . . .

GOLDBERG. Lights!

MCCANN. Right! (*He switches on light.*)

MEG. Clink my glass, Stan.

LULU. Mr. Goldberg—

GOLDBERG. Call me Nat.

MEG (*to McCann*). You clink my glass.

LULU (*to Goldberg*). You're empty. Let me fill you up.

GOLDBERG. It's a pleasure.

LULU. You're a marvellous speaker, Nat, you know that? Where did you learn to speak like that?

GOLDBERG. You liked it, eh?

LULU. Oh yes!

GOLDBERG. Well, my first chance to stand up and give a lecture was at the Ethical Hall, Bayswater. A wonderful opportunity. I'll never forget it. They were all there that night. Charlotte Street was empty. Of course, that's a good while ago.

LULU. What did you speak about?

GOLDBERG. The Necessary and the Possible. It went like a bomb. Since then I always speak at weddings.

(*Stanley is still. Goldberg sits left of table. Meg joins McCann D.R. Lulu D.L. McCann pours more Irish from the bottle, which he carries, into his glass.*)

MEG. Let's have some of yours.

MCCANN. In that?

MEG. Yes.

MCCANN. Are you used to mixing them?

MEG. No.

MCCANN. Sit down. Give me your glass.

(*Meg sits on shoe-box, D.R. Lulu, at table, pours more drink for Goldberg and herself, gives Goldberg his glass.*)

GOLDBERG. Thank you.

MEG (*to McCann*). Do you think I should?

GOLDBERG. Lulu, you're a big bouncy girl. Come and sit on my lap.

MCCANN. Why not?

LULU. Do you think I should?

GOLDBERG. Try it.

MEG (*sipping*). Very nice.

LULU. I'll bounce up to the ceiling.

MCCANN. I don't know how you can mix that stuff.

GOLDBERG. Take a chance.

MEG (*to McCann*). Sit down on this stool.

(*Lulu sits on Goldberg's lap.*)

MCCANN. This?

GOLDBERG. Comfortable?

LULU. Yes, thanks.

MCCANN (*sitting*). It's comfortable.

GOLDBERG. You know, there's a lot in your eyes.

LULU. And in yours too.

GOLDBERG. Do you think so?

LULU (*giggling*). Go on!

MCCANN (*to Meg*). Where'd you get it?

MEG. My father gave it to me.

LULU. I didn't know I was going to meet you here tonight.

MCCANN (*to Meg*). Ever been to Carrikmacross?

MEG (*drinking*). I've been to King's Cross.

LULU. You came right out of the blue, you know that?

GOLDBERG (*as she moves*). Mind how you go. You're cracking a rib.

MEG (*standing*). I want to dance!

(*Lulu and Goldberg look into each other's eyes. McCann drinks. Meg crosses to Stanley.*)

Stanley. Dance.

(*Stanley sits still. Meg dances round the room alone, comes back to McCann, who fills her glass. She sits.*)

LULU (*to Goldberg*). Shall I tell you something?

GOLDBERG. What?

LULU. I trust you.

GOLDBERG (*lifting glass*). Gezunteheit.

LULU. Have you got a wife?

GOLDBERG. I had a wife. What a wife. Listen to this. Friday, of an afternoon, I'd take myself for a little constitutional, down over the park. Eh, do me a favour, just sit on the table a minute, will you? (*Lulu sit on table. He stretches and continues.*) A little constitutional. I'd say hullo to the little boys, the little girls—I never made distinctions—and then back I'd go, back to my bungalow with the flat roof. 'Simey,' my wife used to shout, 'quick, before it gets cold!' And there on the table what would I see? The nicest piece of rollmop and pickled cucumber you could wish to find on a plate.

LULU. I thought your name was Nat.

GOLDBERG. She called me Simey.

LULU. I bet you were a good husband.

GOLDBERG. You should have seen her funeral.

LULU. Why?

GOLDBERG (*draws in breath, wags head*). What a funeral.

MEG (*to McCann*). My father was going to take me to Ireland once. But then he went away by himself.

LULU (*to Goldberg*). Do you think you knew me when I was a little girl?

GOLDBERG. Were you a nice little girl?

LULU. I was.

MEG. I don't know if he went to Ireland.

GOLDBERG. Maybe I played piggy-back with you.

LULU. Maybe you did.

MEG. He didn't take me.

GOLDBERG. Or pop goes the weasel.

LULU. Is that a game?

GOLDBERG. Sure it's a game!

MCCANN. Why didn't he take you to Ireland?

LULU. You're tickling me!

GOLDBERG. You should worry.

LULU. I've always liked older men. They can soothe you.

(*They embrace.*)

MCCANN. I know a place. Roscrea. Mother Nolan's.

MEG. There was a night-light in my room, when I was a little girl.

MCCANN. One time I stayed there all night with the boys. Singing and drinking all night.

MEG. And my Nanny used to sit up with me, and sing songs to me.

MCCANN. And a plate of fry in the morning. Now where am I?

MEG. My little room was pink. I had a pink carpet and pink curtains, and I had musical boxes all over the room. And they played me to sleep. And my father was a very big doctor. That's why I never had any complaints. I was cared for, and I had little sisters and brothers in other rooms, all different colours.

MCCANN. Tullamore, where are you?

MEG (*to McCann*). Give us a drop more.

MCCANN (*filling her glass, singing*). Glorio, Glorio, to the bold Fenian men!

MEG. Oh, what a lovely voice.

GOLDBERG. Give us a song, McCann.

LULU. A love song!

MCCANN (*reciting*). The night that poor Paddy was stretched, the boys they all paid him a visit.

GOLDBERG. A love song!

MCCANN (*in full voice, sings*).

> Oh, the Garden of Eden has vanished, they say,
> But I know the lie of it still.
> Just turn to the left at the foot of Ben Clay
> And stop when halfway to Coote Hill.
> It's there you will find it, I know sure enough,
> And it's whispering over to me:
> Come back, Paddy Reilly, to BallyJamesDuff,
> Come home, Paddy Reilly, to me!

LULU (*to Goldberg*). You're the dead image of the first man I ever loved.

GOLDBERG. It goes without saying.

MEG (*rising*). I want to play a game!

GOLDBERG. A game?

LULU. What game?

MEG. Any game.

LULU (*jumping up*). Yes, let's play a game.

GOLDBERG. What game?

MCCANN. Hide and seek.

LULU. Blind man's buff.

MEG. Yes!

GOLDBERG. You want to play blind man's buff?

LULU and MEG. Yes!

GOLDBERG. All right. Blind man's buff. Come on! Everyone up! (*Rising.*) McCann. Stanley—Stanley!

MEG. Stanley. Up.

GOLDBERG. What's the matter with him?

MEG (*bending over him*). Stanley, we're going to play a game. Oh, come on, don't be sulky, Stan.

(*Stanley rises. McCann rises.*)

GOLDBERG. Right! Now—who's going to be blind first?

LULU. Mrs. Boles.

MEG. Not me.

GOLDBERG. Of course you.

MEG. Who, me?

LULU (*taking scarf from her neck*). Here you are.

MCCANN. How do you play this game?

LULU (*tying scarf round Meg's eyes*). Haven't you ever played blind man's buff? Keep still, Mrs. Boles. You mustn't be touched. But you can't move after she's blind. You must stay where you are after she's blind. And if she touches you then you become blind. Turn round. How many fingers am I holding up?

MEG. I can't see.

LULU. Right.

GOLDBERG. Right! Everyone move about. McCann. Stanley. Now stop. Now still. Off you go!

(*Stanley is D.R. Meg moves about the room. Goldberg fondles Lulu at arm's length. Meg touches McCann.*)

MEG. Caught you!

LULU. Take off your scarf.

MEG. What lovely hair!

LULU (*untying scarf*). There.

MEG. It's you!

GOLDBERG. Put it on, McCann.

LULU (*tying it on McCann*). There. Turn round. How many fingers am I holding up?

MCCANN. I don't know.

GOLDBERG. Right! Everyone move about. Right. Stop! Still!

(*McCann begins to move.*)

MEG. Oh, this is lovely!

GOLDBERG. Quiet! Tch, tch, tch. Now—all move again. Stop! Still!

(*McCann moves about. Goldberg fondles Lulu at arm's length. McCann draws near Stanley. He stretches his arm and touches Stanley's glasses.*)

MEG. It's Stanley!

GOLDBERG (*to Lulu*). Enjoying the game?

MEG. It's your turn, Stan.

(*McCann takes off the scarf.*)

MCCANN (*to Stanley*). I'll take your glasses.

(*McCann takes Stanley's glasses.*)

MEG. Give me the scarf.

GOLDBERG (*holding Lulu*). Tie his scarf, Mrs. Boles.

MEG. That's what I'm doing.

LULU (*to Goldberg*). Kiss me. (*They kiss.*)

MEG (*to Stanley*). Can you see my nose?

GOLDBERG. He can't. Ready? Right! Everyone move. Stop! And still!

(*Stanley stands blindfolded. McCann backs slowly across stage to left. He breaks Stanley's glasses, snapping the frames. Meg is D.L., Lulu and Goldberg U.C., close together. Stanley begins to move, very slowly, across stage to left. McCann picks up drum and places it sideways in Stanley's path. Stanley walks into the drum and falls over with his foot caught in it.*)

MEG. Ooh!

GOLDBERG. Sssh!

(*Stanley rises. He begins to move towards Meg, dragging the drum on his foot. He reaches her and stops. His hands move towards her and they reach her throat. He begins to strangle her. McCann and Goldberg rush forward and throw him off.*)

BLACKOUT

(*There is now no light at all through the window. The stage is in darkness.*)

LULU. The lights!

GOLDBERG. What's happened?

LULU. The lights!

MCCANN. Wait a minute.

GOLDBERG. Where is he?

MCCANN. Let go of me!

LULU. Someone's touching me!

GOLDBERG. Who's this?

MEG. It's me!

MCCANN. Where is he?

MEG. Why has the light gone out?

GOLDBERG. Where's your torch? (*McCann shines torch in Goldberg's face.*) Not on me! (*McCann shifts torch. It is knocked from his hand and falls. It goes out.*)

MCCANN. My torch!

LULU. Oh God!

GOLDBERG. Where's your torch? Pick up your torch!

MCCANN. I can't find it.

LULU. Hold me. Hold me.

GOLDBERG. Get down on your knees. Help him find the torch.

LULU. I can't.

MCCANN. It's gone.

MEG. Why has the light gone out?

GOLDBERG. Everyone quiet! Help him find the torch.

(*Silence. Grunts from McCann and Goldberg on their knees.*)

(*Suddenly a sharp, sustained rat-a-tat on the side of the drum from the back of the room, with a stick. Silence. Whimpers from Lulu.*)

GOLDBERG. Over there. McCann!

MCCANN. Here.

GOLDBERG. Come to me, come to me. Easy. Over there.

(*Goldberg and McCann move up left of the table. Stanley moves down right of the table. Lulu suddenly perceives him moving towards her, screams, faints. Goldberg and McCann turn, stumble against each other.*)

GOLDBERG. What is it?

MCCANN. Who's that?

GOLDBERG. What is it?

(*In the darkness Stanley picks Lulu up and places her on the table.*)

MEG. It's Lulu!

(*Goldberg and McCann move down right.*)

GOLDBERG. Where is she?

MCCANN. She fell.

GOLDBERG. Where?

MCCANN. About here.

GOLDBERG. Help me pick her up.

MCCANN (*moving D.L.*). I can't find her.

GOLDBERG. She must be somewhere.

MCCANN. She's not here.

GOLDBERG (*moving D.L.*). She must be.

MCCANN. She's gone.

(*McCann finds torch on the floor, shines it at table and Stanley, Lulu is lying spread-eagled on the table, Stanley bent over her. Stanley, soon as torchlight hits him, begins to giggle. Goldberg and McCann move towards him. He backs, giggling, the torch on his face. They follow him U.L. He backs against the hatch, giggling. The torch draws closer. His giggle rises and grows as he flattens himself against the wall. Their figures converge upon him.*)

CURTAIN

ACT 3

The next morning. Petey enters left with paper and sits at table. He begins to read. Meg's voice comes through kitchen hatch.

MEG. Is that you, Stan?

(*Pause.*)

Stanny?

PETEY. Yes?

MEG. Is that you?

PETEY. It's me.

MEG (*appearing at hatch*). Oh, it's you. I've run out of corn-flakes.

PETEY. Well, what else have you got?

MEG. Nothing.

PETEY. Nothing?

MEG. Just a minute. (*She leaves hatch and enters by kitchen door.*) You got your paper?

PETEY. Yes.

MEG. Is it good?

PETEY. Not bad.

MEG. The two gentlemen had the last of the fry this morning.

PETEY. Oh, did they?

MEG. There's some tea in the pot though. (*She pours tea for him.*) I'm going out shopping in a minute. Get you something nice.

PETEY. Good.

MEG. Oh, I must sit down a minute. (*Sits right table.*)

PETEY. How are you then, this morning?

MEG. I've got a splitting headache.

PETEY (*reading*). You slept like a log last night.

MEG. Did I?

PETEY. Why don't you have a walk down to the shops? It's fresh out. It'll clear your head.

MEG. Will it?

PETEY. Bound to.

MEG. I will then. Did I sleep like a log?

PETEY. Dead out.

MEG. I must have been tired. (*She looks about the room and sees broken drum in fireplace.*) Oh, look. (*She rises and picks it up.*) The drum's broken. (*Petey looks up.*) Why is it broken?

PETEY. I don't know.

(*She hits it with her hand.*)

MEG. It still makes a noise.

PETEY. You can always get another one.

MEG (*sadly*). It was probably broken in the party. I don't remember it being broken though, in the party. (*She puts it down.*) What a shame.

PETEY. You can always get another one, Meg.

MEG. Well, at least he did have it on his birthday, didn't he? Like I wanted him to.

PETEY (*reading*). Yes.

MEG. Have you seen him down yet? (*Petey does not answer.*) Petey.

PETEY. What?

MEG. Have you seen him down?

PETEY. Who?

MEG. Stanley.

PETEY. No.

MEG. Nor have I. That boy should be up. He's late for his breakfast.

PETEY. There isn't any breakfast.

MEG. Yes, but he doesn't know that. I'm going to call him.

PETEY (*quickly*). No, don't do that, Meg. Let him sleep.

MEG. But you say he stays in bed too much.

PETEY. Let him sleep . . . this morning. Leave him.

MEG. I've been up once, with his cup of tea. But Mr. McCann opened the door. He said they were talking. He said he'd made him one. He must have been up early. I don't know what they were talking about. I was surprised. Because Stanley's usually fast asleep when I wake him. But he wasn't this morning. I heard him talking. (*Pause.*) Do you think they know each other? I think they're old friends. Stanley had a lot of friends. I know he did. (*Pause.*) I didn't give him his tea. He'd already had one. I came down again, and went on with my work. Then, after a bit, they came down to breakfast. Stanley must have gone to sleep again.

(*Pause.*)

PETEY. When are you going to do your shopping, Meg?

MEG. Yes, I must. (*Collecting bag.*) I've got a rotten headache. (*She goes to back door, stops suddenly, turns.*) Did you see what's outside this morning?

PETEY. What?

MEG. That big car.

PETEY. Yes.

MEG. It wasn't there yesterday. Did you . . . did you have a look inside it?

PETEY. I had a peep.

MEG (*coming down tensely, whispering*). Is there anything in it?

PETEY. In it?

MEG. Yes.

PETEY. What do you mean, in it?

MEG. Inside it.

PETEY. What sort of thing?

MEG. Well . . . I mean . . . is there . . . is there a wheelbarrow in it?

PETEY. A wheelbarrow?

MEG. Yes.

PETEY. I didn't see one.

MEG. You didn't? Are you sure?

PETEY. What would Mr. Goldberg want with a wheelbarrow?

MEG. Mr. Goldberg?

PETEY. It's his car.

MEG (*relieved*). His car? Oh, I didn't know it was his car.

PETEY. Of course it's his car.

MEG. Oh, I feel better.

PETEY. What are you on about?

MEG. Oh, I do feel better.

PETEY. You go and get a bit of air.

MEG. Yes, I will. I will. I'll go and get the shopping. (*She goes towards back door. A door slams upstairs. She turns.*) It's Stanley! He's coming down—what am I going to do about his breakfast? (*She rushes into kitchen.*) Petey, what shall I give him? (*She looks through hatch.*) There's no cornflakes. (*They both gaze at door. Enter Goldberg. He halts at door, as he meets their gaze, then smiles.*)

GOLDBERG. A reception committee!

MEG. Oh, I thought it was Stanley.

GOLDBERG. You find a resemblance?

MEG. Oh no. You look quite different.

GOLDBERG (*coming into room*). Different build, of course.

MEG (*entering from kitchen*). I thought he was coming down for his breakfast. He hasn't had his breakfast yet.

GOLDBERG. Your wife makes a very nice cup of tea, Mr. Boles, you know that?

PETEY. Yes, she does sometimes. Sometimes she forgets.

MEG. Is he coming down?

GOLDBERG. Down? Of course he's coming down. On a lovely sunny day like this he shouldn't come down? He'll be up and about in next to no time. (*He sits above table.*) And what a breakfast he's going to get.

MEG. Mr. Goldberg.

GOLDBERG. Yes?

MEG. I didn't know that was your car outside.

GOLDBERG. You like it?

MEG. Are you going to go for a ride?

GOLDBERG (*to Petey*). A smart car, eh?

PETEY. Nice shine on it all right.

GOLDBERG. What is old is good, take my tip. There's room there. Room in the front, and room in the back. (*He strokes teapot.*) The pot's hot. More tea, Mr. Boles?

PETEY. No thanks.

GOLDBERG (*pouring tea*). That car? That car's never let me down.

MEG. Are you going to go for a ride?

GOLDBERG (*ruminatively*). And the boot. A beautiful boot. There's just room . . . for the right amount.

MEG. Well, I'd better be off now. (*She moves to back door, turns.*) Petey, when Stanley comes down . . .

PETEY. Yes?

MEG. Tell him I won't be long.

PETEY. I'll tell him.

MEG (*vaguely*). I won't be long. (*She exits.*)

GOLDBERG (*sipping his tea*). A good woman. A charming woman. My mother was the same. My wife was identical.

PETEY. How is he this morning?

GOLDBERG. Who?

PETEY. Stanley. Is he any better?

GOLDBERG (*a little uncertainly*). Oh . . . a little better, I think, a little better. Of course, I'm not really qualified to say, Mr. Boles. I mean, I haven't got the . . . the qualifications. The best thing would be if someone with the proper . . . mnn . . . qualifications . . . was to have a look at him. Someone with a few letters after his name. It makes all the difference.

PETEY. Yes.

GOLDBERG. Anyway, Dermot's with him at the moment. He's . . . keeping him company.

PETEY. Dermot?

GOLDBERG. Yes.

PETEY. It's a terrible thing.

GOLDBERG (*Sighs*). Yes. The birthday celebration was too much for him.

PETEY. What came over him?

GOLDBERG (*sharply*). What came over him? Breakdown, Mr. Boles. Pure and simple. Nervous breakdown.

PETEY. But what brought it on so suddenly?

GOLDBERG (*rising, moving up*). Well, Mr. Boles, it can happen in all sorts of ways. A friend of mine was telling me about it only the other day. We'd both been concerned with another case—not entirely similar, of course, but . . . quite alike, quite alike. (*He pauses.*) Anyway, he was telling me, you see, this friend of mine, that sometimes it happens gradual—day by day it grows and grows and grows . . . day by day. And then other times it happens all at once. Poof! Like that! The nerves break. There's no guarantee how it's going to happen, but with certain people . . . it's a foregone conclusion.

PETEY. Really?

GOLDBERG. Yes. This friend of mine—he was telling me about it—only the other day. (*He stands uneasily for a moment. He then brings out a cigarette case and takes a cigarette.*) Have an Abdullah.

PETEY. No, no, I don't take them.

GOLDBERG. Once in a while I treat myself to a cigarette. An Abdullah, perhaps, or a . . . (*He snaps his fingers.*)

PETEY. What a night.

(*Goldberg lights his cigarette with a lighter.*)

Came in the front door and all the lights were out. Put a shilling in the slot, came in here and the party was over.

GOLDBERG (*coming down*). You put a shilling in the slot?

PETEY. Yes.

GOLDBERG. And the lights came on.

PETEY. Yes, then I came in here.

GOLDBERG (*with a short laugh*). I could have sworn it was a fuse.

PETEY (*continuing*). There was dead silence. Couldn't hear a thing. So I went upstairs and your friend—Dermot—met me on the landing. And he told me.

GOLDBERG (*sharply*). Who?

PETEY. Your friend—Dermot.

GOLDBERG (*heavily*). Dermot. Yes. (*He sits.*)

PETEY. They get over it sometimes though, don't they? I mean, they can recover from it, can't they?

GOLDBERG. Recover? Yes, sometimes they recover, in one way or another.

PETEY. I mean, he might have recovered by now, mightn't he?

GOLDBERG. It's conceivable. Conceivable.

(*Petey rises and picks up teapot and cup.*)

PETEY. Well, if he's no better by lunchtime I'll go and get hold of a doctor.

GOLDBERG (*briskly*). It's all taken care of, Mr. Boles. Don't worry yourself.

PETEY (*dubiously*). What do you mean?

(*A door slams upstairs. They look towards the door. Enter McCann with two suitcases.*)

Oh, it's you. All packed up?

(*Petey takes teapot and cups into kitchen. McCann crosses left and puts down suitcases. He goes up to window and looks out.*)

GOLDBERG. Well? (*McCann does not answer.*) McCann. I asked you well.

MCCANN (*without turning*). Well what?

GOLDBERG. What's what? (*McCann does not answer.*) What is what?

MCCANN (*turning to look at Goldberg, grimly*). I'm not going up there again.

GOLDBERG. Why not?

MCCANN. I'm not going up there again.

GOLDBERG. What's going on now?

MCCANN (*moving down*). He's quiet now. He stopped all that . . . talking a while ago.

(*Petey appears at kitchen hatch, unnoticed.*)

GOLDBERG. When will he be ready?

MCCANN (*sullenly*). You can go up yourself next time.

GOLDBERG. What's the matter with you?

MCCANN (*quietly*). I gave him . . .

GOLDBERG. What?

MCCANN. I gave him his glasses.

GOLDBERG. Wasn't he glad to get them back?

MCCANN. The frames are bust.

GOLDBERG. How did that happen?

MCCANN. He tried to fit the eyeholes into his eyes. I left him doing it.

PETEY (*at kitchen door*). There's some Sellotape somewhere. We can stick them together.

(*Goldberg and McCann turn to see him. Pause.*)

GOLDBERG. Sellotape? No, no, that's all right, Mr. Boles. It'll keep him quiet for the time being, keep his mind off other things.

PETEY (*moving down*). What about a doctor?

GOLDBERG. It's all taken care of.

(*McCann moves over right to shoe-box, takes out brush and brushes his shoes.*)

PETEY (*in to table*). I think he needs one.

GOLDBERG. I agree with you. It's all taken care of. We'll give him a bit of time to settle down, and then I'll take him to Monty.

PETEY. You're going to take him to a doctor?

GOLDBERG (*staring at him*). Sure. Monty.

(*Pause. McCann brushes his shoes. Petey sits left table.*)

So Mrs. Boles has gone out to get us something nice for lunch?

PETEY. That's right.

GOLDBERG. Unfortunately we may be gone by then.

PETEY. Will you?

GOLDBERG. By then we may be gone.

MCCANN (*breaking in*). You know that girl?

GOLDBERG. What girl?

MCCANN. That girl had nightmares in the night.

GOLDBERG. Those weren't nightmares.

MCCANN. No?

GOLDBERG (*irritably*). I said no.

MCCANN. How do you know?

GOLDBERG. I got up. I went to see what was the matter.

MCCANN. I didn't know that.

GOLDBERG (*sharply*). It may be that you didn't know that. Nevertheless, that's what happened.

MCCANN. Well, what was the matter?

GOLDBERG. Nothing. Nothing at all. She was just having a bit of a sing-song.

MCCANN. A sing-song?

GOLDBERG (*to Petey*). Sure. You know how young girls sing. She was singing.

MCCANN. So what happened then?

GOLDBERG. I joined in. We had a few songs. Yes. We sang a few of the old ballads and then she went to bye-byes.

(*Petey rises.*)

PETEY. Well, I think I'll see how my peas are getting on, in the meantime.

GOLDBERG. The meantime?

PETEY. While we're waiting.

GOLDBERG. Waiting for what? (*Petey walks towards back door.*) Aren't you going back to the beach?

PETEY. No, not yet. Give me a call when he comes down, will you, Mr. Goldberg?

GOLDBERG (*earnestly*). You'll have a crowded beach today . . . on a day like this. They'll be lying on their backs, swimming out to sea. My life. What about the deck-chairs? Are the deck-chairs ready?

PETEY. I put them all out this morning.

GOLDBERG. But what about the tickets? Who's going to take the tickets?

PETEY. That's all right. That'll be all right, Mr. Goldberg. Don't you worry about that. I'll be back.

(*He exits. Goldberg rises, goes to the window, looks after him. McCann crosses to left table, sits, picks up paper and begins to tear it into strips.*)

GOLDBERG. Is everything ready?

MCCANN. Sure.

(*Goldberg walks heavily, brooding, to table. He sits right of it, notices what McCann is doing.*)

GOLDBERG. Stop doing that!

MCCANN. What?

GOLDBERG. Why do you do that all the time? It's childish, it's pointless. It's without a solitary point.

MCCANN. What's the matter with you today?

GOLDBERG. Questions, questions. Stop asking me so many questions. What do you think I am?

(*McCann studies him. He then folds the paper, leaving the strips inside.*)

MCCANN. Well?

(*Pause. Goldberg leans back in the chair, his eyes closed.*)

MCCANN. Well?

GOLDBERG (*with fatigue*). Well what?

MCCANN. What's what?

GOLDBERG. Yes, what is what . . .

MCCANN. Do we wait or do we go and get him?

GOLDBERG (*slowly*). You want to go and get him?

MCCANN. I want to get it over.

GOLDBERG. That's understandable.

MCCANN. So do we wait or do we—?

GOLDBERG (*interrupting*). I don't know why, but I feel knocked out. I feel a bit. . . . It's uncommon for me.

MCCANN. Is that so?

GOLDBERG. It's unusual.

MCCANN (*rising swiftly and going behind Goldberg's chair*). (*Hissing.*) Let's finish and go. Let's get it over and go. Get the thing done. Let's finish the bloody thing. Let's get the thing done and go!

(*Pause.*)

Will I go up?

(*Pause.*)

Nat!

(*Goldberg sits humped. McCann slips to his side.*)

Simey!

GOLDBERG (*opening his eyes, regarding McCann*). What—did—you—call—me?

MCCANN. Who?

GOLDBERG (*murderously*). Don't call me that! (*He seizes McCann by the throat.*) NEVER CALL ME THAT!

MCCANN (*writhing*). Nat, Nat, Nat, NAT! I called you Nat. I was asking you, Nat. Honest to God. Just a question, that's all, just a question, do you see, do you follow me?

GOLDBERG (*jerking him away*). What question?

MCCANN. Will I go up?

GOLDBERG (*violently*). Up? I thought you weren't going to go up there again?

MCCANN. What do you mean? Why not?

GOLDBERG. You said so!

MCCANN. I never said that!

GOLDBERG. No?

MCCANN (*from the floor, to the room at large*). Who said that? I never said that! I'll go up now!

(*He jumps up and rushes to door left.*)

GOLDBERG. Wait!

(*He stretches his arms to the arms of the chair.*)

Come here.

(*McCann approaches him very slowly.*)

I want your opinion. Have a look in my mouth.

(*He opens his mouth wide.*)

Take a good look.

(*McCann looks.*)

You know what I mean?

(*McCann peers.*)

You know what? I've never lost a tooth. Not since the day I was born. Nothing's changed. (*He gets up.*) That's why I've reached my position, McCann. Because I've always been as fit as a fiddle. All my life I've said the same. Play up, play up, and play the game. Honour thy father and thy mother. All along the line. Follow the line, the line, McCann, and you can't go wrong. What do you think, I'm a self-made man? No! I sat where I was told to sit. I kept my eye on the ball. School? Don't talk to me about school. Top in all subjects. And for why? Because I'm telling you, I'm telling you, follow my line? follow my mental? Learn by heart. Never write down a thing. No. And don't go too near the water. And you'll find—that what I say is true.

Because I believe that the world . . . (*Vacant.*) . . .

Because I believe that the world . . . (*Desperate.*) . . .

BECAUSE I BELIEVE THAT THE WORLD . . . (*Lost.*) . . .

(*He sits in chair.*)

Sit down, McCann, sit here where I can look at you.

(*McCann kneels in front of the table.*)

(*Intensely, with growing certainty.*) My father said to me, Benny, Benny, he said, come here. He was dying. I knelt down. By him day and night. Who else was there? Forgive, Benny, he said, and let live. Yes, Dad. Go home to your wife. I will, Dad. Keep an eye open for low-lives, for schnorrers and for layabouts. He didn't mention names. I lost my life in the service of others, he said, I'm not ashamed. Do your duty and keep your observations. Always bid good morning to the neighbours. Never, never forget your family, for they are the rock, the constitution and the core! If you're ever in any difficulties Uncle Barney will see you in the clear. I knelt down. (*He kneels, facing McCann.*) I swore on the good book. And I knew the word I had to remember—Respect! Because McCann—(*Gently.*) Seamus—who came before your father? His father. And who came before him? Before him? . . . (*Vacant—triumphant.*) Who came before your father's father but your father's father's mother! Your great-gran-granny.

(*Silence. He slowly rises.*)

And that's why I've reached my position, McCann. Because I've always been as fit as a fiddle. My motto. Work hard and play hard. Not a day's illness. (*He emits a high-pitched wheeze-whine. He looks round.*) What was that?

MCCANN. What?

GOLDBERG. I heard something.

MCCANN. What was it?

GOLDBERG. A noise. A funny noise.

MCCANN. That was you.

GOLDBERG. Me?

MCCANN. Sure.

GOLDBERG (*interested*). What, you heard it too?

MCCANN. I did.

GOLDBERG. It was me, eh? (*A slight chuckle.*) Huh. What did I do?

MCCANN. You gave . . . you let out a class of a wheeze, like.

GOLDBERG. Go on! (*He laughs. They both laugh.*) (*Suddenly, quickly, anxiously.*) Where's your spoon? You got your spoon?

MCCANN (*producing it*). Here.

GOLDBERG. Test me. (*He opens his mouth and sticks out his tongue.*) Here. (*McCann places spoon on Goldberg's tongue.*) Aaaahhh! Aaaaahhhh!

MCCANN. Perfect condition.

GOLDBERG. You really mean that?

MCCANN. My word of honour.

GOLDBERG. So now you can understand why I occupy such a position, eh?

MCCANN. I can, of course.

(*Goldberg laughs. They both laugh.*)

GOLDBERG (*stopping*). All the same, give me a blow.

(*Pause.*)

Blow in my mouth.

(*McCann stands, puts his hands on his knees, bends, and blows in Goldberg's mouth.*)

GOLDBERG. One for the road.

(*McCann blows again in his mouth. Goldberg breathes deeply, shakes his head, bounds from the chair.*)

Right. We're here. Wait a minute, just a minute. You got everything packed?

MCCANN. I have.

GOLDBERG. The expander?

MCCANN. Yes.

GOLDBERG. Fetch it to me.

MCCANN. Now?

GOLDBERG. At once.

(*McCann goes to suitcase and takes out a chest expander. He gives it to Goldberg, who pulls it playfully, masterfully, bearing down on McCann. They both chuckle. Goldberg pulls it to full stretch. It breaks. He smiles.*)

What did I tell you?

(*He throws it at McCann. Enter left, Lulu.*)

Well, look who's here.

(*McCann looks at them, goes to door.*)

MCCANN (*at door*). I'll give you five minutes. (*He exits with expander.*)

GOLDBERG. Come over here.

LULU. What's going to happen?

GOLDBERG. Come over here.

LULU. No, thank you.

GOLDBERG. What's the matter? You got the needle to Uncle Natey?

LULU. I'm going.

GOLDBERG. Have a game of pontoon first, for old time's sake.

LULU. I've had enough games.

GOLDBERG. A girl like you, at your age, at your time of health, and you don't take to games?

LULU. You're very smart.

GOLDBERG. Anyway, who says you don't take to them?

LULU. Do you think I'm like all the other girls?

GOLDBERG. Are all the other girls like that, too?

LULU. I don't know about any other girls.

GOLDBERG. Nor me. I've never touched another woman.

LULU (*distressed*). What would my father say, if he knew? And what would Eddie say?

GOLDBERG. Eddie?

LULU. He was my first love, Eddie was. And whatever happened, it was pure. With him! He didn't come into my room at night with a briefcase!

GOLDBERG. Who opened the briefcase, me or you?

LULU. You got round me. It was only because I was so upset by last night.

GOLDBERG. Lulu, schmulu, let bygones be bygones, do me a turn. Kiss and make up.

LULU. I wouldn't touch you.

GOLDBERG. And today I'm leaving.

LULU. You're leaving?

GOLDBERG. Today.

LULU (*with growing anger*). You used me for a night. A passing fancy.

GOLDBERG. Who used who?

LULU. You made use of me by cunning when my defences were down.

GOLDBERG. Who took them down?

LULU. That's what you did. You quenched your ugly thirst. You took advantage of me when I was overwrought. I wouldn't do those things again, not even for a Sultan!

GOLDBERG. One night doesn't make a harem.

LULU. You taught me things a girl shouldn't know before she's been married at least three times!

GOLDBERG. Now you're a jump ahead! What are you complaining about?

(*Enter McCann quickly.*)

LULU. You didn't appreciate me for myself. You took all those liberties only to satisfy your appetite.

GOLDBERG. Now you're giving me indigestion.

LULU. And after all that had happened. An old woman nearly killed and a man gone mad—How can I go back behind that counter now? Oh Nat, why did you do it?

GOLDBERG. You wanted me to do it, Lulula, so I did it.

MCCANN. That's fair enough.

LULU (*turning*). Oh!

MCCANN (*advancing*). You had a long sleep, Miss.

LULU (*backing U.L.*). Me?

MCCANN. Your sort, you spend too much time in bed.

LULU. What do you mean?

MCCANN. Have you got anything to confess?

LULU. What?

MCCANN (*savagely*). Confess!

LULU. Confess what?

MCCANN. Down on your knees and confess!

LULU. What does he mean?

GOLDBERG. Confess. What can you lose.

LULU. What, to him?

GOLDBERG. He's only been unfrocked six months.

MCCANN. Kneel down, woman, and tell me the latest!

LULU (*retreating to back door*). I've seen everything that's happened. I know what's going on. I've got a pretty shrewd idea.

MCCANN (*advancing*). I've seen you hanging about the Rock of Cashel, profaning the soil with your goings-on. Out of my sight!

LULU. I'm going.

(*She exits. McCann goes to door left, and goes out. He ushers in Stanley, who is dressed in striped trousers, black jacket, and white collar. He carries a bowler hat in one hand and his broken glasses in the other. He is clean-shaven. McCann follows and closes the door. Goldberg meets Stanley, seats him in chair right and puts his hat on the table.*)

GOLDBERG. How are you, Stan?

(*Pause.*)

Are you feeling any better?

(*Pause.*)

What's the matter with your glasses?

(*Goldberg bends to look.*)

They're broken. A pity.

(*Stanley stares blankly at the floor.*)

MCCANN (*at table*). He looks better, doesn't he?

GOLDBERG. Much better.

MCCANN. A new man.

GOLDBERG. You know what we'll do?

MCCANN. What?

GOLDBERG. We'll buy him another pair.

(*They begin to woo him, gently and with relish. During the following sequence Stanley shows no reaction. He remains with no movement, where he sits.*)

MCCANN. Out of our own pockets.

GOLDBERG. It goes without saying. Between you and me, Stan, it's about time you had a new pair of glasses.

MCCANN. You can't see straight.

GOLDBERG. It's true. You've been cockeyed for years.

MCCANN. Now you're even more cockeyed.

GOLDBERG. He's right. You've gone from bad to worse.

MCCANN. Worse than worse.

GOLDBERG. You need a long convalescence.

MCCANN. A change of air.

GOLDBERG. Somewhere over the rainbow.

MCCANN. Where angels fear to tread.

GOLDBERG. Exactly.

MCCANN. You're in a rut.

GOLDBERG. You look anaemic.

MCCANN. Rheumatic.

GOLDBERG. Myopic.

MCCANN. Epileptic.

GOLDBERG. You're on the verge.

MCCANN. You're a dead duck.

GOLDBERG. But we can save you.

MCCANN. From a worse fate.

GOLDBERG. True.

MCCANN. Undeniable.

GOLDBERG. From now on, we'll be the hub of your wheel.

MCCANN. We'll renew your season ticket.

GOLDBERG. We'll take tuppence off your morning tea.

MCCANN. We'll give you a discount on all inflammable goods.

GOLDBERG. We'll watch over you.

MCCANN. Advise you.

GOLDBERG. Give you proper care and treatment.

MCCANN. Let you use the club bar.

GOLDBERG. Keep a table reserved.

MCCANN. Help you acknowledge the fast days.

GOLDBERG. Bake you cakes.

MCCANN. Help you kneel on kneeling days.

GOLDBERG. Give you a free pass.

MCCANN. Take you for constitutionals.

GOLDBERG. Give you hot tips.

MCCANN. We'll provide the skipping rope.

GOLDBERG. The vest and pants.

MCCANN. The ointment.

GOLDBERG. The hot poultice.

MCCANN. The fingerstall.

GOLDBERG. The abdomen belt.

MCCANN. The ear plugs.

GOLDBERG. The baby powder.

MCCANN. The back scratcher.

GOLDBERG. The spare tyre.

MCCANN. The stomach pump.

GOLDBERG. The oxygen tent.

MCCANN. The prayer wheel.

GOLDBERG. The plaster of Paris.

MCCANN. The crash helmet.

GOLDBERG. The crutches.

MCCANN. A day and night service.

GOLDBERG. All on the house.

MCCANN. That's it.

GOLDBERG. We'll make a man of you.

MCCANN. And a woman.

GOLDBERG. You'll be re-orientated.

MCCANN. You'll be rich.

GOLDBERG. You'll be adjusted.

MCCANN. You'll be our pride and joy.

GOLDBERG. You'll be a mensch.

MCCANN. You'll be a success.

GOLDBERG. You'll be integrated.

MCCANN. You'll give orders.

GOLDBERG. You'll make decisions.

MCCANN. You'll be a magnate.

GOLDBERG. A statesman.

MCCANN. You'll own yachts.

GOLDBERG. Animals.

MCCANN. Animals.

(*Goldberg looks at McCann.*)

GOLDBERG. I said animals. (*He turns back to Stanley.*) You'll be able to make or break, Stan. By my life. (*Silence. Stanley is still.*) Well? What do you say?

(*Stanley's head lifts very slowly and turns in Goldberg's direction.*)

GOLDBERG. What do you think? Eh, boy?

(*Stanley begins to clench and unclench his eyes.*)

MCCANN. What's your opinion, sir? Of this prospect, sir?

GOLDBERG. Prospect. Sure. Sure it's a prospect.

(*Stanley's hands clutching his glasses begin to tremble.*)

What's your opinion of such a prospect? Eh, Stanley?

(*Stanley concentrates, his mouth opens, he attempts to speak, fails, emits sounds from his throat.*)

STAN. Uh-gug . . . uh-gug . . . eeehhh-gag . . . (*On the breath.*) caahh . . . caahh . . .

(*They watch him. He draws a long breath which shudders down his body. He concentrates.*)

GOLDBERG. Well, Stanny boy, what do you say, eh?

(*They watch. He concentrates. His head lowers, his chin draws into his chest, he crouches.*)

STAN. Uh-gughh . . . uh-gughhh . . .

MCCANN. What's your opinion, sir?

STAN. Caaahhh . . . caaahhh . . .

MCCANN. Mr. Webber! What's your opinion?

GOLDBERG. What do you say, Stan? What do you think of the prospect?

MCCANN. What's your opinion of the prospect?

(*Stanley's body shudders, relaxes, his head drops, he becomes still again, stooped. Petey enters from D.L. door.*)

GOLDBERG. Still the same old Stan. Come with us. Come on, boy.

MCCANN. Come along with us.

PETEY. Where are you taking him?

(*They turn. Silence.*)

GOLDBERG. We're taking him to Monty.

PETEY. He can stay here.

GOLDBERG. Don't be silly.

PETEY. We can look after him here.

GOLDBERG. Why do you want to look after him?

PETEY. He's my guest.

GOLDBERG. He needs special treatment.

PETEY. We'll find someone.

GOLDBERG. No. Monty's the best there is. Bring him, McCann.

(*They help Stanley out of the chair. Goldberg puts the bowler hat on Stanley's head. They all three move towards the door L.*)

PETEY. Leave him alone!

(*They stop. Goldberg studies him.*)

GOLDBERG (*insidiously*). Why don't you come with us, Mr. Boles?

MCCANN. Yes, why don't you come with us?

GOLDBERG. Come with us to Monty. There's plenty of room in the car.

(*Petey makes no move. They pass him and reach the door. McCann opens the door, picks up suitcases.*)

PETEY (*broken*). Stan, don't let them tell you what to do!

(*They exit.*)

(*Silence. Petey stands. Front door slams. Sound of car starting. Sound of car going away. Silence. Petey slowly goes to table. He sits chair left. He picks up the paper, opens it. The strips fall to the floor. He looks down at them. Meg comes past window U.L. and enters by back door. Petey studies front page of paper.*)

MEG (*coming down*). The car's gone.

PETEY. Yes.

MEG. Have they gone?

PETEY. Yes.

MEG. Won't they be in for lunch?

PETEY. No.

MEG. Oh, what a shame. (*She puts her bag on the table.*) It's hot out. (*She hangs her coat on a hook.*) What are you doing?

PETEY. Reading.

MEG. Is it good?

PETEY. All right.

(*She sits above table.*)

MEG. Where's Stan?

(*Pause.*)

Is Stan down yet, Petey?

PETEY. No . . . he's . . .

MEG. Is he still in bed?

PETEY. Yes, he's . . . still asleep.

MEG. Still? He'll be late for his breakfast.

PETEY. Let him . . . sleep.

(*Pause.*)

MEG. Wasn't it a lovely party last night?

PETEY. I wasn't there.

MEG. Weren't you?

PETEY. I came in afterwards.

MEG. Oh.

(*Pause.*)

It was a lovely party. I haven't laughed so much for years. We had dancing and singing. And games. You should have been there.

PETEY. It was good, eh?

(*Pause.*)

MEG. I was the belle of the ball.

PETEY. Were you?

MEG. Oh yes. They all said I was.

PETEY. I bet you were, too.

MEG. Oh, it's true. I was.

(*Pause.*)

I know I was.

CURTAIN

TOPICS FOR CRITICAL THINKING AND WRITING

 ### THE PLAY ON THE PAGE

1. Why a birthday party? Would any holiday have done as well, for instance, a New Year's Eve celebration of a patriotic observance? Refer to elements of characterization, plot, setting, and theme in your response.

2. Do you find the seaside setting essential to the overall effect of the play? Could Meg and Petey's boardinghouse just as easily be located in a large city or a suburban community?

3. Taking into account the characters of Meg and Lulu and references to other women by a number of the characters, what view of women do you note in *The Birthday Party*?

4. If you were taking a psychological approach to analyzing the play, what might you say about Stanley? about father-son relationships?

5. In a 1960 newspaper interview in England, Pinter said, "Everything is funny; the greatest earnestness is funny;

even tragedy is funny. And I think what I try to do in my plays is to get to this recognizable reality of the absurdity of what we do and how we behave and how we speak." Comment on the "funny" aspects of *The Birthday Party* and the effect the comedy has for a reader or an audience member.

6. Considering the different ways Pinter uses language—ordinary speeches, quick one-liners, silence, and so forth—what does he seem to imply about human communication and relationships?

7. Harold Clurman, in his introduction to *Nine Plays of the Modern Theater*, refers to the "dis-ease" in *The Birthday Party*. Do you find both dis-ease and disease in the play? Support your opinions with specific reference to characters and moments in the play.

THE PLAY ON THE STAGE

8. Imagine that you are directing a production of *The Birthday Party*. Describe the effect you would wish to achieve in the closing moments of each act. Explain your specific means, such as blocking, lighting, and sound.

9. What are some of the challenges for the actor playing Petey? for the actress playing Lulu?

10. Would you include sound effects in a staging of *The Birthday Party*? Explain your reasoning with reference to four of five different moments in the play.

11. Offer some advice for the actors playing McCann and Goldberg. Following are some questions to consider: Should the actors playing these roles use Irish and Jewish accents, respectively? Should the men seem friendly to each other? Should Goldberg be fatherly toward McCann? Is Goldberg pompous? vulgar? expansive? Should the men have similar physical builds? Do the men make physical contact with each other? (You are encouraged to raise—and answer—other questions along these lines.)

12. Outside of the advice concerning actual delivery of his lines, what advice would you give the actor playing Stanley? How should he stand, walk, sit, hold his head? What changes would be evident as the play proceeds? Choose one segment from each act for close analysis.

13. In a 1994 staging of *The Birthday Party* at Southern Illinois University in Edwardsville, the set designer placed a small, mottled mirror on an upstage wall. What do you think of this choice? What other props or set details would you suggest for a production?

A CONTEXT FOR *THE BIRTHDAY PARTY*

Harold Pinter
INTERVIEW

[In October 1966 Lawrence M. Bensky interviewed Pinter. Following is the material from the interview that relates to *The Birthday Party*.]

Bensky: Has writing always been so easy for you?

Pinter: Well, I had been writing for years, hundreds of poems and short pieces of prose. About a dozen had been published in little magazines. I wrote a novel as well; it's not good enough to be published, really, and never has been. After I wrote *The Room*, which I didn't see performed for a few weeks, I started to work immediately on *The Birthday Party*.

What led you to do that so quickly?

It was the process of writing a play which had started me going. Then I went to see *The Room*, which was a remarkable experience. Since I'd never written a play before, I'd of course never seen one of mine performed, never had an audience sitting there. The only people who'd ever seen what I'd written had been a few friends and my wife. So to sit in the audience—well, I wanted to piss very badly throughout the whole thing, and at the end I dashed out behind the bicycle shed.

What other effect did contact with an audience have on you?

I was very encouraged by the response of that university audience, though no matter what the response had been I would have written *The Birthday Party*, I know that. Watching first nights, though I've seen quite a few by now, is never any better. It's a nerve-racking experience. It's not a question of whether the play goes well or badly. It's not the audience reaction, it's *my* reaction. I'm rather hostile toward audiences—I don't much care for large bodies of people collected together. Everyone knows that audiences vary enormously; it's a mistake to care too much about them. The thing one should be concerned with is whether the performance has expressed what one set out to express in writing the play. It sometimes does.

Do you think that without the impetus provided by your friend at Bristol you would have gotten down to writing plays?

Yes, I think I was going to write *The Room*. I just wrote it a bit quicker under the circumstances; he just triggered something off. *The Birthday Party* had also been in my mind for a long time. It was sparked off from a very distinct situation in digs when I was on tour. In fact, the other day a friend of mine gave me a letter I wrote to him in nineteen-fifty-something, Christ knows when it was. This is what it says: "I have filthy insane digs, a great bulging scrag of a woman with breasts rolling at her belly, an obscene household, cats, dogs, filth, tea strainers, mess, oh bullocks, talk, chat rubbish shit scratch dung poison, infantility, deficient order in the upper fretwork, fucking roll on." Now the thing about this is *that* was *The Birthday Party*—I was in those digs, and this woman was Meg in the play, and there was a fellow staying there in Eastbourne, on the coast. The whole thing remained with me, and three years later I wrote the play.

Why wasn't there a character representing you in the play?

I had—I have—nothing to say about myself, directly. I wouldn't know where to begin. Particularly since I often look at myself in the mirror and say, "Who the hell's that?"

And you don't think being represented as a character on stage would help you find out?

No.

. . .

As an actor, do you find yourself with a compelling sense of how roles in your plays should be performed?

Quite often I have a compelling sense of how a role should be played. And I'm proved—equally as often—quite wrong.

Do you see yourself in each role as you write? And does your acting help you as a playwright?

I read them all aloud to myself while writing. But I don't see myself in each role—I couldn't play most of them. My acting doesn't impede my playwriting because of these limitations. For example, I'd like to write a play—I've frequently thought of this—entirely about women.

Has it ever occurred to you to express political opinions through your characters?

No. Ultimately, politics do bore me, though I recognize they are responsible for a good deal of suffering. I distrust ideological statements of any kind.

But do you think that the picture of personal threat which is sometimes presented on your stage is troubling in a larger sense, a political sense, or doesn't this have any relevance?

I don't feel myself threatened by *any* political body or activity at all. I like living in England. I don't care about political structures—they don't alarm me, but they cause a great deal of suffering to millions of people.

I'll tell you what I really think about politicians. The other night I watched some politicians on television talking about Viet Nam. I wanted very much to burst through the screen with a flamethrower and burn their eyes out and their balls off and then inquire from them how they would assess this action from a political point of view.

Would you ever use this anger in a politically oriented play?

I have occasionally out of irritation thought about writing a play with a satirical point. I once did, actually, a play that no one knows about. A full-length play written after *The Caretaker*. Wrote the whole damn thing in three drafts. It was called *The Hothouse* and was about an institution in which patients were kept: all that was presented was the hierarchy, the people who ran the institution; one never knew what happened to the patients or what they were there for or who they were. It was heavily satirical, and it was quite useless. I never began to like any of the characters, they really didn't live at all. So I discarded the play at once. The characters were so purely cardboard. I was intentionally—for the only time, I think—trying to make a point, an explicit point, that these were nasty people and I disapproved of them. And therefore they didn't begin to live. Whereas in other plays of mine every single character, even a bastard like Goldberg in *The Birthday Party*, I care for.

Edward Albee

THE SANDBOX

Edward Albee (b. 1928) in infancy was adopted by the multimillionaires who owned the chain of Albee theaters. Though surrounded by material comfort, he was an unhappy child who disliked his adoptive parents. The only member of his family with whom he seems to have had an affectionate relationship was his grandmother. His work at school and in college was poor, but he wrote a good deal even as an adolescent; when in 1960 he achieved sudden fame with *Zoo Story* (written in 1958), he had already written plays for more than a decade. Among his other plays are *The Death of Bessie Smith* (1960), *The Sandbox* (1960), *The American Dream* (1961), *Who's Afraid of Virginia Woolf?* (1962), *A Delicate Balance* (1966), *Seascape* (1975), *The Man Who Had Three Arms* (1983), and *Three Tall Women* (written in 1991 but not performed in the United States until 1994). Three of his plays (*A Delicate Balance, Seascape,* and *Three Tall Women*) have won Pulitzer Prizes. A fourth play, *Whose Afraid for Virginia Woolf?*, was so highly regarded that when the committee refused to give it the Pulitzer Prize, two members of the Pulitzer committee resigned in protest.

COMMENTARY

In the middle of the twentieth century, the dominant American playwrights were Tennessee Williams and Arthur Miller, both of whom wrote plays that were basically realistic. Although Williams's dialogue was sometimes a bit "poetic" and Miller's *Death of a Salesman* included unrealistic, expressionistic elements (chiefly in staging Willy's memories), both of these playwrights were in the line of the great realists of the end of the nineteenth century, Ibsen and Chekhov. Their characters moved in settings (usually living rooms or kitchens) that resembled those in which we live, and the characters themselves were believable.

In 1958, Edward Albee arrived on the dramatic scene with *Zoo Story*, a very different sort of play. He was indebted to Beckett and Ionesco, the dramatists of the theater of the absurd (see pp. 690–91) and continued in the new mode. For instance, in *The Sandbox* the set does not allow us to pretend that we are eavesdropping on life, peeking through a window into someone's living room. Here is Albee's opening description:

> THE SCENE: *A bare stage, with only the following: Near the footlights, far stage-right, two simple chairs set side by side, facing the audience; near the footlights, far stage-left, a chair facing stage-right with a music stand before it; farther back, and stage-center, slightly elevated and raked, a large child's sandbox with a toy pail and shovel; the background is the sky, which alters from brightest day to deepest night.*

Conceivably this *could* be a realistic setting, for example, the backyard of a house belonging to a musician who has a small child. However, even if when we first saw the set we drew such an improbable conclusion, the first line of the dialogue would force us to revise our view: "Well, here we are; this is the beach." And as we read the play, encountering characters who are called only "the Musician," "the Young Man," "Mommy," "Daddy," and "Grandma," we realize that Albee is not much interested in giving us complex people responding to each other believably. For one thing, what sort of family is this that transacts its business in the presence of the Musician, who clearly is not a member of the family?

Moreover, Albee seems to go out of his way to tell us (as Ibsen and Chekhov and, for that matter, Williams and Miller would not) that we are witnessing *a play*, not life. Thus, Mommy is a sort of theatrical director, telling the Musician when to play and when to stop, and Grandma on occasion speaks directly to the audience and also to a stagehand. One of Grandma's speeches includes the following passage:

> GRANDMA. I'm not complaining. (*She looks up at the sky, shouts to someone off stage.*) Shouldn't it be getting dark now, dear? . . .

As the time for Grandma's death approaches, Albee tells us that "there is an off-stage rumble," almost a parody of the theatrical hokum that one might find in a melodrama.

Our point is simply this: With Albee, America saw the Americanization of a kind of drama that in the preceding decade had been available only in the imported work of such Europeans as Beckett and Ionesco or the English playwright Harold Pinter. Albee, however, differs notably from his European and English predecessors, if for no other reason than that he is partly the dramatist of American life, or, more accurately, the satirist of American life. To say that he is a satirist is another way of saying that his characters are unrealistic. One does not encounter realistic characters in the work of, for example, Gary Trudeau or, to go beyond the contemporary, Jonathan Swift. One finds caricature, which is to say that one finds such qualities as a delight in exaggeration and in improbability.

Are we saying that unreality, exaggeration, and improbability are characteristic of Albee's work or are characteristic of the theater of the absurd? We will let Albee have the last word. When the *New York Times Magazine* ran an article about Albee (February 25, 1962), the subject of the theater of the absurd came up. Albee talked about his sort of drama. He dismissed the traditional fare of Broadway as inane and suggested that the truly absurd theater was the popular theater of New York. Unlike the Broadway trash, genuine theater, he said, including the new drama that had come to be called the theater of the absurd, seeks to make us "face up to the human condition as it really is."

Edward Albee

THE SANDBOX

The Players

THE YOUNG MAN, *25, a good looking, well-built boy in a bathing suit*
MOMMY, *55, a well-dressed, imposing woman*
DADDY, *60, a small man; gray, thin*
GRANDMA, *86, a tiny, wizened woman with bright eyes*
THE MUSICIAN, *no particular age, but young would be nice*

NOTE: *When, in the course of the play, Mommy and Daddy call each other by these names, there should be no suggestion of regionalism. These names are of empty affection and point up the pre-senility and vacuity of their characters.*

THE SCENE: *A bare stage, with only the following: Near the footlights, far stage-right, two simple chairs set side by side, facing the audience; near the footlights, far stage-left, a chair facing stage-right with a music stand before it; farther back, and stage-center, slightly elevated and raked, a large child's sandbox with a toy pail and shovel; the background is the sky, which alters from brightest day to deepest night.*

At the beginning, it is brightest day, the Young Man is alone on stage, to the rear of the sandbox, and to one side. He is doing calisthenics; he does calisthenics until quite at the very end of the play. These calisthenics, employing the arms only, should suggest the beating and fluttering of wings. The Young Man is, after all, the Angel of Death.

Mommy and Daddy enter from the stage-left, Mommy first.

MOMMY (*motioning to Daddy*). Well, here we are; this is the beach.
DADDY (*whining*). I'm cold.
MOMMY (*dismissing him with a little laugh*). Don't be silly; it's as warm as toast. Look at that nice young man over there: *he* doesn't think it's cold. (*Waves to the Young Man.*) Hello.
YOUNG MAN (*with an endearing smile*). Hi!
MOMMY (*looking about*). This will do perfectly . . . don't you think so, Daddy? There's sand there . . . and the water beyond. What do you think, Daddy?
DADDY (*vaguely*). Whatever you say, Mommy.
MOMMY (*with the same little laugh*). Well, of course . . . whatever I say. Then, it's settled, is it?
DADDY (*shrugs*). She's *your* mother, not mine.
MOMMY. *I* know she's my mother. What do you take me for? (*A pause.*) All right, now; let's get on with it. (*She shouts into the wings, stage-left.*) You! Out there! You can come in now.

The Musician enters, seats himself in the chair, stage-left, places music on the music stand, is ready to play. Mommy nods approvingly.

MOMMY. Very nice; very nice. Are you ready, Daddy? Let's go get Grandma.
DADDY. Whatever you say, Mommy.
MOMMY (*leading the way out, stage-left*). Of course, whatever I say. (*To the Musician.*) You can begin now.

The Musician begins playing; Mommy and Daddy exit; the Musician, all the while playing nods to the Young Man.

YOUNG MAN (*with the same endearing smile*). Hi!

After a moment, Mommy and Daddy re-enter, carrying Grandma. She is borne in by their hands under her armpits; she is quite rigid; her legs are drawn up; her feet do not touch the ground; the expression on her ancient face is that of puzzlement and fear.

DADDY. Where do we put her?
MOMMY (*the same little laugh*). Wherever I say, of course. Let me see . . . well . . . all right, over there . . . in the sandbox. (*Pause.*) Well, what are you waiting for Daddy? . . . The sandbox!

Together they carry Grandma over to the sandbox and more or less dump her in.

GRANDMA (*righting herself to a sitting position; her voice a cross between a baby's laugh and cry*). Ahhhhhh! Graaaaa!
DADDY (*dusting himself*). What do we do now?
MOMMY (*to the MUSICIAN*). You can stop now. (*The Musician stops.*) (*Back to Daddy.*) What do you mean, what do we do now? We go over there and sit down, of course. (*To the Young Man.*) Hello there.
YOUNG MAN (*again smiling*). Hi!

Mommy and Daddy move to the chairs, stage-right, and sit down. A pause.

GRANDMA (*same as before*). Ahhhhhh! Ahhaaaaaa! Graaaaaa!
DADDY. Do you think . . . do you think she's . . . comfortable?
MOMMY (*impatiently*). How would I know?
DADDY (*pause*). What do we do now?
MOMMY (*as if remembering*). We . . . wait. We . . . sit here . . . and we wait . . . that's what we do.
DADDY (*after a pause*). Shall we talk to each other?

743

MOMMY (*with that little laugh; picking something off her dress*). Well, *you* can talk, if you want to . . . if you can think of anything to *say* . . . if you can think of anything *new*.

DADDY (*thinks*). No . . . I suppose not.

MOMMY (*with a triumphant laugh*). Of course not!

GRANDMA (*banging the toy shovel against the pail*). Haaaaaa! Ah-haaaaaa!

MOMMY (*out over the audience*). Be quiet, Grandma . . . just be quiet, and wait.

Grandma throws a shovelful of sand at Mommy.

MOMMY (*still out over the audience*). She's throwing sand at me! You stop that, Grandma; you stop throwing sand at Mommy! (*To Daddy.*) She's throwing sand at me.

Daddy looks around at Grandma, who screams at him.

GRANDMA. GRAAAAAA!

MOMMY. Don't look at her. Just . . . sit here . . . be very still . . . and wait. (*To the Musician.*) You . . . uh . . . you go ahead and do whatever it is you do.

The Musician plays.

Mommy and Daddy are fixed, staring out beyond the audience.

Grandma looks at them, looks at the Musician, looks at the sandbox, throws down the shovel.

GRANDMA. Ah-haaaaaa! Graaaaaa! (*Looks for reaction; gets none. Now . . . directly to the audience.*) Honestly! What a way to treat an old woman! Drag her out of the house . . . stick her in a car . . . bring her out here from the city . . . dump her in a pile of sand . . . and leave her here to set. I'm eighty-six years old! I was married when I was seventeen. To a farmer. He died when I was thirty. (*To the Musician.*) Will you stop that, please?

The Musician stops playing.

I'm a feeble old woman . . . how do you expect anybody to hear me over that peep! peep! peep! (*To herself.*) There's no respect around here. (*To the Young Man.*) There's no respect around here!

YOUNG MAN (*same smile*). Hi!

GRANDMA (*after a pause, a mild double-take, continues, to the audience*). My husband died when I was thirty (*indicates Mommy*), and I had to raise that big cow over there all by my lonesome. You can imagine what *that* was like. Lordy! (*To the Young Man.*) Where'd they get *you*?

YOUNG MAN. Oh . . . I've been around for a while.

GRANDMA. I'll bet you have! Heh, heh, heh. Will you look at you!

YOUNG MAN (*flexing his muscles*). Isn't that something? (*Continues his calisthenics.*)

GRANDMA. Boy, oh boy; I'll say. Pretty good.

YOUNG MAN (*sweetly*). I'll say.

GRANDMA. Where ya from?

YOUNG MAN. Southern California.

GRANDMA (*nodding*). Figgers, figgers. What's your name, honey?

YOUNG MAN. I don't know . . .

GRANDMA (*to the audience*). Bright, too!

YOUNG MAN. I mean . . . I mean, they haven't given me one yet . . . the studio . . .

GRANDMA (*giving him the once-over*). You don't say . . . you don't say. Well . . . uh, I've got to talk some more . . . don't you go 'way.

YOUNG MAN. Oh, no.

GRANDMA (*turning her attention back to the audience*). Fine; fine. (*Then, once more, back to the Young Man.*) You're . . . you're an actor, hunh?

YOUNG MAN (*beaming*). Yes. I am.

GRANDMA (*to the audience again; shrugs*). I'm smart that way. Anyhow, I had to raise . . . *that* over there all by my lonesome; and what's next to her there . . . that's what she married. Rich? I tell you . . . money, money, money. They took me off the *farm* . . . which was real decent of them . . . and they moved me into the big town house with *them* . . . fixed a nice place for me under the stove . . . gave me an army blanket . . . and my own dish . . . my very own dish! So, what have I got to complain about? Nothing, of course. I'm not complaining. (*She looks up at the sky, shouts to someone offstage.*) Shouldn't it be getting dark now, dear?

The lights dim; night comes on. The Musician begins to play; it becomes deepest night. There are spots on all the players, including the Young Man, who is, of course, continuing his calisthenics.

DADDY (*stirring*). It's nighttime.

MOMMY. Shhhh. Be still . . . wait.

DADDY (*whining*). It's so hot.

MOMMY. Shhhhhh. Be still . . . wait.

GRANDMA (*to herself*). That's better. Night. (*To the Musician.*) Honey, do you play all through this part?

The Musician nods.

Well, keep it nice and soft; that's a good boy.

The Musician nods again; plays softly.

That's nice.

There is an off-stage rumble.

DADDY (*starting*). What was that?

MOMMY (*beginning to weep*). It was nothing.

DADDY. It was . . . it was . . . thunder . . . or a wave breaking . . . or something.

MOMMY (*whispering, through her tears*). It was an off-stage rumble . . . and you know what *that* means . . .

DADDY. I forget. . . .

MOMMY (*barely able to talk*). It means the time has come for poor Grandma . . . and I can't bear it!

DADDY (*vacantly*). I . . . I suppose you've got to be brave.

GRANDMA (*mocking*). That's right, kid; be brave. You'll bear up; you'll get over it.

(*Another off-stage rumble . . . louder.*)

MOMMY. Ohhhhhhhhhhh . . . poor Grandma . . . poor Grandma. . . .

GRANDMA (*to Mommy*). I'm fine! I'm all right! It hasn't happened yet!

A violent off-stage rumble. All the lights go out, save the spot on the Young Man; the Musician stops playing.

MOMMY. Ohhhhhhhhhh.... Ohhhhhhhhhh....

Silence.

GRANDMA. Don't put the lights up yet ... I'm not ready; I'm not quite ready. (*Silence.*) All right, dear ... I'm about done.

The lights come up again, to brightest day; the Musician begins to play. Grandma is discovered, still in the sandbox, lying on her side, propped up on an elbow, half covered, busily shoveling sand over herself.

GRANDMA (*muttering*). I don't know how I'm supposed to do anything with this goddam toy shovel....

DADDY. Mommy! It's daylight!

MOMMY (*brightly*). So it is! Well! Our long night is over. We must put away our tears, take off our mourning ... and face the future. It's our duty.

GRANDMA (*still shoveling; mimicking*). ... take off our mourning ... face the future.... Lordy!

Mommy and Daddy rise, stretch. Mommy waves to the young man.

YOUNG MAN (*with that smile*). Hi!

Grandma plays dead. (!) Mommy and Daddy go over to look at her; she is a little more than half buried in the sand; the toy shovel is in her hands, which are crossed on her breast.

MOMMY (*before the sandbox; shaking her head*). Lovely! It's ... it's hard to be sad ... she looks ... so happy. (*With pride and conviction.*) It pays to do things well. (*To the Musician.*) All right, you can stop now, if you want to. I mean, stay around for a swim, or something; it's all right with us. (*She sighs heavily.*) Well, Daddy ... off we go.

DADDY. Brave Mommy!

MOMMY. Brave Daddy!

They exit, stage-left.

GRANDMA (*after they leave; lying quite still*). It pays to do things well.... Boy, oh boy! (*She tries to sit up*) ... well, kids ... (*but she finds she can't*) ... I ... I can't get up, I ... I can't move....

The Young Man stops his calisthenics, nods to the Musician, walks over to Grandma, kneels down by the sandbox.

GRANDMA. I ... can't move....

YOUNG MAN. Shhhhh ... be very still....

GRANDMA. I ... I can't move....

YOUNG MAN. Uh ... ma'am; I ... I have a line here.

GRANDMA. Oh, I'm sorry, sweetie; you go right ahead.

YOUNG MAN. I am ... uh ...

GRANDMA. Take your time, dear.

YOUNG MAN (*prepares; delivers the line like a real amateur*). I am the Angel of Death. I am ... uh ... I am come for you.

GRANDMA. What ... wha ... (*Then, with resignation.*) ... ohhhh ... ohhhh, I see.

The Young Man bends over, kisses Grandma gently on the forehead.

GRANDMA (*her eyes closed, her hands folded on her breast again, the shovel between her hands, a sweet smile on her face*). Well ... that was very nice, dear ...

YOUNG MAN (*still kneeling*). Shhhhhh ... be still....

GRANDMA. What I mean was ... you did that very well, dear....

YOUNG MAN (*blushing*) ... oh ...

GRANDMA. No; I mean it. You've got that ... you've got a quality.

YOUNG MAN (*with his endearing smile*). Oh ... thank you; thank you very much ... ma'am.

GRANDMA (*slowly; softly—as the Young Man puts his hands on top of Grandma's*). You're ... you're welcome ... dear.

Tableau. The Musician continues to play as the curtain slowly comes down.

CURTAIN

TOPICS FOR CRITICAL THINKING AND WRITING

📖 THE PLAY ON THE PAGE

1. In a sentence, characterize Mommy, and in another sentence characterize Daddy. By the way, why doesn't Albee give them names?

2. Of the four speaking characters in the play, which do you find the most sympathetic? Exactly why? Set forth your answer, with supporting evidence, in a paragraph, or perhaps in two paragraphs—the first devoted to the three less sympathetic characters and the second devoted to the most sympathetic character.

3. What do you make of the sandbox? Is it an image of the grave, with suggestions that life is meaningless and sterile? Alternatively, is it an image only of the sterility of life in the United States in the second half of the twentieth century? Does the fact that Grandma was married to a farmer suggest an alternative way of life? Explain.

4. In a longer play, *The American Dream*, Albee uses the same four characters that he uses in *The Sandbox*. Of *The American Dream* he wrote:

> The play . . . is a condemnation of complacency, cruelty, emasculation and vacuity; it is a stand against the fiction that everything in this slipping land of ours is peachy-keen.

To what extent does this statement help you to understand (and to enjoy) *The Sandbox*?

5. In the *New York Times Magazine* (February 25, 1962), Albee protested against the view that his plays, and others of the so-called theater of the absurd, are depressing. He includes a quotation from Martin Esslin's book *The Theatre of the Absurd*:

> Ultimately . . . the Theatre of the Absurd does not reflect despair or a return to dark irrational forces but expresses modern man's endeavor to come to terms with the world in which he lives. It attempts to make him face up to the human condition as it really is, to free him from illusions that are bound to cause constant maladjustment and disappointment. . . . For the dignity of man lies in his reality in all its senselessness; to accept it freely, without fear, without illusions—and to laugh at it.

In what ways do you find this statement helpful? In what ways do you find it not helpful? Explain.

6. In an interview in 1979, Albee said:

> I like to think people are forced to rethink some things as a result of the experience of seeing some of my plays, that they are not left exactly the way they came in.

Has reading *The Sandbox* forced you to rethink anything? If so, what?

THE PLAY ON THE STAGE

7. Why, in your opinion, does Albee insist in the first stage direction that the scene be "a bare stage"? Do you think a realistic setting would in some way diminish the play? Explain.

8. Albee specifies in the opening stage direction that the Young Man "is doing calisthenics; he does calisthenics until quite at the very end of the play." Some viewers and readers who visualize the play find that the calisthenics distract from the lines of the play. If you were directing the play, might you neglect Albee's instruction? If you did omit the calisthenics, what would you have the Young Man do?

9. The Musician plays under two circumstances—when he is asked by Mommy and when he plays unasked. Would you distinguish between these two circumstances by using different kinds of music? What kind or kinds of music would you use?

10. In a stage direction Albee tells us that when the Young Man delivers his big line ("I am the Angel of Death"), he "delivers the line like a real amateur." Furthermore, the Young Man muffs his next line ("I am . . . uh . . . I come for you"). Exactly how would your speak these two sentences and with what (if any) gestures?

A CONTEXT FOR *THE SANDBOX*

Edward Albee
INTERVIEW

[William Flanagan conducted this interview with Albee. It was originally published in *Paris Review*.]

Flanagan: One of your most recent plays was an adaptation of James Purdy's novel Malcolm. *It had as close to one hundred percent bad notices as a play could get. The resultant commercial catastrophe and quick closing of the play apart, how does this affect your own feeling about the piece itself?*

Albee: I see you're starting with the hits. Well, I retain for all my plays, I suppose, a certain amount of enthusiasm. I don't feel intimidated by either the unanimously bad press that *Malcolm* got or the unanimously good press that some of the other plays have received. I haven't changed my feeling about *Malcolm*. I liked doing the adaptation of Purdy's book. I had a number of quarrels with the production, but then I usually end up with quarrels about all of my plays. With the possible exception of the little play *The Sandbox*, which takes thirteen minutes to perform, I don't think anything I've done has worked out to perfection.

While it doesn't necessarily change your feeling, does the unanimously bad critical response open questions in your mind?

I imagine that if we had a college of criticism in this country whose opinions more closely approximated the value of the works of art inspected, it might; but as often as not, I find relatively little relationship between the work of art and the immediate critical response it gets. Every writer's got to pay some attention, I suppose, to what his critics say because theirs is a reflection of what the audience feels about his work. And a playwright, especially a playwright whose work deals very directly with an audience, perhaps he should pay some attention to the nature of the audience response—not necessarily to learn anything about his craft, but as often as not merely to find out about the temper of the time, what is being tolerated, what is being permitted.

. . .

Actually, the final evaluation of a play has nothing to do with immediate audience or critical response. The playwright, along with any writer, composer, painter in this society, has got to have a terribly private view of his own value, of his own work. He's got to listen to his own voice primarily. He's got to watch out for fads, for what might be called the critical aesthetics.

. . .

Since I guess it's fairly imbecilic to ask a writer what he considers to be his best work or his most important work, perhaps I could

ask you this question: which of all of your plays do you feel closest to?

Well, naturally the one I'm writing right now.

Well, excepting that.

I don't know.

There's no one that you feel any special fondness for?

I'm terribly fond of *The Sandbox*. I think it's an absolutely beautiful, lovely, perfect play.

HAPPY DAYS

Samuel Beckett (1906–1989) was born in Dublin of middle-class Protestant parents. He was educated at Trinity College, Dublin, where he took his degree in modern languages, graduating in 1927. He went to Paris the next year where he met James Joyce, a fellow Irishman, and translated parts of *Finnegan's Wake* into French. He stayed in France until 1930, when he returned to Dublin to take up a lectureship in French at Trinity College. He soon decided against teaching and began a number of years of wandering, living in London, traveling about Germany and France, and then settling in Paris in 1937. During World War II, after narrowly escaping capture by the Gestapo for his work in the French Resistance, he fled to Roussillon in southwestern France, where he remained until the end of the war, when he returned to Paris. In 1961, the year he was writing *Happy Days*, he married a French woman, Suzanne Deschevaux-Dumesnil. In 1969 he was awarded the Nobel Prize for literature but refused to go to Stockholm for the ceremonies. His best-known works include the novels *Molloy* (1951), *Malone Dies* (1951), and *The Unnamable* (1953); short stories collected as *More Pricks Than Kicks* (1934); and the plays *Waiting for Godot* (first published in French as *En attendant Godot* in 1952 but translated by Beckett into English and published in 1954), *Endgame* (1957), and *Happy Days* (1961). Numerous shorter works, including scripts for radio and television and even for a movie entitled *Film*, starring Buster Keaton, complete what John Updike called "a single holy book."

COMMENTARY

If you wish to read some background material relevant to *Happy Days*, we suggest that you look at the discussion of the development of modern tragicomedy (pp. 39–40) and "A Note on the Theater of the Absurd" (pp. 690–91). Beckett wrote *Happy Days* in English in 1960–1961. (He sometimes wrote his plays and novels in French, but in *Happy Days*, beyond describing the backdrop as *pompier trompe-l'oeil* ["ordinary illusionistic"], French is implied only in Winnie's uncertainty whether *hair* is "them" or "it," for in French *hair* is plural, *les cheveux*.)

A comment by Ruby Cohn in *Just Play: Beckett's Theater* (1980) may help when reading the play. Cohn reports (p. 253) that Beckett instructed an actress that Winnie should speak in "three main voices—a neutral prattle, high articulation to Willie and childlike intimacy to herself."

Samuel Beckett

HAPPY DAYS

List of Characters

WINNIE, *a woman about fifty*
WILLIE, *a man about sixty*

ACT 1

Expanse of scorched grass rising centre to low mound. Gentle slopes down to front and either side of stage. Back an abrupter fall to stage level. Maximum of simplicity and symmetry.

Blazing light.

Very pompier trompe-l'oeil[1] backcloth to represent unbroken plain and sky receding to meet in far distance.

Imbedded up to above her waist in exact centre of mound, Winnie. About fifty, well preserved, blond for preference, plump, arms and shoulders bare, low bodice, big bosom, pearl necklet. She is discovered sleeping, her arms on the ground before her, her head on her arms. Beside her on ground to her left a capacious black bag, shopping variety, and to her right a collapsible collapsed parasol, beak of handle emerging from sheath.

To her right and rear, lying asleep on ground, hidden by mound, Willie.

Long pause. A bell rings piercingly, say ten seconds, stops. She does not move. Pause. Bell more piercingly, say five seconds. She wakes. Bell stops. She raises her head, gazes front. Long pause. She straightens up, lays her hands flat on ground, throws back her head and gazes at zenith. Long pause.

WINNIE (*gazing at zenith*). Another heavenly day. (*Pause. Head back level, eyes front, pause. She clasps hands to breast, closes eyes. Lips move in inaudible prayer, say ten seconds. Lips still. Hands remain clasped. Low*) For Jesus Christ sake Amen. (*Eyes open, hands unclasp, return to mound. Pause. She clasps hands to breast again, closes eyes, lips move again in inaudible addendum, say five seconds. Low*) World without end Amen. (*Eyes open, hands unclasp, return to mound. Pause.*) Begin, Winnie. (*Pause.*) Begin your day, Winnie. (*Pause. She turns to bag, rummages in it without moving it from its place, brings out toothbrush, rummages again, brings out flat tube of toothpaste, turns back front, unscrews cap of tube, lays cap on ground, squeezes with difficulty small blob of paste on brush, holds tube in one hand and brushes teeth with other. She turns modestly aside and back to her right to spit out behind mound. In this position her eyes rest on Willie. She spits out. She cranes a little further back and down. Loud*) Hoo-

oo! (*Pause. Louder*) Hoo-oo! (*Pause. Tender smile as she turns back front, lays down brush.*) Poor Willie—(*examines tube, smile off*)—running out—(*looks for cap*)—ah well—(*finds cap*)—can't be helped—(*screws on cap*)—just one of those old things—(*lays down tube*)—another of those old things—(*turns towards bag*)—just can't be cured—(*brings out small mirror, turns back front*)—ah yes—(*inspects teeth in mirror*)—poor dear Willie—(*testing upper front teeth with thumb, indistinctly*)—good Lord!—(*pulling back upper lip to inspect gums, do[2]*)—good God!—(*pulling back corner of mouth, mouth open, do*)—ah well—(*other corner, do*)—no worse—(*abandons inspection, normal speech*)—no better, no worse—(*lays down mirror*)—no change—(*wipes fingers on grass*)—no pain—(*looks for toothbrush*)—hardly any—(*takes up toothbrush*)—great thing that—(*examines handle of brush*)—nothing like it—(*examines handle, reads*)—pure . . . what?—(*pause*)—what?—(*lays down brush*)—ah yes—(*turns towards bag*)—poor Willie—(*rummages in bag*)—no zest—(*rummages*)—for anything (*brings out spectacles in case*)—no interest—(*turns back front*)—in life—(*takes spectacles from case*)—poor dear Willie—(*lays down case*)—sleep for ever—(*opens spectacles*)—marvellous gift—(*puts on spectacles*)—nothing to touch it—(*looks for toothbrush*)—in my opinion—(*takes up toothbrush*)—always said so—(*examines handle of brush*)—I wish I had it—(*examines handle, reads*)—genuine . . . pure . . . what?—(*lays down brush*)—blind next—(*takes off spectacles*)—ah well—(*lays down spectacles*)—seen enough—(*feels in bodice for handkerchief*)—I suppose—(*takes out folded handkerchief*)—by now—(*shakes out handkerchief*)—what are those wonderful lines—(*wipes one eye*)—woe woe is me—(*wipes the other*)—to see what I see[3]—(*looks for spectacles*)—ah yes—(*takes up spectacles*)—wouldn't miss it—(*starts polishing spectacles, breathing on lenses*)—or would I?—(*polishes*)—holy light—(*polishes*)—bob up out of dark—(*polishes*)—blaze of hellish light.[4] (*Stops polishing, raises face to sky, pause, head back level, resumes polishing, stops polishing, cranes back to her*

---

[1]*pompier trompe l'oeil* ordinary illusionistic

[2]**do** ditto [3]**woe . . . see** Compare Ophelia, reporting on Hamlet's madness: "O! woe is me,/To have seen what I have seen, see what I see" (3.1.169–70). [4]**holy light . . . blaze of hellish light** In John Milton's *Paradise Lost*, Book 3 begins with a hymn to God, who is associated with light: "Hail holy light, offspring of Heav'n first-born." At the beginning of Act 2, Winnie again alludes to this passage.

right and down.) Hoo-oo! (*Pause. Tender smile as she turns back front and resumes polishing. Smile off.*) Marvellous gift—(*stops polishing, lays down spectacles*)—wish I had it—(*folds handkerchief*)—ah well—(*puts handkerchief back in bodice*)—can't complain—(*looks for spectacles*)—no no—(*takes up spectacles*)—mustn't complain—(*holds up spectacles, looks through lens*)—so much to be thankful for—(*looks through other lens*)—no pain—(*puts on spectacles*)—hardly any—(*looks for toothbrush*)—wonderful thing that—(*takes up toothbrush*)—nothing like it—(*examines handle of brush*)—slight headache sometimes—(*examines handle, reads*)—guaranteed . . . genuine . . . pure . . . what?—(*looks closer*)—genuine pure . . . —(*takes handkerchief from bodice*)—ah yes—(*shakes out handkerchief*)—occasional mild migraine—(*starts wiping handle of brush*)—it comes—(*wipes*)—then goes—(*wiping mechanically*)—ah yes—(*wiping*)—many mercies—(*wiping*)—great mercies—(*stops wiping, fixed lost gaze, brokenly*)—prayers perhaps not for naught—(*pause, do*)—first thing—(*pause, do*)—last thing—(*head down, resumes wiping, stops wiping, head up, calmed, wipes eyes, folds handkerchief, puts it back in bodice, examines handle of brush, reads*)—fully guaranteed . . . genuine pure . . . —(*looks closer*)—genuine pure . . . (*Takes off spectacles, lays them and brush down, gazes before her.*) Old things. (*Pause.*) Old eyes. (*Long pause.*) On, Winnie. (*She casts about her, sees parasol, considers it at length, takes it up and develops from sheath a handle of surprising length. Holding butt of parasol in right hand she cranes back and down to her right to hang over Willie.*) Hoo-oo! (*Pause.*) Willie! (*Pause.*) Wonderful gift. (*She strikes down at him with beak of parasol.*) Wish I had it. (*She strikes again. The parasol slips from her grasp and falls behind mound. It is immediately restored to her by Willie's invisible hand.*) Thank you, dear. (*She transfers parasol to left hand, turns back front and examines right palm.*) Damp. (*Returns parasol to right hand, examines left palm.*) Ah well, no worse. (*Head up, cheerfully*) No better, no worse, no change. (*Pause. Do*) No pain. (*Cranes back to look down at Willie, holding parasol by butt as before.*) Don't go off on me again now dear will you please, I may need you. (*Pause.*) No hurry, no hurry, just don't curl up on me again. (*Turns back front, lays down parasol, examines palms together, wipes them on grass.*) Perhaps a shade off colour just the same. (*Turns to bag, rummages in it, brings out revolver, holds it up, kisses it rapidly, puts it back, rummages, brings out almost empty bottle of red medicine, turns back front, looks for spectacles, puts them on, reads label.*) Loss of spirits . . . lack of keenness . . . want of appetite . . . infants . . . children . . . adults . . . six level . . . tablespoonfuls daily—(*head up, smile*)—the old style!—(*smile off, head down, reads*)—daily . . . before and after . . . meals . . . instantaneous . . . (*looks closer*) . . . improvement. (*Takes off spectacles, lays them down, holds up bottle*

at arm's length to see level, unscrews cap, swigs it off head well back, tosses cap and bottle away in Willie's direction. Sound of breaking glass.*) Ah that's better! (*Turns to bag, rummages in it, brings out lipstick, turns back front, examines lipstick.*) Running out. (*Looks for spectacles.*) Ah well. (*Puts on spectacles, looks for mirror.*) Mustn't complain. (*Takes up mirror, starts doing lips.*) What is that wonderful line? (*Lips.*) Oh fleeting joys—(*lips*)—oh something lasting woe.[5] (*Lips. She is interrupted by disturbance from Willie. He is sitting up. She lowers lipstick and mirror and cranes back and down to look at him. Pause. Top back of Willie's bald head, trickling blood, rises to view above slope, comes to rest. Winnie pushes up her spectacles. Pause. His hand appears with handkerchief, spreads it on skull, disappears. Pause. The hand appears with boater, club ribbon, settles it on head, rakish angle, disappears. Pause. Winnie cranes a little further back and down.*) Slip on your drawers, dear, before you get singed. (*Pause.*) No? (*Pause.*) Oh I see, you still have some of that stuff left. (*Pause.*) Work it well in, dear. (*Pause.*) Now the other. (*Pause. She turns back front, gazes before her. Happy expression.*) Oh this is going to be another happy day! (*Pause. Happy expression off. She pulls down spectacles and resumes lips. Willie opens newspaper, hands invisible. Tops of yellow sheets appear on either side of his head. Winnie finishes lips, inspects them in mirror held a little further away.*) Ensign crimson. (*Willie turns page. Winnie lays down lipstick and mirror, turns towards bag.*) Pale flag.[6]

(*Willie turns page. Winnie rummages in bag, brings out small ornate brimless hat with crumpled feather, turns back front, straightens hat, smooths feather, raises it towards head, arrests gesture as Willie reads.*)

WILLIE. His Grace and Most Reverend Father in God Carolus Hunter dead in tub.

(*Pause.*)

WINNIE (*gazing front, hat in hand, tone of fervent reminiscence*). Charlie Hunter! (*Pause.*) I close my eyes—(*she takes off spectacles and does so, hat in one hand, spectacles in other, Willie turns page*)—and am sitting on his knees again, in the back garden at Borough Green, under the horsebeech. (*Pause. She opens eyes, puts on spectacles, fiddles with hat.*) Oh the happy memories!

(*Pause. She raises hat towards head, arrests gesture as Willie reads.*)

---

[5]**Oh fleeting joys . . . lasting woe** Adam, in John Milton's *Paradise Lost*, remembers with sorrow how by his disobedience he has lost Paradise: "O fleeting joys/Of Paradise, dear bought with lasting woes" (10: 741–2).   [6]**Ensign crimson . . . Pale flag** In *Romeo and Juliet*, Romeo mistakenly thinking that Juliet is dead, expresses wonder that the crimson flag ("ensign") of beauty is still on her cheeks, not the pale flag of death.

WILLIE. Opening for smart youth.

(*Pause. She raises hat towards head, arrests gesture, takes off spectacles, gazes front, hat in one hand, spectacles in other.*)

WINNIE. My first ball! (*Long pause.*) My second ball! (*Long pause. Closes eyes.*) My first kiss! (*Pause. Willie turns page. Winnie opens eyes.*) A Mr. Johnson, or Johnston, or perhaps I should say John*stone*. Very bushy moustache, very tawny. (*Reverently*) Almost ginger! (*Pause.*) Within a toolshed, though whose I cannot conceive. We had no toolshed and he most certainly had no toolshed. (*Closes eyes.*) I see the piles of pots. (*Pause.*) The tangles of bast. (*Pause.*) The shadows deepening among the rafters.

(*Pause. She opens eyes, puts on spectacles, raises hat towards head, arrests gesture as Willie reads.*)

WILLIE. Wanted bright boy.

(*Pause. Winnie puts on hat hurriedly, looks for mirror. Willie turns page. Winnie takes up mirror, inspects hat, lays down mirror, turns toward bag. Paper disappears. Winnie rummages in bag, brings out magnifying-glass, turns back front, looks for toothbrush. Paper reappears, folded, and begins to fan Willie's face, hand invisible. Winnie takes up toothbrush and examines handle through glass.*)

WINNIE. Fully guaranteed . . . (*Willie stops fanning*) . . . genuine pure . . . (*Pause. Willie resumes fanning. Winnie looks closer, reads.*) Fully guaranteed . . . (*Willie stops fanning*) . . . genuine pure . . . (*Pause. Willie resumes fanning. Winnie lays down glass and brush, takes handkerchief from bodice, takes off and polishes spectacles, puts on spectacles, looks for glass, takes up and polishes glass, lays down glass, looks for brush, takes up brush and wipes handle, lays down brush, puts handkerchief back in bodice, looks for glass, takes up glass, looks for brush, takes up brush and examines handle through glass.*) Fully guaranteed . . . (*Willie stops fanning*) . . . genuine pure . . . (*pause, Willie resumes fanning*) . . . hog's (*Willie stops fanning, pause*) . . . setae. (*Pause. Winnie lays down glass and brush, paper disappears, Winnie takes off spectacles, lays them down, gazes front.*) Hog's setae. (*Pause.*) That is what I find so wonderful, that not a day goes by— (*smile*)—to speak in the old style—(*smile off*)—hardly a day, without some addition to one's knowledge however trifling, the addition I mean, provided one takes the pains. (*Willie's hand reappears with a postcard which he examines close to eyes.*) And if for some strange reason no further pains are possible, why then just close the eyes— (*she does so*)—and wait for the day to come—(*opens eyes*)—the happy day to come when flesh melts at so many degrees and the night of the moon has so many hundred hours. (*Pause.*) That is what I find so comforting when I lose heart and envy the brute beast. (*Turning towards Willie*) I hope you are taking in—(*She sees postcard, bends lower.*) What is that you have there, Willie, may I see? (*She reaches down with hand and Willie hands her card. The hairy forearm appears above slope, raised in gesture of giving, the hand open to take back, and remains in this position till card is returned. Winnie turns back front and examines card.*) Heavens what are they up to! (*She looks for spectacles, puts them on and examines card.*) No but this is just genuine pure filth! (*Examines card.*) Make any nice-minded person want to vomit! (*Impatience of Willie's fingers. She looks for glass, takes it up and examines card through glass. Long pause.*) What does that creature in the background think he's doing? (*Looks closer.*) Oh no really! (*Impatience of fingers. Last long look. She lays down glass, takes edge of card between right forefinger and thumb, averts head, takes nose between left forefinger and thumb.*) Pah! (*Drops card.*) Take it away! (*Willie's arm disappears. His hand reappears immediately, holding card. Winnie takes off spectacles, lays them down, gazes before her. During what follows Willie continues to relish card, varying angles and distance from his eyes.*) Hog's setae. (*Puzzled expression.*) What exactly is a hog? (*Pause. Do.*) A sow of course I know, but a hog . . . (*Puzzled expression off*) Oh well what does it matter, that is what I always say, it will come back, that is what I find so wonderful, all comes back. (*Pause.*) All? (*Pause.*) No, not all. (*Smile.*) No no. (*Smile off.*) Not quite. (*Pause.*) A part. (*Pause.*) Floats up, one fine day, out of the blue. (*Pause.*) That is what I find so wonderful. (*Pause. She turns towards bag. Hand and card disappear. She makes to rummage in bag, arrests gesture.*) No. (*She turns back front. Smile.*) No no. (*Smile off.*) Gently Winnie. (*She gazes front. Willie's hand reappears, takes off hat, disappears with hat.*) What then? (*Hand reappears, takes handkerchief from skull, disappears with handkerchief. Sharply, as to one not paying attention.*) Winnie! (*Willie bows head out of sight.*) What is the alternative? (*Pause.*) What is the al— (*Willie blows nose loud and long, head and hands invisible. She turns to look at him. Pause. Head reappears. Pause. Hand reappears with handkerchief, spreads it on skull, disappears. Pause. Hand reappears with boater, settles it on head, rakish angle, disappears. Pause.*) Would I had let you sleep on. (*She turns back front. Intermittent plucking at grass, head up and down, to animate following.*) Ah yes, if only I could bear to be alone, I mean prattle away with not a soul to hear. (*Pause.*) Not that I flatter myself you hear much, no Willie, God forbid. (*Pause.*) Days perhaps when you hear nothing. (*Pause.*) But days too when you answer. (*Pause.*) So that I may say at all times, even when you do not answer and perhaps hear nothing, something of this is being heard, I am not merely talking to myself, that is in the wilderness, a thing I could never bear to do—for any length of time. (*Pause.*) That is what enables me to go on, go on talking that is. (*Pause.*) Whereas if you were to die—(*smile*)—to speak in the old style—(*smile off*)—or go away and leave me, then what would I do, what *could* I do, all day long, I mean between the bell for waking and the bell for sleep? (*Pause.*) Simply gaze before me with compressed lips. (*Long pause while she does so. No more plucking.*) Not another word as long as I drew breath, nothing to break the silence of this place. (*Pause.*) Save possibly, now and then, every now and then, a sigh into my looking-glass. (*Pause.*) Or a brief . . . gale of laughter, should I happen to see the old joke again. (*Pause. Smile appears, broadens and seems about to culminate in laugh when suddenly replaced by expression of anxiety.*) My hair! (*Pause.*) Did I brush and comb my hair? (*Pause.*) I may have done. (*Pause.*) Normally I do. (*Pause.*) There is so little one *can* do. (*Pause.*) One does it all. (*Pause.*) All one can. (*Pause.*) Tis only human. (*Pause.*) Human nature. (*She begins to inspect mound, looks up.*) Human weakness. (*She resumes inspection of mound, looks up.*) Natural weakness. (*She resumes inspection of mound.*) I see no comb. (*Inspects.*) Nor any hairbrush. (*Looks up. Puzzled expression. She turns to bag, rummages in it.*) The comb is here. (*Back front. Puzzled expression. Back to bag. Rummages.*) The brush is here. (*Back front. Puzzled expression.*) Perhaps I put them back, after use. (*Pause. Do.*) But normally I do not put things back, after use, no, I leave them lying about and put them back all together, at the end of the day. (*Smile.*) To speak in the old style. (*Pause.*) The sweet old style. (*Smile off.*) And yet . . . I seem . . . to remember . . . (*Suddenly careless*) Oh well, what does it matter, that is what I always say, I shall simply brush and comb them later on, purely and simply, I have the whole— (*Pause. Puzzled*) Them? (*Pause.*) Or it? (*Pause.*) Brush and comb it? (*Pause.*) Sounds improper somehow. (*Pause. Turning a little towards Willie*) What would you say, Willie? (*Pause. Turning a little further*) What would you say, Willie, speaking of your hair, them or it? (*Pause.*) The hair on your head, I mean. (*Pause. Turning a little further.*) The hair on your head, Willie, what would you say speaking of the hair on your head, them or it?

(*Long pause.*)

WILLIE. It.

WINNIE (*turning back front, joyful*). Oh you are going to talk to me today, this is going to be a happy day! (*Pause. Joy off.*) Another happy day. (*Pause.*) Ah well, where was I, my hair, yes, later on, I shall be thankful for it later on. (*Pause.*) I have my—(*raises hands to hat*)—yes, on, my hat on—(*lowers hands*)—I cannot take it off now. (*Pause.*) To think there are times one cannot take off one's hat, not if one's life were at stake. Times one cannot put it on, times one cannot take it off. (*Pause.*) How often I have said, Put on your hat now, Winnie, there is nothing else for it, take off your hat now, Winnie, like a good girl, it will do you good, and did not. (*Pause.*) Could not. (*Pause. She raises hand, frees a strand of hair from under hat, draws it towards*

eye, *squints at it, lets it go, hand down.*) Golden you called it, that day, when the last guest was gone—(*hand up in gesture of raising a glass*)—to your golden . . . may it never (*voice breaks*) . . . may it never . . . (*Hand down. Head down. Pause. Low*) That day. (*Pause. Do.*) What day? (*Pause. Head up. Normal voice*) What now? (*Pause.*) Words fail, there are times when even they fail. (*Turning a little towards Willie*) Is that not so, Willie? (*Pause. Turning a little further*) Is not that so, Willie, that even words fail, at times? (*Pause. Back front.*) What is one to do then, until they come again? Brush and comb the hair, if it has not been done, or if there is some doubt, trim the nails if they are in need of trimming, these things tide one over. (*Pause.*) That is what I mean. (*Pause.*) That is all I mean. (*Pause.*) That is what I find so wonderful, that not a day goes by—(*smile*)—to speak in the old style—(*smile off*)—without some blessing—(*Willie collapses behind slope, his head disappears, Winnie turns towards event*)—in disguise. (*She cranes back and down.*) Go back into your hole now, Willie, you've exposed yourself enough. (*Pause.*) Do as I say, Willie, don't lie sprawling there in this hellish sun, go back into your hole. (*Pause.*) Go on now, Willie. (*Willie invisible starts crawling left towards hole.*) That's the man. (*She follows his progress with her eyes.*) Not head first, stupid, how are you going to turn? (*Pause.*) That's it . . . right round . . . now . . . back in. (*Pause.*) Oh I know it is not easy, dear, crawling backwards, but it is rewarding in the end. (*Pause.*) You have left your vaseline behind. (*She watches as he crawls back for vaseline.*) The lid! (*She watches as he crawls back towards hole. Irritated*) Not head first, I tell you! (*Pause.*) More to the right. (*Pause.*) The *right*, I said. (*Pause. Irritated*) Keep your tail down, can't you! (*Pause.*) Now. (*Pause.*) There! (*All these directions loud. Now in her normal voice, still turned towards him*) Can you hear me? (*Pause.*) I beseech you, Willie, just yes or no, can you hear me, just yes or nothing.

(*Pause.*)

WILLIE. Yes.

WINNIE (*turning front, same voice*). And now?

WILLIE (*irritated*). Yes.

WINNIE (*less loud*). And now?

WILLIE (*more irritated*). Yes.

WINNIE (*still less loud*). And now? (*A little louder*) And now?

WILLIE (*violently*). Yes!

WINNIE (*same voice*). Fear no more the heat o' the sun.[7] (*Pause.*) Did you hear that?

WILLIE (*irritated*). Yes.

---

[7]**Fear no more the heat o' the sun** This is the first line of a song in Shakespeare's *Cymbeline*, where it is sung as a dirge. In fact, the person who is thought to be dead is still alive.

WINNIE (*same voice*). What? (*Pause.*) What?
WILLIE (*more irritated*). Fear no more.

(*Pause.*)

WINNIE (*same voice*). No more what? (*Pause.*) Fear no more what?
WILLIE (*violently*). Fear no more!
WINNIE (*normal voice, garbled*). Bless you Willie I do appreciate your goodness I know what an effort it costs you, now you may relax I shall not trouble you again unless I am obliged to, by that I mean unless I come to the end of my own resources which is most unlikely, just to know that in theory you can hear me even though in fact you don't is all I need, just to feel you there within earshot and conceivably on the qui vive is all I ask, not to say anything I would not wish you to hear or liable to cause you pain, not to be babbling away on trust as it is were not knowing and something gnawing at me. (*Pause for breath.*) Doubt. (*Places index and second finger on heart area, moves them about, brings them to rest.*) Here. (*Moves them slightly.*) Abouts. (*Hand away.*) Oh no doubt the time will come when before I can utter a word I must make sure you heard the one that went before and then no doubt another come another time when I must learn to talk to myself a thing I could never bear to do such wilderness. (*Pause.*) Or gaze before me with compressed lips. (*She does so.*) All day long. (*Gaze and lips again.*) No. (*Smile.*) No no. (*Smile off.*) There is of course the bag. (*Turns towards it.*) There will always be the bag. (*Back front.*) Yes, I suppose so. (*Pause.*) Even when you are gone, Willie. (*She turns a little towards him.*) You *are* going, Willie, aren't you? (*Pause. Louder*) You *will* be going soon, Willie, won't you? (*Pause. Louder*) Willie! (*Pause. She cranes back and down to look at him.*) So you have taken off your straw, that is wise. (*Pause.*) You do look snug, I must say, with your chin on your hands and the old blue eyes like saucers in the shadows. (*Pause.*) Can you see me from there I wonder, I still wonder. (*Pause.*) No? (*Back front.*) Oh I know it does not follow when two are gathered together—(*faltering*)—in this way—(*normal*)—that because one sees the other the other sees the one, life has taught me that . . . too. (*Pause.*) Yes, life I suppose, there is no other word. (*She turns a little towards him.*) Could you see me, Willie, do you think, from where you are, if you were to raise your eyes in my direction? (*Turns a little further.*) Lift up your eyes to me, Willie, and tell me can you see me, do that for me, I'll lean back as far as I can. (*Does so. Pause.*) No? (*Pause.*) Well never mind. (*Turns back painfully front.*) The earth is very tight today, can it be I have put on flesh, I trust not. (*Pause. Absently, eyes lowered*) The great heat possibly. (*Starts to pat and stroke ground.*) All things expanding, some more than others. (*Pause. Patting and stroking*) Some less. (*Pause. Do.*) Oh I can well imagine what is passing through your mind, it is not enough to have to listen to the woman, now I must look at her as well. (*Pause. Do.*) Well it is very understandable. (*Pause. Do.*) Well it is very understandable. (*Pause. Do.*) Must understandable. (*Pause. Do.*) One does not appear to be asking a great deal, indeed at times it would seem hardly possible—(*voice breaks, falls to a murmur*)—to ask less—of a fellow-creature—to put it mildly—whereas actually—when you think about it—look into your heart—see the other—what he needs—peace—to be left in peace—then perhaps the moon—all this time—asking for the moon. (*Pause. Stroking hand suddenly still. Lively*) Oh I say, what have we here? (*Bending head to ground, incredulous*) Looks like life of some kind! (*Looks for spectacles, puts them on, bends closer. Pause.*) An emmet! (*Recoils. Shrill*) Willie, an emmet, a live emmet! (*Seizes magnifying-glass, bends to ground again, inspects through glass.*) Where's it gone? (*Inspects.*) Ah! (*Follows its progress through grass.*) Has like a little white ball in its arms. (*Follows progress. Hand still. Pause.*) It's gone in. (*Continues a moment to gaze at spot through glass, then slowly straightens up, lays down glass, takes off spectacles and gazes before her, spectacles in hand. Finally*) Like a little white ball.

(*Long pause. Gesture to lay down spectacles.*)

WILLIE. Eggs.
WINNIE (*arresting gesture*). What?

(*Pause.*)

WILLIE. Eggs. (*Pause. Gesture to lay down glasses.*) Formication.
WINNIE (*arresting gesture*). What?

(*Pause.*)

WILLIE. Formication.

(*Pause. She lays down spectacles, gazes before her. Finally.*)

WINNIE (*murmur*). God. (*Pause. Willie laughs quietly. After a moment she joins in. They laugh quietly together. Willie stops. She laughs on a moment alone. Willie joins in. They laugh together. She stops. Willie laughs on a moment alone. He stops. Pause. Normal voice.*) Ah well what a joy in any case to hear you laugh again, Willie, I was convinced I never would, you never would. (*Pause.*) I suppose some people might think us a trifle irreverent, but I doubt it. (*Pause.*) How can one better magnify the Almighty than by sniggering with him at his little jokes, particularly the poorer ones? (*Pause.*) I think you would back me up there, Willie. (*Pause.*) Or were we perhaps diverted by two quite different things? (*Pause.*) Oh well, what does it matter, that is what I always say, so long as one . . . you know . . . what is that wonderful line . . . laughing wild . . . something something laughing wild amid severest woe.[8] (*Pause.*) And now? (*Long pause.*)

[8] **laughing wild amid severest woe** Winnie is recalling a passage from Thomas Gray's "Ode on a Distant Prospect of Eton College" (lines 79–80).

Was I lovable once, Willie? (*Pause.*) Was I ever lovable? (*Pause.*) Do not misunderstand my question, I am not asking you if you loved me, we know all about that, I am asking you if you found me lovable—at one stage. (*Pause.*) No? (*Pause.*) You can't? (*Pause.*) Well I admit it is a teaser. And you have done more than your bit already, for the time being, just lie back now and relax, I shall not trouble you again unless I am compelled to, just to know you are there within hearing and conceivably on the semi-alert is . . . er . . . paradise enow.[9] (*Pause.*) The day is now well advanced. (*Smile.*) To speak in the old style. (*Smile off.*) And yet it is perhaps a little soon for my song. (*Pause.*) To sing too soon is a great mistake, I find. (*Turning towards bag*) There is of course the bag. (*Looking at bag*) The bag. (*Back front.*) Could I enumerate its contents? (*Pause.*) No. (*Pause.*) Could I, if some kind person were to come along and ask, What all have you got in that big black bag, Winnie? give an exhaustive answer? (*Pause.*) No. (*Pause.*) The depths in particular, who knows what treasures. (*Pause.*) What comforts. (*Turns to look at bag.*) Yes, there is the bag. (*Back front.*) But something tells me, Do not overdo the bag, Winnie, make use of it of course, let it help you . . . along, when stuck, by all means, but cast your mind forward, something tells me, cast your mind forward, Winnie, to the time when words must fail—(*she closes eyes, pause, opens eyes*)—and do not overdo the bag. (*Pause. She turns to look at bag.*) Perhaps just one quick dip. (*She turns back front, closes eyes, throws out left arm, plunges hand in bag and brings out revolver. Disgusted.*) You again! (*She opens eyes, brings revolver front and contemplates it. She weighs it in her palm.*) You'd think the weight of this thing would bring it down among the . . . last rounds. But no. It doesn't. Ever uppermost, like Browning. (*Pause.*) Brownie . . . (*Turning a little towards Willie*) Remember Brownie, Willie? (*Pause.*) Remember how you used to keep on at me to take it away from you? Take it away, Winnie, take it away, before I put myself out of my misery. (*Back front. Derisive*) Your misery! (*To revolver*) Oh I suppose it's a comfort to know you're there, but I'm tired of you. (*Pause.*) I'll leave you out, that's what I'll do. (*She lays revolver on ground to her right.*) There, that's your home from this day out. (*Smile.*) The old style! (*Smile off.*) And now? (*Long pause.*) Is gravity what it was, Willie, I fancy not. (*Pause.*) Yes, the feeling more and more that if I were not held—(*gesture*)—in this way, I would simply float up into the blue. (*Pause.*) And that perhaps some day the earth will yield and let me go, the pull is so great, yes, crack all round me and let

me out. (*Pause.*) Don't you ever have that feeling, Willie, of being sucked up? (*Pause.*) Don't you have to cling on sometimes, Willie? (*Pause. She turns a little towards him.*) Willie.

(*Pause.*)

WILLIE. *Sucked* up?

WINNIE. Yes, love, up into the blue, like gossamer. (*Pause.*) No? (*Pause.*) You don't? (*Pause.*) Ah well, natural laws, natural laws, I suppose it's like everything else, it all depends on the creature you happen to be. All I can say is for my part is that for me they are not what they were when I was young and . . . foolish and . . . (*faltering, head down*) . . . beautiful . . . possibly . . . lovely . . . in a way . . . to look at. (*Pause. Head up.*) Forgive me, Willie, sorrow keeps breaking in. (*Normal voice*) Ah well what a joy in any case to know you are there, as usual, and perhaps awake, and perhaps taking all this in, some of all this, what a happy day for me . . . it will have been. (*Pause.*) So far. (*Pause.*) What a blessing nothing grows, imagine if all this stuff were to start growing. (*Pause.*) Imagine. (*Pause.*) Ah yes, great mercies. (*Long pause.*) I can say no more. (*Pause.*) For the moment. (*Pause. Turns to look at bag. Back front. Smile.*) No no. (*Smile off. Looks at parasol.*) I suppose I might—(*takes up parasol*)—yes, I suppose I might . . . hoist this thing now. (*Begins to unfurl it. Following punctuated by mechanical difficulties overcome.*) One keeps putting off—putting up—for fear of putting up—too soon—and the day goes by—quite by—without one's having put up—at all. (*Parasol now fully open. Turned to her right she twirls it idly this way and that.*) Ah yes, so little to say, so little to do, and the fear so great, certain days, of finding oneself . . . left, with hours still to run, before the bell for sleep, and nothing more to say, nothing more to do, that the days go by, certain days go by, quite by, the bell goes, and little or nothing said, little or nothing done. (*Raising parasol*) That is the danger. (*Turning front*) To be guarded against. (*She gazes front, holding up parasol with right hand. Maximum pause.*) I used to perspire freely. (*Pause.*) Now hardly at all. (*Pause.*) The heat is much greater. (*Pause.*) The perspiration much less. (*Pause.*) That is what I find so wonderful. (*Pause.*) The way man adapts himself. (*Pause.*) To changing conditions. (*She transfers parasol to left hand. Long pause.*) Holding up wearies the arm. (*Pause.*) Not if one is going along. (*Pause.*) Only if one is at rest. (*Pause.*) That is a curious observation. (*Pause.*) I hope you heard that, Willie, I should be grieved to think you had not heard that. (*She takes parasol in both hands. Long pause.*) I am weary, holding it up, and I cannot put it down. (*Pause.*) I am worse off with it up than with it down, and I cannot put it down. (*Pause.*) Reason says, Put it down, Winnie, it is not helping you, put the thing down and get on with something else. (*Pause.*) I cannot. (*Pause.*) I cannot move. (*Pause.*) No,

[9] **paradise enow** The phrase is from Edward Fitzgerald's *The Rubaiyat of Omar Khayyam:* "A Book of Verses underneath the Bough, / A Jug of Wine, a Loaf of Bread—and Thou / Beside me singing in the Wilderness— / Oh, Wilderness were Paradise enow!"

something must happen, in the world, take place, some change, I cannot, if I am to move again. (*Pause.*) Willie. (*Mildly*) Help. (*Pause.*) No? (*Pause.*) Bid me put this thing down, Willie, I would obey you instantly, as I have always done, honoured and obeyed. (*Pause.*) Please, Willie. (*Mildly*) For pity's sake. (*Pause.*) No? (*Pause.*) You can't? (*Pause.*) Well I don't blame you, no, it would ill become me, who cannot move, to blame my Willie because he cannot speak. (*Pause.*) Fortunately I am in tongue again. (*Pause.*) That is what I find so wonderful, my two lamps, when one goes out the other burns brighter. (*Pause.*) Oh yes, great mercies. (*Maximum pause. The parasol goes on fire. Smoke, flames if feasible. She sniffs, looks up, throws parasol to her right behind mound, cranes back to watch it burning. Pause.*) Ah earth you old extinguisher. (*Back front.*) I presume this has occurred before, though I cannot recall it. (*Pause.*) Can you, Willie? (*Turns a little towards him.*) Can you recall this having occurred before? (*Pause. Cranes back to look at him.*) Do you know what has occurred, Willie? (*Pause.*) Have you gone off on me again? (*Pause.*) I do not ask if you are alive to all that is going on, I merely ask if you have not gone off on me again. (*Pause.*) Your eyes appear to be closed, but that has no particular significance we know. (*Pause.*) Raise a finger, dear, will you please, if you are not quite senseless. (*Pause.*) Do that for me, Willie please, just the little finger, if you are still conscious. (*Pause. Joyful*) Oh all five, you are a darling today, now I may continue with an easy mind. (*Back front.*) Yes, what ever occurred that did not occur before and yet . . . I wonder, yes, I confess I wonder. (*Pause.*). With the sun blazing so much fiercer down, and hourly fiercer, is it not natural things should go on fire never known to do so, in this way I mean, spontaneous like. (*Pause.*) Shall I myself not melt perhaps in the end, or burn, oh I do not mean necessarily burst into flames, no, just little by little be charred to a black cinder, all this—(*ample gesture of arms*)—visible flesh. (*Pause.*) On the other hand, did I ever know a temperate time? (*Pause.*) No. (*Pause.*) I speak of temperate times and torrid times, they are empty words. (*Pause.*) I speak of when I was not yet caught—in this way—and had my legs and had the use of my legs, and could seek out a shady place, like you, when I was tired of the sun, or a sunny place when I was tired of the shade, like you, and they are all empty words. (*Pause.*) It is no hotter today than yesterday, it will be no hotter tomorrow than today, how could it, and so on back into the far past, forward into the far future. (*Pause.*) And should one day the earth cover my breasts, then I shall never have seen my breasts, no one ever seen my breasts. (*Pause.*) I hope you caught something of that, Willie, I should be sorry to think you had caught nothing of all that, it is not every day I rise to such heights. (*Pause.*) Yes, something seems to have occurred, something to have seemed to occur, and nothing has occurred, nothing at

all, you are quite right, Willie. (*Pause.*) The sunshade will be there again tomorrow, beside me on this mound, to help me through the day. (*Pause. She takes up mirror.*) I take up this little glass, I shiver it on a stone—(*does so*)—I throw it away—(*does so far behind her*)—it will be in the bag again tomorrow, without a scratch, to help me through the day. (*Pause.*) No, one can do nothing. (*Pause.*) That is what I find so wonderful, the way things . . . (*voice breaks, head down*) . . . things . . . so wonderful. (*Long pause, head down. Finally turns, still bowed, to bag, brings out unidentifiable odds and ends, stuffs them back, fumbles deeper, brings out finally musical-box, winds it up, turns it on, listens for a moment holding it in both hands, huddled over it, turns back front, straightens up and listens to tune, holding box to breast with both hands. It plays the Waltz Duet "I Love You So" from* The Merry Widow. *Gradually happy expression. She sways to the rhythm. Music stops. Pause. Brief burst of hoarse song without words—musical-box tune—from Willie. Increase of happy expression. She lays down box.*) Oh this will have been a happy day! (*She claps hands.*) Again, Willie, again! (*Claps.*) Encore, Willie, please! (*Pause. Happy expression off.*) No? You won't do that for me? (*Pause.*) Well it is very understandable, very understandable. One cannot sing just to please someone, however much one loves them, no, song must come from the heart, that is what I always say, pour out from the inmost, like a thrush. (*Pause.*) How often I have said, in evil hours, Sing now, Winnie, sing your song, there is nothing else for it, and did not. (*Pause.*) Could not. (*Pause.*) No, like the thrush, or the bird of dawning,[10] with no thought of benefit, to oneself or anyone else. (*Pause.*) And now? (*Long pause. Low*) Strange feeling. (*Pause. Do.*) Strange feeling that someone is looking at me. I am clear, then dim, then gone, then dim again, then clear again, and so on, back and forth, in and out of someone's eye. (*Pause. Do.*) Strange? (*Pause. Do.*) No, here all is strange. (*Pause. Normal voice*) Something says, Stop talking now, Winnie, for a minute, don't squander all your words for the day, stop talking and do something for a change, will you? (*She raises hands and holds them open before her eyes. Apostrophic*) Do something! (*She closes hands.*) What claws! (*She turns to bag, rummages in it, brings out finally a nailfile, turns back front and begins to file nails. Files for a time in silence, then the following punctuated by filing.*) There floats up—into my thoughts—a Mr. Shower—a Mr. and perhaps a Mrs. Shower—no—they are holding hands—his fiancée then more likely—or just some—loved one. (*Looks closer at nails.*) Very brittle today. (*Resumes filing.*) Shower—Shower—does the

---

[10]**bird of dawning** In *Hamlet*, Marcellus says that on Christmas Eve the cock—"the bird of dawning"—sings all night long, and "no [evil] spirit can walk abroad" (1.1.160–61).

name mean anything—to you, Willie—evoke any reality, I mean—for you, Willie—don't answer if you don't—feel up to it—you have done more—than your bit—already—Shower—Shower. (*Inspects filed nails.*) Bit more like it. (*Raises head, gazes front.*) Keep yourself nice, Winnie, that's what I always say, come what may, keep yourself nice. (*Pause. Resumes filing.*) Yes—Shower—Shower—(*stops filing, raises head, gazes front, pause*)—or Cooker, perhaps I should say Cooker. (*Turning a little towards Willie.*) Cooker, Willie, does Cooker strike a chord? (*Pause. Turns a little further. Louder*) Cooker, Willie, does Cooker ring a bell, the name Cooker? (*Pause. She cranes back to look at him. Pause.*) Oh really! (*Pause.*) Have you no handkerchief, darling? (*Pause.*) Have you no delicacy? (*Pause.*) Oh, Willie, you're not eating it! Spit it out, dear, spit it out! (*Pause. Back front.*) Ah well, I suppose it's only natural. (*Break in voice.*) Human. (*Pause. Do.*) What *is* one to do? (*Head down. Do.*) All day long. (*Pause. Do.*) Day after day. (*Pause. Head up. Smile. Calm*) The old style! (*Smile off. Resumes nails.*) No, done him. (*Passes on to next.*) Should have put on my glasses. (*Pause.*) Too late now. (*Finishes left hand, inspects it.*) Bit more human. (*Starts right hand. Following punctuated as before.*) Well anyway—this man Shower—or Cooker—no matter—and the woman—hand in hand—in the other hands bags—kind of big brown grips—standing there gaping at me—and at last this man Shower—or Cooker—ends in er anyway—stake my life on that—What's she doing? he says—What's the idea? he says—stuck up to her diddies in the bleeding ground—coarse fellow—What does it mean? he says—What's it meant to mean?—and so on—lot more stuff like that—usual drivel—Do you hear me? he says—I do, she says, God help me—What do you mean, he says, God help you? (*Stops filing, raises head, gazes front.*) And you, she says, what's the idea of you, she says, what are you meant to mean? It is because you're still on your two flat feet, with your old ditty full of tinned muck and changes of underwear, dragging me up and down this fornicating wilderness, coarse creature, fit mate—(*with sudden violence*)—let go of my hand and drop for God's sake, she says, drop! (*Pause. Resumes filing.*) Why doesn't he dig her out? he says—referring to you, my dear—What good is she to him like that?—What good is he to her like that?—and so on—usual tosh—Good! she says, have a heart for God's sake—Dig her out, he says, dig her out, no sense in her like that—Dig her out with what? she says—I'd dig her out with my bare hands, he says—must have been man and—wife. (*Files in silence.*) Next thing they're away—hand in hand—and the bags—dim—then gone—last human kind—to stray this way. (*Finishes right hand, inspects it, lays down file, gazes front.*) Strange thing, time like this, drift up into the mind. (*Pause.*) Strange? (*Pause.*) No, here all is strange. (*Pause.*) Thankful for it in any case. (*Voice breaks.*) Most thankful. (*Head down.*

Pause. Head up. Calm) Bow and raise the head, bow and raise, always that. (*Pause.*) And now? (*Long pause. Starts putting things back in bag, toothbrush last. This operation, interrupted by pauses as indicated, punctuates following.*) It is perhaps a little soon—to make ready—for the night—(*stops tidying, head up, smile*)—the old style!—(*smile off, resumes tidying*)—and yet I do—make ready for the night—feeling it at hand—the bell for sleep—saying to myself—Winnie—it will not be long now, Winnie—until the bell for sleep. (*Stops tidying, head up.*) Sometimes I am wrong. (*Smile.*) But not often. (*Smile off.*) Sometimes all is over, for the day, all done, all said, all ready for the night, and the day not over, far from over, the night not ready, far, far from ready. (*Smile.*) But not often. (*Smile off.*) Yes, the bell for sleep, when I feel it at hand, and so make ready for the night—(*gesture*)—in this way, sometimes I am wrong (*smile*)—but not often. (*Smile off. Resumes tidying.*) I used to think—I say I used to think—that all these things—put back into the bag—if too soon—put back too soon—could be taken out again—if necessary—if needed—and so on—indefinitely—back into the bag—back out of the bag—until the bell—went. (*Stops tidying, head up, smile.*) But no. (*Smile broader.*) No no. (*Smile off. Resumes tidying.*) I suppose this—might seem strange—this—what shall I say—this what I have said—yes—(*she takes up revolver*)—strange—(*she turns to put revolver in bag*)—were it not—(*about to put revolver in bag she arrests gesture and turns back front*)—were it not—(*she lays down revolver to her right, stops tidying, head up*)—that all seems strange. (*Pause.*) Most strange. (*Pause.*) Never any change. (*Pause.*) And more and more strange. (*Pause. She bends to mound again, takes up last object, i.e., toothbrush, and turns to put it in bag when her attention is drawn to disturbance from Willie. She cranes back and to her right to see. Pause.*) Weary of your hole, dear? (*Pause.*) Well I can understand that. (*Pause.*) Don't forget your straw. (*Pause.*) Not the crawler you were, poor darling. (*Pause.*) No, not the crawler I gave my heart to. (*Pause.*) The hands and knees, love, try the hands and knees. (*Pause.*) The knees! The knees! (*Pause.*) What a curse, mobility! (*She follows with eyes his progress towards her behind mound, i.e., towards place he occupied at beginning of act.*) Another foot, Willie, and you're home. (*Pause as she observes last foot.*) Ah! (*Turns back front laboriously, rubs neck.*) Crick in my neck admiring you. (*Rubs neck.*) But it's worth it, well worth it. (*Turning slightly towards him*) Do you know what I dream sometimes? (*Pause.*) What I dream sometimes, Willie. (*Pause.*) That you'll come round and live this side where I could see you. (*Pause. Back front.*) I'd be a different woman. (*Pause.*) Unrecognizable. (*Turning slightly towards him*) Or just now and then, come round this side just every now and then and let me feast on you. (*Back front.*) But you can't, I know. (*Head down.*) I know. (*Pause. Head up.*) Well anyway—(*looks at toothbrush in her hand*)—can't be long now—(*looks at brush*)—until the bell. (*Top back of Willie's head appears above slope. Winnie looks closer at brush.*) Fully guaranteed . . . (*head up*) . . . what's this it was? (*Willie's hand appears with handkerchief, spreads it on skull, disappears.*) Genuine pure . . . fully guaranteed . . . (*Willie's hand appears with boater, settles it on head, rakish angle, disappears*) . . . genuine pure . . . ah! hog's setae. (*Pause.*) What is a hog exactly? (*Pause. Turns slightly towards Willie*) What exactly is a hog, Willie, do you know, I can't remember. (*Pause. Turning a little further, pleading*) What *is* a hog, Willie, please!

(*Pause.*)

WILLIE. Castrated male swine. (*Happy expression appears on Winnie's face.*) Reared for slaughter.

(*Happy expression increases. Willie opens newspaper, hands invisible. Tops of yellow sheets appear on either side of his head. Winnie gazes before her with happy expression.*)

WINNIE. Oh this *is* a happy day! (*Pause.*) After all. (*Pause.*) So far.

(*Pause. Happy expression off. Willie turns page. Pause. He turns another page. Pause.*)

WILLIE. Opening for smart youth.

(*Pause. Winnie takes off hat, turns to put it in bag, arrests gesture, turns back front. Smile.*)

WINNIE. No. (*Smile broader.*) No no. (*Smile off. Puts on hat again, gazes front, pause.*) And now? (*Pause.*) Sing. (*Pause.*) Sing your song, Winnie. (*Pause.*) No? (*Pause.*) Then pray. (*Pause.*) Pray your prayer, Winnie.

(*Pause. Willie turns page. Pause.*)

WILLIE. Wanted bright boy.

(*Pause. Winnie gazes before her. Willie turns page. Pause. Newspaper disappears. Long pause.*)

WINNIE. Pray your old prayer, Winnie.

(*Long pause.*)

CURTAIN

ACT 2

Scene as before.

Winnie imbedded up to neck, hat on head, eyes closed. Her head, which she can no longer turn, nor bow, nor raise, faces front motionless throughout act. Movements of eyes as indicated.

Bag and parasol as before. Revolver conspicuous to her right on mound.

Long pause.

Bell rings loudly. She opens eyes at once. Bell stops. She gazes front. Long pause.

WINNIE. Hail, holy light. (*Long pause. She closes her eyes. Bell rings loudly. She opens eyes at once. Bell stops. She gazes front. Long smile. Smile off. Long pause.*) Someone is looking at me still. (*Pause.*) Caring for me still. (*Pause.*) That is what I find so wonderful. (*Pause.*) Eyes on my eyes. (*Pause.*) What is that unforgettable line? (*Pause. Eyes right.*) Willie. (*Pause. Louder*) Willie. (*Pause. Eyes front.*) May one still speak of time? (*Pause.*) Say it is a long time now, Willie, since I saw you. (*Pause.*) Since I heard you. (*Pause.*) May one? (*Pause.*) One does. (*Smile.*) The old style! (*Smile off.*) There is so little one can speak of. (*Pause.*) One speaks of it all. (*Pause.*) All one can. (*Pause.*) I used to think . . . (*pause*) . . . I say I used to think that I would learn to talk alone. (*Pause.*) By that I mean to myself, the wilderness. (*Smile.*) But no. (*Smile broader.*) No no. (*Smile off.*) Ergo you are there. (*Pause.*) Oh no doubt you are dead, like the others, no doubt you have died, or gone away and left me, like the others, it doesn't matter, you are there. (*Pause. Eyes left.*) The bag too is there, the same as ever, I can see it. (*Pause. Eyes right. Louder*) The bag is there, Willie, as good as ever, the one you gave me that day . . . to go to market. (*Pause. Eyes front.*) That day. (*Pause.*) What day? (*Pause.*) I used to pray. (*Pause.*) I say used to pray. (*Pause.*) Yes, I must confess I did. (*Smile.*) Not now. (*Smile broader.*) No no. (*Smile off. Pause.*) Then . . . now . . . what difficulties here, for the mind. (*Pause.*) To have been always what I am—and so changed from what I was. (*Pause.*) I am the one, I say the one, then the other. (*Pause.*) Now the one, then the other (*Pause.*) There is so little one can say, one says it all. (*Pause.*) All one can. (*Pause.*) And no truth in it anywhere. (*Pause.*) My arms. (*Pause.*) My breasts. (*Pause.*) What arms? (*Pause.*) What breasts? (*Pause.*) Willie. (*Pause.*) What Willie? (*Sudden vehement affirmation*) My Willie! (*Eyes right, calling*) Willie! (*Pause. Louder*) Willie! (*Pause. Eyes front.*) Ah well, not to know, not to know for sure, great mercy, all I ask. (*Pause.*) Ah yes . . . then . . . now . . . beechen green[11] . . . this . . . Charlie . . . kisses . . . this . . . all that . . . deep trouble for the mind. (*Pause.*) But it does not trouble mine. (*Smile.*) Not now. (*Smile broader.*) No no. (*Smile off. Long pause. She closes eyes. Bell rings loudly. She opens eyes. Pause.*) Eyes float up that seem to close in peace . . . to see . . . in peace. (*Pause.*) Not mine. (*Smile.*) Not now. (*Smile broader.*) No no. (*Smile off. Long pause.*) Willie. (*Pause.*) Do you think the earth has lost its atmosphere, Willie? (*Pause.*) Do you, Willie? (*Pause.*) You have no opinion? (*Pause.*) Well that

---

[11]**beechen green** The phrase comes from John Keats's "Ode to a Nightingale," a poem about death and immortality.

is like you, you never had any opinion about anything. (*Pause.*) It's understandable. (*Pause.*) Most. (*Pause.*) The earthball. (*Pause.*) I sometimes wonder. (*Pause.*) Perhaps not quite all. (*Pause.*) There always remains something. (*Pause.*) Of everything. (*Pause.*) Some remains. (*Pause.*) If the mind were to go. (*Pause.*) It won't of course. (*Pause.*) Not quite. (*Pause.*) Not mine. (*Smile.*) Not now. (*Smile broader.*) No no. (*Smile off. Long pause.*) It might be the eternal cold. (*Pause.*) Everlasting perishing cold. (*Pause.*) Just chance, I take it, happy chance. (*Pause.*) Oh yes, great mercies, great mercies. (*Pause.*) And now? (*Long pause.*) The face. (*Pause.*) The nose. (*She squints down.*) I can see it . . . (*squinting down*) . . . the tip . . . the nostrils . . . breath of life . . . that curve you so admired . . . (*pouts*) . . . a hint of lip . . . (*pouts again*) . . . if I pout them out . . . (*sticks out tongue*) . . . the tongue of course . . . you so admired . . . if I stick it out . . . (*sticks it out again*) . . . the tip . . . (*eyes up*) . . . suspicion of brow . . . eyebrow . . . imagination possibly . . . (*eyes left*) . . . cheek . . . no . . . (*eyes right*) . . . no . . . (*distends cheeks*) . . . even if I puff them out . . . (*eyes left, distends cheeks again*) . . . no . . . no damask.[12] (*Eyes front.*) That is all. (*Pause.*) The bag of course . . . (*eyes left*) . . . a little blurred perhaps . . . but the bag. (*Eyes front. Offhand*) The earth of course and sky. (*Eyes right.*) The sunshade you gave me . . . that day . . . (*pause*) . . . that day . . . the lake . . . the reeds. (*Eyes front. Pause.*) What day? (*Pause.*) What reeds? (*Long pause. Eyes close. Bell rings loudly. Eyes open. Pause. Eyes right.*) Brownie of course. (*Pause.*) You remember Brownie, Willie, I can see him. (*Pause.*) Brownie is there, Willie, beside me. (*Pause. Loud*) Brownie is there, Willie. (*Pause. Eyes front.*) That is all. (*Pause.*) What would I do without them? (*Pause.*) What would I do without them, when words fail? (*Pause.*) Gaze before me, with compressed lips. (*Long pause while she does so.*) I cannot. (*Pause.*) Ah yes, great mercies, great mercies. (*Long pause. Low*) Sometimes I hear sounds. (*Listening expression. Normal voice*) But not often. (*Pause.*) They are a boon, sounds are a boon, they help me . . . through the day. (*Smile.*) The old style! (*Smile off.*) Yes, those are happy days, when there are sounds. (*Pause.*) When I hear sounds. (*Pause.*) I used to think . . . (*pause*) . . . I say I used to think they were in my head. (*Smile.*) But no. (*Smile broader.*) No no. (*Smile off.*) That was just logic. (*Pause.*) Reason. (*Pause.*) I have not lost my reason. (*Pause.*) Not yet. (*Pause.*) Not all. (*Pause.*) Some remains. (*Pause.*) Sounds. (*Pause.*) Like little . . . sunderings, little falls . . . apart. (*Pause. Low*) It's things, Willie. (*Pause. Normal voice*) In the bag, outside the bag.

[12]**damask** Given the fact that she is speaking of her cheeks, she apparently is quoting from Shakespeare's *Twelfth Night,* in which Viola describes a woman who lost the color from her "damask cheek" (2.2.114).

(*Pause.*) Ah yes, things have their life, that is what I always say, *things* have a life. (*Pause.*) Take my looking-glass, it doesn't need me. (*Pause.*) The bell. (*Pause.*) It hurts like a knife. (*Pause.*) A gouge. (*Pause.*) One cannot ignore it. (*Pause.*) How often . . . (*pause*) . . . I say how often I have said, Ignore it, Winnie, ignore the bell, pay no heed, just sleep and wake, sleep and wake, as you please, open and close the eyes, as you please, or in the way you find most helpful. (*Pause.*) Open and close the eyes, Winnie, open and close, always that. (*Pause.*) But no. (*Smile.*) Not now. (*Smile broader.*) No no. (*Smile off. Pause.*) What now? (*Pause.*) What now, Willie? (*Long pause.*) There is my story of course, when all else fails. (*Pause.*) A life. (*Smile.*) A long life. (*Smile off.*) Beginning in the womb, where life used to begin, Mildred has memories, she will have memories, of the womb, before she dies, the mother's womb. (*Pause.*) She is now four or five already and has recently been given a big waxen dolly. (*Pause.*) Fully clothed, complete outfit. (*Pause.*) Shoes, socks, undies, complete set, frilly frock, gloves. (*Pause.*) White mesh. (*Pause.*) A little white straw hat with a chin elastic. (*Pause.*) Pearly necklet. (*Pause.*) A little picture-book with legends in real print to go under her arm when she takes her walk. (*Pause.*) China blue eyes that open and shut. (*Pause. Narrative*) The sun was not well up when Milly rose, descended the steep . . . (*pause*) . . . slipped on her nightgown, descended all alone the steep wooden stairs, backwards on all fours, though she had been forbidden to do so, entered the . . . (*pause*) . . . tiptoed down the silent passage, entered the nursery and began to undress Dolly. (*Pause.*) Crept under the table and began to undress Dolly. (*Pause.*) Scolding her . . . the while. (*Pause.*) Suddenly a mouse—(*Long pause.*) Gently, Winnie. (*Long pause. Calling*) Willie! (*Pause. Louder*) Willie! (*Pause. Mild reproach*) I sometimes find your attitude a little strange, Willie, all this time, it is not like you to be wantonly cruel. (*Pause.*) Strange? (*Pause.*) No. (*Smile.*) Not here. (*Smile broader.*) Not now. (*Smile off.*) And yet . . . (*Suddenly anxious*) I do hope nothing is amiss. (*Eyes right, loud*) Is all well, dear? (*Pause. Eyes front. To herself*) God grant he did not go in head foremost! (*Eyes right, loud*) You're not stuck, Willie? (*Pause. Do.*) You're not jammed, Willie? (*Eyes front, distressed*) Perhaps he is crying out for help all this time and I do not hear him! (*Pause.*) I do of course hear cries. (*Pause.*) But they are in my head surely. (*Pause.*) Is it possible that . . . (*Pause. With finality*) No no, my head was always full of cries. (*Pause.*) Faint confused cries. (*Pause.*) They come. (*Pause.*) Then go. (*Pause.*) As on a wind. (*Pause.*) That is what I find so wonderful. (*Pause.*) They cease. (*Pause.*) Ah yes, great mercies, great mercies. (*Pause.*) The day is now well advanced. (*Smile. Smile off.*) And yet it is perhaps a little soon for my song. (*Pause.*) To sing too soon is fatal, I always find. (*Pause.*) On the other hand it is possible to leave it too late. (*Pause.*) The bell goes for sleep and one has not sung. (*Pause.*) The whole day has flown—(*smile, smile off*)—flown by, quite by, and no song of any class, kind or description. (*Pause.*) There is a problem here. (*Pause.*) One cannot sing . . . just like that, no. (*Pause.*) It bubbles up, for some unknown reason, the time is ill chosen, one chokes it back. (*Pause.*) One says, Now is the time, it is now or never, and one cannot. (*Pause.*) Simply cannot sing. (*Pause.*) Not a note. (*Pause.*) Another thing, Willie, while we are on this subject. (*Pause.*) The sadness after song. (*Pause.*) Have you run across that, Willie? (*Pause.*) In the course of your experience. (*Pause.*) No? (*Pause.*) Sadness after intimate sexual intercourse one is familiar with of course. (*Pause.*) You would concur with Aristotle there, Willie, I fancy. (*Pause.*) Yes, that one knows and is prepared to face. (*Pause.*) But after song . . . (*Pause.*) It does not last of course. (*Pause.*) That is what I find so wonderful. (*Pause.*) It wears away. (*Pause.*) What are those exquisite lines? (*Pause.*) Go forget me why should something o'er that something shadow fling . . . go forget me . . . why should sorrow . . . brightly smile . . . go forget me . . . never hear me . . . sweetly smile . . . brightly sing[13] . . . (*Pause. With a sigh*) One loses one's classics. (*Pause.*) Oh not all. (*Pause.*) A part. (*Pause.*) A part remains. (*Pause.*) That is what I find so wonderful, a part remains, of one's classics, to help one through the day. (*Pause.*) Oh yes, many mercies, many mercies. (*Pause.*) And now? (*Pause.*) And now, Willie? (*Long pause.*) I call to the eye of the mind[14] . . . Mr. Shower—or Cooker. (*She closes her eyes. Bell rings loudly. She opens her eyes. Pause.*) Hand in hand, in the other hands bags. (*Pause.*) Getting on . . . in life. (*Pause.*) No longer young, not yet old. (*Pause.*) Standing there gaping at me. (*Pause.*) Can't have been a bad bosom, he says, in its day. (*Pause.*) Seen worse shoulders, he says, in my time. (*Pause.*) Does she feel her legs? he says. (*Pause.*) Is there any life in her legs? he says. (*Pause.*) Has she anything on underneath? he says. (*Pause.*) Ask her, he says, I'm shy. (*Pause.*) Ask her what? she says. (*Pause.*) Is there any life in her legs. (*Pause.*) Has she anything on underneath. (*Pause.*) Ask her yourself, she says. (*Pause. With sudden violence*) Let go of me for Christ sake and drop! (*Pause. Do.*) Drop dead! (*Smile.*) But no. (*Smile broader.*) No no. (*Smile off.*) I watch them recede. (*Pause.*) Hand in hand—and the bags. (*Pause.*)

[13]**Go forget me . . . brightly sing** Winnie is quoting from the first stanza of Charles Wolfe's "Go, Forget Me": The stanza runs thus: "Go forget me! Why should sorrow / O'er that brow a shadow fling?/Go, forget me,—and tomorrow/Brightly smile and sweetly sing. / Smile,—though I shall not be near thee. / Sing—though I shall never hear thee. / May thy soul with pleasure shine, / Lasting as the gloom of mine." [14]**I call to the eye of the mind** Winnie quotes the first line of a play by W. B. Yeats, *At the Hawk's Well*. The play contrasts the modern fear of old age with life in ancient heroic Ireland.

Dim. (*Pause.*) Then gone. (*Pause.*) Last human kind—to stray this way. (*Pause.*) Up to date. (*Pause.*) And now? (*Pause. Low*) Help. (*Pause. Do.*) Help, Willie. (*Pause. Do.*) No? (*Long pause. Narrative*) Suddenly a mouse . . . (*Pause.*) Suddenly a mouse ran up her little thigh and Mildred, dropping Dolly in her fright, began to scream—(*Winnie gives a sudden piercing scream*)—and screamed and screamed—(*Winnie screams twice*)—screamed and screamed and screamed and screamed till all came running, in their night attire, papa, mamma, Bibby and . . . old Annie, to see what was the matter . . . (*pause*) . . . what on earth could possibly be the matter. (*Pause.*) Too late. (*Pause.*) Too late. (*Long pause. Just audible*) Willie. (*Pause. Normal voice*) Ah well, not long now, Winnie, can't be long now, until the bell for sleep. (*Pause.*) Then you may close your eyes, then you *must* close your eyes—and keep them closed. (*Pause.*) Why say that again? (*Pause.*) I used to think . . . (*pause*) . . . I say I used to think there was no difference between one fraction of a second and the next. (*Pause.*) I used to say . . . (*pause*) . . . I say I used to say, Winnie, you are changeless, there is never any difference between one fraction of a second and the next. (*Pause.*) Why bring that up again? (*Pause.*) There is so little one can bring up, one brings up all. (*Pause.*) All one can. (*Pause.*) My neck is hurting me. (*Pause. With sudden violence*) My neck is hurting me! (*Pause.*) Ah that's better. (*With mild irritation*) Everything within reason. (*Long pause.*) I can do no more. (*Pause.*) Say no more. (*Pause.*) But I must say more. (*Pause.*) Problem here. (*Pause.*) No, something must move, in the world, I can't any more. (*Pause.*) A zephyr. (*Pause.*) A breath. (*Pause.*) What are those immortal lines? (*Pause.*) It might be the eternal dark. (*Pause.*) Black night without end. (*Pause.*) Just chance, I take it, happy chance. (*Pause.*) Oh yes, abounding mercies. (*Long pause.*) And now? (*Pause.*) And now, Willie? (*Long pause.*) That day. (*Pause.*) The pink fizz. (*Pause.*) The flute glasses. (*Pause.*) The last guest gone. (*Pause.*) The last bumper with the bodies nearly touching. (*Pause.*) The look. (*Long pause.*) What day? (*Long pause.*) What look? (*Long pause.*) I hear cries. (*Pause.*) Sing. (*Pause.*) Sing your old song, Winnie.

(*Long pause. Suddenly alert expression. Eyes switch right. Willie's head appears to her right round corner of mound. He is on all fours, dressed to kill—top hat, morning coat, striped trousers, etc., white gloves in hand. Very long bushy white Battle of Britain moustache. He halts, gazes front, smoothes moustache. He emerges completely from behind mound, turns to his left, halts, looks up at Winnie. He advances on all fours towards centre, halts, turns head front, gazes front, strokes moustache, straightens tie, adjusts hat, advances a little further, halts, takes off hat and looks up at Winnie. He is now not far from centre and within her field of vision. Unable to sustain effort of looking up he sinks head to ground.*)

WINNIE (*mondaine*). Well this is an unexpected pleasure! (*Pause.*) Reminds me of the day you came whining for my hand. (*Pause.*) I worship you, Winnie, be mine. (*He looks up.*) Life a mockery without Win. (*She goes off into a giggle.*) What a get up, you do look a sight! (*Giggles.*) Where are the flowers? (*Pause.*) That smile today.[15] (*Willie sinks head.*) What's that on your neck, an anthrax? (*Pause.*) Want to watch that, Willie, before it gets a hold on you. (*Pause.*) Where were you all this time? (*Pause.*) What were you doing all this time? (*Pause.*) Changing? (*Pause.*) Did you not hear me screaming for you? (*Pause.*) Did you get stuck in your hole? (*Pause. He looks up.*) That's right, Willie, look at me. (*Pause.*) Feast your old eyes, Willie. (*Pause.*) Does anything remain? (*Pause.*) Any remains? (*Pause.*) No? (*Pause.*) I haven't been able to look after it, you know. (*He sinks his head.*) You are still recognizable, in a way. (*Pause.*) Are you thinking of coming to live this side now . . . for a bit maybe? (*Pause.*) No? (*Pause.*) Just a brief call? (*Pause.*) Have you gone deaf, Willie? (*Pause.*) Dumb? (*Pause.*) Oh I know you were never one to talk, I worship you Winnie be mine and then nothing from that day forth only tidbits from Reynold's News. (*Eyes front. Pause.*) Ah well, what matter, that's what I always say, it will have been a happy day, after all, another happy day. (*Pause.*) Not long now, Winnie. (*Pause.*) I hear cries. (*Pause.*) Do you ever hear cries, Willie? (*Pause.*) No? (*Eyes back on Willie.*) Willie. (*Pause.*) Look at me again, Willie. (*Pause.*) Once more, Willie. (*He looks up. Happily*) Ah! (*Pause. Shocked*) What ails you, Willie, I never saw such an expression! (*Pause.*) Put on your hat, dear, it's the sun, don't stand on ceremony, I won't mind. (*He drops hat and gloves and starts to crawl up mound towards her. Gleeful*) Oh I say, this is terrific! (*He halts, clinging to mound with one hand, reaching up with the other.*) Come on, dear, put a bit of jizz into it, I'll cheer you on. (*Pause.*) Is it me you're after, Willie . . . or is it something else? (*Pause.*) Do you want to touch my face . . . again? (*Pause.*) Is it a kiss you're after, Willie . . . or is it something else? (*Pause.*)

There was a time when I could have given you a hand. (*Pause.*) And then a time before that again when I did give you a hand. (*Pause.*) You were always in dire need of a hand, Willie. (*He slithers back to foot of mound and lies with face to ground.*) Brrum! (*Pause. He rises to hands and knees, raises his face towards her.*) Have another go, Willie, I'll cheer you on. (*Pause.*) Don't look at me like that! (*Pause. Vehement*) Don't look at me like that! (*Pause. Low*) Have you gone off your head, Willie? (*Pause. Do.*) Out of your poor old wits, Willie?

(*Pause.*)

WILLIE (*just audible*). Win.

(*Pause. Winnie's eyes front. Happy expression appears, grows.*)

WINNIE. Win! (*Pause.*) Oh this *is* a happy day, this will have been another happy day! (*Pause.*) After all. (*Pause.*) So far.

(*Pause. She hums tentatively beginning of song, then sings softly, musical-box tune.*)

Though I say not
What I may not
Let you hear,
Yet the swaying
Dance is saying,
Love me dear!
Every touch of fingers
Tells me what I know,
Says for you,
It's true, it's true,
You love me so!

(*Pause. Happy expression off. She closes her eyes. Bell rings loudly. She opens her eyes. She smiles, gazing front. She turns her eyes, smiling, to Willie, still on his hands and knees looking up at her. Smile off. They look at each other. Long pause.*)

CURTAIN

TOPICS FOR CRITICAL THINKING AND WRITING

 THE PLAY ON THE PAGE

1. The first director of *Happy Days*, Alan Schneider, said that Beckett originally conceived of Winnie's part as a male part but changed his mind because pockets wouldn't work as well as a handbag. Does the meaning of the present play depend to any degree on the fact that one character is male, the other female?

2. One critic (A. Alvarez, in *Samuel Beckett*) says the play offers "a sour view of a cozy marriage. . . . [Beckett] finds [Winnie] and her manic defenses ludicrous at best." How profitable do you find this line of thinking?

3. Focus your attention on Willie, formulating a thesis about his personality and the function he serves in the play. Why has Beckett given Willie only one line in Act 2?

---

[15]**That smile today** Winnie is quoting from Robert Herrick's "To the Virgins, to Make Much of Time": "Gather ye rosebuds while ye may, / Old Time is still a-flying, / And this same flower that smiles today, / Tomorrow will be dying."

4. The director Peter Brook has said of *Happy Days*, "The optimism of the lady buried in the ground is not a virtue, it is the element that blinds her to the truth of her situation." Evaluate.
5. On page 756 Winnie tells how a man and a woman came by, and she reproduces their conversation:

> WINNIE. . . . What's she doing? he says—What's the idea? he says—stuck up to her diddies in the bleeding ground—coarse fellow—What does it mean?

he says—What's it meant to mean?—and so on—lot more stuff like that—usual drivel—Do you hear me? he says—I do, she says, God help me—What do you mean, he says, God help you? . . . And you, she says, what's the idea of you, she says, what are you meant to mean?

Do you think Beckett here is telling us that the play has no meaning?

THE PLAY ON THE STAGE

6. In another of Beckett's plays, *Endgame*, two characters are in garbage cans. What do you think would be gained or lost if Winnie were in a garbage can instead of in a mound?
7. Is there some dramatic significance or advantage to burying Winnie in a mound, rather than at ground level?
8. Why is Winnie's bag black, rather than, for example, brightly colored or patterned?
9. What do you imagine is the audience's reaction when the parasol goes on fire? How does this reaction compare with Winnie's and Willie's reaction?
10. In the second act, when Winnie is buried up to the chin, gestures of course are fewer than in the first act. Nevertheless, what gestures or movements are there in Act 2?
11. When at the end Willie crawls up the mound and Winnie exclaims, "Don't look at me like that! . . . Have you gone out of your head, Willie?" do you think Willie is expressing renewed love, or is he thinking of shooting her with the revolver? Is it relevant that Willie is said to be "dressed to kill"?
12. The bell that wakes Winnie rings "piercingly." Why not, instead, a cheery cuckoo clock, or a musical sound? Winnie several times mentions "the bell for sleep," but we never hear it, even though it might easily have sounded at the end of Act 1. *Should* we have heard it?
13. In the first act the bell rings twice, at the beginning. In the second act it rings several times, interrupting Winnie's monologues. Is there any meaning to this? Does it perhaps mean that time is moving faster—and what does *that* mean?
14. Consider the first few lines of dialog, and imagine how each is spoken: "Another heavenly day. . . . For Jesus Christ sake Amen. . . . World without end Amen. . . . Begin, Winnie. . . . Begin your day, Winnie."
15. Imagine the final tableau, and describe what emotions you think an audience member would feel.
16. Do you think *Happy Days* would be best acted in a small theater (for example, one with a seating capacity of 150) or a big theater? Provide reasons for your opinion.

THE PLAY IN PERFORMANCE

Although Beckett already had established a reputation as a writer of fiction, he became widely known as a playwright relatively late in life, in 1953, with the production in France of *En attendant Godot* (*Waiting for Godot*). The two-act play—wittily characterized by a reviewer as a play in which nothing happens, twice—was highly controversial. It was hailed by some as a masterpiece and denounced by others as pretentious nonsense or perhaps even a hoax. In the next decade Beckett's reputation continued to grow, yet doubts continued to be expressed.

Happy Days had its world premiere in New York City in September 1961. Inevitably people wondered what Beckett could do with only two characters, especially since one is immobile and the other speaks only a few brief lines. Would *Happy Days* conclusively show that Beckett was perpetrating hoaxes? Edith Oliver, reviewing the play in the *New Yorker* (September 30, 1961), probably expressed the sentiments of many viewers when she said that although she had for some years thought that Beckett was "a murky, self-important bore," *Happy Days* caused her to see that he was not a bore and that he "may be important." She went on to say that Winnie's long monologue was "funny, pathetic, frightened, callous, bawdy, and charming," and that "in this examination of the ins and outs of the mind and heart [there is enough] to more than hold anyone for an evening." John Simon, writing in *Hudson Review* (Winter 1961–62), was a trifle more reserved, wondering "how much the theater can do without and still be theater." Nevertheless, he knew that there was something substantial in the play.

> Beckett the acrobat has hung on to his dramatic thread first by his feet, then by one hand, next by his teeth, and now he proceeds to take out his dentures in mid-air. . . . The play is full of that Beckettian strategy which presents the most innocuous trifles of human existence dripping with blood

and bile, and the most unspeakable horrors rakishly attired and merrily winking.

Of course, not all of the reviews were favorable or even mixed; some were hostile. On the whole, however, *Happy Days* seems to have marked a watershed: Beckett the dramatist has to be taken seriously.

Because the role of Winnie is almost the entire play, producers and directors have been careful to get exceptionally skilled actresses to play the role of a woman who, in Beckett's words, possesses a "kind of profound frivolity." Ruth White, the first Winnie, won praise even from those critics who did not approve of the play; among the later highly praised Winnies were Billie Whitelaw, Irene Worth, Dame Peggy Ashcroft, and (in the French version, *Oh les beaux jours*) Madeleine Renaud. One reviewer praised Renaud for her "transcendent elegance and feathery grace." However, other actresses have been praised for conveying a touch of hearty vulgarity, and still others for conveying more than a touch of desperation.

For interviews with Billie Whitelaw, Dame Peggy Ashcroft, Madeleine Renaud, and several other players of Winnie, see *Women in Beckett*, edited by Linda Ben-zvi, (1990).

Mel Gussow
REVIEW OF *HAPPY DAYS*

Despite her cheerful demeanor, Winnie in "Happy Days" (revived at the CSC Repertory Theater) knows the limits and defeats of her life. Her way to endure the day, and the day after that, is "laughing wild amid severest woe." Laughter shares the stage with sorrow.

As Winnie (Charlotte Rae) primps and fusses over herself, it is as if she is sitting at her dressing table. She is, of course, buried up to her waist in a large mound of earth and, by the second act of Samuel Beckett's masterly existential comedy, she is buried up to her neck. In the unwritten third act, she might have become the distant voice of someone symbolically entombed in life.

Peggy Ashcroft has called the role "a summit part," like Hamlet. Any actress attempting it must find her path through a minefield of detailed stage directions and must single-handedly sustain the drama. Although her husband, Willie, appears, he seldom speaks, leaving the stage to his wife and her one-woman show. Necessarily the role lends itself to interpretation, but no performance should neglect the essential adaptability of Winnie. Though her stage movements are rigidly restricted, emotionally she is unbound.

In Carey Perloff's thoughtful production, Miss Rae holds firmly to the author's inclinations—the pauses, stops and starts and poetic lilt of language. With an ebullience that seems to spring from conviction, she goes about her everyday life, undeterred by the fact of her entrapment. This is a Winnie who is unswerving in her ability to come through wars as well as personal deprivations.

Best known for her comic performances, Miss Rae aims for lightness and achieves it as called for in the first act, which benefits from the actress's expressive face and gestures. She also catches a measure of the second act sobriety, when Winnie's soliloquy begins to resemble the delirium of later Beckett works like "Not I."

For the audience, she becomes a cozy chatterer such as one might encounter in an English pub. She engages us with her refrain, as she tries to recall happy beginnings as well as endings. Other actresses from Ruth White in the original Off Broadway production to Irene Worth have uncovered the gentility beneath the extroverted behavior. That aspect of Winnie eludes Miss Rae, who is most adept at projecting the character's earthy humor.

At the CSC, the audience is seated on three sides of a small stage. Donald Eastman's set places Winnie in the center of a volcanolike hill. The surface looks seared. In the close surroundings, Miss Rae keeps her performance within the framework of intimacy. Bill Moor is apt as Willie, her crusty companion, in top hat and tails looking like a remnant from another, more formal epoch.

Miss Perloff previously directed "Happy Days" (with Miss Rae and Mr. Moor) at the Mark Taper Forum in Los Angeles as part of that company's recent retrospective of plays of the 1950's and 1960's. The production arrives here with a sense of surety, except in one respect. In a sudden flash, Winnie's parasol is supposed to be consumed by flames, but when the moment came during a critics' preview, the fire fizzled. Spontaneous combustion resulted in a puff of smoke.

The director and the actress are careful about keeping the dialogue conversational, even when it is alluding to Milton, Dante and Shakespeare. Ever eclectic, Winnie remembers literary references as a kind of artifact of a cultural heritage she does not possess.

Because of Winnie's persistence, some may regard her as an eternal optimist. Her role is more that of perpetual pragmatist. As she passes the minutes with remembered routines and favorite distractions, "Happy Days" becomes a partial reflection of "Waiting for Godot." Neither salvation nor cessation await her; one dawn is like another. Searchingly, Winnie looks for daily mercies as her helpmate for survival.

W o l e   S o y i n k a

THE STRONG BREED

Wole Soyinka was born in Nigeria in 1934. Soyinka (pronounced *shoy-ING-ka*) received a largely British-style education in primary and secondary schools in Ibadan, Nigeria, and then entered University College, Ibadan. After two years he transferred to the University of Leeds, in England, where he received further training in Western literature. In England he worked for the Royal Court Theatre as a script reader and inevitably witnessed productions of plays and participated in dramatic improvisations. His first play, *The Swamp Dwellers*, was produced at the University of London Drama Festival in 1958 and then in Ibadan the next year. He returned to Nigeria, taught in several universities, and in 1967–1969 during the Nigerian-Biafran War, he was detained (that is, imprisoned, sometimes in solitary confinement) on political grounds.

Soyinka has produced a highly varied body of work, in drama (from comedy to tragedy), poetry, fiction, and autobiography. His work draws both on Western literary traditions (for instance, he has published versions of Euripides' tragedy *The Bacchae* and of Bertolt Brecht's *The Threepenny Opera*) and on African traditions. He set forth some of his thoughts about literature and the theater in *Myth, Literature and the African World* (1975). *The Strong Breed* (published in 1963 and performed in 1966) is rooted in a theme to which Soyinka often returns, the death of a sacrificial figure or scapegoat.

In 1986 Soyinka was awarded the Nobel Prize for Literature.

COMMENTARY

"You will have to make up your mind soon, Eman. The lorry [i.e. the truck] leaves very shortly." With these words the play opens. Sunma, a young woman native to the village, is urging a young man to leave. The man, Eman, came to the village less than a year ago; he does not know that the village has an annual rite in which the sins of the villagers are heaped on a scapegoat—a stranger—who is then destroyed, so that the village may regain health for the next year.

The play is in large part about Eman's making up his mind, even though for much of the play he is not aware that this is his task. When you think about it, many plays deal with this same issue. For instance, in *Trifles* (p. 18) Mrs. Hale and Mrs. Peters have to make up their minds about whether they report the evidence that will incriminate Mrs. Wright in the murder of her husband. In *A Doll's House*, Nora has to decide what she will do once she clearly sees what sort of man Torvald is and what sort of life she has been living.

"Once she clearly sees . . . ." It is all very well to say that one must decide, but frequently one does not realize that a decision must be made or, perhaps, that a decisive decision has already been made, unthinkingly. In our introductory remarks on tragedy (p. 35), we quoted from a poem by William Butler Yeats:

> Even the wisest man grows tense
> With some sort of violence
> Before he can accomplish fate,
> Know his work or choose his mate.

In large measure, *The Strong Breed* is about Eman's growing perception that he is of "the strong breed," that he has a destiny, and that he must willingly accept it. This destiny, we learn in the play, is to serve as a scapegoat, or (to use Soyinka's word) a "carrier," that is, a carrier of the village's pollution.

The word *scapegoat* was given currency by the King James Version of the Bible (1611), where it appears in Leviticus 16.8, though most scholars today believe that the word is a mistranslation of the name of a demon. In any case, the idea was that the sins of the community were transferred to a goat, which was then sacrificed or driven into a wilderness. Presumably the goat was a substitution for a human sacrifice. The gist of the ritual certainly was widespread in the ancient Near East, and, judging from Soyinka's play, it is or was practiced by the Yoruba people in Nigeria.

Soyinka is much interested in ritual (both of ancient Greece and of modern Nigeria), and he has written essays on the connections between ritual and drama. He has also written an adaptation of Euripides' *The Bacchae*, the ancient Greek tragedy that is sometimes invoked as offering support for Aristotle's assertion that Greek drama arose from a ritual connected with the god Dionysus. In *The Strong Breed* Soyinka gives us a play about the importance of a ritual to the community, though the interest is equally in Eman's gradual awareness that he is to become part of the ritual. To a considerable degree the play resembles Sophocles' *Oedipus* (not a surprise, given Soyinka's interest in Greek drama), in which Oedipus comes to realize that he is something other than what he thought he was; we look with deepening interest at Oedipus's reactions to his discovery of his role. If *The Strong Breed* begins with Sunma's urging Eman to make up his mind about whether he will stay or not—she wants him to flee—it ends with Eman having made up his mind not merely to stay, but to do knowingly what he has been destined to do.

What he has been destined to do, we have said, is to take on the role of a sacrificial victim. Fairly early in the play he does indeed take on this role, substituting himself for the idiot boy, Ifada. As the ritual proceeds, he learns that it is easier to say that one will take on the role than it is actually to do so, and he seeks to escape. However, he is discovered by the Girl, who betrays him. In the course of a flashback, his father (who also is one of "the strong breed") tries to save him by urging him to go in a different direction, but Eman at last is able to "know his work" (to use Yeats's words), and he persists in going in the direction that will lead to his death. His father (in the vision) tries to dissuade him, but Eman says (and these are almost his last words), "Wait, father. I am coming with you . . . wait . . . wait for me, father . . . ."

Eman's steps take him to his sacrificial death, for he triggers a trap that hoists him up and hangs him from a tree, a death visually suggestive of the crucifixion of Jesus. And indeed there are several parallels. Eman thirsts, as Jesus did when he was on the cross; Eman, like Jesus, is a teacher; Eman assists the wretched of this world (Ifada), as Jesus did; he is betrayed, as Jesus was; Eman dies not for any faults of his own but for the sins of others. Perhaps one can go even further. A Nigerian student tells us that *Eman* is not a Nigerian name. Perhaps it is meant to be a form of *Emmanuel* or *Immanuel,* Hebrew for "God with us," a name that suggests God's protecting presence and that the early Christians associated with Jesus. (Incidentally, Soyinka was brought up as a Christian, his parents having converted to Christianity.) If Eman is associated with Jesus, he is also associated with the Yoruba deity Ogun. In Yoruba thought, Ogun, patron of craft-workers and god of creation and destruction, is a sacrificial figure who was so distressed by the separation between gods and mortals that he threw himself into the dividing abyss in order to build a bridge toward humanity. (Soyinka discusses Ogun in *Myth, Literature and the African World* [1976] and in *Art, Dialogue, and Outrage* [1993].)

This play about a Yoruba tradition and about the psychological development of a particular "carrier" inevitably raises the question of whether the society for which Eman gives his life is capable of profiting from his sacrifice. Soyinka's plays, essays, and poems clearly indicate his belief that the artist carries a burden and that the arts, and especially drama, can transform their audiences. It is easy, then, to think of Eman, as a symbol of the artist, devoting his life to society. However, given the society depicted in *The Strong Breed*, what is Soyinka saying about the power of the artist to reform society?

Wole Soyinka

THE STRONG BREED

Characters

EMAN, *a stranger*
SUNMA, *Jaguna's daughter*
IFADA, *an idiot*
A GIRL
JAGUNA
OROGE
ATTENDANT STALWARTS, *the villagers*
From Eman's past—
OLD MAN, *his father*
OMAE, *his betrothed*
TUTOR
PRIEST
ATTENDANTS, *the villagers*

The scenes are described briefly, but very often a darkened stage with lit area will not only suffice but is necessary. Except for the one indicated place, there can be no break in the action. A distracting scene-change would be ruinous. A mud house, with space in front of it. Eman, in light buba and trousers, stands at the window, looking out. Inside, Sunma is clearing the table of what looks like a modest clinic, putting the things away in a cupboard. Another rough table in the room is piled with exercise books, two or three worn textbooks, etc. Sunma appears agitated. Outside, just below the window, crouches Ifada. He looks up with a shy smile from time to time, waiting for Eman to notice him.

SUNMA (*hesitant*). You will have to make up your mind soon, Eman. The lorry[1] leaves very shortly.

As Eman does not answer, Sunma continues her work, more nervously. Two villagers, obvious travelers, pass hurriedly in front of the house, the man has a small raffia sack, the woman a cloth-covered basket, the man enters first, turns, and urges the woman who is just emerging to hurry.

SUNMA (*seeing them, her tone is more intense*). Eman, are we going or aren't we? You will leave it till too late.

EMAN (*quietly*). There is still time—if you want to go.

SUNMA. If I want to go . . . and you?

Eman makes no reply.

SUNMA (*bitterly*). You don't really want to leave here. You never want to go away—even for a minute.

[1]**lorry** truck

Ifada continues his antics. Eman eventually pats him on the head and the boy grins happily. Leaps up suddenly and returns with a basket of oranges, which he offers Eman.

EMAN. My gift for today's festival enh?

Ifada nods, grinning.

EMAN. They look ripe—that's a change.

SUNMA (*She has gone inside the room. Looks round the door*). Did you call me?

EMAN. No. (*She goes back.*) And what will you do tonight, Ifada? Will you take part in the dancing? Or perhaps you will mount your own masquerade?

Ifada shakes his head, regretfully.

EMAN. You won't? So you haven't any? But you would like to own one.

Ifada nods eagerly

EMAN. Then why don't you make your own?

Ifada stares, puzzled by this idea.

EMAN. Sunma will let you have some cloth you know. And bits of wool . . .

SUNMA (*coming out*). Who are you talking to, Eman?

EMAN. Ifada. I am trying to persuade him to join the young maskers.

SUNMA (*losing control*). What does he want here? Why is he hanging round us?

EMAN (*amazed*). What . . . ? I said Ifada, Ifada.

SUNMA. Just tell him to go away. Let him go and play somewhere else!

EMAN. What is this? Hasn't he always played here?

SUNMA. I don't want him here. (*Rushes to the window.*) Get away, idiot. Don't bring your foolish face here any more, do you hear? Go on, go away from here . . .

EMAN (*restraining her*). Control yourself, Sunma. What on earth has got into you?

Ifada, hurt and bewildered, backs slowly away.

SUNMA. He comes crawling round here like some horrible insect. I never want to lay my eyes on him again.

EMAN. I don't understand. It *is* Ifada you know, Ifada! The unfortunate one who runs errands for you and doesn't hurt a soul.

SUNMA. I cannot bear the sight of him.

EMAN. You can't do what? It can't be two days since he last fetched water for you.

SUNMA. What else can he do except that? He is useless. Just because we have been kind to him. . . . Others would have put him in an asylum.

EMAN. You are not making sense. He is not a madman, he is just a little more unlucky than other children. (*Looks keenly at her.*) But what is the matter?

SUNMA. It's nothing. I only wish we had sent him off to one of those places for creatures like him.

EMAN. He is quite happy here. He doesn't bother anyone and he makes himself useful.

SUNMA. Useful! Is that one of any use to anybody? Boys of his age are already earning a living but all he can do is hang around and drool at the mouth.

EMAN. But he does work. You know he does a lot for you.

SUNMA. Does he? And what about the farm you started for him! Does he ever work on it? Or have you forgotten that it was really for Ifada you cleared that brush. Now you have to go and work it yourself. You spend all your time on it and you have no room for anything else.

EMAN. That wasn't his fault. I should first have asked him if he was fond of farming.

SUNMA. Oh, so he can choose? As if he shouldn't be thankful for being allowed to live.

EMAN. Sunma!

SUNMA. He does not like farming but he knows how to feast his dumb mouth on the fruits.

EMAN. But I want him to. I encourage him.

SUNMA. Well keep him. I don't want to see him any more.

EMAN (*after some moments*). But why? You cannot be telling all the truth. What has he done?

SUNMA. The sight of him fills me with revulsion.

EMAN (*goes to her and holds her*). What really is it? (*Sunma avoids his eyes.*) It is almost as if you are forcing yourself to hate him. Why?

SUNMA. That is not true. Why should I?

EMAN. Then what is the secret? You've even played with him before.

SUNMA. I have always merely tolerated him. But I cannot any more. Suddenly my disgust won't take him any more. Perhaps . . . perhaps it is the new year. Yes, yes, it must be the new year.

EMAN. I don't believe that.

SUNMA. It must be. I am a woman, and these things matter. I don't want a misshape near me. Surely for one day in the year, I may demand some wholesomeness.

EMAN. I do not understand you.

Sunma is silent.

It was cruel of you. And to Ifada who is so helpless and alone. We are the only friends he has.

SUNMA. No, just you. I have told you, with me it has always been only an act of kindness. And now I haven't any pity left for him.

EMAN. No. He is not a wholesome being.

He turns back to looking through the window.

SUNMA (*half-pleading*). Ifada can rouse your pity. And yet if anything, I need more kindness from you. Every time my weakness betrays me, you close your mind against me . . . Eman . . . Eman . . .

A Girl comes in view, dragging an effigy by a rope attached to one of its legs. She stands for a while gazing at Eman. Ifada, who has crept back shyly to his accustomed position, becomes somewhat excited when he sees the effigy. The Girl is unsmiling. She possesses, in fact, a kind of inscrutability which does not make her hard but is unsettling.

GIRL. Is the teacher in?

EMAN (*smiling*). No.

GIRL. Where is he gone?

EMAN. I don't really know. Shall I ask?

GIRL. Yes, do.

EMAN (*turning slightly*). Sunma, a girl outside wants to know . . .

Sunma turns away, goes into the inside room.

EMAN. Oh. (*Returns to the girl, but his slight gaiety is lost.*) There is no one at home who can tell me.

GIRL. Why are you not in?

EMAN. I don't really know. Maybe I went somewhere.

GIRL. All right. I will wait until you get back.

She pulls the effigy to her, sits down.

EMAN (*slowly regaining his amusement*). So you are ready for the new year.

GIRL (*without turning round*). I am not going to the festival.

EMAN. Then why have you got that?

GIRL. Do you mean my carrier? I am unwell you know. My mother says it will take away my sickness with the old year.

EMAN. Won't you share the carrier with your playmates?

GIRL. Oh, no. Don't you know I play alone? The other children won't come near me. Their mothers would beat them.

EMAN. But I have never seen you here. Why don't you come to the clinic?

GIRL. My mother said No.

Gets up, begins to move off.

EMAN. You are not going away?

GIRL. I must not stay talking to you. If my mother caught me . . .

EMAN. All right, tell me what you want before you go.

GIRL (*stops. For some moments she remains silent*). I must have some clothes for my carrier.

EMAN. Is that all? You wait a moment.

Sunma comes out as he takes down a buba from the wall. She goes to the window and glares almost with hatred at the Girl. The Girl retreats hastily, still impassive.

By the way, Sunma, do you know who that girl is?

SUNMA. I hope you don't really mean to give her that.

EMAN. Why not? I hardly ever use it.

SUNMA. Just the same don't give it to her. She is not a child. She is as evil as the rest of them.

EMAN. What has got into you today?

SUNMA. All right, all right. Do what you wish.

She withdraws. Baffled, Eman returns to the window.

EMAN. Here . . . will this do? Come and look at it.

GIRL. Throw it.

EMAN. What is the matter? I am not going to eat you.

GIRL. No one lets me come near them.

EMAN. But I am not afraid of catching your disease.

GIRL. Throw it.

Eman shrugs and tosses the buba. She takes it without a word and slips it on the effigy, completely absorbed in the task. Eman watches for a while, then joins Sunma in the inner room.

GIRL (*after a long, cool survey of Ifada*). You have a head like a spider's egg, and your mouth dribbles like a roof. But there is no one else. Would you like to play?

Ifada nods eagerly, quite excited.

GIRL. You will have to get a stick.

Ifada rushes around, finds a big stick, and whirls it aloft, bearing down on the carrier.

GIRL. Wait. I don't want you to spoil it. If it gets torn I shall drive you away. Now, let me see how you are going to beat it.

Ifada hits it gently.

GIRL. You may hit harder than that. As long as there is something left to hang at the end.

She appraises him up and down.

You are not very tall . . . will you be able to hang it from a tree?

Ifada nods, grinning happily.

GIRL. You will hang it up and I will set fire to it. (*Then, with surprising venom.*) But just because you are helping me, don't think it is going to cure you. I am the one who will get well at midnight, do you understand? It is my carrier and it is for me alone. (*She pulls at the rope to make sure that it is well attached to the leg.*) Well don't stand there drooling. Let's go.

She begins to walk off, dragging the effigy in the dust. Ifada remains where he is for some moments, seemingly puzzled. Then his face breaks into a large grin and he leaps after the procession, belaboring the effigy with all his strength. The stage remains empty for some moments. Then the horn of a lorry is sounded and Sunma rushes out. The hooting continues for some time with a rhythmic pattern. Eman comes out.

EMAN. I am going to the village . . . I shan't be back before nightfall.

SUNMA (*blankly*). Yes.

EMAN (*hesitates*). Well what do you want me to do?

SUNMA. The lorry was hooting just now.

EMAN. I didn't hear it.

SUNMA. It will leave in a few minutes. And you did promise we could go away.

EMAN. I promised nothing. Will you go home by yourself or shall I come back for you?

SUNMA. You don't even want me here?

EMAN. But you have to go home, haven't you?

SUNMA. I had hoped we would watch the new year together—in some other place.

EMAN. Why do you continue to distress yourself?

SUNMA. Because you will not listen to me. Why do you continue to stay where nobody wants you?

EMAN. That is not true.

SUNMA. It is. You are wasting your life on people who really want you out of their way.

EMAN. You don't know what you are saying.

SUNMA. You think they love you? Do you think they care at all for what you—or I—do for them?

EMAN. *Them?* These are your own people. Sometimes you talk as if you were a stranger too.

SUNMA. I wonder if I really sprang from here. I know they are evil and I am not. From the oldest to the smallest child, they are nourished in evil and unwholesomeness in which I have no part.

EMAN. You knew this when you returned?

SUNMA. You reproach me then for trying at all?

EMAN. I reproach you with nothing. But you must leave me out of your plans. I can have no part in them.

SUNMA (*nearly pleading*). Once I could have run away. I would have gone and never looked back.

EMAN. I cannot listen when you talk like that.

SUNMA. I swear to you, I do not mind what happens afterwards. But you must help me tear myself away from here. I can no longer do it by myself. . . . It is only a little thing. And we have worked so hard this past year . . . surely we can go away for a week . . . even a few days would be enough.

EMAN. I have told you, Sunma . . .

SUNMA (*desperately*). Two days, Eman. Only two days.

EMAN (*distressed*). But I tell you I have no wish to go.

SUNMA (*suddenly angry*). Are you so afraid then?

EMAN. Me? Afraid of what?

SUNMA. You think you will not want to come back.

EMAN (*pitying*). You cannot dare me that way.

SUNMA. Then why won't you leave here, even for an hour? If you are so sure that your life is settled here, why are you afraid to do this thing for me? What is so wrong that you will not go into the next town for a day or two?

EMAN. I don't want to. I do not have to persuade you, or myself, about anything. I simply have no desire to go away.

SUNMA (*his quiet confidence appears to incense her*). You are afraid. You accuse me of losing my sense of mission, but you are afraid to put yours to the test.

EMAN. You are wrong, Sunma. I have no sense of mission. But I have found peace here and I am content with that.

SUNMA. I haven't. For a while I thought that too, but I found there could be no peace in the midst of so much cruelty. Eman, tonight at least, the last night of the old year . . .

EMAN. No, Sunma. I find this too distressing; you should go home now.

SUNMA. It is the time for making changes in one's life, Eman. Let's breathe in the new year away from here.

EMAN. You are hurting yourself.

SUNMA. Tonight. Only tonight. We will come back tomorrow, as early as you like. But let us go away for this one night. Don't let another year break on me in this place . . . you don't know how important it is to me, but I will tell you, I will tell you on the way . . . but we must not be here today, Eman, do this one thing for me.

EMAN (sadly). I cannot.

SUNMA (suddenly calm). I was a fool to think it would be otherwise. The whole village may use you as they will but for me there is nothing. Sometimes I think you believe that doing anything for me makes you unfaithful to some part of your life. If it was a woman then I pity her for what she must have suffered.

Eman winces and hardens slowly. Sunma notices nothing.

Keeping faith with so much is slowly making you inhuman. (*Seeing the change in Eman.*) Eman. Eman. What is it?

As she goes towards him, Eman goes into the house.

SUNMA (apprehensive, follows him). What did I say? Eman, forgive me, forgive me please.

Eman remains facing into the slow darkness of the room. Sunma, distressed, cannot decide what to do.

I swear I didn't know. . . . I would not have said it for all the world.

A lorry is heard taking off somewhere nearby. The sound comes up and slowly fades away into the distance. Sunma starts visibly, goes slowly to the window.

SUNMA (as the sound dies off, to herself). What happens now?

EMAN (joining her at the window). What did you say?

SUNMA. Nothing.

EMAN. Was that not the lorry going off?

SUNMA. It was.

EMAN. I am sorry I couldn't help you.

Sunma, about to speak, changes her mind.

EMAN. I think you ought to go home now.

SUNMA. No, don't send me away. It's the least you can do for me. Let me stay here until all the noise is over.

EMAN. But are you not needed at home? You have a part in the festival.

SUNMA. I have renounced it; I am Jaguna's eldest daughter only in name.

EMAN. Renouncing one's self is not so easy—surely you know that.

SUNMA. I don't want to talk about it. Will you at least let us be together tonight?

EMAN. But . . .

SUNMA. Unless you are afraid my father will accuse you of harboring me.

EMAN. All right, we will go out together.

SUNMA. Go out? I want us to stay here.

EMAN. When there is so much going on outside?

SUNMA. Some day you will wish that you went away when I tried to make you.

EMAN. Are you going back to that?

SUNMA. No. I promise you I will not recall it again. But you must know that it was also for your sake that I tried to get us away.

EMAN. For me? How?

SUNMA. By yourself you can do nothing here. Have you not noticed how tightly we shut out strangers? Even if you lived here for a lifetime, you would remain a stranger.

EMAN. Perhaps that is what I like. There is peace in being a stranger.

SUNMA. For a while perhaps. But they would reject you in the end. I tell you it is only I who stand between you and contempt. And because of this you have earned their hatred. I don't know why I say this now, except that somehow, I feel that it no longer matters. It is only I who have stood between you and much humiliation.

EMAN. Think carefully before you say any more. I am incapable of feeling indebted to you. This will make no difference at all.

SUNMA. I ask for nothing. But you must know it all the same. It is true I hadn't the strength to go by myself. And I must confess this now, if you had come with me, I would have done everything to keep you from returning.

EMAN. I know that.

SUNMA. You see, I bare myself to you. For days I had thought it over, this was to be a new beginning for us. And I placed my fate wholly in your hands. Now the thought will not leave me, I have a feeling which will not be shaken off, that in some way, you have tonight totally destroyed my life.

EMAN. You are depressed, you don't know what you are saying.

SUNMA. Don't think I am accusing you. I say all this only because I cannot help it.

EMAN. We must not remain shut up here. Let us go and be part of the living.

SUNMA. No. Leave them alone.

EMAN. Surely you don't want to stay indoors when the whole town is alive with rejoicing.

SUNMA. Rejoicing! Is that what it seems to you? No, let us remain here. Whatever happens I must not go out until all this is over.

There is silence. It has grown much darker.

EMAN. I shall light the lamp.

SUNMA (*eager to do something*). No, let me do it.

She goes into the inner room. Eman paces the room, stops by a shelf, and toys with the seeds in an "ayo" board, takes down the whole board and places it on a table, playing by himself.

The Girl is now seen coming back, still dragging her "carrier." Ifada brings up the rear as before. As he comes round the corner of the house two men emerge from the shadows. A sack is thrown over Ifada's head, the rope is pulled tight rendering him instantly helpless. The Girl has reached the front of the house before she turns round at the sound of scuffle. She is in time to see Ifada thrown over the shoulders and borne away. Her face betraying no emotion at all, the Girl backs slowly away, turns, and flees, leaving the "carrier" behind. Sunma enters, carrying two kerosene lamps. She hangs one up from the wall.

EMAN. One is enough.

SUNMA. I want to leave one outside.

She goes out, hangs the lamp from a nail just above the door. As she turns she sees the effigy and gasps. Eman rushes out.

EMAN. What is it? Oh, is that what frightened you?

SUNMA. I thought . . . I didn't really see it properly.

Eman goes towards the object, stoops to pick it up.

EMAN. It must belong to that sick girl.

SUNMA. Don't touch it.

EMAN. Let's keep it for her.

SUNMA. Leave it alone. Don't touch it, Eman.

EMAN (*shrugs and goes back*). You are very nervous.

SUNMA. Let's go in.

EMAN. Wait. (*He detains her by the door, under the lamp.*) I know there is something more than you've told me. What are you afraid of tonight?

SUNMA. I was only scared by that thing. There is nothing else.

EMAN. I am not blind, Sunma. It is true I would not run away when you wanted me to, but that doesn't mean I do not feel things. What does tonight really mean that it makes you so helpless?

SUNMA. It is only a mood. And your indifference to me . . . let's go in.

Eman moves aside and she enters; he remains there for a moment and then follows. She fiddles with the lamp, looks vaguely round the room, then goes and shuts the door, bolting it. When she turns, it is to meet Eman's eyes, questioning.

SUNMA. There is a cold wind coming in.

Eman keeps his gaze on her.

SUNMA. It *was* getting cold.

She moves guiltily to the table and stands by the ayo board, rearranging the seeds. Eman remains where he is a few moments, then brings a stool and sits opposite her. She sits down also and they begin to play in silence.

SUNMA. What brought you here at all, Eman? And what makes you stay?

There is another silence.

SUNMA. I am not trying to share your life. I know you too well by now. But at least we have worked together since you came. Is there nothing at all I deserve to know?

EMAN. Let me continue a stranger—especially to you. Those who have much to give fulfill themselves only in total loneliness.

SUNMA. Then there is no love in what you do.

EMAN. There is. Love comes to me more easily with strangers.

SUNMA. That is unnatural.

EMAN. Not for me. I know I find consummation only when I have spent myself for a total stranger.

SUNMA. It seems unnatural to me. But then I am a woman. I have a woman's longings and weaknesses. And the ties of blood are very strong in me.

EMAN (*smiling*). You think I have cut loose from all these—ties of blood.

SUNMA. Sometimes you are so inhuman.

EMAN. I don't know what that means. But I am very much my father's son.

They play in silence. Suddenly Eman pauses, listening.

EMAN. Did you hear that?

SUNMA (*quickly*). I heard nothing . . . it's your turn.

EMAN. Perhaps some of the mummers are coming this way.

Eman, about to play, leaps up suddenly.

SUNMA. What is it? Don't you want to play any more?

Eman moves to the door.

SUNMA. No. Don't go out, Eman.

EMAN. If it's the dancers I want to ask them to stay. At least we won't have to miss everything.

SUNMA. No, no. Don't open the door. Let us keep out everyone tonight.

A terrified and disordered figure bursts suddenly round the corner, past the window and begins hammering at the door. It is Ifada. Desperate with terror, he pounds madly at the door, dumb-moaning all the while.

EMAN. Isn't that Ifada?

SUNMA. They are only fooling about. Don't pay any attention.

EMAN (*looks round the window*). That is Ifada. (*Begins to unbolt the door.*)

SUNMA (*pulling at his hands*). It is only a trick they are playing on you. Don't take any notice, Eman.

EMAN. What are you saying? The boy is out of his senses with fear.

SUNMA. No, no. Don't interfere, Eman. For God's sake don't interfere.

EMAN. Do you know something of this then?

SUNMA. You are a stranger here, Eman. Just leave us alone and go your own way. There is nothing you can do.

EMAN (*he tries to push her out of the way but she clings fiercely to him*). Have you gone mad? I tell you the boy must come in.

SUNMA. Why won't you listen to me, Eman? I tell you it's none of your business. For your own sake do as I say.

Eman pushes her off, unbolts the door. Ifada rushes in, clasps Eman round the knees, dumb-moaning against his legs.

EMAN (*manages to rebolt the door*). What is it, Ifada? What is the matter?

Shouts and voices are heard coming nearer the house.

SUNMA. Before it's too late, let him go. For once, Eman, believe what I tell you. Don't harbor him or you will regret it all your life.

Eman tries to calm Ifada, who becomes more and more abject as the outside voices get nearer.

EMAN. What have they done to him? At least tell me that. What is going on, Sunma?

SUNMA (*with sudden venom*). Monster! Could you not take yourself somewhere else?

EMAN. Stop talking like that.

SUNMA. He could have run into the bush couldn't he? Toad! Why must he follow us with his own disasters!

VOICES OUTSIDE. It's here. . . . Round the back. . . . Spread, spread . . . this way . . . no, head him off . . . use the bush path and head him off . . . get some more lights . . .

Eman listens. Lifts Ifada bodily and carries him into the inner room. Returns at once, shutting the door behind him.

SUNMA (*slumps into a chair, resigned*). You always follow your own way.

JAGUNA (*comes round the corner followed by Oroge and three men, one bearing a torch*). I knew he would come here.

OROGE. I hope our friend won't make trouble.

JAGUNA. He had better not. You, recall all the men and tell them to surround the house.

OROGE. But he may not be in the house after all.

JAGUNA. I know he is here . . . (*To the men.*) . . . go on, do as I say.

He bangs on the door.

Teacher, open your door . . . you two stay by the door. If I need you I will call you.

Eman opens the door.

JAGUNA (*speaks as he enters*). We know he is here.

EMAN. Who?

JAGUNA. Don't let us waste time. We are grown men, teacher. You understand me and I understand you. But we must take back the boy.

EMAN. This is my house.

JAGUNA. Daughter, you'd better tell your friend. I don't think he quite knows our ways. Tell him why he must give up the boy.

SUNMA. Father, I . . .

JAGUNA. Are you going to tell him or aren't you?

SUNMA. Father, I beg you, leave us alone tonight . . .

JAGUNA. I thought you might be a hindrance. Go home then if you will not use your sense.

SUNMA. But there are other ways . . .

JAGUNA (*turning to the men*). See that she gets home. I no longer trust her. If she gives trouble carry her. And see that the women stay with her until all this is over.

Sunma departs, accompanied by one of the men.

JAGUNA. Now, teacher . . .

OROGE (*restrains him*). You see, Mister Eman, it is like this. Right now, nobody knows that Ifada has taken refuge here. No one except us and our men—and they know how to keep their mouths shut. We don't want to have to burn down the house, you see, but if the word gets around, we would have no choice.

JAGUNA. In fact, it may be too late already. A carrier should end up in the bush, not in a house. Anyone who doesn't guard his door when the carrier goes by has himself to blame. A contaminated house should be burnt down.

OROGE. But we are willing to let it pass. Only, you must bring him out quickly.

EMAN. All right. But at least you will let me ask you something.

JAGUNA. What is there to ask? Don't you understand what we have told you?

EMAN. Yes. But why did you pick on a helpless boy? Obviously he is not willing.

JAGUNA. What is the man talking about? Ifada is a godsend. Does he have to be willing?

EMAN. In my home, we believe that a man should be willing.

OROGE. Mister Eman, I don't think you quite understand. This is not a simple matter at all. I don't know what you do, but here, it is not a cheap task for anybody. No one in his senses would do such a job. Why do you think we give refuge to idiots like him? We don't know where he came from. One morning, he is simply there, just like that. From nowhere at all. You see, there is a purpose in that.

JAGUNA. We only waste time.

OROGE. Jaguna, be patient. After all, the man has been with us for some time now and deserves to know. The evil of the old year is no light thing to load on any man's head.

EMAN. I know something about that.

OROGE. You do? (*Turns to Jaguna, who snorts impatiently.*) You see I told you so, didn't I? From the moment you came I saw you were one of the knowing ones.

JAGUNA. Then let him behave like a man and give back the boy.

EMAN. It is you who are not behaving like men.

JAGUNA (*advances aggressively*). That is a quick mouth you have . . .

OROGE. Patience, Jaguna . . . if you want the new year to cushion the land there must be no deeds of anger. What did you mean, my friend?

EMAN. It is a simple thing. A village which cannot produce its own carrier contains no men.

JAGUNA. Enough. Let there be no more talk or this business will be ruined by some rashness. You . . . come inside. Bring the boy out, he must be in the room there.

EMAN. Wait.

The men hesitate.

JAGUNA (*hitting the nearer one and propelling him forward*). Go on. Have you changed masters now that you listen to what he says?

OROGE (*sadly*). I am sorry you would not understand, Mister Eman. But you ought to know that no carrier may return to the village. If he does, the people will stone him to death. It has happened before. Surely it is too much to ask a man to give up his own soil.

EMAN. I know others who have done more.

Ifada is brought out, abjectly dumb-moaning.

EMAN. You can see him with your own eyes. Does it really have meaning to use one as unwilling as that?

OROGE (*smiling*). He shall be willing. Not only willing but actually joyous. I am the one who prepares them all, and I have seen worse. This one escaped before I began to prepare him for the event. But you will see him later tonight, the most joyous creature in the festival. Then perhaps you will understand.

EMAN. Then it is only a deceit. Do you believe the spirit of a new year is so easily fooled?

JAGUNA. Take him out. (*The men carry out Ifada.*) You see, it is so easy to talk. You say there are no men in this village because they cannot provide a willing carrier. And yet I heard Oroge tell you we only use strangers. There is only one other stranger in the village, but I have not heard him offer himself. (*Spits.*) It is so easy to talk is it not?

He turns his back on him. They go off, taking Ifada with them, limp and silent. The only sign of life is that he strains his neck to keep his eyes on Eman till the very moment that he disappears from sight. Eman remains where they left him, staring after the group.

A blackout lasting no more than a minute. The lights come up slowly, and Ifada is seen returning to the house. He stops at the window and looks in. Seeing no one, he bangs on the sill. Appears surprised that there is no response. He slithers down on his favorite spot, then sees the effigy still lying where the Girl had dropped it in her flight. After some hesitation, he goes towards it, begins to strip it of the clothing. Just then the Girl comes in.

GIRL. Hey, leave that alone. You know it's mine.

Ifada pauses, then speeds up his action.

GIRL. I said it is mine. Leave it where you found it. (*She rushes at him and begins to struggle for possession of the carrier.*) Thief! Thief! Let it go, it is mine. Let it go. You animal, just because I let you play with it. Idiot! Idiot!

The struggle becomes quite violent. The Girl is hanging to the effigy and Ifada lifts her with it, flinging her all about. The Girl hangs on grimly.

GIRL. You are spoiling it . . . why don't you get your own? Thief! Let it go, you thief!

Sunma comes in walking very fast, throwing apprehensive glances over her shoulder. Seeing the two children, she becomes immediately angry. Advances on them.

SUNMA. So you've made this place your playground. Get away, you untrained pigs. Get out of here.

Ifada flees at once, the Girl retreats also, retaining possession of the carrier.

Sunma goes to the door. She has her hand on the door when the significance of Ifada's presence strikes her for the first time. She stands rooted to the spot, then turns slowly round.

SUNMA. Ifada! What are you doing here?

Ifada is bewildered. Sunma turns suddenly and rushes into the house, flying into the inner room and out again.

Eman! Eman! Eman!

She rushes outside.

Where did he go? Where did they take him?

Ifada distressed, points. Sunma seizes him by the arm, drags him off.

Take me there at once. God help you if we are too late. You loathsome thing, if you have let him suffer . . .

Her voice fades into other shouts, running footsteps, banged tins, bells, dogs, etc., rising in volume.

It is a narrow passageway between two mudhouses. At the far end one man after another is seen running across the entry, the noise dying off gradually.

About halfway down the passage, Eman is crouching against the wall, tense with apprehension. As the noise dies off, he seems to relax, but the alert, hunted look is still in his eyes, which are ringed in a reddish color. The rest of his body has been whitened with a floury substance. He is naked down to the waist, wears a baggy pair of trousers, calf-length, and around both feet are bangles.

EMAN. I will simply stay here till dawn. I have done enough.

A window is thrown open and a woman empties some slop from a pail. With a startled cry Eman leaps aside to avoid it and the woman puts out her head.

WOMAN. Oh, my head. What have I done! Forgive me, neighbor . . . Eh, it's the carrier! (*Very rapidly she clears her throat and spits on him, flings the pail at him and runs off, shouting.*) He's here. The carrier is hiding in the passage. Quickly, I have found the carrier!

The cry is taken up and Eman flees down the passage. Shortly afterwards his pursuers come pouring down the passage in full cry. After the last of them come Jaguna and Oroge.

OROGE. Wait, wait. I cannot go so fast.

JAGUNA. We will rest a little then. We can do nothing anyway.

OROGE. If only he had let me prepare him.

JAGUNA. They are the ones who break first, these fools who think they were born to carry suffering like a hat. What are we to do now?

OROGE. When they catch him I must prepare him.

JAGUNA. He? It will be impossible now. There can be no joy left in that one.

OROGE. Still, it took him by surprise. He was not expecting what he met.

JAGUNA. Why then did he refuse to listen? Did he think he was coming to sit down to a feast? He had not even gone through one compound before he bolted. Did he think he was taken round the people to be blessed? A woman, that is all he is.

OROGE. No, no. He took the beating well enough. I think he is the kind who would let himself be beaten from night till dawn and not utter a sound. He would let himself be stoned until he dropped dead.

JAGUNA. Then what made him run like a coward?

OROGE. I don't know. I don't really know. It is a night of curses, Jaguna. It is not many unprepared minds will remain unhinged under the load.

JAGUNA. We must find him. It is a poor beginning for a year when our own curses remain hovering over our homes because the carrier refused to take them.

They go. The scene changes. Eman is crouching beside some shrubs, torn and bleeding.

EMAN. They are even guarding my house . . . as if I would go there, but I need water . . . they could at least grant me that . . . I can be thirsty too . . . (*He pricks his ears.*) . . . there must be a stream nearby . . . (*As he looks round him, his eyes widen at a scene he encounters.*)

An Old Man, short and vigorous looking, is seated on a stool. He also is wearing calf-length baggy trousers, white. On his head, a white cap. An attendant is engaged in rubbing his body with oil. Round his eyes, two white rings have already been marked.

OLD MAN. Have they prepared the boat?

ATTENDANT. They are making the last sacrifice.

OLD MAN. Good. Did you send for my son?

ATTENDANT. He's on his way.

OLD MAN. I have never met the carrying of the boat with such a heavy heart. I hope nothing comes of it.

ATTENDANT. The gods will not desert us on that account.

OLD MAN. A man should be at his strongest when he takes the boat, my friend. To be weighed down inside and out is not a wise thing. I hope when the moment comes I shall have found my strength.

Enter Eman, a wrapper round his waist and a danski[2] over it.

OLD MAN. I meant to wait until after my journey to the river, but my mind is so burdened with my own grief and yours I could not delay it. You know I must have all my strength. But I sit here, feeling it all eaten slowly away by my unspoken grief. It helps to say it out. It even helps to cry sometimes.

He signals to the attendant to leave them.

Come nearer . . . we will never meet again, son. Not on this side of the flesh. What I do not know is whether you will return to take my place.

EMAN. I will never come back.

OLD MAN. Do you know what you are saying? Ours is a strong breed, my son. It is only a strong breed that can take this boat to the river year after year and wax stronger on it. I have taken down each year's evils for over twenty years. I hoped you would follow me.

EMAN. My life here died with Omae.

OLD MAN. Omae died giving birth to your child and you think the world is ended. Eman, my pain did not begin when Omae died. Since you sent her to stay with me, son, I lived with the burden of knowing that this child would die bearing your son.

EMAN. Father.

OLD MAN. Don't you know it was the same with you? And me? No woman survives the bearing of the strong ones. Son, it is not the mouth of the boaster that says he belongs to the strong breed. It is the tongue that is red with pain and black with sorrow. Twelve years you were away, my son, and for those twelve years I knew the love of an old man for his daughter and the pain of a man helplessly awaiting his loss.

EMAN. I wish I had stayed away. I wish I never came back to meet her.

OLD MAN. It had to be. But you know now what slowly ate away my strength. I awaited your return with love and fear. Forgive me then if I say that your grief is light. It will pass. This grief may drive you now from home. But you must return.

EMAN. You do not understand. It is not grief alone.

OLD MAN. What is it then? Tell me, I can still learn.

EMAN. I was away twelve years. I changed much in that time.

OLD MAN. I am listening.

EMAN. I am unfitted for your work, father. I wish to say no more. But I am totally unfitted for your call.

OLD MAN. It is only time you need, son. Stay longer and you will answer the urge of your blood.

[2]**danski** a brief garment

EMAN. That I stayed at all was because of Omae. I did not expect to find her waiting. I would have taken her away, but hard as you claim to be, it would have killed you. And I was a tired man. I needed peace. Because Omae was peace, I stayed. Now nothing holds me here.

OLD MAN. Other men would rot and die doing this task year after year. It is strong medicine which only we can take. Our blood is strong like no other. Anything you do in life must be less than this, son.

EMAN. That is not true, father.

OLD MAN. I tell you it is true. Your own blood will betray you, son, because you cannot hold it back. If you make it do less than this, it will rush to your head and burst it open. I say what I know, my son.

EMAN. There are other tasks in life, father. This one is not for me. There are even greater things you know nothing of.

OLD MAN. I am very sad. You only go to give to others what rightly belongs to us. You will use your strength among thieves. They are thieves because they take what is ours, they have no claim of blood to it. They will even lack the knowledge to use it wisely. Truth is my companion at this moment, my son. I know everything I say will surely bring the sadness of truth.

EMAN. I am going, father.

OLD MAN. Call my attendant. And be with me in your strength for this last journey. A-ah, did you hear that? It came out without my knowing it; this is indeed my last journey. But I am not afraid.

Eman goes out. A few moments later, the attendant enters.

ATTENDANT. The boat is ready.

OLD MAN. So am I.

He sits perfectly still for several moments. Drumming begins somewhere in the distance, and the Old Man sways his head almost imperceptibly. Two men come in bearing a miniature boat, containing an indefinable mound. They rush it in and set it briskly down near the Old Man, and stand well back. The Old Man gets up slowly, the attendant watching him keenly. He signs to the men, who lift the boat quickly onto the Old Man's head. As soon as it touches his head, he holds it down with both hands and runs off, the men give him a start, then follow at a trot. As the last man disappears Oroge limps in and comes face to face with Eman—as carrier—who is now seen still standing beside the shrubs, staring into the scene he has just witnessed. Oroge, struck by the look on Eman's face, looks anxiously behind him to see what has engaged Eman's attention. Eman notices him then, and the pair stare at each other. Jaguna enters, sees him and shouts, "Here he is," rushes at Eman, who is whipped back to the immediate and flees, Jaguna in pursuit. Three or four others enter and follow them. Oroge remains where he is, thoughtful.

JAGUNA (*reenters*). They have closed in on him now, we'll get him this time.

OROGE. It is nearly midnight.

JAGUNA. You were standing there looking at him as if he was some strange spirit. Why didn't you shout?

OROGE. You shouted didn't you? Did that catch him?

JAGUNA. Don't worry. We have him now. But things have taken a bad turn. It is no longer enough to drive him past every house. There is too much contamination about already.

OROGE (*not listening*). He saw something. Why may I not know what it was?

JAGUNA. What are you talking about?

OROGE. Hm. What is it?

JAGUNA. I said there is too much harm done already. The year will demand more from this carrier than we thought.

OROGE. What do you mean?

JAGUNA. Do we have to talk with the full mouth?

OROGE. S-sh . . . look!

Jaguna turns just in time to see Sunma fly at him, clawing at his face like a crazed tigress.

SUNMA. Murderer! What are you doing to him? Murderer! Murderer!

Jaguna finds himself struggling really hard to keep off his daughter. He succeeds in pushing her off and striking her so hard on the face that she falls to her knees. He moves on her to hit her again.

OROGE (*comes between*). Think what you are doing, Jaguna, she is your daughter.

JAGUNA. My daughter! Does this one look like my daughter? Let me cripple the harlot for life.

OROGE. That is a wicked thought, Jaguna.

JAGUNA. Don't come between me and her.

OROGE. Nothing in anger—do you forget what tonight is?

JAGUNA. Can you blame me for forgetting?

Draws his hand across his cheek—it is covered with blood.

OROGE. This is an unhappy night for us all. I fear what is to come of it.

JAGUNA. Let's go. I cannot restrain myself in this creature's presence. My own daughter . . . and for a stranger . . .

They go off. Ifada, who came in with Sunma and had stood apart, horror-stricken, comes shyly forward. He helps Sunma up. They go off, he holding Sunma bent and sobbing.

Enter Eman—as carrier. He is physically present in the bounds of this next scene, a side of a round thatched hut. A young girl, about fourteen, runs in, stops beside the hut. She looks carefully to see that she is not observed, puts her mouth to a little hole in the wall.

OMAE. Eman . . . Eman . . .

Eman—as carrier—responds, as he does throughout the scene, but they are unaware of him.

EMAN (*from inside*). Who is it?

OMAE. It is me, Omae.

EMAN. How dare you come here!

Two hands appear at the hole and, pushing outwards, create a much larger hole through which Eman puts out his head. It is Eman as a boy, the same age as the girl.

Go away at once. Are you trying to get me into trouble!

OMAE. What is the matter?

EMAN. You. Go away.

OMAE. But I came to see you.

EMAN. Are you deaf? I say I don't want to see you. Now go before my tutor catches you.

OMAE. All right. Come out.

EMAN. Do what!

OMAE. Come out.

EMAN. You must be mad.

OMAE (*sits on the ground*). All right, if you don't come out I shall simply stay here until your tutor arrives.

EMAN (*about to explode, thinks better of it and the head disappears. A moment later he emerges from behind the hut*). What sort of a devil has got into you?

OMAE. None. I just wanted to see you.

EMAN (*his mimicry is nearly hysterical*). "None. I just wanted to see you." Do you think this place is the stream where you can go and molest innocent people?

OMAE (*coyly*). Aren't you glad to see me?

EMAN. I am not.

OMAE. Why?

EMAN. Why? Do you really ask me why? Because you are a woman and a most troublesome woman. Don't you know anything about this at all? We are not meant to see any woman. So go away before more harm is done.

OMAE (*flirtatious*). What is so secret about it anyway? What do they teach you?

EMAN. Nothing any woman can understand.

OMAE. Ha ha. You think we don't know eh? You've all come to be circumcised.

EMAN. Shut up. You don't know anything.

OMAE. Just think, all this time you haven't been circumcised, and you dared make eyes at us women.

EMAN. Thank you—woman. Now go.

OMAE. Do they give you enough to eat?

EMAN (*testily*). No. We are so hungry that when silly girls like you turn up, we eat them.

OMAE (*feigning tears*). Oh, oh, oh, he's abusing me. He's abusing me.

EMAN (*alarmed*). Don't try that here. Go quickly if you are going to cry.

OMAE. All right, I won't cry.

EMAN. Cry or no cry, go away and leave me alone. What do you think will happen if my tutor turns up now?

OMAE. He won't.

EMAN. (*mimicking*). "He won't." I suppose you are his wife and he tells you where he goes. In fact this is just the time he comes round to our huts. He could be at the next hut this very moment.

OMAE. Ha-ha. You're lying. I left him by the stream, pinching the girls' bottoms. Is that the sort of thing he teaches you?

EMAN. Don't say anything against him or I shall beat you. Isn't it you loose girls who tease him, wiggling your bottoms under his nose?

OMAE (*going tearful again*). A-ah, so I am one of the loose girls, eh?

EMAN. Now don't start accusing me of things I didn't say.

OMAE. But you said it. You said it.

EMAN. I didn't. Look, Omae, someone will hear you and I'll be in disgrace. Why don't you go before anything happens.

OMAE. It's all right. My friends have promised to hold your old rascal tutor till I get back.

EMAN. Then go back right now. I have work to do. (*Going in.*)

OMAE (*runs after and tries to hold him. Eman leaps back, genuinely scared*). What is the matter? I was not going to bite you.

EMAN. Do you know what you nearly did? You almost touched me!

OMAE. Well?

EMAN. Well! Isn't it enough that you let me set my eyes on you? Must you now totally pollute me with your touch? Don't you understand anything?

OMAE. Oh, that.

EMAN (*nearly screaming*). It is not "oh that." Do you think this is only a joke or a little visit like spending the night with your grandmother? This is an important period of my life. Look, these huts, we built them with our own hands. Every boy builds his own. We learn things, do you understand? And we spend much time just thinking. At least, I do. It is the first time I have had nothing to do except think. Don't you see, I am becoming a man. For the first time, I understand that I have a life to fulfill. Has that thought ever worried you?

OMAE. You are frightening me.

EMAN. There. That is all you can say. And what use will that be when a man finds himself alone—like that? (*Points to the hut.*) A man must go on his own, go where no one can help him, and test his strength. Because he may find himself one day sitting alone in a wall as round as that. In there, my mind could hold no other thought. I may never have such moments again to myself. Don't dare to come and steal any more of it.

OMAE (*this time, genuinely tearful*). Oh, I know you hate me. You only want to drive me away.

EMAN (*impatiently*). Yes, yes, I know I hate you—but go.

OMAE (*going, all tears. Wipes her eyes, suddenly all mischief*). Eman.

EMAN. What now?

OMAE. I only want to ask one thing . . . do you promise to tell me?

EMAN. Well, what is it?

OMAE (*gleefully*). Does it hurt?

She turns instantly and flees, landing straight into the arms of the returning tutor.

TUTOR. Te-he-he . . . what have we here? What little mouse leaps straight into the beak of the wise old owl eh?

Omae struggles to free herself, flies to the opposite side, grimacing with distaste.

TUTOR. I suppose you merely came to pick some fruits eh? You did not sneak here to see any of my children.

OMAE. Yes, I came to steal your fruits.

TUTOR. Te-he-he . . . I thought so. And that dutiful son of mine over there. He saw you and came to chase you off my fruit trees didn't he? Te-he-he . . . I'm sure he did, isn't that so, my young Eman?

EMAN. I was talking to her.

TUTOR. Indeed you were. Now be good enough to go into your hut until I decide your punishment (*Eman withdraws.*) Te-he-he . . . now now, my little daughter, you need not be afraid of me.

OMAE (*spiritedly*). I am not.

TUTOR. Good. Very good. We ought to be friendly. (*His voice becomes leering.*) Now this is nothing to worry you, my daughter . . . a very small thing indeed. Although of course if I were to let it slip that your young Eman had broken a strong taboo, it might go hard on him, you know. I am sure you would not like that to happen, would you?

OMAE. No.

TUTOR. Good. You are sensible, my girl. Can you wash clothes?

OMAE. Yes.

TUTOR. Good. If you will come with me now to my hut, I shall give you some clothes to wash, and then we will forget all about this matter eh? Well, come on.

OMAE. I shall wait here. You go and bring the clothes.

TUTOR. Eh? What is that? Now now, don't make me angry. You should know better than to talk back at your elders. Come now.

He takes her by the arm, and tries to drag her off.

OMAE. No no, I won't come to your hut. Leave me. Leave me alone, you shameless old man.

TUTOR. If you don't come I shall disgrace the whole family of Eman, and yours too.

Eman reenters with a small bundle.

EMAN. Leave her alone. Let us go, Omae.

TUTOR. And where do you think you are going?

EMAN. Home.

TUTOR. Te-he-he . . . As easy as that eh? You think you can leave here any time you please? Get right back inside that hut!

Eman takes Omae by the arm and begins to walk off.

TUTOR. Come back at once.

He goes after him and raises his stick. Eman catches it, wrenches it from him, and throws it away.

OMAE (*hopping delightedly*). Kill him. Beat him to death.

TUTOR. Help! Help! He is killing me! Help!

Alarmed, Eman clamps his hand over his mouth.

EMAN. Old tutor, I don't mean you any harm, but you mustn't try to harm me either. (*He removes his hand.*)

TUTOR. You think you can get away with your crime. My report shall reach the elders before you ever get into town.

EMAN. You are afraid of what I will say about you? Don't worry. Only if you try to shame me, then I will speak. I am not going back to the village anyway. Just tell them I have gone, no more. If you say one word more than that I shall hear of it the same day and I shall come back.

TUTOR. You are telling me what to do? But don't think to come back next year because I will drive you away. Don't think to come back here even ten years from now. And don't send your children. (*Goes off with threatening gestures.*)

EMAN. I won't come back.

OMAE. Smoked vulture! But Eman, he says you cannot return next year. What will you do?

EMAN. It is a small thing one can do in the big towns.

OMAE. I thought you were going to beat him that time. Why didn't you crack his dirty hide?

EMAN. Listen carefully, Omae . . . I am going on a journey.

OMAE. Come on. Tell me about it on the way.

EMAN. No, I go that way. I cannot return to the village.

OMAE. Because of that wretched man? Anyway you will first talk to your father.

EMAN. Go and see him for me. Tell him I have gone away for some time. I think he will know.

OMAE. But, Eman . . .

EMAN. I haven't finished. You will go and live with him till I get back. I have spoken to him about you. Look after him!

OMAE. But what is this journey? When will you come back?

EMAN. I don't know. But this is a good moment to go. Nothing ties me down.

OMAE. But, Eman, you want to leave me.

EMAN. Don't forget all I said. I don't know how long I will be. Stay in my father's house as long as you remember me. When you become tired of waiting, you must do as you please. You understand? You must do as you please.

OMAE. I cannot understand anything, Eman. I don't know where you are going or why. Suppose you never came back! Don't go, Eman. Don't leave me by myself.

EMAN. I must go. Now let me see you on your way.

OMAE. I shall come with you.

EMAN. Come with me! And who will look after you? Me? You will only be in my way, you know that! You will hold me back and I shall desert you in a strange place. Go home and do as I say. Take care of my father and let him take care of you. (*He starts going but Omae clings to him.*)

OMAE. But, Eman, stay the night at least. You will only lose your way. Your father, Eman, what will he say? I won't remember what you said . . . come back to the village . . . I cannot return alone, Eman . . . come with me as far as the crossroads.

His face set, Eman strides off and Omae loses balance as he increases his pace. Falling, she quickly wraps her arms around his ankle, but Eman continues unchecked, dragging her along.

OMAE. Don't go, Eman . . . Eman, don't leave me, don't leave me . . . don't leave your Omae . . . don't go, Eman . . . don't leave your Omae . . .

Eman—as carrier—makes a nervous move as if he intends to go after the vanished pair. He stops but continues to stare at the point where he last saw them. There is stillness for a while. Then the Girl enters from the same place and remains looking at Eman. Startled, Eman looks apprehensively round him. The Girl goes nearer but keeps beyond arm's length.

GIRL. Are you the carrier?

EMAN. Yes, I am Eman.

GIRL. Why are you hiding?

EMAN. I really came for a drink of water . . . er . . . is there anyone in front of the house?

GIRL. No.

EMAN. But there might be people in the house. Did you hear voices?

GIRL. There is no one here.

EMAN. Good. Thank you. (*He is about to go, stops suddenly.*) Er . . . would you . . . you will find a cup on the table. Could you bring me the water out here? The water pot is in a corner.

The Girl goes. She enters the house, then, watching Eman carefully, slips out and runs off.

EMAN (*sitting*). Perhaps they have all gone home. It will be good to rest. (*He hears voices and listens hard.*) Too late. (*Moves cautiously nearer the house.*) Quickly, girl, I can hear people coming. Hurry up. (*Looks through the window.*) Where are you? Where is she? (*The truth dawns on him suddenly and he moves off, sadly.*)

Enter Jaguna and Oroge, led by the Girl.

GIRL (*pointing*). He was there.

JAGUNA. Ay, he's gone now. He is a sly one is your friend. But it won't save him forever.

OROGE. What was he doing when you saw him?

GIRL. He asked me for a drink of water.

JAGUNA. } Ah! (*They look at each other.*)
OROGE.

OROGE. We should have thought of that.

JAGUNA. He is surely finished now. If only we had thought of it earlier.

OROGE. It is not too late. There is still an hour before midnight.

JAGUNA. We must call back all the men. Now we need only wait for him—in the right place.

OROGE. Everyone must be told. We don't want anyone heading him off again.

JAGUNA. And it works so well. This is surely the help of the gods themselves, Oroge. Don't you know at once what is on the path to the stream?

OROGE. The sacred trees.

JAGUNA. I tell you it is the very hand of the gods. Let us go.

An overgrown part of the village. Eman wanders in, aimlessly, seemingly uncaring of discovery. Beyond him, an area lights up, revealing a group of people clustered round a spot, all the heads are bowed. One figure stands away and separate from them. Even as Eman looks, the group breaks up and the people disperse, coming down and past him. Only three people are left, a man (Eman) whose back is turned, the village Priest, and the isolated one. They stand on opposite sides of the grave, the man on the mound of earth. The Priest walks round to the man's side and lays a hand on his shoulder.

PRIEST. Come.

EMAN. I will. Give me a few moments here alone.

PRIEST. Be comforted.

They fall silent.

EMAN. I was gone twelve years but she waited. She whom I thought had too much of the laughing child in her. Twelve years I was a pilgrim, seeking the vain shrine of secret strength. And all the time, strange knowledge, this silent strength of my child-woman.

PRIEST. We all saw it. It was a lesson to us; we did not know that such goodness could be found among us.

EMAN. Then why? Why the wasted years if she had to perish giving birth to my child? (*They are both silent.*) I do not really know for what great meaning I searched. When I returned, I could not be certain I had found it. Until I reached my home and I found her a full-grown woman, still a child at heart. When I grew to believe it, I thought, this, after all, is what I sought. It was here all the time. And I threw away my new-gained knowledge. I buried the part of me that was formed in strange places. I made a home in my birthplace.

PRIEST. That was as it should be.

EMAN. Any truth of that was killed in the cruelty of her brief happiness.

PRIEST (*looks up and sees the figure standing away from them, the child in his arms. He is totally still*). Your father—he is over there.

EMAN. I knew he would come. Has he my son with him?

PRIEST. Yes.

EMAN. He will let no one take the child. Go and comfort him, priest. He loved Omae like a daughter, and you all know how well she looked after him. You see how strong we really are. In his heart of hearts the old man's love really awaited a daughter. Go and comfort him. His grief is more than mine.

The Priest goes. The Old Man has stood well away from the burial group. His face is hard and his gaze unswerving from the grave. The Priest goes to him, pauses, but sees that he can make no dent in the man's grief. Bowed, he goes on his way.
Eman, as carrier, walks towards the graveside, the other Eman having gone. His feet sink into the mound and he breaks slowly on to his knees, scooping up the sand in his hands and pouring it on his head. The scene blacks out slowly.
Enter Jaguna and Oroge.

OROGE. We have only a little time.
JAGUNA. He will come. All the wells are guarded. There is only the stream left him. The animal must come to drink.
OROGE. You are sure it will not fail—the trap, I mean.
JAGUNA. When Jaguna sets the trap, even elephants pay homage—their trunks downwards and one leg up in the sky. When the carrier steps on the fallen twigs, it is up in the sacred trees with him.
OROGE. I shall breathe again when this long night is over.

They go out.
Enter Eman—as carrier—from the same direction as the last two entered. In front of him is a still figure, the Old Man as he was, carrying the dwarf boat.

EMAN (*joyfully*). Father.

The figure does not turn round.

EMAN. It is your son. Eman. (*He moves nearer.*) Don't you want to look at me? It is I, Eman. (*He moves nearer still.*)
OLD MAN. You are coming too close. Don't you know what I carry on my head?
EMAN. But, father, I am your son.
OLD MAN. Then go back. We cannot give the two of us.
EMAN. Tell me first where you are going.
OLD MAN. Do *you* ask that? Where else but to the river?
EMAN (*visibly relieved*). I only wanted to be sure. My throat is burning. I have been looking for the stream all night.
OLD MAN. It is the other way.
EMAN. But you said . . .
OLD MAN. I take the longer way, you know how I must do this. It is quicker if you take the other way. Go now.
EMAN. No, I will only get lost again. I shall go with you.
OLD MAN. Go back, my son. Go back.
EMAN. Why? Won't you even look at me?

OLD MAN. Listen to your father. Go back.
EMAN. But, father!

He makes to hold him. Instantly the Old Man breaks into a rapid trot. Eman hesitates, then follows, his strength nearly gone.

EMAN. Wait, father. I am coming with you . . . wait . . . wait for me, father . . .

There is a sound of twigs breaking, of a sudden trembling in the branches. Then silence.
The front of Eman's house. The effigy is hanging from the sheaves. Enter Sunma. Still supported by Ifada, she stands transfixed as she sees the hanging figure. Ifada appears to go mad, rushes at the object, and tears it down. Sunma, her last bit of will gone, crumbles against the wall. Some distance away from them, partly hidden, stands the Girl, impassively watching. Ifada hugs the effigy to him, stands above Sunma. The Girl remains where she is, observing. Almost at once, the villagers begin to return, subdued and guilty. They walk across the front, skirting the house as widely as they can. No word is exchanged. Jaguna and Oroge eventually appear. Jaguna, who is leading, sees Sunma as soon as he comes in view. He stops at once, retreating slightly.

OROGE (*almost whispering*). What is it?
JAGUNA. The viper.

Oroge looks cautiously at the woman.

OROGE. I don't think she will even see you.
JAGUNA. Are you sure? I am in no frame of mind for another meeting with her.
OROGE. Let's go home.
JAGUNA. I am sick to the heart of the cowardice I have seen tonight.
OROGE. That is the nature of men.
JAGUNA. Then it is a sorry world to live in. We did it for them. It was all for their own common good. What did it benefit me whether the man lived or died? But did you see them? One and all they looked up at the man and words died in their throats.
OROGE. It was no common sight.
JAGUNA. Women could not have behaved so shamefully. One by one they crept off like sick dogs. Not one could raise a curse.
OROGE. It was not only him they fled. Do you see how unattended we are?
JAGUNA. There are those who will pay for this night's work!
OROGE. Ay, let us go home.

They go off. Sunma, Ifada, and the Girl remain as they are, the light fading slowly on them.

TOPICS FOR CRITICAL THINKING AND WRITING

THE PLAY ON THE PAGE

1. Early in the play, speaking to Sunma about her hostility to Ifada, Eman says, "It is almost as if you are forcing yourself to hate him." Why is Sunma hostile to Ifada? What is her relationship to him at the end of the play?

2. What do you think of the idea that members of the "strong breed" destroy their mothers?

3. Do you suppose that males and females respond to the play in decidedly different ways? Explain.

4. Oroge and Jaguna talk of "preparing" the carrier, but we do not see them prepare Eman. Why do you suppose Soyinka decided not to include such a scene?

5. If Eman's death is regarded as an attempt to purify the community, exactly what is the impurity that the community suffers from?

6. Do you think the unnamed Girl is symbolic, and, if so, of what?

7. Why do you suppose Soyinka included the episode with the tutor?

8. Briefly sketch the ways in which the following characters respond to Eman's death: Jaguna, Sunma, Ifada, and the Girl. How would you evaluate the report of the way in which the populace responded to Eman's death?

9. Do you think an audience is meant to assume that Eman's sacrifice is redemptive? Does it make sense to say that the society that we see in the play cannot be redeemed and/or does not deserve to be redeemed?

THE PLAY ON THE STAGE

10. In his first stage direction, Soyinka insists that "there can be no break in the action. A distracting scene-change would be ruinous." Do you agree? Explain.

11. The flashbacks may be especially confusing on the stage. What difficulties might an audience have? If you were the director, what steps, if any, might you take (for instance, by using music or lighting) to assist the audience? Alternatively, would you prefer that the audience be confused for a moment? Explain.

A Note on
AFRICAN-AMERICAN THEATER

African-American drama, as the hyphen indicates, has its roots both in Africa and in America. In Africa, public performances of dance, mime, and ritual served specific functions, including political satire, a celebration of social events, and an observation of religious ceremonies. Africans have traditionally celebrated life and death in theater ritual. In the nineteenth century, when Africans were transported to North America as slaves, they brought with them a range of songs and oral drama. Entertainments comprising song, dance, folktales, and music were often performed for white masters and grew into the minstrel shows, which remained popular for many decades. In these shows, both white and black actors appeared in blackface with exaggerated features, and black personalities were stereotyped. Although post-Civil Rights thinking criticizes minstrel characterizations as demeaning to blacks, these shows provided a venue for black performers and writers. The audiences were blacks as well as whites, although in the South audiences were segregated, blacks being confined to the balconies or back rows of theaters.

The first African-American drama company, the African Theatre, was founded in 1821 in New York City by a former West Indian sailor named William Henry Brown. Most of the scripts were adaptations of existing plays. For example, the company opened with a cut version of Shakespeare's *Richard III*. However, Brown was also a playwright, and his *The Drama of King Shotoway* (1823), concerning a rebellion by the Caribs on the island of St. Vincent, is believed to be the first play written and performed by African Americans. From the African Theatre, too, came the internationally praised Shakespearean actor, Ira Aldridge.

William Wells Brown (no relation to William Henry Brown) was an escaped slave who wrote two antislavery plays, *Experience: Or How to Give a Northern Man a Backbone* (1856) and *The Escape: Or a Leap for Freedom* (1858). *Experience* is chiefly a satire on a northern preacher, and *The Escape* is a melodrama indicting slavery and exposing the South as a corrupt society. Brown read the plays on northern Abolitionist platforms, but they did not receive production in his lifetime. Other serious drama written by blacks includes William Edgar Easton's plays on the Haitian revolution and Scott Joplin's opera *Treemonisha* (written in 1911 but unproduced until 1972). W.E.B. Du Bois—the civil rights leader who cofounded the NAACP and who edited an important journal, *The Crisis*—urged the formation of theater companies to present plays "about us, for us, and near us." *The Crisis* and other influential black journals sponsored playwriting contests and published prizewinning entries. Willis Richardson's one-act *The Chip Woman's Fortune* (1923) was the earliest nonmusical black play seen on Broadway. The play celebrates the black family, but it repre-sents hypocritical blacks as well as racist whites as obstacles to black happiness. By the early twentieth century, a number of black theater companies had been established around the nation, and black actors began appearing in Broadway plays, but only in roles calling for blacks. Several plays by white writers offered strong black characters, most notably Eugene O'Neill's *The Emperor Jones* (see p. 567).

A list of black playwrights from the late nineteenth and early twentieth centuries includes Angelina Weld Grimke, Alice Dunbar-Nelson, Bob Cole, Bert Williams, Joseph Seamon Cotter, Wallace Thurman, and Mary Burrill. Much of their output protested racism, violence against black communities, difficult working conditions for blacks, and the economic disparities between white and black workers. On the other hand, *Shuffle Along* (1921), with music and lyrics by Noble Sissle and Eubie Blake, was a genial musical that aimed chiefly to entertain, not to protest. Still, it is important in the history of drama because it presented to a largely white audience images of blacks who were human beings with feelings, not just comic stereotypes. It played to great acclaim in Washington, D.C.; Philadelphia; and New York.

The years 1920–1930, now called the Harlem Renaissance, brought an exciting flowering of black literature extending well beyond the physical boundaries of Harlem. Of special note are plays by Langston Hughes, Theodore Ward, May Miller, Hall Johnson, Maritia Bonner, Eulalie Spence, and Georgia Douglas Johnson.

The American Negro Theater (A.N.T.), established in New York in 1940 by Abram Hill, Frederick O'Neal, and other writer/directors, emphasized training and production. A.N.T. nurtured much talent, including Harry Belafonte, Sidney Poitier, Ruby Dee, and Ossie Davis. After World War II, as the Civil Rights movement began to gain momentum, many black playwrights found recognition. Among a list too long to cite here, we call special attention to Louis Peterson, Alice Childress, Loften Mitchell, Lorraine Hansberry (*A Raisin in the Sun*, 1959, won the New York Drama Critics' Circle Award), Amiri Baraka, James Baldwin, Lonnie Elder, Charles Gordone, Ed Bullins, Adrienne Kennedy (see p. 786), Douglas Turner Ward (who founded the Negro Ensemble Company in 1968), Barbara Ann Tear, and Ron Milner. The most talented black dramatists of the militant 1960s largely turned their backs on white audiences and, in effect, wrote plays aimed at showing blacks that they—not their white oppressors—must change in the sense that they must cease to accept the myths that whites had created. Among many strong scripts in this category are *Dutchman* (1964), a one-act play by LeRoi Jones (Imamu Amiri Baraka), and *The Electronic Nigger* (1968) by Ed Bullins.

A Note on African-American Theater

By the mid-1970s, black dramatists were exploring a full range of modes and themes. As Bullins stated, "the literature has changed from a social-protest oriented form to one of a dialectical nature among black people—Black dialectics—and this new thrust has two main branches, the dialectic of change and the dialectic of experience." In general, more and more opportunities for black writers, actors, and directors became available. For example, Joseph Papp, founder of the New York Shakespeare Festival, cast black performers in roles previously taken by whites. Notable playwrights of the contemporary period include Ntozake Shange, Charles Fuller (who won the Pulitzer Prize for his 1981 *A Soldier's Play*), Sonia Sanchez, Kathleen Collins, August Wilson (see p. 942—two of Wilson's plays have won Pulitzer Prizes), and Anna Deavere Smith. Students will find a number of excellent references and anthologies for continuing an investigation of African-American drama. To start, we recommend:

Bigsby, W. E. *A Critical Introduction to Twentieth-Century American Drama.* Volume I (1982).

Brown-Guillory, Elizabeth. *Their Place on the Stage: Black Women Playwrights in America* (1988).

Bullins, Ed, ed. *The New Lafayette Theatre Presents: Plays with Aesthetic Comments by 6 Black Playwrights* (1974).

Hatch, James V., and Ted Shine. *Black Theater, U.S.A.: Forty-five Plays by Black Americans, 1847–1974* (1974).

Hay, Samuel A. *African-American Theatre: A Historical and Critical Analysis* (1994).

Hill, Earl, ed. *The Theater of Black Americans* (1980).

Keyssar, Helene. *The Curtain and the Veil: Strategies in Black Drama* (1981).

Oliver, Clinton, ed. *Contemporary Black Drama* (1971).

Sanders, Leslie Catherine. *The Development of Black Theater in America* (1988).

Wilkerson, Margaret B., ed. *Nine Plays by Black Women* (1986).

African Americans on the Stage

In the "Note on African-American Theater" (pp. 779–80), we sketch a history of some black theater companies and we mention some major black dramatists, and in the Commentary on Eugene O'Neill's *The Emperor Jones,* we mention the stereotypical roles that white dramatists presented of blacks. Otherwise, we have not discussed black performers. In the following pages we look briefly at blacks in black roles and in white roles.

Many thick (in two senses of the word) books have been written about race. In the late nineteenth century, one finds talk about "the Germanic race," "the Irish race," and so forth. In that context, race is perceived as some sort of complex of distinctive mental traits inherited by members of a group. Today race is usually regarded as a matter of the color of the skin, the color and form of hair, and the shape of the nose. Given this view, there are three races. Caucasoid (pinkish skin, light blond to dark brown hair, high nosebridge); Mongoloid (skin saffron to reddish brown, hair dark and straight, nosebridge usually low or medium); Negroid (skin brown to brown-black, dark hair, usually kinky, nosebridge low and nostrils broad). The genes accounting for any hereditary distinctions among these three races are very few compared to the number of genes common to all human beings. Race, then, is yet another social construction of reality, a way of making sense of the world around us. It has been a very harmful construction, yet it has also been a source of pride. Much depends on who is defining and constructing the category and for what purposes.

In the United States, to talk of race in connection with theater has chiefly been to talk of white and black theater, though in the last few decades we have all become increasingly aware of Asian-American theater. Earlier in the book we comment briefly on the history of African-American theater (pp. 779–80) and on images of African Americans presented in the dramas of whites (p. 567). Here we talk chiefly about black actors and the roles that have been available to them.

First, we want to mention that unless you are attending a predominantly black institution, you probably will not see many black actors or black plays. Whites have become increasingly uneasy about directing productions of plays by and about blacks, and many schools do not have a black director on the faculty. Occasionally, an outside director is invited to direct a campus production, but some black directors will not accept invitations to direct a black play. Stanley Williams, director of the Lorraine Hansberry Theatre in San Francisco, says of such invitations, "That's colonization. I'm the field nigger, and I'm being called up to the big house. I'm not interested in that" (quoted in *American Theatre,* March 1996, p. 16).

Whether or not you get to see black plays on your campus, there is a thriving black drama, and there are talented black actors who perform not only in roles that call for blacks but also in other roles.

Ira Aldridge (c. 1806–1867), an African-American actor who began his theatrical career with the African Grove Theatre in New York, soon found he could not get adequate roles in the United States, and at the age of seventeen or so he went to England, where he achieved fame, especially as a Shakespearean actor. He played Othello (see page 784), as well as another black part that Shakespeare wrote, Aaron (the Moor in *Titus Andronicus*), but Aldridge also played white roles, notably Lear, Macbeth, and Shylock, in whiteface.

Despite Aldridge's fame in England and in Europe, he had no successors. For decades after his death, the role of Othello in England as well as in the United States was almost always played by a white actor. In 1930, however, Paul Robeson (1898–1976) made theatrical history when he played Othello in London (see page 784). The reviews were highly favorable, and there was some talk about bringing the production to the United States, but there was more talk about whether American audiences would tolerate the sight of a black man—a real black man, not a white man wearing blackface—kissing and then killing a white woman. Not until 1942 did Robeson play Othello in the United States, and then it was only in a summer stock production in Cambridge, Boston, and Providence. The reviews again were enthusiastic, and no unpleasant noises were heard, so in 1943 Robeson opened on Broadway in a production that ran an astounding 296 performances. The previous record for a New York *Othello* was 57 performances. It should be added that several reviewers said that Robeson was the first black to play Othello in the United States. In fact, he had been preceded by at least six performers in the late nineteenth century and the early twentieth, but between 1910 and 1943 blacks had been so absent from Broadway—except in minor stereotyped roles—that all memory of serious black performers had been erased.

Despite Robeson's success in the role, Othello was played chiefly by whites for the next twenty or so years. The

Civil Rights movement, however, heightened everyone's awareness of discrimination against blacks, and in the 1960s blacks increasingly played Othello, though whites continued to play it, too. For instance, Laurence Olivier played the part on stage in 1964 and then in a film version (1966) of his stage performance. Although most white actors had played the role pretty much as a white man with a dark skin, Olivier—perhaps responding to the period's emphasis on negritude—gave Othello a distinctive behavior, a sway in his walk and a lilt in his voice. The reviews were mixed, but today (judging from classroom responses) most viewers are disturbed by what they see as racial stereotyping. In any case, Olivier may have been the last white to play the role, at least in the English-speaking world.

African-American actors, of course, cannot subsist on the relatively few available black roles. All or virtually all black theater departments in colleges and universities agree that their students should be immersed in classical drama—let's say the Greeks through Tennessee Williams and Arthur Miller—but questions arise as to whether at least some plays should be interpreted in a distinctive black way. To begin dealing with this issue, we give a quotation from an article in which Philip Kolin discusses black productions of a white play, Tennessee Williams's *The Glass Menagerie.* Most of the productions made no changes in the text, but a few made some small changes, for instance, altering Amanda's membership in the DAR to membership in a black sorority, the Delta Club. Kolin says that "these nontraditional productions address four key issues":

1. Williams's play, as done by African American companies, renegotiates the question of universality as a term of Western aesthetics.
2. The language of ownership, often used in relation to plays and playwrights is also problematized. As Ruby Dee affirms, "I feel Tennessee belongs to me, too."
3. Black and multi-ethnic productions of *The Glass Menagerie* . . . liberate the subtext from racially-imposed constraints . . . .
4. . . . White theatre history has been, a priori, the standard by which Williams's productions are measured. . . . All Amandas are held up to the performances of Laurette Taylor—the original Amanda—or Helen Hayes, or Maureen Stapleton, or Joanne Woodward. Black productions of *The Glass Menagerie,* therefore, free the play from restrictive so-called "prototypical" or "seminal" interpretations of individual roles by white actors.

"Black and Multi-Racial Productions of Tennessee Williams's *The Glass Menagerie,*" *Journal of Dramatic Theory and Criticism* 9 (1995): 97–98

According to Kolin, the first black production of the play was given at Howard University in 1947, less than two years after the Broadway premiere, and a second black production was given in 1950 at the University of Iowa. The first interracial production was given in 1965 at the Karamu

Theatre in Cleveland, Ohio, where the Wingfields were played by African Americans and Jim (the Gentleman Caller) was played by a white (see p. 784). (Karamu House—Swahili for "a place of enjoyment for all"—holds a distinguished place in the history of multiracial theatrical activity. The adult theater group, formed in 1921, originally was called the Gilpin Players, in honor of Charles Gilpin, the African American who created the title role in Eugene O'Neill's *The Emperor Jones.* See p. 567, 581–82.) According to Kolin, none of the reviewers of the Karamu production of *The Glass Menagerie* addressed the issue of a white man calling on a black woman. A question: Should the reviewers have addressed this issue, or were they right to ignore it?

The next interracial production was performed by the Inner City Cultural Center in Los Angeles in 1967, but the audience was unaware that the production was interracial. All of the characters were white, but Jim O'Connor was played by a black actor (Paul Winfield) with "light-skin make-up with an uplifted Irish nose and a red wig" (see p. 785). Reviewers praised Winfield and did raise the issue of the makeup. Kolin remarks, interestingly, "Even in such a disguise Winfield earned high honors." What is interesting about the remark is this: No one would have said of a white actor performing Othello in blackface that "even in such a disguise" he was effective. It has always been assumed that whites would put on the makeup appropriate to the role, whether the role was Othello or Hamlet or Charlie Chan.

In a moment we will continue this brief discussion of makeup, but before we leave productions of *The Glass Menagerie,* we should say that (judging from Kolin's article) black productions are prompted by people who believe that the play speaks to blacks as well as to whites. Very few black directors sought to give a special black twist to the play, but one twist is so interesting that it should be mentioned. When Whitney J. LeBlanc directed it at the Lorraine Hansberry Theatre in 1991, the picture of the missing father was of a white man. LeBlanc used the picture in order to say something about the historic relationship between whites and blacks: "We've always been abandoned by fathers ever since miscegenation" (113).

We can now briefly return to the question of African-American actors in roles that are identifiably white, such as a king of England. Can we have a black King Lear with, for example, a white daughter and two black daughters? If open casting (also called nontraditional casting or color-blind casting) is taken seriously, what effect is produced by having a Lear with, for example, an Asian daughter, a black daughter, and a white or Latino daughter? When the great black actor Canada Lee in 1946 played Bosola in a Jacobean tragedy, *The Duchess of Malfi* (c. 1613), he wore whiteface (really a sort of pinkish greasepaint) and gloves, working within the traditional idea that acting is a matter of impersonation, and theatrical impersonation usually involves makeup. (See p. 785.) If Lee had appeared without makeup, critics doubtless would have said that he shattered the dramatic illusion. On the other hand, the concept of dramatic illusion is very fragile—the audience of course always knows that the actor is an actor, not the role he or she is playing. Stage actors perform chiefly with their voices and their bodies (as opposed to movie actors, who perform chiefly with their faces), and most theatergoers know that with a great actor, costume and makeup are relatively unimportant. On several occasions we have seen performers—John Gielgud, Laurence Olivier, and Michael Redgrave come to mind—in street clothes perform scenes from Shakespeare, and the effect was staggering. No hearer could have wished for costumes and makeup. On the other hand, we are talking about actors of the highest rank, speaking lines that have endured for centuries. Whether lesser actors can be as compelling when they speak lesser lines is another question. With a major actress such as Ruby Dee, who played Amanda in a black production, the color or the makeup probably doesn't matter, but, again, with less skilled actors makeup may be useful. Still, it is now an established convention that actors of color not whiten their faces, and audiences seem able to accept the convention of, for example, a black King Henry V of England (see p. 785) or a black Cordelia, even if the actor playing Lear is white. Just as Desdemona "saw Othello's visage in his mind," if we are properly attuned we can probably ignore a mere matter of pigmentation. Certainly an audience that is used to seeing multicultural productions, such as those that Joseph Papp staged in New York, grew accustomed to color-blind casting. Especially in plays that are not essentially realistic, experience indicates that an audience can disregard race in the casting.

However, what about casting African Americans in a play that is largely realistic, specifically in *Death of a Salesman?* Henry Louis Gates, rejecting the idea that today black artists must work with distinctively black material, in 1994 said in an interview in *Time,* "Discarding the anxieties of a bygone era, [black artists today] presume the universality of the black experience." One understands what Gates

means, and one is not calling into question the competence of black actors, but when black actors perform in *Death of a Salesman,* do they somehow transform the play? Alternatively, does the play somehow overwhelm them?

According to Brenda Murphy in *Miller: Death of a Salesman* (1995), an all-black production at the Center Stage, in Baltimore in 1972, left the critics rather cool. "Willy Loman's values," Mel Gussow wrote in *New York Times,* "are white values—the elevation of personality, congeniality, conformity, salesmanship in the sense of selling oneself." In the all-black production, Gussow said, "Willy becomes a black man embracing the white world as an example to be emulated" (quoted in Murphy, page 86). Two years later an integrated production was scheduled for the Circle in the Square Theatre in New York, with Charley played by a black. Miller was uneasy when he learned of the plan. He cautioned that color-blind casting might work if, for example, Biff were black and Happy were white—that is, if it were evident that race was irrelevant. However, in an essentially realistic play, Miller thought that to cast Charley as the sole black would lead the audience to assume that Willy dares to have a black man for his best friend in the 1930s. The critics were cool toward the production, which was staged in 1975.

The question, again, seems to be this: If the play is chiefly realistic, can a theater audience ignore the pigmentation of the actors? We hope so. However, if not yet, perhaps theater can play a role in helping to bring about a society in which pigmentation is scarcely noticed.

Suggested References

Most of the titles listed at the end of "A Note on African-American Theater" (p. 780) are relevant here. In addition, see Martin B. Duberman, *Paul Robeson* (1989); Herbert Marshall and Mildred Stock, *Ira Aldridge, The Negro Tragedian* (1958); and Kenneth Tynan, *Othello by William Shakespeare: The National Theatre Production* (1966, on Olivier's Othello).

Ira Aldridge, unable to find sufficient work as a Shakespearean actor in the United States, left for England and spent the rest of his life there and in Europe. He was especially famous for his Othello (shown here), but he performed other roles, too, including Shylock, Macbeth, and Lear. When performing white roles, in keeping with the prevailing realism of the theater of the period, he wore white makeup and a wig. ▶

◀ Paul Robeson, an African-American who had achieved fame as an athlete, as a singer, and as an actor—notably in Eugene O'Neill's *The Emperor Jones*—was invited to play the role of Othello at Stratford-upon-Avon in 1930. His performance was enthusiastically received—the reviewer in the London *Morning Post* said, "There has been no Othello on our stage for forty years to compare with his dignity, simplicity, and true passion"—but American producers were unsure about how American audiences would respond to the sight of a black actor kissing a white woman. Not until 1942 could they be persuaded to let Robeson play the role in the United States. The favorable response to the 1942 production led to another production with Robeson in 1943, which was immensely successful.

In l965 the Karamu Theatre in Cleveland, Ohio staged Tennessee Williams's *The Glass Menagerie* with an integrated cast: The Wingfield family was black and Jim O'Connor (the Gentleman Caller) was white. The play has been done fairly often by all-black companies, but the use of one white player made the production unusual. ▶

Paul Winfield, an African-American actor, played the role of Jim O'Connor in whiteface in a 1967 production by the Inner City Cultural Center in Los Angeles. Audiences apparently were unaware that the cast was integrated. The Inner City Cultural Center has been an early innovator in the area now known as "nontraditional casting. It is highly unusual, however, for a black actor today to perform in whiteface. ▶

◀ Canada Lee, a black actor (at the left), in 1946 played the villainous Bosola in John Webster's tragedy, *The Duchess of Malfi*. Doubtless the chief reason for the makeup was the idea that in appearance performers should resemble their roles, but a second reason may possibly have been that if Lee had appeared without white makeup the audience might have mistakenly assumed that the character in the play was black, or that the director was sending a message suggesting that blacks are villainous.

Robert Hooks played Henry V in Joseph Papp's production at the New York Shakespeare Festival's Mobile Theatre in 1965. As the founder of a theatrical enterprise in a highly multicultural city, Papp could hardly ignore the talent of people of color. His principle was to choose the best actors he could find, regardless of color. Although a few reviewers objected that spectators cannot ignore the incongruity of, say, a black actor in a decidedly white role, most viewers did not share the objection. ▶

Adrienne Kennedy

FUNNYHOUSE OF A NEGRO

Adrienne Hawkins Kennedy was born in Pittsburgh in 1931 but spent her childhood in rural Georgia and in Cleveland, Ohio. Kennedy began writing as a young woman and (like most writers) has been influenced by a wide range of factors. Kennedy cites American popular culture, movies and movie stars, religious experiences, several years' residence in Africa, and her own observations of racism. In her memoir, *People Who Led to My Plays*, she recalls that a schoolteacher once discouraged her from considering a career in journalism because of her color. She recalls racial discrimination not only in the South but also at Ohio State University. *Funnyhouse of a Negro*, her first and longest dramatic piece, won an Obie Distinguished Play Award in 1964. Kennedy has received two Rockefeller grants, a Guggenheim fellowship, and several commissions for new plays. Among her plays are *The Owl Answers*, *A Rat's Mass*, *In His Own Write* and *A Spaniard in the Works* (adaptations of John Lennon's writings), *Sun: A Poem for Malcolm X Inspired by His Murder*, and *She Talks to Beethoven*. She has also written poetry, short fiction, two novels, and nonfiction. Adrienne Kennedy was chosen by the Signature Theater in New York City as the sole focus of their 1995–1996 productions.

COMMENTARY

Funnyhouse of a Negro, a disturbing and challenging play for the reader, will most likely strike you as a conspicuous departure from traditional playmaking, and you may be tempted to apply labels such as antirealistic, phantasmagoric, experimental, surrealistic, or absurdist. These labels are all valid and help provide a way of imagining Adrienne Kennedy's play on stage and its impact for audiences.

The on-stage action during a performance of *Funnyhouse of a Negro* gives voice and form to the memories and fears of a young black woman (Sarah), whose mental state has deteriorated to the point that she kills herself. In a traditional play, necessary background information is presented as exposition, usually in the initial scenes. In *Funnyhouse*, the facts are woven through a series of overlapping speeches and lead to our understanding of Sarah's feeling of resentment, despair, guilt, and self-hate. These facts can be summarized as follows: Sarah is a student living in a rented room on the Upper West Side of Manhattan. Her boyfriend, Raymond, is Jewish. Her mother was a light-skinned Negro woman with beautiful, straight hair; her father, darker-skinned, had been raised in Georgia by a devoutly religious mother. Sarah's paternal grandmother had disapproved of her son's marriage to Sarah's mother. The grandmother, wanting her son to become a savior of the black race, urged him to travel to Africa to build a mission in the jungle. It was in Africa that the wife withdrew, emotionally, from the husband; one

night, while drunk, the husband raped his wife. Sarah is the product of this rape. Soon after, the mother's hair began to fall out, and her mental state deteriorated. Losing his sense of mission, the father returned to New York, where he lived alone in a hotel in Harlem. The father visited Sarah to beg her forgiveness, but she spurned him and he then committed suicide.

None of the facts are enacted. Instead, in *Funnyhouse of a Negro* we seem to be inside the mind of the protagonist, Sarah, where we are eerily aware of the unbearable psychological stress that drives her to her final act. Kennedy has said in interviews and in her memoir (*People Who Led to My Plays*) that all her plays are based on her own life—members of her family, her experiences growing up in a racist society, her travels in Africa and Europe, images from films and popular culture. For example, in London she was impressed by the mammoth statue of Queen Victoria in front of Buckingham Palace, and she used a similar statue prominently in *Funnyhouse of a Negro*. The funnyhouse setting is taken from her memories of a place in Cleveland—an amusement park with two huge white figures on either side of the entrance, figures that bobbed back and forth and emitted hysterical laughter. In the play, these figures are Raymond and Sarah's white landlady. Kennedy draws upon the imagery of dreams, choosing distorted effects to project an interior reality onto the stage. On one level, the play uses surreal images to dramatize the anguish of a black woman who feels torn between loyalty and guilt and who is wracked with self-hatred because of her black and white heritage. On a deeper level, the play shows us the terrible consequences of repression (particularly imperialism) on an individual—Sarah as the offspring of both Europe (her mother) and Africa (her father). Sarah's various other "selves"—the Duchess of Hapsburg, Queen Victoria, Jesus Christ, Patrice Lumumba—give personal voice to the larger political and social conflicts embodied in one person.

From the first production of *Funnyhouse of a Negro,* critics and theatergoers have remarked on absurdist components of her work (see pp. 690–91 for a discussion of theater of the absurd). Eugène Ionesco's ideas, written in *Notes and Counternotes* (1964), about how absurdist devices establish an effective theater can help us understand some of Kennedy's techniques in *Funnyhouse of a Negro:*

> To push drama out of that intermediate zone where it is neither theatre nor literature is to restore it to its domain. . . . It was not for me to conceal the devices of the theatre, but rather make them still more evident, deliberately obvious, go all out for caricature and the grotesque. . . . Everything to raised paroxysm, where the source of tragedy lies. A theatre of violence: violently comic, violently dramatic.

Funnyhouse of a Negro is indeed suffused with violence: with fear of rape, with terrifying images of death. Kennedy's opening remarks inform us that the stage curtain is "of a cheap material and a ghastly white, a material that brings to mind the interior of a cheap casket; parts of it are frayed and it looks as if it has been gnawed by rats." As the play builds through its ten episodes (not necessarily marked by the blackouts), the whiteness reinforces Sarah's nightmarish dilemma. Repeated actions (for example, a figure walking), repeated motifs (for example, the central image of falling hair—a symbol of Sarah's self-loathing), and repeated images (for example, of birds) lend unity to the play.

Finally, we must confront the violence inherent in the word *nigger*. In an autobiographical essay, "Becoming a Playwright," Kennedy documents her own struggles with the word. Originally, *nigger* illustrated Sarah's self-hatred, but Kennedy felt unsure of its appropriateness on stage and decided to delete it. Edward Albee (see p. 741), who ran the playwriting workshop in which the script was developed, encouraged her to put it back: "A playwright is someone who lets his guts hang out on the stage and that's what you've done in this play." Thus, even in its language, *Funnyhouse of a Negro* represents the dreadful violence suffered by black people and creates for its audiences and readers a vivid, tortured, dream world. It is a play that is as valid for the 1990s as it was for its first audiences in 1964.

Adrienne Kennedy

FUNNYHOUSE OF A NEGRO

Characters

SARAH, *Negro*
DUCHESS OF HAPSBURG, *one of herselves*
QUEEN VICTORIA, *one of herselves*
PATRICE LUMUMBA, *one of herselves*
JESUS *one of herselves*
THE MOTHER
LANDLADY, *Funnylady*
RAYMOND, *Funnyman*

BEGINNING: *Before the closed curtain a woman dressed in a white nightgown walks across the stage carrying before her a bald head. She moves as one in a trance and is mumbling something inaudible to herself. She appears faceless, wearing a yellow whitish mask over her face, with no apparent eyes. Her hair is wild, straight and black and falls to her waist. As she moves, holding her hands before her, she gives the effect of one in a dream. She crosses the stage from right to left. Before she has barely vanished, the curtain opens. It is a white satin curtain of a cheap material and a ghastly white, a material that brings to mind the interior of a cheap casket; parts of it are frayed and it looks as if it has been gnawed by rats.*

THE SCENE: *Two women are sitting in what appears to be a queen's chamber. It is set in the middle of the stage in a strong white light while the rest of the stage is in strong unnatural blackness. The quality of the white light is unreal and ugly. The queen's chamber consists of a dark monumental bed resembling an ebony tomb, a low dark chandelier with candles and wine-colored walls. Flying about are great black ravens.* QUEEN VICTORIA *is standing before her bed, holding a small mirror in her hand. On the white pillow of her bed is a dark indistinguishable object. The* DUCHESS OF HAPSBURG *is standing at the foot of her bed. Her back is to us as is the Queen's. Throughout the entire scene they do not move. Both women are dressed in royal gowns of white, a white similar to the white of the curtain, the material cheap satin. Their headpieces are white and of a net that falls over their faces. From beneath both their headpieces springs a headful of wild kinky hair. Although in this scene we do not see their faces, they look exactly alike and will wear masks or be made up to appear a whitish yellow. It is an alabaster face, the skin drawn tightly over the high cheekbones, great dark eyes that seem gouged out of the head, a high forehead, a full red mouth and a head of frizzy hair. If the characters do not wear a mask, the face must be highly powdered and possess a hard expressionless quality and a stillness as in the face of death.*

(We hear a knocking.)

VICTORIA *(listening to the knocking).* It is my father. He is arriving again for the night.

(The Duchess makes no reply.)

He comes through the jungle to find me. He never tires of his journey.

DUCHESS. How dare he enter the castle, he who is the darkest of them all, the darkest one. My mother looked like a white woman, hair as straight as any white woman's. And at least I am yellow, but he is black, the blackest one of them all. I hoped he was dead. Yet he still comes through the jungle to find me.

(The knocking is louder.)

VICTORIA. He never tires of the journey, does he, Duchess?

(Looking at herself in the mirror.)

DUCHESS. How dare he enter the castle of Queen Victoria Regina, Monarch of England. It is because of him that my mother died. The wild black beast put his hands on her. She died.

VICTORIA. Why does he keep returning? He keeps returning forever, coming back ever and keeps coming back forever. He is my father.

DUCHESS. He is a black Negro.

VICTORIA. He is my father. I am tied to the black Negro. He came when I was a child in the south, before I was born he haunted my conception, diseased by birth.

DUCHESS. Killed my mother.

VICTORIA. My mother was the light. She was the lightest one. She looked like a white woman.

DUCHESS. We are tied to him unless, of course, he should die.

VICTORIA. But he is dead.

DUCHESS. And he keeps returning.

(The knocking is louder.)

BLACKOUT

The lights go out in the chamber. Onto the stage from the left comes the figure in the white nightgown carrying the bald head. This time we hear her speak.

MOTHER. Black man, black man, I never should have let a black man put his hands on me. The wild black beast raped me and now my skull is shining.

(She disappears to the right. Now the light is focused on a single white square wall that is to the left of the stage that is suspended and stands alone, of about five feet in dimension and width. It stands with the narrow part facing the

audience. A character steps through. She is a faceless dark character with a hangman's rope about her neck and red blood on the part that would be her face. She is the Negro. On first glance she might be a young person but at a closer look the impression of an ancient character is given. The most noticeable aspect of her looks is her wild kinky hair, part of which is missing. It is a ragged head with a crown which the Negro carries in her hand. She is dressed in black. She steps slowly through the wall, stands still before it and begins her monologue.)

NEGRO. Part of the time I live with Raymond, part of the time with God, Prince Charles and Albert Saxe Coburg. I live in my room. It is a small room on the top floor of a brownstone in the West Nineties in New York, a room filled with my dark old volumes, a narrow bed and on the wall old photographs of castles and monarchs of England. It is also Victoria's chamber, Queen Victoria Regina's. Partly because it is consumed by a gigantic plaster statue of Queen Victoria, who is my idol, and partly for other reasons; three steps that I contrived out of boards lead to the statue which I have placed opposite the door as I enter the room. It is a sitting figure, a replica of one in London, and a thing of astonishing whiteness. I found it in a dusty shop on Morningside Heights. Raymond says it is a thing of terror, possessing the quality of nightmares, suggesting large and probable deaths. And of course he is right. When I am the Duchess of Hapsburg, I sit opposite Victoria in my headpiece and we talk. The other time I wear the dress of a student, dark clothes and dark stockings. Victoria always wants me to tell her of whiteness. She wants me to tell her of a royal world where everything and everyone is white and there are no unfortunate black ones. For as we of royal blood know, black is evil and has been from the beginning. Even before my mother's hair started to fall out. Before she was raped by a wild black beast. Black was evil.

When I am not the Duchess of Hapsburg I am myself. As for myself, I long to become even a more pallid Negro than I am now, pallid like Negroes on the covers of American Negro magazines; soulless, educated and irreligious. I want to possess no moral value, particularly value as to my being. I want not to be. I ask nothing except anonymity.

I am an English major, as my mother was when she went to school in Atlanta. My father majored in social work. I am graduated from a city college and have occasional work in libraries, but mostly spend my days preoccupied with the placement and geometric position of words on paper. I write poetry, filling white page after white page with imitations of Edith Sitwell. It is my dream to live in rooms with European antiques and my Queen Victoria, photographs of Roman ruins, walls of books, a piano, oriental carpets, and to eat my meals on a white glass table. I will visit my friends' apartments which will contain books, photographs of Roman ruins, pianos and oriental carpets. My friends will be white. I need them as an embankment to keep me from reflecting too much upon the fact that I am a Negro. For, like all educated Negroes—out of life and death essential—I find it necessary to maintain a stark fortress against recognition of myself. My white friends like myself will be shrewd, intellectual and anxious for death. Anyone's death. I will mistrust them, as I do myself. But if I had not wavered in my opinion of myself then my hair would never have fallen out. And if my hair hadn't fallen out, I wouldn't have bludgeoned my father's head with an ebony mask.

In appearance I am good-looking in a boring way, no glaring Negroid features, medium nose, medium mouth and pale yellow skin. My one defect is that I have a head of frizzy hair, unmistakably Negro kinky hair; and is indisguisable. I would like to lie and say I love Raymond. But I do not. He is a poet and is Jewish. He is very interested in Negroes.

(The Negro stands by the wall and throughout her following speech, the following characters come through the wall, disappearing off into the varying directions in the darkened night of the stage—Duchess, Queen Victoria, Jesus, Patrice Lumumba. Jesus is a hunchback, yellow-skinned dwarf, dressed in white rags and sandals. Patrice Lumumba is a black man. His head appears to be split in two with blood and tissue in eyes. He carries an ebony mask.)

The characters are myself; the Duchess of Hapsburg, Queen Victoria Regina, Jesus, Patrice Lumumba. The rooms are my rooms; a Hapsburg chamber, a chamber in a Victorian castle, the hotel where I killed my father, the jungle. These are the places myselves exist in. I know no places. That is I cannot believe in places. To believe in places is to know hope and to know the emotion of hope is to know beauty. It links us across a horizon and connects us to the world. I find there are no places, only my funnyhouse. Streets are rooms, cities are rooms, eternal rooms. I try to create a space for myselves in cities. New York, the midwest, a southern town but it becomes a lie. I try to give myselves a logical relationship but that too is a lie. For relationships was one of my last religions. I clung loyally to the lie of relationships, again and again seeking to establish a connection between my characters. Jesus is Victoria's son. Mother loved my father before her hair fell out. A loving relationship exists between myself and Jesus but they are lies. You will assume I am trifling with you, teasing your intellect, dealing in subtleties, denying connection then suddenly at a point reveal a startling heartbreaking connection. You are wrong. For the days are past when there are places and characters with connections with themes as in stories you pick up on the shelves of public libraries.

Too, there is no theme. No statements, I might borrow a statement, struggle to fabricate a theme, borrow one from my contemporaries, renew one from the master, hawkishly scan other stories searching for statements, consider the theme then deceive myself that I held such a statement within me, refusing to accept the fact that a statement has to come from an ordered force. I might try to join horizontal elements such as dots on a horizontal line, or create a centrifugal force, or create causes and effects so that they would equal a quantity but it would be a lie. For the statement is the characters and the characters are myself.

BLACKOUT

Then to the right front of the stage comes the white light. It goes to a suspended stairway. At the foot of it stands the Landlady. She is a tall, thin woman dressed in a black hat with red and appears to be talking to someone in a suggested open doorway in a corridor of a rooming house. She laughs like a mad character in a funnyhouse throughout her speech.

LANDLADY (*looking up the stairway*). Ever since her father hung himself in a Harlem hotel when Patrice Lumumba was murdered, she hides in her room. Each night she repeats; he keeps returning. How dare he enter the castle walls, he who is the darkest of them all, the darkest one. My mother looked like a white woman, hair as straight as any white woman's. And I am yellow but he, he is black, the blackest one of them all. I hoped he was dead. Yet still he comes through the jungle.

I tell her: Sarah, honey, the man hung himself. It's not your blame. But, no, she stares at me: No, Mrs. Conrad, he did not hang himself, that is only the way they understand it, they do, but the truth is that I bludgeoned his head with an ebony skull that he carries about with him. Wherever he goes, he carries out black masks and heads.

She's suffering so till her hair has fallen out. But then she did always hide herself in that room with the walls of books and her statues. I always did know she thought she was somebody else, a Queen or something, somebody else.

BLACKOUT

Funnyman's place. The next scene is enacted with the Duchess and Raymond. Raymond's place is suggested as being above the Negro's room, and is etched in with a prop of blinds and a bed . . . behind the blinds are mirrors and when the blinds are opened and closed by Raymond, this is revealed. Raymond turns out to be the Funnyman of the funnyhouse. He is tall, white and ghostly thin and dressed in a black shirt and black trousers in attire suggesting an artist. Throughout his dialogue he laughs. The Duchess is partially disrobed and it is implied from their attitudes of physical intimacy—he is standing and she is sitting before him clinging to his leg. During the scene, Raymond keeps opening and closing the blinds. His face has black sores on

it and he is wearing a black hat. Throughout the scene he strikes her as in affection when he speaks to her.

DUCHESS (*carrying a red paper bag*). My father is arriving, and what am I to do?

(*Raymond walks about the place opening the blinds and laughing.*)

FUNNYMAN. He is arriving from Africa, is he not?

DUCHESS. Yes, yes, he is arriving from Africa.

FUNNYMAN. I always knew your father was African.

DUCHESS. He is an African who lives in the jungle. He is an African who has always lived in the jungle. Yes, he is a nigger who is an African, who is a missionary teacher and is now dedicating his life to the erection of a Christian mission in the middle of the jungle. He is a black man.

FUNNYMAN. He is a black man who shot himself when they murdered Patrice Lumumba.

DUCHESS (*goes on wildly*). Yes, my father is a black man who went to Africa years ago as a missionary teacher, got mixed up in politics, was reviled and is now devoting his foolish life to the erection of a Christian mission in the middle of the jungle in one of those newly freed countries. Hide me.

(*Clinging to his knees.*)

Hide me here so the nigger will not find me.

FUNNYMAN (*laughing*). Your father is in the jungle dedicating his life to the erection of a Christian mission.

DUCHESS. Hide me here so the jungle will not find me. Hide me.

FUNNYMAN. Isn't it cruel of you?

DUCHESS. Hide me from the jungle.

FUNNYMAN. Isn't it cruel?

DUCHESS. No, no.

FUNNYMAN. Isn't it cruel of you?

DUCHESS. No.

(*She screams and opens her red paper bag and draws from it her fallen hair. It is a great mass of dark wild. She holds it up to him. He appears not to understand. He stares at it.*)

It is my hair.

(*He continues to stare at her.*)

When I awakened this morning it had fallen out, not all of it but a mass from the crown of my head that lay on the center of my pillow. I rose and in the greyish winter morning light of my room I stood staring at my hair, dazed by my sleeplessness, still shaken by nightmares of my mother. Was it true, yes, it was my hair. In the mirror I saw that, although my hair remained on both sides, clearly on the crown and at my temples my scalp was bare.

(*She removes her black crown and shows him the top of her head.*)

RAYMOND (*Funnyman*). (*Staring at her.*) Why would your hair fall out? Is it because you are cruel? How could a black father haunt you so.

DUCHESS. He haunted my very conception. He was a black wild beast who raped my mother.

RAYMOND (*Funnyman*). He is a black Negro.

(*Laughing.*)

DUCHESS. Ever since I can remember he's been in a nigger pose of agony. He is the wilderness. He speaks niggerly, grovelling about wanting to touch me with his black hand.

FUNNYMAN. How tormented and cruel you are.

DUCHESS (*as if not comprehending*).

Yes, yes, the man's dark, very dark skinned. He is the darkest, my father is the darkest, my mother is the lightest. I am between. But my father is the darkest. My father is a nigger who drives me to misery. Any time spent with him evolves itself into suffering. He is a black man and the wilderness.

FUNNYMAN. How tormented and cruel you are.

DUCHESS. He is a nigger.

FUNNYMAN. And your mother, where is she?

DUCHESS. She is in the asylum. In the asylum bald. Her father was a white man. And she is the asylum.

(*He takes her in his arms. She responds wildly.*)

BLACKOUT

Knocking is heard, it continues, then somewhere near the center of stage a figure appears in the darkness, a large dark faceless Man carrying a mask in his hand.

MAN. It begins with the disaster of my hair. I awaken. My hair has fallen out, not all of it, but a mass from the crown of my head that lies on the center of my white pillow. I arise and in the greyish winter morning light of my room I stand staring at my hair, dazed by sleeplessness, still shaken by nightmares of my mother. Is it true? Yes. It is my hair. In the mirror I see that although my hair remains on both sides, clearly on the crown and at my temples my scalp is bare. And in my sleep I had been visited by my bald crazy mother who comes to me crying, calling me to her bedside. She lies on the bed watching the strands of her own hair fall out. Her hair fell out after she married and she spent her days lying on the bed watching the strands fall from her scalp, covering the bedspread until she was bald and admitted to the hospital. Black man, black man, my mother says I never should have let a black man put his hands on me. She comes to me, her bald skull shining. Black diseases, Sarah, she says. Black diseases. I run. She follows me, her bald skull shining. That is the beginning.

(*Several Women with white nightgowns on, waistlength black hair, all identical, emerge from the sides of the stage and run into the darkness, toward him shouting—black man, black man. They are carrying bald heads.*)

BLACKOUT

Queen's Chamber. Her hair is in a small pile on the bed and in a small pile on the floor, several other piles of hair are scattered about her and her white gown is covered with fallen out hair.

Queen Victoria acts out the following scene: She awakens (in pantomime) and discovers her hair has fallen. It is on her pillow. She arises and stands at the side of the bed with her back towards us staring at her hair. She opens the red paper bag that she is carrying and takes out her hair, attempting to place it back on her head (for unlike Victoria, she does not wear her headpiece now). Suddenly the women in white gowns come running from the rear of the stage carrying their skulls before them screaming.

(*The unidentified man returns out of the darkness and speaks. He carries the mask.*)

MAN (*Patrice Lumumba*). I am a nigger of two generations. I am Patrice Lumumba. I am a nigger of two generations. I am the black shadow that haunted my mother's conception. I belong to the generation born at the turn of the century and the generation born before the depression. At present I reside in New York City in a brownstone in the West Nineties. I am an English major at a city college. My nigger father majored in social work, so did my mother. I am a student and have occasional work in libraries. But mostly I spend my vile days preoccupied with the placement and geometric position of words on paper. I write poetry filling white page after white page with imitations of Sitwell. It is my vile dream to live in rooms with European antiques and my statues of Queen Victoria, photographs of Roman ruins, walls of books, a piano and oriental carpets and to eat my meals on a white glass table. It is also my nigger dreams for my friends to eat their meals on white glass tables and to live in rooms with European antiques, photographs of Roman ruins, pianos and oriental carpets. My friends will be white. I need them as an embankment to keep me from reflecting too much upon the fact that I am Patrice Lumumba who haunted my mother's conception. They are necessary for me to maintain recognition against myself. My white friends, like myself, will be shrewd intellectuals and anxious for death. Anyone's death. I will despise them as I do myself. For if I did not despise myself then my hair would not have fallen and if my hair had not fallen then I would not have bludgeoned my father's face with the ebony mask.

(*Then another wall is dropped, larger than the first one was. This one is near the front of the stage facing thus. Throughout the following monologue the characters Duchess, Victoria, Jesus go back and forth. As they go in their backs are to us but the Negro faces us speaking.*)

Adrienne Kennedy

NEGRO. I always dreamed of a day when my mother would smile at me. My father—his mother wanted him to be Christ. From the beginning in the lamp of their dark room she said—I want you to be Jesus, to walk in Genesis and save the race. You must return to Africa, find revelation in the midst of golden savannas, nim and white frankopenny trees, white stallions roaming under a blue sky, you must walk with a white dove and heal the race, heal the misery, take us off the cross. She stared at him anguished in the kerosene light . . . at dawn he watched her rise, kill a hen for him to eat at breakfast, then go to work down at the big house till dusk, till she died.

His father told him the race was no damn good. He hated his father and adores his mother. His mother didn't want him to marry my mother and sent a dead chicken to the wedding. I DON'T want you marrying that child, she wrote, she's not good enough for you, I want you to go to Africa. When they first married they lived in New York.

Then they went to Africa where my mother fell out of love with my father. She didn't want him to save the black race and spent her days combing her hair. She would not let him touch her in their wedding bed and called him black. He is black of skin with dark eyes and a great dark square brow. Then in Africa he started to drink and came home drunk one night and raped my mother. The child from the union is me. I clung to my mother. Long after she went to the asylum I wove long dreams of her beauty, her straight hair and fair skin and gray eyes, so identical to mine. How it anguished him. I turned from him, nailing him to the cross, he said, dragging him through grass and nailing him on a cross until he bled. He pleaded with me to help him find Genesis, search for Genesis in the minds of golden savannas, nim and white frankopenny trees and white stallions roaming under a blue sky, help him search for the white dove; he wanted the black man to make a pure statement, he wanted the black man to rise from colonialism. But I sat in the room with my mother, sat by her bedside and helped her comb her straight black hair and wove long dreams of her beauty. She had long since began to curse the place and spoke of herself trapped in blackness. She preferred the company of night owls. Only at night did she rise, walking in the garden among the trees with the owls. When I spoke to her she saw I was a black man's child and she preferred speaking to owls. Nights my father came from his school in the village struggling to embrace me. But I fled and hid under my mother's bed while she screamed of remorse. Her hair was falling badly and after a while we had to return to this country.

He tried to hang himself once. After my mother went to the asylum he had hallucinations, his mother threw a dead chicken at him, his father laughed and said the race was no damn good, my mother appeared in her nightgown screaming she had trapped herself in blackness. No white doves flew. He had left Africa and was again in New York. We lived in Harlem and no white doves flew. Sarah, Sarah, he would say to me, the soldiers are coming and a cross they are placing high on a tree and are dragging me through the grass and nailing me upon the cross. My blood is gushing. I wanted to live in Genesis in the midst of golden savannas, nim and white frankopenny trees and white stallions roaming under a blue sky. I wanted to walk with a white dove. I wanted to be a Christian. Now I am Judas, I betrayed my mother. I sent your mother to the asylum. I created a yellow child who hates me. And he tried to hang himself in a Harlem hotel.

BLACKOUT

(*A bald head is dropped on a string. We hear laughing.*)

DUCHESS'S PLACE: *The next scene is done in the Duchess of Hapsburg's place which is a chandelier ballroom with snow falling, a black and white marble floor, a bench decorated with white flowers, all of this can be made of obviously fake materials as they would be in a funnyhouse. The Duchess is wearing a white dress and as in the previous scene a white headpiece with her kinky hair springing out from under it. In the scene are the Duchess and Jesus. Jesus enters the room which is at first dark, then suddenly brilliant, he starts to cry out at the Duchess who is seated on a bench under the chandelier, and pulls his hair from the red paper bag holding it up for the Duchess to see.*

JESUS. My hair!

(*The Duchess does not speak, Jesus again screams.*)

My hair.

(*Holding the hair up, waiting for a reaction from the Duchess.*)

DUCHESS.

(*As if oblivious.*)

I have something I must show you.

(*She goes quickly to shutters and darkens the room, returning standing before Jesus. She then slowly removes her headpiece and from under it takes a mass of her hair.*)

When I awakened I found it fallen out, not all of it but a mass that lay on my white pillow. I could see, although my hair hung down at the sides, clearly on my white scalp it was missing.

(*Her baldness is identical to Jesus's.*)

BLACKOUT

The light comes back up. They are both sitting on the bench examining each other's hair, running it through their fingers, then slowly the Duchess disappears behind the shutters and returns with a long red comb. She sits on the bench next to Jesus and starts to comb her remaining hair over her baldness. This is done slowly. Jesus then takes the comb and proceeds to do the same to the Duchess of Hapsburg's hair. After they finish they place the Duchess's headpiece back on and we can see the strands of their hair falling to the floor. Jesus then lays down across the bench while the Duchess walks back and forth, the knocking does not cease. They speak in unison as the Duchess walks and Jesus lays on the bench in the falling snow, staring at the ceiling.

DUCHESS and JESUS (*Their hair is falling more now, they are both hideous*). My father isn't going to let us alone.

(*Knocking.*)

Our father isn't going to let us alone, our father is the darkest of us all, my mother was the fairest, I am in between, but my father is the darkest of them all. He is a black man. Our father is the darkest of them all. He is a black man. My father is a dead man.

(*Then they suddenly look up at each other and scream, the lights go to their heads and we see that they are totally bald. There is a knocking. Lights go to the stairs and the Landlady.*)

LANDLADY. He wrote to her saying he loved her and asked for forgiveness. He begged her to take him off the cross. (He had dreamed she would.) Stop them from tormenting him, the one with the chicken and his cursing father. Her mother's hair fell out, the race's hair fell out because he left Africa, he said. He had tried to save them. She must embrace him. He said his existence depended on her embrace. He wrote her from Africa where he is creating his Christian center in the jungle and that is why he came here. I know that he wanted her to return there with him and not desert the race. He came to see her once before he tried to hang himself, appearing in the corridor of my apartment. I had let him in. I found him sitting on a bench in the hallway. He put out his hand to her, tried to take her in his arms, crying out—Forgiveness, Sarah. Is it that you will never forgive me for being black? I know you were a child of torment. But forgiveness. That was before his breakdown. Then, he wrote her and repeated that his mother hoped he would be Christ but he failed. He had married his mother because he could not resist the light. Yet, his mother from the beginning in the kerosene lamp of their dark rooms in Georgia said—I want you to be Jesus, to walk in Genesis and save the race, return to Africa, find revelation in the black. He went away.

But Easter morning, she got to feeling badly and went into Harlem to see him; the streets were filled with vendors selling lilies. He had checked out of that hotel. When she arrived back at my brownstone he was here, dressed badly, rather drunk. I had let him in again. He sat on a bench in the dark hallway, put out his hand to her, trying to take her in his arms, crying out—Forgiveness, Sarah. Forgiveness for my being black, Sarah. I know you are a child of torment. I know on dark winter afternoons you sat alone, weaving stories of your mother's beauty. But, Sarah, answer me, don't turn away, Sarah. Forgive my blackness. She would not answer. He put out his hand to her. She ran past him on the stairs, left him there with his hands out to me, repeating his past, saying his mother hoped he would be Christ. From the beginning in the kerosene lamp of their dark rooms, she said—Wally, I want you to be Jesus, to walk in Genesis and save the race. You must return to Africa, Wally, find revelation in the midst of golden savannas, nim and white frank-openny trees and white stallions roaming under a blue sky. Wally, you must find the white dove and heal the pain of the race, heal the misery of the black man, Wally, take us off the cross, Wally. In the kerosene light she stared at him anguished from her old Negro face . . . but she ran past him leaving him. And now he is dead, she says, now he is dead. He left Africa and now Patrice Lumumba is dead.

(*The next scene is enacted back in the Duchess of Hapsburg's place. Jesus is still in the Duchess's chamber, apparently he has fallen asleep and we see him as he awakes with the Duchess by his side, and sits here as in a trance. He rises terrified and speaks.*)

JESUS. Through my apocalypses and my raging sermons I have tried so to escape him, through God Almighty I have tried to escape being black.

(*He then appears to rouse himself from his thoughts and calls.*)

Duchess, Duchess.

(*He looks about for her, there is no answer. He gets up slowly, walks back into the darkness and there we see that she is hanging on the chandelier, her bald head suddenly drops to the floor and she falls upon Jesus. He screams.*)

I am going to Africa and kill this black man named Patrice Lumumba. Why? Because all my life I believed my Holy Father to be God, but now I know that my father is a black man. I have no fear for whatever I do, I will do in the name of God, I will do in the name of Albert Saxe Godburg, in the name of Victoria, Queen Victoria Regina, the monarch of England, I will.

BLACKOUT

NEXT SCENE: *In the jungle, red run, flying things, wild black grass. The effect of the jungle is that it, unlike the other scenes, is over the entire stage. In time this is the longest scene in the play and is played the slowest as the slow, almost standstill stages of a dream. By lighting the desired effect would be—suddenly the jungle has overgrown the chambers and all the other places with a violence and a dark brightness, a grim yellowness.*

Jesus is the first to appear in the center of the jungle darkness. Unlike in previous scenes, he has a nimbus above his head. As they each successively appear, they all too have nimbuses atop their heads in a manner to suggest that they are saviours.

JESUS. I always believed my father to be God.

(*Suddenly they all appear in various parts of the jungle. Patrice Lumumba, the Duchess, Victoria, wandering about speaking at once. Their speeches are mixed and repeated by one another.*)

ALL. He never tires of the journey, he who is the darkest one, the darkest one of them all. My mother looked like a white woman, hair as straight as any white woman's. I am yellow but he is black, the darkest of us all. How I hoped he was dead, yet he never tires of the journey. It was because of him that my mother died because she let a black man put his hands on her. Why does he keep returning? He keeps returning forever, keeps returning and returning and he is my father. He is a black Negro. They told me my father was God and my father is black. He is my father. I am tied to a black Negro. He returned when I lived in the south back in the twenties, when I was a child, he returned. Before I was born at the turn of the century, he haunted my conception, diseased my birth . . . killed my mother. He killed the light. My mother was the lightest one. I am bound to him unless, of course, he should die.
But he is dead.
And he keeps returning. Then he is not dead.
Then he is not dead.
Yes, he is dead, but dead he comes knocking at my door.

(*This is repeated several times, finally reaching a loud pitch and then all rushing about the grass. They stop and stand perfectly still. All speaking tensely at various times in a chant.*)

I see him. The black ugly thing is sitting in his hallway, surrounded by his ebony masks, surrounded by the black-

ness of himself. My mother comes into the room. He is there with his hand out to me, groveling, saying—Forgiveness, Sarah, is it that you will never forgive me for being black.
Forgiveness, Sarah. I know you are a nigger of torment. Why? Christ would not rape anyone.
You will never forgive me for being black.
Wild beast. Why did you rape my mother? Black beast, Christ would not rape anyone.
He is in grief from that black anguished face of his. Then at once the room will grow bright and my mother will come toward me smiling while I stand before his face and bludgeon him with an ebony head.
Forgiveness, Sarah, I know you are a nigger of torment.

Silence—Victory: Then they suddenly begin to laugh and shout as though they are in. They continue for some minutes running about laughing and shouting.

BLACKOUT

Another wall drops. There is a white plaster of Queen Victoria which represents the Negro's room in the brownstone, the room appears near the staircases highly lit and small. The main prop is the statue but a bed could be suggested. The figure of Victoria is a sitting figure, one of astonishing repulsive whiteness, possessing the quality of nightmares and terror. Sarah's room could be further suggested by dusty volumes of books and old yellowed walls.

The Negro, Sarah, is standing perfectly still, we hear the knocking, the lights come on quickly, her father's black figures with bludgeoned hands rush upon her, the lights black and we see her hanging in the room.

Lights come on the laughing Landlady. And at the same time remain on the hanging figure of the Negro.

LANDLADY. The poor bitch has hung herself.

(*Funnyman, Raymond, appears from his room at the commotion.*)

LANDLADY. The poor bitch has hung herself.
RAYMOND (*observing her hanging figure*). She was a funny little liar.
LANDLADY (*informing him*). Her father hung himself in a Harlem hotel when Patrice Lumumba died.
RAYMOND. She was a funny little liar.
LANDLADY. Her father hung himself in a Harlem hotel when Patrice Lumumba died.
RAYMOND. Her father never hung himself in a Harlem hotel when Patrice Lumumba was murdered.
I know the man. He is a doctor, married to a white whore. He lives in the city in a room with European antiques, photographs of Roman ruins, walls of books and oriental carpets. Her father is a nigger who eats his meals on a white glass table.

TOPICS FOR CRITICAL THINKING AND WRITING

📖 THE PLAY ON THE PAGE

1. *Funnyhouse of a Negro* begins as follows: "Before the closed curtain a woman dressed in a white nightgown walks across the stage carrying before her a bald head. She moves as one in a trance . . . ." Reread the description several times, and then write an interpretation of its meaning, based on your understanding of the entire play.

2. Referring to the Glossary definition of *surrealism* and to your own grasp of the term, select two or three aspects of *Funnyhouse of a Negro* that seem to you to be key surrealistic elements. What effect do you think they would have for an audience?

3. Why does Sarah kill herself? Offer a number of reasons—personal, philosophical, religious, thematic. Could any other ending for this play be substituted?

4. In an essay in *Intersecting Boundaries: The Theatre of Adrienne Kennedy*, edited by Paul K. Bryant-Jackson and Lisa More Overbeck, Robert Scanlan divides the play into ten structural episodes. Try to locate ten distinct units; then give them an appropriate label (for example, "Sarah's first monologue"). Alternatively, propose a different total count and your reasons for so doing. (The marking "Blackout" is used as a stage direction and does not necessarily coincide with starts and ends to the episodes.)

5. Compare and contrast Adrienne Kennedy's characterization of Sarah with Eugene O'Neill's characterization of Jones in *The Emperor Jones*.

6. What do Sarah's different "selves" represent?

7. Do you consider the landlady's speech (p. 793) a key to understanding this play? If so, why? If not, does some other speech serve that function? Why?

🎭 THE PLAY ON THE STAGE

8. In *People Who Led to My Plays*, Adrienne Kennedy remarks:

   > *Vertigo* was perhaps the most influential movie of its time, in the impact it had on my imagination. Watching Kim Novak change identities was enthralling, and it was a contemporary story. I sensed there were elements in Hitchcock's use of the change of identities that, though still then closed off in my mind, might one day open up in my work.

   Pretend that you are the actress cast as Sarah. How does the Hitchcock connection help you prepare for this role? How would you show, on stage, Sarah's change of identities. Do you find Sarah rational? sane? logical?

9. Pretend that you are the lighting director for a full staging of *Funnyhouse of a Negro*. Choose a short segment of the play to demonstrate several ways lighting could be effective, and briefly describe the different approaches. Then select one as the most "true" to your understanding of Kennedy's script, and explain your reasons.

10. For the October 1995 staging by the Signature Theater, original cello music was composed for *Funnyhouse of a Negro*. What other instrument or instruments might be appropriate? Why? Can you also suggest other kinds of sound effects? (In each case, choose one or two speeches from the play to enhance your example.)

11. Choose one or two remarks from the extract from an interview or the review (pp. 795–96), and discuss ways that a director and cast might gain further insight into one of the difficult aspects of staging *Funnyhouse of a Negro*.

THE PLAY IN PERFORMANCE

Funnyhouse of a Negro received its first professional staging at the East End Theatre in New York City in January 1964, directed by Michael Kahn and produced by Joseph Papp. The role of Sarah was played by Billie Allen, who, in an interview with Lisa More Overbeck and Paul K. Bryant-Jackson in *Intersecting Boundaries: The Theatre of Adrienne Kennedy*, provides many interesting comments about the rehearsal process and about the radical aspects of the play, especially for the 1960s. Here is a brief passage from the interview:

Adrienne Kennedy delves into the black psyche, exposing our universal demons to the scrutiny of the light. She forces us to look at them and deal with them.

Hair, for example, had not been dealt with in the theater. Our hair, that grows from us and is a part of us, has always been an ongoing battle: too curly, too straight, too kinky, too thin, too thick.

Sarah, in *Funnyhouse*, says: "My one defect is that I have a head of frizzy hair—unmistakably Negro kinky hair—and is undisguisable." I felt this way about my own hair at the time. Creating the role of Sarah in *Funnyhouse*, I wore my hair long—brushed back and clamped tightly. At a certain point in the play I unleashed it: it sprang forth, gushing from my head like a fountain, alive and visible to the public. Many black women and men were ashamed of my doing this and wondered what "possessed" me. I was possessed by the rhythm, the ancient rituals called up from the depths by Adrienne. I began to love my hair: for me this was a catharsis for life. (223)

Allen herself directed *Funnyhouse of a Negro* in a 1989 New York University production, realizing that the ideas about self, about racism, about Sarah's suffering had remained with her for more than twenty years.

What was the initial reaction to the 1964 staging? Writing in *The Nation*, Harold Clurman said, "The torment of the colored girl in *Funnyhouse of a Negro* parallels that of all people who suffer the pathology of minorities." Howard Taubman, a reviewer for the *New York Times*, remarked that "if nothing much happens according to conventional theatrical tenets, a relatively unknown territory is explored and exposed." And in *The New Yorker*, Edith Oliver called the play "quite strong and original" and emphasized the importance of the theme.

Adrienne Kennedy won an Obie for "most distinguished play" in May 1964 for *Funnyhouse of a Negro*. Additional stagings included the Theater Company of Boston in 1965, as part of a double bill (with a Sam Shepard play) at the Petit Odeon in Paris in 1968, and the English Stage Society of the Royal Court in London in 1968. All the productions have utilized masks; sets and lighting have emphasized the black/white images and analogous thematic motifs. With the Signature Theater's season-long focus (1995–1996) on the works of Adrienne Kennedy, this important, innovative dramatist has been brought to the attention of theater audiences today. Praising the Signature's 1995 staging of *Funnyhouse of a Negro*, Ben Brantley wrote in the *New York Times*, "Ms. Kennedy's language has a fuguelike quality that only deepens in the speaking of it, and the dramatic progression in her seemingly static self-portraits actually becomes much clearer through physical representation."

We reprint key portions from Michael Feingold's review for the *Village Voice* (October 3, 1995).

Michael Feingold

BLAXPRESSIONISM: *FUNNYHOUSE OF A NEGRO*

With Beckett gone, Adrienne Kennedy is probably the boldest artist now writing for the theater, and her boldness—which the Signature Theatre Company is celebrating in a season-long retrospective—is both an exquisite pleasure and an object lesson. Kennedy's plays are the songs of a naked soul in pain, and her expressionist tactic is to let the pain come at you unmediated. Her writing is outspoken and simple—never evasive, inhibited, or cluttered. Her dramaturgy is as free of tricks as it is of theories. The strategies she employs to convey her pain always strike you as products of an inner need, never as devices consciously cooked up.

For an artist with less breadth of spirit, less cultivation, or less courage, her method would probably be both dangerous and foolhardy, but for her it is perfection. With each of her plays, you get the experience of confronting another human soul head-on, and the torment in that soul, for a brief while, becomes yours. You feel that you are the beneficiary of an incredibly precious gift, and only then do you begin to notice how much effort on Kennedy's part has gone into making the song of her torment a thing of beauty. The initial experience is so direct that you hardly realize there is any art in it at all—the best thing one can say about a work of art. Just as a trapeze artist makes triple somersaults in the air seem effortless, Kennedy's plays make total understanding of another human being seem possible.

That it isn't, of course, is the source of her torment, the bitter reality justifying her underlying assumption that her private pain can be the stuff of high tragedy. Kennedy is African American, and ethnicity, like her pain, is her material. Or, viewed another way, her ethnicity is her pain. Few black American writers have explored the inner reality of blackness, the mixture of pride and doubt and wonder and self-hatred and the quest for identity, with the terrifying poet's lucidity she brings to the subject. The deeper she delves in it, the wider its ramifications seem to stretch, implicating all of America, all of Africa, all of the tragic history that binds them. For white theatergoers, used to having black artists talk at them, in friendship or in anger, across a widening chasm, the experience is wholly new. Other black artists' pain is their pain, to be respected, empathized with, commiserated over. Because of her force and directness, Adrienne Kennedy's pain is mine and yours; there is no distance.

Each of the two plays on the Signature's opening bill has many roles but only one character, a young woman writer, named Sarah (or to be precise, Negro-Sarah) in *Funnyhouse of a Negro* and Clara in *A Movie Star Has to Star in Black and White*. The 1964 *Funnyhouse*, Kennedy's first produced play, is dark, violent, frenetic; ironic public figures, like Queen Victoria and Patrice Lumumba, appear, contorted fragments of the heroine's nightmare. Sarah is a woman who hates her blackness and cannot forgive her father, whom she sees as its source, her light-skinned mother ("almost as light as a white woman") has a breakdown and died in an asylum. Mother makes brief, wordless appearances; Father's role is more complexly handled.

We hear several versions of his story: He "majored in Social Work;" he went to Africa to found a Christian mission; he raped Sarah's mother and drove her insane; he hung himself in a Harlem hotel when Lumumba died; Sarah "bludgeoned him to death with an ebony mask;" he died after turning up in the rooming house where Sarah lives and begging her to forgive him, which she refused to do. Her father is also equated with both the crucified Jesus and with Lumumba, murdered leader of a newly awakened Africa. Father does not appear; his role is, in effect, divided between these two figures—both if whom, like all the other characters, speak lines that emanate from Sarah's vision.

Sarah's white landlady, eavesdropping at the door, and her white Jewish boyfriend, Raymond, also appear, representatives of a white world that she fears will never take her seriously. She prefers the fantasy white companionship of "Queen Victoria Regina" and the Duchess of Hapsburg, fragments of herself who endlessly reiterate her deepest terrors. "Victoria . . . wants me to tell her of a royal world where everything and everyone is white and there are no unfortunate black ones. For as we of royal blood know, black is evil and has been from the beginning." From this repudiation of reality, the only ways out are madness and death. Sarah hangs herself, in the play's final moment, the Landlady and Raymond chuckle over the event, and we hear one last version of her father's fate.

A Note on
HISPANIC-AMERICAN THEATER

First we must acknowledge that the word *Hispanic* is unsatisfactory. Although it is commonly used to refer to persons who trace their origin to a Spanish-speaking country (*Hispania* was the Latin name for Spain), many people object that the word overemphasizes the European influence on ethnic identity and neglects the indigenous and black heritages. *Latino* and *Latina* are sometimes used, partly because they are Spanish words, but many people object that these words obscure the unique cultural heritages of, for example, Mexican-Americans (Chicanos), Cuban-Americans, and Puerto Ricans, just as *Hispanic* does. In particular, a single term misleadingly blends Chicano theater, Cuban-American theater, and Nuyorican theater (theater of Puerto Rican migrants in New York). Furthermore, even within these kinds of theater there are differences. For instance, although men have produced most of the plays, women (e.g. Estela Portillo Trambley) have produced important plays that differ in theme and technique from the plays written by men.

Drama in Spanish is nothing new in the New World. As we point out in our comment on the stage history of *The Second Shepherds' Play* (p. 166), Spanish friars performed a play in what is now Mexico City as early as 1526. There are records, too, of a Spanish-language play being performed near what is now El Paso, Texas, in 1598; in fact, the entire area of what we think of as the Southwest of the United States saw a good deal of Spanish-language dramatic activity at least until Mexico was forced to surrender it in the mid-nineteenth century. Even when this region became part of the United States, dramatic activity in Spanish continued, ranging from religious plays to melodramas and musicals. For an eyewitness account of a late-nineteenth-century religious folk play in Texas, along with generous quotations from the play, see an essay reprinted (originally from the *Journal of American Folklore*, 1893) in *Folklore in America*, edited by Tristram P. Coffin and Hennig Cohen (1966), pages 197–204. Furthermore, visiting theatrical companies from Cuba and Mexico helped to keep Spanish-language drama alive in the United States.

Still, in the first half of the twentieth century, despite the persistence of what we can call folkloric drama and of visiting companies, drama in Spanish was thought of as an endangered species. In the 1960s, however, it gained new life when, influenced by the Civil Rights movement, it became highly political. (See the Commentary on Luis

Valdez's play, *Los Vendidos,* p. 799.) It must be understood, however, that although Hispanic theater in the 1960s and later sought to effect political and economic changes (for instance, better working conditions for Chicanos), it also sought to reaffirm cultural identity. Leaders in the movement stressed a dual heritage; for example, Chicanos are rooted in Mexican culture as well as in European or Anglo culture. In Valdez's words:

> We have to rediscover ourselves. There are years and years of discoveries we have to make for our people. People ask me: What is Mexican history in the United States? There is no textbook of the history of La Raza. Yet the history of the Mexican in this country is four hundred years old. We know we predate the landing of the Pilgrims and the American Revolution. But, beyond that? what really happened? No one can tell you. Our history has been lost. . . . Our generation says, Wait! Stop! Let's reconsider our roots.
> QUOTED BY SUSAN BASSNETT-McGUIRE IN *THEATRE QUARTERLY* 9 (SUMMER 1979):20

At least a hundred *teatros* (groups devoted to dramatic representations of Hispanic experience), such as Jorge Huerta's Teatro de la Esperanza (Theater of Hope) in Santa Barbara and Joe Rosenberg's Teatro Bilingüe (Bilingual Theater) in Kingsville, Texas, were active in the late 1960s and 1970s. Many of these theaters continue today. In 1971 a national group, TENAZ (El Teatro Nacional de Aztlan, i.e., the National Theater of Aztlan), was established to sponsor theater festivals across the country. Not surprisingly, given the diversity of the Hispanic theater, this national organization does not speak with one voice.

For further comments on Hispanic theater, see the Commentaries on plays by Luis Valdez (p. 799) and Carlos Morton (p. 809).

For detailed studies, we recommend:

Antush, John. *Puerto Rican Theater: Five Plays from New York* (1991).
Chàvez, Denise, and Linda Feyder. *Shattering the Myth: Plays by Hispanic Women* (1992).
Huerta, Jorge. *Chicano Theater: Themes and Forms* (1982).
Kanellos, Nicolás. A *History of Hispanic Theatre in the United States: The Origins to 1940* (1990).
———, ed. *Mexican American Theatre Then and Now* (1983).

Luis Valdez

LOS VENDIDOS

Luis Valdez was born into a family of migrant farm workers in Delano, California, in 1940. After completing high school, he entered San Jose State College on a scholarship. He wrote his first plays while still an undergraduate, and after receiving his degree (in English and drama) from San Jose in 1964, he joined the San Francisco Mime Troupe, a left-wing group that performed in parks and streets. Revolutionary in technique as well as in political content, the Mime Troupe rejected the traditional forms of drama and instead drew on the traditions of the circus and the carnival.

In 1965 Valdez returned to Delano, California, where Cesar Chavez had organized a strike of farm workers and a boycott against grape growers. It was here, under the wing of the United Farm Workers, that he established El Teatro Campesino (the Farm Workers' Theater), which at first specialized in doing short, improvised, satirical skits called *actos*. When the *teatro* moved to Del Rey, California, it expanded its repertoire beyond farm issues and became part of a cultural center that gave workshops (in English and Spanish) in such subjects as history, drama, and politics.

The *actos*, performed by amateurs on college campuses and on flatbed trucks and at the edges of vineyards, were highly political. Making use of stereotypes (for example, the boss, the scab), the *actos* sought not to present the individual thoughts of a gifted playwright but to present the social vision of ordinary people—the *pueblo*—though it was acknowledged that in an oppressive society the playwright might have to help guide the people to see their own best interests.

Valdez moved from *actos* to *mitos* (myths)—plays that drew on Aztec mythology, Mexican folklore, and Christianity—and then to *Zoot Suit*, a play that ran for many months in California and that became the first Mexican-American play to be produced on Broadway. More recently he wrote and directed a hit movie, *La Bamba*, and in 1991 received an award from the A.T.&T. Foundation for his musical, *Bandido*, to be presented by El Teatro Campesino.

Los Vendidos was written in 1967, when Ronald Reagan was governor of California.

COMMENTARY

As the preceding biographical note indicates, Valdez has not stood still as a dramatist. However, one thread that runs through his career is his vision of drama as politics, a form of art that may be used to help shape society. Such a view is scarcely modern; it can be found as early as Aristophanes (c. 450–c. 385 B.C.), who used comedy as a way of scolding Athens on a variety of matters, from its schools of philosophy to its destructive colonial politics. Closer to our own age, we find Bernard Shaw (1856–1950) and Bertolt Brecht (1898–1956) insisting that they seek not to please us by showing the surface of reality but to change our ways of thinking and, especially, to change the structure of our society.

One form of political theater, *agitprop*, developed in the Soviet Union in the 1920s by the Department of Agitation and Propaganda, consisted of short episodic plays (skits or sketches, we might call them) with a strong Marxist thrust. The playwrights were not interested in presenting rounded, plausible characters, and they were not interested in developing a complicated plot. In short, these works were not at all like the realistic drama of late nineteenth-century Europe, which is still the dominant form of drama in the commercial American theater. Rather, they used stereotypical characters—the worker (good), the boss (bad), the Marxist journalist (good), and so on—and they juxtaposed them in simple (and strong) conflicts. These skits were performed not in well-equipped theaters but in bare halls and in the streets. In the United States agitprop influenced the work of some dramatists in the 1930s, for instance Clifford Odets and Langston Hughes, but probably the closest thing to it in this country was the guerilla theater of the 1960s, which used theater as a working-class weapon against the bourgeoisie.

Valdez was deeply influenced by both the leftist politics and the improvisatory methods of guerilla theater. His *actos*, performed in streets, on flatbed trucks at the edges of vineyards, in meeting halls, and on campuses, were developed with and for the striking workers in the California vineyards. The plays are, he says, "collaborative work," sketches that took shape as he worked with his actors. These actors were not professionals or even trained amateurs; rather, they were unemployed farm workers who were persuaded that they could help their cause by taking roles in the *actos*. Their lack of theatrical training, along with the audience's lack of theatrical experience, meant that the roles had to be drawn fairly broadly, but this was not necessarily a disadvantage, any more than the exaggeration of a caricature is a disadvantage. A caricature (in a newspaper, for instance) can offer us enjoyment, and it may even stimulate us to think and to act in a certain way—it may move us (at least in a tiny degree) to vote against a particular candidate. Such a picture is not to be judged by its realism or, for that matter, by its subtlety.

The stereotypes that Valdez often employed in the *actos* are, he has said, political realities. According to this view, the essence of a person might be, for example, an exploited farm worker or an exploiting grower. Subtle distinctions are unimportant. Thus, a boss may be shown wearing a pig mask and (in pantomime) driving a big car. The facts that few bosses really look like pigs and that many do not drive big cars are said to be irrelevant. The pig-boss, the play implies, is the essence of boss. It should be mentioned, too, that the plays were intended not only to instill political ideas but also to entertain and to keep up the spirits of his audience (chiefly striking workers).

In short, Valdez sought to produce a revolutionary theater for and by workers. A truly revolutionary theater, he believed, could be produced *without* the use of traditional theatrical methods and *with* the aid of workers. In 1966 he wrote:

> If you want unbourgeois theater, find unbourgeois people to do it. Your head could burst open at the simplicity of the *acto* . . . but that's the way it is in Delano. Real theater lies in the excited laughter (or silence) of recognition in the audience, not in all the paraphernalia on the stage. Minus actors, the entire Teatro can be packed into one trunk, and when the Teatro goes on tour, the spirit of the Delano grape strikers goes with it.

Although *Los Vendidos* ("The Sellouts") is no less political than the earlier *actos*, the focus is no longer on striking farm laborers. It is on the Chicano's relationship to Anglo culture. Furthermore, *Los Vendidos* departs from earlier *actos* in not offering a solution to a condition that it reveals. Earlier *actos* had in effect said "Strike" or "Join the union," but *Los Vendidos* seems less concerned with proposing a solution than with showing contrasting kinds of Chicanos, although it is clear where Valdez's sympathies lie.

This photograph is from the 1988 spring tour, in California and in Europe, of El Teatro Ensemble de U.C.S.D. The production, like the text of the play, was highly stylized; here, for instance, stereotypical characters bear labels indicating the stereotypes. On pages 806–08 we include an interview with Professor Jorge A. Huerta of the University of California, San Diego, who directed the play.

Luis Valdez

LOS VENDIDOS*

List of Characters

HONEST SANCHO
SECRETARY
FARM WORKER
JOHNNY
REVOLUCIONARIO
MEXICAN-AMERICAN

SCENE: *Honest Sancho's Used Mexican Lot and Mexican Curio Shop. Three models are on display in Honest Sancho's shop: to the right, there is a Revolucionario, complete with sombrero, car-*

rilleras[1] *and carabina 30-30. At center, on the floor, there is the Farm Worker, under a broad straw sombrero. At stage left is the Pachuco,[2] filero[3] in hand.*

(Honest Sancho *is moving among his models, dusting them off and preparing for another day of business.*)

SANCHO. Bueno, bueno, mis monos, vamos a ver a quien vendemos ahora, ¿no?[4] [*To audience.*] ¡Quihubo! I'm Honest Sancho and this is my shop. Antes fui contratista pero ahora logré tener mi negocito[5] All I need now is a customer. (*A bell rings offstage.*) Ay, a customer!

[1]**carrilleras** cartridge belts   [2]**Pachuco** an urban tough guy   [3]**filero** blade   [4]**Bueno . . . no?** Well, well, darlings, let's see who we can sell now, O.K.?   [5]**Antes . . . negocito** I used to be a contractor, but now I've succeeded in having my little business.

Los Vendidos the sellouts

Luis Valdez

SECRETARY (*entering*). Good morning, I'm Miss Jiménez from—

SANCHO. ¡Ah, una chicana! Welcome, welcome Señorita Jiménez.

SECRETARY (*Anglo pronunciation*). JIM-enez.

SANCHO. ¿Qué?

SECRETARY. My name is Miss JIM-enez. Don't you speak English? What's wrong with you?

SANCHO. Oh, nothing, Señorita JIM-enez. I'm here to help you.

SECRETARY. That's better. As I was starting to say, I'm a secretary from Governor Reagan's office, and we're looking for a Mexican type for the administration.

SANCHO. Well, you come to the right place, lady. This is Honest Sancho's Used Mexican lot, and we got all types here. Any particular type you want?

SECRETARY. Yes, we were looking for somebody suave—

SANCHO. Suave.

SECRETARY. Debonair.

SANCHO. De buen aire.

SECRETARY. Dark.

SANCHO. Prieto.

SECRETARY. But of course not too dark.

SANCHO. No muy prieto.

SECRETARY. Perhaps, beige.

SANCHO. Beige, just the tone. Así como cafecito con leche,[6] ¿no?

SECRETARY. One more thing. He must be hard-working.

SANCHO. That could only be one model. Step right over here to the center of the shop, lady. (*They cross to the Farm Worker.*) This is our standard farm worker model. As you can see, in the words of our beloved Senator George Murphy, he is "built close to the ground." Also take special notice of his four-ply Goodyear huaraches, made from the rain tire. This wide-brimmed sombrero is an extra added feature—keeps off the sun, rain, and dust.

SECRETARY. Yes, it does look durable.

SANCHO. And our farmworker model is friendly. Muy amable.[7] Watch. (*Snaps his fingers.*)

FARM WORKER (*lifts up head*). Buenos días, señorita. (*His head drops.*)

SECRETARY. My, he's friendly.

SANCHO. Didn't I tell you? Loves his patrones! But his most attractive feature is that he's hard working. Let me show you. (*Snaps fingers. Farm Worker stands.*)

FARM WORKER. ¡El jale![8] (*He begins to work.*)

SANCHO. As you can see, he is cutting grapes.

SECRETARY. Oh, I wouldn't know.

SANCHO. He also picks cotton. (*Snap. Farm Worker begins to pick cotton.*)

SECRETARY. Versatile isn't he?

SANCHO. He also picks melons. (*Snap. Farm Worker picks melons.*) That's his slow speed for late in the season. Here's his fast speed. (*Snap. Farm Worker picks faster.*)

SECRETARY. ¡Chihuahua! . . . I mean, goodness, he sure is a hard worker.

SANCHO (*pulls the Farm Worker to his feet*). And that isn't the half of it. Do you see these little holes on his arms that appear to be pores? During those hot sluggish days in the field, when the vines or the branches get so entangled, it's almost impossible to move; these holes emit a certain grease that allow our model to slip and slide right through the crop with no trouble at all.

SECRETARY. Wonderful. But is he economical?

SANCHO. Economical? Señorita, you are looking at the Volkswagen of Mexicans. Pennies a day is all it takes. One plate of beans and tortillas will keep him going all day. That, and chile. Plenty of chile. Chile jalapeños, chile verde, chile colorado. But, of course, if you do give him chile (*Snap. Farm Worker turns left face. Snap. Farm Worker bends over.*) then you have to change his oil filter once a week.

SECRETARY. What about storage?

SANCHO. No problem. You know these new farm labor camps our Honorable Governor Reagan has built out by Parlier or Raisin City? They were designed with our model in mind. Five, six, seven, even ten in one of those shacks will give you no trouble at all. You can also put him in old barns, old cars, river banks. You can even leave him out in the field overnight with no worry!

SECRETARY. Remarkable.

SANCHO. And here's an added feature: Every year at the end of the season, this model goes back to Mexico and doesn't return, automatically, until next Spring.

SECRETARY. How about that. But tell me: does he speak English?

SANCHO. Another outstanding feature is that last year this model was programmed to go out on STRIKE! (*Snap.*)

FARM WORKER. ¡HUELGA! ¡HUELGA! Hermanos, sálganse de esos files.[9] (*Snap. He stops.*)

SECRETARY. No! Oh no, we can't strike in the State Capitol.

SANCHO. Well, he also scabs. (*Snap.*)

FARM WORKER. Me vendo barato, ¿y qué?[10] (*Snap.*)

SECRETARY. That's much better, but you didn't answer my question. Does he speak English?

SANCHO. Bueno . . . no, pero[11] he has other—

SECRETARY. No.

SANCHO. Other features.

SECRETARY. NO! He just won't do!

SANCHO. Okay, okay pues. We have other models.

SECRETARY. I hope so. What we need is something a little more sophisticated.

---

[6]**Así . . . leche** like coffee with milk   [7]**Muy amable** very friendly
[8]**El jale** The job

[9]**Huelga . . . files.** Strike! Strike! Brothers, leave those rows.   [10]**Me . . . qué** I come cheap. So what?   [11]**Bueno . . . no, pero** Well, no but

SANCHO. Sophisti—¿qué?

SECRETARY. An urban model.

SANCHO. Ah, from the city! Step right back. Over here in this corner of the shop is exactly what you're looking for. Introducing our new 1969 JOHNNY PACHUCO model! This is our fast-back model. Streamlined. Built for speed, low-riding, city life. Take a look at some of these features. Mag shoes, dual exhausts, green chartreuse paint-job, dark-tint windshield, a little poof on top. Let me just turn him on. (*Snap. Johnny walks to stage center with a pachuco bounce.*)

SECRETARY. What was that?

SANCHO. That, señorita, was the Chicano shuffle.

SECRETARY. Okay, what does he do?

SANCHO. Anything and everything necessary for city life. For instance, survival: He knife fights. (*Snap. Johnny pulls out switch blade and swings at Secretary.*)

(*Secretary screams.*)

SANCHO. He dances. (*Snap.*)

JOHNNY (*singing*). "Angel Baby, my Angel Baby . . ." (*Snap.*)

SANCHO. And here's a feature no city model can be without. He gets arrested, but not without resisting, of course. (*Snap.*)

JOHNNY. ¡En la madre, la placa![12] I didn't do it! I didn't do it! (*Johnny turns and stands up against an imaginary wall, legs spread out, arms behind his back.*)

SECRETARY. Oh no, we can't have arrests! We must maintain law and order.

SANCHO. But he's bilingual!

SECRETARY. Bilingual?

SANCHO. Simón que yes.[13] He speaks English! Johnny, give us some English. (*Snap.*)

JOHNNY (*comes downstage*). Fuck-you!

SECRETARY (*gasps*). Oh! I've never been so insulted in my whole life!

SANCHO. Well, he learned it in your school.

SECRETARY. I don't care where he learned it.

SANCHO. But he's economical!

SECRETARY. Economical?

SANCHO. Nickels and dimes. You can keep Johnny running on hamburgers, Taco Bell tacos, Lucky Lager beer, Thunderbird wine, yesca—

SECRETARY. Yesca?

SANCHO. Mota.

SECRETARY. Mota?

SANCHO. Leños[14] . . . Marijuana. (*Snap; Johnny inhales on an imaginary joint.*)

SECRETARY. That's against the law!

JOHNNY (*big smile, holding his breath*). Yeah.

SANCHO. He also sniffs glue. (*Snap. Johnny inhales glue, big smile.*)

JOHNNY. That's too much man, ése.[15]

SECRETARY. No, Mr. Sancho, I don't think this—

SANCHO. Wait a minute, he has other qualities I know you'll love. For example, an inferiority complex. (*Snap.*)

JOHNNY (*to Sancho*). You think you're better than me, huh ése? (*Swings switchblade.*)

SANCHO. He can also be beaten and he bruises, cut him and he bleeds; kick him and he—(*He beats, bruises and kicks Pachuco.*) would you like to try it?

SECRETARY. Oh, I couldn't.

SANCHO. Be my guest. He's a great scapegoat.

SECRETARY. No, really.

SANCHO. Please.

SECRETARY. Well, all right. Just once. (*She kicks Pachuco.*) Oh, he's so soft.

SANCHO. Wasn't that good? Try again.

SECRETARY (*kicks Pachuco*). Oh, he's so wonderful! (*She kicks him again.*)

SANCHO. Okay, that's enough, lady. You ruin the merchandise. Yes, our Johnny Pachuco model can give you many hours of pleasure. Why, the L.A.P.D. just bought twenty of these to train their rookie cops on. And talk about maintenance. Señorita, you are looking at an entirely self-supporting machine. You're never going to find our Johnny Pachuco model on the relief rolls. No, sir, this model knows how to liberate.

SECRETARY. Liberate?

SANCHO. He steals. (*Snap. Johnny rushes the Secretary and steals her purse.*)

JOHNNY. ¡Dame esa bolsa, vieja![16] (*He grabs the purse and runs. Snap by Sancho. He stops.*)

(*Secretary runs after Johnny and grabs purse away from him, kicking him as she goes.*)

SECRETARY. No, no, no! We can't have any *more* thieves in the State Administration. Put him back.

SANCHO. Okay, we still got other models. Come on, Johnny, we'll sell you to some old lady. (*Sancho takes Johnny back to his place.*)

SECRETARY. Mr. Sancho, I don't think you quite understand what we need. What we need is something that will attract the women voters. Something more traditional, more romantic.

SANCHO. Ah, a lover. (*He smiles meaningfully.*) Step right over here, señorita. Introducing our standard Revolucionario and/or Early California Bandit type. As you can see he is well-built, sturdy, durable. This is the International Harvester of Mexicans.

SECRETARY. What does he do?

SANCHO. You name it, he does it. He rides horses, stays in the mountains, crosses deserts, plains, rivers, leads revo-

---

[12]¡En . . . la placa! Wow, the cops! [13]Simón que yes. Yea, sure.
[14]Leños joints (marijuana)

[15]ése fellow [16]Dame . . . vieja Give me that bag, old lady!

Luis Valdez

lutions, follows revolutions, kills, can be killed, serves as a martyr, hero, movie star—did I say movie star? Did you ever see *Viva Zapata? Viva Villa? Villa Rides? Pancho Villa Returns? Pancho Villa Goes Back? Pancho Villa Meets Abbott and Costello*—

SECRETARY. I've never seen any of those.

SANCHO. Well, he was in all of them. Listen to this. (*Snap.*)

REVOLUCIONARIO (*Scream*). ¡VIVA VILLAAAAA!

SECRETARY. That's awfully loud.

SANCHO. He has a volume control. (*He adjusts volume. Snap.*)

REVOLUCIONARIO (*mousey voice*). ¡Viva Villa!

SECRETARY. That's better.

SANCHO. And even if you didn't see him in the movies, perhaps you saw him on TV. He makes commercials. (*Snap.*)

REVOLUCIONARIO. Is there a Frito Bandito in your house?

SECRETARY. Oh yes, I've seen that one!

SANCHO. Another feature about this one is that he is economical. He runs on raw horsemeat and tequila!

SECRETARY. Isn't that rather savage?

SANCHO. Al contrario,[17] it makes him a lover. (*Snap.*)

REVOLUCIONARIO (*to Secretary*). ¡Ay, mamasota, cochota, ven pa'ca![18] (*He grabs Secretary and folds her back—Latin-Lover style.*)

SANCHO (*Snap. Revolucionario goes back upright*). Now wasn't that nice?

SECRETARY. Well, it was rather nice.

SANCHO. And finally, there is one outstanding feature about this model I KNOW the ladies are going to love: He's a GENUINE antique! He was made in Mexico in 1910!

SECRETARY. Made in Mexico?

SANCHO. That's right. Once in Tijuana, twice in Guadalajara, three times in Cuernavaca.

SECRETARY. Mr. Sancho, I thought he was an American product.

SANCHO. No, but—

SECRETARY. No, I'm sorry. We can't buy anything but American-made products. He just won't do.

SANCHO. But he's an antique!

SECRETARY. I don't care. You still don't understand what we need. It's true we need Mexican models such as these, but it's more important that he be *American*.

SANCHO. American?

SECRETARY. That's right, and judging from what you've shown me, I don't think you have what we want. Well, my lunch hour's almost over: I better—

SANCHO. Wait a minute! Mexican but American?

SECRETARY. That's correct.

SANCHO. Mexican but . . . (*A sudden flash.*) AMERICAN! Yeah, I think we've got exactly what you want. He just came in today! Give me a minute. (*He exits. Talks from backstage.*) Here he is in the shop. Let me just get some

papers off. There. Introducing our new 1970 Mexican-American! Ta-ra-ra-ra-ra-ra-ra-RA-RAAA!

(*Sancho brings out the Mexican-American model, a clean-shaven middle-class type in a business suit, with glasses.*)

SECRETARY (*impressed*). Where have you been hiding this one?

SANCHO. He just came in this morning. Ain't he a beauty? Feast your eyes on him! Sturdy US STEEL frame, streamlined, modern. As a matter of fact, he is built exactly like our Anglo models except that he comes in a variety of darker shades: naugahyde, leather, or leatherette.

SECRETARY. Naugahyde.

SANCHO. Well, we'll just write that down. Yes, señorita, this model represents the apex of American engineering! He is bilingual, college educated, ambitious! Say the word "acculturate" and he accelerates. He is intelligent, well-mannered, clean—did I say clean? (*Snap. Mexican-American raises his arm.*) Smell.

SECRETARY (*smells*). Old Sobaco, my favorite.

SANCHO (*Snap. Mexican-American turns toward Sancho*). Eric! (*To Secretary.*) We call him Eric García. (*To Eric.*) I want you to meet Miss JIM-enez, Eric.

MEXICAN-AMERICAN. Miss JIM-enez, I am delighted to make your acquaintance. (*He kisses her hand.*)

SECRETARY. Oh, my, how charming!

SANCHO. Did you feel the suction? He has seven especially engineered suction cups right behind his lips. He's a charmer all right!

SECRETARY. How about boards? Does he function on boards?

SANCHO. You name them, he is on them. Parole boards, draft boards, school boards, taco quality control boards, surf boards, two-by-fours.

SECRETARY. Does he function in politics?

SANCHO. Señorita, you are looking at a political MACHINE. Have you ever heard of the OEO, EOC, COD, WAR ON POVERTY? That's our model! Not only that, he makes political speeches.

SECRETARY. May I hear one?

SANCHO. With pleasure. (*Snap.*) Eric, give us a speech.

MEXICAN-AMERICAN. Mr. Congressman, Mr. Chairman, members of the board, honored guests, ladies and gentlemen. (*Sancho and Secretary applaud.*) Please, please. I come before you as a Mexican-American to tell you about the problems of the Mexican. The problems of the Mexican stem from one thing and one thing alone: He's stupid. He's uneducated. He needs to stay in school. He needs to be ambitious, forward-looking, harder-working. He needs to think American, American, American, AMERICAN, AMERICAN, AMERICAN. GOD BLESS AMERICA! GOD BLESS AMERICA! GOD BLESS AMERICA!! (*He goes out of control.*)

(*Sancho snaps frantically and the Mexican-American finally slumps forward, bending at the waist.*)

[17]**Al contrario** On the contrary [18]**Ay . . . pa'ca!** —, get over here!

804

SECRETARY. Oh my, he's patriotic too!

SANCHO. Sí, señorita, he loves his country. Let me just make a little adjustment here. (*Stands Mexican-American up.*)

SECRETARY. What about upkeep? Is he economical?

SANCHO. Well, no, I won't lie to you. The Mexican-American costs a little bit more, but you get what you pay for. He's worth every extra cent. You can keep him running on dry Martinis, Langendorf bread.

SECRETARY. Apple pie?

SANCHO. Only Mom's. Of course, he's also programmed to eat Mexican food on ceremonial functions, but I must warn you: an overdose of beans will plug up his exhaust.

SECRETARY. Fine! There's just one more question: HOW MUCH DO YOU WANT FOR HIM?

SANCHO. Well, I tell you what I'm gonna do. Today and today only, because you've been so sweet, I'm gonna let you steal this model from me! I'm gonna let you drive him off the lot for the simple price of—let's see taxes and license included—$15,000.

SECRETARY. Fifteen thousand DOLLARS? For a MEXICAN!

SANCHO. Mexican? What are you talking, lady? This is a Mexican-AMERICAN! We had to melt down two pachucos, a farm worker and three gabachos[19] to make this model! You want quality, but you gotta pay for it! This is no cheap run-about. He's got class!

SECRETARY. Okay, I'll take him.

SANCHO. You will?

SECRETARY. Here's your money.

SANCHO. You mind if I count it?

SECRETARY. Go right ahead.

SANCHO. Well, you'll get your pink slip in the mail. Oh, do you want me to wrap him up for you? We have a box in the back.

SECRETARY. No, thank you. The Governor is having a luncheon this afternoon, and we need a brown face in the crowd. How do I drive him?

SANCHO. Just snap your fingers. He'll do anything you want.

(*Secretary snaps. Mexican-American steps forward.*)

MEXICAN-AMERICAN. RAZA QUERIDA, ¡VAMOS LEVANTANDO ARMAS PARA LIBERARNOS DE ESTOS DESGRACIADOS GABACHOS QUE NOS EXPLOTAN! VAMOS.[20]

SECRETARY. What did he say?

SANCHO. Something about lifting arms, killing white people, etc.

SECRETARY. But he's not supposed to say that!

SANCHO. Look, lady, don't blame me for bugs from the factory. He's your Mexican-American; you bought him, now drive him off the lot!

SECRETARY. But he's broken!

SANCHO. Try snapping another finger.

(*Secretary snaps. Mexican-American comes to life again.*)

MEXICAN-AMERICAN. ¡ESTA GRAN HUMANIDAD HA DICHO BASTA! Y SE HA PUESTO EN MARCHA! ¡BASTA! ¡BASTA! ¡VIVA LA RAZA! ¡VIVA LA CAUSA! ¡VIVA LA HUELGA! ¡VIVAN LOS BROWN BERETS! ¡VIVAN LOS ESTUDIANTES![21] ¡CHICANO POWER!

(*The Mexican-American turns toward the Secretary, who gasps and backs up. He keeps turning toward the Pachuco, Farm Worker, and Revolucionario, snapping his fingers and turning each of them on, one by one.*)

PACHUCO (*Snap. To Secretary*). I'm going to get you, baby! ¡Viva La Raza!

FARM WORKER (*Snap. To Secretary*). ¡Viva la huelga! ¡Viva la Huelga! ¡VIVA LA HUELGA!

REVOLUCIONARIO (*Snap. To Secretary*). ¡Viva la revolución! ¡VIVA LA REVOLUCIÓN!

(*The three models join together and advance toward the Secretary who backs up and runs out of the shop screaming. Sancho is at the other end of the shop holding his money in his hand. All freeze. After a few seconds of silence, the Pachuco moves and stretches, shaking his arms and loosening up. The Farm Worker and Revolucionario do the same. Sancho stays where he is, frozen to his spot.*)

JOHNNY. Man, that was a long one, ése.[22] (*Others agree with him.*)

FARM WORKER. How did we do?

JOHNNY. Perty good, look at all that lana,[23] man! (*He goes over to Sancho and removes the money from his hand. Sancho stays where he is.*)

REVOLUCIONARIO. En la madre, look at all the money.

JOHNNY. We keep this up, we're going to be rich.

FARM WORKER. They think we're machines.

REVOLUCIONARIO. Burros.

JOHNNY. Puppets.

MEXICAN-AMERICAN. The only thing I don't like is— how come I always got to play the goddamn Mexican-American?

JOHNNY. That's what you get for finishing high school.

FARM WORKER. How about our wages, ése?

JOHNNY. Here it comes right now. $3,000 for you, $3,000 for you, $3,000 for you, and $3,000 for me. The rest we put back into the business.

---

[19]**gabachos** whites [20]**Raza . . . Vamos.** Beloved Raza [persons of Mexican descent], let's take up arms to liberate ourselves from those damned whites who exploit us. Let's get going.

[21]**¡Esta . . . Estudiantes!** This great mass of humanity has said enough! And it has begun to march. Enough! Enough! Long live La Raza! Long live the Cause! Long live the strike! Long live the Brown Berets! Long live the students! [22]**ése** man [23]**lana** money

MEXICAN-AMERICAN. Too much, man. Heh, where you vatos[24] going tonight?

FARM WORKER. I'm going over to Concha's. There's a party.

JOHNNY. Wait a minute, vatos. What about our salesman? I think he needs an oil job.

REVOLUCIONARIO. Leave him to me.

(*The Pachuco, Farm Worker, and Mexican-American exit, talking loudly about their plans for the night. The*

[24]**vatos** guys

Revolucionario goes over to Sancho, removes his derby hat and cigar, lifts him up and throws him over his shoulder. Sancho hangs loose, lifeless.)

REVOLUCIONARIO (*to audience*). He's the best model we got! ¡Ajua![25]

(*Exit.*)

THE END

[25]**Ajua!** Wow!

TOPICS FOR CRITICAL THINKING AND WRITING

📖 THE PLAY ON THE PAGE

1. If you are an Anglo (shorthand for a Caucasian with traditional Northern European values), do you find the play deeply offensive? Why, or why not? If you are a Mexican-American, do you find the play entertaining or do you find parts of it offensive? What might Anglos enjoy in the play, and what might Mexican-Americans find offensive?

2. What stereotypes of Mexican-Americans are presented here? At the end of the play, what image of the Mexican-American is presented? How does it compare with the stereotypes?

3. Putting aside the politics of the play (and your own politics), what do you think are the strengths of *Los Vendidos*? What do you think are the weaknesses?

4. The play was written in 1967. Putting aside a few specific references, for instance to Governor Reagan, do you find it dated? If not, why not?

5. In his short essay, "The Actos," Valdez says that *actos* achieve the following: "Inspire the audience to social action. Illuminate specific points about social problems. Satirize the opposition. Show or hint at a solution. Express what people are feeling." How much of this do you think *Los Vendidos* does?

6. Many people assume that politics gets in the way of serious art. That is, they assume that artists ought to be concerned with issues that transcend politics. Does this point make any sense to you? Why or why not?

🎭 THE PLAY ON THE STAGE

7. In 1971 when *Los Vendidos* was produced by El Teatro de la Esperanza, the group altered the ending by having the men decide to use the money to build a community center. (See the interview with the director, Jorge Huerta, that follows.) Evaluate this ending.

8. On page 807, Jorge Huerta suggests that it was a mistake for Jane Fonda to be cast as Miss Jimenes in the videotape. "Something is lost," he says, "in the realization that this woman is not pretending to be white . . . ." Do you agree? Explain.

9. When the play was videotaped by KNBC in Los Angeles for broadcast in 1973, Valdez changed the ending. In the revised version we discover that a scientist (played by Valdez) masterminds the operation, placing Mexican-American models wherever there are persons of Mexican descent. These models soon will become Chicanos (as opposed to persons with Anglo values) and will aid rather than work against their fellows. Evaluate this ending.

THE PLAY IN PERFORMANCE

Jorge Huerta
DIRECTING *LOS VENDIDOS*

Jorge Huerta is a professor at the University of California, San Diego; a director; critic (among his books is *Chicano Theater: Themes and Forms*); and a founding member of several theatrical groups. In this interview he responds to questions about his production of *Los Vendidos*.

Interviewer: What sort of stage did you use? A proscenium stage? A theater-in-the-round? Do you think that the play works best on one kind of stage?

Huerta: The beauty of *Los Vendidos*, and indeed, any good acto, is that it can be performed virtually anywhere. In a classroom, a theater, outdoors. I have directed this acto on several occasions, under every conceivable condition, touring it to the Southwestern U.S. as well as Western Europe with equal success, regardless of the performance situation.

Do you find that the responses of Anglos differ greatly from the responses of Chicanos?

Definitely. The humor of the piece often comes from the recognition of the stereotypes and if an audience member does not "connect" with a particular type, such as the pachuco, because s/he has no reference point, the humor is diminished. The farce, a vital element of any acto, is a universal comic device, however, and there is enough of that (physicality) in this acto to generate laughter from most audiences. In Europe (Spain, France and what in 1988 was West Germany) our audiences were mostly university students who had been studying the Chicanos and they were therefore familiar with the types. Some of the satire, such as equating the farmworker with the (then economical) Volkswagen, crosses cultures as well.

I have heard that some Chicanos find the acto demeaning. What would you say to them?

If I could dialogue with those people who are offended by the stereotypes, I would explain to them that this acto is exposing the stereotypes, and, in fact, appropriating them for the Chicanos' own purposes, which is to educate them about themselves. *Los Vendidos* is about a very particular Mexican-American who denies her or his Mexican heritage and attempts to "pass." If people are offended by this, perhaps the message is hitting too close to home.

Have you ever used Anglo performers in the play?

Actually, no.

Is this a matter of chance or of principle?

Not chance, and not necessarily "principle." I believe that some theatrical pieces are "ethno-specific" and lose part of their impact if the wrong "type" is cast. However, the Teatro Campesino has a videotape, or film, of this acto with none other than Jane Fonda as Miss Jimenes. But something is lost in the realization that this woman is not pretending to be white; she is white. I have always cast a dark-skinned actress as Miss Jimenes, because the audience can see the irony in her denial. Mexican and Chicano audiences love to see the "vendida/o" type ridiculed and always have, as evidenced in early 20th-century sketches performed in the Southwest, according to the research of Nicolás Kanellos.

In the 1971 production by El Teatro de la Esperanza, the ending was changed—the men decide to use the money to build a community center. How do you personally feel about this change?

We (Teatro de la Esperanza) felt that the original ending/solution was superfluous. We had just become the theatrical arm of a community-based organization, La Casa de la Raza (The Home of the People) in Santa Barbara's Mexican/Chicano community, and we hoped to use the acto as an example to the audiences there. When the characters talked about a community center, they and the audiences were in that very center. The ending should not be about "partying," but, rather, about building communities. By the way, as you know, even Valdez altered the ending for the NBC version of his acto.

In directing the play, did any special problems arise that you had not anticipated? If so, what were they, and how did you handle them?

The 1971 production at La Casa de la Raza generated some discussion among the Mexican-American audience members who felt that we should not be revealing this negative image of our people to non-Chicano audiences. They felt that it was like hanging out one's dirty laundry. At the universities, however, nobody questioned this exposure. It is usually the case that community-based audiences will be less progressive than the younger, student audiences. Other than this minor problem, which did not deter us from performing the play, by the way, I have not encountered any problems with *Los Vendidos*.

Los Vendidos *was first written and produced in 1967. Do you think that it is still valid today?*

Definitely. It is a classic of the genre and is as successful today as it was when first produced in 1967. Every one of the types illustrated still exists. However, as you have noted, some of the contemporary references, such as "Governor Reagan," would have to be up-dated. The Revolucionario's line, "Is there a Frito Bandito in the house?" may no longer resonate, since the television commercial was discontinued long ago, but there are plenty of current equivalents. And the major theme, the problems of assimilation and denial of one's culture are still with us.

Can other culture adapt and perform this acto?

The set-up of a "Used Mexican Lot" is universally understood to mean a used car lot and anybody can buy and sell "cars." A Filipino student of mine adapted *Los Vendidos* to his community, substituting the Mexican and Chicano types with similar models from his own community. I do not know if he ever produced it for his intended audience, but it was quite funny to me. Great fun.

Can anybody write an acto?

Absolutely. All the creator(s) need is a passionate need to educate an audience with their message. If the acto is being created by a group of individuals, they have to have the same agenda. You cannot create a good acto if you do believe in the acto's conclusion or solutions. Once the writer or writers have decided which issue they wish to expose, they need only improvise the conflicts, with clearly delineated heroes and

Luis Valdez

villains and they will have a ready-to-perform acto. Most essential to a good acto, however, is a very clear understanding of the issues involved. This means understanding the enemy as well as the hero. You cannot ridicule your enemy unless you know the enemy very, very well. Finally, the creators of an acto must have fun as they ridicule and expose the enemy's weaknesses. Also, study other actos as well as radical theater of the 1960s for good models.

What are issues that students might want to dramatize in an acto?

I have never given a student an issue to dramatize as an acto. I can't. The idea has to come from the creators. They have to be passionate about something in order to effectively create an acto.

As we point out in our introduction to this acto, Chicano theater is and has been political, leaning particularly to the left. Do the actos have to be radical-left or even liberal?

Not at all. I had an Anglo male student who disliked affirmative action and wanted to write an acto against this concept because of a bad experience he had had with a potential employer. Regardless of how I felt about affirmative action (and he knew how I felt!), I urged him to "Let it all hang out." He did, and although I disagreed with the message philosophically, the writer captured the essence of the acto quite well. I laughed all the way through this acto because the writer knew the situation and had grasped the major features of the acto as expressed in *Los Vendidos* and other actos by Valdez and his Teatro Campesino.

What other issues does the creator of an acto have to consider?

The audience for whom the acto is written. The anti-affirmative action acto would be embraced at the Republican National Convention; a gun-control acto might not be so welcome. Actos are meant to educate and entertain but do not expect an audience of detractors to sit through your acto. Remember that the original actos were created by striking farmworkers for striking farmworkers. They were meant to remind their audiences of the goals of their struggles while also giving them some much-needed comic relief, portraying the boss with a pig-faced mask, etc. Laughter is a very healthy tool and a mediating device as well. So have fun and laugh at your enemy with an acto.

808

Carlos   Morton

THE MANY DEATHS
OF DANNY ROSALES

Carlos Morton, a second generation Mexican-American, was born in Chicago in 1947, and educated at the University of Texas (El Paso), the University of California (San Diego), and the University of Texas (Austin). Among the groups that have performed his plays are the San Francisco Mime Troupe, the Puerto Rican Traveling Theatre, the Denver Center Theatre, and the New York Shakespeare Festival. Morton has been a Fulbright lecturer in Mexico, and he now teaches playwrighting at the University of California, Riverside.

Morton's work is highly varied, ranging from satiric comedy (*El Jardin*) to docudrama. For instance, in *El Jardin* (*The Garden*, 1975) Morton wittily parallels Adam and Eve's loss of paradise with the European conquest of the New World, but in *The Many Deaths of Danny Rosales* (a revision of *Las Many Muertes de Richard Morales*, 1976) there are few laughs and no fantastic elements. Despite this range of dramatic forms, however, Morton is always concerned with the Chicano experience. For example *La Malinche* (1984), his adaptation of the Medea story, is about a historical Mayan woman who aided Cortés, was his lover, and was ultimately rejected by Cortés.

COMMENTARY

It comes as a surprise to most people to learn that the first play staged in what today is the United States was performed in Spanish, *Los moros y los cristianos* (*The Moors and the Christians*). It was produced in 1598 in Nuevo Mexico, somewhere around what is now Santa Fe. Nor is *Los moros y los cristianos* the earliest Spanish play in the New World; as we mention (p. 166) in our comment on the medieval *The Second Shepherds' Play*, Spanish religious plays were performed in Mexico at the beginning of the sixteenth century.

In talking about the early Spanish-language theater in North America, it must be understood that we are not talking about Spanish-speaking people who immigrated into Anglo territory; rather, we refer to Spaniards who preceded the Anglos. Much of what is now the United States (the Southwest, California, Nevada, and Utah) was settled by the Spanish, before the Anglos arrived. After the Mexican War of Independence (1810–1821), this territory ceased to belong to Spain and became a part of Mexico. Then, in the Mexican-American War (1848), Mexico lost the land to the United States. Obviously, even after the land changed hands, the Spanish-speaking residents retained much of their Spanish culture. In the nineteenth century, San Francisco and Los Angeles were centers of Hispanic theater, and there was also a good deal of theatrical activity, such as local ceremonies and occasional visits by troupes from Mexico, in the Southwest.

Today, the facts of immigration and of assimilation have made the Hispanic theater more varied and more diffuse than it was in the nineteenth century. Broadly speaking, there are three chief divisions, although there is some overlap: Chicano (Mexican-American) theater, primarily in the Southwest and West; Cuban-American theater, primarily in Florida and New York; and Nuyorican theater (i.e., the theater of Puerto Ricans who live primarily in New York). Speaking broadly, we can say that although Chicano theater uses Spanish and English as well as a mixture called Spanglish (English words turned into Spanish, such as *boxear*, which means "to box"; *boicot*, which means "*boycott*"; and *esnobismo*, which means "*snobbery*"), the most recent Chicano plays, such as those of Carlos Morton, use far less Spanish than the earlier ones.

The earliest Cuban-American theater, at the end of the nineteenth century, consisted chiefly of melodramas and romantic dramas, performed by immigrants or by theatrical companies visiting from Cuba. In 1959, however, with the Cuban revolution that brought Fidel Castro to power, the Cuban-American theater changed drastically, becoming, in effect, a political theater of exiles. It originally was entirely in Spanish, but many of the younger Cuban-American writers today chiefly use English, as do many of the younger Chicano writers. Similarly, Nuyorican theater (in New York, though not in Puerto Rico) is chiefly in English. All three groups are often highly political. Among the published discussions that can be recommended are Jorge A. Huerta, *Chicano Theatre: Themes and Forms* (1982); and D. Chavez and L. Feyder, *Shattering the Myth: Plays by Hispanic Women* (1992). For collections of plays, see Jorge A. Huerta and

Nicolás Kanellos, eds., *Nuevos Pasos: Chicano and Puerto Rican Drama* (1979); and Jorge A. Huerta, ed., *Necessary Theater: Six Plays about the Chicano Experience* (1989).

Chicano theater (a tradition to which Carlos Morton's play belongs) is highly political, which means that it is a theater committed to social change. (For additional details on political theater, see the Commentary on Valdez's play, p. 799.) Morton's work, as we mention in the biographical note, includes comedies, but these (like those of Valdez) essentially are a matter of joking in earnest.

In *The Many Deaths of Danny Rosales*, Morton puts aside the comic mask and writes a courtroom drama. One thinks of such plays as *The Caine Mutiny Court-Martial*, *Inherit the Wind*, *The Andersonville Trial*, and *Witness for the Prosecution*. One difference between Morton's play and these is that Morton uses flashbacks that often take us out of the courtroom and back to the scene of the crime, and even earlier. When you think about it, it is quite daring for Morton to leave the courtroom. In most courtroom plays, one of the great sources of power is that the witnesses can leave the stand only when the lawyers allow them to, and the action does not let up until each character has been squeezed dry. In contrast, Morton intermingles his hard-hitting court scenes (where lawyers attack witnesses and each other) with a variety of other scenes, some of which let us see the characters as they were before they became locked into a murder trial. *Danny Rosales* has something of the fluidity of a television drama—or even of live televised coverage of a current trial, in which the presentation of the courtroom happening is occasionally interrupted while the narrator provides some background information.

In fact, Carlos Morton derived his basic story from newspaper accounts of an actual happening. In 1975 Frank Hayes (Fred Hall in the play), town marshall in Castroville, Texas, shot to death Ricardo Morales (Danny Rosales). At a trial in 1975, the jury in a Texas court (made up of one Chicano, two blacks, and seven Anglos) found Hayes guilty of aggravated assault, but not of murder, and sentenced him to two to ten years of imprisonment. Two years later, however, a federal court in effect rebuked the Texas judicial system by sentencing Hayes to life imprisonment for violating Morales's civil rights. Carlos Morton wrote the first version of the play (1976) while participating in a graduate seminar in drama. His assignment was to write about a current issue and to find roles for all of the members of the class. When the second trial changed the sentence, Morton rewrote parts of the play, and at a still later date he made further revisions. We give the most recent version.

The sheriff threatens to shoot Danny Rosales, in Carlos Morton's The Many Deaths of Danny Rosales. *The harsh, minimal setting, though essentially realistic, helps to convey the nightmarish quality of the action of the play.*

Carlos Morton

THE MANY DEATHS OF DANNY ROSALES

Characters

BAILIFF/JUDGE, (*voice*)
BERTA ROSALES, *the widow*
ROWENA SALDIVAR, *prosecuting attorney*
DANNY ROSALES, *the victim*
DEPUTY DAVIS, *sheriff's deputy*
HAROLD PEARL, *defense attorney*
KIKI VENTURA, *street dude*
STEVE PETERS, *good old boy*
FRED HALL, *sheriff of Castroville*
GRACE HALL, *sheriff's wife*

DEBBIE HALL, *sheriff's daughter*

SCENE: *Central Texas, 1975–77*

ACT 1

(*Lights up on a courtroom, bare except for a witness stand, where Berta is in the process of being sworn in.*)

BAILIFF (*voice only*). Do you swear to tell the truth, the whole truth, and nothing but the truth, so help you God?

BERTA. I do.

ROWENA (*entering into the scene*). State your name, please.

BERTA. Berta Lopez de Rosales.

ROWENA. Where do you live?

BERTA. Castroville.

ROWENA. How long have you lived there?

BERTA. Almost all of my life. I moved there from Sequin, Texas, where I was born.

ROWENA. How did you first meet Danny Rosales?

BERTA. At "La Rosa Tejana," it's a dance hall off Highway 90. (*As Berta speaks of the dance hall, we hear strains of* conjunto music[1] *being played. "Viva Seguin" would be appropriate.*)

ROWENA. What was your relationship to Danny Rosales?

BERTA. We were living together as man and wife.

ROWENA. Were you legally married?

BERTA. No, when I first met him in 1967 I was too young to get married. So we just started living together. Besides, my parents didn't want us to. They really didn't like Danny because he was from *el otro lado*. (*The* conjunto *music gets louder. Outlines of the dance hall begin to appear.*)

ROWENA. *El otro lado*—"the other side?"

BERTA. Yes, Danny was born in Mexico and came across when he was 12.

ROWENA. Tell us more about your relationship with Danny. (*Rowena fades out of the scene as Danny enters, dressed like a* vaquero norteno, *the Mexican counterpart to the Texas cowboy.*)

BERTA (*walking over to Danny*). He was a really good dancer. He really knew how to move. Much better than the boys from this side. (*They start to dance.*)

ROWENA (*only her voice*). What's the difference between someone born in Mexico and a Chicano born in Texas?

BERTA. I guess you would call it a different culture. (*To Danny.*) You know, my parents want me to marry an *Americano*, some big tall blonde boy.

DANNY. Ah, hah. So they can have *gringo* grandchildren.

BERTA (*teasing*). They don't want you coming around the house anymore.

DANNY. Because I remind them of what they once were!

BERTA. Because you're a *mojado*.

DANNY. A wetback! Not anymore. I got my green card. What is your father, a Border Patrolman or what? (*They both laugh.*)

BERTA. *Dicen que eres muy prieto.*

DANNY. Me, too dark? As if your father was so Spanish! Ask him if, when he wakes up and looks in the mirror, he doesn't see a *nopal* right there in the middle of his forehead.

BERTA. *Nopal?*

DANNY. Cactus. All us *Mexicanos* have a *nopal* stamped right here on our foreheads. And look, we have two *frijoles* for eyes. (*Laughing, jovial.*) So, are you going to marry me?

BERTA. No, but I'll let you take me to San Antonio.

DANNY (*kissing her neck*). When?

BERTA. Whenever you want. (*Danny kisses her on the lips and exits.*) Go on, I'll see you later. (*Berta returns to the witness stand to address Rowena.*) I would practice my Spanish with him, and he would speak English to me.

ROWENA (*entering again*). How long did you live together?

BERTA. Seven years.

ROWENA. That is common law.

BERTA. Yes, I guess that's what you call it.

ROWENA. When was the last time you saw Danny?

BERTA. On September 14, 1975, that Sunday night at our home in Castroville.

ROWENA. Will you please tell the jury what happened that night?

BERTA. We were watching television and getting ready to go to bed when the Deputy Sheriff drove his car up to our driveway and knocked on the front door. (*Flashback. Enter Deputy.*)

DEPUTY. Danny Rosales here?

BERTA. "Just a minute," I said, "I'll call him." (*Going to get Danny.*) Danny, *es la policia!*

ROWENA (*visible, but away from action*). And what did Danny do?

BERTA (*as Danny enters dressing*). He put his shirt on and walked to the door.

DEPUTY. That's a mighty nice stereo and TV you got there, Danny. I'm afraid I'm going to have to take you in.

ROWENA. Do you remember what time of night this was?

BERTA. 10:45 p.m.

ROWENA. What happened then?

BERTA. He handcuffed Danny and took him to the squad car. (*To the Deputy.*) How much is the bail going to be?

DEPUTY. $100.00.

BERTA. Please, Deputy, I don't have a car. Can you give me a ride over to my mother-in-law's so I can borrow the money?

DANNY. Berta, *ellos no tienen dinero.*

BERTA. Deputy, please, can't you give him another break? Can't it wait until the morning?

DANNY (*as the Deputy leads him away to the squad car*). Berta, *callate! Deja de rogar!*

ROWENA. What did Danny say to you?

BERTA. He told me his mother didn't have any money. He also told me not to beg the Deputy. He was very proud.

ROWENA. What happened then?

BERTA. The Deputy put Danny in the squad car and then told me that he had some warrants to search the house.

ROWENA. Can you tell us how Danny was dressed?

BERTA. Red shirt, jeans, black shoes.

ROWENA. Did he have the shoes on when he left the house?

---

[1] **conjunto music** traditional *Tejano* music

BERTA. No, he asked me to get them as he sat handcuffed in the squad car. I put them on, but didn't have time to tie them.

ROWENA. Why?

BERTA. Because the sheriff pulled up in his private car and took him away.

ROWENA. Mrs. Rosales, I will hand you what has been labeled State's Exhibit Number One. Is this Danny's shoe? (*Handing her a black shoe.*)

BERTA. Yes, this is one of the shoes I put on him that night.

ROWENA. And when was the last time you saw it?

BERTA. When I found it the next morning next to a pool of dried blood on the Old Alamo School Road.

ROWENA. No further questions at this time. Your witness, Mr. Pearl.

HAROLD (*entering from the opposite side of Rowena*). Tell us, your husband, or boyfriend, or the man you were living with, did he have a job?

BERTA. Danny had just gotten laid off from construction work.

HAROLD. What kind of education did he have?

BERTA. He started school in Mexico, then got as far as the tenth grade here. He had to quit school to help support his family.

HAROLD. According to his school records, Danny Rosales was a truant who was constantly in trouble, was he not?

ROWENA. I object, irrelevant and immaterial.

HAROLD. I will show the relevancy, your Honor.

JUDGE (*voice only*). Overruled. Answer the question, Mrs. Rosales.

BERTA. My husband was in trouble because none of the teachers understood him. He was put in a special class for slow learners.

HAROLD. Even in his later years—wasn't Danny Rosales in constant trouble with the law?

BERTA. The Sheriff was always hassling and picking on him.

HAROLD. Take a look at this photograph. Is this a fair and accurate representation of what he looked like, Danny Rosales?

BERTA. Yes, it is. But I don't know when this picture was taken.

HAROLD. You don't? You weren't with him? What does it say here?

BERTA. Arroyo County . . .

HAROLD. "Arroyo County Sheriff's Department." He was charged with burglary.

ROWENA. Your Honor, again, I object, irrelevant and immaterial.

HAROLD. Please, your Honor, give me time to show the relevancy.

JUDGE. Overruled, but please get to the point, Mr. Pearl.

HAROLD. Now then, Mrs. Rosales, isn't it a fact that your *husband* was sentenced to three years probation for burglary?

BERTA. Yes, he was.

HAROLD. Wasn't he picked up for questioning about other robberies?

BERTA. Yes.

ROWENA. Your Honor, I object, Danny Rosales is not on trial here, Fred Hall is.

HAROLD. I am establishing that Mr. Rosales had a criminal record and therefore my client had every right to question him.

JUDGE. Overruled.

ROWENA. Your honor, please note my objection to the ruling.

JUDGE. Very well, it will be noted.

HAROLD. Now then, Mrs. Rosales, let's go back to the night Sheriff Hall took your husband away. Where were you?

BERTA. At the front door of the house.

HAROLD. What did the Sheriff say to him?

BERTA. I couldn't hear, I was too far away. But they were shouting.

HAROLD. Did you see the Sheriff push or kick or beat your husband?

BERTA. No, it was too dark.

HAROLD. No further questions. (*Starting to leave.*)

BERTA. But they didn't take him to the jail house like they said they would—they took him in the opposite direction.

HAROLD. I said no further questions, you may be excused. (*Harold steps down.*)

ROWENA. I would like to cross examine the witness. (*Crossing up.*) Now, Berta, this stereo and TV the Deputy was looking at, how long had they been in your house?

BERTA. We had just gotten them that weekend.

ROWENA. How did you acquire these items?

BERTA. Danny and Kiki brought them in Kiki's car.

ROWENA. Who is Kiki?

BERTA. Kiki Ventura. He used to be a friend of Danny's. They came into the house just before dawn. (*As Danny and Kiki enter. Flashback.*) Danny! Where have you been, it's almost morning, I've been worried to death about you.

DANNY. Wouldn't you know, Kiki's car broke down and we spent all night fixing it.

BERTA. Your hands are dirty. Why don't you wash up. I'll make some *chorizo con huevo*.[2] Is that Kiki's car out there? Everytime I see him he's got a different car.

DANNY. *Si,* that's Kiki all right. The Chicano Robin Hood. *Entrale,*[3] Kiki, Berta's not going to bite your head off. (*Kiki sticks his head through the door.*)

KIKI. That's what the black widow spider said to her *viejo*.[4]

BERTA. Why is Kiki the Chicano Robin Hood?

---

[2]**chorizo con huevo** sausage and eggs   [3]**Entrale** Come in   [4]*viejo* old man

KIKI. Because I take from the *gringos* and give to Chicanos like me. Hey man, come on, I'm tired, where do you wanna put the you know what?

DANNY. Shhhhhh!

BERTA. What are you two whispering about?

KIKI. The new stereo and TV. It's a surprise.

DANNY. It was.

BERTA. New stereo and TV?

DANNY. I rented them from a store in San Antonio.

BERTA. Are you sure *Senor* Hood here didn't rip them off? Where did you get the money?

DANNY. Don't worry, *viejita*,[5] I didn't use any of the money for the rent or *la comida*.[6] This is extra *feria*[7] I made picking watermelons.

KIKI. At least he didn't get it picking pockets, eh Berta?

DANNY. Kiki, go get the stuff, will you!

KIKI. O.K. Hey, Berta, *no te pongas*[8] all uptight! (*He exits.*)

BERTA. Danny, I could have paid off the doctor's bills with that money. Give me the receipt, and I'll ride back to *San Anto* with *la comadre*[9] and take it back.

DANNY. Everybody else has a new TV, Berta, why can't we? (*Searching for the receipt.*)

BERTA. But there are more important things. We need to get our telephone turned on again. We need a car that runs. Groceries . . .

DANNY. All right. Ah, I can't find it. I must have left it at the store.

BERTA. Danny, you've got to start saving your receipts! How else are we going to know how much money we spent!

DANNY. Berta!

BERTA. Danny, we'll never get out of this mess we're in unless we save and sacrifice.

DANNY. *Yo se*,[10] every day we get deeper in the hole.

BERTA. Those debts will drag us under.

DANNY (*venting his frustrations*). It's just that everything was going so good and then I got laid off. (*Beat.*) My family never had a TV. I used to go and watch "Lassie" and "Mr. Ed" with this little *gabachito*[11] friend of mine. His mother would make us roast beef sandwiches and say, "poor boy, you probably don't get to eat roast beef at your house, do you?"

BERTA. What is it you want to watch on television?

DANNY. Don't you remember, my brother's going to be in the *Diez Y Seis De Septiembre*[12] Parade in San Antonio? He's going to be dressed like a *charro*[13] riding his horse!

BERTA. Oh, Danny, you're so sentimental. All right, *mi amor*, keep the TV for a while, but what do we need a stereo for?

[5]*viejita* old lady (said affectionately) [6]*la comida* food [7]*feria* income [8]*no te pongas* don't get yourself [9]*la comadre* close friend [10]*Yo se* I know [11]*gabachito* Anglo kid [12]*Diez . . . Septiembre* September 16, celebrating Mexico's independence from Spain [13]*charro* Mexican cowboy

DANNY. That's the surprise, I know how much you like your *conjunto* music. I couldn't get something for me without getting something for you, *tambien*.[14]

BERTA. Danny, you could talk me into anything! (*They embrace.*) *Sabes que?*[15] I have a surprise for you too.

DANNY. What!

BERTA. Well, I, that is, you and I are going . . .

KIKI (*bursting in on them*). Hey man, why don't you surprise me and get that stereo and TV in here. Come on, that stuff is heavy. (*Motioning to Berta that they will talk later. Exit Danny and Kiki.*)

ROWENA. Mrs. Rosales, I want to tell the jury—was Danny telling the truth about having rented that stereo and TV from a firm in San Antonio?

BERTA. Yes, he was. My husband didn't steal anything. He died for nothing! He was murdered!

HAROLD. Your honor, I object, the witness is assuming that a murder has been committed.

JUDGE. Mrs. Rosales, please confine your comments to the questions at hand.

ROWENA. I would like to offer this receipt as evidence to be labeled State's Exhibit Number Two.

HAROLD. I ask that Court verify that receipt for its authenticity.

ROWENA. For our next witness, the State would like to call Steve Peters to the stand.

BAILIFF (*as Steve enters*). Raise your right hand. Do you swear to tell the truth, the whole truth, and nothing but the truth, so help you God?

STEVE. I do.

ROWENA. State your name, please.

STEVE. Steve Earl Peters.

ROWENA. What is your relationship to Mr. Hall?

STEVE. His daughter and I are engaged to be married.

ROWENA. How did he involve you in the shooting of Danny Rosales?

STEVE. I was just keeping him company.

ROWENA. You were keeping him company?

STEVE. I mean, I was just riding around with him. A lot of people ride around with their police friends. They're ain't nothing else to do in Castroville.

ROWENA. Let's go back to the night before shooting. What were you doing on Saturday, September 13, 1975?

STEVE. I was at Mr. Hall's home drinking . . . ice tea . . . and watching the football games on TV. I was also there to ask Debbie for her hand in marriage.

ROWENA. Debbie, Mr. Hall's daughter. Did you ask Mr. Hall for permission?

STEVE. I didn't get a chance to. The Chief kept getting all these calls on his police radio. He was on duty 24

[14]*tambien* also [15]*Sabes que?* You know what?

hours a day. I mean, we were in the middle of the Texas Tech-Baylor when he asked me to go with him on a stakeout!

ROWENA. What was Chief Hall hoping to accomplish?

STEVE. See, he'd gotten a tip from an informant that this Danny Rosales was going to be transporting some stolen merchandise. Mr. Hall wanted to catch him, as he put it, in *flag-grande-dele-ecto*. I guess that means, "in the act."

ROWENA. Did he?

STEVE. No. We waited three hours by the side of the road for a '69 Burgundy Mustang, license plate number BQD195. It was hot and sticky and the skeeters were biting like crazy. All we had to listen to was the police radio squawking all night.

ROWENA. What did you do after the three hours were up?

STEVE. The Chief decided to swing over to "La Rosa Tejana" to see if the informant was there.

ROWENA. "La Rosa Tejana?"

STEVE. It's a Meskin Bar off the Highway 90. The Chief stayed in the squad car and asked me to go in to reconnoiter the situation. He waited outside to block any avenues of escape. (*Flashback. Steve walks into "La Rosa Tejana".*)

KIKI (*drinking a beer*). *Orale!*[16] El Stevie Peters!

STEVE. Hey Kiki!

KIKI. What you doing this side of town, *ese?*[17]

STEVE. Kiki, you better get your ass out of here. The Chief is pissed off as hell. We waited three hours at the side of the road for you!

KIKI. You know what, Stevie, you *gringos* are all hung up on time. Did you know that, *en Espanol, el tiempo anda,* time walks?

STEVE. Chief Hall is right outside, Kiki.

KIKI. Oh shit! Is that his squad car! I better go . . . (*Kiki exits, but runs right into Fred at the back door.*)

FRED. Well, what have we here!

KIKI. Mr. Hall!

FRED. Kiki Ventura. Sit down, Kiki, let me buy you a beer. (*Fred goes to a table. He makes a painful expression as he sits down.*)

KIKI. Sure. I'll take a Longneck.

FRED (*handing Steve some money*). Get him whatever he wants. Gimme a Coke. (*Steve exits.*)

KIKI. Aren't you going to have a beer with me, Fred?

FRED. Not while I'm on duty. All right, what went wrong, what happened to you?

KIKI. Shit, Fred, my generator degenerated on me, man.

FRED. Why can't you Mexicans keep your cars running?

KIKI. 'Cause your *gringos* don't pay us enough! (*Fred just stares at him.*) Look, I'm sorry, I'll make it up to you. (*Steve enters with a beer for Kiki and two sodas.*)

FRED. What's the deal with Rosales?

KIKI. He don't have nothing, Fred, even the *cucarachas* left his house.

FRED. Oh yeah? Well, why is it that everytime a house gets broken into, he's seen in the vicinity. But when I go pick him up for questioning, he's managed to dispose of the goods. Or else he's got a phony alibi. I'm sick and tired of chasing him.

KIKI. I know, I know, somebody's stealing this town blind. I bet you it's them illegals, Fred, they rip stuff off and then go sell it on the other side.

FRED. You better come up with a answer, Kiki, and I mean *pronto*. You're on probation as it is for possession of a controlled substance. All I have to do is make one telephone call to your probation officer and you become property of the Texas Department of Corrections. You hear me, boy?

KIKI. Yes sir.

FRED (*grimacing as he rises*). I don't appreciate being made a fool out of. Let's go, Steve. (*They leave Kiki behind.*)

STEVE. Boy, did you see the look in his face! He's fit to be tied!

FRED. You gotta put the fear of God in them boys.

STEVE. Mr. Hall.

FRED. Yes?

STEVE. Mr. Hall, I've been trying to ask you something all night. Look, I just got promoted to Assistant Manager of the Tasty Freeze. I got my pickup all paid for, and I just saw this out-of-sight apartment near the Cielito Lindo Mall . . .

FRED. I know what you're going to ask me.

STEVE. You do?

FRED. You want permission to take Debbie to the Senior Prom.

STEVE. No, I wanna marry her!

FRED. Take it easy, I'm just funning with you. Now, if you're really going to be my son-in-law . . .

STEVE. Wow! Chief! Do you really mean it!

FRED. Of course, but forget about the Tasty Freeze, Steve. Try something else. How about law enforcement? You can take some courses at the junior college next year. Maybe even become my Deputy. God knows the one I have now ain't worth a damn.

STEVE. I'd be honored, Chief, right honored! (*Exit Fred. Steve returns to the witness stand.*)

HAROLD (*taking his turn with the witness*). So, you were present when Chief Hall interrogated Mr. Ventura, were you not?

STEVE. Yes sir.

HAROLD. The Chief didn't slap the man or beat him or mistreat him in any way, did he?

STEVE. No, Mr. Hall always acted in a very, uh, professional manner.

HAROLD. Thank you. No further questions. You may be excused. (*Exit Steve.*) For the first witness, I would like to

---

[16]**Orale!** Listen!   [17]**ese** you (said contemptuously)

call Mrs. Grace Hall to the stand. (*Fade on Pearl, lights up on Hall home. Debbie is sitting and reading a magazine.*)

GRACE (*entering with a pan*). Debbie! Did you get those pans cleaned?

DEBBIE. Mother, I scoured them until my fingers ached.

GRACE (*showing her the pan*). You just have to scrub harder, dear.

DEBBIE. But, I'm scrapping the finish off the pan, which is why the food sticks to it.

GRACE. Nonsense, you polish it until it shines like a mirror. And you know I don't like you leave all them dirty dishes in the sink. I want them washed after each meal, the table wiped off, the sink shiny white.

DEBBIE. (*She's heard all of this before.*) All right, mother!

GRACE. Stevie is coming over tonight.

DEBBIE. Whooptee do.

GRACE. Aren't you excited?

DEBBIE. Yeah, it just makes me want to stand on my head and shout Hallelujah!

GRACE. Debbie, I thought you were sweet on Stevie, I thought you liked him and wanted to . . .

DEBBIE. Past tense. The Lord didn't create me to spend the rest of my life in a kitchen cooking for Stevie Peters, that's for sure.

GRACE. Why, Debbie, a woman's place is with her man. Why do you think Eve was made from the rib of Adam?

DEBBIE. Mama, you don't understand. I want to go to school, someplace like Chicago or New York!

GRACE. Oh no you don't! Austin is far enough away. Besides, you don't want to go to school with a bunch of Yankees, do you?

DEBBIE. I just don't want to be a dumb old housewife! (*Grace is offended.*) Oh, don't get me wrong. I'm not putting you down. You just don't realize your own worth. Cooking and cleaning and raising a child is a full-time job and you don't even get paid for it.

GRACE. Debbie, of course I get paid. Not with a check, with love. And I'm not just a housewife, I work part-time at the bank. Tell me, who do you think bought this trailer home and everything in it? Including your little foreign Japanese car!

DEBBIE. You and Daddy did of course. And I'm very grateful. I've seen the way some of these Black and Mexican kids live and it just about breaks my heart.

GRACE. The Lord helps those that help themselves, dear.

DEBBIE. I guess what I am trying to say is, I won't have time to be cooking, cleaning and taking care of kids because I'll be too busy working for me.

GRACE. Well, you can always get a Mexican to do your housework. Debbie, listen to me. Stevie told me he's going to ask your father for your hand in marriage—tonight!

DEBBIE. You know what? I hate weddings. They're just like funerals.

GRACE. We thought you'd like to have a June wedding, right after graduation.

DEBBIE. God! Did anybody bother to ask me?

GRACE. Debbie, don't use the Good Lord's name in vain! (*Sound of someone coming through the front door.*) Listen, your Daddy is home.

DEBBIE (*out of earshot*). Jesus Christ!

STEVE. Hi, Mrs. Hall.

GRACE. Hello, Steve dear. (*Grace kisses Fred on the cheek.*)

STEVE. Debbie, can I talk to you for a minute?

DEBBIE (*crossing to her Fred*). How's my Lone Ranger?

FRED. Not too good, honey, Tonto and me let the bad guys get way.

STEVE. Deb . . .

DEBBIE. Did you play Tonto tonight, Steve? Hey, do you know that "Tonto" means "dumb" in Spanish?

FRED. That's pretty funny, eh, *kimo sabe?*

STEVE. Yeah. Hey, Deb, I gotta tell you something.

DEBBIE. What?

STEVE. Your dad said we could get married!

DEBBIE (*deadpan*). Wonderful.

GRACE (*noticing a pained expression on Fred's face as he sits down*). What's the matter, Fred, are you all right?

FRED. I'm O.K. Hand me my pain killers.

GRACE. You've been working too much, Fred.

FRED. Heard anything on the police radio?

GRACE. Can't we turn that thing off, even for one night?

FRED (*very much in pain*). Get me my pain killers!

DEBBIE. I'll get 'em for you, Daddy.

GRACE. Debbie, there's a nice cold pitcher of ice tea in the refrigerator. Fix everybody a tall glass.

STEVE. What's the matter, Chief?

GRACE. Oh, he ain't been the same ever since that shootout with the two Blacks at Del's Liquor Store. (*Harold enters from the side to encourage and coach Grace.*)

STEVE. Oh, yeah, that's right, he was shot three times.

GRACE (*acknowledging Harold*). It was late at night. Fred was on patrol when he noticed this suspicious looking car parked out in front of the liquor store.

FRED (*getting into the act*). One went left and one went right. I caught one guy and handcuffed him when I noticed a colored lady sitting in the car. I ordered her out and was trying to call for a back-up through the dispatcher when the guy who got away snuck up behind me and stuck a knife to my throat.

ROWENA (*interrupting*). Your honor, I object! Didn't we go over this material during the Sanity Hearing? (*The Hall family stays in place.*)

HAROLD. Your honor, I am merely trying to establish my client's state of mind that weekend. The jury should be aware that he was diagnosed as having a chronic brain syndrome. In fact, neurosurgery, even today, is seriously being considered.

ROWENA. You cannot plead Fred Hall not guilty by reason of insanity.

HAROLD. That is not my intention, but there were other factors present that had a direct bearing on the case.

JUDGE. I do want to remind the jury that we did find Fred Hall mentally competent to stand trial at the Sanity Hearing. You may proceed, Mr. Pearl, but let's not cover old ground.

HAROLD. Thank you, your Honor. (*To the Hall family.*) Now then, tell us about the shootout at Del's Liquor Store.

GRACE. Well, the first colored fellow that Fred had apprehended started hitting him on the head with a rock and with the handcuffs.

FRED. I went semi-conscious and hit the ground as one of them took my revolver away.

HAROLD. He took your revolver away?

FRED. Yes, he did.

HAROLD. What happened then?

FRED. He shot me with it! I kept rolling over and over on the ground to avoid the shots.

GRACE. Fred was wounded three times!

FRED. (*Trying to take his shirt off ala L.B.J.*) Here, I'll show you the scars.

GRACE. Fred, please don't!

DEBBIE (*entering*). Oh, Daddy! (*Grace and Debbie embrace Fred.*)

GRACE. And that is why my husband has to take pain killers to this day. (*Debbie leads Fred offstage.*)

HAROLD. Have you noticed anything unusual about your husband since this unfortunate incident occurred?

GRACE. I've noticed that his memory has gotten bad. He has also been depressed, moody, and given to fits of bad temper.

HAROLD. Anything else about your husband involving his line of work?

GRACE. He tended to do things that were extra risky. He would go into a dangerous bar to apprehend a criminal without a backup. Or, he would address a traffic offender in their car out on the highway. One time he even told me he looked forward to being killed in the line of duty.

HAROLD. You were very proud of your husband, weren't you?

GRACE. Oh, everyone in the whole town looked up to him. He would get invitations to speak at the high school and in front of law enforcement classes at the junior college.

HAROLD. Did he take too much of the responsibilities of his office upon himself?

GRACE. Oh yes. After Fred almost died in that shootout he rededicated himself to his career in law. He saw himself as someone saving the community from marital strife, bringing Christ to couples who go into marital conflicts, and cleansing the community of drug addicts . . . .

ROWENA. Your Honor, I am going to object to this! This is nothing more than a barefaced ploy to gain sympathy for the defendant. Mr. Hall's efforts to bring Christ to couples has no bearing on this case whatsoever!

JUDGE. Sustained. Mr. Pearl, I suggest you wrap this testimony up.

HAROLD. Thank you, Mrs. Hall, thank you for telling us what kind of a husband and father Fred Hall was. Your witness, Ms. Saldivar.

ROWENA. I have no questions . . . at this time.

JUDGE. You may step down, Mrs. Hall. (*Exit Grace.*)

BERTA. Aren't you going to question her? She made the Sheriff out to be a saint.

ROWENA. Now is not the time, Berta. We'll get to her and her daughter later.

BERTA. Why isn't that *vieja*[18] on trial? (*Referring to Grace.*)

ROWENA. Because she only pleaded guilty to concealing physical evidence.

BERTA. Physical evidence? What physical evidence?

ROWENA. Danny's body.

BERTA. There, you see, she buried his body in a ditch. What kind of people are they? Why don't they charge her with murder?

ROWENA. *Sientate,*[19] Berta, please—you're going to make it worse for our case.

HAROLD. I would like to call Mr. Kiki Ventura to the stand. (*Enter Kiki with his hat on his head.*)

BAILIFF. Remove your hat, please. (*Kiki removes his hat.*) Do you swear to tell the truth, the whole truth, and nothing but the truth, so help you God?

KIKI. Yeah, I guess so.

JUDGE. You mean, "yes" don't you Mr. Ventura?

KIKI. Yes sir.

HAROLD. Please state your name, age and occupation.

KIKI. Enrique Ignacio Anselmo de Ventura y Rosas. But everybody calls me Kiki. I'm almost 30 years old and, uh, what else did you ask me?

HAROLD. Your occupation.

KIKI. Yeah, well, right now, I'm unemployed.

HAROLD. Mr. Ventura, what was your relationship to the deceased, Danny Rosales?

KIKI (*saddened*). He was my friend.

HAROLD. You were also a business associate of Mr. Rosales, were you not? Didn't you move different items of furniture and things like that from one county to another?

KIKI. Nah, we didn't do any furniture moving.

HAROLD. Mr. Ventura, is it not a proven fact that you have quite an extensive criminal record?

KIKI. That was in the past. I don't do that anymore. Ask my probation officer.

HAROLD. You and Danny were just good buddies, huh?

KIKI. Yeah, we hung out and drank Colorado Koolaid.

HAROLD. Is that all? Weren't you also involved in the sale of narcotics?

KIKI. I refuse to answer on the grounds that it might incriminal me.

HAROLD. Mr. Venture, just answer my question, yes or no.

KIKI. Don't I have the right to talk to my lawyers?

[18]*vieja* old lady   [19]*Sientate* Be quiet

JUDGE. Answer the question, Mr. Ventura.

KIKI. Yes, but I served my time.

HAROLD. Isn't it also a fact that you and Mr. Rosales sold a calf and then did not deliver it?

KIKI. No, that's not true. Danny sold that calf, not me. No, you can't pin that on me. (*Flashback. Enter Danny.*)

DANNY. Kiki, when am I going to get my *dinero*.[20] The farmer wants his money back.

KIKI. Shit, Danny, I'm kind of broke right now. All I got is half a kilo of grass. *Oaxaca Caca!* Worth about $200.

DANNY. No, I don't.

KIKI. You could sell it to some college student for $300 easy.

DANNY. I'm not dealing any drugs.

KIKI. O.K. then, let's smoke it!

DANNY. I'm tired of getting wasted.

KIKI. Hey man, are you turning into a Boy Scout?

DANNY. No, but I'm tired of beating my brains against the wall. From now on I'm going to use my head to think.

KIKI. What are you going to do, man, go to college for something?

DANNY. I could, if I wanted to. I could get my G.E.D. and enroll at the junior college.

KIKI. *Ay si!* Come on, you been talking to your old lady again? She's been telling you how you could have been a *pinche*[21] brain surgeon!

DANNY. No, I've been talking to myself. I've decided that 26 years old is too old to be playing in the streets, man. I don't want to give Berta a bunch of *chavalones*[22] just to watch them do a return of my own life. Look man, remember when Berta said she had a surprise for me? Well, the surprise is that we're going to have a baby!

KIKI. *Hijoles,*[23] another poor *esquincle*[24] in this world!

DANNY. *No ves,*[25] I'm sick of being poor, and the alcohol and the food stamps.

KIKI. Hey, well excuse me. What are you going to do, go live with the *gabachos* in their part of town?

DANNY. No, but I'm not going to live like a punk kid, either.

KIKI. *Simon, vato,*[26] you do your own thing. (*Turning to go.*) Later.

DANNY. Hey, Kiki, we're still friends, *que no?*

KIKI. Sure . . .

DEPUTY (*entering*). Which one of you is Danny Rosales?

KIKI. He is.

DEPUTY. I'm Deputy Davis. I have a warrant for your arrest on the charge that you sold but did not deliver a calf. A farmer named Gonzales signed the complaint.

KIKI. *Hay te watcho,*[27] Danny . . . (*Trying to leave.*)

DANNY. Wait a minute, Kiki, you've got some explaining to do.

DEPUTY. No, I think you better start explaining, Rosales.

DANNY. Well, you see, Deputy, I couldn't deliver the calf because Kiki here killed it.

KIKI. Yes, I killed it, but it was an accident.

DEPUTY. An accident?

KIKI. You see, I was trying to fatten it up for him. It was a little underweight. So, my *Abuelita*[28] says to me, "Kiki, that calf looks a little sickly, maybe you should feed it some of this special grain." So I did. Three weeks passed. One day I woke up and, boom, the calf was *patas para arriba!*[29] Dead! I was feeding it *loco* weed by mistake. (*Beat.*) You don't believe me?

DANNY. Tell him what you did with it, Kiki.

KIKI. I ate it. I was hungry.

DEPUTY. Look, whatever the reason, Rosales, you are still responsible. So, when are you going to give Gonzales his money back?

DANNY. I already gave half of it back last week. And I'm going to give him another fifty tonight. I promise to pay back every penny.

DEPUTY. Why should I believe you?

DANNY. Because I don't want to go to jail. Also, if I'm in jail I can't work. And if I can't work, I'll never pay him back.

DEPUTY. That's a good point. I'll tell you what, if you promise to pay $50 a week until you pay off the entire amount, I'll let you free.

DANNY. Thanks alot, Deputy.

KIKI. Hey man, I wish all the *chotas*[30] could be like you!

DEPUTY. I don't want to lock you up, Rosales, but if you miss just one payment . . .

DANNY. Don't worry, I won't. Thanks for the break, Deputy!

KIKI. *Orale pues!*[31] Let me show you the Chicano handshake. (*Going to the Deputy, who ignores him.*)

DEPUTY. Don't let me down, Rosales. (*Crosses to witness stand.*)

KIKI. *Pinche pig!*

DANNY. *Ya ves,*[32] Kiki, my luck is changing already! *Pero,*[33] now you know how much I really need that money.

KIKI. Don't worry, you'll get it. You'll get every bit of it. (*Exits.*)

ROWENA. Deputy, how did it happen that you went to arrest Danny Rosales at his home that Sunday night?

DEPUTY. Chief Hall had left instructions for me to serve that theft warrant against Rosales.

ROWENA. Wasn't the warrant out-dated? Wasn't it over two weeks old? And under Texas law isn't a warrant only good for 72 hours?

DEPUTY. I told Chief Hall that, but he wouldn't listen to me.

ROWENA. In other words, Chief Hall used the misdemeanor theft warrant as an excuse to take Danny Rosales out to the woods to beat him up and shot him.

---

[20]*dinero* money [21]*pinche* fucking [22]*chavalones* kids [23]*Hicholes* Gee whiz [24]*esquincle* kid [25]*No ves* Don't you see [26]*Simon, vato* All right, dude [27]*Hay te watcho* See you later

[28]*Abuelita* grandma [29]*patas para arriba* hoofs up [30]*chotas* derisive term for police [31]*Orales pues!* All right! [32]*Ya ves* Now you see [33]*Pero* But

HAROLD. Your honor, I object to this line of questioning!

JUDGE. Sustained! Ms. Saldivar, this court is interested in facts, not assumptions.

ROWENA. All right. Deputy, tell us in your own words what transpired that night.

DEPUTY. (*Flashback.*) That's a mighty nice stereo and TV you got there, Danny. Maybe you should have used that money to finish paying off the farmer.

DANNY. I only missed one payment.

DEPUTY. You have the right to remain silent. You have the right to an attorney. Anything you say may be used against you in court of law.

ROWENA. What happened after you read the suspect his rights and finished searching the house?

DEPUTY. I was getting ready to take him in when Chief Hall pulled up in his private car. (*Leading Danny off.*) O.K. Danny, let's go.

FRED (*entering with Steve behind him*). Was the stolen stereo and TV in the house, Davis?

DANNY. Stolen!

DEPUTY. Yes, it was. Who is that with you, Fred?

FRED. None of your damn business. All right, Rosales, where did an unemployed Meskin like you who lives in a broken down shack like this which ain't even got a telephone, get a brand new stereo and TV?

DANNY. I rented them in San Antonio.

FRED. He rented them in San Antonio. Huh. Have you got a receipt?

DANNY. No, I left it at the store . . .

FRED (*striking Danny in the stomach*). You what! You what! Don't lie to me, boy!

DANNY. I'm telling the truth. I rented them from a store.

FRED (*kicking Danny to the floor*). You lying piece of shit! I've had just about enough of your lying and thieving. Stevie, give me that shotgun. (*Jabbing Danny with the barrel.*) Now then, are you going to tell me the truth, are you going to confess? I'll kill you, boy!

DEPUTY. Come on, Danny, tell us the truth. Where did you get them?

DANNY. I told you, I rented them from a store in San Antonio.

FRED. Let the thieving son of a bitch go! Uncuff him and let him run so I can shoot him!

DANNY. I swear to you! I haven't done anything wrong!

FRED. I'm gonna kill you! I'm gonna kill you! (*Beating him.*)

DEPUTY (*pulling Fred off*). Hey, Fred, what the hell's gotten into you?

FRED. You lying to me, boy. You've been lying to me all along! But I got you this time—dead to rights!

DEPUTY. Take it easy, Fred.

FRED. Davis, put him in the squad car. Let's go to the Old Alamo School Road, maybe his tongue will loosen up along the way.

DEPUTY. Couldn't we just lock him up overnight and call the rental place in the morning?

FRED. No, I want this cleared up now! How long you been a law enforcement officer in Arroyo County?

DEPUTY. Six months.

FRED. And you're the dumb son of a bitch who let him go in the first place. What are you, a social worker? I've been doing this for six years.

DEPUTY. But Fred, you can't be beating a prisoner like that.

FRED. Don't you know anything? (*Taking him aside, whispering.*) I'm only trying to scare him into confessing. I used to do this all the time in the C.I.D. Play along with me, tell him I'm going to shoot him if he doesn't tell the truth.

DEPUTY. O.K. Fred, we'll try it your way.

FRED. Tell him I'm a real mean son of a bitch. Tell him I killed me a Meskin before and I'm fixing to kill me another one. Bluff him. I'll follow you in my car.

ROWENA. Then, you actually heard Fred Hall threaten to kill Danny Rosales?

DEPUTY. Yes.

ROWENA. How many times?

DEPUTY. At least five times.

ROWENA. Take note, Deputy Davis heard Fred Hall threaten to kill Danny Rosales at least five times that night. No further questions at this time. I pass the witness.

HAROLD. Deputy, what was your exact title? Didn't you call yourself Assistant Chief Deputy?

DEPUTY. The title was Deputy of Chief of Police.

HAROLD. You had aspirations of becoming Chief of Police, did you not?

DEPUTY. Every police officer has ambitions of bettering himself.

HAROLD. You didn't get along with Chief Hall at all, did you?

DEPUTY. We weren't exactly the best of friends. But I never let this get in the way of our work.

HAROLD. That night at the Rosales home, when you asked Fred who he was with, why did he respond, "none of your damn business?"

DEPUTY. I guess he didn't want me to know.

HAROLD (*sarcastically*). But in no way did your personal feelings for each other get in the way of your professional duties?

DEPUTY. That's what I said.

HAROLD. O.K. Those threats he made to Rosales, things like, "I'm going to kill you" and "I killed me one Mexican and I'm fixin to kill me another one." He told you that was just a ploy to get information out of a suspected burglar, was it not?

DEPUTY. He tried to convince me, but I didn't approve of it.

HAROLD. But you went along with it!

DEPUTY. He ordered me to.

HAROLD. He told you this was an accepted tactic used by him in the Civilian Investigation Division of the United States Air Force, did he not?

DEPUTY. He did, but I really wouldn't know about the legality of that.

HAROLD. You wouldn't know, would you? Were you ever enrolled in a professional Police Training Academy or anything of that sort prior to being hired in Castroville?

DEPUTY. No sir, but I plan to go.

HAROLD. You PLAN to go! No further questions. You may step down. (*As the Deputy leaves the witness stand he encounters Fred coming in.*) I would now like to call Fred Hall to the stand.

BAILIFF. Raise your right hand. Do you swear to tell the truth, the whole truth, and nothing but the truth, so help you God?

FRED. I do.

HAROLD. Tell us your name, please.

FRED. Fred Harold Hall.

HAROLD. Mr. Hall, would you please tell the jury a little about your background, specifically any experience in previous police work.

FRED. I retired from the United States Air Force after 30 years of service. I was a Senior Master Sargeant assigned to the Civilian Investigation Division. I also served in combat in Korea, and the Vietnam conflict . . .

ROWENA. Immaterial and irrelevant.

JUDGE. Sustained.

HAROLD. Let's move on. When were you hired as Police Chief of Castroville?

FRED. When I retired from the Air Force.

HAROLD. And this was done on the basis of your previous experience in police work?

FRED. Correct.

HAROLD. Now then, that Sunday night, September 14, 1975, why did you take your future son-in-law along with you?

FRED. Well, I had been taking him along regularly to show him what police work was like. But that particular night I asked him to come along in case I needed a witness. I wanted to show Deputy Davis' error in police work because he had done so badly in the past.

HAROLD. What about that outstanding theft warrant, that business with the calf? Why did you decide to activate it against Rosales?

FRED. I had hoped to catch him with some stolen property through information provided by an informant.

HAROLD. But you weren't out to "get" Rosales, were you?

FRED. No, but there were all these trails leading to him. And when the informant told me he had a new stereo and TV, I thought I had him with the goodies.

ROWENA. Objection, hearsay.

HAROLD. I'm not going into what the informant said, your Honor, I just want to know if he was reliable.

JUDGE. Proceed.

HAROLD. Now then, was the informant reliable in the past?

FRED. Very reliable.

HAROLD. All right, tell us what happened when you went to arrest Danny Rosales at his home.

FRED. Well, as Stevie and I pulled into the driveway we saw the Deputy struggling to get Rosales into his squad car. (*Flashback. Enter Danny and Deputy.*)

DANNY. God damn it, let me go! Let me go!

DEPUTY. I should have never given you a break, Rosales.

FRED. Have you read the suspect his rights, Deputy?

DEPUTY. Yes sir.

FRED. Good. Now then, Danny, could you please tell us where you got the new stereo and television set?

DANNY. *Que chingados te importa, pinche guey!*[34]

FRED. What did he say, Davis?

DEPUTY. I don't know, Chief, but it don't sound too good.

FRED. Danny, I hate to do this. But I'm afraid we're going to have to take you down to the station and book you for possession of stolen property. Unless, of course, you can show me a receipt for the merchandise.

DANNY. I don't have to show you nothing!

FRED. Put him in the squad car, Davis. Danny Rosales, are you resisting arrest?

DANNY. *Hijos de puta!*[35] Police brutality! (*Struggling with the Deputy.*)

FRED. Deputy, why don't you take him the long way to the jail house? Maybe Danny will calm down by the time we get there.

DEPUTY. Good idea, Chief. (*Exit Deputy and Danny.*)

HAROLD. What happened then?

FRED. Well, half way down there, by the Old Alamo School Road, I got to thinking, "maybe he is telling the truth." So I signaled Davis to stop the car and turn the prisoner over to me. I figured if he was telling the truth I would let him go with a warning.

HAROLD. Now then, there was just you and Rosales out there in the woods, right?

FRED. Yes, the Deputy had left me in charge of the prisoner. Steve was in the car. Rosales and I were by the side of the road. I was still trying to question him.

HAROLD. Now, as a result to this questioning, did he make a gesture towards you?

FRED. Yes, he started coming closer to me and making threatening gestures. I remember pushing him back. At one point, I even went and got my shotgun. You see, he was unhandcuffed.

HAROLD. You had to protect yourself?

ROWENA. I object, defense is leading the witness.

JUDGE. Sustained. Watch your line of questioning, counselor.

---

[34]*Que . . . quey* What the fuck business is it of yours, fucking ass!
[35]*Hijos de puta* Sons of bitches

HAROLD. Tell us in your own words what happened that night.

FRED. He tried to grab a hold of the shotgun.

HAROLD. Show us how Rosales grabbed the shotgun.

FRED. Like this. He grabbed the barrel and tried to yank it away from me. Then he kicked me. At one point I was off my feet. I'd been kicked—just above the pelvis, I was down on one knee.

HAROLD. Mr. Hall, tell us, did you have fear and apprehension for your life?

FRED. Certainly! The thought flashed back in my mind how my gun had been taken away from me before in that liquor store, and how I had been shot three times.

HAROLD. So here was this younger, stronger man kicking you and trying to take your shotgun away, go on.

ROWENA. Your honor, please, the defense is leading the witness again!

JUDGE. Sustained! Cease this line of questioning.

HAROLD. I apologize, your Honor. Mr. Hall, I want you to look right at the jury and tell them exactly what happened that night.

FRED. I was afraid for my life. Thinking about that other fight when I was shot three times made me struggle all the harder. It was dark, he tried to yank the gun away from me and it went off.

HAROLD. Yes?

FRED. Accidentally.

HAROLD. Mr. Hall, I want you to look the jury right in the eye. Did you ever intentionally pull the trigger of that shotgun, sir?

FRED. As God is my witness, I never intended to pull the trigger and hurt that man!

HAROLD. Ladies and gentlemen, I ask you, does this man look capable of murdering in cold blood?

BERTA. He's lying! He's lying! He murdered Danny, he murdered him!

JUDGE. Mrs. Rosales, sit down, or I will be forced to remove you from this court.

BERTA. He's a killer! And you are going to let him get away with it!

JUDGE. Order, order in this court! Bailiff, remove Mrs. Rosales!

BERTA. Try the wife, try the daughter, try the son-in-law, they helped to kill my husband! (*Berta is escorted off by the Deputy.*)

ROWENA. Your Honor, I see no need to have Mrs. Rosales physically removed from this court!

JUDGE. Don't you raise your voice to me, Miss Saldivar! This court will recess for ten minutes.

ROWENA. Your Honor, I have not yet cross examined the witness!

JUDGE. Court is recessed for ten minutes!

ROWENA. Your Honor! Note my objection! Note my objection!

ACT 2

(*Lights up on the courtroom. Harold and Fred on one side, Rowena and Berta on the other.*)

HAROLD. She's going to cross examine you. Stick to the facts, and don't let her rile you.

FRED. Do you think she's going to ask Debbie to testify? My little girl doesn't have any business being up there!

HAROLD. Don't you worry about a thing. You have nothing to be ashamed of. Just stick to your story.

BERTA (*to Rowena*). How can he stand there, swear on the Bible, and lie through his teeth?

ROWENA. The problem is—the Sheriff is the only living witness to the shooting.

BERTA. Well, how's the jury going to know the truth unless you tell them?

ROWENA. Berta, we will. But we must work according to procedure. You can't go up there and try a man without evidence.

BERTA (*pointing to the audience*). But did you see their reaction? The jury believes him. They're all Anglos just like him.

ROWENA. That's because of the change of venue.

BERTA. I don't understand. How could they get away with that!

ROWENA. It's a legitimate tactic on the part of the defense, Berta. At the pre-trial hearings the defense has the right to ask the judge to change the trial from one place to another.

HAROLD. (*Flashback.*) Your Honor, I move for a change of venue on the grounds that biased publicity has made it impossible for my client to receive a fair trial here.

ROWENA. Your Honor, is the defense implying that Fred Hall cannot receive a fair trial in your court?

HAROLD. I am implying no such thing. My motion is based on evidence gathered from this radical Chicano newspaper which pictures my client as a pig and an ogre. There is a climate of racial hatred in Arroyo County that threatens to explode into riot and disorder.

ROWENA. Your Honor, of course the community is indignant. But rather than violence, they have staged some peaceful demonstrations. I fail to see how that can be labeled riot and disorder.

HAROLD. Your Honor, my client has been receiving threatening phone calls.

JUDGE. I will order a change of venue in this case. Unfortunately, there are strong racial overtones in this matter.

ROWENA. Your Honor, I submit that the question deals not so much with race, as it does with justice.

JUDGE. Trial will be held in Jim Bowie County. (*Pounding gavel is heard.*)

ROWENA (*crossing back to Berta*). That's why the trial is being held in a mostly white, Baptist county instead of

Arroyo County which has a high percentage of Mexican American voters.

BERTA. That's why the stores are closed on Sundays.

ROWENA. And then, to top it off, out of the 76 perspective jurors that were called, only three were Chicanos, and the defense rejected them.

BERTA. That's another example of their dirty tricks!

ROWENA. But the lawyers on both sides have the right to exclude or reject any juror they want.

BERTA. Is that why the jury is made up of 11 Anglos and one Black? It's not fair.

ROWENA. That's the way our system works, Berta. If only we would have had more registered voters who were Chicanos in this county. *La Raza* doesn't vote, Berta, *La Raza* doesn't vote.

BERTA. There's no one to vote for, all the politicians are alike.

ROWENA. Don't say that, Berta, the moment you throw away your vote, you lose all rights in this country.

BERTA. That's easy for you to say . . . you went to college . . . I picked crops in the fields.

ROWENA. Berta, it doesn't matter, we're in this together and we're going to win. We have all the evidence we need to convict Hall of first degree murder. We have witnesses that heard Hall threaten to kill Danny, witnesses who saw him beating Danny; we also have witnesses that saw Hall and his wife try and cover up the crime. We can't lose.

BERTA. Rowena, can't you see, I've already lost!

BAILIFF. All rise! (*Everyone stands for the unseen presence of the Judge.*)

JUDGE. Will both sides please approach the bench? (*Harold and Rowena cross to the Judge's space.*) First of all, Mr. Pearl, I want you to desist from leading the witness. Do you understand?

HAROLD. Yes, your Honor.

JUDGE. And, Miss Saldivar, I must warn you that outbursts of the kind you and your client engaged in are not tolerated in a court of law.

ROWENA. Your Honor, I apologize for having raised my voice in court and I assure you that my client will refrain from any further outbursts.

JUDGE. You may proceed, Miss Saldivar. (*Fred makes his way to the witness stand.*)

ROWENA. Now then, Mr. Hall, you told us you worked for the City of Cortezville for six years as Chief of Police. What was your salary at the time you were released, or should I say dismissed.

FRED. $450 per month.

ROWENA. $450 per month. That's not very much for a family of three, even though your wife worked part-time at the bank.

HAROLD. This is irrelevant, your Honor.

ROWENA. I will show the relevancy.

JUDGE. Proceed.

ROWENA. You took that job because you had to supplement your income with your pension from the Air Force, did you not?

FRED. That wasn't the *only* reason.

ROWENA. Now, you never went to a professional police academy prior to being hired by the City of Castroville, did you?

FRED. No.

ROWENA. When you worked for the Civilian Investigation Division you were merely a clerk, were you not?

FRED. Yes, but . . .

ROWENA. You only worked for them two years in a clerical capacity, according to your records. Yet here you were passing yourself off as some kind of secret service man. The Air Force stationed you to different jobs in different places during your 30 year stint, didn't they?

FRED. Yes, they did.

ROWENA. You're not a native Texan, are you, and yet you went around dressed like John Wayne!

HAROLD. Your Honor, irrelevant and immaterial.

ROWENA. Your Honor, I am trying to show that small towns like Castroville hire retired servicemen like Mr. Hall because they are the only ones who can afford to take the relatively low paying jobs.

HAROLD. That is an assumption, not a fact.

JUDGE. Sustained. The jury will ignore that assumption.

ROWENA. Now then, Mr. Hall, in spite of the fact that you had no formal training in police work, you claim that you performed your duties as police chief according to the letter of the law, correct?

FRED. As to the best of my ability.

ROWENA. Then why did you take Danny Rosales to a deserted country road five miles outside of town to interrogate him? Why didn't you take him to your office inside the police station?

FRED. I took him out there because I had every intention of letting him to go. I just did it to scare him.

ROWENA. While you were out there in that woodsy, rural area, did you notice any houses?

FRED. Yes, I did.

ROWENA. There were houses. Is that the reason you didn't want any lights turned on?

FRED. I don't recall that.

ROWENA. You don't recall that?

FRED. No.

ROWENA. You don't recall asking Stevie Peters where you could bury the body before it even got cold?

FRED. No, I don't.

ROWENA. You don't recall talking to your wife about taking the body to East Texas?

FRED. No, I don't.

ROWENA. Do you mean to tell the ladies and gentlemen of this jury that you don't recall driving around town with the body in the back seat of your automobile?

FRED. No, I don't.

ROWENA. Your Honor, please instruct the witness to answer the questions!

JUDGE. Mr. Hall, I don't need to remind you that you are under oath. Do you or do you not remember what happened that night?

FRED. Your Honor, I can't recall anything that happened after the gun went off. My mind is a total blank.

HAROLD. Your Honor, if I may interject a word here. Mrs. Hall testified earlier regarding my client's loss of memory due to the trauma of the wounds which he suffered in that shootout.

ROWENA. I insist that the witness answer my questions in full!

HAROLD. Your Honor, competent physicians have testified that the defendant, Fred Hall, has Alzheimer's Disease or pre-senile dementia. He is a sick man, your Honor.

JUDGE. Mr. Hall, I want you to answer the questions to the best of your ability. Proceed, Ms. Saldivar.

ROWENA. All right, let's talk about this so-called beating on your head, Mr. Hall. Did you have any x-rays taken?

FRED. No, I did not.

ROWENA. You mean to say that the doctor didn't think it was important to take x-rays of your head and yet you claim that this is the cause of your amnesia five years later?

FRED. The bullet wounds to my body were the more serious. The problems with my head turned up later.

ROWENA. Now, you testified, and I quote, "as God is my witness, I did not intend to kill that man." How come your thoughts are so clear on that point, yet on the other points, points that are damaging to your case—you can't recall?

FRED. Well, as I indicated, my thoughts, even right now, are real scrambled because of the medication. I truly believe it was an accident.

ROWENA. You believe it was an accident. Are you saying you don't know for sure?

FRED. I am saying that the whole thing has gone all kinds of ways around my head. I even dream about it. I can't actually say yes or no one way or another, but this is what I feel in my heart.

ROWENA. You only recall the things you think will help you, but you don't recall the things you think will hurt, right?

FRED. No, that is not correct.

ROWENA. That's what it sounds like to me, Mr. Hall!

HAROLD. I will object to her arguing with the witness, your Honor.

JUDGE. Disregard the statement, "It sounds like it."

ROWENA. Very well, Mr. Hall, you may step down. Let me call some witnesses which will help you to refresh your memory. I would like to recall Steve Earl Peters to the stand (*Enter Steve.*) Steve, do you know what an indictment is?

STEVE. That is when someone is charged with a crime.

ROWENA. Are you charged with a crime now by indictment?

STEVE. Yes, I am.

ROWENA. Do you also understand that you are still under oath and that perjury is a punishable offense?

HAROLD. Your Honor, I object, the Prosecution is intimidating the witness.

JUDGE. Objection sustained. Watch your line of questioning, counsel.

ROWENA. Steve, let's go back to that weekend at the home of Fred Hall, prior to Danny Rosales' arrest. (*Flashback.*)

STEVE. Well, we got back from the stakeout late Saturday night. We all sat down and had a cold drink. Of course, I was so excited I could hardly wait to tell Debbie about the wedding. (*Enter Debbie, Fred, and Grace.*)

STEVE. Hey, honey pie, guess what! I talked to your Dad!

DEBBIE. Oh, Steve, you didn't! (*Hugging Steve.*)

STEVE. He said we could get married!

DEBBIE. Wonderful!!! (*Throwing herself in his arms.*)

FRED. This calls for a drink.

GRACE. Is the June wedding on?

ROWENA (*from the side*). How many drinks did you have, Steve?

STEVE. About three or four. Debbie, I'm going to make you the happiest woman alive!

ROWENA. Exactly what were you drinking?

STEVE. Margaritas! Margaritas! How many kids do you want to have, Deb?

DEBBIE. Oh, Stevie, lots and lots!

STEVE. Hey, how about another pitcher of margaritas?

GRACE. Coming right up!

ROWENA. Was Fred drinking margaritas that day?

STEVE (*suddenly realizing what he said*). No, not margaritas, ice tea! We were drinking ice tea.

ROWENA. You're under oath, Stevie.

STEVE. Yes, he was drinking margaritas.

ROWENA. Was he drunk when he went to arrest Danny Rosales?

STEVE. No, he was fine. He could really hold his liquor!

ROWENA. Was Fred Hall consuming anything other than margaritas that weekend?

GRACE. Fred, what are you doing? You know the doctor told you not to drink and take pain killers at the same time! (*Fade on Hall family.*)

ROWENA. Ladies and gentlemen of the jury, take note! Fred Hall was taking pain killers and washing them down with margaritas prior to Danny Rosales' arrest. Now then, Steve, did you, at any time, participate in the beating of Danny Rosales?

STEVE. No, I was just holding the shotgun.

ROWENA. Did you point the shotgun at Rosales?

STEVE. No! In fact, the Chief took the gun away from me and pointed it at Danny's head.

ROWENA. Why did he continue beating him even after Rosales denied stealing anything?

STEVE. I don't know. He just had this thing for Rosales. We talked about it while we were out by the Old Alamo School Road waiting for Davis to bring the prisoner. (*Flashback.*) Hey Chief, how come you hit him so hard?

FRED. I told you Steve, when you're dealing with people like that you gotta be real firm. (*Holding shotgun.*) You got to put the fear of God in them. This is the only language they understand.

STEVE. Yeah, 'sides, they don't talk English none too good.

FRED. Damn people breed like rabbits, end up having 15 kids and living on welfare. And our tax dollars pay for it. Before long they'll out number us and take over. We oughta deport them, don't make no difference if they was born here or not. Now, this particular guy is the worst of the lot. Did I tell you I seen him eyeing Debbie?

STEVE. What do you mean, "eyeing her?"

FRED. He was sniffing around her. One time, after I dropped her off at the bus station, I got back in the car and saw Rosales sitting next to her, grinning at me!

STEVE. That damn greaser! (*Enter Debbie and Danny.*)

DANNY (*seated, as though on the Greyhound bus*). Oh, I've been coming up to the United States since I was a little boy. My family and I picked crops all over the country. Of course, I was never able to get a good education. My father's dream was to settle down in one place so we could go to school.

DEBBIE (*sitting next to him*). I can't imagine what it's like to be so destitute.

DANNY. Destitute?

DEBBIE. You know, poor.

DANNY. Destitute means poor? Well, we were so destitute, we couldn't even afford to use the word destitute.

DEBBIE. You like Texas better than Mexico?

DANNY. Yes, there's more jobs here. Although the people on my father's side immigrated to Mexico from Texas.

DEBBIE. Oh really, how can that be?

DANNY. The Navarros were Tejanos, the original settlers of *Tejas*. My great-great grandfather had a *rancho* around the San Antonio area, but his children moved south to Nuevo Leon, Mexico.

DEBBIE. Really?

DANNY. Remember, it used to be a part of Mexico.

DEBBIE. But of course!

DANNY. What about you? Where were your people from?

DEBBIE. Well, my daddy's an adopted Texan because he was born in the North. But my mother's family all came from Alsace, a region in France, in 1844. They were the first white settlers of Castroville. In fact, that's why Castroville is known as "The Little Alsace of Texas."

DANNY. I didn't know that.

DEBBIE. I was always rather proud of that, knowing that we were "original Texans." (*Fade on flashback.*)

FRED (*to the Deputy as he brings Danny in*). Well, it's about time you got here! Now then, Rosales, where did you get that stereo and TV?

DANNY. Mr. Hall, you're making a big mistake. I rented them from a store in San Antonio.

FRED (*striking Danny*). You're a lying son of a bitch! Unhandcuff him, Davis, let him run so I can shoot him!

DEPUTY. Hey, come on, Fred, that's enough!

FRED. I said, unhandcuff him, that's an order!

DEPUTY. All right, let me have the flashlight so I can see what I am doing.

FRED. No, no flashlights. I don't want no lights.

DEPUTY (*down on his knees trying to unhandcuff Danny*). But I can't see to get the handcuffs off him.

FRED. Steve, close that door! I don't want no car lights, no flashlights, no cigarettes.

DEPUTY. There, I got the handcuffs off of him, now what are you going to do?

FRED (*stage whisper to Deputy*). I'm bluffing! Play along. (*In a louder voice.*) Go back to Castroville, Davis.

DEPUTY. Fred, stop this shit, it ain't working!

FRED (*getting mad now*). Davis, you bastard, I gave you an order!

DEPUTY. He's my prisoner!

FRED (*threatening Deputy with shotgun*). Fuck you! Now, git! (*Deputy exits murder scene, stand off to the side.*) Now then, *Senor* Rosales, this is your last chance . . . (*Leading Danny offstage.*)

ROWENA (*voice only*). Deputy, what was going through your mind when the police chief threatened you with the shotgun and told you to go back to Castroville?

DEPUTY. Being relatively new on the job and all, I was thinking that maybe he was trying to put me through some kind of test to see how sharp I was.

ROWENA. So, you disobeyed his order?

DEPUTY. Yes, I had the feeling, an intuition, that something was wrong. He said he was play acting, but there was something deadly going on.

ROWENA. What did you do?

DEPUTY. I drove about 200 yards or so down the road, cut the radio and lights, and sat there about two or three minutes. Then I heard what sounded like a shot. (*Shot is heard.*)

ROWENA. Steve, you were in the car. Could you see what was happening out there?

STEVE. None too good. The moon was bright that night, but they were both standing behind the car, two or three feet away from each other, arguing back and forth. Mr. Hall pushed him with the butt of the gun, and then with the barrel.

ROWENA. What did Danny Rosales do?

STEVE. He pushed the barrel of the gun away. Mr. Hall went towards him and then I heard the shot. (*Shot is heard.*)

ROWENA (*voice*). Did you see what happened?

STEVE. No, they were in my blind spot. (*To Fred.*) What was that! Fred! Fred!

FRED. He wrestled with the gun, Stevie. It went off . . . and it killed him.

STEVE. Jesus, what are you going to do now?

FRED. I don't know, it was an accident, but nobody will ever believe me.

STEVE. Let's get the hell outa here!

FRED. Wait. There's a light! Somebody's coming. Move away from here. (*They walk in the direction of the Deputy.*)

DEPUTY. What happened? I heard a shot. Fred, where's Rosales? I want to know right now, the bullshit's over.

FRED. Stevie, uh, get back in the car. Come here, Davis, I want to tell you something.

DEPUTY. Just cut the bullshit, Fred. What's going on? Where's Rosales?

FRED. If you shut up, I'll tell you. Well, Davis, I, uh, killed him!

DEPUTY. You what? How did you do it? What happened, where is he?

FRED. No, I don't kill him. I was just blowing smoke at you. I just winged him is all.

DEPUTY. Where did you "wing" him?

FRED. Right up here, under the left armpit. But he's all right.

DEPUTY. What the hell are you talking about?

FRED. I was just joking.

DEPUTY. I said cut the bullshit. What did you do to Rosales?

FRED. I'll tell you the truth. He tripped me and I fell. That's when the gun went off accidentally. Then he ran away.

DEPUTY. Which way did he go?

FRED. He ran into the woods. He's all right. I just scared him.

DEPUTY. God damn it! You better tell me the truth, Fred.

FRED. I am. Look for yourself. This is the spot where he took off from. If he's here, he'd be in that ditch.

DEPUTY. Come on down here, help me look. (*Fred makes no effort to look.*)

FRED. Is he there?

DEPUTY. I don't see anything.

FRED. He's probably on his way home right now.

DEPUTY. Are you telling me the truth? Why did you tell me you killed him?

FRED. I was just testing you to see how you would handle a situation like this. Say, now, what would you tell the Sheriff's office? He was supposed to have been at the county jail 20 minutes ago.

DEPUTY. I don't know, what am I supposed to tell them?

FRED. Well, you could call the dispatcher and tell him that your prisoner escaped somewhere off Highway 90.

DEPUTY. Now, what in the hell am I going to do that for? In the first place, we're not anywhere near Highway 90. In the second place, you had charge of the prisoner.

FRED. You're a jerk, do you know that? You're never gonna make it around this police department or any other police department. When a superior officer gives you an order you obey it!

DEPUTY. Look, first you told me you shot the man, then you told me you didn't. And then you told me something else, I don't know whether to believe you or not. But let me tell you something, I'm not going to lie for you or anybody else.

FRED. O.K. Go on, get the fuck out of here!

DEPUTY. I'll see you back at the county jail, *Chief*. (*Deputy exits, goes to the stand.*)

HAROLD. Now then, Deputy Davis, if you were so certain that Chief Hall killed Danny Rosales, why didn't you arrest him right then and there?

DEPUTY. I couldn't prove anything because there was no body.

HAROLD. Did you actually see Fred Hall shoot Danny Rosales?

DEPUTY. No, but I heard . . .

HAROLD. You were 200 yards away in your squad car. How do you know what was going on out there? Just answer yes or no. Did you see Hall shoot Rosales?

DEPUTY. No, sir.

HAROLD. One more question. Were you granted immunity from prosecution by the State of Texas?

DEPUTY. Yes, sir, I was.

HAROLD. So, in return for this immunity you have agreed to come forward with the most damaging testimony you can think of to bury Fred, isn't that right?

DEPUTY. No, sir, that's not right. The statement I made was written four months before I was granted immunity.

HAROLD. The District Attorney didn't come along at that time and tell you, "now, if you behave and be a good boy and tell us what we want to hear you won't get prosecuted," right?

DEPUTY. No, sir, that's not true. I made an oath at the very beginning to uphold the laws of the State of Texas. That's exactly what I told Mrs. Rosales when she came looking for her husband at the police station the night he was killed. (*Flashback.*)

BERTA. Deputy, where's my husband? They say they haven't seen him at the booking desk and it's way past midnight?

DEPUTY. I honestly don't know where he is, Mrs. Rosales.

BERTA. What do you mean? You arrested him two hours ago.

DEPUTY. Mrs. Rosales, there's nothing I can tell you right now, believe me. If any information comes in you'll be the first to know. Now, if you'll excuse me, there's some problems here at the jail, seems like there's a riot going on or something.

BERTA. You expect us to be treated like this? You arrest my husband and say you're going to take him to jail and he's no where to be found!

DEPUTY. Please, I'm trying to do everything I can to find out what happened to your husband.

BERTA. No you're not, what do you care? To you Danny is just another Mexican.

DEPUTY. That's not true, Mrs. Rosales. Less than a month ago, I gave Danny a break, not because he was brown or green or any other color, but because I believed he'd live up to his word.

BERTA. Where's my husband? Is he hurt? Tell me where to look for him.

DEPUTY. Why don't you ask his *friend*, Kiki Ventura.

BERTA. I don't care about him, all I care about is Danny.

DEPUTY. You better care. The only difference between Kiki and Judas is that Judas hung himself. But I promise you one thing, everybody's going to get what's coming to them, everybody.

DEBBIE (*back at the witness stand, Debbie has been sworn in and has begun her testimony*). It was late, but Mama and I were sitting up talking . . . Mama, what are you doing up so late?

GRACE. Waiting for your father and reading the Good Book.

DEBBIE. Oh, how exciting.

GRACE. It is dear, it's the best seller of all time.

DEBBIE. I thought *Gone with the Wind* was.

GRACE. Do you want to know what passage I was reading?

DEBBIE. Sure.

GRACE. Corinthians 6:19. "Know ye not that your body is the temple of the Holy Spirit?"

DEBBIE. Oh, Mama, not again.

GRACE. The Bible says that thou shalt not defile the body with immorality. Debbie, does Stevie ever touch you?

DEBBIE. Of course he touches me, he touches me all the time.

GRACE. Debbie, you know what I mean. Does he touch you—you know, where he shouldn't?

DEBBIE. Of course not, I wouldn't let him touch me there.

GRACE. I know he kisses you good night, because I've seen the two of you on the front porch, but does he ever, I don't know how to say this—does he ever stick his tongue in your mouth!

DEBBIE. Oh, Mama! Of course not!

GRACE. I know you're a good girl, Debbie, I just want to make sure you save yourself for your wedding night.

DEBBIE. Mama, you know something, I just made up my mind this very night! There will be no wedding!

GRACE. Debbie, you can't be serious. We told all our friends and relatives. (*A car pulls into the driveway, Grace reacts.*) Is that your Daddy and Steve?

DEBBIE. Stevie says he wants to start having lots of kids. Sometimes I think the only reason he wants to get married is so he can sleep with me!

GRACE. Debbie, don't say things like that. (*She is looking out the window.*) (*Steve runs into the house past Grace.*) Hello, Stevie dear.

STEVE. Hello, Mrs. Hall. (*He stands nervously by Debbie's side as she ignores him.*)

GRACE (*opening the screen door and going out to the driveway*). Fred, what are you doing? Did you know there was another disturbance at the county jail? I heard it on the radio.

FRED (*sitting behind the wheel, exhausted*). I can't go.

GRACE. Fred, what's the matter with you? Is your stomach bothering you again? You've been working too hard. You're not going out again, are you?

FRED. Have to.

GRACE. Well, at least let me drive, scoot over. (*Noticing someone is in the back seat.*) My God, is that somebody in the back seat!

STEVE. Debbie, did a guy named Danny Rosales ever speak to you or anything like that?

DEBBIE. Yeah, sure, so what?

STEVE. Just answer my question.

DEBBIE. We talked once on the Greyhound to San Antonio. He was kind of nice, uneducated, but nice.

STEVE. Did Rosales ever touch you or try to make a pass at you?

DEBBIE. Why are you asking me these questions? What are you—my father?

STEVE. Debbie, your father just shot Rosales to death!

DEBBIE (*breaking away from Steve, into a flashback*). Daddy killed Danny!

GRACE (*as Fred enters, followed by Grace*). Answer me. Fred! Where is the Deputy? What did you do, for God's sake! (*Fred sits silently.*) Stevie, what happened?

STEVE. Fred said it was an accident. I don't really know, I didn't see it.

DEBBIE. Daddy, are you all right? You look so pale. What's this on your uniform?

GRACE. Debbie, pour your father a cup of coffee, he needs to think straight.

DEBBIE. Blood stains!

FRED. Get me a beer.

GRACE. No more drinking, Fred. Now tell me, why are you so worried? You said it was an accident.

FRED. Too many witnesses.

STEVE. I think I better go home. Goodnight, Debbie.

GRACE. Stevie Peters, you stay put. Let me tell you something about this family. We stick together, you hear? If you're going to be a part of it you got to stick with us come hell or high water, you hear?

STEVE. Yes 'um.

FRED. Got to get rid of the body.

DEBBIE. Why don't you just take it to the funeral home?

FRED. Give me a drink!

GRACE. I said, no more drinking! Now, listen to me, you and Stevie clean up the back seat of the car and put the body in the trunk. Hurry up, before it gets light.

FRED. You're right, you're right. Come on, Steve. (*They exit.*)

GRACE. Debbie?

DEBBIE. Yes, Mama.

GRACE. You'd do anything for your Daddy, wouldn't you dear?

DEBBIE. Of course.

GRACE. Your father is very sick, you know.

DEBBIE. From the shootout and all?

GRACE. That's right, dear, we have to protect him. Especially when he makes a mistake like he did tonight.

DEBBIE. What are we going to do, Mama?

GRACE. I think we're going to have to go for a little ride, dear. You and I are going to have to help your Daddy dispose of that body.

DEBBIE. What!

STEVE (*entering*). It's all done. We moved the body into the trunk and the Chief's hosing down the back seat. I gotta go now, Mrs. Hall.

DEBBIE. Stevie, Mama needs someone to help her . . . get rid of that body.

STEVE. Listen, I have to go to work tomorrow. I've done more than my share.

DEBBIE. Stevie, she wants me to go with her!

STEVE. Mrs. Hall, can't you just go to the county jail and tell them the truth? Fred's the Chief of Police, they'll protect him.

GRACE. There's a riot going on! That Mexican Independence Day Celebration turned into a riot. This could have something to do with it.

STEVE. Well, I'm sorry, I've got to go. (*Turning to leave.*)

DEBBIE (*blocking his way*). Stevie, go in my place, please!

STEVE. No, I can't deal with this anymore, I just can't.

DEBBIE. Please, Stevie, I love you. I'll do anything, anything. (*Clinging to him.*)

STEVE. They're your parents!

DEBBIE. I don't want nothing to do with it!

STEVE (*flinging her to the floor*). I told you, I done my share! (*Exit Steve.*)

FRED (*coming upon Debbie on the floor, comforting her*). What's going on here!

GRACE. You tell me!

FRED. I don't know.

GRACE. The only place I can think of is my brother's ranch, in Carthage, by the Louisiana Border.

FRED. 500 miles away?

GRACE. Exactly.

FRED. I'll clean up and get started.

GRACE. No, you stay here in case they come looking for you. And take off that blood stained uniform, I'll throw it in the washer.

DEBBIE. Daddy! She wants me to go with her!

FRED. Grace, I don't think this child . . .

GRACE. I need her to help me with the driving. You stay here and go to work in the morning as though nothing had happened. And call in sick for me at the bank.

FRED. I know I could count on you, Grace. (*They embrace and kiss.*)

GRACE. I love you, Fred. (*Fred exits.*)

DEBBIE. I don't want to go!

GRACE. Hush up, girl! From now on we do what I say! (*They exit.*)

KIKI (*on another part of the stage*). Hey, Berta, what are you doing out so late? *Sabes que,*[36] I got some money for Danny! Here, now he can pay off the farmer.

BERTA (*taking the money*). Where did you get this money?

KIKI. My *Abuelita* died and gave it to me.

BERTA. Does your *Abuelita* wear a badge and carry a SHOT-GUN?

KIKI. What are you talking about, Berta?

BERTA. I thought you were Danny's friend.

KIKI. I am. I am his best friend.

BERTA. Then, how could you lie to the police, how could you take their money?

KIKI. Hey now, don't be accusing anybody of being a snitch. People get hurt for less.

BERTA. *Mentiroso!*[37] you told the police that Danny stole a new stereo and TV.

KIKI. That's a lie!

BERTA. And do you know where they took him? To the Old Alamo School Road. You know what they do to Chicanos down there—they beat the hell out of them!

KIKI. *Chingao,*[38] Berta. Is that what they did, *lo llevaron alli? Hijos de puta!*[39]

BERTA. What did you tell them about Danny?

KIKI. Nothing. The sheriff was angry at me for making him wait four hours by the side of the road. All I said was that Danny had a new stereo and TV. I had to tell him *something.*

BERTA. *Madre de Dios!*

KIKI. He wanted to get Danny, I don't know why. I just told him the first crazy thing that came to the top of my head. I swear, Berta, I didn't mean to hurt Danny. The Sheriff was going to beat me, he was going to throw me in jail.

BERTA. So you turned Danny in to take your place!

KIKI. I didn't mean it. They were going to send me away for a long time. *Tu sabes,* I have to survive, I live from day to day, sleeping in the back seat of my car half the time. I ain't got nothing, I never had nothing.

BERTA. Neither did Danny. But at least he was trying to go straight. I hate you! I hope you burn in hell! I wish you were dead!

KIKI. Berta, don't you see, I am dead! (*Exit.*)

DEBBIE (*back at the witness stand*). It was the most horrible experience of my life. There we were, on the expressway in the middle of the morning rush hour with a dead body in the trunk! None of us had much sleep. We didn't know what had caused the accident. Daddy was in a state of shock. He couldn't answer my mother's questions. She had always depended upon him for everything. The drive

---

[36]*Sabes que* You know   [37]*Mentiroso* Liar   [38]*Chingao* Fuck   [39]*lo . . . puta!* they took him there? Bastards!

took six hours. I remember stopping along the way and buying some shovels and a digger. It was the month of September and it was still very hot.

GRACE. The sun is so bright today, like a blinding white disk.

DEBBIE. I never seen so many dead animals on the road in all my life.

GRACE. Look how brown and dried the earth is.

DEBBIE. Just like Danny back there.

GRACE. There's the start of my brother's ranch, 300 acres.

DEBBIE. Mama, what if somebody sees us?

GRACE. Don't worry, I used to play here when I was a little girl. I know a spot no one will ever find.

DEBBIE. I'm not going anywhere near him!

GRACE. Debbie, I didn't expect you to!

DEBBIE. How are you going to bury him all by yourself?

GRACE. Simple. I'll back the car up near the space for the grave, wrap the rope around the body, loop it over a tree branch, and hoist it up out of the car trunk.

DEBBIE. How long do you think it's going to take to dig a grave in this hard clay earth?

GRACE. Don't you worry, I'll do all the digging.

DEBBIE. But Mother, why did you bring two shovels?

GRACE (starting to dig the grave). After all this is over, we'll go up to our cabin at Lake Austin and relax.

DEBBIE. Mama, what happens to a man's spirit when he dies?

GRACE. Well, if he believes that Christ is the Savior, then he'll be with Him. Honey, don't worry yourself about things like that. I know that you're thinking about that boy, but there's nothing we can do to bring him back to life. We have to think of the living.

DEBBIE. But Mama, there's too many witnesses! Even Daddy said so. Maybe we should just tell the truth.

GRACE. What is the truth?

DEBBIE. That it was an accident, that Daddy didn't mean to do it. Don't you see we're just making matters worse by trying to cover it up. Why don't we just go to a police station and tell them the truth?

GRACE. Debbie, I got too many things on my mind to argue with you. Besides, the truth will come out in the end, it always does. Now then, I'm going to dig a small grave and conceal the body. This clay earth will protect it until such a time as we need to retrieve it. Hand me some of those plastic bags.

DEBBIE. What are you going to use them for?

GRACE. To cover up his face and chest and other portions of his body.

DEBBIE. What for?

GRACE. You don't want dirt falling on his face, do you? (Blackout.)

DEPUTY (with Berta at the front door of the Hall home). Fred! Fred! Mrs. Rosales wanted to talk to you and asked me to come along with her.

FRED. Well, good morning, Mrs. Rosales, what can I do for you?

BERTA. I want to know what you did to my husband.

FRED. Well, he's in a lot of trouble. Not only did he escape my custody, but he attempted to assault a law officer.

BERTA. That's a lie. If he had escaped, he would have gotten word to me.

FRED. Maybe he's out having a little drink with the boys.

BERTA. You beat him, didn't you? And then you shot him!

FRED. Mrs. Rosales, I think you'd better get off my property.

BERTA. What have you done to my husband?

FRED. The last time I saw him he was high-tailing it through the woods.

BERTA. Then how do you explain his boot and the pool of dried blood I found near the side of the road?

FRED. Is that true, Davis?

DEPUTY. That's right, Fred, we spent all morning out there. There's dried blood and lots of it.

FRED. Well, that don't prove nothing. The gun did go off accidently, I could have wounded him, but he ran off! Besides, there's no body, where's the body?

DEPUTY. Fred, I think you'd better come down to the station and answer some questions.

FRED. Yeah, sure, I got nothing to hide.

DEPUTY. One more thing, Fred, let's see your sawed off shotgun. (Blackout.)

GRACE (later on that afternoon at Lake Austin). There, you see, we made it, safe and sound.

DEBBIE. It was such a long drive.

GRACE. Texas is a country all unto itself, darling.

DEBBIE. Who would have thought it would have taken six hours to dig that grave.

GRACE. You don't get any blood on your clothes, did you?

DEBBIE. Only on my hands.

GRACE. Now then, we have one more little task to do and then we'll be all done.

DEBBIE. What now?

GRACE. The trunk. First we have to get rid of the shovels and digger. Then we have to scrub it down real good.

DEBBIE. Oh no, not again!

GRACE. We'll scrub it until it's clean as a whistle!

DEBBIE. Mama, I still don't understand why we're going through all of this. You say we have every intention of telling the truth, of going back there and uncovering the body and clearing Daddy's name! Why are we here in Lake Austin hiding from everybody?

GRACE. We're not hiding! (She opens the trunk and takes out the shovels.) We're just waiting until your father can get his wits back together again and explain this unfortunate incident.

DEBBIE. Mother, I'm going to be sick.

GRACE. Hand me the cleaning detergent and that towel. (As she pulls out some plastic bags.)

DEBBIE (covering her face with her hands). What's in those plastic bags!

GRACE. Nothing, now just relax!

DEPUTY (entering rather suddenly). Excuse me! Mrs. Hall?

GRACE. Oh, my goodness, you startled me! What are you doing here, Deputy? Is something the matter?

DEPUTY. Is this your daughter, Debbie?

DEBBIE. No, I'm Berta Rosales.

GRACE. Debbie! These children have no respect nowadays.

DEPUTY. Mind if I take a look at the inside of your trunk?

GRACE. Why, whatever are you looking for?

DEPUTY. Two shovels and digger. (*Commenting on the tools.*) God, what is that awful smell!

GRACE. Well, you see, officer we just got done burying an old dog of ours.

DEBBIE. That's right, and his name was Danny Rosales. Only, you know something, we couldn't get his eyes closed! (*Blackout.*)

JUDGE (*back at the trial*). Ladies and gentlemen of the jury, I want to remind you that this is a two-stage trial and that your first task is to decide on the guilt or innocence of the defendant. Your second task is to assess the punishment. First you must find the defendant, Fred Hall, (1) guilty of murder in the first degree or, (2) guilty of aggravated assault, or (3) not guilty as charged. Proceed with the closing arguments.

ROWENA. Ladies and gentlemen, this is more than just another case of murder in a small Texas town. What is being tried here is the American system of justice and whether or not all the people have the inalienable rights promised to them by the Constitution of the United States.

HAROLD. Ladies and gentlemen of the jury, Ms. Saldivar would have us believe that the American judicial system is on trial here. That is not the case, what is on trial is whether or not an officer of the law has the right to defend himself under attack.

ROWENA. On the eve of my involvement in this case, I reaffirmed my professional commitment not to identify too closely with my client, a rule which we were taught in law school. But the violent manner in which Danny Rosales died tore away the veil of my impartiality.

HAROLD. The prosecutor has admitted being blinded by her emotional involvement in this case. Consequently, she has turned this trial into an arena for her political crusading. But she will find no scapegoat here, no sacrifice to appease the masses.

ROWENA. Danny Rosales was accused of a crime he did not commit, arrested in his home, beaten without cause in his driveway, dragged into the woods, beaten again, and then shot to death at point blank range by the highest ranking law enforcement officer of the town in which he lived. If this could happen to Danny Rosales, it could happen to me or you.

HAROLD. If my client is guilty of anything, he is guilty of being over-zealous in his dedication to duty; a man who served his country for 30 years in the United States Air Force, a God fearing family man who almost gave up his life three years ago in an exchange of gunfire with three suspects in a liquor store. And yet the prosecution paints him as a sadistic racist.

ROWENA. Ladies and gentlemen, if you decide in your wisdom that this was not first degree murder, which I most certainly think it was, then surely Fred Hall can be found guilty of nothing less than an aggravated assault in which he caused the death of Danny Rosales through his negligence. According to the coroner's report, the sawed-off double barreled LeFever shotgun was no more than three and a half feet from the point of impact and wadding from the shell was found imbedded in Danny's chest. Was this negligence? No, this was an execution-style murder.

HAROLD. Let us examine what happened that night. While there is no denying that Fred Hall was carrying a shotgun when he arrested Danny Rosales, there is also no denying that Rosales attacked Hall. There was a struggle; Rosales grabbed the shotgun with both hands, kicked Hall to the ground, and while attempting to seize the weapon, it discharged, accidently. It was self defense, not murder.

ROWENA. Now we come to the gruesome cover up attempt. And please keep in mind that by your actions today we will judge those who helped Fred Hall cover up the crime tomorrow. How could this so-called devoted father and husband allow his wife and daughter to become involved in this macabre affair? And to those of you who say that Fred Hall was temporarily out of his mind, I say, he—with the help of his wife—coldly and calculatingly tried to occult the deed by disposing of the evidence 500 miles from the scene of the crime.

HAROLD. Ladies and gentlemen, if Fred Hall was going to go out there and kill somebody on purpose do you think he would take this boy who was going to be his son-in-law to witness a killing? Does that make any sense?

ROWENA. Why was Danny Rosales killed? Was it because he was born poor? Was it because he was caught stealing in the past? Was it because he was too proud to confess to a crime he did not commit? Or was it because he was a Mexican?

HAROLD. Race had nothing to do with this! We give our police officers the right to bear arms. How can we expect them to perform their duty if they are brought to trial each and every time there is a confrontation with a common criminal? It is time that we stopped coddling and indulging the criminals and started caring more about the police officers.

ROWENA. But does a badge and a uniform give them the license to kill?

HAROLD. Examine your hearts and find the only possible verdict . . .

ROWENA. Guilty!

HAROLD. Not guilty!

FRED. Oh God. They're trying to pin First Degree Murder on me!

GRACE. No, Fred, you're going to be freed!

BERTA. We want justice! *Queremos justicia!*[40]

ROWENA. You'll have it, I promise!

JUDGE. Ladies and gentlemen of the jury, have you arrived at a verdict? Hand it to the Bailiff, Mr. Hall, please rise. (*Fred rises.*) The jury finds the defendant, Fred Hall, guilty . . . of aggravated assault.

FRED (*hugging Grace*). Oh God!

HAROLD (*to Fred and Grace*). It could have been worse.

BERTA. Aggravated assault! Aggravated assault? Rowena . . .

ROWENA. It means that Hall caused Danny's death. But it is a term usually associated with traffic accidents.

BERTA. Traffic accidents!

JUDGE. We have now reached the second point of the trial, which is where you, the jury, deliberate and decide upon the appropriate punishment that should be assessed in this case. Counselors will make their final statements.

ROWENA. Ladies and gentlemen, it is not our place to question the wisdom that you have used in arriving at a verdict of guilty of aggravated assault. But I think that the situation cries out for punishment in this case, and the punishment you have found the defendant guilty of is two to ten years in prison. Now, the defense has filed a motion asking that you consider probation for the defendant. This would be like letting Fred Hall go scot-free for the killing of Danny Rosales. Mr. Pearl made the statement that the law allows a man like Mr. Hall to carry a 12 gauge sawed-off shotgun. That is true, but along with that privilege came the responsibility to use it with discretion and extreme caution. There is a saying, originally in Latin, that goes, "Who will guard the guards?" I am talking about guards who could preserve any type of oppression they care to. Who will guard your liberty and mine? I think your verdict should speak to that question. Do not probate the sentence of two to ten years. Probation is no punishment and without punishment we have no protection. That is our system of justice.

HAROLD. May it please the Court, ladies and gentlemen of the jury, the verdict at which you arrived was probably a very just one. You felt that the gun was not handled properly and that it caused the death of a man. That is now history. When I was selecting you I told you that the defense was going to be looking for the God-like qualities in you. We are created in God's image and we are the only creatures that have the ability to show mercy and compassion, just as God is merciful and compassionate. No matter what we do here today we cannot bring life back to Danny Rosales. Please, we have heard one terrible tragedy, don't cap it with another. Please, for your sakes, don't let another tragedy occur. Each and everyone of us has to look at ourselves in the mirror each morning.

Make sure what you do here today you can be proud of tomorrow. Fred Hall is a man of good reputation who has never been convicted of a felony. I urge you to probate him. Thank you.

JUDGE. Ladies and gentlemen of the jury, have you arrived at a verdict?

BAILIFF. They have, your Honor.

JUDGE. Hand it to the Bailiff, please. I will read the verdict. "The jury, having found the defendant, Fred Hall, guilty of the offense of aggravated assault, a third degree felony, assesses the defendant's punishment as confinement in the Texas Department of Corrections for a period of not less than two nor more than ten years."

GRACE. Oh Jesus! Oh sweet Jesus! (*Embracing Fred, crying.*)

HAROLD. It's the best we could do, Fred.

STEVE. Mr. Hall . . . I'm sorry.

FRED. It's all right, Steve. Just promise me you'll take care of Debbie.

HAROLD (*walking over to Rowena*). Congratulations, counselor.

ROWENA. For what?

HAROLD. For winning the case. My client was found guilty.

ROWENA. You know damn well that with time off for good behavior he could be out in 20 months.

HAROLD. True, but he's going to have to serve some time. Look, why don't we go have a drink and talk about the case?

ROWENA. No thanks, I'm going to be too busy filing for a Department of Justice investigation into this case.

HAROLD. Ms. Saldivar, you know you can't try a man twice for the same crime.

ROWENA. But you can try a man for violating another man's civil rights.

HAROLD. Don't waste your time, counselor, don't waste your time. (*Exits.*)

BERTA. Civil rights? What does that mean, Rowena? What about his life, can they bring back his life?

ROWENA. Berta, listen to me, we're not through yet, we're going to fight this all the way . . .

BERTA. I'm being sued by the funeral home, did you know that! I can't even afford to buy Pampers for the baby!

ROWENA. Berta, listen, we're going to do fund raisers, protest marches, letters to Congress, radio and TV appeals . . .

BERTA. I don't care what you do, Rowena. I've had it with the courts and the police and the *gringos*. Rowena, *crees que todavia estas en* law school?[41] This is Texas, not Harvard! There's no justice for us here. (*Exits.*)

DEPUTY. Miss Saldivar.

ROWENA. Yes, Deputy.

---

[40]*Queremos justicia!* We want justice!

[41]**crees . . . en law school** Do you think that you are still in law school?

DEPUTY. Did you hear? We finally caught the town burglar. Do you know who it was?

ROWENA. No.

DEPUTY. Kiki Ventura!

ROWENA. That figures.

DEPUTY. But what really riles me is that Grace Hall pleaded "no contest" to the charge of concealing physical evidence and was only fined $49.50 in court costs.

ROWENA. Forty-nine dollars and fifty cents! If Danny weighed 154 pounds at the time of his death, that means she got off with about three pounds per dollar! (*Rowena and the Deputy fade into the background as two spots shine on Debbie and Berta.*)

BERTA. They killed my husband many times.

DEBBIE. Stevie and I are getting married next Saturday.

BERTA. Once when he was born poor.

DEBBIE. All our family and friends will be at the wedding.

BERTA. Once when he didn't get a decent education.

DEBBIE. A Country and Western band will be playing.

BERTA. Once with a shotgun on the Old Alamo School Road.

DEBBIE. We'll have *fajitas* and kegs of Lone Star beer.

BERTA. Once with a pick and shovel near the Louisiana border.

DEBBIE. We're going to Las Vegas for our honeymoon.

BERTA. Once in a court of law.

DEBBIE. We plan to have lots of kids.

BERTA. My son will never know his father.

DEBBIE. I'll be dressed in white.

BERTA. I'll be dressed in black.

ROWENA. Two years after Danny Rosales' death, we realized a great victory. Fred and Grace Hall were indicted by a federal grand jury. They were eventually found guilty of violating Danny's civil rights. Fred Hall was sentenced to life in prison, and Grace Hall was sentenced to three years in prison. But was this such a great victory? Did you hear what happened in Mejia, Texas, a couple of years ago? Three black men drowned while in police custody. And just last year in San Antonio they shot another *Mexicano* . . . (*Fade.*)

THE END

TOPICS FOR CRITICAL THINKING AND WRITING

📖 THE PLAY ON THE PAGE

1. Given the evidence that is presented to the jury—the testimony of witnesses in response to questions by lawyers—do you think the decision that the first court reached is clearly wrong? (Remember, a jury is to decide only on the basis of the evidence presented to it, *not* on the basis of its intuitions.)

2. One reviewer of the play said that the characters were too sharply distinguished, good versus bad. Do you agree? Consider the two chief characters. What (if anything) can be said on behalf of Fred Hall, and what (if anything) can be said against Rosales? Also consider two of the lesser characters, for instance, the Judge and Grace.

3. When Grace and Debbie are digging the grave, they talk about the truth. Grace asks, "What is the truth?" and after Debbie's response Grace says, "[T]he truth will come out in the end . . . ." Do you think that Grace means what she says about the truth's coming out, or do you think her words are unconsciously ironic. (On *irony*, see the Glossary.) Is Morton being ironic?

🎭 THE PLAY ON THE STAGE

4. An earlier published version began with this dialogue:

ROWENA. In September 1975, on a moonlit gravel road five miles west of town, Fred Hall, the 52-year-old police chief, put the barrel of a 12-gauge sawed-off shotgun under the left armpit of Danny Rosales and pulled the trigger.

(*Behind scrim, in silhouette, we see Hall struggle with Rosales. Rosales falls, a shot is heard.*)

BAILIFF (*voice, offstage*). All rise! Court is now in session!

If you now glance at the text of the revised version, you will notice that it begins differently. Which beginning do you prefer? Why?

5. The Judge is an offstage voice, not a visible character. Why do you suppose Morton chose to present the judge in this manner? What do you think of Morton's decision?

6. Select two characters, and discuss the special challenges that the roles present for the actors.

A CONTEXT FOR *THE MANY DEATHS OF DANNY ROSALES*

Carlos Morton
TALKING ABOUT *DANNY ROSALES*

[Following is an interview conducted with Carlos Morton in March 1996.]

Interviewer: How did the family respond to the play and the changes you made?

Morton: First of all, I interviewed members of the family, the widow, and the lawyers on both sides. Then I read all the articles I could find on the case, as well as the court transcripts. I even saw actual photos of the crime scene. In terms of research, I approached it from a journalistic point of view. I told everyone I would base the play on the facts, but would also be taking "poetic license." Even then, when the mother came to see a production at the University of Texas in 1982, she told me in no uncertain terms, "that ain't the way it happened." I told her I was sorry, but that's the way I saw it!

I understand that you changed the names? Was this for legal reasons?

For a professional production at the Bilingual Foundation of the Arts (1980) in Los Angeles, the lawyers for the theater company insisted that I change the names to avoid any lawsuits. I had 48 hours to come up with alternate names. In a panic, I used names of actual people I knew in El Paso, Texas, like Stevie Peters, Berta, Rowena, Kiki, Pearl, etc. (Some friends were a little upset.) The protagonist's real name was Richard Morales, but we changed it to Danny Rosales.

Aside from legal reasons, were there other reasons to make changes?

As far as staying with the facts, it's not always possible, try as you may. In the actual case, there were three women (including Grace Hall's sister) who drove 500 miles to bury the body. I didn't have enough actors to fill the parts in the first version written in 1977.

Did the play change as you worked on it?

It began life as a one-act bilingual play entitled *Las Many Muertes de Richard Morales*, as part of a class assignment at the University of California, San Diego. It had to be taken "from the public record," and it had to accommodate all ten actors in my Master of Fine Arts class. Over time, much of the Spanish was translated into English and the work evolved into a two-act play. The title and names were changed, and some scenes were altered or dropped. *Danny Rosales* has been rewritten, in some form or another, half a dozen times. There have been at least a dozen productions—that I know of. Every time I see a production, be it professional or amateur, I get new ideas on how to improve it. The version published here is based on rewrites done after a staged reading at the New York Shakespeare Festival Latino in 1986. Including this version, the play has been published six times in English and Spanish in the U.S., Mexico, and Cuba over a span of twenty years.

Did you write the play with a particular stage or set in mind?

The play can work well on any stage, it all depends upon the directors and their "vision." The less "realistic," the better; that is, getting away from the made-for-TV movie. I would also urge the director to avoid melodrama and "cast against type." For instance, the more personable the Sheriff and his wife, the more frightening they become. Danny and Kiki are opposites, as are the Sheriff and the Deputy. Kiki and Stevie provide "comic relief," while Debbie and Berta embody pathos. The director doesn't need to have the actual Judge (or Bailiff) on stage. A mysterious voice looming over the entire set will suffice. American justice, like God, works in mysterious ways.

The police chief's lawyer is a man, the opposing lawyer a woman. Are you making a point about gender?

Harold can become a woman and Rowena a man, or you can have two female or male lawyers, as long as the director finds some inner conflicts in their style or temperaments.

Do you think Anglos and Chicanos differ in their responses?

I have witnessed different ethnic groups act in various ways, because, on a gut level, the play isn't just the tragedy of Danny Rosales, it is also the story of Fred Hall bringing his house down. To me, this makes it a very American experience for our time. Conservatives and liberals also differ in their reactions. For instance, some audiences identify with the Sheriff and his family, on the side of law and order. This isn't necessarily "bad," but rather an indication that the defense attorney's closing arguments made their mark on the jury. The play loses its strength when it becomes a simple "brown vs. white" issue. There are heroes and villains on both sides. In real life, the "Kiki" character did turn Danny in, and the real life Deputy was instrumental in bringing the Sheriff to justice—which is what the play is really about.

A Note on
ASIAN-AMERICAN THEATER

Although actors and musicians of Asian ancestry have performed in the United States for well over a century, prejudice and exclusionary practices impeded the development of a large body of stage plays. Of course, "mainstream" American plays in the twentieth century have included several with Asian themes—for instance, post–World War II Broadway hits such as *Teahouse of the August Moon, The King and I,* and *South Pacific*—but these were not written by Asian Americans and they did not succeed in removing stereotypical casting from the American stage.

In 1965, dissatisfied with the lack of roles and scripts, a group of Asian-American actors and directors established the East-West Players in Los Angeles, which became a vital force on the West Coast. The players' artistic director, Mako, encouraged a number of Asian-American writers, including Wakako Yamauchi, Momoko Iko, Frank Chin, Genny Lim, and Velina Hasu Houston. In 1982 an interviewer, James F. Dean, asked Mako about those early years.

Dean: Why was East-West Players formed? Because there were actors with unfulfilled needs? Or were there Asian-American plays waiting to be produced?

Mako: I think to answer the question we have to go back to the very beginning. We have to go back to 1965 when our company was formed, founded. Since all of us who were founders at that time were actors, I would have to classify our theater as "actors" theater, as opposed to "directors" theater or "writers" theaters. . . . What is Asian-American art? We do recognize Japanese art or Chinese art or Korean art,

but what is this Asian-American stuff? . . . At the same time, the whole thinking began to evolve much more: Why are we here? What do we have to do? What do we want to do? . . . We needed to educate our own people as well as reaching out to non-Asian audiences. And we had to educate our actors. In order to do that we had to develop writers.

Playwriting contests and grants from the Ford Foundation, the Rockefeller Foundation, and the National Endowment for the Arts all helped encourage Asian-American playwrights. Several other West Coast groups sprang up, among them the Asian American Theater Company in San Francisco, the Asian Exclusion Act (now called the Northwest Asian American Theatre Company), and the Asian American Actors Ensemble in San Diego. Chicago has engendered two Asian-American companies, Angel's Island Theatre Company and Mina-sama-no. In New York City, Tisa Chang established the Pan Asian Repertory Theatre in 1977, which has performed plays by Shakespeare, Ibsen, and Chekhov, as well as many scripts written by Asian-American playwrights. Pan Asian's 1990 production of *And the Soul Shall Dance* toured the United States in 1991.

We provide only a glimpse of Asian-American theater. Perhaps today's most well-known Asian-American playwright is David Henry Hwang, whose early works debuted at New York's Public Theater and whose *M. Butterfly* (1988) won a Tony on Broadway. For one of Hwang's plays, *The Sound of a Voice,* see page 926, and for some of his thoughts about ethnic theater, see page 933.

Wakako Yamauchi

AND THE SOUL SHALL DANCE

Two-time winner of a Rockefeller Playwright's Foundation grant, Wakako Yamauchi (pronounced *Ya-ma-U-chi*), was born in 1924 in California's Imperial Valley to a first-generation Japanese-American farm family, all of whose members suffered internment during World War II. Yamauchi, a painter as well as a writer, turned to plays in the 1970s when she was encouraged to adapt some of her short stories for the theater. Among the plays that followed are *And the Soul Shall Dance* (1974), *The Music Lessons* (1980), *12-1-A* (1982), *The Memento* (1984), *The Chairman's Wife* (1990), and *Not a Through Street* (1991). She has also written one-act plays and several collections of poetry and prose.

COMMENTARY

It is tempting to say that many European playwrights focus on large social problems (we could cite Chekov's *The Cherry Orchard*, Shaw's *Major Barbara*, Ionesco's *The Lesson*) and that many American playwrights focus on domestic matters (we could cite Williams's *The Glass Menagerie*, Miller's *Death of a Salesman*, and Wilson's *Fences*). Although one should be wary of sweeping claims, generalizations can be useful as starting points for discussion. The United States is a relatively new nation, and because we have not had many centuries to evolve complicated community and national social structures, it may be natural for families to loom as dominant, important social units in our plays. Furthermore, a family is often the first bulwark or haven for newcomers—and America is (as is regularly said) a nation of immigrants. Often, of course, the family in an American play serves as a specific illustration for a pervasive social situation. For example, Willie Loman's inadequacies, mistakes, and misfortunes reflect those of many frustrated, tired workers in the 1940s (see *Death of a Salesman*, p. 648); the generational conflicts in Troy Maxson's family are typical of black families that span the Civil Rights era (see *Fences*, p. 944), and, of course, the play calls attention to the out-and-out unfairness of racism.

Wakako Yamauchi's *And the Soul Shall Dance* shares many of the features of Tennessee Williams's *The Glass Menagerie* (p. 617). Both plays are set in the 1930s; both show families beset by emotional and economic pressures; and both show characters who survive and more fragile characters who retreat from the harshness of their respective realities and,

ultimately, are destroyed. Both plays are presented as a series of episodes over the space of a few months. Also, readers, audiences, actors, and directors praise both Williams and Yamauchi for the poetic diction and haunting images of their language.

And the Soul Shall Dance contrasts two Japanese-American families during the depression, both trying to assimilate into American culture and both longing for the culture they left behind. As immigrants learning a new language, raising children, and seeking economic stability, the Japanese Americans shared the struggles of many other immigrant groups in America. However, as Japanese (those born in Japan are called Issei, "first generation"; those born in the United States are Nisei, "second generation"), they faced certain restrictions that other immigrant groups did not. For example, California law forbade them to own their own land; immigrant farmers (such as Murata and Oka in this play) had to sign a two-year lease on the property they tilled and then move on. In short, Japanese Americans were often treated as second-class citizens or worse.

The Muratas (husband, wife Hana, and daughter Masako) are hardy, loving, and resilient. Hana is strong willed and wise. Husband and wife are realistic about both the world they've left behind and the world they've chosen to adopt. Their daughter represents a successful accommodation to American life. In contrast, their neighbors, Oka and his wife, Emiko, are an ill-matched couple. An angry man, Oka is unhappily married to the sister of his deceased first wife. Emiko, trained as a dancer and dreaming of returning to Japan, drinks and rejects her husband. Oka, in turn, becomes brutish and abusive. The scenes between Oka and

Emiko, usually witnessed by the Muratas, are especially powerful. We see Emiko's dreamlike existence, her fragility, snapped by Oka's drunken bluster. Still, we sympathize with Oka, too, for he acts out of loneliness and disappointment.

Hana explains Emiko with a traditional Daoist simile:

HANA. She can't adjust to this life. She can't get over the good times she had in Japan. Well, it's not easy . . . but one has to know when to bend . . . like the bamboo. When the winds blow, bamboo bends. You bend or crack. Remember that. Masako.

And the Soul Shall Dance makes use of a common plot device: Someone new comes to town, in this case, Kiyoko, the fifteen-year-old child of Oka's first marriage. Readers and audiences will recognize this outsider as a catalyst and wonder whether her presence will improve the Okas' marriage, whether she will find a friend in Masako, and whether she will be able to leave behind her Japanese ways. In all the combinations—Masako and Kiyoko, Hana and Masako, Hana and Kiyoko, Hana and Oka, and so forth—Yamauchi's touch is realistic and honest. It's as if she has choreographed a series of duets, trios, and ensemble moments. Scenes of almost dancelike delicacy are juxtaposed against moments of explosive emotion and physical action.

One reviewer called And the Soul Shall Dance "an old-fashioned play." Lest we consider that label an insult, let us consider its implications. Old-fashioned indicates a "well-made play" (see Glossary, p. 1074), one that is structured carefully and builds through several climaxes to a resolution. A well-made play offers a plot that relies on credible, psychologically complex characterizations. It does not trick or dazzle the audience with strobe lights, spinning stages, or high-tech devices. Instead, the set is functional—often, quite simple—and the effects are entirely suitable to mood and nuance. Yamauchi makes use of a number of standard dramatic conventions. Like Shakespeare, she understands the value of dramatic contrasts (for example, quiet scenes followed by emotional outbursts), and like many other American dramatists, she focuses on the family. The narrative structure in And the Soul Shall Dance is simple and chronological, and the painful conflict between Oka and Emiko builds to a searing climax. Because the play is among the first pieces to focus on the experience of Japanese Americans, it occupies a special place in this collection. Yamauchi succeeds in giving us both the vision of a specific group of people at a specific point in time and a sense of the universal.

Wakako Yamauchi

AND THE SOUL SHALL DANCE

ACT 1

SCENE 1

(*Interior of the Murata house, afternoon. The set is spare. There is a kitchen table, four chairs, a bed, and on the wall, a calendar indicating the year and month: June, 1935. There is a doorway leading to the other room. Props are: a bottle of sake, two cups, a dish of chiles, a phonograph, and two towels hanging on pegs on the wall. A wide wooden bench sits outside.*

The bathhouse has just burned to the ground due to the carelessness of Masako, Nisei daughter, eleven. Offstage there are sounds of Murata, forty, Issei farmer, putting out the fire.

Inside the house Hana Murata. Issei wife, in a drab house dress, confronts Masako, who is wearing a summer dress of the era. Masako is sullen and somewhat defiant. Hana breaks the silence.)

HANA. How could you be so careless. Masako? You know you should be extra careful with fire. How often have I told you? Now the whole bathhouse is gone. I told you time and again, when you stoke a fire, you should see that everything is swept into the fireplace.

(*Murata enters. He's dressed in old work clothes. He suffers from heat and exhaustion.*)

MURATA (*coughing*). Shack went up like a matchbox.... This kind of weather dries everything... just takes a spark to make a bonfire out of dry timber.

HANA. Did you save any of it?

MURATA. No. Couldn't...

HANA (*to Masako*). How many times have I told you...

(*Masako moves nervously.*)

MURATA. No use crying about it now. *Shikata ga nai.* It's gone now. No more bathhouse. That's all there is to it.

HANA. But you've got to tell her. Otherwise she'll make the same mistake. You'll be building a bathhouse every year.

(*Murata removes his shirt and wipes off his face. He throws his shirt on a chair and sits at the table.*)

MURATA. *Baka!* Ridiculous!

MASAKO. I didn't do it on purpose. (*She goes to the bed, opens a book!*)

HANA (*follows Masako*). I know that but you know what this means? It means we bathe in a bucket... inside the house. Carry water in from the pond, heat it on the stove ... We'll use more kerosene.

MURATA. Tub's still there. And the fireplace. We can still build a fire under the tub.

HANA (*shocked*). But no walls! Everyone in the country can see us!

MURATA. Wait till dark then. Wait till dark.

HANA. We'll be using a lantern. They'll still see us.

MURATA. Angh! Who? Who'll see us? You think everyone in the country waits to watch us take a bath? Hunh! You know how stupid you sound? Ridiculous!

HANA (*defensively*). It'll be inconvenient.

(*Hana is saved by a rap on the door. Oka, Issei neighbor, forty-five, enters. He is short and stout, dressed in faded work clothes.*)

OKA. Hello! Hello! Oi! What's going on here? Hey! Was there some kind of fire?

(*Hana rushes to the door to let Oka in. He stamps the dust from his shoes and enters.*)

HANA. Oka-san! You just wouldn't believe.... We had a terrible thing happen.

OKA. Yeah. Saw the smoke from down the road. Thought it was your house. Came rushing over. Is the fire out?

(*Murata half rises and sits back again. He's exhausted.*)

MURATA (*gesturing*). Oi, oi. Come in ... sit down. No big problem. It was just our bathhouse.

OKA. Just the *furoba*, eh?

MURATA. Just the bath.

HANA. Our Masako was careless and the *furoba* caught fire. There's nothing left of it but the tub.

(*Masako looks up from her book, pained. She makes a very small sound.*)

OKA. Long as the tub's there, no problem. I'll help you with it. (*He starts to roll up his sleeves. Murata looks at him*)

MURATA. What ... now? Now?

OKA. Long as I'm here.

HANA. Oh, Papa. Aren't we lucky to have such friends?

MURATA (*to Hana*). Hell, we can't work on it now. The ashes are still hot. I just now put the damned fire out. Let me rest awhile. (*To Oka.*) Oi, how about a little sake? (*Gesturing to Hana.*) Make sake for Oka-san.

(*Oka sits at the table. Hana goes to prepare the sake. She heats it, gets out the cups and pours it for the men.*)

I'm tired ... I am *tired*.

HANA. Oka-san has so generously offered his help ...

(*Oka is uncomfortable. He looks around and sees Masako sitting on the bed.*)

OKA. Hello, there, Masako-chan. You studying?

MASAKO. No, it's summer vacation.

MURATA (*sucking in his breath*). Kids nowadays . . . no manners . . .

HANA. She's sulking because I had to scold her.

(*Masako makes a small moan.*)

MURATA. Drink Oka-san.

OKA (*swallowing*). Ahhh, that's good.

MURATA. Eh, you not working today?

OKA. No . . . no . . . I took the afternoon off today. I was driving over to Nagatas' when I saw this big black cloud of smoke coming from your yard.

HANA. It went up so fast . . .

MURATA. What's up at Nagatas'? (*To Hana.*) Get the chiles out. Oka-san loves chiles.

(*Hana opens a jar of chiles and puts them on a plate. She serves the men and gets her mending basket and walks to Masako. Masako makes room for her on the bed.*)

OKA (*helping himself*). Ah, chiles. (*Murata looks at him, the question unanswered.*) Well, I want to see him about my horse. I'm thinking of selling my horse.

MURATA. Sell your horse!

OKA (*scratches his head*). The fact is, I need some money. Nagata-san's the only one around made money this year, and I'm thinking he might want another horse.

MURATA. Yeah, he made a little this year. And he's talking big . . . big. Says he's leasing twenty more acres this fall.

OKA. Twenty acres?

MURATA. Yeah. He might want another horse.

OKA. Twenty acres, eh?

MURATA. That's what he says. But you know his old woman makes all the decisions.

(*Oka scratches his head.*)

HANA. They're doing all right.

MURATA. Henh. Nagata-kun's so hen-pecked, it's pathetic. *Peko-peko.* (*He makes motions of a hen pecking.*)

OKA (*feeling the strain*). I better get over there.

MURATA. Why the hell you selling your horse?

OKA. I need cash.

MURATA. Oh, yeah. I could use some too. Seems like everyone's getting out of the depression but the poor farmers. Nothing changes for us. We go on and on planting our tomatoes and summer squash and eating them. . . . Well, at least it's healthy.

HANA. Papa, do you have lumber?

MURATA. Lumber? For what?

HANA. The bath.

MURATA (*impatiently*). Don't worry about that. We need more sake now.

(*Hana rises to serve him.*)

OKA. You sure Nagata-kun's working twenty more acres?

MURATA. Last I heard. What the hell; if you need a few bucks, I can loan you.

OKA. A few hundred. I need a few hundred dollars.

MURATA. Oh, a few hundred. But what the hell you going to do without a horse? Out here a man's horse is as important as his wife.

OKA (*seriously*). I don't think Nagata will buy my wife.

(*The men laugh, but Hana doesn't find it so funny. Murata glances at her. She fills the cups again. Oka makes a half-hearted gesture to stop her. Masako watches the pantomime carefully. Oka swallows his drink in one gulp.*)

I better get moving.

MURATA. What's the big hurry?

OKA. Like to get the horse business done.

MURATA. Ehhh . . . relax. Do it tomorrow. He's not going to die, is he?

OKA (*laughing*). Hey, he's a good horse. I want to get it settled today. If Nagata-kun won't buy, I got to find someone else. You think maybe Kawaguchi . . . ?

MURATA. Not Kawaguchi. . . . Maybe Yamamoto.

HANA. What is all the money for, Oka-san? Does Emiko-san need an operation?

OKA. Nothing like that . . .

HANA. Sounds very mysterious.

OKA. No mystery, Mrs. No mystery. No sale, no money, no story.

MURATA (*laughing*). That's a good one. "No sale, no money, no. . . ." Eh, Mama.

(*He points to the empty cups. Hana fills the cups and goes back to Masako.*)

HANA (*muttering*). I see we won't be getting any work done today. (*To Masako.*) Are you reading again? Maybe we'd still have a bath if you—

MASAKO. I didn't do it on purpose.

MURATA (*loudly*). I sure hope you know what you're doing, Oka-kun. What'd you do without a horse?

OKA. I was hoping you'd lend me yours now and then . . . (*He looks at Hana.*) I'll pay for some of the feed.

MURATA (*emphatically waving his hand*). Sure! Sure!

OKA. The fact is, I need that money. I got a daughter in Japan and I just got to send for her this year.

(*Coming to life, Hana puts down her mending and sits at the table.*)

HANA. A daughter? You have a daughter in Japan? Why, I didn't know you had children. Emiko-san and you . . . I thought you were childless.

OKA (*scratching his head*). We are. I was married before.

MURATA. You son-of-a-gun!

HANA. Is that so? How old is your daughter?

OKA. Kiyoko must be . . . fifteen now. Yeah, fifteen.

HANA. Fifteen! Oh, that *would* be too old for Emiko-san's child. Is Kiyoko-san living with relatives in Japan?

OKA (*reluctantly*). Yeah, with grandparents. With Shizue's parents. Well, the fact is, Shizue, that's my first wife, and Emiko were sisters. They come from a family with no sons. I was a boy when I went to work for the family . . .

as an apprentice . . . they're blacksmiths. Later I married Shizue and took on the family name—you know, *yoshi*—because they had no sons. My real name is Sakakihara.

MURATA. Sakakihara! That's a great name!

HANA. A magnificent name!

OKA. No one knows me by that here.

MURATA. Should have kept that . . . Sakakihara.

OKA (*muttering*). I don't even know myself by that name.

HANA. And Shizue-san passed away and you married Emiko-san?

OKA. Oh, yeah. Well, Shizue and I lived with the family for a while and we had the baby . . . that's, you know, Kiyoko. . . . (*The liquor has affected him and he's become less inhibited.*) Well, while I was serving apprentice with the family, they always looked down their noses at me. After I married, it got worse. . . . That old man . . . angh! He was terrible! Always pushing me around, making me look bad in front of my wife and kid. That old man was mean . . . ugly!

MURATA. Yeah, I heard about that apprentice work—*detchi-boko*. . . . Heard it was damned humiliating.

OKA. That's the God's truth!

MURATA. Never had to do it myself. I came to America instead. They say *detchi-boko* is bloody hard work.

OKA. The work's all right. I'm not afraid of work. It's the humiliation! I hated them! Pushing me around like I was still a boy. . . . Me, a grown man! And married to their daughter! (*Murata groans in sympathy.*) Well, Shizue and I talked it over and we decided the best thing was to get away. We thought if I came to America and made some money . . . you know, send her money until we had enough, I'd go back and we'd leave the family . . . you know, move to another province . . . start a small business, maybe in the city, a noodle shop or something.

MURATA. That's everyone's dream. Make money, go home and live like a king.

OKA. I worked like a dog. Sent every penny to Shizue. And then she died. She died on me!

(*Hana and Murata observe a moment of silence in respect for Oka's anguish.*)

HANA. And you married Emiko-san.

OKA. I didn't marry her. They married her to me! Right after Shizue died.

HANA. But Oka-san, you were lucky . . .

OKA. Before the body was cold! No respect! By proxy. The old man wrote me they were arranging a marriage by proxy for me and Emiko. They said she'd grown to be a beautiful woman and would serve me well.

HANA. Emiko-san *is* a beautiful woman.

OKA. And they sent her to me. Took care of everything! Immigration, fare, everything.

HANA. But she's your sister-in-law—Kiyoko's aunt. It's good to keep the family together.

OKA. That's what I thought. But hear this: Emiko was the favored one. Shizue was not so pretty, not so smart. They were grooming Emiko for a rich man—his name was Yamoto—lived in a grand house in the village. They sent her to schools, you know, the culture thing: tea ceremony, you know, all that. They didn't even like me, and suddenly they married her to me.

MURATA. Yeah. You don't need all that formal training to make it over here. Just a strong back.

HANA. And a strong will.

OKA. It was all arranged. I couldn't do anything about it.

HANA. It'll be all right. With Kiyoko coming . . .

OKA (*dubiously*). I hope so . . . I never knew human beings could be so cruel. You know how they mistreated my daughter? You know after Emiko came over, things got from bad to worse and I *never* had enough money to send to Kiyoko.

MURATA. They don't know what it's like here. They think money's picked off the ground here.

OKA. And they treated Kiyoko so bad. They told her I forgot about her. They told her I didn't care—they said I abandoned her. Well, she knew better. She wrote to me all the time and I always told her I'd send for her . . . soon as I got the money. (*He shakes his head.*) I just got to do something this year.

HANA. She'll be happier here. She'll know her father cares.

OKA. Kids tormented her for not having parents.

MURATA. Kids are cruel.

HANA. Masako will help her. She'll help her get started at school. She'll make friends . . . she'll be all right.

OKA. I hope so. She'll need friends. (*He considers he might be making a mistake after all.*) What could I say to her? Stay there? It's not what you think over here? I can't help her? I just have to do this thing. I just have to do this one thing for her.

MURATA. Sure . . .

HANA. Don't worry. It'll work out fine.

(*Murata gestures to Hana. She fills the cups.*)

MURATA. You talk about selling your horse, I thought you were pulling out.

OKA. I wish I could. But there's nothing else I can do.

MURATA. Without money, yeah . . .

OKA. You can go into some kind of business with money, but a man like me . . . no education . . . there's no kind of job I can do. I'd starve in the city.

MURATA. Dishwashing, maybe. Janitor . . .

OKA. At least here we can eat. Carrots, maybe, but we can eat.

MURATA. All the carrots we been eating 'bout to turn me into a rabbit.

(*They laugh. Hana starts to pour more wine for Oka but he stops her.*)

OKA. I better not drink any more. Got to drive to Nagata-san's yet. (*He rises and walks over to Masako.*) You study hard, don't you? You'll teach Kiyoko English, eh? When she gets here . . .

HANA. Oh, yes. She will.

MURATA. Kiyoko-san could probably teach her a thing or two.

OKA. She won't know about American ways . . .

MASAKO. I'll help her.

HANA. Don't worry, Oka-san. She'll have a good friend in our Masako.

(*They move toward the door.*)

OKA. Well, thanks for the sake. I guess I talk too much when I drink. (*He scratches his head and laughs.*) Oh. I'm sorry about the fire. By the way, come to my house for your bath . . . until you build yours again.

HANA (*hesitantly*). Oh, uh . . . thank you. I don't know if . . .

MURATA. Good! Good! Thanks a lot. I need a good hot bath tonight.

OKA. Tonight, then.

MURATA. We'll be there.

HANA (*bowing*). Thank you very much. Sayonara.

OKA (*nodding*). See you tonight.

(*Oka leaves. Hana faces her husband as soon as the door closes.*)

HANA. Papa, I don't know about going over there.

MURATA (*surprised*). Why?

HANA. Well, Emiko-san . . .

MURATA (*irritated*). What's the matter with you? We need a bath and Oka's invited us over.

HANA (*to Masako*). Help me clear the table.

(*Masako reluctantly leaves her book and begins to clear the table.*)

Papa, you know we've been neighbors already three, four years and Emiko-san's never been very hospitable.

MURATA. She's shy, that's all.

HANA. Not just shy . . . she's strange. I feel like she's pushing me off . . . she makes me feel like—I don't know—like I'm prying or something.

MURATA. Maybe you are.

HANA. And never puts out a cup of tea. . . . If she had all that training in the graces . . . why, a cup of tea . . .

MURATA. So, if you want tea, ask for it.

HANA. I can't do that, Papa. She's strange . . . I don't know . . . (*To Masako.*) When we go there, be very careful not to say anything wrong.

MASAKO. I never say anything anyway.

HANA (*thoughtfully*). Would you believe the story Oka-san just told? Why I never knew . . .

MURATA. There're lot of things you don't know. Just because a man don't . . . talk about them, don't mean he don't feel . . . don't think about . . .

HANA (*looking around*). We'll have to take something. . . . There's nothing to take. . . . Papa, maybe you can dig up some carrots.

MURATA. God, Mama, be sensible. They got carrots. Everybody's got carrots.

HANA. Something . . . maybe I should make something.

MURATA. Hell, they're not expecting anything.

HANA. It's not good manners to go empty-handed.

MURATA. We'll take the sake.

(*Hana grimaces. Masako sees the record player.*)

MASAKO. I know, Mama. We can take the Victrola! We can play records for Mrs. Oka. Then nobody has to talk.

(*Murata laughs. Fade-out.*)

SCENE 2

(*That evening. We see the exterior wall of Oka's weathered house. There is a workable screen door and a large screened window. Outside there is a wide wooden bench that can accommodate three or four people. There is one separate chair and a lantern stands against the house.*

The last rays of the sun light the area in a soft golden glow. This light grows gray as the scene progresses and it is quite dark at the end of the scene.

Through the screened window, Emiko Oka, Issei woman, thirty, can be seen walking erratically back and forth. She wears a drab cotton dress but her grace and femininity come through. Her hair is in a bun, in the style of Issei women of the era.

Oka sits cross-legged on the bench. He wears a yukata [summer robe] and fans himself with a round Japanese fan.

The Muratas enter. Murata carries towels and a bottle of sake. Hana carries the Victrola, and Masako a package containing their yukatas.)

OKA (*standing to receive the Muratas*). Oh, you've come. Welcome!

MURATA. Yah. . . . Good of you to ask us.

HANA (*bowing*). Yes, thank you very much. (*To Masako.*) Say "hello," Masako.

MASAKO. Hello.

HANA. And "thank you."

MASAKO. Thank you.

(*Oka makes motion of protest. Emiko stops her pacing and watches from the window.*)

HANA (*glancing briefly at the window*). And how is Emiko-san this evening?

OKA (*turning toward the house*). Emi! Emiko!

HANA. That's all right. Don't call her out. She must be busy.

OKA (*half-rising*). Emiko!

(*Emiko comes to the door. Hana starts a deep bow toward the door.*)

MURATA. *Konbanwa* (Good evening)!

HANA. *Konbanwa*, Emiko-san. I feel so bad about this intrusion. Your husband has told you, our bathhouse was destroyed by fire and he graciously invited us to come use yours.

(*Emiko shakes her head.*)

OKA. I didn't have a chance to . . .

HANA (*recovering and nudging Masako*). Say hello to Mrs. Oka.

MASAKO. Hello, Mrs. Oka.

(*Hana lowers the Victrola onto the bench.*)

OKA. What's this? You brought a phonograph?

MASAKO. It's a Victrola.

HANA (*laughing indulgently*). Yes. Masako wanted to bring this over and play some records.

MURATA (*extending the wine*). Brought a little sake too.

OKA (*taking the bottle*). Ah, now that I like. Emiko, bring out the cups.

(*He waves at his wife, but she doesn't move. He starts to ask again, but decides to get them himself. He enters the house and returns with two cups. Emiko seats herself on the single chair. The Muratas unload their paraphernalia; Oka pours the wine, the men drink, Hana chatters and sorts the records. Masako stands by, helping her.*)

HANA. Yes, our Masako loves to play records. I like records too . . . and Papa, he . . .

MURATA (*watching Emiko*). They take me back home. The only way I can get there . . . in my mind.

HANA. Do you like music, Emiko-san? (*Emiko looks vague but smiles faintly.*) Oka-san, you like them, don't you?

OKA. Yeah. But I don't have a player. No chance to hear them.

MURATA. I had to get this for them. They wouldn't leave me alone until I got it. Well . . . a phonograph . . . what the hell, they got to have *some* fun.

HANA. We don't have to play them, if you'd rather not . . .

OKA. Play. Play them.

HANA. I thought we could listen to them and relax. (*She extends some records to Emiko.*) Would you like to look through these, Emiko-san?

(*Emiko doesn't respond. She pulls out a sack of Bull Durham and starts to roll a cigarette. Hana pushes Masako to her.*)

Take these to her.

(*Masako moves toward Emiko with the records. Masako stands watching her as she lights her cigarette.*)

Some of these are very old. You might know them, Emiko-san. (*She sees Masako watching Emiko.*) Masako, bring those over here. (*She laughs uncomfortably.*) You might like this one, Emiko-san . . . (*She starts the player.*) Do you know it?

(*The record whines out "Kago No Tori." Emiko listens with her head cocked. She smokes her cigarette. She becomes wrapped in nostalgia and memories of the past. Masako watches her carefully.*)

MASAKO (*whispering*). Mama, she's crying.

(*Startled, Hana and Murata look toward Emiko.*)

HANA (*pinching Masako*). Shhh. The smoke is in her eyes.

MURATA. Did you bring the record I like, Mama?

(*Emiko rises abruptly and enters the house.*)

MASAKO. They were tears, Mama.

HANA. From yawning, Masako. (*Regretfully, to Oka.*) I'm afraid we've offended her.

OKA (*unaware*). Hunh? Aw . . . no . . . pay no attention . . . no offense . . .

(*Masako looks toward the window. Emiko stands forlornly and slowly drifts into a dance.*)

HANA. I'm very sorry. Children, you know . . . they'll say anything, anything that's on their minds.

MURATA (*notices Masako watching Emiko through the window and tries to divert her attention*). The needles. Masako, where're the needles?

MASAKO (*still watching*). I forgot them.

(*Hana sees what's going on. Oka is unaware.*)

HANA. Masako, go take your bath now. Masako . . .

(*Masako reluctantly picks up her towel and leaves.*)

OKA. Yeah, yeah . . . take your bath.

MURATA (*sees Emiko still dancing*). Change the record, Mama.

OKA (*still unaware*). That's kind of sad.

MURATA. No use to get sick over a record. We're supposed to enjoy.

(*Hana stops the record. Emiko disappears from the window. Hana selects a lively ondo (folk dance)—"Tokyo Ondo."*)

HANA. We'll find something more fun.

(*The three begin to tap their feet to the music.*)

Can't you just see the festival? The dancers, the bright kimonos, the paper lanterns bobbing in the wind, the fireflies . . . how nostalgic. . . . Oh, how nostalgic . . .

(*From the side of the house, Emiko appears. Her hair is down, she wears an old straw hat. She dances in front of the Muratas. They're startled. After the first shock, they watch with frozen smiles. They try to join Emiko's mood but something is missing. Oka is grieved. He finally stands as though he has had enough. Emiko, now close to the door, ducks into the house.*)

That was pretty . . . very nice . . .

(*Oka settles down and grunts. Murata clears his throat and Masako returns from her bath.*)

MURATA. You're done already? (*He's glad to see her.*)

MASAKO. I wasn't very dirty. The water was too hot.

MURATA. Good! Just the way I like it.

HANA. Not dirty?

MURATA (*picking up his towel*). Come on, Mama . . . scrub my back.

HANA (*laughing embarrassedly*). Oh, oh . . . well . . . (*She stops the player.*) Masako, now don't forget . . . crank the machine and change the needle now and then.

MASAKO. I didn't bring them.

HANA. Oh. Oh . . . all right. I'll be back soon . . . don't forget . . . crank.

(*She leaves with her husband. Oka and Masako are alone. Oka is awkward and falsely hearty.*)

OKA. So! So you don't like hot baths, eh?

MASAKO. Not too hot.

OKA (*laughing*). I thought you like it real hot. Hot enough to burn the house down. That's a little joke.

(*Masako busies herself with the records to conceal her annoyance.*)

I hear you're real good in school. Always top of the class.

MASAKO. It's a small class. Only two of us.

OKA. When Kiyoko comes, you'll help her in school, yeah? You'll take care of her . . . a favor for me, eh?

MASAKO. Okay.

OKA. You'll be her friend, eh?

MASAKO. Okay.

OKA. That's good. That's good. You'll like her. She's a nice girl too. (*He stands, yawns, and stretches.*) I'll go for a little walk now. (*He touches his crotch to indicate his purpose.*)

(*Masako turns her attention to the records and selects one—"The Soul Shall Dance"—and begins to sway to the music. The song draws Emiko from the house. She looks out the window, sees Masako is alone and begins to slip into a dance.*)

EMIKO. Do you like that song, Masa-chan?

(*Masako is startled and draws back. She remembers her mother's warning. She doesn't know what to do. She nods.*)

That's one of my favorite songs. I remember in Japan I used to sing it so often . . . my favorite song . . . (*She sings along with the record.*)

    Akai kuchibiru
    Kappu ni yosete
    Aoi sake nomya
    Kokoro ga odoru . . .

Do you know what that means, Masa-chan?

MASAKO. I think so . . . The soul will dance?

EMIKO. Yes, yes, that's right.

    The soul shall dance.
    Red lips against a glass
    Drink the green . . .

MASAKO. Wine?

EMIKO (*nodding*). Drink the green wine.

MASAKO. Green? I thought wine is purple.

EMIKO (*nodding*). Wine is purple . . . but this is a green liqueur. (*She holds up one of the china cups as though it were crystal, and looks at it as though the light were shining through it and she sees the green liquid.*) It's good . . . it warms your heart.

MASAKO. And the soul dances.

EMIKO. Yes.

MASAKO. What does it taste like? The green wine . . .

EMIKO. Oh, it's like . . . it's like . . .

(*The second verse starts. "Kurai yoru no yume / Setsunasa yo / Aoi sake nomya / Yume mo odoru. . . ."*)

MASAKO. In the dark night . . .

EMIKO. Dreams are unbearable . . . insufferable . . . (*She turns sad.*)

MASAKO. Drink the . . .

EMIKO (*nodding*). Drink the green wine . . .

MASAKO. And the dreams will dance.

EMIKO (*softly*). I'll be going back one day . . .

MASAKO. To where?

EMIKO. My home . . . Japan . . . my real home. I'm planning to go back.

MASAKO. By yourself?

EMIKO (*nodding*). Oh, yes. It's a secret. You can keep a secret?

MASAKO. Uh-huh. I have lots of secrets . . . all my own . . .

(*The music stops. Emiko sees Oka approaching and disappears into the house. Masako attends to the record and does not know Emiko is gone.*)

Secrets I never tell anyone.

OKA. Secrets? What kind of secrets? What did she say?

MASAKO. Oh. Nothing.

OKA. What did you talk about?

MASAKO. Nothing. . . . Mrs. Oka was talking about the song. She was telling me what it meant . . . about the soul.

OKA (*scoffing*). Heh! What does she know about soul? (*Calming down.*) Ehhh . . . some people don't have them . . . souls.

MASAKO (*timidly*). I thought . . . I think everyone has a soul. I read in a book . . .

OKA (*laughing*). Maybe . . . maybe you're right. I'm not an educated man, you know . . . I don't know too much about books. When Kiyoko comes you can talk to her about it. Kiyoko is very . . .

(*From inside the house, we hear Emiko begin to sing loudly at the name Kiyoko as though trying to drown it out. Oka stops talking. Then resumes.*)

Kiyoko is very smart. You'll have a good time with her. She'll learn your language fast. How old did you say you are?

MASAKO. Almost twelve.

(*By this time Oka and Masako are shouting, trying to be heard above Emiko's singing.*)

OKA. Kiyoko is fifteen. . . . Kiyoko . . .

(*Oka is exasperated. He rushes into the house seething. Masako hears Oka's muffled rage: "Behave yourself," and "kitchigai" come through. Masako slinks to the window and looks in. Oka slaps Emiko around. Masako reacts to the violence. Oka comes out. Masako returns to the bench*) *in time. He pulls his fingers through his hair and sits next to Masako. She very slightly draws away.*)

Want me to light a lantern?

MASAKO (*shaken*). No . . . ye— . . . okay . . .

OKA. We'll get a little light here . . .

(*He lights the lantern as the Muratas return from their bath. They are in good spirits.*)

MURATA. Ahhhh. . . . Nothing like a good hot bath.

HANA. So refreshing . . .

MURATA. A bath should be taken hot and slow. Don't know how Masako gets through so fast.

HANA. She probably doesn't get in the tub.

MASAKO. I do.

(*Everyone laughs.*)

Well I do.

(*Emiko comes out. She has a large purple welt on her face. She sits on the separate chair, hands folded, quietly watching the Muratas. They look at her with alarm. Oka engages himself with his fan.*)

HANA. Oh! Emiko-san . . . what . . . ah-ah . . . whaa . . . (*She draws a deep breath.*) What a nice bath we had . . . such a lovely bath. We do appreciate your hos . . . pitality. Thank you so much.

EMIKO. Lovely evening, isn't it?

HANA. Very lovely. Very. Ah, a little warm, but nice. . . . Did you get a chance to hear the records? (*Turning to Masako.*) Did you play the records for Mrs. Oka?

MASAKO. Ye— . . . no. . . . The needle was . . .

EMIKO. Yes, she did. We played the records together.

MURATA. Oh, you played the songs together?

EMIKO. Yes . . . yes . . .

MURATA. That's nice. . . . Masako can understand pretty good, eh?

EMIKO. She understands everything . . . everything I say.

MURATA (*withdrawing*). Oh, yeah? Eh, Mama, we ought to be going . . . (*He closes the player.*) Hate to bathe and run but . . .

HANA. Yes, yes. Tomorrow is a busy day. Come, Masako.

EMIKO. Please . . . stay a little longer.

MURATA. Eh, well, we got to be going.

HANA. Why, thank you, but . . .

EMIKO. It's still quite early.

OKA (*indicating he's ready to say good-bye*). Enjoyed the music. And the sake.

EMIKO. The records are very nice. Makes me remember Japan. I sang those songs . . . those very songs. . . . Did you know I used to sing?

HANA (*politely*). Why, no . . . no. I didn't know that. You must have a very lovely voice.

EMIKO. Yes.

HANA. No, I didn't know that. That's very nice.

EMIKO. Yes, I sang. My parents were very strict . . . they didn't like it. They said it was frivolous. Imagine?

HANA. Yes, I can imagine. Things were like that . . . in those days singing was not considered proper or nice . . . I mean, only for women in the profess— . . .

MURATA. We better get home, Mama.

HANA. Yes, yes. What a shame you couldn't continue with it.

EMIKO. In the city I did do some classics: the dance, and the *koto*, and the flower, and of course, the tea . . . (*She makes the proper gesture for the different disciplines.*) All those. Even some singing . . . classics, of course.

HANA (*politely*). Of course.

EMIKO. All of it is so disciplined . . . so disciplined. I was almost a *natori*.

HANA. Oh! How nice.

EMIKO. But everything has changed.

HANA. Oh!

EMIKO. I was sent here to America. (*She glares at Oka.*)

HANA. Oh, too bad . . . I mean, too bad about your *natori*.

MURATA (*loudly to Oka*). So did you see Nagata today?

OKA. Oh, yeah. Yeah.

MURATA. What did he say? Is he interested?

OKA. Yeah. Yeah. He's interested.

MURATA. He likes the horse, eh?

OKA. Ah . . . yeah.

MURATA. I knew he'd like him. I'd buy him myself if I had the money.

OKA. Well, I have to take him over tomorrow. He'll decide then.

MURATA. He'll buy . . . he'll buy. You'd better go straight over to the ticket office and get that ticket. Before you— ha-ha—spend the money.

OKA. Ha-ha. Yeah.

HANA. It'll be so nice when Kiyoko-san comes to join you. I know you're looking forward to it.

EMIKO (*confused*). Oh . . . oh . . .

HANA. Masako is so happy. It'll be good for her too.

EMIKO. I had more freedom in the city . . . I lived with an aunt and she let me. . . . She wasn't so strict.

(*Murata and Masako have their gear together and stand ready to leave.*)

MURATA. Good luck on the horse tomorrow.

OKA. Yeah, thanks.

HANA (*bowing*). Many, many thanks.

OKA (*nodding toward the sake*). Thanks for the sake.

HANA (*bowing again*). Good night, Emiko-san. We'll see you again soon. We'll bring the records too.

EMIKO (*softly*). Those songs . . . those very songs . . .

MURATA. Let's go, Mama.

(*The Muratas pull away. Light follows them and grows dark on the Okas. The Muratas begin walking home.*)

HANA. That was uncomfortable.

MASAKO. What's the matter with—

HANA. Shhhh!

MURATA. I guess Oka has his problems.

MASAKO. Is she really *kitchigai?*

HANA. Of course not. She's not crazy. Don't say that word, Masako.

MASAKO. I heard Mr. Oka call her that.

HANA. He called her that?

MASAKO. I . . . I think so.

HANA. You heard wrong, Masako. Emiko-san isn't crazy. She just likes her drinks. She had too much to drink tonight.

MASAKO. Oh.

HANA. She can't adjust to this life. She can't get over the good times she had in Japan. Well, it's not easy . . . but one has to know when to bend . . . like the bamboo. When the winds blow, bamboo bends. You bend or crack. Remember that, Masako.

MURATA (*laughing wryly*). Bend, eh? Remember that, Mama.

HANA (*softly*). You don't know . . . it isn't ever easy.

MASAKO. Do you want to go back to Japan, Mama?

HANA. Everyone does.

MASAKO. Do you, Papa?

MURATA. I'll have to make some money first.

MASAKO. I don't. Not me. Not Kiyoko . . .

HANA. After Kiyoko-san comes, Emiko will have company and things will straighten out. She has nothing to live on but memories. She doesn't have any friends. At least I have my friends at church . . . at least I have that. She must get awful lonely.

MASAKO. I know that. She tried to make friends with me.

HANA. She did? What did she say?

MASAKO. Well, sort of . . .

HANA. What did she say?

MASAKO. She didn't say anything. I just felt it. Maybe you should be her friend, Mama.

MURATA. Poor woman. We could have stayed longer.

HANA. But you wanted to leave. I tried to be friendly. You saw that. It's not easy to talk to Emiko. She either closes up, you can't pry a word from her, or else she goes on and on . . . all that . . . that . . . about the *koto* and tea and the flower . . . I mean, what am I supposed to say? She's so unpredictable. And the drinking . . .

MURATA. All right, all right, Mama.

MASAKO. Did you see her black eye?

HANA (*calming down*). She probably hurt herself. She wasn't very steady.

MASAKO. Oh, no. Mr. Oka hit her.

HANA. I don't think so.

MASAKO. He hit her. I saw him.

HANA. You saw that? Papa, do you hear that? She saw them. That does it. We're not going there again.

MURATA. Aww . . . Oka wouldn't do that. Not in front of a kid.

MASAKO. Well, they didn't do it in front of me. They were in the house.

MURATA. You see . . .

HANA. That's all right. You just have to fix the bathhouse. Either that or we're going to bathe at home . . . in a bucket.

We're not going . . . we'll bathe at home. (*Murata mutters to himself.*) What?

MURATA. I said all right, it's the bucket then. I'll get to it when I can.

(*Hana passes Murata and walks ahead.*)

SCENE 3

(*Same evening. Lights cross-fade to the exterior of the Oka house. The Muratas have just left. Emiko sits on the bench. Her back is to Oka. Oka, still standing, looks at her contemptuously as she takes the bottle and one of the cups to pour herself a drink.*)

OKA. Nothing more disgusting than a drunk woman. (*Emiko ignores him.*) You made a fool of yourself. *Washi baka ni shite!* You made a fool of me!

(*Emiko doesn't move.*)

EMIKO. One can only make a fool of oneself.

OKA. You learn that in the fancy schools, eh? (*Emiko examines the pattern on her cup.*) Eh? Eh? Answer me! (*Emiko ignores him.*) I'm talking to you. Answer me! (*Menacing.*) You don't get away with that. You think you're so fine . . .

(*Emiko looks off into the horizon. Oka turns her roughly around.*)

When I talk, you listen!

(*Emiko turns away again. Oka pulls the cup from her hand.*)

Goddamnit! What'd you think my friends think of you? What kind of ass they think I am? (*He grabs her shoulders.*)

EMIKO. Don't touch me . . . don't touch me.

OKA. Who the hell you think you are? "Don't touch me, don't touch me." Who the hell! High and mighty, eh? Too good for me, eh? Don't put on the act for me . . . I know who you are.

EMIKO. Tell me who I am, Mister Smart Peasant.

OKA. Shut your fool mouth, goddamnit! Sure! I'll tell you. I know all about you . . . Shizue told me. The whole village knows.

EMIKO. Shizue!

OKA. Yeah! Shizue. Embarrassed the hell out of her, your own sister.

EMIKO. Embarrassed? I have nothing to be ashamed of. I don't know what you're talking about.

OKA (*derisively*). You don't know what I'm talking about. I know. The whole village knows. They're all laughing at you. At me! Stupid Oka got stuck with a secondhand woman. I didn't say anything because . . .

EMIKO. I'm not secondhand!

OKA. Who you trying to fool? I know. Knew long time ago. . . . Shizue wrote me all about your affairs in Tokyo. The men you were mess—

EMIKO. Affairs? Men?

OKA. That man you were messing with . . . I know all along. I didn't say anything because you . . . I . . .

EMIKO. I'm not ashamed of it.

OKA. You're not ashamed! What the hell! Your father thought he was pulling a fast one on me . . . thought I didn't know anything . . . thought I was some kind of dumb ass . . . I didn't say nothing because Shizue's dead . . . Shizue's dead. I was willing to give you a chance.

EMIKO (*laughing*). A chance?

OKA. Yeah! A chance! Laugh! Give a *joro* another chance. Sure, I'm stupid . . . dumb.

EMIKO. I'm not a whore. I'm true . . . he knows I'm true.

OKA. True! Ha!

EMIKO. You think I'm untrue just because I let . . . let you. . . . There's only one man for me.

OKA (*obscene gesture*). You? I can do what I want with you. Your father palmed you off on me—like a dog or cat—an animal . . . couldn't do nothing with you. Even that rich dumb Yamoto wouldn't have you. Your father—greedy father—so proud . . . making big plans for you . . . for himself. Ha! The whole village laughing at him . . . (*Emiko hangs her head.*) Shizue told me. And she was working like a dog . . . trying to keep your goddamn father happy . . . doing my work and yours.

EMIKO. My work?

OKA. Yeah, your work too! She killed herself working! She killed herself . . . (*He has tender memories of his dull, uncomplaining wife.*) Up in the morning getting the fires started, working the bellows, cleaning the furnace, cooking, and late at night working with the sewing . . . tending the baby. . . . (*He mutters.*) The goddamn family killed her. And you . . . you out there in Tokyo with the fancy clothes, doing the (*He sneers.*) dance, the tea, the flower, the *koto*, and the . . . (*Obscene gesture.*)

EMIKO (*hurting*). Achhhh . . .

OKA. Did you have fun? Did you have fun on your sister's blood? (*Emiko doesn't answer.*) Did you? He must have been a son-of-a-bitch. . . . What would make that goddamn greedy old man send his prize mare to a plow horse like me? What kind of bum was he that your father—

EMIKO. He's not a bum . . . he's not a bum.

OKA. Was he Korean? Was he *Etta*? That's the only thing I could figure.

EMIKO. I'm true to him. Only him.

OKA. True? You think he's true to you? You think he waits for you? Remembers you? *Aho!* Think he cares?

EMIKO (*nodding quietly*). He does.

OKA. And waits ten years? *Baka!* Go back to Japan and see. You'll find out. Go back to Japan. *Kaire!*

EMIKO. In time.

OKA. In time? How about now?

EMIKO. I can't now.

OKA. Ha! Now! Go now! Who needs you? Who needs you? You think a man waits ten years for a woman? You think

you're some kind of . . . of . . . diamond . . . treasure . . . he's going to wait his life for you? Go to him. He's probably married with ten kids. Go to him. Get out! Goddamn *joro*. . . . Go! Go!

(*He sweeps Emiko off the bench.*)

EMIKO (*hurting*). Ahhhh! I . . . I don't have the money. Give me money to—

OKA. If I had money I would give it to you ten years ago. You think I been eating this *kuso* for ten years because I like it?

EMIKO. You're selling the horse. . . . Give me the—

OKA (*scoffing*). That's for Kiyoko. I owe you nothing.

EMIKO. Ten years, you owe me.

OKA. Ten years of what? Misery? You gave me nothing. I give you nothing. You want to go, pack your bag and start walking. Try crossing the desert. When you get dry and hungry, think about me.

EMIKO. I'd die out there.

OKA. Die? You think I didn't die here?

EMIKO. I didn't do anything to you.

OKA. No, no you didn't. All I wanted was a little comfort and . . . you . . . no, you didn't. No. So you die. We all die. Shizue died. If she was here, she wouldn't treat me like this. . . . (*He thinks of his poor dead wife.*) Ah. I should have brought her with me. She'd be alive now. We'd be poor but happy . . . like . . . like Murata and his wife . . . and the kid . . .

EMIKO. I wish she were alive too. I'm not to blame for her dying. I didn't know . . . I was away. I loved her. I didn't want her to die . . . I . . .

OKA (*softening*). I know that. I'm not blaming you for that. . . . And it's not my fault what happened to you either . . .

(*Emiko is silent and he mistakes that for a change in attitude. He is encouraged.*)

You understand that, eh? I didn't ask for you. It's not my fault you're here in this desert . . . with . . . with me . . .

(*Emiko weeps. Oka reaches out.*)

I know I'm too old for you. It's hard for me too . . . but this is the way it is. I just ask you be kinder . . . understand it wasn't my fault. Try make it easier for me . . . for yourself too.

(*Oka touches her and she shrinks from his touch.*)

EMIKO. Ach!

OKA (*humiliated again*). Goddamn it! I didn't ask for you! *Aho!* If you were smart you'd done as your father said . . . cut out that *saru shibai* with the *Etta* . . . married the rich Yamoto. Then you'd still be in Japan. Not here to make my life so miserable. (*Emiko is silent.*) And you can have your *Etta* . . . and anyone else you want. Take them all on . . . (*He is worn out. It's hopeless.*) God, why do we do this all the time? Fighting, fighting all the time. There must be a better way to live . . . there must be another way.

(*Oka waits for a response, gives up, and enters the house. Emiko watches him leave and pours herself another drink. The storm has passed, the alcohol takes over. She turns to the door Oka disappeared into.*)

EMIKO. Because I must keep the dream alive . . . the dream is all I live for. I am only in exile now. Because if I give in, all I've lived before . . . will mean nothing . . . will be for nothing. . . . Because if I let you make me believe this is all there is to my life, the dream would die . . . I would die . . . (*She pours another drink and feels warm and good.*)

(*Fade-out.*)

ACT 2

SCENE 1

(*Muratas' kitchen, afternoon. The calendar reads September. Masako is at the kitchen table with several books. She thumbs through a Japanese magazine. Hana is with her, sewing.*)

MASAKO. Do they always wear kimonos in Japan, Mama?

HANA. Most of the time.

MASAKO. I wonder if Kiyoko will be wearing a kimono like this?

HANA (*peering into Masako's magazine*). They don't dress like that . . . not for everyday.

MASAKO. I wonder what she's like.

HANA. Probably a lot like you. What do you think she's like?

MASAKO. She's probably taller.

HANA. Mr. Oka isn't tall.

MASAKO. And pretty.

HANA (*laughing*). Mr. Oka. . . . Well, I don't suppose she'll look like her father.

MASAKO. Mrs. Oka is pretty.

HANA. She isn't Kiyoko-san's real mother, remember.

MASAKO. Oh. That's right.

HANA. But they are related. Well, we'll soon see.

MASAKO. I thought she was coming in September. It's already September.

HANA. Papa said Oka-san went to San Pedro a few days ago. He should be back soon with Kiyoko-san.

MASAKO. Didn't Mrs. Oka go too?

HANA (*glancing toward the Oka house*). I don't think so. I see lights in their house at night.

MASAKO. Will they bring Kiyoko over to see us?

HANA. Of course. First thing, probably. You'll be very nice to her, won't you?

MASAKO (*leaves the table and finds another book*). Sure. I'm glad I'm going to have a friend. I hope she likes me.

HANA. She'll like you. Japanese girls are very polite, you know.

MASAKO. We have to be or our mamas get mad at us.

HANA. Then I should be getting mad at you more often.

MASAKO. It's often enough already, Mama. (*She opens a hardback book.*) Look at this, Mama . . . I'm going to show her this book.

HANA. She won't be able to read at first.

MASAKO. I love this story. Mama, this is about people like us—settlers—it's about the prairie. We live in a prairie, don't we?

HANA. Prairie? Does that mean desert?

MASAKO. I think so.

HANA (*nodding and looking bleak*). We live in a prairie.

MASAKO. It's about the hardships and the floods and droughts and how they have nothing but each other.

HANA (*nodding*). We have nothing but each other. But these people—they're white people.

MASAKO (*nodding*). Sure, Mama. They come from the East. Just like you and Papa came from Japan.

HANA. We come from the Far Far East. That's different. White people are different from us.

MASAKO. I know that.

HANA. White people among white people . . . that's different from Japanese among white people. You know what I'm saying?

MASAKO. I know that. How come they don't write books about us . . . about Japanese people?

HANA. Because we're nobodies here.

MASAKO. If I didn't read these, there'd be nothing for me . . .

HANA. Some of the things you read, you're never going to know.

MASAKO. I can dream though.

HANA (*sighing*). Sometimes the dreaming makes the living harder. Better to keep your head out of the clouds.

MASAKO. That's not much fun.

HANA. You'll have fun when Kiyoko-san comes. You can study together, you can sew, and sometimes you can try some of those fancy American recipes.

MASAKO. Mama, you have to have chocolate and cream and things like that.

HANA. We'll get them.

(*We hear the putt-putt of Oka's old car. Masako and Hana pause and listen. Masako runs to the window.*)

MASAKO. I think it's them!

HANA. The Okas?

MASAKO. It's them! It's them!

(*Hana stands and looks out. She removes her apron and puts away her sewing.*)

HANA. Two of them. Emiko-san isn't with them. Let's go outside.

(*Oka and Kiyoko, fourteen, enter. Oka is wearing his going-out clothes; a sweater, white shirt, dark pants, but no tie. Kiyoko walks behind him. She is short, chunky, broad-chested and very self-conscious. Her hair is straight and banded into two shucks. She wears a conservative cotton dress, white socks and two-inch heels. Oka is proud. He struts in, his chest puffed out.*)

OKA. Hello, hello. . . . We're here. We made it! (*He pushes Kiyoko forward.*) This is my daughter, Kiyoko. (*To Kiyoko.*) Murata-san . . . remember I was talking about? My friends . . .

KIYOKO (*barely audible as she speaks a standard formal greeting, bowing deeply*). *Hajime mashite yoroshiku onegai shimasu . . .*

HANA (*also bowing formally*). I hope your journey was pleasant.

OKA. (*While the women are still bowing, he pushes Kiyoko toward Masako*). This is Masako-chan; I told you about her . . .

(*Masako is shocked at Kiyoko's appearance. The girl she expected is already a woman. She stands with her mouth agape and withdraws noticeably. Hana rushes in to fill the awkwardness.*)

HANA. Say hello, Masako. My goodness, where are your manners? (*She laughs apologetically.*) In this country they don't make much to-do about manners. (*She stands back to examine Kiyoko.*) My, my, I didn't picture you so grown up. My, my. . . . Tell me, how was your trip?

OKA (*proudly*). We just drove in from Los Angeles just this morning. We spent the night in San Pedro and the next two days we spent in Los Angeles . . . you know, Japanese town.

HANA. How nice!

OKA. Kiyoko was so excited. Twisting her head this way and that—couldn't see enough with her big eyes. (*He imitates her fondly.*) She's from the country, you know . . . just a big country girl. Got all excited about the Chinese dinner—we had a Chinese dinner. She never ate it before.

(*Kiyoko covers her mouth and giggles.*)

HANA. Chinese dinner!

OKA. Oh, yeah. Duck, *pakkai*, chow mein, seaweed soup . . . the works!

HANA. A feast!

OKA. Oh, yeah. Like a holiday. Two holidays. Two holidays in one.

HANA (*pushes Masako forward*). Two holidays in one! Kiyoko-san, our Masako has been looking forward to meeting you.

KIYOKO (*bowing again*). *Hajime mashite . . .*

HANA. She's been thinking of all sorts of things she can do with you: sewing, cooking . . .

MASAKO. Oh, Mama.

(*Kiyoko covers her mouth and giggles.*)

HANA. It's true, Kiyoko-san. She's been looking forward to having a best friend.

(*Kiyoko giggles again and Masako pulls away.*)

OKA. Kiyoko, you shouldn't be so shy. The Muratas are my good friends and you should feel free with them. Ask anything, say anything . . . right?

HANA. Of course, of course. (*She is slightly annoyed with Masako.*) Masako, go in and start the tea.

(*Masako enters the house.*)

I'll call Papa. He's in the yard. Papa! Oka-san is here! (*To Kiyoko.*) Now tell me, how was your trip? Did you get seasick?

KIYOKO (*bowing and nodding*). *Eh* [Yes]. A little . . .

OKA. Tell her. Tell her how sick you got.

(*Kiyoko covers her mouth and giggles.*)

HANA. Oh, I know, I know. I was too. That was a long time ago. I'm sure things are improved now. Tell me about Japan . . . what is it like now? They say it's so changed . . . modern . . .

OKA. Kiyoko comes from the country . . . backwoods. Nothing change much there from century to century.

HANA. Ah! That's true. That's why I love Japan. And you wanted to leave. It's unbelievable. To come here!

OKA. She always dreamed about it.

HANA. Well, it's not really that bad.

OKA. No, it's not that bad. Depends on what you make of it.

HANA. That's right. What you make of it. I was just telling Masako today . . .

(*Murata enters. He rubs his hands to take off the soil and comes in grinning. He shakes Oka's hand.*)

MURATA. *Oi, oi . . .*

OKA. Yah . . . I'm back. This is my daughter.

MURATA. No! She's beautiful!

OKA. Finally made it. Finally got her here.

MURATA (*to Kiyoko*). Your father hasn't stopped talking about you all summer.

HANA. And Masako too.

KIYOKO (*bowing*). *Hajime mashite . . .*

MURATA (*acknowledging with a short bow*). Yah. How'd you like the trip?

OKA. I was just telling your wife—had a good time in Los Angeles. Had a couple of great dinners, took in the cinema—Japanese pictures, bought her some American clothes.

HANA. Oh, you bought that in Los Angeles.

MURATA. Got a good price for your horse, eh? Lots of money, eh?

OKA. Nagata's a shrewd bargainer. Heh. It don't take much money to make her happy. She's a country girl.

MURATA. That's all right. Country's all right. Country girl's the best.

OKA. Had trouble on the way back.

MURATA. Yeah?

OKA. Fan belt broke.

MURATA. That'll happen.

OKA. Lucky I was near a gasoline station. We were in the mountains. Waited in a restaurant while it was getting fixed.

HANA. Oh, that was good.

OKA. Guess they don't see Japanese much. Stare? Terrible! Took them a long time to wait on us. Dumb waitress practically threw the food at us. Kiyoko felt bad.

HANA. Ah! That's too bad . . . too bad. That's why I always pack a lunch when we take trips.

MURATA. They'll spoil the day for you . . . those barbarians!

OKA. Terrible food too. Kiyoko couldn't swallow the dry bread and bologna.

HANA. That's the food they eat!

MURATA. Let's go in . . . have a little wine. Mama, we got wine? This is a celebration.

HANA. I think so . . . a little . . .

(*They enter the house talking. Masako has made the tea, and Hana begins to serve the wine.*)

How is your "mother"? Was she happy to see you?

KIYOKO. Oh, she . . . yes . . .

HANA. I just know she was surprised to see you so grown up. Of course, you remember her from Japan, don't you?

KIYOKO (*nodding*). Eh. I can barely remember. I was very young . . .

HANA. Of course. But you do, don't you?

KIYOKO. She was gone most of the time . . . at school in Tokyo. She was very pretty, I remember that.

HANA. She's still very pretty.

KIYOKO. Eh. She was always laughing. She was much younger then.

HANA. Oh now, it hasn't been that long ago.

(*Masako leaves the room to go outside. The following dialogue continues muted as light goes dim in the house and focuses on Masako. Emiko enters, is drawn to the Murata window and listens.*)

OKA. We stayed at an inn on East First Street. *Shizuokaya.* Whole inn filled with Shizuoka people . . . talking the old dialect. Thought I was in Japan again.

MURATA. That right?

OKA. Felt good. Like I was in Japan again.

HANA (*to Kiyoko*). Did you enjoy Los Angeles?

KIYOKO (*nodding*). Eh.

OKA. That's as close as I'll get to Japan.

MURATA. *Mattakuna!* That's for sure.

(*Outside Masako becomes aware of Emiko.*)

MASAKO. Why don't you go in?

EMIKO. Oh. Oh. Why don't you?

MASAKO. They're all grownups in there. I'm not grown up.

EMIKO (*softly*). All grownups. . . . Maybe I'm not either. (*Her mood changes.*) Masa-chan, do you have a boyfriend?

MASAKO. I don't like boys. They don't like me.

EMIKO. Oh, that will change. You will change. I was like that too.

MASAKO. Besides, there're none around here . . . Japanese boys. . . . There are some at school, but they don't like girls.

HANA (*calling from the kitchen*). Masako . . .

(*Masako doesn't answer.*)

EMIKO. Your mother is calling you.

MASAKO (*answering her mother*). *Nani* (What)?

HANA (*from the kitchen*). Come inside now.

EMIKO. You'll have a boyfriend one day.

MASAKO. Not me.

EMIKO. You'll fall in love one day. Someone will make the inside of you light up, and you'll know you're in love. (*She relives her own experience.*) Your life will change . . . grow beautiful. It's good, Masa-chan. And this feeling you'll remember the rest of your life . . . will come back to you . . . haunt you . . . keep you alive . . . five, ten years . . . no matter what happens . . . keep you alive.

HANA (*from the kitchen*). Masako. . . . Come inside now.

(*Masako turns aside to answer and Emiko slips away.*)

MASAKO. What, Mama?

HANA (*coming outside*). Come inside. Don't be so unsociable. Kiyoko wants to talk to you.

MASAKO (*watching Emiko leave*). She doesn't want to talk to me. You're only saying that.

HANA. What's the matter with you? Don't you want to make friends with her?

MASAKO. She's not my friend. She's your friend.

HANA. Don't be silly. She's only fourteen.

MASAKO. Fifteen. They said fifteen. She's your friend. She's an old lady.

HANA. Don't say that.

MASAKO. I don't like her.

HANA. Shhh! Don't say that.

MASAKO. She doesn't like me either.

HANA. Ma-chan. Remember your promise to Mr. Oka? You're going to take her to school, teach her the language, teach her the ways of Americans.

MASAKO. She can do it herself. You did.

HANA. That's not nice, Ma-chan.

MASAKO. I don't like the way she laughs. (*She imitates Kiyoko holding her hand to her mouth and giggling and bowing.*)

HANA. Oh, how awful! Stop that. That's the way the girls do in Japan. Maybe she doesn't like your ways either. That's only a difference in manners. What you're doing now is considered very bad manners. (*She changes tone.*) Ma-chan . . . just wait—when she learns to read and speak, you'll have so much to say to each other. Come on, be a good girl and come inside.

MASAKO. It's just old people in there, Mama. I don't want to go in.

(*Hana calls Kiyoko away from the table and speaks confidentially to her.*)

HANA. Kiyoko-san, please come here a minute. Maybe it's better for you to talk to Masako alone.

(*Kiyoko leaves the table and walks to Hana outside.*)

Masako has a lot of things to tell you about . . . what to expect in school and things . . .

MURATA (*calling from the table*). Mama, put out something . . . chiles . . . for Oka-san.

(*Hana leaves the two girls and enters the house. Kiyoko and Masako stand awkwardly, Kiyoko glancing shyly at Masako.*)

MASAKO. Do you like it here?

KIYOKO (*nodding*). Eh.

(*There's an uncomfortable pause.*)

MASAKO. School will be starting next week . . .

KIYOKO (*nodding*). Eh.

MASAKO. Do you want to walk to school with me?

KIYOKO (*nodding*). Ah.

MASAKO (*rolls her eyes and tries again*). I leave at 7:30.

KIYOKO. Ah.

(*There's a long pause. Masako finally gives up and moves offstage.*)

MASAKO. I have to do something.

(*Kiyoko watches her leave and uncertainly moves back to the house. Hana looks up at Kiyoko coming in alone, sighs, and quietly pulls out a chair for her. Fade-out.*)

SCENE 2

(*November, night. Interior of the Murata house. Lamps are lit. The family is at the kitchen table. Hana sews, Masako does her homework, Murata reads the paper. They're dressed in warm robes and having tea. Outside, thunder rolls in the distance and lightning flashes.*)

HANA. It'll be ohigan (an autumn festival) soon.

MURATA. Something to look forward to.

HANA. We will need sweet rice for omochi (rice cakes).

MURATA. I'll order it next time I go to town.

HANA (*to Masako*). How is school? Getting a little harder?

MASAKO. Not that much. Sometimes the arithmetic is hard.

HANA. How is Kiyoko-san doing? Is she getting along all right?

MASAKO. She's good in arithmetic. She skipped a grade already.

HANA. Already? That's good news. Only November and she skipped a grade! At this rate she'll be through before you.

MASAKO. Well, she's older.

MURATA. Sure, she's older, Mama.

HANA. Has she made any friends?

MASAKO. No. She follows me around all day. She understands okay, but she doesn't talk. She talks like, you know . . . she says "ranchi" for lunch and "ranchi" for ranch

too, and like that. Kids laugh and copy behind her back. It's hard to understand her.

HANA. You understand her, don't you?

MASAKO. I'm used to it.

(*Murata smiles secretly.*)

HANA. You should tell the kids not to laugh; after all, she's trying. Maybe you should help her practice those words . . . show her what she's doing wrong.

MASAKO. I already do. Our teacher told me to do that.

MURATA (*looking up from his paper*). You ought to help her all you can.

HANA. And remember when you started school you couldn't speak English either.

MASAKO. I help her.

(*Murata rises and goes to the window. The night is cold. Lightning flashes and the wind whistles.*)

MURATA. Looks like a storm coming up. Hope we don't have a freeze.

HANA. If it freezes, we'll have another bad year. Maybe we ought to start the smudge pots.

MURATA (*listening*). It's starting to rain. Nothing to do now but pray.

HANA. If praying is the answer, we'd be in Japan now . . . rich.

MURATA (*wryly*). We're not dead yet. We still have a chance. (*Hana glares at this small joke.*) Guess I'll turn in.

HANA. Go to bed . . . go to bed. I'll sit up and worry.

MURATA. If worrying was the answer, we'd be around the world twice and in Japan. Come on, Mama. Let's go to bed. It's too cold tonight to be mad.

(*There's an urgent knock on the door. The family react to it.*)

Dareh da! (*Goes to the door and pauses*) Who is it!

KIYOKO (*weakly*). It's me . . . help me . . .

(*Murata opens the door and Kiyoko enters. She's dressed in a kimono with a shawl thrown over. Her legs are bare except for a pair of straw zori. Her hair is stringy from the rain and she trembles from the cold.*)

MURATA. My God! Kiyoko-san! What's the matter?

HANA. Kiyoko-san! What is it?

MURATA. What happened?

KIYOKO (*gasping*). They're fighting . . . they're fighting.

MURATA. Ah . . . don't worry . . . those things happen. No cause to worry. Mama, make tea for her. Sit down and catch your breath. I'll take you home when you're ready.

HANA. Papa, I'll take care of it.

MURATA. Let me know when you're ready to go home.

HANA. It must be freezing out there. Try to get warm. Try to calm yourself.

MURATA. Kiyoko-san . . . don't worry.

(*Hana waves Masako and Murata off. Murata leaves. Masako goes to her bed in the kitchen.*)

HANA. Papa, I'll take care of it.

KIYOKO (*looking at Murata's retreating form*). I came to ask your help.

HANA. You ran down here without a lantern? You could have fallen and hurt yourself.

KIYOKO. I don't care . . . I don't care.

HANA. You don't know, Kiyoko-san. It's treacherous out there . . . snakes, spiders . . .

KIYOKO. I must go back . . . I . . . I . . . you . . . please come with me.

HANA. First, first, we must get you warm. . . . Drink your tea.

KIYOKO. But they might kill each other. They're fighting like animals. Help me stop them!

HANA (*goes to the stove to warm a pot of soup*). I cannot interfere in a family quarrel.

KIYOKO. It's not a quarrel . . . it's a . . .

HANA. That's all it is. A family squabble. You'll see. Tomorrow . . .

KIYOKO (*rises and puts her hand on Hana's arm*). Not just a squabble . . . please!

(*She starts toward the door but Hana restrains her.*)

HANA. Now listen. Listen to me, Kiyoko-san. I've known your father and mother a little while now. I suspect it's been like this for years. Every family has some kind of trouble.

KIYOKO. Not like this . . . not like this.

HANA. Some have it better—some worse. When you get married, you'll understand. Don't worry. Nothing will happen. (*She takes a towel from the wall and dries Kiyoko's hair.*) You're chilled to the bone. You'll catch your death . . .

KIYOKO. I don't care . . . I want to die.

HANA. Don't be silly. It's not that bad.

KIYOKO. They started drinking early in the afternoon. They make some kind of brew and hide it somewhere in the desert.

HANA. It's illegal to make it. That's why they hide it. That home brew is poison to the body . . . and the mind too.

KIYOKO. It makes them crazy. They drink it all the time and quarrel constantly. I was in the other room studying. I try so hard to keep up with school.

HANA. We were talking about you just this evening. Masako says you're doing so well . . . you skipped a grade?

KIYOKO. It's hard . . . hard . . . I'm too old for the class and the children . . . (*She remembers all her problems and starts to cry again.*)

HANA. It's always hard in a new country.

KIYOKO. They were bickering and quarreling all afternoon. Then something happened. All of a sudden I saw them on the floor . . . hitting and . . . and. . . . He was hitting her in the stomach, the face. . . . I tried to stop them, but they were so . . . drunk.

HANA. There, there. . . . It's probably all over now.

KIYOKO. Why does it happen like this? Nothing is right. Everywhere I go . . . Masa-chan is so lucky. I wish my life was like hers. I can hardly remember my real mother.

HANA. Emiko-san is almost a real mother to you. She's blood kin.

KIYOKO. She hates me. She never speaks to me. She's so cold. I want to love her but she won't let me. She hates me.

HANA. I don't think that's true, Kiyoko-san.

KIYOKO. I know it's true.

HANA. No. I don't think you have anything to do with it. It's this place. She hates it. This place is so lonely and alien.

KIYOKO. Then why didn't she go back? Why did they stay here?

HANA. You don't know. It's not so simple. Sometimes I think—

KIYOKO. Then why don't they make the best of it here? Like you?

HANA. That isn't easy either. Believe me. (*She goes to the stove to stir the soup.*) Sometimes . . . sometimes the longing for homeland fills me with despair. Will I never return again? Will I never see my mother, my father, my sisters again? But what can one do? There are responsibilities here . . . children . . . (*She draws a sharp breath.*) And another day passes . . . another month . . . another year. Eventually everything passes. (*She takes the soup to Kiyoko.*) Did you have supper tonight?

KIYOKO (*bowing gratefully*). Ah. When my . . . my aunt gets like this, she doesn't cook. No one eats. I don't get hungry anymore.

HANA. Cook for yourself. It's important to keep your health.

KIYOKO. I left Japan for a better life here . . .

HANA. It isn't easy for you, is it? But you must remember your final duty.

KIYOKO. It's so hard.

HANA. But you can make the best of it here, Kiyoko-san. And take care of yourself. You owe that to yourself. Eat. Keep well. It'll be better, you'll see. And sometimes it'll seem worse. But you'll survive. We do, you know . . . we do . . . (*She looks around.*) It's getting late.

KIYOKO (*apprehensively*). I don't want to go back.

HANA. You can sleep with Masako tonight. Tomorrow you'll go back. And you'll remember what I told you.

(*She puts her arms around Kiyoko, who is overcome with self-pity and begins to weep quietly.*)

Life is never easy, Kiyoko-san. Endure. Endure. Soon you'll be marrying and going away. Things will not always be this way. And you'll look back on this . . . this night and you'll—

(*There is a rap on the door. Hana exchanges glances with Kiyoko and goes to answer it. She opens it a crack. Oka has come looking for Kiyoko. He's dressed in an overcoat and holds a wet newspaper over his head.*)

OKA. Ah! I'm sorry to bother you so late at night . . . the fact is . . .

HANA. Oka-san . . .

OKA (*jovially*). Good evening, good evening . . . (*He sees Kiyoko.*) Ah . . . there you are. . . . Did you have a nice visit?

HANA (*irritated*). Yes, she's here.

OKA (*still cheerful*). Thought she might be. Ready to come home now?

HANA. She came in the rain.

OKA (*ignoring Hana's tone*). That's foolish of you, Kiyoko. You might catch cold.

HANA. She was frightened by your quarreling. She came for help.

OKA (*laughing with embarrassment*). Oh! Kiyoko, that's nothing to worry about. It's just we had some disagreement . . .

HANA. That's what I told her, but she was frightened all the same.

OKA. Children are—

HANA. Not children, Oka-san. Kiyoko. Kiyoko was terrified. I think that was a terrible thing to do to her.

OKA (*rubbing his head*). Oh, I . . . I . . .

HANA. If you had seen her a few minutes ago . . . hysterical . . . shaking . . . crying . . . wet and cold to the bone . . . out of her mind with worry.

OKA (*rubbing his head*). Oh . . . I . . . don't know what she was so worried about.

HANA. You. You and Emiko fighting like you were going to kill each other.

OKA. (*There's nothing more to hide. He lowers his head in penitence.*) Aaaaaachhhhhhh . . .

HANA. I know I shouldn't tell you this, but there's one or two things I have to say: You sent for Kiyoko-san and now she's here. You said yourself she had a bad time in Japan, and now she's having a worse time. It isn't easy for her in a strange new country; the least you can do is try to keep her from worrying . . . especially about yourselves. I think it's terrible what you're doing to her . . . terrible!

OKA (*bowing in deep humility*). I am ashamed . . .

HANA. I think she deserves better. I think you should think about that.

OKA (*still in his bow*). I thank you for this reminder. It will never happen again. I promise.

HANA. I don't need that promise. Make it to Kiyoko-san.

OKA (*to Kiyoko*). Come with Papa now. He did a bad thing. He'll be a good papa from now on. He won't worry his little girl again. All right? All right?

(*They move to the door.*)

KIYOKO. Thank you so much.

(*Hana puts Murata's robe around Kiyoko, who tries to return it.*)

OKA. Madam. I thank you again.

HANA (*to Kiyoko*). That's all right. You can bring it back tomorrow. (*Aside to Kiyoko.*) Remember . . . remember what we talked about. (*Loudly.*) Good night, Oka-san.

(*They leave. Hana goes to Masako, who lies on the bed, and covers her. Murata appears from the bedroom. He's heard it all. He and Hana exchange a glance and together they retire to their room. Fade-out.*)

SCENE 3

(*The next morning. The Murata house and yard. Hana and Murata have already left the house to examine the rain damage in the fields. Masako prepares to go to school. She puts on a coat and picks up her books and lunch bag. Meanwhile, Kiyoko slips quietly into the yard. She wears a coat and carries Murata's robe. She sets it on the outside bench. Masako walks out and is surprised to see Kiyoko.*)

MASAKO. Hi. I thought you'd be . . . sick today.

KIYOKO. Oh. I woke up late.

MASAKO (*scrutinizing Kiyoko's face*). Your eyes are red.

KIYOKO (*averting her eyes*). Oh, I . . . got . . . sand in it. Yes.

MASAKO. Do you want to use eye drops? We have eye drops in the house.

KIYOKO. Oh . . . no. That's all right.

MASAKO. That's what you call bloodshot.

KIYOKO. Oh.

MASAKO. My father gets it a lot. When he drinks too much.

KIYOKO. Oh . . .

MASAKO (*notices Kiyoko doesn't have her lunch*). Where's your lunch bag?

KIYOKO. I . . . forgot it.

MASAKO. Did you make your lunch today?

KIYOKO. Yes. Yes, I did. But I forgot it.

MASAKO. Do you want to go back and get it?

KIYOKO. No, that's all right.

(*They are silent for a while.*)

We'll be late.

MASAKO. Do you want to practice your words?

KIYOKO (*thoughtfully*). Oh . . .

MASAKO. Say, "My."

KIYOKO. My?

MASAKO. Eyes . . .

KIYOKO. Eyes.

MASAKO. Are . . .

KIYOKO. Are.

MASAKO. Red.

KIYOKO. Red.

MASAKO. Your eyes are red. (*Kiyoko doesn't repeat it.*) I . . . (*Kiyoko doesn't cooperate.*) Say, "I."

KIYOKO. I.

MASAKO. Got . . .

KIYOKO. Got.

MASAKO. Sand . . . (*Kiyoko balks.*) Say, "I."

KIYOKO (*sighing*). I.

MASAKO. Reft . . .

KIYOKO. Reft.

MASAKO. My . . .

KIYOKO. My.

MASAKO. Runch . . .

KIYOKO. Run . . . lunch. (*She stops.*) Masako-san, you are mean. You are hurting me.

MASAKO. It's a joke! I was just trying to make you laugh!

KIYOKO. I cannot laugh today.

MASAKO. Sure you can. You can laugh. Laugh! Like this! (*She makes a hearty laugh.*)

KIYOKO. I cannot laugh when you make fun of me.

MASAKO. Okay, I'm sorry. We'll practice some other words then, okay? (*Kiyoko doesn't answer.*) Say, "Okay."

KIYOKO (*reluctantly*). Okay . . .

MASAKO. Okay, then . . . um . . . um . . . (*She still teases and talks rapidly.*) Say . . . um . . . "She sells sea shells on the sea shore."

(*Kiyoko turns away indignantly.*)

Aw, come on, Kiyoko! It's just a joke. Laugh!

KIYOKO (*imitating sarcastically*). Ha-ha-ha! Now you say, "Kono kyaku waki yoku kaki ku kyaku da (This guest eats a lot of persimmons)!"

MASAKO. Sure! I can say it! *Kono kyaku waki ku kyoku kaku* . . .

KIYOKO. That's not right.

MASAKO. *Koki kuki kya* . . .

KIYOKO. No.

MASAKO. Okay, then. You say, "Sea sells she shells . . . shu . . . sss . . ."

(*They both laugh, Kiyoko with her hands over her mouth. Masako takes Kiyoko's hands from her mouth.*)

Not like that! Like this! (*She gives a big belly laugh.*)

KIYOKO. Like this? (*She imitates Masako.*)

MASAKO. Yeah, that's right! You're not mad anymore?

KIYOKO. I'm not mad anymore.

MASAKO. Okay. You can share my lunch today because we're . . .

KIYOKO. "Flends?"

(*Masako looks at Kiyoko, they giggle and move on. Hana and Murata come in from assessing the storm's damage. They are dressed warmly. Hana is depressed. Murata tries hard to be cheerful.*)

MURATA. It's not so bad, Mama.

HANA. Half the ranch is flooded . . . at least half.

MURATA. No-no. A quarter, maybe. It's sunny today . . . it'll dry.

HANA. The seedlings will rot.

MURATA. No, no. It'll dry. It's all right—better than I expected.

HANA. If we have another bad year, no one will lend us money for the next crop.

MURATA. Don't worry. If it doesn't drain by tomorrow, I'll replant the worst places. We still have some seed left. Yeah, I'll replant . . .

HANA. More work.

MURATA. Don't worry, Mama. It'll be all right.

HANA (*quietly*). Papa, where will it end? Will we always be like this—always at the mercy of the weather—prices—always at the mercy of the gods?

MURATA (*patting Hana's back*). Things will change. Wait and see. We'll be back in Japan by . . . in two years . . . guarantee. . . . Maybe sooner.

HANA (*dubiously*). Two years . . .

MURATA (*finds the robe on the bench*). Ah, look, Mama. Kiyoko-san brought back my robe.

HANA (*sighing*). Kiyoko-san . . . poor Kiyoko-san . . . and Emiko-san.

MURATA. Ah, Mama. We're lucky. We're lucky, Mama.

(*Hana smiles sadly at Murata. Fade-out.*)

SCENE 4

(*The following spring, afternoon. Exterior of the Oka house. Oka is dressed to go out. He wears a sweater, long-sleeved white shirt, dark pants, no tie. He puts his foot on the bench to wipe off his shoe with the palm of his hand. He straightens his sleeve, removes a bit of lint, and runs his fingers through his hair. He hums under his breath. Kiyoko comes from the house. Her hair is frizzled with a permanent wave, she wears a gaudy new dress and a pair of new shoes. She carries a movie magazine—Photoplay or Modern Screen.*)

OKA (*appreciatively*). Pretty. Pretty.

KIYOKO (*turning for him*). It's not too *hadeh?* I feel strange in colors.

OKA. Oh no. Young girls should wear bright colors. There's time enough to wear gray when you get old. Old-lady colors. (*Kiyoko giggles.*) Sure you want to go to the picture show? It's such a nice day . . . shame to waste in a dark hall.

KIYOKO. Where else can we go?

OKA. We can go to the Muratas.

KIYOKO. All dressed up?

OKA. Or Nagatas. I'll show him what I got for my horse.

KIYOKO (*laughing*). Oh, I love the pictures.

OKA. We don't have many nice spring days like this. Here the season is short. Summer comes in like a dragon . . . right behind . . . breathing fire . . . like a dragon. You don't know the summers here. They'll scare you. (*He tousles Kiyoko's hair and pulls a lock of it. It springs back. He shakes his head in wonder.*) Goddamn. Curly hair. Never thought curly hair could make you so happy.

KIYOKO (*giggling*). All the American girls have curly hair.

OKA. Your friend Masako like it?

KIYOKO (*nodding*). She says her mother will never let her get a permanent wave.

851

OKA. She said that, eh? Bet she's wanting one.

KIYOKO. I don't know about that.

OKA. Bet she's wanting some of your pretty dresses too.

KIYOKO. Her mother makes all her clothes.

OKA. Buying is just as good. Buying is better. No trouble that way.

KIYOKO. Masako's not so interested in clothes. She loves the pictures, but her mother won't let her go. Someday, can we take Masako with us?

OKA. If her mother lets her come. Her mother's got a mind of her own . . . a stiff back.

KIYOKO. But she's nice.

OKA (*dubiously*). Oh, yeah. Can't be perfect, I guess. Kiyoko, after the harvest I'll have money and I'll buy you the prettiest dress in town. I'm going to be lucky this year. I feel it.

KIYOKO. You're already too good to me . . . dresses, shoes, permanent wave . . . movies . . .

OKA. That's nothing. After the harvest, just wait . . .

KIYOKO. Magazines. . . . You do enough. I'm happy already.

OKA. You make me happy too, Kiyoko. You make me feel good . . . like a man again. . . . (*That statement bothers him.*) One day you're going to make a young man happy. (*Kiyoko giggles.*) Someday we going to move from here.

KIYOKO. But we have good friends here, Papa.

OKA. Next year our lease will be up and we got to move.

KIYOKO. The ranch is not ours?

OKA. No. In America, Japanese cannot own land. We lease and move every two, three years. Next year we going to go someplace where there's young fellows. There's none good enough for you here. (*He watches Kiyoko giggle.*) Yeah. You going to make a good wife. Already a good cook. I like your cooking.

KIYOKO (*a little embarrassed*). Shall we go now?

OKA. Yeah. Put the magazine away.

KIYOKO. I want to take it with me.

OKA. Take it with you?

KIYOKO. Last time, after we came back, I found all my magazines torn in half.

OKA (*looking toward the house*). Torn?

KIYOKO. This is the only one I have left.

OKA (*not wanting to deal with it*). All right. All right.

(*The two prepare to leave when the door opens. Emiko stands there, her hair is unkempt and she looks wild. She holds an empty can in one hand, the lid in the other.*)

EMIKO. Where is it?

(*Oka tries to make a hasty departure.*)

KIYOKO. Where is what?

(*Oka pushes Kiyoko ahead of him, still trying to make a getaway.*)

EMIKO. Where is it? Where is it? What did you do with it?

(*Emiko moves toward Oka. He can't ignore her and he stops.*)

OKA (*with false unconcern to Kiyoko*). Why don't you walk on ahead to the Muratas?

KIYOKO. We're not going to the pictures?

OKA. We'll go. First you walk to the Muratas. Show them your new dress. I'll meet you there.

(*Kiyoko picks up a small package and exits. Oka sighs and shakes his head.*)

EMIKO (*shaking the can*). Where is it? What did you do with it?

OKA (*feigning surprise*). With what?

EMIKO. You know what. You stole it. You stole my money.

OKA. *Your* money?

EMIKO. I've been saving that money.

OKA. Yeah? Well, where'd you get it? Where'd you get it, eh? You stole it from me! Dollar by dollar. . . . You stole it from me! Out of my pocket.

EMIKO. I saved it!

OKA. From my pocket!

EMIKO. It's mine! I saved for a long time. . . . Some of it I brought from Japan.

OKA. *Bakayuna!* What'd you bring from Japan? Nothing but some useless kimonos.

(*Oka starts to leave but Emiko hangs on to him.*)

EMIKO. Give back my money! Thief!

OKA (*swings around and balls his fists but doesn't strike*). Goddamn! Get off me!

EMIKO (*now pleading*). Please give it back . . . please . . . please . . .

(*She starts to stroke him. Oka pulls her hands away and pushes her from him.*)

Oni!

OKA (*seething*). *Oni?* What does that make you? *Oni baba?* Yeah, that's what you are . . . a devil!

EMIKO. It's mine! Give it back . . .

OKA. The hell! You think you can live off me and steal my money too? How stupid you think I am?

EMIKO (*tearfully*). But I've paid . . . I've paid . . .

OKA. With what?

EMIKO. You know I've paid.

OKA (*scoffing*). You call that paying?

EMIKO. What did you do with it?

OKA. I don't have it.

EMIKO. It's gone? It's gone?

OKA. Yeah! It's gone. I spent it. The hell! Every last cent.

EMIKO. The new clothes . . . the curls . . . restaurants . . . pictures . . . shoes. . . . My money . . . my going-home money . . .

OKA. You through?

EMIKO. What will I do? What will—

OKA. I don't care what you do. Walk. Use your feet. Swim to Japan. I don't care. I give you no more than you gave me. Now I don't want anything. I don't care what you do. (*He walks away.*)

(*Emiko still holds the empty can. Offstage we hear Oka's car door slam and the sound of his old car starting off. Accustomed to crying alone, she doesn't utter a sound. Her shoulders begin to shake, her dry soundless sobs turn to a silent laugh. She wipes the dust gently from the can as though comforting a friend. Her movements become sensuous, her hands move on to her own body, around her throat, over her breasts, to her hips, caressing, soothing, reminding her of her lover's hands. Fade-out.*)

SCENE 5

(*Same day, late afternoon. Exterior of the Murata house. The light is soft. Hana is sweeping the yard; Masako hangs a glass wind chime on the exposed wall.*)

HANA (*directing Masako*). There . . . there. That's a good place.

MASAKO. Here?

HANA (*nodding*). It must catch the slightest breeze. (*Sighing and listening.*) It brings back so much. . . . That's the reason I never hung one before. I guess it doesn't matter much anymore . . .

MASAKO. I thought you liked to think about Japan.

HANA (*laughing sadly*). I didn't want to hear that sound so often . . . get too used to it. Sometimes you hear something too often, after a while you don't hear it anymore. . . . I didn't want that to happen. The same thing happens to feelings too, I guess. After a while you don't feel anymore. You're too young to understand that yet.

MASAKO. I understand, Mama.

HANA. Wasn't it nice of Kiyoko-san to give us the *furin*?

MASAKO. I love it. I don't know anything about Japan, but it makes me feel something too.

HANA. Maybe someday when you're grown up, gone away, you'll hear it and remember yourself as this little girl . . . remember this old house, the ranch, and . . . your old mama . . .

MASAKO. That's kind of scary.

(*Emiko enters unsteadily. She carries a bundle wrapped in a furoshiki [colorful scarf]. In the package are two beautiful kimonos.*)

HANA. Emiko-san! What a pleasant surprise! Please sit down. We were just hanging the *furin*. It was so sweet of Kiyoko-san to give it to Masako. She loves it.

(*Emiko looks mildly interested. She acts as normal as she can throughout the scene, but at times drops her facade, revealing her desperation.*)

EMIKO. Thank you. (*She sets her bundle on the bench but keeps her hand on it.*)

HANA. Your family was here earlier. (*Emiko smiles vaguely.*) On their way to the pictures, I think. (*To Masako.*) Make tea for us. Ma-chan.

EMIKO. Please don't . . .

HANA. Kiyoko-san was looking so nice—her hair all curly. . . . Of course, in our day, straight black hair was desirable. Of course, times change.

EMIKO. Yes.

HANA. But she did look fine. My, my, a colorful new dress, new shoes, a permanent wave—looked like a regular American girl. Did you choose her dress?

EMIKO. No . . . I didn't go.

HANA. You know, I didn't think so. Very pretty though. I liked it very much. Of course, I sew all Masako's clothes. It saves money. It'll be nice for you to make things for Kiyoko-san too. She'd be so pleased. I know she'd be pleased . . .

(*While Hana talks, Emiko plucks nervously at her package. She waits for Hana to stop talking.*)

Emiko-san, is everything all right?

EMIKO (*smiling nervously*). Yes.

HANA. Masako, please go make tea for us. See if there aren't any more of those crackers left. Or did you finish them? (*To Emiko.*) We can't keep anything in this house. She eats everything as soon as Papa brings it home. You'd never know it, she's so skinny. We never have anything left for company.

MASAKO. We hardly ever have company anyway.

(*Hana gives her daughter a strong look, and Masako goes into the house. Emiko is lost in her own thoughts. She strokes her package.*)

HANA. Is there something . . . I can help you with? (*Very gently.*) Emiko-san?

EMIKO (*suddenly frightened*). Oh no. I was thinking . . . Now that . . . now that . . . Masa-chan is growing up . . . older . . .

HANA (*relieved*). Oh, yes. She's growing fast.

EMIKO. I was thinking . . . (*She stops, puts the package on her lap and is lost again.*)

HANA. Yes, she *is* growing. Time goes so fast. I think she'll be taller than me soon. (*She laughs weakly, stops and looks puzzled.*)

EMIKO. Yes.

(*Emiko's depression pervades the atmosphere. Hana is affected by it. The two women sit in silence. A small breeze moves the wind chimes. For a moment light grows dim on the two lonely figures. Masako comes from the house with a tray of tea. The light returns to normal again.*)

HANA (*gently*). You're a good girl.

(*Masako looks first to Emiko then to her mother. She sets the tray on the bench and stands near Emiko, who seems to notice her for the first time.*)

EMIKO. How are you?

HANA (*pours the tea and serves her*). Emiko-san, is there something I can do for you?

EMIKO. There's . . . I was . . . I . . . Masa-chan will be a young lady soon . . .

HANA. Oh, well, now I don't know about "lady."

EMIKO. Maybe she would like a nice . . . nice . . . (*She unwraps her package.*) I have kimonos . . . I wore in Japan for dancing . . . maybe she can . . . if you like, I mean. They'll be nice on her . . . she's so slim . . .

(*Emiko shakes out a robe. Hana and Masako are impressed.*)

HANA. Ohhhh! Beautiful!

MASAKO. Oh, Mama! Pretty!

(*Hana and Masako finger the material.*)

Gold threads, Mama.

HANA. Brocade!

EMIKO. Maybe Masa-chan would like them. I mean for her school programs . . . Japanese school . . .

HANA. Oh, no! Too good for country. People will be envious of us . . . wonder where we got them.

EMIKO. I mean for festivals . . . *Obon, Hana Matsuri* . . .

HANA. Oh, but you have Kiyoko-san now. You should give them to her. Has she seen them?

EMIKO. Oh . . . no . . .

HANA. She'll love them. You should give them to her . . . not our Masako.

EMIKO. I thought . . . I mean I was thinking of . . . if you could give me a little . . . if you could pay . . . manage to give me something for . . .

HANA. But these gowns, Emiko-san—they're worth hundreds.

EMIKO. I know, but I'm not asking for that. Whatever you can give . . . only as much as you can give.

MASAKO. Mama?

HANA. Masako, Papa doesn't have that kind of money.

EMIKO. Anything you can give . . . anything . . .

MASAKO. Ask Papa.

HANA. There's no use asking. I know he can't afford it.

EMIKO (*looking at Masako*). A little at a time.

MASAKO. Mama?

HANA (*firmly*). No, Masako. This is a luxury.

(*Hana folds the gowns and puts them away. Masako is disappointed. Emiko is devastated. Hana sees this and tries to find some way to help.*)

Emiko-san, I hope you understand . . . (*Emiko is silent, trying to gather her resources.*) I know you can sell them and get the full price somewhere. Let's see . . . a family with a lot of growing daughters . . . someone who did well last year. . . . Nagatas have no girls. . . . Umedas have girls but no money. . . . Well, let's see. . . . Maybe not here in this country town. Ah. . . . You can take them to the city, Los Angeles, and sell them to a store . . . or Terminal Island . . . lots of wealthy fishermen there. Yes, that would be the place. Why, it's no problem, Emiko-

san. Have your husband take them there. I know you'll get your money. He'll find a buyer. I know he will.

EMIKO. Yes. (*She finishes folding and ties the scarf. She sits quietly.*)

HANA. Please have your tea. I'm sorry . . . I really would like to take them for Masako but it just isn't possible. You understand, don't you? (*Emiko nods.*) Please don't feel so . . . so bad. It's not really a matter of life or death, is it? Emiko-san?

(*Emiko nods again. Hana sips her tea.*)

MASAKO. Mama? If you could ask Papa . . .

HANA. Oh, the tea is cold. Masako, could you heat the kettle?

EMIKO. No more. I must be going. (*She picks up her package and rises slowly.*)

HANA (*looking helpless*). So soon? Emiko-san, please stay.

(*Emiko starts to go.*)

Masako will walk with you. (*She pushes Masako forward.*)

EMIKO. It's not far.

HANA. Emiko-san? You'll be all right?

EMIKO. Yes . . . yes . . . yes . . . (*She goes.*)

HANA (*calling after her*). I'm sorry, Emiko-san.

EMIKO. Yes . . .

(*Masako and Hana watch as Emiko leaves. The light grows dim as though a cloud passes over. Emiko is gone. Hana strokes Masako's hair.*)

HANA. Your hair is so black and straight . . . nice . . .

(*They stand close. The wind chimes tinkle; light grows dim. Light returns to normal. Murata enters. He sees this tableau of mother and child and is puzzled.*)

MURATA. What's going on here?

(*The two women part.*)

HANA. Oh . . . nothing . . . nothing . . .

MASAKO. Mrs. Oka was here. She had two kimo—

HANA (*putting her hand on Masako's shoulder*). It was nothing . . .

MURATA. *Eh?* What'd she want?

HANA. Later, Papa. Right now, I'd better fix supper.

MURATA (*looking at the sky*). Strange how that sun comes and goes. Maybe I didn't need to irrigate—looks like rain. (*He remembers and is exasperated.*) Ach! I forgot to shut the water.

MASAKO. I'll do it, Papa.

HANA. Masako, that gate's too heavy for you.

MURATA. She can handle it. Take out the pin and let the gate fall all the way down. All the way. And put the pin back. Don't forget to put the pin back.

HANA. And be careful. Don't fall in the canal.

(*Masako leaves.*)

MURATA. What's the matter with that girl?

HANA. Nothing. Why?

MURATA. Usually have to beg her to do . . .

HANA. She's growing up.

MURATA. Must be that time of the month.

HANA. Oh, Papa, she's too young for that yet.

MURATA (*genially as they enter the house*). Got to start sometime. Looks like I'll be outnumbered soon. I'm outnumbered already.

(*Hana glances at him and quietly sets about preparations for supper. Murata removes his shirt and sits at the table with a paper. Light fades slowly.*)

SCENE 6

(*Same evening. Exterior, desert. There is at least one shrub. Masako appears, walking slowly. From a distance we hear Emiko singing the song "And the Soul Shall Dance." Masako looks around, sees the shrub and crouches under it. Emiko appears. She's dressed in one of her beau-* tiful kimonos tied loosely at her waist. She carries a branch of sage. Her hair is loose.*)

EMIKO.

> Akai kichibiru
> Kappu ni yosete
> Aoi sake nomya
> Kokoro ga odoru . . .
> Kurai yoru no yume
> Setsu nasa yo . . .

(*She breaks into a dance, laughs mysteriously, turns round and round, acting out a fantasy. Masako stirs uncomfortably. Emiko senses a presence. She stops, drops her branch and walks offstage, singing as she goes.*)

> Aoi sake nomya
> Yume mo odoru . . .

Masako watches as Emiko leaves. She rises slowly and picks up the branch Emiko has left. She looks at the branch, moves forward a step and looks off to the point where Emiko disappeared. Light slowly fades until only the image of Masako's face remains etched in the mind.*)

TOPICS FOR CRITICAL THINKING AND WRITING

📖 THE PLAY ON THE PAGE

1. *And the Soul Shall Dance* was adapted from Yamauchi's short story, which appears in *Women of the Century*, edited by Regina Barreca (1993). Compare and contrast the two versions, choosing one character that especially interests you for an in-depth analysis.

2. Offer your own character analysis of Hana as mother, wife, and woman.

3. Why does Emiko call her ten years in America a "temporary exile"?

4. What do you make of the title?

5. If you have read Tennessee Williams's *A Streetcar Named Desire*, compare and contrast Blanche and Emiko.

6. Is Oka both tragic and comic?

7. Devise a thesis about Yamauchi's style, and choose three or four different passages to illustrate your points.

8. In what ways is your understanding of *And the Soul Shall Dance* deepened by knowledge of the internment of Japanese Americans during the 1940s?

🎭 THE PLAY ON THE STAGE

9. Concentrate on the first seven speeches in the play. What does Yamauchi accomplish in terms of character and theme? What is established by the setting and situation?

10. Provide sketches of the clothing for all the characters, including details about fabric, color, and texture.

11. Suggest the blocking for Act 2, Scene 3. Include details about the difference in stance and gestures for Kiyoko and Masako, with specific reference to a single word or a pause. Would you cast teenagers to play these two characters?

12. Choose one of the comments from the interviews with either of the directors, Chang or Kuroda (pp. 856–57), and discuss the insights it gave you concerning staging *And the Soul Shall Dance*.

THE PLAY IN PERFORMANCE

And the Soul Shall Dance was developed from Yamauchi's short story of the same title. Its first staging was given by the East-West Players, based in Los Angeles, in 1977. The play was also televised on PBS in that year. Subsequently, *And the Soul Shall Dance* was produced at several universities, and in New York City it was produced by the Pan Asian Repertory Theatre in 1979 and again in 1990.

To give you an idea of two directors' responses to Yamauchi's play, we publish transcripts from telephone interviews conducted by Ren Draya in December 1995.

Tisa Chang
DIRECTING AND THE SOUL SHALL DANCE

Tisa Chang, artistic-producing director of Pan Asian Repertory Theatre in New York City directed the New York premier of *And the Soul Shall Dance* in 1979.

Draya: Why was And the Soul Shall Dance *initially chosen for production?*

Chang: I am an old friend of Mako, who had staged this play with the East-West Players in Los Angeles, and so I learned about the script. I saw at once that it has strong women's roles, which is especially groundbreaking for Asian Americans, and very important social and family issues. Usually, we just don't air those concerns in public—much less on stage. I was drawn to the balanced view Yamauchi presents, exemplified by her treatment of the two families and the two young daughters.

Did you have any conversation or correspondence with the playwright during the rehearsal process?

Yes—Pan Asian Rep likes to be very interactive with playwrights. Yamauchi spoke with me often about her own background and about certain aspects of the characters.

Can you describe your initial approach with the cast—for instance, did you focus on a single image or specific mood?

I think of Emiko's fragility and eroticism as central to the play. Many of the play's symbols—the wind chime, the kimono—represent Emiko and her own longings, her unmet aesthetic needs. We considered music very, very important; the mood of the play is so specific, and the delicate music is crucial in establishing that mood.

Did the approach change during the rehearsals?

Because the actress playing Emiko was a former dancer, she was able to express the character's physical vulnerability in relationship to her emotional vulnerability. As she moved across the stage, I had the image of a bird with a broken wing. One of the important symbols for the Japanese is the white crane; it means good luck, prosperity, fertility—sadly, these attributes are in direct contrast to the reality of Emiko's life.

Can you describe the set?

Quite simple, with the skeletal outlines of the two families' houses.

Which scene or portion of the play proved most challenging during rehearsals?

Oka's rejection of Emiko—his refusal to give her money back.

For the final tableau, what effect did you wish to create?

A vision of enduring serenity, Emiko's walking into the desert is her way of finding a little measure of peace. It's a very Japanese way—suicide is considered a responsible, even noble act. For Emiko, it is a way of returning to Japan.

How did audiences in New York respond to this play?

Oh, very well! Many people commented on the genuinely moving story, and many saluted the play's universality. I'll add that I believe *And the Soul Shall Dance* is one of the seminal works in American theater. It is so well written, it is haunting and poetical—so truthful that audiences and actors say, "These are real people." Yamauchi is in her seventies now, and I am looking forward to the works she will bring to us in the future.

Kati Kuroda
DIRECTING AND THE SOUL SHALL DANCE

[In the second interview, Ren Draya spoke with Kati Kuroda, director for the Pan Asian Repertory Theatre's 1990 revival of Yamauchi's *And the Soul Shall Dance*.]

Draya: When had you first known about And the Soul Shall Dance?

Kuroda: In Hawaii, in 1981, I acted the part of Emiko for a graduate school presentation. Although I had first wanted the part of Hana—seeing myself as homespun and sturdy—I came to love doing Emiko. It was a major part for me in terms of my growth as an actress.

In New York, how did you get involved as director?

Tisa Chang, Artistic-Producing Director at Pan Asian Rep, asked me to direct. And the play is one of my favorite Asian-American scripts—I believe it speaks to one's heart.

Can you describe your initial approach with the cast—for instance, did you focus on a single image or a specific mood?

I felt that the play is very poetical. Emiko's character influenced me a great deal. She is a poetic creature struggling to survive in a barren landscape. She is a beautiful caged bird, an artist who lacks the freedom to leave and to fulfill herself.

The play is presented to us from the perspective of a young girl (Masako). Although all six of the characters are fully developed, I do see this as a woman's play in many ways. I think that as a woman directing *And the Soul Shall Dance*, I could bring a special understanding of Asian women to the rehearsals. Too often, the portrayal of an Asian woman is as the butterfly. But Hana is a woman of strength; she is wise, loving, capable of being tough—a very real person. The relationship of Hana and Masako—mother and daughter—seemed to be very easy for our actors to relate to. And Emiko, although she hardly speaks, has such poetical qualities; we wanted audiences to feel her presence.

Did the approach change during the rehearsals?

We all felt that the characterizations are amazingly accurate. The Japanese-American farmers of that era really did boast and joke as Oka and Murata do. The pattern and rhythms of speech seemed to us very accurate. Some very funny moments emerged—for instance, aspects of Hana and Murata's relationship, as well as Hana and Masako's. We became aware that Yamauchi's play reveals a very intense, emotional side of the Japanese character—a side that is seldom revealed in public. We felt the irony of the play's being set right before the internment, and we came to feel that the Murata family would survive, but that the Okas would be destroyed.

Can you describe the set?

Because this production toured the United States, we needed a "traveling set." It was a simple, two-house arrangement that the actors actually set up during the play's opening moments. The desert was indicated by a painted background, and included a tall, reedlike motif. We wanted to emphasize a beauty amidst the starkness.

Which scene or portion of the play proved most challenging during the rehearsals?

There were two. First, Kiyoko in the rainstorm, having just witnessed Oka's beating of Emiko. The beating itself was not shown on stage. Second, Emiko attempting to sell her lovely kimonos. Just the way the women touch, wrap, fold the cloth—the delicate kimonos, so out of place in the California desert, represent Emiko herself.

For the final tableau, what effect did you wish to create?

I see Emiko as very sexual. For that final moment, she is beautiful but ragged, disheveled. Her kimono (one of the lovely kimonos she had tried to sell) is open—it's a moment of being lost. The audience knows that she's aware of being watched by Masako—not because of any eye contact, but because of Emiko's smile, a slight tilt of her head. This moment represents a passing on of the dream, of aesthetic sensitivity.

How did audiences respond to this play?

Very strongly. People from all sorts of different backgrounds told me they saw the struggles of their own immigrant families in the lives of the Muratas and the Okas.

A n g e l a   J a c k s o n

SHANGO DIASPORA

An African-American Myth of Womanhood and Love

A Chicago writer, Angela Jackson was born in 1951 and graduated from Northwestern University. For many years the chair of Chicago's Organization of Black American Culture Writers Workshops, in 1989 she received the Pushcart Prize for Poetry. She has represented the United States at the World Festival of Black and African Arts and Culture in Lagos, Nigeria.

In addition to writing plays such as *Shango Diaspora* (1980) and *When the Wind Blows* (1984), she has written books of poetry and a novel, *Tremont Stone*, about a young black woman's return to her family's home in Mississippi.

COMMENTARY

We should start our discussion with a few words about Jackson's unusual title. A diaspora is a dispersal of people who are taken from, or forced out of, their homeland. When the word is capitalized, it refers to the scattering of the Jewish people to countries outside of Palestine after the Babylonian captivity. In the Yoruba culture of coastal West Africa, Shango is a god of thunder, lightning, and fire; he is worshiped today by many blacks in North and South America and in the West Indies. Hence, Jackson's title speaks of the loss of a homeland, of a culture that draws from myths and customs in Africa.

Shango, known for his magical powers, was feared because he emitted fire from his mouth when he spoke. According to Yoruba myths, Shango's mother was Yemoja, goddess of the Ogun River in Nigeria. Eventually, Shango became a king and had a number of wives, of whom the most important were goddesses of three rivers named after them: Oya, Oshun, and Oba. The River Oya (also called the Niger) was Shango's most faithful wife; Shango could not fight without Oya, who manifested herself as the strong wind preceding a thunderstorm.

Jackson intermingles Yoruban myths with contemporary African-American references. Her language bounces back and forth between the highly poetical and the abruptly colloquial. For example, although Woman #1 advises the young protagonist, who is experiencing her first sense of desire (fire), "Take some valium and sleep it off," Woman #3 (representing the traditional mother figure, Yemoja),

offers a lyrical description with both American and African echoes:

> WOMAN #3. . . . In autumns what I remember is my father and uncles gathering buckets and rakes doing the earth's duty with a calm and ritual therapy. They worked the wrinkled, sunset leaves into mountains like a sacrifice of lovely and faded women. The men gave leaves to fire. The smoke would rise black and full of husky, sexual smell. The men would lean on their rakes and watch. Their children would flutter and swirl around the smoke and bodies. My father would gather the ashes into buckets and discard them. Now his daughter is fallen, sunsets, and gathering her body for giving. It is a new time, for life, and fire must be fed.

That sense that "fire must be fed"—a metaphor for burning sexual desire—pulsates through the play. It is as if the young girl cannot turn away; she has set out on an unstoppable, inevitable journey. When she reaches Shango's lair, she realizes she is about to leave her childhood behind:

> GIRL. . . . My heart wide as a child's. A woman's aroma at my wrists, at my temples, behind my ears. . . . This craziness of atmosphere. I want to run. I want to stay. I'm wise enough to fear. Fool enough to linger here.

Act I closes with the girl's loss of virginity, suggested by a silhouette that is both erotic and violent. The girl's disillusionment as she bewails her loss of innocence is undercut by

Jackson's deft handling of typically black humor and syntax, as shown in the three women's speeches that are sprinkled with the rhythms and repetition characteristic of colloquial black language.

In Act II the girl embarks on a second journey, this time to be purified—to find herself and to gain knowledge. She must undergo taunting and despair in order to reach the water that will purify her. And in Act III we see the signs of her maturity, of her having left behind youthful naïveté. With the community of women accompanying her, she (now Ms. Waters) is able then to return to Shango and demand what she needs:

MS. WATERS. . . . I want some receiving. I have traveled in the name of love, to find love to beget love.

There is a realization of the "truce" necessary between fire and water (man and woman) in order for each to obtain their desire, in order for babies to be conceived and born. Although *Shango Diaspora: An African-American Myth of Womanhood and Love* uses African symbols and rituals, its story is utterly universal. The need for love, the fear of being hurt, the loss of romantic ideals, the ultimate understanding between woman and man—these are developmental stages common to all.

Angela Jackson

SHANGO DIASPORA

An African-American Myth of Womanhood and Love

Characters

WATERGIRL (MS. WATERS): *a brown-skinned Black woman in her early to mid-twenties; warm and intelligent, but learning herself.*
THE THREE WOMEN: *These three women are like musical energies. #1 and #2 are sopranos, #3 alto, husky, a dreamer. They are three shades and styles of beauty. They are Afros, braids, dreads, nothing extravagant, and nothing too unnatural. They are a trio in different expressions, as the* WOMEN, *the* MAMMIWATERS, *the* VOICES, *the* SISTERS OF SYMPATHY, *and the* WOMEN IN WHITE.

> WOMAN #1: *Black woman from 30 to 45.*
> WOMAN #2: *Black woman a little younger than #1; a shade less aggressive than #1.*
> WOMAN #3: *Black woman from 30 to 45. A Dreamer. A kind woman.*

WOMAN-ALONG-THE-WAY *and* YEMOJA/MOTHER: *the first, a Black woman of seniority; crazy, clipped and harsh.* YEMOJA *is a god. Full of jazz and magic. An ageless, lovely, self-acclaiming, absolutely autonomous, arrogant, and tender deity.*
SHANGO/FIRE: *a god. Black man, virile, in his prime—late thirties to mid-forties, apparently. A Black, lean, Yoruba god of thunder, lightning, and fire. He is a scientist, magician, and ruler, thus has great intellect, stature, and dignity. An African-Diaspora man of brilliance and masks.*
THE FAN: *Black woman of same age as* MS. WATERS, *she is simpering, manipulative, sharp, shallow, and a little sad.*
THE CATS: *three Black women, bitter and sad, of any age. They are primarily dancers. They may have been playing scenery.*
SOLDIER: *Shango's soldier is preferably male, with a forbidding voice.*

SETTING: *A somewhere in the diaspora. A Black space.*

TIME: *The present. What John Wideman calls "African Great Time."*

ACT 1

SCENE 1

SETTING: *A city block. Girl on a porch seated sideways on a bannister, singing along with "Fire," Pointer Sisters' version. Three Women on the street corner coming from*

work. *In hats or scarves, carrying shopping bag, briefcase, basket.*

WOMAN #1 (*yells at Girl aggressively*). Hey, you! Hey, you there singin' "Fire," what you know about it? What you know about Fire?
GIRL (*turns to her. Defensive but firm*). I know enough. I know about him.
WOMAN #1. You know enough to call the Fire Department?
GIRL. I know enough. I learned *something* in school. Isis bathed Osiris in fire for immortality. To build a fire is to burn away the yellow eyes of wolves, to burn the howling out of the night.
GIRL (*pauses, voice softens*). In the kitchen where love is baked in loaves fire heats the stones.
WOMAN #2. Girl, you talking about some kitchen fire. We talking about *Fire.*
WOMAN #1 (*interjects*). Big Fire.
WOMAN #3 (*dreamily*). Fire is the first and final fear. I saw Fire once. It was in a dream.
WOMAN #2 (*has taken out a Dream Book. Points to a section. Reads*). To dream Fire is to dream prosperity, change, good luck, the sweet sex wish.
WOMAN #3. He is a figure of force and fascination in an orange drama.
GIRL (*saunters down steps. While the Women remove hats and baskets, etc.*). Legends I have heard tell of. Stoop-front myths and sermons that made mature women sweat and stir the thick air. Young men shake their heads and touch hands in elaborate fives. Encounters I have watched him through. Flash fire flats housed his concubines. Beautiful and methodical in their wiles. Their kitchens all burned out. Their pots stone cold. I have heard of his hunger. His spirit unharnessed.
WOMAN #1. Once, at a dry feast, drought, he ate three thousand trees.
WOMAN #2. Once, he set a family outside into a freezing winter drift. Flames licked out through gutted windows like horrible children with their tongues stretched out. While a father stood in snow, barefoot, cursing Fire.
WOMAN #3. When he walks he leaves premonitions. When women think of him they store their dreams like secrets poured in Mason Jars, persimmon, marmalade, Sunday morning, and harmonica. They remember the very first fig and the bent heat that swelled from Fire, from him, from them. Delicious!

WOMAN #2. What do you know, girl? You think you an authority on Fire?

WOMAN #3 (*like a robot mother*). Children should not play with Fire.

WOMAN #1 (*bossy*). Give me those matches, that cigarette lighter. Stand back from that stove. That fire'll fall on you.

WOMAN #3 (*to imaginary children*). If you are bad you will burn!

WOMAN #2. Listen at what the mothers tell you. Be careful, girl.

WOMAN #1, 2, and 3. Hot! Hot! Hot!

GIRL (*ignores them*). I'll be alright.

WOMAN #1. Oh, really? Just who do you think you are?

GIRL. It's too late. I already am who I am.

WOMAN #2. Who are you?

WOMAN #3 (*looking into a hand mirror. Curious and crazy*). I know who you are.

(*The Women get busy. #3 begins to braid #2's hair. #1 begins to wash and hang up clothes; she uses a scrub board. All fixtures are imaginary.*)

GIRL (*centerstage*). I am the little girl who plays with the god of Fire. He bites my lips, and scars my hands. "Little girl," he tells me, "Don't you know I'd run through you like a silver knife? Burn down all your trembling houses."

WOMAN #1 (*an aside*). That sound like a warning to me.

GIRL. "Yes," I tell him. "I have watched you a long, long time without winking. I know the cruelty of your ember. I have read your mark on women's eyes."

GIRL (*gestures*). I touch him without squinting. He bites my lips and scars my hands. Full height he draws himself up. He is one flame that flares. Red and blue against the trees. Lightning. Over the sand. Over the houses. "Listen, when I tell you, I am Fire, Little Girl. I am son and father of the sun. I will make you ash and curling smoke."

WOMAN #2 (*an aside*). That sound like warning number two.

GIRL. "I know," I whisper into the deep blue flame. My lips are red with him. "God of Fire who burns poison out of wounds. Son of Fire who bites the ice and makes it sweet. Father of Fire who watches the earth, you are a god of mercy. Have mercy on me. Be tender with my meat. I look into his light and wink.

WOMAN #1 (*an aside*). You better been trying to wink.

GIRL. "Little Girl," he says, "Who owns you? Where is your home?"

WOMAN #1 (*an aside*). He say, "Where this fool come from?"

GIRL. "I am only a child. Water. Early to bed."

WOMAN #2. Early to bed!

WOMAN #1. She ready!

GIRL. River of invisible rises. The beautiful daughter of many people. I strike fire back at the sun and it is glass. Have you never seen the water that holds the fire? Cradles it and rocks it into weaving smoke? You must have something soft against you. You are more child than I. You are thirsty. And will burn yourself out.

WOMAN #1 and #2. You a bold little miss . . .

GIRL. "No," he snaps and hisses. He is full of caprice. He bites my lips and scars my hands. Curses me with thunder. I am too still, without a murmur. He is wary. A muscle of contempt. We watch each other. And we wait. (*Girl stops, pauses. Doesn't want to reveal the rest.*)

WOMAN #3 (*kindly*). Well, then what happened? You not just gone leave us hanging. What happened? Turn yo head around the other way so I can get this part. (*Addresses Girl, then Woman between her knees.*)

GIRL (*getting up enough nerve. Begins quickly, abruptly*). Suddenly. He laughed. He held me up and opened his hand. Seven kinds of stone. Alight. I brushed the flame and fled. Wing-singed. Transformed into a trembling bird: a black wave flying from the sun. Breasts heaving and eyes broken open like lips. Now I know hunger and I am mouths. Who curved dizzy in his palm. I touched his flint and fled.

WOMAN #1 (*sticks clothespin under Girl's nose*). I coulda told you it woulda ended up that way.

WOMAN #3 (*chastises #1*). See there. That's not right. Be telling somebody I told you so. She don't want to hear that. (*To Girl.*) Go on, honey, what was it like when he touched you?

GIRL. Something struck me when he touched me. A déjà vu overwhelming. You were there . . . women ripping their corded hair, shouting my lost name.

WOMAN #3. Did it hurt? His touch.

GIRL. It was like a palmtree hard fell with the fist of its hand; while the earth pit swallowed its own green seeds, all my futures were absorbed by a toothless mouth; everything moving with centrifugal force: this body, a brown paperbag doll, flattened against his wall. It was this terrible, terrible déjà vu I tore loose from, yet could not elude. So here I go down the line of women wounded like a row of moons. And we all look alike crying the same blues.

WOMAN #1 (*working with the clothespin again*). Did you think you'd be any different? Did you think he'd treat you any different than he treated them other women? Did you think you had gold between your legs? And that would make him want you?

GIRL. I didn't think I had anything between my legs because he ain't been between my legs.

WOMAN #2. That's what's wrong with you.

GIRL. He just touched me.

WOMAN #3. Why did you run away?

GIRL. I don't know. I don't remember. I just remember the flirtation dance. The hesitation . . .

WOMAN #3. You were afraid. Weren't you?

GIRL. I guess. The feeling was picking me up. Carrying me away.

WOMAN #3. Why didn't you go with it? You only wishing you *had* gone. You look tired.

GIRL. Every night sleep break me in two. Opens and spreads across the cold. I loiter with my limbs askew and curve around a central heat.

WOMAN #1. Still trying to get next to that heat, huh?

GIRL. "Classic," my sister shakes her head when I tell her. "I did not know such cases were still found." She is not sad for me but marvels at the possibility: a woman so intense, so besieged. The heat a recurring tropical disease. "Tell me who he is." Someone curious inquires. Even though they don't know. They just assume it's got to be a man. How they know it's a man? Got me sleepless. It might be *money*. It just might be lack of money keeping me awake at night. *It might be inflation!*

WOMAN #1. Inflated loneliness.

WOMAN #2. Inflated lust.

WOMAN #3. Love. There is somebody who's stricken you. You're in his aura. He wakes you in the middle of the night. He colors your forehead purple like a royal anointment or a bruise.

WOMAN #2. Valerie Simpson say it's like a mark on you.

WOMAN #1. Then she say, "Don't go, can it wait until tomorrow." Twenty-four more hours before the misery stop or start.

WOMAN #2. Misery stop or start. Miserable he there. You miserable when he gone.

GIRL (*to Woman #3*). What can I do?

WOMAN #1. Take some valium and sleep it off.

WOMAN #2. Do quickies and t.m.

WOMAN #3. You have to go to him. Go to him with a sacrifice. You have to give something up. Go singing. Don't listen to them two filling you with fear. You have to dream with him. Or else you'll be left by yourself. Which wouldn't be bad to be a dreamer by yourself if you didn't want *him*. (*Sends her on her way.*) You have such a pretty voice. Go singing to him.

WOMAN #2. Girl, he is really gonna get you this time.

WOMAN #1. Girl, he is gonna kick your emotional ass.

(*Woman #3 takes up imaginary broom. Sweeps. Humming.*)

(*To Woman #3*). Now, why you send that child on that wild goose chase so he can cook her goose for her?

WOMAN #3. Wasn't no wild goose chase. Something she has to do.

WOMAN #2. She need to be trying to avoid pain.

WOMAN #3. How you avoid pain without avoiding feeling? It's all part of the ritual.

WOMAN #1 and #2. What ritual?

WOMAN #3 (*goes dreamy again*). In autumns what I remember is my father and uncles gathering buckets and rakes doing the earth's duty with a calm and ritual therapy. They worked the wrinkled, sunset leaves into mountains like a sacrifice of lovely and faded women. The men gave leaves to fire. The smoke would rise black and full of husky, sexual smell. The men would lean on their rakes and watch. Their children would flutter and swirl around the smoke and bodies. My father would gather the ashes into buckets and discard them. Now his daughter is fallen,

sunsets, and gathering her body for giving. It is a new time, for life, and fire must be fed.

(*Fade out on Three Women.*)

ACT 1

SCENE 2

SETTING: *Enroute to Fire. Travel is suggested by the dance movements of the Girl, and by, possibly, having trees move. Stones move. A fence moves. Roadsigns move. Dancers may take these parts. She stops at a fence. An old Woman is working in a garden behind a low fence. She wears a huge sunhat, carries a cane, is initially on her knees. Rises.*

GIRL (*friendly. Respectful*). Morning. I hate to disturb you. You look so busy. Your garden is so beautiful. Okra, tomatoes, bright sun corn, look like you growing a pot of gumbo right out of the ground. You must have a special gift.

WOMAN-ALONG-THE-WAY (*abrupt, but not unkind*). It's a hot day. I suppose you want water? Where you on your way to?

(*Goes to a pail of water.*)

My plantings know I love them. Not everything responds the way fruits and vegetables do to good loving. (*Hands Girl dipper.*) Here's water. Nice and chilly.

GIRL. Oh, it's well water. Good. Thank you. (*Drinks politely.*)

WOMAN-ALONG-THE-WAY. Not everybody like well water. Some say they can taste the rust in it. I shouldn't have asked. I know where you going. (*Works with spade or hoe all the while.*)

GIRL. You do?

WOMAN-ALONG-THE-WAY. You going to see Him. Ain't you? Don't answer. I know you are.

GIRL. How do you know when I haven't even said so. And who is *Him*?

WOMAN-ALONG-THE-WAY (*mumbles*). They come and go. (*Aloud.*) I can tell these things. You got that look about you. You got fire in your eyes. Flame in yo cheeks. No use blushing all over.

GIRL. I can't help it.

WOMAN-ALONG-THE-WAY. Well, if you blushing that means you ain't been to his firebed yet. It's soft as feathers that burn to the bone. He ain't made you his. Yet. You can still turn around and high tail it out of here.

GIRL. O, I think I know best what I have to do.

WOMAN-ALONG-THE-WAY. Girl, O.K. I was hard-headed too. Just like you. Nobody could tell me anything. I was under his spell. (*Is overtaken by memory.*) I was one entranced. Violated by flame. I stared too long into the roar. Music took my hands. I circled myself in wild paint and watched my body move into heat. I was hungry all the time. Fire was delicious: an inflammatory statement. You know he was. I loved his devastation, continuing combustion. I indulged him too much. He raged unchecked, petulant, spoiled. I swear. His language was abusive. His expressions cruel grimace and scowls. Let me give you a caution: give him only the animal exchange of energy. He doesn't know the sacrament of the heart. His is a bleeding ulcer. But who am I to say a thing or two? I have grown old. I have a loose mouth. Once my cheeks were round and fire swelled inside me until I burst.

GIRL (*disbelieving*). Nobody tells the same story twice. Tell it to me again.

WOMAN-ALONG-THE-WAY. O.K., I'll put it to you simply. Woman is a language of no more than tree; he roots, he branches, he breaks, he leaves.

GIRL. How he leave after he breaks? Nothing leaves after it's broken.

WOMAN-ALONG-THE-WAY. You know what I mean. What is man will lay you waste. Gods such as they are. Will open you, rotate a crop of jubilee and suicide, then will lay you waste, will lay you waste. Am I right or wrong?

GIRL. I don't like to make general statements about love. Every love don't turn sour in the mouth.

WOMAN-ALONG-THE-WAY. When you come back here spitting out the insides of a used vinegar douche bag you'll be whistling another tune.

GIRL. I have to go. Thank you for the drink. (*Prepares to continue her journey. Walks.*)

WOMAN-ALONG-THE-WAY (*hollers after her*). Answer me this, Miss Fearless-won't-listen-at-good-advice-know-it-all: Who is gone pick up your body? (*Mumbles to self.*) I probably have to call the Fire Department. Where is that number for the Burn Unit? (*Goes about her tasks.*) Why don't they listen? Why don't the young ones listen to the old ones? Why didn't I listen when they tried to tell me? Well, we'll see. We shall see. Where is that number for the Burn Unit?

(*Fade on scene.*)

ACT 1

SCENE 3

SETTING: *Smoke in the distance from a high place. That is Shango's lair/palace. The Girl is journeying. Again, trees walk and stones move. Birds in flight. Bird signal songs. Flight from a big wind, a movement.*

GIRL (*watching the signs of animal flight. Worried. Muses*). When Fire struts/ bewildered beasts scurry. From miles away birds set out a flurry of fear.

(*A flurry among the trees. She cringes.*)

I smell the skin of smoke. I sense his presence near. His teeth that mark the barks of trees; his eyes peeling a path of leaves leaving the bones of slow bedazzled beasts set-

tled beneath his feet. (*Hesitantly approaches a gate at the foot of a suggested stairwell. The stairwell has steps that are really landings. The steps curve. The steps are in darkness. She listens.*) I hear his breathing. The soft rending of cloth. The soft tearing of the hair of air. (*She looks around her, warily.*) A craziness of atmosphere, near his lair of brilliance and intrigue. (*Measures herself to meet the task.*) My heart wide as a child's. A woman's aroma at my wrists, at my temples, behind my ears. (*Takes out perfume from her carrying basket. Carrying basket is full of goodies.*) This craziness of atmosphere. I want to run. I want to stay. I'm wise enough to fear. Fool enough to linger here.

(*Girl, having decided to face Fire, prepares by dressing up. Adds a skirt of bright-colored veils, jewelry. All this from her basket of goodies. A bowl is also in the basket.*)

A VOICE (*a warning voice, deep and stern, comes from nowhere and everywhere*). Who enters his electromagnetic field is polarized, pulled apart, limb from limb, shocked, wild in the head.

(*Girl pauses with hand outstretched toward the suggestion of a door/gate.*)

VOICE OF WOMAN #3. You must go to him with a sacrifice. Go singing. If you don't you'll never be free.

(*Girl still hesitates.*)

You want a good night's sleep, don't you?

(*Girl opens door/gate. Girl mounts the long, wide steps that are more like platforms. Lights go up on Shango on high. He is close to a cloud. Clouds are stones. Shango Fire Diaspora sits in a Huey P. Newton, big-backed, bamboo chair. He reclines. Arrogantly. He remains in shadow, although all around him is illuminated. Perhaps he is flanked by drummers who are at a distance. He has one Soldier, at least. He is being fanned by a woman. All in Shango's palace wear African dress. Flamboyant fire colors. A great glaring light falls on the Girl's face. Blinds her.*)

SOLDIER. Who comes?

GIRL. Only . . . a girl sleepless with praises. (*Shields her eyes.*)

SOLDIER. Then praise.

(*Light softens as Girl kneels and bows deeply.*)

GIRL (*begins tremulously. Gains confidence. It gets good to her. She is downright cocky by the end*). Most Excellent Lord Shango. You were a god before music/ fell and broke/ into voices. Before the tribes were marked limb from limb, eye from eye, skin from skin, heart from heart, and brain before desire was formed out of hormone, mucus, and marrow. Before Osiris/ you were a god. Before the market of salt, and spices and trade/ beads before rice rose out of mud. Before brute force/ you were a god before the death howl/ before the Chain/ before the Coffle . . .

THE FAN (*bored and jealous*). My. My. My girl is so extravagant. Sweet child.

GIRL (*loud and determined*). You were born before Hallelujah, as old as Hosanna! Before the plain and orange breasted lizard made marriage patterns in the sand./ Before the funeral of justice, before mercy, before '27, the flood, when the house was torn from its roots and twins were birthed on the roof./ Before the river ran wild before the anger of water/ before the beacon, and the lighthouse. (*Is so excited she rises in her speech. Soldier and The Fan gesture her down. She ignores them.*) You were a being before the Hawk and the Holy Ghost danced as one on the corner of Celebration and Sanctuary, before women of the creme sachet and toilet water lay with porcelain gods and works of art./ You were there in the Time of the North Star/ in the Time of Moss that hugs the Tree of Memory. You are as old as the longing for Messiah. Your lifetime equatorial and your heart bleeds back from the long tunnel of the First God. You have accumulated more pain than I. I have heard of you. I know that I am young. Magician of two thousand smoke screens, griot of light years, people say that I am aglow, a star has set upon me. And I am patient as the moon.

SHANGO (*in shadow. Bored. Matter-of-factly*). You are a fool.

GIRL (*before he can complete the sentence*). Beyond a shadow . . . I am ready for giving. I have come singing. I know that I am young.

THE FAN. Is that all, *little girl?*

GIRL (*feisty*). I wasn't talking to you. (*To Fire.*) May we have privacy? I have brought an offering. (*Shango snaps his fingers. All retreat to lower platforms. They watch and listen.*)

(*The Fan takes centerstage. She narrates the actions of the Girl and Fire. Fire and the Girl do dance actions in the shadows. A hot, hot, hot dance done in shadows with sparks shooting out.*)

THE FAN (*blasé. Delighting in the Girl's fate*). She prepared a lamb for him. A sacrifice floating in herbs and blood and water seasoned with salt of camouflaged tears, onions, and three kinds of peppers, enough to kill a goat. (*She fans herself all the while.*) Her mouth shaped half a plate of triumph. She held murder in her hands. He sat on his throne, a luxuriating storm. His neck was stiff as an eagle's. He watched the sway of her hips, heavy, widened as she walked with design. He took the dish and tasted it. He ground West African pepper with his teeth. He lulled his tongue inside the heat. Then he said, "This is not sweet enough. There is not enough salt." (*Gleefully.*) He crushed her eyes for salt. He opened her veins for syrup and let her laughter over lamb. Devoured it. *His teeth cracked bone.* Devoured it. *He sucked the marrow.* Then, he roared for more. She gave him her mouth. He pulled her kisses til she was gaunt. Her joints grew thin as spider tapestries. Still. He said he was not satisfied. She fell behind her mask. Inscrutable. Wall of water. Silent hieroglyphic of hurt. Reflecting, she watched his fine teeth glisten while he laughed.

(*A deep bass growl-laugh descends from the shadow and sparks. The two figures now tangled in erotic and subtly violent embrace. A low fade on couple coupling. Then Girl descends. Like a sleepwalker. She is off her center.*)

GIRL (*more to self than to others. Disoriented*). Fire is absolute. You were absolutely right. I should have known. I had no ways. I had no means enough to know. I, who have always been water. More or less. Fire burns. Grates the eyes. Peels/ flesh and sears. (*Gestures back toward Fire. Turns to shout to Him.*) Fire: you are absolute. There is no defense. A woman who loves Fire/ who meddles with flame/ who flirts with tongues/ will burn/ will be/ consumed.

(*On a lower platform the village women appear. They are doing a Fire Dance. Girl descends toward them.*)

In the village, on the street corners, the women raised their skirts and only fanned the flame. Fire rose around their thighs. Went through them and blossomed between their breasts. Fire licked their ankles and they danced. Fire: you are music/ nobody has business listening to alone. *And when I touched you you were warm. I cupped the heat and laughed into the colored shadows you cast across my skin.* I was laughing, people say. Not like a little girl. They say, I raised my skirts delicately, like a lady, and danced. Til they only saw the smoke.

(*Girl goes up in fire and smoke. The Fan fans on like this happens everyday.*)

(*Black out. Quick.*)

ACT 2

SCENE 1

SETTING: *Same as initial setting. The Girl's porch is lighted but past it, within the house, is in darkness. The Three Women are outside. Doing woman's work, i.e., household service chores that women usually get stuck with.*

WOMAN #1. How's that singing girl doin'? I ain't seen her in a while.

WOMAN #2. Ask her. She in the know. (*Points to Woman #3.*)

WOMAN #1. How's that girl doin'? She takin' it bad?

WOMAN #3. How else can she take it? I know it was for me. I didn't think it would be that way for her. I don't know exactly how it was for her. She don't talk. I know how it was for me. After a session of such sorcery: the tongue becomes a feather dipped in blood. The bones begin to dance. In leave of reason. The body goes bare and all of the air is familiar. Is a house of flesh as warm as breath is. His loa. His spirit. His power turns tongues to feathers. Bones to dance. Body to bare familiar air. Fire finds his house of flesh. What tongue once feather will speak again? What bones be still after the dance? What body be clothed in the stranger house of cold after his loa has taken hold . . . ?

(*While she is talking #1 and #2 spice her monologue with "Here she goes again. . . ." "You'd think that burned out memory be cold by now."*)

WOMAN #2. You make too much of it. It was only *sex*. Birds do it. Bees do it. Hippopotamuses . . .

WOMAN #1. Hippopotami . . .

WOMAN #2. Yeah, well, they do and ain't got to cry about it.

WOMAN #3. How you know they don't cry about it? And if they don't, why shouldn't I? Or *her*?

WOMAN #1 (*hesitating at first step of Girl's home*). How long is she gone stay in that room suffering so? That night-cryin' is drivin' me crazy. Some nights I stay awake on the other side of the wall. She be night-cryin' and tears come standin' in my eyes like some soldiers of some goddamned misery warring with my good sense. I thought they was dead. She raisin' my tears from the dead. Why don't she come out? How long is this National Day of Mourning going on?

WOMAN #3. I don't know. Seems like the pain goes up and down like a pot over a gas flame. Flame going up and down.

WOMAN #2. How long can anything sit on the stove and still be good?

WOMAN #1. I'm tired of cryin' for that girl. I told her not to go. Though I hoped deep inside it would turn out a happy ending. I need a happy ending.

WOMAN #2. Well, I ain't gone cry her tears for her. Shit, my eyes allergic to my own tears.

WOMAN #3 (*angry. Distressed, turns on #2*). I guess you happy now. When she sit in a circle of women, now she can show off her wounds, a review of miseries like cats shedding hair. Don't shed on me, she-cat.

(*Fade on the group as light opens on Girl and her surroundings.*)

ACT 2

SCENE 2

SETTING: *The Girl's house. Porch is illuminated. So is inside. There is only a bed. The Girl is on it. Smoke rises from the bed suggesting smouldering ashes. The Three Women appear transformed into benevolent spirits all. They are the Sisters of Sympathy. All in dresses and headrags and/or gelees of royal blue, sky blue, and turquoise. There is little initial dialogue. Intense movement. They sweep into the Girl's house. They make a semicircle around her. Shaking their heads. One ministers to the Girl. One goes to sweep the porch. Another builds a fire with a pot over it. They begin throwing things into the fire. Reciting.*

SISTER #1 (*as she throws said item into pot*). Black cat bones. Mojo root. Essence of Van Van. Jasmine Perfume.

SISTER #2 (*accepts an invisible something from #3 who ministers to the Girl. #2 gives the invisible thing to #1*). Pining from a young girl's heart. And bad news.

(*Sister #1 stirs the mixture. Then all move swiftly to Girl.*)

GIRL (*sitting up in bed. Watching amazed and looking scared*). Who are you?

(*The Sisters speak almost simultaneously. One behind the other. They could be one person.*)

SISTER #1. Sisters of

SISTER #2. Sympathy

SISTER #3. But not too much.

ALL SISTERS. Too much sympathy not good for you.

SISTER #1. We interested in curing.

SISTER #2. Self-sufficiency.

SISTER #3. We have come to cure impurities. We've mixed water and magic over a tame fire. Anything can happen. We are in control.

SISTER #2. You have been out of your element.

SISTER #3. You have taken leave of your senses.

SISTER #1. Let Fire get the best of you, huh?

SISTER #3. He was a sweet child.

SISTER #2. Known him since he was a boy.

SISTER #1. But look at you random with assault. Disconcerted. Nearly anonymous with the fate's surprise, and such fabulous, fabulous misery.

SISTER #3. Hair all over your head!

SISTER #2. Eyes looking like hot peppers!

SISTER #1. You are tone-deaf and stupid. While he has danced inside your inner mirror. Settled his sediment. You can't see.

SISTER #3. You would see if you knew *your* eyes, your central equations, your orisha, your deity.

SISTER #2. You must go to meet her.

GIRL (*reluctantly*). Is this another wild goose chase?

SISTER #1. Do you want a good night's sleep?

(*Light begins to fade and Girl rises and they help her prepare for her journey. Whispering all the while.*)

ALL SISTERS. Believe her. Believe only her.

(*Light continues to fade.*)

SISTER #3. How you gone sing for him if you don't know your own song?

ALL SISTERS. Believe her.

GIRL. Who is she?

ALL SISTERS. You'll know.

(*Total fade as Girl stands on porch. Ready to go. Black stage. Except for one spot on Girl, a blue spot, on Girl at centerstage. She sing-speaks.*)

GIRL. (*half singing. Half talking*).

He's a deep sea diver/ c.c. rider.

He's a deep sea diver/ c.c. rider.
Dipped his hand in water/ turned to cider.

Heard of a woman/ hoodoo in her hand.
Heard of a woman/ hoodoo in her hand.
She live across forest/ and burning sand.

I am the one with a burn/ in my throat.
I am the woman/ a burn in my throat.
Lightning scorched my music/ couldn't save a note.

I simmered my gumbo/ seasoned it hot.
I simmered my gumbo/ seasoned it hot.
Dipped his hand in gumbo/ stuck to the pot.

Heard of a woman/ hoodoo in her hand.
Heard of a woman/ hoodoo in her hand.
Her house past bamboo/ and glistening sand.

(*Slow fade on Girl.*)

ACT 2

SCENE 3

SETTING: *A swamp area. Leafy. Steamy. Initially, the MammiWaters are camouflaged. They reveal themselves. They look downright whorish, villainous, powerful. They wear wet satin that clings. They smoke reefer through cigarette holders. They are portrayed by the Three Women.*

    Because they hate elegantly, and are slinkily powerful and above everything including themselves, they narrate their own actions like malicious observers. They punctuate their narration with awful laughter. Girl appears, weary, and confused, talking to herself.

GIRL. Past bamboo boulevards and neon avenues, icy moons and madness . . . and it is so far! Where is this elusive Water Mother-Hoodoo Woman-Deity who gone make it all right? Am I on another wild goose chase?

MAMMIWATER #1 (*comes as a voice from behind Girl. Startling as it is meant to be*). Could be. Could be a wild goose chase.

MAMMIWATER #2. Could be the goose that laid the golden egg.

(*MammiWaters all laugh happily.*)

GIRL. Who are you?

MAMMIWATER #3. Who are who?

GIRL. You. Three. The three of you.

MAMMIWATER #1 (*begins narration of their action*). The MammiWaters crossed/ their legs were scarred by crocodile teeth. And when they cried/ they cried crocodile tears.

MAMMIWATER #2. Three figurines they sat/ one/ she see no evil. One/ she hear no evil. One/ she speak no evil. They all do a little of each.

MAMMIWATER #3. One/ she played a waterreed. Two/ made nets of waterweeds/ chanting/ while they worked.

GIRL. Who are you? Your voices sound like the worst nightwinds on a cold, cold night. Your faces nearly hidden behind a costume of temptations, bull rushes, and lily leaves.

(*Girl touches MammiWater #1's frock.*)

MAMMIWATER #1 (*slaps Girl's hand back*). If you please! Don't touch the fabric.

MAMMIWATER #2. Yeah. Hands off the merchandise. Some poor sucker worked his fingers down to the bone to pay for these happy rags.

MAMMIWATER #3. Even the clothes on we back is happy cause they on we back!

MAMMIWATER #2 (*leans her head toward Girl*). Feel we do. Madame Ag Onee. Dare you. Touch it.

MAMMIWATER #1 (*again narrates*). They dare a man to lay with them, and he will disappear. Be devoured by their hidden faces. Their taboo embraces.

MAMMIWATER #3 (*continues narration*). They drain his scrotum, and seal the veins that make his memory his dream. They draw him down like quicksand, like whirlpool with poisons of the stagnant pool they/ lay wait for him.

ALL MAMMIWATERS (*almost as one voice, more like a double echo chamber*). They are sisters of tragedy, accomplices, for grief they remove their masks and smile.

MAMMIWATER #2 (*leans over again*). You look plum tuckered out, girlie. Where you from?

MAMMIWATER #3. She don't know. She don't know where she comin' from.

MAMMIWATER #1. Well, where you been, bitch?

GIRL (*intimidated. Momentarily despairing. Feeling a little sorry for herself*). It was through a rain forest I travelled. This is how old my heart is: it is broken in the numbers of rice and rain.

MAMMIWATER #2 (*an aside*). This broad is poetic.

GIRL. My eyes form flat faced leaves/ traces with chains around their ankles. Welts. (*The MammiWaters are unruly all the while she speaks. She really doesn't notice. She is all wrapped up in her journey.*) I watched the earth unwind. Blackbirds that spun like arrows. Insects of a fat season of appendages and poisons.

MAMMIWATER #1 (*to other MammiWaters*). What this fool talkin' about?

GIRL. It was through a rain forest I travelled. The path cut through anguish and wish so ripe to be rank, spoiled. Sprawling insurmountable, insatiably wanton, a garden of funeral and soiled solitudes.

MAMMIWATER #3. Hard times, huh?

MAMMIWATER #2. The hoe is cracked.

(*The MammiWaters come to phoney sympathetic attention.*)

MAMMIWATER #1 (*snaps to attention*). Who sent you?

GIRL. Friends with their good advice. A coterie of women. A chorus of sympathy grown weary of me. And who exactly are you? Are you the one the sisters sent me to? The three of you? They sent me to *you*? You smelling like rainy autumns, asafetida Grandmama wrapped around my neck to keep out the cold virus and everything else alive. You smelling like perpetual reefer smell your sex simply hovers. And your eyes—faithless castaway, and cunning . . . Can I trust you?

(*MammiWaters laugh until they cry.*)

MAMMIWATER #2. You trusted *him*!

GIRL. Who?

MAMMIWATER #3. The S.O.B. got you in this sorry way in the first place

GIRL (*whispers*). Fire.

MAMMIWATER #3. Yeah, sweet piece, we know about him.

ALL MAMMIWATERS (*sensuously. Obscenely*). Fire!

MAMMIWATER #1. Longed/ to wrap their thighs around him. Fire! To pull him down into wet hurricanes, whirlpools, to eat his echo and chew his maleness. Longed/ to pull him down into the dank forest of forever. To swallow him whole.

MAMMIWATER #2. Well, you gone join us?

MAMMIWATER #3. The pickings is good.

MAMMIWATER #1. Or you gone be a pretty, pious Earth-Mother, Good Sister, or whatever. Getting fire in yo face at the drop of a hat.

MAMMIWATER #2. Getting *peed* on in the name of Water.

GIRL. I don't think I can hang. I ain't got the proper attitude. I don't believe this was meant for me.

MAMMIWATER #1. Worst that can happen is folks talk bad about you.

MAMMIWATER #2. Yeah, we just a lot of evil rumor, mythologizing, and hypothetomizing on femininity.

MAMMIWATER #3. Yeah. In other words, they talking about yo mama.

MAMMIWATER #1 (*talking about the other two MammiWaters*). Girl, don't mind them. They on they period.

MAMMIWATER #2. Unh. Uh. Labor pains. We breedin' discontent and fomenting revolution.

GIRL. I heard that! But, tell me, how do you sleep at night?

ALL MAMMIWATERS. Who sleeps at night?

(*Girl is moving away. Still fascinated by, aware of their madness.*)

MAMMIWATER #1. Reconsider.

MAMMIWATER #2. Send that fire here, to rest, ours is the deep hotel.

MAMMIWATER #3. We'll give him a sleep.

(*The awful laughter of the MammiWaters reverberates.*)

(*Slow fade.*)

ACT 2

SCENE 4

SETTING: *The moon hangs in the sky. Is replaced by sun. Sun descends. The Girl travels through a field. A pool of water is at centerstage. Girl enters. Very much alone.*

GIRL (*looking around wonderingly*). Now where in the world am I? I shouldn't be far. I should be almost there. Shouldn't I?

VOICE #1 (*a voice from an unseen source. Frail. Timid*). Ask me anything. I am only ash. A product of burn. Set into a hollowed out hole.

GIRL. Who is that?

VOICE #1. Here. Behind this tree.

(*Girl runs to tree. Finds nothing.*)

GIRL. Where?

VOICE #1, #2, and #3. Ask us, we balance on nothing. We laugh on nothing. Shadow. And indifferent act. Vacant image in a dark man's eye. A movie image. Mammie. Mamie, Sapphire. Empty idea in lipstick and headrag.

GIRL. Where are you?

VOICE #2. Here beneath this rock.

VOICE #1, #2, and #3. Here. Here. Here. The heart hurts.

GIRL. Who are you? I feel like a stupid owl always asking "Who?"

VOICE #1. Call me anything. He is not the only hurt in the world.

GIRL. Who is he? Are you talking about Fire? Are you talking about me? Now where are you?

VOICE #1, #2, and #3. Our face is wind opening its hand. There are other women-mysteries besides the Mammi-Waters who have their drink of murder and laughter. Our face is wind, voice the edge of nothing. Strictly a product of burn and pale, indifferent imagination. Give us a glass of sparkling pity. We thirst like, better than, bearded Jesus on the cross.

GIRL. Where are you? Maybe I can help you . . .

VOICE #1, #2, and #3. We're nowhere. Don't you know? We don't exist.

GIRL (*first kneels, then sits at the pool. Worn out. Talking into the pool*). I give up. Talking to crazy women want me to come wallow in the swamp with them. Now here come some women so pitiful they don't even exist. I just want to find the WaterMother. That's all. Water. I'm thirsty. Look at me. I need to wash my face and hands. Look at me. Embers eaten my eyes. I just want to see. And sleep whole at night. Have a good night's rest. Replenish my heart fibrillating, and womb like a broken silken bubble, frail and frivolous with my female trouble. (*Girl goes to sleep.*)

(*Enter Women in ritual dress, all white, carrying baskets on their heads. They circle Girl. Entrap her. It is the Three Women again.*)

WOMEN IN WHITE (*whispering. A sonorous chant*). Oba. Water. Oya. Water. Oshun. Water. Omi.

(*They make washing gestures over the Girl, who is still sleeping.*)

WOMAN IN WHITE #1 (*over the head of the sleeping Girl, makes gestures*). The washing of the beads. The washing of her leaves. The washing of the whispers of her name. The plucking of the eyes of the sorrow.

(*Girl opens eyes. Is unafraid. Submissive to ritual.*)

The shaving of the head til her hair is an ebony skullcap, shorn immaculate. The washing of the herbs. The washing of the whisper-ring, white-gowned circling. Til the air sings nutmeg and perfumes unknown/ the girl unknown to herself/ fingers the beads/ washes her prayers/ into immaculate sleep.

(*Girl again sleeps. Fade out on smiling Women still circling her.*)

ACT 3

SCENE 1

SETTING: *A ritual line. Seven women bearing gifts. All in immaculate white. The Girl, however, wears color, perhaps brilliant green. The scene is only blue—indigo, royal blue, azure. Sky, water large and looming. Three male drummers. Girl brings up the rear of the line with her arms full of gifts. She also wears an ivory mask.*

WOMAN IN WHITE #3. I'm taking all my cares to Yemoja, Yemanja, the WaterMother.

WOMAN IN WHITE #2. What you bring her?

WOMAN IN WHITE #3. A fertility doll to bring me babies. A bag of Susan B. Anthony dollars spending like quarters. I'm prayin' she'll multiply my cash.

WOMAN IN WHITE #2. What you bring for her to eat? The orisha must be fed.

WOMAN IN WHITE #3. Red, Black, and Green beans over Brown and wild rice.

WOMAN IN WHITE #2. That'll please her. The national dish. (*She calls back to the Girl.*) And what are you bringing Yemoja, Yemanja. The WaterMother, besides your problems, girl?

GIRL (*looks into her basket*). A dish of okra and dried shrimp, many colored beads of sweat, a rosary, perfume, honey, avocado, broken melons, and groundnuts. Ointments and perennial blood.

WOMAN IN WHITE #2. That should definitely please her. She'll look on you with favor. She'll know you serious about fixin' your problem.

WOMAN IN WHITE #3 (*to Girl solicitously*). Tell me this, honey, why you got on that mask of ivory serenity made of white clay. You not gonna fool her. Everything is not cool.

WOMAN IN WHITE #2. Girl, she just gonna break yo face.

WOMAN IN WHITE #1. Silence. The gift giving begins.

(*All in turn take gifts to the water's edge. They pray at the water's edge. The Girl is last to come forward. When she sets down her offerings and looks out into the suggested sea, something begins to happen. A sparkling mist lifts from the water. It spreads out. A Woman is shrouded in the sparkling mist. Jazz music comes up with her. She is it!*)

YEMOJA. Girl, you look like death.

(*Girl draws back.*)

You wearin' that white like death. Child, like a hurt on you. Step out from behind the mask and be a woman. The Mardi Gras of Pain is over. Let me see your hands.

(*Girl extends hands.*)

Let me see your face.

(*Girl drops mask. Lifts face.*)

Uh huh. You come just to the right place. Glad you passed the test.

GIRL. What test? There was a test?

YEMOJA. Why you think you have to walk this far to find me? Anybody, whining and worthless, cain't come to me. Very few/ but people/ know my address. Know where I can be reached. Very few/ have crossed the bridge my mouth makes or swings shut. Know how to get past the water that swallows blues. Only a select few recognize my call letters—W-O-M-A-N or W-A-T-E-R, whichever you please. Very few/ outside of human beings, know how to get in touch with me or touch me past a laugh of tea leaves loose in the bottom in the cup of the water that swallows blues.

(*All the worshippers become involved with her talk. They clap and sway. Woman in White #2 praisefully mimics the gestures of Yemoja. The Women are all joyful and sassy like the Mother.*)

WOMAN IN WHITE #1 (*pleased with Girl. At Girl's shoulder*). She laughs fat and fabulous!

GIRL (*mesmerized*). Tender. Like a wish inside a cage. So beautiful. Her face—what I can see, is an instrument of music.

WOMAN IN WHITE #1. But isn't her face familiar.

YEMOJA. Music, huh? Thank you, child. But do you really know who I am? I know you don't because you don't know who you are.

WOMAN IN WHITE #1. She is the first birthfluid and the last afterbirth. She is the root of the watertree.

YEMOJA. So you're a child of mine.

GIRL (*shyly*). I think so. I believe we're related.

YEMOJA (*amused*). Tell me how.

GIRL. By way of the river and the man who grows dreams that are plucked before winter, yet frostbitten. From the bluesdelta by way of cousins and kitchenette whippings. I have seen the falling sunsets and the MammiWaters.

YEMOJA. My lost daughters!

WOMEN IN WHITE ALL. Those creatures. She has seen the MammiWaters.

YEMOJA (*raises her hand and all is silence*). Let me see your hands again. Yes. You have touched fire. The trauma of the burn is over. Mother's here now. This is the mass dedicated to you. The mass of the snake newly wise finding skin.

(*The encounter between Yemoja and the Girl is lengthy. The static quality is broken by the activity of the other Women. They make preparations for a ritual. Bring candles, etc. There is a surreal, quick quality to their movements. They pantomime water activities: washing, bathing, etc. One boils water . . .*)

You've been held by Fire. I know his name.

GIRL. How do you know?

YEMOJA. His flame still flickers in your eyes. I know his name is Fire. I know him well. And what's he done for you?

GIRL. He infected me with laughing sickness. He taught me the miracle of death. I walked the third rail. He put his eyes on me. I'm in his hot shadow. I can't get a good night's sleep.

YEMOJA. Come here.

(*Girl hesitates.*)

WOMAN IN WHITE #1. She will rinse you in cool water and medicines. She will bandage you in honey and herbs.

(*Yemoja throws a net/shawl which may be imaginary over the Girl's shoulders.*)

YEMOJA. That's a net of sympathy. But, not too much. Giving or getting. Too much sympathy not good for you. You have to understand . . .

(*Light fades . . .*)

Let's talk about him first. Get him out the way. You know what's wrong with Fire?

GIRL. He crazy!

(*Girl wails.*)

YEMOJA (*matter-of-factly*). Besides the obvious. He's walking in the danger zone and he got his sentry up twenty-four hours a day. He's got his guard up and it ain't standing against you alone.

GIRL. Who?

YEMOJA. I don't wanna name no names. They're afraid he'll break out of his diamond and burn their greedy fingers.

GIRL. If he broke out for me would he burn me—again?

YEMOJA. If you let him. He got some bad habits he gotta break. He think all that actin' out is interestin'.

GIRL. It's too much. All this is keeping me awake nights.

YEMOJA. He sleepin' like a baby.

GIRL. With his mama no doubt.

YEMOJA. Uh uh. The baby sitter.

(*Girl begins to laugh.*)

YEMOJA. I knew I could get a laugh outta you. Honey, that story he tellin' is funny. You have to holler. He jumpin' around acting out like he got his penis caught in a zipper.

GIRL. I hope he didn't break it.

YEMOJA. What?

YEMOJA (*laughs*). Now you got it. But you know he know better than the way he acts. He an adult. He know his childhood is over, but he hanging on. Anyway, you know what I'm about to do? I'm getting ready to jump in this dish of Red, Black, and Green beans, with that okra and shrimp ya brought me on the side. You know talking about these men is that old nervous talk, make you hungry. (*Girl nods. Yemoja yells to Woman in White #1.*) Bring this child a plate!

(*Black out. Scene does not end. Slowly the setting that the Women have arranged comes alive. A circle of candles is lighted. A strong female singing, twailing and a scatting. The Women are dancing in a half-circle. The Yemoja leads their chanting.*)

YEMOJA. Woman, child, you were born before his touch. Listen. Listen. You were born before his touch.

WOMAN IN WHITE #1. Centuries.

WOMAN IN WHITE #2. Millenniums.

WOMAN IN WHITE #3. Eons before.

YEMOJA. His is the theater. Showboat and star stage. He calls down exclamations and hawks applause.

WOMEN IN WHITE ALL. It is you. It is you. The power rests with.

YEMOJA. Yours is subtle and sophisticated. The massive understatement. The magic that moves too slow for the eye. The eloquence of the curve and the deep.

WOMAN IN WHITE #1. It is the weight of you

WOMAN IN WHITE #2. and the waiting, heavy holding,

WOMAN IN WHITE #3. the body of water that can put him still.

YEMOJA. Don't cup your hand too heavy on him. You have the mother's power to caress and smother. He presides over his fear of your extinguishing love and loathing.

WOMAN IN WHITE #1. God/woman, what you can do to him.

WOMAN IN WHITE #2. God/woman, what you can do to him.

YEMOJA. He goes out in the image of a snake, smoke in the hiss before it strikes the abyss that holds all things that are gone. You go over him. Hold, in hungry folds.

WOMEN IN WHITE ALL AND YEMOJA. Do not cup your hand too heavy on him.

(*All Women withdraw. Leaving only Girl centerstage. The rest linger in the darkness. Spotlight on Girl, blue, green, yellow, red.*)

GIRL. My face of accusatory eyes. Steam me. Polish me. Mist, take me, til I unfold my eyes that know the language of the high rains that wore grooves in mountains til they bled roads that rose like singers in the sun. My face of lullabye eyes, mist, take me, til I unfold my eyes so soft so on the edge of water and rose so knowing, so soft so on the edge of water and rose so knowing.

(*The Women return. They encircle Girl again. They bow to her, or they genuflect, kneel.*)

YEMOJA. She knows. This one. She knows, and becomes and is and was. She was.

GIRL (*to Yemoja, the WaterMother*). I am as you are. My face is your face. Your face is my power and my grace. (*To others.*) I am a simple being believing in small rituals. Bathwater flung out of tubs into the streets of Soweto. The child's Saturday night gaiety, a lake, in the cold flat. I am a simple being believing in small rituals. Lovers who bathe after Creation. Mine is a merciful killing/ the cotton chillsoft cloth, unwanted kittens hidden in my blue velvet gelee. Out of each family I have taken a son, testing his method, his trim muscle against the drift. I taste his marrow. And hold his music in my eyes. Until I untie the tides and old slave bones sing while scavengers swoop and swallow songless air. Mine is a merciful killing. The serious suicide's quiet celebration. Ballooning lungs that fatten the chest to bursting. Feel the water fill the mouth. Feel the water fill the nostrils. Feel the water rise, cover the black iris of the eyes.

(*This testimony must be a dance as well as a talk. A church scene of fierce, powerful, swift movements.*)

GIRL (*to all*). I've learned the word, the key, the tone, and sealed it here (*points to her own chest*) to breathe into his mouth.

(*Some Women are weeping for joy. Dancing. Girl gathers herself, triumphantly, prepares to leave.*)

YEMOJA. Wait. One last lesson before you forget. Don't meet that fool more than half way. He has to learn to reach. He gotta be above where he is and brave enough to show it. Remember? Let him take a risk.

(*Girl nods.*)

Fold this leaf of music between the lifted bridges of your breast, above the uncalibrated heartbeat. Listen to this one note: If he ever said something crazy like "No." If he acted like he was loving as a favor to a friend; or he a member of an anti-cruelty society; or if he has nothing in him or sees nothing in you he wants or needs—never mind. You need you. You have some thing for yourself. Poor thing. He out of luck.

(*Yemoja and Girl exchange farewell embrace.*)

(*Blackout.*)

ACT 3

SCENE 2

SETTING: *On the way home. Women in White accompany Girl. Each Woman in White wears an identifying band of*

color—*red, yellow, purple. Girl is now Omi Oshun Oba Oya, or Ms. Waters for short.*

WOMAN IN WHITE #1. Wooo. My goodness! This is one traveling woman!

WOMAN IN WHITE #2. Where are we now, Ms. Waters.

MS. WATERS. Not far from the strain of the MammiWaters. Can't you smell them?

(*Ms. Waters and Women pause. Cat sounds are heard. Ms. Waters and Women are mystified. Cat dancers appear, making cat noises. Dancers wear eye patches over one eye. They parade before the Women. They are similar to the MammiWaters in their outcast quality, but they lack personal power.*)

CHIEF CAT. Welcome to the Festival of the One Eye.

ALL CATS. He open her nose. He got her mind. He piss in her bread. He mess with her head.

(*All Cats cry through their one eye.*)

WOMAN IN WHITE #2. We better move on. I don't like the smell of things here.

WOMAN IN WHITE #3 (*horrified*). How do they spend their nights?

CHIEF CAT. We suck our solitudes and our whiskey. We sleep a slippery eyed dream. Most of all we lick our wounds miserably. Join us.

MS. WATERS. The Mardi Gras of Pain is over. Haven't you heard? At the festival of widows, wives of complaint, and 3:30 A.M. weepers I will not perform.

CHIEF CAT. Well, you ain't got to be snooty about it.

SECOND CAT. Hey, you! Wipe that smile off yo face!

MS. WATERS. Don't you get tired of crying the blues, crying the blues, instead of weeping and laughing yo personal joy? My sisters, I share your pain but don't you grow weary of wasting yo water in a whiskey glass?

CHIEF CAT (*to other Cats, then Ms. Waters*). Listen at her. She think she free. Who you on yo way to see now, Mama, since you been baptized? What you gone do if he, whoever he be, don't want you?

SECOND CAT. Yeah, you gone shout for joy?

MS. WATERS. No. Yes. Why, Yes, I will! I will just be me and . . .

CHIEF CAT. Shit. . . .

ALL CATS (*chanting*). You a female you can't be free. You a woman you can't be free. You a womb, girl, you can't be free. You a female you can't be free.

(*Women in White having withdrawn, resurge, form a line behind Ms. Waters.*)

MS. WATERS. I got a line of believers behind me to prove you a lie. My genealogy speaks in butt strut, under satin slightly wrinkled, like one of Duke's songs in this rough, dry material of my African tongue.

(*Snaps out a gorgeous fan. All Women fan.*)

WOMEN IN WHITE ALL. Smoke it, Mama. You sizzling, woman. Go head on.

MS. WATERS. I'm so happy I wanta sing for everybody. (*Embraces each Woman.*) I love, love, love, I even love his Mama. She a sister. I bear her bowls of African mimosa and violet. I have charity for her and her husband and hers . . .

WOMEN IN WHITE. Woman, you just loving everybody.

MS. WATERS. That's cause I love me. I am about love. I ain't all giving, either. I want some receiving. I have traveled in the name of love, to find love to beget love.

(*Cats are licking their wounds as lights fade.*)

ACT 3

SCENE 3

SETTING: *Shango in his palace is mixing pots and potions. He is doing math, magic, and science. He is busy and talking to himself; The Fan thinks he's talking to her. She is rapping.*

THE FAN. Feel the breeze? I am only here to please. Am I too high? I don't want to trouble the flame. I am only here to please.

SHANGO (*musing while working*). In my ordinary life as a man, before I tamed thunder and caught lightning in a jar like lightning bugs and sealed it. In that life I was just a man.

THE FAN. You are man. You are all man.

SHANGO. Without my divine complexity, I was all that I am now and less wise. Oba and man of science, magic, and mathematics. In that life in my land we celebrated the first yam and plantains grew long and thick as Eshu's member. (*Shango gestures vaguely.*)

THE FAN (*coy and coolly lascivious*). How big is Eshu's member? Feel the breeze. I am only here to please.

SHANGO (*ignores her*). In that time of the giant baobab before I messed in the magic pots of Creation I made love and war. Three wives loved me and I husbanded them. I savored each one of them and listened to the music they spread throughout my house.

THE FAN. There is music in this breeze. Listen. (*She fans furiously.*)

SHANGO. No. Not my house. It was *our* house. (*Having finished mixing, he pours his mixture in a tall chalice. Moves to his throne and begins to sip pensively.*) I poured myself into three women and they grew children from the vines of their bellies. A field of children, a harvest of honey and blackberry flesh and laughter high as grasses. Children. (*He begins to laugh.*) I remember when Awotunde hid in the belly of the old baobab and his mothers could not find him for a day. When he stepped out into the sunlight they reached out for him singing. All three singing. Oya, Oba, Oshun. Three wives.

(*Shadows beside and behind his throne dance as three women.*)

THE FAN (*sarcastic*). What perfection rested in the palm of your hand.

SHANGO. What perfect peace! I lost it and them. I didn't know my magic, the second face it could turn. (*Rises, looks at The Fan directly for the first time. Puts down chalice. Takes centerstage, looks up, flings out arms, as if he were trying to reach the sun.*) I didn't say my prayers before I joined in the feast. I simply gorged myself like a barbarian. Taking knowledge, pleasure, and plenty without a word of thanks. I messed up. At last, the pulse of the Ancestors beat against me because I did not bless them.

THE FAN (*bored*). Feel the breeze? The only aim is to please.

SHANGO. And it all went up in the last magic that raged against me. Lightning shaped in a terrible boomerang. I lost it all. I lost it all. Wives, children. What was left but Death? I took Death. Death is the teacher the Ancestors sent me to.

THE FAN (*interested*). Teaching what?

SHANGO. Loss. I learned loss. You know what lessons I have brought to this lifetime? Never to have what it hurts too much to lose. So I see a dish and I taste. I taste but not too much. (*He is trying to convince himself.*)

THE FAN. Taste. Taste me.

SHANGO. Go away.

THE FAN. My only aim is to please. (*All over him. Whining.*)

SHANGO. Is that all?

THE FAN. Yes. Oh. Yes. Only to please you.

SHANGO (*a slow realization*). Your only aim is me? Do you sing?

(*The Fan shakes her head.*)

You don't have a life song to sing for yourself? Don't you have a god of your own inside you, flowing like the rivers of Oba, or Oya, or Oshun?

THE FAN. I am a tame breeze at your holy feet. (*She falls to his feet.*)

SHANGO. Get up. I'm too old for this. I know the treachery of all this servility. There were other women after my three.

THE FAN. My veins are fragile glass tubes hot and breaking from the heat.

SHANGO. Woman, are you empty?

THE FAN. I'm filled only with you.

SHANGO. Or whoever is available to . . . What is your name?

THE FAN. I have no *name*. I am only The Fan, handle me. Feel the breeze, my only aim is to please. (*She backs away into darkness.*)

SHANGO (*back on his throne. Talks to himself*). Three wives— they were. Oba, the first and always ready for battle; Oya, the loyal always at my side even into Death who went with me to face the Ancestors; Oshun, the coy and beautiful, playful one dancing behind her own fan.

(*Three shadows again.*)

And then, after these centuries and so many mistakes . . . a girl with lush, fruit-filled hips, breasts, mouth, and eyes wide open, always for giving. A girl singing self-sacrifice she should have saved. After all . . . What do I have to give? What did I give besides anger and loss? Oba, Oya, Oshun—that girl I tasted, (admit it, man!) I devoured her and demanded more, the delicacy was so tender. I wonder, that girl, who came singing, does she have a name?

(*Slow fade into black.*)

ACT 3

SCENE 4

SETTING: *Women arrive at Shango's gate. Ms. Waters is in foreground, we see shadow of Fire busy on high.*

WOMAN IN WHITE #1. He has sent away his sentry.

WOMAN IN WHITE #2. And his fan.

WOMAN IN WHITE #3. Are you sure . . . ? And what if he?

MS. WATERS. Then I am Ms. Waters. I'm still Ms. Waters. And I'll always sing. (*Knocking at gate/door. Yelling.*) I believe good things are in you. Beyond your fire. Things with no passion in them, torn things of the child you once were, and the hidden face of the god you are. (*Pauses to watch his reaction. He is being coy.*) Tho fire is good I will touch you without heat, remarking only on the simple bone of air you are.

WOMAN IN WHITE #1 (*in background*). He ain't changed. What good is her change if he ain't changed too. She just be broke. He still the same.

(*Fire is acting like he hears none of this.*)

MS. WATERS. Listen, open this door, fool.

(*He opens door majestically, forcefully.*)

WOMAN IN WHITE #3. She has come singing. Singing.

SHANGO (*sullen. Reserved. Watching her*). Well. I'm busy. I got a lot ta do.

MS. WATERS. That's fine. I do too. I was on my way home. Thought I'd drop you a line . . . How's tricks? (*She takes his seat. Crosses her legs.*) I want to speak to him.

SHANGO. Only person here is me.

MS. WATERS. Fine. I want to speak to your secret face.

SHANGO. I ain't got no secrets. My business is in the streets.

MS. WATERS (*rises. Stands on side of seat*). Have a seat.

(*He sits. Tries to assume his original stance. She toys with him. Touches him.*)

I am willing to be kind. Call a truce. I'll keep it. I am absolutely fierce with honey on the verge of falling. I have forever been one who has given/ charity I found delicious. Too much giving. The ceremony of gifts I was enchanted with. Now I want to receive. I am hungry for draughts of blood and fire.

(*She caresses him.*)

Now I am the Fire Eater. Nourish me. Here is the painted vase that holds your soulpiece. I break you, sunder, and carefully collect: I pull out your organs, the suggestion of mango and papaya. My teeth go deep. I suck your crystals of strength. Now I am the Fire Eater. Nourish me.

SHANGO (*His talk counters hers. They speak in turns*). I know the treacheries of waters. Dark sailors who set sail across centuries. Men lost in sudden squalls at sea.

MS. WATERS. Now I am the Fire Eater. Nourish me.

WOMEN IN WHITE (*husky whispers*). Now she is the Fire Eater. Nourish her.

SHANGO. I know the hunger of the fishing villages that turned to scratch the rocks when the ocean gave up empty nets. I know the treacheries of waters. Men are lost in sudden squalls at sea.

MS. WATERS. I part the fur on your chest. Split your chords of thunder and treble. You are a disembodied voice, hidden, aloof, I claim you, Flamboyant Flame, Fastidious Deity. Now I am the Fire Eater.

WOMEN IN WHITE. Nourish her. Nourish her.

SHANGO. I know the mysteries of waters. A man losing his voice in the fog. The storm, sudden and evil, breaking the body, taking the soul away . . .

(*Fire tries to break away.*)

I've aged and been through many lives. Wives. I know the *under*-side of oceans.

WOMEN IN WHITE (*disgustedly*).

So you been a poor judge of character?
Don't judge her by your error.
Listen to her, my brother.

MS. WATERS. Have you never seen the fire reflected in the water? Its edges are softened, blur into a flame easy on the eye.

SHANGO. I've seen rivers rise over their banks. Wash away flesh and dream until every valley is filled with missing links that cannot connect, again. I know the treacheries of water. I never swim alone.

MS. WATERS. Take this thigh bone for wish. And this mouth to sail inside. Mouth made of mist. Break my breasts like bread. I am the end of all drought and famine. (*She rises.*)

WOMEN IN WHITE.

She is sincere as spring water.
She is the movement of honey and the passion of fruit.
Be tender with her.

MS. WATERS. I am the end of all drought and famine. Don't fool around and miss this, brother. There's only one *me* per lifetime.

SHANGO. Only one, huh?

MS. WATERS. Only one smile.

SHANGO. One smile. Milk and easy.

MS. WATERS. One kiss.

SHANGO. One kiss. Like berries breaking.

MS. WATERS. One touch.

SHANGO. One touch. Cool. A dance of feathers.

MS. WATERS. One faith. Believe me.

SHANGO. One faith.

MS. WATERS. One hope. One purpose.

SHANGO. One hope.

MS. WATERS. One charity.

SHANGO. One charity. That means love.

MS. WATERS. Uh huh.

SHANGO. One love. By the way. What's your name, woman?

(*They circle around and around each other tentatively act-ing out each other's spoken promises and hesitations. Bar-riers are breaking as they do. They mesmerize each other.*)

MS. WATERS. Omi. Omi Oya Oba Oshun. Ms. Waters for short.

SHANGO (*secretly joyous*). That's enough name for three women. How can you be three women?

MS. WATERS. I'm a riddle like the sphinx. Only one.

SHANGO. Only one. (*Issues his last resistance.*) I'm not looking to be hurt by no woman. This is the way it's gonna be . . . I get restless some time. I gotta have money to burn . . . I flare up now and then. (*He draws her into his lap.*)

MS. WATERS. Fire, hush.

(*Spotlight on the circle of their faces.*)

RECESSIONAL

SETTING: *An African wedding. Much color. Shango and Ms. Waters are at the head of a reception area. Ms. Waters is sing-speaking. This scene is used to spotlight the players for applause. It is inside and outside the play proper.*

MS. WATERS. Three wives I come to you. Three wise. My lord he comes like the lightning. My love he is the thun-der king.

(*She and Shango receive the guests.*)

WOMAN #1. Watch him, Ms. Waters. Don't let him get too high and mighty.

WOMAN #2. Be tender with him. Tender never hurt nobody, Omi.

WOMAN #3. Be yourself. Just be yourself and you two will make it.

WOMAN #2 (*looking off stage*). Did somebody call the Fire Department? Burn Unit? They outside.

WOMAN #3. Tell them to go away. We just burning bad bridges here. We have crossed over to the other side.

WOMAN #1 (*to Ms. Waters*). Woman, just be strong and love that man. Ain't no harm in that. And be sure he got his-self together when he go in the water.

(*All laugh.*)

SHANGO. I'm always together.

WOMAN #2. We hate for somethin' to happen to him.

WOMAN #3. Water can be dangerous. Like he say.

MS. WATERS. My love he calls me. He calls me by the love of God.

WOMAN #2. You know this don't guarantee no happy end-ing.

WOMAN #3. How come it don't?

WOMAN #1. Well, I hope she don't put him out when she get tired of his high jinks.

WOMAN #3. What high jinks? He looks right secure to me.

WOMAN #1. Water can be dangerous.

WOMAN #2. So can Fire.

SHANGO. Women, hush.

MS. WATERS (*to Shango*). Three wives of love are singing to you. Three women singing as one.

TOPICS FOR CRITICAL THINKING AND WRITING

📖 THE PLAY ON THE PAGE

1. What aspects of the Girl strike you as universal? Cite links to other works of literature (for example, a poem by Rita Dove, a play by William Shakespeare, a con-temporary song) to support your ideas.

2. Thematically, what is the importance of Act 2, Scene 4?

3. In Act 3, Scene 1, the Girl learns that she has passed the test. Just what was the test? Which of her actions proved her worthy? What character traits of the Girl are thus revealed?

4. Thematically, what is the importance of Act 3, Scene 2?

5. Locate several puns in the play, and analyze their effec-tiveness and appropriateness. Do the same thing for hyperboles, for similes, and for passages that seem to you especially lyrical.

6. Look up four allusions or references (for example, in Act 1, Scene 3, Huey P. Newton), and briefly explain them. In what ways does each allusion strengthen your understanding of the play?

7. Provide an analysis of Yemoja, and include one speech of hers that seems to you to epitomize her role in the play.

8. Analyze the three journeys of the Girl from a social-psychological point of view.

Angela Jackson

9. Pretend that you are directing a full production of *Shango Diaspora*. Choose one scene and indicate its choreography, explaining the effects you wish to achieve.

10. The second speaker in Act 1, Scene 3 is indicated simply as "A Voice." Should this be a male voice or a female voice? Explain your choice.

11. Propose music for Act 3, Scene 1—titles of actual songs, artists' names, and/or musical instruments. Are there places in this scene that would require sound effects other than music? Explain your choices.

12. What are the special challenges for the actress playing The Fan? Can you suggest someone—a contemporary stage or film actress, or someone from your own circle— who would be well cast as The Fan? Why?

THE PLAY IN PERFORMANCE

Shango Diaspora was first produced in New York in 1982 and was then performed by a number of black theater groups across the United States. A strong production in 1992 by the ETA Creative Arts Foundation in Chicago emphasized its lyrical and musical elements. Many of the speeches by the three MammiWater women were chanted, keened, or howled. All the performers utilized dance or dancelike movements based on African rhythms. A reviewer, Sid Smith of the *Chicago Tribune*, called Jackson's play "a parable about love, with song and dance" and praised the play's experimental qualities.

Athol Fugard

"MASTER HAROLD" . . . AND THE BOYS

Athol Fugard, whose full name is Athol Harold Lannigan Fugard, was born in 1932 in Cape Province, South Africa. In 1958 he organized a multiracial theater, for which he wrote plays (*A Lesson of Aloes* won the New York Drama Critics' Circle Award as the best play of 1980) and also served as a director and an actor. In addition to writing plays, he has written a novel and an autobiographical volume entitled *Notebooks 1960–1977. "MASTER HAROLD"* . . . *and the boys* was first produced in 1982 at the Yale Repertory Theatre.

COMMENTARY

The origins of a play, as with those of any other work of art, are ultimately mysterious. Perhaps the best that one can say is what Lady Murasaki said almost a thousand years ago, in a long Japanese book that is often called the first novel, *The Tale of Genji*:

> Again and again something in one's own life or in that around one will seem so important that one cannot bear to let it pass into oblivion. There must never come a time, the writer feels, when people do not know about this.

"Something in one's own life or in that around one" includes the reading and play going that an author does. For instance, before Shakespeare wrote his *King Lear*, he must have seen the old play *King Leir*—which ends happily, with Leir restored to the throne—and felt, "Well, there is much of interest here, but the way it *really* ought to go, if it is to be true to life, is. . . ." Similarly, the ancient Greek writers began with traditional myths, but each writer shaped the myth in a distinctive way, presumably in accordance with his insight into experience.

Some plays arise more obviously out of the life around the writer. Consider Ibsen's *A Doll's House*, for example. Ibsen's wife was a vigorous champion of women's causes, and she must have influenced his thinking. More specifically, *A Doll's House* is partly based on the experience of a woman whom Ibsen knew—someone who had forged a check to pay for a vacation that her husband's health required. However, Ibsen changed a good deal of the story. For instance, Ibsen's Nora leaves her husband, whereas the woman whom Ibsen knew was thrust out of the house (and into an insane asylum, in fact) by her husband, though ultimately the couple was more or less reconciled for the sake of their children. Rather as Shakespeare must have felt that the anonymous author of *King Leir* didn't quite get the story right, so Ibsen must have felt that real life was a bit muddled and that the story—to be enduring—should have gone this way: . . .

With Athol Fugard's *"MASTER HAROLD"* . . . *and the boys* (1982), however, we are pretty close to real life, if an entry for 1961 in Fugard's *Notebooks* can be trusted. Fugard, who was called Hally, was ashamed of his father, a lame man with a drinking problem. The boy found a surrogate father in Sam Semela, a black man who worked in the café that the boy's parents operated. If after reading the play you read the account in the *Notebooks* (reprinted here on p. 895), you will see how close the play is to certain of Fugard's experiences.

On the other hand, Fugard does not simply transcribe what really happened. For instance, Fugard was in fact fourteen at the time of the chief episode, but he makes his character Hally seventeen. Furthermore, the episode in which Hally spits did not take place in the café but when Hally was bicycling. Similarly, Sam in fact was a skilled dancer, but so were Fugard and his sister, who were junior ballroom dancing champions during their teenage years. In writing the play, Fugard drew on his experience as a dancer and his consequent insight into the dance, but he does not endow Hally with his own passion, understanding, and skill.

Out of his own experience Fugard shaped a play that in many ways closely resembles his experience on the one hand but that also departs from it on the other. What has he done with this material? Fugard clearly has very strong views about South African society, particularly about the injustice of apartheid (racial segregation). It is significant, however, that the word *apartheid* never appears in the play. Neither readers nor viewers feel that they are receiving a lecture on politics or on human decency. The closest we come to hearing a lecture is perhaps when Sam explains that dancing "is . . . like being in a dream about a world where accidents don't happen." What we are saying is that if "*MASTER HAROLD*" is a "problem play"—that is, a play that calls attention to a social problem—it does not degenerate into a propaganda play, a play in which the author's passionate convictions overshadow everything else, including believ-

able human beings. "*MASTER HAROLD*" seems to us to be rooted in what happened rather than in the urge to make an abstract political point, though of course the "what happened" is for Fugard immensely important because it is a personal experience that goes far beyond the merely personal. In any case, one can say that for the most part Fugard allows his characters to remain characters; he does not turn them into spokespersons for opposing political points of view. If "*MASTER HAROLD*" were only a thesis play, it would already be obsolete now that the "Whites Only" signs are coming down in South Africa. However, it remains because it is a play about human relationships.

Athol Fugard

"MASTER HAROLD"
. . . AND THE BOYS

The St. George's Park Tea Room on a wet and windy Port Elizabeth[1] afternoon.

Tables and chairs have been cleared and are stacked on one side except for one which stands apart with a single chair. On this table a knife, fork, spoon and side plate in anticipation of a simple meal, together with a pile of comic books.

Other elements: a serving counter with a few stale cakes under glass and a not very impressive display of sweets, cigarettes and cool drinks, etc.; a few cardboard advertising handouts—Cadbury's Chocolate, Coca-Cola—and a blackboard on which an untrained hand has chalked up the prices of Tea, Coffee, Scones, Milkshakes—all flavors—and Cool Drinks; a few sad ferns in pots; a telephone; an old-style jukebox.

There is an entrance on one side and an exit into a kitchen on the other.

Leaning on the solitary table, his head cupped in one hand as he pages through one of the comic books, is Sam. A black man in his mid-forties. He wears the white coat of a waiter. Behind him on his knees, mopping down the floor with a bucket of water and a rag, is Willie. Also black and about the same age as Sam. He has his sleeves and trousers rolled up.

The year: 1950

WILLIE (*singing as he works*).

"She was scandalizin' my name,
She took my money
She called me honey
But she was scandalizin' my name.
Called it love but was playin' a game . . ."

He gets up and moves the bucket. Stands thinking for a moment, then, raising his arms to hold an imaginary partner, he launches into an intricate ballroom dance step. Although a mildly comic figure, he reveals a reasonable degree of accomplishment.

Hey, Sam.

Sam, absorbed in the comic book, does not respond.

Hey, Boet[2] Sam!

Sam looks up.

[1]**Port Elizabeth** city in South Africa   [2]**Boet** Buddy, Brother

I'm getting it. The quickstep. Look now and tell me. (*He repeats the step.*) Well?

SAM (*encouragingly*). Show me again.

WILLIE. Okay, count for me.

SAM. Ready?

WILLIE. Ready.

SAM. Five, six, seven, eight . . . (*Willie starts to dance.*) A-n-d one two three four . . . and one two three four. . . . (*Ad libbing as Willie dances.*) Your shoulders, Willie . . . your shoulders! Don't look down! Look happy, Willie! Relax, Willie!

WILLIE (*desperate but still dancing*). I am relax.

SAM. No, you're not.

WILLIE. (*He falters.*) Ag no man, Sam! Mustn't talk. You make me make mistakes.

SAM. But you're too stiff.

WILLIE. Yesterday I'm not straight . . . today I'm too stiff!

SAM. Well, you are. You asked me and I'm telling you.

WILLIE. Where?

SAM. Everywhere. Try to glide through it.

WILLIE. Glide?

SAM. Ja, make it smooth. And give it more style. It must look like you're enjoying yourself.

WILLIE (*emphatically*). I wasn't.

SAM. Exactly.

WILLIE. How can I enjoy myself? Not straight, too stiff and now it's also glide, give it more style, make it smooth. . . . Haai! Is hard to remember all those things, Boet Sam.

SAM. That's your trouble. You're trying too hard.

WILLIE. I try hard because it *is* hard.

SAM. But don't let me see it. The secret is to make it look easy. Ballroom must look happy, Willie, not like hard work. It must . . . Ja! . . . it must look like romance.

WILLIE. Now another one! What's romance?

SAM. Love story with happy ending. A handsome man in tails, and in his arms, smiling at him, a beautiful lady in evening dress!

WILLIE. Fred Astaire, Ginger Rogers.

SAM. You got it. Tapdance or ballroom, it's the same. Romance. In two weeks' time when the judges look at you and Hilda, they must see a man and a woman who are dancing their way to a happy ending. What I saw was you holding her like you were frightened she was going to run away.

WILLIE. Ja! Because that is what she wants to do! I got no romance left for Hilda anymore, Boet Sam.

SAM. Then pretend. When you put your arms around Hilda, imagine she is Ginger Rogers.

WILLIE. With no teeth? You try.

SAM. Well, just remember, there's only two weeks left.

WILLIE. I know, I know! (*To the jukebox.*) I do it better with music. You got sixpence for Sarah Vaughan?[3]

SAM. That's a slow foxtrot. You're practicing the quickstep.

WILLIE. I'll practice slow foxtrot.

SAM (*shaking his head*). It's your turn to put money in the jukebox.

WILLIE. I only got bus fare to go home. (*He returns disconsolately to his work.*) Love story and happy ending! She's doing it all right, Boet Sam, but is not me she's giving happy endings. Fuckin' whore! Three nights now she doesn't come practice. I wind up gramophone, I get record ready and I sit and wait. What happens? Nothing. Ten o'clock I start dancing with my pillow. You try and practice romance by yourself, Boet Sam. Struesgod, she doesn't come tonight I take back my dress and ballroom shoes and I find me new partner. Size twenty-six. Shoes size seven. And now she's also making trouble for me with the baby again. Reports me to Child Wellfed, that I'm not giving her money. She lies! Every week I am giving her money for milk. And how do I know is my baby? Only his hair looks like me. She's fucking around all the time I turn my back. Hilda Samuels is a bitch! (*Pause.*) Hey, Sam!

SAM. Ja.

WILLIE. You listening?

SAM. Ja.

WILLIE. So what you say?

SAM. About Hilda?

WILLIE. Ja.

SAM. When did you last give her a hiding?

WILLIE (*reluctantly*). Sunday night.

SAM. And today is Thursday.

WILLIE. (*He knows what's coming.*) Okay.

SAM. Hiding on Sunday night, then Monday, Tuesday and Wednesday she doesn't come to practice . . . and you are asking me why?

WILLIE. I said okay, Boet Sam!

SAM. You hit her too much. One day she's going to leave you for good.

WILLIE. So? She makes me the hell-in too much.

SAM (*emphasizing his point*). *Too* much and *too* hard. You had the same trouble with Eunice.

WILLIE. Because she also make the hell-in, Boet Sam. She never got the steps right. Even the waltz.

SAM. Beating her up every time she makes a mistake in the waltz? (*Shaking his head.*) No, Willie! That takes the pleasure out of ballroom dancing.

WILLIE. Hilda is not too bad with the waltz, Boet Sam. Is the quickstep where the trouble starts.

SAM (*teasing him gently*). How's your pillow with the quickstep?

WILLIE (*ignoring the tease*). Good! And why? Because it got no legs. That's her trouble. She can't move them quick enough, Boet Sam. I start the record and before halfway Count Basie[4] is already winning. Only time we catch up with him is when gramophone runs down.

Sam laughs.

Haaikona, Boet Sam, is not funny.

SAM (*snapping his fingers*). I got it! Give her a handicap.

WILLIE. What's that?

SAM. Give her a ten-second start and then let Count Basie go. Then I put my money on her. Hot favorite in the Ballroom Stakes: Hilda Samuels ridden by Willie Malopo.

WILLIE (*turning away*). I'm not talking to you no more.

SAM (*relenting*). Sorry, Willie . . .

WILLIE. It's finish between us.

SAM. Okay, okay . . . I'll stop.

WILLIE. You can also fuck off.

SAM. Willie, listen! I want to help you!

WILLIE. No more jokes?

SAM. I promise.

WILLIE. Okay. Help me.

SAM (*his turn to hold an imaginary partner*). Look and learn. Feet together. Back straight. Body relaxed. Right hand placed gently in the small of her back and wait for the music. Don't start worrying about making mistakes or the judges or the other competitors. It's just you, Hilda and the music, and you're going to have a good time. What Count Basie do you play?

WILLIE. "You the cream in my coffee, you the salt in my stew."

SAM. Right. Give it to me in strict tempo.

WILLIE. Ready?

SAM. Ready.

WILLIE. A-n-d . . . (*Singing.*)

> "You the cream in my coffee.
> You the salt in my stew.
> You will always be my necessity.
> I'd be lost without you. . . ." (*etc.*)

Sam launches into the quickstep. He is obviously a much more accomplished dancer than Willie. Hally enters. A

---

[3]**Sarah Vaughan** American jazz singer, born in 1924

[4]**Count Basie** William Basie (1904–1984), American jazz pianist, band leader, and composer

seventeen-year-old white boy. Wet raincoat and school case. He stops and watches Sam. The demonstration comes to an end with a flourish. Applause from Hally and Willie.

HALLY. Bravo! No question about it. First place goes to Mr. Sam Semela.

WILLIE (in total agreement). You was gliding with style, Boet Sam.

HALLY (cheerfully). How's it, chaps?

SAM. Okay, Hally.

WILLIE (springing to attention like a soldier and saluting). At your service, Master Harold!

HALLY. Not long to the big event, hey!

SAM. Two weeks.

HALLY. You nervous?

SAM. No.

HALLY. Think you stand a chance?

SAM. Let's just say I'm ready to go out there and dance.

HALLY. It looked like it. What about you, Willie?

Willie groans.

What's the matter?

SAM. He's got leg trouble.

HALLY (innocently). Oh, sorry to hear that, Willie.

WILLIE. Boet Sam! You promised. (Willie returns to his work.)

Hally deposits his school case and takes off his raincoat. His clothes are a little neglected and untidy: black blazer with school badge, gray flannel trousers in need of an ironing, khaki shirt and tie, black shoes. Sam has fetched a towel for Hally to dry his hair.

HALLY. God, what a lousy bloody day. It's coming down cats and dogs out there. Bad for business, chaps . . . (Conspiratorial whisper.) . . . but it also means we're in for a nice quiet afternoon.

SAM. You can speak loud, Your Mom's not here.

HALLY. Out shopping?

SAM. No. The hospital.

HALLY. But it's Thursday. There's no visiting on Thursday afternoons. Is my Dad okay?

SAM. Sounds like it. In fact, I think he's going home.

HALLY (stopped short by Sam's remark). What do you mean?

SAM. The hospital phoned.

HALLY. To say what?

SAM. I don't know. I just heard your Mom talking.

HALLY. So what makes you say he's going home?

SAM. It sounded as if they were telling her to come and fetch him.

Hally thinks about what Sam has said for a few seconds.

HALLY. When did she leave?

SAM. About an hour ago. She said she would phone you. Want to eat?

Hally doesn't respond.

Hally, want your lunch?

HALLY. I suppose so. (His mood has changed.) What's on the menu? . . . as if I don't know.

SAM. Soup, followed by meat pie and gravy.

HALLY. Today's?

SAM. No.

HALLY. And the soup?

SAM. Nourishing pea soup.

HALLY. Just the soup. (The pile of comic books on the table.) And these?

SAM. For your Dad. Mr. Kempston brought them.

HALLY. You haven't been reading them, have you?

SAM. Just looking.

HALLY (examining the comics). Jungle Jim . . . Batman and Robin . . . Tarzan . . . God, what rubbish! Mental pollution. Take them away.

Sam exits waltzing into the kitchen. Hally turns to Willie.

HALLY. Did you hear my Mom talking on the telephone, Willie?

WILLIE. No, Master Hally. I was at the back.

HALLY. And she didn't say anything to you before she left?

WILLIE. She said I must clean the floors.

HALLY. I mean about my Dad.

WILLIE. She didn't say nothing to me about him, Master Hally.

HALLY (with conviction). No! It can't be. They said he needed at least another three weeks of treatment. Sam's definitely made a mistake. (Rummages through his school case, finds a book and settles down at the table to read.) So, Willie!

WILLIE. Yes, Master Hally! Schooling okay today?

HALLY. Yes, okay. . . . (He thinks about it.) . . . No, not really. Ag, what's the difference? I don't care. And Sam says you've got problems.

WILLIE. Big problems.

HALLY. Which leg is sore?

Willie groans.

Both legs.

WILLIE. There is nothing wrong with my legs. Sam is just making jokes.

HALLY. So then you will be in the competition.

WILLIE. Only if I can find me a partner.

HALLY. But what about Hilda?

SAM (returning with a bowl of soup). She's the one who's got trouble with her legs.

HALLY. What sort of trouble, Willie?

SAM. From the way he describes it, I think the lady has gone a bit lame.

HALLY. Good God! Have you taken her to see a doctor?

SAM. I think a vet would be better.

HALLY. What do you mean?

SAM. What do you call it again when a racehorse goes very fast?

HALLY. Gallop?

SAM. That's it!

WILLIE. Boet Sam!

HALLY. "A gallop down the homestretch to the winning post." But what's that got to do with Hilda?

SAM. Count Basie always gets there first.

Willie lets fly with his slop rag. It misses Sam and hits Hally.

HALLY (*furious*). For Christ's sake, Willie! What the hell do you think you're doing!

WILLIE. Sorry, Master Hally, but it's him. . . .

HALLY. Act your bloody age! (*Hurls the rag back at Willie.*) Cut out the nonsense now and get on with your work. And you too, Sam. Stop fooling around.

Sam moves away.

No. Hang on. I haven't finished! Tell me exactly what my Mom said.

SAM. I have. "When Hally comes, tell him I've gone to the hospital and I'll phone him."

HALLY. She didn't say anything about taking my Dad home?

SAM. No. It's just that when she was talking on the phone . . .

HALLY (*interrupting him*). No, Sam. They can't be discharging him. She would have said so if they were. In any case, we saw him last night and he wasn't in good shape at all. Staff nurse even said there was talk about taking more X-rays. And now suddenly today he's better? If anything, it sounds more like a bad turn to me . . . which I sincerely hope it isn't. Hang on . . . how long ago did you say she left?

SAM. Just before two . . . (*His wrist watch.*) . . . hour and a half.

HALLY. I know how to settle it. (*Behind the counter to the telephone. Talking as he dials.*) Let's give her ten minutes to get to the hospital, ten minutes to load him up, another ten, at the most, to get home and another ten to get him inside. Forty minutes. They should have been home for at least half an hour already. (*Pause—he waits with the receiver to his ear.*) No reply, chaps. And you know why? Because she's at his bedside in hospital helping him pull through a bad turn. You definitely heard wrong.

SAM. Okay.

As far as Hally is concerned, the matter is settled. He returns to his table, sits down and divides his attention between the book and his soup. Sam is at his school case and picks up a textbook "Modern Graded Mathematics for Standards Nine and Ten." Opens it at random and laughs at something he sees.

Who is this supposed to be?

HALLY. Old fart-face Prentice.

SAM. Teacher?

HALLY. Thinks he is. And believe me, that is not a bad likeness.

SAM. Has he seen it?

HALLY. Yes.

SAM. What did he say?

HALLY. Tried to be clever, as usual. Said I was no Leonardo da Vinci and that bad art had to be punished. So, six of the best, and his are bloody good.

SAM. On your bum?

HALLY. Where else? The days when I got them on my hands are gone forever, Sam.

SAM. With your trousers down!

HALLY. No. He's not quite that barbaric.

SAM. That's the way they do it in jail.

HALLY (*flicker of morbid interest*). Really?

SAM. Ja. When the magistrate sentences you to "strokes with a light cane."

HALLY. Go on.

SAM. They make you lie down on a bench. One policeman pulls down your trousers and holds your ankles, another one pulls your shirt over your head and holds your arms . . .

HALLY. Thank you! That's enough.

SAM. . . . and the one that gives you the strokes talks to you gently and for a long time between each one. (*He laughs.*)

HALLY. I've heard enough, Sam! Jesus! It's a bloody awful world when you come to think of it. People can be real bastards.

SAM. That's the way it is, Hally.

HALLY. It doesn't *have* to be that way. There is something called progress, you know. We don't exactly burn people at the stake anymore.

SAM. Like Joan of Arc.

HALLY. Correct. If she was captured today, she'd be given a fair trial.

SAM. And then the death sentence.

HALLY (*a world-weary sigh*). I know, I know! I oscillate between hope and despair for this world as well, Sam. But things will change, you wait and see. One day somebody is going to get up and give history a kick up the backside and get it going again.

SAM. Like who?

HALLY (*after thought*). They're called social reformers. Every age, Sam, has got its social reformer. My history book is full of them.

SAM. So where's ours?

HALLY. Good question. And I hate to say it, but the answer is: I don't know. Maybe he hasn't even been born yet. Or is still only a babe in arms at his mother's breast. God, what a thought.

SAM. So we just go on waiting.

HALLY. Ja, looks like it. (*Back to his soup and the book.*)

SAM (*reading from the textbook*). "Introduction: In some mathematical problems only the magnitude . . ." (*He mispronounces the word "magnitude."*)

HALLY (*correcting him without looking up*). Magnitude.

SAM. What's it mean?

HALLY. How big it is. The size of the thing.

SAM (*reading*). ". . . a magnitude of the quantities is of importance. In other problems we need to know whether these quantities are negative or positive. For example, whether there is a debit or credit bank balance . . ."

HALLY. Whether you're broke or not.

SAM. ". . . whether the temperature is above or below Zero . . ."

HALLY. Naught degrees. Cheerful state of affairs! No cash and you're freezing to death. Mathematics won't get you out of that one.

SAM. "All these quantities are called . . ." (*Spelling the word.*) . . . s-c-a-l . . .

HALLY. Scalars.

SAM. Scalars! (*Shaking his head with a laugh.*) You understand all that?

HALLY (*turning a page*). No. And I don't intend to try.

SAM. So what happens when the exams come?

HALLY. Failing a maths exam isn't the end of the world, Sam. How many times have I told you that examination results don't measure intelligence?

SAM. I would say about as many times as you've failed one of them.

HALLY (*mirthlessly*). Ha, ha, ha.

SAM (*simultaneously*). Ha, ha, ha.

HALLY. Just remember Winston Churchill didn't do particularly well at school.

SAM. You've also told me that one many times.

HALLY. Well, it just so happens to be the truth.

SAM (*enjoying the word*). Magnitude! Magnitude! Show me how to use it.

HALLY (*after thought*). An intrepid social reformer will not be daunted by the magnitude of the task he has undertaken.

SAM (*impressed*). Couple of jaw-breakers in there!

HALLY. I gave you three for the price of one. Intrepid, daunted and magnitude. I did that once in an exam. Put five of the words I had to explain in one sentence. It was half a page long.

SAM. Well, I'll put my money on you in the English exam.

HALLY. Piece of cake. Eighty percent without even trying.

SAM (*another textbook from Hally's case*). And history?

HALLY. So-so. I'll scrape through. In the fifties if I'm lucky.

SAM. You didn't do too badly last year.

HALLY. Because we had World War One. That at least had some action. You try to find that in the South African Parliamentary system.

SAM (*reading from the history textbook*). "Napoleon and the principle of equality." Hey! This sounds interesting. "After concluding peace with Britain in 1802, Napoleon used a brief period of calm to in-sti-tute . . ."

HALLY. Introduce.

SAM. ". . . many reforms. Napoleon regarded all people as equal before the law and wanted them to have equal opportunities for advancement. All ves-ti-ges of the feudal system with its oppression of the poor were abol-

ished." Vestiges, feudal system and abolished. I'm all right on oppression.

HALLY. I'm thinking. He swept away . . . abolished . . . the last remains . . . vestiges . . . of the bad old days . . . feudal system.

SAM. Ha! There's the social reformer we're waiting for. He sounds like a man of some magnitude.

HALLY. I'm not so sure about that. It's a damn good title for a book, though. A man of magnitude!

SAM. He sounds pretty big to me, Hally.

HALLY. Don't confuse historical significance with greatness. But maybe I'm being a bit prejudiced. Have a look in there and you'll see he's two chapters long. And hell! . . . has he only got dates, Sam, all of which you've got to remember! This campaign and that campaign, and then, because of all the fighting, the next thing is we get Peace Treaties all over the place. And what's the end of the story? Battle of Waterloo, which he loses. Wasn't worth it. No, I don't know about him as a man of magnitude.

SAM. Then who would you say was?

HALLY. To answer that, we need a definition of greatness, and I suppose that would be somebody who . . . somebody who benefited all mankind.

SAM. Right. But like who?

HALLY. (*He speaks with total conviction.*) Charles Darwin. Remember him? That big book from the library. *The Origin of the Species.*

SAM. Him?

HALLY. Yes. For his Theory of Evolution.

SAM. You didn't finish it.

HALLY. I ran out of time. I didn't finish it because my two weeks was up. But I'm going to take it out again after I've digested what I read. It's safe. I've hidden it away in the Theology section. Nobody ever goes in there. And anyway who are you to talk? You hardly even looked at it.

SAM. I tried. I looked at the chapters in the beginning and I saw one called "The Struggle for an Existence." Ah ha, I thought. At last! But what did I get? Something called the mistletoe which needs the apple tree and there's too many seeds and all are going to die except one . . . ! No, Hally.

HALLY (*intellectually outraged*). What do you mean, No! The poor man had to start somewhere. For God's sake, Sam, he revolutionized science. Now we know.

SAM. What?

HALLY. Where we come from and what it all means.

SAM. And that's a benefit to mankind? Anyway, I still don't believe it.

HALLY. God, you're impossible. I showed it to you in black and white.

SAM. Doesn't mean I got to believe it.

HALLY. It's the likes of you that kept the Inquisition in business. It's called bigotry. Anyway, that's my man of magnitude. Charles Darwin! Who's yours?

SAM (*without hesitation*). Abraham Lincoln.

Athol Fugard

HALLY. I might have guessed as much. Don't get sentimental, Sam. You've never been a slave, you know. And anyway we freed your ancestors here in South Africa long before the Americans. But if you want to thank somebody on their behalf, do it to Mr. William Wilberforce.[5] Come on. Try again. I want a real genius. (*Now enjoying himself, and so is Sam. Hally goes behind the counter and helps himself to a chocolate.*)

SAM. William Shakespeare.

HALLY (*no enthusiasm*). Oh. So you're also one of them, are you? You're basing that opinion on only one play, you know. You've only read my *Julius Caesar* and even I don't understand half of what they're talking about. They should do what they did with the old Bible: bring the language up to date.

SAM. That's all you've got. It's also the only one *you've* read.

HALLY. I know. I admit it. That's why I suggest we reserve our judgment until we've checked up on a few others. I've got a feeling, though, that by the end of this year one is going to be enough for me, and I can give you the names of twenty-nine other chaps in the Standard Nine class of the Port Elizabeth Technical College who feel the same. But if you want him, you can have him. My turn now. (*Pacing.*) This is a damned good exercise, you know! It started off looking like a simple question and here it's got us really probing into the intellectual heritage of our civilization.

SAM. So who is it going to be?

HALLY. My next man . . . and he gets the title on two scores: social reform and literary genius . . . is Leo Nikolaevich Tolstoy.

SAM. That Russian.

HALLY. Correct. Remember the picture of him I showed you?

SAM. With the long beard.

HALLY (*trying to look like Tolstoy*). And those burning, visionary eyes. My God, the face of a social prophet if ever I saw one! And remember my words when I showed it to you? Here's a *man*, Sam!

SAM. Those were words, Hally.

HALLY. Not many intellectuals are prepared to shovel manure with the peasants and then go home and write a "little book" called *War and Peace*. Incidentally, Sam, he was somebody else who, to quote, ". . . did not distinguish himself scholastically."

SAM. Meaning?

HALLY. He was also no good at school.

SAM. Like you and Winston Churchill.

HALLY (*mirthlessly*). Ha, ha, ha.

SAM (*simultaneously*). Ha, ha, ha.

HALLY. Don't get clever, Sam. That man freed his serfs of his own free will.

---

[5]**William Wilberforce** English abolitionist (1759–1833)

SAM. No argument. He was a somebody, all right. I accept him.

HALLY. I'm sure Count Tolstoy will be very pleased to hear that. Your turn. Shoot. (*Another chocolate from behind the counter.*) I'm waiting, Sam.

SAM. I've got him.

HALLY. Good. Submit your candidate for examination.

SAM. Jesus.

HALLY (*stopped dead in his tracks*). Who?

SAM. Jesus Christ.

HALLY. Oh, come on, Sam!

SAM. The Messiah.

HALLY. Ja, but still . . . No, Sam. Don't let's get started on religion. We'll just spend the whole afternoon arguing again. Suppose I turn around and say Mohammed?

SAM. All right.

HALLY. You can't have them both on the same list!

SAM. Why not? You like Mohammed, I like Jesus.

HALLY. I *don't* like Mohammed. I never have. I was merely being hypothetical. As far as I'm concerned, the Koran is as bad as the Bible. No. Religion is out! I'm not going to waste my time again arguing with you about the existence of God. You know perfectly well I'm an atheist . . . and I've got homework to do.

SAM. Okay, I take him back.

HALLY. You've got time for one more name.

SAM (*after thought*). I've got one I know we'll agree on. A simple straightforward great Man of Magnitude . . . and no arguments. And *he* really *did* benefit all mankind.

HALLY. I wonder. After your last contribution I'm beginning to doubt whether anything in the way of an intellectual agreement is possible between the two of us. Who is he?

SAM. Guess.

HALLY. Socrates? Alexandre Dumas? Karl Marx? Dostoevsky? Nietzsche?

Sam shakes his head after each name.

Give me a clue.

SAM. The letter P is important . . .

HALLY. Plato!

SAM. . . . and his name begins with an F.

HALLY. I've got it. Freud and Psychology.

SAM. No. I didn't understand him.

HALLY. That makes two of us.

SAM. Think of mouldy apricot jam.

HALLY (*after a delighted laugh*). Penicillin and Sir Alexander Fleming! And the title of the book: *The Microbe Hunters*. (*Delighted.*) Splendid, Sam! Splendid. For once we are in total agreement. The major breakthrough in medical science in the Twentieth Century. If it wasn't for him, we might have lost the Second World War. It's deeply gratifying, Sam, to know that I haven't been wasting my time in talking to you. (*Strutting around proudly.*) Tolstoy may have educated his peasants, but I've educated you.

SAM. Standard Four to Standard Nine.

HALLY. Have we been at it as long as that?

SAM. Yep. And my first lesson was geography.

HALLY (*intrigued*). Really? I don't remember.

SAM. My room there at the back of the old Jubilee Boarding House. I had just started working for your Mom. Little boy in short trousers walks in one afternoon and asks me seriously: "Sam, do you want to see South Africa?" Hey man! Sure I wanted to see South Africa!

HALLY. Was that me?

SAM. . . . So the next thing I'm looking at a map you had just done for homework. It was your first one and you were very proud of yourself.

HALLY. Go on.

SAM. Then came my first lesson. "Repeat after me, Sam: Gold in the Transvaal, mealies in the Free State, sugar in Natal and grapes in the Cape." I still know it!

HALLY. Well, I'll be buggered. So that's how it all started.

SAM. And your next map was one with all the rivers and the mountains they came from. The Orange, the Vaal, the Limpopo, the Zambezi . . .

HALLY. You've got a phenomenal memory!

SAM. You should be grateful. That is why you started passing your exams. You tried to be better than me.

They laugh together. Willie is attracted by the laughter and joins them.

HALLY. The old Jubilee Boarding House. Sixteen rooms with board and lodging, rent in advance and one week's notice. I haven't thought about it for donkey's years . . . and I don't think that's an accident. God, was I glad when we sold it and moved out. Those years are not remembered as the happiest ones of an unhappy childhood.

WILLIE (*knocking on the table and trying to imitate a woman's voice*). "Hally, are you there?"

HALLY. Who's that supposed to be?

WILLIE. "What you doing in there, Hally? Come out at once!"

HALLY (*to Sam*). What's he talking about?

SAM. Don't you remember?

WILLIE. "Sam, Willie . . . is he in there with you boys?"

SAM. Hiding away in our room when your mother was looking for you.

HALLY (*another good laugh*). Of course! I used to crawl and hide under your bed! But finish the story, Willie. Then what used to happen? You chaps would give the game away by telling her I was in there with you. So much for friendship.

SAM. We couldn't lie to her. She knew.

HALLY. Which meant I got another rowing for hanging around the "servants' quarters." I think I spent more time in there with you chaps than anywhere else in that dump. And do you blame me? Nothing but bloody misery wherever you went. Somebody was always complaining about the food, or my mother was having a fight with Micky

Nash because she'd caught her with a petty officer in her room. Maud Meiring was another one. Remember those two? They were prostitutes, you know. Soldiers and sailors from the troopships. Bottom fell out of the business when the war ended. God, the flotsam and jetsam that life washed up on our shores! No joking, if it wasn't for your room, I would have been the first certified ten-year-old in medical history. Ja, the memories are coming back now. Walking home from school and thinking: "What can I do this afternoon?" Try out a few ideas, but sooner or later I'd end up in there with you fellows. I bet you I could still find my way to your room with my eyes closed. (*He does exactly that.*) Down the corridor . . . telephone on the right, which my Mom keeps locked because somebody is using it on the sly and not paying . . . past the kitchen and unappetizing cooking smells . . . around the corner into the backyard, hold my breath again because there are more smells coming when I pass your lavatory, then into that little passageway, first door on the right and into your room. How's that?

SAM. Good. But, as usual, you forgot to knock.

HALLY. Like that time I barged in and caught you and Cynthia . . . at it. Remember? God, was I embarrassed! I didn't know what was going on at first.

SAM. Ja, that taught you a lesson.

HALLY. And about a lot more than knocking on doors, I'll have you know, and I don't mean geography either. Hell, Sam, couldn't you have waited until it was dark?

SAM. No.

HALLY. Was it that urgent?

SAM. Yes, and if you don't believe me, wait until your time comes.

HALLY. No, thank you. I am not interested in girls. (*Back to his memories . . . Using a few chairs he recreates the room as he lists the items.*) A gray little room with a cold cement floor. Your bed against that wall . . . and I now know why the mattress sags so much! . . . Willie's bed . . . it's propped up on bricks because one leg is broken . . . that wobbly little table with the washbasin and jug of water . . . Yes! . . . stuck to the wall above it are some pin-up pictures from magazines. Joe Louis[6] . . .

WILLIE. Brown Bomber. World Title. (*Boxing pose.*) Three rounds and knockout.

HALLY. Against who?

SAM. Max Schmeling.

HALLY. Correct. I can also remember Fred Astaire and Ginger Rogers, and Rita Hayworth in a bathing costume which always made me hot and bothered when I looked at it. Under Willie's bed is an old suitcase with all his

---

[6]**Joe Louis** In 1938 the African-American prizefighter Joe Louis (1914–1981), known as the Brown Bomber, defeated the heavyweight champion, Max Schmeling.

clothes in a mess, which is why I never hide there. Your things are neat and tidy in a trunk next to your bed, and on it there is a picture of you and Cynthia in your ballroom clothes, your first silver cup for third place in a competition and an old radio which doesn't work anymore. Have I left out anything?

SAM. No.

HALLY. Right, so much for the stage directions. Now the characters. (*Sam and Willie move to their appropriate positions in the bedroom.*) Willie is in bed, under his blankets with his clothes on, complaining nonstop about something, but we can't make out a word of what he's saying because he's got his head under the blankets as well. You're on your bed trimming your toenails with a knife—not a very edifying sight—and as for me . . . What am I doing?

SAM. You're sitting on the floor giving Willie a lecture about being a good loser while you get the checker board and pieces ready for a game. Then you go to Willie's bed, pull off the blankets and make him play with you first because you know you're going to win, and that gives you the second game with me.

HALLY. And you certainly were a bad loser, Willie!

WILLIE. Haai!

HALLY. Wasn't he, Sam? And so slow! A game with you almost took the whole afternoon. Thank God I gave up trying to teach you how to play chess.

WILLIE. You and Sam cheated.

HALLY. I never saw Sam cheat, and mine were mostly the mistakes of youth.

WILLIE. Then how is it you two was always winning?

HALLY. Have you ever considered the possibility, Willie, that it was because we were better than you?

WILLIE. Every time better?

HALLY. Not every time. There were occasions when we deliberately let you win a game so that you would stop sulking and go on playing with us. Sam used to wink at me when you weren't looking to show me it was time to let you win.

WILLIE. So then you two didn't play fair.

HALLY. It was for your benefit, Mr. Malopo, which is more than being fair. It was an act of self-sacrifice. (*To Sam.*) But you know what my best memory is, don't you?

SAM. No.

HALLY. Come on, guess. If your memory is so good, you must remember it as well.

SAM. We got up to a lot of tricks in there, Hally.

HALLY. This one was special, Sam.

SAM. I'm listening.

HALLY. It started off looking like another of those useless nothing-to-do afternoons. I'd already been down to Main Street looking for adventure, but nothing had happened. I didn't feel like climbing trees in the Donkin Park or pretending I was a private eye and following a stranger . . . so as usual: See what's cooking in Sam's room. This

time it was you on the floor. You had two thin pieces of wood and you were smoothing them down with a knife. It didn't look particularly interesting, but when I asked you what you were doing, you just said, "Wait and see, Hally. Wait . . . and see" . . . in that secret sort of way of yours, so I knew there was a surprise coming. You teased me, you bugger, by being deliberately slow and not answering my questions!

Sam laughs.

And whistling while you worked away! God, it was infuriating! I could have brained you! It was only when you tied them together in a cross and put that down on the brown paper that I realized what you were doing. "Sam is making a kite?" And when I asked you and you said "Yes" . . . ! (*Shaking his head with disbelief.*) The sheer audacity of it took my breath away. I mean, seriously, what the hell does a black man know about flying a kite? I'll be honest with you, Sam, I had no hopes for it. If you think I was excited and happy, you got another guess coming. In fact, I was shit-scared that we were going to make fools of ourselves. When we left the boarding house to go up onto the hill, I was praying quietly that there wouldn't be any other kids around to laugh at us.

SAM (*enjoying the memory as much as Hally*). Ja, I could see that.

HALLY. I made it obvious, did I?

SAM. Ja. You refused to carry it.

HALLY. Do you blame me? Can you remember what the poor thing looked like? Tomato-box wood and brown paper! Flour and water for glue! Two of my mother's old stockings for a tail, and then all those bits and pieces of string you made me tie together so that we could fly it! Hell, no, that was now only asking for a miracle to happen.

SAM. Then the big argument when I told you to hold the string and run with it when I let go.

HALLY. I was prepared to run, all right, but straight back to the boarding house.

SAM (*knowing what's coming*). So what happened?

HALLY. Come on, Sam, you remember as well as I do.

SAM. I want to hear it from you.

Hally pauses. He wants to be as accurate as possible.

HALLY. You went a little distance from me down the hill, you held it up ready to let it go. . . . "This is it," I thought. "Like everything else in my life, here comes another fiasco." Then you shouted, "Go, Hally!" and I started to run. (*Another pause.*) I don't know how to describe it, Sam. Ja! The miracle happened! I was running, waiting for it to crash to the ground, but instead suddenly there was something alive behind me at the end of the string, tugging at it as if it wanted to be free. I looked back . . . (*Shakes his head.*) . . . I still can't believe my eyes. It was flying! Looping around and trying to climb even higher into the sky. You shouted to me to let it have more string. I did, until there was none left and I was just holding that piece of wood we had tied it to. You came up and joined me. You were laughing.

SAM. So were you. And shouting, "It works, Sam! We've done it!"

HALLY. And we had! I was so proud of us! It was the most splendid thing I had ever seen. I wished there were hundreds of kids around to watch us. The part that scared me, though, was when you showed me how to make it dive down to the ground and then just when it was on the point of crashing, swoop up again!

SAM. You didn't want to try yourself.

HALLY. Of course not! I would have been suicidal if anything had happened to it. Watching you do it made me nervous enough. I was quite happy just to see it up there with its tail fluttering behind it. You left me after that, didn't you? You explained how to get it down, we tied it to the bench so that I could sit and watch it, and you went away. I wanted you to stay, you know. I was a little scared of having to look after it by myself.

SAM (quietly). I had work to do, Hally.

HALLY. It was sort of sad bringing it down, Sam. And it looked sad again when it was lying there on the ground. Like something that had lost its soul. Just tomato-box wood, brown paper and two of my mother's old stockings! But, hell, I'll never forget that first moment when I saw it up there. I had a stiff neck the next day from looking up so much.

Sam laughs. Hally turns to him with a question he never thought of asking before.

Why did you make that kite, Sam?

SAM (evenly). I can't remember.

HALLY. Truly?

SAM. Too long ago, Hally.

HALLY. Ja, I suppose it was. It's time for another one, you know.

SAM. Why do you say that?

HALLY. Because it feels like that. Wouldn't be a good day to fly it, though.

SAM. No. You can't fly kites on rainy days.

HALLY. (He studies Sam. Their memories have made him conscious of the man's presence in his life.) How old are you, Sam?

SAM. Two score and five.

HALLY. Strange, isn't it?

SAM. What?

HALLY. Me and you.

SAM. What's strange about it?

HALLY. Little white boy in short trousers and a black man old enough to be his father flying a kite. It's not every day you see that.

SAM. But why strange? Because the one is white and the other black?

HALLY. I don't know. Would have been just as strange, I suppose, if it had been me and my Dad . . . cripple man and a

little boy! Nope! There's no chance of me flying a kite without it being strange. (*Simple statement of fact—no self-pity.*) There's a nice little short story there. "The Kite-Flyers." But we'd have to find a twist in the ending.

SAM. Twist?

HALLY. Yes. Something unexpected. The way it ended with us was too straightforward . . . me on the bench and you going back to work. There's no drama in that.

WILLIE. And me?

HALLY. You?

WILLIE. Yes me.

HALLY. You want to get into the story as well, do you? I got it! Change the title: "Afternoons in Sam's Room" . . . expand it and tell all the stories. It's on its way to being a novel. Our days in the old Jubilee. Sad in a way that they're over. I almost wish we were still in that little room.

SAM. We're still together.

HALLY. That's true. It's just that life felt the right size in there . . . not too big and not too small. Wasn't so hard to work up a bit of courage. It's got so bloody complicated since then.

The telephone rings. Sam answers it.

SAM. St. George's Park Tea Room . . . Hello, Madam . . . Yes, Madam, he's here . . . Hally, it's your mother.

HALLY. Where is she phoning from?

SAM. Sounds like the hospital. It's a public telephone.

HALLY (relieved). You see! I told you. (*The telephone.*) Hello, Mom . . . Yes . . . Yes no fine. Everything's under control here. How's things with poor old Dad? . . . Has he had a bad turn? . . . What? . . . Oh, God! . . . Yes, Sam told me, but I was sure he'd made a mistake, But what's this all about, Mom? He didn't look at all good last night. How can he get better so quickly? . . . Then very obviously you must say no. Be firm with him. You're the boss. . . . You know what it's going to be like if he comes home. . . . Well, then, don't blame me when I fail my exams at the end of the year. . . . Yes! How am I expected to be fresh for school when I spend half the night massaging his gammy leg? . . . So am I! . . . So tell him a white lie. Say Dr. Colley wants more X-rays of his stump. Or bribe him. We'll sneak in double tots of brandy in future. . . . What? . . . Order him to get back into bed at once! If he's going to behave like a child, treat him like one. . . . All right, Mom! I was just trying to . . . I'm sorry. . . . I said I'm sorry. . . . Quick, give me your number. I'll phone you back. (*He hangs up and waits a few seconds.*) Here we go again! (*He dials.*) I'm sorry, Mom. . . . Okay . . . But now listen to me carefully. All it needs is for you to put your foot down. Don't take no for an answer. . . . Did you hear me? And whatever you do, don't discuss it with him. . . . Because I'm frightened you'll give in to him. . . . Yes, Sam gave me lunch. . . . I ate all of it! . . . No, Mom not a soul. It's still raining here. . . . Right, I'll tell them. I'll just do some homework and then lock up. . . . But remember now, Mom. Don't listen to anything he says. And phone me back and let me know what happens. . . . Okay. Bye, Mom. (*He hangs up. The men are staring at him.*) My Mom says that when you're finished with the floors you must do the windows. (*Pause.*) Don't misunderstand me, chaps. All I want is for him to get better. And if he was, I'd be the first person to say: "Bring him home." But he's not, and we can't give him the medical care and attention he needs at home. That's what hospitals are there for. (*Brusquely.*) So don't just stand there! Get on with it!

Sam clears Hally's table.

You heard right. My Dad wants to go home.

SAM. Is he better?

HALLY. (*sharply.*) No! How the hell can he be better when last night he was groaning with pain? This is not an age of miracles!

SAM. Then he should stay in hospital.

HALLY (*seething with irritation and frustration*). Tell me something I don't know, Sam. What the hell do you think I was saying to my Mom? All I can say is fuck-it-all.

SAM. I'm sure he'll listen to your Mom.

HALLY. You don't know what she's up against. He's already packed his shaving kit and pajamas and is sitting on his bed with his crutches, dressed and ready to go. I know him when he gets in that mood. If she tries to reason with him, we've had it. She's no match for him when it comes to a battle of words. He'll tie her up in knots. (*Trying to hide his true feelings.*)

SAM. I suppose it gets lonely for him in there.

HALLY. With all the patients and nurses around? Regular visits from the Salvation Army? Balls! It's ten times worse for him at home. I'm at school and my mother is here in the business all day.

SAM. He's at least got you at night.

HALLY (*before he can stop himself*). And we've got him! Please! I don't want to talk about it anymore. (*Unpacks his school case, slamming down books on the table.*) Life is just a plain bloody mess, that's all. And people are fools.

SAM. Come on, Hally.

HALLY. Yes, they are! They bloody well deserve what they get.

SAM. Then don't complain.

HALLY. Don't try to be clever, Sam. It doesn't suit you. Anybody who thinks there's nothing wrong with this world needs to have his head examined. Just when things are going along all right, without fail someone or something will come along and spoil everything. Somebody should write that down as a fundamental law of the Universe. The principle of perpetual disappointment. If there is a God who created this world, he should scrap it and try again.

SAM. All right, Hally, all right. What you got for homework?

HALLY. Bullshit, as usual. (*Opens an exercise book and reads.*) "Write five hundred words describing an annual event of cultural or historical significance."

SAM. That should be easy enough for you.

HALLY. And also plain bloody boring. You know what he wants, don't you? One of their useless old ceremonies. The commemoration of the landing of the 1820 Settlers,[7] or if it's going to be culture, Carols by Candlelight every Christmas.

SAM. It's an impressive sight. Make a good description, Hally. All those candles glowing in the dark and the people singing hymns.

HALLY. And it's called religious hysteria. (*Intense irritation.*) Please, Sam! Just leave me alone and let me get on with it. I'm not in the mood for games this afternoon. And remember my Mom's orders . . . you're to help Willie with the windows. Come on now, I don't want any more nonsense in here.

SAM. Okay, Hally, okay.

Hally settles down to his homework; determined preparations . . . pen, ruler, exercise book, dictionary, another cake . . . all of which will lead to nothing. (Sam waltzes over to Willie and starts to replace tables and chairs. He practices a ballroom step while doing so. Willie watches. When Sam is finished, Willie tries.)

Good! But just a little bit quicker on the turn and only move in to her after she's crossed over. What about this one?

Another step. When Sam is finished, Willie again has a go.

Much better. See what happens when you just relax and enjoy yourself? Remember that in two weeks' time and you'll be all right.

WILLIE. But I haven't got partner, Boet Sam.

SAM. Maybe Hilda will turn up tonight.

WILLIE. No, Boet Sam. (*Reluctantly.*) I gave her a good hiding.

SAM. You mean a bad one.

WILLIE. Good bad one.

SAM. Then you mustn't complain either. Now you pay the price for losing your temper.

WILLIE. I also pay two pounds ten shilling entrance fee.

SAM. They'll refund you if you withdraw now.

WILLIE (*appalled*). You mean, don't dance?

SAM. Yes.

WILLIE. No! I wait too long and I practice too hard. If I find me new partner, you think I can be ready in two weeks? I ask Madam for my leave now and we practice every day.

SAM. Quickstep non-stop for two weeks. World record, Willie, but you'll be mad at the end.

WILLIE. No jokes, Boet Sam.

---

[7]**1820 Settlers** In 1820 the British government paid 4,000 Britons to travel to the Cape and allotted each family 100 acres.

SAM. I'm not joking.

WILLIE. So then what?

SAM. Find Hilda. Say you're sorry and promise you won't beat her again.

WILLIE. No.

SAM. Then withdraw. Try again next year.

WILLIE. No.

SAM. Then I give up.

WILLIE. Haaikona, Boet Sam, you can't.

SAM. What do you mean, I can't? I'm telling you: I give up.

WILLIE (*adamant*). No! (*Accusingly.*) It was you who start me ballroom dancing.

SAM. So?

WILLIE. Before that I use to be happy. And is you and Miriam who bring me to Hilda and say here's partner for you.

SAM. What are you saying, Willie?

WILLIE. You!

SAM. But me what? To blame?

WILLIE. Yes.

SAM. Willie . . . ? (*Bursts into laughter.*)

WILLIE. And now all you do is make jokes at me. You wait. When Miriam leaves you is my turn to laugh. Ha! Ha! Ha!

SAM. (*He can't take Willie seriously any longer.*) She can leave me tonight! I know what to do. (*Bowing before an imaginary partner*). May I have the pleasure? (*He dances and sings.*)

"Just a fellow with his pillow . . .
Dancin' like a willow . . .
In an autumn breeze . . ."

WILLIE. There you go again!

Sam goes on dancing and singing.

Boet Sam!

SAM. There's the answer to your problem! Judges' announcement in two weeks' time: "Ladies and gentlemen, the winner in the open section . . . Mr. Willie Malopo and his pillow!"

This is too much for a now really angry Willie. He goes for Sam, but the latter is too quick for him and puts Hally's table between the two of them.

HALLY (*exploding*). For Christ's sake, you two!

WILLIE (*still trying to get at Sam*). I donner you, Sam! Struesgod!

SAM (*still laughing*). Sorry, Willie . . . Sorry . . .

HALLY. Sam! Willie! (*Grabs his ruler and gives Willie a vicious whack on the bum.*) How the hell am I supposed to concentrate with the two of you behaving like bloody children!

WILLIE. Hit him too!

HALLY. Shut up, Willie.

WILLIE. He started jokes again.

HALLY. Get back to your work. You too, Sam. (*His ruler.*) Do you want another one, Willie?

Sam and Willie return to their work. Hally uses the opportunity to escape from his unsuccessful attempt at homework. He struts around like a little despot, ruler in hand, giving vent to his anger and frustration.

Suppose a customer had walked in then? Or the Park Superintendent. And seen the two of you behaving like a pair of hooligans. That would have been the end of my mother's license, you know. And your jobs! Well, this is the end of it. From now on there will be no more of your ballroom nonsense in here. This is a business establishment, not a bloody New Brighton dancing school. I've been far too lenient with the two of you. (*Behind the counter for a green cool drink and a dollop of ice cream. He keeps up his tirade as he prepares it.*) But what really makes me bitter is that I allow you chaps a little freedom in here when business is bad and what do you do with it? The foxtrot! Specially you, Sam. There's more to life than trotting around a dance floor and I thought at least you knew it.

SAM. It's a harmless pleasure, Hally. It doesn't hurt anybody.

HALLY. It's also a rather simple one, you know.

SAM. You reckon so? Have you ever tried?

HALLY. Of course not.

SAM. Why don't you? Now.

HALLY. What do you mean? Me dance?

SAM. Yes. I'll show you a simple step—the waltz—then you try it.

HALLY. What will that prove?

SAM. That it might not be as easy as you think.

HALLY. I didn't say it was easy. I said it was simple—like in simple-minded, meaning mentally retarded. You can't exactly say it challenges the intellect.

SAM. It does other things.

HALLY. Such as?

SAM. Make people happy.

HALLY (*the glass in his hand*). So do American cream sodas with ice cream. For God's sake, Sam, you're not asking me to take ballroom dancing serious, are you?

SAM. Yes.

HALLY (*sigh of defeat*). Oh, well, so much for trying to give you a decent education. I've obviously achieved nothing.

SAM. You still haven't told me what's wrong with admiring something that's beautiful and then trying to do it yourself.

HALLY. Nothing. But we happen to be talking about a foxtrot, not a thing of beauty.

SAM. But that is just what I'm saying. If you were to see two champions doing, two masters of the art . . . !

HALLY. Oh, God, I give up. So now it's also art!

SAM. Ja.

HALLY. There's a limit, Sam. Don't confuse art and entertainment.

SAM. So then what is art?

HALLY. You want a definition?

SAM. Ja.

HALLY. (*He realizes he has got to be careful. He gives the matter a lot of thought before answering.*) Philosophers have been trying to do that for centuries. What is Art? What is Life? But basically I suppose it's . . . the giving of meaning to matter.

SAM. Nothing to do with beautiful?

HALLY. It goes beyond that. It's the giving of form to the formless.

SAM. Ja, well, maybe it's not art, then. But I still say it's beautiful.

HALLY. I'm sure the word you mean to use is entertaining.

SAM (*adamant*). No. Beautiful. And if you want proof, come along to the Centenary Hall in New Brighton in two weeks' time.

The mention of the Centenary Hall draws Willie over to them.

HALLY. What for? I've seen the two of you prancing around in here often enough.

SAM. (*He laughs.*) This isn't the real thing, Hally. We're just playing around in here.

HALLY. So? I can use my imagination.

SAM. And what do you get?

HALLY. A lot of people dancing around and having a so-called good time.

SAM. That all?

HALLY. Well, basically it is that, surely.

SAM. No, it isn't. Your imagination hasn't helped you at all. There's a lot more to it than that. We're getting ready for the championships, Hally, not just another dance. There's going to be a lot of people, all right, and they're going to have a good time, but they'll only be spectators, sitting around and watching. It's just the competitors out there on the dance floor. Party decorations and fancy lights all around the walls! The ladies in beautiful evening dresses!

HALLY. My mother's got one of those, Sam, and quite frankly, it's an embarrassment every time she wears it.

SAM (*undeterred*). Your imagination left out the excitement.

Hally scoffs.

Oh, yes. The finalists are not going to be out there just to have a good time. One of those couples will be the 1950 Eastern Province Champions. And your imagination left out the music.

WILLIE. Mr. Elijah Gladman Guzana and his Orchestral Jazzonions.

SAM. The sound of the big band, Hally. Trombone, trumpet, tenor and alto sax. And then, finally, your imagination also left out the climax of the evening when the dancing is finished, the judges have stopped whispering among themselves and the Master of Ceremonies collects their scorecards and goes up onto the stage to announce the winners.

HALLY. All right. So you make it sound like a bit of a do. It's an occasion. Satisfied?

SAM (*victory*). So you admit that!

HALLY. Emotionally yes, intellectually no.

SAM. Well, I don't know what you mean by that, all I'm telling you is that it is going to be *the* event of the year in New Brighton. It's been sold out for two weeks already. There's only standing room left. We've got competitors coming from Kingwilliamstown, East London, Port Alfred.

Hally starts pacing thoughtfully.

HALLY. Tell me a bit more.

SAM. I thought you weren't interested . . . intellectually.

HALLY (*mysteriously*). I've got my reasons.

SAM. What do you want to know?

HALLY. It takes place every year?

SAM. Yes. But only every third year in New Brighton. It's East London's turn to have the championships next year.

HALLY. Which, I suppose, makes it an even more significant event.

SAM. Ah ha! We're getting somewhere. Our "occasion" is now a "significant event."

HALLY. I wonder.

SAM. What?

HALLY. I wonder if I would get away with it.

SAM. But what?

HALLY (*to the table and his exercise book*). "Write five hundred words describing an annual event of cultural or historical significance." Would I be stretching poetic license a little too far if I called your ballroom championships a cultural event?

SAM. You mean . . . ?

HALLY. You think we could get five hundred words out of it, Sam?

SAM. Victor Sylvester has written a whole book on ballroom dancing.

WILLIE. You going to write about it, Master Hally?

HALLY. Yes, gentlemen, that is precisely what I am considering doing. Old Doc Bromely—he's my English teacher—is going to argue with me, of course. He doesn't like natives. But I'll point out to him that in strict anthropological terms the culture of a primitive black society includes its dancing and singing. To put my thesis in a nutshell: The war-dance has been replaced by the waltz. But it still amounts to the same thing: the release of primitive emotions through movement. Shall we give it a go?

SAM. I'm ready.

WILLIE. Me also.

HALLY. Ha! This will teach the old bugger a lesson. (*Decision taken.*) Right. Let's get ourselves organized. (*This means another cake on the table. He sits.*) I think you've given me enough general atmosphere, Sam, but to build the tension and suspense I need facts. (*Pencil poised.*)

WILLIE. Give him facts, Boet Sam.

HALLY. What you called the climax . . . how many finalists?

SAM. Six couples.

HALLY (*making notes*). Go on. Give me the picture.

SAM. Spectators seated right around the hall. (*Willie becomes a spectator.*)

HALLY. . . . and it's a full house.

SAM. At one end, on the stage, Gladman and his Orchestral Jazzonions. At the other end is a long table with the three judges. The six finalists go onto the dance floor and take up their positions. When they are ready and the spectators have settled down, the Master of Ceremonies goes to the microphone. To start with, he makes some jokes to get the people laughing . . .

HALLY. Good touch! (*As he writes.*) " . . . creating a relaxed atmosphere which will change to one of tension and drama as the climax is approached."

SAM (*onto a chair to act out the M.C.*). "Ladies and gentlemen, we come now to the great moment you have all been waiting for this evening. . . . The finals of the 1950 Eastern Province Open Ballroom Dancing Championships. But first let me introduce the finalists! Mr. and Mrs. Welcome Tchabalala from Kingwilliamstown . . ."

WILLIE. (*He applauds after every name.*) Is when the people clap their hands and whistle and make a lot of noise, Master Hally.

SAM. "Mr. Mulligan Njikelane and Miss Nomhle Nkonyeni of Grahamstown; Mr. and Mrs. Norman Nchinga from Port Alfred; Mr. Fats Bokolane and Miss Dina Plaatjies from East London; Mr. Sipho Dugu and Mrs. Mable Magada from Peddie; and from New Brighton our very own Mr. Willie Malopo and Miss Hilda Samuels."

Willie can't believe his ears. He abandons his role as spectator and scrambles into position as a finalist.

WILLIE. Relaxed and ready to romance!

SAM. The applause dies down. When everybody is silent, Gladman lifts up his sax, nods at the Orchestral Jazzonions . . .

WILLIE. Play the jukebox please, Boet Sam!

SAM. I also only got bus fare, Willie.

HALLY. Hold it, everybody. (*Heads for the cash register behind the counter.*) How much is in the till, Sam?

SAM. Three shillings. Hally . . . your Mom counted it before she left.

Hally hesitates.

HALLY. Sorry, Willie. You know how she carried on the last time I did it. We'll just have to pool our combined imaginations and hope for the best. (*Returns to the table.*) Back to work. How are the points scored, Sam?

SAM. Maximum of ten points each for individual style, deportment, rhythm and general appearance.

WILLIE. Must I start?

HALLY. Hold it for a second, Willie. And penalties?

SAM. For what?

HALLY. For doing something wrong. Say you stumble or bump into somebody . . . do they take off any points?

SAM (*aghast*). Hally . . . !

HALLY. When you're dancing. If you and your partner collide into another couple.

Hally can get no further. Sam has collapsed with laughter. He explains to Willie.

SAM. If me and Miriam bump into you and Hilda . . .

Willie joins him in another good laugh.

Hally, Hally . . . !

HALLY (*perplexed*). Why? What did I say?

SAM. There's no collisions out there, Hally. Nobody trips or stumbles or bumps into anybody else. That's what that moment is all about. To be one of those finalists on that dance floor is like . . . like being in a dream about a world in which accidents don't happen.

HALLY (*genuinely moved by Sam's image*). Jesus, Sam! That's beautiful!

WILLIE (*can endure waiting no longer*). I'm starting! (*Willie dances while Sam talks.*)

SAM. Of course it is. That's what I've been trying to say to you all afternoon. And it's beautiful because that is what we want life to be like. But instead, like you said, Hally, we're bumping into each other all the time. Look at the three of us this afternoon: I've bumped into Willie, the two of us have bumped into you, you've bumped into your mother, she bumping into your Dad. . . . None of us knows the steps and there's no music playing. And it doesn't stop with us. The whole world is doing it all the time. Open a newspaper and what do you read? America has bumped into Russia, England is bumping into India, rich man bumps into poor man. Those are big collisions, Hally. They make for a lot of bruises. People get hurt in all that bumping, and we're sick and tired of it now. It's been going on for too long. Are we never going to get it right? . . . Learn to dance life like champions instead of always being just a bunch of beginners at it?

HALLY (*deep and sincere admiration of the man*). You've got a vision, Sam!

SAM. Not just me. What I'm saying to you is that everybody's got it. That's why there's only standing room left for the Centenary Hall in two weeks' time. For as long as the music lasts, we are going to see six couples get it right, the way we want life to be.

HALLY. But is that the best we can do, Sam . . . watch six finalists dreaming about the way it should be?

SAM. I don't know. But it starts with that. Without the dream we won't know what we're going for. And anyway I reckon there are a few people who have got past just dreaming about it and are trying for something real. Remember that thing we read once in the paper about the Mahatma Gandhi? Going without food to stop those riots in India?

HALLY. You're right. He certainly was trying to teach people to get the steps right.

SAM. And the Pope.

HALLY. Yes, he's another one. Our old General Smuts as well, you know. He's also out there dancing. You know, Sam, when you come to think of it, that's what the United Nations boils down to . . . a dancing school for politicians!

SAM. And let's hope they learn.

HALLY (*a little surge of hope*). You're right. We mustn't despair. Maybe there's some hope for mankind after all. Keep it up, Willie. (*Back to his table with determination.*) This is a lot bigger than I thought. So what have we got? Yes, our title: "A World Without Collisions."

SAM. That sounds good! "A World Without Collisions."

HALLY. Subtitle: "Global Politics on the Dance Floor." No. A bit too heavy, hey? What about "Ballroom Dancing as a Political Vision"?

The telephone rings. Sam answers it.

SAM. St. George's Park Tea Room . . . Yes, Madam . . . Hally, it's your Mom.

HALLY (*back to reality*). Oh, God, yes! I'd forgotten all about that. Shit! Remember my words, Sam? Just when you're enjoying yourself, someone or something will come along and wreck everything.

SAM. You haven't heard what she's got to say yet.

HALLY. Public telephone?

SAM. No.

HALLY. Does she sound happy or unhappy?

SAM. I couldn't tell. (*Pause.*) She's waiting, Hally.

HALLY (*to the telephone*). Hello, Mom . . . No, everything is okay here. Just doing my homework. . . . What's your news? . . . You've what? . . . (*Pause. He takes the receiver away from his ear for a few seconds. In the course of Hally's telephone conversation, Sam and Willie discretely position the stacked tables and chairs. Hally places the receiver back to his ear.*) Yes, I'm still here. Oh, well, I give up now. Why did you do it, Mom? . . . Well, I just hope you know what you've let us in for. . . . (*Loudly.*) I said I hope you know what you've let us in for! It's the end of the peace and quiet we've been having. (*Softly.*) Where is he? (*Normal voice.*) He can't hear us from in there. But for God's sake, Mom, what happened? I told you to be firm with him. . . . Then you and the nurses should have held him down, taken his crutches away. . . . I know only too well he's my father! . . . I'm not being disrespectful, but I'm sick and tired of emptying stinking chamberpots full of phlegm and piss. . . . Yes, I do! When you're not there, he asks *me* to do it. . . . If you really want to know the truth, that's why I've got no appetite for my food. . . . Yes! There's a lot of things you don't know about. For your information, I still haven't got that science textbook I need. And you know why? He borrowed the money you gave me for it. . . . Because I didn't want to start another fight between you two. . . . He says that every time. . . . All right, Mom! (*Viciously.*) Then just remember to start hiding your bag away again, because he'll be at your purse before long for money for booze. And when he's well enough to come down here, you better keep an eye on the till as well, because that is also going to develop a leak. . . . Then don't complain to me when he starts his old tricks. . . . Yes, you do. I get it from you on one side and from him on the other, and it makes life hell for me. I'm not going to be the peacemaker anymore. I'm warning you now: when the two of you start fighting again, I'm leaving home. . . . Mom, if you start crying, I'm going to put down the receiver. . . . Okay . . . (*Lowering his voice to a vicious whisper.*) Okay, Mom. I heard you. (*Desperate.*) No. . . . Because I don't want to. I'll see him when I get home! Mom! . . . (*Pause. When he speaks again, his tone changes completely. It is not simply pretense. We sense a genuine emotional conflict.*) Welcome home, chum! . . . What's that? . . . Don't be silly, Dad. You being home is just about the best news in the world. . . . I bet you are. Bloody depressing there with everybody going on about their ailments, hey! . . . How you feeling? . . . Good . . . Here as well, pal. Coming down cats and dogs. . . . That's right. Just the day for a kip and a toss in your old Uncle Ned. . . . Everything's just hunky-dory on my side, Dad. . . . Well, to start with, there's a nice pile of comics for you on the counter. . . . Yes, old Kemple brought them in. *Batman and Robin, Submariner* . . . just your cup of tea . . . I will. . . . Yes, we'll spin a few yarns tonight. . . . Okay, chum, see you in a little while. . . . No, I promise. I'll come straight home. . . . (*Pause—his mother comes back on the phone.*) Mom? Okay. I'll lock up now. . . . What? . . . Oh, the brandy . . . Yes, I'll remember! . . . I'll put it in my suitcase now, for God's sake. I know well enough what will happen if he doesn't get it. . . . (*Places a bottle of brandy on the counter.*) I *was* kind to him, Mom. I didn't say anything nasty! . . . All right. Bye. (*End of telephone conversation. A desolate Hally doesn't move. A strained silence.*)

SAM (*quietly*). That sounded like a bad bump, Hally.

HALLY (*having a hard time controlling his emotions. He speaks carefully*). Mind your own business, Sam.

SAM. Sorry. I wasn't trying to interfere. Shall we carry on? Hally? (*He indicates the exercise book. No response from Hally.*)

WILLIE (*also trying*). Tell him about when they give out the cups, Boet Sam.

SAM. Ja! That's another big moment. The presentation of the cups after the winners have been announced. You've got to put that in.

Still no response from Hally.

WILLIE. A big silver one, Master Hally, called floating trophy for the champions.

SAM. We always invite some big-shot personality to hand them over. Guest of honor this year is going to be His Holiness Bishop Jabulani of the All African Free Zionist Church.

Hally gets up abruptly, goes to his table and tears up the page he was writing on.

HALLY. So much for a bloody world without collisions.

SAM. Too bad. It was on its way to being a good composition.

HALLY. Let's stop bullshitting ourselves, Sam.

SAM. Have we been doing that?

HALLY. Yes! That's what all our talk about a decent world has been . . . just so much bullshit.

SAM. We did say it was still only a dream.

HALLY. And a bloody useless one at that. Life's a fuck-up and it's never going to change.

SAM. Ja, maybe that's true.

HALLY. There's no maybe about it. It's a blunt and brutal fact. All we've done this afternoon is waste our time.

SAM. Not if we'd got your homework done.

HALLY. I don't give a shit about my homework, so, for Christ's sake, just shut up about it. (*Slamming books viciously into his school case.*) Hurry up now and finish your work. I want to lock up and get out of here. (*Pause.*) And then go where? Home-sweet-fucking-home. Jesus, I hate that word.

Hally goes to the counter to put the brandy bottle and comics in his school case. After a moment's hesitation, he smashes the bottle of brandy. He abandons all further attempts to hide his feelings. Sam and Willie work away as unobtrusively as possible.

Do you want to know what is really wrong with your lovely little dream, Sam? It's not just that we are all bad dancers. That does happen to be perfectly true, but there's more to it than just that. You left out the cripples.

SAM. Hally!

HALLY (*now totally reckless*). Ja! Can't leave them out, Sam. That's why we always end up on our backsides on the dance floor. They're also out there dancing . . . like a bunch of broken spiders trying to do the quickstep! (*An ugly attempt at laughter.*) When you come to think of it, it's a bloody comical sight. I mean, it's bad enough on two legs . . . but one and a pair of crutches! Hell, no, Sam. That's guaranteed to turn that dance floor into a shambles. Why you shaking your head? Picture it, man. For once this afternoon let's use our imaginations sensibly.

SAM. Be careful, Hally.

HALLY. Of what? The truth? I seem to be the only one around here who is prepared to face it. We've had the pretty dream, it's time now to wake up and have a good long look at the way things really are. Nobody knows the steps, there's no music, the cripples are also out there tripping up everybody and trying to get into the act, and it's all called the All-Comers-How-to-Make-a-Fuckup-of-Life Championships. (*Another ugly laugh.*) Hang on, Sam! The best bit is still coming. Do you know what the winner's trophy is? A beautiful big chamber-pot with roses on the side, and it's full to the brim with piss. And guess who I think is going to be this year's winner.

SAM (*almost shouting*). Stop now!

HALLY (*suddenly appalled by how far he has gone*). Why?

SAM. Hally? It's your father you're talking about.

HALLY. So?

SAM. Do you know what you've been saying?

Hally can't answer. He is rigid with shame. Sam speaks to him sternly.

No, Hally, you mustn't do it. Take back those words and ask for forgiveness! It's a terrible sin for a son to mock his father with jokes like that. You'll be punished if you carry on. Your father is your father, even if he is a . . . cripple man.

WILLIE. Yes, Master Hally. Is true what Sam say.

SAM. I understand how you are feeling, Hally, but even so . . .

HALLY. No, you don't!

SAM. I think I do.

HALLY. And I'm telling you you don't. Nobody does. (*Speaking carefully as his shame turns to rage at Sam.*) It's your turn to be careful, Sam. Very careful! You're treading on dangerous ground. Leave me and my father alone.

SAM. I'm not the one who's been saying things about him.

HALLY. What goes on between me and my Dad is none of your business!

SAM. Then don't tell me about it. If that's all you've got to say about him, I don't want to hear.

For a moment Hally is at loss for a response.

HALLY. Just get on with your bloody work and shut up.

SAM. Swearing at me won't help you.

HALLY. Yes, it does! Mind your own fucking business and shut up!

SAM. Okay. If that's the way you want it, I'll stop trying.

He turns away. This infuriates Hally even more.

HALLY. Good. Because what you've been trying to do is meddle in something you know nothing about. All that concerns you in here, Sam, is to try and do what you get paid for—keep the place clean and serve the customers. In plain words, just get on with your job. My mother is right. She's always warning me about allowing you to get too familiar. Well, this time you've gone too far. It's going to stop right now.

No response from Sam.

You're only a servant in here, and don't forget it.

Still no response. Hally is trying hard to get one.

And as far as my father is concerned, all you need to remember is that he is your boss.

SAM (*needled at last*). No, he isn't. I get paid by your mother.

HALLY. Don't argue with me, Sam!

SAM. Then don't say he's my boss.

HALLY. He's a white man and that's good enough for you.

SAM. I'll try to forget you said that.

HALLY. Don't! Because you won't be doing me a favor if you do. I'm telling you to remember it.

A pause. Sam pulls himself together and makes one last effort.

SAM. Hally, Hally . . . ! Come on now. Let's stop before it's too late. You're right. We *are* on dangerous ground. If we're not careful, somebody is going to get hurt.

HALLY. It won't be me.

SAM. Don't be so sure.

HALLY. I don't know what you're talking about, Sam.

SAM. Yes, you do.

HALLY (*furious*). Jesus, I wish you would stop trying to tell me what I do and what I don't know.

Sam gives up. He turns to Willie.

SAM. Let's finish up.

HALLY. Don't turn your back on me! I haven't finished talking.

He grabs Sam by the arm and tries to make him turn around. Sam reacts with a flash of anger.

SAM. Don't do that, Hally! (*Facing the boy.*) All right, I'm listening. Well? What do you want to say to me?

HALLY (*pause as Hally looks for something to say*). To begin with, why don't you also start calling me Master Harold, like Willie.

SAM. Do you mean that?

HALLY. Why the hell do you think I said it?

SAM. And if I don't.

HALLY. You might just lose your job.

SAM (*quietly and very carefully*). If you make me say it once, I'll never call you anything else again.

HALLY. So? (*The boy confronts the man.*) Is that meant to be a threat?

SAM. Just telling you what will happen if you make me do that. You must decide what it means to you.

HALLY. Well, I have. It's good news. Because that is exactly what Master Harold wants from now on. Think of it as a little lesson in respect, Sam, that's long overdue, and I hope you remember it as well as you do your geography. I can tell you now that somebody who will be glad to hear I've finally given it to you will be my Dad. Yes! He agrees with my Mom. He's always going on about it as well. "You must teach the boys to show you more respect, my son."

SAM. So now you can stop complaining about going home. Everybody is going to be happy tonight.

HALLY. That's perfectly correct. You see, you mustn't get the wrong idea about me and my Dad, Sam. We also have our good times together. Some bloody good laughs. He's got a marvelous sense of humor. Want to know what our favorite joke is? He gives out a big groan, you see, and says: "It's not fair, is it, Hally?" Then I have to ask: "What, chum?" And then he says: "A nigger's arse" . . . and we both have a good laugh.

The men stare at him with disbelief.

What's the matter, Willie? Don't you catch the joke? You always were a bit slow on the uptake. It's what is called a pun. You see, fair means both light in color and to be just and decent. (*He turns to Sam.*) I thought *you* would catch it, Sam.

SAM. Oh ja, I catch it all right.

HALLY. But it doesn't appeal to your sense of humor.

SAM. Do you really laugh?

HALLY. Of course.

SAM. To please him? Make him feel good?

HALLY. No, for heaven's sake! I laugh because I think it's a bloody good joke.

SAM. You're really trying hard to be ugly, aren't you? And why drag poor old Willie into it? He's done nothing to you except show you the respect you want so badly. That's also not being fair, you know . . . and I mean just or decent.

WILLIE. It's all right, Sam. Leave it now.

SAM. It's me you're after. You should just have said "Sam's arse" . . . because that's the one you're trying to kick. Anyway, how do you know it's not fair? You've never seen it. Do you want to? (*He drops his trousers and underpants and presents his backside for Hally's inspection.*) Have a good look. A real Basuto[8] arse . . . which is about as nigger as they can come. Satisfied? (*Trousers up.*) Now you can make your Dad even happier when you go home tonight. Tell him I showed you my arse and he is quite right. It's not fair. And if it will give him an even better laugh next time, I'll also let *him* have a look. Come, Willie, let's finish up and go.

Sam and Willie start to tidy up the tea room. Hally doesn't move. He waits for a moment when Sam passes him.

HALLY (*quietly*). Sam . . .

Sam stops and looks expectantly at the boy. Hally spits in his face. A long and heartfelt groan from Willie. For a few seconds Sam doesn't move.

SAM (*taking out a handkerchief and wiping his face*). It's all right, Willie.

To Hally.

Ja, well, you've done it . . . Master Harold. Yes, I'll start calling you that from now on. It won't be difficult anymore. You've hurt yourself, Master Harold. I saw it coming. I warned you, but you wouldn't listen. You've just hurt yourself *bad*. And you're a coward, Master Harold. The face you should be spitting in is your father's . . . but you used mine, because you think you're safe inside your fair skin . . . and this time I don't mean just or decent. (*Pause, then moving violently towards Hally.*) Should I hit him, Willie?

WILLIE (*stopping Sam*). No, Boet Sam.

SAM (*violently*). Why not?

WILLIE. It won't help, Boet Sam.

SAM. I don't want to help! I want to hurt him.

WILLIE. You also hurt yourself.

[8]**Basuto** The Basuto are Africans living in Basutoland in southeast Africa.

SAM. And if he had done it to you, Willie?

WILLIE. Me? Spit at me like I was a dog? (*A thought that had not occurred to him before. He looks at Hally.*) Ja. Then I want to hit him. I want to hit him hard!

A dangerous few seconds as the men stand staring at the boy. Willie turns away, shaking his head.

But maybe all I do is go cry at the back. He's little boy, Boet Sam. Little *white* boy. Long trousers now, but he's still little boy.

SAM (*his violence ebbing away into defeat as quickly as it flooded*). You're right. So go on, then: groan again, Willie. You do it better than me. (*To Hally.*) You don't know all of what you've just done . . . Master Harold. It's not just that you've made me feel dirtier than I've ever been in my life . . . I mean, how do I wash off yours and your father's filth? . . . I've also failed. A long time ago I promised myself I was going to try and do something, but you've just shown me . . . Master Harold . . . that I've failed. (*Pause.*) I've also got a memory of a little white boy when he was still wearing short trousers and a black man, but they're not flying a kite. It was the old Jubilee days, after dinner one night. I was in my room. You came in and just stood against the wall, looking down at the ground, and only after I'd asked you what you wanted, what was wrong, I don't know how many times, did you speak and even then so softly I almost didn't hear you. "Sam, please help me to go and fetch my Dad." Remember? He was dead drunk on the floor of the Central Hotel Bar. They'd phoned for your Mom, but you were the only one at home. And do you remember how we did it? You went in first by yourself to ask permission for me to go into the bar. Then I loaded him onto my back like a baby and carried him back to the boarding house with you following behind carrying his crutches. (*Shaking his head as he remembers.*) A crowded Main Street with all the people watching a little white boy following his drunk father on a nigger's back! I felt for that little boy . . . Master Harold. I felt for him. After that we still had to clean him up, remember? He'd messed in his trousers, so we had to clean him up and get him into bed.

HALLY (*great pain*). I love him, Sam.

SAM. I know you do. That's why I tried to stop you from saying these things about him. It would have been so simple if you could have just despised him for being a weak man. But he's your father. You love him and you're ashamed of him. You're ashamed of so much! . . . And now that's going to include yourself. That was the promise I made to myself: to try and stop that happening. (*Pause.*) After we got him to bed you came back with me to my room and sat in a corner and carried on just looking down at the ground. And for days after that! You hadn't done anything wrong, but you went around as if you owed the world an apology for being alive. I didn't like seeing that! That's not the way a boy grows up to be a man! . . . But the one person who should have been teaching you what that means was the cause of your shame. If you really want to know, that's why I made you that kite. I wanted you to look up, be proud of something, of yourself . . . (*Bitter smile at the memory.*) . . . and you certainly were that when I left you with it up there on the hill. Oh, ja . . . something else! . . . If you ever do write it as a short story, there *was* a twist in our ending. I couldn't sit down there and stay with you. It was a "Whites Only" bench. You were too young, too excited to notice then. But not anymore. If you're not careful . . . Master Harold . . . you're going to be sitting up there by yourself for a long time to come, and there won't be a kite in the sky. (*Sam has got nothing more to say. He exits into the kitchen, taking off his waiter's jacket.*)

WILLIE. Is bad. Is all all bad in here now.

HALLY (*books into his school case, raincoat on*). Willie . . . (*It is difficult to speak.*) Will you lock up for me and look after the keys?

WILLIE. Okay.

Sam returns. Hally goes behind the counter and collects the few coins in the cash register. As he starts to leave . . .

SAM. Don't forget the comic books.

Hally returns to the counter and puts them in his case. He starts to leave again.

SAM (*to the retreating back of the boy*). Stop . . . Hally . . .

Hally stops, but doesn't turn to face him.

Hally . . . I've got no right to tell you what being a man means if I don't behave like one myself, and I'm not doing so well at that this afternoon. Should we try again, Hally?

HALLY. Try what?

SAM. Fly another kite, I suppose. It worked once, and this time I need it as much as you do.

HALLY. It's still raining, Sam. You can't fly kites on rainy days, remember.

SAM. So what do we do? Hope for better weather tomorrow?

HALLY (*helpless gesture*). I don't know. I don't know anything anymore.

SAM. You sure of that, Hally? Because it would be pretty hopeless if that was true. It would mean nothing has been learnt in here this afternoon, and there was a hell of a lot of teaching going on . . . one way or the other. But anyway, I don't believe you. I reckon there's one thing you know. You don't *have* to sit up there by yourself. You know what that bench means now, and you can leave it any time you choose. All you've got to do is stand up and walk away from it.

Hally leaves. Willie goes up quietly to Sam.

WILLIE. Is okay, Boet Sam. You see. Is . . . (*He can't find any better words.*) . . . is going to be okay tomorrow. (*Changing his tone.*) Hey, Boet Sam! (*He is trying hard.*) You right. I think about it and you right. Tonight I find Hilda and say sorry. And make promise I won't beat her no more. You hear me, Boet Sam?

SAM. I hear you, Willie.

WILLIE. And when we practice I relax and romance with her from beginning to end. Non-stop! You watch! Two weeks' time: "First prize for promising newcomers: Mr. Willie Malopo and Miss Hilda Samuels." (*Sudden impulse.*) To hell with it! I walk home. (*He goes to the jukebox, puts in a coin and selects a record. The machine comes to life in the gray twilight, blushing its way through a spectrum of soft, romantic colors.*) How did you say it, Boet Sam? Let's dream. (*Willie sways with the music and gestures for Sam to dance.*)

Sarah Vaughan sings.

"Little man you're crying,
I know why you're blue,
Someone took your kiddy car away;
Better go to sleep now,
Little ma you've had a busy day." (*etc. etc.*)

You lead. I follow.

The men dance together.

"Johnny won your marbles,
Tell you what we'll do;
Dad will get you new ones right away;
Better go to sleep now,
Little man you've had a busy day."

TOPICS FOR CRITICAL THINKING AND WRITING

📖 THE PLAY ON THE PAGE

1. Exactly what do you think is implied in the title? Why is "MASTER HAROLD" in capital letters and in quotation marks, while *and the boys* (separated by three dots from *Harold*) is in lowercase letters? Why *Harold* rather than *Hally,* even though he is called Hally in the play? Why "*boys*" instead of *grown men?*

2. Compare Sam and Willie, making specific references to the text in order to support your characterizations.

3. Characterize Hally, taking account of his relationships to his parents as well as to Sam and Willie. In his autobiographical volume, *Notebooks,* Fugard tells how as an adolescent he spat at Sam "out of a spasm of acute loneliness." In your characterization of Hally you may want to discuss the degree (if any) to which loneliness helps to explain the boy's behavior.

4. The play is set in Fugard's native country, South Africa, in the 1950s. How closely does that world resemble that of the United States in the 1950s?

5. Can it be argued that the relationship dramatized in this play is not limited to South Africa in the 1950s but is essentially rooted in the situation, that is, in the relationship of employees to the child of the employer?

6. Early in the play, when Sam describes policemen whipping a prisoner, Hally says "People can be real bastards,"

and Sam replies, "That's the way it is, Hally." Does the play as a whole suggest that hostility and cruelty are "the way it is," despite Hally's belief that "there is something called progress, you know"? Later (p. 886), speaking of his father's plan to leave the hospital, Hally says, "This is not an age of miracles!" Is it legitimate to connect these passages and to relate them to the theme of the play?

7. Why does Fugard introduce the episode of the kite?

8. Sam cautions Hally, "Be careful." Exactly what is he cautioning Hally against? And what is Hally cautioning Sam against when he says, "Very careful! You're treading on dangerous ground"?

9. "Reversal" (Aristotle's *peripeteia*) and "recognition" (Aristotle's *anagnorisis*) are discussed in Part One, and in the Glossary. Consider the relevance of these terms to this play.

10. In Mary McCarthy's novel *A Charmed Life,* one of the characters says that tragedies depict "growing pains." How apt a characterization is this of other tragedies that you have read and of this play?

11. In your opinion, why does Fugard end the play not with Hally's final exit but with three speeches and a song?

🎭 THE PLAY ON THE STAGE

12. If you were directing a production, exactly what gestures and facial responses would you suggest for Hally when he first hears that his father may be coming home from the hospital?

13. How would you direct the line, "There are no collisions out there, Hally"? (Consider not only the speaker but also Hally's reaction.)

14. How would you speak Sam's speech about his "arse," just before Hally spits in Sam's face?

A CONTEXT FOR "MASTER HAROLD" . . . and the boys

Athol Fugard
NOTEBOOKS 1960–1977

[The following entry from Fugard's notebook is dated March 1961.]

Sam Semela—Basuto—with the family fifteen years. Meeting him again when he visited Mom set off string of memories.

The kite which he produced for me one day during those early years when Mom ran the Jubilee Hotel and he was a waiter there. He had made it himself: brown paper, its ribs fashioned from thin strips of tomato-box plank which he had smoothed down, a paste of flour and water for glue. I was surprised and bewildered that he had made it for me.

I vaguely recall shyly 'haunting' the servants' quarters in the well of the hotel—cold, cement-grey world—the pungent mystery of the dark little rooms—a world I didn't understand. Frightened to enter any of the rooms. Sam, broad-faced, broader based—he smelled of woodsmoke. The 'kaffir smell' of South Africa is the smell of poverty—woodsmoke and sweat.

Later, when he worked for her at the Park café, Mom gave him the sack: '. . . he became careless. He came late for work. His work went to hell. He didn't seem to care no more.' I was about thirteen and served behind the counter while he waited on table.

Realise now he was the most significant—the only—friend of my boyhood years. On terrible windy days when no-one came to swim or walk in the park, we would sit together and talk. Or I was reading—Introductions to Eastern Philosophy or Plato and Socrates—and when I had finished he would take the book back to New Brighton.

Can't remember now what precipitated it, but one day there was a rare quarrel between Sam and myself. In a truculent silence we closed the café, Sam set off home to New Brighton on foot and I followed a few minutes later on my bike. I saw him walking ahead of me and, coming out of a spasm of acute loneliness, as I rode up behind him I called his name, he turned in mid-stride to look back and, as I cycled past, I spat in his face. Don't suppose I will ever deal with the shame that overwhelmed me the second after I had done that.

Now he is thin. We had a long talk. He told about the old woman ('Ma') whom he and his wife have taken in to look after their house while he goes to work—he teaches ballroom dancing. 'Ma' insists on behaving like a domestic—making Sam feel guilty and embarrassed. She brings him an early morning cup of coffee. Sam: 'No, Ma, you mustn't, man.' Ma: 'I must.' Sam: 'Look, Ma, if I want it, I can make it.' Ma: 'No, I must.'

Occasionally, when she is doing something, Sam feels like a cup of tea but is too embarrassed to ask her, and daren't make one for himself. Similarly, with his washing. After three days or a week away in other towns, giving dancing lessons, he comes back with under-clothes that are very dirty. He is too shy to give them out to be washed so washes them himself. When Ma sees this she goes and complains to Sam's wife that he doesn't trust her, that it's all wrong for him to do the washing.

Of tsotsis, he said: 'They grab a old man, stick him with a knife and ransack him. And so he must go to hospital and his kids is starving with hungry.' Of others: 'He's got some little moneys. So he is facing starvation for the weekend.'

Of township snobs, he says there are the educational ones: 'If you haven't been to the big school, like Fort Hare, what you say isn't true.' And the money ones: 'If you aren't selling shops or got a business or a big car, man, you're nothing.'

Sam's incredible theory about the likeness of those 'with the true seed of love.' Starts with Plato and Socrates—they were round. 'Man is being shrinking all the time. An Abe Lincoln, him too, taller, but that's because man is shrinking.' Basically, those with the true seed of love look the same—'It's in the eyes.'

He spoke admiringly of one man, a black lawyer in East London, an educated man—university background—who was utterly without snobbery, looking down on no-one—any man, educated or ignorant, rich or poor, was another *man* to him, another human being, to be respected, taken seriously, to be talked to, listened to.

'They' won't allow Sam any longer to earn a living as a dancing teacher. 'You must get a job!' One of his fellow teachers was forced to work at Fraser's Quarries.

A Note on
WOMEN'S THEATER

The earliest surviving plays in Western dramatic literature, written in the fifth century B.C., are from ancient Greece. Of course, they include female characters, some of whom (for instance, Antigone) are heroic, but all of the plays were written by men and the female roles were acted by men. It is even possible that the plays were seen only by men, since the evidence that women attended the Greek dramatic festivals is inconclusive. Not until the tenth century A.D. do we find dramatic work written by a woman, six Latin plays by Hrotsvit of Gandersheim (also called Hrotsvitha or Roswith, c. 935–973). She was a German noblewoman who imitated the Roman dramatist Terence. In the preface she says that her "object is to glorify to the best of [her] poor ability the praiseworthy chastity of Christian virgins in the same form [i.e., in dramatic form] that has been used to describe the indecent acts of licentious women." It is not known whether her plays were performed in her lifetime, though at least some of them have been performed recently in academic surroundings.

Until about 1960 most people probably thought it was "natural" that there were not many plays by women. In fact, there *were* many plays by women, but the older ones had been forgotten. For instance, in England Aphra Behn (1640–1689), a professional writer, had written at least sixteen plays, one of which, *The Rover* (1677), held the stage for almost a century. (We reprint it on p. 355.) In the mid-nineteenth century another woman, Anna Cora Mowatt (1819–1870), wrote an immensely popular play, *Fashion* (1845), spoofing the infatuation of the nouveaux riches with English and European culture. Somewhat closer to our own time, Susan Glaspell (1876–1948), cofounder of the influential Provincetown Players (1915–1929), wrote several important plays, including *Trifles* (1916, reprinted on p. 18); and Anne Nichols (1891–1966) wrote *Abie's Irish Rose* (1922), which ran on Broadway for 2,327 consecutive performances. It would be easy to add at least a dozen comparable names—Lillian Hellman (1906–1984) and Lorraine Hansberry (1930–1965) for starters—but it is also true that however notable the achievements of all of these women as playwrights were, they were not seen as forming a distinctive "women's theater." Similarly, those relatively few women who were active in the theater in other capacities—for instance, as directors (Margo Jones [1913–1955] and Eve Le Gallienne [1899–1991] are the best-known examples) or producers—worked in an essentially male world.

Honor Moore, in *The New Women's Theatre* (1977), suggests an explanation: Theater (unlike writing fiction or poetry) is a communal activity, and men have not welcomed women into this community. "Male exclusion of women," she says, "perhaps more than any other single factor, has

been responsible for the lack of a female tradition in playwriting similar to that which exists in both fiction and poetry." Then, too, working for the theater requires larger chunks of time (for instance, whole days at early rehearsals) than most women in the past were able to spare, because they were tied to households. (Nevertheless, performers—that is, actresses—managed to find the time, and so one must conclude that it was not simply domestic obligations that kept women from serving as directors in the theater.)

Feminist critics looked at the past, noticed that the dramatic canon assumed that the spectator was male and that the subject matter often concerned fathers and sons (for example, *Oedipus, Hamlet, Death of a Salesman*). Was this pattern "natural," or was there a further explanation? Elaine Showalter, writing in *Signs* 1:2 (Winter 1975) put it this way, "Feminist criticism has allowed us to see meaning in what previously has been empty space" (435). The most obvious meaning of the emptiness was, of course, that the theater reinforced the ideals of patriarchal cultures.

In any case, despite the achievements of the women we have already mentioned, it was not until the late 1960s, as part of the women's movement, that a substantial number of women begin to set forth on the stage a drama of feminine sensibility. These plays are not just plays by women; they are plays about the experiences of women, especially about the difficult business of surviving as a woman in a man's world. As Eve Merriam said in 1976, surveying the plays written by women since 1960, "First you had to write an Arthur Miller play, then you had to write an absurd play. Now there is a new freedom—you can write empathetic women characters."

Once alerted to political realities, what sorts of theatrical activities would enlightened women engage in and what kinds of plays would women write? In the 1960s, seeing the gains made by the Civil Rights movement, many women engaged in consciousness-raising sessions: Women were the equals of men, and they should have the rights that men had long enjoyed. In the 1970s, a shift in thinking occurred: Women should, of course, have the opportunities that men have had, but women and men are *different*—not only biologically but also by virtue of their life experiences. Why, then, should the art of women resemble the art of men? Men might engage in painting and sculpture, but women might (for instance) use their bodies as their medium and as their subject, and this they did in a form now called performance art. Although performance art uses language and sometimes music and pictures, an equally important medium is the performer's body. For instance, in *Sally's Rape*, an episode in a longer work called *Confessions of a Black Working Class Woman*, Robbie McCauley, an African-American woman, strips off all of her clothing and stands on a bench, representing a slave on the auction block. Her white partner urges the audience to participate by chanting, "Bid em in, bid em in." While the audience chants, McCauley says,

> They take off my sack dress
> and order me onto the block with my socks rolled down.
> On the auction block, they put
> their hands all down yr body
> the men smell ya, feel ya. . . .

Raewyn Whyte, who describes the performance in *Acting Out: Feminist Performances*, edited by Lynda Hart and Peggy Phelan (1993), goes on to say that

> [a]s she speaks, she flinches at the invisible, probing fingers, which assess her soundness for childbearing. . . . For the onlooker there is an awe-ful fascination in this representation of the slave auction, this scene of victimage. The pleasure of looking at the naked body of the black woman caught in the spotlight is made guilty by the awareness of being inescapably positioned as a potential buyer in the slave market, yet the urge to look away is countered by the seductive intensity of the scene. Similarly, whether or not you join the chanting you are trapped by the sympathetic magic of sound, which reanimates the past, and, no matter how much you tell yourself you had nothing to do with this scene, you are made vicariously complicit in the auction system that McCauley's staging represents. (278)

Clearly this sort of performance is a kind of drama that is remote from such canonical dramas as *Oedipus the King* and *Death of a Salesman*. Broadly speaking, feminists have characterized canonical drama as Aristotelian, male, and linear. In canonical drama, a plot is developed—we might say the plot advances—in a fairly consistent way. Most critics, from Aristotle to the present, have held that a plot should be unified, the actions of the characters should be convincingly motivated, and the end should be implicit in the beginning, that is, the end should not be arbitrary but should (at least in retrospect) seem inevitable. Some feminist critics, however, have characterized this view of plot as masculine. Sue-Ellen Case in *Feminism and Theatre* (1988) puts it this way:

> Within the study of the theatre, several versions of masculine and feminine morphology have taken hold. For example, some feminist critics have described the form of tragedy as a replication of the male sexual experience. Tragedy is composed of foreplay, excitation and ejaculation (catharsis). The broader organisation of plot—complication, crisis and resolution—is also tied to this phallic experience. The central focus in male forms is labelled phallocentric, reflecting the nature of the male's sexual physiology. A female form might embody her sexual mode, aligned with multiple orgasms, with no dramatic focus on ejaculation or necessity to build to a single climax. The contiguous organisation would replace this ejaculatory form. The feminist critic might analyse the plays of Adrienne Kennedy, women's performance-art pieces or witches' cyclic rituals using this notion. (129)

If you have read Kennedy's *Funnyhouse of a Negro* (p. 788), you know that the episodes in her play are indeed better described as "contiguous" than as interdependent and leading to a single climax. However, Case does not suggest that the feminist view she has just sketched is incontestable. She goes on to point out that other feminists, objecting to this "biologizing" or "essentializing" of gender, argue that this particular "feminine morphology" neglects the enormous influence of social forces. Proponents of this counterview, of course, recognize that there are biological distinctions between the sexes, but they distinguish between "sex" and "gender." Gender, they argue, concerns such qualities as masculinity and femininity, and these are largely a matter of cultural practice. In this view, the biological material is shaped by human intervention. If at first this sounds odd, perhaps it will become convincing when you consider Susan Brownmiller's witty formulation, "Women are all female impersonators to some degree." From this it is an easy step to seeing that men are male impersonators to some degree. Some feminists argue, Case points out, that the biological or essentialist approach may discount the products of women who chose to work in what is alleged to be a male form. And, to complicate matters, Adrienne Kennedy herself, a woman working in what is characterized as a woman's mode, seems to think that playwrighting is essentially a masculine form. This is supported by her comment (*New York Times*, May 13, 1973, section 2, page 3) that playwrighting is "an arena of glory and power like bullfighting, like boxing."

Kennedy's provocative statement forces us to realize that no single formulation of drama, or of feminist drama, can be entirely satisfactory. Certainly it is now evident that the feminism of the 1960s, which most often asserted the equality of men with women, yielded to a much more radical feminism in the 1970s and 1980s, which emphasized the distinctiveness of women, even to the extent of banishing *man* from *woman* and *men* from *women,* by adopting such spellings as *womon, wimmin,* and *womyn.* The radical feminists held the view that gender roles—created not by nature but by patriarchal oppression—can be changed only by a revolutionary restructuring of power. Plays, or, better, performances, created in this spirit tend *not* to use the linear structure of canonical plays but find some precedent in the work of Bertolt Brecht's "epic drama" (see p. 584). As in the plays of Brecht, the actors do not seek to generate dramatic illusion, but rather they break through the proscenium and confront the audience directly.

Interestingly, at the very time that radical feminist theater was perhaps at its height, women were winning prizes on Broadway with plays that from a radical feminist point of view left much to be desired. In the 1980s three plays by women were awarded Pulitzer Prizes: Beth Henley's *Crimes of the Heart* (1981), Marsha Norman's *'night, Mother* (1983), and Wendy Wasserstein's *The Heidi Chronicles* (1989). All are fairly traditional in form and in content. Let's look briefly at the comments about one of these plays, Marsha Norman's, since we include 'night, Mother on page 905.

Most critics for major newspapers and magazines—which means most male critics—reviewed 'night, Mother favorably. Robert Brustein, for instance, said that it reveals "an authentic, universal playwright—not a woman playwright, mind you, not a regional playwright, not an ethnic playwright, but one who speaks to the concerns and experiences of all humankind" (The New Republic, May 2, 1983). However, this talk about universals is exactly what many advocates of women's theater object to; they say that for too many centuries male critics have praised as "universal" dramas by and about males that do not in fact recognize that males and females are very different, whether because of biology or because of social pressures. In this view, females confronted with a play such as Death of a Salesman are forced to reject their own experiences and to adopt (for the sake of participating in an alleged "universal" experience) a male way of seeing or thinking. Jill Dolan, for instance, in the first issue of Women and Performance Journal (1983) and again in her book, The Feminist Spectator as Critic (1988), said that Brustein was obscuring Marsha Norman's gender. By coopting her—by making her (so to speak) an honorary man—he was dishonoring her female vision. Several other feminist critics expressed displeasure with the play, arguing that it depicted a self-destructive woman. In celebrating a loser, they said, it did not at all deal with the prototypical female experience. Helene Keyssar, writing in Encyclopedia of Literature and Criticism, edited by Martin Coyle and others (1991), said that the play "obscures feminist issues such as victimization, and in form and style poses no serious alternative to dominant theatre. It is, in fact, a prime example of the unthreatening kind of gendered dramas that make it into the canon of 'good' American drama" (499–500).

In short, not all women are willing to welcome as "women's theater" a prize-winning play by a woman. Furthermore, in the last twenty years or so, it has become evident that one cannot speak about "women" as though they constitute a group with a single vision. Perhaps the first great division in the feminist movement occurred around 1970, when women of color, especially African Americans, pointed out that the feminist movement at that time was chiefly white and middle class. The movement, falsely assuming a uniformity of experience, did not speak for the poor or for blacks, Asian Americans, or Latinas. Nor (it was

soon pointed out) did it speak for lesbians; in fact, with its middle-class values, its celebration of the achievements of Aphra Behn and Virginia Woolf and other notable white women, it seemed almost as narrow and as self-satisfied as the patriarchal structure that it opposed.

Looking back on the years since 1970, then, one should speak not of women's theater but of women's theaters. There can be no doubt that women are now playing much more active roles in the theater than they did in the past, partly because we now all recognize that indeed there are many mansions in the house of the drama; the Aristotelian dramatists may still occupy the royal suite, but the achievements of other kinds of dramatists, as well as the achievements of producers, directors, and actors in these other kinds of play have enriched not only women's theater but (and here we slip into universalizing) all theater. A recommended reading list includes the following:

Austin, G., Feminist Theories for Drama Criticism (1990).

Betsko, Kathleen, and Rachel Koenig, Interviews with Contemporary Women Playwrights (1987).

Brater, Enoch, ed., The New Women Playwrights (1989).

Brown-Guillory, Elizabeth, Their Place on the Stage: Black Women Playwrights in America (1988).

Case, Sue-Ellen, Feminism and Theatre (1988).

Chinoy, Helen Krich, and Lynda Walsh Jenkins, eds., Women in American Theatre, rev. ed. (1981).

Dolan, Jill, The Feminist Spectator as Critic (1988).

Hart, Lynda, ed., Making a Spectacle: Feminist Essays on Contemporary Women's Theatre (1989).

Kennedy, Adrienne, People Who Led to My Plays (1987).

Keyssar, Helene, Feminist Theatre, rev. ed. (1990).

Leavitt, Dinah, Feminist Theatre Groups (1980).

Yarbro-Bejarano, Yvonne, "The Female Subject in Chicano Theatre," in Sue-Ellen Case, Performing Feminisms (1990).

For anthologies of plays, see Plays by Women (ten volumes, with various editors, 1983). See also Women's Work: Five New Plays from The Women's Project, edited by Julia Miles (1989); two collections by Honor Moore, Women's Theatre (1972) and The New Women's Theatre: Ten Plays by Contemporary American Women (1977); and Black Female Playwrights: An Anthology of Plays before 1950, edited by Kathy A. Perkins (1989).

Representations of Gender in the Theater

In "A Note on Women's Theater" (p. 896), we briefly discuss some of the reasons why women were not strongly represented as dramatists in earlier centuries. In the following pages we discuss other aspects of gender in the theater.

Contemporary thinking divides between two views of gender. The "essentialist" view holds that our species has a biologically fixed sex division between male and female (a matter of chromosomes, hormones, and anatomical differences) and that the masculine and feminine roles we live out are natural, or innate—part of our very essence. In this sense, they are "essential." The "constructivist" view on the other hand, distinguishes between sex and gender. This second view holds that although there is a fixed sex division (again, a matter of biology), our patterns of gender (masculinity, femininity) are largely produced by cultural interpretation. Parents, siblings, advertisements, and so forth, teach us that males are masculine (strong, active, rational) and that females are feminine (weak, passive, emotional). According to this view, we (or at least most of us) play male or female roles in a social performance, "constructing" ourselves into what society expects of us. This is not exactly what Shakespeare meant when he said, "All the world's a stage," but the phrase is apt enough; we are all performers, playing many roles—for example, students, athletes, lovers, siblings, workers, dutiful (or perhaps rebellious) children, sober citizens, hearty friends, and so on.

Here are two statements setting forth the two positions. The first is by an essentialist.

> Every mother who has held a girl child in her arms has known that she was different from a boy child and that she would approach the reality around her in a different way. . . . She is a female and she will die female, and though many centuries should pass, archaeologists would identify her skeleton as the remains of a female creature.
>
> Germaine Greer, *The Change* (1991)

The second statement is by a constructivist, although he lived two centuries before the word was invented.

> The multitude will hardly believe the excessive force of education, and in the difference of modesty between men and women, [they] ascribe that to nature which is altogether owing to early instruction. *Miss* is scarce three years old, but she's spoke to every day to hide her leg, and rebuked in good earnest if she shows it; whilst *little*

Master at the same age is bid to take up his coats and piss like a man.
>
> Bernard Mandeville, *The Fable of the Bees* (1723)

With these competing views as background, let's now quickly survey the presence of women in drama.

In ancient Greece, plays were written only by men, and female roles in plays were performed by men who wore female costumes and masks. (See p. 902.) Possibly women attended the dramatic festivals, but the evidence is unclear. From the point of view of many feminist scholars, real women were in effect erased—they were mere household aids and machines for producing children—and their images were constructed by the male dramatists who wrote the roles and the male actors who performed the roles. One feminist scholar, Sue-Ellen Case, in *Feminism and Theatre* (1988) suggests that female readers or spectators may find that the female roles in Greek drama are mere male fantasies, images that have nothing to do with the experience of real women. Of course, when Greek plays are staged today, women perform these roles, but Case suggests that these "classic drag" roles (5) should perhaps today be performed by men, just as they were performed in ancient Greece. If they were performed by men, she says, we could all clearly see how "Other" they are.

> The feminist theatre-practitioner might, for instance, understand *Lysistrata* not as a good play for women, but as a male drag show, with burlesque jokes about breasts and phalluses playing well in the drag tradition. The feminist director might cast a man in the role of Medea, underscoring the patriarchal prejudice of ownership and jealousy and the ownership of children as male concerns. The feminist actor may no longer regard these roles as desirable for her career. (19)

By the way, notice that in Case's last sentence she uses the word *actor,* whereas other writers might use *actress*. Many people today find *actress* (like *hostess* and *stewardess*) demeaning and prefer to use *actor* for a woman as well as a man.

In the Elizabethan theater, too, female roles were played by males, in this case by boys whose voices had not yet changed. As with Greek plays, these roles today are played by women. We might ask ourselves whether the roles have, therefore, necessarily changed, whether, for example, Hippolyta, Helena, Hermia, and Titania in *A Midsummer Night's Dream* and Goneril, Regan, and Cordelia in *King*

Lear must be different today from what they were in Shakespeare's day by virtue of the fact that today the parts are enacted by female bodies and female voices. (For an extreme example, see p. 902.) One view is that they are different and they are better, since they now truly have a woman's imprint. A different view holds that the biology of the actor is irrelevant to the way in which the role is performed. A third view resembles Case's view of Greek drama—that is, one might argue that the parts (no matter who speaks them) remain "classic drag."

The fact that originally the roles were performed by boys dressed as girls has provoked much speculation about the spectators' responses. Were some spectators (knowing of course that the performers were boys) erotically aroused? Conversely, did the fact that the performers were boys provide a sort of "aesthetic distance," allowing the spectators (at least the straight ones) to enjoy the play *as a play,* free from any fantasized physical involvement with the female roles they watched on the stage? Perhaps no one gave the matter any thought, one way or another. Perhaps it was a convention they were so used to that they gave it no more thought than we give the fact that when we see Ibsen's *A Doll's House* acted in a box set, we are looking at the strangest imaginable room—a room that is realistic in countless details except that—crazy though this sounds—the fourth wall is missing.

Cross-dressing is a convention in the theater in other cultures, notably China and Japan, where it is still used in certain kinds of plays. (See p. 902.) Theorists sometimes argue, in fact, that a man can play a woman better than a woman can, because he *is acting* whereas she may be behaving naturally, and acting is something quite different from natural behavior. Of course, by this logic, women ought to play men's roles better than men can, but one rarely hears this assertion.

Cross-dressing affords women a chance to play male roles. (See p. 903.) Alternatively, roles can simply be changed, for example, from King Lear to Queen Lear. In our brief essay on Shakespearean production, we reproduce a photograph of a production of *King Lear* (p. 225) in which the roles were altered, and we can now quote a comment by the director of the production concerning Ruth Maleczech's desire to play Lear:

> It took me a while to understand that there were certain political imperatives inherent in that desire. What's one of the first things you see? That Lear's story, at least in part, is about the relationship between power and love. A man can be powerful and still be loved, but it's rare to see a woman loved for her power—women must be powerless. So as women gain power in our society, they also find love more difficult to attain.

Quoted in Lesley Ferris, ed., *Crossing the Stage* (1993), 3.

Cross-dressing—a female in a male role, or a male in a female role—is used (chiefly by feminists) as a critique of society's construction of gender.

We use cross-gender performances to challenge traditional representations, to illuminate gender-as-construction, and to provide actors (especially women) with access to a broader range of roles than they would otherwise have. Cross-gender casting expands a director's range in conceptualizing a production and can subvert conventional representation and realism. Crossing genders is also simply a way to increase the pleasure and fun of theatrical work.

Rhonda Blair, in *Upstaging Big Daddy,* ed. Ellen Donkin and Susan Clements (1993), 291.

At least two other things ought to be said about cross-dressing. First, some playwrights vehemently oppose it. Samuel Beckett, for instance, refused to allow his plays to be produced with women taking male roles. Second, much cross-dressing, for instance in Brandon Thomas's venerable classic, *Charley's Aunt* (1892), and in films such as *Tootsie, Some Like It Hot,* and *Mrs. Doubtfire,* seems largely based on the idea that it is funny for a man to be dressed as a woman. What is offered is light entertainment, not a searching examination of gender roles. The humor perhaps is rooted in the assumption that a man dressed as a woman is in some sort of inferior and inherently demeaning position. Understandably, many women resent these images. A related instance is illustrated on p. 903, where an older woman in Molière's *The Misanthrope* is played by a man. Because women are expected (at least by most male viewers) to add beauty to the stage, an older (and implicitly therefore unattractive) woman may be played comically by a male.

Something should be said here about gay and lesbian theater. In the introduction to Harvey Fierstein's *On Tidy Endings* (p. 973), we very briefly sketch the history of representations of male homosexuality in English and American drama, but here we should add the obvious point that until the 1960s homosexual writers could not write openly about their experience. It is a significant fact that three of the four chief American dramatists of the middle of the century—Tennessee Williams, William Inge, and Edward Albee—were gay but could not directly put gay characters on the stage. In looking at some of their works, it now is evident (and indeed it was evident even then to those who were in the know) that they were writing about homosexual experience and that they voiced their concerns through various disguises. Thus, in Inge's *Bus Stop,* the professor (like Inge) is an alcoholic, but the professor's problem is a fondness for young girls, whereas Inge's was a forbidden fondness for men. These gay writers sometimes expressed their concerns through some of their female characters. In discussing *A Streetcar Named Desire,* it is a rare commentator today who does not say that Tennessee Williams was voicing a private concern when Blanche DuBois said, "I don't want realism. I want magic!" The usual interpretation is that this is the voice of a gay man crying out for freedom from current oppressive conventions.

Although male gay drama was common (if sufficiently disguised) on the stage from the 1920s through the 1950s, lesbian drama is almost invisible before the late 1960s. The absence of lesbian voices in the theater is not surprising, given the fact that until recently very few women wrote for the theater. (See "A Note on Women's Theater," p. 896.) True, the topic occasionally was introduced in a play, for instance in Lillian Hellman's *The Children's Hour* (1934), but the author was straight, and within the play the charge of being a lesbian is unfounded. Not until the 1970s do we get a significant number of plays (presumably addressed to a predominantly straight audience) speaking openly about lesbianism. Beginning with the 1980s there seems to be something of a shift from defensiveness to celebration, and the audience (for instance in Ellen Galford's *The Fires of Bride* [1990]) seems to have changed from straights to lesbians. One final point, and it repeats one we have already made. Many feminists argue that the great body of dramatic literature, at least from Greece through Arthur Miller, falsifies the experience of women. For instance, after talking about playwrights of the 1970s, Linda Ben-Zvi continues thus:

> The depiction of women by playwrights of the preceding generation is often no better. One need only think of Arthur Miller's handling of Linda Loman in *Death of a Salesman*. She is wife, she is mother, but she is never a person in her own right. . . . Unlike Winnie [in Beckett's *Happy Days*] she is never allowed to articulate her dreams, memories, or thoughts. She functions entirely as a cipher for the men in her life. Her signs are the laundry basket and the darned socks, just as the signs of the woman in the hotel room—another stereotyped figure at the other end of the gender spectrum—are her raucous laughter and her unclothed body. Both are images of women seen entirely from a male perspective. At the Loman family table only three places are set.
>
> *Women in Beckett* (1990), xiv.

There is much to think about here, but we want to suggest three points. First, the men in the Loman family are hardly such that one would want them in one's own family. Second, Linda ultimately throws out her sons ("Get out of here, both of you, and don't come back. . . . Pick up this stuff, I'm not your maid any more. Pick it up, you bum, you!"). Third, the most memorable speech in the play is spoken not by any of the men but by Linda:

> Willy Loman never made a lot of money. His name was never in the paper. He's not the finest character that ever lived. But he's a human being, and a terrible thing is happening to him. So attention must be paid. He's not to be allowed to fall into his grave like an old dog. Attention, attention must be finally paid to such a person.

Of course the speech is *about* Willy, but we can never forget the speaker. If the Loman table is set with only three places—if, in effect, Linda is an outsider—Linda nevertheless is the most impressive figure in the play. (See p. 903.)

SUGGESTED REFERENCES

Most of the titles listed at the end of "A Note on Women's Theater" (p. 898) are relevant here, but in addition see Vern L. Burrough, *Cross Dressing, Sex, and Gender* (1993); and Marjorie Garber, *Vested Interests: Cross-Dressing and Cultural Anxiety* (1992).

This marble relief sculpture shows the Greek comic dramatist Menander holding the mask of a young man. On the table are the mask of a woman and the grotesque mask of a slave. All of the roles were played by males. Given the great size of Greek theaters, subtle facial gestures of live actors would be invisible to most spectators, so masks were used to convey the essential type of the role. One of the questions that feminist scholars have raised is this: Can male playwrights and male actors adequately give voice to the experience of women? ▶

◀ In a 1961 production of Christopher Marlowe's *Doctor Faustus,* Helen was nude. Obviously, nudity was impossible in the Elizabethan theater, when boys played the female roles. This production raises, in an extreme form, the question of whether the use of female actors in female roles has substantially changed those roles from what they were in Elizabethan times.

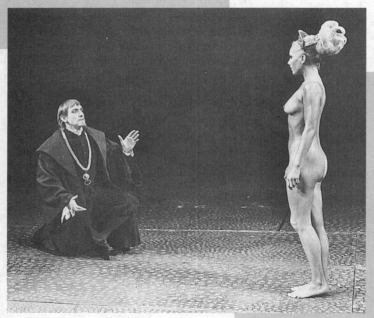

A woman invented the Japanese Kabuki drama in the seventeenth century, and initially women performed in the plays. Soon, however, women were banned on grounds of immorality, and men performed female as well as male roles. The *onnagata* (female impersonator) shown here, Masakado, has been honored with the title of Living National Treasure. In Kabuki, the acting is highly stylized. Fight scenes, for instance, are almost balletic. Furthermore, stage hands, usually dressed in black, are conceived as invisible. Despite the high degree of stylization, devotees of Kabuki insist that the *onnagata* is more feminine than a real woman. ▶

◀ Sarah Bernhardt (1844–1923), widely regarded as the greatest performer in nineteenth-century France, occasionally played what are called *breeches parts,* that is, male roles designed to be played by women. She also played some male roles originally written for males, for example, Napoleon's son in Rostand's *L'Aiglon* (1900) and Hamlet. Special circumstances helped to make these roles acceptable. In the case of *L'Aiglon,* the play is something of a romantic costume piece about Napoleon's son, a fragile youth who died when he was twenty-one; in the case of *Hamlet,* the protagonist is sometimes regarded (wrongly) as unmanly.

A common explanation for nineteenth-century breeches parts is that they gave women a chance to show their legs, or, rather, they gave men a chance to admire women's legs. However, these explanations may trivialize the matter. The fact is that women, because of their sex, were in effect barred from performing many great parts. Think, for example, of Greek tragedy. *Oedipus the King* has seven speaking parts for men but only one for a woman; even *Antigone* has five speaking parts for males and only three for females. In *Hamlet,* there are more than twenty speaking parts for males and only two for females. Bernhardt may well have been more interested in playing the role of Hamlet than in displaying her body for the delight of men.

Linda Loman, in Arthur Miller's *Death of a Salesman,* has come in for severe criticism from some feminist writers, but others have held that she is the most decent and the most sensible character in the play. If the Loman family is essentially the father and two sons, her apartness from the family suggests her superiority. ▶

◀ An old theatrical tradition allows a man to play the part of an older woman, a so-called *dame part.* Probably the nasty underlying idea is that if a woman is not sexually attractive, she is a figure of fun. In this scene from Moliére's *The Misanthrope,* the older woman, Arsinoë, is played by a man, who emphasizes the character's awkwardness (notice the position of the feet) and stridency (notice the wide-open mouth).

Marsha Norman

'NIGHT, MOTHER

Marsha Norman was born in Louisville, Kentucky, in 1947. After receiving a bachelor's degree from Agnes Scott College and a master of arts in teaching from the University of Louisville, she taught gifted children and disturbed children. Her reputation as a playwright was established with a two-act play, *Getting Out*, which was produced in Louisville (1977) and subsequently in New York (1978). *'night, Mother*, which had its world premiére in Cambridge, Massachusetts, in 1983, won the Pulitzer Prize for drama in that year.

COMMENTARY

In our introductory words to *Death of a Salesman* (pp. 648–49), in which we sketch the rise of the middle class and we mention that the ideas of Copernicus, Darwin, and Freud have contributed to the view that human beings are "lust-ridden, soulless creatures in a terrifying materialistic universe." In contrast to this somewhat despairing view, Marsha Norman gives us a figure whom she sees as very strong. In an interview published in *Interviews with Contemporary Women Playwrights*, edited by Kathleen Betsko and Rachel Koenig (1987), Norman said that Jessie achieves a "nearly total triumph. Jessie is able to get what she feels she needs. . . . It may look despairing from the outside, but it has cost her everything she has. If Jessie says it is worth it, then it is."

In this quotation Norman is pretty much saying that Jessie is a traditional tragic hero, someone who ventures boldly and, in a way, turns apparent material defeat into some sort of spiritual triumph. Interestingly, the very success of Norman's play brought fairly widespread criticism from persons interested in the development of women's theater. The two chief objections are somewhat contradictory: (1) *'night, Mother* suggests that women are self-destructive neurotics; (2) *'night, Mother* is just another drama in the male tradition—that is, it emphasizes the heroism of the isolated individual but ignores the strength born out of communal action, a kind of action that many women today regard as necessary if they are to escape from the assigned roles of housewife and sexual object. (Many feminist theater groups reject the usual hierarchical structure—a director dominating actors, designers, and technicians—in favor of a leaderless group.)

Marsha Norman

'NIGHT, MOTHER

List of Characters

JESSIE CATES, *in her late thirties or early forties, is pale and vaguely unsteady physically. It is only in the last year that Jessie has gained control of her mind and body, and tonight she is determined to hold on to that control. She wears pants and a long black sweater with deep pockets, which contain scraps of paper, and there may be a pencil behind her ear or a pen clipped to one of the pockets of the sweater.*

As a rule, Jessie doesn't feel much like talking. Other people have rarely found her quirky sense of humor amusing. She has a peaceful energy on this night, a sense of purpose, but is clearly aware of the time passing moment by moment. Oddly enough, Jessie has never been as communicative or as enjoyable as she is on this evening, but we must know she has not always been this way. There is a familiarity between these two women that comes from having lived together for a long time. There is a shorthand to the talk and a sense of routine comfort in the way they relate to each other physically. Naturally, there are also routine aggravations.

THELMA CATES, *"Mama," is Jessie's mother, in her late fifties or early sixties. She has begun to feel her age and so takes it easy when she can, or when it serves her purpose to let someone help her. But she speaks quickly and enjoys talking. She believes that things are what she says they are. Her sturdiness is more a mental quality than a physical one, finally. She is chatty and nosy, and this is her house.*

The play takes place in a relatively new house built way out on a country road, with a living room and connecting kitchen, and a center hall that leads off to the bedrooms. A pull cord in the hall ceiling releases a ladder which leads to the attic. One of these bedrooms opens directly onto the hall, and its entry should be visible to everyone in the audience. It should be, in fact, the focal point of the entire set, and the lighting should make it disappear completely at times and draw the entire set into it at others. It is a point of both threat and promise. It is an ordinary door that opens onto absolute nothingness. That door is the point of all the action, and the utmost care should be given to its design and construction.

The living room is cluttered with magazines and needlework catalogues, ashtrays and candy dishes. Examples of Mama's needlework are everywhere—pillows, afghans, and quilts, doilies and rugs, and they are quite nice examples. The house is more comfortable than messy, but there is quite a lot to keep in place here. It is more personal than charming. It is not quaint. Under no circumstances should the set and its dressing make a judgment about the intelligence or taste of Jessie and Mama. It should simply indicate that they are very specific real people who happen to live in a particular part of the country. Heavy accents, which would further distance the audience from Jessie and Mama, are also wrong.

The time is the present, with the action beginning about 8:15. Clocks onstage in the kitchen and on a table in the living room should run throughout the performance and be visible to the audience.

There will be no intermission.

> *Mama stretches to reach the cupcakes in a cabinet in the kitchen. She can't see them, but she can feel around for them, and she's eager to have one, so she's working pretty hard at it. This may be the most serious exercise Mama ever gets. She finds a cupcake, the coconut-covered, raspberry-and-marshmallow-filled kind known as a snowball, but sees that there's one missing from the package. She calls to Jessie, who is apparently somewhere else in the house.*

MAMA (*unwrapping the cupcake*). Jessie, it's the last snowball, sugar. Put it on the list, O.K.? And we're out of Hershey bars, and where's that peanut brittle? I think maybe Dawson's been in it again. I ought to put a big mirror on the refrigerator door. That'll keep him out of my treats, won't it? You hear me, honey? (*Then more to herself.*) I hate it when the coconut falls off. Why does the coconut fall off?

> *Jessie enters from her bedroom, carrying a stack of newspapers.*

JESSIE. We got any old towels?

MAMA. There you are!

JESSIE (*holding a towel that was on the stack of newspapers*). Towels you don't want anymore. (*Picking up Mama's snowball wrapper.*) How about this swimming towel Loretta gave us? Beach towel, that's the name of it. You want it? (*Mama shakes her head no.*)

MAMA. What have you been doing in there?

JESSIE. And a big piece of plastic like a rubber sheet or something. Garbage bags would do if there's enough.

MAMA. Don't go making a big mess, Jessie. It's eight o'clock already.

JESSIE. Maybe an old blanket or towels we got in a soap box sometime?

MAMA. I said don't make a mess. Your hair is black enough, hon.

JESSIE (*continuing to search the kitchen cabinets, finding two or three more towels to add to her stack*). It's not for my hair, Mama. What about some old pillows anywhere, or a foam cushion out of a yard chair would be real good.

MAMA. You haven't forgot what night it is, have you? (*Holding up her fingernails.*) They're all chipped, see? I've been waiting all week, Jess. It's Saturday night, sugar.

JESSIE. I know. I got it on the schedule.

MAMA (*crossing to the living room*). You want me to wash 'em now or are you making your mess first? (*Looking at the snowball.*) We're out of these. Did I say that already?

JESSIE. There's more coming tomorrow. I ordered you a whole case.

MAMA (*checking the* TV Guide). A whole case will go stale, Jessie.

JESSIE. They can go in the freezer till you're ready for them. Where's Daddy's gun?

MAMA. In the attic.

JESSIE. Where in the attic? I looked your whole nap and couldn't find it anywhere.

MAMA. One of his shoeboxes, I think.

JESSIE. Full of shoes. I looked already.

MAMA. Well, you didn't look good enough, then. There's that box from the ones he wore to the hospital. When he died, they told me I could have them back, but I never did like those shoes.

JESSIE (*pulling them out of her pocket*). I found the bullets. They were in an old milk can.

MAMA (*as Jessie starts for the hall*). Dawson took the shotgun, didn't he? Hand me that basket, hon.

JESSIE (*getting the basket for her*). Dawson better not've taken that pistol.

MAMA (*stopping her again*). Now my glasses, please. (*Jessie returns to get the glasses.*) I told him to take those rubber boots, too, but he said they were for fishing. I told him to take up fishing.

Jessie reaches for the cleaning spray, and cleans Mama's glasses for her.

JESSIE. He's just too lazy to climb up there, Mama. Or maybe he's just being smart. That floor's not very steady.

MAMA (*getting out a piece of knitting*). It's not a floor at all, hon, it's a board now and then. Measure this for me. I need six inches.

JESSIE (*as she measures*). Dawson could probably use some of those clothes up there. Somebody should have them. You ought to call the Salvation Army before the whole thing falls in on you. Six inches exactly.

MAMA. It's plenty safe! As long as you don't go up there.

JESSIE (*turning to go again*). I'm careful.

MAMA. What do you want the gun for, Jess?

JESSIE (*not returning this time. Opening the ladder in the hall*). Protection. (*She steadies the ladder as Mama talks.*)

MAMA. You take the TV way too serious, hon. I've never seen a criminal in my life. This is way too far to come for what's out here to steal. Never seen a one.

JESSIE (*taking her first step up*). Except for Ricky.

MAMA. Ricky is mixed up. That's not a crime.

JESSIE. Get your hands washed. I'll be right back. And get 'em real dry. You dry your hands till I get back or it's no go, all right?

MAMA. I thought Dawson told you not to go up those stairs.

JESSIE (*going up*). He did.

MAMA. I don't like the idea of a gun, Jess.

JESSIE (*calling down from the attic*). Which shoebox, do you remember?

MAMA. Black.

JESSIE. The box was black?

MAMA. The shoes were black.

JESSIE. That doesn't help much, Mother.

MAMA. I'm not trying to help, sugar. (*No answer.*) We don't have anything anybody'd want, Jessie. I mean, I don't even want what we got, Jessie.

JESSIE. Neither do I. Wash your hands. (*Mama gets up and crosses to stand under the ladder.*)

MAMA. You come down from there before you have a fit. I can't come up and get you, you know.

JESSIE. I know.

MAMA. We'll just hand it over to them when they come, how's that? Whatever they want, the criminals.

JESSIE. That's a good idea, Mama.

MAMA. Ricky will grow out of this and be a real fine boy, Jess. But I have to tell you, I wouldn't want Ricky to know we had a gun in the house.

JESSIE. Here it is. I found it.

MAMA. It's just something Ricky's going through. Maybe he's in with some bad people. He just needs some time, sugar. He'll get back in school or get a job or one day you'll get a call and he'll say he's sorry for all the trouble he's caused and invite you out for supper someplace dress-up.

JESSIE (*coming back down the steps*). Don't worry. It's not for him, it's for me.

MAMA. I didn't think you would shoot your own boy, Jessie. I know you've felt like it, well, we've all felt like shooting somebody, but we don't do it. I just don't think we need . . .

JESSIE (*interrupting*). Your hands aren't washed. Do you want a manicure or not?

MAMA. Yes, I do, but . . .

JESSIE (*crossing to the chair*). Then wash your hands and don't talk to me any more about Ricky. Those two rings he took were the last valuable things I had, so now he's started in on other people, door to door. I hope they put him away sometime. I'd turn him in myself if I knew where he was.

MAMA. You don't mean that.

JESSIE. Every word. Wash your hands and that's the last time I'm telling you.

Jessie sits down with the gun and starts cleaning it, pushing the cylinder out, checking to see that the chambers and barrel are empty, then putting some oil on a small patch of cloth and pushing it through the barrel with the push rod that was in the box. Mama goes to the kitchen and washes her hands, as instructed, trying not to show her concern about the gun.

MAMA. I shoulda got you to bring down that milk can. Agnes Fletcher sold hers to somebody with a flea market for forty dollars apiece.

JESSIE. I'll go back and get it in a minute. There's a wagon wheel up there, too. There's even a churn. I'll get it all if you want.

MAMA (*coming over, now, taking over now*). What are you doing?

JESSIE. The barrel has to be clean, Mama. Old powder, dust gets in it . . .

MAMA. What for?

JESSIE. I told you.

MAMA (*reaching for the gun*). And I told you, we don't get criminals out here.

JESSIE (*quickly pulling it to her*). And I told you . . . (*Then trying to be calm.*) The gun is for me.

MAMA. Well, you can have it if you want. When I die, you'll get it all, anyway.

JESSIE. I'm going to kill myself, Mama.

MAMA (*returning to the sofa*). Very funny. Very funny.

JESSIE. I am.

MAMA. You are not! Don't even say such a thing, Jessie.

JESSIE. How would you know if I didn't say it? You want it to be a surprise? You're lying there in your bed or maybe you're just brushing your teeth and you hear this . . . noise down the hall?

MAMA. Kill yourself.

JESSIE. Shoot myself. In a couple of hours.

MAMA. It must be time for your medicine.

JESSIE. Took it already.

MAMA. What's the matter with you?

JESSIE. Not a thing. Feel fine.

MAMA. You feel fine. You're just going to kill yourself.

JESSIE. Waited until I felt good enough, in fact.

MAMA. Don't make jokes, Jessie. I'm too old for jokes.

JESSIE. It's not a joke, Mama.

Mama watches for a moment in silence.

MAMA. That gun's no good, you know. He broke it right before he died. He dropped it in the mud one day.

JESSIE. Seems O.K. (*She spins the chamber, cocks the pistol, and pulls the trigger. The gun is not yet loaded, so all we hear is the click, but it will definitely work. It's also obvious that Jessie knows her way around a gun. Mama cannot speak.*) I had Cecil's all ready in there, just in case I couldn't find this one, but I'd rather use Daddy's.

MAMA. Those bullets are at least fifteen years old.

JESSIE (*pulling out another box*). These are from last week.

MAMA. Where did you get those?

JESSIE. Feed store Dawson told me about.

MAMA. Dawson!

JESSIE. I told him I was worried about prowlers. He said he thought it was a good idea. He told me what kind to ask for.

MAMA. If he had any idea . . .

JESSIE. He took it as a compliment. He thought I might be taking an interest in things. He got through telling me all about the bullets and then he said we ought to talk like this more often.

MAMA. And where was I while this was going on?

JESSIE. On the phone with Agnes. About the milk can, I guess. Anyway, I asked Dawson if he thought they'd send me some bullets and he said he'd just call for me, because he knew they'd send them if he told them to. And he was absolutely right. Here they are.

MAMA. How could he do that?

JESSIE. Just trying to help, Mama.

MAMA. And then I told you where the gun was.

JESSIE (*smiling, enjoying this joke*). See? Everybody's doing what they can.

MAMA. You told me it was for protection!

JESSIE. It *is*! I'm still doing your nails, though. Want to try that new Chinaberry color?

MAMA. Well, I'm calling Dawson right now. We'll just see what he has to say about this little stunt.

JESSIE. Dawson doesn't have any more to do with this.

MAMA. He's your brother.

JESSIE. And that's all.

MAMA (*stands up, moves toward the phone*). Dawson will put a stop to this. Yes he will. He'll take the gun away.

JESSIE. If you call him, I'll just have to do it before he gets here. Soon as you hang up the phone, I'll just walk in the bedroom and lock the door. Dawson will get here just in time to help you clean up. Go ahead, call him. Then call the police. Then call the funeral home. Then call Loretta and see if *she'll* do your nails.

MAMA. You will not! This is crazy talk, Jessie!

Mama goes directly to the telephone and starts to dial, but Jessie is fast, coming up behind her and taking the receiver out of her hand, putting it back down.

JESSIE (*firm and quiet*). I said no. This is private. Dawson is not invited.

MAMA. Just me.

JESSIE. I don't want anybody else over here. Just you and me. If Dawson comes over, it'll make me feel stupid for not doing it ten years ago.

MAMA. I think we better call the doctor. Or how about the ambulance. You like that one driver, I know. What's his name, Timmy? Get you somebody to talk to.

JESSIE (*going back to her chair*). I'm through talking, Mama. You're it. No more.

MAMA. We're just going to sit around like every other night in the world and then you're going to kill yourself? (*Jessie doesn't answer.*) You'll miss. (*Again there is no response.*) You'll just wind up a vegetable. How would you like that? Shoot your ear off? You know what the doctor said about getting excited. You'll cock the pistol and have a fit.

JESSIE. I think I can kill myself, Mama.

MAMA. You're not going to kill yourself, Jessie. You're not even upset! (*Jessie smiles, or laughs quietly, and Mama tries a different approach.*) People don't really kill themselves, Jessie. No, mam, doesn't make sense, unless you're retarded or deranged, and you're as normal as they come, Jessie, for the most part. We're all *afraid* to die.

JESSIE. I'm not, Mama. I'm cold all the time, anyway.

MAMA. That's ridiculous.

JESSIE. It's exactly what I want. It's dark and quiet.

MAMA. So is the back yard, Jessie! Close your eyes. Stuff cotton in your ears. Take a nap! It's quiet in your room. I'll leave the TV off all night.

JESSIE. So quiet I don't know it's quiet. So nobody can get me.

MAMA. You don't know what dead is like. It might not be quiet at all. What if it's like an alarm clock and you can't wake up so you can't shut it off. Ever.

JESSIE. Dead is everybody and everything I ever knew, gone. Dead is dead quiet.

MAMA. It's a sin. You'll go to hell.

JESSIE. Uh-huh.

MAMA. You will!

JESSIE. Jesus was a suicide, if you ask me.

MAMA. You'll go to hell just for saying that. Jessie!

JESSIE (*with genuine surprise*). I didn't know I thought that.

MAMA. Jessie!

Jessie doesn't answer. She puts the now-loaded gun back in the box and crosses to the kitchen. But Mama is afraid she's headed for the bedroom.

MAMA (*in a panic*). You can't use my towels! They're my towels. I've had them for a long time. I like my towels.

JESSIE. I asked you if you wanted that swimming towel and you said you didn't.

MAMA. And you can't use your father's gun, either. It's mine now, too. And you can't do it in my house.

JESSIE. Oh, come on.

MAMA. No. You can't do it. I won't let you. The house is in my name.

JESSIE. I have to go in the bedroom and lock the door behind me so they won't arrest you for killing me. They'll probably test your hands for gunpowder, anyway, but you'll pass.

MAMA. Not in my house!

JESSIE. If I'd known you were going to act like this, I wouldn't have told you.

MAMA. How am I supposed to act? Tell you to go ahead? O.K. by me, sugar? Might try it myself. What took you so long?

JESSIE. There's just no point in fighting me over it, that's all. Want some coffee?

MAMA. Your birthday's coming up, Jessie. Don't you want to know what we got you?

JESSIE. You got me dusting powder, Loretta got me a new housecoat, pink probably, and Dawson got me new slippers, too small, but they go with the robe, he'll say. (*Mama cannot speak.*) Right? (*Apparently Jessie is right.*) Be back in a minute.

Jessie takes the gun box, puts it on top of the stack of towels and garbage bags, and takes them into her bedroom. Mama, alone for a moment, goes to the phone, picks up the receiver, looks toward the bedroom, starts to dial, and then replaces the receiver in its cradle as Jessie walks back into the room. Jessie wonders, silently. They have lived together for so long there is very rarely any reason for one to ask what the other was about to do.

MAMA. I started to, but I didn't. I didn't call him.

JESSIE. Good. Thank you.

MAMA (*starting over, a new approach*). What's this all about, Jessie?

JESSIE. About?

Jessie now begins the next task she had "on the schedule," which is refilling all the candy jars, taking the empty papers out of the boxes of chocolates, etc. Mama generally snitches when Jessie does this. Not tonight, though. Nevertheless, Jessie offers.

MAMA. What did I do?

JESSIE. Nothing. Want a caramel?

MAMA (*ignoring the candy*). You're mad at me.

JESSIE. Not a bit. I am worried about you, but I'm going to do what I can before I go. We're not just going to sit around tonight. I made a list of things.

MAMA. What things?

JESSIE. How the washer works. Things like that.

MAMA. I know how the washer works. You put the clothes in. You put the soap in. You turn it on. You wait.

JESSIE. You do something else. You don't just wait.

MAMA. Whatever else you find to do, you're still mainly waiting. The waiting's the worst part of it. The waiting's what you pay somebody else to do, if you can.

JESSIE (*nodding*). O.K. Where do we keep the soap?

MAMA. I could find it.

JESSIE. See?

MAMA. If you're mad about doing the wash, we can get Loretta to do it.

JESSIE. Oh now, that might be worth staying to see.

MAMA. She'd never in her life, would she?

JESSIE. Nope.

MAMA. What's the matter with her?

JESSIE. She thinks she's better than we are. She's not.

MAMA. Maybe if she didn't wear that yellow all the time.

JESSIE. The washer repair number is on a little card taped to the side of the machine.

MAMA. Loretta doesn't ever have to come over here again. Dawson can just leave her at home when he comes. And we don't ever have to see Dawson either if he bothers you. Does he bother you?

JESSIE. Sure he does. Be sure you clean out the lint tray every time you use the dryer. But don't ever put your house shoes in, it'll melt the soles.

MAMA. What does Dawson do, that bothers you?

JESSIE. He just calls me Jess like he knows who he's talking to. He's always wondering what I do all day. I mean, I wonder that myself, but it's my day, so it's mine to wonder about, not his.

MAMA. Family is just accident, Jessie. It's nothing personal, hon. They don't mean to get on your nerves. They don't even mean to be your family, they just are.

JESSIE. They know too much.

MAMA. About what?

JESSIE. They know things about you, and they learned it before you had a chance to say whether you wanted them to know it or not. They were there when it happened and it don't belong to them, it belongs to you, only they got it. Like my mail-order bra got delivered to their house.

MAMA. By accident!

JESSIE. All the same . . . they opened it. They saw the little rosebuds on it. (Offering her another candy.) Chewy mint?

MAMA (shaking her head no). What do they know about you? I'll tell them never to talk about it again. Is it Ricky or Cecil or your fits or your hair is falling out or you drink too much coffee or you never go out of the house or what?

JESSIE. I just don't like their talk. The account at the grocery is in Dawson's name when you call. The number's on a whole list of numbers on the back cover of the phone book.

MAMA. Well! Now we're getting somewhere. They're none of them ever setting foot in this house again.

JESSIE. It's not them, Mother. I wouldn't kill myself just to get away from them.

MAMA. You leave the room when they come over, anyway.

JESSIE. I stay as long as I can. Besides, it's you they come to see.

MAMA. That's because I stay in the room when they come.

JESSIE. It's not them.

MAMA. Then what is it?

JESSIE (checking the list on her note pad). The grocery won't deliver on Saturday anymore. And if you want your order the same day, you have to call before ten. And they won't deliver less than fifteen dollars' worth. What I do is tell them what we need and tell them to add on cigarettes until it gets to fifteen dollars.

MAMA. It's Ricky. You're trying to get through to him.

JESSIE. If I thought I could do that, I would stay.

MAMA. Make him sorry he hurt you, then. That's it, isn't it?

JESSIE. He's hurt me, I've hurt him. We're about even.

MAMA. You'll be telling him killing is O.K. with you, you know. Want him to start killing next? Nothing wrong with it. Mom did it.

JESSIE. Only a matter of time, anyway, Mama. When the call comes, you let Dawson handle it.

MAMA. Honey, nothing says those calls are always going to be some new trouble he's into. You could get one that he's got a job, that he's getting married, or how about he's joined the army, wouldn't that be nice?

JESSIE. If you call the Sweet Tooth before you call the grocery, that Susie will take your fudge next door to the grocery and it'll all come out together. Be sure you talk to Susie, though. She won't let them put it in the bottom of a sack like that one time, remember?

MAMA. Ricky could come over, you know. What if he calls us?

JESSIE. It's not Ricky, Mama.

MAMA. Or anybody could call us, Jessie.

JESSIE. Not on Saturday night, Mama.

MAMA. Then what is it? Are you sick? If your gums are swelling again, we can get you to the dentist in the morning.

JESSIE. No. Can you order your medicine or do you want Dawson to? I've got a note to him. I'll add that to it if you want.

MAMA. Your eyes don't look right. I thought so yesterday.

JESSIE. That was just the ragweed. I'm not sick.

MAMA. Epilepsy is sick, Jessie.

JESSIE. It won't kill me. (A pause.) If it would, I wouldn't have to.

MAMA. You don't have to.

JESSIE. No, I don't. That's what I like about it.

MAMA. Well, I won't let you!

JESSIE. It's not up to you.

MAMA. Jessie!

JESSIE. I want to hang a big sign around my neck, like Daddy's on the barn. GONE FISHING.

MAMA. You don't like it here.

JESSIE (smiling). Exactly.

MAMA. I meant here in my house.

JESSIE. I know you did.

MAMA. You never should have moved back in here with me. If you'd kept your little house or found another place when Cecil left you, you'd have made some new friends at least. Had a life to lead. Had your own things around you. Give Ricky a place to come see you. You never should've come here.

JESSIE. Maybe.

MAMA. But I didn't force you, did I?

JESSIE. If it was a mistake, we made it together. You took me in. I appreciate that.

MAMA. You didn't have any business being by yourself right then, but I can see how you might want a place of your own. A grown woman should . . .

JESSIE. Mama . . . I'm just not having a very good time and I don't have any reason to think it'll get anything but worse. I'm tired. I'm hurt. I'm sad. I feel used.

MAMA. Tired of what?

JESSIE. It all.

MAMA. What does that mean?

JESSIE. I can't say it any better.

MAMA. Well, you'll have to say it better because I'm not letting you alone till you do. What were those other things? Hurt . . . (Before Jessie can answer.) You had this all ready to say to me, didn't you? Did you write this down? How long have you been thinking about this?

JESSIE. Off and on, ten years. On all the time, since Christmas.

MAMA. What happened at Christmas?

JESSIE. Nothing.

MAMA. So why Christmas?

JESSIE. That's it. On the nose.

A pause. Mama knows exactly what Jessie means. She was there, too, after all.

JESSIE (*putting the candy sacks away*). See where all this is? Red hots up front, sour balls and horehound mixed together in this one sack. New packages of toffee and licorice right in back there.

MAMA. Go back to your list. You're hurt by what?

JESSIE (*Mama knows perfectly well*). Mama . . .

MAMA. O.K. Sad about what? There's nothing real sad going on right now. If it was after your divorce or something, that would make sense.

JESSIE (*looking at her list, then opening the drawer*). Now, this drawer has everything in it that there's no better place for. Extension cords, batteries for the radio, extra lighters, sandpaper, masking tape, Elmer's glue, thumbtacks, that kind of stuff. The mousetraps are under the sink, but you call Dawson if you've got one and let him do it.

MAMA. Sad about what?

JESSIE. The way things are.

MAMA. Not good enough. What things?

JESSIE. Oh, everything from you and me to Red China.

MAMA. I think we can leave the Chinese out of this.

JESSIE (*crosses back into the living room*). There's extra light bulbs in a box in the hall closet. And we've got a couple of packages of fuses in the fuse box. There's candles and matches in the top of the broom closet, but if the lights go out, just call Dawson and sit tight. But don't open the refrigerator door. Things will stay cool in there as long as you keep the door shut.

MAMA. I asked you a question.

JESSIE. I read the paper. I don't like how things are. And they're not any better out there than they are in here.

MAMA. If you're doing this because of the newspapers, I can sure fix that!

JESSIE. There's just more of it on TV.

MAMA (*kicking the television set*). Take it out, then!

JESSIE. You wouldn't do that.

MAMA. Watch me.

JESSIE. What would you do all day?

MAMA (*desperately*). Sing. (*Jessie laughs.*) I would, too. You want to watch? I'll sing till morning to keep you alive, Jessie, please!

JESSIE. No. (*Then affectionately.*) It's a funny idea, though. What do you sing?

MAMA (*has no idea how to answer this*). We've got a good life here!

JESSIE (*going back into the kitchen*). I called this morning and canceled the papers, except for Sunday, for your puzzles; you'll still get that one.

MAMA. Let's get another dog, Jessie! You liked a big dog, now, didn't you? That King dog, didn't you?

JESSIE (*washing her hands*). I did like that King dog, yes.

MAMA. I'm so dumb. He's the one run under the tractor.

JESSIE. That makes him dumb, not you.

MAMA. For bringing it up.

JESSIE. It's O.K. Handi-Wipes and sponges under the sink.

MAMA. We could get a new dog and keep him in the house. Dogs are cheap!

JESSIE (*getting big pill jars out of the cabinet*). No.

MAMA. Something for you to take care of.

JESSIE. I've had you, Mama.

MAMA (*frantically starting to fill pill bottles*). You do too much for me. I can fill pill bottles all day, Jessie, and change the shelf paper and wash the floor when I get through. You just watch me. You don't have to do another thing in this house if you don't want to. You don't have to take care of me, Jessie.

JESSIE. I know that. You've just been letting me do it so I'll have something to do, haven't you?

MAMA (*realizing this was a mistake*). I don't do it as well as you. I just meant if it tires you out or makes you feel used . . .

JESSIE. Mama, I know you used to ride the bus. Riding the bus and it's hot and bumpy and crowded and too noisy and more than anything in the world you want to get off and the only reason in the world you don't get off is it's still fifty blocks from where you're going? Well, I can get off right now if I want to, because even if I ride fifty more years and get off then, it's the same place when I step down to it. Whenever I feel like it, I can get off. As soon as I've had enough, it's my stop. I've had enough.

MAMA. You're feeling sorry for yourself!

JESSIE. The plumber's helper is under the sink, too.

MAMA. You're not having a good time! Whoever promised you a good time? Do you think I've had a good time?

JESSIE. I think you're pretty happy, yeah. You have things you like to do.

MAMA. Like what?

JESSIE. Like crochet.

MAMA. I'll teach you to crochet.

JESSIE. I can't do any of that nice work, Mama.

MAMA. Good time don't come looking for you, Jessie. You could work some puzzles or put in a garden or go to the store. Let's call a taxi and go to the A&P!

JESSIE. I shopped you up for about two weeks already. You're not going to need toilet paper till Thanksgiving.

MAMA (*interrupting*). You're acting like some little brat, Jessie. You're mad and everybody's boring and you don't have anything to do and you don't like me and you don't like going out and you don't like staying in and you never talk on the phone and you don't watch TV and you're miserable and it's your own sweet fault.

JESSIE. And it's time I did something about it.

MAMA. Not something like killing yourself. Something like . . . buying us all new dishes! I'd like that. Or maybe the doctor would let you get a driver's license now, or I know what let's do right this minute, let's rearrange the furniture.

JESSIE. I'll do that. If you want. I always thought if the TV was somewhere else, you wouldn't get such a glare on it during the day. I'll do whatever you want before I go.

MAMA (*badly frightened by those words*). You could get a job!

JESSIE. I took that telephone sales job and I didn't even make enough money to pay the phone bill, and I tried to work at the gift shop at the hospital and they said I made people real uncomfortable smiling at them the way I did.

MAMA. You could keep books. You kept your dad's books.

JESSIE. But nobody ever checked them.

MAMA. When he died, they checked them.

JESSIE. And that's when they took the books away from me.

MAMA. That's because without him there wasn't any business, Jessie!

JESSIE (*putting the pill bottles away*). You know I couldn't work. I can't do anything. I've never been around people my whole life except when I went to the hospital. I could have a seizure any time. What good would a job do? The kind of job I could get would make me feel worse.

MAMA. Jessie!

JESSIE. It's true!

MAMA. It's what you think is true!

JESSIE (*struck by the clarity of that*). That's right. It's what I think is true.

MAMA (*hysterically*). But I can't do anything about that!

JESSIE (*quietly*). No. You can't. (*Mama slumps, if not physically, at least emotionally*.) And I can't do anything either, about my life, to change it, make it better, make me feel better about it. Like it better, make it work. But I can stop it. Shut it down, turn it off like the radio when there's nothing on I want to listen to. It's all I really have that belongs to me and I'm going to say what happens to it. And it's going to stop. And I'm going to stop it. So. Let's just have a good time.

MAMA. Have a good time.

JESSIE. We can't go on fussing all night. I mean, I could ask you things I always wanted to know and you could make me some hot chocolate. The old way.

MAMA (*in despair*). It takes cocoa, Jessie.

JESSIE (*gets it out of the cabinet*). I bought cocoa, Mama. And I'd like to have a caramel apple and do your nails.

MAMA. You didn't eat a bite of supper.

JESSIE. Does that mean I can't have a caramel apple?

MAMA. Of course not. I mean . . . (*Smiling a little.*) Of course you can have a caramel apple.

JESSIE. I thought I could.

MAMA. I make the best caramel apples in the world.

JESSIE. I know you do.

MAMA. Or used to. And you don't get cocoa like mine anywhere anymore.

JESSIE. It takes time, I know, but . . .

MAMA. The salt is the trick.

JESSIE. Trouble and everything.

MAMA (*backing away toward the stove*). It's no trouble. What trouble? You put it in the pan and stir it up. All right. Fine. Caramel apples. Cocoa. O.K.

Jessie walks to the counter to retrieve her cigarettes as Mama looks for the right pan. There are brief near-smiles, and maybe Mama clears her throat. We have a truce, for the moment. A genuine but nevertheless uneasy one. Jessie, who has been in constant motion since the beginning, now seems content to sit.

Mama starts looking for a pan to make the cocoa, getting out all the pans in the cabinets in the process. It looks like she's making a mess on purpose so Jessie will have to put them all away again. Mama is buying time, or trying to, and entertaining.

JESSIE. You talk to Agnes today?

MAMA. She's calling me from a pay phone this week. God only knows why. She has a perfectly good Trimline at home.

JESSIE (*laughing*). Well, how is she?

MAMA. How is she every day, Jessie? Nuts.

JESSIE. Is she really crazy or just silly?

MAMA. No, she's really crazy. She was probably using the pay phone because she had another little fire problem at home.

JESSIE. Mother . . .

MAMA. I'm serious! Agnes Fletcher's burned down every house she ever lived in. Eight fires, and she's due for a new one any day now.

JESSIE (*laughing*). No!

MAMA. Wouldn't surprise me a bit.

JESSIE (*laughing*). Why didn't you tell me this before? Why isn't she locked up somewhere?

MAMA. 'Cause nobody ever got hurt, I guess. Agnes woke everybody up to watch the fires as soon as she set 'em. One time she set out porch chairs and served lemonade.

JESSIE (*shaking her head*). Real lemonade?

MAMA. The houses they lived in, you knew they were going to fall down anyway, so why wait for it, is all I could ever make out about it. Agnes likes a feeling of accomplishment.

JESSIE. Good for her.

MAMA (*finding the pan she wants*). Why are you asking about Agnes? One cup or two?

JESSIE. One. She's your friend. No marshmallows.

MAMA (*getting the milk, etc.*). You have to have marshmallows. That's the old way, Jess. Two or three? Three is better.

JESSIE. Three, then. Her whole house burns up? Her clothes and pillows and everything? I'm not sure I believe this.

MAMA. When she was a girl, Jess, not now. Long time ago. But she's still got it in her, I'm sure of it.

JESSIE. She wouldn't burn her house down now. Where would she go? She can't get Buster to build her a new one, he's dead. How could she burn it up?

MAMA. Be exciting, though, if she did. You never know.

JESSIE. You do too know, Mama. She wouldn't do it.

MAMA (*forced to admit, but reluctant*). I guess not.

JESSIE. What else? Why does she wear all those whistles around her neck?

MAMA. Why does she have a house full of birds?

JESSIE. I didn't know she had a house full of birds!

MAMA. Well, she does. And she says they just follow her home. Well, I know for a fact she's still paying on the last parrot she bought. You gotta keep your life filled up, she says. She says a lot of stupid things. (*Jessie laughs, Mama continues, convinced she's getting somewhere.*) It's all that okra she eats. You can't just willy-nilly eat okra two meals a day and expect to get away with it. Made her crazy.

JESSIE. She really eats okra twice a day? Where does she get it in the winter?

MAMA. Well, she eats it a lot. Maybe not two meals, but . . .

JESSIE. More than the average person.

MAMA (*beginning to get irritated*). I don't know how much okra the average person eats.

JESSIE. Do you know how much okra Agnes eats?

MAMA. No.

JESSIE. How many birds does she have?

MAMA. Two.

JESSIE. Then what are the whistles for?

MAMA. They're not real whistles. Just little plastic ones on a necklace she won playing Bingo, and I only told you about it because I thought I might get a laugh out of you

for once even if it wasn't the truth, Jessie. Things don't have to be true to talk about 'em, you know.

JESSIE. Why won't she come over here?

Mama is suddenly quiet, but the cocoa and milk are in the pan now, so she lights the stove and starts stirring.

MAMA. Well now, what a good idea. We should've had more cocoa. Cocoa is perfect.

JESSIE. Except you don't like milk.

MAMA (*another attempt, but not as energetic*). I hate milk. Coats your throat as bad as okra. Something just downright disgusting about it.

JESSIE. It's because of me, isn't it?

MAMA. No, Jess.

JESSIE. Yes, Mama.

MAMA. O.K. Yes, then, but she's crazy. She's as crazy as they come. She's a lunatic.

JESSIE. What is it exactly? Did I say something, sometime? Or did she see me have a fit and's afraid I might have another one if she came over, or what?

MAMA. I guess.

JESSIE. You guess what? What's she ever said? She must've given you some reason.

MAMA. Your hands are cold.

JESSIE. What difference does that make?

MAMA. "Like a corpse," she says, "and I'm gonna be one soon enough as it is."

JESSIE. That's crazy.

MAMA. That's Agnes. "Jessie's shook the hand of death and I can't take the chance it's catching, Thelma, so I ain't comin 'over, and you can understand or not, but I ain't comin'. I'll come up the driveway, but that's as far as I go."

JESSIE (*laughing, relieved*). I thought she didn't like me! She's scared of me! How about that! Scared of me.

MAMA. I could make her come over here, Jessie. I could call her up right now and she could bring the birds and come visit. I didn't know you ever thought about her at all. I'll tell her she just has to come and she'll come, all right. She owes me one.

JESSIE. No, that's all right. I just wondered about it. When I'm in the hospital, does she come over here?

MAMA. Her kitchen is just a tiny thing. When she comes over here, she feels like . . . (*Toning it down a little.*) Well, we all like a change of scene, don't we?

JESSIE (*playing along*). Sure we do. Plus there's no birds diving around.

MAMA. I hate those birds. She says I don't understand them. What's there to understand about birds?

JESSIE. Why Agnes likes them, for one thing. Why they stay with her when they could be outside with the other birds. What their singing means. How they fly. What they think Agnes is.

MAMA. Why do you have to know so much about things, Jessie? There's just not that much *to* things that I could ever see.

JESSIE. That you could ever *tell*, you mean. You didn't have to lie to me about Agnes.

MAMA. I didn't lie. You never asked before!

JESSIE. You lied about setting fire to all those houses and about how many birds she has and how much okra she eats and why she won't come over here. If I have to keep dragging the truth out of you, this is going to take all night.

MAMA. That's fine with me. I'm not a bit sleepy.

JESSIE. Mama . . .

MAMA. All right. Ask me whatever you want. Here.

They come to an awkward stop, as the cocoa is ready and Mama pours it into the cups Jessie has set on the table.

JESSIE (*as Mama takes her first sip*). Did you love Daddy?

MAMA. No.

JESSIE (*pleased that Mama understands the rules better now*). I didn't think so. Were you really fifteen when you married him?

MAMA. The way he told it? I'm sitting in the mud, he comes along, drags me in the kitchen, "She's been there ever since"?

JESSIE. Yes.

MAMA. No. It was a big fat lie, the whole thing. He just thought it was funnier that way. God, this milk in here.

JESSIE. The cocoa helps.

MAMA (*pleased that they agree on this, at least*). Not enough, though, does it? You can still taste it, can't you?

JESSIE. Yeah, it's pretty bad. I thought it was my memory that was bad, but it's not. It's the milk, all right.

MAMA. It's a real waste of chocolate. You don't have to finish it.

JESSIE (*putting her cup down*). Thanks, though.

MAMA. I should've known not to make it. I knew you wouldn't like it. You never did like it.

JESSIE. You didn't ever love him, or he did something and you stopped loving him, or what?

MAMA. He felt sorry for me. He wanted a plain country woman and that's what he married, and then he held it against me the rest of my life like I was supposed to change and surprise him somehow. Like I remember this one day he was standing on the porch and I told him to get a shirt on and he went in and got one and then he said, real peaceful, but to the point, "You're right, Thelma. If God had meant for people to go around without any clothes on, they'd have been born that way."

JESSIE (*sees Mama's hurt*). He didn't mean anything by that, Mama.

MAMA. He never said a word he didn't have to, Jessie. That was probably all he'd said to me all day, Jessie. So if he said it, there was something to it, but I never did figure that one out. What did that mean?

JESSIE. I don't know. I liked him better than you did, but I didn't know him any better.

MAMA. How could I love him, Jessie. I didn't have a thing he wanted. (*Jessie doesn't answer.*) He got his share,

though. You loved him enough for both of us. You followed him around like some . . . Jessie, all the man ever did was farm and sit . . . and try to think of somebody to sell the farm to.

JESSIE. Or make me a boyfriend out of pipe cleaners and sit back and smile like the stick man was about to dance and wasn't I going to get a kick out of that. Or sit up with a sick cow all night and leave me a chain of sleepy stick elephants on my bed in the morning.

MAMA. Or just sit.

JESSIE. I liked him sitting. Big old faded blue man in the chair. Quiet.

MAMA. Agnes gets more talk out of her birds than I got from the two of you. He could've had that GONE FISHING sign around his neck in that chair. I saw him stare off at the water. I saw him look at the weather rolling in. I got where I could practically see that boat myself. But you, you knew what he was thinking about and you're going to tell me.

JESSIE. I don't know, Mama! His life, I guess. His corn. His boots. Us. Things. You know.

MAMA. No, I don't know, Jessie! You had those quiet little conversations after supper every night. What were you whispering about?

JESSIE. We weren't whispering, you were just across the room.

MAMA. What did you talk about?

JESSIE. We talked about why black socks are warmer than blue socks. Is that something to go tell Mother? You were just jealous because I'd rather talk to him than wash the dishes with you.

MAMA. I was jealous because you'd rather talk to him than anything! (*Jessie reaches across the table for the small clock and starts to wind it.*) If I had died instead of him, he wouldn't have taken you in like I did.

JESSIE. I wouldn't have expected him to.

MAMA. Then what would you have done?

JESSIE. Come visit.

MAMA. Oh, I see. He died and left you stuck with me and you're mad about it.

JESSIE (*getting up from the table*). Not anymore. He didn't mean to. I didn't have to come here. We've been through this.

MAMA. He felt sorry for you, too, Jessie, don't kid yourself about that. He said you were a runt and he said it from the day you were born and he said you didn't have a chance.

JESSIE (*getting the canister of sugar and starting to refill the sugar bowl*). I know he loved me.

MAMA. What if he did? It didn't change anything.

JESSIE. It didn't have to. I miss him.

MAMA. He never really went fishing, you know. Never once. His tackle box was full of chewing tobacco and all he ever did was drive out to the lake and sit in his car. Dawson told me. And Bennie at the bait shop, he told Dawson. They all laughed about it. And he'd come back from fishing and all he'd have to show for it was a . . . a whole pipe cleaner *family*—chickens, pigs, a dog with a bad leg—it was creepy strange. It made me sick to look at them and I hid his pipe cleaners a couple of times but he always had more somewhere.

JESSIE. I thought it might be better for you after he died. You'd get interested in things. Breathe better. Change somehow.

MAMA. Into what? The Queen? A clerk in a shoe store? Why should I? Because he said to? Because you said to? (*Jessie shakes her head.*) Well I wasn't here for his entertainment and I'm not here for yours either, Jessie. I don't know what I'm here for, but then I don't think about it. (*Realizing what all this means.*) But I bet you wouldn't be killing yourself if he were still alive. That's a fine thing to figure out, isn't it?

JESSIE (*filling the honey jar now*). That's not true.

MAMA. Oh no? Then what were you asking about him for? Why did you want to know if I loved him?

JESSIE. I didn't think you did, that's all.

MAMA. Fine then. You were right. Do you feel better now?

JESSIE (*cleaning the honey jar carefully*). It feels good to be right about it.

MAMA. It didn't matter whether I loved him. It didn't matter to me and it didn't matter to him. And it didn't mean we didn't get along. It wasn't important. We didn't talk about it. (*Sweeping the pots off the cabinet.*) Take all these pots out to the porch!

JESSIE. What for?

MAMA. Just leave me this one pan. (*She jerks the silverware drawer open.*) Get me one knife, one fork, one big spoon, and the can opener, and put them out where I can get them. (*Starts throwing knives and forks in one of the pans.*)

JESSIE. Don't do that! I just straightened that drawer!

MAMA (*throwing the pan in the sink*). And throw out all the plates and cups. I'll use paper. Loretta can have what she wants and Dawson can sell the rest.

JESSIE (*calmly*). What are you doing?

MAMA. I'm not going to cook. I never liked it, anyway. I like candy. Wrapped in plastic or coming in sacks. And tuna. I'll eat tuna, thank you.

JESSIE (*taking the pan out of the sink*). What if you want to make apple butter? You can't make apple butter in that little pan. What if you leave carrots on cooking and burn up that pan?

MAMA. I don't like carrots.

JESSIE. What if the strawberries are good this year and you want to go picking with Agnes.

MAMA. I'll tell her to bring a pan. You said you would do whatever I wanted! I don't want a bunch of pans cluttering up my cabinets I can't get down to, anyway. Throw them out. Every last one.

JESSIE (*gathering up the pots*). I'm putting them all back in. I'm not taking them to the porch. If you want them, they'll be here. You'll bend down and get them, like you got the one for the cocoa. And if somebody else comes over here to cook, they'll have something to cook in, and that's the end of it!

MAMA. Who's going to come cook here?

JESSIE. Agnes.

MAMA. In my pots. Not on your life.

JESSIE. There's no reason why the two of you couldn't just live here together. Be cheaper for both of you and somebody to talk to. And if the birds bothered you, well, one day when Agnes is out getting her hair done, you could take them all for a walk!

MAMA (*as Jessie straightens the silverware*). So that's why you're pestering me about Agnes. You think you can rest easy if you get me a new babysitter? Well, I don't want to live with Agnes. I barely want to talk with Agnes. She's just around. We go back, that's all. I'm not letting Agnes near this place. You don't get off as easy as that, child.

JESSIE. O.K., then. It's just something to think about.

MAMA. I don't like things to think about. I like things to go on.

JESSIE (*closing the silverware drawer*). I want to know what Daddy said to you the night he died. You came storming out of his room and said I could wait it out with him if I wanted to, but you were going to watch *Gunsmoke*. What did he say to you?

MAMA. He didn't have *anything* to say to me, Jessie. That's why I left. He didn't say a thing. It was his last chance not to talk to me and he took full advantage of it.

JESSIE (*after a moment*). I'm sorry you didn't love him. Sorry for you, I mean. He seemed like a nice man.

MAMA (*as Jessie walks to the refrigerator*). Ready for your apple now?

JESSIE. Soon as I'm through here, Mama.

MAMA. You won't like the apple, either. It'll be just like the cocoa. You never liked eating at all, did you? Any of it! What have you been living on all these years, toothpaste?

JESSIE (*as she starts to clean out the refrigerator*). Now, you know the milkman comes on Wednesdays and Saturdays, and he leaves the order blank in an egg box, and you give the bills to Dawson once a month.

MAMA. Do they still make that orangeade?

JESSIE. It's not orangeade, it's just orange.

MAMA. I'm going to get some. I thought they stopped making it. You just stopped ordering it.

JESSIE. You should drink milk.

MAMA. Not anymore, I'm not. That hot chocolate was the last. Hooray.

JESSIE (*getting the garbage can from under the sink*). I told them to keep delivering a quart a week no matter what you said. I told them you'd run out of Cokes and you'd have to drink it. I told them I knew you wouldn't pour it on the ground . . .

MAMA (*finishing her sentence*). And you told them you weren't going to be ordering anymore?

JESSIE. I told them I was taking a little holiday and to look after you.

MAMA. And they didn't think something was funny about that? You who doesn't go to the front steps? You, who only sees the driveway looking down from a stretcher passed out cold?

JESSIE (*enjoying this, but not laughing*). They said it was about time, but why didn't I take you with me? And I said I didn't think you'd want to go, and they said, "Yeah, everybody's got their own idea of vacation."

MAMA. I guess you think that's funny.

JESSIE (*pulling jars out of the refrigerator*). You know there never was any reason to call the ambulance for me. All they ever did for me in the emergency room was let me wake up. I could've done that here. Now, I'll just call them out and you say yes or no. I know you like pickles. Ketchup?

MAMA. Keep it.

JESSIE. We've had this since last Fourth of July.

MAMA. Keep the ketchup. Keep it all.

JESSIE. Are you going to drink ketchup from the bottle or what? How can you want your food and not want your pots to cook it in? This stuff will all spoil in here, Mother.

MAMA. Nothing I ever did was good enough for you and I want to know why.

JESSIE. That's not true.

MAMA. And I want to know why you've lived here this long feeling the way you do.

JESSIE. You have no earthly idea how I feel.

MAMA. Well, how could I? You're real far back there, Jessie.

JESSIE. Back where?

MAMA. What's it like over there, where you are? Do people always say the right thing or get whatever they want, or what?

JESSIE. What are you talking about?

MAMA. Why do you read the newspaper? Why don't you wear that sweater I made for you? Do you remember how I used to look, or am I just any old woman now? When you have a fit, do you see stars or what? How did you fall off the horse, really? Why did Cecil leave you? Where did you put my old glasses?

JESSIE (*stunned by Mama's intensity*). They're in the bottom drawer of your dresser in an old Milk of Magnesia box. Cecil left me because he made me choose between him and smoking.

MAMA. Jessie, I know he wasn't that dumb.

JESSIE. I never understood why he hated it so much when it's so good. Smoking is the only thing I know that's always just what you think it's going to be. Just like it was the last time, right there when you want it and real quiet.

MAMA. Your fits made him sick and you know it.

JESSIE. Say seizures, not fits. Seizures.

MAMA. It's the same thing. A seizure in the hospital is a fit at home.

JESSIE. They didn't bother him at all. Except he did feel responsible for it. It *was* his idea to go horseback riding that day. It was his idea I could do *anything* if I just made

up my mind to. I fell off the horse because I didn't know how to hold on. Cecil left for pretty much the same reason.

MAMA. He had a girl, Jessie. I walked right in on them in the toolshed.

JESSIE (*after a moment*). O.K. That's fair. (*Lighting another cigarette.*) Was she very pretty?

MAMA. She was Agnes's girl, Carlene. Judge for yourself.

JESSIE (*as she walks to the living room*). I guess you and Agnes had a good talk about that, huh?

MAMA. I never thought he was good enough for you. They moved here from Tennessee, you know.

JESSIE. What are you talking about? You liked him better than I did. You flirted him out here to build your porch or I'd never even met him at all. You thought maybe he'd help you out around the place, come in and get some coffee and talk to you. God knows what you thought. All that curly hair.

MAMA. He's the best carpenter I ever saw. That little house of yours will still be standing at the end of the world, Jessie.

JESSIE. You didn't need a porch, Mama.

MAMA. All right! I wanted you to have a husband.

JESSIE. And I couldn't get one on my own, of course.

MAMA. How were you going to get a husband never opening your mouth to a living soul?

JESSIE. So I was quiet about it, so what?

MAMA. So I should have let you just sit here? Sit like your daddy? Sit here?

JESSIE. Maybe.

MAMA. Well, I didn't think so.

JESSIE. Well, what did you know?

MAMA. I never said I knew much. How was I supposed to learn anything living out here? I didn't know enough to do half the things I did in my life. Things happen. You do what you can about them and you see what happens next. I married you off to the wrong man, I admit that. So I took you in when he left, I'm sorry.

JESSIE. He wasn't the wrong man.

MAMA. He didn't love you, Jessie, or he wouldn't have left.

JESSIE. He wasn't the wrong man, Mama. I loved Cecil so much. And I tried to get more exercise and I tried to stay awake. I tried to learn to ride a horse. And I tried to stay outside with him, but he always knew I was trying, so it didn't work.

MAMA. He was a selfish man. He told me once he hated to see people move into his houses after he built them. He knew they'd mess them up.

JESSIE. I loved that bridge he built over the creek in back of the house. It didn't have to be anything special, a couple of boards would have been just fine, but he used that yellow pine and rubbed it so smooth . . .

MAMA. He had responsibilities here. He had a wife and son here and he failed you.

JESSIE. Or that baby bed he built for Ricky. I told him he didn't have to spend so much time on it, but he said it had to last, and the thing ended up weighing two hundred pounds and I couldn't move it. I said, "How long does a baby bed have to last, anyway?" But maybe he thought if it was strong enough, it might keep Ricky a baby.

MAMA. Ricky is too much like Cecil.

JESSIE. He is not. Ricky is as much like me as it's possible for any human to be. We even wear the same size pants. These are his, I think.

MAMA. That's just the same size. That's not you're the same person.

JESSIE. I see it on his face. I hear it when he talks. We look out at the world and we see the same thing: Not Fair. And the only difference between us is Ricky's out there trying to get even. And he knows not to trust anybody and he got it straight from me. And he knows not to try to get work, and guess where he got that. He walks around like there's loose boards in the floor, and you know who laid that floor, I did.

MAMA. Ricky isn't through yet. You don't know how he'll turn out!

JESSIE (going back to the kitchen). Yes I do and so did Cecil. Ricky is the two of us together for all time in too small a space. And we're tearing each other apart, like always, inside that boy, and if you don't see it, then you're just blind.

MAMA. Give him time, Jess.

JESSIE. Oh, he'll have plenty of that. Five years for forgery, ten years for armed assault . . .

MAMA (furious). Stop that! (Then pleading.) Jessie, Cecil might be ready to try it again, honey, that happens sometimes. Go downtown. Find him. Talk to him. He didn't know what he had in you. Maybe he sees things different now, but you're not going to know that till you see him. Or call him up! Right now! He might be home.

JESSIE. And say what? Nothing's changed, Cecil, I'd just like to look at you, if you don't mind? No. He loved me, Mama. He just didn't know how things fall down around me like they do. I think he did the right thing. He gave himself another chance, that's all. But I did beg him to take me with him. I did tell him I would leave Ricky and you and everything I loved out here if only he would take me with him, but he couldn't and I understood that. (Pause.) I wrote that note I showed you. I wrote it. Not Cecil. I said "I'm sorry, Jessie, I can't fix it all for you." I said I'd always love me, not Cecil. But that's how he felt.

MAMA. Then he should've taken you with him!

JESSIE (picking up the garbage bag she has filled). Mama, you don't pack your garbage when you move.

MAMA. You will not call yourself garbage, Jessie.

JESSIE (taking the bag to the big garbage can near the back door). Just a way of saying it, Mama. Thinking about my list, that's all. (Opening the can, putting the garbage in, then securing the lid.) Well, a little more than that. I was trying to say it's all right that Cecil left. It was . . . a relief in a way. I never was what he wanted to see, so it was better when he wasn't looking at me all the time.

MAMA. I'll make your apple now.

JESSIE. No thanks. You get the manicure stuff and I'll be right there.

Jessie ties up the big garbage bag in the can and replaces the small garbage bag under the sink, all the time trying desperately to regain her calm. Mama watches, from a distance, her hand reaching unconsciously for the phone. Then she has a better idea. Or rather she thinks of the only other thing left and is willing to try it. Maybe she is even convinced it will work.

MAMA. Jessie, I think your daddy had little . . .

JESSIE (interrupting her). Garbage night is Tuesday. Put it out as late as you can. The Davis's dogs get in it if you don't. (Replacing the garbage bag in the can under the sink.) And keep ordering the heavy black bags. It doesn't pay to buy the cheap ones. And I've got all the ties here with the hammers and all. Take them out of the box as soon as you open a new one and put them in this drawer. They'll get lost if you don't, and rubber bands or something else won't work.

MAMA. I think your daddy had fits, too. I think he sat in his chair and had little fits. I read this a long time ago in a magazine, how little fits go, just little blackouts where maybe their eyes don't even close and people just call them "thinking spells."

JESSIE (getting the slipcover out of the laundry basket). I don't think you want this manicure we've been looking forward to. I washed this cover for the sofa, but it'll take both of us to get it back on.

MAMA. I watched his eyes. I know that's what it was. The magazine said some people don't even know they've had one.

JESSIE. Daddy would've known if he'd had fits, Mama.

MAMA. The lady in this story had kept track of hers and she'd had eighty thousand of them in the last eleven years.

JESSIE. Next time you wash this cover, it'll dry better if you put it on wet.

MAMA. Jessie, listen to what I'm telling you. This lady had anywhere between five and five hundred fits a day and they lasted maybe fifteen seconds apiece, so that out of her life, she'd only lost about two weeks altogether, and she had a full-time secretary job and an IQ of 120.

JESSIE (amused by Mama's approach). You want to talk about the fits, is that it?

MAMA. Yes. I do. I want to say . . .

JESSIE (interrupting). Most of the time I wouldn't even know I'd had one, except I wake up with different clothes on, feeling like I've been run over. Sometimes I feel my head start to turn around or hear myself scream. And sometimes there is this dizzy stupid feeling a little before it, but if the TV's on, well, it's easy to miss.

As Jessie and Mama replace the slipcover on the sofa and the afghan on the chair, the physical struggle somehow mirrors the emotional one in the conversation.

MAMA. I can tell when you're about to have one. Your eyes get this big! But, Jessie, you haven't . . .

JESSIE (*taking charge of this*). What do they look like? The seizures.

MAMA (*reluctant*). Different each time, Jess.

JESSIE. O.K. Pick one, then. A good one. I think I want to know now.

MAMA. There's not much to tell. You just . . . crumple, in a heap, like a puppet and somebody cut the strings all at once, or like the firing squad in some Mexican movie, you just slide down the wall, you know. You don't know what happens? How can you not know what happens?

JESSIE. I'm busy.

MAMA. That's not funny.

JESSIE. I'm not laughing. My head turns around and I fall down and then what?

MAMA. Well, your chest squeezes in and out, and you sound like you're gagging, sucking air in and out like you can't breathe.

JESSIE. Do it for me. Make the sound for me.

MAMA. I will not. It's awful-sounding.

JESSIE. Yeah. It felt like it might be. What's next?

MAMA. Your mouth bites down and I have to get your tongue out of the way fast, so you don't bite yourself.

JESSIE. Or you. I bite you, too, don't I?

MAMA. You got me once real good. I had to get a tetanus! But I know what to watch for now. And then you turn blue and the jerks start up. Like I'm standing there poking you with a cattle prod or you're sticking your finger in a light socket as fast as you can . . .

JESSIE. Foaming like a mad dog the whole time.

MAMA. It's bubbling, Jess, not foam like the washer overflowed, for God's sake; it's bubbling like a baby spitting up. I go get a wet washcloth, that's all. And then the jerks slow down and you wet yourself and it's over. Two minutes tops.

JESSIE. How do I get to bed?

MAMA. How do you think?

JESSIE. I'm too heavy for you now. How do you do it?

MAMA. I call Dawson. But I get you cleaned up before he gets here and I make him leave before you wake up.

JESSIE. You could just leave me on the floor.

MAMA. I want you to wake up someplace nice, O.K.? (*Then making a real effort.*) But, Jessie, and this is the reason I even brought this up! You haven't had a seizure for a solid year. A whole year, do you realize that?

JESSIE. Yeah, the phenobarb's about right now, I guess.

MAMA. You bet it is. You might never have another one, ever! You might be through with it for all time!

JESSIE. Could be.

MAMA. You are. I know you are!

JESSIE. I sure am feeling good. I really am. The double vision's gone and my gums aren't swelling. No rashes or anything. I'm feeling as good as I ever felt in my life. I'm even feeling like worrying or getting mad and I'm not afraid it will start a fit if I do, I just go ahead.

MAMA. Of course you do! You can even scream at me, if you want to. I can take it. You don't have to act like you're just visiting here, Jessie. This is your house, too.

JESSIE. The best part is, my memory's back.

MAMA. Your memory's always been good. When couldn't you remember things? You're always reminding me what . . .

JESSIE. Because I've made lists for everything. But now I remember what things mean on my lists. I see "dish towels," and I used to wonder whether I was supposed to wash them, buy them, or look for them because I wouldn't remember where I put them after I washed them, but now I know it means wrap them up, they're a present for Loretta's birthday.

MAMA (*finished with the sofa now*). You used to go looking for your lists, too, I've noticed that. You always know where they are now! (*Then suddenly worried.*) Loretta's birthday isn't coming up, is it?

JESSIE. I made a list of all the birthdays for you. I even put yours on it. (*A small smile.*) So you can call Loretta and remind her.

MAMA. Let's take Loretta to Howard Johnson's and have those fried clams. I *know* you love that clam roll.

JESSIE (*slight pause*). I won't be here, Mama.

MAMA. What have we just been talking about? You'll be here. You're well, Jessie. You're starting all over. You said it yourself. You're remembering things and . . .

JESSIE. I won't be here. If I'd ever had a year like this, to think straight and all, before now, I'd be gone already.

MAMA (*not pleading, commanding*). No, Jessie.

JESSIE (*folding the rest of the laundry*). Yes, Mama. Once I started remembering, I could see what it all added up to.

MAMA. The fits are over!

JESSIE. It's not the fits, Mama.

MAMA. Then it's me for giving them to you, but I didn't do it!

JESSIE. It's not the fits! You said it yourself, the medicine takes care of the fits.

MAMA (*interrupting*). Your daddy gave you those fits, Jessie. He passed it down to you like your green eyes, and your straight hair. It's not my fault!

JESSIE. So what if he had little fits? It's not inherited. I fell off the horse. It was an accident.

MAMA. The horse wasn't the first time, Jessie. You had a fit when you were five years old.

JESSIE. I did not.

MAMA. You did! You were eating a popsicle and down you went. He gave it to you. It's *his* fault, not mine.

JESSIE. Well, you took your time telling me.

MAMA. How do you tell that to a five-year-old?

917

JESSIE. What did the doctor say?

MAMA. He said kids have them all the time. He said there wasn't anything to do but wait for another one.

JESSIE. But I didn't have another one.

Now there is a real silence.

JESSIE. You mean to tell me I had fits all the time as a kid and you just told me I fell down or something and it wasn't till I had the fit when Cecil was looking that anybody bothered to find out what was the matter with me?

MAMA. It wasn't *all the time*, Jessie. And they changed when you started to school. More like your daddy's. Oh, that was some swell time, sitting here with the two of you turning off and on like light bulbs some nights.

JESSIE. How many fits did I have?

MAMA. You never hurt yourself. I never let you out of my sight. I caught you every time.

JESSIE. But you didn't tell anybody.

MAMA. It was none of their business.

JESSIE. You were ashamed.

MAMA. I didn't want anybody to know. Least of all you.

JESSIE. Least of all me. Oh, right. That was mine to know, Mama, not yours. Did Daddy know?

MAMA. He thought you were . . . you fell down a lot. That's what he thought. You were careless. Or maybe he thought I beat you. I don't know what he thought. He didn't think about it.

JESSIE. Because you didn't tell him!

MAMA. If I told him about you, I'd have to tell him about him!

JESSIE. I don't like this. I don't like this one bit.

MAMA. I didn't think you'd like it. That's why I didn't tell you.

JESSIE. If I'd known I was an epileptic, Mama, I wouldn't have ridden any horses.

MAMA. Make you feel like a freak, is that what I should have done?

JESSIE. Just get the manicure tray and sit down!

MAMA (*throwing it to the floor*). I don't want a manicure!

JESSIE. Doesn't look like you do, no.

MAMA. Maybe I did drop you, you don't know.

JESSIE. If you say you didn't, you didn't.

MAMA (*beginning to break down*). Maybe I fed you the wrong thing. Maybe you had a fever sometime and I didn't know it soon enough. Maybe it's a punishment.

JESSIE. For what?

MAMA. I don't know. Because of how I felt about your father. Because I didn't want any more children. Because I smoked too much or didn't eat right when I was carrying you. It has to be something I did.

JESSIE. It does not. It's just a sickness, not a curse. Epilepsy doesn't mean anything. It just is.

MAMA. I'm not talking about the fits here, Jessie! I'm talking about this killing yourself. It has to be me that's the matter here. You wouldn't be doing this if it wasn't. I didn't

tell you things or I married you off to the wrong man or I took you in and let your life get away from you or all of it put together. I don't know what I did, but I did it, I know. This is all my fault, Jessie, but I don't know what to do about it now!

JESSIE (*exasperated at having to say this again*). It doesn't have anything to do with you!

MAMA. Everything you do has to do with me, Jessie. You can't do *anything*, wash your face or cut your finger, without doing it to me. That's right! You might as well kill me as you, Jessie, it's the same thing. This has to do with me, Jessie.

JESSIE. Then what if it does! What if it has everything to do with you! What if you are all I have and you're not enough? What if I could take all the rest of it if only I didn't have you here? What if the only way I can get away from you for good is to kill myself? What if it is? I can *still* do it!

MAMA (*in desperate tears*). Don't leave me, Jessie! (*Jessie stands for a moment, then turns for the bedroom.*) No! (*She grabs Jessie's arm.*)

JESSIE (*carefully taking her arm away*). I have a box of things I want people to have. I'm just going to go get it for you. You . . . just rest a minute.

Jessie is gone. Mama heads for the telephone, but she can't even pick up the receiver this time and, instead, stoops to clean up the bottles that have spilled out of the manicure tray.

Jessie returns, carrying a box that groceries were delivered in. It probably says Hershey Kisses or Starkist Tuna. Mama is still down on the floor cleaning up, hoping that maybe if she just makes it look nice enough, Jessie will stay.

MAMA. Jessie, how can I live here without you? I need you! You're supposed to tell me to stand up straight and say how nice I look in my pink dress, and drink my milk. You're supposed to go around and lock up so I know we're safe for the night, and when I wake up, you're supposed to be out there making the coffee and watching me get older every day, and you're supposed to help me die when the time comes. I can't do that by myself, Jessie. I'm not like you, Jessie. I hate the quiet and I don't want to die and I don't want you to go, Jessie. How can I . . . (*Has to stop a moment.*) How can I get up every day knowing you had to kill yourself to make it stop hurting and I was here all the time and I never even saw it. And then you gave me this chance to make it better, convince you to stay alive, and I couldn't do it. How can I live with myself after this, Jessie?

JESSIE. I only told you so I could explain it, so you wouldn't blame yourself, so you wouldn't feel bad. There wasn't anything you could say to change my mind. I didn't want you to save me. I just wanted you to know.

MAMA. Stay with me just a little longer. Just a few more years. I don't have that many more to go, Jessie. And as soon as I'm dead, you can do whatever you want. Maybe with me gone, you'll have all the quiet you want, right here in the house. And maybe one day you'll put in some begonias up the walk and get just the right rain for them all summer. And Ricky will be married by then and he'll bring your grandbabies over and you can sneak them a piece of candy when their daddy's not looking and then be real glad when they've gone home and left you to your quiet again.

JESSIE. Don't you see, Mama, everything I do winds up like this. How could I think you would understand? How could I think you would want a manicure? We could hold hands for an hour and then I could go shoot myself? I'm sorry about tonight, Mama, but it's exactly why I'm doing it.

MAMA. If you've got the guts to kill yourself, Jessie, you've got the guts to stay alive.

JESSIE. I know that. So it's really just a matter of where I'd rather be.

MAMA. Look, maybe I can't think of what you should do, but that doesn't mean there isn't something that would help. *You* find it. *You* think of it. You can keep trying. You can get brave and try some more. You don't have to give up!

JESSIE. I'm *not* giving up! This *is* the other thing I'm trying. And I'm sure there are some other things that might work, but *might* work isn't good enough anymore. I need something that *will* work. *This* will work. That's why I picked it.

MAMA. But something might happen. Something that could change everything. Who knows what it might be, but it might be worth waiting for! (*Jessie doesn't respond.*) Try it for two more weeks. We could have more talks like tonight.

JESSIE. No, Mama.

MAMA. I'll pay more attention to you. Tell the truth when you ask me. Let you have your say.

JESSIE. No, Mama! We wouldn't have more talks like tonight, because it's this next part that's made this last part so good, Mama. No, Mama. *This* is how I have my say. This is how I say what I thought about it *all* and I say no. To Dawson and Loretta and the Red Chinese and epilepsy and Ricky and Cecil and you. And me. And hope. I say no! (*Then going to Mama on the sofa.*) Just let me go easy, Mama.

MAMA. How can I let you go?

JESSIE. You can because you have to. It's what you've always done.

MAMA. You are my child!

JESSIE. I am what became of your child. (*Mama cannot answer.*) I found an old baby picture of me. And it was somebody else, not me. It was somebody pink and fat who never heard of sick or lonely, somebody who cried and got fed, and reached up and got held and kicked but didn't hurt anybody, and slept whenever she wanted to, just by closing her eyes. Somebody who mainly just laid there and laughed at the colors waving around over her head and chewed on a polka-dot whale and woke up knowing some new trick nearly every day, and rolled over and drooled on the sheet and felt your hand pulling my quilt back up over me. That's who I started out and this is who is left. (*There is no self-pity here.*) That's what this is about. It's somebody I lost, all right, it's my own self. Who I never was. Or who I tried to be and never got there. Somebody I waited for who never came. And never will. So, see, it doesn't much matter what else happens in the world or in this house, even. I'm what was worth waiting for and I didn't make it. Me . . . who might have made a difference to me . . . I'm not going to show up, so there's no reason to stay, except to keep you company . . . not reason enough because I'm not . . . very good company. (*Pause.*) Am I?

MAMA (*knowing she must tell the truth*). No. And neither am I.

JESSIE. I had this strange little thought, well, maybe it's not so strange. Anyway, after Christmas, after I decided to do this, I would wonder, sometimes, what might keep me here, what might be worth staying for, and you know what it was? It was maybe if there was something I really liked, like maybe if I really liked rice pudding or cornflakes for breakfast or something, that might be enough.

MAMA. Rice pudding is good.

JESSIE. Not to me.

MAMA. And you're not afraid?

JESSIE. Afraid of what?

MAMA. I'm afraid of it, for me, I mean. When my time comes. I know it's coming, but . . .

JESSIE. You don't know when. Like in a scary movie.

MAMA. Yeah, sneaking up on me like some killer on the loose, hiding out in the back yard just waiting for me to have my hands full someday and how am I supposed to protect myself anyhow when I don't know what he looks like and I don't know how he sounds coming up behind me like that or if it will hurt or take very long or what I don't get done before it happens.

JESSIE. You've got plenty of time left.

MAMA. I forget what for, right now.

JESSIE. For whatever happens, I don't know. For the rest of your life. For Agnes burning down one more house or Dawson losing his hair or . . .

MAMA (*quickly*). Jessie. I can't just sit here and say O.K., kill yourself if you want to.

JESSIE. Sure you can. You just did. Say it again.

MAMA (*really startled*). Jessie! (*Quiet horror.*) How dare you! (*Furious.*) How dare you! You think you can just leave whenever you want, like you're watching television here? No, you can't, Jessie. You make me feel like a fool for being alive, child, and you are so wrong! I like it here, and I will stay here until they make me go, until they drag me screaming and I mean screeching into my grave, and you're real smart to get away before then because, I mean, honey, you've never heard noise like that in your life. (*Jessie turns away.*) Who am I talking to? You're gone already, aren't you? I'm looking right through you! I can't stop you because you're already gone! I guess you think they'll all have to talk about you now! I guess you think this will really confuse them. Oh yes, ever since Christmas you've been laughing to yourself and thinking, "Boy, are they all in for a surprise." Well, nobody's going to be a bit surprised, sweetheart. This is just like you. Do it the hard way, that's my girl, all right. (*Jessie gets up and goes into the kitchen, but Mama follows her.*) You know who they're going to feel sorry for? Me! How about that! Not you, me! They're going to be *ashamed* of you. Yes. *Ashamed!* If somebody asks Dawson about it, he'll change the subject as fast as he can. He'll talk about how much he has to pay to park his car these days.

JESSIE. Leave me alone.

MAMA. It's the truth!

JESSIE. I should've just left you a note!

MAMA (*screaming*). Yes! (*Then suddenly understanding what she has said, nearly paralyzed by the thought of it, she turns slowly to face Jessie, nearly whispering.*) No. No. I . . . might not have thought of all the things you've said.

JESSIE. It's O.K., Mama.

Mama is nearly unconscious from the emotional devastation of these last few moments. she sits down at the kitchen table, hurt and angry and desperately afraid. But she looks almost numb. She is so far beyond what is known as pain that she is virtually unreachable and Jessie knows this, and talks quietly, watching for signs of recovery.

JESSIE (*washes her hands in the sink*). I remember you liked that preacher who did Daddy's, so if you want to ask him to do the service, that's O.K. with me.

MAMA (*not an answer, just a word*). What.

JESSIE (*putting on hand lotion as she talks*). And pick some songs you like or let Agnes pick, she'll know exactly which ones. Oh, and I had your dress cleaned that you wore to Daddy's. You looked real good in that.

MAMA. I don't remember, hon.

JESSIE. And it won't be so bad once your friends start coming to the funeral home. You'll probably see people you haven't seen for years, but I thought about what you should say to get you over that nervous part when they first come in.

MAMA (*simply repeating*). Come in.

JESSIE. Take them up to see their flowers, they'd like that. And when they say, "I'm so sorry, Thelma," you just say, "I appreciate your coming, Connie." And then ask how their garden was this summer or what they're doing for Thanksgiving or how their children . . .

MAMA. I don't think I should ask about their children. I'll talk about what they have on, that's always good. And I'll have some crochet work with me.

JESSIE. And Agnes will be there, so you might not have to talk at all.

MAMA. Maybe if Connie Richards does come, I can get her to tell me where she gets that Irish yarn, she calls it. I know it doesn't come from Ireland. I think it just comes with a green wrapper.

JESSIE. And be sure to invite enough people home afterward so you get enough food to feed them all and have some left for you. But don't let anybody take anything home, especially Loretta.

MAMA. Loretta will get all the food set up, honey. It's only fair to let her have some macaroni or something.

JESSIE. No, mama. You have to be more selfish from now on. (*Sitting at the table with Mama.*) Now, somebody's bound to ask you why I did it and you just say you don't know. That you loved me and you know I loved you and we just sat around tonight like every other night of our lives, and then I came over and kissed you and said, " 'Night, Mother," and you heard me close my bedroom door and the next thing you heard was the shot. And whatever reasons I had, well, you guess I just took them with me.

MAMA (*quietly*). It was something personal.

JESSIE. Good. That's good, Mama.

MAMA. That's what I'll say, then.

JESSIE. Personal. Yeah.

MAMA. Is that what I tell Dawson and Loretta, too? We sat around, you kissed me, " 'Night, Mother"? They'll want to know more, Jessie. They won't believe it.

JESSIE. Well, then, tell them what we did. I filled up the candy jars. I cleaned out the refrigerator. We made some hot chocolate and put the cover back on the sofa. You had no idea. All right? I really think it's better that way. If they know we talked about it, they really won't understand how you let me go.

MAMA. I guess not.

JESSIE. It's private. Tonight is private, yours and mine, and I don't want anybody else to have any of it.

MAMA. O.K., then.

JESSIE (*standing behind Mama now, holding her shoulders*). Now, when you hear the shot, I don't want you to come in. First of all, you won't be able to get in by yourself, but I don't want you trying. Call Dawson, then call the police, and then call Agnes. And then you'll need something to do till somebody gets here, so wash the hot-chocolate pan. You wash that pan till you hear the doorbell ring and I don't care if it's an hour, you keep washing that pan.

MAMA. I'll make my calls and then I'll just sit. I won't need something to do. What will the police say?

JESSIE. They'll do that gunpowder test, I guess, and ask you what happened, and by that time, the ambulance will be here and they'll come in and get me and you know how that goes. You stay out here with Dawson and Loretta. You keep Dawson out here. I want the police in the room first, not Dawson, O.K.?

MAMA. What if Dawson and Loretta want me to go home with them?

JESSIE (*returning to the living room*). That's up to you.

MAMA. I think I'll stay here. All they've got is Sanka.

JESSIE. Maybe Agnes could come stay with you for a few days.

MAMA (*standing up, looking into the living room*). I'd rather be by myself, I think. (*Walking toward the box Jessie brought in earlier.*) You want me to give people those things?

JESSIE (*they sit down on the sofa, Jessie holding the box on her lap*). I want Loretta to have my little calculator. Dawson bought it for himself, you know, but then he saw one he liked better and he couldn't bring both of them home with Loretta counting every penny the way she does, so he gave the first one to me. Be funny for her to have it now, don't you think? And all my house slippers are in a sack for her in my closet. Tell her I know they'll fit and I've never worn any of them, and make sure Dawson hears you tell her that. I'm glad he loves Loretta so much, but I wish he knew not everybody has her size feet.

MAMA (*taking the calculator*). O.K.

JESSIE (*reaching into the box again*). This letter is for Dawson, but it's mostly about you, so read it if you want. There's a list of presents for you for at least twenty more Christmases and birthdays, so if you want anything special you better add it to this list before you give it to him. Or if you want to be surprised, just don't read that page. This Christmas, you're getting mostly stuff for the house, like a new rug in your bathroom and needlework, but next Christmas, you're really going to cost him next Christmas. I think you'll like it a lot and you'd never think of it.

MAMA. And you think he'll go for it?

JESSIE. I think he'll feel like a real jerk if he doesn't. Me telling him to, like this and all. Now, this number's where you call Cecil. I called it last week and he answered, so I know he still lives there.

MAMA. What do you want me to tell him?

JESSIE. Tell him we talked about him and I only had good things to say about him, but mainly tell him to find Ricky and tell him what I did, and tell Ricky you have something for him, out here, from me, and to come get it. (*Pulls a sack out of the box.*)

MAMA (*the sack feels empty*). What is it?

JESSIE (*taking it off*). My watch. (*Putting it in the sack and taking a ribbon out of the sack to tie around the top of it.*)

MAMA. He'll sell it!

JESSIE. That's the idea. I appreciate him not stealing it already. I'd like to buy him a good meal.

MAMA. He'll buy dope with it!

JESSIE. Well, then, I hope he gets some good dope with it, Mama. And the rest of this is for you. (*Handing Mama the box now. Mama picks up the things and looks at them.*)

MAMA (*surprised and pleased*). When did you do all this? During my naps, I guess.

JESSIE. I guess. I tried to be quiet about it. (*As Mama is puzzled by the presents.*) Those are just little presents. For whenever you need one. They're not bought presents, just things I thought you might like to look at, pictures or things you think you've lost. Things you didn't know you had, even. You'll see.

MAMA. I'm not sure I want them. They'll make me think of you.

JESSIE. No they won't. They're just things, like a free tube of toothpaste I found hanging on the door one day.

MAMA. Oh. All right, then.

JESSIE. Well, maybe there's one nice present in there somewhere. It's Granny's ring she gave me and I thought you might like to have it, but I didn't think you'd wear it if I gave it to you right now.

MAMA (*taking the box to a table nearby*). No. Probably not. (*Turning back to face her.*) I'm ready for my manicure, I guess. Want me to wash my hands again?

JESSIE (*standing up*). It's time for me to go, Mama.

MAMA (*starting for her*). No, Jessie, you've got all night!

JESSIE (*as Mama grabs her*). No, Mama.

MAMA. It's not even ten o'clock.

JESSIE (*very calm*). Let me go, Mama.

MAMA. I can't. You can't go. You can't do this. You didn't say it would be so soon, Jessie. I'm scared. I love you.

JESSIE (*takes her hands away*). Let go of me, Mama. I've said everything I had to say.

MAMA (*standing still a minute*). You said you wanted to do my nails.

JESSIE (*taking a small step backward*). I can't. It's too late.

MAMA. It's not too late!

JESSIE. I don't want you to wake Dawson and Loretta when you call. I want them to still be up and dressed so they can get right over.

MAMA (*As Jessie backs up, Mama moves in on her, but carefully*). They wake up fast, Jessie, if they have to. They don't matter here, Jessie. You do. I do. We're not through yet. We've got a lot of things to take care of here. I don't know where my prescriptions are and you didn't tell me what to tell Dr. Davis when he calls or how much you want me to tell Ricky or who I call to rake the leaves or . . .

JESSIE. Don't try and stop me, Mama, you can't do it.

MAMA (*grabbing her again, this time hard*). I can too! I'll stand in front of this hall and you can't get past me. (*They struggle.*) You'll have to knock me down to get away from me, Jessie. I'm not about to let you . . .

Mama struggles with Jessie at the door and in the struggle Jessie gets away from her and—

JESSIE (*almost a whisper*). 'Night, Mother. (*She vanishes into her bedroom and we hear the door lock just as Mama gets to it.*)

MAMA (*screams*). Jessie! (*Pounding on the door.*) Jessie, you let me in there. Don't you do this, Jessie. I'm not going to stop screaming until you open this door, Jessie. Jessie! Jessie! What if I don't do any of the things you told me to do! I'll tell Cecil what a miserable man he was to make you feel the way he did and I'll give Ricky's watch to Dawson if I feel like it and the only way you can make sure I do what you want is you come out here and make me, Jessie! (*Pounding again.*) Jessie! Stop this! I didn't know! I was here with you all the time. How could I know you were so alone?

And Mama stops for a moment, breathless and frantic, putting her ear to the door, and when she doesn't hear anything, she stands up straight again and screams once more.

Jessie! Please!

And we hear the shot, and it sounds like an answer, it sounds like No.

Mama collapses against the door, tears streaming down her face, but not screaming anymore. In shock now.

Jessie, Jessie, child . . . Forgive me. (*Pause.*) I thought you were mine.

And she leaves the door and makes her way through the living room, around the furniture, as though she didn't know where it was, not knowing what to do. Finally, she goes to the stove in the kitchen and picks up the hot-chocolate pan and carries it with her to the telephone, and holds on to it while she dials the number. She looks down at the pan, holding it tight like her life depended on it. She hears Loretta answer.

MAMA. Loretta, let me talk to Dawson, honey.

TOPICS FOR CRITICAL THINKING AND WRITING

📖 THE PLAY ON THE PAGE

1. Early in the play, on page 906, Jessie says she wants the gun for "protection." In the context of the entire play, what does this mean?
2. On page 907 Jessie says she would rather use her father's gun than her husband's. Why?
3. Jessie insists (p. 916) that Ricky is like her and not like his father Cecil. Exactly what do you think she is getting at?
4. On page 908 Mama says, "People don't really kill themselves, Jessie. No, mam, doesn't make sense, unless you're retarded or deranged. . . ." Specify the various reasons that Mama assumes are the motives for Jessie's suicide.
5. Most theories of suicide can be classified into one of two groups, psychoanalytical and sociological. Psychoanalytical theories (usually rooted in Freud) assume that human beings have dual impulses, *eros* (life instinct) and *thanatos* (death instinct). When the death instinct, expressed as hostility and aggression, is turned against others, it takes the form of homicide; when it is turned against the self, it takes the form of suicide. Most sociological theories assume that suicide occurs among three types of people: egoistic suicides, people who are excessively individualistic (i.e., who are not integrated into society); altruistic suicides, people who have an excessive sense of duty to society and who die willingly to serve society; and anomic suicides, people who find their usual lifestyles disrupted by sudden social changes such as the loss of a job during an economic depression. Do any of these theories strike you as helpful in explaining Jessie's suicide? Exactly why does Jessie kill herself? (You may want to do some research on suicide by consulting, for instance, Freud, *Civilization and Its Discontents*; or Andrew F. Henry and James F. Short, *Homicide and Suicide*; or Edwin S. Scheidman, ed., *Essays in Self-Destruction*; or A. Alvarez, *The Savage God*.)

6. The greatest tragedies somehow suggest that the tragic figures not only are particular individuals—Oedipus, Lear, and so forth—but also are universal figures who somehow embody our own hopes and fears. Another way of putting it is to say that the greatest plays are not case histories but are visions of a central aspect of life. To what extent do you think '*night, Mother* meets this criterion?

🎭 THE PLAY ON THE STAGE

7. In describing the set, at the start of the play, Marsha Norman emphasizes numerous details, saying, for instance, that "The living room is cluttered with magazines and needlework catalogs, ashtrays, and candy dishes." Do you think the play can be effectively staged without abundant realistic detail? Explain?

8. Although Norman gives abundant stage directions, she cannot indicate how every sentence is to be enacted on the stage. Take a group of a dozen or so speeches—the single lines will do nicely—and describe exactly how you would direct the performers to speak these lines.
9. What well-known actors would you cast in these two roles? Explain your choices.

A CONTEXT FOR 'night MOTHER

Marsha Norman
INTERVIEW

[We reprint part of an interview from an important collection, *Interviews with Contemporary Women Playwrights*, ed. Kathleen Betsko and Rachel Koenig (1987).]

Norman. . . . I'm also always exploring the rules. I want to know which ones are breakable and which ones are not. I'm convinced that there are absolutely unbreakable rules in the theater, and that it doesn't matter how good you are, you can't break them.

Do you care to list them?

Sure. It's real easy, you could put this on the back of a cereal box! You must state the issue at the beginning of the play. The audience must know what is at stake; they must know when they will be able to go home: "This is a story of a little boy who lost his marbles." They must know, when the little boy either gets his marbles back or finds something that is better than his marbles, or kills himself because he can't live without his marbles, that the play will end and they can applaud and go home. He can't *not* care about the marbles. He has to want them with such a passion that you are interested, that you connect to that passion. The theater is all about wanting things that you can or can't have or you do or do not get. Now, the boy himself has to be likable. It has to matter to you whether he gets his marbles or not. The other things—language, structure, et cetera—are variables. One other thing: You can't stop the action for detours. On the way to finding his marbles, the boy can't stop and go swimming. He might do that in a novel, but not in a play.

I like to talk about plays as pieces of machinery. A ski lift. When you get in it, you must feel absolutely secure; you must know that this thing can hold you up. And the first movement of it must be so smooth that whatever residual fears you had about the machine or the mountain are allayed. The journey up the mountain on the ski lift must be continuous. You can't stop and just dangle. If you do, people will realize how far down it is, and they will suddenly get afraid and start grasping the corners of their chairs, which you don't want them to do.

You've said the main character must want something. Is 'night, Mother, then, Thelma's play? It seems that Jessie, the suicidal daughter, has lost all desire.

Well, Jessie certainly doesn't want to have anything more to do with *her* life, but she does want Mama to be able to go on, and that's a very strong desire on Jessie's part. She *wants* Mama to be able to do the wash and know where everything is. She wants Mama to live, and to live free of the guilt that

Mama might have felt had Jessie just left her a note. Jessie's desires are so strong in the piece. The play exists because Jessie wants something for Mama. Then, of course, Mama wants Jessie to stay. So you have two conflicting goals. And at that point it is a real struggle. It might as well be armed warfare. Only very late in the piece do they realize that both goals are achievable given some moderation. What Mama does understand, finally, is that there wasn't anything she could do. And so Jessie does win. Mama certainly loses in the battle to keep her alive, but Mama does gain other things in the course of the evening.

Why doesn't Thelma go a bit further? Why doesn't she attack her daughter physically to prevent the suicide?

Well, there is that final moment at the door, and it posed an interesting dilemma. At that moment in the script, Thelma is reaching for something to hit Jessie with. In the early versions of the script, there was a line that said, "I'll knock you out cold before I'll let you . . ." In my mind I saw Thelma reaching for the frying pan. Like, "I am going to hurt you now. And we will straighten this out when you wake up." [Laughter] Then Tom Moore, the director, pointed out that while it may be tragedy to pick up a frying pan, it is farce when you put it down.

You weren't willing then to risk humor at that point?

Right. And you can't leave Thelma standing there at the door holding the frying pan.

But did you try it that way during rehearsal?

We tried to make the fight as violent as we could. Thelma only has one thing left to try and that is physical harm. But I don't know if the audience ever understands that effort.

Did the fact that you could not demonstrate Thelma's passion in a physical way put more weight on her final verbal plea to Jessie?

The struggle at the door is one of the most difficult moments for both of them. The actress, Anne Pitoniak, as a human being inside that character, realizes she must fight and she must lose.

Does she let go of Jessie in that moment?

Thelma's crucial letting go has occurred earlier in the piece. This fight is pure instinct. This has nothing to do with thinking or feeling, this is just physical. This is that last moment when you realize you're cornered, and you're not going to try to talk to the grizzly bear anymore. . . . She *does* know that she has lost. Jessie is simply too powerful. But that doesn't mean that Thelma is just going to stand there.

The play is due to go to Japan soon, where I believe that suicide is considered a civil right. I should think the audiences there will experience your story very differently than a Western audience.

It's going to be fascinating, isn't it? I thought the same thing. I have no idea. Americans have a life-at-all-costs attitude. It's a very privileged point of view, actually. My sense of *'night, Mother* is that it is, by my own definitions of these words, a play of nearly total triumph. Jessie is able to get what she feels she needs. That is not a despairing act. It may look despairing from the outside, but it has cost her everything she has. If Jessie says it's worth it, then it is.

But suicide is not survival. That's what I'm questioning.

But see, by Jessie's definition of survival, it is. As Jessie says, "My life is all I really have that belongs to me, and I'm going to say what happens to it." . . . Jessie has taken an action on her own behalf that for her is the final test of all that she has been. That's how I see it. Now you don't have to see it that way; nor does anybody else have to see it that way.

Better death with honor than a life of humiliation?

Right. I think that the question the play asks is, "What does it take to survive? What does it take to save your life?" Now Jessie's answer is "It takes killing myself." Mama's answer is "It takes cocoa and marshmallows and doilies and the *TV Guide* and Agnes and the birds and trips to the grocery." Jessie feels, "No, I'm sorry. That's not enough."

THE PLAY IN PERFORMANCE

Norman's *'night, Mother* opened in January 1983 at the American Repertory Theater in Cambridge, Massachusetts, where it received strong reviews. It then went to New York the same year, opening on March 31. *'night, Mother* won the Pulitzer Prize for drama, and in the ensuing years it has been staged in several dozen countries in Europe, Latin America, Africa, and Australia.

Of course, not every review has been favorable. For example, Douglas Watt, reviewing the play in the *New York Daily News* complained that "the final cap-pistol report from behind a bedroom door is as weak as the play's premise," which raises an interesting question in production: How loud should the shot be?

WOMAN. Yokiko.

MAN. That's your name?

WOMAN. It's what you may call me.

MAN. Goodnight, Yokiko. You are very kind.

WOMAN. You are very smart. Goodnight. (*Man exits. Hanako[1] goes to the mat. She tidies it, brushes it off. She goes to the vase. She picks up the flowers, studies them. She carries them out of the room with her. Man re-enters. He takes off his outer clothing. He glimpses the spot where the vase used to sit. He reaches into his clothing, pulls out the stolen flower. He studies it. He puts it underneath his head as he lies down to sleep, like a pillow. He starts to fall asleep. Suddenly, a start. He picks up his head. He listens.*)

SCENE 2. *Dawn. Man is getting dressed. Woman enters with food.*

WOMAN. Good morning.

MAN. Good morning, Yokiko.

WOMAN. You weren't planning to leave?

MAN. I have quite a distance to travel today.

WOMAN. Please. (*She offers him food.*)

MAN. Thank you.

WOMAN. May I ask where you're travelling to?

MAN. It's far.

WOMAN. I know this region well.

MAN. Oh? Do you leave the house often?

WOMAN. I used to. I used to travel a great deal. I know the region from those days.

MAN. You probably wouldn't know the place I'm headed.

WOMAN. Why not?

MAN. It's new. A new village. It didn't exist in "those days." (*Pause.*)

WOMAN. I thought you said you wouldn't deceive me.

MAN. I didn't. You don't believe me, do you?

WOMAN. No.

MAN. Then I didn't deceive you. I'm travelling. That much is true.

WOMAN. Are you in such a hurry?

MAN. Travelling is a matter of timing. Catching the light. (*Woman exits; Man finishes eating, puts down his bowl. Woman re-enters with the vase of flowers.*) Where did you find those? They don't grow native around these parts, do they?

WOMAN. No; they've all been brought in. They were brought in by visitors. Such as yourself. They were left here. In my custody.

MAN. But—they look so fresh, so alive.

WOMAN. I take care of them. They remind me of the people and places outside this house.

MAN. May I touch them?

WOMAN. Certainly.

MAN. These have just blossomed.

WOMAN. No; they were in bloom yesterday. If you'd noticed them before, you would know that.

MAN. You must have received these very recently. I would guess—within five days.

WOMAN. I don't know. But I wouldn't trust your estimate. It's all in the amount of care you show to them. I create a world which is outside the realm of what you know.

MAN. What do you do?

WOMAN. I can't explain. Words are too inefficient. It takes hundreds of words to describe a single act of caring. With hundreds of acts, words become irrelevant. (*Pause.*) But perhaps you can stay.

MAN. How long?

WOMAN. As long as you'd like.

MAN. Why?

WOMAN. To see how I care for them.

MAN. I *am* tired.

WOMAN. Rest.

MAN. The light?

WOMAN. It will return.

SCENE 3. *Man is carrying chopped wood. He is stripped to the waist. Woman enters.*

WOMAN. You're very kind to do that for me.

MAN. I enjoy it, you know. Chopping wood. It's clean. No questions. You take your axe, you stand up the log, you aim—pow!—you either hit it or you don't. Success or failure.

WOMAN. You seem to have been very successful today.

MAN. Why shouldn't I be? It's a beautiful day. I can see to those hills. The trees are cool. The sun is gentle. Ideal. If a man can't be successful on a day like this, he might as well kick the dust up into his own face. (*Man notices Woman staring at him. Man pats his belly, looks at her.*) Protection from falls.

WOMAN. What? (*Man pinches his belly, showing some fat.*) Oh. Don't be silly. (*Man begins slapping the fat on his belly to a rhythm.*)

MAN. Listen—I can make music—see?—that wasn't always possible. But now—that I've developed this—whenever I need entertainment.

WOMAN. You shouldn't make fun of your body.

MAN. Why not? I saw you. You were staring.

WOMAN. I wasn't making fun. (*Man inflates his cheeks.*) I was just—stop that!

MAN. Then why were you staring?

WOMAN. I was—

MAN. Laughing?

WOMAN. No.

MAN. Well?

WOMAN. I was—Your body. It's . . . strong. (*Pause.*)

MAN. People say that. But they don't know. I've heard that age brings wisdom. That's a laugh. The years don't accumulate here. They accumulate here. (*Pause; he pinches his*

[1]**Hanako** the woman

David Henry Hwang

belly.) But today is a day to be happy, right? The woods. The sun. Blue. It's a happy day. I'm going to chop wood.

WOMAN. There's nothing left to chop. Look.

MAN. Oh. I guess . . . that's it.

WOMAN. Sit. Here.

MAN. But—

WOMAN. There's nothing left. (*Man sits; Woman stares at his belly.*) Learn to love it.

MAN. Don't be ridiculous.

WOMAN. Touch it.

MAN. It's flabby.

WOMAN. It's strong.

MAN. It's weak.

WOMAN. And smooth.

MAN. Do you mind if I put on my shirt?

WOMAN. Of course not. Shall I get it for you?

MAN. No. No. Just sit there. (*Man starts to put on his shirt. He pauses, studies his body.*) You think it's cute, huh?

WOMAN. I think you should learn to love it. (*Man pats his belly, talks to it.*)

MAN (*to belly*). You're okay, sir. You hang onto my body like a great horseman.

WOMAN. Not like that.

MAN (*Ibid.*). You're also faithful. You'll never leave me for another man.

WOMAN. No.

MAN. What do you want me to say? (*Woman walks over to Man. She touches his belly with her hand. They look at each other.*)

SCENE 4. *Night. Man is alone. Flowers are gone from stand. Mat is unrolled. Man lies on it, sleeping. Suddenly, he starts. He lifts up his head. He listens. Silence. He goes back to sleep. Another start. He lifts up his head, strains to hear. Slowly, we begin to make out the strains of a single shakuhachi[2] playing a haunting line. It is very soft. He strains to hear it. The instrument slowly fades out. He waits for it to return, but it does not. He takes out the stolen flower. He stares into it.*

SCENE 5. *Day. Woman is cleaning, while Man relaxes. She is on her hands and knees, scrubbing. She is dressed in a simple outfit, for working. Her hair is tied back. Man is sweating. He has not, however, removed his shirt.*

MAN. I heard your playing last night.

WOMAN. My playing?

MAN. *Shakuhachi.*

WOMAN. Oh.

MAN. You played very softly. I had to strain to hear it. Next time, don't be afraid. Play out. Fully. Clear. It must've been very beautiful, if only I could've heard it clearly. Why don't you play for me sometime?

[2]**shakuhachi** a Japanese bamboo flute

928

WOMAN. I'm very shy about it.

MAN. Why?

WOMAN. I play for my own satisfaction. That's all. It's something I developed on my own. I don't know if it's at all acceptable by outside standards.

MAN. Play for me. I'll tell you.

WOMAN. No; I'm sure you're too knowledgeable in the arts.

MAN. Who? Me?

WOMAN. You being from the city and all.

MAN. I'm ignorant, believe me.

WOMAN. I'd play, and you'd probably bite your cheek.

MAN. Ask me a question about music. Any question. I'll answer incorrectly. I guarantee it.

WOMAN. Look at this.

MAN. What?

WOMAN. A stain.

MAN. Where?

WOMAN. Here? See? I can't get it out.

MAN. Oh. I hadn't noticed it before.

WOMAN. I notice it every time I clean.

MAN. Here. Let me try.

WOMAN. Thank you.

MAN. Ugh. It's tough.

WOMAN. I know.

MAN. How did it get here?

WOMAN. It's been there as long as I've lived here.

MAN. I hardly stand a chance. (*Pause.*) But I'll try. Uh—one—two—three—four! One—two—three—four! See, you set up . . . gotta set up . . . a rhythm—two—three—four. Like fighting! Like battle! One—two—three—four! Used to practice with a rhythm . . . beat . . . battle! Yes! (*The stain starts to fade away.*) Look—it's—yes!—whoo!—there it goes—got the sides—the edges—yes!—fading quick—fading away—ooo—here we come—towards the center—to the heart—two—three—four—slow—slow death—tough—dead! (*Man rolls over in triumphant laughter.*)

WOMAN. Dead.

MAN. I got it! I got it! Whoo! A little rhythm! All it took! Four! Four!

WOMAN. Thank you.

MAN. I didn't think I could do it—but there—it's gone—I did it!

WOMAN. Yes. You did.

MAN. And you—you were great.

WOMAN. No—I was carried away.

MAN. We were a team! You and me!

WOMAN. I only provided encouragement.

MAN. You were great! You were! (*Man grabs Woman. Pause.*)

WOMAN. It's gone. Thank you. Would you like to hear me play *shakuhachi*?

MAN. Yes I would.

WOMAN. I don't usually play for visitors. It's so . . . I'm not sure. I developed it—all by myself—in times when I was alone. I heard nothing—no human voice. So I learned to play *shakuhachi*. I tried to make these sounds resemble the human voice. The *shakuhachi* became my weapon. To ward off the air. It kept me from choking on many a silent evening.

MAN. I'm here. You can hear my voice.

WOMAN. Speak again.

MAN. I will.

SCENE 6. *Night. Man is sleeping. Suddenly, a start. He lifts his head up. He listens. Silence. He strains to hear. The shakuhachi melody rises up once more. This time, however, it becomes louder and more clear than before. He gets up. He cannot tell from what direction the music is coming. He walks around the room, putting his ear to different places in the wall, but he cannot locate the sound. It seems to come from all directions at once, as omnipresent as the air. Slowly, he moves towards the wall with the sliding panel through which the Woman enters and exits. He puts his ear against it, thinking the music may be coming from there. Slowly, he slides the door open just a crack, ever so carefully. He peeks through the crack. As he peeks through, the Upstage wall of the set becomes transparent, and through the scrim, we are able to see what he sees. Woman is Upstage of the scrim. She is tending a room filled with potted and vased flowers of all variety. The lushness and beauty of the room Upstage of the scrim stands out in stark contrast to the barrenness of the main set. She is also transformed. She is a young woman. She is beautiful. She wears a brightly colored kimono. Man observes this scene for a long time. He then slides the door shut. The scrim returns to opaque. The music continues. He returns to his mat. He picks up the stolen flower. It is brown and wilted, dead. He looks at it. The music slowly fades out.*

SCENE 7. *Morning. Man is half-dressed. He is practicing sword maneuvers. He practices with the feel of a man whose spirit is willing, but the flesh is inept. He tries to execute deft movements, but is dissatisfied with his efforts. He curses himself, and returns to basic exercises. Suddenly, he feels something buzzing around his neck—a mosquito. He slaps his neck, but misses it. He sees it flying near him. He swipes at it with his sword. He keeps missing. Finally, he thinks he's hit it. He runs over, kneels down to recover the fallen insect. He picks up two halves of a mosquito on two different fingers. Woman enters the room. She looks as she normally does. She is carrying a vase of flowers, which she places on its shelf.*

MAN. Look.

WOMAN. I'm sorry?

MAN. Look.

WOMAN. What? (*He brings over the two halves of mosquito to show her.*)

MAN. See?

WOMAN. Oh.

MAN. I hit it—chop!

WOMAN. These are new forms of target practice?

MAN. Huh? Well—yes—in a way.

WOMAN. You seem to do well at it.

MAN. Thank you. For last night. I heard your *shakuhachi*. It was very loud, strong—good tone.

WOMAN. Did you enjoy it? I wanted you to enjoy it. If you wish, I'll play it for you every night.

MAN. Every night!

WOMAN. If you wish.

MAN. No—I don't—I don't want you to treat me like a baby.

WOMAN. What? I'm not.

MAN. Oh, yes. Like a baby. Who you must feed in the middle of the night or he cries. Waaah! Waaah!

WOMAN. Stop that!

MAN. You need your sleep.

WOMAN. I don't mind getting up for you. (*Pause.*) I would enjoy playing for you. Every night. While you sleep. It will make me feel—like I'm shaping your dreams. I go through long stretches when there is no one in my dreams. It's terrible. During those times, I avoid my bed as much as possible. I paint. I weave. I play *shakuhachi*. I sit on mats and rub powder into my face. Anything to keep from facing a bed with no dreams. It is like sleeping on ice.

MAN. What do you dream of now?

WOMAN. Last night—I dreamt of you. I don't remember what happened. But you were very funny. Not in a mocking way. I wasn't laughing at you. But you made me laugh. And you were very warm. I remember that. (*Pause.*) What do you remember about last night?

MAN. Just your playing. That's all. I got up, listened to it, and went back to sleep. (*Man gets up, resumes practicing with his sword.*)

WOMAN. Another mosquito bothering you?

MAN. Just practicing. Ah! Weak! Too weak! I tell you, it wasn't always like this. I'm telling you, there were days when I could chop the fruit from a tree without ever taking my eyes off the ground. (*He continues practicing.*) You ever use one of these?

WOMAN. I've had to pick one up, yes.

MAN. Oh?

WOMAN. You forget—I live alone—out here—there is . . . not much to sustain me but what I manage to learn myself. It wasn't really a matter of choice.

MAN. I used to be very good, you know. Perhaps I can give you some pointers.

WOMAN. I'd really rather not.

MAN. C'mon—a woman like you—you're absolutely right. You need to know how to defend yourself.

WOMAN. As you wish.

MAN. Do you have something to practice with?

WOMAN. Yes. Excuse me. (*She exits. He practices more. She re-enters with two wooden sticks. He takes one of them.*) Will these do?

MAN. Nice. Now, show me what you can do.

WOMAN. I'm sorry?

MAN. Run up and hit me.

WOMAN. Please.

MAN. Go on—I'll block it.

WOMAN. I feel so . . . undignified.

MAN. Go on. (*She hits him playfully with stick.*) Not like that!

WOMAN. I'll try to be gentle.

MAN. What?

WOMAN. I don't want to hurt you.

MAN. You won't—Hit me! (*Woman charges at Man, quickly, deftly. She scores a hit.*) Oh!

WOMAN. Did I hurt you?

MAN. No—you were—let's try that again. (*They square off again. Woman rushes forward. She appears to attempt a strike. He blocks that apparent strike, which turns out to be a feint. She scores.*) Huh?

WOMAN. Did I hurt you? I'm sorry.

MAN. No.

WOMAN. I hurt you.

MAN. No.

WOMAN. Do you wish to hit me?

MAN. No.

WOMAN. Do you want me to try again?

MAN. No.

WOMAN. Thank you.

MAN. Just practice there—by yourself—let me see you run through some maneuvers.

WOMAN. Must I?

MAN. Yes! Go! (*She goes to an open area.*) My greatest strength was always as a teacher. (*Woman executes a series of deft movements. Her whole manner is transformed. Man watches with increasing amazement. Her movements end. She regains her submissive manner.*)

WOMAN. I'm so embarrassed. My skills—they're so—inappropriate. I look like a man.

MAN. Where did you learn that?

WOMAN. There is much time to practice here.

MAN. But you—the techniques.

WOMAN. I don't know what's fashionable in the outside world. (*Pause.*) Are you unhappy?

MAN. No.

WOMAN. Really?

MAN. I'm just . . . surprised.

WOMAN. You think it's unbecoming for a woman.

MAN. No, no. Not at all.

WOMAN. You want to leave.

MAN. No!

WOMAN. All visitors do. I know. I've met many. They say they'll stay. And they do. For a while. Until they see too much. Or they learn something new. There are boundaries outside of which visitors do not want to see me step. Only who knows what those boundaries are? Not I. They change with every visitor. You have to be careful not to cross them, but you never know where they are. And one day, inevitably, you step outside the lines. The visitor knows.

You don't. You didn't know that you'd done anything different. You thought it was just another part of you. The visitor sneaks away. The next day, you learn that you had stepped outside his heart. I'm afraid you've seen too much.

MAN. There are stories.

WOMAN. What?

MAN. People talk.

WOMAN. Where? We're two days from the nearest village.

MAN. Word travels.

WOMAN. What are you talking about?

MAN. There are stories about you. I heard them. They say that your visitors never leave this house.

WOMAN. That's what you heard?

MAN. They say you imprison them.

WOMAN. Then you were a fool to come here.

MAN. Listen.

WOMAN. Me? Listen? You. Look! Where are these prisoners? Have you seen any?

MAN. They told me you were very beautiful.

WOMAN. Then they are blind as well as ignorant.

MAN. You are.

WOMAN. What?

MAN. Beautiful.

WOMAN. Stop that! My skin feels like seaweed.

MAN. I didn't realize it at first. I must confess—I didn't. But over these few days—your face has changed for me. The shape of it. The feel of it. The color. All changed. I look at you now, and I'm no longer sure you are the same woman who had poured tea for me just a week ago. And because of that I remembered—how little I know about a face that changes in the night. (*Pause.*) Have you heard those stories?

WOMAN. I don't listen to old wives' tales.

MAN. But have you heard them?

WOMAN. Yes. I've heard them. From other visitors—young—hotblooded—or old—who came here because they were told great glory was to be had by killing the witch in the woods.

MAN. I was told that no man could spend time in this house without falling in love.

WOMAN. Oh? So why did you come? Did you wager gold that you could come out untouched? The outside world is so flattering to me. And you—are you like the rest? Passion passing through your heart so powerfully that you can't hold onto it?

MAN. No! I'm afraid!

WOMAN. Of what?

MAN. Sometimes—when I look into the flowers, I think I hear a voice—from inside—a voice beneath the petals. A human voice.

WOMAN. What does it say? "Let me out"?

MAN. No. Listen. It hums. It hums with the peacefulness of one who is completely imprisoned.

WOMAN. I understand that if you listen closely enough, you can hear the ocean.

MAN. No. Wait. Look at it. See the layers? Each petal—hiding the next. Try and see where they end. You can't. Follow them down, further down, around—and as you come down—faster and faster—the breeze picks up. The breeze becomes a wail. And in that rush of air—in the silent midst of it—you can hear a voice.

WOMAN (*Woman grabs flower from Man*). So, you believe I water and prune my lovers? How can you be so foolish? (*She snaps the flower in half, at the stem. She throws it to the ground.*) Do you come only to leave again? To take a chunk of my heart, then leave with your booty on your belt, like a prize? You say that I imprison hearts in these flowers? Well, bits of my heart are trapped with travellers across this land. I can't even keep track. So kill me. If you came here to destroy a witch, kill me now. I can't stand to have it happen again.

MAN. I won't leave you.

WOMAN. I believe you. (*She looks at the flower that she has broken, bends to pick it up. He touches her. They embrace.*)

SCENE 8. *Day. Woman wears a simple undergarment, over which she is donning a brightly colored kimono, the same one we saw her wearing Upstage of the scrim. Man stands apart.*

WOMAN. I can't cry. I don't have the capacity. Right from birth, I didn't cry. My mother and father were shocked. They thought they'd given birth to a ghost, a demon. Sometimes I've thought myself that. When great sadness has welled up inside me, I've prayed for a means to release the pain from my body. But my prayers went unanswered. The grief remained inside me. It would sit like water, still. (*Pause; she models her kimono.*) Do you like it?

MAN. Yes, it's beautiful.

WOMAN. I wanted to wear something special today.

MAN. It's beautiful. Excuse me. I must practice.

WOMAN. Shall I get you something?

MAN. No.

WOMAN. Some tea, maybe?

MAN. No. (*Man resumes swordplay.*)

WOMAN. Perhaps later today—perhaps we can go out—just around here. We can look for flowers.

MAN. All right.

WOMAN. We don't have to.

MAN. No. Let's.

WOMAN. I just thought if—

MAN. Fine. Where do you want to go?

WOMAN. There are very few recreational activities around here, I know.

MAN. All right. We'll go this afternoon. (*Pause.*)

WOMAN. Can I get you something?

MAN (*turning around*). What?

WOMAN. You might be—

MAN. I'm not hungry or thirsty or cold or hot.

WOMAN. Then what are you?

MAN. Practicing. (*Man resumes practicing; Woman exits. As soon as she exits, he rests. He sits down. He examines his*

sword. *He runs his finger along the edge of it. He takes the tip, runs it against the soft skin under his chin. He places the sword on the ground with the tip pointed directly upwards. He keeps it from falling by placing the tip under his chin. He experiments with different degrees of pressure. Woman re-enters. She sees him in this precarious position. She jerks his head upward; the sword falls.*)

WOMAN. Don't do that!

MAN. What?

WOMAN. You can hurt yourself!

MAN. I was practicing!

WOMAN. You were playing!

MAN. I was practicing!

WOMAN. It's dangerous.

MAN. What do you take me for—a child?

WOMAN. Sometimes wise men do childish things.

MAN. I knew what I was doing!

WOMAN. It scares me.

MAN. Don't be ridiculous. (*He reaches for the sword again.*)

WOMAN. Don't! Don't do that!

MAN. Get back! (*He places the sword back in its previous position, suspended between the floor and his chin, upright.*)

WOMAN. But—

MAN. Sssssh!

WOMAN. I wish—

MAN. Listen to me! The slightest shock, you know—the slightest shock—surprise—it might make me jerk or—something—and then . . . so you must be perfectly still and quiet.

WOMAN. But I—

MAN. Sssssh! (*Silence.*) I learned this exercise from a friend—I can't even remember his name—good swordsman—many years ago. He called it his meditation position. He said, like this, he could feel the line between this world and the others because he rested on it. If he saw something in another world that he liked better, all he would have to do is let his head drop, and he'd be there. Simple. No fuss. One day, they found him with the tip of his sword run clean out the back of his neck. He was smiling. I guess he saw something he liked. Or else he'd fallen asleep.

WOMAN. Stop that.

MAN. Stop what?

WOMAN. Tormenting me.

MAN. I'm not.

WOMAN. Take it away!

MAN. You don't have to watch, you know.

WOMAN. Do you want to die that way—an accident?

MAN. I was doing this before you came in.

WOMAN. If you do, all you need to do is tell me.

MAN. What?

WOMAN. I can walk right over. Lean on the back of your head.

MAN. Don't try to threaten—

WOMAN. Or jerk your sword up.

MAN. Or scare me. You can't threaten—

WOMAN. I'm not. But if that's what you want.

MAN. You can't threaten me. You wouldn't do it.

WOMAN. Oh?

MAN. Then I'd be gone. You wouldn't let me leave that easily.

WOMAN. Yes, I would.

MAN. You'd be alone.

WOMAN. No. I'd follow you. Forever. (*Pause.*) Now, let's stop this nonsense.

MAN. No! I can do what I want! Don't come any closer!

WOMAN. Then release your sword.

MAN. Come any closer and I'll drop my head.

WOMAN (*Woman slowly approaches Man. She grabs the hilt of the sword. She looks into his eyes. She pulls it out from under his chin.*) There will be no more of this. (*She exits with the sword. He starts to follow her, then stops. He touches under his chin. On his finger, he finds a drop of blood.*)

SCENE 9. *Night. Man is leaving the house. He is just about out, when he hears a shakuhachi playing. He looks around, trying to locate the sound. Woman appears in the doorway to the outside. Shakuhachi slowly fades out.*

WOMAN. It's time for you to go?

MAN. Yes. I'm sorry.

WOMAN. You're just going to sneak out? A thief in the night? A frightened child?

MAN. I care about you.

WOMAN. You express it strangely.

MAN. I leave in shame because it is proper. (*Pause.*) I came seeking glory.

WOMAN. To kill me? You can say it. You'll be surprised at how little I blanche. As if you'd said, "I came for a bowl of rice," or "I came seeking love" or "I came to kill you."

MAN. Weakness. All weakness. Too weak to kill you. Too weak to kill myself. Too weak to do anything but sneak away in shame. (*Woman brings out Man's sword.*)

WOMAN. Were you even planning to leave without this? (*He takes sword.*) Why not stay here?

MAN. I can't live with someone who's defeated me.

WOMAN. I never thought of defeating you. I only wanted to take care of you. To make you happy. Because that made me happy and I was no longer alone.

MAN. You defeated me.

WOMAN. Why do you think that way?

MAN. I came here with a purpose. The world was clear. You changed the shape of your face, the shape of my heart—rearranged everything—created a world where I could do nothing.

WOMAN. I only tried to care for you.

MAN. I guess that was all it took. (*Pause.*)

WOMAN. You still think I'm a witch. Just because old women gossip. You are so cruel. Once you arrived, there were only two possibilities: I would die or you would leave. (*Pause.*) If you believe I'm a witch, then kill me. Rid the province of one more evil.

MAN. I can't—

WOMAN. Why not? If you believe that about me, then it's the right thing to do.

MAN. You know I can't.

WOMAN. Then stay.

MAN. Don't try and force me.

WOMAN. I won't force you to do anything. (*Pause.*) All I wanted was an escape—for both of us. The sound of a human voice—the simplest thing to find, and the hardest to hold onto. This house—my loneliness is etched into the walls. Kill me, but don't leave. Even in death, my spirit would rest here and be comforted by your presence.

MAN. Force me to stay.

WOMAN. I won't. (*Man starts to leave.*) Beware.

MAN. What?

WOMAN. The ground on which you walk is weak. It could give way at any moment. The crevice beneath is dark.

MAN. Are you talking about death? I'm ready to die.

WOMAN. Fear for what is worse than death.

MAN. What?

WOMAN. Falling. Falling through the darkness. Waiting to hit the ground. Picking up speed. Waiting for the ground. Falling faster. Falling alone. Waiting. Falling. Waiting. Falling.

(*Woman wails and runs out through the door to her room. Man stands, confused, not knowing what to do. He starts to follow her, then hesitates, and rushes out the door to the outside. Silence. Slowly, he re-enters from the outside. He looks for her in the main room. He goes slowly towards the panel to her room. He throws down his sword. He opens the panel. He goes inside. He comes out. He unrolls his mat. He sits on it, cross-legged. He looks out into space. He notices near him a shakuhachi. He picks it up. He begins to blow into it. He tries to make sounds. He continues trying through the end of the play. The Upstage scrim lights up. Upstage, we see the Woman. She is young. She is hanging from a rope suspended from the roof. She has hung herself. Around her are scores of vases with flowers in them whose blossoms have been blown off. Only the stems remain in the vases. Around her swirl the thousands of petals from the flowers. They fill the Upstage scrim area like a blizzard of color. Man continues to attempt to play. Lights fade to black.*)

TOPICS FOR CRITICAL THINKING AND WRITING

 THE PLAY ON THE PAGE

1. Choose one speech (or stage direction) that seems to you to encapsulate the meaning of the play. Explain the reasons for your choice.
2. Why has the man come to this house? Propose several reasons, some practical and some philosophical.
3. What do you make of the title?
4. Do you think there is a point in the play at which you sense a turning in the relationship between the man and the woman? If so, cite the exact words and the reasons you have selected them.

THE PLAY ON THE STAGE

7. If you were the costume director, in what colors would you dress the man and the woman?
8. Referring only to Scene 1, make a list of all the traits of the man that you can deduce from his words, actions, or other determinants (for instance, the fact that it is he who speaks first); make a similar list for the woman. Then go through Scene 1 again, and indicate any place—the exact word—where you believe the two performers should make eye contact. Explain your reasons. If you believe there should be no eye contact at all, explain this decision.
9. One group of students discussing *The Sound of a Voice*

5. In Scene 9 the man contradicts himself. In response to the woman's pleas for him to stay, he says, "Don't try and force me!" And a moment later, he asks her, "Force me to stay." Provide a psychological analysis for this contradiction.
6. If you think the play is a parable, provide an interpretation of the ending.

had a heated debate over the look of the vase (its shape, texture, dimensions, color, etc.) and the kind of flowers. What seems "right" to you? Why?
10. What well-known (or more easily obtained) musical instrument would you substitute for a *shakuhatchi*? Why?
11. Assume that you are directing a production of *The Sound of a Voice* in a theater-in-the-round that seats two hundred. Provide line-by-line blocking for Scene 7.
12. David Henry Hwang describes the setting as "a remote corner of a forest." Would you advise a set designer to indicate the forest? Why? How? If not, why not?

A CONTEXT FOR *THE SOUND OF A VOICE*

David Henry Hwang
THOUGHTS ABOUT "ETHNIC THEATER"

[On June 28, 1989, Jean W. Ross interviewed David Henry Hwang on behalf of *Contemporary Authors*.]

CA: *You told Jeremy Gerard for the* New York Times *Magazine that when you were growing up, you thought being Chinese was "a minor detail, like having red hair." How did you begin to feel otherwise and to start exploring your heritage?*

Hwang: A lot of that happened in college. I was in college in the mid- to late 1970s, and whereas most people seem to associate collegiate life in the seventies with [actor] John Travolta, there was at that time a third-world consciousness, a third-world power movement, in the universities, particularly among Hispanics and Asians. The blacks really started it in the late sixties and early seventies, and it took a while

to trickle down into the other third-world communities. Asians probably picked it up last; we got interested in the late seventies, when many of the other ethnic communities had become less politicized. I think my political consciousness, such as it is, evolved out of that third-world, Marxist setting at the university. While I was never a very ardent Marxist, I studied the ideas and I was interested in the degree to which we all may have been affected by certain prejudices in the society without having realized it, and to what degree we had incorporated that into our persons by the time we'd reached our early twenties.

The other thing that I think fascinated me about exploring my Chineseness at that time was consistent with my interest in playwriting. I had become very interested in Sam Shepard, particularly in the way in which Shepard likes to create a sort of American mythology. In his case it's the cowboy mythology, but nonetheless it's something that is larger than simply our present-day, fast-food existence. In my context, creating a mythology, creating a past for myself, involved going into Chinese history and Chinese-American history. I think the combination of wanting to delve into those things for artistic reasons and being exposed to an active third-world-consciousness movement was what started to get me interested in my roots when I was in college.

You've told earlier interviewers how the amazing true story of a French diplomat and his Chinese lover, a Beijing Opera star who turned out to be a man, called to your mind the Puccini opera Madama Butterfly *and became your award-winning play* M. Butterfly. *Earlier you had felt some concern about "riding the hyphen," as Jeremy Gerard titled his article—becoming stereotyped as a Chinese-American writer. Has* M. Butterfly *helped you overcome that worry to some extent?*

I first became aware of the simplistic nature of this stereotyping when I did the two Japanese plays *The Sound of a Voice* and *The House of Sleeping Beauties.* I thought this work was a departure because these were the first plays I'd written that didn't deal with being Chinese-American, with race and assimilation; I felt that they were really tragic love stories. Yet they were not perceived as being a departure, because they had Asian actors. So I realized that the stereotyping is based on the color of the actors. . . .

I wonder if there will come a time when the expression "ethnic theater" won't have any meaning.

I'm hopeful that there will be a time at some point, but I think it's going to be fifty years or so down the road. The whole idea of being ethnic only applies when it's clear what the dominant culture is. Once it becomes less clear and the culture is acknowledged to be more multicultural, then the idea of what's ethnic becomes irrelevant. I think even today we're starting to see that. The mono-ethnic theaters—that is, the Asian theaters, the black theaters, the Hispanic theaters—are really useful; they serve a purpose. But I think, if we do our jobs correctly, we will phase out our own need for existence and the future of theaters will be in multicultural theaters, theaters that do a black play and a Jewish play and a classic and whatever. That sort of thing is already starting to happen. In San Francisco, for example, there's now a coalition being built between the Oakland Ensemble Theater, which is a black theater; Teatro Campesino, which is Hispanic; and the Asian-American Theater Company. They will pool their resources and do a season. I think that sort of thing is great.

There are so many people now who can't be labeled. I know a couple in which the man is Japanese and Jewish and the woman is Haitian and Filipino. They have a child, and sociologists have told them that a child of that stock probably hasn't existed before. When someone like that becomes a writer, what do we call him? Do we say he's an Asian writer, or what? As those distinctions become increasingly muddled, the whole notion of what is ethnic as opposed to what is mainstream is going to become more and more difficult to define.

THE PLAY IN PERFORMANCE

Originally, David Henry Hwang wrote *The Sound of a Voice* in the Japanese *onnagata* tradition, in which a female character is acted by a man who specializes in acting women's roles. The playwright thought that this casting would give a great deal of dramatic power to the staging. Then, finding it difficult to find a suitable *onnagata* performer, he chose a Japanese-American actress. *The Sound of a Voice* was first presented in October 1983 at the Public Theater in New York, under the sponsorship of Joseph Papp's New York

Shakespeare Festival. John Lone, who had won an Obie in 1981 for his acting in Hwang's *FOB*, directed *The Sound of a Voice* and played the role of the Man. The run was sold out and extended twice.

Since 1983 the play has been staged at a number of university and community theaters. The review printed here describes a Chicago production done by the Oasis Theatre Collective in January 1990.

Sid Smith
REVIEW OF *THE SOUND OF A VOICE*

David Henry Hwang is a young playwright of growing interest thanks to the smash success of his M. *Butterfly.*

A new group called the Oasis Theatre Collective has been enterprising enough to rummage around and dig up an earlier Hwang offering, his 1983 *The Sound of a Voice.* The

company's production, at the Blue Rider Theater, 1822 N Halsted St., allows a glimpse of an important writer and at the same time represents an enterprising collaborative effort.

Oasis worked with Hwang and obtained his permission to change the script to conform to its own original concept of the piece. His story tells of a dreamy, other-worldly encounter between a traveling warrior and his temporary host, a woman who may be a witch. Oriental in flavor and philosophy, it is also fable-like and remote, set in a faraway land and probably in the medieval era.

But director Mark Wohlgenani cast his production nontraditionally, pitting black actor William King as the warrior and Austrian-American Louise Freistadt as the woman—playing two characters who, if anything, would seem to be Oriental in extraction. But the strategy pays off, since Hwang's play is deliberately threadbare and symbolic, a kind of Everyman-Everywoman struggle for communication and love. Hwang intentionally leaves much of the specifics unexplained, blending theatrical haiku and allegory to reach for larger truths. The multi-racial elements only add to the work's poetic reverberations.

Wendy Wasserstein

THE MAN IN A CASE

Wendy Wasserstein, the daughter of immigrants from central Europe, was born in Brooklyn, New York, in 1950. After graduating from Mount Holyoke College, she took creative writing courses at the City College of New York and then completed a degree program at the Yale School of Drama. Wasserstein has had a highly successful career as a playwright (*The Heidi Chronicles* won a Pulitzer Prize in 1989), and she has also achieved recognition for her television screenplays and a book of essays.

The Man in a Case is based on a short story by Anton Chekhov, one of her favorite writers.

COMMENTARY

In our introductory comments about comedy, we suggest that comedy often shows the absurdity of ideals. The miser, the puritan, the health faddist, and so on, are people of ideals, but their ideals are suffocating. In his famous essay on comedy (1884), Henri Bergson suggested that an organism is comic when it behaves like a mechanism, that is, when instead of responding freely, flexibly, resourcefully—one might almost say intuitively and also intelligently—to the vicissitudes of life, it responds in a predictable, mechanical (and, given life's infinite variety, often inappropriate) way. It is not surprising that the first line in Wasserstein's comedy, spoken by a pedant to his betrothed, is "You are ten minutes late." This is not the way that Demetrius and Lysander speak in *A Midsummer Night's Dream*. True, a Shakespearean lover may fret about time when he is not in the presence of his mistress, but when he sees her, all thoughts of the clock disappear and he is nothing but lover. The Shakespearean lover is, in his way, mechanical too, but the audience feels a degree of sympathy for him that it does not feel for the pedantic clock-watcher.

The very title, *The Man in a Case*, alerts us to a man who is imprisoned—a man, it turns out, who lives in a prison of his own making. Byelinkov says, "I don't like change very much." His words could be said by many other butts of satire—jealous husbands or misers, for example. Of course, the comic writer takes such figures and places them where they will be subjected to maximum change. The dramatist puts the jealous husband, for instance, into a plot in which a stream of men visit the house, and every new visitor is (in the eyes of the comic figure) a potential seducer, or the miser into a plot in which every caller is a potential thief. In *The Man in a Case*, we meet a man of highly disciplined habits who is confronted by an uninhibited woman. The inevitable result of this juxtaposition is comic.

In this play we have a pedant who unaccountably has fallen in love with a vivacious young woman. (In Chekhov's story, Byelinkov's acquaintances have decided that it is time for him to get married, so they conspire to persuade him that he is in love.) The pedant is a stock comic character, who can be traced back to the "doctor" (*il dottore*, not a medical doctor but a pedant) of Renaissance Italian comedy. Such a figure values Latin more than life. True, Byelinkov is in love, but (as his first line shows) he remains the precise schoolmaster. Later, when Varinka says, "It is time for tea," he replies, "It is too early for tea. Tea is at half past the hour." Perhaps tea regularly is served at half past the hour, but again, a lover does not talk this way; a true lover will take every opportunity to have tea with his mistress.

We are not surprised to hear that Byelinkov describes his career as the teaching of "the discipline and contained beauty of the classics." "Discipline" and containment are exactly what we expect from this sort of comic figure, a man who tells us that he smiles three times every day and that in twenty years of teaching he has never been late to school. The speech that begins "I don't like change very much," goes on thus: "If one works out the arithmetic, the final fraction of improvement is at best less than an eighth of value over the total damage caused by disruption."

Why, then, is this man talking to Varinka? Because he has fallen in love. Love conquers all, even mathematicians and classicists. For the most part, when such monomaniacs fall in love, they are, as we have said, comic, objects of satire. However, since audiences approve of love, these figures—if young and genuinely in love—also can generate some sympathy from the audience. Thus, when Byelinkov says he will put a lilac in Varinka's hair, he almost becomes sympathetic. However, when he makes an entry in his notebook reminding him to do this again next year, he reverts to the pedant whom we find ridiculous.

Is Byelinkov only a comic figure, or does he sometimes evoke at least a little pathos? In seeing the play in your mind's eye, try to envision his final action at the end of the play. You might think about how, if you were directing a production of *The Man in a Case,* you would have him perform the action specified in the last stage direction. In fact, you might from the very start of this short play set yourself the pleasant task of mentally directing the actors. The first stage direction tells us that "Byelinkov is pacing," but exactly how does he pace? Does he have his arms behind his back? Does he pace regularly, or does he occasionally stop, perhaps to look at his watch? His first line of dialogue, when Varinka enters, is, "You are ten minutes late." Does he take out a pocket watch when he first sees her or when she is close to him? Does he replace it before speaking? The choices are yours.

Wendy Wasserstein

THE MAN IN A CASE

List of Characters

BYELINKOV

VARINKA

SCENE: *A small garden in the village of Mironitski. 1898.*

(*Byelinkov is pacing. Enter Varinka out of breath.*)

BYELINKOV. You are ten minutes late.

VARINKA. The most amazing thing happened on my way over here. You know the woman who runs the grocery store down the road. She wears a black wig during the week, and a blond wig on Saturday nights. And she has the daughter who married an engineer in Moscow who is doing very well thank you and is living, God bless them, in a three-room apartment. But he really is the most boring man in the world. All he talks about is his future and his station in life. Well, she heard we were to be married and she gave me this basket of apricots to give to you.

BYELINKOV. That is a most amazing thing!

VARINKA. She said to me, Varinka, you are marrying the most honorable man in the entire village. In this village he is the only man fit to speak with my son-in-law.

BYELINKOV. I don't care for apricots. They give me hives.

VARINKA. I can return them. I'm sure if I told her they give you hives she would give me a basket of raisins or a cake.

BYELINKOV. I don't know this woman or her pompous son-in-law. Why would she give me her cakes?

VARINKA. She adores you!

BYELINKOV. She is emotionally loose.

VARINKA. She adores you by reputation. Everyone adores you by reputation. I tell everyone I am to marry Byelinkov, the finest teacher in the country.

BYELINKOV. You tell them this?

VARINKA. If they don't tell me first.

BYELINKOV. Pride can be an imperfect value.

VARINKA. It isn't pride. It is the truth. You are a great man!

BYELINKOV. I am the master of Greek and Latin at a local school at the end of the village of Mironitski.

(*Varinka kisses him.*)

VARINKA. And I am to be the master of Greek and Latin's wife!

BYELINKOV. Being married requires a great deal of responsibility. I hope I am able to provide you with all that a married man must properly provide a wife.

VARINKA. We will be very happy.

BYELINKOV. Happiness is for children. We are entering into a social contract, an amicable agreement to provide us with a secure and satisfying future.

VARINKA. You are so sweet! You are the sweetest man in the world!

BYELINKOV. I'm a man set in his ways who saw a chance to provide himself with a small challenge.

VARINKA. Look at you! Look at you! Your sweet round spectacles, your dear collar always starched, always raised, your perfectly pressed pants always creasing at right angles perpendicular to the floor, and my most favorite part, the sweet little galoshes, rain or shine, just in case. My Byelinkov, never taken by surprise. Except by me.

BYELINKOV. You speak about me as if I were your pet.

VARINKA. You are my pet! My little school mouse.

BYELINKOV. A mouse?

VARINKA. My sweetest dancing bear with galoshes, my little stale babka.[1]

BYELINKOV. A stale babka?

VARINKA. I am not Pushkin.[2]

BYELINKOV (*laughs*). That depends what you think of Pushkin.

VARINKA. You're smiling. I knew I could make you smile today.

BYELINKOV. I am a responsible man. Every day I have for breakfast black bread, fruit, hot tea, and every day I smile three times. I am halfway into my translation of the *Aeneid*[3] from classical Greek hexameter into Russian alexandrines. In twenty years I have never been late to school. I am a responsible man, but no dancing bear.

VARINKA. Dance with me.

BYELINKOV. Now? It is nearly four weeks before the wedding!

VARINKA. It's a beautiful afternoon. We are in your garden. The roses are in full bloom.

BYELINKOV. The roses have beetles.

VARINKA. Dance with me!

BYELINKOV. You are a demanding woman.

VARINKA. You chose me. And right. And left. And turn. And right. And left.

[1]**babka** cake with almonds and raisins [2]**Pushkin** Alexander Pushkin (1799–1837), Russian poet [3]**Aeneid** Latin epic poem by the Roman poet Virgil (70–19 B.C.)

BYELINKOV. And turn. Give me your hand. You dance like a school mouse. It's a beautiful afternoon! We are in my garden. The roses are in full bloom! And turn. And turn. (*Twirls Varinka around.*)

VARINKA. I am the luckiest woman!

(*Byelinkov stops dancing.*)

Why are you stopping?

BYELNKOV. To place a lilac in your hair. Every year on this day I will place a lilac in your hair.

VARINKA. Will you remember?

BYELINKOV. I will write it down. (*Takes a notebook from his pocket.*) Dear Byelinkov, don't forget the day a young lady, your bride, entered your garden, your peace, and danced on the roses. On that day every year you are to place a lilac in her hair.

VARINKA. I love you.

BYELINKOV. It is convenient we met.

VARINKA. I love you.

BYELINKOV. You are a girl.

VARINKA. I am thirty.

BYELINKOV. But you think like a girl. That is an attractive attribute.

VARINKA. Do you love me?

BYELINKOV. We've never spoken about housekeeping.

VARINKA. I am an excellent housekeeper. I kept house for my family on the farm in Gadyatchsky. I can make a beetroot soup with tomatoes and aubergines which is so nice. Awfully awfully nice.

BYELINKOV. You are fond of expletives.

VARINKA. My beet soup, sir, is excellent!

BYELINKOV. Please don't be cross. I too am an excellent housekeeper. I have a place for everything in the house. A shelf for each pot, a cubby for every spoon, a folder for favorite recipes. I have cooked for myself for twenty years. Though my beet soup is not outstanding, it is sufficient.

VARINKA. I'm sure it's very good.

BYELINKOV. No. It is awfully, awfully not. What I am outstanding in, however, what gives me greatest pleasure, is preserving those things which are left over. I wrap each tomato slice I haven't used in a wet cloth and place it in the coolest corner of the house. I have had my shoes for seven years because I wrap them in the galoshes you are so fond of. And every night before I go to sleep I wrap my bed in quilts and curtains so I never catch a draft.

VARINKA. You sleep with curtains on your bed?

BYELINKOV. I like to keep warm.

VARINKA. I will make you a new quilt.

BYELINKOV. No. No new quilt. That would be hazardous.

VARINKA. It is hazardous to sleep under curtains.

BYELINKOV. Varinka, I don't like change very much. If one works out the arithmetic the final fraction of improvement is at best less than an eighth of value over the total damage caused by disruption. I never thought of marrying till I saw your eyes dancing among the familiar faces at the headmaster's tea. I assumed I would grow old preserved like those which are left over, wrapped suitably in my case of curtains and quilts.

VARINKA. Byelinkov, I want us to have dinners with friends and summer country visits. I want people to say, "Have you spent time with Varinka and Byelinkov? He is so happy now that they are married. She is just what he needed."

BYELINKOV. You have already brought me some happiness. But I never was a sad man. Don't ever think I thought I was a sad man.

VARINKA. My sweetest darling, you can be whatever you want! If you are sad, they'll say she talks all the time, and he is softspoken and kind.

BYELINKOV. And if I am difficult?

VARINKA. Oh, they'll say he is difficult because he is highly intelligent. All great men are difficult. Look at Lermontov, Tchaikovsky, Peter the Great.

BYELINKOV. Ivan the Terrible.[4]

VARINKA. Yes, him too.

BYELINKOV. Why are you marrying me? I am none of these things.

VARINKA. To me you are.

BYELINKOV. You have imagined this. You have constructed an elaborate romance for yourself. Perhaps you are the great one. You are the one with the great imagination.

VARINKA. Byelinkov, I am a pretty girl of thirty. You're right, I am not a woman. I have not made myself into a woman because I do not deserve that honor. Until I came to this town to visit my brother I lived on my family's farm. As the years passed I became younger and younger in fear that I would never marry. And it wasn't that I wasn't pretty enough or sweet enough, it was just that no man ever looked at me and saw a wife. I was not the woman who would be there when he came home. Until I met you I thought I would lie all my life and say I never married because I never met a man I loved. I will love you, Byelinkov. And I will help you to love me. We deserve the life everyone else has. We deserve not to be different.

BYELINKOV. Yes. We are the same as everyone else.

VARINKA. Tell me you love me.

BYELINKOV. I love you.

VARINKA (*takes his hands*). We will be very happy. I am very strong. (*Pauses.*) It is time for tea.

---

[4]**Lermontov . . . Ivan the Terrible** Mikhail Lermontov (1814–1841), poet and novelist; Peter Ilich Tchaikovsky (1840–1893), composer; Peter the Great (1672–1725) and Ivan the Terrible (1530–1584), czars credited with making Russia a great European power

BYELINKOV. It is too early for tea. Tea is at half past the hour.

VARINKA. Do you have heavy cream? It will be awfully nice with apricots.

BYELINKOV. Heavy cream is too rich for teatime.

VARINKA. But today is special. Today you placed a lilac in my hair. Write in your note pad. Every year we will celebrate with apricots and heavy cream. I will go to my brother's house and get some.

BYELINKOV. But your brother's house is a mile from here.

VARINKA. Today it is much shorter. Today my brother gave me his bicycle to ride. I will be back very soon.

BYELINKOV. You rode to my house by bicycle! Did anyone see you!

VARINKA. Of course. I had such fun. I told you I saw the grocery store lady with the son-in-law who is doing very well thank you in Moscow, and the headmaster's wife.

BYELINKOV. You saw the headmaster's wife!

VARINKA. She smiled at me.

BYELINKOV. Did she laugh or smile?

VARINKA. She laughed a little. She said, "My dear, you are very progressive to ride a bicycle." She said you and your fiancé Byelinkov must ride together sometime. I wonder if he'll take off his galoshes when he rides a bicycle.

BYELINKOV. She said that?

VARINKA. She adores you. We had a good giggle.

BYELINKOV. A woman can be arrested for riding a bicycle. That is not progressive, it is a premeditated revolutionary act. Your brother must be awfully, awfully careful on behalf of your behavior. He has been careless—oh so careless—in giving you the bicycle.

VARINKA. Dearest Byelinkov, you are wrapping yourself under curtains and quilts! I made friends on the bicycle.

BYELINKOV. You saw more than the headmaster's wife and the idiot grocery woman.

VARINKA. She is not an idiot.

BYELINKOV. She is a potato-vending, sausage-armed fool!

VARINKA. Shhhh! My school mouse. Shhh!

BYELINKOV. What other friends did you make on this bicycle?

VARINKA. I saw students from my brother's classes. They waved and shouted, "Anthropos in love! Anthropos in love!!"

BYELINKOV. Where is that bicycle?

VARINKA. I left it outside the gate. Where are you going?

BYELINKOV (muttering as he exits). Anthropos in love, anthropos in love.

VARINKA. They were cheering me on. Careful, you'll trample the roses.

BYELINKOV (returning with the bicycle). Anthropos is the Greek singular for man. Anthropos in love translates as the Greek and Latin master in love. Of course they cheered you. Their instructor, who teaches them the discipline and contained beauty of the classics, is in love with a sprite on a bicycle. It is a good giggle, isn't it? A

very good giggle! I am returning this bicycle to your brother.

VARINKA. But it is teatime.

BYELINKOV. Today we will not have tea.

VARINKA. But you will have to walk back a mile.

BYELINKOV. I have my galoshes on. (Gets on the bicycle.) Varinka, we deserve not to be different. (Begins to pedal. The bicycle doesn't move.)

VARINKA. Put the kickstand up.

BYELINKOV. I beg your pardon.

VARINKA (giggling). Byelinkov, to make the bicycle move, you must put the kickstand up.

(Byelinkov puts it up and awkwardly falls off the bicycle as it moves.)

(Laughing.) Ha ha ha. My little school mouse. You look so funny! You are the sweetest dearest man in the world. Ha ha ha!

(Pause.)

BYELINKOV. Please help me up. I'm afraid my galosh is caught.

VARINKA (trying not to laugh). Your galosh is caught! (Explodes in laughter again.) Oh, you are so funny! I do love you so. (Helps Byelinkov up.) You were right, my pet, as always. We don't need heavy cream for tea. The fraction of improvement isn't worth the damage caused by the disruption.

BYELINKOV. Varinka, it is still too early for tea. I must complete two stanzas of my translation before late afternoon. That is my regular schedule.

VARINKA. Then I will watch while you work.

BYELINKOV. No. You had a good giggle. That is enough.

VARINKA. Then while you work I will work too. I will make lists of guests for our wedding.

BYELINKOV. I can concentrate only when I am alone in my house. Please take your bicycle home to your brother.

VARINKA. But I don't want to leave you. You look so sad.

BYELINKOV. I never was a sad man. Don't ever think I was a sad man.

VARINKA. Byelinkov, it's a beautiful day, we are in your garden. The roses are in bloom.

BYELINKOV. Allow me to help you on to your bicycle. (Takes Varinka's hand as she gets on the bike.)

VARINKA. You are such a gentleman. We will be very happy.

BYELINKOV. You are very strong. Good day, Varinka.

(Varinka pedals off. Byelinkov, alone in the garden, takes out his pad and rips up the note about the lilac, strews it over the garden, then carefully picks up each piece of paper and places them all in a small envelope as lights fade to black.

TOPICS FOR CRITICAL THINKING AND WRITING

📖 THE PLAY ON THE PAGE

1. You will probably agree that the scene in which Byelinkov gets on the bicycle and pedals and goes nowhere is funny. But *why* is it funny? Can you formulate some sort of theory of comedy based on this episode?

🎭 THE PLAY ON THE STAGE

2. At the end of the play, Byelinkov tears up the note but then collects the pieces. If you were directing the play, exactly what gestures and actions would you suggest here? (Obviously, your directions will be based on how you interpret the episode.)

August Wilson

FENCES

August Wilson, the son of a black woman and a white man, was born in Pittsburgh in 1945. After dropping out of school at the age of fifteen, Wilson took various odd jobs, such as stock clerk and short-order cook, in his spare time, while educating himself in the public library, chiefly by reading works by such black writers as Richard Wright, Ralph Ellison, Langston Hughes, and Imamu Amiri Baraka (LeRoi Jones). In 1978 the director of a black theater in St. Paul, Minnesota, who had known Wilson in Pittsburgh, invited him to write a play for the theater. Six months later Wilson moved permanently to St. Paul.

The winner of the Pulitzer Prize for drama in 1987, Wilson's *Fences* was first presented as a staged reading in 1983 and was later performed in Chicago, Seattle, Rochester (New York), and New Haven (Connecticut) before reaching New York City in 1987. An earlier play, *Ma Rainey's Black Bottom*, was voted Best Play of the Year 1984–1985 by the New York Drama Critics' Circle. In 1981 when *Ma Rainey* was first read at the O'Neill Center in Waterford, Connecticut, Wilson met Lloyd Richards, a black director with whom he has continued to work closely.

COMMENTARY

In 1926 W.E.B. DuBois, a black leader, organized a black theater in Harlem and enunciated his vision of a new black drama:

> The plays of a real Negro theatre must be: 1. About us. That is, they must have plots that reveal Negro life as it is. 2. By us; they must be written by Negro authors who understand from birth and continued association just what it means to be a Negro today. 3. For us; that is, the Negro theatre must cater primarily to Negro audiences and be supported by their entertainment and approval. 4. Near us. The theatre must be in a neighborhood near the mass of Negro people.

However, when it came to putting ink on paper, not every black writer was quite sure how to proceed. In 1928, in an article titled "The Dilemma of the Negro Artist," James Weldon Johnson wrote:

> The moment a Negro writer picks up his pen and sits down to his typewriter he is immediately called upon to solve, consciously or unconsciously, this problem of the double audience. To whom shall he address himself, to his own black group or to white America?

Johnson in fact went on to assert that the black writer's audience "is always both white America and black America," but, as we shall see in a moment, in the 1960s—the period when "black" displaced "Negro"—not all black writers agreed.

The plays written by blacks from, say, 1920 to the early 1960s fit rather comfortably into the mainstream of American drama. Two plays by and about blacks, Langston Hughes's *Mulatto* (1935) and Lorraine Hansberry's *A Raisin in the Sun*

(1959), enjoyed long runs on Broadway, which is to say that much of their support came from whites. These plays are not fundamentally different from, say, Philip Yordan's *Anna Lucasta*, which is by a white playwright and originally dealt with a working-class Polish family in Philadelphia but was altered for a black cast and then became a Broadway hit. With the growth of the Civil Rights movement in the 1960s, however, black theater changed decisively, helping to form the black power movement.

The most talented black dramatists, including Imamu Amiri Baraka (LeRoi Jones) and Ed Bullins, largely turned their backs on white audiences and, in effect, wrote plays aimed at showing blacks that *they*—not their white oppressors—must change, must cease to accept the myths that whites had created. Today, however, strongly revolutionary plays by and about blacks have difficulty getting a hearing. Instead, the newest black writers seem to be concerned less with raising the consciousness of blacks than with depicting black life and with letting both blacks and whites respond aesthetically rather than politically. Baraka has attributed the change to a desire by many blacks to become assimilated in today's society, and surely there is much to his view. One might also say, however, that black dramatists may for other reasons have come to assume that the business of drama is not to preach but to show, and that a profound, honest depiction—in a traditional, realistic dramatic form—of things as they are, or in Wilson's play, things as they were in the 1950s—will touch audiences whatever their color. "Part of the reason I wrote *Fences*," Wilson has said, "was to illuminate that generation, which shielded its children from all of the indignities they went through."

This is not to say, of course, that *Fences* is a play about people who just happen to be black. The Polish family of *Anna Lucasta* could easily be converted to a black family (though perhaps blacks may feel that there is something unconvincing about this family), but Troy Maxson's family cannot be whitewashed. The play is very much about persons who are what they are because they are blacks living in an unjust society run by whites. We are not allowed to forget this. Troy is a baseball player who was too old to join a white team when the major leagues began to hire blacks. For Troy's friend, Bono, "Troy just came along too early," to which Troy pungently replies, "There ought not never have been no time called too early." Blacks of Troy's day were expected to subscribe to American ideals—for instance, to serve in the army in time of war—but they were also expected to sit in the back of the bus and to accept the fact that they were barred from decent jobs. Wilson shows us the scars that such treatment left. Troy is no paragon. Although he has a deep sense of responsibility to his family, his behavior toward them is deeply flawed: he oppresses his son Cory; he is unfaithful to his wife, Rose; and he exploits his brother Gabriel.

Wilson, as we have seen, calls attention to racism in baseball, and he indicates that Troy turned to crime because he could not earn money. However, Wilson does not allow *Fences* to become a prolonged protest against white oppression—though one can never quite forget that Troy insists on a high personal ideal in a world that has cheated him. The interest in the play is in Troy as a human being, or, rather, in all of the characters as human beings rather than as representatives of white victimization. As Troy sees it, by preventing Cory from engaging in athletics (the career that frustrated Troy), he is helping rather than oppressing Cory: "I don't want him to be like me. I want him to move as far from me as he can." Wilson also makes it clear, however, that Troy has other (very human) motives, of which Troy perhaps is unaware.

August Wilson

FENCES

for Lloyd Richards,
who adds to whatever he touches
When the sins of our fathers visit us
We do not have to play host.
We can banish them with forgiveness
As God, in His Largeness and Laws.
—*August Wilson*

List of Characters

TROY MAXSON

JIM BONO, *Troy's friend*

ROSE, *Troy's wife*

LYONS, *Troy's oldest son by previous marriage*

GABRIEL, *Troy's brother*

CORY, *Troy and Rose's son*

RAYNELL, *Troy's daughter*

SETTING: *The setting is the yard which fronts the only entrance to the Maxson household, an ancient two-story brick house set back off a small alley in a big-city neighborhood. The entrance to the house is gained by two or three steps leading to a wooden porch badly in need of paint.*

A relatively recent addition to the house and running its full width, the porch lacks congruence. It is a sturdy porch with a flat roof. One or two chairs of dubious value sit at one end where the kitchen window opens onto the porch. An old-fashioned icebox stands silent guard at the opposite end.

The yard is a small dirt yard, partially fenced, except for the last scene, with a wooden saw horse, a pile of lumber, and other fence-building equipment set off to the side. Opposite is a tree from which hangs a ball made of rags. A baseball bat leans against the tree. Two oil drums serve as garbage receptacles and sit near the house at right to complete the setting.

THE PLAY: *Near the turn of the century, the destitute of Europe sprang on the city with tenacious claws and an honest and solid dream. The city devoured them. They swelled its belly until it burst into a thousand furnaces and sewing machines, a thousand butcher shops and bakers' ovens, a thousand churches and hospitals and funeral parlors and money-lenders. The city grew. It nourished itself and offered each man a partnership limited only by his talent, his guile, and his willingness and capacity for hard work. For the immigrants of Europe, a dream dared and won true.*

The descendants of African slaves were offered no such welcome or participation. They came from places called the Carolinas and the Virginias, Georgia, Alabama, Mississippi, and Tennessee. They came strong, eager, searching. The city rejected them and they fled and settled along the riverbanks and under bridges in shallow, ramshackle houses made of sticks and tarpaper. They collected rags and wood. They sold the use of their muscles and their bodies. They cleaned houses and washed clothes, they shined shoes, and in quiet desperation and vengeful pride, they stole, and lived in pursuit of their own dream. That they could breathe free, finally, and stand to meet life with the force of dignity and whatever eloquence the heart could call upon.

By 1957, the hard-won victories of the European immigrants had solidified the industrial might of America. War had been confronted and won with new energies that used loyalty and patriotism as its fuel. Life was rich, full, and flourishing. The Milwaukee Braves won the World Series, and the hot winds of change that would make the sixties a turbulent, racing, dangerous, and provocative decade had not yet begun to blow full.

ACT 1

SCENE 1

It is 1957. Troy and Bono enter the yard, engaged in conversation. Troy is fifty-three years old, a large man with thick, heavy hands; it is this largeness that he strives to fill out and make an accommodation with. Together with his blackness, his largeness informs his sensibilities and the choices he has made in his life.

Of the two men, Bono is obviously the follower. His commitment to their friendship of thirty-odd years is rooted in his admiration of Troy's honesty, capacity for hard work, and his strength, which Bono seeks to emulate.

It is Friday night, payday, and the one night of the week the two men engage in a ritual of talk and drink. Troy is usually the most talkative and at times he can be crude and almost vulgar, though he is capable of rising to profound heights of expression. The men carry lunch buckets and wear or carry burlap aprons and are dressed in clothes suitable to their jobs as garbage collectors.

BONO. Troy, you ought to stop that lying!

TROY. I ain't lying! The nigger had a watermelon this big. (*He indicates with his hands.*) Talking about . . . "What watermelon, Mr. Rand?" I liked to fell out! "What watermelon, Mr. Rand?" . . . And it sitting there big as life.

BONO. What did Mr. Rand say?

TROY. Ain't said nothing. Figure if the nigger too dumb to know he carrying a watermelon, he wasn't gonna get much sense out of him. Trying to hide that great big old watermelon under his coat. Afraid to let the white man see him carry it home.

BONO. I'm like you . . . I ain't got no time for them kind of people.

TROY. Now what he look like getting mad cause he see the man from the union talking to Mr. Rand?

BONO. He come to me talking about . . . "Maxson gonna get us fired." I told him to get away from me with that. He walked away from me calling you a troublemaker. What Mr. Rand say?

TROY. Ain't said nothing. He told me to go down the Commissioner's office next Friday. They called me down there to see them.

BONO. Well, as long as you got your complaint filed, they can't fire you. That's what one of them white fellows tell me.

TROY. I ain't worried about them firing me. They gonna fire me cause I asked a question? That's all I did. I went to Mr. Rand and asked him, "Why? Why you got the white mens driving and the colored lifting?" Told him, "what's the matter, don't I count? You think only white fellows got sense enough to drive a truck. That ain't no paper job! Hell, anybody can drive a truck. How come you got all whites driving and the colored lifting?" He told me "take it to the union." Well, hell, that's what I done! Now they wanna come up with this pack of lies.

BONO. I told Brownie if the man come and ask him any questions . . . just tell the truth! It ain't nothing but something they done trumped up on you cause you filed a complaint on them.

TROY. Brownie don't understand nothing. All I want them to do is change the job description. Give everybody a chance to drive the truck. Brownie can't see that. He ain't got that much sense.

BONO. How you figure he be making out with that gal be up at Taylor's all the time . . . that Alberta gal?

TROY. Same as you and me. Getting just as much as we is. Which is to say nothing.

BONO. It is, huh? I figure you doing a little better than me . . . and I ain't saying what I'm doing.

TROY. Aw, nigger, look here . . . I know you. If you had got anywhere near that gal, twenty minutes later you be looking to tell somebody. And the first one you gonna tell . . . that you gonna want to brag to . . . is me.

BONO. I ain't saying that. I see where you be eyeing her.

TROY. I eye all the women. I don't miss nothing. Don't never let nobody tell you Troy Maxson don't eye the women.

BONO. You been doing more than eyeing her. You done bought her a drink or two.

TROY. Hell yeah, I bought her a drink! What that mean? I bought you one, too. What that mean cause I buy her a drink? I'm just being polite.

BONO. It's all right to buy her one drink. That's what you call being polite. But when you wanna be buying two or three . . . that's what you call eyeing her.

TROY. Look here, as long as you known me . . . you ever known me to chase after women?

BONO. Hell yeah! Long as I done known you. You forgetting I knew you when.

TROY. Naw, I'm talking about since I been married to Rose?

BONO. Oh, not since you been married to Rose. Now, that's the truth, there. I can say that.

TROY. All right then! Case closed.

BONO. I see you be walking up around Alberta's house. You supposed to be at Taylors' and you be walking up around there.

TROY. What you watching where I'm walking for? I ain't watching after you.

BONO. I seen you walking around there more than once.

TROY. Hell, you liable to see me walking anywhere! That don't mean nothing cause you see me walking around there.

BONO. Where she come from anyway? She just kinda showed up one day.

TROY. Tallahassee. You can look at her and tell she one of them Florida gals. They got some big healthy women down there. Grow them right up out the ground. Got a little bit of Indian in her. Most of them niggers down in Florida got some Indian in them.

BONO. I don't know about that Indian part. But she damn sure big and healthy. Woman wear some big stockings. Got them great big old legs and hips as wide as the Mississippi River.

TROY. Legs don't mean nothing. You don't do nothing but push them out of the way. But them hips cushion the ride!

BONO. Troy, you ain't got no sense.

TROY. It's the truth! Like you riding on Goodyears!

Rose enters from the house. She is ten years younger than Troy, her devotion to him stems from her recognition of the possibilities of her life without him: a succession of abusive men and their babies, a life of partying and running the streets, the Church, or aloneness with its attendant pain and frustration. She recognizes Troy's spirit as a fine and illuminating one and she either ignores or forgives his faults, only some of which she recognizes. Though she doesn't drink, her presence is an integral part of the Friday night rituals. She alternates between the porch and the kitchen, where supper preparations are under way.

ROSE. What you all out here getting into?

TROY. What you worried about what we getting into for? This is men talk, woman.

ROSE. What I care what you all talking about? Bono, you gonna stay for supper?

BONO. No, I thank you, Rose. But Lucille say she cooking up a pot of pigfeet.

TROY. Pigfeet! Hell, I'm going home with you! Might even stay the night if you got some pigfeet. You got something in there to top them pigfeet, Rose?

ROSE. I'm cooking up some chicken. I got some chicken and collard greens.

TROY. Well, go on back in the house and let me and Bono finish what we was talking about. This is men talk. I got some talk for you later. You know what kind of talk I mean. You go on and powder it up.

ROSE. Troy Maxson, don't you start that now!

TROY (*puts his arm around her*). Aw, woman . . . come here. Look here, Bono . . . when I met this woman . . . I got out that place, say, "Hitch up my pony, saddle up my mare . . . there's a woman out there for me somewhere. I looked here. Looked there. Saw Rose and latched on to her." I latched on to her and told her—I'm gonna tell you the truth—I told her, "Baby, I don't wanna marry, I just wanna be your man." Rose told me . . . tell him what you told me, Rose.

ROSE. I told him if he wasn't the marrying kind, then move out the way so the marrying kind could find me.

TROY. That's what she told me. "Nigger, you in my way. You blocking the view! Move out the way so I can find me a husband." I thought it over two or three days. Come back—

ROSE. Ain't no two or three days nothing. You was back the same night.

TROY. Come back, told her . . . "Okay, baby . . . but I'm gonna buy me a banty rooster and put him out there in the backyard . . . and when he see a stranger come, he'll flap his wings and crow . . . ." Look here, Bono, I could watch the front door by myself . . . it was that back door I was worried about.

ROSE. Troy, you ought not talk like that. Troy ain't doing nothing but telling a lie.

TROY. Only thing is . . . when we first got married . . . forget the rooster . . . we ain't had no yard!

BONO. I hear you tell it. Me and Lucille was staying down there on Logan Street. Had two rooms with the outhouse in the back. I ain't mind the outhouse none. But when that goddamn wind blow through there in the winter . . . that's what I'm talking about! To this day I wonder why in the hell I ever stayed down there for six long years. But see, I didn't know I could do no better. I thought only white folks had inside toilets and things.

ROSE. There's a lot of people don't know they can do no better than they doing now. That's just something you got to learn. A lot of folks still shop at Bella's.

TROY. Ain't nothing wrong with shopping at Bella's. She got fresh food.

ROSE. I ain't said nothing about if she got fresh food. I'm talking about what she charge. She charge ten cents more than the A&P.

TROY. The A&P ain't never done nothing for me. I spends my money where I'm treated right. I go down to Bella, say, "I need a loaf of bread, I'll pay you Friday." She give it to me. What sense that make when I got money to go and spend it somewhere else and ignore the person who done right by me? That ain't in the Bible.

ROSE. We ain't talking about what's in the Bible. What sense it make to shop there when she overcharge?

TROY. You shop where you want to. I'll do my shopping where the people been good to me.

ROSE. Well, I don't think it's right for her to overcharge. That's all I was saying.

BONO. Look here . . . I got to get on. Lucille going be raising all kind of hell.

TROY. Where you going, nigger? We ain't finished this pint. Come here, finish this pint.

BONO. Well, hell, I am . . . if you ever turn the bottle loose.

TROY (*hands him the bottle*). The only thing I say about the A&P is I'm glad Cory got that job down there. Help him take care of his school clothes and things. Gabe done moved out and things getting tight around here. He got that job. . . . He can start to look out for himself.

ROSE. Cory done went and got recruited by a college football team.

TROY. I told that boy about that football stuff. The white man ain't gonna let him get nowhere with that football. I told him when he first come to me with it. Now you come telling me he done went and got more tied up in it. He ought to go and get recruited in how to fix cars or something where he can make a living.

ROSE. He ain't talking about making no living playing football. It's just something the boys in school do. They gonna send a recruiter by to talk to you. He'll tell you he ain't talking about making no living playing football. It's a honor to be recruited.

TROY. It ain't gonna get him nowhere. Bono'll tell you that.

BONO. If he be like you in the sports . . . he's gonna be all right. Ain't but two men ever played baseball as good as you. That's Babe Ruth and Josh Gibson.[1] Them's the only two men ever hit more home runs than you.

TROY. What it ever get me? Ain't got a pot to piss in or a window to throw it out of.

---

[1]African-American ballplayer (1911–47), known as the Babe Ruth of the Negro leagues

ROSE. Times have changed since you was playing baseball, Troy. That was before the war. Times have changed a lot since then.

TROY. How in hell they done changed?

ROSE. They got lots of colored boys playing ball now. Baseball and football.

BONO. You right about that, Rose. Times have changed, Troy. You just come along too early.

TROY. There ought not never have been no time called too early! Now you take that fellow . . . what's that fellow they had playing right field for the Yankees back then? You know who I'm talking about, Bono. Used to play right field for the Yankees.

ROSE. Selkirk?

TROY. Selkirk! That's it! Man batting .269, understand? .269. What kind of sense that make? I was hitting .432 with thirty-seven home runs! Man batting .269 and playing right field for the Yankees! I saw Josh Gibson's daughter yesterday. She walking around with raggedy shoes on her feet. Now I bet you Selkirk's daughter ain't walking around with raggedy shoes on the feet! I bet you that!

ROSE. They got a lot of colored baseball players now. Jackie Robinson[2] was the first. Folks had to wait for Jackie Robinson.

TROY. I done seen a hundred niggers play baseball better than Jackie Robinson. Hell, I know some teams Jackie Robinson couldn't even make! What you talking about Jackie Robinson. Jackie Robinson wasn't nobody. I'm talking about if you could play ball then they ought to have let you play. Don't care what color you were. Come telling me I come along too early. If you could play . . . then they ought to have let you play.

Troy takes a long drink from the bottle.

ROSE. You gonna drink yourself to death. You don't need to be drinking like that.

TROY. Death ain't nothing. I done seen him. Done wrassled with him. You can't tell me nothing about death. Death ain't nothing but a fastball on the outside corner. And you know what I'll do to that! Lookee here, Bono . . . am I lying? You get one of them fastballs, about waist high, over the outside corner of the plate where you can get the meat of the bat on it . . . and good god! You can kiss it goodbye. Now, am I lying?

BONO. Naw, you telling the truth there. I seen you do it.

TROY. If I'm lying . . . that 450 feet worth of lying! (*Pause.*) That's all death is to me. A fastball on the outside corner.

ROSE. I don't know why you want to get on talking about death.

TROY. Ain't nothing wrong with talking about death. That's part of life. Everybody gonna die. You gonna die, I'm gonna die. Bono's gonna die. Hell, we all gonna die.

ROSE. But you ain't got to talk about it. I don't like to talk about it.

TROY. You the one brought it up. Me and Bono was talking about baseball . . . you tell me I'm gonna drink myself to death. Ain't that right, Bono? You know I don't drink this but one night out of the week. That's Friday night. I'm gonna drink just enough to where I can handle it. Then I cuts it loose. I leave it alone. So don't you worry about me drinking myself to death. 'Cause I ain't worried about Death. I done seen him. I done wrestled with him.

Look here, Bono . . . I looked up one day and Death was marching straight at me. Like Soldiers on Parade! The Army of Death was marching straight at me. The middle of July, 1941. It got real cold just like it be winter. It seem like Death himself reached out and touched me on the shoulder. He touch me just like I touch you. I got cold as ice and Death standing there grinning at me.

ROSE. Troy, why don't you hush that talk.

TROY. I say . . . what you want, Mr. Death? You be wanting me? You done brought your army to be getting me? I looked him dead in the eye. I wasn't fearing nothing. I was ready to tangle. Just like I'm ready to tangle now. The Bible say be ever vigilant. That's why I don't get but so drunk. I got to keep watch.

ROSE. Troy was right down there in Mercy Hospital. You remember he had pneumonia? Laying there with a fever talking plumb out of his head.

TROY. Death standing there staring at me . . . carrying that sickle in his hand. Finally he say, "You want bound over for another year?" See, just like that . . . "You want bound over for another year?" I told him, "Bound over hell! Let's settle this now!"

It seem like he kinda fell back when I said that, and all the cold went out of me. I reached down and grabbed that sickle and threw it just as far as I could throw it . . . and me and him commenced to wrestling.

We wrestled for three days and three nights. I can't say where I found the strength from. Everytime it seemed like he was gonna get the best of me, I'd reach way down deep inside myself and find the strength to do him one better.

ROSE. Everytime Troy tell that story he find different ways to tell it. Different things to make up about it.

TROY. I ain't making up nothing. I'm telling you the facts of what happened. I wrestled with Death for three days and three nights and I'm standing here to tell you about it. (*Pause.*) All right. At the end of the third night we done weakened each other to where we can't hardly move. Death stood up, throwed on his robe . . . had him a white robe with a hood on it. He throwed on that robe and went off to look for his sickle. Say, "I'll be back." Just like that. "I'll be back." I told him, say, "Yeah, but . . . you

---

[2]In 1947 Robinson (1919–72) became the first African-American to play baseball in the major leagues.

gonna have to find me!" I wasn't no fool. I wasn't going looking for him. Death ain't nothing to play with. And I know he's gonna get me. I know I got to join his army . . . his camp followers. But as long as I keep my strength and see him coming . . . as long as I keep up my vigilance . . . he's gonna have to fight to get me. I ain't going easy.

BONO. Well, look here, since you got to keep up your vigilance . . . let me have the bottle.

TROY. Aw hell, I shouldn't have told you that part. I should have left out that part.

ROSE. Troy be talking that stuff and half the time don't even know what he be talking about.

TROY. Bono know me better than that.

BONO. That's right. I know you. I know you got some Uncle Remus[3] in your blood. You got more stories than the devil got sinners.

TROY. Aw hell, I done seen him too! Done talked with the devil.

ROSE. Troy, don't nobody wanna be hearing all that stuff.

Lyons enters the yard from the street. Thirty-four years old, Troy's son by a previous marriage, he sports a neatly trimmed goatee, sport coat, white shirt, tieless and buttoned at the collar. Though he fancies himself a musician, he is more caught up in the rituals and "idea" of being a musician than in the actual practice of the music. He has come to borrow money from Troy, and while he knows he will be successful, he is uncertain as to what extent his lifestyle will be held up to scrutiny and ridicule.

LYONS. Hey, Pop.

TROY. What you come "Hey, Popping" me for?

LYONS. How you doing, Rose? (*He kisses her.*) Mr. Bono. How you doing?

BONO. Hey, Lyons . . . how you been?

TROY. He must have been doing all right. I ain't seen him around here last week.

ROSE. Troy, leave your boy alone. He come by to see you and you wanna start all that nonsense.

TROY. I ain't bothering Lyons. (*Offers him the bottle.*) Here . . . get you a drink. We got an understanding. I know why he come by to see me and he know I know.

LYONS. Come on, Pop . . . I just stopped by to say hi . . . see how you was doing.

TROY. You ain't stopped by yesterday.

ROSE. You gonna stay for supper, Lyons? I got some chicken cooking in the oven.

LYONS. No, Rose . . . thanks. I was just in the neighborhood and thought I'd stop by for a minute.

TROY. You was in the neighborhood all right, nigger. You telling the truth there. You was in the neighborhood cause it's my payday.

[3]Narrator of traditional black tales in a book by Joel Chandler Harris.

LYONS. Well, hell, since you mentioned it . . . let me have ten dollars.

TROY. I'll be damned! I'll die and go to hell and play blackjack with the devil before I give you ten dollars.

BONO. That's what I wanna know about . . . that devil you done seen.

LYONS. What . . . Pop done seen the devil? You too much, Pops.

TROY. Yeah, I done seen him. Talked to him too!

ROSE. You ain't seen no devil. I done told you that man ain't had nothing to do with the devil. Anything you can't understand, you want to call it the devil.

TROY. Look here, Bono . . . I went down to see Hertzberger about some furniture. Got three rooms for two-ninety-eight. That what it say on the radio. "Three rooms . . . two-ninety-eight." Even made up a little song about it. Go down there . . . man tell me I can't get no credit. I'm working every day and can't get no credit. What to do? I got an empty house with some raggedy furniture in it. Cory ain't got no bed. He's sleeping on a pile of rags on the floor. Working every day and can't get no credit. Come back here—Rose'll tell you—madder than hell. Sit down . . . try to figure what I'm gonna do. Come a knock on the door. Ain't been living here but three days. Who know I'm here? Open the door . . . devil standing there bigger than life. White fellow . . . white fellow . . . got on good clothes and everything. Standing there with a clipboard in his hand. I ain't had to say nothing. First words come out of his mouth was . . . "I understand you need some furniture and can't get no credit." I liked to fell over. He say, "I'll give you all the credit you want, but you got to pay the interest on it." I told him, "Give me three rooms worth and charge whatever you want." Next day a truck pulled up here and two men unloaded them three rooms. Man what drove the truck give me a book. Say send ten dollars, first of every month to the address in the book and every thing will be all right. Say if I miss a payment the devil was coming back and it'll be hell to pay. That was fifteen years ago. To this day . . . the first of the month I send my ten dollars, Rose'll tell you.

ROSE. Troy lying.

TROY. I ain't never seen that man since. Now you tell me who else that could have been but the devil? I ain't sold my soul or nothing like that, you understand. Naw, I wouldn't have truck with the devil about nothing like that. I got my furniture and pays my ten dollars the first of the month just like clockwork.

BONO. How long you say you been paying this ten dollars a month?

TROY. Fifteen years!

BONO. Hell, ain't you finished paying for it yet? How much the man done charged you?

TROY. Ah hell, I done paid for it. I done paid for it ten times over! The fact is I'm scared to stop paying it.

ROSE. Troy lying. We got that furniture from Mr. Glickman. He ain't paying no ten dollars a month to nobody.

TROY. Aw hell, woman. Bono know I ain't that big a fool.

LYONS. I was just getting ready to say . . . I know where there's a bridge for sale.

TROY. Look here, I'll tell you this . . . it don't matter to me if he was the devil. It don't matter if the devil give credit. Somebody has got to give it.

ROSE. It ought to matter. You going around talking about having truck with the devil . . . God's the one you gonna have to answer to. He's the one gonna be at the Judgment.

LYONS. Yeah, well, look here, Pop . . . Let me have that ten dollars. I'll give it back to you. Bonnie got a job working at the hospital.

TROY. What I tell you, Bono? The only time I see this nigger is when he wants something. That's the only time I see him.

LYONS. Come on, Pop, Mr. Bono don't want to hear all that. Let me have the ten dollars. I told you Bonnie working.

TROY. What that mean to me? "Bonnie working." I don't care if she working. Go ask her for the ten dollars if she working. Talking about "Bonnie working." Why ain't you working?

LYONS. Aw, Pop, you know I can't find no decent job. Where am I gonna get a job at? You know I can't get no job.

TROY. I told you I know some people down there. I can get you on the rubbish if you want to work. I told you that the last time you came by here asking me for something.

LYONS. Naw, Pop . . . thanks. That ain't for me. I don't wanna be carrying nobody's rubbish. I don't wanna be punching nobody's time clock.

TROY. What's the matter, you too good to carry people's rubbish? Where you think that ten dollars you talking about come from? I'm just supposed to haul people's rubbish and give my money to you cause you too lazy to work. You too lazy to work and wanna know why you ain't got what I got.

ROSE. What hospital Bonnie working at? Mercy?

LYONS. She's down at Passavant working in the laundry.

TROY. I ain't got nothing as it is. I give you that ten dollars and I got to eat beans the rest of the week. Naw . . . you ain't getting no ten dollars here.

LYONS. You ain't got to be eating no beans. I don't know why you wanna say that.

TROY. I ain't got no extra money. Gabe done moved over to Miss Pearl's paying her the rent and things done got tight around here. I can't afford to be giving you every payday.

LYONS. I ain't asked you to give me nothing. I asked you to loan me ten dollars. I know you got ten dollars.

TROY. Yeah, I got it. You know why I got it? Cause I don't throw my money away out there in the streets. You living the fast life . . . wanna be a musician . . . running around in them clubs and things . . . then, you learn to take care of yourself. You ain't gonna find me going and asking nobody for nothing. I done spent too many years without.

LYONS. You and me is two different people, Pop.

TROY. I done learned my mistake and learned to do what's right by it. You still trying to get something for nothing. Life don't owe you nothing. You owe it to yourself. Ask Bono. He'll tell you I'm right.

LYONS. You got your way of dealing with the world . . . I got mine. The only thing that matters to me is the music.

TROY. Yeah, I can see that! It don't matter how you gonna eat . . . where your next dollar is coming from. You telling the truth there.

LYONS. I know I got to eat. But I got to live too. I need something that gonna help me to get out of the bed in the morning. Make me feel like I belong in the world. I don't bother nobody. I just stay with the music cause that's the only way I can find to live in the world. Otherwise there ain't no telling what I might do. Now I don't come criticizing you and how you live. I just come by to ask you for ten dollars. I don't wanna hear all that about how I live.

TROY. Boy, your mamma did a hell of a job raising you.

LYONS. You can't change me, Pop. I'm thirty-four years old. If you wanted to change me, you should have been there when I was growing up. I come by to see you . . . ask for ten dollars and you want to talk about how I was raised. You don't know nothing about how I was raised.

ROSE. Let the boy have ten dollars, Troy.

TROY (to Lyons). What the hell you looking at me for? I ain't got no ten dollars. You know what I do with my money. (To Rose.) Give him ten dollars if you want him to have it.

ROSE. I will. Just as soon as you turn it loose.

TROY (handing Rose the money). There it is. Seventy-six dollars and forty-two cents. You see this, Bono? Now, I ain't gonna get but six of that back.

ROSE. You ought to stop telling that lie. Here, Lyons. (She hands him the money.)

LYONS. Thanks, Rose. Look . . . I got to run . . . I'll see you later.

TROY. Wait a minute. You gonna say, "thanks, Rose" and ain't gonna look to see where she got that ten dollars from? See how they do me, Bono?

LYONS. I know she got it from you, Pop. Thanks. I'll give it back to you.

TROY. There he go telling another lie. Time I see that ten dollars . . . he'll be owing me thirty more.

LYONS. See you, Mr. Bono.

BONO. Take care, Lyons!

LYONS. Thanks, Pop. I'll see you again.

Lyons exits the yard.

TROY. I don't know why he don't go and get him a decent job and take care of that woman he got.

BONO. He'll be all right, Troy. The boy is still young.

TROY. The *boy* is thirty-four years old.

ROSE. Let's not get off into all that.

BONO. Look here . . . I got to be going. I got to be getting on. Lucille gonna be waiting.

TROY (*puts his arm around Rose*). See this woman, Bono? I love this woman. I love this woman so much it hurts. I love her so much . . . I done run out of ways of loving her. So I got to go back to basics. Don't you come by my house Monday morning talking about time to go to work . . . 'cause I'm still gonna be stroking!

ROSE. Troy! Stop it now!

BONO. I ain't paying him no mind, Rose. That ain't nothing but gin-talk. Go on, Troy. I'll see you Monday.

TROY. Don't you come by my house, nigger! I done told you what I'm gonna be doing.

The lights go down to black.

SCENE 2

The lights come up on Rose hanging up clothes. She hums and sings softly to herself. It is the following morning.

ROSE (*sings*).

Jesus, be a fence all around me every day
Jesus, I want you to protect me as I travel on my way.
Jesus, be a fence all around me every day.

Troy enters from the house.

Jesus, I want you to protect me
As I travel on my way.

(*To Troy.*) 'Morning. You ready for breakfast? I can fix it soon as I finish hanging up these clothes?

TROY. I got the coffee on. That'll be all right. I'll just drink some of that this morning.

ROSE. That 651 hit yesterday. That's the second time this month. Miss Pearl hit for a dollar . . . seem like those that need the least always get lucky. Poor folks can't get nothing.

TROY. Them numbers don't know nobody. I don't know why you fool with them. You and Lyons both.

ROSE. It's something to do.

TROY. You ain't doing nothing but throwing your money away.

ROSE. Troy, you know I don't play foolishly. I just play a nickel here and a nickel there.

TROY. That's two nickels you done thrown away.

ROSE. Now I hit sometimes . . . that makes up for it. It always comes in handy when I do hit. I don't hear you complaining then.

TROY. I ain't complaining now. I just say it's foolish. Trying to guess out of six hundred ways which way the number gonna come. If I had all the money niggers, these

Negroes, throw away on numbers for one week—just one week—I'd be a rich man.

ROSE. Well, you wishing and calling it foolish ain't gonna stop folks from playing numbers. That's one thing for sure. Besides . . . some good things come from playing numbers. Look where Pope done bought him that restaurant off of numbers.

TROY. I can't stand niggers like that. Man ain't had two dimes to rub together. He walking around with his shoes all run over bumming money for cigarettes. All right. Got lucky there and hit the numbers . . .

ROSE. Troy, I know all about it.

TROY. Had good sense, I'll say that for him. He ain't throwed his money away. I seen niggers hit the numbers and go through two thousand dollars in four days. Man bought him that restaurant down there . . . fixed it up real nice . . . and then didn't want nobody to come in it! A Negro go in there and can't get no kind of service. I seen a white fellow come in there and order a bowl of stew. Pope picked all the meat out of the pot for him. Man ain't had nothing but a bowl of meat! Negro come behind him and ain't got nothing but the potatoes and carrots. Talking about what numbers do for people, you picked a wrong example. Ain't done nothing but make a worser fool out of him than he was before.

ROSE. Troy, you ought to stop worrying about what happened at work yesterday.

TROY. I ain't worried. Just told me to be down there at the Commissioner's office on Friday. Everybody think they gonna fire me. I ain't worried about them firing me. You ain't got to worry about that. (*Pause.*) Where's Cory? Cory in the house? (*Calls.*) Cory?

ROSE. He gone out.

TROY. Out, huh? He gone out 'cause he know I want him to help me with this fence. I know how he is. That boy scared of work.

Gabriel enters. He comes halfway down the alley and, hearing Troy's voice, stops.

TROY (*continues*). He ain't done a lick of work in his life.

ROSE. He had to go to football practice. Coach wanted them to get in a little extra practice before the season start.

TROY. I got his practice . . . running out of here before he get his chores done.

ROSE. Troy, what is wrong with you this morning? Don't nothing set right with you. Go on back in there and go to bed . . . get up on the other side.

TROY. Why something got to be wrong with me? I ain't said nothing wrong with me.

ROSE. You got something to say about everything. First it's the numbers . . . then it's the way the man runs his restaurant . . . then you done got on Cory. What's it gonna be next? Take a look up there and see if the weather suits you . . . or is it gonna be how you gonna put up the fence with the clothes hanging in the yard.

TROY. You hit the nail on the head then.

ROSE. I know you like I know the back of my hand. Go on in there and get you some coffee . . . see if that straighten you up. 'Cause you ain't right this morning.

Troy starts into the house and sees Gabriel. Gabriel starts singing. Troy's brother, he is seven years younger than Troy. Injured in World War II, he has a metal plate in his head. He carries an old trumpet tied around his waist and believes with every fiber of his being that he is the Archangel Gabriel. He carries a chipped basket with an assortment of discarded fruits and vegetables he has picked up in the strip district and which he attempts to sell.

GABRIEL (*singing*).

> Yes, ma'am I got plums
> You ask me how I sell them
> Oh ten cents apiece
> Three for a quarter
> Come and buy now
> 'Cause I'm here today
> And tomorrow I'll be gone

Gabriel enters.

> Hey, Rose!

ROSE. How you doing Gabe?

GABRIEL. There's Troy . . . Hey, Troy!

TROY. Hey, Gabe.

Exit into kitchen.

ROSE (*to Gabriel*). What you got there?

GABRIEL. You know what I got, Rose. I got fruits and vegetables.

ROSE (*looking in basket*). Where's all these plums you talking about?

GABRIEL. I ain't got no plums today, Rose. I was just singing that. Have some tomorrow. Put me in a big order for plums. Have enough plums tomorrow for St. Peter and everybody.

Troy reenters from kitchen, crosses to steps.

(*To Rose.*) Troy's mad at me.

TROY. I ain't mad at you. What I got to be mad at you about? You ain't done nothing to me.

GABRIEL. I just moved over to Miss Pearl's to keep out from in your way. I ain't mean no harm by it.

TROY. Who said anything about that? I ain't said anything about that.

GABRIEL. You ain't mad at me, is you?

TROY. Naw . . . I ain't mad at you, Gabe. If I was mad at you I'd tell you about it.

GABRIEL. Got me two rooms. In the basement. Got my own door too. Wanna see my key? (*He holds up a key.*) That's my own key! My two rooms!

TROY. Well, that's good, Gabe. You got your own key . . . that's good.

ROSE. You hungry, Gabe? I was just fixing to cook Troy his breakfast.

GABRIEL. I'll take some biscuits. You got some biscuits? Did you know when I was in heaven . . . every morning me and St. Peter would sit down by the gate and eat some big fat biscuits? Oh, yeah! We had us a good time. We'd sit there and eat us them biscuits and then St. Peter would go off to sleep and tell me to wake him up when it's time to open the gates for the judgment.

ROSE. Well, come on . . . I'll make up a batch of biscuits.

Rose exits into the house.

GABRIEL. Troy . . . St. Peter got your name in the book. I seen it. It say . . . Troy Maxson. I say . . . I know him! He got the same name like what I got. That's my brother!

TROY. How many times you gonna tell me that, Gabe?

GABRIEL. Ain't got my name in the book. Don't have to have my name. I done died and went to heaven. He got your name though. One morning St. Peter was looking at his book . . . marking it up for the judgment . . . and he let me see your name. Got it in there under M. Got Rose's name . . . I ain't seen it like I seen yours . . . but I know it's in there. He got a great big book. Got everybody's name what was ever been born. That's what he told me. But I seen your name. Seen it with my own eyes.

TROY. Go on in the house there. Rose going to fix you something to eat.

GABRIEL. Oh, I ain't hungry. I done had breakfast with Aunt Jemimah. She come by and cooked me up a whole mess of flapjacks. Remember how we used to eat them flapjacks?

TROY. Go on in the house and get you something to eat now.

GABRIEL. I got to sell my plums. I done sold some tomatoes. Got me two quarters. Wanna see? (*He shows Troy his quarters.*) I'm gonna save them and buy me a new horn so St. Peter can hear me when it's time to open the gates. (*Gabriel stops suddenly. Listens.*) Hear that? That's the hellhounds. I got to chase them out of here. Go on get out of here! Get out!

Gabriel exits singing.

> Better get ready for the judgment
> Better get ready for the judgment
> My Lord is coming down

Rose enters from the house.

TROY. He's gone off somewhere.

GABRIEL (*offstage*).

> Better get ready for the judgment
> Better get ready for the judgment morning
> Better get ready for the judgment
> My God is coming down

ROSE. He ain't eating right. Miss Pearl say she can't get him to eat nothing.

TROY. What you want me to do about it, Rose? I done did everything I can for the man. I can't make him get well. Man got half his head blown away . . . what you expect?

ROSE. Seem like something ought to be done to help him.

TROY. Man don't bother nobody. He just mixed up from that metal plate he got in his head. Ain't no sense for him to go back into the hospital.

ROSE. Least he be eating right. They can help him take care of himself.

TROY. Don't nobody wanna be locked up, Rose. What you wanna lock him up for? Man go over there and fight the war . . . messin' around with them Japs, get half his head blow off . . . and they give him a lousy three thousand dollars. And I had to swoop down on that.

ROSE. Is you fixing to go into that again?

TROY. That's the only way I got a roof over my head . . . cause of that metal plate.

ROSE. Ain't no sense you blaming yourself for nothing. Gabe wasn't in no condition to manage that money. You done what was right by him. Can't nobody say you ain't done what was right by him. Look how long you took care of him . . . till he wanted to have his own place and moved over there with Miss Pearl.

TROY. That ain't what I'm saying, woman! I'm just stating the facts. If my brother didn't have that metal plate in his head . . . I wouldn't have a pot to piss in or a window to throw it out of. And I'm fifty-three years old. Now see if you can understand that!

Troy gets up from the porch and starts to exit the yard.

ROSE. Where you going off to? You been running out of here every Saturday for weeks. I thought you was gonna work on this fence?

TROY. I'm gonna walk down to Taylor's. Listen to the ball game. I'll be back in a bit. I'll work on it when I get back.

He exits the yard. The lights go to black.

SCENE 3

The lights come up on the yard. It is four hours later. Rose is taking down the clothes from the line. Cory enters carrying his football equipment.

ROSE. Your daddy like to had a fit with you running out of here this morning without doing your chores.

CORY. I told you I had to go to practice.

ROSE. He say you were supposed to help him with this fence.

CORY. He been saying that the last four or five Saturdays, and then he don't never do nothing, but go down to Taylors'. Did you tell him about the recruiter?

ROSE. Yeah, I told him.

CORY. What he say?

ROSE. He ain't said nothing too much. You get in there and get started on your chores before he gets back. Go on and scrub down them steps before he gets back here hollering and carrying on.

CORY. I'm hungry. What you got to eat, Mama?

ROSE. Go on and get started on your chores. I got some meat loaf in there. Go on and make you a sandwich . . . and don't leave no mess in there.

Cory exits into the house. Rose continues to take down the clothes. Troy enters the yard and sneaks up and grabs her from behind.

Troy! Go on, now. You liked to scared me to death. What was the score of the game? Lucille had me on the phone and I couldn't keep up with it.

TROY. What I care about the game? Come here, woman. (*He tries to kiss her.*)

ROSE. I thought you went down Taylors' to listen to the game. Go on, Troy! You supposed to be putting up this fence.

TROY (*attempting to kiss her again*). I'll put it up when I finish with what is at hand.

ROSE. Go on, Troy. I ain't studying you.

TROY (*chasing after her*). I'm studying you . . . fixing to do my homework!

ROSE. Troy, you better leave me alone.

TROY. Where's Cory? That boy brought his butt home yet?

ROSE. He's in the house doing his chores.

TROY (*calling*). Cory! Get your butt out here, boy!

Rose exits into the house with the laundry. Troy goes over to the pile of wood, picks up a board, and starts sawing. Cory enters from the house.

TROY. You just now coming in here from leaving this morning?

CORY. Yeah, I had to go to football practice.

TROY. Yeah, what?

CORY. Yessir.

TROY. I ain't but two seconds off you noway. The garbage sitting in there overflowing . . . you ain't done none of your chores . . . and you come in here talking about "Yeah."

CORY. I was just getting ready to do my chores now, Pop . . .

TROY. Your first chore is to help me with this fence on Saturday. Everything else come after that. Now get that saw and cut them boards.

Cory takes the saw and begins cutting the boards. Troy continues working. There is a long pause.

CORY. Hey, Pop . . . why don't you buy a TV?

TROY. What I want with a TV? What I want one of them for?

CORY. Everybody got one. Earl, Ba Bra . . . Jesse!

TROY. I ain't asked you who had one. I say what I want with one?

CORY. So you can watch it. They got lots of things on TV. Baseball games and everything. We could watch the World Series.

TROY. Yeah . . . and how much this TV cost?

CORY. I don't know. They got them on sale for around two hundred dollars.

TROY. Two hundred dollars, huh?

CORY. That ain't that much, Pop.

TROY. Naw, it's just two hundred dollars. See that roof you got over your head at night? Let me tell you something about that roof. It's been over ten years since that roof was last tarred. See now . . . the snow come this winter and sit up there on that roof like it is . . . and it's gonna seep inside. It's just gonna be a little bit . . . ain't gonna hardly notice it. Then the next thing you know, it's gonna be leaking all over the house. Then the wood rot from all that water and you gonna need a whole new roof. Now, how much you think it cost to get that roof tarred?

CORY. I don't know.

TROY. Two hundred and sixty-four dollars . . . cash money. While you thinking about a TV, I got to be thinking about the roof . . . and whatever else go wrong here. Now if you had two hundred dollars, what would you do . . . fix the roof or buy a TV?

CORY. I'd buy a TV. Then when the roof started to leak . . . when it needed fixing . . . I'd fix it.

TROY. Where you gonna get the money from? You done spent it for a TV. You gonna sit up and watch the water run all over your brand new TV.

CORY. Aw, Pop. You got money. I know you do.

TROY. Where I got it at, huh?

CORY. You got it in the bank.

TROY. You wanna see my bankbook? You wanna see that seventy-three dollars and twenty-two cents I got sitting up in there?

CORY. You ain't got to pay for it all at one time. You can put a down payment on it and carry it on home with you.

TROY. Not me. I ain't gonna owe nobody nothing if I can help it. Miss a payment and they come and snatch it right out of your house. Then what you got? Now, soon as I get two hundred dollars clear, then I'll buy a TV. Right now, as soon as I get two hundred and sixty-four dollars, I'm gonna have this roof tarred.

CORY. Aw . . . Pop!

TROY. You go on and get you two hundred dollars and buy one if ya want it. I got better things to do with my money.

CORY. I can't get no two hundred dollars. I ain't never seen two hundred dollars.

TROY. I'll tell you what . . . you get you a hundred dollars and I'll put the other hundred with it.

CORY. All right, I'm gonna show you.

TROY. You gonna show me how you can cut them boards right now.

Cory begins to cut the boards. There is a long pause.

CORY. The Pirates won today. That makes five in a row.

TROY. I ain't thinking about the Pirates. Got an all-white team. Got that boy . . . that Puerto Rican boy . . . Clemente. Don't even half-play him. That boy could be something if they give him a chance. Play him one day and sit him on the bench the next.

CORY. He gets a lot of chances to play.

TROY. I'm talking about playing regular. Playing every day so you can get your timing. That's what I'm talking about.

CORY. They got some white guys on the team that don't play every day. You can't play everybody at the same time.

TROY. If they got a white fellow sitting on the bench . . . you can bet your last dollar he can't play! The colored guy got to be twice as good before he get on the team. That's why I don't want you to get all tied up in them sports. Man on the team and what it get him? They got colored on the team and don't use them. Same as not having them. All them teams the same.

CORY. The Braves got Hank Aaron and Wes Covington. Hank Aaron hit two home runs today. That makes forty-three.

TROY. Hank Aaron ain't nobody. That what you supposed to do. That's how you supposed to play the game. Ain't nothing to it. It's just a matter of timing . . . getting the right follow-through. Hell, I can hit forty-three home runs right now!

CORY. Not off no major-league pitching, you couldn't.

TROY. We had better pitching in the Negro leagues. I hit seven home runs off of Satchel Paige.[4] You can't get no better than that!

CORY. Sandy Koufax. He's leading the league in strikeouts.

TROY. I ain't thinking of no Sandy Koufax.

CORY. You got Warren Spahn and Lew Burdette. I bet you couldn't hit no home runs off of Warren Spahn.

TROY. I'm through with it now. You go on and cut them boards. (*Pause.*) Your mama tell me you done got recruited by a college football team? Is that right?

CORY. Yeah. Coach Zellman say the recruiter gonna be coming by to talk to you. Get you to sign the permission papers.

TROY. I thought you supposed to be working down there at the A&P. Ain't you suppose to be working down there after school?

CORY. Mr. Stawicki say he gonna hold my job for me until after the football season. Say starting next week I can work weekends.

TROY. I thought we had an understanding about this football stuff? You suppose to keep up with your chores and hold that job down at the A&P. Ain't been around here all day on a Saturday. Ain't none of your chores done . . . and now you telling me you done quit your job.

---

[4]Paige (1906–82) was a pitcher in the Negro leagues.

CORY. I'm going to be working weekends.

TROY. You damn right you are! And ain't no need for nobody coming around here to talk to me about signing nothing.

CORY. Hey, Pop . . . you can't do that. He's coming all the way from North Carolina.

TROY. I don't care where he coming from. The white man ain't gonna let you get nowhere with that football noway. You go on and get your book-learning so you can work yourself up in that A&P or learn how to fix cars or build houses or something, get you a trade. That way you have something can't nobody take away from you. You go on and learn how to put your hands to some good use. Besides hauling people's garbage.

CORY. I get good grades, Pop. That's why the recruiter wants to talk with you. You got to keep up your grades to get recruited. This way I'll be going to college. I'll get a chance . . .

TROY. First you gonna get your butt down there to the A&P and get your job back.

CORY. Mr. Stawicki done already hired somebody else 'cause I told him I was playing football.

TROY. You a bigger fool than I thought . . . to let somebody take away your job so you can play some football. Where you gonna get your money to take out your girlfriend and whatnot? What kind of foolishness is that to let somebody take away your job?

CORY. I'm still gonna be working weekends.

TROY. Naw . . . naw. You getting your butt out of here and finding you another job.

CORY. Come on, Pop! I got to practice. I can't work after school and play football too. The team needs me. That's what Coach Zellman say . . .

TROY. I don't care what nobody else say. I'm the boss . . . you understand? I'm the boss around here. I do the only saying what counts.

CORY. Come on, Pop!

TROY. I asked you . . . did you understand?

CORY. Yeah . . .

TROY. What?!

CORY. Yessir.

TROY. You go on down there to that A&P and see if you can get your job back. If you can't do both . . . then you quit the football team. You've got to take the crookeds with the straights.

CORY. Yessir. (Pause.) Can I ask you a question?

TROY. What the hell you wanna ask me? Mr. Stawicki the one you got the questions for.

CORY. How come you ain't never liked me?

TROY. Liked you? Who the hell say I got to like you? What law is there say I got to like you? Wanna stand up in my face and ask a damn foolass question like that. Talking about liking somebody. Come here, boy, when I talk to you.

Cory comes over to where Troy is working. He stands slouched over and Troy shoves him on his shoulder.

Straighten up, goddammit! I asked you a question . . . what law is there say I got to like you?

CORY. None.

TROY. Well, all right then! Don't you eat every day? (Pause.) Answer me when I talk to you! Don't you eat every day?

CORY. Yeah.

TROY. Nigger, as long as you in my house, you put that sir on the end of it when you talk to me.

CORY. Yes . . . sir.

TROY. You eat every day.

CORY. Yessir!

TROY. Got a roof over your head.

CORY. Yessir!

TROY. Got clothes on your back.

CORY. Yessir.

TROY. Why you think that is?

CORY. Cause of you.

TROY. Ah, hell I know it's cause of me . . . but why do you think that is?

CORY (hesitant). Cause you like me.

TROY. Like you? I go out of here every morning . . . bust my butt . . . putting up with them crackers every day . . . cause I like you? You are the biggest fool I ever saw. (Pause.) It's my job. It's my responsibility! You understand that? A man got to take care of his family. You live in my house . . . sleep you behind on my bedclothes . . . fill you belly up with my food . . . cause you my son. You my flesh and blood. Not cause I like you! Cause it's my duty to take care of you. I owe a responsibility to you! Let's get this straight right here . . . before it go along any further . . . I ain't got to like you. Mr. Rand don't give me my money come payday cause he likes me. He gives me cause he owe me. I done give you everything I had to give you. I gave you your life! Me and your mama worked that out between us. And liking your black ass wasn't part of the bargain. Don't you try and go through life worrying about if somebody like you or not. You best be making sure they doing right by you. You understand what I'm saying boy?

CORY. Yessir.

TROY. Then get the hell out of my face, and get on down to that A&P.

Rose has been standing behind the screen door for much of the scene. She enters as Cory exits.

ROSE. Why don't you let the boy go ahead and play football, Troy? Ain't no harm in that. He's just trying to be like you with the sports.

TROY. I don't want him to be like me! I want him to move as far away from my life as he can get. You the only decent thing that ever happened to me. I wish him that. But I don't wish him a thing else from my life. I decided seventeen years ago that boy wasn't getting involved in no sports. Not after what they did to me in the sports.

ROSE. Troy, why don't you admit you was too old to play in the major leagues? For once . . . why don't you admit that?

TROY. What do you mean too old? Don't come telling me I was too old. I just wasn't the right color. Hell, I'm fifty-three years old and can do better than Selkirk's .269 right now!

ROSE. How's was you gonna play ball when you were over forty? Sometimes I can't get no sense out of you.

TROY. I got good sense, woman. I got sense enough not to let my boy get hurt over playing no sports. You been mothering that boy too much. Worried about if people like him.

ROSE. Everything that boy do . . . he do for you. He wants you to say "Good job, son." That's all.

TROY. Rose, I ain't got time for that. He's alive. He's healthy. He's got to make his own way. I made mine. Ain't nobody gonna hold his hand when he get out there in that world.

ROSE. Times have changed from when you was young, Troy. People change. The world's changing around you and you can't even see it.

TROY (slow, methodical). Woman . . . I do the best I can do. I come in here every Friday. I carry a sack of potatoes and a bucket of lard. You all line up at the door with your hands out. I give you the lint from my pockets. I give you my sweat and my blood. I ain't got no tears. I done spent them. We go upstairs in that room at night . . . and I fall down on you and try to blast a hole into forever. I get up Monday morning . . . find my lunch on the table. I go out. Make my way. Find my strength to carry me through to the next Friday. (Pause.) That's all I got, Rose. That's all I got to give. I can't give nothing else.

Troy exits into the house. The lights go down to black.

SCENE 4

It is Friday. Two weeks later. Cory starts out of the house with his football equipment. The phone rings.

CORY (calling). I got it! (He answers the phone and stands in the screen door talking.) Hello? Hey, Jesse. Naw . . . I was just getting ready to leave now.

ROSE (calling). Cory!

CORY. I told you, man, them spikes is all tore up. You can use them if you want, but they ain't no good. Earl got some spikes.

ROSE (calling). Cory!

CORY (calling to Rose). Mam? I'm talking to Jesse. (Into phone.) When she say that? (Pause.) Aw, you lying, man. I'm gonna tell her you said that.

ROSE (calling). Cory, don't you go nowhere!

CORY. I got to go to the game, Ma! (Into the phone.) Yeah, hey, look, I'll talk to you later. Yeah, I'll meet you over Earl's house. Later. Bye, Ma.

Cory exits the house and starts out the yard.

ROSE. Cory, where you going off to? You got that stuff all pulled out and thrown all over your room.

CORY (in the yard). I was looking for my spikes. Jesse wanted to borrow my spikes.

ROSE. Get up there and get that cleaned up before your daddy get back in here.

CORY. I got to go to the game! I'll clean it up *when I get back.*

Cory exits.

ROSE. That's all he need to do is see that room all messed up.

Rose exits into the house. Troy and Bono enter the yard. Troy is dressed in clothes other than his work clothes.

BONO. He told him the same thing he told you. Take it to the union.

TROY. Brownie ain't got that much sense. Man wasn't thinking about nothing. He wait until I confront them on it . . . then he wanna come crying seniority. (Calls.) Hey, Rose!

BONO. I wish I could have seen Mr. Rand's face when he told you.

TROY. He couldn't get it out of his mouth! Liked to bit his tongue! When they called me down there to the Commissioner's office . . . he thought they was gonna fire me. Like everybody else.

BONO. I didn't think they was gonna fire you. I thought they was gonna put you on the warning paper.

TROY. Hey, Rose! (To Bono.) Yeah, Mr. Rand like to bit his tongue.

Troy breaks the seal on the bottle, takes a drink, and hands it to Bono.

BONO. I see you run right down to Taylors' and told that Alberta gal.

TROY (calling). Hey Rose! (To Bono.) I told everybody. Hey, Rose! I went down there to cash my check.

ROSE (entering from the house). Hush all that hollering, man! I know you out here. What they say down there at the Commissioner's office?

TROY. You supposed to come when I call you, woman. Bono'll tell you that. (To Bono.) Don't Lucille come when you call her?

ROSE. Man, hush your mouth. I ain't no dog . . . talk about "come when you call me."

TROY (puts his arm around Rose). You hear this, Bono? I had me an old dog used to get uppity like that. You say, "C'mere, Blue!" . . . and he just lay there and look at you. End up getting a stick and chasing him away trying to make him come.

ROSE. I ain't studying you and your dog. I remember you used to sing that old song.

TROY (*he sings*).

> Hear it ring! Hear it ring! I had a dog his name was
> Blue.

ROSE. Don't nobody wanna hear you sing that old song.

TROY (*sings*).

> You know Blue was mighty true.

ROSE. Used to have Cory running around here singing that
song.

BONO. Hell, I remember that song myself.

TROY (*sings*).

> You know Blue was a good old dog.
> Blue treed a possum in a hollow log.

That was my daddy's song. My daddy made up that song.

ROSE. I don't care who made it up. Don't nobody wanna
hear you sing it.

TROY (*makes a song like calling a dog*). Come here, woman.

ROSE. You come in here carrying on, I reckon they ain't
fired you. What they say down there at the Commissioner's office?

TROY. Look here, Rose . . . Mr. Rand called me into his
office today when I got back from talking to them people
down there . . . it come from up top . . . he called me in
and told me they was making me a driver.

ROSE. Troy, you kidding!

TROY. No I ain't. Ask Bono.

ROSE. Well, that's great, Troy. Now you don't have to hassle
them people no more.

Lyons enters from the street.

TROY. Aw hell, I wasn't looking to see you today. I thought
you was in jail. Got it all over the front page of the *Courier*
about them raiding Sefus's place . . . where you be hanging out with all them thugs.

LYONS. Hey, Pop . . . that ain't got nothing to do with me. I
don't go down there gambling. I go down there to sit in
with the band. I ain't got nothing to do with the gambling part. They got some good music down there.

TROY. They got some rogues . . . is what they got.

LYONS. How you been, Mr. Bono? Hi, Rose.

BONO. I see where you playing down at the Crawford Grill
tonight.

ROSE. How come you ain't brought Bonnie like I told you?
You should have brought Bonnie with you, she ain't been
over in a month of Sundays.

LYONS. I was just in the neighborhood . . . thought I'd stop by.

TROY. Here he come . . .

BONO. Your daddy got a promotion on the rubbish. He's
gonna be the first colored driver. Ain't got to do nothing
but sit up there and read the paper like them white fellows.

LYONS. Hey, Pop . . . if you knew how to read you'd be all right.

BONO. Naw . . . naw . . . you mean if the nigger knew how
to drive he'd be all right. Been fighting with them people

about driving and ain't even got a license. Mr. Rand
know you ain't got no driver's license?

TROY. Driving ain't nothing. All you do is point the truck
where you want it to go. Driving ain't nothing.

BONO. Do Mr. Rand know you ain't got no driver's license?
That's what I'm talking about. I ain't asked if driving was
easy. I asked if Mr. Rand know you ain't got no driver's
license.

TROY. He ain't got to know. The man ain't got to know my
business. Time he find out, I have two or three driver's
licenses.

LYONS (*going into his pocket*). Say, look here, Pop . . .

TROY. I knew it was coming. Didn't I tell you, Bono? I know
what kind of "Look here, Pop" that was. The nigger fixing to ask me for some money. It's Friday night. It's my
payday. All them rogues down there on the avenue . . .
the ones that ain't in jail . . . and Lyons is hopping in his
shoes to get down there with them.

LYONS. See, Pop . . . if you give somebody else a chance to
talk sometimes, you'd see that I was fixing to pay you
back your ten dollars like I told you. Here . . . I told you
I'd pay you when Bonnie got paid.

TROY. Naw . . . you go ahead and keep that ten dollars. Put
it in the bank. The next time you feel like you wanna
come by here and ask me for something . . . you go on
down there and get that.

LYONS. Here's your ten dollars, Pop. I told you I don't want you
to give me nothing. I just wanted to borrow ten dollars.

TROY. Naw . . . you go on and keep that for the next time
you want to ask me.

LYONS. Come on, Pop . . . here go your ten dollars.

ROSE. Why don't you go on and let the boy pay you back,
Troy?

LYONS. Here you go, Rose. If you don't take it I'm gonna
have to hear about it for the next six months. (*He hands
her the money.*)

ROSE. You can hand yours over here too, Troy.

TROY. You see this, Bono. You see how they do me.

BONO. Yeah, Lucille do me the same way.

Gabriel is heard singing off stage. He enters.

GABRIEL. Better get ready for the Judgment! Better get ready
for . . . Hey! . . . Hey! . . . There's Troy's boy!

LYONS. How are you doing, Uncle Gabe?

GABRIEL. Lyons . . . The King of the Jungle! Rose . . . hey,
Rose. Got a flower for you. (*He takes a rose from his pocket.*)
Picked it myself. That's the same rose like you is!

ROSE. That's right nice of you, Gabe.

LYONS. What you been doing, Uncle Gabe?

GABRIEL. Oh, I been chasing hellhounds and waiting on the
time to tell St. Peter to open the gates.

LYONS. You been chasing hellhounds, huh? Well . . . you
doing the right thing, Uncle Gabe. Somebody got to
chase them.

GABRIEL. Oh, yeah . . . I know it. The devil's strong. The
devil ain't no pushover. Hellhounds snipping at every-

body's heels. But I got my trumpet waiting on the judgment time.

LYONS. Waiting on the Battle of Armageddon, huh?

GABRIEL. Ain't gonna be too much of a battle when God get to waving that Judgment sword. But the people's gonna have a hell of a time trying to get into heaven if them gates ain't open.

LYONS (*putting his arm around Gabriel*). You hear this, Pop. Uncle Gabe, you all right!

GABRIEL (*laughing with Lyons*). Lyons! King of the Jungle.

ROSE. You gonna stay for supper, Gabe? Want me to fix you a plate?

GABRIEL. I'll take a sandwich, Rose. Don't want no plate. Just wanna eat with my hands. I'll take a sandwich.

ROSE. How about you, Lyons? You staying? Got some short ribs cooking.

LYONS. Naw, I won't eat nothing till after we finished playing. (*Pause.*) You ought to come down and listen to me play, Pop.

TROY. I don't like that Chinese music. All that noise.

ROSE. Go on in the house and wash up, Gabe . . . I'll fix you a sandwich.

GABRIEL (*to Lyons, as he exits*). Troy's mad at me.

LYONS. What you mad at Uncle Gabe for, Pop?

ROSE. He thinks Troy's mad at him cause he moved over to Miss Pearl's.

TROY. I ain't mad at the man. He can live where he want to live at.

LYONS. What he move over there for? Miss Pearl don't like nobody.

ROSE. She don't mind him none. She treats him real nice. She just don't allow all that singing.

TROY. She don't mind that rent he be paying . . . that's what she don't mind.

ROSE. Troy, I ain't going through that with you no more. He's over there cause he want to have his own place. He can come and go as he please.

TROY. Hell, he could come and go as he please here. I wasn't stopping him. I ain't put no rules on him.

ROSE. It ain't the same thing, Troy. And you know it.

Gabriel comes to the door.

Now, that's the last I wanna hear about that. I don't wanna hear nothing else about Gabe and Miss Pearl. And next week . . .

GABRIEL. I'm ready for my sandwich, Rose.

ROSE. And next week . . . when that recruiter come from that school . . . I want you to sign that paper and go on and let Cory play football. Then that'll be the last I have to hear about that.

TROY (*to Rose as she exits into the house*). I ain't thinking about Cory nothing.

LYONS. What . . . Cory got recruited? What school he going to?

TROY. That boy walking around here smelling his piss . . . thinking he's grown. Thinking he's gonna do what he want, irrespective of what I say. Look here, Bono . . . I left the Commissioner's office and went down to the A&P . . . that boy ain't working down there. He lying to me. Telling me he got his job back . . . telling me he working weekends . . . telling me he working after school . . . Mr. Stawicki tell me he ain't working down there at all!

LYONS. Cory just growing up. He's just busting at the seams trying to fill out your shoes.

TROY. I don't care what he's doing. When he get to the point where he wanna disobey me . . . then it's time for him to move on. Bono'll tell you that. I bet he ain't never disobeyed his daddy without paying the consequences.

BONO. I ain't never had a chance. My daddy came on through . . . but I ain't never knew him to see him . . . or what he had on his mind or where he went. Just moving on through. Searching out the New Land. That's what the old folks used to call it. See a fellow moving around from place to place . . . woman to woman . . . called it searching out the New Land. I can't say if he ever found it. I come along, didn't want no kids. Didn't know if I was gonna be in one place long enough to fix on them right as their daddy. I figured I was going searching too. As it turned out I been hooked up with Lucille near about as long as your daddy been with Rose. Going on sixteen years.

TROY. Sometimes I wish I hadn't known my daddy. He ain't cared nothing about no kids. A kid to him wasn't nothing. All he wanted was for you to learn how to walk so he could start you to working. When it come time for eating . . . he ate first. If there was anything left over, that's what you got. Man would sit down and eat two chickens and give you the wing.

LYONS. You ought to stop that, Pop. Everybody feed their kids. No matter how hard times is . . . everybody care about their kids. Make sure they have something to eat.

TROY. The only thing my daddy cared about was getting them bales of cotton in to Mr. Lubin. That's the only thing that mattered to him. Sometimes I used to wonder why he was living. Wonder why the devil hadn't come and got him. "Get them bales of cotton in to Mr. Lubin" and find out he owe him money . . .

LYONS. He should have just went on and left when he saw he couldn't get nowhere. That's what I would have done.

TROY. How he gonna leave with eleven kids? And where he gonna go? He ain't knew how to do nothing but farm. No, he was trapped and I think he knew it. But I'll say this for him . . . he felt a responsibility toward us. Maybe he ain't treated us the way I felt he should have . . . but without that responsibility he could have walked off and left us . . . made his own way.

BONO. A lot of them did. Back in those days what you talking about . . . they walk out their front door and just take on down one road or another and keep on walking.

LYONS. There you go! That's what I'm talking about.

BONO. Just keep on walking till you come to something else. Ain't you never heard of nobody having the walking blues? Well, that's what you call it when you just take off like that.

TROY. My daddy ain't had them walking blues! What you talking about? He stayed right there with his family. But he was just as evil as he could be. My mama couldn't stand him. Couldn't stand that evilness. She run off when I was about eight. She sneaked off one night after he had gone to sleep. Told me she was coming back for me. I ain't never seen her no more. All his women run off and left him. He wasn't good for nobody.

When my turn come to head out, I was fourteen and got to sniffing around Joe Canewell's daughter. Had us an old mule we called Greyboy. My daddy sent me out to do some plowing and I tied up Greyboy and went to fooling around with Joe Canewell's daughter. We done found us a nice little spot, got real cozy with each other. She about thirteen and we done figured we was grown anyway . . . so we down there enjoying ourselves . . . ain't thinking about nothing. We didn't know Greyboy had got loose and wandered back to the house and my daddy was looking for me. We down there by the creek enjoying ourselves when my daddy come up on us. Surprised us. He had them leather straps off the mule and commenced to whupping me like there was no tomorrow. I jumped up, mad and embarrassed. I was scared of my daddy. When he commenced to whupping on me . . . quite naturally I run to get out of the way. (*Pause.*) Now I thought he was mad cause I ain't done my work. But I see where he was chasing me off so he could have the gal for himself. When I see what the matter of it was, I lost all fear of my daddy. Right there is where I become a man . . . at fourteen years of age. (*Pause.*) Now it was my turn to run him off. I picked up them same reins that he had used on me. I picked up them reins and commenced to whupping on him. The gal jumped up and run off . . . and when my daddy turned to face me, I could see why the devil had never come to get him . . . cause he was the devil himself. I don't know what happened. When I woke up, I was laying right there by the creek, and Blue . . . this old dog we had . . . was licking my face. I thought I was blind. I couldn't see nothing. Both my eyes were swollen shut. I laid there and cried. I didn't know what I was gonna do. The only thing I knew was the time had come for me to leave my daddy's house. And right there the world suddenly got big. And it was a long time before I could cut it down to where I could handle it.

Part of that cutting down was when I got to the place where I could feel him kicking in my blood and knew that the only thing that separated us was the matter of a few years.

Gabriel enters from the house with a sandwich.

LYONS. What you got there, Uncle Gabe?

GABRIEL. Got me a ham sandwich. Rose gave me a ham sandwich.

TROY. I don't know what happened to him. I done lost touch with everybody except Gabriel. But I hope he's dead. I hope he found some peace.

LYONS. That's a heavy story, Pop. I didn't know you left home when you was fourteen.

TROY. And didn't know nothing. The only part of the world I knew was the forty-two acres of Mr. Lubin's land. That's all I knew about life.

LYONS. Fourteen's kinda young to be out on your own. (*Phone rings.*) I don't even think I was ready to be out on my own at fourteen. I don't know what I would have done.

TROY. I got up from the creek and walked on down to Mobile. I was through with farming. Figured I could do better in the city. So I walked the two hundred miles to Mobile.

LYONS. Wait a minute . . . you ain't walked no two hundred miles, Pop. Ain't nobody gonna walk no two hundred miles. You talking about some walking there.

BONO. That's the only way you got anywhere back in them days.

LYONS. Shhh. Damn if I wouldn't have hitched a ride with somebody!

TROY. Who you gonna hitch it with? They ain't had no cars and things like they got now. We talking about 1918.

ROSE (*entering*). What you all out here getting into?

TROY (*to Rose*). I'm telling Lyons how good he got it. He don't know nothing about this I'm talking.

ROSE. Lyons, that was Bonnie on the phone. She say you supposed to pick her up.

LYONS. Yeah, okay, Rose.

TROY. I walked on down to Mobile and hitched up with some of them fellows that was heading this way. Got up here and found out . . . not only couldn't you get a job . . . you couldn't find no place to live. I thought I was in freedom. Shhh. Colored folks living down there on the riverbanks in whatever kind of shelter they could find for themselves. Right down there under the Brady Street Bridge. Living in shacks made of sticks and tarpaper. Messed around there and went from bad to worse. Started stealing. First it was food. Then I figured, hell, if I steal money I can buy me some food. Buy me some shoes too! One thing led to another. Met your mama. I was young and anxious to be a man. Met your mama and had you. What I do that for? Now I got to worry about feeding you and her. Got to steal three times as much. Went out one day looking for somebody to rob . . . that's what I was, a robber. I'll tell you the truth. I'm ashamed of it today. But it's the truth. Went to rob this fellow . . . pulled out my knife . . . and he pulled out a gun. Shot me in the chest. I felt just like somebody had taken a hot branding iron and laid it on me. When he shot me I jumped at him with my knife. They told me I killed him and they put me in the penitentiary and locked me up for fifteen years. That's where I met Bono. That's where I learned how to play baseball. Got out that place and your mama had taken you and went on to make life without me. Fifteen years was a long time for her to wait. But that fifteen years cured me of that robbing stuff. Rose'll tell you. She asked me when I met her if I had gotten all that foolishness out of my system. And I told her, "Baby, it's you and baseball all what count with me." You hear me, Bono? I meant it too. She say, "Which one comes first?" I told her, "Baby, ain't no doubt it's baseball . . . but you stick and get old with me and we'll both outlive this baseball." Am I right, Rose? And it's true.

ROSE. Man, hush your mouth. You ain't said no such thing. Talking about, "Baby you know you'll always be number one with me." That's what you was talking.

TROY. You hear that, Bono. That's why I love her.

BONO. Rose'll keep you straight. You get off the track, she'll straighten you up.

ROSE. Lyons, you better get on up and get Bonnie. She waiting on you.

LYONS (gets up to go). Hey, Pop, why don't you come on down to the Grill and hear me play?

TROY. I ain't going down there. I'm too old to be sitting around in them clubs.

BONO. You got to be good to play down at the Grill.

LYONS. Come on, Pop . . .

TROY. I got to get up in the morning.

LYONS. You ain't got to stay long.

TROY. Naw, I'm gonna get my supper and go on to bed.

LYONS. Well, I got to go. I'll see you again.

TROY. Don't you come around my house on my payday.

ROSE. Pick up the phone and let somebody know you coming. And bring Bonnie with you. You know I'm always glad to see her.

LYONS. Yeah, I'll do that, Rose. You take care now. See you, Pop. See you, Mr. Bono. See you, Uncle Gabe.

GABRIEL. Lyons! King of the Jungle!

Lyons exits.

TROY. Is supper ready, woman? Me and you got some business to take care of. I'm gonna tear it up too.

ROSE. Troy, I done told you now!

TROY (puts his arm around Bono). Aw hell, woman . . . this is Bono. Bono like family. I done known this nigger since . . . how long I done know you?

BONO. It's been a long time.

TROY. I done know this nigger since Skippy was a pup. Me and him done been through some times.

BONO. You sure right about that.

TROY. Hell, I done know him longer than I known you. And we still standing shoulder to shoulder. Hey, look here, Bono . . . a man can't ask for no more than that. (Drinks to him.) I love you, nigger.

BONO. Hell, I love you too . . . I got to get home see my woman. You got yours in hand. I got to get mine.

Bono starts to exit as Cory enters the yard, dressed in his football uniform. He gives Troy a hard, uncompromising look.

CORY. What you do that for, Pop?

He throws his helmet down in the direction of Troy.

ROSE. What's the matter? Cory . . . what's the matter?

CORY. Papa done went up to the school and told Coach Zellman I can't play football no more. Wouldn't even let me play the game. Told him to tell the recruiter not to come.

ROSE. Troy . . .

TROY. What you Troying me for. Yeah, I did it. And the boy know why I did it.

CORY. Why you wanna do that to me? That was the one chance I had.

ROSE. Ain't nothing wrong with Cory playing football, Troy.

TROY. The boy lied to me. I told the nigger if he wanna play football . . . to keep up his chores and hold down that job at the A&P. That was the conditions. Stopped down there to see Mr. Stawicki . . .

CORY. I can't work after school during the football season, Pop! I tried to tell you that Mr. Stawicki's holding my job for me. You don't never want to listen to nobody. And then you wanna go and do this to me!

TROY. I ain't done nothing to you. You done it to yourself.

CORY. Just cause you didn't have a chance! You just scared I'm gonna be better than you, that's all.

TROY. Come here.

ROSE. Troy . . .

Cory reluctantly crosses over to Troy.

TROY. All right! See. You done made a mistake.

CORY. I didn't even do nothing!

TROY. I'm gonna tell you what your mistake was. See . . . you swung at the ball and didn't hit it. That's strike one. See, you in the batter's box now. You swung and you missed. That's strike one. Don't you strike out!

Lights fade to black.

ACT 2

SCENE 1

The following morning. Cory is at the tree hitting the ball with the bat. He tries to mimic Troy, but his swing is awkward, less sure. Rose enters from the house.

ROSE. Cory, I want you to help me with this cupboard.

CORY. I ain't quitting the team. I don't care what Poppa say.

ROSE. I'll talk to him when he gets back. He had to go see about your Uncle Gabe. The police done arrested him. Say he was disturbing the peace. He'll be back directly. Come on in here and help me clean out the top of this cupboard.

Cory exits into the house. Rose sees Troy and Bono coming down the alley.

Troy . . . what they say down there?

TROY. Ain't said nothing. I give them fifty dollars and they let him go. I'll talk to you about it. Where's Cory?

ROSE. He's in there helping me clean out these cupboards.

TROY. Tell him to get his butt out here.

Troy and Bono go over to the pile of wood. Bono picks up the saw and begins sawing.

TROY (*to Bono*). All they want is the money. That makes six or seven times I done went down there and got him. See me coming they stick out their hands.

BONO. Yeah. I know what you mean. That's all they care about . . . that money. They don't care about what's right. (*Pause.*) Nigger, why you got to go and get some hard wood? You ain't doing nothing but building a little old fence. Get you some soft pine wood. That's all you need.

TROY. I know what I'm doing. This is outside wood. You put pine wood inside the house. Pine wood is inside wood. This here is outside wood. Now you tell me where the fence is gonna be?

BONO. You don't need this wood. You can put it up with pine wood and it'll stand as long as you gonna be here looking at it.

TROY. How you know how long I'm gonna be here, nigger? Hell, I might just live forever. Live longer than old man Horsely.

BONO. That's what Magee used to say.

TROY. Magee's damn fool. Now you tell me who you ever heard of gonna pull their own teeth with a pair of rusty pliers.

BONO. The old folks . . . my granddaddy used to pull his teeth with pliers. They ain't had no dentists for the colored folks back then.

TROY. Get clean pliers! You understand? Clean pliers! Sterilize them! Besides we ain't living back then. All Magee had to do was walk over to Doc Goldblum's.

BONO. I see where you and that Tallahassee gal . . . that Alberta . . . I see where you all done got tight.

TROY. What you mean "got tight"?

BONO. I see where you be laughing and joking with her all the time.

TROY. I laughs and jokes with all of them, Bono. You know me.

BONO. That ain't the kind of laughing and joking I'm talking about.

Cory enters from the house.

CORY. How you doing. Mr. Bono?

TROY. Cory? Get that saw from Bono and cut some wood. He talking about the wood's too hard to cut. Stand back there, Jim, and let that young boy show you how it's done.

BONO. He's sure welcome to it.

Cory takes the saw and begins to cut the wood.

Whew-e-e! Look at that. Big old strong boy. Look like Joe Louis. Hell, must be getting old the way I'm watching that boy whip through that wood.

CORY. I don't see why Mama want a fence around the yard noways.

TROY. Damn if I know either. What the hell she keeping out with it? She ain't got nothing nobody want.

BONO. Some people build fences to keep people out . . . and other people build fences to keep people in. Rose wants to hold on to you all. She loves you.

TROY. Hell, nigger, I don't need nobody to tell me my wife loves me. Cory . . . go on in the house and see if you can find that other saw.

CORY. Where's it at?

TROY. I said find it! Look for it till you find it!

Cory exits into the house.

What's that supposed to mean? Wanna keep us in?

BONO. Troy . . . I done known you seem like damn near my whole life. You and Rose both. I done know both of you all for a long time. I remember when you met Rose. When you was hitting them baseball out the park. A lot of them old gals was after you then. You had the pick of the litter. When you picked Rose, I was happy for you. That was the first time I knew you had any sense. I said . . . My man Troy knows what he's doing . . . I'm gonna follow this nigger . . . he might take me somewhere. I been following you too. I done learned a whole heap of things about life watching you. I done learned how to tell where the shit lies. How to tell it from the alfalfa. You done learned me a lot of things. You showed me how to not make the same mistakes . . . to take life as it comes along and keep putting one foot in front of the other. (*Pause.*) Rose a good woman, Troy.

TROY. Hell, nigger, I know she a good woman. I been married to her for eighteen years. What you got on your mind, Bono?

BONO. I just say she a good woman. Just like I say anything. I ain't got to have nothing on my mind.

TROY. You just gonna say she a good woman and leave it hanging out there like that? Why you telling me she a good woman?

BONO. She loves you, Troy. Rose loves you.

TROY. You saying I don't measure up. That's what you trying to say. I don't measure up cause I'm seeing this other gal. I know what you trying to say.

BONO. I know what Rose means to you, Troy. I'm just trying to say I don't want to see you mess up.

TROY. Yeah, I appreciate that, Bono. If you was messing around on Lucille I'd be telling you the same thing.

BONO. Well, that's all I got to say. I just say that because I love you both.

TROY. Hell, you know me . . . I wasn't out there looking for nothing. You can't find a better woman than Rose. I know that. But seems like this woman just stuck onto me where I can't shake her loose. I done wrestled with it, tried to throw her off me . . . but she just stuck on tighter. Now she's stuck on for good.

BONO. You's in control . . . that's what you tell me all the time. You responsible for what you do.

TROY. I ain't ducking the responsibility of it. As long as it sets right in my heart . . . then I'm okay. Cause that's all I listen to. It'll tell me right from wrong every time. And I ain't talking about doing Rose no bad turn. I love Rose. She done carried me a long ways and I love and respect her for that.

BONO. I know you do. That's why I don't want to see you hurt her. But what you gonna do when she find out? What you got then? If you try and juggle both of them . . . sooner or later you gonna drop one of them. That's common sense.

TROY. Yeah, I hear what you saying, Bono. I been trying to figure a way to work it out.

BONO. Work it out right, Troy. I don't want to be getting all up between you and Rose's business . . . but work it so it come out right.

TROY. Ah hell, I get all up between you and Lucille's business. When you gonna get that woman that refrigerator she been wanting? Don't tell me you ain't got no money now. I know who your banker is. Mellon don't need that money bad as Lucille want that refrigerator. I'll tell you that.

BONO. Tell you what I'll do . . . when you finish building this fence for Rose . . . I'll buy Lucille that refrigerator.

TROY. You done stuck your foot in your mouth now!

Troy grabs up a board and begins to saw. Bono starts to walk out the yard.

Hey, nigger . . . where you going?

BONO. I'm going home. I know you don't expect me to help you now. I'm protecting my money. I wanna see you put that fence up by yourself. That's what I want to see. You'll be here another six months without me.

TROY. Nigger, you ain't right.

BONO. When it comes to my money . . . I'm right as fireworks on the Fourth of July.

TROY. All right, we gonna see now. You better get out your bankbook.

Bono exits, and Troy continues to work. Rose enters from the house.

ROSE. What they say down there? What's happening with Gabe?

TROY. I went down there and got him out. Cost me fifty dollars. Say he was disturbing the peace. Judge set up a hearing for him in three weeks. Say to show cause why he shouldn't be recommitted.

ROSE. What was he doing that cause them to arrest him?

TROY. Some kids was teasing him and he run them off home. Say he was howling and carrying on. Some folks seen him and called the police. That's all it was.

ROSE. Well, what's you say? What'd you tell the judge?

TROY. Told him I'd look after him. It didn't make no sense to recommit the man. He stuck out his big greasy palm and told me to give him fifty dollars and take him on home.

ROSE. Where's he at now? Where'd he go off to?

TROY. He's gone about his business. He don't need nobody to hold his hand.

ROSE. Well, I don't know. Seem like that would be the best place for him if they did put him into the hospital. I know what you're gonna say. But that's what I think would be best.

TROY. The man done had his life ruined fighting for what? And they wanna take and lock him up. Let him be free. He don't bother nobody.

ROSE. Well, everybody got their own way of looking at it I guess. Come on and get your lunch. I got a bowl of lima beans and some cornbread in the oven. Come and get something to eat. Ain't no sense you fretting over Gabe.

Rose turns to go into the house.

TROY. Rose . . . got something to tell you.

ROSE. Well, come on . . . wait till I get this food on the table.

TROY. Rose!

She stops and turns around.

I don't know how to say this. (*Pause.*) I can't explain it none. It just sort of grows on you till it gets out of hand. It starts out like a little bush . . . and the next thing you know it's a whole forest.

ROSE. Troy . . . what is you talking about?

TROY. I'm talking, woman, let me talk. I'm trying to find a way to tell you . . . I'm gonna be a daddy. I'm gonna be somebody's daddy.

ROSE. Troy . . . you're not telling me this? You're gonna be . . . what?

TROY. Rose . . . now . . . see . . .

ROSE. You telling me you gonna be somebody's daddy? You telling your *wife* this?

Gabriel enters from the street. He carries a rose in his hand.

GABRIEL. Hey, Troy! Hey, Rose!

ROSE. I have to wait eighteen years to hear something like this.

GABRIEL. Hey, Rose . . . I got a flower for you. (*He hands it to her.*) That's a rose. Same rose like you is.

ROSE. Thanks, Gabe.

GABRIEL. Troy, you ain't mad at me is you? Them bad mens come and put me away. You ain't mad at me is you?

TROY. Naw, Gabe, I ain't mad at you.

ROSE. Eighteen years and you wanna come with this.

GABRIEL (*takes a quarter out of his pocket*). See what I got? Got a brand new quarter.

TROY. Rose . . . it's just . . .

ROSE. Ain't nothing you can say, Troy. Ain't no way of explaining that.

GABRIEL. Fellow that give me this quarter had a whole mess of them. I'm gonna keep this quarter till it stop shining.

ROSE. Gabe, go on in the house there. I got some watermelon in the Frigidaire. Go on and get you a piece.

GABRIEL. Say, Rose . . . you know I was chasing hellhounds and them bad mens come and get me and take me away. Troy helped me. He come down there and told them they better let me go before he beat them up. Yeah, he did!

ROSE. You go on and get you a piece of watermelon, Gabe. Them bad mens is gone now.

GABRIEL. Okay, Rose . . . gonna get me some watermelon. The kind with the stripes on it.

Gabriel exits into the house.

ROSE. Why, Troy? Why? After all these years to come dragging this in to me now. It don't make no sense at your age. I could have expected this ten or fifteen years ago, but not now.

TROY. Age ain't got nothing to do with it, Rose.

ROSE. I done tried to be everything a wife should be. Everything a wife could be. Been married eighteen years and I got to live to see the day you tell me you been seeing another woman and done fathered a child by her. And you know I ain't never wanted no half nothing in my family. My whole family is half. Everybody got different fathers and mothers . . . my two sisters and my brother. Can't hardly tell who's who. Can't never sit down and talk about Papa and Mama. It's your papa and your mama and my papa and my mama . . .

TROY. Rose . . . stop it now.

ROSE. I ain't never wanted that for none of my children. And now you wanna drag your behind in here and tell me something like this.

TROY. You ought to know. It's time for you to know.

ROSE. Well, I don't want to know, goddamn it!

TROY. I can't just make it go away. It's done now. I can't wish the circumstance of the thing away.

ROSE. And you don't want to either. Maybe you want to wish me and my boy away. Maybe that's what you want? Well, you can't wish us away. I've got eighteen years of my life invested in you. You ought to have stayed upstairs in my bed where you belong.

TROY. Rose . . . now listen to me . . . we can get a handle on this thing. We can talk this out . . . come to an understanding.

ROSE. All of a sudden it's "we." Where was "we" at when you was down there rolling around with some godforsaken woman? "We" should have come to an understanding before you started making a damn fool of yourself. You're a day late and a dollar short when it comes to an understanding with me.

TROY. It's just . . . She gives me a different idea . . . a different understanding about myself. I can step out of this house and get away from the pressures and problems . . . be a different man. I ain't got to wonder how I'm gonna pay the bills or get the roof fixed. I can just be a part of myself that I ain't never been.

ROSE. What I want to know . . . is do you plan to continue seeing her. That's all you can say to me.

TROY. I can sit up in her house and laugh. Do you understand what I'm saying. I can laugh out loud . . . and it feels good. It reaches all the way down to the bottom of my shoes. (*Pause.*) Rose, I can't give that up.

ROSE. Maybe you ought to go on and stay down there with her . . . if she's a better woman than me.

TROY. It ain't about nobody being a better woman or nothing. Rose, you ain't the blame. A man couldn't ask for no woman to be a better wife than you've been. I'm responsible for it. I done locked myself into a pattern trying to take care of you all that I forgot about myself.

ROSE. What the hell was I there for? That was my job, not somebody else's.

TROY. Rose, I done tried all my life to live decent . . . to live a clean . . . hard . . . useful life. I tried to be a good husband to you. In every way I knew how. Maybe I come into the world backwards, I don't know. But . . . you born with two strikes on you before you come to the plate. You got to guard it closely . . . always looking for the curve ball on the inside corner. You can't afford to let none get past you. You can't afford a call strike. If you going down . . . you going down swinging. Everything lined up against you. What you gonna do. I fooled them, Rose. I bunted. When I found you and Cory and a halfway decent job . . . I was safe. Couldn't nothing touch me. I wasn't gonna strike out no more. I wasn't going back to the penitentiary. I wasn't gonna lay in the streets with a bottle of wine. I was safe. I had me a family. A job. I wasn't gonna get that last strike. I was on first looking for one of them boys to knock me in. To get me home.

ROSE. You should have stayed in my bed, Troy.

TROY. Then when I saw that gal . . . she firmed up my backbone. And I got to thinking that if I tried . . . I just might be able to steal second. Do you understand after eighteen years I wanted to steal second.

ROSE. You should have held me tight. You should have grabbed me and held on.

TROY. I stood on first base for eighteen years and I thought . . . well, goddamn it . . . go on for it!

ROSE. We're not talking about baseball! We're talking about you going off to lay in bed with another woman . . . and then bring it home to me. That's what we're talking about. We ain't talking about no baseball.

TROY. Rose, you're not listening to me. I'm trying the best I can to explain it to you. It's not easy for me to admit that I been standing in the same place for eighteen years.

ROSE. I been standing with you! I been right here with you, Troy. I got a life too. I gave eighteen years of my life to stand in the same spot with you. Don't you think I ever wanted other things? Don't you think I had dreams and hopes? What about my life? What about me. Don't you think it ever crossed my mind to want to know other men? That I wanted to lay up somewhere and forget about my responsibilities? That I wanted someone to make me laugh so I could feel good? You not the only one who's got wants and needs. But I held on to you, Troy. I took all my feelings, my wants and needs, my dreams . . . and I buried them inside you. I planted a seed and watched and prayed over it. I planted myself inside you and waited to bloom. And it didn't take me no eighteen years to find out the soil was hard and rocky and it wasn't never gonna bloom.

But I held on to you, Troy. I held you tighter. You was my husband. I owed you everything I had. Every part of me I could find to give you. And upstairs in that room . . . with the darkness falling in on me . . . I gave everything I had to try and erase the doubt that you wasn't the finest man in the world. And wherever you was going . . . I wanted to be there with you. Cause you was my husband. Cause that's the only way I was gonna survive as your wife. You always talking about what you give . . . and what you don't have to give. But you take too. You take . . . and don't even know nobody's giving!

Rose turns to exit into the house; Troy grabs her arm.

TROY. You say I take and don't give!

ROSE. Troy! You're hurting me!

TROY. You say I take and don't give!

ROSE. Troy . . . you're hurting my arm! Let go!

TROY. I done give you everything I got. Don't you tell that lie on me.

ROSE. Troy!

TROY. Don't you tell that lie on me!

Cory enters from the house.

CORY. Mama!

ROSE. Troy. You're hurting me.

TROY. Don't you tell me about no taking and giving.

Cory comes up behind Troy and grabs him. Troy, surprised, is thrown off balance just as Cory throws a glancing blow that catches him on the chest and knocks him down. Troy is stunned, as is Cory.

ROSE. Troy. Troy. No!

Troy gets to his feet and starts at Cory.

Troy . . . no. Please! Troy!

Rose pulls on Troy to hold him back. Troy stops himself.

TROY (*to Cory*). All right. That's strike two. You stay away from around me, boy. Don't you strike out. You living with a full count. Don't you strike out.

Troy exits out the yard as the lights go down.

SCENE 2

It is six months later, early afternoon. Troy enters from the house and starts to exit the yard. Rose enters from the house.

ROSE. Troy, I want to talk to you.

TROY. All of a sudden, after all this time, you want to talk to me, huh? You ain't wanted to talk to me for months. You ain't wanted to talk to me last night. You ain't wanted no part of me then. What you wanna talk to me about now?

ROSE. Tomorrow's Friday.

TROY. I know what day tomorrow is. You think I don't know tomorrow's Friday? My whole life I ain't done nothing but look to see Friday coming and you got to tell me it's Friday.

ROSE. I want to know if you're coming home.

TROY. I always come home, Rose. You know that. There ain't never been a night I ain't come home.

ROSE. That ain't what I mean . . . and you know it. I want to know if you're coming straight home after work.

TROY. I figure I'd cash my check . . . hang out at Taylors' with the boys . . . maybe play a game of checkers . . .

ROSE. Troy, I can't live like this. I won't live like this. You livin' on borrowed time with me. It's been going on six months now you ain't been coming home.

TROY. I be here every night. Every night of the year. That's 365 days.

ROSE. I want you to come home tomorrow after work.

TROY. Rose . . . I don't mess up my pay. You know that now. I take my pay and I give it to you. I don't have no money but what you give me back. I just want to have a little time to myself . . . a little time to enjoy life.

ROSE. What about me? When's my time to enjoy life?

TROY. I don't know what to tell you, Rose. I'm doing the best I can.

ROSE. You ain't been home from work but time enough to change your clothes and run out . . . and you wanna call that the best you can do?

TROY. I'm going over to the hospital to see Alberta. She went into the hospital this afternoon. Look like she might have the baby early. I won't be gone long.

ROSE. Well, you ought to know. They went over to Miss Pearl's and got Gabe today. She said you told them to go ahead and lock him up.

TROY. I ain't said no such thing. Whoever told you that is telling a lie. Pearl ain't doing nothing but telling a big fat lie.

ROSE. She ain't had to tell me. I read it on the papers.

TROY. I ain't told them nothing of the kind.

ROSE. I saw it right there on the papers.

TROY. What it say, huh?

ROSE. It said you told them to take him.

TROY. Then they screwed that up, just the way they screw up everything. I ain't worried about what they got on the paper.

ROSE. Say the government send part of his check to the hospital and the other part to you.

TROY. I ain't got nothing to do with that if that's the way it works. I ain't made up the rules about how it work.

ROSE. You did Gabe just like you did Cory. You wouldn't sign the paper for Cory . . . but you signed for Gabe. You signed that paper.

The telephone is heard ringing inside the house.

TROY. I told you I ain't signed nothing, woman! The only thing I signed was the release form. Hell, I can't read, I don't know what they had on that paper! I ain't signed nothing about sending Gabe away.

ROSE. I said send him to the hospital . . . you said let him be free . . . now you done went down there and signed him to the hospital for half his money. You went back on yourself, Troy. You gonna have to answer for that.

TROY. See now . . . you been over there talking to Miss Pearl. She done got mad cause she ain't getting Gabe's rent money. That's all it is. She's liable to say anything.

ROSE. Troy, I seen where you signed the paper.

TROY. You ain't seen nothing I signed. What she doing got papers on my brother anyway? Miss Pearl telling a big fat lie. And I'm gonna tell her about it too! You ain't seen nothing I signed. Say . . . you ain't seen nothing I signed.

Rose exits into the house to answer the telephone. Presently she returns.

ROSE. Troy . . . that was the hospital. Alberta had the baby.

TROY. What she have? What is it?

ROSE. It's a girl.

TROY. I better get on down to the hospital to see her.

ROSE. Troy . . .

TROY. Rose . . . I got to go see her now. That's only right . . . what's the matter . . . the baby's all right, ain't it?

ROSE. Alberta died having the baby.

TROY. Died . . . you say she's dead? Alberta's dead?

ROSE. They said they done all they could. They couldn't do nothing for her.

TROY. The baby? How's the baby?

ROSE. They say it's healthy. I wonder who's gonna bury her.

TROY. She had family, Rose. She wasn't living in the world by herself.

ROSE. I know she wasn't living in the world by herself.

TROY. Next thing you gonna want to know if she had any insurance.

ROSE. Troy, you ain't got to talk like that.

TROY. That's the first thing that jumped out your mouth. "Who's gonna bury her?" Like I'm fixing to take on that task for myself.

ROSE. I am your wife. Don't push me away.

TROY. I ain't pushing nobody away. Just give me some space. That's all. Just give me some room to breathe.

Rose exists into the house. Troy walks about the yard.

TROY (*with a quiet rage that threatens to consume him*). All right . . . Mr. Death. See now . . . I'm gonna tell you what I'm gonna do. I'm gonna take and build me a fence around this yard. See? I'm gonna build me a fence around what belongs to me. And then I want you to stay on the other side. See? You stay over there until you're ready for me. Then you come on. Bring your army. Bring your sickle. Bring your wrestling clothes. I ain't gonna fall down on my vigilance this time. You ain't gonna sneak up on me no more. When you ready for me . . . when the top of your list say Troy Maxson . . . that's when you come around here. You come up and knock on the front door. Ain't nobody else got nothing to do with this. This is between you and me. Man to man. You stay on the other side of that fence until you ready for me. Then you come up and knock on the front door. Anytime you want. I'll be ready for you.

The lights go down to black.

SCENE 3

The lights come up on the porch. It is late evening three days later. Rose sits listening to the ball game waiting for Troy. The final out of the game is made and Rose switches off the radio. Troy enters the yard carrying an infant wrapped in blankets. He stands back from the house and calls.

Rose enters and stands on the porch. There is a long, awkward silence, the weight of which grows heavier with each passing second.

TROY. Rose . . . I'm standing here with my daughter in my arms. She ain't but a wee bittie little old thing. She don't know nothing about grownups' business. She innocent . . . and she ain't got no mama.

ROSE. What you telling me for, Troy?

She turns and exits into the house.

TROY. Well . . . I guess we'll just sit out here on the porch.

He sits down on the porch. There is an awkward indelicateness about the way he handles the baby. His largeness engulfs and seems to swallow it. He speaks loud enough for Rose to hear.

A man's got to do what's right for him. I ain't sorry for nothing I done. It felt right in my heart. (*To the baby.*) What you smiling at? Your daddy's a big man. Got these great big old hands. But sometimes he's scared. And right now your daddy's scared cause we sitting out here and ain't got no home. Oh, I been homeless before. I ain't had no little baby with me. But I been homeless. You just be out on the road by your lonesome and you see one of them trains coming and you just kinda go like this . . .

He sings as a lullaby.

Please, Mr. Engineer let a man ride the line

Please, Mr. Engineer let a man ride the line
I ain't got no ticket please let me ride the blinds.

Rose enters from the house. Troy, hearing her steps behind him, stands and faces her.

She's my daughter, Rose. My own flesh and blood. I can't deny her no more than I can deny them boys. (*Pause.*) You and them boys is my family. You and them and this child is all I got in the world. So I guess what I'm saying is . . . I'd appreciate it if you'd help me take care of her.

ROSE. Okay, Troy . . . you're right. I'll take care of your baby for you . . . cause . . . like you say . . . she's innocent . . . and you can't visit the sins of the father upon the child. A motherless child has got a hard time. (*She takes the baby from him.*) From right now . . . this child got a mother. But you a womanless man.

Rose turns and exits into the house with the baby. Lights go down to black.

SCENE 4

It is two months later. Lyons enters the street. He knocks on the door and calls.

LYONS. Hey, Rose! (*Pause.*) Rose!
ROSE (*from inside the house*). Stop that yelling. You gonna wake up Raynell. I just got her to sleep.
LYONS. I just stopped by to pay Papa this twenty dollars I owe him. Where's Papa at?
ROSE. He should be here in a minute. I'm getting ready to go down to the church. Sit down and wait on him.
LYONS. I got to go pick up Bonnie over her mother's house.
ROSE. Well, sit it down there on the table. He'll get it.
LYONS (*enters the house and sets the money on the table*). Tell Papa I said thanks. I'll see you again.
ROSE. All right, Lyons. We'll see you.

Lyons starts to exit as Cory enters.

CORY. Hey, Lyons.
LYONS. What's happening, Cory? Say man, I'm sorry I missed your graduation. You know I had a gig and couldn't get away. Otherwise, I would have been there, man. So what you doing?
CORY. I'm trying to find a job.
LYONS. Yeah I know how that go, man. It's rough out here. Jobs are scarce.
CORY. Yeah, I know.
LYONS. Look here, I got to run. Talk to Papa . . . he know some people. He'll be able to help get you a job. Talk to him . . . see what he say.
CORY. Yeah . . . all right, Lyons.
LYONS. You take care. I'll talk to you soon. We'll find some time to talk.

Lyons exits the yard. Cory wanders over to the tree, picks up the bat, and assumes a batting stance. He studies an imaginary pitcher and swings. Dissatisfied with the result,

he tries again. Troy enters. They eye each other for a beat. Cory puts the bat down and exits the yard. Troy starts into the house as Rose exits with Raynell. She is carrying a cake.

TROY. I'm coming in and everybody's going out.
ROSE. I'm taking this cake down to the church for the bake sale. Lyons was by to see you. He stopped by to pay you your twenty dollars. It's laying in there on the table.
TROY (*going into his pocket*). Well . . . here go this money.
ROSE. Put it in there on the table, Troy. I'll get it.
TROY. What time you coming back?
ROSE. Ain't no use in you studying me. It don't matter what time I come back.
TROY. I just asked you a question, woman. What's the matter . . . can't I ask you a question?
ROSE. Troy, I don't want to go into it. Your dinner's in there on the stove. All you got to do is heat it up. And don't you be eating the rest of them cakes in there. I'm coming back for them. We having a bake sale at the church tomorrow.

Rose exits the yard. Troy sits down on the steps, takes a pint bottle from his pocket, opens it, and drinks. He begins to sing.

TROY.

    Hear it ring! Hear it ring!
    Had an old dog his name was Blue
    You know Blue was mighty true
    You know Blue as a good old dog
    Blue trees a possum in a hollow log
    You know from that he was a good old dog.

Bono enters the yard.

BONO. Hey, Troy.
TROY. Hey, what's happening, Bono?
BONO. I just thought I'd stop by to see you.
TROY. What you stop by and see me for? You ain't stopped by in a month of Sundays. Hell, I must owe you money or something.
BONO. Since you got your promotion I can't keep up with you. Used to see you every day. Now I don't even know what route you working.
TROY. They keep switching me around. Got me out in Greentree now . . . hauling white folks' garbage.
BONO. Greentree, huh? You lucky, at least you ain't got to be lifting them barrels. Damn if they ain't getting heavier. I'm gonna put in my two years and call it quits.
TROY. I'm thinking about retiring myself.
BONO. You got it easy. You can drive for another five years.
TROY. It ain't the same, Bono. It ain't like working the back of the truck. Ain't got nobody to talk to . . . feel like you working by yourself. Naw, I'm thinking about retiring. How's Lucille?
BONO. She all right. Her arthritis get to acting up on her sometime. Saw Rose on my way in. She going down to the church, huh?

TROY. Yeah, she took up going down there. All them preachers looking for somebody to fatten their pockets. (*Pause.*) Got some gin here.

BONO. Naw, thanks. I just stopped by to say hello.

TROY. Hell, nigger . . . you can take a drink. I ain't never known you to say no to a drink. You ain't got to work tomorrow.

BONO. I just stopped by. I'm fixing to go over to Skinner's. We got us a domino game going over his house every Friday.

TROY. Nigger, you can't play no dominoes. I used to whup you four games out of five.

BONO. Well, that learned me. I'm getting better.

TROY. Yeah? Well, that's all right.

BONO. Look here . . . I got to be getting on. Stop by sometime, huh?

TROY. Yeah, I'll do that, Bono. Lucille told Rose you bought her a new refrigerator.

BONO. Yeah, Rose told Lucille you had finally built your fence . . . so I figured we'd call it even.

TROY. I knew you would.

BONO. Yeah . . . okay. I'll be talking to you.

TROY. Yeah, take care, Bono. Good to see you. I'm gonna stop over.

BONO. Yeah. Okay, Troy.

Bono exits. Troy drinks from the bottle.

TROY.

> Old Blue died and I dig his grave
> Let him down with a golden chain
> Every night when I hear old Blue bark
> I know Blue treed a possum in Noah's Ark.
> Hear it ring! Hear it ring!

Cory enters the yard. They eye each other for a beat. Troy is sitting in the middle of the steps. Cory walks over.

CORY. I got to get by.

TROY. Say what? What's you say?

CORY. You in my way. I got to get by.

TROY. You got to get by where? This is my house. Bought and paid for. In full. Took me fifteen years. And if you wanna go in my house and I'm sitting on the steps . . . you say excuse me. Like your mama taught you.

CORY. Come on, Pop . . . I got to get by.

Cory starts to maneuver his way past Troy. Troy grabs his leg and shoves him back.

TROY. You just gonna walk over top of me?

CORY. I live here too!

TROY (*advancing toward him*). You just gonna walk over top of me in my own house?

CORY. I ain't scared of you.

TROY. I ain't asked if you was scared of me. I asked you if you was fixing to walk over top of me in my own house? That's the question. You ain't gonna say excuse me? You just gonna walk over top of me?

CORY. If you wanna put it like that.

TROY. How else am I gonna put it?

CORY. I was walking by you to go into the house cause you sitting on the steps drunk, singing to yourself. You can put it like that.

TROY. Without saying excuse me???

Cory doesn't respond.

I asked you a question. Without saying excuse me???

CORY. I ain't got to say excuse me to you. You don't count around here no more.

TROY. Oh, I see . . . I don't count around here no more. You ain't got to say excuse me to your daddy. All of a sudden you done got so grown that your daddy don't count around here no more . . . Around here in his own house and yard that he done paid for with the sweat of his brow. You done got so grown to where you gonna take over. You gonna take over my house. Is that right? You gonna wear my pants. You gonna go in there and stretch out on my bed. You ain't got to say excuse me cause I don't count around here no more. Is that right?

CORY. That's right. You always talking this dumb stuff. Now, why don't you just get out my way?

TROY. I guess you got someplace to sleep and something to put in your belly. You got that, huh? You got that? That's what you need. You got that, huh?

CORY. You don't know what I got. You ain't got to worry about what I got.

TROY. You right! You one hundred percent right! I done spent the last seventeen years worrying about what you got. Now it's your turn, see? I'll tell you what to do. You grown . . . we done established that. You a man. Now, let's see you act like one. Turn your behind around and walk out this yard. And when you get out there in the alley . . . you can forget about this house. See? Cause this is my house. You go on and be a man and get your own house. You can forget about this. Cause this is mine. You go on and get yours cause I'm through with doing for you.

CORY. You talking about what you did for me . . . what'd you ever give me?

TROY. Them feet and bones! That pumping heart, nigger! I give you more than anybody else is ever gonna give you.

CORY. You ain't never gave me nothing! You ain't never done nothing but hold me back. Afraid I was gonna be better than you. All you ever did was try and make me scared of you. I used to tremble every time you called my name. Every time I heard your footsteps in the house. Wondering all the time . . . what's Papa gonna say if I do this? . . . What's he gonna say if I do that? . . . What's Papa gonna say if I turn on the radio? And Mama, too . . . she tries . . . but she's scared of you.

TROY. You leave your mama out of this. She ain't got nothing to do with this.

CORY. I don't know how she stand you . . . after what you did to her.

TROY. I told you to leave your mama out of this!

He advances toward Cory.

CORY. What you gonna do . . . give me a whupping? You can't whup me no more. You're too old. You just an old man.

TROY (*shoves him on his shoulder*). Nigger! That's what you are. You just another nigger on the street to me!

CORY. You crazy! You know that?

TROY. Go on now! You got the devil in you. Get on away from me!

CORY. You just a crazy old man . . . talking about I got the devil in me.

TROY. Yeah, I'm crazy! If you don't get on the other side of that yard . . . I'm gonna show you how crazy I am! Go on . . . get the hell out of my yard.

CORY. It ain't your yard. You took Uncle Gabe's money he got from the army to buy this house and then you put him out.

TROY (*advances on Cory*). Get your black ass out of my yard!

Troy's advance backs Cory up against the tree. Cory grabs up the bat.

CORY. I ain't going nowhere! Come on . . . put me out! I ain't scared of you.

TROY. That's my bat!

CORY. Come on!

TROY. Put my bat down!

CORY. Come on, put me out.

Cory swings at Troy, who backs across the yard.

What's the matter? You so bad . . . put me out!

Troy advances toward Cory.

CORY (*backing up*). Come on! Come on!

TROY. You're gonna have to use it! You wanna draw that bat back on me . . . you're gonna have to use it.

CORY. Come on! . . . Come on!

Cory swings the bat at Troy a second time. He misses. Troy continues to advance toward him.

TROY. You're gonna have to kill me! You wanna draw that bat back on me. You're gonna have to kill me.

Cory, backed up against the tree, can go no farther. Troy taunts him. He sticks out his head and offers him a target.

Come on! Come on!

Cory is unable to swing the bat. Troy grabs it.

TROY. Then I'll show you.

Cory and Troy struggle over the bat. The struggle is fierce and fully engaged. Troy ultimately is the stronger and takes the bat from Cory and stands over him ready to swing. He stops himself.

Go on and get away from around my house.

Cory, stung by his defeat, picks himself up, walks slowly out of the yard and up the alley.

CORY. Tell Mama I'll be back for my things.

TROY. They'll be on the other side of that fence.

Cory exits.

TROY. I can't taste nothing. Helluljah! I can't taste nothing no more. (*Troy assumes a batting posture and begins to taunt Death, the fastball on the outside corner.*) Come on! It's between you and me now! Come on! Anytime you want! Come on! I be ready for you . . . but I ain't gonna be easy.

The lights go down on the scene.

SCENE 5

The time is 1965. The lights come up in the yard. It is the morning of Troy's funeral. A funeral plaque with a light hangs beside the door. There is a small garden plot off to the side. There is noise and activity in the house as Rose, Lyons, and Bono have gathered. The door opens and Raynell, seven years old, enters dressed in a flannel night-gown. She crosses to the garden and pokes around with a stick. Rose calls from the house.

ROSE. Raynell!

RAYNELL. Mam?

ROSE. What you doing out there?

RAYNELL. Nothing.

Rose comes to the door.

ROSE. Girl, get in here and get dressed. What you doing?

RAYNELL. Seeing if my garden growed.

ROSE. I told you it ain't gonna grow overnight. You got to wait.

RAYNELL. It don't look like it never gonna grow. Dag!

ROSE. I told you a watched pot never boils. Get in here and get dressed.

RAYNELL. This ain't even no pot, Mama.

ROSE. You just have to give it a chance. It'll grow. Now you come on and do what I told you. We got to be getting ready. This ain't no morning to be playing around. You hear me?

RAYNELL. Yes, mam.

Rose exits into the house. Raynell continues to poke at her garden with a stick. Cory enters. He is dressed in a Marine corporal's uniform, and carries a duffelbag. His posture is that of a military man, and his speech has a clipped sternness.

CORY (*to Raynell*). Hi. (*Pause.*) I bet your name is Raynell.

RAYNELL. Uh huh.

CORY. Is your mama home?

Raynell runs up on the porch and calls through the screen door.

RAYNELL. Mama . . . there's some man out here. Mama?

Rose comes to the door.

ROSE. Cory? Lord have mercy! Look here, you all!

Rose and Cory embrace in a tearful reunion as Bono and Lyons enter from the house dressed in funeral clothes.

BONO. Aw, looka here . . .

ROSE. Done got all grown up!

CORY. Don't cry, Mama. What you crying about?

ROSE. I'm just so glad you made it.

CORY. Hey Lyons. How you doing, Mr. Bono.

Lyons goes to embrace Cory.

LYONS. Look at you, man. Look at you. Don't he look good, Rose. Got them Corporal stripes.

ROSE. What took you so long?

CORY. You know how the Marines are, Mama. They got to get all their paperwork straight before they let you do anything.

ROSE. Well, I'm sure glad you made it. They let Lyons come. Your Uncle Gabe's still in the hospital. They don't know if they gonna let him out or not. I just talked to them a little while ago.

LYONS. A Corporal in the United States Marines.

BONO. Your daddy knew you had it in you. He used to tell me all the time.

LYONS. Don't he look good, Mr. Bono?

BONO. Yeah, he remind me of Troy when I first met him. (*Pause.*) Say, Rose, Lucille's down at the church with the choir. I'm gonna go down and get the pallbearers lined up. I'll be back to get you all.

ROSE. Thanks, Jim.

CORY. See you, Mr. Bono.

LYONS (*with his arm around Raynell*). Cory . . . look at Raynell. Ain't she precious? She gonna break a whole lot of hearts.

ROSE. Raynell, come and say hello to your brother. This is your brother, Cory. You remember Cory.

RAYNELL. No, Mam.

CORY. She don't remember me, Mama.

ROSE. Well, we talk about you. She heard us talk about you. (*To Raynell.*) This is your brother, Cory. Come on and say hello.

RAYNELL. Hi.

CORY. Hi. So you're Raynell. Mama told me a lot about you.

ROSE. You all come on into the house and let me fix you some breakfast. Keep up your strength.

CORY. I ain't hungry, Mama.

LYONS. You can fix me something, Rose. I'll be in there in a minute.

ROSE. Cory, you sure you don't want nothing? I know they ain't feeding you right.

CORY. No, Mama . . . thanks. I don't feel like eating. I'll get something later.

ROSE. Raynell . . . get on upstairs and get that dress on like I told you.

Rose and Raynell exit into the house.

LYONS. So . . . I hear you thinking about getting married.

CORY. Yeah, I done found the right one, Lyons. It's about time.

LYONS. Me and Bonnie been split up about four years now. About the time Papa retired. I guess she just got tired of all them changes I was putting her through. (*Pause.*) I always knew you was gonna make something out yourself. Your head was always in the right direction. So . . . you gonna stay in . . . make it a career . . . put in your twenty years?

CORY. I don't know. I got six already, I think that's enough.

LYONS. Stick with Uncle Sam and retire early. Ain't nothing out here. I guess Rose told you what happened with me. They got me down the workhouse. I thought I was being slick cashing other people's checks.

CORY. How much time you doing?

LYONS. They give me three years. I got that beat now. I ain't got but nine more months. It ain't so bad. You learn to deal with it like anything else. You got to take the crookeds with the straights. That's what Papa used to say. He used to say that when he struck out. I seen him strike out three times in a row . . . and the next time up he hit the ball over the grandstand. Right out there in Homestead Field. He wasn't satisfied hitting in the seats . . . he want to hit it over everything! After the game he had two hundred people standing around waiting to shake his hand. You got to take the crookeds with the straights. Yeah, Papa was something else.

CORY. You still playing?

LYONS. Cory . . . you know I'm gonna do that. There's some fellows down there we got us a band . . . we gonna try and stay together when we get out . . . but yeah, I'm still playing. It still helps me to get out of bed in the morning. As long as it do that I'm gonna be right there playing and trying to make some sense out of it.

ROSE (*calling*). Lyons, I got these eggs in the pan.

LYONS. Let me go on and get these eggs, man. Get ready to go bury Papa. (*Pause.*) How you doing? You doing all right?

Cory nods. Lyons touches him on the shoulder and they share a moment of silent grief. Lyons exits into the house. Cory wanders about the yard. Raynell enters.

RAYNELL. Hi.

CORY. Hi.

RAYNELL. Did you used to sleep in my room?

CORY. Yeah . . . that used to be my room.

RAYNELL. That's what Papa call it. "Cory's room." It got your football in the closet.

Rose comes to the door.

ROSE. Raynell, get in there and get them good shoes on.

RAYNELL. Mama, can't I wear these? Them other one hurt my feet.

ROSE. Well, they just gonna have to hurt your feet for a while. You ain't said they hurt your feet when you went down to the store and got them.

RAYNELL. They didn't hurt then. My feet done got bigger.

ROSE. Don't you give me no backtalk now. You get in there and get them shoes on.

Raynell exits into the house.

Ain't too much changed. He still got that piece of rag tied to that tree. He was out here swinging that bat. I was just ready to go back in the house. He swung that bat and then he just fell over. Seem like he swung it and stood there with this grin on his face . . . and then he just fell over. They carried him on down to the hospital, but I knew there wasn't no need . . . why don't you come on in the house?

CORY. Mama . . . I got something to tell you. I don't know how to tell you this . . . but I've got to tell you . . . I'm not going to Papa's funeral.

ROSE. Boy, hush your mouth. That's your daddy you talking about. I don't want hear that kind of talk this morning. I done raised you to come to this? You standing there all healthy and grown talking about you ain't going to your daddy's funeral?

CORY. Mama . . . listen . . .

ROSE. I don't want to hear it, Cory. You just get that thought out of your head.

CORY. I can't drag Papa with me everywhere I go. I've got to say no to him. One time in my life I've got to say no.

ROSE. Don't nobody have to listen to nothing like that. I know you and your daddy ain't seen eye to eye, but I ain't got to listen to that kind of talk this morning. Whatever was between you and your daddy . . . the time has come to put it aside. Just take it and set it over there on the shelf and forget about it. Disrespecting your daddy ain't gonna make you a man, Cory. You got to find a way to come to that on your own. Not going to your daddy's funeral ain't gonna make you a man.

CORY. The whole time I was growing up . . . living in his house . . . Papa was like a shadow that followed you everywhere. It weighed on you and sunk into your flesh. It would wrap around you and lay there until you couldn't tell which one was you anymore. That shadow digging in your flesh. Trying to crawl in. Trying to live through you. Everywhere I looked, Troy Maxson was staring back at me . . . hiding under the bed . . . in the closet. I'm just saying I've got to find a way to get rid of that shadow, Mama.

ROSE. You just like him. You got him in you good.

CORY. Don't tell me that, Mama.

ROSE. You Troy Maxson all over again.

CORY. I don't want to be Troy Maxson. I want to be me.

ROSE. You can't be nobody but who you are, Cory. That shadow wasn't nothing but you growing into yourself. You either got to grow into it or cut it down to fit you. But that's all you got to make life with. That's all you got to measure yourself against that world out there. Your daddy wanted you to be everything he wasn't . . . and at the same time he tried to make you into everything he was. I don't know if he was right or wrong . . . but I do know he meant to do more good than he meant to do harm. He wasn't always right. Sometimes when he

touched he bruised. And sometimes when he took me in his arms he cut.

When I first met your daddy I thought . . . Here is a man I can lay down with and make a baby. That's the first thing I thought when I seen him. I was thirty years old and had done seen my share of men. But when he walked up to me and said, "I can dance a waltz that'll make you dizzy," I thought, Rose Lee, here is a man that you can open yourself up to and be filled to bursting. Here is a man that can fill all them empty spaces you been tipping around the edges of. One of them empty spaces was being somebody's mother.

I married your daddy and settled down to cooking his supper and keeping clean sheets on the bed. When your daddy walked through the house he was so big he filled it up. That was my first mistake. Not to make him leave some room for me. For my part in the matter. But at that time I wanted that. I wanted a house that I could sing in. And that's what your daddy gave me. I didn't know to keep up his strength I had to give up little pieces of mine. I did that. I took on his life as mine and mixed up the pieces so that you couldn't hardly tell which was which anymore. It was my choice. It was my life and I didn't have to live it like that. But that's what life offered me in the way of being a woman and I took it. I grabbed hold of it with both hands.

By the time Raynell came into the house, me and your daddy had done lost touch with one another. I didn't want to make my blessing off of nobody's misfortune . . . but I took on to Raynell like she was all them babies I had wanted and never had.

The phone rings.

Like I'd been blessed to relive a part of my life. And if the Lord see fit to keep up my strength . . . I'm gonna do her just like your daddy did you . . . I'm gonna give her the best of what's in me.

RAYNELL (*entering, still with her old shoes*). Mama . . . Reverend Tollivier on the phone.

Rose exits into the house.

RAYNELL. Hi.

CORY. Hi.

RAYNELL. You in the Army or the Marines?

CORY. Marines.

RAYNELL. Papa said it was the Army. Did you know Blue?

CORY. Blue? Who's Blue?

RAYNELL. Papa's dog what he sing about all the time.

CORY (*singing*).

Hear it ring! Hear it ring!
I had a dog his name was Blue
You know Blue was mighty true
You know Blue was a good old dog
Blue treed a possum in a hollow log
You know from that he was a good old dog.
Hear it ring! Hear it ring!

Raynell joins in singing.

CORY AND RAYNELL.

> Blue treed a possum out on a limb
> Blue looked at me and I looked at him
> Grabbed that possum and put him in a sack
> Blue stayed there till I came back
> Old Blue's feets was big and round
> Never allowed a possum to touch the ground.

> Old Blue died and I dug his grave
> I dug his grave with a silver spade
> Let him down with a golden chain
> And every night I call his name
> Go on Blue, you good dog you
> Go on Blue, you good dog you.

RAYNELL.

> Blue laid down and died like a man
> Blue laid down and died . . .

BOTH.

> Blue laid down and died like a man
> Now he's treeing possums in the Promised Land
> I'm gonna tell you this to let you know
> Blue's gone where the good dogs go
> When I hear old Blue bark
> When I hear old Blue bark
> Blue treed a possum in Noah's Ark
> Blue treed a possum in Noah's Ark.

Rose comes to the screen door.

ROSE. Cory, we gonna be ready to go in a minute.
CORY (*to Raynell*). You go on in the house and change them shoes like Mama told you so we can go to Papa's funeral.
RAYNELL. Okay, I'll be back.

Raynell exits into the house. Cory gets up and crosses over to the tree. Rose stands in the screen door watching him. Gabriel enters from the alley.

GABRIEL (*calling*). Hey, Rose!
ROSE. Gabe?
GABRIEL. I'm here, Rose. Hey Rose, I'm here!

Rose enters from the house.

ROSE. Lord . . . Look here, Lyons!
LYONS. See, I told you, Rose . . . I told you they'd let him come.
CORY. How you doing, Uncle Gabe?
LYONS. How you doing, Uncle Gabe?
GABRIEL. Hey, Rose. It's time. It's time to tell St. Peter to open the gates. Troy, you ready? You ready, Troy. I'm gonna tell St. Peter to open the gates. You get ready now.

Gabriel, with great fanfare, braces himself to blow. The trumpet is without a mouthpiece. He puts the end of it into his mouth and blows with great force, like a man who has been waiting some twenty-odd years for this single moment. No sound comes out of the trumpet. He braces himself and blows again with the same result. A third time he blows. There is a weight of impossible description that falls away and leaves him bare and exposed to a frightful realization. It is a trauma that a sane and normal mind would be unable to withstand. He begins to dance. A slow, strange dance, eerie and life-giving. A dance of atavistic signature and ritual. Lyons attempts to embrace him. Gabriel pushes Lyons away. He begins to howl in what is an attempt at song, or perhaps a song turning back into itself in an attempt at speech. He finishes his dance and the gates of heaven stand open as wide as God's closet.

> That's the way that go!

BLACKOUT

TOPICS FOR CRITICAL THINKING AND WRITING

📖 THE PLAY ON THE PAGE

1. What do you think Bono means when he says, early in Act 2, "Some people build fences to keep people out . . . and some people build fences to keep people in"? Why is the play called *Fences*? What has fenced Troy in? What is Troy fencing in? (Take account of Troy's last speech in Act 2, Scene 2, but do not limit your discussion to this speech.)

2. What do you think Troy's reasons are—conscious and unconscious—for not wanting Cory to play football at college?

3. Compare and contrast Cory and Lyons. Consider, too, in what ways they resemble Troy and in what ways they differ from him.

4. In what ways is Troy like his father, and in what ways unlike him?

5. What do you make out of the prominence given to the song about Blue?

6. There is a good deal of anger in the play, but there is also humor. Which passages do you find humorous, and why?

7. Characterize Rose Maxson.

🎭 THE PLAY ON THE STAGE

8. How would Wilson's remarks in the 1987 interview (see below) help a director in staging *Fences?* For example, his assertion that every person (except Raynell) is institutionalized at the end of the play might suggest a certain tone or mood for a production.

9. In what ways is the role of Gabriel a challenge for an actor? What advice might you give to the other actors on stage during Gabriel's appearances?

10. Some scenes begin by specifying that "the lights come up." Others do not, presumably beginning with an illuminated stage. All scenes except the last one end with the lights going down to blackness. Explain Wilson's use of lighting.

A CONTEXT FOR *FENCES*

August Wilson
TALKING ABOUT *FENCES*

[Following is part of an interview conducted with David Savran on March 13, 1987.]

Savran: In reading Fences, *I came to view Troy more and more critically as the play progressed, sharing Rose's point of view. We see that Troy has been crippled by his father. That's being replayed in Troy's relationship with Cory. Do you think there's a way out of that cycle?*

Wilson: Surely. First of all, we're all like our parents. The things we are taught early in life, how to respond to the world, our sense of morality—everything, we get from them. Now you can take that legacy and do with it anything you want to do. It's in your hands. Cory is Troy's son. How can he be Troy's son without sharing Troy's values? I was trying to get at why Troy made the choices he made, how they have influenced his values and how he attempts to pass those along to his son. Each generation gives the succeeding generation what they think they need. One question in the play is, "Are the tools we are given sufficient to compete in a world that is different from the one our parents knew?" I think they are—it's just that we have to do different things with the tools. That's all Troy has to give. Troy's flaw is that he does not recognize that the world was changing. That's because he spent fifteen years in a penitentiary.

As African-Americans, we should demand to participate in society as Africans. That's the way out of the vicious cycle of poverty and neglect that exists in 1987 in America, where you have a huge percentage of blacks living in the equivalent of South African townships, in housing projects. No one is inviting these people to participate in society. Look at the poverty levels—$8,500 for a family of four, if you have $8,501 you're not counted. Those statistics would go up enormously if we had an honest assessment of the cost of living in America. I don't know how anybody can support a family of four on $8,500. What I'm saying is that 85 or 90 percent of blacks in America are living in abject poverty and, for the most part, are crowded into what amount to concentration camps. The situation for blacks in America is worse than it was forty years ago. Some sociologists will tell you about the tremendous progress we've made. They didn't put me out when I walked in the door. And you can always point to someone who works on Wall Street, or is a doctor. But they don't count in the larger scheme of things.

Do you have any idea how these political changes could take place?

I'm not sure. I know that blacks must be allowed their cultural differences. I think the process of assimilation to white American society was a big mistake. We don't want to be like you. Blacks living in housing projects are isolated from the society, for the most part—living as they choose, as Africans. Only they don't realize the value in what they're doing because they have accepted their victimization. They've marked themselves as victims. Once they recognize that, they can begin to move through society in a different manner, from a stronger position, and claim what is theirs.

A project of yours is to point up what happens when oppression is internalized.

Yes, transfer of aggression to the wrong target. I think it's interesting that the two roads open to blacks for "full participation" are entertainment and sports. *Ma Rainey* and *Fences*, and I didn't plan it that way. I don't think that they're the correct roads. I think Troy's right. Now with the benefit of historical perspective, I can say that the athletic scholarship was actually a way of exploiting. Now you've got two million kids who think they're going to play in the NBA. In the sixties the universities made a lot of money off of athletics. You had kids playing for free who, by and large, were not getting educated, were taking courses in basketweaving. Some of them could barely read.

Troy may be right about that issue, but it seems that he has passed on certain destructive traits in spite of himself. Take the hostility between father and son.

I think every generation says to the previous generation: you're in my way. I've got to get by. The father-son conflict is actually a normal generational conflict that happens all the time.

So it's a healthy and a good thing?

Oh, sure. Troy is seeing this boy walk around, smelling his piss. Two men cannot live in the same household. Troy would have been tremendously disappointed if Cory had not challenged him. Troy knows that this boy has to go out and do battle with that world: "So I had best prepare him because I know that's a harsh, cruel place out there. But that's going to be easy compared to what he's getting here. Ain't nobody gonna whip your ass like I'm gonna whip it." He has a tremendous love for the kid. But he's not going to say, "I love you," he's going to demonstrate it. He's carrying garbage for seventeen years just for the kid. The only world Troy knows is the one that he made. Cory's going to go on to find another one, he's going to arrive at the same place as Troy. I think one of the most important lines in the play is when Troy is talking about his father: "I got to the place where I could feel him kicking in my blood and knew that the only thing that separated us was the matter of a few years."

Hopefully, Cory will do things a bit differently with his son. For Troy, sports was not the way to go, the white man wouldn't let him get away with that. "Get you a job, with your hands, something that nobody can take away from you." The idea of school—he doesn't know what that is. That's for white folks. Very few blacks had paperwork jobs. But if you knew how to fix cars, you could always make some money. That's what Troy wants for Cory. There aren't many people who ever jumped up in Troy's face. So he's proud of the kid at the same time that he expresses a hurt that all

men feel. You got to cut your kid loose at some point. There's that sense of loss and separation. You find out how Troy left his father's house and you see how Cory leaves his house. I suspect with Cory it will repeat with some differences and maybe, after five or six generations, they'll find a different way to do it.

Where Cory ends up is very ambiguous, as a marine in 1965.

Yes. For the average black kid on the street, that was an alternative. You went into the army because you could learn how to do something. I can remember my parents talking about the son of some friends: "He's in the navy. He *did* something"—as opposed to standing on the street corner, shooting drugs, drinking wine, and robbing stores. Lyons says to Cory, "I always knew you were going to make something out of yourself." It really wounds me. He's a corporal in the marines. For blacks, that is a sense of accomplishment. Therein lies one of the tragedies of blacks in America. Cory says, "I don't know. I put in six years. That's enough." Anyone who goes into the army and makes a career out of it is a loser. They sit there and are nurtured by the army and they don't have to confront life. Then they get out of the army and find there's nothing to do. They didn't learn any skills. And if they did, they can't find a job. Four months later, they're shooting dope. In the sixties a whole bunch of blacks went over, fought and died in the Vietnam War. The survivors came back to the same street corners and found out nothing had changed. They still couldn't get a job.

At the end of *Fences* every person, with the exception of Raynell, is institutionalized. Rose is in a church. Lyons is in a penitentiary. Gabriel's in a mental hospital and Cory's in the marines. The only free person is the girl, Troy's daughter, the hope for the future. That was conscious on my part because in '57 that's what I saw. Blacks have relied on institutions which are really foreign—except for the black church, which has been our saving grace. I have some problems with it but I recognize it as a central social organization and sometimes an economic organization for the black community. I would like to see blacks develop their own institutions that respond to their needs.

Harvey Fierstein

On Tidy Endings

Harvey Fierstein was born in Brooklyn, New York, in 1954, the son of parents who had emigrated from Eastern Europe. While studying painting at Pratt Institute, he acted in plays and revues, and one of his plays was produced in 1973. He did not achieve fame until his *Torch Song Trilogy* (1976–1979) moved from off-Broadway to Broadway in 1982. *Torch Song Trilogy* won the Theatre World Award, the Tony Award, and the Drama Desk Award. In addition, Fierstein won the Best Actor Tony Award and the Best Actor Drama Desk Award. He later received a third Tony Award for the book for the musical version of *La Cage aux Folles* (1983).

COMMENTARY

Beginning with the 1970s, plays about homosexuality became fairly common, but before that the topic was hardly mentioned in drama. For instance, in all of Greek and Elizabethan drama, there are only a few brief gibes at the homosexual proclivities of some people, and certainly there were no sympathetic portraits of homosexuals, nor was homosexuality the chief or central subject matter of any play.

The first play in English that was seen widely on the stage and that was built on a homosexual relationship was Mordaunt Shairp's *The Green Bay Tree* (1933). The wealthy, witty, sinister Mr. Dulcimer—whom we first see arranging flowers—has adopted Julian (played by the young Laurence Olivier), a handsome working-class youth, and brought him up in a life of idle luxury. Julian's girlfriend tries to free Julian from the influence of Dulcimer, but she fails. Julian's father resorts to a desperate measure: he kills Dulcimer, thus freeing Julian to marry his girlfriend. However, even in death Dulcimer triumphs, for at the end of the play, the wealthy young man rejects the girl and (like Dulcimer in the first scene) sets about arranging flowers. The interesting thing is that, so far as we can find, none of the contemporary reviewers mentioned homosexuality, although they did talk about "corruption" and about "abominable people." In a period when homosexuality was for most people unmentionable and even unthinkable, the play *could* be taken, and apparently *was* widely taken, as a play about the triumph of materialism over love.

In the following year, 1934, Lillian Hellman's *The Children's Hour* was produced. Here, homosexuality—lesbianism—was clearly part of the subject. For most of the play the audience sympathizes with women who, it believes, are falsely accused of lesbianism. Late in the play we learn that one of the women is in fact a lesbian, and so the play at the last minute shifts from a condemnation of a society that harasses the innocent to a condemnation of a society that harasses lesbians (the lesbian commits suicide). The thrust of the play, in any case, is about society's treatment of the individual, not about sexuality. Somewhat similarly, Robert Anderson's *Tea and Sympathy* (1953) can be said to deal with homosexuality but doesn't really, since the play is about a boy who fears he may be gay but who in fact is straight. ("Thank God," most people in the audience must have thought.)

In 1958 Shelagh Delaney's *A Taste of Honey* appeared, a comedy in which the unmarried pregnant heroine sets up house with her mother, the mother's drunken husband, and a homosexual art student. Homosexuality is not central to the play, but it is conspicuously there, treated comically but sympathetically. (The pregnant woman, who shares a bedroom with the painter, is curious: "What d'you do? Go on—what d'you do?").

Thus far we have omitted mention of the plays of Noel Coward, who from the late 1920s to the early 1940s almost always had a comedy on Broadway. The plays dealt ostensibly with witty heterosexual couples, but reviewers usually described these plays with such words as "frothy," "witty," "brittle," "bohemian," "frivolous"—words that, in fact, called up the stock image of the irresponsible male homosexual. Probably most members of the audience regarded the plays as sophisticated comedies of heterosexual love and marriage, but those who knew that Coward was gay could easily see the plays' characters as gay.

The 1960s brought Vietnam, antiwar demonstrations, and the Civil Rights movement, and, on the stage, a theater of political commitment. The extension of interest to previously marginalized groups, which produced the women's theater, black theater, and Chicano theater, also produced gay theater. Many of the early gay plays, that is, those of the 1960s, were campy, out-of-the-closet self-parodies that were political in their assertion of a lifestyle that previously had been concealed. Ronald Tavel's *Gorilla Queen* (1967), for instance, consisted of musical skits about a gay King Kong, called Queen Kong; most of the female parts were played by men in drag. Since the 1980s, however, most gay plays have been more evidently serious, though they usually include a good deal of wit. Usually they are tragicomedies, witty (gay?) but bitter plays about AIDS.

Harvey Fierstein seems to have been the first writer of gay plays to have achieved the respectability implied by public awards. (Other gay playwrights, such as Tennessee Williams and Edward Albee, had been honored long before Fierstein, but their works were about the straight world.) In 1982 Fierstein's *Torch Song Trilogy* played on Broadway (it had appeared off-Broadway in 1978), won a Tony Award, was voted best play of the year by the Dramatists' Guild, and was made into a film. One might say that *On Tidy Endings* (part of a later trilogy) is, in large measure, about AIDS, but to say so might make it sound like an Ibsen-derived problem play or discussion play. It is not, and that is one of the things that makes it remarkable. It does not raise such issues as whether AIDS is a divine punishment, whether the government is spending enough on medical research, or whether

health workers should undergo mandatory testing. Rather, although AIDS is central to the play, the play is not really *about* AIDS. It is about people, about personal relationships that keep shifting as the play proceeds. As Fierstein said in an interview, "This is not a play about disease, it's a play about life."

These people—four characters appear in the play, but two do most of the talking—engage in action in the sense that, as Elizabeth Bowen has said, dialogue is action: "Dialogue is what the characters *do* to each other." And one aspect of the dialogue—the comedy—perhaps requires special mention. Consider dialogue in the following exchange. Arthur has just said that he has gained a lot of weight since the death of his lover. The deceased lover's ex-wife, Marion, says "You'd never know," and Arthur replies:

ARTHUR. Marion, *you'd* never know, but ask my belt. Ask my pants. Ask my underwear. Even my stretch socks have stretch marks.

AIDS and all of the grief associated with it are scarcely laughing matters, and indeed one writer has said, "If art is to confront AIDS more honestly than the media have done, it must begin in fact, avoid humor, and end in anger." The point (in this view) is that humor must be avoided because it "domesticates terror." But of course we are all familiar with the fact that laughter may be defensive, a way of dealing with extreme grief. In Byron's words, "And if I laugh at any mortal thing, / Tis that I may not weep." One might reply that it is for this very reason—that humor makes us put up with the intolerable—that anyone writing about AIDS must avoid humor. We leave it to readers of *On Tidy Endings* to decide for themselves.

Harvey Fierstein

ON TIDY ENDINGS

The curtain rises on a deserted, modern Upper West Side apartment. In the bright daylight that pours in through the windows we can see the living room of the apartment. Far Stage Right is the galley kitchen, next to it the multilocked front door with intercom. Stage Left reveals a hallway that leads to the two bedrooms and baths.

Though the room is still fully furnished (couch, coffee table, etc.), there are boxes stacked against the wall and several photographs and paintings are on the floor leaving shadows on the wall where they once hung. Obviously someone is moving out. From the way the boxes are neatly labeled and stacked, we know that this is an organized person.

From the hallway just outside the door we hear the rattling of keys and two arguing voices:

JIM (*offstage*). I've got to be home by four. I've got practice.

MARION (*offstage*). I'll get you to practice, don't worry.

JIM (*offstage*). I don't want to go in there.

MARION (*offstage*). Jimmy, don't make Mommy crazy, alright? We'll go inside, I'll call Aunt Helen and see if you can go down and play with Robbie.

(*The door opens. Marion is a handsome woman of forty. Dressed in a business suit, her hair conservatively combed, she appears to be going to a business meeting. Jim is a boy of eleven. His playclothes are typical, but someone has obviously just combed his hair. Marion recovers the key from the lock.*)

JIM. Why can't I just go down and ring the bell?

MARION. Because I said so.

(*As Marion steps into the room she is struck by some unexpected emotion. She freezes in her path and stares at the empty apartment. Jim lingers by the door.*)

JIM. I'm going downstairs.

MARION. Jimmy, please.

JIM. This place gives me the creeps.

MARION. This was your father's apartment. There's nothing creepy about it.

JIM. Says you.

MARION. You want to close the door, please?

(*Jim reluctantly obeys.*)

MARION. Now, why don't you go check your room and make sure you didn't leave anything.

JIM. It's empty.

MARION. Go look.

JIM. I looked last time.

MARION (*trying to be patient*). Honey, we sold the apartment. You're never going to be here again. Go make sure you have everything you want.

JIM. But Uncle Arthur packed everything.

MARION (*less patiently*). Go make sure.

JIM. There's nothing in there.

MARION (*exploding*). I said make sure!

(*Jim jumps, then realizing that she's not kidding, obeys.*)

MARION. Everything's an argument with that one. (*She looks around the room and breathes deeply. There is sadness here. Under her breath:*) I can still smell you. (*Suddenly not wanting to be alone.*) Jimmy? Are you okay?

JIM (*returning*). Nothing. Told you so.

MARION. Uncle Arthur must have worked very hard. Make sure you thank him.

JIM. What for? Robbie says, (*fey mannerisms*) "They love to clean up things!"

MARION. Sometimes you can be a real joy.

JIM. Did you call Aunt Helen?

MARION. Do I get a break here? (*Approaching the boy understandingly.*) Wouldn't you like to say good-bye?

JIM. To who?

MARION. To the apartment. You and your daddy spent a lot of time here together. Don't you want to take one last look around?

JIM. Ma, get a real life.

MARION. "Get a real life." (*Going for the phone.*) Nice. Very nice.

JIM. Could you call already?

MARION (*dialing*). Jimmy, what does this look like I'm doing?

(*Jim kicks at the floor impatiently. Someone answers the phone at the other end.*)

MARION (*into the phone*). Helen? Hi, we're upstairs. . . . No, we just walked in the door. Jimmy wants to know if he can come down. . . . Oh, thanks.

(*Hearing that, Jim breaks for the door.*)

MARION (*yelling after him*). Don't run in the halls! And don't play with the elevator buttons!

(*The door slams shut behind him.*)

MARION (*back to the phone*). Hi. . . . No, I'm okay. It's a little weird being here. . . . No. Not since the funeral, and then there were so many people. Jimmy told me to get "a real life." I don't think I could handle anything realer. . . . No, please. Stay where you are. I'm fine. The doorman said Arthur would be right back and my lawyer should have been here already. . . . Well, we've got the papers to sign and a few other odds and ends to clean up. Shouldn't take long.

(*The intercom buzzer rings.*)

MARION. Hang on, that must be her. (*Marion goes to the intercom and speaks*) Yes? . . . Thank you. (*Back to the phone.*) Helen? Yeah, it's the lawyer. I'd better go. . . . Well, I could use a stiff drink, but I drove down. Listen, I'll stop by on my way out. Okay? Okay. 'Bye.

(*She hangs up the phone, looks around the room. That uncomfortable feeling returns to her quickly. She gets up and goes to the front door, opens it and looks out. No one there yet. She closes the door, shakes her head knowing that she's being silly and starts back into the room. She looks around, can't make it and retreats to the door. She opens it, looks out, closes it, but stays right there, her hand on the doorknob. The bell rings. She throws open the door.*)

MARION. That was quick.

(*June Lowell still has her finger on the bell. Her arms are loaded with contracts. Marion's contemporary, June is less formal in appearance and more hyper in her manner.*)

JUNE. *That* was quicker. What, were you waiting by the door?

MARION (*embarrassed*). No. I was just passing it. Come on in.

JUNE. Have you got your notary seal?

MARION. I think so.

JUNE. Great. Then you can witness. I left mine at the office and thanks to gentrification I'm double-parked downstairs. (*Looking for a place to dump her load.*) Where?

MARION (*definitely pointing to the coffee table*). Anywhere. You mean you're not staying?

JUNE. If you really think you need me I can go down and find a parking lot. I think there's one over on Columbus. So, I can go down, park the car in the lot and take a cab back if you really think you need me.

MARION. Well . . . ?

JUNE. But you shouldn't have any problems. The papers are about as straightforward as papers get. Arthur is giving you power of attorney to sell the apartment and you're giving him a check for half the purchase price. Everything else is just signing papers that state that you know that you signed the other papers. Anyway, he knows the deal, his lawyers have been over it all with him, it's just a matter of signatures.

MARION (*not fine*). Oh, fine.

JUNE. Unless you just don't want to be alone with him . . . ?

MARION. With Arthur? Don't be silly.

JUNE (*laying out the papers*). Then you'll handle it solo? Great. My car thanks you, the parking lot thanks you, and the cab driver that wouldn't have gotten a tip thanks you. Come have a quick look-see.

MARION (*joining her on the couch*). There are a lot of papers here.

JUNE. Copies. Not to worry. Start here.

(*Marion starts to read.*)

JUNE. I ran into Jimmy playing Elevator Operator.

(*Marion jumps.*)

JUNE. I got him off at the sixth floor. Read on.

MARION. This is definitely not my day for dealing with him.

(*June gets up and has a look around.*)

JUNE. I don't believe what's happening to this neighborhood. You made quite an investment when you bought this place.

MARION. Collin was always very good at figuring out those things.

JUNE. Well, he sure figured this place right. What, have you tripled your money in ten years?

MARION. More.

JUNE. It's a shame to let it go.

MARION. We're not ready to be a two-dwelling family.

JUNE. So, sublet it again.

MARION. Arthur needs the money from the sale.

JUNE. Arthur got plenty already. I'm not crying for Arthur.

MARION. I don't hear you starting in again, do I?

JUNE. Your interests and your wishes are my only concern.

MARION. Fine.

JUNE. I still say we should contest Collin's will.

MARION. June . . . !

JUNE. You've got a child to support.

MARION. And a great job, and a husband with a great job. Tell me what Arthur's got.

JUNE. To my thinking, half of everything that should have gone to you. And more. All of Collin's personal effects, his record collection . . .

MARION. And I suppose their three years together meant nothing.

JUNE. When you compare them to your sixteen-year marriage? Not nothing, but not half of everything.

MARION (*trying to change the subject*). June, who gets which copies?

JUNE. Two of each to Arthur. One you keep. The originals and anything else come back to me. (*Looking around.*) I still say you should've sublet the apartment for a year and then sold it. You would've gotten an even better price. Who wants to buy an apartment when they know someone died in it. No one. And certainly no one wants to buy an apartment when they know the person died of AIDS.

MARION (*snapping*). June. Enough!

JUNE (*catching herself*). Sorry. That was out of line. Sometimes my mouth does that to me. Hey, that's why I'm a lawyer. If my brain worked as fast as my mouth I would have gotten a real job.

MARION (*holding out a stray paper*). What's this?

JUNE. I forgot. Arthur's lawyer sent that over yesterday. He found it in Collin's safety-deposit box. It's an insurance policy that came along with some consulting job he did in Japan. He either forgot about it when he made out his will or else he wanted you to get the full payment. Either way, it's yours.

MARION. Are you sure we don't split this?

JUNE. Positive.

MARION. But everything else . . . ?

JUNE. Hey, Arthur found it, his lawyer sent it to me. Relax, it's all yours. Minus my commission, of course. Go out and buy yourself something. Anything else before I have to use my cut to pay the towing bill?

MARION. I guess not.

JUNE (*starting to leave*). Great. Call me when you get home. (*Stopping at the door and looking back.*) Look, I know that I'm attacking this a little coldly. I am aware that someone you loved has just died. But there's a time and place for everything. This is about tidying up loose ends, not holding hands. I hope you'll remember that when Arthur gets here. Call me.

(*And she's gone.*)

(*Marion looks ill at ease to be alone again. She nervously straightens the papers into neat little piles, looks at them and then remembers:*)

MARION. Pens. We're going to need pens.

(*At last a chore to be done. She looks in her purse and finds only one. She goes to the kitchen and opens a drawer where she finds two more. She starts back to the table with them but suddenly remembers something else. She returns to the kitchen and begins going through the cabinets until she finds what she's looking for: a blue Art Deco teapot. Excited to find it, she takes it back to the couch. Guilt strikes. She stops, considers putting it back, wavers, then:*)

MARION (*to herself*). Oh, he won't care. One less thing to pack.

(*She takes the teapot and places it on the couch next to her purse. She is happier. Now she searches the room with her eyes for any other treasures she may have overlooked. Nothing here. She wanders off into the bedroom. We hear keys outside the front door. Arthur lets himself into the apartment carrying a load of empty cartons and a large shopping bag. Arthur is in his mid-thirties, pleasant looking though sloppily dressed in work clothes and slightly overweight. Arthur enters the apartment just as Marion comes out of the bedroom carrying a framed watercolor painting. They jump at the sight of each other.*)

MARION. Oh, hi, Arthur. I didn't hear the door.

ARTHUR (*staring at the painting*). Well hello, Marion.

MARION (*guiltily*). I was going to ask you if you were thinking of taking this painting because if you're not going to then I'll take it. Unless, of course, you want it.

ARTHUR. No. You can have it.

MARION. I never really liked it, actually. I hate cats. I didn't even like the show. I needed something for my college dorm room. I was never the rock star poster type. I kept it in the back of a closet for years until Collin moved in here and took it. He said he liked it.

ARTHUR. I do too.

MARION. Well, then you keep it.

ARTHUR. No. Take it.

MARION. We've really got no room for it. You keep it.

ARTHUR. I don't want it.

MARION. Well, if you're sure.

ARTHUR (*seeing the teapot*). You want the teapot?

MARION. If you don't mind.

ARTHUR. One less thing to pack.

MARION. Funny, but that's exactly what I thought. One less thing to pack. You know, my mother gave it to Collin and me when we moved in to our first apartment. Silly sentimental piece of junk, but you know.

ARTHUR. That's not the one.

MARION. Sure it is. Hall used to make them for Westinghouse back in the thirties. I see them all the time at antiques shows and I always wanted to buy another, but they ask such a fortune for them.

ARTHUR. We broke the one your mother gave you a couple of years ago. That's a reproduction. You can get them almost anywhere in the Village for eighteen bucks.

MARION. Really? I'll have to pick one up.

ARTHUR. Take this one. I'll get another.

MARION. No, it's yours. You bought it.

ARTHUR. One less thing to pack.

MARION. Don't be silly. I didn't come here to raid the place.

ARTHUR. Well, was there anything else of Collin's that you thought you might like to have?

MARION. Now I feel so stupid, but actually I made a list. Not for me. But I started thinking about different people; friends, relatives, you know, that might want to have something of Collin's to remember him by. I wasn't sure just what you were taking and what you were throwing out. Anyway, I brought the list. (*Gets it from her purse.*) Of course these are only suggestions. You probably thought of a few of these people yourself. But I figured it couldn't hurt to write it all down. Like I said, I don't know what you are planning on keeping.

ARTHUR (*taking the list*). I was planning on keeping it all.

MARION. Oh, I know. But most of these things are silly. Like his high school yearbooks. What would you want with them?

ARTHUR. Sure. I'm only interested in his Gay period.

MARION. I didn't mean it that way. Anyway, you look it over. They're only suggestions. Whatever you decide to do is fine with me.

ARTHUR (*folding the list*). It would have to be, wouldn't it. I mean, it's all mine now. He did leave this all to me.

(*Marion is becoming increasingly nervous, but tries to keep a light approach as she takes a small bundle of papers from her bag.*)

MARION. While we're on the subject of what's yours. I brought a batch of condolence cards that were sent to you care of me. Relatives mostly.

ARTHUR (*taking them*). More cards? I'm going to have to have another printing of thank-you notes done.

MARION. I answered these last week, so you don't have to bother. Unless you want to.

ARTHUR. Forge my signature?

MARION. Of course not. They were addressed to both of us and they're mostly distant relatives or friends we haven't seen in years. No one important.

ARTHUR. If they've got my name on them, then I'll answer them myself.

MARION. I wasn't telling you not to, I was only saying that you don't have to.

ARTHUR. I understand.

(*Marion picks up the teapot and brings it to the kitchen.*)

MARION. Let me put this back.

ARTHUR. I ran into Jimmy in the lobby.

MARION. Tell me you're joking.

ARTHUR. I got him to Helen's.

MARION. He's really racking up the points today.

ARTHUR. You know, he still can't look me in the face.

MARION. He's reacting to all of this in strange ways. Give him time. He'll come around. He's really very fond of you.

ARTHUR. I know. But he's at that awkward age: under thirty. I'm sure in twenty years we'll be the best of friends.

MARION. It's not what you think.

ARTHUR. What do you mean?

MARION. Well, you know.

ARTHUR. No I don't know. Tell me.

MARION. I thought that you were intimating something about his blaming you for Collin's illness and I was just letting you know that it's not true. (*Foot in mouth, she braves on.*) We discussed it a lot and . . . uh . . . he understands that his father was sick before you two ever met.

ARTHUR. I don't believe this.

MARION. I'm just trying to say that he doesn't blame you.

ARTHUR. First of all, who asked you? Second of all, that's between him and me. And third and most importantly, of course he blames me. Marion, he's eleven years old. You can discuss all you want, but the fact is that his father died of a "fag" disease and I'm the only fag around to finger.

MARION. My son doesn't use that kind of language.

ARTHUR. Forget the language. I'm talking about what he's been through. Can you imagine the kind of crap he's taken from his friends? That poor kid's been chased and chastised from one end of town to the other. He's got to have someone to blame just to survive. He can't blame you, you're all he's got. He can't blame his father; he's dead. So, Uncle Arthur gets the shaft. Fine, I can handle it.

MARION. You are so wrong, Arthur. I know my son and that is not the way his mind works.

ARTHUR. I don't know what you know. I only know what I know. And all I know is what I hear and see. The snide remarks, the little smirks. . . . And it's not just the illness. He's been looking for a scapegoat since the day you and Collin first split up. Finally he has one.

MARION (*getting very angry now*). Wait. Are you saying that if he's going to blame someone it should be me?

ARTHUR. I think you should try to see things from his point of view.

MARION. Where do you get off thinking you're privy to my son's point of view?

ARTHUR. It's not that hard to imagine. Life's rolling right along, he's having a happy little childhood, when suddenly one day his father's moving out. No explanations, no reasons, none of the fights that usually accompany such things. Divorce is hard enough for a kid to understand when he's listened to years of battles, but yours?

MARION. So what should we have done? Faked a few months' worth of fights before Collin moved out?

ARTHUR. You could have told him the truth, plain and simple.

MARION. He was seven years old at the time. How the hell do you tell a seven-year-old that his father is leaving his mother to go sleep with other men?

ARTHUR. Well, not like that.

MARION. You know, Arthur, I'm going to say this as nicely as I can: Butt out. You're not his mother and you're not his father.

ARTHUR. Thank you. I wasn't acutely aware of that fact. I will certainly keep that in mind from now on.

MARION. There's only so much information a child that age can handle.

ARTHUR. So it's best that he reach his capacity on the street.

MARION. He knew about the two of you. We talked about it.

ARTHUR. Believe me, he knew before you talked about it. He's young, not stupid.

MARION. It's very easy for you to stand here and criticize, but there are aspects that you will just never be able to understand. You weren't there. You have no idea what it was like for me. You're talking to someone who thought that a girl went to college to meet a husband. I went to protest rallies because I liked the music. I bought a guitar because I thought it looked good on the bed! This lifestyle, this knowledge that you take for granted, was all a little out of left field for me.

ARTHUR. I can imagine.

MARION. No, I don't think you can. I met Collin in college, married him right after graduation and settled down for a nice quiet life of Kids and Careers. You think I had any idea about this? Talk about life's little surprises. You live with someone for sixteen years, you share your life, your bed, you have a child together, and then you wake up one day and he tells you that to him it's all been a lie. A lie. Try that on for size. Here you are the happiest couple you know, fulfilling your every life fantasy and he tells you he's living a lie.

ARTHUR. I'm sure he never said that.

MARION. Don't be so sure. There was a lot of new ground being broken back then and plenty of it was muddy.

ARTHUR. You know that he loved you.

MARION. What's that supposed to do, make things easier? It doesn't. I was brought up to believe, among other things, that if you had love that was enough. So what if I wasn't everything he wanted. Maybe he wasn't exactly everything I wanted either. So, you know what? You count your blessings and you settle.

ARTHUR. No one has to settle. Not him. Not you.

MARION. Of course not. You can say, "Up yours!" to everything and everyone who depends and needs you, and go off to make yourself happy.

ARTHUR. It's not that simple.

MARION. No. This is simpler. Death is simpler. (Yelling out:) Happy now?

(They stare at each other. Marion calms the rage and catches her breath. Arthur holds his emotions in check.)

ARTHUR. How about a nice hot cup of coffee? Tea with lemon? Hot cocoa with a marshmallow floating in it?

MARION. (laughs). I was wrong. You are a mother.

(Arthur goes into the kitchen and starts preparing things. Marion loafs by the doorway.)

MARION. I lied before. He was everything I ever wanted.

(Arthur stops, looks at her, and then changes the subject as he goes on with his work.)

ARTHUR. When I came into the building and saw Jimmy in the lobby I absolutely freaked for a second. It's amazing how much they look alike. It was like seeing a little miniature Collin standing there.

MARION. I know. He's like Collin's clone. There's nothing of me in him.

ARTHUR. I always kinda hoped that when he grew up he'd take after me. Not much chance, I guess.

MARION. Don't do anything fancy in there.

ARTHUR. Please. Anything we can consume is one less thing to pack.

MARION. So you've said.

ARTHUR. So we've said.

MARION. I want to keep seeing you and I want you to see Jim. You're still part of this family. No one's looking to cut you out.

ARTHUR. Ah, who'd want a kid to grow up looking like me anyway. I had enough trouble looking like this. Why pass on the misery?

MARION. You're adorable.

ARTHUR. Is that like saying I have a good personality?

MARION. I think you are one of the most naturally handsome men I know.

ARTHUR. Natural is right, and the bloom is fading.

MARION. All you need is a few good nights' sleep to kill those rings under your eyes.

ARTHUR. Forget the rings under my eyes, (grabbing his middle) . . . how about the rings around my moon?

MARION. I like you like this.

ARTHUR. From the time that Collin started using the wheelchair until he died, about six months, I lost twenty-three pounds. No gym, no diet. In the last seven weeks I've gained close to fifty.

MARION. You're exaggerating.

ARTHUR. I'd prove it on the bathroom scale, but I sold it in working order.

MARION. You'd never know.

ARTHUR. Marion, you'd never know, but ask my belt. Ask my pants. Ask my underwear. Even my stretch socks have stretch marks. I called the ambulance at five A.M., he was gone at nine and by nine-thirty, I was on a firstname basis with Sara Lee. I can quote the business hours of every ice-cream parlor, pizzeria and bakery on the island of Manhattan. I know the location of every twenty-four-hour grocery in the greater New York area, and I have memorized the phone numbers of every Mandarin, Szechuan and Hunan restaurant with free delivery.

MARION. At least you haven't wasted your time on useless hobbies.

ARTHUR. Are you kidding? I'm opening my own Overeater's Hotline. We'll have to start small, but expansion is guaranteed.

MARION. You're the best, you know that? If I couldn't be everything that Collin wanted then I'm grateful that he found someone like you.

ARTHUR (turning on her without missing a beat). Keep your goddamned gratitude to yourself. I didn't go through any of this for you. So your thanks are out of line. And he didn't find "someone like" me. It was me.

MARION (frightened). I didn't mean . . .

ARTHUR. And I wish you'd remember one thing more: He died in my arms, not yours.

(Marion is totally caught off guard. She stares disbelieving, openmouthed. Arthur walks past her as he leaves the kitchen with place mats. He puts them on the coffee table. As he arranges the papers and place mats he speaks, never looking at her.)

ARTHUR. Look, I know you were trying to say something supportive. Don't waste your breath. There's nothing you can say that will make any of this easier for me. There's no way for you to help me get through this. And that's your fault. After three years you still have no idea or understanding of who I am. Or maybe you do know but refuse to accept it. I don't know and I don't care. But at least understand, from my point of view, who you are: You are my husband's *ex-wife*. If you like, the mother of *my* stepson. Don't flatter yourself into thinking you're any more than that. And whatever you are, you're certainly not my friend.

(*He stops, looks up at her, then passes her again as he goes back to the kitchen. Marion is shaken, working hard to control herself. She moves toward the couch.*)

MARION. Why don't we just sign these papers and I'll be out of your way.

ARTHUR. Shouldn't you say *I'll* be out of *your* way? After all, I'm not just signing papers. I'm signing away my home.

MARION (*resolved not to fight, she gets her purse*). I'll leave the papers here. Please have them notarized and returned to my lawyer.

ARTHUR. Don't forget my painting.

MARION (*exploding*). What do you want from me, Arthur?

ARTHUR (*yelling back*). I want you the hell out of my apartment! I want you out of my life! And I want you to leave Collin alone!

MARION. The man's dead. I don't know how much more alone I can leave him.

(*Arthur laughs at the irony, but behind the laughter is something much more desperate.*)

ARTHUR. Lots more, Marion. You've got to let him go.

MARION. For the life of me, I don't know what I did or what you think I did, for you to treat me like this. But you're not going to get away with it. You will not take your anger out on me. I will not stand here and be badgered and insulted by you. I know you've been hurt and I know you're hurting but you're not the only one who lost someone here.

ARTHUR (*topping her*). Yes I am! You didn't just lose him. I did! You lost him five years ago when he divorced you. This is not your moment of grief and loss, it's mine! (*Picking up the bundle of cards and throwing it toward her.*) These condolences do not belong to you, they're mine. (*Tossing her list back to her.*) His things are not yours to give away, they're mine! This death does not belong to you, it's mine! Bought and paid for outright. I suffered for it, I bled for it.

I was the one who cooked his meals. I was the one who spoon-fed them. I pushed his wheelchair. I carried and bathed him. I wiped his backside and changed his diapers. I breathed life into and wrestled fear out of his heart. I kept him alive for two years longer than any doctor thought possible and when it was time I was the one who prepared him for death.

I paid in full for my place in his life and I will *not* share it with you. We are not the two widows of Collin Redding. Your life was not here. Your husband didn't just die. You've got a son and a life somewhere else. Your husband's sitting, waiting for you at home, wondering, as I am, what the hell you're doing here and why you can't let go.

(*Marion leans back against the couch. She's blown away. Arthur stands staring at her.*)

ARTHUR (*quietly*). Let him go, Marion. He's mine. Dead or alive; mine.

(*The teakettle whistles. Arthur leaves the room, goes to the kitchen and pours the water as Marion pulls herself together. Arthur carries the loaded tray back into the living room and sets it down on the coffee table. He sits and pours a cup.*)

ARTHUR. One marshmallow or two?

(*Marion stares, unsure as to whether the attack is really over or not.*)

ARTHUR (*placing them in her cup*). Take three, they're small.

(*Marion smiles and takes the offered cup.*)

ARTHUR (*campily*). Now let me tell you how I *really* feel.

(*Marion jumps slightly, then they share a small laugh. Silence as they each gather themselves and sip their refreshments*)

MARION (*calmly*). Do you think that I sold the apartment just to throw you out?

ARTHUR. I don't care about the apartment . . .

MARION. . . . Because I really didn't. Believe me.

ARTHUR. I know.

MARION. I knew the expenses here were too much for you, and I knew you couldn't afford to buy out my half . . . I figured if we sold it, that you'd at least have a nice chunk of money to start over with.

ARTHUR. You could've given me a little more time.

MARION. Maybe. But I thought the sooner you were out of here, the sooner you could go on with your life.

ARTHUR. Or the sooner you could go on with yours.

MARION. Maybe. (*Pauses to gather her thoughts.*) Anyway, I'm not going to tell you that I have no idea what you're talking about. I'd have to be worse than deaf and blind not to have seen the way you've been treated. Or mistreated. When I read Collin's obituary in the newspaper and saw my name and Jimmy's name and no mention of you. . . . (*Shakes her head, not knowing what to say.*) You know that his secretary was the one who wrote that up and sent it in. Not me. But I should have done something about it and I didn't. I know.

ARTHUR. Wouldn't have made a difference. I wrote my own obituary for him and sent it to the smaller papers. They edited me out.

MARION. I'm sorry. I remember, at the funeral, I was surrounded by all of Collin's family and business associates while you were left with your friends. I knew it was wrong. I knew I should have said something but it felt good to have them around me and you looked like you were holding up. . . . Wrong. But saying that it's all my fault for not letting go . . . ? There were other people involved.

ARTHUR. Who took their cue from you.

MARION. Arthur, you don't understand. Most people that we knew as a couple had no idea that Collin was Gay right up to his death. And even those that did know only found out when he got sick and the word leaked out that it was AIDS. I don't think I have to tell you how stupid and ill-informed most people are about homosexuality. And AIDS . . . ? The kinds of insane behavior that word inspires . . . ?

Those people at the funeral, how many times did they call to see how he was doing over these years? How many of them ever went to see him in the hospital? Did any of them even come here? So, why would you expect them to act any differently after his death?

So, maybe that helps to explain their behavior, but what about mine, right? Well, maybe there is no explanation. Only excuses. And excuse number one is that you're right, I have never really let go of him. And I am jealous of you. Hell, I was jealous of anyone that Collin ever talked to, let alone slept with . . . let alone loved.

The first year, after he moved out, we talked all the time about the different men he was seeing. And I always listened and advised. It was kind of fun. It kept us close. It kept me a part of his intimate life. And the bottom line was always that he wasn't happy with the men he was meeting. So, I was always allowed to hang on to the hope that one day he'd give it all up and come home. Then he got sick.

He called me, told me he was in the hospital and asked if I'd come see him. I ran. When I got to his door there was a sign, INSTRUCTIONS FOR VISITORS OF AN AIDS PATIENT. I nearly died.

ARTHUR. He hadn't told you?

MARION. No. And believe me, a sign is not the way to find these things out. I was so angry. . . . And he was so sick . . . I was sure that he'd die right then. If not from the illness then from the hospital staff's neglect. No one wanted to go near him and I didn't bother fighting with them because I understood that they were scared. I was scared. That whole month in the hospital I didn't let Jimmy visit him once.

You learn.

Well, as you know, he didn't die. And he asked if he could come stay with me until he was well. And I said yes. Of course, yes. Now, here's something I never thought I'd ever admit to anyone: had he asked to stay with me for a few weeks I would have said no. But he asked to stay with me until he was well and knowing there was no cure I said yes. In my craziness I said yes because to me that meant forever. That he was coming back to me forever. Not that I wanted him to die, but I assumed from everything I'd read. . . . And we'd be back together for whatever time he had left. Can you understand that?

(Arthur nods.)

MARION (gathers her thoughts again). Two weeks later he left. He moved in here. Into this apartment that we had bought as an investment. Never to live in. Certainly never to live apart in. Next thing I knew, the name Arthur starts appearing in every phone call, every dinner conversation.

"Did you see the doctor?"

"Yes. Arthur made sure I kept the appointment."

"Are you going to your folks for Thanksgiving?"

"No. Arthur and I are having some friends over."

I don't know which one of us was more of a coward, he for not telling or me for not asking about you. But eventually you became a given. Then, of course, we met and became what I had always thought of as friends.

(Arthur winces in guilt.)

MARION. I don't care what you say, how could we not be friends with someone so great in common: love for one of the most special human beings there ever was. And don't try and tell me there weren't times when you enjoyed me being around as an ally. I can think of a dozen occasions when we ganged up on him, teasing him with our intimate knowledge of his personal habits.

(Arthur has to laugh.)

MARION. Blanket stealing? Snoring? Excess gas, no less? (Takes a moment to enjoy this truce.) I don't think that my loving him threatened your relationship. Maybe I'm not being truthful with myself. But I don't. I never tried to step between you. Not that I ever had the opportunity. Talk about being joined at the hip! And that's not to say I wasn't jealous. I was. Terribly. Hatefully. But always lovingly. I was happy for Collin because there was no way to deny that he was happy. With everything he was facing, he was happy. Love did that. You did that.

He lit up with you. He came to life. I envied that and all the time you spent together, but more, I watched you care for him (sometimes overcare for him), and I was in awe. I could never have done what you did. I never would have survived. I really don't know how you did.

ARTHUR. Who said I survived?

MARION. Don't tease. You did an absolutely incredible thing. It's not as if you met him before he got sick. You entered a relationship that you knew in all probability would end this way and you never wavered.

ARTHUR. Of course I did. Don't have me sainted, Marion. But sometimes you have no choice. Believe me, if I could've gotten away from him I would've. But I was a prisoner of love.

(*He makes a campy gesture and pose.*)

MARION. Stop.

ARTHUR. And there were lots of pluses. I got to quit a job I hated, stay home all day and watch game shows. I met a lot of doctors and learned a lot of big words. (*Arthur jumps up and goes to the pile of boxes where he extracts one and brings it back to the couch.*)

And then there was all the exciting traveling I got to do. This box has a souvenir from each one of our trips. Wanna see? (*Marion nods. He opens the box and pulls things out one by one. Holding up an old bottle.*)

This is from the house we rented in Reno when we went to clear out his lungs. (*Holding handmade potholders.*)

This is from the hospital in Reno. Collin made them. They had a great arts and crafts program. (*Copper bracelets.*)

These are from a faith healer in Philly. They don't do much for a fever, but they look great with a green sweater. (*Glass ashtrays.*)

These are from our first visit to the clinic in France. Such lovely people. (*A Bible.*)

This is from our second visit to the clinic in France. (*A bead necklace.*)

A Voodoo doctor in New Orleans. Next time we'll have to get there earlier in the year. I think he sold all the pretty ones at Mardi Gras. (*A tiny piñata.*)

Then there was Mexico. Black market drugs and empty wallets. (*Now pulling things out at random.*)

L.A., San Francisco, Houston, Boston. . . . We traveled everywhere they offered hope for sale and came home with souvenirs. (*Arthur quietly pulls a few more things out and then begins to put them all back into the box slowly. Softly as he works:*) Marion, I would have done anything, traveled anywhere to avoid . . . or delay. . . . Not just because I loved him so desperately, but when you've lived the way we did for three years . . . the battle becomes your life. (*He looks at her and then away.*) His last few hours were beyond any scenario I had imagined. He hadn't walked in nearly six months. He was totally incontinent. If he spoke two words in a week I was thankful. Days went by without his eyes ever focusing on me. He just stared out at I don't know what. Not the meals as I fed him. Not the TV I played constantly for company. Just out. Or maybe in.

It was the middle of the night when I heard his breathing become labored. His lungs were filling with fluid again. I knew the sound. I'd heard it a hundred times before. So, I called the ambulance and got him to the hospital.

They hooked him up to the machines, the oxygen, shot him with morphine and told me that they would do what they could to keep him alive.

But, Marion, it wasn't the machines that kept him breathing. He did it himself. It was that incredible will and strength inside him. Whether it came from his love of life or fear of death, who knows. But he'd been counted out a hundred times and a hundred times he fought his way back.

I got a magazine to read him, pulled a chair up to the side of his bed and holding his hand, I wondered whether I should call Helen to let the cleaning lady in or if he'd fall asleep and I could sneak home for an hour. I looked up from the page and he was looking at me. Really looking right into my eyes. I patted his cheek and said, "Don't worry, honey, you're going to be fine."

But there was something else in his eyes. He wasn't satisfied with that. And I don't know why, I have no idea where it came from, I just heard the words coming out of my mouth, "Collin, do you want to die?"

His eyes filled and closed, he nodded his head.

I can't tell you what I was thinking, I'm not sure I was. I slipped off my shoes, lifted his blanket and climbed into bed next to him. I helped him to put his arms around me, and mine around him, and whispered as gently as I could into his ear, "It's alright to let go now. It's time to go on." And he did.

Marion, you've got your life and your son. All I have is an intangible place in a man's history. Leave me that. Respect that.

MARION. I understand.

(*Arthur suddenly comes to life, running to get the shopping bag that he'd left at the front door.*)

ARTHUR. Jeez! With all the screamin' and sad storytelling I forgot something. (*He extracts a bouquet of flowers from the bag.*) I brung you flowers and everything.

MARION. You brought *me* flowers?

ARTHUR. Well, I knew you'd never think to bring me flowers and I felt that on an occasion such as this somebody oughta get flowers from somebody.

MARION. You know, Arthur, you're really making me feel like a worthless piece of garbage.

ARTHUR. So what else is new? (*He presents the flowers.*) Just promise me one thing: Don't press one in a book. Just stick them in a vase and when they fade just toss them out. No more memorabilia.

MARION. Arthur, I want to do something for you and I don't know what. Tell me what you want.

ARTHUR. I want little things. Not much. I want to be remembered. If you get a Christmas card from Collin's mother make sure she sent me one too. If his friends call to see how you are, ask if they've called me. Have me to dinner so I can see Jimmy. Let me take him out now and then. Invite me to his wedding. (*They both laugh.*)

MARION. You've got it.

ARTHUR (*clearing the table*). Let me get all this cold cocoa out of the way. We still have the deed to do.

MARION (*checking her watch*). And I've got to get Jimmy home in time for practice.

ARTHUR. Band practice?

MARION. Baseball. (*Picking her list off the floor.*) About this list, you do what you want.

ARTHUR. Believe me, I will. But I promise to consider your suggestions. Just don't rush me. I'm not ready to give it all away. (*Arthur is off to the kitchen with his tray and the phone rings. He answers in the kitchen.*) "Hello? . . . Just a minute." (*Calling out.*) It's your eager Little Leaguer.

(*Marion picks up the living room extension and Arthur hangs his up*)

MARION (*into phone*). Hello, honey. . . . I'll be down in five minutes. No. You know what? You come up here and get me. . . . No, I said you should come up here. . . . I said I want you to come up here. . . . Because I said so. . . . Thank you. (*She hangs the receiver.*)

ARTHUR (*rushing to the papers*). Alright, where do we start on these?

MARION (*getting out her seal*). I guess you should just start signing everything and I'll stamp along with you. Keep one of everything on the side for yourself.

ARTHUR. Now I feel so rushed. What am I signing?

MARIOM. You want to do this another time?

ARTHUR. No. Let's get it over with. I wouldn't survive another session like this.

(*He starts to sign and she starts her job.*)

MARION. I keep meaning to ask you; how are you?

ARTHUR (*at first puzzled and then:*) Oh, you mean my health? Fine. No. I'm fine. I've been tested, and nothing. We were very careful. We took many precautions. Collin used to make jokes about how we should invest in rubber futures.

MARION. I'll bet.

ARTHUR (*Stops what he's doing*). It never occurred to me until now. How about you?

MARION (*not stopping*). Well, we never had sex after he got sick.

ARTHUR. But before?

MARION (*stopping but not looking up*). I have the antibodies in my blood. No signs that it will ever develop into anything else. And it's been five years so my chances are pretty good that I'm just a carrier.

ARTHUR. I'm so sorry. Collin never told me.

MARION. He didn't know. In fact, other than my husband and the doctors, you're the only one I've told.

ARTHUR. You and your husband . . . ?

MARION. Have invested in rubber futures. There'd only be a problem if we wanted to have a child. Which we do. But we'll wait. Miracles happen every day.

ARTHUR. I don't know what to say.

MARION. Tell me you'll be be there if I ever need you.

(*Arthur gets up, goes to her and puts his arm around her. They hold each other. He gently pushes her away to make a joke.*)

ARTHUR. Sure! Take something else that should have been mine.

MARION. Don't even joke about things like that.

(*The doorbell rings. They pull themselves together.*)

ARTHUR. You know we'll never get these done today.

MARION. So, tomorrow.

(*Arthur goes to open the door as Marion gathers her things. He opens the doors and Jimmy is standing in the hall.*)

JIM. C'mon, Ma. I'm gonna be late.

ARTHUR. Would you like to come inside?

JIM. We've gotta go.

MARION. Jimmy, come on.

JIM. Ma!

(*She glares. He comes in. Arthur closes the door.*)

MARION (*holding out the flowers*). Take these for Mommy.

JIM (*taking them*). Can we go?

MARION (*picking up the painting*). Say good-bye to your Uncle Arthur.

JIM. 'Bye, Arthur. Come on.

MARION. Give him a kiss.

ARTHUR. Marion, don't.

MARION. Give your uncle a kiss good-bye.

JIM. He's not my uncle.

MARION. No. He's a hell of a lot more than your uncle.

ARTHUR (*offering his hand*). A handshake will do.

MARION. Tell Uncle Arthur what your daddy told you.

JIM. About what?

MARION. Stop playing dumb. You know.

ARTHUR. Don't embarrass him.

MARION. Jimmy, please.

JIM (*He regards his mother's softer tone and then speaks*). He said that after me and Mommy he loved you the most.

MARION (*standing behind him*). Go on.

JIM. And that I should love you too. And make sure that you're not lonely or very sad.

ARTHUR. Thank you.

(*Arthur reaches down to the boy and they hug. Jim gives him a little peck on the cheek and then breaks away.*)

MARION (*going to open the door*). Alright, kid, you done good. Now let's blow this joint before you muck it up.

(*Jim rushes out the door. Marion turns to Arthur.*)

MARION. A child's kiss is magic. Why else would they be so stingy with them. I'll call you.

(*Arthur nods understanding. Marion pulls the door closed behind her. Arthur stands quietly as the lights fade to black.*)

THE END

NOTE: *If being performed on film, the final image should be of Arthur leaning his back against the closed door on the inside of the apartment and Marion leaning on the outside of the door. A moment of thought and then they both move on.*

TOPICS FOR CRITICAL THINKING AND WRITING

📖 THE PLAY ON THE PAGE

1. We first hear about AIDS on page 976. Were you completely surprised, or did you think the play might introduce the subject? That is, did the author in any way prepare you for the subject? If so, how?

2. As far as the basic story goes, June (the lawyer) is not necessary. Marion could have brought the papers with her. Why do you suppose Fierstein introduces June? What function or functions does she serve? How would you characterize her?

3. On page 977 Marion says of the teapot, "One less thing to pack." Arthur says the same words a moment later, and then he repeats them yet again. A little later, while drinking cocoa, he repeats the words, and Marion says, "So you've said," to which Arthur replies, "So *we've* said." Exactly what tone do you think should be used when Marion first says these words? When Arthur says them? What significance, if any, do you attach to the fact that both characters speak these words?

4. Arthur says that Jimmy blames him for Collin's death, but Marion denies it. Who do you think is right? Can a reader be sure? Why or why not?

🎭 THE PLAY ON THE STAGE

9. A reviewer of the play said that Arthur is "bitchy" in many of his responses to Marion. What do you suppose the reviewer meant by this? Does the term imply that Fierstein presents a stereotype of the homosexual? If so, what is this stereotype? If you think that the term applies (even though you might not use such a word

5. When Arthur tells Marion that she should have told Jimmy why Collin left her, Marion says, "How the hell do you tell a seven-year-old that his father is leaving his mother to go sleep with other men?" Arthur replies, "[W]ell, not like that." What does Arthur mean? How might Marion have told Jimmy? Do you think she should have told Jimmy?

6. Do you agree with a reader who found Marion an unconvincing character because she is "so passive and unquestioningly loving in her regard for her ex-husband"? If you disagree, how would you argue your case?

7. During the course of the play, what (if anything) does Marion learn? What (if anything) does Arthur learn? What (if anything) does Jimmy learn? What (if anything) does the reader or viewer learn from the play?

8. One reader characterized the play as "propaganda." Do you agree? Why or why not? And if you think *On Tidy Endings* is propaganda, are you implying that it is, therefore, deficient as a work of art?

yourself), do you think that Fierstein's portrayal of Arthur is stereotypical? If it is stereotypical, is this a weakness in the play?

10. What well-known actors would you cast in the roles? Explain your choices.

D a v i d   M a m e t

OLEANNA

David Mamet was born in Chicago in 1947, and educated at Goddard College. A screenwriter and director as well as a playwright, he has occasionally taught courses in film. In 1976 his play *American Buffalo* won the New York Drama Critics Circle Award for the best American play, and in 1984 *Glengarry Glen Ross* won the Pulitzer Prize. *Oleanna* was first produced in 1992. "All my plays," Mamet has said, "attempt to bring out the poetry in the plain, everyday language people use."

COMMENTARY

Commenting on a school of writers who, in his opinion, merely said what they felt rather than shaped their material into artistic form, Truman Capote said, "That's not writing; it's typing." Capote was voicing memorably what many people vaguely think when they hear dialogue that seems to be nothing more than a transcription of what we daily hear on the bus or at the mall. It all seems so ordinary, so *artless*. However, perhaps the first thing to notice is that, in fact, ordinary speech is *not* artless. If you listen closely to conversations, you will notice that they often are amazingly rich in some of the qualities that we associate with poetry, for instance, in metaphor but especially in rhythm (recurrences at more or less regular intervals). The recurrences may be of words (repetition), of initial sounds of words (alliteration, as in "strong, silent type"), or of stresses. For instance:

1. Good morning.
2. Good morning.
1. How are you?
2. Fine, and you?

These words are not very inspiring, but they do show two people maintaining a relationship. Notice, too, that the second speaker repeats the words of the first speaker, and then, in the second speech, uses the same number of words (three) as in the speech being responded to. Furthermore, the second speech ends with a repetition of the final word ("you") of the preceding speech.

Now consider this line, spoken by Carol, in *Oleanna*:

CAROL. I don't *understand*. I don't *understand*. I don't understand what anything means.

It sounds pretty much like ordinary speech, and it probably *is* close to ordinary speech. If we were to scan Carol's first sentence, we would probably describe the pattern of stresses (here indicated by italic type) thus:

I *don't* under*stand*.

That is, we have an unaccented syllable, an accented syllable, two unaccented syllables, and finally another accented syllable. The second sentence is identical, and (not surprisingly) we would probably scan it the same way—an unaccented syllable, an accented syllable, two unaccented syllables, and an accented syllable. What is perhaps a bit surprising is that the third sentence, which repeats the first three words but adds three new ones, probably scans the same way:

I *don't* under*stand* what *anything means*.

Our daily speech often *does* have rhythms—but, of course, Mamet invented rather than transcribed his dialogue, and he must be given credit for his ability to catch the rhythms of ordinary speech. Mamet perhaps had this quality in mind when he said, "All my plays attempt to bring out the poetry in the plain, everyday language people use. That's the only way to put art back into the theater."

In fact, the rhythms and repetitions illustrated in this scrap of Carol's dialogue in *Oleanna* can also be found in larger units, that is to say, in the overall plot. As you will see when you read the play, *Oleanna* begins with John (a professor) in a position of power and with Carol (a student) in a position of weakness. Most noticeably, John is articulate, and Carol inarticulate. During the course of the play, the relationship undergoes a reversal; as one character goes up, the other goes down, giving us an almost visible symmetry or pattern, although this pattern does not continue to the very end. Parenthetically, we can mention that Mamet is fond of the two-person play, perhaps precisely because it so neatly lends itself to symmetry. Of course, an evident pattern—particularly one involving a reversal—is not unique to Mamet; it is at the heart of much drama. In the words of Arthur Miller (in an essay called "The Shadow of the Gods"), "The structure of a play is always the story of how the birds come home to roost."

A second quality that sets *Oleanna* apart from mere typing—a second quality that makes it a work of art that holds our interest—is the submerged element of mystery in it. Significant works of art never fully give up their secrets, and in drama the mystery is especially rooted in the nature of the characters. Tennessee Williams, in a stage direction in *Cat on a Hot Tin Roof*, put it this way: "Some mystery should be left in the revelation of character in a play, just as a great deal of mystery is always left in the revelation of character in life, even in one's own character to himself." P. G. James, an English writer of murder mysteries, has remarked that most stories (she cites the social novels of Jane Austen) are, at their heart, mysteries; we read them in order to discover a certain truth.

Oleanna is easy enough to follow, and it all seems "real" enough, but we probably cannot quite explain everything in it, and its ambiguities are part of its power. For example, in the early part of the play, Carol, a not-too-sophisticated student, is baffled by some of the professor's language. She is unfamiliar with such words as *predilection* and *indictment*, and she is a bit confused by metaphoric statements, such as John's assertion that academic tests are a form of *hazing* and that our current educational system is merely a matter of *warehousing the young*. Later in the play, however, she herself uses comparable language, and we are not quite sure whether her friends have given her a crash course in vocabulary and in argumentation or whether she has naturally

matured once she has decided not to let herself be bullied. In one delightful exchange in the latter part of the play, she is still somewhat puzzled when John uses the word *transpire*. (This passage, incidentally, also illustrates our first point about patterns in prose.)

CAROL. Transpire?
JOHN. Yes.
CAROL. "Happen?"
JOHN. Yes.

And now comes the evidence of her growth:

CAROL. Then *say* it.

Our two points, briefly, are these: Under the prosaic dialogue, or, rather, *by means of it*, Mamet presents the exciting and ultimately mysterious spectacle of people hammering out their destinies—and that is pretty much what we see in, for example, the plays of Shakespeare. Of course, Shakespeare does not hesitate to write poetry in a higher vein. Macbeth, for instance, imagines that his bloody hand (Macbeth has fatally stabbed the king) would turn the ocean red; in Macbeth's kingly idiom, his hand would "the multitudinous seas incarnadine." He follows these words, however, with simpler language; the hand that would "incarnadine" the sea would make "the green one red." If we remember some of Shakespeare's lofty language, we also remember much of his simple language. In the passage just quoted, the simple words are no less powerful than the unusual words. Consider also Lady Macbeth, who a moment later tries to dismiss her husband's fears by saying, "A little water clears us of this deed." Her line is simple, almost proselike, yet it, too, is iambic pentameter (that is, ten syllables with the stress on every other syllable). Near the end of the play we remember her simple, common-sensical statement, when we see her going through the motions of washing her hands while she is sleepwalking and sense a mysterious pattern in her life.

We are not saying that *Oleanna* is *Macbeth*, or that Mamet is Shakespeare, but we are saying that Mamet's prosaic language perhaps should be seen as the poetry of today's theater.

Oleanna, *a two-person play, is rich in verbal violence, a fine example of Elizabeth Bowen's assertion that "Dialogue is what characters do to each other." (In* Oleanna *a jangling telephone adds to the auditory assault.) This photograph shows Rebecca Pidgeon (Carol) and William H. Macy (John) as the student and the professor. In this production, Carol's apparent change in character from a shy girl to an assertive woman was given visible form by a change in her costume from a girlish outfit to trousers and a vest.*

David Mamet

OLEANNA

The want of fresh air does not seem much to affect the happiness of children in a London alley: the greater part of them sing and play as though they were on a moor in Scotland. So the absence of a genial mental atmosphere is not commonly recognized by children who have never known it. Young people have a marvelous faculty of either dying or adapting themselves to circumstances. Even if they are unhappy—very unhappy—it is astonishing how easily they can be prevented from finding it out, or at any rate from attributing it to any other cause than their own sinfulness.
—Samuel Butler, The Way of All Flesh

"Oh, to be in Oleanna,
That's where I would rather be.
Than be bound in Norway
And drag the chains of slavery."
—Folk Song

David Mamet

Characters

CAROL, *a woman of twenty*
JOHN, *a man in his forties*

The play takes place in John's office.

1

John is talking on the phone. Carol is seated across the desk from him.

JOHN (*on phone*). And what about the land. (*Pause*) The land. And what about the land? (*Pause*) What about it? (*Pause*) No. I don't understand. Well, yes, I'm I'm . . . no, I'm *sure* it's signif . . . I'm sure it's significant. (*Pause*) Because it's significant to mmmmmm . . . did you call Jerry? (*Pause*) Because . . . no, no, no, no, no. What did they say . . . ? Did you speak to the *real* estate . . . where *is* she . . . ? Well, well, all right. Where are her notes? Where are the notes we took with her. (*Pause*) I thought you were? No. No, I'm sorry, I didn't mean that, I just thought that I saw you, when we were there . . . what . . . ? I thought I saw you with a *pencil*. WHY NOW? is what I'm say . . . well, that's why I say "call Jerry." Well, I can't right now, be . . . no, I *didn't* schedule any . . . Grace: I *didn't* . . . I'm well aware . . . Look: Look. Did you call Jerry? Will you call Jerry . . . ? Because I can't now. I'll be there, I'm sure I'll be there in fifteen, in twenty. I intend to. No, we aren't *going* to lose the, we aren't *going* to lose the house. Look: Look, I'm not minimizing it. The "easement." Did she say "easement"? (*Pause*) What did she *say*; *is* it a "term of art," are we *bound* by it . . . I'm sorry . . . (*Pause*) are: we: yes. *Bound* by . . . Look: (*He checks his watch.*) before the other side *goes* home, all right? "a term of art." Because: that's right (*Pause*) The yard for the boy. Well, that's the whole . . . Look: I'm going to meet you there . . . (*He checks his watch.*) Is the realtor there? All right, tell her to show you the basement again. Look at the *this* because . . . Bec . . . I'm leaving in, I'm leaving in ten or fifteen . . . Yes. No, no, I'll meet you at the new . . . That's a good. If he thinks it's necc . . . you tell Jerry to meet . . . All right? We *aren't* going to lose the deposit. All right? I'm sure it's going to be . . . (*Pause*) I hope so. (*Pause*) I love you, too. (*Pause*) I love you, too. As soon as . . . I will.

   (*He hangs up.*) (*He bends over the desk and makes a note.*) (*He looks up.*) (*To Carol:*) I'm sorry . . .

CAROL. (*Pause*) What is a "term of art"?

JOHN. (*Pause*) I'm sorry . . . ?

CAROL. (*Pause*) What is a "term of art"?

JOHN. Is that what you want to talk about?

CAROL. . . . to talk about . . . ?

JOHN. Let's take the mysticism out of it, shall we? Carol? (*Pause*) Don't you think? I'll tell you: when you have some "thing." Which must be broached. (*Pause*) Don't you think . . . ? (*Pause*)

CAROL. . . . don't I think . . . ?

JOHN. Mmm?

CAROL. . . . did I . . . ?

JOHN. . . . what?

CAROL. Did . . . did I . . . did I say something wr . . .

JOHN. (*Pause*) No. I'm sorry. No. You're right. I'm very sorry. I'm somewhat rushed. As you see. I'm sorry. You're right. (*Pause*) What is a "term of art"? It seems to mean a *term*, which has come, through its use, to mean something *more specific* than the words would, to someone *not acquainted* with them . . . indicate. That, I believe, is what a "term of art," would mean. (*Pause*)

CAROL. You don't know what it means . . . ?

JOHN. I'm not sure that I know what it means. It's one of those things, perhaps you've had them, that, you look them up, or have someone explain them to you, and you say "aha," and, you immediately *forget* what . . .

CAROL. You don't do that.

JOHN. . . . I . . . ?

CAROL. You don't do . . .

JOHN. . . . I don't, what . . . ?

CAROL. . . . for . . .

JOHN. . . . I don't for . . .

CAROL. . . . no . . .

JOHN. . . . forget things? Everybody does that.

CAROL. No, they don't.

JOHN. They don't . . .

CAROL. No.

JOHN. (*Pause*) No. Everybody does that.

CAROL. Why would they do that . . . ?

JOHN. Because. I don't know. Because it doesn't interest them.

CAROL. No.

JOHN. I think so, though. (*Pause*) I'm sorry that I was distracted.

CAROL. You don't have to say that to me.

JOHN. You paid me the compliment, or the "obeisance"—all right—of coming in here . . . All right. *Carol*. I find that I am at a *standstill*. I find that I . . .

CAROL. . . . what . . .

JOHN. . . . one moment. In regard to your . . . to your . . .

CAROL. Oh, oh. You're buying a new house!

JOHN. No, let's get on with it.

CAROL. "Get on"? (*Pause*)

JOHN. I know how . . . *believe* me. I know how . . . potentially *humiliating* these . . . I have no desire to . . . I have no desire other than to help you. But: (*He picks up some papers on his desk.*) I won't even say "but." I'll say that as I go back over the . . .

CAROL. I'm just, I'm just trying to . . .

JOHN. . . . no, it will not do.

CAROL. . . . what? What will . . . ?

JOHN. No. I see, I see what you, it . . . (*He gestures to the papers.*) but your work . . .

CAROL. I'm just: I sit in class I . . . (*She holds up her notebook.*) I take notes . . .

JOHN. (*simultaneously with* "notes"). Yes. I understand. What I am trying to *tell* you is that some, some basic . . .

CAROL. . . . I . . .

JOHN. . . . one moment: some basic missed communi . . .

CAROL. I'm doing what I'm told. I bought your book, I read your . . .

JOHN. No, I'm sure you . . .

CAROL. No, no, no. I'm doing what I'm told. It's *difficult* for me. It's *difficult* . . .

JOHN. . . . but . . .

CAROL. I don't . . . lots of the *language* . . .

JOHN. . . . please . . .

CAROL. The *language*, the "things" that you say . . .

JOHN. I'm sorry. No. I don't think that that's true.

CAROL. It *is* true. I . . .

JOHN. I think . . .

CAROL. It *is* true.

JOHN. . . . I . . .

CAROL. Why would I . . . ?

JOHN. I'll tell you why: you're an incredibly bright girl.

CAROL. . . . I . . .

JOHN. You're an incredibly . . . you have no problem with the . . . Who's kidding who?

CAROL. . . . I . . .

JOHN. No. No. I'll tell you why. I'll tell. . . . I think you're *angry*, I . . .

CAROL. . . . why would I . . .

JOHN. . . . wait one moment. I . . .

CAROL. It *is* true. I have *problems* . . .

JOHN. . . . every . . .

CAROL. . . . I come from a different *social* . . .

JOHN. . . . ev . . .

CAROL. a different economic . . .

JOHN. . . . Look:

CAROL. No. I: when I *came* to this school:

JOHN. Yes. Quite . . . (*Pause*)

CAROL. . . . does that mean nothing . . . ?

JOHN. . . . but look: look . . .

CAROL. . . . I . . .

JOHN. (*Picks up paper.*) Here: Please: Sit down. (*Pause*) Sit down. (*Reads from her paper.*) "I think that the ideas contained in this work express the author's feelings in a way that he intended, based on his results." What can that mean? Do you see? What . . .

CAROL. I, the best that I . . .

JOHN. I'm saying, that perhaps this course . . .

CAROL. No, no, no, you can't, you can't . . . I have to . . .

JOHN. . . . how . . .

CAROL. . . . I have to pass it . . .

JOHN. Carol, I:

CAROL. I *have* to pass this course, I . . .

JOHN. Well.

CAROL. . . . don't you . . .

JOHN. Either the . . .

CAROL. . . . I . . .

JOHN. . . . either the, I . . . either the *criteria* for judging progress in the class are . . .

CAROL. No, no, no, no, I have to pass it.

JOHN. Now, look: I'm a human being, I . . .

CAROL. I did what you told me. I did, I did everything that, I read your *book,* you told me to buy your book and read it. Everything you *say* I . . . (*She gestures to her notebook.*) (*The phone rings.*) I do. . . . Ev . . .

JOHN. . . . look:

CAROL. . . . everything I'm told . . .

JOHN. Look. Look. I'm not your *father.* (*Pause*)

CAROL. What?

JOHN. I'm.

CAROL. Did I say you were my father?

JOHN. . . . no . . .

CAROL. Why did you say that . . . ?

JOHN. I . . .

CAROL. . . . why . . . ?

JOHN. . . . in class I . . . (*He picks up the phone.*) (*Into phone:*) Hello. I can't talk now. Jerry? Yes? I underst . . . I can't talk now. I know . . . I know . . . Jerry. I can't *talk* now. Yes, I. Call me back in . . . Thank you. (*He hangs up.*) (*To Carol:*) What do you want me to do? We are two people, all right? Both of whom have subscribed to . . .

CAROL. No, no . . .

JOHN. . . . certain arbitrary . . .

CAROL. No. You have to help me.

JOHN. Certain institutional . . . you tell me what you want me to do. . . . You tell me what you want me to . . .

CAROL. How can I go back and tell them the *grades* that I . . .

JOHN. . . . what can I do . . . ?

CAROL. *Teach* me. *Teach* me.

JOHN. . . . I'm trying to teach you.

CAROL. I read your book. I read it. I don't under . . .

JOHN. . . . you don't understand it.

CAROL. No.

JOHN. Well, perhaps it's not well *written* . . .

CAROL (*simultaneously with* "written"). No. No. No. I want to *understand* it.

JOHN. What don't you understand? (*Pause*)

CAROL. Any of it. What you're trying to say. When you talk about . . .

JOHN. . . . yes . . . ? (*She consults her notes.*)

CAROL. "Virtual warehousing of the young" . . .

JOHN. "Virtual warehousing of the young." If we artificially prolong adolescence . . .

David Mamet

CAROL. . . . and about "The Curse of Modern Education."

JOHN. . . . well . . .

CAROL. I don't . . .

JOHN. Look. It's just a *course*, it's just a *book*, it's just a . . .

CAROL. No. No. There are *people* out there. People who came *here*. To know something they didn't *know*. Who *came* here. To be *helped*. To be *helped*. So someone would *help* them. To *do* something. To *know* something. To get, what do they say? "To get on in the world." How can I do that if I don't, if I fail? But I don't *understand*. I don't *understand*. I don't understand what anything means . . . and I walk around. From morning 'til night: with this one thought in my head. I'm *stupid*.

JOHN. No one thinks you're stupid.

CAROL. No? What am I . . . ?

JOHN. I . . .

CAROL. . . . what am I, then?

JOHN. I think you're angry. Many people are. I have a *telephone* call that I have to make. And an *appointment*, which is rather *pressing*; though I sympathize with your concerns, and though I wish I had the time, this was not a previously scheduled meeting and I . . .

CAROL. . . . you think I'm nothing . . .

JOHN. . . . have an appointment with a *realtor*, and with my wife and . . .

CAROL. You think that I'm stupid.

JOHN. No. I certainly don't.

CAROL. You said it.

JOHN. No. I did not.

CAROL. You did.

JOHN. When?

CAROL. . . . you . . .

JOHN. No. I never did, or never would say that to a student, and . . .

CAROL. You said, "What can that mean?" (*Pause*) "What can that mean?" . . . (*Pause*)

JOHN. . . . and what did that mean to you . . . ?

CAROL. That meant I'm stupid. And I'll never learn. That's what that meant. And you're right.

JOHN. . . . I . . .

CAROL. But then. But then, what am I doing here . . . ?

JOHN. . . . if you thought that I . . .

CAROL. . . . when nobody wants me, and . . .

JOHN. . . . if you interpreted . . .

CAROL. Nobody *tells* me anything. And I *sit* there . . . in the *corner*. In the *back*. And everybody's talking about "this" all the time. And "concepts," and "precepts" and, and, and, and, and, WHAT IN THE WORLD ARE YOU *TALKING* ABOUT? And I read your book. And they said, "Fine, go in that class." Because you talked about responsibility to the young. I DON'T KNOW WHAT IT MEANS AND I'M *FAILING* . . .

JOHN. May . . .

CAROL. No, you're right. "Oh, hell." I failed. Flunk me out of it. It's garbage. Everything I do. "The ideas contained in this work express the author's feelings." That's right. That's right. I know I'm stupid. I know what I am. (*Pause*) I know what I am, Professor. You don't have to tell me. (*Pause*) It's pathetic. Isn't it?

JOHN. . . . Aha . . . (*Pause*) Sit down. Sit down. Please. (*Pause*) Please sit down.

CAROL. Why?

JOHN. I want to talk to you.

CAROL. Why?

JOHN. Just sit down. (*Pause*) Please. Sit down. Will you, please . . . ? (*Pause. She does so.*) Thank you.

CAROL. What?

JOHN. I want to tell you something.

CAROL. (*Pause*) What?

JOHN. Well, I know what you're talking about.

CAROL. No. You don't.

JOHN. I think I do. (*Pause*)

CAROL. How can you?

JOHN. I'll tell you a story about myself. (*Pause*) Do you mind? (*Pause*) I was raised to think myself stupid. That's what I want to tell you. (*Pause*)

CAROL. What do you mean?

JOHN. Just what I said. I was brought up, and my earliest, and most persistent memories are of being told that I was stupid. "You have such *intelligence*. Why must you behave so *stupidly*?" Or, "Can't you *understand*? Can't you *understand*?" And I could *not* understand. I could *not* understand.

CAROL. What?

JOHN. The simplest problem. Was beyond me. It was a mystery.

CAROL. What was a mystery?

JOHN. How people learn. How *I* could learn. Which is what I've been speaking of in class. And of *course* you can't hear it. Carol. Of *course* you can't. (*Pause*) I used to speak of "real people," and wonder what the *real* people did. The *real* people. Who were they? *They* were the people other than myself. The *good* people. The *capable* people. The people who could do the things, *I* could not do: learn, study, retain . . . all that *garbage*—which is what I have been talking of in class, and that's *exactly* what I have been talking of—If you are told . . . Listen to this. If the young child is told he cannot understand. Then he takes it as a *description* of himself. What am I? I am *that which can not understand*. And I saw you out there, when we were speaking of the concepts of . . .

CAROL. I can't understand any of them.

JOHN. Well, then, that's *my* fault. That's not your fault. And that is not verbiage. That's what I firmly hold to be the truth. And I am sorry, and I owe you an apology.

CAROL. Why?

JOHN. And I suppose that I have had some *things* on my mind. . . . We're buying a *house*, and . . .

CAROL. People said that you were stupid . . . ?

JOHN. Yes.

CAROL. When?

JOHN. I'll tell you when. Through my life. In my childhood; and, perhaps, they stopped. But I heard them continue.

CAROL. And what did they say?

JOHN. They said I was incompetent. Do you see? And when I'm tested the, the, the *feelings* of my youth about the *very subject of learning* come up. And I . . . I become, I feel "unworthy," and "unprepared." . . .

CAROL. . . . yes.

JOHN. . . . eh?

CAROL. . . . yes.

JOHN. And I feel that I must fail. (*Pause*)

CAROL. . . . but then you *do* fail. (*Pause*) You have to. (*Pause*) Don't you?

JOHN. A *pilot*. Flying a plane. The pilot is flying the plane. He thinks: Oh, my *God*, my mind's been drifting! Oh, my God! What kind of a cursed imbecile am I, that I, with this so precious cargo of *Life* in my charge, would allow my attention to wander. Why was I born? How deluded are those who put their trust in me, . . . et cetera, so on, and he crashes the plane.

CAROL. (*Pause*) He could just . . .

JOHN. That's right.

CAROL. He could say:

JOHN. My attention *wandered* for a moment . . .

CAROL. . . . uh huh . . .

JOHN. I had a *thought* I did not like . . . but now:

CAROL. . . . but now it's . . .

JOHN. That's what I'm telling you. It's time to put my attention . . . see: it is not: this is what I learned. It is Not Magic. Yes. Yes. *You.* You are going to be frightened. When faced with what may or may not be but which you are going to perceive as a test. You will become frightened. And you will say: "I am incapable of . . ." and everything *in* you will think these two things. "I must. But I can't." And you will think: Why was I born to be the laughingstock of a world in which everyone is better than I? In which I am entitled to nothing. Where I can not learn.

(*Pause*)

CAROL. Is that . . . (*Pause*) Is that what I have . . . ?

JOHN. Well. I don't know if I'd put it that way. Listen: I'm talking to you as I'd talk to my son. Because that's what I'd like him to have that I never had. I'm talking to you the way I wish that someone had talked to me. I don't know how to do it, other than to be *personal*, . . . but . . .

CAROL. Why would you want to be personal with me?

JOHN. Well, you see? That's what I'm saying. We can only interpret the behavior of others through the screen we . . . (*The phone rings.*) Through . . . (*To phone:*) Hello . . . ? (*To Carol:*) Through the screen we create. (*To phone:*) Hello. (*To Carol:*) Excuse me a moment. (*To phone:*) Hello? No, I can't talk nnn . . . I know I did. In a few . . .

I'm . . . is he coming to the . . . yes. I talked to him. We'll meet you at the No, because I'm with a *student*. It's going to be fff . . . This is important, too. I'm with a *student,* Jerry's going to . . . Listen: the sooner I get off, the sooner I'll be down, all right. I love you. Listen, listen, I said "I love you," it's going to work *out* with the, because I feel that it is, I'll be right down. All right? Well, then it's going to take as long as it takes. (*He hangs up.*) (*To Carol:*) I'm sorry.

CAROL. What was that?

JOHN. There are some problems, as there usually are, about the final agreements for the new house.

CAROL. You're buying a new house.

JOHN. That's right.

CAROL. Because of your promotion.

JOHN. Well, I suppose that that's right.

CAROL. Why did you stay here with me?

JOHN. Stay here.

CAROL. Yes. When you should have gone.

JOHN. Because I like you.

CAROL. You like me.

JOHN. Yes.

CAROL. Why?

JOHN. Why? Well? Perhaps we're similar. (*Pause*) Yes. (*Pause*)

CAROL. You said "everyone has problems."

JOHN. Everyone has problems.

CAROL. Do they?

JOHN. Certainly.

CAROL. You do?

JOHN. Yes.

CAROL. What are they?

JOHN. Well. (*Pause*) Well, you're perfectly right. (*Pause*) If we're going to take off the Artificial *Stricture,* of "Teacher," and "Student," why should *my* problems be any more a mystery than your own? Of *course* I have problems. As you saw.

CAROL. . . . with what?

JOHN. With my *wife* . . . with *work* . . .

CAROL. With work?

JOHN. Yes. And, and, perhaps my problems are, do you see? *Similar* to yours.

CAROL. Would you tell me?

JOHN. All right. (*Pause*) I came *late* to teaching. And I found it Artificial. The notion of "I know and you do not"; and I saw an *exploitation* in the education process. I told you. I hated school, I hated teachers. I hated everyone who was in the position of a "boss" because I *knew*—I didn't *think*, mind you, I *knew* I was going to fail. Because I was a fuck-up. I was just no goddamned good. When I . . . late in life . . . (*Pause*) When I *got out from under* . . . when I worked my way out of the need to fail. When I . . .

CAROL. How do you do that? (*Pause*)

JOHN. You have to look at what you are, and what you feel, and how you act. And, finally, you have to look at how

David Mamet

you act. And say: If that's what I *did*, that must be how I think of myself.

CAROL. I don't understand.

JOHN. If I fail all the time, it must be that I think of myself as a failure. If I do not want to think of myself as a failure, perhaps I should begin by *succeeding* now and again. Look. The tests, you see, which you encounter, in school, in college, in life, were designed, in the most part, for idiots. *By* idiots. There is no need to fail at them. They are not a test of your worth. They are a test of your ability to retain and spout back misinformation. Of *course* you fail them. They're *nonsense*. And I . . .

CAROL. . . . no . . .

JOHN. Yes. They're *garbage*. They're a *joke*. Look at me. Look at me. The Tenure Committee. The Tenure Committee. Come to judge me. The Bad Tenure Committee. The "Test." Do you see? They put me to the test. Why, they had people voting on me I wouldn't employ to wax my car. And yet, I go before the Great Tenure Committee, and I have an urge, to *vomit*, to, to, to puke my *badness* on the table, to show them: "I'm no good. Why would you pick *me*?"

CAROL. They granted you tenure.

JOHN. Oh no, they announced it, but they haven't *signed*. Do you see? "At any moment . . ."

CAROL. . . . mmm . . .

JOHN. "They might not *sign*" . . . I might not . . . the *house* might not go through . . . Eh? Eh? They'll find out my "dark secret." (*Pause*)

CAROL. . . . what is it . . . ?

JOHN. There *isn't* one. But *they* will find an index of my badness . . .

CAROL. Index?

JOHN. A ". . . pointer." A "Pointer." You see? Do you see? I *understand* you. I. Know. That. Feeling. Am I entitled to my job, and my nice *home*, and my *wife*, and my *family*, and so on. This is what I'm saying: That theory of education which, that *theory*:

CAROL. I . . . I . . . (*Pause*)

JOHN. What?

CAROL. I . . .

JOHN. What?

CAROL. I want to know about my grade. (*Long pause*)

JOHN. Of course you do.

CAROL. Is that bad?

JOHN. No.

CAROL. Is it bad that I asked you that?

JOHN. No.

CAROL. Did I upset you?

JOHN. No. And I apologize. Of *course* you want to know about your grade. And, of course, you can't concentrate on anyth . . . (*The telephone starts to ring.*) Wait a moment.

CAROL. I should go.

JOHN. I'll make you a deal.

CAROL. No, you have to . . .

JOHN. Let it ring. I'll make you a deal. You stay here. We'll start the whole course over. I'm going to say it was not you, it was I who was not paying attention. We'll start the whole course over. Your grade is an "A." Your final grade is an "A." (*The phone stops ringing.*)

CAROL. But the class is only half over . . .

JOHN (*simultaneously with* "over"). Your grade for the whole term is an "A." If you will come back and meet with me. A few more times. Your grade's an "A." Forget about the paper. You didn't like it, you didn't like writing it. It's not important. What's important is that I awake your interest, if I can, and that I answer your questions. Let's start over. (*Pause*)

CAROL. Over. With what?

JOHN. Say this is the beginning.

CAROL. The beginning.

JOHN. Yes.

CAROL. Of what?

JOHN. Of the class.

CAROL. But we can't start over.

JOHN. I say we can. (*Pause*) I say we can.

CAROL. But I don't believe it.

JOHN. Yes, I know that. But it's true. What is The Class but you and me? (*Pause*)

CAROL. There are rules.

JOHN. Well. We'll break them.

CAROL. How can we?

JOHN. We won't tell anybody.

CAROL. Is that all right?

JOHN. I say that it's fine.

CAROL. Why would you do this for me?

JOHN. I like you. Is that so difficult for you to . . .

CAROL. Um . . .

JOHN. There's no one here but you and me. (*Pause*)

CAROL. All right. I did not understand. When you referred . . .

JOHN. All right, yes?

CAROL. When you referred to hazing.

JOHN. Hazing.

CAROL. You wrote, in your book. About the comparative . . . the comparative . . . (*She checks her notes.*)

JOHN. Are you checking your notes . . . ?

CAROL. Yes.

JOHN. Tell me in your own . . .

CAROL. I want to make sure that I have it right.

JOHN. No. Of course. You want to be exact.

CAROL. I want to know everything that went on.

JOHN. . . . that's good.

CAROL. . . . so I . . .

JOHN. That's very good. But I was suggesting, many times, that that which we wish to retain is retained oftentimes, I think, *better* with less expenditure of effort.

CAROL. (Of notes) Here it is: you wrote of *hazing*.

JOHN. . . . that's correct. Now: I said "hazing." It means ritualized annoyance. We shove this book at you, we say read it. Now, you say you've read it? I think that you're *lying*. I'll *grill* you, and when I find you've lied, you'll be disgraced, and your life will be ruined. It's a sick game. Why do we do it? Does it educate? In no sense. Well, then, what is higher education? It is something-other-than-useful.

CAROL. What is "something-other-than-useful?"

JOHN. It has become a ritual, it has become an article of faith. That all must be subjected to, or to put it differently, that all are entitled to Higher Education. And my point . . .

CAROL. You disagree with that?

JOHN. Well, let's address that. What do you think?

CAROL. I don't know.

JOHN. What do you think, though? (*Pause*)

CAROL. I don't know.

JOHN. I spoke of it in class. Do you remember my example?

CAROL. Justice.

JOHN. Yes. Can you repeat it to me? (*She looks down at her notebook.*) Without your notes? I ask you as a favor to me, so that I can see if my idea was interesting.

CAROL. You said "justice" . . .

JOHN. Yes?

CAROL. . . . that all are entitled . . . (*Pause*) I . . . I . . . I . . .

JOHN. Yes. To a speedy trial. To a fair trial. But they needn't be given a trial *at all* unless they stand accused. Eh? Justice is their right, should they choose to avail themselves of it, they should have a fair trial. It does not follow, of necessity, a person's life is incomplete without a trial in it. Do you see? My point is a confusion between equity and *utility* arose. So we confound the *usefulness* of higher education with our, granted, right to equal access to the same. We, in effect, create a *prejudice* toward it, completely independent of . . .

CAROL. . . . that it is prejudice that we should go to school?

JOHN. Exactly. (*Pause*)

CAROL. How can you say that? How . . .

JOHN. Good. Good. *Good.* That's right! Speak up! What is a prejudice? An unreasoned belief. We are all subject to it. None of us is not. When it is threatened, or opposed, we feel anger, and feel, do we not? As you do now. Do you not? Good.

CAROL. . . . but how can you . . .

JOHN. . . . let us examine. Good.

CAROL. How . . .

JOHN. Good. Good. When . . .

CAROL. I'M SPEAKING . . . (*Pause*)

JOHN. I'm sorry.

CAROL. How can you . . .

JOHN. . . . I beg your pardon.

CAROL. That's all right.

JOHN. I beg your pardon.

CAROL. That's all right.

JOHN. I'm sorry I interrupted you.

CAROL. That's all right.

JOHN. You were saying?

CAROL. I was saying . . . I was saying . . . (*She checks her notes.*) How can you say in a class. Say in a college class, that college education is prejudice?

JOHN. I said that our predilection for it . . .

CAROL. Predilection . . .

JOHN. . . . you know what that means.

CAROL. Does it mean "liking"?

JOHN. Yes.

CAROL. But how can you say that? That College . . .

JOHN. . . . that's my *job*, don't you know.

CAROL. What is?

JOHN. To provoke you.

CAROL. No.

JOHN. Oh. Yes, though.

CAROL. To provoke me?

JOHN. That's right.

CAROL. To make me mad?

JOHN. That's right. To force you . . .

CAROL. . . . to make me mad is your job?

JOHN. To force you to . . . listen: (*Pause*) Ah. (*Pause*) When I was young somebody told me, are you ready, the rich copulate less often than the poor. But when they do, they take more of their clothes off. Years. Years, mind you, I would compare experiences of my own to this dictum, saying, aha, this fits the norm, or ah, this is a variation from it. What did it mean? Nothing. It was some jerk thing, some school kid told me that took up room inside my head. (*Pause*)

Somebody told *you*, and you hold it as an article of faith, that higher education is an unassailable good. This notion is so dear to you that when I question it you become angry. Good. Good, I say. Are not those the very things which we should question? I say college education, since the war, has become so a matter of course, and such a fashionable necessity, for those either of or aspiring *to* the new vast middle class, that we *espouse* it, as a matter of right, and have ceased to ask, "What is it good for?" (*Pause*)

What might be some reasons for pursuit of higher education?

One: A love of learning.

Two: The wish for mastery of a skill.

Three: For economic betterment.

(*Stops. Makes a note.*)

CAROL. I'm keeping you.

JOHN. One moment. I have to make a note . . .

CAROL. It's something that I said?

JOHN. No, we're buying a house.

CAROL. You're buying the new house.

JOHN. To go with the tenure. That's right. Nice *house*, close to the *private school* . . . (*He continues making his note.*) . . . We were talking of economic *betterment* (*Carol writes in her notebook.*) . . . I was thinking of the School Tax. (*He continues writing.*) (*To himself:*) . . . *where is it written* that I have to send my child to public school. . . . Is it a law that I have to improve the City Schools at the expense of my own interest? And, is this not simply *The White Man's Burden*? Good. And (*Looks up to Carol*) . . . does this interest you?

CAROL. No. I'm taking notes . . .

JOHN. You don't have to take notes, you know, you can just listen.

CAROL. I want to make sure I remember it. (*Pause*)

JOHN. I'm not lecturing you, I'm just trying to tell you some things I think.

CAROL. What do you think?

JOHN. Should all kids go to college? *Why* . . .

CAROL. (*Pause*) To learn.

JOHN. But if he does not learn.

CAROL. If the child does not learn?

JOHN. Then why is he in college? Because he was told it was his "right"?

CAROL. Some might find college instructive.

JOHN. I would hope so.

CAROL. But how do they feel? Being told they are wasting their time?

JOHN. I don't think I'm telling them that.

CAROL. You said that education was "prolonged and systematic hazing."

JOHN. Yes. It can be so.

CAROL. . . . if education is so *bad*, why do you do it?

JOHN. I do it because I love it. (*Pause*) Let's. . . . I suggest you look at the demographics, wage-earning capacity, college- and non-college-educated men and women, 1855 to 1980, and let's see if we can wring some worth from the statistics. Eh? And . . .

CAROL. No.

JOHN. What?

CAROL. I can't understand them.

JOHN. . . . you . . . ?

CAROL. . . . the "charts." The *Concepts*, the . . .

JOHN. "Charts" are simply . . .

CAROL. When I leave here . . .

JOHN. Charts, do you see . . .

CAROL. No, I can't . . .

JOHN. You can, though.

CAROL. NO, NO—I DON'T UNDERSTAND. DO YOU SEE??? I DON'T *UNDERSTAND* . . .

JOHN. What?

CAROL. Any of it. Any of it. I'm *smiling* in class, I'm *smiling*, the whole time. What are you *talking* about? What is everyone *talking* about? I don't *understand*. I don't know

what it *means*. I don't know what it means to *be* here . . . you tell me I'm intelligent, and then you tell me I should not be *here*, what do you *want* with me? What does it *mean*? Who should I *listen* to . . . I . . .

(*He goes over to her and puts his arm around her shoulder.*)

NO! (*She walks away from him.*)

JOHN. Sshhhh.

CAROL. No, I don't under . . .

JOHN. Sshhhh.

CAROL. I don't know what you're *saying* . . .

JOHN. Sshhhhh. It's all right.

CAROL. . . . I have no . . .

JOHN. Sshhhhh. Sshhhhh. Let it go a moment. (*Pause*) Sshhhhh . . . let it go. (*Pause*) Just let it go. (*Pause*) Just let it go. It's all right. (*Pause*) Sshhhhh. (*Pause*) I understand . . . (*Pause*) What do you feel?

CAROL. I feel bad.

JOHN. I know. It's all right.

CAROL. I . . . (*Pause*)

JOHN. What?

CAROL. I . . .

JOHN. What? Tell me.

CAROL. I don't understand you.

JOHN. I know. It's all right.

CAROL. I . . .

JOHN. What? (*Pause*) What? *Tell* me.

CAROL. I can't tell you.

JOHN. No, you must.

CAROL. I can't.

JOHN. No. Tell me. (*Pause*)

CAROL. I'm bad. (*Pause*) Oh, God. (*Pause*)

JOHN. It's all right.

CAROL. I'm . . .

JOHN. It's all right.

CAROL. I can't talk about this.

JOHN. It's all right. Tell me.

CAROL. Why do you want to know this?

JOHN. I don't want to know. I want to know whatever you . . .

CAROL. I always . . .

JOHN. . . . good . . .

CAROL. I always . . . all my life . . . I have never told anyone this . . .

JOHN. Yes. Go on. (*Pause*) Go on.

CAROL. All of my life . . . (*The phone rings.*) (*Pause. John goes to the phone and picks it up.*)

JOHN (*into phone*). I can't talk now. (*Pause*) What? (*Pause*) Hmm. (*Pause*) All right, I . . . I. Can't. Talk. Now. No, no, no, I *Know* I did, but. . . . What? Hello. What? She *what*? She *can't*, she said the agreement is void? How, how is the agreement *void*? *That's Our House*.

I have the *paper*; when we come down, next week, with the payment, and the paper, that house is . . . wait,

wait, wait, wait, wait, wait, wait: Did Jerry . . . is Jerry there? (*Pause*) Is *she* there . . . ? Does she have a *lawyer* . . . ? How the *hell*, how the *Hell*. That is . . . it's a question, you said, of the *easement*. I don't underst . . . it's not the *whole agreement*. It's just the *easement*, why would she? Put, put, put, *Jerry* on. (*Pause*) Jer, *Jerry*: What the *Hell* . . . that's my *house*. That's . . . Well, I'm no, no, no, I'm *not* coming ddd . . . List, *Listen*, *screw* her. You *tell* her. You, listen: I want you to take *Grace*, you take Grace, and get out of that house. You *leave* her there. Her and her lawyer, and you *tell* them, we'll see them in court next . . . no. No. Leave her there, leave her to *stew* in it: You tell her, we're *getting* that house, and we are going to . . . No. I'm *not* coming down. I'll be damned if I'll sit in the same rrr . . . the next, you tell her the next time I *see* her is in court . . . I . . . (*Pause*) What? (*Pause*) What? I don't understand. (*Pause*) Well, what about the house? (*Pause*) There isn't any problem with the hhh . . . (*Pause*) No, no, no, that's all right. All ri . . . All right . . . (*Pause*) Of course. Tha . . . Thank you. No, I will. Right away. (*He hangs up.*) (*Pause*)

CAROL. What is it? (*Pause*)

JOHN. It's a surprise party.

CAROL. It is.

JOHN. Yes.

CAROL. A party for you.

JOHN. Yes.

CAROL. Is it your birthday?

JOHN. No.

CAROL. What is it?

JOHN. The tenure announcement.

CAROL. The tenure announcement.

JOHN. They're throwing a party for us in our new house.

CAROL. Your new house.

JOHN. The house that we're buying.

CAROL. You have to go.

JOHN. It seems that I do.

CAROL. (*Pause*) They're proud of you.

JOHN. Well, there are those who would say it's a form of aggression.

CAROL. What is?

JOHN. A surprise.

2

John and Carol seated across the desk from each other.

JOHN. You see, (*pause*) I love to teach. And flatter myself I am *skilled* at it. And I love the, the aspect of *performance*. I think I must confess that.

When I found I loved to teach I swore that I would not become that cold, rigid automation of an instructor which I had encountered as a child.

Now, I was not unconscious that it was given me to err upon the other side. And, so, I asked and *ask* myself if

I engaged in heterodoxy, I will not say "gratuitously" for I do not care to posit orthodoxy as a given good—but, "to the detriment of, of my students." (*Pause*)

As I said. When the possibility of tenure opened, and, of course, I'd long pursued it, I was, of course *happy*, and *covetous* of it.

I asked myself if I was wrong to covet it. And thought about it long, and, I hope, truthfully, and saw in myself several things in, I think, no particular order. (*Pause*)

That I *would* pursue it. That I *desired* it, that I was not pure of longing for security, and that that, perhaps, was not reprehensible in me. That I had duties *beyond* the school, and that my duty to my home, for instance, was, or should be, if it were not, of an equal weight. That tenure, and security, and yes, and *comfort*, were not, of themselves, to be scorned; and were even worthy of honorable pursuit. And that it was given me. Here, in this place, which I enjoy, and in which I find comfort, to assure myself of—as far as it rests in The Material—a continuation of that joy and comfort. In exchange for what? Teaching. Which I love.

What was the price of this security? To obtain *tenure*. Which tenure the committee is in the process of granting me. And on the basis of which I contracted to purchase a house. Now, as you don't have your own family, at this point, you may not know what that means. But to me it is important. A home. A Good Home. To raise my family. Now: The Tenure Committee will meet. This is the process, and a *good* process. Under which the school has functioned for quite a long time. They will meet, and hear your complaint—which you have the right to make; and they will dismiss it. They will *dismiss* your complaint; and, in the intervening period, I will lose my house. I will not be able to close on my house. I will lose my *deposit*, and the home I'd picked out for my wife and son will go by the boards. Now: I see I have angered you. I understand your anger at teachers. I was angry with mine. I felt hurt and humiliated by them. Which is one of the reasons that I went into education.

CAROL. What do you want of me?

JOHN. (*Pause*) I was hurt. When I received the report. Of the tenure committee. I was shocked. And I was hurt. No, I don't mean to subject you to my weak sensibilities. All right. Finally, I didn't understand. Then I thought: is it not always at those points at which we reckon ourselves unassailable that we are most vulnerable and . . . (*Pause*) Yes. All right. You find me pedantic. Yes. I am. By nature, by *birth*, by profession, I don't know . . . I'm always looking for a *paradigm* for . . .

CAROL. I don't know what a paradigm is.

JOHN. It's a model.

CAROL. Then why can't you use that word? (*Pause*)

JOHN. If it is important to you. Yes, all right. I was looking for a model. To continue: I feel that one point . . .

David Mamet

CAROL. I . . .

JOHN. One second . . . upon which I am unassailable is my unflinching concern for my students' dignity. I asked you here to . . . in the spirit of *investigation*, to ask you . . . to ask . . . (*Pause*) What have I done to you? (*Pause*) And, and, I suppose, how I can make amends. Can we not settle this now? It's pointless, really, and I want to know.

CAROL. What you can do to force me to retract?

JOHN. That is not what I meant at all.

CAROL. To bribe me, to convince me . . .

JOHN. . . . No.

CAROL. To retract . . .

JOHN. That is not what I meant at all. I think that you know it is not.

CAROL. That is not what I know. I *wish* I . . .

JOHN. I do not want to . . . you wish what?

CAROL. No, you said what amends can you make. To force me to retract.

JOHN. That is not what I said.

CAROL. I have my notes.

JOHN. Look. Look. The Stoics say . . .

CAROL. The Stoics?

JOHN. The Stoical Philosophers say if you remove the phrase "I have been injured," you have removed the injury. Now: Think: I know that you're upset. Just tell me. Literally. Literally: what wrong have I done you?

CAROL. Whatever you have done to me—to the extent that you've done it to *me*, do you know, rather than to me as a *student*, and, so, to the student body, is contained in my report. To the tenure committee.

JOHN. Well, all right. (*Pause*) Let's see. (*He reads.*) I find that I am sexist. That I am *elitist*. I'm not sure I know what that means, other than it's a derogatory word, meaning "bad." That I . . . That I insist on wasting time, in nonprescribed, in self-aggrandizing and theatrical *diversions* from the prescribed *text* . . . that these have taken both sexist and pornographic forms . . . here we find listed . . . (*Pause*) Here we find listed . . . instances ". . . closeted with a student" . . . "Told a rambling, sexually explicit story, in which the frequency and attitudes of fornication of the poor and rich are, it would seem, the central point . . . moved to *embrace* said student and . . . all part of a pattern . . ." (*Pause*)

(*He reads.*) That I used the phrase "The White Man's Burden" . . . that I told you how I'd asked you to my room because I quote like you. (*Pause*)

(*He reads.*) "He said he 'liked' me. That he 'liked being with me.' He'd let me write my examination paper over, if I could come back oftener to see him in his office." (*Pause*) (*To Carol:*) It's *ludicrous*. Don't you know that? It's not *necessary*. It's going to *humiliate* you, and it's going to cost me my *house*, and . . .

CAROL. It's "*ludicrous* . . ."?

(*John picks up the report and reads again.*)

JOHN. "He told me he had problems with his wife; and that he wanted to take off the artificial stricture of Teacher and Student. He put his arm around me . . ."

CAROL. Do you deny it? Can you deny it . . . ? Do you see? (*Pause*) Don't you see? You don't see, do you?

JOHN. I don't see . . .

CAROL. You think, you think you can deny that these things happened; or, if they *did*, if they *did*, that they meant what you *said* they meant. Don't you see? You drag me in here, you drag us, to listen to you "go on"; and "go on" about this, or that, or we don't "express" ourselves very well. We don't say what we mean. Don't we? Don't we? We *do* say what we mean. And you say that "I don't understand you . . .": Then *you* . . . (*Points.*)

JOHN. "Consult the Report"?

CAROL. . . . that's right.

JOHN. You see. You see. Can't you. . . . You see what I'm saying? Can't you tell me in your own words?

CAROL. Those are my own words. (*Pause*)

JOHN. (*He reads.*) "He told me that if I would stay alone with him in his office, he would change my grade to an A." (*To Carol:*) What have I done to you? Oh. My God, are you so hurt?

CAROL. What I "feel" is irrelevant. (*Pause*)

JOHN. Do you know that I tried to help you?

CAROL. What I know I have reported.

JOHN. I would like to help you now. I would. Before this escalates.

CAROL (*simultaneously with* "escalates"). You see. I don't think that I need your help. I don't think I need anything you have.

JOHN. I feel . . .

CAROL. I don't *care* what you feel. Do you see? DO YOU SEE? You can't *do* that anymore. You. Do. Not. Have. The. Power. Did you misuse it? *Someone* did. Are you part of that group? *Yes. Yes.* You Are. You've *done* these things. And to say, and to say, "Oh. Let me help you with your problem . . ."

JOHN. Yes. I understand. I understand. You're *hurt*. You're *angry*. Yes. I think your *anger* is *betraying* you. Down a path which helps no one.

CAROL. I don't *care* what you think.

JOHN. You don't? (*Pause*) But you talk of *rights*. Don't you see? *I* have rights too. Do you see? I have a *house* . . . part of the *real* world; and The Tenure Committee, Good Men and True . . .

CAROL. . . . Professor . . .

JOHN. . . . Please: *Also* part of that world: you understand? This is my *life*. I'm not a *bogeyman*. I don't "stand" for something, I . . .

CAROL. . . . Professor . . .

JOHN. . . . . I . . .

CAROL. Professor. I came here as a *favor*. At your personal request. Perhaps I should not have done so. But I did. On my behalf, and on behalf of my group. And you speak of the tenure committee, one of whose members is a woman, as you know. And though you might call it Good Fun, or An Historical Phrase, or An Oversight, or, All of the Above, to refer to the committee as Good Men and True, it is a demeaning remark. It is a sexist remark, and to overlook it is to countenance continuation of that method of thought. It's a remark . . .

JOHN. OH COME ON. Come on. . . . Sufficient to deprive a family of . . .

CAROL. Sufficient? Sufficient? Sufficient? Yes. It is a *fact* . . . and that story, which I quote, is *vile* and *classist*, and *manipulative* and *pornographic*. It . . .

JOHN. . . . it's pornographic . . . ?

CAROL. What gives you the *right*. Yes. To speak to a *woman* in your private . . . Yes. Yes. I'm sorry. I'm sorry. You feel yourself empowered . . . you say so yourself. To *strut*. To *posture*. To "perform." To "Call me in here . . ." Eh? You say that higher education is a joke. And treat it as such, you *treat* it as such. And *confess* to a taste to play the *Patriarch* in your class. To grant *this*. To deny *that*. To embrace your students.

JOHN. How can you assert. How can you stand there and . . .

CAROL. How can you *deny* it. You did it to me. *Here*. You did. . . . You *confess*. You love the Power. To *deviate*. To *invent*, to transgress . . . to *transgress* whatever norms have been established for us. And you think it's charming to "question" in yourself this taste to mock and destroy. But you should question it. Professor. And you pick those things which you feel *advance* you: publication, *tenure*, and the steps to get them you call "harmless rituals." And you perform those steps. Although you say it is hypocrisy. But to the aspirations of your students. Of *hardworking students*, who come here, who *slave* to come here—you have no idea what it cost me to come to this school—you *mock* us. You call education "hazing," and from your so-protected, so-elitist seat you hold our confusion as a *joke*, and our hopes and efforts with it. Then you sit there and say "what have I done?" And ask me to understand that *you* have aspirations too. But I tell you. I tell you. That you are vile. And that you are exploitative. And if you possess one ounce of that inner honesty you describe in your book, you can look in yourself and see those things that I see. And you can find revulsion equal to my own. Good day. (*She prepares to leave the room.*)

JOHN. Wait a second, will you, just one moment. (*Pause*) Nice day today.

CAROL. What?

JOHN. You said "Good day." I think that it is a nice day today.

CAROL. *Is it?*

JOHN. Yes, I think it is.

CAROL. And why is that important?

JOHN. Because it is the essence of all human communication. I say something conventional, you respond, and the information we exchange is not about the "weather," but that we both agree to converse. In effect, we agree that we are both human. (*Pause*)

I'm not a . . . "exploiter," and you're not a . . . "deranged," what? *Revolutionary* . . . that we may, that we may have . . . positions, and that we may have . . . desires, which are in *conflict*, but that we're just human. (*Pause*) That means that sometimes we're *imperfect*. (*Pause*) Often we're in conflict . . . (*Pause*) *Much* of what we do, you're right, in the name of "principles" is *self-serving* . . . much of what we do is *conventional*. (*Pause*) You're right. (*Pause*) You said you came in the class because you wanted to learn about *education*. I don't know that I can teach you about education. But I know that I can tell you what I *think* about education, and then *you* decide. And you don't have to fight with me. *I'm* not the subject. (*Pause*) And where I'm *wrong* . . . perhaps it's not your job to "fix" me. I don't want to fix *you*. I would like to tell you what I *think*, because that *is* my job, conventional as it is, and flawed as I may be. And then, if you can show me some better *form*, then we can proceed from there. But, just like "nice day, isn't it . . . ?" I don't think we can proceed until we accept that each of us is human. (*Pause*) And we still can have difficulties. We *will* have them . . . that's all right too. (*Pause*) Now:

CAROL. . . . wait . . .

JOHN. Yes. I want to hear it.

CAROL. . . . the . . .

JOHN. Yes. Tell me frankly.

CAROL. . . . my position . . .

JOHN. I want to hear it. In your own words. What you want. And what you feel.

CAROL. . . . I . . .

JOHN. . . . yes . . .

CAROL. My Group.

JOHN. Your "Group" . . . ? (*Pause*)

CAROL. The people I've been talking to . . .

JOHN. There's no shame in that. Everybody needs advisers. Everyone needs to expose themselves. To various points of view. It's not wrong. It's essential. Good. Good. Now: You and I . . . (*The phone rings.*)

You and I . . .

(*He hesitates for a moment, and then picks it up.*) (*Into phone*) Hello. (*Pause*) Um . . . no, I know they do. (*Pause*) I know she does. Tell her that I . . . can I call you back? . . . Then tell her that I think it's going to be fine. (*Pause*) Tell her just, just hold on, I'll . . . can I get back to you? . . . Well . . . no, no, no, we're *taking* the house . . .

we're . . . no, no, nn . . . no, she will nnn, it's not a *question* of refunding the dep . . . no . . . it's not a *question* of the deposit . . . will you call Jerry? Babe, baby, will you just call Jerry? Tell him, nnn . . . tell him they, well, they're to keep the deposit, because the deal, be . . . because the deal is going to go *through* . . . because I know . . . be . . . will you please? Just *trust* me. Be . . . well, I'm dealing with the complaint. Yes. Right *Now*. Which is why I . . . yes, no, no, it's really, I can't *talk* about it now. Call Jerry, and I can't talk now. Ff . . . fine. Gg . . . good-bye. (*Hangs up.*) (*Pause*) I'm sorry we were interrupted.

CAROL. No . . .

JOHN. I . . . I was saying:

CAROL. You said that we should agree to talk about my complaint.

JOHN. That's correct.

CAROL. But we *are* talking about it.

JOHN. Well, that's correct too. You see? This is the *gist* of education.

CAROL. No, no. I mean, we're talking about it at the Tenure Committee Hearing. (*Pause*)

JOHN. Yes, but I'm saying: we can talk about it *now*, as easily as . . .

CAROL. No. I think that we should stick to the process . . .

JOHN. . . . wait a . . .

CAROL. . . . the "conventional" process. As you said. (*She gets up.*) And you're right, I'm sorry if I was, um, if I was "discourteous" to you. You're right.

JOHN. Wait, wait a . . .

CAROL. I really should go.

JOHN. Now, look, granted. I have an interest. In the status quo. All right? Everyone does. But what I'm saying is that the *committee* . . .

CAROL. Professor, you're right. Just don't impinge on me. We'll take our differences, and . . .

JOHN. You're going to make a . . . look, look, look, you're going to . . .

CAROL. I shouldn't have come here. They told me . . .

JOHN. One moment. No. No. There are *norms*, here, and there's no reason. Look: I'm trying to *save* you . . .

CAROL. No one *asked* you to . . . you're trying to save *me*? Do me the courtesy to . . .

JOHN. I *am* doing you the courtesy. I'm talking *straight* to you. We can settle this *now*. And I want you to sit *down* and . . .

CAROL. You must excuse me . . . (*She starts to leave the room.*)

JOHN. Sit down, it seems we each have a . . . . Wait one moment. Wait one moment . . . just do me the courtesy to . . .

(*He restrains her from leaving.*)

CAROL. LET ME GO.

JOHN. I have no desire to *hold* you, I just want to *talk* to you . . .

CAROL. LET ME GO. LET ME GO. WOULD SOMEBODY *HELP* ME? WOULD SOMEBODY *HELP* ME PLEASE . . . ?

3

(*At rise, Carol and John are seated.*)

JOHN. I have asked you here. (*Pause*) I have asked you here against, against my . . .

CAROL. I was most surprised you asked me.

JOHN. . . . against my better *judgment*, against . . .

CAROL. I was most surprised . . .

JOHN. . . . against the . . . yes. I'm sure.

CAROL. . . . If you would like me to leave, I'll leave. I'll go right now . . . (*She rises.*)

JOHN. Let us begin *correctly*, may we? I feel . . .

CAROL. That is what I wished to do. That's why I came here, but now . . .

JOHN. . . . I feel . . .

CAROL. But now perhaps you'd like me to leave . . .

JOHN. I don't want you to leave. I asked you to come . . .

CAROL. I didn't have to come here.

JOHN. No. (*Pause*) Thank you.

CAROL. All right. (*Pause*) (*She sits down.*)

JOHN. Although I feel that it *profits*, it would *profit* you something, to . . .

CAROL. . . . what I . . .

JOHN. If you would hear me out, if you would hear me out.

CAROL. I came here to, the court officers told me not to come.

JOHN. . . . the "court" officers . . . ?

CAROL. I was shocked that you asked.

JOHN. . . . wait . . .

CAROL. Yes. But I did *not* come here to hear what it "profits" me.

JOHN. The "court" officers . . .

CAROL. . . . no, no, perhaps I should leave . . . (*She gets up.*)

JOHN. Wait.

CAROL. No. I shouldn't have . . .

JOHN. . . . wait. Wait. Wait a moment.

CAROL. Yes? What is it you want? (*Pause*) What is it you want?

JOHN. I'd like you to stay.

CAROL. You want me to stay.

JOHN. Yes.

CAROL. You do.

JOHN. Yes. (*Pause*) Yes. I would like to have you hear me out. If you would. (*Pause*) Would you please? If you would do that I would be in your debt. (*Pause*) (*She sits.*) Thank You. (*Pause*)

CAROL. What is it you wish to tell me?

JOHN. All right. I cannot . . . (*Pause*) I cannot help but feel you are owed an apology. (*Pause*) (*Of papers in his hands*) I have read. (*Pause*) And reread these accusations.

CAROL. What "accusations"?

JOHN. The, the tenure comm . . . what other accusations . . . ?

CAROL. The tenure committee . . . ?

JOHN. Yes.

CAROL. Excuse me, but those are not accusations. They have been *proved*. They are facts.

JOHN. . . . I . . .

CAROL. No. Those are not "accusations."

JOHN. . . . those?

CAROL. . . . the committee (*The phone starts to ring.*) the committee has . . .

JOHN. . . . All right . . .

CAROL. . . . those are not accusations. The Tenure Committee.

JOHN. ALL RIGHT. ALL RIGHT. ALL RIGHT. (*He picks up the phone.*) Hello. Yes. No. I'm here. Tell Mister . . . No, I can't talk to him now . . . I'm sure he has, but I'm fff . . . I know . . . No, I have no time t . . . tell Mister . . . tell Mist . . . tell Jerry that I'm *fine* and that I'll call him right aw . . . (*Pause*) My wife . . . Yes. I'm sure she has. Yes, thank you. Yes, I'll call her too. I cannot talk to you now. (*He hangs up.*) (*Pause*) All right. It was good of you to come, Thank you. I have studied. I have spent some time studying the indictment.

CAROL. You will have to explain that word to me.

JOHN. An "indictment" . . .

CAROL. Yes.

JOHN. Is a "bill of particulars." A . . .

CAROL. All right. Yes.

JOHN. In which is alleged . . .

CAROL. No. I cannot allow that. I cannot allow that. Nothing is alleged. Everything is proved . . .

JOHN. Please, wait a sec . . .

CAROL. I cannot *come* to allow . . .

JOHN. If I may . . . If I may, from whatever you feel is "established," by . . .

CAROL. The issue here is not what I "feel." It is not my "feelings," but the feelings of women. And men. Your superiors, who've been "polled," do you see? To whom *evidence* has been presented, who have *ruled*, do you see? Who have weighed the testimony and the evidence, and have *ruled*, do you see? That you are *negligent*. That you are *guilty*, that you are found *wanting*, and in *error*; and are *not*, for the reasons so-told, to be given tenure. That you are to be disciplined. For facts. For *facts*. Not "alleged," what is the word? But *proved*. Do you see? By *your own actions*.

That is what the tenure committee has said. That is what my lawyer said. For what you did in class. For what you did *in this office*.

JOHN. They're going to discharge me.

CAROL. As full well they should. You don't understand? You're angry? What has *led* you to this place? Not your sex. Not your race. Not your class. YOUR OWN ACTIONS. And you're *angry*. You *ask* me here. What *do* you want? You want to "charm" me. You want to "convince" me. You want me to recant. I will *not* recant. Why should I . . . ? What I say is right. You tell me, you are going to tell me that you have a wife and child. You are going to say that you have a career and that you've worked for twenty years for this. Do you know what you've *worked* for? *Power*. For *power*. Do you understand? And you sit there, and you tell me *stories*. About your *house*, about all the private *schools*, and about *privilege*, and how you are entitled. To *buy*, to *spend*, to *mock*, to *summon*. All your stories. All your silly weak *guilt*, it's all about *privilege*; and you won't know it. Don't you see? You worked twenty years for the right to *insult* me. And you feel entitled to be *paid* for it. Your Home. Your Wife . . . Your sweet "deposit" on your house . . .

JOHN. Don't you have feelings?

CAROL. That's my point. You see? Don't you have feelings? Your final argument. What is it that has no feelings. *Animals*. I don't take your side, you question if I'm Human.

JOHN. Don't you have feelings?

CAROL. I have a responsibility. I . . .

JOHN. . . . to . . . ?

CAROL. To? This institution. To the *students*. To my *group*.

JOHN. . . . your "group." . . .

CAROL. Because I speak, yes, not for myself. But for the group; for those who suffer what I suffer. On behalf of whom, even if I, were, inclined, to what, forgive? Forget? What? Overlook your . . .

JOHN. . . . my behavior?

CAROL. . . . it would be wrong.

JOHN. Even if you were inclined to "forgive" me.

CAROL. It would be wrong.

JOHN. And what would transpire.

CAROL. Transpire?

JOHN. Yes.

CAROL. "Happen?"

JOHN. Yes.

CAROL. Then *say* it. For Christ's sake. Who the *hell* do you think that you are? You want a post. You want unlimited power. To do and to say what you want. As it pleases you—Testing, Questioning, Flirting . . .

JOHN. I never . . .

CAROL. Excuse me, one moment, will you?

(*She reads from her notes.*)

The twelfth: "Have a good day, dear."
The fifteenth: "Now, don't *you* look fetching . . ."
April seventeenth: "If you girls would come over here . . ." I saw you. I saw you, Professor. For two semesters sit there, stand there and exploit our, as you thought, "paternal prerogative," and what is that but rape; I swear

to God. You asked me in here to explain something to me, as a child, that I did not understand. But I came to explain something to you. You Are Not God. You ask me why I came? I came here to instruct you.

(*She produces his book.*)

And your book? You think you're going to show me some "light"? You "*maverick.*" Outside of tradition. No, no, (*She reads from the book's liner notes.*) "*of that fine tradition of inquiry. Of Polite skepticism*" . . . and you say you believe in free intellectual discourse. YOU BELIEVE IN NOTHING. YOU BELIEVE IN NOTHING AT ALL.

JOHN. I believe in freedom of thought.

CAROL. Isn't that fine. *Do* you?

JOHN. Yes. I do.

CAROL. Then why do you question, for one moment, the committee's decision refusing your tenure? Why do you question your suspension? You believe in what *you call* freedom of thought. Then, fine. *You* believe in freedom-of-thought *and* a home, and, *and* prerogatives for your kid, *and* tenure. And I'm going to tell you. You believe *not* in "freedom of thought," but in an elitist, in, in a protected hierarchy which rewards you. And for whom you are the clown. And you mock and exploit the system which pays your rent. You're wrong. I'm not wrong. You're wrong. You think that I'm full of hatred. I know what you think I am.

JOHN. Do you?

CAROL. You think I'm a, of course I do. You think I am a frightened, repressed, confused, I don't know, abandoned young thing of some doubtful sexuality, who wants, power and revenge. (*Pause*) *Don't* you? (*Pause*)

JOHN. Yes. I do. (*Pause*)

CAROL. Isn't that better? And I feel that that is the first moment which you've treated me with respect. For you told me the truth. (*Pause*) I did not come here, as you are assured, to gloat. Why would I want to gloat? I've profited nothing from your, your, as you say, your "misfortune." I came here, as you did me the honor to *ask* me here, I came here to *tell* you something.

    (*Pause*) That I think . . . that I think you've been wrong. That I think you've been terribly wrong. Do you hate me now? (*Pause*)

JOHN. Yes.

CAROL. Why do you hate me? Because you think me wrong? No. Because I have, you think, *power* over you. Listen to me. Listen to me, Professor. (*Pause*) It is the power that you hate. So deeply that, that any atmosphere of free discussion is impossible. It's not "unlikely." It's *impossible.* Isn't it?

JOHN. Yes.

CAROL. *Isn't* it . . . ?

JOHN. Yes. I suppose.

CAROL. Now. The thing which you find so cruel is the self-same process of selection I, and my group, go through

every day of our lives. In admittance to school. In our tests, in our class rankings. . . . Is it unfair? I can't tell you. But, if it is fair. Or even if it is "unfortunate but necessary" for us, then, by God, so must it be for you. (*Pause*) You write of your "responsibility to the young." Treat us with respect, and that will *show* you your responsibility. You write that education is just hazing. (*Pause*) But we worked to get to this school. (*Pause*) And some of us. (*Pause*) Overcame prejudices. Economic, sexual, you cannot begin to imagine. And endured humiliations I *pray* that you and those you love never will encounter. (*Pause*) To gain admittance here. To pursue that same dream of security *you* pursue. We, who, who are, at any moment, in danger of being deprived of it. By . . .

JOHN. . . . by . . . ?

CAROL. By the administration. By the teachers. By *you*. By, say, one low grade, that keeps us out of graduate school; by one, say, one capricious or inventive answer on our parts, which, perhaps, you don't find amusing. Now you *know*, do you see? What it is to be subject to that power. (*Pause*)

JOHN. I don't understand. (*Pause*)

CAROL. My charges are not trivial. You see that in the haste, I think, with which they were accepted. A *joke* you have told, with a sexist tinge. The language you use, a verbal or physical caress, yes, yes, I know, you say that it is meaningless. I understand. I differ from you. To lay a hand on someone's shoulder.

JOHN. It was devoid of sexual content.

CAROL. I say it was not. I SAY IT WAS NOT. Don't you begin to *see* . . . ? Don't you begin to understand? IT'S NOT FOR YOU TO SAY.

JOHN. I take your point, and I see there is much good in what you refer to.

CAROL. . . . do you think so . . . ?

JOHN. . . . but, and this is not to say that I cannot change, in those things in which I am deficient . . . But, the . . .

CAROL. Do you hold yourself harmless from the charge of sexual exploitativeness . . . ? (*Pause*)

JOHN. Well, I . . . I . . . I . . . You know I, as I said. I . . . think I am not too old to *learn*, and I *can* learn, I . . .

CAROL. Do you hold yourself innocent of the charge of . . .

JOHN. . . . wait, wait, wait . . . All right, let's go back to . . .

CAROL. YOU FOOL. Who do you think I am? To come here and be taken in by a *smile*. You little yapping fool. You think I want "revenge." I don't want revenge. I WANT UNDERSTANDING.

JOHN. . . . do you?

CAROL. I do. (*Pause*)

JOHN. What's the use. It's over.

CAROL. Is it? What is?

JOHN. My job.

CAROL. Oh. Your job. That's what you want to talk about. (*Pause*) (*She starts to leave the room. She steps and turns back to him.*) All right. (*Pause*) What if it were possible that my Group withdraws its complaint. (*Pause*)

JOHN. What?

CAROL. That's right. (*Pause*)

JOHN. Why.

CAROL. Well, let's say as an act of friendship.

JOHN. An act of friendship.

CAROL. Yes. (*Pause*)

JOHN. In exchange for what.

CAROL. Yes. But I don't think, "exchange." Not "in exchange." For what do we derive from it? (*Pause*)

JOHN. "Derive."

CAROL. Yes.

JOHN. (*Pause*) Nothing. (*Pause*)

CAROL. That's right. We derive nothing. (*Pause*) Do you see that?

JOHN. Yes.

CAROL. That is a little word, Professor. "Yes." "I see that." But you will.

JOHN. And you might speak to the committee . . . ?

CAROL. To the committee?

JOHN. Yes.

CAROL. Well. Of course. That's on your mind. We might.

JOHN. "If" what?

CAROL. "Given" what. Perhaps. I think that that is more friendly.

JOHN. GIVEN WHAT?

CAROL. And, believe me, I understand your rage. It is not that I don't feel it. But I do not see that it is deserved, so I do not resent it. . . . All right. I have a list.

JOHN. . . . a list.

CAROL. Here is a list of books, which we . . .

JOHN. . . . a list of books . . . ?

CAROL. That's right. Which we find questionable.

JOHN. What?

CAROL. Is this so bizarre . . . ?

JOHN. I can't believe . . .

CAROL. It's not necessary you believe it.

JOHN. Academic freedom . . .

CAROL. Someone chooses the books. If you can choose them, others can. What are you, "God"?

JOHN. . . . no, no, the "dangerous." . . .

CAROL. You have an agenda, we have an agenda. I am not interested in your feelings or your motivation, but your actions. If you would like me to speak to the Tenure Committee, here is my list. You are a Free Person, you decide. (*Pause*)

JOHN. Give me the list. (*She does so. He reads.*)

CAROL. I think you'll find . . .

JOHN. I'm capable of reading it. Thank you.

CAROL. We have a number of *texts* we need re . . .

JOHN. I see that.

CAROL. We're amenable to . . .

JOHN. Aha. Well, let me look over the . . . (*He reads.*)

CAROL. I think that . . .

JOHN. LOOK. I'm reading your demands. All right?! (*He reads*) (*Pause*) You want to ban my book?

CAROL. We do not . . .

JOHN (*of list*). It says here . . .

CAROL. . . . We want it removed from inclusion as a representative example of the university.

JOHN. Get out of here.

CAROL. If you put aside the issues of personalities.

JOHN. Get the fuck out of my office.

CAROL. No, I think I would reconsider.

JOHN. . . . you think you can.

CAROL. We can and we *will*. Do you want our support? That is the only quest . . .

JOHN. . . . to ban my *book* . . . ?

CAROL. . . . that is correct . . .

JOHN. . . . this . . . this is a *university* . . . we . . .

CAROL. . . . and we have a statement . . . which we need you to . . . (*She hands him a sheet of paper.*)

JOHN. No, no. It's out of the question. I'm sorry. I don't know what I was thinking of. I want to tell you something. I'm a teacher. I am a teacher. Eh? It's my *name* on the door, and *I* teach the class, and that's what I do. I've got a book with my name on it. And my son will *see* that book someday. And I have a respon . . . No, I'm sorry I have a *responsibility* . . . to *myself*, to my *son*, to my *profession*. . . . I haven't been *home* for two days, do you know that? Thinking this out.

CAROL. . . . you haven't?

JOHN. I've been, no. If it's of interest to you. I've been in a *hotel. Thinking.* (*The phone starts ringing.*) *Thinking* . . .

CAROL. . . . you haven't been home?

JOHN. . . . *thinking,* do you see.

CAROL. Oh.

JOHN. And, and, I owe you a debt, I see that now. (*Pause*) You're *dangerous,* you're *wrong* and it's my *job* . . . to say no to you. That's my job. You are absolutely right. You want to ban my book? Go to *hell,* and they can do whatever they want to me.

CAROL. . . . you haven't been home in two days . . .

JOHN. I think I told you that.

CAROL. . . . you'd better get that phone. (*Pause*) I think that you should pick up the phone. (*Pause*)

(*John picks up the phone.*)

JOHN (*on phone*). Yes. (*Pause*) Yes. Wh . . . I. I. I had to be away. All ri . . . did they wor . . . did they worry ab . . . No. I'm all right, now, Jerry. I'm f . . . I got a little turned *around,* but I'm *sitting* here and . . . I've got it figured out. I'm fine. I'm fine don't worry about me. I got a little bit mixed up. But I am not sure that it's not a blessing. It cost me my job? Fine. Then the job was not worth having. Tell Grace that I'm coming home and everything is fff . . . . (*Pause*) What? (*Pause*) *What?* (*Pause*) What do you mean? WHAT? Jerry . . . Jerry. They . . . Who, who, what can they do . . . ? (*Pause*) NO. (*Pause*) NO. They can't do th . . . What do you mean? (*Pause*) But how . . . (*Pause*) She's, she's, she's *here* with me. To . . . Jerry. I don't underst . . . (*Pause*) (*He hangs up.*) (*To Carol:*) What does this mean?

CAROL. I thought you knew.

JOHN. What. (*Pause*) What does it mean. (*Pause*)

CAROL. You tried to rape me. (*Pause*) According to the law. (*Pause*)

JOHN. . . . what . . . ?

CAROL. You tried to rape me. I was leaving this office, you "pressed" yourself into me. You "pressed" your body into me.

JOHN. . . . I . . .

CAROL. My Group has told your lawyer that we may pursue criminal charges.

JOHN. . . . no . . .

CAROL. . . . under the statute. I am told. It was battery.

JOHN. . . . no . . .

CAROL. Yes. And attempted rape. That's right. (*Pause*)

JOHN. I think that you should go.

CAROL. Of course. I thought you knew.

JOHN. I have to talk to my lawyer.

CAROL. Yes. Perhaps you should.

(*The phone rings again.*) (*Pause*)

JOHN. (*Picks up phone. Into phone:*) Hello? I . . . Hello . . . ? I . . . Yes, he just called. No . . . I. I can't talk to you now, Baby. (*To Carol:*) Get out.

CAROL. . . . your wife . . . ?

JOHN. . . . who it is is no concern of yours. Get out. (*To phone:*) No, no, it's going to be all right. I. I can't talk now, Baby. (*To Carol:*) Get out of here.

CAROL. I'm going.

JOHN. Good.

CAROL (*exiting*). . . . and don't call your wife "baby."

JOHN. What?

CAROL. Don't call your wife baby. You heard what I said.

(*Carol starts to leave the room. John grabs her and begins to beat her.*)

JOHN. You vicious little bitch. You think you can come in here with your political correctness and destroy my life?

(*He knocks her to the floor.*)

After how I treated you . . . ? You should be . . . *Rape you* . . . ? Are you kidding me . . . ?

(*He picks up a chair, raises it above his head, and advances on her.*)

I wouldn't touch you with a ten-foot pole. You little *cunt* . . .

(*She cowers on the floor below him. Pause. He looks down at her. He lowers the chair. He moves to his desk, and arranges the papers on it. Pause. He looks over at her.*)

. . . well . . .

(*Pause. She looks at him.*)

CAROL. Yes. That's right.

(*She looks away from him, and lowers her head. To herself:*) . . . yes. That's right.

END

TOPICS FOR CRITICAL THINKING AND WRITING

 ### THE PLAY ON THE PAGE

1. Did you find that, on the whole, you were on the side of one character rather than the other, or did your sympathies change? If they changed, did they change once and for all? (Incidentally, Mamet in an interview said that both characters are "altogether right" and both are "altogether wrong." Does this statement help you?)

2. Toward the end of the first scene, John tells Carol that it is his job (as a professor) to "provoke" her, that is, to stimulate students to question traditional values. Reread the play, paying close attention to all of the comments on education, especially to Carol's comments in Scene 2, for instance to her charge that by saying that education may be a form of "hazing," he mocks "*hardworking students,* who come here." Summarize, if it is possible, John's view of education and Carol's. In your opinion, how much validity is there to what either character says about education? Explain.

3. Near the end of the first scene, we hear one side of a telephone conversation, which at first seems to suggest that John is in danger of losing the house he is about to buy. It turns out that this is a friendly ruse to get him to come to the house, where he will find a party in his honor. Why do you suppose Mamet included this bit?

4. Although in much of the third scene Carol is dominant, the play ends with her cowering on the floor and saying—indeed repeating—"That's right." Mamet said, in an interview, "I think that people are generally more happy with a mystery than with an explanation." Is the ending mysterious? If so, do you agree with Mamet's generalization about mystery? Explain.

5. What do you take to be the relevance of the quotation from Samuel Butler (p. 987). (By the way, we strongly recommend Butler's *The Way of All Flesh*, a witty, highly autobiographical and often moving novel published in 1903, a year after Butler's death.)

6. "Oleanna" is never mentioned in the play, but (as you know) the printed version includes as a sort of preface a quotation from a song, mentioning Oleanna, where it is contrasted with an oppressive Norwegian state. A student tells us of another stanza:

> So if you'd like a happy life,
> To Oleanna you must go,
> The poorest man from the old country
> Becomes a king in a year or so.

Judging from this stanza. Oleanna is a never-never land, a dream world. We have also heard that Oleanna was the name of a nineteenth-century Norwegian-American utopian community and that as a youth Mamet once went camping on the site. In any case, what do you think of the title?

🎭 THE PLAY ON THE STAGE

7. Each of the three scenes begins with a stage direction informing the reader that the two characters are seated. In the first two scenes, they are "seated across the desk." The third scene does not specify the desk. How would you begin the third scene? Explain your decision.

8. Nothing is said of the costumes. How would you dress the two performers? Would you have them wear the same clothing in all three scenes or different costumes in each scene? Why? What colors and styles do you suggest? Why? Should either character wear (or carry) eyeglasses?

9. Pretend that you are directing *Oleanna*. Provide a description of the blocking for the last scene (p. 998–1002), giving specific details for each character's tone of voice, emphases, stage action, and gestures. Do you have any suggestions for the lighting crew?

A CONTEXT FOR OLEANNA

David Mamet
TALKING ABOUT DRAMA

[Following is part of an interview conducted with David Savran on February 11, 1987.]

Savran: In your plays the through-line is so strong that the characters can be saying things that are very, very different from what is really being communicated in the subtext.

Mamet: That's why theatre's like life, don't you think? No one really says what they mean, but they always mean what they mean.

Also, in acting, subtext is usually defined as a power dynamic.

I've been teaching acting for about twenty years now, and I love it. It's all about two people who want something different. If the two people don't want something different, what the hell is the scene about? Stay home. The same is true for writing. If two people don't want something from each other, then why are you having the scene? Throw the goddam scene out—which might seem like an overly strict lesson to be learned in a schoolroom but is awfully helpful in the theatre. If the two people don't want something different, the audience is going to go to sleep. Power, that's another way of putting it.

All of us are trying all the time to create the best setting and the best expression we can, not to communicate our wishes to each other, but to *achieve* our wishes *from* each other. I think awareness of this is the difference between good and bad playwriting. Whether it's a politician trying to get votes or a guy trying to go to bed with a girl or somebody trying to get a good table at a restaurant, the point is not to speak the desire but to speak that which is most likely to bring about the desire.

Your plays are confrontational only indirectly, insofar as they're about asking questions rather than providing answers or delineating a mystery.

In *Writing in Restaurants* I say that the purpose of the theatre is to deal with things that can't be dealt with rationally. If they can be dealt with rationally, they probably don't belong in my theatre. There are other people who feel differently and who work that way brilliantly. One of them is Arthur Miller. *Incident at Vichy*, *The Crucible*, also his new play, *Clara*. Or Wally Shawn, in *Aunt Dan and Lemon*. Or Fugard, for example.

Timberlake Wertenbaker

OUR COUNTRY'S GOOD

If there were a term "*Internationalist*," Timberlake Wertenbaker would deserve it. She was raised in the Basque region of France, educated in the United States, and is a resident of Great Britain. Wertenbaker spent the early part of her career working in New York, first as a freelance journalist and later as an editor at Time Life, Inc. She wrote her first plays for children when she was teaching English in Greece in the late 1970s. Moving to London, she began writing plays for fringe theaters (comparable to off- and off-off Broadway theaters) and in 1984–1985 was a resident writer at the Royal Court Theatre. In addition to writing a dozen or so plays, including several commissioned by the Royal Court, Wertenbaker has translated French drama. *Our Country's Good* won the Olivier Prize for best play in 1988. Wertenbaker's most recent play, *The Break of Day*, opened in London in December 1995.

COMMENTARY

Our Country's Good is a fitting play with which to conclude this anthology because it celebrates the ways in which theater can ennoble and transform our lives. The situation Timberlake Wetenbaker chooses is unusual. Set in the penal colony of Sydney, Australia, in the late 1780s, the play brings us a motley group of British convicts—both men and women, many quite young, most of them arrested for petty thefts—who left their country for "their country's good" (hence, the title). The story revolves around the effort on the part of the colony's head, Governor Arthur Phillip, and a handful of sympathetic officers to overcome the brutalities of the prison system. Both convicts and officers face desperate shortages of food and other basic necessities; resentments, violence, and despair seem likely to overwhelm this fledgling society.

Based on *The Playmaker*, a novel by Thomas Keneally, *Our Country's Good* is strongly rooted in historical fact, and the characters are all based on actual officers and convicts. Ranging from the comic to the tender to the cruel, the play makes us consider questions such as the following: Is poverty—not being a pickpocket—the real crime? Are people born depraved? Does society have a responsibility to educate as it punishes? And, of course: Can the arts transform us? Consider the following conversation among the officers, men who represent the British government and thus hold all the power.

HARRY. The convicts laugh at hangings, Sir. They watch them all the time.

TENCH. It's their favourite form of entertainment, I should say.

PHILLIP. Perhaps because they've never been offered anything else.

TENCH. Perhaps we should build an opera house for the convicts.

PHILLIP. We learned to love such things because they were offered to us when we were children or young men. Surely no one is born naturally cultured? I'll have the gun now.

COLLINS. We don't even have any books here, apart from the odd play and a few Bibles. And most of the convicts can't read, so let us return to the matter in hand, which is the punishment of the convicts, not their education.

Two centuries later, the questions central to their quarrel still rage: Punishment or education? Punishment and education? Education during punishment? For this ragtag group, the "odd play" turns out to be a 1708 comedy, *The Recruiting Officer*, by George Farquhar. Governor Phillip decides the convicts will stage it, directed by the ambitious second lieutenant, Ralph Clark. Phillip believes:

PHILLIP. The theatre is an expression of civilisation. . . . The convicts will be speaking a refined, literate language and expressing sentiments of a delicacy they are not used to. It will remind them that there is more to life than crime, punishment. And we, this colony of a few hundred will be watching this together, for a few hours we will no longer be despised prisoners and hated gaolers. We will laugh, we may be moved, we many even think a little. Can you suggest something else that will provide such an evening . . . ?

Radical notions, indeed. However, after some five months of frustrations and wrangling, several of the key performers are in chains and Lieutenant Clark, worried that many of the superior officers are against the play, is about ready to give up. Governor Phillip tells him of a dialogue by Socrates, in which Socrates demonstrates that a slave boy can learn the principles of geometry as well as a gentleman can.

PHILLIP. In other words, he shows that human beings have an intelligence which has nothing to do with the circumstances into which they are born.

RALPH. Sir—

PHILLIP. Sit down, Lieutenant. It is a matter of reminding the slave of what he knows, of his own intelligence. And by intelligence you may read goodness, talent, the innate qualities of human beings.

RALPH. I see—Sir.

PHILLIP. When he treats the slave boy as a rational human being, the boy becomes one, he loses his fear, and he becomes a competent mathematician. A little more encouragement and he might become an extraordinary mathematician. Who knows? You must see your actors in that light.

RALPH. I can see some of them, Sir, but there are others . . . John Arscott—

PHILLIP. He has been given 200 lashes for trying to escape. It will take time for him to see himself as a human being again.

It is this uneasy combination—punishment *and* education—that provides the thematic tensions and conflicts in *Our Country's Good.*

Wertenbaker includes the technique called "a play within a play," by which readers and audiences are aware of scenes from another story within the larger drama. This device can serve a number of purposes. For example, it provides a chance for a different narrative perspective or a change in characterization. In Shakespeare's *Hamlet,* for instance, a troupe of visiting players stage "The Mousetrap," with extra lines inserted by Hamlet because he hopes to "catch the conscience of a king." The play being rehearsed in *Our Country's Good* is *The Recruiting Officer,* a sentimental comedy that involves upper-class flirtations; thus, its content provides an ironic contrast to the actual squalor and degradation in the lives of the prisoners (who are, of course, the actors). Nonetheless, *doing* the play—saying the words, taking on the attributes of the characters, pretending to be highborn, being actively immersed in language—changes their lives. As Michele La Rue commented in *Theatre Arts* (March 1991), "This is not a play about history; it is a play about putting on a play, and the freeing of suppressed human spirit through the creative process."

In 1988 Timberlake Wertenbaker's Our Country's Good won London's Olivier Award for the Best Play. In 1990 the Repertory Theatre of St. Louis staged an effective production, directed by Edward Stern. The play is based on an odd fact: In 1789 English men and women convicts serving prison time in Australia staged a production of an English comedy, George Farquhar's The Recruiting Officer (1706). Wertenbaker uses this historical incident as a way of discussing the role of the theater in society. In the St. Louis production, Andrew Jackness's set used movable sheets of cloth to establish spaces.

Timberlake Wertenbaker

OUR COUNTRY'S GOOD

based on the novel *The Playmaker* by Thomas Keneally

CAPTAIN ARTHUR PHILLIP, RN (*Governor-in-Chief
of New South Wales*)
MAJOR ROBBIE ROSS, RM
CAPTAIN DAVID COLLINS, RM (*Advocate General*)
CAPTAIN WATKIN TENCH, RM
CAPTAIN JEMMY CAMPBELL, RM
REVEREND JOHNSON
LIEUTENANT GEORGE JOHNSTON, RM
LIEUTENANT WILL DAWES, RM
SECOND LIEUTENANT RALPH CLARK, RM
SECOND LIEUTENANT WILLIAM FADDY, RM
MIDSHIPMAN HARRY BREWER, RN (*Provost Marshal*)

AN ABORIGINAL AUSTRALIAN
JOHN ARSCOTT
BLACK CAESAR
KETCH FREEMAN
ROBERT SIDEWAY
JOHN WISEHAMMER
MARY BRENHAM
DABBY BRYANT
LIZ MORDEN
DUCKLING SMITH
MEG LONG

The play takes place in Sydney, Australia in 1788/9.

ACT 1

SCENE 1

THE VOYAGE OUT

The hold of a convict ship bound for Australia, 1787. The convicts huddle together in the semi-darkness. On deck, the convict Robert Sideway is being flogged. Second Lieutenant Ralph Clark counts the lashes in a barely audible, slow and monotonous voice.

RALPH CLARK. Forty-four, forty-five, forty-six, forty-seven, forty-eight, forty-nine, fifty.

Sideway is untied and dumped with the rest of the convicts. He collapses. No one moves. A short silence.

JOHN WISEHAMMER. At night? The sea cracks against the ship. Fear whispers, screams, falls silent, hushed. Spewed from our country, forgotten, bound to the dark edge of the earth, at night what is there to do but seek English cunt, warm, moist, soft, oh the comfort, the comfort of the lick, the thrust into the nooks, the crannies of the crooks of England. Alone, frightened, nameless in this stinking hole of hell, take me, take me inside you, whoever you are. Take me, my comfort and we'll remember England together.

JOHN ARSCOTT. Hunger. Funny. Doesn't start in the stomach, but in the mind. A picture flits in and out of a corner. Something you've eaten long ago. Roast beef with salt and grated horseradish.

MARY. I don't know why I did it. Love, I suppose.

SCENE 2

A LONE ABORIGINAL AUSTRALIAN DESCRIBES THE ARRIVAL OF THE FIRST CONVICT FLEET IN BOTANY BAY ON JANUARY 20, 1788

THE ABORIGINE. A giant canoe drifts onto the sea, clouds billowing from upright oars. This is a dream which has lost its way. Best to leave it alone.

SCENE 3

PUNISHMENT

Sydney Cove. Governor Arthur Phillip, Judge David Collins, Captain Watkin Tench, Midshipman Harry Brewer. The men are shooting birds.

PHILLIP. Was it necessary to cross fifteen thousand miles of ocean to erect another Tyburn?[1]

TENCH. I should think it would make the convicts feel at home.

COLLINS. This land is under English law. The court found them guilty and sentenced them accordingly. There: a bald-eyed corella.

PHILLIP. But hanging?

COLLINS. Only the three who were found guilty of stealing from the colony's stores. And that, over there on the Eucalyptus, is a flock of "cacatua galerita"—the sulphur-crested cockatoo. You have been made Governor-in-Chief of a paradise of birds, Arthur.

PHILLIP. And I hope not of a human hell, Davey. Don't shoot yet, Watkin, let's observe them. Could we not be more humane?

TENCH. Justice and humaneness have never gone hand in hand. The law is not a sentimental comedy.

PHILLIP. I am not suggesting they go without punishment. It is the spectacle of hanging I object to. The convicts will feel nothing has changed and will go back to their old ways.

TENCH. The convicts never left their old ways, Governor, nor do they intend to.

PHILLIP. Three months is not long enough to decide that. You're speaking too loud, Watkin.

COLLINS. I commend your endeavour to oppose the baneful influence of vice with the harmonising arts of civilisation, Governor, but I suspect your edifice will collapse without the mortar of fear.

PHILLIP. Have these men lost all fear of being flogged?

COLLINS. John Arscott has already been sentenced to 150 lashes for assault.

TENCH. The shoulder-blades are exposed at about 100 lashes and I would say that somewhere between 250 and 500 lashes you are probably condemning a man to death anyway.

COLLINS. With the disadvantage that the death is slow, unobserved and cannot serve as a sharp example.

PHILLIP. Harry?

HARRY. The convicts laugh at hangings, Sir. They watch them all the time.

TENCH. It's their favourite form of entertainment, I should say.

PHILLIP. Perhaps because they've never been offered anything else.

TENCH. Perhaps we should build an opera house for the convicts.

PHILLIP. We learned to love such things because they were offered to us when we were children or young men. Surely no one is born naturally cultured? I'll have the gun now.

---

[1]**Tyburn** site of public hangings in eighteenth-century London

COLLINS. We don't even have any books here, apart from the odd play and a few Bibles. And most of the convicts can't read, so let us return to the matter in hand, which is the punishment of the convicts, not their education.

PHILLIP. Who are the condemned men, Harry?

HARRY. Thomas Barrett, age 17. Transported seven years for stealing one ewe sheep.

PHILLIP. Seventeen!

TENCH. It does seem to prove that the criminal tendency is innate.

PHILLIP. It proves nothing.

HARRY. James Freeman, age 25, Irish, transported fourteen years for assault on a sailor at Shadwell Dock.

COLLINS. I'm surprised he wasn't hanged in England.

HARRY. Handy Baker, marine and the thieves' ringleader.

COLLINS. He pleaded that it was wrong to put the convicts and the marines on the same rations and that he could not work on so little food. He almost swayed us.

TENCH. I do think that was an unfortunate decision. My men are in a ferment of discontent.

COLLINS. Our Governor-in-Chief would say it is justice, Tench, and so it is. It is also justice to hang these men.

TENCH. The sooner the better, I believe. There is much excitement in the colony about the hangings. It's their theatre, Governor, you cannot change that.

PHILLIP. I would prefer them to see real plays: fine language, sentiment.

TENCH. No doubt Garrick[2] would relish the prospect of eight months at sea for the pleasure of entertaining a group of criminals and the odd savage.

PHILLIP. I never liked Garrick, I always preferred Macklin.

COLLINS. I'm a Kemble man myself. We will need a hangman.

PHILLIP. Harry, you will have to organise the hanging and eventually find someone who agrees to fill that hideous office.

Phillip shoots.

COLLINS. Shot.

TENCH. Shot.

HARRY. Shot, Sir.

COLLINS. It is my belief the hangings should take place tomorrow. The quick execution of justice for the good of the colony, Governor.

PHILLIP. The good of the colony? Oh, look! We've frightened a kankaroo.

They look.

ALL. Ah!

---

[2]**Garrick** David Garrick (1717–1779), actor and manager of Drury Lane theatre; Macklin and Kemble, mentioned in the next lines, are Charles Macklin (1700–1797) and John Philip Kemble (1757–1823), both famous Shakespearean actors.

HARRY. There is also Dorothy Handland, 82, who stole a biscuit from Robert Sideway.

PHILLIP. Surely we don't have to hang an 82-year-old woman?

COLLINS. That will be unnecessary. She hanged herself this morning.

SCENE 4

THE LONELINESS OF MEN

Ralph Clark's tent. It is late at night. Ralph stands, composing and speaking his diary.

RALPH. Dreamt, my beloved Alicia, that I was walking with you and that you was in your riding-habit—oh my dear woman when shall I be able to hear from you—

All the officers dined with the Governor—I never heard of any one single person having so great a power vested in him as Captain Phillip has by his commission as Governor-in-Chief of New South Wales—dined on a cold collation but the Mutton which had been killed yesterday morning was full of maggots—nothing will keep 24 hours in this dismal country I find—

Went out shooting after breakfast—I only shot one cockatoo—they are the most beautiful birds—

Major Ross ordered one of the Corporals to flog with a rope Elizabeth Morden for being impertinent to Captain Campbell—the Corporal did not play with her but laid it home which I was very glad to see—she has long been fishing for it—

On Sunday as usual, kissed your dear beloved image a thousand times—was very much frightened by the lightning as it broke very near my tent—several of the convicts have run away.

He goes to his table and writes in his journal.

If I'm not made 1st Lieutenant soon . . .

Harry Brewer has come in.

RALPH. Harry—

HARRY. I saw the light in your tent—

RALPH. I was writing my journal.

Silence.

Is there any trouble?

HARRY. No. (*Pause.*) I just came.

Talk, you know. If I wrote a journal about my life it would fill volumes. Volumes. My travels with the Captain—His Excellency now, no less, Governor-in-Chief, power to raise armies, build cities—I still call him plain Captain Phillip. He likes it from me. The war in America[3] and before that, Ralph, my life in London. That

---

[3]**war in America** the American Revolution

would fill a volume on its own. Not what you would call a good life.

Pause.

Sometimes I look at the convicts and I think, one of those could be you, Harry Brewer, if you hadn't joined the navy when you did. The officers may look down on me now, but what if they found out that I used to be an embezzler?

RALPH. Harry, you should keep these things to yourself.

HARRY. You're right, Ralph.

Pause.

I think the Captain suspects, but he's a good man and he looks for different things in a man—

RALPH. Like what?

HARRY. Hard to say. He likes to see something unusual. Ralph, I saw Handy Baker last night.

RALPH. You hanged him a month ago, Harry.

HARRY. He had a rope—Ralph, he's come back.

RALPH. It was a dream. Sometimes I think my dreams are real—But they're not.

HARRY. We used to hear you on the ship, Ralph, calling for your Betsey Alicia.

RALPH. Don't speak her name on this iniquitous shore!

HARRY. Duckling's gone silent on me again. I know it's because of Handy Baker. I saw him as well as I see you. Duckling wants me, he said, even if you've hanged me. At least your poker's danced its last shindy, I said. At least it's young and straight, he said, she likes that. I went for him but he was gone. But he's going to come back, I know it. I didn't want to hang him, Ralph, I didn't.

RALPH. He did steal that food from the stores.

Pause.

I voted with the rest of the court those men should be hanged, I didn't know His Excellency would be against it.

HARRY. Duckling says she never feels anything. How do I know she didn't feel something when she was with him? She thinks I hanged him to get rid of him, but I didn't, Ralph.

Pause.

Do you know I saved her life? She was sentenced to be hanged at Newgate[4] for stealing two candlesticks but I got her name put on the transport lists. But when I remind her of that she says she wouldn't have cared. Eighteen years old, and she didn't care if she was turned off.

Pause.

These women are sold before they're ten. The Captain says we should treat them with kindness.

RALPH. How can you treat such women with kindness? Why does he think that?

HARRY. Not all the officers find them disgusting, Ralph—haven't you ever been tempted?

RALPH. Never! (*Pause.*) His Excellency never seems to notice me.

Pause.

He finds time for Davey Collins, Lieutenant Dawes.

HARRY. That's because Captain Collins is going to write about the customs of the Indians here—and Lieutenant Dawes is recording the stars.

RALPH. I could write about the Indians.

HARRY. He did suggest to Captain Tench that we do something to educate the convicts, put on a play or something, but Captain Tench just laughed. He doesn't like Captain Tench.

RALPH. A play? Who would act in a play?

HARRY. The convicts of course. He is thinking of talking to Lieutenant Johnston, but I think Lieutenant Johnston wants to study the plants.

RALPH. I read *The Tragedy of Lady Jane Grey*[5] on the ship. It is such a moving and uplifting play. But how could a whore play Lady Jane?

HARRY. Some of those women are good women, Ralph, I believe my Duckling is good. It's not her fault—if only she would look at me, once, react. Who wants to fuck a corpse!

Silence.

I'm sorry. I didn't mean to shock you, Ralph, I have shocked you, haven't I? I'll go.

RALPH. Is His Excellency serious about putting on a play?

HARRY. When the Captain decides something, Ralph.

RALPH. If I went to him—no. It would be better if you did, Harry, you could tell His Excellency how much I like the theatre.

HARRY. I didn't know that Ralph, I'll tell him.

RALPH. Duckling could be in it, if you wanted.

HARRY. I wouldn't want her to be looked at by all the men.

RALPH. If His Excellency doesn't like *Lady Jane* we could find something else.

Pause.

A comedy perhaps . . .

HARRY. I'll speak to him, Ralph. I like you.

Pause.

It's good to talk . . .

Pause.

You don't think I killed him then?

---

[4]**Newgate** London prison; *turned off,* later in the speech, means *hanged*

[5]**Lady Jane Grey** at the age of fifteen Lady Jane Grey (1537–1554) was proclaimed Queen of England; she ruled for nine days, was then imprisoned, and within a year was beheaded.

RALPH. Who?

HARRY. Handy Baker.

RALPH. No, Harry. You did not kill Handy Baker.

HARRY. Thank you, Ralph.

RALPH. Harry, you won't forget to talk to His Excellency about the play?

SCENE 5

AN AUDITION

Ralph Clark, Meg Long. Meg Long is very old and very smelly. She hovers over Ralph.

MEG. We heard you was looking for some women, Lieutenant. Here I am.

RALPH. I've asked to see some women to play certain parts in a play.

MEG. I can play, Lieutenant, I can play with any part you like. There ain't nothing puts Meg off. That's how I got my name: Shitty Meg.

RALPH. The play has four particular parts for young women.

MEG. You don't want a young woman for your peculiar,[6] Lieutenant, they don't know nothing. Shut your eyes and I'll play you as tight as a virgin.

RALPH. You don't understand, Long. Here's the play. It's called *The Recruiting Officer*.

MEG. Oh, I can do that too.

RALPH. What?

MEG. Recruiting. Anybody you like. (*She whispers.*) You want women: you ask Meg. Who do you want?

RALPH. I want to try some out.

MEG. Good idea, Lieutenant, good idea. Ha! Ha! Ha!

RALPH. Now if you don't mind—

Meg doesn't move.

Long!

MEG (*frightened but still holding her ground*). We thought you was a madge cull.[7]

RALPH. What?

MEG. You know, a fluter, a mollie. (*Impatiently.*) A prissy cove, a girl! You having no she-lag[8] on the ship. Nor here, neither. On the ship maybe you was seasick. But all these months here. And now we hear how you want a lot of women, all at once. Well, I'm glad to hear that, Lieutenant, I am. You let me know when you want Meg, old Shitty Meg.

She goes off quickly and Robert Sideway comes straight on.

SIDEWAY. Ah, Mr Clark.

He does a flourish.[9]

I am calling you Mr Clark as one calls Mr Garrick Mr Garrick, we have not had the pleasure of meeting before.

RALPH. I've seen you on the ship.

SIDEWAY. Different circumstances, Mr Clark, best forgotten. I was once a gentleman. My fortune has turned. The wheel . . . You are doing a play, I hear, ah, Drury Lane, Mr Garrick, the lovely Peg Woffington.[10] (*Conspiratorially.*) He was so cruel to her. She was so pale—

RALPH. You say you were a gentleman, Sideway?

SIDEWAY. Top of my profession, Mr Clark, pickpocket, born and bred in Bermondsey. Do you know London, Sir, don't you miss it? In these my darkest hours, I remember my happy days in that great city. London Bridge at dawn—hand on cold iron for good luck. Down Cheapside with the market traders—never refuse a mince pie. Into St Paul's churchyard—I do love a good church—and begin work in Bond Street. There, I've spotted her, rich, plump, not of the best class, stands in front of the shop, plucking up courage, I pluck her. Time for coffee until five o'clock and the pinnacle, the glory of the day: Drury Lane. The coaches, the actors scuttling, the gentlemen watching, the ladies tittering, the perfumes, the clothes, the handkerchiefs.

He hands Ralph the handkerchief he has just stolen from him.

Here, Mr Clark, you see the skill. Ah, Mr Clark, I beg you, I entreat you, to let me perform on your stage, to let me feel once again the thrill of a play about to begin. Ah, I see ladies approaching: our future Woffingtons, Siddons.[11]

Dabby Bryant comes on, with a shrinking Mary Brenham in tow. Sideways bows.

Ladies.

I shall await your word of command, Mr Clark, I shall be in the wings.

Sideway scuttles off.

DABBY. You asked to see Mary Brenham, Lieutenant. Here she is.

RALPH. Yes—the Governor has asked me to put on a play. (*To Mary.*) You know what a play is?

DABBY. I've seen lots of plays, Lieutenant, so has Mary.

RALPH. Have you, Brenham?

---

[6]**your peculiar** your mistress   [7]**a madge cull** a homosexual (also in Meg's next speech, *fluter, mollie,* and *prissy cove*)   [8]**she-lag** female convict

[9]**flourish** elaborate bow   [10]**Peg Woffington** an actress (1718–1760)   [11]**Siddons** Sarah Siddons (1755–1831), tragic actress, the brother of John Philip Kemble

MARY (*inaudibly*). Yes.

RALPH. Can you remember which plays you've seen?

MARY (*inaudibly*). No.

DABBY. I can't remember what they were called, but I always knew when they were going to end badly. I knew right from the beginning. How does this one end, Lieutenant?

RALPH. It ends happily. It's called *The Recruiting Officer*.[12]

DABBY. Mary wants to be in your play, Lieutenant, and so do I.

RALPH. Do you think you have a talent for acting, Brenham?

DABBY. Of course she does, and so do I. I want to play Mary's friend.

RALPH. Do you know *The Recruiting Officer*, Bryant?

DABBY. No, but in all those plays, there's always a friend. That's because a girl has to talk to someone and she talks to her friend. So I'll be Mary's friend.

RALPH. Silvia—that's the part I want to try Brenham for— doesn't have a friend. She has a cousin. But they don't like each other.

DABBY. Oh. Mary doesn't always like me.

RALPH. The Reverend Johnson told me you can read and write, Brenham?

DABBY. She went to school until she was ten. She used to read to us on the ship. We loved it. It put us to sleep.

RALPH. Shall we try reading some of the play?

Ralph hands her the book. Mary reads silently, moving her lips.

I mean read it aloud. As you did on the ship. I'll help you, I'll read Justice Balance. That's your father.

DABBY. Doesn't she have a sweetheart?

RALPH. Yes, but this scene is with her father.

DABBY. What's the name of her lover?

RALPH. Captain Plume.

DABBY. A Captain! Mary!

RALPH. Start here, Brenham.

Mary begins to read.

MARY. "Whilst there is life there is hope, Sir."

DABBY. Oh, I like that, Lieutenant. This is a good play, I can tell.

RALPH. Shht. She hasn't finished. Start again, Brenham, that's good.

MARY. "Whilst there is life there is hope, Sir; perhaps my brother may recover."

RALPH. That's excellent, Brenham, very fluent. You could read a little louder. Now I'll read.

"We have but little reason to expect it. Poor Owen! But the decree is just; I was pleased with the death of my

father, because he left me an estate, and now I'm punished with the loss of an heir to inherit mine."

Pause. He laughs a little.

This is a comedy. They don't really mean it. It's to make people laugh. "The death of your brother makes you sole heiress to my estate, which you know is about twelve hundred pounds a year."

DABBY. Twelve hundred pounds! It must be a comedy.

MARY. "My desire of being punctual in my obedience requires that you would be plain in your commands, Sir."

DABBY. Well said, Mary, well said.

RALPH. I think that's enough. You read very well, Brenham. Would you also be able to copy the play? We have only two copies.

DABBY. Course she will. Where do I come in, Lieutenant? The cousin.

RALPH. Can you read, Bryant?

DABBY. Not those marks in the books, Lieutenant, but I can read other things. I read dreams very well, Lieutenant. Very well.

RALPH. I don't think you're right for Melinda. I'm thinking of someone else. And if you can't read . . .

DABBY. Mary will read me the lines, Lieutenant.

RALPH. There's Rose . . .

DABBY. Rose. I like the name. I'll be Rose. Who is she?

RALPH. She's a country girl . . .

DABBY. I grew up in Devon, Lieutenant. I'm perfect for Rose. What does she do?

RALPH. She—well, it's complicated. She falls in love with Silvia.

Mary begins to giggle but tries to hold it back.

But it's because she thinks Silvia's a man. And she— they—she sleeps with her. Rose. With Silvia. Euh. Silvia too. With Rose. But nothing happens.

DABBY. It doesn't? Nothing?

Dabby bursts out laughing.

RALPH. Because Silvia is pretending to be a man, but of course she can't—

DABBY. Play the flute? Ha! She's not the only one around here. I'll do Rose.

RALPH. I would like to hear you.

DABBY. I don't know my lines yet, Lieutenant. When I know my lines, you can hear me do them. Come on, Mary—

RALPH. I didn't say you could—I'm not certain you're the right—Bryant, I'm not certain I want you in the play.

DABBY. Yes you do, Lieutenant. Mary will read me the lines and I, Lieutenant, will read you your dreams.

There's a guffaw. It's Liz Morden.

RALPH. Ah. Here's your cousin.

There is a silence. Mary shrinks away. Dabby and Liz stare at each other, each holding her ground, each ready to pounce.

Melinda. Silvia's cousin.

---

[12]**The Recruiting Officer** a comedy (1706) by the Irish-born actor and playwright, George Farquhar (1677–1707); the basic plot concerns Capt. Plume, who makes love to women in order to recruit their suitors.

DABBY. You can't have her in the play, Lieutenant.

RALPH. Why not?

DABBY. You don't have to be able to read the future to know that Liz Morden is going to be hanged.

Liz looks briefly at Dabby, as if to strike, then changes her mind.

LIZ. I understand you want me in your play, Lieutenant. Is that it?

She snatches the book from Ralph and strides off.

I'll look at it and let you know.

SCENE 6

THE AUTHORITIES DISCUSS THE MERITS OF THE THEATRE

Governor Arthur Phillip, Major Robbie Ross, Judge David Collins, Captain Watkin Tench, Captain Jemmy Campbell, Reverend Johnson, Lieutenant George Johnston, Lieutenant Will Dawes, Second Lieutenant Ralph Clark, Second Lieutenant William Faddy.

It is late at night, the men have been drinking, tempers are high. They interrupt each other, overlap, make jokes under and over the conversation but all engage in it with the passion for discourse and thought of eighteenth-century men.

ROSS. A play! A f—

REVD. JOHNSON. Mmhm.

ROSS. A frippery frittering play!

CAMPBELL. Aheeh, aeh, here?

RALPH (*timidly*). To celebrate the King's birthday, on June the 4th.

ROSS. If a frigating ship doesn't appear soon, we'll all be struck with stricturing starvation—and you—you—a play!

COLLINS. Not putting on the play won't bring us a supply ship, Robbie.

ROSS. And you say you want those contumelious convicts to act in this play. The convicts!

CAMPBELL. Eh, kev, weh, discipline's bad. Very bad.

RALPH. The play has several parts for women. We have no other women here.

COLLINS. Your wife excepted, Reverend.

REVD. JOHNSON. My wife abhors anything of that nature. After all, actresses are not famed for their morals.

COLLINS. Neither are our women convicts.

REVD. JOHNSON. How can they be when some of our officers set them up as mistresses.

He looks pointedly at Lieutenant George Johnston.

ROSS. Filthy, thieving, lying whores and now we have to watch them flout their flitty wares on the stage!

PHILLIP. No one will be forced to watch the play.

DAWES. I believe there's a partial lunar eclipse that night. I shall have to watch that. The sky of this southern hemisphere is full of wonders. Have you looked at the constellations?

Short pause.

ROSS. Constellations. Plays! This is a convict colony, the prisoners are here to be punished and we're here to make sure they get punished. Constellations! Jemmy? Constellations!

He turns to Jemmy Campbell for support.

CAMPBELL. Tss, weh, marines, marines: war, phoo, discipline. Eh? Service—His Majesty.

PHILLIP. We are indeed here to supervise the convicts who are already being punished by their long exile. Surely they can also be reformed?

TENCH. We are talking about criminals, often hardened criminals. They have a habit of vice and crime. Many criminals seem to have been born that way. It is in their nature.

PHILLIP. Rousseau[13] would say that we have made them that way, Watkin: "Man is born free, and everywhere he is in chains."

REVD. JOHNSON. But Rousseau was a Frenchman.

ROSS. A Frenchman! What can you expect? We're going to listen to a foraging Frenchman now—

COLLINS. He was Swiss actually.

CAMPBELL. Eeh, eyeh, good soldiers, the Swiss.

PHILLIP. Surely you believe man can be redeemed, Reverend?

REVD. JOHNSON. By the grace of God and a belief in the true church, yes. But Christ never proposed putting on plays to his disciples. However, he didn't forbid it either. It must depend on the play.

JOHNSTON. He did propose treating sinners, especially women who have sinned, with compassion. Most of the convict women have committed small crimes, a tiny theft—

COLLINS. We know about your compassion, not to say passion, for the women convicts, George.

TENCH. A crime is a crime. You commit a crime or you don't. If you commit a crime, you are a criminal. Surely that is logical? It's like the savages here. A savage is a savage because he behaves in a savage manner. To expect anything else is foolish. They can't even build a proper canoe.

PHILLIP. They can be educated.

COLLINS. Actually, they seem happy enough as they are. They do not want to build canoes or houses, nor do they suffer from greed and ambition.

---

[13]**Rousseau** Jean Jacques Rousseau (1712–1778), French philosopher; Phillip goes on to quote Rousseau's most famous line.

FADDY (*looking at Ralph*). Unlike some.

TENCH. Which can't be said of our convicts. But really, I don't see what this has to do with a play. It is at most a passable diversion, an entertainment to wile away the hours of the idle.

CAMPBELL. Ttts, weh, heh, the convicts, bone idle.

DAWES. We're wiling away precious hours now. Put the play on, don't put it on, it won't change the shape of the universe.

RALPH. But it could change the nature of our little society.

FADDY. Second Lieutenant Clark change society!

PHILLIP. William!

TENCH. My dear Ralph, a bunch of convicts making fools of themselves, mouthing words written no doubt by some London ass, will hardly change our society.

RALPH. George Farquhar was not an ass! And he was from Ireland.

ROSS. An Irishman! I have to sit there and listen to an Irishman!

CAMPBELL. Tss, tt. Irish. Wilde.[14] Wilde.

REVD. JOHNSON. The play doesn't propagate Catholic doctrine, does it, Ralph?

RALPH. He was also an officer.

FADDY. Crawling for promotion.

RALPH. Of the Grenadiers.

ROSS. Never liked the Grenadiers myself.

CAMPBELL. Ouah, pheuee, grenades, pho. Throw and run.[15] Eh. Backs.

RALPH. The play is called *The Recruiting Officer*.

COLLINS. I saw it in London I believe. Yes. Very funny if I remember. Sergeant Kite. The devious ways he used to serve his Captain . . .

FADDY. Your part, Ralph.

COLLINS. William, if you can't contribute anything useful to the discussion, keep quiet!

Silence.

REVD. JOHNSON. What is the plot, Ralph?

RALPH. It's about this recruiting officer and his friend, and they are in love with these two young ladies from Shrewsbury and after some difficulties, they marry them.

REVD. JOHNSON. It sanctions Holy Matrimony then?

RALPH. Yes, yes, it does.

REVD. JOHNSON. That wouldn't do the convicts any harm. I'm having such trouble getting them to marry instead of this sordid cohabitation they're so used to.

ROSS. Marriage, plays, why not a ball for the convicts!

CAMPBELL. Euuh. Boxing.

PHILLIP. Some of these men will have finished their sentence in a few years. They will become members of society again, and help create a new society in this colony. Should we not encourage them now to think in a free and responsible manner?

TENCH. I don't see how a comedy about two lovers will do that, Arthur.

PHILLIP. The theatre is an expression of civilisation. We belong to a great country which has spawned great playwrights: Shakespeare, Marlowe, Jonson, and even in our own time, Sheridan. The convicts will be speaking a refined, literate language and expressing sentiments of a delicacy they are not used to. It will remind them that there is more to life than crime, punishment. And we, this colony of a few hundred will be watching this together, for a few hours we will no longer be despised prisoners and hated gaolers. We will laugh, we may be moved, we may even think a little. Can you suggest something else that will provide such an evening, Watkin?

DAWES. Mapping the stars gives me more enjoyment, personally.

TENCH. I'm not sure it's a good idea having the convicts laugh at officers, Arthur.

CAMPBELL. No. Pheeoh, insubordination, heh, ehh, no discipline.

ROSS. You want this vice-ridden vermin to enjoy themselves?

COLLINS. They would only laugh at Sergeant Kite.

RALPH. Captain Plume is a most attractive, noble fellow.

REVD. JOHNSON. He's not loose, is he Ralph? I hear many of these plays are about rakes and encourage loose morals in women. They do get married? Before,[16] that is, before. And for the right reasons.

RALPH. They marry for love and to secure wealth.

REVD. JOHNSON. That's all right.

TENCH. I would simply say that if you want to build a civilisation there are more important things than a play. If you want to teach the convicts something, teach them to farm, to build houses, teach them a sense of respect for property, teach them thrift so they don't eat a week's rations in one night, but above all, teach them how to work, not how to sit around laughing at a comedy.

PHILLIP. The Greeks believed that it was a citizen's duty to watch a play. It was a kind of work in that it required attention, judgement, patience, all social virtues.

TENCH. And the Greeks were conquered by the more practical Romans, Arthur.

COLLINS. Indeed, the Romans built their bridges, but they also spent many centuries wishing they were Greeks. And they, after all, were conquered by barbarians, or by their own corrupt and small spirits.

TENCH. Are you saying Rome would not have fallen if the theatre had been better?

---

[14]**Wilde** a pun on the name of the later Irish playwright, Oscar Wilde (1854–1900) [15]**Throw and run** The job of a grenadier was to throw a grenade.

[16]**Before** That is, they should marry before they have sex.

RALPH (*very loud*). Why not? (*Everyone looks at him and he continues, fast and nervously.*) In my own small way, in just a few hours, I have seen something change. I asked some of the convict women to read me some lines, these women who behave often no better than animals. And it seemed to me, as one or two—I'm not saying all of them, not at all—but one or two, saying those well-balanced lines of Mr Farquhar, they seemed to acquire a dignity, they seemed—they seemed to lose some of their corruption. There was one, Mary Brenham, she read so well, perhaps this play will keep her from selling herself to the first marine who offers her bread—

FADDY (*under his breath*). She'll sell herself to him, instead.

ROSS. So that's the way the wind blows—

CAMPBELL. Hooh. A tempest. Hooh.

RALPH (*over them*). I speak about her, but in a small way this could affect all the convicts and even ourselves, we could forget our worries about the supplies, the hangings and the floggings, and think of ourselves at the theatre, in London with our wives and children, that is, we could, euh—

PHILLIP. Transcend—

RALPH. Transcend the darker, euh—transcend the—

JOHNSTON. Brutal—

RALPH. The brutality—remember our better nature and remember—

COLLINS. England.

RALPH. England.

A moment.

ROSS. Where did the wee Lieutenant learn to speak?

FADDY. He must have had one of his dreams.

TENCH (*over them*). You are making claims that cannot be substantiated, Ralph. It's two hours, possibly of amusement, possibly of boredom, and we will lose the labour of the convicts during the time they are learning the play. It's a waste, an unnecessary waste.

REVD. JOHNSON. I'm still concerned about the content.

TENCH. The content of a play is irrelevant.

ROSS. Even if it teaches insubordination, disobedience, revolution?

COLLINS. Since we have agreed it can do no harm, since it might, possibly, do some good, since the only person violently opposed to it is Major Ross for reasons he has not made quite clear, I suggest we allow Ralph to rehearse his play. Does anyone disagree?

ROSS. I—I—

COLLINS. We have taken your disagreement into account, Robbie.

CAMPBELL. Ah, eeh, I—I—(*He stops.*)

COLLINS. Thank you, Captain Campbell. Dawes? Dawes, do come back to earth and honour us with your attention for a moment.

DAWES. What? No? Why not? As long as I don't have to watch it.

COLLINS. Johnston?

JOHNSTON. I'm for it.

COLLINS. Faddy?

FADDY. I'm against it.

COLLINS. Could you tell us why?

FADDY. I don't trust the director.

COLLINS. Tench?

TENCH. Waste of time.

COLLINS. The Reverend, our moral guide, has no objections.

REVD. JOHNSON. Of course I haven't read it.

TENCH. Davey, this is not an objective summing up, this is typical of your high-handed manner—

COLLINS (*angrily*). I don't think you're the one to accuse others of a high-handed manner, Watkin.

PHILLIP. Gentlemen, please.

COLLINS. Your Excellency, I believe, is for the play and I myself am convinced it will prove a most interesting experiment. So let us conclude with our good wishes to Ralph for a successful production.

ROSS. I will not accept this. You willy-wally wobbly words, Greeks, Romans, experiment, to get your own way. You don't take anything seriously, but I know this play—this play—order will become disorder. The theatre leads to threatening theory and you, Governor, you have His Majesty's commission to build castles, cities, raise armies, administer a military colony, not fandangle about with a lewdy play! I am going to write to the Admiralty about this. (*He goes.*)

PHILLIP. You're out of turn, Robbie.

CAMPBELL. Aah—eeh—a. Confusion. (*He goes.*)

DAWES. Why is Robbie so upset? So much fuss over a play.

JOHNSTON. Major Ross will never forgive you, Ralph.

COLLINS. I have summed up the feelings of the assembled company, Arthur, but the last word must be yours.

PHILLIP. The last word will be the play, gentlemen.

SCENE 7

HARRY AND DUCKLING GO ROWING

Harry Brewer, Duckling Smith. Harry is rowing, Duckling is sulking.

HARRY. It's almost beginning to look like a town. Look, Duckling, there's the Captain's house. I can see him in his garden.

Harry waves. Duckling doesn't turn around.

Sydney. He could have found a better name. Mobsbury. Lagtown. Duckling Cove, eh?

Harry laughs. Duckling remains morose.

The Captain said it had to be named after the Home Secretary.[17] The courthouse looks impressive all in brick. There's Lieutenant Dawes' observatory. Why don't you look, Duckling?

Duckling glances, then turns back.

The trees look more friendly from here. Did you know the Eucalyptus tree can't be found anywhere else in the world? Captain Collins told me that. Isn't that interesting? Lieutenant Clark says the three orange trees on his island are doing well. It's the turnips he's worried about, he thinks they're being stolen and he's too busy with his play to go and have a look. Would you like to see the orange trees, Duckling?

Duckling glowers.

I thought you'd enjoy rowing to Ralph's island. I thought it would remind you of rowing on the Thames. Look how blue the water is. Duckling. Say something. Duckling!

DUCKLING. If I was rowing on the Thames, I'd be free.

HARRY. This isn't Newgate, Duckling.

DUCKLING. I wish it was.

HARRY. Duckling!

DUCKLING. At least the gaoler of Newgate left you alone and you could talk to people.

HARRY. I let you talk to the women.

DUCKLING (*with contempt*). Esther Abrahams, Mary Brenham!

HARRY. They're good women.

DUCKLING. I don't have anything to say to those women, Harry. My friends are in the women's camp—

HARRY. It's not the women you're after in the women's camp, it's the marines who come looking for buttock, I know you, who do you have your eye on now, who, a soldier? Another marine, a Corporal? Who, Duckling, who?

Pause.

You've found someone already, haven't you? Where do you go, on the beach? In my tent, like with Handy Baker, eh? Where, under the trees?

DUCKLING. You know I hate trees, don't be so filthy.

HARRY. Filthy, you're filthy, you filthy whore.

Pause.

I'm sorry, Duckling, please. Why can't you?—can't you just be with me? Don't be angry. I'll do anything for you, you know that. What do you want, Duckling?

DUCKLING. I don't want to be watched all the time. I wake up in the middle of the night and you're watching me. What do you think I'm going to do in my sleep, Harry? Watching, watching, watching. JUST STOP WATCHING ME.

HARRY. You want to leave me. All right, go and live in the women's camp, sell yourself to a convict for a biscuit. Leave if you want to. You're filthy, filthy, opening your legs to the first marine—

DUCKLING. Why are you so angry with your Duckling, Harry? Don't you like it when I open my legs wide to you? Cross them over you—the way you like? What will you do when your little Duckling isn't there anymore to touch you with her soft fingertips, Harry, where you like it? First the left nipple and then the right. Your Duckling doesn't want to leave you, Harry.

HARRY. Duckling . . .

DUCKLING. I need freedom sometimes, Harry.

HARRY. You have to earn your freedom with good behavior.

DUCKLING. Why didn't you let them hang me and take my corpse with you, Harry? You could have kept that in chains. I wish I was dead. At least when you're dead, you're free.

Silence.

HARRY. You know Lieutenant Clark's play?

Duckling is silent.

Do you want to be in it?

Duckling laughs.

Dabby Bryant is in it too and Liz Morden. Do you want to be in it? You'd rehearse in the evenings with Lieutenant Clark.

DUCKLING. And he can watch over me instead of you.

HARRY. I'm trying to make you happy, Duckling, if you don't want to—

DUCKLING. I'll be in the play.

Pause.

How is Lieutenant Clark going to manage Liz Morden?

HARRY. The Captain wanted her to be in it.

DUCKLING. On the ship we used to see who could make Lieutenant Clark blush first. It didn't take long, haha.

HARRY. Duckling, you won't try anything with Lieutenant Clark, will you?

DUCKLING. With that Mollie? No.

HARRY. You're talking to me again. Will you kiss your Harry?

They kiss.

I'll come and watch the rehearsals.

[17]**Home Secretary** the government official responsible for law

SCENE 8

THE WOMEN LEARN THEIR LINES

Dabby Bryant is sitting on the ground muttering to herself with concentration. She could be counting. Mary Brenham comes on.

MARY. Are you remembering your lines, Dabby?

DABBY. What lines? No. I was remembering Devon. I was on my way back to Bigbury Bay.

MARY. You promised Lieutenant Clark you'd learn your lines.

DABBY. I want to go back. I want to see a wall of stone. I want to hear the Atlantic breaking into the estuary. I can bring a boat into any harbour, in any weather. I can do it as well as the Governor.

MARY. Dabby, what about your lines?

DABBY. I'm not spending the rest of my life in this flat, brittle burnt-out country. Oh, give me some English rain.

MARY. It rains here.

DABBY. It's not the same. I could recognise English rain anywhere. And Devon rain, Mary, Devon rain is the softest in England. As soft as your breasts, as soft as Lieutenant Clark's dimpled cheeks.

MARY. Dabby, don't!

DABBY. You're wasting time, girl, he's ripe for the plucking. You can always tell with men, they begin to walk sideways. And if you don't—

MARY. Don't start. I listened to you once before.

DABBY. What would you have done without that lanky sailor drooling over you?

MARY. I would have been less of a whore.

DABBY. Listen, my darling, you're only a virgin once. You can't go to a man and say, I'm a virgin except for this one lover I had. After that, it doesn't matter how many men go through you.

MARY. I'll never wash the sin away.

DABBY. If God didn't want women to be whores he shouldn't have created men who pay for their bodies. While you were with your little sailor there were women in that stinking pit of a hold who had three men on them at once, men with the pox, men with the flux,[18] men biting like dogs.

MARY. But if you don't agree to it, then you're not a whore, you're a martyr.

DABBY. You have to be a virgin to be a martyr, Mary, and you didn't come on that ship a virgin. "A.H. I love thee to the heart", ha, tattooed way up there—

Dabby begins to lift Mary's skirt to reveal a tattoo high up on the inner thigh. Mary leaps away.

MARY. That was different. That was love.

[18] **flux** dysentery

DABBY. The second difficulty with being a martyr is that you have to be dead to qualify. Well, you didn't die, thanks to me, you had three pounds of beef a week instead of two, two extra ounces of cheese.

MARY. Which you were happy to eat!

DABBY. We women have to look after each other. Let's learn the lines.

MARY. You sold me that first day so you and your husband could eat!

DABBY. Do you want me to learn these lines or not?

MARY. How can I play Silvia? She's brave and strong. She couldn't have done what I've done.

DABBY. She didn't spend eight months and one week on a convict ship. Anyway, you can pretend you're her.

MARY. No. I have to be her.

DABBY. Why?

MARY. Because that's acting.

DABBY. No way I'm being Rose, she's an idiot.

MARY. It's not such a big part, it doesn't matter so much.

DABBY. You didn't tell me that before.

MARY. I hadn't read it carefully. Come on, let's do the scene between Silvia and Rose. (*She reads.*) "I have rested but indifferently, and I believe my bedfellow was as little pleased; poor Rose! Here she comes"—

DABBY. I could have done something for Rose. Ha! I should play Silvia.

MARY. "Good morrow, my dear, how d'ye this morning?" Now you say: "Just as I was last night, neither better nor worse for you."

Liz Morden comes on.

LIZ. You can't do the play without me. I'm in it! Where's the Lieutenant?

DABBY. She's teaching me some lines.

LIZ. Why aren't you teaching me the lines?

MARY. We're not doing your scenes.

LIZ. Well do them.

DABBY. You can read. You can read your own lines.

LIZ. I don't want to learn them on my own.

Liz thrusts Dabby away and sits by Mary.

I'm waiting.

DABBY. What are you waiting for, Liz Morden, a blind man to buy your wares?

MARY (*quickly*). We'll do the first scene between Melinda and Silvia, all right?

LIZ. Yea. The first scene.

Mary gives Liz the book.

MARY. You start.

Liz looks at the book.

You start. "Welcome to town, cousin Silvia"—

LIZ. "Welcome to town, cousin Silvia"—

MARY. Go on—"I envied you"—

LIZ. "I envied you"—You read it first.

MARY. Why?

LIZ. I want to hear how you do it.

MARY. Why?

LIZ. Cause then I can do it different.

MARY. "I envied you your retreat in the country; for Shrews-bury, methinks, and all your heads of shires"—

DABBY. Why don't you read it? You can't read!

LIZ. What?

She lunges at Dabby.

MARY. I'll teach you the lines.

DABBY. Are you her friend now, is that it? Mary the holy innocent and thieving bitch—

Liz and Dabby seize each other. Ketch Freeman appears.

KETCH (*with nervous affability*). Good morning, ladies. And why aren't you at work instead of at each other's throats?

Liz and Dabby turn on him.

LIZ. I wouldn't talk of throats if I was you, Mr Hangman Ketch Freeman.

DABBY. Crap merchant.[19]

LIZ. Crapping cull. Switcher.

MARY. Roper.

KETCH. I was only asking what you were doing, you know, friendly like.

LIZ. Stick to your ropes, my little galler, don't bother the actresses.

KETCH. Actresses? You're doing a play?

LIZ. Better than dancing the Paddington frisk[20] in your arms—noser!

KETCH. I'll nose[21] on you, Liz, if you're not careful.

LIZ. I'd take a leap in the dark sooner than turn off my own kind. Now take your whirligigs out of our sight, we have lines to learn.

Ketch slinks away as Liz and Dabby spit him off.

DABBY (*after him*). Don't hang too many people, Ketch, we need an audience!

MARY. "Welcome to town, cousin Silvia." It says you salute.

LIZ (*giving a military salute*). "Welcome to town, cousin—Silvia."

SCENE 9

RALPH CLARK TRIES TO KISS HIS DEAR WIFE'S PICTURE

Ralph's tent. Candlelight. Ralph paces.

RALPH. Dreamt my beloved Betsey that I was with you and that I thought I was going to be arrested.

---

[19]**Crap merchant** hangman (similarly, in the next speeches, *Crapping cull, Switcher,* and *Roper*)   [20]**the Paddington frisk** Tyburn was in Paddington, so a hanged person was said to do the Paddington frisk.   [21]**nose** spy

He looks at his watch.

I hope to God that there is nothing the matter with you my tender Alicia or that of our dear boy—

He looks at his watch.

My darling tender wife I am reading Proverbs waiting till midnight, the Sabbath, that I might kiss your picture as usual.

He takes his Bible and kneels. Looks at his watch.

The Patrols caught three seamen and a boy in the women's camp.

He reads.

"Let thy fountain be blessed: and rejoice with the wife of thy youth."

Good God what a scene of whoredom is going on there in the women's camp.

He looks at his watch. Gets up. Paces.

Very hot this night.

       Captain Shea killed today one of the kankaroos—it is the most curious animal I ever saw.

He looks at his watch.

Almost midnight, my Betsey, the Lord's day—

He reads.

"And behold, there met him a woman with the attire of an harlot, and subtle of heart.
So she caught him, and kissed him with an impudent face."

Felt ill with the toothache my dear wife my God what pain.

Reads.

"So she caught him and kissed him with an impudent face . . ."

I have perfumed my bed with myrrh, aloes, cinnamon—

       Sarah McCormick was flogged today for calling the doctor a c—midnight—

       This being Sunday took your picture out of its prison and kissed it—God bless you my sweet woman.

He now proceeds to do so. That is, he goes down on his knees and brings the picture to himself. Ketch Freeman comes into the tent. Ralph jumps.

KETCH. Forgive me, Sir, please forgive me, I didn't want to disturb your prayers. I say fifty Hail Mary's myself every night, and 200 on the days when—I'll wait outside, Sir.

RALPH. What do you want?

KETCH. I'll wait quietly, Sir, don't mind me.

RALPH. Why aren't you in the camp at this hour?

KETCH. I should be, God forgive me, I should be. But I'm not. I'm here. I have to have a word with you, Sir.

RALPH. Get back to the camp immediately, I'll see you in the morning, Ketch.

KETCH. Don't call me that, Sir, I beg you, don't call me by that name, that's what I came to see you about, Sir.

RALPH. I was about to go to sleep.

KETCH. I understand, Sir, and your soul in peace, I won't take up your time, Sir, I'll be brief.

Pause.

RALPH. Well?

KETCH. Don't you want to finish your prayers? I can be very quiet. I used to watch my mother, may her poor soul rest in peace, I used to watch her say her prayers, every night.

RALPH. Get on with it!

KETCH. When I say my prayers I have a terrible doubt. How can I be sure God is forgiving me? What if he will forgive me, but hasn't forgiven me yet? That's why I don't want to die, Sir. That's why I can't die. Not until I am sure. Are you sure?

RALPH. I'm not a convict: I don't sin.

KETCH. To be sure. Forgive me, Sir. But if we're in God's power, then surely he makes us sin. I was given a guardian angel when I was born, like all good Catholics, why didn't my guardian angel look after me better? But I think he must've stayed in Ireland. I think the devil tempted my mother to London and both our guardian angels stayed behind. Have you ever been to Ireland, Sir? It's a beautiful country. If I'd been an angel I wouldn't have left it either. And when we came within six fields of Westminister, the devils took over. But it's God's judgement I'm frightened of. And the women's. They're so hard. Why is that?

RALPH. Why have you come here?

KETCH. I'm coming to that, Sir.

RALPH. Hurry up, then.

KETCH. I'm speaking as fast as I can, Sir—

RALPH. Ketch—

KETCH. James, Sir, James, Daniel, Patrick, after my three uncles. Good men they were too, didn't go to London. If my mother hadn't brought us to London, may God give peace to her soul and breathe pity into the hearts of hard women—because the docks are in London and if I hadn't worked on the docks, on that day, May 23rd, 1785, do you remember it, Sir? Shadwell Dock. If only we hadn't left, then I wouldn't have been there, then nothing would have happened, I wouldn't have become a coal heaver on Shadwell Dock and been there on the 23rd of May when we refused to unload because they were paying us so badly, Sir. I wasn't even near the sailor who got killed. He shouldn't have done the unloading, that was wrong of the sailors, but I didn't kill him, maybe one blow, not to look stupid, you know, just to show I was with the lads, even if I wasn't, but I didn't kill him. And they caught five at random, Sir, and I was among the five, and they found the cudgel, but I just had that to look good, that's all, and when they said to me later you can hang or you can give the names, what was I to do, what would you have done, Sir?

RALPH. I wouldn't have been in that situation, Freeman.

KETCH. To be sure, forgive me, Sir. I only told on the ones I saw, I didn't tell anything that wasn't true, death is a horrible thing, that poor sailor.

RALPH. Freeman, I'm going to go to bed now—

KETCH. I understand, Sir, I understand. And when it happened again, here! And I had hopes of making a good life here. It's because I'm so friendly, see, so I go along, and then I'm the one who gets caught. That theft, I didn't do it, I was just there, keeping a look out, just to help some friends, you know. But when they say to you, hang or be hanged, what do you do? Someone has to do it. I try to do it well. God had mercy on the whore, the thief, the lame, surely he'll forgive the hang—it's the women—they're without mercy—not like you and me, Sir, men. What I wanted to say, Sir, is that I heard them talking about the play.

Pause.

Some players came into our village once. They were loved like the angels, Lieutenant, like the angels. And the way the women watched them—the light of a spring dawn in their eyes.

Lieutenant—

I want to be an actor.

SCENE 10

JOHN WISEHAMMER AND MARY BRENHAM EXCHANGE WORDS

Mary is copying The Recruiting Officer in the afternoon light. John Wisehammer is carrying bricks and piling them to one side. He begins to hover over her.

MARY. "I would rather counsel than command; I don't propose this with the authority of a parent, but as the advice of your friend"—

WISEHAMMER. Friend. That's a good word. Short, but full of promise.

MARY. "That you would take the coach this moment and go into the country."

WISEHAMMER. Country can mean opposite things. It renews you with trees and grass, you go rest in the country, or it crushes you with power: you die for your country, your country doesn't want you, you're thrown out of your country.

Pause.

I like words.

Pause.

My father cleared the houses of the dead to sell the old clothes to the poor houses by the Thames. He found a dictionary—Johnson's dictionary—it was as big as a

Bible. It went from A to L. I started with the A's. Abecedarian: someone who teaches the alphabet or rudiments of literature. Abject: a man without hope.

MARY. What does indulgent mean?

WISEHAMMER. How is it used?

MARY (*reads*). "You have been so careful, so indulgent to me"—

WISEHAMMER. It means ready to overlook faults.

Pause.

You have to be careful with words that begin with 'in'. It can turn everything upside down. Injustice. Most of that word is taken up with justice, but the 'in' twists it inside out and makes it the ugliest word in the English language.

MARY. Guilty is an uglier word.

WISEHAMMER. Innocent ought to be a beautiful word, but it isn't, it's full of sorrow. Anguish.

Mary goes back to her copying.

MARY. I don't have much time. We start this in a few days.

Wisehammer looks over her shoulder.

I have the biggest part.

WISEHAMMER. You have a beautiful hand.

MARY. There is so much to copy. So many words.

WISEHAMMER. I can write.

MARY. Why don't you tell Lieutenant Clark? He's doing it.

WISEHAMMER. No . . . no . . . I'm—

MARY. Afraid?

WISEHAMMER. Diffident.

MARY. I'll tell him. Well, I won't. My friend Dabby will. She's—

WISEHAMMER. Bold.

Pause.

Shy is not a bad word, it's soft.

MARY. But shame is a hard one.

WISEHAMMER. Words with two L's are the worst. Lonely, loveless.

MARY. Love is a good word.

WISEHAMMER. That's because it only has one L. I like words with one L: Luck. Latitudinarian.[22]

Mary laughs.

Laughter.

SCENE 11

THE FIRST REHEARSAL

Ralph Clark, Robert Sideway, John Wisehammer, Mary Brenham, Liz Morden, Dabby Bryant, Duckling Smith, Ketch Freeman.

RALPH. Good afternoon, ladies and gentlemen—

DABBY. We're ladies now. Wait till I tell my husband I've become a lady.

MARY. Sshht.

RALPH. It is with pleasure that I welcome you—

SIDEWAY. Our pleasure, Mr Clark, our pleasure.

RALPH. We have many days of hard work ahead of us.

LIZ. Work! I'm not working. I thought we was acting.

RALPH. Now, let me introduce the company—

DABBY. We've all met before, Lieutenant, you could say we know each other, you could say we'd know each other in the dark.

SIDEWAY. It's a theatrical custom, the company is formally introduced to each other, Mrs Bryant.

DABBY. Mrs Bryant? Who's Mrs Bryant?

SIDEWAY. It's the theatrical form of address, Madam. You may call me Mr Sideway.

RALPH. If I may proceed—

KETCH. Shhh! You're interrupting the director.

DABBY. So we are, Mr Hangman.

The women all hiss and spit at Ketch.

RALPH. The ladies first: Mary Brenham who is to play Silvia. Liz Morden who is to play Melinda. Duckling Smith who is to play Lucy, Melinda's maid.

DUCKLING. I'm not playing Liz Morden's maid.

RALPH. Why not?

DUCKLING. I live with an officer. He wouldn't like it.

DABBY. Just because she lives chained up in that old toss pot's garden.

DUCKLING. Don't you dare talk of my Harry—

RALPH. You're not playing Morden's maid, Smith, you're playing Melinda's. And Dabby Bryant, who is to play Rose, a country girl.

DABBY. From Devon.

DUCKLING (*to Dabby*). Screw jaws!

DABBY (*to Duckling*). Salt bitch!

RALPH. That's the ladies. Now, Captain Plume will be played by Henry Kable.

He looks around.

Who seems to be late. That's odd. I saw him an hour ago and he said he was going to your hut to learn some lines, Wisehammer?

Wisehammer is silent.

Sergeant Kite is to be played by John Arscott, who did send a message to say he would be kept at work an extra hour.

DABBY. An hour! You won't see him in an hour!

LIZ (*under her breath*). You're not the only one with new wrinkles in your arse,[23] Dabby Bryant.

RALPH. Mr Worthy will be played by Mr Sideway.

---

[22]**Latitudinarian** a liberal, and especially someone who cares little about specific religious creeds

[23]**new wrinkles in your arse** special knowledge (Liz alludes to Arscott's escape.)

Sideway takes a vast bow.

SIDEWAY. I'm here.

RALPH. Justice Balance by James Freeman.

DUCKLING. No way I'm doing a play with a hangman. The words would stick in my throat.

More hisses and spitting. Ketch shrinks.

RALPH. You don't have any scenes with him, Smith. Now if I could finish the introductions. Captain Brazen is to be played by John Wisehammer.

   The small parts are still to be cast. Now. We can't do the first scene until John Arscott appears.

DABBY. There won't be a first scene.

RALPH. Bryant, will you be quiet please! The second scene. Wisehammer, you could read Plume.

Wisehammer comes forward eagerly.

No, I'll read Plume myself. So, Act One, Scene Two, Captain Plume and Mr Worthy.

SIDEWAY. That's me. I'm at your command.

RALPH. The rest of you can watch and wait for your scenes. Perhaps we should begin by reading it.

SIDEWAY. No need, Mr Clark. I know it.

RALPH. Ah, I'm afraid I shall have to read Captain Plume.

SIDEWAY. I know that part too. Would you like me to do both?

RALPH. I think it's better if I do it. Shall we begin? Kite, that's John Arscott, has just left—

DABBY. Running.

RALPH. Bryant! I'll read the line before Worthy's entrance: "None at present. 'Tis indeed the picture of Worthy, but the life's departed." Sideway? Where's he gone?

Sideway has scuttled off. He shouts from the wings.

SIDEWAY. I'm preparing my entrance, Mr Clark, I won't be a minute. Could you read the line again, slowly?

RALPH. "'Tis indeed the picture of Worthy, but the life's departed. What, arms-a-cross, Worthy!"

Sideway comes on, walking sideways, arms held up in a grandiose eighteenth-century theatrical pose. He suddenly stops.

SIDEWAY. Ah, yes, I forgot. Arms-a-cross. I shall have to start again.

He goes off again and shouts.

Could you read the line again louder please?

RALPH. "What, arms-a-cross, Worthy!"

Sideway rushes on.

SIDEWAY. My wiper! Someone's buzzed my wiper![24] There's a wipe drawer in this crew, Mr Clark.

RALPH. What's the matter?

SIDEWAY. There's a pickpocket in the company.

DABBY. Talk of the pot calling the kettle black.

Sideway stalks around the company threateningly.

SIDEWAY. My handkerchief. Who prigged[25] my handkerchief?

RALPH. I'm sure it will turn up, Sideway, let's go on.

SIDEWAY. I can't do my entrance without my handkerchief. (*Furious.*) I've been practising it all night. If I get my mittens on the rum diver[26] I'll—

He lungs at Liz, who fights back viciously. They jump apart, each taking threatening poses and Ralph intervenes with speed.

RALPH. Let's assume Worthy has already entered, Sideway. Now, I say: "What arms-a-cross, Worthy! Methinks you should hold 'em open when a friend's so near. I must expel this melancholy spirit."

Sideway has dropped to his knees and is sobbing in a pose of total sorrow.

What are you doing down there, Sideway?

SIDEWAY. I'm being melancholy. I saw Mr Garrick being melancholy once. That is what he did. Hamlet it was.

He stretches his arms to the ground and begins to repeat.

"Oh that this too, too solid flesh would melt. Oh that this too too solid flesh would melt. Oh that this too too—"

RALPH. This is a comedy. It is perhaps a little lighter. Try simply to stand normally and look melancholy. I'll say the line again. (*Sideway is still sobbing.*) The audience won't hear Captain Plume's lines if your sobs are so loud, Sideway.

SIDEWAY. I'm still establishing my melancholy.

RALPH. A comedy needs to move quite fast. In fact, I think we'll cut that line and the two verses that follow and go straight to Worthy greeting Plume.

WISEHAMMER. I like the word melancholy.

SIDEWAY. A greeting. Yes. A greeting looks like this.

He extends his arms high and wide.

"Plume!" Now I'll change to say the next words. "My dear Captain", that's affection isn't it? If I put my hands on my heart, like this. Now, "Welcome." I'm not quite sure how to do "Welcome."

RALPH. I think if you just say the line.

SIDEWAY. Quite. Now.

He feels Ralph.

RALPH. Sideway! What are you doing?

SIDEWAY. I'm checking that you're safe and sound returned. That's what the line says: "Safe and sound returned."

RALPH. You don't need to touch him. You can see that!

SIDEWAY. Yes, yes. I'll check his different parts with my eyes. Now, I'll put it all together, "Plume! My dear Captain, welcome. Safe and sound returned!"

---

[24]**buzzed my wiper** stole my handkerchief

[25]**prigged** stole [26]**rum diver** smooth pickpocket

He does this with appropriate gestures.

RALPH. Sideway—it's a very good attempt. It's very theatrical. But you could try to be a little more—euh—natural.

SIDEWAY. Natural! On the stage! But Mr Clark!

RALPH. People must—euh—believe you. Garrick after all is admired for his naturalness.

SIDEWAY. Of course. I thought I was being Garrick—but never mind. Natural. Quite. You're the director, Mr Clark.

RALPH. Perhaps you could look at me while you're saying the lines.

SIDEWAY. But the audience won't see my face.

RALPH. The lines are said to Captain Plume. Let's move on. Plume says: "I 'scaped safe from Germany," shall we say— America? It will make it more contemporary—

WISEHAMMER. You can't change the words of the playwright.

RALPH. Mm, well, "and sound, I hope, from London: you see I have—"

Black Caesar rushes on.

RALPH. Caesar, we're rehearsing—would you—

CAESAR. I see that well, Monsieur Lieutenant. I see it is a piece of theatre, I have seen many pieces of theatre in my beautiful island of Madagascar so I have decided to play in your piece of theatre.

RALPH. There's no part for you.

CAESAR. There is always a part for Caesar.

SIDEWAY. All the parts have been taken.

CAESAR. I will play his servant.

He stands next to Sideway.

RALPH. Farquhar hasn't written a servant for Worthy.

DUCKLING. He can have my part. I want to play something else.

CAESAR. There is always a black servant in a play, Monsieur Lieutenant. And Caesar is that servant. So, now I stand here just behind him and I will be his servant.

RALPH. There are no lines for it, Caesar.

CAESAR. I speak in French. That makes him a more high up gentleman if he has a French servant, and that is good. Now he gets the lady with the black servant. Very chic.

RALPH. I'll think about it. Actually, I would like to rehearse the ladies now. They have been waiting patiently and we don't have much time left. Freeman, would you go and see what's happened to Arscott. Sideway, we'll come back to this scene another time, but that was very good, very good. A little, a little euh, but very good.

Sideway bows out, followed by Caesar.

Now we will rehearse the first scene between Melinda and Silvia. Morden and Brenham, if you would come and stand here. Now the scene is set in Melinda's apartments. Silvia is already there. So, if you stand here, Morden. Brenham, you stand facing her.

LIZ (*very, very fast*). "Welcome to town cousin Silvia I envied you your retreat in the country for Shrewsbury methinks and all your heads of shires are the most irregular places for living—"

RALPH. Euh, Morden—

LIZ. Wait, I haven't finished yet. "Here we have smoke noise scandal affectation and pretension in short everything to give the spleen and nothing to divert it then the air is intolerable—"

RALPH. Morden, you know the lines very well.

LIZ. Thank you, Lieutenant Clark.

RALPH. But you might want to try and act them.

Pause.

Let's look at the scene.

Liz looks.

You're a rich lady. You're at home. Now a rich lady would stand in a certain way. Try to stand like a rich lady. Try to look at Silvia with a certain assurance.

LIZ. Assurance.

WISEHAMMER. Confidence.

RALPH. Like this. You've seen rich ladies, haven't you?

LIZ. I robbed a few.

RALPH. How did they behave?

LIZ. They screamed.

RALPH. I mean before you—euh—robbed them.

LIZ. I don't know. I was watching their purses.

RALPH. Have you ever seen a lady in her own house?

LIZ. I used to climb into the big houses when I was a girl, and just stand there, looking. I didn't take anything. I just stood. Like this.

RALPH. But if it was your own house, you would think it was normal to live like that.

WISEHAMMER. It's not normal. It's not normal when others have nothing.

RALPH. When acting, you have to imagine things. You have to imagine you're someone different. So, now, think of a rich lady and imagine you're her.

Liz begins to masticate.

What are you doing?

LIZ. If I was rich I'd eat myself sick.

DABBY. Me too, potatoes.

The convicts speak quickly and over each other.

SIDEWAY. Roast beef and Yorkshire pudding.

CAESAR. Hearts of palm.

WISEHAMMER. Four fried eggs, six fried eggs, eight fried eggs.

LIZ. Eels, oysters—

RALPH. Could we get on with the scene, please? Brenham, it's your turn to speak.

MARY. "Oh, Madam, I have heard the town commended for its air."

LIZ. "But you don't consider Silvia how long I have lived in't."

RALPH (*to Liz*). I believe you would look at her.

LIZ. She didn't look at me.

RALPH. Didn't she? She will now.

LIZ. "For I can assure you that to a lady the least nice in her constitution no air can be good above half a year change of air I take to be the most agreeable of any variety in life."

MARY. "But prithee, my dear Melinda, don't put on such an air to me."

RALPH. Excellent, Brenham. You could be a little more sharp on the "don't."

MARY. "Don't." (*Mary now tries a few gestures.*) "Your education and mine were just the same, and I remember the time when we never troubled our heads about air, but when the sharp air from the Welsh mountains made our noses drop in a cold morning at the boarding-school."

RALPH. Good! Good! Morden?

LIZ. "Our education cousin was the same but our temperaments had nothing alike."

RALPH. That's a little better, Morden, but you needn't be quite so angry with her. Now go on Brenham.

LIZ. I haven't finished my speech!

RALPH. You're right, Morden, please excuse me.

LIZ (*embarrassed*). No, no, there's no need for that, Lieutenant. I only meant—I don't have to.

RALPH. Please do.

LIZ. "You have the constitution of a horse."

RALPH. Much better, Morden. But you must always remember you're a lady. What can we do to help you? Lucy.

DABBY. That's you, Duckling.

RALPH. See that little piece of wood over there? Take it to Melinda. That will be your fan.

DUCKLING. I'm not fetching nothing for Liz.

RALPH. She's not Morden, she's Melinda, your mistress. You're her servant, Lucy. In fact, you should be in this scene. Now take her that fan.

DUCKLING (*gives the wood to Liz*). Here.

LIZ. Thank you, Lucy, I do much appreciate your effort.

RALPH. No, you would nod your head.

WISEHAMMER. Don't add any words to the play.

RALPH. Now, Lucy, stand behind Morden.

DUCKLING. What do I say?

RALPH. Nothing.

DUCKLING. How will they know I'm here? Why does she get all the lines? Why can't I have some of hers?

RALPH. Brenham, it's your speech.

MARY. "So far as to be troubled with neither spleen, colic, nor vapours—"

The convicts slink away and sink down, trying to make themselves invisible as Major Ross, followed by Captain Campbell, come on.

"I need no salt for my stomach, no—"

She sees the officers herself and folds in with the rest of the convicts.

RALPH. Major Ross, Captain Campbell, I'm rehearsing.

ROSS. Rehearsing! Rehearsing!

CAMPBELL. Tssaach. Rehearsing.

ROSS. Lieutenant Clark is rehearsing. Lieutenant Clark asked us to give the prisoners two hours so he could rehearse, but what has he done with them? What?

CAMPBELL. Eeeh. Other things, eh.

ROSS. Where are the prisoners Kable and Arscott, Lieutenant?

CAMPBELL. Eh?

RALPH. They seem to be late.

ROSS. While you were rehearsing, Arscott and Kable slipped into the woods with three others, so five men have run away and it's all because of your damned play and your so-called thespists. And not only have your thespists run away, they've stolen food from the stores for their renegade escapade, that's what your play has done.

RALPH. I don't see what the play—

ROSS. I said it from the beginning. The play will bring down calamity on this colony.

RALPH. I don't see—

ROSS. The devil, Lieutenant, always comes through the mind, here, worms its way, idleness and words.

RALPH. Major Ross, I can't agree—

ROSS. Listen to me, my lad, you're a Second Lieutenant and you don't agree or disagree with Major Ross.

CAMPBELL. No discipline, tcchhha.

Ross looks over the convicts.

ROSS. Caesar! He started going with them and came back.

RALPH. That's all right, he's not in the play.

CAESAR. Yes I am, please Lieutenant, I am a servant.

ROSS. John Wisehammer!

WISEHAMMER. I had nothing to do with it!

ROSS. You're Jewish, aren't you? You're guilty. Kable was last seen near Wisehammer's hut. Liz Morden! She was observed next to the colony's stores late last night in the company of Kable who was supposed to be repairing the door. (*To Liz.*) Liz Morden, you will be tried for stealing from the stores. You know the punishment? Death by hanging. (*Pause.*) And now you may continue to rehearse, Lieutenant.

Ross goes. Campbell lingers, looking at the book.

CAMPBELL. Ouusstta. *The Recruiting Officer.* Good title. Arara. But a play, tss, a play.

He goes. Ralph and the convicts are left in the shambles of their rehearsal. A silence.

ACT 2

SCENE 1

VISITING HOURS

Liz, Wisehammer, Arscott, Caesar all in chains. Arscott is bent over, facing away.

LIZ. Luck? Don't know the word. Shifts its bob[27] when I comes near. Born under a ha'penny planet I was. Dad's a nibbler, don't want to get crapped. Mum leaves. Five brothers, I'm the only titter. I takes in washing. Then. My own father. Lady's walking down the street, he takes her wiper. She screams, he's shoulder-clapped, says, it's not me, Sir, it's Lizzie, look, she took it. I'm stripped, beaten in the street, everyone watching. That night, I take my dad's cudgel and try to kill him, I prig all his clothes and go to my older brother. He don't want me. Liz, he says, why trine for a make, when you can wap for a winne? I'm no dimber mort, I says. Don't ask you to be a swell mollisher, Sister, men want Miss Laycock, don't look at your mug. So I begin to sell my mother of saints. I thinks I'm in luck when I meet the swell cove. He's a bobcull: sports a different wiper every day of the week. He says to me, it's not enough to sell your mossie face, Lizzie, it don't bring no shiners no more. Shows me how to spice the swells. So. Swell has me up the wall, flashes a pocket watch, I lifts it. But one time, I stir my stumps too slow, the swell squeaks beef, the snoozie hears, I'm nibbed. It's up the ladder to rest, I thinks when I goes up before the fortune teller, but no, the judge's a bobcull, I nap the King's pardon and it's seven years across the herring pond. Jesus Christ the hunger on the ship, sailors won't touch me: no rantum scantum, no food. But here, the Governor says, new life. You could nob it here, Lizzie, I thinks, bobcull Gov, this niffynaffy play, not too much work, good crew of rufflers, Kable, Arscott, but no, Ross don't like my mug, I'm nibbed again and now it's up the ladder to rest for good. Well. Lizzie Morden's life. And you, Wisehammer, how did you get here?

WISEHAMMER. Betrayal. Barbarous falsehood. Intimidation. Injustice.

LIZ. Speak in English, Wisehammer.

WISEHAMMER. I am innocent. I didn't do it and I'll keep saying I didn't.

LIZ. It doesn't matter what you say. If they say you're a thief, you're a thief.

WISEHAMMER. I am not a thief. I'll go back to England to the snuff shop of Rickett and Loads and say, see, I'm back, I'm innocent.

LIZ. They won't listen.

WISEHAMMER. You can't live if you think that way.

---

[27]**Shifts its bob** moves away; other canting terms in this speech are: **ha'penny planet** unlucky star; **nibbler** petty thief; **crapped** hanged; **titter** daughter; **wiper** handkerchief; **shoulder-clapped** arrested; **trine for a make . . . wap for a winner,** why hang for a ha'penny when you can whore for a penny; **dimber mort . . . swell mollisher** beautiful woman (the terms mean the same thing); **mother of saints** vagina; **swell cove** gentleman; **bobcull** easy-going fellow; **mossie face** genitals; **shiners** bright coins; **spice the swells** cheat rich people; **snoozie** night watchman; **nibbed** arrested; **up the ladder to rest** hanging; **nap the King's pardon** get pardoned; **rantum scantum** sex; **nob it** do well; **rufflers** crooks

---

Pause.

I'm sorry. Seven years and I'll go back.

LIZ. What do you want to go back to England for? You're not English.

WISEHAMMER. I was born in England. I'm English. What do I have to do to make people believe I'm English?

LIZ. You have to think English. I hate England. But I think English. And him, Arscott, he's not said anything since they brought him in but he's thinking English, I can tell.

CAESAR. I don't want to think English. If I think English I will die. I want to go back to Madagascar and think Malagasy. I want to die in Madagascar and join my ancestors.

LIZ. It doesn't matter where you die when you're dead.

CAESAR. If I die here, I will have no spirit. I want to go home. I will escape again.

ARSCOTT. There's no escape!

CAESAR. This time I lost my courage, but next time I ask my ancestors and they will help me escape.

ARSCOTT (*shouts*). There's no escape!

LIZ. See. That's English. You know things.

CAESAR. My ancestors will know the way.

ARSCOTT. There's no escape I tell you.

Pause.

You go in circles out there, that's all you do. You go out there and you walk and walk and you don't reach China. You come back on your steps if the savages don't get you first. Even a compass doesn't work in this foreign upside-down desert. Here. You can read. Why didn't it work? What does it say?

He hands Wisehammer a carefully folded, wrinkled piece of paper.

WISEHAMMER. It says north.

ARSCOTT. Why didn't it work then? It was supposed to take us north to China, why did I end up going in circles?

WISEHAMMER. Because it's not a compass.

ARSCOTT. I gave my only shilling to a sailor for it. He said it was a compass.

WISEHAMMER. It's a piece of paper with north written on it. He lied. He deceived you, he betrayed you.

Sideway, Mary and Duckling come on.

SIDEWAY. Madam, gentlemen, fellow players, we have come to visit, to commiserate, to offer our humble services.

LIZ. Get out!

MARY. Liz, we've come to rehearse the play.

WISEHAMMER. Rehearse the play?

DUCKLING. The Lieutenant has gone to talk to the Governor. Harry said we could come see you.

MARY. The Lieutenant has asked me to stand in his place so we don't lose time. We'll start with the first scene between Melinda and Brazen.

WISEHAMMER. How can I play Captain Brazen in chains?

MARY. This is the theatre. We will believe you.

ARSCOTT. Where does Kite come in?

SIDEWAY (*bowing to Liz*). Madam, I have brought you your fan. (*He hands her the "fan", which she takes.*)

SCENE 2

HIS EXCELLENCY EXHORTS RALPH

Phillip, Ralph.

PHILLIP. I hear you want to stop the play, Lieutenant.

RALPH. Half of my cast is in chains, Sir.

PHILLIP. That is a difficulty, but it can be overcome. Is that your only reason, Lieutenant?

RALPH. So many people seem against it, Sir.

PHILLIP. Are you afraid?

RALPH. No, Sir, but I do not wish to displease my superior officers.

PHILLIP. If you break conventions, it's inevitable you make enemies, Lieutenant. This play irritates them.

RALPH. Yes and I—

PHILLIP. Socrates[28] irritated the state of Athens and was put to death for it.

RALPH. Sir—

PHILLIP. Would you have a world without Socrates?

RALPH. Sir, I—

PHILLIP. In the Meno, one of Plato's[29] great dialogues, have you read it, Lieutenant, Socrates demonstrates that a slave boy can learn the principles of geometry as well as a gentleman.

RALPH. Ah—

PHILLIP. In other words, he shows that human beings have an intelligence which has nothing to do with the circumstances into which they are born.

RALPH. Sir—

PHILLIP. Sit down, Lieutenant. It is a matter of reminding the slave of what he knows, of his own intelligence. And by intelligence you may read goodness, talent, the innate qualities of human beings.

RALPH. I see—Sir.

PHILLIP. When he treats the slave boy as a rational human being, the boy becomes one, he loses his fear, and he becomes a competent mathematician. A little more encouragement and he might become an extraordinary mathematician. Who knows? You must see your actors in that light.

RALPH. I can see some of them, Sir, but there are others . . . John Arscott—

PHILLIP. He has been given 200 lashes for trying to escape. It will take time for him to see himself as a human being again.

[28]**Socrates** Greek philosopher (469–399 B.C.) [29]**Plato** Greek philosopher (429–347 B.C.), student of Socrates, and the author of dialogues in which Socrates is the chief figure

RALPH. Liz Morden—

PHILLIP. Liz Morden—(*He pauses.*) I had a reason for asking you to cast her as Melinda. Morden is one of the most difficult women in the colony.

RALPH. She is indeed, Sir.

PHILLIP. Lower than a slave, full of loathing, foul mouthed, desperate.

RALPH. Exactly, Sir. And violent.

PHILLIP. Quite. To be made an example of.

RALPH. By hanging?

PHILLIP. No, Lieutenant, by redemption.

RALPH. The Reverend says he's given up on her, Sir.

PHILLIP. The Reverend's an ass, Lieutenant. I am speaking of redeeming her humanity.

RALPH. I am afraid there may not be much there, Sir.

PHILLIP. How do we know what humanity lies hidden under the rags and filth of a mangled life? I have seen soldiers given up for dead, limbs torn, heads cut open, come back to life. If we treat her as a corpse, of course she will die. Try a little kindness, Lieutenant.

RALPH. But will she be hanged, Sir?

PHILLIP. I don't want a woman to be hanged. You will have to help, Ralph.

RALPH. Sir!

PHILLIP. I had retired from His Majesty's Service, Ralph. I was farming. I don't know why they asked me to rule over this colony of wretched souls, but I will fulfil my responsibility. No one will stop me.

RALPH. No, Sir, but I don't see—

PHILLIP. What is a statesman's responsibility? To ensure the rule of law. But the citizens must be taught to obey that law of their own will. I want to rule over responsible human beings, not tyrannise over a group of animals. I want there to be a contract between us, not a whip on my side, terror and hatred on theirs. And you must help me, Ralph.

RALPH. Yes, Sir. The play—

PHILLIP. Won't change much, but it is the diagram in the sand that may remind—just remind the slave boy—Do you understand?

RALPH. I think so.

PHILLIP. We may fail. I may have a mutiny on my hands. They are trying to convince the Admiralty that I am mad.

RALPH. Sir!

PHILLIP. And they will threaten you. You don't want to be a Second Lieutenant all your life.

RALPH. No, sir!

PHILLIP. I cannot go over the head of Major Ross in the matter of promotion.

RALPH. I see.

PHILLIP. But we have embarked, Ralph, we must stay afloat. There is a more serious threat and it may capsize us all. If a ship does not come within three months, the supplies will be exhausted. In a month, I will cut the rations again. (*Pause.*) Harry is not well. Can you do something? Good luck with the play, Lieutenant. Oh, and Ralph—

RALPH. Sir—

PHILLIP. Unexpected situations are often matched by unexpected virtues in people, are they not?

RALPH. I believe they are, Sir.

PHILLIP. A play is a world in itself, a tiny colony we could almost say.

Pause.

And you are in charge of it. That is a great responsibility.

RALPH. I will lay down my life if I have to, Sir.

PHILLIP. I don't think it will come to that, Lieutenant. You need only do your best.

RALPH. Yes, Sir, I will, Sir.

PHILLIP. Excellent.

RALPH. It's a wonderful play, Sir. I wasn't sure at first, as you know, but now—

PHILLIP. Good, Good. I shall look forward to seeing it. I'm sure it will be a success.

RALPH. Thank you, Sir. Thank you.

SCENE 3

HARRY BREWER SEES THE DEAD

Harry Brewer's tent. Harry sits, drinking rum, speaking in the different voices of his tormenting ghosts and answering in his own.

HARRY. Duckling! Duckling! "She's on the beach, Harry, waiting for her young Handy Baker." Go away, Handy, go away! "The dead never go away, Harry. You thought you'd be the only one to dance the buttock ball with your trull,[30] but no one owns a whore's cunt, Harry, you rent." I didn't hang you. "You wanted me dead." I didn't. "You wanted me hanged." All right, I wanted you hanged. Go away! (*Pause.*) "Death is horrible, Mr Brewer, it's dark, there's nothing." Thomas Barrett! You were hanged because you stole from the stores. "I was seventeen, Mr Brewer." You lived a very wicked life. "I didn't." That's what you said that morning, "I have led a very wicked life." "I had to say something, Mr Brewer, and make sense of dying. I'd heard the Reverend say we were all wicked, but it was horrible, my body hanging, my tongue sticking out." You shouldn't have stolen that food! "I wanted to live, go back to England, I'd only be twenty-four. I hadn't done it much, not like you." Duckling! "I wish I wasn't dead, Mr Brewer I had plans. I was going to have my farm, drink with friends and feel the strong legs of a girl around me—" You shouldn't have stolen. "Didn't you ever steal?" No! Yes. But that was different. Duckling!

[30]**trull** whore

"Why should you be alive after what you've done?" Duckling! Duckling!

Duckling rushes on.

DUCKLING. What's the matter, Harry?

HARRY. I'm seeing them.

DUCKLING. Who?

HARRY. All of them. The dead. Help me.

DUCKLING. I heard your screams from the beach. You're having another bad dream.

HARRY. No. I see them.

Pause.

Let me come inside you.

DUCKLING. Now?

HARRY. Please.

DUCKLING. Will you forget your nightmares?

HARRY. Yes.

DUCKLING. Come then.

HARRY. Duckling . . .

She lies down and lifts her skirts. He begins to go down over her and stops.

What were you doing on the beach? You were with him, he told me, you were with Handy Baker.

SCENE 4

THE ABORIGINE MUSES ON THE NATURE OF DREAMS

THE ABORIGINE. Some dreams lose their way and wander over the earth, lost. But this is a dream no one wants. It has stayed. How can we befriend this crowded, hungry and disturbed dream?

SCENE 5

THE SECOND REHEARSAL

Ralph Clark, Mary Brenham and Robert Sideway are waiting. Major Ross and Captain Campbell bring the three prisoners Caesar, Wisehammer and Liz Morden. They are still in chains. Ross shoves them forward.

ROSS. Here is some of your caterwauling cast, Lieutenant.

CAMPBELL. The Governor, chht, said, release, tssst. Prisoners.

ROSS. Unchain Wisehammer and the savage, Captain Campbell. (*Points to Liz.*) She stays in chains. She's being tried tomorrow, we don't want her sloping off.

RALPH. I can't rehearse with one of my players in chains, Major.

CAMPBELL. Eeh. Difficult. Mmmm.

ROSS. We'll tell the Governor you didn't need her and take her back to prison.

RALPH. No. We shall manage. Sideway, go over the scene you rehearsed in prison with Melinda, please.

CAESAR. I'm in that scene too, Lieutenant.

RALPH. No you're not.

LIZ and SIDEWAY. Yes he is, Lieutenant.

SIDEWAY. He's my servant.

Ralph nods and Liz, Sideway and Caesar move to the side and stand together, ready to rehearse, but waiting.

RALPH. The rest of us will go from Silvia's entrance as Wilful. Where's Arscott?

ROSS. We haven't finished with Arscott yet, Lieutenant.

CAMPBELL. Punishment, eeeh, for escape. Fainted. Fifty-three lashes left. Heeeh.

ROSS (*pointing to Caesar*). Caesar's next. After Morden's trial.

Caesar cringes.

RALPH. Brenham, are you ready? Wisehammer? I'll play Captain Plume.

ROSS. The wee Lieutenant wants to be in the play too. He wants to be promoted to convict. We'll have you in the chain gang soon, Mr Clark, haha. (*A pause. Ross and Campbell stand, watching. The Convicts are frozen.*)

RALPH. Major, we will rehearse now.

Pause. No one moves.

We wish to rehearse.

ROSS. No one's stopping you, Lieutenant.

Silence.

RALPH. Major, rehearsals need to take place in the utmost euh—privacy, secrecy you might say. The actors are not yet ready to be seen by the public.

ROSS. Not ready to be seen?

RALPH. Major, there is a modesty attached to the process of creation which must be respected.

ROSS. Modesty? Modesty! Sideway, come here.

RALPH. Major. Sideway—stay—

ROSS. Lieutenant, I would not try to countermand the orders of a superior officer.

CAMPBELL. Obedience. Ehh, first euh, rule.

ROSS. Sideway.

Sideway comes up to Ross.

Take your shirt off.

Sideway obeys. Ross turns him and shows his scarred back to the company.

One hundred lashes on the Sirius for answering an officer. Remember, Sideway? Three hundred lashes for trying to strike the same officer.

I have seen the white of this animal's bones, his wretched blood and reeky convict urine have spilled on my boots and he's feeling modest? Are you feeling modest, Sideway?

He shoves Sideway aside.

Modesty.

Bryant. Here.

Dabby comes forward.

On all fours.

Dabby goes down on all fours.

Now wag your tail and bark, and I'll throw you a biscuit. What? You've forgotten? Isn't that how you begged for your food on the ship? Wag your tail, Bryant, bark! We'll wait.

Brenham.

Mary comes forward.

Where's your tattoo, Brenham? Show us. I can't see it. Show us.

Mary tries to obey, lifting her skirt a little.

If you can't manage, I'll help you. (*Mary lifts her skirt a little higher.*) I can't see it.

But Sideway turns to Liz and starts acting, boldly, across the room, across everyone.

SIDEWAY. "What pleasures I may receive abroad are indeed uncertain; but this I am sure of, I shall meet with less cruelty among the most barbarous nations than I have found at home."

LIZ. "Come, Sir, you and I have been jangling a great while; I fancy if we made up our accounts, we should the sooner come to an agreement."

SIDEWAY. "Sure, Madam, you won't dispute your being in my debt—my fears, sighs, vows, promises, assiduities, anxieties, jealousies, have run on for a whole year, without any payment."

CAMPBELL. Mmhem, good, that. Sighs, vows, promises, hehem, mmm. Anxieties.

ROSS. Captain Campbell, start Arscott's punishment.

Campbell goes.

LIZ. "A year! Oh Mr Worthy, what you owe to me is not to be paid under a seven years' servitude. How did you use me the year before—"

The shouts of Arscott are heard.

"How did you use me the year before—"

She loses her lines. Sideway tries to prompt her.

SIDEWAY. "When taking advantage—"

LIZ. "When taking the advantage of my innocence and necessity—"

But she stops and drops down, defeated. Silence, except for the beating and Arscott's cries.

SCENE 6

THE SCIENCE OF HANGING

Harry, Ketch Freeman, Liz, sitting, staring straight ahead of her.

KETCH. I don't want to do this.

HARRY. Get on with it, Freeman.

KETCH (*to Liz*). I have to measure you.

Pause.

I'm sorry.

Liz doesn't move.

You'll have to stand, Liz.

Liz doesn't move.

Please.

Pause.

I won't hurt you. I mean, now. And if I have the measurements right, I can make it quick. Very quick. Please.

Liz doesn't move.

She doesn't want to get up, Mr Brewer. I could come back later.

HARRY. Hurry up.

KETCH. I can't. I can't measure her unless she gets up. I have to measure her to judge the drop. If the rope's too short, it won't hang her and if the rope is too long, it could pull her head off. It's very difficult, Mr Brewer, I've always done my best.

Pause.

But I've never hung a woman.

HARRY (*in Tom Barrett's voice*). "You've hung a boy." (*To Ketch.*) You've hung a boy.

KETCH. That was a terrible mess, Mr Brewer, don't you remember. It took twenty minutes and even then he wasn't dead. Remember how he danced and everyone laughed. I don't want to repeat something like that, Mr Brewer, not now. Someone had to get hold of his legs to weigh him down and then—

HARRY. Measure her, Freeman!

KETCH. Yes, Sir. Could you tell her to get up. She'll listen to you.

HARRY (*shouts*). Get up, you bitch.

Liz doesn't move.

Get up!

He seizes her and makes her stand.

Now measure her!

KETCH (*measuring the neck, etc., of Liz*). The Lieutenant is talking to the Governor again, Liz, maybe he'll change his mind. At least he might wait until we've done the play.

Pause.

I don't want to do this.

I know, you're thinking in my place you wouldn't. But somebody will do it, if I don't, and I'll be gentle. I won't hurt you.

Liz doesn't move, doesn't look at him.

It's wrong, Mr Brewer. It's wrong.

HARRY (*in Tom Barrett's voice*). "It's wrong. Death is horrible." (*In his own voice to Ketch.*) There's no food left in the colony and she steals it and gives it to Kable to run away.

KETCH. That's true, Liz, you shouldn't have stolen that food. Especially when the Lieutenant trusted us. That was wrong, Liz. Actors can't behave like normal people, not even like normal criminals. Still, I'm sorry. I'll do my best.

HARRY. "I had plans." (*To Ketch.*) Are you finished?

KETCH. Yes, yes. I have all the measurements I need. No, one more. I need to lift her. You don't mind, do you, Liz?

He lifts her.

She's so light. I'll have to use a very long rope. The fig tree would be better, it's higher. When will they build me some gallows, Mr Brewer? Nobody will laugh at you, Liz, you won't be shamed, I'll make sure of that.

HARRY. "You could hang yourself." Come on, Freeman. Let's go.

KETCH. Goodbye, Liz. You were a very good Melinda. No one will be as good as you.

They begin to go.

LIZ. Mr Brewer.

HARRY. "You wanted me dead." I didn't. You shouldn't've stolen that food!

KETCH. Speak to her, please, Mr Brewer.

HARRY. What?

LIZ. Tell Lieutenant Clark I didn't steal the food. Tell him—afterwards. I want him to know.

HARRY. Why didn't you say that before? Why are you lying now?

LIZ. Tell the Lieutenant.

HARRY. "Another victim of yours, another body. I was so frightened, so alone."

KETCH. Mr Brewer.

HARRY. "It's dark. There's nothing." Get away, get away!

LIZ. Please tell the Lieutenant.

HARRY. "First fear, then a pain at the back of the neck. Then nothing." I can't see. It's dark. It's dark.

Harry screams and falls.

SCENE 7

THE MEANING OF PLAYS

THE ABORIGINE. Ghosts in a multitude have spilled from the dream. Who are they? A swarm of ancestors comes through unmended cracks in the sky. But why? What do they need? If we can satisfy them, they will go back. How can we satisfy them?

Mary, Ralph, Dabby, Wisehammer, Arscott. Mary and Ralph are rehearsing. The others are watching.

RALPH. "For I swear, Madam, by the honour of my profession, that whatever dangers I went upon, it was with the hope of making myself more worthy of your esteem, and if I ever had thoughts of preserving my life, 'twas for the pleasure of dying at your feet."

MARY. "Well, well, you shall die at my feet, or where you will; but you know, Sir, there is a certain will and testament to be made beforehand."

I don't understand why Silvia has asked Plume to make a will.

DABBY. It's a proof of his love, he wants to provide for her.

MARY. A will is a proof of love?

WISEHAMMER. No. She's using will in another sense. He must show his willingness to marry her. Dying is used in another sense, too.

RALPH. He gives her his will to indicate that he intends to take care of her.

DABBY. That's right, Lieutenant, marriage is nothing, but will you look after her?

WISEHAMMER. Plume is too ambitious to marry Silvia.

MARY. If I had been Silvia, I would have trusted Plume.

DABBY. When dealing with men, always have a contract.

MARY. Love is a contract.

DABBY. Love is the barter of perishable goods. A man's word for a woman's body.

WISEHAMMER. Dabby is right. If a man loves a woman, he should marry her.

RALPH. Sometimes he can't.

WISEHAMMER. Then she should look for someone who can.

DABBY. A woman should look after her own interests, that's all.

MARY. Her interest is to love.

DABBY. A girl will love the first man who knows how to open her legs. She's called a whore and ends up here. I could write scenes, Lieutenant, women with real lives, not these Shrewsbury prudes.

WISEHAMMER. I've written something. The prologue of this play won't make any sense to the convicts: "In ancient times, when Helen's fatal charms" and so on. I've written another one. Will you look at it, Lieutenant?

Ralph does so and Wisehammer takes Mary aside.

You mustn't trust the wrong people, Mary. We could make a new life together, here. I would marry you, Mary, think about it, you would live with me, in a house. He'll have to put you in a hut at the bottom of his garden and call you his servant in public, that is, his whore. Don't do it, Mary.

DABBY. Lieutenant, are we rehearsing or not? Arscott and I have been waiting for hours.

RALPH. It seems interesting, I'll read it more carefully later.

WISEHAMMER. You don't like it.

RALPH. I do like it. Perhaps it needs a little more work. It's not Farquhar.

WISEHAMMER. It would mean more to the convicts.

RALPH. We'll talk about it another time.

WISEHAMMER. Do you think it should be longer?

RALPH. I'll think about it.

WISEHAMMER. Shorter? Do you like the last two lines? Mary helped me with them.

RALPH. Ah.

WISEHAMMER. The first lines took us days, didn't they, Mary?

RALPH. We'll rehearse Silvia's entrance as Jack Wilful. You're in the scene, Wisehammer. We'll come to your scenes in a minute, Bryant. Now, Brenham, remember what I showed you yesterday about walking like a gentleman? I've ordered breeches to be made for you, you can practise in them tomorrow.

MARY. I'll tuck my skirt in. (*She does so and takes a masculine pose.*) "Save ye, save ye, gentlemen."

WISEHAMMER. "My dear, I'm yours."

He kisses her.

RALPH (*angrily*). It doesn't say Silvia is kissed in the stage directions!

WISEHAMMER. Plume kisses her later and there's the line about men kissing in the army. I thought Brazen would kiss her immediately.

RALPH. It's completely wrong.

WISEHAMMER. It's right for the character of Brazen.

RALPH. No it isn't. I'm the director, Wisehammer.

WISEHAMMER. Yes, but I have to play the part. They're equal in this scene. They're both Captains and in the end fight for her. Who's playing Plume in our performance?

RALPH. I will have to, as Kable hasn't come back. It's your line.

WISEHAMMER. Will I be given a sword?

RALPH. I doubt it. Let's move on to Kite's entrance, Arscott has been waiting too long.

ARSCOTT (*delighted, launches straight in*). "Sir, if you please—"

RALPH. Excellent, Arscott, but we should just give you our last lines so you'll know when to come in. Wisehammer.

WISEHAMMER. "The fellow dare not fight."

RALPH. That's when you come in.

ARSCOTT. "Sir, if you please—"

DABBY. What about me? I haven't done anything either. You always rehearse the scenes with Silvia.

RALPH. Let's rehearse the scene where Rose comes on with her brother Bullock. It's a better scene for you Arscott. Do you know it?

ARSCOTT. Yes.

RALPH. Good. Wisehammer, you'll have to play the part of Bullock.

WISEHAMMER. What? Play two parts?

RALPH. Major Ross won't let any more prisoners off work. Some of you will have to play several parts.

WISEHAMMER. It'll confuse the audience. They'll think Brazen is Bullock and Bullock Brazen.

RALPH. Nonsense, if the audience is paying attention, they'll know that Bullock is a country boy and Brazen a Captain.

WISEHAMMER. What if they aren't paying attention?

RALPH. People who can't pay attention should not go to the theatre.

MARY. If you act well, they will have to pay attention.

WISEHAMMER. It will ruin my entrance as Captain Brazen.

RALPH. We have no choice and we must turn this necessity into an advantage. You will play two very different characters and display the full range of your abilities.

WISEHAMMER. Our audience won't be that discerning.

RALPH. Their imagination will be challenged and trained. Let's start the scene. Bryant?

DABBY. I think *The Recruiting Officer* is a silly play. I want to be in a play that has more interesting people in it.

MARY. I like playing Silvia. She's bold, she breaks rules out of love for her Captain and she's not ashamed.

DABBY. She hasn't been born poor, she hasn't had to survive, and her father's a Justice of the Peace. I want to play myself.

ARSCOTT. I don't want to play myself. When I say Kite's lines I forget everything else. I forget the judge said I'm going to have to spend the rest of my natural life in this place getting beaten and working like a slave. I can forget that out there it's trees and burnt grass, spiders that kill you in four hours and snakes. I don't have to think about what happened to Kable, I don't have to remember the things I've done, when I speak Kite's lines I don't hate any more. I'm Kite. I'm in Shrewsbury. Can we get on with the scene, Lieutenant, and stop talking?

DABBY. I want to see a play that shows life as we know it.

WISEHAMMER. A play should make you understand something new. If it tells you what you already know, you leave it as ignorant as you went in.

DABBY. Why can't we do a play about now?

WISEHAMMER. It doesn't matter when a play is set. It's better if it's set in the past, it's clearer. It's easier to understand Plume and Brazen than some of the officers we know here.

RALPH. Arscott, would you start the scene?

ARSCOTT. "Captain, Sir, look yonder, a-coming this way, 'tis the prettiest, cleanest, little tit."

RALPH. Now Worthy—He's in this scene. Where's Sideway?

MARY. He's so upset about Liz he won't rehearse.

RALPH. I am going to talk to the Governor, but he has to rehearse. We must do the play, whatever happens. We've been rehearsing for five months! Let's go on. "Here she comes, and what is that great country fellow with her?"

ARSCOTT. "I can't tell, Sir."

WISEHAMMER. I'm not a great country fellow.

RALPH. Act it, Wisehammer.

DABBY. "Buy chickens, young and tender, young and tender chickens." This is a very stupid line and I'm not saying it.

RALPH. It's written by the playwright and you have to say it. "Here, you chickens!"

DABBY. "Who calls?"

RALPH. Bryant, you're playing a pretty country wench who wants to entice the Captain. You have to say these lines with charm and euh—blushes.

DABBY. I don't blush.

RALPH. I can't do this scene without Sideway. Let's do another scene.

Pause.

Arscott, let's work on your big speeches, I haven't heard them yet. I still need Sideway. This is irresponsible, he wanted the part. Somebody go and get Sideway.

No one moves.

ARSCOTT. I'll do the first speech anyway, Sir. "Yes, Sir, I understand my business, I will say it; you must know, Sir, I was born a gypsy, and bred among that crew till I was ten years old, there I learned canting[31] and lying;—"

DABBY. That's about me!

ARSCOTT. "I was bought from my mother Cleopatra by a certain nobleman, for three guineas, who liking my beauty made me his page—"

DABBY. That's my story. Why do I have to play a silly milkmaid? Why can't I play Kite?

MARY. You can't play a man, Dabby.

DABBY. You're playing a man: Jack Wilful.

MARY. Yes, but in the play, I know I'm a woman, whereas if you played Kite, you would have to think you were a man.

DABBY. If Wisehammer can think he's a big country lad, I can think I'm a man. People will use their imagination and people with no imagination shouldn't go to the theatre.

RALPH. Bryant, you're muddling everything.

DABBY. No. I see things very clearly and I'm making you see clearly, Lieutenant. I want to play Kite.

ARSCOTT. You can't play Kite! I'm playing Kite! You can't steal my part!

RALPH. You may have to play Melinda.

DABBY. All she does is marry Sideway, that's not interesting.

Dabby stomps off. Ketch comes on.

KETCH. I'm sorry I'm late, Lieutenant, but I know all my lines.

RALPH. We'll rehearse the first scene between Justice Balance and Silvia. Brenham.

Arscott stomps off.

MARY. "Whilst there is life there is hope, Sir; perhaps my brother may recover."

---

[31]**canting** talking in the secret language of a group

KETCH. "We have but little reason to expect it—"

MARY. I can't. Not with him. Not with Liz—I can't.

She runs off.

RALPH. One has to transcend personal feelings in the theatre.

Wisehammer runs after Mary.

(*To Ketch.*) We're not making much progress today, let's end this rehearsal.

He goes. Ketch is left alone, bewildered.

SCENE 8

DUCKLING MAKES VOWS

Night. Harry, ill. Duckling.

DUCKLING. If you live, I will never again punish you with my silence. If you live, I will never again turn away from you. If you live, I will never again imagine another man when you make love to me. If you live, I will never tell you I want to leave you. If you live, I will speak to you. If you live, I will be tender with you. If you live, I will look after you. If you live, I will stay with you. If you live, I will be wet and open to your touch. If you live, I will answer all your questions. If you live, I will look at you. If you live, I will love you.

Pause.

If you die, I will never forgive you.

She leans over him. Listens. Touches. Harry is dead.

I hate you.

    No. I love you.

She crouches into a foetal position, cries out.

How could you do this?

SCENE 9

A LOVE SCENE

The beach. Night. Mary, then Ralph.

MARY (*to herself*). "Captain Plume, I despise your listing-money; if I do serve, 'tis purely for love—of that wench I mean. For you must know," etc—

    "So you only want an opportunity for accomplishing your designs upon her?"

    "Well, Sir, I'm satisfied as to the point in debate; but now let me beg you to lay aside your recruiting airs, put on the man of honour, and tell me plainly what usage I must expect when I'm under your command."

She tries that again, with a stronger and lower voice. Ralph comes on, sees her. She sees him, but continues.

"And something tells me, that if you do discharge me 'twill be the greatest punishment you can inflict; for were we this moment to go upon the greatest dangers in your profession, they would be less terrible to me than to stay behind you. And now your hand—this lists me—and now you are my Captain."

RALPH (*as Plume*). "Your friend." (*Kisses her.*) "'Sdeath! There's something in this fellow that charms me."

MARY. "One favour I must beg—this affair will make some noise—"

RALPH. Silvia—

He kisses her again.

MARY. "I must therefore take care to be impressed by the Act of Parliament—"

RALPH. "What you please as to that. Will you lodge at my quarters in the meantime? You shall have part of my bed." Silvia. Mary.

MARY. Am I doing it well? It's difficult to play a man. It's not the walk, it's the way you hold your head. A man doesn't bow his head so much and never at an angle. I must face you without lowering my head. Let's try it again.

RALPH. "What you please as to that.—Will you lodge at my quarters in the meantime? You shall have part of my bed." Mary!

She holds her head straight. Pause.

Will you?

Pause.

MARY. Yes.

They kiss.

RALPH. Don't lower your head. Silvia wouldn't.

She begins to undress, from the top.

I've never looked at the body of a woman before.

MARY. Your wife?

RALPH. It wasn't right to look at her.

    Let me see you.

MARY. Yes.

    Let me see you.

RALPH. Yes.

He begins to undress himself.

SCENE 10

THE QUESTION OF LIZ

Ralph, Ross, Phillip, Collins, Campbell.

COLLINS. She refused to defend herself at the trial. She didn't say a word. This was taken as an admission of guilt and she was condemned to be hanged. The evidence against her, however, is flimsy.

ROSS. She was seen with Kable next to the food stores. That is a fingering fact.

COLLINS. She was seen by a drunken soldier in the dark. He admitted he was drunk and that he saw her at a distance. He knew Kable was supposed to be repairing the door and she's known to be friends with Kable and Arscott. She won't speak, she won't say where she was. That is our difficulty.

ROSS. She won't speak because she's guilty.

PHILLIP. Silence has many causes, Robbie.

RALPH. She won't speak, Your Excellency, because of the convict code of honour. She doesn't want to beg for her life.

ROSS. Convict code of honour. This pluming play has muddled the muffy Lieutenant's mind.

COLLINS. My only fear, Your Excellency, is that she may have refused to speak because she no longer believes in the process of justice. If that is so, the courts here will become travesties. I do not want that.

PHILLIP. But if she won't speak, there is nothing more we can do. You cannot get at the truth through silence.

RALPH. She spoke to Harry Brewer.

PHILLIP. But Harry never regained consciousness before he died.

RALPH. James Freeman was there and told me what she said.

PHILLIP. Wasn't this used in the trial?

COLLINS. Freeman's evidence wasn't very clear and as Liz Morden wouldn't confirm what he said, it was dismissed.

ROSS. You can't take the word of a crooked crawling hangman.

PHILLIP. Why won't she speak?

ROSS. Because she's guilty.

PHILLIP. Robbie, we may be about to hang the first woman in this colony. I do not want to hang the first innocent woman.

RALPH. We must get at the truth.

ROSS. Truth! We have 800 thieves, perjurers, forgers, murderers, liars, escapers, rapists, whores, coiners in this scrub-ridden, dust-driven, thunder-bolted, savage-run, cretinous colony. My marines who are trained to fight are turned into gouly gaolers, fed less than the prisoners—

PHILLIP. The rations, Major, are the same for all, prisoners and soldiers.

ROSS. They have a right to more so that makes them have less. Not a ship shifting into sight, the prisoners running away, stealing, drinking and the wee ductile Lieutenant talks about the truth.

PHILLIP. Truth is indeed a luxury, but its absence brings about the most abject poverty in a civilisation. That is the paradox.

ROSS. This is a profligate prison for us all, it's a hellish hole we soldiers have been hauled to because they blame us for losing the war in America. This is a hateful, hary-scary, topsy-turvy outpost, this is not a civilisation. I hate this possumy place.

COLLINS. Perhaps we could return to the question of Liz Morden. (Calls.) Captain Campbell.

Campbell brings in Liz Morden.

Morden, if you don't speak, we will have to hang you; if you can defend yourself, His Excellency can overrule the court. We would not then risk a miscarriage of justice. But you must speak. Did you steal that food with the escaped prisoner Kable?

A long silence.

RALPH. She—

COLLINS. It is the accused who must answer.

PHILLIP. Liz Morden. You must speak the truth.

COLLINS. We will listen to you.

Pause.

RALPH. Morden. No one will despise you for telling the truth.

PHILLIP. That is not so, Lieutenant. Tell the truth and accept the contempt. That is the history of great men. Liz, you may be despised, but you will have shown courage.

RALPH. If that soldier has lied—

ROSS. There, there, he's accusing my soldiers of lying. It's that play, it makes fun of officers, it shows an officer lying and cheating. It shows a corrupt justice as well, Collins—

CAMPBELL. Good scene that, very funny, hah, scchhh.

COLLINS. Et tu,[32] Campbell?

CAMPBELL. What? Meant only. Hahah. If he be so good at gunning he shall have enough—he may be of use against the French, for he shoots flying, hahaha. Good, and then there's this Constable ha—

ROSS. Campbell!

PHILLIP. The play seems to be having miraculous effects already. Don't you want to be in it, Liz?

RALPH. Morden, you must speak.

COLLINS. For the good of the colony.

PHILLIP. And of the play.

A long silence.

LIZ. I didn't steal the food.

COLLINS. Were you there when Kable stole it?

LIZ. No. I was there before.

ROSS. And you knew he was going to steal it?

LIZ. Yes.

ROSS. Guilty. She didn't report it.

COLLINS. Failure to inform is not a hangable offence.

ROSS. Conspiracy.

COLLINS. We may need a retrial.

PHILLIP. Why wouldn't you say any of this before?

ROSS. Because she didn't have time to invent a lie.

COLLINS. Major, you are demeaning the process of law.

PHILLIP. Why, Liz?

LIZ. Because it wouldn't have mattered.

PHILLIP. Speaking the truth?

LIZ. Speaking.

---

[32]**Et tu** Latin for "and you," spoken by the dying Julius Caesar when he recognized Brutus among his assassins

ROSS. You are taking the word of a convict against the word of a soldier—

COLLINS. A soldier who was drunk and uncertain of what he saw.

ROSS. A soldier is a soldier and has a right to respect. You will have revolt on your hands, Governor.

PHILLIP. I'm sure I will, but let us see the play first. Liz, I hope you are good in your part.

RALPH. She will be, Your Excellency, I promise that.

LIZ. Your Excellency, I will endeavour to speak Mr Farquhar's lines with the elegance and clarity their own worth commands.

SCENE 11

BACKSTAGE

Night. The Aborigine.

THE ABORIGINE. Look: oozing pustules on my skin, heat on my forehead. Perhaps we have been wrong all this time and this is not a dream at all.

The Actors come on. They begin to change and make up. The Aborigine drifts off.

MARY. Are the savages coming to see the play as well?

KETCH. They come around the camp because they're dying: smallpox.

MARY. Oh.

SIDEWAY. I hope they won't upset the audience.

MARY. Everyone is here. All the officers too.

LIZ (*to Duckling*). Dabby could take your part.

DUCKLING. No. I will do it. I will remember the lines.

MARY. I've brought you an orange from Lieutenant Clark's island. They've thrown her out of Harry Brewer's tent.

WISEHAMMER. Why? He wouldn't have wanted that.

DUCKLING. Major Ross said a whore was a whore and I was to go into the women's camp. They've taken all of Harry's things.

She bursts into tears.

MARY. I'll talk to the Lieutenant.

LIZ. Let's go over your lines. And if you forget them, touch my foot and I'll whisper them to you.

SIDEWAY (*who has been practising on his own*). We haven't rehearsed the bow. Garrick used to take his this way: you look up to the circle,[33] to the sides, down, make sure everyone thinks you're looking at them. Get in a line.

They do so.

ARSCOTT. I'll be in the middle. I'm the tallest.

MARY. No, Arscott. (*Mary places herself in the middle.*)

[33]**the circle** the upper tier in a theater

SIDEWAY. Dabby, you should be next to Mary.

DABBY. I won't take the bow.

SIDEWAY. It's not the biggest part, Dabby, but you'll be noticed.

DABBY. I don't want to be noticed.

SIDEWAY. Let's get this right. If we don't all do the same thing, it will look a mess.

They try. Dabby is suddenly transfixed.

DABBY. Hurray, hurray, hurray.

SIDEWAY. No, they will be shouting bravo, but we're not in a line yet.

DABBY. I wasn't looking at the bow, I saw the whole play, and we all knew our lines, and Mary, you looked so beautiful, and after that, I saw Devon and they were shouting bravo, bravo Dabby, hurray, you've escaped, you've sailed thousands and thousands of miles on the open sea and you've come back to your Devon, bravo Dabby, bravo.

MARY. When are you doing this, Dabby?

DABBY. Tonight.

MARY. You can't.

DABBY. I'll be in the play till the end, then in the confusion, when it's over, we can slip away. The tide is up, the night will be dark, everything's ready.

MARY. The Lieutenant will be blamed, I won't let you.

DABBY. If you say anything to the Lieutenant, I'll refuse to act in the play.

ARSCOTT. When I say my lines, I think of nothing else. Why can't you do the same?

DABBY. Because it's only for one night. I want to grow old in Devon.

MARY. They'll never let us do another play, I'm telling the Lieutenant.

ALL. No, you're not.

DABBY. Please, I want to go back to Devon.

WISEHAMMER. I don't want to go back to England now. It's too small and they don't like Jews. Here, no one has more of a right than anyone else to call you a foreigner. I want to become the first famous writer.

MARY. You can't become a famous writer until you're dead.

WISEHAMMER. You can if you're the only one.

SIDEWAY. I'm going to start a theatre company. Who wants to be in it?

WISEHAMMER. I will write you a play about justice.

SIDEWAY. Only comedies, my boy, only comedies.

WISEHAMMER. What about a comedy about unrequited love?

LIZ. I'll be in your company, Mr Sideway.

KETCH. And so will I. I'll play all the parts that have dignity and gravity.

SIDEWAY. I'll hold auditions tomorrow.

DABBY. Tomorrow.

DUCKLING. Tomorrow.

MARY. Tomorrow.

LIZ. Tomorrow.

A long silence. (Un ange passe.)

MARY. Where are my shoes?

Ralph comes in.

RALPH. Arscott, remember to address the soldiers when you talk of recruiting. Look at them: you are speaking to them. And don't forget, all of you, to leave a space for people to laugh.

ARSCOTT. I'll kill anyone who laughs at me.

RALPH. They're not laughing at you, they're laughing at Farquhar's lines. You must expect them to laugh.

ARSCOTT. That's all right, but if I see Major Ross or any other officer laughing at me, I'll kill them.

MARY. No more violence. By the way, Arscott, when you carry me off the stage as Jack Wilful, could you be a little more gentle? I don't think he'd be so rough with a young gentleman.

RALPH. Where's Caesar?

KETCH. I saw him walking towards the beach earlier. I thought he was practising his lines.

ARSCOTT. Caesar!

He goes out.

WISEHAMMER (*to Liz*). When I say "Do you love fishing, Madam?", do you say something then?—

RALPH (*goes over to Duckling*). I am so sorry, Duckling. Harry was my friend.

DUCKLING. I loved him. But now he'll never know that. I thought that if he knew he would become cruel.

RALPH. Are you certain you don't want Dabby to take your part?

DUCKLING. No! I will do it. I want to do it.

Pause.

He liked to hear me say my lines.

RALPH. He will be watching from somewhere. (*He goes to Mary.*) How beautiful you look.

MARY. I dreamt I had a necklace of pearls and three children.

RALPH. If we have a boy we will call him Harry.

MARY. And if we have a girl?

RALPH. She will be called Betsey Alicia.

Arscott comes in with Caesar drunk and dishevelled.

ARSCOTT. Lying on the beach, dead drunk.

CAESAR (*to Ralph, pleading*). I can't. All those people. My ancestors are angry, they do not want me to be laughed at by all those people.

RALPH. You wanted to be in this play and you will be in this play—

KETCH. I'm nervous too, but I've overcome it. You have to be brave to be an actor.

CAESAR. My ancestors will kill me.

He swoons. Arscott hits him.

ARSCOTT. You're going to ruin my first scene.

CAESAR. Please, Lieutenant, save me.

RALPH. Caesar, if I were back home, I wouldn't be in this play either. My ancestors wouldn't be very pleased to see me here—But our ancestors are thousands of miles away.

CAESAR. I cannot be a disgrace to Madagascar.

ARSCOTT. You will be more of a disgrace if you don't come out with me on that stage. NOW.

MARY. Think of us as your family.

SIDEWAY (*to Ralph*). What do you think of this bow?

RALPH. Caesar, I am your Lieutenant and I command you to go on that stage. If you don't, you will be tried and hanged for treason.

KETCH. And I'll tie the rope in such a way you'll dangle there for hours full of piss and shit.

RALPH. What will your ancestors think of that, Caesar?

Caesar cries but pulls himself together.

KETCH (*to Liz*). I couldn't have hanged you.

LIZ. No?

RALPH. Dabby, have you got your chickens?

DABBY. My chickens? Yes. Here.

RALPH. Are you all right?

DABBY. Yes. (*Pause.*) I was dreaming.

RALPH. Of your future success?

DABBY. Yes. Of my future success.

RALPH. And so is everyone here, I hope. Now, Arscott.

ARSCOTT. Yes. Sir!

RALPH. Calm.

ARSCOTT. I have been used to danger, Sir.

SIDEWAY. Here.

LIZ. What's that?

SIDEWAY. Salt. For good luck.

RALPH. Where did you get that from?

SIDEWAY. I have been saving it from my rations. I have saved enough for each of us to have some.

They all take a little salt.

WISEHAMMER. Lieutenant?

RALPH. Yes, Wisehammer.

WISEHAMMER. There's—there's—

MARY. There's his prologue.

RALPH. The prologue. I forgot.

Pause.

Let me hear it again.

WISEHAMMER.

> From distant climes o'er wide-spread seas we come,
> Though not with much éclat or beat of drum,
> True patriots all; for be it understood,
> We left our country for our country's good;
> No private views disgraced our generous zeal,
> What urg'd our travels was our country's weal,
> And none will doubt but that our emigration
> Has prov'd most useful to the British nation.

Silence.

RALPH. When Major Ross hears that, he'll have an apoplectic fit.

MARY. I think it's very good.

DABBY. So do I. And true.

SIDEWAY. But not theatrical.

RALPH. It is very good, Wisehammer, it's very well written, but it's too—too political. It will be considered provocative.

WISEHAMMER. You don't want me to say it.

RALPH. Not tonight. We have many people against us.

WISEHAMMER. I could tone it down. I could omit "We left our country for our country's good."

DABBY. That's the best line.

RALPH. It would be wrong to cut it.

WISEHAMMER. I worked so hard on it.

LIZ. It rhymes.

SIDEWAY. We'll use it in the Sideway Theatre.

RALPH. You will get much praise as Brazen, Wisehammer.

WISEHAMMER. It isn't the same as writing.

RALPH. The theatre is like a small republic, it requires private sacrifices for the good of the whole. That is something you should agree with, Wisehammer.

Pause.

And now, my actors, I want to say what a pleasure it has been to work with you. You are on your own tonight and you must do your utmost to provide the large audience out there with a pleasurable, intelligible and memorable evening.

LIZ. We will do our best, Mr Clark.

MARY. I love this!

RALPH. Arscott.

ARSCOTT (*to Caesar*). You walk three steps ahead of me. If you stumble once, you know what will happen to you later? Move!

RALPH. You're on.

Arscott is about to go on, then remembers.

ARSCOTT. Halberd! Halberd!

He is handed his halberd and goes upstage and off, preceded by Caesar beating the drum. Backstage, the remaining actors listen with trepidation to Kite's first speech.

ARSCOTT. "If any gentlemen soldiers, or others, have a mind to serve Her Majesty, and pull down the French King; if any prentices have severe masters, any children have undutiful parents; if any servants have too little wages or any husband too much wife; let them repair to the noble Sergeant Kite, at the Sign of the Raven, in this good town of Shrewsbury, and they shall receive present relief and entertainment" . . .

And to the triumphant music of Beethoven's Fifth Symphony *and the sound of applause and laughter from the First Fleet audience, the first Australian performance of* The Recruiting Officer *begins.*

TOPICS FOR CRITICAL THINKING AND WRITING

📖 THE PLAY ON THE PAGE

1. What does Wertenbaker accomplish in the first three scenes of Act One?

2. Explain the pun in the title.

3. Offer a character analysis of Ralph Clark. How do Harry, Mary, and some of the other characters provide contrasts to Ralph? What does he learn about himself over the course of the play?

4. Why is Scene Six of Act One so important? What are the different reasons proposed for putting on a play?

5. Choose one of the shorter scenes, and describe its importance—in terms of theme and character to the overall play.

6. Although popular in the eighteenth century, George Farquhar's *The Recruiting Officer* is not often staged today. Relying merely on the scenes being rehearsed in *Our Country's Good*, what is your sense about the Farquhar play? Under the unusual circumstances at the prison colony, do you think it a "suitable" script? Does the process of rehearsing accomplish any of Governor Phillip's objectives?

7. Devise a thesis to explain the characterizations of Liz Morden and John Wisehammer.

8. Write an essay discussing the relationships between men and women throughout the play.

9. Scene Seven of Act Two is subtitled "The Meaning of Plays." Summarize the conflicts and emotions in this scene. Then, try to describe a few ways of interpreting "The Meaning of Plays." You may wish to include illustrations from a number of the plays in this volume of *Types of Drama.*

10. Do you find the appearances and speeches of the Aborigine necessary to the play, or are they a distraction? Explain your opinions.

11. Do you consider Governor Arthur Phillip the play's protagonist? If so, why? If not, propose an alternative. In either case, who or what serves as the play's antagonist?

♦♦ THE PLAY ON THE STAGE

12. In a number of the recent stagings of *Our Country's Good*, the officers have worn powdered wigs and well-tailored, red military jackets—in other words, the garb of a late eighteenth-century British soldier. The convicts, of course, have been dressed in virtual rags. Do you agree with this visual distinction? Or, Alterna should the officers' clothing appear almost as tattered as the convicts? Supply reasons for your opinions.

13. Choose one scene, and discuss the ways in which you would use lighting to create the appropriate dramatic effects.

14. Discuss costuming, blocking, and any special effects for the scenes in which the Aborigine appears.

15. Draw up a possible ten-person cast list—doubling and tripling roles will be necessary.

16. Which two consecutive scenes in *Our Country's Good* seem to you to be excellent examples of effective dra-matic contrast? What general techniques of blocking does your example prove?

17. When asked about her primary visual image for *Our Country's Good*, Wertenbaker replied, "A sandy beach." If you were the set designer, would you try to create a sandy beach? If so, how? If not, what alternative seems to you to be more effective?

18. To what extent would you simulate or suggest violence on stage? Give a specific example from one scene.

19. Choose three instances, from three different scenes, in which both Lieutenant Clark and Mary are on stage (alone or with other characters). Pretend that you are directing a production of *Our Country's Good*, and offer advice for the two actors. For example, on which words might there be eye contact or a glance or a voice change. Add any specifics that you wish.

THE PLAY IN PERFORMANCE

In 1988, two hundred years after the original fifteen hundred British convicts and their keepers—the founders of present-day Australia—landed at Botany Bay, London's Royal Court Theatre premiered Timberlake Wertenbaker's *Our Country's Good*. The circumstances of this first production are interesting. Wertenbaker had been commissioned by the theater to adapt Thomas Keneally's 1987 novel, *The Playmaker*, in order to commemorate the 1789 performance of *The Recruiting Officer* by a barely literate cast of convicts. The two plays, Wertenbaker's and Farquhar's, were performed in daily rotation by the Royal Court Theatre.

Preparation for the play involved weeks of improvisatory workshops for the dramatist and her actors, as well as a number of meetings with British prisoners. Wertenbaker's research included learning eighteenth-century slang and reading the diaries of convicts (past and present). Much of the script was written in three months, with another two months of additions and changes sparked by the rehearsal process. The Royal Court production subsequently played the British provinces, Toronto, Warsaw, and the West End (London's equivalent of Broadway) and won England's Olivier Award (equivalent to the Tony Award in the United States) for best play.

Our Country's Good premiered in the United States in 1989, with a mostly British production team at Los Angeles' Mark Taper Forum. The 1990–1991 season included full stagings by Repertory Theatre of St. Louis, Remains Theatre in Chicago, Hartford Stage Company, Berkeley Repertory Theatre, and Arena Stage in Washington, D.C. Since then the play has been offered each year by community, university, and professional companies nationwide. Edward Stern, who directed the production at the Repertory Theatre of St. Louis, comments on the play: "I was attracted by the way the play deals with issues that are so personal. The playwright steadfastly refuses to let the audience pigeonhole the play as a comedy, or history, or a straight drama." A number of directors, reviewers, and producers cited connections between national cutbacks to the arts and the uplifting message of *Our Country's Good*.

Obviously, *Our Country's Good* does not require a fussy or complicated set, for the Australian landscape of 1789 was bleak and barren. The play can be performed on a bare stage, and there are only a few necessary props. The original Royal Court double production (*Our Country's Good* and *The Recruiting Officer*) had only two hours between performances; the staging was Spartan, on a space about twenty-one feet across and twenty-three feet deep (with a seven-foot forestage area). Christopher Barreca, scenic designer for the Hartford production, devised three set elements: the beached shell of a ship, an overhanging forest of nooses, and a mud-colored and puddle-bespattered deck. Barreca commented that the ship conveyed both "romanticism and loss, a constant reminder that the convicts couldn't get away." Set changes were indicated only by lighting and simple furniture. For the rowing scene, a pair of oars was inserted in the center of the deck, and the actors positioned themselves as if in a dinghy.

Andrew Jackness, designer for the set at Repertory Theatre of St. Louis, raked his stage in order to provide a variety of acting areas and levels and to create the illusion of a distant horizon, which he dubbed, "[a] barrier to the beautiful sky beyond." He chose weathered wood for its texture and authenticity (aside from mud or sand, the eighteenth-century British colony had virtually no building materials at hand) and laid sections of twelve-inch boards at odd angles, "as though the floor had been upheaved and come together again." Because Jackness wanted actors, not props, to dominate the stage, he used only a few, simple objects—trestle tables, stools.

Hartwell, set designer for both the Royal Court and the Mark Taper productions, utilized one central element: a tan-colored ground cloth that covered the entire stage; the cloth was made of flax and painted to look like a cross between a beach and a moldy canvas sail. The cloth covered three low, boxlike shapes upstage—levels for sitting. The only furniture had a military look (folding chairs, crude table, a few crates, and barrels). Hartwell also created a strong vertical line by planting a ship's mast upstage, right of center.

And what of lighting for this play? Representing the pitiless, bleak landscape of Our Country's Good places complicated demands on a lighting designer. Kevin Rigdon (for the Mark Taper production in Los Angeles), for example, chose harsh and colorless lighting in order to replicate the searing Australian sunlight. Peter Kaczorowski (for the Repertory Theatre of St. Louis production) used strong banks of directional lights, relying on whites and steel blue tints. On the other hand, Mimi Jordan Sherin (for the Hartford production) did use color, including "bright oranges and really strong blues." In addition, the episodic nature of the script poses special challenges for a lighting team. Sherin commented that lighting "is the key to swift movement"; she tried to make the transitions interesting and clear by alternating between creating a sense of a big space and a sense of a small space. For the last scene, when the convicts make

their entrance in The Recruiting Officer, all the productions managed to simulate some kind of footlights—the sparkle and brightness very appropriate to the play's exuberant conclusion.

A lone aborigine recurs in the script. The person is both a witness to the arrival of the British and, ultimately, a victim of their imperialism. Andrew Jackness (at St. Louis) sought to portray this figure as spectral, always seen in silhouette, always heard as a voice-over.

Because the historical convicts arrived in tatters, costume designers for Our Country's Good have dressed the actors and actresses in appropriately seedy clothing: plain fabrics, begrimed uniforms, undergarments, makeshift accessories. Many of the convicts are shoeless. Candice Donnelly (for the St. Louis production) researched the lower-class images of Hogarth and other late eighteenth-century artists. She stated, "The officers as well as the prisoners should be disheveled and dirty because of the blurred distinctions between convicts and jailers created by their isolated situation."

Finally, a word needs to be said about the characters themselves. A cast of ten (four women and six men) plays twenty-two roles. Except for the role of Second Lieutenant Ralph Clark, played by one actor, all others are double or triple cast. For example, in the Repertory Theatre of St. Louis staging, one actress played Mary Brenham (a key role), Meg Long, and Lieutenant Will Dawes; one actor played Black Caesar, Captain Watkin Tench, and the Aborigine.

The above quotations are taken from Michele La Rue's thorough discussion of three stagings of Our Country's Good. We recommend her article to students interested in further details (Theatre Arts, March 1991). Reviews of the Royal Court Theatre production are reprinted in London Theatre Record for September 9–22, 1988, and July 30–August 12, 1989.

PART THREE

Writing

WRITING ABOUT DRAMA

BASIC MATTERS

Why Write?

People write about plays because they to clarify and to account for their responses to works that interest, excite, or frustrate them. In order to put words on paper, we have to take a second and a third look at what is in front of us and at what is within us. Writing, then is a way of learning. The last word is never said about complex thoughts and feelings, but when we write, we hope to make at least a little progress in the difficult but rewarding job of talking about our responses. We learn, and then we hope to interest our reader because we are communicating our responses to something that for one reason or another is worth talking about.

This communication is, in effect, teaching. You may think that you are writing for the teacher, but such a belief is a misconception; when you write, *you* are the teacher. An essay on a play is an attempt to help someone see the play as you do. If this chapter had to be boiled down to a single sentence of advice, that sentence would be: Because you are teaching, your essay should embody those qualities that you value in teachers—probably intelligence, open-mindedness, effort, and certainly a desire to offer what help you can.

Analysis

Analysis is, literally, a separation into parts in order to understand. An analysis commonly considers one part and the relation of this part to the whole. For example, it may consider only the functions of the setting in *The Sandbox*, of the Fool in *King Lear*, or of the music in *Happy Days*.

Analysis is not a process used only in talking about literature. It is commonly applied in thinking about almost any complex matter. Steffi Graf plays a deadly game of tennis; what makes it so good? How does her backhand contribute to her game? What does her serve do to the opponent? Because a play is usually long and complicated, in a paper written for a college course you probably do not have enough space to analyze all aspects of the play, and so you will probably choose only one and relate it to the whole. Of course, all of the parts are related; a study of one character, for example, will have to take some account of other characters and of the plot and perhaps even of the setting. Nevertheless, an analysis may legitimately devote most of its space to one part, taking account of other parts only insofar as they are relevant to the topic.

Finding a Topic

If a work is fairly long and complex and if you are writing only a few pages, almost surely you will write an analysis of some part. Unless you have an enormous amount of time for reflection and revision, you cannot write a meaningful essay of five hundred or even a thousand words on *Oedipus* or *The Cherry Orchard*. You cannot even write on "Character in *Oedipus*" or "Symbolism in *The Cherry Orchard*." In any case, you probably won't want to write on such topics anyway. Probably *one* character or *one* symbol has caught your interest. Trust your feelings; you are probably onto something interesting, and it will be best to think about this smaller topic for the relatively few hours that you have.

A "smaller" topic need not be dull or trivial; treated properly, it may illuminate the entire work, or, to change the metaphor, it may serve as a mine shaft that gives entry to the work. "The Dramatic Function of the Gloucester Subplot in *King Lear*," carefully thought about, will in five hundred or a thousand words tell a reader more (and will have taught its author more) than will "*King Lear* as a Tragedy." Similarly, "Imagery of Blindness in *King Lear*" is a better topic than "Imagery in *King Lear*," and "The Meanings of 'Nature' in *King Lear*" is a better topic than "The Meaning of *King Lear*."

Every play affords its own topics for analysis, and every essayist must set forth his or her own thesis, but a few useful generalizations may be made. You can often find a thesis by asking one of two questions:

- **What is this doing?** That is, why is this scene in the play? Why is the Fool in *King Lear*? Why the music in *Happy Days*? Why are these lines verse and those lines prose? Why is a certain action reported to us rather than represented on the stage? What is the significance of the parts of the work? (Titles are often highly significant parts of the work: Ibsen's *A Doll's House* and Chekhov's *The Cherry Orchard* would be slightly different if they had other titles.)
- **Why do I have this response?** Why do I find this scene clever, moving, or puzzling? How did the author make this character funny, dignified, or pathetic? How did he or she communicate the idea that this character is a bore without boring me?

The first of these questions, "What is this doing?" requires that you identify yourself with the dramatist, wondering, for example, whether this opening scene is the best possible for this story. The second question, "Why do I have this response?" requires that you trust your feelings. If you are amused, bored, puzzled, or annoyed, assume that these responses are appropriate and follow them up, at least until a rereading of the play provides other responses.

On pages 1046–1048 we suggest many questions that you can ask yourself in order to stimulate ideas for an essay, but here we briefly suggest a few topics:

- Compare two somewhat similar characters.
- Discuss the function of a relatively minor character.

- Compare a play with a film version of the play (what has been added, what omitted, and why?).
- Write the director's notes for one scene.

From Topic to Thesis

How do you find a topic and then turn it into a thesis, that is, a point you want to make? An idea may hit you suddenly. For example, as you are reading you may find yourself jotting in the margin, "Contrast with Nora's earlier response," or "Note the change of costume," or "too heavy irony," or "ugh." Alternatively, an idea may come slowly on rereading. For example, perhaps you gradually become aware that in *Antigone* the chorus may not be a static character but changes its views as the play progresses. At this point, then, you have a thesis—an angle—as well as a topic.

Think of it this way: A topic is a subject, and a thesis is an assertion about a subject. "Imagery in *King Lear*" is a topic, but it can be turned into a thesis thus: "Imagery helps to distinguish the characters in *King Lear*." Once you can formulate a thesis, you are well on the way to writing a good paper. Note that the more precise the formulation of the thesis, the better the paper will probably be. After all, "Imagery in *King Lear* is interesting" is a thesis, but such a vague assertion gives you little to go on. Not until you can turn it into something such as "Imagery in *King Lear* serves three important purposes" are you anywhere near being able to draft your essay.

Following is a short essay written by a student. The student told us privately that when she began work on the paper she was planning to write on the irrationality of the fairies in *A Midsummer Night's Dream* as a sort of mirror of the irrationality of the young lovers, but when she searched

the play for supporting detail she found, to her surprise, that she had to revise her thesis.

Her earliest jottings—a sort of preliminary outline and guide to rereading the play—looked like this:

> fairies--like lovers, irrational?
>   Puck
>   mischievous
>   Titania and Oberon
>   equally quarrelsome?
>   quarrel disturbs human world
>   Titania wants Indian boy
>   isn't she right?
>   if so, she's not irrational
>   Oberon
>   jealous
>   cruel to Titania?
>   unfaithful?
>   Other fairies
>   do they do anything?
>   T's different from O's?

In rereading the play and in jotting down notes, she came to see that the supernatural characters were not as malicious and irrational as she had thought, and so she changed the focus of her thesis. She wrote her notes on 3-by-5-inch index cards, but many students prefer to use a word processor. Beginning on page 1049 we offer suggestions about using a word processor.

A Sample Analysis

Title is informative.

Opening paragraph leads into the subject.

> Fairy Mischief and Morality and
>
> A Midsummer Night's Dream
>
>   If we read A Midsummer Night's Dream casually, or
> come away from a delightful performance, we may have the
> vague impression that the fairies are wild, mischievous,
> willful creatures who perhaps represent the irrational quali-
> ties of mankind. But in fact the text lends only a little
> support to this view. The irrationality of mankind is really
> represented chiefly by the human beings in the play--we are
> told in the first scene, for example, that Demetrius used to
> love Helena, but now loves Hermia--and the fairies are really
> largely responsible for the happy ending finally achieved.

It is, of course, easy to see why we may think of the fairies as wild and mischievous. Titania and Oberon have quarreled over a little Indian boy, and their quarrel has led to fogs, floods, and other disorders in nature. Moreover, Titania accuses Oberon of infidelity, and Oberon returns the charge:

> How canst thou thus for shame, Titania
> Glance at my credit with Hippolyta,
> Knowing I know thy love to Theseus?
> (2.1.74-76)[1]

Short quotation provides evidence.

Titania rejects this countercharge, saying "These are the forgeries of jealousy" (2.1.81), but we are not convinced of her innocence. It would be easy to give additional examples of speeches in which the king and queen of fairyland present unflattering pictures of each other, but probably one of the strongest pieces of evidence of their alleged irrationality is the fact that Oberon causes Titania to fall in love with the asinine Bottom. We should not forget, however, that later Oberon will take pity on her: "Her dotage now I do begin to pity" (4.1.46).

Citation in parentheses reduces the number of footnotes.

In fact, it is largely through Oberon's sense of pity--this time for the quarreling young lovers in the forest--that the lovers finally are successfully paired off. And we should remember, too, before we claim that the fairies are consistently quarrelsome and mischievous, that at the very end of the play Oberon and Titania join in a song and dance blessing the newlyweds and promising healthy offspring. The fairies, though quarrelsome, are fundamentally benevolent spirits.

But what of Robin Goodfellow, the Puck of this play? Is he not mischievous? One of the fairies says Robin is a "shrewd and knavish sprite" (2.1.33) who frightens maids and plays tricks on housewives; Robin admits the charge, saying

The main point having been set forth, essayist now turns to an apparent exception.

Essayist concedes a point but then goes on in the rest of the paragraph to argue that the main point nevertheless still holds.

[1]All quotations from this play are from the text reprinted in Sylvan Barnet et al., <u>Types of Drama</u>, 7th ed. (New York: Longman, 1997). Further references to the play will be given parenthetically, within the text of the essay.

Footnote gives source and explains that other footnotes will not be necessary.

"Thou speakest aright" (2.1.42), and two lines later he says "I jest to Oberon, and make him smile," and then he goes on to describe some of his practical jokes, including his fondness for neighing to tease a horse, and pulling a stool from under an old lady. But this is not quite the whole story. The fact is, despite this speech, that we do not see Robin engage in any mischievous pranks. After all, he does not deliberately anoint the eyes of the wrong Athenian lover. Oberon tells Robin that he will recognize the young man by his Athenian clothing, and when Puck encounters a young man in Athenian clothing he anoints the youth's eyes. The fault is really Oberon's, though of course Oberon meant well when he instructed Robin:

> A sweet Athenian lady is in love
> With a disdainful youth. Anoint his eyes;
> But do it when the next thing he espies
> May be the lady.
>
> (2.1.260-263)

So Robin's error is innocent. He is speaking honestly when he says, "Believe me, king of shadows, I mistook" (3.2.347). Of course he does enjoy the confusion he mistakenly causes, but we can hardly blame him severely for that. After all, we enjoy it, too.

The fairies, by their very nature, of course suggest a mysterious, irrational world, but--even though, as we have just seen, Oberon is called the "king of shadows"--they are not to be confused with "ghosts, wand'ring here and there," "damnèd spirits" who "willfully themselves exile from light/ And must for aye consort with black-browed night" (3.2.386-392). Oberon explicitly says, after this speech, "But we are spirits of another sort," and his speech is filled with references not to darkness but to light: "morning," "eastern gate," "blessèd beams." The closer we observe them in the play, then, the closer their behavior is to that of normal, decent human beings. There is plenty of irrationality in the play, but it is found for the most part in the mortals.

Concluding paragraph summarizes, but it does not merely repeat what has come before; it offers a few brief new quotations. The paragraph ends by setting the conclusion (fairies are decent) in a fresh context (it's the mortals who are irrational).

Notice that this first-rate essay:

- Has a thesis
- Develops the thesis effectively

Notice also that:

- The title gives the reader some idea of what is coming.
- The first paragraph clearly sets forth the thesis.
- The essay next takes up the evidence that might seem to contradict the thesis—Oberon and Titania, and Robin Goodfellow—and it shows that this evidence is not decisive.
- The essay continues to move the thesis forward, substantiating it, especially with well-chosen quotations.
- The last paragraph slightly restates the thesis in light of what the essay has demonstrated.

Writing a Review

Your instructor may ask you to write a review of a local production. A review requires analytic skill, but it is not identical to an analysis. First of all, a reviewer normally assumes that the reader is unfamiliar with the production being reviewed and unfamiliar with the play if the play is not a classic. Thus, the first paragraph usually provides a helpful introduction, such as the following:

> Marsha Norman's new play, 'night, Mother, a tragedy with only two actors and one set, shows us a woman's preparation for suicide. Jessie has concluded that she no longer wishes to live, and so she tries to put her affairs into order, which chiefly means preparing her rather uncomprehending mother to get along without her.

Inevitably some retelling of the plot is necessary if the play is new, and a summary of a sentence or two is acceptable even for a familiar play. However, the focus of the review is on:

- Describing
- Analyzing
- Evaluating (most especially)

(By the way, don't confuse description with analysis. Description tells what something—for instance, the set or the cos-tumes—looks like; analysis tells how it works, what it adds up to, and what it contributes to the total effect.) If the play is new, much of the evaluation may center on the play itself, but if the play is a classic, the evaluation probably will be devoted chiefly to the acting, the set, and the direction.

Here are other points to consider:

- **Save the playbill;** it will give you the names of the actors, and perhaps a brief biography of the author, a synopsis of the plot, and a photograph of the set, all of which may be helpful.
- **Draft your review as soon as possible,** while the performance is still fresh in your mind. If you can't draft it immediately after seeing the play, at least jot down some notes about the setting and the staging, the acting, and the audience's response.
- If possible, **read the play**—ideally, before the performance and again after it.
- **In your first draft, don't worry about limitations of space;** write as long a review as you can, putting down everything that comes to mind. Later you can cut it to the required length, retaining only the chief points and the necessary supporting details. In your first draft, try to produce a fairly full record of the performance and your response to it, so that a day or two later, when you are working on a revision, you won't have to trust a fading memory for details.

If you read reviews of plays in Time, Newsweek, or a newspaper, you will soon develop a sense of what reviews normally do.

The following example, an undergraduate's review of a college production of Macbeth, is typical except in one respect: Because Macbeth is so widely known, the reviewer has chosen not to risk offending her readers by telling them that Macbeth is a tragedy by Shakespeare. If it were a review of a new play it would customarily include a few sentences summarizing the plot and classifying the play (a tragedy, a farce, a rock musical, or whatever), perhaps briefly putting it into the context of the author's other works.

A Sample Review

An Effective Macbeth

Title implies thesis.

Macbeth at the University Theater is a thoughtful and occasionally exciting production, partly because the director, Mark Urice, has trusted Shakespeare and has not imposed a gimmick on the play. The characters do not wear cowboy costumes as they did in last year's production of A Midsummer Night's Dream.

Opening paragraph is informative, letting the reader know the reviewer's overall attitude.

Probably the chief problem confronting a director of Macbeth is how to present the witches so that they are pow-

Reviewer promptly turns to a major issue.

erful supernatural forces and not silly things that look as though they came from a Halloween party. Urice gives us ugly but not absurdly grotesque witches, and he introduces them most effectively. The stage seems to be a bombed-out battlefield littered with rocks and great chunks of earth, but some of these begin to stir--the earth seems to come alive-- and the clods move, unfold, and become the witches, dressed in brown and dark gray rags. The suggestion is that the witches are a part of nature, elemental forces that can hardly be escaped. This effect is increased by the moans and creaking noises that they make, all of which could be comic but which in this production are impressive.

The witches' power over Macbeth is further emphasized by their actions. When the witches first meet Macbeth, they encircle him, touch him, caress him, even embrace him, and he seems helpless, almost their plaything. Moreover, in the scene in which he imagines that he sees a dagger, the director has arranged for one of the witches to appear, stand near Macbeth, and guide his hand toward the invisible dagger. This is, of course, not in the text, but the interpretation is reasonable rather than intrusive. Finally, near the end of the play, just before Macduff kills Macbeth, a witch appears and laughs at Macbeth as Macduff explains that he was not "born of woman." There is no doubt that throughout the tragedy Macbeth has been a puppet of the witches.

First sentence of this paragraph provides an effective transition.

Stephen Beers (Macbeth) and Tina Peters (Lady Macbeth) are excellent. Beers is sufficiently brawny to be convincing as a battlefield hero, but he also speaks the lines sensitively, so the audience feels that in addition to being a hero, he is a man of gentleness. One can believe Lady Macbeth when she says that she fears he is "too full o' the milk of human kindness" to murder Duncan. Lady Macbeth is especially effective in the scene in which she asks the spirits to "unsex her." During this speech she is reclining on a bed and as she delivers the lines she becomes increasingly sexual in her bodily motions, deriving excitement from her own stimulating words. Her attachment to Macbeth is strongly sexual, and so is his attraction to her. The scene when she persuades him to kill Duncan ends with them passionately em-

Paragraph begins with a broad assertion and then offers supporting details.

Reference is made to a particular scene.

bracing. The strong attraction of each for the other, so evident in the early part of the play, disappears after the murder, when Macbeth keeps his distance from Lady Macbeth and does not allow her to touch him. The acting of the other performers is effective, except for John Berens (Duncan), who recites the lines mechanically and seems not to take much account of their meaning.

Reviewer provides description and analysis.

The set consists of a barren plot at the rear of which stands a spidery framework of piping of the sort used by construction companies, supporting a catwalk. This framework fits with the costumes (lots of armor, leather, heavy boots), suggesting a sort of elemental, primitive, and somewhat sadistic world. The catwalk, though effectively used when Macbeth goes off to murder Duncan (whose room is presumably upstairs and offstage) is not much used in later scenes. For the most part it is an interesting piece of scenery but it is not otherwise helpful. For instance, there is no reason why the scene with Macduff's wife and children is staged on it. The costumes are not in any way Scottish—no plaids—but in several scenes the sound of a bagpipe is heard, adding another weird or primitive tone to the production.

Concrete details support evaluation.

This <u>Macbeth</u> appeals to the eye, the ear, and the mind. The director has given us a unified production that makes sense and that is faithful to the spirit of Shakespeare's play.

Summary is given.

Much of what we want to say about this review we have already said in our marginal notes, but three additional points should be made:

• The reviewer's feelings and evaluations are clearly expressed, not in such expressions as "furthermore, I feel," or "it is also my opinion," but in such expressions as "a thoughtful and occasionally exciting production," "excellent," and "appeals to the eye, the ear, and the mind."
• The evaluations are supported by details. For instance, the evaluation that the witches are effectively presented is supported by a brief description of their appearance.
• The reviewer is courteous, even when (as in the discussion of the catwalk, in the next-to-last paragraph) she is talking about aspects of the production she doesn't care for.

Writing a Comparison

Something should be said about an essay organized around a comparison or a contrast between, for example, two characters (in one play or even in two plays). Probably a student's first thought, after making some notes, is to discuss half of the comparison and then go on to the second half. Instructors and textbooks usually condemn such an organization, arguing that the essay breaks into two parts and that the second part involves a good deal of repetition of categories set up in the first part. Usually they recommend that the student organize his or her thoughts differently, somewhat along these lines:

1. First similarity
   a. First work (or character, or characteristic)

    b. Second work
2. Secondary similarity
    a. First work
    b. Second work
3. First difference
    a. First work
    b. Second work
4. Second difference
    a. First work
    b. Second work

The pattern would continue for as many additional differences as are considered relevant. For example, if one wishes to compare King Lear with King Oedipus, one may organize the material in this way:

1. Each figure is a person of great authority (first similarity)
    a. Lear
    b. Oedipus
2. Each figure is ignorant (second similarity)
    a. Lear's ignorance of his daughters
    b. Oedipus's ignorance of his birth
3. Stage at which the character attains self-knowledge (first difference)
    a. Lear's early recognition
    b. Oedipus's continuing ignorance until late in the play

Another way of organizing a comparison and contrast is to do so by presenting the information one point at a time. For example, if we use the same example that focuses on King Lear and King Oedipus, the organization of the material might look like this:

1. Lack of self-knowledge (first point)
    a. Similarities between Lear and Oedipus
    b. Differences between Lear and Oedipus
2. The corrupt world (second point)
    a. Similarities between the worlds in *King Lear* and *Oedipus*
    b. Differences between the worlds in *King Lear* and *Oedipus*
3. Degree of attainment of self-knowledge (third point)
    a. Similarities between Lear and Oedipus
    b. Differences between Lear and Oedipus

A Simple, Effective Organization for a Comparison

However, a comparison need not employ either of these structures. There is even the danger that an essay employing either of them may not come into focus until the essayist stands back from the seven-layer cake and announces, in the concluding paragraph, that the odd layers taste better. In your preparatory thinking, you may want to make comparisons in pairs (Faults: Lear and Oedipus; Children: Lear's daughters, Oedipus's sons; Comments by others: the Fool on Lear, the Chorus on Oedipus . . .), but you must come to

some conclusions about what these add up to before writing the final version. This final version should not duplicate your thought processes; rather, it should be organized to make the point clearly and effectively. After reflection, you may believe that although there are superficial similarities between Lear and Oedipus, there are essential differences; then in the finished essay you probably will not wish to obscure the main point by jumping back and forth from play to play, working through a series of similarities and differences. It may be better to discuss King Lear and then point out that, although Oedipus resembles him in *A, B,* and *C,* Oedipus in *D, E,* and *F* does *not* resemble Lear. Some repetition in the second half of the essay (for example, "Oedipus comes very late to the deep self-knowledge that we see Lear achieve by the middle of the play") will serve to bind the two halves into a meaningful whole, making clear the degree of similarity or difference.

The point of the essay presumably is not to list pairs of similarities or differences but to illuminate a work, or works, by making a thoughtful comparison. Although in a long essay you cannot postpone until page 30 a discussion of the second half of the comparison, in an essay of, say, fewer than ten pages nothing is wrong with setting forth the first half of the comparison and then, in light of it, the second half. The essay will break into two unrelated parts if the second half makes no use of the first or if it fails to modify the first half, but this will not happen if the second half looks back to the first half and calls attention to differences that the new material reveals.

Communicating Judgments

Because a critical essay on a play is a judicious attempt to help a reader understand what is going on in a work or in a part of a work, the voice of the critic sounds, on first hearing, impartial. However, good criticism includes—at least implicitly—evaluation. You can say not only that the setting changes (a neutral expression) but also that "the playwright aptly shifts the setting" or "unconvincingly introduces a new character," or "effectively juxtaposes . . ." Support these evaluations with evidence. As we have already pointed out in our discussion of the review of *Macbeth,* reveal your feelings about the work under discussion, not by continually saying "I feel" and "this moves me," but by calling attention to the degree of success or failure you perceive. Nothing is wrong with occasionally using "I." In fact, noticeable avoidance of it—using instead passives such as "this writer," "we," and the like—suggests an offensive sham modesty, but too much talk of "I" makes a writer sound like an egomaniac.

Asking Questions to Get Answers

The next two pages are devoted to helping you to find topics to write about. We have already suggested that you can often find a thesis by asking two questions: "What is this doing?"

and "Why do I have this response?" In the sections following we suggest many additional questions, but first we want to mention that the editorial apparatus throughout this book is intended to help you to read, enjoy, and discuss drama as fully as possible. When you are sitting down to write about a play, you may want to reread some parts of this apparatus for guidance on your topic, perhaps paying special attention to the Glossary entries on **character, convention, dialogue, diction, foil, irony, motivation, plot, suspense,** and **unity.** You may also want to reread some of the earlier material in the book, especially "The Language of Drama" and the questions that follow each play.

Following are additional questions that may help you to find topics and to sharpen them into these.

Plot and Conflict

• Does the exposition introduce elements that will be ironically fulfilled? During the exposition, do you perceive things differently from the way the characters do?

• Are certain happenings or situations recurrent? If so, what significance do you attach to them?

• If there is more than one plot, do the plots seem to you to be related? Is one plot clearly the main plot and another plot a sort of subplot, a minor variation on the theme?

• Do any scenes strike you as irrelevant?

• Are certain scenes so strongly foreshadowed that you anticipated them? If so, did the happenings in these scenes merely fulfill your expectations, or did they also in some way surprise you?

• What kinds of conflict are there—for example, one character against another, one group against another, one part of a personality against another part in the same person?

• How is the conflict resolved? Is it resolved by an unambiguous triumph of one side or by a triumph that is also in some degree a loss for the triumphant side? Do you find the resolution satisfying, unsettling, or what? Why?

Character

• A dramatic character is not likely to be thoroughly realistic, a copy of someone we might know. Still, we can ask whether the character is consistent and coherent. We can also ask whether the character is complex or is, on the other hand, a rather simple representative of some human type.

• How is the character defined? Consider what the character says and does and what others say about him or her and do to him or her. Also consider other characters who more or less resemble the character in question, because the similarities—and the differences—may be significant.

• How trustworthy are the characters when they characterize themselves? when they characterize others?

• Do characters change as the play goes on, or do we simply know them better at the end?

• What do you make of the minor characters? Are they merely necessary to the plot, or are they foils to other characters? Do they perhaps serve some other functions?

• If a character is tragic, does the tragedy seem to you to proceed from a moral flaw, from an intellectual error, from the malice of others, from sheer chance, or from some combination of these?

• What are the character's goals? To what degree do you sympathize with them? If a character is comic, do you laugh *with* or *at* the character?

• Do you think the characters are adequately motivated?

• Is a given character so meditative that you feel he or she is engaged less in a dialogue with others than in a dialogue with the self? If so, do you feel that this character is in large degree a spokesperson for the author, commenting not only on the world of the play but also on the outside world?

Tragedy

• What causes the tragedy? Is it a flaw in the central character? a mistake (*not* the same thing as a flaw) made by this character? an outside force, such as another character or fate?

• Is the tragic character defined partly by other characters, for instance by characters who help us to sense what the character *might* have done, or who in some other way reveal the strengths or weaknesses of the protagonist?

• Does a viewer know more than the tragic figure knows? more than most or all of the characters know?

• Does the tragic character achieve any sort of wisdom at the end of the play?

• To what degree do you sympathize with the tragic character?

• Is the play depressing? If not, why not?

Comedy

• Do the comic complications arise chiefly out of the personalities of the characters (for instance, pretentiousness or amorousness) or out of the situations (for instance, mistaken identity)?

• What are the chief goals of the figures? Do we sympathize with these goals, or do we laugh at persons who pursue them? If we laugh, *why* do we laugh?

• What are the personalities of those who oppose the central characters? Do we laugh at them, or do we sympathize with them?

• What is funny about the play? Is the comedy high (including verbal comedy) or chiefly situational and physical?

• Is the play predominantly genial, or is there a strong satiric tone?

• Does the comedy have any potentially tragic elements in it? Might the plot be slightly rewritten so that it would become a tragedy?

• What, if anything, do the characters learn by the end of the play?

Nonverbal Language

• If the playwright does not provide full stage directions, try to imagine for at least one scene what gestures, facial expressions, and tones might accompany each speech. Consider, too, pauses that characters might make in delivering speeches.

• Consider the physical positions characters take on the stage in relationship to other characters.
• What do you make of the setting? Does it help to reveal character? Do changes of scene strike you as symbolic? If so, symbolic of what?
• Do certain costumes (dark suits, flowery shawls, stiff collars, etc.) or certain properties (books, pictures, toys, candlesticks, etc.) strike you as symbolic? If so, symbolic of what?

The Play on Film

Often we can gain a special pleasure from, or insight into, a dramatic work when we actually see it produced onstage or made into a film. This manifestation gives us an opportunity to think about the choices that the director has made, and, even more, it may prompt us to imagine and ponder how we would direct the play for the theater or make a film version of it ourselves.

• If you have seen the play in a film version, what has been added? What has been omitted? Why?
• In the case of a film, has the film medium been used to advantage—for example, in focusing attention through close-ups or reaction shots (shots showing not the speaker but a person reacting to the speaker)?
• Do certain plays seem to be especially suited—maybe *only* suited—to the stage? Would they not work effectively as films? Is the reverse true—that is, are some plays best presented and best understood when they are done as films?
• Critics have sometimes said about this or that play that it cannot really be staged successfully or presented well on film—that the best way to appreciate and understand it is as something to be *read*, such as a poem or novel. Are there plays you have studied for which this observation appears to be true? Which features of the work—its characters, settings, dialogue, central themes—might make it difficult to transfer the play from the page to the movie screen or to the stage?
• Imagine that you are directing a film version. What would be the important decisions you would have to make about character, setting, and pacing of the action? Would you be inclined to omit certain scenes? Would you, alternatively, add new scenes that are not in the work itself? What kinds of advice would you give to the performers about their roles?

Organizing an Essay

Like a play, an essay on a play should be organized, and one can hardly go wrong in saying (as Aristotle said of plays) that an essay should have a beginning, a middle, and an end.

In the *beginning*, probably in the first paragraph, it's usually a good idea to state your thesis. You don't have to state it in the first sentence (you may, for example, want to open with a quotation from the play), but state it early and clearly.

In the *middle*, support your thesis with evidence, probably including some brief quotations from the play. The middle, like the essay as a whole, should be organized. For example, if you are discussing the development of a character, you will probably want to move through the play act by act. If you are discussing symbolism—maybe blindness in *King Lear*—you may first want to discuss literal blindness (Gloucester's eyes are put out) and then figurative blindness (Lear doesn't "see" what he is doing). Probably you'll move from the obvious to the less obvious or from the less important to the more important in order to avoid a sense of anticlimax.

In the *end*, or conclusion, it's helpful to recapitulate briefly, but try also (lest your conclusion strike the reader as nothing more than an unnecessary restatement of what you said a moment ago) to set your findings in a larger context, the context of the entire play.

Summary: How to Write an Effective Essay

All writers must work out their own procedures and rituals (John C. Calhoun liked to plough his farm before writing), but the following suggestions provide some help.

If you use a word processor (and we hope that you do, because it makes the job of writing easier), we suggest that you read these pages even though they assume that the writer is using pen and index cards. For further suggestions, read "Suggestions for Writing with a Word Processor," page 1049.

1. **Read the play carefully.**
2. **Choose a worthwhile and manageable topic,** something that interests you and is not so big that your handling of it must be superficial. As you work, shape your topic into a thesis, moving, for example, from "The Character of King Lear" to "Change in King Lear."
3. **Reread the play, jotting down notes** of all relevant matters. As you read, reflect on your reading and record your reflections. If you have a feeling or an idea, jot it down; don't assume that you will remember it when you get around to writing your essay. The margins of this book are a good place for initial notes, but many people find that in the long run it is best to transfer these notes to 3-by-5-inch cards, writing on one side only. (Easiest of all is to use a word processor.)
4. **Sort out your cards** into some kind of reasonable division, and reject cards irrelevant to your topic. If you have adequately formulated your thesis (for example, "Tom, not Laura, is the central character in *The Glass Menagerie*"), you ought to be able to work out a tentative organization. As you work you may discover a better way to group your notes. If so, start reorganizing. Speaking generally, it is a good idea

to organize your essay from the lesser material to the greater (to avoid anticlimax) or from the simple to the complex (to ensure intelligibility). If, for example, you are discussing the roles of three characters, it may be best to build up to the one of the three that you think is the most important. If you are comparing two characters, it may be best to move from the most obvious contrasts to the least obvious ones. (In your opening paragraph, which will probably be almost the last thing you will write, you should, of course, give the reader an idea of the scope of the paper, but at this stage you are organizing the material chiefly for yourself and so you need not yet worry about an introductory paragraph.) When you have arranged your notes into a meaningful sequence of packets, you have approximately divided your material into paragraphs.

5. **Get it down on paper.** Most essayists find it useful to jot down some sort of outline, indicating the main idea of each paragraph and, under each main idea, supporting details that give it substance. An outline—not necessarily anything highly formal with capital and lowercase letters and Roman and Arabic numerals but merely key phrases in some sort of order—will help you to overcome the paralysis called writer's block that commonly afflicts professionals as well as students. A page of paper with ideas in some sort of sequence, however rough, ought to assure you that you do have something to say. You should feel encouraged that, despite the temptation to sharpen another pencil, the best thing to do is to sit down and start writing.

If you don't feel that you can work from note cards and a rough outline, try another method: Get something down on paper, writing freely, sloppily, automatically, or whatever, but allow your ideas about what the work means to you and how it conveys its meaning—rough as they may be—to begin to take visible form. If you are like most people, you can't do much precise thinking until you have committed to paper at least a rough sketch of your initial ideas. Later you can push and polish your ideas into shape, perhaps even deleting all of them and starting over, but it's a lot easier to improve your ideas once you see them in front of you than it is to do the job in your head. On paper (or on a computer screen) one word leads to another; in your head one word often blocks another.

Just keep going; you may realize, as you near the end of a sentence, that you no longer believe it. OK; be glad that your first idea led you to a better one, and pick up your better one and keep going with it. What you are doing is, in a sense, is using trial and error to push your way not only toward clear expression but also toward sharper ideas and richer responses.

6. If there is time, **reread the play,** looking for additional material that strengthens or weakens your main point; take account of it in your outline or draft.

7. **With your outline or draft in front of you, write a more lucid version,** checking your notes for fuller details, such as supporting quotations. If, as you work, you find that some of the points in your earlier jottings are no longer rele-

vant, eliminate them; it is important that the argument flows from one point to the next. As you write, your ideas will doubtless become clearer; some may prove to be poor ideas. (We rarely know exactly what our ideas are until we have them set down on paper. As the little girl said, replying to the suggestion that she should think before she spoke, "How do I know what I think until I say it?") Not until you have written a draft do you really have a strong sense of how good your essay may be.

8. After a suitable interval, preferably a few days, **read the draft with a view toward revising it,** not with a view toward congratulating yourself. A revision, after all, is a revision, a second (and presumably sharper) view. When you revise, you will be in the company of Picasso, who said that in painting a picture he advanced by a series of destructions. A revision—such as the addition of an example, the reorganization of the sequence of examples, or even the substitution of a precise word for an imprecise one—is not a matter of prettying but of thinking. As you read, correct things that disturb you (for example, awkward repetitions that bore, inflated utterances that grate), add supporting detail where the argument is undeveloped (a paragraph of only one or two sentences is usually an undeveloped paragraph), and ruthlessly delete irrelevancies however well written they may be. Remember though that a deletion probably requires some adjustment in the preceding and subsequent material. Make sure that the opening paragraph gives the readers some sense of where they will be going and that between the opening and the closing paragraphs the argument, aided by transition terms (such as *furthermore, on the other hand, in the next scene*), runs smoothly. The details should be relevant, the organization reasonable, and the argument clear. Check all quotations for accuracy. Quotations are evidence, usually intended to support your assertions, and you should not alter the evidence, even unintentionally. If there is time (there almost never is), put the revision aside, reread it in a day or two, and revise it again, especially with a view toward shortening it.

9. **Keyboard or write a clean copy,** following the principles concerning margins, pagination, footnotes, and so on set forth on page 1051. If you have borrowed any ideas, be sure to give credit, usually in footnotes, to your sources. Remember that plagiarism is not limited to the unacknowledged borrowing of words; a borrowed idea, even when put into your own words, requires acknowledgment.

10. **Proofread and make corrections.**

Suggestions for Writing with a Word Processor

If possible, write your paper on a word processor. Writing a first draft on a word processor is physically easier than writing by hand or by typewriter, and revising the draft is incomparably easier. (You can almost effortlessly move material around or insert new material.) Furthermore, for many people the screen is less intimidating than a sheet of paper, and when you do put words down, they look a lot better than handwritten or typed material. In addition, if your paper includes footnotes or endnotes and a list of Works Cited, your software probably will automatically format them.

A word processor may not save you time, but it will allow you to use your time efficiently. In the past, writers had to spend a great deal of time on the tedious job of typing a clean copy. The more they revised, the more they doomed themselves to hours of retyping. With a word processor, you can spend all of your time reading, writing, and rewriting, and you can virtually leave to the printer the job of typing.

Prewriting

Your first notes probably will be in the margins of your text, but once you go beyond these, you can use a word processor to brainstorm, for instance. By means of *free association*—writing down whatever comes to mind, without fretting about spelling, punctuation, or logic—you will probably find that you can generate ideas, at least some of which will lead to something. Alternatively, you can try *listing*, jotting down key terms (for instance the names of characters in a play or technical terms such as *tragedy, pathos, hamartia, irony*) and then inserting further thoughts about each. Produce a print-out, and then start *linking* or *clustering* (with circles and connecting lines) related items. Then return to your screen, and reorganize the material, moving *this* word or phrase over to connect it with *that* one.

Many students find *dialoguing* helpful. After writing a sentence or two, they imagine a somewhat skeptical critic who asks questions such as, "What examples can you give?" "What counterevidence might be offered?" and "Have you defined your terms?" In answering such questions, writers get additional ideas.

Back up your material. Don't run the risk of losing your work. Write on a hard drive (it's faster), and keep a floppy disk nearby for making backups at the close of each work session.

Taking Notes

Write into one file all of your notes for a paper. If the notes are for a paper on, for example, Marsha Norman, you will probably name the file "Norman." The name does not matter, so long as you remember it.

Put all bibliographic references in one place. If you are using written sources, you will want to keep a record of each source. Some programs, for instance, *Fifty-Third Street Writer*, automatically alphabetize each entry. However, even if your program does not alphabetize bibliographic entries, you can easily insert a new entry by scrolling down through the existing references to the appropriate alphabetic place where you can then insert the new reference, last name first.

When taking notes, be sure to check the accuracy of your transcription. If you quote directly, make certain that you have quoted exactly. Use three periods (ellipsis points) to indicate any omissions within a quotation, and use square brackets to enclose any addition that you make within a quotation. (See pp. 1052–1053.) As we discuss below, when you are drafting your paper you may want to block some of this material and move it into the draft.

It's a good idea to print out all of your notes before you prepare a first draft. Because the screen shows very little of the material that constitutes your notes, print it all out so that you can survey it as a whole. Cut apart the various notes, and discard material that no longer seems helpful. Next, arrange the surviving material into a tentative sequence, just as you would arrange index cards with handwritten notes. (The word processor is a great help, but don't hesitate to produce hard copy at various stages and to work with the printed material. The screen is too small to give you a feel of the whole.)

Many writers find it helpful to put this selection of material, now in a sequence, back into the computer. They do this by *blocking* and moving the useful material. Do *not* delete the unused material; as you work on the essay, you may realize that you can use some of this material in the final version. It's advisable to copy this selected and arranged material into a new file, named "draft" or some such thing. If you simply add it to the end of the file containing all of the notes, you may sometimes find yourself working with the unselected notes when you mean to work with the selected notes.

Writing a First Draft

Even if you did not take notes on a computer, you can, of course, write your drafts and ultimately the final paper on a word processor. Use double-spacing to allow room for handwritten additions on a printed version of the draft, and start writing.

Some writers find it useful to start writing on the computer by setting down a rough outline—perhaps phrases in a sequence that, at least for the moment, seems reasonable. They then go back and fill in the outline, expanding words or phrases into detailed sentences and paragraphs. Of course, as they write they may find that they want to rearrange some of the material, which they can easily do by cut-and-paste commands.

Let's assume, however, that you do have notes on the word processor and that you have arranged them in a sequence. You may want to begin by looking at the first note and writing an opening paragraph that will lead into it, and then go on to the next note. Of course, as you work you will find that some of the notes are unneeded. Don't delete them, since they may come in handy later. Just block them and move them (cut-and-paste) to the end of the file.

Because it is so easy to produce a clean final copy (with a keystroke or two you can tell the printer to print the file), don't hesitate in your draft to incorporate comments that you know you won't retain in the final version, such as "CHECK QUOTATION" or "GET BETTER EXAMPLE."

(Use capitals or boldface for such comments so that you will focus on them when you read the draft and so you cannot overlook them when the time comes to delete them.)

When you think you have come to the end of your draft, you will probably want to read it on the screen, from the beginning, to correct typos and to make other obvious corrections. That's fine, but remember that because the screen is small you cannot get a good sense of the entire essay. You won't be able to see, for instance, if a paragraph is much too long. Even when you scroll through the draft, you will not experience the material in the way that the reader of a printed copy will experience it. What you need to do at this stage is to print your draft.

Revising a Draft

Read the printed draft, making necessary revisions in pen or pencil. Probably you will find that some of the quoted material can be abridged, or even deleted, and that in some places better transitions are needed. It is also likely that you will see the need to add details and to reorganize some of the material. Try to read the draft from the point of view of someone new to the material. Keep asking yourself, "Will my reader understand *why* I am making this point at this stage in the essay?" If you ask this question, you probably will find yourself not only adding helpful transitions ("An apparent exception is . . .") but also occasionally reorganizing. Make these changes on the printed copy, incorporate them into the computer, and print the revised version.

Read the revised version with a critical eye; you probably will find that you can extensively revise even this version. You may get some help from a computer program. For instance, if you are using *Fifty-Third Street Writer*, which includes the *Scott, Foresman Handbook*, and you are uncertain about the use of the semicolon, you can consult the index to the *Handbook* and then bring up the material on semicolons. Similarly, if you are writing a book review, you can find the material on reviews by consulting the index and can then bring to the screen the discussion of the qualities that make for a good review. Among other software programs that many writers find useful are *Grammatik*, *Word Plus*, *Right Writer*, and *Writer's Workbench*. Some of these will alert you to such matters as spelling errors, clichés, split infinitives, overuse of the passive voice, and certain kinds of grammatical errors. For instance, *Writer's Workbench* (and some of the others) lets you check troublesome pairs of words (for example, (*affect/effect*), flags words and phrases that are potentially sexist, detects most split infinitives and misspellings, and gives (among other things) help with transitions. You cannot rely entirely on these programs, but they do offer considerable help.

When you get a version that seems to you the best that you can do without further assistance, ask a friend to read it. **Prepare a copy for peer review.** Print your text—double-spaced and in letter quality, of course—and give it to your reader.

When the paper is returned to you, respond to the suggestions appropriately. Be sure to give credit in your paper to your reader (something such as, "I want to thank Tina Lee for valuable suggestions," or "Martin Baratz suggested the comparison with Adrienne Kennedy's play"), and then print out this new version. Do not rely on reading the paper on the screen; you will need to read the hard copy, with an eye toward making further revisions.

Producing the Final Version

After you print out the version you have prepared in response to the comments by your reviewer, read it to see whether you can make any further improvements. (Even at this late date, you may think of a better title or you may sense that a quotation doesn't sound quite right.) You can make small changes in ink, but if you make a substantial number of changes, print out a clean copy. Your paper will be neater, and there is little labor involved.

Basic Manuscript Form

Much of what follows regarding basic manuscript form is nothing more than common sense.

- Use $8\frac{1}{2}$-by-11-inch paper of good weight.
- If you use a word processor, be sure to use a reasonably fresh ribbon, double-space, and print on one side of the page only. If you submit a handwritten copy, use lined paper and write on one side of the page only, in ink, on every other line. Most instructors do *not* want papers to be enclosed in any sort of binder. Most prefer papers to be stapled in the upper left corner; do not crimp or crease corners and expect them to hold together.
- Leave an adequate margin—1 or $1\frac{1}{2}$ inches—at top, bottom, and sides.
- Number the pages consecutively, using Arabic numerals in the upper right-hand corner.
- Put your name and class or course number in the upper left-hand corner of the first page. It is a good idea to put your name in the upper right corner of each subsequent page so that your essay can be easily reassembled if a page gets separated.
- Create your own title, one that reflects your topic or thesis. For example, a paper on *The Glass Menagerie* should not be called "*The Glass Menagerie*" but might be called "Tom's Romanticization of Laura: A View of *The Glass Menagerie*."
- Center the title of your essay below the top margin of the first page. Begin the first word of the title with a capital, and capitalize each subsequent word except articles (*the*, *a*, *an*) and prepositions (*in*, *on*, *or*, *with*, and so forth). For example:

```
The Truth of Dreams in

A Midsummer Night's Dream
```

- Begin the essay 1 or 2 inches below the title.

• Your extensive revisions should have been made in your drafts, but minor last-minute revisions may be made—neatly—on the finished copy. Proofreading may catch some typographical errors, and you may notice some small weaknesses. Additions should be made *above* the line, with a caret (^) *below* the line to indicate placement of the correction. Mark deletions by drawing a horizontal line through the word or words you wish to delete. Delete a single letter by drawing a vertical line through it. Use a vertical line, too, to separate words that should not have been run together.

Quotations and Quotation Marks

Excerpts from the plays you are writing about are indispensable. Such quotations not only let the reader know what you are talking about, but they also present the material you are responding to, thus letting the reader share your responses.

Here are some mechanical matters regarding the presentation of quotations:

• **Identify the speaker or writer of the quotation** so that the reader is not left with a sense of uncertainty. Usually this identification precedes the quoted material (for example, "Smith says . . .") in accordance with the principle of letting readers know where they are going, but occasionally it may follow the quotation, especially if it will provide something of a pleasant surprise. For instance, in a discussion of Williams's *The Glass Menagerie*, you might quote a comment that seems to belittle the play and then reveal that Williams himself was the speaker.

• **The quotation must fit grammatically into your sentence.** Suppose you want to use Lear's line, addressed to the Fool, "In boy; go first." Do *not* say:

```
    In 3.4, in response to Lear's command,
the Fool "go first."
```

You'll have to say something like this:

```
    In 3.4, in response to Lear's command to
"go first," the Fool enters the hovel.
```

Of course, you can say,

```
    In 3.4, Lear says to the Fool, "In boy;
go first," and the Fool obeys.
```

• The quotation must be exact. **Any material that you add—even one or two words—must be in square brackets,** as shown in this example:

```
    When Lear says, "In boy; go [into the
hovel] first," he shows a touch of humility.
```

If you wish to omit material from within a quotation, indicate the ellipsis by three spaced periods. If a sentence ends in an omission, add a closed-up period and then three

spaced periods to indicate the omission. The following example is based on a quotation from the sentences immediately above this one:

```
    The instructions say that "if you . . .
omit material from within a quotation, [you
must] indicate the ellipsis. . . . If a sen-
tence ends in an omission, add a closed-up
period and then three spaced periods. . . ."
```

Notice that although material preceded "If you," periods are not needed to indicate the omission because "If you" began a sentence in the original. Customarily, initial and terminal omissions are indicated only when they are part of the sentence you are quoting. Even such omissions need not be indicated when the quoted material is obviously incomplete—when, for instance, it is a word or phrase. Notice, too, that although quotations must be given word for word, the initial capitalization can be adapted, as here where "If" is changed to "if."

When a line or more of verse is omitted from a passage that is set off, the three spaced periods are printed on a separate line:

```
    If we shadows have offended,
    Think but this, and all is mended;
              . . .
    Give me your hands, if we be friends,
    And Robin shall restore amends.
```

• **Distinguish between short and long quotations,** and treat each appropriately. Short quotations (usually defined as fewer than three lines of verse or five lines of prose) are enclosed within quotation marks and run into the text (rather than set off, without quotation marks). The following examples can be run in with text:

```
    Near the end of Oedipus Rex, the Chorus
reminds the audience that Oedipus "solved the
famous riddle," but it does not tell us what
the riddle was.
```

```
    King Lear's first long speech begins au-
thoritatively: "Meantime we shall express our
darker purpose. / Give me the map there. Know
that we have divided / In three our kingdom."
His authoritative manner is evident through-
out the act.
```

Notice in the first passage that although only four words are being quoted, quotation marks are used, indicating that these are Sophocles' words, not the essayist's. Notice that in the second example a slash (diagonal line, or virgule) is used to indicate the end of a line of verse other than the last line quoted. The slash is, of course, not used for prose, and it is not used if poetry is set off, indented, and printed as verse, as shown here:

```
King Lear's first long speech begins authori-

tatively:

    Meantime we shall express our darker

        purpose.

    Give me the map there. Know that we

        have divided

    In three our kingdom; and 'tis our

        fast intent

    To shake all cares and business

        from our age,

    Conferring them on younger

        strengths, while we

    Unburthened crawl toward death.
```

Material that is set off (usually three or more lines of verse, five or more lines of prose) is *not* enclosed within quotation marks. To set it off, indent the quotation ten spaces from the left margin. **Poetry should be centered.** (Be sparing in your use of long quotations.) Use quotations as evidence, not as padding. Do not bore the reader with material that can be effectively reduced either by paraphrase or by cutting. If you cut, indicate ellipses as explained above.

• **Commas and periods go inside the quotation marks.** (An exception is if the quotation is immediately followed by material in parentheses or in square brackets. If that is the case, close the quotation, give the parenthetic or bracketed material, and then—after the closing parenthesis or bracket—put the comma or period.)

Semicolons, colons, and dashes go outside quotation marks. Question marks and exclamation points go inside if they are part of the quotation, outside if they are your own. In the following example, the first two question marks are Shakespeare's, so they go *inside* the quotation marks. The third question mark, however, is the essayist's, so it goes *outside* the quotation marks.

```
    Lear asks the beggar, "Dids't thou give

all to thy daughters?" The beggar's reply is,

"Who gives anything to Poor Tom?" Are we sur-

prised when he goes on to say, "Do Poor Tom

some charity, whom the foul fiend vexes"?
```

• **Use *single* quotation marks for material contained within a quotation that itself is within quotation marks.** For example:

```
    The editors of Types of Drama say, "With

Puck we look at the antics in the forest,

smile tolerantly, and say with a godlike per-

spective, 'Lord, what fools these mortals

be!'"
```

• **Use quotation marks around titles of short works,** that is, for titles of chapters in books and for essays that might not be published by themselves. Unpublished works, even book-length dissertations, are also enclosed in quotation marks. **Use italics (indicated by underlining) for books, that is, for plays, periodicals, novels, and collections of essays.**

A Note on Footnotes and Endnotes

You may wish to use a footnote or endnote, telling the reader that the passage you are quoting is found in this book on such and such a page. Let us assume that you have already mentioned the author and the title of the play and have just quoted a passage. At the end of the sentence that includes the quotation, or at the end of the quotation if you are offering it as an independent sentence, following the period add the number *1*, elevating it slightly above the line. Do not put a period after the digit. Near the bottom of the paper, indent five spaces and insert the number *1*, elevated and without a period. Then write the appropriate information. For example:

```
    ¹Reprinted in Sylvan Barnet et al.,

Types of Drama, 7th ed. (New York: Long-

man, 1997), p. 236.
```

Notice that the abbreviation for *page* is *p.*, not *pg.*; the abbreviation for *pages* is *pp.* (for example, pp. 236–237). For verse plays whose lines are numbered, the usual procedure is not to cite a page but to cite act, scene, and line numbers in parentheses after the quotation. The old method was to give the act in capital Roman numerals, the scene in small roman numerals, and the line in Arabic numerals, with periods following the act and scene (for example, V.i.7–11), but the preferred method today is to give the act, scene, and line (if numbered in the text) in Arabic numerals, with periods but no extra spaces.

```
    The lunatic, the lover and the poet

    Are of imagination all compact.

    One sees more devils than vast hell can

        hold,

    That is the madman. The lover, all as

        frantic,
```

```
     Sees Helen's beauty in a brow of Egypt.
                              (5.1.7-11)¹
```

The corresponding footnote would read:

```
¹All quotations from A Midsummer
Night's Dream are from the text
reprinted in Sylvan Barnet et al., Types
of Drama, 7th ed. (New York: Longman,
1997).
```

If you have not mentioned the author or title of the work quoted, you need to give that information in the note, as follows:

```
¹William Shakespeare, A Midsummer
Night's Dream, reprinted in Sylvan Bar-
net et al., Types of Drama, 7th ed. (New
York: Longman, 1997).
```

If you have mentioned the author, but not the work, the note would follow this pattern:

```
¹A Midsummer Night's Dream,
reprinted in Sylvan Barnet et al., Types
of Drama, 7th ed. (New York: Longman,
1997).
```

In short, you need not give information in the note that is already given in the main body of the essay.

In order to eliminate writing many footnotes, each one merely citing the page of a quotation, you can write in the first footnote after giving the bibliographical information as above something such as this:

```
     All further references to this work will
be given parenthetically, within the text of
the essay.
```

Thus, when you quote the next passage from the play, at the end of the sentence—just before the period—you need only insert a pair of parentheses enclosing the page number or the act, scene, and line number. Here is an example:

```
     At this point Lear goes out, saying, "O
Fool, I shall go mad!" (p. 208).
```

or

```
     At this point Lear goes out, saying, "O
Fool, I shall go mad!" (2.4.282).
```

Notice that in the sample analysis on pages 1040–1042 the author used only one footnote and then cited all of the other quotations parenthetically.

A Note on Internal Citations

If you use secondary sources, your instructor may want you to cite your source (usually an authority you are quoting or summarizing) parenthetically within the body of your paper. Here is an example, citing page 29 of a book:

```
     In Comic Women, Tragic Men, Linda Bamber
says that in Shakespeare's plays, "The nat-
ural order, the status quo, is for men to
rule women" (29).
```

or

```
     In Shakespeare's plays "the natural or-
der," Bamber says, "is for men to rule women"
(29), but she goes on to modify this state-
ment.
```

At the end of your paper, on **a separate page with the heading "Works Cited,"** list all of your sources, alphabetically by author, with last name first, then the title (underlined, to indicate italics), then the place of publication, the publisher, and the date. After the date, type a period.

```
Bamber, Linda. Comic Women, Tragic Men. Stan-
     ford. Stanford UP, 1982.
```

For details on how to cite journals, books published in more than one volume, translations, and dozens of other troublesome works, see Joseph Gibaldi, *MLA Handbook for Writers of Research Papers,* 4th ed. (New York: MLA, 1995). (By the way, MLA stands for Modern Language Association.)

WRITING DRAMA

SCENES AND PLAYS

Your instructor may ask you to write some dialogue, such as might constitute one scene in a realistic play. Alternatively, you may be asked to turn some classic short story into a one-act play or even to write an original one-act play.

Writing a Scene

If you are asked to write a scene that might be part of a longer work, once you have settled on the situation, try to get your characters fairly clearly in mind even before you begin writing (though, of course, once you start writing you will doubtless revise your view of them).

Where do you start? Where do you find your characters? All writers are asked where they get their ideas, and the answers vary greatly. Some writers draw on their family and friends. Others begin with something they glimpsed on the street (a well-dressed woman accompanied by a disheveled man) or with a scrap of conversation they overheard on the bus ("So I told him I'd do what I could, but I wouldn't do *that*"), and from this they imagine a relationship and invent dialogue.

Whether you start with some such sight or sound or whether you begin by imagining characters, think hard about who these people are. Let's say that your scene concerns a college student who tells her parents that she is dropping out of college. These are the kinds of questions you should ask yourself about your characters:

What is their race and ethnic background?
What do they wear?
What sort of furnishings surround them?
What kinds of food do they eat?
How old are they?
How much money do they have?
What are their attitudes toward education? Why?
Is the student immature, mature, troubled, timid, adventurous, or what?
What gestures do the characters use?
How do they stand or sit?
How do they speak (thoughtfully, hesitantly, vigorously)?
What sort of vocabulary do they use? What are their speech rhythms?
What sorts of people are the parents? Is the father intolerant but the mother sympathetic, is the father baffled and the mother hostile, or what?

Furthermore, if (for instance) you conceive of the mother as intolerant of the daughter's goals, *why* is she intolerant? Is it because she is afraid that the daughter will excel her? Is it because, on the contrary, she strongly feels her own limitations and is so eager for her daughter to transcend them that she cannot understand the daughter's choice of what seems to the mother to be a very limited goal. To overstate a bit, a viewer ought to be able to imagine the entire history of this family from the dialogue that you create for this scene. Difficult? Yes, but exciting, too.

Following is a list of encounters you might want to set forth in a scene of two or three pages. First, however, we want to add three points:

- We leave to you the challenging job of creating the particular personalities who are in these situations. In your introductory stage directions, you can describe and briefly characterize the speakers and the setting, but remember that an audience will not be aware of these comments. The audience will understand the characters only through the language, gestures (stage business), and setting.
- Your characters should be believable individuals, not mere stereotypes, though, of course, even a highly individualized character is in some degree representative of some aspect of a culture—let's say the bourgeois parent (or the neglectful father) or the rebellious adolescent (or the dutiful son). That is, each character will be a coherent personality, and at the same time each will in some degree stand for something. Each will be a concrete embodiment (but not a flat or abstract vision) of a point of view and also of a type of person in a given culture.
- Among the most interesting confrontations in drama are those of one right against another right, rather than of right against wrong.

Here are the sample encounters:

- A female college student tells her drama instructor (a male) that she wants to stage Wendy Wasserstein's *The Man in a Case*. (How does he respond, and why?)
- A person responding to an ad offering to sell a car comes to talk to the owner. (Your dialogue should give the reader a strong sense of what sort of person each one is.)
- A young woman seeking a job as a driver is interviewed by the male owner of a taxi cab company.
- A Chicano or Asian American is telling a friend of similar ethnic background about a job interview that he or she has just had with an Anglo employer.
- A young white man tells his parents (or some white friends) that he plans to marry a young black woman.
- A young black woman tells her parents (or some black friends) that she plans to marry a white man.
- A middle-aged married woman, assuming that her older unmarried sister must be unhappy, tells her that marriage isn't so great.
- A character wants something (perhaps money, a job, or approval) that another character does not want to give.
- A member of some minority group is talking with a friend who makes what is supposed to be an amusing ethnic slur.

- Choose two characters from some play—perhaps from Molière's *The Misanthrope*, Ibsen's *A Doll's House*, or Wilson's *Fences*—and let them continue the issue in today's terms. Alternatively, write a monologue, for instance by Linda Loman five years after the death of Willy Loman.

Two additional points:

- Before you set to work, please read the rest of this discussion; it concerns the importance of giving a shape or pattern to a scene.
- After you have drafted and revised your scene, ask some friends to take the roles and to read the dialogue aloud. Listen as impartially as possible, and then revise your work where necessary, making the dialogue more convincing and the dramatic conflict more effective.

Your instructor may want not just a scene but a play, perhaps your dramatized version of a short story, such as one by Poe, Updike, or Sandra Cisneros. If so, your plot and characters (and some of your lines) are already established for you, but you will still have to invent much of the dialogue and the gestures. Almost surely you will have to arrange the dialogue to include exposition that a storyteller may simply tell the reader directly, and probably you will have to omit some episodes and combine some others into one episode. The author of the original story will doubtless have given it a significant structure, but you may have to reshape it at least slightly, since you are converting a story into a play.

Construction in Drama

At this point we digress for a moment to talk about construction in drama. A playwright (not "playwrite") is a *wright*, that is, a maker—a maker of plays, just as a shipwright is a maker of ships. A play is made with characters engaged in a plot. The word *plot* itself suggests the importance of "making" or "building" or "constructing," since the original meaning of the word was a parcel of land (as in "a plot of ground"); the plot originally was the area staked out on which one might then build. When one looks closely at a good play, one always sees that it has been designed carefully and built well. Consider, for instance, the basic pattern, or ground plan, of *A Midsummer Night's Dream*.

- The play begins (1.1) and ends (5.1) in Athens.
- Just after the first scene, and then again just before the last scene, Shakespeare gives us scenes of the comic workers (1.2 and 4.2).
- In between these scenes we are in the forest (2.1–4.1).

A close analysis reveals numerous contrasts and similarities between scenes. Few if any viewers are conscious of the pattern—of the architecture, we might say—but the pattern probably makes its effect nevertheless. In the words of the dramatist Friedrich Hebbel:

A genuine drama is comparable to one of those big buildings which have almost as many rooms and corridors below ground as above ground. People in general are aware only of the latter; the master builder is aware of the former as well.

For example, consider the structure not of an entire play but of a single scene, the first in *King Lear*, where Lear makes the enormous mistake of giving his kingdom to two of his daughters and of banishing the third. If (so to speak) we stand back from the scene, we notice that it falls into three parts, which we can characterize as:

- A prologue (lines 1–32, in prose)
- A central portion (Lear's decisions)
- An epilogue (lines 270–309, the latter part of it in prose)

The prologue is rather intimate; Gloucester and Kent begin the play by chatting about public affairs, and then their conversation turns to talk about Gloucester's sons. The epilogue, too (which is about the same length as the prologue), is relatively intimate or private; it begins with the banished sister taking her farewell of her two wicked sisters, and it ends with the two wicked sisters, speaking prose, plotting against Lear. Between these two passages, beginning with Lear's entrance at line 33 and ending with Lear's exit at line 269, is, of course, the highly ceremonial scene of Lear inviting his three daughters to speak, their speeches, and his responses. Within this central part of the scene, the speeches of the three daughters fall into patterns, but here we need not go into that.

The One-Act Play

Your instructor may ask you to write a one-act play of your own invention. A distinction is often made between the one-act play and the full-length play, but the terms are a bit misleading. A one-act play, like a three-act play or a five-act play, is full length in the sense that it treats its material as fully as is appropriate. Usually, of course, the material of the one-act play is more limited than that of a longer play. For instance, it usually covers less time and deals with fewer characters. Thus, if the piece really is a one-act play and not just a short play with two or more scenes, the time covered by the play usually corresponds closely to real time, perhaps twenty to forty minutes. The action probably involves only a few characters; indeed, some one-act plays are monologues, although most use two or three characters.

Generally only a single incident is dramatized. For example, two strangers exchange words on a park bench, and one ends up dead (Albee, *The Zoo Story*); an angry man goes to a woman to collect an overdue payment and ends up courting her (Chekhov, *The Boor*); sailors on a ship during war suspect a fellow sailor of being a spy, break into his locker, and find not incriminating documents but a letter concerning a failed love affair (O'Neill, *In the Zone*). None of these plays has the scope of, say, *King Lear*, which covers several months and is rich in parallels and contrasts. For instance, in *Lear* the stories of Cordelia, Kent, and Edgar all involve persons whose love is so deep that they can forgive actions that others might think intolerable.

A one-act play cannot have the complexity of a three- or five-act play; still, we will see something of the subtlety that even a one-act play can convey if we think about Susan Glaspell's *Trifles* (p. 18). To take perhaps the two most obvious examples: (1) the men form a contrast to the women (though the two women are by no means interchangeable), and (2) the broken hinge of the bird cage, the broken neck of the bird, the broken neck of the man, and the broken spirit of the wife are all part of a pattern.

Most writers of one-act plays do not try to pack a three-act play into one act; rather, as we have already said, they severely limit the time covered and the number of characters, usually concentrating on one or two figures involved in a single episode. What sort of structure does a one-act play have? In the late nineteenth century, and in the first half of the twentieth, it was commonplace to say that a play, whether in three acts or in one, has a pyramidal structure; that is, it rises to a climax, and it then descends or unknots. A variation was to say that the structure of a play is like an arch, with the turning point in the plot resembling the keystone. If we go back more than two thousand years, in Aristotle's terms a play has a beginning, a middle, and an end. Although some plays since the 1950s have seemed to use a different structure (a wit has said that in Beckett's *Waiting for Godot*—a play in two acts—nothing happens, twice), the old pattern is still often used effectively, and indeed it may be found even in many works that, at first glance, seem not to use it.

There are other ways of expressing the idea: one ancient formula (speaking of the three-act play, but applicable also to the structure of a one-act play) goes thus: In the first act, get your people up a tree, in the second act throw stones at them, and in the third act get them down. In romantic comedy this formula often takes the shape of "Boy meets girl, boy loses girl, boy gets girl." With a little thought it is evident that such formulas are versions of Aristotle's beginning, middle, and end—or, as Peter De Vries cleverly put it,

"beginning, muddle, and end." That is, a stable situation (the beginning) is disrupted (the middle) and then resolved (the end).

Almost every scene or act in a long play has something of this structure, at least to the extent that a scene or act develops. Line by line it may seem to be simply adding a unit to a unit, but in retrospect the whole has a unity, a definite shape. Even a scene that consists of a single speech is likely to move from (in effect), "What am I to do?" to "I'll do X," to "Now I feel better (or worse)"; that is, the scene builds to a climax in complexity or tension and then settles toward a resolution or relaxation.

Almost surely your first few drafts of a scene or an act will not have an effective pattern—but then comes the job of rewriting the material so that it becomes not mere dialogue but drama. You can test your scene by rewriting it in a few sentences as a scenario, that is, without any dialogue. Does the summary of the encounter have a shape—a beginning, a middle, and an end?

Last Words

We come now to our final point: An effective scene, or an effective one-act play, gives us characters in whom we are interested—characters whose ideas or passions hold our attention—but it also gives a shape to the presentation of those ideas or passions. Aristotle said that the arts arise from two impulses, *the impulse to imitate,* and *the impulse toward harmony.* The first of these (except in certain forms, such as farce) requires fairly realistic dialogue and convincing characterization; we listen to the characters speak and we say, "Yes, that is how people sound, that's the way they behave." Obviously, however, works of art do not simply offer language that imitates the language we can hear on the campus or in a bus. Works of art—songs are the most obvious example—put language into a harmonious shape. They impose a pattern (songs use meter, melody, and rhyme), and here we get to Aristotle's second point, that works of art arise partly from the human instinct for harmony. The impulse toward harmony requires a shapely "plot," a territory staked out, and then a blueprint, or plan, that is converted into a well-ordered construction.

A GLOSSARY OF DRAMATIC TERMS

absurd, theater of the. Drama of such writers as Eugène Ionesco and Samuel Beckett in France and Harold Pinter in England imitates the absurdity of our existence. "Everything, as I see it, is an aberration," Ionesco has said. Among the basic themes are loneliness in a world without God, inability to communicate, dehumanization at the hands of mass media, and impotence in the face of society and of death. Though the plays are serious, they may contain extravagantly comic scenes to depict a reality that is absurd, illogical, and senseless—a world of futility and meaningless clichés. In Ionesco's *The Chairs* (1951) an elderly couple rush about, filling a room with chairs for nonexistent visitors. Old age is a fact, but an absurdity, too, and old people are incomprehensible. At the end of *The Chairs*, an orator who is to deliver a solemn talk about the truths of life turns out to be deaf and dumb and merely makes unintelligible noises and gestures to the invisible crowd. Ionesco summarizes the theme of *The Chairs* (*New York Times*, June 1, 1958): "I have tried to deal . . . with emptiness, with frustration, with this world, at once fleeting and crushing. The characters I have used are not fully conscious of their spiritual rootlessness, but they feel it instinctively and emotionally." One basis of the inability to communicate, and one that the "absurd" dramatists seize upon, is the corruption of language. The absurdity of trying to communicate by means of a debased language is dramatized by Ionesco in *The Bald Soprano* (1948), in which the characters speak in clichés. Because the characters are incomprehensible and the happenings illogical and baffling, the spectators cannot simply sit back in ease but are continually challenged to grasp the play's meaning. The theater of the absurd can be said to be a descendent of expressionism (see p. 558). Consult M. Esslin, *The Theatre of the Absurd*. See pages 38–40, 690–91.

act. A main division in drama or opera. Act divisions probably arose in Roman theory and derive ultimately from the Greek practice of separating episodes in a play by choral interludes, but Greek (and probably Roman) plays were performed without interruption, for the choral interludes were part of the plays themselves. The division of Elizabethan plays into five acts is often the work of editors rather than authors. No play of Shakespeare's was published in his lifetime with divisions into five acts. Today an act division is commonly indicated by lowering the curtain and turning up the houselights. A **scene** is a smaller unit, either (1) a division with no change of locale and no abrupt shift of time, or (2) a division consisting of an actor or a group of actors on the stage. According to the second definition, the departure or entrance of an actor changes the composition of the group and thus produces a new scene. In an entirely different sense, the scene is the locale where a work is set. The first speech in *Romeo and Juliet* informs the audience of the play's locale: "In fair Verona, where we lay our scene." Often

the décor lets the spectator know where the play is set, but during the last hundred years playwrights have tended, for the convenience of readers, to write long stage directions describing the scene. Here is the beginning of the first stage direction in Shaw's *Candida*: "A fine morning in October 1894 in the north east quarter of London, a vast district miles away from the London of Mayfair and St. James's, and much less narrow, squalid, fetid and airless in its slums."

acting. The imitation by one person of another. The two extreme views of the actor's methods are, on the one hand, that acting is a craft, a matter of developing the technical skill to arouse certain feelings in an audience by means of gesture and voice, and, on the other hand, that acting is a matter of psychologically exploring the character, playing (so to speak) from the heart rather than the head. The first view is especially identified with Denis Diderot, who in *The Paradox of Acting* (1773–1788) said, "Actors impress the public not when they are impassioned but when they effectively imitate passion." The second view is especially associated with Constantin Stanislavski (1863–1938), who insisted that the actor must "sense" the "inner state" of the role. In America in the 1930s and 1940s, a school of acting called *The Method* was greatly influenced by Stanislavski.

action. (1) The physical movement of an actor, whether, for example, he is leaping into Ophelia's grave or speaking softly to himself. That talk is action is easily seen in the Bastard's remark (*King John*, 2.1.466): "Zounds! I was never so bethumped with words / Since I first called my brother's father dad." (2) An incident in the plot; an episode. Aristotle's statement that a drama is an "imitation of an action" (*praxis*) has provoked considerable controversy; recently there has been a tendency to regard this action as the motive underlying the outward deeds of the plot. Francis Fergusson says (in *The Human Image in Dramatic Literature*, p. 116), for example, that the action of *Oedipus the King* "is the quest for Laius's slayer, . . . which persists through the changing circumstances of the play."

acto. A short dramatic sketch, written in a mixture of Spanish and English, often with stereotyped characters satirizing the Anglo establishment. The form, developed by Luis Valdez in 1965 during a strike by farm workers in California, aims at stimulating Chicanos to value their culture and to unite against exploitation (see pages 799, 808). Consult *The Drama Review* 11:4 (1967).

aesthetic distance, or **sychical distance.** The detachment between the receptor and the work of art. The concept is chiefly associated with Edward Bullough (see the essay in his *Aesthetics*, reprinted in Melvin Rader, *A Modern Book of Aesthetics*). Bullough explains that there must be some sort of psychical "distance" (gap) between our practical self (our personal needs) and the work of art. Thus, an old man who has been treated harshly by his children may be unable to divorce his personal feelings from *King Lear*. He may be too involved with the piece as life to see it as art. However, "distance" does not mean that receptors are totally detached or objective. Rather, they are detached from their usual personal involvements, and because of this detachment they can look with a new vigorous interest—a new sort of passion born of a new personality—at the work of art as art. Persons who do not understand the need for distance between themselves and a work, Bullough explains, commonly say that they do not wish to see a tragedy because there is enough suffering in real life. However, the more sophisticated spectator at a tragedy realizes that as a picture is distanced by the frame, a play is distanced from the audience (the characters may speak verse, they perform behind footlights, and their deeds cohere to make a unified harmonious pattern); the feelings a play evokes are not the feelings evoked by an equivalent event in real life. In the theater we feel "rapturous awe" at what in life would be depressing. See also *dramatic illusion, empathy, epic drama*.

agit-prop. Propaganda theater. The term is derived from the Department of Agitation and Propaganda, formed in the former Soviet Union in 1920.

agon (Greek, "contest"). A debate in a Greek comedy. See page 123. In the last few decades the term has been used (e.g., by Francis Fergusson, *The Idea of a Theater*) to designate a scene of conflict in tragedy, such as the agonizing struggle between Oedipus and Teiresias.

agroikos. See *character.*

alazon. See *character.*

alienation effect. See *epic drama.*

allegory. Often a narrative in which abstractions (e.g., virtue, fear) are made concrete (Mr. Virtue, Giant Fear), for the purpose of effectively communicating a moral. In essence, an allegory is merely a system of equivalents. Though allegory need not personify abstractions, allegoric drama almost always does. *Everyman* (c. 1500), an allegoric morality play, includes among its dramatis personae Death; Good Deeds; Beauty; and of course, Everyman. But morality plays may also include allegoric castles (standing for strength or chastity), roses (standing for love or virtue), and so on. Consult Bernard Spivack, *Shakespeare and the Allegory of Evil*. (See also *symbolism*.)

alternative theater. The theater that sees itself in opposition to the established bourgeois theater. For example, The Living Theatre, an experimental company founded in New York in 1951 and influential in the 1960s, held anarchist and pacifist goals and often sought to arouse the hostility of the audience. Another example is the Teatro Campesino of Luis Valdez, on which see page 799. See T. Shank, *American Alternative Theatre*.

anagnorisis, or **disclosure, discovery, recognition.** For Aristotle the "recognition," or "disclosure," seemed to be merely a recognition of who is who, by such tokens as birthmarks, clothes, and so on, but the term has been extended to include the tragic hero's recognition of his or her nature and/or the essence of life. Thus Othello, having murdered his faithful wife, learns he was beguiled into thinking her dishonest and finally recognizes himself as "one not easily jealous, but being wrought / Perplexed in the extreme"; and he exacts justice from himself by suicide. For examples from *King Lear, Hamlet,* and *Macbeth* see page 34.

antagonist. See *plot, protagonist.*

antecedent action. See *plot.*

anticlimax. A descent, the lines or happenings being markedly less important or less impressive than those that precede. In melodrama, a decrease in tension may cause disappointment and loss of interest; in comedy, a sharp descent (as when the beautiful princess opens her mouth and sounds like a burlesque queen) may get a desirable laugh. On the desirability of a gradual decrease in tension in tragedy (i.e., a "quiet ending"), consult Max Beerbohm, "Last Acts," in *Around Theatres*.

anti-hero. A central character who, reversing the conventional idea of a hero (attractive, brave, high-minded), forces the audience to examine its conception of heroism and indeed of society. An example is Samuel Beckett's tramps.

antimasque. See *masque.*

Apollonian. See *Dionysus.*

arena stage. (1) In British usage, a stage with a back wall and with an audience on three sides. (2) In American usage, a playing space surrounded by spectators, a **theater-in-the-round.** Proponents of arena staging (in the American sense) stress the intimacy afforded by having actors in the midst of the audience, but opponents suggest that at least for some plays the intimacy ought not to be very great. (See *aesthetic distance*.) It has been noted, too, that even in arena staging the audience normally feels set apart from the actors, for the audience is in the dark while the actors are in an illuminated playing area. Critics of arena staging cite the following difficulties: soliloquies, asides, and direct addresses are hard to deliver in such a theater; directors, aware that the back of an actor's head is not very expressive, tend to have the actors gyrate disturbingly and meaninglessly; entrances and exits are cumbersome; and little use can be made of elevation and of groupings of actors.

arras. See page 186.

aside. See *convention, soliloquy.*

atmosphere. The mood created by setting, language, and happenings.

blocking. The director's organization of the movement on the stage in order to form effective stage positions and groupings.

bombast. Rant; speech that is too inflated for the occasion; from a word meaning "cotton stuffing." In Marlowe's *Tamburlaine* (c. 1587) Tamburlaine brags thus:

Our quivering lances, shaking in the air,
And bullets, like Jove's dreadful thunderbolts,
Enrolled in flames and fiery smoldering mists,
Shall threat the gods more than Cyclopian wars:
And with our sun-bright armor as we march,
Will chase the stars from Heaven and dim their eyes
That stand and muse at our admirèd arms.

bomolochos. See *character.*

bourgeois drama. A serious play with middle-class dramatis personae. There are a few Elizabethan tragedies of middle-class life, but bourgeois drama, with its emphasis on pathos, is more or less an eighteenth-century invention. Bourgeois dramas were written in the eighteenth and nineteenth centuries, apparently in response to the middle class's desire to see itself on the stage; the bourgeoisie by the eighteenth century regarded themselves as a suitable replacement for the nobleborn of earlier tragedy. Speaking generally, the characteristics of these plays are middle-class dramatis personae, virtue in distress, sentimentality, and an unreasonably high moral tone. Eighteenth-century critics, not sure what to do with pathetic plays on middle-class life, used the terms *drame, drame bourgeois, comédie larmoyante* (tearful comedy), *tragédie bourgeoise,* and *bürgerliches Trauerspiel* (bourgeois tragedy) interchangeably. (Note that a *comédie larmoyante* need not end happily, nor a *tragédie bourgeoise* end sadly.) In England, George Lillo's *The London Merchant* (1731), "a tale of private woe. A London 'prentice ruined," depicted an apprentice who murdered his benefactor. Bourgeois drama in the nineteenth century became melodrama in many hands but tragedy in Ibsen's hands. Consult Fred O. Nolte, *Early Middle Class Drama*; and Eric Auerbach, *Mimesis*, Chapter 17. On Ibsen as a bourgeois dramatist, consult Eric Bentley, *The Playwright as Thinker*. See *domestic tragedy, sentimental*, and pages 648–49, 686–88.

box set. Flats connected to form three walls with movable doors and windows. The box set, developed in the mid-nineteenth century, replaced sliding wings and canvas backdrops on which windows, doors, and even pieces of furniture were painted. See *realism.*

burla. See *commedia dell'arte.*

burlesque. Any imitation that, by distortion, aims to amuse. Its subject matter is sometimes said to be faults rather than vices, and its tone is neither shrill nor savage. Thus, in distinction from satire it can be defined as a comic imitation of a mannerism or a minor fault (either in style or subject matter), contrived to arouse amusement rather than indignation. In the theater, a burlesque may be a play that amusingly criticizes another play by grotesquely imitating aspects of it, as Gay's *The Beggar's Opera* (1728) mimicked serious operas. In England, a burlesque may be a musical extravaganza in which fantasy has almost entirely ousted criticism. In America, burlesque (especially popular in the late nine-

teenth and first half of the twentieth century) is usually a sort of vaudeville or variety show stressing bawdy humor and sex. The sexual theme is most fully revealed in the striptease, introduced about 1920. See *comedy, satire.*

catastrophe. See *plot.*

catharsis. Aristotle and countless followers said that tragedy evokes pity and fear and that it produces in the spectator a catharsis (purgation, or, some scholars hold, purification) of these emotions; it drains or perhaps refines or modifies these emotions, and thus tragedy is socially useful. (Aristotle's *Poetics* is the subject of much controversy; one cannot with security assert that Aristotle said anything without a counterargument being offered. For various views of catharsis, consult F. L. Lucas, *Tragedy*; and Gerald F. Else's monumental *Aristotle's Poetics*.)

character. (1) One of the dramatis personae, for example, King Lear. (2) The personality of such a figure. Characters are sometimes divided into **flat** and **round characters.** The former have only one "side," representing a single trait (e.g., the faithful wife, the genial drunkard); the latter have many traits and are seen, as it were, from all sides, in the round. The behavior of flat characters is thoroughly predictable; that of round characters is sometimes unexpected though credible. A **stock character** is a type that recurs in many works. For example, from Greek comedy to the present there have been numerous braggart soldiers, stubborn fathers, jealous husbands. Northrop Frye finds four chief types of comic figures: (1) the *alazon,* the imposter, boaster, hypocrite; (2) the *eiron* (see *irony*), the man who deprecates himself and exposes the boaster; (3) the *bomolochos,* the buffoon, or, more generally, the man who entertains by his mannerisms and talk; and (4) the *agroikos,* the straight man who is the unwitting butt of humor. Each of these types appears in many dresses. The *alazon,* for example, is most commonly the braggart soldier (*in Latin miles gloriosus*), but he is also the pedant, the crank, or anyone who is full of ideas that have no relation to reality. (See *commedia dell'arte;* consult Northrop Frye, *Anatomy of Criticism*, pp. 171–176, and R. L. Hunter, *The New Comedy of Greece and Rome*.) Stock characters are not limited to comedy. The proud tragic hero is a stock character, as are, for example, the cruel stepmother and the son who wishes to avenge his father. See also *motivation, plot.* Consult J. L. Styan, *The Elements of Drama*, Chapter 8.

chorus. In Greek drama, a group of singers and dancers (*khoros* in Greek means "dancer") who play a role, for example, Old Men of Corinth. (The chorus leader is the *koryphaios.*) In Aeschylus's *The Suppliants* (c. 490 B.C.), perhaps the earliest extant play, the chorus consists of the heroines, but in most Greek plays the chorus consists of subsidiary figures who comment rather helplessly on what is happening to the important people. Aeschylus reduced the chorus of fifty to twelve; Sophocles increased it to fifteen, where it remained. The Greek chorus, it is often said, is a sort of middleman between the unusual main figures and the humdrum spectators. Elizabethan dramas occasionally had a chorus of one actor who, not a participant in the story, commented on it. The Chorus (or prologue) in Shakespeare's *Henry V* urges the audience to

> Think when we talk of horses that you see them
> Printing their proud hoofs i' the receiving earth;
> For 'tis your thoughts that now must deck our kings.
> Carry them here and there, jumping o'er times,
> Turning the accomplishment of many years
> Into an hour-glass: for the which supply,
> Admit me Chorus to this history:
> Who prologue-like your humble patience pray,
> Gently to hear, kindly to judge, our play.

A **chorus character,** or *raisonneur,* however, such as Enobarbus in *Antony and Cleopatra,* is a character who participates in the story yet seems to be the author's mouthpiece, intelligently commenting (often with irony) on the actions of the other characters. However, Alfred Harbage, in *As They Liked It,* skeptically and aptly calls such a figure "The Unreliable Spokesman." The use of the chorus, in one form or another, continues into our times. For example, in T. S. Eliot's *Murder in the Cathedral,* the "Chorus of Women of Canterbury," like a Greek chorus and like the audience, "are forced to bear witness"; and in Tennessee William's *The Glass Menagerie,* Tom Wingfield tells the audience he is "the narrator of the play, and also a character in it." See also *plot.*

climax. See *plot.*

closet drama. A play suited only for reading, not for acting. Most nineteenth-century English poetic dramas (e.g., Coleridge's, Shelley's, Tennyson's) fit into this category, although Byron's plays have recently been moving out of the closet. Consult Moody Prior, *The Language of Tragedy.*

comedy. Most broadly, anything amusing, whether a literary work or a situation. More specifically, comedy is (in Dr. Johnson's words) "such a dramatic representation of human life, as may excite mirth." Dramatic comedies generally depict a movement from unhappiness to happiness, from (for example) young lovers frustrated by their parents to young lovers happily married. The unhappy situation is so presented that it entertains rather than distresses the spectator; it is ridiculous or diverting rather than painful.

Comic drama seems related to fertility rituals; it celebrates generation, renewal, variety (laughing away any narrow-minded persons who seek to limit life's abundance), and it celebrates human triumphs over the chances of life. Irate parents and shipwrecks cannot prevent journeys from ending with lovers' meeting. For the kinds of Greek comedy (Old, Middle, and New) see pages 123–25. For the stock characters in Greek comedy see *character.* Consult C. Hoy, *The Hyacinth Room; Theories of Comedy,* edited by P. Lauter; and L. J. Potts, *Comedy.*

comedy of humors. A term sometimes applied to plays—notably those of Ben Jonson—in which the characters,

though somewhat individualized, obviously represent types of moods (for example, the jealous husband, the witless pedant). A humor was a bodily liquid (such as blood [Latin: *sanguis*], phlegm, yellow bile, black bile) thought to control one's behavior. Allegedly, a proper mixture produced a well-adjusted person, but a preponderance of any one humor produced a distorted personality. The old sense of the word survives in the phrase, "He is in a bad humor"; *sanguine, phlegmatic,* and *bilious* are also modern survivals of the old psychology of humors. **Humor characters** are common in **situational comedy;** they are engineered by a clever plot into a situation that displays their absurdity. For example, the man who craves silence is confronted with a talkative woman, or the coward is confronted by the braggart.

comedy of manners, comedy of wit. See *high comedy.*

comic relief. Humorous episodes in tragedy, alleged to alleviate or lighten the tragic effect. Some comic scenes in tragedy, however, not only provide "relief" but enlarge the canvas of tragedy, showing us a fuller picture of life. The clown who brings Cleopatra the poisonous asp sets her tragedy against the daily world. Critics have increasingly noted that the comic scenes (such as the macabre comments of the gravediggers in *Hamlet*) often deepen rather than alleviate the tragic effect. See *tragicomedy.* Consult A. P. Rossiter, *Angel with Horns,* Chapter 14.

commedia dell'arte. Italian drama, more or less improvised, performed by professionals in Italy and abroad, mostly in the sixteenth century but still alive in the early eighteenth century. In contrast to the classically inspired written drama (**commedia erudita**) performed by actors who memorized their lines, *commedia dell'arte* (perhaps best translated "professional drama") employed sketches of plots (**scenario;** plural: **scenarii**) specifying entrances and exits and the gist of the dialogue. In performance these *scenarii* were fleshed out with stock bits of comic stage business (**lazzi**) or larger pieces of business (**burle**) such as practical jokes. (The singulars are **lazzo** and **burla,** respectively.) Thus a *scenario* may call for the *lazzo* of anger or the *burla* of chasing a fly and leave it to the actor to work out the swats and the smile when at last he munches the fly. Though these plays are said to have been improvised, the stock characters, stock situations, and stock stage business make them something more—or less—than improvised. The chief characters—most of whom wore masks—are Pantolone, an elderly Venetian merchant wearing a little cap, a red jacket, loose trousers (hence our word *pants*), and slippers; his age, amours, and avarice make him ridiculous; Dottore, a Bolognese doctor wearing a black academic gown, his age and his pedantry making him ridiculous; Capitano, a soldier, ridiculous in being a braggart and a coward; several servants called *zanne* (singular: *zanni,* from *Gianni,* "Johnny"), including Arlecchino (later Harlequin), who in the sixteenth century wore patches that in the next century were represented by triangles or diamonds; Brighella, a rather cruel and crafty rogue; Pulcinella, noted for his resourcefulness and his disguises; Pedrolino, a naive valet who becomes the melancholy Pagliacci and Pierrot; Colombina, who later becomes Columbine and loves Harlequin. Furthermore, there are usually four lovers, children of the two Old Men. Consult Allardyce Nicoll, *Masks, Mimes and Miracles*, and *The World of Harliquin*; and K. M. Lea, *Italian Popular Comedy*.

complication. See *plot*.

confidant (feminine: **confidante**). A character in whom a principal character confides, revealing his state of mind and often furthering the exposition. Horatio is Hamlet's confidant; Oenone is Phèdre's. Although Horatio and Oenone are memorable, the confidant is sometimes absurdly vapid. Though the French defended the device as more plausible than the soliloquy, the confidant may be more trouble than he is worth. In *The Critic* (1779), Sheridan ridiculed it thus: "Enter Tilburina stark mad in white satin, and her confidante stark mad in white linen."

conflict. See *plot*.

convention. An unrealistic device that the public agrees to tolerate. Thus, a character in a drama may express her thoughts aloud and not be heard by other characters (the **aside**), or she may speak her thoughts aloud on the empty stage (the **soliloquy**). Italian characters (e.g., Desdemona and Iago) speak English, yet are understood to be speaking Italian. In motion pictures, one image fades out and another fades in, and through this convention the audience knows that there is a shift in time or place. More generally any character type, any theme or motif (e.g., the suspected butler), widely used in literature or drama is a convention. Similarly, **realism**, though apparently opposed to conventions, has its own conventions. For instance, a realistic set showing a room is, when one thinks about it, highly conventional since the room lacks a fourth wall. Consult Harry Levin, *Refractions*; M. C. Bradbrook, *Themes and Conventions of Elizabethan Tragedy*.

cosmic irony. See *irony*.

cothurnus. See *sock and buskin*.

coup de théatre. A surprise, especially a striking turn of events in the plot. Consult Alan R. Thompson, *The Anatomy of Drama*.

crisis. See *plot*.

cruelty, theater of. Antonin Artaud (1896–1948) used the term in 1933 to refer to a drama that, working rather like a plague, would shock people out of the bonds of their "logical" or "civilized" conceptions and would release the suppressed primitive or prelogical powers within them, such as criminal instincts and erotic obsessions, revealing the "cruelty" or terrible mystery of existence. This drama, relying more on gestures, shapes, music, and light than on words (Artaud was immensely impressed by Balinese drama although he did not understand Indonesian), bypasses mere realism (i.e., psychology) and makes manifest the truly real supernatural, creating in the spectator a "kind of terror" or a purifying delirium. Artaud, a poet, actor, and director, published relatively little, but his metaphysics and his emphasis

on an antirealistic theater in various ways have influenced Sartre, Camus, Beckett, Ionesco, Genet, and others. Language sometimes becomes gibberish, and madness and violence are presented in order to jolt spectators out of their comfortable false view of humankind and of the universe— or, in less metaphysical plays, in order to reflect on the stage the cruelty of the modern world. Consult Artaud's *The Theater and Its Double*; several articles in *Tulane Drama Review*, 8 (Winter 1963); and the "Conclusion" in Jacques Guicharnaud and June Beckelman, *Modern French Theatre*.

dénouement. See *plot*.

deus ex machina. Literally, a god out of a machine. (1) In Greek drama a god who descends by a cranelike arrangement and solves a problem in the story, thus allowing the play to end. It was much used by Euripides; Sophocles in his old age borrowed the idea and introduced Heracles at the end of *Philoctetes* to induce the title character to go to Troy. (2) Any unexpected and improbable device (e.g., an unexpected inheritance from a long-lost uncle in Australia) used to unknot a problem and thus conclude the work.

deuteragonist. See *protagonist*.

dialogue. The speech exchanged between characters or, loosely, even the speech of a single character. Dialogue is sometimes contrasted to action, but Elizabeth Bowen aptly says that dialogue is what the characters *do* to each other, and Shaw aptly says that his plays are all talk just as Beethoven's symphonies are all music. *Stichomythia* is a special form of dialogue, wherein two speakers in a verbal duel thrust and parry in alternating lines or fragments of lines. For example:

QUEEN.
Hamlet, thou hast thy father much offended.
HAMLET.
Mother, you have my father much offended.
QUEEN.
Come, come, you answer with an idle tongue.
HAMLET.
Go, go, you question with a wicked tongue.

See *action, soliloquy*. Consult J. L. Styan, *The Elements of Drama*, Chapters 1–2; and Eric Bentley, *The Life of the Drama*.

diction. (1) Choice of words, wording. Dr. Johnson objected to the "knife" ("an instrument used by butchers and cooks," he said) that Lady Macbeth says she will use to murder the king. "Words too familiar, or too remote," Johnson said, "defeat the purpose of a poet." Consult Moody Prior, *The Language of Tragedy*. (2) A performer's manner or style of speaking, including pronunciation and phrasing.

Dionysus. Greek god of wine, the phallus, the surge of growth, and (to join all these) irrational impulse. It is commonly held that Greek tragedy grew from choral celebrations in his honor. In any case, from the sixth century B.C. tragedies were performed in Athens at the **Great** (or **Greater,** or **City**) **Dionysia,** a festival in Dionysus's honor.

(For a survey of theories of the origin of tragedy, see A. W. Pickard-Cambridge, *Dithyramb, Tragedy and Comedy*, 2nd ed., revised by T. B. L. Webster. For a brief rejection of the theory that drama originated in Dionysian festivals, see H. D. F. Kitto, in *Theatre Survey*, 1 [1960], 3–17.) Friedrich Nietzsche suggested in *The Birth of Tragedy* (1872) that Greek tragedy, usually considered calm and poised, was not the product of quiet minds. If tragedy, Nietzsche said, showed light and beauty (over which the god Apollo presided), it was nevertheless also indebted to Dionysus, who represented the frenzied, buried self-assertions of the mind. That is, Greek tragedy was the product of **Dionysian** ecstatic and violent self-assertion tamed by (or fused with) the **Apollonian** sense of reason, of moderation, and of external order. *Apollonian* is often associated with classicism, and "*Dionysian*" with romanticism.

direct address. See *soliloquy*.

disclosure, discovery. See *anagnorisis*.

disguising. See *masque*.

domestic tragedy. A serious play showing the misfortunes (especially within the family) of a private citizen rather than of a person of high rank who is involved in events that shake a realm. See *bourgeois drama*. Consult Henry H. Adams, *English Domestic or Homiletic Tragedy 1575 to 1642*.

double plot. See *plot*.

downstage. The front half of the stage, or any part of the stage considered in relationship to someone or something further from the audience.

drama (from Greek: *dran*, "to do"). (1) A play; a work that tells a story by means of impersonators. (2) The whole body of work written for the theater. (3) A serious but untragic play (see *drame*). (4) Events containing conflict, tension, surprise ("life is full of drama"; "the first act lacks drama"). See *closet drama, comedy, melodrama, tragedy*. A play is written by a **dramatist;** the art of writing plays is **dramaturgy.** A person who writes plays is also a **playwright.** (Note that the last syllable is not *-write* but *-wright*, denoting a maker, as a shipwright is a maker of ships.) Consult Kenneth T. Rowe, *Write That Play*; Walter Kerr, *How Not to Write a Play*; and Bernard Grebanier, *Playwriting*.

drama of ideas. See *pièce à thèse*.

dramatic illusion. The state between delusion (the spectators think the world on the stage is real) and full awareness (the spectators never forget they are looking at scenery and actors). In *A Midsummer Night's Dream*, Bottom fears that delusion will occur unless the audience is carefully warned: "Write me a prologue, and let the prologue seem to say we will do no harm with our swords, and that Pyramus is not killed indeed. And, for the more better assurance, tell them that I Pyramus am not Pyramus, but Bottom the Weaver. This will put them out of fear." See *aesthetic distance*.

George Henry Lewes (1817–1878) introduced into English dramatic criticism the term *optique du théâtre,* taken from the French actor François René Molé (1734–1802). Spectators must have this "theater view," this understanding of "scenic illusion," if they are to enjoy the theater. If they lack it, they will complain that Hamlet ought to be speaking Danish (see *convention*). *Optique du théâtre* requires that we be given not reality but a symbolic representation of it. A stage miser should finger his gold differently from a real miser; a stage character must be heard, even though in real life the character might speak inaudibly.

Staging that aims at delusion or a high degree of illusion is **representational** staging. With this kind of staging, characters eat real food on stage, speak with their backs to the audience, and so on. (See *naturalism, realism*.) When David Belasco staged *The Governor's Lady* in 1912, he was representational, placing on the stage an exact duplicate of a particular (Child's) restaurant. On the other hand, **presentational** staging is antirealistic; in Thornton Wilder's *Our Town* (1938), a drugstore counter, for example, consisted of a board across the backs of two chairs. The staging in musical comedies, ballets, and puppet shows is, of course, presentational. Presentational staging is sometimes called **theatrical** staging. **Theatricalism,** by its unreality, continually reminds us that we are in the theater, not in the street. On theatricalism, see *style*. A derogatory way of saying a work is theatrical is to say it is "**stagy.**"

dramatic irony. See *irony*.

dramatist. See *drama*.

dramaturgy. See *drama*.

drame. A solemn but untragic play, especially an eighteenth-century play that, quietly glorifying the bourgeois virtues, preaches and appeals to the audience's emotions. See *bourgeois drama*. Consult Alan R. Thompson, *The Anatomy of Drama*, which classifies most naturalistic and realistic plays (e.g., Ibsen's and Chekhov's) as *drames*.

eiron. See *character*.

Elizabethan playhouse. See page 186.

empathy. The projection of one's feelings into a perceived object. The Germans call it *Einfühlung*—"a feeling into." Vernon Lee, one of the formulators of the idea, claimed that when we say "the mountain rises," we do so not because the mountain rises (it doesn't) but because we have often raised our eyes, head, and total muscular structure to look at mountains or other tall objects. In perceiving a mountain, we merge (unaware) its image with the previously accumulated idea of rising. We are said to empathize with characters if we flinch at a blow directed at them or if we feel bowed with their grief—if, in short, we *experience* as well as *see* their behavior. Empathy is often distinguished from **sympathy:** we empathize if we feel *with* the character; we sympathize if we feel *for* the character. See *aesthetic distance*. Consult Vernon Lee's essay in *A Modern Book of Aesthetics*, edited by Melvin Rader; and Herbert S. Langfield, *The Aesthetic Attitude*.

epic drama. Bertolt Brecht (1898–1956) labeled "Aristotelian" most drama before his own. He held that it aimed at enthralling the spectators by building up to a climax, thus arousing and then purging their emotions. In contrast, Brecht said, epic drama (he borrowed the phrase from Erwin

Piscator) aims at arousing the audience's detached thought; it teaches, keeping the spectators alert by preventing any emotional involvement. The epic drama (probably so-called because it resembles the epic in its abundance of loosely connected scenes and its tendency to deal with a society rather than merely with a few individuals) achieves this estrangement, or **alienation effect** (German: ***Verfremdungs-effekt***), by many means. For example, the epic play (e.g., Brecht's *The Good Woman of Setzuan* or his *Mother Courage*) commonly consists of a series of loosely connected scenes rather than a tightly organized plot with a climax; the settings are not realistic but merely suggest the locale, and they are often changed in full view of the audience, preventing any entrancing illusion (a night scene may be done on an illuminated stage, again to prevent the audience from emotionally entering into the play); the actor may address the audience directly, sometimes in song, aiming not at becoming the character but at presenting the character, or, to put it differently, making a comment on the character, as we might do when we put aside a cigarette and say, "He said to me, '. . .'"; loudspeakers, films, and placards may be used; and the whole is something of a lecture-demonstration, aimed not at arousing and then quieting the audience's emotions but at making things somewhat strange to the audience so that the audience will look sharply and will think (see p. 584–85). Consult Bertolt Brecht, "A Short Organum," in *Playwrights on Playwriting*, edited by Toby Cole; *Brecht on Theatre*, translated by John Willett; and R. Gray "Brecht," *The Tulane Drama Review*, 6 (Sept. 1961).

epilogue. (1) An appendix (usually a concluding address) to a play. (2) The actor who recites such an appendix (e.g., Puck, at the close of Shakespeare's *A Midsummer Night's Dream*).

exposition. See *plot*.

expressionism. An antinaturalistic movement chiefly associated with Germany just after World War I. It was foreshadowed by Strindberg, notably in his trilogy *To Damascus* (1898–1904) and in his *A Dream Play* (1902). Expressionism does not seek to "hold the mirror up to nature" (Hamlet's words) or to present reality dispassionately; rather, it seeks to show the world as we feel (rather than literally see) it. (See p. 558.) Thus, when Mr. Zero shakes his employer (in Elmer Rice's *The Adding Machine* [1923]), the office spins; when he is on trial, the walls of the courtroom veer crazily. In other words, the dramatist makes visible the symbolic, subjective experience of the characters (or of the dramatist) by distorting objective or literal reality. Speaking broadly, expressionist plays (in addition to being unrealistic) usually (1) depict types or classes (Rice's Mr. Zero; the Man, the Woman, the Nameless One in Ernst Toller's *Man and Masses* [1921]), (2) employ dream sequences, and (3) assume that society is responsible for our troubles. Though Arthur Miller's *Death of a Salesman* (see p. 650) is in many ways "realistic," it also is indebted to expressionism, especially in the scenes involving Willy's memories. (Miller originally

planned to call the play *The Inside of His Head*.) Note, too, the name of Miller's hero—Loman, that is, low man. Tennessee Williams's *The Glass Menagerie* (see p. 619) similarly reveals a modified—one might say Americanized—expressionism. Consult John Willett, *Expressionism*.

falling action. See *plot*.

farce. A sort of comedy based not on clever language or subtleties of character but on broadly humorous situations (for example, a man mistakenly enters the ladies' locker room). Farce is lucidly defended by Eric Bentley in his introduction to *"Let's Get a Divorce" and Other Plays*, in which he suggests that farce, like dreams, shows "the disguised fulfillment of repressed wishes." Farce is usually filled with surprise, with swift physical action, and with assault. The characters are physically and intellectually insensitive, and characterization is subordinated to plot. See also Bentley's *The Life of the Drama*. **Slapstick,** named for an implement made of two slats that resound when slapped against a posterior, is farce that relies on physical assault. Farce and slapstick are **low comedy,** as is comedy that depends on obscenity.

feminist theater. A movement that seeks to expand the opportunities for women in the theater and to heighten the public's awareness of women, especially by concentrating on female experience. See page 896 and H. Keysaar, *Feminist Theatre*.

foil. A character who sets off another, as Laertes and Fortinbras—young men who, like Hamlet, have lost a father—help to set off Hamlet, or as a braggart soldier helps to set off a courageous one.

foreshadowing. See *suspense*.

Great Dionysia. See *Dionysus*.

Greek theater. See A Note on the Greek Theater, page 44.

groundlings. See A Note on the Elizabethan Theater, page 186.

guerilla theater. Dramatic performances, especially in the 1960s, seeking to help the populace throw off what was said to be an oppressive bourgeois government. Theater was viewed not as a means of producing beauty or of exploring ideas but as a weapon in a class war. Performances were given in such places as streets, fields, and gymnasiums rather than in conventional theaters. Thus, the traditional separation of players from audience was broken down. Moreover, the audience itself might be in some degree assaulted, by, for instance, obscenities or the spectacle of nudity, offered in an effort to shock the spectators into an awareness of new ideals. Furthermore, *performance* and *drama* were loosely interpreted. For example, Luis Valdez, founder of El Teatro Campesino (1965) in *Actos* wrote, "A demonstration with a thousand Chicanos, all carrying flags and picket signs, shouting 'Chicano Power!' is . . . theater." (See p. 799.) Consult Henry Lesnik, ed., *Guerilla Street Theatre*; and (especially for El Teatro Campesino) C. W. E. Bigsby, *A Critical Introduction to Twentieth-Century American Drama*, volume 3.

hamartia. A Greek word variously translated as "tragic flaw," "error," "shortcoming," or "weakness." In many plays it is a flaw or even a vice such as *hybris* (also *hubris*)—a word that in classical Greek meant bullying or even assault and battery, but that in discussions of tragedy means overweening pride, arrogance, excessive confidence. In other plays, however, it is merely a misstep, such as a choice that turns out badly. Indeed, the tragic hero may be undone by his virtue—his courage, for example, when others are not merely prudent but cowardly. See pages 33–34. On *hamartia* and *hybris* see Richmond Lattimore, *Story Patterns in Greek Tragedy*.

Hellenistic theater. Theaters of, say, the third and second centuries B.C. erected in towns to which Greek culture had been spread by Alexander's conquests seem to have been much like the Greek theater, though the *proskenion* was apparently more highly decorated, having pillars a few feet in front of it and being fitted with painted panels called *pinakes*. And the *skene*, now of stone rather than of wood, may have had projections at the sides (*paraskenia*) and a upper story (*episkenion*). The playing area on this upper level is the *logeion*. Consult Margarete Bieber, *The History of the Greek and Roman Theater*.

hero, heroine. The protagonist in a drama. Until the rise of middle-class drama in the late eighteenth century, heroes were usually persons of high rank (King Oedipus, King Lear) and therefore of political power. Heroines too were sometimes politically powerful (Clytemnestra, in Aeschylus's *Agamemnon*), but more often their power was moral (Desdemona, in Shakespeare's *Othello*). When heroines have exerted physical power, they have often been regarded—at least by men—as wicked. See T. H. Henn, "The Woman's Part," in Henn's *The Harvest of Tragedy*.

high comedy. Intellectual rather than physical, a type of comedy that requires the close attention of a sophisticated audience, flourishing (says George Meredith in his *Essay on Comedy* [1877]) in a "society of cultivated men and women . . . wherein ideas are current, and the perceptions quick." Etherege, Wycherley, Congreve, and other playwrights of the decades following the Restoration of Charles II to the throne of England (1660) wrote **Restoration comedy,** high comedy of a particular sort, often called **comedy of manners** or **comedy of wit.** Their plays abound in witty **repartee** (what Dr. Johnson called "gay remarks and unexpected answers") and often strike modern audiences as cynical. Restoration comedy has no precise terminal date but can be said to have ended about 1700 with the development of sentimental comedy, plays of venerable parents and middle-class dutiful sons who love pure young things. An example is Richard Steele's *The Conscious Lovers* (1722). Consult Thomas H. Fujimura, *The Restoration Comedy of Wit*; Louis Kronenberger, *The Thread of Laughter*; and Norman N. Holland, *The First Modern Comedies*.

hubris (*hybris*). See *hamartia*.

humor character. See *comedy of humors*.

imitation (Greek: *mimesis*). Not a pejorative term in much criticism, for it often implies a "making" or "re-creat-

ing" or "representing" of a form in a substance not natural to it. Thus, Michelangelo reproduced or imitated the form of Moses, in stone. For Aristotle, tragedy was the imitation (i.e., representation, re-creation) by means of words, gesture, music, and scenery, of an important action.

irony. Irony is of several sorts. **Socratic irony,** named for Socrates, who commonly feigned more ignorance than he possessed, denotes understatement. The *eiron* (see *character*) is the cunning fellow who plays the underdog. **Dramatic irony,** or **Sophoclean irony,** or **tragic irony** refers to a condition of affairs that is the tragic reverse of what the participants think. Thus, it is ironic that Macbeth kills Duncan, thinking he will achieve happiness, because he later finds he loses all that makes life worth living. Oedipus accuses the blind prophet of corruption, but by the end of the play Oedipus learns (as the audience knew at the outset) that he himself is corrupt, that he has been mentally blind (ignorant), and that the prophet has had vision (knowledge). Oedipus meant what he said, but his words have proved to be ironic. (Aristotle's word for reversal is *peripeteia*.) We have dramatic irony, it can be said, when a speech or action is more fully understood by the spectators than by the characters. This sort of irony, based on misunderstanding, or partial knowledge, is common in tragedy, but comedy too has its misunderstandings; comic speeches or actions are ironic if they bring about the opposite of what is intended. More generally, the contrast implied in irony need be neither tragic nor comic. For example, it is ironic that the strong man is overthrown by the weak man and that the liar unknowingly tells the truth. **Irony of fate** (a phrase that H. W. Fowler's *Modern English Usage* aptly says is hackneyed), or **cosmic irony,** denotes the view that God, or fate, or some sort of supernatural figure is amused to manipulate human beings as a puppeteer manipulates puppets. Thus, by an irony of fate, the messenger delivers the prisoner's pardon an instant too late. Consult Garnett G. Sedgewick, *Of Irony*; and Alan R. Thompson, *The Dry Mock*.

koryphaios. See *chorus*.

kothurnus. See *sock and buskin*.

lazzo. See *commedia dell'arte*.

Lenaea. See A Note on the Greek Theater, page 44.

liturgical drama. A play that is part of the church service or liturgy. In the tenth century the churchmen put on a playlet of a few lines as part of the Easter liturgy. The text was based on Mark 16:1–7. Clerics dressed as the Three Marys approached the "tomb" of Christ (the altar) and were asked by a cleric, disguised as an angel, whom they sought. When they replied that they sought Christ, he told them that Christ had risen and showed them the empty "tomb." The performers were all male, and the Latin dialogue was chanted; probably the gestures were stylized. See p. 4.

low comedy. See *farce*.

masque, mask, disguising. An entertainment (apparently derived from an ancient ritual) in the Renaissance court, wherein noblemen performed a dignified playlet, usually allegorical and mythological. The masque was lavishly produced, but its basic structure was generally simple: the masquers (costumed and masked noble performers) entered (supposedly having come from afar), danced with the ladies of the court, and then departed. Because the masquers were of the same rank as the ladies and because performers and audience joined in a dance, the masque was very close to the masked ball. Ben Jonson (1572–1637) popularized what he called the **antimasque** (a grotesque dance of monsters or clowns), performed by professionals representing chaos, who were dispelled by the courtly performers. (*Anti*, from *antic*, meaning "a grotesque caper" or "a fool," is sometimes written *ante* because the antimasque precedes the masque.) Consult Enid Welsford, *The Court Masque*; E. K. Chambers, *The Elizabethan Stage*; Stephen Orgel, *The Jonsonian Masque*.

melodrama. Originally, in Renaissance Italy, an opera; later, a drama with occasional songs or with music (*melos* is Greek for "song") expressing a character's thoughts, much as in films today. In the early nineteenth century plays with musical accompaniment became so stereotyped that the word *melodrama* acquired a second (and now dominant) meaning: a play wherein characters clearly virtuous or vicious are pitted against each other in sensational situations filled with suspense, until justice triumphs. The situations, not the characters, are exciting. The exotic horror (castles and dungeons) dominant in early nineteenth-century melodramas was often replaced later in the century by local horror (the cruel landlord), but whether exotic or local, melodrama is improbable, and virtue—unsullied by any touch of guilt—triumphs over unlikely circumstances. Melodrama is sometimes said to be tragedy with character left out (i.e., it contains serious happenings), but by virtue of its happy ending and its one-sided characters, it can better be described as comedy with good humor left out. Some critics use *melodrama* without any pejorative connotation to describe such serious, often sensational, plays as Emlyn Williams's *Night Must Fall* (1935), Robert Ardrey's *Thunder Rock* (1939), and Arthur Miller's *All My Sons*. Consult Robert B. Heilman, *Tragedy and Melodrama*.

miracle play, mystery play. Interchangeable terms for a medieval play on a biblical episode or a saint's life. The term *mystery play* derives from the French *métier* ("work," "occupation," "ministry") from the Latin *ministerium* ("attendant," "servant"). The plays were sponsored by *mysteries*, that is, trades or guilds. Consult Arnold Williams, *The Drama of Medieval England*. See pages 149–51.

monologue. See *soliloquy*.

morality play. A late medieval development, popular well into the sixteenth century, allegorically dramatizing some aspect of the moral life, including such characters as Everyman, Good Deeds, and Avarice. It usually showed the conflict between good and evil or the way in which the Christian faces death. Consult Arnold Williams, *The Drama of Medieval England*; Bernard Spivack, *Shakespeare and the Allegory of Evil*; and R. Potter, *The English Morality Play*. See pages 167–68.

motivation. Grounds based on character and situation that make behavior plausible. Such grounds are not always present, even in great drama. For example, when Othello asks why Iago "hath thus ensnared my soul," Iago replies, "Demand me nothing: what you know, you know." See *character*. Consult J. I. M. Stewart, *Character and Motive in Shakespeare*.

naturalism. Sometimes defined, like realism, as the portrayal of "a scientifically accurate, detached picture of life, including everything and selecting nothing." The spectators looking through the peephole of the proscenium, as a scientist looks through the eyepiece of a microscope, are to feel they are witnessing life rather than a symbolic representation of life. More commonly, however, naturalism alludes neither to a panoramic view nor to the detailed presentation of a narrow **slice of life** (French: *tranche de vie*) but to a particular attitude held by some writers since the middle of the nineteenth century. Though claiming to be dispassionate observers, they were influenced by evolutionary thought and regarded humans as creatures determined by their heredity and environment rather than as possessed of a soul and of free will. The movement in drama can be said to have begun with the Goncourt brothers' unsuccessful *Henriette Maréchal* (1865), but it is usual to say that the opening gun in the battle for naturalism was fired in Émile Zola's dramatization (1873) of his novel *Thérèse Raquin*. Thérèse and her lover drown her husband but are then so guilt-ridden that they poison themselves. In his preface Zola urged that the theater be brought "into closer relation with the great movement toward truth and experimental science which has since the last century been on the increase. . . . I have chosen characters who were completely dominated by their nerves and blood." In Paris, André Antoine opened his Théâtre Libre in 1887, devoting it mostly to plays showing the power of instincts and the influence of heredity and environment. These plays were staged as untheatrically as possible; for example, the actors turned their backs to the audience. In Germany, Otto Brahm opened the Freie Bühne in 1889, and in England J. T. Grein opened the Independent Theatre in 1891, both with Ibsen's *Ghosts* (1881), a play showing the destruction of a young man by inherited syphilis. Ibsen's greatness does not allow him to be pinned down by the label "naturalist," but he can be said to be naturalistic (among other things) by virtue of his serious interests in the effects of heredity and environment. Other dramatists who wrote naturalistic plays include August Strindberg (e.g., his *Miss Julie* [1888]) and Gerhart Hauptmann (early in his career with *The Weavers* [1892]), and Eugene O'Neill (again, the early plays such as *The Rope* [1918] and *Diff'rent* [1920]). Note, however, that the major naturalistic writers usually are more than naturalistic. Strindberg's *Miss Julie*, for example, has a preface that talks about the influence of heredity and environment. It deals with sordid aspects of reality, but it also has symbolic overtones, notably in Julie's and Jean's dreams. Consult Mordecai Gorelik, *New Theatres for Old*;

TDR: *The Drama Review* 13 (Winter 1968); and (for Strindberg, O'Neill, and the sources of their ideas) Oscar Cargill, *Intellectual America.*

nuntius. See *Senecan tragedy.*

obligatory scene. See *scène à faire.*

optique du théâtre. See *dramatic illusion.*

orchestra. See A Note on the Greek Theater, page 44.

pathos. The quality that evokes pity. The pathetic is often distinguished from the tragic. In the former, the suffering is experienced by the passive and the innocent (especially women and children), while in the latter it is experienced by persons who act, struggle, and are in some measure responsible for their sufferings. Discussing Aeschylus's *The Suppliants,* H. D. F. Kitto says in *Greek Tragedy* (2nd ed.): "The Suppliants are not only pathetic, as the victims of outrage, but also tragic, as the victims of their own misconceptions." See *bourgeois drama.*

performance theater. A movement in the 1960s and early 1970s especially associated with Julian Beck, a cofounder of the Living Theatre. Influenced by Antonin Artaud's **theater of cruelty,** performance theater rejected the gap between performers and spectators (performers moving on stage, spectators impassively sitting in the dark); it therefore necessarily minimized the role of the playwright and gave the actors freedom to improvise. Verbal and visual assaults (for instance nudity) on the audience, as well as physical contact with it, supposedly gave actor and spectator freedom to celebrate bodily and spiritual unity and liberation. Consult Julian Beck, *The Life of the Theatre,* and for a critical and historical survey, see part 2 of the third volume of C. W. E. Bigsby, *A Critical Introduction to Twentieth-Century American Drama.*

peripeteia (anglicized to **peripety,** meaning "reversal"). The reversal occurs when an action produces the opposite of what was intended or expected, and it is, therefore, a kind of irony. An example of *peripeteia* occurs in *Julius Caesar;* Brutus kills Caesar in order to free Rome from tyranny, but the deed introduces tyranny into Rome. See *irony, plot.*

picture-frame stage. See *proscenium stage.*

pièce à thèse. A play with a thesis; a play in which the dramatist argues a point. Commonly the thesis is not about, for example, the benevolence of God, but about the merits or defects of some social institution; a play dealing with a social institution may also be called a **problem play** or a **drama of ideas.** Some critics distinguish between the terms, saying that a problem play merely poses a social problem, as Galsworthy does in *Strife* (1909), while a thesis play propounds a solution. Shaw says that "the material of the dramatist is always some conflict of human feeling with circumstances"; when the circumstances are "human institutions" (e.g., divorce laws, penal codes) rather than unchanging facts of life (e.g., death) and the audience is forced to meditate on the value of the institutions, we have a problem play. Shaw's essay, "The Problem Play," is reprinted in *Shaw on Theatre,* edited by E. J. West, a volume that also contains

Shaw's "The Play of Ideas." Consult also Walter Kerr, *How Not to Write a Play,* Chapter 5.

pièce bien faite, or **well-made play.** Of course, all good plays are "well-made," but the term has come to mean a play with much suspense and with little depth of characterization that relies on a cleverly constructed plot—first developing a situation, then building the crisis to a climax, and then resolving the business. The type, which perhaps can be described as melodrama with the fisticuffs left out, is chiefly associated with Victorien Sardou (1831–1908), but Sardou was indebted to Eugène Scribe (1791–1861), who indeed coined the term *pièce bien faite* in describing his farces and melodramas. Shaw called their plays clockwork mice, and Sardoodledom, but the influence of Sardou on Shaw's hero, Ibsen, is undeniable. See *plot,* and consult Walter Kerr, *How Not to Write a Play,* Chapter 10; Eric Bentley, "Homage to Scribe," *What Is Theatre?*; C. E. Montague, *Dramatic Values,* pages 63–74; and *Camille and Other Plays,* edited by Stephen S. Stanton.

plot and **character.** The plot is sometimes the "story," that is the "narrative," but usually it is the happenings *as the author arranges them.* In *Hamlet,* for example, the story involves the poisoning of Hamlet's father, but Shakespeare omits this scene from his plot. Aristotle, in Chapter 6 of the *Poetics,* calls plot "the whole structure of the incidents," and he speaks of plot as the "soul of tragedy," thus making it more important than character. By *character* he means the personalities of the figures in the story. Menander (a Greek comic dramatist) is said to have told a friend that he had finished a comedy, though he had not yet written a line of dialogue. The anecdote implies that Menander had completed his idea of *what happens* (action) and in *what order* (plot), and he would find it easy then to write the lines of the characters necessary to his plot. The separation, however, between plot and character is misleading, for the two usually interplay. Although it is true that there may be much plot and little character (as in a thriller), in most great plays there is such a fusion between what is done and the personality of the doer that we feel the truth of Henry James's questions: "What is character but the determination of incident? What is incident but the illustration of character?" (See also *character.*)

Most plots entail a **conflict,** in which the protagonist is somehow opposed. If the protagonist is opposed chiefly by another person rather than by a force such as fate, God, or by an aspect of himself or herself, the opposing figure is the **antagonist.** The German critic Gustav Freytag, in *Technique of the Drama* (1863), held that a play dramatizes "the rushing forth of will power from the depths of man's soul toward the external world" and "the coming into being of a deed and its consequences on the human soul." The five-act play, he said, commonly arranged such an action into a **pyramidal structure,** consisting of a **rising action,** a **climax,** and **falling action.** (In Peter de Vries's witty formulation, a plot has a beginning, a muddle, and an end.) The rising action begins with the **exposition,** in which is given essential information, especially about the **antecedent action** (what has occurred before this piece of action begins). For example, the two gossiping servants who tell each other that after a year away in Paris the young master is coming home today with his new wife are giving the audience the exposition. The action rises through a **complication** (the protagonist is opposed) to a high point, or **crisis,** or **climax** (a moment at which tension is high and which is a decisive turning point). The falling action goes through a **reversal** (if a tragedy, the protagonist loses power), and then into a **catastrophe,** also called a **dénouement** (unknotting) or resolution. (Aristotle's word for the reversal is *peripeteia,* anglicized to *peripety,* and, translated as "irony of events," would in a comedy be a change from bad fortune to good, and the catastrophe would thus be happy.) The dénouement frequently involves what Aristotle called an *anagnorisis* (**recognition, disclosure, discovery**). This recognition may be as simple as the identification of a long-lost brother by a birth mark, or it may involve a character's recognition of his own true condition. Shakespeare sometimes used a pyramidal structure, placing his climax neatly in the middle of what seems to us to be the third of five acts. In *Julius Caesar,* for example, Brutus rises in the first half of the play, reaching his height in 3.1 with the death of Caesar; later in this scene he gives Marc Antony permission to speak at Caesar's funeral and thus sets in motion his own fall, which occupies the second half of the play. In *Macbeth,* the protagonist attains his height in 3.1 ("Thou hast it now: King"), but he soon perceives that he is going downhill:

> I am in blood
> Stepped in so far that, should I wade no more,
> Returning were as tedious as go o'er.

Some works have a **double plot,** that is, two plots, usually with some sort of relationship. For example, the **subplot** or **underplot** (the secondary narrative) might be a grotesque version of the serious main plot. In Shakespeare's *The Tempest,* the main plot and subplot both deal with usurpation. In *King Lear,* the main plot concerns Lear's relationship with his daughters, while the parallel subplot concerns Gloucester's relationship with his sons. For another aspect of the subplot, see *comic relief.* Consult William Empson, *Some Versions of Pastoral,* Chapter 2. On plotting, see *pièce bien faite* and *scène à faire.*

poetic justice. A term coined by Thomas Rymer in 1678, denoting the reward of the virtuous and the punishment of the vicious. Aristotle had said or implied that the tragic hero is undone partly by some sort of personal flaw—that is, he is at least partly responsible for the suffering he later encounters. (See *hamartia* and p. 33.) Poetic justice, with its idea that all characters reap the harvest of their just deserts, is a hardening of Aristotle's suggestion. Consult M. A. Quinlan, *Poetic Justice in the Drama.*

poor theater. A term associated with the Polish director Jerzy Grotowski (1933–). Unlike the "rich" theater, which uses elaborate lighting, scenery, and costumes, the poor theater rejects technology and concentrates on the involvement of actor and audience in "a living collaboration." The actors' faces are the only "masks," and their voices are the only "sound effects." Gestures, at least in moments of strong emotion, tend to be stylized rather than naturalistic. See J. Grotowski, *Towards a Poor Theatre.*

presentational theater. A type of theater in which there is little or no illusionism in the acting and staging (as opposed to realistic or naturalistic or representational theater). Communication is achieved by means of evident conventions, such as direct address to the audience (which acknowledges the existence of the audience), the soliloquy, and the aside. Similarly, a voyage in a boat may be indicated by pantomiming the motion of rowing. Virtually all drama before the middle of the nineteenth century was highly presentational, if only because of the inability to produce illusionistic lighting effects. However, a largely presentational theater, such as Shakespeare's (where, on the open-air stage, a night scene might be indicated in daylight by the presence of characters holding torches), also might aim at realism. For instance, in Shakespeare's *The Tempest* a stage direction specifies that the sailors are "wet." On the other hand, even highly illusionistic sets of the later nineteenth century also employ conventions; for instance, the audience agrees to pretend that there is a fourth wall for the living room it sees exposed on the stage. On one form of twentieth-century presentational theater, see *expressionism.*

problem play. See *pièce à thèse.*

prologue. (1) A preface or introduction. For the Greeks the *prologos* was the first scene, which gave the exposition. Elizabethan prologues commonly summarize the plot, as the Chorus does in the prologue to *Romeo and Juliet,* but in the English theater of the late seventeenth century, the prologue was almost an independent verse essay spoken before the play began. (2) The actor who speaks a piece of the sort described above.

properties, props. Objects used on the stage, other than scenery and costumes. Examples include umbrellas, books, and food.

proscenium stage, or **picture-frame stage.** A playing area framed in the front, and thus separated from the audience. This frame is the *proscenium arch* or the *proscenium;* the empty space it contains, sometimes filled with a curtain, is the *proscenium opening.* Basically a proscenium theater has two rooms, one for the audience and another (with a hole in the mutual wall) for the performers. Such a theater is at least as old as the early seventeenth century, when the Farnese Theater was built in Parma. Consult Allardyce Nicoll, *The Development of the Theatre.* See page 322.

protagonist. The chief figure in a play. In Greek, the word means literally the "first contender," that is, the chief actor (*protos,* meaning "first"). The second role was given to the **deuteragonist,** and the third to the **tritagonist.** The protagonist is commonly opposed by the **antagonist,** played by the deuteragonist. For the relationship between the protagonist and the antagonist, see *plot*.

psychical distance. See *aesthetic distance*.

pyramidal structure. See *plot*.

raisonneur. See *chorus*.

realism. The reproduction of life, especially as it appears to the eye and ear; the illusion of nature. Usually realism deals with ordinary people in ordinary situations, moving in scenery that closely imitates reality. In England, T. W. Robertson (1829–1871) insisted, for example, that doorknobs not be painted on the doors but be three-dimensional. Wings and a backcloth (i.e., projecting flats at the sides and a painted cloth at the rear) were increasingly replaced by the box set (a room with the front wall missing, containing real furniture) for interior scenes. Gas lighting, introduced to the stage about 1820, soon became capable of producing effects of sunlight, moonlight, and so on. The dialogue, as well as the sets, came closer to what the senses perceive. Realistic plays (in prose, of course) avoid soliloquies, asides, and declamation. (On the other hand, realism makes use of its conventions. See the entry on *convention*.) The great playwrights of the movement are Ibsen and Chekhov. As Mary McCarthy says of American realistic drama (*On the Contrary*), "realism is a depreciation of the real," for in "its resolve to tell the whole truth" it tends to deflate, to reveal human littleness. (It doesn't believe in exceptional, heroic people; when it treats the upper classes, it usually tends toward satire.) The oppressive box set of realistic plays, McCarthy points out, "is the box or 'coffin' of average middle-class life opened at one end to reveal the corpse within." That realism shades into naturalism is clear; that in Ibsen it shades into symbolism is less obvious but is well demonstrated by John Northam, *Ibsen's Dramatic Method*. A simple example of Ibsen's symbolism occurs in *Hedda Gabler*. Hedda's hair is "not particularly ample," but Thea's is "unusually rich and wavy," suggesting Hedda's barrenness and Thea's fertility. Consult Mordecai Gorelik, *New Theatres for Old*; A. Nicholas Vardac, *Stage to Screen*, Chapters 4 and 9; and Ernest B. Watson, *Sheridan to Robertson*. In **selective realism,** some of the scenery (e.g., a window and a door) closely reproduce reality, but some (e.g., a framework *suggesting* a roof) does not.

recognition. See *anagnorisis*.

repartee. See *high comedy*.

Restoration comedy. See *high comedy*.

revenge play. See *Senecan tragedy*.

reversal. See *peripeteia*.

rising action. See *plot*.

Roman theater. A permanent theater was not built at Rome until the first century B.C. The plays of Plautus (254?–184 B.C.) and Terence (190?–159? B.C.) were performed on temporary stages erected in the Circus Maximus and the Forum during holidays. In the permanent Roman theater, the enormous audience (40,000 or more) sat in a semicircle around a level space that was a vestige of what had been called the *orchestra* ("dancing place") of the Greek theater. Behind this vestige was the stage, running through what would have been the diameter of the circle. The long, slightly elevated stage was backed by a facade (painted to resemble two or three houses) with several doors through which actors made some of their exits and entrances, the others being made at the ends of the stage. Behind the façade was the dressing-room. The Roman theater, unlike the Greek and Hellenistic theaters, was a self-enclosed structure, built on level ground, not against a hillside. Consult Margarete Bieber, *The History of the Greek and Roman Theater*.

satire. A work ridiculing aspects of human behavior and seeking to arouse in the audience contempt for its object. Satirists almost always justify their attacks by claiming that satire is therapeutic. Shaw says, in the preface to his *Complete Plays*, "If I make you laugh at yourself remember that my business as a classic writer of comedies is to 'chasten morals with ridicule'; and if I sometimes make you feel like a fool, remember that I have by the same action cured your folly." Satire, however, is sometimes distinguished from comedy on the grounds that satire aims to correct by ridiculing, while comedy aims simply to evoke amusement. Among notable satires are the plays of Aristophanes; Gay's *The Beggar's Opera* (1728); Brecht's *The Threepenny Opera* (1928); and Kaufman, Ryskind, and Gershwin's *Of Thee I Sing* (1931)—though Kaufman himself has defined satire as "that which closes on Saturday night." See *burlesque, comedy.* Consult Northrop Frye, *Anatomy of Criticism*.

satyr-play. A piece in which there is a chorus of lewd satyrs (creatures half-man and half either horse or goat). The Greek tragic playwrights of the fifth century B.C. presented three tragedies and a satyr-play for the dramatic festival. Apparently the satyr-play often burlesqued a hero, showing him in a ludicrous situation. Only one complete satyr-play (Euripides' *The Cyclops*) is extant; it travesties the legend of Odysseus's encounter with Polyphemus. Consult Philip W. Harsh, *A Handbook of Classical Drama*.

scenario. See *commedia dell'arte*.

scene. See *act*.

scène à faire, or (in William Archer's translation of Francisque Sarcey's term) **obligatory scene.** "An obligatory scene [Archer says] is one which the audience (more or less clearly and consciously) foresees and desires, and the absence of which it may with reason resent." For example, a familiar legend may make a scene obligatory, or a dramatist may cause the audience to expect a certain scene. In Hamlet the play-within-the-play (3.2) has been called such a scene: Hamlet has doubted the ghost, and we must see the ghost's words verified. Most often, however, an obligatory scene is an expected critical confrontation in which information previously hidden from a character or from the audience is revealed. Consult William Archer, *Play-making*.

scenery. The carpentry and painted cloths (and projected images) used on a stage. Scenery may be used to conceal parts of the stage, to decorate, to imitate or suggest locales, to establish time, or to evoke mood. For comments on early scenery, see A Note on the Greek Theater, page 44, and A Note on the Elizabethan Theater, page 186. The Elizabethan public theater did not use much scenery. In *Twelfth Night*, when Viola asks, "What country, friends, is this?" she is told, "This is Illyria, lady," and the audience knows all that carpenters and painters can tell it. But even before Shakespeare's birth, Renaissance Italians had placed buildings, probably of lath and cloth, at the right and left of the stage. Behind the buildings, which were three-dimensional and embellished with moldings, projected flat pieces cut and painted to look like other buildings at a distance, and behind these flat pieces were yet other flats, still smaller.

selective realism. See *realism*.

Senecan tragedy. Any of the serious plays by the Roman author Seneca (4 B.C.–A.D. 65), or imitations of them. Of the ten extant Roman tragedies, nine are attributed to Seneca, and these were probably written not for the stage but for private readings. The heroes seem to us to be almost madmen, but perhaps they are to be regarded sympathetically as people overwhelmed by passion. Seneca's influence on the Elizabethan dramatists was considerable; the **revenge play,** with its ghosts and its deranged hero who seeks vengeance, doubtless would have been different had Seneca not existed. Among the signs of Seneca's influence are ghosts, revenge, deeds of horror (e.g., children stewed and served to their parents), occasional stoical speeches but a predominance of passionate speeches, use of *stichomythia* (see *dialogue*), and a *nuntius* (messenger) who recites in a heightened style an off-stage happening (e.g., the wounded soldier in *Macbeth*, 1.1). Of course, not every use of any of these characteristics is necessarily attributable to Seneca's influence, and there are differences. For example, the horrors in Seneca are narrated, but in *King Lear* Gloucester is blinded on the stage. Consult F. L. Lucas, *Seneca and Elizabethan Tragedy*; Madeleine Doran, *Endeavors of Art*; and Willard Farnham, *The Medieval Heritage of Elizabethan Tragedy*. Howard Baker, in *Induction to Tragedy*, minimizes Seneca's influence.

sensibility. See *sentimental*.

sentimental. Generally a pejorative word in criticism, indicating a superabundance of tender emotion, a disproportionate amount of sentiment (feeling). It is sentimental to be intensely distressed because one has stepped on a flower. A character, for example, Hamlet, may display deep emotions, but they are sentimental only if they are in excess of what the situation warrants. More specifically, "sentimental" writing refers to writing in which evil is facilely conquered, denied, overlooked, or bathed in a glow of forgiving tenderness. In the eighteenth century the ability to respond emotionally (usually tearfully) to acts of benevolence or malevolence was called **sensibility.** In **sentimental drama** there is at the expense of reason an emphasis on tearful situations; people's benevolent emotions are overestimated, for they are assumed to be innately good, and villains reform, usually in bursts of repenting tears. There is little wit, the characters are usually of the middle class, and they demonstrate their virtue by weeping at the sight of distress. In his "Comparison between Sentimental and Laughing Comedy" (1772), Oliver Goldsmith attacked sentimental comedy, saying that in it

> the virtues of private life are exhibited, rather than the vices exposed; and the distresses rather than the faults of mankind make our interest in the piece. . . . Almost all the characters are good, . . . and though they want humor, have abundance of sentiment and feeling. If they happen to have faults or foibles, the spectator is taught, not only to pardon, but to applaud them, in consideration of the goodness of their hearts; so that folly, instead of being ridiculed, is commended, and the comedy aims at touching our passions, without the power of being truly pathetic.

See *bourgeois drama*. Consult Ernest Bernbaum, *The Drama of Sensibility*; and Arthur Sherbo, *English Sentimental Drama*.

sets. The scenery constructed for a theatrical performance, especially the three-dimensional environment (as opposed to two-dimensional wings) in which the characters move.

situational comedy. See *comedy of humors*.

slapstick. See *farce*.

slice of life. See *naturalism*.

sock and **buskin.** Performers of Latin comedy wore a light slipper or sandal called the *soccus*. The sock is either this piece of footwear or comedy itself. The high boot worn by Greek tragic actors was the *cothurnus* or *kothurnus*. In Hellenistic times it acquired a very thick sole, giving the performer the height appropriate to a great man. In English this footgear (or tragic drama in general) is called the buskin, apparently from Old French *broissequin*, from Middle Dutch *brosekin*, "a small leather boot." Consult Margarete Bieber, *The History of the Greek and Roman Theater*.

Socratic irony. See *irony*.

soliloquy. A monologue in which a character utters his or her thoughts aloud while alone. An **aside** is a speech in which a character utters his or her thoughts in words audible to the spectators but supposedly unheard by the other stage characters present. Both were important conventions in Elizabethan drama and, later, in melodrama, but the late nineteenth century sought so vigorously to present on the stage the illusion of real life that both techniques were banished. They have, however, been revived in the twentieth century, as in Eugene O'Neill's *Strange Interlude*, in which the asides represent the characters' thoughts and unspoken desires. In **direct address,** a character turns from the world on the stage and speaks directly to the audience, telling it, for instance, to watch closely. Consult Una Ellis-Fermor, *The Frontiers of Drama*, Chapter 6; George E. Duckworth, *The Nature of Roman Comedy*; and Max Beerbohm,

"Soliloquies in Drama," *Around Theatres*. The soliloquy, the aside, and direct address are all monologues, but more often a **monologue** is either a long speech delivered by one character, which may be heard but not interrupted by others in his presence, or a performance by a single actor.

Sophoclean irony. See *irony*.

sound effect. An imitative noise, usually produced by simple machinery. Though a sound effect may be a mere imitation of nature, it may also be a richly symbolic suggestion. Chekhov's *The Cherry Orchard* (1904) concludes, "There is a far-off sound as if out of the sky, the sound of a snapped string, dying away, sad. A stillness falls, and there is only the thud of an ax on a tree, far away in the orchard." Consult Frank Napier, *Noises Off*.

spectacle. The last of Aristotle's six elements of drama, spectacle denotes what appeals to the eye, such as costume and scenery. Greek drama was splendidly costumed and made some use of scenery. Aeschylus especially seems to have contrived moments that caught the eye, such as Agamemnon's entrance in a chariot. The Elizabethan stage, though sparse in scenery, apparently was architecturally impressive, and doubtless military scenes were embellished with waving banners. In the Restoration, spectacle sometimes got the upper hand. Alexander Pope complained:

> The play stands still; damn action and discourse,
> Back fly the scenes, and enter foot and horse;
> Pageants on pageants, in long order drawn,
> Peers, heralds, bishops, ermine, gold, and lawn.

In the nineteenth century the development of gas light and then electric light made possible elaborate sunrises and twilights, and at the end of the century (especially in Russia) there was an emphasis on ensemble acting that gave a tableau effect. Pictorial effects in late-nineteenth-century productions of Shakespeare were often achieved at the cost of Shakespeare's lines. At the very end of the century, William Poel rejected spectacle and helped establish a trend to stage Shakespeare in what was thought to be an Elizabethan manner: an uncluttered stage, allowing the action to proceed rapidly. Consult James Laver, *Drama*; and A. Nicholas Vardac, *Stage to Screen*, Chapters 3–4.

stage. A platform or space for theatrical performances. See *arena stage*, *Hellenistic theater*, *proscenium stage*, and *thrust stage*. See also A Note on the Elizabethan Theater, page 186, and A Note on the Greek Theater, page 44.

stage business. Minor physical action—including posture and facial expression—by a performer. Business ranges from head scratching to an addition Henry Irving made to *The Merchant of Venice*, 2.4. In Shakespeare's scene, Jessica and Lorenzo elope and the scene ends quietly; Irving added business in which Shylock entered and knocked on the door of his empty house while the curtain fell. Irving's successors amplified his business by having Shylock enter the house, cry out, reappear, and so on. Consult Arthur C. Sprague, *Shakespeare and the Actors*.

stichomythia. See *dialogue*.

stock character. See *character*.

structure. The arrangement of episodes.

style. The mode of expression. Cardinal Newman, talking of the writer's style, called it "a thinking out into language." This idea of "a thinking out" (but not into language) is applicable also to the style of the scene designer, the costume designer, and so on. Kenneth Tynan in *Curtains* defines good style as "a happy consonance of manner with matter, of means with end, of tools with job." To **stylize** a play commonly means to present it with a noticeable artful manner rather than to present it realistically, though in fact realism itself is a style. A **stylized production** usually is presentational or anti-illusionistic rather than representational (*see dramatic illusion*). Consult George R. Kernodle, "Style, Stylization, and Styles of Acting," *Educational Theatre Journal*, 12 (1960), 251–261.

subplot. See *plot*.

subtext. Constantin Stanislavski's term for a text assumed to be hidden beneath the surface. Thus, Stanislavski wanted his actors to discover and communicate the character's unspoken but felt life.

surprise. See *suspense*.

surrealism. A literary movement, especially vigorous in France in the 1920s and 1930s, that insisted that reality is grasped by the unconscious, the irrational, rather than by the conscious. The best art, it is held, is the dream. Among the forerunners were Alfred Jarry, whose *Ubu Roi* (1896) combined grotesque farce with antibourgeois satire; August Strindberg, whose *To Damascus* (three parts, 1898–1904) and *The Dream Play* (1902) had presented dreamlike worlds; and Guillaume Apollinaire, whose *Breasts of Tiresias* (1917) was called a *"drame surréaliste"* (the first use of the word) by the author. Perhaps the chief surrealist dramatist is Jean Cocteau, notably in his *Orpheus* (1926), in which a glazier is an angel and a horse dictates prophetic words. Consult Georges E. Lemaître, *From Cubism to Surrealism in French Literature*.

suspense. Uncertainty, often characterized by anxiety. Suspense is usually a curious mixture of pain and pleasure, as Gwendolen, in Oscar Wilde's *The Importance of Being Earnest*, implies: "This suspense is terrible. I hope it will last." Most great art relies more heavily on suspense than on **surprise** (the unexpected). One can rarely sit twice through a play depending on surprise; when the surprise is gone, the interest is gone. Suspense is usually achieved in part by **foreshadowing**—hints of what is to come. Dumas *fils* put it this way: "The art of the theater is the art of preparations." Coleridge, who held that Shakespeare gives us not surprise but expectation and then the satisfaction of perfect knowledge, once wrote: "As the feeling with which we startle at a shooting star, compared with that of watching the sunrise at the pre-established moment, such and so low is surprise compared with expectation." Thus, in *Hamlet*, the ghost does not pop up surprisingly but satisfies the eager expectations that have been aroused by references to "this thing," "this dreaded sight," and "this apparition." Often, in fact, Shakespeare—like the Greek dramatists—used traditional stories. For example, the audience presumably was not surprised by the deaths of Caesar and Brutus, and it enjoyed the suspense of anticipating them. Suspense is thus related to tragic irony. The tragic character moves closer and closer to his or her doom, and though the character may be surprised by it, we are not; we are held by suspense. On surprise, consult David L. Grossvogel, *The Self-Conscious Stage in Modern French Drama* (reprinted in paperback as *Twentieth-Century French Drama*).

symbolism. Derived from Greek *symballein*, "to throw together," which thus suggests the essential quality of symbolism, the drawing together of two worlds; it presents the concrete material world of roses, toads, caves, stars, and so on, and through them reveals an otherwise invisible world. Thus, the storm in *King Lear* symbolizes both the disorder in Lear's kingdom (brother against brother, etc.) and also the disorder in Lear's mind. The strangled canary in Glaspell's *Trifles* symbolizes the maltreatment that Minnie Wright experienced from her husband.

Symbolism is often distinguished from **allegory.** Where the allegorist commonly invents a world (the author of *Everyman* [c. 1500] invents a figure called Everyman, who seeks aid from figures called Goods, Kindred, etc.) in order to talk about the real world, the symbolist commonly presents the phenomena of what we usually call the real world in order to reveal a "higher," eternal world of which the symbol is a part. The allegorist is free to invent any number of imaginary worlds to talk about the real world, but the symbolist feels that there is only one way by which he or she can present the "higher" real world he or she envisions. The everyday world is often considered by symbolists as a concrete but transient version of a more important realm, and the symbolist who presents, for example, a rose, is (the symbolist might hold) speaking about a rose and also about the eternal beauty of womanhood in the only possible way.

In the second half of the nineteenth century, there arose in France the so-called **Symbolist Movement,** but it must be emphasized that symbolism of a sort is probably as old as literature. An author's insistence on some object may cause us to regard it as more than its apparent nature. For example, the forest or greenwood in *As You Like It* suggests a benevolent nature that restores humans to their best part. On the whole, however, Shakespeare's plays do not leave the world of sensible reality. The plays of the Symbolists do. The Symbolist writer presents a world that seems to be a dream world, a world that is not the usual world enriched, but a new world. In his preface to *The Dream Play* (1902), Strindberg says he "has tried to imitate the disconnected but seemingly logical form of the dream. Anything may happen. . . . The characters split, double, multiply, vanish, solidify, blur, clarify." A play is the expression of a "soul-state" (Stéphane Mallarmé's term) rather than an imitation of an external action. See *surrealism*.

The best naturalists (Ibsen, Chekhov, Strindberg, and Hauptmann) at times wrote symbolic works, but the chief Symbolic dramatists are the French (if we include the Belgian Maurice Maeterlinck) and William Butler Yeats. In Maeterlinck's *The Intruder* (1890) a blind old man sees with his soul the approach of Death. In *The Blind* (1896) a group of blind men are lost in a forest; their leader was a priest, but he has died. Maeterlinck occasionally said some of his plays were for marionettes, and though his statement is sometimes held to be a mildly self-deprecating joke, in fact there is much in the plays that belongs to the realm of impassive, other-worldly dolls, not surprising in the work of a writer who said he wished to study man "in the presence of eternity and mystery." Paul Claudel's *Tidings Brought to Mary* (written in 1892, revised in 1899 and 1912) was acted in 1912. Claudel, who said he had gained from Arthur Rimbaud (one of the leading Symbolists) "an almost physical impression of the supernatural," in this play envelops his medieval characters in a divine world and dramatizes salvation. In Ireland, Yeats, who compared an artistic work to a magic talisman ("it entangles . . . a part of the Divine essence") wrote verse plays of Irish supernatural creatures and heroes. In *On Baile's Strand* (1903), for instance, Cuchulain, the protagonist, is said to have been sired by a hawk. The bird imagery is insisted on; Cuchulain's associates are called chicks and nestlings, and the Fool (who represents Cuchulain on another level) is delighted with feathers. Near the conclusion of the play, Cuchulain rushes out to fight the waves, literally doing what Hamlet spoke metaphorically of doing.

In Russia, Meyerhold in 1906 staged Ibsen's *Hedda Gabler* (1890) as symbolically as possible, turning what had been a naturalistic play into a vision suggestive of another world, something (in the words of a hostile critic) "halfway between metaphysics and ballet." (Consult Nikolai Gorchakov, *The Theater in Soviet Russia*.) For symbolism in the sense of richly suggestive images, consult Alan S. Downer, "The Life of Our Design: The Function of Imagery in the Poetic Drama," *The Hudson Review*, 2 (Summer 1949), 242–260. On the Symbolist Movement, consult William Butler Yeats, *Essays and Introductions*; Arthur Symons, *The Symbolist Movement in Literature*; *Yale French Studies*, No. 9; Eric Bentley, *The Playwright as Thinker*; and John Gassner, *Form and Idea in the Modern Theatre*.

sympathy. See *empathy*.

theater-in-the-round. See *arena stage*.

theater of the absurd. See *absurd, theater of the*.

theatrical. Literally, characteristic of the theater, but often (unfortunately) used pejoratively, to suggest artificially contrived, melodramatic, implausible.

theme. The underlying idea, such as the triumph of love or the failure of idealism. A *theme* can thus be distinguished from a *thesis*, which is a message, such as "Love ought to triumph" or "Idealism is short-sighted."

three unities. See *unity*.

thrust stage. A stage that projects into the auditorium. It encourages direct address to the spectators because even a large audience can be fairly close to the actors. On the other hand, since some members of the audience will be to the side of, or even behind, the performers, there may be acoustical problems.

total theater. The idea that the theater should not try to imitate realistically an aspect of life but should embody a synthesis of all of the expressive arts—music, movement, speech, lighting, and so on. The expression *total theater* is probably derived from Richard Wagner's *Gesamtkunstwerk*, "united" or "total artwork." Consult *Total Theatre*, edited by E. T. Kirby.

tragedy. For Aristotle, tragedy was a dramatic imitation (representation) of an "action of high importance." A Greek tragedy was serious, but it did not necessarily end unhappily. Aeschylus's *Eumenides*, for example, ends on a note of solemn joy. For us a tragedy is generally a play that faces evil, depicts suffering, and ends with death or (especially in the naturalistic tragedies since the latter part of the nineteenth century) ends with the hero alive but spiritually crushed. Tragedy's essence, Alfred North Whitehead says (*Science and the Modern World*, Chapter 1), resides not in unhappiness but "in the solemnity of the remorseless working of things." H. D. F. Kitto says (*The Greeks*, Ch. 4) that Greek tragedy—and perhaps one might add the great tragedy of other countries—was in part the product of intellectualism and humanism. Intellectualism let the Greeks see that human life must be lived within a great framework of what might be called the will of the gods, or Necessity: "Actions must have their consequences; ill-judged actions must have uncomfortable results." Humanism denied the Greeks an easy view of a heavenly life and gave them an "almost fierce joy in life, the exultation in human achievement and in human personality." The tragic note, Kitto suggests, is produced by a tension between this unalterable framework and this passionate delight in life. Consult R. Sewall, *The Vision of Tragedy*; T. R. Henn, *The Harvest of Tragedy*; and H. J. Muller, *The Spirit of Tragedy*.

tragic irony. See *irony*.

tragicomedy. Renaissance critical theorists, embroidering on Aristotle's *Poetics*, assumed that tragedy dealt with noble (important) figures and ended with a death; comedy dealt with trivial (laughable) figures and ended with a celebration. A tragicomedy was some sort of mixture: high characters in a play ending happily, a mingling of deaths and feasts, or, most often (as in many American films), threats of death that are happily—and unconvincingly—evaded. John Fletcher (1579–1625), who with his collaborator Francis Beaumont wrote graceful dramas relying heavily on passionate outbursts and surprising turns of plot, defined a tragicomedy as a play that lacks deaths (and thus is no tragedy) but "brings some near it, which is enough to make it no comedy." One of the speakers in John Dryden's *Essay of Dramatick Poesie* (1668) says: "There is no theater in the world has anything so absurd as the English tragicomedy; . . . here a course of mirth, there another of sadness and passion, and a third of honor and a duel: thus, in two hours and a half, we run through all the fits of Bedlam." Consult Eugene Waith, *The Pattern of Tragi-Comedy*. On what can roughly be called the bitter or ironic comedy of the nineteenth and twentieth centuries, consult K. S. Guthke, *Modern Tragicomedy*; C. Hoy, *The Hyacinth Room*; and Eric Bentley, *The Life of the Drama*.

trilogy. A unit of three works. Though Greek tragic dramatists submitted three tragedies at a time, the plays are only a trilogy if they have an internal unity. Aeschylus's *Oresteia* (458 B.C.) is the only extant complete Greek trilogy; Sophocles's three plays on the Oedipus legend—*Antigone* (c. 422 B.C.), *Oedipus the King* (c. 425), and *Oedipus at Colonus* (c. 406) are not properly a trilogy because they were written at widely separated times and do not cohere into a consistent, unified whole. An example of a modern trilogy is O'Neill's *Mourning Becomes Electra* (1931).

tritagonist. See *protagonist*.

underplot. See *plot*.

unity. Generally means something like "coherence" or "congruence"; in a unified piece the parts work together and jointly contribute to the whole. The subplot of a play may parallel the main plot, or one character may be a foil to another. In any case, unity suggests "completeness" or "pattern" resulting from a controlling intelligence. In the *Poetics*, Aristotle said that a tragedy should have a unified action, and he mentioned that most tragedies cover a period of twenty-four hours. Italian critics, making his comments rigid, in the late sixteenth century established the **Three Unities** of Time, Place, and Action: a play (1) must not cover more than twenty-four hours, (2) must be set in one locale only or, at worst, in various parts of a single city, and (3) must be either entirely tragic or entirely comic, rather than a mixture of (as Sir Philip Sidney said) "hornpipes and funerals." (Consult H. B. Charlton, *Castelvetro's Theory of Poetry*.) Actually, the time covered by Greek tragedies is vague, and characters come from distant places in the space of relatively few lines. For example, in *Oedipus the King*, a shepherd who lives in the "farthest" fields from Corinth is sent for in line 863 and arrives in line 1108. Nor is unity of place invariable in Greek tragedy; there are violations of it in, for example, Aeschylus's *The Eumenides* and Sophocles's *Ajax*.

upstage. The back half of the acting area, or any part of the stage considered in relation to someone or something nearer the audience.

well-made play. See *pièce bien faite*.

ACKNOWLEDGMENTS

Edward Albee. *The Sandbox*, reprinted by permission of the Putnam Publishing Group from *The Sandbox* by Edward Albee. Copyright © 1960 by Edward Albee. *The Sandbox* is sole property of the author and is fully protected by copyright. It may not be acted either by professionals or amateurs without written consent. Public readings, radio and television broadcasts likewise are forbidden. All inquiries concerning the rights should be addressed to the William Morris Agency, 1325 Avenue of the Americas, New York, NY 10019; excerpt from "Interview with Edward Albee" by William Flanagan from *Paris Review*. Reprinted by permission of The Paris Review.

Aristophanes. *Lysistrata* by Aristophanes from *Aristophanes: Four Comedies*, translated by Dudley Fitts. Copyright 1954 by Harcourt Brace & Company, renewed © 1982 by Cornelia Fitts, Daniel H. Fitts, and Deborah W. Fitts. Reprinted by permission of Harcourt Brace & Company. CAUTION: Professionals and amateurs are hereby warned that all titles included in this volume, being fully protected under the copyright laws of the United States of America, Canada, The British Empire and all other countries which are signatories to the Universal Copyright Convention and the International Copyright Union, are subject to royalty. All rights, including professional, amateur, motion picture, recitation, lecturing, public reading, radio broadcasting, television, and the rights of translation into foreign languages are strictly reserved. Inquiries on professional rights should be addressed to Lucy Kroll Agency, 390 West End Avenue, New York, NY 10024. Inquiries on all other rights should be addressed to Harcourt Brace & Company, Permissions Department, Orlando, FL 32887.

Aristotle. *The Poetics*, from *Aristotle on the Art of Fiction* by L. J. Potts, ed. Copyright © 1953 by Cambridge University Press. Reprinted with the permission of Cambridge University Press.

John Astington. "*Everyman* in Toronto" by John Astington from *Everyman*, edited by John Astington. Reprinted by permission of Poculi Ludique Societas and John H. Astington.

Samuel Beckett. *Happy Days*, copyright © 1961, 1989 by Samuel Beckett. Used by permission of Grove Press, Inc.; review of *Happy Days*, "Beckett Heroine Laughs as She Suffers" by Mel Gussow from *The New York Times*, October 13, 1990. Copyright © 1990 by The New York Times Company. Reprinted by permission.

Bertolt Brecht. *The Good Woman of Szechuan* from *Parables for Theatre: Two Plays by Bertolt Brecht*, translated and revised by Eric Bentley. Copyright © 1947, 1948, 1956, 1961, Epilogue Copyright © 1965 by Eric Bentley. Reprinted by permission of the University of Minnesota Press.

Anton Chekhov. *The Cherry Orchard*. Revised translation copyright © 1985 by Laurence Senelick. Used by permission; "Stage: Brook's 'Cherry Orchard' " by Frank Rich from the *New York Times*, January 25, 1988. Copyright © 1988 by The New York Times Company. Reprinted by permission; interview on directing *The Cherry Orchard* with Alan MacVey. Reprinted by permission of Alan MacVey.

Euripides. *Medea* by Euripides, translated by Mary-Kay Gamel. Originally appeared in *Quarterly West* (Spring–Summer 1995). Reprinted by permission of the translator and *Quarterly West*; "Amid Pain, Blood and Din, Diana Rigg Rises as a Mighty Medea" by David Richards from the *New York Times*, April 8, 1994. Copyright © 1994 by The New York Times Company. Reprinted by permission; interview on directing *Medea* with L. L. West. Reprinted by permission of L. L. West.

Harvey Fierstein. *On Tidy Endings* by Harvey Fierstein from *Safe Sex*. Copyright © 1987 by Harvey Fierstein. Reprinted by permission of Scribner, a Division of Simon & Schuster. This play may not be reproduced in whole or in part without the written permission of the publisher. No performance of any kind, including readings may be given without permission in writing from the author's agent, William Morris Agency, 1325 Avenue of the Americas, New York, NY 10019.

Athol Fugard. "*MASTER HAROLD*" . . . *and the boys* by Athol Fugard. Copyright © 1982 by Athol Fugard; excerpts from *Notebooks 1960–1977* by Athol Fugard. Copyright © 1983 by Athol Fugard. Play and excerpts reprinted by permission of Alfred A. Knopf, Inc.

David Henry Hwang. *The Sound of a Voice* by David Henry Hwang from *FOB and Other Plays*. Copyright © 1990 by David Henry Hwang. Reprinted by permission of Dutton Signet, a division of Penguin Books USA; "Sound of a Voice with Hint of Orient," by Sid Smith. *Chicago Tribune*, January 1990. Copyright © 1990 by the Chicago Tribune Company. All rights reserved. Used with permission of Tribune Media Services; excerpt from "Thoughts about Ethnic Theatre" by David Henry Hwang from *Contemporary Authors*, June 28, 1989, edited by Jean W. Ross. Reprinted by permission of Gale Research.

Henrik Ibsen. *A Doll's House* from *Ghosts and Other Plays* by Henrik Ibsen, translated by Michael Meyer. Reprinted by permission of Harold Ober Associates Incorporated. Copyright © 1966 by Michael Meyer. CAUTION: These plays are fully protected in whole, in part, or in any form under the copyright laws of the United States of America, the British Empire including the Dominion of Canada, and all other countries of the Copyright Union, and are subject to royalty. All rights including motion picture, radio, television, recitation, public reading, are strictly reserved. For professional rights and amateur rights all inquiries should be addressed to the Author's Agent: Robert A. Freedman Dramatic Agency Inc., 1501 Broadway, New York, NY 10036; "Notes for the Tragedy of Modern Times" and "Alternative Ending for *A Doll's House*" reprinted from *Oxford Ibsen*, Volume 5, edited by J. W. Macfarlane with the permission of Oxford University Press; interview on directing *A Doll's House* with Carol Elliot MacVey. Reprinted by permission of Carol Elliot MacVey; "Speech at the Banquet of the Norwegian League for Women's Rights" by Henrik Ibsen from *Ibsen: Letters and Speeches*, edited by Evert Sprinchorn. Copyright © 1964 by Evert Sprinchorn. Reprinted by permission of Hill and Wang, a division of Farrar, Straus & Giroux, Inc.

Eugène Ionesco. *The Lesson* from *The Bald Soprano and Other Plays* by Eugène Ionesco, translated by Donald M. Allen. Copyright © 1958 by Grove Press, Inc. Used by permission of Grove/Atlantic, Inc.; "Ionesco: Man of Destiny" by Kenneth Tynan from *The Observer*, June 22, 1958, and "A Reply to Kenneth Tynan" by Eugène Ionesco from *The Observer*, July 29, 1958. Copyright © 1958 by Guardian News Service Limited, a division of Guardian Media Group. Reprinted by permission of Guardian Media Group.

Angela Jackson. *Shango Diaspora* by Angela Jackson. Copyright © 1980 by Angela Jackson. Also appears in *The Woman That I Am*, edited by D. Soyini Madison. Reprinted by permission of the author.

Adrienne Kennedy. *Funnyhouse of a Negro* by Adrienne Kennedy. Reprinted by permission of the author; excerpt from "Blaxpressionism: Funnyhouse of a Negro" by Michael Feingold from *The Village Voice*, October 3, 1995. Reprinted by permission of the author and *The Village Voice*.

Carol Elliot MacVey. Interview on directing *The Rover* with Carol Elliot MacVey. Reprinted by permission of Carol Elliot MacVey.

David Mamet. *Oleanna*. Copyright © 1992 by David Mamet. Reprinted by permission of Vintage Books, a Division of Random House Inc.; excerpt from interview with David Mamet from *In Their Own Words: Contemporary Playwrights*, conducted by David Savran. Copyright © 1988 by David Savran. Used by permission of Theatre Communications Group.

Christopher Marlowe. *Dr. Faustus* by Christopher Marlowe, edited with an introduction by Sylvan Barnet. Copyright © 1969 by Sylvan Barnet. Used by permission of Dutton Signet, a division of Penguin Books USA Inc.; excerpt from "The Royal Shakespeare Company Production of Dr. Faustus" by Gareth Lloyd Evans from *Shakespeare Survey*, Volume 22, 1969. Copyright © 1969 by Gareth Lloyd Evans. Reprinted by permission of Barbara Lloyd Evans.

Arthur Miller. *Death of a Salesman* by Arthur Miller. Copyright 1949, renewed © 1977 by Arthur Miller; "Tragedy and the Common Man," from *The Theater Essays of Arthur Miller* by Arthur Miller, edited by Robert A. Martin. Copyright 1949, renewed © 1977 by Arthur Miller. Used by permission of Viking Penguin, a division of Penguin Books USA Inc.; "Willy Loman's Ideals" [editor's title] from

Conversations with Arthur Miller, edited by Matthew C. Roudane, 1987. Reprinted by permission of the University Press of Mississippi.

Molière. *The Misanthrope* by Molière, translated by Richard Wilbur. Copyright 1955 and renewed © 1983 by Richard Wilbur. Reprinted by permission of Harcourt Brace & Company. CAUTION: Professionals and amateurs are hereby warned that this translation, being fully protected under the copyright laws of the United States of America, the British Commonwealth, including the Dominion of Canada, and all other countries which are signatories to the Universal Copyright Convention and the International Copyright Convention, is subject to royalty. All rights, including professional, amateur, motion picture, recitation, lecturing, public reading, radio broadcasting, and television, are strictly reserved. Particular emphasis is laid on the question of readings, permission for which must be secured from the author's agent in writing. Inquiries on professional rights (except for amateur rights) should be addressed to Mr. Gilbert Parker, William Morris Agency, 1325 Avenue of the Americas, New York, NY 10019; inquiries on translation rights should be addressed to Permissions Department, Harcourt Brace & Company, 6th Floor, Orlando, FL 32887–6777. The amateur acting rights of *The Misanthrope* are controlled exclusively by the Dramatists Play Service, Inc., 440 Park Avenue South, New York, NY 10016. No amateur performance of the play may be given without obtaining in advance the written permission of the Dramatists Play Service, Inc., and paying the requisite fee.

Carlos Morton. *The Many Deaths of Danny Rosales* by Carlos Morton. Copyright © 1983 by Arte Público Press. Reprinted by permission of Arte Público Press–University of Houston; "A Context for *The Many Deaths of Danny Rosales*" by Carlos Morton. Reprinted by permission of Carlos Morton.

Marsha Norman. *'night, Mother* by Marsha Norman. Copyright © 1983 by Marsha Norman. CAUTION: Professionals and amateurs are hereby warned that *'night Mother*, being fully protected under the Copyright Laws of the United States of America and other countries of the Berne and Universal Copyright Conventions, is subject to a royalty. All rights, including but not limited to, professional, amateur, recording, motion picture, recitation, lecturing, public reading, radio and television broadcasting, video or sound taping, photocopying, all other forms of mechanical or electronic reproduction, and the rights of translation into foreign languages are expressly reserved. All inquiries concerning rights (other than stock and amateur rights) should be addressed to the author's agent, Charmaine Ferenezi, The Tantleff Office, 375 Greenwich Street, Suite 700, New York, NY 10013. The stock and amateur production rights for *'night Mother* are controlled exclusively by the Dramatists Play Service, Inc., 440 Park Avenue South, New York, NY 10016. No amateur performance of the play may be given without obtaining in advance the written permission of the Dramatists Play Service, Inc., and paying the requisite fee;

interview with Marsha Norman from *Interviews with Contemporary Women Playwrights*, edited by Kathleen Betsko and Rachel Koenig. Copyright © 1986 by Kathleen Betsko and Rachel Koenig. Reprinted by permission of William Morrow & Company, Inc.

Eugene O'Neill. *Emperor Jones* by Eugene O'Neill from *Selected Plays of Eugene O'Neill* by Eugene O'Neill. Copyright 1925, renewed © 1953 by Eugene O'Neill. Reprinted by permission of Random House, Inc.; "Review of *Emperor Jones*" by Heywood Broun from the *New York Herald Tribune*, November 4, 1920. Copyright 1920 by the New York Herald Tribune. All rights reserved. Reproduced by permission.

Harold Pinter. *The Birthday Party* by Harold Pinter. Copyright © 1959, renewed 1987 by Harold Pinter. Used by permission of Grove/Atlantic, Inc.; excerpt from "Interview with Harold Pinter" by Lawrence M. Bensky from *Paris Review*. Reprinted by permission of The Paris Review.

William Shakespeare. *A Midsummer Night's Dream* and *The Tragedy of King Lear* from *The Complete Works of Shakespeare*, 4th Edition, by William Shakespeare, edited by David Bevington. Copyright © 1992 by HarperCollins Publishers. Reprinted by permission of HarperCollins Publishers; interviews on directing *A Midsummer Night's Dream* and *The Tragedy of King Lear* with Alan MacVey. Reprinted by permission of Alan MacVey.

Bernard Shaw. *Major Barbara*. Reprinted by permission of The Society of Authors on behalf of the Estate of Bernard Shaw.

Sophocles. *Antigone* by Sophocles from *The Oedipus Rex of Sophocles: An English Version* translated by Dudley Fitts and Robert Fitzgerald. Copyright 1939 by Harcourt Brace & Company and renewed © 1967 by Dudley Fitts and Robert Fitzgerald. CAUTION: All rights, including professional, amateur, motion picture, recitation, lecturing, performance, public reading, radio broadcasting, and television are strictly reserved. Inquiries on all rights should be addressed to Harcourt Brace & Company, Permissions Department, Orlando, FL 32887; "*Antigone* in Modern Dress" by Michael Billington from *The Guardian*, May 18, 1984. Reprinted by permission of Michael Billington, drama critic for *The Guardian*.

Sophocles. *Oedipus Rex* by Sophocles from *The Oedipus Rex of Sophocles: An English Version*, translated by Dudley Fitts and Robert Fitzgerald. Copyright 1949 by Harcourt Brace & Company and renewed © 1977 by Cornelia Fitts and Robert Fitzgerald. Reprinted by permission of Harcourt Brace & Company. CAUTION: All rights, including professional, amateur, motion picture, recitation, lecturing, performance, public reading, radio broadcasting, and television are strictly reserved. Inquiries on all rights should be addressed to Harcourt Brace & Company, Permissions Department, Orlando, FL 32887; "Directing *Oedipus* in Canada" by Tyrone Guthrie from *World Theatre*, 6:4 (Winter 1957).

Reprinted by permission of The Tyrone Guthrie Centre, Annaghmakerrig, Newbliss, Co. Menaghan, Ireland; interview on directing *Oedipus Rex* with Alan MacVey. Reprinted by permission of Alan MacVey.

Wole Soyinka. *The Strong Breed* by Wole Soyinka from *Collected Plays 1* (1973). Copyright © 1964 by Wole Soyinka. Reprinted by permission of Oxford University Press.

August Strindberg. *Miss Julie* by August Strindberg from *Strindberg: Five Plays*, translated/edited by Harry Carlson; excerpt to preface of *Strindberg: Five Plays* by Harry Carlson. Copyright © 1983 by The Regents of the University of California. Play and excerpts reprinted by permission of the University of California Press and the author.

Luis Valdez. *Los Vendidos* and "The Actos" from *Actos* by Luis Valdez. Reprinted by permission of Arte Público Press–University of Houston; interview on directing *Los Vendidos* with Jorge Huerta. Reprinted by permission of Jorge Huerta, Ph.D.–Chancellor's Associates Endowed Chair Professor of Theatre, University of California, San Diego.

Wendy Wasserstein. "The Man in a Case" from *Orchards* by Anton Chekhov et al. Copyright © 1986 by Wendy Wasserstein. Reprinted by permission of Alfred A. Knopf, Inc.

Timberlake Wertenbaker. *Our Country's Good* by Timberlake Wertenbaker. Copyright © 1988 by The Dramatic Publishing Company by Timberlake Wertenbaker, revised © 1989. Based on the novel *The Playmaker* by Thomas Keneally. All rights reserved. Printed in the United States. All inquiries regarding performance rights should be addressed to Dramatic Publishing Company, 311 Washington Street, Woodstock, IL 60098.

Tennessee Williams. *The Glass Menagerie* and "Production Notes" from *The Glass Menagerie* by Tennessee Williams. Copyright 1945 by Tennessee Williams and Edwina D. Williams, renewed © 1973 by Tennessee Williams. Reprinted by Random House, Inc.; interview on directing *The Glass Menagerie* with L. L. West. Reprinted by permission of L. L. West.

August Wilson. *Fences* by August Wilson. Copyright © 1986 by August Wilson. Used by permission of Dutton Signet, a division of Penguin Books USA Inc.; excerpt from August Wilson interview in *In Their Own Words: Contemporary American Playwrights* by David Savran. Copyright © 1988 by David Savran. Reprinted by permission of Theatre Communications Group.

Wakako Yamauchi. *And the Soul Shall Dance* by Wakako Yamauchi. Copyright © 1974 by Wakako Yamauchi. Reprinted by permission of Darhansoff/Verrill Agency; interview on directing *And the Soul Shall Dance* with Tisa Chang. Reprinted by permission of Tisa Chang, Artistic/Producing Director for Pan Asian Repertory Theatre; interview on directing *And the Soul Shall Dance* with Kati Kuroda. Reprinted by permission of Kati Kuroda.

PHOTO CREDITS